GEAC
X

ASHIRE
LIB.

AUTHOR	CLASS 796.358

TITLE WISDEN cricketers' almanack. 1996.

D0540608

133rd Year

WISDEN

CRICKETERS' ALMANACK

1996

EDITED BY MATTHEW ENGEL

PUBLISHED BY JOHN WISDEN & CO LTD

06670928

© John Wisden & Co Ltd 1996

Cased edition ISBN 0 947766 31 6   £24.50
Soft cover edition ISBN 0 947766 32 4   £24.50
Leather bound edition ISBN 0 947766 33 2   £200
(Limited edition of 150)

JOHN WISDEN & CO LTD
25 Down Road, Merrow, Guildford, Surrey GU1 2PY
Tel: 01483 570358   Fax: 01483 33153

WISDEN CRICKETERS' ALMANACK

Editor: Matthew Engel, The Oaks, Newton St Margarets, Herefordshire HR2 0QN.
Assistant editor: Harriet Monkhouse. Production editor: Christine Forrest.
General manager: Christopher Lane. Advertisement manager: Colin Ackehurst.

Computer typeset by Spottiswoode Ballantyne Ltd, Colchester

Printed and bound in Great Britain by Clays Ltd, St Ives plc
Distributed by The Penguin Group

PREFACE

Nothing in four years of editing *Wisden* has given me quite as much job-satisfaction as the establishment of the Cricket Round the World feature, which has now become an established part of the Almanack.

Forty-six different countries (or groups of countries, or territories, or dots on the ocean) have now appeared in this section. These are in addition to the 13 cricketing nations that have their own sections in *Wisden* as of right (nine Test teams, Holland and Denmark plus Scotland and Ireland, which these days have their cricketing independence, whatever the constitutional position might be), making 59 in all.

This is being written during the fraught countdown to cricket's largest-ever World Cup, including 12 of these countries. The tournament will be reported fully in the 1997 *Wisden*, along, I hope, with news from parts of the world the Almanack has not yet discovered.

It is in the nature of the late 20th century that we are beginning to run out of places that would seem truly exotic, though I believe this year's evocative reports from Ascension Island and Western Samoa still have the thrill of the really remote. And we still await news from, for instance, North Korea and Albania. I did go to Albania myself two years ago but, alas, could find no trace of cricket; how different it would have been if C. B. Fry ever had taken up the famous offer of kingship.

Many of the reports – and these are usually the jolliest – merely concern larky matches between expats, often floating populations of businessmen and diplomats. In other places, there are serious attempts to give the game local roots: Italy is especially energetic; and Hong Kong's latest report is an anguished account of how a once confident and self-absorbed cricketing community is struggling to cope with new political realities.

The Empire-building British first spread the game round the world. Now exiled workers from the subcontinent are producing what might be cricket's second wave, to places as improbable as Iran (see *Wisden* 1995) and as obvious as North America, cricket's Lost Continent. There has been a big influx recently into both Canada and the US. Organisation there remains patchy and confused. But one day, maybe, one day . . . Cricket keeps growing as it is, and the 133rd *Wisden* is, yet again, the biggest ever. By ancient tradition, the editor grumbles about this but, as a member of our management committee recently pointed out, the time to get worried is if we ever get the reverse problem, so I will keep quiet. There are no significant changes in the structure of this year's *Wisden*, for which some readers will be grateful.

My thanks, as usual, go in particular to the board and management committee of John Wisden & Co; to Harriet Monkhouse, Christine Forrest, Christopher Lane and Colin Ackehurst of the *Wisden* staff; to Peter Bather and Mike Smith of Spottiswoode Ballantyne, our typesetters; to our distributors Penguin, especially Alastair Rolfe, Shaun Snow and Fiona Davidson; to Gordon Burling, Bill Frindall, John Kitchin, Andrew Radd and Roy Smart; and to Hilary and Laurie, my wife and son, for all their support. I would also like to thank all our contributors and our readers, whose support for the institution of *Wisden* has allowed it to flourish for one and a third centuries.

MATTHEW ENGEL

Newton St Margarets, Herefordshire,
February 1996

LIST OF CONTRIBUTORS

Jonathan Agnew
Jack Arlidge
Chris Aspin
Jack Bailey
Philip Bailey
Mark Baldwin
Jack Bannister
Brian Bearshaw
Tony Becca
Mike Berry
Scyld Berry
Edward Bevan
J. Watson Blair
Paul Bolton
Shaun Botterill
Robert Brooke
Colin Bryden
John Callaghan
D. J. Cameron
Mike Coward
Tony Cozier
Robert Craddock
John Curtis
Gareth A. Davies
Geoffrey Dean
Peter Deeley
Tim de Lisle
Norman de Mesquita
Patrick Eagar
John Etheridge
Paton Fenton

David Foot
Bill Frindall
David Frith
Nigel Fuller
Andrew Gidley
Chris Goddard
Gideon Haigh
David Hallett
David Hardy
Peter Hargreaves
Norman Harris
Murray Hedgcock
Eric Hill
Philip Hoare
Derek Hodgson
Grenville Holland
David Hopps
Gerald Howat
John Jameson
Peter Johnson
Abid Ali Kazi
Ken Kelly
John Kitchin
Alan Lee
David Llewellyn
David Lloyd
Andrew Longmore
Nick Lucy
Steven Lynch
John MacKinnon
Peter Mason

Robert Mills
R. Mohan
Graham Morris
Gerald Mortimer
Brian Murgatroyd
Pat Murphy
Adrian Murrell
Rebecca Naden
Mike Neasom
Terry Power
Qamar Ahmed
Andrew Radd
Amanda Ripley
Peter Robinson
Alan Ross
Carol Salmon
Andrew Samson
Derek Scott
Mike Selvey
Bill Smith
Ivo Tennant
Sa'adi Thawfeeq
John Thicknesse
Bob Thomas
Sudhir Vaidya
Gerry Vaidyasekera
Waheed Khan
John Ward
Tim Wellock
Graeme Wright
Terry Yates-Round

Round the World: Nasir F. M. Akram, Bob Barlow, Charlie Chelliah, Brian Fell, T. J. Finlayson, Tony Fisher, Simone Gambino, Joe Grimberg, Maurice F. Hankey, Simon Hewitt, John Kaminsky, Peter Knight, Russell Mawhinney, Bryan Pattison, Stanley Perlman, Jimmy Powell, Ahmad Saidullah, Ian Malcolm Scott, Fraser M. Simm, Andrew Simpson-Parker, Jasmer Singh, Mark Stafford, Tanjeeb Ahsan Saad, Derek Thursby, Nicholas Turner, Richard Walker, Colin Wolfe and Clive Woodbridge.

Thanks are accorded to the following for checking the scorecards of first-class matches: Keith Booth, Caroline Byatt, Len Chandler, Bill Davies, Alex Davis, Byron Denning, Jack Foley, Peter Gordon, Brian Hunt, Vic Isaacs, Bert Jenkins, David Kendix, Tony Kingston, Reg May, David Oldam, Tony Smith, Gordon Stringfellow, Stan Tacey, Tony Weld, Roy Wilkinson, Gordon Wood and Graham York.

The editor also acknowledges with gratitude assistance from the following: David Armstrong, Brian Austin, Anthony Baines-Walker, Trevor Bailey, June Bayliss, Chris Bowden, Dick Brittenden, Andrew Burgess-Tupling, Donald Carr, Michael Chandler, Marion Collin, Geoffrey Copinger, D. G. Crampton, Brian Croudy, Prakash Dahatonde, Ian Davidson, Andrew Dawson, Christopher Douglas, Robert Eastaway, Clive Everton, Ben Fenton, Ric Finlay, Shyam Sundar Ghosh, Ghulam Mustafa Khan, Pat Gibson, Robin Gordon-Walker, John Harms, Bob Harragan, T. F. Harrison, Les Hatton, Col. Malcolm Havergal, Lt-Col. K. Hitchcock, Ken Ingman, M. A. Jafri, Kate Jenkins, Ian Jobling, Frank Keating, Ian Keresey, Rajesh Kumar, Derek Lodge, Malcolm Lorimer, Mervyn Mansell, M. P. Mapagunaratne, Tony Marcovecchio, Robin Marlar, Mohandas Menon, Peter Mensforth, Allan Miller, Jeff Morris, Don Moyes, Pat Mullins, D. J. Newton, Andrew Nickolds, Michael Owen-Smith, Peter Paylor, Francis Payne, S. S. Perera, S. Pervez Qaiser, Simon Rae, Brian Reynolds, Rex Roberts, Geoffrey Saulez, Philip Snow, Karen Spink, Richard Streeton, David J. Taverner, Nancy Tomkins, Mike Turner, Keith Walmsley, David Walsh, Donna Wilkinson, Wendy Wimbush and John Woodcock.

The production of *Wisden* would not be possible without the support and co-operation of many other cricket officials, writers and lovers of the game. To them all, many thanks.

CONTENTS

Part Four: Overseas Cricket in 1994-95

Part Five: Administration and Laws

Part Six: Miscellaneous

Addresses of first-class and minor counties can now be found on pages 1300-1301.

A more detailed index to Cricket Records appears on pages 101-105. The index to the Laws may be found on pages 1304-1305 and an index of Test matches played in 1995-96 on pages 1417-1418.

Index of Fillers and Inserts

PART ONE: COMMENT

NOTES BY THE EDITOR

The process by which the great port-wine makers decide whether or not a vintage is to be declared in any given year is a complex one, involving repeated tastings and a 12-month wait. Some years are unanimously considered great; some are arguable; others are undeniably duds. There is no formal process for making the same declaration for cricket seasons, but everyone who follows the game with any kind of historical perspective will have a sense of which years are vintage and which are not.

The English season of 1995 cannot be ranked with the greatest summers, like 1947 and 1981. It may not be recalled in future quite as often as 1948, 1956 or 1975. But it was a wonderfully rich and satisfying summer as it occurred, and perhaps the memories still need more time to mature before we can decide how long they will last. At the heart of it all was a classic Test series between England and West Indies, who traded punches like battered heavyweights (an analogy which sums up the state of both teams) before collapsing in a heap at 2-2. In the background was a tremendous battle for the County Championship. Above everything, after the first few weeks, there was a hot, hot sun which shone with the intensity of 1959 and 1976. At various moments of the Test match TV commentary, I swear I heard Geoff Boycott complain that a batsman was boring and David Gower that someone had got out to an irresponsible shot. The heat must have been doing strange things to the imagination.

In the end, 1995 was short of just one element; the catharsis that would have come from England actually winning the series and the Wisden Trophy changing hands, the kind of historic shift that made 1953 so unforgettable. This is not a question of an Englishman's bias (not entirely, anyway). When John Wisden and Co. gave the trophy to mark this Almanack's centenary in 1963, no one would have envisaged that the same team could win it on 12 consecutive occasions. There was no injustice in a drawn series: the teams were well-matched and, even in their present reduced circumstances, West Indies will always be very difficult to beat when Brian Lara strikes the kind of form he did in the last three matches. But it was exceptionally disappointing that the final Test should have been played on a surface which, unless one side performed quite incompetently, could never have provided a result.

When the Edgbaston Test finished in little more than two days, Warwickshire were attacked for producing an over-fiery pitch, and rightly so. The Oval would hardly have arrived at a natural finish in less than a fortnight, yet the criticism of Surrey hardly amounted to more than a little light chuntering. Since they have the time-honoured right to host the last Test of a summer, the ground authority at The Oval have a special obligation to offer an appropriate stage for the occasion, particularly when a series is level. Over-conservatism is as wrong in these circumstances as taking risks or trying to favour one side or the other. It is all too easy for those of us with a little half-digested knowledge of loam and aeration to start criticising groundsmen. But it is hard to avoid the conclusion that Surrey did the game and the public a disservice.

A New World Order

Before West Indies arrived in England they had lost a series that was seen as a turning-point. Their defeat at home to Australia, their first in any series in 15 years, led to a general declaration that the Australians were now world champions. And it could not have happened to a more deserving team. Mark Taylor's leadership has been forceful but sporting; the batting positive; and Shane Warne's bowling has been among the most welcome developments cricket has had in years. These Notes are being written just before the 1996 World Cup. By the time they are read, it will (fingers crossed) have taken place and people will loosely be declaring someone or other – possibly even England – world champions.

Well, world one-day champions, yes. But even with that proviso, it will be a happy accident if the winners of the World Cup are the planet's best team. The nature of one-day cricket is that any set of capable professionals can beat any other, depending on who performs on the day. And the format chosen for the 1996 World Cup – three weeks of shadow-boxing to reduce 12 teams, including three makeweights, to eight followed by nine days of straight knockouts – was particularly ill-designed for the purpose. The case for a true Test match World Championship, with minimum disruption to the existing structure, was stated here last year and I will not bang on again – yet. The response from round the world was enthusiastic. The authorities did nothing. It is an idea whose time will come.

Muck and brass

Fifteen years ago, Dennis Lillee and Rodney Marsh handed over a couple of notes to a gopher and instructed him to place them on the 500 to 1 available against England in the betting tent at Headingley. They were playing for the opposition. The most famous odds in the history of cricket produced the most famous win and, in the case of those two, the most disgraceful pay-out.

If the sport were baseball and the country America, they would have been banned forever. Australia and cricket did nothing. Indeed, the Aussies tended to laugh the matter off, as though a pair of lovable larrikins had been caught playing a slightly illegal game of two-up during the factory lunch-hour. So one cannot resist a slightly malicious chuckle at the mess in which Australian cricket has lately found itself.

David Hopps gives the background to the bribery scandal on page 17. Some conclusions are easy to draw. There really is no more serious allegation possible within the game than the one Warne, Mark Waugh and Tim May made against Salim Malik. If Malik tried to bribe Warne to throw a match, he is a cheat; alternatively the other three are liars. Whoever is guilty should not be allowed to continue in the game. But which?

There is no point in having an International Cricket Council if it is not to investigate a situation like this, adjudicate on it and issue penalties as appropriate. Who cares how many overs are bowled in a day's cricket, if the overs and the day are tainted? Most outside observers believe the power exists, inherently. The ICC's chief executive, David Richards, believes it should exist, and hopes to get more authority to deal with emergencies, but he was warned against precipitate action by the lawyers. In the old days, the world's great fears were war, famine and pestilence; these days litigation sometimes seems have superseded the lot.

Instead, the only investigation was the one conducted by the retired Pakistani judge Fakhruddin G. Ebrahim. The three Australians, perhaps arrogantly, declined to travel to Pakistan. But if they had no faith in Pakistani justice, they were vindicated. The judge said their allegations were concocted. Now there are still countries in the world where judges sometimes reach a verdict without listening to the defence; it is pretty unusual to get there without listening to the prosecution. Judicial ignorance ("Who are the Beatles?") is a well-known phenomenon, though it is a little baffling that any judge could produce a nine-page summary while apparently ignorant of the relevance of gambling to this case. Judicial pique is less well-documented but it shines through this judge's attitude to the Australians.

Cricket is a splendidly designed game for betting: its mixture of the individual and the general gives an unparalleled range of opportunities for enthusiasts to back their judgments. But, as the northern saying ought to go, where there's brass, there's muck. In Britain, where betting is legal and bookmakers are inclined to cowardice rather than corruption, the problem appears to be controllable; any unusual betting patterns would be spotted at once, and publicly exposed. In the subterranean world of subcontinental betting, too illegal to be subject to the public gaze, too narrowly-based to form a mature market, the same checks do not apply. The ICC Code of Conduct belatedly lays down the law and bans players from betting: the sound of stable doors slamming is heard across the globe.

The Henderson Affair (1)

In its July 1995 issue, the magazine *Wisden Cricket Monthly* made the mistake of publishing the views of one Robert Henderson on the subject of race and cricket under the headline "Is It In The Blood?" Henderson speculated that foreign-born and, most specifically, black cricketers as "a matter of biology" were subconsciously incapable of trying whole-heartedly when they play for England. The libel action threatened by players named in the article was settled out of court. Since the magazine is under the same ultimate ownership as this Almanack, it was a peculiarly painful episode for us.

The Henderson thesis is, in essence, piffle. He is not qualified to analyse anyone's subconscious. Let's try to separate two issues here. Firstly, there can be no support – there is no support – for the idea that England teams should discriminate against black players. Apartheid in South Africa is only just dead; the idea that it could appear here instead is abhorrent and unthinkable. For the first time, a significant number of British-born blacks are beginning to make their mark in county cricket; it would be surprising if some of them are not in the Test team in the next two years. Of course, they must and will be judged on their merits, as were the migrant generation that preceded them.

There remains a related matter that is a legitimate area of discussion. Let me repeat: it is nothing to do with race. Many cricketers, black and white, can in effect choose their nationality through ancestral or residential qualification. However, it is not a fair choice. The UK has the only cricketing circuit that offers players of a wide range of ability the chance of a career. Only the most brilliant can have that career without being qualified for England.

It is reasonable to believe that not everyone who has chosen to regard himself as English has done so out of any deep patriotic commitment. I am not casting aspersions on any individual's motivation, still less his subconscious. But there is a widespread belief – not least among the players – that the qualification rules should be tightened, to prevent the merest suspicion that anyone might be flying a flag of convenience. And I support that.

England, Illy's England

The calendar year 1995 was not a bad one for the England team. They played 13 Test matches, all against strong teams, won three, lost three and drew seven. The year was immediately preceded by a decisive defeat in Melbourne and followed by one in Cape Town, after which came a 6-1 defeat in a set of one-day internationals against South Africa. The team was then weary, in the way that only cricket teams who have lost an overseas Test series can be weary. Two youngish quality fast bowlers have emerged: Darren Gough was followed by Dominic Cork. They have hardly yet played together in Test cricket, still less played well together. But the potential is there.

The TCCB's decision last March to sack Keith Fletcher and make Ray Illingworth manager as well as chairman of selectors was the only sensible response to the situation that had developed. In the short run, it has been successful. With fewer internal tensions, England's affairs were mostly conducted with more dignity than had been the case beforehand, especially on the hopelessly-run 1994-95 tour of Australia. The South African tour, with Illingworth in charge, was mostly harmonious and the arrival of the diplomatic John Barclay as assistant manager was extremely helpful. The handling of gifted but problematic individuals remained woeful. It was hard to fathom what Illingworth thought he was achieving in his dealings with Mark Ramprakash and Devon Malcolm. Other teams are deeply into sports psychology; Illingworth expresses his contempt for the very idea.

Theoretically, Illingworth had more power than anyone has ever had over the national team. And he would regularly flex his muscles, laying down iron principles for the untrammelled exercise of his power and for selecting the team. Then, suddenly, those principles would prove unexpectedly changeable. Ultimately, it became clear that teams were being chosen much as they had been before, by a coalition in which the captain's voice was extremely important. And Mike Atherton's reputation, as a cricketer and captain, had recovered after his difficult 1994; indeed, it was sky-high – both because of the way he held the batting together (saving the Johannesburg Test was merely the most dramatic example) and because of the sensible manner in which he appeared to deal with his master. There was something rather endearing about Illy's claims to total power, which became a great deal less insistent when things were going wrong. It is clear, though, that if the counties are ever to agree to let the England selectors have a say in the way they handle their players, it will come only when Illingworth gives way to a more emollient figure.

To me, the biggest disappointment of Illingworth's reign so far is not that he has exercised too much power but the reverse: he would insist on citing form as a justification for selection instead of backing his judgment about a player's quality and then sticking with it, and facing the consequences. The style of leadership has changed dramatically; the sense that England selection policy will be blown around by the most fickle of winds has not.

On the small screen

For some of us, 1995 was the Ceefax summer. The Press Association/TCCB scores computer, after an appalling start in 1993, began to provide an efficient service, enabling Championship scores to be updated every few balls instead of every half-hour. The upshot was that watching a game on teletext could be almost as exciting as being there: Northamptonshire's marvellous matches against Warwickshire and Nottinghamshire were as draining on the screen as they must have been for the players. (Note to the BBC: this summer, can you just mention how many overs are left, please?)

It was a remarkable Championship season. Middlesex and Northamptonshire had records that would have made them easy champions in a normal year. But Warwickshire were outstanding: in terms of win percentages, their 14 wins, two defeats and a draw out of 17 fractionally beat Surrey's benchmark season of 1955, when they won 23, lost five and drew none.

Certainly, no one has won so much and received so little credit as Warwickshire in the past two years. And many of Northamptonshire's wins were truly epic: Allan Lamb strutting about the field, all but giving orders to the opposition, was one of the most memorable sights of 1995. The combination of dry weather, four-day matches played on three-day pitches and the absence of any kind of incentive for struggling teams to try and hold out for a draw made for some one-sided matches. The evidence of the year suggests a case for introducing points for a draw, but these could easily make for a lot of drab cricket in a year when pitches were flatter and the weather wetter.

The best teams expected to beat the worst in 1995 with greater certainty than for many years past. If anything, this ought to have increased the clamour for a two-division Championship, but eventually this ill-considered argument died away as suddenly as it had flared up. Among the panaceas for the reform of English cricket that replaced it was the suggestion that county groundsmen ought to be employed centrally to prevent them preparing pitches for home advantage.

I suppose it could take as long as three seconds for the averagely intelligent person to realise the unworkability of this scheme. Imagine the glowering between committee and dressing-rooms and the enemy on their square. How would anyone exercise control? How can London give orders about the soil in Scarborough? What if the groundsman were incompetent or drunk? If the club complained, he would go to Lord's and announce that they were trying to interfere with his sacred duty.

The Henderson Affair (2)

Michael Henderson (no known relation to Robert) is the cricket writer on *The Times* whose attack on the competition coming from former players turned journalists provided a rather less serious diversion in 1995 than the other Henderson business. The story is dealt with by Tim de Lisle in his media article on page 1371. Basically, this Henderson is also wrong. The public is best served by variety in its newspapers and in its writers. Anyone who plays first-class cricket acquires an understanding of the game that the rest of us cannot possibly hope to match. But cricket also has to be reported by people who have broader perspectives. Cricket needs both Hendo and the people he abuses.

What no one seems to realise is that none of this is remotely new. The generation of cricketers just retired happened to contain a number of gifted writers. But during the Ashes series of 1934 the *Daily Herald* was said to be the only daily paper with a journalist reporting the game; the best seats in the press boxes all went to ex-players, who were employed solely for their names, and their ghost writers. The *Sunday Referee*, which also stood out against the trend, had the headline "A Straightforward Account of Yesterday's Play in the Test Match at Lord's Written by Professional Sports Reporters".

Editors of other papers said they had to get big names as a defence against the "Johnnie Walker" scoreboards, recording every run, which the whisky firm put up in seaside resorts. The 1934 Press First XI read: J. B. Hobbs (*The Star*), C. B. Fry (*Evening Standard*), P. F. Warner (*Daily Telegraph*), D. R. Jardine (*Evening Standard*), P. G. H. Fender (*Evening News*), Lord Tennyson (*News of the World*, if you please), A. E. R. Gilligan (*News Chronicle*), A. W. Carr (*Nottingham Journal*), J. C. White (*Sunday Pictorial*), B. J. T. Bosanquet (*Daily Mail*) and R. C. Robertson-Glasgow (*Morning Post*). A notional match between that side and a modern press box XI headed by Roebuck, Marks, Pringle, Bannister and Selvey – to take only those ex-players who are front-rank correspondents rather than columnists or commentators – would probably be a walkover for the ancients, even if that side is a bit short of pace. But, Robertson-Glasgow aside, the moderns could write the other lot off the park.

Sixes and Symonds

I am not convinced that many of the current generation of players are ever going to enlighten us much about the way cricket is and should be played. I was lucky enough to be at Abergavenny to see the 16th six of Andrew Symonds's innings sail over the outfield, a hawthorn bush and a patch of bindweed and on to a nearby tennis court, giving him a world record. Most of the interest centred on Symonds's nationality. English-born, Australian-bred, he decided, with refreshing originality, not to take the easy option of declaring himself English at once, and set out to prove himself in Australia, the country to which he felt he owed most allegiance.

It was something else that bothered me. Interviewed later, he said he was entirely unconcerned by the record; what mattered was playing the best he could for his team etc. etc. This is supposed to be the sort of thing one says in these circumstances. What was so worrying was that he sounded sincere. Since the definition of a six-hit was regularised in 1910, there must have been – what? – over a million innings played in first-class cricket. Not one of these had ever before brought forth a six, the ultimate expression of a batsman's power and dominance, 16 times. Did it really mean nothing to Symonds? If so, it is dispiriting that such gifts could have been given to someone with so little appreciation of what they mean to the rest of us.

At Lord's

During the Benson and Hedges Cup final, someone was spotted in the Lord's pavilion wearing an AIDS ribbon. It was a reminder, besides anything else, that MCC is no longer, if it ever was, an exclusive club for irascible colonels. All kinds and conditions of men belong, though not many young ones, as is inevitable in a club where the main qualification for membership is the patience to endure 20 years on the waiting list.

Many people have noticed that attitudes at the club have lately become a little less narrow too. This has been a gradual process but it has accelerated since Roger Knight became secretary. There are imaginative rebuilding plans. And the atmosphere for non-members seems less intimidating; a little more in keeping with a place of entertainment at the end of the 20th century and less with the glasshouse at Catterick circa 1942. Perhaps eventually this mood will reach the membership as a whole and they will realise the extent to which their attitude towards the half of the human race excluded by birth from MCC makes not just them but the whole game look stupid.

But the most urgent problem, at Lord's as at other major grounds, is not getting into the pavilion but into the ground itself. In perhaps the bravest piece of cricket reporting last summer, Andrew Longmore of *The Times* discovered that it was indeed possible, just about, to buy a ticket on the day. He queued four hours for returns at the back of the Mound Stand. So did dozens of others. By the time Longmore was saved by a friendly passer-by with a spare, the grand total of two people had gained admission. After all that, he was rather angry to discover that the person in the seat in front of him, an MCC member, spent the afternoon reading *The Spectator* instead of being one.

It was noticeable in 1995 that West Indian supporters were virtually absent from the Tests. Spontaneous enthusiasm now is out; buy a ticket months in advance or stay at home is the message. There is a danger that soon the disadvantaged, the unconnected and – worst of all – the young will all be missing. This needs coherent thought and care from the game's authorities. Why not a couple of thousand tickets for the Saturday and Sunday of a Test match kept back and sold at affordable prices? The small loss of short-term revenue would be more than cancelled out by long-term gains. How many of today's cricket fans got hooked because they were able to get a glimpse of some big game when they were young? And how many of tomorrow's?

Newlands for Old

It used to be generally – and, I think, rightly – said that the two most beautiful Test grounds in the world were the Adelaide Oval and Newlands, Cape Town. That, however, was in the days when Newlands was not actually staging Test cricket. Now it is, and has been revamped. No one has yet moved Table Mountain. But the cricket ground itself is no longer beautiful.

The local association had a difficult task. If the facilities and the capacity had not been improved, Tests might have been taken away. And officials say that the oak trees that were the ground's chief glory were mostly dying. Now there are capacious but uninspiring stands instead. More imaginative solutions could have been found to preserve one of cricket's great shrines. In England or Australia they would have been, because public opinion would have insisted. In South Africa, where democracy is a novelty, there was hardly a peep. It is a rotten shame.

A novel theory

The formation of the English Cricket Board is not an especially thrilling subject for most followers of the game. And the arguments over it have now become bogged down in detail so that the handover from the existing bodies has been postponed at least until later this year. Officials from a group styling itself "the Big Five" – the Test ground counties excluding Middlesex – did try and hijack the process with an unsubtle plan to give their counties the bulk of the power and money, based on a wrong-headed analysis of their own importance, but this merely united everyone else against them.

Part of the urge for change comes from the people who attend TCCB meetings getting fed up with the discomfort of being crammed in a small conference room containing 60 people. There is also a genuine belief among administrators that the new Board will lead to better government. One's worry is still that what emerges will be even less responsive to the concerns of ordinary players and spectators.

It will obviously require a genius to run the new Board. But the present TCCB chief executive may have been under-rated. *The Guardian* recently reported that Sir Arthur Conan Doyle used to play in goal for Portsmouth FC under the alias A. C. Smith. It said nothing about keeping wicket for Warwickshire. But is it possible that, in addition to holding English cricket together, which he has done with great skill, A.C. also found time to write the Sherlock Holmes stories? When he retires later this year, he should clearly be succeeded either by Sherlock himself or his cleverer brother, Mycroft.

The missing centurion

I probably ought to say something in these Notes about Laws 24 and 42, and Brian Lara's battles against the problems of mega-stardom, mixed in with some perceptive thoughts on Sky TV, the Internet and Darren Gough's left foot. Some other time, maybe. It is gratifying (though occasionally alarming) to know how many *Wisden* readers rummage conscientiously even through the mustiest corner of the Almanack. Several have noted that Cota Ramaswami of Madras is apparently due to celebrate his 100th birthday this year, a feat not yet achieved by any Test cricketer. His date of birth is recorded as June 18, 1896, and there is no record of his death.

Ramaswami toured England in 1936, played two Tests on the tour though he was already over 40, and indeed scored rather well: 40, 60, 29 and 41 not out. And his centenary falls just two days before the start of this year's Lord's Test against India. Unfortunately, the odds seem to be against him being around to enjoy it. In 1985, aged 89, Ramaswami left his home, wearing shorts, T-shirt and slippers, and has never been seen since. He had already tried to commit suicide several times. But no body has ever been found, and some people believe he must still be alive. In *Wisden*, though, he will now have to be "presumed dead".

The Case of the Kanpur Fifty

Some *Wisden* problems are less weighty. Salim Durani is listed in the Records section as having scored the second-fastest fifty in Test history: 29 minutes for India against England at Kanpur in February 1964, against the unchallenging little leggers of Colin Cowdrey and Jim Parks. More than thirty years on there was an attempt to strip Durani of full honours on the same grounds as the contrived fifties and hundreds in the first-class list were relegated to footnotes.

But Durani's innings was slightly different. The match was already dead, the fifth draw in a five-Test series, played on horribly flat pitches. The bowlers may have been clubbable and not trying very hard to be anything else, but that is not the same as actively conniving with the batsman. Parks was particularly miffed by any suggestion to the contrary since Durani was dropped in his leg-trap, though he does admit this was actually set on the deep square boundary. So Durani stays. And let us give thanks for a game that, among its endless and multifaceted delights, throws up historical conundrums like this one that manage simultaneously to be absurdly trivial and desperately important.

THE BRIBES CRISIS

By DAVID HOPPS

Australia's chief executive, Graham Halbish, called it "cricket's greatest crisis for 20 years". If the Salim Malik Affair is ultimately survived without excessive disorder, it will be largely due to the game's inclination to suppress a scandal rather than investigate it. When three Australian players allege that the captain of Pakistan offered them bribes to throw matches, and when talk is rife of illegal betting scams throughout Asia, which have burgeoned since the introduction of satellite TV coverage, then crisis is a reasonable word.

The International Cricket Council's failure to take a central role by conducting an immediate inquiry – preferring instead to act as a conduit between the two nations involved – identified it as a body hopelessly unempowered to manage the international game convincingly. In an increasingly litigious world, governing bodies in many sports are reluctant to act, for fear that their authority will be undermined in a civil court. There must be a measure of sympathy for their predicament. But ICC's policy of damage limitation leaves most questions in this affair unanswered, and leaves Salim Malik's reputation forever besmirched by assumptions and innuendo.

Malik *was* cleared of the allegations by an independent inquiry in Pakistan. Frustrated by ICC's failure to take control, the Pakistan Board placed matters in the hands of Fakhruddin G. Ebrahim, a former Pakistani supreme court judge, and one-time attorney-general and governor of Sindh province. Ebrahim's investigation was hampered by Australia's unwillingness to subject their three players – Shane Warne, Tim May and Mark Waugh – to cross-examination in Pakistan, saying they feared for their welfare, and that they would be prepared to travel to London for any ICC inquiry. That left Ebrahim's investigation strictly limited. After studying a sworn statement from the three Australians, and cross-examining Malik, who was represented by counsel, at length, Judge Ebrahim concluded on October 21, 1995: "The allegations against Saleem (*sic*) Malik are not worthy of any credence and must be rejected as unfounded."

He angered the Australian Cricket Board with his final remark, suggesting that the allegations "appear to have been concocted for reasons best known to the accusers". The ACB, a week later, condemned such comments as "extraordinary and damaging". The Board also contended that ICC should have conducted an inquiry and was empowered to do so, under Rule 2 of its Code of Conduct. That states: "Players and team officials shall not at any time engage in conduct unbecoming to an international player or team official which could bring them or the game into disrepute."

The allegations arose from Australia's tour of Pakistan in late 1994. Warne's sworn statement contended that, on the fourth evening of the Test at Karachi (where Pakistan had never lost a Test, and where illegal bookmakers appear to wield considerable power) he received a phone call from Malik, in the presence of his room-mate, May. According to Warne, he visited Malik's room, whereupon Malik offered him $US200,000 (about £130,000) to bowl badly on the final day. Warne's affidavit assumed the money was to be shared between them; May interpreted it as $200,000 each. Ebrahim refused to believe "that Malik should offer a large sum of money not for any direct personal gain, but for the sake of the nation's pride". The judge appeared unaware of any suggestion that betting might be involved.

Warne's second charge in his affidavit concerned a conversation between Malik and Mark Waugh at a presidential reception before a one-day international in Rawalpindi. It was alleged that Waugh was "offered $200,000 for four or five Australian players not to play well the next day". Incredibly, Pakistan did not hear of Australia's accusations for five months, and then only because the facts were deliberately leaked in finest Deep Throat tradition to Phil Wilkins of the *Sydney Morning Herald*. By that time, rumours of corruption on Pakistan's tours of South Africa and Zimbabwe were rife and two players, Rashid Latif and Basit Ali, went into temporary retirement, reportedly to bring matters to a head. Pakistan's loss to Zimbabwe in the First Test in Harare had been one of the greatest upsets in Test history. Before the match, Zimbabwe had been quoted at 40 to 1 with some Asian bookmakers, but went on to record their first win since becoming a full Test nation.

Intikhab Alam, Pakistan's team manager, confirmed that his team had been asked to swear on the Koran after the series against Australia that they were not involved with any betting syndicates. "I think that people have gone mad," he claimed. "There is no truth in it. It is terrible. These are very serious charges against the Pakistan team." Nevertheless, more than one Pakistani player intimated that bribery and betting activities were out of control and must be addressed. That Judge Ebrahim made no reference to Asia's illegal betting market was a regrettable omission. Betting syndicates in Bombay and the Gulf were credited with enormous influence. Bets were taken not just on the result of matches, but on the toss, individual scores and even the number of runs scored in an over. Ladbrokes thought that their level of cricket betting in England was minuscule by comparison.

The crisis spread its tentacles far and wide. Mushtaq Mohammad said his question to Australia's captain, Allan Border, about how he would react if someone offered him £500,000 to throw the 1993 Edgbaston Test against England had been purely hypothetical, a joke that had been misunderstood. Sarfraz Nawaz, the former Pakistani pace bowler, who had re-emerged as a sports adviser to the Pakistani prime minister, Benazir Bhutto, claimed an anti-corruption committee had launched an investigation the previous year into "six or seven" players, including Malik. Imran Khan broke off from his wedding preparations with a vehement denial of reports that he had called for any perpetrators, if found guilty, to be hanged. He said the word he used was "banned".

Salim Malik was replaced as captain, and suspended, pending investigation, only for him to return as a batsman on Pakistan's tour of Australia in November 1995. Warne dismissed him, fourth ball, in the First Test in Brisbane. "It shows there is justice in the game," he said.

David Hopps is a cricket writer on The Guardian.

HAS THE GAME GOT WORSE?

Interviews by PAT MURPHY

NORMAN GIFFORD

Born 1940. Worcestershire 1960-1982; Warwickshire 1983-1988; Sussex coach/cricket manager 1989-1995; Durham coach 1996- . 710 first-class matches; 15 England caps.

It's so much more competitive now, and you can't expect it to be otherwise with all that extra prize money and prestige being dangled in front of the players. The extra emphasis on winning made me a casualty at Sussex. Winning a trophy gives you breathing space – look at Kent after winning the Sunday League last year – otherwise people say you're a load of rubbish. When I first started, you weren't expected to win anything, and as long as Worcestershire did OK in the two local derbies against Warwickshire, you didn't get much grief. I think the standard of wickets overall could be better and that's tied up with the emphasis on winning. They aren't conducive to the long-term development of cricketers. I'm also saddened by the reluctance of batsmen to walk any more. When I began my career, you walked if you knew you'd hit it, but now they leave it to the umpire. The emphasis on medical care and fitness is much greater now and the fielding is fantastic. Look at Trevor Penney: you can consider a batsman/fielder like him as an all-rounder. The players deserve the extra money now because of all the media pressure that's on them, getting their techniques dissected every day on the box. I wish the younger ones would talk more about the game, though. There are exceptions – like Jamie Hall at Sussex and Warwickshire's Andy Moles when he first started – but generally, they don't stand at the bar and drink in knowledge as well as beer, like we used to. Perhaps they spend too much time in a car, travelling to games.

JOHN EMBUREY

Born 1952. Middlesex 1973-1995; Northamptonshire coach 1996- . 499 first-class matches; 64 England caps.

The behaviour of players on the field has changed enormously in my time. All the hand-slapping and "high fives" have got out of hand. I noticed it in particular when I came back into the England side at Old Trafford last year, yet I still preferred to slap people on the back and say "well done" instead of risking a hernia with all that "high five" stuff. I get well paid to do my job and we should tell ourselves we're only doing our jobs when we do well, it's nothing out of the ordinary. I don't approve of close fielders shouting "well bowled" when someone is pitching the ball outside the off stump and the batsman isn't being troubled. It's unprofessional if you aren't bowling at the stumps or troubling the batsman in some way. I don't like to see players on match days walking around in public wearing shorts or T-shirts – that to me suggests a lack of pride in one's profession. Whites or blazers are respectable and show a respect for the job. The four-day game is a big plus for English cricket, but there are still too many under-prepared pitches. Too many matches are finishing prematurely due to poor wickets and that's not helping to develop spinners. I made my first-class debut in the era of uncovered wickets and that allowed greater variety: you had to bowl at different speeds, a different line and length according to the conditions. You had to learn how to bowl, but now spinners lack variety. The first-class game is less friendly than it was and captains are often responsible for that. Too much emphasis on winning. The media doesn't help. If you can't relax off the field because of the close attention of the media, the players are tensed up and aggressive and they take that out on the opposition on the field of play. But I believe that coaching is now more imaginative and thorough. There's more preparation involved and someone like Bob Woolmer was tremendous at getting his players to relax and to think more about their game. Dermot Reeve has carried that philosophy on at Warwickshire and they are now way ahead of other clubs in terms of talking out a game plan and at stretching their players, making a team of average players a highly successful unit. Other clubs, note.

EDDIE HEMMINGS

Born 1949. Warwickshire 1966-1978; Nottinghamshire 1979-1992; Sussex 1993-1995. 518 first-class matches; 16 England caps.

One of the big pluses is that at last proper wages are now being paid, so that you don't have to worry so much about getting work in the winter and you can go abroad and try to improve your cricket, without going broke. I've got two teenage sons who have professional ambitions in cricket and they can see an attractive career there. The fitness levels and fielding are far better. The running between the wickets is fantastic now: when the ball goes to third man, they're all thinking, "Is there two to him?" One-day cricket is a big plus and players ought to be grateful to that for bringing cricket to a wider public. It's exciting, it stretches you mentally and the public love it, so let's not be snooty. I like the increased media awareness about cricket and I think the TV coverage is beneficial, apart from the action replays affecting umpires' decisions. The game was fine enough without that artificiality. But I like the talk and speculation about the wicket before the game starts – that's good for those who are just coming into the game and the rest of us can just smile and listen. The product is now being marketed as positively as it was in Australia in the early eighties, and about time too. It means more money for the top players and that's something for the ambitious youngsters to aim for. Some of the young players are too complacent, though. They expect their sponsored cars on the first of April, instead of having to earn them. The same goes for first and second eleven caps. I don't see enough players enjoying themselves on the field as they used to – more slagging off than cracking jokes. Money matters, I suppose. For the same reason, sportsmanship has declined in my time. Sad – you're only cheating your fellow pros. I believe pitches nowadays don't help bowlers to learn their trade. They were far more accurate when bowling on flat wickets. Patience has gone from the Championship game. Batters don't wait for the bad ball; they're looking to

[Patrick Eagar

Above: 1965 – John Edrich hits Bryan Yuile for four on his way to 310 not out in the Headingley Test against New Zealand. No helmets, no advertising – and most of the spectators are wearing ties. *Below:* 1995 – Modern cricket at its most typical in a Headingley Test 30 years on. Graeme Hick sways away from a bouncer from Kenny Benjamin.

[Patrick Eagar

score all the time, taking risks, messing with their techniques. In my last three years at Sussex, all I did was bowl line and length, and the batters got themselves out. And bowlers aren't patient enough now – they don't seem to want to bowl three or four maidens in a row, lulling the batsman. They think that keeping it tight is boring; too many of them want close fielders round the bat, rather than thinking the batters out. Let the batsmen struggle, don't make it easy by putting all those slips in, leaving gaps all over the place.

CHRIS BROAD

Born 1957. Gloucestershire 1979-1983 and 1993-1994; Nottinghamshire 1984-1992. 340 first-class matches; 25 England caps.

At county level, the game is still run by amateurs; all those corporate hospitality people don't know about first-class cricket and its particular problems. I don't think playing standards have dropped in my time, and I'm pleased that the counties can now have only one overseas player registered. When I started with Gloucestershire, they were playing Procter, Sadiq and Zaheer, which didn't exactly help in the development of home-grown talent. The quality of wickets still concerns me – as you'd expect from a batsman – and it's hampering the prospects of unearthing bowlers of variety. Where are all the swing bowlers? Poor pitches mean bowlers don't have to work all that hard for success, but they get found out at Test level. The extra hype from TV is good for the game. I like all that coloured clothing razzmatazz; it shows the game is starting to move with the times and attracting different people. I don't think more cricket on TV is harming English cricket – crowds for Premiership soccer matches are up every season, even though there is so much of it on satellite TV now. My nine-year-old son has lots of cricket heroes and I'm sure that's because he watches them on television. Every sport needs its heroes. I am sad, though, that all the beneficial changes to cricket seem to be coming from whizz-kids in the southern hemisphere. Why can't England, the so-called home of cricket, move with the times and come up with some progressive ideas? At Lord's they just seem to sit back, rake in the money and don't develop a radical enough approach to safeguard the game.

JOHN CHILDS

Born 1951. Gloucestershire 1975-1984; Essex 1985- . 375 first-class matches; two England caps.

I suppose the generation gap is a problem – or in my case, the double generation gap. I do miss talking as a team about cricket at close of play. These days, the Essex youngsters go smartly back to our hotel, get their gear on and head for the liveliest place in town. That just leaves me and Graham Gooch to mull over the game and its pleasures over a quiet beer. I still enjoy county cricket a great deal, although the absence of walking and the extra harshness is a bit sad. Like Goochie, I find the fielding rather taxing now, and when I bat and have to face the likes of Wasim Akram or Allan Donald, that can be a little embarrassing. It's times like that when I envy the slow bowlers of yesteryear, whose job was solely to take wickets. They must have got more fun out of it in those less stressful days. All that sliding and throwing off-balance in the field is thrilling to watch, but I know I'd end up in a heap with a torn muscle if I tried it. Having said that, I don't think the quality of close catching is as good as it was when I started. Blokes like Keith Fletcher and Sadiq Mohammad made it look so easy, whereas today there seems rather more fuss. Perhaps they copy what they see on television; there certainly seems to be a lot of hysteria whenever a wicket falls in a Test match. The longer I play, the more aware I become of what the game involves and I do still cherish it. Lulling a batsman out of the crease and getting him stumped gives me so much more pleasure than slapping hands in the middle. I'm sad to see craftsmen like Eddie Hemmings retiring. How can the spinner survive? It has to be in pairs, and that's why I've been lucky with Peter Such at Essex. He's a similar cricketer to me – a specialist, who hasn't stunned anyone with fielding and batting skills – but loves the spider/fly aspect of slow bowling. For me six for 60 has always been preferable to keeping it tight and getting four for 35, and I would hate to think that flight bowlers will soon be gone from the game.

GEOFF COOK

Born 1951. Northamptonshire 1971-1990; Durham director of cricket 1991- . 460 first-class matches; seven England caps.

The most disappointing area of change is in the quality of pitches and the level of what is deemed acceptable now. That started with the covering of wickets and today the four-day games are being played on surfaces that are cynically prepared. Deduction of points seems draconian, but is the only way. I feel sorry for the umpires, who have to get the initial investigations under way. Umpires have a hell of a job nowadays, because pressures on their own careers make their lives harder. So much stems from cash considerations and the need to win. That reflects the society in which we live. I wouldn't like to be a county captain nowadays because of the demands of the players, the club and sponsors. Players are far more ambitious earlier in their career than they used to be, and they become disenchanted earlier, so that rumours of transfers to other counties get stronger. Soccer-style sackings of coaches and captains are more prevalent in cricket and I was very sad to see what happened to Norman Gifford at Sussex. He's a great man of cricket with a youthful, positive attitude to the game still, and you just can't dispense with such experience. The game is much less sentimental; it's a case of survival of the fittest. It's much more hard-nosed on the field, and the camaraderie isn't there any more. From a skills point of view much has changed in my time. When I started as an opening batsman, the swinging ball was something that had to be faced early on from the likes of Peter Lever, Ken Shuttleworth and Chris Old. Now it usually doesn't swing until it's about 30 overs old. The areas in which batsmen score are now so much wider, compared to the days when you'd play "through the V", through the covers or between mid-on and mid-wicket. Now batsmen play with greater virtuosity, partly through necessity because of the brilliant fielding and greater insight from captains into their field-placing.

BOB WOOLMER

Born 1948. Kent 1968-1984; Warwickshire director of coaching 1991-1994; South Africa coach 1994- . 350 first-class matches; 19 England caps.

The players of today are every bit as good as they were when I first started, but in a different way. Sports science is still in its infancy, but the players I've dealt with are very receptive: they're becoming more aware of what they're doing. The current crop are 50 per cent fitter than any of those I started with, but the intensity of international cricket now is huge. One-day cricket has decreased the life expectancy of an English professional, and increased injury problems. It's an exciting spectacle and hasn't altered techniques detrimentally, they just play differently. At Test level the game is being stifled. It's very difficult to play at such high intensity without showing emotion, and the introduction of a match referee has neutered the umpire's influence. The huge media coverage has blown up emotional responses to more than they really are and the standard of umpiring doesn't help. There aren't enough high-quality umpires coming through, the standards needed haven't kept up with the times and that leads to mistrust in the game.

ROBIN MARLAR

Born 1931. Cambridge University 1951-1953; Sussex 1951-1968. 289 first-class matches. Cricket correspondent, Sunday Times *1970-1996.*

What really annoys me is that the players don't have the command of the essential aspects of the game. You have bowlers who don't swing the ball, just bang it into the ground, spinners who don't turn it and just stop in their delivery stride, no bad-wicket experts in batting, no deftness in batsmanship because of the absence of uncovered wickets and using a plank of wood rather than a light bat. I do think batting has become more difficult because of the growth of extremely nasty fast bowlers who have formed a frightening challenge to the art of batting. The fast bowlers are taller, fitter, bouncier and it's very hard to score quickly when the ball is aimed between the left chest and left eye. The introduction of the helmet encapsulates that – a very stark event in cricket history. Coaching in English cricket is appalling. So many mediocrities are appointed to these jobs, and they're content with mediocrity. Why haven't we produced another world-class swing bowler since Ian Botham? The Test and County Cricket Board is a mess. It has to be reorganised like any other corporate activity. Any organisation that develops as much paperwork as the TCCB is in trouble. Committees are a form of non-organisation. The whole thing should be centralised like it is in South Africa, where Ali Bacher as the Board's managing director is publicly accountable, making quick decisions. At least he's decisive, for good or ill. All these county chairmen aren't qualified to talk about important issues concerning the game in England. But they do!

Pat Murphy joined the BBC in 1974 and is now BBC Radio's Midlands sports correspondent. He is the author of numerous cricket books including The Centurions *and* The Spinner's Turn.

FIFTY YEARS OF POST-WAR CRICKET

By MATTHEW ENGEL and PHILIP BAILEY

Had anyone but known it, there was a thrilling little contest going on at the end of the last English Championship season aside from the tight race to determine the destination of the 1995 title. Middlesex's last-gasp, one-run win over Leicestershire failed, in the end, to make them county champions. But it had an extra significance. That victory was their 434th in the fifty seasons of cricket that began in 1946 when the game resumed after Hitler stopped play. It was enough to squeeze them ahead of Surrey in the Wisden championship table of the past fifty years. Thus Middlesex can be declared county champions of the half-century in domestic cricket, with West Indies the world champions of the half-century.

The race in Test cricket was almost as close as among the counties. Australia's series victory in the West Indies and their sequence of home Test wins at the end of 1995 took them very near to the top of the fifty-year Test match table. Three further wins anywhere in 384 Tests would have made the difference. Indeed, three strategic runs would have made the difference: if the result of West Indies' one-run win at Adelaide in 1992-93 were reversed and if Australia had won either of the two Tests – against West Indies and India – they have tied, then they could be declared post-war champions. Better luck next half-century.

The contest for third place was even tighter. At the end of the 1995 English season, England were fourth behind South Africa. But the four draws at the start of the 1995-96 series between South Africa and England meant the teams reversed places – through a statistical quirk. Because South Africa have played fewer matches, the four draws dragged down their win percentage more than England's.

The Fifth Test at Newlands, which South Africa won, does not count in this table, because it took place after New Year 1996 and is thus in the next half-century. Had it been held in 1995, South Africa would have been back in third place.

Both these tables have been worked out using percentage of wins as the fairest basis for determining the champions. But since West Indies have also lost a smaller proportion of their matches than any of the other countries, there can be no dispute about their dominance. Splitting the fifty years up into decades, the durability of West Indies cricket emerges again. They were the leading team of the second, fourth and fifth decades of the period.

But teams have to play each other to prove anything conclusively, and the international cricketing programme has been (and to some extent remains) very haphazard. For most of this period South Africa were absent; before that they did not play three of their six possible opponents. Australia did not deign to play New Zealand for almost 28 years after the very first post-war Test match in March 1946 (which itself was granted Test status only retrospectively); and West Indies did not play for almost 19 months between Frank Worrell's triumphal tour of England in 1963 and Australia's visit to the Caribbean in 1964-65. Had that great team been playing some of the weaker countries of the era more often, their position in the table could have been even more impressive.

And the sight of South Africa at the head of the table of the next decade (dependent wholly on two series against Australia) is enough to re-open the most achingly unanswered question of modern cricket. What would have happened if a team including the Pollock brothers, Richards, Procter and Barlow had played against Lillee and Thomson's Australia or the pace-led West Indies that emerged in the late 1970s? We shall not find out this side of Elysium.

England's record remains dismal. Although they were almost certainly the strongest team in the world for most of the 1950s, they cannot be considered as champions of any period, even if one turns the tables around and divides the era into conventional decades. Seen that way, the figures show that Australia were champions of the 1950s (30 wins out of 58 between 1950 and 1959 compared to England's 39 out of 83) as well as the 1940s; with West Indies on top in the 1960s and 1980s; and South Africa (on the basis of four wins out of four) leading Australia in the 1970s.

The 1990s are turning into the tightest decade of all. At the end of the 1995 English season, Pakistan would have been on top. Since then Australia have taken the lead (29 wins out of 62 to Pakistan's 20 out of 43). West Indies and South Africa are both within range.

The English domestic tables provide more reliable indicators in the sense that everyone at least plays the same number of matches – except between 1960 and 1962 when counties had the choice of arranging 28 fixtures or 32, which explains the small discrepancy in the number of matches played. No statistics can rectify the built-in handicapping system of the Championship caused by the absence of players at Test matches, though they can at least confirm some ancient grumbles about the weather: Lancashire are the only county to have drawn more than half their matches.

The points system was changed too many times up to the mid-1970s to be helpful, so percentage of wins, as in Test cricket, is the only sensible guide to merit. Some rather surprising features do emerge. The gap between the top three in the fifty-year table and the rest is so enormous that, even if Essex or Warwickshire should walk away with the Championship for the next ten years, they would probably be unable to bridge the chasm. The eight teams from Essex in fourth place to Kent in 11th are fairly tightly bunched. Then there is another gap, before the next group of five. And it does come as a shock to find Nottinghamshire – champions twice in the 1980s – so far behind the other 16 established counties, with a win percentage not all that much better than Durham's. But their record between 1956 and 1975, when they averaged barely three and a half wins a year, was truly horrendous, even taking into account their brief flowering at the end of the 1960s when Gary Sobers arrived to inaugurate the age of instantly-qualified overseas professionals in county cricket.

This led to a much more egalitarian era and in the nine years from 1968 to 1976 nine different teams were champions; Yorkshire, who maintained their strict county-born policy until 1992, faded away. The record of the middle post-war decade, 1966-1975, reflects this. All but the bottom three counties are very tightly grouped, with only 27 wins separating the best, Kent, from the 14th, Essex.

Finally, there was another shift, as restrictions on imports slowly tightened again. In the past twenty years, only six counties have won the Championship. And although no one has come near to dominating the competition in the way Yorkshire and Surrey once did, there has been a clear distinction between the teams who played the game most combatively and the rest.

The five decades produce five different champions: Surrey, Yorkshire, Kent, Middlesex and Essex. And re-shuffling the figures into conventional decades produces similar results: Middlesex were champions of the 1940s, Surrey (naturally) of the 1950s, Yorkshire of the 1960s, Kent of the 1970s, when widespread overseas players brought about greater equality between the counties, Essex of the 1980s. So far, Warwickshire are the best of the 1990s.

But three teams emerge clearly as the best. Middlesex, Surrey and Yorkshire have, between them, won half the post-war Championships. But two of these teams have gone into eclipse, and it is Middlesex – where the leadership of Brearley and Gatting revived the successes of the Compton and Edrich days – who most justly embody the post-war era. The executives of the Test ground counties, excluding Middlesex, tried to band together last year, calling themselves The Big Five. Looking at these figures, it would be more realistic to talk about The Big Three. Or, if Middlesex really insist on being boastful, The Big One.

TEST MATCHES, 1946-1995

		P	W	L	D	T	% W	% L	% D
1	West Indies	298	120	65	112	1	40.26	21.81	37.58
2	Australia	384	152	99	131	2	39.58	25.78	34.11
3	England	479	146	132	201	0	30.48	27.55	41.96
4	South Africa	109	33	35	41	0	30.27	32.11	37.61
5	Pakistan	228	62	53	113	0	27.19	23.24	49.56
6	India	288	54	92	141	1	18.75	31.94	48.95
7	New Zealand	227	33	95	99	0	14.53	41.85	43.61
8	Sri Lanka	65	7	30	28	0	10.76	46.15	43.07
9	Zimbabwe	14	1	7	6	0	7.14	50.00	42.85
		2,092	608	608	872	4	29.06	29.06	41.68

COUNTY CHAMPIONSHIP, 1946-95

		P	W	L	D	T	% W	% L	% D
1	Middlesex	1,221	434	275	509	3	35.54	22.52	41.68
2	Surrey	1,221	433	259	529	0	35.46	21.21	43.32
3	Yorkshire	1,233	427	239	565	2	34.63	19.38	45.82
4	Essex	1,221	361	301	555	4	29.56	24.65	45.45
5	Warwickshire	1,233	352	333	547	1	28.54	27.00	44.36
6	Worcestershire	1,233	351	329	552	1	28.46	26.68	44.76
7	Northamptonshire	1,221	339	308	571	3	27.76	25.22	46.76
8	Gloucestershire	1,221	335	388	496	2	27.43	31.77	40.62
9	Lancashire	1,233	337	277	617	2	27.33	22.46	50.04
10	Hampshire	1,233	334	351	544	4	27.08	28.46	44.12
11	Kent	1,221	330	364	523	4	27.02	29.81	42.83
12	Derbyshire	1,221	301	354	565	1	24.65	28.99	46.27
13	Somerset	1,233	301	414	518	0	24.41	33.57	42.01
14	Leicestershire	1,221	293	392	535	1	23.99	32.10	43.81
15	Glamorgan	1,233	294	363	576	0	23.84	29.44	46.71
16	Sussex	1,233	290	399	539	5	23.51	32.36	43.71
17	Nottinghamshire	1,221	256	391	573	1	20.96	32.02	46.92
18	Durham	73	12	43	18	0	16.43	58.90	24.65
		20,926	5,780	5,780	9,332	34	27.62	27.62	44.59

TEST MATCHES

Figures exclude matches abandoned without a ball bowled. Tests included are those up to and including the end of the calendar year 1995. In a ten-year split, a match is included under the year in which it finished.

1946-55		P	W	L	D	% W	% L	% D
1	Australia	51	30	8	13	58.82	15.68	25.49
2	England	83	28	24	31	33.73	28.91	37.34
3	West Indies	35	11	10	14	31.42	28.57	40.00
4	South Africa	37	10	17	10	27.02	45.94	27.02
5	Pakistan	17	4	3	10	23.52	17.64	58.82
6	India	40	4	12	24	10.00	30.00	60.00
7	New Zealand	25	0	13	12	0.00	52.00	48.00
		288	87	87	114	30.20	30.20	39.58

1956-65		P	W	L	D	T	% W	% L	% D
1	West Indies	47	21	12	13	1	44.68	25.53	27.65
2	England	95	36	17	42	0	37.89	17.89	44.21
3	Australia	63	23	11	28	1	36.50	17.46	44.44
4	Pakistan	33	6	11	16	0	18.18	33.33	48.48
5	South Africa	36	6	12	18	0	16.66	33.33	50.00
6	India	47	6	18	23	0	12.76	38.29	48.93
7	New Zealand	37	3	20	14	0	8.10	54.05	37.83
		358	101	101	154	2	28.21	28.21	43.01

1966-75		P	W	L	D	% W	% L	% D
1	South Africa	9	7	1	1	77.77	11.11	11.11
2	Australia	70	30	18	22	42.85	25.71	31.42
3	England	93	28	18	47	30.10	19.35	50.53
4	India	43	11	21	11	25.58	48.83	25.58
5	West Indies	57	14	16	27	24.56	28.07	47.36
6	New Zealand	40	5	15	20	12.50	37.50	50.00
7	Pakistan	26	1	7	18	3.84	26.92	69.23
		338	96	96	146	28.40	28.40	43.19

1976-85		P	W	L	D	% W	% L	% D
1	West Indies	80	35	10	35	43.75	12.50	43.75
2	England	103	35	28	40	33.98	27.18	38.83
3	Pakistan	78	24	17	37	30.76	21.79	47.43
4	Australia	104	31	42	31	29.80	40.38	29.80
5	New Zealand	57	15	22	20	26.31	38.59	35.08
6	India	94	15	27	52	15.95	28.72	55.31
7	Sri Lanka	18	1	10	7	5.55	55.55	38.88
		534	156	156	222	29.21	29.21	41.57

1986-95		P	W	L	D	T	% W	% L	% D
1	West Indies	79	39	17	23	0	49.36	21.51	29.11
2	Australia	96	38	20	37	1	39.58	20.83	38.54
3	South Africa	27	10	5	12	0	37.03	18.51	44.44
4	Pakistan	74	27	15	32	0	36.48	20.27	43.24
5	India	64	18	14	31	1	28.12	21.87	48.43
6	England	105	19	45	41	0	18.09	42.85	39.04
7	New Zealand	68	10	25	33	0	14.70	36.76	48.52
8	Sri Lanka	47	6	20	21	0	12.76	42.55	44.68
9	Zimbabwe	14	1	7	6	0	7.14	50.00	42.85
		574	168	168	236	2	29.26	29.26	41.11

COUNTY CHAMPIONSHIP

1946-55		P	W	L	D	T	% W	% L	% D
1	Surrey	272	135	60	77	0	49.63	22.05	28.30
2	Yorkshire	272	133	35	103	1	48.89	12.86	37.86
3	Middlesex	272	119	69	83	1	43.75	25.36	30.51
4	Lancashire	272	104	37	129	2	38.23	13.60	47.42
5	Warwickshire	272	92	78	101	1	33.82	28.67	37.13
6	Gloucestershire	272	89	80	103	0	32.72	29.41	37.86
7	Derbyshire	272	86	86	100	0	31.61	31.61	36.76
8	Glamorgan	272	84	65	123	0	30.88	23.89	45.22
9	Sussex	272	74	91	105	2	27.20	33.45	38.60
10	Hampshire	272	72	100	97	3	26.47	36.76	35.66
11	Worcestershire	272	71	106	95	0	26.10	38.97	34.92
12	Kent	272	66	118	87	1	24.26	43.38	31.98
13	Leicestershire	272	62	107	102	1	22.79	39.33	37.50
14 {	Essex	272	59	86	125	2	21.69	31.61	45.95
	Nottinghamshire	272	59	84	129	0	21.69	30.88	47.42
16	Northamptonshire	272	58	81	131	2	21.32	29.77	48.16
17	Somerset	272	56	136	80	0	20.58	50.00	29.41
		4,624	1,419	1,419	1,770	16	30.68	30.68	38.27

1956-65		P	W	L	D	T	% W	% L	% D
1	Yorkshire	292	123	48	121	0	42.12	16.43	41.43
2	Surrey	280	108	53	119	0	38.57	18.92	42.50
3	Middlesex	280	97	70	113	0	34.64	25.00	40.35
4	Northamptonshire	280	96	63	121	0	34.28	22.50	43.21
5	Worcestershire	292	100	67	125	0	34.24	22.94	42.80
6	Gloucestershire	280	89	99	91	1	31.78	35.35	32.50
7	Hampshire	292	90	74	128	0	30.82	25.34	43.83
8	Glamorgan	292	87	97	108	0	29.79	33.21	36.98
9	Somerset	292	86	109	97	0	29.45	37.32	33.21
10	Essex	280	81	69	129	1	28.92	24.64	46.07
11	Warwickshire	292	84	75	133	0	28.76	25.68	45.54
12	Derbyshire	280	80	83	117	0	28.57	29.64	41.78
13	Lancashire	292	80	88	124	0	27.39	30.13	42.46
14	Sussex	292	79	90	123	0	27.05	30.82	42.12
15	Kent	280	71	88	121	0	25.35	31.42	43.21
16	Nottinghamshire	280	44	126	110	0	15.71	45.00	39.28
17	Leicestershire	280	41	137	102	0	14.64	48.92	36.42
		4,856	1,436	1,436	1,982	2	29.57	29.57	40.81

1966-75		P	W	L	D	T	% W	% L	% D
1	Kent	236	78	52	106	0	33.05	22.03	44.91
2	Yorkshire	236	74	51	110	1	31.35	21.61	46.61
3	Surrey	236	70	37	129	0	29.66	15.67	54.66
4 {	Leicestershire	236	68	48	120	0	28.81	20.33	50.84
	Worcestershire	236	68	50	118	0	28.81	21.18	50.00
	Hampshire	236	66	49	120	1	27.96	20.76	50.84
6 {	Northamptonshire	236	66	62	108	0	27.96	26.27	45.76
	Warwickshire	236	66	58	112	0	27.96	24.57	47.45
9	Glamorgan	236	58	62	116	0	24.57	26.27	49.15
10	Somerset	236	57	64	115	0	24.15	27.11	48.72
11	Middlesex	236	56	55	123	2	23.72	23.30	52.11
12	Lancashire	236	55	39	142	0	23.30	16.52	60.16
13	Gloucestershire	236	52	75	109	0	22.03	31.77	46.18
14	Essex	236	51	60	124	1	21.61	25.42	52.54
15	Derbyshire	236	39	66	131	0	16.52	27.96	55.50
16	Sussex	236	38	96	101	1	16.10	40.67	42.79
17	Nottinghamshire	236	29	67	140	0	12.28	28.38	59.32
		4,012	991	991	2,024	6	24.70	24.70	50.44

1976-85		P	W	L	D	T	% W	% L	% D
1	Middlesex	224	92	40	92	0	41.07	17.85	41.07
2	Essex	224	87	36	101	0	38.83	16.07	45.08
3 {	Kent	224	62	46	114	2	27.67	20.53	50.89
	Leicestershire	224	62	37	125	0	27.67	16.51	55.80
5	Surrey	224	59	50	115	0	26.33	22.32	51.33
6	Sussex	224	58	54	111	1	25.89	24.10	49.55
7	Nottinghamshire	224	57	60	107	0	25.44	26.78	47.76
8	Somerset	224	56	51	117	0	25.00	22.76	52.23
9	Hampshire	224	52	70	102	0	23.21	31.25	45.53
10 {	Northamptonshire	224	50	51	122	1	22.32	22.76	54.46
	Yorkshire	224	50	43	131	0	22.32	19.19	58.48
12	Gloucestershire	224	48	60	116	0	21.42	26.78	51.78
13	Worcestershire	224	43	65	116	0	19.19	29.01	51.78
14	Derbyshire	224	41	56	127	0	18.30	25.00	56.69
15	Warwickshire	224	40	68	116	0	17.85	30.35	51.78
16	Lancashire	224	32	56	136	0	14.28	25.00	60.71
17	Glamorgan	224	27	73	124	0	12.05	32.58	55.35
		3,808	916	916	1,972	4	24.05	24.05	51.78

1986-95		P	W	L	D	T	% W	% L	% D
1	Essex	209	83	50	76	0	39.71	23.92	36.36
2 {	Middlesex	209	70	41	98	0	33.49	19.61	46.88
	Warwickshire	209	70	54	85	0	33.49	25.83	40.66
4 {	Northamptonshire	209	69	51	89	0	33.01	24.40	42.58
	Worcestershire	209	69	41	98	1	33.01	19.61	46.88
6	Nottinghamshire	209	67	54	87	1	32.05	25.83	41.62
7	Lancashire	209	66	57	86	0	31.57	27.27	41.14
8	Surrey	209	61	59	89	0	29.18	28.22	42.58
9	Leicestershire	209	60	63	86	0	28.70	30.14	41.14
10	Gloucestershire	209	57	74	77	1	27.27	35.40	36.84
11	Derbyshire	209	55	63	90	1	26.31	30.14	43.06
12	Hampshire	209	54	58	97	0	25.83	27.75	46.41
13	Kent	209	53	60	95	1	25.35	28.70	45.45
14	Yorkshire	209	47	62	100	0	22.48	29.66	47.84
15	Somerset	209	46	54	109	0	22.00	25.83	52.15
16	Sussex	209	41	68	99	1	19.61	32.53	47.36
17	Glamorgan	209	38	66	105	0	18.18	31.57	50.23
18	Durham	73	12	43	18	0	16.43	58.90	24.65
		3,626	1,018	1,018	1,584	6	28.07	28.07	43.68

All abandoned matches are included as draws.

Champions: In the 50 years since the war Surrey and Yorkshire have been outright champions 8 times, Middlesex 7, Essex 6, Worcestershire 5, Warwickshire 4, Glamorgan, Hampshire, Kent and Nottinghamshire 2 and Leicestershire 1. Middlesex have been joint champions twice, Kent, Lancashire, Surrey and Yorkshire once.

Wooden spoons: Since the war Nottinghamshire have finished bottom of the table 8 times, Somerset 7, Glamorgan 6, Leicestershire and Sussex 5, Derbyshire and Gloucestershire 4, Northamptonshire 3, Durham and Warwickshire 2, and Essex, Hampshire, Kent and Yorkshire once.

THE LAST OF THE LINE

By DAVID FRITH

The generations slip gently away. All the Edwardian Golden Age cricketers are gone. And in 1995, within 93 days, the last two truly eminent English survivors of the 1920s and 1930s died. R. E. S. Wyatt and Harold Larwood were not the last living pre-war Test cricketers, but they were clearly the most outstanding of the oldest soldiers, and symbolic of the two English divisions, the two castes: amateur and professional, Gentleman and Player.

All about them was contrast: their backgrounds, their speech, their education, their financial standing. Yet united they stood as two of the toughest and most resilient cricketers ever to have represented England: Larwood (H.), the Nottinghamshire express bowler, and Mr R. E. S. Wyatt, the very serious Warwickshire and later Worcestershire captain, who was vice-captain during England's notorious 1932-33 "Bodyline" tour of Australia.

The former miner finished that explosive venture with a broken foot, which might have been coupled with a broken heart had he been made of lesser stuff, for he was expected to shoulder all the blame when those who ran English cricket finally came to comprehend the malodorous nature of D. R. Jardine's strategy.

Larwood was accessible in his Sydney home, where he spent more than half his life after emigrating in 1950 with his wife Lois and their five daughters. In short-sleeved shirt, braces and slippers, liberated from the drudgery of a sweet-shop in Blackpool, he would tell visitors of his pride in his achievements as a cricketer, of his respect for his vilified skipper, of his undying love for his homeland and his gratitude to Australia, where he had once been hated and abused during that acrimonious 1932-33 tour, when his bumpers crashed into Australian flesh. He never lost that sense of wonder at the warmth of welcome extended to him by his former adversaries, though in truth Australia was proud to accommodate a sporting icon of such dimension and vintage. England had been the losers, not just in their refusal to open the way for Larwood's return to the Test side later in the 1930s.

In a faintly anachronistic panama hat, and latterly in need of sturdy walking-sticks, Mr Wyatt was also accessible whenever he left his remote home in Cornwall to watch cricket or attend functions in the metropolis. In spite of his physical discomfort he journeyed till the end with his wife Mollie – South Africa in 1989, Lord's summer after summer, at ease in Paul Getty's box in the new Mound Stand. From that vantage-point, the action out in the middle gradually became a blur, though the memory – of olden days if not of last week – never failed. Didn't Percy Chapman make a century here against Australia in 1930 when Bob Wyatt was not playing? Yes – missed before he'd scored a run!

The nonagenarian with the basset-hound eyes and slightly glottal voice, in common with the old fast bowler who now lived on the other side of the world, was firm in his opinions. Mr Wyatt loved theory. He would talk at length and with passionate conviction on the iniquities of the lbw law (among other things, he believed it discouraged backplay).

[*Popperfoto*

HAROLD LARWOOD, 1934

[*Popperfoto*

BOB WYATT, 1935

[*Patrick Eagar*

HAROLD LARWOOD, 1977

[*Patrick Eagar*

BOB WYATT, 1980

Larwood, for his part, was good on whether a batsman stood up to fast bowling or revealed a shortfall in courage. At his most animated he could still be scathing in the matter of Australian "heart" in that particular Test series with which, alas, he will always be linked. Always, though, he referred to his old captain as Mr Jardine (or "the Skipper") and to the MCC vice-captain as Mr Wyatt. Decades in Australia's egalitarian environment came too late for him to throw off the code of etiquette into which he had been born in 1904.

These two old cricketers were characteristic of the two classes of pre-war English life which coalesced into an often formidable Test team, rather as a horse and jockey become one for the purpose of their challenge. Those who made the acquaintance of Larwood and Mr Wyatt over the past half-century could only study photographs or close their eyes to imagine what they were like all those years ago.

For Mr Wyatt, one would fancy a bright blazer, an upturned shirt collar, a period cottage adorned with climbing roses, a pair of red setters reclining on the lawn, and a fairly fine motor-car in the garage. There might also, among the mail on his hall carpet, have been some sort of medical report following the latest of his countless injuries. And a disputatious letter from a club committeeman.

For Larwood, picture a foaming tankard of beer and a cigarette, a respectable suit and a respectable trilby hat, and a virile ease among his fellow professionals which might quickly tense up when any of the "officer class" came by. It would take little imagination to discern for which political party each of them might have voted.

Mr Wyatt and Larwood, at opposite ends of the social and economic scales in the 1920s, when both were first chosen to play for England, could scarcely have been further apart physically from 1950 onwards, with the Larwood family resident 12,000 miles away, where so many of the disillusioned have thrown off their shackles.

That they held each other in deep respect is beyond question. Visualise cricket's 1995 Legion of the Departed as they shuffled up the steps of the Greatest Pavilion: "After you, Lol . . ." "Naw, after you, Mr Wyatt . . ."

If there was any final imbalance, it was that Prime Minister John Major, he who wished to create a classless society, gave Harold Larwood an MBE by way of long-overdue atonement. Bob Wyatt was never thus recognised. It was as illogical and unjust as Larwood's ostracism by Lord's following Bodyline.

David Frith founded Wisden Cricket Monthly *in 1979 and edited the magazine until 1996. He is the author of a number of cricket books, including* The Fast Men.

MIRACLE IN QUEENSLAND
(SOMEWHAT BELATED)

By GIDEON HAIGH

"It behoves the young players of the present day to prove themselves throughout the cricket struggles that are ahead of them, to be worthy in every way of the honour conferred on their association by the conference of the Sheffield Shield States in the year 1926." – E. H. Hutcheon, Queensland cricketer and historian.

It took 68 years and nearly 500 matches before Queensland cricketers proved equal to their behoving: at 3.52 p.m. precisely, Tuesday March 28, 1995, was transformed into VQ Day, when the state beat South Australia by an innings and 101 runs and finally took custody of Australia's symbol of interstate cricket supremacy.

To make himself audible above the celebratory din of his "Banana Army" of supporters, and to adjust to the sensation of victory, captain Stuart Law enunciated his post-match remarks carefully: "We have won the Shield. It does sound strange saying it. It's just a fantastic feeling to finally have that thing in our room, to hold it up above our heads and feel really proud. It's been the longest week ever. We've won it. Now we can get on with enjoying life again."

Law's team was still encircled by 1,000 revellers at midnight. Nobody the next day would have pissed a fatness test. Given the 14 occasions the state have been runners-up in the Shield, Queensland have always been wary of the Ides of March. They have traditionally been sombre and self-recriminatory times: Where did we go wrong this time? Whom should we sack this time? Is our state cursed? Should the captain/coach/groundsman/Premier go?

The last time Queensland were in possession of the Shield was before their opening match in 1926, when it was borrowed from New South Wales for a shop window display. In the meantime, the nearest they had come was winning the Bougainville Sheffield Shield, contested by Australian soldiers in the South Pacific who were awaiting repatriation after VJ Day. This Shield was actually the casing of a military shell.

In 1995, however, the real Shield arrived. The players took it on a three-day tour in a Government plane round the state's vast hinterland. There was a ticker-tape parade in Brisbane itself, a vintage car cavalcade in Mackay, an escort by Harley-Davidson bikers in Mount Isa, and a quick trip to Kynuna (population: 25). It was all such a novelty that in one town they left it behind.

Fortune toyed with Queensland from their admission to join New South Wales, Victoria and South Australia in the Shield in 1926-27. Set 400 to win in their first match by NSW's Alan Kippax, local captain Leo O'Connor was run out by debutant Gordon Amos for 196, only 19 short of victory, and he saw his side lose by a paltry eight runs. O'Connor was presented with engraved gold cufflinks in honour of his resistance, but there were precious few other spoils before the Second World War: Queensland won only a dozen Shield matches and lost 53.

Having established a tradition of wretched defeat for Queensland, it was fitting that Amos should establish another: he crossed the border to play for

Queensland in 1927-28. (Poignantly, Amos died, aged 90, ten days after the final.) In that first match, ten of the Queensland team had been born in the state. But an amazing squad could be assembled from Queensland's VIPs (Very Imported Players): extra-colonials Colin McCool, Ray Lindwall, Greg Chappell, Jeff Thomson, Dirk Wellham, Ian Davis, Ray Phillips, Allan Border and Paul Jackson; extra-continentals Kepler Wessels, Majid Khan, Vivian Richards, Tom Graveney, Graeme Hick, Alvin Kallicharran, Rusi Surti, Ian Botham and Wes Hall.

It is a squad to beat the world, but not the rest of Australia. While a few gave their all, others gave only some and at least a handful provided precious little. Queensland seemed in some seasons likelier to win the FA Cup than the Sheffield Shield. And that the most consciously patriotic and occasionally separatist Australian state should acquire such a dependency struck many as eccentric. The Olympic swimming coach Laurie Lawrence wrote, after Queensland crumbled again a couple of years ago: "Imports are not the answer, or at least they are not the answer that will give any Queenslander any satisfaction."

Year after year, John Morton, the sports editor of the now defunct Brisbane *Telegraph*, used to run the same headline at the start of the season: "This is the Year." And people were intoning the words this time. But otherwise Queensland's 1994-95 campaign drew an altogether different feel, from its investment in homespun talent. Law's squad were, if not native, at least long resident in the state: Border's career with NSW and left-arm spinner Jackson's prior duties in Victoria are now some yellow books back.

Blown in from such outposts as Toowoomba, Wondai, Bileola, Kingaroy, Innisfail and Mundubberra, and mingling the born-again Border and the indestructible Carl Rackemann with the supple skills of tyros like Martin Love, Jim Maher, Wade Seccombe and Andrew Symonds, they played with resource and without regret.

The Gabba was being refurbished and the schedule proved too inflexible to allow the Sir Leslie Wilson Stand a few days' grace for the final, though spectators enlisted the debris in their visions of victory. The Brisbane bard, "Rupert" McCall – a modern-day Albert Craig – wrote this pre-match doggerel for the Brisbane *Courier-Mail*:

> Let's get out there and win 'cos we're the best team in the land,
> Let's demolish South Australia like the Leslie Wilson Stand.

Which Queensland did. Their 664 was more than enough to overwhelm South Australia and, since a draw was going to be enough anyway, locals were able to savour the prospect of victory for at least three days before its arrival. Grown men – as they do in all the best sports stories – wept. John Maclean, chairman of the Queensland Cricket Association, greeted century-maker and player-of-the-season Trevor Barsby with tears of joy running down his face saying: "You don't know what you've done." He probably didn't. And that may have been why he and his team-mates were able to do it.

Gideon Haigh is an Australian author and freelance journalist.

Major Tim Bible, collector of cricketing pub signs, outside The Cricketers, Southampton.

BAT, BALL AND BITTER: CRICKET AND PUBS

The connection between cricket and alcohol is probably as old as the game itself. Innkeepers were among the first promoters of organised cricket. But it is reasonable to imagine that even before then, the shepherd boys who played on the downs had a quick noggin after the game, and very probably during it too.

The tie-up is reflected in that very British form of everyday history: the inn sign. Hundreds of pubs all over England have cricketing names, sometimes reflecting a link dating back into the mists of mediaeval times, sometimes reflecting some modern marketing man's half-baked idea for a trendy theme pub.

Tim Bible, an army major from Romsey, Hampshire, has turned this arcane but fascinating subject into his hobby. He has a collection of 250 photos of signs with cricketing connections, and knows there are dozens more he has yet to photograph; cricket is represented on a surprisingly high proportion of the nation's 50,000-odd pubs. Bible has logged more than thirty Cricketers, Cricketers Arms, Cricketers Inns (breweries don't seem to worry about apostrophes much) and related titles in his home county alone. They are equally thick on the ground in the other counties of cricket's ancient heartland – Kent, Surrey and Sussex. Yorkshire is well-stocked too. But other places, where the game is popular but perhaps a little less old, have surprisingly few: Bible has found only one in each of Gloucestershire and Devon.

The inn sign in Britain dates back to the Roman invasion, according to Alan Wright, secretary of the Inn Signs Society. "Alehouse keepers had to give illiterate customers an indication of what they were selling and it would become known that you could get a good drink at the sign of whatever it was," he said. "As soon as religious signs gave way to everyday signs, sport became a popular subject, often because the game could be played on the premises. Usually The Cricketers used to mean there was a green nearby, and some of them would have functioned as pavilions."

The most famous of all cricketing pubs was the home of Hambledon: the Bat and Ball at Broadhalfpenny Down in Hampshire. But this has recently had to overcome a bizarre attempt to change its name to Natterjacks. Since 1993 the pub has in effect been using both names, but there are hopes that cricket and history will eventually emerge triumphant. Outside Sevenoaks, there is a Bat and Ball railway station. The trains still stop, but the pub is reported to have closed.

The tradition, however, is a durable one. And for every cricketing pub that vanishes or changes its name, another one seems to pop up. The drearily named New Inn in West Meon, Hampshire, became the Thomas Lord in 1952 to commemorate the founder of Lord's, who is buried in the village. And in Dewsbury, Yorkshire, there is now the "Sir" Geoffrey Boycott OBE. It was originally called The Park, then reopened in 1995 under its new name, with a sign depicting Boycott taking strike in his England gear. The owner, Bernard Poulter, has been collecting memorabilia and books, has organised his own pub team, and is hoping for a visit from the great man shortly.

On the Darnall estate in Sheffield is the Fiery Fred, opened by Fred Trueman about 15 years ago. Unfortunately, the actual sign was stolen by souvenir hunters and has never been replaced. Other pubs noted by Major Bible as being named after players include two Dr W. G. Graces (in London and Chesterfield), The Spofforth in Liverpool, The Larwood in Mansfield, and a bar called Sobers (which may be an elaborate pun) in Derby. His own favourite signs include the Cricketers at Wrecclesham, Surrey, which depicts Billy Beldham, the Cricketers Arms at Keighley, with the young Len Hutton, and the Maiden Over in Earley, Reading, showing a girl jumping over the stumps.

Some names are not necessarily connected with cricket, but the sign-painter has chosen to emphasise the cricketing side of a double meaning – as at the Dog and Duck in Bristol, the Last Man Inn in the Cumberland village of Plumbland and the First In, Last Out in Bath. There is also the Tommy Wass in Leeds – apparently named after a local landowner, not the Nottinghamshire bowler, though there is a cricketer on the coat of arms on the sign. Most bizarre perhaps is Le Toad and Stumps (formerly The Lamb) at Eversley Cross in Hampshire. The landlord, Tim Paine, had intended to call it Le Toad and Stump, meaning a tree-stump. But an artist did him a really nice cartoon involving cricket stumps. So the most English of games crept on to the sign along with the strange franglais. The pub is, after all, next to the village ground.

You would expect some pubs to have cricketing names, like The Sussex Cricketer, right by the Hove ground, and the Larwood and Voce Tavern at Trent Bridge. But it is good to report that the game survives in the most improbable places: there is a Cricketers Arms right by the rugby league stadium in Widnes, and the supporters traditionally go there to discuss the afternoon's mayhem.

NEXT – SCHOOLBOYS IN PYJAMAS?

BY ANDREW LONGMORE

It was only a matter of time before the last barricades of "proper" cricket came tumbling down. In the West Country in the summer of 1995, seven public schools formed their own 55-overs league, marking a significant move away from the traditional game in the schools. The league produced some bright, positive cricket too, with masters reporting a greater sense of involvement within teams and increased enthusiasm for the game.

"There was a real buzz about the place when we had an overs game," Ray Codd, head of games at King's College in Taunton, said. This was bad news for those who believe that overs cricket will poison tender minds just as surely as it has ruined professional techniques.

Five months earlier, in late spring, Codd had sat in the Long Room at Lord's, underneath the portrait of W. G. Grace and alongside 140 other cricket masters and school representatives listening to a lament delivered by Dr Tim Woods of Trent College at a forum organised by MCC. Dr Woods warned that cricket was losing credibility in the schools because the timed game produced too many dull draws. Cricket was therefore regarded as boring by many teenagers, who were turning to sports offering more instant excitement. The game, he added, had to become brighter and sharper to capture the more demanding imaginations of the young.

Dr Woods advocated matches of 110 overs, split 60-50 in favour of the side batting first, as a way of eliminating stalemate and stimulating competition. The idea triggered a lively discussion about the pros and cons of limited-overs cricket for schools. On the one hand: bad batting habits, defensive bowling and unambitious field placing – the formulaic cricket which had ruined many of the leagues in Yorkshire and Lancashire. On the other hand: improved standards of fielding, better running between the wickets and more aggressive batting. The arguments on both sides were largely adapted from the county game. The real message of the evening, though, was more fundamental.

The assembled cricket masters – consciences clicking, excuses whirring – stood accused of the professional vice of elevating the result above the game, of deliberately playing not to lose. Some, privately, defended their negative attitudes on the grounds that, like football managers, they would be dismissed if their teams lost too often; success at sport is one of the best ways for schools to attract publicity in a competitive market. Others scoured their souls and found no guilt. "Me? Negative? Ah yes, but we were 20 for four and the wicket was poor and, goodness, did we bat that long? Well, we were playing Harrow and the previous year they'd batted on after tea . . ." Feuds are surprisingly commonplace in schools cricket.

David Walsh, of Tonbridge School, who chaired the meeting, said that it did not matter whether the game was limited-overs or timed, attitude was all-important. "Challenge your cricketers," he said. "Give them a sense of enjoyment and adventure." He saw no harm in having a balance of fixtures, some limited-overs, some timed, which would satisfy the twin – and often conflicting – aims of attracting the young to cricket, boys and girls, while developing the best of them into potential Test cricketers.

The idea of the West Country league arose after King's, Taunton, toured Western Australia. The league was not quite as limited as it seemed. Imaginative use of bonus points encouraged sides not to defend too quickly and a match could end in a draw, the side batting first automatically earning eight points for a "winning" draw, their opponents four points for a "losing" draw. Bonus points were awarded in the first innings for every 25 runs scored over 125 up to a maximum of four, and for the third wicket and every two thereafter. An outright win was worth 16 points. The seven schools (King's, Taunton were joined by Millfield, Clifton, Blundell's, Taunton School, Sherborne and King's School, Bruton) played each other at six different levels: three senior, Under-16, Under-15 and Under-14. All except the first team played 40 overs a side.

One game, in particular, brought out the best of overs cricket. At 98 for five at lunch after 34 overs against Sherborne, Clifton had no option but to force the pace in the afternoon; they made 212 and won the match by 60 runs. "Based on previous experience, I could have envisaged a dull draw," wrote Mike Nurton, the Sherborne cricket master. "The match was an endorsement of limited-overs cricket at school level."

Overs cricket, though, has a habit of starting brightly only to stagnate as tactics become more sophisticated. Cricket masters and coaches must know where to draw the line, or Eton will soon be strolling out to play Harrow at Lord's dressed in light blue pyjamas and sponsored by a brewery.

Andrew Longmore is a sports feature writer on The Times.

FIFTY YEARS OF THE CRICKET WRITERS' CLUB

By DEREK HODGSON

In the autumn of 1946, as the MCC touring team, under Walter Hammond, arrived at Perth aboard a ship containing 14 British cricket correspondents and 600 war brides, there appeared a gap in the schedule of about a month before the first post-war tour of Australia began, a delay caused by the necessity of having to adhere to transport schedules disrupted by what was still described as "the late emergency".

To fill the time the correspondents, joined by Australian writers from the eastern cities, formed a cricket club. Arthur Mailey proposed it should be named the "Empire Cricket Writers' Club" and its first club tie – believed to be the only one immediately available in bulk – featured a skull and crossbones.

The old ECWC could field a formidable XI, including Fingleton, Whitington, Grimmett, Richardson, Mailey, O'Reilly, Oldfield, Sellers, Bowes, Duckworth and Wellings. At St Kilda they attracted a crowd of 15,000 to watch them play Victoria Past and Present and the public address announcer (a racing man) delighted the dressing-room by announcing how pleased he was to see "Bill O'Reilly bowling again, all arms and legs". It was Bill Bowes.

The notion of such a club was too good to be discarded. At the Trent Bridge Test the following summer, 1947, a more permanent structure was erected: the Cricket Writers' Club, with E. W. Swanton as chairman,

Charles Bray secretary and Archie Ledbrooke treasurer. The CWC thus became the forerunner of many other clubs in different branches of sports writing. National prominence was achieved in 1948, when Bradman and his Australians were invited to a dinner attended by the Duke of Edinburgh. There were six speeches, and those by Bradman and Sir Norman Birkett were broadcast by the BBC, causing the nine o'clock radio news to be delayed.

Club dinners in those days were lavish affairs, often held in liveried halls. Not that dinners were always formal and polite. Basil Easterbrook, chairman in 1965, remembered before he died how "an attempt was made to ban drinking until after the AGM which used to precede the annual dinner. There was much noise, calls for order and the singing of a ribald chorus of 'On Rosenwater's doorstep, down Leytonstone way' to the tune of *Mother Kelly*. Irving Rosenwater was a leading member at that time and some of the club's elder statesmen were angry enough to walk out." Dicky Rutnagur believes John Arlott was the chairman at that meeting and, as was his custom, had taken the odd sip of wine: "John tried hard to bring some order to the proceedings by banging the table with a spoon, but he missed the table."

The serious work consists largely of consultation, now on almost a weekly basis, with the TCCB, MCC and the first-class counties. The club's most famous contribution has been the Young Cricketer of the Year award, started in 1950 at the instigation of Archie Ledbrooke, who was to die in the Munich air crash. Out of 47 winners (there was a tie in 1986) only six have failed to become England players, though Andrew Symonds, the 1995 choice, might be a seventh if he opts to play for Australia instead.

A newer award is named after a former much-loved chairman, Peter Smith, and is presented "for services to the presentation of cricket to the public". The chairman of the sub-committee making the award is the editor of this Almanack and recipients so far have been David Gower, John Woodcock, Brian Lara and Mark Taylor.

The Club now has a "home" in the press box at Lord's, marked by a handsome Honours Board and by portraits of past luminaries, presented by MCC. Plaques have been placed to commemorate such rich local characters as Dick Williamson and Fred Speakman, at Headingley and Northampton. Another plaque, at Lord's, will honour Reg Hayter.

In 1952 there were 58 members, of whom 16 were still with us at the start of 1996. Now there are 244, ninety per cent of everyone working in the cricket media. A recent nomination for membership was dismissed by one senior member with the words: "We can't possibly have him. The man's a prat." When this was reported to the chairman, Jack Bannister, he commented: "Sadly, if that were a disqualification we would have many fewer members." While we can continue to laugh at ourselves, we shall prosper.

Derek Hodgson has written on cricket for most national newspapers and currently writes for The Independent. *He has been secretary of the Cricket Writers' Club since 1986.*

FIVE CRICKETERS OF THE YEAR

DOMINIC CORK

Very rarely in recent times has an English cricketer burst on to the Test scene in a manner that suggested that it was always his destiny to succeed at the highest level. David Gower announced himself with a languid pull for four off the first delivery he received. Ian Botham took five wickets the first time he bowled and it was obvious to everyone that there was much more to come.

But the arrival of Dominic Cork last summer was, without question, the most explosive entrance in living memory. His seven for 43 in the second innings of the Lord's Test against West Indies are the best figures ever achieved by an Englishman on his debut. Two matches later Cork seized the first hat-trick taken by an England bowler in a Test match since Peter Loader in 1957. In June, while England were losing the First Test at Headingley, Cork was still simply a young and promising county cricketer with eight one-day internationals behind him, hoping that consistent performances for Derbyshire would catch the eye of the Test selectors. Less than two months later, he was handing over the cheque for £21 million to the winner of the National Lottery.

DOMINIC GERALD CORK was born on August 7, 1971 in Newcastle-under-Lyme, the third son of Gerald Cork, a pace bowler of some repute in the North Staffordshire and South Cheshire League. His mother, Mary, rated Dad a shade faster than Dominic – and she should know, because cricket in the Cork household meant a family day out. While the three boys were all involved in the Under-14s, Dad umpired and Mum made the teas. On occasions, all three Cork boys played under Gerald's captaincy in the Betley Cricket Club Second Eleven.

Perhaps it is because he is the youngest of three brothers that Dominic Cork has been moulded into the intensely competitive individual that he is today. Another reason could very well be that his childhood hero was Ian Botham, who "played his own natural, aggressive game even if England were losing. It did not always work, but at least he never gave up." The Botham influence was a major factor in Cork's development. Cork's smooth, short run-up might have a suggestion of Sir Richard Hadlee about it, but it was modelled on the early Botham. And what about that appeal? That raucous screech with back arched and both arms flung skywards, delivered with such ferocity that the umpire might fear being blown into the sightscreen? Again, Botham has been copied to some degree. But there is also a contribution from Hadlee (the bending of the knees bit) and, to make the whole performance particularly terrifying, a pinch of Ole Mortensen has been thrown in, although Cork has wisely decided not to attempt the accompanying Danish expletives.

Cork could easily have played for England before he finally broke through last summer. He toured with England A four times after making his Championship debut in 1990 against Leicestershire at Derby (my own final match). It would be nice to think that the national selectors had embarked on a deliberate policy and had decided that Cork, however promising, should not be rushed into the England team until he was absolutely ready. It is more likely they felt, unfairly, that Cork had prospered on helpful, green pitches at Derby and Chesterfield and that he would have to prove himself on surfaces which required greater patience and skill before being trusted in Tests.

Cork might not have made his dramatic entrance at Lord's had he not taken nine for 43 against Northamptonshire a week before the selection meeting. (Should anybody think that Cork enjoyed more than his fair share of fortune during 1995, it should be remembered that he claimed the first nine wickets in that match and watched, aghast, as the tenth was dropped off his bowling.) His first Test return for England was hardly devastating – Ian Bishop was his only victim – but in the second innings, as West Indies chased 296, Cork, roaring in from the Nursery End, bowled England to a 72-run victory. When Alec Stewart safely pouched an edge from the last man, Courtney Walsh, Cork was a national hero.

West Indies had regained the lead by the time the series moved north to Old Trafford and, at the start of the fourth day, were 159 for three. By the end of the first over they were 161 for six. Richie Richardson played the fourth ball on to his stumps, Junior Murray fell palpably leg before wicket to bring in Carl Hooper whom Cork had dismissed as the final wicket in his hat-trick for Derbyshire against Kent the previous summer.

"It's amazing how many hat-trick balls are not bowled in the right place," Cork said. "For Hooper I knew that I had to pitch it right up, almost half-volley length, and get it straight because he is an lbw candidate early on." The plan worked. Hooper was struck plumb in front, Cork vented an ear-splitting appeal and, after a moment's delay, umpire Mitchley raised his right index finger. "I just knew he was going to give it out," Cork said. "I have watched the replay a thousand times to check if there was any way that it couldn't have been given, but there definitely wasn't."

Half a dozen young all-rounders have been given a chance to succeed the irreplaceable Ian Botham, but none has managed to make that position in the England team his own. Dominic Cork, with his tireless out-swingers and in-duckers, coupled with a natural eye for a cricket ball, is the latest to try on his hero's crown. His batting caught public attention when he pulverised the Lancashire bowling in the 1993 Benson and Hedges final. At Test level it has more potential than achievement, but he knows what needs to be done. "I am determined not to be one of those England cricketers who has had a good start and then not gone on," he says through gritted teeth. And, looking on as he goes about his daily business of training and practising, one is left in no doubt whatever that Cork means every word. – Jonathan Agnew.

ARAVINDA DE SILVA

It was the biting southeaster that so discomforted him at the start of last summer. The layers of thermal garments and sweaters reached right down to Aravinda de Silva's bandy legs as he ruminated at third man over whether a season of county cricket was really for him. He spoke, when he arrived, of the need for adrenalin in his game. A one-day final at Lord's, he felt, would be his ideal stage.

Indeed it was. His 112 off 95 balls in the Benson and Hedges final was arguably the finest innings played in England last summer. De Silva demonstrated all too vividly that top-class batsmen need not be constricted by the artificiality of one-day cricket. Even when the asking-rate was reaching absurd proportions, he did not have to resort to slogging. This was as felicitous a piece of batting seen in a limited-overs final since Asif Iqbal made 89 for the same county, Kent, against the same opposition, Lancashire, in 1971. Neither of these innings could have been played by an Englishman, for the ball was feathered, not bludgeoned, persuaded, not carved. Throughout the season, de Silva batted in this manner. In the first-class game, he scored 1,781 runs at an average of 59.36. Around him nothing was happening and Kent finished bottom of the County Championship table. But his standards never wavered.

De Silva took to Lord's early in his career. He was 18 when he made his Test debut there, going in at No. 7. He did not have particular cause to remember his own contribution – 19 runs in two innings – but this was Sri Lanka's inaugural Test at Lord's and they marked the occasion by comprehensively out-batting England. Three of de Silva's colleagues made centuries and the whole side won over a predominantly English gathering. And yet, 11 years on, there was to be no Test at Lord's or anywhere else in England for him and his country. De Silva, by now regarded as a world-class batsman, unashamedly used his innings in the Benson and Hedges final as a platform to air his grievances. "Since 1984 Sri Lanka has always played a one-off Test against England after each West Indian tour, but in 1995 we were dropped. It is disappointing because we won the last time we played England, we feel we deserve a three-Test series and, given the opportunity, we would prove good value," he said. After the way de Silva batted when the two countries last met – his innings of 80 was an important factor in Sri Lanka's victory in Colombo in 1992-93 – the marketing men ought to think likewise.

PINNADUWAGE ARAVINDA DE SILVA was born in Colombo on October 17, 1965, and, in spite of his size (5 ft 3½ in) was soon demonstrating that he possessed an exceptional talent. Like many small men, he learned to cut and hook proficiently. He started attacking the ball while playing weekend club cricket that scarcely differed in approach from the Sunday League in England. Hence de Silva's fondness for the one-day game (it was no coincidence that Kent won the League during his one season with them) and his desire early in his career not to let anything go by outside off stump. As a 19-year-old, he took part in his country's first victory, against India in Colombo, making 75 in the second innings. A decade later, he was part of the side that beat New Zealand in Napier, Sri Lanka's first victory outside their own country. It might conceivably have come earlier had England not deigned to play Sri Lanka only five times since they achieved Test status in 1981. Other issues have affected de Silva's motivation and concentration: "When the troubles were at their height in my country, the game did well just to survive. I lost my best years. It was not easy to remain motivated, training all year to play, perhaps, in just one Test."

Yet de Silva would seem to have had little difficulty in playing the long innings. At the age of 30 and after more than 50 Tests, he has a batting average that has not veered much from 40, the bench-mark of the very good batsman. His highest score, 267, was made against New Zealand in 1990-91. In addition to these accomplishments, he bowls passable off-spin that can be effective in the one-day game. His failings, indeed, have less to do with technique and character than cakes (in England) and fast cars (at home) both of which, of course, are an integral part of the game.

De Silva did not want his season with Kent to end. He would have preferred to have seen their triumph in the Sunday League through to completion rather than leave England a few days before the end of the season to rejoin Sri Lanka for the last two Tests of their series in Pakistan. "I cannot believe any player, anywhere, has been so popular," said Graham Cowdrey, his county colleague. "Ari was an inspiration to me and the whole side felt the same. When he packed his bags, he hugged each of us and I have never known a professional sports team so close to tears." – Ivo Tennant.

ANGUS FRASER

It is a sight as familiar now as once was Trueman's surge, Botham's bull-charge or Willis's manic flapping. Angus Fraser's trundle begins with a shuffle, and gathers momentum as he picks up his size thirteens and leans forward like a trawlerman breasting a brisk nor'easter. It is all rather inelegant and unathletic: a man trampling through a nettle-bed pursued by a swarm of bees.

This is only the prelude, though. He hits the crease with the minimum of elevation, and his delivery stride – short by any standard, let alone a man approaching six and a half feet – scarcely spans the width of the crease. There is no resistance in his action and he bowls through his run rather than setting himself. Nor does he bend his back.

Not much for the purist so far. But now something happens. His front arm reaches out and inscribes an imaginary line to a point just outside the batsman's off stump, tugging his bowling arm after it in a replica arc so high that his knuckles could snag on the clouds and pull them down. Unencumbered by being yanked out of plane, the ball can only follow the line. The geometry of it all is simple, and the result predictable, but it is a gift given to few.

Fraser deals in parsimony and red-faced effort. He is perennially grumpy, kicks savage lumps from the turf at a conceded leg-bye, and could murder a misfielder: the opposite to the millionaire spendthrifts who buy their wickets with boundaries. Somewhere, he believes, he can always get a cheaper deal. Runs are a commodity to be hoarded, not frittered away on the undeserving. This is Scrooge in flannels. Batsmen? Bah! Humbug! There is a rationale here, though: he can dart and jag the ball around with the best of them on a sappy pitch, but when the going is tough and others do not want to know, he has another, more torturing, weapon: length and line. Throttle the lifeblood supply of runs with a garotte of accuracy and patience and you create anxiety, he will say. And where that exists so do wickets.

ANGUS ROBERT CHARLES FRASER was born on August 8, 1965, in Billinge, Lancashire, rugby league country, but the family came south when he was two, before his brother Alastair was born. Both went to play cricket for Stanmore and Middlesex. Alastair did not quite make the grade in county cricket. His brother is, as a succession of leaders will confirm, a captain's dream. Ever since he found his way, belatedly, into the England side at Edgbaston in 1989 and announced himself by bowling Steve Waugh at a time when the batsman was beginning to appear invincible, he has given control. Sometimes the deeds are unsung, not obvious to anyone except those in the game itself. On other occasions they manifest themselves gloriously. At Jamaica in 1990, when Gordon Greenidge and Desmond Haynes were threatening to destroy English morale terminally on the first morning of the series, it was Fraser, in only his fourth Test, who first of all held them in check and then tore them out with a spell of five for six. England won famously. Then four years on, he conjured figures of eight for 75 from the Bridgetown pitch when all around were wilting. England won again.

And yet the fates have conspired against him almost as much as his expression suggests. From his debut until the end of the 1995 season, England played a total of 65 Tests but Fraser took the field in just 29. Injury has played a large part, not least the debilitating hip ailment that manifested itself in Melbourne over Christmas of 1990, and which took two frustrating years from his cricket life. He missed 24 consecutive Tests, although when he did return for the final match of the 1993 Ashes series his match figures of eight for 131 helped bring England a consolation win at the end of a trying summer.

More mystifying, however, has been the reluctance of selectors to recognise his virtues as a thoroughbred Test match bowler, mistaking his downcast demeanour – Eeyore without the *joie de vivre* – for lack of spark. In particular, Ray Illingworth's decision not to include him in the party to Australia in 1994-95 amounted to nothing less than a dereliction of the chairman's duty. He had, said Illingworth, not bowled well in county matches. The Australians could scarcely contain their delight and pummelled England mercilessly in the first two Tests until injury to others and circumstance demanded Fraser's recall to the team. He promptly all but bowled England to victory in Sydney.

Fraser only learned of his original omission when the side was announced on the television. The captain, Mike Atherton – who, possibly through embarrassment, had not contacted Fraser prior to the announcement – confessed only to "disappointment", but it carried the flavour of hospital bulletins which describe the condition of multiple fracture patients as "comfortable". For his part, Fraser admits he was devastated. "I was just so disappointed at the way it was done," he says. "Playing for England means such a lot and if people treat you like that it makes it seem like it's not such a big deal after all."

Even then, the lesson was not heeded. At Headingley, for the first Test of the West Indies series, Fraser was in the squad but left out on the morning of the match. Rudderless, England were pulverised. Fraser returned next match to take five for 66 in the win at Lord's.

There may not be much left now and the best has undoubtedly gone. The hip injury blunted the edge, anyone can see that. But he has still been too good, too rare a commodity, too wholeheartedly English to ignore. And for all his talent, his confidence has been dented and his pride hurt. "All along," he says, "I feel people have been doubting me. I'm proving myself all the time. Mostly I feel that I have to prove myself more than anyone else. It's a bit sad." – Mike Selvey.

ANIL KUMBLE

The summer of 1995 saw a pleasing contrast between international cricket and the domestic game. The Test series between England and West Indies was so dominated by pace bowlers, on both sides, that spinners took less than a tenth of the wickets. In first-class cricket, on the other hand, the two leading wicket-takers were Asian leg-spinners: Mushtaq Ahmed with 95 wickets, and Anil Kumble with 105.

Kumble thus became the first bowler to take 100 wickets since 1991; the first spinner to do so since 1983; and the first leg-spinner since 1971. But only nominally can Kumble be classified as a leg-spinner, for he does not specialise in temptations that end in a stumping, or a catch at long-off, and a deceived bat slammed against pad. He is a bowler of his own kind: a brisk top-spin bowler, making the ball turn a little both ways; tall at six foot two and dangerously bouncy on a hard pitch; and as persistently accurate in finding his target as a mosquito. Not one of his 105 victims was stumped. Twenty were leg-before and 21 bowled, most of them making the mistake of thinking they had time to play back to this "leg-spinner." All the rest were caught, seldom in the deep, largely by Richard Montgomerie at short leg, David Capel at slip, Rob Bailey at silly point and Kevin Curran at gully. Kumble paid tribute to them all, and to Bob Carter who conducted their practices, for fulfilling such a demanding task without previous experience of such bowling.

Over the first-class season he conceded 2.3 runs per over, and then the bat's edge was frequently the scorer: at times a whole session would pass without Kumble conceding a boundary in front of the wicket. He bowled more overs than anyone else as well, except Mushtaq; and as his Indian compatriots at Gloucestershire and Durham, Javagal Srinath and Manoj Prabhakar, were equally hard-working, together they did much to change the perception of Indian players, hitherto not renowned for their stamina, in county cricket. After the NatWest Trophy final at Lord's, when Kumble turned on what he thought was his best one-day bowling of the season, Warwickshire's captain Dermot Reeve summarised the impression of all English cricket when he declared that Kumble was "a fabulous bowler".

There is only one bowler of the last generation to whom he could be compared. But as ANIL KUMBLE was born on October 17, 1970, in Bangalore, he was too young to have studied Bhagwat Chandrasekhar and did not take him as a model. However, the conditions which prompted Chandrasekhar to bowl medium-paced top-spinners and googlies were those that governed Kumble's development. Club cricket in Bangalore is played on matting spread over baked mud (Kumble still occasionally turns out for his club, Young Cricketers), and the springy rather than fast surface can make a top-spinner bounce exceptionally. Kumble smiles at the recollection of wicket-keepers who were apprehensive about standing up to him. As in the case of Chandra, the batsman can sometimes hear the ball fizz after leaving Kumble's hand – although it is no easier to play for being audible as well as visible.

Kumble's father, a management consultant, had not played the game formally. Anil began by playing tennis ball cricket in the streets outside his house, a form of the game which has organised tournaments there. He moved on to bowl medium-pace until his conversion at 15, when for one reason or another, his elder brother Dinesh persuaded him to try leg-spin as a novelty, even in southern India. "There was no one to guide me or coach me or show me how to grip the ball," Kumble remembers. But with a long and energetic arm-swing, and powerful shoulders, he could soon make it bounce like a tennis ball.

He was rapidly selected for Karnataka Schools Under-15, then for Karnataka in 1989-90, when Chandra was in his last year as a state selector. On the 1990 tour of England he made his Test debut at Old Trafford, aged 19, as a bespectacled No. 10 (he has since shed the glasses for lenses, and his lowly status in the order, making hundreds for Karnataka). His first Test wicket was Allan Lamb, caught at silly point, which had long-term consequences.

His 100th came in his 21st Test, on his home ground in Bangalore. In home Tests he often had turning pitches to bowl on, and large Tendulkar-fed totals to bowl at, but that is still a fine record: Shane Warne took two more Tests to reach his 100. His Indian captain, Mohammad Azharuddin, phoned Lamb to recommend Kumble when Northamptonshire wanted to replace Curtly Ambrose; and when the county contacted him at a Madras hotel, he accepted without even discussing terms.

Kumble's aim in undertaking county cricket was to develop his variety and to learn more about pitches, with a view to India's tour of England in 1996. This ambition he fulfilled. While he kept to his lower trajectory and faster speed for one-day matches, in the Championship he bowled more slowly than hitherto, and turned the ball sideways both further and more often, not just fizzing it through. He would bowl six googlies in an over against a left-hander.

His county did their best to make Northampton's pitches as similar as possible to Bangalore. He took 64 wickets at 16 runs apiece at Northampton, and 41 wickets at 27 elsewhere. If he sometimes had to come on before the seam bowlers had taken a wicket, he was always accurate, and calm, as native Kannada-speakers are reputed to be.

"I'm very satisfied with my season," he declared afterwards, and so were the county, who failed to win that elusive Championship through no fault of their overseas signing. Unmarried, teetotal and vegetarian, a graduate in mechanical engineering and speaking excellent English, Kumble would join in with his team-mates at the bar, even if taking soft drinks. They would have him back any time he can get away from his public relations job for Triton Watches, his employers in Bangalore; and from the Test match game so dominated by seam. – Scyld Berry.

DERMOT REEVE

Very occasionally in the game of cricket, a player emerges to defy conventional categorisation. Dermot Reeve is one such. By the accepted benchmarks of batting, bowling and fielding, he falls short of excellence and yet the sum of the parts compels attention and admiration. The same, of course, can be said of the Warwickshire side, whose unprecedented success over the past two seasons owes so much to Reeve's inspiration.

They have been good for each other. Warwickshire, a big club with resources and ambitions, gave Reeve the broad canvas he required when they made him captain in 1993; in return, he gave them the success they craved by instilling in the players a confidence, almost a joy, in free expression. The outcome is unarguable; by winning the Championship and the NatWest Trophy in 1995, they raised the trophy count to six in Reeve's three seasons of stewardship. In the Lord's final, he was Man of the Match, and not just for his perky batting. Nobody, now, is putting it all down to coincidence.

FIVE CRICKETERS OF THE YEAR

DOMINIC CORK

FIVE CRICKETERS OF THE YEAR

[*Patrick Eagar*

ARAVINDA DE SILVA

FIVE CRICKETERS OF THE YEAR

[*Patrick Eagar*

ANGUS FRASER

FIVE CRICKETERS OF THE YEAR

[*Bob Thomas/Popperfoto*]

ANIL KUMBLE

FIVE CRICKETERS OF THE YEAR

[*Graham Morris*

DERMOT REEVE

ON TOP OF THE WORLD

[*Shaun Botterill/Allsport*]

The Australian players hold their captain Mark Taylor aloft after their victory over West Indies at Sabina Park, which made them, by general consent, world champions.

THE ACCUSER AND THE ACCUSED

[*Shaun Botterill/Allsport*]

Salim Malik, the former Pakistan captain, pictured at the Sydney Test in December 1995 with Shane Warne, the man who said Malik offered him a bribe to throw a match.

OURS – AGAIN

[Rebecca Naden/PA

West Indies captain Richie Richardson at The Oval with the Wisden Trophy, which his team won for the 12th consecutive time after drawing 2-2 in the series against England. David Gower, who was acting as master of ceremonies, is on the left.

TARGET PRACTICE

[Adrian Murrell/Allsport]

Robin Smith avoids a West Indian bouncer in the first innings of the Old Trafford Test. He was less fortunate when facing Ian Bishop in the second innings, and fractured a cheekbone.

[Shaun Botterill/Allsport]

Sri Lankan off-spinner Muttiah Muralitharan, seen in action in the Perth Test against Australia, two weeks before he was called for throwing by umpire Darrell Hair.

BEHIND BARS . . .

[Adrian Murrell/Allsport

England manager Ray Illingworth, wrapped against the cold, watching his team go down to defeat in the Headingley Test.

. . . OUT OF JAIL

[Patrick Eagar

England captain Mike Atherton being embraced by Robin Smith as he reaches the century that saved the Johannesburg Test.

LIGHTNING STRIKES

[*Patrick Eagar*

The scene at Centurion Park as England's first Test in South Africa for more than 30 years heads towards a watery finish.

If this past season was the best of his career, it is because he was fulfilled by the esteem of his peers. Previously, it had often been grudgingly given, and then with stinging caveats. But as 1995 progressed and it became clear even to the most starstruck that there was, after all, more to Warwickshire's rise than the presence of Brian Lara, the significance of Reeve's input received due acknowledgement and genuine respect.

He had a decent enough season with bat and ball, fractionally improving his career batting average to 34 and taking 38 wickets at 17.39 to finish second, to his team-mate Allan Donald, in the first-class bowling averages. But bald statistics are not the measure of this man, whose greatest quality as a cricketer is contributing crucially when it is most urgently needed and whose gift as a captain is convincing others around him that they are capable of the same.

Donald, the South African fast bowler whose seamless takeover from Lara was critical to Reeve's strategy, sums up his captain: "Nobody should ever take Dermot for granted. He may seem to be taking the mickey and bubbling all the time but he is a very focused man and a great disciplinarian. He never lets us take our mind off the job and he has brought an arrogant, cocky attitude to the team. I wouldn't like to play against him, though, because he is such a niggling character on the field." Some say it was ever thus. Reeve's nature is to be extrovert, even confrontational, and it has not always endeared him to opponents. Many have accused him of possessing a swollen head; probably, many did so even during his schooldays.

DERMOT ALEXANDER REEVE was born in Kowloon, Hong Kong, on April 2, 1963, perhaps a day late to be truly appropriate. He was brought up in the colony by his parents, Alexander and Monica, and educated at King George V School in Kowloon. In his teens, he became something of a sporting celebrity within the local expatriate community and he represented Hong Kong in the ICC Trophy of 1982. By then, however, he was on the Lord's groundstaff and, the following season, he made his county debut for Sussex.

His five seasons at Hove were not a spectacular success, although in 1986 he did play a significant role in the winning of the NatWest Trophy, taking four for 20 in the final against Lancashire. For this, he received the first of his three Man of the Match awards in NatWest finals, an unparalleled feat. He left Sussex claiming that their conditions did not suit his swing bowling. This was only part of the truth. Reeve was intensely ambitious and wanted to play for a club that demonstrably shared his ambitions; he did not feel Sussex were proceeding in the right direction. He joined Warwickshire and played for five years under the leadership of Andy Lloyd, for whom he has an oft-repeated regard. For at least the last two of them, however, it was plain that Reeve was the captain in waiting.

His accession will not have pleased everyone. Reeve is the sort of person who never will please everyone, nor seek to. But at least by then he had ticked off a number of ambitions, having played Test cricket for England and appeared in the 1992 World Cup. He fared moderately in three Tests against New Zealand, with a top score of 59 on debut, but showed himself to be an effective one-day player, especially on sluggish pitches where his stealthy swing bowling, now augmented by outrageous changes of pace, could frustrate and infuriate batsmen of all abilities.

On the second of his England tours, to India and Sri Lanka in 1992-93, his mother became the England team scorer when the official appointee, Clem Driver, fell ill. That Monica was on hand should be no surprise, for she scarcely misses a match in which her son is playing. She is Dermot's greatest fan. Those who are not presumably include Curtly Ambrose, who bowled him three beamers in swift succession during his career-best innings of 202 not out at Northampton in 1990. A certain county coach also falls into Ambrose's camp. Against himself, Reeve tells how this coach accused him, last summer, "of setting out to upset his players on a regular basis". Reeve insists: "It was a misunderstanding. I don't set out to upset people but I will be aggressive on the field. I remember at Hove going in to bat against Somerset. Ian Botham was at slip and he gave me a lot of lip, but when we walked off he clapped me on the back and said 'well played'. That's the way I play too."

It is not, however, quite as simplistic as that. Reeve is a deep thinker on the game, with a formidable memory for situations and for the weaknesses of individuals. His bowling and field changes reflect this. His analysis of each game is pressed upon his team at meetings before every session. Warwickshire have also shunned recent trends and gone back to talking cricket, as a team, when out socially or in the dressing-room.

That is the strategist within Reeve. Then there is the showman, who will do the unorthodox, notably reverse-sweeping, as much for irritation as gain. And the man who will roll around in the outfield engaged in complex calisthenics for what seems an age. "I think," he says, "I am a visual cricketer." Recently, it has been unwise to take one's eyes off him, for fear of missing some new gem. – Alan Lee.

TRAGEDY AT NAGPUR

Nine people were killed and 50 injured when a wall collapsed at the Vidarbha Cricket Association Ground at Nagpur during a one-day international between India and New Zealand on November 26, 1995.

The disaster happened during the lunch interval when, according to reports, spectators from the third tier of the East Stand were rushing down and those from the second tier were going up to try to get a better view. The staircase wall gave way under the pressure of people. Three youngsters were killed immediately when they plunged 15 metres to the ground. Six more died in hospital. Among the dead was a female engineering student. Some reports spoke of up to 12 dead and 70 injured but these figures were not confirmed. Four cricket fans had already been killed in a car crash while on their way to the ground.

The wall had only just been built as part of an extension constructed in preparation for the World Cup. It had been built without reinforcement and four people, including the architect and contractor, were charged with negligence. VCA officials decided to continue the match, despite protests from some members of the city council. The players were not told and New Zealand went on to win.

PART TWO: RECORDS

TEST CRICKETERS

FULL LIST FROM 1877 TO AUGUST 28, 1995

These lists have been compiled on a home and abroad basis, appearances abroad being printed in *italics*.

Abbreviations. E: England. A: Australia. SA: South Africa. WI: West Indies. NZ: New Zealand. In: India. P: Pakistan. SL: Sri Lanka. Z: Zimbabwe.

All appearances are placed in this order of seniority. Hence, any England cricketer playing against Australia in England has that achievement recorded first and the remainder of his appearances at home (if any) set down before passing to matches abroad. The figures immediately following each name represent the total number of appearances in *all* Tests.

No Tests from the 1995-96 season have been included.

Where the season embraces two different years, the first year is given; i.e. 1876 indicates 1876-77.

ENGLAND

Number of Test cricketers: 576

Abel, R. 13: v A 1888 (3) 1896 (3) 1902 (2); *v A 1891 (3); v SA 1888 (2)*

Absolom, C. A. 1: *v A 1878*

Agnew, J. P. 3: v A 1985 (1); v WI 1984 (1); v SL 1984 (1)

Allen, D. A. 39: v A 1961 (4) 1964 (1); v SA 1960 (2); v WI 1963 (2) 1966 (1); v P 1962 (4); *v A 1962 (1) 1965 (4); v SA 1964 (4); v WI 1959 (5); v NZ 1965 (3); v In 1961 (5); v P 1961 (3)*

Allen, G. O. B. 25: v A 1930 (1) 1934 (2); v WI 1933 (1); v NZ 1931 (3); v In 1936 (3); *v A 1932 (5) 1936 (5); v WI 1947 (3); v NZ 1932 (2)*

Allom, M. J. C. 5: *v SA 1930 (1); v NZ 1929 (4)*

Allott, P. J. W. 13: v A 1981 (1) 1985 (4); v WI 1984 (1); v In 1982 (2); v SL 1984 (1); *v In 1981 (1); v SL 1981 (1)*

Ames, L. E. G. 47: v A 1934 (5) 1938 (2); v SA 1929 (1) 1935 (4); v WI 1933 (3); v NZ 1931 (3) 1937 (3); v In 1932 (1); *v A 1932 (5) 1936 (5); v SA 1938 (5); v WI 1929 (4) 1934 (4); v NZ 1932 (2)*

Amiss, D. L. 50: v A 1968 (1) 1975 (2) 1977 (2); v WI 1966 (1) 1973 (3) 1976 (1); v NZ 1973 (3); v In 1967 (2) 1971 (1) 1974 (3); v P 1967 (1) 1971 (3) 1974 (3); *v A 1974 (5) 1976 (1); v WI 1973 (5) v 1974 (2); v In 1972 (3) 1976 (5); v P 1972 (3)*

Andrew, K. V. 2: v WI 1963 (1); *v A 1954 (1)*

Appleyard, R. 9: v A 1956 (1); v SA 1955 (1); v P 1954 (1); *v A 1954 (4); v NZ 1954 (2)*

Archer, A. G. 1: *v SA 1898*

Armitage, T. 2: *v A 1876 (2)*

Arnold, E. G. 10: v A 1905 (4); v SA 1907 (2); *v A 1903 (4)*

Arnold, G. G. 34: v A 1972 (3) 1975 (1); v WI 1973 (3); v NZ 1969 (1) 1973 (3); v In 1974 (2); v P 1967 (2) 1974 (3); *v A 1974 (4); v WI 1973 (3); v NZ 1974 (2); v In 1972 (4); v P 1972 (3)*

Arnold, J. 1: v NZ 1931

Astill, W. E. 9: *v SA 1927 (5); v WI 1929 (4)*

Atherton, M. A. 51: v A 1989 (2) 1993 (6); v SA 1994 (3); v WI 1991 (5) 1995 (6); v NZ 1990 (3) 1994 (3); v In 1990 (3); v P 1992 (3); *v A 1990 (5) 1994 (5); v WI 1993 (5); v In 1992 (1); v SL 1992 (1)*

Athey, C. W. J. 23: v A 1980 (1); v WI 1988 (1); v NZ 1986 (3); v In 1986 (2); v P 1987 (4); *v A 1986 (5) 1987 (1); v WI 1980 (2); v NZ 1987 (1); v P 1987 (3)*

Attewell, W. 10: v A 1890 (1); *v A 1884 (5) 1887 (1) 1891 (3)*

Bailey, R. J. 4: v WI 1988 (1); *v A 1989 (3)*

Bailey, T. E. 61: v A 1953 (5) 1956 (4); v SA 1951 (2) 1955 (5); v WI 1950 (2) 1957 (4); v NZ 1949 (4) 1958 (4); v P 1954 (3); *v A 1950 (4) 1954 (5) 1958 (5); v SA 1956 (5); v WI 1953 (5); v NZ 1950 (2) 1954 (2)*

Bairstow, D. L. 4: v A 1980 (1); v WI 1980 (1); v In 1979 (1); *v WI 1980 (1)*
Bakewell, A. H. 6: v SA 1935 (2); v WI 1933 (1); v NZ 1931 (2); *v In 1933 (1)*
Balderstone, J. C. 2: v WI 1976 (2)
Barber, R. W. 28: v A 1964 (1) 1968 (1); v SA 1960 (1) 1965 (3); v WI 1966 (2); v NZ 1965 (3); *v A 1965 (5); v SA 1964 (4); v In 1961 (5); v P 1961 (3)*
Barber, W. 2: v SA 1935 (2)
Barlow, G. D. 3: v A 1977 (1); *v In 1976 (2)*
Barlow, R. G. 17: v A 1882 (1) 1884 (3) 1886 (3); *v A 1881 (4) 1882 (4) 1886 (2)*
Barnes, S. F. 27: v A 1902 (1) 1909 (2) 1912 (3); v SA 1912 (3); *v A 1901 (3) 1907 (5) 1911 (5); v SA 1913 (4)*
Barnes, W. 21: v A 1880 (1) 1882 (1) 1884 (2) 1886 (2) 1888 (3) 1890 (2); *v A 1882 (4) 1884 (5) 1886 (1)*
Barnett, C. J. 20: v A 1938 (3) 1948 (1); v SA 1947 (3); v WI 1933 (1); v NZ 1937 (3); v In 1936 (1); *v A 1936 (5); v In 1933 (3)*
Barnett, K. J. 4: v A 1989 (3); v SL 1988 (1)
Barratt, F. 5: v A 1929 (1); *v NZ 1929 (4)*
Barrington, K. F. 82: v A 1961 (5) 1964 (5) 1968 (3); v SA 1955 (2) 1960 (4) 1965 (3); v WI 1963 (5) 1966 (2); v NZ 1965 (2); v In 1959 (5) 1967 (3); v P 1962 (4) 1967 (3); *v A 1962 (5) 1965 (5); v SA 1964 (5) 1967 (5); v WI 1959 (5) 1967 (5); v NZ 1962 (3); v In 1961 (5) 1963 (1); v P 1961 (2)*
Barton, V. A. 1: *v SA 1891*
Bates, W. 15: *v A 1881 (4) 1882 (4) 1884 (5) 1886 (2)*
Bean, G. 3: *v A 1891 (3)*
Bedser, A. V. 51: v A 1948 (5) 1953 (5); v SA 1947 (2) 1951 (5) 1955 (1); v WI 1950 (3); v NZ 1949 (2); v In 1946 (3) 1952 (4); v P 1954 (2); *v A 1946 (5) 1950 (5) 1954 (1); v SA 1948 (5); v NZ 1946 (1) 1950 (2)*
Benjamin, J. E. 1: v SA 1994
Benson, M. R. 1: v In 1986
Berry, R. 2: v WI 1950 (2)
Bicknell, M. P. 2: v A 1993 (2)
Binks, J. G. 2: *v In 1963 (2)*
Bird, M. C. 10: *v SA 1909 (5) 1913 (5)*
Birkenshaw, J. 5: *v WI 1973 (2); v In 1972 (2); v P 1972 (1)*
Blakey, R. J. 2: *v In 1992 (2)*
Bligh, Hon. I. F. W. 4: *v A 1882 (4)*
Blythe, C. 19: v A 1905 (1) 1909 (2); v SA 1907 (3); *v A 1901 (5) 1907 (1); v SA 1905 (5) 1909 (2)*
Board, J. H. 6: *v SA 1898 (2) 1905 (4)*
Bolus, J. B. 7: v WI 1963 (2); *v In 1963 (5)*
Booth, M. W. 2: *v SA 1913 (2)*
Bosanquet, B. J. T. 7: v A 1905 (2); *v A 1903 (4)*
Botham, I. T. 102: v A 1977 (2) 1980 (1) 1981 (6) 1985 (6) 1989 (3); v WI 1980 (5) 1984 (5) 1991 (1); v NZ 1978 (3) 1983 (4) 1986 (1); v In 1979 (4) 1982 (3); v P 1978 (3) 1982 (3) 1987 (5) 1992 (2); v SL 1984 (1) 1991 (1); *v A 1978 (6) 1979 (3) 1982 (5) 1986 (4); v WI 1980 (4) 1985 (5); v NZ 1977 (3) 1983 (1) 1991 (1); v In 1979 (1) 1981 (6); v P 1983 (1); v SL 1981 (1)*
Bowden, M. P. 2: *v SA 1888 (2)*
Bowes, W. E. 15: v A 1934 (3) 1938 (2); v SA 1935 (4); v WI 1939 (2); v In 1932 (1) 1946 (1); *v A 1932 (1); v NZ 1932 (1)*
Bowley, E. H. 5: v SA 1929 (2); *v NZ 1929 (3)*
Boycott, G. 108: v A 1964 (4) 1968 (3) 1972 (2) 1977 (5) 1980 (1) 1981 (6); v SA 1965 (2); v WI 1966 (4) 1969 (3) 1973 (3) 1980 (5); v NZ 1965 (2) 1969 (2) 1973 (3) 1978 (2); v In 1967 (2) 1971 (1) 1974 (1) 1979 (4); v P 1967 (1) 1971 (2); *v A 1965 (5) 1970 (5) 1978 (6) 1979 (3); v SA 1964 (5); v WI 1967 (5) 1973 (5) 1980 (4); v NZ 1965 (2) 1977 (3); v In 1979 (1) 1981 (4); v P 1977 (3)*
Bradley, W. M. 2: v A 1899 (2)
Braund, L. C. 23: v A 1902 (5); v SA 1907 (3); *v A 1901 (5) 1903 (5) 1907 (5)*
Brearley, J. M. 39: v A 1977 (5) 1981 (4); v WI 1976 (2); v NZ 1978 (3); v In 1979 (4); *v P 1978 (3); v A 1976 (1) 1978 (6) 1979 (3); v In 1976 (5) 1979 (1); v P 1977 (2)*
Brearley, W. 4: v A 1905 (2) 1909 (1); v SA 1912 (1)
Brennan, D. V. 2: v SA 1951 (2)
Briggs, John 33: v A 1886 (1) 1888 (3) 1893 (2) 1896 (1) 1899 (1); *v A 1884 (5) 1886 (2) 1887 (1) 1891 (3) 1894 (5) 1897 (5); v SA 1888 (2)*
Broad, B. C. 25: v A 1989 (2); v WI 1984 (2) 1988 (2); v P 1987 (4); v SL 1984 (1); *v A 1986 (5) 1987 (1); v NZ 1987 (3); v P 1987 (3)*
Brockwell, W. 7: v A 1893 (1) 1899 (1); *v A 1894 (5)*

Bromley-Davenport, H. R. 4: *v SA 1895* (3) *1898* (1)

Brookes, D. 1: *v WI 1947*

Brown, A. 2: *v In 1961* (1); *v P 1961* (1)

Brown, D. J. 26: *v A 1968* (4); *v SA 1965* (2); *v WI 1966* (1) *1969* (3); *v NZ 1969* (1); *v In 1967* (2): *v A 1965* (4); *v WI 1967* (4); *v NZ 1965* (2); *v P 1968* (3)

Brown, F. R. 22: *v A 1953* (1); *v WI 1950* (1); *v NZ 1931* (2) *1937* (1) *1949* (2); *v In 1932* (1); *v A 1950* (5); *v NZ 1932* (2) *1950* (2)

Brown, G. 7: *v A 1921* (3); *v SA 1922* (4)

Brown, J. T. 8: *v A 1896* (2) *1899* (1); *v A 1894* (5)

Buckenham, C. P. 4: *v SA 1909* (4)

Butcher, A. R. 1: *v In 1979*

Butcher, R. O. 3: *v WI 1980* (3)

Butler, H. J. 2: *v SA 1947* (1); *v WI 1947* (1)

Butt, H. R. 3: *v SA 1895* (3)

Caddick, A. R. 8: *v A 1993* (4); *v WI 1993* (4)

Calthorpe, Hon. F. S. G. 4: *v WI 1929* (4)

Capel, D. J. 15: *v A 1989* (1); *v WI 1988* (2); *v P 1987* (1); *v A 1987* (1); *v WI 1989* (4); *v NZ 1987* (3); *v P 1987* (3)

Carr, A. W. 11: *v A 1926* (4); *v SA 1929* (2); *v SA 1922* (5)

Carr, D. B. 2: *v In 1951* (2)

Carr, D. W. 1: *v A 1909*

Cartwright, T. W. 5: *v A 1964* (2); *v SA 1965* (1); *v NZ 1965* (1); *v SA 1964* (1)

Chapman, A. P. F. 26: *v A 1926* (4) *1930* (4); *v SA 1924* (2); *v WI 1928* (3); *v A 1924* (4) *1928* (4); *v SA 1930* (5)

Charlwood, H. R. J. 2: *v A 1876* (2)

Chatterton, W. 1: *v SA 1891*

Childs, J. H. 2: *v WI 1988* (2)

Christopherson, S. 1: *v A 1884*

Clark, E. W. 8: *v A 1934* (2); *v SA 1929* (1); *v WI 1933* (2); *v In 1933* (3)

Clay, J. C. 1: *v SA 1935*

Close, D. B. 22: *v A 1961* (1); *v SA 1955* (1); *v WI 1957* (2) *1963* (5) *1966* (1) *1976* (3); *v NZ 1949* (1); *v In 1959* (1) *1967* (3); *v P 1967* (3); *v A 1950* (1)

Coldwell, L. J. 7: *v A 1964* (2); *v P 1962* (2); *v A 1962* (2); *v NZ 1962* (1)

Compton, D. C. S. 78: *v A 1938* (4) *1948* (5) *1953* (5) *1956* (1); *v SA 1947* (5) *1951* (4) *1955* (5); *v WI 1939* (1) *1950* (1); *v NZ 1937* (1) *1949* (4); *v In 1946* (3) *1952* (2); *v P 1954* (4); *v A 1946* (5) *1950* (4) *1954* (4); *v SA 1948* (5) *1956* (5); *v WI 1953* (5); *v NZ 1946* (1) *1950* (2)

Cook, C. 1: *v SA 1947*

Cook, G. 7: *v In 1982* (3); *v A 1982* (3); *v SL 1981* (1)

Cook, N. G. B. 15: *v A 1989* (3); *v WI 1984* (3); *v NZ 1983* (2); *v NZ 1983* (1); *v P 1983* (3) *1987* (2)

Cope, G. A. 3: *v P 1977* (3)

Copson, W. H. 3: *v SA 1947* (1); *v WI 1939* (2)

Cork, D. G. 5: *v WI 1995* (5)

Cornford, W. L. 4: *v NZ 1929* (4)

Cottam, R. M. H. 4: *v In 1972* (2); *v P 1968* (2)

Coventry, Hon. C. J. 2: *v SA 1888* (2)

Cowans, N. G. 19: *v A 1985* (1); *v WI 1984* (1); *v NZ 1983* (4); *v A 1982* (4); *v NZ 1983* (2); *v In 1984* (5); *v P 1983* (2)

Cowdrey, C. S. 6: *v WI 1988* (1); *v In 1984* (5)

Cowdrey, M. C. 114: *v A 1956* (5) *1961* (4) *1964* (3) *1968* (4); *v SA 1955* (1) *1960* (5) *1965* (3); *v WI 1957* (5) *1963* (2) *1966* (4); *v NZ 1958* (4) *1965* (3); *v In 1959* (5); *v P 1962* (4) *1967* (1); *v A 1954* (5) *1958* (5) *1962* (5) *1965* (4) *1970* (3) *1974* (5); *v SA 1956* (5); *v WI 1959* (5) *1967* (5); *v NZ 1954* (2) *1958* (2) *1962* (3) *1965* (3) *1970* (1); *v In 1963* (3); *v P 1968* (3)

Coxon, A. 1: *v A 1948*

Cranston, J. 1: *v A 1890*

Cranston, K. 8: *v A 1948* (1); *v SA 1947* (3); *v WI 1947* (4)

Crapp, J. F. 7: *v A 1948* (3); *v SA 1948* (4)

Crawford, J. N. 12: *v SA 1907* (2); *v A 1907* (5); *v SA 1905* (5)

Crawley, J. P. 9: *v SA 1994* (3); *v WI 1995* (2); *v A 1994* (3)

Curtis, T. S. 5: *v A 1989* (3); *v WI 1988* (2)

Cuttell, W. R. 2: *v SA 1898* (2)

Dawson, E. W. 5: *v SA 1927 (1); v NZ 1929 (4)*

Dean, H. 3: v A 1912 (2); v SA 1912 (1)

DeFreitas, P. A. J. 44: v A 1989 (1) 1993 (1); v SA 1994 (3); v WI 1988 (3) 1991 (5) 1995 (1); v NZ 1990 (2) 1994 (3); v P 1987 (1) 1992 (2); v SL 1991 (1); *v A 1986 (4) 1990 (3) 1994 (4); v WI 1989 (2); v NZ 1987 (2) 1991 (3); v In 1992 (1); v P 1987 (2)*

Denness, M. H. 28: v A 1975 (1); v NZ 1969 (1); v In 1974 (3); v P 1974 (3); *v A 1974 (5); v WI 1973 (1); v NZ 1974 (2); v In 1972 (5); v P 1972 (3)*

Denton, D. 11: v A 1905 (1); *v SA 1905 (5) 1909 (5)*

Dewes, J. G. 5: v A 1948 (1); v WI 1950 (1); *v A 1950 (2)*

Dexter, E. R. 62: v A 1961 (5) 1964 (5) 1968 (2); v SA 1960 (5); v WI 1963 (5); v NZ 1958 (1) 1965 (2); v In 1959 (2); v P 1962 (5); *v A 1958 (2) 1962 (5); v SA 1964 (5); v WI 1959 (5); v NZ 1958 (2) 1962 (5); v In 1961 (5); v P 1961 (3)*

Dilley, G. R. 41: v A 1981 (3) 1989 (2); v WI 1980 (3) 1988 (4); v NZ 1983 (1) 1986 (2); v In 1986 (2); v P 1987 (4); *v A 1979 (2) 1986 (4) 1987 (1); v WI 1980 (4); v NZ 1987 (3); v In 1981 (4); v P 1983 (1) 1987 (1)*

Dipper, A. E. 1: v A 1921

Doggart, G. H. G. 2: v WI 1950 (2)

D'Oliveira, B. L. 44: v A 1968 (2) 1972 (5); v WI 1966 (4) 1969 (3); v NZ 1969 (3); v In 1967 (2) 1971 (3); v P 1967 (3) 1971 (3); *v A 1970 (6); v WI 1967 (5); v NZ 1970 (2); v P 1968 (3)*

Dollery, H. E. 4: v A 1948 (2); v SA 1947 (1); v WI 1950 (1)

Dolphin, A. 1: *v A 1920*

Douglas, J. W. H. T. 23: v A 1912 (1) 1921 (5); v SA 1924 (1); *v A 1911 (5) 1920 (5) 1924 (1); v SA 1913 (5)*

Downton, P. R. 30: v A 1981 (1) 1985 (6); v WI 1984 (5) 1988 (3); v In 1986 (1); v SL 1984 (1); *v WI 1980 (3) 1985 (5); v In 1984 (5)*

Druce, N. F. 5: *v A 1897 (5)*

Ducat, A. 1: v A 1921

Duckworth, G. 24: v A 1930 (5); v SA 1924 (1) 1929 (4) 1935 (1); v WI 1928 (1); v In 1936 (3); *v A 1928 (5); v SA 1930 (3); v NZ 1932 (1)*

Duleepsinhji, K. S. 12: v A 1930 (4); v SA 1929 (1); v NZ 1931 (3); *v NZ 1929 (4)*

Durston, F. J. 1: v A 1921

Edmonds, P. H. 51: v A 1975 (2) 1985 (5); v NZ 1978 (3) 1983 (2) 1986 (3); v In 1979 (4) 1982 (3) 1986 (2); v P 1978 (3) 1987 (5); *v A 1978 (1) 1986 (5); v WI 1985 (3); v NZ 1977 (3); v In 1984 (5); v P 1977 (2)*

Edrich, J. H. 77: v A 1964 (5) 1968 (5) 1972 (5) 1975 (4); v SA 1965 (1); v WI 1963 (3) 1966 (1) 1969 (3) 1976 (2); v NZ 1965 (1) 1969 (3); v In 1967 (2) 1971 (3) 1974 (3); v P 1971 (3) 1974 (3); *v A 1965 (5) 1970 (6) 1974 (4); v WI 1967 (5); v NZ 1965 (3) 1970 (2) 1974 (2); v In 1963 (2); v P 1968 (3)*

Edrich, W. J. 39: v A 1938 (4) 1948 (5) 1953 (3); v SA 1947 (4); v WI 1950 (2); v NZ 1949 (4); v In 1946 (1); v P 1954 (1); *v A 1946 (5) 1954 (4); v SA 1938 (5); v NZ 1946 (1)*

Elliott, H. 4: v WI 1928 (1); *v SA 1927 (1); v In 1933 (2)*

Ellison, R. M. 11: v A 1985 (2); v WI 1984 (1); v In 1986 (1); v SL 1984 (1); *v WI 1985 (3); v In 1984 (5)*

Emburey, J. E. 64: v A 1980 (1) 1981 (4) 1985 (6) 1989 (3) 1993 (1); v WI 1980 (3) 1988 (5) 1995 (1); v NZ 1978 (3) 1986 (2); v In 1986 (3); v P 1987 (4); v SL 1988 (1); *v A 1978 (4) 1986 (5) 1987 (1); v WI 1980 (4) 1985 (4); v NZ 1987 (3); v In 1979 (1) 1981 (3) 1992 (1); v P 1987 (3); v SL 1981 (1) 1992 (1)*

Emmett, G. M. 1: v A 1948

Emmett, T. 7: *v A 1876 (2) 1878 (1) 1881 (4)*

Evans, A. J. 1: v A 1921

Evans, T. G. 91: v A 1948 (5) 1953 (5) 1956 (5); v SA 1947 (5) 1951 (3) 1955 (3); v WI 1950 (3) 1957 (5); v NZ 1949 (4) 1958 (5); v In 1946 (1) 1952 (4) 1959 (2); v P 1954 (4); *v A 1946 (4) 1950 (5) 1954 (4) 1958 (3); v SA 1948 (3) 1956 (5); v WI 1947 (4) 1953 (4); v NZ 1946 (1) 1950 (2) 1954 (2)*

Fagg, A. E. 5: v WI 1939 (1); v In 1936 (1); *v A 1936 (2)*

Fairbrother, N. H. 10: v NZ 1990 (3); v P 1987 (1); *v NZ 1987 (2); v In 1992 (2); v P 1987 (1); v SL 1992 (1)*

Fane, F. L. 14: *v A 1907 (4); v SA 1905 (5) 1909 (5)*

Farnes, K. 15: v A 1934 (2) 1938 (4); *v A 1936 (2); v SA 1938 (5); v WI 1934 (2)*

Farrimond, W. 4: v SA 1935 (1); *v SA 1930 (2); v WI 1934 (1)*

Fender, P. G. H. 13: v A 1921 (2); v SA 1924 (2) 1929 (1); *v A 1920 (3); v SA 1922 (5)*

Ferris, J. J. 1: *v SA 1891*

Fielder, A. 6: *v A 1903 (2) 1907 (4)*

Fishlock, L. B. 4: v In 1936 (2) 1946 (1); *v A 1946 (1)*

Flavell, J. A. 4: v A 1961 (2) 1964 (2)

Fletcher, K. W. R. 59: v A 1968 (1) 1972 (1) 1975 (2); v WI 1973 (3); v NZ 1969 (2) 1973 (3); v In 1971 (2) 1974 (3); *v A 1970/1 (2) 1974 (3); v P 1974 (3); v A 1974/5 (2) 1976 (1); v WI 1973 (4); v NZ 1970 (1) 1974 (2); v In 1972 (3) 1976 (3) 1981 (6); v P 1968 (3) 1972 (3); v SL 1981 (1)*

Flowers, W. 8: v A 1893 (1); *v A 1884 (5) 1886 (2)*

Ford, F. G. J. 5: *v A 1894 (5)*

Foster, F. R. 11: v A 1912 (3); v SA 1912 (3); *v A 1911 (5)*

Foster, N. A. 29: v A 1985 (1) 1989 (3) 1993 (1); v WI 1984 (1) 1988 (2); v NZ 1983 (1) 1986 (2); v In 1986 (1); v P 1987 (5); v SL 1988 (2); *v A 1987 (1); v WI 1985 (3); v NZ 1983 (2); v In 1984 (2); v P 1983 (2) 1987 (2)*

Foster, R. E. 8: v SA 1907 (3); *v A 1903 (5)*

Fothergill, A. J. 2: *v SA 1888 (2)*

Fowler, G. 21: v WI 1984 (5); v NZ 1983 (2); v P 1982 (1); v SL 1984 (1); *v A 1982 (3); v NZ 1983 (2); v In 1984 (2); v P 1983 (2)*

Fraser, A. R. C. 29: v A 1989 (3) 1993 (1); v SA 1994 (2); v WI 1995 (5); v NZ 1994 (3); v In 1990 (3); *v A 1990 (3) 1994 (3); v WI 1989 (2) 1993 (4)*

Freeman, A. P. 12: v SA 1929 (3); v WI 1928 (3); *v A 1924 (2); v SA 1927 (4)*

French, B. N. 16: v NZ 1986 (3); v In 1986 (2); v P 1987 (4); *v A 1987 (1); v NZ 1987 (3); v P 1987 (2)*

Fry, C. B. 26: v A 1899 (5) 1902 (3) 1905 (4) 1909 (3) 1912 (3); v SA 1907 (3) 1912 (3); *v SA 1895 (2)*

Gallian, J. E. R. 2: v WI 1995 (2)

Gatting, M. W. 79: v A 1980 (1) 1981 (6) 1985 (6) 1989 (1) 1993 (2); v WI 1980 (4) 1984 (1) 1988 (2); v NZ 1983 (2) 1986 (3); v In 1986 (3); v P 1982 (1) 1987 (5); *v A 1986 (5) 1987 (1) 1994 (5); v WI 1980 (1) 1985 (1); v NZ 1977 (1) 1983 (2) 1987 (3); v In 1981 (5) 1984 (5) 1992 (3); v P 1977 (1) 1983 (3) 1987 (3); v SL 1992 (1)*

Gay, L. H. 1: *v A 1894*

Geary, G. 14: v A 1926 (2) 1930 (1) 1934 (2); v SA 1924 (1) 1929 (1); *v A 1928 (4); v SA 1927 (2)*

Gibb, P. A. 8: v In 1946 (2); *v A 1946 (1); v SA 1938 (5)*

Gifford, N. 15: v A 1964 (2) 1972 (3); v NZ 1973 (2); v In 1971 (2); v P 1971 (2); *v In 1972 (2); v P 1972 (2)*

Gilligan, A. E. R. 11: v SA 1924 (4); *v A 1924 (5); v SA 1922 (2)*

Gilligan, H. H. 4: *v NZ 1929 (4)*

Gimblett, H. 3: v WI 1939 (1); v In 1936 (2)

Gladwin, C. 8: v SA 1947 (2); v NZ 1949 (1); *v SA 1948 (5)*

Goddard, T. W. 8: v A 1930 (1); v WI 1939 (2); v NZ 1937 (2); *v SA 1938 (3)*

Gooch, G. A. 118: v A 1975 (2) 1980 (1) 1981 (5) 1985 (6) 1989 (5) 1993 (6); v SA 1994 (3); v WI 1980 (5) 1988 (5) 1991 (5); v NZ 1978 (3) 1986 (3) 1990 (3) 1994 (3); v In 1979 (4) 1986 (3) 1990 (3); v P 1978 (2) 1992 (5); v SL 1988 (1) 1991 (1); *v A 1978 (6) 1979 (2) 1990 (4) 1994 (5); v WI 1980 (4) 1985 (5) 1989 (2); v NZ 1991 (3); v In 1979 (1) 1981 (6) 1992 (2); v P 1987 (3); v SL 1981 (1)*

Gough, D. 10: v SA 1994 (3); v WI 1995 (3); v NZ 1994 (1); *v A 1994 (3)*

Gover, A. R. 4: v A 1937 (2); v In 1936 (1) 1946 (1)

Gower, D. I. 117: v A 1980 (1) 1981 (5) 1985 (6) 1989 (6); v WI 1980 (1) 1984 (5) 1988 (4); v NZ 1978 (3) 1983 (4) 1986 (3); v In 1979 (4) 1982 (3) 1986 (2) 1990 (3); v P 1978 (3) 1982 (3) 1987 (5) 1992 (5); v SL 1984 (1); *v A 1978 (6) 1979 (3) 1982 (5) 1986 (5) 1990 (5); v WI 1980 (4) 1985 (5); v NZ 1983 (3); v In 1979 (1) 1981 (6) 1984 (5); v P 1983 (3); v SL 1981 (1)*

Grace, E. M. 1: v A 1880

Grace, G. F. 1: v A 1880

Grace, W. G. 22: v A 1880 (1) 1882 (1) 1884 (3) 1886 (3) 1888 (3) 1890 (2) 1893 (2) 1896 (3) 1899 (1); *v A 1891 (3)*

Graveney, T. W. 79: v A 1953 (5) 1956 (2) 1968 (5); v SA 1951 (1) 1955 (5); v WI 1957 (4) 1966 (4) 1969 (1); v NZ 1958 (4); v In 1952 (4) 1967 (3); v P 1954 (3) 1962 (4) 1967 (3); *v A 1954 (2) 1958 (5) 1962 (3); v WI 1953 (4) 1967 (5); v NZ 1954 (3) 1958 (2); v In 1951 (4); v P 1968 (3)*

Greenhough, T. 4: v SA 1960 (1); v In 1959 (3)

Greenwood, A. 2: *v A 1876 (2)*

Greig, A. W. 58 : v A 1972 (5) 1975 (4) 1977 (5); v WI 1973 (3) 1976 (5); v NZ 1973 (3); v In 1974 (3); v P 1974 (3); *v A 1974 (6) 1976 (1); v WI 1973 (5); v NZ 1974 (2); v In 1972 (5) 1976 (5); v P 1972 (3)*

Greig, I. A. 2 : v P 1982 (2)

Grieve, B. A. F. 2 : *v SA 1888 (2)*

Griffith, S. C. 3 : *v SA 1948 (1); v WI 1947 (1)*

Gunn, G. 15 : v A 1909 (1); *v A 1907 (5) 1911 (5); v WI 1929 (4)*

Gunn, J. 6 : v A 1905 (1); *v A 1901 (5)*

Gunn, W. 11 : v A 1888 (2) 1890 (2) 1893 (3) 1896 (1) 1899 (1); *v A 1886 (2)*

Haig, N. E. 5 : v A 1921 (1); *v WI 1929 (4)*

Haigh, S. 11 : v A 1905 (2) 1909 (1) 1912 (1); *v SA 1898 (2) 1905 (5)*

Hallows, C. 2 : v A 1921 (1); v WI 1928 (1)

Hammond, W. R. 85 : v A 1930 (5) 1934 (5) 1938 (4); v SA 1929 (4) 1935 (5); v WI 1928 (3) 1933 (3) 1939 (3); v NZ 1931 (3) 1937 (3); v In 1932 (1) 1936 (2) 1946 (3); *v A 1928 (5) 1932 (5) 1936 (5) 1946 (4); v SA 1927 (5) 1930 (5) 1938 (5); v WI 1934 (4); v NZ 1932 (2) 1946 (1)*

Hampshire, J. H. 8 : v A 1972 (1) 1975 (1); v WI 1969 (2); *v A 1970 (3); v NZ 1970 (2)*

Hardinge, H. T. W. 1 : v A 1921

Hardstaff, J. 5 : *v A 1907 (5)*

Hardstaff, J. jun. 23 : v A 1938 (2) 1948 (1); v SA 1935 (1); v WI 1939 (1); v NZ 1937 (3); v In 1936 (2) 1946 (2); *v A 1936 (5) 1946 (1); v WI 1947 (3)*

Harris, Lord 4 : v A 1880 (1) 1884 (2); *v A 1878 (1)*

Hartley, J. C. 2 : *v SA 1905 (2)*

Hawke, Lord 5 : *v SA 1895 (3) 1898 (2)*

Hayes, E. G. 5 : v A 1909 (1); v SA 1912 (1); *v SA 1905 (3)*

Hayes, F. C. 9 : v WI 1973 (3) 1976 (2); *v WI 1973 (4)*

Hayward, T. W. 35 : v A 1896 (2) 1899 (2) 1902 (1) 1905 (5) 1909 (1); v SA 1907 (3); *v A 1897 (5) 1901 (5) 1903 (5); v SA 1895 (3)*

Hearne, A. 1 : *v SA 1891*

Hearne, F. 2 : *v SA 1888 (2)*

Hearne, G. G. 1 : *v SA 1891*

Hearne, J. T. 12 : v A 1896 (3) 1899 (3); *v A 1897 (5); v SA 1891 (1)*

Hearne, J. W. 24 : v A 1912 (3) 1921 (1) 1926 (1); v SA 1912 (2) 1924 (3); *v A 1911 (5) 1920 (2) 1924 (4); v SA 1913 (3)*

Hemmings, E. E. 16 : v A 1989 (1); v NZ 1990 (3); v In 1990 (3); v P 1982 (2); *v A 1982 (3) 1987 (1) 1990 (1); v NZ 1987 (1); v P 1987 (1)*

Hendren, E. H. 51 : v A 1921 (2) 1926 (5) 1930 (2) 1934 (4); v SA 1924 (5) 1929 (4); v WI 1928 (1); *v A 1920 (5) 1924 (5) 1928 (5); v SA 1930 (5); v WI 1929 (4) 1934 (4)*

Hendrick, M. 30 : v A 1977 (3) 1980 (1) 1981 (2); v WI 1976 (2) 1980 (2); v NZ 1978 (2); v In 1974 (3) 1979 (1); v P 1974 (2); *v A 1974 (2) 1978 (5); v NZ 1974 (1) 1977 (1)*

Heseltine, C. 2 : *v SA 1895 (2)*

Hick, G. A. 37 : v A 1993 (3); v SA 1994 (3); v WI 1991 (4) 1995 (5); v NZ 1994 (3); v P 1992 (4); *v A 1994 (3); v WI 1993 (5); v NZ 1991 (3); v In 1992 (3); v SL 1992 (1)*

Higgs, K. 15 : v A 1968 (1); v WI 1966 (5); v SA 1965 (1); v In 1967 (1); v P 1967 (3); *v A 1965 (1); v NZ 1965 (3)*

Hill, A. 2 : *v A 1876 (2)*

Hill, A. J. L. 3 : *v SA 1895 (3)*

Hilton, M. J. 4 : v SA 1951 (1); v WI 1950 (1); *v In 1951 (2)*

Hirst, G. H. 24 : v A 1899 (1) 1902 (5) 1905 (3) 1909 (4); v SA 1907 (3); *v A 1897 (4) 1903 (5)*

Hitch, J. W. 7 : v A 1912 (1) 1921 (1); v SA 1912 (1); *v A 1911 (3) 1920 (1)*

Hobbs, J. B. 61 : v A 1909 (3) 1912 (3) 1921 (1) 1926 (5) 1930 (5); v SA 1912 (3) 1924 (4) 1929 (5); v WI 1928 (2); *v A 1907 (4) 1911 (5) 1920 (5) 1924 (5) 1928 (5); v SA 1909 (5) 1913 (5)*

Hobbs, R. N. S. 7 : v In 1967 (3); v P 1967 (1) 1971 (1); *v WI 1967 (1); v P 1968 (1)*

Hollies, W. E. 13 : v A 1948 (1); v SA 1947 (3); v WI 1950 (2); v NZ 1949 (4); *v WI 1934 (4)*

Holmes, E. R. T. 5 : v SA 1935 (1); *v WI 1934 (4)*

Holmes, P. 7 : v A 1921 (1); v In 1932 (1); *v SA 1927 (5)*

Hone, L. 1 : *v A 1878*

Hopwood, J. L. 2 : v A 1934 (2)

Hornby, A. N. 3 : v A 1882 (1) 1884 (1); *v A 1878 (1)*

Horton, M. J. 2 : v In 1959 (2)

Howard, N. D. 4 : *v In 1951 (4)*

Howell, H. 5 : v A 1921 (1); v SA 1924 (1); *v A 1920 (3)*

Howorth, R. 5: v SA 1947 (1); *v WI 1947 (4)*
Humphries, J. 3: *v A 1907 (3)*
Hunter, J. 5: *v A 1884 (5)*
Hussain, N. 7: v A 1993 (4); *v WI 1989 (3)*
Hutchings, K. L. 7: v A 1909 (2); *v A 1907 (5)*
Hutton, L. 79: v A 1938 (3) 1948 (4) 1953 (5); v SA 1947 (5) 1951 (5); v WI 1939 (3) 1950 (3); v NZ 1937 (3) 1949 (4); v In 1946 (3) 1952 (4); v P 1954 (2); *v A 1946 (5) 1950 (5) 1954 (5); v SA 1938 (4) 1948 (5); v WI 1947 (2) 1953 (5); v NZ 1950 (2) 1954 (2)*
Hutton, R. A. 5: v In 1971 (3); v P 1971 (2)

Iddon, J. 5: v SA 1935 (1); *v WI 1934 (4)*
Igglesden, A. P. 3: v A 1989 (1); *v WI 1993 (2)*
Ikin, J. T. 18: v SA 1951 (3) 1955 (1); v In 1946 (2) 1952 (2); *v A 1946 (3); v NZ 1946 (1); v WI 1947 (4)*
Illingworth, R. 61: v A 1961 (2) 1968 (3) 1972 (5); v SA 1960 (4); v WI 1966 (2) 1969 (3) 1973 (3); v NZ 1958 (1) 1965 (1) 1969 (3) 1973 (3); v In 1959 (2) 1967 (3) 1971 (3); v P 1962 (1) 1967 (1) 1971 (3); *v A 1962 (2) 1970 (6); v WI 1959 (3); v NZ 1962 (3) 1970 (2)*
Illingworth, R. K. 6: v WI 1991 (2) 1995 (4)
Ilott, M. C. 3: v A 1993 (3)
Insole, D. J. 9: v A 1956 (1); v SA 1955 (1); v WI 1950 (1) 1957 (1); *v SA 1956 (5)*

Jackman, R. D. 4: v P 1982 (2); *v WI 1980 (2)*
Jackson, F. S. 20: v A 1893 (3) 1896 (3) 1899 (5) 1902 (5) 1905 (5)
Jackson, H. L. 2: v A 1961 (1); v NZ 1949 (1)
Jameson, J. A. 4: v In 1971 (2); *v WI 1973 (2)*
Jardine, D. R. 22: v WI 1928 (2) 1933 (2); v NZ 1931 (3); v In 1932 (1); *v A 1928 (5) 1932 (5); v NZ 1932 (1); v In 1933 (3)*
Jarvis, P. W. 9: v A 1989 (2); v WI 1988 (2); *v NZ 1987 (2); v In 1992 (2), v SL 1992 (1)*
Jenkins, R. O. 9: v WI 1950 (2); v In 1952 (2); *v SA 1948 (5)*
Jessop, G. L. 18: v A 1899 (1) 1902 (4) 1905 (1) 1909 (2); v SA 1907 (3) 1912 (2); *v A 1901 (5)*
Jones, A. O. 12: v A 1899 (1) 1905 (2) 1909 (2); *v A 1901 (5) 1907 (2)*
Jones, I. J. 15: v WI 1966 (2); *v A 1965 (4); v WI 1967 (5); v NZ 1965 (3); v In 1963 (1)*
Jupp, H. 2: *v A 1876 (2)*
Jupp, V. W. C. 8: v A 1921 (2); v WI 1928 (2); *v SA 1922 (4)*

Keeton, W. W. 2: v A 1934 (1); v WI 1939 (1)
Kennedy, A. S. 5: *v SA 1922 (5)*
Kenyon, D. 8: v A 1953 (2); v SA 1955 (3); *v In 1951 (3)*
Killick, E. T. 2: v SA 1929 (2)
Kilner, R. 9: v A 1926 (4); v SA 1924 (2); *v A 1924 (3)*
King, J. H. 1: v A 1909
Kinneir, S. P. 1: *v A 1911*
Knight, A. E. 3: *v A 1903 (3)*
Knight, B. R. 29: v A 1968 (2); v WI 1966 (1) 1969 (3); v NZ 1969 (2); v P 1962 (1); *v A 1962 (1) 1965 (2); v NZ 1962 (3) 1965 (2); v In 1961 (4) 1963 (5); v P 1961 (2)*
Knight, D. J. 2: v A 1921 (2)
Knight, N. V. 2: v WI 1995 (2)
Knott, A. P. E. 95: v A 1968 (5) 1972 (5) 1975 (4) 1977 (5) 1981 (2); v WI 1969 (3) 1973 (3) 1976 (5) 1980 (4); v NZ 1969 (3) 1973 (3); v In 1971 (3) 1974 (3); v P 1967 (2) 1971 (3) 1974 (3); *v A 1970 (6) 1974 (6) 1976 (1); v WI 1967 (2) 1973 (5); v NZ 1970 (1) 1974 (2); v In 1972 (5) 1976 (5); v P 1968 (3) 1972 (3)*
Knox, N. A. 2: v SA 1907 (2)

Laker, J. C. 46: v A 1948 (3) 1953 (3) 1956 (5); v SA 1951 (2) 1955 (1); v WI 1950 (1) 1957 (4); v NZ 1949 (1) 1958 (4); v In 1952 (4); v P 1954 (1); *v A 1958 (4); v SA 1956 (5); v WI 1947 (4) 1953 (4)*
Lamb, A. J. 79: v A 1985 (6) 1989 (1); v WI 1984 (5) 1988 (4) 1991 (4); v NZ 1983 (4) 1986 (1) 1990 (3); v In 1982 (3) 1986 (2) 1990 (3); v P 1982 (3) 1992 (2); v SL 1984 (1) 1988 (1); *v A 1982 (5) 1986 (5) 1990 (5); v WI 1985 (5) 1989 (4); v NZ 1983 (3) 1991 (3); v In 1984 (5); v P 1983 (3)*
Langridge, James 8: v SA 1935 (1); v WI 1933 (2); v In 1936 (1) 1946 (1); *v In 1933 (3)*
Larkins, W. 13: v A 1981 (1); v WI 1980 (3); *v A 1979 (1) 1990 (3); v WI 1989 (4); v In 1979 (1)*
Larter, J. D. F. 10: v SA 1965 (2); v NZ 1965 (1); v P 1962 (1); *v NZ 1962 (3); v In 1963 (3)*

Larwood, H. 21 : v A 1926 (2) 1930 (3); v SA 1929 (3); v WI 1928 (2); v NZ 1931 (1); *v A 1928 (5) 1932 (5)*

Lathwell, M. N. 2: v A 1993 (2)

Lawrence, D. V. 5: v WI 1991 (2); v SL 1988 (1) 1991 (1); *v NZ 1991 (1)*

Leadbeater, E. 2: *v In 1951 (2)*

Lee, H. W. 1: *v SA 1930*

Lees, W. S. 5: *v SA 1905 (5)*

Legge, G. B. 5: *v SA 1927 (1); v NZ 1929 (4)*

Leslie, C. F. H. 4: *v A 1882 (4)*

Lever, J. K. 21 : v A 1977 (3); v WI 1980 (1); v In 1979 (1) 1986 (1); *v A 1976 (1) 1978 (1) 1979 (1); v NZ 1977 (1); v In 1976 (5) 1979 (1) 1981 (2); v P 1977 (3)*

Lever, P. 17: v A 1972 (1) 1975 (1); v In 1971 (1); v P 1971 (3); *v A 1970 (5) 1974 (2); v NZ 1970 (2) 1974 (2)*

Leveson Gower, H. D. G. 3: *v SA 1909 (3)*

Levett, W. H. V. 1: *v In 1933*

Lewis, A. R. 9: v In 1972 (5); *v P 1972 (3)*

Lewis, C. C. 27: v A 1993 (2); v WI 1991 (2); v NZ 1990 (1); v In 1990 (2); v P 1992.(5); v SL 1991 (1); *v A 1990 (1) 1994 (2); v WI 1993 (5); v NZ 1991 (2); v In 1992 (3); v SL 1992 (1)*

Leyland, M. 41: v A 1930 (3) 1934 (5) 1938 (1); v SA 1929 (5) 1935 (4); v WI 1928 (5) 1933 (1); v In 1936 (2); *v A 1928 (1) 1932 (5) 1936 (5); v SA 1930 (5); v WI 1934 (3)*

Lilley, A. A. 35: v A 1896 (3) 1899 (4) 1902 (5) 1905 (5) 1909 (5); v SA 1907 (3); *v A 1901 (5) 1903 (5)*

Lillywhite, James jun. 2: *v A 1876 (2)*

Lloyd, D. 9: v In 1974 (2); v P 1974 (3); *v A 1974 (4)*

Lloyd, T. A. 1: v WI 1984

Loader, P. J. 13: v SA 1955 (1); v WI 1957 (2); v NZ 1958 (3); v P 1954 (1); *v A 1958 (2); v SA 1956 (4)*

Lock, G. A. R. 49: v A 1953 (2) 1956 (4) 1961 (3); v SA 1955 (3); v WI 1957 (3) 1963 (3); v NZ 1958 (5); v In 1952 (2); v P 1962 (3); *v A 1958 (4); v SA 1956 (1); v WI 1953 (5) 1967 (2); v NZ 1958 (2); v In 1961 (5); v P 1961 (3)*

Lockwood, W. H. 12: v A 1893 (2) 1899 (1) 1902 (4); *v A 1894 (5)*

Lohmann, G. A. 18: v A 1886 (3) 1888 (3) 1890 (2) 1896 (1); *v A 1886 (2) 1887 (1) 1891 (3); v SA 1895 (3)*

Lowson, F. A. 7: v SA 1951 (2) 1955 (1); *v In 1951 (4)*

Lucas, A. P. 5: v A 1880 (1) 1882 (1) 1884 (2); *v A 1878 (1)*

Luckhurst, B. W. 21: v A 1972 (4); v WI 1973 (2); v In 1971 (3); v P 1971 (3); *v A 1970 (5) 1974 (2); v NZ 1970 (2)*

Lyttelton, Hon. A. 4: v A 1880 (1) 1882 (1) 1884 (2)

Macaulay, G. G. 8: v A 1926 (1); v SA 1924 (1); v WI 1933 (2); *v SA 1922 (4)*

MacBryan, J. C. W. 1: v SA 1924

McCague, M. J. 3: v A 1993 (2); *v A 1994 (1)*

McConnon, J. E. 2: v P 1954 (2)

McGahey, C. P. 2: *v A 1901 (2)*

MacGregor, G. 8: v A 1890 (2) 1893 (3); *v A 1891 (3)*

McIntyre, A. J. W. 3: v SA 1955 (1); v WI 1950 (1); *v A 1950 (1)*

MacKinnon, F. A. 1: *v A 1878*

MacLaren, A. C. 35: v A 1896 (2) 1899 (4) 1902 (5) 1905 (4) 1909 (5); *v A 1894 (5) 1897 (5) 1901 (5)*

McMaster, J. E. P. 1: *v SA 1888*

Makepeace, J. W. H. 4: *v A 1920 (4)*

Malcolm, D. E. 34: v A 1989 (1) 1993 (1); v SA 1994 (1); v WI 1991 (2) 1995 (2); v NZ 1990 (3) 1994 (1); v In 1990 (3); v P 1992 (3); *v A 1990 (5) 1994 (4); v WI 1989 (1) 1993 (1); v In 1992 (2); v SL 1992 (1)*

Mallender, N. A. 2: v P 1992 (2)

Mann, F. G. 7: v NZ 1949 (2); *v SA 1948 (5)*

Mann, F. T. 5: *v SA 1922 (5)*

Marks, V. J. 6: v NZ 1983 (1); v P 1982 (1); *v NZ 1983 (1); v P 1983 (3)*

Marriott, C. S. 1: v WI 1933

Martin, F. 2: v A 1890 (1); *v SA 1891 (1)*

Martin, J. W. 1: v SA 1947

Martin, P. J. 3: v WI 1995 (3)

Mason, J. R. 5: *v A 1897 (5)*

Matthews, A. D. G. 1: v NZ 1937

May, P. B. H. 66: v A 1953 (2) 1956 (5) 1961 (4); v SA 1951 (2) 1955 (5); v WI 1957 (5); v NZ 1958 (5); v In 1952 (4) 1959 (3); v P 1954 (4); *v A 1954 (5) 1958 (5); v SA 1956 (5); v WI 1953 (5) 1959 (3); v NZ 1954 (2) 1958 (2)*

Maynard, M. P. 4: v A 1993 (2); v WI 1988 (1); *v WI 1993 (1)*

Mead, C. P. 17: v A 1921 (2); *v A 1911 (4) 1928 (1); v SA 1913 (5) 1922 (5)*

Mead, W. 1: v A 1899

Midwinter, W. E. 4: *v A 1881 (4)*

Milburn, C. 9: v A 1968 (2); v WI 1966 (4); v In 1967 (1); v P 1967 (1); *v P 1968 (1)*

Miller, A. M. 1: *v SA 1895*

Miller, G. 34: v A 1977 (2); v WI 1976 (1) 1984 (2); v NZ 1978 (2); v In 1979 (3) 1982 (1); v P 1978 (3) 1982 (1); *v A 1978 (6) 1979 (1) 1982 (5); v WI 1980 (1); v NZ 1977 (3); v P 1977 (3)*

Milligan, F. W. 2: *v SA 1898 (2)*

Millman, G. 6: v P 1962 (2); *v In 1961 (2); v P 1961 (2)*

Milton, C. A. 6: v NZ 1958 (2); v In 1959 (2); *v A 1958 (2)*

Mitchell, A. 6: v SA 1935 (2); v In 1936 (1); *v In 1933 (3)*

Mitchell, F. 2: *v SA 1898 (2)*

Mitchell, T. B. 5: v A 1934 (2); v SA 1935 (1); *v A 1932 (1); v NZ 1932 (1)*

Mitchell-Innes, N. S. 1: v SA 1935

Mold, A. W. 3: v A 1893 (3)

Moon, L. J. 4: *v SA 1905 (4)*

Morley, F. 4: v A 1880 (1); *v A 1882 (3)*

Morris, H. 3: v WI 1991 (2); v SL 1991 (1)

Morris, J. E. 3: v In 1990 (3)

Mortimore, J. B. 9: v A 1964 (1); v In 1959 (2); *v A 1958 (1); v NZ 1958 (2); v In 1963 (3)*

Moss, A. E. 9: v A 1956 (1); v SA 1960 (2); v In 1959 (3); *v WI 1953 (1) 1959 (2)*

Moxon, M. D. 10: v A 1989 (1); v WI 1988 (2); v NZ 1986 (2); v P 1987 (1); *v A 1987 (1); v NZ 1987 (3)*

Munton, T. A. 2: v P 1992 (2)

Murdoch, W. L. 1: *v SA 1891*

Murray, J. T. 21: v A 1961 (5); v WI 1966 (1); v In 1967 (3); v P 1962 (3) 1967 (1); *v A 1962 (1); v SA 1964 (1); v NZ 1962 (1) 1965 (1); v In 1961 (3); v P 1961 (1)*

Newham, W. 1: *v A 1887*

Newport, P. J. 3: v A 1989 (1); v SL 1988 (1); *v A 1990 (1)*

Nichols, M. S. 14: v A 1930 (1); v SA 1935 (4); v WI 1933 (1) 1939 (1); *v NZ 1929 (4); v In 1933 (3)*

Oakman, A. S. M. 2: v A 1956 (2)

O'Brien, Sir T. C. 5: v A 1884 (1) 1888 (1); *v SA 1895 (3)*

O'Connor, J. 4: v SA 1929 (1); *v WI 1929 (3)*

Old, C. M. 46: v A 1975 (3) 1977 (2) 1980 (1) 1981 (2); v WI 1973 (1) 1976 (2) 1980 (1); v NZ 1973 (2) 1978 (1); v In 1974 (3); v P 1974 (3) 1978 (3); *v A 1974 (2) 1976 (1) 1978 (1); v WI 1973 (4) 1980 (1); v NZ 1974 (1) 1977 (2); v In 1972 (4) 1976 (4); v P 1972 (1) 1977 (1)*

Oldfield, N. 1: v WI 1939

Padgett, D. E. V. 2: v SA 1960 (2)

Paine, G. A. E. 4: *v WI 1934 (4)*

Palairet, L. C. H. 2: v A 1902 (2)

Palmer, C. H. 1: *v WI 1953*

Palmer, K. E. 1: *v SA 1964*

Parfitt, P. H. 37: v A 1964 (4) 1972 (3); v SA 1965 (2); v WI 1969 (1); v NZ 1965 (2); v P 1962 (5); *v A 1962 (4) 1964 (5); v NZ 1962 (3) 1965 (3); v In 1961 (2) 1963 (3); v P 1961 (2)*

Parker, C. W. L. 1: v A 1921

Parker, P. W. G. 1: v A 1981

Parkhouse, W. G. A. 7: v WI 1950 (2); v In 1959 (2); *v A 1950 (2); v NZ 1950 (1)*

Parkin, C. H. 10: v A 1921 (4); v SA 1924 (1); *v A 1920 (5)*

Parks, J. H. 1: v NZ 1937

Parks, J. M. 46: v A 1964 (5); v SA 1960 (5) 1965 (3); v WI 1963 (4) 1966 (4); v NZ 1965 (3); v P 1954 (1); *v A 1965 (5); v SA 1964 (5); v WI 1959 (1) 1967 (3); v NZ 1965 (2); v In 1963 (5)*

Pataudi sen., Nawab of, 3: v A 1934 (1); *v A 1932 (2)*

Paynter, E. 20: v A 1938 (4); v WI 1939 (2); v NZ 1931 (1) 1937 (2); v In 1932 (1); *v A 1932 (3); v SA 1938 (5); v NZ 1932 (2)*

Peate, E. 9: v A 1882 (1) 1884 (2) 1886 (1); *v A 1881 (4)*

Peebles, I. A. R. 13: v A 1930 (2); v NZ 1931 (3); *v SA 1927 (4) 1930 (4)*

Peel, R. 20: v A 1888 (3) 1890 (1) 1893 (1) 1896 (1); *v A 1884 (5) 1887 (1) 1891 (3) 1894 (5)*

Penn, F. 1: v A 1880

Perks, R. T. D. 2: v WI 1939 (1); *v SA 1938 (1)*

Philipson, H. 5: *v A 1891 (1) 1894 (4)*

Pigott, A. C. S. 1: *v NZ 1983*

Pilling, R. 8: v A 1884 (1) 1886 (1) 1888 (1); *v A 1881 (4) 1887 (1)*

Place, W. 3: *v WI 1947 (3)*

Pocock, P. I. 25: v A 1968 (1); v WI 1976 (2) 1984 (2); v SL 1984 (1); *v WI 1967 (2) 1973 (4); v In 1972 (4) 1984 (5); v P 1968 (1) 1972 (3)*

Pollard, R. 4: v A 1948 (2); v In 1946 (1); *v NZ 1946 (1)*

Poole, C. J. 3: *v In 1951 (3)*

Pope, G. H. 1: v SA 1947

Pougher, A. D. 1: *v SA 1891*

Price, J. S. E. 15: v A 1964 (2) 1972 (1); v In 1971 (3); v P 1971 (1); *v SA 1964 (4); v In 1963 (4)*

Price, W. F. F. 1: v A 1938

Prideaux, R. M. 3: v A 1968 (1); *v P 1968 (2)*

Pringle, D. R. 30: v A 1989 (2); v WI 1984 (3) 1988 (4) 1991 (4); v NZ 1986 (1); v In 1982 (3) 1986 (3); v P 1982 (1) 1992 (3); v SL 1988 (1); *v A 1982 (3); v NZ 1991 (2)*

Pullar, G. 28: v A 1961 (5); v SA 1960 (3); v In 1959 (4); v P 1962 (2); *v A 1962 (4); v WI 1959 (5); v In 1961 (3); v P 1961 (3)*

Quaife, W. G. 7: v A 1899 (2); *v A 1901 (5)*

Radford, N. V. 3: v NZ 1986 (1); v In 1986 (1); *v NZ 1987 (1)*

Radley, C. T. 8: v NZ 1978 (3); v P 1978 (3); *v NZ 1977 (2)*

Ramprakash, M. R. 17: v A 1993 (1); v WI 1991 (5) 1995 (2); v P 1992 (3); v SL 1991 (1); *v A 1994 (1); v WI 1993 (4)*

Randall, D. W. 47: v A 1977 (5); v WI 1984 (1); v NZ 1983 (3); v In 1979 (3) 1982 (3); v P 1982 (3); *v A 1976 (1) 1978 (6) 1979 (2) 1982 (4); v NZ 1977 (3) 1983 (3); v In 1976 (4); v P 1977 (3) 1983 (3)*

Ranjitsinhji, K. S. 15: v A 1896 (2) 1899 (5) 1902 (3); *v A 1897 (5)*

Read, H. D. 1: v SA 1935

Read, J. M. 17: v A 1882 (1) 1890 (1) 1893 (1); *v A 1884 (5) 1886 (2) 1887 (1) 1891 (3); v SA 1888 (2)*

Read, W. W. 18: v A 1884 (2) 1886 (3) 1888 (3) 1890 (2) 1893 (2); *v A 1882 (4) 1887 (1); v SA 1891 (1)*

Reeve, D. A. 3: *v NZ 1991 (3)*

Relf, A. E. 13: v A 1909 (1); *v A 1903 (2); v SA 1905 (5) 1913 (5)*

Rhodes, H. J. 2: v In 1959 (2)

Rhodes, S. J. 11: v SA 1994 (3); v NZ 1994 (3); *v A 1994 (5)*

Rhodes, W. 58: v A 1899 (3) 1902 (5) 1905 (4) 1909 (4) 1912 (3) 1921 (1) 1926 (1); v SA 1912 (3); *v A 1903 (5) 1907 (5) 1911 (5) 1920 (5); v SA 1909 (5) 1913 (5); v WI 1929 (4)*

Richards, C. J. 8: v WI 1988 (2); v P 1987 (1); *v A 1986 (5)*

Richardson, D. W. 1: v WI 1957

Richardson, P. E. 34: v A 1956 (5); v WI 1957 (5) 1963 (1); v NZ 1958 (4); *v A 1958 (4); v SA 1956 (5); v NZ 1958 (2); v In 1961 (5); v P 1961 (3)*

Richardson, T. 14: v A 1893 (1) 1896 (3); *v A 1894 (5) 1897 (5)*

Richmond, T. L. 1: v A 1921

Ridgway, F. 5: *v In 1951 (5)*

Robertson, J. D. 11: v SA 1947 (1); v NZ 1949 (1); *v WI 1947 (4); v In 1951 (5)*

Robins, R. W. V. 19: v A 1930 (2); v SA 1929 (1) 1935 (3); v WI 1933 (2); v NZ 1931 (1) 1937 (3); v In 1932 (1) 1936 (2); *v A 1936 (4)*

Robinson, R. T. 29: v A 1985 (6) 1989 (1); v In 1986 (1); v P 1987 (5); v SL 1988 (1); *v A 1987 (1); v WI 1985 (4); v NZ 1987 (3); v In 1984 (5); v P 1987 (2)*

Roope, G. R. J. 21: v A 1975 (1) 1977 (2); v WI 1973 (1); v NZ 1973 (1) 1978 (1); v P 1978 (3); *v NZ 1977 (3); v In 1972 (2); v P 1972 (2) 1977 (3)*

Root, C. F. 3: v A 1926 (3)

Rose, B. C. 9: v WI 1980 (3); *v WI 1980 (1); v NZ 1977 (2); v P 1977 (3)*

Royle, V. P. F. A. 1: *v A 1878*

Rumsey, F. E. 5: v A 1964 (1); v SA 1965 (1); v NZ 1965 (3)

Russell, A. C. 10: v A 1921 (2); *v A 1920 (4); v SA 1922 (4)*

Russell, R. C. 39: v A 1989 (6); v WI 1991 (4) 1995 (3); v NZ 1990 (3); v In 1990 (3); v P 1992 (3); v SL 1988 (1) 1991 (1); *v A 1990 (3); v WI 1989 (4) 1993 (5); v NZ 1991 (3)*

Russell, W. E. 10: v SA 1965 (1); v WI 1966 (2); v P 1967 (1); *v A 1965 (1); v NZ 1965 (3); v In 1961 (1); v P 1961 (1)*

Salisbury, I. D. K. 7: v SA 1994 (1); v P 1992 (2); *v WI 1993 (2); v In 1992 (2)*

Sandham, A. 14: v A 1921 (1); v SA 1924 (2); *v A 1924 (2); v SA 1922 (5); v WI 1929 (4)*

Schultz, S. S. 1: *v A 1878*

Scotton, W. H. 15: v A 1884 (1) 1886 (3); *v A 1881 (4) 1884 (5) 1886 (2)*

Selby, J. 6: *v A 1876 (2) 1881 (4)*

Selvey, M. W. W. 3: v WI 1976 (2); v In 1976 (1)

Shackleton, D. 7: v SA 1951 (1); v WI 1950 (1) 1963 (4); *v In 1951 (1)*

Sharp, J. 3: v A 1909 (3)

Sharpe, J. W. 3: v A 1890 (1); *v A 1891 (2)*

Sharpe, P. J. 12: v A 1964 (2); v WI 1963 (3) 1969 (3); v NZ 1969 (3); *v In 1963 (1)*

Shaw, A. 7: v A 1880 (1); *v A 1876 (2) 1881 (4)*

Sheppard, Rev. D. S. 22: v A 1956 (2); v WI 1950 (1) 1957 (2); v In 1952 (2); v P 1954 (2) 1962 (2); *v A 1950 (2) 1962 (5); v NZ 1950 (1) 1963 (3)*

Sherwin, M. 3: v A 1888 (1); *v A 1886 (2)*

Shrewsbury, A. 23: v A 1884 (3) 1886 (3) 1890 (2) 1893 (3); *v A 1881 (4) 1884 (5) 1886 (2) 1887 (1)*

Shuter, J. 1: v A 1888

Shuttleworth, K. 5: v P 1971 (1); *v A 1970 (2); v NZ 1970 (2)*

Sidebottom, A. 1: v A 1985

Simpson, R. T. 27: v A 1953 (2); v SA 1951 (3); v WI 1950 (3); v NZ 1949 (2); v In 1952 (2); v P 1954 (3); *v A 1950 (5) 1954 (1); v SA 1948 (1); v NZ 1950 (2) 1954 (2)*

Simpson-Hayward, G. H. 5: *v SA 1909 (5)*

Sims, J. M. 4: v SA 1935 (1); v In 1936 (1); *v A 1936 (2)*

Sinfield, R. A. 1: v A 1938

Slack, W. N. 3: v In 1986 (1); *v WI 1985 (2)*

Smailes, T. F. 1: v In 1946

Small, G. C. 17: v A 1989 (1); v WI 1988 (1); v NZ 1986 (2) 1990 (3); *v A 1986 (2) 1990 (4); v WI 1989 (4)*

Smith, A. C. 6: *v A 1962 (4); v NZ 1962 (2)*

Smith, C. A. 1: *v SA 1888*

Smith, C. I. J. 5: v NZ 1937 (1); *v WI 1934 (4)*

Smith, C. L. 8: v NZ 1983 (2); v In 1986 (1); *v NZ 1983 (2); v P 1983 (3)*

Smith, D. 2: v SA 1935 (2)

Smith, D. M. 2: *v WI 1985 (2)*

Smith, D. R. 5: *v In 1961 (5)*

Smith, D. V. 3: v WI 1957 (3)

Smith, E. J. 11: v A 1912 (3); v SA 1912 (3); *v A 1911 (4); v SA 1913 (1)*

Smith, H. 1: v WI 1928

Smith, M. J. K. 50: v A 1961 (1) 1972 (3); v SA 1960 (4) 1965 (3); v WI 1966 (1); v NZ 1958 (3) 1965 (3); v In 1959 (2); *v A 1965 (5); v SA 1964 (5); v WI 1959 (5); v NZ 1965 (3); v In 1961 (4) 1963 (5); v P 1961 (3)*

Smith, R. A. 57: v A 1989 (5) 1993 (5); v WI 1988 (2) 1991 (4) 1995 (4); v NZ 1990 (3) 1994 (3); v In 1990 (3); v P 1992 (5); v SL 1988 (1) 1991 (1); *v A 1990 (5); v WI 1989 (4) 1993 (5); v NZ 1991 (3); v In 1992 (3); v SL 1992 (1)*

Smith, T. P. B. 4: v In 1946 (1); *v A 1946 (2); v NZ 1946 (1)*

Smithson, G. A. 2: *v WI 1947 (2)*

Snow, J. A. 49: v A 1968 (5) 1972 (5) 1975 (4); v SA 1965 (1); v WI 1966 (3) 1969 (3) 1973 (1) 1976 (3); v NZ 1965 (1) 1969 (2) 1973 (3); v In 1967 (3) 1971 (2); v P 1967 (1); *v A 1970 (6); v WI 1967 (4); v P 1968 (2)*

Southerton, J. 2: *v A 1876 (2)*

Spooner, R. H. 10: v A 1905 (2) 1909 (2) 1912 (3); v SA 1912 (3)

Spooner, R. T. 7: v A 1955 (1); *v In 1951 (5); v WI 1953 (1)*

Stanyforth, R. T. 4: *v SA 1927 (4)*

Staples, S. J. 3: *v SA 1927 (3)*

Statham, J. B. 70: v A 1953 (1) 1956 (3) 1961 (4); v SA 1951 (2) 1955 (4) 1960 (5) 1965 (1); v WI 1957 (3) 1963 (2); v NZ 1958 (2); v In 1959 (3); v P 1954 (2) 1962 (3); *v A 1954 (5) 1958 (4) 1962 (5); v SA 1956 (4); v WI 1953 (4) 1959 (3); v NZ 1950 (1) 1954 (2); v In 1951 (5)*

Steel, A. G. 13: v A 1880 (1) 1882 (1) 1884 (3) 1886 (3) 1888 (1); *v A 1882 (4)*

Steele, D. S. 8: v A 1975 (3); v WI 1976 (5)

Stephenson, J. P. 1: v A 1989

Stevens, G. T. S. 10: v A 1926 (2); *v SA 1922 (1) 1927 (5); v WI 1929 (2)*

Stevenson, G. B. 2: *v WI 1980 (1); v In 1979 (1)*

Stewart, A. J. 48: v A 1993 (6); v SA 1994 (3); v WI 1991 (1) 1995 (3); v NZ 1990 (3) 1994 (3); v P 1992 (5); v SL 1991 (1); *v A 1990 (5) 1994 (2); v WI 1989 (4) 1993 (5); v NZ 1991 (3); v In 1992 (3); v SL 1992 (1)*

Stewart, M. J. 8: v WI 1963 (4); v P 1962 (2); *v In 1963 (2)*

Stoddart, A. E. 16: v A 1893 (3) 1896 (2); *v A 1887 (1) 1891 (3) 1894 (5) 1897 (2)*

Storer, W. 6: v A 1899 (1); *v A 1897 (5)*

Street, G. B. 1: *v SA 1922*

Strudwick, H. 28: v A 1921 (2) 1926 (5); v SA 1924 (5); *v A 1911 (1) 1920 (4) 1924 (5); v SA 1909 (5) 1913 (5)*

Studd, C. T. 5: v A 1882 (1); *v A 1882 (4)*

Studd, G. B. 4: *v A 1882 (4)*

Subba Row, R. 13: v A 1961 (5); v SA 1960 (4); v NZ 1958 (1); v In 1959 (1); *v WI 1959 (2)*

Such, P. M. 8: v A 1993 (5); v NZ 1994 (3)

Sugg, F. H. 2: v A 1888 (2)

Sutcliffe, H. 54: v A 1926 (5) 1930 (4) 1934 (4); v SA 1924 (5) 1929 (5) 1935 (2); v WI 1928 (3) 1933 (2); v NZ 1931 (2); v In 1932 (1); *v A 1924 (5) 1928 (4) 1932 (5); v SA 1927 (5); v NZ 1932 (2)*

Swetman, R. 11: v In 1959 (3); *v A 1958 (2); v WI 1959 (4); v NZ 1958 (2)*

Tate, F. W. 1: v A 1902

Tate, M. W. 39: v A 1926 (5) 1930 (5); v SA 1924 (5) 1929 (3) 1935 (1); v WI 1928 (3); v NZ 1931 (1); *v A 1924 (5) 1928 (5); v SA 1930 (5); v NZ 1932 (1)*

Tattersall, R. 16: v A 1953 (1); v SA 1951 (5); v P 1954 (1); *v A 1950 (2); v NZ 1950 (2); v In 1951 (2)*

Tavaré, C. J. 31: v A 1981 (2) 1989 (1); v WI 1980 (2) 1984 (1); v NZ 1983 (4); v In 1982 (3); v P 1982 (3); v SL 1984 (1); *v A 1982 (5); v NZ 1983 (2); v In 1981 (6); v SL 1981 (1)*

Taylor, J. P. 2: v NZ 1994 (1); *v In 1992 (1)*

Taylor, K. 3: v A 1964 (1); v In 1959 (2)

Taylor, L. B. 2: v A 1985 (2)

Taylor, R. W. 57: v A 1981 (3); v NZ 1978 (3) 1983 (4); v In 1979 (3) 1982 (3); v P 1978 (3) 1982 (3); *v A 1978 (6) 1979 (3) 1982 (5); v NZ 1970 (1) 1977 (3) 1983 (3); v In 1979 (1) 1981 (6); v P 1977 (3) 1983 (3); v SL 1981 (1)*

Tennyson, Hon. L. H. 9: v A 1921 (4); *v SA 1913 (5)*

Terry, V. P. 2: v WI 1984 (2)

Thomas, J. G. 5: v NZ 1986 (1); *v WI 1985 (4)*

Thompson, G. J. 6: v A 1909 (1); *v SA 1909 (5)*

Thomson, N. I. 5: *v SA 1964 (5)*

Thorpe, G. P. 21: v A 1993 (3); v SA 1994 (2); v WI 1995 (6); *v A 1994 (5); v WI 1993 (5)*

Titmus, F. J. 53: v A 1964 (5); v SA 1955 (2) 1965 (3); v WI 1963 (4) 1966 (3); v NZ 1965 (3); v P 1962 (2) 1967 (2); *v A 1962 (5) 1965 (5) 1974 (4); v SA 1964 (5); v WI 1967 (2); v NZ 1962 (3); v In 1963 (5)*

Tolchard, R. W. 4: *v In 1976 (4)*

Townsend, C. L. 2: v A 1899 (2)

Townsend, D. C. H. 3: *v WI 1934 (3)*

Townsend, L. F. 4: *v WI 1929 (1); v In 1933 (3)*

Tremlett, M. F. 3: *v WI 1947 (3)*

Trott, A. E. 2: *v SA 1898 (2)*

Trueman, F. S. 67: v A 1953 (1) 1956 (2) 1961 (4) 1964 (4); v SA 1955 (1) 1960 (5); v WI 1957 (5) 1963 (5); v NZ 1958 (5) 1965 (2); v In 1952 (4) 1959 (5); v P 1962 (4); *v A 1958 (3) 1962 (5); v WI 1953 (3) 1959 (5); v NZ 1958 (2) 1962 (2)*

Tufnell, N. C. 1: *v SA 1909*

Tufnell, P. C. R. 22: v A 1993 (2); v SA 1994 (1); v WI 1991 (1); v P 1992 (1); v SL 1991 (1); *v A 1990 (4); v WI 1993 (2); v NZ 1991 (3); v In 1992 (2); v SL 1992 (1)*

Turnbull, M. J. 9: v WI 1933 (1); v In 1936 (1); *v SA 1930 (5); v NZ 1929 (1)*

Tyldesley, E. 14: v A 1921 (3) 1926 (1); v SA 1924 (1); v WI 1928 (3); *v A 1928 (1); v SA 1927 (5)*

Tyldesley, J. T. 31: v A 1899 (2) 1902 (5) 1905 (5) 1909 (4); v SA 1907 (3); *v A 1901 (5) 1903 (5); v SA 1898 (2)*

Tyldesley, R. K. 7: v A 1930 (2); v SA 1924 (4); *v A 1924 (1)*

Tylecote, E. F. S. 6: v A 1886 (2); *v A 1882 (4)*

Tyler, E. J. 1: *v SA 1895*

Tyson, F. H. 17: v A 1956 (1); v SA 1955 (2); v P 1954 (1); *v A 1954 (5) 1958 (2); v SA 1956 (2); v NZ 1954 (2) 1958 (2)*

Ulyett, G. 25: v A 1882 (1) 1884 (3) 1886 (3) 1888 (2) 1890 (1); *v A 1876 (2) 1878 (1) 1881 (4) 1884 (5) 1887 (1); v SA 1888 (2)*

Underwood, D. L. 86: v A 1968 (4) 1972 (2) 1975 (4) 1977 (5); v WI 1966 (2) 1969 (2) 1973 (3) 1976 (5) 1980 (1); v NZ 1969 (3) 1973 (1); v In 1971 (1) 1974 (3); v P 1967 (2) 1971 (1) 1974 (3); *v A 1970 (5) 1974 (5) 1976 (1) 1979 (3); v WI 1973 (4); v NZ 1970 (2) 1974 (2); v In 1972 (4) 1976 (5) 1979 (1) 1981 (6); v P 1968 (3) 1972 (2); v SL 1981 (1)*

Valentine, B. H. 7: *v SA 1938 (5); v In 1933 (2)*

Verity, H. 40: v A 1934 (5) 1938 (4); v SA 1935 (4); v WI 1933 (2) 1939 (1); v NZ 1931 (2) 1937 (1); v In 1936 (3); *v A 1932 (4) 1936 (5); v SA 1938 (5); v NZ 1932 (1); v In 1933 (3)*

Vernon, G. F. 1: *v A 1882*

Vine, J. 2: *v A 1911 (2)*

Voce, W. 27: v NZ 1931 (1) 1937 (1); v In 1932 (1) 1936 (1) 1946 (1); *v A 1932 (4) 1936 (5) 1946 (2); v SA 1930 (5); v WI 1929 (4); v NZ 1932 (2)*

Waddington, A. 2: *v A 1920 (2)*

Wainwright, E. 5: v A 1893 (1); *v A 1897 (4)*

Walker, P. M. 3: v SA 1960 (3)

Walters, C. F. 11: v A 1934 (5); v WI 1933 (3); *v In 1933 (3)*

Ward, A. 5: v WI 1976 (1); v NZ 1969 (3); v P 1971 (1)

Ward, A. 7: v A 1893 (2); *v A 1894 (5)*

Wardle, J. H. 28: v A 1953 (3) 1956 (1); v SA 1951 (2) 1955 (3); v WI 1950 (1) 1957 (1); v P 1954 (4); *v A 1954 (4); v SA 1956 (4); v WI 1947 (1) 1953 (2); v NZ 1954 (2)*

Warner, P. F. 15: v A 1909 (1) 1912 (3); v SA 1912 (1); *v A 1903 (5); v SA 1898 (2) 1905 (5)*

Warr, J. J. 2: *v A 1950 (2)*

Warren, A. R. 1: v A 1905

Washbrook, C. 37: v A 1948 (4) 1956 (3); v SA 1947 (5); v WI 1950 (2); v NZ 1937 (1) 1949 (2); v In 1946 (3); *v A 1946 (5) 1950 (5); v SA 1948 (5); v NZ 1946 (1) 1950 (1)*

Watkin, S. L. 3: v A 1993 (1); v WI 1991 (2)

Watkins, A. J. 15: v A 1948 (1); v NZ 1949 (1); v In 1952 (3); *v SA 1948 (5); v In 1951 (5)*

Watkinson, M. 3: v WI 1995 (3)

Watson, W. 23: v A 1953 (3) 1956 (2); v SA 1951 (5) 1955 (1); v NZ 1958 (2); v In 1952 (1); *v A 1958 (2); v WI 1953 (5); v NZ 1958 (2)*

Webbe, A. J. 1: *v A 1878*

Wellard, A. W. 2: v A 1938 (1); v NZ 1937 (1)

Wells, A. P. 1: v WI 1995

Wharton, A. 1: v NZ 1949

Whitaker, J. J. 1: *v A 1986*

White, C. 6: v SA 1994 (1); v WI 1995 (2); v NZ 1994 (3)

White, D. W. 2: *v P 1961 (2)*

White, J. C. 15: v A 1921 (1) 1930 (1); v SA 1929 (3); v WI 1928 (1); *v A 1928 (5); v SA 1930 (4)*

Whysall, W. W. 4: v A 1930 (1); *v A 1924 (3)*

Wilkinson, L. L. 3: *v SA 1938 (3)*

Willey, P. 26: v A 1980 (1) 1981 (4) 1985 (1); v WI 1976 (2) 1980 (5); v NZ 1986 (1); v In 1979 (1); *v A 1979 (3); v WI 1980 (4) 1985 (4)*

Williams, N. F. 1: v In 1990

Willis, R. G. D. 90: v A 1977 (5) 1981 (6); v WI 1973 (1) 1976 (2) 1980 (4) 1984 (3); v NZ 1978 (3) 1983 (4); v In 1974 (1) 1979 (3) 1982 (3); v P 1974 (1) 1978 (3) 1982 (2); *v A 1970 (4) 1974 (5) 1976 (1) 1978 (6) 1979 (3) 1982 (5); v WI 1973 (3); v NZ 1970 (1) 1977 (3) 1983 (3); v In 1976 (5) 1981 (5); v P 1977 (3) 1983 (1); v SL 1981 (1)*

Wilson, C. E. M. 2: *v SA 1898 (2)*

Wilson, D. 6: *v NZ 1970 (1); v In 1963 (5)*

Wilson, E. R. 1: *v A 1920*
Wood, A. 4: v A 1938 (1); v WI 1939 (3)
Wood, B. 12: v A 1972 (1) 1975 (3); v WI 1976 (1); v P 1978 (1); *v NZ 1974 (2); v In 1972 (3); v P 1972 (1)*
Wood, G. E. C. 3: v SA 1924 (3)
Wood, H. 4: v A 1888 (1); *v SA 1888 (2) 1891 (1)*
Wood, R. 1: *v A 1886*
Woods, S. M. J. 3: *v SA 1895 (3)*
Woolley, F. E. 64: v A 1909 (1) 1912 (3) 1921 (5) 1926 (5) 1930 (2) 1934 (1); v SA 1912 (3) 1924 (5) 1929 (3); v NZ 1931 (1); v In 1932 (1); *v A 1911 (5) 1920 (5) 1924 (5); v SA 1909 (5) 1913 (5) 1922 (5); v NZ 1929 (4)*
Woolmer, R. A. 19: v A 1975 (2) 1977 (5) 1981 (2); v WI 1976 (5) 1980 (2); *v A 1976 (1); v In 1976 (2)*
Worthington, T. S. 9: v In 1936 (2); *v A 1936 (3); v NZ 1929 (4)*
Wright, C. W. 3: *v SA 1895 (3)*
Wright, D. V. P. 34: v A 1938 (3) 1948 (1); v SA 1947 (4); v WI 1939 (3) 1950 (1); v NZ 1949 (1); v In 1946 (2); *v A 1946 (5) 1950 (5); v SA 1938 (3) 1948 (3); v NZ 1946 (1) 1950 (2)*
Wyatt, R. E. S. 40: v A 1930 (1) 1934 (4); v SA 1929 (2) 1935 (5); v WI 1933 (2); v In 1936 (1); *v A 1932 (5) 1936 (2); v SA 1927 (5) 1930 (5); v WI 1929 (2) 1934 (4); v NZ 1932 (2)*
Wynyard, E. G. 3: v A 1896 (1); *v SA 1905 (2)*

Yardley, N. W. D. 20: v A 1948 (5); v SA 1947 (5); v WI 1950 (3); *v A 1946 (5); v SA 1938 (1); v NZ 1946 (1)*
Young, H. I. 2: v A 1899 (2)
Young, J. A. 8: v A 1948 (3); v SA 1947 (1); v NZ 1949 (2); *v SA 1948 (2)*
Young, R. A. 2: *v A 1907 (2)*

AUSTRALIA

Number of Test cricketers: 364

a'Beckett, E. L. 4: v E 1928 (2); v SA 1931 (1); *v E 1930 (1)*
Alderman, T. M. 41: v E 1982 (1) 1990 (4); v WI 1981 (2) 1984 (3) 1988 (2); v NZ 1989 (1); v P 1981 (3) 1989 (2); v SL 1989 (2); *v E 1981 (6) 1989 (6); v WI 1983 (3) 1990 (1); v NZ 1981 (3) 1989 (1); v P 1982 (1)*
Alexander, G. 2: v E 1884 (1); *v E 1880 (1)*
Alexander, H. H. 1: v E 1932
Allan, F. E. 1: v E 1878
Allan, P. J. 1: v E 1965
Allen, R. C. 1: v E 1886
Andrews, T. J. E. 16: v E 1924 (3); *v E 1921 (5) 1926 (5); v SA 1921 (3)*
Angel, J. 4: v E 1994 (1); v WI 1992 (1); *v P 1994 (2)*
Archer, K. A. 5: v E 1950 (3); v WI 1951 (2)
Archer, R. G. 19: v E 1954 (4); v SA 1952 (1); *v E 1953 (3) 1956 (5); v WI 1954 (5); v P 1956 (1)*
Armstrong, W. W. 50: v E 1901 (4) 1903 (3) 1907 (5) 1911 (5) 1920 (5); v SA 1910 (5); *v E 1902 (5) 1905 (5) 1909 (5) 1921 (5); v SA 1902 (3)*

Badcock, C. L. 7: v E 1936 (3); *v E 1938 (4)*
Bannerman, A. C. 28: v E 1878 (1) 1881 (3) 1882 (4) 1884 (4) 1886 (1) 1887 (1) 1891 (3); *v E 1880 (1) 1882 (1) 1884 (3) 1888 (3) 1893 (3)*
Bannerman, C. 3: v E 1876 (2) 1878 (1)
Bardsley, W. 41: v E 1911 (4) 1920 (5) 1924 (3); v SA 1910 (5); *v E 1909 (5) 1912 (3) 1921 (5) 1926 (5); v SA 1912 (3) 1921 (3)*
Barnes, S. G. 13: v E 1946 (4); v In 1947 (3); *v E 1938 (1) 1948 (4); v NZ 1945 (1)*
Barnett, B. A. 4: *v E 1938 (4)*
Barrett, J. E. 2: *v E 1890 (2)*
Beard, G. R. 3: *v P 1979 (3)*
Benaud, J. 3: v P 1972 (2); *v WI 1972 (1)*
Benaud, R. 63: v E 1954 (5) 1958 (5) 1962 (5); v SA 1952 (4) 1963 (4); v WI 1951 (1) 1960 (5); *v E 1953 (3) 1956 (5) 1961 (4); v SA 1957 (5); v WI 1954 (5); v In 1956 (3) 1959 (5); v P 1956 (1) 1959 (3)*

Bennett, M. J. 3: v WI 1984 (2); *v E 1985 (1)*

Bevan, M. G. 6: v E 1994 (3); *v P 1994 (3)*

Blackham, J. McC. 35: v E 1876 (2) 1878 (1) 1881 (4) 1882 (4) 1884 (2) 1886 (1) 1887 (1) 1891 (3) 1894 (1); *v E 1880 (1) 1882 (1) 1884 (3) 1886 (3) 1888 (3) 1890 (2) 1893 (3)*

Blackie, D. D. 3: v E 1928 (3)

Blewett, G. S. 6: v E 1994 (2); *v WI 1994 (4)*

Bonnor, G. J. 17: v E 1882 (4) 1884 (3); *v E 1880 (1) 1882 (1) 1884 (3) 1886 (2) 1888 (3)*

Boon, D. C. 101: v E 1986 (4) 1987 (1) 1990 (5) 1994 (5); v SA 1993 (3); v WI 1984 (3) 1988 (5) 1992 (5); v NZ 1985 (3) 1987 (3) 1989 (1) 1993 (3); v In 1985 (3) 1991 (5); v P 1989 (2); v SL 1987 (1) 1989 (2); *v E 1985 (4) 1989 (6) 1993 (6); v SA 1993 (3); v WI 1990 (5) 1994 (4); v NZ 1985 (3) 1989 (1) 1992 (3); v In 1986 (3); v P 1988 (3) 1994 (3); v SL 1992 (3)*

Booth, B. C. 29: v E 1962 (5) 1965 (3); v SA 1963 (4); v P 1964 (1); *v E 1961 (2) 1964 (5); v WI 1964 (5); v In 1964 (3); v P 1964 (1)*

Border, A. R. 156: v E 1978 (3) 1979 (3) 1982 (5) 1986 (5) 1987 (1) 1990 (5); v SA 1993 (3); v WI 1979 (3) 1981 (3) 1984 (5) 1988 (5) 1992 (5); v NZ 1980 (3) 1985 (3) 1987 (3) 1989 (1) 1993 (3); v In 1980 (3) 1985 (3) 1991 (5); v P 1978 (2) 1981 (3) 1983 (5) 1989 (3); v SL 1987 (1) 1989 (2); *v E 1980 (1) 1981 (6) 1985 (6) 1989 (6) 1993 (6); v SA 1993 (3); v WI 1983 (5) 1990 (5); v NZ 1981 (3) 1985 (3) 1989 (1) 1992 (3); v In 1979 (6) 1986 (3); v P 1979 (3) 1982 (3) 1988 (3); v SL 1982 (1) 1992 (3)*

Boyle, H. F. 12: v E 1878 (1) 1881 (4) 1882 (1) 1884 (1); *v E 1880 (1) 1882 (1) 1884 (3)*

Bradman, D. G. 52: v E 1928 (4) 1932 (4) 1936 (5) 1946 (5); v SA 1931 (5); v WI 1930 (5); v In 1947 (5); *v E 1930 (5) 1934 (5) 1938 (4) 1948 (5)*

Bright, R. J. 25: v E 1979 (1); v WI 1979 (1); v NZ 1985 (1); v In 1985 (3); *v E 1977 (3) 1980 (1) 1981 (5); v NZ 1985 (2); v In 1986 (3); v P 1979 (3) 1982 (2)*

Bromley, E. H. 2: v E 1932 (1); *v E 1934 (1)*

Brown, W. A. 22: v E 1936 (2); v In 1947 (3); *v E 1934 (5) 1938 (4) 1948 (2); v SA 1935 (5); v NZ 1945 (1)*

Bruce, W. 14: v E 1884 (2) 1891 (3) 1894 (4); *v E 1886 (2) 1893 (3)*

Burge, P. J. P. 42: v E 1954 (1) 1958 (1) 1962 (3) 1965 (4); v SA 1963 (5); v WI 1960 (2); *v E 1956 (3) 1961 (5) 1964 (5); v SA 1957 (1); v WI 1954 (1); v In 1956 (3) 1959 (2) 1964 (3); v P 1959 (2) 1964 (1)*

Burke, J. W. 24: v E 1950 (2) 1954 (2) 1958 (5); v WI 1951 (1); *v E 1956 (5); v SA 1957 (5); v In 1956 (3); v P 1956 (1)*

Burn, K. E. 2: *v E 1890 (2)*

Burton, F. J. 2: v E 1886 (1) 1887 (1)

Callaway, S. T. 3: v E 1891 (2) 1894 (1)

Callen, I. W. 1: v In 1977

Campbell, G. D. 4: v P 1989 (1); v SL 1989 (1); *v E 1989 (1); v NZ 1989 (1)*

Carkeek, W. 6: *v E 1912 (3); v SA 1912 (3)*

Carlson, P. H. 2: v E 1978 (2)

Carter, H. 28: v E 1907 (5) 1911 (5) 1920 (2); v SA 1910 (5); *v E 1909 (5) 1921 (4); v SA 1921 (2)*

Chappell, G. S. 87: v E 1970 (5) 1974 (6) 1976 (1) 1979 (3) 1982 (5); v WI 1975 (6) 1979 (3) 1981 (3); v NZ 1973 (3) 1980 (3); v In 1980 (3); v P 1972 (3) 1976 (3) 1981 (3) 1983 (5); *v E 1972 (5) 1975 (4) 1977 (5) 1980 (1); v WI 1972 (5); v NZ 1973 (3) 1976 (2) 1981 (3); v P 1979 (3); v SL 1982 (1)*

Chappell, I. M. 75: v E 1965 (2) 1970 (6) 1974 (6) 1979 (2); v WI 1968 (5) 1975 (6) 1979 (1); v NZ 1973 (3); v In 1967 (4); v P 1964 (1) 1972 (3); *v E 1968 (5) 1972 (5) 1975 (4); v SA 1966 (5) 1969 (4); v WI 1972 (5); v NZ 1973 (3); v In 1969 (5)*

Chappell, T. M. 3: *v E 1981 (3)*

Charlton, P. C. 2: *v E 1890 (2)*

Chipperfield, A. G. 14: v E 1936 (3); *v E 1934 (5) 1938 (1); v SA 1935 (5)*

Clark, W. M. 10: v In 1977 (5); v P 1978 (1); *v WI 1977 (4)*

Colley, D. J. 3: *v E 1972 (3)*

Collins, H. L. 19: v E 1920 (5) 1924 (5); *v E 1921 (3) 1926 (3); v SA 1921 (3)*

Coningham, A. 1: v E 1894

Connolly, A. N. 29: v E 1965 (1) 1970 (1); v SA 1963 (3); v WI 1968 (5); v In 1967 (3); *v E 1968 (5); v SA 1969 (4); v In 1964 (2) 1969 (5)*

Cooper, B. B. 1: v E 1876

Cooper, W. H. 2: v E 1881 (1) 1884 (1)

Corling, G. E. 5: *v E 1964 (5)*

Cosier, G. J. 18: v E 1976 (1) 1978 (2); v WI 1975 (3); v In 1977 (4); v P 1976 (3); *v WI 1977 (3); v NZ 1976 (2)*

Cottam, J. T. 1: v E 1886

Cotter, A. 21: v E 1903 (2) 1907 (2) 1911 (4); v SA 1910 (5); *v E 1905 (3) 1909 (5)*

Coulthard, G. 1: v E 1881

Cowper, R. M. 27: v E 1965 (4); v In 1967 (4); v P 1964 (1); *v E 1964 (1) 1968 (4); v SA 1966 (5); v WI 1964 (5); v In 1964 (2); v P 1964 (1)*

Craig, I. D. 11: v SA 1952 (1); *v E 1956 (2); v SA 1957 (5); v In 1956 (2); v P 1956 (1)*

Crawford, W. P. A. 4: *v E 1956 (1); v In 1956 (3)*

Darling, J. 34: v E 1894 (5) 1897 (5) 1901 (3); *v E 1896 (3) 1899 (5) 1902 (5) 1905 (5); v SA 1902 (3)*

Darling, L. S. 12: v E 1932 (2) 1936 (1); *v E 1934 (4); v SA 1935 (5)*

Darling, W. M. 14: v E 1978 (4); v In 1977 (1); v P 1978 (1); *v WI 1977 (3); v In 1979 (5)*

Davidson, A. K. 44: v E 1954 (3) 1958 (5) 1962 (5); v WI 1960 (4); *v E 1953 (5) 1956 (2) 1961 (5); v SA 1957 (5); v In 1956 (1) 1959 (5); v P 1956 (1) 1959 (3)*

Davis, I. C. 15: v E 1976 (1); v NZ 1973 (3); v P 1976 (3); *v E 1977 (3); v NZ 1973 (3) 1976 (2)*

Davis, S. P. 1: *v NZ 1985*

De Courcy, J. H. 3: *v E 1953 (3)*

Dell, A. R. 2: v E 1970 (1); v NZ 1973 (1)

Dodemaide, A. I. C. 10: v E 1987 (1); v WI 1988 (2); v NZ 1987 (1); v SL 1987 (1); *v P 1988 (3); v SL 1992 (2)*

Donnan, H. 5: v E 1891 (2); *v E 1896 (3)*

Dooland, B. 3: v E 1946 (2); v In 1947 (1)

Duff, R. A. 22: v E 1901 (4) 1903 (5); *v E 1902 (5) 1905 (5); v SA 1902 (3)*

Duncan, J. R. F. 1: v E 1970

Dyer, G. C. 6: v E 1986 (1) 1987 (1); v NZ 1987 (3); v SL 1987 (1)

Dymock, G. 21: v E 1974 (1) 1978 (3) 1979 (3); v WI 1979 (2); v NZ 1973 (1); v P 1978 (1); *v NZ 1973 (2); v In 1979 (5); v P 1979 (3)*

Dyson, J. 30: v E 1982 (5); v WI 1981 (2) 1984 (3); v In 1977 (3) 1980 (3); *v E 1981 (5); v NZ 1981 (3); v P 1982 (3)*

Eady, C. J. 2: v E 1901 (1); *v E 1896 (1)*

Eastwood, K. H. 1: v E 1970

Ebeling, H. I. 1: *v E 1934*

Edwards, J. D. 3: *v E 1888 (3)*

Edwards, R. 20: v E 1974 (5); v P 1972 (2); *v E 1972 (4) 1975 (4); v WI 1972 (5)*

Edwards, W. J. 3: v E 1974 (3)

Emery, P. A. 1: *v P 1994*

Emery, S. H. 4: *v E 1912 (2); v SA 1912 (2)*

Evans, E. 6: v E 1881 (2) 1882 (1) 1884 (1); *v E 1886 (2)*

Fairfax, A. G. 10: v E 1928 (1); v WI 1930 (5); *v E 1930 (4)*

Favell, L. E. 19: v E 1954 (4) 1958 (2); v WI 1960 (4); *v WI 1954 (2); v In 1959 (4); v P 1959 (3)*

Ferris, J. J. 8: v E 1886 (2) 1887 (1); *v E 1888 (3) 1890 (2)*

Fingleton, J. H. 18: v E 1932 (3) 1936 (5); v SA 1931 (1); *v E 1938 (4); v SA 1935 (5)*

Fleetwood-Smith, L. O'B. 10: v E 1936 (3); *v E 1938 (4); v SA 1935 (5)*

Fleming, D. W. 4: v E 1994 (3); *v P 1994 (1)*

Francis, B. C. 3: *v E 1972 (3)*

Freeman, E. W. 11: v WI 1968 (4); v In 1967 (3); *v E 1968 (2); v SA 1969 (2); v In 1969 (1)*

Freer, F. W. 1: v E 1946

Gannon, J. B. 3: v In 1977 (3)

Garrett, T. W. 19: v E 1876 (2) 1878 (1) 1881 (3) 1882 (3) 1884 (3) 1886 (2) 1887 (1); *v E 1882 (1) 1886 (3)*

Gaunt, R. A. 3: v SA 1963 (1); *v E 1961 (1); v SA 1957 (1)*

Gehrs, D. R. A. 6: v E 1903 (2); v SA 1910 (4); *v E 1905 (1)*

Giffen, G. 31: v E 1881 (3) 1882 (4) 1884 (3) 1891 (3) 1894 (5); *v E 1882 (1) 1884 (3) 1886 (3) 1893 (3) 1896 (3)*

Giffen, W. F. 3: v E 1886 (1) 1891 (2)

Gilbert, D. R. 9: v NZ 1985 (3); v In 1985 (2); *v E 1985 (1); v NZ 1985 (1); v In 1986 (2)*

Gilmour, G. J. 15: v E 1976 (1); v WI 1975 (5); v NZ 1973 (1); v P 1976 (3); *v E 1975 (1); v NZ 1973 (1) 1976 (2)*

Gleeson, J. W. 29: v E 1970 (5); v WI 1968 (5); v In 1967 (4); *v E 1968 (5) 1972 (3); v SA 1969 (4); v In 1969 (3)*

Graham, H. 6: v E 1894 (2); *v E 1893 (3) 1896 (1)*

Gregory, D. W. 3: v E 1876 (2) 1878 (1)

Gregory, E. J. 1: v E 1876

Gregory, J. M. 24: v E 1920 (5) 1924 (5) 1928 (1); *v E 1921 (5) 1926 (5); v SA 1921 (3)*

Gregory, R. G. 2: v E 1936 (2)

Gregory, S. E. 58: v E 1891 (1) 1894 (5) 1897 (5) 1901 (5) 1903 (4) 1907 (2) 1911 (1); *v E 1890 (2) 1893 (3) 1896 (3) 1899 (5) 1902 (5) 1905 (3) 1909 (5) 1912 (3); v SA 1902 (3) 1912 (3)*

Grimmett, C. V. 37: v E 1924 (1) 1928 (5) 1932 (5); v SA 1931 (5); v WI 1930 (5); *v E 1926 (3) 1930 (5) 1934 (5); v SA 1935 (5)*

Groube, T. U. 1: *v E 1880*

Grout, A. T. W. 51: v E 1958 (5) 1962 (2) 1965 (5); v SA 1963 (5); v WI 1960 (5); *v E 1961 (5) 1964 (5); v SA 1957 (5); v WI 1964 (5); v In 1959 (4) 1964 (1); v P 1959 (3) 1964 (1)*

Guest, C. E. J. 1: v E 1962

Hamence, R. A. 3: v E 1946 (1); v In 1947 (2)

Hammond, J. R. 5: *v WI 1972 (5)*

Harry, J. 1: v E 1894

Hartigan, R. J. 2: v E 1907 (2)

Hartkopf, A. E. V. 1: v E 1924

Harvey, M. R. 1: v E 1946

Harvey, R. N. 79: v E 1950 (5) 1954 (5) 1958 (5) 1962 (5); v SA 1952 (5); v WI 1951 (5) 1960 (4); v In 1947 (2); *v E 1948 (2) 1953 (5) 1956 (5) 1961 (5); v SA 1949 (5) 1957 (4); v WI 1954 (5); v In 1956 (3) 1959 (5); v P 1956 (1) 1959 (3)*

Hassett, A. L. 43: v E 1946 (5) 1950 (5); v SA 1952 (5); v WI 1951 (4); v In 1947 (4); *v E 1938 (4) 1948 (5) 1953 (5); v SA 1949 (5); v NZ 1945 (1)*

Hawke, N. J. N. 27: v E 1962 (1) 1965 (4); v SA 1963 (4); v In 1967 (1); v P 1964 (1); *v E 1964 (5) 1968 (2); v SA 1966 (2); v WI 1964 (5); v In 1964 (1); v P 1964 (1)*

Hayden, M. L. 1: *v SA 1993*

Hazlitt, G. R. 9: v E 1907 (2) 1911 (1); *v E 1912 (3); v SA 1912 (3)*

Healy, I. A. 73: v E 1990 (5) 1994 (5); v SA 1993 (3); v WI 1988 (5) 1992 (5); v NZ 1989 (1) 1993 (3); v In 1991 (5); v P 1989 (3); v SL 1989 (2); *v E 1989 (6) 1993 (6); v SA 1993 (3); v WI 1990 (5) 1994 (4); v NZ 1989 (1) 1992 (3); v P 1988 (3) 1994 (2); v SL 1992 (3)*

Hendry, H. S. T. L. 11: v E 1924 (1) 1928 (4); *v E 1921 (4); v SA 1921 (2)*

Hibbert, P. A. 1: v In 1977

Higgs, J. D. 22: v E 1978 (5) 1979 (1); v WI 1979 (1); v NZ 1980 (3); v In 1980 (2); *v WI 1977 (4); v In 1979 (6)*

Hilditch, A. M. J. 18: v E 1978 (1); v WI 1984 (2); v NZ 1985 (1); v P 1978 (2); *v E 1985 (6); v In 1979 (6)*

Hill, C. 49: v E 1897 (5) 1901 (5) 1903 (5) 1907 (5) 1911 (5); v SA 1910 (5); *v E 1896 (3) 1899 (3) 1902 (5) 1905 (5); v SA 1902 (3)*

Hill, J. C. 3: *v E 1953 (2); v WI 1954 (1)*

Hoare, D. E. 1: v WI 1960

Hodges, J. R. 2: v E 1876 (2)

Hogan, T. G. 7: v P 1983 (1); *v WI 1983 (5); v SL 1982 (1)*

Hogg, R. M. 38: v E 1978 (6) 1982 (3); v WI 1979 (2) 1984 (4); v NZ 1980 (2); v In 1980 (2); v P 1978 (2) 1983 (4); *v E 1981 (2); v WI 1983 (4); v In 1979 (6); v SL 1982 (1)*

Hohns, T. V. 7: v WI 1988 (2); *v E 1989 (5)*

Hole, G. B. 18: v E 1950 (1) 1954 (3); v SA 1952 (4); v WI 1951 (5); *v E 1953 (5)*

Holland, R. G. 11: v WI 1984 (3); v NZ 1985 (3); v In 1985 (1); *v E 1985 (4)*

Hookes, D. W. 23: v E 1976 (1) 1982 (5); v WI 1979 (1); v NZ 1985 (2); v In 1985 (2); *v E 1977 (5); v WI 1983 (5); v P 1979 (1); v SL 1982 (1)*

Hopkins, A. J. Y. 20: v E 1901 (2) 1903 (5); *v E 1902 (5) 1905 (3) 1909 (2); v SA 1902 (3)*

Horan, T. P. 15: v E 1876 (1) 1878 (1) 1881 (4) 1882 (4) 1884 (4); *v E 1882 (1)*

Hordern, H. V. 7: v E 1911 (5); v SA 1910 (2)

Hornibrook, P. M. 6: v E 1928 (1); *v E 1930 (5)*

Howell, W. P. 18: v E 1897 (3) 1901 (4) 1903 (3); *v E 1899 (5) 1902 (1); v SA 1902 (2)*

Hughes, K. J. 70: v E 1978 (6) 1979 (3) 1982 (5); v WI 1979 (3) 1981 (3) 1984 (4); v NZ 1980 (3); v In 1977 (2) 1980 (3); v P 1978 (2) 1981 (3) 1983 (5); *v E 1977 (1) 1980 (1) 1981 (6); v WI 1983 (5); v NZ 1981 (3); v In 1979 (6); v P 1979 (3) 1982 (3)*

Hughes, M. G. 53: v E 1986 (4) 1990 (4); v WI 1988 (4) 1992 (5); v NZ 1987 (1) 1989 (1); v In 1985 (1) 1991 (5); v P 1989 (3); v SL 1987 (1) 1989 (2); *v E 1989 (6) 1993 (6); v SA 1993 (2); v WI 1990 (5); v NZ 1992 (3)*

Hunt, W. A. 1: v SA 1931

Hurst, A. G. 12: v E 1978 (6); v NZ 1973 (1); v In 1977 (1); v P 1978 (2); *v In 1979 (2)*

Hurwood, A. 2: v WI 1930 (2)

Inverarity, R. J. 6: v WI 1968 (1); *v E 1968 (2) 1972 (3)*

Iredale, F. A. 14: v E 1894 (5) 1897 (4); *v E 1896 (2) 1899 (3)*

Ironmonger, H. 14: v E 1928 (2) 1932 (4); v SA 1931 (4); v WI 1930 (4)

Iverson, J. B. 5: v E 1950 (5)

Jackson, A. A. 8: v E 1928 (2); v WI 1930 (4); *v E 1930 (2)*

Jarman, B. N. 19: v E 1962 (3); v WI 1968 (1); v In 1967 (4); v P 1964 (1); *v E 1968 (4); v In 1959 (1) 1964 (2)*

Jarvis, A. H. 11: v E 1884 (2) 1894 (4); *v E 1886 (2) 1888 (2)*

Jenner, T. J. 9: v E 1970 (2) 1974 (2); v WI 1975 (1); *v WI 1972 (4)*

Jennings, C. B. 6: *v E 1912 (3); v SA 1912 (3)*

Johnson I. W. 45: v E 1946 (4) 1950 (5) 1954 (4); v SA 1952 (1); v WI 1951 (4); v In 1947 (4); *v E 1948 (4) 1956 (5); v SA 1949 (5); v WI 1954 (5); v NZ 1945 (1); v In 1956 (2); v P 1956 (1)*

Johnson, L. J. 1: v In 1947

Johnston W. A. 40: v E 1950 (5) 1954 (4); v SA 1952 (5); v WI 1951 (5); v In 1947 (4); *v E 1948 (5) 1953 (3); v SA 1949 (5); v WI 1954 (4)*

Jones, D. M. 52: v E 1986 (5) 1987 (1) 1990 (5); v WI 1988 (3); v NZ 1987 (3) 1989 (1); v In 1991 (5); v P 1989 (3); v SL 1987 (1) 1989 (2); *v E 1989 (6); v WI 1983 (2) 1990 (5); v NZ 1989 (1); v In 1986 (3); v P 1988 (3); v SL 1992 (3)*

Jones, E. 19: v E 1894 (1) 1897 (1) 1901 (2); *v E 1896 (3) 1899 (5) 1902 (2); v SA 1902 (1)*

Jones, S. P. 12: v E 1881 (2) 1884 (4) 1886 (1) 1887 (1); *v E 1882 (1) 1886 (3)*

Joslin, L. R. 1: v In 1967

Julian, B. P. 6: *v E 1993 (2); v WI 1994 (4)*

Kelleway, C. 26: v E 1911 (4) 1920 (5) 1924 (5) 1928 (1); v SA 1910 (5); *v E 1912 (3); v SA 1912 (3)*

Kelly, J. J. 36: v E 1897 (5) 1901 (5) 1903 (5); *v E 1896 (3) 1899 (5) 1902 (5) 1905 (5); v SA 1902 (3)*

Kelly, T. J. D. 2: v E 1876 (1) 1878 (1)

Kendall, T. 2: v E 1876 (2)

Kent, M. F. 3: *v E 1981 (3)*

Kerr, R. B. 2: v NZ 1985 (2)

Kippax, A. F. 22: v E 1924 (1) 1928 (5) 1932 (1); v SA 1931 (4); v WI 1930 (5); *v E 1930 (5) 1934 (1)*

Kline L. F. 13: v E 1958 (2); v WI 1960 (2); *v SA 1957 (5); v In 1959 (3); v P 1959 (1)*

Laird, B. M. 21: v E 1979 (2); v WI 1979 (3) 1981 (3); v P 1981 (3); *v E 1980 (1); v NZ 1981 (3); v P 1979 (3) 1982 (3)*

Langer, J. L. 6: v WI 1992 (2); *v NZ 1992 (3); v P 1994 (1)*

Langley, G. R. A. 26: v E 1954 (2); v SA 1952 (5); v WI 1951 (5); *v E 1953 (4) 1956 (3); v WI 1954 (4); v In 1956 (2); v P 1956 (1)*

Laughlin, T. J. 3: v E 1978 (1); *v WI 1977 (2)*

Laver, F. 15: v E 1901 (1) 1903 (1); *v E 1899 (4) 1905 (5) 1909 (4)*

Lawry, W. M. 67: v E 1962 (5) 1965 (5) 1970 (5); v SA 1963 (5); v WI 1968 (5); v In 1967 (4); v P 1964 (1); *v E 1961 (5) 1964 (5) 1968 (4); v SA 1966 (5) 1969 (4); v WI 1964 (5); v In 1964 (3) 1969 (5); v P 1964 (1)*

Lawson, G. F. 46: v E 1982 (5) 1986 (1); v WI 1981 (1) 1984 (5) 1988 (1); v NZ 1980 (1) 1985 (2) 1989 (1); v P 1983 (5); v SL 1989 (1); *v E 1981 (3) 1985 (6) 1989 (6); v WI 1983 (5); v P 1982 (3)*

Lee, P. K. 2: v E 1932 (1); v SA 1931 (1)

Lillee, D. K. 70: v E 1970 (2) 1974 (6) 1976 (1) 1979 (3) 1982 (3); v WI 1975 (5) 1979 (3) 1981 (3); v NZ 1980 (3); v P 1972 (3) 1976 (3) 1981 (3) 1983 (5); *v E 1972 (5) 1975 (4) 1980 (1) 1981 (6); v WI 1972 (1); v NZ 1976 (2) 1981 (3); v P 1979 (3); v SL 1982 (1)*

Lindwall, R. R. 61: v E 1946 (4) 1950 (5) 1954 (4) 1958 (2); v SA 1952 (4); v WI 1951 (5); v In 1947 (5); *v E 1948 (5) 1953 (5) 1956 (4); v SA 1949 (4); v WI 1954 (5); v NZ 1945 (1); v In 1956 (3) 1959 (2); v P 1956 (1) 1959 (2)*

Love, H. S. B. 1: v E 1932

Loxton, S. J. E. 12: v E 1950 (3); v In 1947 (1); *v E 1948 (3); v SA 1949 (5)*

Lyons, J. J. 14: v E 1886 (1) 1891 (3) 1894 (3) 1897 (1); *v E 1888 (1) 1890 (2) 1893 (3)*

McAlister, P. A. 8: v E 1903 (2) 1907 (4); *v E 1909 (2)*

Macartney, C. G. 35: v E 1907 (5) 1911 (1) 1920 (2); v SA 1910 (4); *v E 1909 (5) 1912 (3) 1921 (5) 1926 (5); v SA 1912 (3) 1921 (2)*

McCabe, S. J. 39: v E 1932 (5) 1936 (5); v SA 1931 (5); v WI 1930 (5); *v E 1930 (5) 1934 (5) 1938 (4); v SA 1935 (5)*

McCool, C. L. 14: v E 1946 (5); v In 1947 (3); *v SA 1949 (5) v NZ 1945 (1)*

McCormick, E. L. 12: v E 1936 (4); *v E 1938 (3); v SA 1935 (5)*

McCosker, R. B. 25: v E 1974 (3) 1976 (1) 1979 (2); v WI 1975 (4) 1979 (1); v P 1976 (3); *v E 1975 (4) 1977 (5); v NZ 1976 (2)*

McDermott, C. J. 65: v E 1986 (1) 1987 (1) 1990 (2) 1994 (5); v SA 1993 (3); v WI 1984 (2) 1988 (2) 1992 (5); v NZ 1985 (2) 1987 (3) 1993 (3); v In 1985 (2) 1991 (5); v SL 1987 (1); *v E 1985 (6) 1993 (2); v SA 1993 (3); v WI 1990 (5); v NZ 1985 (2) 1992 (3); v In 1986 (2); v P 1994 (2); v SL 1992 (3)*

McDonald, C. C. 47: v E 1954 (2) 1958 (5); v SA 1952 (5); v WI 1951 (1) 1960 (5); *v E 1956 (5) 1961 (3); v SA 1957 (5); v WI 1954 (5); v In 1956 (2) 1959 (5); v P 1956 (1) 1959 (3)*

McDonald, E. A. 11: v E 1920 (3); *v E 1921 (5); v SA 1921 (3)*

McDonnell, P. S. 19: v E 1881 (4) 1882 (3) 1884 (2) 1886 (2) 1887 (1); *v E 1880 (1) 1884 (3) 1888 (3)*

McGrath, G. D. 13: v E 1994 (2); v SA 1993 (1); v NZ 1993 (2); *v SA 1993 (2); v WI 1994 (4); v P 1994 (2)*

McIlwraith, J. 1: *v E 1886*

McIntyre, P. E. 1: v E 1994

Mackay K. D. 37: v E 1958 (5) 1962 (3); v WI 1960 (5); *v E 1956 (3) 1961 (5); v SA 1957 (3); v In 1956 (3) 1959 (5); v P 1959 (3)*

McKenzie, G. D. 60: v E 1962 (5) 1965 (4) 1970 (3); v SA 1963 (5); v WI 1968 (5); v In 1967 (2); v P 1964 (1); *v E 1961 (3) 1964 (5) 1968 (5); v SA 1966 (5) 1969 (3); v WI 1964 (5); v In 1964 (3) 1969 (5); v P 1964 (1)*

McKibbin, T. R. 5: v E 1894 (1) 1897 (2); *v E 1896 (2)*

McLaren, J. W. 1: v E 1911

Maclean, J. A. 4: v E 1978 (4)

McLeod, C. E. 17: v E 1894 (1) 1897 (5) 1901 (2) 1903 (3); *v E 1899 (1) 1905 (5)*

McLeod, R. W. 6: v E 1891 (3); *v E 1893 (3)*

McShane, P. G. 3: v E 1884 (1) 1886 (1) 1887 (1)

Maddocks, L. V. 7: v E 1954 (3); *v E 1956 (2); v WI 1954 (1); v In 1956 (1)*

Maguire, J. N. 3: v P 1983 (1); *v WI 1983 (2)*

Mailey, A. A. 21: v E 1920 (5) 1924 (5); *v E 1921 (3) 1926 (5); v SA 1921 (3)*

Mallett, A. A. 38: v E 1970 (2) 1974 (5) 1979 (1); v WI 1968 (1) 1975 (6) 1979 (1); v NZ 1973 (3); v P 1972 (2); *v E 1968 (1) 1972 (2) 1975 (4) 1980 (1); v SA 1969 (1); v NZ 1973 (3); v In 1969 (5)*

Malone, M. F. 1: *v E 1977*

Mann, A. L. 4: v In 1977 (4)

Marr, A. P. 1: v E 1884

Marsh, G. R. 50: v E 1986 (5) 1987 (1) 1990 (5); v WI 1988 (5); v NZ 1987 (3); v In 1985 (3) 1991 (4); v P 1989 (2); v SL 1987 (1); *v E 1989 (6); v WI 1990 (5); v NZ 1985 (3) 1989 (1); v In 1986 (3); v P 1988 (3)*

Marsh, R. W. 96: v E 1970 (6) 1974 (6) 1976 (1) 1979 (3) 1982 (5); v WI 1975 (6) 1979 (3) 1981 (3); v NZ 1973 (3) 1980 (3); v P 1972 (3) 1976 (3) 1981 (3) 1983 (5); *v E 1972 (5) 1975 (4) 1977 (5) 1980 (1) 1981 (6); v WI 1972 (5); v NZ 1973 (3) 1976 (2) 1981 (3); v P 1979 (3) 1982 (3)*

Martin, J. W. 8: v SA 1963 (1); v WI 1960 (3); *v SA 1966 (1); v In 1964 (2); v P 1964 (1)*

Martyn, D. R. 7: v SA 1993 (2); v WI 1992 (4); *v NZ 1992 (1)*

Massie, H. H. 9: v E 1881 (4) 1882 (3) 1884 (1); *v E 1882 (1)*

Massie, R. A. L. 6: v P 1972 (2); *v E 1972 (4)*

Matthews, C. D. 3: v E 1986 (2); v WI 1988 (1)

Matthews, G. R. J. 33: v E 1986 (4) 1990 (5); v WI 1984 (2) 1992 (1); v NZ 1985 (3); v In 1985 (3); v P 1983 (2); *v E 1985 (1); v WI 1983 (1) 1990 (2); v NZ 1985 (3); v In 1986 (3); v SL 1992 (3)*

Matthews, T. J. 8: v E 1911 (2); *v E 1912 (3); v SA 1912 (3)*

May, T. B. A. 24: v E 1994 (3); v SA 1993 (3); v WI 1988 (3) 1992 (1); v NZ 1987 (1) 1993 (2); *v E 1993 (5); v SA 1993 (1); v P 1988 (3) 1994 (2)*

Mayne, E. R. 4: *v E 1912 (1); v SA 1912 (1) 1921 (2)*

Mayne, L. C. 6: *v SA 1969 (2); v WI 1964 (3); v In 1969 (1)*

Meckiff, I. 18: v E 1958 (4); v SA 1963 (1); v WI 1960 (2); *v SA 1957 (4); v In 1959 (5); v P 1959 (2)*

Meuleman, K. D. 1: *v NZ 1945*

Midwinter, W. E. 8: v E 1876 (2) 1882 (1) 1886 (2); *v E 1884 (3)*

Miller, K. R. 55: v E 1946 (5) 1950 (5) 1954 (4); v SA 1952 (4); v WI 1951 (5); v In 1947 (5); *v E 1948 (5) 1953 (5) 1956 (5); v SA 1949 (5); v WI 1954 (5); v NZ 1945 (1); v P 1956 (1)*

Minnett, R. B. 9: v E 1911 (5); *v E 1912 (1); v SA 1912 (3)*

Misson, F. M. 5: v WI 1960 (3); *v E 1961 (2)*

Moody, T. M. 8: v NZ 1989 (1); v In 1991 (1); v P 1989 (1); v SL 1989 (2); *v SL 1992 (3)*

Moroney, J. R. 7: v E 1950 (1); v WI 1951 (1); *v SA 1949 (5)*

Morris, A. R. 46: v E 1946 (5) 1950 (5) 1954 (4); v SA 1952 (5); v WI 1951 (4); v In 1947 (4); *v E 1948 (5) 1953 (5); v SA 1949 (5); v WI 1954 (4)*

Morris, S. 1: v E 1884

Moses, H. 6: v E 1886 (2) 1887 (1) 1891 (2) 1894 (1)

Moss, J. K. 1: v P 1978

Moule, W. H. 1: *v E 1880*

Murdoch, W. L. 18: v E 1876 (1) 1878 (1) 1881 (1) 1882 (4) 1884 (1); *v E 1880 (1) 1882 (1) 1884 (3) 1890 (2)*

Musgrove, H. 1: v E 1884

Nagel, L. E. 1: v E 1932

Nash, L. J. 2: v E 1936 (1); v SA 1931 (1)

Nitschke, H. C. 2: v SA 1931 (2)

Noble, M. A. 42: v E 1897 (4) 1901 (5) 1903 (5) 1907 (5); *v E 1899 (5) 1902 (5) 1905 (5) 1909 (5); v SA 1902 (3)*

Noblet, G. 3: v SA 1952 (1); v WI 1951 (1); *v SA 1949 (1)*

Nothling, O. E. 1: v E 1928

O'Brien, L. P. J. 5: v E 1932 (2) 1936 (1); *v SA 1935 (2)*

O'Connor, J. D. A. 4: v E 1907 (3); *v E 1909 (1)*

O'Donnell, S. P. 6: v NZ 1985 (1); *v E 1985 (5)*

Ogilvie, A. D. 5: v In 1977 (3); *v WI 1977 (2)*

O'Keeffe, K. J. 24: v E 1970 (2) 1976 (1); v NZ 1973 (3); v P 1972 (2) 1976 (3); *v E 1977 (3); v WI 1972 (5); v NZ 1973 (3) 1976 (5)*

Oldfield, W. A. 54: v E 1920 (3) 1924 (5) 1928 (5) 1932 (4) 1936 (5); v SA 1931 (5); v WI 1930 (5); *v E 1921 (5) 1926 (5) 1930 (5) 1934 (5); v SA 1921 (1) 1935 (5)*

O'Neill, N. C. 42: v E 1958 (5) 1962 (5); v SA 1963 (4); v WI 1960 (5); *v E 1961 (5) 1964 (4); v WI 1964 (3); v In 1959 (5) 1964 (2); v P 1959 (3)*

O'Reilly, W. J. 27: v E 1932 (5) 1936 (5); v SA 1931 (2); *v E 1934 (5) 1938 (4); v SA 1935 (5); v NZ 1945 (1)*

Oxenham, R. K. 7: v E 1928 (3); v SA 1931 (1); v WI 1930 (3)

Palmer, G. E. 17: v E 1881 (4) 1882 (4) 1884 (2); *v E 1880 (1) 1884 (3) 1886 (3)*

Park, R. L. 1: v E 1920

Pascoe, L. S. 14: v E 1979 (2); v WI 1979 (1) 1981 (1); v NZ 1980 (3); v In 1980 (3); *v E 1977 (3) 1980 (1)*

Pellew, C. E. 10: v E 1920 (4); *v E 1921 (5); v SA 1921 (1)*

Phillips, W. B. 27: v WI 1984 (2); v NZ 1985 (3); v In 1985 (3); v P 1983 (5); *v E 1985 (6); v WI 1983 (5); v NZ 1985 (3)*

Phillips, W. N. 1: v In 1991

Philpott, P. I. 8: v E 1965 (3); *v WI 1964 (5)*

Ponsford, W. H. 29: v E 1924 (5) 1928 (2) 1932 (3); v SA 1931 (4); v WI 1930 (5); *v E 1926 (2) 1930 (4) 1934 (4)*

Pope, R. J. 1: v E 1884

Rackemann, C. G. 12: v E 1982 (1) 1990 (1); v WI 1984 (1); v NZ 1989 (1); v P 1983 (2) 1989 (3); v SL 1989 (1); *v WI 1983 (1); v NZ 1989 (1)*

Ransford, V. S. 20: v E 1907 (5) 1911 (5); v SA 1910 (5); *v E 1909 (5)*

Redpath, I. R. 66: v E 1965 (1) 1970 (6) 1974 (6); v SA 1963 (1); v WI 1968 (5) 1975 (6); v In 1967 (3); v P 1972 (5); *v E 1964 (5) 1968 (5); v SA 1966 (5) 1969 (4); v WI 1972 (5); v NZ 1973 (3); v In 1964 (2) 1969 (5); v P 1964 (1)*

Reedman, J. C. 1: v E 1894
Reid, B. A. 27: v E 1986 (5) 1990 (4); v WI 1992 (1); v NZ 1987 (2); v In 1985 (3) 1991 (2); *v WI 1990 (2); v NZ 1985 (3); v In 1986 (2); v P 1988 (3)*
Reiffel, P. R. 16: v SA 1993 (2); v NZ 1993 (2); v In 1991 (1); *v E 1993 (3); v SA 1993 (1); v WI 1994 (4); v NZ 1992 (1)*
Renneberg, D. A. 8: v In 1967 (3); *v SA 1966 (5)*
Richardson, A. J. 9: v E 1924 (4); *v E 1926 (5)*
Richardson, V. Y. 19: v E 1924 (3) 1928 (2) 1932 (5); *v E 1930 (4); v SA 1935 (5)*
Rigg, K. E. 8: v E 1936 (3); v SA 1931 (4); v WI 1930 (1)
Ring, D. T. 13: v SA 1952 (5); v WI 1951 (5); v In 1947 (1); *v E 1948 (1) 1953 (1)*
Ritchie, G. M. 30: v E 1986 (4); v WI 1984 (1); v NZ 1985 (3); v In 1985 (2); *v E 1985 (6); v In 1983 (5); v NZ 1985 (3); v In 1986 (3); v P 1982 (3)*
Rixon, S. J. 13: v WI 1984 (3); v In 1977 (5); *v WI 1977 (5)*
Robertson, W. R. 1: v E 1884
Robinson, R. D. 3: *v E 1977 (3)*
Robinson, R. H. 1: v E 1936
Rorke, G. F. 4: v E 1958 (2); *v In 1959 (2)*
Rutherford, J. W. 1: *v In 1956*
Ryder, J. 20: v E 1920 (5) 1924 (3) 1928 (5); *v E 1926 (4); v SA 1921 (3)*

Saggers, R. A. 6: *v E 1948 (1); v SA 1949 (5)*
Saunders, J. V. 14: v E 1901 (1) 1903 (2) 1907 (5); *v E 1902 (4); v SA 1902 (2)*
Scott, H. J. H. 8: v E 1884 (2); *v E 1884 (3) 1886 (3)*
Sellers, R. H. D. 1: *v In 1964*
Serjeant, C. S. 12: v In 1977 (4); *v E 1977 (3); v WI 1977 (5)*
Sheahan, A. P. 31: v E 1970 (2); v WI 1968 (5); v NZ 1973 (2); v In 1967 (4); v P 1972 (2); *v E 1968 (5) 1972 (2); v SA 1969 (4); v In 1969 (5)*
Shepherd, B. K. 9: v E 1962 (2); v SA 1963 (4); v P 1964 (1); *v WI 1964 (2)*
Sievers, M. W. 3: v E 1936 (3)
Simpson, R. B. 62: v E 1958 (1) 1962 (5) 1965 (3); v SA 1963 (5); v WI 1960 (5); v In 1967 (3) 1977 (5); v P 1964 (1); *v E 1961 (5) 1964 (5); v SA 1957 (5) 1966 (5); v WI 1964 (5) 1977 (5); v In 1964 (3); v P 1964 (1)*
Sincock, D. J. 3: v E 1965 (1); v P 1964 (1); *v WI 1964 (1)*
Slater, K. N. 1: v E 1958
Slater, M. J. 27: v E 1994 (5); v SA 1993 (3); v NZ 1993 (2); *v E 1993 (6); v SA 1993 (3); v WI 1994 (4); v P 1994 (3)*
Sleep, P. R. 14: v E 1986 (3) 1987 (1); v NZ 1987 (3); v P 1978 (1) 1989 (1); v SL 1989 (1); *v In 1979 (2); v P 1982 (1) 1988 (1)*
Slight, J. 1: *v E 1880*
Smith, D. B. M. 2: *v E 1912 (2)*
Smith, S. B. 3: *v WI 1983 (3)*
Spofforth, F. R. 18: v E 1876 (1) 1878 (1) 1881 (1) 1882 (4) 1884 (3) 1886 (1); *v E 1882 (1) 1884 (3) 1886 (3)*
Stackpole, K. R. 43: v E 1965 (2) 1970 (6); v WI 1968 (5); v NZ 1973 (3); v P 1972 (1); *v E 1972 (5); v SA 1966 (5) 1969 (4); v WI 1972 (4); v NZ 1973 (3); v In 1969 (5)*
Stevens, G. B. 4: *v In 1959 (2); v P 1959 (2)*

Taber, H. B. 16: v WI 1968 (1); *v E 1968 (1); v SA 1966 (5) 1969 (4); v In 1969 (5)*
Tallon, D. 21: v E 1946 (5) 1950 (5); v In 1947 (5); *v E 1948 (4) 1953 (4); v NZ 1945 (1)*
Taylor, J. M. 20: v E 1920 (5) 1924 (5); *v E 1921 (5) 1926 (3); v SA 1921 (2)*
Taylor, M. A. 66: v E 1990 (5) 1994 (5); v SA 1993 (3); v WI 1988 (2) 1992 (4); v NZ 1989 (1) 1993 (3); v In 1991 (5); v P 1989 (3); v SL 1989 (2); *v E 1989 (6) 1993 (6); v SA 1993 (2); v WI 1990 (5) 1994 (4); v NZ 1989 (1) 1992 (3); v P 1994 (3); v SL 1992 (3)*
Taylor, P. L. 13: v E 1986 (1) 1987 (1); v WI 1988 (2); v In 1991 (2); v P 1989 (2); v SL 1987 (1); *v WI 1990 (1); v NZ 1989 (1); v P 1988 (2)*
Thomas, G. 8: v E 1965 (3); *v WI 1964 (5)*
Thoms, G. R. 1: v WI 1951
Thomson, A. L. 4: v E 1970 (4)
Thomson, J. R. 51: v E 1974 (5) 1979 (1) 1982 (4); v WI 1975 (6) 1979 (1) 1981 (2); v In 1977 (5); v P 1972 (1) 1976 (1) 1981 (3); *v E 1975 (4) 1977 (5) 1985 (2); v WI 1977 (5); v NZ 1981 (3); v P 1982 (3)*
Thomson, N. F. D. 2: v E 1876 (2)

Thurlow, H. M. 1: v SA 1931

Toohey, P. M. 15: v E 1978 (5) 1979 (1); v WI 1979 (1); v In 1977 (5); *v WI 1977 (3)*

Toshack, E. R. H. 12: v E 1946 (5); v In 1947 (2); *v E 1948 (4); v NZ 1945 (1)*

Travers, J. P. F. 1: v E 1901

Tribe, G. E. 3: v E 1946 (3)

Trott, A. E. 3: v E 1894 (3)

Trott, G. H. S. 24: v E 1891 (3) 1894 (5) 1897 (5); *v E 1888 (3) 1890 (2) 1893 (3) 1896 (3)*

Trumble, H. 32: v E 1894 (1) 1897 (5) 1901 (5) 1903 (4); *v E 1890 (2) 1893 (3) 1896 (3) 1899 (5) 1902 (3); v SA 1902 (1)*

Trumble, J. W. 7: v E 1884 (4); *v E 1886 (3)*

Trumper, V. T. 48: v E 1901 (5) 1903 (5) 1907 (5) 1911 (5); v SA 1910 (5); *v E 1899 (5) 1902 (5) 1905 (5) 1909 (5); v SA 1902 (3)*

Turner, A. 14: v WI 1975 (6); v P 1976 (3); *v E 1975 (3); v NZ 1976 (2)*

Turner, C. T. B. 17: v E 1886 (2) 1887 (1) 1891 (3) 1894 (3); *v E 1888 (3) 1890 (2) 1893 (3)*

Veivers, T. R. 21: v E 1965 (4); v SA 1963 (3); v P 1964 (1); *v E 1964 (5); v SA 1966 (4); v In 1964 (3); v P 1964 (1)*

Veletta, M. R. J. 8: v E 1987 (1); v WI 1988 (2); v NZ 1987 (3); v P 1989 (1); v SL 1987 (1)

Waite, M. G. 2: *v E 1938 (2)*

Walker, M. H. N. 34: v E 1974 (6) 1976 (1); v WI 1975 (3); v NZ 1973 (1); v P 1972 (2) 1976 (2); *v E 1975 (4) 1977 (5); v WI 1972 (5); v NZ 1973 (3) 1976 (2)*

Wall, T. W. 18: v E 1928 (1) 1932 (4); v SA 1931 (3); v WI 1930 (1); *v E 1930 (5) 1934 (4)*

Walters, F. H. 1: v E 1884

Walters, K. D. 74: v E 1965 (5) 1970 (6) 1974 (6) 1976 (1); v WI 1968 (4); v NZ 1973 (3) 1980 (3); v In 1967 (2) 1980 (3); v P 1972 (1) 1976 (3); *v E 1968 (5) 1972 (4) 1975 (4) 1977 (5); v SA 1969 (4); v WI 1972 (5); v NZ 1973 (3) 1976 (2); v In 1969 (5)*

Ward, F. A. 4: v E 1936 (3); *v E 1938 (1)*

Warne, S. K. 38: v E 1994 (5); v SA 1993 (3); v WI 1992 (4); v NZ 1993 (3); v In 1991 (2); *v E 1993 (6); v SA 1993 (3); v WI 1994 (4); v NZ 1992 (3); v P 1994 (3); v SL 1992 (2)*

Watkins, J. R. 1: v P 1972

Watson, G. D. 5: *v E 1972 (2); v SA 1966 (3)*

Watson, W. J. 4: v E 1954 (1); *v WI 1954 (3)*

Waugh, M. E. 48: v E 1990 (2) 1994 (5); v SA 1993 (3); v WI 1992 (5); v NZ 1993 (3); v In 1991 (4); *v E 1993 (6); v SA 1993 (3); v WI 1990 (5) 1994 (4); v NZ 1992 (2); v P 1994 (3); v SL 1992 (2)*

Waugh, S. R. 76: v E 1986 (5) 1987 (1) 1990 (3) 1994 (5); v SA 1993 (1); v WI 1988 (5) 1992 (5); v NZ 1987 (3) 1989 (1) 1993 (3); v In 1985 (2); v P 1989 (1); v SL 1987 (1) 1989 (2); *v E 1989 (6) 1993 (6); v SA 1993 (3); v WI 1990 (2) 1994 (4); v NZ 1985 (3) 1989 (1) 1992 (3); v In 1986 (3); v P 1988 (3) 1994 (2)*

Wellham, D. M. 6: v E 1986 (1); v WI 1981 (1); v P 1981 (2); *v E 1981 (1) 1985 (1)*

Wessels, K. C. 24: v E 1982 (4); v WI 1984 (5); v NZ 1985 (1); v P 1983 (5); *v E 1985 (6); v WI 1983 (2); v SL 1982 (1)*

Whatmore, D. F. 7: v P 1978 (2); *v In 1979 (5)*

Whitney, M. R. 12: v E 1988 (1) 1992 (1); v NZ 1987 (1); v In 1991 (3); *v E 1981 (2); v WI 1990 (2); v SL 1992 (2)*

Whitty, W. J. 14: v E 1911 (2); v SA 1910 (5); *v E 1909 (1) 1912 (1); v SA 1912 (3)*

Wiener, J. M. 6: v E 1979 (2); v WI 1979 (2); *v P 1979 (2)*

Wilson, J. W. 1: *v In 1956*

Wood, G. M. 59: v E 1978 (6) 1982 (1); v WI 1981 (3) 1984 (5) 1988 (3); v NZ 1980 (3); v In 1977 (1) 1980 (3); v P 1978 (1) 1981 (3); *v E 1980 (1) 1981 (6) 1985 (5); v WI 1977 (5) 1983 (1); v NZ 1981 (3); v In 1979 (2); v P 1982 (3) 1988 (3); v SL 1982 (1)*

Woodcock, A. J. 1: v NZ 1973

Woodfull, W. M. 35: v E 1928 (5) 1932 (5); v SA 1931 (5); v WI 1930 (5); *v E 1926 (5) 1930 (5) 1934 (5)*

Woods, S. M. J. 3: *v E 1888 (3)*

Woolley, R. D. 2: *v WI 1983 (1); v SL 1982 (1)*

Worrall, J. 11: v E 1884 (1) 1887 (1) 1894 (1) 1897 (1); *v E 1888 (3) 1899 (2)*

Wright, K. J. 10: v E 1978 (2); v P 1978 (2); *v In 1979 (6)*

Yallop, G. N. 39: v E 1978 (6); v WI 1975 (3) 1984 (1); v In 1977 (1); v P 1978 (1) 1981 (1) 1983 (5); *v E 1980 (1) 1981 (6); v WI 1977 (4); v In 1979 (6); v P 1979 (3); v SL 1982 (1)*

Yardley, B. 33: v E 1978 (4) 1982 (5); v WI 1981 (3); v In 1977 (1) 1980 (2); v P 1978 (1) 1981 (3); *v WI 1977 (5); v NZ 1981 (3); v In 1979 (3); v P 1982 (2); v SL 1982 (1)*

Zoehrer, T. J. 10: v E 1986 (4); *v NZ 1985 (3); v In 1986 (3)*

SOUTH AFRICA

Number of Test cricketers: 260

Adcock, N. A. T. 26: v E 1956 (5); v A 1957 (5); v NZ 1953 (5) 1961 (2); *v E 1955 (4) 1960 (5)*
Anderson, J. H. 1: v A 1902
Ashley, W. H. 1: v E 1888

Bacher, A. 12: v A 1966 (5) 1969 (4); *v E 1965 (3)*
Balaskas, X. C. 9: v E 1930 (2) 1938 (1); v A 1935 (3); *v E 1935 (1); v NZ 1931 (2)*
Barlow, E. J. 30: v E 1964 (5); v A 1966 (5) 1969 (4); v NZ 1961 (5); *v E 1965 (3); v A 1963 (5); v NZ 1963 (3)*
Baumgartner, H. V. 1: v E 1913
Beaumont, R. 5: v E 1913 (2); *v E 1912 (1); v A 1912 (2)*
Begbie, D. W. 5: v E 1948 (3); v A 1949 (2)
Bell, A. J. 16: v E 1930 (3); *v E 1929 (3) 1935 (3); v A 1931 (5); v NZ 1931 (2)*
Bisset, M. 3: v E 1898 (2) 1909 (1)
Bissett, G. F. 4: v E 1927 (4)
Blanckenberg, J. M. 18: v E 1913 (5) 1922 (5); v A 1921 (3); *v E 1924 (5)*
Bland, K. C. 21: v E 1964 (5); v A 1966 (1); v NZ 1961 (5); *v E 1965 (3); v A 1963 (4); v NZ 1963 (3)*
Bock, E. G. 1: v A 1935
Bond, G. E. 1: v E 1938
Bosch, T. 1: *v WI 1991*
Botten, J. T. 3: *v E 1965 (3)*
Brann, W. H. 3: v E 1922 (3)
Briscoe, A. W. 2: v E 1938 (1); v A 1935 (1)
Bromfield, H. D. 9: v E 1964 (3); v NZ 1961 (5); *v E 1965 (1)*
Brown, L. S. 2: *v A 1931 (1); v NZ 1931 (1)*
Burger, C. G. de V. 2: v A 1957 (2)
Burke, S. F. 2: v E 1964 (1); v NZ 1961 (1)
Buys, I. D. 1: v E 1922

Cameron, H. B. 26: v E 1927 (5) 1930 (5); *v E 1929 (4) 1935 (5); v A 1931 (5); v NZ 1931 (2)*
Campbell, T. 5: v E 1909 (4); *v E 1912 (1)*
Carlstein, P. R. 8: v A 1957 (1); *v E 1960 (5); v A 1963 (2)*
Carter, C. P. 10: v E 1913 (2); v A 1921 (3); *v E 1912 (2) 1924 (3)*
Catterall, R. H. 24: v E 1922 (5) 1927 (5) 1930 (4); *v E 1924 (5) 1929 (5)*
Chapman, H. W. 2: v E 1913 (1); v A 1921 (1)
Cheetham, J. E. 24: v E 1948 (1); v A 1949 (3); v NZ 1953 (5); *v E 1951 (5) 1955 (3); v A 1952 (5); v NZ 1952 (7)*
Chevalier, G. A. 1: v A 1969
Christy, J. A. J. 10: v E 1930 (1); *v E 1929 (2); v A 1931 (5); v NZ 1931 (2)*
Chubb, G. W. A. 5: *v E 1951 (5)*
Cochran, J. A. K. 1: v E 1930
Coen, S. K. 2: v E 1927 (2)
Commaille, J. M. M. 12: v E 1909 (5) 1927 (2); *v E 1924 (5)*
Commins, J. B. 3: v NZ 1994 (2); v P 1994 (1)
Conyngham, D. P. 1: v E 1922
Cook, F. J. 1: v E 1895
Cook, S. J. 3: v In 1992 (2); *v SL 1993 (1)*
Cooper, A. H. C. 1: v E 1913
Cox, J. L. 3: v E 1913 (3)
Cripps, G. 1: v E 1891
Crisp, R. J. 9: v A 1935 (4); *v E 1935 (5)*

Cronje, W. J. 21: v A 1993 (3); v NZ 1994 (3); v In 1992 (3); v P 1994 (1); *v E 1994 (3); v A 1993 (3); v WI 1991 (1); v NZ 1994 (1); v SL 1993 (3)*

Cullinan, D. J. 13: v NZ 1994 (3); v In 1992 (1); v P 1994 (1); *v E 1994 (1); v A 1993 (3); v NZ 1994 (1); v SL 1993 (3)*

Curnow, S. H. 7: v E 1930 (3); *v A 1931 (4)*

Dalton, E. L. 15: v E 1930 (1) 1938 (4); v A 1935 (1); *v E 1929 (1) 1935 (4); v A 1931 (2); v NZ 1931 (2)*

Davies, E. Q. 5: v E 1938 (3); v A 1935 (2)

Dawson, O. C. 9: v E 1948 (4); *v E 1947 (5)*

Deane, H. G. 17: v E 1927 (5) 1930 (2); *v E 1924 (5) 1929 (5)*

de Villiers, P. S. 14: v A 1993 (3); v NZ 1994 (3); v P 1994 (1); *v E 1994 (3); v A 1993 (3); v NZ 1994 (1)*

Dixon, C. D. 1: v E 1913

Donald, A. A. 19: v A 1993 (3); v In 1992 (4); v P 1994 (1); *v E 1994 (3); v A 1993 (3); v WI 1991 (1); v NZ 1994 (1); v SL 1993 (3)*

Dower, R. R. 1: v E 1898

Draper, R. G. 2: v A 1949 (2)

Duckworth, C. A. R. 2: v E 1956 (2)

Dumbrill, R. 5: v A 1966 (2); *v E 1965 (3)*

Duminy, J. P. 3: v E 1927 (2); *v E 1929 (1)*

Dunell, O. R. 2: v E 1888 (2)

Du Preez, J. H. 2: v A 1966 (2)

Du Toit, J. F. 1: v E 1891

Dyer, D. V. 3: *v E 1947 (3)*

Eksteen, C. E. 5: v NZ 1994 (2); v P 1994 (1); *v NZ 1994 (1); v SL 1993 (1)*

Elgie, M. K. 3: v NZ 1961 (3)

Endean, W. R. 28: v E 1956 (5); v A 1957 (5); v NZ 1953 (5); *v E 1951 (1) 1955 (5); v A 1952 (5); v NZ 1952 (2)*

Farrer, W. S. 6: v NZ 1961 (3); *v NZ 1963 (3)*

Faulkner, G. A. 25: v E 1905 (5) 1909 (5); *v E 1907 (3) 1912 (3) 1924 (1); v A 1910 (5) 1912 (3)*

Fellows-Smith, J. P. 4: *v E 1960 (4)*

Fichardt, C. G. 2: v E 1891 (1) 1895 (1)

Finlason, C. E. 1: v E 1888

Floquet, C. E. 1: v E 1909

Francis, H. H. 2: v E 1898 (2)

Francois, C. M. 5: v E 1922 (5)

Frank, C. N. 3: v A 1921 (3)

Frank, W. H. B. 1: v E 1895

Fuller, E. R. H. 7: v A 1957 (1); *v E 1955 (2); v A 1952 (2); v NZ 1952 (2)*

Fullerton, G. M. 7: v A 1949 (2); *v E 1947 (2) 1951 (3)*

Funston, K. J. 18: v E 1956 (3); v A 1957 (5); v NZ 1953 (3); *v A 1952 (5); v NZ 1952 (2)*

Gamsy, D. 2: v A 1969 (2)

Gleeson, R. A. 1: v E 1895

Glover, G. K. 1: v E 1895

Goddard, T. L. 41: v E 1956 (5) 1964 (5); v A 1957 (5) 1966 (5) 1969 (3); *v E 1955 (5) 1960 (5); v A 1963 (5); v NZ 1963 (3)*

Gordon, N. 5: v E 1938 (5)

Graham, R. 2: v E 1898 (2)

Grieveson, R. E. 2: v E 1938 (2)

Griffin, G. M. 2: *v E 1960 (2)*

Hall, A. E. 7: v E 1922 (4) 1927 (2) 1930 (1)

Hall, G. G. 1: v E 1964

Halliwell, E. A. 8: v E 1891 (1) 1895 (3) 1898 (1); v A 1902 (3)

Halse, C. G. 3: *v A 1963 (3)*

Hands, P. A. M. 7: v E 1913 (5); v A 1921 (1); *v E 1924 (1)*

Hands, R. H. M. 1: v E 1913

Hanley, M. A. 1: v E 1948

Harris, T. A. 3: v E 1948 (1); *v E 1947 (2)*
Hartigan, G. P. D. 5: v E 1913 (3); *v E 1912 (1); v A 1912 (1)*
Harvey, R. L. 2: v A 1935 (2)
Hathorn, C. M. H. 12: v E 1905 (5); v A 1902 (3); *v E 1907 (3); v A 1910 (1)*
Hearne, F. 4: v E 1891 (1) 1895 (3)
Hearne, G. A. L. 3: v E 1922 (3); *v E 1924 (1)*
Heine, P. S. 14: v E 1956 (5); v A 1957 (4); v NZ 1961 (1); *v E 1955 (4)*
Henry, O. 3: v In 1992 (3)
Hime, C. F. W. 1: v E 1895
Hudson, A. C. 19: v A 1993 (3); v NZ 1994 (2); v In 1992 (4); *v E 1994 (2); v A 1993 (3); v WI 1991 (1); v NZ 1994 (1); v SL 1993 (3)*
Hutchinson, P. 2: v E 1888 (2)

Ironside, D. E. J. 3: v NZ 1953 (3)
Irvine, B. L. 4: v A 1969 (4)

Jack, S. D. 2: v NZ 1994 (2)
Johnson, C. L. 1: v E 1895

Keith, H. J. 8: v E 1956 (3); *v E 1955 (4); v A 1952 (1)*
Kempis, G. A. 1: v E 1888
Kirsten, G. 14: v A 1993 (3); v NZ 1994 (3); v P 1994 (1); *v E 1994 (3); v A 1993 (3); v NZ 1994 (1)*
Kirsten, P. N. 12: v A 1993 (3); v In 1992 (4); *v E 1994 (3); v A 1993 (1); v WI 1991 (1)*
Kotze, J. J. 3: v A 1902 (2); *v E 1907 (1)*
Kuiper, A. P. 1: *v WI 1991*
Kuys, F. 1: v E 1898

Lance, H. R. 13: v A 1966 (5) 1969 (3); v NZ 1961 (2); *v E 1965 (3)*
Langton, A. B. C. 15: v E 1938 (5); v A 1935 (5); *v E 1935 (5)*
Lawrence, G. B. 5: v NZ 1961 (5)
le Roux, F. L. 1: v E 1913
Lewis, P. T. 1: v E 1913
Lindsay, D. T. 19: v E 1964 (3); v A 1966 (5) 1969 (3); *v E 1965 (3); v A 1963 (3); v NZ 1963 (3)*
Lindsay, J. D. 3: *v E 1947 (3)*
Lindsay, N. V. 1: v A 1921
Ling, W. V. S. 6: v E 1922 (3); v A 1921 (3)
Llewellyn, C. B. 15: v E 1895 (1) 1898 (1); v A 1902 (3); *v E 1912 (3); v A 1910 (5) 1912 (2)*
Lundie, E. B. 1: v E 1913

Macaulay, M. J. 1: v E 1964
McCarthy, C. N. 15: v E 1948 (5); v A 1949 (5); *v E 1951 (5)*
McGlew, D. J. 34: v E 1956 (1); v A 1957 (5); v NZ 1953 (5) 1961 (5); *v E 1951 (2) 1955 (5) 1960 (5); v A 1952 (4); v NZ 1952 (2)*
McKinnon, A. H. 8: v E 1964 (2); v A 1966 (2); v NZ 1961 (1); *v E 1960 (1) 1965 (2)*
McLean, R. A. 40: v E 1956 (5) 1964 (5); v A 1957 (4); v NZ 1953 (4) 1961 (5); *v E 1951 (3) 1955 (5) 1960 (5); v A 1952 (5); v NZ 1952 (2)*
McMillan, B. M. 17: v A 1993 (3); v NZ 1994 (3); v In 1992 (4); v P 1994 (1); *v E 1994 (3); v A 1993 (1); v SL 1993 (2)*
McMillan, Q. 13: v E 1930 (5); *v E 1929 (2); v A 1931 (4); v NZ 1931 (2)*
Mann, N. B. F. 19: v E 1948 (5); v A 1949 (5); *v E 1947 (5) 1951 (4)*
Mansell, P. N. F. 13: *v E 1951 (2) 1955 (4); v A 1952 (5); v NZ 1952 (2)*
Markham, L. A. 1: v E 1948
Marx, W. F. E. 3: v A 1921 (3)
Matthews, C. R. 14: v A 1993 (3); v NZ 1994 (2); v In 1992 (3); *v E 1994 (3); v A 1993 (2); v NZ 1994 (1)*
Meintjes, D. J. 2: v E 1922 (2)
Melle, M. G. 7: v A 1949 (2); *v E 1951 (1); v A 1952 (4)*
Melville, A. 11: v E 1938 (5) 1948 (1); *v E 1947 (5)*
Middleton, J. 6: v E 1895 (2) 1898 (2); v A 1902 (2)
Mills, C. 1: v E 1891
Milton, W. H. 3: v E 1888 (2) 1891 (1)

Mitchell, B. 42: v E 1930 (5) 1938 (5) 1948 (5); v A 1935 (5); *v E 1929 (5) 1935 (5) 1947 (5); v A 1931 (5); v NZ 1931 (2)*
Mitchell, F. 3: *v E 1912 (1); v A 1912 (2)*
Morkel, D. P. B. 16: v E 1927 (5); *v E 1929 (5); v A 1931 (5); v NZ 1931 (1)*
Murray, A. R. A. 10: v NZ 1953 (4); *v A 1952 (4); v NZ 1952 (2)*

Nel, J. D. 6: v A 1949 (5) 1957 (1)
Newberry, C. 4: v E 1913 (4)
Newson, E. S. 3: v E 1930 (1) 1938 (2)
Nicholson, F. 4: v A 1935 (4)
Nicolson, J. F. W. 3: v E 1927 (3)
Norton, N. O. 1: v E 1909
Nourse, A. D. 34: v E 1938 (5) 1948 (5); v A 1935 (5) 1949 (5); *v E 1935 (4) 1947 (5) 1951 (5)*
Nourse, A. W. 45: v E 1905 (5) 1909 (5) 1913 (5) 1922 (5); v A 1902 (3) 1921 (3); *v E 1907 (3) 1912 (3) 1924 (5); v A 1910 (5) 1912 (3)*
Nupen, E. P. 17: v E 1922 (4) 1927 (5) 1930 (3); v A 1921 (2) 1935 (1); *v E 1924 (2)*

Ochse, A. E. 2: v E 1888 (2)
Ochse, A. L. 3: v E 1927 (1); *v E 1929 (2)*
O'Linn, S. 7: v NZ 1961 (2); *v E 1960 (5)*
Owen-Smith, H. G. 5: *v E 1929 (5)*

Palm, A. W. 1: v E 1927
Parker, G. M. 2: *v E 1924 (2)*
Parkin, D. C. 1: v E 1891
Partridge, J. T. 11: v E 1964 (3); *v A 1963 (5); v NZ 1963 (3)*
Pearse, O. C. 3: *v A 1910 (3)*
Pegler, S. J. 16: v E 1909 (1); *v E 1912 (3) 1924 (5); v A 1910 (4) 1912 (3)*
Pithey, A. J. 17: v E 1956 (3) 1964 (5); *v E 1960 (2); v A 1963 (4); v NZ 1963 (3)*
Pithey, D. B. 8: v A 1966 (2); *v A 1963 (3); v NZ 1963 (3)*
Plimsoll, J. B. 1: *v E 1947*
Pollock, P. M. 28: v E 1964 (5); v A 1966 (5) 1969 (4); v NZ 1961 (3); *v E 1965 (3); v A 1963 (3); v NZ 1963 (3)*
Pollock, R. G. 23: v E 1964 (5); v A 1966 (5) 1969 (4); *v E 1965 (3); v A 1963 (5); v NZ 1963 (1)*
Poore, R. M. 3: v E 1895 (3)
Pothecary, J. E. 3: *v E 1960 (3)*
Powell, A. W. 1: v E 1898
Prince, C. F. H. 1: v E 1898
Pringle, M. W. 3: v In 1992 (2); *v WI 1991 (1)*
Procter, M. J. 7: v A 1966 (3) 1969 (4)
Promnitz, H. L. E. 2: v E 1927 (2)

Quinn, N. A. 12: v E 1930 (1); *v E 1929 (4); v A 1931 (5); v NZ 1931 (2)*

Reid, N. 1: v A 1921
Rhodes, J. N. 21: v A 1993 (3); v NZ 1994 (3); v In 1992 (4); v P 1994 (1); *v E 1994 (3); v A 1993 (3); v NZ 1994 (1); v SL 1993 (3)*
Richards, A. R. 1: v E 1895
Richards, B. A. 4: v A 1969 (4)
Richards, W. H. 1: v E 1888
Richardson, D. J. 22: v A 1993 (3); v NZ 1994 (3); v In 1992 (4); v P 1994 (1); *v E 1994 (3); v A 1993 (3); v WI 1991 (1); v NZ 1994 (1); v SL 1993 (3)*
Robertson, J. B. 3: v A 1935 (3)
Rose-Innes, A. 2: v E 1888 (2)
Routledge, T. W. 4: v E 1891 (1) 1895 (3)
Rowan, A. M. B. 15: v E 1948 (5); *v E 1947 (5) 1951 (5)*
Rowan, E. A. B. 26: v E 1938 (4) 1948 (4); v A 1935 (3) 1949 (5); *v E 1935 (4) 1951 (5)*
Rowe, G. A. 5: v E 1895 (2) 1898 (2); v A 1902 (1)
Rushmere, M. W. 1: *v WI 1991*

Samuelson, S. V. 1: v E 1909
Schultz, B. N. 5: v In 1992 (2); *v SL 1993 (3)*

Schwarz, R. O. 20: v E 1905 (5) 1909 (4); *v E 1907 (3) 1912 (I); v A 1910 (5) 1912 (2)*
Seccull, A. W. 1: v E 1895
Seymour, M. A. 7: v E 1964 (2); v A 1969 (1); *v A 1963 (4)*
Shalders, W. A. 12: v E 1898 (1) 1905 (5); v A 1902 (3); *v E 1907 (3)*
Shepstone, G. H. 2: v E 1895 (1) 1898 (1)
Sherwell, P. W. 13: v E 1905 (5); *v E 1907 (3); v A 1910 (5)*
Siedle, I. J. 18: v E 1927 (1) 1930 (5); v A 1935 (5); *v E 1929 (3) 1935 (4)*
Sinclair, J. H. 25: v E 1895 (3) 1898 (2) 1905 (5) 1909 (4); v A 1902 (3); *v E 1907 (3); v A 1910 (5)*
Smith, C. J. E. 3: v A 1902 (3)
Smith, F. W. 3: v E 1888 (2) 1895 (1)
Smith, V. I. 9: v A 1949 (3) 1957 (1); *v E 1947 (4) 1955 (I)*
Snell, R. P. 5: v NZ 1994 (1); *v A 1993 (I); v WI 1991 (I); v SL 1993 (2)*
Snooke, S. D. 1: *v E 1907*
Snooke, S. J. 26: v E 1905 (5) 1909 (5) 1922 (3); *v E 1907 (3) 1912 (3); v A 1910 (5) 1912 (2)*
Solomon, W. R. 1: v E 1898
Stewart, R. B. 1: v E 1888
Steyn, P. J. R. 3: v NZ 1994 (1); *v P 1994 (1); v NZ 1994 (I)*
Stricker, L. A. 13: v E 1909 (4); *v E 1912 (2); v A 1910 (5) 1912 (2)*
Susskind, M. J. 5: *v E 1924 (5)*
Symcox, P. L. 5: *v A 1993 (2); v SL 1993 (3)*

Taberer, H. M. 1: v A 1902
Tancred, A. B. 2: v E 1888 (2)
Tancred, L. J. 14: v E 1905 (5) 1913 (1); v A 1902 (3); *v E 1907 (I) 1912 (2); v A 1912 (2)*
Tancred, V. M. 1: v E 1898
Tapscott, G. L. 1: v E 1913
Tapscott, L. E. 2: v E 1922 (2)
Tayfield, H. J. 37: v E 1956 (5); v A 1949 (5) 1957 (5); v NZ 1953 (5); *v E 1955 (5) 1960 (5); v A 1952 (5); v NZ 1952 (2)*
Taylor, A. I. 1: v E 1956
Taylor, D. 2: v E 1913 (2)
Taylor, H. W. 42: v E 1913 (5) 1922 (5) 1927 (5) 1930 (4); v A 1921 (3); *v E 1912 (3) 1924 (5) 1929 (3); v A 1912 (3) 1931 (5); v NZ 1931 (I)*
Theunissen, N. H. C. de J. 1: v E 1888
Thornton, P. G. 1: v A 1902
Tomlinson, D. S. 1: *v E 1935*
Traicos, A. J. 3: v A 1969 (3)
Trimborn, P. H. J. 4: v A 1966 (3) 1969 (1)
Tuckett, L. 9: v E 1948 (4); *v E 1947 (5)*
Tuckett, L. R. 1: v E 1913
Twentyman-Jones, P. S. 1: v A 1902

van der Bijl, P. G. V. 5: v E 1938 (5)
Van der Merwe, E. A. 2: v A 1935 (1); *v E 1929 (I)*
Van der Merwe, P. L. 15: v E 1964 (2); v A 1966 (5); *v E 1965 (3); v A 1963 (3); v NZ 1963 (2)*
Van Ryneveld, C. B. 19: v E 1956 (5); v A 1957 (4); v NZ 1953 (5); *v E 1951 (5)*
Varnals, G. D. 3: v E 1964 (3)
Viljoen, K. G. 27: v E 1930 (3) 1938 (4) 1948 (2); v A 1935 (4); *v E 1935 (4) 1947 (5); v A 1931 (4); v NZ 1931 (I)*
Vincent, C. L. 25: v E 1927 (5) 1930 (5); *v E 1929 (4) 1935 (4); v A 1931 (5); v NZ 1931 (2)*
Vintcent, C. H. 3: v E 1888 (2) 1891 (1)
Vogler, A. E. E. 15: v E 1905 (5) 1909 (5); *v E 1907 (3); v A 1910 (2)*

Wade, H. F. 10: v A 1935 (5); *v E 1935 (5)*
Wade, W. W. 11: v E 1938 (3) 1948 (5); v A 1949 (3)
Waite, J. H. B. 50: v E 1956 (5) 1964 (2); v NZ 1953 (5) 1961 (5); *v E 1951 (4) 1955 (5) 1960 (5); v A 1952 (5) 1963 (4); v NZ 1952 (2) 1963 (3)*
Walter, K. A. 2: v NZ 1961 (2)
Ward, T. A. 23: v E 1913 (5) 1922 (5); v A 1921 (3); *v E 1912 (2) 1924 (5); v A 1912 (3)*
Watkins, J. C. 15: v E 1956 (2); v A 1949 (3); v NZ 1953 (5); *v A 1952 (5); v NZ 1952 (2)*
Wesley, C. 3: *v E 1960 (3)*

Wessels, K. C. 16: v A 1993 (3); v In 1992 (4); *v E 1994 (3); v A 1993 (2); v WI 1991 (1); SL 1993 (3)*
Westcott, R. J. 5: v A 1957 (2); v NZ 1953 (3)
White, G. C. 17: v E 1905 (5) 1909 (4); *v E 1907 (3) 1912 (2); v A 1912 (3)*
Willoughby, J. T. I. 2: v E 1895 (2)
Wimble, C. S. 1: v E 1891
Winslow, P. L. 5: v A 1949 (2); *v E 1955 (3)*
Wynne, O. E. 6: v E 1948 (3); v A 1949 (3)

Zulch, J. W. 16: v E 1909 (5) 1913 (3); v A 1921 (3); *v A 1910 (5)*

WEST INDIES

Number of Test cricketers: 210

Achong, E. 6: v E 1929 (1) 1934 (2); *v E 1933 (3)*
Adams, J. C. 22: v E 1993 (5); v A 1994 (4); v SA 1991 (1); *v E 1995 (4); v A 1992 (3); v NZ 1994 (2); v In 1994 (3)*
Alexander, F. C. M. 25: v E 1959 (5); v P 1957 (5); *v E 1957 (2); v A 1960 (5); v In 1958 (5); v P 1958 (3)*
Ali, Imtiaz 1: v In 1975
Ali, Inshan 12: v E 1973 (2); v A 1972 (3); v In 1970 (1); v P 1976 (1); v NZ 1971 (3); *v E 1973 (1); v A 1975 (1)*
Allan, D. W. 5: v A 1964 (1); v In 1961 (2); *v E 1966 (2)*
Allen, I. B. A. 2: *v E 1991 (2)*
Ambrose, C. E. L. 59: v E 1989 (3) 1993 (5); v A 1990 (5) 1994 (4); v SA 1991 (1); v In 1988 (4); v P 1987 (3) 1992 (3); *v E 1988 (5) 1991 (5) 1995 (5); v A 1988 (5) 1992 (5); v NZ 1994 (2); v P 1990 (3); v SL 1993 (1)*
Arthurton, K. L. T. 33: v E 1993 (5); v A 1994 (3); v SA 1991 (1); v In 1988 (4); v P 1992 (3); *v E 1988 (1) 1992 (5); v A 1992 (5); v NZ 1994 (2); v In 1994 (3); v SL 1993 (1)*
Asgarali, N. 2: *v E 1957 (2)*
Atkinson, D. St E. 22: v E 1953 (4); v A 1954 (4); v P 1957 (1); *v E 1957 (2); v A 1951 (3); v NZ 1951 (1) 1955 (4); v In 1948 (4)*
Atkinson, E. St E. 8: v P 1957 (3); *v In 1958 (3); v P 1958 (2)*
Austin, R. A. 2: v A 1977 (2)

Bacchus, S. F. A. F. 19: v A 1977 (2); *v E 1980 (5); v A 1981 (2); v In 1978 (6); v P 1980 (4)*
Baichan, L. 3: *v A 1975 (1); v P 1974 (2)*
Baptiste, E. A. E. 10: v E 1989 (1); v A 1983 (3); *v E 1984 (5); v In 1983 (1)*
Barrett, A. G. 6: v E 1973 (2); v In 1970 (2); *v In 1974 (2)*
Barrow, I. 11: v E 1929 (1) 1934 (1); *v E 1933 (3) 1939 (1); v A 1930 (5)*
Bartlett, E. L. 5: *v E 1928 (1); v A 1930 (4)*
Benjamin, K. C. G. 21: v E 1993 (5); v A 1994 (4); v SA 1991 (1); *v E 1995 (5); v A 1992 (1); v NZ 1994 (2); v In 1994 (3)*
Benjamin, W. K. M. 21: v E 1993 (5); v A 1994 (4); v In 1988 (1); v P 1987 (3) 1992 (3); *v E 1988 (3); v NZ 1994 (1); v In 1987 (1); v SL 1993 (1)*
Best, C. A. 8: v E 1985 (3) 1989 (3); *v P 1990 (2)*
Betancourt, N. 1: v E 1929
Binns, A. P. 5: v A 1954 (1); v In 1952 (1); *v NZ 1955 (3)*
Birkett, L. S. 4: *v A 1930 (4)*
Bishop, I. R. 24: v E 1989 (4); v In 1988 (4); v P 1992 (2); *v E 1995 (6); v A 1992 (5); v P 1990 (3)*
Boyce, K. D. 21: v E 1973 (4); v A 1972 (4); v In 1970 (1); *v E 1973 (5); v A 1975 (4); v In 1974 (3); v P 1974 (2)*
Browne, C. O. 3: v A 1994 (1); *v E 1995 (2)*
Browne, C. R. 4: v E 1929 (2); *v E 1928 (2)*
Butcher, B. F. 44: v E 1959 (1) 1967 (5); v A 1964 (5); *v E 1963 (5) 1966 (5) 1969 (5); v A 1968 (5); v NZ 1968 (3); v In 1958 (5) 1966 (3); v P 1958 (3)*
Butler, L. 1: v A 1954
Butts, C. G. 7: v NZ 1984 (1); *v NZ 1986 (1); v In 1987 (3); v P 1986 (2)*
Bynoe, M. R. 4: *v In 1966 (3); v P 1958 (1)*

Camacho, G. S. 11: v E 1967 (5); v In 1970 (2); *v E 1969 (2); v A 1968 (2)*

Cameron, F. J. 5: *v In 1948 (5)*

Cameron, J. H. 2: *v E 1939 (2)*

Campbell, S. L. 9: v A 1994 (1); *v E 1995 (6); v NZ 1994 (2)*

Carew, G. M. 4: v E 1934 (1) 1947 (2); *v In 1948 (1)*

Carew, M. C. 19: v E 1967 (1); v NZ 1971 (3); v In 1970 (3); *v E 1963 (2) 1966 (1) 1969 (1); v A 1968 (5); v NZ 1968 (3)*

Challenor, G. 3: *v E 1928 (3)*

Chanderpaul, S. 9: v E 1993 (4); *v E 1995 (2); v NZ 1994 (2); v In 1994 (1)*

Chang, H. S. 1: *v In 1978*

Christiani, C. M. 4: v E 1934 (4)

Christiani, R. J. 22: v E 1947 (4) 1953 (1); v In 1952 (2); *v E 1950 (4); v A 1951 (5); v NZ 1951 (1); v In 1948 (5)*

Clarke, C. B. 3: *v E 1939 (3)*

Clarke, S. T. 11: v A 1977 (1); *v A 1981 (1); v In 1978 (5); v P 1980 (4)*

Constantine, L. N. 18: v E 1929 (3) 1934 (3); *v E 1928 (3) 1933 (1) 1939 (3); v A 1930 (5)*

Croft, C. E. H. 27: v E 1980 (4); v A 1977 (2); v P 1976 (5); *v E 1980 (3); v A 1979 (3) 1981 (3); v NZ 1979 (3); v P 1980 (4)*

Cuffy, C. E. 2: *v In 1994 (2)*

Cummins, A. C. 5: v P 1992 (2); *v A 1992 (1); v In 1994 (2)*

Da Costa, O. C. 5: v E 1929 (1) 1934 (1); *v E 1933 (3)*

Daniel, W. W. 10: v A 1983 (2); v In 1975 (1); *v E 1976 (4); v In 1983 (3)*

Davis, B. A. 4: v E 1964 (4)

Davis, C. A. 15: v A 1972 (3); v NZ 1971 (5); v In 1970 (4); *v E 1969 (3); v A 1968 (1)*

Davis, W. W. 15: v A 1983 (1); v NZ 1984 (2); v In 1982 (1); *v E 1984 (1); v In 1983 (6) 1987 (4)*

De Caires, F. I. 3: v E 1929 (3)

Depeiza, C. C. 5: v A 1954 (3); *v NZ 1955 (2)*

Dewdney, T. 9: v A 1954 (2); v P 1957 (1); *v E 1957 (1); v NZ 1955 (3)*

Dhanraj, R. 3: *v E 1995 (1); v NZ 1994 (1); v In 1994 (1)*

Dowe, U. G. 4: v A 1972 (1); v NZ 1971 (1); v In 1970 (2)

Dujon, P. J. L. 81: v E 1985 (4) 1989 (4); v A 1983 (5) 1990 (5); v NZ 1984 (4); v In 1982 (5) 1988 (4); v P 1987 (3); *v E 1984 (5) 1988 (5) 1991 (2); v A 1981 (3) 1984 (5) 1988 (5); v NZ 1986 (3); v In 1983 (6) 1987 (4); v P 1986 (3) 1990 (3)*

Edwards, R. M. 5: *v A 1968 (2); v NZ 1968 (3)*

Ferguson, W. 8: v E 1947 (4) 1953 (1); *v In 1948 (3)*

Fernandes, M. P. 2: v E 1929 (1); *v E 1928 (1)*

Findlay, T. M. 10: v A 1972 (1); v NZ 1971 (5); v In 1970 (2); *v E 1969 (2)*

Foster, M. L. C. 14: v E 1973 (1); v A 1972 (4) 1977 (1); v NZ 1971 (3); v In 1970 (2); v P 1976 (1); *v E 1969 (1) 1973 (1)*

Francis, G. N. 10: v E 1929 (1); *v E 1928 (3) 1933 (1); v A 1930 (5)*

Frederick, M. C. 1: v E 1953

Fredericks, R. C. 59: v E 1973 (5); v A 1972 (5); v NZ 1971 (5); v In 1970 (4) 1975 (4); v P 1976 (5); *v E 1969 (3) 1973 (3) 1976 (5); v A 1968 (4) 1975 (6); v NZ 1968 (3); v In 1974 (3); v P 1974 (2)*

Fuller, R. L. 1: v E 1934

Furlonge, H. A. 3: v A 1954 (1); *v NZ 1955 (2)*

Ganteaume, A. G. 1: v E 1947

Garner, J. 58: v E 1980 (4) 1985 (5); v A 1977 (2) 1983 (5); v NZ 1984 (4); v In 1982 (4); v P 1976 (5); *v E 1980 (5) 1984 (5); v A 1979 (3) 1981 (3) 1984 (5); v NZ 1979 (3) 1986 (2); v P 1980 (3)*

Gaskin, B. B. M. 2: v E 1947 (2)

Gibbs, G. L. R. 1: v A 1954

Gibbs, L. R. 79: v E 1967 (5) 1973 (5); v A 1964 (5) 1972 (5); v NZ 1971 (2); v In 1961 (5) 1970 (1); v P 1957 (4); *v E 1963 (5) 1966 (5) 1969 (3) 1973 (3); v A 1960 (3) 1968 (5) 1975 (6); v NZ 1968 (3); v In 1958 (1) 1966 (3) 1974 (5); v P 1958 (3) 1974 (2)*

Gibson, O. D. 1: *v E 1995*

Gilchrist, R. 13: v P 1957 (5); *v E 1957 (4); v In 1958 (4)*

Gladstone, G. 1: v E 1929

Goddard, J. D. C. 27: v E 1947 (4); *v E 1950 (4) 1957 (5); v A 1951 (4); v NZ 1951 (2) 1955 (3); v In 1948 (5)*

Gomes, H. A. 60: v E 1980 (4) 1985 (5); v A 1977 (3) 1983 (2); v NZ 1984 (4); v In 1982 (5); *v E 1976 (2) 1984 (5); v A 1981 (3) 1984 (5); v NZ 1986 (3); v In 1978 (6) 1983 (6); v P 1980 (4) 1986 (3)*

Gomez, G. E. 29: v E 1947 (4) 1953 (4); v In 1952 (4); *v E 1939 (2) 1950 (4); v A 1951 (5); v NZ 1951 (1); v In 1948 (5)*

Grant, G. C. 12: v E 1934 (4); *v E 1933 (3); v A 1930 (5)*

Grant, R. S. 7: v E 1934 (4); *v E 1939 (3)*

Gray, A. H. 5: *v NZ 1986 (2); v P 1986 (3)*

Greenidge, A. E. 6: *v A 1977 (2); v In 1978 (4)*

Greenidge, C. G. 108: v E 1980 (4) 1985 (5) 1989 (4); v A 1977 (2) 1983 (5) 1990 (5); v NZ 1984 (4); v In 1982 (5) 1988 (4); v P 1976 (5) 1987 (3); *v E 1976 (5) 1980 (5) 1984 (5) 1988 (4); v A 1975 (2) 1979 (3) 1981 (2) 1984 (5) 1988 (5); v NZ 1979 (3) 1986 (3); v In 1974 (5) 1983 (6) 1987 (3); v P 1986 (3) 1990 (3)*

Greenidge, G. A. 5: v A 1972 (3); v NZ 1971 (2)

Grell, M. G. 1: v E 1929

Griffith, C. C. 28: v E 1959 (1) 1967 (4); v A 1964 (5); *v E 1963 (5) 1966 (5); v A 1968 (3); v NZ 1968 (2); v In 1966 (3)*

Griffith, H. C. 13: v E 1929 (3); *v E 1928 (3) 1933 (2); v A 1930 (5)*

Guillen, S. C. 5: *v A 1951 (3); v NZ 1951 (2)*

Hall, W. W. 48: v E 1959 (5) 1967 (4); v A 1964 (5); v In 1961 (5); *v E 1963 (5) 1966 (5); v A 1960 (5) 1968 (2); v NZ 1968 (1); v In 1958 (5) 1966 (3); v P 1958 (3)*

Harper, R. A. 25: v E 1985 (2); v A 1983 (4); v NZ 1984 (1); *v E 1984 (2) 1988 (3); v A 1984 (2) 1988 (1); v In 1983 (2) 1987 (1); v P 1986 (3); v SL 1993 (1)*

Haynes, D. L. 116: v E 1980 (4) 1985 (5) 1989 (4) 1993 (4); v A 1977 (2) 1983 (5) 1990 (5); v SA 1991 (1); v NZ 1984 (4); v In 1982 (5) 1988 (4); v P 1987 (3) 1992 (3); *v E 1980 (5) 1984 (5) 1988 (4) 1991 (5); v A 1979 (3) 1981 (3) 1984 (5) 1988 (5) 1992 (5); v NZ 1979 (3) 1986 (3); v In 1983 (6) 1987 (4); v P 1980 (4) 1986 (3) 1990 (3); v SL 1993 (1)*

Headley, G. A. 22: v E 1929 (4) 1934 (4) 1947 (1) 1953 (1); *v E 1933 (3) 1939 (3); v A 1930 (5); v In 1948 (1)*

Headley, R. G. A. 2: *v E 1973 (2)*

Hendriks, J. L. 20: v A 1964 (4); v In 1961 (1); *v E 1966 (3) 1969 (1); v A 1968 (5); v NZ 1968 (1); v In 1966 (3)*

Hoad, E. L. G. 4: v E 1929 (1); *v E 1928 (1) 1933 (2)*

Holder, V. A. 40: v E 1973 (1); v A 1972 (3) 1977 (3); v NZ 1971 (4); v In 1970 (3) 1975 (1); v P 1976 (1); *v E 1969 (3) 1973 (2) 1976 (4); v A 1975 (3); v In 1974 (4) 1978 (6); v P 1974 (2)*

Holding, M. A. 60: v E 1980 (4) 1985 (4); v A 1983 (3); v NZ 1984 (3); v In 1975 (4) 1982 (5); *v E 1976 (4) 1980 (5) 1984 (4); v A 1975 (5) 1979 (3) 1981 (3) 1984 (3); v NZ 1979 (3) 1986 (1); v In 1983 (6)*

Holford, D. A. J. 24: v E 1967 (4); v NZ 1971 (5); v In 1970 (1) 1975 (2); v P 1976 (1); *v E 1966 (5); v A 1968 (2); v NZ 1968 (3); v In 1966 (1)*

Holt, J. K. 17: v E 1953 (5); v A 1954 (5); *v In 1958 (5); v P 1958 (2)*

Hooper, C. L. 52: v E 1989 (3); v A 1990 (5) 1994 (4); v P 1987 (3) 1992 (3); *v E 1988 (5) 1991 (5) 1995 (5); v A 1988 (5) 1992 (4); v In 1987 (3) 1994 (3); v P 1990 (3); v SL 1993 (1)*

Howard, A. B. 1: v NZ 1971

Hunte, C. C. 44: v E 1959 (5); v A 1964 (5); v In 1961 (5); v P 1957 (5); *v E 1963 (5) 1966 (5); v A 1960 (5); v In 1958 (5) 1966 (3); v P 1958 (1)*

Hunte, E. A. C. 3: v E 1929 (3)

Hylton, L. G. 6: v E 1934 (4); *v E 1939 (2)*

Johnson, H. H. H. 3: v E 1947 (1); *v E 1950 (2)*

Johnson, T. F. 1: *v E 1939*

Jones, C. M. 4: v E 1929 (1) 1934 (3)

Jones, P. E. 9: v E 1947 (1); *v E 1950 (2); v A 1951 (1); v In 1948 (5)*

Julien, B. D. 24: v E 1973 (5); v In 1975 (4); v P 1976 (1); *v E 1973 (3) 1976 (2); v A 1975 (3); v In 1974 (4); v P 1974 (2)*

Jumadeen, R. R. 12: v A 1972 (1) 1977 (2); v NZ 1971 (1); v In 1975 (4); v P 1976 (1); *v E 1976 (1); v In 1978 (2)*

Kallicharran, A. I. 66: v E 1973 (5); v A 1972 (5) 1977 (5); v NZ 1971 (2); v In 1975 (4); v P 1976 (5); *v E 1973 (3) 1976 (3) 1980 (5); v A 1975 (6) 1979 (3); v NZ 1979 (3); v In 1974 (5) 1978 (6); v P 1974 (2) 1980 (4)*

Kanhai, R. B. 79: v E 1959 (5) 1967 (5) 1973 (5); v A 1964 (5) 1972 (5); v In 1961 (5) 1970 (5); v P 1957 (5); *v E 1957 (5) 1963 (5) 1966 (5) 1973 (3); v A 1960 (5) 1968 (5); v In 1958 (5) 1966 (3); v P 1958 (3)*

Kentish, E. S. M. 2: v E 1947 (1) 1953 (1)

King, C. L. 9: v P 1976 (1); *v E 1976 (3) 1980 (1); v A 1979 (1); v NZ 1979 (3)*

King, F. M. 14: v E 1953 (3); v A 1954 (4); v In 1952 (5); *v NZ 1955 (3)*

King, L. A. 2: v E 1967 (1); v In 1961 (1)

Lambert, C. B. 1: *v E 1991*

Lara, B. C. 31: v E 1993 (5); v A 1994 (4); v SA 1991 (1); v P 1992 (3); *v E 1995 (6); v A 1992 (5); v NZ 1994 (2); v In 1994 (3); v P 1990 (1); v SL 1993 (1)*

Lashley, P. D. 4: *v E 1966 (2); v A 1960 (2)*

Legall, R. 4: v In 1952 (4)

Lewis, D. M. 3: v In 1970 (3)

Lloyd, C. H. 110: v E 1967 (5) 1973 (5) 1980 (4); v A 1972 (3) 1977 (2) 1983 (4); v NZ 1971 (2); v In 1970 (5) 1975 (4) 1982 (5); v P 1976 (5); *v E 1969 (3) 1973 (3) 1976 (5) 1980 (4) 1984 (5); v A 1968 (4) 1975 (6) 1979 (2) 1981 (3) 1984 (5); v NZ 1968 (3) 1979 (3); v In 1966 (3) 1974 (5) 1983 (6); v P 1974 (2) 1980 (4)*

Logie, A. L. 52: v E 1989 (3); v A 1983 (1) 1990 (5); v NZ 1984 (4); v In 1982 (5) 1988 (4); v P 1987 (3); *v E 1988 (5) 1991 (4); v A 1988 (5); v NZ 1986 (3); v In 1983 (3) 1987 (4); v P 1990 (3)*

McMorris, E. D. A. St J. 13: v E 1959 (4); v In 1961 (4); v P 1957 (1); *v E 1963 (2) 1966 (2)*

McWatt, C. A. 6: v E 1953 (5); v A 1954 (1)

Madray, I. S. 2: v P 1957 (2)

Marshall, M. D. 81: v E 1980 (1) 1985 (5) 1989 (2); v A 1983 (4) 1990 (5); v NZ 1984 (4); v In 1982 (5) 1988 (3); v P 1987 (2); *v E 1980 (4) 1984 (4) 1988 (5) 1991 (5); v A 1984 (5) 1988 (5); v NZ 1986 (3); v In 1978 (3) 1983 (6); v P 1980 (4) 1986 (3) 1990 (3)*

Marshall, N. E. 1: v A 1954

Marshall, R. E. 4: *v A 1951 (2); v NZ 1951 (2)*

Martin, F. R. 9: v E 1929 (1); *v E 1928 (3); v A 1930 (5)*

Martindale, E. A. 10: v E 1934 (4); *v E 1933 (3) 1939 (3)*

Mattis, E. H. 4: v E 1980 (4)

Mendonca, I. L. 2: v In 1961 (2)

Merry, C. A. 2: *v E 1933 (2)*

Miller, R. 1: v In 1952

Moodie, G. H. 1: v E 1934

Moseley, E. A. 2: v E 1989 (2)

Murray, D. A. 19: v E 1980 (4); v A 1977 (3); *v A 1981 (2); v In 1978 (6); v P 1980 (4)*

Murray, D. L. 62: v E 1967 (5) 1973 (5); v A 1972 (4) 1977 (2); v In 1975 (4); v P 1976 (5); *v E 1963 (5) 1973 (3) 1976 (5) 1980 (5); v A 1975 (6) 1979 (3); v NZ 1979 (3); v In 1974 (5); v P 1974 (2)*

Murray, J. R. 24: v E 1993 (5); v A 1994 (3); v P 1992 (3); *v E 1995 (4); v A 1992 (3); v NZ 1994 (2); v In 1994 (3); v SL 1993 (1)*

Nanan, R. 1: *v P 1980*

Neblett, J. M. 1: v E 1934

Noreiga, J. M. 4: v In 1970 (4)

Nunes, R. K. 4: v E 1929 (1); *v E 1928 (3)*

Nurse, S. M. 29: v E 1959 (1) 1967 (5); v A 1964 (4); v In 1961 (1); *v E 1966 (5); v A 1960 (3) 1968 (5); v NZ 1968 (3); v In 1966 (2)*

Padmore, A. L. 2: v In 1975 (1); *v E 1976 (1)*

Pairaudeau, B. H. 13: v E 1953 (2); v In 1952 (5); *v E 1957 (2); v NZ 1955 (4)*

Parry, D. R. 12: v A 1977 (5); *v NZ 1979 (1); v In 1978 (6)*

Passailaigue, C. C. 1: v E 1929

Patterson, B. P. 28: v E 1985 (2) 1989 (1); v A 1990 (5); v SA 1991 (1); v P 1987 (1); *v E 1988 (2) 1991 (3); v A 1988 (4) 1992 (1); v In 1987 (4); v P 1986 (1)*

Payne, T. R. O. 1: v E 1985

Phillip, N. 9: v A 1977 (3); *v In 1978 (6)*

Pierre, L. R. 1: v E 1947

Rae, A. F. 15: v In 1952 (2); *v E 1950 (4); v A 1951 (3); v NZ 1951 (1); v In 1948 (5)*

Ramadhin, S. 43: v E 1953 (5) 1959 (4); v A 1954 (4); v In 1952 (4); *v E 1950 (4) 1957 (5); v A 1951 (5) 1960 (2); v NZ 1951 (2) 1955 (4); v In 1958 (2); v P 1958 (2)*

Richards, I. V. A. 121: v E 1980 (4) 1985 (5) 1989 (3); v A 1977 (2) 1983 (5) 1990 (5); v NZ 1984 (4); v In 1975 (4) 1982 (5) 1988 (4); v P 1976 (5) 1987 (2); *v E 1976 (4) 1980 (5) 1984 (5) 1988 (5) 1991 (5); v A 1975 (6) 1979 (3) 1981 (3) 1984 (3) 1988 (5); v NZ 1986 (3); v In 1974 (5) 1983 (6) 1987 (4); v P 1974 (2) 1980 (4) 1986 (3)*

Richardson, R. B. 86: v E 1985 (5) 1989 (4) 1993 (4); v A 1983 (5) 1990 (5) 1994 (4); v SA 1991 (1); v NZ 1984 (4); v In 1988 (4); v P 1987 (3) 1992 (3); *v E 1988 (3) 1991 (5) 1995 (6); v A 1984 (5) 1988 (5) 1992 (5); v NZ 1986 (3); v In 1983 (1) 1987 (4); v P 1986 (3) 1990 (3); v SL 1993 (1)*

Rickards, K. R. 2: v E 1947 (1); *v A 1951 (1)*

Roach, C. A. 16: v E 1929 (4) 1934 (1); *v E 1928 (3) 1933 (3); v A 1930 (5)*

Roberts, A. M. E. 47: v E 1973 (1) 1980 (3); v A 1977 (2); v In 1975 (2) 1982 (5); v P 1976 (5); *v E 1976 (5) 1980 (3); v A 1975 (3) 1979 (3) 1981 (2); v NZ 1979 (2); v In 1974 (5) 1983 (2); v P 1974 (2)*

Roberts, A. T. 1: *v NZ 1955*

Rodriguez, W. V. 5: v E 1967 (1); v A 1964 (1); v In 1961 (2); *v E 1963 (1)*

Rowe, L. G. 30: v E 1973 (5); v A 1972 (3); v NZ 1971 (4); v In 1975 (4); *v E 1976 (2); v A 1975 (6) 1979 (3); v NZ 1979 (3)*

St Hill, E. L. 2: v E 1929 (2)

St Hill, W. H. 3: v E 1929 (1); *v E 1928 (2)*

Scarlett, R. O. 3: v E 1959 (3)

Scott, A. P. H. 1: v In 1952

Scott, O. C. 8: v E 1929 (1); *v E 1928 (2); v A 1930 (5)*

Sealey, B. J. 1: *v E 1933*

Sealey, J. E. D. 11: v E 1929 (2) 1934 (4); *v E 1939 (3); v A 1930 (2)*

Shepherd, J. N. 5: v In 1970 (2); *v E 1969 (3)*

Shillingford, G. C. 7: v NZ 1971 (2); v In 1970 (3); *v E 1969 (2)*

Shillingford, I. T. 4: v A 1977 (1); *v P 1976 (3)*

Shivnarine, S. 8: v A 1977 (3); *v In 1978 (5)*

Simmons, P. V. 22:·v E 1993 (2); v SA 1991 (1); v P 1987 (1) 1992 (3); *v E 1991 (5); v A 1992 (5); v In 1987 (1) 1994 (3); v SL 1993 (1)*

Singh, C. K. 2: v E 1959 (2)

Small, J. A. 3: v E 1929 (1); *v E 1928 (2)*

Small, M. A. 2: v A 1983 (1); *v E 1984 (1)*

Smith, C. W. 5: v In 1961 (1); *v A 1960 (4)*

Smith, O. G. 26: v A 1954 (4); v P 1957 (5); *v E 1957 (5); v NZ 1955 (4); v In 1958 (5); v P 1958 (3)*

Sobers, G. S. 93: v E 1953 (1) 1959 (5) 1967 (5) 1973 (4); v A 1954 (4) 1964 (5); v NZ 1971 (5); v In 1961 (5) 1970 (5); v P 1957 (5); *v E 1957 (5) 1963 (5) 1966 (5) 1969 (3) 1973 (3); v A 1960 (5) 1968 (5); v NZ 1955 (4) 1968 (3); v In 1958 (5) 1966 (3); v P 1958 (3)*

Solomon, J. S. 27: v E 1959 (2); v A 1964 (4); v In 1961 (4); *v E 1963 (5); v A 1960 (5); v In 1958 (4); v P 1958 (3)*

Stayers, S. C. 4: v In 1961 (4)

Stollmeyer, J. B. 32: v E 1947 (2) 1953 (5); v A 1954 (2); v In 1952 (5); *v E 1939 (3) 1950 (4); v A 1951 (5); v NZ 1951 (2); v In 1948 (4)*

Stollmeyer, V. H. 1: *v E 1939*

Taylor, J. 3: v P 1957 (1); *v In 1958 (1); v P 1958 (1)*

Trim, J. 4: v E 1947 (1); *v A 1951 (1); v In 1948 (2)*

Valentine, A. L. 36: v E 1953 (3); v A 1954 (3); v In 1952 (5) 1961 (2); v P 1957 (1); *v E 1950 (4) 1957 (2); v A 1951 (5) 1960 (5); v NZ 1951 (2) 1955 (4)*

Valentine, V. A. 2: *v E 1933 (2)*

Walcott, C. L. 44: v E 1947 (4) 1953 (5) 1959 (2); v A 1954 (5); v In 1952 (5); v P 1957 (4); *v E 1950 (4) 1957 (5); v A 1951 (3); v NZ 1951 (2); v In 1948 (5)*

Walcott, L. A. 1: v E 1929

Walsh, C. A. 80: v E 1985 (1) 1989 (3) 1993 (5); v A 1990 (5) 1994 (4); v SA 1991 (1); v NZ 1984 (1); v In 1988 (4); v P 1987 (3) 1992 (3); *v E 1988 (5) 1991 (5) 1995 (6); v A 1984 (5) 1988 (5) 1992 (5); v NZ 1986 (3) 1994 (2); v In 1987 (4) 1994 (3); v P 1986 (3) 1990 (3); v SL 1993 (1)*

Watson, C. 7: v E 1959 (5); v In 1961 (1); *v A 1960 (1)*

Weekes, E. D. 48: v E 1947 (4) 1953 (4); v A 1954 (5) v In 1952 (5); v P 1957 (5); *v E 1950 (4) 1957 (5); v A 1951 (5); v NZ 1951 (2) 1955 (4); v In 1948 (5)*
Weekes, K. H. 2: *v E 1939 (2)*
White, W. A. 2: v A 1964 (2)
Wight, C. V. 2: v E 1929 (1); *v E 1928 (1)*
Wight, G. L. 1: v In 1952
Wiles, C. A. 1: *v E 1933*
Willett, E. T. 5: v A 1972 (3); *v In 1974 (2)*
Williams, A. B. 7: v A 1977 (3); *v In 1978 (4)*
Williams, D. 3: v SA 1991 (1); *v A 1992 (2)*
Williams, E. A. V. 4: v E 1947 (3); *v E 1939 (1)*
Williams, S. C. 12: v E 1993 (1); v A 1994 (4); *v E 1995 (2); v NZ 1994 (2); v In 1994 (3)*
Wishart, K. L. 1: v E 1934
Worrell, F. M. M. 51: v E 1947 (3) 1953 (4) 1959 (4); v A 1954 (4); v In 1952 (5) 1961 (5); *v E 1950 (4) 1957 (5) 1963 (5); v A 1951 (5) 1960 (5); v NZ 1951 (2)*

NEW ZEALAND

Number of Test cricketers: 192

Alabaster, J. C. 21: v E 1962 (2); v WI 1955 (1); v In 1967 (4); *v E 1958 (2); v SA 1961 (5); v WI 1971 (2); v In 1955 (4); v P 1957 (1)*
Allcott, C. F. W. 6: v E 1929 (2); v SA 1931 (1); *v E 1931 (3)*
Anderson, R. W. 9: v E 1977 (3); *v E 1978 (3); v P 1976 (3)*
Anderson, W. M. 1: v A 1945
Andrews, B. 2: *v A 1973 (2)*

Badcock, F. T. 7: v E 1929 (3) 1932 (2); v SA 1931 (2)
Barber, R. T. 1: v WI 1955
Bartlett, G. A. 10: v E 1965 (2); v In 1967 (2); v P 1964 (1); *v SA 1961 (5)*
Barton, P. T. 7: v E 1962 (3); *v SA 1961 (4)*
Beard, D. D. 4: v WI 1951 (2) 1955 (2)
Beck, J. E. F. 8: v WI 1955 (4); *v SA 1953 (4)*
Bell, W. 2: *v SA 1953 (2)*
Bilby, G. P. 2: v E 1965 (2)
Blain, T. E. 11: v A 1992 (2); v P 1993 (3); *v E 1986 (1); v A 1993 (3); v In 1988 (2)*
Blair, R. W. 19: v E 1954 (1) 1958 (2) 1962 (2); v SA 1952 (2) 1963 (3); v WI 1955 (2); *v E 1958 (3); v SA 1953 (4)*
Blunt, R. C. 9: v E 1929 (4); v SA 1931 (2); *v E 1931 (3)*
Bolton, B. A. 2: v E 1958 (2)
Boock, S. L. 30: v E 1977 (3) 1983 (2) 1987 (1); v WI 1979 (3) 1986 (2); v P 1978 (3) 1984 (2) 1988 (1); *v E 1978 (3); v A 1985 (1); v WI 1984 (3); v P 1984 (3); v SL 1983 (3)*
Bracewell, B. P. 6: v P 1978 (1) 1984 (1); *v E 1978 (3); v A 1980 (1)*
Bracewell, J. G. 41: v E 1987 (3); v A 1985 (2) 1989 (1); v WI 1986 (1); v In 1980 (1) 1989 (2); v P 1988 (2); *v E 1983 (4) 1986 (3) 1990 (3); v A 1980 (3) 1985 (2) 1987 (3); v WI 1984 (1); v In 1988 (3); v P 1984 (2) 1986 (1)*
Bradburn, G. E. 5: v SL 1990 (1); *v P 1990 (3); v SL 1992 (1)*
Bradburn, W. P. 2: v SA 1963 (2)
Brown, V. R. 2: *v A 1985 (2)*
Burgess, M. G. 50: v E 1970 (1) 1977 (3); v A 1973 (1) 1976 (2); v WI 1968 (2); v In 1967 (4) 1975 (3); v P 1972 (3) 1978 (3); *v E 1969 (2) 1973 (3) 1978 (3); v A 1980 (3); v WI 1971 (5); v In 1969 (3) 1976 (3); v P 1969 (3) 1976 (3)*
Burke, C. 1: v A 1945
Burtt, T. B. 10: v E 1946 (1) 1950 (2); v SA 1952 (1); v WI 1951 (2); *v E 1949 (4)*
Butterfield, L. A. 1: v A 1945

Cairns, B. L. 43: v E 1974 (1) 1977 (1) 1983 (3); v A 1976 (1) 1981 (3); v WI 1979 (3); v In 1975 (1) 1980 (3); v P 1978 (3) 1984 (3); v SL 1982 (2); *v E 1978 (2) 1983 (4); v A 1973 (1) 1980 (3) 1985 (1); v WI 1984 (2); v In 1976 (2); v P 1976 (2); v SL 1983 (2)*
Cairns, C. L. 10: v E 1991 (3); v A 1992 (2); v P 1993 (1); v SL 1990 (1); *v A 1989 (1) 1993 (2)*

Cameron, F. J. 19: v E 1962 (3); v SA 1963 (3); v P 1964 (3); *v E 1965 (2); v SA 1961 (5); v In 1964 (1); v P 1964 (2)*

Cave, H. B. 19: v E 1954 (2); v WI 1955 (3); *v E 1949 (4) 1958 (2); v In 1955 (5); v P 1955 (3)*

Chapple, M. E. 14: v E 1954 (1) 1965 (1); v SA 1952 (1) 1963 (3); v WI 1955 (1); *v SA 1953 (5) 1961 (2)*

Chatfield, E. J. 43: v E 1974 (1) 1977 (1) 1983 (3) 1987 (3); v A 1976 (2) 1981 (1) 1985 (3); v WI 1986 (3); v P 1984 (3) 1988 (2); v SL 1982 (2); *v E 1983 (3) 1986 (1); v A 1985 (2) 1987 (2); v WI 1984 (4); v In 1988 (3); v P 1984 (1); v SL 1983 (2) 1986 (1)*

Cleverley, D. C. 2: v SA 1931 (1); v A 1945 (1)

Collinge, R. O. 35: v E 1970 (2) 1974 (2) 1977 (3); v A 1973 (3); v In 1967 (2) 1975 (3); v P 1964 (3) 1972 (2); *v E 1965 (3) 1969 (1) 1973 (3) 1978 (1); v In 1964 (2) 1976 (1); v P 1964 (2) 1976 (2)*

Colquhoun, I. A. 2: v E 1954 (2)

Coney, J. V. 52: v E 1983 (3); v A 1973 (3) 1981 (3) 1985 (3); v WI 1979 (3) 1986 (3); v In 1980 (3); v P 1978 (3) 1984 (3); v SL 1982 (2); *v E 1983 (4) 1986 (3); v A 1973 (2) 1980 (2) 1985 (3); v WI 1984 (4); v P 1984 (3); v SL 1983 (3)*

Congdon, B. E. 61: v E 1965 (3) 1970 (2) 1974 (2) 1977 (3); v A 1973 (3) 1976 (2); v WI 1968 (3); v In 1967 (2) 1975 (3); v P 1964 (3) 1972 (3); *v E 1965 (3) 1969 (3) 1973 (3) 1978 (3); v A 1973 (3); v WI 1971 (5); v In 1964 (3) 1969 (3); v P 1964 (1) 1969 (3)*

Cowie, J. 9: v E 1946 (1); v A 1945 (1); *v E 1937 (3) 1949 (4)*

Cresswell, G. F. 3: v E 1950 (2); *v E 1949 (1)*

Cromb, I. B. 5: v SA 1931 (3); *v E 1931 (2)*

Crowe, J. J. 39: v E 1983 (3) 1987 (3); v A 1989 (1); v WI 1986 (3); v P 1984 (3) 1988 (2); v SL 1982 (2); *v E 1983 (2) 1986 (3); v A 1985 (3) 1987 (3) 1989 (1); v WI 1984 (4); v P 1984 (3); v SL 1983 (3) 1986 (1)*

Crowe, M. D. 74: v E 1983 (3) 1987 (3) 1991 (3); v A 1981 (3) 1985 (3) 1992 (3); v SA 1994 (1); v WI 1986 (3); v In 1989 (3); v P 1984 (3) 1988 (2); v SL 1990 (2); *v E 1983 (4) 1986 (3) 1990 (3) 1994 (3); v A 1985 (3) 1987 (3) 1989 (1) 1993 (1); v WI 1984 (4); v P 1984 (3) 1990 (3); v SL 1983 (3) 1986 (1) 1992 (2)*

Cunis, R. S. 20: v E 1965 (3) 1970 (2); v SA 1963 (1); v WI 1968 (3); *v E 1969 (1); v WI 1971 (5); v In 1969 (3); v P 1969 (2)*

D'Arcy, J. W. 5: *v E 1958 (5)*

Davis, H. T. 1: *v E 1994*

de Groen, R. P. 5: v P 1993 (2); *v A 1993 (2); v SA 1994 (1)*

Dempster, C. S. 10: v E 1929 (4) 1932 (2); v SA 1931 (2); *v E 1931 (2)*

Dempster, E. W. 5: v SA 1952 (1); *v SA 1953 (4)*

Dick, A. E. 17: v E 1962 (3); v SA 1963 (2); v P 1964 (2); *v E 1965 (3); v SA 1961 (5); v P 1964 (3)*

Dickinson, G. R. 3: v E 1929 (2); v SA 1931 (1)

Donnelly, M. P. 7: *v E 1937 (3) 1949 (4)*

Doull, S. B. 11: v WI 1994 (2); v P 1993 (3); *v A 1993 (2); v SA 1994 (3); v Z 1992 (1)*

Dowling, G. T. 39: v E 1962 (3) 1970 (2); v SA 1963 (1); v WI 1968 (3); v In 1967 (4); v P 1964 (2); *v E 1965 (3) 1969 (3); v SA 1961 (4); v WI 1971 (2); v In 1964 (4) 1969 (3); v P 1964 (2) 1969 (3)*

Dunning, J. A. 4: v E 1932 (1); *v E 1937 (3)*

Edgar, B. A. 39: v E 1983 (3); v A 1981 (3) 1985 (3); v WI 1979 (3); v In 1980 (3); v P 1978 (3); v SL 1982 (2); *v E 1978 (3) 1983 (4) 1986 (3); v A 1980 (3) 1985 (3); v P 1984 (3)*

Edwards, G. N. 8: v E 1977 (1); v A 1976 (2); v In 1980 (1); *v E 1978 (2)*

Emery, R. W. G. 2: v WI 1951 (2)

Fisher, F. E. 1: v SA 1952

Fleming, S. P. 12: v SA 1994 (1); v WI 1994 (2); v In 1993 (1); v SL 1994 (2); *v E 1994 (3); SA 1994 (3)*

Foley, H. 1: v E 1929

Franklin, T. J. 21: v E 1987 (3); v A 1985 (1) 1989 (1); v In 1989 (3); v SL 1990 (3); *v E 1983 (1) 1990 (3); v In 1988 (3); v P 1990 (3)*

Freeman, D. L. 2: v E 1932 (2)

Gallichan, N. 1: *v E 1937*

Gedye, S. G. 4: v SA 1963 (3); v P 1964 (1)

Gillespie, S. R. 1: *v A 1985*

Gray, E. J. 10: v E 1983 (2) 1986 (3); v A 1987 (1); v In 1988 (1); v P 1984 (2); v SL 1986 (1)
Greatbatch, M. J. 36: v E 1987 (2) 1991 (1); v A 1989 (1) 1992 (3); v In 1989 (3) 1993 (1); v P 1988 (1) 1992 (1) 1993 (3); v SL 1990 (2) 1994 (2); v E 1990 (3) 1994 (1); v A 1989 (1) 1993 (3); v In 1988 (3); v P 1990 (3); v Z 1992 (2)
Guillen, S. C. 3: v WI 1955 (3)
Guy, J. W. 12: v E 1958 (2); v WI 1955 (2); v SA 1961 (2); v In 1955 (5); v P 1955 (1)

Hadlee, D. R. 26: v E 1974 (2) 1977 (1); v A 1973 (3) 1976 (1); v In 1975 (3); v P 1972 (2); v E 1969 (2) 1973 (3); v A 1973 (3); v In 1969 (3); v P 1969 (3)
Hadlee, R. J. 86: v E 1977 (3) 1983 (3) 1987 (1); v A 1973 (2) 1976 (2) 1981 (3) 1985 (3) 1989 (1); v WI 1979 (3) 1986 (3); v In 1975 (2) 1980 (3) 1989 (3); v P 1972 (1) 1978 (3) 1984 (3) 1988 (2); v SL 1982 (2); v E 1973 (1) 1978 (3) 1983 (4) 1986 (3) 1990 (3); v A 1973 (3) 1980 (3) 1985 (3) 1987 (3); v In 1976 (3) 1988 (3); v P 1976 (3); v SL 1983 (3) 1986 (1)
Hadlee, W. A. 11: v E 1946 (1) 1950 (2); v A 1945 (1); v E 1937 (3) 1949 (4)
Harford, N. S. 8: v E 1958 (4); v In 1955 (2); v P 1955 (2)
Harford, R. I. 3: v In 1967 (3)
Harris, C. Z. 5: v A 1992 (1); v P 1992 (1); v A 1993 (1); v SL 1992 (2)
Harris, P. G. Z. 9: v P 1964 (1); v SA 1961 (5); v In 1955 (1); v P 1955 (2)
Harris, R. M. 2: v E 1958 (2)
Hart, M. N. 12: v SA 1994 (1); v WI 1994 (2); v In 1993 (1); v P 1993 (2); v E 1994 (3); v SA 1994 (3)
Hartland, B. R. 9: v E 1991 (3); v In 1993 (1); v P 1992 (1) 1993 (1); v E 1994 (1); v SL 1992 (2)
Haslam, M. J. 2: v Z 1992 (2)
Hastings, B. F. 31: v E 1974 (2); v A 1973 (3); v WI 1968 (3); v In 1975 (1); v P 1972 (3); v E 1969 (3) 1973 (3); v A 1973 (3); v WI 1971 (5); v In 1969 (2); v P 1969 (3)
Hayes, J. A. 15: v E 1950 (2) 1954 (1); v WI 1951 (2); v E 1958 (4); v In 1955 (5); v P 1955 (1)
Henderson, M. 1: v E 1929
Horne, P. A. 4: v WI 1986 (1); v A 1987 (1); v P 1990 (1); v SL 1986 (1)
Hough, K. W. 2: v E 1958 (2)
Howarth, G. P. 47: v E 1974 (2) 1977 (3) 1983 (3); v A 1976 (2) 1981 (3); v WI 1979 (3); v In 1980 (3); v P 1978 (3) 1983 (3); v SL 1982 (2); v E 1978 (3) 1983 (4); v A 1980 (2); v WI 1984 (4); v In 1976 (2); v P 1976 (2); v SL 1983 (3)
Howarth, H. J. 30: v E 1970 (2) 1974 (2); v A 1973 (3) 1976 (2); v In 1975 (2); v P 1972 (3); v E 1969 (3) 1973 (2); v WI 1971 (5); v In 1969 (3); v P 1969 (3)

James, K. C. 11: v E 1929 (4) 1932 (2); v SA 1931 (2); v E 1931 (3)
Jarvis, T. W. 13: v E 1965 (1); v P 1972 (3); v WI 1971 (4); v In 1964 (2); v P 1964 (3)
Jones, A. H. 39: v E 1987 (1) 1991 (3); v A 1989 (1) 1992 (3); v WI 1994 (2); v In 1989 (3); v P 1988 (2) 1992 (1) 1993 (3); v SL 1990 (3); v E 1990 (3); v A 1987 (3) 1993 (3); v In 1988 (3); v SL 1986 (1) 1992 (2); v Z 1992 (2)

Kerr, J. L. 7: v E 1932 (2); v SA 1931 (1); v E 1931 (2) 1937 (2)
Kuggeleijn, C. M. 2: v In 1988 (2)

Larsen, G. R. 4: v SA 1994 (1); v SL 1994 (2); v E 1994 (1)
Latham, R. T. 4: v E 1991 (1); v P 1992 (1); v Z 1992 (2)
Lees, W. K. 21: v E 1977 (2); v A 1976 (1); v WI 1979 (3); v P 1978 (3); v SL 1982 (2); v E 1983 (2); v A 1980 (2); v In 1976 (3); v P 1976 (3)
Leggat, I. B. 1: v SA 1953
Leggat, J. G. 9: v E 1954 (1); v SA 1952 (1); v WI 1951 (1) 1955 (1); v In 1955 (3); v P 1955 (2)
Lissette, A. F. 2: v WI 1955 (2)
Lowry, T. C. 7: v E 1929 (4); v E 1931 (3)

MacGibbon, A. R. 26: v E 1950 (2) 1954 (2); v SA 1952 (1); v WI 1955 (3); v E 1958 (5); v SA 1953 (5); v In 1955 (5); v P 1955 (3)
McEwan, P. E. 4: v WI 1979 (1); v A 1980 (2); v P 1984 (1)
McGirr, H. M. 2: v E 1929 (2)
McGregor, S. N. 25: v E 1954 (2) 1958 (2); v SA 1963 (3); v WI 1955 (4); v P 1964 (2); v SA 1961 (5); v In 1955 (4); v P 1955 (3)
McLeod, E. G. 1: v E 1929
McMahon, T. G. 5: v WI 1955 (1); v In 1955 (3); v P 1955 (1)
McRae, D. A. N. 1: v A 1945
Matheson, A. M. 2: v E 1929 (1); v E 1931 (1)

Meale, T. 2: v E 1958 (2)
Merritt, W. E. 6: v E 1929 (4); v E 1931 (2)
Meuli, E. M. 1: v SA 1952
Milburn, B. D. 3: v WI 1968 (3)
Miller, L. S. M. 13: v SA 1952 (2); v WI 1955 (3); v E 1958 (4); v SA 1953 (4)
Mills, J. E. 7: v E 1929 (2) 1932 (1); v E 1931 (3)
Moir, A. M. 17: v E 1950 (2) 1954 (2) 1958 (2); v SA 1952 (1); v WI 1951 (2) 1955 (1); v E 1958
     (2); v In 1955 (2); v P 1955 (3)
Moloney, D. A. R. 3: v E 1937 (3)
Mooney, F. L. H. 14: v E 1950 (2); v SA 1952 (2); v WI 1951 (2); v E 1949 (3); v SA 1953 (5)
Morgan, R. W. 20: v E 1965 (2) 1970 (2); v WI 1968 (1); v P 1964 (2); v E 1965 (3); v WI 1971 (3);
     v In 1964 (4); v P 1964 (3)
Morrison, B. D. 1: v E 1962
Morrison, D. K. 41: v E 1987 (3) 1991 (3); v A 1989 (1) 1992 (3); v SA 1994 (1); v WI 1994 (2);
     v In 1989 (3) 1993 (1); v P 1988 (1) 1992 (1) 1993 (2); v SL 1990 (3) 1994 (1); v E 1990 (3);
     v A 1987 (3) 1989 (1) 1993 (3); v SA 1994 (2); v In 1988 (1); v P 1990 (3)
Morrison, J. F. M. 17: v E 1974 (2); v A 1973 (3) 1981 (3); v In 1975 (3); v A 1973 (3); v In 1976
     (1); v P 1976 (2)
Motz, R. C. 32: v E 1962 (2) 1965 (3); v SA 1963 (2); v WI 1968 (3); v In 1967 (4); v P 1964 (3);
     v E 1965 (3) 1969 (3); v SA 1961 (5); v In 1964 (3); v P 1964 (1)
Murray, B. A. G. 13: v E 1970 (1); v In 1967 (4); v E 1969 (2); v In 1969 (3); v P 1969 (3)
Murray, D. J. 8: v SA 1994 (1); v WI 1994 (2); v SL 1994 (2); v SA 1994 (3)

Nash, D. J. 10: v SA 1994 (1); v WI 1994 (1); v In 1993 (1); v SL 1994 (1); v E 1994 (3); v SA 1994
     (1); v SL 1992 (1); v Z 1992 (1)
Newman J. 3: v E 1932 (2); v SA 1931 (1)

O'Sullivan, D. R. 11: v In 1975 (1); v P 1972 (1); v A 1973 (3); v In 1976 (3); v P 1976 (3)
Overton, G. W. F. 3: v SA 1953 (3)
Owens, M. B. 8: v A 1992 (2); v P 1992 (1) 1993 (1); v E 1994 (2); v SL 1992 (2)

Page, M. L. 14: v E 1929 (4) 1932 (2); v SA 1931 (2); v E 1931 (3) 1937 (3)
Parker, J. M. 36: v E 1974 (2) 1977 (3); v A 1973 (3) 1976 (2); v WI 1979 (3); v In 1975 (3); v P
     1972 (1) 1978 (2); v E 1973 (3) 1978 (2); v A 1973 (3) 1980 (3); v In 1976 (3); v P 1976 (3)
Parker, N. M. 3: v In 1976 (2); v P 1976 (1)
Parore, A. C. 20: v E 1991 (1); v A 1992 (1); v SA 1994 (1); v WI 1994 (2); v In 1993 (1); v P 1992
     (1); v SL 1994 (2); v E 1990 (1) 1994 (3); v SA 1994 (3); v SL 1992 (2); v Z 1992 (2)
Patel, D. N. 27: v E 1991 (3); v A 1992 (3); v SA 1994 (1); v WI 1986 (3); v P 1988 (1) 1992 (1);
     v SL 1990 (2) 1994 (1); v A 1987 (3) 1989 (1) 1993 (3); v P 1990 (3); v Z 1992 (2)
Petherick, P. J. 6: v A 1976 (1); v In 1976 (3); v P 1976 (2)
Petrie, E. C. 14: v E 1958 (2) 1965 (3); v E 1958 (5); v In 1955 (2); v P 1955 (2)
Playle, W. R. 8: v E 1962 (3); v E 1958 (5)
Pocock, B. A. 6: v P 1993 (2); v E 1994 (1); v A 1993 (3)
Pollard, V. 32: v E 1965 (3) 1970 (1); v WI 1968 (3); v In 1967 (4); v P 1972 (1); v E 1965 (3) 1969
     (3) 1973 (3); v In 1964 (4) 1969 (1); v P 1964 (3) 1969 (3)
Poore, M. B. 14: v E 1954 (1); v SA 1952 (1); v SA 1953 (5); v In 1955 (4); v P 1955 (3)
Priest, M. W. 1: v E 1990
Pringle, C. 14: v E 1991 (1); v In 1993 (1); v P 1993 (1); v SL 1990 (2) 1994 (1); v E 1994 (2); v SA
     1994 (2); v P 1990 (3); v SL 1992 (1)
Puna, N. 3: v E 1965 (3)

Rabone, G. O. 12: v E 1954 (2); v SA 1952 (1); v WI 1951 (2); v E 1949 (4); v SA 1953 (3)
Redmond, R. E. 1: v P 1972
Reid, J. F. 19: v A 1985 (3); v In 1980 (3); v P 1978 (1) 1984 (3); v A 1985 (3); v P 1984 (3); v SL
     1983 (3)
Reid, J. R. 58: v E 1950 (2) 1954 (2) 1958 (2) 1962 (3); v SA 1952 (2) 1963 (3); v WI 1951 (2) 1955
     (4); v P 1964 (3); v E 1949 (2) 1958 (5) 1965 (3); v SA 1953 (5) 1961 (5); v In 1955 (5) 1964 (4);
     v P 1955 (3) 1964 (3)
Roberts, A. D. G. 7: v In 1976 (3); v P 1976 (2)
Roberts, A. W. 5: v E 1929 (1); v SA 1931 (2); v E 1937 (2)
Robertson, G. K. 1: v A 1985
Rowe, C. G. 1: v A 1945

Rutherford, K. R. 56: v E 1987 (2) 1991 (2); v A 1985 (3) 1989 (1) 1992 (3); v SA 1994 (1); v WI 1986 (2) 1994 (2); v In 1989 (3) 1993 (1); v P 1992 (1) 1993 (3); v SL 1990 (3) 1994 (2); *v E 1986 (1) 1990 (2) 1994 (3); v A 1987 (1) 1993 (3); v SA 1994 (3); v WI 1984 (4); v In 1988 (2); v P 1990 (3); v SL 1986 (1) 1992 (2) v Z 1992 (2)*

Scott, R. H. 1: v E 1946
Scott, V. J. 10: v E 1946 (1) 1950 (2); v A 1945 (1); v WI 1951 (2); *v E 1949 (4)*
Shrimpton, M. J. F. 10: v E 1962 (2) 1965 (3) 1970 (2); v SA 1963 (1); *v A 1973 (2)*
Sinclair, B. W. 21: v E 1962 (3) 1965 (3); v SA 1963 (3); v In 1967 (2); v P 1964 (2); *v E 1965 (3); v In 1964 (2) v P 1964 (3)*
Sinclair, I. M. 2: v WI 1955 (2)
Smith, F. B. 4: v E 1946 (1); v WI 1951 (1); *v E 1949 (2)*
Smith, H. D. 1: v E 1932
Smith, I. D. S. 63: v E 1983 (3) 1987 (3) 1991 (2); v A 1981 (3) 1985 (3) 1989 (1); v WI 1986 (3); v In 1980 (3) 1989 (3); v P 1984 (3) 1988 (2); v SL 1990 (3); *v E 1983 (2) 1986 (2) 1990 (2); v A 1980 (1) 1985 (3) 1987 (3) 1989 (1); v WI 1984 (4); v In 1988 (3); v P 1984 (3) 1990 (3); v SL 1983 (3) 1986 (1)*
Snedden, C. A. 1: v E 1946
Snedden, M. C. 25: v E 1983 (1) 1987 (2); v A 1981 (3) 1989 (1); v WI 1986 (1); v In 1980 (3) 1989 (3); v SL 1982 (1); *v E 1983 (1) 1990 (3); v A 1985 (1) 1987 (1) 1989 (1); v In 1988 (1); v SL 1986 (1)*
Sparling, J. T. 11: v E 1958 (2) 1962 (1); v SA 1963 (2); *v E 1958 (3); v SA 1961 (3)*
Stirling, D. A. 6: *v E 1986 (2); v WI 1984 (1); v P 1984 (3)*
Su'a, M. L. 13: v E 1991 (2); v A 1992 (2); v WI 1994 (1); v P 1992 (1); v SL 1994 (1); *v A 1993 (2); v SL 1992 (2); v Z 1992 (2)*
Sutcliffe, B. 42: v E 1946 (1) 1950 (2) 1954 (2) 1958 (2); v SA 1952 (2); v WI 1951 (2) 1955 (2); *v E 1949 (4) 1958 (4) 1965 (1); v SA 1953 (5); v In 1955 (5) 1964 (4); v P 1955 (3) 1964 (3)*

Taylor, B. R. 30: v E 1965 (1); v WI 1968 (3); v In 1967 (3); v P 1972 (3); *v E 1965 (2) 1969 (2) 1973 (3); v WI 1971 (4); v In 1964 (3) 1969 (2); v P 1964 (3) 1969 (1)*
Taylor, D. D. 3: v E 1946 (1); v WI 1955 (2)
Thomson, K. 2: v In 1967 (2)
Thomson, S. A. 17: v E 1991 (1); v WI 1994 (2); v In 1989 (1) 1993 (1); v SL 1990 (3) 1994 (1); *v E 1994 (3); v SA 1994 (3)*
Tindill, E. W. T. 5: v E 1946 (1); v A 1945 (1); *v E 1937 (3)*
Troup, G. B. 15: v A 1981 (2) 1985 (2); v WI 1979 (3); v In 1980 (2); v P 1978 (2); *v A 1980 (2); v WI 1984 (1); v In 1976 (1)*
Truscott, P. B. 1: v P 1964
Turner, G. M. 41: v E 1970 (2) 1974 (2); v A 1973 (3) 1976 (2); v WI 1968 (3); v In 1975 (3); v P 1972 (3); v SL 1982 (2); *v E 1969 (2) 1973 (3); v A 1973 (2); v WI 1971 (5); v In 1969 (3) 1976 (3); v P 1969 (1) 1976 (2)*

Vance, R. H. 4: v E 1987 (1); v P 1988 (2); *v A 1989 (1)*
Vaughan, J. T. C. 1: *v SL 1992*
Vivian, G. E. 5: *v WI 1971 (4); v In 1964 (1)*
Vivian, H. G. 7: v E 1932 (1); v SA 1931 (1); *v E 1931 (2) 1937 (3)*

Wadsworth, K. J. 33: v E 1970 (2) 1974 (2); v A 1973 (3); v In 1975 (3); v P 1972 (3); *v E 1969 (3) 1973 (3); v A 1973 (3); v WI 1971 (5); v In 1969 (3); v P 1969 (3)*
Wallace, W. M. 13: v E 1946 (1) 1950 (2); v A 1945 (1); v SA 1952 (2); *v E 1937 (3) 1949 (4)*
Walmsley, K. P. 2: v SL 1994 (2)
Ward, J. T. 8: v SA 1963 (1); v In 1967 (1); v P 1964 (1); *v E 1965 (1); v In 1964 (4)*
Watson, W. 15: v E 1991 (1); v A 1992 (2); v SL 1990 (3); *v E 1986 (2); v A 1989 (1) 1993 (1); v P 1990 (3); v Z 1992 (2)*
Watt, L. 1: v E 1954
Webb, M. G. 3: v E 1970 (1); v A 1973 (1); *v WI 1971 (1)*
Webb, P. N. 2: v WI 1979 (2)
Weir, G. L. 11: v E 1929 (3) 1932 (2); v SA 1931 (2); *v E 1931 (3) 1937 (1)*
White, D. J. 2: *v P 1990 (2)*
Whitelaw, P. E. 2: v E 1932 (2)

Wright, J. G. 82: v E 1977 (3) 1983 (3) 1987 (3) 1991 (3); v A 1981 (3) 1985 (2) 1989 (1) 1992 (3);
v WI 1979 (3) 1986 (3); v In 1980 (3) 1989 (3); v P 1978 (3) 1984 (3) 1988 (2); v SL 1982 (2)
1990 (3); *v E 1978 (2) 1983 (3) 1986 (3) 1990 (3); v A 1980 (3) 1985 (3) 1987 (3) 1989 (1); v WI
1984 (4); v In 1988 (3); v P 1984 (3); v SL 1983 (3) 1992 (2)*

Young, B. A. 16: v SA 1994 (1); v WI 1994 (2); v In 1993 (1); v P 1993 (3); v SL 1994 (2); *v E 1994
(3); v A 1993 (1); v SA 1994 (3)*
Yuile, B. W. 17: v E 1962 (2); v WI 1968 (3); v In 1967 (1); v P 1964 (3); *v E 1965 (1); v In 1964 (3)
1969 (1); v P 1964 (1) 1969 (2)*

INDIA

Number of Test cricketers: 201

Abid Ali, S. 29: v E 1972 (4); v A 1969 (1); v WI 1974 (2); v NZ 1969 (3); *v E 1971 (3) 1974 (3);
v A 1967 (4); v WI 1970 (5); v NZ 1967 (4)*
Adhikari, H. R. 21: v E 1951 (3); v A 1956 (2); v WI 1948 (5) 1958 (1); v P 1952 (2); *v E 1952 (3);
v A 1947 (5)*
Amarnath, L. 24: v E 1933 (3) 1951 (3); v WI 1948 (5); v P 1952 (5); *v E 1946 (3); v A 1947 (5)*
Amarnath, M. 69: v E 1976 (2) 1984 (5); v A 1969 (1) 1979 (1) 1986 (3); v WI 1978 (2) 1983 (3)
1987 (3); v NZ 1976 (3); v P 1983 (2) 1986 (5); v SL 1986 (2); *v E 1979 (2) 1986 (2); v A 1977 (5)
1985 (3); v WI 1975 (4) 1982 (5); v NZ 1975 (3); v P 1978 (3) 1982 (6) 1984 (2); v SL 1985 (2)*
Amarnath, S. 10: v E 1976 (2); *v WI 1975 (2); v NZ 1975 (3); v P 1978 (3)*
Amar Singh 7: v E 1933 (3); *v E 1932 (1) 1936 (3)*
Amir Elahi 1: *v A 1947*
Amre, P. K. 11: v E 1992 (3); v Z 1992 (1); *v SA 1992 (4); v SL 1993 (3)*
Ankola, S. A. 1: *v P 1989*
Apte, A. L. 1: *v E 1959*
Apte, M. L. 7: v P 1952 (2); *v WI 1952 (5)*
Arshad Ayub 13: v WI 1987 (4); v NZ 1988 (3); *v WI 1988 (4); v P 1989 (2)*
Arun, B. 2: v SL 1986 (2)
Arun Lal 16: v WI 1987 (4); v NZ 1988 (3); v P 1986 (1); v SL 1982 (1); *v WI 1988 (4); v P
1982 (3)*
Azad, K. 7: v E 1981 (3); v WI 1983 (2); v P 1983 (1); *v NZ 1980 (1)*
Azharuddin, M. 65: v E 1984 (3) 1992 (3); v A 1986 (3); v WI 1987 (3) 1994 (3); v NZ 1988 (3);
v P 1986 (5); v SL 1986 (1) 1990 (1) 1993 (3); v Z 1992 (1); *v E 1986 (3) 1990 (3); v A 1985 (3)
1991 (5); v SA 1992 (4); v WI 1988 (3); v NZ 1989 (3) 1993 (1); v P 1989 (4); v SL 1985 (3)
1993 (3); v Z 1992 (1)*

Baig, A. A. 10: v A 1959 (3); v WI 1966 (2); v P 1960 (3); *v E 1959 (2)*
Banerjee, S. A. 1: v WI 1948
Banerjee, S. N. 1: v WI 1948
Banerjee, S. T. 1: *v A 1991*
Baqa Jilani, M. 1: *v E 1936*
Bedi, B. S. 67: v E 1972 (5) 1976 (5); v A 1969 (5); v WI 1966 (2) 1974 (4) 1978 (3); v NZ 1969 (3)
1976 (3); *v E 1967 (3) 1971 (3) 1974 (3) 1979 (3); v A 1967 (2) 1977 (5); v WI 1970 (5) 1975 (4);
v NZ 1967 (4) 1975 (2); v P 1978 (3)*
Bhandari, P. 3: v A 1956 (1); v NZ 1955 (1); *v P 1954 (1)*
Bhat, A. R. 2: v WI 1983 (1); v P 1983 (1)
Binny, R. M. H. 27: v E 1979 (1); v WI 1983 (6); v P 1979 (6) 1983 (2) 1986 (3); *v E 1986 (3); v A
1980 (1) 1985 (2); v NZ 1980 (1); v P 1984 (1); v SL 1985 (1)*
Borde, C. G. 55: v E 1961 (5) 1963 (5); v A 1959 (3) 1964 (3) 1969 (1); v WI 1958 (4) 1966 (3);
v NZ 1964 (4); v P 1960 (5); *v E 1959 (4) 1967 (3); v A 1967 (4); v WI 1961 (5); v NZ 1967 (4)*

Chandrasekhar, B. S. 58: v E 1963 (4) 1972 (5) 1976 (5); v A 1964 (2); v WI 1966 (3) 1974 (4) 1978
(4); v NZ 1964 (2) 1976 (3); *v E 1967 (3) 1971 (3) 1974 (2) 1979 (1); v A 1967 (2) 1977 (5); v WI
1975 (4); v NZ 1975 (3); v P 1978 (3)*
Chauhan, C. P. S. 40: v E 1972 (2); v A 1969 (1) 1979 (6); v WI 1978 (6); v NZ 1969 (2); v P 1979
(6); *v E 1979 (4); v A 1977 (4) 1980 (3); v NZ 1980 (3); v P 1978 (3)*
Chauhan, R. K. 13: v E 1992 (3); v WI 1994 (2); v SL 1993 (3); v Z 1992 (1); *v NZ 1993 (1); v SL
1993 (3)*

Chowdhury, N. R. 2: v E 1951 (1); v WI 1948 (1)

Colah, S. H. M. 2: v E 1933 (1); *v E 1932 (1)*

Contractor, N. J. 31: v E 1961 (5); v A 1956 (1) 1959 (5); v WI 1958 (5); v NZ 1955 (4); v P 1960 (5); *v E 1959 (4); v WI 1961 (2)*

Dani, H. T. 1: v P 1952

Desai, R. B. 28: v E 1961 (4) 1963 (2); v A 1959 (3); v WI 1958 (1); v NZ 1964 (3); v P 1960 (5); *v E 1959 (5); v A 1967 (1); v WI 1961 (3); v NZ 1967 (1)*

Dilawar Hussain 3: v E 1933 (2); *v E 1936 (1)*

Divecha, R. V. 5: v E 1951 (2); v P 1952 (1); *v E 1952 (2)*

Doshi, D. R. 33: v E 1979 (1) 1981 (6); v A 1979 (6); v P 1979 (6) 1983 (1); v SL 1982 (1); *v E 1982 (3); v A 1980 (3); v NZ 1980 (2); v P 1982 (4)*

Durani, S. A. 29: v E 1961 (5) 1963 (5) 1972 (3); v A 1959 (1) 1964 (3); v WI 1966 (1); v NZ 1964 (3); *v WI 1961 (5) 1970 (3)*

Engineer, F. M. 46: v E 1961 (4) 1972 (5); v A 1969 (5); v WI 1966 (1) 1974 (5); v NZ 1964 (4) 1969 (2); *v E 1967 (3) 1971 (3) 1974 (3); v A 1967 (4); v WI 1961 (3); v NZ 1967 (4)*

Gadkari, C. V. 6: *v WI 1952 (3); v P 1954 (3)*

Gaekwad, A. D. 40: v E 1976 (4) 1984 (3); v WI 1974 (3) 1978 (5) 1983 (6); v NZ 1976 (3); v P 1983 (3); *v A 1977 (1); v WI 1975 (3) 1982 (5); v P 1984 (2)*

Gaekwad, D. K. 11: v WI 1958 (1); v P 1952 (2) 1960 (1); *v E 1952 (1) 1959 (1); v WI 1952 (2)*

Gaekwad, H. G. 1: v P 1952

Gandotra, A. 2: v A 1969 (1); v NZ 1969 (1)

Gavaskar, S. M. 125: v E 1972 (5) 1976 (5) 1979 (1) 1981 (6) 1984 (5); v A 1979 (6) 1986 (3); v WI 1974 (2) 1978 (6) 1983 (6); v NZ 1976 (3); v P 1979 (6) 1983 (3) 1986 (4); v SL 1982 (1) 1986 (3); *v E 1971 (3) 1974 (3) 1979 (4) 1982 (3) 1986 (3); v A 1977 (5) 1980 (3) 1985 (3); v WI 1970 (4) 1975 (4) 1982 (5); v NZ 1975 (3) 1980 (3); v P 1978 (3) 1982 (6) 1984 (2); v SL 1985 (3)*

Ghavri, K. D. 39: v E 1976 (3) 1979 (1); v A 1979 (6); v WI 1974 (3) 1978 (6); v NZ 1976 (2); v P 1979 (6); *v E 1979 (4); v A 1977 (3) 1980 (3); v NZ 1980 (1); v P 1978 (1)*

Ghorpade, J. M. 8: v A 1956 (1); v WI 1958 (1); v NZ 1955 (1); *v E 1959 (3); v WI 1952 (2)*

Ghulam Ahmed 22: v E 1951 (2); v A 1956 (2); v WI 1948 (3) 1958 (2); v NZ 1955 (1); v P 1952 (4); *v E 1952 (2); v P 1954 (4)*

Gopalan, M. J. 1: v E 1933

Gopinath, C. D. 8: v E 1951 (3); v A 1959 (1); v P 1952 (1); *v E 1952 (1); v P 1954 (2)*

Guard, G. M. 2: v A 1959 (1); v WI 1958 (1)

Guha, S. 4: v A 1969 (3); *v E 1967 (1)*

Gul Mahomed 8: v P 1952 (2); *v E 1946 (1); v A 1947 (5)*

Gupte, B. P. 3: v E 1963 (1); v NZ 1964 (1); v P 1960 (1)

Gupte, S. P. 36: v E 1951 (1) 1961 (2); v A 1956 (3); v WI 1958 (5); v NZ 1955 (5); v P 1952 (2) 1960 (3); *v E 1959 (5); v WI 1952 (5); v P 1954 (5)*

Gursharan Singh 1: v NZ 1989

Hafeez, A. 3: *v E 1946 (3)*

Hanumant Singh 14: v E 1963 (2); v A 1964 (3); v WI 1966 (2); v NZ 1964 (4) 1969 (1); *v E 1967 (2)*

Hardikar, M. S. 2: v WI 1958 (2)

Hazare, V. S. 30: v E 1951 (5); v WI 1948 (5); v P 1952 (3); *v E 1946 (3) 1952 (4); v A 1947 (5); v WI 1952 (5)*

Hindlekar, D. D. 4: *v E 1936 (1) 1946 (3)*

Hirwani, N. D. 14: v WI 1987 (1); v NZ 1988 (3); v SL 1990 (1); *v E 1990 (3); v WI 1988 (3); v NZ 1989 (3)*

Ibrahim, K. C. 4: v WI 1948 (4)

Indrajitsinhji, K. S. 4: v A 1964 (3); v NZ 1969 (1)

Irani, J. K. 2: *v A 1947 (2)*

Jadeja, A. D. 3: *v SA 1992 (3)*

Jahangir Khan, M. 4: *v E 1932 (1) 1936 (3)*

Jai, L. P. 1: v E 1933

Jaisimha, M. L. 39: v E 1961 (5) 1963 (5); v A 1959 (1) 1964 (3); v WI 1966 (2); v NZ 1964 (4) 1969 (1); v P 1960 (4); *v E 1959 (1); v A 1967 (2); v WI 1961 (4) 1970 (3); v NZ 1967 (4)*

Jamshedji, R. J. 1: v E 1933
Jayantilal, K. 1: *v WI 1970*
Joshi, P. G. 12: v E 1951 (2); v A 1959 (1); v WI 1958 (1); v P 1952 (1) 1960 (1); *v E 1959 (3); v WI 1952 (3)*

Kambli, V. G. 14: v E 1992 (3); v WI 1994 (3); v SL 1993 (3); v Z 1992 (1); *v NZ 1993 (1); v SL 1993 (3)*
Kanitkar, H. S. 2: v WI 1974 (2)
Kapil Dev 131: v E 1979 (1) 1981 (6) 1984 (4) 1992 (3); v A 1979 (6) 1986 (3); v WI 1978 (6) 1983 (6) 1987 (4); v NZ 1988 (3); v P 1979 (6) 1983 (3) 1986 (5); v SL 1982 (1) 1986 (3) 1990 (1) 1993 (3); v Z 1992 (1); *v E 1979 (4) 1982 (3) 1986 (3) 1990 (3); v A 1980 (3) 1985 (3) 1991 (5); v SA 1992 (4); v WI 1982 (5) 1988 (4); v NZ 1980 (3) 1989 (3) 1993 (1); v P 1978 (3) 1982 (6) 1984 (2) 1989 (4); v SL 1985 (3) 1993 (3); v Z 1992 (1)*
Kapoor, A. R. 1: v WI 1994
Kardar, A. H. (*see* Hafeez)
Kenny, R. B. 5: v A 1959 (4); v WI 1958 (1)
Kirmani, S. M. H. 88: v E 1976 (5) 1979 (1) 1981 (6) 1984 (5); v A 1979 (6); v WI 1978 (6) 1983 (6); v NZ 1976 (3); v P 1979 (6) 1983 (3) 1986 (5); v SL 1982 (1); *v E 1982 (3); v A 1977 (5) 1980 (3) 1985 (3); v WI 1975 (4) 1982 (5); v NZ 1975 (3) 1980 (3); v P 1978 (3) 1982 (6) 1984 (2)*
Kischenchand, G. 5: v P 1952 (1); *v A 1947 (4)*
Kripal Singh, A. G. 14: v E 1961 (3) 1963 (2); v A 1956 (2) 1964 (1); v WI 1958 (1); v NZ 1955 (4); *v E 1959 (1)*
Krishnamurthy, P. 5: *v WI 1970 (5)*
Kulkarni, R. R. 3: v A 1986 (1); v P 1986 (2)
Kulkarni, U. N. 4: *v A 1967 (3); v NZ 1967 (1)*
Kumar, V. V. 2: v E 1961 (1); v P 1960 (1)
Kumble, A. 20: v E 1992 (3); v WI 1994 (3); v SL 1993 (3); v Z 1992 (1); *v E 1990 (1); v SA 1992 (4); v NZ 1993 (1); v SL 1993 (3); v Z 1992 (1)*
Kunderan, B. K. 18: v E 1961 (1) 1963 (5); v A 1959 (1); v WI 1966 (2); v NZ 1964 (1); v P 1960 (2); *v E 1961 (2); v WI 1961 (2)*

Lall Singh 1: *v E 1932*
Lamba, R. 4: v WI 1987 (1); v SL 1986 (3)

Madan Lal 39: v E 1976 (2) 1981 (6); v WI 1974 (1) 1983 (3); v NZ 1976 (1); v P 1983 (3); v SL 1982 (1); *v E 1974 (2) 1982 (3) 1986 (1); v A 1977 (2); v WI 1975 (4) 1982 (2); v NZ 1975 (3); v P 1982 (3) 1984 (1)*
Maka, E. S. 2: v P 1952 (1); *v WI 1952 (1)*
Malhotra, A. 7: v E 1981 (2) 1984 (1); v WI 1983 (3); *v E 1982 (1)*
Maninder Singh 35: v A 1986 (3); v WI 1983 (4) 1987 (3); v P 1986 (4); v SL 1986 (3); v Z 1992 (1); *v E 1986 (3); v WI 1982 (3); v P 1982 (5) 1984 (1) 1989 (1); v SL 1985 (3)*
Manjrekar, S. V. 33: v WI 1987 (1) 1994 (3); v SL 1990 (1) 1993 (3); *v E 1990 (3); v A 1991 (5); v SA 1992 (4); v WI 1988 (4); v NZ 1989 (3) 1993 (1); v P 1989 (4); v Z 1992 (1)*
Manjrekar, V. L. 55: v E 1951 (2) 1961 (5) 1963 (4); v A 1956 (2) 1964 (3); v WI 1958 (1); v NZ 1955 (4) 1964 (1); v P 1952 (3) 1960 (5); *v E 1952 (4) 1959 (2); v WI 1952 (4) 1961 (5); v P 1954 (5)*
Mankad, A. V. 22: v E 1976 (1); v A 1969 (5); v WI 1974 (1); v NZ 1969 (2) 1976 (1); *v E 1971 (3) 1974 (1); v A 1977 (3); v WI 1970 (3)*
Mankad, V. 44: v E 1951 (5); v A 1956 (3); v WI 1948 (5) 1958 (2); v NZ 1955 (4); v P 1952 (4); *v E 1946 (3) 1952 (3); v A 1947 (5); v WI 1952 (5); v P 1954 (5)*
Mansur Ali Khan (*see* Pataudi)
Mantri, M. K. 4: v E 1951 (1); *v E 1952 (2); v P 1954 (1)*
Meherhomji, K. R. 1: *v E 1936*
Mehra, V. L. 8: v E 1961 (1) 1963 (2); v NZ 1955 (2); *v WI 1961 (3)*
Merchant, V. M. 10: v E 1933 (3) 1951 (1); *v E 1936 (3) 1946 (3)*
Milkha Singh, A. G. 4: v E 1961 (1); v A 1959 (1); v P 1960 (2)
Modi, R. S. 10: v E 1951 (1); v WI 1948 (5); v P 1952 (1); *v E 1946 (3)*
Mongia, N. R. 7: v WI 1994 (3); v SL 1993 (3); *v NZ 1993 (1)*
More, K. S. 49: v E 1992 (3); v WI 1987 (4); v NZ 1988 (3); v P 1986 (5); v SL 1986 (3) 1990 (1); *v E 1986 (3) 1990 (3); v A 1991 (5); v SA 1992 (4); v WI 1988 (4); v NZ 1989 (3); v P 1989 (4); v SL 1993 (3); v Z 1992 (1)*
Muddiah, V. M. 2: v A 1959 (1); v P 1960 (1)

Mushtaq Ali, S. 11: v E 1933 (2) 1951 (1); v WI 1948 (3); *v E 1936 (3) 1946 (2)*

Nadkarni, R. G. 41: v E 1961 (1) 1963 (5); v A 1959 (5) 1964 (3); v WI 1958 (1) 1966 (1); v NZ 1955 (1) 1964 (4); v P 1960 (4); *v E 1959 (4); v A 1967 (3); v WI 1961 (5); v NZ 1967 (4)*
Naik, S. S. 3: v WI 1974 (2); *v E 1974 (1)*
Naoomal Jeoomal 3: v E 1933 (2); *v E 1932 (1)*
Narasimha Rao, M. V. 4: v A 1979 (2); v WI 1978 (2)
Navle, J. G. 2: v E 1933 (1); *v E 1932 (1)*
Nayak, S. V. 2: *v E 1982 (2)*
Nayudu, C. K. 7: v E 1933 (3); *v E 1932 (1) 1936 (3)*
Nayudu, C. S. 11: v E 1933 (2) 1951 (1); *v E 1936 (2) 1946 (2); v A 1947 (4)*
Nazir Ali, S. 2: v E 1933 (1); *v E 1932 (1)*
Nissar, Mahomed 6: v E 1933 (2); *v E 1932 (1) 1936 (3)*
Nyalchand, S. 1: v P 1952

Pai, A. M. 1: v NZ 1969
Palia, P. E. 2: *v E 1932 (1) 1936 (1)*
Pandit, C. S. 5: v A 1986 (2); *v E 1986 (1); v A 1991 (2)*
Parkar, G. A. 1: *v E 1982*
Parkar, R. D. 2: v E 1972 (2)
Parsana, D. D. 2: v WI 1978 (2)
Patankar, C. T. 1: v NZ 1955
Pataudi sen., Nawab of, 3: *v E 1946 (3)*
Pataudi jun., Nawab of (now Mansur Ali Khan) 46: v E 1961 (1) 1963 (5) 1972 (3); v A 1964 (3) 1969 (5); v WI 1966 (3) 1974 (4); v NZ 1964 (4) 1969 (3); *v E 1967 (3); v A 1967 (3); v WI 1961 (3); v NZ 1967 (4)*
Patel, B. P. 21: v E 1976 (5); v WI 1974 (3); v NZ 1976 (3); *v E 1974 (2); v A 1977 (2); v WI 1975 (3); v NZ 1975 (3)*
Patel, J. M. 7: v A 1956 (2) 1959 (3); v NZ 1955 (1); *v P 1954 (1)*
Patel, R. 1: v NZ 1988
Patiala, Yuvraj of, 1: v E 1933
Patil, S. M. 29: v E 1979 (1) 1981 (4) 1984 (2); v WI 1983 (2); v P 1979 (2) 1983 (3); v SL 1982 (1); *v E 1982 (2); v A 1980 (3); v NZ 1980 (3); v P 1982 (4) 1984 (2)*
Patil, S. R. 1: v NZ 1955
Phadkar, D. G. 31: v E 1951 (4); v A 1956 (1); v WI 1948 (4) 1958 (1); v NZ 1955 (4); v P 1952 (2); *v E 1952 (4); v A 1947 (4); v WI 1952 (4); v P 1954 (3)*
Prabhakar, M. 36: v E 1984 (2) 1992 (3); v WI 1994 (3); v SL 1990 (1) 1993 (3); v Z 1992 (1); *v E 1990 (3); v A 1991 (5); v SA 1992 (4); v NZ 1989 (3); v P 1989 (4); v SL 1993 (3); v Z 1992 (1)*
Prasanna, E. A. S. 49: v E 1961 (1) 1972 (3) 1976 (4); v A 1969 (5); v WI 1966 (1) 1974 (5); v NZ 1969 (3); *v E 1967 (3) 1974 (2); v A 1967 (4) 1977 (4); v WI 1961 (1) 1970 (3) 1975 (1); v NZ 1967 (4) 1975 (3); v P 1978 (2)*
Punjabi, P. H. 5: *v P 1954 (5)*

Rai Singh, K. 1: *v A 1947*
Rajinder Pal 1: v E 1963
Rajindernath, V. 1: v P 1952
Rajput, L. S. 2: *v SL 1985 (2)*
Raju, S. L. V. 21: v E 1992 (3); v WI 1994 (3); v SL 1990 (1) 1993 (3); *v A 1991 (4); v SA 1992 (2); v NZ 1989 (2) 1993 (1); v SL 1993 (1); v Z 1992 (1)*
Raman, W. V. 8: v WI 1987 (1); v NZ 1988 (1); *v SA 1992 (1); v WI 1988 (1); v NZ 1989 (3); v Z 1992 (1)*
Ramaswami, C. 2: *v E 1936 (2)*
Ramchand, G. S. 33: v A 1956 (1) 1959 (5); v WI 1958 (3); v NZ 1955 (5); v P 1952 (3); *v E 1952 (4); v WI 1952 (5); v P 1954 (5)*
Ramji, L. 1: v E 1933
Rangachary, C. R. 4: v WI 1948 (2); *v A 1947 (2)*
Rangnekar, K. M. 3: *v A 1947 (3)*
Ranjane, V. B. 7: v E 1961 (3) 1963 (1); v A 1964 (1); v WI 1958 (1); *v WI 1961 (1)*
Razdan, V. 2: *v P 1989 (2)*
Reddy, B. 4: *v E 1979 (4)*
Rege, M. R. 1: v WI 1948
Roy, A. 4: v A 1969 (2); v NZ 1969 (2)

Roy, Pankaj 43: v E 1951 (5); v A 1956 (3) 1959 (5); v WI 1958 (5); v NZ 1955 (3); v P 1952 (3) 1960 (1); *v E 1952 (4) 1959 (5); v WI 1952 (4); v P 1954 (5)*
Roy, Pranab 2: v E 1981 (2)

Sandhu, B. S. 8: v WI 1983 (1); *v WI 1982 (4); v P 1982 (3)*
Sardesai, D. N. 30: v E 1961 (1) 1963 (5) 1972 (1); v A 1964 (3) 1969 (1); v WI 1966 (2); v NZ 1964 (3); *v E 1967 (1) 1971 (3); v A 1967 (2); v WI 1961 (3) 1970 (5)*
Sarwate, C. T. 9: v E 1951 (1); v WI 1948 (2); *v E 1946 (1); v A 1947 (5)*
Saxena, R. C. 1: *v E 1967*
Sekar, T. A. P. 2: *v P 1982 (2)*
Sen, P. 14: v E 1951 (2); v WI 1948 (5); v P 1952 (2); *v E 1952 (2); v A 1947 (3)*
Sengupta, A. K. 1: v WI 1958
Sharma, Ajay 1: v WI 1987
Sharma, Chetan 23: v E 1984 (3); v A 1986 (2); v WI 1987 (3); v SL 1986 (2); *v E 1986 (2); v A 1985 (2); v WI 1988 (4); v P 1984 (2); v SL 1985 (3)*
Sharma, Gopal 5: v E 1984 (1); v P 1986 (2); v SL 1990 (1); *v SL 1985 (1)*
Sharma, P. 5: v E 1976 (2); v WI 1974 (2); *v P 1975 (1)*
Sharma, Sanjeev 2: v NZ 1988 (1); *v E 1990 (1)*
Shastri, R. J. 80: v E 1981 (6) 1984 (5); v A 1986 (3); v WI 1983 (6) 1987 (4); v NZ 1988 (3); v P 1983 (2) 1986 (5); v SL 1986 (3) 1990 (1); *v E 1982 (3) 1986 (3) 1990 (3); v A 1985 (3) 1991 (3); v SA 1992 (3); v WI 1982 (5) 1988 (4); v NZ 1980 (3); v P 1982 (2) 1984 (2) 1989 (4); v SL 1985 (3); v Z 1992 (1)*
Shinde, S. G. 7: v E 1951 (3); v WI 1948 (1); *v E 1946 (1) 1952 (2)*
Shodhan, R. H. 3: v P 1952 (1); *v WI 1952 (2)*
Shukla, R. C. 1: v SL 1982
Sidhu, N. S. 34: v E 1992 (3); v WI 1983 (2) 1994 (3); v NZ 1988 (3); v SL 1993 (3); v Z 1992 (1); *v E 1990 (3); v A 1991 (3); v WI 1988 (4); v NZ 1989 (1) 1993 (1); v P 1989 (4); v SL 1993 (3)*
Sivaramakrishnan, L. 9: v E 1984 (5); *v A 1985 (2); v WI 1982 (1); v SL 1985 (1)*
Sohoni, S. W. 4: v E 1951 (1); *v E 1946 (2); v A 1947 (1)*
Solkar, E. D. 27: v E 1972 (5) 1976 (1); v A 1969 (4); v WI 1974 (4); v NZ 1969 (1); *v E 1971 (3) 1974 (3); v WI 1970 (5) 1975 (1)*
Sood, M. M. 1: v A 1959
Srikkanth, K. 43: v E 1981 (4) 1984 (2); v A 1986 (3); v WI 1987 (4); v NZ 1988 (3); v P 1986 (5); v SL 1986 (3); *v E 1986 (3); v A 1985 (3) 1991 (4); v P 1982 (2) 1989 (4); v SL 1985 (3)*
Srinath, J. 15: v WI 1994 (3); *v A 1991 (5); v SA 1992 (3); v NZ 1993 (1); v SL 1993 (2); v Z 1992 (1)*
Srinivasan, T. E. 1: *v NZ 1980*
Subramanya, V. 9: v WI 1966 (2); v NZ 1964 (1); *v E 1967 (2); v A 1967 (2); v NZ 1967 (2)*
Sunderram, G. 2: v NZ 1955 (2)
Surendranath, R. 11: v A 1959 (2); v WI 1958 (5); v P 1960 (2); *v E 1959 (5)*
Surti, R. F. 26: v E 1963 (1); v A 1964 (2) 1969 (1); v WI 1966 (2); v NZ 1964 (1) 1969 (2); *v P 1960 (2); v E 1967 (2); v A 1967 (4); v WI 1961 (5); v NZ 1967 (4)*
Swamy, V. N. 1: v NZ 1955

Tamhane, N. S. 21: v A 1956 (3) 1959 (1); v WI 1958 (4); v NZ 1955 (4); v P 1960 (2); *v E 1959 (2); v P 1954 (5)*
Tarapore, K. K. 1: v WI 1948
Tendulkar, S. R. 35: v E 1992 (3); v WI 1994 (3); v SL 1990 (1) 1993 (3); v Z 1992 (1); *v E 1990 (3); v A 1991 (5); v SA 1992 (4); v NZ 1989 (3) 1993 (1); v P 1989 (4); v SL 1993 (3); v Z 1992 (1)*

Umrigar, P. R. 59: v E 1951 (5) 1961 (4); v A 1956 (3) 1959 (3); v WI 1948 (1) 1958 (5); v NZ 1955 (5); v P 1952 (5) 1960 (5); *v E 1952 (4) 1959 (4); v WI 1952 (5) 1961 (5); v P 1954 (5)*

Vengsarkar, D. B. 116: v E 1976 (1) 1979 (1) 1981 (6) 1984 (5); v A 1979 (6) 1986 (2); v WI 1978 (6) 1983 (5) 1987 (3); v NZ 1988 (3); v P 1979 (5) 1983 (1) 1986 (5); v SL 1982 (1) 1986 (3) 1990 (1); *v E 1979 (4) 1982 (3) 1986 (3) 1990 (3); v A 1977 (5) 1980 (3) 1985 (3) 1991 (5); v WI 1975 (2) 1982 (5) 1988 (4); v NZ 1975 (3) 1980 (3) 1989 (2); v P 1978 (3) 1982 (6) 1984 (2); v SL 1985 (3)*
Venkataraghavan, S. 57: v E 1972 (2) 1976 (1); v A 1969 (5) 1979 (3); v WI 1966 (2) 1974 (2) 1978 (6); v NZ 1964 (4) 1969 (2) 1976 (3); v P 1983 (2); *v E 1967 (1) 1971 (3) 1974 (2) 1979 (4); v A 1977 (1); v WI 1970 (5) 1975 (3) 1982 (5); v NZ 1975 (1)*
Venkataramana, M. 1: *v WI 1988*

Viswanath, G. R. 91 : v E 1972 (5) 1976 (5) 1979 (1) 1981 (6); v A 1969 (4) 1979 (6); v WI 1974 (5) 1978 (6); v NZ 1976 (3); v P 1979 (6); v SL 1982 (1); *v E 1971 (3) 1974 (3) 1979 (4) 1982 (3); v A 1977 (5) 1980 (3); v WI 1970 (3) 1975 (4); v NZ 1975 (3) 1980 (3); v P 1978 (3) 1982 (6)*

Viswanath, S. 3: *v SL 1985 (3)*

Vizianagram, Maharaj Kumar of, Sir Vijay A. 3: *v E 1936 (3)*

Wadekar, A. L. 37: v E 1972 (5); v A 1969 (5); v WI 1966 (2); v NZ 1969 (3); *v E 1967 (3) 1971 (3) 1974 (3); v A 1967 (4); v WI 1970 (5); v NZ 1967 (4)*

Wassan, A. S. 4: *v E 1990 (1); v NZ 1989 (3)*

Wazir Ali, S. 7: v E 1933 (3); *v E 1932 (1) 1936 (3)*

Yadav, N. S. 35: v E 1979 (1) 1981 (1) 1984 (4); v A 1979 (5) 1986 (3); v WI 1983 (3); v P 1979 (5) 1986 (4); v SL 1986 (2); *v A 1980 (2) 1985 (3); v NZ 1980 (1); v P 1984 (1)*

Yadav, V. S. 1: *v NZ 1992*

Yajurvindra Singh 4: v E 1976 (2); v A 1979 (1); *v E 1979 (1)*

Yashpal Sharma 37: v E 1979 (1) 1981 (2); v A 1979 (6); v WI 1983 (1); v P 1979 (6) 1983 (3); v SL 1982 (1); *v E 1979 (3) 1982 (3); v A 1980 (3); v WI 1982 (5); v NZ 1980 (1); v P 1982 (2)*

Yograj Singh 1: *v NZ 1980*

Note: Hafeez, on going later to Oxford University, took his correct name, Kardar.

PAKISTAN

Number of Test cricketers: 132

Aamer Malik 14: v E 1987 (2); v A 1988 (1) 1994 (1); v WI 1990 (1); v In 1989 (4); *v A 1989 (2); v WI 1987 (1); v NZ 1988 (2)*

Aamir Nazir 5: *v SA 1994 (1); v WI 1992 (1); v NZ 1993 (1); v Z 1994 (2)*

Aamir Sohail 23: v A 1994 (3); v Z 1993 (3); *v E 1992 (5); v SA 1994 (1); v WI 1992 (1); v NZ 1992 (1) 1993 (3); v SL 1994 (2); v Z 1994 (3)*

Abdul Kadir 4: v In 1964 (1); *v A 1964 (1); v NZ 1964 (2)*

Abdul Qadir 67: v E 1977 (3) 1983 (3) 1987 (3); v A 1982 (3) 1988 (3); v WI 1980 (2) 1986 (3) 1990 (2); v NZ 1984 (3) 1990 (2); v In 1982 (5) 1984 (1) 1989 (4); v SL 1985 (3); *v E 1982 (3) 1987 (4); v A 1983 (5); v WI 1987 (3); v NZ 1984 (2) 1988 (2); v In 1979 (3) 1986 (3); v SL 1985 (2)*

Afaq Hussain 2: v E 1961 (1); *v A 1964 (1)*

Aftab Baloch 2: v WI 1974 (1); *v NZ 1969 (1)*

Aftab Gul 6: v E 1968 (2); v NZ 1969 (1); *v E 1971 (3)*

Agha Saadat Ali 1: v NZ 1955

Agha Zahid 1: v WI 1974

Akram Raza 9: v A 1994 (2); v WI 1990 (1); v In 1989 (1); v SL 1991 (1); *v NZ 1993 (2); v SL 1994 (1); v Z 1994 (1)*

Alim-ud-Din 25: v E 1961 (1); v A 1956 (1) 1959 (1); v WI 1958 (1); v NZ 1955 (3); v In 1954 (5); *v E 1954 (3) 1962 (3); v WI 1957 (5); v In 1960 (1)*

Amir Elahi 5: *v In 1952 (5)*

Anil Dalpat 9: v E 1983 (3); v NZ 1984 (3); *v NZ 1984 (3)*

Anwar Hussain 4: *v In 1952 (4)*

Anwar Khan 1: *v NZ 1978*

Aqib Javed 18: v A 1994 (1); v NZ 1990 (1); v SL 1991 (3); *v E 1992 (5); v A 1989 (1); v SA 1994 (1); v NZ 1988 (1) 1992 (1); v Z 1994 (2)*

Arif Butt 3: *v A 1964 (1); v NZ 1964 (2)*

Ashfaq Ahmed 1: v Z 1993

Ashraf Ali 8: v E 1987 (3); v In 1984 (2); v SL 1981 (2) 1985 (1)

Asif Iqbal 58: v E 1968 (3) 1972 (3); v A 1964 (1); v WI 1974 (2); v NZ 1964 (3) 1969 (3) 1976 (3); v In 1978 (3); *v E 1967 (3) 1971 (3) 1974 (3); v A 1964 (1) 1972 (3) 1976 (3) 1978 (2); v WI 1976 (5); v NZ 1964 (3) 1972 (3) 1978 (2); v In 1979 (6)*

Asif Masood 16: v E 1968 (2) 1972 (1); v WI 1974 (2); v NZ 1969 (1); *v E 1971 (3) 1974 (3); v A 1972 (3) 1976 (1)*

Asif Mujtaba 21: v E 1987 (1); v WI 1986 (2); v Z 1993 (3); *v E 1992 (5); v SA 1994 (1); v WI 1992 (3); v NZ 1992 (1) 1993 (2); v SL 1994 (2); v Z 1994 (1)*

Ata-ur-Rehman 9: v Z 1993 (3); *v E 1992 (1); v WI 1992 (3); v NZ 1993 (2)*

Atif Rauf 1: *v NZ 1993*

Azeem Hafeez 18: v E 1983 (2); v NZ 1984 (3); v In 1984 (2); *v A 1983 (5); v NZ 1984 (3); v In 1983 (3)*

Azhar Khan 1: v A 1979

Azmat Rana 1: v A 1979

Basit Ali 14: v A 1994 (2); v Z 1993 (3); *v WI 1992 (3); v NZ 1993 (3); v SL 1994 (2); v Z 1994 (1)*

Burki, J. 25: v E 1961 (3); v A 1964 (1); v NZ 1964 (3) 1969 (1); *v E 1962 (5) 1967 (3); v A 1964 (1); v NZ 1964 (3); v In 1960 (5)*

D'Souza, A. 6: v E 1961 (2); v WI 1958 (1); *v E 1962 (3)*

Ehtesham-ud-Din 5: v A 1979 (1); *v E 1982 (1); v In 1979 (3)*

Farooq Hamid 1: *v A 1964*

Farrukh Zaman 1: v NZ 1976

Fazal Mahmood 34: v E 1961 (1); v A 1956 (1) 1959 (2); v WI 1958 (3); v NZ 1955 (2); v In 1954 (4); *v E 1954 (4) 1962 (2); v WI 1957 (5); v In 1952 (5) 1960 (5)*

Ghazali, M. E. Z. 2: *v E 1954 (2)*

Ghulam Abbas 1: *v E 1967*

Gul Mahomed 1: v A 1956

Hanif Mohammad 55: v E 1961 (3) 1968 (3); v A 1956 (1) 1959 (3) 1964 (1); v WI 1958 (1); v NZ 1955 (3) 1964 (3) 1969 (1); v In 1954 (5); *v E 1954 (4) 1962 (5) 1967 (3); v A 1964 (1); v WI 1957 (5); v NZ 1964 (3); v In 1952 (5) 1960 (5)*

Haroon Rashid 23: v E 1977 (3); v A 1979 (2) 1982 (3); v In 1982 (1); v SL 1981 (2); *v E 1978 (3) 1982 (1); v A 1976 (1) 1978 (1); v WI 1976 (5); v NZ 1978 (1)*

Haseeb Ahsan 12: v E 1961 (2); v A 1959 (1); v WI 1958 (1); *v WI 1957 (3); v In 1960 (5)*

Ibadulla, K. 4: v A 1964 (1); *v E 1967 (2); v NZ 1964 (1)*

Ijaz Ahmed 24: v A 1988 (3) 1994 (1); v WI 1990 (3); *v E 1987 (4); v A 1989 (3); v SA 1994 (1); v WI 1987 (2); v In 1986 (1); v Z 1994 (3)*

Ijaz Butt 8: v A 1959 (2); v WI 1958 (3); *v E 1962 (3)*

Ijaz Faqih 5: v WI 1980 (1); *v A 1981 (1); v WI 1987 (2); v In 1986 (1)*

Imran Khan 88: v A 1979 (2) 1982 (3); v WI 1980 (4) 1986 (3) 1990 (3); v NZ 1976 (3); v In 1978 (3) 1982 (6) 1989 (2); v SL 1981 (1) 1985 (3) 1991 (3); *v E 1971 (1) 1974 (3) 1982 (3) 1987 (5); v A 1976 (3) 1978 (2) 1981 (3) 1983 (2) 1989 (3); v WI 1976 (5) 1987 (3); v NZ 1978 (2) 1988 (2); v In 1979 (3) 1986 (5); v SL 1985 (3)*

Imtiaz Ahmed 41: v E 1961 (3); v A 1956 (1) 1959 (3); v WI 1958 (3); v NZ 1955 (3); v In 1954 (5); *v E 1954 (4) 1962 (4); v WI 1957 (5); v In 1952 (5) 1960 (5)*

Intikhab Alam 47: v E 1961 (2) 1968 (3) 1972 (3); v A 1959 (1) 1964 (1); v WI 1974 (2); v NZ 1964 (3) 1969 (3) 1976 (3); *v E 1962 (3) 1967 (3) 1971 (3) 1974 (3); v A 1964 (1) 1972 (3); v WI 1976 (1); v NZ 1964 (3) 1972 (3); v In 1960 (3)*

Inzamam-ul-Haq 23: v A 1994 (3); v Z 1993 (3); *v E 1992 (4); v SA 1994 (1); v WI 1992 (3); v NZ 1992 (1) 1993 (3); v SL 1994 (2); v Z 1994 (3)*

Iqbal Qasim 50: v E 1977 (3) 1987 (3); v A 1979 (3) 1982 (2) 1988 (3); v WI 1980 (4); v NZ 1984 (3); v In 1978 (3) 1982 (2); *v E 1978 (3); v A 1976 (3) 1981 (2); v WI 1976 (2); v NZ 1984 (1); v In 1979 (6) 1983 (1) 1986 (3)*

Israr Ali 4: v A 1959 (2); *v In 1952 (2)*

Jalal-ud-Din 6: v A 1982 (1); v In 1982 (2) 1984 (2); v SL 1985 (1)

Javed Akhtar 1: *v E 1962*

Javed Miandad 124: v E 1977 (3) 1987 (3); v A 1979 (3) 1982 (3) 1988 (3); v WI 1980 (4) 1986 (3) 1990 (2); v NZ 1976 (3) 1984 (3) 1990 (3); v In 1978 (3) 1982 (6) 1984 (2) 1989 (4); v SL 1981 (3) 1985 (3) 1991 (3); v Z 1993 (3); *v E 1978 (3) 1982 (3) 1987 (5) 1992 (5); v A 1976 (3) 1978 (2) 1981 (3) 1983 (5) 1989 (3); v WI 1976 (1) 1987 (3) 1992 (3); v NZ 1978 (3) 1984 (3) 1988 (2) 1992 (1); v In 1979 (6) 1983 (3) 1986 (4); v SL 1985 (3)*

Kabir Khan 4: *v SA 1994 (1); v SL 1994 (1); v Z 1994 (2)*

Kardar, A. H. 23: v A 1956 (1); v NZ 1955 (3); v In 1954 (5); *v E 1954 (4); v WI 1957 (5); v In 1952 (5)*

Khalid Hassan 1: *v E 1954*

Khalid Wazir 2: *v E 1954 (2)*

Khan Mohammad 13: v A 1956 (1); v NZ 1955 (3); v In 1954 (4); *v E 1954 (2); v WI 1957 (2); v In 1952 (1)*

Liaqat Ali 5: v E 1977 (2); v WI 1974 (1); *v E 1978 (2)*

Mahmood Hussain 27: v E 1961 (1); v WI 1958 (3); v NZ 1955 (1); v In 1954 (5); *v E 1954 (2) 1962 (3); v WI 1957 (3); v In 1952 (4) 1960 (5)*

Majid Khan 63: v E 1968 (3) 1972 (3); v A 1964 (1) 1979 (3); v WI 1974 (2) 1980 (4); v NZ 1964 (3) 1976 (3); v In 1978 (3) 1982 (1); v SL 1981 (1); *v E 1967 (3) 1971 (2) 1974 (3) 1982 (1); v A 1972 (3) 1976 (3) 1978 (2) 1981 (3); v WI 1976 (5); v NZ 1972 (3) 1978 (2); v In 1979 (6)*

Mansoor Akhtar 19: v A 1982 (3); v WI 1980 (2); v In 1982 (3); v SL 1981 (1); *v E 1982 (3) 1987 (5); v A 1981 (1) 1989 (1)*

Manzoor Elahi 6: v NZ 1984 (1); v In 1984 (1); *v In 1986 (2); v Z 1994 (2)*

Maqsood Ahmed 16: v NZ 1955 (2); v In 1954 (5); *v E 1954 (4); v In 1952 (5)*

Masood Anwar 1: v WI 1990

Mathias, Wallis 21: v E 1961 (1); v A 1956 (1) 1959 (2); v WI 1958 (3); v NZ 1955 (1); *v E 1962 (3); v WI 1957 (5); v In 1960 (5)*

Miran Bux 2: v In 1954 (2)

Mohammad Aslam 1: *v E 1954*

Mohammad Farooq 7: v NZ 1964 (3); *v E 1962 (2); v In 1960 (2)*

Mohammad Ilyas 10: v E 1968 (2); v NZ 1964 (3); *v E 1967 (1); v A 1964 (1); v NZ 1964 (3)*

Mohammad Munaf 4: v E 1961 (2); v A 1959 (2)

Mohammad Nazir 14: v E 1972 (1); v WI 1980 (4); v NZ 1969 (3); *v A 1983 (3); v In 1983 (3)*

Mohsin Kamal 9: v E 1983 (1); v A 1994 (3); v SL 1985 (1); *v E 1987 (4); v SL 1985 (1)*

Mohsin Khan 48: v E 1977 (1) 1983 (3); v A 1982 (3); v WI 1986 (3); v NZ 1984 (2); v In 1982 (6) 1984 (2); v SL 1981 (2) 1985 (2); *v E 1978 (3) 1982 (3); v A 1978 (1) 1981 (2) 1983 (5); v NZ 1978 (1) 1984 (3); v In 1983 (3); v SL 1985 (3)*

Moin Khan 13: v A 1994 (1); v WI 1990 (2); v SL 1991 (3); *v E 1992 (4); v SA 1994 (1); v WI 1992 (2)*

Mudassar Nazar 76: v E 1977 (3) 1983 (1) 1987 (3); v A 1979 (3) 1982 (3) 1988 (3); v WI 1986 (2); v NZ 1984 (3); v In 1978 (2) 1982 (6) 1984 (2); v SL 1981 (1) 1985 (3); *v E 1978 (3) 1982 (3) 1987 (5); v A 1976 (1) 1978 (1) 1981 (3) 1983 (3); v WI 1987 (3); v NZ 1978 (1) 1984 (3) 1988 (2); v In 1979 (5) 1983 (3); v SL 1985 (3)*

Mufasir-ul-Haq 1: *v NZ 1964*

Munir Malik 3: v A 1959 (1); *v E 1962 (2)*

Mushtaq Ahmed 18: v A 1994 (3); v WI 1990 (2); v Z 1993 (2); *v E 1992 (5); v A 1989 (1); v WI 1992 (1); v NZ 1992 (1) 1993 (1); v SL 1994 (2)*

Mushtaq Mohammad 57: v E 1961 (1) 1968 (3) 1972 (3); v WI 1958 (1) 1974 (2); v NZ 1969 (2) 1976 (3); v In 1978 (3); *v E 1962 (5) 1967 (3) 1971 (3) 1974 (3); v A 1972 (3) 1976 (3) 1978 (2); v WI 1976 (5); v NZ 1972 (2) 1978 (3); v In 1960 (5)*

Nadeem Abbasi 3: v In 1989 (3)

Nadeem Ghauri 1: *v A 1989*

Nadeem Khan 1: *v WI 1992*

Nasim-ul-Ghani 29: v E 1961 (2); v A 1959 (2) 1964 (3); v WI 1958 (3); *v E 1962 (5) 1967 (2); v A 1964 (1) 1972 (1); v WI 1957 (5); v NZ 1964 (3); v In 1960 (4)*

Naushad Ali 6: v NZ 1964 (3); *v NZ 1964 (3)*

Naved Anjum 2: v NZ 1990 (1); v In 1989 (1)

Nazar Mohammad 5: *v In 1952 (5)*

Nazir Junior (*see* Mohammad Nazir)

Niaz Ahmed 2: v E 1968 (1); *v E 1967 (1)*

Pervez Sajjad 19: v E 1968 (1) 1972 (2); v A 1964 (1); v NZ 1964 (3) 1969 (3); *v E 1971 (3); v NZ 1964 (3) 1972 (3)*

Qasim Omar 26: v E 1983 (3); v WI 1986 (3); v NZ 1984 (2); v In 1984 (2); v SL 1985 (3); *v A 1983 (5); v NZ 1984 (3); v In 1983 (1); v SL 1985 (3)*

Ramiz Raja 48: v E 1983 (2) 1987 (3); v A 1988 (3); v WI 1986 (3) 1990 (2); v NZ 1990 (3); v In 1989 (4); v SL 1985 (1) 1991 (3); *v E 1987 (2) 1992 (5); v A 1989 (2); v WI 1987 (3) 1992 (3); v NZ 1992 (1); v In 1986 (5); v SL 1985 (3)*

Rashid Khan 4: v SL 1981 (2); *v A 1983 (1)*; *v NZ 1984 (1)*

Rashid Latif 16: v A 1994 (2); v Z 1993 (3); *v E 1992 (1)*; *v WI 1992 (1)*; *v NZ 1992 (1) 1993 (3); v SL 1994 (2)*; *v Z 1994 (3)*

Rehman, S. F. 1: *v WI 1957*

Rizwan-uz-Zaman 11: v WI 1986 (1); v SL 1981 (2); *v A 1981 (1)*; *v NZ 1988 (2)*; *v In 1986 (5)*

Sadiq Mohammad 41: v E 1972 (3) 1977 (2); v WI 1974 (1) 1980 (3); v NZ 1969 (3) 1976 (3); v In 1978 (1); *v E 1971 (3) 1974 (3) 1978 (3)*; *v A 1972 (3) 1976 (2)*; *v WI 1976 (5)*; *v NZ 1972 (3)*; *v In 1979 (3)*

Saeed Ahmed 41: v E 1961 (3) 1968 (3); v A 1959 (3) 1964 (1); v WI 1958 (3); v NZ 1964 (3); *v E 1962 (5) 1967 (3) 1971 (1)*; *v A 1964 (1) 1972 (2)*; *v WI 1957 (5)*; *v NZ 1964 (3)*; *v In 1960 (5)*

Saeed Anwar 12: v A 1994 (2); v WI 1990 (1); *v SA 1994 (1)*; *v NZ 1993 (3)*; *v SL 1994 (2)*; *v Z 1994 (2)*

Salah-ud-Din 5: v E 1968 (1); v NZ 1964 (3) 1969 (1)

Saleem Jaffer 14: v E 1987 (1); v A 1988 (2); v WI 1986 (1); v NZ 1990 (2); v In 1989 (1); v SL 1991 (2); *v WI 1987 (1)*; *v NZ 1988 (2)*; *v In 1986 (2)*

Salim Altaf 21: v E 1972 (3); v NZ 1969 (3); v In 1978 (1); *v E 1967 (2) 1971 (2)*; *v A 1972 (3) 1976 (2)*; *v WI 1976 (3)*; *v NZ 1972 (3)*

Salim Malik 84: v E 1983 (3) 1987 (3); v A 1988 (3) 1994 (3); v WI 1986 (1) 1990 (3); v NZ 1984 (3) 1990 (3); v In 1982 (6) 1984 (2) 1989 (4); v SL 1981 (2) 1985 (3) 1991 (3); *v E 1987 (5) 1992 (5)*; *v A 1983 (3) 1989 (1)*; *v SA 1994 (1)*; *v WI 1987 (3)*; *v NZ 1984 (3) 1988 (2) 1992 (1) 1993 (3)*; *v In 1983 (2) 1986 (5)*; *v SL 1985 (3) 1994 (2)*; *v Z 1994 (3)*

Salim Yousuf 32: v A 1988 (3); v WI 1986 (3) 1990 (1); v NZ 1990 (3); v In 1989 (1); v SL 1981 (1) 1985 (2); *v E 1987 (5)*; *v A 1989 (3)*; *v WI 1987 (3)*; *v NZ 1988 (2)*; *v In 1986 (5)*

Sarfraz Nawaz 55: v E 1968 (1) 1972 (2) 1977 (2) 1983 (2); v A 1979 (3); v WI 1974 (2) 1980 (2); v NZ 1976 (3); v In 1978 (3) 1982 (6); *v E 1974 (3) 1978 (2) 1982 (1)*; *v A 1972 (2) 1976 (2) 1978 (2) 1981 (3) 1983 (2)*; *v WI 1976 (4)*; *v NZ 1972 (3) 1978 (3)*

Shafiq Ahmed 6: v E 1977 (3); v WI 1980 (2); *v E 1974 (1)*

Shafqat Rana 5: v E 1968 (2); v A 1964 (1); v NZ 1969 (2)

Shahid Israr 1: v NZ 1976

Shahid Mahboob 1: v In 1989

Shahid Mahmood 1: *v E 1962*

Shahid Saeed 1: v In 1989

Shakeel Ahmed 3: *v WI 1992 (1)*; *v Z 1994 (2)*

Sharpe, D. 3: v A 1959 (3)

Shoaib Mohammad 42: v E 1983 (1) 1987 (1); v A 1988 (3); v WI 1990 (3); v NZ 1984 (1) 1990 (3); v In 1985 (1) 1991 (3); v Z 1993 (3); *v E 1987 (4) 1992 (1)*; *v A 1989 (3)*; *v WI 1987 (3)*; *v NZ 1984 (1) 1988 (2)*; *v In 1983 (2) 1986 (3)*

Shuja-ud-Din 19: v E 1961 (2); v A 1959 (3); v WI 1958 (3); v NZ 1955 (3); v In 1954 (5); *v E 1954 (3)*

Sikander Bakht 26: v E 1977 (2); v WI 1980 (1); v NZ 1976 (1); v In 1978 (2) 1982 (1); *v E 1978 (3) 1982 (2)*; *v A 1978 (2) 1981 (3)*; *v WI 1976 (1)*; *v NZ 1978 (3)*; *v In 1979 (5)*

Tahir Naqqash 15: v A 1982 (3); v In 1982 (2); v SL 1981 (3); *v E 1982 (2)*; *v A 1983 (1)*; *v NZ 1984 (1)*; *v In 1983 (3)*

Talat Ali 10: v E 1972 (3); *v E 1978 (2)*; *v A 1972 (1)*; *v NZ 1972 (1) 1978 (3)*

Taslim Arif 6: v A 1979 (3); v WI 1980 (2); *v In 1979 (1)*

Tauseef Ahmed 34: v E 1983 (2) 1987 (2); v A 1979 (3) 1988 (3); v WI 1986 (3); v NZ 1984 (1) 1990 (2); v In 1984 (1); v SL 1981 (3) 1985 (1); v Z 1993 (1); *v E 1987 (2)*; *v A 1989 (3)*; *v NZ 1988 (1)*; *v In 1986 (4)*; *v SL 1985 (2)*

Waqar Hassan 21: v A 1956 (1) 1959 (3); v WI 1958 (1); v NZ 1955 (3); v In 1954 (5); *v E 1954 (4)*; *v WI 1957 (1)*; *v In 1952 (5)*

Waqar Younis 33: v A 1994 (2); v WI 1990 (3); v NZ 1990 (3); v In 1989 (2); v SL 1991 (3); v Z 1993 (3); *v E 1992 (5)*; *v A 1989 (3)*; *v WI 1992 (3)*; *v NZ 1992 (1) 1993 (3)*; *v SL 1994 (2)*

Wasim Akram 61: v E 1987 (2); v A 1994 (2); v WI 1986 (2) 1990 (3); v NZ 1990 (2); v In 1989 (4); v SL 1985 (3) 1991 (3); v Z 1993 (2); *v E 1987 (5) 1992 (4)*; *v A 1989 (3)*; *v SA 1994 (1)*; *v WI 1987 (3) 1992 (3)*; *v NZ 1984 (2) 1992 (1) 1993 (3)*; *v In 1986 (5)*; *v SL 1985 (3) 1994 (2)*; *v Z 1994 (3)*

Wasim Bari 81: v E 1968 (3) 1972 (3) 1977 (3); v A 1982 (3); v WI 1974 (2) 1980 (2); v NZ 1969 (3) 1976 (2); v In 1978 (3) 1982 (6); *v E 1967 (3) 1971 (3) 1974 (3) 1978 (3) 1982 (3)*; *v A 1972 (3) 1976 (3) 1978 (2) 1981 (3) 1983 (5)*; *v WI 1976 (5)*; *v NZ 1972 (3) 1978 (3)*; *v In 1979 (6) 1983 (3)*

Wasim Raja 57: v E 1972 (1) 1977 (3) 1983 (3); v A 1979 (3); v WI 1974 (2) 1980 (4); v NZ 1976 (1) 1984 (1); v In 1982 (1) 1984 (1); v SL 1981 (3); *v E 1974 (2) 1978 (3) 1982 (1); v A 1978 (1) 1981 (3) 1983 (2); v WI 1976 (5); v NZ 1972 (3) 1978 (3) 1984 (2); v In 1979 (6) 1983 (3)*

Wazir Mohammad 20: v A 1956 (1) 1959 (1); v WI 1958 (3); v NZ 1955 (2); v In 1954 (5); *v E 1954 (2); v WI 1957 (5); v In 1952 (1)*

Younis Ahmed 4: v NZ 1969 (2); *v In 1986 (2)*

Zaheer Abbas 78: v E 1972 (2) 1983 (3); v A 1979 (2) 1982 (3); v WI 1974 (2) 1980 (3); v NZ 1969 (1) 1976 (3) 1984 (3); v In 1978 (3) 1982 (6) 1984 (2); v SL 1981 (1) 1985 (2); *v E 1971 (3) 1974 (3) 1982 (3); v A 1972 (3) 1976 (3) 1978 (2) 1981 (2) 1983 (5); v WI 1976 (3); v NZ 1972 (3) 1978 (2) 1984 (2); v In 1979 (5) 1983 (3)*

Zahid Fazal 8: v A 1994 (2); v WI 1990 (2); v SL 1991 (3)

Zakir Khan 2: v In 1989 (1); *v SL 1985 (1)*

Zulfiqar Ahmed 9: v A 1956 (1); v NZ 1955 (3); *v E 1954 (2); v In 1952 (3)*

Zulqarnain 3: *v SL 1985 (3)*

SRI LANKA

Number of Test cricketers: 64

Ahangama, F. S. 3: v In 1985 (3)

Amalean, K. N. 2: v P 1985 (1); *v A 1987 (1)*

Amerasinghe, A. M. J. G. 2: v NZ 1983 (2)

Anurasiri, S. D. 17: v A 1992 (3); v WI 1993 (1); v NZ 1986 (1) 1992 (2); v P 1985 (2); *v E 1991 (1); v In 1986 (1) 1993 (3); v P 1991 (3)*

Atapattu, M. S. 3: v A 1992 (1); *v In 1990 (1) 1993 (1)*

Dassanayake, P. B. 11: v SA 1993 (3); v WI 1993 (1); v P 1994 (2); *v In 1993 (3); v Z 1994 (2)*

de Alwis, R. G. 11: v A 1982 (1); v NZ 1983 (3); v P 1985 (2); *v A 1987 (1); v NZ 1982 (1); v In 1986 (3)*

de Mel, A. L. F. 17: v E 1981 (1); v A 1982 (1); v In 1985 (3); v P 1985 (3); *v E 1984 (1); v In 1982 (1) 1986 (1); v P 1981 (3) 1985 (3)*

de Silva, A. M. 3: v E 1992 (1); v In 1993 (2)

de Silva, D. S. 12: v E 1981 (1); v A 1982 (1); v NZ 1983 (3); *v E 1984 (1); v NZ 1982 (2); v In 1982 (1); v P 1981 (3)*

de Silva, E. A. R. 10: v In 1985 (1); v P 1985 (1); *v A 1989 (2); v NZ 1990 (3); v In 1986 (3)*

de Silva, G. R. A. 4: v E 1981 (1); *v In 1982 (1); v P 1981 (2)*

de Silva, P. A. 48: v E 1992 (1); v A 1992 (1); v SA 1993 (3); v WI 1993 (1); v NZ 1992 (2); v In 1985 (3) 1993 (3); v P 1985 (3) 1994 (2); *v E 1984 (1) 1988 (1) 1991 (1); v A 1987 (1) 1989 (2); v NZ 1990 (3) 1994 (2); v In 1986 (3) 1990 (1) 1993 (3) 1991 (3); v P 1985 (3) 1991 (3); v Z 1994 (3)*

Dharmasena, H. D. P. K. 6: v SA 1993 (2); v P 1994 (2); *v Z 1994 (2)*

Dias, R. L. 20: v E 1981 (1); v A 1982 (1); v NZ 1983 (2) 1986 (1); v In 1985 (3); v P 1985 (1); *v E 1984 (1); v In 1982 (1) 1986 (3); v P 1981 (3) 1985 (3)*

Dunusinghe, C. I. 2: *v NZ 1994 (2)*

Fernando, E. R. N. S. 5: v A 1982 (1); v NZ 1983 (2); *v NZ 1982 (2)*

Goonatillake, H. M. 5: v E 1981 (1); *v In 1982 (1); v P 1981 (3)*

Gunasekera, Y. 2: *v NZ 1982 (2)*

Guneratne, R. P. W. 1: v A 1982

Gurusinha, A. P. 33: v E 1992 (1); v A 1992 (1); v SA 1993 (1); v NZ 1986 (1) 1992 (2); v In 1993 (3); v P 1985 (2) 1994 (1); *v E 1991 (1); v A 1989 (2); v NZ 1990 (3) 1994 (2); v In 1986 (3) 1990 (1); v P 1985 (3); v Z 1994 (3)*

Hathurusinghe, U. C. 18: v E 1992 (1); v A 1992 (3); v SA 1993 (1); v NZ 1992 (2); v In 1993 (3); *v E 1991 (1); v NZ 1990 (2); v P 1991 (3)*

Jayasekera, R. S. A. 1: *v P 1981*

Jayasuriya S. T. 16: v E 1992 (1); v A 1992 (2); v SA 1993 (2); v WI 1993 (1); v In 1993 (1); v P 1994 (1); *v E 1991 (1); v NZ 1990 (2); v In 1993 (1); v P 1991 (3); v Z 1994 (1)*

Jeganathan, S. 2: *v NZ 1982* (2)
John, V. B. 6: *v NZ 1983* (3); *v E 1984* (*1*); *v NZ 1982* (2)
Jurangpathy, B. R. 2: v In 1985 (1); *v In 1986* (*1*)

Kalpage, R. S. 8: *v SA 1993* (1); *v WI 1993* (1); v In 1993 (1); *v P 1994* (1); *v In 1993* (3); *v Z 1994* (*1*)
Kaluperuma, L. W. 2: v E 1981 (1); *v P 1981* (*1*)
Kaluperuma, S. M. S. 4: v NZ 1983 (3); *v A 1987* (*1*)
Kaluwitharana, R. S. 3: v A 1992 (2); v In 1993 (1)
Kuruppu, D. S. B. P. 4: v NZ 1986 (1); *v E 1988* (*1*) *1991* (*1*); *v A 1987* (*1*)
Kuruppuarachchi, A. K. 2: v NZ 1986 (1); v P 1985 (1)

Labrooy, G. F. 9: *v E 1988* (*1*); *v A 1987* (*1*) *1989* (2); *v NZ 1990* (3); *v In 1986* (*1*) *1990* (*1*)
Liyanage, D. K. 8: v A 1992 (2); v SA 1993 (1); v NZ 1992 (2); v In 1993 (2); *v In 1993* (*1*)

Madugalle, R. S. 21: v E 1981 (1); v A 1982 (1); v NZ 1983 (3) 1986 (1); v In 1985 (3); *v E 1984* (*1*) *1988* (*1*); *v A 1987* (*1*); *v NZ 1982* (2); *v In 1982* (*1*) *1986* (3) *1985* (3)
Madurasinghe, A. W. R. 3: v A 1992 (1); *v E 1988* (*1*); *v In 1990* (*1*)
Mahanama, R. S. 32: v E 1992 (1); v A 1992 (3); v SA 1993 (3); v WI 1993 (1); v NZ 1986 (1) 1992 (2); v In 1993 (3); v P 1985 (2) 1994 (2); *v E 1991* (*1*); *v A 1987* (*1*) *1989* (2); *v NZ 1990* (*1*); *v In 1990* (*1*) *1993* (3); *v P 1991* (2); *v Z 1994* (3)
Mendis, L. R. D. 24: v E 1981 (1); v A 1982 (1); v NZ 1983 (3) 1986 (1); v In 1985 (3); v P 1985 (3); *v E 1984* (*1*) *1988* (*1*); *v In 1982* (*1*) *1986* (3); *v P 1981* (3) *1985* (3)
Muralitharan, M. 18: v E 1992 (1); v A 1992 (2); v SA 1993 (1); v WI 1993 (1); v NZ 1992 (1); v In 1993 (2); v P 1994 (1); *v NZ 1994* (2); *v In 1993* (3); *v Z 1994* (2)

Pushpakumara, K. R. 5: v P 1994 (1); *v NZ 1994* (2); *v Z 1994* (2)

Ramanayake, C. P. H. 18: v E 1992 (1); v A 1992 (3); v SA 1993 (2); v NZ 1992 (1); v In 1993 (1); *v E 1988* (*1*) *1991* (*1*); *v A 1987* (*1*) *1989* (2); *v NZ 1990* (3); *v P 1991* (2)
Ranasinghe, A. N. 2: *v In 1982* (*1*); *v P 1981* (*1*)
Ranatunga, A. 56: v E 1981 (1) 1992 (1); v A 1982 (1) 1992 (3); v SA 1993 (3); v WI 1993 (1); v NZ 1983 (3) 1986 (1) 1992 (2); v In 1985 (3) 1993 (3); v P 1985 (3) 1994 (2); *v E 1984* (*1*) *1988* (*1*); *v A 1987* (*1*) *1989* (2); *v NZ 1990* (3) *1994* (2); *v In 1982* (*1*) *1986* (3) *1990* (*1*) *1993* (3); *v P 1981* (2) *1985* (3) *1991* (3); *v Z 1994* (3)
Ranatunga, D. 2: *v A 1989* (2)
Ranatunga, S. 6: v P 1994 (1); *v NZ 1994* (2); *v Z 1994* (3)
Ratnayake, R. J. 23: v A 1982 (1); v NZ 1983 (1) 1986 (1); v In 1985 (3); v P 1985 (1); *v E 1991* (*1*); *v A 1989* (*1*); *v NZ 1982* (2) *1990* (3); *v In 1986* (2) *1990* (*1*); *v P 1985* (3) *1991* (3)
Ratnayeke, J. R. 22: v NZ 1983 (2) 1986 (1); v P 1985 (3); *v E 1984* (*1*) *1988* (*1*); *v A 1987* (*1*) *1989* (2); *v NZ 1982* (2); *v In 1982* (*1*) *1986* (3); *v P 1981* (3) *1985* (3)

Samarasekera, M. A. R. 4: *v E 1988* (*1*); *v A 1989* (*1*); *v In 1990* (*1*); *v P 1991* (*1*)
Samaraweera, D. P. 7: v WI 1993 (1); v P 1994 (1); *v NZ 1994* (2); *v In 1993* (3)
Senanayake, C. P. 3: *v NZ 1990* (3)
Silva, S. A. R. 9: v In 1985 (3); v P 1985 (1); *v E 1984* (*1*) *1988* (*1*); *v NZ 1982* (*1*); *v P 1985* (2)

Tillekeratne, H. P. 30: v E 1992 (1); v A 1992 (1); v SA 1993 (3); v WI 1993 (1); v NZ 1992 (2); v In 1993 (3); v P 1994 (2); *v E 1991* (*1*); *v A 1989* (*1*); *v NZ 1990* (3) *1994* (2); *v In 1990* (*1*) *1993* (3); *v P 1991* (3); *v Z 1994* (3)

Vaas, W. P. U. J. C. 6: v P 1994 (1); *v NZ 1994* (2); *v Z 1994* (3)

Warnapura, B. 4: v E 1981 (1); *v In 1982* (*1*); *v P 1981* (2)
Warnaweera, K. P. J. 10: v E 1992 (1); v NZ 1992 (2); v In 1993 (3); v P 1985 (1) 1994 (1); *v NZ 1990* (*1*); *v In 1990* (*1*)
Weerasinghe, C. D. U. S. 1: v In 1985
Wettimuny, M. D. 2: *v NZ 1982* (2)
Wettimuny, S. 23: v E 1981 (1); v A 1982 (1); v NZ 1983 (3); v In 1985 (3); v P 1985 (3); *v E 1984* (*1*); *v NZ 1982* (2); *v In 1986* (3); *v P 1981* (3) *1985* (3)
Wickremasinghe, A. G. D. 3: v NZ 1992 (2); *v A 1989* (*1*)
Wickremasinghe, G. P. 17: v A 1992 (1); v SA 1993 (2); v WI 1993 (1); v In 1993 (3); v P 1994 (1); *v NZ 1994* (2); *v In 1993* (3); *v P 1991* (3); *v Z 1994* (2)
Wijegunawardene, K. I. W. 2: *v E 1991* (*1*); *v P 1991* (*1*)
Wijesuriya, R. G. C. E. 4: *v P 1981* (*1*) *1985* (3)
Wijetunge, P. K. 1: v SA 1993

ZIMBABWE

Number of Test cricketers: 27

Arnott, K. J. 4: v NZ 1992 (2); v In 1992 (1); *v In 1992 (1)*
Brain, D. H. 9: v NZ 1992 (1); v P 1994 (3); v SL 1994 (2); *v In 1992 (1); v P 1993 (2)*
Brandes, E. A. 6: v NZ 1992 (1); v In 1992 (1); *v In 1992 (1); v P 1993 (3)*
Briant, G. A. 1: *v In 1992*
Bruk-Jackson, G. K. 2: *v P 1993 (2)*
Burmester, M. G. 3: v NZ 1992 (2); v In 1992 (1)
Butchart, I. P. 1: v P 1994
Campbell, A. D. R. 13: v NZ 1992 (2); v In 1992 (1); v P 1994 (3); v SL 1994 (3); *v In 1992 (1); v P 1993 (3)*
Carlisle, S. V. 3: v P 1994 (3)
Crocker, G. J. 3: v NZ 1992 (2); v In 1992 (1)
Dekker, M. H. 8: v P 1994 (2); v SL 1994 (3); *v P 1993 (3)*
Flower, A. 13: v NZ 1992 (2); v In 1992 (1); v P 1994 (3); v SL 1994 (3); *v In 1992 (1); v P 1993 (3)*
Flower, G. W. 13: v NZ 1992 (2); v In 1992 (1); v P 1994 (3); v SL 1994 (3); *v In 1992 (1); v P 1993 (3)*
Houghton, D. L. 13: v NZ 1992 (2); v In 1992 (1); v P 1994 (3); v SL 1994 (3); *v In 1992 (1); v P 1993 (3)*
James, W. R. 4: v SL 1994 (3); *v P 1993 (1)*
Jarvis, M. P. 5: v NZ 1992 (1); v In 1992 (1); v SL 1994 (3)
Olonga, H. K. 1: v P 1994
Peall, S. G. 4: v SL 1994 (2); *v P 1993 (2)*
Pycroft, A. J. 3: v NZ 1992 (2); v In 1992 (1)
Ranchod, U. 1: *v In 1992*
Rennie, J. A. 3: v SL 1994 (1); *v P 1993 (2)*
Shah, A. H. 2: v NZ 1992 (1); *v In 1992 (1)*
Strang, B. C. 2: v P 1994 (2)
Strang, P. A. 4: v P 1994 (3); v SL 1994 (1)
Streak, H. H. 9: v P 1994 (3); v SL 1994 (3); *v P 1993 (3)*
Traicos, A. J. 4: v NZ 1992 (2); v In 1992 (1); *v In 1992 (1)*
Whittall, G. J. 9: v P 1994 (3); v SL 1994 (3); *v P 1993 (3)*

TWO COUNTRIES

Fourteen cricketers have appeared for two countries in Test matches, namely:

Amir Elahi, *India and Pakistan.*
J. J. Ferris, *Australia and England.*
S. C. Guillen, *West Indies and NZ.*
Gul Mahomed, *India and Pakistan.*
F. Hearne, *England and South Africa.*
A. H. Kardar, *India and Pakistan.*
W. E. Midwinter, *England and Australia.*

F. Mitchell, *England and South Africa.*
W. L. Murdoch, *Australia and England.*
Nawab of Pataudi, sen., *England and India.*
A. J. Traicos, *South Africa and Zimbabwe.*
A. E. Trott, *Australia and England.*
K. C. Wessels, *Australia and South Africa.*
S. M. J. Woods, *Australia and England.*

ENGLAND v REST OF THE WORLD

In 1970, owing to the cancellation of the South African tour to England, a series of matches was arranged, with the trappings of a full Test series, between England and the Rest of the World. It was played for the Guinness Trophy.

The following were awarded England caps for playing against the Rest of the World in that series, although the five matches played are now generally considered not to have rated as full Tests: D. L. Amiss (1), G. Boycott (2), D. J. Brown (2), M. C. Cowdrey (4), M. H. Denness (1), B. L. D'Oliveira (4), J. H. Edrich (1), K. W. R. Fletcher (4), A. W. Greig (3), R. Illingworth (5), A. Jones (1), A. P. E. Knott (5), P. Lever (1), B. W. Luckhurst (5), C. M. Old (2), P. J. Sharpe (1), K. Shuttleworth (1), J. A. Snow (5), D. L. Underwood (3), A. Ward (1), D. Wilson (2).

The following players represented the Rest of the World: E. J. Barlow (5), F. M. Engineer (2), L. R. Gibbs (4), Intikhab Alam (5), R. B. Kanhai (5), C. H. Lloyd (5), G. D. McKenzie (3), D. L. Murray (3), Mushtaq Mohammad (2), P. M. Pollock (1), R. G. Pollock (5), M. J. Procter (5), B. A. Richards (5), G. S. Sobers (5).

LIMITED-OVERS INTERNATIONAL CRICKETERS

The following players have appeared in limited-overs internationals but had not represented their countries in Test matches by August 28, 1995:

England I. J. Gould, G. W. Humpage, T. E. Jesty, J. D. Love, M. A. Lynch, M. J. Smith, S. D. Udal, C. M. Wells.

Australia G. A. Bishop, S. F. Graf, S. G. Law, R. J. McCurdy, K. H. MacLeay, R. T. Ponting, G. D. Porter, G. R. Robertson, J. D. Siddons, G. S. Trimble, A. K. Zesers.

South Africa D. J. Callaghan, D. N. Crookes, C. E. B. Rice, M. J. R. Rindel, D. B. Rundle, T. G. Shaw, E. O. Simons, E. L. R. Stewart, C. J. P. G. van Zyl, M. Yachad.

West Indies B. St A. Browne, V. C. Drakes, R. S. Gabriel, R. C. Haynes, R. I. C. Holder, M. R. Pydanna, P. A. Wallace.

New Zealand N. J. Astle, B. R. Blair, P. G. Coman, M. W. Douglas, L. K. Germon, B. G. Hadlee, R. T. Hart, R. L. Hayes, B. J. McKechnie, E. B. McSweeney, J. P. Millmow, R. G. Petrie, R. B. Reid, S. J. Roberts, L. W. Stott, R. J. Webb, J. W. Wilson.

G. R. Larsen appeared for New Zealand in 55 limited-overs internationals before making his Test debut.

India A. C. Bedade, Bhupinder Singh, sen., G. Bose, V. B. Chandrasekhar, U. Chatterjee, S. C. Ganguly, R. S. Ghai, S. C. Khanna, S. P. Mukherjee, A. K. Patel, B. K. V. Prasad, Randhir Singh, R. P. Singh, R. R. Singh, Sudhakar Rao, P. S. Vaidya.

Pakistan Aamer Hameed, Aamer Hanif, Arshad Khan, Arshad Pervez, Ghulam Ali, Haafiz Shahid, Hasan Jamil, Iqbal Sikandar, Irfan Bhatti, Javed Qadir, Mahmood Hamid, Mansoor Rana, Maqsood Rana, Masood Iqbal, Moin-ul-Atiq, Naeem Ahmed, Naeem Ashraf, Naseer Malik, Parvez Mir, Saadat Ali, Sajid Ali, Sajjad Akbar, Salim Pervez, Shakil Khan, Sohail Fazal, Tanvir Mehdi, Wasim Haider, Zafar Iqbal, Zahid Ahmed.

Sri Lanka U. U. Chandana, D. L. S. de Silva, G. N. de Silva, E. R. Fernando, T. L. Fernando, U. N. K. Fernando, J. C. Gamage, F. R. M. Goonatillake, A. A. W. Gunawardene, P. D. Heyn, S. A. Jayasinghe, S. H. U. Karnain, C. Mendis, M. Munasinghe, A. R. M. Opatha, S. P. Pasqual, K. G. Perera, H. S. M. Pieris, S. K. Ranasinghe, N. Ranatunga, N. L. K. Ratnayake, K. J. Silva, A. P. B. Tennekoon, M. H. Tissera, D. M. Vonhagt, A. P. Weerakkody, S. R. de S. Wettimuny, R. P. A. H. Wickremaratne.

Zimbabwe R. D. Brown, K. M. Curran, K. G. Duers, E. A. Essop-Adam, C. N. Evans, D. A. G. Fletcher, J. G. Heron, V. R. Hogg, G. C. Martin, M. A. Meman, G. A. Paterson, G. E. Peckover, P. W. E. Rawson, A. C. Waller.

CRICKET RECORDS

Amended by BILL FRINDALL to end of the 1995 season in England

Unless stated to be of a minor character, all records apply only to first-class cricket. This is traditionally considered to have started in 1815, after the Napoleonic War.

* Denotes not out or an unbroken partnership.

(A), (SA), (WI), (NZ), (I), (P), (SL) or (Z) indicates either the nationality of the player, or the country in which the record was made.

FIRST-CLASS RECORDS

BATTING RECORDS

BOWLING RECORDS

ALL-ROUND RECORDS

WICKET-KEEPING RECORDS

FIELDING RECORDS

TEAM RECORDS

TEST MATCH RECORDS

BATTING RECORDS

BOWLING RECORDS

ALL-ROUND RECORDS

WICKET-KEEPING RECORDS

FIELDING RECORDS

TEAM RECORDS

CAPTAINCY

UMPIRING

TEST SERIES

LIMITED-OVERS INTERNATIONAL RECORDS

MISCELLANEOUS

FIRST-CLASS RECORDS

BATTING RECORDS

HIGHEST INDIVIDUAL SCORES

501*	B. C. Lara	Warwickshire v Durham at Birmingham	1994
499	Hanif Mohammad	Karachi v Bahawalpur at Karachi	1958-59
452*	D. G. Bradman	NSW v Queensland at Sydney	1929-30
443*	B. B. Nimbalkar	Maharashtra v Kathiawar at Poona	1948-49

437	W. H. Ponsford	Victoria v Queensland at Melbourne	1927-28
429	W. H. Ponsford	Victoria v Tasmania at Melbourne	1922-23
428	Aftab Baloch	Sind v Baluchistan at Karachi	1973-74
424	A. C. MacLaren	Lancashire v Somerset at Taunton	1895
405*	G. A. Hick	Worcestershire v Somerset at Taunton	1988
385	B. Sutcliffe	Otago v Canterbury at Christchurch	1952-53
383	C. W. Gregory	NSW v Queensland at Brisbane	1906-07
377	S. V. Manjrekar	Bombay v Hyderabad at Bombay	1990-91
375	B. C. Lara	West Indies v England at St John's	1993-94
369	D. G. Bradman	South Australia v Tasmania at Adelaide	1935-36
366	N. H. Fairbrother	Lancashire v Surrey at The Oval	1990
366	M. V. Sridhar	Hyderabad v Andhra at Secunderabad	1993-94
365*	C. Hill	South Australia v NSW at Adelaide	1900-01
365*	G. S. Sobers	West Indies v Pakistan at Kingston	1957-58
364	L. Hutton	England v Australia at The Oval	1938
359*	V. M. Merchant	Bombay v Maharashtra at Bombay	1943-44
359	R. B. Simpson	NSW v Queensland at Brisbane	1963-64
357*	R. Abel	Surrey v Somerset at The Oval	1899
357	D. G. Bradman	South Australia v Victoria at Melbourne	1935-36
356	B. A. Richards	South Australia v Western Australia at Perth	1970-71
355*	G. R. Marsh	Western Australia v South Australia at Perth	1989-90
355	B. Sutcliffe	Otago v Auckland at Dunedin	1949-50
352	W. H. Ponsford	Victoria v NSW at Melbourne	1926-27
350	Rashid Israr	Habib Bank v National Bank at Lahore	1976-77
345	C. G. Macartney	Australians v Nottinghamshire at Nottingham	1921
344*	G. A. Headley	Jamaica v Lord Tennyson's XI at Kingston	1931-32
344	W. G. Grace	MCC v Kent at Canterbury	1876
343*	P. A. Perrin	Essex v Derbyshire at Chesterfield	1904
341	G. H. Hirst	Yorkshire v Leicestershire at Leicester	1905
340*	D. G. Bradman	NSW v Victoria at Sydney	1928-29
340	S. M. Gavaskar	Bombay v Bengal at Bombay	1981-82
338*	R. C. Blunt	Otago v Canterbury at Christchurch	1931-32
338	W. W. Read	Surrey v Oxford University at The Oval	1888
337*	Pervez Akhtar	Railways v Dera Ismail Khan at Lahore	1964-65
337*	D. J. Cullinan	Transvaal v Northern Transvaal at Johannesburg	1993-94
337†	Hanif Mohammad	Pakistan v West Indies at Bridgetown	1957-58
336*	W. R. Hammond	England v New Zealand at Auckland	1932-33
336	W. H. Ponsford	Victoria v South Australia at Melbourne	1927-28
334	D. G. Bradman	Australia v England at Leeds	1930
333	K. S. Duleepsinhji	Sussex v Northamptonshire at Hove	1930
333	G. A. Gooch	England v India at Lord's	1990
332	W. H. Ashdown	Kent v Essex at Brentwood	1934
331*	J. D. Robertson	Middlesex v Worcestershire at Worcester	1949
325*	H. L. Hendry	Victoria v New Zealanders at Melbourne	1925-26
325	A. Sandham	England v West Indies at Kingston	1929-30
325	C. L. Badcock	South Australia v Victoria at Adelaide	1935-36
324*	D. M. Jones	Victoria v South Australia at Melbourne	1994-95
324	J. B. Stollmeyer	Trinidad v British Guiana at Port-of-Spain	1946-47
324	Waheed Mirza	Karachi Whites v Quetta at Karachi	1976-77
323	A. L. Wadekar	Bombay v Mysore at Bombay	1966-67
322	E. Paynter	Lancashire v Sussex at Hove	1937
322	I. V. A. Richards	Somerset v Warwickshire at Taunton	1985
321	W. L. Murdoch	NSW v Victoria at Sydney	1881-82
320	R. Lamba	North Zone v West Zone at Bhilai	1987-88
319	Gul Mahomed	Baroda v Holkar at Baroda	1946-47
318*	W. G. Grace	Gloucestershire v Yorkshire at Cheltenham	1876
317	W. R. Hammond	Gloucestershire v Nottinghamshire at Gloucester	1936
317	K. R. Rutherford	New Zealanders v D. B. Close's XI at Scarborough	1986
316*	J. B. Hobbs	Surrey v Middlesex at Lord's	1926
316*	V. S. Hazare	Maharashtra v Baroda at Poona	1939-40
316	R. H. Moore	Hampshire v Warwickshire at Bournemouth	1937
315*	T. W. Hayward	Surrey v Lancashire at The Oval	1898

315*	P. Holmes	Yorkshire v Middlesex at Lord's	1925
315*	A. F. Kippax	NSW v Queensland at Sydney	1927-28
314*	C. L. Walcott	Barbados v Trinidad at Port-of-Spain	1945-46
313*	S. J. Cook	Somerset v Glamorgan at Cardiff	1990
313	H. Sutcliffe	Yorkshire v Essex at Leyton	1932
313	W. V. Raman	Tamil Nadu v Goa at Panjim	1988-89
312*	W. W. Keeton	Nottinghamshire v Middlesex at The Oval‡	1939
312*	J. M. Brearley	MCC Under-25 v North Zone at Peshawar	1966-67
312	R. Lamba	Delhi v Himachal Pradesh at Delhi	1994-95
311*	G. M. Turner	Worcestershire v Warwickshire at Worcester	1982
311	J. T. Brown	Yorkshire v Sussex at Sheffield	1897
311	R. B. Simpson	Australia v England at Manchester	1964
311	Javed Miandad	Karachi Whites v National Bank at Karachi	1974-75
310*	J. H. Edrich	England v New Zealand at Leeds	1965
310	H. Gimblett	Somerset v Sussex at Eastbourne	1948
309	V. S. Hazare	The Rest v Hindus at Bombay	1943-44
308*	F. M. M. Worrell	Barbados v Trinidad at Bridgetown	1943-44
307*	T. N. Lazard	Boland v W. Province at Worcester, Cape Province	1993-94
307	M. C. Cowdrey	MCC v South Australia at Adelaide	1962-63
307	R. M. Cowper	Australia v England at Melbourne	1965-66
306*	A. Ducat	Surrey v Oxford University at The Oval	1919
306*	E. A. B. Rowan	Transvaal v Natal at Johannesburg	1939-40
306*	D. W. Hookes	South Australia v Tasmania at Adelaide	1986-87
305*	F. E. Woolley	MCC v Tasmania at Hobart	1911-12
305*	F. R. Foster	Warwickshire v Worcestershire at Dudley	1914
305*	W. H. Ashdown	Kent v Derbyshire at Dover	1935
304*	A. W. Nourse	Natal v Transvaal at Johannesburg	1919-20
304*	P. H. Tarilton	Barbados v Trinidad at Bridgetown	1919-20
304*	E. D. Weekes	West Indians v Cambridge University at Cambridge	1950
304	R. M. Poore	Hampshire v Somerset at Taunton	1899
304	D. G. Bradman	Australia v England at Leeds	1934
303*	W. W. Armstrong	Australians v Somerset at Bath	1905
303*	Mushtaq Mohammad	Karachi Blues v Karachi University at Karachi	1967-68
303*	Abdul Azeem	Hyderabad v Tamil Nadu at Hyderabad	1986-87
302*	P. Holmes	Yorkshire v Hampshire at Portsmouth	1920
302*	W. R. Hammond	Gloucestershire v Glamorgan at Bristol	1934
302*	Arjan Kripal Singh	Tamil Nadu v Goa at Panjim	1988-89
302	W. R. Hammond	Gloucestershire v Glamorgan at Newport	1939
302	L. G. Rowe	West Indies v England at Bridgetown	1973-74
301*	E. H. Hendren	Middlesex v Worcestershire at Dudley	1933
301	W. G. Grace	Gloucestershire v Sussex at Bristol	1896
300*	V. T. Trumper	Australians v Sussex at Hove	1899
300*	F. B. Watson	Lancashire v Surrey at Manchester	1928
300*	Imtiaz Ahmed	PM's XI v Commonwealth XI at Bombay	1950-51
300	J. T. Brown	Yorkshire v Derbyshire at Chesterfield	1898
300	D. C. S. Compton	MCC v N. E. Transvaal at Benoni	1948-49
300	R. Subba Row	Northamptonshire v Surrey at The Oval	1958
300	Ramiz Raja	Allied Bank v Habib Bank at Lahore	1994-95

† *Hanif Mohammad batted for 16 hours 10 minutes – the longest innings in first-class cricket.*
‡ *Played at The Oval because Lord's was required for Eton v Harrow.*
Note: W. V. Raman (313) and Arjan Kripal Singh (302*) provide the only instance of two triple-hundreds in the same innings.

HIGHEST SCORE FOR EACH FIRST-CLASS COUNTY

Derbyshire	274	G. Davidson v Lancashire at Manchester	1896
Durham	204	J. E. Morris v Warwickshire at Birmingham	1994
Essex	343*	P. A. Perrin v Derbyshire at Chesterfield	1904
Glamorgan	287*	D. E. Davies v Gloucestershire at Newport	1939
Gloucestershire	318*	W. G. Grace v Yorkshire at Cheltenham	1876

Hampshire	316	R. H. Moore v Warwickshire at Bournemouth	1937
Kent	332	W. H. Ashdown v Essex at Brentwood	1934
Lancashire	424	A. C. MacLaren v Somerset at Taunton	1895
Leicestershire	261	P. V. Simmons v Northamptonshire at Leicester ..	1994
Middlesex	331*	J. D. Robertson v Worcestershire at Worcester....	1949
Northamptonshire	300	R. Subba Row v Surrey at The Oval	1958
Nottinghamshire	312*	W. W. Keeton v Middlesex at The Oval†	1939
Somerset	322	I. V. A. Richards v Warwickshire at Taunton	1985
Surrey	357*	R. Abel v Somerset at The Oval	1899
Sussex	333	K. S. Duleepsinhji v Northamptonshire at Hove ..	1930
Warwickshire	501*	B. C. Lara v Durham at Birmingham	1994
Worcestershire	405*	G. A. Hick v Somerset at Taunton	1988
Yorkshire	341	G. H. Hirst v Leicestershire at Leicester	1905

† *Played at The Oval because Lord's was required for Eton v Harrow.*

HIGHEST SCORE AGAINST EACH FIRST-CLASS COUNTY

Derbyshire	343*	P. A. Perrin (Essex) at Chesterfield	1904
Durham	501*	B. C. Lara (Warwickshire) at Birmingham	1994
Essex	332	W. H. Ashdown (Kent) at Brentwood	1934
Glamorgan	313*	S. J. Cook (Somerset) at Cardiff	1990
Gloucestershire	296	A. O. Jones (Nottinghamshire) at Nottingham	1903
Hampshire	302*	P. Holmes (Yorkshire) at Portsmouth............	1920
Kent	344	W. G. Grace (MCC) at Canterbury	1876
Lancashire	315*	T. W. Hayward (Surrey) at The Oval........	1898
Leicestershire	341	G. H. Hirst (Yorkshire) at Leicester	1905
Middlesex	316*	J. B. Hobbs (Surrey) at Lord's	1926
Northamptonshire	333	K. S. Duleepsinhji (Sussex) at Hove	1930
Nottinghamshire	345	C. G. Macartney (Australians) at Nottingham	1921
Somerset	424	A. C. MacLaren (Lancashire) at Taunton	1895
Surrey	366	N. H. Fairbrother (Lancashire) at The Oval	1990
Sussex	322	E. Paynter (Lancashire) at Hove	1937
Warwickshire	322	I. V. A. Richards (Somerset) at Taunton	1985
Worcestershire	331*	J. D. Robertson (Middlesex) at Worcester	1949
Yorkshire	318*	W. G. Grace (Gloucestershire) at Cheltenham	1876

DOUBLE-HUNDRED ON DEBUT

227	T. Marsden	Sheffield & Leicester v Nottingham at Sheffield ..	1826
207	N. F. Callaway†	New South Wales v Queensland at Sydney	1914-15
240	W. F. E. Marx	Transvaal v Griqualand West at Johannesburg ..	1920-21
200*	A. Maynard	Trinidad v MCC at Port-of-Spain..............	1934-35
232*	S. J. E. Loxton	Victoria v Queensland at Melbourne	1946-47
215*	G. H. G. Doggart	Cambridge University v Lancashire at Cambridge	1948
202	J. Hallebone	Victoria v Tasmania at Melbourne	1951-52
230	G. R. Viswanath	Mysore v Andhra at Vijayawada	1967-68
260	A. A. Muzumdar	Bombay v Haryana at Faridabad	1993-94

† *In his only first-class innings. He was killed in action in France in 1917.*

TWO SEPARATE HUNDREDS ON DEBUT

148	and 111	A. R. Morris	New South Wales v Queensland at Sydney ..	1940-41
152	and 102*	N. J. Contractor	Gujarat v Baroda at Baroda	1952-53
132*	and 110	Aamer Malik	Lahore "A" v Railways at Lahore	1979-80

Notes: J. S. Solomon, British Guiana, scored a hundred in each of his first three innings in first-class cricket: 114* v Jamaica; 108 v Barbados in 1956-57; 121 v Pakistanis in 1957-58.

R. Watson-Smith, Border, scored 310 runs before he was dismissed in first-class cricket, including not-out centuries in his first two innings: 183* v Orange Free State and 125* v Griqualand West in 1969-70.

G. R. Viswanath and D. M. Wellham alone have scored a hundred on their debut in both first-class cricket and Test cricket. Viswanath scored 230 for Mysore v Andhra in 1967-68 and 137 for India v Australia in 1969-70. Wellham scored 100 for New South Wales v Victoria in 1980-81 and 103 for Australia v England in 1981.

HUNDRED ON DEBUT IN BRITAIN

(The following list does not include instances of players who have previously appeared in first-class cricket outside the British Isles or who performed the feat before 1965. Full lists of earlier instances are in *Wisdens* prior to 1984.)

108	D. R. Shepherd	Gloucestershire v Oxford University at Oxford.....	1965
110*	A. J. Harvey-Walker†	Derbyshire v Oxford University at Burton upon Trent	1971
173	J. Whitehouse	Warwickshire v Oxford University at Oxford......	1971
106	J. B. Turner	Minor Counties v Pakistanis at Jesmond..........	1974
112	J. A. Claughton†	Oxford University v Gloucestershire at Oxford.....	1976
100*	A. W. Lilley†	Essex v Nottinghamshire at Nottingham...........	1978
146*	J. S. Johnson	Minor Counties v Indians at Wellington	1979
110	N. R. Taylor	Kent v Sri Lankans at Canterbury...............	1979
146*	D. G. Aslett	Kent v Hampshire at Bournemouth	1981
116	M. D. Moxon†	Yorkshire v Essex at Leeds.....................	1981
100	D. A. Banks	Worcestershire v Oxford University at Oxford	1983
122	A. A. Metcalfe	Yorkshire v Nottinghamshire at Bradford	1983
117*	K. T. Medlycott‡ }	Surrey v Cambridge University at Banstead	1984
101*	N. J. Falkner ‡ }		
106	A. C. Storie†	Northamptonshire v Hampshire at Northampton ...	1985
102	M. P. Maynard	Glamorgan v Yorkshire at Swansea	1985
117*	R. J. Bartlett	Somerset v Oxford University at Oxford	1986
100*	P. D. Bowler	Leicestershire v Hampshire at Leicester	1986
145	I. L. Philip	Scotland v Ireland at Glasgow	1986
114*	P. D. Atkins	Surrey v Cambridge University at The Oval.......	1988
100	B. M. W. Patterson	Scotland v Ireland at Dumfries.................	1988
116*	J. J. B. Lewis	Essex v Surrey at The Oval....................	1990
117	J. D. Glendenen	Durham v Oxford University at Oxford	1992
109	J. R. Wileman	Nottinghamshire v Cambridge U. at Nottingham ..	1992
123	A. J. Hollioake†	Surrey v Derbyshire at Ilkeston	1993

† *In his second innings.*
‡ *The only instance in England of two players performing the feat in the same match.*

TWO DOUBLE-HUNDREDS IN A MATCH

A. E. Fagg........	244	202*	Kent v Essex at Colchester		1938

TRIPLE-HUNDRED AND HUNDRED IN A MATCH

G. A. Gooch	333	123	England v India at Lord's		1990

DOUBLE-HUNDRED AND HUNDRED IN A MATCH

C. B. Fry	125	229	Sussex v Surrey at Hove		1900
W. W. Armstrong	157*	245	Victoria v South Australia at Melbourne	.	1920-21
H. T. W. Hardinge	207	102*	Kent v Surrey at Blackheath	.	1921
C. P. Mead	113	224	Hampshire v Sussex at Horsham		1921
K. S. Duleepsinhji	115	246	Sussex v Kent at Hastings		1929
D. G. Bradman	124	225	Woodfull's XI v Ryder's XI at Sydney		1929-30
B. Sutcliffe	243	100*	New Zealanders v Essex at Southend	...	1949
M. R. Hallam	210*	157	Leicestershire v Glamorgan at Leicester	.	1959
M. R. Hallam	203*	143*	Leicestershire v Sussex at Worthing	....	1961
Hanumant Singh	109	213*	Rajasthan v Bombay at Bombay	...	1966-67
Salah-ud-Din	256	102*	Karachi v East Pakistan at Karachi	...	1968-69
K. D. Walters	242	103	Australia v West Indies at Sydney	....	1968-69
S. M. Gavaskar	124	220	India v West Indies at Port-of-Spain	...	1970-71
L. G. Rowe	214	100*	West Indies v New Zealand at Kingston		1971-72
G. S. Chappell	247*	133	Australia v New Zealand at Wellington	.	1973-74
L. Baichan	216*	102	Berbice v Demerara at Georgetown	....	1973-74
Zaheer Abbas	216*	156*	Gloucestershire v Surrey at The Oval	...	1976
Zaheer Abbas	230*	104*	Gloucestershire v Kent at Canterbury	...	1976
Zaheer Abbas	205*	108*	Gloucestershire v Sussex at Cheltenham	.	1977
Saadat Ali	141	222	Income Tax v Multan at Multan	....	1977-78
Talat Ali	214*	104	PIA v Punjab at Lahore	....	1978-79
Shafiq Ahmad	129	217*	National Bank v MCB at Karachi	...	1978-79
D. W. Randall	209	146	Notts. v Middlesex at Nottingham	...	1979
Zaheer Abbas	215*	150*	Gloucestershire v Somerset at Bath	....	1981
Qasim Omar	210*	110	MCB v Lahore at Lahore	....	1982-83
A. I. Kallicharran	200*	117*	Warwicks. v Northants at Birmingham	.	1984
Rizwan-uz-Zaman	139	217*	PIA v PACO at Lahore	....	1989-90
G. A. Hick	252*	100*	Worcs. v Glamorgan at Abergavenny	.	1990
N. R. Taylor	204	142	Kent v Surrey at Canterbury	......	1990
N. R. Taylor	111	203*	Kent v Sussex at Hove	....	1991
W. V. Raman	226	120	Tamil Nadu v Haryana at Faridabad	.	1991-92
A. J. Lamb	209	107	Northants v Warwicks. at Northampton	.	1992
G. A. Gooch	101	205	Essex v Worcestershire at Worcester	....	1994
P. A. de Silva	255	116	Kent v Derbyshire at Maidstone	....	1995

TWO SEPARATE HUNDREDS IN A MATCH

Eight times: Zaheer Abbas.

Seven times: W. R. Hammond.

Six times: J. B. Hobbs, G. M. Turner.

Five times: C. B. Fry, G. A. Gooch.

Four times: D. G. Bradman, G. S. Chappell, J. H. Edrich, L. B. Fishlock, T. W. Graveney, C. G. Greenidge, H. T. W. Hardinge, E. H. Hendren, Javed Miandad, G. L. Jessop, H. Morris, P. A. Perrin, B. Sutcliffe, H. Sutcliffe.

Three times: Agha Zahid, L. E. G. Ames, G. Boycott, I. M. Chappell, D. C. S. Compton, S. J. Cook, M. C. Cowdrey, D. Denton, K. S. Duleepsinhji, R. E. Foster, R. C. Fredericks, S. M. Gavaskar, W. G. Grace, G. Gunn, M. R. Hallam, Hanif Mohammad, M. J. Harris, T. W. Hayward, V. S. Hazare, D. W. Hookes, L. Hutton, A. Jones, D. M. Jones, P. N. Kirsten, R. B. McCosker, P. B. H. May, C. P. Mead, Rizwan-uz-Zaman, R. T. Robinson, A. C. Russell, Sadiq Mohammad, J. T. Tyldesley, K. C. Wessels.

Twice: Ali Zia, D. L. Amiss, C. W. J. Athey, L. Baichan, Basit Ali, D. C. Boon, A. R. Border, B. J. T. Bosanquet, R. J. Boyd-Moss, A. R. Butcher, M. D. Crowe, C. C. Dacre, G. M. Emmett, A. E. Fagg, L. E. Favell, H. Gimblett, C. Hallows, R. A. Hamence, A. L. Hassett, M. L. Hayden, D. L. Haynes, G. A. Headley, G. A. Hick, D. M. Jones, A. I. Kallicharran, J. H. King, A. F. Kippax, A. J. Lamb, J. G. Langridge, S. G. Law, H. W. Lee, E. Lester, C. B. Llewellyn, C. G. Macartney, M. P. Maynard, C. A. Milton, T. M. Moody, A. R. Morris, P. H. Parfitt, M. H. Parmar, Nawab of Pataudi jun., E. Paynter, C. Pinch, R. G. Pollock, R. M. Prideaux, Qasim Omar, M. R. Ramprakash, W. Rhodes, B. A. Richards, I. V. A. Richards, Pankaj Roy, Salim Malik, James Seymour, Shafiq Ahmad, R. B. Simpson, C. L. Smith, G. S. Sobers, M. A. Taylor, N. R. Taylor, E. Tyldesley, C. L. Walcott, T. R. Ward, W. W. Whysall, G. N. Yallop.

Notes: W. Lambert scored 107 and 157 for Sussex v Epsom at Lord's in 1817 and it was not until W. G. Grace made 130 and 102* for South of the Thames v North of the Thames at Canterbury in 1868 that the feat was repeated.

C. J. B. Wood, 107* and 117* for Leicestershire v Yorkshire at Bradford in 1911, and S. J. Cook, 120* and 131* for Somerset v Nottinghamshire at Nottingham in 1989, are alone in carrying their bats and scoring hundreds in each innings.

FOUR HUNDREDS OR MORE IN SUCCESSION

Six in succession: D. G. Bradman 1938-39; C. B. Fry 1901; M. J. Procter 1970-71.

Five in succession: B. C. Lara 1993-94/1994; E. D. Weekes 1955-56.

Four in succession: C. W. J. Athey 1987; M. Azharuddin 1984-85; M. G. Bevan 1990-91; A. R. Border 1985; D. G. Bradman 1931-32, 1948/1948-49; D. C. S. Compton 1946-47; N. J. Contractor 1957-58; S. J. Cook 1989; K. S. Duleepsinhji 1931; C. B. Fry 1911; C. G. Greenidge 1986; W. R. Hammond 1936-37, 1945/1946; H. T. W. Hardinge 1913; T. W. Hayward 1906; J. B. Hobbs 1920, 1925; D. W. Hookes 1976-77; Ijaz Ahmed, jun. 1994-95; P. N. Kirsten 1976-77; J. G. Langridge 1949; C. G. Macartney 1921; K. S. McEwan 1977; P. B. H. May 1956-57; V. M. Merchant 1941-42; A. Mitchell 1933; Nawab of Pataudi sen. 1931; Rizwan-uz-Zaman 1989-90; L. G. Rowe 1971-72; Pankaj Roy 1962-63; Sadiq Mohammad 1976; Saeed Ahmed 1961-62; M. V. Sridhar 1990-91/1991-92; H. Sutcliffe 1931, 1939; S. R. Tendulkar 1994-95; E. Tyldesley 1926; W. W. Whysall 1930; F. E. Woolley 1929; Zaheer Abbas 1970-71, 1982-83.

Notes: T. W. Hayward (Surrey v Nottinghamshire and Leicestershire) and D. W. Hookes (South Australia v Queensland and New South Wales) are the only players listed above to score two hundreds in two successive matches. Hayward scored his in six days, June 4-9, 1906.

The most fifties in consecutive innings is ten – by E. Tyldesley in 1926, by D. G. Bradman in the 1947-48 and 1948 seasons and by R. S. Kaluwitharana in 1994-95.

MOST HUNDREDS IN A SEASON

Eighteen: D. C. S. Compton 1947.

Sixteen: J. B. Hobbs 1925.

Fifteen: W. R. Hammond 1938.

Fourteen: H. Sutcliffe 1932.

Thirteen: G. Boycott 1971, D. G. Bradman 1938, C. B. Fry 1901, W. R. Hammond 1933 and 1937, T. W. Hayward 1906, E. H. Hendren 1923, 1927 and 1928, C. P. Mead 1928, H. Sutcliffe 1928 and 1931.

Since 1969 (excluding G. Boycott – above)

Twelve: G. A. Gooch 1990.

Eleven: S. J. Cook 1991, Zaheer Abbas 1976.

Ten: G. A. Hick 1988, H. Morris 1990, M. R. Ramprakash 1995, G. M. Turner 1970, Zaheer Abbas 1981.

MOST DOUBLE-HUNDREDS IN A SEASON

Six: D. G. Bradman 1930.

Five: K. S. Ranjitsinhji 1900; E. D. Weekes 1950.

Four: Arun Lal 1986-87; C. B. Fry 1901; W. R. Hammond 1933, 1934; E. H. Hendren 1929-30; V. M. Merchant 1944-45; G. M. Turner 1971-72.

Three: L. E. G. Ames 1933; Arshad Pervez 1977-78; D. G. Bradman 1930-31, 1931-32, 1934, 1935-36, 1936-37, 1938, 1939-40; W. J. Edrich 1947; C. B. Fry 1903, 1904; M. W. Gatting 1994; G. A. Gooch 1994; W. R. Hammond 1928, 1928-29, 1932-33, 1938; J. Hardstaff jun. 1937, 1947; V. S. Hazare 1943-44; E. H. Hendren 1925; J. B. Hobbs 1914, 1926; L. Hutton 1949; D. M. Jones 1991-92; A. I. Kallicharran 1982; V. G. Kambli 1992-93; P. N. Kirsten 1980; R. S. Modi 1944-45; Nawab of Pataudi sen. 1933; W. H. Ponsford 1927-28, 1934; W. V. Raman 1988-89; M. R. Ramprakash 1995; K. S. Ranjitsinhji 1901; I. V. A. Richards 1977; R. B. Simpson 1963-64; P. R. Umrigar 1952, 1959; F. B. Watson 1928.

MOST HUNDREDS IN A CAREER

(35 or more)

		100s	Total Inns	100th 100 Season	100th 100 Inns	400+	300+	200+
1	J. B. Hobbs	197	1,315	1923	821	0	1	16
2	E. H. Hendren	170	1,300	1928-29	740	0	1	22
3	W. R. Hammond	167	1,005	1935	679	0	4	36
4	C. P. Mead	153	1,340	1927	892	0	0	13
5	G. Boycott	151	1,014	1977	645	0	0	10
6	H. Sutcliffe	149	1,088	1932	700	0	1	17
7	F. E. Woolley	145	1,532	1929	1,031	0	1	9
8	L. Hutton	129	814	1951	619	0	1	11
9	W. G. Grace	126	1,493	1895	1,113	0	3	13
10	D. C. S. Compton	123	839	1952	552	0	1	9
11	T. W. Graveney	122	1,223	1964	940	0	0	7
12	**G. A. Gooch**	**120**	**941**	**1992-93**	**820**	**0**	**1**	**12**
13	D. G. Bradman	117	338	1947-48	295	1	6	37
14	I. V. A. Richards	114	796	1988-89	658	0	1	10
15	Zaheer Abbas	108	768	1982-83	658	0	0	10
16	A. Sandham	107	1,000	1935	871	0	1	11
	M. C. Cowdrey	107	1,130	1973	1,035	0	1	3
18	T. W. Hayward	104	1,138	1913	1,076	0	1	8
19	J. H. Edrich	103	979	1977	945	0	1	4
	G. M. Turner	103	792	1982	779	0	1	10
21	E. Tyldesley	102	961	1934	919	0	0	7
	L. E. G. Ames	102	951	1950	915	0	0	9
	D. L. Amiss	102	1,139	1986	1,081	0	0	3

*E. H. Hendren, D. G. Bradman and I. V. A. Richards scored their 100th hundreds in Australia,
G. A. Gooch scored his in India. His record includes his century in South Africa in 1981-82, which is
no longer accepted by ICC. Zaheer Abbas scored his in Pakistan. Zaheer Abbas and G. Boycott did
so in Test matches.*

Most double-hundreds scored by batsmen not included in the above list:

Sixteen: C. B. Fry.
Fourteen: C. G. Greenidge, K. S. Ranjitsinhji.
Thirteen: W. H. Ponsford (including two 400s and two 300s), J. T. Tyldesley.
Twelve: P. Holmes, Javed Miandad, R. B. Simpson.
Eleven: J. W. Hearne, V. M. Merchant.
Ten: S. M. Gavaskar, J. Hardstaff, jun., V. S. Hazare, A. Shrewsbury, R. T. Simpson.

J. W. Hearne	96	
C. B. Fry	94	
C. G. Greenidge	92	
M. W. Gatting	**89**	
A. J. Lamb	**89**	
A. I. Kallicharran	87	
W. J. Edrich	86	
G. S. Sobers	86	
J. T. Tyldesley	86	
P. B. H. May	85	
R. E. S. Wyatt	85	
G. A. Hick	**84**	
J. Hardstaff, jun.	83	
R. B. Kanhai	83	
S. M. Gavaskar	81	
Javed Miandad	80	
M. Leyland	80	
B. A. Richards	80	
C. H. Lloyd	79	
K. F. Barrington	76	
J. G. Langridge	76	
C. Washbrook	76	
H. T. W. Hardinge	75	
R. Abel	74	
G. S. Chappell	74	
D. Kenyon	74	
K. S. McEwan	74	
Majid Khan	73	
Mushtaq Mohammad	72	
J. O'Connor	72	
W. G. Quaife	72	
K. S. Ranjitsinhji	72	
D. Brookes	71	
A. C. Russell	71	
A. R. Border	**70**	
M. D. Crowe	**69**	
D. Denton	69	
M. J. K. Smith	69	
R. E. Marshall	68	
R. N. Harvey	67	
P. Holmes	67	
J. D. Robertson	67	

P. A. Perrin	66	
S. J. Cook	**64**	
R. G. Pollock	64	
R. T. Simpson	64	
K. W. R. Fletcher	63	
G. Gunn	62	
D. L. Haynes	**60**	
V. S. Hazare	60	
G. H. Hirst	60	
R. B. Simpson	60	
P. F. Warner	60	
I. M. Chappell	59	
A. L. Hassett	59	
W. Larkins	**59**	
A. Shrewsbury	59	
J. G. Wright	59	
A. E. Fagg	58	
P. H. Parfitt	58	
W. Rhodes	58	
R. T. Robinson	**58**	
K. C. Wessels	**58**	
M. E. Waugh	**57**	
L. B. Fishlock	56	
A. Jones	56	
C. A. Milton	56	
D. C. Boon	**55**	
C. Hallows	55	
Hanif Mohammad	55	
D. B. Vengsarkar	55	
W. Watson	55	
D. J. Insole	54	
W. W. Keeton	54	
W. Bardsley	53	
B. F. Davison	53	
A. E. Dipper	53	
D. I. Gower	53	
G. L. Jessop	53	
P. N. Kirsten	**53**	
James Seymour	53	
Shafiq Ahmad	53	
E. H. Bowley	52	
D. B. Close	52	
A. Ducat	52	
D. W. Randall	52	
C. W. J. Athey	**51**	
E. R. Dexter	51	
J. M. Parks	51	
W. W. Whysall	51	
B. C. Broad	50	
G. Cox, jun.	50	
H. E. Dollery	50	
K. S. Duleepsinhji	50	
H. Gimblett	50	
W. M. Lawry	50	
Sadiq Mohammad	50	
F. B. Watson	50	
C. G. Macartney	49	
M. J. Stewart	49	
K. G. Suttle	49	
P. R. Umrigar	49	

W. M. Woodfull	49	
C. J. Barnett	48	
M. R. Benson	**48**	
W. Gunn	48	
E. G. Hayes	48	
B. W. Luckhurst	48	
M. J. Procter	48	
C. E. B. Rice	48	
R. A. Smith	**48**	
C. J. Tavaré	48	
A. C. MacLaren	47	
P. W. G. Parker	47	
W. H. Ponsford	47	
C. L. Smith	47	
K. J. Barnett	**46**	
A. R. Butcher	46	
J. Iddon	46	
A. R. Morris	46	
C. T. Radley	46	
Younis Ahmed	46	
W. W. Armstrong	45	
Asif Iqbal	45	
L. G. Berry	45	
J. M. Brearley	45	
A. W. Carr	45	
C. Hill	45	
N. C. O'Neill	45	
E. Paynter	45	
Rev. D. S. Sheppard	45	
K. D. Walters	45	
H. H. I. Gibbons	44	
V. M. Merchant	44	
A. Mitchell	44	
P. E. Richardson	44	
B. Sutcliffe	44	
G. R. Viswanath	44	
P. Willey	44	
E. J. Barlow	43	
B. L. D'Oliveira	43	
J. H. Hampshire	43	
D. M. Jones	**43**	
A. F. Kippax	43	
J. W. H. Makepeace	43	
T. M. Moody	**43**	
H. Morris	**43**	
James Langridge	42	
J. E. Morris	**42**	
Mudassar Nazar	42	
H. W. Parks	42	
T. F. Shepherd	42	
N. R. Taylor	**42**	
V. T. Trumper	42	
M. J. Harris	41	
G. D. Mendis	41	
K. R. Miller	41	
M. D. Moxon	**41**	
A. D. Nourse	41	
J. H. Parks	41	
R. M. Prideaux	41	
G. Pullar	41	

W. E. Russell	41	
A. P. Wells	**41**	
M. Azharuddin	**40**	
R. C. Fredericks	40	
J. Gunn	40	
M. J. Smith	40	
C. L. Walcott	40	
D. M. Young	40	
Arshad Pervez	39	
W. H. Ashdown	39	
J. B. Bolus	39	
W. A. Brown	39	
R. J. Gregory	39	
M. A. Lynch	**39**	
W. R. D. Payton	39	
J. R. Reid	39	
F. M. M. Worrell	39	
M. A. Atherton	**38**	
R. J. Bailey	**38**	
I. T. Botham	38	
F. L. Bowley	38	
P. J. Burge	38	
J. F. Crapp	38	
D. Lloyd	38	
V. L. Manjrekar	38	
A. W. Nourse	38	
N. Oldfield	38	
Rev. J. H. Parsons	38	
W. W. Read	38	
J. Sharp	38	
V. P. Terry	**38**	
L. J. Todd	38	
J. Arnold	37	
G. Brown	37	
G. Cook	37	
T. S. Curtis	**37**	
G. M. Emmett	37	
H. W. Lee	37	
M. A. Noble	37	
B. P. Patel	37	
R. B. Richardson	**37**	
Salim Malik	**37**	
H. S. Squires	37	
R. T. Virgin	37	
C. J. B. Wood	37	
N. F. Armstrong	36	
G. Fowler	36	
M. C. J. Nicholas	**36**	
E. Oldroyd	36	
W. Place	36	
Rizwan-uz-Zaman	**36**	
A. L. Wadekar	36	
E. D. Weekes	36	
C. S. Dempster	35	
D. R. Jardine	35	
T. E. Jesty	35	
B. H. Valentine	35	
G. M. Wood	35	

Bold type denotes those who played in 1994-95 and 1995 seasons.

3,000 RUNS IN A SEASON

	Season	I	NO	R	HS	100s	Avge
D. C. S. Compton	1947	50	8	3,816	246	18	90.85
W. J. Edrich	1947	52	8	3,539	267*	12	80.43
T. W. Hayward	1906	61	8	3,518	219	13	66.37
L. Hutton	1949	56	6	3,429	269*	12	68.58
F. E. Woolley........	1928	59	4	3,352	198	12	60.94
H. Sutcliffe	1932	52	7	3,336	313	14	74.13
W. R. Hammond.....	1933	54	5	3,323	264	13	67.81
E. H. Hendren	1928	54	7	3,311	209*	13	70.44
R. Abel.............	1901	68	8	3,309	247	7	55.15
W. R. Hammond.....	1937	55	5	3,252	217	13	65.04
M. J. K. Smith	1959	67	11	3,245	200*	8	57.94
E. H. Hendren	1933	65	9	3,186	301*	11	56.89
C. P. Mead	1921	52	6	3,179	280*	10	69.10
T. W. Hayward	1904	63	5	3,170	203	11	54.65
K. S. Ranjitsinhji....	1899	58	8	3,159	197	8	63.18
C. B. Fry	1901	43	3	3,147	244	13	78.67
K. S. Ranjitsinhji....	1900	40	5	3,065	275	11	87.57
L. E. G. Ames	1933	57	5	3,058	295	9	58.80
J. T. Tyldesley	1901	60	5	3,041	221	9	55.29
C. P. Mead	1928	50	10	3,027	180	13	75.67
J. B. Hobbs	1925	48	5	3,024	266*	16	70.32
E. Tyldesley	1928	48	10	3,024	242	10	79.57
W. E. Alley	1961	64	11	3,019	221*	11	56.96
W. R. Hammond.....	1938	42	2	3,011	271	15	75.27
E. H. Hendren	1923	51	12	3,010	200*	13	77.17
H. Sutcliffe	1931	42	11	3,006	230	11	96.96
J. H. Parks	1937	63	4	3,003	168	11	50.89
H. Sutcliffe	1928	44	5	3,002	228	13	76.97

Notes: W. G. Grace scored 2,739 runs in 1871 – the first batsman to reach 2,000 runs in a season. He made ten hundreds and twice exceeded 200, with an average of 78.25 in all first-class matches.

The highest aggregate in a season since the reduction of County Championship matches in 1969 is 2,755 by S. J. Cook (42 innings) in 1991.

2,000 RUNS IN A SEASON

Since Reduction of Championship Matches in 1969

Five times: G. A. Gooch 2,746 (1990), 2,559 (1984), 2,324 (1988), 2,208 (1985), 2,023 (1993).
Three times: D. L. Amiss 2,239 (1984), 2,110 (1976), 2,030 (1978); S. J. Cook 2,755 (1991), 2,608 (1990), 2,241 (1989); M. W. Gatting 2,257 (1984), 2,057 (1991), 2,000 (1992); G. A. Hick 2,713 (1988), 2,347 (1990), 2,004 (1986); G. M. Turner 2,416 (1973), 2,379 (1970), 2,101 (1981).
Twice: G. Boycott 2,503 (1971), 2,051 (1970); J. H. Edrich 2,238 (1969), 2,031 (1971); A. I. Kallicharran 2,301 (1984), 2,120 (1982); Zaheer Abbas 2,554 (1976), 2,306 (1981).
Once: M. Azharuddin 2,016 (1991); J. B. Bolus 2,143 (1970); P. D. Bowler 2,044 (1992); B. C. Broad 2,226 (1990); A. R. Butcher 2,116 (1990); C. G. Greenidge 2,035 (1986); M. J. Harris 2,238 (1971); D. L. Haynes 2,346 (1990); Javed Miandad 2,083 (1981); A. J. Lamb 2,049 (1981); B. C. Lara 2,066 (1994); K. S. McEwan 2,176 (1983); Majid Khan 2,074 (1972); A. A. Metcalfe 2,047 (1990); H. Morris 2,276 (1990); M. R. Ramprakash 2,258 (1995); D. W. Randall 2,151 (1985); I. V. A. Richards 2,161 (1977); R. T. Robinson 2,032 (1984); M. A. Roseberry 2,044 (1992); C. L. Smith 2,000 (1985); R. T. Virgin 2,223 (1970); D. M. Ward 2,072 (1990); M. E. Waugh 2,072 (1990).

1,000 RUNS IN A SEASON MOST TIMES

(Includes Overseas Tours and Seasons)

28 times: W. G. Grace 2,000 (6); F. E. Woolley 3,000 (1), 2,000 (12).

27 times: M. C. Cowdrey 2,000 (2); C. P. Mead 3,000 (2), 2,000 (9).

26 times: G. Boycott 2,000 (3); J. B. Hobbs 3,000 (1), 2,000 (16).

25 times: E. H. Hendren 3,000 (3), 2,000 (12).

24 times: D. L. Amiss 2,000 (3); W. G. Quaife 2,000 (1); H. Sutcliffe 3,000 (3), 2,000 (12).

23 times: A. Jones.

22 times: T. W. Graveney 2,000 (7); W. R. Hammond 3,000 (3), 2,000 (9).

21 times: D. Denton 2,000 (5); J. H. Edrich 2,000 (6); W. Rhodes 2,000 (2).

20 times: D. B. Close; K. W. R. Fletcher; G. A. Gooch 2,000 (5); G. Gunn; T. W. Hayward 3,000 (2), 2,000 (8); James Langridge 2,000 (1); J. M. Parks 2,000 (3); A. Sandham 2,000 (8); M. J. K. Smith 3,000 (1), 2,000 (5); C. Washbrook 2,000 (2).

19 times: J. W. Hearne 2,000 (4); G. H. Hirst 2,000 (3); D. Kenyon 2,000 (7); E. Tyldesley 3,000 (1), 2,000 (5); J. T. Tyldesley 3,000 (1), 2,000 (4).

18 times: L. G. Berry 2,000 (1); M. W. Gatting 2,000 (2); H. T. W. Hardinge 2,000 (5); R. E. Marshall 2,000 (6); P. A. Perrin; G. M. Turner 2,000 (3); R. E. S. Wyatt 2,000 (5).

17 times: L. E. G. Ames 3,000 (1), 2,000 (5); T. E. Bailey 2,000 (1); D. Brookes 2,000 (6); D. C. S. Compton 3,000 (1), 2,000 (5); G. A. Greenidge 2,000 (1); L. Hutton 3,000 (1), 2,000 (8); J. G. Langridge 2,000 (11); M. Leyland 2,000 (3); I. V. A. Richards 2,000 (1); K. G. Suttle 2,000 (1); Zaheer Abbas 2,000 (2).

16 times: D. G. Bradman 2,000 (4); D. E. Davies 2,000 (1); E. G. Hayes 2,000 (2); C. A. Milton 2,000 (1); J. O'Connor 2,000 (4); C. T. Radley; James Seymour 2,000 (1); C. J. Tavaré.

15 times: G. Barker; K. F. Barrington 2,000 (1); E. H. Bowley 2,000 (4); M. H. Denness; A. E. Dipper 2,000 (5); H. E. Dollery 2,000 (2); W. J. Edrich 3,000 (1), 2,000 (8); J. H. Hampshire; P. Holmes 2,000 (7); Mushtaq Mohammad; R. B. Nicholls 2,000 (1); P. H. Parfitt 2,000 (3); W. G. A. Parkhouse 2,000 (1); B. A. Richards 2,000 (1); J. D. Robertson 2,000 (9); G. S. Sobers; M. J. Stewart 2,000 (1).

Notes: F. E. Woolley reached 1,000 runs in 28 consecutive seasons (1907-1938), C. P. Mead in 27 (1906-1936).

Outside England, 1,000 runs in a season has been reached most times by D. G. Bradman (in 12 seasons in Australia).

Three batsmen have scored 1,000 runs in a season in each of four different countries: G. S. Sobers in West Indies, England, India and Australia; M. C. Cowdrey and G. Boycott in England, South Africa, West Indies and Australia.

HIGHEST AGGREGATES OUTSIDE ENGLAND

	Season	I	NO	R	HS	100s	Avge
In Australia D. G. Bradman	1928-29	24	6	1,690	340*	7	93.88
In South Africa J. R. Reid	1961-62	30	2	1,915	203	7	68.39
In West Indies E. H. Hendren	1929-30	18	5	1,765	254*	6	135.76
In New Zealand M. D. Crowe	1986-87	21	3	1,676	175*	8	93.11
In India C. G. Borde	1964-65	28	3	1,604	168	6	64.16
In Pakistan Saadat Ali	1983-84	27	1	1,649	208	4	63.42
In Sri Lanka P. A. de Silva	1992-93	22	1	1,308	231	3	62.28

In Zimbabwe	Season	I	NO	R	HS	100s	Avge
G. W. Flower........	1994-95	20	3	983	201*	4	57.82

Note: In more than one country, the following aggregates of over 2,000 runs have been recorded:

M. Amarnath (P/I/WI)	1982-83	34	6	2,234	207	9	79.78
J. R. Reid (SA/A/NZ).	1961-62	40	2	2,188	203	7	57.57
S. M. Gavaskar (I/P) .	1978-79	30	6	2,121	205	10	88.37
R. B. Simpson							
(I/P/A/WI)	1964-65	34	4	2,063	201	8	68.76

LEADING BATSMEN IN AN ENGLISH SEASON

(Qualification: 8 completed innings)

Season	Leading scorer	Runs	Avge	Top of averages	Runs	Avge
1946	D. C. S. Compton ...	2,403	61.61	W. R. Hammond ...	1,783	84.90
1947	D. C. S. Compton ...	3,816	90.85	D. C. S. Compton ...	3,816	90.85
1948	L. Hutton	2,654	64.73	D. G. Bradman.....	2,428	89.92
1949	L. Hutton	3,429	68.58	J. Hardstaff........	2,251	72.61
1950	R. T. Simpson......	2,576	62.82	E. Weekes	2,310	79.65
1951	J. D. Robertson	2,917	56.09	P. B. H. May	2,339	68.79
1952	L. Hutton	2,567	61.11	D. S. Sheppard	2,262	64.62
1953	W. J. Edrich	2,557	47.35	R. N. Harvey	2,040	65.80
1954	D. Kenyon	2,636	51.68	D. C. S. Compton ...	1,524	58.61
1955	D. J. Insole	2,427	42.57	D. J. McGlew	1,871	58.46
1956	T. W. Graveney	2,397	49.93	K. Mackay	1,103	52.52
1957	T. W. Graveney	2,361	49.18	P. B. H. May	2,347	61.76
1958	P. B. H. May	2,231	63.74	P. B. H. May	2,231	63.74
1959	M. J. K. Smith	3,245	57.94	V. L. Manjrekar ...	755	68.63
1960	M. J. K. Smith	2,551	45.55	R. Subba Row	1,503	55.66
1961	W. E. Alley	3,019	56.91	W. M. Lawry	2,019	61.18
1962	J. H. Edrich	2,482	51.70	R. T. Simpson......	867	54.18
1963	J. B. Bolus..........	2,190	41.32	G. S. Sobers	1,333	47.60
1964	T. W. Graveney	2,385	54.20	K. F. Barrington....	1,872	62.40
1965	J. H. Edrich	2,319	62.67	M. C. Cowdrey	2,093	63.42
1966	A. R. Lewis	2,198	41.47	G. S. Sobers	1,349	61.31
1967	C. A. Milton	2,089	46.42	K. F. Barrington....	2,059	68.63
1968	B. A. Richards	2,395	47.90	G. Boycott.........	1,487	64.65
1969	J. H. Edrich	2,238	69.93·	J. H. Edrich	2,238	69.93
1970	G. M. Turner	2,379	61.00	G. S. Sobers	1,742	75.73
1971	G. Boycott.........	2,503	100.12	G. Boycott.........	2,503	100.12
1972	Majid Khan	2,074	61.00	G. Boycott.........	1,230	72.35
1973	G. M. Turner	2,416	67.11	G. M. Turner	2,416	67.11
1974	R. T. Virgin	1,936	56.94	C. H. Lloyd	1,458	63.39
1975	G. Boycott.........	1,915	73.65	R. B. Kanhai	1,073	82.53
1976	Zaheer Abbas	2,554	75.11	Zaheer Abbas	2,554	75.11
1977	I. V. A. Richards ...	2,161	65.48	G. Boycott.........	1,701	68.04
1978	D. L. Amiss	2,030	53.42	C. E. B. Rice	1,871	66.82
1979	K. C. Wessels	1,800	52.94	G. Boycott.........	1,538	102.53
1980	P. N. Kirsten	1,895	63.16	A. J. Lamb	1,797	66.55
1981	Zaheer Abbas	2,306	88.69	Zaheer Abbas	2,306	88.69
1982	A. I. Kallicharran...	2,120	66.25	G. M. Turner	1,171	90.07
1983	K. S. McEwan	2,176	64.00	I. V. A. Richards ...	1,204	75.25
1984	G. A. Gooch.......	2,559	67.34	C. G. Greenidge	1,069	82.23
1985	G. A. Gooch.......	2,208	71.22	I. V. A. Richards ...	1,836	76.50
1986	C. G. Greenidge	2,035	67.83	C. G. Greenidge	2,035	67.83

Season	Leading scorer	Runs	Avge	Top of averages	Runs	Avge
1987	G. A. Hick	1,879	52.19	M. D. Crowe	1,627	67.79
1988	G. A. Hick	2,713	77.51	R. A. Harper	622	77.75
1989	S. J. Cook	2,241	60.56	D. M. Jones	1,510	88.82
1990	G. A. Gooch	2,746	101.70	G. A. Gooch	2,746	101.70
1991	S. J. Cook	2,755	81.02	C. L. Hooper	1,501	93.81
1992	P. D. Bowler	2,044	65.93	Salim Malik	1,184	78.93
	M. A. Roseberry	2,044	56.77			
1993	G. A. Gooch	2,023	63.21	D. C. Boon	1,437	75.63
1994	B. C. Lara	2,066	89.82	J. D. Carr	1,543	90.76
1995	M. R. Ramprakash . .	2,258	77.86	M. R. Ramprakash. .	2,258	77.86

Notes: The highest average recorded in an English season was 115.66 (2,429 runs, 26 innings) by D. G. Bradman in 1938.

In 1953 W. A. Johnston averaged 102.00 from 17 innings, 16 not out.

25,000 RUNS IN A CAREER

Dates in italics denote the first half of an overseas season; i.e. *1945* denotes the 1945-46 season.

		Career	R	I	NO	HS	100s	Avge
1	J. B. Hobbs.	1905-34	61,237	1,315	106	316*	197	50.65
2	F. E. Woolley	1906-38	58,969	1,532	85	305*	145	40.75
3	E. H. Hendren	1907-38	57,611	1,300	166	301*	170	50.80
4	C. P. Mead	1905-36	55,061	1,340	185	280*	153	47.67
5	W. G. Grace.	1865-1908	54,896	1,493	105	344	126	39.55
6	W. R. Hammond	1920-51	50,551	1,005	104	336*	167	56.10
7	H. Sutcliffe.	1919-45	50,138	1,088	123	313	149	51.95
8	G. Boycott	1962-86	48,426	1,014	162	261*	151	56.83
9	T. W. Graveney	1948-71	47,793	1,223	159	258	122	44.91
10	T. W. Hayward	1893-1914	43,551	1,138	96	315*	104	41.79
11	D. L. Amiss	1960-87	43,423	1,139	126	262*	102	42.86
12	M. C. Cowdrey	1950-76	42,719	1,130	134	307	107	42.89
13	**G. A. Gooch**	**1973-95**	**42,528**	**941**	**73**	**333**	**120**	**48.99**
14	A. Sandham	1911-37	41,284	1,000	79	325	107	44.82
15	L. Hutton	1934-60	40,140	814	91	364	129	55.51
16	M. J. K. Smith.	1951-75	39,832	1,091	139	204	69	41.84
17	W. Rhodes	1898-1930	39,802	1,528	237	267*	58	30.83
18	J. H. Edrich	1956-78	39,790	979	104	310*	103	45.47
19	R. E. S. Wyatt	1923-57	39,405	1,141	157	232	85	40.04
20	D. C. S. Compton	1936-64	38,942	839	88	300	123	51.85
21	E. Tyldesley	1909-36	38,874	961	106	256*	102	45.46
22	J. T. Tyldesley	1895-1923	37,897	994	62	295*	86	40.66
23	K. W. R. Fletcher	1962-88	37,665	1,167	170	228*	63	37.77
24	C. G. Greenidge.	1970-92	37,354	889	75	273*	92	45.88
25	J. W. Hearne	1909-36	37,252	1,025	116	285*	96	40.98
26	L. E. G. Ames	1926-51	37,248	951	95	295	102	43.51
27	D. Kenyon	1946-67	37,002	1,159	59	259	74	33.63
28	W. J. Edrich	1934-58	36,965	964	92	267*	86	42.39
29	J. M. Parks	1949-76	36,673	1,227	172	205*	51	34.76
30	D. Denton	1894-1920	36,479	1,163	70	221	69	33.37
31	G. H. Hirst	1891-1929	36,323	1,215	151	341	60	34.13
32	I. V. A. Richards	*1971-93*	36,212	796	63	322	114	49.40
33	A. Jones	1957-83	36,049	1,168	72	204*	56	32.89
34	W. G. Quaife	1894-1928	36,012	1,203	185	255*	72	35.37
35	R. E. Marshall	*1945*-72	35,725	1,053	59	228*	68	35.94
36	G. Gunn	1902-32	35,208	1,061	82	220	62	35.96

		Career	R	I	NO	HS	100s	Avge
37	D. B. Close	1949-86	34,994	1,225	173	198	52	33.26
38	Zaheer Abbas	1965-86	34,843	768	92	274	108	51.54
39	J. G. Langridge	1928-55	34,380	984	66	250*	76	37.45
40	G. M. Turner	1964-82	34,346	792	101	311*	103	49.70
41	C. Washbrook	1933-64	34,101	906	107	251*	76	42.67
42	M. Leyland	1920-48	33,660	932	101	263	80	40.50
43	H. T. W. Hardinge	1902-33	33,519	1,021	103	263*	75	36.51
44	**M. W. Gatting**	**1975-95**	**33,456**	**778**	**118**	**258**	**89**	**50.69**
45	R. Abel	1881-1904	33,124	1,007	73	357*	74	35.46
46	A. I. Kallicharran	1966-90	32,650	834	86	243*	87	43.64
47	**A. J. Lamb**	**1972-95**	**32,502**	**772**	**108**	**294**	**89**	**48.94**
48	C. A. Milton	1948-74	32,150	1,078	125	170	56	33.73
49	J. D. Robertson	1937-59	31,914	897	46	331*	67	37.50
50	J. Hardstaff, jun.	1930-55	31,847	812	94	266	83	44.35
51	James Langridge	1924-53	31,716	1,058	157	167	42	35.20
52	K. F. Barrington	1953-68	31,714	831	136	256	76	45.63
53	C. H. Lloyd	1963-86	31,232	730	96	242*	79	49.26
54	Mushtaq Mohammad	1956-85	31,091	843	104	303*	72	42.07
55	C. B. Fry	1892-1921	30,886	658	43	258*	94	50.22
56	D. Brookes	1934-59	30,874	925	70	257	71	36.10
57	P. Holmes	1913-35	30,573	810	84	315*	67	42.11
58	R. T. Simpson	1944-63	30,546	852	55	259	64	38.32
59 {	L. G. Berry	1924-51	30,225	1,056	57	232	45	30.25
	K. G. Suttle	1949-71	30,225	1,064	92	204*	49	31.09
61	P. A. Perrin	1896-1928	29,709	918	91	343*	66	35.92
62	P. F. Warner	1894-1929	29,028	875	75	244	60	36.28
63	R. B. Kanhai	1954-81	28,774	669	82	256	83	49.01
64	J. O'Connor	1921-39	28,764	903	79	248	72	34.90
65	Javed Miandad	1973-93	28,647	631	95	311	80	53.44
66	T. E. Bailey	1945-67	28,641	1,072	215	205	28	33.42
67	D. W. Randall	1972-93	28,456	827	81	237	52	38.14
68	E. H. Bowley	1912-34	28,378	859	47	283	52	34.94
69	B. A. Richards	1964-82	28,358	576	58	356	80	54.74
70	G. S. Sobers	1952-74	28,315	609	93	365*	86	54.87
71	A. E. Dipper	1908-32	28,075	865	69	252*	53	35.27
72	D. G. Bradman	1927-48	28,067	338	43	452*	117	95.14
73	J. H. Hampshire	1961-84	28,059	924	112	183*	43	34.55
74	P. B. H. May	1948-63	27,592	618	77	285*	85	51.00
75	B. F. Davison	1967-87	27,453	766	79	189	53	39.96
76	Majid Khan	1961-84	27,444	700	62	241	73	43.01
77	A. C. Russell	1908-30	27,358	717	59	273	71	41.57
78	E. G. Hayes	1896-1926	27,318	896	48	276	48	32.21
79	A. E. Fagg	1932-57	27,291	803	46	269*	58	36.05
80	James Seymour	1900-26	27,237	911	62	218*	53	32.08
81	**W. Larkins**	**1972-95**	**27,142**	**842**	**54**	**252**	**59**	**34.44**
82	P. H. Parfitt	1956-73	26,924	845	104	200*	58	36.33
83	G. L. Jessop	1894-1914	26,698	855	37	286	53	32.63
84	K. S. McEwan	1972-91	26,628	705	67	218	74	41.73
85	D. E. Davies	1924-54	26,564	1,032	80	287*	32	27.90
86	A. Shrewsbury	1875-1902	26,505	813	90	267	59	36.65
87	M. J. Stewart	1954-72	26,492	898	93	227*	49	32.90
88	**A. R. Border**	**1976-94**	**26,462**	**608**	**96**	**205**	**70**	**51.68**
89	C. T. Radley	1964-87	26,441	880	134	200	46	35.44
90	D. I. Gower	1975-93	26,339	727	70	228	53	40.08
91	C. E. B. Rice	1969-93	26,331	766	123	246	48	40.95
92	Younis Ahmed	1961-86	26,073	762	118	221*	46	40.48
93	P. E. Richardson	1949-65	26,055	794	41	185	44	34.60
94	M. H. Denness	1959-80	25,886	838	65	195	33	33.48
95	S. M. Gavaskar	1966-87	25,834	563	61	340	81	51.46
96	J. W. H. Makepeace	1906-30	25,799	778	66	203	43	36.23

		Career	R	I	NO	HS	100s	Avge
97	W. Gunn...............	1880-1904	25,691	850	72	273	48	33.02
98	W. Watson.............	1939-64	25,670	753	109	257	55	39.86
99	G. Brown	1908-33	25,649	1,012	52	232*	37	26.71
100	G. M. Emmett	1936-59	25,602	865	50	188	37	31.41
101	J. B. Bolus	1956-75	25,598	833	81	202*	39	34.03
102	W. E. Russell	1956-72	25,525	796	64	193	41	34.87
103	C. J. Barnett..........	1927-53	25,389	821	45	259	48	32.71
104	L. B. Fishlock	1931-52	25,376	699	54	253	56	39.34
105	D. J. Insole...........	1947-63	25,241	743	72	219*	54	37.61
106	**G. A. Hick**	**1983-95**	**25,194**	**492**	**50**	**405***	**84**	**57.00**
107	J. M. Brearley.........	1961-83	25,185	768	102	312*	45	37.81
108	J. Vine	1896-1922	25,171	920	79	202	34	29.92
109	R. M. Prideaux	1958-74	25,136	808	75	202*	41	34.29
110	J. H. King	1895-1925	25,122	988	69	227*	34	27.33
111	J. G. Wright	1975-92	25,073	636	44	192	59	42.35
112	**D. L. Haynes**	**1976-94**	**25,027**	**612**	**70**	**255***	**60**	**46.17**

Bold type denotes those who played in 1994-95 and 1995 seasons.

Note: Some works of reference provide career figures which differ from those in this list, owing to the exclusion or inclusion of matches recognised or not recognised as first-class by *Wisden*.

Current Players with 20,000 Runs

	Career	R	I	NO	HS	100s	Avge
R. T. Robinson	1978-95	24,365	637	76	220*	58	43.43
C. W. J. Athey	1976-95	23,680	730	69	184	51	35.82
K. C. Wessels.......	1973-94	21,954	482	43	254	58	50.00
K. J. Barnett	1979-95	21,816	612	57	239*	46	39.30
P. N. Kirsten	1973-94	21,270	535	58	271	53	44.59
S. J. Cook	1972-94	21,143	475	57	313*	64	50.58

CAREER AVERAGE OVER 50

(Qualification: 10,000 runs)

Avge		Career	I	NO	R	HS	100s
95.14	D. G. Bradman	1927-48	338	43	28,067	452*	117
71.22	V. M. Merchant	1929-51	229	43	13,248	359*	44
65.18	W. H. Ponsford	1920-34	235	23	13,819	437	47
64.99	W. M. Woodfull	1921-34	245	39	13,388	284	49
58.24	A. L. Hassett	1932-53	322	32	16,890	232	59
58.19	V. S. Hazare	1934-66	365	45	18,621	316*	60
57.22	A. F. Kippax	1918-35	256	33	12,762	315*	43
57.00	**G. A. Hick**	**1983-95**	**492**	**50**	**25,194**	**405***	**84**
56.83	G. Boycott	1962-86	1,014	162	48,426	261*	151
56.55	C. L. Walcott	1941-63	238	29	11,820	314*	40
56.37	K. S. Ranjitsinhji	1893-1920	500	62	24,692	285*	72
56.22	R. B. Simpson	1952-77	436	62	21,029	359	60
56.10	W. R. Hammond	1920-51	1,005	104	50,551	336*	167
56.03	**M. D. Crowe**	**1979-94**	**406**	**61**	**19,333**	**299**	**69**
55.67	**M. E. Waugh**	**1985-95**	**356**	**46**	**17,260**	**229***	**57**
55.51	L. Hutton	1934-60	814	91	40,140	364	129
55.34	E. D. Weekes	1944-64	241	24	12,010	304*	36
54.87	G. S. Sobers	1952-74	609	93	28,315	365*	86
54.74	B. A. Richards	1964-82	576	58	28,358	356	80
54.67	R. G. Pollock	1960-86	437	54	20,940	274	64

Avge		Career	I	NO	R	HS	100s
54.24	F. M. M. Worrell	*1941-64*	326	49	15,025	308*	39
53.78	R. M. Cowper	*1959-69*	228	31	10,595	307	26
53.67	A. R. Morris	*1940-63*	250	15	12,614	290	46
53.44	Javed Miandad	*1973-93*	631	95	28,647	311	80
52.86	D. B. Vengsarkar	*1975-91*	390	52	17,868	284	55
52.80	**D. M. Jones**	*1981-94*	**316**	**35**	**14,837**	**324***	**43**
52.32	Hanif Mohammad	*1951-75*	371	45	17,059	499	55
52.27	P. R. Umrigar	*1944-67*	350	41	16,154	252*	49
52.20	G. S. Chappell	*1966-83*	542	72	24,535	247*	74
52.11	**M. Azharuddin**	*1981-94*	**256**	**28**	**11,882**	**226**	**40**
51.95	H. Sutcliffe	*1919-45*	1,088	123	50,138	313	149
51.85	D. C. S. Compton	*1936-64*	839	88	38,942	300	123
51.68	**A. R. Border**	*1976-94*	**608**	**96**	**26,462**	**205**	**70**
51.54	Zaheer Abbas	*1965-86*	768	92	34,843	274	108
51.53	A. D. Nourse	*1931-52*	269	27	12,472	260*	41
51.46	S. M. Gavaskar	*1966-87*	563	61	25,834	340	81
51.44	W. A. Brown	*1932-49*	284	15	13,838	265*	39
51.00	P. B. H. May	*1948-63*	618	77	27,592	285*	85
50.95	N. C. O'Neill	*1955-67*	306	34	13,859	284	45
50.93	R. N. Harvey	*1946-62*	461	35	21,699	231*	67
50.90	W. M. Lawry	*1955-71*	417	49	18,734	266	50
50.90	A. V. Mankad	*1963-82*	326	71	12,980	265	31
50.80	E. H. Hendren	*1907-38*	1,300	166	57,611	301*	170
50.69	**M. W. Gatting**	*1975-95*	**778**	**118**	**33,456**	**258**	**89**
50.65	J. B. Hobbs	*1905-34*	1,315	106	61,237	316*	197
50.58	**S. J. Cook**	*1972-94*	**475**	**57**	**21,143**	**313***	**64**
50.54	**S. R. Waugh**	*1984-94*	**304**	**55**	**12,585**	**216***	**34**
50.22	C. B. Fry	*1892-1921*	658	43	30,886	258*	94
50.01	Shafiq Ahmad	*1967-90*	449	58	19,555	217*	53
50.00	**K. C. Wessels**	*1973-94*	**482**	**43**	**21,954**	**254**	**58**

Bold type denotes those who played in 1994-95 and 1995 seasons.

FASTEST FIFTIES

Minutes

11	C. I. J. Smith (66)	Middlesex v Gloucestershire at Bristol............	1938
14	S. J. Pegler (50)	South Africans v Tasmania at Launceston	1910-11
14	F. T. Mann (53)	Middlesex v Nottinghamshire at Lord's..........	1921
14	H. B. Cameron (56)	Transvaal v Orange Free State at Johannesburg....	1934-35
14	C. I. J. Smith (52)	Middlesex v Kent at Maidstone	1935

Note: The following fast fifties were scored in contrived circumstances when runs were given from full tosses and long hops to expedite a declaration: C. C. Inman (8 minutes), Leicestershire v Nottinghamshire at Nottingham, 1965; G. Chapple (10 minutes), Lancashire v Glamorgan at Manchester, 1993; T. M. Moody (11 minutes), Warwickshire v Glamorgan at Swansea, 1990; A. J. Stewart (14 minutes), Surrey v Kent at Dartford, 1986; M. P. Maynard (14 minutes), Glamorgan v Yorkshire at Cardiff, 1987.

FASTEST HUNDREDS

Minutes

35	P. G. H. Fender (113*)	Surrey v Northamptonshire at Northampton ...	1920
40	G. L. Jessop (101)	Gloucestershire v Yorkshire at Harrogate	1897
40	Ahsan-ul-Haq (100*)	Muslims v Sikhs at Lahore	1923-24
42	G. L. Jessop (191)	Gentlemen of South v Players of South at Hastings.................................	1907
43	A. H. Hornby (106)	Lancashire v Somerset at Manchester	1905
43	D. W. Hookes (107)	South Australia v Victoria at Adelaide........	1982-83
44	R. N. S. Hobbs (100)	Essex v Australians at Chelmsford	1975

Notes: The fastest recorded authentic hundred in terms of balls received was scored off 34 balls by D. W. Hookes (above).

Research of the scorebook has shown that P. G. H. Fender scored his hundred from between 40 and 46 balls. He contributed 113 to an unfinished sixth-wicket partnership of 171 in 42 minutes with H. A. Peach.

E. B. Alletson (Nottinghamshire) scored 189 out of 227 runs in 90 minutes against Sussex at Hove in 1911. It has been estimated that his last 139 runs took 37 minutes.

The following fast hundreds were scored in contrived circumstances when runs were given from full tosses and long hops to expedite a declaration: G. Chapple (21 minutes), Lancashire v Glamorgan at Manchester, 1993; T. M. Moody (26 minutes), Warwickshire v Glamorgan at Swansea, 1990; S. J. O'Shaughnessy (35 minutes), Lancashire v Leicestershire at Manchester, 1983; C. M. Old (37 minutes), Yorkshire v Warwickshire at Birmingham, 1977; N. F. M. Popplewell (41 minutes), Somerset v Gloucestershire at Bath, 1983.

FASTEST DOUBLE-HUNDREDS

Minutes

113	R. J. Shastri (200*)	Bombay v Baroda at Bombay	1984-85
120	G. L. Jessop (286)	Gloucestershire v Sussex at Hove	1903
120	C. H. Lloyd (201*)	West Indians v Glamorgan at Swansea	1976
130	G. L. Jessop (234)	Gloucestershire v Somerset at Bristol	1905
131	V. T. Trumper (293)	Australians v Canterbury at Christchurch	1913-14

FASTEST TRIPLE-HUNDREDS

Minutes

181	D. C. S. Compton (300)	MCC v N. E. Transvaal at Benoni	1948-49
205	F. E. Woolley (305*)	MCC v Tasmania at Hobart	1911-12
205	C. G. Macartney (345)	Australians v Nottinghamshire at Nottingham	1921
213	D. G. Bradman (369)	South Australia v Tasmania at Adelaide	1935-36

300 RUNS IN ONE DAY

390*	B. C. Lara	Warwickshire v Durham at Birmingham	1994
345	C. G. Macartney	Australians v Nottinghamshire at Nottingham	1921
334	W. H. Ponsford	Victoria v New South Wales at Melbourne	1926-27
333	K. S. Duleepsinhji	Sussex v Northamptonshire at Hove	1930
331*	J. D. Robertson	Middlesex v Worcestershire at Worcester	1949
325*	B. A. Richards	S. Australia v W. Australia at Perth	1970-71
322†	E. Paynter	Lancashire v Sussex at Hove	1937
322	I. V. A. Richards	Somerset v Warwickshire at Taunton	1985
318	C. W. Gregory	New South Wales v Queensland at Brisbane	1906-07
317	K. R. Rutherford	New Zealanders v D. B. Close's XI at Scarborough	1986
316†	R. H. Moore	Hampshire v Warwickshire at Bournemouth	1937
315*	R. C. Blunt	Otago v Canterbury at Christchurch	1931-32
312*	J. M. Brearley	MCC Under-25 v North Zone at Peshawar	1966-67
311*	G. M. Turner	Worcestershire v Warwickshire at Worcester	1982
311*	N. H. Fairbrother	Lancashire v Surrey at The Oval	1990
309*	D. G. Bradman	Australia v England at Leeds	1930
307*	W. H. Ashdown	Kent v Essex at Brentwood	1934
306*	A. Ducat	Surrey v Oxford University at The Oval	1919
305*	F. R. Foster	Warwickshire v Worcestershire at Dudley	1914

† E. Paynter's 322 and R. H. Moore's 316 were scored on the same day: July 28, 1937.

These scores do not necessarily represent the complete innings. See pages 105-107.

1,000 RUNS IN MAY

		Runs	Avge
W. G. Grace, May 9 to May 30, 1895 (22 days):			
13, 103, 18, 25, 288, 52, 257, 73*, 18, 169		1,016	112.88
Grace was within two months of completing his 47th year.			
W. R. Hammond, May 7 to May 31, 1927 (25 days):			
27, 135, 108, 128, 17, 11, 99, 187, 4, 30, 83, 7, 192, 14		1,042	74.42
Hammond scored his 1,000th run on May 28, thus equalling Grace's record of 22 days.			
C. Hallows, May 5 to May 31, 1928 (27 days):			
100, 101, 51*, 123, 101*, 22, 74, 104, 58, 34*, 232		1,000	125.00

1,000 RUNS IN APRIL AND MAY

		Runs	Avge
T. W. Hayward, April 16 to May 31, 1900:			
120*, 55, 108, 131*, 55, 193, 120, 5, 6, 3, 40, 146, 92		1,074	97.63
D. G. Bradman, April 30 to May 31, 1930:			
236, 185*, 78, 9, 48*, 66, 4, 44, 252*, 32, 47*		1,001	143.00
On April 30 Bradman was 75 not out.			
D. G. Bradman, April 30 to May 31, 1938:			
258, 58, 137, 278, 2, 143, 145*, 5, 30*		1,056	150.85
Bradman scored 258 on April 30, and his 1,000th run on May 27.			
W. J. Edrich, April 30 to May 31, 1938:			
104, 37, 115, 63, 20*, 182, 71, 31, 53*, 45, 15, 245, 0, 9, 20*		1,010	84.16
Edrich was 21 not out on April 30. All his runs were scored at Lord's.			
G. M. Turner, April 24 to May 31, 1973:			
41, 151*, 143, 85, 7, 8, 17*, 81, 13, 53, 44, 153*, 3, 2, 66*, 30, 10*, 111		1,018	78.30
G. A. Hick, April 17 to May 29, 1988:			
61, 37, 212, 86, 14, 405*, 8, 11, 6, 7, 172		1,019	101.90
Hick scored a record 410 runs in April, and his 1,000th run on May 28.			

1,000 RUNS IN TWO SEPARATE MONTHS

Only four batsmen, C. B. Fry, K. S. Ranjitsinhji, H. Sutcliffe and L. Hutton, have scored over 1,000 runs in each of two months in the same season. L. Hutton, by scoring 1,294 in June 1949, made more runs in a single month than anyone else. He also made 1,050 in August 1949.

MOST RUNS SCORED OFF ONE OVER

(All instances refer to six-ball overs)

36	G. S. Sobers	off M. A. Nash, Nottinghamshire v Glamorgan at Swansea (six sixes)	1968
36	R. J. Shastri	off Tilak Raj, Bombay v Baroda at Bombay (six sixes) . . .	1984-85
34	E. B. Alletson	off E. H. Killick, Nottinghamshire v Sussex at Hove (46604446; including two no-balls)	1911
34	F. C. Hayes	off M. A. Nash, Lancashire v Glamorgan at Swansea (646666)	1977
32	I. T. Botham	off I. R. Snook, England XI v Central Districts at Palmerston North (466466)	1983-84
32	P. W. G. Parker	off A. I. Kallicharran, Sussex v Warwickshire at Birmingham (466664)	1982
32	I. R. Redpath	off N. Rosendorff, Australians v Orange Free State at Bloemfontein (666644)	1969-70
32	C. C. Smart	off G. Hill, Glamorgan v Hampshire at Cardiff (664664) .	1935

Notes: The following instances have been excluded from the above table because of the bowlers' compliance: 34 – M. P. Maynard off S. A. Marsh, Glamorgan v Kent at Swansea, 1992; 34 – G. Chapple off P. A. Cottey, Lancashire v Glamorgan at Manchester, 1993; 32 – C. C. Inman off N. W. Hill, Leicestershire v Nottinghamshire at Nottingham, 1965; 32 – T. E. Jesty off R. J. Boyd-Moss, Hampshire v Northamptonshire at Southampton, 1984; 32 – G. Chapple off P. A. Cottey, Lancashire v Glamorgan at Manchester, 1993. Chapple's 34 and 32 came off successive overs from Cottey.

The greatest number of runs scored off an eight-ball over is 34 (40446664) by R. M. Edwards off M. C. Carew, Governor-General's XI v West Indians at Auckland, 1968-69.

In a Shell Trophy match against Canterbury at Christchurch in 1989-90, R. H. Vance (Wellington), acting on the instructions of his captain, deliberately conceded 77 runs in an over of full tosses which contained 17 no-balls and, owing to the umpire's understandable miscalculation, only five legitimate deliveries.

MOST SIXES IN AN INNINGS

16	A. Symonds (254*)	Gloucestershire v Glamorgan at Abergavenny .	1995
15	J. R. Reid (296)	Wellington v N. Districts at Wellington	1962-63
14	Shakti Singh (128)	Himachal Pradesh v Haryana at Dharmsala . . .	1990-91
13	Majid Khan (147*)	Pakistanis v Glamorgan at Swansea	1967
13	C. G. Greenidge (273*)	D. H. Robins' XI v Pakistanis at Eastbourne . .	1974
13	C. G. Greenidge (259)	Hampshire v Sussex at Southampton	1975
13	G. W. Humpage (254)	Warwickshire v Lancashire at Southport	1982
13	R. J. Shastri (200*)	Bombay v Baroda at Bombay	1984-85
12	Gulfraz Khan (207)	Railways v Universities at Lahore	1976-77
12	I. T. Botham (138*)	Somerset v Warwickshire at Birmingham	1985
12	R. A. Harper (234)	Northamptonshire v Gloucestershire at Northampton	1986
12	D. M. Jones (248)	Australians v Warwickshire at Birmingham . . .	1989
12	D. N. Patel (204)	Auckland v Northern Districts at Auckland . . .	1991-92
12	W. V. Raman (206)	Tamil Nadu v Kerala at Madras	1991-92
11	C. K. Nayudu (153)	Hindus v MCC at Bombay	1926-27
11	C. J. Barnett (194)	Gloucestershire v Somerset at Bath	1934
11	R. Benaud (135)	Australians v T. N. Pearce's XI at Scarborough	1953
11	R. Bora (126)	Assam v Tripura at Gauhati	1987-88
11	G. A. Hick (405*)	Worcestershire v Somerset at Taunton	1988

MOST SIXES IN A MATCH

20	A. Symonds (254*, 76)	Gloucestershire v Glamorgan at Abergavenny .	1995
17	W. J. Stewart (155, 125)	Warwickshire v Lancashire at Blackpool	1959

MOST SIXES IN A SEASON

80	I. T. Botham	1985		49	I. V. A. Richards	1985
66	A. W. Wellard	1935		48	A. W. Carr	1925
57	A. W. Wellard	1936		48	J. H. Edrich	1965
57	A. W. Wellard	1938		48	A. Symonds	1995
51	A. W. Wellard	1933				

MOST BOUNDARIES IN AN INNINGS

	4s/6s			
72	62/10	B. C. Lara (501*)	Warwickshire v Durham at Birmingham	1994
68	68/–	P. A. Perrin (343*)	Essex v Derbyshire at Chesterfield	1904
64	64/–	Hanif Mohammad (499)	Karachi v Bahawalpur at Karachi	1958-59
63	62/1	A. C. MacLaren (424)	Lancashire v Somerset at Taunton	1895
57	52/5	J. H. Edrich (310*)	England v New Zealand at Leeds	1965
55	55/–	C. W. Gregory (383)	NSW v Queensland at Brisbane	1906-07

	4s/6s			
55	53/2	G. R. Marsh (355*)	W. Australia v S. Australia at Perth ..	1989-90
54	53/1	G. H. Hirst (341)	Yorkshire v Leicestershire at Leicester .	1905
54	51/2†	S. V. Manjrekar (377)	Bombay v Hyderabad at Bombay.....	1990-91
53	53/–	A. W. Nourse (304*)	Natal v Transvaal at Johannesburg ..	1919-20
53	45/8	K. R. Rutherford (317)	New Zealanders v D. B. Close's XI at	
			Scarborough	1986
52	47/5	N. H. Fairbrother (366)	Lancashire v Surrey at The Oval	1990
51	47/4	C. G. Macartney (345)	Australians v Notts. at Nottingham ..	1921
51	50/1	B. B. Nimbalkar (443*)	Maharashtra v Kathiawar at Poona ..	1948-49
50	46/4	D. G. Bradman (369)	S. Australia v Tasmania at Adelaide ..	1935-36
50	47/–‡	A. Ducat (306*)	Surrey v Oxford U. at The Oval......	1919
50	35/15	J. R. Reid (296)	Wellington v N. Districts at Wellington	1962-63
50	42/8	I. V. A. Richards (322)	Somerset v Warwickshire at Taunton .	1985

† Plus one five.
‡ Plus three fives.

HIGHEST PARTNERSHIPS

577 V. S. Hazare (288) and Gul Mahomed (319), fourth wicket, Baroda v Holkar at
Baroda 1946-47
574* F. M. M. Worrell (255*) and C. L. Walcott (314*), fourth wicket, Barbados v
Trinidad at Port-of-Spain 1945-46
561 Waheed Mirza (324) and Mansoor Akhtar (224*), first wicket, Karachi Whites
v Quetta at Karachi 1976-77
555 P. Holmes (224*) and H. Sutcliffe (313), first wicket, Yorkshire v Essex at
Leyton 1932
554 J. T. Brown (300) and J. Tunnicliffe (243), first wicket, Yorkshire v Derbyshire
at Chesterfield 1898
502* F. M. M. Worrell (308*) and J. D. C. Goddard (218*), fourth wicket, Barbados
v Trinidad at Bridgetown 1943-44
490 E. H. Bowley (283) and J. G. Langridge (195), first wicket, Sussex v Middlesex
at Hove 1933
487* G. A. Headley (344*) and C. C. Passailaigue (261*), sixth wicket, Jamaica v
Lord Tennyson's XI at Kingston 1931-32
475 Zahir Alam (257) and L. S. Rajput (239), second wicket, Assam v Tripura at
Gauhati 1991-92
470 A. I. Kallicharran (230*) and G. W. Humpage (254), fourth wicket,
Warwickshire v Lancashire at Southport 1982

HIGHEST PARTNERSHIPS FOR EACH WICKET

The following lists include all stands above 400; otherwise the top ten for each wicket.

First Wicket

561	Waheed Mirza and Mansoor Akhtar, Karachi Whites v Quetta at Karachi	1976-77
555	P. Holmes and H. Sutcliffe, Yorkshire v Essex at Leyton.................	1932
554	J. T. Brown and J. Tunnicliffe, Yorkshire v Derbyshire at Chesterfield	1898
490	E. H. Bowley and J. G. Langridge, Sussex v Middlesex at Hove	1933
464	R. Sehgal and R. Lamba, Delhi v Himachal Pradesh at Delhi	1994-95
456	E. R. Mayne and W. H. Ponsford, Victoria v Queensland at Melbourne ...	1923-24
451*	S. Desai and R. M. H. Binny, Karnataka v Kerala at Chikmagalur	1977-78
431	M. R. J. Veletta and G. R. Marsh, Western Australia v South Australia at Perth	1989-90
428	J. B. Hobbs and A. Sandham, Surrey v Oxford University at The Oval.....	1926
424	I. J. Siedle and J. F. W. Nicolson, Natal v Orange Free State at Bloemfontein	1926-27
421	S. M. Gavaskar and G. A. Parkar, Bombay v Bengal at Bombay.........	1981-82
418	Kamal Najamuddin and Khalid Alvi, Karachi v Railways at Karachi	1980-81
413	V. Mankad and Pankaj Roy, India v New Zealand at Madras	1955-56
405	C. P. S. Chauhan and M. S. Gupte, Maharashtra v Vidarbha at Poona ...	1972-73

Second Wicket

475	Zahir Alam and L. S. Rajput, Assam v Tripura at Gauhati	1991-92
465*	J. A. Jameson and R. B. Kanhai, Warwicks. v Gloucestershire at Birmingham	1974
455	K. V. Bhandarkar and B. B. Nimbalkar, Maharashtra v Kathiawar at Poona	1948-49
451	W. H. Ponsford and D. G. Bradman, Australia v England at The Oval ...	1934
446	C. C. Hunte and G. S. Sobers, West Indies v Pakistan at Kingston	1957-58
429*	J. G. Dewes and G. H. G. Doggart, Cambridge U. v Essex at Cambridge .	1949
426	Arshad Pervez and Mohsin Khan, Habib Bank v Income Tax at Lahore ..	1977-78
415	A. D. Jadeja and S. V. Manjrekar, Indians v Bowl XI at Springs.........	1992-93
403	G. A. Gooch and P. J. Prichard, Essex v Leicestershire at Chelmsford	1990
398	A. Shrewsbury and W. Gunn, Nottinghamshire v Sussex at Nottingham ...	1890

Third Wicket

467	A. H. Jones and M. D. Crowe, New Zealand v Sri Lanka at Wellington ..	1990-91
456	Khalid Irtiza and Aslam Ali, United Bank v Multan at Karachi	1975-76
451	Mudassar Nazar and Javed Miandad, Pakistan v India at Hyderabad	1982-83
445	P. E. Whitelaw and W. N. Carson, Auckland v Otago at Dunedin	1936-37
434	J. B. Stollmeyer and G. E. Gomez, Trinidad v British Guiana at Port-of-Spain	1946-47
424*	W. J. Edrich and D. C. S. Compton, Middlesex v Somerset at Lord's	1948
413	D. J. Bicknell and D. M. Ward, Surrey v Kent at Canterbury	1990
410*	R. S. Modi and L. Amarnath, India in England v The Rest at Calcutta ...	1946-47
405	A. D. Jadeja and A. S. Kaypee, Haryana v Services at Faridabad	1991-92
399	R. T. Simpson and D. C. S. Compton, MCC v N. E. Transvaal at Benoni .	1948-49

Fourth Wicket

577	V. S. Hazare and Gul Mahomed, Baroda v Holkar at Baroda............	1946-47
574*	C. L. Walcott and F. M. M. Worrell, Barbados v Trinidad at Port-of-Spain	1945-46
502*	F. M. M. Worrell and J. D. C. Goddard, Barbados v Trinidad at Bridgetown	1943-44
470	A. I. Kallicharran and G. W. Humpage, Warwicks. v Lancs. at Southport .	1982
462*	D. W. Hookes and W. B. Phillips, South Australia v Tasmania at Adelaide	1986-87
448	R. Abel and T. W. Hayward, Surrey v Yorkshire at The Oval	1899
425*	A. Dale and I. V. A. Richards, Glamorgan v Middlesex at Cardiff	1993
424	I. S. Lee and S. O. Quin, Victoria v Tasmania at Melbourne	1933-34
411	P. B. H. May and M. C. Cowdrey, England v West Indies at Birmingham .	1957
410	G. Abraham and P. Balan Pandit, Kerala v Andhra at Palghat	1959-60
402	W. Watson and T. W. Graveney, MCC v British Guiana at Georgetown ..	1953-54
402	R. B. Kanhai and K. Ibadulla, Warwicks. v Notts. at Nottingham	1968

Fifth Wicket

464*	M. E. Waugh and S. R. Waugh, New South Wales v Western Australia at Perth	1990-91
405	S. G. Barnes and D. G. Bradman, Australia v England at Sydney	1946-47
397	W. Bardsley and C. Kelleway, New South Wales v South Australia at Sydney	1920-21
393	E. G. Arnold and W. B. Burns, Worcestershire v Warwickshire at Birmingham.	1909
360	U. M. Merchant and M. N. Raiji, Bombay v Hyderabad at Bombay......	1947-48
355	Altaf Shah and Tariq Bashir, HBFC v Multan at Multan	1976-77
355	A. J. Lamb and J. J. Strydom, OFS v Eastern Province at Bloemfontein ..	1987-88
347	D. Brookes and D. W. Barrick, Northamptonshire v Essex at Northampton	1952
344	M. C. Cowdrey and T. W. Graveney, MCC v South Australia at Adelaide .	1962-63
343	R. I. Maddocks and J. Hallebone, Victoria v Tasmania at Melbourne	1951-52

Sixth Wicket

487*	G. A. Headley and C. C. Passailaigue, Jamaica v Lord Tennyson's XI at Kingston	1931-32
428	W. W. Armstrong and M. A. Noble, Australians v Sussex at Hove	1902
411	R. M. Poore and E. G. Wynyard, Hampshire v Somerset at Taunton	1899
376	R. Subba Row and A. Lightfoot, Northamptonshire v Surrey at The Oval .	1958
371	V. M. Merchant and R. S. Modi, Bombay v Maharashtra at Bombay	1943-44
356	W. V. Raman and A. Kripal Singh, Tamil Nadu v Goa at Panjim	1988-89

353	Salah-ud-Din and Zaheer Abbas, Karachi v East Pakistan at Karachi	1968-69
346	J. H. W. Fingleton and D. G. Bradman, Australia v England at Melbourne	1936-37
337	R. R. Montgomerie and D. J. Capel, Northamptonshire v Kent at Canterbury	1995
332	N. G. Marks and G. Thomas, New South Wales v South Australia at Sydney	1958-59

Seventh Wicket

460	Bhupinder Singh, jun. and P. Dharmani, Punjab v Delhi at Delhi	1994-95
347	D. St E. Atkinson and C. C. Depeiza, West Indies v Australia at Bridgetown	1954-55
344	K. S. Ranjitsinhji and W. Newham, Sussex v Essex at Leyton	1902
340	K. J. Key and H. Philipson, Oxford University v Middlesex at Chiswick Park	1887
336	F. C. W. Newman and C. R. N. Maxwell, Sir J. Cahn's XI v Leicestershire	
	at Nottingham	1935
335	C. W. Andrews and E. C. Bensted, Queensland v New South Wales at Sydney	1934-35
325	G. Brown and C. H. Abercrombie, Hampshire v Essex at Leyton	1913
323	E. H. Hendren and L. F. Townsend, MCC v Barbados at Bridgetown	1929-30
308	Waqar Hassan and Imtiaz Ahmed, Pakistan v New Zealand at Lahore	1955-56
301	C. C. Lewis and B. N. French, Nottinghamshire v Durham at Chester-le-Street	1993

Eighth Wicket

433	V. T. Trumper and A. Sims, A. Sims' Aust. XI v Canterbury at Christchurch	1913-14
292	R. Peel and Lord Hawke, Yorkshire v Warwickshire at Birmingham	1896
270	V. T. Trumper and E. P. Barbour, New South Wales v Victoria at Sydney .	1912-13
263	D. R. Wilcox and R. M. Taylor, Essex v Warwickshire at Southend	1946
255	E. A. V. Williams and E. A. Martindale, Barbados v Trinidad at Bridgetown	1935-36
249*	Shaukat Mirza and Akram Raza, Habib Bank v PNSC at Lahore	1993-94
246	L. E. G. Ames and G. O. B. Allen, England v New Zealand at Lord's	1931
243	R. J. Hartigan and C. Hill, Australia v England at Adelaide	1907-08
242*	T. J. Zoehrer and K. H. MacLeay, W. Australia v New South Wales at Perth	1990-91
240	Gulfraz Khan and Raja Sarfraz, Railways v Universities at Lahore	1976-77

Ninth Wicket

283	J. Chapman and A. Warren, Derbyshire v Warwickshire at Blackwell	1910
268	J. B. Commins and N. Boje, South Africa A v Mashonaland at Harare	1994-95
251	J. W. H. T. Douglas and S. N. Hare, Essex v Derbyshire at Leyton	1921
245	V. S. Hazare and N. D. Nagarwalla, Maharashtra v Baroda at Poona	1939-40
244*	Arshad Ayub and M. V. Ramanamurthy, Hyderabad v Bihar at Hyderabad	1986-87
239	H. B. Cave and I. B. Leggat, Central Districts v Otago at Dunedin	1952-53
232	C. Hill and E. Walkley, South Australia v New South Wales at Adelaide	1900-01
231	P. Sen and J. Mitter, Bengal v Bihar at Jamshedpur	1950-51
230	D. A. Livingstone and A. T. Castell, Hampshire v Surrey at Southampton .	1962
226	C. Kelleway and W. A. Oldfield, New South Wales v Victoria at Melbourne	1925-26

Tenth Wicket

307	A. F. Kippax and J. E. H. Hooker, New South Wales v Victoria at Melbourne	1928-29
249	C. T. Sarwate and S. N. Banerjee, Indians v Surrey at The Oval	1946
235	F. E. Woolley and A. Fielder, Kent v Worcestershire at Stourbridge	1909
233	Ajay Sharma and Maninder Singh, Delhi v Bombay at Bombay	1991-92
230	R. W. Nicholls and W. Roche, Middlesex v Kent at Lord's	1899
228	R. Illingworth and K. Higgs, Leicestershire v Northamptonshire at Leicester	1977
218	F. H. Vigar and T. P. B. Smith, Essex v Derbyshire at Chesterfield	1947
211	M. Ellis and T. J. Hastings, Victoria v South Australia at Melbourne	1902-03
196*	Nadim Yousuf and Maqsood Kundi, MCB v National Bank at Lahore	1981-82
192	H. A. W. Bowell and W. H. Livsey, Hampshire v Worcs. at Bournemouth . .	1921

Note: Three of the above partnerships were affected by TCCB or ACB regulations governing no-balls. The stand between A. Dale and I. V. A. Richards (fourth wicket) included 13 runs for no-balls instead of the five that would have applied under the Laws of Cricket; between M. E. and S. R. Waugh (fifth wicket) 20 instead of seven; between R. R. Montgomerie and D. J. Capel (sixth wicket) nine instead of four.

UNUSUAL DISMISSALS

Handled the Ball

J. Grundy	MCC v Kent at Lord's	1857
G. Bennett	Kent v Sussex at Hove	1872
W. H. Scotton	Smokers v Non-Smokers at East Melbourne	1886-87
C. W. Wright	Nottinghamshire v Gloucestershire at Bristol	1893
E. Jones	South Australia v Victoria at Melbourne	1894-95
A. W. Nourse	South Africans v Sussex at Hove	1907
E. T. Benson	MCC v Auckland at Auckland	1929-30
A. W. Gilbertson	Otago v Auckland at Auckland	1952-53
W. R. Endean	South Africa v England at Cape Town	1956-57
P. J. Burge	Queensland v New South Wales at Sydney	1958-59
Dildar Awan	Services v Lahore at Lahore	1959-60
M. Mehra	Railways v Delhi at Delhi	1959-60
Mahmood-ul-Hasan	Karachi University v Railways-Quetta at Karachi	1960-61
Ali Raza	Karachi Greens v Hyderabad at Karachi	1961-62
Mohammad Yusuf	Rawalpindi v Peshawar at Peshawar	1962-63
A. Rees	Glamorgan v Middlesex at Lord's	1965
Pervez Akhtar	Multan v Karachi Greens at Sahiwal.....................	1971-72
Javed Mirza	Railways v Punjab at Lahore	1972-73
R. G. Pollock	Eastern Province v Western Province at Cape Town	1973-74
C. I. Dey	Northern Transvaal v Orange Free State at Bloemfontein .	1973-74
Nasir Valika	Karachi Whites v National Bank at Karachi	1974-75
Haji Yousuf	National Bank v Railways at Lahore	1974-75
Masood-ul-Hasan	PIA v National Bank B at Lyallpur......................	1975-76
D. K. Pearse	Natal v Western Province at Cape Town	1978-79
A. M. J. Hilditch	Australia v Pakistan at Perth	1978-79
Musleh-ud-Din	Railways v Lahore at Lahore	1979-80
Jalal-ud-Din	IDBP v Habib Bank at Bahawalpur	1981-82
Mohsin Khan	Pakistan v Australia at Karachi	1982-83
D. L. Haynes	West Indies v India at Bombay	1983-84
K. Azad	Delhi v Punjab at Amritsar	1983-84
Athar A. Khan	Allied Bank v HBFC at Sialkot	1983-84
A. N. Pandya	Saurashtra v Baroda at Baroda	1984-85
G. L. Linton	Barbados v Windward Islands at Bridgetown	1985-86
R. B. Gartrell	Tasmania v Victoria at Melbourne	1986-87
R. Nayyar	Himachal Pradesh v Punjab at Una	1988-89
R. Weerawardene	Moratuwa v Nomads SC at Colombo	1988-89
A. M. Kane	Vidarbha v Railways at Nagpur..........................	1989-90
P. Bali	Jammu and Kashmir v Services at Delhi	1991-92
M. J. Davis	Northern Transvaal B v OFS B at Bloemfontein	1991-92
J. T. C. Vaughan	Emerging Players v England XI at Hamilton	1991-92
G. A. Gooch	England v Australia at Manchester	1993
A. C. Waller	Mashonaland CD v Mashonaland Under-24 at Harare	1994-95

Obstructing the Field

C. A. Absolom	Cambridge University v Surrey at The Oval.............	1868
T. Straw	Worcestershire v Warwickshire at Worcester	1899
T. Straw	Worcestershire v Warwickshire at Birmingham	1901
J. P. Whiteside	Leicestershire v Lancashire at Leicester.................	1901
L. Hutton	England v South Africa at The Oval	1951
J. A. Hayes	Canterbury v Central Districts at Christchurch	1954-55
D. D. Deshpande	Madhya Pradesh v Uttar Pradesh at Benares	1956-57
K. Ibadulla	Warwickshire v Hampshire at Coventry	1963
Qaiser Khan	Dera Ismail Khan v Railways at Lahore	1964-65
Ijaz Ahmed	Lahore Greens v Lahore Blues at Lahore	1973-74

Qasim Feroze	Bahawalpur v Universities at Lahore	1974-75
T. Quirk	Northern Transvaal v Border at East London	1978-79
Mahmood Rashid	United Bank v Muslim Commercial Bank at Bahawalpur	1981-82
Arshad Ali	Sukkur v Quetta at Quetta	1983-84
H. R. Wasu	Vidarbha v Rajasthan at Akola	1984-85
Khalid Javed	Railways v Lahore at Lahore	1985-86
C. Binduhewa	Singha SC v Sinhalese SC at Colombo	1990-91
S. J. Kalyani	Bengal v Orissa at Calcutta	1994-95

Hit the Ball Twice

H. E. Bull	MCC v Oxford University at Lord's	1864
H. R. J. Charlwood	Sussex v Surrey at Hove	1872
R. G. Barlow	North v South at Lord's	1878
P. S. Wimble	Transvaal v Griqualand West at Kimberley	1892-93
G. B. Nicholls	Somerset v Gloucestershire at Bristol	1896
A. A. Lilley	Warwickshire v Yorkshire at Birmingham	1897
J. H. King	Leicestershire v Surrey at The Oval	1906
A. P. Binns	Jamaica v British Guiana at Georgetown	1956-57
K. Bhavanna	Andhra v Mysore at Guntur	1963-64
Zaheer Abbas	PIA A v Karachi Blues at Karachi	1969-70
Anwar Miandad	IDBP v United Bank at Lahore	1979-80
Anwar Iqbal	Hyderabad v Sukkur at Hyderabad	1983-84
Iqtidar Ali	Allied Bank v Muslim Commercial Bank at Lahore	1983-84
Aziz Malik	Lahore Division v Faisalabad at Sialkot	1984-85
Javed Mohammad	Multan v Karachi Whites at Sahiwal	1986-87
Shahid Pervez	Jammu and Kashmir v Punjab at Srinigar	1986-87

BOWLING RECORDS

TEN WICKETS IN AN INNINGS

	O	M	R		
E. Hinkly (Kent)				v England at Lord's	1848
*J. Wisden (North)				v South at Lord's	1850
V. E. Walker (England)	43	17	74	v Surrey at The Oval	1859
V. E. Walker (Middlesex)	44.2	5	104	v Lancashire at Manchester	1865
G. Wootton (All England)	31.3	9	54	v Yorkshire at Sheffield	1865
W. Hickton (Lancashire)	36.2	19	46	v Hampshire at Manchester	1870
S. E. Butler (Oxford)	24.1	11	38	v Cambridge at Lord's	1871
James Lillywhite (South)	60.2	22	129	v North at Canterbury	1872
A. Shaw (MCC)	36.2	8	73	v North at Lord's	1874
E. Barratt (Players)	29	11	43	v Australians at The Oval	1878
G. Giffen (Australian XI)	26	10	66	v The Rest at Sydney	1883-84
W. G. Grace (MCC)	36.2	17	49	v Oxford University at Oxford . . .	1886
G. Burton (Middlesex)	52.3	25	59	v Surrey at The Oval	1888
†A. E. Moss (Canterbury)	21.3	10	28	v Wellington at Christchurch . . .	1889-90
S. M. J. Woods (Cambridge U.) . .	31	6	69	v Thornton's XI at Cambridge . .	1890
T. Richardson (Surrey)	15.3	3	45	v Essex at The Oval	1894
H. Pickett (Essex)	27	11	32	v Leicestershire at Leyton	1895
E. J. Tyler (Somerset)	34.3	15	49	v Surrey at Taunton	1895
W. P. Howell (Australians)	23.2	14	28	v Surrey at The Oval	1899
C. H. G. Bland (Sussex)	25.2	10	48	v Kent at Tonbridge	1899
J. Briggs (Lancashire)	28.5	7	55	v Worcestershire at Manchester .	1900
A. E. Trott (Middlesex)	14.2	5	42	v Somerset at Taunton	1900
A. Fielder (Players)	24.5	1	90	v Gentlemen at Lord's	1906
E. G. Dennett (Gloucestershire) . .	19.4	7	40	v Essex at Bristol	1906
A. E. E. Vogler (E. Province) . . .	12	2	26	v Griqualand W. at Johannesburg	1906-07

	O	M	R		
C. Blythe (Kent)	16	7	30	v Northants at Northampton....	1907
A. Drake (Yorkshire)	8.5	0	35	v Somerset at Weston-s-Mare ...	1914
W. Bestwick (Derbyshire)......	19	2	40	v Glamorgan at Cardiff	1921
A. A. Mailey (Australians)	28.4	5	66	v Gloucestershire at Cheltenham	1921
C. W. L. Parker (Glos.)	40.3	13	79	v Somerset at Bristol	1921
T. Rushby (Surrey)	17.5	4	43	v Somerset at Taunton	1921
J. C. White (Somerset)	42.2	11	76	v Worcestershire at Worcester ...	1921
G. C. Collins (Kent)	19.3	4	65	v Nottinghamshire at Dover	1922
H. Howell (Warwickshire)	25.1	5	51	v Yorkshire at Birmingham.....	1923
A. S. Kennedy (Players)	22.4	10	37	v Gentlemen at The Oval	1927
G. O. B. Allen (Middlesex) ...	25.3	10	40	v Lancashire at Lord's	1929
A. P. Freeman (Kent)	42	9	131	v Lancashire at Maidstone	1929
G. Geary (Leicestershire)	16.2	8	18	v Glamorgan at Pontypridd ...	1929
C. V. Grimmett (Australians) ...	22.3	8	37	v Yorkshire at Sheffield	1930
A. P. Freeman (Kent)	30.4	8	53	v Essex at Southend	1930
H. Verity (Yorkshire)	18.4	6	36	v Warwickshire at Leeds	1931
A. P. Freeman (Kent)	36.1	9	79	v Lancashire at Manchester	1931
V. W. C. Jupp (Northants)	39	6	127	v Kent at Tunbridge Wells	1932
H. Verity (Yorkshire)	19.4	16	10	v Nottinghamshire at Leeds	1932
T. W. Wall (South Australia) ...	12.4	2	36	v New South Wales at Sydney ..	1932-33
T. B. Mitchell (Derbyshire)....	19.1	4	64	v Leicestershire at Leicester	1935
J. Mercer (Glamorgan)	26	10	51	v Worcestershire at Worcester ...	1936
T. W. J. Goddard (Glos.)	28.4	4	113	v Worcestershire at Cheltenham .	1937
T. F. Smailes (Yorkshire)	17.1	5	47	v Derbyshire at Sheffield	1939
E. A. Watts (Surrey)	24.1	8	67	v Warwickshire at Birmingham .	1939
*W. E. Hollies (Warwickshire)..	20.4	4	49	v Notts. at Birmingham......	1946
J. M. Sims (East)	18.4	2	90	v West at Kingston	1948
T. E. Bailey (Essex)	39.4	9	90	v Lancashire at Clacton	1949
J. K. Graveney (Glos.)	18.4	2	66	v Derbyshire at Chesterfield ...	1949
R. Berry (Lancashire)	36.2	9	102	v Worcestershire at Blackpool...	1953
S. P. Gupte (President's XI) ...	24.2	7	78	v Combined XI at Bombay ...	1954-55
J. C. Laker (Surrey)	46	18	88	v Australians at The Oval	1956
J. C. Laker (England)	51.2	23	53	v Australia at Manchester	1956
G. A. R. Lock (Surrey)	29.1	18	54	v Kent at Blackheath	1956
K. Smales (Nottinghamshire) ...	41.3	20	66	v Gloucestershire at Stroud	1956
P. M. Chatterjee (Bengal)	19	11	20	v Assam at Jorhat	1956-57
J. D. Bannister (Warwickshire) .	23.3	11	41	v Comb. Services at Birmingham‡	1959
A. J. G. Pearson (Cambridge U.)	30.3	8	78	v Leics. at Loughborough	1961
N. I. Thomson (Sussex)	34.2	19	49	v Warwickshire at Worthing	1964
P. J. Allan (Queensland)	15.6	3	61	v Victoria at Melbourne	1965-66
I. J. Brayshaw (W. Australia) ...	17.6	4	44	v Victoria at Perth	1967-68
Shahid Mahmood (Karachi Whites)	25	5	58	v Khairpur at Karachi......	1969-70
E. E. Hemmings (International XI)...........	49.3	14	175	v West Indies XI at Kingston ...	1982-83
P. Sunderam (Rajasthan)	22	5	78	v Vidarbha at Jodhpur	1985-86
S. T. Jefferies (W. Province)....	22.5	7	59	v Orange Free State at Cape Town	1987-88
Imran Adil (Bahawalpur)	22.5	3	92	v Faisalabad at Faisalabad	1989-90
G. P. Wickremasinghe (Sinhalese SC)	19.2	5	41	v Kalutara at Colombo (SSC) ...	1991-92
R. L. Johnson (Middlesex)	18.5	6	45	v Derbyshire at Derby	1994

Note: The following instances were achieved in 12-a-side matches:

E. M. Grace (MCC)	32.2	7	69	v Gents of Canterbury at Canterbury	1862
W. G. Grace (MCC)	46.1	15	92	v Kent at Canterbury......	1873
†D. C. S. Hinds (A. B. St Hill's XII)	19.1	6	36	v Trinidad at Port-of-Spain	1900-01

*J. Wisden and W. E. Hollies achieved the feat without the direct assistance of a fielder. Wisden's ten
were all bowled; Hollies bowled seven and had three lbw.*

† *On debut in first-class cricket.* ‡ *Mitchells & Butlers Ground.*

OUTSTANDING ANALYSES

	O	M	R	W		
H. Verity (Yorkshire)	19.4	16	10	10	v Nottinghamshire at Leeds	1932
G. Elliott (Victoria)	19	17	2	9	v Tasmania at Launceston	1857-58
Ahad Khan (Railways)	6.3	4	7	9	v Dera Ismail Khan at Lahore	1964-65
J. C. Laker (England)	14	12	2	8	v The Rest at Bradford	1950
D. Shackleton (Hampshire)	11.1	7	4	8	v Somerset at Weston-s-Mare	1955
E. Peate (Yorkshire)	16	11	5	8	v Surrey at Holbeck	1883
F. R. Spofforth (Australians)	8.3	6	3	7	v England XI at Birmingham	1884
W. A. Henderson (N.E. Transvaal)	9.3	7	4	7	v Orange Free State at Bloemfontein	1937-38
Rajinder Goel (Haryana)	7	4	4	7	v Jammu and Kashmir at Chandigarh	1977-78
V. I. Smith (South Africans)	4.5	3	1	6	v Derbyshire at Derby	1947
S. Cosstick (Victoria)	21.1	20	1	6	v Tasmania at Melbourne	1868-69
Israr Ali (Bahawalpur)	11	10	1	6	v Dacca U. at Bahawalpur	1957-58
A. D. Pougher (MCC)	3	3	0	5	v Australians at Lord's	1896
G. R. Cox (Sussex)	6	6	0	5	v Somerset at Weston-s-Mare	1921
R. K. Tyldesley (Lancashire)	5	5	0	5	v Leicestershire at Manchester	1924
P. T. Mills (Gloucestershire)	6.4	6	0	5	v Somerset at Bristol	1928

MOST WICKETS IN A MATCH

19-90	J. C. Laker	England v Australia at Manchester	1956
17-48	C. Blythe	Kent v Northamptonshire at Northampton	1907
17-50	C. T. B. Turner	Australians v England XI at Hastings	1888
17-54	W. P. Howell	Australians v Western Province at Cape Town	1902-03
17-56	C. W. L. Parker	Gloucestershire v Essex at Gloucester	1925
17-67	A. P. Freeman	Kent v Sussex at Hove	1922
17-89	W. G. Grace	Gloucestershire v Nottinghamshire at Cheltenham	1877
17-89	F. C. L. Matthews	Nottinghamshire v Northants at Nottingham	1923
17-91	H. Dean	Lancashire v Yorkshire at Liverpool	1913
17-91	H. Verity	Yorkshire v Essex at Leyton	1933
17-92	A. P. Freeman	Kent v Warwickshire at Folkestone	1932
17-103	W. Mycroft	Derbyshire v Hampshire at Southampton	1876
17-106	G. R. Cox	Sussex v Warwickshire at Horsham	1926
17-106	T. W. J. Goddard	Gloucestershire v Kent at Bristol	1939
17-119	W. Mead	Essex v Hampshire at Southampton	1895
17-137	W. Brearley	Lancashire v Somerset at Manchester	1905
17-159	S. F. Barnes	England v South Africa at Johannesburg	1913-14
17-201	G. Giffen	South Australia v Victoria at Adelaide	1885-86
17-212	J. C. Clay	Glamorgan v Worcestershire at Swansea	1937

SIXTEEN OR MORE WICKETS IN A DAY

17-48	C. Blythe	Kent v Northamptonshire at Northampton	1907
17-91	H. Verity	Yorkshire v Essex at Leyton	1933
17-106	T. W. J. Goddard	Gloucestershire v Kent at Bristol	1939
16-38	T. Emmett	Yorkshire v Cambridgeshire at Hunslet	1869
16-52	J. Southerton	South v North at Lord's	1875
16-69	T. G. Wass	Nottinghamshire v Lancashire at Liverpool	1906
16-38	A. E. E. Vogler	E. Province v Griqualand West at Johannesburg	1906-07
16-103	T. G. Wass	Nottinghamshire v Essex at Nottingham	1908
16-83	J. C. White	Somerset v Worcestershire at Bath	1919

FOUR WICKETS WITH CONSECUTIVE BALLS

J. Wells	Kent v Sussex at Brighton	1862
G. Ulyett	Lord Harris's XI v New South Wales at Sydney	1878-79
G. Nash	Lancashire v Somerset at Manchester	1882
J. B. Hide	Sussex v MCC and Ground at Lord's	1890
F. J. Shacklock	Nottinghamshire v Somerset at Nottingham	1893
A. D. Downes	Otago v Auckland at Dunedin.......................	1893-94
F. Martin	MCC and Ground v Derbyshire at Lord's	1895
A. W. Mold	Lancashire v Nottinghamshire at Nottingham..........	1895
W. Brearley†	Lancashire v Somerset at Manchester.................	1905
S. Haigh	MCC v Army XI at Pretoria	1905-06
A. E. Trott‡	Middlesex v Somerset at Lord's.....................	1907
F. A. Tarrant	Middlesex v Gloucestershire at Bristol	1907
A. Drake	Yorkshire v Derbyshire at Chesterfield	1914
S. G. Smith	Northamptonshire v Warwickshire at Birmingham......	1914
H. A. Peach	Surrey v Sussex at The Oval	1924
A. F. Borland	Natal v Griqualand West at Kimberley	1926-27
J. E. H. Hooker†	New South Wales v Victoria at Sydney	1928-29
R. K. Tyldesley†	Lancashire v Derbyshire at Derby	1929
R. J. Crisp	Western Province v Griqualand West at Johannesburg ..	1931-32
R. J. Crisp	Western Province v Natal at Durban	1933-34
A. R. Gover	Surrey v Worcestershire at Worcester	1935
W. H. Copson	Derbyshire v Warwickshire at Derby	1937
W. A. Henderson	N.E. Transvaal v Orange Free State at Bloemfontein....	1937-38
F. Ridgway	Kent v Derbyshire at Folkestone	1951
A. K. Walker§	Nottinghamshire v Leicestershire at Leicester	1956
S. N. Mohol	President's XI v Combined XI at Poona	1965-66
P. I. Pocock	Surrey v Sussex at Eastbourne......................	1972
S. S. Saini†	Delhi v Himachal Pradesh at Delhi	1988-89
D. Dias	W. Province (Suburbs) v Central Province at Colombo ..	1990-91
Ali Gauhar	Karachi Blues v United Bank at Peshawar	1994-95

† *Not all in the same innings.*

‡ *Trott achieved another hat-trick in the same innings of this, his benefit match.*

§ *Having bowled Firth with the last ball of the first innings, Walker achieved a unique feat by dismissing Lester, Tompkin and Smithson with the first three balls of the second.*

Notes: In their match with England at The Oval in 1863, Surrey lost four wickets in the course of a four-ball over from G. Bennett.

Sussex lost five wickets in the course of the final (six-ball) over of their match with Surrey at Eastbourne in 1972. P. I. Pocock, who had taken three wickets in his previous over, captured four more, taking in all seven wickets with 11 balls, a feat unique in first-class matches. (The eighth wicket fell to a run-out.)

HAT-TRICKS

Double Hat-Trick

Besides Trott's performance, which is given in the preceding section, the following instances are recorded of players having performed the hat-trick twice in the same match, Rao doing so in the same innings.

A. Shaw	Nottinghamshire v Gloucestershire at Nottingham	1884
T. J. Matthews	Australia v South Africa at Manchester	1912
C. W. L. Parker	Gloucestershire v Middlesex at Bristol	1924
R. O. Jenkins	Worcestershire v Surrey at Worcester	1949
J. S. Rao	Services v Northern Punjab at Amritsar	1963-64
Amin Lakhani	Combined XI v Indians at Multan	1978-79

Five Wickets in Six Balls

W. H. Copson	Derbyshire v Warwickshire at Derby	1937
W. A. Henderson	N.E. Transvaal v Orange Free State at Bloemfontein	1937-38
P. I. Pocock	Surrey v Sussex at Eastbourne	1972

Most Hat-Tricks

Seven times: D. V. P. Wright.

Six times: T. W. J. Goddard, C. W. L. Parker.

Five times: S. Haigh, V. W. C. Jupp, A. E. G. Rhodes, F. A. Tarrant.

Four times: R. G. Barlow, J. T. Hearne, J. C. Laker, G. A. R. Lock, G. G. Macaulay, T. J. Matthews, M. J. Procter, T. Richardson, F. R. Spofforth, F. S. Trueman.

Three times: W. M. Bradley, H. J. Butler, S. T. Clarke, W. H. Copson, R. J. Crisp, J. W. H. T. Douglas, J. A. Flavell, A. P. Freeman, G. Giffen, K. Higgs, A. Hill, W. A. Humphreys, R. D. Jackman, R. O. Jenkins, A. S. Kennedy, W. H. Lockwood, E. A. McDonald, T. L. Pritchard, J. S. Rao, A. Shaw, J. B. Statham, M. W. Tate, H. Trumble, D. Wilson, G. A. Wilson.

Twice (current players only): D. G. Cork, E. E. Hemmings, M. D. Marshall, Shahid Ali Khan, P. A. Smith.

HAT-TRICK ON DEBUT

H. Hay	South Australia v Lord Hawke's XI at Unley, Adelaide . .	1902-03
H. A. Sedgwick	Yorkshire v Worcestershire at Hull	1906
V. B. Ranjane	Maharashtra v Saurashtra at Poona	1956-57
J. S. Rao	Services v Jammu & Kashmir at Delhi	1963-64
R. O. Estwick	Barbados v Guyana at Bridgetown	1982-83
S. A. Ankola	Maharashtra v Gujarat at Poona	1988-89
J. Srinath	Karnataka v Hyderabad at Secunderabad	1989-90
S. P. Mukherjee	Bengal v Hyderabad at Secunderabad	1989-90

Notes: R. R. Phillips (Border) took a hat-trick in his first over in first-class cricket (v Eastern Province at Port Elizabeth, 1939-40) having previously played in four matches without bowling.

J. S. Rao took two more hat-tricks in his next match.

250 WICKETS IN A SEASON

	Season	O	M	R	W	Avge
A. P. Freeman	1928	1,976.1	423	5,489	304	18.05
A. P. Freeman	1933	2,039	651	4,549	298	15.26
T. Richardson	1895‡	1,690.1	463	4,170	290	14.37
C. T. B. Turner**	1888†	2,427.2	1,127	3,307	283	11.68
A. P. Freeman	1931	1,618	360	4,307	276	15.60
A. P. Freeman	1930	1,914.3	472	4,632	275	16.84
T. Richardson	1897‡	1,603.4	495	3,945	273	14.45
A. P. Freeman	1929	1,670.5	381	4,879	267	18.27
W. Rhodes	1900	1,553	455	3,606	261	13.81
J. T. Hearne	1896	2,003.1	818	3,670	257	14.28
A. P. Freeman	1932	1,565.5	404	4,149	253	16.39
W. Rhodes	1901	1,565	505	3,797	251	15.12

† *Indicates 4-ball overs;* ‡ *5-ball overs.*

** *Exclusive of matches not reckoned as first-class.*

Notes: In four consecutive seasons (1928-31), A. P. Freeman took 1,122 wickets, and in eight consecutive seasons (1928-35), 2,090 wickets. In each of these eight seasons he took over 200 wickets.

T. Richardson took 1,005 wickets in four consecutive seasons (1894-97).

In 1896, J. T. Hearne took his 100th wicket as early as June 12. In 1931, C. W. L. Parker did the same and A. P. Freeman obtained his 100th wicket a day later.

LEADING BOWLERS IN AN ENGLISH SEASON

(Qualification: 10 wickets in 10 innings)

Season	Leading wicket-taker	Wkts	Avge	Top of averages	Wkts	Avge
1946	W. E. Hollies	184	15.60	A. Booth	111	11.61
1947	T. W. J. Goddard	238	17.30	J. C. Clay	65	16.44
1948	J. E. Walsh	174	19.56	J. C. Clay	41	14.17
1949	R. O. Jenkins	183	21.19	T. W. J. Goddard	160	19.18
1950	R. Tattersall	193	13.59	R. Tattersall	193	13.59
1951	R. Appleyard	200	14.14	R. Appleyard	200	14.14
1952	J. H. Wardle	177	19.54	F. S. Trueman	61	13.78
1953	B. Dooland	172	16.58	C. J. Knott	38	13.71
1954	B. Dooland	196	15.48	J. B. Statham	92	14.13
1955	G. A. R. Lock	216	14.49	R. Appleyard	85	13.01
1956	D. J. Shepherd	177	15.36	G. A. R. Lock	155	12.46
1957	G. A. R. Lock	212	12.02	G. A. R. Lock	212	12.02
1958	G. A. R. Lock	170	12.08	H. L. Jackson	143	10.99
1959	D. Shackleton	148	21.55	J. B. Statham	139	15.01
1960	F. S. Trueman	175	13.98	J. B. Statham	135	12.31
1961	J. A. Flavell	171	17.79	J. A. Flavell	171	17.79
1962	D. Shackleton	172	20.15	C. Cook	58	17.13
1963	D. Shackleton	146	16.75	C. C. Griffith	119	12.83
1964	D. Shackleton	142	20.40	J. A. Standen	64	13.00
1965	D. Shackleton	144	16.08	H. J. Rhodes	119	11.04
1966	D. L. Underwood	157	13.80	D. L. Underwood	157	13.80
1967	T. W. Cartwright	147	15.52	D. L. Underwood	136	12.39
1968	R. Illingworth	131	14.36	O. S. Wheatley	82	12.95
1969	R. M. H. Cottam	109	21.04	A. Ward	69	14.82
1970	D. J. Shepherd	106	19.16	Majid Khan	11	18.81
1971	L. R. Gibbs	131	18.89	G. G. Arnold	83	17.12
1972	{ T. W. Cartwright	98	18.64	I. M. Chappell	10	10.60
	{ B. Stead	98	20.38			
1973	B. S. Bedi	105	17.94	T. W. Cartwright	89	15.84
1974	A. M. E. Roberts	119	13.62	A. M. E. Roberts	119	13.62
1975	P. G. Lee	112	18.45	A. M. E. Roberts	57	15.80
1976	G. A. Cope	93	24.13	M. A. Holding	55	14.38
1977	M. J. Procter	109	18.04	R. A. Woolmer	19	15.21
1978	D. L. Underwood	110	14.49	D. L. Underwood	110	14.49
1979	{ D. L. Underwood	106	14.85	J. Garner	55	13.83
	{ J. K. Lever	106	17.30			
1980	R. D. Jackman	121	15.40	J. Garner	49	13.93
1981	R. J. Hadlee	105	14.89	R. J. Hadlee	105	14.89
1982	M. D. Marshall	134	15.73	R. J. Hadlee	61	14.57
1983	{ J. K. Lever	106	16.28	Imran Khan	12	7.16
	{ D. L. Underwood	106	19.28			
1984	R. J. Hadlee	117	14.05	R. J. Hadlee	117	14.05
1985	N. V. Radford	101	24.68	R. M. Ellison	65	17.20
1986	C. A. Walsh	118	18.17	M. D. Marshall	100	15.08
1987	N. V. Radford	109	20.81	R. J. Hadlee	97	12.64
1988	F. D. Stephenson	125	18.31	M. D. Marshall	42	13.16
1989	{ D. R. Pringle	94	18.64	T. M. Alderman	70	15.64
	{ S. L. Watkin	94	25.09			
1990	N. A. Foster	94	26.61	I. R. Bishop	59	19.05
1991	Waqar Younis	113	14.65	Waqar Younis	113	14.65
1992	C. A. Walsh	92	15.96	C. A. Walsh	92	15.96
1993	S. L. Watkin	92	22.80	Wasim Akram	59	19.27
1994	M. M. Patel	90	22.86	C. E. L. Ambrose	77	14.45
1995	A. Kumble	105	20.40	A. A. Donald	89	16.07

100 WICKETS IN A SEASON

Since Reduction of Championship Matches in 1969

Five times: D. L. Underwood 110 (1978), 106 (1979), 106 (1983), 102 (1971), 101 (1969).

Four times: J. K. Lever 116 (1984), 106 (1978), 106 (1979), 106 (1983).

Twice: B. S. Bedi 112 (1974), 105 (1973); T. W. Cartwright 108 (1969), 104 (1971); N. A. Foster 105 (1986), 102 (1991); N. Gifford 105 (1970), 104 (1983); R. J. Hadlee 117 (1984), 105 (1981); P. G. Lee 112 (1975), 101 (1973); M. D. Marshall 134 (1982), 100 (1986); M. J. Procter 109 (1977), 108 (1969); N. V. Radford 109 (1987), 101 (1985); F. J. Titmus 105 (1970), 104 (1971).

Once: J. P. Agnew 101 (1987); I. T. Botham 100 (1978); K. E. Cooper 101 (1988); R. M. H. Cottam 109 (1969); D. R. Doshi 101 (1980); J. E. Emburey 103 (1983); L. R. Gibbs 131 (1971); R. N. S. Hobbs 102 (1970); Intikhab Alam 104 (1971); R. D. Jackman 121 (1980); A. Kumble 105 (1995); A. M. E. Roberts 119 (1974); P. J. Sainsbury 107 (1971); Sarfraz Nawaz 101 (1975); M. W. W. Selvey 101 (1978); D. J. Shepherd 106 (1970); F. D. Stephenson 125 (1988); C. A. Walsh 118 (1986); Waqar Younis 113 (1991); D. Wilson 102 (1969).

100 WICKETS IN A SEASON MOST TIMES

(Includes Overseas Tours and Seasons)

23 times: W. Rhodes 200 wkts (3).

20 times: D. Shackleton (In successive seasons – 1949 to 1968 inclusive).

17 times: A. P. Freeman 300 wkts (1), 200 wkts (7).

16 times: T. W. J. Goddard 200 wkts (4), C. W. L. Parker 200 wkts (5), R. T. D. Perks, F. J. Titmus.

15 times: J. T. Hearne 200 wkts (3), G. H. Hirst 200 wkts (1), A. S. Kennedy 200 wkts (1).

14 times: C. Blythe 200 wkts (1), W. E. Hollies, G. A. R. Lock 200 wkts (2), M. W. Tate 200 wkts (3), J. C. White.

13 times: J. B. Statham.

12 times: J. Briggs, E. G. Dennett 200 wkts (1), C. Gladwin, D. J. Shepherd, N. I. Thomson, F. S. Trueman.

11 times: A. V. Bedser, G. Geary, S. Haigh, J. C. Laker, M. S. Nichols, A. E. Relf.

10 times: W. Attewell, W. G. Grace, R. Illingworth, H. L. Jackson, V. W. C. Jupp, G. G. Macaulay 200 wkts (1), W. Mead, T. B. Mitchell, T. Richardson 200 wkts (3), J Southerton 200 wkts (1), R. K. Tyldesley, D. L. Underwood, J. H. Wardle, T. G. Wass, D. V. P. Wright.

9 times: W. E. Astill, T. E. Bailey, W. E. Bowes, C. Cook, R. Howorth, J. Mercer, A. W. Mold 200 wkts (2), J. A. Newman, C. F. Root 200 wkts (1), A. Shaw 200 wkts (1), H. Verity 200 wkts (3).

8 times: T. W. Cartwright, H. Dean, J. A. Flavell, A. R. Gover 200 wkts (2), H. Larwood, G. A. Lohmann 200 wkts (3), R. Peel, J. M. Sims, F. A. Tarrant, R. Tattersall, G. J. Thompson, G. E. Tribe, A. W. Wellard, F. E. Woolley, J. A. Young.

100 WICKETS IN A SEASON OUTSIDE ENGLAND

W		Season	Country	R	Avge
116	M. W. Tate	1926-27	India/Ceylon	1,599	13.78
107	Ijaz Faqih	1985-86	Pakistan	1,719	16.06
106	C. T. B. Turner	1887-88	Australia	1,441	13.59
106	R. Benaud	1957-58	South Africa	2,056	19.39
104	S. F. Barnes	1913-14	South Africa	1,117	10.74
104	Sajjad Akbar	1989-90	Pakistan	2,328	22.38
103	Abdul Qadir	1982-83	Pakistan	2,367	22.98

1,500 WICKETS IN A CAREER

Dates in italics denote the first half of an overseas season; i.e. *1970* denotes the 1970-71 season.

		Career	W	R	Avge
1	W. Rhodes	1898-1930	4,187	69,993	16.71
2	A. P. Freeman	1914-36	3,776	69,577	18.42
3	C. W. L. Parker	1903-35	3,278	63,817	19.46
4	J. T. Hearne	1888-1923	3,061	54,352	17.75
5	T. W. J. Goddard	1922-52	2,979	59,116	19.84
6	W. G. Grace	1865-1908	2,876	51,545	17.92
7	A. S. Kennedy	1907-36	2,874	61,034	21.23
8	D. Shackleton	1948-69	2,857	53,303	18.65
9	G. A. R. Lock	1946-*70*	2,844	54,709	19.23
10	F. J. Titmus	1949-82	2,830	63,313	22.37
11	M. W. Tate	1912-37	2,784	50,571	18.16
12	G. H. Hirst	1891-1929	2,739	51,282	18.72
13	C. Blythe	1899-1914	2,506	42,136	16.81
14	D. L. Underwood	1963-87	2,465	49,993	20.28
15	W. E. Astill	1906-39	2,431	57,783	23.76
16	J. C. White	1909-37	2,356	43,759	18.57
17	W. E. Hollies	1932-57	2,323	48,656	20.94
18	F. S. Trueman	1949-69	2,304	42,154	18.29
19	J. B. Statham	1950-68	2,260	36,999	16.37
20	R. T. D. Perks	1930-55	2,233	53,770	24.07
21	J. Briggs	1879-1900	2,221	35,431	15.95
22	D. J. Shepherd	1950-72	2,218	47,302	21.32
23	E. G. Dennett	1903-26	2,147	42,571	19.82
24	T. Richardson	1892-1905	2,104	38,794	18.43
25	T. E. Bailey	1945-67	2,082	48,170	23.13
26	R. Illingworth	1951-83	2,072	42,023	20.28
27	{ N. Gifford	1960-88	2,068	48,731	23.56
	{ F. E. Woolley	1906-38	2,068	41,066	19.85
29	G. Geary	1912-38	2,063	41,339	20.03
30	D. V. P. Wright	1932-57	2,056	49,307	23.98
31	J. A. Newman	1906-30	2,032	51,111	25.15
32	†A. Shaw	1864-97	2,027	24,580	12.12
33	S. Haigh	1895-1913	2,012	32,091	15.94
34	H. Verity	1930-39	1,956	29,146	14.90
35	W. Attewell	1881-1900	1,951	29,896	15.32
36	J. C. Laker	1946-*64*	1,944	35,791	18.41
37	A. V. Bedser	1939-60	1,924	39,279	20.41
38	W. Mead	1892-1913	1,916	36,388	18.99
39	A. E. Relf	1900-21	1,897	39,724	20.94
40	P. G. H. Fender	1910-36	1,894	47,458	25.05
41	J. W. H. T. Douglas	1901-30	1,893	44,159	23.32
42	J. H. Wardle	1946-*67*	1,846	35,027	18.97
43	G. R. Cox	1895-1928	1,843	42,136	22.86
44	G. A. Lohmann	1884-*97*	1,841	25,295	13.73
45	J. W. Hearne	1909-36	1,839	44,926	24.42
46	G. G. Macaulay	1920-35	1,837	32,440	17.65
47	M. S. Nichols	1924-39	1,833	39,666	21.63
48	J. B. Mortimore	1950-75	1,807	41,904	23.18
49	C. Cook	1946-64	1,782	36,578	20.52
50	R. Peel	1882-99	1,752	28,442	16.23
51	H. L. Jackson	1947-63	1,733	30,101	17.36
52	J. K. Lever	1967-89	1,722	41,772	24.25
53	T. P. B. Smith	1929-52	1,697	45,059	26.55
54	J. Southerton	1854-79	1,681	24,290	14.44
55	A. E. Trott	*1892*-1911	1,674	35,317	21.09
56	A. W. Mold	1889-1901	1,673	26,010	15.54

		Career	W	R	Avge
57	T. G. Wass	1896-1920	1,666	34,092	20.46
58	V. W. C. Jupp..........	1909-38	1,658	38,166	23.01
59	C. Gladwin	1939-58	1,653	30,265	18.30
60	W. E. Bowes	1928-47	1,639	27,470	16.76
61	**M. D. Marshall**	*1977-94*	**1,637**	**31,145**	**19.02**
62	A. W. Wellard..........	1927-50	1,614	39,302	24.35
63	P. I. Pocock	1964-86	1,607	42,648	26.53
64	N. I. Thomson..........	1952-72	1,597	32,867	20.58
65	J. Mercer	1919-47	1,591	37,210	23.38
	G. J. Thompson	1897-1922	1,591	30,058	18.89
67	J. M. Sims	1929-53	1,581	39,401	24.92
68	**J. E. Emburey**	*1973-95*	**1,577**	**40,657**	**25.78**
69	T. Emmett	1866-88	1,571	21,314	13.56
	Intikhab Alam..........	*1957-82*	1,571	43,474	27.67
71	B. S. Bedi.............	*1961-81*	1,560	33,843	21.69
72	W. Voce...............	1927-52	1,558	35,961	23.08
73	A. R. Gover	1928-48	1,555	36,753	23.63
74	T. W. Cartwright	1952-77	1,536	29,357	19.11
	K. Higgs	1958-86	1,536	36,267	23.61
76	James Langridge	1924-53	1,530	34,524	22.56
77	J. A. Flavell...........	1949-67	1,529	32,847	21.48
78	**E. E. Hemmings**	*1966-95*	**1,515**	**44,403**	**29.30**
79	C. F. Root	1910-33	1,512	31,933	21.11
	F. A. Tarrant...........	*1898-1936*	1,512	26,450	17.49
81	R. K. Tyldesley	1919-35	1,509	25,980	17.21

Bold type denotes those who played in 1994-95 and 1995 seasons.

† *The figures for A. Shaw exclude one wicket for which no analysis is available.*

Note: Some works of reference provide career figures which differ from those in this list, owing to the exclusion or inclusion of matches recognised or not recognised as first-class by *Wisden*.

Current Players with 1,000 Wickets

	Career	W	R	Avge
C. A. Walsh	*1981-95*	1,305	29,200	22.37
J. H. Childs........	1975-95	1,009	29,835	29.56

ALL-ROUND RECORDS

HUNDRED AND TEN WICKETS IN AN INNINGS

V. E. Walker, England v Surrey at The Oval; 20*, 108, ten for 74, and four for 17.   1859
W. G. Grace, MCC v Oxford University at Oxford; 104, two for 60, and ten for 49.   1886

Note: E. M. Grace, for MCC v Gentlemen of Kent in a 12-a-side match at Canterbury in 1862, scored 192* and took five for 77 and ten for 69.

TWO HUNDRED RUNS AND SIXTEEN WICKETS

G. Giffen, South Australia v Victoria at Adelaide; 271, nine for 96, and seven for 70.   1891-92

HUNDRED IN EACH INNINGS AND FIVE WICKETS TWICE

G. H. Hirst, Yorkshire v Somerset at Bath; 111, 117*, six for 70, and five for 45.   1906

HUNDRED IN EACH INNINGS AND TEN WICKETS

B. J. T. Bosanquet, Middlesex v Sussex at Lord's; 103, 100*, three for 75, and
eight for 53 1905
F. D. Stephenson, Nottinghamshire v Yorkshire at Nottingham; 111, 117, four for
105, and seven for 117 1988

HUNDRED AND HAT-TRICK

G. Giffen, Australians v Lancashire at Manchester; 13, 113, and six for 55 including
hat-trick 1884
W. E. Roller, Surrey v Sussex at The Oval; 204, four for 28 including hat-trick, and
two for 16. (Unique instance of 200 and hat-trick.) 1885
W. B. Burns, Worcestershire v Gloucestershire at Worcester; 102*, three for 56
including hat-trick, and two for 21 1913
V. W. C. Jupp, Sussex v Essex at Colchester; 102, six for 61 including hat-trick, and
six for 78 1921
R. E. S. Wyatt, MCC v Ceylon at Colombo; 124 and five for 39 including hat-trick. 1926-27
L. N. Constantine, West Indians v Northamptonshire at Northampton; seven for 45
including hat-trick, 107, and six for 67 1928
D. E. Davies, Glamorgan v Leicestershire at Leicester; 139, four for 27, and three for
31 including hat-trick 1937
V. M. Merchant, Dr C. R. Pereira's XI v Sir Homi Mehta's XI at Bombay; 1, 142,
three for 31 including hat-trick, and no wicket for 17 1946-47
M. J. Procter, Gloucestershire v Essex at Westcliff-on-Sea; 51, 102, three for 43, and
five for 30 including hat-trick (all lbw) 1972
M. J. Procter, Gloucestershire v Leicestershire at Bristol; 122, no wkt for 32, and
seven for 26 including hat-trick 1979

Note: W. G. Grace, for MCC v Kent in a 12-a-side match at Canterbury in 1874, scored 123 and
took five for 82 and six for 47 including a hat-trick.

SEASON DOUBLES

2,000 Runs and 200 Wickets

1906   G. H. Hirst   2,385 runs and 208 wickets

3,000 Runs and 100 Wickets

1937   J. H. Parks   3,003 runs and 101 wickets

2,000 Runs and 100 Wickets

	Season	R	W		Season	R	W
W. G. Grace	1873	2,139	106	F. E. Woolley	1914	2,272	125
W. G. Grace	1876	2,622	129	J. W. Hearne	1920	2,148	142
C. L. Townsend	1899	2,440	101	V. W. C. Jupp	1921	2,169	121
G. L. Jessop	1900	2,210	104	F. E. Woolley	1921	2,101	167
G. H. Hirst	1904	2,501	132	F. E. Woolley	1922	2,022	163
G. H. Hirst	1905	2,266	110	F. E. Woolley	1923	2,091	101
W. Rhodes	1909	2,094	141	L. F. Townsend	1933	2,268	100
W. Rhodes	1911	2,261	117	D. E. Davies	1937	2,012	103
F. A. Tarrant	1911	2,030	111	James Langridge	1937	2,082	101
J. W. Hearne	1913	2,036	124	T. E Bailey	1959	2,011	100
J. W. Hearne	1914	2,116	123				

1,000 Runs and 200 Wickets

	Season	R	W		Season	R	W
A. E. Trott	1899	1,175	239	M. W. Tate	1923	1,168	219
A. E. Trott	1900	1,337	211	M. W. Tate	1924	1,419	205
A. S. Kennedy ...	1922	1,129	205	M. W. Tate	1925	1,290	228

1,000 Runs and 100 Wickets

Sixteen times: W. Rhodes.
Fourteen times: G. H. Hirst.
Ten times: V. W. C. Jupp.
Nine times: W. E. Astill.
Eight times: T. E. Bailey, W. G. Grace, M. S. Nichols, A. E. Relf, F. A. Tarrant, M. W. Tate†, F. J. Titmus, F. E. Woolley.
Seven times: G. E. Tribe.
Six times: P. G. H. Fender, R. Illingworth, James Langridge.
Five times: J. W. H. T. Douglas, J. W. Hearne, A. S. Kennedy, J. A. Newman.
Four times: E. G. Arnold, J. Gunn, R. Kilner, B. R. Knight.
Three times: W. W. Armstrong (Australians), L. C. Braund, G. Giffen (Australians), N. E. Haig, R. Howorth, C. B. Llewellyn, J. B. Mortimore, Ray Smith, S. G. Smith, L. F. Townsend, A. W. Wellard.

† *M. W. Tate also scored 1,193 runs and took 116 wickets for MCC in first-class matches on the 1926-27 MCC tour of India and Ceylon.*

Note: R. J. Hadlee (1984) and F. D. Stephenson (1988) are the only players to perform the feat since the reduction of County Championship matches. A complete list of those performing the feat before then will be found on p. 202 of the 1982 *Wisden.*

Wicket-Keeper's Double

	Season	R	D
L. E. G. Ames	1928	1,919	122
L. E. G. Ames	1929	1,795	128
L. E. G. Ames	1932	2,482	104
J. T. Murray	1957	1,025	104

20,000 RUNS AND 2,000 WICKETS IN A CAREER

	Career	R	Avge	W	Avge	Doubles
W. E. Astill	1906-39	22,731	22.55	2,431	23.76	9
T. E. Bailey	1945-67	28,641	33.42	2,082	23.13	8
W. G. Grace	1865-1908	54,896	39.55	2,876	17.92	8
G. H. Hirst	1891-1929	36,323	34.13	2,739	18.72	14
R. Illingworth	1951-83	24,134	28.06	2,072	20.28	6
W. Rhodes	1898-1930	39,802	30.83	4,187	16.71	16
M. W. Tate........	1912-37	21,717	25.01	2,784	18.16	8
F. J. Titmus	1949-82	21,588	23.11	2,830	22.37	8
F. E. Woolley	1906-38	58,969	40.75	2,068	19.85	8

WICKET-KEEPING RECORDS

MOST DISMISSALS IN AN INNINGS

9 (8ct, 1st)	Tahir Rashid	Habib Bank v PACO at Gujranwala	1992-93
8 (all ct)	A. T. W. Grout	Queensland v Western Australia at Brisbane	1959-60
8 (all ct)†	D. E. East	Essex v Somerset at Taunton	1985
8 (all ct)	S. A. Marsh‡	Kent v Middlesex at Lord's.	1991
8 (6ct, 2st)	T. J. Zoehrer	Australians v Surrey at The Oval	1993
7 (4ct, 3st)	E. J. Smith	Warwickshire v Derbyshire at Birmingham	1926
7 (6ct, 1st)	W. Farrimond	Lancashire v Kent at Manchester.	1930
7 (all ct)	W. F. F. Price	Middlesex v Yorkshire at Lord's.	1937
7 (3ct, 4st)	D. Tallon	Queensland v Victoria at Brisbane	1938-39
7 (all ct)	R. A. Saggers	New South Wales v Combined XI at Brisbane	1940-41
7 (1ct, 6st)	H. Yarnold	Worcestershire v Scotland at Dundee	1951
7 (4ct, 3st)	J. Brown	Scotland v Ireland at Dublin	1957
7 (6ct, 1st)	N. Kirsten	Border v Rhodesia at East London	1959-60
7 (all ct)	M. S. Smith	Natal v Border at East London	1959-60
7 (all ct)	K. V. Andrew	Northamptonshire v Lancashire at Manchester . . .	1962
7 (all ct)	A. Long	Surrey v Sussex at Hove	1964
7 (all ct)	R. M. Schofield	Central Districts v Wellington at Wellington	1964-65
7 (all ct)	R. W. Taylor	Derbyshire v Glamorgan at Derby	1966
7 (6ct, 1st)	H. B. Taber	New South Wales v South Australia at Adelaide . .	1968-69
7 (6ct, 1st)	E. W. Jones	Glamorgan v Cambridge University at Cambridge.	1970
7 (6ct, 1st)	S. Benjamin	Central Zone v North Zone at Bombay	1973-74
7 (all ct)	R. W. Taylor	Derbyshire v Yorkshire at Chesterfield	1975
7 (6ct, 1st)	Shahid Israr	Karachi Whites v Quetta at Karachi	1976-77
7 (4ct, 3st)	Wasim Bari	PIA v Sind at Lahore	1977-78
7 (all ct)	J. A. Maclean	Queensland v Victoria at Melbourne	1977-78
7 (5ct, 2st)	Taslim Arif	National Bank v Punjab at Lahore	1978-79
7 (all ct)	Wasim Bari	Pakistan v New Zealand at Auckland	1978-79
7 (all ct)	R. W. Taylor	England v India at Bombay	1979-80
7 (all ct)	D. L. Bairstow	Yorkshire v Derbyshire at Scarborough	1982
7 (6ct, 1st)	R. B. Phillips	Queensland v New Zealanders at Bundaberg	1982-83
7 (3ct, 4st)	Masood Iqbal	Habib Bank v Lahore at Lahore	1982-83
7 (3ct, 4st)	Arif-ud-Din	United Bank v PACO at Sahiwal.	1983-84
7 (6ct, 1st)	R. J. East	OFS v Western Province B at Cape Town	1984-85
7 (all ct)	B. A. Young	Northern Districts v Canterbury at Christchurch . .	1986-87
7 (all ct)	D. J. Richardson	Eastern Province v OFS at Bloemfontein	1988-89
7 (6ct, 1st)	Dildar Malik	Multan v Faisalabad at Sahiwal	1988-89
7 (all ct)	W. K. Hegg	Lancashire v Derbyshire at Chesterfield	1989
7 (all ct)	Imran Zia	Bahawalpur v Faisalabad at Faisalabad.	1989-90
7 (all ct)	I. D. S. Smith	New Zealand v Sri Lanka at Hamilton	1990-91
7 (all ct)	J. F. Holyman	Tasmania v Western Australia at Hobart	1990-91
7 (all ct)	P. J. L. Radley	OFS v Western Province at Cape Town	1990-91
7 (all ct)	C. P. Metson	Glamorgan v Derbyshire at Chesterfield	1991
7 (all ct)	H. M. de Vos	W. Transvaal v E. Transvaal at Potchefstroom . . .	1993-94
7 (all ct)	P. Kirsten	Griqualand West v W. Transvaal at Potchefstroom	1993-94
7 (6ct, 1st)	S. A. Marsh	Kent v Durham at Canterbury	1994
7 (all ct)	K. J. Piper	Warwickshire v Essex at Birmingham	1994
7 (6ct, 1st)	K. J. Piper	Warwickshire v Derbyshire at Chesterfield	1994

† *The first eight wickets to fall.*   ‡ *S. A. Marsh also scored 108*.*

WICKET-KEEPERS' HAT-TRICKS

W. H. Brain, Gloucestershire v Somerset at Cheltenham, 1893 – three stumpings off successive balls from C. L. Townsend.

G. O. Dawkes, Derbyshire v Worcestershire at Kidderminster, 1958 – three catches off successive balls from H. L. Jackson.

R. C. Russell, Gloucestershire v Surrey at The Oval, 1986 – three catches off successive balls from C. A. Walsh and D. V. Lawrence (2).

MOST DISMISSALS IN A MATCH

12 (8ct, 4st)	E. Pooley	Surrey v Sussex at The Oval	1868
12 (9ct, 3st)	D. Tallon	Queensland v New South Wales at Sydney	1938-39
12 (9ct, 3st)	H. B. Taber	New South Wales v South Australia at Adelaide.	1968-69
11 (all ct)	A. Long	Surrey v Sussex at Hove	1964
11 (all ct)	R. W. Marsh	Western Australia v Victoria at Perth	1975-76
11 (all ct)	D. L. Bairstow	Yorkshire v Derbyshire at Scarborough	1982
11 (all ct)	W. K. Hegg	Lancashire v Derbyshire at Chesterfield	1989
11 (all ct)	A. J. Stewart	Surrey v Leicestershire at Leicester	1989
11 (all ct)	T. J. Nielsen	South Australia v Western Australia at Perth . .	1990-91
11 (10ct, 1st)	I. A. Healy	Australians v N. Transvaal at Verwoerdburg . .	1993-94
11 (10ct, 1st)	K. J. Piper	Warwickshire v Derbyshire at Chesterfield	1994

MOST DISMISSALS IN A SEASON

128 (79ct, 49st)	L. E. G. Ames	Kent	1929
122 (70ct, 52st)	L. E. G. Ames	Kent	1928
110 (63ct, 47st)	H. Yarnold	Worcestershire	1949
107 (77ct, 30st)	G. Duckworth	Lancashire	1928
107 (96ct, 11st)	J. G. Binks	Yorkshire	1960
104 (40ct, 64st)	L. E. G. Ames	Kent	1932
104 (82ct, 22st)	J. T. Murray	Middlesex	1957
102 (69ct, 33st)	F. H. Huish	Kent	1913
102 (95ct, 7st)	J. T. Murray	Middlesex	1960
101 (62ct, 39st)	F. H. Huish	Kent	1911
101 (85ct, 16st)	R. Booth	Worcestershire	1960
100 (91ct, 9st)	R. Booth	Worcestershire	1964

MOST DISMISSALS IN A CAREER

Dates in italics denote the first half of an overseas season; i.e. *1914* denotes the 1914-15 season.

		Career	M	Ct	St	Total
1	R. W. Taylor	1960-88	639	1,473	176	1,649
2	J. T. Murray	1952-75	635	1,270	257	1,527
3	H. Strudwick	1902-27	675	1,242	255	1,497
4	A. P. E. Knott	1964-85	511	1,211	133	1,344
5	F. H. Huish	1895-*1914*	497	933	377	1,310
6	B. Taylor	1949-73 . . . .;. . .	572	1,083	211	1,294
7	D. Hunter	1889-1909	548	906	347	1,253
8	H. R. Butt	1890-1912	550	953	275	1,228
9	J. H. Board	1891-*1914*	525	852	355	1,207
10	H. Elliott	1920-47	532	904	302	1,206
11	J. M. Parks	1949-76	739	1,088	93	1,181
12	R. Booth	1951-70	468	948	178	1,126
13	L. E. G. Ames	1926-51	593	703	418†	1,121
14	D. L. Bairstow	1970-90	459	961	138	1,099
15	G. Duckworth	1923-47	504	753	343	1,096
16	H. W. Stephenson	1948-64	462	748	334	1,082
17	J. G. Binks	1955-75	502	895	176	1,071
18	T. G. Evans	1939-69	465	816	250	1,066
19	A. Long	1960-80	452	922	124	1,046
20	G. O. Dawkes	1937-61	482	895	148	1,043
21	R. W. Tolchard	1965-83	483	912	125	1,037
22	W. L. Cornford	1921-47	496	675	342	1,017

† *Record.*

Current Players with 500 Dismissals

	Career	M	Ct	St	Total
B. N. French	1976-95	360	817	100	917
R. C. Russell	1981-95	318	751	96	847
S. J. Rhodes	1981-95	289	733	96	829
C. P. Metson	1981-95	221	538	48	586
S. A. Marsh	1982-95	227	529	42	571
D. Ripley	1984-95	219	473	67	540
D. J. Richardson	1977-94	166	481	33	514

FIELDING RECORDS

(Excluding wicket-keepers)

MOST CATCHES IN AN INNINGS

7	M. J. Stewart	Surrey v Northamptonshire at Northampton	1957
7	A. S. Brown	Gloucestershire v Nottinghamshire at Nottingham	1966

MOST CATCHES IN A MATCH

10	W. R. Hammond†	Gloucestershire v Surrey at Cheltenham	1928
8	W. B. Burns	Worcestershire v Yorkshire at Bradford	1907
8	F. G. Travers	Europeans v Parsees at Bombay	1923-24
8	A. H. Bakewell	Northamptonshire v Essex at Leyton	1928
8	W. R. Hammond	Gloucestershire v Worcestershire at Cheltenham	1932
8	K. J. Grieves	Lancashire v Sussex at Manchester	1951
8	C. A. Milton	Gloucestershire v Sussex at Hove	1952
8	G. A. R. Lock	Surrey v Warwickshire at The Oval	1957
8	J. M. Prodger	Kent v Gloucestershire at Cheltenham	1961
8	P. M. Walker	Glamorgan v Derbyshire at Swansea	1970
8	Masood Anwar	Rawalpindi v Lahore Division at Rawalpindi	1983-84
8	M. C. J. Ball	Gloucestershire v Yorkshire at Cheltenham	1994

† *Hammond also scored a hundred in each innings.*

MOST CATCHES IN A SEASON

78	W. R. Hammond	1928
77	M. J. Stewart	1957
73	P. M. Walker	1961
71	P. J. Sharpe	1962
70	J. Tunnicliffe	1901
69	J. G. Langridge	1955
69	P. M. Walker	1960
66	J. Tunnicliffe	1895
65	W. R. Hammond	1925
65	P. M. Walker	1959

65	D. W. Richardson	1961
64	K. F. Barrington	1957
64	G. A. R. Lock	1957
63	J. Tunnicliffe	1896
63	J. Tunnicliffe	1904
63	K. J. Grieves	1950
63	C. A. Milton	1956
61	J. V. Wilson	1955
61	M. J. Stewart	1958

Note: The most catches by a fielder since the reduction of County Championship matches in 1969 is 49 by C. J. Tavaré in 1978.

MOST CATCHES IN A CAREER

Dates in italics denote the first half of an overseas season; i.e. *1970* denotes the 1970-71 season.

1,018	F. E. Woolley (1906-38)		784	J. G. Langridge (1928-55)
887	W. G. Grace (1865-1908)		764	W. Rhodes (1898-1930)
830	G. A. R. Lock (1946-*70*)		758	C. A. Milton (1948-74)
819	W. R. Hammond (1920-51)		754	E. H. Hendren (1907-38)
813	D. B. Close (1949-86)			

Most Catches by Current Players

525	G. A. Gooch (1973-95)		441	M. W. Gatting (1975-95)
452	J. E. Emburey (1973-95)		405	C. W. J. Athey (1976-95)

TEAM RECORDS

HIGHEST TOTALS

1,107	Victoria v New South Wales at Melbourne	1926-27
1,059	Victoria v Tasmania at Melbourne	1922-23
951-7 dec.	Sind v Baluchistan at Karachi	1973-74
944-6 dec.	Hyderabad v Andhra at Secunderabad	1993-94
918	New South Wales v South Australia at Sydney	1900-01
912-8 dec.	Holkar v Mysore at Indore	1945-46
912-6 dec.†	Tamil Nadu v Goa at Panjim	1988-89
910-6 dec.	Railways v Dera Ismail Khan at Lahore	1964-65
903-7 dec.	England v Australia at The Oval	1938
887	Yorkshire v Warwickshire at Birmingham	1896
868†	North Zone v West Zone at Bhilai	1987-88
863	Lancashire v Surrey at The Oval	1990
855-6 dec.†	Bombay v Hyderabad at Bombay	1990-91
849	England v West Indies at Kingston	1929-30
843	Australians v Oxford & Cambridge U P & P at Portsmouth	1893
839	New South Wales v Tasmania at Sydney	1898-99
826-4	Maharashtra v Western India States at Poona	1948-49
824	Lahore Greens v Bahawalpur at Lahore	1965-66
821-7 dec.	South Australia v Queensland at Adelaide	1939-40
815	New South Wales v Victoria at Sydney	1908-09
811	Surrey v Somerset at The Oval	1899
810-4 dec.	Warwickshire v Durham at Birmingham	1994
807	New South Wales v South Australia at Adelaide	1899-1900
805	New South Wales v Victoria at Melbourne	1905-06
803-4 dec.	Kent v Essex at Brentwood	1934
803	Non-Smokers v Smokers at East Melbourne	1886-87
802-8 dec.	Karachi Blues v Lahore City at Peshawar	1994-95
802	New South Wales v South Australia at Sydney	1920-21
801	Lancashire v Somerset at Taunton	1895

† *Tamil Nadu's total of 912-6 dec. included 52 penalty runs from their opponents' failure to meet the required bowling rate. North Zone's total of 868 included 68 and Bombay's total of 855-6 dec. included 48.*

HIGHEST FOR EACH FIRST-CLASS COUNTY

Derbyshire	645	v Hampshire at Derby	1898
Durham	625-6 dec.	v Derbyshire at Chesterfield	1994
Essex	761-6 dec.	v Leicestershire at Chelmsford	1990
Glamorgan	587-8 dec.	v Derbyshire at Cardiff	1951
Gloucestershire	653-6 dec.	v Glamorgan at Bristol	1928
Hampshire	672-7 dec.	v Somerset at Taunton	1899
Kent	803-4 dec.	v Essex at Brentwood	1934
Lancashire	863	v Surrey at The Oval	1990
Leicestershire	701-4 dec.	v Worcestershire at Worcester	1906
Middlesex	642-3 dec.	v Hampshire at Southampton	1923
Northamptonshire	781-7 dec.	v Nottinghamshire at Northampton	1995
Nottinghamshire	739-7 dec.	v Leicestershire at Nottingham	1903
Somerset	675-9 dec.	v Hampshire at Bath	1924
Surrey	811	v Somerset at The Oval	1899
Sussex	705-8 dec.	v Surrey at Hastings	1902
Warwickshire	810-4 dec.	v Durham at Birmingham	1994
Worcestershire	670-7 dec.	v Somerset at Worcester	1995
Yorkshire	887	v Warwickshire at Birmingham	1896

HIGHEST AGAINST EACH FIRST-CLASS COUNTY

Derbyshire	662	by Yorkshire at Chesterfield	1898
Durham	810-4 dec.	by Warwickshire at Birmingham	1994
Essex	803-4 dec.	by Kent at Brentwood	1934
Glamorgan	657-7 dec.	by Warwickshire at Birmingham	1994
Gloucestershire	774-7 dec.	by Australians at Bristol	1948
Hampshire	742	by Surrey at The Oval	1909
Kent	676	by Australians at Canterbury	1921
Lancashire	707-9 dec.	by Surrey at The Oval	1990
Leicestershire	761-6 dec.	by Essex at Chelmsford	1990
Middlesex	665	by West Indians at Lord's	1939
Northamptonshire	670-9 dec.	by Sussex at Hove	1921
Nottinghamshire	781-7 dec.	by Northamptonshire at Northampton	1995
Somerset	811	by Surrey at The Oval	1899
Surrey	863	by Lancashire at The Oval	1990
Sussex	726	by Nottinghamshire at Nottingham	1895
Warwickshire	887	by Yorkshire at Birmingham	1896
Worcestershire	701-4 dec.	by Leicestershire at Worcester	1906
Yorkshire	630	by Somerset at Leeds	1901

LOWEST TOTALS

12	Oxford University v MCC and Ground at Oxford	†1877
12	Northamptonshire v Gloucestershire at Gloucester	1907
13	Auckland v Canterbury at Auckland	1877-78
13	Nottinghamshire v Yorkshire at Nottingham	1901
14	Surrey v Essex at Chelmsford	1983
15	MCC v Surrey at Lord's	1839
15	Victoria v MCC at Melbourne	†1903-04
15	Northamptonshire v Yorkshire at Northampton	†1908
15	Hampshire v Warwickshire at Birmingham	1922

(Following on, Hampshire scored 521 and won by 155 runs.)

16	MCC and Ground v Surrey at Lord's	1872
16	Derbyshire v Nottinghamshire at Nottingham	1879
16	Surrey v Nottinghamshire at The Oval	1880
16	Warwickshire v Kent at Tonbridge	1913
16	Trinidad v Barbados at Bridgetown	1942-43
16	Border v Natal at East London (first innings)	1959-60
17	Gentlemen of Kent v Gentlemen of England at Lord's	1850
17	Gloucestershire v Australians at Cheltenham	1896
18	The Bs v England at Lord's	1831
18	Kent v Sussex at Gravesend	†1867
18	Tasmania v Victoria at Melbourne	1868-69
18	Australians v MCC and Ground at Lord's	†1896
18	Border v Natal at East London (second innings)	1959-60
19	Sussex v Surrey at Godalming	1830
19	Sussex v Nottinghamshire at Hove	†1873
19	MCC and Ground v Australians at Lord's	1878
19	Wellington v Nelson at Nelson	1885-86

† *Signifies that one man was absent.*

Note: At Lord's in 1810, The Bs, with one man absent, were dismissed by England for 6.

LOWEST TOTAL IN A MATCH

| 34 | (16 and 18) Border v Natal at East London | 1959-60 |
| 42 | (27 and 15) Northamptonshire v Yorkshire at Northampton | 1908 |

Note: Northamptonshire batted one man short in each innings.

LOWEST FOR EACH FIRST-CLASS COUNTY

Derbyshire	16	v Nottinghamshire at Nottingham	1879
Durham	83	v Lancashire at Manchester	1993
Essex	30	v Yorkshire at Leyton	1901
Glamorgan	22	v Lancashire at Liverpool	1924
Gloucestershire	17	v Australians at Cheltenham	1896
Hampshire	15	v Warwickshire at Birmingham	1922
Kent	18	v Sussex at Gravesend	1867
Lancashire	25	v Derbyshire at Manchester	1871
Leicestershire	25	v Kent at Leicester	1912
Middlesex	20	v MCC at Lord's	1864
Northamptonshire	12	v Gloucestershire at Gloucester	1907
Nottinghamshire	13	v Yorkshire at Nottingham	1901
Somerset	25	v Gloucestershire at Bristol	1947
Surrey	14	v Essex at Chelmsford	1983
Sussex	19	v Nottinghamshire at Hove	1873
Warwickshire	16	v Kent at Tonbridge	1913
Worcestershire	24	v Yorkshire at Huddersfield	1903
Yorkshire	23	v Hampshire at Middlesbrough	1965

LOWEST AGAINST EACH FIRST-CLASS COUNTY

Derbyshire	23	by Hampshire at Burton upon Trent	1958
Durham	73	by Oxford University at Oxford	1994
Essex	14	by Surrey at Chelmsford	1983
Glamorgan	33	by Leicestershire at Ebbw Vale	1965
Gloucestershire	12	by Northamptonshire at Gloucester	1907

Hampshire	23	by Yorkshire at Middlesbrough	1965
Kent	16	by Warwickshire at Tonbridge	1913
Lancashire	22	by Glamorgan at Liverpool	1924
Leicestershire	24	by Oxford University at Oxford	1985
Middlesex	31	by Gloucestershire at Bristol	1924
Northamptonshire	33	by Lancashire at Northampton	1977
Nottinghamshire {	16	by Derbyshire at Nottingham	1879
	16	by Surrey at The Oval	1880
Somerset	22	by Gloucestershire at Bristol	1920
Surrey	16	by MCC at Lord's	1872
Sussex	18	by Kent at Gravesend	1867
Warwickshire	15	by Hampshire at Birmingham	1922
Worcestershire	30	by Hampshire at Worcester	1903
Yorkshire	13	by Nottinghamshire at Nottingham	1901

HIGHEST MATCH AGGREGATES

2,376 for 37 wickets	Maharashtra v Bombay at Poona	1948-49
2,078 for 40 wickets	Bombay v Holkar at Bombay	1944-45
1,981 for 35 wickets	England v South Africa at Durban	1938-39
1,945 for 18 wickets	Canterbury v Wellington at Christchurch	1994-95
1,929 for 39 wickets	New South Wales v South Australia at Sydney	1925-26
1,911 for 34 wickets	New South Wales v Victoria at Sydney	1908-09
1,905 for 40 wickets	Otago v Wellington at Dunedin	1923-24

In Britain

1,808 for 20 wickets	Sussex v Essex at Hove	1993
1,723 for 31 wickets	England v Australia at Leeds	1948
1,650 for 19 wickets	Surrey v Lancashire at The Oval	1990
1,642 for 29 wickets	Nottinghamshire v Kent at Nottingham	1995
1,641 for 16 wickets	Glamorgan v Worcestershire at Abergavenny	1990
1,614 for 30 wickets	England v India at Manchester	1990
1,603 for 28 wickets	England v India at Lord's	1990
1,601 for 29 wickets	England v Australia at Lord's	1930
1,601 for 35 wickets	Kent v Surrey at Canterbury	1995

LOWEST AGGREGATE IN A COMPLETED MATCH

105 for 31 wickets   MCC v Australians at Lord's 1878

Note: The lowest aggregate since 1900 is 158 for 22 wickets, Surrey v Worcestershire at The Oval, 1954.

HIGHEST FOURTH-INNINGS TOTALS

(Unless otherwise stated, the side making the runs won the match.)

| 654-5 | England v South Africa at Durban | 1938-39 |

(After being set 696 to win. The match was left drawn on the tenth day.)

| 604 | Maharashtra v Bombay at Poona | 1948-49 |

(After being set 959 to win.)

| 576-8 | Trinidad v Barbados at Port-of-Spain | 1945-46 |

(After being set 672 to win. Match drawn on fifth day.)

| 572 | New South Wales v South Australia at Sydney | 1907-08 |

(After being set 593 to win.)

| 529-9 | Combined XI v South Africans at Perth | 1963-64 |

(After being set 579 to win. Match drawn on fourth day.)

518	Victoria v Queensland at Brisbane	1926-27
	(After being set 753 to win.)	
507-7	Cambridge University v MCC and Ground at Lord's	1896
506-6	South Australia v Queensland at Adelaide......................	1991-92
502-6	Middlesex v Nottinghamshire at Nottingham	1925
	(Game won by an unfinished stand of 271; a county record.)	
502-8	Players v Gentlemen at Lord's	1900
500-7	South African Universities v Western Province at Stellenbosch	1978-79

LARGEST VICTORIES

Largest Innings Victories

Inns and 851 runs:	Railways (910-6 dec.) v Dera Ismail Khan (Lahore)	1964-65
Inns and 666 runs:	Victoria (1,059) v Tasmania (Melbourne)	1922-23
Inns and 656 runs:	Victoria (1,107) v New South Wales (Melbourne)	1926-27
Inns and 605 runs:	New South Wales (918) v South Australia (Sydney).......	1900-01
Inns and 579 runs:	England (903-7 dec.) v Australia (The Oval)............	1938
Inns and 575 runs:	Sind (951-7 dec.) v Baluchistan (Karachi).............	1973-74
Inns and 527 runs:	New South Wales (713) v South Australia (Adelaide)	1908-09
Inns and 517 runs:	Australians (675) v Nottinghamshire (Nottingham)	1921

Largest Victories by Runs Margin

685 runs:	New South Wales (235 and 761-8 dec.) v Queensland (Sydney)......	1929-30
675 runs:	England (521 and 342-8 dec.) v Australia (Brisbane)	1928-29
638 runs:	New South Wales (304 and 770) v South Australia (Adelaide)	1920-21
625 runs:	Sargodha (376 and 416) v Lahore Municipal Corporation (Faisalabad)	1978-79
609 runs:	Muslim Commercial Bank (575 and 282-0 dec.) v WAPDA (Lahore).	1977-78
573 runs:	Sinhalese SC (395-7 dec. and 350-2 dec.) v Sebastianites C and AC (63 and 109) at Colombo	1990-91
571 runs:	Victoria (304 and 649) v South Australia (Adelaide).............	1926-27
562 runs:	Australia (701 and 327) v England (The Oval)	1934

Victory Without Losing a Wicket

Lancashire (166-0 dec. and 66-0) beat Leicestershire by ten wickets (Manchester)	1956
Karachi A (277-0 dec.) beat Sind A by an innings and 77 runs (Karachi)	1957-58
Railways (236-0 dec. and 16-0) beat Jammu and Kashmir by ten wickets (Srinagar)	1960-61
Karnataka (451-0 dec.) beat Kerala by an innings and 186 runs (Chikmagalur)..	1977-78

TIED MATCHES IN FIRST-CLASS CRICKET

Since 1948 a tie has been recognised only when the scores are level with all the wickets down in the fourth innings.

The following are the instances since then:

D. G. Bradman's XI v A. L. Hassett's XI at Melbourne.....................	1948-49
Hampshire v Kent at Southampton	1950
Sussex v Warwickshire at Hove.......................................	1952
Essex v Lancashire at Brentwood	1952
Northamptonshire v Middlesex at Peterborough	1953
Yorkshire v Leicestershire at Huddersfield	1954
Sussex v Hampshire at Eastbourne	1955
Victoria v New South Wales at Melbourne	1956-57
T. N. Pearce's XI v New Zealanders at Scarborough	1958
Essex v Gloucestershire at Leyton	1959
Australia v West Indies (First Test) at Brisbane	1960-61
Bahawalpur v Lahore B at Bahawalpur.................................	1961-62
Hampshire v Middlesex at Portsmouth	1967
England XI v England Under-25 XI at Scarborough	1968

Yorkshire v Middlesex at Bradford	1973
Sussex v Essex at Hove	1974
South Australia v Queensland at Adelaide	1976-77
Central Districts v England XI at New Plymouth	1977-78
Victoria v New Zealanders at Melbourne	1982-83
Muslim Commercial Bank v Railways at Sialkot	1983-84
Sussex v Kent at Hastings	1984
Northamptonshire v Kent at Northampton	1984
Eastern Province B v Boland at Albany SC, Port Elizabeth	1985-86
Natal B v Eastern Province B at Pietermaritzburg	1985-86
India v Australia (First Test) at Madras	1986-87
Gloucestershire v Derbyshire at Bristol	1987
Bahawalpur v Peshawar at Bahawalpur	1988-89
Wellington v Canterbury at Wellington	1988-89
Sussex v Kent at Hove	†1991
Nottinghamshire v Worcestershire at Nottingham	1993

† *Sussex (436) scored the highest total to tie a first-class match.*

MATCHES BEGUN AND FINISHED ON FIRST DAY

Since 1900. A fuller list may be found in the Wisden *of 1981 and preceding editions.*

Yorkshire v Worcestershire at Bradford, May 7	1900
MCC and Ground v London County at Lord's, May 20	1903
Transvaal v Orange Free State at Johannesburg, December 30	1906
Middlesex v Gentlemen of Philadelphia at Lord's, July 20	1908
Gloucestershire v Middlesex at Bristol, August 26	1909
Eastern Province v Orange Free State at Port Elizabeth, December 26	1912
Kent v Sussex at Tonbridge, June 21	1919
Lancashire v Somerset at Manchester, May 21	1925
Madras v Mysore at Madras, November 4	1934
Ireland v New Zealanders at Dublin, September 11	1937
Derbyshire v Somerset at Chesterfield, June 11	1947
Lancashire v Sussex at Manchester, July 12	1950
Surrey v Warwickshire at The Oval, May 16	1953
Somerset v Lancashire at Bath, June 6 (H. F. T. Buse's benefit)	1953
Kent v Worcestershire at Tunbridge Wells, June 15	1960

TEST MATCH RECORDS

Note: This section covers all Tests up to August 28, 1995.

BATTING RECORDS

HIGHEST INDIVIDUAL INNINGS

375	B. C. Lara	West Indies v England at St John's	1993-94
365*	G. S. Sobers	West Indies v Pakistan at Kingston	1957-58
364	L. Hutton	England v Australia at The Oval	1938
337	Hanif Mohammad	Pakistan v West Indies at Bridgetown	1957-58
336*	W. R. Hammond	England v New Zealand at Auckland	1932-33
334	D. G. Bradman	Australia v England at Leeds	1930
333	G. A. Gooch	England v India at Lord's	1990
325	A. Sandham	England v West Indies at Kingston	1929-30
311	R. B. Simpson	Australia v England at Manchester	1964
310*	J. H. Edrich	England v New Zealand at Leeds	1965
307	R. M. Cowper	Australia v England at Melbourne	1965-66
304	D. G. Bradman	Australia v England at Leeds	1934
302	L. G. Rowe	West Indies v England at Bridgetown	1973-74
299*	D. G. Bradman	Australia v South Africa at Adelaide	1931-32
299	M. D. Crowe	New Zealand v Sri Lanka at Wellington	1990-91
291	I. V. A. Richards	West Indies v England at The Oval	1976
287	R. E. Foster	England v Australia at Sydney	1903-04
285*	P. B. H. May	England v West Indies at Birmingham	1957
280*	Javed Miandad	Pakistan v India at Hyderabad	1982-83
278	D. C. S. Compton	England v Pakistan at Nottingham	1954
277	B. C. Lara	West Indies v Australia at Sydney	1992-93
274	R. G. Pollock	South Africa v Australia at Durban	1969-70
274	Zaheer Abbas	Pakistan v England at Birmingham	1971
271	Javed Miandad	Pakistan v New Zealand at Auckland	1988-89
270*	G. A. Headley	West Indies v England at Kingston	1934-35
270	D. G. Bradman	Australia v England at Melbourne	1936-37
268	G. N. Yallop	Australia v Pakistan at Melbourne	1983-84
267	P. A. de Silva	Sri Lanka v New Zealand at Wellington	1990-91
266	W. H. Ponsford	Australia v England at The Oval	1934
266	D. L. Houghton	Zimbabwe v Sri Lanka at Bulawayo	1994-95
262*	D. L. Amiss	England v West Indies at Kingston	1973-74
261	F. M. M. Worrell	West Indies v England at Nottingham	1950
260	C. C. Hunte	West Indies v Pakistan at Kingston	1957-58
260	Javed Miandad	Pakistan v England at The Oval	1987
259	G. M. Turner	New Zealand v West Indies at Georgetown . .	1971-72
258	T. W. Graveney	England v West Indies at Nottingham	1957
258	S. M. Nurse	West Indies v New Zealand at Christchurch . .	1968-69
256	R. B. Kanhai	West Indies v India at Calcutta	1958-59
256	K. F. Barrington	England v Australia at Manchester	1964
255*	D. J. McGlew	South Africa v New Zealand at Wellington . . .	1952-53
254	D. G. Bradman	Australia v England at Lord's	1930
251	W. R. Hammond	England v Australia at Sydney	1928-29
250	K. D. Walters	Australia v New Zealand at Christchurch	1976-77
250	S. F. A. F. Bacchus . . .	West Indies v India at Kanpur	1978-79

The highest individual innings for India is:

236*	S. M. Gavaskar	India v West Indies at Madras	1983-84

HUNDRED ON TEST DEBUT

C. Bannerman (165*)	Australia v England at Melbourne	1876-77
W. G. Grace (152)	England v Australia at The Oval	1880
H. Graham (107)	Australia v England at Lord's	1893

†K. S. Ranjitsinhji (154*)....	England v Australia at Manchester............	1896
†P. F. Warner (132*)......	England v South Africa at Johannesburg......	1898-99
†R. A. Duff (104)........	Australia v England at Melbourne............	1901-02
R. E. Foster (287).......	England v Australia at Sydney..............	1903-04
G. Gunn (119)...........	England v Australia at Sydney..............	1907-08
†R. J. Hartigan (116)......	Australia v England at Adelaide............	1907-08
†H. L. Collins (104).......	Australia v England at Sydney..............	1920-21
W. H. Ponsford (110).....	Australia v England at Sydney..............	1924-25
A. A. Jackson (164)......	Australia v England at Adelaide............	1928-29
†G. A. Headley (176)......	West Indies v England at Bridgetown........	1929-30
J. E. Mills (117).........	New Zealand v England at Wellington........	1929-30
Nawab of Pataudi sen. (102)	England v Australia at Sydney..............	1932-33
B. H. Valentine (136).....	England v India at Bombay................	1933-34
†L. Amarnath (118).......	India v England at Bombay................	1933-34
†P. A. Gibb (106)........	England v South Africa at Johannesburg......	1938-39
S. C. Griffith (140)......	England v West Indies at Port-of-Spain......	1947-48
A. G. Ganteaume (112)....	West Indies v England at Port-of-Spain......	1947-48
†J. W. Burke (101*)......	Australia v England at Adelaide............	1950-51
P. B. H. May (138).......	England v South Africa at Leeds............	1951
R. H. Shodhan (110)......	India v Pakistan at Calcutta..............	1952-53
B. H. Pairaudeau (115)....	West Indies v India at Port-of-Spain........	1952-53
†O. G. Smith (104).......	West Indies v Australia at Kingston........	1954-55
A. G. Kripal Singh (100*)..	India v New Zealand at Hyderabad..........	1955-56
C. C. Hunte (142)........	West Indies v Pakistan at Bridgetown......	1957-58
C. A. Milton (104*)......	England v New Zealand at Leeds............	1958
†A. A. Baig (112)........	India v England at Manchester............	1959
Hanumant Singh (105)....	India v England at Delhi..................	1963-64
Khalid Ibadulla (166).....	Pakistan v Australia at Karachi............	1964-65
B. R. Taylor (105)........	New Zealand v India at Calcutta............	1964-65
K. D. Walters (155).......	Australia v England at Brisbane............	1965-66
J. H. Hampshire (107)....	England v West Indies at Lord's............	1969
†G. R. Viswanath (137)....	India v Australia at Kanpur..............	1969-70
G. S. Chappell (108)......	Australia v England at Perth..............	1970-71
‡L. G. Rowe (214, 100*)..	West Indies v New Zealand at Kingston......	1971-72
A. I. Kallicharran (100*)..	West Indies v New Zealand at Georgetown....	1971-72
R. E. Redmond (107).....	New Zealand v Pakistan at Auckland	1972-73
†F. C. Hayes (106*).......	England v West Indies at The Oval..........	1973
†C. G. Greenidge (107).....	West Indies v India at Bangalore..........	1974-75
†L. Baichan (105*)........	West Indies v Pakistan at Lahore..........	1974-75
G. J. Cosier (109)........	Australia v West Indies at Melbourne........	1975-76
S. Amarnath (124)........	India v New Zealand at Auckland	1975-76
Javed Miandad (163)......	Pakistan v New Zealand at Lahore..........	1976-77
†A. B. Williams (100)......	West Indies v Australia at Georgetown......	1977-78
†D. M. Wellham (103)......	Australia v England at The Oval............	1981
†Salim Malik (100*).......	Pakistan v Sri Lanka at Karachi............	1981-82
K. C. Wessels (162).......	Australia v England at Brisbane............	1982-83
W. B. Phillips (159).......	Australia v Pakistan at Perth..............	1983-84
§M. Azharuddin (110).....	India v England at Calcutta..............	1984-85
D. S. B. P. Kuruppu (201*).	Sri Lanka v New Zealand at Colombo (CCC)..	1986-87
†M. J. Greatbatch (107*)..	New Zealand v England at Auckland	1987-88
M. E. Waugh (138).......	Australia v England at Adelaide............	1990-91
A. C. Hudson (163).......	South Africa v West Indies at Bridgetown....	1991-92
R. S. Kaluwitharana (132*).	Sri Lanka v Australia at Colombo (SSC)......	1992-93
D. L. Houghton (121).....	Zimbabwe v India at Harare..............	1992-93
P. K. Amre (103).........	India v South Africa at Durban............	1992-93
†G. P. Thorpe (114*)......	England v Australia at Nottingham..........	1993
G. S. Blewett (102*)......	Australia v England at Adelaide............	1994-95

† *In his second innings of the match.*

‡ *L. G. Rowe is the only batsman to score a hundred in each innings on debut.*

§ *M. Azharuddin is the only batsman to score hundreds in each of his first three Tests.*

Note: L. Amarnath and S. Amarnath were father and son.

300 RUNS IN FIRST TEST

314	L. G. Rowe (214, 100*)	West Indies v New Zealand at Kingston	1971-72
306	R. E. Foster (287, 19)	England v Australia at Sydney	1903-04

TWO SEPARATE HUNDREDS IN A TEST

Three times: S. M. Gavaskar v West Indies (1970-71), v Pakistan (1978-79), v West Indies (1978-79).

Twice in one series: C. L. Walcott v Australia (1954-55).

Twice: H. Sutcliffe v Australia (1924-25), v South Africa (1929); G. A. Headley v England (1929-30 and 1939); G. S. Chappell v New Zealand (1973-74), v West Indies (1975-76); ‡A. R. Border v Pakistan (1979-80), v New Zealand (1985-86).

Once: W. Bardsley v England (1909); A. C. Russell v South Africa (1922-23); W. R. Hammond v Australia (1928-29); E. Paynter v South Africa (1938-39); D. C. S. Compton v Australia (1946-47); A. R. Morris v England (1946-47); A. Melville v England (1947); B. Mitchell v England (1947); D. G. Bradman v India (1947-48); V. S. Hazare v Australia (1947-48); E. D. Weekes v India (1948-49); J. Moroney v South Africa (1949-50); G. S. Sobers v Pakistan (1957-58); R. B. Kanhai v Australia (1960-61); Hanif Mohammad v England (1961-62); R. B. Simpson v Pakistan (1964-65); K. D. Walters v West Indies (1968-69); †L. G. Rowe v New Zealand (1971-72); I. M. Chappell v New Zealand (1973-74); G. M. Turner v Australia (1973-74); C. G. Greenidge v England (1976); G. P. Howarth v England (1977-78); L. R. D. Mendis v India (1982-83); Javed Miandad v New Zealand (1984-85); D. M. Jones v Pakistan (1989-90); G. A. Gooch v India (1990); A. H. Jones v Sri Lanka (1990-91); A. P. Gurusinha v New Zealand (1990-91); A. J. Stewart v West Indies (1993-94).

   † *L. G. Rowe's two hundreds were on his Test debut.*
   ‡ *A. R. Border scored 150* and 153 against Pakistan to become the first batsman to score 150 in each innings of a Test match.*

TRIPLE-HUNDRED AND HUNDRED IN SAME TEST

G. A. Gooch (England)	333 and 123 v India at Lord's	1990

   The only instance in first-class cricket.

DOUBLE-HUNDRED AND HUNDRED IN SAME TEST

K. D. Walters (Australia)	242 and 103 v West Indies at Sydney	1968-69
S. M. Gavaskar (India)	124 and 220 v West Indies at Port-of-Spain	1970-71
†L. G. Rowe (West Indies)	214 and 100* v New Zealand at Kingston	1971-72
G. S. Chappell (Australia)	247* and 133 v New Zealand at Wellington	1973-74

   † *On Test debut.*

MOST RUNS IN A SERIES

	T	I	NO	R	HS	100s	Avge		
D. G. Bradman ...	5	7	0	974	334	4	139.14	A v E	1930
W. R. Hammond .	5	9	1	905	251	4	113.12	E v A	1928-29
M. A. Taylor	6	11	1	839	219	2	83.90	A v E	1989
R. N. Harvey	5	9	0	834	205	4	92.66	A v SA	1952-53
I. V. A. Richards .	4	7	0	829	291	3	118.42	WI v E	1976
C. L. Walcott	5	10	0	827	155	5	82.70	WI v A	1954-55

	T	I	NO	R	HS	100s	Avge		
G. S. Sobers......	5	8	2	824	365*	3	137.33	WI v P	1957-58
D. G. Bradman ...	5	9	0	810	270	3	90.00	A v E	1936-37
D. G. Bradman ...	5	5	1	806	299*	4	201.50	A v SA	1931-32
B. C. Lara	5	8	0	798	375	2	99.75	WI v E	1993-94
E. D. Weekes	5	7	0	779	194	4	111.28	WI v I	1948-49
†S. M. Gavaskar ..	4	8	3	774	220	4	154.80	I v WI	1970-71
B. C. Lara	6	10	1	765	179	3	85.00	WI v E	1995
Mudassar Nazar ..	6	8	2	761	231	4	126.83	P v I	1982-83
D. G. Bradman ...	5	8	0	758	304	2	94.75	A v E	1934
D. C. S. Compton .	5	8	0	753	208	4	94.12	E v SA	1947
‡G. A. Gooch	3	6	0	752	333	3	125.33	E v I	1990

† Gavaskar's aggregate was achieved in his first Test series.

‡ G. A. Gooch is alone in scoring 1,000 runs in Test cricket during an English season with 1,058 runs in 11 innings against New Zealand and India in 1990.

MOST TEST RUNS IN A CALENDAR YEAR

	T	I	NO	R	HS	100s	Avge	Year
I. V. A. Richards (WI)........	11	19	0	1,710	291	7	90.00	1976
S. M. Gavaskar (I)	18	27	1	1,555	221	5	59.80	1979
G. R. Viswanath (I)	17	26	3	1,388	179	5	60.34	1979
R. B. Simpson (A)	14	26	3	1,381	311	3	60.04	1964
D. L. Amiss (E)	13	22	2	1,379	262*	5	68.95	1974
S. M. Gavaskar (I)	18	32	4	1,310	236*	5	46.78	1983
G. A. Gooch (E).............	9	17	1	1,264	333	4	79.00	1990
D. C. Boon (A)	16	25	5	1,241	164*	4	62.05	1993
B. C. Lara (WI)	12	20	2	1,220	179	4	67.77	1995
M. A. Taylor (A)............	11	20	1	1,219	219	4	64.15	1989†

† The year of his debut.

Notes: M. Amarnath reached 1,000 runs in 1983 on May 3.

The only batsman to score 1,000 runs in a year before World War II was C. Hill of Australia: 1,061 in 1902.

MOST RUNS IN A CAREER

(Qualification: 2,000 runs)

ENGLAND

		T	I	NO	R	HS	100s	Avge
1	**G. A. Gooch**	**118**	**215**	**6**	**8,900**	**333**	**20**	**42.58**
2	D. I. Gower	117	204	18	8,231	215	18	44.25
3	G. Boycott	108	193	23	8,114	246*	22	47.72
4	M. C. Cowdrey	114	188	15	7,624	182	22	44.06
5	W. R. Hammond.....	85	140	16	7,249	336*	22	58.45
6	L. Hutton	79	138	15	6,971	364	19	56.67
7	K. F. Barrington	82	131	15	6,806	256	20	58.67
8	D. C. S. Compton	78	131	15	5,807	278	17	50.06
9	J. B. Hobbs	61	102	7	5,410	211	15	56.94
10	I. T. Botham	102	161	6	5,200	208	14	33.54
11	J. H. Edrich	77	127	9	5,138	310*	12	43.54
12	T. W. Graveney......	79	123	13	4,882	258	11	44.38
13	A. J. Lamb	79	139	10	4,656	142	14	36.09
14	H. Sutcliffe	54	84	9	4,555	194	16	60.73
15	P. B. H. May	66	106	9	4,537	285*	13	46.77
16	E. R. Dexter	62	102	8	4,502	205	9	47.89
17	**M. W. Gatting**	**79**	**138**	**14**	**4,409**	**207**	**10**	**35.55**

		T	I	NO	R	HS	100s	Avge
18	A. P. E. Knott	95	149	15	4,389	135	5	32.75
19	**R. A. Smith**	**57**	**105**	**15**	**3,982**	**175**	**9**	**44.24**
20	**M. A. Atherton**	**51**	**96**	**1**	**3,812**	**151**	**8**	**40.12**
21	D. L. Amiss	50	88	10	3,612	262*	11	46.30
22	A. W. Greig	58	93	4	3,599	148	8	40.43
23	E. H. Hendren	51	83	9	3,525	205*	7	47.63
24	F. E. Woolley	64	98	7	3,283	154	5	36.07
25	K. W. R. Fletcher	59	96	14	3,272	216	7	39.90
26	**A. J. Stewart**	**48**	**87**	**6**	**3,168**	**190**	**7**	**39.11**
27	M. Leyland	41	65	5	2,764	187	9	46.06
28	C. Washbrook	37	66	6	2,569	195	6	42.81
29	B. L. D'Oliveira	44	70	8	2,484	158	5	40.06
30	D. W. Randall	47	79	5	2,470	174	7	33.37
31	W. J. Edrich	39	63	2	2,440	219	6	40.00
32	T. G. Evans	91	133	14	2,439	104	2	20.49
33	L. E. G. Ames	47	72	12	2,434	149	8	40.56
34	**G. A. Hick**	**37**	**66**	**4**	**2,336**	**178**	**3**	**37.67**
35	W. Rhodes	58	98	21	2,325	179	2	30.19
36	T. E. Bailey	61	91	14	2,290	134*	1	29.74
37	M. J. K. Smith	50	78	6	2,278	121	3	31.63
38	P. E. Richardson	34	56	1	2,061	126	5	37.47

AUSTRALIA

		T	I	NO	R	HS	100s	Avge
1	A. R. Border	156	265	44	11,174	205	27	50.56
2	**D. C. Boon**	**101**	**181**	**20**	**7,111**	**200**	**20**	**44.16**
3	G. S. Chappell	87	151	19	7,110	247*	24	53.86
4	D. G. Bradman	52	80	10	6,996	334	29	99.94
5	R. N. Harvey	79	137	10	6,149	205	21	48.41
6	K. D. Walters	74	125	14	5,357	250	15	48.26
7	I. M. Chappell	75	136	10	5,345	196	14	42.42
8	W. M. Lawry	67	123	12	5,234	210	13	47.15
9	**M. A. Taylor**	**66**	**119**	**8**	**5,005**	**219**	**13**	**45.09**
10	R. B. Simpson	62	111	7	4,869	311	10	46.81
11	I. R. Redpath	66	120	11	4,737	171	8	43.45
12	**S. R. Waugh**	**76**	**117**	**23**	**4,440**	**200**	**8**	**47.23**
13	K. J. Hughes	70	124	6	4,415	213	9	37.41
14	R. W. Marsh	96	150	13	3,633	132	—	26.51
15	D. M. Jones	52	89	11	3,631	216	11	46.55
16	A. R. Morris	46	79	3	3,533	206	12	46.48
17	C. Hill	49	89	2	3,412	191	7	39.21
18	G. M. Wood	59	112	6	3,374	172	9	31.83
19	V. T. Trumper	48	89	8	3,163	214*	8	39.04
20	C. C. McDonald	47	83	4	3,107	170	5	39.32
21	A. L. Hassett	43	69	3	3,073	198*	10	46.56
22	**M. E. Waugh**	**48**	**77**	**4**	**3,072**	**140**	**8**	**42.08**
23	K. R. Miller	55	87	7	2,958	147	7	36.97
24	W. W. Armstrong	50	84	10	2,863	159*	6	38.68
25	G. R. Marsh	50	93	7	2,854	138	4	33.18
26	K. R. Stackpole	43	80	5	2,807	207	7	37.42
27	N. C. O'Neill	42	69	8	2,779	181	6	45.55
28	G. N. Yallop	39	70	3	2,756	268	8	41.13
29	S. J. McCabe	39	62	5	2,748	232	6	48.21
30	**I. A. Healy**	**73**	**109**	**14**	**2,557**	**113***	**2**	**26.91**
31	W. Bardsley	41	66	5	2,469	193*	6	40.47
32	W. M. Woodfull	35	54	4	2,300	161	7	46.00
33	P. J. Burge	42	68	8	2,290	181	4	38.16
34	S. E. Gregory	58	100	7	2,282	201	4	24.53
35	R. Benaud	63	97	7	2,201	122	3	24.45
36	**M. J. Slater**	**27**	**47**	**2**	**2,163**	**176**	**6**	**48.06**
37	C. G. Macartney	35	55	4	2,131	170	7	41.78
38	W. H. Ponsford	29	48	4	2,122	266	7	48.22
39	R. M. Cowper	27	46	2	2,061	307	5	46.84

SOUTH AFRICA

		T	I	NO	R	HS	100s	Avge
1	B. Mitchell	42	80	9	3,471	189*	8	48.88
2	A. D. Nourse	34	62	7	2,960	231	9	53.81
3	H. W. Taylor	42	76	4	2,936	176	7	40.77
4	E. J. Barlow	30	57	2	2,516	201	6	45.74
	T. L. Goddard	41	78	5	2,516	112	1	34.46
6	D. J. McGlew	34	64	6	2,440	255*	7	42.06
7	J. H. B. Waite	50	86	7	2,405	134	4	30.44
8	R. G. Pollock	23	41	4	2,256	274	7	60.97
9	A. W. Nourse	45	83	8	2,234	111	1	29.78
10	R. A. McLean	40	73	3	2,120	142	5	30.28

K. C. Wessels scored 2,788 runs in 40 Tests: 1,761 (average 42.95) in 24 Tests for Australia, and 1,027 (average 38.03) in 16 Tests for South Africa.

WEST INDIES

		T	I	NO	R	HS	100s	Avge
1	I. V. A. Richards	121	182	12	8,540	291	24	50.23
2	G. S. Sobers	93	160	21	8,032	365*	26	57.78
3	C. G. Greenidge	108	185	16	7,558	226	19	44.72
4	C. H. Lloyd	110	175	14	7,515	242*	19	46.67
5	D. L. Haynes	116	202	25	7,487	184	18	42.29
6	R. B. Kanhai	79	137	6	6,227	256	15	47.53
7	**R. B. Richardson**	**86**	**146**	**12**	**5,949**	**194**	**16**	**44.39**
8	E. D. Weekes	48	81	5	4,455	207	15	58.61
9	A. I. Kallicharran	66	109	10	4,399	187	12	44.43
10	R. C. Fredericks	59	109	7	4,334	169	8	42.49
11	F. M. M. Worrell	51	87	9	3,860	261	9	49.48
12	C. L. Walcott	44	74	7	3,798	220	15	56.68
13	P. J. L. Dujon	81	115	11	3,322	139	5	31.94
14	C. C. Hunte	44	78	6	3,245	260	8	45.06
15	H. A. Gomes	60	91	11	3,171	143	9	39.63
16	B. F. Butcher	44	78	6	3,104	209*	7	43.11
17	**B. C. Lara**	**31**	**52**	**2**	**3,048**	**375**	**7**	**60.96**
18	**C. L. Hooper**	**52**	**87**	**7**	**2,548**	**178***	**5**	**31.85**
19	S. M. Nurse	29	54	1	2,523	258	6	47.60
20	A. L. Logie	52	78	9	2,470	130	2	35.79
21	G. A. Headley	22	40	4	2,190	270*	10	60.83
22	J. B. Stollmeyer	32	56	5	2,159	160	4	42.33
23	L. G. Rowe	30	49	2	2,047	302	7	43.55

NEW ZEALAND

		T	I	NO	R	HS	100s	Avge
1	**M. D. Crowe**	**74**	**128**	**11**	**5,394**	**299**	**17**	**46.10**
2	J. G. Wright	82	148	7	5,334	185	12	37.82
3	B. E. Congdon	61	114	7	3,448	176	7	32.22
4	J. R. Reid	58	108	5	3,428	142	6	33.28
5	R. J. Hadlee	86	134	19	3,124	151*	2	27.16
6	G. M. Turner	41	73	6	2,991	259	7	44.64
7	**A. H. Jones**	**39**	**74**	**8**	**2,922**	**186**	**7**	**44.27**
8	B. Sutcliffe	42	76	8	2,727	230*	5	40.10
9	M. G. Burgess	50	92	6	2,684	119*	5	31.20
10	J. V. Coney	52	85	14	2,668	174*	3	37.57
11	G. P. Howarth	47	83	5	2,531	147	6	32.44
12	**K. R. Rutherford**	**56**	**99**	**8**	**2,465**	**107***	**3**	**27.08**
13	G. T. Dowling	39	77	3	2,306	239	3	31.16

INDIA

		T	I	NO	R	HS	100s	Avge
1	S. M. Gavaskar	125	214	16	10,122	236*	34	51.12
2	D. B. Vengsarkar	116	185	22	6,868	166	17	42.13
3	G. R. Viswanath	91	155	10	6,080	222	14	41.93
4	Kapil Dev	131	184	15	5,248	163	8	31.05
5	M. Amarnath	69	113	10	4,378	138	11	42.50
6	**M. Azharuddin**	**65**	**94**	**4**	**4,198**	**199**	**14**	**46.64**
7	R. J. Shastri	80	121	14	3,830	206	11	35.79
8	P. R. Umrigar	59	94	8	3,631	223	12	42.22
9	V. L. Manjrekar	55	92	10	3,208	189*	7	39.12
10	C. G. Borde	55	97	11	3,061	177*	5	35.59
11	Nawab of Pataudi jun.	46	83	3	2,793	203*	6	34.91
12	S. M. H. Kirmani	88	124	22	2,759	102	2	27.04
13	F. M. Engineer	46	87	3	2,611	121	2	31.08
14	Pankaj Roy	43	79	4	2,442	173	5	32.56
15	**S. R. Tendulkar**	**35**	**51**	**5**	**2,425**	**179**	**8**	**52.71**
16	V. S. Hazare	30	52	6	2,192	164*	7	47.65
17	A. L. Wadekar	37	71	3	2,113	143	1	31.07
18	V. Mankad	44	72	5	2,109	231	5	31.47
19	C. P. S. Chauhan	40	68	2	2,084	97	0	31.57
20	K. Srikkanth	43	72	3	2,062	123	2	29.88
21	M. L. Jaisimha	39	71	4	2,056	129	3	30.68
22	**N. S. Sidhu**	**34**	**52**	**2**	**2,013**	**124**	**6**	**40.26**
23	D. N. Sardesai	30	55	4	2,001	212	5	39.23

PAKISTAN

		T	I	NO	R	HS	100s	Avge
1	Javed Miandad	124	189	21	8,832	280*	23	52.57
2	Zaheer Abbas	78	124	11	5,062	274	12	44.79
3	**Salim Malik**	**84**	**124**	**19**	**4,804**	**237**	**13**	**45.75**
4	Mudassar Nazar	76	116	8	4,114	231	10	38.09
5	Majid Khan	63	106	5	3,931	167	8	38.92
6	Hanif Mohammad	55	97	8	3,915	337	12	43.98
7	Imran Khan	88	126	25	3,807	136	6	37.69
8	Mushtaq Mohammad	57	100	7	3,643	201	10	39.17
9	Asif Iqbal	58	99	7	3,575	175	11	38.85
10	Saeed Ahmed	41	78	4	2,991	172	5	40.41
11	Wasim Raja	57	92	14	2,821	125	4	36.16
12	Mohsin Khan	48	79	6	2,709	200	7	37.10
13	Shoaib Mohammad	42	63	7	2,622	203*	7	46.82
14	Sadiq Mohammad	41	74	2	2,579	166	5	35.81
15	Ramiz Raja	48	78	5	2,243	122	2	30.72
16	Imtiaz Ahmed	41	72	1	2,079	209	3	29.28

SRI LANKA

		T	I	NO	R	HS	100s	Avge
1	**A. Ranatunga**	**56**	**94**	**5**	**3,134**	**135***	**4**	**35.21**
2	**P. A. de Silva**	**48**	**83**	**4**	**2,965**	**267**	**7**	**37.93**

ZIMBABWE: The highest aggregate is 912, average 48.00, by **D. L. Houghton** in 13 Tests.

Bold type denotes those who played Test cricket in 1994-95 and 1995 seasons.

HIGHEST CAREER AVERAGES

(Qualification: 20 innings)

Avge		T	I	NO	R	HS	100s
99.94	D. G. Bradman (A)	52	80	10	6,996	334	29
62.15	**J. C. Adams (WI)**	**22**	**34**	**8**	**1,616**	**174***	**4**
60.97	R. G. Pollock (SA)	23	41	4	2,256	274	7
60.96	**B. C. Lara (WI)**	**31**	**52**	**2**	**3,048**	**375**	**7**
60.83	G. A. Headley (WI)	22	40	4	2,190	270*	10
60.73	H. Sutcliffe (E)	54	84	9	4,555	194	16
59.23	E. Paynter (E)	20	31	5	1,540	243	4
58.67	K. F. Barrington (E)	82	131	15	6,806	256	20
58.61	E. D. Weekes (WI).........	48	81	5	4,455	207	15
58.45	W. R. Hammond (E)	85	140	16	7,249	336*	22
57.78	G. S. Sobers (WI)	93	160	21	8,032	365*	26
56.94	J. B. Hobbs (E)............	61	102	7	5,410	211	15
56.68	C. L. Walcott (WI)	44	74	7	3,798	220	15
56.67	L. Hutton (E)	79	138	15	6,971	364	19
55.00	E. Tyldesley (E)	14	20	2	990	122	3
54.20	C. A. Davis (WI)	15	29	5	1,301	183	4
53.86	G. S. Chappell (A)	87	151	19	7,110	247*	24
53.81	A. D. Nourse (SA)	34	62	7	2,960	231	9
52.71	**S. R. Tendulkar (I)**	**35**	**51**	**5**	**2,425**	**179**	**8**
52.57	Javed Miandad (P)	124	189	21	8,832	280*	23
51.62	J. Ryder (A)	20	32	5	1,394	201*	3
51.12	S. M. Gavaskar (I)	125	214	16	10,122	236*	34
50.56	A. R. Border (A)...........	156	265	44	11,174	205	27
50.23	I. V. A. Richards (WI)....	121	182	12	8,540	291	24
50.06	D. C. S. Compton (E)	78	131	15	5,807	278	17

Bold type denotes those who played Test cricket in 1994-95 and 1995 seasons.

MOST HUNDREDS

							Opponents					
	Total	*200+*	*Inns*	*E*	*A*	*SA*	*WI*	*NZ*	*I*	*P*	*SL*	*Z*
S. M. Gavaskar (I) ..	34	4	214	4	8	–	13	2	–	5	2	–
D. G. Bradman (A)..	29	12	80	19	–	4	2	–	4	–	–	–
A. R. Border (A)	27	2	265	8	–	–	3	5	4	6	1	–
G. S. Sobers (WI) ...	26	2	160	10	4	–	–	1	8	3	–	–
G. S. Chappell (A) ..	24	4	151	9	–	–	5	3	1	6	0	–
I. V. A. Richards (WI)	24	3	182	8	5	–	–	1	8	2	–	–
Javed Miandad (P) ..	23	6	189	2	6	–	2	7	5	–	1	–
G. Boycott (E)	22	1	193	–	7	1	5	2	4	3	–	–
M. C. Cowdrey (E) ..	22	0	188	–	5	3	6	2	3	3	–	–
W. R. Hammond (E).	22	7	140	–	9	6	1	4	2	–	–	–
R. N. Harvey (A)	21	2	137	6	–	8	3	–	4	0	–	–
K. F. Barrington (E) .	20	1	131	–	5	2	3	3	3	4	–	–
D. C. Boon (A)......	**20**	**1**	**181**	**7**	**–**	**–**	**3**	**3**	**6**	**1**	**0**	**–**
G. A. Gooch (E).....	**20**	**2**	**215**	**–**	**4**	**–**	**5**	**4**	**5**	**1**	**1**	**–**
C. G. Greenidge (WI)	19	4	185	7	4	–	–	2	5	1	–	–
L. Hutton (E)	19	4	138	–	5	4	5	3	2	0	–	–
C. H. Lloyd (WI)....	19	1	175	5	6	–	–	0	7	1	–	–
D. I. Gower (E).....	18	2	204	–	9	–	1	4	2	2	0	–
D. L. Haynes (WI)..	18	0	202	5	5	0	–	3	2	3	–	–
D. C. S. Compton (E)	17	2	131	–	5	7	2	2	0	1	–	–
M. D. Crowe (NZ)..	**17**	**1**	**128**	**5**	**3**	**–**	**3**	**–**	**1**	**2**	**2**	**1**
D. B. Vengsarkar (I).	17	0	185	5	2	–	6	0	–	2	2	–
R. B. Richardson (WI)	**16**	**0**	**122**	**4**	**9**	**0**	**–**	**1**	**2**	**0**	**–**	**–**
H. Sutcliffe (E).......	16	0	84	–	8	6	0	2	0	–	–	–

	Total	200+	Inns	Opponents								
				E	A	SA	WI	NZ	I	P	SL	Z
J. B. Hobbs (E)	15	1	102	–	12	2	1	–	–	–	–	–
R. B. Kanhai (WI) . .	15	2	137	5	5	–	–	–	4	1	–	–
C. L. Walcott (WI) . .	15	1	74	4	5	–	–	1	4	1	–	–
K. D. Walters (A) . . .	15	2	125	4	–	0	6	3	1	1	–	–
E. D. Weekes (WI) . .	15	2	81	3	1	–	–	3	7	1	–	–

Notes: The most hundreds for Sri Lanka is 7 by **P. A. de Silva** in 83 innings and for Zimbabwe 3 by **D. L. Houghton** in 20 innings.

The most double-hundreds by batsmen not qualifying for the above list is four by Zaheer Abbas (12 hundreds for Pakistan) and three by R. B. Simpson (10 hundreds for Australia).

Bold type denotes those who played Test cricket in 1994-95 and 1995 seasons. Dashes indicate that a player did not play against the country concerned.

CARRYING BAT THROUGH TEST INNINGS

(Figures in brackets show side's total)

A. B. Tancred	26*	(47)	South Africa v England at Cape Town . .	1888-89
J. E. Barrett	67*	(176)	Australia v England at Lord's	1890
R. Abel	132*	(307)	England v Australia at Sydney	1891-92
P. F. Warner	132*	(237)	England v South Africa at Johannesburg .	1898-99
W. W. Armstrong . .	159*	(309)	Australia v South Africa at Johannesburg	1902-03
J. W. Zulch	43*	(103)	South Africa v England at Cape Town . .	1909-10
W. Bardsley	193*	(383)	Australia v England at Lord's	1926
W. M. Woodfull	30*	(66)‡	Australia v England at Brisbane	1928-29
W. M. Woodfull	73*	(193)†	Australia v England at Adelaide	1932-33
W. A. Brown	206*	(422)	Australia v England at Lord's	1938
L. Hutton	202*	(344)	England v West Indies at The Oval	1950
L. Hutton	156*	(272)	England v Australia at Adelaide	1950-51
Nazar Mohammad . .	124*	(331)	Pakistan v India at Lucknow	1952-53
F. M. M. Worrell . . .	191*	(372)	West Indies v England at Nottingham . . .	1957
T. L. Goddard	56*	(99)	South Africa v Australia at Cape Town . .	1957-58
D. J. McGlew	127*	(292)	South Africa v New Zealand at Durban . .	1961-62
C. C. Hunte	60*	(131)	West Indies v Australia at Port-of-Spain .	1964-65
G. M. Turner	43*	(131)	New Zealand v England at Lord's	1969
W. M. Lawry	49*	(107)	Australia v India at Delhi	1969-70
W. M. Lawry	60*	(116)†	Australia v England at Sydney	1970-71
G. M. Turner	223*	(386)	New Zealand v West Indies at Kingston . .	1971-72
I. R. Redpath	159*	(346)	Australia v New Zealand at Auckland . . .	1973-74
G. Boycott	99*	(215)	England v Australia at Perth	1979-80
S. M. Gavaskar	127*	(286)	India v Pakistan at Faisalabad	1982-83
Mudassar Nazar . . .	152*	(323)	Pakistan v India at Lahore	1982-83
S. Wettimuny	63*	(144)	Sri Lanka v New Zealand at Christchurch	1982-83
D. C. Boon	58*	(103)	Australia v New Zealand at Auckland . . .	1985-86
D. L. Haynes	88*	(211)	West Indies v Pakistan at Karachi	1986-87
G. A. Gooch	154*	(252)	England v West Indies at Leeds	1991
D. L. Haynes	75*	(176)	West Indies v England at The Oval	1991
A. J. Stewart	69*	(175)	England v Pakistan at Lord's	1992
D. L. Haynes	143*	(382)	West Indies v Pakistan at Port-of-Spain .	1992-93
M. H. Dekker	68*	(187)	Zimbabwe v Pakistan at Rawalpindi	1993-94

† *One man absent.*   ‡ *Two men absent.*

Notes: G. M. Turner (223*) holds the record for the highest score by a player carrying his bat through a Test innings. He is also the youngest player to do so, being 22 years 63 days old when he first achieved the feat (1969).

G. A. Gooch (61.11%) holds the record for the highest percentage of a side's total by anyone carrying his bat throughout a Test innings.

Nazar Mohammad and Mudassar Nazar were father and son.

D. L. Haynes, who is alone in achieving this feat on three occasions, also opened the batting and was last man out in each innings for West Indies v New Zealand at Dunedin, 1979-80.

FASTEST FIFTIES

Minutes

28	J. T. Brown	England v Australia at Melbourne	1894-95
29	S. A. Durani	India v England at Kanpur	1963-64
30	E. A. V. Williams. .	West Indies v England at Bridgetown	1947-48
30	B. R. Taylor	New Zealand v West Indies at Auckland	1968-69
33	C. A. Roach	West Indies v England at The Oval	1933
34	C. R. Browne	West Indies v England at Georgetown	1929-30

The fastest fifties in terms of balls received (where recorded) are:

Balls

30	Kapil Dev	India v Pakistan at Karachi (2nd Test)	1982-83
32	I. V. A. Richards . .	West Indies v India at Kingston	1982-83
32	I. T. Botham	England v New Zealand at The Oval	1986
33	R. C. Fredericks . .	West Indies v Australia at Perth.	1975-76
33	Kapil Dev	India v Pakistan at Karachi	1978-79
33	Kapil Dev	India v England at Manchester	1982
33	A. J. Lamb	England v New Zealand at Auckland	1991-92

FASTEST HUNDREDS

Minutes

70	J. M. Gregory	Australia v South Africa at Johannesburg	1921-22
75	G. L. Jessop	England v Australia at The Oval	1902
78	R. Benaud	Australia v West Indies at Kingston	1954-55
80	J. H. Sinclair	South Africa v Australia at Cape Town	1902-03
81	I. V. A. Richards . .	West Indies v England at St John's	1985-86
86	B. R. Taylor	New Zealand v West Indies at Auckland	1968-69

The fastest hundreds in terms of balls received (where recorded) are:

Balls

56	I. V. A. Richards . .	West Indies v England at St John's	1985-86
67	J. M. Gregory	Australia v South Africa at Johannesburg	1921-22
71	R. C. Fredericks . .	West Indies v Australia at Perth	1975-76
74	Majid Khan.	Pakistan v New Zealand at Karachi	1976-77
74	Kapil Dev	India v Sri Lanka at Kanpur.	1986-87
76	G. L. Jessop	England v Australia at The Oval	1902

FASTEST DOUBLE-HUNDREDS

Minutes

214	D. G. Bradman. . . .	Australia v England at Leeds	1930
223	S. J. McCabe	Australia v England at Nottingham	1938
226	V. T. Trumper	Australia v South Africa at Adelaide	1910-11
234	D. G. Bradman. . . .	Australia v England at Lord's	1930
240	W. R. Hammond . .	England v New Zealand at Auckland	1932-33
241	S. E. Gregory	Australia v England at Sydney	1894-95
245	D. C. S. Compton . .	England v Pakistan at Nottingham.	1954

The fastest double-hundreds in terms of balls received (where recorded) are:

Balls

220	I. T. Botham	England v India at The Oval.	1982
232	C. G. Greenidge . . .	West Indies v England at Lord's	1984
240	C. H. Lloyd	West Indies v India at Bombay.	1974-75
241	Zaheer Abbas	Pakistan v India at Lahore	1982-83
242	D. G. Bradman. . . .	Australia v England at The Oval	1934
242	I. V. A. Richards . .	West Indies v Australia at Melbourne	1984-85

FASTEST TRIPLE-HUNDREDS

Minutes

288	W. R. Hammond ..	England v New Zealand at Auckland	1932-33
336	D. G. Bradman....	Australia v England at Leeds	1930

MOST RUNS IN A DAY BY A BATSMAN

309	D. G. Bradman	Australia v England at Leeds	1930
295	W. R. Hammond	England v New Zealand at Auckland	1932-33
273	D. C. S. Compton	England v Pakistan at Nottingham...........	1954
271	D. G. Bradman	Australia v England at Leeds	1934

SLOWEST INDIVIDUAL BATTING

2* in	81 minutes	P. C. R. Tufnell, England v India at Bombay	1992-93
3* in	100 minutes	J. T. Murray, England v Australia at Sydney	1962-63
5 in	102 minutes	Nawab of Pataudi jun., India v England at Bombay	1972-73
7 in	123 minutes	G. Miller, England v Australia at Melbourne	1978-79
9 in	132 minutes	R. K. Chauhan, India v Sri Lanka at Ahmedabad	1993-94
10* in	133 minutes	T. G. Evans, England v Australia at Adelaide	1946-47
16* in	147 minutes	D. B. Vengsarkar, India v Pakistan at Kanpur	1979-80
17* in	166 minutes	G. M. Ritchie, Australia v India at Sydney	1985-86
18 in	194 minutes	W. R. Playle, New Zealand v England at Leeds	1958
19 in	217 minutes	M. D. Crowe, New Zealand v Sri Lanka at Moratuwa ...	1983-84
25 in	242 minutes	D. K. Morrison, New Zealand v Pakistan at Faisalabad ..	1990-91
28* in	250 minutes	J. W. Burke, Australia v England at Brisbane..........	1958-59
31 in	264 minutes	K. D. Mackay, Australia v England at Lord's	1956
34* in	271 minutes	Younis Ahmed, Pakistan v India at Ahmedabad	1986-87
35 in	332 minutes	C. J. Tavaré, England v India at Madras	1981-82
55 in	336 minutes	B. A. Edgar, New Zealand v Australia at Wellington	1981-82
57 in	346 minutes	G. S. Camacho, West Indies v England at Bridgetown ...	1967-68
58 in	367 minutes	Ijaz Butt, Pakistan v Australia at Karachi	1959-60
60 in	390 minutes	D. N. Sardesai, India v West Indies at Bridgetown	1961-62
62 in	408 minutes	Ramiz Raja, Pakistan v West Indies at Karachi	1986-87
68 in	458 minutes	T. E. Bailey, England v Australia at Brisbane..........	1958-59
99 in	505 minutes	M. L. Jaisimha, India v Pakistan at Kanpur	1960-61
105 in	575 minutes	D. J. McGlew, South Africa v Australia at Durban	1957-58
114 in	591 minutes	Mudassar Nazar, Pakistan v England at Lahore	1977-78
120* in	609 minutes	J. J. Crowe, New Zealand v Sri Lanka, Colombo (CCC) .	1986-87
146* in	655 minutes	M. J. Greatbatch, New Zealand v Australia at Perth.....	1989-90
163 in	720 minutes	Shoaib Mohammad, Pakistan v New Zealand at Wellington	1988-89
201* in	777 minutes	D. S. B. P. Kuruppu, Sri Lanka v New Zealand at Colombo (CCC)	1986-87
337 in	970 minutes	Hanif Mohammad, Pakistan v West Indies at Bridgetown.	1957-58

Note: The longest any batsman in all first-class innings has taken to score his first run is 97 minutes by T. G. Evans for England against Australia at Adelaide, 1946-47.

SLOWEST HUNDREDS

557 minutes	Mudassar Nazar, Pakistan v England at Lahore	1977-78
545 minutes	D. J. McGlew, South Africa v Australia at Durban	1957-58
535 minutes	A. P. Gurusinha, Sri Lanka v Zimbabwe at Harare	1994-95
516 minutes	J. J. Crowe, New Zealand v Sri Lanka at Colombo (CCC)	1986-87
500 minutes	S. V. Manjrekar, India v Zimbabwe at Harare	1992-93
488 minutes	P. E. Richardson, England v South Africa at Johannesburg	1956-57

Notes: The slowest hundred for any Test in England is 458 minutes (329 balls) by K. W. R. Fletcher, England v Pakistan, The Oval, 1974.

The slowest double-hundred in a Test was scored in 777 minutes (548 balls) by D. S. B. P. Kuruppu for Sri Lanka v New Zealand at Colombo (CCC), 1986-87, on his debut. It is also the slowest-ever first-class double-hundred.

HIGHEST PARTNERSHIPS FOR EACH WICKET

413 for 1st	V. Mankad (231)/Pankaj Roy (173)........	I v NZ	Madras	1955-56
451 for 2nd	W. H. Ponsford (266)/D. G. Bradman (244).	A v E	The Oval	1934
467 for 3rd	A. H. Jones (186)/M. D. Crowe (299).....	NZ v SL	Wellington	1990-91
411 for 4th	P. B. H. May (285*)/M. C. Cowdrey (154)..	E v WI	Birmingham	1957
405 for 5th	S. G. Barnes (234)/D. G. Bradman (234) ...	A v E	Sydney	1946-47
346 for 6th	J. H. W. Fingleton (136)/D. G. Bradman (270)	A v E	Melbourne	1936-37
347 for 7th	D. St E. Atkinson (219)/C. C. Depeiza (122)	WI v A	Bridgetown	1954-55
246 for 8th	L. E. G. Ames (137)/G. O. B. Allen (122) .	E v NZ	Lord's	1931
190 for 9th	Asif Iqbal (146)/Intikhab Alam (51)	P v E	The Oval	1967
151 for 10th	B. F. Hastings (110)/R. O. Collinge (68*)...	NZ v P	Auckland	1972-73

PARTNERSHIPS OF 300 AND OVER

467 for 3rd	A. H. Jones (186)/M. D. Crowe (299)	NZ v SL	Wellington	1990-91
451 for 2nd	W. H. Ponsford (266)/D. G. Bradman (244) ..	A v E	The Oval	1934
451 for 3rd	Mudassar Nazar (231)/Javed Miandad (280*) .	P v I	Hyderabad	1982-83
446 for 2nd	C. C. Hunte (260)/G. S. Sobers (365*)	WI v P	Kingston	1957-58
413 for 1st	V. Mankad (231)/Pankaj Roy (173)	I v NZ	Madras	1955-56
411 for 4th	P. B. H. May (285*)/M. C. Cowdrey (154)	E v WI	Birmingham	1957
405 for 5th	S. G. Barnes (234)/D. G. Bradman (234)	A v E	Sydney	1946-47
399 for 4th	G. S. Sobers (226)/F. M. M. Worrell (197*) ..	WI v E	Bridgetown	1959-60
397 for 3rd	Qasim Omar (206)/Javed Miandad (203*)	P v SL	Faisalabad	1985-86
388 for 4th	W. H. Ponsford (181)/D. G. Bradman (304) ..	A v E	Leeds	1934
387 for 1st	G. M. Turner (259)/T. W. Jarvis (182)........	NZ v WI	Georgetown	1971-72
382 for 2nd	L. Hutton (364)/M. Leyland (187)..........	E v A	The Oval	1938
382 for 1st	W. M. Lawry (210)/R. B. Simpson (201)	A v WI	Bridgetown	1964-65
370 for 3rd	W. J. Edrich (189)/D. C. S. Compton (208)....	E v SA	Lord's	1947
369 for 4th	J. H. Edrich (310*)/K. F. Barrington (163)	E v NZ	Leeds	1965
359 for 1st	L. Hutton (158)/C. Washbrook (195)	E v SA	Johannesburg	1948-49
351 for 2nd	G. A. Gooch (196)/D. I. Gower (157)	E v A	The Oval	1985
350 for 4th	Mushtaq Mohammad (201)/Asif Iqbal (175) ..	P v NZ	Dunedin	1972-73
347 for 7th	D. St E. Atkinson (219)/C. C. Depeiza (122)...	WI v A	Bridgetown	1954-55
346 for 6th	J. H. Fingleton (136)/D. G. Bradman (270) ...	A v E	Melbourne	1936-37
344* for 3rd	S. M. Gavaskar (182*)/D. B. Vengsarkar (157*)	I v WI	Calcutta	1978-79
341 for 3rd	E. J. Barlow (201)/R. G. Pollock (175)........	SA v A	Adelaide	1963-64
338 for 3rd	E. D. Weekes (206)/F. M. M. Worrell (167) ...	WI v E	Port-of-Spain	1953-54
336 for 4th	W. M. Lawry (151)/K. D. Walters (242)	A v WI	Sydney	1968-69
332* for 5th	A. R. Border (200*)/S. R. Waugh (157*)	A v E	Leeds	1993
331 for 2nd	R. T. Robinson (148)/D. I. Gower (215)	E v A	Birmingham	1985
329 for 1st	G. R. Marsh (138)/M. A. Taylor (219)........	A v E	Nottingham	1989
323 for 1st	J. B. Hobbs (178)/W. Rhodes (179)	E v A	Melbourne	1911-12
322 for 4th	Javed Miandad (153*)/Salim Malik (165)	P v E	Birmingham	1992
319 for 3rd	A. Melville (189)/A. D. Nourse (149)	SA v E	Nottingham	1947
316† for 3rd	G. R. Viswanath (222)/Yashpal Sharma (140)..	I v E	Madras	1981-82
308 for 7th	Waqar Hassan (189)/Imtiaz Ahmed (209)	P v NZ	Lahore	1955-56
308 for 3rd	R. B. Richardson (154)/I. V. A. Richards (178).	WI v A	St John's	1983-84
308 for 3rd	G. A. Gooch (333)/A. J. Lamb (139)	E v I	Lord's	1990
303 for 3rd	I. V. A. Richards (232)/A. I. Kallicharran (97).	WI v E	Nottingham	1976
303 for 3rd	M. A. Atherton (135)/R. A. Smith (175)	E v WI	St John's	1993-94
301 for 2nd	A. R. Morris (182)/D. G. Bradman (173*).....	A v E	Leeds	1948

† 415 runs were scored for this wicket in two separate partnerships: D. B. Vengsarkar retired hurt when he and Viswanath had added 99 runs.

BOWLING RECORDS

MOST WICKETS IN AN INNINGS

10-53	J. C. Laker	England v Australia at Manchester	1956
9-28	G. A. Lohmann	England v South Africa at Johannesburg	1895-96
9-37	J. C. Laker	England v Australia at Manchester	1956
9-52	R. J. Hadlee	New Zealand v Australia at Brisbane	1985-86
9-56	Abdul Qadir	Pakistan v England at Lahore	1987-88
9-57	D. E. Malcolm	England v South Africa at The Oval	1994
9-69	J. M. Patel	India v Australia at Kanpur	1959-60
9-83	Kapil Dev	India v West Indies at Ahmedabad	1983-84
9-86	Sarfraz Nawaz	Pakistan v Australia at Melbourne	1978-79
9-95	J. M. Noreiga	West Indies v India at Port-of-Spain	1970-71
9-102	S. P. Gupte	India v West Indies at Kanpur	1958-59
9-103	S. F. Barnes	England v South Africa at Johannesburg	1913-14
9-113	H. J. Tayfield	South Africa v England at Johannesburg	1956-57
9-121	A. A. Mailey	Australia v England at Melbourne	1920-21
8-7	G. A. Lohmann	England v South Africa at Port Elizabeth	1895-96
8-11	J. Briggs	England v South Africa at Cape Town	1888-89
8-29	S. F. Barnes	England v South Africa at The Oval	1912
8-29	C. E. H. Croft	West Indies v Pakistan at Port-of-Spain	1976-77
8-31	F. Laver	Australia v England at Manchester	1909
8-31	F. S. Trueman	England v India at Manchester	1952
8-34	I. T. Botham	England v Pakistan at Lord's	1978
8-35	G. A. Lohmann	England v Australia at Sydney	1886-87
8-38	L. R. Gibbs	West Indies v India at Bridgetown	1961-62
8-43†	A. E. Trott	Australia v England at Adelaide	1894-95
8-43	H. Verity	England v Australia at Lord's	1934
8-43	R. G. D. Willis	England v Australia at Leeds	1981
8-45	C. E. L. Ambrose	West Indies v England at Bridgetown	1989-90
8-51	D. L. Underwood	England v Pakistan at Lord's	1974
8-52	V. Mankad	India v Pakistan at Delhi	1952-53
8-53	G. B. Lawrence	South Africa v New Zealand at Johannesburg	1961-62
8-53†	R. A. L. Massie	Australia v England at Lord's	1972
8-55	V. Mankad	India v England at Madras	1951-52
8-56	S. F. Barnes	England v South Africa at Johannesburg	1913-14
8-58	G. A. Lohmann	England v Australia at Sydney	1891-92
8-58	Imran Khan	Pakistan v Sri Lanka at Lahore	1981-82
8-59	C. Blythe	England v South Africa at Leeds	1907
8-59	A. A. Mallett	Australia v Pakistan at Adelaide	1972-73
8-60	Imran Khan	Pakistan v India at Karachi	1982-83
8-61†	N. D. Hirwani	India v West Indies at Madras	1987-88
8-65	H. Trumble	Australia v England at The Oval	1902
8-68	W. Rhodes	England v Australia at Melbourne	1903-04
8-69	H. J. Tayfield	South Africa v England at Durban	1956-57
8-69	Sikander Bakht	Pakistan v India at Delhi	1979-80
8-70	S. J. Snooke	South Africa v England at Johannesburg	1905-06
8-71	G. D. McKenzie	Australia v West Indies at Melbourne	1968-69
8-71	S. K. Warne	Australia v England at Brisbane	1994-95
8-72	S. Venkataraghavan	India v New Zealand at Delhi	1964-65
8-75†	N. D. Hirwani	India v West Indies at Madras	1987-88
8-75	A. R. C. Fraser	England v West Indies at Bridgetown	1993-94
8-76	E. A. S. Prasanna	India v New Zealand at Auckland	1975-76
8-79	B. S. Chandrasekhar	India v England at Delhi	1972-73
8-81	L. C. Braund	England v Australia at Melbourne	1903-04
8-83	J. R. Ratnayeke	Sri Lanka v Pakistan at Sialkot	1985-86
8-84†	R. A. L. Massie	Australia v England at Lord's	1972
8-85	Kapil Dev	India v Pakistan at Lahore	1982-83
8-86	A. W. Greig	England v West Indies at Port-of-Spain	1973-74
8-87	M. G. Hughes	Australia v West Indies at Perth	1988-89

8-92	M. A. Holding	West Indies v England at The Oval	1976
8-94	T. Richardson	England v Australia at Sydney	1897-98
8-97	C. J. McDermott ...	Australia v England at Perth................	1990-91
8-103	I. T. Botham	England v West Indies at Lord's...........	1984
8-104†	A. L. Valentine	West Indies v England at Manchester	1950
8-106	Kapil Dev	India v Australia at Adelaide	1985-86
8-107	B. J. T. Bosanquet .	England v Australia at Nottingham	1905
8-107	N. A. Foster	England v Pakistan at Leeds	1987
8-112	G. F. Lawson	Australia v West Indies at Adelaide	1984-85
8-126	J. C. White	England v Australia at Adelaide	1928-29
8-141	C. J. McDermott ...	Australia v England at Manchester........	1985
8-143	M. H. N. Walker ..	Australia v England at Melbourne	1974-75

† *On Test debut.*
Note: The best for Zimbabwe is 6-90 by **H. H. Streak** against Pakistan at Harare in 1994-95.

OUTSTANDING ANALYSES

	O	M	R	W		
J. C. Laker (E)	51.2	23	53	10	v Australia at Manchester	1956
G. A. Lohmann (E)	14.2	6	28	9	v South Africa at Johannesburg.	1895-96
J. C. Laker (E)	16.4	4	37	9	v Australia at Manchester	1956
G. A. Lohmann (E)	9.4	5	7	8	v South Africa at Port Elizabeth	1895-96
J. Briggs (E)	14.2	5	11	8	v South Africa at Cape Town ..	1888-89
J. Briggs (E)	19.1	11	17	7	v South Africa at Cape Town ..	1888-89
M. A. Noble (A)	7.4	2	17	7	v England at Melbourne	1901-02
W. Rhodes (E)	11	3	17	7	v Australia at Birmingham	1902
A. E. R. Gilligan (E)	6.3	4	7	6	v South Africa at Birmingham .	1924
S. Haigh (E)	11.4	6	11	6	v South Africa at Cape Town ..	1898-99
D. L. Underwood (E)	11.6	7	12	6	v New Zealand at Christchurch.	1970-71
S. L. V. Raju (I)	17.5	13	12	6	v Sri Lanka at Chandigarh	1990-91
H. J. Tayfield (SA)	14	7	13	6	v New Zealand at Johannesburg.	1953-54
C. T. B. Turner (A)	18	11	15	6	v England at Sydney...........	1886-87
M. H. N. Walker (A)	16	8	15	6	v Pakistan at Sydney	1972-73
E. R. H. Toshack (A)	2.3	1	2	5	v India at Brisbane	1947-48
H. Ironmonger (A)	7.2	5	6	5	v South Africa at Melbourne ...	1931-32
T. B. A. May (E)	6.5	3	9	5	v West Indies at Adelaide	1992-93
Pervez Sajjad (P)	12	8	5	4	v New Zealand at Rawalpindi..	1964-65
K. Higgs (E)	9	7	5	4	v New Zealand at Christchurch.	1965-66
P. H. Edmonds (E)	8	6	6	4	v Pakistan at Lord's	1978
J. C. White (E)	6.3	2	7	4	v Australia at Brisbane........	1928-29
J. H. Wardle (E)	5	2	7	4	v Australia at Manchester	1953
R. Appleyard (E)	6	3	7	4	v New Zealand at Auckland ...	1954-55
R. Benaud (A)	3.4	3	0	3	v India at Delhi	1959-60

MOST WICKETS IN A MATCH

19-90	J. C. Laker	England v Australia at Manchester	1956
17-159	S. F. Barnes......	England v South Africa at Johannesburg	1913-14
16-136†	N. D. Hirwani ..	India v West Indies at Madras	1987-88
16-137†	R. A. L. Massie ..	Australia v England at Lord's	1972
15-28	J. Briggs.........	England v South Africa at Cape Town	1888-89
15-45	G. A. Lohmann...	England v South Africa at Port Elizabeth	1895-96
15-99	C. Blythe	England v South Africa at Leeds	1907
15-104	H. Verity	England v Australia at Lord's	1934
15-123	R. J. Hadlee	New Zealand v Australia at Brisbane	1985-86
15-124	W. Rhodes.......	England v Australia at Melbourne	1903-04
14-90	F. R. Spofforth ...	Australia v England at The Oval..............	1882

14-99	A. V. Bedser	England v Australia at Nottingham	1953
14-102	W. Bates	England v Australia at Melbourne.	1882-83
14-116	Imran Khan.	Pakistan v Sri Lanka at Lahore.	1981-82
14-124	J. M. Patel.	India v Australia at Kanpur	1959-60
14-144	S. F. Barnes	England v South Africa at Durban	1913-14
14-149	M. A. Holding. . . .	West Indies v England at The Oval	1976
14-199	C. V. Grimmett. . .	Australia v South Africa at Adelaide	1931-32

† *On Test debut.*

Notes: The best for South Africa is 13-165 by H. J. Tayfield against Australia at Melbourne, 1952-53, for Sri Lanka 9-125 by R. J. Ratnayake against India at Colombo (PSS), 1985-86, for Zimbabwe 9-105 by H. H. Streak against Pakistan at Harare, 1994-95.

MOST WICKETS IN A SERIES

	T	R	W	Avge		
S. F. Barnes	4	536	49	10.93	England v South Africa.	1913-14
J. C. Laker.	5	442	46	9.60	England v Australia. . . .	1956
C. V. Grimmett	5	642	44	14.59	Australia v South Africa	1935-36
T. M. Alderman	6	893	42	21.26	Australia v England. . . .	1981
R. M. Hogg	6	527	41	12.85	Australia v England. . . .	1978-79
T. M. Alderman	6	712	41	17.36	Australia v England. . . .	1989
Imran Khan	6	558	40	13.95	Pakistan v India	1982-83
A. V. Bedser	5	682	39	17.48	England v Australia. . . .	1953
D. K. Lillee	6	870	39	22.30	Australia v England. . . .	1981
M. W. Tate	5	881	38	23.18	England v Australia. . . .	1924-25
W. J. Whitty	5	632	37	17.08	Australia v South Africa	1910-11
H. J. Tayfield	5	636	37	17.18	South Africa v England.	1956-57
A. E. E. Vogler	5	783	36	21.75	South Africa v England.	1909-10
A. A. Mailey	5	946	36	26.27	Australia v England. . . .	1920-21
G. A. Lohmann	3	203	35	5.80	England v South Africa.	1895-96
B. S. Chandrasekhar . .	5	662	35	18.91	India v England	1972-73
M. D. Marshall	5	443	35	12.65	West Indies v England .	1988

Notes: The most for New Zealand is 33 by R. J. Hadlee against Australia in 1985-86, for Sri Lanka 20 by R. J. Ratnayake against India in 1985-86, and for Zimbabwe 22 by H. H. Streak against Pakistan in 1994-95.

MOST WICKETS IN A CAREER

(Qualification: 100 wickets)

ENGLAND

		T	Balls	R	W	Avge	5W/i	10W/m
1	I. T. Botham	102	21,815	10,878	383	28.40	27	4
2	R. G. D. Willis	90	17,357	8,190	325	25.20	16	—
3	F. S. Trueman	67	15,178	6,625	307	21.57	17	3
4	D. L. Underwood	86	21,862	7,674	297	25.83	17	6
5	J. B. Statham	70	16,056	6,261	252	24.84	9	1
6	A. V. Bedser	51	15,918	5,876	236	24.89	15	5
7	J. A. Snow	49	12,021	5,387	202	26.66	8	1
8	J. C. Laker.	46	12,027	4,101	193	21.24	9	3
9	S. F. Barnes	27	7,873	3,106	189	16.43	24	7
10	G. A. R. Lock	49	13,147	4,451	174	25.58	9	3
11	M. W. Tate	39	12,523	4,055	155	26.16	7	1
12	F. J. Titmus	53	15,118	4,931	153	32.22	7	—
13	**J. E. Emburey . . . . . .**	**64**	**15,391**	**5,646**	**147**	**38.40**	**6**	**—**

		T	Balls	R	W	Avge	5W/i	10W/m
14	H. Verity	40	11,173	3,510	144	24.37	5	2
15	C. M. Old	46	8,858	4,020	143	28.11	4	—
16	A. W. Greig	58	9,802	4,541	141	32.20	6	2
17	P. A. J. DeFreitas	44	9,838	4,700	140	33.57	4	—
18	G. R. Dilley	41	8,192	4,107	138	29.76	6	—
19	T. E. Bailey	61	9,712	3,856	132	29.21	5	1
20	W. Rhodes	58	8,231	3,425	127	26.96	6	1
21	P. H. Edmonds	51	12,028	4,273	125	34.18	2	—
22 ⎰	D. A. Allen	39	11,297	3,779	122	30.97	4	—
⎱	R. Illingworth	61	11,934	3,807	122	31.20	3	—
24	J. Briggs	33	5,332	2,095	118	17.75	9	4
25	D. E. Malcolm	34	7,580	4,246	116	36.60	5	2
26	G. G. Arnold	34	7,650	3,254	115	28.29	6	—
27	A. R. C. Fraser	29	7,571	3,322	115	28.88	8	—
28	G. A. Lohmann	18	3,821	1,205	112	10.75	9	5
29	D. V. P. Wright	34	8,135	4,224	108	39.11	6	1
30	J. H. Wardle	28	6,597	2,080	102	20.39	5	1
31	R. Peel	20	5,216	1,715	101	16.98	5	1
32	C. Blythe	19	4,546	1,863	100	18.63	9	4

AUSTRALIA

		T	Balls	R	W	Avge	5W/i	10W/m
1	D. K. Lillee	70	18,467	8,493	355	23.92	23	7
2	C. J. McDermott	65	15,385	7,697	270	28.50	13	2
3	R. Benaud	63	19,108	6,704	248	27.03	16	1
4	G. D. McKenzie	60	17,681	7,328	246	29.78	16	3
5	R. R. Lindwall	61	13,650	5,251	228	23.03	12	—
6	C. V. Grimmett	37	14,513	5,231	216	24.21	21	7
7	M. G. Hughes	53	12,285	6,017	212	28.38	7	1
8	J. R. Thomson	51	10,535	5,601	200	28.00	8	—
9	A. K. Davidson	44	11,587	3,819	186	20.53	14	2
10	G. F. Lawson	46	11,118	5,501	180	30.56	11	2
11	S. K. Warne	38	11,440	4,239	176	24.08	9	2
12 ⎰	K. R. Miller	55	10,461	3,906	170	22.97	7	1
⎱	T. M. Alderman	41	10,181	4,616	170	27.15	14	1
14	W. A. Johnston	40	11,048	3,826	160	23.91	7	—
15	W. J. O'Reilly	27	10,024	3,254	144	22.59	11	3
16	H. Trumble	32	8,099	3,072	141	21.78	9	3
17	M. H. N. Walker	34	10,094	3,792	138	27.47	6	—
18	A. A. Mallett	38	9,990	3,940	132	29.84	6	1
19	B. Yardley	33	8,909	3,986	126	31.63	6	1
20	R. M. Hogg	38	7,633	3,503	123	28.47	6	2
21	M. A. Noble	42	7,159	3,025	121	25.00	9	2
22	B. A. Reid	27	6,244	2,784	113	24.63	5	2
23	I. W. Johnson	45	8,780	3,182	109	29.19	3	—
24	G. Giffen	31	6,457	2,791	103	27.09	7	1
25	A. N. Connolly	29	7,818	2,981	102	29.22	4	—
26	C. T. B. Turner	17	5,179	1,670	101	16.53	11	2

SOUTH AFRICA

		T	Balls	R	W	Avge	5W/i	10W/m
1	H. J. Tayfield	37	13,568	4,405	170	25.91	14	2
2	T. L. Goddard	41	11,736	3,226	123	26.22	5	—
3	P. M. Pollock	28	6,522	2,806	116	24.18	9	1
4	N. A. T. Adcock	26	6,391	2,195	104	21.10	5	—

WEST INDIES

		T	Balls	R	W	Avge	5W/i	10W/m
1	M. D. Marshall	81	17,584	7,876	376	20.94	22	4
2	L. R. Gibbs	79	27,115	8,989	309	29.09	18	2
3	**C. A. Walsh**	**80**	**17,093**	**7,534**	**301**	**25.02**	**11**	**2**
4	J. Garner	58	13,169	5,433	259	20.97	7	—
5	**C. E. L. Ambrose**	**59**	**13,870**	**5,493**	**258**	**21.29**	**13**	**3**
6	M. A. Holding	60	12,680	5,898	249	23.68	13	2
7	G. S. Sobers	93	21,599	7,999	235	34.03	6	—
8	A. M. E. Roberts.....	47	11,136	5,174	202	25.61	11	2
9	W. W. Hall	48	10,421	5,066	192	26.38	9	1
10	S. Ramadhin	43	13,939	4,579	158	28.98	10	1
11	A. L. Valentine	36	12,953	4,215	139	30.32	8	2
12	C. E. H. Croft	27	6,165	2,913	125	23.30	3	—
13	**I. R. Bishop**	**24**	**5,373**	**2,347**	**110**	**21.33**	**6**	—
14	V. A. Holder	40	9,095	3,627	109	33.27	3	—

NEW ZEALAND

		T	Balls	R	W	Avge	5W/i	10W/m
1	R. J. Hadlee........	86	21,918	9,612	431	22.29	36	9
2	**D. K. Morrison**......	**41**	**8,893**	**4,795**	**143**	**33.53**	**9**	—
3	B. L. Cairns	43	10,628	4,280	130	32.92	6	1
4	E. J. Chatfield	43	10,360	3,958	123	32.17	3	1
5	R. O. Collinge	35	7,689	3,392	116	29.24	3	—
6	B. R. Taylor........	30	6,334	2,953	111	26.60	4	—
7	J. G. Bracewell	41	8,403	3,653	102	35.81	4	1
8	R. C. Motz..........	32	7,034	3,148	100	31.48	5	—

INDIA

		T	Balls	R	W	Avge	5W/i	10W/m
1	Kapil Dev	131	27,740	12,867	434	29.64	23	2
2	B. S. Bedi...........	67	21,364	7,637	266	28.71	14	1
3	B. S. Chandrasekhar ..	58	15,963	7,199	242	29.74	16	2
4	E. A. S. Prasanna	49	14,353	5,742	189	30.38	10	2
5	V. Mankad..........	44	14,686	5,236	162	32.32	8	2
6	S. Venkataraghavan ..	57	14,877	5,634	156	36.11	3	1
7	R. J. Shastri	80	15,751	6,185	151	40.96	2	—
8	S. P. Gupte	36	11,284	4,403	149	29.55	12	1
9	D. R. Doshi	33	9,322	3,502	114	30.71	6	—
10	K. D. Ghavri	39	7,042	3,656	109	33.54	4	—
11	N. S. Yadav.........	35	8,349	3,580	102	35.09	3	—

PAKISTAN

		T	Balls	R	W	Avge	5W/i	10W/m
1	Imran Khan	88	19,458	8,258	362	22.81	23	6
2	**Wasim Akram**	**61**	**14,057**	**6,057**	**261**	**23.20**	**18**	**3**
3	Abdul Qadir........	67	17,126	7,742	236	32.80	15	5
4	**Waqar Younis**	**33**	**6,857**	**3,640**	**190**	**19.15**	**19**	**4**
5	Sarfraz Nawaz	55	13,927	5,798	177	32.75	4	1
6	Iqbal Qasim	50	13,019	4,807	171	28.11	8	2
7	Fazal Mahmood......	34	9,834	3,434	139	24.70	13	4
8	Intikhab Alam	47	10,474	4,494	125	35.95	5	2

SRI LANKA: The highest aggregate is 73 wickets, average 35.10, by R. J. Ratnayake in 23 Tests.

ZIMBABWE: The highest aggregate is 43 wickets, average 20.60, by **H. H. Streak** in nine Tests.

Bold type denotes those who played Test cricket in 1994-95 and 1995 seasons.

WICKET WITH FIRST BALL IN TEST CRICKET

	Batsman dismissed			
A. Coningham	A. C. MacLaren	A v E	Melbourne	1894-95
W. M. Bradley	F. Laver	E v A	Manchester	1899
E. G. Arnold	V. T. Trumper	E v A	Sydney	1903-04
G. G. Macaulay	G. A. L. Hearne	E v SA	Cape Town	1922-23
M. W. Tate	M. J. Susskind	E v SA	Birmingham	1924
M. Henderson	E. W. Dawson	NZ v E	Christchurch	1929-30
H. D. Smith	E. Paynter	NZ v E	Christchurch	1932-33
T. F. Johnson	W. W. Keeton	WI v E	The Oval	1939
R. Howorth	D. V. Dyer	E v SA	The Oval	1947
Intikhab Alam	C. C. McDonald	P v A	Karachi	1959-60
R. K. Illingworth	P. V. Simmons	E v WI	Nottingham	1991

HAT-TRICKS

F. R. Spofforth	Australia v England at Melbourne	1878-79
W. Bates	England v Australia at Melbourne	1882-83
J. Briggs	England v Australia at Sydney	1891-92
G. A. Lohmann	England v South Africa at Port Elizabeth	1895-96
J. T. Hearne	England v Australia at Leeds	1899
H. Trumble	Australia v England at Melbourne	1901-02
H. Trumble	Australia v England at Melbourne	1903-04
T. J. Matthews† ⎫	Australia v South Africa at Manchester	1912
T. J. Matthews ⎭		
M. J. C. Allom‡	England v New Zealand at Christchurch	1929-30
T. W. J. Goddard	England v South Africa at Johannesburg	1938-39
P. J. Loader	England v West Indies at Leeds	1957
L. F. Kline	Australia v South Africa at Cape Town	1957-58
W. W. Hall	West Indies v Pakistan at Lahore	1958-59
G. M. Griffin	South Africa v England at Lord's	1960
L. R. Gibbs	West Indies v Australia at Adelaide	1960-61
P. J. Petherick‡	New Zealand v Pakistan at Lahore	1976-77
C. A. Walsh§	West Indies v Australia at Brisbane	1988-89
M. G. Hughes§	Australia v West Indies at Perth	1988-89
D. W. Fleming‡	Australia v Pakistan at Rawalpindi	1994-95
S. K. Warne	Australia v England at Melbourne	1994-95
D. G. Cork	England v West Indies at Manchester	1995

† *T. J. Matthews did the hat-trick in each innings of the same match.*
‡ *On Test debut.*
§ *Not all in the same innings.*

FOUR WICKETS IN FIVE BALLS

M. J. C. Allom	England v New Zealand at Christchurch	1929-30
	On debut, in his eighth over: W-WWW	
C. M. Old	England v Pakistan at Birmingham	1978
	Sequence interrupted by a no-ball: WW-WW	
Wasim Akram	Pakistan v West Indies at Lahore (*WW-WW*)	1990-91

MOST BALLS BOWLED IN A TEST

S. Ramadhin (West Indies) sent down 774 balls in 129 overs against England at Birmingham, 1957. It was the most delivered by any bowler in a Test, beating H. Verity's 766 for England against South Africa at Durban, 1938-39. In this match Ramadhin also bowled the most balls (588) in any single first-class innings, including Tests.

ALL-ROUND RECORDS

100 RUNS AND FIVE WICKETS IN AN INNINGS

England

A. W. Greig	148	6-164	v West Indies	Bridgetown	1973-74
I. T. Botham	103	5-73	v New Zealand	Christchurch	1977-78
I. T. Botham	108	8-34	v Pakistan	Lord's	1978
I. T. Botham	114	6-58 7-48 }	v India	Bombay	1979-80
I. T. Botham	149*	6-95	v Australia	Leeds	1981
I. T. Botham	138	5-59	v New Zealand	Wellington	1983-84

Australia

C. Kelleway	114	5-33	v South Africa	Manchester	1912
J. M. Gregory	100	7-69	v England	Melbourne	1920-21
K. R. Miller	109	6-107	v West Indies	Kingston	1954-55
R. Benaud	100	5-84	v South Africa	Johannesburg	1957-58

South Africa

J. H. Sinclair	106	6-26	v England	Cape Town	1898-99
G. A. Faulkner	123	5-120	v England	Johannesburg	1909-10

West Indies

D. St E. Atkinson	219	5-56	v Australia	Bridgetown	1954-55
O. G. Smith	100	5-90	v India	Delhi	1958-59
G. S. Sobers	104	5-63	v India	Kingston	1961-62
G. S. Sobers	174	5-41	v England	Leeds	1966

New Zealand

B. R. Taylor†	105	5-86	v India	Calcutta	1964-65

India

V. Mankad	184	5-196	v England	Lord's	1952
P. R. Umrigar	172*	5-107	v West Indies	Port-of-Spain	1961-62

Pakistan

Mushtaq Mohammad	201	5-49	v New Zealand	Dunedin	1972-73
Mushtaq Mohammad	121	5-28	v West Indies	Port-of-Spain	1976-77
Imran Khan	117	6-98 5-82 }	v India	Faisalabad	1982-83
Wasim Akram	123	5-100	v Australia	Adelaide	1989-90

† *On debut.*

100 RUNS AND FIVE DISMISSALS IN AN INNINGS

D. T. Lindsay	182	6ct	SA v A	Johannesburg	1966-67
I. D. S. Smith	113*	4ct, 1st	NZ v E	Auckland	1983-84
S. A. R. Silva	111	5ct	SL v I	Colombo (PSS)	1985-86

100 RUNS AND TEN WICKETS IN A TEST

A. K. Davidson	44 80	5-135 6-87 }	A v WI	Brisbane..........	1960-61
I. T. Botham	114	6-58 7-48 }	E v I	Bombay	1979-80
Imran Khan	117	6-98 5-82 }	P v I	Faisalabad	1982-83

1,000 RUNS AND 100 WICKETS IN A CAREER

	Tests	Runs	Wkts	Tests for Double
England				
T. E. Bailey..............	61	2,290	132	47
†I. T. Botham	102	5,200	383	21
J. E. Emburey	**64**	**1,713**	**147**	**46**
A. W. Greig	58	3,599	141	37
R. Illingworth	61	1,836	122	47
W. Rhodes...............	58	2,325	127	44
M. W. Tate	39	1,198	155	33
F. J. Titmus	53	1,449	153	40
Australia				
R. Benaud	63	2,201	248	32
A. K. Davidson	44	1,328	186	34
G. Giffen.................	31	1,238	103	30
M. G. Hughes	53	1,032	212	52
I. W. Johnson	45	1,000	109	45
R. R. Lindwall	61	1,502	228	38
K. R. Miller	55	2,958	170	33
M. A. Noble	42	1,997	121	27
South Africa				
T. L. Goddard............	41	2,516	123	36
West Indies				
M. D. Marshall...........	81	1,810	376	49
†G. S. Sobers	93	8,032	235	48
New Zealand				
J. G. Bracewell	41	1,001	102	41
R. J. Hadlee	86	3,124	431	28
India				
Kapil Dev	131	5,248	434	25
V. Mankad	44	2,109	162	23
R. J. Shastri	80	3,830	151	44
Pakistan				
Abdul Qadir	67	1,029	236	62
Imran Khan	88	3,807	362	30
Intikhab Alam	47	1,493	125	41
Sarfraz Nawaz	55	1,045	177	55
Wasim Akram..............	**61**	**1,401**	**261**	**45**

Bold type denotes those who played Test cricket in 1994-95 and 1995 seasons.

† I. T. Botham (120 catches) and G. S. Sobers (109) are the only players to have achieved the treble of 1,000 runs, 100 wickets and 100 catches.

WICKET-KEEPING RECORDS

Most Dismissals in an Innings

7 (all ct)	Wasim Bari	Pakistan v New Zealand at Auckland . . .	1978-79
7 (all ct)	R. W. Taylor	England v India at Bombay	1979-80
7 (all ct)	I. D. S. Smith	New Zealand v Sri Lanka at Hamilton . .	1990-91
6 (all ct)	A. T. W. Grout	Australia v South Africa at Johannesburg	1957-58
6 (all ct)	D. T. Lindsay	South Africa v Australia at Johannesburg	1966-67
6 (all ct)	J. T. Murray	England v India at Lord's	1967
6 (5ct, 1st)	S. M. H. Kirmani . .	India v New Zealand at Christchurch . . .	1975-76
6 (all ct)	R. W. Marsh	Australia v England at Brisbane	1982-83
6 (all ct)	S. A. R. Silva	Sri Lanka v India at Colombo (SSC)	1985-86
6 (all ct)	R. C. Russell	England v Australia at Melbourne	1990-91

Note: The most stumpings in an innings is 5 by K. S. More for India v West Indies at Madras in 1987-88.

Most Dismissals in a Test

10 (all ct)	R. W. Taylor	England v India at Bombay	1979-80
9 (8ct, 1st)	G. R. A. Langley . .	Australia v England at Lord's	1956
9 (all ct)	D. A. Murray	West Indies v Australia at Melbourne . . .	1981-82
9 (all ct)	R. W. Marsh	Australia v England at Brisbane	1982-83
9 (all ct)	S. A. R. Silva	Sri Lanka v India at Colombo (SSC)	1985-86
9 (8ct, 1st)	S. A. R. Silva	Sri Lanka v India at Colombo (PSS)	1985-86
9 (all ct)	D. J. Richardson . . .	South Africa v India at Port Elizabeth . . .	1992-93
9 (all ct)	Rashid Latif	Pakistan v New Zealand at Auckland . . .	1993-94
9 (all ct)	I. A. Healy	Australia v England at Brisbane	1994-95
9 (all ct)	C. O. Browne	West Indies v England at Nottingham . . .	1995

Notes: S. A. R. Silva made 18 dismissals in two successive Tests.

The most stumpings in a match is 6 by K. S. More for India v West Indies at Madras in 1987-88.

J. J. Kelly (8ct) for Australia v England in 1901-02 and L. E. G. Ames (6ct, 2st) for England v West Indies in 1933 were the only wicket-keepers to make eight dismissals in a Test before World War II.

Most Dismissals in a Series

(Played in 5 Tests unless otherwise stated)

28 (all ct)	R. W. Marsh	Australia v England	1982-83
26 (23ct, 3st)	J. H. B. Waite	South Africa v New Zealand	1961-62
26 (all ct)	R. W. Marsh	Australia v West Indies (6 Tests)	1975-76
26 (21ct, 5st)	I. A. Healy	Australia v England (6 Tests)	1993
25 (23ct, 2st)	I. A. Healy	Australia v England	1994-95
24 (22ct, 2st)	D. L. Murray	West Indies v England	1963
24 (all ct)	D. T. Lindsay	South Africa v Australia	1966-67
24 (21ct, 3st)	A. P. E. Knott	England v Australia (6 Tests)	1970-71
24 (all ct)	I. A. Healy	Australia v England	1990-91
23 (16ct, 7st)	J. H. B. Waite	South Africa v New Zealand	1953-54
23 (22ct, 1st)	F. C. M. Alexander	West Indies v England	1959-60
23 (20ct, 3st)	A. T. W. Grout . . .	Australia v West Indies	1960-61
23 (21ct, 2st)	A. E. Dick	New Zealand v South Africa	1961-62
23 (21ct, 2st)	R. W. Marsh	Australia v England	1972
23 (22ct, 1st)	A. P. E. Knott	England v Australia (6 Tests)	1974-75
23 (all ct)	R. W. Marsh	Australia v England (6 Tests)	1981
23 (all ct)	P. J. L. Dujon	West Indies v Australia	1990-91
23 (19ct, 4st)	I. A. Healy	Australia v West Indies	1992-93
22 (all ct)	S. J. Rixon	Australia v India	1977-78
22 (21ct, 1st)	S. A. R. Silva	Sri Lanka v India (3 Tests)	1985-86

Notes: G. R. A. Langley made 20 dismissals (16ct, 4st) in four Tests for Australia v West Indies in 1954-55.

H. Strudwick, with 21 (15ct, 6st) for England v South Africa in 1913-14, was the only wicket-keeper to make as many as 20 dismissals in a series before World War II.

Most Dismissals in a Career

		T	Ct	St	Total
1	R. W. Marsh (Australia)	96	343	12	355
2	P. J. L. Dujon (West Indies)	81	267	5	272
3	A. P. E. Knott (England)	95	250	19	269
4	**I. A. Healy (Australia)**	**73**	**231**	**17**	**248**
5	Wasim Bari (Pakistan).....................	81	201	27	228
6	T. G. Evans (England).....................	91	173	46	219
7	S. M. H. Kirmani (India)	88	160	38	198
8	D. L. Murray (West Indies)	62	181	8	189
9	A. T. W. Grout (Australia)	51	163	24	187
10	I. D. S. Smith (New Zealand)..............	63	168	8	176
11	R. W. Taylor (England)..................	57	167	7	174
12	J. H. B. Waite (South Africa)	50	124	17	141
13 {	K. S. More (India)	49	110	20	130
	W. A. S. Oldfield (Australia)...............	54	78	52	130
15	J. M. Parks (England)	46	103	11	114
16	**R. C. Russell (England)**	**39**	**99**	**9**	**108**
17	Salim Yousuf (Pakistan)	32	91	13	104

Notes: The records for P. J. L. Dujon and J. M. Parks each include two catches taken when not keeping wicket in two and three Tests respectively.

The most dismissals for other countries are Sri Lanka 34 (S. A. R. Silva 33ct, 1st in 9 Tests) and Zimbabwe 26 (**A. Flower** 24ct, 2st in 9 Tests as wicket-keeper).

Bold type denotes those who played Test cricket in 1994-95 and 1995 seasons.

FIELDING RECORDS

(Excluding wicket-keepers)

Most Catches in an Innings

5	V. Y. Richardson	Australia v South Africa at Durban	1935-36
5	Yajurvindra Singh.....	India v England at Bangalore	1976-77
5	M. Azharuddin	India v Pakistan at Karachi	1989-90
5	K. Srikkanth	India v Australia at Perth	1991-92

Most Catches in a Test

7	G. S. Chappell........	Australia v England at Perth................	1974-75
7	Yajurvindra Singh.....	India v England at Bangalore	1976-77
7	H. P. Tillekeratne	Sri Lanka v New Zealand at Colombo (SSC) ...	1992-93
6	A. Shrewsbury	England v Australia at Sydney	1887-88
6	A. E. E. Vogler	South Africa v England at Durban	1909-10
6	F. E. Woolley	England v Australia at Sydney	1911-12
6	J. M. Gregory	Australia v England at Sydney	1920-21
6	B. Mitchell	South Africa v Australia at Melbourne	1931-32
6	V. Y. Richardson	Australia v South Africa at Durban	1935-36
6	R. N. Harvey	Australia v England at Sydney	1962-63
6	M. C. Cowdrey	England v West Indies at Lord's............	1963
6	E. D. Solkar	India v West Indies at Port-of-Spain	1970-71
6	G. S. Sobers.........	West Indies v England at Leeds	1973
6	I. M. Chappell........	Australia v New Zealand at Adelaide	1973-74
6	A. W. Greig	England v Pakistan at Leeds	1974
6	D. F. Whatmore	Australia v India at Kanpur	1979-80
6	A. J. Lamb	England v New Zealand at Lord's	1983
6	G. A. Hick	England v Pakistan at Leeds	1992
6	B. A. Young	New Zealand v Pakistan at Auckland	1993-94
6	J. C. Adams	West Indies v England at Kingston	1993-94

Most Catches in a Series

15	J. M. Gregory	Australia v England	1920-21
14	G. S. Chappell	Australia v England (6 Tests)	1974-75
13	R. B. Simpson	Australia v South Africa	1957-58
13	R. B. Simpson	Australia v West Indies	1960-61

Most Catches in a Career

A. R. Border (Australia)	156 in 156 matches
G. S. Chappell (Australia)	122 in 87 matches
I. V. A. Richards (West Indies)	122 in 121 matches
I. T. Botham (England)	120 in 102 matches
M. C. Cowdrey (England)	120 in 114 matches
R. B. Simpson (Australia)	110 in 62 matches
W. R. Hammond (England)	110 in 85 matches
G. S. Sobers (West Indies)	109 in 93 matches
S. M. Gavaskar (India)	108 in 125 matches
I. M. Chappell (Australia)	105 in 75 matches
G. A. Gooch (England)	**103 in 118 matches**

Bold type denotes those who played Test cricket in 1994-95 and 1995 seasons.

TEAM RECORDS

HIGHEST INNINGS TOTALS

903-7 dec.	England v Australia at The Oval	1938
849	England v West Indies at Kingston	1929-30
790-3 dec.	West Indies v Pakistan at Kingston	1957-58
758-8 dec.	Australia v West Indies at Kingston	1954-55
729-6 dec.	Australia v England at Lord's	1930
708	Pakistan v England at The Oval	1987
701	Australia v England at The Oval	1934
699-5	Pakistan v India at Lahore	1989-90
695	Australia v England at The Oval	1930
692-8 dec.	West Indies v England at The Oval	1995
687-8 dec.	West Indies v England at The Oval	1976
681-8 dec.	West Indies v England at Port-of-Spain	1953-54
676-7	India v Sri Lanka at Kanpur	1986-87
674-6	Pakistan v India at Faisalabad	1984-85
674	Australia v India at Adelaide	1947-48
671-4	New Zealand v Sri Lanka at Wellington	1990-91
668	Australia v West Indies at Bridgetown	1954-55
660-5 dec.	West Indies v New Zealand at Wellington	1994-95
659-8 dec.	Australia v England at Sydney	1946-47
658-8 dec.	England v Australia at Nottingham	1938
657-8 dec.	Pakistan v West Indies at Bridgetown	1957-58
656-8 dec.	Australia v England at Manchester	1964
654-5	England v South Africa at Durban	1938-39
653-4 dec.	England v India at Lord's	1990
653-4 dec.	Australia v England at Leeds	1993
652-7 dec.	England v India at Madras	1984-85
652-8 dec.	West Indies v England at Lord's	1973
652	Pakistan v India at Faisalabad	1982-83
650-6 dec.	Australia v West Indies at Bridgetown	1964-65

The highest innings for the countries not mentioned above are:

622-9 dec.	South Africa v Australia at Durban	1969-70
547-8 dec.	Sri Lanka v Australia at Colombo (SSC)	1992-93
544-4 dec.	Zimbabwe v Pakistan at Harare	1994-95

HIGHEST FOURTH-INNINGS TOTALS

To win

406-4	India (needing 403) v West Indies at Port-of-Spain	1975-76
404-3	Australia (needing 404) v England at Leeds	1948
362-7	West Indies (needing 359) v Australia at Georgetown	1977-78
348-5	West Indies (needing 345) v New Zealand at Auckland	1968-69
344-1	West Indies (needing 342) v England at Lord's....................	1984

To tie

347	India v Australia at Madras...................................	1986-87

To draw

654-5	England (needing 696 to win) v South Africa at Durban	1938-39
429-8	India (needing 438 to win) v England at The Oval................	1979
423-7	South Africa (needing 451 to win) v England at The Oval	1947
408-5	West Indies (needing 836 to win) v England at Kingston	1929-30

To lose

445	India (lost by 47 runs) v Australia at Adelaide	1977-78
440	New Zealand (lost by 38 runs) v England at Nottingham............	1973
417	England (lost by 45 runs) v Australia at Melbourne	1976-77
411	England (lost by 193 runs) v Australia at Sydney....................	1924-25

MOST RUNS IN A DAY (BOTH SIDES)

588	England (398-6), India (190-0) at Manchester (2nd day)	1936
522	England (503-2), South Africa (19-0) at Lord's (2nd day)	1924
508	England (221-2), South Africa (287-6) at The Oval (3rd day)	1935

MOST RUNS IN A DAY (ONE SIDE)

503	England (503-2) v South Africa at Lord's (2nd day)	1924
494	Australia (494-6) v South Africa at Sydney (1st day).................	1910-11
475	Australia (475-2) v England at The Oval (1st day)....................	1934
471	England (471-8) v India at The Oval (1st day)......................	1936
458	Australia (458-3) v England at Leeds (1st day).....................	1930
455	Australia (455-1) v England at Leeds (2nd day).....................	1934

MOST WICKETS IN A DAY

27	England (18-3 to 53 out and 62) v Australia (60) at Lord's (2nd day)	1888
25	Australia (112 and 48-5) v England (61) at Melbourne (1st day)	1901-02

HIGHEST MATCH AGGREGATES

Runs	Wkts			Days played
1,981	35	South Africa v England at Durban	1938-39	10†
1,815	34	West Indies v England at Kingston	1929-30	9‡
1,764	39	Australia v West Indies at Adelaide	1968-69	5
1,753	40	Australia v England at Adelaide	1920-21	6

Runs	Wkts			Days played
1,723	31	England v Australia at Leeds	1948	5
1,661	36	West Indies v Australia at Bridgetown...............	1954-55	6

† *No play on one day.*   ‡ *No play on two days.*

LOWEST INNINGS TOTALS

26	New Zealand v England at Auckland............................	1954-55
30	South Africa v England at Port Elizabeth	1895-96
30	South Africa v England at Birmingham	1924
35	South Africa v England at Cape Town.........................	1898-99
36	Australia v England at Birmingham...........................	1902
36	South Africa v Australia at Melbourne........................	1931-32
42	Australia v England at Sydney...............................	1887-88
42	New Zealand v Australia at Wellington........................	1945-46
42†	India v England at Lord's..................................	1974
43	South Africa v England at Cape Town.........................	1888-89
44	Australia v England at The Oval.............................	1896
45	England v Australia at Sydney...............................	1886-87
45	South Africa v Australia at Melbourne........................	1931-32
46	England v West Indies at Port-of-Spain	1993-94
47	South Africa v England at Cape Town.........................	1888-89
47	New Zealand v England at Lord's............................	1958

The lowest innings for the countries not mentioned above are:

53	West Indies v Pakistan at Faisalabad	1986-87
62	Pakistan v Australia at Perth...............................	1981-82
71	Sri Lanka v Pakistan at Kandy..............................	1994-95
134	Zimbabwe v Pakistan at Karachi (DS).........................	1993-94

† *Batted one man short.*

FEWEST RUNS IN A FULL DAY'S PLAY

95 At Karachi, October 11, 1956. Australia 80 all out; Pakistan 15 for two (first day, 5½ hours).

104 At Karachi, December 8, 1959. Pakistan 0 for no wicket to 104 for five v Australia (fourth day, 5½ hours).

106 At Brisbane, December 9, 1958. England 92 for two to 198 all out v Australia (fourth day, 5 hours). *England were dismissed five minutes before the close of play, leaving no time for Australia to start their second innings.*

112 At Karachi, October 15, 1956. Australia 138 for six to 187 all out; Pakistan 63 for one (fourth day, 5½ hours).

115 At Karachi, September 19, 1988. Australia 116 for seven to 165 all out and 66 for five following on v Pakistan (fourth day, 5½ hours).

117 At Madras, October 19, 1956. India 117 for five v Australia (first day, 5½ hours).

117 At Colombo (SSC), March 21, 1984. New Zealand 6 for no wicket to 123 for four (fifth day, 5 hours 47 minutes).

In England

151 At Lord's, August 26, 1978. England 175 for two to 289 all out; New Zealand 37 for seven (third day, 6 hours).

159 At Leeds, July 10, 1971. Pakistan 208 for four to 350 all out; England 17 for one (third day, 6 hours).

LOWEST MATCH AGGREGATES

(For a completed match)

Runs	Wkts			Days played
234	29	Australia v South Africa at Melbourne................	1931-32	3†
291	40	England v Australia at Lord's	1888	2

Runs	Wkts			Days played
295	28	New Zealand v Australia at Wellington...............	1945-46	2
309	29	West Indies v England at Bridgetown	1934-35	3
323	30	England v Australia at Manchester...................	1888	2

† *No play on one day.*

YOUNGEST TEST PLAYERS

Years	Days			
15	124	Mushtaq Mohammad.....	Pakistan v West Indies at Lahore	1958-59
16	189	Aqib Javed	Pakistan v New Zealand at Wellington	1988-89
16	205	S. R. Tendulkar	India v Pakistan at Karachi	1989-90
16	221	Aftab Baloch...........	Pakistan v New Zealand at Dacca	1969-70
16	248	Nasim-ul-Ghani	Pakistan v West Indies at Bridgetown .	1957-58
16	352	Khalid Hassan	Pakistan v England at Nottingham ...	1954
17	5	Zahid Fazal	Pakistan v West Indies at Karachi....	1990-91
17	69	Ata-ur-Rehman.........	Pakistan v England at Birmingham ...	1992
17	118	L. Sivaramakrishnan	India v West Indies at St John's....	1982-83
17	122	J. E. D. Sealy	West Indies v England at Bridgetown .	1929-30
17	189	C. D. U. S. Weerasinghe .	Sri Lanka v India at Colombo (PSS) ..	1985-86
17	193	Maninder Singh	India v Pakistan at Karachi	1982-83
17	239	I. D. Craig	Australia v South Africa at Melbourne.	1952-53
17	245	G. S. Sobers	West Indies v Australia at Kingston ...	1953-54
17	265	V. L. Mehra	India v New Zealand at Bombay	1955-56
17	300	Hanif Mohammad	Pakistan v India at Delhi	1952-53
17	341	Intikhab Alam	Pakistan v Australia at Karachi	1959-60
17	364	Waqar Younis...........	Pakistan v India at Karachi	1989-90

Note: The youngest Test players for countries not mentioned above are: England – D. B. Close, 18 years 149 days, v New Zealand at Manchester, 1949; New Zealand – D. L. Freeman, 18 years 197 days, v England at Christchurch, 1932-33; South Africa – A. E. Ochse, 19 years 1 day, v England at Port Elizabeth, 1888-89; Zimbabwe – H. R. Olonga, 18 years 212 days, v Pakistan at Harare, 1994-95.

OLDEST PLAYERS ON TEST DEBUT

Years	Days			
49	119	J. Southerton.....	England v Australia at Melbourne	1876-77
47	284	Miran Bux.......	Pakistan v India at Lahore	1954-55
46	253	D. D. Blackie....	Australia v England at Sydney	1928-29
46	237	H. Ironmonger ...	Australia v England at Brisbane	1928-29
42	242	N. Betancourt....	West Indies v England at Port-of-Spain .	1929-30
41	337	E. R. Wilson.....	England v Australia at Sydney	1920-21
41	27	R. J. D. Jamshedji	India v England at Bombay...........	1933-34
40	345	C. A. Wiles	West Indies v England at Manchester ..	1933
40	295	O. Henry........	South Africa v India at Durban	1992-93
40	216	S. P. Kinneir ...	England v Australia at Sydney	1911-12
40	110	H. W. Lee.......	England v South Africa at Johannesburg	1930-31
40	56	G. W. A. Chubb ..	South Africa v England at Nottingham .	1951
40	37	C. Ramaswami ...	India v England at Manchester	1936

Note: The oldest Test player on debut for New Zealand was H. M. McGirr, 38 years 101 days, v England at Auckland, 1929-30; for Sri Lanka, D. S. de Silva, 39 years 251 days, v England at Colombo (PSS), 1981-82; for Zimbabwe, M. P. Jarvis, 36 years 317 days, v India at Harare, 1992-93. A. J. Traicos was 45 years 154 days old when he made his debut for Zimbabwe (v India at Harare, 1992-93) having played 3 Tests for South Africa in 1969-70.

OLDEST TEST PLAYERS

(Age on final day of their last Test match)

Years	Days			
52	165	W. Rhodes..........	England v West Indies at Kingston ...	1929-30
50	327	H. Ironmonger	Australia v England at Sydney	1932-33
50	320	W. G. Grace	England v Australia at Nottingham ...	1899
50	303	G. Gunn	England v West Indies at Kingston ...	1929-30
49	139	J. Southerton	England v Australia at Melbourne ...	1876-77
47	302	Miran Bux	Pakistan v India at Peshawar	1954-55
47	249	J. B. Hobbs	England v Australia at The Oval	1930
47	87	F. E. Woolley	England v Australia at The Oval	1934
46	309	D. D. Blackie	Australia v England at Adelaide ..	1928-29
46	206	A. W. Nourse	South Africa v England at The Oval ..	1924
46	202	H. Strudwick	England v Australia at The Oval	1926
46	41	E. H. Hendren	England v West Indies at Kingston ...	1934-35
45	304	A. J. Traicos	Zimbabwe v India at Delhi	1992-93
45	245	G. O. B. Allen	England v West Indies at Kingston ...	1947-48
45	215	P. Holmes	England v India at Lord's	1932
45	140	D. B. Close	England v West Indies at Manchester .	1976

MOST TEST APPEARANCES

156	A. R. Border (Australia)		116	D. B. Vengsarkar (India)
131	Kapil Dev (India)		114	M. C. Cowdrey (England)
125	S. M. Gavaskar (India)		110	C. H. Lloyd (West Indies)
124	Javed Miandad (Pakistan)		108	G. Boycott (England)
121	I. V. A. Richards (West Indies)		108	C. G. Greenidge (West Indies)
118	**G. A. Gooch (England)**		102	I. T. Botham (England)
117	D. I. Gower (England)		**101**	**D. C. Boon (Australia)**
116	D. L. Haynes (West Indies)			

The most appearances for New Zealand is 86 by R. J. Hadlee, for South Africa 50 by J. H. B. Waite, for Sri Lanka 56 by **A. Ranatunga** and for Zimbabwe 13 by **A. D. R. Campbell, A. Flower, G. W. Flower** and **D. L. Houghton**.

Bold type denotes those who played Test cricket in 1994-95 and 1995 seasons.

MOST CONSECUTIVE TEST APPEARANCES

153	A. R. Border (Australia)	March 1979 to March 1994
106	S. M. Gavaskar (India)	January 1975 to February 1987
87	G. R. Viswanath (India)	March 1971 to February 1983
85	G. S. Sobers (West Indies)......	April 1955 to April 1972
72	D. L. Haynes (West Indies)	December 1979 to June 1988
71	I. M. Chappell (Australia)	January 1966 to February 1976
66	Kapil Dev (India).............	October 1978 to December 1984
65	I. T. Botham (England)	February 1978 to March 1984
65	Kapil Dev (India).............	January 1985 to March 1994
65	A. P. E. Knott (England).......	March 1971 to August 1977

The most consecutive Test appearances for the countries not mentioned above are:

58†	J. R. Reid (New Zealand)	July 1949 to July 1965
53	Javed Miandad (Pakistan)	December 1977 to January 1984
45†	A. W. Nourse (South Africa)....	October 1902 to August 1924
35*	P. A. de Silva (Sri Lanka)	February 1988 to March 1995

The most for Zimbabwe is 13 (as above).

* *Sequence still in progress.*
† *Indicates complete Test career.*

CAPTAINCY

MOST TESTS AS CAPTAIN

	P	W	L	D		P	W	L	D
A. R. Border (A)	93	32	22	38*	Javed Miandad (P)	34	14	6	14
C. H. Lloyd (WI)	74	36	12	26	Kapil Dev (I)	34	4	7	22*
I. V. A. Richards (WI)	50	27	8	15	J. R. Reid (NZ)	34	3	18	13
G. S. Chappell (A)	48	21	13	14	D. I. Gower (E)	32	5	18	9
Imran Khan (P)	48	14	8	26	**M. Azharuddin (I)**	**31**	**10**	**8**	**13**
S. M. Gavaskar (I)	47	9	8	30	J. M. Brearley (E)	31	18	4	9
P. B. H. May (E)	41	20	10	11	R. Illingworth (E)	31	12	5	14
Nawab of Pataudi jun. (I)	40	9	19	12	I. M. Chappell (A)	30	15	5	10
R. B. Simpson (A)	39	12	12	15	E. R. Dexter (E)	30	9	7	14
G. S. Sobers (WI)	39	9	10	20	G. P. Howarth (NZ)	30	11	7	12
G. A. Gooch (E)	34	10	12	12					

* *One match tied.*

Most Tests as captain of countries not mentioned above:

	P	W	L	D
A. Ranatunga (SL)	**29**	**3**	**10**	**16**
H. W. Taylor (SA)	18	1	10	7
A. Flower (Z)	**9**	**1**	**4**	**4**

Notes: A. R. Border captained Australia in 93 consecutive Tests.

W. W. Armstrong (Australia) captained his country in the most Tests without being defeated: ten matches with eight wins and two draws.

I. T. Botham (England) captained his country in the most Tests without ever winning: 12 matches with eight draws and four defeats.

Bold type denotes those who were captains in the 1994-95 season.

UMPIRING

MOST TEST MATCHES

		First Test	*Last Test*
63	**H. D. Bird (England)**	**1973**	**1995**
48	F. Chester (England)	1924	1955
42	C. S. Elliott (England)	1957	1974
36	D. J. Constant (England)	1971	1988
33	J. S. Buller (England)	1956	1969
33	A. R. Crafter (Australia)	1978-79	1991-92
32	R. W. Crockett (Australia)	1901-02	1924-25
31	D. Sang Hue (West Indies)	1961-62	1980-81
31	**Khizar Hayat (Pakistan)**	**1979-80**	**1994-95**

Bold type indicates an umpire who stood in 1994-95 or 1995 seasons.

SUMMARY OF ALL TEST MATCHES

To August 28, 1995

	Opponents	Tests	\<Won by\> E	A	SA	WI	NZ	I	P	SL	Z	Tied	Drawn
England	v Australia	285	90	111	–	–	–	–	–	–	–	–	84
	v South Africa	105	47	–	19	–	–	–	–	–	–	–	39
	v West Indies	115	27	–	–	48	–	–	–	–	–	–	40
	v New Zealand	75	34	–	–	–	4	–	–	–	–	–	37
	v India	81	31	–	–	–	–	14	–	–	–	–	36
	v Pakistan	52	14	–	–	–	–	–	7	–	–	–	31
	v Sri Lanka	5	3	–	–	–	–	–	–	1	–	–	1
Australia	v South Africa	59	–	31	13	–	–	–	–	–	–	–	15
	v West Indies	81	–	32	–	27	–	–	–	–	–	1	21
	v New Zealand	32	–	13	–	–	7	–	–	–	–	–	12
	v India	50	–	24	–	–	–	8	–	–	–	1	17
	v Pakistan	37	–	12	–	–	–	–	10	–	–	–	15
	v Sri Lanka	7	–	4	–	–	–	–	–	0	–	–	3
South Africa	v West Indies	1	–	–	0	1	–	–	–	–	–	–	–
	v New Zealand	21	–	–	12	–	3	–	–	–	–	–	6
	v India	4	–	–	1	–	–	0	–	–	–	–	3
	v Pakistan	1	–	–	1	–	–	–	0	–	–	–	–
	v Sri Lanka	3	–	–	1	–	–	–	–	0	–	–	2
West Indies	v New Zealand	26	–	–	–	9	4	–	–	–	–	–	13
	v India	65	–	–	–	27	–	7	–	–	–	–	31
	v Pakistan	31	–	–	–	12	–	–	7	–	–	–	12
	v Sri Lanka	1	–	–	–	0	–	–	–	0	–	–	1
New Zealand	v India	32	–	–	–	–	6	12	–	–	–	–	14
	v Pakistan	36	–	–	–	–	4	–	16	–	–	–	16
	v Sri Lanka	13	–	–	–	–	4	–	–	2	–	–	7
	v Zimbabwe	2	–	–	–	–	1	–	–	–	0	–	1
India	v Pakistan	44	–	–	–	–	–	4	7	–	–	–	33
	v Sri Lanka	14	–	–	–	–	–	7	–	1	–	–	6
	v Zimbabwe	2	–	–	–	–	–	1	–	–	0	–	1
Pakistan	v Sri Lanka	14	–	–	–	–	–	–	8	1	–	–	5
	v Zimbabwe	6	–	–	–	–	–	–	4	–	1	–	1
Sri Lanka	v Zimbabwe	3	–	–	–	–	–	–	–	0	0	–	3
		1,303	246	227	47	124	33	53	59	5	1	2	506

	Tests	Won	Lost	Drawn	Tied	Toss Won
England	718	246	204	268	–	355
Australia	551	227	155	167	2	274
South Africa	194	47	82	65	–	93
West Indies	320	124	77	118	1	167
New Zealand	237	33	98	106	–	121
India	292	53	97	141	1	146
Pakistan	221	59	49	113	–	111
Sri Lanka	60	5	27	28	–	30
Zimbabwe	13	1	6	6	–	6

ENGLAND v AUSTRALIA

Captains

Season	England		Australia	T	E	A	D
1876-77	James Lillywhite		D. W. Gregory	2	1	1	0
1878-79	Lord Harris		D. W. Gregory	1	0	1	0
1880	Lord Harris		W. L. Murdoch	1	1	0	0
1881-82	A. Shaw		W. L. Murdoch	4	0	2	2
1882	A. N. Hornby		W. L. Murdoch	1	0	1	0

THE ASHES

Captains

Season	England		Australia	T	E	A	D	Held by
1882-83	Hon. Ivo Bligh		W. L. Murdoch	4*	2	2	0	E
1884	Lord Harris[1]		W. L. Murdoch	3	1	0	2	E
1884-85	A. Shrewsbury		T. P. Horan[2]	5	3	2	0	E
1886	A. G. Steel		H. J. H. Scott	3	3	0	0	E

Captains

Season	England	Australia	T	E	A	D	Held by
1886-87	A. Shrewsbury	P. S. McDonnell	2	2	0	0	E
1887-88	W. W. Read	P. S. McDonnell	1	1	0	0	E
1888	W. G. Grace[3]	P. S. McDonnell	3	2	1	0	E
1890†	W. G. Grace	W. L. Murdoch	2	2	0	0	E
1891-92	W. G. Grace	J. McC. Blackham	3	1	2	0	A
1893	W. G. Grace[4]	J. McC. Blackham	3	1	0	2	E
1894-95	A. E. Stoddart	G. Giffen[5]	5	3	2	0	E
1896	W. G. Grace	G. H. S. Trott	3	2	1	0	E
1897-98	A. E. Stoddart[6]	G. H. S. Trott	5	1	4	0	A
1899	A. C. MacLaren[7]	J. Darling	5	0	1	4	A
1901-02	A. C. MacLaren	J. Darling[8]	5	1	4	0	A
1902	A. C. MacLaren	J. Darling	5	1	2	2	A
1903-04	P. F. Warner	M. A. Noble	5	3	2	0	E
1905	Hon. F. S. Jackson	J. Darling	5	2	0	3	E
1907-08	A. O. Jones[9]	M. A. Noble	5	1	4	0	A
1909	A. C. MacLaren	M. A. Noble	5	1	2	2	A
1911-12	J. W. H. T. Douglas	C. Hill	5	4	1	0	E
1912	C. B. Fry	S. E. Gregory	3	1	0	2	E
1920-21	J. W. H. T. Douglas	W. W. Armstrong	5	0	5	0	A
1921	Hon. L. H. Tennyson[10]	W. W. Armstrong	5	0	3	2	A
1924-25	A. E. R. Gilligan	H. L. Collins	5	1	4	0	A
1926	A. W. Carr[11]	H. L. Collins[12]	5	1	0	4	E
1928-29	A. P. F. Chapman[13]	J. Ryder	5	4	1	0	E
1930	A. P. F. Chapman[14]	W. M. Woodfull	5	1	2	2	A
1932-33	D. R. Jardine	W. M. Woodfull	5	4	1	0	E
1934	R. E. S. Wyatt[15]	W. M. Woodfull	5	1	2	2	A
1936-37	G. O. B. Allen	D. G. Bradman	5	2	3	0	A
1938†	W. R. Hammond	D. G. Bradman	4	1	1	2	A
1946-47	W. R. Hammond[16]	D. G. Bradman	5	0	3	2	A
1948	N. W. D. Yardley	D. G. Bradman	5	0	4	1	A
1950-51	F. R. Brown	A. L. Hassett	5	1	4	0	A
1953	L. Hutton	A. L. Hassett	5	1	0	4	E
1954-55	L. Hutton	I. W. Johnson[17]	5	3	1	1	E
1956	P. B. H. May	I. W. Johnson	5	2	1	2	E
1958-59	P. B. H. May	R. Benaud	5	0	4	1	A
1961	P. B. H. May[18]	R. Benaud[19]	5	1	2	2	A
1962-63	E. R. Dexter	R. Benaud	5	1	1	3	A
1964	E. R. Dexter	R. B. Simpson	5	0	1	4	A
1965-66	M. J. K. Smith	R. B. Simpson[20]	5	1	1	3	A
1968	M. C. Cowdrey[21]	W. M. Lawry[22]	5	1	1	3	A
1970-71†	R. Illingworth	W. M. Lawry[23]	6	2	0	4	E
1972	R. Illingworth	I. M. Chappell	5	2	2	1	E
1974-75	M. H. Denness[24]	I. M. Chappell	6	1	4	1	A
1975	A. W. Greig[25]	I. M. Chappell	4	0	1	3	A
1976-77‡	A. W. Greig	G. S. Chappell	1	0	1	0	—
1977	J. M. Brearley	G. S. Chappell	5	3	0	2	E
1978-79	J. M. Brearley	G. N. Yallop	6	5	1	0	E
1979-80‡	J. M. Brearley	G. S. Chappell	3	0	3	0	—
1980‡	I. T. Botham	G. S. Chappell	1	0	0	1	—
1981	J. M. Brearley[26]	K. J. Hughes	6	3	1	2	E
1982-83	R. G. D. Willis	G. S. Chappell	5	1	2	2	A
1985	D. I. Gower	A. R. Border	6	3	1	2	E
1986-87	M. W. Gatting	A. R. Border	5	2	1	2	E
1987-88‡	M. W. Gatting	A. R. Border	1	0	0	1	—
1989	D. I. Gower	A. R. Border	6	0	4	2	A
1990-91	G. A. Gooch[27]	A. R. Border	5	0	3	2	A
1993	G. A. Gooch[28]	A. R. Border	6	1	4	1	A
1994-95	M. A. Atherton	M. A. Taylor	5	1	3	1	A

	In Australia		150	52	73	25	
	In England		135	38	38	59	
	Totals		285	90	111	84	

* *The Ashes were awarded in 1882-83 after a series of three matches which England won 2-1. A fourth match was played and this was won by Australia.*

† *The matches at Manchester in 1890 and 1938 and at Melbourne (Third Test) in 1970-71 were abandoned without a ball being bowled and are excluded.*

‡ *The Ashes were not at stake in these series.*

Notes: The following deputised for the official touring captain or were appointed by the home authority for only a minor proportion of the series:

[1]A. N. Hornby (First). [2]W. L. Murdoch (First), H. H. Massie (Third), J. McC. Blackham (Fourth). [3]A. G. Steel (First). [4]A. E. Stoddart (First). [5]J. McC. Blackham (First). [6]A. C. MacLaren (First, Second and Fifth). [7]W. G. Grace (First). [8]H. Trumble (Fourth and Fifth). [9]F. L. Fane (First, Second and Third). [10]J. W. H. T. Douglas (First and Second). [11]A. P. F. Chapman (Fifth). [12]W. Bardsley (Third and Fourth). [13]J. C. White (Fifth). [14]R. E. S. Wyatt (Fifth). [15]C. F. Walters (First). [16]N. W. D. Yardley (Fifth). [17]A. R. Morris (Second). [18]M. C. Cowdrey (First and Second). [19]R. N. Harvey (Second). [20]B. C. Booth (First and Third). [21]T. W. Graveney (Fourth). [22]B. N. Jarman (Fourth). [23]I. M. Chappell (Seventh). [24]J. H. Edrich (Fourth). [25]M. H. Denness (First). [26]I. T. Botham (First and Second). [27]A. J. Lamb (First). [28]M. A. Atherton (Fifth and Sixth).

HIGHEST INNINGS TOTALS

For England in England: 903-7 dec. at The Oval	....	1938
in Australia: 636 at Sydney	....	1928-29
For Australia in England: 729-6 dec. at Lord's	....	1930
in Australia: 659-8 dec. at Sydney	....	1946-47

LOWEST INNINGS TOTALS

For England in England: 52 at The Oval	....	1948
in Australia: 45 at Sydney	....	1886-87
For Australia in England: 36 at Birmingham	....	1902
in Australia: 42 at Sydney	....	1887-88

INDIVIDUAL HUNDREDS

For England (201)

R. Abel (1)
132*‡ Sydney 1891-92
L. E. G. Ames (1)
120   Lord's 1934
M. A. Atherton (1)
105   Sydney 1990-91
R. W. Barber (1)
185   Sydney 1965-66
W. Barnes (1)
134   Adelaide ... 1884-85
C. J. Barnett (2)
129   Adelaide ... 1936-37
126   Nottingham . 1938
K. F. Barrington (5)
132* Adelaide ... 1962-63
101   Sydney 1962-63
256   Manchester.. 1964

102   Adelaide 1965-66
115   Melbourne .. 1965-66
I. T. Botham (4)
119* Melbourne .. 1979-80
149* Leeds 1981
118   Manchester .. 1981
138   Brisbane ... 1986-87
G. Boycott (7)
113   The Oval.... 1964
142* Sydney 1970-71
119* Adelaide 1970-71
107   Nottingham . 1977
191   Leeds 1977
128* Lord's 1980
137   The Oval.... 1981
L. C. Braund (2)
103* Adelaide 1901-02
102   Sydney 1903-04

J. Briggs (1)
121   Melbourne .. 1884-85
B. C. Broad (4)
162   Perth....... 1986-87
116   Adelaide 1986-87
112   Melbourne .. 1986-87
139   Sydney 1987-88
J. T. Brown (1)
140   Melbourne .. 1894-95
A. P. F. Chapman (1)
121   Lord's 1930
D. C. S. Compton (5)
102† Nottingham . 1938
147   ⎫
103* ⎬ Adelaide 1946-47
184   Nottingham . 1948
145* Manchester . 1948

M. C. Cowdrey (5)
102 Melbourne .. 1954-55
100* Sydney 1958-59
113 Melbourne .. 1962-63
104 Melbourne .. 1965-66
104 Birmingham . 1968

M. H. Denness (1)
188 Melbourne .. 1974-75

E. R. Dexter (2)
180 Birmingham . 1961
174 Manchester.. 1964

B. L. D'Oliveira (2)
158 The Oval.... 1968
117 Melbourne .. 1970-71

K. S. Duleepsinhji (1)
173† Lord's 1930

J. H. Edrich (7)
120† Lord's 1964
109 Melbourne .. 1965-66
103 Sydney 1965-66
164 The Oval.... 1968
115* Perth...... 1970-71
130 Adelaide 1970-71
175 Lord's 1975

W. J. Edrich (2)
119 Sydney 1946-47
111 Leeds 1948

K. W. R. Fletcher (1)
146 Melbourne .. 1974-75

R. E. Foster (1)
287† Sydney 1903-04

C. B. Fry (1)
144 The Oval.... 1905

M. W. Gatting (4)
160 Manchester.. 1985
100* Birmingham . 1985
100 Adelaide 1986-87
117 Adelaide 1994-95

G. A. Gooch (4)
196 Melbourne .. 1985
117 Adelaide 1990-91
133 Manchester.. 1993
120 Nottingham . 1993

D. I. Gower (9)
102 Perth...... 1978-79
114 Adelaide 1982-83
166 Nottingham . 1985
215 Birmingham . 1985
157 The Oval.... 1985
136 Perth...... 1986-87
106 Lord's 1989
100 Melbourne .. 1990-91
123 Sydney 1990-91

W. G. Grace (2)
152† The Oval.... 1880
170 The Oval.... 1886

T. W. Graveney (1)
111 Sydney 1954-55

A. W. Greig (1)
110 Brisbane 1974-75

G. Gunn (2)
119† Sydney 1907-08
122* Sydney 1907-08

W. Gunn (1)
102* Manchester.. 1893

W. R. Hammond (9)
251 Sydney 1928-29
200 Melbourne .. 1928-29
119* ⎫ Adelaide .. 1928-29
177 ⎭
113 Leeds 1930
112 Sydney 1932-33
101 Sydney 1932-33
231* Sydney 1936-37
240 Lord's 1938

J. Hardstaff jun. (1)
169* The Oval.... 1938

T. W. Hayward (2)
130 Manchester.. 1899
137 The Oval.... 1899

J. W. Hearne (1)
114 Melbourne .. 1911-12

E. H. Hendren (3)
127† Lord's 1926
169 Brisbane 1928-29
132 Manchester.. 1934

J. B. Hobbs (12)
126* Melbourne .. 1911-12
187 Adelaide 1911-12
178 Melbourne .. 1911-12
107 Lord's 1912
122 Melbourne .. 1920-21
123 Adelaide 1920-21
115 Sydney 1924-25
154 Melbourne .. 1924-25
119 Adelaide 1924-25
119 Lord's 1926
100 The Oval.... 1926
142 Melbourne .. 1928-29

K. L. Hutchings (1)
126 Melbourne .. 1907-08

L. Hutton (5)
100† Nottingham . 1938
364 The Oval.... 1938
122* Sydney 1946-47
156*‡ Adelaide 1950-51
145 Lord's 1953

Hon. F. S. Jackson (5)
103 The Oval.... 1893
118 The Oval.... 1899
128 Manchester.. 1902
144* Leeds 1905
113 Manchester.. 1905

G. L. Jessop (1)
104 The Oval.... 1902

A. P. E. Knott (2)
106* Adelaide 1974-75
135 Nottingham . 1977

A. J. Lamb (1)
125 Leeds 1989

M. Leyland (7)
137† Melbourne .. 1928-29
109 Lord's 1934
153 Manchester.. 1934
110 The Oval.... 1934
126 Brisbane 1936-37
111* Melbourne .. 1936-37
187 The Oval.... 1938

B. W. Luckhurst (2)
131 Perth...... 1970-71
109 Melbourne .. 1970-71

A. C. MacLaren (5)
120 Melbourne .. 1894-95
109 Sydney 1897-98
124 Adelaide 1897-98
116 Sydney 1901-02
140 Nottingham . 1905

J. W. H. Makepeace (1)
117 Melbourne .. 1920-21

P. B. H. May (3)
104 Sydney 1954-55
101 Leeds 1956
113 Melbourne .. 1958-59

C. P. Mead (1)
182* The Oval.... 1921

Nawab of Pataudi sen. (1)
102† Sydney 1932-33

E. Paynter (1)
216* Nottingham . 1938

D. W. Randall (3)
174† Melbourne .. 1976-77
150 Sydney 1978-79
115 Perth...... 1982-83

K. S. Ranjitsinhji (2)
154*† Manchester.. 1896
175 Sydney 1897-98

W. W. Read (1)
117 The Oval.... 1884

W. Rhodes (1)
179 Melbourne .. 1911-12

C. J. Richards (1)
133 Perth...... 1986-87

P. E. Richardson (1)
104 Manchester.. 1956

R. T. Robinson (2)
175† Leeds 1985
148 Birmingham . 1985

A. C. Russell (3)
135* Adelaide 1920-21
101 Manchester.. 1921
102* The Oval.... 1921

R. C. Russell (1)
128* Manchester.. 1989

J. Sharp (1)
105 The Oval.... 1909

Rev. D. S. Sheppard (2)
113 Manchester.. 1956
113 Melbourne .. 1962-63

A. Shrewsbury (3)
105* Melbourne .. 1884-85
164 Lord's 1886
106 Lord's 1893

R. T. Simpson (1)
156* Melbourne .. 1950-51

R. A. Smith (2)
143 Manchester.. 1989
101 Nottingham . 1989

A. G. Steel (2)
135* Sydney 1882-83
148 Lord's 1884

A. E. Stoddart (2)
134	Adelaide	1891-92
173	Melbourne .	1894-95

R. Subba Row (2)
112†	Birmingham .	1961
137	The Oval	1961

H. Sutcliffe (8)
115†	Sydney	1924-25
176	} Melbourne ..	1924-25
127		
143	Melbourne ..	1924-25
161	The Oval	1926
135	Melbourne ..	1928-29
161	The Oval....	1930
194	Sydney	1932-33

G. P. Thorpe (2)
114*†	Nottingham .	1993
123	Perth.......	1994-95

J. T. Tyldesley (3)
138	Birmingham .	1902
100	Leeds	1905
112*	The Oval	1905

G. Ulyett (1)
149	Melbourne ..	1881-82

A. Ward (1)
117	Sydney	1894-95

C. Washbrook (2)
112	Melbourne ..	1946-47
143	Leeds	1948

W. Watson (1)
109†	Lord's	1953

F. E. Woolley (2)
133*	Sydney	1911-12
123	Sydney	1924-25

R. A. Woolmer (3)
149	The Oval....	1975
120	Lord's	1977
137	Manchester..	1977

† Signifies hundred on first appearance in England–Australia Tests.
‡ Carried his bat.

For Australia (232)

W. W. Armstrong (4)
133*	Melbourne ..	1907-08
158	Sydney	1920-21
121	Adelaide	1920-21
123*	Melbourne ..	1920-21

C. L. Badcock (1)
118	Melbourne ..	1936-37

C. Bannerman (1)
165*†	Melbourne ..	1876-77

W. Bardsley (3)
136	} The Oval	1909
130		
193*‡	Lord's	1926

S. G. Barnes (2)
234	Sydney	1946-47
141	Lord's	1948

G. S. Blewett (2)
102*†	Adelaide	1994-95
115	Perth.......	1994-95

G. J. Bonnor (1)
128	Sydney	1884-85

D. C. Boon (7)
103	Adelaide	1986-87
184*	Sydney	1987-88
121	Adelaide	1990-91
164*	Lord's	1993
101	Nottingham .	1993
107	Leeds	1993
131	Melbourne ..	1994-95

B. C. Booth (2)
112	Brisbane	1962-63
103	Melbourne ..	1962-63

A. R. Border (8)
115	Perth.......	1979-80
123*	Manchester..	1981
106*	The Oval	1981
196	Lord's	1985
146*	Manchester..	1985
125	Perth.......	1986-87
100*	Adelaide	1986-87
200*	Leeds	1993

D. G. Bradman (19)
112	Melbourne ..	1928-29
123	Melbourne ..	1928-29
131	Nottingham .	1930
254	Lord's	1930
334	Leeds	1930
232	The Oval	1930
103*	Melbourne ..	1932-33
304	Leeds	1934
244	The Oval	1934
270	Melbourne ..	1936-37
212	Adelaide	1936-37
169	Melbourne ..	1936-37
144*	Nottingham .	1938
102*	Lord's	1938
103	Leeds	1938
187	Brisbane	1946-47
234	Sydney	1946-47
138	Nottingham .	1948
173*	Leeds	1948

W. A. Brown (3)
105	Lord's	1934
133	Nottingham .	1938
206*‡	Lord's	1938

P. J. Burge (4)
181	The Oval	1961
103	Sydney	1962-63
160	Leeds	1964
120	Melbourne ..	1965-66

J. W. Burke (1)
101*†	Adelaide	1950-51

G. S. Chappell (9)
108†	Perth.......	1970-71
131	Lord's	1972
113	The Oval ...	1972
144	Sydney	1974-75
102	Melbourne ..	1974-75
112	Manchester..	1977
114	Melbourne ..	1979-80
117	Perth.......	1982-83
115	Adelaide	1982-83

I. M. Chappell (4)
111	Melbourne ..	1970-71
104	Adelaide	1970-71
118	The Oval	1972
192	The Oval	1975

H. L. Collins (3)
104†	Sydney	1920-21
162	Adelaide	1920-21
114	Sydney	1924-25

R. M. Cowper (1)
307	Melbourne ..	1965-66

J. Darling (3)
101	Sydney	1897-98
178	Adelaide	1897-98
160	Sydney	1897-98

R. A. Duff (2)
104†	Melbourne ..	1901-02
146	The Oval	1905

J. Dyson (1)
102	Leeds	1981

R. Edwards (2)
170*	Nottingham .	1972
115	Perth.......	1974-75

J. H. Fingleton (2)
100	Brisbane	1936-37
136	Melbourne ..	1936-37

G. Giffen (1)
161	Sydney	1894-95

H. Graham (2)
107†	Lord's	1893
105	Sydney	1894-95

J. M. Gregory (1)
100	Melbourne ..	1920-21

S. E. Gregory (4)
201	Sydney	1894-95
103	Lord's	1896
117	The Oval	1899
112	Adelaide	1903-04

R. J. Hartigan (1)
116†	Adelaide	1907-08

R. N. Harvey (6)

112†	Leeds	1948
122	Manchester..	1953
162	Brisbane	1954-55
167	Melbourne ..	1958-59
114	Birmingham .	1961
154	Adelaide	1962-63

A. L. Hassett (4)

128	Brisbane	1946-47
137	Nottingham .	1948
115	Nottingham .	1953
104	Lord's	1953

I. A. Healy (1)

102*	Manchester..	1993

H. S. T. L. Hendry (1)

112	Sydney	1928-29

A. M. J. Hilditch (1)

119	Leeds	1985

C. Hill (4)

188	Melbourne ..	1897-98
135	Lord's	1899
119	Sheffield ...	1902
160	Adelaide	1907-08

T. P. Horan (1)

124	Melbourne ..	1881-82

K. J. Hughes (3)

129	Brisbane	1978-79
117	Lord's	1980
137	Sydney	1982-83

F. A. Iredale (2)

140	Adelaide	1894-95
108	Manchester..	1896

A. A. Jackson (1)

164†	Adelaide	1928-29

D. M. Jones (3)

184*	Sydney	1986-87
157	Birmingham .	1989
122	The Oval....	1989

C. Kelleway (1)

147	Adelaide	1920-21

A. F. Kippax (1)

100	Melbourne ..	1928-29

W. M. Lawry (7)

130	Lord's	1961
102	Manchester..	1961
106	Manchester..	1964
166	Brisbane	1965-66
119	Adelaide	1965-66
108	Melbourne ..	1965-66
135	The Oval....	1968

R. R. Lindwall (1)

100	Melbourne ..	1946-47

J. J. Lyons (1)

134	Sydney	1891-92

C. G. Macartney (5)

170	Sydney	1920-21
115	Leeds	1921
133*	Lord's	1926
151	Leeds	1926
109	Manchester..	1926

S. J. McCabe (4)

187*	Sydney	1932-33
137	Manchester..	1934
112	Melbourne ..	1936-37
232	Nottingham .	1938

C. L. McCool (1)

104*	Melbourne ..	1946-47

R. B. McCosker (2)

127	The Oval....	1975
107	Nottingham .	1977

C. C. McDonald (2)

170	Adelaide	1958-59
133	Melbourne ..	1958-59

P. S. McDonnell (3)

147	Sydney	1881-82
103	The Oval....	1884
124	Adelaide	1884-85

C. E. McLeod (1)

112	Melbourne ..	1897-98

G. R. Marsh (2)

110†	Brisbane	1986-87
138	Nottingham .	1989

R. W. Marsh (1)

110*	Melbourne ..	1976-77

G. R. J. Matthews (1)

128	Sydney	1990-91

K. R. Miller (3)

141*	Adelaide	1946-47
145*	Sydney	1950-51
109	Lord's	1953

A. R. Morris (8)

155	Melbourne ..	1946-47
122 ⎫	Adelaide	1946-47
124* ⎭		
105	Lord's	1948
182	Leeds	1948
196	The Oval....	1948
206	Adelaide	1950-51
153	Brisbane	1954-55

W. L. Murdoch (2)

153*	The Oval....	1880
211	The Oval....	1884

M. A. Noble (1)

133	Sydney	1903-04

N. C. O'Neill (2)

117	The Oval....	1961
100	Adelaide	1962-63

C. E. Pellew (2)

116	Melbourne ..	1920-21
104	Adelaide	1920-21

W. H. Ponsford (5)

110†	Sydney	1924-25
128	Melbourne ..	1924-25
110	The Oval....	1930
181	Leeds	1934
266	The Oval....	1934

V. S. Ransford (1)

143*	Lord's	1909

I. R. Redpath (2)

171	Perth.......	1970-71
105	Sydney	1974-75

A. J. Richardson (1)

100	Leeds	1926

V. Y. Richardson (1)

138	Melbourne ..	1924-25

G. M. Ritchie (1)

146	Nottingham .	1985

J. Ryder (2)

201*	Adelaide	1924-25
112	Melbourne ..	1928-29

H. J. H. Scott (1)

102	The Oval....	1884

R. B. Simpson (2)

311	Manchester..	1964
225	Adelaide	1965-66

M. J. Slater (4)

152	Lord's	1993
176	Brisbane	1994-95
103	Sydney	1994-95
124	Perth.......	1994-95

K. R. Stackpole (3)

207	Brisbane	1970-71
136	Adelaide	1970-71
114	Nottingham .	1972

J. M. Taylor (1)

108	Sydney	1924-25

M. A. Taylor (5)

136†	Leeds	1989
219	Nottingham .	1989
124	Manchester.	1993
111	Lord's	1993
113	Sydney	1994-95

G. H. S. Trott (1)

143	Lord's	1896

V. T. Trumper (6)

135*	Lord's	1899
104	Manchester..	1902
185*	Sydney	1903-04
113	Adelaide	1903-04
166	Sydney	1907-08
113	Sydney	1911-12

K. D. Walters (4)

155†	Brisbane	1965-66
115	Melbourne ..	1965-66
112	Brisbane	1970-71
103	Perth.......	1974-75

M. E. Waugh (3)

138†	Adelaide	1990-91
137	Birmingham .	1993
140	Brisbane	1994-95

S. R. Waugh (3)

177*	Leeds	1989
152*	Lord's	1989
157*	Leeds	1993

D. M. Wellham (1)

103†	The Oval....	1981

K. C. Wessels (1)

162†	Brisbane	1982-83

G. M. Wood (3)

100	Melbourne ..	1978-79
112	Lord's	1980
172	Nottingham .	1985

W. M. Woodfull (6)						**G. N. Yallop (3)**		
141	Leeds	1926		107	Melbourne .. 1928-29	102†	Brisbane	1978-79
117	Manchester..	1926		102	Melbourne .. 1928-29	121	Sydney	1978-79
111	Sydney	1928-29		155	Lord's 1930	114	Manchester..	1981

† Signifies hundred on first appearance in England–Australia Tests.
‡ Carried his bat.

RECORD PARTNERSHIPS FOR EACH WICKET

For England

323 for 1st	J. B. Hobbs and W. Rhodes at Melbourne	1911-12
382 for 2nd†	L. Hutton and M. Leyland at The Oval	1938
262 for 3rd	W. R. Hammond and D. R. Jardine at Adelaide	1928-29
222 for 4th	W. R. Hammond and E. Paynter at Lord's	1938
206 for 5th	E. Paynter and D. C. S. Compton at Nottingham	1938
215 for 6th	{ L. Hutton and J. Hardstaff jun. at The Oval	1938
	{ G. Boycott and A. P. E. Knott at Nottingham	1977
143 for 7th	F. E. Woolley and J. Vine at Sydney	1911-12
124 for 8th	E. H. Hendren and H. Larwood at Brisbane...............	1928-29
151 for 9th	W. H. Scotton and W. W. Read at The Oval	1884
130 for 10th†	R. E. Foster and W. Rhodes at Sydney	1903-04

For Australia

329 for 1st	G. R. Marsh and M. A. Taylor at Nottingham............	1989
451 for 2nd†	W. H. Ponsford and D. G. Bradman at The Oval	1934
276 for 3rd	D. G. Bradman and A. L. Hassett at Brisbane	1946-47
388 for 4th†	W. H. Ponsford and D. G. Bradman at Leeds	1934
405 for 5th†‡	S. G. Barnes and D. G. Bradman at Sydney	1946-47
346 for 6th†	J. H. Fingleton and D. G. Bradman at Melbourne..........	1936-37
165 for 7th	C. Hill and H. Trumble at Melbourne	1897-98
243 for 8th†	R. J. Hartigan and C. Hill at Adelaide	1907-08
154 for 9th†	S. E. Gregory and J. McC. Blackham at Sydney	1894-95
127 for 10th†	J. M. Taylor and A. A. Mailey at Sydney	1924-25

† Denotes record partnership against all countries.
‡ Record fifth-wicket partnership in first-class cricket.

MOST RUNS IN A SERIES

England in England	732 (average 81.33)	D. I. Gower.......	1985
England in Australia	905 (average 113.12)	W. R. Hammond ..	1928-29
Australia in England	974 (average 139.14)	D. G. Bradman....	1930
Australia in Australia........	810 (average 90.00)	D. G. Bradman....	1936-37

TEN WICKETS OR MORE IN A MATCH

For England (36)

13-163 (6-42, 7-121)	S. F. Barnes, Melbourne.............................	1901-02
14-102 (7-28, 7-74)	W. Bates, Melbourne................................	1882-83
10-105 (5-46, 5-59)	A. V. Bedser, Melbourne	1950-51
14-99 (7-55, 7-44)	A. V. Bedser, Nottingham	1953

11-102 (6-44, 5-58)	C. Blythe, Birmingham	1909
11-176 (6-78, 5-98)	I. T. Botham, Perth	1979-80
10-253 (6-125, 4-128)	I. T. Botham, The Oval	1981
11-74 (5-29, 6-45)	J. Briggs, Lord's	1886
12-136 (6-49, 6-87)	J. Briggs, Adelaide	1891-92
10-148 (5-34, 5-114)	J. Briggs, The Oval	1893
10-104 (6-77, 4-27)†	R. M. Ellison, Birmingham	1985
10-179 (5-102, 5-77)†	K. Farnes, Nottingham	1934
10-60 (6-41, 4-19)	J. T. Hearne, The Oval	1896
11-113 (6-58, 6-55)	J. C. Laker, Leeds	1956
19-90 (9-37, 10-53)	J. C. Laker, Manchester	1956
10-124 (5-96, 5-28)	H. Larwood, Sydney	1932-33
11-76 (6-48, 5-28)	W. H. Lockwood, Manchester	1902
12-104 (7-36, 5-68)	G. A. Lohmann, The Oval	1886
10-87 (8-35, 2-52)	G. A. Lohmann, Sydney	1886-87
10-142 (8-58, 2-84)	G. A. Lohmann, Sydney	1891-92
12-102 (6-50, 6-52)†	F. Martin, The Oval	1890
11-68 (7-31, 4-37)	R. Peel, Manchester	1888
15-124 (7-56, 8-68)	W. Rhodes, Melbourne	1903-04
10-156 (5-49, 5-107)†	T. Richardson, Manchester	1893
11-173 (6-39, 5-134)	T. Richardson, Lord's	1896
13-244 (7-168, 6-76)	T. Richardson, Manchester	1896
10-204 (8-94, 2-110)	T. Richardson, Sydney	1897-98
11-228 (6-130, 5-98)†	M. W. Tate, Sydney	1924-25
11-88 (5-58, 6-30)	F. S. Trueman, Leeds	1961
10-130 (4-45, 6-85)	F. H. Tyson, Sydney	1954-55
10-82 (4-37, 6-45)	D. L. Underwood, Leeds	1972
11-215 (7-113, 4-102)	D. L. Underwood, Adelaide	1974-75
15-104 (7-61, 8-43)	H. Verity, Lord's	1934
10-57 (6-41, 4-16)	W. Voce, Brisbane	1936-37
13-256 (5-130, 8-126)	J. C. White, Adelaide	1928-29
10-49 (5-29, 5-20)	F. E. Woolley, The Oval	1912

For Australia (39)

10-151 (5-107, 5-44)	T. M. Alderman, Leeds	1989
10-239 (4-129, 6-110)	L. O'B. Fleetwood-Smith, Adelaide	1936-37
10-160 (4-88, 6-72)	G. Giffen, Sydney	1891-92
11-82 (5-45, 6-37)†	C. V. Grimmett, Sydney	1924-25
10-201 (5-107, 5-94)	C. V. Grimmett, Nottingham	1930
10-122 (5-65, 5-57)	R. M. Hogg, Perth	1978-79
10-66 (5-30, 5-36)	R. M. Hogg, Melbourne	1978-79
12-175 (5-85, 7-90)†	H. V. Hordern, Sydney	1911-12
10-161 (5-95, 5-66)	H. V. Hordern, Sydney	1911-12
10-164 (7-88, 3-76)	E. Jones, Lord's	1899
11-134 (6-47, 5-87)	G. F. Lawson, Brisbane	1982-83
10-181 (5-58, 5-123)	D. K. Lillee, The Oval	1972
11-165 (6-26, 5-139)	D. K. Lillee, Melbourne	1976-77
11-138 (6-60, 5-78)	D. K. Lillee, Melbourne	1979-80
11-159 (7-89, 4-70)	D. K. Lillee, The Oval	1981
11-85 (7-58, 4-27)	C. G. Macartney, Leeds	1909
11-157 (8-97, 3-60)	C. J. McDermott, Perth	1990-91
10-302 (5-160, 5-142)	A. A. Mailey, Adelaide	1920-21
13-236 (4-115, 9-121)	A. A. Mailey, Melbourne	1920-21
16-137 (8-84, 8-53)†	R. A. L. Massie, Lord's	1972
10-152 (5-72, 5-80)	K. R. Miller, Lord's	1956
13-77 (7-17, 6-60)	M. A. Noble, Melbourne	1901-02
11-103 (5-51, 6-52)	M. A. Noble, Sheffield	1902
10-129 (5-63, 5-66)	W. J. O'Reilly, Melbourne	1932-33
11-129 (4-75, 7-54)	W. J. O'Reilly, Nottingham	1934
10-122 (5-66, 5-56)	W. J. O'Reilly, Leeds	1938

11-165 (7-68, 4-97)	G. E. Palmer, Sydney	1881-82
10-126 (7-65, 3-61)	G. E. Palmer, Melbourne	1882-83
13-148 (6-97, 7-51)	B. A. Reid, Melbourne	1990-91
13-110 (6-48, 7-62)	F. R. Spofforth, Melbourne	1878-79
14-90 (7-46, 7-44)	F. R. Spofforth, The Oval	1882
11-117 (4-73, 7-44)	F. R. Spofforth, Sydney	1882-83
10-144 (4-54, 6-90)	F. R. Spofforth, Sydney	1884-85
12-89 (6-59, 6-30)	H. Trumble, The Oval	1896
10-128 (4-75, 6-53)	H. Trumble, Manchester	1902
12-173 (8-65, 4-108)	H. Trumble, The Oval	1902
12-87 (5-44, 7-43)	C. T. B. Turner, Sydney	1887-88
10-63 (5-27, 5-36)	C. T. B. Turner, Lord's	1888
11-110 (3-39, 8-71)	S. K. Warne, Brisbane	1994-95

† *Signifies ten wickets or more on first appearance in England–Australia Tests.*

Note: J. Briggs, J. C. Laker, T. Richardson in 1896, R. M. Hogg, A. A. Mailey, H. Trumble and C. T. B. Turner took ten wickets or more in successive Tests. J. Briggs was omitted, however, from the England team for the first Test match in 1893.

MOST WICKETS IN A SERIES

England in England	46 (average 9.60)	J. C. Laker	1956
England in Australia	38 (average 23.18)	M. W. Tate	1924-25
Australia in England	42 (average 21.26)	T. M. Alderman (6 Tests)	1981
Australia in Australia	41 (average 12.85)	R. M. Hogg (6 Tests)	1978-79

WICKET-KEEPING – MOST DISMISSALS

	M	Ct	St	Total
†R. W. Marsh (Australia)	42	141	7	148
A. P. E. Knott (England)	34	97	8	105
†W. A. Oldfield (Australia)	38	59	31	90
I. A. Healy (Australia)	22	82	7	89
A. A. Lilley (England)	32	65	19	84
A. T. W. Grout (Australia)	22	69	7	76
T. G. Evans (England)	31	63	12	75

† *The number of catches by R. W. Marsh (141) and stumpings by W. A. Oldfield (31) are respective records in England–Australia Tests.*

SCORERS OF OVER 2,000 RUNS

	T		I		NO		R		HS		Avge
D. G. Bradman	37	..	63	..	7	..	5,028	..	334	..	89.78
J. B. Hobbs	41	..	71	..	4	..	3,636	..	187	..	54.26
A. R. Border	47	..	82	..	19	..	3,548	..	200*	..	56.31
D. I. Gower	42	..	77	..	4	..	3,269	..	215	..	44.78
G. Boycott	38	..	71	..	9	..	2,945	..	191	..	47.50
W. R. Hammond	33	..	58	..	3	..	2,852	..	251	..	51.85
H. Sutcliffe	27	..	46	..	5	..	2,741	..	194	..	66.85
C. Hill	41	..	76	..	1	..	2,660	..	188	..	35.46
J. H. Edrich	32	..	57	..	3	..	2,644	..	175	..	48.96
G. A. Gooch	42	..	79	..	0	..	2,632	..	196	..	33.31
G. S. Chappell	35	..	65	..	8	..	2,619	..	144	..	45.94
M. C. Cowdrey	43	..	75	..	4	..	2,433	..	113	..	34.26
L. Hutton	27	..	49	..	6	..	2,428	..	364	..	56.46

	T		I		NO		R		HS		Avge
R. N. Harvey	37	..	68	..	5	..	2,416	..	167	..	38.34
V. T. Trumper	40	..	74	..	5	..	2,263	..	185*	..	32.79
D. C. Boon	31	..	57	..	8	..	2,237	..	184*	..	45.65
W. M. Lawry	29	..	51	..	5	..	2,233	..	166	..	48.54
S. E. Gregory	52	..	92	..	7	..	2,193	..	201	..	25.80
W. W. Armstrong	42	..	71	..	9	..	2,172	..	158	..	35.03
I. M. Chappell	30	..	56	..	4	..	2,138	..	192	..	41.11
K. F. Barrington	23	..	39	..	6	..	2,111	..	256	..	63.96
A. R. Morris	24	..	43	..	2	..	2,080	..	206	..	50.73

BOWLERS WITH 100 WICKETS

	T		Balls		R		W		5W/i		Avge
D. K. Lillee	29	..	8,516	..	3,507	..	167	..	11	..	21.00
I. T. Botham	36	..	8,479	..	4,093	..	148	..	9	..	27.65
H. Trumble	31	..	7,895	..	2,945	..	141	..	9	..	20.88
R. G. D. Willis	35	..	7,294	..	3,346	..	128	..	7	..	26.14
M. A. Noble	39	..	6,845	..	2,860	..	115	..	9	..	24.86
R. R. Lindwall	29	..	6,728	..	2,559	..	114	..	6	..	22.44
W. Rhodes	41	..	5,791	..	2,616	..	109	..	6	..	24.00
S. F. Barnes	20	..	5,749	..	2,288	..	106	..	12	..	21.58
C. V. Grimmett	22	..	9,224	..	3,439	..	106	..	11	..	32.44
D. L. Underwood	29	..	8,000	..	2,770	..	105	..	4	..	26.38
A. V. Bedser	21	..	7,065	..	2,859	..	104	..	7	..	27.49
G. Giffen	31	..	6,457	..	2,791	..	103	..	7	..	27.09
W. J. O'Reilly	19	..	7,864	..	2,587	..	102	..	8	..	25.36
R. Peel	20	..	5,216	..	1,715	..	101	..	5	..	16.98
C. T. B. Turner	17	..	5,195	..	1,670	..	101	..	11	..	16.53
T. M. Alderman	17	..	4,717	..	2,117	..	100	..	11	..	21.17
J. R. Thomson	21	..	4,951	..	2,418	..	100	..	5	..	24.18

RESULTS ON EACH GROUND

In England

THE OVAL (31)

England (14) 1880, 1886, 1888, 1890, 1893, 1896, 1902, 1912, 1926, 1938, 1953, 1968, 1985, 1993.

Australia (5) 1882, 1930, 1934, 1948, 1972.

Drawn (12) 1884, 1899, 1905, 1909, 1921, 1956, 1961, 1964, 1975, 1977, 1981, 1989.

MANCHESTER (26)

England (7) 1886, 1888, 1905, 1956, 1972, 1977, 1981.

Australia (6) 1896, 1902, 1961, 1968, 1989, 1993.

Drawn (13) 1884, 1893, 1899, 1909, 1912, 1921, 1926, 1930, 1934, 1948, 1953, 1964, 1985.

The scheduled matches in 1890 and 1938 were abandoned without a ball bowled and are excluded.

LORD'S (30)

England (5) 1884, 1886, 1890, 1896, 1934.

Australia (12) 1888, 1899, 1909, 1921, 1930, 1948, 1956, 1961, 1972, 1985, 1989, 1993.

Drawn (13) 1893, 1902, 1905, 1912, 1926, 1938, 1953, 1964, 1968, 1975, 1977, 1980, 1981.

NOTTINGHAM (17)

England (3) 1905, 1930, 1977.

Australia (5) 1921, 1934, 1948, 1981, 1989.

Drawn (9) 1899, 1926, 1938, 1953, 1956, 1964, 1972, 1985, 1993.

LEEDS (21)

England (6)	1956, 1961, 1972, 1977, 1981, 1985.
Australia (7)	1909, 1921, 1938, 1948, 1964, 1989, 1993.
Drawn (8)	1899, 1905, 1926, 1930, 1934, 1953, 1968, 1975.

BIRMINGHAM (9)

England (3)	1909, 1981, 1985.
Australia (2)	1975, 1993.
Drawn (4)	1902, 1961, 1968, 1989.

SHEFFIELD (1)

Australia (1)	1902.

In Australia

MELBOURNE (50)

England (18)	*1876, 1882, 1884*(2), *1894*(2), *1903, 1907, 1911*(2), *1924, 1928, 1950, 1954, 1962, 1974, 1982, 1986.*
Australia (25)	*1876, 1878, 1882, 1891, 1897*(2), *1901*(2), *1903, 1907, 1920*(2), *1924, 1928, 1932, 1936*(2), *1950, 1958*(2), *1976, 1978, 1979, 1990, 1994.*
Drawn (7)	*1881*(2), *1946, 1965*(2), *1970, 1974.*

One scheduled match in 1970-71 was abandoned without a ball bowled and is excluded.

SYDNEY (50)

England (20)	*1882, 1886*(2), *1887, 1894, 1897, 1901, 1903*(2), *1911, 1928, 1932*(2), *1936, 1954, 1965, 1970*(2), *1978*(2).
Australia (23)	*1881*(2), *1882, 1884*(2), *1891, 1894, 1897, 1901, 1907*(2), *1911, 1920*(2), *1924*(2), *1946*(2), *1950, 1962, 1974, 1979, 1986.*
Drawn (7)	*1954, 1958, 1962, 1982, 1987, 1990, 1994.*

ADELAIDE (26)

England (8)	*1884, 1891, 1911, 1928, 1932, 1954, 1978, 1994.*
Australia (13)	*1894, 1897, 1901, 1903, 1907, 1920, 1924, 1936, 1950, 1958, 1965, 1974, 1982.*
Drawn (5)	*1946, 1962, 1970, 1986, 1990.*

BRISBANE Exhibition Ground (1)

England (1)	*1928.*

BRISBANE Woolloongabba (15)

England (4)	*1932, 1936, 1978, 1986.*
Australia (8)	*1946, 1950, 1954, 1958, 1974, 1982, 1990, 1994.*
Drawn (3)	*1962, 1965, 1970.*

PERTH (8)

England (1)	*1978.*
Australia (4)	*1974, 1979, 1990, 1994.*
Drawn (3)	*1970, 1982, 1986.*

For Tests in Australia the first year of the season is given in italics; i.e. *1876* denotes the 1876-77 season.

ENGLAND v SOUTH AFRICA

Season	England	South Africa	T	E	SA	D
		Captains				
1888-89	C. A. Smith[1]	O. R. Dunell[2]	2	2	0	0
1891-92	W. W. Read	W. H. Milton	1	1	0	0
1895-96	Lord Hawke[3]	E. A. Halliwell[4]	3	3	0	0
1898-99	Lord Hawke	M. Bisset	2	2	0	0
1905-06	P. F. Warner	P. W. Sherwell	5	1	4	0
1907	R. E. Foster	P. W. Sherwell	3	1	0	2
1909-10	H. D. G. Leveson Gower[5]	S. J. Snooke	5	2	3	0
1912	C. B. Fry	F. Mitchell[6]	3	3	0	0
1913-14	J. W. H. T. Douglas	H. W. Taylor	5	4	0	1
1922-23	F. T. Mann	H. W. Taylor	5	2	1	2
1924	A. E. R. Gilligan[7]	H. W. Taylor	5	3	0	2
1927-28	R. T. Stanyforth[8]	H. G. Deane	5	2	2	1
1929	J. C. White[9]	H. G. Deane	5	2	0	3
1930-31	A. P. F. Chapman	H. G. Deane[10]	5	0	1	4
1935	R. E. S. Wyatt	H. F. Wade	5	0	1	4
1938-39	W. R. Hammond	A. Melville	5	1	0	4
1947	N. W. D. Yardley	A. Melville	5	3	0	2
1948-49	F. G. Mann	A. D. Nourse	5	2	0	3
1951	F. R. Brown	A. D. Nourse	5	3	1	1
1955	P. B. H. May	J. E. Cheetham[11]	5	3	2	0
1956-57	P. B. H. May	C. B. van Ryneveld[12]	5	2	2	1
1960	M. C. Cowdrey	D. J. McGlew	5	3	0	2
1964-65	M. J. K. Smith	T. L. Goddard	5	1	0	4
1965	M. J. K. Smith	P. L. van der Merwe	3	0	1	2
1994	M. A. Atherton	K. C. Wessels	3	1	1	1
	In South Africa		58	25	13	20
	In England		47	22	6	19
	Totals		105	47	19	39

Notes: The following deputised for the official touring captain or were appointed by the home authority for only a minor proportion of the series:

[1]M. P. Bowden (Second). [2]W. H. Milton (Second). [3]Sir T. C. O'Brien (First). [4]A. R. Richards (Third). [5]F. L. Fane (Fourth and Fifth). [6]L. J. Tancred (Second and Third). [7]J. W. H. T. Douglas (Fourth). [8]G. T. S. Stevens (Fifth). [9]A. W. Carr (Fourth and Fifth). [10]E. P. Nupen (First), H. B. Cameron (Fourth and Fifth). [11]D. J. McGlew (Third and Fourth). [12]D. J. McGlew (Second).

HIGHEST INNINGS TOTALS

For England in England: 554-8 dec. at Lord's	....	1947
in South Africa: 654-5 at Durban	....	1938-39
For South Africa in England: 538 at Leeds	....	1951
in South Africa: 530 at Durban	....	1938-39

LOWEST INNINGS TOTALS

For England in England: 76 at Leeds 1907
    in South Africa: 92 at Cape Town 1898-99

For South Africa in England: 30 at Birmingham 1924
      in South Africa: 30 at Port Elizabeth 1895-96

INDIVIDUAL HUNDREDS

For England (88)

R. Abel (1)
120 Cape Town . . 1888-89
L. E. G. Ames (2)
148* The Oval 1935
115 Cape Town . . 1938-39
K. F. Barrington (2)
148* Durban 1964-65
121 Johannesburg 1964-65
G. Boycott (1)
117 Pt Elizabeth . 1964-65
L. C. Braund (1)
104† Lord's 1907
D. C. S. Compton (7)
163† Nottingham .. 1947
208 Lord's 1947
115 Manchester.... 1947
113 The Oval.... 1947
114 Johannesburg 1948-49
112 Nottingham . 1951
158 Manchester . 1955
M. C. Cowdrey (3)
101 Cape Town . 1956-57
155 The Oval.... 1960
105 Nottingham . 1965
D. Denton (1)
104 Johannesburg 1909-10
E. R. Dexter (1)
172 Johannesburg 1964-65
J. W. H. T. Douglas (1)
119† Durban 1913-14
W. J. Edrich (3)
219 Durban 1938-39
189 Lord's 1947
191 Manchester.. 1947
F. L. Fane (1)
143 Johannesburg 1905-06
C. B. Fry (1)
129 The Oval.... 1907
P. A. Gibb (2)
106† Johannesburg 1938-39
120 Durban 1938-39
W. R. Hammond (6)
138* Birmingham . 1929
101* The Oval.... 1929
136* Durban 1930-31

181 Cape Town . . 1938-39
120 Durban 1938-39
140 Durban 1938-39
T. W. Hayward (1)
122 Johannesburg 1895-96
E. H. Hendren (1)
132 Leeds 1924
142 The Oval.... 1924
G. A. Hick (1)
110 Leeds 1994
A. J. L. Hill (1)
124 Cape Town . . 1895-96
J. B. Hobbs (2)
187 Cape Town . . 1909-10
211 Lord's 1924
L. Hutton (4)
100 Leeds 1947
158 Johannesburg 1948-49
123 Johannesburg 1948-49
100 Leeds 1951
D. J. Insole (1)
110* Durban 1956-57
M. Leyland (2)
102 Lord's 1929
161 The Oval.... 1935
F. G. Mann (1)
136* Pt Elizabeth . 1948-49
P. B. H. May (3) .
138† Leeds 1951
112 Lord's 1955
117 Manchester.. 1955
C. P. Mead (3)
102 Johannesburg 1913-14
117 Pt Elizabeth . 1913-14
181 Durban 1922-23
P. H. Parfitt (1)
122* Johannesburg 1964-65
J. M. Parks (1)
108* Durban 1964-65
E. Paynter (3)
117 ⎫
100 ⎬†Johannesburg 1938-39
243 Durban 1938-39
G. Pullar (1)
175 The Oval.... 1960

W. Rhodes (1)
152 Johannesburg 1913-14
P. E. Richardson (1)
117† Johannesburg 1956-57
R. W. V. Robins (1)
108 Manchester.. 1935
A. C. Russell (2)
140 ⎫
111 ⎬Durban 1922-23
R. T. Simpson (1)
137 Nottingham . 1951
M. J. K. Smith (1)
121 Cape Town . . 1964-65
R. H. Spooner (1)
119† Lord's 1912
H. Sutcliffe (6)
122 Lord's 1924
102 Johannesburg 1927-28
114 Birmingham . 1929
100 Lord's 1929
104 ⎫
109* ⎬The Oval.... 1929
M. W. Tate (1)
100* Lord's 1929
E. Tyldesley (2)
122 Johannesburg 1927-28
100 Durban 1927-28
J. T. Tyldesley (1)
112 Cape Town . . 1898-99
B. H. Valentine (1)
112 Cape Town . . 1938-39
P. F. Warner (1)
132*†‡Johannesburg 1898-99
C. Washbrook (1)
195 Johannesburg 1948-49
A. J. Watkins (1)
111 Johannesburg 1948-49
H. Wood (1)
134* Cape Town . . 1891-92
F. E. Woolley (3)
115* Johannesburg 1922-23
134* Lord's 1924
154 Manchester.. 1929
R. E. S. Wyatt (2)
113 Manchester.. 1929
149 Nottingham . 1935

For South Africa (60)

E. J. Barlow (1)
138   Cape Town . . 1964-65

K. C. Bland (2)
144* Johannesburg 1964-65
127   The Oval 1965

R. H. Catterall (3)
120   Birmingham .   1924
120   Lord's 1924
119   Durban 1927-28

E. L. Dalton (2)
117   The Oval 1935
102   Johannesburg 1938-39

W. R. Endean (1)
116* Leeds 1955

G. A. Faulkner (1)
123   Johannesburg 1909-10

T. L. Goddard (1)
112   Johannesburg 1964-65

C. M. H. Hathorn (1)
102   Johannesburg 1905-06

P. N. Kirsten (1)
104   Leeds 1994

D. J. McGlew (2)
104* Manchester . . 1955
133   Leeds 1955

R. A. McLean (3)
142   Lord's 1955
100   Durban 1956-57
109   Manchester . . 1960

A. Melville (4)
103   Durban 1938-39

189 ⎫
104* ⎭ Nottingham .   1947
117   Lord's 1947

B. Mitchell (7)
123   Cape Town . . 1930-31
164* Lord's 1935
128   The Oval 1935
109   Durban 1938-39
120 ⎫
189* ⎭ The Oval . . . 1947
120   Cape Town . . 1948-49

A. D. Nourse (7)
120   Cape Town . . 1938-39
103   Durban 1938-39
149   Nottingham .   1947
115   Manchester . . 1947
112   Cape Town . . 1948-49
129* Johannesburg 1948-49
208   Nottingham .   1951

H. G. Owen-Smith (1)
129   Leeds 1929

A. J. Pithey (1)
154   Cape Town . . 1964-65

R. G. Pollock (2)
137   Pt Elizabeth . 1964-65
125   Nottingham .   1965

E. A. B. Rowan (2)
156* Johannesburg 1948-49
236   Leeds 1951

P. W. Sherwell (1)
115   Lord's 1907

I. J. Siedle (1)
141   Cape Town . . 1930-31

J. H. Sinclair (1)
106   Cape Town . . 1898-99

H. W. Taylor (7)
109   Durban 1913-14
176   Johannesburg 1922-23
101   Johannesburg 1922-23
102   Durban 1922-23
101   Johannesburg 1927-28
121   The Oval 1929
117   Cape Town . . 1930-31

P. G. V. van der Bijl (1)
125   Durban 1938-39

K. G. Viljoen (1)
124   Manchester . . 1935

W. W. Wade (1)
125   Pt Elizabeth 1948-49

J. H. B. Waite (1)
113   Manchester . . 1955

K. C. Wessels (1)
105† Lord's 1994

G. C. White (2)
147   Johannesburg 1905-06
118   Durban 1909-10

P. L. Winslow (1)
108   Manchester . . 1955

† *Signifies hundred on first appearance in England–South Africa Tests. K. C. Wessels had earlier scored 162 on his Test debut for Australia against England at Brisbane in 1982-83.*
‡ *P. F. Warner carried his bat through the second innings.*
A. Melville's four hundreds were made in successive Test innings.
H. Wood scored the only hundred of his career in a Test match.

RECORD PARTNERSHIP FOR EACH WICKET

For England

359	for 1st†	L. Hutton and C. Washbrook at Johannesburg	1948-49
280	for 2nd	P. A. Gibb and W. J. Edrich at Durban	1938-39
370	for 3rd†	W. J. Edrich and D. C. S. Compton at Lord's	1947
197	for 4th	W. R. Hammond and L. E. G. Ames at Cape Town	1938-39
237	for 5th	D. C. S. Compton and N. W. D. Yardley at Nottingham	1947
206*	for 6th	K. F. Barrington and J. M. Parks at Durban	1964-65
115	for 7th	J. W. H. T. Douglas and M. C. Bird at Durban	1913-14
154	for 8th	C. W. Wright and H. R. Bromley-Davenport at Johannesburg	1895-96
71	for 9th	H. Wood and J. T. Hearne at Cape Town	1891-92
92	for 10th	A. C. Russell and A. E. R. Gilligan at Durban	1922-23

For South Africa

260	for 1st†	B. Mitchell and I. J. Siedle at Cape Town	1930-31
198	for 2nd†	E. A. B. Rowan and C. B. van Ryneveld at Leeds	1951
319	for 3rd	A. Melville and A. D. Nourse at Nottingham	1947
214	for 4th†	H. W. Taylor and H. G. Deane at The Oval	1929
157	for 5th†	A. J. Pithey and J. H. B. Waite at Johannesburg	1964-65
171	for 6th	J. H. B. Waite and P. L. Winslow at Manchester	1955
123	for 7th	H. G. Deane and E. P. Nupen at Durban	1927-28

109* for 8th	B. Mitchell and L. Tuckett at The Oval....................	1947
137 for 9th†	E. L. Dalton and A. B. C. Langton at The Oval..............	1935
103 for 10th†	H. G. Owen-Smith and A. J. Bell at Leeds	1929

   † *Denotes record partnership against all countries.*

MOST RUNS IN A SERIES

England in England	753 (average 94.12)	D. C. S. Compton..	1947
England in South Africa	653 (average 81.62)	E. Paynter	1938-39
South Africa in England	621 (average 69.00)	A. D. Nourse	1947
South Africa in South Africa..	582 (average 64.66)	H. W. Taylor......	1922-23

TEN WICKETS OR MORE IN A MATCH

For England (24)

11-110 (5-25, 6-85)†	S. F. Barnes, Lord's	1912
10-115 (6-52, 4-63)	S. F. Barnes, Leeds..............................	1912
13-57 (5-28, 8-29)	S. F. Barnes, The Oval...........................	1912
10-105 (5-57, 5-48)	S. F. Barnes, Durban............................	1913-14
17-159 (8-56, 9-103)	S. F. Barnes, Johannesburg.......................	1913-14
14-144 (7-56, 7-88)	S. F. Barnes, Durban............................	1913-14
12-112 (7-58, 5-54)	A. V. Bedser, Manchester	1951
11-118 (6-68, 5-50)	C. Blythe, Cape Town............................	1905-06
15-99 (8-59, 7-40)	C. Blythe, Leeds................................	1907
10-104 (7-46, 3-58)	C. Blythe, Cape Town............................	1909-10
15-28 (7-17, 8-11)	J. Briggs, Cape Town............................	1888-89
13-91 (6-54, 7-37)†	J. J. Ferris, Cape Town..........................	1891-92
10-207 (7-115, 3-92)	A. P. Freeman, Leeds	1929
12-171 (7-71, 5-100)	A. P. Freeman, Manchester	1929
12-130 (7-70, 5-60)	G. Geary, Johannesburg..........................	1927-28
11-90 (6-7, 5-83)	A. E. R. Gilligan, Birmingham	1924
10-119 (4-64, 6-55)	J. C. Laker, The Oval	1951
15-45 (7-38, 8-7)†	G. A. Lohmann, Port Elizabeth	1895-96
12-71 (9-28, 3-43)	G. A. Lohmann, Johannesburg.....................	1895-96
10-138 (1-81, 9-57)	D. E. Malcolm, The Oval	1994
11-97 (6-63, 5-34)	J. B. Statham, Lord's	1960
12-101 (7-52, 5-49)	R. Tattersall, Lord's	1951
12-89 (5-53, 7-36)	J. H. Wardle, Cape Town.........................	1956-57
10-175 (5-95, 5-80)	D. V. P. Wright, Lord's	1947

For South Africa (6)

11-112 (4-49, 7-63)†	A. E. Hall, Cape Town...........................	1922-23
11-150 (5-63, 6-87)	E. P. Nupen, Johannesburg........................	1930-31
10-87 (5-53, 5-34)	P. M. Pollock, Nottingham	1965
12-127 (4-57, 8-70)	S. J. Snooke, Johannesburg	1905-06
13-192 (4-79, 9-113)	H. J. Tayfield, Johannesburg......................	1956-57
12-181 (5-87, 7-94)	A. E. E. Vogler, Johannesburg	1909-10

   † *Signifies ten wickets or more on first appearance in England–South Africa Tests.*

Note: S. F. Barnes took ten wickets or more in his first five Tests v South Africa and in six of his seven Tests v South Africa. A. P. Freeman and G. A. Lohmann took ten wickets or more in successive matches.

MOST WICKETS IN A SERIES

England in England	34 (average 8.29)	S. F. Barnes	1912
England in South Africa	49 (average 10.93)	S. F. Barnes	1913-14
South Africa in England	26 (average 21.84)	H. J. Tayfield	1955
South Africa in England	26 (average 22.57)	N. A. T. Adcock ...	1960
South Africa in South Africa..	37 (average 17.18)	H. J. Tayfield	1956-57

ENGLAND v WEST INDIES

		Captains				
Season	England	West Indies	T	E	WI	D
1928	A. P. F. Chapman	R. K. Nunes	3	3	0	0
1929-30	Hon. F. S. G. Calthorpe	E. L. G. Hoad[1]	4	1	1	2
1933	D. R. Jardine[2]	G. C. Grant	3	2	0	1
1934-35	R. E. S. Wyatt	G. C. Grant	4	1	2	1
1939	W. R. Hammond	R. S. Grant	3	1	0	2
1947-48	G. O. B. Allen[3]	J. D. C. Goddard[4]	4	0	2	2
1950	N. W. D. Yardley[5]	J. D. C. Goddard	4	1	3	0
1953-54	L. Hutton	J. B. Stollmeyer	5	2	2	1
1957	P. B. H. May	J. D. C. Goddard	5	3	0	2
1959-60	P. B. H. May[6]	F. C. M. Alexander	5	1	0	4

THE WISDEN TROPHY

		Captains					
Season	England	West Indies	T	E	WI	D	Held by
1963	E. R. Dexter	F. M. M. Worrell	5	1	3	1	WI
1966	M. C. Cowdrey[7]	G. S. Sobers	5	1	3	1	WI
1967-68	M. C. Cowdrey	G. S. Sobers	5	1	0	4	E
1969	R. Illingworth	G. S. Sobers	3	2	0	1	E
1973	R. Illingworth	R. B. Kanhai	3	0	2	1	WI
1973-74	M. H. Denness	R. B. Kanhai	5	1	1	3	WI
1976	A. W. Greig	C. H. Lloyd	5	0	3	2	WI
1980	I. T. Botham	C. H. Lloyd[8]	5	0	1	4	WI
1980-81†	I. T. Botham	C. H. Lloyd	4	0	2	2	WI
1984	D. I. Gower	C. H. Lloyd	5	0	5	0	WI
1985-86	D. I. Gower	I. V. A. Richards	5	0	5	0	WI
1988	J. E. Emburey[9]	I. V. A. Richards	5	0	4	1	WI
1989-90‡	G. A. Gooch[10]	I. V. A. Richards[11]	4	1	2	1	WI
1991	G. A. Gooch	I. V. A. Richards	5	2	2	1	WI
1993-94	M. A. Atherton	R. B. Richardson[12]	5	1	3	1	WI
1995	M. A. Atherton	R. B. Richardson	6	2	2	2	WI
	In England		65	18	28	19	
	In West Indies		50	9	20	21	
	Totals.....................		115	27	48	40	

† *The Second Test, at Georgetown, was cancelled owing to political pressure and is excluded.*
‡ *The Second Test, at Georgetown, was abandoned without a ball being bowled and is excluded.*

Notes: The following deputised for the official touring captain or were appointed by the home authority for only a minor proportion of the series:
[1]N. Betancourt (Second), M. P. Fernandes (Third), R. K. Nunes (Fourth). [2]R. E. S. Wyatt (Third). [3]K. Cranston (First). [4]G. A. Headley (First), G. E. Gomez (Second). [5]F. R. Brown (Fourth). [6]M. C. Cowdrey (Fourth and Fifth). [7]M. J. K. Smith (First), D. B. Close (Fifth). [8]I. V. A. Richards (Fifth). [9]M. W. Gatting (First), C. S. Cowdrey (Fourth), G. A. Gooch (Fifth). [10]A. J. Lamb (Fourth and Fifth). [11]D. L. Haynes (Third). [12]C. A. Walsh (Fifth).

HIGHEST INNINGS TOTALS

For England in England: 619-6 dec. at Nottingham	1957
in West Indies: 849 at Kingston	1929-30
For West Indies in England: 692-8 dec. at The Oval	1995
in West Indies: 681-8 dec. at Port-of-Spain	1953-54

LOWEST INNINGS TOTALS

For England in England: 71 at Manchester 1976
          in West Indies: 46 at Port-of-Spain 1993-94

For West Indies in England: 86 at The Oval 1957
          in West Indies: 102 at Bridgetown 1934-35

INDIVIDUAL HUNDREDS

For England (95)

L. E. G. Ames (3)
105 Port-of-Spain 1929-30
149 Kingston.... 1929-30
126 Kingston.... 1934-35

D. L. Amiss (4)
174 Port-of-Spain 1973-74
262* Kingston.... 1973-74
118 Georgetown . 1973-74
203 The Oval.... 1976

M. A. Atherton (3)
144 Georgetown . 1993-94
135 St John's.... 1993-94
113 Nottingham . 1995

A. H. Bakewell (1)
107† The Oval.... 1933

K. F. Barrington (3)
128† Bridgetown . 1959-60
121 Port-of-Spain 1959-60
143 Port-of-Spain 1967-68

G. Boycott (5)
116 Georgetown . 1967-68
128 Manchester.. 1969
106 Lord's 1969
112 Port-of-Spain 1973-74
104* St John's.... 1980-81

D. C. S. Compton (2)
120† Lord's 1939
133 Port-of-Spain 1953-54

M. C. Cowdrey (6)
154* Birmingham . 1957
152 Lord's 1957
114 Kingston.... 1959-60
119 Port-of-Spain 1959-60
101 Kingston.... 1967-68
148 Port-of-Spain 1967-68

E. R. Dexter (2)
136*† Bridgetown .. 1959-60
110 Georgetown . 1959-60

J. H. Edrich (1)
146 Bridgetown . 1967-68

T. G. Evans (1)
104 Manchester.. 1950

K. W. R. Fletcher (1)
129* Bridgetown .. 1973-74

G. Fowler (1)
106 Lord's 1984

G. A. Gooch (5)
123 Lord's 1980
116 Bridgetown .. 1980-81
153 Kingston.... 1980-81
146 Nottingham . 1988
154*‡ Leeds 1991

D. I. Gower (1)
154* Kingston.... 1980-81

T. W. Graveney (5)
258 Nottingham . 1957
164 The Oval.... 1957
109 Nottingham . 1966
165 The Oval.... 1966
118 Port-of-Spain 1967-68

A. W. Greig (3)
148 Bridgetown . 1973-74
121 Georgetown . 1973-74
116 Leeds 1976

S. C. Griffith (1)
140† Port-of-Spain 1947-48

W. R. Hammond (1)
138 The Oval.... 1939

J. H. Hampshire (1)
107† Lord's 1969

F. C. Hayes (1)
106*† The Oval.... 1973

E. H. Hendren (2)
205* Port-of-Spain 1929-30
123 Georgetown . 1929-30

G. A. Hick (1)
118* Nottingham . 1995

J. B. Hobbs (1)
159 The Oval.... 1928

L. Hutton (5)
196† Lord's 1939
165* The Oval.... 1939
202*‡ The Oval.... 1950
169 Georgetown . 1953-54
205 Kingston.... 1953-54

R. Illingworth (1)
113 Lord's 1969

D. R. Jardine (1)
127 Manchester.. 1933

A. P. E. Knott (1)
116 Leeds 1976

A. J. Lamb (6)
110 Lord's 1984
100 Leeds 1984

G. A. Gooch (5) 100* Manchester.. 1984
113 Lord's 1988
132 Kingston.... 1989-90
119 Bridgetown . 1989-90

P. B. H. May (3)
135 Port-of-Spain 1953-54
285* Birmingham . 1957
104 Nottingham . 1957

C. Milburn (1)
126* Lord's 1966

J. T. Murray (1)
112† The Oval.... 1966

J. M. Parks (1)
101*† Port-of-Spain 1959-60

W. Place (1)
107 Kingston.... 1947-48

P. E. Richardson (2)
126 Nottingham . 1957
107 The Oval.... 1957

J. D. Robertson (1)
133 Port-of-Spain 1947-48

A. Sandham (2)
152† Bridgetown . 1929-30
325 Kingston.... 1929-30

M. J. K. Smith (1)
108 Port-of-Spain 1959-60

R. A. Smith (3)
148* Lord's 1991
109 The Oval ... 1991
175 St John's.... 1993-94

D. S. Steele (1)
106† Nottingham . 1976

A. J. Stewart (2)
118 ⎫
143 ⎬ Bridgetown . 1993-94
    ⎭

R. Subba Row (1)
100† Georgetown . 1959-60

E. Tyldesley (1)
122† Lord's 1928

C. Washbrook (2)
114† Lord's 1950
102 Nottingham . 1950

W. Watson (1)
116† Kingston.... 1953-54

P. Willey (1)
100* The Oval.... 1980
102* St John's.... 1980-81

For West Indies (107)

J. C. Adams (1)
137   Georgetown . 1993-94

K. L. T. Arthurton (1)
126   Kingston ... 1993-94

I. Barrow (1)
105   Manchester.. 1933

C. A. Best (1)
164   Bridgetown .. 1989-90

B. F. Butcher (2)
133   Lord's 1963
209* Nottingham . 1966

G. M. Carew (1)
107   Port-of-Spain 1947-48

C. A. Davis (1)
103   Lord's 1969

P. J. L. Dujon (1)
101   Manchester.. 1984

R. C. Fredericks (3)
150   Birmingham . 1973
138   Lord's 1976
109   Leeds 1976

A. G. Ganteaume (1)
112† Port-of-Spain 1947-48

H. A. Gomes (2)
143   Birmingham . 1984
104* Leeds 1984

C. G. Greenidge (7)
134 ⎫
101 ⎬ Manchester.. 1976
115   Leeds 1976
214* Lord's 1984
223   Manchester.. 1984
103   Lord's 1988
149   St John's ... 1989-90

D. L. Haynes (5)
184   Lord's 1980
125   The Oval ... 1984
131   St John's ... 1985-86
109   Bridgetown .. 1989-90
167   St John's ... 1989-90

G. A. Headley (8)
176† Bridgetown . 1929-30
114 ⎫
112 ⎬ Georgetown . 1929-30
223   Kingston 1929-30
169* Manchester.. 1933
270* Kingston 1934-35

106 ⎫
107 ⎬ Lord's 1939

D. A. J. Holford (1)
105* Lord's 1966

J. K. Holt (1)
166   Bridgetown .. 1953-54

C. L. Hooper (2)
111   Lord's 1991
127   The Oval ... 1995

C. C. Hunte (3)
182   Manchester.. 1963
108* The Oval.... 1963
135   Manchester.. 1966

B. D. Julien (1)
121   Lord's 1973

A. I. Kallicharran (2)
158   Port-of-Spain 1973-74
119   Bridgetown .. 1973-74

R. B. Kanhai (5)
110   Port-of-Spain 1959-60
104   The Oval.... 1966
153   Port-of-Spain 1967-68
150   Georgetown . 1967-68
157   Lord's 1973

B. C. Lara (5)
167   Georgetown . 1993-94
375   St John's ... 1993-94
145   Manchester.. 1995
152   Nottingham . 1995
179   The Oval ... 1995

C. H. Lloyd (5)
118† Port-of-Spain 1967-68
113* Bridgetown .. 1967-68
132   The Oval.... 1973
101   Manchester.. 1980
100   Bridgetown .. 1980-81

S. M. Nurse (2)
137   Leeds 1966
136   Port-of-Spain 1967-68

A. F. Rae (2)
106   Lord's 1950
109   The Oval.... 1950

I. V. A. Richards (8)
232† Nottingham . 1976
135   Manchester.. 1976
291   The Oval ... 1976
145   Lord's 1980
182* Bridgetown .. 1980-81

St John's ... 1980-81
117   Birmingham . 1984
110* St John's ... 1985-86

R. B. Richardson (4)
102   Port-of-Spain 1985-86
160   Bridgetown .. 1985-86
104   Birmingham . 1991
121   The Oval ... 1991

C. A. Roach (2)
122   Bridgetown .. 1929-30
209   Georgetown . 1929-30

L. G. Rowe (3)
120   Kingston 1973-74
302   Bridgetown .. 1973-74
123   Port-of-Spain 1973-74

O. G. Smith (2)
161† Birmingham . 1957
168   Nottingham . 1957

G. S. Sobers (10)
226   Bridgetown .. 1959-60
147   Kingston 1959-60
145   Georgetown . 1959-60
102   Leeds 1963
161   Manchester.. 1966
163* Lord's 1966
174   Leeds 1966
113* Kingston 1967-68
152   Georgetown . 1967-68
150* Lord's 1973

C. L. Walcott (4)
168* Lord's 1950
220   Bridgetown .. 1953-54
124   Port-of-Spain 1953-54
116   Kingston 1953-54

E. D. Weekes (3)
141   Kingston 1947-48
129   Nottingham . 1950
206   Port-of-Spain 1953-54

K. H. Weekes (1)
137   The Oval.... 1939

F. M. M. Worrell (6)
131* Manchester.. 1947-48
261   Nottingham . 1950
138   The Oval.... 1950
167   Port-of-Spain 1953-54
191*‡ Nottingham . 1957
197* Bridgetown .. 1959-60

114   St John's 1980-81

† *Signifies hundred on first appearance in England–West Indies Tests. S. C. Griffith provides the only instance for England of a player hitting his maiden century in first-class cricket in his first Test.*
‡ *Carried his bat.*

RECORD PARTNERSHIPS FOR EACH WICKET

For England

212	for 1st	C. Washbrook and R. T. Simpson at Nottingham	1950
266	for 2nd	P. E. Richardson and T. W. Graveney at Nottingham	1957
303	for 3rd	M. A. Atherton and R. A. Smith at St John's	1993-94

411	for 4th†	P. B. H. May and M. C. Cowdrey at Birmingham	1957
150	for 5th	A. J. Stewart and G. P. Thorpe at Bridgetown	1993-94
163	for 6th	A. W. Greig and A. P. E. Knott at Bridgetown	1973-74
197	for 7th†	M. J. K. Smith and J. M. Parks at Port-of-Spain	1959-60
217	for 8th	T. W. Graveney and J. T. Murray at The Oval	1966
109	for 9th	G. A. R. Lock and P. I. Pocock at Georgetown	1967-68
128	for 10th	K. Higgs and J. A. Snow at The Oval	1966

For West Indies

298	for 1st†	C. G. Greenidge and D. L. Haynes at St John's	1989-90
287*	for 2nd	C. G. Greenidge and H. A. Gomes at Lord's	1984
338	for 3rd†	E. D. Weekes and F. M. M. Worrell at Port-of-Spain	1953-54
399	for 4th†	G. S. Sobers and F. M. M. Worrell at Bridgetown	1959-60
265	for 5th†	S. M. Nurse and G. S. Sobers at Leeds	1966
274*	for 6th†	G. S. Sobers and D. A. J. Holford at Lord's	1966
155*	for 7th‡	G. S. Sobers and B. D. Julien at Lord's	1973
99	for 8th	C. A. McWatt and J. K. Holt at Georgetown	1953-54
150	for 9th	E. A. E. Baptiste and M. A. Holding at Birmingham	1984
67*	for 10th	M. A. Holding and C. E. H. Croft at St John's	1980-81

† *Denotes record partnership against all countries.*

‡ *231 runs were added for this wicket in two separate partnerships: G. S. Sobers retired ill and was replaced by K. D. Boyce when 155 had been added.*

TEN WICKETS OR MORE IN A MATCH

For England (11)

11-98 (7-44, 4-54)	T. E. Bailey, Lord's	1957
10-93 (5-54, 5-39)	A. P. Freeman, Manchester	1928
13-156 (8-86, 5-70)	A. W. Greig, Port-of-Spain	1973-74
11-48 (5-28, 6-20)	G. A. R. Lock, The Oval	1957
10-137 (4-60, 6-77)	D. E. Malcolm, Port-of-Spain	1989-90
11-96 (5-37, 6-59)†	C. S. Marriott, The Oval	1933
10-142 (4-82, 6-60)	J. A. Snow, Georgetown	1967-68
10-195 (5-105, 5-90)†	G. T. S. Stevens, Bridgetown	1929-30
11-152 (6-100, 5-52)	F. S. Trueman, Lord's	1963
12-119 (5-75, 7-44)	F. S. Trueman, Birmingham	1963
11-149 (4-79, 7-70)	W. Voce, Port-of-Spain	1929-30

For West Indies (14)

10-127 (2-82, 8-45)	C. E. L. Ambrose, Bridgetown	1989-90
11-84 (5-60, 6-24)	C. E. L. Ambrose, Port-of-Spain	1993-94
10-174 (5-105, 5-69)	K. C. G. Benjamin, Nottingham	1995
11-147 (5-70, 6-77)†	K. D. Boyce, The Oval	1973
11-229 (5-137, 6-92)	W. Ferguson, Port-of-Spain	1947-48
11-157 (5-59, 6-98)†	L. R. Gibbs, Manchester	1963
10-106 (5-37, 5-69)	L. R. Gibbs, Manchester	1966
14-149 (8-92, 6-57)	M. A. Holding, The Oval	1976
10-96 (5-41, 5-55)†	H. H. H. Johnson, Kingston	1947-48
10-92 (6-32, 4-60)	M. D. Marshall, Lord's	1988
11-152 (5-66, 6-86)	S. Ramadhin, Lord's	1950
10-123 (5-63, 5-63)	A. M. E. Roberts, Lord's	1976
11-204 (8-104, 3-100)†	A. L. Valentine, Manchester	1950
10-160 (4-121, 6-39)	A. L. Valentine, The Oval	1950

† *Signifies ten wickets or more on first appearance in England–West Indies Tests.*

Note: F. S. Trueman took ten wickets or more in successive matches.

ENGLAND v NEW ZEALAND

Captains

Season	England	New Zealand	T	E	NZ	D
1929-30	A. H. H. Gilligan	T. C. Lowry	4	1	0	3
1931	D. R. Jardine	T. C. Lowry	3	1	0	2
1932-33	D. R. Jardine[1]	M. L. Page	2	0	0	2
1937	R. W. V. Robins	M. L. Page	3	1	0	2
1946-47	W. R. Hammond	W. A. Hadlee	1	0	0	1
1949	F. G. Mann[2]	W. A. Hadlee	4	0	0	4
1950-51	F. R. Brown	W. A. Hadlee	2	1	0	1
1954-55	L. Hutton	G. O. Rabone	2	2	0	0
1958	P. B. H. May	J. R. Reid	5	4	0	1
1958-59	P. B. H. May	J. R. Reid	2	1	0	1
1962-63	E. R. Dexter	J. R. Reid	3	3	0	0
1965	M. J. K. Smith	J. R. Reid	3	3	0	0
1965-66	M. J. K. Smith	B. W. Sinclair[3]	3	0	0	3
1969	R. Illingworth	G. T. Dowling	3	2	0	1
1970-71	R. Illingworth	G. T. Dowling	2	1	0	1
1973	R. Illingworth	B. E. Congdon	3	2	0	1
1974-75	M. H. Denness	B. E. Congdon	2	1	0	1
1977-78	G. Boycott	M. G. Burgess	3	1	1	1
1978	J. M. Brearley	M. G. Burgess	3	3	0	0
1983	R. G. D. Willis	G. P. Howarth	4	3	1	0
1983-84	R. G. D. Willis	G. P. Howarth	3	0	1	2
1986	M. W. Gatting	J. V. Coney	3	0	1	2
1987-88	M. W. Gatting	J. J. Crowe[4]	3	0	0	3
1990	G. A. Gooch	J. G. Wright	3	1	0	2
1991-92	G. A. Gooch	M. D. Crowe	3	2	0	1
1994	M. A. Atherton	K. R. Rutherford	3	1	0	2
	In New Zealand		35	13	2	20
	In England		40	21	2	17
	Totals.........................		75	34	4	37

Notes: The following deputised for the official touring captain or were appointed by the home authority for only a minor proportion of the series:
[1]R. E. S. Wyatt (Second). [2]F. R. Brown (Third and Fourth). [3]M. E. Chapple (First). [4]J. G. Wright (Third).

HIGHEST INNINGS TOTALS

For England in England: 567-8 dec. at Nottingham	1994
in New Zealand: 593-6 dec. at Auckland	1974-75
For New Zealand in England: 551-9 dec. at Lord's.........................	1973
in New Zealand: 537 at Wellington	1983-84

LOWEST INNINGS TOTALS

For England in England: 158 at Birmingham	1990
in New Zealand: 64 at Wellington	1977-78
For New Zealand in England: 47 at Lord's	1958
in New Zealand: 26 at Auckland	1954-55

INDIVIDUAL HUNDREDS

For England (79)

G. O. B. Allen (1)		
122†	Lord's	1931
L. E. G. Ames (2)		
137†	Lord's	1931
103	Christchurch.	1932-33
D. L. Amiss (2)		
138*†	Nottingham .	1973
164*	Christchurch.	1974-75
M. A. Atherton (3)		
151†	Nottingham .	1990
101	Nottingham .	1994
111	Manchester. .	1994
T. E. Bailey (1)		
134*	Christchurch.	1950-51
K. F. Barrington (3)		
126†	Auckland . . .	1962-63
137	Birmingham .	1965
163	Leeds	1965
I. T. Botham (3)		
103	Christchurch.	1977-78
103	Nottingham .	1983
138	Manchester . .	1983-84
E. H. Bowley (1)		
109	Auckland . . .	1929-30
G. Boycott (2)		
115	Leeds	1973
131	Nottingham .	1978
B. C. Broad (1)		
114†	Christchurch.	1987-88
D. C. S. Compton (2)		
114	Leeds	1949
116	Lord's	1949
M. C. Cowdrey (2)		
128*	Wellington .	1962-63
119	Lord's	1965
M. H. Denness (1)		
181	Auckland . . .	1974-75
E. R. Dexter (1)		
141	Christchurch.	1958-59
B. L. D'Oliveira (1)		
100	Christchurch.	1970-71
K. S. Duleepsinhji (2)		
117	Auckland . . .	1929-30
109	The Oval. . . .	1931
J. H. Edrich (3)		
310*†	Leeds	1965
115	Lord's	1969
155	Nottingham .	1969
W. J. Edrich (1)		
100	The Oval. . . .	1949
K. W. R. Fletcher (2)		
178	Lord's	1973
216	Auckland . . .	1974-75
G. Fowler (1)		
105†	The Oval. . . .	1983
M. W. Gatting (1)		
121	The Oval. . . .	1986
G. A. Gooch (4)		
183	Leeds	1986
154	Birmingham .	1990
114	Auckland . . .	1991-92
210	Nottingham .	1994
D. I. Gower (4)		
111†	The Oval. . . .	1978
112*	Leeds	1983
108	Lord's	1983
131	The Oval. . . .	1986
A. W. Greig (1)		
139†	Nottingham .	1973
W. R. Hammond (4)		
100*	The Oval. . . .	1931
227	Christchurch.	1932-33
336*	Auckland . . .	1932-33
140	Lord's	1937
J. Hardstaff jun. (2)		
114†	Lord's	1937
103	The Oval. . . .	1937
L. Hutton (3)		
100	Manchester. .	1937
101	Leeds	1949
206	The Oval. . . .	1949
B. R. Knight (1)		
125†	Auckland . . .	1962-63
A. P. E. Knott (1)		
101	Auckland . . .	1970-71
A. J. Lamb (3)		
102*†	The Oval. . . .	1983
137*	Nottingham .	1983
142	Wellington .	1991-92
G. B. Legge (1)		
196	Auckland . . .	1929-30
P. B. H. May (3)		
113*	Leeds	1958
101	Manchester . .	1958
124*	Auckland . . .	1958-59
C. A. Milton (1)		
104*†	Leeds	1958
P. H. Parfitt (1)		
131*†	Auckland . . .	1962-63
C. T. Radley (1)		
158	Auckland . . .	1977-78
D. W. Randall (2)		
164	Wellington .	1983-84
104	Auckland . . .	1983-84
P. E. Richardson (1)		
100†	Birmingham .	1958
J. D. Robertson (1)		
121†	Lord's	1949
P. J. Sharpe (1)		
111	Nottingham .	1969
R. T. Simpson (1)		
103†	Manchester. .	1949
A. J. Stewart (3)		
148	Christchurch.	1991-92
107	Wellington . .	1991-92
119	Lord's	1994
H. Sutcliffe (2)		
117†	The Oval. . . .	1931
109*	Manchester. .	1931
C. J. Tavaré (1)		
109†	The Oval. . . .	1983
C. Washbrook (1)		
103*	Leeds	1949

For New Zealand (38)

J. G. Bracewell (1)		
110	Nottingham .	1986
M. G. Burgess (2)		
104	Auckland . . .	1970-71
105	Lord's	1973
J. V. Coney (1)		
174*	Wellington .	1983-84
B. E. Congdon (3)		
104	Christchurch.	1965-66
176	Nottingham .	1973
175	Lord's	1973
J. J. Crowe (1)		
128	Auckland . . .	1983-84
M. D. Crowe (5)		
100	Wellington .	1983-84
106	Lord's	1986
143	Wellington .	1987-88
142	Lord's	1994
115	Manchester . .	1994
C. S. Dempster (2)		
136	Wellington .	1929-30
120	Lord's	1931
M. P. Donnelly (1)		
206	Lord's	1949
T. J. Franklin (1)		
101	Lord's	1990
M. J. Greatbatch (1)		
107*†	Auckland . . .	1987-88
W. A. Hadlee (1)		
116	Christchurch.	1946-47
G. P. Howarth (3)		
122	⎫	
102	⎬ Auckland . . .	1977-78
123	Lord's	1978
A. H. Jones (1)		
143	Wellington . .	1991-92

J. E. Mills (1)		**J. R. Reid** (1)		**B. Sutcliffe** (2)	
117† Wellington .. 1929-30		100 Christchurch. 1962-63		101 Manchester.. 1949	
M. L. Page (1)		**K. R. Rutherford** (1)		116 Christchurch. 1950-51	
104 Lord's 1931		107* Wellington ... 1987-88		**J. G. Wright** (4)	
J. M. Parker (1)		**B. W. Sinclair** (1)		130 Auckland ... 1983-84	
121 Auckland ... 1974-75		114 Auckland ... 1965-66		119 The Oval 1986	
V. Pollard (2)		**I. D. S. Smith** (1)		103 Auckland ... 1987-88	
116 Nottingham .. 1973		113* Auckland ... 1983-84		116 Wellington .. 1991-92	
105* Lord's 1973					

† *Signifies hundred on first appearance in England–New Zealand Tests.*

RECORD PARTNERSHIPS FOR EACH WICKET

For England

223	for 1st	G. Fowler and C. J. Tavaré at The Oval	1983
369	for 2nd	J. H. Edrich and K. F. Barrington at Leeds	1965
245	for 3rd	J. Hardstaff jun. and W. R. Hammond at Lord's	1937
266	for 4th	M. H. Denness and K. W. R. Fletcher at Auckland	1974-75
242	for 5th	W. R. Hammond and L. E. G. Ames at Christchurch	1932-33
240	for 6th†	P. H. Parfitt and B. R. Knight at Auckland	1962-63
149	for 7th	A. P. E. Knott and P. Lever at Auckland	1970-71
246	for 8th†	L. E. G. Ames and G. O. B. Allen at Lord's	1931
163*	for 9th†	M. C. Cowdrey and A. C. Smith at Wellington	1962-63
59	for 10th	A. P. E. Knott and N. Gifford at Nottingham	1973

For New Zealand

276	for 1st	C. S. Dempster and J. E. Mills at Wellington	1929-30
241	for 2nd†	J. G. Wright and A. H. Jones at Wellington	1991-92
210	for 3rd	B. A. Edgar and M. D. Crowe at Lord's	1986
155	for 4th	M. D. Crowe and M. J. Greatbatch at Wellington	1987-88
180	for 5th	M. D. Crowe and S. A. Thomson at Lord's	1994
141	for 6th	M. D. Crowe and A. C. Parore at Manchester	1994
117	for 7th	D. N. Patel and C. L. Cairns at Christchurch	1991-92
104	for 8th	D. A. R. Moloney and A. W. Roberts at Lord's	1937
118	for 9th	J. V. Coney and B. L. Cairns at Wellington	1983-84
57	for 10th	F. L. H. Mooney and J. Cowie at Leeds	1949

† *Denotes record partnership against all countries.*

TEN WICKETS OR MORE IN A MATCH

For England (8)

11-140 (6-101, 5-39)	I. T. Botham, Lord's	1978
10-149 (5-98, 5-51)	A. W. Greig, Auckland	1974-75
11-65 (4-14, 7-51)	G. A. R. Lock, Leeds	1958
11-84 (5-31, 6-53)	G. A. R. Lock, Christchurch	1958-59
11-147 (4-100, 7-47)†	P. C. R. Tufnell, Christchurch	1991-92
11-70 (4-38, 7-32)†	D. L. Underwood, Lord's	1969
12-101 (6-41, 6-60)	D. L. Underwood, The Oval	1969
12-97 (6-12, 6-85)	D. L. Underwood, Christchurch	1970-71

For New Zealand (5)

10-144 (7-74, 3-70)	B. L. Cairns, Leeds	1983
10-140 (4-73, 6-67)	J. Cowie, Manchester	1937
10-100 (4-74, 6-26)	R. J. Hadlee, Wellington	1977-78
10-140 (6-80, 4-60)	R. J. Hadlee, Nottingham	1986
11-169 (6-76, 5-93)	D. J. Nash, Lord's	1994

† *Signifies ten wickets or more on first appearance in England–New Zealand Tests.*

Note: D. L. Underwood took 12 wickets in successive matches against New Zealand in 1969 and 1970-71.

HAT-TRICK AND FOUR WICKETS IN FIVE BALLS

M. J. C. Allom, in his first Test match, v New Zealand at Christchurch in 1929-30, dismissed C. S. Dempster, T. C. Lowry, K. C. James, and F. T. Badcock to take four wickets in five balls (w-www).

ENGLAND v INDIA

	Captains					
Season	*England*	*India*	*T*	*E*	*I*	*D*
1932	D. R. Jardine	C. K. Nayudu	1	1	0	0
1933-34	D. R. Jardine	C. K. Nayudu	3	2	0	1
1936	G. O. B. Allen	Maharaj of Vizianagram	3	2	0	1
1946	W. R. Hammond	Nawab of Pataudi sen.	3	1	0	2
1951-52	N. D. Howard[1]	V. S. Hazare	5	1	1	3
1952	L. Hutton	V. S. Hazare	4	3	0	1
1959	P. B. H. May[2]	D. K. Gaekwad[3]	5	5	0	0
1961-62	E. R. Dexter	N. J. Contractor	5	0	2	3
1963-64	M. J. K. Smith	Nawab of Pataudi jun.	5	0	0	5
1967	D. B. Close	Nawab of Pataudi jun.	3	3	0	0
1971	R. Illingworth	A. L. Wadekar	3	0	1	2
1972-73	A. R. Lewis	A. L. Wadekar	5	1	2	2
1974	M. H. Denness	A. L. Wadekar	3	3	0	0
1976-77	A. W. Greig	B. S. Bedi	5	3	1	1
1979	J. M. Brearley	S. Venkataraghavan	4	1	0	3
1979-80	J. M. Brearley	G. R. Viswanath	1	1	0	0
1981-82	K. W. R. Fletcher	S. M. Gavaskar	6	0	1	5
1982	R. G. D. Willis	S. M. Gavaskar	3	1	0	2
1984-85	D. I. Gower	S. M. Gavaskar	5	2	1	2
1986	M. W. Gatting[4]	Kapil Dev	3	0	2	1
1990	G. A. Gooch	M. Azharuddin	3	1	0	2
1992-93	G. A. Gooch[5]	M. Azharuddin	3	0	3	0
	In England		38	21	3	14
	In India.		43	10	11	22
	Totals.		81	31	14	36

Notes: The 1932 Indian touring team was captained by the Maharaj of Porbandar but he did not play in the Test match.

The following deputised for the official touring captain or were appointed by the home authority for only a minor proportion of the series:
[1]D. B. Carr (Fifth). [2]M. C. Cowdrey (Fourth and Fifth). [3]Pankaj Roy (Second). [4]D. I. Gower (First). [5]A. J. Stewart (Second).

HIGHEST INNINGS TOTALS

For England in England: 653-4 dec. at Lord's	1990
in India: 652-7 dec. at Madras.	1984-85
For India in England: 606-9 dec. at The Oval	1990
in India: 591 at Bombay	1992-93

LOWEST INNINGS TOTALS

For England in England: 101 at The Oval	1971
in India: 102 at Bombay.	1981-82
For India in England: 42 at Lord's	1974
in India: 83 at Madras	1976-77

INDIVIDUAL HUNDREDS

For England (72)

D. L. Amiss (2)
188 Lord's 1974
179 Delhi....... 1976-77
M. A. Atherton (1)
131 Manchester.. 1990
K. F. Barrington (3)
151* Bombay 1961-62
172 Bombay 1961-62
113* Delhi....... 1961-62
I. T. Botham (5)
137 Leeds 1979
114 Bombay 1979-80
142 Kanpur 1981-82
128 Manchester.. 1982
208 The Oval 1982
G. Boycott (4)
246*† Leeds 1967
155 Birmingham . 1979
125 The Oval 1979
105 Delhi....... 1981-82
M. C. Cowdrey (3)
160 Leeds 1959
107 Calcutta 1963-64
151 Delhi 1963-64
M. H. Denness (2)
118 Lord's 1974
100 Birmingham . 1974
E. R. Dexter (1)
126* Kanpur 1961-62
B. L. D'Oliveira (1)
109† Leeds 1967
J. H. Edrich (1)
100* Manchester.. 1974
T. G. Evans (1)
104 Lord's 1952
K. W. R. Fletcher (2)
113 Bombay 1972-73
123* Manchester.. 1974

G. Fowler (1)
201 Madras 1984-85
M. W. Gatting (3)
136 Bombay 1984-85
207 Madras 1984-85
183* Birmingham . 1986
G. A. Gooch (5)
127 Madras 1981-82
114 Lord's 1986
333 } Lord's 1990
123 }
116 Manchester.. 1990
D. I. Gower (2)
200*† Birmingham . 1979
157* The Oval 1990
T. W. Graveney (2)
175† Bombay 1951-52
151 Lord's 1967
A. W. Greig (3)
148 Bombay 1972-73
106 Lord's 1974
103 Calcutta 1976-77
W. R. Hammond (2)
167 Manchester.. 1936
217 The Oval 1936
J. Hardstaff jun. (1)
205* Lord's 1946
G. A. Hick (1)
178 Bombay 1992-93
L. Hutton (2)
150 Lord's 1952
104 Manchester.. 1952
R. Illingworth (1)
107 Manchester.. 1971
B. R. Knight (1)
127 Kanpur 1963-64
A. J. Lamb (3)
107 The Oval 1982

139 Lord's 1990
109 Manchester.. 1990
A. R. Lewis (1)
125 Kanpur 1972-73
C. C. Lewis (1)
117 Madras 1992-93
D. Lloyd (1)
214* Birmingham . 1974
B. W. Luckhurst (1)
101 Manchester.. 1971
P. B. H. May (1)
106 Nottingham . 1959
P. H. Parfitt (1)
121 Kanpur 1963-64
G. Pullar (2)
131 Manchester.. 1959
119 Kanpur 1961-62
D. W. Randall (1)
126 Lord's 1982
R. T. Robinson (1)
160 Delhi 1984-85
D. S. Sheppard (1)
119 The Oval 1952
M. J. K. Smith (1)
100† Manchester.. 1959
R. A. Smith (2)
100*† Lord's 1990
121* Manchester.. 1990
C. J. Tavaré (1)
149 Delhi 1981-82
B. H. Valentine (1)
136† Bombay 1933-34
C. F. Walters (1)
102 Madras 1933-34
A. J. Watkins (1)
137*† Delhi....... 1951-52
T. S. Worthington (1)
128 The Oval 1936

For India (60)

L. Amarnath (1)
118† Bombay 1933-34
M. Azharuddin (6)
110† Calcutta 1984-85
105 Madras 1984-85
122 Kanpur 1984-85
121 Lord's 1990
179 Manchester.. 1990
182 Calcutta 1992-93
A. A. Baig (1)
112† Manchester.. 1959
F. M. Engineer (1)
121 Bombay 1972-73
S. M. Gavaskar (4)
101 Manchester.. 1974

108 Bombay 1976-77
221 The Oval 1979
172 Bangalore ... 1981-82
Hanumant Singh (1)
105† Delhi....... 1963-64
V. S. Hazare (2)
164* Delhi....... 1951-52
155 Bombay 1951-52
M. L. Jaisimha (2)
127 Delhi....... 1961-62
129 Calcutta 1963-64
V. G. Kambli (1)
224 Bombay 1992-93
Kapil Dev (2)
116 Kanpur 1981-82
110 The Oval ... 1990

S. M. H. Kirmani (1)
102 Bombay 1984-85
B. K. Kunderan (2)
192 Madras 1963-64
100 Delhi....... 1963-64
V. L. Manjrekar (3)
133 Leeds 1952
189* Delhi....... 1961-62
108 Madras 1963-64
V. Mankad (1)
184 Lord's 1952
V. M. Merchant (3)
114 Manchester.. 1936
128 The Oval 1946
154 Delhi....... 1951-52

Mushtaq Ali (1)		**R. J. Shastri** (4)		**D. B. Vengsarkar** (5)	
112 Manchester.. 1936		142 Bombay 1984-85		103 Lord's 1979	
R. G. Nadkarni (1)		111 Calcutta 1984-85		157 Lord's 1982	
122* Kanpur 1963-64		100 Lord's 1990		137 Kanpur 1984-85	
Nawab of Pataudi jun. (3)		187 The Oval ... 1990		126* Lord's 1986	
103 Madras 1961-62		**N. S. Sidhu** (1)		102* Leeds 1986	
203* Delhi....... 1963-64		106 Madras 1992-93		**G. R. Viswanath** (4)	
148 Leeds 1967		**S. R. Tendulkar** (2)		113 Bombay 1972-73	
S. M. Patil (1)		119* Manchester.. 1990		113 Lord's 1979	
129* Manchester.. 1982		165 Madras 1992-93		107 Delhi....... 1981-82	
D. G. Phadkar (1)		**P. R. Umrigar** (3)		222 Madras 1981-82	
115 Calcutta 1951-52		130* Madras 1951-52		**Yashpal Sharma** (1)	
Pankaj Roy (2)		118 Manchester.. 1959		140 Madras 1981-82	
140 Bombay 1951-52		147* Kanpur 1961-62			
111 Madras 1951-52					

† *Signifies hundred on first appearance in England–India Tests.*

Notes: G. A. Gooch's match aggregate of 456 (333 and 123) for England at Lord's in 1990 is the record in Test matches and provides the only instance of a batsman scoring a triple-hundred and a hundred in the same first-class match. His 333 is the highest innings in any match at Lord's.

    M. Azharuddin scored hundreds in each of his first three Tests.

RECORD PARTNERSHIPS FOR EACH WICKET

For England

225 for 1st	G. A. Gooch and M. A. Atherton at Manchester	1990
241 for 2nd	G. Fowler and M. W. Gatting at Madras	1984-85
308 for 3rd	G. A. Gooch and A. J. Lamb at Lord's	1990
266 for 4th	W. R. Hammond and T. S. Worthington at The Oval.........	1936
254 for 5th†	K. W. R. Fletcher and A. W. Greig at Bombay	1972-73
171 for 6th	I. T. Botham and R. W. Taylor at Bombay	1979-80
125 for 7th	D. W. Randall and P. H. Edmonds at Lord's	1982
168 for 8th	R. Illingworth and P. Lever at Manchester.................	1971
83 for 9th	K. W. R. Fletcher and N. Gifford at Madras	1972-73
70 for 10th	P. J. W. Allott and R. G. D. Willis at Lord's.............	1982

For India

213 for 1st	S. M. Gavaskar and C. P. S. Chauhan at The Oval	1979
192 for 2nd	F. M. Engineer and A. L. Wadekar at Bombay	1972-73
316 for 3rd†‡	G. R. Viswanath and Yashpal Sharma at Madras	1981-82
222 for 4th†	V. S. Hazare and V. L. Manjrekar at Leeds	1952
214 for 5th†	M. Azharuddin and R. J. Shastri at Calcutta	1984-85
130 for 6th	S. M. H. Kirmani and Kapil Dev at The Oval	1982
235 for 7th†	R. J. Shastri and S. M. H. Kirmani at Bombay	1984-85
128 for 8th	R. J. Shastri and S. M. H. Kirmani at Delhi	1981-82
104 for 9th	R. J. Shastri and Madan Lal at Delhi	1981-82
51 for 10th {	R. G. Nadkarni and B. S. Chandrasekhar at Calcutta	1963-64
	S. M. H. Kirmani and Chetan Sharma at Madras.............	1984-85

† *Denotes record partnership against all countries.*

‡ *415 runs were added between the fall of the 2nd and 3rd wickets: D. B. Vengsarkar retired hurt when he and Viswanath had added 99 runs.*

TEN WICKETS OR MORE IN A MATCH

For England (7)

10-78 (5-35, 5-43)†	G. O. B. Allen, Lord's	1936
11-145 (7-49, 4-96)†	A. V. Bedser, Lord's	1946
11-93 (4-41, 7-52)	A. V. Bedser, Manchester	1946
13-106 (6-58, 7-48)	I. T. Botham, Bombay	1979-80
11-163 (6-104, 5-59)†	N. A. Foster, Madras	1984-85
10-70 (7-46, 3-24)†	J. K. Lever, Delhi	1976-77
11-153 (7-49, 4-104)	H. Verity, Madras	1933-34

For India (4)

10-177 (6-105, 4-72)	S. A. Durani, Madras	1961-62
12-108 (8-55, 4-53)	V. Mankad, Madras	1951-52
10-188 (4-130, 6-58)	Chetan Sharma, Birmingham	1986
12-181 (6-64, 6-117)†	L. Sivaramakrishnan, Bombay	1984-85

† *Signifies ten wickets or more on first appearance in England–India Tests.*

Note: A. V. Bedser took 11 wickets in a match in each of the first two Tests of his career.

ENGLAND v PAKISTAN

Captains

Season	England	Pakistan	T	E	P	D
1954	L. Hutton[1]	A. H. Kardar	4	1	1	2
1961-62	E. R. Dexter	Imtiaz Ahmed	3	1	0	2
1962	E. R. Dexter[2]	Javed Burki	5	4	0	1
1967	D. B. Close	Hanif Mohammad	3	2	0	1
1968-69	M. C. Cowdrey	Saeed Ahmed	3	0	0	3
1971	R. Illingworth	Intikhab Alam	3	1	0	2
1972-73	A. R. Lewis	Majid Khan	3	0	0	3
1974	M. H. Denness	Intikhab Alam	3	0	0	3
1977-78	J. M. Brearley[3]	Wasim Bari	3	0	0	3
1978	J. M. Brearley	Wasim Bari	3	2	0	1
1982	R. G. D. Willis[4]	Imran Khan	3	2	1	0
1983-84	R. G. D. Willis[5]	Zaheer Abbas	3	0	1	2
1987	M. W. Gatting	Imran Khan	5	0	1	4
1987-88	M. W. Gatting	Javed Miandad	3	0	1	2
1992	G. A. Gooch	Javed Miandad	5	1	2	2
	In England		34	13	5	16
	In Pakistan		18	1	2	15
	Totals		52	14	7	31

Notes: The following deputised for the official touring captain or were appointed by the home authority for only a minor proportion of the series:
[1]D. S. Sheppard (Second and Third). [2]M. C. Cowdrey (Third). [3]G. Boycott (Third). [4]D. I. Gower (Second). [5]D. I. Gower (Second and Third).

HIGHEST INNINGS TOTALS

For England in England: 558-6 dec. at Nottingham	1954
in Pakistan: 546-8 dec. at Faisalabad	1983-84
For Pakistan in England: 708 at The Oval	1987
in Pakistan: 569-9 dec. at Hyderabad	1972-73

LOWEST INNINGS TOTALS

For England in England: 130 at The Oval 1954
         in Pakistan: 130 at Lahore 1987-88

For Pakistan in England: 87 at Lord's 1954
        in Pakistan: 191 at Faisalabad 1987-88

INDIVIDUAL HUNDREDS

For England (44)

D. L. Amiss (3)	182 The Oval.... 1962	**B. W. Luckhurst (1)**
112 Lahore 1972-73	100 Lahore 1968-69	108*† Birmingham . 1971
158 Hyderabad . 1972-73	**E. R. Dexter (2)**	**C. Milburn (1)**
183 The Oval.... 1974	205 Karachi ... 1961-62	139 Karachi 1968-69
C. W. J. Athey (1)	172 The Oval.... 1962	**P. H. Parfitt (4)**
123 Lord's 1987	**B. L. D'Oliveira (2)**	111 Karachi 1961-62
K. F. Barrington (4)	114* Dacca 1968-69	101* Birmingham . 1962
139† Lahore 1961-62	**K. W. R. Fletcher (1)**	119 Leeds 1962
148 Lord's 1967	122 The Oval.... 1974	101* Nottingham . 1962
109* Nottingham . 1967	**M. W. Gatting (2)**	**G. Pullar (1)**
142 The Oval.... 1967	124 Birmingham . 1987	165 Dacca 1961-62
I. T. Botham (2)	150* The Oval.... 1987	**C. T. Radley (1)**
100† Birmingham . 1978	**G. A. Gooch (1)**	106† Birmingham . 1978
108 Lord's 1978	135 Leeds 1992	**D. W. Randall (1)**
G. Boycott (3)	**D. I. Gower (2)**	105 Birmingham . 1982
121* Lord's 1971	152 Faisalabad .. 1983-84	**R. T. Robinson (1)**
112 Leeds 1971	173* Lahore 1983-84	166† Manchester.. 1987
100* Hyderabad .. 1977-78	**T. W. Graveney (3)**	**R. T. Simpson (1)**
B. C. Broad (1)	153 Lord's 1962	101 Nottingham . 1954
116 Faisalabad .. 1987-88	114 Nottingham . 1962	**R. A. Smith (1)**
D. C. S. Compton (1)	105 Karachi 1968-69	127† Birmingham . 1992
278 Nottingham . 1954	**A. P. E. Knott (1)**	**A. J. Stewart (1)**
M. C. Cowdrey (3)	116 Birmingham . 1971	190† Birmingham . 1992
159† Birmingham . 1962		

For Pakistan (33)

Aamir Sohail (1)	**Intikhab Alam (1)**	**Mushtaq Mohammad (3)**
205 Manchester.. 1992	138 Hyderabad .. 1972-73	100* Nottingham . 1962
Alim-ud-Din (1)	**Javed Burki (3)**	100 Birmingham . 1971
109 Karachi 1961-62	138† Lahore 1961-62	157 Hyderabad .. 1972-73
Asif Iqbal (3)	140 Dacca 1961-62	**Nasim-ul Ghani (1)**
146 The Oval.... 1967	101 Lord's 1962	101 Lord's 1962
104* Birmingham . 1971	**Javed Miandad (2)**	**Sadiq Mohammad (1)**
102 Lahore 1972-73	260 The Oval.... 1987	119 Lahore 1972-73
Hanif Mohammad (3)	153* Birmingham . 1992	**Salim Malik (3)**
111 }Dacca 1961-62	**Mohsin Khan (2)**	116 Faisalabad .. 1983-84
104 }	200 Lord's 1982	102 The Oval.... 1987
187* Lord's 1967	104 Lahore 1983-84	165 Birmingham . 1992
Haroon Rashid (2)	**Mudassar Nazar (3)**	**Wasim Raja (1)**
122† Lahore 1977-78	114† Lahore 1977-78	112 Faisalabad .. 1983-84
108 Hyderabad .. 1977-78	124 Birmingham . 1987	**Zaheer Abbas (2)**
Imran Khan (1)	120 Lahore 1987-88	274† Birmingham . 1971
118 The Oval.... 1987		240 The Oval.... 1974

† *Signifies hundred on first appearance in England–Pakistan Tests.*

Note: Three batsmen – Majid Khan, Mushtaq Mohammad and D. L. Amiss – were dismissed for 99 at Karachi, 1972-73: the only instance in Test matches.

RECORD PARTNERSHIPS FOR EACH WICKET

For England

198	for 1st	G. Pullar and R. W. Barber at Dacca	1961-62
248	for 2nd	M. C. Cowdrey and E. R. Dexter at The Oval................	1962
227	for 3rd	A. J. Stewart and R. A. Smith at Birmingham.................	1992
188	for 4th	E. R. Dexter and P. H. Parfitt at Karachi	1961-62
192	for 5th	D. C. S. Compton and T. E. Bailey at Nottingham.............	1954
153*	for 6th	P. H. Parfitt and D. A. Allen at Birmingham.................	1962
167	for 7th	D. I. Gower and V. J. Marks at Faisalabad	1983-84
99	for 8th	P. H. Parfitt and D. A. Allen at Leeds	1962
76	for 9th	T. W. Graveney and F. S. Trueman at Lord's	1962
79	for 10th	R. W. Taylor and R. G. D. Willis at Birmingham.............	1982

For Pakistan

173	for 1st	Mohsin Khan and Shoaib Mohammad at Lahore..............	1983-84
291	for 2nd†	Zaheer Abbas and Mushtaq Mohammad at Birmingham........	1971
180	for 3rd	Mudassar Nazar and Haroon Rashid at Lahore	1977-78
322	for 4th	Javed Miandad and Salim Malik at Birmingham..............	1992
197	for 5th	Javed Burki and Nasim-ul-Ghani at Lord's..................	1962
145	for 6th	Mushtaq Mohammad and Intikhab Alam at Hyderabad........	1972-73
89	for 7th	Ijaz Ahmed and Salim Yousuf at The Oval..................	1987
130	for 8th†	Hanif Mohammad and Asif Iqbal at Lord's	1967
190	for 9th†	Asif Iqbal and Intikhab Alam at The Oval..................	1967
62	for 10th	Sarfraz Nawaz and Asif Masood at Leeds	1974

† *Denotes record partnership against all countries.*

TEN WICKETS OR MORE IN A MATCH

For England (2)

11-83 (6-65, 5-18)†	N. G. B. Cook, Karachi	1983-84
13-71 (5-20, 8-51)	D. L. Underwood, Lord's...........................	1974

For Pakistan (6)

10-194 (5-84, 5-110)	Abdul Qadir, Lahore	1983-84
13-101 (9-56, 4-45)	Abdul Qadir, Lahore	1987-88
10-186 (5-88, 5-98)	Abdul Qadir, Karachi	1987-88
10-211 (7-96, 3-115)	Abdul Qadir, The Oval	1987
12-99 (6-53, 6-46)	Fazal Mahmood, The Oval	1954
10-77 (3-37, 7-40)	Imran Khan, Leeds	1987

† *Signifies ten wickets or more on first appearance in England–Pakistan Tests.*

FOUR WICKETS IN FIVE BALLS

C. M. Old, v Pakistan at Birmingham in 1978, dismissed Wasim Raja, Wasim Bari, Iqbal Qasim and Sikander Bakht to take four wickets in five balls (ww-ww).

ENGLAND v SRI LANKA

Captains

Season	England	Sri Lanka	T	E	SL	D
1981-82	K. W. R. Fletcher	B. Warnapura	1	1	0	0
1984	D. I. Gower	L. R. D. Mendis	1	0	0	1
1988	G. A. Gooch	R. S. Madugalle	1	1	0	0
1991	G. A. Gooch	P. A. de Silva	1	1	0	0
1992-93	A. J. Stewart	A. Ranatunga	1	0	1	0
	In England		3	2	0	1
	In Sri Lanka		2	1	1	0
	Totals..........................		5	3	1	1

HIGHEST INNINGS TOTALS

For England in England: 429 at Lord's.................................... 1988
in Sri Lanka: 380 at Colombo (SSC)........................... 1992-93

For Sri Lanka in England: 491-7 dec. at Lord's.......................... 1984
in Sri Lanka: 469 at Colombo (SSC) 1992-93

LOWEST INNINGS TOTALS

For England in England: 282 at Lord's.................................... 1991
in Sri Lanka: 223 at Colombo (PSS)........................... 1981-82

For Sri Lanka in England: 194 at Lord's 1988
in Sri Lanka: 175 at Colombo (PSS) 1981-82

INDIVIDUAL HUNDREDS

For England (4)

G. A. Gooch (1)			**R. A. Smith** (1)		
174	Lord's	1991	128	Colombo (SSC)	1992-93
A. J. Lamb (1)			**A. J. Stewart** (1)		
107†	Lord's	1984	113*†	Lord's	1991

For Sri Lanka (3)

L. R. D. Mendis (1)			**S. A. R. Silva** (1)			**S. Wettimuny** (1)		
111	Lord's	1984	102*†	Lord's	1984	190	Lord's	1984

† *Signifies hundred on first appearance in England–Sri Lanka Tests.*

BEST BOWLING

Best bowling in an innings for England: 7-70 by P. A. J. DeFreitas at Lord's ... 1991
for Sri Lanka: 5-69 by R. J. Ratnayake at Lord's.... 1991

RECORD PARTNERSHIPS FOR EACH WICKET

For England

78 for 1st	G. A. Gooch and H. Morris at Lord's	1991
139 for 2nd	G. A. Gooch and A. J. Stewart at Lord's	1991
112 for 3rd	R. A. Smith and G. A. Hick at Colombo (SSC)	1992-93
122 for 4th	R. A. Smith and A. J. Stewart at Colombo (SSC)...........	1992-93

40 for 5th	A. J. Stewart and I. T. Botham at Lord's	1991
87 for 6th	A. J. Lamb and R. M. Ellison at Lord's	1984
63 for 7th	A. J. Stewart and R. C. Russell at Lord's	1991
20 for 8th	J. E. Emburey and P. W. Jarvis at Colombo (SSC)	1992-93
37 for 9th	P. J. Newport and N. A. Foster at Lord's	1988
40 for 10th	J. E. Emburey and D. E. Malcolm at Colombo (SSC)	1992-93

For Sri Lanka

99 for 1st	R. S. Mahanama and U. C. Hathurusinghe at Colombo (SSC) .	1992-93
83 for 2nd	B. Warnapura and R. L. Dias at Colombo (PSS)	1981-82
101 for 3rd	S. Wettimuny and R. L. Dias at Lord's	1984
148 for 4th	S. Wettimuny and A. Ranatunga at Lord's	1984
150 for 5th†	S. Wettimuny and L. R. D. Mendis at Lord's	1984
138 for 6th†	S. A. R. Silva and L. R. D. Mendis at Lord's	1984
74 for 7th	U. C. Hathurusinghe and R. J. Ratnayake at Lord's	1991
29 for 8th	R. J. Ratnayake and C. P. H. Ramanayake at Lord's	1991
83 for 9th†	H. P. Tillekeratne and M. Muralitharan at Colombo (SSC)	1992-93
64 for 10th†	J. R. Ratnayeke and G. F. Labrooy at Lord's	1988

† *Denotes record partnership against all countries.*

AUSTRALIA v SOUTH AFRICA

		Captains				
Season	*Australia*	*South Africa*	*T*	*A*	*SA*	*D*
1902-03*S*	J. Darling	H. M. Taberer[1]	3	2	0	1
1910-11*A*	C. Hill	P. W. Sherwell	5	4	1	0
1912*E*	S. E. Gregory	F. Mitchell[2]	3	2	0	1
1921-22*S*	H. L. Collins	H. W. Taylor	3	1	0	2
1931-32*A*	W. M. Woodfull	H. B. Cameron	5	5	0	0
1935-36*S*	V. Y. Richardson	H. F. Wade	5	4	0	1
1949-50*S*	A. L. Hassett	A. D. Nourse	5	4	0	1
1952-53*A*	A. L. Hassett	J. E. Cheetham	5	2	2	1
1957-58*S*	I. D. Craig	C. B. van Ryneveld[3]	5	3	0	2
1963-64*A*	R. B. Simpson[4]	T. L. Goddard	5	1	1	3
1966-67*S*	R. B. Simpson	P. L. van der Merwe	5	1	3	1
1969-70*S*	W. M. Lawry	A. Bacher	4	0	4	0
1993-94*A*	A. R. Border	K. C. Wessels[5]	3	1	1	1
1993-94*S*	A. R. Border	K. C. Wessels	3	1	1	1
	In South Africa		33	16	8	9
	In Australia		23	13	5	5
	In England		3	2	0	1
	Totals		59	31	13	15

S Played in South Africa.   A Played in Australia.   E Played in England.

Notes: The following deputised for the official touring captain or were appointed by the home authority for only a minor proportion of the series:
[1]J. H. Anderson (Second), E. A. Halliwell (Third). [2]L. J. Tancred (Third). [3]D. J. McGlew (First). [4]R. Benaud (First). [5]W. J. Cronje (Third).

HIGHEST INNINGS TOTALS

For Australia in Australia: 578 at Melbourne	1910-11
in South Africa: 549-7 dec. at Port Elizabeth	1949-50
For South Africa in Australia: 595 at Adelaide	1963-64
in South Africa: 622-9 dec. at Durban	1969-70

LOWEST INNINGS TOTALS

For Australia in Australia: 111 at Sydney 1993-94
          in South Africa: 75 at Durban 1949-50

For South Africa in Australia: 36† at Melbourne 1931-32
          in South Africa: 85‡ at Johannesburg 1902-03
                    85‡ at Cape Town..................... 1902-03

† Scored 45 in the second innings giving the smallest aggregate of 81 (12 extras) in Test cricket.
‡ In successive innings.

INDIVIDUAL HUNDREDS

For Australia (58)

W. W. Armstrong (2)
159*‡   Johannesburg   1902-03
132   Melbourne ..   1910-11
W. Bardsley (3)
132†   Sydney   1910-11
121   Manchester .   1912
164   Lord's   1912
R. Benaud (2)
122   Johannesburg   1957-58
100   Johannesburg   1957-58
B. C. Booth (2)
169†   Brisbane   1963-64
102*   Sydney   1963-64
D. G. Bradman (4)
226‡   Brisbane   1931-32
112   Sydney   1931-32
167   Melbourne ..   1931-32
299*   Adelaide   1931-32
W. A. Brown (1)
121   Cape Town ..   1935-36
J. W. Burke (1)
189   Cape Town ..   1957-58
A. G. Chipperfield (1)
109‡   Durban   1935-36
H. L. Collins (1)
203   Johannesburg   1921-22
J. H. Fingleton (3)
112   Cape Town ..   1935-36
108   Johannesburg   1935-36
118   Durban   1935-36

J. M. Gregory (1)
119   Johannesburg   1921-22
R. N. Harvey (8)
178   Cape Town .   1949-50
151*   Durban   1949-50
100   Johannesburg   1949-50
116   Pt Elizabeth .   1949-50
109   Brisbane   1952-53
190   Sydney   1952-53
116   Adelaide   1952-53
205   Melbourne ..   1952-53
A. L. Hassett (3)
112‡   Johannesburg   1949-50
167   Pt Elizabeth .   1949-50
163   Adelaide   1952-53
C. Hill (3)
142†   Johannesburg   1902-03
191   Sydney   1910-11
100   Melbourne ..   1910-11
C. Kelleway (2)
114   Manchester..   1912
102   Lord's   1912
W. M. Lawry (1)
157   Melbourne ..   1963-64
S. J. E. Loxton (1)
101†   Johannesburg   1949-50
C. G. Macartney (2)
137   Sydney   1910-11
116   Durban   1921-22

S. J. McCabe (2)
149   Durban   1935-36
189*   Johannesburg   1935-36
C. C. McDonald (1)
154   Adelaide   1952-53
J. Moroney (2)
118 ⎫
101*⎭   Johannesburg   1949-50
A. R. Morris (2)
111   Johannesburg   1949-50
157   Pt Elizabeth .   1949-50
K. E. Rigg (1)
127†   Sydney   1931-32
J. Ryder (1)
142   Cape Town ..   1921-22
R. B. Simpson (1)
153   Cape Town ..   1966-67
K. R. Stackpole (1)
134   Cape Town ..   1966-67
M. A. Taylor (1)
170†   Melbourne ..   1993-94
V. T. Trumper (2)
159   Melbourne ..   1910-11
214*   Adelaide   1910-11
M. E. Waugh (1)
113*   Durban   1993-94
S. R. Waugh (1)
164‡   Adelaide   1993-94
W. M. Woodfull (1)
161   Melbourne ..   1931-32

For South Africa (38)

E. J. Barlow (5)
114†   Brisbane   1963-64
109   Melbourne ..   1963-64
201   Adelaide   1963-64
127   Cape Town ..   1969-70
110   Johannesburg   1969-70
K. C. Bland (1)
126   Sydney   1963-64
W. J. Cronje (1)
122   Johannesburg   1993-94
W. R. Endean (1)
162*   Melbourne ..   1952-53
G. A. Faulkner (3)
204   Melbourne ..   1910-11

115   Adelaide   1910-11
122*   Manchester..   1912
C. N. Frank (1)
152   Johannesburg   1921-22
A. C. Hudson (1)
102   Cape Town ..   1993-94
B. L. Irvine (1)
102   Pt Elizabeth .   1969-70
D. T. Lindsay (3)
182   Johannesburg   1966-67
137   Durban   1966-67
131   Johannesburg   1966-67
D. J. McGlew (2)
108   Johannesburg   1957-58

105   Durban   1957-58
A. D. Nourse (2)
231   Johannesburg   1935-36
114   Cape Town ..   1949-50
A. W. Nourse (1)
111   Johannesburg   1921-22
R. G. Pollock (5)
122   Sydney   1963-64
175   Adelaide   1963-64
209   Cape Town ..   1966-67
105   Pt Elizabeth .   1966-67
274   Durban   1969-70
B. A. Richards (2)
140   Durban   1969-70

126	Pt Elizabeth . 1969-70	**S. J. Snooke** (1)		134	Durban 1957-58
E. A. B. Rowan (1)		103	Adelaide 1910-11	**J. W. Zulch** (2)	
143	Durban 1949-50	**K. G. Viljoen** (1)		105	Adelaide 1910-11
J. H. Sinclair (2)		111	Melbourne .. 1931-32	150	Sydney 1910-11
101	Johannesburg 1902-03	**J. H. B. Waite** (2)			
104	Cape Town .. 1902-03	115	Johannesburg 1957-58		

† *Signifies hundred on first appearance in Australia–South Africa Tests.*
‡ *Carried his bat.*

RECORD PARTNERSHIPS FOR EACH WICKET

For Australia

233 for 1st	J. H. Fingleton and W. A. Brown at Cape Town	1935-36
275 for 2nd	C. C. McDonald and A. L. Hassett at Adelaide	1952-53
242 for 3rd	C. Kelleway and W. Bardsley at Lord's	1912
169 for 4th	M. A. Taylor and M. E. Waugh at Melbourne	1993-94
208 for 5th	A. R. Border and S. R. Waugh at Adelaide	1993-94
108 for 6th	S. R. Waugh and I. A. Healy at Cape Town	1993-94
160 for 7th	R. Benaud and G. D. McKenzie at Sydney	1963-64
83 for 8th	A. G. Chipperfield and C. V. Grimmett at Durban	1935-36
78 for 9th {	D. G. Bradman and W. J. O'Reilly at Adelaide	1931-32
{	K. D. Mackay and I. Meckiff at Johannesburg	1957-58
82 for 10th	V. S. Ransford and W. J. Whitty at Melbourne	1910-11

For South Africa

176 for 1st	D. J. McGlew and T. L. Goddard at Johannesburg	1957-58
173 for 2nd	L. J. Tancred and C. B. Llewellyn at Johannesburg	1902-03
341 for 3rd†	E. J. Barlow and R. G. Pollock at Adelaide	1963-64
206 for 4th	C. N. Frank and A. W. Nourse at Johannesburg	1921-22
129 for 5th	J. H. B. Waite and W. R. Endean at Johannesburg	1957-58
200 for 6th†	R. G. Pollock and H. R. Lance at Durban	1969-70
221 for 7th	D. T. Lindsay and P. L. van der Merwe at Johannesburg ...	1966-67
124 for 8th†	A. W. Nourse and E. A. Halliwell at Johannesburg	1902-03
85 for 9th	R. G. Pollock and P. M. Pollock at Cape Town	1966-67
53 for 10th	L. A. Stricker and S. J. Pegler at Adelaide	1910-11

† *Denotes record partnership against all countries.*

TEN WICKETS OR MORE IN A MATCH

For Australia (6)

14-199 (7-116, 7-83)	C. V. Grimmett, Adelaide	1931-32
10-88 (5-32, 5-56)	C. V. Grimmett, Cape Town	1935-36
10-110 (3-70, 7-40)	C. V. Grimmett, Johannesburg	1935-36
13-173 (7-100, 6-73)	C. V. Grimmett, Durban	1935-36
11-24 (5-6, 6-18)	H. Ironmonger, Melbourne	1931-32
12-128 (7-56, 5-72)	S. K. Warne, Sydney	1993-94

For South Africa (3)

10-123 (4-80, 6-43)	P. S. de Villiers, Sydney	1993-94
10-116 (5-43, 5-73)	C. B. Llewellyn, Johannesburg	1902-03
13-165 (6-84, 7-81)	H. J. Tayfield, Melbourne	1952-53

Note: C. V. Grimmett took ten wickets or more in three consecutive matches in 1935-36.

AUSTRALIA v WEST INDIES

Captains

Season	Australia	West Indies	T	A	WI	T	D
1930-31*A*	W. M. Woodfull	G. C. Grant	5	4	1	0	0
1951-52*A*	A. L. Hassett[1]	J. D. C. Goddard[2]	5	4	1	0	0
1954-55*W*	I. W. Johnson	D. St E. Atkinson[3]	5	3	0	0	2
1960-61*A*	R. Benaud	F. M. M. Worrell	5	2	1	1	1

THE FRANK WORRELL TROPHY

Captains

Season	Australia	West Indies	T	A	WI	T	D	Held by
1964-65*W*	R. B. Simpson	G. S. Sobers	5	1	2	0	2	WI
1968-69*A*	W. M. Lawry	G. S. Sobers	5	3	1	0	1	A
1972-73*W*	I. M. Chappell	R. B. Kanhai	5	2	0	0	3	A
1975-76*A*	G. S. Chappell	C. H. Lloyd	6	5	1	0	0	A
1977-78*W*	R. B. Simpson	A. I. Kallicharran[4]	5	1	3	0	1	WI
1979-80*A*	G. S. Chappell	C. H. Lloyd[5]	3	0	2	0	1	WI
1981-82*A*	G. S. Chappell	C. H. Lloyd	3	1	1	0	1	WI
1983-84*W*	K. J. Hughes	C. H. Lloyd[6]	5	0	3	0	2	WI
1984-85*A*	A. R. Border[7]	C. H. Lloyd	5	1	3	0	1	WI
1988-89*A*	A. R. Border	I. V. A. Richards	5	1	3	0	1	WI
1990-91*W*	A. R. Border	I. V. A. Richards	5	1	2	0	2	WI
1992-93*A*	A. R. Border	R. B. Richardson	5	1	2	0	2	WI
1994-95*W*	M. A. Taylor	R. B. Richardson	4	2	1	0	1	A

	T	A	WI	T	D
In Australia	47	22	16	1	8
In West Indies	34	10	11	0	13
Totals	81	32	27	1	21

A Played in Australia. W Played in West Indies.

Notes: The following deputised for the official touring captain or were appointed by the home authority for only a minor proportion of the series:
[1]A. R. Morris (Third). [2]J. B. Stollmeyer (Fifth). [3]J. B. Stollmeyer (Second and Third). [4]C. H. Lloyd (First and Second). [5]D. L. Murray (First). [6]I. V. A. Richards (Second). [7]K. J. Hughes (First and Second).

HIGHEST INNINGS TOTALS

For Australia in Australia: 619 at Sydney		1968-69
in West Indies: 758-8 dec. at Kingston		1954-55
For West Indies in Australia: 616 at Adelaide		1968-69
in West Indies: 573 at Bridgetown		1964-65

LOWEST INNINGS TOTALS

For Australia in Australia: 76 at Perth		1984-85
in West Indies: 90 at Port-of-Spain		1977-78
For West Indies in Australia: 78 at Sydney		1951-52
in West Indies: 109 at Georgetown		1972-73

INDIVIDUAL HUNDREDS

For Australia (76)

R. G. Archer (1)
128   Kingston 1954-55
R. Benaud (1)
121   Kingston 1954-55
D. C. Boon (3)
149   Sydney 1988-89
109*   Kingston 1990-91
111   Brisbane 1992-93
B. C. Booth (1)
117   Port-of-Spain 1964-65
A. R. Border (3)
126   Adelaide 1981-82
100*   Port-of-Spain 1983-84
110   Melbourne .. 1992-93
D. G. Bradman (2)
223   Brisbane 1930-31
152   Melbourne .. 1930-31
G. S. Chappell (5)
106   Bridgetown .. 1972-73
123 ⎫
109* ⎬ ‡Brisbane ... 1975-76
182*   Sydney 1975-76
124   Brisbane 1979-80

I. M. Chappell (5)
117†   Brisbane 1968-69
165   Melbourne 1968-69
106*   Bridgetown .. 1972-73
109   Georgetown . 1972-73
156   Perth 1975-76
G. J. Cosier (1)
109†   Melbourne .. 1975-76
R. M. Cowper (2)
143   Port-of-Spain 1964-65
102   Bridgetown .. 1964-65

J. Dyson (1)
127*† Sydney 1981-82
R. N. Harvey (3)
133 Kingston 1954-55
133 Port-of-Spain 1954-55
204 Kingston 1954-55
A. L. Hassett (2)
132 Sydney 1951-52
102 Melbourne .. 1951-52
A. M. J. Hilditch (1)
113† Melbourne 1984-85
K. J. Hughes (2)
130*† Brisbane 1979-80
100* Melbourne .. 1981-82
D. M. Jones (1)
216 Adelaide 1988-89
A. F. Kippax (1)
146† Adelaide 1930-31
W. M. Lawry (4)
210 Bridgetown .. 1964-65
105 Brisbane 1968-69
205 Melbourne .. 1968-69
151 Sydney 1968-69
R. R. Lindwall (1)
118 Bridgetown .. 1954-55
R. B. McCosker (1)
109* Melbourne .. 1975-76

C. C. McDonald (2)
110 Port-of-Spain 1954-55
127 Kingston 1954-55
K. R. Miller (4)
129 Sydney 1951-52
147 Kingston 1954-55
137 Bridgetown .. 1954-55
109 Kingston 1954-55
A. R. Morris (1)
111 Port-of-Spain 1954-55
N. C. O'Neill (1)
181† Brisbane 1960-61
W. B. Phillips (1)
120 Bridgetown .. 1983-84
W. H. Ponsford (2)
183 Sydney 1930-31
109 Brisbane 1930-31
I. R. Redpath (4)
132 Sydney 1968-69
102 Melbourne .. 1975-76
103 Adelaide 1975-76
101 Melbourne .. 1975-76
C. S. Serjeant (1)
124 Georgetown . 1977-78
R. B. Simpson (1)
201 Bridgetown .. 1964-65

K. R. Stackpole (1)
142 Kingston 1972-73
M. A. Taylor (1)
144 St John's.... 1990-91
P. M. Toohey (1)
122 Kingston 1977-78
A. Turner (1)
136 Adelaide 1975-76
K. D. Walters (6)
118 Sydney 1968-69
110 Adelaide 1968-69
242 ⎫Sydney 1968-69
103 ⎭
102* Bridgetown .. 1972-73
112 Port-of-Spain 1972-73
M. E. Waugh (3)
139* St John's.... 1990-91
112 Melbourne .. 1992-93
126 Kingston 1994-95
S. R. Waugh (2)
100 Sydney 1992-93
200 Kingston 1994-95
K. C. Wessels (1)
173 Sydney 1984-85
G. M. Wood (2)
126 Georgetown . 1977-78
111 Perth........ 1988-89

For West Indies (78)

F. C. M. Alexander (1)
108 Sydney 1960-61
K. L. T. Arthurton (1)
157*† Brisbane 1992-93
D. St E. Atkinson (1)
219 Bridgetown .. 1954-55
B. F. Butcher (3)
117 Port-of-Spain 1964-65
101 Sydney 1968-69
118 Adelaide 1968-69
C. C. Depeiza (1)
122 Bridgetown .. 1954-55
P. J. L. Dujon (2)
130 Port-of-Spain 1983-84
139 Perth 1984-85
M. L. C. Foster (1)
125† Kingston 1972-73
R. C. Fredericks (1)
169 Perth........ 1975-76
H. A. Gomes (6)
101† Georgetown . 1977-78
115 Kingston 1977-78
126 Sydney 1981-82
124* Adelaide 1981-82
127 Perth........ 1984-85
120* Adelaide 1984-85
C. G. Greenidge (4)
120* Georgetown . 1977-78
127 Kingston 1983-84
104 Adelaide 1988-89
226 Bridgetown .. 1990-91

D. L. Haynes (5)
103* Georgetown . 1983-84
145 Bridgetown .. 1983-84
100 Perth........ 1988-89
143 Sydney 1988-89
111 Georgetown . 1990-91
G. A. Headley (2)
102* Brisbane 1930-31
105 Sydney 1930-31
C. C. Hunte (1)
110 Melbourne .. 1960-61
A. I. Kallicharran (4)
101 Brisbane 1975-76
127 Port-of-Spain 1977-78
126 Kingston 1977-78
106 Adelaide 1979-80
R. B. Kanhai (5)
117 ⎫
115 ⎭Adelaide 1960-61
129 Bridgetown .. 1964-65
121 Port-of-Spain 1964-65
105 Bridgetown .. 1972-73
B. C. Lara (1)
277 Sydney 1992-93
C. H. Lloyd (6)
129† Brisbane 1968-69
178 Georgetown . 1972-73
149 Perth........ 1975-76
102 Melbourne .. 1975-76
121 Adelaide 1979-80
114 Brisbane 1984-85

F. R. Martin (1)
123* Sydney 1930-31
S. M. Nurse (2)
201 Bridgetown .. 1964-65
137 Sydney 1968-69
I. V. A. Richards (5)
101 Adelaide 1975-76
140 Brisbane 1979-80
178 St John's.... 1983-84
208 Melbourne .. 1984-85
146 Perth........ 1988-89
R. B. Richardson (9)
131* Bridgetown .. 1983-84
154 St John's.... 1983-84
138 Brisbane 1984-85
122 Melbourne .. 1988-89
106 Adelaide 1988-89
104* Kingston 1990-91
182 Georgetown . 1990-91
109 Sydney 1992-93
100 Kingston 1994-95
L. G. Rowe (1)
107 Brisbane 1975-76
P. V. Simmons (1)
110 Melbourne .. 1992-93
O. G. Smith (1)
104† Kingston 1954-55
G. S. Sobers (4)
132 Brisbane 1960-61
168 Sydney 1960-61
110 Adelaide 1968-69
113 Sydney 1968-69

J. B. Stollmeyer (1)
104   Sydney 1951-52

C. L. Walcott (5)
108   Kingston.... 1954-55
126
110 } Port-of-Spain 1954-55

155
110 } Kingston.... 1954-55

E. D. Weekes (1)
139   Port-of-Spain 1954-55

A. B. Williams (1)
100†   Georgetown . 1977-78

F. M. M. Worrell (1)
108   Melbourne .. 1951-52

  † *Signifies hundred on first appearance in Australia–West Indies Tests.*
  ‡ *G. S. Chappell is the only player to score hundreds in both innings of his first Test as captain.*

Note: F. C. M. Alexander and C. C. Depeiza scored the only hundreds of their careers in a Test match.

RECORD PARTNERSHIPS FOR EACH WICKET

For Australia

382 for 1st†	W. M. Lawry and R. B. Simpson at Bridgetown............	1964-65
298 for 2nd	W. M. Lawry and I. M. Chappell at Melbourne............	1968-69
295 for 3rd†	C. C. McDonald and R. N. Harvey at Kingston	1954-55
336 for 4th	W. M. Lawry and K. D. Walters at Sydney	1968-69
220 for 5th	K. R. Miller and R. G. Archer at Kingston	1954-55
206 for 6th	K. R. Miller and R. G. Archer at Bridgetown	1954-55
134 for 7th	A. K. Davidson and R. Benaud at Brisbane	1960-61
137 for 8th	R. Benaud and I. W. Johnson at Kingston	1954-55
114 for 9th	D. M. Jones and M. G. Hughes at Adelaide	1988-89
97 for 10th	T. G. Hogan and R. M. Hogg at Georgetown............	1983-84

For West Indies

250* for 1st	C. G. Greenidge and D. L. Haynes at Georgetown	1983-84
297 for 2nd	D. L. Haynes and R. B. Richardson at Georgetown	1990-91
308 for 3rd	R. B. Richardson and I. V. A. Richards at St John's	1983-84
198 for 4th	L. G. Rowe and A. I. Kallicharran at Brisbane	1975-76
210 for 5th	R. B. Kanhai and M. L. C. Foster at Kingston	1972-73
165 for 6th	R. B. Kanhai and D. L. Murray at Bridgetown	1972-73
347 for 7th†‡	D. St E. Atkinson and C. C. Depeiza at Bridgetown	1954-55
87 for 8th	P. J. L. Dujon and C. E. L. Ambrose at Port-of-Spain	1990-91
122 for 9th	D. A. J. Holford and J. L. Hendriks at Adelaide	1968-69
56 for 10th	J. Garner and C. E. H. Croft at Brisbane	1979-80

  † *Denotes record partnership against all countries.*
  ‡ *Record seventh-wicket partnership in first-class cricket.*

TEN WICKETS OR MORE IN A MATCH

For Australia (11)

11-96 (7-46, 4-50)	A. R. Border, Sydney	1988-89
11-222 (5-135, 6-87)†	A. K. Davidson, Brisbane	1960-61
11-183 (7-87, 4-96)†	C. V. Grimmett, Adelaide	1930-31
10-115 (6-72, 4-43)	N. J. N. Hawke, Georgetown	1964-65
10-144 (6-54, 4-90)	R. G. Holland, Sydney	1984-85
13-217 (5-130, 8-87)	M. G. Hughes, Perth	1988-89
11-79 (7-23, 4-56)	H. Ironmonger, Melbourne	1930-31
11-181 (8-112, 3-69)	G. F. Lawson, Adelaide	1984-85
10-127 (7-83, 3-44)	D. K. Lillee, Melbourne	1981-82
10-159 (8-71, 2-88)	G. D. McKenzie, Melbourne	1968-69
10-185 (3-87, 7-98)	B. Yardley, Sydney	1981-82

For West Indies (4)

10-120 (6-74, 4-46)	C. E. L. Ambrose, Adelaide	1992-93
10-113 (7-55, 3-58)	G. E. Gomez, Sydney..........................	1951-52
11-107 (5-45, 6-62)	M. A. Holding, Melbourne	1981-82
10-107 (5-69, 5-38)	M. D. Marshall, Adelaide	1984-85

† *Signifies ten wickets or more on first appearance in Australia–West Indies Tests.*

AUSTRALIA v NEW ZEALAND

		Captains				
Season	*Australia*	*New Zealand*	*T*	*A*	*NZ*	*D*
1945-46N	W. A. Brown	W. A. Hadlee	1	1	0	0
1973-74A	I. M. Chappell	B. E. Congdon	3	2	0	1
1973-74N	I. M. Chappell	B. E. Congdon	3	1	1	1
1976-77N	G. S. Chappell	G. M. Turner	2	1	0	1
1980-81A	G. S. Chappell	G. P. Howarth[1]	3	2	0	1
1981-82N	G. S. Chappell	G. P. Howarth	3	1	1	1

TRANS-TASMAN TROPHY

		Captains					
Season	*Australia*	*New Zealand*	*T*	*A*	*NZ*	*D*	*Held by*
1985-86A	A. R. Border	J. V. Coney	3	1	2	0	NZ
1985-86N	A. R. Border	J. V. Coney	3	0	1	2	NZ
1987-88A	A. R. Border	J. J. Crowe	3	1	0	2	A
1989-90A	A. R. Border	J. G. Wright	1	0	0	1	A
1989-90N	A. R. Border	J. G. Wright	1	0	1	0	NZ
1992-93N	A. R. Border	M. D. Crowe	3	1	1	1	NZ
1993-94A	A. R. Border	M. D. Crowe[2]	3	2	0	1	A
	In Australia		16	8	2	6	
	In New Zealand		16	5	5	6	
	Totals.........................		32	13	7	12	

A Played in Australia. N Played in New Zealand.

Note: The following deputised for the official touring captain: [1]M. G. Burgess (Second). [2]K. R. Rutherford (Second and Third).

HIGHEST INNINGS TOTALS

For Australia in Australia: 607-6 dec. at Brisbane......................		1993-94
in New Zealand: 552 at Christchurch		1976-77
For New Zealand in Australia: 553-7 dec. at Brisbane		1985-86
in New Zealand: 484 at Wellington		1973-74

LOWEST INNINGS TOTALS

For Australia in Australia: 162 at Sydney...................		1973-74
in New Zealand: 103 at Auckland..........................		1985-86
For New Zealand in Australia: 121 at Perth		1980-81
in New Zealand: 42 at Wellington		1945-46

INDIVIDUAL HUNDREDS

For Australia (30)

D. C. Boon (3)	**G. J. Gilmour** (1)	**K. R. Stackpole** (1)
143 Brisbane 1987-88	101 Christchurch. 1976-77	122† Melbourne .. 1973-74
200 Perth 1989-90	**I. A. Healy** (1)	**M. A. Taylor** (1)
106 Hobart 1993-94	113* Perth 1993-94	142* Perth 1993-94
A. R. Border (5)	**G. R. Marsh** (1)	**K. D. Walters** (3)
152* Brisbane 1985-86	118 Auckland ... 1985-86	104* Auckland ... 1973-74
140 }Christchurch. 1985-86	**R. W. Marsh** (1)	250 Christchurch. 1976-77
114*	132 Adelaide 1973-74	107 Melbourne .. 1980-81
205 Adelaide 1987-88	**G. R. J. Matthews** (2)	**M. E. Waugh** (1)
105 Brisbane 1993-94	115† Brisbane 1985-86	111 Hobart 1993-94
G. S. Chappell (3)	130 Wellington .. 1985-86	**S. R. Waugh** (1)
247* }Wellington .. 1973-74	**I. R. Redpath** (1)	147* Brisbane 1993-94
133	159*‡ Auckland ... 1973-74	**G. M. Wood** (2)
176 Christchurch. 1981-82	**M. J. Slater** (1)	111† Brisbane 1980-81
I. M. Chappell (2)	168 Hobart 1993-94	100 Auckland ... 1981-82
145 }Wellington .. 1973-74		
121		

For New Zealand (19)

J. V. Coney (1)	**M. J. Greatbatch** (1)	**J. F. Reid** (1)
101* Wellington .. 1985-86	146*† Perth 1989-90	108† Brisbane 1985-86
B. E. Congdon (2)	**B. F. Hastings** (1)	**K. R. Rutherford** (1)
132 Wellington .. 1973-74	101 Wellington .. 1973-74	102 Christchurch. 1992-93
107* Christchurch. 1976-77	**A. H. Jones** (2)	**G. M. Turner** (2)
M. D. Crowe (3)	150 Adelaide 1987-88	101 }Christchurch. 1973-74
188 Brisbane 1985-86	143 Perth 1993-94	110*
137 Christchurch. 1985-86	**J. F. M. Morrison** (1)	**J. G. Wright** (2)
137 Adelaide 1987-88	117 Sydney 1973-74	141 Christchurch. 1981-82
B. A. Edgar (1)	**J. M. Parker** (1)	117* Wellington .. 1989-90
161 Auckland ... 1981-82	108 Sydney 1973-74	

† *Signifies hundred on first appearance in Australia–New Zealand Tests.*
‡ *Carried his bat.*

Notes: G. S. and I. M. Chappell at Wellington in 1973-74 provide the only instance in Test matches of brothers both scoring a hundred in each innings and in the same Test.

RECORD PARTNERSHIPS FOR EACH WICKET

For Australia

198 for 1st	M. J. Slater and M. A. Taylor at Perth	1993-94
235 for 2nd	M. J. Slater and D. C. Boon at Hobart	1993-94
264 for 3rd	I. M. Chappell and G. S. Chappell at Wellington	1973-74
150 for 4th	M. E. Waugh and A. R. Border at Hobart	1993-94
213 for 5th	G. M. Ritchie and G. R. J. Matthews at Wellington...........	1985-86
197 for 6th	A. R. Border and G. R. J. Matthews at Brisbane	1985-86
217 for 7th†	K. D. Walters and G. J. Gilmour at Christchurch.............	1976-77
93 for 8th	G. J. Gilmour and K. J. O'Keeffe at Auckland	1976-77
69 for 9th	I. A. Healy and C. J. McDermott at Perth	1993-94
60 for 10th	K. D. Walters and J. D. Higgs at Melbourne	1980-81

For New Zealand

111	for 1st	M. J. Greatbatch and J. G. Wright at Wellington	1992-93
128*	for 2nd	J. G. Wright and A. H. Jones at Wellington	1989-90
224	for 3rd	J. F. Reid and M. D. Crowe at Brisbane	1985-86
229	for 4th†	B. E. Congdon and B. F. Hastings at Wellington	1973-74
88	for 5th	J. V. Coney and M. G. Burgess at Perth	1980-81
109	for 6th	K. R. Rutherford and J. V. Coney at Wellington	1985-86
132*	for 7th	J. V. Coney and R. J. Hadlee at Wellington	1985-86
88*	for 8th	M. J. Greatbatch and M. C. Snedden at Perth	1989-90
73	for 9th	H. J. Howarth and D. R. Hadlee at Christchurch	1976-77
124	for 10th	J. G. Bracewell and S. L. Boock at Sydney	1985-86

† *Denotes record partnership against all countries.*

TEN WICKETS OR MORE IN A MATCH

For Australia (2)

10-174 (6-106, 4-68)	R. G. Holland, Sydney	1985-86
11-123 (5-51, 6-72)	D. K. Lillee, Auckland	1976-77

For New Zealand (4)

10-106 (4-74, 6-32)	J. G. Bracewell, Auckland	1985-86
15-123 (9-52, 6-71)	R. J. Hadlee, Brisbane	1985-86
11-155 (5-65, 6-90)	R. J. Hadlee, Perth	1985-86
10-176 (5-109, 5-67)	R. J. Hadlee, Melbourne	1987-88

AUSTRALIA v INDIA

		Captains					
Season	Australia	India	T	A	I	T	D
1947-48*A*	D. G. Bradman	L. Amarnath	5	4	0	0	1
1956-57*I*	I. W. Johnson[1]	P. R. Umrigar	3	2	0	0	1
1959-60*I*	R. Benaud	G. S. Ramchand	5	2	1	0	2
1964-65*I*	R. B. Simpson	Nawab of Pataudi jun.	3	1	1	0	1
1967-68*A*	R. B. Simpson[2]	Nawab of Pataudi jun.[3]	4	4	0	0	0
1969-70*I*	W. M. Lawry	Nawab of Pataudi jun.	5	3	1	0	1
1977-78*A*	R. B. Simpson	B. S. Bedi	5	3	2	0	0
1979-80*I*	K. J. Hughes	S. M. Gavaskar	6	0	2	0	4
1980-81*A*	G. S. Chappell	S. M. Gavaskar	3	1	1	0	1
1985-86*A*	A. R. Border	Kapil Dev	3	0	0	0	3
1986-87*I*	A. R. Border	Kapil Dev	3	0	0	1	2
1991-92*A*	A. R. Border	M. Azharuddin	5	4	0	0	1
	In Australia		25	16	3	0	6
	In India		25	8	5	1	11
	Totals		50	24	8	1	17

A Played in Australia. I Played in India.

Notes: The following deputised for the official touring captain or were appointed by the home authority for only a minor proportion of the series:
[1]R. R. Lindwall (Second). [2]W. M. Lawry (Third and Fourth). [3]C. G. Borde (First).

HIGHEST INNINGS TOTALS

For Australia in Australia: 674 at Adelaide 1947-48
      in India: 574-7 dec. at Madras 1986-87

For India in Australia: 600-4 dec. at Sydney 1985-86
     in India: 517-5 dec. at Bombay 1986-87

LOWEST INNINGS TOTALS

For Australia in Australia: 83 at Melbourne 1980-81
      in India: 105 at Kanpur 1959-60

For India in Australia: 58 at Brisbane 1947-48
     in India: 135 at Delhi 1959-60

INDIVIDUAL HUNDREDS

For Australia (51)

S. G. Barnes (1)
112	Adelaide	1947-48

D. C. Boon (6)
123†	Adelaide	1985-86
131	Sydney	1985-86
122	Madras	1986-87
129*	Sydney	1991-92
135	Adelaide	1991-92
107	Perth	1991-92

A. R. Border (4)
162†	Madras	1979-80
124	Melbourne	1980-81
163	Melbourne	1985-86
106	Madras	1986-87

D. G. Bradman (4)
185†	Brisbane	1947-48
132		
127* }	Melbourne	1947-48
201	Adelaide	1947-48

J. W. Burke (1)
161	Bombay	1956-57

G. S. Chappell (1)
204†	Sydney	1980-81

I. M. Chappell (2)
151	Melbourne	1967-68
138	Delhi	1969-70

R. M. Cowper (2)
108	Adelaide	1967-68
165	Sydney	1967-68

L. E. Favell (1)
101	Madras	1959-60

R. N. Harvey (4)
153	Melbourne	1947-48
140	Bombay	1956-57
114	Delhi	1959-60
102	Bombay	1959-60

A. L. Hassett (1)
198*	Adelaide	1947-48

K. J. Hughes (2)
100	Madras	1979-80
213	Adelaide	1980-81

D. M. Jones (2)
210†	Madras	1986-87
150*	Perth	1991-92

W. M. Lawry (1)
100	Melbourne	1967-68

A. L. Mann (1)
105	Perth	1977-78

G. R. Marsh (1)
101	Bombay	1986-87

G. R. J. Matthews (1)
100*	Melbourne	1985-86

T. M. Moody (1)
101†	Perth	1991-92

A. R. Morris (1)
100*	Melbourne	1947-48

N. C. O'Neill (2)
163	Bombay	1959-60
113	Calcutta	1959-60

G. M. Ritchie (1)
128†	Adelaide	1985-86

A. P. Sheahan (1)
114	Kanpur	1969-70

R. B. Simpson (4)
103	Adelaide	1967-68
109	Melbourne	1967-68
176	Perth	1977-78
100	Adelaide	1977-78

K. R. Stackpole (1)
103†	Bombay	1969-70

M. A. Taylor (1)
100	Adelaide	1991-92

K. D. Walters (1)
102	Madras	1969-70

G. M. Wood (1)
125	Adelaide	1980-81

G. N. Yallop (2)
121†	Adelaide	1977-78
167	Calcutta	1979-80

For India (35)

M. Amarnath (2)		**M. L. Jaisimha** (1)	
100	Perth......	1977-78	101	Brisbane	1967-68
138	Sydney	1985-86	**Kapil Dev** (1)	
M. Azharuddin (1)			119	Madras	1986-87
106	Adelaide	1991-92	**S. M. H. Kirmani** (1)	
N. J. Contractor (1)			101*	Bombay	1979-80
108	Bombay ...	1959-60	**V. Mankad** (2)	
S. M. Gavaskar (8)			116	Melbourne ..	1947-48
113†	Brisbane ...	1977-78	111	Melbourne ..	1947-48
127	Perth......	1977-78	**Nawab of Pataudi jun.** (1)	
118	Melbourne ..	1977-78	128*†	Madras	1964-65
115	Delhi......	1979-80	**S. M. Patil** (1)	
123	Bombay	1979-80	174	Adelaide	1980-81
166*	Adelaide	1985-86	**D. G. Phadkar** (1)	
172	Sydney	1985-86	123	Adelaide	1947-48
103	Bombay	1986-87	**G. S. Ramchand** (1)	
V. S. Hazare (2)			109	Bombay	1956-57

R. J. Shastri (2)		
121*	Bombay	1986-87
206	Sydney	1991-92
K. Srikkanth (1)		
116	Sydney	1985-86
S. R. Tendulkar (2)		
148*	Sydney	1991-92
114	Perth.......	1991-92
D. B. Vengsarkar (2)		
112	Bangalore ...	1979-80
164*	Bombay	1986-87
G. R. Viswanath (4)		
137†	Kanpur	1969-70
161*	Bangalore ...	1979-80
131	Delhi.......	1979-80
114	Melbourne ..	1980-81
Yashpal Sharma (1)		
100*	Delhi	1979-80

116 ⎫ Adelaide 1947-48
145 ⎭

† *Signifies hundred on first appearance in Australia–India Tests.*

RECORD PARTNERSHIPS FOR EACH WICKET

For Australia

217	for 1st	D. C. Boon and G. R. Marsh at Sydney	1985-86
236	for 2nd	S. G. Barnes and D. G. Bradman at Adelaide	1947-48
222	for 3rd	A. R. Border and K. J. Hughes at Madras	1979-80
178	for 4th	D. M. Jones and A. R. Border at Madras	1986-87
223*	for 5th	A. R. Morris and D. G. Bradman at Melbourne............	1947-48
151	for 6th	T. R. Veivers and B. N. Jarman at Bombay	1964-65
66	for 7th	G. R. J. Matthews and R. J. Bright at Melbourne	1985-86
73	for 8th	T. R. Veivers and G. D. McKenzie at Madras	1964-65
87	for 9th	I. W. Johnson and W. P. A. Crawford at Madras	1956-57
77	for 10th	A. R. Border and D. R. Gilbert at Melbourne	1985-86

For India

192	for 1st	S. M. Gavaskar and C. P. S. Chauhan at Bombay	1979-80
224	for 2nd	S. M. Gavaskar and M. Amarnath at Sydney	1985-86
159	for 3rd	S. M. Gavaskar and G. R. Viswanath at Delhi	1979-80
159	for 4th	D. B. Vengsarkar and G. R. Viswanath at Bangalore	1979-80
196	for 5th	R. J. Shastri and S. R. Tendulkar at Sydney	1991-92
298*	for 6th†	D. B. Vengsarkar and R. J. Shastri at Bombay	1986-87
132	for 7th	V. S. Hazare and H. R. Adhikari at Adelaide.............	1947-48
127	for 8th	S. M. H. Kirmani and K. D. Ghavri at Bombay	1979-80
81	for 9th	S. R. Tendulkar and K. S. More at Perth	1991-92
94	for 10th	S. M. Gavaskar and N. S. Yadav at Adelaide.............	1985-86

† *Denotes record partnership against all countries.*

TEN WICKETS OR MORE IN A MATCH

For Australia (11)

11-105 (6-52, 5-53)	R. Benaud, Calcutta	1956-57
12-124 (5-31, 7-93)	A. K. Davidson, Kanpur	1959-60

12-166 (5-99, 7-67)	G. Dymock, Kanpur	1979-80
10-168 (5-76, 5-92)	C. J. McDermott, Adelaide	1991-92
10-91 (6-58, 4-33)†	G. D. McKenzie, Madras	1964-65
10-151 (7-66, 3-85)	G. D. McKenzie, Melbourne	1967-68
10-144 (5-91, 5-53)	A. A. Mallett, Madras	1969-70
10-249 (5-103, 5-146)	G. R. J. Matthews, Madras	1986-87
12-126 (6-66, 6-60)	B. A. Reid, Melbourne	1991-92
11-31 (5-2, 6-29)†	E. R. H. Toshack, Brisbane	1947-48
11-95 (4-68, 7-27)	M. R. Whitney, Perth	1991-92

For India (6)

10-194 (5-89, 5-105)	B. S. Bedi, Perth	1977-78
12-104 (6-52, 6-52)	B. S. Chandrasekhar, Melbourne	1977-78
10-130 (7-49, 3-81)	Ghulam Ahmed, Calcutta	1956-57
11-122 (5-31, 6-91)	R. G. Nadkarni, Madras	1964-65
14-124 (9-69, 5-55)	J. M. Patel, Kanpur	1959-60
10-174 (4-100, 6-74)	E. A. S. Prasanna, Madras	1969-70

† *Signifies ten wickets or more on first appearance in Australia–India Tests.*

AUSTRALIA v PAKISTAN

		Captains				
Season	Australia	Pakistan	T	A	P	D
1956-57 P	I. W. Johnson	A. H. Kardar	1	0	1	0
1959-60 P	R. Benaud	Fazal Mahmood[1]	3	2	0	1
1964-65 P	R. B. Simpson	Hanif Mohammad	1	0	0	1
1964-65 A	R. B. Simpson	Hanif Mohammad	1	0	0	1
1972-73 A	I. M. Chappell	Intikhab Alam	3	3	0	0
1976-77 A	G. S. Chappell	Mushtaq Mohammad	3	1	1	1
1978-79 A	G. N. Yallop[2]	Mushtaq Mohammad	2	1	1	0
1979-80 P	G. S. Chappell	Javed Miandad	3	0	1	2
1981-82 A	G. S. Chappell	Javed Miandad	3	2	1	0
1982-83 P	K. J. Hughes	Imran Khan	3	0	3	0
1983-84 A	K. J. Hughes	Imran Khan[3]	5	2	0	3
1988-89 P	A. R. Border	Javed Miandad	3	0	1	2
1989-90 A	A. R. Border	Imran Khan	3	1	0	2
1994-95 P	M. A. Taylor	Salim Malik	3	0	1	2
	In Pakistan		17	2	7	8
	In Australia		20	10	3	7
	Totals		37	12	10	15

A Played in Australia. P Played in Pakistan.

Notes: The following deputised for the official touring captain or were appointed by the home authority for only a minor proportion of the series:
[1]Imtiaz Ahmed (Second). [2]K. J. Hughes (Second). [3]Zaheer Abbas (First, Second and Third).

HIGHEST INNINGS TOTALS

For Australia in Australia: 585 at Adelaide		1972-73
in Pakistan: 617 at Faisalabad		1979-80
For Pakistan in Australia: 624 at Adelaide		1983-84
in Pakistan: 537 at Rawalpindi		1994-95

LOWEST INNINGS TOTALS

For Australia in Australia: 125 at Melbourne 1981-82
     in Pakistan: 80 at Karachi 1956-57

For Pakistan in Australia: 62 at Perth 1981-82
     in Pakistan: 134 at Dacca 1959-60

INDIVIDUAL HUNDREDS

For Australia (39)

J. Benaud (1)
142 Melbourne .. 1972-73
D. C. Boon (1)
114* Karachi 1994-95
A. R. Border (6)
105† Melbourne .. 1978-79
150* ⎫
153 ⎬Lahore 1979-80
118 Brisbane 1983-84
117* Adelaide 1983-84
113* Faisalabad .. 1988-89
G. S. Chappell (6)
116* Melbourne .. 1972-73
121 Melbourne .. 1976-77
235 Faisalabad .. 1979-80
201 Brisbane 1981-82
150* Brisbane 1983-84
182 Sydney 1983-84
I. M. Chappell (1)
196 Adelaide 1972-73
G. J. Cosier (1)
168 Melbourne .. 1976-77

I. C. Davis (1)
105† Adelaide 1976-77
K. J. Hughes (2)
106 Perth....... 1981-82
106 Adelaide 1983-84
D. M. Jones (2)
116 ⎫
121* ⎬Adelaide 1989-90
R. B. McCosker (1)
105 Melbourne.. 1976-77
R. W. Marsh (1)
118† Adelaide 1972-73
N. C. O'Neill (1)
134 Lahore...... 1959-60
W. B. Phillips (1)
159† Perth....... 1983-84
I. R. Redpath (1)
135 Melbourne.. 1972-73
G. M. Ritchie (1)
106* Faisalabad .. 1982-83

A. P. Sheahan (1)
127 Melbourne .. 1972-73
R. B. Simpson (2)
153 ⎫
115 ⎬†Karachi 1964-65
M. J. Slater (1)
110 Rawalpindi.. 1994-95
M. A. Taylor (2)
101† Melbourne .. 1989-90
101* Sydney 1989-90
K. D. Walters (1)
107 Melbourne .. 1976-77
K. C. Wessels (1)
179 Adelaide 1983-84
G. M. Wood (1)
100 Melbourne .. 1981-82
G. N. Yallop (3)
172 Faisalabad .. 1979-80
141 Perth 1983-84
268 Melbourne .. 1983-84

For Pakistan (35)

Aamir Sohail (1)
105 Lahore 1994-95
Asif Iqbal (3)
152* Adelaide 1976-77
120 Sydney 1976-77
134* Perth 1978-79
Hanif Mohammad (2)
101* Karachi 1959-60
104 Melbourne .. 1964-65
Ijaz Ahmed (2)
122 Faisalabad .. 1988-89
121 Melbourne .. 1989-90
Imran Khan (1)
136 Adelaide 1989-90
Javed Miandad (6)
129* Perth 1978-79
106* Faisalabad .. 1979-80
138 Lahore 1982-83

131 Adelaide 1983-84
211 Karachi 1988-89
107 Faisalabad .. 1988-89
Khalid Ibadulla (1)
166† Karachi 1964-65
Majid Khan (3)
158 Melbourne .. 1972-73
108 Melbourne .. 1978-79
110* Lahore 1979-80
Mansoor Akhtar (1)
111 Faisalabad .. 1982-83
Mohsin Khan (3)
135 Lahore 1982-83
149 Adelaide 1983-84
152 Melbourne .. 1983-84
Moin Khan (1)
115*† Lahore 1994-95

Mushtaq Mohammad (1)
121 Sydney 1972-73
Qasim Omar (1)
113 Adelaide 1983-84
Sadiq Mohammad (2)
137 Melbourne .. 1972-73
105 Melbourne .. 1976-77
Saeed Ahmed (1)
166 Lahore 1959-60
Salim Malik (2)
237 Rawalpindi.. 1994-95
143 Lahore 1994-95
Taslim Arif (1)
210* Faisalabad .. 1979-80
Wasim Akram (1)
123 Adelaide 1989-90
Zaheer Abbas (2)
101 Adelaide 1976-77
126 Faisalabad .. 1982-83

† *Signifies hundred on first appearance in Australia–Pakistan Tests.*

RECORD PARTNERSHIPS FOR EACH WICKET

For Australia

176 for 1st	M. A. Taylor and M. J. Slater at Rawalpindi...............	1994-95
259 for 2nd	W. B. Phillips and G. N. Yallop at Perth.................	1983-84
203 for 3rd	G. N. Yallop and K. J. Hughes at Melbourne.............	1983-84
217 for 4th	G. S. Chappell and G. N. Yallop at Faisalabad..........	1979-80
171 for 5th	{ G. S. Chappell and G. J. Cosier at Melbourne.........	1976-77
	{ A. R. Border and G. S. Chappell at Brisbane...........	1983-84
139 for 6th	R. M. Cowper and T. R. Veivers at Melbourne..........	1964-65
185 for 7th	G. N. Yallop and G. R. J. Matthews at Melbourne......	1983-84
117 for 8th	G. J. Cosier and K. J. O'Keeffe at Melbourne..........	1976-77
83 for 9th	J. R. Watkins and R. A. L. Massie at Sydney............	1972-73
52 for 10th	{ D. K. Lillee and M. H. N. Walker at Sydney...........	1976-77
	{ G. F. Lawson and T. M. Alderman at Lahore...........	1982-83

For Pakistan

249 for 1st†	Khalid Ibadulla and Abdul Kadir at Karachi............	1964-65
233 for 2nd	Mohsin Khan and Qasim Omar at Adelaide..............	1983-84
223* for 3rd	Taslim Arif and Javed Miandad at Faisalabad...........	1979-80
155 for 4th	Mansoor Akhtar and Zaheer Abbas at Faisalabad.......	1982-83
186 for 5th	Javed Miandad and Salim Malik at Adelaide............	1983-84
196 for 6th	Salim Malik and Aamir Sohail at Lahore...............	1994-95
104 for 7th	Intikhab Alam and Wasim Bari at Adelaide.............	1972-73
111 for 8th	Majid Khan and Imran Khan at Lahore.................	1979-80
56 for 9th	Intikhab Alam and Afaq Hussain at Melbourne..........	1964-65
87 for 10th	Asif Iqbal and Iqbal Qasim at Adelaide................	1976-77

† *Denotes record partnership against all countries.*

TEN WICKETS OR MORE IN A MATCH

For Australia (3)

10-111 (7-87, 3-24)†	R. J. Bright, Karachi..........................	1979-80
10-135 (6-82, 4-53)	D. K. Lillee, Melbourne........................	1976-77
11-118 (5-32, 6-86)†	C. G. Rackemann, Perth........................	1983-84

For Pakistan (6)

11-218 (4-76, 7-142)	Abdul Qadir, Faisalabad........................	1982-83
13-114 (6-34, 7-80)†	Fazal Mahmood, Karachi.......................	1956-57
12-165 (6-102, 6-63)	Imran Khan, Sydney...........................	1976-77
11-118 (4-69, 7-49)	Iqbal Qasim, Karachi..........................	1979-80
11-125 (2-39, 9-86)	Sarfraz Nawaz, Melbourne......................	1978-79
11-160 (6-62, 5-98)†	Wasim Akram, Melbourne......................	1989-90

† *Signifies ten wickets or more on first appearance in Australia–Pakistan Tests.*

AUSTRALIA v SRI LANKA

Captains

Season	Australia	Sri Lanka	T	A	SL	D
1982-83S	G. S. Chappell	L. R. D. Mendis	1	1	0	0
1987-88A	A. R. Border	R. S. Madugalle	1	1	0	0
1989-90A	A. R. Border	A. Ranatunga	2	1	0	1
1992-93S	A. R. Border	A. Ranatunga	3	1	0	2
	In Australia....................		3	2	0	1
	In Sri Lanka...................		4	2	0	2
	Totals......................		7	4	0	3

A Played in Australia. S Played in Sri Lanka.

INNINGS TOTALS

Highest innings total for Australia: 514-4 dec. at Kandy 1982-83
for Sri Lanka: 547-8 dec. at Colombo (SSC) 1992-93

Lowest innings total for Australia: 224 at Hobart 1989-90
for Sri Lanka: 153 at Perth 1987-88

INDIVIDUAL HUNDREDS

For Australia (10)

A. R. Border (1)
106   Moratuwa... 1992-93
D. W. Hookes (1)
143*† Kandy....... 1982-83
D. M. Jones (3)
102†   Perth....... 1987-88

118*   Hobart 1989-90
100*   Colombo (KS) 1992-93
T. M. Moody (1)
106†   Brisbane 1989-90
M. A. Taylor (2)
164†   Brisbane 1989-90
108   Hobart 1989-90

S. R. Waugh (1)
134*   Hobart 1989-90
K. C. Wessels (1)
141†   Kandy....... 1982-83

For Sri Lanka (4)

P. A. de Silva (1)
167   Brisbane 1989-90
A. P. Gurusinha (1)
137   Colombo (SSC) 1992-93

A. Ranatunga (1)
127   Colombo (SSC) 1992-93
R. S. Kaluwitharana (1)
132*† Colombo (SSC) 1992-93

† *Signifies hundred on first appearance in Australia–Sri Lanka Tests.*

RECORD PARTNERSHIPS FOR EACH WICKET

For Australia

120	for 1st	G. R. Marsh and D. C. Boon at Perth......................	1987-88
170	for 2nd	K. C. Wessels and G. N. Yallop at Kandy	1982-83
158	for 3rd	T. M. Moody and A. R. Border at Brisbane	1989-90
163	for 4th	M. A. Taylor and A. R. Border at Hobart..................	1989-90
155*	for 5th	D. W. Hookes and A. R. Border at Kandy	1982-83
260*	for 6th	D. M. Jones and S. R. Waugh at Hobart	1989-90
129	for 7th	G. R. J. Matthews and I. A. Healy at Moratuwa	1992-93
56	for 8th	G. R. J. Matthews and C. J. McDermott at Colombo (SSC)....	1992-93
45	for 9th	I. A. Healy and S. K. Warne at Colombo (SSC)............	1992-93
49	for 10th	I. A. Healy and M. R. Whitney at Colombo (SSC)	1992-93

For Sri Lanka

110	for 1st	R. S. Mahanama and U. C. Hathurusinghe at Colombo (KS) ...	1992-93
92	for 2nd	R. S. Mahanama and A. P. Gurusinha at Colombo (SSC).....	1992-93
107	for 3rd	{ U. C. Hathurusinghe and P. A. de Silva at Colombo (KS) ...	1992-93
		R. S. Mahanama and P. A. de Silva at Moratuwa	1992-93
230	for 4th	A. P. Gurusinha and A. Ranatunga at Colombo (SSC)	1992-93
116	for 5th	H. P. Tillekeratne and A. Ranatunga at Moratuwa	1992-93
96	for 6th	A. Ranatunga and R. S. Kaluwitharana at Colombo (SSC)	1992-93
144	for 7th†	P. A. de Silva and J. R. Ratnayeke at Brisbane	1989-90
33	for 8th	A. Ranatunga and C. P. H. Ramanayake at Perth	1987-88
44*	for 9th	R. S. Kaluwitharana and A. W. R. Madurasinghe at Colombo (SSC)	1992-93
27	for 10th	P. A. de Silva and C. P. H. Ramanayake at Brisbane	1989-90

† *Denotes record partnership against all countries.*

BEST MATCH BOWLING ANALYSES
For Australia
8-156 (3-68, 5-88) M. G. Hughes, Hobart 1989-90

For Sri Lanka
8-157 (5-82, 3-75) C. P. H. Ramanayake, Moratuwa 1992-93

SOUTH AFRICA v WEST INDIES

Season	South Africa	Captains West Indies	T	SA	WI	D
1991-92 W	K. C. Wessels	R. B. Richardson	1	0	1	0

W Played in West Indies.

HIGHEST INNINGS TOTALS

For South Africa: 345 at Bridgetown 1991-92

For West Indies: 283 at Bridgetown 1991-92

INDIVIDUAL HUNDREDS
For South Africa (1)
A. C. Hudson (1)
163† Bridgetown .. 1991-92

Highest score for West Indies: 79* by J. C. Adams.
† *Signifies hundred on first appearance in South Africa–West Indies Tests.*

HIGHEST PARTNERSHIPS
For South Africa
125 for 2nd A. C. Hudson and K. C. Wessels at Bridgetown.............. 1991-92

For West Indies
99 for 1st D. L. Haynes and P. V. Simmons at Bridgetown 1991-92

BEST MATCH BOWLING ANALYSES
For South Africa
8-158 (4-84, 4-74) R. P. Snell, Bridgetown 1991-92

For West Indies
8-81 (2-47, 6-34) C. E. L. Ambrose, Bridgetown 1991-92

SOUTH AFRICA v NEW ZEALAND

Season	South Africa	*Captains* New Zealand	T	SA	NZ	D
1931-32*N*	H. B. Cameron	M. L. Page	2	2	0	0
1952-53*N*	J. E. Cheetham	W. M. Wallace	2	1	0	1
1953-54*S*	J. E. Cheetham	G. O. Rabone[1]	5	4	0	1
1961-62*S*	D. J. McGlew	J. R. Reid	5	2	2	1
1963-64*N*	T. L. Goddard	J. R. Reid	3	0	0	3
1994-95*S*	W. J. Cronje	K. R. Rutherford	3	2	1	0
1994-95*N*	W. J. Cronje	K. R. Rutherford	1	1	0	0
	In New Zealand		8	4	0	4
	In South Africa		13	8	3	2
	Totals..........................		21	12	3	6

N Played in New Zealand. S Played in South Africa.

Note: The following deputised for the official touring captain:
[1]B. Sutcliffe (Fourth and Fifth).

HIGHEST INNINGS TOTALS

For South Africa in South Africa: 464 at Johannesburg 1961-62
in New Zealand: 524-8 at Wellington 1952-53

For New Zealand in South Africa: 505 at Cape Town 1953-54
in New Zealand: 364 at Wellington 1931-32

LOWEST INNINGS TOTALS

For South Africa in South Africa: 148 at Johannesburg 1953-54
in New Zealand: 223 at Dunedin 1963-64

For New Zealand in South Africa: 79 at Johannesburg 1953-54
in New Zealand: 138 at Dunedin 1963-64

INDIVIDUAL HUNDREDS

For South Africa (14)

X. C. Balaskas (1)
122* Wellington .. 1931-32
J. A. J. Christy (1)
103† Christchurch. 1931-32
W. J. Cronje (2)
112   Cape Town . 1994-95
101   Auckland .. 1994-95
W. R. Endean (1)
116   Auckland ... 1952-53

D. J. McGlew (3)
255*† Wellington .. 1952-53
127*‡ Durban 1961-62
120   Johannesburg 1961-62
R. A. McLean (2)
101   Durban 1953-54
113   Cape Town . 1961-62
B. Mitchell (1)
113† Christchurch. 1931-32

A. R. A. Murray (1)
109† Wellington .. 1952-53
D. J. Richardson (1)
109   Cape Town . 1994-95
J. H. B. Waite (1)
101   Johannesburg 1961-62

For New Zealand (7)

P. T. Barton (1)	**J. R. Reid** (2)	**H. G. Vivian** (1)
109 Pt Elizabeth . 1961-62	135 Cape Town .. 1953-54	100† Wellington .. 1931-32
P. G. Z. Harris (1)	142 Johannesburg 1961-62	
101 Cape Town.. 1961-62	**B. W. Sinclair** (1)	
G. O. Rabone (1)	138 Auckland ... 1963-64	
107 Durban..... 1953-54		

† *Signifies hundred on first appearance in South Africa–New Zealand Tests.*
‡ *Carried his bat.*

RECORD PARTNERSHIPS FOR EACH WICKET

For South Africa

196 for 1st	J. A. J. Christy and B. Mitchell at Christchurch	1931-32
97 for 2nd	G. Kirsten and J. B. Commins at Durban	1994-95
112 for 3rd	D. J. McGlew and R. A. McLean at Johannesburg	1961-62
135 for 4th	K. J. Funston and R. A. McLean at Durban	1953-54
130 for 5th	W. R. Endean and J. E. Cheetham at Auckland	1952-53
83 for 6th	K. C. Bland and D. T. Lindsay at Auckland	1963-64
246 for 7th†	D. J. McGlew and A. R. A. Murray at Wellington	1952-53
95 for 8th	J. E. Cheetham and H. J. Tayfield at Cape Town	1953-54
60 for 9th	P. M. Pollock and N. A. T. Adcock at Port Elizabeth	1961-62
47 for 10th	D. J. McGlew and H. D. Bromfield at Port Elizabeth	1961-62

For New Zealand

126 for 1st	G. O. Rabone and M. E. Chapple at Cape Town	1953-54
72 for 2nd	D. J. Murray and S. P. Fleming at Johannesburg	1994-95
94 for 3rd	M. B. Poore and B. Sutcliffe at Cape Town	1953-54
171 for 4th	B. W. Sinclair and S. N. McGregor at Auckland	1963-64
174 for 5th	J. R. Reid and J. E. F. Beck at Cape Town	1953-54
100 for 6th	H. G. Vivian and F. T. Badcock at Wellington	1931-32
84 for 7th	J. R. Reid and G. A. Bartlett at Johannesburg	1961-62
74 for 8th	S. A. Thomson and D. J. Nash at Johannesburg	1994-95
69 for 9th	C. F. W. Allcott and I. B. Cromb at Wellington	1931-32
57 for 10th	S. B. Doull and R. P. de Groen at Johannesburg	1994-95

† *Denotes record partnership against all countries.*

TEN WICKETS OR MORE IN A MATCH

For South Africa (1)

11-196 (6-128, 5-68)†   S. F. Burke, Cape Town............................ 1961-62

† *Signifies ten wickets or more on first appearance in South Africa–New Zealand Tests.*
Note: The best match figures by a New Zealand bowler are 8-134 (3-57, 5-77), M. N. Hart at Johannesburg, 1994-95.

SOUTH AFRICA v INDIA

		Captains				
Season	*South Africa*		*India*	*T*	*SA*	*I*	*D*
1992-93*S*	K. C. Wessels		M. Azharuddin	4	1	0	3

S Played in South Africa.

HIGHEST INNINGS TOTALS

For South Africa: 360-9 dec. at Cape Town.............................. 1992-93

For India: 277 at Durban... 1992-93

INDIVIDUAL HUNDREDS

For South Africa (2)

W. J. Cronje (1) | **K. C. Wessels** (1)
135   Pt Elizabeth . 1992-93 | 118†   Durban 1992-93

For India (3)

P. K. Amre (1) | **Kapil Dev** (1) | **S. R. Tendulkar** (1)
103†   Durban ..... 1992-93 | 129   Pt Elizabeth . 1992-93 | 111   Johannesburg 1992-93

    † *Signifies hundred on first appearance in South Africa–India Tests.*

HUNDRED PARTNERSHIPS

For South Africa

117 for 2nd   A. C. Hudson and W. J. Cronje at Port Elizabeth 1992-93

For India

101 for 8th   P. K. Amre and K. S. More at Durban 1992-93

TEN WICKETS OR MORE IN A MATCH

For South Africa (1)

12-139 (5-55, 7-84)   A. A. Donald at Port Elizabeth...................... 1992-93

Note: The best match figures by an Indian bowler are 8-113 (2-60, 6-53), A. Kumble at Johannesburg, 1992-93.

SOUTH AFRICA v PAKISTAN

| Season | South Africa | Captains | | | | | |
		Pakistan	T	SA	P	D
1994-95S	W. J. Cronje	Salim Malik	1	1	0	0

S Played in South Africa.

HIGHEST INNINGS TOTALS

For South Africa: 460 at Johannesburg.................................... 1994-95

For Pakistan: 230 at Johannesburg 1994-95

INDIVIDUAL HUNDREDS

For South Africa (1)

B. M. McMillan (1)
113†   Johannesburg   1994-95

Highest score for Pakistan: 99 by Salim Malik at Johannesburg 1994-95

† Signifies hundred on first appearance in South Africa–Pakistan Tests.

HUNDRED PARTNERSHIP

For South Africa

157 for 6th   J. N. Rhodes and B. M. McMillan at Johannesburg   1994-95

Note: The highest partnership for Pakistan is 93 for the 4th wicket between Asif Mujtaba and Inzamam-ul-Haq at Johannesburg, 1994-95.

TEN WICKETS OR MORE IN A MATCH

For South Africa (1)

10-108 (6-81, 4-27)†   P. S. de Villiers, Johannesburg   1994-95

Note: The best match figures for Pakistan are 5-184 (3-102, 2-82), Aqib Javed at Johannesburg, 1994-95.

† Signifies ten wickets or more on first appearance in South Africa–Pakistan Tests.

SOUTH AFRICA v SRI LANKA

Season	South Africa	*Captains*	Sri Lanka	T	SA	SL	D
1993-94*SL*	K. C. Wessels		A. Ranatunga	3	1	0	2

SL Played in Sri Lanka.

HIGHEST INNINGS TOTALS

For South Africa: 495 at Colombo (SSC)   1993-94

For Sri Lanka: 331 at Moratuwa   1993-94

INDIVIDUAL HUNDREDS

For South Africa (3)

W. J. Cronje (1)	**D. J. Cullinan** (1)	**J. N. Rhodes** (1)
122 Colombo (SSC) 1993-94	102 Colombo (PSS) 1993-94	101*† Moratuwa ... 1993-94

For Sri Lanka (1)

A. Ranatunga (1)
131†   Moratuwa ...   1993-94

† Signifies hundred on first appearance in South Africa–Sri Lanka Tests.

HUNDRED PARTNERSHIPS

For South Africa

137 for 1st	K. C. Wessels and A. C. Hudson at Colombo (SSC)	1993-94
122 for 6th	D. J. Cullinan and D. J. Richardson at Colombo (PSS).......	1993-94
105 for 3rd	W. J. Cronje and D. J. Cullinan at Colombo (SSC)	1993-94
104 for 1st	K. C. Wessels and A. C. Hudson at Moratuwa...............	1993-94

For Sri Lanka

121 for 5th	P. A. de Silva and A. Ranatunga at Moratuwa...............	1993-94
103 for 6th	A. Ranatunga and H. P. Tillekeratne at Moratuwa	1993-94
101 for 4th	P. A. de Silva and A. Ranatunga at Colombo (PSS)..........	1993-94

BEST MATCH BOWLING ANALYSES

For South Africa

9-106 (5-48, 4-58)	B. N. Schultz, Colombo (SSC)........................	1993-94

For Sri Lanka

6-152 (5-104, 1-48)	M. Muralitharan, Moratuwa	1993-94

WEST INDIES v NEW ZEALAND

		Captains				
Season	West Indies	New Zealand	T	WI	NZ	D
1951-52N	J. D. C. Goddard	B. Sutcliffe	2	1	0	1
1955-56N	D. St E. Atkinson	J. R. Reid[1]	4	3	1	0
1968-69N	G. S. Sobers	G. T. Dowling	3	1	1	1
1971-72W	G. S. Sobers	G. T. Dowling[2]	5	0	0	5
1979-80N	C. H. Lloyd	G. P. Howarth	3	0	1	2
1984-85W	I. V. A. Richards	G. P. Howarth	4	2	0	2
1986-87N	I. V. A. Richards	J. V. Coney	3	1	1	1
1993-94N	C. A. Walsh	K. R. Rutherford	2	1	0	1
	In New Zealand		17	7	4	6
	In West Indies		9	2	0	7
	Totals..........................		26	9	4	13

N Played in New Zealand.   W Played in West Indies.

Notes: The following deputised for the official touring captain or were appointed by the home authority for only a minor proportion of the series:
[1]H. B. Cave (First). [2]B. E. Congdon (Third, Fourth and Fifth).

HIGHEST INNINGS TOTALS

For West Indies in West Indies: 564-8 at Bridgetown........................		1971-72
in New Zealand: 660-5 dec. at Wellington		1994-95
For New Zealand in West Indies: 543-3 dec. at Georgetown		1971-72
in New Zealand: 460 at Christchurch		1979-80

LOWEST INNINGS TOTALS

For West Indies in West Indies: 133 at Bridgetown 1971-72
                 in New Zealand: 77 at Auckland 1955-56

For New Zealand in West Indies: 94 at Bridgetown 1984-85
               in New Zealand: 74 at Dunedin 1955-56

INDIVIDUAL HUNDREDS

By West Indies (28)

J. C. Adams (1)
151   Wellington . . 1994-95
M. C. Carew (1)
109† Auckland . . 1968-69
C. A. Davis (1)
183   Bridgetown . . 1971-72
R. C. Fredericks (1)
163   Kingston 1971-72
C. G. Greenidge (2)
100   Port-of-Spain 1984-85
213   Auckland . . . 1986-87
D. L. Haynes (3)
105† Dunedin 1979-80
122   Christchurch . 1979-80
121   Wellington . . 1986-87

A. I. Kallicharran (2)
100*† Georgetown . 1971-72
101   Port-of-Spain 1971-72
C. L. King (1)
100* Christchurch . 1979-80
B. C. Lara (1)
147   Wellington . . 1994-95
J. R. Murray (1)
101* Wellington . . 1994-95
S. M. Nurse (2)
168† Auckland . . . 1968-69
258   Christchurch . 1968-69
I. V. A. Richards (1)
105   Bridgetown . . 1984-85
R. B. Richardson (1)
185   Georgetown . 1984-85

L. G. Rowe (3)
214   †Kingston . . . 1971-72
100* }
100   Christchurch . 1979-80
G. S. Sobers (1)
142   Bridgetown . . 1971-72
J. B. Stollmeyer (1)
152   Auckland . . . 1951-52
C. L. Walcott (1)
115   Auckland . . . 1951-52
E. D. Weekes (3)
123   Dunedin 1955-56
103   Christchurch . 1955-56
156   Wellington . . 1955-56
F. M. M. Worrell (1)
100   Auckland . . . 1951-52

By New Zealand (18)

M. G. Burgess (1)
101   Kingston 1971-72
B. E. Congdon (2)
166* Port-of-Spain 1971-72
126   Bridgetown . . 1971-72
J. J. Crowe (1)
112   Kingston 1984-85
M. D. Crowe (3)
188   Georgetown . 1984-85
119   Wellington . . 1986-87

104   Auckland . . . 1986-87
B. A. Edgar (1)
127   Auckland . . . 1979-80
R. J. Hadlee (1)
103   Christchurch . 1979-80
B. F. Hastings (2)
117* Christchurch . 1968-69
105   Bridgetown . . 1971-72
G. P. Howarth (1)
147   Christchurch . 1979-80

T. W. Jarvis (1)
182   Georgetown . 1971-72
A. C. Parore (1)
100*† Christchurch . 1994-95
B. R. Taylor (1)
124† Auckland . . . 1968-69
G. M. Turner (2)
223*‡ Kingston 1971-72
259   Georgetown . 1971-72
J. G. Wright (1)
138   Wellington . . 1986-87

† *Signifies hundred on first appearance in West Indies–New Zealand Tests.*
‡ *Carried his bat.*

Notes: E. D. Weekes in 1955-56 made three hundreds in consecutive innings.
    L. G. Rowe and A. I. Kallicharran each scored hundreds in their first two innings in Test cricket, Rowe being the only batsman to do so in his first match.

RECORD PARTNERSHIPS FOR EACH WICKET

For West Indies

225 for 1st   C. G. Greenidge and D. L. Haynes at Christchurch 1979-80
269 for 2nd R. C. Fredericks and L. G. Rowe at Kingston 1971-72
221 for 3rd   B. C. Lara and J. C. Adams at Wellington 1994-95
162 for 4th { E. D. Weekes and O. G. Smith at Dunedin 1955-56
            { C. G. Greenidge and A. I. Kallicharran at Christchurch 1979-80
189 for 5th   F. M. M. Worrell and C. L. Walcott at Auckland 1951-52
254 for 6th   C. A. Davis and G. S. Sobers at Bridgetown 1971-72
143 for 7th   D. St E. Atkinson and J. D. C. Goddard at Christchurch 1955-56
83 for 8th   I. V. A. Richards and M. D. Marshall at Bridgetown 1984-85
70 for 9th   M. D. Marshall and J. Garner at Bridgetown 1984-85
31 for 10th T. M. Findlay and G. C. Shillingford at Bridgetown 1971-72

For New Zealand

387	for 1st†	G. M. Turner and T. W. Jarvis at Georgetown	....	1971-72
210	for 2nd	G. P. Howarth and J. J. Crowe at Kingston	....	1984-85
241	for 3rd	J. G. Wright and M. D. Crowe at Wellington	....	1986-87
175	for 4th	B. E. Congdon and B. F. Hastings at Bridgetown	....	1971-72
142	for 5th	M. D. Crowe and J. V. Coney at Georgetown	....	1984-85
220	for 6th	G. M. Turner and K. J. Wadsworth at Kingston	....	1971-72
143	for 7th	M. D. Crowe and I. D. S. Smith at Georgetown	....	1984-85
136	for 8th†	B. E. Congdon and R. S. Cunis at Port-of-Spain	....	1971-72
62*	for 9th	V. Pollard and R. S. Cunis at Auckland	....	1968-69
41	for 10th	B. E. Congdon and J. C. Alabaster at Port-of-Spain	....	1971-72

† *Denotes record partnership against all countries.*

TEN WICKETS OR MORE IN A MATCH

For West Indies (2)

11-120 (4-40, 7-80)	M. D. Marshall, Bridgetown	....	1984-85
13-55 (7-37, 6-18)	C. A. Walsh, Wellington	....	1994-95

For New Zealand (3)

10-124 (4-51, 6-73)†	E. J. Chatfield, Port-of-Spain	....	1984-85
11-102 (5-34, 6-68)†	R. J. Hadlee, Dunedin	....	1979-80
10-166 (4-71, 6-95)	G. B. Troup, Auckland	....	1979-80

† *Signifies ten wickets or more on first appearance in West Indies–New Zealand Tests.*

WEST INDIES v INDIA

Season	West Indies	*Captains* India	T	WI	I	D
1948-49*I*	J. D. C. Goddard	L. Amarnath	5	1	0	4
1952-53*W*	J. B. Stollmeyer	V. S. Hazare	5	1	0	4
1958-59*I*	F. C. M. Alexander	Ghulam Ahmed[1]	5	3	0	2
1961-62*W*	F. M. M. Worrell	N. J. Contractor[2]	5	5	0	0
1966-67*I*	G. S. Sobers	Nawab of Pataudi jun.	3	2	0	1
1970-71*W*	G. S. Sobers	A. L. Wadekar	5	0	1	4
1974-75*I*	C. H. Lloyd	Nawab of Pataudi jun.[3]	5	3	2	0
1975-76*W*	C. H. Lloyd	B. S. Bedi	4	2	1	1
1978-79*I*	A. I. Kallicharran	S. M. Gavaskar	6	0	1	5
1982-83*W*	C. H. Lloyd	Kapil Dev	5	2	0	3
1983-84*I*	C. H. Lloyd	Kapil Dev	6	3	0	3
1987-88*I*	I. V. A. Richards	D. B. Vengsarkar[4]	4	1	1	2
1988-89*I*	I. V. A. Richards	D. B. Vengsarkar	4	3	0	1
1994-95*I*	C. A. Walsh	M. Azharuddin	3	1	1	1
	In India		37	14	5	18
	In West Indies		28	13	2	13
	Totals		65	27	7	31

I Played in India. W Played in West Indies.

Notes: The following deputised for the official touring captain or were appointed by the home authority for only a minor proportion of the series: [1]P. R. Umrigar (First), V. Mankad (Fourth), H. R. Adhikari (Fifth). [2]Nawab of Pataudi jun. (Third, Fourth and Fifth). [3]S. Venkataraghavan (Second). [4]R. J. Shastri (Fourth).

HIGHEST INNINGS TOTALS

For West Indies in West Indies: 631-8 dec. at Kingston 1961-62
                in India: 644-8 dec. at Delhi 1958-59

For India in West Indies: 469-7 at Port-of-Spain 1982-83
          in India: 644-7 dec. at Kanpur 1978-79

LOWEST INNINGS TOTALS

For West Indies in West Indies: 214 at Port-of-Spain 1970-71
              in India: 127 at Delhi 1987-88

For India in West Indies: 97† at Kingston 1975-76
          in India: 75 at Delhi 1987-88

   † *Five men absent hurt. The lowest with 11 men batting is 98 at Port-of-Spain, 1961-62.*

INDIVIDUAL HUNDREDS

For West Indies (78)

J. C. Adams (2)	**A. I. Kallicharran** (3)	**R. B. Richardson** (2)
125* Nagpur 1994-95	124† Bangalore ... 1974-75	194 Georgetown . 1988-89
174* Mohali 1994-95	103* Port-of-Spain 1975-76	156 Kingston .. 1988-89
S. F. A. F. Bacchus (1)	187 Bombay 1978-79	**O. G. Smith** (1)
250 Kanpur 1978-79	**R. B. Kanhai** (4)	100 Delhi 1958-59
B. F. Butcher (2)	256 Calcutta 1958-59	**G. S. Sobers** (8)
103 Calcutta 1958-59	138 Kingston ... 1961-62	142*† Bombay 1958-59
142 Madras 1958-59	139 Port-of-Spain 1961-62	198 Kanpur 1958-59
R. J. Christiani (1)	158* Kingston ... 1970-71	106* Calcutta 1958-59
107† Delhi 1948-49	**C. H. Lloyd** (7)	153 Kingston ... 1961-62
C. A. Davis (2)	163 Bangalore ... 1974-75	104 Kingston ... 1961-62
125* Georgetown . 1970-71	242* Bombay 1974-75	108* Georgetown . 1970-71
105 Port-of-Spain 1970-71	102 Bridgetown . 1975-76	178* Bridgetown . 1970-71
P. J. L. Dujon (1)	143 Port-of-Spain 1982-83	132 Port-of-Spain 1970-71
110 St John's 1982-83	106 St John's 1982-83	**J. S. Solomon** (1)
R. C. Fredericks (2)	161* Calcutta 1983-84	100* Delhi 1958-59
100 Calcutta 1974-75	**A. L. Logie** (2)	**J. B. Stollmeyer** (2)
104 Bombay 1974-75	130 Bridgetown . 1982-83	160 Madras 1948-49
H. A. Gomes (1)	101 Calcutta 1987-88	104* Port-of-Spain 1952-53
123 Port-of-Spain 1982-83	**E. D. A. McMorris** (1)	**C. L. Walcott** (4)
G. E. Gomez (1)	125† Kingston ... 1961-62	152† Delhi 1948-49
101† Delhi 1948-49	**B. H. Pairaudeau** (1)	108 Calcutta 1948-49
C. G. Greenidge (5)	115† Port-of-Spain 1952-53	125 Georgetown . 1952-53
107† Bangalore ... 1974-75	**A. F. Rae** (2)	118 Kingston ... 1952-53
154* St John's 1982-83	104 Bombay 1948-49	**E. D. Weekes** (7)
194 Kanpur 1983-84	109 Madras 1948-49	128† Delhi 1948-49
141 Calcutta 1987-88	**I. V. A. Richards** (8)	194 Bombay 1948-49
117 Bridgetown . 1988-89	192* Delhi 1974-75	162 ⎫ Calcutta ... 1948-49
D. L. Haynes (2)	142 Bridgetown . 1975-76	101 ⎭
136 St John's 1982-83	130 Port-of-Spain 1975-76	207 Port-of-Spain 1952-53
112* Bridgetown . 1988-89	177 Port-of-Spain 1975-76	161 Port-of-Spain 1952-53
J. K. Holt (1)	109 Georgetown . 1982-83	109 Kingston ... 1952-53
123 Delhi 1958-59	120 Bombay 1983-84	**A. B. Williams** (1)
C. L. Hooper (1)	109* Delhi 1987-88	111 Calcutta 1978-79
100* Calcutta 1987-88	110 Kingston ... 1988-89	**F. M. M. Worrell** (1)
C. C. Hunte (1)		237 Kingston ... 1952-53
101 Bombay 1966-67		

For India (58)

H. R. Adhikari (1)			120	Delhi	1978-79	112	Port-of-Spain	1970-71
114*†	Delhi	1948-49	147*	Georgetown	1982-83	150	Bridgetown	1970-71
M. Amarnath (3)			121	Delhi	1983-84	**R. J. Shastri** (2)		
101*	Kanpur	1978-79	236*	Madras	1983-84	102	St John's	1982-83
117	Port-of-Spain	1982-83	**V. S. Hazare** (2)			107	Bridgetown	1988-89
116	St John's	1982-83	134*	Bombay	1948-49	**N. S. Sidhu** (2)		
M. L. Apte (1)			122	Bombay	1948-49	116	Kingston	1988-89
163*	Port-of-Spain	1952-53	**Kapil Dev** (3)			107	Nagpur	1994-95
C. G. Borde (3)			126*	Delhi	1978-79	**E. D. Solkar** (1)		
109	Delhi	1958-59	100*	Port-of-Spain	1982-83	102	Bombay	1974-75
121	Bombay	1966-67	109	Madras	1987-88	**S. R. Tendulkar** (1)		
125	Madras	1966-67	**S. V. Manjrekar** (1)			179	Nagpur	1994-95
S. A. Durani (1)			108	Bridgetown	1988-89	**P. R. Umrigar** (3)		
104	Port-of-Spain	1961-62	**V. L. Manjrekar** (1)			130	Port-of-Spain	1952-53
F. M. Engineer (1)			118	Kingston	1952-53	117	Kingston	1952-53
109	Madras	1966-67	**R. S. Modi** (1)			172*	Port-of-Spain	1961-62
A. D. Gaekwad (1)			112	Bombay	1948-49	**D. B. Vengsarkar** (6)		
102	Kanpur	1978-79	**Mushtaq Ali** (1)			157*	Calcutta	1978-79
S. M. Gavaskar (13)			106†	Calcutta	1948-49	109	Delhi	1978-79
116	Georgetown	1970-71	**B. P. Patel** (1)			159	Delhi	1983-84
117*	Bridgetown	1970-71	115*	Port-of-Spain	1975-76	100	Bombay	1983-84
124 ⎫	Port-of-Spain	1970-71	**M. Prabhakar** (1)			102	Delhi	1987-88
220 ⎭			120	Mohali	1994-95	102*	Calcutta	1987-88
156	Port-of-Spain	1975-76	**Pankaj Roy** (1)			**G. R. Viswanath** (4)		
102	Port-of-Spain	1975-76	150	Kingston	1952-53	139	Calcutta	1974-75
205	Bombay	1978-79	**D. N. Sardesai** (3)			112	Port-of-Spain	1975-76
107 ⎫	Calcutta	1978-79	212	Kingston	1970-71	124	Madras	1978-79
182* ⎭						179	Kanpur	1978-79

† *Signifies hundred on first appearance in West Indies–India Tests.*

RECORD PARTNERSHIPS FOR EACH WICKET

For West Indies

296	for 1st	C. G. Greenidge and D. L. Haynes at St John's	....	1982-83
255	for 2nd	E. D. A. McMorris and R. B. Kanhai at Kingston	....	1961-62
220	for 3rd	I. V. A. Richards and A. I. Kallicharran at Bridgetown	....	1975-76
267	for 4th	C. L. Walcott and G. E. Gomez at Delhi	....	1948-49
219	for 5th	E. D. Weekes and B. H. Pairaudeau at Port-of-Spain	..	1952-53
250	for 6th	C. H. Lloyd and D. L. Murray at Bombay	....	1974-75
130	for 7th	C. G. Greenidge and M. D. Marshall at Kanpur	....	1983-84
124	for 8th†	I. V. A. Richards and K. D. Boyce at Delhi	....	1974-75
161	for 9th†	C. H. Lloyd and A. M. E. Roberts at Calcutta	....	1983-84
98*	for 10th	F. M. M. Worrell and W. W. Hall at Port-of-Spain	....	1961-62

For India

153	for 1st	S. M. Gavaskar and C. P. S. Chauhan at Bombay	....	1978-79
344*	for 2nd†	S. M. Gavaskar and D. B. Vengsarkar at Calcutta	....	1978-79
177	for 3rd	N. S. Sidhu and S. R. Tendulkar at Nagpur	....	1994-95
172	for 4th	G. R. Viswanath and A. D. Gaekwad at Kanpur	....	1978-79
204	for 5th	S. M. Gavaskar and B. P. Patel at Port-of-Spain	....	1975-76
170	for 6th	S. M. Gavaskar and R. J. Shastri at Madras	....	1983-84
186	for 7th	D. N. Sardesai and E. D. Solkar at Bridgetown	....	1970-71
107	for 8th	Yashpal Sharma and B. S. Sandhu at Kingston	....	1982-83
143*	for 9th	S. M. Gavaskar and S. M. H. Kirmani at Madras	....	1983-84
64	for 10th	J. Srinath and S. L. V. Raju at Mohali	....	1994-95

† *Denotes record partnership against all countries.*

TEN WICKETS OR MORE IN A MATCH

For West Indies (4)

11-126 (6-50, 5-76)	W. W. Hall, Kanpur	1958-59
11-89 (5-34, 6-55)	M. D. Marshall, Port-of-Spain	1988-89
12-121 (7-64, 5-57)	A. M. E. Roberts, Madras	1974-75
10-101 (6-62, 4-39)	C. A. Walsh, Kingston	1988-89

For India (4)

11-235 (7-157, 4-78)†	B. S. Chandrasekhar, Bombay	1966-67
10-223 (9-102, 1-121)	S. P. Gupte, Kanpur	1958-59
16-136 (8-61, 8-75)†	N. D. Hirwani, Madras	1987-88
10-135 (1-52, 9-83)	Kapil Dev, Ahmedabad	1983-84

† *Signifies ten wickets or more on first appearance in West Indies–India Tests.*

WEST INDIES v PAKISTAN

	Captains					
Season	West Indies	Pakistan	T	WI	P	D
1957-58W	F. C. M. Alexander	A. H. Kardar	5	3	1	1
1958-59P	F. C. M. Alexander	Fazal Mahmood	3	1	2	0
1974-75P	C. H. Lloyd	Intikhab Alam	2	0	0	2
1976-77W	C. H. Lloyd	Mushtaq Mohammad	5	2	1	2
1980-81P	C. H. Lloyd	Javed Miandad	4	1	0	3
1986-87P	I. V. A. Richards	Imran Khan	3	1	1	1
1987-88W	I. V. A. Richards[1]	Imran Khan	3	1	1	1
1990-91P	D. L. Haynes	Imran Khan	3	1	1	1
1992-93W	R. B. Richardson	Wasim Akram	3	2	0	1
	In West Indies		16	8	3	5
	In Pakistan		15	4	4	7
	Totals		31	12	7	12

P Played in Pakistan. W Played in West Indies.

Note: The following was appointed by the home authority for only a minor proportion of the series:

[1]C. G. Greenidge (First).

HIGHEST INNINGS TOTALS

For West Indies in West Indies: 790-3 dec. at Kingston	1957-58
in Pakistan: 493 at Karachi	1974-75
For Pakistan in West Indies: 657-8 dec. at Bridgetown	1957-58
in Pakistan: 406-8 dec. at Karachi	1974-75

LOWEST INNINGS TOTALS

For West Indies in West Indies: 127 at Port-of-Spain	1992-93
in Pakistan: 53 at Faisalabad	1986-87
For Pakistan in West Indies: 106 at Bridgetown	1957-58
in Pakistan: 77 at Lahore	1986-87

INDIVIDUAL HUNDREDS

For West Indies (24)

L. Baichan (1)

105*†	Lahore	1974-75

P. J. L. Dujon (1)

106*	Port-of-Spain	1987-88

R. C. Fredericks (1)

120	Port-of-Spain	1976-77

C. G. Greenidge (1)

100	Kingston	1976-77

D. L. Haynes (3)

117	Karachi	1990-91
143*‡	Port-of-Spain	1992-93
125	Bridgetown . .	1992-93

C. L. Hooper (2)

134	Lahore	1990-91
178*	St John's . . .	1992-93

C. C. Hunte (3)

142†	Bridgetown . .	1957-58
260	Kingston	1957-58
114	Georgetown . .	1957-58

B. D. Julien (1)

101	Karachi	1974-75

A. I. Kallicharran (1)

115	Karachi	1974-75

R. B. Kanhai (1)

217	Lahore	1958-59

C. H. Lloyd (1)

157	Bridgetown . .	1976-77

I. V. A. Richards (2)

120*	Multan	1980-81
123	Port-of-Spain	1987-88

I. T. Shillingford (1)

120	Georgetown .	1976-77

G. S. Sobers (3)

365*	Kingston	1957-58
125	} Georgetown .	1957-58
109*		

C. L. Walcott (1)

145	Georgetown .	1957-58

E. D. Weekes (1)

197†	Bridgetown . .	1957-58

For Pakistan (18)

Asif Iqbal (1)

135	Kingston	1976-77

Hanif Mohammad (2)

337†	Bridgetown . .	1957-58
103	Karachi	1958-59

Imtiaz Ahmed (1)

122	Kingston	1957-58

Imran Khan (1)

123	Lahore	1980-81

Inzamam-ul-Haq (1)

123	St John's	1992-93

Javed Miandad (2)

114	Georgetown .	1987-88
102	Port-of-Spain	1987-88

Majid Khan (2)

100	Karachi	1974-75
167	Georgetown .	1976-77

Mushtaq Mohammad (2)

123	Lahore	1974-75
121	Port-of-Spain	1976-77

Saeed Ahmed (1)

150	Georgetown .	1957-58

Salim Malik (1)

102	Karachi	1990-91

Wasim Raja (2)

107*	Karachi	1974-75
117*	Bridgetown . .	1976-77

Wazir Mohammad (2)

106	Kingston	1957-58
189	Port-of-Spain	1957-58

† *Signifies hundred on first appearance in West Indies–Pakistan Tests.*
‡ *Carried his bat.*

RECORD PARTNERSHIPS FOR EACH WICKET

For West Indies

182	for 1st	R. C. Fredericks and C. G. Greenidge at Kingston	1976-77
446	for 2nd†	C. C. Hunte and G. S. Sobers at Kingston	1957-58
169	for 3rd	D. L. Haynes and B. C. Lara at Port-of-Spain	1992-93
188*	for 4th	G. S. Sobers and C. L. Walcott at Kingston	1957-58
185	for 5th	E. D. Weekes and O. G. Smith at Bridgetown	1957-58
151	for 6th	C. H. Lloyd and D. L. Murray at Bridgetown	1976-77
70	for 7th	C. H. Lloyd and J. Garner at Bridgetown	1976-77
60	for 8th	C. L. Hooper and A. C. Cummins at St John's	1992-93
61*	for 9th	P. J. L. Dujon and W. K. M. Benjamin at Bridgetown	1987-88
106	for 10th†	C. L. Hooper and C. A. Walsh at St John's	1992-93

For Pakistan

159	for 1st[1]	Majid Khan and Zaheer Abbas at Georgetown	1976-77
178	for 2nd	Hanif Mohammad and Saeed Ahmed at Karachi	1958-59
169	for 3rd	Saeed Ahmed and Wazir Mohammad at Port-of-Spain	1957-58
174	for 4th	Shoaib Mohammad and Salim Malik at Karachi	1990-91
88	for 5th	Basit Ali and Inzamam-ul-Haq at St John's	1992-93
166	for 6th	Wazir Mohammad and A. H. Kardar at Kingston	1957-58
128	for 7th[2]	Wasim Raja and Wasim Bari at Karachi	1974-75

94 for 8th	Salim Malik and Salim Yousuf at Port-of-Spain	1987-88
96 for 9th	Inzamam-ul-Haq and Nadeem Khan at St John's.............	1992-93
133 for 10th†	Wasim Raja and Wasim Bari at Bridgetown.................	1976-77

† *Denotes record partnership against all countries.*

[1] *219 runs were added for this wicket in two separate partnerships: Sadiq Mohammad retired hurt and was replaced by Zaheer Abbas when 60 had been added. The highest partnership by two opening batsmen is 152 by Hanif Mohammad and Imtiaz Ahmed at Bridgetown, 1957-58.*

[2] *Although the seventh wicket added 168 runs against West Indies at Lahore in 1980-81, this comprised two partnerships with Imran Khan adding 72* with Abdul Qadir (retired hurt) and a further 96 with Sarfraz Nawaz.*

TEN WICKETS OR MORE IN A MATCH

For Pakistan (2)

12-100 (6-34, 6-66)	Fazal Mahmood, Dacca	1958-59
11-121 (7-80, 4-41)	Imran Khan, Georgetown	1987-88

Note: The best match figures by a West Indian bowler are 9-95 (8-29, 1-66) by C. E. H. Croft at Port-of-Spain, 1976-77.

WEST INDIES v SRI LANKA

	Captains					
Season	*West Indies*	*Sri Lanka*	*T*	*WI*	*SL*	*D*
1993-94*S*	R. B. Richardson	A. Ranatunga	1	0	0	1

S Played in Sri Lanka.

HIGHEST INNINGS TOTALS

For West Indies: 204 at Moratuwa		1993-94
For Sri Lanka: 190 at Moratuwa		1993-94

Highest score for West Indies: 62 by C. L. Hooper at Moratuwa.
Highest score for Sri Lanka: 53 by P. A. de Silva at Moratuwa.

HIGHEST PARTNERSHIPS

For West Indies

84 for 5th	R. B. Richardson and C. L. Hooper at Moratuwa	1993-94

For Sri Lanka

51 for 7th	R. S. Kalpage and P. B. Dassanayake at Moratuwa	1993-94

BEST MATCH BOWLING ANALYSES

For West Indies

5-51 (4-46, 1-5)	W. K. M. Benjamin, Moratuwa......................	1993-94

For Sri Lanka

4-47 (4-47)	M. Muralitharan, Moratuwa	1993-94

NEW ZEALAND v INDIA

Captains

Season	New Zealand	India	T	NZ	I	D
1955-56*I*	H. B. Cave	P. R. Umrigar[1]	5	0	2	3
1964-65*I*	J. R. Reid	Nawab of Pataudi jun.	4	0	1	3
1967-68*N*	G. T. Dowling[2]	Nawab of Pataudi jun.	4	1	3	0
1969-70*I*	G. T. Dowling	Nawab of Pataudi jun.	3	1	1	1
1975-76*N*	G. M. Turner	B. S. Bedi[3]	3	1	1	1
1976-77*I*	G. M. Turner	B. S. Bedi	3	0	2	1
1980-81*N*	G. P. Howarth	S. M. Gavaskar	3	1	0	2
1988-89*I*	J. G. Wright	D. B. Vengsarkar	3	1	2	0
1989-90*N*	J. G. Wright	M. Azharuddin	3	1	0	2
1993-94*N*	K. R. Rutherford	M. Azharuddin	1	0	0	1
	In India		18	2	8	8
	In New Zealand		14	4	4	6
	Totals		32	6	12	14

I Played in India. N Played in New Zealand.

Notes: The following deputised for the official touring captain or were appointed by the home authority for a minor proportion of the series:

[1]Ghulam Ahmed (First). [2]B. W. Sinclair (First). [3]S. M. Gavaskar (First).

HIGHEST INNINGS TOTALS

For New Zealand in New Zealand: 502 at Christchurch 1967-68
in India: 462-9 dec. at Calcutta 1964-65

For India in New Zealand: 482 at Auckland 1989-90
in India: 537-3 dec. at Madras 1955-56

LOWEST INNINGS TOTALS

For New Zealand in New Zealand: 100 at Wellington 1980-81
in India: 124 at Hyderabad 1988-89

For India in New Zealand: 81 at Wellington 1975-76
in India: 88 at Bombay 1964-65

INDIVIDUAL HUNDREDS

For New Zealand (21)

M. D. Crowe (1)
113 Auckland ... 1989-90
G. T. Dowling (3)
129 Bombay 1964-65
143 Dunedin 1967-68
239 Christchurch. 1967-68
J. W. Guy (1)
102† Hyderabad .. 1955-56
G. P. Howarth (1)
137* Wellington . 1980-81
A. H. Jones (1)
170* Auckland ... 1989-90

J. M. Parker (1)
104 Bombay 1976-77
J. F. Reid (1)
123* Christchurch. 1980-81
J. R. Reid (2)
119* Delhi 1955-56
120 Calcutta 1955-56
I. D. S. Smith (1)
173 Auckland ... 1989-90
B. Sutcliffe (3)
137*† Hyderabad .. 1955-56

230* Delhi 1955-56
151* Calcutta 1964-65
B. R. Taylor (1)
105† Calcutta 1964-65
G. M. Turner (2)
117 Christchurch. 1975-76
113 Kanpur 1976-77
J. G. Wright (3)
110 Auckland ... 1980-81
185 Christchurch. 1989-90
113* Napier 1989-90

For India (22)

S. Amarnath (1)	177 Delhi 1955-56	**D. N. Sardesai** (2)
124† Auckland ... 1975-76	102* Madras 1964-65	200* Bombay ... 1964-65
M. Azharuddin (1)	**V. Mankad** (2)	106 Delhi 1964-65
192 Auckland ... 1989-90	223 Bombay 1955-56	**N. S. Sidhu** (1)
C. G. Borde (1)	231 Madras 1955-56	116† Bangalore ... 1988-89
109 Bombay 1964-65	**Nawab of Pataudi jun.** (2)	**P. R. Umrigar** (1)
S. M. Gavaskar (2)	153 Calcutta 1964-65	223† Hyderabad .. 1955-56
116† Auckland ... 1975-76	113 Delhi 1964-65	**G. R. Viswanath** (1)
119 Bombay 1976-77	**G. S. Ramchand** (1)	103* Kanpur 1976-77
A. G. Kripal Singh (1)	106* Calcutta 1955-56	**A. L. Wadekar** (1)
100*† Hyderabad .. 1955-56	**Pankaj Roy** (2)	143 Wellington .. 1967-68
V. L. Manjrekar (3)	100 Calcutta 1955-56	
118† Hyderabad .. 1955-56	173 Madras 1955-56	

† *Signifies hundred on first appearance in New Zealand–India Tests. B. R. Taylor provides the only instance for New Zealand of a player scoring his maiden hundred in first-class cricket in his first Test.*

RECORD PARTNERSHIPS FOR EACH WICKET

For New Zealand

149	for 1st	T. J. Franklin and J. G. Wright at Napier	1989-90
155	for 2nd	G. T. Dowling and B. E. Congdon at Dunedin	1967-68
222*	for 3rd	B. Sutcliffe and J. R. Reid at Delhi	1955-56
125	for 4th	J. G. Wright and M. J. Greatbatch at Christchurch	1989-90
119	for 5th	G. T. Dowling and K. Thomson at Christchurch	1967-68
87	for 6th	J. W. Guy and A. R. MacGibbon at Hyderabad	1955-56
163	for 7th	B. Sutcliffe and B. R. Taylor at Calcutta	1964-65
103	for 8th	R. J. Hadlee and I. D. S. Smith at Auckland	1989-90
136	for 9th†	I. D. S. Smith and M. C. Snedden at Auckland	1989-90
61	for 10th	J. T. Ward and R. O. Collinge at Madras	1964-65

For India

413	for 1st†	V. Mankad and Pankaj Roy at Madras	1955-56
204	for 2nd	S. M. Gavaskar and S. Amarnath at Auckland	1975-76
238	for 3rd	P. R. Umrigar and V. L. Manjrekar at Hyderabad	1955-56
171	for 4th	P. R. Umrigar and A. G. Kripal Singh at Hyderabad	1955-56
127	for 5th	V. L. Manjrekar and G. S. Ramchand at Delhi	1955-56
193*	for 6th	D. N. Sardesai and Hanumant Singh at Bombay	1964-65
128	for 7th	S. R. Tendulkar and K. S. More at Napier....................	1989-90
143	for 8th†	R. G. Nadkarni and F. M. Engineer at Madras	1964-65
105	for 9th {	S. M. H. Kirmani and B. S. Bedi at Bombay	1976-77
	{	S. M. H. Kirmani and N. S. Yadav at Auckland	1980-81
57	for 10th	R. B. Desai and B. S. Bedi at Dunedin	1967-68

† *Denotes record partnership against all countries.*

TEN WICKETS OR MORE IN A MATCH

For New Zealand (2)

11-58 (4-35, 7-23)	R. J. Hadlee, Wellington	1975-76
10-88 (6-49, 4-39)	R. J. Hadlee, Bombay	1988-89

For India (2)

11-140 (3-64, 8-76)	E. A. S. Prasanna, Auckland	1975-76
12-152 (8-72, 4-80)	S. Venkataraghavan, Delhi	1964-65

NEW ZEALAND v PAKISTAN

Captains

Season	New Zealand	Pakistan	T	NZ	P	D
1955-56*P*	H. B. Cave	A. H. Kardar	3	0	2	1
1964-65*N*	J. R. Reid	Hanif Mohammad	3	0	0	3
1964-65*P*	J. R. Reid	Hanif Mohammad	3	0	2	1
1969-70*P*	G. T. Dowling	Intikhab Alam	3	1	0	2
1972-73*N*	B. E. Congdon	Intikhab Alam	3	0	1	2
1976-77*P*	G. M. Turner[1]	Mushtaq Mohammad	3	0	2	1
1978-79*N*	M. G. Burgess	Mushtaq Mohammad	3	0	1	2
1984-85*P*	J. V. Coney	Zaheer Abbas	3	0	2	1
1984-85*N*	G. P. Howarth	Javed Miandad	3	2	0	1
1988-89*N*†	J. G. Wright	Imran Khan	2	0	0	2
1990-91*P*	M. D. Crowe	Javed Miandad	3	0	3	0
1992-93*N*	K. R. Rutherford	Javed Miandad	1	0	1	0
1993-94*N*	K. R. Rutherford	Salim Malik	3	1	2	0
	In Pakistan		18	1	11	6
	In New Zealand		18	3	5	10
	Totals...........................		36	4	16	16

N Played in New Zealand.   P Played in Pakistan.
  † The First Test at Dunedin was abandoned without a ball being bowled and is excluded.

Note: The following deputised for the official touring captain:
¹J. M. Parker (Third).

HIGHEST INNINGS TOTALS

For New Zealand in New Zealand 492 at Wellington.......................	1984-85
in Pakistan: 482-6 dec. at Lahore.......................	1964-65
For Pakistan in New Zealand: 616-5 dec. at Auckland.......................	1988-89
in Pakistan: 565-9 dec. at Karachi	1976-77

LOWEST INNINGS TOTALS

For New Zealand in New Zealand: 93 at Hamilton	1992-93
in Pakistan: 70 at Dacca	1955-56
For Pakistan in New Zealand: 169 at Auckland	1984-85
in Pakistan: 102 at Faisalabad	1990-91

INDIVIDUAL HUNDREDS

For New Zealand (21)

M. G. Burgess (2)
119* Dacca 1969-70
111 Lahore 1976-77
J. V. Coney (1)
111* Dunedin 1984-85
M. D. Crowe (2)
174 Wellington .. 1988-89
108* Lahore 1990-91
B. A. Edgar (1)
129† Christchurch. 1978-79
M. J. Greatbatch (1)
133 Hamilton .. 1992-93
B. F. Hastings (1)
110 Auckland ... 1972-73

G. P. Howarth (1)
114 Napier 1978-79
W. K. Lees (1)
152 Karachi 1976-77
S. N. McGregor (1)
111 Lahore 1955-56
R. E. Redmond (1)
107† Auckland ... 1972-73
J. F. Reid (3)
106 Hyderabad .. 1984-85
148 Wellington .. 1984-85
158* Auckland ... 1984-85
J. R. Reid (1)
128 Karachi 1964-65

B. W. Sinclair (1)
130 Lahore 1964-65
S. A. Thomson (1)
120* Christchurch 1993-94
G. M. Turner (1)
110† Dacca 1969-70
J. G. Wright (1)
107 Karachi 1984-85
B. A. Young (1)
120 Christchurch 1993-94

For Pakistan (37)

Asif Iqbal (3)		104	} Hyderabad .. 1984-85
175 Dunedin 1972-73		103*	}
166 Lahore 1976-77		118 Wellington .. 1988-89	
104 Napier 1978-79		271 Auckland ... 1988-89	
Basit Ali (1)		**Majid Khan** (3)	
103 Christchurch 1993-94		110 Auckland ... 1972-73	
Hanif Mohammad (3)		112 Karachi 1976-77	
103 Dacca 1955-56		119* Napier 1978-79	
100* Christchurch. 1964-65		**Mohammad Ilyas** (1)	
203* Lahore 1964-65		126 Karachi 1964-65	
Imtiaz Ahmed (1)		**Mudassar Nazar** (1)	
209 Lahore 1955-56		106 Hyderabad .. 1984-85	
Inzamam-ul-Haq (1)		**Mushtaq Mohammad** (3)	
135* Wellington .. 1993-94		201 Dunedin 1972-73	
Javed Miandad (7)		101 Hyderabad .. 1976-77	
163† Lahore 1976-77		107 Karachi 1976-77	
206 Karachi 1976-77		**Sadiq Mohammad** (2)	
160* Christchurch. 1978-79		166 Wellington .. 1972-73	

103* Hyderabad .. 1976-77	
Saeed Ahmed (1)	
172 Karachi 1964-65	
Saeed Anwar (1)	
169 Wellington . 1993-94	
Salim Malik (2)	
119* Karachi 1984-85	
140 Wellington . 1993-94	
Shoaib Mohammad (5)	
163 Wellington .. 1988-89	
112 Auckland ... 1988-89	
203* Karachi 1990-91	
105 Lahore 1990-91	
142 Faisalabad .. 1990-91	
Waqar Hassan (1)	
189 Lahore 1955-56	
Zaheer Abbas (1)	
135 Auckland ... 1978-79	

† *Signifies hundred on first appearance in New Zealand–Pakistan Tests.*

Notes: Mushtaq and Sadiq Mohammad, at Hyderabad in 1976-77, provide the fourth instance in Test matches, after the Chappells (thrice), of brothers each scoring hundreds in the same innings.

RECORD PARTNERSHIPS FOR EACH WICKET

For New Zealand

159 for 1st	R. E. Redmond and G. M. Turner at Auckland	1972-73
195 for 2nd	J. G. Wright and G. P. Howarth at Napier..................	1978-79
178 for 3rd	B. W. Sinclair and J. R. Reid at Lahore	1964-65
128 for 4th	B. F. Hastings and M. G. Burgess at Wellington	1972-73
183 for 5th†	M. G. Burgess and R. W. Anderson at Lahore	1976-77
145 for 6th	J. F. Reid and R. J. Hadlee at Wellington	1984-85
186 for 7th†	W. K. Lees and R. J. Hadlee at Karachi.................	1976-77
100 for 8th	B. W. Yuile and D. R. Hadlee at Karachi.................	1969-70
96 for 9th	M. G. Burgess and R. S. Cunis at Dacca.................	1969-70
151 for 10th†	B. F. Hastings and R. O. Collinge at Auckland	1972-73

For Pakistan

172 for 1st	Ramiz Raja and Shoaib Mohammad at Karachi	1990-91
114 for 2nd	Mohammad Ilyas and Saeed Ahmed at Rawalpindi	1964-65
248 for 3rd	Shoaib Mohammad and Javed Miandad at Auckland........	1988-89
350 for 4th†	Mushtaq Mohammad and Asif Iqbal at Dunedin	1972-73
281 for 5th†	Javed Miandad and Asif Iqbal at Lahore.................	1976-77
217 for 6th†	Hanif Mohammad and Majid Khan at Lahore..............	1964-65
308 for 7th†	Waqar Hassan and Imtiaz Ahmed at Lahore................	1955-56
89 for 8th	Anil Dalpat and Iqbal Qasim at Karachi.................	1984-85
52 for 9th	Intikhab Alam and Arif Butt at Auckland.................	1964-65
65 for 10th	Salah-ud-Din and Mohammad Farooq at Rawalpindi..........	1964-65

† *Denotes record partnership against all countries.*

TEN WICKETS OR MORE IN A MATCH

For New Zealand (1)

11-152 (7-52, 4-100)   C. Pringle, Faisalabad   1990-91

For Pakistan (7)

10-182 (5-91, 5-91)	Intikhab Alam, Dacca	1969-70
11-130 (7-52, 4-78)	Intikhab Alam, Dunedin	1972-73
10-106 (3-20, 7-86)	Waqar Younis, Lahore	1990-91
12-130 (7-76, 5-54)	Waqar Younis, Faisalabad	1990-91
10-128 (5-56, 5-72)	Wasim Akram, Dunedin	1984-85
11-179 (4-60, 7-119)	Wasim Akram, Wellington	1993-94
11-79 (5-37, 6-42)†	Zulfiqar Ahmed, Karachi	1955-56

† *Signifies ten wickets or more on first appearance in New Zealand–Pakistan Tests.*

Note: Waqar Younis's performances were in successive matches.

NEW ZEALAND v SRI LANKA

		Captains				
Season	*New Zealand*	*Sri Lanka*	*T*	*NZ*	*SL*	*D*
1982-83*N*	G. P. Howarth	D. S. de Silva	2	2	0	0
1983-84*S*	G. P. Howarth	L. R. D. Mendis	3	2	0	1
1986-87*S*†	J. J. Crowe	L. R. D. Mendis	1	0	0	1
1990-91*N*	M. D. Crowe[1]	A. Ranatunga	3	0	0	3
1992-93*S*	M. D. Crowe	A. Ranatunga	2	0	1	1
1994-95*N*	K. R. Rutherford	A. Ranatunga	2	0	1	1
	In New Zealand		7	2	1	4
	In Sri Lanka		6	2	1	3
	Totals........................		13	4	2	7

N Played in New Zealand. S Played in Sri Lanka.

† *The Second and Third Tests were cancelled owing to civil disturbances.*

Note: The following was appointed by the home authority for only a minor proportion of the series:

[1] I. D. S. Smith (Third).

HIGHEST INNINGS TOTALS

For New Zealand in New Zealand: 671-4 at Wellington 1990-91
        in Sri Lanka: 459 at Colombo (CCC) 1983-84

For Sri Lanka in New Zealand: 497 at Wellington 1990-91
        in Sri Lanka: 397-9 dec. at Colombo (CCC) 1986-87

LOWEST INNINGS TOTALS

For New Zealand in New Zealand: 109 at Napier 1994-95
        in Sri Lanka: 102 at Colombo (SSC) 1992-93

For Sri Lanka in New Zealand: 93 at Wellington 1982-83
        in Sri Lanka: 97 at Kandy 1983-84

INDIVIDUAL HUNDREDS

For New Zealand (10)

J. J. Crowe (1)
120* Colombo
      (CCC) 1986-87

M. D. Crowe (2)
299   Wellington .. 1990-91
107   Colombo (SSC) 1992-93

R. J. Hadlee (1)
151* Colombo
      (CCC) 1986-87

A. H. Jones (3)
186   Wellington .. 1990-91
122 ⎫ Hamilton ... 1990-91
100* ⎭

J. F. Reid (1)
180   Colombo
      (CCC) 1983-84

K. R. Rutherford (1)
105   Moratuwa ... 1992-93

J. G. Wright (1)
101   Hamilton ... 1990-91

For Sri Lanka (10)

P. A. de Silva (2)
267† Wellington .. 1990-91
123   Auckland ... 1990-91

R. L. Dias (1)
108† Colombo
      (SSC) 1983-84

A. P. Gurusinha (3)
119 ⎫ Hamilton ... 1990-91
102 ⎭
127   Dunedin 1994-95

D. S. B. P. Kuruppu (1)
201*† Colombo
      (CCC) 1986-87

R. S. Mahanama (2)
153   Moratuwa ... 1992-93
109   Colombo
      (SSC) 1992-93

H. P. Tillekeratne (1)
108   Dunedin 1994-95

† *Signifies hundred on first appearance in New Zealand–Sri Lanka Tests.*

Note: A. P. Gurusinha and A. H. Jones at Hamilton in 1990-91 provided the second instance of a player on each side hitting two separate hundreds in a Test match.

RECORD PARTNERSHIPS FOR EACH WICKET

For New Zealand

161 for 1st	T. J. Franklin and J. G. Wright at Hamilton	1990-91
76 for 2nd	J. G. Wright and A. H. Jones at Auckland	1990-91
467 for 3rd†‡	A. H. Jones and M. D. Crowe at Wellington	1990-91
82 for 4th	J. F. Reid and S. L. Boock at Colombo (CCC)	1983-84
151 for 5th	K. R. Rutherford and C. Z. Harris at Moratuwa	1992-93
246* for 6th†	J. J. Crowe and R. J. Hadlee at Colombo (CCC)	1986-87
47 for 7th	D. N. Patel and M. L. Su'a at Dunedin	1994-95
79 for 8th	J. V. Coney and W. K. Lees at Christchurch	1982-83
42 for 9th	W. K. Lees and M. C. Snedden at Christchurch	1982-83
52 for 10th	W. K. Lees and E. J. Chatfield at Christchurch	1982-83

For Sri Lanka

102 for 1st	R. S. Mahanama and U. C. Hathurusinghe at Colombo (SSC)	1992-93
138 for 2nd	R. S. Mahanama and A. P. Gurusinha at Moratuwa	1992-93
159* for 3rd†[1]	S. Wettimuny and R. L. Dias at Colombo (SSC)	1983-84
192 for 4th	A. P. Gurusinha and H. P. Tillekeratne at Dunedin	1994-95
130 for 5th	R. S. Madugalle and D. S. de Silva at Wellington	1982-83
109* for 6th[2]	R. S. Madugalle and A. Ranatunga at Colombo (CCC)	1983-84
89 for 7th	C. I. Dunusinghe and W. P. U. J. C. Vaas at Napier	1994-95
69 for 8th	H. P. Tillekeratne and S. D. Anurasiri at Colombo (SSC)	1992-93
31 for 9th ⎧	G. F. Labrooy and R. J. Ratnayake at Auckland	1990-91
⎩	S. T. Jayasuriya and R. J. Ratnayake at Auckland	1990-91
60 for 10th	V. B. John and A. M. J. G. Amerasinghe at Kandy	1983-84

† *Denotes record partnership against all countries.*

‡ *Record third-wicket partnership in first-class cricket.*

[1] *163 runs were added for this wicket in two separate partnerships: S. Wettimuny retired hurt and was replaced by L. R. D. Mendis when 159 had been added.*

[2] *119 runs were added for this wicket in two separate partnerships: R. S. Madugalle retired hurt and was replaced by D. S. de Silva when 109 had been added.*

TEN WICKETS OR MORE IN A MATCH

For New Zealand (1)

10-102 (5-73, 5-29) R. J. Hadlee, Colombo (CCC) 1983-84

For Sri Lanka (1)

10-90 (5-47, 5-43)† W. P. U. J. C. Vaas, Napier........................ 1994-95

† *Signifies ten wickets or more on first appearance in New Zealand–Sri Lanka Tests.*

NEW ZEALAND v ZIMBABWE

Season	New Zealand	Captains Zimbabwe	T	NZ	Z	D
1992-93Z	M. D. Crowe	D. L. Houghton	2	1	0	1

Z Played in Zimbabwe.

HIGHEST INNINGS TOTALS

For New Zealand: 335 at Harare 1992-93

For Zimbabwe: 283-9 dec. at Harare 1992-93

INDIVIDUAL HUNDREDS

For New Zealand (2)

M. D. Crowe (1) | **R. T. Latham** (1)
140 Harare ..... 1992-93 | 119† Bulawayo ... 1992-93

For Zimbabwe (1)

K. J. Arnott (1)
101*† Bulawayo ... 1992-93

† *Signifies hundred on first appearance in New Zealand–Zimbabwe Tests.*

HUNDRED PARTNERSHIPS

For New Zealand

116 for 1st	M. J. Greatbatch and R. T. Latham at Bulawayo.............	1992-93
102 for 1st	M. J. Greatbatch and R. T. Latham at Bulawayo.............	1992-93
127 for 2nd	R. T. Latham and A. H. Jones at Bulawayo	1992-93
168 for 4th	M. D. Crowe and K. R. Rutherford at Harare	1992-93
130 for 5th	K. R. Rutherford and D. N. Patel at Harare................	1992-93

For Zimbabwe

107 for 2nd	K. J. Arnott and A. D. R. Campbell at Harare	1992-93
105* for 2nd	K. J. Arnott and A. D. R. Campbell at Bulawayo	1992-93

BEST MATCH BOWLING ANALYSES

For New Zealand

8-131 (2-81, 6-50) D. N. Patel, Harare 1992-93

For Zimbabwe

4-101 (3-49, 1-52) D. H. Brain, Harare 1992-93

INDIA v PAKISTAN

		Captains				
Season	*India*	*Pakistan*	*T*	*I*	*P*	*D*
1952-53*I*	L. Amarnath	A. H. Kardar	5	2	1	2
1954-55*P*	V. Mankad	A. H. Kardar	5	0	0	5
1960-61*I*	N. J. Contractor	Fazal Mahmood	5	0	0	5
1978-79*P*	B. S. Bedi	Mushtaq Mohammad	3	0	2	1
1979-80*I*	S. M. Gavaskar[1]	Asif Iqbal	6	2	0	4
1982-83*P*	S. M. Gavaskar	Imran Khan	6	0	3	3
1983-84*I*	Kapil Dev	Zaheer Abbas	3	0	0	3
1984-85*P*	S. M. Gavaskar	Zaheer Abbas	2	0	0	2
1986-87*I*	Kapil Dev	Imran Khan	5	0	1	4
1989-90*P*	K. Srikkanth	Imran Khan	4	0	0	4
	In India		24	4	2	18
	In Pakistan		20	0	5	15
	Totals........................		44	4	7	33

I Played in India.   P Played in Pakistan.

Note: The following was appointed by the home authority for only a minor proportion of the series:

[1]G. R. Viswanath (Sixth).

HIGHEST INNINGS TOTALS

For India in India: 539-9 dec. at Madras 1960-61
       in Pakistan: 509 at Lahore 1989-90

For Pakistan in India: 487-9 dec. at Madras 1986-87
       in Pakistan: 699-5 at Lahore 1989-90

LOWEST INNINGS TOTALS

For India in India: 106 at Lucknow 1952-53
       in Pakistan: 145 at Karachi 1954-55

For Pakistan in India: 116 at Bangalore 1986-87
       in Pakistan: 158 at Dacca 1954-55

INDIVIDUAL HUNDREDS

For India (31)

M. Amarnath (4)	166 Madras 1979-80	**K. Srikkanth (1)**
109* Lahore 1982-83	127*‡ Faisalabad .. 1982-83	123 Madras 1986-87
120 Lahore 1982-83	103* Bangalore ... 1983-84	**P. R. Umrigar (5)**
103* Karachi ... 1982-83	**V. S. Hazare (1)**	102 Bombay ... 1952-53
101* Lahore 1984-85	146* Bombay ... 1952-53	108 Peshawar ... 1954-55
M. Azharuddin (3)	**S. V. Manjrekar (2)**	115 Kanpur 1960-61
141 Calcutta ... 1986-87	113*† Karachi 1989-90	117 Madras 1960-61
110 Jaipur 1986-87	218 Lahore 1989-90	112 Delhi 1960-61
109 Faisalabad . 1989-90	**S. M. Patil (1)**	**D. B. Vengsarkar (2)**
C. G. Borde (1)	127 Faisalabad .. 1984-85	146* Delhi 1979-80
177* Madras 1960-61	**R. J. Shastri (3)**	109 Ahmedabad . 1986-87
A. D. Gaekwad (1)	128 Karachi 1982-83	**G. R. Viswanath (1)**
201 Jullundur ... 1983-84	139 Faisalabad .. 1984-85	145† Faisalabad .. 1978-79
S. M. Gavaskar (5)	125 Jaipur 1986-87	
111 } Karachi 1978-79	**R. H. Shodhan (1)**	
137 }	110† Calcutta 1952-53	

For Pakistan (41)

Aamer Malik (2)	126 Faisalabad .. 1982-83	**Saeed Ahmed (2)**
117 Faisalabad .. 1989-90	280* Hyderabad .. 1982-83	121† Bombay 1960-61
113 Lahore 1989-90	145 Lahore 1989-90	103 Madras 1960-61
Alim-ud-Din (1)	**Mohsin Khan (1)**	**Salim Malik (3)**
103* Karachi ... 1954-55	101*† Lahore 1982-83	107 Faisalabad . 1982-83
Asif Iqbal (1)	**Mudassar Nazar (6)**	102* Faisalabad .. 1984-85
104† Faisalabad .. 1978-79	126 Bangalore .. 1979-80	102* Karachi 1989-90
Hanif Mohammad (2)	119 Karachi 1982-83	**Shoaib Mohammad (2)**
142 Bahawalpur . 1954-55	231 Hyderabad .. 1982-83	101 Madras 1986-87
160 Bombay 1960-61	152*‡ Lahore 1982-83	203* Lahore 1989-90
Ijaz Faqih (1)	152 Karachi 1982-83	**Wasim Raja (1)**
105† Ahmedabad . 1986-87	199 Faisalabad .. 1984-85	125 Jullundur ... 1983-84
Imtiaz Ahmed (1)	**Mushtaq Mohammad (1)**	**Zaheer Abbas (6)**
135 Madras 1960-61	101 Delhi 1960-61	176† Faisalabad .. 1978-79
Imran Khan (3)	**Nazar Mohammad (1)**	235* Lahore 1978-79
117 Faisalabad .. 1982-83	124*‡ Lucknow 1952-53	215 Lahore 1982-83
135* Madras 1986-87	**Qasim Omar (1)**	186 Karachi 1982-83
109* Karachi 1989-90	210 Faisalabad .. 1984-85	168 Faisalabad .. 1982-83
Javed Miandad (5)	**Ramiz Raja (1)**	168* Lahore 1984-85
154*† Faisalabad .. 1978-79	114 Jaipur 1986-87	
100 Karachi 1978-79		

† *Signifies hundred on first appearance in India–Pakistan Tests.*
‡ *Carried his bat.*

RECORD PARTNERSHIPS FOR EACH WICKET

For India

200 for 1st	S. M. Gavaskar and K. Srikkanth at Madras	1986-87
135 for 2nd	N. S. Sidhu and S. V. Manjrekar at Karachi.................	1989-90
190 for 3rd	M. Amarnath and Yashpal Sharma at Lahore	1982-83
186 for 4th	S. V. Manjrekar and R. J. Shastri at Lahore................	1989-90
200 for 5th	S. M. Patil and R. J. Shastri at Faisalabad	1984-85
143 for 6th	M. Azharuddin and Kapil Dev at Calcutta	1986-87
155 for 7th	R. M. H. Binny and Madan Lal at Bangalore	1983-84
122 for 8th	S. M. H. Kirmani and Madan Lal at Faisalabad	1982-83
149 for 9th†	P. G. Joshi and R. B. Desai at Bombay	1960-61
109 for 10th†	H. R. Adhikari and Ghulam Ahmed at Delhi	1952-53

For Pakistan

162 for 1st	Hanif Mohammad and Imtiaz Ahmed at Madras	1960-61
250 for 2nd	Mudassar Nazar and Qasim Omar at Faisalabad	1984-85
451 for 3rd†	Mudassar Nazar and Javed Miandad at Hyderabad	1982-83
287 for 4th	Javed Miandad and Zaheer Abbas at Faisalabad	1982-83
213 for 5th	Zaheer Abbas and Mudassar Nazar at Karachi	1982-83
207 for 6th	Salim Malik and Imran Khan at Faisalabad	1982-83
154 for 7th	Imran Khan and Ijaz Faqih at Ahmedabad	1986-87
112 for 8th	Imran Khan and Wasim Akram at Madras	1986-87
60 for 9th	Wasim Bari and Iqbal Qasim at Bangalore	1979-80
104 for 10th	Zulfiqar Ahmed and Amir Elahi at Madras	1952-53

† *Denotes record partnership against all countries.*

TEN WICKETS OR MORE IN A MATCH

For India (3)

11-146 (4-90, 7-56)	Kapil Dev, Madras	1979-80
10-126 (7-27, 3-99)	Maninder Singh, Bangalore	1986-87
13-131 (8-52, 5-79)†	V. Mankad, Delhi	1952-53

For Pakistan (5)

12-94 (5-52, 7-42)	Fazal Mahmood, Lucknow	1952-53
11-79 (3-19, 8-60)	Imran Khan, Karachi	1982-83
11-180 (6-98, 5-82)	Imran Khan, Faisalabad	1982-83
10-175 (4-135, 6-40)	Iqbal Qasim, Bombay	1979-80
11-190 (8-69, 3-121)	Sikander Bakht, Delhi	1979-80

† *Signifies ten wickets or more on first appearance in India–Pakistan Tests.*

INDIA v SRI LANKA

		Captains				
Season	*India*	*Sri Lanka*	*T*	*I*	*SL*	*D*
1982-83*I*	S. M. Gavaskar	B. Warnapura	1	0	0	1
1985-86*S*	Kapil Dev	L. R. D. Mendis	3	0	1	2
1986-87*I*	Kapil Dev	L. R. D. Mendis	3	2	0	1
1990-91*I*	M. Azharuddin	A. Ranatunga	1	1	0	0
1993-94*S*	M. Azharuddin	A. Ranatunga	3	1	0	2
1993-94*I*	M. Azharuddin	A. Ranatunga	3	3	0	0
	In India		8	6	0	2
	In Sri Lanka		6	1	1	4
	Totals........................		14	7	1	6

I Played in India.   S Played in Sri Lanka.

HIGHEST INNINGS TOTALS

For India in India: 676-7 at Kanpur.....................................	1986-87
in Sri Lanka: 446 at Colombo (PSS)	1993-94
For Sri Lanka in India: 420 at Kanpur...............................	1986-87
in Sri Lanka: 385 at Colombo (PSS)	1985-86

LOWEST INNINGS TOTALS

For India in India: 288 at Chandigarh	1990-91
in Sri Lanka: 198 at Colombo (PSS)	1985-86
For Sri Lanka in India: 82 at Chandigarh	1990-91
in Sri Lanka: 198 at Kandy	1985-86

INDIVIDUAL HUNDREDS

For India (17)

M. Amarnath (2)
116*   Kandy......   1985-86
131   Nagpur ...   1986-87
M. Azharuddin (3)
199   Kanpur   1986-87
108   Bangalore ...   1993-94
152   Ahmedabad .   1993-94
S. M. Gavaskar (2)
155†   Madras   1982-83

176   Kanpur   1986-87
V. G. Kambli (2)
125   Colombo (SSC) 1993-94
120   Colombo (PSS) 1993-94
Kapil Dev (1)
163   Kanpur   1986-87
S. M. Patil (1)
114*†   Madras   1982-83

N. S. Sidhu (2)
104   Colombo (SSC) 1993-94
124   Lucknow.... 1993-94
S. R. Tendulkar (2)
104*   Colombo (SSC) 1993-94
142   Lucknow.... 1993-94
D. B. Vengsarkar (2)
153   Nagpur   1986-87
166   Cuttack..... 1986-87

For Sri Lanka (9)

P. A. de Silva (1)
148   Colombo (PSS) 1993-94
R. L. Dias (1)
106   Kandy...... 1985-86
R. S. Madugalle (1)
103   Colombo
     (SSC) 1985-86

R. S. Mahanama (1)
151   Colombo (PSS) 1993-94
L. R. D. Mendis (3)
105 ⎫
105 ⎬†Madras 1982-83
124   Kandy...... 1985-86

A. Ranatunga (1)
111   Colombo
     (SSC) 1985-86
S. A. R. Silva (1)
111   Colombo
     (PSS)....... 1985-86

† *Signifies hundred on first appearance in India–Sri Lanka Tests.*

RECORD PARTNERSHIPS FOR EACH WICKET

For India

171	for 1st	M. Prabhakar and N. S. Sidhu at Colombo (SSC)	1993-94
173	for 2nd	S. M. Gavaskar and D. B. Vengsarkar at Madras	1982-83
173	for 3rd	M. Amarnath and D. B. Vengsarkar at Nagpur	1986-87
163	for 4th	S. M. Gavaskar and M. Azharuddin at Kanpur	1986-87
87	for 5th	M. Azharuddin and S. V. Manjrekar at Bangalore	1993-94
272	for 6th	M. Azharuddin and Kapil Dev at Kanpur..................	1986-87
78*	for 7th	S. M. Patil and Madan Lal at Madras	1982-83
70	for 8th	Kapil Dev and L. Sivaramakrishnan at Colombo (PSS).......	1985-86
67	for 9th	M. Azharuddin and R. K. Chauhan at Ahmedabad	1993-94
29	for 10th	Kapil Dev and Chetan Sharma at Colombo (PSS)	1985-86

For Sri Lanka

159	for 1st†	S. Wettimuny and J. R. Ratnayeke at Kanpur	1986-87
95	for 2nd	S. A. R. Silva and R. S. Madugalle at Colombo (PSS)	1985-86
153	for 3rd	R. L. Dias and L. R. D. Mendis at Madras	1982-83
216	for 4th	R. L. Dias and L. R. D. Mendis at Kandy	1985-86.
144	for 5th	R. S. Madugalle and A. Ranatunga at Colombo (SSC).........	1985-86
89	for 6th	L. R. D. Mendis and A. N. Ranasinghe at Madras	1982-83
77	for 7th	R. S. Madugalle and D. S. de Silva at Madras	1982-83
40*	for 8th	P. A. de Silva and A. L. F. de Mel at Kandy	1985-86
60	for 9th	H. P. Tillekeratne and A. W. R. Madurasinghe at Chandigarh .	1990-91
44	for 10th	R. J. Ratnayake and E. A. R. de Silva at Nagpur	1986-87

† *Denotes record partnership against all countries.*

TEN WICKETS OR MORE IN A MATCH

For India (3)

11-128 (4-69, 7-59)	A. Kumble, Lucknow	1993-94
10-107 (3-56, 7-51)	Maninder Singh, Nagpur	1986-87
11-125 (5-38, 6-87)	S. L. V. Raju, Ahmedabad	1993-94

Note: The best match figures by a Sri Lankan bowler are 9-125 (4-76, 5-49) by R. J. Ratnayake against India at Colombo (PSS), 1985-86.

INDIA v ZIMBABWE

		Captains				
Season	*India*	*Zimbabwe*	*T*	*I*	*Z*	*D*
1992-93*Z*	M. Azharuddin	D. L. Houghton	1	0	0	1
1992-93*I*	M. Azharuddin	D. L. Houghton	1	1	0	0
	In India		1	1	0	0
	In Zimbabwe		1	0	0	1
	Totals		2	1	0	1

I Played in India. Z Played in Zimbabwe.

HIGHEST INNINGS TOTALS

For India: 536-7 dec. at Delhi 1992-93

For Zimbabwe: 456 at Harare 1992-93

INDIVIDUAL HUNDREDS

For India (2)

V. G. Kambli (1)	**S. V. Manjrekar** (1)
227† Delhi 1992-93	104† Harare 1992-93

For Zimbabwe (2)

A. Flower (1)	**D. L. Houghton** (1)
115 Delhi 1992-93	121† Harare 1992-93

† *Signifies hundred on first appearance in India–Zimbabwe Tests.*

HUNDRED PARTNERSHIPS

For India

107 for 2nd	N. S. Sidhu and V. G. Kambli at Delhi	1992-93
137 for 3rd	V. G. Kambli and S. R. Tendulkar at Delhi	1992-93
107 for 4th	V. G. Kambli and M. Azharuddin at Delhi	1992-93

For Zimbabwe

100 for 1st	K. J. Arnott and G. W. Flower at Harare	1992-93
192 for 4th	G. W. Flower and A. Flower at Delhi	1992-93
165 for 6th†	D. L. Houghton and A. Flower at Harare	1992-93

† *Denotes record partnership against all countries.*

BEST MATCH BOWLING ANALYSES

For India

8-160 (3-90, 5-70)   A. Kumble, Delhi 1992-93

For Zimbabwe

5-86 (5-86)   A. J. Traicos, Harare 1992-93

PAKISTAN v SRI LANKA

Season	Pakistan	Sri Lanka	T	P	SL	D
		Captains				
1981-82P	Javed Miandad	B. Warnapura[1]	3	2	0	1
1985-86P	Javed Miandad	L. R. D. Mendis	3	2	0	1
1985-86S	Imran Khan	L. R. D. Mendis	3	1	1	1
1991-92P	Imran Khan	P. A. de Silva	3	1	0	2
1994-95S†	Salim Malik	A. Ranatunga	2	2	0	0
	In Pakistan		9	5	0	4
	In Sri Lanka		5	3	1	1
	Totals............................		14	8	1	5

P Played in Pakistan. S Played in Sri Lanka.

† *One Test was cancelled owing to the threat of civil disturbances following a general election.*
Note: The following deputised for the official touring captain:
[1]L. R. D. Mendis (Second).

HIGHEST INNINGS TOTALS

For Pakistan in Pakistan: 555-3 at Faisalabad 1985-86
　　　　　　in Sri Lanka: 390 at Colombo (PSS).......................... 1994-95

For Sri Lanka in Pakistan: 479 at Faisalabad 1985-86
　　　　　　in Sri Lanka: 323-3 at Colombo (PSS) 1985-86

LOWEST INNINGS TOTALS

For Pakistan in Pakistan: 221 at Faisalabad 1991-92
　　　　　　in Sri Lanka: 132 at Colombo (CCC)........................ 1985-86

For Sri Lanka in Pakistan: 149 at Karachi 1981-82
　　　　　　in Sri Lanka: 71 at Kandy 1994-95

INDIVIDUAL HUNDREDS

For Pakistan (10)

Haroon Rashid (1)	**Qasim Omar** (1)	**Salim Malik** (2)
153† Karachi 1981-82	206† Faisalabad .. 1985-86	100*† Karachi 1981-82
Inzamam-ul-Haq (1)	**Ramiz Raja** (1)	101 Sialkot 1991-92
100* Kandy...... 1994-95	122 Colombo	**Zaheer Abbas** (1)
Javed Miandad (1)	(PSS)....... 1985-86	134† Lahore 1981-82
203* Faisalabad .. 1985-86	**Saeed Anwar** (1)	
Mohsin Khan (1)	136† Colombo	
129 Lahore 1981-82	(PSS)....... 1994-95	

For Sri Lanka (7)

P. A. de Silva (3)	**R. L. Dias** (1)	**A. Ranatunga** (1)
122† Faisalabad .. 1985-86	109 Lahore 1981-82	135* Colombo
105 Karachi 1985-86	**A. P. Gurusinha** (1)	(PSS)....... 1985-86
127 Colombo	116* Colombo	**S. Wettimuny** (1)
(PSS)....... 1994-95	(PSS)....... 1985-86	157 Faisalabad .. 1981-82

† *Signifies hundred on first appearance in Pakistan–Sri Lanka Tests.*

RECORD PARTNERSHIPS FOR EACH WICKET

For Pakistan

128 for 1st	{ Ramiz Raja and Shoaib Mohammad at Sialkot..............	1991-92
	{ Saeed Anwar and Aamir Sohail at Colombo (PSS).........	1994-95
151 for 2nd	Mohsin Khan and Majid Khan at Lahore...................	1981-82
397 for 3rd	Qasim Omar and Javed Miandad at Faisalabad	1985-86
162 for 4th	Salim Malik and Javed Miandad at Karachi................	1981-82
132 for 5th	Salim Malik and Imran Khan at Sialkot	1991-92
100 for 6th	Zaheer Abbas and Imran Khan at Lahore..................	1981-82
104 for 7th	Haroon Rashid and Tahir Naqqash at Karachi	1981-82
33 for 8th	Inzamam-ul-Haq and Wasim Akram at Kandy	1994-95
127 for 9th	Haroon Rashid and Rashid Khan at Karachi	1981-82
48 for 10th	Rashid Khan and Tauseef Ahmed at Faisalabad	1981-82

For Sri Lanka

81 for 1st	R. S. Mahanama and U. C. Hathurusinghe at Faisalabad	1991-92
217 for 2nd†	S. Wettimuny and R. L. Dias at Faisalabad	1981-82
85 for 3rd	S. Wettimuny and R. L. Dias at Faisalabad	1985-86
240* for 4th†	A. P. Gurusinha and A. Ranatunga at Colombo (PSS)	1985-86
119 for 5th	P. A. de Silva and H. P. Tillekeratne at Colombo (PSS)	1994-95
121 for 6th	A. Ranatunga and P. A. de Silva at Faisalabad	1985-86
131 for 7th	H. P. Tillekeratne and R. S. Kalpage at Kandy	1994-95
61 for 8th†	R. S. Madugalle and D. S. de Silva at Faisalabad	1981-82
52 for 9th	P. A. de Silva and R. J. Ratnayake at Faisalabad	1985-86
36 for 10th	R. J. Ratnayake and R. G. C. E. Wijesuriya at Faisalabad.....	1985-86

† *Denotes record partnership against all countries.*

TEN WICKETS OR MORE IN A MATCH

For Pakistan (2)

14-116 (8-58, 6-58)	Imran Khan, Lahore	1981-82
11-119 (6-34, 5-85)	Waqar Younis, Kandy	1994-95

Note: The best match figures by a Sri Lankan bowler are 9-162 (4-103, 5-59), D. S. de Silva at Faisalabad, 1981-82.

PAKISTAN v ZIMBABWE

Captains

Season	Pakistan	Zimbabwe	T	P	Z	D
1993-94P	Wasim Akram[1]	A. Flower	3	2	0	1
1994-95Z	Salim Malik	A. Flower	3	2	1	0
	In Pakistan		3	2	0	1
	In Zimbabwe		3	2	1	0
	Totals		6	4	1	1

P Played in Pakistan. Z Played in Zimbabwe.

Note: The following was appointed by the home authority for only a minor proportion of the series:

[1]Waqar Younis (First).

HIGHEST INNINGS TOTALS

For Pakistan in Pakistan: 423-8 dec. at Karachi (DS) 1993-94
in Zimbabwe: 322 at Harare 1994-95

For Zimbabwe in Pakistan: 289 at Karachi (DS) 1993-94
in Zimbabwe: 544-4 dec. at Harare 1994-95

LOWEST INNINGS TOTALS

For Pakistan in Pakistan: 147 at Lahore 1993-94
in Zimbabwe: 158 at Harare 1994-95

For Zimbabwe in Pakistan: 134 at Karachi (DS) 1993-94
in Zimbabwe: 139 at Harare 1994-95

INDIVIDUAL HUNDREDS

For Pakistan (1)

Inzamam-ul-Haq (1)
101   Harare 1994-95

For Zimbabwe (3)

A. Flower (1)	**G. W. Flower** (1)	**G. J. Whittall** (1)
156 Harare 1994-95	201* Harare 1994-95	113* Harare 1994-95

RECORD PARTNERSHIPS FOR EACH WICKET

For Pakistan

95	for 1st	Aamir Sohail and Shoaib Mohammad at Karachi (DS)	1993-94
118*	for 2nd	Shoaib Mohammad and Asif Mujtaba at Lahore	1993-94
83	for 3rd	Shoaib Mohammad and Javed Miandad at Karachi (DS)	1993-94
116	for 4th	Inzamam-ul-Haq and Ijaz Ahmed at Harare	1994-95
76	for 5th	Ijaz Ahmed and Inzamam-ul-Haq at Harare	1994-95
96	for 6th	Inzamam-ul-Haq and Rashid Latif at Harare	1994-95
120	for 7th	Ijaz Ahmed and Inzamam-ul-Haq at Harare	1994-95
46	for 8th	Inzamam-ul-Haq and Wasim Akram at Harare	1994-95
60*	for 9th	Rashid Latif and Tausif Ahmed at Karachi (DS)	1993-94
28	for 10th	Inzamam-ul-Haq and Aamir Nazir at Harare	1994-95

For Zimbabwe

20	for 1st	G. W. Flower and S. V. Carlisle at Harare	1994-95
135	for 2nd†	M. H. Dekker and A. D. R. Campbell at Rawalpindi	1993-94
61	for 3rd	A. D. R. Campbell and D. L. Houghton at Karachi (DS)	1993-94
269	for 4th†	G. W. Flower and A. Flower at Harare	1994-95
233*	for 5th†	G. W. Flower and G. J. Whittall at Harare	1994-95
72	for 6th	M. H. Dekker and G. J. Whittall at Harare	1993-94
48	for 7th	A. D. R. Campbell and P. A. Strang at Bulawayo	1994-95
46	for 8th	A. Flower and D. H. Brain at Lahore	1993-94
40	for 9th	P. A. Strang and D. H. Brain at Harare	1994-95
29	for 10th	E. A. Brandes and S. G. Peall at Rawalpindi	1993-94

† *Denotes record partnership against all countries.*

TEN WICKETS OR MORE IN A MATCH

For Pakistan (1)

13-135 (7-91, 6-44)†   Waqar Younis, Karachi (DS)   1993-94

Note: The best match figures for Zimbabwe are 9-105 (6-90, 3-15) by H. H. Streak at Harare, 1994-95.

† *Signifies ten wickets or more on first appearance in Pakistan–Zimbabwe Tests.*

SRI LANKA v ZIMBABWE

Season	Sri Lanka	*Captains* Zimbabwe	T	P	Z	D
1994-95Z	A. Ranatunga	A. Flower	3	0	0	3

Z Played in Zimbabwe.

HIGHEST INNINGS TOTALS

For Sri Lanka: 402 at Harare 1994-95
For Zimbabwe: 462-9 dec. at Bulawayo 1994-95

LOWEST INNINGS TOTALS

For Sri Lanka: 218 at Bulawayo 1994-95
For Zimbabwe: 375 at Harare 1994-95

INDIVIDUAL HUNDREDS

For Sri Lanka (4)

A. P. Gurusinha (1)
128† Harare 1994-95

S. Ranatunga (2)
118† Harare 1994-95
100* Bulawayo . . . 1994-95

H. P. Tillekeratne (1)
116   Harare 1994-95

For Zimbabwe (2)

D. L. Houghton (2)
266   Bulawayo . . . 1994-95
142   Harare 1994-95

† *Signifies hundred on first appearance in Sri Lanka–Zimbabwe Tests.*

HUNDRED PARTNERSHIPS

For Sri Lanka

217 for 2nd†	A. P. Gurusinha and S. Ranatunga at Harare	1994-95

For Zimbabwe

113 for 1st†	G. W. Flower and M. H. Dekker at Harare	1994-95
194 for 3rd†	A. D. R. Campbell and D. L. Houghton at Harare	1994-95
121 for 4th	D. L. Houghton and A. Flower at Bulawayo	1994-95
100 for 6th	D. L. Houghton and W. R. James at Bulawayo	1994-95

† *Denotes record partnership against all countries.*

BEST MATCH BOWLING ANALYSES

For Sri Lanka

7-116 (7-116)	K. R. Pushpakumara, Harare	1994-95

For Zimbabwe

5-129 (4-97, 1-32)	H. H. Streak, Harare	1994-95

TEST MATCH GROUNDS

In Chronological Sequence

City and Ground	First Test Match		Tests
1. Melbourne, Melbourne Cricket Ground	March 15, 1877	A v E	87
2. London, Kennington Oval	September 6, 1880	E v A	78
3. Sydney, Sydney Cricket Ground (No. 1)	February 17, 1882	A v E	81
4. Manchester, Old Trafford	July 11, 1884	E v A	62
5. London, Lord's	July 21, 1884	E v A	93
6. Adelaide, Adelaide Oval	December 12, 1884	A v E	53
7. Port Elizabeth, St George's Park	March 12, 1889	SA v E	13
8. Cape Town, Newlands	March 25, 1889	SA v E	27
9. Johannesburg, Old Wanderers	March 2, 1896	SA v E	22
Now the site of Johannesburg Railway Station.			
10. Nottingham, Trent Bridge	June 1, 1899	E v A	43
11. Leeds, Headingley	June 29, 1899	E v A	57
12. Birmingham, Edgbaston	May 29, 1902	E v A	31
13. Sheffield, Bramall Lane	July 3, 1902	E v A	1
Sheffield United Football Club have built a stand over the cricket pitch.			
14. Durban, Lord's	January 21, 1910	SA v E	4
Ground destroyed and built on.			
15. Durban, Kingsmead	January 18, 1923	SA v E	22
16. Brisbane, Exhibition Ground	November 30, 1928	A v E	2
No longer used for cricket.			
17. Christchurch, Lancaster Park	January 10, 1930	NZ v E	33
18. Bridgetown, Kensington Oval	January 11, 1930	WI v E	31
19. Wellington, Basin Reserve	January 24, 1930	NZ v E	30
20. Port-of-Spain, Queen's Park Oval	February 1, 1930	WI v E	44
21. Auckland, Eden Park	February 17, 1930	NZ v E	37
22. Georgetown, Bourda	February 21, 1930	WI v E	23
23. Kingston, Sabina Park	April 3, 1930	WI v E	31
24. Brisbane, Woolloongabba	November 27, 1931	A v SA	37
25. Bombay, Gymkhana Ground	December 15, 1933	I v E	1
No longer used for first-class cricket.			

	City and Ground	First Test Match		Tests
26.	Calcutta, Eden Gardens	January 5, 1934	I v E	27
27.	Madras, Chepauk (Chidambaram Stadium)	February 10, 1934	I v E	21
28.	Delhi, Feroz Shah Kotla	November 10, 1948	I v WI	23
29.	Bombay, Brabourne Stadium	December 9, 1948	I v WI	17
	Rarely used for first-class cricket.			
30.	Johannesburg, Ellis Park	December 27, 1948	SA v E	6
	Mainly a rugby stadium, no longer used for cricket.			
31.	Kanpur, Green Park (Modi Stadium)	January 12, 1952	I v E	16
32.	Lucknow, University Ground	October 25, 1952	I v P	1
	Ground destroyed, now partly under a river bed.			
33.	Dacca, Dacca Stadium	January 1, 1955	P v I	7
	Ceased staging Tests after East Pakistan seceded and became Bangladesh.			
34.	Bahawalpur, Dring (now Bahawal) Stadium	January 15, 1955	P v I	1
	Still used for first-class cricket.			
35.	Lahore, Lawrence Gardens (Bagh-i-Jinnah)	January 29, 1955	P v I	3
	Still used for club and occasional first-class matches.			
36.	Peshawar, Services Ground	February 13, 1955	P v I	1
	Superseded by new stadium.			
37.	Karachi, National Stadium	February 26, 1955	P v I	30
38.	Dunedin, Carisbrook	March 11, 1955	NZ v E	9
39.	Hyderabad, Fateh Maidan (Lal Bahadur Stadium)	November 19, 1955	I v NZ	3
40.	Madras, Corporation Stadium	January 6, 1956	I v NZ	9
	Superseded by rebuilt Chepauk Stadium.			
41.	Johannesburg, Wanderers	December 24, 1956	SA v E	15
42.	Lahore, Gaddafi Stadium	November 21, 1959	P v A	27
43.	Rawalpindi, Pindi Club Ground	March 27, 1965	P v NZ	1
	Superseded by new stadium.			
44.	Nagpur, Vidarbha C.A. Ground	October 3, 1969	I v NZ	4
45.	Perth, Western Australian C.A. Ground	December 11, 1970	A v E	22
46.	Hyderabad, Niaz Stadium	March 16, 1973	P v E	5
47.	Bangalore, Karnataka State C.A. Ground (Chinnaswamy Stadium)	November 22, 1974	I v WI	10
48.	Bombay, Wankhede Stadium	January 23, 1975	I v WI	15
49.	Faisalabad, Iqbal Stadium	October 16, 1978	P v I	16
50.	Napier, McLean Park	February 16, 1979	NZ v P	3
51.	Multan, Ibn-e-Qasim Bagh Stadium	December 30, 1980	P v WI	1
52.	St John's (Antigua), Recreation Ground	March 27, 1981	WI v E	9
53.	Colombo, P. Saravanamuttu Stadium	February 17, 1982	SL v E	6
54.	Kandy, Asgiriya Stadium	April 22, 1983	SL v A	6
55.	Jullundur, Burlton Park	September 24, 1983	I v P	1
56.	Ahmedabad, Gujarat Stadium	November 12, 1983	I v WI	3
57.	Colombo, Sinhalese Sports Club Ground	March 16, 1984	SL v NZ	7
58.	Colombo, Colombo Cricket Club Ground	March 24, 1984	SL v NZ	3
59.	Sialkot, Jinnah Stadium	October 27, 1985	P v SL	3
60.	Cuttack, Barabati Stadium	January 4, 1987	I v SL	1
61.	Jaipur, Sawai Mansingh Stadium	February 21, 1987	I v P	1
62.	Hobart, Bellerive Oval	December 16, 1989	A v SL	2
63.	Chandigarh, Sector 16 Stadium	November 23, 1990	I v SL	1
	Superseded by Mohali ground			
64.	Hamilton, Trust Bank (Seddon) Park	February 22, 1991	NZ v SL	3
65.	Gujranwala, Municipal Stadium	December 20, 1991	P v SL	1
66.	Colombo, R. Premadasa (Khettarama) Stadium	August 28, 1992	SL v A	1
67.	Moratuwa, Tyronne Fernando Stadium	September 8, 1992	SL v A	4
68.	Harare, Harare Sports Club	October 18, 1992	Z v I	6
69.	Bulawayo, Bulawayo Athletic Club	November 1, 1992	Z v NZ	1
70.	Karachi, Defence Stadium	December 1, 1993	P v Z	2
71.	Rawalpindi, Rawalpindi Cricket Stadium	December 9, 1993	P v Z	2
72.	Lucknow, K. D. "Babu" Singh Stadium	January 18, 1994	I v SL	1
73.	Bulawayo, Queens Sports Club	October 20, 1994	Z v SL	2
74.	Mohali, Punjab Cricket Association Stadium	December 10, 1994	I v WI	1

FAMILIES IN TEST CRICKET

FATHERS AND SONS

England
M. C. Cowdrey (114 Tests, 1954-55–1974-75) and C. S. Cowdrey (6 Tests, 1984-85–1988).
J. Hardstaff (5 Tests, 1907-08) and J. Hardstaff jun. (23 Tests, 1935–1948).
L. Hutton (79 Tests, 1937–1954-55) and R. A. Hutton (5 Tests, 1971).
F. T. Mann (5 Tests, 1922-23) and F. G. Mann (7 Tests, 1948-49–1949).
J. H. Parks (1 Test, 1937) and J. M. Parks (46 Tests, 1954–1967-68).
M. J. Stewart (8 Tests, 1962–1963-64) and A. J. Stewart (48 Tests, 1989-90–1995).
F. W. Tate (1 Test, 1902) and M. W. Tate (39 Tests, 1924–1935).
C. L. Townsend (2 Tests, 1899) and D. C. H. Townsend (3 Tests, 1934-35).

Australia
E. J. Gregory (1 Test, 1876-77) and S. E. Gregory (58 Tests, 1890–1912).

South Africa
F. Hearne (4 Tests, 1891-92–1895-96) and G. A. L. Hearne (3 Tests, 1922-23–1924).
  F. Hearne also played 2 Tests for England in 1888-89.
J. D. Lindsay (3 Tests, 1947) and D. T. Lindsay (19 Tests, 1963-64–1969-70).
A. W. Nourse (45 Tests, 1902-03–1924) and A. D. Nourse (34 Tests, 1935–1951).
L. R. Tuckett (1 Test, 1913-14) and L. Tuckett (9 Tests, 1947–1948-49).

West Indies
G. A. Headley (22 Tests, 1929-30–1953-54) and R. G. A. Headley (2 Tests, 1973).
O. C. Scott (8 Tests, 1928–1930-31) and A. P. H. Scott (1 Test, 1952-53).

New Zealand
W. M. Anderson (1 Test, 1945-46) and R. W. Anderson (9 Tests, 1976-77–1978).
W. P. Bradburn (2 Tests, 1963-64) and G. E. Bradburn (4 Tests, 1990-91).
B. L. Cairns (43 Tests, 1973-74–1985-86) and C. L. Cairns (10 Tests, 1989-90–1993-94).
W. A. Hadlee (11 Tests, 1937–1950-51) and D. R. Hadlee (26 Tests, 1969–1977-78);
  R. J. Hadlee (86 Tests, 1972-73–1990).
P. G. Z. Harris (9 Tests, 1955-56–1964-65) and C. Z. Harris (5 Tests, 1993-94).
H. G. Vivian (7 Tests, 1931–1937) and G. E. Vivian (5 Tests, 1964-65–1971-72).

India
L. Amarnath (24 Tests, 1933-34–1952-53) and M. Amarnath (69 Tests, 1969-70–1987-88);
  S. Amarnath (10 Tests, 1975-76–1978-79).
D. K. Gaekwad (11 Tests, 1952–1960-61) and A. D. Gaekwad (40 Tests, 1974-75–1984-85).
Nawab of Pataudi (Iftikhar Ali Khan) (3 Tests, 1946) and Nawab of Pataudi (Mansur Ali
  Khan) (46 Tests, 1961-62–1974-75).
  Nawab of Pataudi sen. also played 3 Tests for England, 1932-33–1934.
V. L. Manjrekar (55 Tests, 1951-52–1964-65) and S. V. Manjrekar (33 Tests, 1987-88–1994-95).
V. Mankad (44 Tests, 1946–1958-59) and A. V. Mankad (22 Tests, 1969-70–1977-78).
Pankaj Roy (43 Tests, 1951-52–1960-61) and Pranab Roy (2 Tests, 1981-82).

India and Pakistan
M. Jahangir Khan (4 Tests, 1932–1936) and Majid Khan (63 Tests, 1964-65–1982-83).
S. Wazir Ali (7 Tests, 1932–1936) and Khalid Wazir (2 Tests, 1954).

Pakistan
Hanif Mohammad (55 Tests, 1954–1969-70) and Shoaib Mohammad (42 Tests, 1983-84–
  1993-94).
Nazar Mohammad (5 Tests, 1952-53) and Mudassar Nazar (76 Tests, 1976-77–
  1988-89).

GRANDFATHERS AND GRANDSONS

Australia
V. Y. Richardson (19 Tests, 1924-25–1935-36) and G. S. Chappell (87 Tests, 1970-71–1983-84);
I. M. Chappell (75 Tests, 1964-65–1979-80); T. M. Chappell (3 Tests, 1981).

GREAT-GRANDFATHER AND GREAT-GRANDSON

Australia
W. H. Cooper (2 Tests, 1881-82 and 1884-85) and A. P. Sheahan (31 Tests, 1967-68–1973-74).

BROTHERS IN SAME TEST TEAM

England
E. M., G. F. and W. G. Grace: 1 Test, 1880.
C. T. and G. B. Studd: 4 Tests, 1882-83.
A. and G. G. Hearne: 1 Test, 1891-92.
   F. Hearne, their brother, played in this match for South Africa.
D. W. and P. E. Richardson: 1 Test, 1957.

Australia
E. J. and D. W. Gregory: 1 Test, 1876-77.
C. and A. C. Bannerman: 1 Test, 1878-79.
G. and W. F. Giffen: 2 Tests, 1891-92.
G. H. S. and A. E. Trott: 3 Tests, 1894-95.
I. M. and G. S. Chappell: 43 Tests, 1970-71–1979-80.
S. R. and M. E. Waugh: 33 Tests, 1990-91–1994-95 – the first instance of twins appearing
   together.

South Africa
S. J. and S. D. Snooke: 1 Test, 1907.
D. and H. W. Taylor: 2 Tests, 1913-14.
R. H. M. and P. A. M. Hands: 1 Test, 1913-14.
E. A. B. and A. M. B. Rowan: 9 Tests, 1948-49–1951.
P. M. and R. G. Pollock: 23 Tests, 1963-64–1969-70.
A. J. and D. B. Pithey: 5 Tests, 1963-64.
P. N. and G. Kirsten: 7 Tests, 1993-94–1994.

West Indies
G. C. and R. S. Grant: 4 Tests, 1934-35.
J. B. and V. H. Stollmeyer: 1 Test, 1939.
D. St E. and E. St E. Atkinson: 1 Test, 1957-58.

New Zealand
D. R. and R. J. Hadlee: 10 Tests, 1973–1977-78.
H. J. and G. P. Howarth: 4 Tests, 1974-75–1976-77.
J. M. and N. M. Parker: 3 Tests, 1976-77.
B. P. and J. G. Bracewell: 1 Test, 1980-81.
J. J. and M. D. Crowe: 34 Tests, 1983–1989-90.

India
S. Wazir Ali and S. Nazir Ali: 2 Tests, 1932–1933-34.
L. Ramji and Amar Singh: 1 Test, 1933-34.
C. K. and C. S. Nayudu: 4 Tests, 1933-34–1936.
A. G. Kripal Singh and A. G. Milkha Singh: 1 Test, 1961-62.
S. and M. Amarnath: 8 Tests, 1975-76–1978-79.

Pakistan

Wazir and Hanif Mohammad: 18 Tests, 1952-53–1959-60.
Wazir and Mushtaq Mohammad: 1 Test, 1958-59.
Hanif and Mushtaq Mohammad: 19 Tests, 1960-61–1969-70.
Hanif, Mushtaq and Sadiq Mohammad: 1 Test, 1969-70.
Mushtaq and Sadiq Mohammad: 26 Tests, 1969-70–1978–79.
Wasim and Ramiz Raja: 2 Tests, 1983-84.

Sri Lanka

M. D. and S. Wettimuny: 2 Tests, 1982-83.
A. and D. Ranatunga: 2 Tests, 1989-90.
A. and S. Ranatunga: 6 Tests, 1994-95.

Zimbabwe

A. and G. W. Flower: 13 Tests, 1992-93–1994-95.
P. A. and B. C. Strang: 2 Tests, 1994-95.

LIMITED-OVERS INTERNATIONAL RECORDS

Note: Limited-overs international matches do not have first-class status.

SUMMARY OF ALL LIMITED-OVERS INTERNATIONALS

1970-71 to 1995 inclusive

	Opponents	Matches	Won by													Tied	NR
			E	A	SA	WI	NZ	I	P	SL	Z	B	C	EA	UAE		
England	Australia	57	26	29	–	–	–	–	–	–	–	–	–	–	–	1	1
	South Africa	4	4	–	0	–	–	–	–	–	–	–	–	–	–	–	–
	West Indies	51	22	–	–	27	–	–	–	–	–	–	–	–	–	–	2
	New Zealand	41	21	–	–	–	17	–	–	–	–	–	–	–	–	–	3
	India	29	16	–	–	–	–	13	–	–	–	–	–	–	–	–	–
	Pakistan	36	23	–	–	–	–	–	12	–	–	–	–	–	–	–	1
	Sri Lanka	11	8	–	–	–	–	–	–	3	–	–	–	–	–	–	–
	Zimbabwe	3	1	–	–	–	–	–	–	–	2	–	–	–	–	–	–
	Canada	1	1	–	–	–	–	–	–	–	–	–	0	–	–	–	–
	East Africa	1	1	–	–	–	–	–	–	–	–	–	–	0	–	–	–
Australia	South Africa	20	–	12	8	–	–	–	–	–	–	–	–	–	–	–	–
	West Indies	74	–	27	–	45	–	–	–	–	–	–	–	–	–	1	1
	New Zealand	62	–	43	–	–	17	–	–	–	–	–	–	–	–	–	2
	India	43	–	24	–	–	–	16	–	–	–	–	–	–	–	–	3
	Pakistan	42	–	21	–	–	–	–	18	–	–	–	–	–	–	1	2
	Sri Lanka	26	–	18	–	–	–	–	–	6	–	–	–	–	–	–	2
	Zimbabwe	7	–	6	–	–	–	–	–	–	1	–	–	–	–	–	–
	Bangladesh	1	–	1	–	–	–	–	–	–	–	0	–	–	–	–	–
	Canada	1	–	1	–	–	–	–	–	–	–	–	0	–	–	–	–
South Africa	West Indies	8	–	–	4	4	–	–	–	–	–	–	–	–	–	–	–
	New Zealand	7	–	–	3	–	4	–	–	–	–	–	–	–	–	–	–
	India	14	–	–	8	–	–	6	–	–	–	–	–	–	–	–	–
	Pakistan	11	–	–	4	–	–	–	7	–	–	–	–	–	–	–	–
	Sri Lanka	7	–	–	3	–	–	–	–	3	–	–	–	–	–	–	1
	Zimbabwe	2	–	–	1	–	–	–	–	–	0	–	–	–	–	–	1
West Indies	New Zealand	19	–	–	–	15	2	–	–	–	–	–	–	–	–	–	2
	India	50	–	–	–	32	–	17	–	–	–	–	–	–	–	1	–
	Pakistan	73	–	–	–	50	–	–	21	–	–	–	–	–	–	2	–
	Sri Lanka	19	–	–	–	16	–	–	–	2	–	–	–	–	–	–	1
	Zimbabwe	4	–	–	–	4	–	–	–	–	0	–	–	–	–	–	–
New Zealand	India	36	–	–	–	–	16	20	–	–	–	–	–	–	–	–	–
	Pakistan	36	–	–	–	–	14	–	20	–	–	–	–	–	–	1	1
	Sri Lanka	32	–	–	–	–	22	–	–	8	–	–	–	–	–	–	2
	Zimbabwe	5	–	–	–	–	5	–	–	–	0	–	–	–	–	–	–
	Bangladesh	1	–	–	–	–	1	–	–	–	–	0	–	–	–	–	–
	East Africa	1	–	–	–	–	1	–	–	–	–	–	–	0	–	–	–
India	Pakistan	41	–	–	–	–	–	12	27	–	–	–	–	–	–	–	2
	Sri Lanka	37	–	–	–	–	–	24	–	11	–	–	–	–	–	–	2
	Zimbabwe	10	–	–	–	–	–	9	–	–	0	–	–	–	–	1	–
	Bangladesh	3	–	–	–	–	–	3	–	–	–	0	–	–	–	–	–
	East Africa	1	–	–	–	–	–	1	–	–	–	–	–	0	–	–	–
	U A Emirates	1	–	–	–	–	–	1	–	–	–	–	–	–	0	–	–
Pakistan	Sri Lanka	49	–	–	–	–	–	–	38	10	–	–	–	–	–	–	1
	Zimbabwe	9	–	–	–	–	–	–	7	–	1	–	–	–	–	1	–
	Bangladesh	3	–	–	–	–	–	–	3	–	–	0	–	–	–	–	–
	Canada	1	–	–	–	–	–	–	1	–	–	–	0	–	–	–	–
	U A Emirates	1	–	–	–	–	–	–	1	–	–	–	–	–	0	–	–
Sri Lanka	Zimbabwe	6	–	–	–	–	–	–	–	5	1	–	–	–	–	–	–
	Bangladesh	4	–	–	–	–	–	–	–	4	–	0	–	–	–	–	–
		1,001	123	182	31	193	99	122	155	52	5	0	0	0	0	9	30

RESULTS SUMMARY OF ALL LIMITED-OVERS INTERNATIONALS

1970-71 to 1995 inclusive

	Matches	Won	Lost	Tied	No Result	% Won (excl. NR)
West Indies	298	193	95	4	6	66.09
Australia	333	182	137	3	11	56.52
England	234	123	103	1	7	54.18
Pakistan	302	155	135	5	7	52.54
India	265	122	134	2	7	47.28
South Africa	73	31	40	–	2	43.66
New Zealand	240	99	130	1	10	43.04
Sri Lanka	191	52	130	–	9	28.57
Zimbabwe	46	5	38	2	1	11.11
Bangladesh	12	–	12	–	–	–
Canada	3	–	3	–	–	–
East Africa	3	–	3	–	–	–
United Arab Emirates	2	–	2	–	–	–

MOST RUNS

	M	I	NO	R	HS	100s	Avge
D. L. Haynes (West Indies)	238	237	28	8,648	152*	17	41.37
Javed Miandad (Pakistan)	228	215	40	7,327	119*	8	41.86
I. V. A. Richards (West Indies)	187	167	24	6,721	189*	11	47.00
A. R. Border (Australia)	273	252	39	6,524	127*	3	30.62
D. M. Jones (Australia)	164	161	25	6,068	145	7	44.61
D. C. Boon (Australia)	181	177	16	5,964	122	5	37.04
R. B. Richardson (West Indies)	206	199	27	5,689	122	5	33.07
M. Azharuddin (India)	194	179	35	5,288	108*	3	36.72
Salim Malik (Pakistan)	210	190	27	5,271	102	5	32.33
C. G. Greenidge (West Indies)	128	127	13	5,134	133*	11	45.03
Ramiz Raja (Pakistan)	159	158	11	4,915	119*	8	33.43
A. Ranatunga (Sri Lanka)	164	157	29	4,536	101*	1	35.43
M. D. Crowe (New Zealand)	139	137	18	4,517	105*	3	37.95
P. A. de Silva (Sri Lanka)	156	152	14	4,389	107*	3	31.80
G. R. Marsh (Australia)	117	115	6	4,357	126*	9	39.97
G. A. Gooch (England)	125	122	6	4,290	142	8	36.98
K. Srikkanth (India)	146	145	4	4,092	123	4	29.02
A. J. Lamb (England)	122	118	16	4,010	118	4	39.31

Leading aggregates for other Test-playing countries:

W. J. Cronje (South Africa)	68	65	11	1,975	112	2	36.57
D. L. Houghton (Zimbabwe)	45	43	1	1,246	142	1	29.66

HIGHEST INDIVIDUAL SCORES

189*	I. V. A. Richards	West Indies v England at Manchester	1984
181	I. V. A. Richards	West Indies v Sri Lanka at Karachi.............	1987-88
175*	Kapil Dev	India v Zimbabwe at Tunbridge Wells	1983
171*	G. M. Turner	New Zealand v East Africa at Birmingham	1975
169*	D. J. Callaghan	South Africa v New Zealand at Verwoerdburg	1994-95
167*	R. A. Smith	England v Australia at Birmingham	1993
158	D. I. Gower	England v New Zealand at Brisbane	1982-83
153*	I. V. A. Richards	West Indies v Australia at Melbourne	1979-80
153	B. C. Lara	West Indies v Pakistan at Sharjah	1993-94
152*	D. L. Haynes	West Indies v India at Georgetown	1988-89

Highest individual scores for other Test-playing countries:

145	D. M. Jones	Australia v England at Brisbane	1990-91
142	D. L. Houghton	Zimbabwe v New Zealand at Hyderabad, India ...	1987-88
140	S. T. Jayasuriya	Sri Lanka v New Zealand at Bloemfontein	1994-95
137*	Inzamam-ul-Haq	Pakistan v New Zealand at Sharjah	1993-94

MOST HUNDREDS

Total		E	A	SA	WI	NZ	I	P	SL	Z
17	D. L. Haynes (West Indies)	2	6	0	–	2	2	4	1	0
11	C. G. Greenidge (West Indies) ..	0	1	–	–	3	3	2	1	1
11	I. V. A. Richards (West Indies)..	3	3	–	–	1	3	0	1	0
9	G. R. Marsh (Australia)	1	–	0	2	2	3	1	0	0
8	G. A. Gooch (England)	–	4	0	1	1	1	1	0	0
8	Javed Miandad (Pakistan)	1	0	1	1	0	3	–	2	0
8	Ramiz Raja (Pakistan)	1	0	0	1	3	0	–	3	0
8	Saeed Anwar (Pakistan)	–	1	1	1	0	–	0	4	1
7	D. I. Gower (England)	–	2	–	0	3	0	1	1	–
7	D. M. Jones (Australia)	3	–	0	0	2	0	1	1	0
7	Zaheer Abbas (Pakistan)	0	2	–	0	1	3	–	1	–

HIGHEST PARTNERSHIP FOR EACH WICKET

212 for 1st	G. R. Marsh and D. C. Boon	A v I	Jaipur	1986-87
263 for 2nd	Aamir Sohail and Inzamam-ul-Haq	P v NZ	Sharjah	1993-94
224* for 3rd	D. M. Jones and A. R. Border	A v SL	Adelaide	1984-85
173 for 4th	D. M. Jones and S. R. Waugh	A v P	Perth	1986-87
152 for 5th	I. V. A. Richards and C. H. Lloyd	WI v SL	Brisbane	1984-85
154 for 6th	R. B. Richardson and P. J. L. Dujon	WI v P	Sharjah	1991-92
115 for 7th	P. J. L. Dujon and M. D. Marshall	WI v P	Gujranwala	1986-87
119 for 8th	P. R. Reiffel and S. K. Warne	A v SA	Port Elizabeth	1993-94
126* for 9th	Kapil Dev and S. M. H. Kirmani	I v Z	Tunbridge Wells	1983
106* for 10th	I. V. A. Richards and M. A. Holding	WI v E	Manchester	1984

MOST WICKETS

	M	Balls	R	W	BB	4W/i	Avge
Wasim Akram (Pakistan)	189	9,800	6,164	273	5-15	15	22.57
Kapil Dev (India)	224	11,202	6,946	253	5-43	4	27.45
C. J. McDermott (Australia).......	129	7,023	4,733	190	5-44	5	24.91
Imran Khan (Pakistan)	175	7,461	4,845	182	6-14	4	26.62
Waqar Younis (Pakistan)	104	5,231	3,800	176	6-26	15	21.59
S. R. Waugh (Australia)	185	7,332	5,415	162	4-33	2	33.42
R. J. Hadlee (New Zealand)......	115	6,182	3,407	158	5-25	6	21.56
C. A. Walsh (West Indies)	142	7,470	4,778	158	5-1	6	30.24
M. D. Marshall (West Indies)	136	7,175	4,233	157	4-18	6	26.96
C. E. L. Ambrose (West Indies)....	114	6,095	3,571	154	5-17	8	23.18
M. Prabhakar (India)	120	5,958	4,188	147	5-35	5	28.48
J. Garner (West Indies)...........	98	5,330	2,752	146	5-31	5	18.84
I. T. Botham (England)...........	116	6,271	4,139	145	4-31	3	28.54
M. A. Holding (West Indies)	102	5,473	3,034	142	5-26	6	21.36
E. J. Chatfield (New Zealand)	114	6,065	3,618	140	5-34	4	25.84
Abdul Qadir (Pakistan)	104	5,100	3,453	132	5-44	6	26.15
R. J. Shastri (India).............	150	6,613	4,650	129	5-15	3	36.04
C. L. Hooper (West Indies)	133	5,398	3,921	126	4-34	1	31.11

	M	Balls	R	W	BB	4W/i	Avge
Aqib Javed (Pakistan).............	110	5,572	3,760	123	7-37	3	30.56
I. V. A. Richards (West Indies)....	187	5,644	4,228	118	6-41	3	35.83
M. C. Snedden (New Zealand)......	93	4,525	3,237	114	4-34	1	28.39
J. Srinath (India).................	77	3,941	2,814	112	5-24	3	25.12
Mudassar Nazar (Pakistan)........	122	4,855	3,431	111	5-28	2	30.90
S. P. O'Donnell (Australia)........	87	4,350	3,102	108	5-13	6	28.72
P. A. J. DeFreitas (England)	93	5,213	3,401	105	4-35	1	32.39
D. K. Lillee (Australia)...........	63	3,593	2,145	103	5-34	6	20.82
C. Pringle (New Zealand)..........	64	3,314	2,455	103	5-45	3	23.83
W. K. M. Benjamin (West Indies)..	85	4,442	3,079	100	5-22	1	30.79

Leading aggregates for other Test-playing countries:

	M	Balls	R	W	BB	4W/i	Avge
J. R. Ratnayeke (Sri Lanka).......	78	3,573	2,866	85	4-23	1	33.71
A. A. Donald (South Africa)	50	2,660	1,764	67	5-29	2	26.32
E. A. Brandes (Zimbabwe)........	24	1,235	1,016	29	4-21	1	35.03

BEST ANALYSES

7-37	Aqib Javed	Pakistan v India at Sharjah..................	1991-92
7-51	W. W. Davis	West Indies v Australia at Leeds	1983
6-12	A. Kumble	India v West Indies at Calcutta	1993-94
6-14	G. J. Gilmour	Australia v England at Leeds	1975
6-14	Imran Khan	Pakistan v India at Sharjah	1984-85
6-15	C. E. H. Croft	West Indies v England at Arnos Vale	1980-81
6-26	Waqar Younis	Pakistan v Sri Lanka at Sharjah	1989-90
6-29	B. P. Patterson	West Indies v India at Nagpur	1987-88
6-29	S. T. Jayasuriya	Sri Lanka v England at Moratuwa	1992-93
6-30	Waqar Younis	Pakistan v New Zealand at Auckland	1993-94
6-39	K. H. Macleay	Australia v India at Nottingham.............	1983
6-41	I. V. A. Richards	West Indies v India at Delhi	1989-90
6-50	A. H. Gray	West Indies v Australia at Port-of-Spain	1990-91

Best analyses for other Test-playing countries:

5-20	V. J. Marks	England v New Zealand at Wellington	1983-84
5-22	M. N. Hart	New Zealand v West Indies at Margao	1994-95
5-29	A. A. Donald	South Africa v India at Calcutta..............	1991-92
4-21	E. A. Brandes	Zimbabwe v England at Albury	1991-92

HAT-TRICKS

Jalal-ud-Din	Pakistan v Australia at Hyderabad	1982-83
B. A. Reid	Australia v New Zealand at Sydney	1985-86
Chetan Sharma	India v New Zealand at Nagpur	1987-88
Wasim Akram	Pakistan v West Indies at Sharjah....................	1989-90
Wasim Akram	Pakistan v Australia at Sharjah	1989-90
Kapil Dev	India v Sri Lanka at Calcutta	1990-91
Aqib Javed	Pakistan v India at Sharjah	1991-92
D. K. Morrison	New Zealand v India at Napier	1993-94
Waqar Younis	Pakistan v New Zealand at East London	1994-95

MOST DISMISSALS IN AN INNINGS

5 (all ct)	R. W. Marsh	Australia v England at Leeds	1981
5 (all ct)	R. G. de Alwis	Sri Lanka v Australia at Colombo (PSS)	1982-83
5 (all ct)	S. M. H. Kirmani	India v Zimbabwe at Leicester	1983
5 (3ct, 2st)	S. Viswanath	India v England at Sydney	1984-85
5 (3ct, 2st)	K. S. More	India v New Zealand at Sharjah	1987-88
5 (all ct)	H. P. Tillekeratne	Sri Lanka v Pakistan at Sharjah	1990-91
5 (3ct, 2st)	N. R. Mongia	India v New Zealand at Auckland	1993-94
5 (3ct, 2st)	A. C. Parore	New Zealand v West Indies at Margao	1994-95
5 (all ct)	D. J. Richardson	South Africa v Pakistan at Johannesburg	1994-95
5 (all ct)	Moin Khan	Pakistan v Zimbabwe at Harare	1994-95
5 (4ct, 1st)	R. S. Kaluwitharana	Sri Lanka v Pakistan at Sharjah	1994-95

MOST DISMISSALS IN A CAREER

	M	*Ct*	*St*	*Total*
P. J. L. Dujon (West Indies)	169	183	21	204
I. A. Healy (Australia)	129	155	27	182
R. W. Marsh (Australia)	92	120	4	124
Salim Yousuf (Pakistan)	86	81	22	103
D. J. Richardson (South Africa)	69	83	12	95
K. S. More (India)	94	63	27	90
I. D. S. Smith (New Zealand)	98	81	5	86
Rashid Latif (Pakistan)	66	64	18	82

MOST CATCHES IN AN INNINGS

(Excluding wicket-keepers)

5	J. N. Rhodes	South Africa v West Indies at Bombay	1993-94
4	Salim Malik	Pakistan v New Zealand at Sialkot	1984-85
4	S. M. Gavaskar	India v Pakistan at Sharjah	1984-85
4	R. B. Richardson	West Indies v England at Birmingham	1991
4	K. C. Wessels	South Africa v West Indies at Kingston	1991-92
4	M. A. Taylor	Australia v West Indies at Sydney	1992-93
4	C. L. Hooper	West Indies v Pakistan at Durban	1992-93
4	K. R. Rutherford	New Zealand v India at Napier	1994-95

Note: While fielding as substitute, J. G. Bracewell held 4 catches for New Zealand v Australia at Adelaide, 1980-81.

MOST CATCHES IN A CAREER

	M	*Ct*
A. R. Border (A)	273	127
I. V. A. Richards (WI)	187	101
M. Azharuddin (I)	194	80
Kapil Dev (I)	220	71
R. B. Richardson (WI)	206	70

ALL-ROUND

1,000 Runs and 100 Wickets

	M	R	W
I. T. Botham (England)............	116	2,113	145
R. J. Hadlee (New Zealand).......	115	1,751	158
C. L. Hooper (West Indies)	133	3,071	126
Imran Khan (Pakistan)............	175	3,709	182
Kapil Dev (India)	224	3,783	253
Mudassar Nazar (Pakistan)	122	2,653	111
S. P. O'Donnell (Australia)........	87	1,242	108
M. Prabhakar (India)	120	1,699	147
I. V. A. Richards (West Indies)....	187	6,721	118
R. J. Shastri (India)..............	150	3,108	129
Wasim Akram (Pakistan)	189	1,680	273
S. R. Waugh (Australia)	185	3,852	162

1,000 Runs and 100 Dismissals

	M	R	D
P. J. L. Dujon (West Indies)	169	1,945	204
I. A. Healy (Australia)	129	1,341	182
R. W. Marsh (Australia)..........	92	1,225	124

TEAM RECORDS

HIGHEST INNINGS TOTALS

363-7	(55 overs)	England v Pakistan at Nottingham.................	1992
360-4	(50 overs)	West Indies v Sri Lanka at Karachi...............	1987-88
338-4	(50 overs)	New Zealand v Bangladesh at Sharjah..............	1989-90
338-5	(60 overs)	Pakistan v Sri Lanka at Swansea	1983
334-4	(60 overs)	England v India at Lord's	1975
333-8	(45 overs)	West Indies v India at Jamshedpur	1983-84
333-9	(60 overs)	England v Sri Lanka at Taunton..................	1983
332-3	(50 overs)	Australia v Sri Lanka at Sharjah.................	1989-90
330-6	(60 overs)	Pakistan v Sri Lanka at Nottingham	1975

Highest totals by other Test-playing countries:

314-7	(50 overs)	South Africa v New Zealand at Verwoerdburg	1994-95
313-7	(49.2 overs)	Sri Lanka v Zimbabwe at New Plymouth	1991-92
312-4	(50 overs)	Zimbabwe v Sri Lanka at New Plymouth	1991-92
299-4	(40 overs)	India v Sri Lanka at Bombay	1986-87

HIGHEST TOTALS BATTING SECOND

Winning

313-7	(49.2 overs)	Sri Lanka v Zimbabwe at New Plymouth	1991-92
298-6	(54.5 overs)	New Zealand v England at Leeds.................	1990
297-6	(48.5 overs)	New Zealand v England at Adelaide	1982-83

Losing

289-7	(40 overs)	Sri Lanka v India at Bombay	1986-87
288-9	(60 overs)	Sri Lanka v Pakistan at Swansea	1983
288-8	(50 overs)	Sri Lanka v Pakistan at Adelaide	1989-90
288-8	(50 overs)	Sri Lanka v Zimbabwe at Harare	1994-95

HIGHEST MATCH AGGREGATES

626-14	(120 overs)	Pakistan v Sri Lanka at Swansea	1983
625-11	(99.2 overs)	Sri Lanka v Zimbabwe at New Plymouth	1991-92
619-19	(118 overs)	England v Sri Lanka at Taunton	1983
604-9	(120 overs)	Australia v Sri Lanka at The Oval	1975
603-11	(100 overs)	Pakistan v Sri Lanka at Adelaide	1989-90

LOWEST INNINGS TOTALS

43	(19.5 overs)	Pakistan v West Indies at Cape Town	1992-93
45	(40.3 overs)	Canada v England at Manchester	1979
55	(28.3 overs)	Sri Lanka v West Indies at Sharjah	1986-87
63	(25.5 overs)	India v Australia at Sydney	1980-81
64	(35.5 overs)	New Zealand v Pakistan at Sharjah	1985-86
69	(28 overs)	South Africa v Australia at Sydney	1993-94
70	(25.2 overs)	Australia v England at Birmingham	1977
70	(26.3 overs)	Australia v New Zealand at Adelaide	1985-86

Note: This section does not take into account those matches in which the number of overs was reduced.

Lowest totals by other Test-playing counties:

87	(29.3 overs)	West Indies v Australia at Sydney	1992-93
93	(36.2 overs)	England v Australia at Leeds	1975
99	(36.3 overs)	Zimbabwe v West Indies at Hyderabad, India	1993-94

LARGEST VICTORIES

232 runs   Australia (323-2 in 50 overs) v Sri Lanka (91 in 35.5 overs) at Adelaide... 1984-85

206 runs   New Zealand (276-7 in 50 overs) v Australia (70 in 26.3 overs) at Adelaide... 1985-86

202 runs   England (334-4 in 60 overs) v India (132-3 in 60 overs) at Lord's 1975

By ten wickets: There have been nine instances of victory by ten wickets.

TIED MATCHES

West Indies 222-5 (50 overs) v Australia 222-9 (50 overs) at Melbourne........	1983-84
England 226-5 (55 overs) v Australia 226-8 (55 overs) at Nottingham..........	1989
West Indies 186-5 (39 overs) v Pakistan 186-9 (39 overs) at Lahore	1991-92
India 126 (47.4 overs) v West Indies 126 (41 overs) at Perth	1991-92
Australia 228-7 (50 overs) v Pakistan 228-9 (50 overs) at Hobart	1992-93
Pakistan 244-6 (50 overs) v West Indies 244-5 (50 overs) at Georgetown	1992-93
India 248-5 (50 overs) v Zimbabwe 248 (50 overs) at Indore	1993-94
Pakistan 161-9 (50 overs) v New Zealand 161 (49.4 overs) at Auckland	1993-94

MOST APPEARANCES

(200 or more)

	Total	E	A	SA	WI	NZ	I	P	SL	Z	C	B	UAE
A. R. Border (A).......	273	43	–	15	61	52	38	34	23	5	1	1	–
D. L. Haynes (WI)	238	35	64	8	–	13	36	65	14	3	–	–	–
Javed Miandad (P).....	228	26	35	3	64	23	34	–	35	6	1	1	–
Kapil Dev (I)	224	23	41	13	42	29	–	32	33	9	–	2	–
Salim Malik (P)	210	21	24	11	45	31	28	–	40	8	–	1	1
R. B. Richardson (WI)..	206	35	46	8	–	11	31	59	14	2	–	–	–

Most appearances for other Test-playing countries:

	Total	E	A	SA	WI	NZ	I	P	SL	Z	C	B	UAE
A. Ranatunga (SL)	164	9	21	7	15	27	33	43	–	6	–	3	–
J. G. Wright (NZ)	149	30	42	–	11	–	21	18	24	2	–	1	–
G. A. Gooch (E)	125	–	32	1	32	16	18	16	6	3	1	–	–
D. J. Richardson (SA) ..	69	4	20	–	6	6	14	10	7	2	–	–	–
D. L. Houghton (Z)	45	2	7	2	4	5	10	9	6	–	–	–	–

CAPTAINCY

LIMITED-OVERS INTERNATIONAL CAPTAINS

England (234 matches; 19 captains)

G. A. Gooch 50; M. W. Gatting 37; R. G. D. Willis 29; J. M. Brearley 25; D. I. Gower 24; M. A. Atherton 15; M. H. Denness 12; I. T. Botham 9; A. J. Stewart 6; K. W. R. Fletcher 5; J. E. Emburey 4; A. J. Lamb 4; D. B. Close 3; R. Illingworth 3; G. Boycott 2; N. Gifford 2; A. W. Greig 2; J. H. Edrich 1; A. P. E. Knott 1.

Australia (333 matches; 11 captains)

A. R. Border 178; G. S. Chappell 49; K. J. Hughes 49; M. A. Taylor 33; I. M. Chappell 11; G. R. Marsh 4; G. N. Yallop 4; R. B. Simpson 2; R. J. Bright 1; D. W. Hookes 1; W. M. Lawry 1.

South Africa (73 matches; 3 captains)

K. C. Wessels 52; W. J. Cronje 18; C. E. B. Rice 3.

West Indies (298 matches; 12 captains)

I. V. A. Richards 108; C. H. Lloyd 81; R. B. Richardson 69; C. A. Walsh 15; C. G. Greenidge 8; D. L. Haynes 7; M. A. Holding 2; R. B. Kanhai 2; B. C. Lara 2; D. L. Murray 2; P. J. L. Dujon 1; A. I. Kallicharran 1.

New Zealand (240 matches; 11 captains)

G. P. Howarth 60; M. D. Crowe 44; K. R. Rutherford 37; J. G. Wright 31; J. V. Coney 25; J. J. Crowe 16; M. G. Burgess 8; B. E. Congdon 7; G. M. Turner 7; G. R. Larsen 1; A. H. Jones 2.

India (265 matches; 12 captains)

M. Azharuddin 96; Kapil Dev 74; S. M. Gavaskar 37; D. B. Vengsarkar 18; K. Srikkanth 13; R. J. Shastri 11; S. Venkataraghavan 7; B. S. Bedi 4; A. L. Wadekar 2; M. Amarnath 1; S. M. H. Kirmani 1; G. R. Viswanath 1.

Pakistan (302 matches; 16 captains)

Imran Khan 139; Javed Miandad 62; Salim Malik 34; Wasim Akram 23; Zaheer Abbas 13; Asif Iqbal 6; Abdul Qadir 5; Wasim Bari 5; Mushtaq Mohammad 4; Intikhab Alam 3; Majid Khan 2; Moin Khan 2; Ramiz Raja 1; Saeed Anwar 1; Sarfraz Nawaz 1; Waqar Younis 1.

Sri Lanka (191 matches; 9 captains)

A. Ranatunga 88; L. R. D. Mendis 61; P. A. de Silva 13; R. S. Madugalle 13; B. Warnapura 8; A. P. B. Tennekoon 4; R. S. Mahanama 2; D. S. de Silva 1; J. R. Ratnayeke 1.

Zimbabwe (46 matches; 4 captains)

A. Flower 17; D. L. Houghton 17; D. A. G. Fletcher 6; A. J. Traicos 6.

Others (20 matches; 7 captains)

Gazi Ashraf (Bangladesh) 7; B. M. Mauricette (Canada) 3; Harilal R. Shah (East Africa) 3; Akram Khan (Bangladesh) 2; Minhaz-ul-Abedin (Bangladesh) 2; Sultan M. Zarawani (United Arab Emirates) 2; Athar Ali Khan (Bangladesh) 1.

MISCELLANEOUS

LARGE ATTENDANCES

Test Series

943,000	Australia v England (5 Tests)	1936-37
In England		
549,650	England v Australia (5 Tests)	1953

Test Matches

†350,534	Australia v England, Melbourne (Third Test)	1936-37
325,000+	India v England, Calcutta (Second Test)	1972-73
In England		
158,000+	England v Australia, Leeds (Fourth Test)	1948
137,915	England v Australia, Lord's (Second Test)	1953

Test Match Day

90,800	Australia v West Indies, Melbourne (Fifth Test, 2nd day)	1960-61

Other First-Class Matches in England

93,000	England v Australia, Lord's (Fourth Victory Match, 3 days) ..	1945
80,000+	Surrey v Yorkshire, The Oval (3 days)	1906
78,792	Yorkshire v Lancashire, Leeds (3 days)	1904
76,617	Lancashire v Yorkshire, Manchester (3 days)	1926

Limited-Overs Internationals

‡90,000	India v Pakistan, Calcutta...........................	1986-87
‡90,000	India v South Africa, Calcutta	1991-92
‡90,000	India v South Africa, Calcutta	1993-94
‡90,000	India v West Indies, Calcutta	1993-94
87,182	England v Pakistan, Melbourne (World Cup final)........	1991-92
86,133	Australia v West Indies, Melbourne	1983-84

† *Although no official figures are available, the attendance at the Fourth Test between India and England at Calcutta, 1981-82, was thought to have exceeded this figure.*

‡ *No official attendance figures were issued for these games, but 90,000 seats were believed to be occupied. Press reports which gave much higher figures included security guards, food vendors etc., as well as paying spectators.*

LORD'S CRICKET GROUND

Lord's and the MCC were founded in 1787. The Club has enjoyed an uninterrupted career since that date, but there have been three grounds known as Lord's. The first (1787-1810) was situated where Dorset Square now is; the second (1809-13), at North Bank, had to be abandoned owing to the cutting of the Regent's Canal; and the third, opened in 1814, is the present one at St John's Wood. It was not until 1866 that the freehold of Lord's was secured by the MCC. The present pavilion was erected in 1890 at a cost of £21,000.

HIGHEST INDIVIDUAL SCORES MADE AT LORD'S

333	G. A. Gooch	England v India	1990
316*	J. B. Hobbs	Surrey v Middlesex	1926
315*	P. Holmes	Yorkshire v Middlesex	1925

Note: The longest innings in a first-class match at Lord's was played by S. Wettimuny (636 minutes, 190 runs) for Sri Lanka v England, 1984.

HIGHEST TOTALS AT LORD'S

First-Class Matches

729-6 dec.	Australia v England	1930
665	West Indians v Middlesex	1939
653-4 dec.	England v India	1990
652-8 dec.	West Indies v England	1973

Minor Match

735-9 dec.	MCC and Ground v Wiltshire	1888

BIGGEST HIT AT LORD'S

The only known instance of a batsman hitting a ball over the present pavilion at Lord's occurred when A. E. Trott, appearing for MCC against Australians on July 31, August 1, 2, 1899, drove M. A. Noble so far and high that the ball struck a chimney pot and fell behind the building.

MINOR CRICKET

HIGHEST INDIVIDUAL SCORES

628*	A. E. J. Collins, Clark's House v North Town at Clifton College. (A Junior House match. His innings of 6 hours 50 minutes was spread over four afternoons.)	1899
566	C. J. Eady, Break-o'-Day v Wellington at Hobart	1901-02
515	D. R. Havewalla, B.B. and C.I. Rly v St Xavier's at Bombay	1933-34
506*	J. C. Sharp, Melbourne GS v Geelong College at Melbourne	1914-15
502*	Chaman Lal, Mehandra Coll., Patiala v Government Coll., Rupar at Patiala	1956-57
485	A. E. Stoddart, Hampstead v Stoics at Hampstead	1886
475*	Mohammad Iqbal, Muslim Model HS v Islamia HS, Sialkot at Lahore	1958-59
466*	G. T. S. Stevens, Beta v Lambda (University College School House match) at Neasden	1919
459	J. A. Prout, Wesley College v Geelong College at Geelong	1908-09

Note: The highest score in a Minor County match is 323* by F. E. Lacey for Hampshire v Norfolk at Southampton in 1887; the highest in the Minor Counties Championship is 282 by E. Garnett for Berkshire v Wiltshire at Reading in 1908.

HIGHEST PARTNERSHIP

664* for 3rd   V. G. Kambli and S. R. Tendulkar, Sharadashram Vidyamandir
              School v St Xavier's High School at Bombay 1987-88

RECORD HIT

The Rev. W. Fellows, while at practice on the Christ Church ground at Oxford in 1856, drove
a ball bowled by Charles Rogers 175 yards from hit to pitch.

THROWING THE CRICKET BALL

140 yards 2 feet, Robert Percival, on the Durham Sands racecourse, Co. Durham   c1882
140 yards 9 inches, Ross Mackenzie, at Toronto 1872
140 yards, "King Billy" the Aborigine at Clermont, Queensland 1872

Note: Extensive research has shown that these traditional records are probably authentic, if not
necessarily wholly accurate. Modern competitions have failed to produce similar distances
although Ian Pont, the Essex all-rounder who also played baseball, was reported to have thrown
138 yards in Cape Town in 1981. There have been speculative reports attributing throws of 150
yards or more to figures as diverse at the South African Test player Colin Bland, the Latvian
javelin thrower Janis Lusis, who won a gold medal for the Soviet Union in the 1968 Olympics,
and the British sprinter Charley Ransome. The definitive record is still awaited.

DATES OF FORMATION OF COUNTY CLUBS NOW FIRST-CLASS

County	First known county organisation	Present Club Original date	Reorganisation, if substantial
Derbyshire	November 4, 1870	November 4, 1870	—
Durham	January 24, 1874	May 10, 1882	March, 1991
Essex	By May, 1790	January 14, 1876	—
Glamorgan........	August 5, 1861	July 6, 1888	—
Gloucestershire	November 3, 1863	1871	—
Hampshire........	April 3, 1849	August 12, 1863	July, 1879
Kent..............	August 6, 1842	March 1, 1859	December 6, 1870
Lancashire........	January 12, 1864	January 12, 1864	—
Leicestershire.......	By August, 1820	March 25, 1879	—
Middlesex	December 15, 1863	February 2, 1864	—
Northamptonshire....	1820†	July 31, 1878	—
Nottinghamshire	March/April, 1841	March/April, 1841	December 11, 1866
Somerset	October 15, 1864	August 18, 1875	—
Surrey.............	August 22, 1845	August 22, 1845	—
Sussex	June 16, 1836	March 1, 1839	August, 1857
Warwickshire......	May, 1826	1882	—
Worcestershire......	1844	March 5, 1865	—
Yorkshire.........	March 7, 1861	January 8, 1863	December 10, 1891

† *Town club.*

DATES OF FORMATION OF CLUBS IN THE CURRENT MINOR COUNTIES CHAMPIONSHIP

County	First known county organisation	Present Club
Bedfordshire	May, 1847	November 3, 1899
Berkshire	By May, 1841	March 17, 1895
Buckinghamshire	November, 1864	January 15, 1891
Cambridgeshire	March 13, 1844	June 6, 1891
Cheshire	1819	September 29, 1908
Cornwall	1813	November 12, 1894
Cumberland	January 2, 1884	April 10, 1948
Devon	1824	November 26, 1899
Dorset	1862 *or* 1871	February 5, 1896
Herefordshire	July 13, 1836	January 9, 1991
Hertfordshire	1838	March 8, 1876
Lincolnshire	1853	September 28, 1906
Norfolk	January 11, 1827	October 14, 1876
Northumberland	1834	December, 1895
Oxfordshire	1787	December 14, 1921
Shropshire	1819 or 1829	June 28, 1956
Staffordshire	November 24, 1871	November 24, 1871
Suffolk	July 27, 1864	August, 1932
Wales Minor Counties	1988	May 3, 1988
Wiltshire	February 24, 1881	January, 1893

CONSTITUTION OF COUNTY CHAMPIONSHIP

There are references in the sporting press to a champion county as early as 1825, but the list is not continuous and in some years only two counties contested the title. The earliest reference in any cricket publication is from 1864, and at this time there were eight leading counties who have come to be regarded as first-class from that date – Cambridgeshire, Hampshire, Kent, Middlesex, Nottinghamshire, Surrey, Sussex and Yorkshire. The newly formed Lancashire club began playing inter-county matches in 1865, Gloucestershire in 1870 and Derbyshire in 1871, and they are therefore regarded as first-class from these respective dates. Cambridgeshire dropped out after 1871, Hampshire, who had not played inter-county matches in certain seasons, after 1885, and Derbyshire after 1887. Somerset, who had played matches against the first-class counties since 1879, were regarded as first-class from 1882 to 1885, and were admitted formally to the Championship in 1891. In 1894, Derbyshire, Essex, Leicestershire and Warwickshire were granted first-class status, but did not compete in the Championship until 1895 when Hampshire returned. Worcestershire, Northamptonshire and Glamorgan were admitted to the Championship in 1899, 1905 and 1921 respectively and are regarded as first-class from these dates. An invitation in 1921 to Buckinghamshire to enter the Championship was declined, owing to the lack of necessary playing facilities, and an application by Devon in 1948 was unsuccessful. Durham were admitted to the Championship in 1992 and were granted first-class status prior to their pre-season tour of Zimbabwe.

MOST COUNTY CHAMPIONSHIP APPEARANCES

762	W. Rhodes	Yorkshire	1898-1930
707	F. E. Woolley	Kent	1906-38
668	C. P. Mead	Hampshire	1906-36
617	N. Gifford	Worcestershire (484), Warwickshire (133)	1960-88
611	W. G. Quaife	Warwickshire	1895-1928
601	G. H. Hirst	Yorkshire	1891-1921

The most appearances for counties not mentioned singly above are:

594	F. J. Titmus	Middlesex	1949-82
591	W. E. Astill	Leicestershire	1906-39
589	D. J. Shepherd	Glamorgan	1950-72
571	C. W. L. Parker	Gloucestershire	1905-35
561	J. Langridge	Sussex	1924-53
544	G. Gunn	Nottinghamshire	1902-32
538	D. Kenyon	Worcestershire	1946-67
536	J. B. Hobbs	Surrey	1905-34
529	K. W. R. Fletcher	Essex	1962-88
526	E. Tyldesley	Lancashire	1909-36
506	D. C. Morgan	Derbyshire	1950-69
479	B. A. Langford	Somerset	1953-74
464	D. Brookes	Northamptonshire	1934-59
66	S. J. E. Brown	Durham	1992-95

Notes: F. J. Titmus also played one match for Surrey (1978). The most appearances by a captain is 407 by Lord Hawke for Yorkshire (1883-1909), by a wicket-keeper 506 by H. Strudwick for Surrey (1902-27) and by an amateur 496 by P. A. Perrin for Essex (1896-1928).

MOST CONSECUTIVE COUNTY CHAMPIONSHIP APPEARANCES

423	K. G. Suttle	Sussex	1954-69
412	J. G. Binks	Yorkshire	1955-69
399	J. Vine	Sussex	1899-1914
344	E. H. Killick	Sussex	1898-1912
326	C. N. Woolley	Northamptonshire	1913-31
305	A. H. Dyson	Glamorgan	1930-47
301	B. Taylor	Essex	1961-72

Notes: J. Vine made 417 consecutive appearances for Sussex in all first-class matches between July 1900 and September 1914.

J. G. Binks did not miss a Championship match for Yorkshire between making his debut in June 1955 and retiring at the end of the 1969 season.

UMPIRES

MOST COUNTY CHAMPIONSHIP APPEARANCES

569	T. W. Spencer	1950-1980
533	F. Chester	1922-1955
516	H. G. Baldwin	1932-1962
481	**P. B. Wight**	**1966-1995**
457	A. Skelding	1931-1958

Bold type denotes an umpire who stood in the 1995 season.

MOST SEASONS ON FIRST-CLASS LIST

31	T. W. Spencer	1950-1980
30	**P. B. Wight**	**1966-1995**
28	F. Chester	1922-1955
27	**D. J. Constant**	**1969-1995**
27	J. Moss	1899-1929
26	**H. D. Bird**	**1970-1995**
26	W. A. J. West	1896-1925
26	**A. G. T. Whitehead**	**1970-1995**
25	H. G. Baldwin	1932-1962
25	A. Jepson	1960-1984
25	J. G. Langridge	1956-1980

Bold type denotes umpires who stood in the 1995 season.

WISDEN'S CRICKETERS OF THE YEAR, 1889-1996

1889	*Six Great Bowlers of the Year:* J. Briggs, J. J. Ferris, G. A. Lohmann, R. Peel, C. T. B. Turner, S. M. J. Woods.
1890	*Nine Great Batsmen of the Year:* R. Abel, W. Barnes, W. Gunn, L. Hall, R. Henderson, J. M. Read, A. Shrewsbury, F. H. Sugg, A. Ward.
1891	*Five Great Wicket-Keepers:* J. McC. Blackham, G. MacGregor, R. Pilling, M. Sherwin, H. Wood.
1892	*Five Great Bowlers:* W. Attewell, J. T. Hearne, F. Martin, A. W. Mold, J. W. Sharpe.
1893	*Five Batsmen of the Year:* H. T. Hewett, L. C. H. Palairet, W. W. Read, S. W. Scott, A. E. Stoddart.
1894	*Five All-Round Cricketers:* G. Giffen, A. Hearne, F. S. Jackson, G. H. S. Trott, E. Wainwright.
1895	*Five Young Batsmen of the Season:* W. Brockwell, J. T. Brown, C. B. Fry, T. W. Hayward, A. C. MacLaren.
1896	W. G. Grace.
1897	*Five Cricketers of the Season:* S. E. Gregory, A. A. Lilley, K. S. Ranjitsinhji, T. Richardson, H. Trumble.
1898	*Five Cricketers of the Year:* F. G. Bull, W. R. Cuttell, N. F. Druce, G. L. Jessop, J. R. Mason.
1899	*Five Great Players of the Season:* W. H. Lockwood, W. Rhodes, W. Storer, C. L. Townsend, A. E. Trott.
1900	*Five Cricketers of the Season:* J. Darling, C. Hill, A. O. Jones, M. A. Noble, Major R. M. Poore.
1901	*Mr R. E. Foster and Four Yorkshiremen:* R. E. Foster, S. Haigh, G. H. Hirst, T. L. Taylor, J. Tunnicliffe.
1902	L. C. Braund, C. P. McGahey, F. Mitchell, W. G. Quaife, J. T. Tyldesley.
1903	W. W. Armstrong, C. J. Burnup, J. Iremonger, J. J. Kelly, V. T. Trumper.
1904	C. Blythe, J. Gunn, A. E. Knight, W. Mead, P. F. Warner.
1905	B. J. T. Bosanquet, E. A. Halliwell, J. Hallows, P. A. Perrin, R. H. Spooner.
1906	D. Denton, W. S. Lees, G. J. Thompson, J. Vine, L. G. Wright.
1907	J. N. Crawford, A. Fielder, E. G. Hayes, K. L. Hutchings, N. A. Knox.
1908	A. W. Hallam, R. O. Schwarz, F. A. Tarrant, A. E. E. Vogler, T. G. Wass.
1909	*Lord Hawke and Four Cricketers of the Year:* W. Brearley, Lord Hawke, J. B. Hobbs, A. Marshal, J. T. Newstead.
1910	W. Bardsley, S. F. Barnes, D. W. Carr, A. P. Day, V. S. Ransford.
1911	H. K. Foster, A. Hartley, C. B. Llewellyn, W. C. Smith, F. E. Woolley.
1912	*Five Members of the MCC's Team in Australia:* F. R. Foster, J. W. Hearne, S. P. Kinneir, C. P. Mead, H. Strudwick.
1913	John Wisden: Personal Recollections.
1914	M. W. Booth, G. Gunn, J. W. Hitch, A. E. Relf, Hon. L. H. Tennyson.
1915	J. W. H. T. Douglas, P. G. H. Fender, H. T. W. Hardinge, D. J. Knight, S. G. Smith.
1916-17	No portraits appeared.
1918	*School Bowlers of the Year:* H. L. Calder, J. E. D'E. Firth, C. H. Gibson, G. A. Rotherham, G. T. S. Stevens.
1919	*Five Public School Cricketers of the Year:* P. W. Adams, A. P. F. Chapman, A. C. Gore, L. P. Hedges, N. E. Partridge.
1920	*Five Batsmen of the Year:* A. Ducat, E. H. Hendren, P. Holmes, H. Sutcliffe, E. Tyldesley.
1921	P. F. Warner.
1922	H. Ashton, J. L. Bryan, J. M. Gregory, C. G. Macartney, E. A. McDonald.
1923	A. W. Carr, A. P. Freeman, C. W. L. Parker, A. C. Russell, A. Sandham.
1924	*Five Bowlers of the Year:* A. E. R. Gilligan, R. Kilner, G. G. Macaulay, C. H. Parkin, M. W. Tate.
1925	R. H. Catterall, J. C. W. MacBryan, H. W. Taylor, R. K. Tyldesley, W. W. Whysall.

1926	J. B. Hobbs.
1927	G. Geary, H. Larwood, J. Mercer, W. A. Oldfield, W. M. Woodfull.
1928	R. C. Blunt, C. Hallows, W. R. Hammond, D. R. Jardine, V. W. C. Jupp.
1929	L. E. G. Ames, G. Duckworth, M. Leyland, S. J. Staples, J. C. White.
1930	E. H. Bowley, K. S. Duleepsinhji, H. G. Owen-Smith, R. W. V. Robins, R. E. S. Wyatt.
1931	D. G. Bradman, C. V. Grimmett, B. H. Lyon, I. A. R. Peebles, M. J. Turnbull.
1932	W. E. Bowes, C. S. Dempster, James Langridge, Nawab of Pataudi sen., H. Verity.
1933	W. E. Astill, F. R. Brown, A. S. Kennedy, C. K. Nayudu, W. Voce.
1934	A. H. Bakewell, G. A. Headley, M. S. Nichols, L. F. Townsend, C. F. Walters.
1935	S. J. McCabe, W. J. O'Reilly, G. A. E. Paine, W. H. Ponsford, C. I. J. Smith.
1936	H. B. Cameron, E. R. T. Holmes, B. Mitchell, D. Smith, A. W. Wellard.
1937	C. J. Barnett, W. H. Copson, A. R. Gover, V. M. Merchant, T. S. Worthington.
1938	T. W. J. Goddard, J. Hardstaff jun., L. Hutton, J. H. Parks, E. Paynter.
1939	H. T. Bartlett, W. A. Brown, D. C. S. Compton, K. Farnes, A. Wood.
1940	L. N. Constantine, W. J. Edrich, W. W. Keeton, A. B. Sellers, D. V. P. Wright.
1941-46	No portraits appeared.
1947	A. V. Bedser, L. B. Fishlock, V. (M. H.) Mankad, T. P. B. Smith, C. Washbrook.
1948	M. P. Donnelly, A. Melville, A. D. Nourse, J. D. Robertson, N. W. D. Yardley.
1949	A. L. Hassett, W. A. Johnston, R. R. Lindwall, A. R. Morris, D. Tallon.
1950	T. E. Bailey, R. O. Jenkins, J. G. Langridge, R. T. Simpson, B. Sutcliffe.
1951	T. G. Evans, S. Ramadhin, A. L. Valentine, E. D. Weekes, F. M. M. Worrell.
1952	R. Appleyard, H. E. Dollery, J. C. Laker, P. B. H. May, E. A. B. Rowan.
1953	H. Gimblett, T. W. Graveney, D. S. Sheppard, W. S. Surridge, F. S. Trueman.
1954	R. N. Harvey, G. A. R. Lock, K. R. Miller, J. H. Wardle, W. Watson.
1955	B. Dooland, Fazal Mahmood, W. E. Hollies, J. B. Statham, G. E. Tribe.
1956	M. C. Cowdrey, D. J. Insole, D. J. McGlew, H. J. Tayfield, F. H. Tyson.
1957	D. Brookes, J. W. Burke, M. J. Hilton, G. R. A. Langley, P. E. Richardson.
1958	P. J. Loader, A. J. W. McIntyre, O. G. Smith, M. J. Stewart, C. L. Walcott.
1959	H. L. Jackson, R. E. Marshall, C. A. Milton, J. R. Reid, D. Shackleton.
1960	K. F. Barrington, D. B. Carr, R. Illingworth, G. Pullar, M. J. K. Smith.
1961	N. A. T. Adcock, E. R. Dexter, R. A. McLean, R. Subba Row, J. V. Wilson.
1962	W. E. Alley, R. Benaud, A. K. Davidson, W. M. Lawry, N. C. O'Neill.
1963	D. Kenyon, Mushtaq Mohammad, P. H. Parfitt, P. J. Sharpe, F. J. Titmus.
1964	D. B. Close, C. C. Griffith, C. C. Hunte, R. B. Kanhai, G. S. Sobers.
1965	G. Boycott, P. J. P. Burge, J. A. Flavell, G. D. McKenzie, R. B. Simpson.
1966	K. C. Bland, J. H. Edrich, R. C. Motz, P. M. Pollock, R. G. Pollock.
1967	R. W. Barber, B. L. D'Oliveira, C. Milburn, J. T. Murray, S. M. Nurse.
1968	Asif Iqbal, Hanif Mohammad, K. Higgs, J. M. Parks, Nawab of Pataudi jun.
1969	J. G. Binks, D. M. Green, B. A. Richards, D. L. Underwood, O. S. Wheatley.
1970	B. F. Butcher, P. E. E. Knott, Majid Khan, M. J. Procter, D. J. Shepherd.
1971	J. D. Bond, C. H. Lloyd, B. W. Luckhurst, G. M. Turner, R. T. Virgin.
1972	G. G. Arnold, B. S. Chandrasekhar, L. R. Gibbs, B. Taylor, Zaheer Abbas.
1973	G. S. Chappell, D. K. Lillee, R. A. L. Massie, J. A. Snow, K. R. Stackpole.
1974	K. D. Boyce, B. E. Congdon, K. W. R. Fletcher, R. C. Fredericks, P. J. Sainsbury.
1975	D. L. Amiss, M. H. Denness, N. Gifford, A. W. Greig, A. M. E. Roberts.
1976	I. M. Chappell, P. G. Lee, E. B. McCosker, D. S. Steele, R. A. Woolmer.
1977	J. M. Brearley, C. G. Greenidge, M. A. Holding, I. V. A. Richards, R. W. Taylor.
1978	I. T. Botham, M. Hendrick, A. Jones, K. S. McEwan, R. G. D. Willis.
1979	D. I. Gower, J. K. Lever, C. M. Old, C. T. Radley, J. N. Shepherd.
1980	J. Garner, S. M. Gavaskar, A. A. Gooch, D. W. Randall, B. C. Rose.
1981	K. J. Hughes, R. D. Jackman, A. J. Lamb, C. E. B. Rice, V. A. P. van der Bijl.
1982	T. M. Alderman, A. R. Border, R. J. Hadlee, Javed Miandad, R. W. Marsh.
1983	Imran Khan, T. E. Jesty, A. I. Kallicharran, Kapil Dev, M. D. Marshall.
1984	M. Amarnath, J. V. Coney, J. E. Emburey, M. W. Gatting, C. L. Smith.
1985	M. D. Crowe, H. A. Gomes, G. W. Humpage, J. Simmons, S. Wettimuny.
1986	P. Bainbridge, R. M. Ellison, C. J. McDermott, N. V. Radford, R. T. Robinson.
1987	J. H. Childs, G. A. Hick, D. B. Vengsarkar, C. A. Walsh, J. J. Whitaker.

1988 J. P. Agnew, N. A. Foster, D. P. Hughes, P. M. Roebuck, Salim Malik.
1989 K. J. Barnett, P. J. L. Dujon, P. A. Neale, F. D. Stephenson, S. R. Waugh.
1990 S. J. Cook, D. M. Jones, R. C. Russell, R. A. Smith, M. A. Taylor.
1991 M. A. Atherton, M. Azharuddin, A. R. Butcher, D. L. Haynes, M. E. Waugh.
1992 C. E. L. Ambrose, P. A. J. DeFreitas, A. A. Donald, R. B. Richardson, Waqar Younis.
1993 N. E. Briers, M. D. Moxon, I. D. K. Salisbury, A. J. Stewart, Wasim Akram.
1994 D. C. Boon, I. A. Healy, M. G. Hughes, S. K. Warne, S. L. Watkin.
1995 B. C. Lara, D. E. Malcolm, T. A. Munton, S. J. Rhodes, K. C. Wessels.
1996 D. G. Cork, P. A. de Silva, A. R. C. Fraser, A. Kumble, D. A. Reeve.

POST-WAR CRICKETERS OF THE YEAR

The five players chosen to be Cricketers of the Year for 1996 bring the number chosen since selection resumed in 1947 after the wartime hiatus to exactly 250. The 250 have been chosen from 26 different teams as follows:

Derbyshire	7	Lancashire	12	Sussex	8	South Africans	11
Durham	–	Leicestershire	4	Warwickshire	13	West Indians	21
Essex	12	Middlesex	11	Worcestershire	11	New Zealanders	5
Glamorgan	7	Northants	9	Yorkshire	13	Indians	8
Gloucestershire	7	Nottinghamshire	7	Oxford Univ.	1	Pakistanis	8
Hampshire	9	Somerset	10	Cambridge Univ.	2	Sri Lankans	1
Kent	10	Surrey	15	Australians	33	Zimbabweans	–

Note: The total of sides comes to 255 because five players played regularly for two teams in the year for which they were chosen: K. D. Boyce (Essex and West Indians), Imran Khan (Sussex and Pakistanis), Kapil Dev (Northamptonshire and Indians), P. B. H. May (Surrey and Cambridge University) and D. S. Sheppard (Sussex and Cambridge University).

Types of players

Of the 250 Cricketers of the Year, 137 are best classified as batsmen, 72 as bowlers, 25 as all-rounders and 16 as wicket-keepers.

Ages

On April 1 in year of selection

Youngest: 19-130 Mushtaq Mohammad (1963); 20-136 Waqar Younis (1992); 20-313 G. A. Hick (1987); 20-337 A. L. Valentine (1951); 20-352 C. J. McDermott (1986); 21-336 S. Ramadhin (1951); 22-0 D. I. Gower (1979).

Note: The youngest Cricketer of the Year ever was H. L. Calder, chosen in 1918 aged 17 years and 67 days.

Oldest: 44-4 J. Simmons (1985); 43-57 W. E. Alley (1962); 42-300 W. E. Hollies (1955); 42-232 D. J. Shepherd (1970); 42-52 E. A. B. Rowan (1952); 41-154 D. Brookes (1957).

Note: The oldest Cricketer of the Year ever was Lord Hawke, chosen in 1909 aged 48 years and 257 days.

BIRTHS AND DEATHS OF CRICKETERS

The qualifications for inclusion are as follows:

1. All players who have appeared in a Test match or a one-day international for a Test-match playing country.

2. English county players who have appeared in 50 or more first-class matches during their careers and, if dead, were still living ten years ago.

3. Players who appeared in 15 or more first-class matches in the 1995 English season.

4. English county captains, county caps and captains of Oxford and Cambridge Universities who, if dead, were still living ten years ago.

5. All players chosen as *Wisden* Cricketers of the Year, including the Public Schoolboys chosen for the 1918 and 1919 Almanacks. Cricketers of the Year are identified by the italic notation *CY* and year of appearance. A list of the Cricketers of the Year from 1889 to 1996 appears on pages 267-269.

6. Players or personalities not otherwise qualified who are thought to be of sufficient interest to merit inclusion.

Key to abbreviations and symbols

CUCC – Cambridge University, OUCC – Oxford University.

Australian states: NSW – New South Wales, Qld – Queensland, S. Aust. – South Australia, Tas. – Tasmania, Vic. – Victoria, W. Aust. – Western Australia.

Indian teams: Guj. – Gujarat, H'bad – Hyderabad, Ind. Rlwys – Indian Railways, Ind. Serv. – Indian Services, J/K – Jammu and Kashmir, Karn. – Karnataka (Mysore to 1972-73), M. Pradesh – Madhya Pradesh (Central India [C. Ind.] to 1939-40, Holkar to 1954-55, Madhya Bharat to 1956-57), M'tra – Maharashtra, Naw. – Nawanagar, Raja. – Rajasthan, S'tra – Saurashtra (West India [W. Ind.] to 1945-46, Kathiawar to 1949-50), S. Punjab – Southern Punjab (Patiala to 1958-59, Punjab since 1968-69), TC – Travancore-Cochin (Kerala since 1956-57), TN – Tamil Nadu (Madras to 1959-60), U. Pradesh – Uttar Pradesh (United Provinces [U. Prov.] to 1948-49), Vidarbha (CP & Berar to 1949-50, Madhya Pradesh to 1956-57).

New Zealand provinces: Auck. – Auckland, Cant. – Canterbury, C. Dist. – Central Districts, N. Dist. – Northern Districts, Wgtn – Wellington.

Pakistani teams: ADBP – Agricultural Development Bank of Pakistan, B'pur – Bahawalpur, F'bad – Faisalabad, HBFC – House Building Finance Corporation, HBL – Habib Bank Ltd, I'bad – Islamabad, IDBP – Industrial Development Bank of Pakistan, Kar. – Karachi, MCB – Muslim Commercial Bank, NBP – National Bank of Pakistan, NWFP – North-West Frontier Province, PACO – Pakistan Automobile Corporation, Pak. Rlwys – Pakistan Railways, Pak. Us – Pakistan Universities, PIA – Pakistan International Airlines, PNSC – Pakistan National Shipping Corporation, PWD – Public Works Department, R'pindi – Rawalpindi, UBL – United Bank Ltd, WAPDA – Water and Power Development Authority.

South African provinces: E. Prov. – Eastern Province, E. Tvl – Eastern Transvaal, Griq. W. – Griqualand West, N. Tvl – Northern Transvaal, NE Tvl – North-Eastern Transvaal, OFS – Orange Free State, Rhod. – Rhodesia, Tvl – Transvaal, W. Prov. – Western Province, W. Tvl – Western Transvaal.

Sri Lankan teams: Ant. – Antonians, Bloom. – Bloomfield Cricket and Athletic Club, BRC – Burgher Recreation Club, CCC – Colombo Cricket Club, Mor. – Moratuwa Sports Club, NCC – Nondescripts Cricket Club, Pan. – Panadura Sports Club, Seb. – Sebastianites, SLAF – Air Force, SSC – Sinhalese Sports Club, TU – Tamil Union Cricket and Athletic Club, Under-23 – Board Under-23 XI, WPN – Western Province (North), WPS – Western Province (South).

West Indies islands: B'dos – Barbados, BG – British Guiana (Guyana since 1966), Comb. Is. – Combined Islands, Jam. – Jamaica, T/T – Trinidad & Tobago.

Zimbabwean teams: Mash. – Mashonaland, Mat. – Matabeleland, MCD – Mashonaland Country Districts, Under-24 – Mashonaland Under-24, Zimb. – Zimbabwe.

* *Denotes Test player.* ** *Denotes appeared for two countries. There is a list of Test players country by country from page 51.*

† *Denotes also played for team under its previous name.*

Aamer Hameed (Pak. Us, Lahore, Punjab & OUCC) b Oct. 18, 1954

Aamer Hanif (Kar., PACO & Allied Bank) b Oct. 4, 1971

*Aamer Malik (ADBP, PIA, Multan & Lahore) b Jan. 3, 1963

*Aamir Nazir (I'bad, Lahore & Allied Bank) b Jan. 2, 1971

*Aamir Sohail (HBL, Sargodha & Lahore) b Sept. 14, 1966

Abberley, R. N. (Warwicks.) b April 22, 1944

*a'Beckett, E. L. (Vic.) b Aug. 11, 1907, d June 2, 1989

*Abdul Kadir (Kar. & NBP) b May 10, 1944

*Abdul Qadir (HBL, Lahore & Punjab) b Sept. 15, 1955

*Abel, R. (Surrey; *CY 1890*) b Nov. 30, 1857, d Dec. 10, 1936

Abell, Sir G. E. B. (OUCC, Worcs. & N. Ind.) b June 22, 1904, d Jan. 11, 1989

Aberdare, 3rd Lord (*see* Bruce, Hon. C. N.)

*Abid Ali, S. (H'bad) b Sept. 9, 1941

Abrahams, J. (Lancs.) b July 21, 1952

*Absolom, C. A. (CUCC & Kent) b June 7, 1846, d July 30, 1889

Acfield D. L. (CUCC & Essex) b July 24, 1947

*Achong, E. (T/T) b Feb. 16, 1904, d Aug. 29, 1986

Ackerman, H. M. (Border, NE Tvl, Northants, Natal & W. Prov.) b April 28, 1947

A'Court, D. G. (Glos.) b July 27, 1937

Adam, Sir Ronald, 2nd Bt (Pres. MCC 1946-47) b Oct. 30, 1885, d Dec. 26, 1982

Adams, C. J. (Derbys.) b May 6, 1970

*Adams, J. C. (Jam. & Notts.) b Jan. 9, 1968

Adams, P. W. (Cheltenham & Sussex; *CY 1919*) b Sept. 5, 1900, d Sept. 28, 1962

*Adcock, N. A. T. (Tvl & Natal; *CY 1961*) b March 8, 1931

*Adhikari, H. R. (Guj., Baroda & Ind. Serv.) b July 31, 1919

*Afaq Hussain (Kar., Pak. Us, PIA & PWD) b Dec. 31, 1939

Afford, J. A. (Notts.) b May 12, 1964

Aftab Baloch (PWD, Kar., Sind, NBP & PIA) b April 1, 1953

*Aftab Gul (Punjab U., Pak. Us & Lahore) b March 31, 1946

*Agha Saadat Ali (Pak. Us, Punjab, B'pur & Lahore) b June 21, 1929, d Oct. 26, 1995

*Agha Zahid (Pak. Us, Punjab, Lahore & HBL) b Jan. 7, 1953

*Agnew, J. P. (Leics; *CY 1988*) b April 4, 1960

*Ahangama, F. S. (SSC) b Sept. 14, 1959

Aird, R. (CUCC & Hants; Sec. MCC 1953-62, Pres. MCC 1968-69) b May 4, 1902, d Aug. 16, 1986

Aislabie, B. (Surrey, Hants, Kent & Sussex; Sec. MCC 1822-42) b Jan. 14, 1774, d June 2, 1842

Aitchison, Rev. J. K. (Scotland) b May 26, 1920, d Feb. 13, 1994

*Akram Raza (Lahore, Sargodha, WAPDA & HBL) b Nov. 22, 1964

*Alabaster, J. C. (Otago) b July 11, 1930

Alcock, C. W. (Sec. Surrey CCC 1872-1907, Editor *Cricket* 1882-1907) b Dec. 2, 1842, d Feb. 26, 1907

Alderman, A. E. (Derbys.) b Oct. 30, 1907, d June 4, 1990

*Alderman, T. M. (W. Aust., Kent & Glos.; *CY 1982*) b June 12, 1956

Aldridge, K. J. (Worcs & Tas.) b March 13, 1935

Alexander of Tunis, 1st Lord (Pres. MCC 1955-56) b Dec. 10, 1891, d June 16, 1969

*Alexander, F. C. M. (CUCC & Jam.) b Nov. 2, 1928

*Alexander, G. (Vic.) b April 22, 1851, d Nov. 6, 1930

*Alexander, H. H. (Vic.) b June 9, 1905, d April 15, 1993

Alikhan, R. I. (Sussex, PIA, Surrey & PNSC) b Dec. 28, 1962

*Alim-ud-Din (Rajputana, Guj., Sind, B'pur, Kar. & PWD) b Dec. 15, 1930

*Allan, D. W. (B'dos) b Nov. 5, 1937

*Allan, F. E. (Vic.) b Dec. 2, 1849, d Feb. 9, 1917

Allan, J. M. (OUCC, Kent, Warwicks. & Scotland) b April 2, 1932

*Allan, P. J. (Qld) b Dec. 31, 1935

*Allcott, C. F. W. (Auck.) b Oct. 7, 1896, d Nov. 19, 1973

Allen, A. W. (CUCC & Northants) b Dec. 22, 1912

*Allen, D. A. (Glos.) b Oct. 29, 1935

*Allen, Sir G. O. B. (CUCC & Middx; Pres. MCC 1963-64; *special portrait 1987*) b July 31, 1902, d Nov. 29, 1989

*Allen, I. B. A. (Windwards) b Oct. 6, 1965

Allen, M. H. J. (Northants & Derbys.) b Jan. 7, 1933, d Oct. 6, 1995

*Allen, R. C. (NSW) b July 2, 1858, d May 2, 1952

Alletson, E. B. (Notts.) b March 6, 1884, d July 5, 1963

Alley, W. E. (NSW & Som.; *CY 1962*) b Feb. 3, 1919

Alleyne, H. L. (B'dos, Worcs., Natal & Kent) b Feb. 28, 1957

Alleyne, M. W. (Glos.) b May 23, 1968

*Allom, M. J. C. (CUCC & Surrey; Pres. MCC 1969-70) b March 23, 1906, d April 8, 1995

*Allott, P. J. W. (Lancs. & Wgtn) b Sept. 14, 1956

Altham, H. S. (OUCC, Surrey & Hants; Pres. MCC 1959-60) b Nov. 30, 1888, d March 11, 1965

*Amalean, K. N. (SL) b April 7, 1965

*Amarnath, Lala (N. Ind., S. Punjab, Guj., Patiala, U. Pradesh & Ind. Rlwys) b Sept. 11, 1911

*Amarnath, M. (Punjab & Delhi; *CY 1984*) b Sept. 24, 1950

*Amarnath, S. (Punjab & Delhi) b Dec. 30, 1948

*Amar Singh, L. (Patiala, W. Ind. & Naw.) b Dec. 4, 1910, d May 20, 1940

*Ambrose, C. E. L. (Leewards & Northants; *CY 1992*) b Sept. 21, 1963

*Amerasinghe, A. M. J. G. (Nomads & Ant.) b Feb. 2, 1954

*Ames, L. E. G. (Kent; *CY 1929*) b Dec. 3, 1905, d Feb. 26, 1990

**Amir Elahi (Baroda, N. Ind., S. Punjab & B'pur) b Sept. 1, 1908, d Dec. 28, 1980

*Amiss, D. L. (Warwicks.; *CY 1975*) b April 7, 1943

*Amre, P. K. (Ind. Rlwys & Raja.) b Aug. 14, 1968

Anderson, I. S. (Derbys. & Boland) b April 24, 1960

*Anderson, J. H. (W. Prov.) b April 26, 1874, d March 11, 1926

*Anderson, R. W. (Cant., N. Dist., Otago & C. Dist.) b Oct. 2, 1948

*Anderson, W. McD. (Otago, C. Dist. & Cant.) b Oct. 8, 1919, d Dec. 21, 1979

Andrew, C. R. (CUCC) b Feb. 18, 1963

*Andrew, K. V. (Northants) b Dec. 15, 1929

Andrew, S. J. W. (Hants & Essex) b Jan. 27, 1966

*Andrews, B. (Cant., C. Dist. & Otago) b April 4, 1945

*Andrews, T. J. E. (NSW) b Aug. 26, 1890, d Jan. 28, 1970

Andrews, W. H. R. (Som.) b April 14, 1908, d Jan. 9, 1989

*Angel, J. (W. Aust.) b April 22, 1968

Angell, F. L. (Som.) b June 29, 1922

*Anil Dalpat (Kar. & PIA) b Sept. 20, 1963

*Ankola, S. A. (M'tra & Bombay) b March 1, 1968

Anthony, H. A. G. (Leewards & Glam.) b Jan. 16, 1971

*Anurasiri, S. D. (Pan.) b Feb. 25, 1966

*Anwar Hussain (N. Ind., Bombay, Sind & Kar.) b July 16, 1920

*Anwar Khan (Kar., Sind & NBP) b Dec. 24, 1955

*Appleyard, R. (Yorks.; *CY 1952*) b June 27, 1924

*Apte, A. L. (Ind. Us, Bombay & Raja.) b Oct. 24, 1934

*Apte, M. L. (Bombay & Bengal) b Oct. 5, 1932

*Aqib Javed (Lahore, PACO, Hants, I'bad & Allied Bank) b Aug. 5, 1972

*Archer, A. G. (Worcs.) b Dec. 6, 1871, d July 15, 1935

Archer, G. F. (Notts.) b Sept. 26, 1970

*Archer, K. A. (Qld) b Jan. 17, 1928

*Archer, R. G. (Qld) b Oct. 25, 1933

*Arif Butt (Lahore & Pak. Rlwys) b May 17, 1944

Arlott, John (Writer & Broadcaster) b Feb. 25, 1914, d Dec. 14, 1991

*Armitage, T. (Yorks.) b April 25, 1848, d Sept. 21, 1922

Armstrong, N. F. (Leics.) b Dec. 22, 1892, d Jan. 19, 1990

Armstrong, T. R. (Derbys.) b Oct. 13, 1909

*Armstrong, W. W. (Vic.; *CY 1903*) b May 22, 1879, d July 13, 1947

Arnold, A. P. (Cant. & Northants) b Oct. 16, 1924

*Arnold, E. G. (Worcs.) b Nov. 7, 1876, d Oct. 25, 1942

*Arnold, G. G. (Surrey & Sussex; *CY 1972*) b Sept. 3, 1944

*Arnold, J. (Hants) b Nov. 30, 1907, d April 4, 1984

*Arnott, K. J. (MCD) b March 8, 1961

*Arshad Ayub (H'bad) b Aug. 2, 1958

Arshad Khan (Peshawar, I'bad & Pak. Rlwys) b March 22, 1971

Arshad Pervez (Sargodha, Lahore, Pak. Us, Servis Ind., HBL & Punjab) b Oct. 1, 1952

*Arthurton, K. L. T. (Leewards) b Feb. 21, 1965

*Arun, B. (TN) b Dec. 14, 1962

*Arun Lal (Delhi & Bengal) b Aug. 1, 1955

*Asgarali, N. (T/T) b Dec. 28, 1920

Ashdown, W. H. (Kent) b Dec. 27, 1898, d Sept. 15, 1979

*Ashfaq Ahmed (PACO & PIA) b June 6, 1973

Ashley, W. H. (W. Prov.) b Feb. 10, 1862, d July 14, 1930

*Ashraf Ali (Lahore, Income Tax, Pak Us, Pak Rlwys & UBL) b April 22, 1958

Ashton, C. T. (CUCC & Essex) b Feb. 19, 1901, d Oct. 31, 1942

Ashton, G. (CUCC & Worcs.) b Sept. 27, 1896, d Feb. 6, 1981

Ashton, Sir H. (CUCC & Essex; *CY 1922*; Pres. MCC 1960-61) b Feb. 13, 1898, d June 17, 1979

Asif Din, M. (Warwicks.) b Sept. 21, 1960

*Asif Iqbal (H'bad, Kar., Kent, PIA & NBP; *CY 1968*) b June 6, 1943

*Asif Masood (Lahore, Punjab U. & PIA) b Jan. 23, 1946

*Asif Mujtaba (Kar. & PIA) b Nov. 4, 1967

Aslett, D. G. (Kent) b Feb. 12, 1958

Aspinall, R. (Yorks.) b Nov. 26, 1918

*Astill, W. E. (Leics.; *CY 1933*) b March 1, 1888, d Feb. 10, 1948

Astle, N. J. (Cant.) b Sept. 15, 1971

*Atapattu, M. S. (SSC) b Nov. 22, 1972

*Ata-ur-Rehman (Lahore, PACO & Allied Bank) b March 28, 1975

Atherton, M. A. (CUCC & Lancs.; *CY 1991*) b March 23, 1968

*Athey, C. W. J. (Yorks., Glos. & Sussex) b Sept. 27, 1957

*Atif Rauf (I'bad & ADBP) b March 3, 1964

Atkinson, C. R. M. (Som.) b July 23, 1931, d June 25, 1991

*Atkinson, D. St E. (B'dos & T/T) b Aug. 9, 1926

*Atkinson, E. St E. (B'dos) b Nov. 6, 1927

Atkinson, G. (Som. & Lancs.) b March 29, 1938

Atkinson, J. C. M. (Som. & CUCC) b July 10, 1968

Atkinson, T. (Notts.) b Sept. 27, 1930, d Sept. 2, 1990

*Attewell, W. (Notts.; *CY 1892*) b June 12, 1861, d June 11, 1927

Austin, Sir H. B. G. (B'dos) b July 15, 1877, d July 27, 1943

Austin, I. D. (Lancs.) b May 30, 1966

*Austin, R. A. (Jam.) b Sept. 5, 1954

Avery, A. V. (Essex) b Dec. 19, 1914

Aworth, C. J. (CUCC & Surrey) b Feb. 19, 1953

Ayling, J. R. (Hants) b June 13, 1967

Aylward, J. (Hants & All-England) b 1741, d Dec. 27, 1827

Aymes, A. N. (Hants) b June 4, 1964

*Azad, K. (Delhi) b Jan. 2, 1959

*Azeem Hafeez (Kar., Allied Bank & PIA) b July 29, 1963

*Azhar Khan (Lahore, Punjab, Pak. Us., PIA & HBL) b Sept. 7, 1955

*Azharuddin, M. (H'bad & Derbys.; *CY 1991*) b Feb. 8, 1963

*Azmat Rana (B'pur, PIA, Punjab, Lahore & MCB) b Nov. 3, 1951

Babington, A. M. (Sussex & Glos.) b July 22, 1963

*Bacchus, S. F. A. F. (Guyana, W. Prov. & Border) b Jan. 31, 1954

*Bacher, Dr A. (Tvl) b May 24, 1942

*Badcock, C. L. (Tas. & S. Aust.) b April 10, 1914, d Dec. 13, 1982

*Badcock, F. T. (Wgtn & Otago) b Aug. 9, 1895, d Sept. 19, 1982

*Baichan, L. (Guyana) b May 12, 1946

*Baig, A. A. (H'bad, OUCC & Som.) b March 19, 1939

Bailey, Sir D. T. L. (Glos.) b Aug. 5, 1918

Bailey, J. (Hants) b April 6, 1908, d Feb. 9, 1988

Bailey, J. A. (Essex & OUCC; Sec. MCC 1974-87) b June 22, 1930

*Bailey, R. J. (Northants) b Oct. 28, 1963

*Bailey, T. E. (Essex & CUCC; *CY 1950*) b Dec. 3, 1923

Baillie, A. W. (Sec. MCC 1858-63) b June 22, 1830, d May 10, 1867

Bainbridge, P. (Glos. & Durham; *CY 1986*) b April 16, 1958

*Bairstow, D. L. (Yorks. & Griq. W.) b Sept. 1, 1951

Baker, R. P. (Surrey) b April 9, 1954

*Bakewell, A. H. (Northants; *CY 1934*) b Nov. 2, 1908, d Jan. 23, 1983

Bakker, P. J. (Hants) b Aug. 19, 1957

*Balaskas, X. C. (Griq. W., Border, W. Prov., Tvl & NE Tvl) b Oct. 15, 1910, d May 12, 1994

*Balderstone, J. C. (Yorks. & Leics.) b Nov. 16, 1940

Baldry, D. O. (Middx & Hants) b Dec. 26, 1931

Ball, M. C. J. (Glos.) b April 26, 1970

*Banerjee, S. A. (Bengal & Bihar) b Nov. 1, 1919, d Sept. 14, 1992

*Banerjee, S. N. (Bengal, Naw., Bihar & M. Pradesh) b Oct. 3, 1911, d Oct. 14, 1980

*Banerjee, S. T. (Bihar) b Feb. 13, 1969

*Bannerman, A. C. (NSW) b March 22, 1854, d Sept. 19, 1924

*Bannerman, Charles (NSW) b July 23, 1851, d Aug. 20, 1930

Bannister, J. D. (Warwicks.; Writer & Broadcaster) b Aug. 23, 1930

*Baptiste, E. A. E. (Kent, Leewards, Northants & E. Prov.) b March 12, 1960

*Baqa Jilani, M. (N. Ind.) b July 20, 1911, d July 2, 1941

Barber, A. T. (OUCC & Yorks.) b June 17, 1905, d March 10, 1985

*Barber, R. T. (Wgtn & C. Dist.) b June 23, 1925

*Barber, R. W. (Lancs., CUCC & Warwicks.; *CY 1967*) b Sept. 26, 1935

*Barber, W. (Yorks.) b April 18, 1901, d Sept. 10, 1968

Barclay, J. R. T. (Sussex & OFS) b Jan. 22, 1954

*Bardsley, W. (NSW; *CY 1910*) b Dec. 6, 1882, d Jan. 20, 1954

Baring, A. E. G. (Hants) b Jan. 21, 1910, d Aug. 29, 1986

Barker, G. (Essex) b July 6, 1931

Barling, H. T. (Surrey) b Sept. 1, 1906, d Jan. 2, 1993

*Barlow, E. J. (Tvl, E. Prov., W. Prov., Derbys. & Boland) b Aug. 12, 1940

*Barlow, G. D. (Middx) b March 26, 1950

*Barlow, R. G. (Lancs.) b May 28, 1851, d July 31, 1919

Barnard, H. M. (Hants) b July 18, 1933

Barnes, A. R. (Sec. Aust. Cricket Board 1960-81) b Sept. 12, 1916, d March 14, 1989

Barnes, S. F. (Warwicks. & Lancs.; *CY 1910*) b April 19, 1873, d Dec. 26, 1967

*Barnes, S. G. (NSW) b June 5, 1916, d Dec. 16, 1973

*Barnes, W. (Notts.; *CY 1890*) b May 27, 1852, d March 24, 1899

Barnett, A. A. (Middx & Lancs.) b Sept. 11, 1970

*Barnett, B. A. (Vic.) b March 23, 1908, d June 29, 1979

*Barnett, C. J. (Glos.; *CY 1937*) b July 3, 1910, d May 28, 1993

*Barnett, K. J. (Derbys. & Boland; *CY 1989*) b July 17, 1960

Barnwell, C. J. P. (Som.) b June 23, 1914

Baroda, Maharaja of (Manager, Ind. in Eng., 1959) b April 2, 1930, d Sept. 1, 1988

*Barratt, F. (Notts.) b April 12, 1894, d Jan. 29, 1947

*Barratt, R. J. (Leics.) b May 3, 1942, d Feb. 1995

*Barrett, A. G. (Jam.) b April 5, 1942

Barrett, B. J. (Auck., C. Dist., Worcs. & N. Dist.) b Nov. 16, 1966

*Barrett, J. E. (Vic.) b Oct. 15, 1866, d Feb. 6, 1916

Barrick, D. W. (Northants) b April 28, 1926

*Barrington, K. F. (Surrey; *CY 1960*) b Nov. 24, 1930, d March 14, 1981

Barron, W. (Lancs. & Northants) b Oct. 26, 1917

*Barrow, I. (Jam.) b Jan. 6, 1911, d April 2, 1979

*Bartlett, E. L. (B'dos) b March 18, 1906, d Dec. 21, 1976

*Bartlett, G. A. (C. Dist. & Cant.) b Feb. 3, 1941

Bartlett, H. T. (CUCC, Surrey & Sussex; *CY 1939*) b Oct. 7, 1914, d June 26, 1988

Bartlett, R. J. (Som.) b Oct. 8, 1966

Bartley, T. J. (Umpire) b March 19, 1908, d April 2, 1964

Barton, M. R. (OUCC & Surrey) b Oct. 14, 1914

*Barton, P. T. (Wgtn) b Oct. 9, 1935

*Barton, V. A. (Kent & Hants) b Oct. 6, 1867, d March 23, 1906

Barwick, S. R. (Glam.) b Sept. 6, 1960

Base, S. J. (W. Prov., Glam., Derbys., Boland & Border) b Jan. 2, 1960

*Basit Ali (Kar. & UBL) b Dec. 13, 1970

Bates, D. L. (Sussex) b May 10, 1933

*Bates, W. (Yorks.) b Nov. 19, 1855, d Jan. 8, 1900

Batty, J. D. (Yorks. & Som.) b May 15, 1971

*Baumgartner, H. V. (OFS & Tvl) b Nov. 17, 1883, d April 8, 1938

Baxter, A. D. (Devon, Lancs., Middx & Scotland) b Jan. 20, 1910, d Jan. 28, 1986

*Bean, G. (Notts & Sussex) b March 7, 1864, d March 16, 1923

Bear, M. J. (Essex & Cant.) b Feb. 23, 1934

*Beard, D. D. (C. Dist. & N. Dist.) b Jan. 14, 1920, d July 15, 1982

*Beard, G. R. (NSW) b Aug. 19, 1950

Beauclerk, Lord Frederick (Middx, Surrey & MCC) b May 8, 1773, d April 22, 1850

Beaufort, 10th Duke of (Pres. MCC 1952-53) b April 4, 1900, d Feb. 5, 1984

*Beaumont, R. (Tvl) b Feb. 4, 1884, d May 25, 1958

*Beck, J. E. F. (Wgtn) b Aug. 1, 1934

Bedade, A. C. (Baroda) b Sept. 24, 1966

*Bedi, B. S. (N. Punjab, Delhi & Northants) b Sept. 25, 1946

*Bedser, A. V. (Surrey; *CY 1947*) b July 4, 1918

Bedser, E. A. (Surrey) b July 4, 1918

Beet, G. (Derbys.; Umpire) b April 24, 1886, d Dec. 13, 1946

*Begbie, D. W. (Tvl) b Dec. 12, 1914

Beldham, W. (Hambledon & Surrey) b Feb. 5, 1766, d Feb. 20, 1862

*Bell, A. J. (W. Prov. & Rhod.) b April 15, 1906, d Aug. 2, 1985

Bell, R. V. (Middx & Sussex) b Jan. 7, 1931, d Oct. 26, 1989

*Bell, W. (Cant.) b Sept. 5, 1931

*Benaud, J. (NSW) b May 11, 1944

*Benaud, R. (NSW; *CY 1962*) b Oct. 6, 1930

*Benjamin, J. E. (Warwicks. & Surrey) b Feb. 2, 1961

*Benjamin, K. C. G. (Leewards & Worcs.) b April 8, 1967

*Benjamin, W. K. M. (Leewards, Leics. & Hants) b Dec. 31, 1964

Bennett, D. (Middx) b Dec. 18, 1933

*Bennett, M. J. (NSW) b Oct. 16, 1956

Bennett, N. H. (Surrey) b Sept. 23, 1912

Bennett, R. (Lancs.) b June 16, 1940

Benson, J. D. R. (Leics.) b March 1, 1967

*Benson, M. R. (Kent) b July 6, 1958

Bernard, J. R. (CUCC & Glos.) b Dec. 7, 1938

Berry, L. G. (Leics.) b April 28, 1906, d Feb. 5, 1985

*Berry, R. (Lancs., Worcs. & Derbys.) b Jan. 29, 1926

*Best, C. A. (B'dos & W. Prov.) b May 14, 1959

*Betancourt, N. (T/T) b June 4, 1887, d Oct. 12, 1947

*Bevan, M. G. (NSW & Yorks.) b May 8, 1970

Bhalekar, R. B. (M'tra) b Feb. 17, 1952

*Bhandari, P. (Delhi & Bengal) b Nov. 27, 1935

*Bhat, A. R. (Karn.) b April 16, 1958

Bhupinder Singh (Punjab) b April 1, 1965

Bick, D. A. (Middx) b Feb. 22, 1936, d Jan. 13, 1992

Bicknell, D. J. (Surrey) b June 24, 1967

*Bicknell, M. P. (Surrey) b Jan. 14, 1969

Biddulph, K. D. (Som.) b May 29, 1932

*Bilby, G. P. (Wgtn) b May 7, 1941

*Binks, J. G. (Yorks.; *CY 1969*) b Oct. 5, 1935

*Binns, A. P. (Jam.) b July 24, 1929

*Binny, R. M. H. (Karn.) b July 19, 1955

Birch, J. D. (Notts.) b June 18, 1955

Bird, H. D. (Yorks. & Leics.; Umpire) b April 19, 1933

*Bird, M. C. (Lancs. & Surrey) b March 25, 1888, d Dec. 9, 1933

*Birkenshaw, J. (Yorks., Leics. & Worcs.) b Nov. 13, 1940

*Birkett, L. S. (B'dos, BG & T/T) b April 14, 1904

Birrell, H. B. (E. Prov., Rhod. & OUCC) b Dec. 1, 1927

Bishop, G. A. (S. Aust.) b Feb. 25, 1960

*Bishop, I. R. (T/T & Derbys.) b Oct. 24, 1967

*Bisset, Sir Murray (M.) (W. Prov.) b April 14, 1876, d Oct. 24, 1931

*Bissett, G. F. (Griq. W., W. Prov. & Tvl) b Nov. 5, 1905, d Nov. 14, 1965

Bissex, M. (Glos.) b Sept. 28, 1944

*Blackham, J. McC. (Vic.; *CY 1891*) b May 11, 1854, d Dec. 28, 1932

*Blackie, D. D. (Vic.) b April 5, 1882, d April 18, 1955

Blackledge, J. F. (Lancs.) b April 15, 1928

*Blain, T. E. (C. Dist.) b Feb. 17, 1962

Blair, B. R. (Otago) b Dec. 27, 1957

*Blair, R. W. (Wgtn & C. Dist.) b June 23, 1932

Blake, D. E. (Hants) b April 27, 1925

Blake, Rev. P. D. S. (OUCC & Sussex) b May 23, 1927

*Blakey, R. J. (Yorks.) b Jan. 15, 1967

*Blanckenberg, J. M. (W. Prov. & Natal) b Dec. 31, 1893, dead

*Bland, K. C. (Rhod., E. Prov. & OFS; *CY 1966*) b April 5, 1938

Blenkiron, W. (Warwicks.) b July 21, 1942

*Blewett, G. S. (S. Aust.) b Oct. 29, 1971

Bligh, Hon. Ivo (*see* 8th Earl of Darnley)

Blundell, Sir E. D. (CUCC & NZ) b May 29, 1907, d Sept. 24, 1984

*Blunt, R. C. (Cant. & Otago; *CY 1928*) b Nov. 3, 1900, d June 22, 1966

*Blythe, C. (Kent; *CY 1904*) b May 30, 1879, d Nov. 8, 1917

*Board, J. H. (Glos.) b Feb. 23, 1867, d April 16, 1924

*Bock, E. G. (Griq. W., Tvl & W. Prov.) b Sept. 17, 1908, d Sept. 5, 1961

Bodkin, P. E. (CUCC) b Sept. 15, 1924, d Sept. 18, 1994

Boiling, J. (Surrey & Durham) b April 8, 1968

*Bolton, B. A. (Cant. & Wgtn) b May 31, 1935

*Bolus, J. B. (Yorks., Notts. & Derbys.) b Jan. 31, 1934

*Bond, G. E. (W. Prov.) b April 5, 1909, d Aug. 27, 1965

Bond, J. D. (Lancs. & Notts.; *CY 1971*) b May 6, 1932

*Bonnor, G. J. (Vic. & NSW) b Feb. 25, 1855, d June 27, 1912

*Boock, S. L. (Otago & Cant.) b Sept. 20, 1951

*Boon, D. C. (Tas.; *CY 1994*) b Dec. 29, 1960

Boon, T. J. (Leics.) b Nov. 1, 1961

*Booth, B. C. (NSW) b Oct. 19, 1933

Booth, B. J. (Lancs. & Leics.) b Dec. 3, 1935

*Booth, M. W. (Yorks.; *CY 1914*) b Dec. 10, 1886, d July 1, 1916

Booth, P. (Leics.) b Nov. 2, 1952

Booth, P. A. (Yorks. & Warwicks.) b Sept. 5, 1965

Booth, R. (Yorks. & Worcs.) b Oct. 1, 1926

*Borde, C. G. (Baroda & M'tra) b July 21, 1934

*Border, A. R. (NSW, Glos, Qld & Essex; *CY 1982*) b July 27, 1955

Bore, M. K. (Yorks. & Notts.) b June 2, 1947

Borrington, A. J. (Derbys.) b Dec. 8, 1948

*Bosanquet, B. J. T. (OUCC & Middx; *CY 1905*) b Oct. 13, 1877, d Oct. 12, 1936

*Bosch T. (N. Tvl & Natal) b March 14, 1966

Bose, G. (Bengal) b May 20, 1947

Boshier, B. S. (Leics.) b March 6, 1932

*Botham, I. T. (Som., Worcs., Durham & Qld; *CY 1978*) b Nov. 24, 1955

*Botten, J. T. (NE Tvl & N. Tvl) b June 21, 1938

Boucher, J. C. (Ireland) b Dec. 22, 1910

Bourne, W. A. (B'dos & Warwicks.) b Nov. 15, 1952

*Bowden, M. P. (Surrey & Tvl) b Nov. 1, 1865, d Feb. 19, 1892

*Bowes, W. E. (Yorks.; *CY 1932*) b July 25, 1908, d Sept. 5, 1987

Bowler, P. D. (Leics., Tas., Derbys. & Som.) b July 30, 1963

*Bowley, E. H. (Sussex & Auck.; *CY 1930*) b June 6, 1890, d July 9, 1974

Bowley, F. L. (Worcs.) b Nov. 9, 1873, d May 31, 1943

Box, T. (Sussex) b Feb. 7, 1808, d July 12, 1876

*Boyce, K. D. (B'dos & Essex; *CY 1974*) b Oct. 11, 1943

*Boycott, G. (Yorks. & N. Tvl; *CY 1965*) b Oct. 21, 1940

Boyd-Moss, R. J. (CUCC & Northants) b Dec. 16, 1959

Boyes, G. S. (Hants) b March 31, 1899, d Feb. 11, 1973

*Boyle, H. F. (Vic.) b Dec. 10, 1847, d Nov. 21, 1907

*Bracewell, B. P. (C. Dist., Otago & N. Dist.) b Sept. 14, 1959

*Bracewell, J. G. (Otago & Auck.) b April 15, 1958

*Bradburn, G. E. (N. Dist.) b May 26, 1966

*Bradburn, W. P. (N. Dist.) b Nov. 24, 1938

Bradley, W. M. (Kent) b Jan. 2, 1875, d June 19, 1944

*Bradman, Sir D. G. (NSW & S. Aust.; *CY 1931*) b Aug. 27, 1908

Brain, B. M. (Worcs. & Glos.) b Sept. 13, 1940

*Brain, D. H. (Mash.) b Oct. 4, 1964

Bramall, Field-Marshal The Lord (Pres. MCC 1988-89) b Dec. 18, 1923

*Brandes, E. A. (MCD) b March 5, 1963

*Brann, W. H. (E. Prov.) b April 4, 1899, d Sept. 22, 1953

Brassington, A. J. (Glos.) b Aug. 9, 1954

*Braund, L. C. (Surrey & Som.; *CY 1902*) b Oct. 18, 1875, d Dec. 23, 1955

Bray, C. (Essex) b April 6, 1898, d Sept. 12, 1993

Brayshaw, I. J. (W. Aust.) b Jan. 14, 1942

Brazier, A. F. (Surrey & Kent) b Dec. 7, 1924

Breakwell, D. (Northants & Som.) b July 2, 1948

*Brearley, J. M. (CUCC & Middx; *CY 1977*) b April 28, 1942

*Brearley, W. (Lancs.; *CY 1909*) b March 11, 1876, d Jan. 13, 1937

*Brennan, D. V. (Yorks.) b Feb. 10, 1920, d Jan. 9, 1985

*Briant, G. A. (Zimb.) b April 11, 1969

Bridge, W. B. (Warwicks.) b May 29, 1938

Bridger, Rev. J. R. (Hants) b April 8, 1920, d July 14, 1986

Brierley, T. L. (Glam., Lancs. & Canada) b June 15, 1910, d Jan. 7, 1989

Briers, N. E. (Leics.; *CY 1993*) b Jan. 15, 1955

*Briggs, John (Lancs.; *CY 1889*) b Oct. 3, 1862, d Jan. 11, 1902

*Bright, R. J. (Vic.) b July 13, 1954

*Briscoe, A. W. (Tvl) b Feb. 6, 1911, d April 22, 1941

*Broad, B. C. (Glos. & Notts.) b Sept. 29, 1957

Broadbent, R. G. (Worcs.) b June 21, 1924, d April 26, 1993

Brocklehurst, B. G. (Som.) b Feb. 18, 1922

*Brockwell, W. (Kimberley & Surrey; *CY 1895*) b Jan. 21, 1865, d June 30, 1935

Broderick, V. (Northants) b Aug. 17, 1920

Brodhurst, A. H. (CUCC & Glos.) b July 21, 1916

Bromfield, H. D. (W. Prov.) b June 26, 1932

*Bromley, E. H. (W. Aust. & Vic.) b Sept. 2, 1912, d Feb. 1, 1967

*Bromley-Davenport, H. R. (CUCC, Bombay Eur. & Middx) b Aug. 18, 1870, d May 23, 1954

*Brookes, D. (Northants; *CY 1957*) b Oct. 29, 1915

Brookes, W. H. (Editor of *Wisden* 1936-39) b Dec. 5, 1894, d May 28, 1955

*Brown, A. (Kent) b Oct. 17, 1935

Brown, A. D. (Surrey) b Feb. 11, 1970

Brown, A. S. (Glos.) b June 24, 1936

*Brown, D. J. (Warwicks.) b Jan. 30, 1942

Brown, D. R. (Scotland & Warwicks.) b Oct. 29, 1969

Brown, D. W. J. (Glos.) b Feb. 26, 1942

*Brown, F. R. (CUCC, Surrey & Northants; *CY 1933*; Pres. MCC 1971-72) b Dec. 16, 1910, d July 24, 1991

*Brown, G. (Hants) b Oct. 6, 1887, d Dec. 3, 1964

Brown, J. (Scotland) b Sept. 24, 1931

*Brown, J. T. (Yorks.; *CY 1895*) b Aug. 20, 1869, d Nov. 4, 1904

Brown, K. R. (Middx) b March 18, 1963

*Brown, L. S. (Tvl, NE Tvl & Rhod.) b Nov. 24, 1910, d Sept. 1, 1983

Brown, R. D. (Zimb.) b March 11, 1951

Brown, S. J. E. (Northants & Durham) b June 29, 1969

Brown, S. M. (Middx) b Dec. 8, 1917, d Dec. 28, 1987

*Brown, V. R. (Cant. & Auck.) b Nov. 3, 1959

*Brown, W. A. (NSW & Qld; *CY 1939*) b July 31, 1912

Brown, W. C. (Northants) b Nov. 13, 1900, d Jan. 20, 1986

Browne, B. St A. (Guyana) b Sept. 16, 1967

*Browne, C. O. (B'dos) b Dec. 7, 1970

*Browne, C. R. (B'dos & BG) b Oct. 8, 1890, d Jan. 12, 1964

Bruce, Hon. C. N. (3rd Lord Aberdare) (OUCC & Middx) b Aug. 2, 1885, d Oct. 4, 1957

*Bruce, W. (Vic.) b May 22, 1864, d Aug. 3, 1925

*Bruk-Jackson, G. K. (MCD) b April 25, 1969

Bryan, G. J. (Kent) b Dec. 29, 1902, d April 4, 1991

Bryan, J. L. (CUCC & Kent; *CY 1922*) b May 26, 1896, d April 23, 1985

Bryan, R. T. (Kent) b July 30, 1898, d July 27, 1970

*Buckenham, C. P. (Essex) b Jan. 16, 1876, d Feb. 23, 1937

Buckingham, J. (Warwicks.) b Jan. 21, 1903, d Jan. 25, 1987

Budd, E. H. (Middx & All-England) b Feb. 23, 1785, d March 29, 1875

Budd, W. L. (Hants) b Oct. 25, 1913, d Aug. 23, 1986

Bull, F. G. (Essex; *CY 1898*) b April 2, 1875, d Sept. 16, 1910

Buller, J. S. (Yorks. & Worcs.; Umpire) b Aug. 23, 1909, d Aug. 7, 1970

Burden, M. D. (Hants) b Oct. 4, 1930, d Nov. 9, 1987

*Burge, P. J. P. (Qld; *CY 1965*) b May 17, 1932

*Burger, C. G. de V. (Natal) b July 12, 1935

Burgess, G. I. (Som.) b May 5, 1943

*Burgess, M. G. (Auck.) b July 17, 1944

*Burke, C. (Auck.) b March 22, 1914

*Burke, J. W. (NSW; *CY 1957*) b June 12, 1930, d Feb. 2, 1979

*Burke, S. F. (NE Tvl & OFS) b March 11, 1934

*Burki, Javed (Pak. Us, OUCC, Punjab, Lahore, Kar., R'pindi & NWFP) b May 8, 1938

*Burmester, M. G. (Mash.) b Jan. 24, 1968

*Burn, E. J. K. (K. E.) (Tas.) b Sept. 17, 1862, d July 20, 1956

Burnet, J. R. (Yorks.) b Oct. 11, 1918

Burns, N. D. (Essex, W. Prov. & Som.) b Sept. 19, 1965

Burnup, C. J. (CUCC & Kent; *CY 1903*) b Nov. 21, 1875, d April 5, 1960

Burrough, H. D. (Som.) b Feb. 6, 1909, d April 9, 1994

*Burton, F. J. (Vic. & NSW) b Nov. 2, 1865, d Aug. 25, 1929

*Burtt, T. B. (Cant.) b Jan. 22, 1915, d May 24, 1988

Buse, H. F. T. (Som.) b Aug. 5, 1910, d Feb. 23, 1992

Bushby, M. H. (CUCC) b July 29, 1931

Buss, A. (Sussex) b Sept. 1, 1939

Buss, M. A. (Sussex & OFS) b Jan. 24, 1944

Buswell, J. E. (Northants) b July 3, 1909

*Butchart, I. P. (MCD) b May 9, 1960

*Butcher, A. R. (Surrey & Glam.; *CY 1991*) b Jan. 7, 1954

*Butcher, B. F. (Guyana; *CY 1970*) b Sept. 3, 1933

Butcher, I. P. (Leics. & Glos.) b July 1, 1962

Butcher, M. A. (Surrey) b Aug. 23, 1972

*Butcher, R. O. (Middx, B'dos & Tas.) b Oct. 14, 1953

*Butler, H. J. (Notts.) b March 12, 1913, d July 17, 1991

*Butler, L. S. (T/T) b Feb. 9, 1929

*Butt, H. R. (Sussex) b Dec. 27, 1865, d Dec. 21, 1928

*Butterfield, L. A. (Cant.) b Aug. 29, 1913

*Butts, C. G. (Guyana) b July 8, 1957

Buxton, I. R. (Derbys.) b April 17, 1938

*Buys, I. D. (W. Prov.) b Feb. 3, 1895, dead

Byas, D. (Yorks.) b Aug. 26, 1963

*Bynoe, M. R. (B'dos) b Feb. 23, 1941

Caccia, Lord (Pres. MCC 1973-74) b Dec. 21, 1905, d Oct. 31, 1990

*Caddick, A. R. (Som.) b Nov. 21, 1968

Caesar, Julius (Surrey & All-England) b March 25, 1830, d March 6, 1878

Caffyn, W. (Surrey & NSW) b Feb. 2, 1828, d Aug. 28, 1919

Caine, C. Stewart (Editor of *Wisden* 1926-33) b Oct. 28, 1861, d April 15, 1933

*Cairns, B. L. (C. Dist., Otago & N. Dist.) b Oct. 10, 1949

*Cairns, C. L. (N. Dist., Notts. & Cant.) b June 13, 1970

Calder, H. L. (Cranleigh; *CY 1918*) b Jan. 24, 1901, d Sept. 15, 1995

Callaghan, D. J. (E. Prov.) b Feb. 1, 1965

*Callaway, S. T. (NSW & Cant.) b Feb. 6, 1868, d Nov. 25, 1923

*Callen, I. W. (Vic. & Boland) b May 2, 1955

*Calthorpe, Hon. F. S. Gough- (CUCC, Sussex & Warwicks.) b May 27, 1892, d Nov. 19, 1935

*Camacho, G. S. (Guyana) b Oct. 15, 1945

*Cameron, F. J. (Jam.) b June 22, 1923, d Feb. 1995

*Cameron, F. J. (Otago) b June 1, 1932

*Cameron, H. B. (Tvl, E. Prov. & W. Prov.; *CY 1936*) b July 5, 1905, d Nov. 2, 1935

*Cameron, J. H. (CUCC, Jam. & Som.) b April 8, 1914

*Campbell, A. D. R. (MCD) b Sept. 23, 1972

*Campbell, G. D. (Tas.) b March 10, 1964

*Campbell, S. L. (B'dos) b Nov. 1, 1970

*Campbell, T. (Tvl) b Feb. 9, 1882, d Oct. 5, 1924

Cannings, V. H. D. (Warwicks. & Hants) b April 3, 1919

*Capel, D. J. (Northants & E. Prov.) b Feb. 6, 1963

Caple, R. G. (Middx & Hants) b Dec. 8, 1939

Cardus, Sir Neville (Cricket Writer) b April 3, 1888, d Feb. 27, 1975

*Carew, G. McD. (B'dos) b June 4, 1910, d Dec. 9, 1974

*Carew, M. C. (T/T) b Sept. 15, 1937

*Carkeek, W. (Vic.) b Oct. 17, 1878, d Feb. 20, 1937

Carlisle, S. V. (Under-24) b May 10, 1972

*Carlson, P. H. (Qld) b Aug. 8, 1951

*Carlstein, P. R. (OFS, Tvl, Natal & Rhod.) b Oct. 28, 1938

Carpenter, D. (Glos.) b Sept. 12, 1935

Carpenter, R. (Cambs. & Utd England XI) b Nov. 18, 1830, d July 13, 1901

*Carr, A. W. (Notts.; *CY 1923*) b May 21, 1893, d Feb. 7, 1963

*Carr, D. B. (OUCC & Derbys.; *CY 1960*; Sec. TCCB 1974-86) b Dec. 28, 1926

*Carr, D. W. (Kent; *CY 1910*) b March 17, 1872, d March 23, 1950

Carr, J. D. (OUCC & Middx) b June 15, 1963

Carrick, P. (Yorks. & E. Prov.) b July 16, 1952

Carrington, E. (Derbys.) b March 25, 1914

Carse, J. A. (Rhod., W. Prov., E. Prov. & Northants) b Dec. 13, 1958

*Carter, C. P. (Natal & Tvl) b April 23, 1881, d Nov. 8, 1952

*Carter, H. (NSW) b Halifax, Yorks. March 15, 1878, d June 8, 1948

Carter, R. G. (Warwicks.) b April 14, 1933

Carter, R. G. M. (Worcs.) b July 11, 1937

Carter, R. M. (Northants & Cant.) b May 25, 1960

Cartwright, H. (Derbys.) b May 12, 1951

*Cartwright, T. W. (Warwicks., Som. & Glam.) b July 22, 1935

Cass, G. R. (Essex, Worcs. & Tas.) b April 23, 1940

Castell, A. T. (Hants) b Aug. 6, 1943

Catt, A. W. (Kent & W. Prov.) b Oct. 2, 1933

*Catterall, R. H. (Tvl, Rhod., Natal & OFS; *CY 1925*) b July 10, 1900, d Jan. 2, 1961

*Cave, H. B. (Wgtn & C. Dist.) b Oct. 10, 1922, d Sept. 15, 1989

Chalk, F. G. H. (OUCC & Kent) b Sept. 7, 1910, d Feb. 17, 1943

*Challenor, G. (B'dos) b June 28, 1888, d July 30, 1947

Chamberlain, W. R. F. (Northants; Chairman TCCB 1990-94) b April 13, 1925

Chandana, U. U. (TU) b May 7, 1972

*Chanderpaul, S. (Guyana) b Aug. 18, 1974

*Chandrasekhar, B. S. (†Karn.; *CY 1972*) b May 17, 1945

Chandrasekhar, V. B. (TN) b Aug. 21, 1961

*Chang, H. S. (Jam.) b July 22, 1952

*Chapman, A. P. F. (Uppingham, OUCC & Kent; *CY 1919*) b Sept. 3, 1900, d Sept. 16, 1961

*Chapman, H. W. (Natal) b June 30, 1890, d Dec. 1, 1941

*Chappell, G. S. (S. Aust., Som. & Qld; *CY 1973*) b Aug. 7, 1948

*Chappell, I. M. (S. Aust. & Lancs.; *CY 1976*) b Sept. 26, 1943

*Chappell, T. M. (S. Aust., W. Aust. & NSW) b Oct. 21, 1952

Chapple, G. (Lancs.) b Jan. 23, 1974

*Chapple, M. E. (Cant. & C. Dist.) b July 25, 1930, d July 31, 1985

*Charlton, P. C. (NSW) b April 9, 1867, d Sept. 30, 1954

*Charlwood, H. R. J. (Sussex) b Dec. 19, 1846, d June 6, 1888

*Chatfield, E. J. (Wgtn) b July 3, 1950

Chatterjee, U. (Bengal) b July 13, 1964

*Chatterton, W. (Derbys.) b Dec. 27, 1861, d March 19, 1913

*Chauhan, C. P. S. (M'tra & Delhi) b July 21, 1947

*Chauhan, R. K. (M. Pradesh) b Dec. 19, 1966

Cheatle, R. G. L. (Sussex & Surrey) b July 31, 1953

*Cheetham, J. E. (W. Prov.) b May 26, 1920, d Aug. 21, 1980

Chester, F. (Worcs.; Umpire) b Jan. 20, 1895, d April 8, 1957

Chesterton, G. H. (OUCC & Worcs.) b July 15, 1922

*Chevalier, G. A. (W. Prov.) b March 9, 1937

*Childs, J. H. (Glos. & Essex; *CY 1987*) b Aug. 15, 1951

*Chipperfield, A. G. (NSW) b Nov. 17, 1905, d July 29, 1987

Chisholm, R. H. E. (Scotland) b May 22, 1927

*Chowdhury, N. R. (Bihar & Bengal) b May 23, 1923, d Dec. 14, 1979

*Christiani, C. M. (BG) b Oct. 28, 1913, d April 4, 1938

*Christiani, R. J. (BG) b July 19, 1920

*Christopherson, S. (Kent; Pres. MCC 1939-45) b Nov. 11, 1861, d April 6, 1949

*Christy, J. A. J. (Tvl & Qld) b Dec. 12, 1904, d Feb. 1, 1971

*Chubb, G. W. A. (Border & Tvl) b April 12, 1911, d Aug. 28, 1982

Clark, D. G. (Kent; Pres. MCC 1977-78) b Jan. 27, 1919

Clark, E. A. (Middx) b April 15, 1937

*Clark, E. W. (Northants) b Aug. 9, 1902, d April 28, 1982

Clark, L. S. (Essex) b March 6, 1914

*Clark, W. M. (W. Aust.) b Sept. 19, 1953

*Clarke, Dr C. B. (B'dos, Northants & Essex) b April 7, 1918, d Oct. 14, 1993

*Clarke, S. T. (B'dos, Surrey, Tvl, OFS & N. Tvl) b Dec. 11, 1954

Clarke, William (Notts.; founded All-England XI & Trent Bridge ground) b Dec. 24, 1798, d Aug. 25, 1856

Clarkson, A. (Yorks. & Som.) b Sept. 5, 1939

*Claughton, J. A. (OUCC & Warwicks.) b Sept. 17, 1956

*Clay, J. C. (Glam.) b March 18, 1898, d Aug. 12, 1973

Clay, J. D. (Notts.) b Oct. 15, 1924

Clayton, G. (Lancs. & Som.) b Feb. 3, 1938

Clements, S. M. (OUCC) b April 19, 1956

*Cleverley, D. C. (Auck.) b Dec. 23, 1909

Clift, Patrick B. (Rhod., Leics. & Natal) b July 14, 1953

Clift, Philip B. (Glam.) b Sept. 3, 1918

Clinton, G. S. (Kent, Surrey & Zimb.-Rhod.) b May 5, 1953

*Close, D. B. (Yorks. & Som.; *CY 1964*) b Feb. 24, 1931

Cobb, R. A. (Leics. & Natal) b May 18, 1961

Cobham, 10th Visct (Hon. C. J. Lyttelton) (Worcs.; Pres. MCC 1954) b Aug. 8, 1909, d March 20, 1977

*Cochrane, J. A. K. (Tvl & Griq. W.) b July 15, 1909, d June 15, 1987

Cock, D. F. (Essex) b Oct. 22, 1914, d Sept. 26, 1992

*Coen, S. K. (OFS, W. Prov., Tvl & Border) b Oct. 14, 1902, d Jan. 28, 1967

*Colah, S. M. H. (Bombay, W. Ind. & Naw.) b Sept. 22, 1902, d Sept. 11, 1950

Colchin, Robert ("Long Robin") (Kent & All-England) b Nov. 1713, d April 1750

*Coldwell, L. J. (Worcs.) b Jan. 10, 1933

*Colley, D. J. (NSW) b March 15, 1947

Collin, T. (Warwicks.) b April 7, 1911

*Collinge, R. O. (C. Dist., Wgtn & N. Dist.) b April 2, 1946

Collins, A. E. J. (Clifton Coll. & Royal Engineers) b Aug. 18, 1885, d Nov. 11, 1914

*Collins, H. L. (NSW) b Jan. 21, 1888, d May 28, 1959

Collins, R. (Lancs.) b March 10, 1934

*Colquhoun, I. A. (C. Dist.) b June 8, 1924

Coman, P. G. (Cant.) b April 13, 1943

*Commaille, J. M. M. (W. Prov., Natal, OFS & Griq. W.) b Feb. 21, 1883, d July 27, 1956

Commins, J. B. (Boland) b Feb. 19, 1965

*Compton, D. C. S. (Middx & Holkar; *CY 1939*) b May 23, 1918

*Coney, J. V. (Wgtn; *CY 1984*) b June 21, 1952

*Congdon, B. E. (C. Dist., Wgtn, Otago & Cant.; *CY 1974*) b Feb. 11, 1938

*Coningham, A. (NSW & Qld) b July 14, 1863, d June 13, 1939

*Connolly, A. N. (Vic. & Middx) b June 29, 1939

Connor, C. A. (Hants) b March 24, 1961

Constable, B. (Surrey) b Feb. 19, 1921

*Constant, D. J. (Kent & Leics.; Umpire) b Nov. 9, 1941

*Constantine, Lord L. N. (T/T & B'dos; *CY 1940*) b Sept. 21, 1902, d July 1, 1971

Constantine, L. S. (T/T) b May 25, 1874, d Jan. 5, 1942

*Contractor, N. J. (Guj. & Ind. Rlwys) b March 7, 1934

*Conyngham, D. P. (Natal, Tvl & W. Prov.) b May 10, 1897, d July 7, 1979

*Cook, C. (Glos.) b Aug. 23, 1921

*Cook, F. J. (E. Prov.) b 1870, d Nov. 30, 1914

*Cook, G. (Northants & E. Prov.) b Oct. 9, 1951

*Cook, N. G. B. (Leics. & Northants) b June 17, 1956

*Cook, S. J. (Tvl & Som.; *CY 1990*) b July 31, 1953

Cook, T. E. R. (Sussex) b Jan. 5, 1901, d Jan. 15, 1950

*Cooper, A. H. C. (Tvl) b Sept 2, 1893, d July 18, 1963

*Cooper, B. B. (Middx, Kent & Vic.) b March 15, 1844, d Aug. 7, 1914

Cooper, F. S. Ashley- (Cricket Historian) b March 17, 1877, d Jan. 31, 1932

Cooper, G. C. (Sussex) b Sept. 2, 1936

Cooper, H. P. (Yorks. & N. Tvl) b April 17, 1949

Cooper, K. E. (Notts. & Glos.) b Dec. 27, 1957

*Cooper, W. H. (Vic.) b Sept. 11, 1849, d April 5, 1939

*Cope, G. A. (Yorks.) b Feb. 23, 1947

*Copson, W. H. (Derbys.; *CY 1937*) b April 27, 1908, d Sept. 14, 1971

Cordle, A. E. (Glam.) b Sept. 21, 1940

*Cork, D. G. (Derbys.; *CY 1996*) b Aug. 7, 1971

*Corling, G. E. (NSW) b July 13, 1941

Cornford, J. H. (Sussex) b Dec. 9, 1911, d June 17, 1985

*Cornford, W. L. (Sussex) b Dec. 25, 1900, d Feb. 6, 1964

Corrall, P. (Leics.) b July 16, 1906, d Feb. 1994

Corran, A. J. (OUCC & Notts.) b Nov. 25, 1936

*Cosier, G. J. (Vic., S. Aust. & Qld) b April 25, 1953

*Cottam, J. T. (NSW) b Sept. 5, 1867, d Jan. 30, 1897

*Cottam, R. M. H. (Hants & Northants) b Oct. 16, 1944

*Cotter, A. (NSW) b Dec. 3, 1884, d Oct. 31, 1917

Cottey, P. A. (Glam. & E. Tvl) b June 2, 1966

Cotton, J. (Notts. & Leics.) b Nov. 7, 1940

Cottrell, G. A. (CUCC) b March 23, 1945

*Coulthard, G. (Vic.) b Aug. 1, 1856, d Oct. 22, 1883

*Coventry, Hon. C. J. (Worcs.) b Feb. 26, 1867, d June 2, 1929

Coverdale, S. P. (CUCC, Yorks., & Northants) b Nov. 20, 1954

Cowan, M. J. (Yorks.) b June 10, 1933

*Cowans, N. G. (Middx & Hants) b April 17, 1961

*Cowdrey, C. S. (Kent & Glam.) b Oct. 20, 1957

Cowdrey, G. R. (Kent) b June 27, 1964

*Cowdrey, Sir M. C. (OUCC & Kent; *CY 1956*; Pres. MCC 1986-87) b Dec. 24, 1932

*Cowie, J. (Auck.) b March 30, 1912, d June 3, 1994

Cowley, N. G. (Hants & Glam.) b March 1, 1953

*Cowper, R. M. (Vic. & W. Aust.) b Oct. 5, 1940

Cox, A. L. (Northants) b July 22, 1907, d Nov. 1986

Cox, G., jun. (Sussex) b Aug. 23, 1911, d March 30, 1985

Cox, G. R. (Sussex) b Nov. 29, 1873, d March 24, 1949

*Cox, J. L. (Natal) b June 28, 1886, d July 4, 1971

*Coxon, A. (Yorks.) b Jan. 18, 1916

Craig, E. J. (CUCC & Lancs.) b March 26, 1942

*Craig, I. D. (NSW) b June 12, 1935

Cranfield, L. M. (Glos.) b Aug. 29, 1909, d Nov. 18, 1993

Cranmer, P. (Warwicks.) b Sept. 10, 1914, d May 29, 1994

*Cranston, J. (Glos.) b Jan. 9, 1859, d Dec. 10, 1904

*Cranston, K. (Lancs.) b Oct. 20, 1917

*Crapp, J. F. (Glos.) b Oct. 14, 1912, d Feb. 15, 1981

*Crawford, J. N. (Surrey, S. Aust., Wgtn & Otago; *CY 1907*) b Dec. 1, 1886, d May 2, 1963

*Crawford, P. (NSW) b Aug. 3, 1933

Crawley, A. M. (OUCC & Kent; Pres. MCC 1972-73) b April 10, 1908, d Nov. 3, 1993

*Crawley, J. P. (Lancs. & CUCC) b Sept. 21, 1971

Crawley, M. A. (OUCC, Lancs. & Notts.) b Dec. 16, 1967

Cray, S. J. (Essex) b May 29, 1921

*Cresswell, G. F. (Wgtn & C. Dist.) b March 22, 1915, d Jan. 10, 1966

*Cripps, G. (W. Prov.) b Oct. 19, 1865, d July 27, 1943

*Crisp, R. J. (Rhod., W. Prov. & Worcs.) b May 28, 1911, d March 3, 1994

*Crocker, G. J. (MCD) b May 16, 1962

*Croft, C. E. H. (Guyana & Lancs.) b March 15, 1953

Croft, R. D. B. (Glam.) b May 25, 1970

*Cromb, I. B. (Cant.) b June 25, 1905, d March 6, 1984

*Cronje, W. J. (OFS & Leics.) b Sept. 25, 1969

Crookes, D. N. (Natal) b March 5, 1969

Crookes, N. S. (Natal) b Nov. 15, 1935

Cross, G. F. (Leics.) b Nov. 15, 1943

*Crowe, J. J. (S. Aust. & Auck.) b Sept. 14, 1958

*Crowe, M. D. (Auck., C. Dist., Som. & Wgtn; *CY 1985*) b Sept. 22, 1962

Crump, B. S. (Northants) b April 25, 1938

Crush, E. (Kent) b April 25, 1917

*Cuffy, C. E. (Windwards & Surrey) b Feb. 8, 1970

*Cullinan, D. J. (Border, W. Prov., Tvl & Derbys.) b March 4, 1967

Cumbes, J. (Lancs., Surrey, Worcs. & Warwicks.) b May 4, 1944

*Cummins, A. C. (B'dos & Durham) b May 7, 1966

*Cunis, R. S. (Auck. & N. Dist.) b Jan. 5, 1941

*Curnow, S. H. (Tvl) b Dec. 16, 1907, d July 28, 1986

Curran, K. M. (Glos., Zimb, Natal, Northants & Boland) b Sept. 7, 1959

*Curtis, T. S. (Worcs. & CUCC) b Jan. 15, 1960

Cuthbertson, G. B. (Middx, Sussex & Northants) b March 23, 1901, d August 9, 1993

*Cuttell, W. R. (Lancs.; *CY 1898*) b Sept. 13, 1864, d Dec. 9, 1929

*Da Costa, O. C. (Jam.) b Sept. 11, 1907, d Oct. 1, 1936

Dacre, C. C. (Auck. & Glos.) b May 15, 1899, d Nov. 2, 1975

Daft, Richard (Notts. & All-England) b Nov. 2, 1835, d July 18, 1900

Dakin, G. F. (E. Prov.) b Aug. 13, 1935

Dale, A. (Glam.) b Oct. 24, 1968

*Dalton, E. L. (Natal) b Dec. 2, 1906, d June 3, 1981

*Dani, H. T. (M'tra & Ind. Serv.) b May 24, 1933

*Daniel, W. W. (B'dos, Middx & W. Aust.) b Jan. 16, 1956

*D'Arcy, J. W. (Cant., Wgtn & Otago) b April 23, 1936

Dare, R. (Hants) b Nov. 26, 1921

*Darling, J. (S. Aust.; *CY 1900*) b Nov. 21, 1870, d Jan. 2, 1946

*Darling, L. S. (Vic.) b Aug. 14, 1909, d June 24, 1992

*Darling, W. M. (S. Aust.) b May 1, 1957

*Darnley, 8th Earl of (Hon. Ivo Bligh) (CUCC & Kent; Pres. MCC 1900) b March 13, 1859, d April 10, 1927

*Dassanayake, P. B. (Colts, Under-23 & Bloom.) b July 11, 1970

Davey, J. (Glos.) b Sept. 4, 1944

*Davidson, A. K. (NSW; *CY 1962*) b June 14, 1929

Davies, Dai (Glam.; Umpire) b Aug. 26, 1896, d July 16, 1976

Davies, Emrys (Glam.; Umpire) b June 27, 1904, d Nov. 10, 1975

*Davies, E. Q. (E. Prov., Tvl & NE Tvl) b Aug. 26, 1909, d Nov. 11, 1976

Davies, H. D. (Glam.) b July 23, 1932

Davies, H. G. (Glam.) b April 23, 1912, d Sept. 4, 1993

Davies, J. G. W. (CUCC & Kent; Pres. MCC 1985-86) b Sept. 10, 1911, d Nov. 5, 1992

Davies, T. (Glam.) b Oct. 25, 1960

*Davis, B. A. (T/T & Glam.) b May 2, 1940

*Davis, C. A. (T/T) b Jan. 1, 1944

Davis, E. (Northants) b March 8, 1922

*Davis, H. T. (Wgtn) b Nov. 30, 1971

*Davis, I. C. (NSW & Qld) b June 25, 1953

Davis, M. R. (Som.) b Feb. 26, 1962

Davis, P. C. (Northants) b May 24, 1915

Davis, R. C. (Glam.) b Jan. 1, 1946

Davis, R. P. (Kent & Warwicks.) b March 18, 1966

*Davis, S. P. (Vic.) b Nov. 8, 1959

*Davis, W. W. (Windwards, Glam., Tas., Northants & Wgtn) b Sept. 18, 1958

Davison, B. F. (Rhod., Leics, Tas. & Glos.) b Dec. 21, 1946

Davison, I. J. (Notts.) b Oct. 4, 1937

Dawkes, G. O. (Leics. & Derbys.) b July 19, 1920

*Dawson, E. W. (CUCC & Leics.) b Feb. 13, 1904, d June 4, 1979

*Dawson, O. C. (Natal & Border) b Sept. 1, 1919

Day, A. P. (Kent; *CY 1910*) b April 10, 1885, d Jan. 22, 1969

*de Alwis, R. G. (SSC) b Feb. 15, 1959

Dean, H. (Lancs.) b Aug. 13, 1884, d March 12, 1957

*Deane, H. G. (Natal & Tvl) b July 21, 1895, d Oct. 21, 1939

*De Caires, F. I. (BG) b May 12, 1909, d Feb. 2, 1959

*De Courcy, J. H. (NSW) b April 18, 1927

*DeFreitas, P. A. J. (Leics., Lancs., Boland & Derbys.; *CY 1992*) b Feb. 18, 1966

*de Groen, R. P. (Auck. & N. Dist.) b Aug. 5, 1962

*Dekker, M. H. (Mat.) b Dec. 5, 1969

Delisle, G. P. S. (OUCC & Middx) b Dec. 25, 1934

*Dell, A. R. (Qld) b Aug. 6, 1947

*de Mel, A. L. F. (SL) b May 9, 1959

*Dempster, C. S. (Wgtn, Leics., Scotland & Warwicks.; *CY 1932*) b Nov. 15, 1903, d Feb. 14, 1974

*Dempster, E. W. (Wgtn) b Jan. 25, 1925

*Denness, M. H. (Scotland, Kent & Essex; *CY 1975*) b Dec. 1, 1940

Dennett, E. G. (Glos.) b April 27, 1880, d Sept. 14, 1937

Denning, P. W. (Som.) b Dec. 16, 1949

Dennis, F. (Yorks.) b June 11, 1907

Dennis, S. J. (Yorks., OFS & Glam.) b Oct. 18, 1960

*Denton, D. (Yorks.; *CY 1906*) b July 4, 1874, d Feb. 16, 1950

Deodhar, D. B. (M'tra) b Jan. 14, 1892, d Aug. 24, 1993

*Depeiza, C. C. (B'dos) b Oct. 10, 1928, d Nov. 10, 1995

Derrick, J. (Glam.) b Jan. 15, 1963

*Desai, R. B. (Bombay) b June 20, 1939

*de Silva, A. M. (CCC) b Dec. 3, 1963

de Silva, D. L. S. (SL) b Nov. 17, 1956, d April 12, 1980

*de Silva, D. S. (Bloom.) b June 11, 1942

*de Silva, E. A. R. (NCC & Galle) b March 28, 1956

de Silva, G. N. (SL) b March 12, 1955

*de Silva, G. R. A. (SL) b Dec. 12, 1952

*de Silva, P. A. (NCC & Kent; *CY 1996*) b Oct. 17, 1965

de Smidt, R. W. (W. Prov., longest-lived known first-class cricketer) b Nov. 24, 1883, d Aug. 3, 1986

Devereux, L. N. (Middx, Worcs. & Glam.) b Oct. 20, 1931

*de Villiers, P. S. (N. Tvl & Kent) b Oct. 12, 1964

*Dewdney, C. T. (Jam.) b Oct. 23, 1933

*Dewes, J. G. (CUCC & Middx) b Oct. 11, 1926

Dews, G. (Worcs.) b June 5, 1921

*Dexter, E. R. (CUCC & Sussex; *CY 1961*) b May 15, 1935

*Dhanraj, R. (T&T) b Feb. 6, 1969

*Dharmasena, H. D. P. K. (TU, Ant. & Bloom.) b April 24, 1971

*Dias, R. L. (CCC) b Oct. 18, 1952

Dibbs, A. H. A. (Pres. MCC 1983-84) b Dec. 9, 1918, d Nov. 28, 1985

*Dick, A. E. (Otago & Wgtn) b Oct. 10, 1936

*Dickinson, G. R. (Otago) b March 11, 1903, d March 17, 1978

*Dilley, G. R. (Kent, Natal & Worcs.) b May 18, 1959

Diment, R. A. (Glos. & Leics.) b Feb. 9, 1927

*Dipper, A. E. (Glos.) b Nov. 9, 1885, d Nov. 7, 1945

*Divecha, R. V. (Bombay, OUCC, Northants, Vidarbha & S'tra) b Oct. 18, 1927

Diver, A. J. D. (Cambs., Middx, Notts. & All-England) b June 6, 1824, d March 25, 1876

Dixon, A. L. (Kent) b Nov. 27, 1933

*Dixon, C. D. (Tvl) b Feb. 12, 1891, d Sept. 9, 1969

Dodds, T. C. (Essex) b May 29, 1919

*Dodemaide, A. I. C. (Vic. & Sussex) b Oct. 5, 1963

*Doggart, G. H. G. (CUCC & Sussex; Pres. MCC 1981-82) b July 18, 1925

D'Oliveira, B. L. (Worcs.; *CY 1967*) b Oct. 4, 1931

D'Oliveira, D. B. (Worcs.) b Oct. 19, 1960

*Dollery, H. E. (Warwicks. & Wgtn; *CY 1952*) b Oct. 14, 1914, d Jan. 20, 1987

Dollery, K. R. (Qld., Auck., Tas. & Warwicks.) b Dec. 9, 1924

*Dolphin, A. (Yorks.) b Dec. 24, 1885, d Oct. 23, 1942

*Donald, A. A. (OFS & Warwicks.; *CY 1992*) b Oct. 20, 1966

Donelan, B. T. P. (Sussex & Som.) b Jan. 3, 1968

*Donnan, H. (NSW) b Nov. 12, 1864, d Aug. 13, 1956

*Donnelly, M. P. (Wgtn, Cant., Middx, Warwicks. & OUCC; *CY 1948*) b Oct. 17, 1917

*Dooland, B. (S. Aust. & Notts.; *CY 1955*) b Nov. 1, 1923, d Sept. 8, 1980

Dorrinton, W. (Kent & All-England) b April 29, 1809, d Nov. 8, 1848

Dorset, 3rd Duke of (Kent) b March 24, 1745, d July 19, 1799

*Doshi, D. R. (Bengal, Notts., Warwicks. & S'tra) b Dec. 22, 1947

*Douglas, J. W. H. T. (Essex; *CY 1915*) b Sept. 3, 1882, d Dec. 19, 1930

Douglas, M. W. (C. Dist. & Wgtn) b Oct. 20, 1968

*Doull, S. B. (N. Dist.) b Aug. 6, 1969

Dowding, A. L. (OUCC) b April 4, 1929

*Dowe, U. G. (Jam.) b March 29, 1949

*Dower, R. R. (E. Prov.) b June 4, 1876, d Sept. 15, 1964

*Dowling, G. T. (Cant.) b March 4, 1937

*Downton, P. R. (Kent & Middx) b April 4, 1957

Drakes, V. C. (B'dos) b Aug. 5, 1969

*Draper, R. G. (E. Prov. & Griq. W.) b Dec. 24, 1926

Dredge, C. H. (Som.) b Aug. 4, 1954

*Druce, N. F. (CUCC & Surrey; *CY 1898*) b Jan. 1, 1875, d Oct. 27, 1954

Drybrough, C. D. (OUCC & Middx) b Aug. 31, 1938

*D'Souza, A. (Kar., Peshawar & PIA) b Jan. 17, 1939

*Ducat, A. (Surrey; *CY 1920*) b Feb. 16, 1886, d July 23, 1942

*Duckworth, C. A. R. (Natal & Rhod.) b March 22, 1933

*Duckworth, G. (Lancs.; *CY 1929*) b May 9, 1901, d Jan. 5, 1966

Dudleston, B. (Leics., Glos. & Rhod.) b July 16, 1945

Duers, K. G. (Mash.) b June 30, 1960

*Duff, R. A. (NSW) b Aug. 17, 1878, d Dec. 13, 1911

*Dujon, P. J. L. (Jam.; *CY 1989*) b May 28, 1956

*Duleepsinhji, K. S. (CUCC & Sussex; *CY 1930*) b June 13, 1905, d Dec. 5, 1959

*Dumbrill, R. (Natal & Tvl) b Nov. 19, 1938

*Duminy, J. P. (OUCC, W. Prov. & Tvl) b Dec. 16, 1897, d Jan. 31, 1980

*Duncan, J. R. F. (Qld & Vic.) b March 25, 1944

*Dunell, O. R. (E. Prov.) b July 15, 1856, d Oct. 21, 1929

*Dunning, J. A. (Otago & OUCC) b Feb. 6, 1903, d June 24, 1971

*Dunusinghe, C. I. (Ant.) b Oct. 19, 1970

*Du Preez, J. H. (Rhod. & Zimb.) b Nov. 14, 1942

*Durani, S. A. (S'tra, Guj. & Raja.) b Dec. 11, 1934

Durose, A. J. (Northants) b Oct. 10, 1944

*Durston, F. J. (Middx) b July 11, 1893, d April 8, 1965

*Du Toit, J. F. (SA) b April 5, 1868, d July 10, 1909

Dye, J. C. J. (Kent, Northants & E. Prov.) b July 24, 1942

Dyer, D. D. (Natal & Tvl) b Dec. 3, 1946

*Dyer, D. V. (Natal) b May 2, 1914, d June 18, 1990

*Dyer, G. C. (NSW) b March 16, 1959

Dyer, R. I. H. B. (Warwicks.) b Dec. 22, 1958

*Dymock, G. (Qld) b July 21, 1945

Dyson, A. H. (Glam.) b July 10, 1905, d June 7, 1978

Dyson, J. (Lancs.) b July 8, 1934

*Dyson, John (NSW) b June 11, 1954

*Eady, C. J. (Tas.) b Oct. 29, 1870, d Dec. 20, 1945

Eagar, E. D. R. (OUCC, Glos. & Hants) b Dec. 8, 1917, d Sept. 13, 1977

Eagar, M. A. (OUCC & Glos.) b March 20, 1934

Eaglestone, J. T. (Middx & Glam.) b July 24, 1923

Ealham, A. G. E. (Kent) b Aug. 30, 1944

Ealham, M. A. (Kent) b Aug. 27, 1969

East, D. E. (Essex) b July 27, 1959

East, R. E. (Essex) b June 20, 1947

Eastman, G. F. (Essex) b April 7, 1903, d March 15, 1991

Eastman, L. C. (Essex & Otago) b June 3, 1897, d April 17, 1941

*Eastwood, K. H. (Vic.) b Nov. 23, 1935

*Ebeling, H. I. (Vic.) b Jan. 1, 1905, d Jan. 12, 1980

Eckersley, P. T. (Lancs.) b July 2, 1904, d Aug. 13, 1940

*Edgar, B. A. (Wgtn) b Nov. 23, 1956

Edinburgh, HRH Duke of (Pres. MCC 1948-49, 1974-75) b June 10, 1921

Edmeades, B. E. A. (Essex) b Sept. 17, 1941

*Edmonds, P. H. (CUCC, Middx & E. Prov.) b March 8, 1951

Edmonds, R. B. (Warwicks.) b March 2, 1941

Edrich, B. R. (Kent & Glam.) b Aug. 18, 1922

Edrich, E. H. (Lancs.) b March 27, 1914, d July 9, 1993

Edrich, G. A. (Lancs.) b July 13, 1918

*Edrich, J. H. (Surrey; *CY 1966*) b June 21, 1937

*Edrich, W. J. (Middx; *CY 1940*) b March 26, 1916, d April 24, 1986

*Edwards, G. N. (C. Dist.) b May 27, 1955

*Edwards, J. D. (Vic.) b June 12, 1862, d July 31, 1911

Edwards, M. J. (CUCC & Surrey) b March 1, 1940

*Edwards, R. (W. Aust. & NSW) b Dec. 1, 1942

*Edwards, R. M. (B'dos) b June 3, 1940

*Edwards, W. J. (W. Aust.) b Dec. 23, 1949

Eele, P. J. (Som.) b Jan. 27, 1935

*Ehtesham-ud-Din (Lahore, Punjab, PIA, NBP & UBL) b Sept. 4, 1950

*Eksteen, C. E. (Tvl) b Dec. 2, 1966

*Elgie, M. K. (Natal) b March 6, 1933

Elliott, C. S. (Derbys.) b April 24, 1912

*Elliott, H. (Derbys.) b Nov. 2, 1891, d Feb. 2, 1976

Ellis, G. P. (Glam.) b May 24, 1950

Ellis, R. G. P. (OUCC & Middx) b Oct. 20, 1960

*Ellison, R. M. (Kent & Tas.; *CY 1986*) b Sept. 21, 1959

Elms, R. B. (Kent & Hants) b April 5, 1949

*Emburey, J. E. (Middx & W. Prov.; *CY 1984*) b Aug. 20, 1952

*Emery, P. A. (NSW) b June 25, 1964

Emery, R. W. G. (Auck. & Cant.) b March 28, 1915, d Dec. 18, 1982

*Emery, S. H. (NSW) b Oct. 16, 1885, d Jan. 7, 1967

*Emmett, G. M. (Glos.) b Dec. 2, 1912, d Dec. 18, 1976

*Emmett, T. (Yorks.) b Sept. 3, 1841, d June 30, 1904

*Endean, W. R. (Tvl) b May 31, 1924

*Engineer, F. M. (Bombay & Lancs.) b Feb. 25, 1938

Essop-Adam, E. A. (Mash.) b Nov. 16, 1968

*Evans, A. J. (OUCC, Hants & Kent) b May 1, 1889, d Sept. 18, 1960

Evans, C. N. (Mash.) b Nov. 29, 1969

Evans, D. G. L. (Glam.; Umpire) b July 27, 1933, d March 25, 1990

*Evans, E. (NSW) b March 26, 1849, d July 2, 1921

Evans, G. (OUCC, Glam. & Leics.) b Aug. 13, 1915

Evans, J. B. (Glam.) b Nov. 9, 1936

Evans, K. P. (Notts.) b Sept. 10, 1963

*Evans, T. G. (Kent; *CY 1951*) b Aug. 18, 1920

Every, T. (Glam.) b Dec. 19, 1909, d Jan. 20, 1990

Eyre, T. J. P. (Derbys.) b Oct. 17, 1939

Faber, M. J. J. (OUCC & Sussex) b Aug. 15, 1950, d Dec. 10, 1991

*Fagg, A. E. (Kent) b June 18, 1915, d Sept. 13, 1977

Fairbairn, A. (Middx) b Jan. 25, 1923

*Fairbrother, N. H. (Lancs. & Tvl) b Sept. 9, 1963

*Fairfax, A. G. (NSW) b June 16, 1906, d May 17, 1955

Fairservice, C. (Kent & Middx) b Aug. 21, 1909

*Fane, F. L. (OUCC & Essex) b April 27, 1875, d Nov. 27, 1960

Fantham, W. E. (Warwicks.) b May 14, 1918

*Farnes, K. (CUCC & Essex; *CY 1939*) b July 8, 1911, d Oct. 20, 1941

*Farooq Hamid (Lahore & PIA) b March 3, 1945

*Farrer, W. S. (Border) b Dec. 8, 1936

*Farrimond, W. (Lancs.) b May 23, 1903, d Nov. 14, 1979

*Farrukh Zaman (Peshawar, NWFP, Punjab & MCB) b April 2, 1956

*Faulkner, G. A. (Tvl) b Dec. 17, 1881, d Sept. 10, 1930

*Favell, L. E. (S. Aust.) b Oct. 6, 1929, d June 14, 1987

*Fazal Mahmood (N. Ind., Punjab & Lahore; *CY 1955*) b Feb. 18, 1927

Fearnley, C. D. (Worcs.) b April 12, 1940

Featherstone, N. G. (Tvl, N. Tvl, Middx & Glam.) b Aug. 20, 1949

'Felix', N. (Wanostrocht) (Kent, Surrey & All-England) b Oct. 4, 1804, d Sept. 3, 1876

*Fellows-Smith, J. P. (OUCC, Tvl & Northants) b Feb. 3, 1932

Feltham, M. A. (Surrey & Middx) b June 26, 1963

Felton, N. A. (Som. & Northants) b Oct. 24, 1960

*Fender, P. G. H. (Sussex & Surrey; *CY 1915*) b Aug. 22, 1892, d June 15, 1985

*Ferguson, W. (T/T) b Dec. 14, 1917, d Feb. 23, 1961

*Fernandes, M. P. (BG) b Aug. 12, 1897, d May 8, 1981

Fernando, E. R. (SL) b Feb. 22, 1944

*Fernando, E. R. N. S. (SLAF) b Dec. 19, 1955

Fernando, T. L. (Colts & BRC) b Dec. 27, 1962

Fernando, U. N. K. (SSC) b March 10, 1970

Ferreira, A. M. (N. Tvl & Warwicks.) b April 13, 1955

Ferris, G. J. F. (Leics. & Leewards) b Oct. 18, 1964

**Ferris, J. J. (NSW, Glos. & S. Aust.; *CY 1889*) b May 21, 1867, d Nov. 21, 1900

*Fichardt, C. G. (OFS) b March 20, 1870, d May 30, 1923

Fiddling, K. (Yorks. & Northants) b Oct. 13, 1917, d June 19, 1992

*Fielder, A. (Kent; *CY 1907*) b July 19, 1877, d Aug. 30, 1949

*Findlay, T. M. (Comb. Is. & Windwards) b Oct. 19, 1943

Findlay, W. (OUCC & Lancs.; Sec. Surrey CCC, Sec. MCC 1926-36) b June 22, 1880, d June 19, 1953

*Fingleton, J. H. (NSW) b April 28, 1908, d Nov. 22, 1981

*Finlason, C. E. (Tvl & Griq. W.) b Feb. 19, 1860, d July 31, 1917

Finney, R. J. (Derbys.) b Aug. 2, 1960

Firth, Rev. Canon J. D'E. E. (Winchester, OUCC & Notts.; *CY 1918*) b Jan. 21, 1900, d Sept. 21, 1957

*Fisher, F. E. (Wgtn & C. Dist.) b July 28, 1924

Fisher, P. B. (OUCC, Middx & Worcs.) b Dec. 19, 1954

*Fishlock, L. B. (Surrey; *CY 1947*) b Jan. 2, 1907, d June 26, 1986

Fitton, J. D. (Lancs.) b Aug. 24, 1965

Fitzgerald, R. A. (CUCC & Middx; Sec. MCC 1863-76) b Oct. 1, 1834, d Oct. 28, 1881

*Flavell, J. A. (Worcs.; *CY 1965*) b May 15, 1929

*Fleetwood-Smith, L. O'B. (Vic.) b March 30, 1908, d March 16, 1971

*Fleming, D. W. (Vic.) b April 24, 1970

Fleming, M. V. (Kent) b Dec. 12, 1964

*Fleming, S. P. (Cant.) b April 1, 1973

Fletcher, D. A. G. (Rhod. & Zimb.) b Sept. 27, 1948

Fletcher, D. G. W. (Surrey) b July 6, 1924

*Fletcher, K. W. R. (Essex; *CY 1974*) b May 20, 1944

Fletcher, S. D. (Yorks. & Lancs.) b June 8, 1964

*Floquet, C. E. (Tvl) b Nov. 3, 1884, d Nov. 22, 1963

*Flower, A. (Mash.) b April 28, 1968

*Flower, G. W. (Under-24) b Dec. 20, 1970

*Flowers, W. (Notts.) b Dec. 7, 1856, d Nov. 1, 1926

Foat, J. C. (Glos.) b Nov. 21, 1952

*Foley, H. (Wgtn) b Jan. 28, 1906, d Oct. 16, 1948

Folley, I. (Lancs. & Derbys.) b Jan. 9, 1963, d Aug. 30, 1993

Foord, C. W. (Yorks.) b June 11, 1924

Forbes, C. (Notts.) b Aug. 9, 1936

*Ford, F. G. J. (CUCC & Middx) b Dec. 14, 1866, d Feb. 7, 1940

Ford, N. M. (OUCC, Derbys. & Middx) b Nov. 18, 1906

Fordham, A. (Northants) b Nov. 9, 1964

Foreman, D. J. (W. Prov. & Sussex) b Feb. 1, 1933

*Foster, F. R. (Warwicks.; *CY 1912*) b Jan. 31, 1889, d May 3, 1958

Foster, G. N. (OUCC, Worcs. & Kent) b Oct. 16, 1884, d Aug. 11, 1971

Foster, H. K. (OUCC & Worcs.; *CY 1911*) b Oct. 30, 1873, d June 23, 1950

Foster, M. K. (Worcs.) b Jan. 1, 1889, d Dec. 3, 1940

*Foster, M. L. C. (Jam.) b May 9, 1943

*Foster, N. A. (Essex & Tvl; *CY 1988*) b May 6, 1962

*Foster, R. E. (OUCC & Worcs.; *CY 1901*) b April 16, 1878, d May 13, 1914

*Fothergill, A. J. (Som.) b Aug. 26, 1854, d Aug. 1, 1932

Fotheringham, H. R. (Natal & Tvl) b April 4, 1953

*Fowler, G. (Lancs. & Durham) b April 20, 1957

Fowler, W. P. (Derbys., N. Dist. & Auck.) b March 13, 1959

*Francis, B. C. (NSW & Essex) b Feb. 18, 1948

Francis, D. A. (Glam.) b Nov. 29, 1953

*Francis, G. N. (B'dos) b Dec. 11, 1897, d Jan. 7, 1942

*Francis, H. H. (Glos. & W. Prov.) b May 26, 1868, d Jan. 7, 1936

Francke, F. M. (SL & Qld) b March 29, 1941

*Francois, C. M. (Griq. W.) b June 20, 1897, d May 26, 1944

*Frank, C. N. (Tvl) b Jan. 27, 1891, d Dec. 26, 1961

*Frank, W. H. B. (SA) b Nov. 23, 1872, d Feb. 16, 1945

*Franklin, T. J. (Auck.) b March 18, 1962

*Fraser, A. R. C. (Middx; *CY 1996*) b Aug. 8, 1965

*Frederick, M. C. (B'dos, Derbys. & Jam.) b May 6, 1927

*Fredericks, R. C. (†Guyana & Glam.; *CY 1974*) b Nov. 11, 1942

*Freeman, A. P. (Kent; *CY 1923*) b May 17, 1888, d Jan. 28, 1965

*Freeman, D. L. (Wgtn) b Sept. 8, 1914, d May 31, 1994

*Freeman, E. W. (S. Aust.) b July 13, 1944

*Freer, F. W. (Vic.) b Dec. 4, 1915

*French, B. N. (Notts.) b Aug. 13, 1959

Frost, G. (Notts.) b Jan. 15, 1947

Frost, M. (Surrey & Glam.) b Oct. 21, 1962

Fry, C. A. (OUCC, Hants & Northants) b Jan. 14, 1940

*Fry, C. B. (OUCC, Sussex & Hants; *CY 1895*) b April 25, 1872, d Sept. 7, 1956

*Fuller, E. R. H. (W. Prov.) b Aug. 2, 1931

*Fuller, R. L. (Jam.) b Jan. 30, 1913, d May 3, 1987

*Fullerton, G. M. (Tvl) b Dec. 8, 1922

Funston, G. K. (NE Tvl & Griq. W.) b Nov. 21, 1948

*Funston, K. J. (NE Tvl, OFS & Tvl) b Dec. 3, 1925

*Furlonge, H. A. (T/T) b June 19, 1934

Gabriel, R. S. (T/T) b June 5, 1952

*Gadkari, C. V. (M'tra & Ind. Serv.) b Feb. 3, 1928

*Gaekwad, A. D. (Baroda) b Sept. 23, 1952

*Gaekwad, D. K. (Baroda) b Oct. 27, 1928

*Gaekwad, H. G. (†M. Pradesh) b Aug. 29, 1923

Gale, R. A. (Middx) b Dec. 10, 1933

*Gallian, J. E. R. (Lancs. & OUCC) b June 25, 1971

*Gallichan, N. (Wgtn) b June 3, 1906, d March 25, 1969

*Gamage, J. C. (Colts & Galle) b April 17, 1964

*Gamsy, D. (Natal) b Feb. 17, 1940

*Gandotra, A. (Delhi & Bengal) b Nov. 24, 1948

Ganguly, S. C. (Bengal) b July 8, 1966

*Gannon, J. B. (W. Aust.) b Feb. 8, 1947

*Ganteaume, A. G. (T/T) b Jan. 22, 1921

Gard, T. (Som.) b June 2, 1957

Gardner, L. R. (Leics.) b Feb. 23, 1934

Garland-Wells, H. M. (OUCC & Surrey) b Nov. 14, 1907, d May 28, 1993

Garlick, R. G. (Lancs. & Northants) b April 11, 1917, d May 16, 1988

*Garner, J. (B'dos, Som. & S. Aust.; *CY 1980*) b Dec. 16, 1952

Garnham, M. A. (Glos., Leics. & Essex) b Aug. 20, 1960

*Garrett, T. W. (NSW) b July 26, 1858, d Aug. 6, 1943

*Gaskin, B. B. MacG. (BG) b March 21, 1908, d May 1, 1979

*Gatting, M. W. (Middx; *CY 1984*) b June 6, 1957

*Gaunt, R. A. (W. Aust. & Vic.) b Feb. 26, 1934

*Gavaskar, S. M. (Bombay & Som.; *CY 1980*) b July 10, 1949

*Gay, L. H. (CUCC, Hants & Som.) b March 24, 1871, d Nov. 1, 1949

Geary, A. C. T. (Surrey) b Sept. 11, 1900, d Jan. 23, 1989

*Geary, G. (Leics.; *CY 1927*) b July 9, 1893, d March 6, 1981

*Gedye, S. G. (Auck.) b May 2, 1929

*Gehrs, D. R. A. (S. Aust.) b Nov. 29, 1880, d June 25, 1953

Germon, L. K. (Cant.) b Nov. 4, 1968

Ghai, R. S. (Punjab) b June 12, 1960

*Ghavri, K. D. (S'tra & Bombay) b Feb. 28, 1951

*Ghazali, M. E. Z. (M'tra & Pak. Serv.) b June 15, 1924

*Ghorpade, J. M. (Baroda) b Oct. 2, 1930, d March 29, 1978

*Ghulam Abbas (Kar., NBP & PIA) b May 1, 1947

*Ghulam Ahmed (H'bad) b July 4, 1922

Ghulam Ali (Kar. & PACO) b Sept. 8, 1966

*Gibb, P. A. (CUCC, Scotland, Yorks. & Essex) b July 11, 1913, d Dec. 7, 1977

Gibbons, H. H. (Worcs.) b Oct. 10, 1904, d Feb. 16, 1973

*Gibbs, G. L. (BG) b Dec. 27, 1925, d Feb. 21, 1979

*Gibbs, L. R. (†Guyana, S. Aust. & Warwicks.; *CY 1972*) b Sept. 29, 1934

Gibbs, P. J. K. (OUCC & Derbys.) b Aug. 17, 1944

Gibson, C. H. (Eton, CUCC & Sussex; *CY 1918*) b Aug. 23, 1900, d Dec. 31, 1976

Gibson, D. (Surrey) b May 1, 1936

*Gibson, O. D. (B'dos, Border & Glam.) b March 16, 1969

Giddins, E. S. H. (Sussex), b July 20, 1971

*Giffen, G. (S. Aust.; *CY 1894*) b March 27, 1859, d Nov. 29, 1927

*Giffen, W. F. (S. Aust.) b Sept. 20, 1861, d June 29, 1949

*Gifford, N. (Worcs. & Warwicks.; *CY 1975*) b March 30, 1940

*Gilbert, D. R. (NSW, Tas. & Glos.) b Dec. 29, 1960

*Gilchrist, R. (Jam. & H'bad) b June 28, 1934

Giles, R. J. (Notts.) b Oct. 17, 1919

Gilhouley, K. (Yorks. & Notts.) b Aug. 8, 1934

Gill, A. (Notts.) b Aug. 4, 1940

*Gillespie, S. R. (Auck.) b March 2, 1957

Gilliat, R. M. C. (OUCC & Hants) b May 20, 1944

*Gilligan, A. E. R. (CUCC, Surrey & Sussex; *CY 1924*; Pres. MCC 1967-68) b Dec. 23, 1894, d Sept. 5, 1976

*Gilligan, A. H. H. (Sussex) b June 29, 1896, d May 5, 1978

Gilligan, F. W. (OUCC & Essex) b Sept. 20, 1893, d May 4, 1960

*Gilmour, G. J. (NSW) b June 26, 1951

*Gimblett, H. (Som.; *CY 1953*) b Oct. 19, 1914, d March 30, 1978

Gladstone, G. (*see* Marais, G. G.)

Gladwin, Chris (Essex & Derbys.) b May 10, 1962

*Gladwin, Cliff (Derbys.) b April 3, 1916, d April 10, 1988

*Gleeson, J. W. (NSW & E. Prov.) b March 14, 1938

*Gleeson, R. A. (E. Prov.) b Dec. 6, 1873, d Sept. 27, 1919

Glendenen, J. D. (Durham) b June 20, 1965

*Glover, G. K. (Kimberley & Griq. W.) b May 13, 1870, d Nov. 15, 1938

Glover, T. R. (OUCC) b Nov. 26, 1951

Goddard, G. F. (Scotland) b May 19, 1938

*Goddard, J. D. C. (B'dos) b April 21, 1919, d Aug. 26, 1987

*Goddard, T. L. (Natal & NE Tvl) b Aug. 1, 1931

*Goddard, T. W. J. (Glos.; *CY 1938*) b Oct. 1, 1900, d May 22, 1966

Goel, R. (Patiala & Haryana) b Sept. 29, 1942

Goldsmith, S. C. (Kent & Derbys.) b Dec. 19, 1964

Goldstein, F. S. (OUCC, Northants, Tvl & W. Prov.) b Oct. 14, 1944

*Gomes, H. A. (T/T & Middx; *CY 1985*) b July 13, 1953

*Gomez, G. E. (T/T) b Oct. 10, 1919

*Gooch, G. A. (Essex & W. Prov.; *CY 1980*) b July 23, 1953

Goodway, C. C. (Warwicks.) b July 10, 1909, d May 22, 1991

Goodwin, K. (Lancs.) b June 25, 1938

Goodwin, T. J. (Leics.) b Jan. 22, 1929

Goonatillake, F. R. M. de S. (SL) b Aug. 15, 1951

*Goonatillake, H. M. (SL) b Aug. 16, 1952

Goonesena, G. (Ceylon, Notts., CUCC & NSW) b Feb. 16, 1931

*Gopalan, M. J. (Madras) b June 6, 1909

*Gopinath, C. D. (Madras) b March 1, 1930

*Gordon, N. (Tvl) b Aug. 6, 1911

Gore, A. C. (Eton & Army; *CY 1919*) b May 14, 1900, d June 7, 1990

*Gough, D. (Yorks.) b Sept. 18, 1970

Gould, I. J. (Middx, Auck. & Sussex) b Aug. 19, 1957

*Gover, A. R. (Surrey; *CY 1937; oldest surviving CY*) b Feb. 29, 1908

*Gower, D. I. (Leics. & Hants; *CY 1979*) b April 1, 1957

Gowrie, 1st Lord (Pres. MCC 1948-49) b July 6, 1872, d May 2, 1955

Grace, Dr Alfred b May 17, 1840, d May 24, 1916

Grace, Dr Alfred H. (Glos.) b March 10, 1866, d Sept. 16, 1929

Grace, C. B. (Clifton) b March 1882, d June 6, 1938

*Grace, Dr E. M. (Glos.) b Nov. 28, 1841, d May 20, 1911

Grace, Dr Edgar M. (MCC) (son of E. M. Grace) b Oct. 6, 1886, d Nov. 24, 1974

*Grace, G. F. (Glos.) b Dec. 13, 1850, d Sept. 22, 1880

Grace, Dr Henry (Glos.) b Jan. 31, 1833, d Nov. 15, 1895

Grace, Dr H. M. (father of W. G., E. M. and G. F.) b Feb. 21, 1808, d Dec. 23, 1871

Grace, Mrs H. M. (mother of W. G., E. M. and G. F.) b July 18, 1812, d July 25, 1884

*Grace, Dr W. G. (Glos.; *CY 1896*) b July 18, 1848, d Oct. 23, 1915

Grace, W. G., jun. (CUCC & Glos.) b July 6, 1874, d March 2, 1905

Graf, S. F. (Vic., W. Aust. & Hants) b May 19, 1957

*Graham, H. (Vic. & Otago) b Nov. 22, 1870, d Feb. 7, 1911

Graham, J. N. (Kent) b May 8, 1943

*Graham, R. (W. Prov.) b Sept. 16, 1877, d April 21, 1946

*Grant, G. C. (CUCC, T/T & Rhod.) b May 9, 1907, d Oct. 26, 1978

*Grant, R. S. (CUCC & T/T) b Dec. 15, 1909, d Oct. 18, 1977

Graveney, D. A. (Glos., Som. & Durham) b Jan. 2, 1953

Graveney, J. K. (Glos.) b Dec. 16, 1924

*Graveney, T. W. (Glos., Worcs. & Qld; *CY 1953*) b June 16, 1927

Graves, P. J. (Sussex & OFS) b May 19, 1946

*Gray, A. H. (T/T, Surrey & W. Tvl) b May 23, 1963

*Gray, E. J. (Wgtn) b Nov. 18, 1954

Gray, J. R. (Hants) b May 19, 1926

Grayson, A. P. (Yorks.) b March 31, 1971

Greasley, D. G. (Northants) b Jan. 20, 1926

*Greatbatch, M. J. (C. Dist.) b Dec. 11, 1963

*Green, A. M. (Sussex & OFS) b May 28, 1960

Green, D. J. (Derbys. & CUCC) b Dec. 18, 1935

Green, D. M. (OUCC, Lancs. & Glos.; *CY 1969*) b Nov. 10, 1939

Greenfield, K. (Sussex) b Dec. 6, 1968

*Greenhough, T. (Lancs.) b Nov. 9, 1931

*Greenidge, A. E. (B'dos) b Aug. 20, 1956

*Greenidge, C. G. (Hants & B'dos; *CY 1977*) b May 1, 1951

*Greenidge, G. A. (B'dos & Sussex) b May 26, 1948

Greensmith, W. T. (Essex) b Aug. 16, 1930

*Greenwood, A. (Yorks.) b Aug. 20, 1847, d Feb. 12, 1889

Greenwood, P. (Lancs.) b Sept. 11, 1924

Greetham, C. (Som.) b Aug. 28, 1936

*Gregory, David W. (NSW; first Australian captain) b April 15, 1845, d Aug. 4, 1919

*Gregory, E. J. (NSW) b May 29, 1839, d April 22, 1899

*Gregory, J. M. (NSW; *CY 1922*) b Aug. 14, 1895, d Aug. 7, 1973

*Gregory, R. G. (Vic.) b Feb. 28, 1916, d June 10, 1942

*Gregory, S. E. (NSW; *CY 1897*) b April 14, 1870, d August 1, 1929

*Greig, A. W. (Border, E. Prov. & Sussex; *CY 1975*) b Oct. 6, 1946

*Greig, I. A. (CUCC, Border, Sussex & Surrey) b Dec. 8, 1955

*Grell, M. G. (T/T) b Dec. 18, 1899, d Jan. 11, 1976

*Grieve, B. A. F. (Eng.) b May 28, 1864, d Nov. 19, 1917

Grieves, K. J. (NSW & Lancs.) b Aug. 27, 1925, d Jan. 3, 1992

Grieveson, R. E. (Tvl) b Aug. 24, 1909

*Griffin, G. M. (Natal & Rhod.) b June 12, 1939

*Griffith, C. C. (B'dos; *CY 1964*) b Dec. 14, 1938

Griffith, G. ("Ben") (Surrey & Utd England XI) b Dec. 20, 1833, d May 3, 1879

*Griffith, H. C. (B'dos) b Dec. 1, 1893, d March 18, 1980

Griffith, M. G. (CUCC & Sussex) b Nov. 25, 1943

*Griffith, S. C. (CUCC, Surrey & Sussex; Sec. MCC 1962-74; Pres. MCC 1979-80) b June 16, 1914, d April 7, 1993

Griffiths, B. J. (Northants) b June 13, 1949

Griffiths, Rt Hon. The Lord (W. H.) (CUCC & Glam.; Pres. MCC 1990-91) b Sept. 26, 1923

*Grimmett, C. V. (Wgtn, Vic. & S. Aust.; *CY 1931*) b Dec. 25, 1891, d May 2, 1980

Grimshaw, N. (Northants) b May 5, 1911

*Groube, T. U. (Vic.) b Sept. 2, 1857, d Aug. 5, 1927

*Grout, A. T. W. (Qld) b March 30, 1927, d Nov. 9, 1968

Grover, J. N. (OUCC) b Oct. 15, 1915, d Dec. 17, 1990

Groves, M. G. M. (OUCC, Som. & W. Prov.) b Jan. 14, 1943

Grundy, J. (Notts. & Utd England XI) b March 5, 1824, d Nov. 24, 1873

*Guard, G. M. (Bombay & Guj.) b Dec. 12, 1925, d March 13, 1978

*Guest, C. E. J. (Vic. & W. Aust.) b Oct. 7, 1937

*Guha, S. (Bengal) b Jan. 31, 1946

**Guillen, S. C. (T/T & Cant.) b Sept. 24, 1924

Guise, J. L. (OUCC & Middx) b Nov. 25, 1903, d June 29, 1991

**Gul Mahomed (N. Ind., Baroda, H'bad, Punjab & Lahore) b Oct. 15, 1921, d May 8, 1992

*Gunasekera, Y. (SL) b Nov. 8, 1957

Gunawardene, A. A. W. (SSC) b March 31, 1969

*Guneratne, R. P. W. (Nomads) b Jan. 26, 1962

*Gunn, G. (Notts.; *CY 1914*) b June 13, 1879, d June 29, 1958

Gunn, G. V. (Notts.) b June 21, 1905, d Oct. 14, 1957

*Gunn, J. (Notts.; *CY 1904*) b July 19, 1876, d Aug. 21, 1963

Gunn, T. (Sussex) b Sept. 27, 1935

*Gunn, William (Notts.; *CY 1890*) b Dec. 4, 1858, d Jan. 29, 1921

*Gupte, B. P. (Bombay, Bengal & Ind. Rlwys) b Aug. 30, 1934

*Gupte, S. P. (Bombay, Bengal, Raja. & T/T) b Dec. 11, 1929

*Gursharan Singh (Punjab) b March 8, 1963

*Gurusinha, A. P. (SSC & NCC) b Sept. 16, 1966

*Guy, J. W. (C. Dist., Wgtn, Northants, Cant., Otago & N. Dist.) b Aug. 29, 1934

Haafiz Shahid (WAPDA) b May 10, 1963

Hacker, P. J. (Notts., Derbys. & OFS) b July 16, 1952

*Hadlee, B. G. (Cant.) b Dec. 14, 1941

*Hadlee, D. R. (Cant.) b Jan. 6, 1948

*Hadlee, Sir R. J. (Cant., Notts. & Tas.; *CY 1982*) b July 3, 1951

*Hadlee, W. A. (Cant. & Otago) b June 4, 1915

Hafeez, A. (*see* Kardar)

*Haig, N. E. (Middx) b Dec. 12, 1887, d Oct. 27, 1966

*Haigh, S. (Yorks.; *CY 1901*) b March 19, 1871, d Feb. 27, 1921

Halfyard, D. J. (Kent & Notts.) b April 3, 1931

*Hall, A. E. (Tvl & Lancs.) b Jan. 23, 1896, d Jan. 1, 1964

*Hall, G. G. (NE Tvl & E. Prov.) b May 24, 1938, d June 26, 1987

Hall, I. W. (Derbys.) b Dec. 27, 1939

Hall, J. W. (Sussex) b March 30, 1968

Hall, Louis (Yorks.; *CY 1890*) b Nov. 1, 1852, d Nov. 19, 1915

*Hall, W. W. (B'dos, T/T & Qld) b Sept. 12, 1937

Hallam, A. W. (Lancs. & Notts.; *CY 1908*) b Nov. 12, 1869, d July 24, 1940

Hallam, M. R. (Leics.) b Sept. 10, 1931

*Halliwell, E. A. (Tvl & Middx; *CY 1905*) b Sept. 7, 1864, d Oct. 2, 1919

*Hallows, C. (Lancs.; *CY 1928*) b April 4, 1895, d Nov. 10, 1972

Hallows, J. (Lancs.; *CY 1905*) b Nov. 14, 1873, d May 20, 1910

*Halse, C. G. (Natal) b Feb. 28, 1935

*Hamence, R. A. (S. Aust.) b Nov. 25, 1915

Hamer, A. (Yorks. & Derbys.) b Dec. 8, 1916, d Nov. 3, 1993

*Hammond, J. R. (S. Aust.) b April 19, 1950

*Hammond, W. R. (Glos.; *CY 1928*) b June 19, 1903, d July 1, 1965

Hampshire, J. H. (Yorks., Derbys. & Tas.; Umpire) b Feb. 10, 1941

Hancock, T. H. C. (Glos.) b April 20, 1972

*Hands, P. A. M. (W. Prov.) b March 18, 1890, d April 27, 1951

*Hands, R. H. M. (W. Prov.) b July 26, 1888, d April 20, 1918

*Hanif Mohammad (B'pur, Kar. & PIA; *CY 1968*) b Dec. 21, 1934

*Hanley, M. A. (Border & W. Prov.) b Nov. 10, 1918

Hanley, R. W. (E. Prov., OFS, Tvl & Northants) b Jan. 29, 1952

*Hanumant Singh (M. Pradesh & Raja.) b March 29, 1939

Harbord, W. E. (Yorks. & OUCC) b Dec. 15, 1908, d July 28, 1992

Harden, R. J. (Som. & C. Dist.) b Aug. 16, 1965

Hardie, B. R. (Scotland & Essex) b Jan. 14, 1950

*Hardikar, M. S. (Bombay) b Feb. 8, 1936, d Feb. 4, 1995

*Hardinge, H. T. W. (Kent; *CY 1915*) b Feb. 25, 1886, d May 8, 1965

*Hardstaff, J. (Notts.) b Nov. 9, 1882, d April 2, 1947

*Hardstaff, J., jun. (Notts. & Auck.; *CY 1938*) b July 3, 1911, d Jan. 1, 1990

Hardy, J. J. E. (Hants, Som., W. Prov. & Glos.) b Oct. 2, 1960

*Harford, N. S. (C. Dist. & Auck.) b Aug. 30, 1930, d March 30, 1981

*Harford, R. I. (Auck.) b May 30, 1936

Harman, R. (Surrey) b Dec. 28, 1941

*Haroon Rashid (Kar., Sind, NBP, PIA & UBL) b March 25, 1953

*Harper, R. A. (Guyana & Northants) b March 17, 1963

*Harris, 4th Lord (OUCC & Kent; Pres. MCC 1895) b Feb. 3, 1851, d March 24, 1932

*Harris, C. Z. (Cant.) b Nov. 20, 1969

Harris, David (Hants & All-England) b 1755, d May 19, 1803

Harris, M. J. (Middx, Notts., E. Prov. & Wgtn) b May 25, 1944

*Harris, P. G. Z. (Cant.) b July 18, 1927, d Dec. 1, 1991

*Harris, R. M. (Auck.) b July 27, 1933

*Harris, T. A. (Griq. W. & Tvl) b Aug. 27, 1916, d March 7, 1993

Harrison, L. (Hants) b June 8, 1922

*Harry, J. (Vic.) b Aug. 1, 1857, d Oct. 27, 1919

Hart, G. E. (Middx) b Jan. 13, 1902, d April 11, 1987

*Hart, M. N. (N. Dist.) b May 16, 1972

Hart, R. T. (C. Dist. & Wgtn) b Nov. 7, 1961

*Hartigan, G. P. D. (Border) b Dec. 30, 1884, d Jan. 7, 1955

*Hartigan, R. J. (NSW & Qld) b Dec. 12, 1879, d June 7, 1958

*Hartkopf, A. E. V. (Vic.) b Dec. 28, 1889, d May 20, 1968

*Hartland, B. R. (Cant.) b Oct. 22, 1966

Hartley, A. (Lancs.; *CY 1911*) b April 11, 1879, d Oct. 9, 1918

*Hartley, J. C. (OUCC & Sussex) b Nov. 15, 1874, d March 8, 1963

Hartley, P. J. (Warwicks. & Yorks.) b April 18, 1960

Hartley, S. N. (Yorks. & OFS) b March 18, 1956

Harvey, J. F. (Derbys.) b Sept. 27, 1939

*Harvey, M. R. (Vic.) b April 29, 1918, d March 20, 1995

Harvey, P. F. (Notts.) b Jan. 15, 1923

*Harvey, R. L. (Natal) b Sept. 14, 1911

*Harvey, R. N. (Vic. & NSW; *CY 1954*) b Oct. 8, 1928

Harvey-Walker, A. J. (Derbys.) b July 21, 1944

Hasan Jamil (Kalat, Kar., Pak. Us & PIA) b July 25, 1952

*Haseeb Ahsan (Peshawar, Pak. Us, Kar. & PIA) b July 15, 1939

Haslam, M. J. (Auck.) b Sept. 26, 1972

Hassan, B. (Notts.) b March 24, 1944

*Hassett, A. L. (Vic.; *CY 1949*) b Aug. 28, 1913, d June 16, 1993

Hastings, B. F. (Wgtn, C. Dist. & Cant.) b March 23, 1940

*Hathorn, C. M. H. (Tvl) b April 7, 1878, d May 17, 1920

Hathurusinghe, U. C. (TU) b Sept. 13, 1968

*Hawke, 7th Lord (CUCC & Yorks.; *CY 1909*; Pres. MCC 1914-18) b Aug. 16, 1860, d Oct. 10, 1938

*Hawke, N. J. N. (W. Aust., S. Aust. & Tas.) b June 27, 1939

Hawker, Sir Cyril (Essex; Pres. MCC 1970-71) b July 21, 1900, d Feb. 22, 1991

Hawkins, D. G. (Glos.) b May 18, 1935

*Hayden, M. L. (Qld) b Oct. 29, 1971

*Hayes, E. G. (Surrey & Leics.; *CY 1907*) b Nov. 6, 1876, d Dec. 2, 1953

Hayes, F. C. (Lancs.) b Dec. 6, 1946

*Hayes, J. A. (Auck. & Cant.) b Jan. 11, 1927

Hayes, K. A. (OUCC & Lancs.) b Sept. 26, 1962

Hayes, R. L. (N. Dist.) b May 9, 1971

Haygarth, A. (Sussex; Historian) b Aug. 4, 1825, d May 1, 1903

Hayhurst, A. N. (Lancs. & Som.) b Nov. 23, 1962

*Haynes, D. L. (B'dos, Middx & W. Prov.; *CY 1991*) b Feb. 15, 1956

Haynes, G. R. (Worcs.) b Sept. 29, 1969

Haynes, R. C. (Jam.) b Nov. 11, 1964

Haysman, M. D. (S. Aust., Leics. & N. Tvl) b April 22, 1961

Hayward, T. (Cambs. & All-England) b March 21, 1835, d July 21, 1876

*Hayward, T. W. (Surrey; *CY 1895*) b March 29, 1871, d July 19, 1939

Haywood, P. R. (Leics.) b March 30, 1947

*Hazare, V. S. (M'tra, C. Ind. & Baroda) b March 11, 1915

Hazell, H. L. (Som.) b Sept. 30, 1909, d March 31, 1990

Hazlerigg, Lord, formerly Hon. A. G. (CUCC & Leics.) b Feb. 24, 1910

*Hazlitt, G. R. (Vic. & NSW) b Sept. 4, 1888, d Oct. 30, 1915

Headley, D. W. (Middx & Kent) b Jan. 27, 1970

*Headley, G. A. (Jam.; *CY 1934*) b May 30, 1909, d Nov. 30, 1983

*Headley, R. G. A. (Worcs. & Jam.) b June 29, 1939

*Healy, I. A. (Qld; *CY 1994*) b April 30, 1964

Hearn, P. (Kent) b Nov. 18, 1925

*Hearne, Alec (Kent; *CY 1894*) b July 22, 1863, d May 16, 1952

**Hearne, Frank (Kent & W. Prov.) b Nov. 23, 1858, d July 14, 1949

*Hearne, G. A. L. (W. Prov.) b March 27, 1888, d Nov. 13, 1978

*Hearne, George G. (Kent) b July 7, 1856, d Feb. 13, 1932

*Hearne, J. T. (Middx; *CY 1892*) b May 3, 1867, d April 17, 1944

*Hearne, J. W. (Middx; *CY 1912*) b Feb. 11, 1891, d Sept. 14, 1965

Hearne, Thos. (Middx) b Sept. 4, 1826, d May 13, 1900

Hearne, Thos., jun. (Lord's Ground Superintendent) b Dec. 29, 1849, d Jan. 29, 1910

Heath, G. E. M. (Hants) b Feb. 20, 1913

Heath, M. (Hants) b March 9, 1934

Hedges, B. (Glam.) b Nov. 10, 1927

Hedges, L. P. (Tonbridge, OUCC, Kent & Glos.; *CY 1919*) b July 13, 1900, d Jan. 12, 1933

Hegg, W. K. (Lancs.) b Feb. 23, 1968

*Heine, P. S. (NE Tvl, OFS & Tvl) b June 28, 1928

*Hemmings, E. E. (Warwicks., Notts. & Sussex) b Feb. 20, 1949

Hemp, D. L. (Glam.) b Nov. 15, 1970

Hemsley, E. J. O. (Worcs.) b Sept. 1, 1943

*Henderson, M. (Wgtn) b Aug. 2, 1895, d June 17, 1970

Henderson, R. (Surrey; *CY 1890*) b March 30, 1865, d Jan. 29, 1931

Henderson, S. P. (CUCC, Worcs. & Glam.) b Sept. 24, 1958

*Hendren, E. H. (Middx; *CY 1920*) b Feb. 5, 1889, d Oct. 4, 1962

*Hendrick, M. (Derbys. & Notts.; *CY 1978*) b Oct. 22, 1948

*Hendriks, J. L. (Jam.) b Dec. 21, 1933

*Hendry, H. S. T. L. (NSW & Vic.) b May 24, 1895, d Dec. 16, 1988

*Henry, O. (W. Prov., Boland, OFS & Scotland) b Jan. 23, 1952

Hepworth, P. N. (Leics.) b May 4, 1967

Herman, O. W. (Hants) b Sept. 18, 1907, d June 24, 1987

Herman, R. S. (Middx, Border, Griq. W. & Hants) b Nov. 30, 1946

Heron, J. G. (Zimb.) b Nov. 8, 1948

*Heseltine, C. (Hants) b Nov. 26, 1869, d June 13, 1944

Hever, N. G. (Middx & Glam.) b Dec. 17, 1924, d Sept. 11, 1987

*Hewett, H. T. (OUCC & Som.; *CY 1893*) b May 25, 1864, d March 4, 1921

Heyhoe-Flint, Rachael (England Women) b June 11, 1939

Heyn, P. D. (SL) b June 26, 1945

*Hibbert, P. A. (Vic.) b July 23, 1952

*Hick, G. A. (Worcs., Zimb., N. Dist. & Qld; *CY 1987*) b May 23, 1966

Higgs, J. D. (Vic.) b July 11, 1950

*Higgs, K. (Lancs. & Leics.; *CY 1968*) b Jan. 14, 1937

Hignell, A. J. (CUCC & Glos.) b Sept. 4, 1955

*Hilditch, A. M. J. (NSW & S. Aust.) b May 20, 1956

Hill, Alan (Derbys. & OFS) b June 29, 1950

*Hill, Allen (Yorks.) b Nov. 14, 1843, d Aug. 29, 1910

*Hill, A. J. L. (CUCC & Hants) b July 26, 1871, d Sept. 6, 1950

*Hill, C. (S. Aust.; *CY 1900*) b March 18, 1877, d Sept. 5, 1945

Hill, E. (Som.) b July 9, 1923

Hill, G. (Hants) b April 15, 1913

*Hill, J. C. (Vic.) b June 25, 1923, d Aug. 11, 1974

Hill, L. W. (Glam.) b April 14, 1942

Hill, M. (Notts., Derbys & Som.) b Sept. 14, 1935

Hill, N. W. (Notts.) b Aug. 22, 1935

Hill, W. A. (Warwicks.) b April 27, 1910, d Aug. 11, 1995

Hills, R. W. (Kent) b Jan. 8, 1951

Hill-Wood, C. K. (OUCC & Derbys.) b June 5, 1907, d Sept. 21, 1988

Hilton, C. (Lancs. & Essex) b Sept. 26, 1937

Hilton, J. (Lancs. & Som.) b Dec. 29, 1930

*Hilton, M. J. (Lancs.; *CY 1957*) b Aug. 2, 1928, d July 8, 1990

Hime, C. F. W. (Natal) b Oct. 24, 1869, d Dec. 6, 1940

*Hindlekar, D. D. (Bombay) b Jan. 1, 1909, d March 30, 1949

Hindson, J. E. (Notts.) b Sept. 13, 1973

Hinks, S. G. (Kent & Glos.) b Oct. 12, 1960

*Hirst, G. H. (Yorks.; *CY 1901*) b Sept. 7, 1871, d May 10, 1954

*Hirwani, N. D. (M. Pradesh) b Oct. 18, 1968

*Hitch, J. W. (Surrey; *CY 1914*) b May 7, 1886, d July 7, 1965

Hitchcock, R. E. (Cant. & Warwicks.) b Nov. 28, 1929

*Hoad, E. L. G. (B'dos) b Jan. 29, 1896, d March 5, 1986

*Hoare, D. E. (W. Aust.) b Oct. 19, 1934

*Hobbs, Sir J. B. (Surrey; *CY 1909, special portrait 1926*) b Dec. 16, 1882, d Dec. 21, 1963

*Hobbs, R. N. S. (Essex & Glam.) b May 8, 1942

*Hodges, J. R. (Vic.) b Aug. 11, 1855, death unknown

Hodgkinson, G. F. (Derbys.) b Feb. 19, 1914, d Jan. 7, 1987

Hodgson, A. (Northants) b Oct. 27, 1951

Hodgson, G. D. (Glos.) b Oct. 22, 1966

Hofmeyr, M. B. (OUCC & NE Tvl) b Dec. 9, 1925

*Hogan, T. G. (W. Aust.) b Sept. 23, 1956

*Hogg, R. M. (S. Aust.) b March 5, 1951

Hogg, W. (Lancs. & Warwicks.) b July 12, 1955

*Hohns, T. V. (Qld) b Jan. 23, 1954

Holder, J. W. (Hants; Umpire) b March 19, 1945

Holder, R. I. C. (B'dos) b Dec. 22, 1967

*Holder, V. A. (B'dos, Worcs. & OFS) b Oct. 8, 1945

*Holding, M. A. (Jam., Lancs., Derbys., Tas. & Cant.; *CY 1977*) b Feb. 16, 1954

*Hole, G. B. (NSW & S. Aust.) b Jan. 6, 1931, d Feb. 14, 1990

*Holford, D. A. J. (B'dos & T/T) b April 16, 1940

*Holland, R. G. (NSW & Wgtn) b Oct. 19, 1946

*Hollies, W. E. (Warwicks.; *CY 1955*) b June 5, 1912, d April 16, 1981

Hollingdale, R. A. (Sussex) b March 6, 1906, d Aug. 1989

Holloake, A. J. (Surrey) b Sept. 5, 1971

Holmes, Gp Capt. A. J. (Sussex) b June 30, 1899, d May 21, 1950

*Holmes, E. R. T. (OUCC & Surrey; *CY 1936*) b Aug. 21, 1905, d Aug. 16, 1960

Holmes, G. C. (Glam.) b Sept. 16, 1958

*Holmes, P. (Yorks.; *CY 1920*) b Nov. 25, 1886, d Sept. 3, 1971

Holt, A. G. (Hants) b April 8, 1911, d July 28, 1994

*Holt, J. K., jun. (Jam.) b Aug. 12, 1923

Home of the Hirsel, Lord (Middx; Pres. MCC 1966-67) b July 2, 1903, d Oct. 9, 1995

*Hone, L. (MCC) b Jan. 30, 1853, d Dec. 31, 1896

Hooker, R. W. (Middx) b Feb. 22, 1935

*Hookes, D. W. (S. Aust.) b May 3, 1955

*Hooper, C. L. (Guyana & Kent) b Dec. 15, 1966

Hopkins, A. J. Y. (NSW) b May 3, 1874, d April 25, 1931

Hopkins, J. A. (Glam. & E. Prov.) b June 16, 1953

*Hopwood, J. L. (Lancs.) b Oct. 30, 1903, d June 15, 1985

*Horan, T. P. (Vic.) b March 8, 1854, d April 16, 1916

*Hordern, H. V. (NSW & Philadelphia) b Feb. 10, 1884, d June 17, 1938

*Hornby, A. N. (Lancs.) b Feb. 10, 1847, d Dec. 17, 1925

*Horne, P. A. (Auck.) b Jan. 21, 1960

Horner, N. F. (Yorks. & Warwicks.) b May 10, 1926

*Hornibrook, P. M. (Qld) b July 27, 1899, d Aug. 25, 1976

Horton, H. (Worcs. & Hants) b April 18, 1923

Horton, J. (Worcs.) b Aug. 12, 1916

*Horton, M. J. (Worcs. & N. Dist.) b April 21, 1934

Hossell, J. J. (Warwicks.) b May 25, 1914

*Hough, K. W. (Auck.) b Oct. 24, 1928

*Houghton, D. L. (Mash.) b June 23, 1957

*Howard, A. B. (B'dos) b Aug. 27, 1946

Howard, A. R. (Glam.) b Dec. 11, 1909, d March, 1993

Howard, B. J. (Lancs.) b May 21, 1926

Howard, K. (Lancs.) b June 29, 1941

*Howard, N. D. (Lancs.) b May 18, 1925, d May 31, 1979

Howard, Major R. (Lancs.; MCC Team Manager) b April 17, 1890, d Sept. 10, 1967

*Howarth, G. P. (Auck., Surrey & N. Dist.) b March 29, 1951

*Howarth, H. J. (Auck.) b Dec. 25, 1943

*Howell, H. (Warwicks.) b Nov. 29, 1890, d July 9, 1932

*Howell, W. P. (NSW) b Dec. 29, 1869, d July 14, 1940

Howland, C. B. (CUCC, Sussex & Kent) b Feb. 6, 1936

*Howorth, R. (Worcs.) b April 26, 1909, d April 2, 1980

*Hudson, A. C. (Natal) b March 17, 1965

Hughes, D. P. (Lancs. & Tas.; *CY 1988*) b May 13, 1947

*Hughes, K. J. (W. Aust. & Natal; *CY 1981*) b Jan. 26, 1954

*Hughes, M. G. (Vic. & Essex; *CY 1994*) b Nov. 23, 1961

Hughes, S. P. (Middx, N. Tvl & Durham) b Dec. 20, 1959

Huish, F. H. (Kent) b Nov. 15, 1869, d March 16, 1957

Hulme, J. H. A. (Middx) b Aug. 26, 1904, d Sept. 26, 1991

Human, J. H. (CUCC & Middx) b Jan. 13, 1912, d July 22, 1991

Humpage, G. W. (Warwicks. & OFS; *CY 1985*) b April 24, 1954

Humphries, D. J. (Leics. & Worcs.) b Aug. 6, 1953

*Humphries, J. (Derbys.) b May 19, 1876, d May 7, 1946

Hunt, A. V. (Scotland & Bermuda) b Oct. 1, 1910

*Hunt, W. A. (NSW) b Aug. 26, 1908, d Dec. 30, 1983

*Hunte, C. C. (B'dos; *CY 1964*) b May 9, 1932

*Hunte, E. A. C. (T/T) b Oct. 3, 1905, d June 26, 1967

Hunter, David (Yorks.) b Feb. 23, 1860, d Jan. 11, 1927

*Hunter, Joseph (Yorks.) b Aug. 3, 1855, d Jan. 4, 1891

Hurd, A. (CUCC & Essex) b Sept. 7, 1937

*Hurst, A. G. (Vic.) b July 15, 1950

Hurst, R. J. (Middx) b Dec. 29, 1933

*Hurwood, A. (Qld) b June 17, 1902, d Sept. 26, 1982

*Hussain, M. Dilawar (C. Ind. & U. Prov.) b March 19, 1907, d Aug. 26, 1967

*Hussain, N. (Essex) b March 28, 1968

*Hutchings, K. L. (Kent; *CY 1907*) b Dec. 7, 1882, d Sept. 3, 1916

Hutchinson, J. M. (Derbys.) (oldest known living county cricketer) b Nov. 29, 1896

*Hutchinson, P. (SA) b Jan. 26, 1862, d Sept. 30, 1925

Hutton, Sir Leonard (Yorks.; *CY 1938*) b June 23, 1916, d Sept. 6, 1990

*Hutton, R. A. (CUCC, Yorks. & Tvl) b Sept. 6, 1942

*Hylton, L. G. (Jam.) b March 29, 1905, d May 17, 1955

*Ibadulla, K. (Punjab, Warwicks., Tas. & Otago) b Dec. 20, 1935

*Ibrahim, K. C. (Bombay) b Jan. 26, 1919

*Iddon, J. (Lancs.) b Jan. 8, 1902, d April 17, 1946

*Igglesden, A. P. (Kent & W. Prov.) b Oct. 8, 1964

*Ijaz Ahmed (Gujranwala, PACO, HBL, I'bad & Lahore) b Sept. 20, 1968

*Ijaz Butt (Pak. Us, Punjab, Lahore, R'pindi & Multan) b March 10, 1938

*Ijaz Faqih (Kar., Sind, PWD & MCB) b March 24, 1956

*Ikin, J. T. (Lancs.) b March 7, 1918, d Sept. 15, 1984

*Illingworth, R. (Yorks. & Leics.; *CY 1960*) b June 8, 1932

*Illingworth, R. K. (Worcs. & Natal) b Aug. 23, 1963

*Ilott, M. C. (Essex) b Aug. 27, 1970

*Imran Khan (Lahore, Dawood, Worcs., OUCC, PIA, Sussex & NSW; *CY 1983*) b Nov. 25, 1952

*Imtiaz Ahmed (N. Ind., Comb. Us, NWFP, Pak. Serv., Peshawar & PAF) b Jan. 5, 1928

*Imtiaz Ali (T/T) b July 28, 1954

Inchmore, J. D. (Worcs. & N. Tvl) b Feb. 22, 1949

*Indrajitsinhji, K. S. (S'tra & Delhi) b June 15, 1937

*Ingle, R. A. (Som.) b Nov. 5, 1903, d Dec. 19, 1992

Ingleby-Mackenzie, A. C. D. (Hants) b Sept. 15, 1933

Inman C. C. (Ceylon & Leics.) b Jan. 29, 1936

*Inshan Ali (T/T) b Sept. 25, 1949, d June 24, 1995

*Insole, D. J. (CUCC & Essex; *CY 1956*) b April 18, 1926

*Intikhab Alam (Kar., PIA, Surrey, PWD, Sind & Punjab) b Dec. 28, 1941

*Inverarity, R. J. (W. Aust. & S. Aust.) b Jan. 31, 1944

*Inzamam-ul-Haq (Multan & UBL) b March 3, 1970

*Iqbal Qasim (Kar., Sind & NBP) b Aug. 6, 1953

Iqbal Sikandar (Karachi & PIA) b Dec. 19, 1958

*Irani, J. K. (Sind) b Aug. 18, 1923, d Feb. 25, 1982

Irani, R. C. (Lancs. & Essex) b Oct. 26, 1971

*Iredale, F. A. (NSW) b June 19, 1867, d April 15, 1926

*Iremonger, J. (Notts.; *CY 1903*) b March 5, 1876, d March 25, 1956

Irfan Bhatti (R'pindi) b Sept. 28, 1964

*Ironmonger, H. (Qld & Vic.) b April 7, 1882, d June 1, 1971

*Ironside, D. E. J. (Tvl) b May 2, 1925

*Irvine, B. L. (W. Prov., Natal, Essex & Tvl) b March 9, 1944

*Israr Ali (S. Punjab, B'pur & Multan) b May 1, 1927

*Iverson, J. B. (Vic.) b July 27, 1915, d Oct. 24, 1973

*Jack, S. D. (Tvl) b Aug. 4, 1970
*Jackman, R. D. (Surrey, W. Prov. & Rhod.; *CY 1981*) b Aug. 13, 1945
*Jackson, A. A. (NSW) b Sept. 5, 1909, d Feb. 16, 1933
Jackson, A. B. (Derbys.) b Aug. 21, 1933
*Jackson, Rt Hon. Sir F. S. (CUCC & Yorks.; *CY 1894*; Pres. MCC 1921) b Nov. 21, 1870, d March 9, 1947
Jackson, G. R. (Derbys.) b June 23, 1896, d Feb. 21, 1966
*Jackson, H. L. (Derbys.; *CY 1959*) b April 5, 1921
Jackson, John (Notts. & All-England) b May 21, 1833, d Nov. 4, 1901
Jackson, P. F. (Worcs.) b May 11, 1911
Jacques, T. A. (Yorks.) b Feb. 19, 1905, d Feb. 23, 1995
*Jadeja, A. D. (Haryana) b Feb. 1, 1971
*Jahangir Khan (N. Ind. & CUCC) b Feb. 1, 1910, d July 23, 1988
*Jai, L. P. (Bombay) b April 1, 1902, d Jan. 29, 1968
*Jaisimha, M. L. (H'bad) b March 3, 1939
Jakeman, F. (Yorks. & Northants) b Jan. 10, 1920, d May 18, 1986
*Jalal-ud-Din (PWD, Kar., IDBP & Allied Bank) b June 12, 1959
James, A. E. (Sussex) b Aug. 7, 1924
James, C. L. R. (Writer) b Jan. 4, 1901, d May 31, 1989
*James, K. C. (Wgtn & Northants) b March 12, 1904, d Aug. 21, 1976
James, K. D. (Middx, Hants & Wgtn) b March 18, 1961
James, R. M. (CUCC & Wgtn) b Oct. 2, 1934
James, S. P. (Glam., CUCC & Mash.) b Sept. 7, 1967
*James, W. R. (Mat.) b Aug. 27, 1965
Jameson, J. A. (Warwicks.) b June 30, 1941
Jamshedji, R. J. D. (Bombay) b Nov. 18, 1892, d April 5, 1976
*Jardine, D. R. (OUCC & Surrey; *CY 1928*) b Oct. 23, 1900, d June 18, 1958
*Jarman, B. N. (S. Aust.) b Feb. 17, 1936
Jarrett, D. W. (OUCC & CUCC) b April 19, 1952
*Jarvis, A. H. (S. Aust.) b Oct. 19, 1860, d Nov. 15, 1933
Jarvis, K. B. S. (Kent & Glos.) b April 23, 1953
*Jarvis, M. P. (Mash.) b Dec. 6, 1955
*Jarvis, P. W. (Yorks. & Sussex) b June 29, 1965
*Jarvis, T. W. (Auck. & Cant.) b July 29, 1944
*Javed Akhtar (R'pindi & Pak. Serv.) b Nov. 21, 1940

*Javed Miandad (Kar., Sind, Sussex, HBL & Glam.; *CY 1982*) b June 12, 1957
Javed Qadir (PIA) b Aug. 25, 1976
*Jayantilal, K. (H'bad) b Jan. 13, 1948
Jayasekera, R. S. A. (SL) b Dec. 7, 1957
Jayasinghe, S. (Ceylon & Leics.) b Jan. 19, 1931
Jayasinghe, S. A. (SL) b July 15, 1955, d April 20, 1995
*Jayasuriya, S. T. (CCC & Bloom.) b June 30, 1969
Jean-Jacques, M. (Derbys. & Hants) b July 2, 1960
Jeeves, P. (Warwicks.) b March 5, 1888, d July 22, 1916
Jefferies, S. T. (W. Prov., Derbys., Lancs., Hants & Boland) b Dec. 8, 1959
Jefferson, R. I. (CUCC & Surrey) b Aug. 15, 1941
*Jeganathan, S. (SL) b July 11, 1951
*Jenkins, R. O. (Worcs.; *CY 1950*) b Nov. 24, 1918, d July 21, 1995
Jenkins, V. G. J. (OUCC & Glam.) b Nov. 2, 1911
*Jenner, T. J. (W. Aust. & S. Aust.) b Sept. 8, 1944
*Jennings, C. B. (S. Aust.) b June 5, 1884, d June 20, 1950
Jennings, K. F. (Som.) b Oct. 5, 1953
Jennings, R. V. (Tvl & N. Tvl) b Aug. 9, 1954
Jepson, A. (Notts.) b July 12, 1915
*Jessop, G. L. (CUCC & Glos.; *CY 1898*) b May 19, 1874, d May 11, 1955
Jesty, T. E. (Hants, Border, Griq. W., Cant., Surrey & Lancs.; *CY 1983*) b June 2, 1948
*John, V. B. (SL) b May 27, 1960
Johnson, C. (Yorks.) b Sept. 5, 1947
*Johnson, C. L. (Tvl) b 1871, d May 31, 1908
Johnson, G. W. (Kent & Tvl) b Nov. 8, 1946
*Johnson, H. H. H. (Jam.) b July 17, 1910, d June 24, 1987
Johnson, H. L. (Derbys.) b Nov. 8, 1927
*Johnson, I. W. (Vic.) b Dec. 8, 1917
Johnson, L. A. (Northants) b Aug. 12, 1936
*Johnson, L. J. (Qld) b March 18, 1919, d April 20, 1977
Johnson, P. (Notts.) b April 24, 1965
Johnson, P. D. (CUCC & Notts.) b Nov. 12, 1949
*Johnson, T. F. (T/T) b Jan. 10, 1917, d April 5, 1985
Johnston, Brian A. (Broadcaster) b June 24, 1912, d Jan. 5, 1994
*Johnston, W. A. (Vic.; *CY 1949*) b Feb. 26, 1922
Jones, A. (Glam., W. Aust., N. Tvl & Natal; *CY 1978*) b Nov. 4, 1938
Jones, A. A. (Sussex, Som., Middx, Glam., N. Tvl & OFS) b Dec. 9, 1947

*Jones, A. H. (Wgtn & C. Dist.) b May 9, 1959

Jones, A. L. (Glam.) b June 1, 1957

Jones, A. N. (Sussex, Border & Som.) b July 22, 1961

*Jones, A. O. (Notts. & CUCC; *CY 1900*) b Aug. 16, 1872, d Dec. 21, 1914

Jones, B. J. R. (Worcs.) b Nov. 2, 1955

*Jones, C. M. (C. E. L.) (BG) b Nov. 3, 1902, d Dec. 10, 1959

*Jones, D. M. (Vic. & Durham; *CY 1990*) b March 24, 1961

*Jones, Ernest (S. Aust. & W. Aust.) b Sept. 30, 1869, d Nov. 23, 1943

Jones, E. C. (Glam.) b Dec. 14, 1912, d April 14, 1989

Jones, E. W. (Glam.) b June 25, 1942

*Jones, I. J. (Glam.) b Dec. 10, 1941

Jones, K. V. (Middx) b March 28, 1942

*Jones, P. E. (T/T) b June 6, 1917, d Nov. 20, 1991

Jones, P. H. (Kent) b June 19, 1935

*Jones, S. P. (NSW, Qld & Auck.) b Aug. 1, 1861, d July 14, 1951

Jones, W. E. (Glam.) b Oct. 31, 1916

Jordan, J. M. (Lancs.) b Feb. 7, 1932

Jorden, A. M. (CUCC & Essex) b Jan. 28, 1947

Jordon, R. C. (Vic.) b Feb. 17, 1937

*Joshi, P. G. (M'tra) b Oct. 27, 1926, d Jan. 8, 1987

Joshi, U. C. (S'tra, Ind. Rlwys, Guj. & Sussex) b Dec. 23, 1944

*Joslin, L. R. (Vic.) b Dec. 13, 1947

Jowett, D. C. P. R. (OUCC) b Jan. 24, 1931

Judd, A. K. (CUCC & Hants) b Jan. 1, 1904, d Feb. 15, 1988

Judge, P. F. (Middx, Glam. & Bengal) b May 23, 1916, d March 4, 1992

*Julian, B. P. (W. Aust.) b Aug. 10, 1970

Julian, R. (Leics.) b Aug. 23, 1936

*Julien, B. D. (T/T & Kent) b March 13, 1950

*Jumadeen, R. R. (T/T) b April 12, 1948

*Jupp, H. (Surrey) b Nov. 19, 1841, d April 8, 1889

*Jupp, V. W. C. (Sussex & Northants; *CY 1928*) b March 27, 1891, d July 9, 1960

*Jurangpathy, B. R. (CCC) b June 25, 1967

*Kabir Khan (HBFC) b April 12, 1974

*Kallicharran, A. I. (Guyana, Warwicks., Qld, Tvl & OFS; *CY 1983*) b March 21, 1949

*Kalpage, R. S. (NCC & Bloom.) b Feb. 19, 1970

*Kaluperuma, L. W. (SL) b May 25, 1949

*Kaluperuma, S. M. S. (SL) b Oct. 22, 1961

*Kaluwitharana, R. S. (Seb. & Galle) b Nov. 24, 1969

*Kambli, V. G. (Bombay) b Jan. 18, 1972

*Kanhai, R. B. (†Guyana, T/T, W. Aust., Warwicks. & Tas.; *CY 1964*) b Dec. 26, 1935

*Kanitkar, H. S. (M'tra) b Dec. 8, 1942

*Kapil Dev (Haryana, Northants & Worcs.; *CY 1983*) b Jan. 6, 1959

*Kapoor, A. R. (Punjab) b March 25, 1971

**Kardar, A. H. (formerly Abdul Hafeez) (N. Ind., OUCC, Warwicks. & Pak. Serv.) b Jan. 17, 1925

Karnain, S. H. U. (NCC & Moors) b Aug. 11, 1962

Kasprowicz, M. S. (Qld & Essex) b Feb. 10, 1972

*Keeton, W. W. (Notts.; *CY 1940*) b April 30, 1905, d Oct. 10, 1980

Keighley, W. G. (OUCC & Yorks.) b Jan. 10, 1925

*Keith, H. J. (Natal) b Oct. 25, 1927

Kelleher, H. R. A. (Surrey & Northants) b March 3, 1929

Kellett, S. A. (Yorks.) b Oct. 16, 1967

*Kelleway, C. (NSW) b April 25, 1886, d Nov. 16, 1944

Kelly, J. (Notts.) b Sept. 15, 1930

*Kelly, J. J. (NSW; *CY 1903*) b May 10, 1867, d Aug. 14, 1938

*Kelly, T. J. D. (Vic.) b May 3, 1844, d July 20, 1893

*Kempis, G. A. (Natal) b Aug. 4, 1865, d May 19, 1890

*Kendall, T. (Vic. & Tas.) b Aug. 24, 1851, d Aug. 17, 1924

Kendrick, N. M. (Surrey & Glam.) b Nov. 11, 1967

Kennedy, A. (Lancs.) b Nov. 4, 1949

*Kennedy, A. S. (Hants; *CY 1933*) b Jan. 24, 1891, d Nov. 15, 1959

*Kenny, R. B. (Bombay & Bengal) b Sept. 29, 1930, d Nov. 21, 1985

*Kent, M. F. (Qld) b Nov. 23, 1953

*Kentish, E. S. M. (Jam. & OUCC) b Nov. 21, 1916

*Kenyon, D. (Worcs.; *CY 1963*) b May 15, 1924

*Kerr, J. L. (Cant.) b Dec. 28, 1910

Kerr, K. J. (Tvl & Warwicks.) b Sept. 11, 1961

*Kerr, R. B. (Qld) b June 16, 1961

Kersey, G. J. (Surrey) b May 19, 1971

Kerslake, R. C. (CUCC & Som.) b Dec. 26, 1942

Kettle, M. K. (Northants) b March 18, 1944

*Khalid Hassan (Punjab & Lahore) b July 14, 1937

*Khalid Wazir (Pak.) b April 27, 1936

*Khan Mohammad (N. Ind., Pak. Us, Som., B'pur, Sind, Kar. & Lahore) b Jan. 1, 1928

Khanna, S. C. (Delhi) b June 3, 1956

Kilborn, M. J. (OUCC) b Sept. 20, 1962

*Killick, Rev. E. T. (CUCC & Middx) b May 9, 1907, d May 18, 1953

Kilner, Norman (Yorks. & Warwicks.) b July 21, 1895, d April 28, 1979

*Kilner, Roy (Yorks.; *CY 1924*) b Oct. 17, 1890, d April 5, 1928

Kimpton, R. C. M. (OUCC & Worcs.) b Sept. 21, 1916

*King, C. L. (B'dos, Glam., Worcs. & Natal) b June 11, 1951

*King, F. McD. (B'dos) b Dec. 14, 1926, d Dec. 23, 1990

King, I. M. (Warwicks. & Essex) b Nov. 10, 1931

King, J. B. (Philadelphia) b Oct. 19, 1873, d Oct. 17, 1965

*King, J. H. (Leics.) b April 16, 1871, d Nov. 18, 1946

*King, L. A. (Jam. & Bengal) b Feb. 27, 1939

Kingsley, Sir P. G. T. (OUCC) b May 26, 1908

*Kinneir, S. P. (Warwicks.; *CY 1912*) b May 13, 1871, d Oct. 16, 1928

Kippax, A. F. (NSW) b May 25, 1897, d Sept. 4, 1972

Kirby, D. (CUCC & Leics.) b Jan. 18, 1939

*Kirmani, S. M. H. (†Karn.) b Dec. 29, 1949

*Kirsten, G. (W. Prov.) b Nov. 23, 1967

*Kirsten, P. N. (W. Prov., Sussex, Derbys. & Border) b May 14, 1955

*Kischenchand, G. (W. Ind., Guj. & Baroda) b April 14, 1925

Kitchen, M. J. (Som.; Umpire) b Aug. 1, 1940

*Kline, L. F. (Vic.) b Sept. 29, 1934

*Knight, A. E. (Leics.; *CY 1904*) b Oct. 8, 1872, d April 25, 1946

*Knight, B. R. (Essex & Leics.) b Feb. 18, 1938

*Knight, D. J. (OUCC & Surrey; *CY 1915*) b May 12, 1894, d Jan. 5, 1960

*Knight, N. V. (Essex & Warwicks.) b Nov. 28, 1969

Knight, R. D. V. (CUCC, Surrey, Glos. & Sussex; Sec. MCC 1994-   ) b Sept. 6, 1946

Knight, W. H. (Editor of *Wisden* 1870-79) b Nov. 29, 1812, d Aug. 16, 1879

*Knott, A. P. E. (Kent & Tas.; *CY 1970*) b April 9, 1946

Knott, C. H. (OUCC & Kent) b March 20, 1901, d June 18, 1988

Knott, C. J. (Hants) b Nov. 26, 1914

Knowles, J. (Notts.) b March 25, 1910

Knox, G. K. (Lancs.) b April 22, 1937

*Knox, N. A. (Surrey; *CY 1907*) b Oct. 10, 1884, d March 3, 1935

Kortright, C. J. (Essex) b Jan. 9, 1871, d Dec. 12, 1952

*Kotze, J. J. (Tvl & W. Prov.) b Aug. 7, 1879, d July 7, 1931

Krikken, K. M. (Derbys.) b April 9, 1969

*Kripal Singh, A. G. (Madras & H'bad) b Aug. 6, 1933, d July 23, 1987

*Krishnamurthy, P. (H'bad) b July 12, 1947

*Kuggeleijn, C. M. (N. Dist.) b May 10, 1956

*Kuiper, A. P. (W. Prov. & Derbys.) b Aug. 24, 1959

*Kulkarni, R. R. (Bombay) b Sept. 25, 1962

*Kulkarni, U. N. (Bombay) b March 7, 1942

*Kumar, V. V. (†TN) b June 22, 1935

*Kumble, A. (Karn. & Northants; *CY 1996*) b Oct. 17, 1970

*Kunderan, B. K. (Ind. Rlwys & Mysore) b Oct. 2, 1939

*Kuruppu, D. S. B. P. (BRC) b Jan. 5, 1962

*Kuruppuarachchi, A. K. (NCC) b Nov. 1, 1964

*Kuys, F. (W. Prov.) b March 21, 1870, d Sept. 12, 1953

Kynaston, R. (Middx; Sec. MCC 1846-58) b Nov. 5, 1805, d June 21, 1874

*Labrooy, G. F. (CCC) b June 7, 1964

Lacey, Sir F. E. (CUCC & Hants; Sec MCC 1898-1926) b Oct. 19, 1859, d May 26, 1946

*Laird, B. M. (W. Aust.) b Nov. 21, 1950

*Laker, J. C. (Surrey, Auck. & Essex; *CY 1952*) b Feb. 9, 1922, d April 23, 1986

*Lall Singh (S. Punjab) b Dec. 16, 1909, d Nov. 19, 1985

*Lamb, A. J. (W. Prov., Northants & OFS; *CY 1981*) b June 20, 1954

Lamb, Hon. T. M. (OUCC, Middx & Northants; Cricket Sec., TCCB 1987-   ) b March 24, 1953

*Lamba, R. (Delhi) b Jan. 2, 1958

*Lambert, C. B. (Guyana & N. Tvl) b Feb. 2, 1962

Lambert, G. E. E. (Glos. & Som.) b May 11, 1918, d Oct. 31, 1991

Lambert, R. H. (Ireland) b July 18, 1874, d March 24, 1956

Lambert, Wm (Surrey) b 1779, d April 19, 1851

Lampitt, S. R. (Worcs.) b July 29, 1966

*Lance, H. R. (NE Tvl & Tvl) b June 6, 1940

*Langer, J. L. (W. Aust.) b Nov. 21, 1970

Langford, B. A. (Som.) b Dec. 17, 1935

Langley, G. R. A. (S. Aust.; *CY 1957*) b Sept. 14, 1919

*Langridge, James (Sussex; *CY 1932*) b July 10, 1906, d Sept. 10, 1966

Langridge, J. G. (John) (Sussex; *CY 1950*) b Feb. 10, 1910

Langridge, R. J. (Sussex) b April 13, 1939

*Langton, A. B. C. (Tvl) b March 2, 1912, d Nov. 27, 1942

*Lara, B. C. (T/T & Warwicks.; *CY 1995*) b May 2, 1969

*Larkins, W. (Northants, E. Prov. & Durham) b Nov. 22, 1953

*Larsen, G. R. (Wgtn) b Sept. 27, 1962

*Larter, J. D. F. (Northants) b April 24, 1940

*Larwood, H. (Notts.; *CY 1927*) b Nov. 14, 1904, d July 22, 1995

*Lashley, P. D. (B'dos) b Feb. 11, 1937

Latchman, H. C. [A. H.] (Middx & Notts.) b July 26, 1943

*Latham, R. T. (Cant.) b June 12, 1961

*Lathwell, M. N. (Som.) b Dec. 26, 1971

*Laughlin, T. J. (Vic.) b Jan. 30, 1951

*Laver, F. (Vic.) b Dec. 7, 1869, d Sept. 24, 1919

Law, S. G. (Qld) b Oct. 18, 1968

Lawrence, D. V. (Glos.) b Jan. 28, 1964

*Lawrence, G. B. (Rhod. & Natal) b March 31, 1932

Lawrence, J. (Som.) b March 29, 1914, d Dec. 10, 1988

*Lawry, W. M. (Vic.; *CY 1962*) b Feb. 11, 1937

*Lawson, G. F. (NSW & Lancs.) b Dec. 7, 1957

Leadbeater, B. (Yorks.) b Aug. 14, 1943

*Leadbeater, E. (Yorks. & Warwicks.) b Aug. 15, 1927

Leary, S. E. (Kent) b April 30, 1933, d Aug. 21, 1988

Leatherdale, D. A. (Worcs.) b Nov. 26, 1967

Lee, C. (Yorks. & Derbys.) b March 17, 1924

Lee, F. S. (Middx & Som.; Umpire) b July 24, 1905, d March 30, 1982

*Lee, H. W. (Middx) b Oct. 26, 1890, d April 21, 1981

Lee, J. W. (Middx & Som.) b Feb. 1, 1904, d June 20, 1944

Lee, P. G. (Northants & Lancs.; *CY 1976*) b Aug. 27, 1945

*Lee, P. K. (S. Aust.) b Sept. 14, 1904, d Aug. 9, 1980

*Lees, W. K. (Otago) b March 19, 1952

*Lees, W. S. (Surrey; *CY 1906*) b Dec. 25, 1875, d Sept. 10, 1924

Leese, Sir Oliver, Bt (Pres. MCC 1965-66) b Oct. 27, 1894, d Jan. 20, 1978

Lefebvre, R. P. (Holland, Som., Cant. & Glam.) b Feb. 7, 1963

*Legall, R. A. (B'dos & T/T) b Dec. 1, 1925

Legard, E. (Warwicks.) b Aug. 23, 1935

*Leggat, I. B. (C. Dist.) b June 7, 1930

*Leggat, J. G. (Cant.) b May 27, 1926, d March 8, 1973

*Legge, G. B. (OUCC & Kent) b Jan. 26, 1903, d Nov. 21, 1940

Lenham, L. J. (Sussex) b May 24, 1936

Lenham, N. J. (Sussex) b Dec. 17, 1965

*le Roux, F. L. (Tvl & E. Prov.) b Feb. 5, 1882, d Sept. 22, 1963

le Roux, G. S. (W. Prov. & Sussex) b Sept. 4, 1955

*Leslie, C. F. H. (OUCC & Middx) b Dec. 8, 1861, d Feb. 12, 1921

Lester, E. (Yorks.) b Feb. 18, 1923

Lester, G. (Leics.) b Dec. 27, 1915

Lester, Dr J. A. (Philadelphia) b Aug. 1, 1871, d Sept. 3, 1969

Lethbridge, C. (Warwicks.) b June 23, 1961

*Lever, J. K. (Essex & Natal; *CY 1979*) b Feb. 24, 1949

*Lever, P. (Lancs. & Tas.) b Sept. 17, 1940

*Leveson Gower, Sir H. D. G. (OUCC & Surrey) b May 8, 1873, d Feb. 1, 1954

*Levett, W. H. V. (Kent) b Jan. 25, 1908, d Nov. 30, 1995

Lewington, P. J. (Warwicks.) b Jan. 30, 1950

*Lewis, A. R. (CUCC & Glam.) b July 6, 1938

Lewis, C. (Kent) b July 27, 1908, d April 26, 1993

*Lewis, C. C. (Leics. & Notts.) b Feb. 14, 1968

*Lewis, D. M. (Jam.) b Feb. 21, 1946

Lewis, E. J. (Glam. & Sussex) b Jan. 31, 1942

Lewis, J. J. B. (Essex) b May 21, 1970

*Lewis, P. T. (W. Prov.) b Oct. 2, 1884, d Jan. 30, 1976

Lewis, R. V. (Hants) b Aug. 6, 1947

*Leyland, M. (Yorks.; *CY 1929*) b July 20, 1900, d Jan. 1, 1967

*Liaqat Ali (Kar., Sind, HBL & PIA) b May 21, 1955

Lightfoot, A. (Northants) b Jan. 8, 1936

*Lillee, D. K. (W. Aust., Tas. & Northants; *CY 1973*) b July 18, 1949

*Lilley, A. A. (Warwicks.; *CY 1897*) b Nov. 28, 1866, d Nov. 17, 1929

Lilley, A. W. (Essex) b May 8, 1959

Lilley, B. (Notts.) b Feb. 11, 1895, d Aug. 4, 1950

Lillywhite, Fred (Sussex; Editor of *Lillywhite's Guide to Cricketers*) b July 23, 1829, d Sept. 15, 1866

Lillywhite, F. W. ("William") (Sussex) b June 13, 1792, d Aug. 21, 1854

*Lillywhite, James, jun. (Sussex) b Feb. 23, 1842, d Oct. 25, 1929

*Lindsay, D. T. (NE Tvl, N. Tvl & Tvl) b Sept 4, 1939

*Lindsay, J. D. (Tvl & NE Tvl) b Sept. 8, 1909, d Aug. 31, 1990

*Lindsay, N. V. (Tvl & OFS) b July 30, 1886, d Feb. 2, 1976

*Lindwall, R. R. (NSW & Qld; *CY 1949*) b Oct. 3, 1921

*Ling, W. V. S. (Griq. W. & E. Prov.) b Oct. 3, 1891, d Sept. 26, 1960

*Lissette, A. F. (Auck. & N. Dist.) b Nov. 6, 1919, d Jan. 24, 1973

Lister, J. (Yorks. & Worcs.) b May 14, 1930, d Jan. 28, 1991

Lister, W. H. L. (Lancs.) b Oct. 7, 1911

Livingston, L. (NSW & Northants) b May 3, 1920

Livingstone, D. A. (Hants) b Sept. 21, 1933, d Sept. 8, 1988

*Liyanage, D. K. (Colts) b June 6, 1972

*Llewellyn, C. B. (Natal & Hants; *CY 1911*) b Sept. 26, 1876, d June 7, 1964

Llewellyn, M. J. (Glam.) b Nov. 27, 1953

Llong, N. J. (Kent) b Feb. 11, 1969

Lloyd, B. J. (Glam.) b Sept. 6, 1953

*Lloyd, C. H. (†Guyana & Lancs.; *CY 1971*) b Aug. 31, 1944

*Lloyd, D. (Lancs.) b March 18, 1947

Lloyd, G. D. (Lancs.) b July 1, 1969

*Lloyd, T. A. (Warwicks. & OFS) b Nov. 5, 1956

Lloyds, J. W. (Som., OFS & Glos.) b Nov. 17, 1954

*Loader, P. J. (Surrey and W. Aust.; *CY 1958*) b Oct. 25, 1929

Lobb, B. (Warwicks. & Som.) b Jan. 11, 1931

*Lock, G. A. R. (Surrey, Leics. & W. Aust.; *CY 1954*) b July 5, 1929, d March 29, 1995

Lockwood, Ephraim (Yorks.) b April 4, 1845, d Dec. 19, 1921

*Lockwood, W. H. (Notts. & Surrey; *CY 1899*) b March 25, 1868, d April 26, 1932

Lockyer, T. (Surrey & All-England) b Nov. 1, 1826, d Dec. 22, 1869

Logan, J. D. (SA) b June 24, 1880, d Jan. 3, 1960

*Logie, A. L. (T/T) b Sept. 28, 1960

*Lohmann, G. A. (Surrey, W. Prov. & Tvl; *CY 1889*) b June 2, 1865, d Dec. 1, 1901

Lomax, J. G. (Lancs. & Som.) b May 5, 1925, d May 21, 1992

Long, A. (Surrey & Sussex) b Dec. 18, 1940

Lord, G. J. (Warwicks. & Worcs.) b April 25, 1961

Lord, Thomas (Middx; founder of Lord's) b Nov. 23, 1755, d Jan. 13, 1832

*Love, H. S. B. (NSW & Vic.) b Aug. 10, 1895, d July 22, 1969

Love, J. D. (Yorks.) b April 22, 1955

Lovell, G. B. T. (OUCC) b July 11, 1966

*Lowry, T. C. (Wgtn, CUCC & Som.) b Feb. 17, 1898, d July 20, 1976

*Lowson, F. A. (Yorks.) b July 1, 1925, d Sept. 8, 1984

*Loxton, S. J. E. (Vic.) b March 29, 1921

Loye, M. B. (Northants) b Sept. 27, 1972

*Lucas, A. P. (CUCC, Surrey, Middx & Essex) b Feb. 20, 1857, d Oct. 12, 1923

*Luckhurst, B. W. (Kent; *CY 1971*) b Feb. 5, 1939

Lumb, R. G. (Yorks.) b Feb. 27, 1950

*Lundie, E. B. (E. Prov., W. Prov. & Tvl) b March 15, 1888, d Sept. 12, 1917

Lynch, M. A. (Surrey, Guyana & Glos.) b May 21, 1958

Lyon, B. H. (OUCC & Glos.; *CY 1931*) b Jan. 19, 1902, d June 22, 1970

Lyon, J. (Lancs.) b May 17, 1951

Lyon, M. D. (CUCC & Som.) b April 22, 1898, d Feb. 17, 1964

*Lyons, J. J. (S. Aust.) b May 21, 1863, d July 21, 1927

Lyons, K. J. (Glam.) b Dec. 18, 1946

*Lyttelton, Rt Hon. Alfred (CUCC & Middx; Pres. MCC 1898) b Feb. 7, 1857, d July 5, 1913

Lyttelton, Rev. Hon. C. F. (CUCC & Worcs.) b Jan. 26, 1887, d Oct. 3, 1931

Lyttelton, Hon. C. G. (CUCC) b Oct. 27, 1842, d June 9, 1922

Lyttelton, Hon. C. J. (*see* 10th Visct Cobham)

*McAlister, P. A. (Vic.) b July 11, 1869, d May 10, 1938

*Macartney, C. G. (NSW & Otago; *CY 1922*) b June 27, 1886, d Sept. 9, 1958

*Macaulay, G. G. (Yorks.; *CY 1924*) b Dec. 7, 1897, d Dec. 13, 1940

*Macaulay, M. J. (Tvl, W. Prov., OFS, NE Tvl & E. Prov.) b April 19, 1939

*MacBryan, J. C. W. (CUCC & Som.; *CY 1925*) b July 22, 1892, d July 14, 1983

*McCabe, S. J. (NSW; *CY 1935*) b July 16, 1910, d Aug. 25, 1968

*McCague, M. J. (Kent & W. Aust.) b May 24, 1969

McCanlis, M. A. (OUCC, Surrey & Glos.) b June 17, 1906, d Sept. 27, 1991

*McCarthy, C. N. (Natal & CUCC) b March 24, 1929

*McConnon, J. E. (Glam.) b June 21, 1922

*McCool, C. L. (NSW, Qld & Som.) b Dec. 9, 1916, d April 5, 1986

McCorkell, N. T. (Hants) b March 23, 1912

*McCormick, E. L. (Vic.) b May 16, 1906, d June 28, 1991

*McCosker, R. B. (NSW; *CY 1976*) b Dec. 11, 1946

McCurdy, R. J. (Vic., Derbys., S. Aust., E. Prov. & Natal) b Dec. 30, 1959

*McDermott, C. J. (Qld; *CY 1986*) b April 14, 1965

*McDonald, C. C. (Vic.) b Nov. 17, 1928

*McDonald, E. A. (Tas., Vic. & Lancs.; *CY 1922*) b Jan. 6, 1891, d July 22, 1937

*McDonnell, P. S. (Vic., NSW & Qld) b Nov. 13, 1858, d Sept. 24, 1896

McEvoy, M. S. A. (Essex & Worcs.) b Jan. 25, 1956

McEwan, K. S. (E. Prov., W. Prov., Essex & W. Aust; *CY 1978*) b July 16, 1952

*McEwan, P. E. (Cant.) b Dec. 19, 1953

McEwan, S. M. (Worcs. & Durham) b May 5, 1962

McFarlane, L. L. (Northants, Lancs. & Glam.) b Aug. 19, 1952

*McGahey, C. P. (Essex; *CY 1902*) b Feb. 12, 1871, d Jan. 10, 1935

*MacGibbon, A. R. (Cant.) b Aug. 28, 1924

*McGirr, H. M. (Wgtn) b Nov. 5, 1891, d April 14, 1964

*McGlew, D. J. (Natal; *CY 1956*) b March 11, 1929

*McGrath, G. D. (NSW) b Feb. 9, 1970

*MacGregor, G. (CUCC & Middx; *CY 1891*) b Aug. 31, 1869, d Aug. 20, 1919

*McGregor, S. N. (Otago) b Dec. 18, 1931

McHugh, F. P. (Yorks. & Glos.) b Nov. 15, 1925

*McIlwraith, J. (Vic.) b Sept. 7, 1857, d July 5, 1938

Macindoe, D. H. (OUCC) b Sept. 1, 1917, d March 3, 1986

*McIntyre, A. J. W. (Surrey; *CY 1958*) b May 14, 1918

*McIntyre, P. E. (S. Aust.) b April 27, 1966

*Mackay, K. D. (Qld) b Oct. 24, 1925, d June 13, 1982

McKechnie, B. J. (Otago) b Nov. 6, 1953

*McKenzie, G. D. (W. Aust. & Leics.; *CY 1965*) b June 24, 1941

*McKibbin, T. R. (NSW) b Dec. 10, 1870, d Dec. 15, 1939

*McKinnon, A. H. (E. Prov. & Tvl) b Aug. 20, 1932, d Dec. 2, 1983

*MacKinnon, F. A. (CUCC & Kent) b April 9, 1848, d Feb. 27, 1947

*MacLaren, A. C. (Lancs.; *CY 1895*) b Dec. 1, 1871, d Nov. 17, 1944

*McLaren, J. W. (Qld) b Dec. 24, 1887, d Nov. 17, 1921

*Maclean, J. A. (Qld) b April 27, 1946

Maclean, J. F. (Worcs. & Glos.) b March 1, 1901, d March 9, 1986

*McLean, R. A. (Natal; *CY 1961*) b July 9, 1930

MacLeay, K. H. (W. Aust. & Som.) b April 2, 1959

*McLeod, C. E. (Vic.) b Oct. 24, 1869, d Nov. 26, 1918

*McLeod, E. G. (Auck. & Wgtn) b Oct. 14, 1900, d Sept. 14, 1989

*McLeod, R. W. (Vic.) b Jan. 19, 1868, d June 14, 1907

McMahon, J. W. (Surrey & Som.) b Dec. 28, 1919

*McMahon, T. G. (Wgtn) b Nov. 8, 1929

*McMaster, J. E. P. (Eng.) b March 16, 1861, d June 7, 1929

*McMillan, B. M. (Tvl, W. Prov. & Warwicks.) b Dec. 22, 1963

Macmillan, G. I. (OUCC & Leics.) b Aug. 7, 1969

*McMillan, Q. (Tvl) b June 23, 1904, d July 3, 1948

*McMorris, E. D. A. (Jam.) b April 4, 1935

*McRae, D. A. N. (Cant.) b Dec. 25, 1912, d Aug. 10, 1986

*McShane, P. G. (Vic.) b 1857, d Dec. 11, 1903

McSweeney, E. B. (C. Dist. & Wgtn) b March 8, 1957

McVicker, N. M. (Warwicks. & Leics.) b Nov. 4, 1940

*McWatt, C. A. (BG) b Feb. 1, 1922

*Madan Lal (Punjab & Delhi) b March 20, 1951

*Maddocks, L. V. (Vic. & Tas.) b May 24, 1926

*Madray, I. S. (BG) b July 2, 1934

*Madugalle, R. S. (NCC) b April 22, 1959

*Madurasinghe, A. W. R. (Kurunegala) b Jan. 30, 1961

*Maguire, J. N. (Qld, E. Prov. & Leics.) b Sept. 15, 1956

*Mahanama, R. S. (CCC & Bloom.) b May 31, 1966

Maher, B. J. M. (Derbys.) b Feb. 11, 1958

Mahmood Hamid (Kar. & UBL) b Jan. 19, 1969

*Mahmood Hussain (Pak. Us, Punjab, Kar., E. Pak. & NTB) b April 2, 1932, d Dec. 25, 1991

*Mailey, A. A. (NSW) b Jan. 3, 1886, d Dec. 31, 1967

*Majid Khan (Lahore, Pak. Us, CUCC, Glam., PIA, Qld & Punjab; *CY 1970*) b Sept. 28, 1946

*Maka, E. S. (Bombay) b March 5, 1922

*Makepeace, J. W. H. (Lancs.) b Aug. 22, 1881, d Dec. 19, 1952

*Malcolm, D. E. (Derbys.; *CY 1995*) b Feb. 22, 1963

*Malhotra, A. (Haryana & Bengal) b Jan. 26, 1957

*Mallender, N. A. (Northants, Otago & Som.) b Aug. 13, 1961

*Mallett, A. A. (S. Aust.) b July 13, 1945

Mallett, A. W. H. (OUCC & Kent) b Aug. 29, 1924, d Dec. 10, 1994

*Malone, M. F. (W. Aust. & Lancs.) b Oct. 9, 1950

Malone, S. J. (Essex, Hants & Glam.) b Oct. 19, 1953

*Maninder Singh (Delhi) b June 13, 1965

*Manjrekar, S. V. (Bombay) b July 12, 1965

*Manjrekar, V. L. (Bombay, Bengal, Andhra, U. Pradesh, Raja. & M'tra) b Sept. 26, 1931, d Oct. 18, 1983

*Mankad, A. V. (Bombay) b Oct. 12, 1946

*Mankad, V. (M. H.) (W. Ind., Naw., M'tra, Guj., Bengal, Bombay & Raja.; *CY 1947*) b April 12, 1917, d Aug. 21, 1978

*Mann, A. L. (W. Aust.) b Nov. 8, 1945

*Mann, F. G. (CUCC; Middx; Pres. MCC 1984-85) b Sept. 6, 1917

*Mann, F. T. (CUCC & Middx) b March 3, 1888, d Oct. 6, 1964

Mann, J. P. (Middx) b June 13, 1919

*Mann, N. B. F. (Natal & E. Prov.) b Dec. 28, 1920, d July 31, 1952

Manning, J. S. (S. Aust. & Northants) b June 11, 1924, d May 5, 1988

*Mansell, P. N. F. (Rhod.) b March 16, 1920, d May 9, 1995

*Mansoor Akhtar (Kar., UBL & Sind) b Dec. 25, 1956

Mansoor Rana (ADBP & Lahore) b Dec. 27, 1962

Mansur Ali Khan (*see* Pataudi, Mansur Ali, Nawab of)

Mantri, M. K. (Bombay & M'tra) b Sept. 1, 1921

*Manzoor Elahi (Multan, Pak. Rlwys & IDBP) b April 15, 1963

*Maqsood Ahmed (S. Punjab, R'pindi & Kar.) b March 26, 1925

Maqsood Rana (Lahore & NBP) b Aug. 1, 1972

*Marais, G. G. ("G. Gladstone") (Jam.) b Jan. 14, 1901, d May 19, 1978

Marie, G. V. (OUCC) b Feb. 17, 1945

*Markham, L. A. (Natal) b Sept. 12, 1924

*Marks, V. J. (OUCC, Som. & W. Aust.) b June 25, 1955

Marlar, R. G. (CUCC & Sussex) b Jan. 2, 1931

Marner, P. T. (Lancs. & Leics.) b March 31, 1936

*Marr, A. P. (NSW) b March 28, 1862, d March 15, 1904

*Marriott, C. S. (CUCC, Lancs. & Kent) b Sept. 14, 1895, d Oct. 13, 1966

Marsden, Tom (Eng.) b 1805, d Feb. 27, 1843

Marsh, F. E. (Derbys.) b July 7, 1920

*Marsh, G. R. (W. Aust.) b Dec. 31, 1958

*Marsh, R. W. (W. Aust.; *CY 1982*) b Nov. 4, 1947

Marsh, S. A. (Kent) b Jan. 27, 1961

Marshal, Alan (Qld & Surrey; *CY 1909*) b June 12, 1883, d July 23, 1915

Marshall, J. M. A. (Warwicks.) b Oct. 26, 1916

*Marshall, M. D. (B'dos, Hants & Natal; *CY 1983*) b April 18, 1958

*Marshall, N. E. (B'dos & T/T) b Feb. 27, 1924

*Marshall, R. E. (B'dos & Hants; *CY 1959*) b April 25, 1930, d Oct. 27, 1992

Martin, E. J. (Notts.) b Aug. 17, 1925

*Martin, F. (Kent; *CY 1892*) b Oct. 12, 1861, d Dec. 13, 1921

*Martin, F. R. (Jam.) b Oct. 12, 1893, d Nov. 23, 1967

Martin, G. C. (Mash.) b May 30, 1966

Martin, J. D. (OUCC & Som.) b Dec. 23, 1941

*Martin, J. W. (NSW & S. Aust.) b July 28, 1931, d July 16, 1992

*Martin, J. W. (Kent) b Feb. 16, 1917, d Jan. 4, 1987

*Martin, P. J. (Lancs.) b Nov. 15, 1968

Martin, S. H. (Worcs., Natal & Rhod.) b Jan. 11, 1909, d Feb. 1988

Martindale, D. J. R. (Notts.) b Dec 13, 1963

*Martindale, E. A. (B'dos) b Nov. 25, 1909, d March 17, 1972

*Martyn, D. R. (W. Aust.) b Oct. 21, 1971

Maru, R. J. (Middx & Hants) b Oct. 28, 1962

*Marx, W. F. E. (Tvl) b July 4, 1895, d June 2, 1974

*Mason, J. R. (Kent; *CY 1898*) b March 26, 1874, d Oct. 15, 1958

*Masood Anwar (UBL, Multan & F'bad) b Dec. 12, 1967

Masood Iqbal (Lahore, Punjab U., Pak. Us & HBL) b April 17, 1952

*Massie, H. H. (NSW) b April 11, 1854, d Oct. 12, 1938

*Massie, R. A. L. (W. Aust.; *CY 1973*) b April 14, 1947

*Matheson, A. M. (Auck.) b Feb. 27, 1906, d Dec. 31, 1985

*Mathias, Wallis (Sind, Kar. & NBP) b Feb. 4, 1935, d Sept. 1, 1994

*Matthews, A. D. G. (Northants & Glam.) b May 3, 1904, d July 29, 1977

*Matthews, C. D. (W. Aust. & Lancs.) b Sept. 22, 1962

*Matthews, C. R. (W. Prov.) b Feb. 15, 1965

Matthews, C. S. (Notts.) b Oct. 17, 1931, d March 15, 1990

*Matthews, G. R. J. (NSW) b Dec. 15, 1959

*Matthews, T. J. (Vic.) b April 3, 1884, d Oct. 14, 1943

*Mattis, E. H. (Jam.) b April 11, 1957

*May, P. B. H. (CUCC & Surrey; *CY 1952*; Pres. MCC 1980-81) b Dec. 31, 1929, d Dec. 27, 1994

*May, T. B. A. (S. Aust.) b Jan. 26, 1962

Mayer, J. H. (Warwicks.) b March 2, 1902, d Sept. 6, 1981

Mayes, R. (Kent) b Oct. 7, 1921

Maynard, C. (Warwicks. & Lancs.) b April 8, 1958

*Maynard, M. P. (Glam. & N. Dist.) b March 21, 1966

*Mayne, E. R. (S. Aust. & Vic.) b July 2, 1882, d Oct. 26, 1961

*Mayne, L. C. (W. Aust.) b Jan. 23, 1942

*Mead, C. P. (Hants; *CY 1912*) b March 9, 1887, d March 26, 1958

*Mead, W. (Essex; *CY 1904*) b March 25, 1868, d March 18, 1954

Meads, E. A. (Notts.) b Aug. 17, 1916

*Meale, T. (Wgtn) b Nov. 11, 1928

*Meckiff, I. (Vic.) b Jan. 6, 1935

Medlycott, K. T. (Surrey & N. Tvl) b May 12, 1965

*Meher-Homji, K. R. (W. Ind. & Bombay) b Aug. 9, 1911, d Feb. 10, 1982

*Mehra, V. L. (E. Punjab, Ind. Rlwys & Delhi) b March 12, 1938

*Meintjes, D. J. (Tvl) b June 9, 1890, d July 17, 1979

*Melle, M. G. (Tvl & W. Prov.) b June 3, 1930

Melluish, M. E. L. (CUCC & Middx; Pres. MCC 1991-92) b June 13, 1932

*Melville, A. (OUCC, Sussex, Natal & Tvl; *CY 1948*) b May 19, 1910, d April 18, 1983

Mence, M. D. (Warwicks. & Glos.) b April 13, 1944

Mendis, G. D. (Sussex & Lancs.) b April 20, 1955

*Mendis, L. R. D. (SSC) b Aug. 25, 1952

Mendis, M. C. (Colts) b Dec. 28, 1968

Mendonca, I. L. (BG) b July 13, 1934

Mercer, J. (Sussex, Glam. & Northants; *CY 1927*) b April 22, 1895, d Aug. 31, 1987

*Merchant, V. M. (Bombay; *CY 1937*) b Oct. 12, 1911, d Oct. 27, 1987

Merrick, T. A. (Leewards, Warwicks. & Kent) b June 10, 1963

*Merritt, W. E. (Cant. & Northants) b Aug. 18, 1908, d June 9, 1977

*Merry, C. A. (T/T) b Jan. 20, 1911, d April 19, 1964

Metcalfe, A. A. (Yorks. & OFS) b Dec. 25, 1963

Metson, C. P. (Middx & Glam.) b July 2, 1963

*Meuleman, K. D. (Vic. & W. Aust.) b Sept. 5, 1923

*Meuli, E. M. (C. Dist.) b Feb. 20, 1926

Meyer, B. J. (Glos.; Umpire) b Aug. 21, 1932

Meyer, R. J. O. (CUCC, Som. & W. Ind.) b March 15, 1905, d March 9, 1991

Mian Mohammad Saaed (N. Ind. Patiala & S. Punjab; Pak.'s first captain) b Aug. 31, 1910, d Aug. 23, 1979

*Middleton, J. (W. Prov.) b Sept. 30, 1865, d Dec. 23, 1913

Middleton, T. C. (Hants) b Feb. 1, 1964

**Midwinter, W. E. (Vic. & Glos.) b June 19, 1851, d Dec. 3, 1890

*Milburn, B. D. (Otago) b Nov. 24, 1943

*Milburn, C. (Northants & W. Aust.; *CY 1967*) b Oct. 23, 1941, d Feb. 28, 1990

*Milkha Singh, A. G. (Madras) b Dec. 31, 1941

Miller, A. J. T. (OUCC & Middx) b May 30, 1963

*Miller, A. M. (Eng.) b Oct. 19, 1869, d June 26, 1959

*Miller, G. (Derbys., Natal & Essex) b Sept. 8, 1952

*Miller, K. R. (Vic., NSW & Notts.; *CY 1954*) b Nov. 28, 1919

*Miller, L. S. M. (C. Dist. & Wgtn) b March 31, 1923

Miller, R. (Warwicks.) b Jan. 6, 1941

*Miller, R. C. (Jam.) b Dec. 24, 1924

*Milligan, F. W. (Yorks.) b March 19, 1870, d March 31, 1900

*Millman, G. (Notts.) b Oct. 2, 1934

Millmow, J. P. (Wgtn) b Sept. 22, 1967

Millns, D. J. (Notts. & Leics.) b Feb. 27, 1965

*Mills, C. H. (Surrey, Kimberley & W. Prov.) b Nov. 26, 1867, d July 26, 1948

*Mills, J. E. (Auck.) b Sept. 3, 1905, d Dec. 11, 1972

Mills, J. M. (CUCC & Warwicks.) b July 27, 1921

Mills, J. P. C. (CUCC & Northants) b Dec. 6, 1958

Milner, J. (Essex) b Aug. 22, 1937

*Milton, C. A. (Glos.; *CY 1959*) b March 10, 1928

*Milton, W. H. (W. Prov.) b Dec. 3, 1854, d March 6, 1930

*Minnett, R. B. (NSW) b June 13, 1888, d Oct. 21, 1955

"Minshull", John (scorer of first recorded century) b *circa* 1741, d Oct. 1793

*Miran Bux (Pak. Serv., Punjab & R'pindi) b April 20, 1907, d Feb. 8, 1991

*Misson, F. M. (NSW) b Nov. 19, 1938

*Mitchell, A. (Yorks.) b Sept. 13, 1902, d Dec. 25, 1976

*Mitchell, B. (Tvl; *CY 1936*) b Jan. 8, 1909, d July 1, 1995

Mitchell, C. G. (Som.) b Jan. 27, 1929

**Mitchell, F. (CUCC, Yorks. & Tvl; *CY 1902*) b Aug. 13, 1872, d Oct. 11, 1935

*Mitchell, T. B. (Derbys.) b Sept. 4, 1902, d Jan. 27, 1996

*Mitchell-Innes, N. S. (OUCC & Som.) b Sept. 7, 1914

*Modi, R. S. (Bombay) b Nov. 11, 1924

*Mohammad Aslam (N. Ind. & Pak. Rlwys) b Jan. 5, 1920

*Mohammad Farooq (Kar.) b April 8, 1938

*Mohammad Ilyas (Lahore & PIA) b March 19, 1946

*Mohammad Munaf (Sind, E. Pak., Kar. & PIA) b Nov. 2, 1935

*Mohammad Nazir (Pak. Rlwys) b March 8, 1946

*Mohsin Kamal (Lahore, Allied Bank & PNSC) b June 16, 1963

*Mohsin Khan (Pak. Rlwys, Kar., Sind, Pak. Us & HBL) b March 15, 1955

*Moin Khan (Karachi & PIA) b Sept. 23, 1971

Moin-ul-Atiq (UBL, Karachi & HBL) b Aug. 5, 1964

*Moir, A. McK. (Otago) b July 17, 1919

Moir, D. G. (Derbys. & Scotland) b April 13, 1957

*Mold, A. W. (Lancs.; *CY 1892*) b May 27, 1863, d April 29, 1921

Moles, A. J. (Warwicks. & Griq. W.) b Feb. 12, 1961

*Moloney, D. A. R. (Wgtn, Otago & Cant.) b Aug. 11, 1910, d July 15, 1942

Monckton of Brenchley, 1st Lord (Pres. MCC 1956-57) b Jan. 17, 1891, d Jan. 9, 1965

*Mongia, N. R. (Baroda) b Dec. 19, 1969

Monkhouse, G. (Surrey) b April 26, 1954

Montgomerie, R. R. (OUCC & Northants) b July 3, 1971

*Moodie, G. H. (Jam.) b Nov. 25, 1915

*Moody, T. M. (W. Aust., Warwicks. & Worcs.) b Oct. 2, 1965

*Moon, L. J. (CUCC & Middx) b Feb. 9, 1878, d Nov. 23, 1916

*Mooney, F. L. H. (Wgtn) b May 26, 1921

Moore, D. N. (OUCC & Glos.) b Sept. 26, 1910

Moore, H. I. (Notts.) b Feb. 28, 1941

Moore, R. H. (Hants) b Nov. 14, 1913

Moores, P. (Worcs., Sussex & OFS) b Dec. 18, 1962

*More, K. S. (Baroda) b Sept. 4, 1962

Morgan, D. C. (Derbys.) b Feb. 26, 1929

Morgan, M. (Notts.) b May 21, 1936

Morgan, R. W. (Auck.) b Feb. 12, 1941

*Morkel, D. P. B. (W. Prov.) b Jan. 25, 1906, d Oct. 6, 1980

*Morley, F. (Notts.) b Dec. 16, 1850, d Sept. 28, 1884

Morley, J. D. (Sussex) b Oct. 20, 1950

*Moroney, J. (NSW) b July 24, 1917

*Morris, A. R. (NSW; *CY 1949*) b Jan. 19, 1922

*Morris, H. (Glam.) b Oct. 5, 1963

*Morris, J. E. (Derbys, Griq. W. & Durham) b April 1, 1964

Morris, R. E. (OUCC) b June 8, 1967

*Morris, S. (Vic.) b June 22, 1855, d Sept. 20, 1931

*Morrison, B. D. (Wgtn) b Dec. 17, 1933

*Morrison, D. K. (Auck. & Lancs.) b Feb. 3, 1966

*Morrison, J. F. M. (C. Dist. & Wgtn) b Aug. 27, 1947

Mortensen, O. H. (Denmark & Derbys.) b Jan. 29, 1958

*Mortimore, J. B. (Glos.) b May 14, 1933

Mortlock, W. (Surrey & Utd Eng. XI) b July 18, 1832, d Jan. 23, 1884

*Moseley, E. A. (B'dos, Glam., E. Prov. & N. Tvl) b Jan. 5, 1958

Moseley, H. R. (B'dos & Som.) b May 28, 1948

*Moses, H. (NSW) b Feb. 13, 1858, d Dec. 7, 1938

*Moss, A. E. (Middx) b Nov. 14, 1930

*Moss, J. K. (Vic.) b June 29, 1947

*Motz, R. C. (Cant.; *CY 1966*) b Jan. 12, 1940

Moulding, R. P. (OUCC & Middx) b Jan. 3, 1958

*Moule, W. H. (Vic.) b Jan. 31, 1858, d Aug. 24, 1939

*Moxon, M. D. (Yorks. & Griq. W.; *CY 1993*) b May 4, 1960

*Mudassar Nazar (Lahore, Punjab, Pak. Us, HBL, PIA & UBL) b April 6, 1956

*Muddiah, V. M. (Mysore & Ind. Serv.) b June 8, 1929

*Mufasir-ul-Haq (Kar., Dacca, PWD, E. Pak. & NBP) b Aug. 16, 1944, d July 27, 1983

Mukherjee, S. P. (Bengal) b Oct. 5, 1964

Mullally, A. D. (W. Aust., Vic., Hants & Leics.) b July 12, 1969

Munasinghe, M. (SSC) b Dec. 10, 1971

Munden, V. S. (Leics.) b Jan. 2, 1928

*Munir Malik (Punjab, R'pindi, Pak. Serv. & Kar.) b July 10, 1934

*Munton, T. A. (Warwicks; *CY 1995*) b July 30, 1965

Muralitharan, M. (TU) b April 17, 1972

**Murdoch, W. L. (NSW & Sussex) b Oct. 18, 1854, d Feb. 18, 1911

Murphy, A. J. (Lancs. & Surrey) b Aug. 6, 1962

*Murray, A. R. A. (E. Prov.) b April 30, 1922, d April 17, 1995

*Murray, B. A. G. (Wgtn) b Sept. 18, 1940

*Murray, D. A. (B'dos) b Sept. 29, 1950

*Murray, D. J. (Cant.) b Sept. 4, 1967

*Murray, D. L. (T/T, CUCC, Notts. & Warwicks.) b May 20, 1943

Murray, J. R. (Windwards) b Jan. 20, 1968

*Murray, J. T. (Middx; *CY 1967*) b April 1, 1935

Murray-Willis, P. E. (Worcs. & Northants) b July 14, 1910, d Jan. 7, 1995

Murrell, H. R. (Kent & Middx) b Nov. 19, 1879, d Aug. 15, 1952

Murrills, T. J. (CUCC) b Dec. 22, 1953

*Musgrove, H. (Vic.) b Nov. 27, 1860, d Nov. 2, 1931

*Mushtaq Ahmed (UBL, Multan & Som.) b June 28, 1970

*Mushtaq Ali, S. (C. Ind., Guj., †M. Pradesh & U. Pradesh) b Dec. 17, 1914

*Mushtaq Mohammad (Kar., Northants & PIA; *CY 1963*) b Nov. 22, 1943

Mynn, Alfred (Kent & All-Eng.) b Jan. 19, 1807, d Oct. 31, 1861

*Nadkarni, R. G. (M'tra & Bombay) b April 4, 1932

*Nadeem Abbasi (R'pindi) b April 15, 1964

*Nadeem Ghauri (Lahore, Pak. Rlways & HBL) b Oct 12, 1962

*Nadeem Khan (Kar. & NBP) b Dec. 10, 1969

Naeem Ahmed (Kar., Pak. Us, NBP, UBL & PIA) b Sept. 20, 1952

Naeem Ahmed (Sargodha & HBL) b April 14, 1971

Naeem Ashraf (Lahore & NBP) b Nov. 10, 1972

*Nagel, L. E. (Vic.) b March 6, 1905, d Nov. 23, 1971

*Naik, S. S. (Bombay) b Feb. 21, 1945

*Nanan, R. (T/T) b May 29, 1953

*Naoomal Jaoomal, M. (N. Ind. & Sind) b April 17, 1904, d July 18, 1980

*Narasimha Rao, M. V. (H'bad) b Aug. 11, 1954

Naseer Malik (Khairpair & NBP) b Feb. 1, 1950

*Nash, D. J. (N. Dist., Otago & Middx) b Nov. 20, 1971

*Nash, L. J. (Tas. & Vic.) b May 2, 1910, d July 24, 1986

Nash, M. A. (Glam.) b May 9, 1945

*Nasim-ul-Ghani (Kar., Pak. Us, Dacca, E. Pak., PWD & NBP) b May 14, 1941

*Naushad Ali (Kar., E. Pak., R'pindi, Peshawar, NWFP, Punjab & Pak. Serv.) b Oct. 1, 1943

*Naved Anjum (Lahore, UBL & HBL) b July 27, 1963

*Navle, J. G. (Rajputna, C. Ind., Holkar & Gwalior) b Dec. 7, 1902, d Sept. 7, 1979

*Nayak, S. V. (Bombay) b Oct. 20, 1954

*Nayudu, Col. C. K. (C. Ind., Andhra, U. Pradesh & Holkar; *CY 1933*) b Oct. 31, 1895, d Nov. 14, 1967

*Nayudu, C. S. (C. Ind., Holkar, Baroda, Bengal, Andhra & U. Pradesh) b April 18, 1914

*Nazar Mohammad (N. Ind. & Punjab) b March 5, 1921

*Nazir Ali, S. (S. Punjab & Sussex) b June 8, 1906, d Feb. 18, 1975

Neale, P. A. (Worcs.; *CY 1989*) b June 5, 1954

*Neblett, J. M. (B'dos & BG) b Nov. 13, 1901, d March 28, 1959

Needham, A. (Surrey & Middx) b March 23, 1957

*Nel, J. D. (W. Prov.) b July 10, 1928

Nevell, W. T. (Middx, Surrey & Northants) b June 13, 1916

*Newberry, C. (Tvl) b 1889, d Aug. 1, 1916

Newell, M. (Notts.) b Feb. 25, 1965

*Newham, W. (Sussex) b Dec 12, 1860, d June 26, 1944

Newland, Richard (Sussex) b *circa* 1718, d May 29, 1791

*Newman, Sir J. (Wgtn & Cant.) b July 3, 1902

Newman, J. A. (Hants & Cant.) b Nov. 12, 1884, d Dec. 21, 1973

Newman, P. G. (Derbys.) b Jan. 10, 1959

*Newport, P. J. (Worcs., Boland & N. Tvl) b Oct. 11, 1962

*Newson, E. S. (Tvl & Rhod.) b Dec. 2, 1910, d April 24, 1988

Newstead, J. T. (Yorks.; *CY 1909*) b Sept. 8, 1877, d March 25, 1952

*Niaz Ahmed (Dacca, PWD, E. Pak. & Pak. Rlwys) b Nov. 11, 1945

Nicholas, M. C. J. (Hants) b Sept. 29, 1957

Nicholls, D. (Kent) b Dec. 8, 1943

Nicholls, R. B. (Glos.) b Dec. 4, 1933, d July 21, 1994

*Nichols, M. S. (Essex; *CY 1934*) b Oct. 6, 1900, d Jan. 26, 1961

*Nicholson, F. (Griq. W.) b Sept. 17, 1909, d July 30, 1982

*Nicholson, J. F. W. (Natal & OUCC) b July 19, 1899, d Dec. 13, 1935

*Nissar, Mahomed (Patiala, S. Punjab & U. Pradesh) b Aug. 1, 1910, d March 11, 1963

Nixon, P. A. (Leics.) b Oct. 21, 1970

*Noble, M. A. (NSW; *CY 1900*) b Jan. 28, 1873, d June 22, 1940

*Noblet, G. (S. Aust.) b Sept. 14, 1916

Noon, W. M. (Northants & Notts.) b Feb. 5, 1971

*Noreiga, J. M. (T/T) b April 15, 1936

Norfolk, 16th Duke of (Pres. MCC 1957-58) b May 30, 1908, d Jan. 31, 1975

Norman, M. E. J. C. (Northants & Leics.) b Jan. 19, 1933

*Norton, N. O. (W. Prov. & Border) b May 11, 1881, d June 27, 1968

*Nothling, O. E. (NSW & Qld) b Aug. 1, 1900, d Sept. 26, 1965

*Nourse, A. D. ("Dudley") (Natal; *CY 1948*) b Nov. 12, 1910, d Aug. 14, 1981

*Nourse, A. W. ("Dave") (Natal, Tvl & W. Prov.) b Jan. 26, 1878, d July 8, 1948

Nugent, 1st Lord (Pres. MCC 1962-63) b Aug. 11, 1895, d April 27, 1973

*Nunes, R. K. (Jam.) b June 7, 1894, d July 22, 1958

*Nupen, E. P. (Tvl) b Jan. 1, 1902, d Jan. 29, 1977

*Nurse, S. M. (B'dos; *CY 1967*) b Nov. 10, 1933

Nutter, A. E. (Lancs. & Northants) b June 28, 1913

*Nyalchand, S. (W. Ind., Kathiawar, Guj. & S'tra) b Sept. 14, 1919

Nye, J. K. (Sussex) b May 23, 1914

Nyren, John (Hants) b Dec. 15, 1764, d June 28, 1837

Nyren, Richard (Hants & Sussex) b 1734, d April 25, 1797

Oakes, C. (Sussex) b Aug. 10, 1912

Oakes, J. (Sussex) b March 3, 1916
*Oakman, A. S. M. (Sussex) b April 20, 1930
Oates, T. W. (Notts.) b Aug. 9, 1875, d June 18, 1949
Oates, W. F. (Yorks. & Derbys.) b June 11, 1929
O'Brien, F. P. (Cant. & Northants) b Feb. 11, 1911, d Oct. 22, 1991
*O'Brien, L. P. J. (Vic.) b July 2, 1907
*O'Brien, Sir T. C. (OUCC & Middx) b Nov. 5, 1861, d Dec. 9, 1948
*Ochse, A. E. (Tvl) b March 11, 1870, d April 11, 1918
*Ochse, A. L. (E. Prov.) b Oct. 11, 1899, d May 6, 1949
*O'Connor, J. (Essex) b Nov. 6, 1897, d Feb. 22, 1977
*O'Connor, J. D. A. (NSW & S. Aust.) b Sept. 9, 1875, d Aug. 23, 1941
*O'Donnell, S. P. (Vic.) b Jan. 26, 1963
*Ogilvie, A. D. (Qld) b June 3, 1951
O'Gorman, T. J. G. (Derbys.) b May 15, 1967
*O'Keeffe, K. J. (NSW & Som.) b Nov. 25, 1949
*Old, C. M. (Yorks., Warwicks. & N. Tvl; *CY 1979*) b Dec. 22, 1948
*Oldfield, N. (Lancs. & Northants) b April 30, 1911
*Oldfield, W. A. (NSW; *CY 1927*) b Sept. 9, 1894, d Aug. 10, 1976
Oldham, S. (Yorks. & Derbys.) b July 26, 1948
Oldroyd, E. (Yorks.) b Oct. 1, 1888, d Dec. 27, 1964
*O'Linn, S. (Kent, W. Prov. & Tvl) b May 5, 1927
Oliver, P. R. (Warwicks.) b May 9, 1956
*Olonga, H. K. (Mat.) b July 3, 1976
*O'Neill, N. C. (NSW; *CY 1962*) b Feb. 19, 1937
Ontong, R. C. (Border, Tvl, N. Tvl & Glam.) b Sept. 9, 1955
Opatha, A. R. M. (SL) b Aug. 5, 1947
Ord, J. S. (Warwicks.) b July 12, 1912
*O'Reilly, W. J. (NSW; *CY 1935*) b Dec. 20, 1905, d Oct. 6, 1992
O'Riordan, A. J. (Ireland) b July 20, 1940
Ormrod, J. A. (Worcs. & Lancs.) b Dec. 22, 1942
O'Shaughnessy, S. J. (Lancs. & Worcs.) b Sept. 9, 1961
Oslear, D. O. (Umpire) b March 3, 1929
Ostler, D. P. (Warwicks.) b July 15, 1970
*O'Sullivan, D. R. (C. Dist. & Hants) b Nov. 16, 1944
Outschoorn, L. (Worcs.) b Sept. 26, 1918, d Jan. 9, 1994
*Overton, G. W. F. (Otago) b June 8, 1919, d. Sept. 7, 1993
*Owens, M. B. (Cant.) b Nov. 11, 1969

*Owen-Smith, H. G. (W. Prov., OUCC & Middx; *CY 1930*) b Feb. 18, 1909, d Feb. 28, 1990
Owen-Thomas, D. R. (CUCC & Surrey) b Sept. 20, 1948
*Oxenham, R. K. (Qld) b July 28, 1891, d Aug. 16, 1939

*Padgett, D. E. V. (Yorks.) b July 20, 1934
*Padmore, A. L. (B'dos) b Dec. 17, 1946
Page, H. A. (Tvl, Essex & Griq. W.) b July 3, 1962
Page, J. C. T. (Kent) b May 20, 1930, d Dec. 14, 1990
Page, M. H. (Derbys.) b June 17, 1941
*Page, M. L. (Cant.) b May 8, 1902, d Feb. 13, 1987
*Pai, A. M. (Bombay) b April 28, 1945
*Paine, G. A. E. (Middx & Warwicks.; *CY 1935*) b June 11, 1908, d March 30, 1978
*Pairaudeau, B. H. (BG & N. Dist.) b April 14, 1931
*Palairet, L. C. H. (OUCC & Som.; *CY 1893*) b May 27, 1870, d March 27, 1933
Palairet, R. C. N. (OUCC & Som.; Joint-Manager MCC in Australia 1932-33) b June 25, 1871, d Feb. 11, 1955
*Palm, A. W. (W. Prov.) b June 8, 1901, d Aug. 17, 1966
*Palmer, C. H. (Worcs. & Leics.; Pres. MCC 1978-79) b May 15, 1919
*Palmer, G. E. (Vic. & Tas.) b Feb. 22, 1859, d Aug. 22, 1910
Palmer, G. V. (Som.) b Nov. 1, 1965
*Palmer, K. E. (Som.; Umpire) b April 22, 1937
Palmer, R. (Som.) b July 12, 1942
*Pandit, C. S. (Bombay) b Sept. 30, 1961
Pardon, Charles Frederick (Editor of *Wisden* 1887-90) b March 28, 1850, d April 18, 1890
Pardon, Sydney H. (Editor of *Wisden* 1891-1925) b Sept. 23, 1855, d Nov. 20, 1925
*Parfitt, P. H. (Middx; *CY 1963*) b Dec. 8, 1936
Paris, C. G. A. (Hants; Pres. MCC 1975-76) b Aug. 20, 1911
Parish, R. J. (Aust. Administrator) b May 7, 1916
*Park, R. L. (Vic.) b July 30, 1892, d Jan. 23, 1947
*Parkar, G. A. (Bombay) b Oct. 24, 1955
*Parkar, R. D. (Bombay) b Oct. 31, 1946
Parkar, Z. (Bombay) b Nov. 22, 1957
*Parker, C. W. L. (Glos.; *CY 1923*) b Oct. 14, 1882, d July 11, 1959
*Parker, G. M. (SA) b May 27, 1899, d May 1, 1969
Parker, G. W. (CUCC & Glos.) b Feb. 11, 1912, d Nov. 11, 1995
Parker, J. F. (Surrey) b April 23, 1913, d Jan. 27, 1983

*Parker, J. M. (N. Dist. & Worcs.) b Feb. 21, 1951

*Parker, N. M. (Otago & Cant.) b Aug. 28, 1948

*Parker, P. W. G. (CUCC, Sussex, Natal & Durham) b Jan. 15, 1956

*Parkhouse, W. G. A. (Glam.) b Oct. 12, 1925

*Parkin, C. H. (Yorks. & Lancs.; *CY 1924*) b Feb. 18, 1886, d June 15, 1943

*Parkin, D. C. (E. Prov., Tvl & Griq. W.) b Feb. 18, 1870, d March 20, 1936

Parks, H. W. (Sussex) b July 18, 1906, d May 7, 1984

*Parks, J. H. (Sussex & Cant.; *CY 1938*) b May 12, 1903, d Nov. 21, 1980

*Parks, J. M. (Sussex & Som.; *CY 1968*) b Oct. 21, 1931

Parks, R. J. (Hants & Kent) b June 15, 1959

*Parore, A. C. (Auck.) b Jan. 23, 1971

Parr, F. D. (Lancs.) b June 1, 1928

Parr, George (Notts. & All-England) b May 22, 1826, d June 23, 1891

*Parry, D. R. (Comb. Is. & Leewards) b Dec. 22, 1954

*Parsana, D. D. (S'tra, Ind. Rlwys & Guj.) b Dec. 2, 1947

Parsons, A. B. D. (CUCC & Surrey) b Sept. 20, 1933

Parsons, A. E. W. (Auck. & Sussex) b Jan. 9, 1949

Parsons, G. J. (Leics., Warwicks., Boland, Griq. W. & OFS) b Oct. 17, 1959

Parsons, Canon J. H. (Warwicks.) b May 30, 1890, d Feb. 2, 1981

Parsons, K. A. (Som.) b May 2, 1973

*Partridge, J. T. (Rhod.) b Dec. 9, 1932, d June 7, 1988

Partridge, N. E. (Malvern, CUCC & Warwicks.; *CY 1919*) b Aug. 10, 1900, d March 10, 1982

Partridge, R. J. (Northants) b Feb. 11, 1912

Parvez Mir (R'pindi, Lahore, Punjab, Pak. Us, Derbys., HBL & Glam.) b Sept. 24, 1953

*Pascoe, L. S. (NSW) b Feb. 13, 1950

Pasqual, S. P. (SL) b Oct. 15, 1961

*Passailaigue, C. C. (Jam.) b Aug. 1902, d Jan. 7, 1972

*Patankar, C. T. (Bombay) b Nov. 24, 1930

**Pataudi, Iftikhar Ali, Nawab of (OUCC, Worcs., Patiala, N. Ind. & S. Punjab; *CY 1932*) b March 16, 1910, d Jan. 5, 1952

*Pataudi, Mansur Ali, Nawab of (Sussex, OUCC, Delhi & H'bad; *CY 1968*) b Jan. 5, 1941

Patel, A. K. (S'tra) b March 6, 1957

*Patel, B. P. (Karn.) b Nov. 24, 1952

*Patel, D. N. (Worcs. & Auck.) b Oct. 25, 1958

*Patel, J. M. (Guj.) b Nov. 26, 1924, d Dec. 12, 1992

Patel, M. M. (Kent) b July 7, 1970

*Patel, R. (Baroda) b June 1, 1964

Pathmanathan, G. (OUCC, CUCC & SL) b Jan. 23, 1954

*Patil, S. M. (Bombay & M. Pradesh) b Aug. 18, 1956

*Patil, S. R. (M'tra) b Oct. 10, 1933

*Patterson, B. P. (Jam., Tas. & Lancs.) b Sept. 15, 1961

Pauline, D. B. (Surrey & Glam.) b Dec. 15, 1960

Pawson, A. G. (OUCC & Worcs.) b May 30, 1888, d Feb. 25, 1986

Pawson, H. A. (OUCC & Kent) b Aug. 22, 1921

Payn, L. W. (Natal) b May 6, 1915, d May 2, 1992

*Payne, T. R. O. (B'dos) b Feb. 13, 1957

*Paynter, E. (Lancs.; *CY 1938*) b Nov. 5, 1901, d Feb. 5, 1979

Payton, W. R. D. (Notts.) b Feb. 13, 1882, d May 2, 1943

*Peall, S. G. (MCD) b Sept. 2, 1969

Pearce, G. (Sussex) b Oct. 27, 1908, d June 16, 1986

Pearce, T. N. (Essex) b Nov. 3, 1905, d April 10, 1994

*Pearse, C. O. C. (Natal) b Oct. 10, 1884, d May 7, 1953

Pearson, D. B. (Worcs.) b March 29, 1937

*Peate, E. (Yorks.) b March 2, 1855, d March 11, 1900

Peck, I. G. (CUCC & Northants) b Oct. 18, 1957

*Peebles, I. A. R. (OUCC, Middx & Scotland; *CY 1931*) b Jan. 20, 1908, d Feb. 28, 1980

*Peel, R. (Yorks.; *CY 1889*) b Feb. 12, 1857, d Aug. 12, 1941

*Pegler, S. J. (Tvl) b July 28, 1888, d Sept. 10, 1972

*Pellew, C. E. (S. Aust.) b Sept. 21, 1893, d May 9, 1981

Penberthy, A. L. (Northants) b Sept. 1, 1969

Penn, C. (Kent) b June 19, 1963

*Penn, F. (Kent) b March 7, 1851, d Dec. 26, 1916

Penney, T. L. (Boland, Warwicks. & Mash.) b June 11, 1968

*Pepper, C. G. (NSW & Aust. Serv.; Umpire) b Sept. 15, 1916, d March 24, 1993

Perera, K. G. (Mor.) b May 22, 1964

Perkins, G. C. (Northants) b June 4, 1911

Perkins, H. (CUCC & Cambs.; Sec. MCC 1876-97) b Dec. 10, 1832, d May 6, 1916

*Perks, R. T. D. (Worcs.) b Oct. 4, 1911, d Nov. 22, 1977

Perrin, P. A. (Essex; *CY 1905*) b May 26, 1876, d Nov. 20, 1945

Perryman, S. P. (Warwicks. & Worcs.) b Oct. 22, 1955

*Pervez Sajjad (Lahore, PIA & Kar.) b Aug. 30, 1942

*Petherick, P. J. (Otago & Wgtn) b Sept. 25, 1942

*Petrie, E. C. (Auck. & N. Dist.) b May 22, 1927

Petrie, R. G. (Cant. & Wgtn) b Aug. 23, 1967

*Phadkar, D. G. (M'tra, Bombay, Bengal & Ind. Rlwys) b Dec. 10, 1925, d March 17, 1985

Phebey, A. H. (Kent) b Oct. 1, 1924

Phelan, P. J. (Essex) b Feb. 9, 1938

*Philipson, H. (OUCC & Middx) b June 8, 1866, d Dec. 4, 1935

*Phillip, N. (Comb. Is., Windwards & Essex) b June 12, 1948

Phillips, R. B. (NSW & Qld) b May 23, 1954

*Phillips, W. B. (S. Aust.) b March 1, 1958

*Phillips, W. N. (Vic.) b Nov. 7, 1962

Phillipson, C. P. (Sussex) b Feb. 10, 1952

Phillipson, W. E. (Lancs.) b Dec. 3, 1910, d Aug. 24, 1991

*Philpott, P. I. (NSW) b Nov. 21, 1934

Piachaud, J. D. (OUCC, Hants & Ceylon) b March 1, 1937

Pick, R. A. (Notts. & Wgtn) b Nov. 19, 1963

Pickles, C. S. (Yorks.) b Jan. 30, 1966

Pickles, L. (Som.) b Sept. 17, 1932

Pienaar, R. F. (Tvl, W. Prov., N. Tvl & Kent) b July 17, 1961

Pieris, H. S. M. (SL) b Feb. 16, 1946

*Pierre, L. R. (T/T) b June 5, 1921, d April 14, 1989

Pierson, A. R. K. (Warwicks. & Leics.) b July 21, 1963

*Pigott, A. C. S. (Sussex, Wgtn & Surrey) b June 4, 1958

Pilch, Fuller (Norfolk & Kent) b March 17, 1804, d May 1, 1870

Pilling, H. (Lancs.) b Feb. 23, 1943

*Pilling, R. (Lancs.; *CY 1891*) b July 5, 1855, d March 28, 1891

Piper, K. J. (Warwicks.) b Dec. 18, 1969

*Pithey, A. J. (Rhod. & W. Prov.) b July 17, 1933

*Pithey, D. B. (Rhod., OUCC, Northants, W. Prov., Natal & Tvl) b Oct. 4, 1936

Pitman, R. W. C. (Hants) b Feb. 21, 1933

*Place, W. (Lancs.) b Dec 7, 1914

Platt, R. K. (Yorks. & Northants) b Dec. 21, 1932

*Playle, W. R. (Auck. & W. Aust.) b Dec. 1, 1938

Pleass, J. E. (Glam.) b May 21, 1923

*Plimsoll, J. B. (W. Prov. & Natal) b Oct. 27, 1917

*Pocock, B. A. (N. Dist.) b June 18, 1971

Pocock, N. E. J. (Hants) b Dec. 15, 1951

*Pocock, P. I. (Surrey & N. Tvl) b Sept. 24, 1946

Pollard, P. R. (Notts.) b Sept. 24, 1968

*Pollard, R. (Lancs.) b June 19, 1912, d Dec. 16, 1985

*Pollard, V. (C. Dist. & Cant.) b Burnley Sept. 7, 1945

Pollock, A. J. (CUCC) b April 19, 1962

*Pollock, P. M. (E. Prov.; *CY 1966*) b June 30, 1941

*Pollock, R. G. (E. Prov. & Tvl; *CY 1966*) b Feb. 27, 1944

*Ponsford, W. H. (Vic.; *CY 1935*) b Oct. 19, 1900, d April 6, 1991

Pont, K. R. (Essex) b Jan. 16, 1953

Ponting, R. T. (Tas.) b Dec. 19, 1974

*Poole, C. J. (Notts.) b March 13, 1921

Pooley, J. C. (Middx) b Aug. 8, 1969

Pooley, E. (Surrey & first England tour) b Feb. 13, 1838, d July 18, 1907

*Poore, M. B. (Cant.) b June 1, 1930

*Poore, Brig-Gen. R. M. (Hants & SA; *CY 1900*) b March 20, 1866, d July 14, 1938

Pope, A. V. (Derbys.) b Aug. 15, 1909

*Pope, G. H. (Derbys.) b Jan. 27, 1911, d Oct. 29, 1993

*Pope, R. J. (NSW) b Feb. 18, 1864, d July 27, 1952

Popplewell, N. F. M. (CUCC & Som.) b Aug. 8, 1957

Portal of Hungerford, 1st Lord (Pres. MCC 1958-59) b May 21, 1893, d April 22, 1971

Porter, A. (Glam.) b March 25, 1914, d Feb. 20, 1994

Porter, G. D. (W. Aust.) b March 18, 1955

Pothecary, A. E. (Hants) b March 1, 1906, d May 21, 1991

*Pothecary, J. E. (W. Prov.) b Dec. 6, 1933

Potter, G. (Sussex) b Oct. 26, 1931

Potter, L. (Kent, Griq. W., Leics. & OFS) b Nov. 7, 1962

*Pougher, A. D. (Leics.) b April 19, 1865, d May 20, 1926

Pountain, F. R. (Sussex) b April 23, 1941

*Powell, A. W. (Griq. W.) b July 18, 1873, d Sept. 11, 1948

*Prabhakar, M. (Delhi & Durham) b April 15, 1963

Prasad, B. K. V. (Karn.) b Aug. 5, 1969

*Prasanna, E. A. S. (†Karn.) b May 22, 1940

Pratt, R. L. (Leics.) b Nov. 15, 1938

Pressdee, J. S. (Glam. & NE Tvl) b June 19, 1933

Preston, Hubert (Editor of *Wisden* 1944-51) b Dec. 16, 1868, d Aug. 6, 1960

Preston, K. C. (Essex) b Aug. 22, 1925

Preston, Norman (Editor of *Wisden* 1952-80) b March 18, 1903, d March 6, 1980

Pretlove, J. F. (CUCC & Kent) b Nov. 23, 1932

Price, D. G. (CUCC) b Feb. 7, 1965

Price, E. J. (Lancs. & Essex) b Oct. 27, 1918

*Price, J. S. E. (Middx) b July 22, 1937

*Price, W. F. F. (Middx) b April 25, 1902, d Jan. 13, 1969

Prichard, P. J. (Essex) b Jan. 7, 1965

*Prideaux, R. M. (CUCC, Kent, Northants, Sussex & OFS) b July 31, 1939

Pridgeon, A. P. (Worcs.) b Feb. 22, 1954

*Priest, M. W. (Cant.) b Aug. 12, 1961

*Prince, C. F. H. (W. Prov., Border & E. Prov.) b Sept. 11, 1874, d March 5, 1948

*Pringle, C. (Auck.) b Jan. 26, 1968

*Pringle, D. R. (CUCC & Essex) b Sept. 18, 1958

*Pringle, M. W. (W. Prov.) b June 22, 1966

Pritchard, T. L. (Wgtn, Warwicks. & Kent) b March 10, 1917

*Procter, M. J. (Glos., Natal, W. Prov., Rhod. & OFS; *CY 1970*) b Sept. 15, 1946

Prodger, J. M. (Kent) b Sept. 1, 1935

*Promnitz, H. L. E. (Border, Griq. W. & OFS) b Feb. 23, 1904, d Sept. 7, 1983

Prouton, R. O. (Hants) b March 1, 1926

Pugh, C. T. M. (Glos.) b March 13, 1937

Pullan, D. A. (Notts.) b May 1, 1944

*Pullar, G. (Lancs. & Glos.; *CY 1960*) b Aug. 1, 1935

*Puna, N. (N. Dist.) b Oct. 28, 1929

*Punjabi, P. H. (Sind & Guj.) b Sept. 20, 1921

*Pushpakumara, K. R. (NCC) b July 21, 1975

*Pycroft, A. J. (Zimb.) b June 6, 1956

Pydanna, M. R. (Guyana), b Jan. 27, 1950

*Qasim Omar (Kar. & MCB) b Feb. 9, 1957

Quaife, B. W. (Warwicks. & Worcs.) b Nov. 24, 1899, d Nov. 28, 1984

*Quaife, William (W. G.) (Warwicks. & Griq. W.; *CY 1902*) b March 17, 1872, d Oct. 13, 1951

*Quinn, N. A. (Griq. W. & Tvl) b Feb. 21, 1908, d Aug. 5, 1934

*Rabone, G. O. (Wgtn & Auck.) b Nov. 6, 1921

*Rackemann, C. G. (Qld & Surrey) b June 3, 1960

*Radford, N. V. (Lancs., Tvl & Worcs.; *CY 1986*) b June 7, 1957

*Radley, C. T. (Middx; *CY 1979*) b May 13, 1944

Rae, A. F. (Jam.) b Sept. 30, 1922

Raees Mohammad (Kar.) b Dec. 24, 1932

*Rai Singh, K. (S. Punjab & Ind. Serv.) b Feb. 24, 1922

Rait Kerr, Col. R. S. (Sec. MCC 1936-52) b April 13, 1891, d April 2, 1961

Rajadurai, B. E. A. (SSC) b Aug. 24, 1965

*Rajindernath, V. (N. Ind., U. Prov., S. Punjab, Bihar & E. Punjab) b Jan. 7, 1928, d Nov. 22, 1989

*Rajinder Pal (Delhi, S. Punjab & Punjab) b Nov. 18, 1937

*Rajput, L. S. (Bombay) b Dec. 18, 1961

*Raju, S. L. V. (H'bad) b July 9, 1969

Ralph, L. H. R. (Essex) b May 22, 1920

*Ramadhin, S. (T/T & Lancs.; *CY 1951*) b May 1, 1929

*Raman, W. V. (TN) b May 23, 1965

*Ramanayake, C. P. H. (TU) b Jan. 8, 1965

*Ramaswami, C. (Madras) b June 18, 1896, presumed dead

*Ramchand, G. S. (Sind, Bombay & Raja.) b July 26, 1927

*Ramiz Raja (Lahore, Allied Bank, PNSC & I'bad) b July 14, 1962

*Ramji, L. (W. Ind.) b 1902 d Dec. 20, 1948

*Ramprakash, M. R. (Middx) b Sept. 5, 1969

Ramsamooj, D. (T/T & Northants) b July 5, 1932, d May 24, 1994

*Ranasinghe, A. N. (BRC) b Oct. 13, 1956

Ranasinghe, S. K. (SL) b July 4, 1962

*Ranatunga, A. (SSC) b Dec. 1, 1963

*Ranatunga, D. (SSC) b Oct. 12, 1962

Ranatunga, N. (Colts) b Jan. 22, 1966

*Ranatunga, S. (Colts & NCC) b April 25, 1969

*Ranchod, U. (Mash.) b May 17, 1969

*Randall, D. W. (Notts.; *CY 1980*) b Feb. 24, 1951

Randhir Singh (Orissa & Bihar) b Aug. 16, 1957

*Rangachari, C. R. (Madras) b April 14, 1916, d Oct. 9, 1993

*Rangnekar, K. M. (M'tra, Bombay & †M. Pradesh) b June 27, 1917, d Oct. 11, 1984

*Ranjane, V. B. (M'tra & Ind. Rlwys) b July 22, 1937

*Ranjitsinhji, K. S., afterwards H. H. the Jam Sahib of Nawanagar (CUCC & Sussex; *CY 1897*) b Sept. 10, 1872, d April 2, 1933

*Ransford, V. S. (Vic.; *CY 1910*) b March 20, 1885, d March 19, 1958

Ransom, V. J. (Hants & Surrey) b March 17, 1918

*Rashid Khan (PWD, Kar. & PIA) b Dec. 15, 1959

*Rashid Latif (Kar. & UBL) b Oct. 14, 1968

Ratcliffe, J. D. (Warwicks. & Surrey) b June 19, 1969

Ratcliffe, R. M. (Lancs.) b Oct. 29, 1951

Ratnayake, N. L. K. (SSC) b Nov. 22, 1968

*Ratnayake, R. J. (NCC) b Jan. 2, 1964

*Ratnayeke, J. R. (NCC) b May 2, 1960

Rawson, P. W. E. (Zimb. & Natal) b May 25, 1957

Rayment, A. W. H. (Hants) b May 29, 1928
*Razdan, V. (Delhi) b Aug. 25, 1969
*Read, H. D. (Surrey & Essex) b Jan. 28, 1910
*Read, J. M. (Surrey; *CY 1890*) b Feb. 9, 1859, d Feb. 17, 1929
*Read, W. W. (Surrey; *CY 1893*) b Nov. 23, 1855, d Jan. 6, 1907
*Reddy, B. (TN) b Nov. 12, 1954
*Redmond, R. E. (Wgtn & Auck.) b Dec. 29, 1944
Redpath, I. R. (Vic.) b May 11, 1941
Reed, B. L. (Hants) b Sept. 17, 1937
*Reedman, J. C. (S. Aust.) b Oct. 9, 1865, d March 25, 1924
Rees, A. (Glam.) b Feb. 17, 1938
*Reeve, D. A. (Sussex & Warwicks.; *CY 1996*) b April 2, 1963
Reeves, W. (Essex; Umpire) b Jan. 22, 1875, d March 22, 1944
*Rege, M. R. (M'tra) b March 18, 1924
*Rehman, S. F. (Punjab, Pak. Us & Lahore) b June 11, 1935
*Reid, B. A. (W. Aust.) b March 14, 1963
*Reid, J. F. (Auck.) b March 3, 1956
*Reid, J. R. (Wgtn & Otago; *CY 1959*) b June 3, 1928
*Reid, N. (W. Prov.) b Dec. 26, 1890, d June 6, 1947
Reid, R. B. (Wgtn & Auck.) b Dec. 3, 1958
Reidy, B. W. (Lancs.) b Sept. 18, 1953
*Reiffel, P. R. (Vic.) b April 19, 1966
*Relf, A. E. (Sussex & Auck.; *CY 1914*) b June 26, 1874, d March 26, 1937
*Renneburg, D. A. (NSW) b Sept. 23, 1942
*Rennie, J. A. (Mat.) b July 29, 1970
Revill, A. C. (Derbys. & Leics.) b March 27, 1923
Reynolds, B. L. (Northants) b June 10, 1932
Rhodes, A. E. G. (Derbys.) b Oct. 10, 1916, d Oct. 18, 1983
*Rhodes, H. J. (Derbys.) b July 22, 1936
*Rhodes, J. N. (Natal) b July 26, 1969
Rhodes, S. D. (Notts.) b March 24, 1910, d Jan. 7, 1989
*Rhodes, S. J. (Yorks. & Worcs.; *CY 1995*) b June 17, 1964
*Rhodes, W. (Yorks.; *CY 1899*) b Oct. 29, 1877, d July 8, 1973
Rice, C. E. B. (Tvl & Notts.; *CY 1981*) b July 23, 1949
Rice, J. M. (Hants) b Oct. 23, 1949
*Richards, A. R. (W. Prov.) b 1868, d Jan. 9, 1904
*Richards, B. A. (Natal, Glos., Hants & S. Aust.; *CY 1969*) b July 21, 1945
*Richards, C. J. (Surrey & OFS) b Aug. 10, 1958
Richards, D. L. (Chief Exec. ICC 1993–) b July 28, 1946
Richards, G. (Glam.) b Nov. 29, 1951

*Richards, I. V. A. (Comb. Is., Leewards, Som., Qld & Glam.; *CY 1977*) b March 7, 1952
*Richards, W. H. M. (SA) b Aug. 1862, d Jan. 4, 1903
*Richardson, A. J. (S. Aust.) b July 24, 1888, d Dec. 23, 1973
*Richardson, D. J. (E. Prov. & N. Tvl) b Sept. 16, 1959
*Richardson, D. W. (Worcs.) b Nov. 3, 1934
Richardson, G. W. (Derbys.) b April 26, 1938
*Richardson, P. E. (Worcs. & Kent; *CY 1957*) b July 4, 1931
*Richardson, R. B. (Leewards & Yorks.; *CY 1992*) b Jan. 12, 1962
*Richardson, T. (Surrey & Som.; *CY 1897*) b Aug. 11, 1870, d July 2, 1912
*Richardson, V. Y. (S. Aust.) b Sept. 7, 1894, d Oct. 29, 1969
*Richmond, T. L. (Notts.) b June 23, 1890, d Dec. 29, 1957
*Rickards, K. R. (Jam. & Essex) b Aug. 23, 1923, d Aug. 21, 1995
Riddington, A. (Leics.) b Dec. 22, 1911
*Ridgway, F. (Kent) b Aug. 10, 1923
*Rigg, K. E. (Vic.) b May 21, 1906, d Feb. 28, 1995
Riley, H. (Leics.) b Oct. 3, 1902, d Jan. 24, 1989
Rindel, M. J. R. (N. Tvl) b Feb. 9, 1963
*Ring, D. T. (Vic.) b Oct. 14, 1918
Ripley, D. (Northants) b Sept. 13, 1966
Rist, F. H. (Essex) b March 30, 1914
*Ritchie, G. M. (Qld) b Jan. 23, 1960
*Rixon, S. J. (NSW) b Feb. 25, 1954
*Rizwan-uz-Zaman (Kar. & PIA) b Sept. 4, 1962
*Roach, C. A. (T/T) b March 13, 1904, d April 16, 1988
*Roberts, A. D. G. (N. Dist.) b May 6, 1947, d Oct. 26, 1989
*Roberts, A. M. E. (Comb. Is., Leewards, Hants, NSW & Leics.; *CY 1975*) b Jan. 29, 1951
Roberts, A. R. (Northants & Wgtn) b April 16, 1971
*Roberts, A. T. (Windwards) b Sept. 18, 1937
*Roberts, A. W. (Cant. & Otago) b Aug. 20, 1909, d May 13, 1978
Roberts, B. (Tvl & Derbys.) b May 30, 1962
Roberts, The Hon. Sir Denys (Pres. MCC 1989-90) b Jan. 19, 1923
Roberts, S. J. (Cant.) b March 22, 1965
Roberts, W. B. (Lancs. & Victory Tests) b Sept. 27, 1914, d Aug. 24, 1951
*Robertson, G. K. (C. Dist.) b July 15, 1960
Robertson, G. R. (NSW) b May 28, 1966
*Robertson, J. B. (W. Prov.) b June 5, 1906, d July 5, 1985

*Robertson, J. D. (Middx; *CY 1948*) b Feb. 22, 1917

*Robertson, W. R. (Vic.) b Oct. 6, 1861, d June 24, 1938

Robertson-Glasgow, R. C. (OUCC & Som.; Writer) b July 15, 1901, d March 4, 1965

Robins, D. H. (Warwicks.) b June 26, 1914

Robins, R. V. C. (Middx) b March 13, 1935

*Robins, R. W. V. (CUCC & Middx; *CY 1930*) b June 3, 1906, d Dec. 12, 1968

Robinson, A. L. (Yorks.) b Aug. 17, 1946

Robinson, D. D. J. (Essex) b March 2, 1973

Robinson, Emmott (Yorks.) b Nov. 16, 1883, d Nov. 17, 1969

Robinson, Ellis P. (Yorks. & Som.) b Aug. 10, 1911

Robinson, H. B. (OUCC & Canada) b March 3, 1919

Robinson, M. (Glam., Warwicks., H'bad & Madras) b July 16, 1921, d Aug. 8, 1994

Robinson, M. A. (Northants & Yorks.) b Nov. 23, 1966

Robinson, P. E. (Yorks. & Leics.) b Aug. 3, 1963

Robinson, P. J. (Worcs. & Som.) b Feb. 9, 1943

*Robinson, R. D. (Vic.) b June 8, 1946

*Robinson, R. H. (NSW, S. Aust. & Otago) b March 26, 1914, d Aug. 10, 1965

*Robinson, R. T. (Notts.; *CY 1986*) b Nov. 21, 1958

Robson, E. (Som.) b May 1, 1870, d May 23, 1924

Rochford, P. (Glos.) b Aug. 27, 1928, d June 18, 1992

*Rodriguez, W. V. (T/T) b June 25, 1934

Roe, B. (Som.) b Jan. 27, 1939

Roebuck, P. M. (CUCC & Som.; *CY 1988*) b March 6, 1956

Rogers, N. H. (Hants) b March 9, 1918

Rollins, A. S. (Derbys.) b Feb. 8, 1972

Rollins, R. J. (Essex) b Jan. 30, 1974

Romaines, P. W. (Northants, Glos. & Griq. W.) b Dec. 25, 1955

*Roope, G. R. J. (Surrey & Griq. W.) b July 12, 1946

*Root, C. F. (Derbys. & Worcs.) b April 16, 1890, d Jan. 20, 1954

*Rorke, G. F. (NSW) b June 27, 1938

*Rose, B. C. (Som.; *CY 1980*) b June 4, 1950

Rose, G. D. (Middx & Som.) b April 12, 1964

Roseberry, M. A. (Middx & Durham) b Nov. 28, 1966

*Rose-Innes, A. (Kimberley & Tvl) b Feb. 16, 1868, d Nov. 22, 1946

Ross, C. J. (Wgtn & OUCC) b June 24, 1954

Rotherham, G. A. (Rugby, CUCC, Warwicks. & Wgtn; *CY 1918*) b May 28, 1899, d Jan. 31, 1985

Rouse, S. J. (Warwicks.) b Jan. 20, 1949

Routledge, R. (Middx) b June 12, 1920

*Routledge, T. W. (W. Prov. & Tvl) b April 18, 1867, d May 9, 1927

*Rowan, A. M. B. (Tvl) b Feb. 7, 1921

*Rowan, E. A. B. (Tvl; *CY 1952*) b July 20, 1909, d April 30, 1993

*Rowe, C. G. (Wgtn & C. Dist.) b June 30, 1915, d June 9, 1995

Rowe, C. J. C. (Kent & Glam.) b Nov. 11, 1951

Rowe, E. J. (Notts.) b July 21, 1920, d Dec. 17, 1989

*Rowe, G. A. (W. Prov.) b June 15, 1874, d Jan. 8, 1950

*Rowe, L. G. (Jam. & Derbys.) b Jan. 8, 1949

*Roy, A. (Bengal) b June 5, 1945

*Roy, Pankaj (Bengal) b May 31, 1928

*Roy, Pranab (Bengal) b Feb. 10, 1957

*Royle, Rev. V. P. F. A. (OUCC & Lancs.) b Jan. 29, 1854, d May 21, 1929

*Rumsey, F. E. (Worcs., Som. & Derbys.) b Dec. 4, 1935

Rundle, D. B. (W. Prov.) b Sept. 25, 1965

*Rushmere, M. W. (E. Prov. & Tvl) b Jan. 7, 1965

*Russell, A. C. [C. A. G.] (Essex; *CY 1923*) b Oct. 7, 1887, d March 23, 1961

Russell, P. E. (Derbys.) b May 9, 1944

*Russell, R. C. (Glos.; *CY 1990*) b Aug. 15, 1963

Russell, S. E. J. (Middx & Glos.) b Oct. 4, 1937, d June 18, 1994

*Russell, W. E. (Middx) b July 3, 1936

Russom, N. (CUCC & Som.) b Dec. 3, 1958

Rutherford, I. A. (Worcs. & Otago) b June 30, 1957

*Rutherford, J. W. (W. Aust.) b Sept. 25, 1929

*Rutherford, K. R. (Otago) b Oct. 26, 1965

Ryan, M. (Yorks.) b June 23, 1933

*Ryder, J. (Vic.) b Aug. 8, 1889, d April 3, 1977

Saadat Ali (Lahore, UBL & HBFC) b Feb. 6, 1955

*Sadiq Mohammad (Kar., PIA, Tas., Essex, Glos. & UBL) b May 3, 1945

*Saeed Ahmed (Punjab, Pak. Us, Lahore, PIA, Kar., PWD & Sind) b Oct. 1, 1937

*Saeed Anwar (Kar., UBL & ADBP) b Sept. 6, 1968

*Saggers, R. A. (NSW) b May 15, 1917, d March 1987

Sainsbury, G. E. (Essex & Glos.) b Jan. 17, 1958

Sainsbury, P. J. (Hants; *CY 1974*) b June 13, 1934

*St Hill, E. L. (T/T) b March 9, 1904, d May 21, 1957

*St Hill, W. H. (T/T) b July 6, 1893, d c1957

Sajid Ali (Kar. & NBP) b July 1, 1963

Sajjad Akbar (Lahore, PNSC & Sargodha) b March 1, 1961

*Salah-ud-Din (Kar., PIA & Pak. Us) b Feb. 14, 1947

Sale, R., jun. (OUCC, Warwicks. & Derbys.) b Oct. 4, 1919, d Feb. 3, 1987

*Saleem Altaf (Lahore & PIA) b April 19, 1944

*Saleem Jaffer (Kar. & UBL) b Nov. 19, 1962

*Salim Malik (Lahore, HBL & Essex; *CY 1988*) b April 16, 1963

Salim Pervez (NBP) b Sept. 9, 1947

*Salim Yousuf (Sind, Kar., IDBP, Allied Bank & Customs) b Dec. 7, 1959

*Salisbury, I. D. K. (Sussex; *CY 1993*) b Jan. 21, 1970

Samaranayake, A. D. A. (SL) b Feb. 25, 1962

*Samarasekera, M. A. R. (CCC) b Aug. 5, 1961

*Samaraweera, D. P. (Colts) b Feb. 12, 1972

Sampson, H. (Yorks. & All-England) b March 13, 1813, d March 29, 1885

*Samuelson, S. V. (Natal) b Nov. 21, 1883, d Nov. 18, 1958

*Sandham, A. (Surrey; *CY 1923*) b July 6, 1890, d April 20, 1982

*Sandhu, B. S. (Bombay) b Aug. 3, 1956

*Sardesai, D. N. (Bombay) b Aug. 8, 1940

*Sarfraz Nawaz (Lahore, Punjab, Northants, Pak. Rlwys & UBL) b Dec. 1, 1948

Sargeant, N. F. (Surrey) b Nov. 8, 1965

*Sarwate, C. T. (CP & B, M'tara, Bombay & †M. Pradesh) b June 22, 1920

*Saunders, J. V. (Vic. & Wgtn) b March 21, 1876, d Dec. 21, 1927

Savage, J. S. (Leics. & Lancs.) b March 3, 1929

Savage, R. Le Q. (OUCC & Warwicks.) b Dec. 10, 1955

Savill, L. A. (Essex) b June 30, 1935

Saville, G. J. (Essex) b Feb. 5, 1944

Saxelby, K. (Notts.) b Feb. 23, 1959

Saxelby, M. (Notts. & Durham) b Jan. 4, 1969

*Saxena, R. C. (Delhi & Bihar) b Sept. 20, 1944

Sayer, D. M. (OUCC & Kent) b Sept. 19, 1936

*Scarlett, R. O. (Jam.) b Aug. 15, 1934

*Schultz, B. N. (E. Prov.) b Aug. 26, 1970

*Schultz, S. S. (CUCC & Lancs.) b Aug. 29, 1857, d Dec. 18, 1937

*Schwarz, R. O. (Middx & Natal; *CY 1908*) b May 4, 1875, d Nov. 18, 1918

*Scott, A. P. H. (Jam.) b July 29, 1934

Scott, Christopher J. (Lancs.) b Sept. 16, 1959

Scott, Colin J. (Glos.) b May 1, 1919, d Nov. 22, 1992

Scott, C. W. (Notts. & Durham) b Jan. 23, 1964

*Scott, H. J. H. (Vic.) b Dec. 26, 1858, d Sept. 23, 1910

Scott, M. E. (Northants) b May 8, 1936

*Scott, O. C. (Jam.) b Aug. 25, 1893, d June 16, 1961

*Scott, R. H. (Cant.) b March 6, 1917

Scott, R. J. (Hants & Glos.) b Nov. 2, 1963

Scott, S. W. (Middx; *CY 1893*) b March 24, 1854, d Dec. 8, 1933

*Scott, V. J. (Auck.) b July 31, 1916, d Aug. 2, 1980

*Scotton, W. H. (Notts.) b Jan. 15, 1856, d July 9, 1893

*Sealey, B. J. (T/T) b Aug. 12, 1899, d Sept. 12, 1963

*Sealy, J. E. D. (B'dos & T/T) b Sept. 11, 1912, d Jan. 3, 1982

Seamer, J. W. (Som. & OUCC) b June 23, 1913

*Seccull, A. W. (Kimberley, W. Prov. & Tvl) b Sept. 14, 1868, d July 20, 1945

*Sekar, T. A. P. (TN) b March 28, 1955

*Selby, J. (Notts.) b July 1, 1849, d March 11, 1894

Sellers, A. B. (Yorks.; *CY 1940*) b March 5, 1907, d Feb. 20, 1981

*Sellers, R. H. D. (S. Aust.) b Aug. 20, 1940

*Selvey, M. W. W. (CUCC, Surrey, Middx, Glam. & OFS) b April 25, 1948

*Sen, P. (Bengal) b May 31, 1926, d Jan. 27, 1970

*Sen Gupta, A. K. (Ind. Serv.) b Aug. 3, 1939

*Senanayake, C. P. (CCC) b Dec. 19, 1962

*Serjeant, C. S. (W. Aust.) b Nov. 1, 1951

Seymour, James (Kent) b Oct. 25, 1879, d Sept. 30, 1930

*Seymour, M. A. (W. Prov.) b June 5, 1936

*Shackleton, D. (Hants.; *CY 1959*) b Aug. 12, 1924

*Shafiq Ahmad (Lahore, Punjab, NBP & UBL) b March 28, 1949

*Shafqat Rana (Lahore & PIA) b Aug. 10, 1943

*Shah, A. H. (Mash.) b Aug. 7, 1959

*Shahid Israr (Kar. & Sind) b March 1, 1950

*Shahid Mahboob (Kar., Quetta, R'pindi, PACO & Allied Bank) b Aug. 25, 1962

*Shahid Mahmood (Kar., Pak. Us & PWD) b March 17, 1939

Shahid, N. (Essex & Surrey) b April 23, 1969

*Shahid Saeed (HBFC, Lahore & PACO) b Jan. 6, 1966

*Shakeel Ahmed (B'pur, HBL & I'bad) b Nov. 12, 1971

Shakil Khan (WAPDA, HBL, R'pindi & I'bad) b May 28, 1968

*Shalders, W. A. (Griq. W. & Tvl) b Feb. 12, 1880, d March 18, 1917

*Sharma, Ajay (Delhi) b April 3, 1964

*Sharma, Chetan (Haryana & Bengal) b Jan. 3, 1966

*Sharma, Gopal (U. Pradesh) b Aug. 3, 1960

*Sharma, P. (Raja.) b Jan. 5, 1948

Sharma, R. (Derbys.) b June 27, 1962

Sharma, Sanjeev (Delhi) b Aug. 25, 1965

Sharp, G. (Northants) b March 12, 1950

Sharp, H. P. H. (Middx; Middx scorer) b Oct. 6, 1917, d Jan. 15, 1995

*Sharp, J. (Lancs.) b Feb. 15, 1878, d Jan. 28, 1938

Sharp, K. (Yorks. & Griq. W.) b April 6, 1959

*Sharpe, D. (Punjab, Pak. Rlwys, Lahore & S. Aust.) b Aug. 3, 1937

*Sharpe, J. W. (Surrey & Notts.; *CY 1892*) b Dec. 9, 1866, d June 19, 1936

*Sharpe, P. J. (Yorks. & Derbys.; *CY 1963*) b Dec. 27, 1936

*Shastri, R. J. (Bombay & Glam.) b May 27, 1962

*Shaw, Alfred (Notts. & Sussex) b Aug. 29, 1842, d Jan. 16, 1907

Shaw, C. (Yorks.) b Feb. 17, 1964

Shaw, T. G. (E. Prov.) b July 5, 1959

*Sheahan, A. P. (Vic.) b Sept. 30, 1946

Sheffield, J. R. (Essex & Wgtn) b Nov. 19, 1906

*Shepherd, B. K. (W. Aust.) b April 23, 1937

Shepherd, D. J. (Glam.; *CY 1970*) b Aug. 12, 1927

Shepherd, D. R. (Glos.; Umpire) b Dec. 27, 1940

*Shepherd, J. N. (B'dos, Kent, Rhod. & Glos.; *CY 1979*) b Nov. 9, 1943

Shepherd, T. F. (Surrey) b Dec. 5, 1889, d Feb. 13, 1957

*Sheppard, Rt Rev. D. S. (Bishop of Liverpool) (CUCC & Sussex; *CY 1953*) b March 6, 1929

*Shepstone, G. H. (Tvl) b April 8, 1876, d July 3, 1940

*Sherwell, P. W. (Tvl) b Aug. 17, 1880, d April 17, 1948

*Sherwin, M. (Notts.; *CY 1891*) b Feb. 26, 1851, d July 3, 1910

*Shillingford, G. C. (Comb. Is. & Windwards) b Sept. 25, 1944

*Shillingford, I. T. (Comb. Is. & Windwards) b April 18, 1944

*Shinde, S. G. (Baroda, M'tra & Bombay) b Aug. 18, 1923, d June 22, 1955

Shine, K. J. (Hants & Middx) b Feb. 22, 1969

Shirreff, A. C. (CUCC, Hants, Kent & Som.) b Feb. 12, 1919

*Shivnarine, S. (Guyana) b May 13, 1952

Shoaib Mohammad (Kar. & PIA) b Jan. 8, 1961

*Shodhan, R. H. (Guj. & Baroda) b Oct. 18, 1928

*Shrewsbury, Arthur (Notts.; *CY 1890*) b April 11, 1856, d May 19, 1903

*Shrimpton, M. J. F. (C. Dist. & N. Dist.) b June 23, 1940

*Shuja-ud-Din, Col. (N. Ind., Pak. Us, Pak. Serv., B'pur & R'pindi) b April 10, 1930

*Shukla, R. C. (Bihar & Delhi) b Feb. 4, 1948

*Shuter, J. (Kent & Surrey) b Feb. 9, 1855, d July 5, 1920

*Shuttleworth, K. (Lancs. & Leics.) b Nov. 13, 1944

Siddons, J. D. (Vic. & S. Aust.) b April 25, 1964

*Sidebottom, A. (Yorks. & OFS) b April 1, 1954

*Sidhu, N. S. (Punjab) b Oct. 20, 1963

*Siedle, I. J. (Natal) b Jan. 11, 1903, d Aug. 24, 1982

*Sievers, M. W. (Vic.) b April 13, 1912, d May 10, 1968

*Sikander Bakht (PWD, PIA, Sind, Kar. & UBL) b Aug. 25, 1957

Silk, D. R. W. (CUCC & Som.; Pres. MCC 1992-1994, Chairman TCCB 1994-) b Oct. 8, 1931

Silva, K. J. (Bloom.) b June 2, 1973

*Silva, S. A. R. (NCC) b Dec. 12, 1960

*Simmons, J. (Lancs. & Tas.; *CY 1985*) b March 28, 1941

*Simmons, P. V. (T/T, Border & Leics.) b April 18, 1963

Simons, E. O. (W. Prov.) b March 9, 1962

*Simpson, R. B. (NSW & W. Aust.; *CY 1965*) b Feb. 3, 1936

*Simpson, R. T. (Notts. & Sind; *CY 1950*) b Feb. 27, 1920

Simpson-Hayward, G. H. (Worcs.) b June 7, 1875, d Oct. 2, 1936

Sims, Sir Arthur (Cant.) b July 22, 1877, d April 27, 1969

*Sims, J. M. (Middx) b May 13, 1903, d April 27, 1973

*Sinclair, B. W. (Wgtn) b Oct. 23, 1936

Sinclair, I. McK. (Cant.) b June 1, 1933

*Sinclair, J. H. (Tvl) b Oct. 16, 1876, d Feb. 23, 1913

*Sincock, D. J. (S. Aust.) b Feb. 1, 1942

*Sinfield, R. A. (Glos.) b Dec. 24, 1900, d March 17, 1988

*Singh, Charan K. (T/T) b Nov. 27, 1935

Singh, "Robin" [R. R.] (TN) b Sept. 14, 1963

Singh, R. P. (U. Pradesh) b Jan. 6, 1963

Singh, Swaranjit (CUCC, Warwicks., E. Punjab & Bengal) b July 18, 1931

Singleton, A. P. (OUCC, Worcs. & Rhod.) b Aug. 5, 1914

*Sivaramakrishnan, L. (TN) b Dec. 31, 1965

Skelding, A. (Leics.; Umpire) b Sept. 5, 1886, d April 17, 1960

Skinner, D. A. (Derbys.) b March 22, 1920

Skinner, L. E. (Surrey & Guyana) b Sept. 7, 1950

*Slack, W. N. (Middx & Windwards) b Dec. 12, 1954, d Jan. 15, 1989

Slade, D. N. F. (Worcs.) b Aug. 24, 1940

Slade, W. D. (Glam.) b Sept. 27, 1941

*Slater, K. N. (W. Aust.) b March 12, 1935

*Slater, M. J. (NSW) b Feb. 21, 1970

*Sleep, P. R. (S. Aust.) b May 4, 1957

*Slight, J. (Vic.) b Oct. 20, 1855, d Dec. 9, 1930

Slocombe, P. A. (Som.) b Sept. 6, 1954

*Smailes, T. F. (Yorks.) b March 27, 1910, d Dec. 1, 1970

Smales, K. (Yorks. & Notts.) b Sept. 15, 1927

*Small, G. C. (Warwicks. & S. Aust.) b Oct. 18, 1961

Small, John, sen. (Hants & All-England) b April 19, 1737, d Dec. 31, 1826

*Small, J. A. (T/T) b Nov. 3, 1892, d April 26, 1958

*Small, M. A. (B'dos) b Feb. 12, 1964

Smedley, M. J. (Notts.) b Oct. 28, 1941

*Smith, A. C. (OUCC & Warwicks.; Chief Exec. TCCB 1987-   ) b Oct. 25, 1936

Smith, A. M. (Glos.) b Oct. 1, 1967

Smith, B. F. (Leics.) b April 3, 1972

*Smith, Sir C. Aubrey (CUCC, Sussex & Tvl) b July 21, 1863, d Dec. 20, 1948

*Smith, C. I. J. (Middx; CY 1935) b Aug. 25, 1906, d Feb. 9, 1979

*Smith, C. J. E. (Tvl) b Dec. 25, 1872, d March 27, 1947

*Smith, C. L. (Natal, Glam. & Hants; CY 1984) b Oct. 15, 1958

*Smith, C. W. (B'dos) b July 29, 1933

*Smith, Denis (Derbys.; CY 1936) b Jan. 24, 1907, d Sept. 12, 1979

*Smith, D. B. M. (Vic.) b Sept. 14, 1884, d July 29, 1963

Smith, D. H. K. (Derbys. & OFS) b June 29, 1940

*Smith, D. M. (Surrey, Worcs. & Sussex) b Jan. 9, 1956

*Smith, D. R. (Glos.) b Oct. 5, 1934

*Smith, D. V. (Sussex) b June 14, 1923

Smith, Edwin (Derbys.) b Jan. 2, 1934

*Smith, E. J. (Warwicks.) b Feb. 6, 1886, d Aug. 31, 1979

*Smith, F. B. (Cant.) b March 13, 1922

*Smith, F. W. (Tvl) No details of birth or death known

Smith, G. (Kent) b Nov. 30, 1915

Smith, G. J. (Essex) b April 2, 1935

*Smith, Harry (Glos.) b May 21, 1890, d Nov. 12, 1937

*Smith, H. D. (Otago & Cant.) b Jan. 8, 1913, d Jan. 25, 1986

Smith, I. (Glam. & Durham) b March 11, 1967

*Smith, I. D. S. (C. Dist. & Auck.) b Feb. 28, 1957

Smith, K. D. (Warwicks.) b July 9, 1956

Smith, M. J. (Middx) b Jan. 4, 1942

*Smith, M. J. K. (OUCC, Leics. & Warwicks.; CY 1960) b June 30, 1933

Smith, N. (Yorks. & Essex) b April 1, 1949

Smith, N. M. K. (Warwicks.) b July 27, 1967

*Smith, O. G. (Jam.; CY 1958) b May 5, 1933, d Sept. 9, 1959

Smith, P. A. (Warwicks.) b April 5, 1964

Smith, Ray (Essex) b Aug. 10, 1914

Smith, Roy (Som.) b April 14, 1930

*Smith, R. A. (Natal & Hants; CY 1990) b Sept. 13, 1963

Smith, R. C. (Leics.) b Aug. 3, 1935

*Smith, S. B. (NSW & Tvl) b Oct. 18, 1961

Smith, S. G. (T/T, Northants & Auck.; CY 1915) b Jan. 15, 1881, d Oct. 25, 1963

*Smith, T. P. B. (Essex; CY 1947) b Oct. 30, 1908, d Aug. 4, 1967

Smith, V. I. (Natal) b Feb. 23, 1925

Smith, W. A. (Surrey) b Sept. 15, 1937

Smith, W. C. (Surrey; CY 1911) b Oct. 4, 1877, d July 16, 1946

Smithson, G. A. (Yorks. & Leics.) b Nov. 1, 1926, d Sept. 6, 1970

*Snedden, C. A. (Auck.) b Jan. 7, 1918, d May 19, 1993

*Snedden, M. C. (Auck.) b Nov. 23, 1958

Snell, R. P. (Tvl & Som.) b Sept. 12, 1968

Snellgrove, K. L. (Lancs.) b Nov. 12, 1941

*Snooke, S. D. (W. Prov. & Tvl) b Nov. 11, 1878, d April 4, 1959

*Snooke, S. J. (Border, W. Prov. & Tvl) b Feb. 1, 1881, d Aug. 14, 1966

*Snow, J. A. (Sussex; CY 1973) b Oct. 13, 1941

Snowden, W. (CUCC) b Sept. 27, 1952

*Sobers, Sir G. S. (B'dos, S. Aust. & Notts.; CY 1964) b July 28, 1936

Sohail Fazal (Lahore & HBL) b Nov. 11, 1967

*Sohoni, S. W. (M'tra, Baroda & Bombay) b March 5, 1918, d May 19, 1993

Solanky, J. W. (E. Africa & Glam.) b June 30, 1942

*Solkar, E. D. (Bombay & Sussex) b March 18, 1948

*Solomon, J. S. (BG) b Aug. 26, 1930

*Solomon, W. R. T. (Tvl & E. Prov.) b April 23, 1872, d July 12, 1964

*Sood, M. M. (Delhi) b July 6, 1939

Southern, J. W. (Hants) b Sept. 2, 1952

*Southerton, James (Surrey, Hants & Sussex) b Nov. 16, 1827, d June 16, 1880

Southerton, S. J. (Editor of Wisden 1934-35) b July 7, 1874, d March 12, 1935

*Sparling, J. T. (Auck.) b July 24, 1938

Speak, N. J. (Lancs.) b Nov. 21, 1966

Speight, M. P. (Sussex & Wgtn) b Oct. 24, 1967

Spencer, C. T. (Leics.) b Aug. 18, 1931

Spencer, J. (CUCC & Sussex) b Oct. 6, 1949

Spencer, T. W. (Kent) b March 22, 1914

Sperry, J. (Leics.) b March 19, 1910

*Spofforth, F. R. (NSW & Vic.) b Sept. 9, 1853, d June 4, 1926

*Spooner, R. H. (Lancs.; *CY 1905*) b Oct. 21, 1880, d Oct. 2, 1961

*Spooner, R. T. (Warwicks.) b Dec. 30, 1919

Springall, J. D. (Notts.) b Sept. 19, 1932

*Srikkanth, K. (TN) b Dec. 21, 1959

*Srinath, J. (Karn. & Glos.) b Aug. 31, 1969

Srinivasan, T. E. (TN) b Oct. 26, 1950

*Stackpole, K. R. (Vic.; *CY 1973*) b July 10, 1940

Standen, J. A. (Worcs.) b May 30, 1935

Standing, D. K. (Sussex) b Oct. 21, 1963

Stansfield-Smith, Sir Colin (CUCC & Lancs.) b Oct. 1, 1932

Stanworth, J. (Lancs.) b Sept. 30, 1960

*Stanyforth, Lt.-Col. R. T. (Yorks.) b May 30, 1892, d Feb. 20, 1964

*Staples, S. J. (Notts.; *CY 1929*) b Sept. 18, 1892, d June 4, 1950

Starkie, S. (Northants) b April 4, 1926

*Statham, J. B. (Lancs.; *CY 1955*) b June 17, 1930

*Stayers, S. C. (†Guyana & Bombay) b June 9, 1937

*Steel, A. G. (CUCC & Lancs.; Pres. MCC 1902) b Sept. 24, 1858, d June 15, 1914

*Steele, D. S. (Northants & Derbys.; *CY 1976*) b Sept. 29, 1941

Steele, J. F. (Leics., Natal & Glam.) b July 23, 1946

Stemp, R. D. (Worcs. & Yorks.) b Dec. 11, 1967

Stephenson, F. D. (B'dos, Glos., Tas., Notts., Sussex & OFS; *CY 1989*) b April 8, 1959

Stephenson, G. R. (Derbys. & Hants) b Nov. 19, 1942

Stephenson, H. H. (Surrey & All-England) b May 3, 1832, d Dec. 17, 1896

Stephenson, H. W. (Som.) b July 18, 1920

*Stephenson, J. P. (Essex, Boland & Hants) b March 14, 1965

Stephenson, Lt.-Col. J. R. (Sec. MCC 1987-93) b Feb. 25, 1931

Stevens, Edward ("Lumpy") (Hants) b *circa* 1735, d Sept. 7, 1819

*Stevens, G. B. (S. Aust.) b Feb. 29, 1932

*Stevens, G. T. S. (UCS, OUCC & Middx; *CY 1918*) b Jan. 7, 1901, d Sept. 19, 1970

*Stevenson, G. B. (Yorks. & Northants) b Dec. 16, 1955

Stevenson, K. (Derbys. & Hants) b Oct. 6, 1950

Stevenson, M. H. (CUCC & Derbys.) b June 13, 1927, d Sept. 19, 1994

*Stewart, A. J. (Surrey; *CY 1993*) b April 8, 1963

Stewart, E. L. R. (Natal) b July 30, 1969

*Stewart, M. J. (Surrey; *CY 1958*) b Sept. 16, 1932

*Stewart, R. B. (SA) b Sept. 3, 1856, d Sept. 12, 1913

Stewart, R. W. (Glos. & Middx) b Feb. 28, 1945

Stewart, W. J. (Warwicks. & Northants) b Oct. 31, 1934

*Steyn, P. J. R. (OFS) b June 30, 1967

*Stirling, D. A. (C. Dist.) b Oct. 5, 1961

Stocks, F. W. (Notts.) b Nov. 6, 1917

*Stoddart, A. E. (Middx; *CY 1893*) b March 11, 1863, d April 3, 1915

*Stollmeyer, J. B. (T/T) b April 11, 1921, d Sept. 10, 1989

*Stollmeyer, V. H. (T/T) b Jan. 24, 1916

*Storer, W. (Derbys.; *CY 1899*) b Jan. 25, 1867, d Feb. 28, 1912

Storey, S. J. (Surrey & Sussex) b Jan. 6, 1941

Storie, A. C. (Northants, Warwicks., OFS, OUCC & Scotland) b July 25, 1965

Stott, L. W. (Auck.) b Dec. 8, 1946

Stott, W. B. (Yorks.) b July 18, 1934

Stovold, A. W. (Glos. & OFS) b March 19, 1953

*Strang, B. C. (MCD) b June 9, 1972

*Strang, P. A. (MCD) b July 28, 1970

*Streak, H. H. (Mat. & Hants) b March 16, 1974

*Street, G. B. (Sussex) b Dec. 6, 1889, d April 24, 1924

*Stricker, L. A. (Tvl) b May 26, 1884, d Feb. 5, 1960

Stringer, P. M. (Yorks. & Leics.) b Feb. 23, 1943

*Strudwick, H. (Surrey; *CY 1912*) b Jan. 28, 1880, d Feb. 14, 1970

*Studd, C. T. (CUCC & Middx) b Dec. 2, 1860, d July 16, 1931

*Studd, G. B. (CUCC & Middx) b Oct. 20, 1859, d Feb. 13, 1945

Studd, Sir Peter M. (CUCC) b Sept. 15, 1916

Sturt, M. O. C. (Middx) b Sept. 12, 1940

*Su'a, M. L. (N. Dist. & Auck.) b Nov. 7, 1966

*Subba Row, R. (CUCC, Surrey & Northants; *CY 1961*) b Jan. 29, 1932

*Subramanya, V. (Mysore) b July 16, 1936

*Such, P. M. (Notts., Leics. & Essex) b June 12, 1964

Sudhakar Rao, R. (Karn.) b Aug. 8, 1952

Sueter, T. (Hants & Surrey) b *circa* 1749, d Feb. 17, 1827

*Sugg, F. H. (Yorks., Derbys. & Lancs.; *CY 1890*) b Jan. 11, 1862, d May 29, 1933

Sullivan, J. (Lancs.) b Feb. 5, 1945
Sully, H. (Som. & Northants) b Nov. 1, 1939
*Sunderram, G. R. (Bombay & Raja.) b March 29, 1930
Sunnucks, P. R. (Kent) b June 22, 1916
*Surendranath, R. (Ind. Serv.) b Jan. 4, 1937
Surridge, W. S. (Surrey; *CY 1953*) b Sept. 3, 1917, d April 13, 1992
*Surti, R. F. (Guj., Raja. & Qld) b May 25, 1936
*Susskind, M. J. (CUCC, Middx & Tvl) b June 8, 1891, d July 9, 1957
*Sutcliffe, B. (Auck., Otago & N. Dist.; *CY 1950*) b Nov. 17, 1923
*Sutcliffe, H. (Yorks.; *CY 1920*) b Nov. 24, 1894, d Jan. 22, 1978
Sutcliffe, S. P. (OUCC & Warwicks.) b May 22, 1960
Sutcliffe, W. H. H. (Yorks.) b Oct. 10, 1926
Suttle, K. G. (Sussex) b Aug. 25, 1928
Swallow, I. G. (Yorks. & Som.) b Dec. 18, 1962
*Swamy, V. N. (Ind. Serv.) b May 23, 1924, d May 1, 1983
Swanton, E. W. (Middx; Writer) b Feb. 11, 1907
Swarbrook, F. W. (Derbys., Griq. W. & OFS) b Dec. 17, 1950
Swart, P. D. (Rhod., W. Prov., Glam. & Boland) b April 27, 1946
*Swetman, R. (Surrey, Notts & Glos.) b Oct. 25, 1933
Sydenham, D. A. D. (Surrey) b April 6, 1934
*Symcox, P. L. (Natal) b April 14, 1960
Symington, S. J. (Leics.) b Sept. 16, 1926
Symonds, A. (Qld & Glos.) b June 9, 1975

*Taber, H. B. (NSW) b April 29, 1940
*Taberer, H. M. (OUCC & Natal) b Oct. 7, 1870, d June 5, 1932
*Tahir Naqqash (Servis Ind., MCB, Punjab & Lahore) b July 6, 1959
Tait, A. (Northants & Glos.) b Dec. 27, 1953
*Talat Ali (Lahore, PIA & UBL) b May 29, 1950
*Tallon, D. (Qld; *CY 1949*) b Feb. 17, 1916, d Sept. 7, 1984
*Tamhane, N. S. (Bombay) b Aug. 4, 1931
*Tancred, A. B. (Kimberley, Griq. W. & Tvl) b Aug. 20, 1865, d Nov. 23, 1911
*Tancred, L. J. (Tvl) b Oct. 7, 1876, d July 28, 1934
*Tancred, V. M. (Tvl) b July 7, 1875, d June 3, 1904
Tanvir Mehdi (Lahore & UBL) b Nov. 7, 1972
*Tapscott, G. L. (Griq. W.) b Nov. 7, 1889, d Dec. 13, 1940

*Tapscott, L. E. (Griq. W.) b March 18, 1894, d July 7, 1934
*Tarapore, K. K. (Bombay) b Dec. 17, 1910, d June 15, 1986
Tarrant, F. A. (Vic., Middx & Patiala; *CY 1908*) b Dec. 11, 1880, d Jan. 29, 1951
Tarrant, George F. (Cambs. & All-England) b Dec. 7, 1838, d July 2, 1870
*Taslim Arif (Kar., Sind & NBP) b May 1, 1954
Tate, F. W. (Sussex) b July 24, 1867, d Feb. 24, 1943
*Tate, M. W. (Sussex; *CY 1924*) b May 30, 1895, d May 18, 1956
*Tattersall, R. (Lancs.) b Aug. 17, 1922
*Tauseef Ahmed (PWD, UBL & Kar.) b May 10, 1958
*Tavaré, C. J. (OUCC, Kent & Som.) b Oct. 27, 1954
*Tayfield, H. J. (Natal, Rhod. & Tvl; *CY 1956*) b Jan. 30, 1929, d Feb. 25, 1994
*Taylor, A. I. (Tvl) b July 25, 1925
*Taylor, B. (Essex; *CY 1972*) b June 19, 1932
*Taylor, B. R. (Cant. & Wgtn) b July 12, 1943
*Taylor, Daniel (Natal) b Jan. 9, 1887, d Jan. 24, 1917
*Taylor, D. D. (Auck. & Warwicks.) b March 2, 1923, d Dec. 5, 1980
Taylor, D. J. S. (Surrey, Som. & Griq. W.) b Nov. 12, 1942
Taylor, G. R. (Hants) b Nov. 25, 1909, d Oct. 31, 1986
*Taylor, H. W. (Natal, Tvl & W. Prov.; *CY 1925*) b May 5, 1889, d Feb. 8, 1973
*Taylor, J. M. (NSW) b Oct. 10, 1895, d May 12, 1971
*Taylor, J. O. (T/T) b Jan. 3, 1932
*Taylor, J. P. (Derbys. & Northants) b Aug. 8, 1964
*Taylor, K. (Yorks. & Auck.) b Aug. 21, 1935
Taylor, K. A. (Warwicks.) b Sept. 29, 1916
*Taylor, L. B. (Leics. & Natal) b Oct. 25, 1953
*Taylor, M. A. (NSW; *CY 1990*) b Oct 27, 1964
Taylor, M. N. S. (Notts & Hants) b Nov. 12, 1942
Taylor, N. R. (Kent) b July 21, 1959
*Taylor, P. L. (NSW & Qld) b Aug. 22, 1956
*Taylor, R. W. (Derbys.; *CY 1977*) b July 17, 1941
Taylor, T. L. (CUCC & Yorks.; *CY 1901*) b May 25, 1878, d March 16, 1960
Taylor, W. (Notts.) b Jan. 24, 1947
Tedstone, G. A. (Warwicks. & Glos.) b Jan. 19, 1961
*Tendulkar, S. R. (Bombay & Yorks.) b April 24, 1973
Tennekoon, A. P. B. (SL) b Oct. 29, 1946

*Tennyson, 3rd Lord (Hon. L. H.) (Hants; *CY 1914*) b Nov. 7, 1889, d June 6, 1951

*Terry, V. P. (Hants) b Jan. 14, 1959

*Theunissen, N. H. (W. Prov.) b May 4, 1867, d Nov. 9, 1929

Thomas, D. J. (Surrey, N. Tvl & Glos.) b June 30, 1959

*Thomas, G. (NSW) b March 21, 1938

*Thomas, J. G. (Glam., Border, E. Prov. & Northants) b Aug. 12, 1960

Thompson, A. W. (Middx) b April 17, 1916

*Thompson, G. J. (Northants; *CY 1906*) b Oct. 27, 1877, d March 3, 1943

Thompson, J. R. (CUCC & Warwicks.) b May 10, 1918

Thompson, R. G. (Warwicks.) b Sept. 26, 1932

*Thoms, G. R. (Vic.) b March 22, 1927

*Thomson, A. L. (Vic.) b Dec. 2, 1945

*Thomson, J. R. (NSW, Qld & Middx) b Aug. 16, 1950

*Thomson, K. (Cant.) b Feb. 26, 1941

*Thomson, N. F. D. (NSW) b May 29, 1839, d Sept. 2, 1896

*Thomson, N. I. (Sussex) b Jan. 23, 1929

*Thomson, S. A. (N. Dist.) b Jan. 27, 1969

Thorne, D. A. (Warwicks & OUCC) b Dec. 12, 1964

*Thornton, C. I. (CUCC, Kent & Middx) b March 20, 1850, d Dec. 10, 1929

*Thornton, P. G. (Yorks., Middx & SA) b Dec. 24, 1867, d Jan. 31, 1939

*Thorpe, G. P. (Surrey) b Aug. 1, 1969

*Thurlow, H. M. (Qld) b Jan. 10, 1903, d Dec. 3, 1975

*Tillekeratne, H. P. (NCC) b July 14, 1967

Tilly, H. W. (Middx) b May 25, 1932

Timms, B. S. V. (Hants & Warwicks.) b Dec. 17, 1940

Timms, J. E. (Northants) b Nov. 3, 1906, d May 18, 1980

Timms, W. W. (Northants) b Sept. 28, 1902, d Sept. 30, 1986

Tindall, M. (CUCC & Middx) b March 31, 1914, d July 10, 1994

Tindall, R. A. E. (Surrey) b Sept. 23, 1935

*Tindill, E. W. T. (Wgtn) b Dec. 18, 1910

Tissera, M. H. (SL) b March 23, 1939

Titchard, S. P. (Lancs.) b Dec. 17, 1967

*Titmus, F. J. (Middx, Surrey & OFS; *CY 1963*) b Nov. 24, 1932

Todd, L. J. (Kent) b June 19, 1907, d Aug. 20, 1967

Todd, P. A. (Notts. & Glam.) b March 12, 1953

Tolchard, J. G. (Leics.) b March 17, 1944

*Tolchard, R. W. (Leics.) b June 15, 1946

Tolley, C. M. (Worcs.) b Dec. 30, 1967

Tomlins, K. P. (Middx & Glos.) b Oct. 23, 1957

*Tomlinson, D. S. (Rhod. & Border) b Sept. 4, 1910, d July 11, 1993

Tompkin, M. (Leics.) b Feb. 17, 1919, d Sept. 27, 1956

Toogood, G. J. (OUCC) b Nov. 19, 1961

*Toohey, P. M. (NSW) b April 20, 1954

Tooley, C. D. M. (OUCC) b April 19, 1964

Topley, P. A. (Surrey, Essex & Griq. W.) b Feb. 25, 1964

Tordoff, G. G. (CUCC & Som.) b Dec. 6, 1929

*Toshack, E. R. H. (NSW) b Dec. 15, 1914

Townsend, A. (Warwicks.) b Aug. 26, 1921

Townsend, A. F. (Derbys.) b March 29, 1912, d Feb. 25, 1994

*Townsend, C. L. (Glos.; *CY 1899*) b Nov. 7, 1876, d Oct. 17, 1958

*Townsend, D. C. H. (OUCC) b April 20, 1912

*Townsend, L. F. (Derbys. & Auck.; *CY 1934*) b June 8, 1903, d Feb. 17, 1993

*Travers, J. P. F. (S. Aust.) b Jan. 10, 1871, d Sept. 15, 1942

*Tremlett, M. F. (Som. & C. Dist.) b July 5, 1923, d July 30, 1984

Tremlett, T. M. (Hants) b July 26, 1956

*Tribe, G. E. (Vic. & Northants; *CY 1955*) b Oct. 4, 1920

*Trim, J. (BG) b Jan. 24, 1915, d Nov. 12, 1960

Trimble, G. S. (Qld) b Jan. 1, 1963

*Trimborn, P. H. J. (Natal) b May 18, 1940

**Trott, A. E. (Vic., Middx & Hawkes Bay; *CY 1899*) b Feb. 6, 1873, d July 30, 1914

*Trott, G. H. S. (Vic.; *CY 1894*) b Aug. 5, 1866, d Nov. 10, 1917

*Troup, G. B. (Auck.) b Oct. 3, 1952

*Trueman, F. S. (Yorks.; *CY 1953*) b Feb. 6, 1931

*Trumble, H. (Vic.; *CY 1897*) b May 12, 1867, d Aug. 14, 1938

*Trumble, J. W. (Vic.) b Sept. 16, 1863, d Aug. 17, 1944

Trump, H. R. J. (Som.) b Oct. 11, 1968

*Trumper, V. T. (NSW; *CY 1903*) b Nov. 2, 1877, d June 28, 1915

*Truscott, P. B. (Wgtn) b Aug. 14, 1941

*Tuckett, L. (OFS) b Feb. 6, 1919

*Tuckett, L. R. (Natal & OFS) b April 19, 1885, d April 8, 1963

*Tufnell, N. C. (CUCC & Surrey) b June 13, 1887, d Aug. 3, 1951

*Tufnell, P. C. R. (Middx) b April 29, 1966

Tuke, Sir Anthony (Pres. MCC 1982-83) b Aug. 22, 1920

Tunnicliffe, C. J. (Derbys.) b Aug. 11, 1951

Tunnicliffe, H. T. (Notts.) b March 4, 1950

*Tunnicliffe, J. (Yorks.; *CY 1901*) b Aug. 26, 1866, d July 11, 1948

*Turnbull, M. J. (CUCC & Glam.; *CY 1931*) b March 16, 1906, d Aug. 5, 1944

*Turner, A. (NSW) b July 23, 1950

*Turner, C. T. B. (NSW; *CY 1889*) b Nov. 16, 1862, d Jan. 1, 1944
Turner, D. R. (Hants & W. Prov.) b Feb. 5, 1949
Turner, F. M. (Leics.) b Aug. 8, 1934
Turner, G. J. (W. Prov., N. Tvl & OUCC) b Aug. 5, 1964
*Turner, G. M. (Otago, N. Dist. & Worcs.; *CY 1971*) b May 26, 1947
Turner, R. J. (CUCC & Som.) b Nov. 25, 1967
Turner, S. (Essex & Natal) b July 18, 1943
*Twentyman-Jones, P. S. (W. Prov.) b Sept. 13, 1876, d March 8, 1954
Twining, R. H. (OUCC & Middx; Pres. MCC 1964-65) b Nov. 3, 1889, d Jan. 3, 1979
Twose, R. G. (Warwicks., N. Dist., C. Dist. & Wgtn) b April 17, 1968
*Tyldesley, E. (Lancs.; *CY 1920*) b Feb. 5, 1889, d May 5, 1962
*Tyldesley, J. T. (Lancs.; *CY 1902*) b Nov. 22, 1873, d Nov. 27, 1930
*Tyldesley, R. K. (Lancs.; *CY 1925*) b March 11, 1897, d Sept. 17, 1943
*Tylecote, E. F. S. (OUCC & Kent) b June 23, 1849, d March 15, 1938
*Tyler, E. J. (Som.) b Oct. 13, 1864, d Jan. 25, 1917
*Tyson, F. H. (Northants; *CY 1956*) b June 6, 1930

Udal, S. D. (Hants) b March 18, 1969
Ufton, D. G. (Kent) b May 31, 1928
*Ulyett, G. (Yorks.) b Oct. 21, 1851, d June 18, 1898
*Umrigar, P. R. (Bombay & Guj.) b March 28, 1926
*Underwood, D. L. (Kent; *CY 1969*) b June 8, 1945
Unwin, F. St G. (Essex) b April 23, 1911, d Oct. 4, 1990

*Vaas, W. P. U. J. C. (Colts) b Jan. 27, 1975
Vaidya, P. S. (Bengal) b Sept. 23, 1967
*Valentine, A. L. (Jam.; *CY 1951*) b April 29, 1930
*Valentine, B. H. (CUCC & Kent) b Jan. 17, 1908, d Feb. 2, 1983
*Valentine, V. A. (Jam.) b April 4, 1908, d July 6, 1972
*Vance, R. H. (Wgtn) b March 31, 1955
*van der Bijl, P. G. (W. Prov. & OUCC) b Oct. 21, 1907, d Feb. 16, 1973
van der Bijl, V. A. P. (Natal, Middx & Tvl; *CY 1981*) b March 19, 1948
Van der Gucht, P. I. (Glos. & Bengal) b Nov. 2, 1911, d Dec. 15, 1993
*Van der Merwe, E. A. (Tvl) b Nov. 9, 1904, d Feb. 26, 1971
*Van der Merwe, P. L. (W. Prov. & E. Prov.) b March 14, 1937

van Geloven, J. (Yorks. & Leics.) b Jan. 4, 1934
*Van Ryneveld, C. B. (W. Prov. & OUCC) b March 19, 1928
van Troost, A. P. (Holland & Som.) b Oct. 2, 1972
van Zyl, C. J. P. G. (OFS & Glam.) b Oct. 1, 1961
Varachia, R. (First Pres. SA Cricket Union) b Oct. 12, 1915, d Dec. 11, 1981
Varey, D. W. (CUCC & Lancs.) b Oct. 15, 1961
*Varnals, G. D. (E. Prov., Tvl & Natal) b July 24, 1935
Vaughan, M. P. (Yorks.) b Oct. 29, 1974
*Vaughan, J. T. C. (Auck.) b Aug. 30, 1967
Vaulkhard, P. (Notts. & Derbys.) b Sept. 15, 1911, d April 1, 1995
*Veivers, T. R. (Qld) b April 6, 1937
*Veletta, M. R. J. (W. Aust.) b Oct. 30, 1963
*Vengsarkar, D. B. (Bombay; *CY 1987*) b April 6, 1956
*Venkataraghavan, S. (†TN & Derbys.) b April 21, 1946
*Venkataramana, M. (TN) b April 24, 1966
*Verity, H. (Yorks.; *CY 1932*) b May 18, 1905, d July 31, 1943
*Vernon, G. F. (Middx) b June 20, 1856, d Aug. 10, 1902
Vigar, F. H. (Essex) b July 7, 1917
*Viljoen, K. G. (Griq. W., OFS & Tvl) b May 14, 1910, d Jan. 21, 1974
*Vincent, C. L. (Tvl) b Feb. 16, 1902, d Aug. 24, 1968
*Vine, J. (Sussex; *CY 1906*) b May 15, 1875, d April 25, 1946
*Vintcent, C. H. (Tvl & Griq. W.) b Sept. 2, 1866, d Sept. 28, 1943
Virgin, R. T. (Som., Northants & W. Prov.; *CY 1971*) b Aug. 26, 1939
*Viswanath, G. R. (†Karn.) b Feb. 12, 1949
*Viswanath, S. (Karn.) b Nov. 29, 1962
*Vivian, G. E. (Auck.) b Feb. 28, 1946
*Vivian, H. G. (Auck.) b Nov. 4, 1912, d Aug. 12, 1983
*Vizianagram, Maharaj Kumar of, Sir Vijay A. (U. Prov.) b Dec. 28, 1905, d Dec. 2, 1965
*Voce, W. (Notts.; *CY 1933*) b Aug. 8, 1909, d June 6, 1984
*Vogler, A. E. E. (Middx, Natal, Tvl & E. Prov.; *CY 1908*) b Nov. 28, 1876, d Aug. 9, 1946
Vonhagt, D. M. (Moors) b March 31, 1965

*Waddington, A. (Yorks.) b Feb. 4, 1893, d Oct. 28, 1959
Waddington, J. E. (Griq. W.) b Dec. 30, 1918, d Nov. 24, 1985
*Wade, H. F. (Natal) b Sept. 14, 1905, d Nov. 22, 1980

Wade, T. H. (Essex) b Nov. 24, 1910, d July 25, 1987

*Wade, W. W. (Natal) b June 18, 1914

*Wadekar, A. L. (Bombay) b April 1, 1941

*Wadsworth, K. J. (C. Dist. & Cant.) b Nov. 30, 1946, d Aug. 19, 1976

*Wainwright, E. (Yorks.; *CY 1894*) b April 8, 1865, d Oct. 28, 1919

*Waite, J. H. B. (E. Prov. & Tvl) b Jan. 19, 1930

*Waite, M. G. (S. Aust.) b Jan. 7, 1911, d Dec. 16, 1985

*Walcott, Sir C. L. (B'dos & BG; *CY 1958*) b Jan. 17, 1926

*Walcott, L. A. (B'dos) b Jan. 18, 1894, d Feb. 27, 1984

Walden, F. I. (Northants; Umpire) b March 1, 1888, d May 3, 1949

Walford, M. M. (OUCC & Som.) b Nov. 27, 1915

Walker, A. (Northants & Durham) b July 7, 1962

Walker, A. K. (NSW & Notts.) b Oct. 4, 1925

Walker, C. (Yorks. & Hants) b June 27, 1919, d Dec. 3, 1992

Walker, I. D. (Middx) b Jan. 8, 1844, d July 6, 1898

*Walker, M. H. N. (Vic.) b Sept. 12, 1948

*Walker, P. M. (Glam., Tvl & W. Prov.) b Feb. 17, 1936

Walker, V. E. (Middx) b April 20, 1837, d Jan. 3, 1906

Walker, W. (Notts.) b Nov. 24, 1892, d Dec. 3, 1991

*Wall, T. W. (S. Aust.) b May 13, 1904, d March 25, 1981

Wallace, P. A. (B'dos) b Aug. 2, 1970

*Wallace, W. M. (Auck.) b Dec. 19, 1916

Waller, A. C. (MCD) b Sept. 25, 1959

Waller, C. E. (Surrey & Sussex) b Oct. 3, 1948

*Walmsley, K. P. (Auck.) b Aug. 23, 1973

*Walsh, C. A. (Jam. & Glos.; *CY 1987*) b Oct. 30, 1962

Walsh, J. E. (NSW & Leics.) b Dec. 4, 1912, d May 20, 1980

*Walter, K. A. (Tvl) b Nov. 5, 1939

*Walters, C. F. (Glam. & Worcs.; *CY 1934*) b Aug. 28, 1905, d Dec. 23, 1992

*Walters, F. H. (Vic. & NSW) b Feb. 9, 1860, d June 1, 1922

Walters, J. (Derbys.) b Aug. 7, 1949

*Walters, K. D. (NSW) b Dec. 21, 1945

Walton, A. C. (OUCC & Middx) b Sept. 26, 1933

*Waqar Hassan (Pak. Us, Punjab, Pak. Serv. & Kar.) b Sept. 12, 1932

*Waqar Younis (Multan, UBL & Surrey; *CY 1992*) b Nov. 16, 1971

*Ward, Alan (Derbys., Leics. & Border) b Aug. 10, 1947

*Ward, Albert (Yorks. & Lancs.; *CY 1890*) b Nov. 21, 1865, d Jan. 6, 1939

Ward, B. (Essex) b Feb. 28, 1944

Ward, D. (Glam.) b Aug. 30, 1934

Ward, D. M. (Surrey) b Feb. 10, 1961

*Ward, F. A. (S. Aust.) b Feb. 23, 1906, d March 25, 1974

*Ward, J. T. (Cant.) b March 11, 1937

*Ward, T. A. (Tvl) b Aug. 2, 1887, d Feb. 16, 1936

Ward, T. R. (Kent) b Jan. 18, 1968

Ward, William (MCC & Hants) b July 24, 1787, d June 30, 1849

*Wardle, J. H. (Yorks.; *CY 1954*) b Jan. 8, 1923, d July 23, 1985

*Warnapura, B. (SL) b March 1, 1953

*Warnaweera, K. P. J. (Galle) b Nov. 23, 1960

*Warne, F. B. (Worcs., Vic. & Tvl) b Oct. 3, 1906, d May 29, 1994

*Warne, S. K. (Vic.; *CY 1994*) b Sept. 13, 1969

Warner, A. E. (Worcs. & Derbys.) b May 12, 1959

*Warner, Sir P. F. (OUCC & Middx; *CY 1904, special portrait 1921*; Pres. MCC 1950-51) b Oct. 2, 1873, d Jan. 30, 1963

*Warr, J. J. (CUCC & Middx; Pres. MCC 1987-88) b July 16, 1927

*Warren, A. R. (Derbys.) b April 2, 1875, d Sept. 3, 1951

Warren, R. J. (Northants) b Sept. 10, 1971

*Washbrook, C. (Lancs.; *CY 1947*) b Dec. 6, 1914

*Wasim Akram (Lahore, PACO, PNSC, PIA & Lancs.; *CY 1993*) b June 3, 1966

*Wasim Bari (Kar., PIA & Sind) b March 23, 1948

Wasim Haider (Faisalabad & PIA) b June 6, 1967

*Wasim Raja (Lahore, Sargodha, Pak. Us, PIA, Punjab & NBP) b July 3, 1952

Wass, T. G. (Notts.; *CY 1908*) b Dec. 26, 1873, d Oct. 27, 1953

*Wassan, A. S. (Delhi) b March 23, 1968

Wassell, A. (Hants) b April 15, 1940

*Watkin, S. L. (Glam.; *CY 1994*) b Sept. 15, 1964

*Watkins, A. J. (Glam.) b April 21, 1922

*Watkins, J. C. (Natal) b April 10, 1923

*Watkins, J. R. (NSW) b April 16, 1943

*Watkinson, M. (Lancs.) b Aug. 1, 1961

*Watson, C. (Jam. & Delhi) b July 1, 1938

Watson, F. B. (Lancs.) b Sept. 17, 1898, d Feb. 1, 1976

*Watson, G. D. (Vic., W. Aust. & NSW) b March 8, 1945

Watson, G. G. (NSW, W. Aust. & Worcs.) b Jan. 29, 1955

*Watson, W. (Yorks. & Leics.; *CY 1954*) b March 7, 1920

*Watson, W. (Auck.) b Aug. 31, 1965

*Watson, W. J. (NSW) b Jan. 3i, 1931

Watson, W. K. (Border, N. Tvl, E. Prov. & Notts.) b May 21, 1955

*Watt, L. (Otago) b Sept. 17, 1924

Watts, H. E. (CUCC & Som.) b March 4, 1922, d Dec. 27, 1993

Watts, P. D. (Northants & Notts.) b March 31, 1938

Watts, P. J. (Northants) b June 16, 1940

*Waugh, M. E. (NSW & Essex; *CY 1991*) b June 2, 1965

*Waugh, S. R. (NSW & Som.; *CY 1989*) b June 2, 1965

*Wazir Ali, S. (C. Ind., S. Punjab & Patiala) b Sept. 15, 1903, d June 17, 1950

*Wazir Mohammad (B'pur & Kar.) b Dec. 22, 1929

*Webb, M. G. (Otago & Cant.) b June 22, 1947

*Webb, P. N. (Auck.) b July 14, 1957

Webb, R. J. (Otago) b Sept. 15, 1952

Webb, R. T. (Sussex) b July 11, 1922

*Webbe, A. J. (OUCC & Middx) b Jan. 16, 1855, d Feb. 19, 1941

Webster, J. (CUCC & Northants) b Oct. 28, 1917

Webster, Dr R. V. (Warwicks. & Otago) b June 10, 1939

Webster, W. H. (CUCC & Middx; Pres. MCC 1976-77) b Feb. 22, 1910, d June 19, 1986

*Weekes, Sir E. D. (B'dos; *CY 1951*) b Feb. 26, 1925

*Weekes, K. H. (Jam.) b Jan. 24, 1912

Weekes, P. N. (Middx) b July 8, 1969

Weeks, R. T. (Warwicks.) b April 30, 1930

Weerakkody, A. P. (NCC) b Oct. 1, 1970

*Weerasinghe, C. D. U. S. (TU & NCC) b March 1, 1968

*Weir, G. L. (Auck.) b June 2, 1908

*Wellard, A. W. (Som.; *CY 1936*) b April 8, 1902, d Dec. 31, 1980

*Wellham, D. M. (NSW, Tas. & Qld) b March 13, 1959

Wellings, E. M. (OUCC & Surrey) b April 6, 1909, d Sept. 10, 1992

*Wells, A. P. (Sussex & Border) b Oct. 2, 1961

Wells, B. D. (Glos. & Notts.) b July 27, 1930

Wells, C. M. (Sussex, Border, W. Prov. & Derbys.) b March 3, 1960

Wells, V. J. (Kent & Leics.) b Aug. 6, 1965

Wenman, E. G. (Kent & England) b Aug. 18, 1803, d Dec. 31, 1879

Wensley, A. F. (Sussex) b May 23, 1898, d June 17, 1970

*Wesley, C. (Natal) b Sept. 5, 1937

**Wessels, K. C. (OFS, W. Prov., N. Tvl, Sussex, Qld & E. Prov.; *CY 1995*) b Sept. 14, 1957

West, G. H. (Editor of *Wisden* 1880-86) b 1851, d Oct. 6, 1896

*Westcott, R. J. (W. Prov.) b Sept. 19, 1927

Weston, M. J. (Worcs.) b April 8, 1959

Weston, W. P. C. (Worcs.) b June 16, 1973

*Wettimuny, M. D. (SL) b June 11, 1951

*Wettimuny, S. (SL; *CY 1985*) b Aug. 12, 1956

Wettimuny, S. R. de S. (SL) b Feb. 7, 1949

*Wharton, A. (Lancs. & Leics.) b April 30, 1923, d Aug. 26, 1993

*Whatmore, D. F. (Vic.) b March 16, 1954

Wheatley, K. J. (Hants) b Jan. 20, 1946

Wheatley, O. S. (CUCC, Warwicks. & Glam.; *CY 1969*) b May 28, 1935

Whitaker, Haddon (Editor of *Wisden* 1940-43) b Aug. 30, 1908, d Jan. 5, 1982

*Whitaker, J. J. (Leics.; *CY 1987*) b May 5, 1962

Whitcombe, P. A. (OUCC & Middx) b April 23, 1923

White, A. F. T. (CUCC, Warwicks. & Worcs.) b Sept. 5, 1915, d March 16, 1993

*White, C. (Vic. & Yorks.) b Dec. 16, 1969

*White, D. J. (N. Dist.) b June 26, 1961

*White, D. W. (Hants & Glam.) b Dec. 14, 1935

White, E. C. S. (NSW) b July 14, 1913

*White, G. C. (Tvl) b Feb. 5, 1882, d Oct. 17, 1918

White, G. W. (Som. & Hants) b March 23, 1972

*White, J. C. (Som.; *CY 1929*) b Feb. 19, 1891, d May 2, 1961

White, Hon. L. R. (5th Lord Annaly) (Middx & Victory Test) b March 15, 1927, d Sept. 30, 1990

White, R. A. (Middx & Notts.; Umpire) b Oct. 6, 1936

White, R. C. (CUCC, Glos. & Tvl) b Jan. 29, 1941

*White, W. A. (B'dos) b Nov. 20, 1938

Whitehead, J. P. (Yorks. & Worcs.) b Sept. 3, 1925

Whitehouse, J. (Warwicks.) b April 8, 1949

*Whitelaw, P. E. (Auck.) b Feb. 10, 1910, d Aug. 28, 1988

Whitfield, B. J. (Natal) b March 14, 1959

Whitfield, E. W. (Surrey & Northants) b May 31, 1911

Whiting, N. H. (Worcs.) b Oct. 2, 1920

Whitington, R. S. (S. Aust. & Victory Tests; Writer) b June 30, 1912, d March 13, 1984

*Whitney, M. R. (NSW & Glos.) b Feb. 24, 1959

Whittaker, G. J. (Surrey) b May 29, 1916

Whittall, A. R. (CUCC) b March 28, 1973

*Whittall, G. J. (Mat.) b Sept. 5, 1972

Whitticase, P. (Leics.) b March 15, 1965

Whittingham, N. B. (Notts.) b Oct. 22, 1940

*Whitty, W. J. (S. Aust.) b Aug. 15, 1886, d Jan. 30, 1974

*Whysall, W. W. (Notts.; *CY 1925*) b Oct. 31, 1887, d Nov. 11, 1930

Wickremaratne, R. P. A. H. (SSC) b Feb. 21, 1971

*Wickremasinghe, A. G. D. (NCC) b Dec. 27, 1965

*Wickremasinghe, G. P. (BRC & SSC) b Aug. 14, 1971

*Wiener, J. M. (Vic.) b May 1, 1955

*Wight, C. V. (BG) b July 28, 1902, d Oct. 4, 1969

*Wight, G. L. (BG) b May 28, 1929

Wight, P. B. (BG, Som., & Cant.) b June 25, 1930

*Wijegunawardene, K. I. W. (CCC) b Nov. 23, 1964

*Wijesuriya, R. G. C. E. (Mor. & Colts) b Feb. 18, 1960

*Wijetunge, P. K. (SSC) b Aug. 6, 1971

Wild, D. J. (Northants) b Nov. 28, 1962

*Wiles, C. A. (B'dos & T/T) b Aug. 11, 1892, d Nov. 4, 1957

Wilkins, A. H. (Glam., Glos. & N. Tvl) b Aug. 22, 1953

Wilkins, C. P. (Derbys., Border, E. Prov. & Natal) b July 31, 1944

*Wilkinson, L. L. (Lancs.) b Nov. 5, 1916

Wilkinson, P. A. (Notts.) b Aug. 23, 1951

Willatt, G. L. (CUCC, Notts. & Derbys.) b May 7, 1918

Willett, E. T. (Comb. Is. & Leewards) b May 1, 1953

Willett, M. D. (Surrey) b April 21, 1933

*Willey, P. (Northants, E. Prov. & Leics.) b Dec. 6, 1949

*Williams, A. B. (Jam.) b Nov. 21, 1949

Williams, C. C. P. (Lord Williams of Elvet) (OUCC & Essex) b Feb. 9, 1933

*Williams, D. (T/T) b Nov. 4, 1963

Williams, D. L. (Glam.) b Nov. 20, 1946

*Williams, E. A. V. (B'dos) b April 10, 1914

*Williams, N. F. (Middx, Windwards, Tas. & Essex) b July 2, 1962

Williams, R. G. (Northants) b Aug. 10, 1957

*Williams, R. J. (Natal) b April 12, 1912, d May 14, 1984

*Williams, S. C. (Leewards) b Aug. 12, 1969

Williamson, J. G. (Northants) b April 4, 1936

*Willis, R. G. D. (Surrey, Warwicks. & N. Tvl; *CY 1978*) b May 30, 1949

*Willoughby, J. T. (SA) b Nov. 7, 1874, d circa 1955

Willsher, E. (Kent & All-England) b Nov. 22, 1828, d Oct. 7, 1885

Wilmot, K. (Warwicks.) b April 3, 1911

Wilson, A. (Lancs.) b April 24, 1921

Wilson, A. E. (Middx & Glos.) b May 18, 1910

*Wilson, Rev. C. E. M. (CUCC & Yorks.) b May 15, 1875, d Feb. 8, 1944

*Wilson, D. (Yorks. & MCC) b Aug. 7, 1937

*Wilson, E. R. (CUCC & Yorks.) b March 25, 1879, d July 21, 1957

Wilson, J. V. (Yorks.; *CY 1961*) b Jan. 17, 1921

Wilson, J. W. (Otago) b Oct. 24, 1973

*Wilson, J. W. (Vic. & S. Aust.) b Aug. 20, 1921, d Oct. 13, 1985

Wilson, P. H. L. (Surrey, Som. & N. Tvl) b Aug. 17, 1958

Wilson, R. C. (Kent) b Feb. 18, 1928

*Wimble, C. S. (Tvl) b Jan. 9, 1864, d Jan. 28, 1930

Windows, A. R. (Glos. & CUCC) b Sept. 25, 1942

Winfield, H. M. (Notts.) b June 13, 1933

Wingfield Digby, Rev. A. R. (OUCC) b July 25, 1950

Winn, C. E. (OUCC & Sussex) b Nov. 13, 1926

*Winslow, P. L. (Sussex, Tvl & Rhod.) b May 21, 1929

Wisden, John (Sussex; founder John Wisden and Co. and *Wisden's Cricketers' Almanack*) b Sept. 5, 1826, d April 5, 1884

*Wishart, K. L. (BG) b Nov. 28, 1908, d Oct. 18, 1972

Wolton, A. V. G. (Warwicks.) b June 12, 1919, d Sept. 9, 1990

*Wood, A. (Yorks.; *CY 1939*) b Aug. 25, 1898, d April 1, 1973

*Wood, B. (Yorks., Lancs., Derbys. & E. Prov.) b Dec. 26, 1942

Wood, C. J. B. (Leics.) b Nov. 21, 1875, d June 5, 1960

Wood, D. J. (Sussex) b May 19, 1914, d March 12, 1989

*Wood, G. E. C. (CUCC & Kent) b Aug. 22, 1893, d March 18, 1971

*Wood, G. M. (W. Aust.) b Nov. 6, 1956

*Wood, H. (Kent & Surrey; *CY 1891*) b Dec. 14, 1854, d April 30, 1919

Wood, J. (Durham) b July 22, 1970

*Wood, R. (Lancs. & Vic.) b March 7, 1860, d Jan. 6, 1915

*Woodcock, A. J. (S. Aust.) b Feb. 27, 1948

Woodcock, John C. (Editor of *Wisden* 1981-86) b Aug. 7, 1926

*Woodfull, W. M. (Vic.; *CY 1927*) b Aug. 22, 1897, d Aug. 11, 1965

Woodhead, F. G. (Notts.) b Oct. 30, 1912, d May 24, 1991

Woodhouse, G. E. S. (Som.) b Feb. 15, 1924, d Jan. 19, 1988

**Woods, S. M. J. (CUCC & Som.; *CY 1889*) b April 13, 1867, d April 30, 1931

Wookey, S. M. (CUCC & OUCC) b Sept. 2, 1954

Wooler, C. R. D. (Leics. & Rhod.) b June 30, 1930

Wooller, W. (CUCC & Glam.) b Nov. 20, 1912

Woolley, C. N. (Glos. & Northants) b May 5, 1886, d Nov. 3, 1962

*Woolley, F. E. (Kent; *CY 1911*) b May 27, 1887, d Oct. 18, 1978

*Woolley, R. D. (Tas.) b Sept. 16, 1954

*Woolmer, R. A. (Kent, Natal & W. Prov.; *CY 1976*) b May 14, 1948

*Worrall, J. (Vic.) b June 21, 1861, d Nov. 17, 1937

*Worrell, Sir F. M. M. (B'dos & Jam.; *CY 1951*) b Aug. 1, 1924, d March 13, 1967

Worsley, D. R. (OUCC & Lancs.) b July 18, 1941

Worsley, Sir W. A. 4th Bt (Yorks.; Pres. MCC 1961-62) b April 5, 1890, d Dec. 4, 1973

*Worthington, T. S. (Derbys.; *CY 1937*) b Aug. 21, 1905, d Aug. 31, 1973

Wright, A. (Warwicks.) b Aug. 25, 1941

Wright, A. J. (Glos.) b July 27, 1962

*Wright, C. W. (CUCC & Notts.) b May 27, 1863, d Jan. 10, 1936

*Wright, D. V. P. (Kent; *CY 1940*) b Aug. 21, 1914

Wright, Graeme A. (Editor of *Wisden* 1987-92) b April 23, 1943

*Wright, J. G. (N. Dist., Derbys., Cant. & Auck.) b July 5, 1954

*Wright, K. J. (W. Aust. & S. Aust.) b Dec. 27, 1953

Wright, L. G. (Derbys.; *CY 1906*) b June 15, 1862, d Jan. 11, 1953

Wyatt, J. G. (Som.) b June 19, 1963

*Wyatt, R. E. S. (Warwicks. & Worcs.; *CY 1930*) b May 2, 1901, d April 20, 1995

*Wynne, O. E. (Tvl & W. Prov.) b June 1, 1919, d July 13, 1975

*Wynyard, E. G. (Hants) b April 1, 1861, d Oct. 30, 1936

Yachad, M. (N. Tvl & Tvl) b Nov. 17, 1960

*Yadav, N. S. (H'bad) b Jan. 26, 1957

*Yadav, V. S. (Haryana) b March 14, 1967

*Yajurvindra Singh (M'tra & S'tra) b Aug. 1, 1952

*Yallop, G. N. (Vic.) b Oct. 7, 1952

*Yardley, B. (W. Aust.) b Sept. 5, 1947

*Yardley, N. W. D. (CUCC & Yorks.; *CY 1948*) b March 19, 1915, d Oct. 4, 1989

Yardley, T. J. (Worcs. & Northants) b Oct. 27, 1946

Yarnold, H. (Worcs.) b July 6, 1917, d Aug. 13, 1974

*Yashpal Sharma (Punjab) b Aug. 11, 1954

Yates, G. (Lancs.) b Sept. 20, 1967

Yawar Saeed (Som. & Punjab) b Jan. 22, 1935

*Yograj Singh (Haryana & Punjab) b March 25, 1958

*Young, B. A. (N. Dist.) b Nov. 3, 1964

*Young, D. M. (Worcs. & Glos.) b April 15, 1924, d June 18, 1993

*Young, H. I. (Essex) b Feb. 5, 1876, d Dec. 12, 1964

*Young, J. A. (Middx) b Oct. 14, 1912, d Feb. 5, 1993

*Young, R. A. (CUCC & Sussex) b Sept. 16, 1885, d July 1, 1968

*Younis Ahmed (Lahore, Kar., Surrey, PIA, S. Aust., Worcs. & Glam.) b Oct. 20, 1947

*Yuile, B. W. (C. Dist.) b Oct. 29, 1941

Zafar Iqbal (Kar., NBP & Lahore) b March 6, 1969

*Zaheer Abbas (Kar., Glos., PWD, Dawood Indust., Sind & PIA; *CY 1972*) b July 24, 1947

Zahid Ahmed (PIA, Peshawar & F'bad) b Nov. 15, 1961

*Zahid Fazal (PACO, PIA & Lahore) b Nov. 10, 1973

*Zakir Khan (Sind, Peshawar & ADBP) b April 3, 1963

Zesers, A. K. (S. Aust.) b March 11, 1967

*Zoehrer, T. J. (W. Aust.) b Sept. 25, 1961

*Zulch, J. W. (Tvl) b Jan. 2, 1886, d May 19, 1924

*Zulfiqar Ahmed (B'pur & PIA) b Nov. 22, 1926

*Zulqarnain (Pak. Rlwys, Lahore, HBFC & PACO) b May 25, 1962

PART THREE: ENGLISH CRICKET IN 1995

FEATURES OF 1995

Double-Hundreds (15)

255	P. A. de Silva§......	Kent v Derbyshire at Maidstone.
254*	A. Symonds	Gloucestershire v Glamorgan at Abergavenny.
235	M. R. Ramprakash§ ..	Middlesex v Yorkshire at Leeds.
230*	S. P. James.........	Glamorgan v Leicestershire at Leicester.
228*	D. J. Bicknell.......	Surrey v Nottinghamshire at Guildford.
225	P. A. de Silva§......	Kent v Nottinghamshire at Nottingham.
216	C. J. Adams.........	Derbyshire v Kent at Maidstone.
214	M. R. Ramprakash§ ..	Middlesex v Surrey at Lord's.
213	D. Byas.............	Yorkshire v Worcestershire at Scarborough.
213	W. J. Cronje	Leicestershire v Somerset at Weston-super-Mare.
209	R. T. Robinson	Nottinghamshire v Northamptonshire at Northampton.
208	D. P. Ostler	Warwickshire v Surrey at Birmingham.
205	M. R. Ramprakash§ ..	Middlesex v Sussex at Lord's.
203*	M. D. Moxon.......	Yorkshire v Kent at Leeds.
200*	A. S. Rollins........	Derbyshire v Gloucestershire at Bristol.

§ M. R. Ramprakash scored three double-hundreds; P. A. de Silva scored two.

Hundred on First-Class Debut in Britain

181	M. L. Love..........	Young Australia v Somerset at Taunton.
161*	A. Symonds	Gloucestershire v Surrey at The Oval.
122	A. C. Gilchrist.......	Young Australia v Somerset at Taunton.
113*	M. G. Bevan	Yorkshire v Cambridge University at Cambridge.
110	S. Young............	Young Australia v Somerset at Taunton.

Three Hundreds in Successive Innings

M. W. Gatting (Middlesex) ....108 v Gloucestershire at Bristol, 101 v Sussex at Lord's, 148 v Nottinghamshire at Lord's.

T. M. Moody (Worcestershire)..157 and 106 v Nottinghamshire at Nottingham, 110 v Lancashire at Worcester.

M. R. Ramprakash (Middlesex).158 and 111* v Leicestershire at Uxbridge, 115 v Somerset at Taunton.

Hundred in Each Innings of a Match

R. J. Bailey	157	119	Northamptonshire v Middlesex at Uxbridge.
J. P. Crawley	182	108	Lancashire v Glamorgan at Manchester.
P. A. de Silva	255	116	Kent v Derbyshire at Maidstone.
M. A. Lynch	108	114	Gloucestershire v Kent at Canterbury.
T. M. Moody.......	157	106	Worcestershire v Nottinghamshire at Nottingham.
H. Morris..........	166*	104*	Glamorgan v Nottinghamshire at Cardiff.
M. R. Ramprakash..	158	111*	Middlesex v Leicestershire at Uxbridge.
P. V. Simmons	112	139*	West Indians v Essex at Chelmsford.
M. E. Waugh	121*	121	Essex v Derbyshire at Chelmsford.
A. P. Wells	107	136	Sussex v Kent at Hove.

Fastest Hundred

C. L. Cairns .... 65 balls (76 minutes) Nottinghamshire v Cambridge University at Cambridge.

Hundred Before Lunch

G. A. Hick	27*-144*	Worcestershire v Lancashire at Worcester (2nd day).
C. L. Hooper.	105*	West Indians v Combined Universities at Oxford (1st day).
J. C. Pooley.	100*	Middlesex v Nottinghamshire at Lord's (1st day).
M. R. Ramprakash. .	111*	Middlesex v Leicestershire at Uxbridge (4th day).
N. R. Taylor	101*	Kent v Leicestershire at Canterbury (1st day).

Most Sixes in an Innings

16   A. Symonds† . . . .   Gloucestershire v Glamorgan at Abergavenny.

   † *World record.*

Most Sixes in a Match

20   A. Symonds† . . . .   Gloucestershire v Glamorgan at Abergavenny.

   † *World record.*

First to 1,000 Runs

D. Byas (Yorkshire) on June 29.

2,000 Runs

M. R. Ramprakash (Middlesex, England and England A) on September 11.

Carrying Bat Through Completed Innings

N. E. Briers	175*	Leicestershire (359) v Worcestershire at Worcester.
T. S. Curtis	75*	Worcestershire (177) v Warwickshire at Birmingham.
J. C. Pooley	85*	Middlesex (174) v Derbyshire at Lord's.
A. S. Rollins.	200*	Derbyshire (463) v Gloucestershire at Bristol (*one man retired hurt*).
T. R. Ward	114*	Kent (215) v Northamptonshire at Canterbury.

Unusual Dismissals – Stumped by a Substitute

A. P. Grayson by M. J. Birks, Cambridge University v Yorkshire at Cambridge.
R. J. Blakey by M. J. Birks, Cambridge University v Yorkshire at Cambridge.

First-Wicket Partnership of 100 in Each Innings

107   103   M. P. Dowman/R. T. Robinson, Nottinghamshire v Essex at Nottingham.
123   106*   J. E. R. Gallian/N. J. Speak, Lancashire v Essex at Manchester.

Other Notable Partnerships

First Wicket
362   A. J. Wright/G. D. Hodgson, Gloucestershire v Nottinghamshire at Bristol.
283   C. M. Gupte/I. J. Sutcliffe, Oxford University v Hampshire at Oxford.
263   N. J. Lenham/K. Newell, Sussex v West Indians at Hove.
260*   S. Chanderpaul/P. V. Simmons, West Indians v Essex at Chelmsford.

Second Wicket
294   R. T. Robinson/G. F. Archer, Nottinghamshire v Northamptonshire at Northampton.
260   D. J. Bicknell/G. P. Thorpe, Surrey v Kent at Canterbury.

Third Wicket
306   D. L. Hemp/M. P. Maynard, Glamorgan v Gloucestershire at Abergavenny.
259   V. P. Terry/R. A. Smith, Hampshire v Sussex at Portsmouth.
253   M. R. Ramprakash/J. D. Carr, Middlesex v Hampshire at Lord's.
250   G. A. Hick/T. M. Moody, Worcestershire v Lancashire at Worcester.

Fourth Wicket
368†   P. A. de Silva/G. R. Cowdrey, Kent v Derbyshire at Maidstone.
261   M. L. Hayden/J. L. Langer, Young Australia v Sussex at Hove.

Fifth Wicket
282   A. J. Lamb/K. M. Curran, Northamptonshire v Surrey at Northampton.
237   J. P. Crawley/W. K. Hegg, Lancashire v Northamptonshire at Manchester.
225   S. P. Titchard/M. Watkinson, Lancashire v Essex at Manchester.

Sixth Wicket
337   R. R. Montgomerie/D. J. Capel, Northamptonshire v Kent at Canterbury.
315†   P. A. de Silva/M. A. Ealham, Kent v Nottinghamshire at Nottingham.

Tenth Wicket
122   N. E. Briers/A. R. K. Pierson, Leicestershire v Worcestershire at Worcester.
100   A. J. Hollioake/J. E. Benjamin, Surrey v Warwickshire at Birmingham.

     * *Unbroken partnership.*   † *County record for that wicket.*

Twelve or More Wickets in a Match

15-83	C. L. Cairns	Nottinghamshire v Sussex at Arundel.
14-105	M. C. Ilott	Essex v Northamptonshire at Luton.
14-177	A. Walker	Durham v Essex at Chelmsford.
13-93	D. G. Cork	Derbyshire v Northamptonshire at Derby.
13-150	J. Srinath	Gloucestershire v Glamorgan at Abergavenny.
13-192	A. Kumble	Northamptonshire v Hampshire at Northampton.
12-68	J. N. B. Bovill...	Hampshire v Durham at Stockton-on-Tees.
12-157	J. E. Emburey ...	Middlesex v Yorkshire at Leeds.
12-165	Wasim Akram....	Lancashire v Leicestershire at Leicester.
12-178	P. M. Such	Essex v Worcestershire at Chelmsford.

Eight or More Wickets in an Innings

9-19	M. C. Ilott	Essex v Northamptonshire at Luton.
9-41	P. J. Hartley	Yorkshire v Derbyshire at Chesterfield.
9-43	D. G. Cork	Derbyshire v Northamptonshire at Derby.
9-76	J. Srinath	Gloucestershire v Glamorgan at Abergavenny.
8-47	C. L. Cairns	Nottinghamshire v Sussex at Arundel.
8-69	A. R. Caddick....	Somerset v Durham at Chester-le-Street.
8-93	P. M. Such	Essex v Hampshire at Colchester.
8-118	A. Walker	Durham v Essex at Chelmsford.

Hat-Tricks

D. G. Cork	....	England v West Indies (Fourth Test) at Manchester.
D. Gough†	....	Yorkshire v Kent at Leeds.
P. J. Hartley‡	....	Yorkshire v Derbyshire at Chesterfield.
M. C. Ilott§	....	Essex v Northamptonshire at Luton.
M. E. Trescothick	....	Somerset v Young Australia at Taunton.

† Also four wickets in five balls.   ‡ Also five wickets in nine balls.   § All lbw.

100 Wickets

A. Kumble (Northamptonshire) on September 9.

Most Runs Conceded in an Innings

41–4–223–3 ..	J. A. Afford	Nottinghamshire v Northamptonshire at Northampton.
59.5–10–206–6	M. M. Patel	Kent v Surrey at Canterbury.

Most Overs Bowled in an Innings

60–17–192–2 ..	Mushtaq Ahmed	Somerset v Worcestershire at Worcester.

Nine or More Wicket-Keeping Dismissals in a Match

7 ct, 3 st	A. C. Gilchrist	Young Australia v TCCB XI at Birmingham.
9 ct	C. O. Browne	West Indies v England (Fifth Test) at Nottingham.
9 ct	C. P. Metson	Glamorgan v Surrey at The Oval.
8 ct, 1 st	K. J. Piper	Warwickshire v Hampshire at Southampton.

Six Wicket-Keeping Dismissals in an Innings

4 ct, 2 st	A. C. Gilchrist	Young Australia v TCCB XI at Birmingham.
6 ct	W. K. Hegg	Lancashire v Derbyshire at Derby.
6 ct	K. M. Krikken	Derbyshire v Oxford University at Oxford.
6 ct	K. J. Piper	Warwickshire v Gloucestershire at Birmingham.
6 ct	R. J. Turner	Somerset v West Indians at Taunton.

Eight Catches in a Match in the Field

J. D. Carr ..... Middlesex v Warwickshire at Birmingham.

Six Catches in an Innings in the Field

J. D. Carr ..... Middlesex v Warwickshire at Birmingham.

No Byes Conceded in Total of 500 or More

W. M. Noon ...	Nottinghamshire v Middlesex (587) at Lord's.
P. Whitticase...	Leicestershire v Kent (575) at Canterbury.
S. A. Marsh....	Kent v Surrey (559) at Canterbury.
W. M. Noon	Nottinghamshire v Kent (533) at Nottingham.
G. J. Kersey ...	Surrey v Leicestershire (503) at Leicester.

Highest Innings Totals

781-7 dec.†... Northamptonshire v Nottinghamshire at Northampton.
696-6 dec..... West Indians v Hampshire at Southampton.
692-8 dec..... West Indies v England (Sixth Test) at The Oval.
670-7 dec.†... Worcestershire v Somerset at Worcester.
662-7 dec..... Essex v Hampshire at Colchester.
652-9 dec..... Surrey v Durham at The Oval.
637-5 dec..... West Indians v Combined Universities at Oxford.
603-6 dec..... Derbyshire v Sussex at Derby.
602-7 dec..... Middlesex v Sussex at Lord's.
600-4 dec..... Yorkshire v Worcestershire at Scarborough.
587......... Middlesex v Nottinghamshire at Lord's.
580-8 dec..... Young Australia v Sussex at Hove.
575......... Kent v Leicestershire at Canterbury.
564......... Northamptonshire v Leicestershire at Northampton.
561-8 dec..... Northamptonshire v Kent at Canterbury.
560......... Hampshire v Northamptonshire at Northampton.
559......... Surrey v Kent at Canterbury.

   † *County record.*

Highest Fourth-Innings Totals

467-9 .... Worcestershire v Derbyshire at Kidderminster (set 517).
430......... Somerset v Young Australia at Taunton (set 461).
413......... Worcestershire v Hampshire at Southampton (set 484).
404-5 .... Leicestershire v Oxford University at Oxford (set 404).

Lowest Innings Totals

46......... Northamptonshire v Essex at Luton.
59......... Northamptonshire v Surrey at Northampton.
67†........ Leicestershire v Warwickshire at Leicester.
83†........ Leicestershire v Worcestershire at Worcester.
85......... Durham v Kent at Chester-le-Street.
87......... Somerset v West Indians at Taunton.
88......... Middlesex v Lancashire at Lord's.
89†........ England v West Indies (Third Test) at Birmingham.
91......... Cambridge University v Nottinghamshire at Cambridge.
95......... Kent v West Indians at Canterbury.
96......... Yorkshire v Warwickshire at Birmingham.
97......... Oxford University v Derbyshire at Oxford.

   † *One man absent.*

Match Aggregates of 1,400 Runs

Runs-Wkts
1,642-29 ..... Nottinghamshire v Kent at Nottingham.
1,601-35 ..... Kent v Surrey at Canterbury.
1,587-32 ..... Kent v Derbyshire at Maidstone.
1,559-39 ..... Glamorgan v Gloucestershire at Abergavenny.
1,502-32 ..... Somerset v Young Australia at Taunton.
1,478-39 ..... Surrey v Glamorgan at The Oval.
1,474-35 ..... Hampshire v Worcestershire at Southampton.
1,473-17 ..... Yorkshire v Worcestershire at Scarborough.
1,465-27 ..... Northamptonshire v Nottinghamshire at Northampton.
1,463-29 ..... Lancashire v Glamorgan at Manchester.
1,451-33 ..... Worcestershire v Derbyshire at Kidderminster.

Batsman's Match

86.64 runs per wicket . . . . Yorkshire (600-4 dec., 231-3 dec.) v Worcestershire (453-5 dec., 189-5) at Scarborough.

Victory after Following On

Surrey (217, 475) beat Gloucestershire (392, 207) at The Oval.
Somerset (189, 434) beat Derbyshire (376, 168) at Derby.

Four Hundreds in an Innings

West Indians (637-5 dec.) v Combined Universities at Oxford:
  C. L. Hooper 118, S. C. Williams 114, J. C. Adams 114*, K. L. T. Arthurton 102*.
Northamptonshire (781-7 dec.) v Nottinghamshire at Northampton:
  A. Fordham 130, A. J. Lamb 115, R. J. Warren 154, D. J. Capel 114*.

Most Extras in an Innings

b	l-b	w	n-b	
71	8	18	0	45	Warwickshire (462) v Worcestershire at Birmingham.
69	1	10	1	57	Somerset (374) v West Indians at Taunton.
67	2	13	1	51	Durham (364-8 dec.) v West Indians at Chester-le-Street.
64	10	14	2	38	Nottinghamshire (364) v Leicestershire at Leicester.
64	18	11	1	34	England (437) v West Indies (Fourth Test) at Manchester.
64	8	22	2	32	Yorkshire (505) v Lancashire at Manchester.
64	9	21	10	24	Northamptonshire (781-7 dec.) v Nottinghamshire at Northampton.

Under TCCB regulations, two extras were scored for every no-ball, excluding runs scored off the delivery, except in Tests. There were 14 further instances of 50 or more extras in an innings.

Career Aggregate Milestones†

25,000 runs	G. A. Hick.
15,000 runs	M. P. Maynard, M. E. Waugh.
10,000 runs	P. D. Bowler, J. D. Carr, P. A. de Silva, M. R. Ramprakash, R. C. Russell, G. P. Thorpe.
1,000 wickets	J. H. Childs.
500 wickets	M. P. Bicknell, D. J. Capel, C. A. Connor, A. R. C. Fraser, R. J. Maru, P. M. Such.

† *Achieved since September 1994.*

FIRST-CLASS AVERAGES, 1995

BATTING

(Qualification: 8 completed innings)

Signifies not out.   † Denotes a left-handed batsman.

		M	I	NO	R	HS	100s	50s	Avge
1	M. R. Ramprakash (*Middx*)	20	32	3	2,258	235	10	7	77.86
2	M. D. Moxon (*Yorks.*)	13	23	8	1,145	203*	3	8	76.33
3	†A. C. Gilchrist (*Young Australia*) .	8	11	3	495	122	2	2	61.87
4	P. A. de Silva (*Kent*)	16	30	0	1,781	255	7	7	59.36
5	†B. C. Lara (*West Indians*)	13	20	1	1,126	179	3	7	59.26
6	†S. Chanderpaul (*West Indians*) ...	15	25	8	1,003	140*	4	5	59.00
7	†J. L. Langer (*Young Australia*) ...	7	12	3	516	149	2	2	57.33
8	†K. L. T. Arthurton (*West Indians*)	15	23	4	1,077	146	3	6	56.68
9	†D. Byas (*Yorks.*)	20	37	3	1,913	213	4	10	56.26
10	A. J. Lamb (*Northants*)	16	24	4	1,237	166	3	6	56.22
11	A. Symonds (*Glos.*)	18	31	5	1,438	254*	4	9	55.30
12	T. M. Moody (*Worcs.*)	18	31	2	1,600	168	5	7	55.17
13	†M. G. Bevan (*Yorks.*)	20	34	5	1,598	153*	6	7	55.10
14	N. Hussain (*Essex*)	19	35	1	1,854	186	6	10	54.52
15	A. P. Wells (*Sussex*)	18	30	2	1,524	178	7	4	54.42
16	M. W. Gatting (*Middx*)	16	22	1	1,139	148	5	3	54.23
17	R. T. Robinson (*Notts.*)	18	32	0	1,728	209	7	5	54.00
18	P. D. Bowler (*Somerset*)	19	33	3	1,619	196	6	5	53.96
19	†P. C. L. Holloway (*Somerset*)	12	22	6	863	129*	2	6	53.93
20	R. A. Smith (*Hants*)	12	23	2	1,117	172	3	4	53.19
21	†H. Morris (*Glam.*)	18	33	3	1,574	166*	6	8	52.46
22	M. E. Waugh (*Essex & NSW*) ...	16	29	2	1,392	173	5	6	51.55
23	†J. C. Pooley (*Middx*)	18	30	4	1,335	136	5	6	51.34
24	G. A. Gooch (*Essex*)	18	34	1	1,669	165	7	6	50.57
25	W. J. Cronje (*Leics.*)	16	28	1	1,362	213	4	7	50.44
26	T. L. Penney (*Warwicks.*)	19	27	3	1,198	144	4	4	49.91
27	†W. G. Khan (*Warwicks.*)	13	23	6	847	181	1	6	49.82
28	G. A. Hick (*Worcs.*)	16	27	3	1,193	152	4	5	49.70
29	†N. V. Knight (*Warwicks.*)	13	23	5	887	174	1	7	49.27
30	R. J. Harden (*Somerset*)	19	35	6	1,429	129*	5	6	49.27
31	P. A. Cottey (*Glam.*)	19	33	3	1,465	130	5	7	48.83
32	J. D. Carr (*Middx*)	20	29	6	1,098	129	4	3	47.73
33	J. P. Crawley (*Lancs.*)	18	31	2	1,377	182	3	10	47.48
34	†S. C. Ecclestone (*Somerset*)	7	12	2	472	81	0	3	47.20
35	S. L. Campbell (*West Indians*) ...	16	26	0	1,225	172	3	6	47.11
36	A. J. Wright (*Glos.*)	18	34	4	1,401	193	4	5	46.70
37	R. Q. Cake (*CUCC*)	7	14	3	511	101	1	2	46.45
38	M. L. Love (*Young Australia*) ...	7	13	2	510	181	2	1	46.36
39	C. L. Hooper (*West Indians*)	15	25	2	1,063	195	5	2	46.21
40	R. T. Ponting (*Young Australia*) ..	7	12	2	460	103*	1	4	46.00
41	†M. L. Hayden (*Young Australia*) .	7	14	2	551	178	2	1	45.91
42	†R. G. Twose (*Warwicks.*)	19	30	4	1,186	191	4	3	45.61
43	D. J. Cullinan (*Derbys.*)	14	26	4	1,003	161	5	1	45.59
44	M. P. Maynard (*Glam.*)	20	36	1	1,590	164	3	12	45.42
45	C. O. Browne (*West Indians*) ...	12	16	5	498	102*	2	1	45.27
46	K. J. Barnett (*Derbys.*)	17	31	3	1,251	169	2	7	44.67
47	†R. C. Russell (*Glos.*)	17	26	4	977	91	0	8	44.40
48	A. J. Moles (*Warwicks.*)	9	16	0	710	131	1	6	44.37

		M	I	NO	R	HS	100s	50s	Avge
49	G. R. Cowdrey (*Kent*)	13	22	1	930	137	2	6	44.28
50	S. G. Law (*Young Australia*)	7	11	2	397	134	1	1	44.11
51	M. A. Atherton (*Lancs.*)	18	31	1	1,323	155*	4	6	44.10
52	†J. C. Adams (*West Indians*)	13	22	5	741	114*	1	5	43.58
53	J. A. Daley (*Durham*)	7	12	2	435	55	0	4	43.50
54	I. J. Sutcliffe (*OUCC & Leics.*)...	14	24	4	847	163*	1	5	42.35
55	J. J. Whitaker (*Leics.*)	15	25	0	1,055	127	3	5	42.20
56	K. R. Brown (*Middx*)	19	27	4	970	147*	1	7	42.17
57	A. D. Brown (*Surrey*)	16	29	4	1,054	187	3	3	42.16
58	N. R. Taylor (*Kent*)	7	12	2	421	127	1	2	42.10
59	N. E. Briers (*Leics.*)	15	27	2	1,046	175*	3	3	41.84
60	R. J. Warren (*Northants*)	16	27	5	914	154	1	5	41.54
61	D. P. Ostler (*Warwicks.*)	18	26	2	983	208	2	6	40.95
62	†G. P. Thorpe (*Surrey*)	16	30	0	1,223	152	2	9	40.76
63	S. J. Rhodes (*Worcs.*)	20	33	8	1,018	122*	1	7	40.72
64	T. S. Curtis (*Worcs.*)	20	35	5	1,221	169*	2	5	40.70
65	C. J. Adams (*Derbys.*)	15	27	0	1,096	216	3	5	40.59
66	S. P. James (*Glam.*)	15	28	3	1,011	230*	3	2	40.44
67	{ C. L. Cairns (*Notts.*)	17	30	1	1,171	115	2	7	40.37
	G. F. Archer (*Notts.*)	17	32	3	1,171	158	3	4	40.37
69	M. C. J. Nicholas (*Hants*)	19	33	3	1,210	147	4	4	40.33
70	R. B. Richardson (*West Indians*) .	15	23	3	804	101*	1	5	40.20
71	†D. J. Bicknell (*Surrey*)	15	28	3	997	228*	2	4	39.88
72	†M. T. G. Elliott (*Young Australia*)	6	12	3	357	89*	0	3	39.66
73	N. J. Lenham (*Sussex*)	15	25	3	867	128	2	4	39.40
74	N. Shahid (*Surrey*)	14	25	2	900	139	2	5	39.13
75	S. C. Williams (*West Indians*) ...	13	20	0	770	137	3	3	38.50
76	R. J. Bailey (*Northants*)	18	30	3	1,038	157	4	2	38.44
77	J. E. Morris (*Durham*)	19	35	1	1,297	169	3	6	38.14
78	A. J. Stewart (*Surrey*)	10	18	1	647	151	2	2	38.05
79	M. A. Lynch (*Glos.*)	17	29	2	1,026	114	5	2	38.00
80	J. E. R. Gallian (*Lancs.*)	18	33	3	1,122	158	2	4	37.40
81	D. A. Leatherdale (*Worcs.*)	18	30	3	993	93	0	8	36.77
82	†M. A. Butcher (*Surrey*)	18	34	1	1,210	167	2	10	36.66
83	A. J. Hollioake (*Surrey*)	18	32	2	1,099	117*	1	8	36.63
84	A. Fordham (*Northants*)	16	29	1	1,025	130	4	4	36.60
85	R. C. Irani (*Essex*)	18	34	2	1,165	108	1	9	36.40
86	D. A. Reeve (*Warwicks.*)	16	22	4	652	77*	0	5	36.22
87	C. M. Wells (*Derbys.*)	16	30	3	976	115	2	6	36.14
88	K. M. Curran (*Northants*)	17	27	3	863	117	1	4	35.95
89	C. W. J. Athey (*Sussex*)	15	27	1	929	163*	2	5	35.73
90	D. J. Capel (*Northants*)	19	29	3	926	175	3	3	35.61
91	G. I. Macmillan (*OUCC & Leics.*)	17	26	3	817	122	3	3	35.52
92	†W. P. C. Weston (*Worcs.*)	20	35	4	1,207	111	3	7	35.50
93	C. M. Gupte (*OUCC*)	10	18	2	554	119	1	3	34.62
94	A. N. Hayhurst (*Somerset*)	17	29	5	825	107	1	5	34.37
95	P. Johnson (*Notts.*)	17	30	1	996	120*	1	8	34.34
96	†P. N. Weekes (*Middx*)	20	31	2	995	143	2	6	34.31
97	J. P. Stephenson (*Hants*)	17	30	4	892	127	1	6	34.30
98	†M. P. Dowman (*Notts.*)	9	18	2	548	107	2	2	34.25
99	A. S. Rollins (*Derbys.*)	17	33	1	1,095	200*	2	5	34.21
100	W. A. Dessaur (*Derbys.*)	8	16	2	478	119*	1	2	34.14
101	M. Watkinson (*Lancs.*)	18	29	3	887	161	2	3	34.11
102	P. J. Prichard (*Essex*)	18	33	1	1,080	109	2	5	33.75
103	†N. J. Llong (*Kent*)	9	16	0	538	118	2	1	33.62
104	M. W. Alleyne (*Glos.*)	19	32	2	1,007	141	1	7	33.56
105	D. P. Fulton (*Kent*)	8	16	1	502	116	1	4	33.46
106	†M. R. Benson (*Kent*)	13	21	0	702	192	2	1	33.42
107	N. J. Speak (*Lancs.*)	17	30	2	919	116	1	7	32.82

		M	I	NO	R	HS	100s	50s	Avge
108	M. P. Vaughan (*Yorks.*)	21	39	1	1,244	88	0	10	32.73
109	W. S. Kendall (*OUCC*)	11	16	2	457	94	0	3	32.64
110	R. A. Battye (*CUCC*)	8	14	2	391	70*	0	5	32.58
111	J. D. Ratcliffe (*Surrey*)	9	17	0	550	75	0	5	32.35
112	W. Larkins (*Durham*)	13	23	0	737	121	2	1	32.04
113	M. Prabhakar (*Durham*)	17	31	3	896	101	1	5	32.00
114	S. P. Titchard (*Lancs.*)	13	24	2	697	130	1	5	31.68
115	K. A. Parsons (*Somerset*)	16	28	2	821	105	1	6	31.57
116	M. N. Lathwell (*Somerset*)	17	33	0	1,033	111	2	5	31.30
117	C. White (*Yorks.*)	19	33	5	874	110	3	3	31.21
118	R. J. Turner (*Somerset*)	19	30	7	717	106*	1	4	31.17
119	B. F. Smith (*Leics.*)	18	31	5	802	112	1	6	30.84
120	G. D. Rose (*Somerset*)	16	25	0	771	84	0	6	30.84
121	G. D. Hodgson (*Glos.*)	9	17	0	524	148	1	2	30.82
122	V. P. Terry (*Hants*)	20	35	2	1,012	170	2	3	30.66
123	†N. H. Fairbrother (*Lancs.*)	14	23	3	602	132	2	1	30.10
124	†S. D. Thomas (*Glam.*)	11	15	4	331	78*	0	2	30.09
125	T. R. Ward (*Kent*)..........	18	32	1	932	114*	2	6	30.06
126	A. N. Aymes (*Hants*)	20	33	9	720	62*	0	5	30.00
126	F. D. Stephenson (*Sussex*) ...	13	23	0	690	106	1	3	30.00
128	W. M. Noon (*Notts.*)	17	31	6	745	66	0	5	29.80
128	M. V. Fleming (*Kent*)	10	16	1	447	100	1	2	29.80
130	†P. R. Pollard (*Notts.*)	11	19	2	506	120	1	2	29.76
131	†P. R. Whitaker (*Hants*)	13	21	0	624	119	1	3	29.71
132	M. A. Ealham (*Kent*)	18	31	1	891	121	1	4	29.70
133	†J. M. Dakin (*Leics.*)	8	13	2	326	101*	1	2	29.63
134	A. Dale (*Glam.*)	12	23	2	622	133	2	2	29.61
135	G. J. Kersey (*Surrey*)	15	28	4	708	83	0	6	29.50
136	K. Newell (*Sussex*)	10	19	2	500	135	1	2	29.41
137	J. S. Laney (*Hants*)	9	17	1	470	73	0	2	29.37
138	C. Banton (*Notts.*)...........	7	14	4	292	80*	0	2	29.20
139	†S. Hutton (*Durham*)	12	23	1	634	98	0	4	28.81
140	V. J. Wells (*Leics.*)	14	24	1	654	124	1	5	28.43
141	D. R. Brown (*Warwicks.*)	15	20	2	506	85	0	4	28.11
142	A. McGrath (*Yorks.*)	5	10	0	280	84	0	1	28.00
143	W. K. Hegg (*Lancs.*)	18	28	4	669	101	1	2	27.87
143	†D. A. Blenkiron (*Durham*)	9	17	1	446	145	1	1	27.87
145	G. D. Lloyd (*Lancs.*)	14	23	2	584	117	1	3	27.80
146	J. N. Snape (*Northants*)	13	16	3	361	55	0	2	27.76
147	O. D. Gibson (*West Indians*)	11	13	2	303	101*	1	0	27.54
148	S. A. Marsh (*Kent*)	16	28	3	688	67*	0	4	27.52
149	K. Greenfield (*Sussex*)	19	32	1	853	121	1	5	27.51
150	J. R. Murray (*West Indians*) ...	12	19	3	440	100	1	1	27.50
151	R. R. Montgomerie (*Northants*) ..	14	24	1	632	192	1	2	27.47
152	†D. L. Hemp (*Glam.*)	18	32	0	872	157	1	4	27.25
153	P. J. Newport (*Worcs.*)	18	23	8	404	50	0	1	26.93
154	F. A. Griffith (*Derbys.*)	8	13	4	240	53	0	1	26.66
155	K. M. Krikken (*Derbys.*)	11	16	5	288	61	0	1	26.18
156	C. W. Scott (*Durham*)	7	13	1	311	56	0	2	25.91
157	S. R. Lampitt (*Worcs.*)	17	25	6	488	97	0	1	25.68
158	†D. J. Millns (*Leics.*)	8	14	2	307	70	0	2	25.58
159	R. J. Rollins (*Essex*)	19	35	3	809	133*	1	4	25.28
160	G. W. White (*Hants*)	15	24	2	554	62	0	3	25.18
161	A. C. Ridley (*OUCC*)	10	16	1	375	71	0	2	25.00
161	J. E. Owen (*Derbys.*)	4	8	0	200	65	0	2	25.00
163	M. A. Roseberry (*Durham*)......	16	29	2	669	90	0	4	24.77
163	†R. C. J. Williams (*Glos.*)	5	9	0	223	90	0	2	24.77
165	J. I. Longley (*Durham*)	9	18	1	420	58	0	2	24.70
166	G. R. Haynes (*Worcs.*)	18	30	0	737	78	0	4	24.56

		M	I	NO	R	HS	100s	50s	Avge
167	J. W. Hall (*Sussex*)	12	22	0	537	100	1	2	24.40
168 {	R. I. Dawson (*Glos.*)	9	16	1	355	101	1	3	23.66
	M. P. Bicknell (*Surrey*)	9	12	3	213	61	0	1	23.66
170	K. P. Evans (*Notts.*)	7	13	2	260	78*	0	2	23.63
171	K. J. Piper (*Warwicks.*)	16	19	2	398	99	0	2	23.41
172	N. M. K. Smith (*Warwicks.*)	18	23	2	486	75	0	4	23.14
173	T. H. C. Hancock (*Glos.*)	8	13	1	275	79*	0	1	22.91
174	†I. D. Austin (*Lancs.*)	13	22	4	412	80*	0	1	22.88
175 {	†S. Young (*Young Australia*)	7	10	0	228	110	1	0	22.80
	S. A. Kellett (*Yorks.*)	6	11	1	228	86	0	1	22.80
177	J. P. Carroll (*CUCC*)	8	15	2	292	42	0	0	22.46
178 {	R. D. B. Croft (*Glam.*)	20	36	4	716	143	1	1	22.37
	J. Ratledge (*CUCC*)	8	16	0	358	67	0	3	22.37
180 {	R. T. Ragnauth (*CUCC*)	8	16	1	335	82	0	3	22.33
	A. J. Dalton (*Glam.*)	5	10	1	201	46	0	0	22.33
182	†Wasim Akram (*Lancs.*)	14	22	3	423	61	0	4	22.26
183	D. D. J. Robinson (*Essex*)	17	32	0	712	123	2	1	22.25
184	I. D. K. Salisbury (*Sussex*)	18	30	3	599	74	0	2	22.18
185	P. Moores (*Sussex*)	19	32	2	660	94	0	5	22.00
186	M. C. J. Ball (*Glos.*)	18	28	9	417	48	0	0	21.94
187	†M. T. E. Peirce (*Sussex*)	6	10	0	219	60	0	1	21.90
188	†J. P. Taylor (*Northants*)	18	21	8	284	86	0	2	21.84
189	D. G. Cork (*Derbys.*)	18	31	4	589	84*	0	3	21.81
190	J. J. B. Lewis (*Essex*)	7	14	0	299	75	0	1	21.35
191	A. W. Smith (*Surrey*)	9	13	0	272	88	0	1	20.92
192	M. G. N. Windows (*Glos.*)	9	17	2	313	56	0	2	20.86
193	D. J. Nash (*Middx*)	19	25	4	433	67	0	3	20.61
194	P. A. J. DeFreitas (*Derbys.*)	16	26	3	474	94*	0	2	20.60
195	T. A. Tweats (*Derbys.*)	8	16	1	308	78*	0	2	20.53
196	J. I. D. Kerr (*Somerset*)	13	19	2	349	80	0	1	20.52
197	S. D. Udal (*Hants*)	18	29	4	512	85	0	3	20.48
198	R. S. M. Morris (*Hants*)	10	18	0	368	47	0	0	20.44
199	J. E. Emburey (*Middx*)	17	20	1	387	87	0	1	20.36
200	N. C. Phillips (*Sussex*)	6	10	1	183	53	0	3	20.33
201	A. Kumble (*Northants*)	17	21	5	321	40*	0	0	20.06
202	P. J. Martin (*Lancs.*)	13	17	2	300	71	0	1	20.00
203	G. Chapple (*Lancs.*)	15	21	6	292	58	0	1	19.46
204	†G. J. Parsons (*Leics.*)	18	28	2	501	73	0	1	19.26
205	K. C. G. Benjamin (*West Indians*)	11	12	4	154	44	0	0	19.25
206	J. R. Wileman (*Notts.*)	8	16	4	230	43	0	0	19.16
207	D. R. Law (*Sussex*)	8	13	0	248	115	1	0	19.07
208	†M. E. Trescothick (*Somerset*)	12	22	0	417	151	1	1	18.95
209	†K. D. James (*Hants*)	12	21	3	341	53	0	1	18.94
210	A. E. Warner (*Derbys.*)	14	22	8	265	43	0	0	18.92
211	V. S. Solanki (*Worcs.*)	6	9	1	150	36	0	0	18.75
212	D. Gough (*Yorks.*)	14	19	1	332	60	0	1	18.44
213	†P. A. Nixon (*Leics.*)	18	30	5	461	79	0	2	18.44
214	M. J. McCague (*Kent*)	14	25	6	344	59	0	1	18.10
215	A. P. Grayson (*Yorks.*)	9	14	1	235	73	0	2	18.07
216	C. P. Metson (*Glam.*)	17	23	9	253	26*	0	0	18.07
217	H. A. G. Anthony (*Glam.*)	14	25	1	433	91	0	2	18.04
218	†R. A. Pick (*Notts.*)	17	26	4	395	50*	0	1	17.95
219	†M. Saxelby (*Durham*)	7	14	0	251	68	0	1	17.92
220	A. R. K. Pierson (*Leics.*)	20	32	10	392	50	0	1	17.81
221	H. S. Malik (*OUCC*)	8	10	1	160	64	0	1	17.77
222	A. A. Donald (*Warwicks.*)	15	16	5	194	44	0	0	17.63
223	R. J. Blakey (*Yorks.*)	20	29	6	398	77*	0	1	17.30
224	H. R. J. Trump (*Somerset*)	16	22	10	207	47	0	0	17.25
225	N. M. Kendrick (*Glam.*)	15	21	4	291	59	0	1	17.11
226	A. R. Whittall (*CUCC*)	8	13	2	185	81*	0	1	16.81

		M	I	NO	R	HS	100s	50s	Avge
227	D. L. Maddy (*Leics.*)	9	17	1	264	131	1	0	16.50
228	M. M. Patel (*Kent*)	18	29	6	376	56	0	2	16.34
229	P. W. Jarvis (*Sussex*)	9	13	2	177	38	0	0	16.09
230 {	C. A. Connor (*Hants*)	17	27	6	336	33	0	0	16.00
	R. K. Illingworth (*Worcs.*)	14	19	9	160	23*	0	0	16.00
231	D. G. C. Ligertwood (*Durham*)	12	21	2	303	40	0	0	15.94
233	M. J. Church (*Worcs.*)	5	9	1	126	35	0	0	15.75
234	J. Srinath (*Glos.*)	15	24	4	314	44	0	0	15.70
235	T. J. G. O'Gorman (*Derbys.*)	5	8	0	125	39	0	0	15.62
236	H. H. Streak (*Hants*)	19	28	3	378	69	0	1	15.12
237	C. G. Rackemann (*Surrey*)	13	20	12	120	20*	0	0	15.00
238	R. L. Johnson (*Middx*)	12	13	2	164	29*	0	0	14.90
239	M. B. Loye (*Northants*)	7	10	1	134	51*	0	1	14.88
240	Mushtaq Ahmed (*Somerset*)	17	23	2	311	62*	0	1	14.80
241	J. D. Ricketts (*OUCC*)	10	11	1	148	63	0	1	14.80
242 {	T. J. Boon (*Leics.*)	6	12	0	177	38	0	0	14.75
	V. C. Drakes (*West Indians*)	6	9	1	118	48*	0	0	14.75
244	N. V. Radford (*Worcs.*)	10	11	2	130	50	0	1	14.44
245	D. W. Headley (*Kent*)	14	24	6	253	54	0	1	14.05
246	†M. C. Ilott (*Essex*)	17	29	4	350	60	0	1	14.00
247	N. Killeen (*Durham*)	7	13	3	137	48	0	0	13.70
248	A. J. Tudor (*Surrey*)	5	9	0	123	56	0	1	13.66
249	P. J. Hartley (*Yorks.*)	18	23	4	256	38	0	0	13.47
250	J. E. Hindson (*Notts.*)	17	28	5	309	53*	0	1	13.43
251	†U. Afzaal (*Notts.*)	7	12	2	134	37	0	0	13.40
252	J. Boiling (*Durham*)	18	32	7	312	69	0	1	12.48
253	†M. J. Walker (*Kent*)	9	14	1	162	53	0	1	12.46
254 {	J. E. Benjamin (*Surrey*)	12	18	4	174	49	0	0	12.42
	S. L. Watkin (*Glam.*)	16	23	9	174	30	0	0	12.42
256	D. R. H. Churton (*CUCC*)	6	10	0	118	39	0	0	11.80
257	S. J. E. Brown (*Durham*)	18	30	6	278	36	0	0	11.58
258	†T. W. Harrison (*Derbys.*)	5	10	1	102	61*	0	1	11.33
259	C. A. Walsh (*West Indians*)	11	11	1	111	40	0	0	11.10
260	M. A. Feltham (*Middx*)	14	15	4	115	25	0	0	10.45
261	A. P. van Troost (*Somerset*)	7	11	3	82	34	0	0	10.25
262	I. R. Bishop (*West Indians*)	10	11	1	102	25	0	0	10.20
263	D. M. Cousins (*Essex*)	9	16	4	121	18*	0	0	10.08
264	†J. D. Lewry (*Sussex*)	12	19	4	150	34	0	0	10.00
265	R. J. Chapman (*Notts.*)	8	11	3	78	22	0	0	9.75
266	P. M. Such (*Essex*)	18	30	8	214	32	0	0	9.72
267	E. S. H. Giddins (*Sussex*)	18	27	12	137	34	0	0	9.13
268	N. F. Williams (*Essex*)	8	12	2	90	17	0	0	9.00
269	R. D. Stemp (*Yorks.*)	21	25	4	179	22*	0	0	8.52
270	S. P. Griffiths (*Derbys.*)	5	9	0	75	20	0	0	8.33
271	P. C. R. Tufnell (*Middx*)	17	15	7	65	23*	0	0	8.12
272	R. Dhanraj (*West Indians*)	15	13	3	81	22	0	0	8.10
273	P. Aldred (*Derbys.*)	7	12	0	97	33	0	0	8.08
274	†A. Walker (*Durham*)	11	16	3	102	29	0	0	7.84
275	A. C. S. Pigott (*Surrey*)	6	11	1	76	19	0	0	7.60
276	†R. W. Nowell (*Surrey*)	11	20	2	134	27	0	0	7.44
277	D. E. Malcolm (*Derbys.*)	14	21	4	125	25*	0	0	7.35
278	A. R. C. Fraser (*Middx*)	17	21	8	95	20	0	0	7.30
279	†J. H. Childs (*Essex*)	17	28	11	113	18	0	0	6.64
280 {	A. D. Mullally (*Leics.*)	19	30	6	150	22	0	0	6.25
	M. A. Robinson (*Yorks.*)	18	20	8	75	23	0	0	6.25
282	M. M. Betts (*Durham*)	9	15	5	55	14	0	0	5.50
283	A. Sheriyar (*Leics.*)	8	12	1	59	19	0	0	5.36
284	P. A. Thomas (*Worcs.*)	14	15	4	57	25	0	0	5.18
285	P. Mirza (*Worcs.*)	6	10	2	39	18*	0	0	4.87
286	A. M. Smith (*Glos.*)	11	11	2	37	11	0	0	4.11

BOWLING

(Qualification: 10 wickets in 10 innings)

† *Denotes a left-arm bowler.*

		O	M	R	W	BB	5W/i	Avge
1	A. A. Donald (*Warwicks.*)	535.3	134	1,431	89	6-56	6	16.07
2	D. A. Reeve (*Warwicks.*)	312	117	661	38	5-30	1	17.39
3	J. Srinath (*Glos.*)	568.4	147	1,661	87	9-76	5	19.09
4	†Wasim Akram (*Lancs.*)	518.1	108	1,598	81	7-52	7	19.72
5	T. A. Munton (*Warwicks.*)	373.5	111	952	48	5-37	3	19.83
6	C. L. Cairns (*Notts.*)	375.5	89	1,035	52	8-47	3	19.90
7	D. G. Cork (*Derbys.*)	587	111	1,800	90	9-43	4	20.00
8	R. L. Johnson (*Middx*)	301.4	79	812	40	5-48	2	20.30
9	A. Kumble (*Northants*)	899.4	265	2,143	105	7-82	8	20.40
10	K. C. G. Benjamin (*West Indians*)	284.1	71	923	43	5-52	3	21.46
11	†A. M. Smith (*Glos.*)	415.3	104	1,275	59	5-70	4	21.61
12	†P. C. R. Tufnell (*Middx*)	678.1	207	1,634	74	6-111	5	22.08
13	†A. F. Giles (*Warwicks.*)	146.5	46	354	16	5-23	1	22.12
14	M. S. Kasprowicz (*Young Australia*)	175.1	42	599	27	5-19	1	22.18
15	S. Young (*Young Australia*)	128	36	359	16	3-23	0	22.43
16	P. J. Newport (*Worcs.*)	548	148	1,551	69	5-45	4	22.47
17	P. J. Hartley (*Yorks.*)	549	120	1,861	81	9-41	4	22.97
18	J. E. Emburey (*Middx*)	708.4	198	1,701	74	7-82	5	22.98
19	V. J. Wells (*Leics.*)	139.3	33	438	19	3-28	0	23.05
20	D. J. Capel (*Northants*)	358.2	70	1,206	51	7-44	2	23.64
21	M. P. Bicknell (*Surrey*)	285	65	978	41	5-61	3	23.85
22	†M. C. Ilott (*Essex*)	582.4	126	1,897	78	9-19	6	24.32
23	P. Aldred (*Derbys.*)	108.2	22	375	15	3-47	0	25.00
24	J. E. Benjamin (*Surrey*)	420.4	85	1,326	53	5-37	3	25.01
25	N. A. Mallender (*Northants*)	142.2	32	427	17	4-49	0	25.11
26	I. D. Austin (*Lancs.*)	363.4	111	889	35	4-50	0	25.40
27	A. R. Caddick (*Somerset*)	183.1	34	613	24	8-69	1	25.54
28	†M. T. Brimson (*Leics.*)	110	24	310	12	2-11	0	25.83
29	†J. H. Childs (*Essex*)	678.2	184	1,757	68	6-36	2	25.83
30	I. R. Bishop (*West Indians*)	334	69	983	38	5-32	1	25.86
31	D. E. Malcolm (*Derbys.*)	461.4	82	1,692	65	6-61	3	26.03
32	R. Dhanraj (*West Indians*)	475.3	79	1,596	61	6-50	4	26.16
33	J. Angel (*Young Australia*)	179.5	39	709	27	4-31	0	26.25
34	P. J. Martin (*Lancs.*)	338.5	96	922	35	4-51	0	26.34
35	†J. D. Lewry (*Sussex*)	350.1	62	1,247	47	6-43	3	26.53
36	D. Gough (*Yorks.*)	414.5	89	1,365	51	7-28	1	26.76
37	P. M. Such (*Essex*)	748.4	174	2,064	77	8-93	6	26.80
38	A. P. Igglesden (*Kent*)	171.2	37	563	21	5-92	1	26.80
39	A. E. Warner (*Derbys.*)	375.1	90	1,050	39	6-21	3	26.92
40	†R. K. Illingworth (*Worcs.*)	524	172	1,212	45	4-30	0	26.93
41	S. L. Watkin (*Glam.*)	590.4	144	1,755	65	7-49	2	27.00
	M. A. Feltham (*Middx*)	273.1	72	783	29	6-41	1	27.00
43	J. N. B. Bovill (*Hants*)	251.3	62	814	30	6-29	2	27.13
44	D. R. Brown (*Warwicks.*)	311.4	71	1,011	37	4-24	0	27.32
45	R. G. Twose (*Warwicks.*)	108	29	301	11	3-50	0	27.36
46	†A. Sheriyar (*Leics.*)	189	27	799	29	6-30	2	27.55
47	P. W. Jarvis (*Sussex*)	228.4	45	719	26	5-55	1	27.65
48	S. R. Lampitt (*Worcs.*)	494.1	124	1,524	55	4-34	0	27.70
49	M. Prabhakar (*Durham*)	579.1	163	1,439	51	7-65	1	28.21
50	†A. D. Mullally (*Leics.*)	583.4	172	1,700	59	6-50	2	28.81
51	C. A. Walsh (*West Indians*)	384.2	76	1,124	39	5-45	1	28.82
52	D. W. Headley (*Kent*)	430.5	101	1,276	44	7-58	3	29.00

		O	M	R	W	BB	5W/i	Avge
53	†J. P. Taylor (*Northants*)	573.4	122	1,713	59	7-50	2	29.03
54	D. J. Nash (*Middx*)	460.1	90	1,512	52	5-35	2	29.07
55	M. J. McCague (*Kent*)	424.2	79	1,457	50	5-47	2	29.14
56	A. R. C. Fraser (*Middx*)	592.1	156	1,632	56	5-56	2	29.14
57	P. A. J. DeFreitas (*Derbys.*)	591.1	127	1,751	60	6-35	2	29.18
58	M. Watkinson (*Lancs.*)	622.4	158	1,910	65	7-140	2	29.38
59	E. E. Hemmings (*Sussex*)	177.5	51	442	15	4-33	0	29.46
60	E. S. H. Giddins (*Sussex*)	605.4	110	2,004	68	6-73	4	29.47
61	G. J. Parsons (*Leics.*)	579.2	179	1,570	53	4-46	0	29.62
62	Mushtaq Ahmed (*Somerset*)	952	286	2,821	95	6-38	7	29.69
63	C. E. L. Ambrose (*West Indians*)	262.1	70	744	25	5-96	1	29.76
64	C. G. Rackemann (*Surrey*)	457	114	1,430	48	6-60	1	29.79
65	G. C. Small (*Warwicks.*)	182.5	48	507	17	5-71	1	29.82
66	M. A. Robinson (*Yorks.*)	483.1	134	1,375	46	4-46	0	29.89
67	P. E. McIntyre (*Young Australia*)	307	70	1,018	34	5-38	1	29.94
68	A. C. S. Pigott (*Surrey*)	209.3	50	667	22	6-91	2	30.31
69	A. R. K. Pierson (*Leics.*)	637.1	131	2,115	69	5-48	2	30.65
70	H. H. Streak (*Hants*)	516.2	115	1,629	53	4-40	0	30.73
71	A. Walker (*Durham*)	285.3	53	958	31	8-118	2	30.90
72	I. D. K. Salisbury (*Sussex*)	558.2	130	1,674	54	7-72	5	31.00
73	O. D. Gibson (*West Indians*)	242.4	36	966	31	4-32	0	31.16
74	R. A. Pick (*Notts.*)	490.2	105	1,602	51	5-82	2	31.41
75	B. A. Williams (*Young Australia*)	134.3	26	443	14	4-79	0	31.64
76	F. D. Stephenson (*Sussex*)	361.2	73	1,113	35	5-64	1	31.80
77	H. A. G. Anthony (*Glam.*)	397.5	70	1,402	44	6-77	2	31.86
78	K. M. Curran (*Northants*)	357.1	84	1,202	37	4-78	0	32.48
79	C. M. Wells (*Derbys.*)	110	25	326	10	4-29	0	32.60
80	J. E. R. Gallian (*Lancs.*)	129.5	17	533	16	3-14	0	33.31
81	S. D. Udal (*Hants*)	628.2	137	1,864	55	6-65	3	33.89
82	C. A. Connor (*Hants*)	554.2	115	1,944	57	6-44	3	34.10
83	†T. N. Wren (*Kent*)	205.4	31	785	23	5-148	1	34.13
84	†J. E. Hindson (*Notts.*)	692	165	2,219	65	5-67	2	34.13
85	G. Chapple (*Lancs.*)	380.1	81	1,229	36	4-44	0	34.13
86	†S. J. E. Brown (*Durham*)	589.3	117	1,951	57	6-69	4	34.22
87	A. J. Hollioake (*Surrey*)	230.3	46	721	21	4-22	0	34.33
88	R. D. B. Croft (*Glam.*)	847	210	2,353	68	6-104	4	34.60
89	S. C. Ecclestone (*Somerset*)	105	20	383	11	2-31	0	34.81
90	C. E. W. Silverwood (*Yorks.*)	147.1	23	630	18	5-62	1	35.00
91	N. M. K. Smith (*Warwicks.*)	460	105	1,375	39	6-72	3	35.25
92	M. C. J. Ball (*Glos.*)	577.2	144	1,481	42	5-49	2	35.26
93	N. F. Williams (*Essex*)	188.4	31	743	21	5-93	1	35.38
94	†M. M. Patel (*Kent*)	788	194	2,336	66	6-74	3	35.39
95	N. V. Radford (*Worcs.*)	220.1	46	780	22	5-45	1	35.45
96	G. D. Rose (*Somerset*)	426	93	1,402	39	5-78	1	35.94
97	F. A. Griffith (*Derbys.*)	190.4	42	614	17	4-89	0	36.11
98	N. J. Haste (*CUCC*)	197	41	655	18	5-73	1	36.38
99	J. P. Stephenson (*Hants*)	358	62	1,316	36	7-51	1	36.55
100	A. R. Whittall (*CUCC*)	328.4	85	1,064	29	6-46	2	36.68
101	K. P. Sheeraz (*Glos.*)	225.1	35	888	24	6-67	2	37.00
102	C. White (*Yorks.*)	273.4	49	934	25	4-40	0	37.36
103	†M. A. Harrity (*Young Australia*)	135.2	33	497	13	4-37	0	38.23
104	M. A. Ealham (*Kent*)	384.2	95	1,151	30	3-37	0	38.36
105	†R. P. Davis (*Warwicks.*)	216.4	58	576	15	5-118	1	38.40
106	A. P. van Troost (*Somerset*)	145.3	23	624	16	5-120	1	39.00
107	J. N. Snape (*Northants*)	231	53	747	19	5-65	1	39.31
108	D. P. Mather (*OUCC*)	227.1	49	710	18	4-65	0	39.44
109	†R. W. Nowell (*Surrey*)	424.5	117	1,264	32	4-43	0	39.50
110	K. J. Barnett (*Derbys.*)	218.2	42	635	16	3-51	0	39.68
111	M. P. Vaughan (*Yorks.*)	272.4	64	876	22	3-32	0	39.81
112	G. R. Haynes (*Worcs.*)	272	76	840	21	4-33	0	40.00
113	†G. Keedy (*Lancs.*)	505	128	1,498	37	4-35	0	40.48

		O	M	R	W	BB	5W/i	Avge
114	J. I. D. Kerr (*Somerset*)	280.1	53	1,134	28	5-82	1	40.50
115	D. J. Millns (*Leics.*)	205.2	27	792	19	3-47	0	41.68
116	K. P. Evans (*Notts.*)	238.1	60	590	14	3-66	0	42.14
117	M. W. Alleyne (*Glos.*)	421.5	125	1,228	29	3-59	0	42.34
118	M. A. Butcher (*Surrey*)	234.5	37	935	22	4-72	0	42.50
119	J. D. Ricketts (*OUCC*)	224.5	35	732	17	3-30	0	43.05
120	H. R. J. Trump (*Somerset*)	596.2	173	1,745	40	5-85	1	43.62
121	G. Yates (*Lancs.*)................	136	33	494	11	4-67	0	44.90
122	N. Killeen (*Durham*)	195.3	30	767	17	5-118	1	45.11
123	R. C. Irani (*Essex*)	361.5	71	1,222	27	5-62	1	45.25
124	†K. D. James (*Hants*)	235.2	47	867	19	6-38	1	45.63
125	W. J. Cronje (*Leics.*)............	256.2	82	688	15	3-42	0	45.86
126	†R. D. Stemp (*Yorks.*)	721.1	226	1,929	42	4-68	0	45.92
127	M. E. Waugh (*Essex*)	256	61	789	17	4-76	0	46.41
128	†N. M. Kendrick (*Glam.*)	389.5	102	1,255	27	4-70	0	46.48
129	A. D. MacRobert (*OUCC*)	264	37	843	18	4-41	0	46.83
130	P. A. Thomas (*Worcs.*)	386.4	67	1,554	33	5-70	1	47.09
131	†J. A. Afford (*Notts.*)	314.5	69	991	21	4-58	0	47.19
132	P. Mirza (*Worcs.*)	175.1	40	661	14	5-110	1	47.21
133	C. L. Hooper (*West Indians*)......	267.4	54	821	17	3-22	0	48.29
134	S. D. Thomas (*Glam.*)	303.3	51	1,356	28	5-99	1	48.42
135	S. R. Barwick (*Glam.*)...........	233.4	58	681	14	4-116	0	48.64
136	M. M. Betts (*Durham*)	194.5	31	853	17	3-35	0	50.17
137	A. N. Hayhurst (*Somerset*)	139.2	21	519	10	2-39	0	51.90
138	P. N. Weekes (*Middx*)	258.4	55	679	13	3-26	0	52.23
139	D. M. Cousins (*Essex*)	176	23	640	12	3-73	0	53.33
140	V. J. Pike (*Glos.*)................	195.3	39	592	11	3-72	0	53.81
141	J. Boiling (*Durham*).............	599	149	1,702	27	5-73	2	63.03
142	A. W. Smith (*Surrey*)	165.3	27	647	10	3-112	0	64.70
143	R. J. Chapman (*Notts.*)...........	179.2	23	777	11	3-119	0	70.63
144	A. N. Janisch (*CUCC*)	185	21	723	10	3-38	0	72.30
145	D. B. Pennett (*Notts.*)...........	208.1	35	811	10	3-136	0	81.10

The following bowlers took ten wickets but bowled in fewer than ten innings:

	O	M	R	W	BB	5W/i	Avge
J. Lewis (*Glos.*)	67.4	12	209	12	4-34	0	17.41
K. E. Cooper (*Glos.*).............	103	32	228	13	4-34	0	17.53
S. M. Milburn (*Yorks.*)...........	69	15	204	10	4-68	0	20.40
J. Wood (*Durham*)	97.4	25	303	14	4-54	0	21.64
A. J. Tudor (*Surrey*)	83.3	7	320	14	5-32	1	22.85
V. C. Drakes (*West Indians*).......	106	17	400	16	5-20	1	25.00
A. J. Harris (*Derbys.*)	85.5	16	354	14	4-84	0	25.28
R. T. Bates (*Notts.*)..............	115.1	32	369	10	5-88	1	36.90
†D. M. Cox (*Durham*)	129.5	28	422	11	4-141	0	38.36

INDIVIDUAL SCORES OF 100 AND OVER

There were 347 three-figure innings in 201 first-class matches in 1995, 69 more than in 1994 when 200 matches were played. Of these, 15 were double-hundreds, compared with 24 in 1994. The list includes 260 hundreds hit in the County Championship, compared with 213 in 1994.

   * *Signifies not out.*

M. R. Ramprakash (10)

163*	Middx v Hants, Lord's
214	Middx v Surrey, Lord's
133	Middx v Glos., Bristol
205	Middx v Sussex, Lord's
155	Middx v Durham, Chester-le-Street
235	Middx v Yorks., Leeds
111	Middx v Northants, Uxbridge
158 111* }	Middx v Leics., Uxbridge
115	Middx v Somerset, Taunton

P. A. de Silva (7)

117	Kent v Sussex, Hove
135	Kent v Glam., Tunbridge Wells
115	Kent v Yorks., Leeds
225	Kent v Notts., Nottingham
255 116 }	Kent v Derbys., Maidstone
102	Kent v West Indians, Canterbury

G. A. Gooch (7)

139	Essex v Leics., Chelmsford
165	Essex v Worcs., Chelmsford
123	Essex v Lancs., Manchester
142	Essex v Hants, Colchester
102	Essex v Glam., Swansea
109*	Essex v West Indians, Chelmsford
106	Essex v Kent, Canterbury

R. T. Robinson (7)

101	Notts. v Cambridge U., Cambridge
136	Notts. v Lancs., Liverpool
101	Notts. v Essex, Nottingham
196	Notts. v Kent, Nottingham
134	Notts. v Somerset, Nottingham
124	Notts. v Yorks., Nottingham
209	Notts. v Northants, Northampton

A. P. Wells (7)

178	England A v Warwicks., Birmingham
107 136 }	Sussex v Kent, Hove
106	Sussex v Somerset, Bath
142	Sussex v Leics., Hove
105	Sussex v Lancs., Lytham
108	Sussex v Worcs., Eastbourne

M. G. Bevan (6)

113*	Yorks. v Cambridge U., Cambridge
108	Yorks. v Lancs., Leeds
102	Yorks. v Glos., Middlesbrough
107	Yorks. v Hants, Southampton
153*	Yorks. v Surrey, The Oval
105	Yorks. v West Indians, Scarborough

P. D. Bowler (6)

136	Somerset v Glos., Taunton
176	Somerset v Warwicks., Birmingham
132*	Somerset v Surrey, The Oval
138	Somerset v Derbys., Derby
196	Somerset v Essex, Southend
130*	Somerset v Worcs., Worcester

N. Hussain (6)

100	Essex v Leics., Chelmsford
106	Essex v Notts., Nottingham
137	Essex v Surrey, The Oval
145	Essex v Hants, Colchester
103	Essex v Glam., Swansea
186	Essex v Kent, Canterbury

H. Morris (6)

125	Glam. v Oxford U., Oxford
109	Glam. v Northants, Cardiff
114	Glam. v Kent, Tunbridge Wells
106	Glam. v Durham, Swansea
166* 104* }	Glam. v Notts., Cardiff

P. A. Cottey (5)

116	Glam. v Northants, Cardiff
124	Glam. v Lancs., Manchester
125	Glam. v Surrey, The Oval
130	Glam. v Durham, Swansea
123*	Glam. v Young Australia, Neath

D. J. Cullinan (5)

134	Derbys. v Sussex, Derby
131	Derbys. v Notts., Nottingham
161	Derbys. v Somerset, Derby
101*	Derbys. v Worcs., Kidderminster
121	Derbys. v Warwicks., Birmingham

M. W. Gatting (5)

108	Middx v Glos., Bristol
101	Middx v Sussex, Lord's
148	Middx v Notts., Lord's
136	Middx v Kent, Lord's
122*	Middx v Somerset, Taunton

R. J. Harden (5)
113   Somerset v Glam., Taunton
103   Somerset v Glos., Taunton
129* Somerset v Yorks., Taunton
100* Somerset v Durham, Chester-le-Street
124   Somerset v Leics., Weston-super-Mare

C. L. Hooper (5)
176   West Indians v Somerset, Taunton
118   West Indians v Combined Univs, Oxford
195   West Indians v Hants, Southampton
127   West Indies v England, The Oval
105   West Indians v Yorks., Scarborough

M. A. Lynch (5)
105   Glos. v Somerset, Taunton
108 }
114 } Glos. v Kent, Canterbury
111   Glos. v Essex, Cheltenham
104   Glos. v Northants, Northampton

T. M. Moody (5)
157 }
106 } Worcs. v Notts., Nottingham
110   Worcs. v Lancs., Worcester
168   Worcs. v Derbys., Kidderminster
155   Worcs. v Somerset, Worcester

J. C. Pooley (5)
121   Middx v Worcs., Worcester
125   Middx v Glam., Colwyn Bay
100* Middx v Oxford U., Oxford
136   Middx v Glos., Bristol
133   Middx v Notts., Lord's

M. E. Waugh (5)
126   Essex v Surrey, The Oval
173   Essex v Somerset, Southend
136   Essex v Hants, Colchester
121* }
121 } Essex v Derbys., Chelmsford

M. A. Atherton (4)
129   Lancs. v Yorks., Leeds
155* Lancs. v Durham, Manchester
113   England v West Indies, Nottingham
100   Lancs. v Yorks., Manchester

R. J. Bailey (4)
111   Northants v Yorks., Sheffield
132   Northants v Durham, Northampton
157 }
119 } Northants v Middx, Uxbridge

D. Byas (4)
181   Yorks. v Cambridge U., Cambridge
193   Yorks. v Lancs., Leeds
108   Yorks. v Glos., Middlesbrough
213   Yorks. v Worcs., Scarborough

J. D. Carr (4)
129   Middx v Hants, Lord's
116* Middx v Cambridge U., Cambridge
129   Middx v Glam., Colwyn Bay
115   Middx v West Indians, Lord's

S. Chanderpaul (4)
140* West Indians v Leics., Leicester
100   West Indians v Somerset, Taunton
103* West Indians v Essex, Chelmsford
132* West Indians v Yorks., Scarborough

W. J. Cronje (4)
124   Leics. v Kent, Canterbury
113   Leics. v Notts., Leicester
163   Leics. v Surrey, Leicester
213   Leics. v Somerset, Weston-super-Mare

A. Fordham (4)
120   Northants v Hants, Northampton
101   Northants v Warwicks., Birmingham
130   Northants v Notts., Northampton
126   Northants v Worcs., Northampton

G. A. Hick (4)
120   Worcs. v Surrey, Worcester
152   Worcs. v Lancs., Worcester
118* England v West Indies, Nottingham
128   Worcs. v Somerset, Worcester

M. C. J. Nicholas (4)
120   Hants v Oxford U., Oxford
138* Hants v Worcs., Southampton
147   Hants v Yorks., Southampton
120   Hants v Northants, Northampton

T. L. Penney (4)
101* Warwicks. v Somerset, Birmingham
141   Warwicks. v Essex, Ilford
144   Warwicks. v Notts., Nottingham
137* Warwicks. v Derbys., Birmingham

A. Symonds (4)
161* Glos. v Surrey, The Oval
102   Glos. v Somerset, Taunton
123* Glos. v Essex, Cheltenham
254* Glos. v Glam., Abergavenny

R. G. Twose (4)
131* Warwicks. v Sussex, Birmingham
140   Warwicks. v Northants, Birmingham
191   Warwicks. v Worcs., Birmingham
109* Warwicks. v Kent, Canterbury

A. J. Wright (4)
193   Glos. v Notts., Bristol
139   Glos. v Sussex, Hove
107* Glos. v Yorks., Middlesbrough
117   Glos. v Durham, Bristol

C. J. Adams (3)
111	Derbys. v Sussex, Derby
216	Derbys. v Kent, Maidstone
101	Derbys. v Surrey, Derby

G. F. Archer (3)
122*	Notts. v Leics., Leicester
158	Notts. v Northants, Northampton
110	Notts. v Glam., Cardiff

K. L. T. Arthurton (3)
146	West Indians v Leics., Leicester
121*	West Indians v Northants, Northampton
102*	West Indians v Combined Univs, Oxford

N. E. Briers (3)
114	Leics. v Essex, Chelmsford
175*	Leics. v Worcs., Worcester
125	Leics. v Sussex, Hove

A. D. Brown (3)
187	Surrey v Glos., The Oval
103	Surrey v Essex, The Oval
124*	Surrey v Kent, Canterbury

S. L. Campbell (3)
113	West Indians v Durham, Chester-le-Street
102	West Indians v Middx, Lord's
172	West Indians v Hants, Southampton

D. J. Capel (3)
167	Northants v Kent, Canterbury
175	Northants v Leics., Northampton
114*	Northants v Notts., Northampton

J. P. Crawley (3)
182	Lancs. v Glam., Manchester
108	Lancs. v Glam., Manchester
173	Lancs. v Northants, Manchester

S. P. James (3)
116	Glam. v Young Australia, Neath
230*	Glam. v Leics., Leicester
101*	Glam. v Notts., Cardiff

A. J. Lamb (3)
124	Northants v Glam., Cardiff
166	Northants v Surrey, Northampton
115	Northants v Notts., Northampton

B. C. Lara (3)
145	West Indies v England, Manchester
152	West Indies v England, Nottingham
179	West Indies v England, The Oval

G. I. Macmillan (3)
113*	Oxford U. v Cambridge U., Lord's
103	Leics. v Sussex, Hove
122	Leics. v Surrey, Leicester

M. P. Maynard (3)
138	Glam. v Lancs., Manchester
164	Glam. v Glos., Abergavenny
103	Glam. v Leics., Leicester

J. E. Morris (3)
169	Durham v Lancs., Manchester
128	Durham v Warwicks., Chester-le-Street
109	Durham v Notts., Chester-le-Street

M. D. Moxon (3)
130	Yorks. v Cambridge U., Cambridge
203*	Yorks. v Kent, Leeds
104	Yorks. v Middx, Leeds

R. A. Smith (3)
120	Hants v Sussex, Portsmouth
136	Hants v Glos., Bristol
172	Hants v Northants, Northampton

W. P. C. Weston (3)
100	Worcs. v Oxford U., Oxford
105	Worcs. v Notts., Nottingham
111	Worcs. v Sussex, Eastbourne

J. J. Whitaker (3)
120	Leics. v Derbys., Leicester
127	Leics. v Notts., Leicester
103	Leics. v Young Australia, Leicester

C. White (3)
107	Yorks. v Leics., Leicester
110	Yorks. v Northants, Sheffield
107*	Yorks. v Worcs., Scarborough

S. C. Williams (3)
114	West Indians v Combined Univs, Oxford
137	West Indians v Kent, Canterbury
119	West Indians v Somerset, Taunton

C. W. J. Athey (2)
163*	Sussex v Glos., Hove
108	Sussex v Durham, Hartlepool

K. J. Barnett (2)
164	Derbys. v Sussex, Derby
169	Derbys. v Worcs., Kidderminster

M. R. Benson (2)
192	Kent v Leics., Canterbury
102	Kent v Glos., Canterbury

D. J. Bicknell (2)
228*	Surrey v Notts., Guildford
146	Surrey v Kent, Canterbury

C. O. Browne (2)
102*	West Indians v Durham, Chester-le-Street
102	West Indians v Yorks., Scarborough

M. A. Butcher (2)
167   Surrey v Durham, The Oval
102   Surrey v Somerset, The Oval

C. L. Cairns (2)
110   Notts. v Cambridge U., Cambridge
115   Notts. v Middx, Lord's

G. R. Cowdrey (2)
137   Kent v Derbys., Maidstone
103   Kent v Warwicks., Canterbury

T. S. Curtis (2)
169* Worcs. v Yorks., Scarborough
129   Worcs. v Somerset, Worcester

A. Dale (2)
121   Glam. v Oxford U., Oxford
133   Glam. v Kent, Tunbridge Wells

M. P. Dowman (2)
102* Notts. v Cambridge U., Cambridge
107   Notts. v Oxford U., Oxford

N. H. Fairbrother (2)
129   Lancs. v Warwicks., Manchester
132   Lancs. v Somerset, Taunton

J. E. R. Gallian (2)
158   Lancs. v Glam., Manchester
110   Lancs. v Surrey, The Oval

A. C. Gilchrist (2)
122   Young Australia v Somerset,
      Taunton
105* Young Australia v Derbys.,
      Chesterfield

M. L. Hayden (2)
146   Young Australia v Hants,
      Southampton
178   Young Australia v Sussex, Hove

P. C. L. Holloway (2)
129* Somerset v Sussex, Bath
117   Somerset v Leics., Weston-super-
      Mare

J. L. Langer (2)
111* Young Australia v Glam., Neath
149   Young Australia v Sussex, Hove

W. Larkins (2)
112   Durham v Northants, Northampton
121   Durham v Notts., Chester-le-Street

M. N. Lathwell (2)
111   Somerset v Yorks., Taunton
110   Somerset v Notts., Nottingham

N. J. Lenham (2)
128   Sussex v West Indians, Hove
104   Sussex v Durham, Hartlepool

N. J. Llong (2)
118   Kent v Surrey, Canterbury
100   Kent v Somerset, Taunton

M. L. Love (2)
181   Young Australia v Somerset,
      Taunton
108   Young Australia v Derbys.,
      Chesterfield

D. P. Ostler (2)
208   Warwicks. v Surrey, Birmingham
116   Warwicks. v Essex, Ilford

P. J. Prichard (2)
109   Essex v Notts., Nottingham
104   Essex v Yorks., Chelmsford

D. D. J. Robinson (2)
110   Essex v Durham, Chelmsford
123   Essex v Glos., Cheltenham

A. S. Rollins (2)
118   Derbys. v Glam., Derby
200* Derbys. v Glos., Bristol

N. Shahid (2)
125   Surrey v Glam., The Oval
139   Surrey v Yorks., The Oval

P. V. Simmons (2)
112 ⎫
139* ⎬ West Indians v Essex, Chelmsford

A. J. Stewart (2)
151   Surrey v Durham, The Oval
150   Surrey v Sussex, Horsham

V. P. Terry (2)
170   Hants v Sussex, Portsmouth
104   Hants v Young Australia,
      Southampton

G. P. Thorpe (2)
110   Surrey v Sussex, Horsham
152   Surrey v Kent, Canterbury

T. R. Ward (2)
114* Kent v Northants, Canterbury
101   Kent v Surrey, Canterbury

M. Watkinson (2)
108   Lancs. v Durham, Manchester
161   Lancs. v Essex, Manchester

P. N. Weekes (2)
143   Middx v Oxford U., Oxford
127* Middx v Northants, Uxbridge

C. M. Wells (2)
115   Derbys. v Oxford U., Oxford
106   Derbys. v Glam., Derby

The following each played one three-figure innings:

J. C. Adams, 114*, West Indians v Combined Univs, Oxford; M. W. Alleyne, 141, Glos. v Essex, Cheltenham.

D. A. Blenkiron, 145, Durham v Glam., Swansea; K. R. Brown, 147*, Middx v Glam., Colwyn Bay.

R. Q. Cake, 101, Cambridge U. v Oxford U., Lord's; R. D. B. Croft, 143, Glam. v Somerset, Taunton; R. J. Cunliffe, 190*, Glos. v Oxford U., Bristol; K. M. Curran, 117, Northants v Surrey, Northampton.

J. M. Dakin, 101*, Leics. v Notts., Leicester; R. I. Dawson, 101, Glos. v Worcs., Gloucester; W. A. Dessaur, 119*, Derbys. v Oxford U., Oxford.

M. A. Ealham, 121, Kent v Notts., Nottingham.

M. V. Fleming, 100, Kent v Cambridge U., Folkestone; D. P. Fulton, 116, Kent v Cambridge U., Folkestone.

O. D. Gibson, 101*, West Indians v Somerset, Taunton; K. Greenfield, 121, Sussex v Essex, Hove; C. M. Gupte, 119, Oxford U. v Hants, Oxford.

A. Habib, 174*, Leics. v Oxford U., Oxford; J. W. Hall, 100, Sussex v Durham, Hartlepool; J. C. Hallett, 111*, Somerset v Hants, Taunton; A. N. Hayhurst, 107, Somerset v Durham, Chester-le-Street; W. K. Hegg, 101, Lancs. v Northants, Manchester; D. L. Hemp, 157, Glam. v Glos., Abergavenny; G. D. Hodgson, 148, Glos. v Notts., Bristol; A. J. Hollioake, 117*, Surrey v Warwicks., Birmingham.

R. C. Irani, 108, Essex v Surrey, The Oval.

P. Johnson, 120*, Notts. v Warwicks., Nottingham.

W. G. Khan, 181, Warwicks. v Hants, Southampton; N. V. Knight, 174, Warwicks. v Kent, Canterbury.

D. R. Law, 115, Sussex v Young Australia, Hove; S. G. Law, 134, Young Australia v Hants, Southampton; G. D. Lloyd, 117, Lancs. v Cambridge U., Cambridge.

D. L. Maddy, 131, Leics. v Oxford U., Oxford; A. A. Metcalfe, 100, Yorks. v West Indians, Scarborough; A. J. Moles, 131, Warwicks. v Somerset, Birmingham; R. R. Montgomerie, 192, Northants v Kent, Canterbury; J. R. Murray, 100, West Indians v Combined Univs, Oxford.

K. Newell, 135, Sussex v West Indians, Hove.

K. A. Parsons, 105, Somerset v Young Australia, Taunton; P. R. Pollard, 120, Notts. v Somerset, Nottingham; R. T. Ponting, 103*, Young Australia v Worcs., Worcester; M. Prabhakar, 101, Durham v Glam., Swansea.

S. J. Rhodes, 122*, Worcs. v Young Australia, Worcester; R. B. Richardson, 101*, West Indians v Durham, Chester-le-Street; R. J. Rollins, 133*, Essex v Glam., Swansea.

B. F. Smith, 112, Leics. v Northants, Northampton; N. J. Speak, 116, Lancs. v Cambridge U., Cambridge; F. D. Stephenson, 106, Sussex v Glos., Hove; J. P. Stephenson, 127, Hants v Lancs., Portsmouth; I. J. Sutcliffe, 163*, Oxford U. v Hants, Oxford.

N. R. Taylor, 127, Kent v Leics., Canterbury; S. P. Titchard, 130, Lancs. v Essex, Manchester; M. E. Trescothick, 151, Somerset v Northants, Northampton; R. J. Turner, 106*, Somerset v Derbys., Derby.

R. J. Warren, 154, Northants v Notts., Northampton; V. J. Wells, 124, Leics. v Middx, Uxbridge; P. R. Whitaker, 119, Hants v Worcs., Southampton.

S. Young, 110, Young Australia v Somerset, Taunton.

TEN WICKETS IN A MATCH

There were 44 instances of bowlers taking ten or more wickets in a match in first-class cricket in 1995, 15 more than in 1994. The list includes 38 in the County Championship.

Wasim Akram (3)
10-172, Lancs. v Northants, Manchester; 12-165, Lancs. v Leics., Leicester; 10-156, Lancs. v Hants, Portsmouth.
J. E. Emburey (2)
10-98, Middx v Surrey, Lord's; 12-157, Middx v Yorks., Leeds.
J. E. Hindson (2)
10-197, Notts. v Essex, Nottingham; 10-145, Notts. v Somerset, Nottingham.

M. C. Ilott (2)
10-157, Essex v Sussex, Hove; 14-105, Essex v Northants, Luton.
A. Kumble (2)
13-192, Northants v Hants, Northampton; 10-151, Northants v Warwicks., Birmingham.
Mushtaq Ahmed (2)
10-116, Somerset v Sussex, Bath; 11-144, Somerset v Kent, Taunton.
J. Srinath (2)
10-97, Glos. v Yorks., Middlesbrough; 13-150, Glos. v Glam., Abergavenny.
P. M. Such (2)
12-178, Essex v Worcs., Chelmsford; 11-160, Essex v Hants, Colchester.

The following each took ten wickets in a match on one occasion:

K. C. G. Benjamin, 10-174, West Indies v England, Nottingham; J. N. B. Bovill, 12-68, Hants v Durham, Stockton-on-Tees; S. J. E. Brown, 11-192, Durham v Warwicks., Chester-le-Street.

A. R. Caddick, 10-131, Somerset v Durham, Chester-le-Street; C. L. Cairns, 15-83, Notts. v Sussex, Arundel; C. A. Connor, 10-127, Hants v Leics., Basingstoke; D. G. Cork, 13-93, Derbys. v Northants, Derby; R. D. B. Croft, 10-191, Glam. v Essex, Swansea.

A. A. Donald, 10-136, Warwicks. v Northants, Birmingham.

E. S. H. Giddins, 10-144, Sussex v Durham, Hartlepool; D. Gough, 10-80, Yorks. v Lancs., Leeds.

P. J. Hartley, 11-68, Yorks. v Derbys., Chesterfield.

R. L. Johnson, 10-98, Middx v Durham, Chester-le-Street.

D. E. Malcolm, 10-179, Derbys. v Worcs., Kidderminster; T. A. Munton, 10-116, Warwicks. v Notts., Nottingham.

M. M. Patel, 10-117, Kent v Cambridge U., Folkestone; A. C. S. Pigott, 11-111, Surrey v Northants, Northampton.

I. D. K. Salisbury, 11-171, Sussex v Leics., Hove; K. P. Sheeraz, 11-111, Glos. v West Indians, Bristol; A. Sheriyar, 10-85, Leics. v Young Australia, Leicester; A. M. Smith, 10-125, Glos v Worcs., Gloucester.

P. C. R. Tufnell, 10-202, Middx v Leics., Uxbridge.

S. D. Udal, 11-170, Hants v Notts., Nottingham.

A. Walker, 14-177, Durham v Essex, Chelmsford; S. L. Watkin, 10-104, Glam. v Somerset, Taunton; M. Watkinson, 10-222, Lancs. v Sussex, Lytham; A. R. Whittall, 11-113, Cambridge U. v Essex, Cambridge.

PROFESSIONALS' AWARDS, 1995

The Cricketers' Association chose Dominic Cork of Derbyshire as the winner of the Reg Hayter Award for Player of the Year in 1995. The John Arlott Award for Young Player of the Year went to Andrew Symonds of Gloucestershire.

THE WEST INDIANS IN ENGLAND, 1995

England and West Indies contested a fascinating, fluctuating series watched by packed houses in a gloriously hot summer. For a variety of reasons, they were more evenly matched than for some time and, fittingly, they shared it 2-2.

If West Indies enjoyed the better of the last two drawn, high-scoring Tests, and had the satisfaction of retaining the Wisden Trophy they have held through 22 years and 12 series, captain Richie Richardson's assessment that they performed below their potential was self-evident. In every department their cricket was inconsistent. England showed great spirit to recover from heavy defeats at Headingley and, especially, Edgbaston (where they were routed for 147 and 89) to draw level twice and then bat through difficult last days to safety at Trent Bridge and The Oval when West Indies held the upper hand. The home team overcame injuries that were mainly responsible for the use of 21 players in the six Tests – the longest series ever scheduled between the two teams – and could take considerable comfort from the authoritative leadership of Mike Atherton.

Only a year earlier, the England captain's position was under a cloud following the ball-tampering controversy in the Lord's Test against South Africa. He had returned from a disappointing Ashes campaign in Australia despondent and with his relationship with team manager and chief selector Ray Illingworth unsettled. Now West Indies manager Wes Hall reflected general opinion when, in choosing Atherton as England's Man of the Series, he identified him as "the defining difference to the result of this series". Atherton had, observed Hall, led from the front, "taking the fire of the West Indies pace bowlers unflinchingly". His influence was established in the one-day international matches which England won 2-1; he was also Man of the Series for those games, as he was in 1991. If there were occasional differences of opinion over selection during the summer, Illingworth acknowledged at the end that he and Atherton had become closer – "we're thinking of getting out the Bowie knife and becoming blood brothers" – and that team spirit was "in good shape".

In contrast, Richardson was a captain always under pressure. The 2-1 defeat by Australia in the Caribbean in the preceding series had ended a proud West Indian record of 15 years' invincibility; returning to the helm after his medically enforced rest the previous year, Richardson was made the principal scapegoat by a disenchanted public. A calm, undemonstrative individual, he often let the game take its course and seemed out of touch with his men. His indifferent form that yielded a modest Test average of 34.37 did nothing to dispel the widespread criticism of his leadership. The trauma of the Australian defeat was evident. During that series the new cricket manager, Andy Roberts, the great fast bowler of an earlier era, had publicly charged some of his players with having "attitude problems" and complained that his fast bowlers would not heed his advice. Yet everyone who played against Australia was chosen for the England tour.

It was soon clear that all was still not well. Between the Second and Third Tests, Hall, another legendary fast bowler, returning as team manager after ten years as a Barbadian cabinet minister, announced the expulsion of Winston Benjamin on disciplinary and fitness grounds. Defeat by an innings and 121 runs by Sussex, the heaviest ever inflicted by a

THE WEST INDIAN TOURING PARTY

[Patrick Eagar

Back row: D. J. M. Waight (*physiotherapist*), S. Chanderpaul, J. R. Murray, J. C. Adams, C. O. Browne, K. C. G. Benjamin, I. R. Bishop, O. D. Gibson, K. L. T. Arthurton, S. C. Williams, S. L. Campbell, R. Dhanraj, *Front row*: A. M. E. Roberts (*coach*), W. K. M. Benjamin, C. A. Walsh, R. B. Richardson (*captain*), W. W. Hall (*manager*), C. E. L. Ambrose, B. C. Lara, C. L. Hooper.

county on an official West Indian team, immediately followed. But at Edgbaston, a pitch of astonishing appearance and menacing behaviour, ideally suited to their fast bowlers, allowed them to regroup within a week, with one of Test cricket's swiftest victories, before lunch on the third day. Yet there was always the feeling that the management had their hands full maintaining control over their charges, especially some of the most eminent. That impression was confirmed when the West Indies Cricket Board of Control, acting on the manager's report, subsequently summoned four players before its disciplinary committee: Brian Lara and Carl Hooper for being absent without leave, Curtly Ambrose and Kenny Benjamin for more general failings of behaviour and attitude. All were fined 10 per cent of their tour earnings. Lara was sufficiently angered to pull out of the World Series in Australia, putting his entire future in question.

The team's packed international schedule over the previous ten months was another consideration in West Indies' erratic performances. From the previous October, they had played nine Tests and 18 one-day internationals in India, New Zealand and the Caribbean, arriving in England for the long, hot summer only five days after they succumbed to Australia in Kingston. By August, they had to summon Phil Simmons and Andy Cummins from the English leagues to shore up a team diminished by injury and fatigue.

As against Australia, the West Indian batting was unreliable and too heavily dependent on the phenomenal Lara, who only found his true touch midway through the season. While Ian Bishop's successful and courageous return to international cricket, after a break of two years, waiting for the second stress fracture of his back to heal, was a definite boost to their attack, there were unmistakable signs that Ambrose and Courtney Walsh were beginning to feel the strain of advancing years and too much cricket. In the first innings of each of the last three Tests, England passed 400, a feat last achieved against West Indies by Australia in 1975-76.

Lara's early failures included his first pair in a first-class match when he was dismissed twice by Julian Thompson, a Kent part-timer whose more regular employment is as a surgeon at the Royal Berkshire Hospital. It was not until late July, in the Fourth Test, that he batted with his accustomed dominance. England had already drawn level in the series once, through a victory at Lord's which was virtually assured when Lara was out half an hour into the final day. At Old Trafford, even his 87 and 145 were not sufficient to prevent England's second victory as most of his team-mates – only one other reached 40 – surrendered their wickets with wanton strokes on a true pitch in the brilliant sunshine. What the admiring public did not know was that Lara was in bitter dispute within the dressing-room and disappeared from the tour for several days after the Test. However, he returned with a flourish, delighting the crowds that packed Trent Bridge and The Oval, as they did everywhere else, with further hundreds, both compiled at the staggering rate of over 80 runs per 100 balls. But these were made on surfaces so unsympathetic to bowlers that run-filled draws were always likely, even though England had their moments of anxiety in holding on. Lara's superiority was emphasised by the statistics. His 765 runs were 259 more than the next highest on either side, Graham Thorpe's 506 for England, and 311 more than his nearest team-mate, Sherwin Campbell.

Campbell's advance was arguably the most encouraging development for the tourists. In his first full series and on his first tour of England, the little opener passed 40 in one innings of each Test and soon adapted to different conditions and situations with his quick footwork and straight-batted technique. He stayed over five hours for 93 in a vain attempt to steer his team home at Lord's, an approach in contrast to his 69 off 101 balls in the First Test and 89 off 152 balls in the last, when he matched Lara stroke for stroke in a partnership of 108. West Indies could be optimistic that they had eased one half of a headache which had afflicted them since Desmond Haynes followed Gordon Greenidge out of the team. Campbell was also a fast and sure-handed fielder, claiming nine catches in the Tests, so that it was undeserving bad luck that the only one that got away, on the final afternoon of the Fifth Test, denied him and his fellow batsmen the chance of a reasonable target for victory.

The latest of several opening partnerships West Indies have tried since Greenidge and Haynes's golden days involved matching Campbell with Hooper, in the hope that the added responsibility would eliminate Hooper's exasperating underachievement. But Hooper continued to add to his list of irrational methods of dismissal, and the experiment came to nothing; he was in his accustomed position in the middle order when he finally showed his class with a hundred in the final Test. The original adjustment meant there was no place for the second young specialist opener, Stuart Williams, until the Fifth Test, which Hooper missed with a fractured finger. Given his chance, Williams batted with more confidence in his two innings than he had shown in his previous ten Tests. Like Campbell, his value was enhanced by his flawless, often spectacular, work in the slips where he snared 11 catches, six as substitute.

Injury and loss of form also prompted the replacement of three established players late in the series. The left-handed Jimmy Adams was not the batsman whose solidity had been such a vital element as a foil to the strokemakers around him. He was unable to play a significant innings before his tour was ended in early August by a blow from Somerset's fast bowler Andre van Troost that fractured his right cheekbone. Keith Arthurton, one of the four middle-order left-handers, secured his place at No. 6 on the basis of his heavy scoring in the early county matches but fell away after an accomplished 75 at Lord's and was dropped. So, too, was Junior Murray, when his wicket-keeping became increasingly untidy and his batting erratic.

The changes allowed the introduction of younger players, all on their first tours of England. Williams, 26, came back to his accredited position, Shivnarine Chanderpaul, 21, finally reclaimed his place after an absence of eight Tests and Courtney Browne, 24, was installed as wicket-keeper. Williams fashioned an attractive half-century in his first innings, the left-handed Chanderpaul recorded his highest Test score, 80, at The Oval and Browne's nine catches at Trent Bridge equalled the West Indian Test record. Along with Campbell's consistency, these were encouraging signs for the future.

There were distinctly fewer in the bowling which, except in the helpful conditions of Edgbaston, lacked its customary bite. The amazing Walsh, in his 11th year of Test cricket, continued to defy the effects of *anno domini*, uncomplainingly bowling more overs (290) than anyone else on either side and, at The Oval, claiming his 300th Test wicket, joining Malcolm Marshall and Lance Gibbs as the only West Indians to have reached the landmark. Yet he could not be expected to maintain such a workload for much longer; he turned 33 in October. Ambrose, a year younger, was always capable of a spell of incisive, too, quality bowling, even on the featherbed at The Oval, but his body, too, was beginning to react to the demands placed on it over the years. Injuries restricted him to 7.5 overs at Edgbaston and scratched him from Trent Bridge altogether. As he prematurely left the ground on the final day of the series with a leg strain, his arm-waving farewell indicated an uncertain future.

Obliged to alter his action in deference to his fragile back, so that he was more front-on in delivery, Bishop was still capable of out-swing and genuine pace and his 27 wickets – 21 in the first four Tests – were the most by a bowler on either side. His return, as player and influential team man, was a bonus for West Indies but, given his medical history, he is likely to be handled with care. The fourth member of the fast bowling quartet, Kenny Benjamin, made a distinct advance once he finally heeded Roberts's advice to observe a fuller length and more direct line. His probing out-swing and complementary off-cut placed him top of both the Test and tour averages, enhancing his status. Yet, at 28, he continued to be bothered by injury, missing the Second Test and the entire last day of the Sixth when his presence would have made England's fight for survival more difficult.

The two reserve fast bowlers, Barbadians Ottis Gibson and Vasbert Drakes, Winston Benjamin's replacement, achieved nothing of note and, while the leg-spinner Rajindra Dhanraj was given every chance against the counties, claiming 61 first-class wickets, he was found wanting when called up for the Trent Bridge Test. He failed to take a wicket in 55 overs and compounded West Indian doubts about the need for spin bowlers.

If the proliferation of injuries never allowed England to keep a settled team – only Atherton and Thorpe appeared in all six Tests – Illingworth regarded it as an opportunity "to look at one or two other players". He said: "We have tried to go for people who have a bit of ticker, a bit of character, and we have seen enough to show there is plenty of fighting spirit there".

No one epitomised that spirit more than Dominic Cork. The ebullient Derbyshire all-rounder, only 24 but for some time on the fringe of selection, won a Test for England on debut with his second-innings seven for 43 at Lord's and set the seal on the Old Trafford triumph in his first over of the fourth day with the first Test hat-trick by an Englishman since 1957. Positive and aggressive in everything he did, not least his appealing, he also contributed important runs lower in the order and quickly had the unenviable tag of the "new Botham" stamped all over him. Such a heady comparison had been attached to another spirited cricketer only a few months earlier. But Darren Gough, overwhelmed by an abundance of adulation and advice and a shortage of form and fitness, disappeared from the scene after the Third Test. Cork would have heeded the warning but, while neither he nor Gough is likely to match Botham's feats, he certainly brought a Bothamesque vitality to the team.

In a less demonstrative way, the left-handed Thorpe also filled Illingworth's requirements of character. He became the first Englishman to pass 500 runs in a home series against West Indies, albeit in six rather than five Tests, batting with determination and combativeness throughout. In 13 successive Tests since his recall to the team against South Africa the previous summer, Thorpe had accumulated 1,189 runs at an average just under 50, enough to establish a permanence at No. 4. Graeme Hick also went a long way towards a settled place. He removed justifiable doubts about his temperament and technique with 118 not out, 96 and 51 not out in three of his last four innings, though the pitches involved, at Trent Bridge and The Oval, were benign. It was significant that this run followed a straight-talking, face-to-face meeting with Illingworth, initiated by the usually taciturn Hick himself after he was upset by his omission from the final eleven at Old Trafford.

His success was counterbalanced by the unconvincing performances of the younger brigade, Mark Ramprakash, John Crawley, Jason Gallian and Nick Knight, and Alan Wells's first-ball duck in his debut Test innings for which, at 33, he had waited so long.

Illingworth had his way in the use of Alec Stewart as wicket-keeper for the first half of the series. While his breathtaking catch to dismiss Lara in the second innings proved decisive in the Lord's victory, he did little with the bat, either at No. 5 or in his more accustomed role as Atherton's partner. Finally, fingers that had been repeatedly damaged in Australia could not stand up to the pounding they took in front of and behind the stumps; he did not play again for the summer after sustaining a fracture in the Third Test. It would be a blessing in disguise if it finally ended the selectors' policy of landing him with the difficult dual role, especially as Jack Russell, regaining his place after a year and a half, not only kept with his old aplomb but also frustrated the opposition with his unorthodox left-handed batting. Injury also cut short Robin Smith's series. His proven record against West Indian fast bowling earned him his place back after a year's absence, initially as opening batsman, and he was as effective as ever. He top-scored in both innings at Lord's and Edgbaston. But, like Adams a week later, he was forced out when his cheekbone was shattered by a delivery from Bishop that deflected from his bat. He required an operation and was thus denied the chance of batting on the flattest pitches of the summer.

If Cork's success was reason for unquestionable optimism, England ended the series with the future composition of their bowling unresolved. Phillip DeFreitas's dismissal after the first Test appeared to signal the end of his chequered career for England – though it has seemed so many times before – and Devon Malcolm's speed was again only grudgingly trusted for the first and last Tests. Angus Fraser, inexplicably omitted from the First Test, where conditions would have ideally suited his method, was as persistent as ever in the remaining five. Peter Martin, the tall fast-medium out-swinger, was one of the many to succumb to injury after a promising start in his first Test series.

Cork and Martin were fresh, new fast bowlers but England's approach to spin disregarded the future. Mike Watkinson, the Lancashire captain, batsman and off-spinner, gained his first England cap at 33, played a match-saving, unbeaten 82 at Trent Bridge and bowled reasonably but scarcely had long-term prospects in Test cricket. Nor did left-arm spinner Richard Illingworth, almost 32, back in the team four years after his previous two Tests against West Indies, and certainly not John Emburey, summoned in his 43rd year for his 64th and, one assumes, last Test at Old Trafford. He did not take a wicket. Younger men who had been tried already, such as Shaun Udal, Peter Such and Ian Salisbury, were bypassed, as was Phil Tufnell, whose mercurial temperament weighed more heavily with the selectors than his proven left-arm spin.

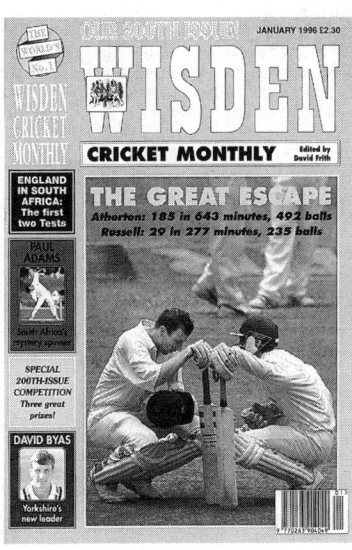

After the finale at The Oval, there were contrasting reactions to the outcome from Richardson, who expressed his disappointment, and from Atherton and Illingworth, who both pronounced themselves satisfied. It was an understandable reflection of the contrasting records of the two teams in the recent past for, while there were signs that England were emerging from a lengthy trough, the series confirmed the end of West Indies' unprecedented period of domination. – Tony Cozier.

WEST INDIAN TOURING PARTY

R. B. Richardson (Leeward Islands) (*captain*), C. A. Walsh (Jamaica) (*vice-captain*), J. C. Adams (Jamaica), C. E. L. Ambrose (Leeward Islands), K. L. T. Arthurton (Leeward Islands), K. C. G. Benjamin (Leeward Islands), W. K. M. Benjamin (Leeward Islands), I. R. Bishop (Trinidad & Tobago), C. O. Browne (Barbados), S. L. Campbell (Barbados), S. Chanderpaul (Guyana), R. Dhanraj (Trinidad & Tobago), O. D. Gibson (Barbados), C. L. Hooper (Guyana), B. C. Lara (Trinidad & Tobago), J. R. Murray (Windward Islands), S. C. Williams (Leeward Islands).

V. C. Drakes (Barbados) replaced W. K. M. Benjamin, who was sent home for reasons of discipline and fitness. A. C. Cummins (Barbados) and P. V. Simmons (Trinidad & Tobago) joined the party for two matches in August.

Manager: W. W. Hall.   *Coach:* A. M. E. Roberts.

WEST INDIAN TOUR RESULTS

Test matches – Played 6: Won 2, Lost 2, Drawn 2.
First-class matches – Played 20: Won 6, Lost 3, Drawn 11.
Wins – England (2), Leicestershire, Kent, Somerset, Gloucestershire.
Losses – England (2), Sussex.
Draws – England (2), Worcestershire, Somerset, Northamptonshire, Durham, Combined Universities, Middlesex, Hampshire, Essex, Yorkshire.
One-day internationals – Played 3: Won 1, Lost 2.
Other non-first-class matches – Played 7: Won 3, Lost 3, Drawn 1. *Wins* – Lavinia, Duchess of Norfolk's XI, Scotland, Warwickshire. *Losses* – Hampshire, Minor Counties, Yorkshire. *Draw* – Ireland.

TEST MATCH AVERAGES

ENGLAND – BATTING

	T	I	NO	R	HS	100s	Avge	Ct/St
M. Watkinson	3	4	1	156	82*	0	52.00	1
G. A. Hick.........	5	10	2	403	118*	1	50.37	5
R. C. Russell	3	5	1	199	91	0	49.75	9/1
R. A. Smith	4	8	1	305	90	0	43.57	0
G. P. Thorpe	6	12	0	506	94	0	42.16	2
M. A. Atherton	6	12	0	488	113	1	40.66	3
D. G. Cork	5	8	1	197	56*	0	28.14	1
R. K. Illingworth ...	4	8	5	69	17*	0	23.00	2
A. J. Stewart	3	5	0	113	37	0	22.60	9
N. V. Knight	2	4	0	89	57	0	22.25	5
J. P. Crawley	3	6	1	100	50	0	20.00	4
D. Gough	3	6	0	73	29	0	12.16	2
P. J. Martin	3	6	0	52	29	0	8.66	4
J. E. R. Gallian	2	4	0	32	25	0	8.00	1
C. White..........	2	4	0	26	23	0	6.50	0
M. R. Ramprakash ..	2	4	0	22	18	0	5.50	1
A. R. C. Fraser	5	8	4	22	10*	0	5.50	1

Played in two Tests: D. E. Malcolm 0, 5, 10. Played in one Test: P. A. J. DeFreitas 23, 1; J. E. Emburey 8 (1 ct); A. P. Wells 0, 3*.

* *Signifies not out.*

BOWLING

	O	M	R	W	BB	5W/i	Avge
D. G. Cork	184.2	30	661	26	7-43	1	25.42
A. R. C. Fraser	187.5	52	563	16	5-66	1	35.18
R. K. Illingworth....	100	40	215	6	4-96	0	35.83
M. Watkinson	93	21	289	8	3-64	0	36.12
D. Gough	70	6	255	6	3-79	0	42.50
D. E. Malcolm......	50.3	7	220	5	3-160	0	44.00
P. J. Martin	84	21	241	5	2-65	0	48.20

Also bowled: P. A. J. DeFreitas 27-3-115-2; J. E. Emburey 30-7-82-0; J. E. R. Gallian 12-1-56-0; G. A. Hick 18-4-64-1; C. White 16-0-76-0.

WEST INDIES – BATTING

	T	I	NO	R	HS	100s	Avge	Ct
B. C. Lara	6	10	1	765	179	3	85.00	4
S. L. Campbell......	6	10	0	454	93	0	45.40	9
C. L. Hooper	5	8	1	310	127	1	44.28	4
R. B. Richardson....	6	8	0	275	93	0	34.37	4
J. C. Adams	4	6	0	160	58	0	26.66	1
C. E. L. Ambrose ...	5	7	4	77	23*	0	25.66	2
K. L. T. Arthurton ..	5	7	0	172	75	0	24.57	6
K. C. G. Benjamin ..	5	6	2	74	20	0	18.50	0
J. R. Murray	4	6	0	84	26	0	14.00	14
C. A. Walsh........	6	7	1	61	19	0	10.16	1
I. R. Bishop	6	8	1	71	16	0	10.14	0

Played in two Tests: C. O. Browne 34, 1*, 27* (13 ct); S. Chanderpaul 18, 5*, 80; S. C. Williams 62, 30 (5 ct). Played in one Test: R. Dhanraj 3; O. D. Gibson 29, 14.

* Signifies not out.

BOWLING

	O	M	R	W	BB	5W/i	Avge
K. C. G. Benjamin....	158.2	33	506	23	5-69	2	22.00
I. R. Bishop	242.3	49	649	27	5-32	1	24.03
C. E. L. Ambrose.....	185.1	43	506	21	5-96	1	24.09
C. A. Walsh	290	57	786	26	5-45	1	30.23

Also bowled: J. C. Adams 12-1-32-0; K. L. T. Arthurton 33.5-6-76-0; S. Chanderpaul 6-0-22-0; R. Dhanraj 55-8-191-0; O. D. Gibson 34-3-132-2; C. L. Hooper 68-22-149-3; B. C. Lara 1-1-0-0.

WEST INDIAN TOUR AVERAGES

BATTING

	M	I	NO	R	HS	100s	Avge	Ct/St
B. C. Lara	13	20	1	1,126	179	3	59.26	14
S. Chanderpaul	15	25	8	1,003	140*	4	59.00	11
K. L. T. Arthurton ..	15	23	4	1,077	146	3	56.68	8
S. L. Campbell......	16	26	0	1,225	172	3	47.11	15
C. L. Hooper	15	25	2	1,063	195	5	46.21	10
C. O. Browne.......	12	16	5	498	102*	2	45.27	47/7

	M	I	NO	R	HS	100s	Avge	Ct/St
J. C. Adams........	13	22	5	741	114*	1	43.58	5
R. B. Richardson....	15	23	3	804	101*	1	40.20	12
S. C. Williams	13	20	0	770	137	3	38.50	13
O. D. Gibson.......	11	13	2	303	101*	1	27.54	5
J. R. Murray	12	19	3	440	100	1	27.50	27/3
C. E. L. Ambrose ...	10	13	7	147	27*	0	24.50	8
K. C. G. Benjamin ..	11	12	4	154	44	0	19.25	0
V. C. Drakes	6	9	1	118	48*	0	14.75	2
C. A. Walsh........	11	11	1	111	40	0	11.10	3
I. R. Bishop	10	11	1	102	25	0	10.20	5
R. Dhanraj.........	15	13	3	81	22	0	8.10	5

Played in three matches: W. K. M. Benjamin 4, 7 (1 ct). Played in two matches: A. C. Cummins 16; P. V. Simmons 10, 112, 139*.

* Signifies not out.

BOWLING

	O	M	R	W	BB	5W/i	Avge
K. C. G. Benjamin....	284.1	71	923	43	5-52	3	21.46
J. C. Adams	42.1	9	114	5	3-41	0	22.80
V. C. Drakes	106	17	400	16	5-20	1	25.00
A. C. Cummins	42	4	180	7	5-60	1	25.71
I. R. Bishop	334	69	983	38	5-32	1	25.86
R. Dhanraj	475.3	79	1,596	61	6-50	4	26.16
C. A. Walsh	384.2	76	1,124	39	5-45	1	28.82
C. E. L. Ambrose.....	262.1	70	744	25	5-96	1	29.76
O. D. Gibson	242.4	36	966	31	4-32	0	31.16
K. L. T. Arthurton....	88.5	17	264	6	2-19	0	44.00
C. L. Hooper	267.4	54	821	17	3-22	0	48.29

Also bowled: W. K. M. Benjamin 33–10–73–1; C. O. Browne 2–0–16–0; S. Chanderpaul 42–5–154–2; B. C. Lara 9–1–45–0; P. V. Simmons 39–9–121–1; S. C. Williams 1–0–2–0.

Note: Matches in this section which were not first-class are signified by a dagger.

†LAVINIA, DUCHESS OF NORFOLK'S XI v WEST INDIANS

At Arundel, May 13. West Indians won by 102 runs. Toss: West Indians.

The West Indians made a slightly disorganised entrance – they arrived without their scorebook and left without their flag – but took easy command on the field. The mostly retired county players representing the Duchess could not contain Hooper, who scored 173 from 140 balls, dominating century stands with Campbell and Richardson. Hughes, whose first ball he hit for one of nine sixes, later resorted to bowling under-arm. The only significant response came from Randall, who completed a century after a let-off on 98. The Barbadian Drakes had a decent all-round game, and he was later drafted from Sussex's second team into the touring party.

West Indians

C. L. Hooper not out................173		K. L. T. Arthurton not out	3
S. L. Campbell b Graveney 38		L-b 8, w 4, n-b 6............	18
*R. B. Richardson c Cowans b James.. 53			—
J. C. Adams lbw b James............ 13		1/104 2/237 3/276 (3 wkts, 50 overs)	298

S. Chanderpaul, †C. O. Browne, O. D. Gibson, I. R. Bishop, K. C. G. Benjamin and R. Dhanraj did not bat.

Bowling: Cowans 10–0–42–0; Drakes 10–4–33–0; Hughes 10–0–71–0; Murphy 3–1–6–0; Graveney 10–0–69–1; James 7–0–69–2.

Lavinia, Duchess of Norfolk's XI

M. H. Richardson c Bishop b Gibson	18	S. P. Hughes not out	2
*P. W. G. Parker c Richardson b Bishop	7	N. G. Cowans not out	4
K. D. James c and b Dhanraj	5		
V. C. Drakes lbw b Arthurton	26	B 1, l-b 2, w 3, n-b 4	10
D. W. Randall c Bishop b Chanderpaul	101		
P. R. Downton b Adams	16	1/21 2/33 3/47 (8 wkts, 50 overs)	196
†R. J. Parks b Arthurton	3	4/73 5/125 6/149	
D. A. Graveney lbw b Chanderpaul	4	7/186 8/189	

A. J. Murphy did not bat.

Bowling: Benjamin 6–1–8–0; Bishop 5–0–13–1; Gibson 5–0–16–1; Arthurton 10–1–48–2; Dhanraj 10–0–41–1; Chanderpaul 10–2–39–2; Adams 4–0–28–1.

Umpires: J. C. Balderstone and T. E. Jesty.

†HAMPSHIRE v WEST INDIANS

At Southampton, May 14. Hampshire won by 43 runs. Toss: West Indians.

The visitors showed little appetite for a chilly May day and Hampshire were scarcely stretched in recording a much-needed victory. Their only victims in eight previous games in 1995 had been Combined Universities. The problems which were to dog the West Indian bowlers showed up as they conceded 31 in no-balls, with Ambrose having particular trouble. Both Morris and White made solid half-centuries for the county; in reply, only a late, cavalier fifty by Gibson, who hit three sixes and three fours in 46 balls, threatened to deny Hampshire.

Hampshire

V. P. Terry c and b Benjamin	9	S. D. Udal not out	28
R. S. M. Morris b Benjamin	62		
R. A. Smith c Lara b Bishop	21	L-b 4, w 9, n-b 31	44
G. W. White not out	68		
*M. C. J. Nicholas b Gibson	28	1/43 2/95 3/121 (5 wkts, 55 overs)	268
†A. N. Aymes c Murray b Ambrose	8	4/201 5/226	

M. J. Thursfield, H. H. Streak, C. A. Connor and N. G. Cowans did not bat.

Bowling: Ambrose 11–1–59–1; Bishop 11–2–58–1; Benjamin 11–1–33–2; Gibson 11–0–63–1; Hooper 7–0–23–0; Arthurton 4–0–28–0.

West Indians

S. C. Williams lbw b Cowans	3	O. D. Gibson c Nicholas b Streak	57
C. L. Hooper c Terry b Udal	35	I. R. Bishop c Aymes b Connor	12
B. C. Lara b Cowans	14	C. E. L. Ambrose not out	4
J. C. Adams lbw b Streak	6	L-b 10, w 4, n-b 2	16
*R. B. Richardson c Aymes b Udal	17		
K. L. T. Arthurton c White b Connor	36	1/19 2/52 3/59 (52.1 overs)	225
†J. R. Murray c White b Udal	2	4/85 5/88 6/98	
W. K. M. Benjamin c White b Streak	23	7/139 8/154 9/219	

Bowling: Connor 9.1–1–39–2; Cowans 11–1–47–2; Streak 10–0–51–3; Thursfield 11–1–44–0; Udal 11–2–34–3.

Umpires: J. H. Hampshire and N. T. Plews.

WORCESTERSHIRE v WEST INDIANS

At Worcester, May 16, 17, 18. Drawn. Toss: West Indians. First-class debut: P. A. Thomas.

The tourists' traditional opening first-class fixture was blighted by rain, which returned in the final session to deny them probable victory. The game did provide pace bowler Paul Thomas with a promising first-class debut. He took a wicket with his fifth ball, although an onslaught by Lara gave him overnight figures of 5–0–44–1. Following a second-day washout, however, Thomas found his length and finished with five for 70. After Lara's 78 off 80 balls had illuminated the gloom, two forfeitures set Worcestershire a challenge of 242 in 48 overs. Bishop, Gibson and Benjamin bowled lively spells and Worcestershire slumped to 86 for five before the rain swept across New Road with more than 21 overs remaining.

Close of play: First day, West Indians 114-2 (B. C. Lara 29*, J. C. Adams 3*); Second day, No play.

West Indians

S. C. Williams c Weston b Thomas	23	W. K. M. Benjamin c Church b Thomas	4
S. L. Campbell b Lampitt	46	O. D. Gibson c Church b Thomas	4
B. C. Lara st Rhodes b Illingworth	78	I. R. Bishop c Weston b Illingworth	1
J. C. Adams c Leatherdale b Thomas	25	B 5, l-b 11, n-b 8	24
*R. B. Richardson st Rhodes			
b Illingworth	1	1/59 2/93 3/181	(9 wkts dec.) 241
S. Chanderpaul not out	9	4/193 5/199 6/227	
†J. R. Murray c Haynes b Thomas	26	7/231 8/239 9/241	

R. Dhanraj did not bat.

Bowling: Newport 12–2–48–0; Radford 7–1–28–0; Lampitt 16–1–49–1; Thomas 16–4–70–5; Illingworth 14.3–4–30–3.

West Indians forfeited their second innings.

Worcestershire

Worcestershire forfeited their first innings.

W. P. C. Weston b Gibson	1	†S. J. Rhodes c Murray b Dhanraj	13
*T. S. Curtis not out	37	S. R. Lampitt not out	5
M. J. Church b Williams b Gibson	5		
G. R. Haynes st Murray b Dhanraj	12	N-b 12	12
D. A. Leatherdale c Richardson			
b Benjamin	1	1/11 2/35 3/57 4/60 5/79	(5 wkts) 86

P. J. Newport, R. K. Illingworth, N. V. Radford and P. A. Thomas did not bat.

Bowling: Bishop 6.3–0–24–0; Gibson 7–0–33–2; Benjamin 7–3–10–1; Dhanraj 6–1–19–2.

Umpires: H. D. Bird and D. R. Shepherd.

SOMERSET v WEST INDIANS

At Taunton, May 19, 20, 21. Drawn. Toss: West Indians.

The most impressive innings of a batsman's match came at the start: Hooper scored a magnificent 176 from 179 balls, with seven sixes and 24 fours. He was supported by near-centuries from Campbell, with whom he shared a first-wicket stand of 242, and Adams. Somerset's openers both fell early, but Bowler and Harden then added 150 to give their reply its base, though nine wickets fell – four of them to Walsh – in saving the follow-on. Hayhurst declared and Campbell and Chanderpaul helped the West Indians to extend their lead to 324. Several of their bowlers were suffering from small injuries (blamed by coach Andy Roberts on over-soft beds) and Lathwell and Parsons were able to score briskly, though without making an attempt on the target.

Close of play: First day, West Indians 398-5 (J. C. Adams 63*, C. O. Browne 13*); Second day, Somerset 301-9 (R. J. Turner 12*, H. R. J. Trump 1*).

West Indians

C. L. Hooper c Mushtaq Ahmed b Parsons	176		
S. L. Campbell c Trump b Hayhurst	93	– st Turner b Trump	80
*R. B. Richardson c Trescothick			
b Mushtaq Ahmed	4	– (1) lbw b Rose	0
J. C. Adams c Lathwell b Mushtaq Ahmed	 91	– (5) not out	7
K. L. T. Arthurton c Turner b Ecclestone	9	– (3) c Rose b Trump	38
S. Chanderpaul c and b Trump	30	– (4) not out	50
†C. O. Browne c Turner b Hayhurst	17		
C. E. L. Ambrose not out	19		
C. A. Walsh b Mushtaq Ahmed	0		
L-b 8, w 2	10	L-b 1	1

1/242 2/251 3/287 4/315 5/370   (8 wkts dec.) 449   1/0 2/88 3/164   (3 wkts dec.) 176
6/409 7/449 8/449

K. C. G. Benjamin and R. Dhanraj did not bat.

Bowling: *First Innings*—Rose 15–5–37–0; Ecclestone 22–2–113–1; Hayhurst 14–0–83–2; Mushtaq Ahmed 16–3–77–3; Parsons 15–2–51–1; Trump 19–4–70–1; Trescothick 5–2–10–0. *Second Innings*—Rose 10–2–53–1; Parsons 6–1–20–0; Trescothick 5–1–23–0; Hayhurst 3–0–19–0; Mushtaq Ahmed 8–2–28–0; Trump 12.4–3–32–2.

Somerset

M. N. Lathwell b Walsh	7	– c Richardson b Dhanraj	76
M. E. Trescothick c Browne b Benjamin	24	– c Hooper b Walsh	0
P. D. Bowler c Browne b Benjamin	84		
R. J. Harden c and b Dhanraj	78		
*A. N. Hayhurst hit wkt b Walsh	7		
K. A. Parsons c Browne b Walsh	0	– (3) not out	52
G. D. Rose c Browne b Walsh	15		
S. C. Ecclestone b Dhanraj	6		
†R. J. Turner not out	12	– (4) not out	15
Mushtaq Ahmed c Chanderpaul b Dhanraj	 12		
H. R. J. Trump not out	1		
L-b 3, n-b 52	55	B 8, n-b 8	16

1/13 2/60 3/210 4/238 5/238   (9 wkts dec.) 301   1/20 2/125   (2 wkts) 159
6/254 7/268 8/276 9/292

Bowling: *First Innings*—Ambrose 9–1–64–0; Walsh 18–2–77–4; Benjamin 17–4–56–2; Hooper 15–1–47–0; Dhanraj 20–5–49–3; Arthurton 4–1–5–0. *Second Innings*—Ambrose 10–1–49–0; Walsh 6–2–17–1; Arthurton 4–1–8–0; Dhanraj 12–0–32–1; Hooper 3–0–17–0; Chanderpaul 8–0–28–0.

Umpires: K. E. Palmer and R. Palmer.

†ENGLAND v WEST INDIES

First One-Day International

At Nottingham, May 24, 25. West Indies won by five wickets. Toss: West Indies.

West Indies' victory was their first in limited-overs internationals in England since 1984, and would have been far more crushing but for careless batting towards the end. But the home batsmen's failings counted for more. Only Stewart, who scored 74, and Ramprakash, with 32 from 36 balls, passed 15. Walsh bowled tightly, conceding 28 in ten overs, and his third wicket made him the leading West Indian wicket-taker in one-day internationals. A target of 200 was too easy. West Indies were well on course when rain ended play – though they could not have been declared winners, as they were one ball short of the 20 overs needed for a result. Next morning, Lara and Campbell took them to 180 for one before

Gough dismissed Lara, caught over his shoulder by a running Atherton, and Richardson. Two more wickets quickly followed, but it was too late to make much difference – except by giving England hope for the rest of the series.

Man of the Match: C. A. Walsh.   *Attendance*: 13,003; *receipts* £335,686.

Close of play: West Indies 76-1 (19.5 overs) (S. L. Campbell 34*, B. C. Lara 6*).

England

*M. A. Atherton c Lara b Walsh	8	S. D. Udal not out	5
†A. J. Stewart b Hooper	74	A. R. C. Fraser not out	4
G. A. Hick c Murray b Benjamin	8	L-b 11, w 5, n-b 1	17
G. P. Thorpe c Murray b Walsh	7		
N. H. Fairbrother b Bishop	12	1/25 (1) 2/60 (3) (9 wkts, 55 overs) 199	
M. R. Ramprakash b Walsh	32	3/85 (4) 4/121 (5)	
P. A. J. DeFreitas run out	15	5/125 (2) 6/157 (7)	
D. G. Cork b Arthurton	14	7/186 (6) 8/190 (8)	
D. Gough run out	3	9/191 (9)	

Bowling: Ambrose 8–1–33–0; Walsh 10–1–28–3; Bishop 11–2–30–1; Benjamin 8–1–22–1; Hooper 10–0–45–1; Arthurton 8–0–30–1.

West Indies

C. L. Hooper b Cork	34	†J. R. Murray not out	7
S. L. Campbell run out	80	L-b 1, w 4, n-b 1	6
B. C. Lara c Atherton b Gough	70		
*R. B. Richardson c DeFreitas b Gough	1	1/66 (1) 2/180 (3) (5 wkts, 52.4 overs) 201	
J. C. Adams lbw b Cork	2	3/183 (4) 4/191 (5)	
K. L. T. Arthurton not out	1	5/194 (2)	

W. K. M. Benjamin, I. R. Bishop, C. E. L. Ambrose and C. A. Walsh did not bat.

Bowling: DeFreitas 10.4–1–44–0; Fraser 10–2–29–0; Gough 11–1–30–2; Cork 11–0–48–2; Udal 8–0–37–0; Hick 2–0–12–0.

Umpires: N. T. Plews and D. R. Shepherd.   Referee: J. R. Reid (New Zealand).

†ENGLAND v WEST INDIES

Second One-Day International

At The Oval, May 26. England won by 25 runs. Toss: West Indies. International debut: P. J. Martin.

England won the 1,000th official limited-overs international to level the series, thanks to a total of 306 for five, the most West Indies had ever conceded in this form of cricket. But their real hero was Peter Martin, the Lancashire seamer, who took four wickets on his England debut. Afterwards, he said it hadn't quite sunk in that he was in the team, but he radiated amiable delight. West Indies' determined assault had brought them 69 for one when he came on, in the 13th over, and dismissed Campbell with his fifth delivery. He soon added Adams and, as the *coup de grâce*, Lara, bowled for 39 off 36 balls. But Murray revived the faltering innings, with 86 from 77, and England could not feel quite safe until he was run out with two overs to spare. Atherton and Hick had launched their massive total with a stand of 144 in 28 overs, making the most of Walsh's absence with a back injury, and the last 15 overs brought England 118 as Fairbrother raced to 61 in 52 balls.

Man of the Match: P. J. Martin.   *Attendance*: 16,051; *receipts* £434,068.

England

*M. A. Atherton b Benjamin	92	D. Gough not out	8
†A. J. Stewart c Murray b Bishop	16	B 6, l-b 5, w 6, n-b 4	21
G. A. Hick run out	66		
G. P. Thorpe run out	26	1/33 (2) 2/177 (3) (5 wkts, 55 overs) 306	
N. H. Fairbrother not out	61	3/188 (1) 4/243 (4)	
M. R. Ramprakash c Adams b Hooper	16	5/295 (6)	

P. A. J. DeFreitas, D. G. Cork, P. J. Martin and S. D. Udal did not bat.

Bowling: Ambrose 10–1–47–0; Walsh 5.2–0–17–0; Bishop 11–0–60–1; Benjamin 10.4–0–55–1; Arthurton 8–0–48–0; Hooper 10–0–68–1.

West Indies

C. L. Hooper c Atherton b Gough	17	I. R. Bishop run out	18
S. L. Campbell c Thorpe b Martin	20	C. E. L. Ambrose b Martin	10
B. C. Lara b Martin	39	C. A. Walsh not out	5
J. C. Adams lbw b Martin	2	L-b 6, w 7	13
*R. B. Richardson c and b Cork	15		
K. L. T. Arthurton run out	39	1/25 (1) 2/69 (2) 3/77 (4) (53 overs) 281	
†J. R. Murray run out	86	4/88 (3) 5/114 (5) 6/166 (6)	
W. K. M. Benjamin c Ramprakash		7/213 (8) 8/261 (9)	
b DeFreitas	17	9/275 (10) 10/281 (7)	

Bowling: Gough 11–0–62–1; DeFreitas 10–0–73–1; Cork 11–0–56–1; Udal 11–0–40–0; Martin 10–1–44–4.

Umpires: H. D. Bird and R. Palmer.   Referee: J. R. Reid (New Zealand).

†ENGLAND v WEST INDIES

Third One-Day International

At Lord's, May 28. England won by 73 runs. Toss: West Indies. International debuts: A. P. Wells; O. D. Gibson.

Atherton had just missed his maiden one-day international hundred at The Oval; here he played a triumphant, series-clinching 127, striking 14 fours in 160 balls and lifting Bishop for six. Though England's selectors had once judged him unsuited to limited-overs cricket, he passed 1,000 runs in his 25th game at an average of 46.43. He had to weather early difficulties, when Richardson put England in for the third time, on a damp and lively pitch. It took Atherton 27 balls to get off the mark. But though his first 50 occupied 96 balls, his second needed only 48 and the rest 16. His team-mates were reduced to supporting roles and Wells, making his England debut at 33, had to walk out for a ten-minute thrash after Atherton finally departed to a standing ovation. Set to score just over five an over, none of the West Indians could play the major innings required. Hooper batted for 34 overs before becoming Cork's third victim, but no one else reached 40 and they were all out with more than six overs left.

Man of the Match: M. A. Atherton.   *Attendance:* 25,441; *receipts* £763,322.

Men of the Series: M. A. Atherton and J. R. Murray.

England

*M. A. Atherton c Adams b Gibson	127	P. J. Martin not out	4
†A. J. Stewart c Lara b Bishop	8		
G. A. Hick b Hooper	24	B 4, l-b 13, w 9, n-b 7	33
G. P. Thorpe c Hooper b Gibson	28		
M. R. Ramprakash not out	29	1/12 (2) 2/79 (3) (7 wkts, 55 overs) 276	
A. P. Wells b Gibson	15	3/152 (4) 4/244 (1)	
D. Gough b Benjamin	8	5/263 (6) 6/272 (7)	
D. G. Cork lbw b Benjamin	4	7/272 (8)	

S. D. Udal and A. R. C. Fraser did not bat.

Bowling: Ambrose 11–1–45–0; Bishop 11–2–53–1; Benjamin 10–0–61–2; Gibson 11–0–51–3; Hooper 11–0–38–1; Arthurton 1–0–11–0.

West Indies

S. C. Williams c Atherton b Cork	21	I. R. Bishop not out	1
C. L. Hooper c Gough b Cork	40	C. E. L. Ambrose b Martin	1
B. C. Lara c Stewart b Cork	11	L-b 13, w 11	24
J. C. Adams c Stewart b Martin	29		
K. L. T. Arthurton c Stewart b Gough	35	1/29 (1) 2/44 (3) (48.2 overs) 203	
*R. B. Richardson lbw b Gough	23	3/94 (4) 4/128 (2)	
†J. R. Murray b Fraser	5	5/171 (5) 6/184 (6)	
O. D. Gibson c Atherton b Fraser	7	7/190 (7) 8/198 (8)	
W. K. M. Benjamin b Fraser	6	9/201 (9) 10/203 (11)	

Bowling: Fraser 11–3–34–3; Martin 9.2–1–36–2; Cork 9–2–27–3; Gough 10–0–31–2; Udal 8–0–52–0; Hick 1–0–10–0.

Umpires: J. H. Hampshire and M. J. Kitchen. Referee: J. R. Reid (New Zealand).

LEICESTERSHIRE v WEST INDIANS

At Leicester, May 30, 31, June 1. West Indians won by 287 runs. Toss: Leicestershire. County debuts: V. P. Clarke, A. Habib.

Two marvellous centuries from left-handers Arthurton and Chanderpaul set up an easy win. They put on 223 in 51 overs and Arthurton cracked 24 fours and four sixes on the opening day; Chanderpaul reached his hundred next morning and hit 23 fours before Richardson, who had himself made his first fifty since Arundel, declared at 468. Then the leg-spinner, Dhanraj, destroyed the Leicestershire batting, which was missing several injured players, including Briers and Cronje, who was absent on a delayed honeymoon. Acting-captain Whitaker, however, made a remarkable 75 from 82 balls. The tourists declined to enforce the follow-on, instead taking their lead to 417 before putting the county back in with 60 overs left. Nine overs of pace from Gibson and Kenny Benjamin reduced Leicestershire to a humiliating 25 for six, from which they limped on to 130. Benjamin had been in trouble with umpire Jones on the second day, when he bowled two successive bouncers and was then no-balled twice for over-stepping the crease. He responded by running in without releasing the ball at all.

Close of play: First day, West Indians 389-5 (S. Chanderpaul 97*, C. O. Browne 3*); Second day, West Indians 16-1 (S. C. Williams 11*, R. B. Richardson 4*).

West Indians

S. C. Williams c Nixon b Parsons	13	– (2) st Nixon b Clarke	54
C. L. Hooper c Maddy b Dakin	29	– (1) c Dakin b Sheriyar	1
*R. B. Richardson lbw b Parsons	60	– lbw b Parsons	16
J. C. Adams c Nixon b Sheriyar	2	– c and b Pierson	42
K. L. T. Arthurton c Parsons b Dakin	146	– not out	16
S. Chanderpaul not out	140	– not out	6
†C. O. Browne b Sheriyar	19		
W. K. M. Benjamin c Nixon b Millns	7		
O. D. Gibson not out	7		
B 5, l-b 4, w 4, n-b 32	45	B 4, l-b 1, w 1, n-b 2	8

1/19 2/60 3/72 4/154 5/377 (7 wkts dec.) 468   1/1 2/42 (4 wkts dec.) 143
6/429 7/445   3/100 4/130

R. Dhanraj and K. C. G. Benjamin did not bat.

Bowling: *First Innings*—Millns 18–2–67–1; Parsons 21–9–23–2; Sheriyar 24–1–146–2; Dakin 20–2–94–2; Pierson 18–2–80–0; Clarke 7–0–49–0. *Second Innings*—Parsons 9–3–20–1; Sheriyar 9–0–41–1; Dakin 6–1–27–0; Clarke 8.1–0–35–1; Pierson 4–2–15–1.

Leicestershire

D. L. Maddy c Williams b K. C. G. Benjamin	8	– lbw b K. C. G. Benjamin	4
B. F. Smith b Dhanraj	18	– c Williams b K. C. G. Benjamin	6
*J. J. Whitaker c Chanderpaul b Dhanraj	75	– c Browne b Gibson	4
A. Habib b Dhanraj	4	– c Williams b K. C. G. Benjamin	0
†P. A. Nixon c Browne b Dhanraj	7	– c Browne b K. C. G. Benjamin	10
J. M. Dakin c and b Dhanraj	1	– c Browne b Gibson	0
V. P. Clarke c Richardson b Gibson	5	– c and b Gibson	10
G. J. Parsons c Richardson b K. C. G. Benjamin	19	– c Browne b Hooper	16
D. J. Millns lbw b Dhanraj	20	– c W. K. M. Benjamin b Hooper	28
A. R. K. Pierson not out	0	– not out	19
A. Sheriyar b K. C. G. Benjamin	0	– st Browne b Hooper	19
L-b 4, w 1, n-b 38	43	B 4, l-b 2, n-b 8	14

1/42 2/96 3/108 4/118 5/130   194   1/4 2/11 3/11 4/15 5/19   130
6/135 7/154 8/194 9/194   6/25 7/45 8/79 9/92

Bowling: *First Innings*—W. K. M. Benjamin 11–3–27–0; Gibson 12–2–55–1; K. C. G. Benjamin 9.2–2–58–3; Dhanraj 15–3–50–6. *Second Innings*—K. C. G. Benjamin 11–3–50–4; Gibson 8–1–26–3; Dhanraj 6–1–25–0; W. K. M. Benjamin 1–0–1–0; Hooper 8–1–22–3.

Umpires: T. E. Jesty and A. A. Jones.

NORTHAMPTONSHIRE v WEST INDIANS

At Northampton, June 3, 4, 5. Drawn. Toss: Northamptonshire.

The captains could not agree terms for a meaningful contest after the loss of the first day to rain. But the tourists were more concerned with settling their line-up for the First Test. Most encouraging for them was the form of Arthurton, who scored his second century in successive matches, with three sixes and 20 fours. He batted fluently to add 206 in 65 overs with Adams, after Taylor and Capel had removed the first three men in the space of seven balls. Lara, rejoining the squad after a brief business trip to Trinidad, played on to the second delivery he faced, aiming a loose drive. On the previous day, Bishop had proved by far the most threatening of the West Indian bowlers, although Northamptonshire battled their way to a respectable total, thanks largely to Penberthy and Warren, and then to Mallender with a late flourish.

Close of play: First day, No play; Second day, Northamptonshire 281.

Northamptonshire

R. R. Montgomerie c Lara b Bishop	27	†D. Ripley b Bishop	3
A. Fordham c Chanderpaul b Walsh	0	N. A. Mallender not out	49
*R. J. Bailey c Chanderpaul b Bishop	30	J. P. Taylor c Walsh b Adams	7
T. C. Walton b Dhanraj	0		
R. J. Warren lbw b Walsh	37	L-b 3, w 1, n-b 22	26
D. J. Capel c Adams b Bishop	12		
A. L. Penberthy c Murray b Adams	73	1/1 2/67 3/68 4/70 5/88	281
J. N. Snape lbw b Dhanraj	17	6/157 7/190 8/197 9/243	

Bowling: Ambrose 13–6–28–0; Walsh 15–4–43–2; Bishop 23–7–64–4; Arthurton 2–0–9–0; Dhanraj 33–5–113–2; Adams 11.1–4–21–2.

West Indians

S. C. Williams lbw b Taylor	25	†J. R. Murray not out	0
S. L. Campbell c Mallender b Capel	25		
B. C. Lara b Taylor	0	B 2, l-b 1	3
J. C. Adams c Mallender b Bailey	93		
K. L. T. Arthurton not out	121	1/50 2/50 3/52 (5 wkts dec.) 268
S. Chanderpaul c Bailey b Fordham	1	4/258 5/268	

I. R. Bishop, C. E. L. Ambrose, *C. A. Walsh and R. Dhanraj did not bat.

Bowling: Taylor 15–4–28–2; Mallender 12–3–45–0; Capel 11–1–37–1; Penberthy 11–1–36–0; Snape 19–6–66–0; Bailey 8–1–27–1; Walton 8–2–26–0; Fordham 1–1–0–1.

Umpires: J. C. Balderstone and J. D. Bond.

ENGLAND v WEST INDIES

First Cornhill Test

At Leeds, June 8, 9, 10, 11. West Indies won by nine wickets. Toss: West Indies. Test debut: P. J. Martin.

The notion that defeat by Australia had left West Indian cricket on a life-support machine proved a trifle far-fetched. But for repeated interference by mid-winter weather, victory in what England regarded as the vital, trend-setting Test would have been wrapped up in three embarrassing days. Individual weaknesses in Richardson's side were easy to identify, more difficult to exploit for an England team that got its balance and its strategy badly wrong.

The close-season sacking of manager Keith Fletcher made this the first Test in which chairman of the selectors Ray Illingworth assumed total power and, by inference, accepted all the blame. His determination to play five bowlers gave Lancashire's Peter Martin his Test debut but forced the reluctant Stewart to keep wicket and bat down the order. Strangely, his position as opener was entrusted to Smith. As Smith had rarely done the specialist job, was playing his first Test for 11 months, and was still finding his form after a shoulder operation, he hardly seemed the perfect choice. And so it proved when Richardson – winning the toss for the eighth time in successive Tests – asked England to bat, something, it transpired, they would have done anyway. Smith, dropped in the slips by Hooper's chilled fingers when he was three, survived for 69 minutes before his obsession with cutting the uncuttable gave Richardson a slip catch.

Atherton, on trial again after being given the captaincy for only three Tests, had already focused his immense powers of concentration on the brand of innings Headingley pitches demand. His 81 was not so much a masterpiece as a priceless collection of miniatures. Statistically, it lasted 214 minutes but, in fact, it spread from the first to the last ball of a rain-wrecked day – another shower started before Ramprakash could take guard. As squall upon squall hit the ground, Atherton played himself in seven times – on each occasion looking as if he had never been away. Until an away-swinging peach from Bishop gave wicket-keeper Murray a diving catch, he drove and pulled at anything off-line with the certainty of a batsman nearing a peak many believed he might never scale.

Maybe it was he who told his team not to cower before the West Indian attack, as so many of their predecessors had done. Wise advice, but, like the order to the Light Brigade, it was misinterpreted. The promise of 142 for two shortly before the end of the first day became 199 all out as batsmen swung wildly at enticingly short balls. Wistful dreams about aging, sulking, half-pace bowlers were shattered. Walsh, ageless and tireless, was as combative as ever. Ambrose rediscovered his rhythm and his scowling enthusiasm and, by bowling Malcolm in the second innings, claimed his 100th Test wicket against England. Injury restricted Kenny Benjamin later, but his five wickets warned against taking liberties with his erratic speed. However, the revelation was Bishop, devout Christian and born-again fast bowler. He collected seven wickets in his first Test since a back injury threatened his career two years earlier. His remodelled action did not generate the old pace, but he had become the thinking man's giant, able to hit the right spot from a great height and move the ball both ways. His first-innings five for 32 included a spell of five for five in 18 balls.

England's apologists blamed Headingley's unreadable bounce. That understated the artfulness of the bowling as well as the naïveté of some of the batting. Nothing could have made that point more savagely than Lara's assault upon England's bowlers. He launched into his spectacular, irreverent 53 after Malcolm's first delivery had been dollied to slip by Hooper – like Smith, an unfamiliar Test opener. But players of Lara's calibre tend to be oblivious to crises. He hit Malcolm with such nimble-footed abandon that England's spearhead was withdrawn after his first two overs cost 24. He was rarely called upon again and not trusted with the new ball in the second innings. Fraser's weary-looking accuracy would have been useful, but England's most dependable bowler had been omitted from the twelve. Without him, the attack never recovered from a ragged, indisciplined start as Lara outpaced the fluent Campbell in a partnership worth 95 runs and plenty more psychologically. He had hit ten fours in 55 balls when a huge swing at left-arm spinner Richard Illingworth gave Hick a leaping catch at slip. Like the steady Martin, Illingworth kept his nerve under heavy fire. He had played his only two previous Tests on West Indies' last visit in 1991 and, at 31, was recalled only because younger spinners had not lived up to expectations. Yet England leaned heavily on him, especially after Gough strained his back delivering his second ball. Gough had only a walk-on part for the rest of the match.

After Lara's half-century was followed by calmer ones from Campbell and Adams, West Indies could throw away wickets and still lead by 83. It was too many for England batsmen intent on using the square cut as a razor across their own throats. Smith and Stewart perished that way, and Hick pulled crudely. But England's spirit was really lowered to half-mast at 55, when Atherton edged Walsh to Murray. Thorpe's sound 61 was too late and too isolated to do more than prolong matters.

West Indies made up for lost time when Hooper and Lara, going hell-for-leather for the necessary 126, indulged in the kind of strokeplay that stays for ever in a spectator's memory and permanently scars the bowler's. Hooper hit four sixes and nine fours in his 73, Lara eight fours in 48 off just 40 balls. Neither could ever have had more fun in the schoolyard. Could this really have been the team who, according to coach Andy Roberts, had to be "cajoled on to the field" to face Australia only six weeks earlier? – Peter Johnson.

Man of the Match: I. R. Bishop.   *Attendance:* 63,770; *receipts* £1,193,138.

Close of play: First day, England 148-4 (A. J. Stewart 1*, M. R. Ramprakash 0*); Second day, West Indies 236-5 (K. L. T. Arthurton 36*, J. R. Murray 14*); Third day, England 109-4 (G. P. Thorpe 37*, M. R. Ramprakash 12*).

England

R. A. Smith c Richardson b Benjamin	16	– c Arthurton b Ambrose ... 6
*M. A. Atherton c Murray b Bishop	81	– c Murray b Walsh ... 17
G. A. Hick c Campbell b Benjamin	18	– b Walsh b Bishop ... 27
G. P. Thorpe lbw b Bishop	20	– c Campbell b Walsh ... 61
†A. J. Stewart c Hooper b Bishop	2	– c Murray b Benjamin ... 4
M. R. Ramprakash c Campbell b Bishop	4	– b Walsh ... 18
P. A. J. DeFreitas c Murray b Benjamin	23	– c sub (S. Chanderpaul) b Walsh . 1
D. Gough c Ambrose b Bishop	0	– c sub (S. C. Williams)
		b Ambrose . 29
P. J. Martin c Murray b Ambrose	2	– c Lara b Bishop ... 19
R. K. Illingworth not out	17	– not out ... 10
D. E. Malcolm b Benjamin	0	– b Ambrose ... 5
B 1, n-b 15	16	B 1, l-b 3, n-b 7 ... 11

1/52 (1) 2/91 (3) 3/142 (4) 4/148 (2)   199   1/6 (1) 2/55 (2) 3/55 (3)   208
5/153 (6) 6/154 (5) 7/154 (8)   4/82 (5) 5/130 (6) 6/136 (7)
8/157 (9) 9/199 (7) 10/199 (11)   7/152 (4) 8/193 (8)
     9/193 (9) 10/208 (11)

Bowling: *First Innings*—Ambrose 17-4-56-1; Walsh 13-2-50-0; Bishop 16-2-32-5; Benjamin 13.5-2-60-4. *Second Innings*—Ambrose 20.2-6-44-3; Walsh 22-4-60-4; Bishop 19-3-81-2; Benjamin 6-1-19-1.

West Indies

C. L. Hooper c Thorpe b Malcolm	0	– not out ... 73
S. L. Campbell run out	69	– c Atherton b Martin ... 2
B. C. Lara c Hick b Illingworth	53	– not out ... 48
J. C. Adams c Martin b Hick	58	
K. L. T. Arthurton c Stewart b DeFreitas	42	
*R. B. Richardson lbw b Martin	0	
†J. R. Murray c Illingworth b DeFreitas	20	
I. R. Bishop run out	5	
C. E. L. Ambrose c Gough b Malcolm	15	
C. A. Walsh c Stewart b Gough	4	
K. C. G. Benjamin not out	0	
B 4, l-b 11, n-b 1	16	B 1, l-b 3, n-b 2 ... 6

1/0 (1) 2/95 (3) 3/141 (2) 4/216 (4)   282   1/11 (2)   (1 wkt) 129
5/219 (6) 6/243 (7) 7/254 (5)
8/254 (8) 9/275 (10) 10/282 (9)

Bowling: *First Innings*—Malcolm 7.3-0-48-2; Gough 5-1-24-1; DeFreitas 23-3-82-2; Martin 27-9-48-1; Illingworth 24-9-50-1; Hick 4-0-15-1. *Second Innings*—Martin 8-2-49-1; DeFreitas 4-0-33-0; Illingworth 3-0-31-0; Malcolm 4-0-12-0.

Umpires: S. Venkataraghavan (India) and H. D. Bird.
Referee: J. R. Reid (New Zealand).

†SCOTLAND v WEST INDIES

At Raeburn Place, Edinburgh, June 15. West Indians won by 47 runs. Toss: West Indians.

Relaxing in warm Scottish sunshine after the chill of Leeds, the West Indians ran up more than five and a half an over. Williams, omitted from the Test, hit back with 132 off 135 balls, including 22 fours and a six. He added 134 in only 78 minutes with Adams. But the Scots built two brave partnerships of their own: Philip and Smith put on 90 in 67 minutes and Salmond and Williamson 117 in 54, exploiting occasional spinners Adams and Chanderpaul. Williamson's dismissal prompted a crowd invasion and the final two balls of Scotland's innings were never bowled. Three streakers joined the many cavorting across the outfields in 1995.

West Indians

S. L. Campbell b Thomson	0	W. K. M. Benjamin c Allingham	
S. C. Williams c Salmond b Williamson	132	b Williamson	1
*R. B. Richardson c Philip b Allingham	21	O. D. Gibson b Thomson	24
J. C. Adams c Govan b Williamson	57	B 5, l-b 2, w 4, n-b 12	23
K. L. T. Arthurton c Philip b Stanger	9		
S. Chanderpaul run out	0	1/8 2/69 3/203 4/237 (8 wkts, 55 overs)	305
†C. O. Browne not out	38	5/238 6/244 7/246 8/305	

C. A. Walsh and R. Dhanraj did not bat.

Bowling: Cowan 6–0–40–0; Thomson 11–1–43–2; Stanger 11–1–60–1; Allingham 11–1–48–1; Govan 7–0–39–0; Williamson 9–0–68–3.

Scotland

*A. C. Storie lbw b Benjamin	7	J. G. Williamson c Walsh b Campbell	57
†I. L. Philip b Adams	65	B 1, l-b 2, w 3, n-b 14	20
M. J. Smith c Richardson b Gibson	43		
G. B. J. McGurk lbw b Dhanraj	5	1/30 2/120 3/127 (5 wkts, 54.4 overs)	258
G. Salmond not out	61	4/141 5/258	

M. J. D. Allingham, I. M. Stanger, J. W. Govan, D. Cowan and K. Thomson did not bat.

Bowling: Gibson 9–1–37–1; Benjamin 5–1–9–1; Arthurton 8–0–30–0; Walsh 3–0–22–0; Dhanraj 8–0–29–1; Adams 11–0–62–1; Chanderpaul 10–0–60–0; Campbell 0.4–0–6–1.

Umpires: H. Blackburn and A. W. Wood.

DURHAM v WEST INDIES

At Chester-le-Street, June 17, 18, 19. Drawn. Toss: Durham. First-class debut: N. Killeen.

Having slipped to the bottom of the Championship, Durham dared not risk opening bowlers Brown and Prabhakar, while the tourists rested most of their Test attack. The result was a feast of runs. For Durham, Roseberry's vigilance contrasted with Morris's fluency. Three West Indians made centuries and Lara stroked 91 off 90 balls – a trifle to the 501 he took off the county in 1994. Campbell impressed Durham enough to earn, three months later, an invitation to join them. Richardson made his first big score of the tour and wicket-keeper Browne hit his maiden hundred. He gave Richardson 90 minutes' start but reached three figures in the same over, in an unbroken stand of 170. Winston Benjamin withdrew after one day because of injury, but Bishop bowled superbly on the final morning and Durham collapsed to 65 for five. Boiling led the rescue with 69, doubling his previous best, while Killeen, who had toured the West Indies with England Under-19 a few months earlier, made a confident 35.

Close of play: First day, West Indians 18-0 (S. C. Williams 4*, S. L. Campbell 12*); Second day, Durham 31-0 (J. I. Longley 7*, M. A. Roseberry 20*).

Durham

J. I. Longley c Lara b Bishop	0	– c Browne b Bishop	7
*M. A. Roseberry lbw b Bishop	79	– c Lara b Gibson	20
J. E. Morris b Bishop	75	– c Browne b Bishop	0
S. Hutton c Lara b Hooper	39	– c Lara b Hooper	8
M. Saxelby c Lara b Hooper	29	– c Hooper b Gibson	7
†D. G. C. Ligertwood c Campbell b Hooper	40	– c Browne b Hooper	38
D. A. Blenkiron b Dhanraj	24	– (11) c Bishop b Hooper	9
J. Boiling not out	8	– (7) b Gibson	69
N. Killeen c Campbell b Gibson	2	– (8) c Bishop b Dhanraj	35
A. Walker not out	1	– (9) c Chanderpaul b Gibson	29
M. M. Betts (did not bat)	–	(10) not out	11
B 2, l-b 13, w 1, n-b 51	67	L-b 2, n-b 24	26

1/0 2/149 3/226 4/266 5/294	(8 wkts dec.) 364	1/31 2/31 3/31 4/38 5/65 259
6/341 7/353 8/361		6/102 7/171 8/237 9/248

Bowling: *First Innings*—Bishop 17–3–71–3; Gibson 13.1–3–56–1; Benjamin 14–4–35–0; Dhanraj 23–1–77–1; Hooper 26–3–103–3; Chanderpaul 1–0–7–0. *Second Innings*—Gibson 24–5–64–4; Bishop 19–6–65–2; Hooper 23.4–3–79–3; Dhanraj 12–2–39–1; Chanderpaul 2–0–10–0.

West Indians

S. C. Williams lbw b Betts	27		
S. L. Campbell c Killeen b Betts	113	– c Walker b Betts	11
B. C. Lara lbw b Betts	91		
*R. B. Richardson not out	101		
S. Chanderpaul lbw b Walker	13	– (3) not out	2
C. L. Hooper c Morris b Killeen	4	– (1) not out	3
†C. O. Browne not out	102		
L-b 7, n-b 4	11		

1/68 2/219 3/252 4/278 5/292	(5 wkts dec.) 462	1/14 (1 wkt) 16

W. K. M. Benjamin, O. D. Gibson, I. R. Bishop and R. Dhanraj did not bat.

Bowling: *First Innings*—Walker 24–7–100–1; Killeen 20–2–109–1; Boiling 21–6–91–0; Betts 16–1–112–3; Saxelby 13–3–38–0; Roseberry 1–0–5–0. *Second Innings*—Walker 3–1–8–0; Betts 3–1–8–1.

Umpires: J. W. Holder and R. Julian.

ENGLAND v WEST INDIES

Second Cornhill Test

At Lord's, June 22, 23, 24, 25, 26. England won by 72 runs. Toss: England. Test debuts: D. G. Cork; O. D. Gibson.

A match of startling fluctuations and compelling cricket was finally settled by a historic bowling performance. Dominic Cork, the 23-year-old Derbyshire bowler, returned an analysis of seven for 43, the best by an England player on Test debut and fifth on the list for any country. England levelled the series with the sort of aggression, determination and plain good sense that were so woefully lacking in the First Test. For West Indies, it was their third defeat in six Tests – a sequence of failure unknown during their two decades of world dominance – and their first at Lord's since 1957.

The match began with an undercurrent of disharmony between Ray Illingworth, England's overlord, and Mike Atherton, his captain. The full selection panel decided at its regular Saturday meeting that Steve Rhodes would keep wicket, Stewart return to his favoured place at the head of the order and Smith bat at No. 5 after opening at Headingley. Then, on the eve of the match, Illingworth unilaterally overturned this central plank of team strategy and inflicted on Atherton a line-up he strongly opposed. To cram in five specialist bowlers, Illingworth coerced Stewart into the all-rounder's role of wicket-keeper/opening batsman, with Smith on standby to go in first if Stewart was too tired after a stint in the field. Rhodes was omitted from the 13, as was DeFreitas. It was an unprecedented display of autocracy by Illingworth and the manner in which he did it outraged many. Yet he was appointed to make such decisions and his vindication came with victory – which also, as if by magic, brought public unity with Atherton.

The game's balance of power shifted so frequently that all three results were quoted by bookmakers at 4 to 1 or longer at various times. England were around 70 runs short of par in their first innings. A fourth-wicket stand of 111 between Thorpe, who completed his ninth half-century in his last nine Tests, and Smith sustained them, although both were dropped by Richardson early on. Cork, who cut his first ball in Test cricket for four, and Martin added 50 for the eighth wicket, but too many batsmen surrendered to ill-disciplined shots. West Indies were restricted to a first-innings lead of 41, however. Fraser, the foot-slogging yeoman omitted from the defeat at Headingley, took his 100th Test wicket when Lara was lbw, added four more and bowled with his customary control and loathing for conceding runs. Several West Indian batsmen became established, without going on to play a substantial innings. The top scorer was Arthurton, with 75; he was last out to a thrilling, acrobatic catch by Gough on the long-leg boundary, giving Fraser his fifth wicket.

After the second day, West Indies coach Andy Roberts claimed the pitch had been "deliberately under-prepared" in England's favour, and was later reprimanded for his comments by match referee John Reid. In the event, the parched and cracked surface became easier and offered less sideways movement as the match progressed.

SEVEN OR MORE WICKETS IN AN INNINGS ON TEST DEBUT

8-43	A. E. Trott, Australia v England at Adelaide	1894-95
8-53	R. A. L. Massie, Australia v England at Lord's	1972
8-61	N. D. Hirwani, India v West Indies at Madras	1987-88
8-75	N. D. Hirwani, India v West Indies at Madras	1987-88
8-84	R. A. L. Massie, Australia v England at Lord's	1972
8-104	A. L. Valentine, West Indies v England at Manchester	1950
7-43	**D. G. Cork, England v West Indies at Lord's**	**1995**
7-46	J. K. Lever, England v India at Delhi	1976-77
7-49	A. V. Bedser, England v India at Lord's	1946
7-55	T. Kendall, Australia v England at Melbourne	1876-77
7-56	James Langridge, England v West Indies at Manchester	1933
7-63	A. E. Hall, South Africa v England at Cape Town	1922-23
7-95	W. H. Ashley, South Africa v England at Cape Town	1888-89
7-99	Mohammad Nazir, Pakistan v New Zealand at Karachi	1969-70
7-103	J. C. Laker, England v West Indies at Bridgetown	1947-48

Stewart struck a flurry of early boundaries in the second innings but, at 52 for two, only 11 ahead, with Thorpe on his way to hospital, England were long shots. Yet they recovered to a second-innings total of 336, which became the bedrock of victory. Thorpe had been struck on the helmet by his first ball, another of Walsh's unintentional slow beamers. Several England batsmen complained that the tall West Indian fast bowlers' arms emerged from the dark of the trees above the sightscreen at the Nursery End, and Thorpe did not see the ball as it hurtled towards his head. Groggy, he was treated for five minutes on the pitch and spent a night under observation in St Mary's, Paddington. Hick and Smith, though, added 98 and Thorpe, proving that he numbers courage among his qualities, returned the following day after Ramprakash completed a pair. His partnership of 85 with Smith took England towards a position from which they could sense victory. Before the game, Smith admitted failure could end his Test career. But he was the hustling, hyper, bobbing and weaving embodiment of raw desire. He scored just 29 in each of the first two sessions of the fourth day, but he was damned if he was getting out. Eventually, after six hours, Ambrose nipped one back. Like every other key moment, it was replayed on the giant screen perched above the Edrich Stand and in use for the first time at Lord's.

Requiring 296 to win, West Indies lost Hooper early, but Lara tore into the bowling. He played and missed and struck boundaries in equal quantity as he raced to 38 not out, with eight fours, from 44 balls on the fourth evening. The destiny of the match rested in his hands of genius. But, after two more fours the next day, he was superbly caught by Stewart, plunging to his left, off Gough. This was the crucial dismissal of the game. Campbell hung on for over five hours, until he was eighth out for 93, but no other batsmen passed 14. Most of them fell to Cork, from the Nursery End, bowling wicket-to-wicket with enough out-swing to cause problems. His virtues were old-fashioned – line, length and movement – coupled with a fierce and demonstrable will. His final analysis was three runs better than that of John Lever, with seven for 46 on his debut against India at Delhi in 1976-77; J. J. Ferris took seven for 37 against South Africa, at Cape Town in 1891-92, but he had already played Test cricket for Australia.

The crowd swelled to more than 10,000 on the final afternoon after four full houses. They saw a classic Test, which England won by playing resourceful, brick-by-brick cricket over five days. – John Etheridge.

Man of the Match: D. G. Cork.   *Attendance:* 111,938; *receipts* £2,412,793.

Close of play: First day, England 255-8 (P. J. Martin 22*); Second day, West Indies 209-6 (K. L. T. Arthurton 14*, O. D. Gibson 12*); Third day, England 155-3 (R. A. Smith 31*, M. R. Ramprakash 0*); Fourth day, West Indies 68-1 (S. L. Campbell 14*, B. C. Lara 38*).

England

*M. A. Atherton b Ambrose	21	– c Murray b Walsh 9
†A. J. Stewart c Arthurton b Gibson	34	– c Murray b Walsh 36
G. A. Hick c Lara b Bishop	13	– b Bishop 67
G. P. Thorpe c Lara b Ambrose	52	– c Richardson b Ambrose 42
R. A. Smith b Hooper	61	– lbw b Ambrose 90
M. R. Ramprakash c Campbell b Hooper	0	– c sub (S. C. Williams) b Bishop . 0
D. G. Cork b Walsh	30	– c Murray b Bishop 23
D. Gough c Campbell b Gibson	11	– b Ambrose 20
P. J. Martin b Walsh	29	– c Arthurton b Ambrose 1
R. K. Illingworth not out	16	– lbw b Walsh 4
A. R. C. Fraser lbw b Walsh	1	– not out 2
B 1, l-b 10, n-b 4	15	B 6, l-b 27, w 2, n-b 7 ... 42

1/29 (1) 2/70 (3) 3/74 (2) 4/185 (5)   283   1/32 (1) 2/51 (2) 3/150 (3)   336
5/187 (6) 6/191 (4) 7/205 (8)   4/155 (6) 5/240 (4) 6/290 (7)
8/255 (7) 9/281 (9) 10/283 (11)   7/320 (5) 8/329 (8)
                                                           9/334 (9) 10/336 (10)

In the second innings G. P. Thorpe, when 0, retired hurt at 52 and resumed at 155.

Bowling: *First Innings*—Ambrose 26–6–72–2; Walsh 22.4–6–50–3; Gibson 20–2–81–2; Bishop 17–4–33–1; Hooper 14–3–36–2. *Second Innings*—Ambrose 24–5–70–4; Walsh 28.1–10–91–3; Gibson 14–1–51–0; Bishop 22–5–56–3; Hooper 9–1–31–0; Adams 2–0–4–0.

West Indies

S. L. Campbell c Stewart b Gough	5	– (2) c Stewart b Cork 93
C. L. Hooper b Martin	40	– (1) c Martin b Gough 14
B. C. Lara lbw b Fraser	6	– c Stewart b Gough 54
J. C. Adams lbw b Fraser	54	– c Hick b Cork 13
*R. B. Richardson c Stewart b Fraser	49	– lbw b Cork 0
K. L. T. Arthurton c Gough b Fraser	75	– c sub (P. N. Weekes) b Cork ... 0
†J. R. Murray c and b Martin	16	– c sub (P. N. Weekes) b Gough.. 9
O. D. Gibson lbw b Gough	29	– lbw b Cork 14
I. R. Bishop b Cork	8	– not out 10
C. E. L. Ambrose c Ramprakash b Fraser	12	– c Illingworth b Cork 11
C. A. Walsh not out	11	– c Stewart b Cork 0
B 8, l-b 11	19	L-b 5 5

1/6 (1) 2/23 (3) 3/88 (2) 4/166 (5)   324   1/15 (1) 2/99 (3) 3/124 (4)   223
5/169 (4) 6/197 (7) 7/246 (8)   4/130 (5) 5/138 (6) 6/177 (7)
8/272 (9) 9/305 (10) 10/324 (6)   7/198 (8) 8/201 (2)
                                                           9/223 (10) 10/223 (11)

Bowling: *First Innings*—Gough 27–2–84–2; Fraser 33–13–66–5; Cork 22–4–72–1; Martin 23–5–65–2; Illingworth 7–2–18–0. *Second Innings*—Fraser 25–9–57–0; Gough 20–0–79–3; Illingworth 7–0–30–0; Martin 7–0–30–0; Cork 19.3–5–43–7.

Umpires: S. Venkataraghavan (India) and D. R. Shepherd.
Referee: J. R. Reid (New Zealand).

COMBINED UNIVERSITIES v WEST INDIANS

At Oxford, June 28, 29, 30. Drawn. Toss: West Indians. First-class debuts: A. D. Edwards, S. W. K. Ellis, S. J. Renshaw.

The tourists convalesced after their defeat at Lord's by milking the student attack for more than five an over. Hooper and Williams scored 200 in the first session – Hooper was 105 at lunch. After Adams was third to a hundred before going off, citing a stomach bug, Lara smashed 83 in 65 balls, mostly in a second-morning blitz, but it was Arthurton who stayed in to become the fourth century-maker of the innings. Had they not been replying to 637, the Universities' 310, dominated by the Oxford batsmen on their home ground, might have looked a good total. The West Indians preferred not to field again in the almost unbearable heat of the final day and let Murray compile their fifth hundred of the match before putting the students back in for a couple of hours. But the last day was over-shadowed by the announcement that the tour management were sending Winston Benjamin home "on grounds of discipline and fitness". Not for the first time, he had pulled out minutes before the game, pleading illness, and forced Walsh to forgo his rest.

Close of play: First day, West Indians 493-4 (K. L. T. Arthurton 38*, B. C. Lara 12*); Second day, Combined Universities 310.

West Indians

S. C. Williams c Trimby b Macmillan	114	– lbw b Ellis 19
C. L. Hooper c Edwards b Renshaw	118	– (4) c Trimby b Ellis 4
S. Chanderpaul c and b Macmillan	79	
J. R. Murray c Macmillan b Renshaw	1	– (2) c Macmillan b Ellis 100
J. C. Adams retired ill	114	– (7) not out 24
K. L. T. Arthurton not out	102	
B. C. Lara c Ellis b Windows	83	
†C. O. Browne not out	5	– (3) c Windows b Ellis 16
R. Dhanraj (did not bat)		– (5) c Batty b Ellis............. 1
*C. A. Walsh (did not bat)		– (6) c Edwards b Windows 40
B 5, l-b 4, n-b 12	21	B 4, l-b 2, n-b 6 12

1/225 2/254 3/255 4/408 5/614 (5 wkts dec.) 637   1/37 2/71 3/97 (6 wkts dec.) 216
4/129 5/166 6/216

K. C. G. Benjamin did not bat.

In the first innings J. C. Adams retired ill at 466.

Bowling: *First Innings*—Renshaw 24-3-135-2; Edwards 20-0-136-0; Ellis 19-2-87-0; Trimby 18-0-110-0; Macmillan 29-0-108-2; Kendall 5-0-22-0; Windows 7-1-30-1. *Second Innings*—Renshaw 16-2-56-0; Edwards 4-0-23-0; Ellis 16-1-59-5; Trimby 7-0-46-0; Sutcliffe 3-0-20-0; Windows 0.3-0-6-1.

Combined Universities

C. M. Gupte (*Oxford*) c sub (S. L. Campbell) b Dhanraj	56	– c Adams b Dhanraj 26
I. J. Sutcliffe (*Oxford*) c Browne b Benjamin	48	– not out..................... 63
M. G. N. Windows (*Durham*) lbw b Dhanraj	30	– not out..................... 27
*G. I. Macmillan (*Oxford*) c Lara b Adams	71	
W. S. Kendall (*Oxford*) lbw b Walsh	15	
M. E. Harvey (*Loughborough*) c Hooper b Adams	23	
†J. N. Batty (*Durham*) not out	31	
A. D. Edwards (*Loughborough*) c Walsh b Adams	15	
S. W. K. Ellis (*Warwick*) c Lara b Dhanraj	0	
S. J. Renshaw (*Leeds*) c Browne b Dhanraj	0	
P. W. Trimby (*Liverpool*) st Browne b Dhanraj	5	
B 4, n-b 12	16	B 1, l-b 3, n-b 16 20

1/92 2/144 3/144 4/222 5/248   310   1/73   (1 wkt) 136
6/267 7/297 8/298 9/302

Bowling: *First Innings*—Benjamin 12–4–49–1; Walsh 10–2–39–1; Hooper 15–5–61–0; Dhanraj 32.3–7–87–5; Adams 16–3–41–3; Arthurton 4–0–29–0. *Second Innings*—Benjamin 7–1–27–0; Walsh 2–1–3–0; Arthurton 2–0–10–0; Dhanraj 13–3–33–1; Lara 7–0–40–0; Hooper 4–0–19–0; Adams 1–1–0–0.

Umpires: G. I. Burgess and J. F. Steele.

SUSSEX v WEST INDIANS

At Hove, July 1, 2, 3. Sussex won by an innings and 121 runs. Toss: Sussex.

Vasbert Drakes had expected to make his first-class debut for Sussex in this game. Instead, he found himself in the West Indian team, replacing the disgraced Winston Benjamin. But he could not change their luck: they suffered their heaviest ever defeat by an English county. No county had beaten them in a first-class match since Middlesex in 1976. Sussex certainly had the better of the conditions. They piled up 446 for nine, thanks to a sparkling opening partnership of 263 between Lenham and Newell. Both took full advantage of wayward bowling, sloppy fielding and a fast outfield, with Newell recording a maiden hundred. Sussex declared on a rain-affected second day and their bowlers reduced the tourists to 97 for seven in steamy conditions. Only Arthurton denied them into the third day. When he and the obdurate Dhanraj, who held on for two hours, departed, Sussex needed only 41.3 overs to bowl them out again. Lewry and Stephenson nipped out the top order, then veteran off-spinner Hemmings took four for 33 to rout the West Indians and earn Sussex £7,500 from sponsors Tetley.

Close of play: First day, Sussex 390-5 (P. Moores 19*, F. D. Stephenson 3*); Second day, West Indians 167-7 (K. L. T. Arthurton 70*, R. Dhanraj 17*).

Sussex

N. J. Lenham c Murray b Dhanraj	128	P. W. Jarvis c and b Dhanraj	0
K. Newell c Campbell b Dhanraj	135	J. D. Lewry not out	0
K. Greenfield c Richardson b Dhanraj	29		
*A. P. Wells st Murray b Dhanraj	21	B 3, l-b 5, w 1, n-b 4	13
D. R. Law c Richardson b Arthurton	43		
†P. Moores c Arthurton b Gibson	45	1/263 2/292 3/303	(9 wkts dec.) 446
F. D. Stephenson c Drakes b Dhanraj	32	4/338 5/378 6/436	
I. D. K. Salisbury c Murray b Gibson	0	7/437 8/438 9/446	

E. E. Hemmings did not bat.

Bowling: Benjamin 11–2–30–0; Gibson 25.3–1–110–2; Arthurton 7–1–37–1; Drakes 21–6–59–0; Dhanraj 36–5–144–6; Hooper 13–3–58–0.

West Indians

C. L. Hooper c Moores b Stephenson	9	b Lewry	3
S. L. Campbell c Moores b Stephenson	13	b Stephenson	32
*R. B. Richardson lbw b Jarvis	34	b Stephenson	11
J. C. Adams c Stephenson b Jarvis	2	c Moores b Lewry	28
K. L. T. Arthurton b Jarvis	75	c Law b Hemmings	17
S. C. Williams b Lewry	4	c Law b Hemmings	0
†J. R. Murray lbw b Lewry	3	c Stephenson b Hemmings	6
O. D. Gibson lbw b Law	4	(9) c Wells b Lewry	8
R. Dhanraj c and b Salisbury	21	(11) not out	0
V. C. Drakes b Salisbury	9	(8) lbw b Lewry	22
K. C. G. Benjamin not out	1	(10) c Lenham b Hemmings	4
B 4, l-b 5, n-b 2	11	B 2, l-b 4, n-b 2	8

1/23 2/32 3/37 4/82 5/88   186   1/11 2/30 3/53 4/79 5/81   139
6/92 7/97 8/173 9/183   6/95 7/118 8/129 9/134

Bowling: *First Innings*—Stephenson 9–1–21–2; Lewry 21–6–62–2; Jarvis 16–4–51–3; Law 10–5–11–1; Salisbury 8–2–25–2; Hemmings 3–1–7–0. *Second Innings*—Stephenson 6–1–23–2; Lewry 10.3–2–38–4; Jarvis 10–2–39–0; Hemmings 15–4–33–4.

Umpires: D. J. Constant and P. Willey.

ENGLAND v WEST INDIES

Third Cornhill Test

At Birmingham, July 6, 7, 8. West Indies won by an innings and 64 runs. Toss: England. Test debut: J. E. R. Gallian.

Test pitch controversies are normally the preserve of Headingley. But all the talk before, during and after this one-sided contest was of an Edgbaston strip of unusual appearance – shaved at each end and grassy in the middle – which was ultimately lethal to England. West Indies won by an innings and 64 runs, at 12.18 on the third day of a match which lasted for only 172.2 overs. The aftermath was queues of disgruntled ticket-holders arguing over where to direct their anger (Ray Illingworth, Mike Atherton and groundsman Steve Rouse were the candidates) amid claims and counter-claims about who was to blame for a fast pitch of variable bounce which played into the hands of the West Indian pace bowlers. They used it with ruthless efficiency.

This was not quite the expected script. The tourists came into the match in some turbulence, having lost at Lord's and then, by a humiliating innings margin, to Sussex, while one member of the party had been sent home in disgrace. The optimistic English view was that they were on the point of reaching for the oxygen masks; a win here would be enough to shatter brittle morale for good. England dropped Ramprakash, after his pair at Lord's, and brought in Australian-born Lancastrian Jason Gallian for his Test debut; with Kenny Benjamin fit again, West Indies omitted Ottis Gibson and reverted to the side which had won at Leeds.

Long before the end of the first day, there had to be a drastic reappraisal of the balance of power. Ambrose's first delivery after Atherton had elected to bat caused consternation in the England camp – it was a huge leg-side bouncer which flew for four wides. Three balls later, Atherton fell to a poor stroke. That set the pattern for a dismal first innings of 147 in 44.2 overs, which owed more to their suspicions about the pitch than to what was actually happening. The exception was Thorpe, who batted with zest to hit five fours in 46 minutes before a ball of spiteful lift from Ambrose flew off his glove into gully's hands. He departed nursing a bruised thumb, the first name on a disruptive injury list. The next, more serious casualty was Gallian, who suffered a hairline fracture of the finger just before playing on to Benjamin. Smith was bravely defiant for 144 minutes and 46 runs, England's best effort of the day. By the time he was eighth out, at 141, they were in disarray. The only consolation was that it could have been worse; Ambrose had broken down with a groin strain in his eighth hostile over and did not bowl again in either innings.

England's only success on the first evening came when Hooper was caught down the leg side by Stewart, immediately after the appearance of two male streakers, ending an opening stand of 73. Stewart then suffered further damage to his suspect right index finger in trying to take a bouncer from Gough. He needed pain-killing injections to get through the second day.

That began with Cork giving England sight of a competitive position by removing Lara, Adams and Campbell, with West Indies' lead only nine. Campbell had struck a bristling 79 from 140 balls, with 16 fours, which earned him the match award. But a tenacious 69 from Richardson, spanning just over four hours, had at least equal value. Richardson had moments of good fortune, but showed such concentration and patience in his side's cause that he was unmoved by being stuck on seven for 75 minutes, or by a score of 16 after two hours of the sort of dogged occupation not normally associated with the West Indian captain. He had precious support from Bishop and Benjamin, who between them batted for more than two hours.

England went in again 153 behind, with a testing 17 overs to negotiate on the second evening. Memories of Trinidad in March 1994 were soon revived as Atherton was speared out by Walsh, Hick timidly fended a catch into the slips off Bishop and Thorpe surrendered his wicket to one of the poorest strokes of the match. That was 26 for three; they closed on 59, but night-watchman Cork's fighting talk became a mockery the following morning, when they were blown away for the addition of 30 runs in a little over an hour. Bishop, achieving vicious lift from a wide angle at the crease, claimed Smith as his 100th Test victim in his 21st match. Smith's 41, a score probably matched by the number of bruises on his arms and body from the ruthless assault, was described by Atherton as worth a hundred on any other pitch. Again, he was eighth out, having been promoted to open because Stewart was unable to bat and Gallian, who had not fielded, could not appear until No. 7.

The final blow came when Richard Illingworth broke a knuckle in the hopelessly lost cause. England's theme so far had been their need for five bowlers; their destruction was completed by two, Walsh and Bishop.

Atherton said it was the worst Test pitch he had encountered and that the blame for the early finish lay with Warwickshire. Ray Illingworth, annoyed by suggestions that it was prepared to his specifications, said that he had wanted even bounce but had not got it. He called for a return to the use of lighter soils; reporters were not quite in the mood for such niceties. Warwickshire added a touch of cheek to the drama by filling in one of the missing days with a challenge match between the county and the West Indians on the same pitch – they lost by 22 runs, but the pitch behaved. – Robert Mills.

Man of the Match: S. L. Campbell.　　　　*Attendance*: 62,544; *receipts* £1,141,201.

Close of play: First day, West Indies 104-1 (S. L. Campbell 38*, B. C. Lara 21*); Second day, England 59-3 (R. A. Smith 33*, D. G. Cork 15*).

England

*M. A. Atherton c Murray b Ambrose	0	– b Walsh	4
†A. J. Stewart lbw b Benjamin	37	– absent hurt	
G. A. Hick c Richardson b Walsh	3	– c Hooper b Bishop	3
G. P. Thorpe c Campbell b Ambrose	30	– c Murray b Bishop	0
R. A. Smith c Arthurton b Bishop	46	– b Bishop	41
J. E. R. Gallian b Benjamin	7	– (7) c Murray b Walsh	0
D. G. Cork lbw b Walsh	4	– (5) c sub (S. C. Williams) b Walsh	16
D. Gough c Arthurton b Bishop	1	– c Campbell b Walsh	12
P. J. Martin c sub (S. C. Williams) b Walsh	1	– (6) lbw b Bishop	0
R. K. Illingworth b Bishop	0	– (9) c Hooper b Bishop	0
A. R. C. Fraser not out	0	– (10) not out	1
L-b 4, w 4, n-b 10	18	N-b 12	12
	147		**89**

1/4 (1) 2/9 (3) 3/53 (4) 4/84 (2) 5/100 (6) 6/109 (7) 7/124 (8) 8/141 (9) 9/147 (9) 10/147 (10)

1/17 (1) 2/20 (3) 3/26 (4) 4/61 (5) 5/62 (6) 6/63 (7) 7/88 (8) 8/88 (2) 9/89 (9)

Bowling: First Innings—Ambrose 7.5–1–26–2; Walsh 17.1–4–54–3; Bishop 6.2–0–18–3; Benjamin 13–4–45–2. *Second Innings*—Walsh 15–2–45–5; Bishop 13–3–29–4; Benjamin 2–0–15–0.

West Indies

C. L. Hooper c Stewart b Cork	40	C. A. Walsh run out	0
S. L. Campbell b Cork	79	C. E. L. Ambrose not out	4
B. C. Lara lbw b Cork	21		
J. C. Adams lbw b Cork	10	B 5, l-b 5, n-b 6	16
*R. B. Richardson b Fraser	69		
K. L. T. Arthurton lbw b Fraser	8		**300**
†J. R. Murray c Stewart b Martin	26		
I. R. Bishop c Martin b Illingworth	16		
K. C. G. Benjamin run out	11		

1/73 (1) 2/105 (3) 3/141 (4) 4/156 (2) 5/171 (6) 6/198 (7) 7/260 (8) 8/292 (9) 9/292 (10) 10/300 (5)

Bowling: Fraser 31–7–93–2; Gough 18–3–68–0; Cork 22–5–69–4; Martin 19–5–49–1; Illingworth 8–4–11–1.

Umpires: I. D. Robinson (Zimbabwe) and M. J. Kitchen.
Referee: J. R. Reid (New Zealand).

†At Birmingham, July 10. West Indians won by 22 runs. Toss: Warwickshire. West Indians 220 for seven (40 overs) (J. C. Adams 86 not out, B. C. Lara 51; D. R. Brown three for 52); Warwickshire 198 (38.5 overs) (D. P. Ostler 63; O. D. Gibson three for 25, R. Dhanraj four for 25).

†MINOR COUNTIES v WEST INDIANS

At Reading, July 13. Minor Counties won by four wickets. Toss: West Indians.

Another dramatic swing of fortune saw the tourists lose to a team of part-timers with more than three overs to spare. Manager Wes Hall held a 90-minute team talk afterwards to discuss their failings – including 78 extras, nearly 30 per cent of the Minor Counties' total. Newman gave the West Indians an early shock, dismissing Campbell and Richardson, the heroes of Edgbaston, at 22. Though Williams and Hooper scored fifties, and Lara a run-a-ball 44, no one took complete control. The man of the match was Dean of Staffordshire, who scored 91 in 134 balls, with ten fours, and added 107 in 21 overs with Fell.

West Indians

S. C. Williams run out	61	O. D. Gibson b Potter	17
S. L. Campbell hit wkt b Newman	7	K. C. G. Benjamin not out	8
*R. B. Richardson c Humphries b Newman	0	R. Dhanraj not out	1
J. C. Adams c Evans b Sharp	13	L-b 11, w 4, n-b 6	21
C. L. Hooper c Newman b Sharp	54		
B. C. Lara c Fell b Sharp	44	1/22 2/22 3/76 (9 wkts, 55 overs) 266
†C. O. Browne c Humphries b Arnold	19	4/111 5/186 6/204
V. C. Drakes c Fell b Arnold	21	7/223 8/239 9/258

Bowling: Newman 11–3–31–2; Arnold 10–0–53–2; Laudat 11–0–61–0; Sharp 11–1–38–3; Potter 5–0–18–1; Evans 5–0–32–0; Marvell 2–0–22–0.

Minor Counties

L. Potter st Browne b Dhanraj	21	M. J. Marvell c Campbell b Benjamin	7
S. J. Dean b Drakes	91	P. G. Newman not out	4
S. V. Laudat c Adams b Hooper	5	B 8, l-b 10, w 15, n-b 45	78
M. A. Fell b Gibson	50		
*I. Cockbain b Gibson	2	1/83 2/122 3/229 (6 wkts, 51.5 overs) 270
†M. I. Humphries not out	12	4/239 5/240 6/266

R. A. Evans, M. A. Sharp and K. A. Arnold did not bat.

Bowling: Benjamin 10.4–0–41–1; Gibson 10–0–76–2; Drakes 10–1–43–1; Dhanraj 11–1–50–1; Hooper 10–2–38–1; Lara 0.1–0–4–0.

Umpires: M. P. Moran and J. M. Tythcott.

†IRELAND v WEST INDIANS

At Castle Avenue, Dublin, July 15. Drawn. Toss: Ireland.

The West Indians, reminded on every trip to Ireland of their famous defeat in 1969, made sure that there would be no further upsets. Chanderpaul scored a dazzling hundred, from 84 balls with 17 fours, and Arthurton 94 in 95 balls; he and Richardson took the tourists' total past 300 before declaring. A rain-break of 70 minutes left Ireland only two hours to bat. They lost their first three wickets for 26, but Smyth and Benson added 161, with Benson, formerly of Leicestershire, benefiting from some occasional bowling to hit three sixes and nine fours in his 74 from 62 balls.

West Indians

S. C. Williams c Smyth b Doak	34	C. L. Hooper not out	1
S. Chanderpaul st Ogilby b Harrison	101	L-b 7, w 1, n-b 2	10
B. C. Lara c and b Doak	9		
K. L. T. Arthurton c Doak b Eagleson	94	1/99 2/117 (4 wkts dec.) 306
*R. B. Richardson c Doak b Eagleson	57	3/187 4/301

O. D. Gibson, I. R. Bishop, †C. O. Browne, V. C. Drakes and R. Dhanraj did not bat.

Bowling: Eagleson 11–1–75–1; Patterson 5–0–33–0; Graham 6–0–37–0; Doak 12.3–1–63–2; Harrison 10–0–54–1; Lewis 8–0–37–0.

Ireland

S. J. S. Warke c Bishop b Gibson	0	J. D. R. Benson not out	74
J. A. M. Molins b Gibson	0	L-b 2, w 2, n-b 3	7
S. G. Smyth not out	98		
*D. A. Lewis c Williams b Drakes	8	1/0 2/5 3/26 (3 wkts)	187

N. G. Doak, G. D. Harrison, S. Graham, R. L. Eagleson, M. W. Patterson and †S. Ogilby did not bat.

Bowling: Gibson 5–1–19–2; Bishop 5–4–1–0; Drakes 3–1–16–1; Dhanraj 5–0–35–0; Chanderpaul 4–0–36–0; Williams 6–0–46–0; Lara 5–0–32–0.

Umpires: L. P. Hogan and P. L. O'Hara.

KENT v WEST INDIANS

At Canterbury, July 19, 20, 21. West Indians won by six wickets. Toss: West Indians.

Julian Thompson, Kent's cricketing doctor, got his third first-class match off to a sensational start, dismissing Campbell and Lara in five deliveries without a run on the board. Thompson also had Lara lbw in the second innings, for the first pair of his career. But on the first day Williams and Adams put the West Indians back on course with 223 in 55 overs. Williams was dropped twice – Kent spilled six catches – but reached an impressive century. Kent's first innings began just as badly, when Gibson quickly claimed Fulton and Ward. They were bowled out inside 19 overs and, by lunch on the second day, were 21 for two following on. But Fulton and de Silva put on 141 in 25 overs, which took the match into a third day and averted a corporate hospitality disaster. De Silva reached his fifth hundred in seven first-class innings in 98 balls, with 16 fours and two sixes. Chasing 90, the West Indians suffered early alarms but completed only their second win in seven county matches on the stroke of lunch.

Close of play: First day, West Indians 337; Second day, Kent 307-8 (M. M. Patel 3*, M. J. McCague 7*).

West Indians

S. C. Williams c Marsh b Fleming	137	– c Fulton b McCague	8
S. L. Campbell b Thompson	0	– c Marsh b Thompson	36
B. C. Lara c Marsh b Thompson	0	– lbw b Thompson	0
J. C. Adams run out	77	– not out	34
S. Chanderpaul c Cowdrey b Wren	29	– c Marsh b Wren	0
R. B. Richardson not out	48	– not out	6
†C. O. Browne b Ealham	4		
V. C. Drakes lbw b Ealham	0		
O. D. Gibson c Marsh b Ealham	0		
R. Dhanraj b McCague	9		
*C. A. Walsh b McCague	10		
B 1, l-b 8, w 2, n-b 12	23	B 2, l-b 5, w 1	8

1/0 2/0 3/223 4/235 5/276   337   1/37 2/38 3/53 4/66 (4 wkts) 92
6/282 7/282 8/286 9/315

Bowling: *First Innings*—McCague 16.4–7–64–2; Thompson 11–1–72–2; Wren 16–1–67–1; Ealham 17–4–37–3; Patel 20–5–43–0; Fleming 15–0–41–1; de Silva 1–0–4–0. *Second Innings*—McCague 6–1–29–1; Thompson 7–3–23–2; Wren 3–0–17–1; Patel 2.3–0–13–0; de Silva 1–0–3–0.

Kent

D. P. Fulton c Browne b Gibson	5	– c Williams b Walsh	89
T. R. Ward c Browne b Gibson	3	– b Drakes	0
M. V. Fleming b Walsh	8	– c Browne b Drakes	4
G. R. Cowdrey c Lara b Drakes	20	– c Chanderpaul b Dhanraj	43
P. A. de Silva b Drakes	18	– lbw b Drakes	102
M. A. Ealham c Browne b Drakes	5	– st Browne b Dhanraj	26
*†S. A. Marsh c Campbell b Gibson	3	– st Browne b Dhanraj	12
J. B. D. Thompson b Gibson	4	– c Campbell b Walsh	5
M. M. Patel c Browne b Drakes	5	– not out	12
M. J. McCague not out	0	– c sub (K. L. T. Arthurton) b Dhanraj	17
T. N. Wren b Drakes	0	– c Browne b Drakes	4
B 4, l-b 4, n-b 16	24	B 1, l-b 4, w 2, n-b 10	17
	95		**331**

1/7 2/20 3/34 4/76 5/77   1/8 2/12 3/89 4/230 5/269
6/82 7/86 8/88 9/95   6/284 7/297 8/297 9/324

Bowling: *First Innings*—Walsh 5–0–20–1; Gibson 9–1–47–4; Drakes 4.4–0–20–5. *Second Innings*—Walsh 21.2–6–77–3; Drakes 17–1–78–3; Gibson 13–1–75–0; Dhanraj 25–5–88–4; Adams 1–0–8–0.

Umpires: J. H. Harris and B. J. Meyer.

MIDDLESEX v WEST INDIANS

At Lord's, July 22, 23, 24. Drawn. Toss: West Indians.

With Richardson and Walsh resting, the tourists were led by Lara, who did not quite manage the long innings everyone was awaiting from him. Arthurton, in particular, shone brightly. Tufnell took advantage of the absence of Fraser and Emburey to claim five wickets for the first time this season, but the rest of the Middlesex bowling was mundane; the West Indians easily passed 450. Benjamin and Ambrose were too good for a top order which lacked the injured Gatting, and Middlesex were soon 78 for five. But Carr was in fine form and completed his fourth century of 1995. As the innings progressed, the West Indians grew cynical, bowling as few overs as they could and then, despite a 219-run lead, batting again, using the final day for an extended net. Though Feltham returned a career-best six for 41, it showed little respect for an above average Monday crowd, who had paid £7 a head.

Close of play: First day, West Indians 346-6 (K. L. T. Arthurton 49*, O. D. Gibson 4*); Second day, Middlesex 215-7 (J. D. Carr 99*, R. L. Johnson 29*).

West Indians

C. L. Hooper lbw b Shine	24	– c Weekes b Feltham	53
S. L. Campbell b Tufnell	102		
S. Chanderpaul b Tufnell	71	– lbw b Feltham	4
*B. C. Lara b Tufnell	62	– st Brown b Weekes	17
K. L. T. Arthurton c Radford b Tufnell	83	– not out	55
J. C. Adams c Weekes b Nash	27	– lbw b Feltham	8
†J. R. Murray lbw b Shine	1	– (2) c Feltham b Shine	21
O. D. Gibson c Carr b Tufnell	33	– c Weekes b Feltham	3
C. E. L. Ambrose c Nash b Tufnell	11	– c Carr b Feltham	2
K. C. G. Benjamin not out	26	– b Ramprakash	44
R. Dhanraj run out	6	– (7) b Feltham	0
L-b 10	10	L-b 6	6
	456	**(9 wkts dec.)**	**213**

1/68 2/161 3/261 4/268 5/338   1/60 2/76 3/85   (9 wkts dec.)
6/339 7/390 8/410 9/441   4/113 5/132 6/132
                            7/142 8/148 9/213

Bowling: *First Innings*—Nash 24.5–4–93–1; Johnson 24–3–84–0; Shine 14–1–65–2; Feltham 5–1–22–0; Tufnell 40–8–111–6; Weekes 24–4–71–0. *Second Innings*—Johnson 8–2–33–0; Shine 6–0–42–1; Weekes 19–2–74–1; Feltham 19–5–41–6; Ramprakash 2.2–0–17–1.

THE ENGLAND SQUAD FOR THE OLD TRAFFORD TEST

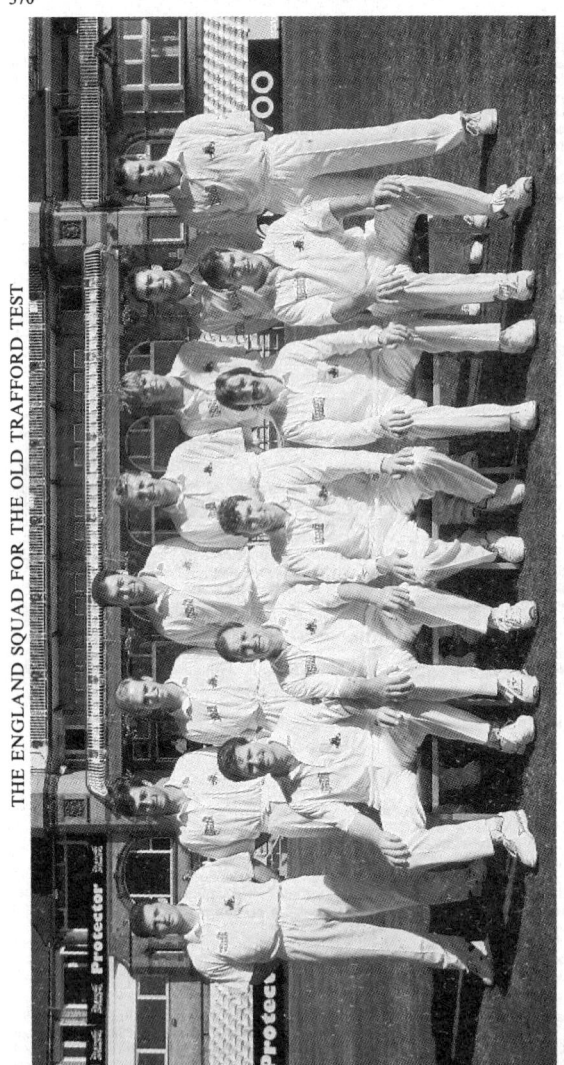

[*Patrick Eagar*

Back row: D. Gough, M. Watkinson, J. P. Crawley, A. R. C. Fraser, D. G. Cork, N. V. Knight, G. P. Thorpe, C. White. *Front row*: R. A. Smith, J. E. Emburey, M. A. Atherton (*captain*), R. C. Russell, G. A. Hick.

Middlesex

P. N. Weekes b Ambrose	0	– not out	23
T. A. Radford lbw b Gibson	12	– not out	26
M. R. Ramprakash c Ambrose b Benjamin	10		
J. C. Harrison c Murray b Gibson	5		
*J. D. Carr st Murray b Dhanraj	115		
†K. R. Brown c Chanderpaul b Dhanraj	6		
D. J. Nash c Adams b Hooper	29		
M. A. Feltham lbw b Gibson	10		
R. L. Johnson c Ambrose b Dhanraj	29		
K. J. Shine c Hooper b Dhanraj	0		
P. C. R. Tufnell not out	0		
B 1, l-b 2, n-b 12	15	L-b 1, n-b 2	3

1/0 2/15 3/27 4/59 5/78   237   (no wkt) 52
6/135 7/146 8/215 9/229

Bowling: *First Innings*—Ambrose 10–6–20–1; Benjamin 16–8–31–1; Gibson 14–5–45–3; Hooper 15–0–60–1; Dhanraj 17.5–1–66–4; Adams 1–0–12–0. *Second Innings*—Ambrose 4–3–1–0; Benjamin 4–2–11–0; Chanderpaul 4–1–18–0; Dhanraj 5–1–16–0; Lara 1–0–5–0.

Umpires: A. Clarkson and K. J. Lyons.

ENGLAND v WEST INDIES

Fourth Cornhill Test

At Manchester, July 27, 28, 29, 30. England won by six wickets. Toss: West Indies. Test debuts: N. V. Knight, M. Watkinson.

To the West Indians, the Fourth Test was a disappointment. To England, however, it was an occasion to celebrate; and to cricket fans of any nationality – those who love the game for the game's sake – it was a match to remember. England won by six wickets in four days and levelled the series at 2–2, to set up a potentially glorious finish.

But the Test was set apart from those that had preceded it and transformed into an unforgettable experience, firstly by the way England recovered from their mauling at Edgbaston and then by the magnificent performances of Dominic Cork and Brian Lara. The England pace bowler continued his astonishing entry to Test cricket with a devastating hat-trick and the West Indian batting ace displayed his class with a solid 87 followed by a superb 145.

Battered and bruised in Birmingham, England made six changes, mostly because of injuries; Hick was left out by choice. Stewart's opening role was taken over by Nick Knight of Warwickshire while Russell returned to take the gloves. Crawley and White were recalled and there were two off-spinners, the 42-year-old Emburey, selected for his 64th Test, and Mike Watkinson, playing his first, on home ground, a few days before his 34th birthday. West Indies fielded the same high-riding eleven who had won at Leeds and Birmingham, and many expected them to take a stranglehold on the series.

To the surprise of their most ardent supporters, however, England came out like tigers. By the end of the first day of a Test bathed in sunshine – tea was taken 15 minutes early because the light off a glass roof was dazzling the batsmen – they had routed West Indies for 216. Only Lara passed 24 as Fraser and Cork led the assault with some lively, accurate and testing seam bowling, and earned four wickets each, backed up by fielders who caught almost everything in sight. Resuming next morning on 65 for two, England batted with a beautifully effective mixture of resolve and panache. Thorpe, who just missed the distinction of scoring the first century of the series when he was caught behind for 94, was the star as they eased to 437, their best against West Indies at Old Trafford, and ample reflection of their fighting spirit. The West Indian attack bowled far too short throughout the match – so short in fact that it annoyed even their own supporters – and umpire Bird warned Walsh after Atherton was hit over the heart. But the England batsmen stood their ground and then reeled off some wonderful strokes, culminating in an undefeated 56 from Cork. Further evidence that Cork leads a charmed life occurred early on Saturday when his

[Patrick Eagar

The celebrations start at Old Trafford as Dominic Cork becomes the first England player in 38 years to take a Test hat-trick. Carl Hooper, out lbw, is the victim.

foot dislodged a bail as he set off for an all-run four; none of the fielders noticed and he replaced the bail himself on his return. A total of 64 extras, 34 from no-balls, was equal to the fourth-highest in a Test innings.

Trailing by 221, West Indies had pulled back to 159 for three by the fourth morning. With the enigmatic Hooper, pushed down the order after chipping a finger, the only specialist bat to come, their fate depended heavily on their most gifted batsman, Lara, and their most experienced, Richardson. When Richardson stroked the third ball of the morning confidently to long leg for a single and Lara steered the fourth – a no-ball – comfortably past gully for another, the West Indians appeared ready for the fight. But in one of the most stunning starts to a day's play in any Test match, Cork knocked them flat; the once unbeatable world champions dropped from 161 for three to 161 for six in three balls.

Bowling from the Stretford End, Cork picked off Richardson, Murray and Hooper to become only the eighth England bowler to do the hat-trick – the first since Peter Loader surprised West Indies at Headingley in 1957 – and, following T. J. Matthews's double hat-trick for Australia against South Africa in 1912, only the second bowler to achieve it in an Old Trafford Test. Richardson was bowled, the ball bouncing off his pads, on to the bat and then on to the stumps as he attempted to pull his bat away; Murray was leg before, going inside and playing across the line of the ball; and Hooper was also lbw, beaten for pace and struck on the pad as he attempted to play forward.

With the West Indian batting in ruins and England scenting an innings win, Lara, then 60, made a brilliant effort to rescue his team, parading his repertoire of strokes as he went for the bowling in a bold and beautiful counter-attack. He reached his first first-class hundred since the Second Test against New Zealand, in February, in 151 balls, and went on to 145 from 216, with 16 fours. The odds were always against even his amazing talent, however. When he went, caught by Knight at square leg with the persistent Fraser, after scoring 85 of the last 122 runs, only the formalities were left – or so it seemed.

Left to score only 94 to win, with Atherton stroking the ball effortlessly, England appeared to be heading for an emphatic victory. But after Atherton was carelessly run out with the score on 39, Bishop and Benjamin pulled the throttle. In a last kick, they removed Knight, Thorpe and White. England were 48 for four, effectively five, as a short-pitched ball from Bishop had fractured Smith's cheekbone and sent him off to hospital. It was left to Crawley and a gutsy Russell to inch their way to victory.

Invasions by streakers reached epidemic proportions during this Test. They caused seven interruptions, five on Saturday afternoon, though not all managed to finish removing their underwear before being tackled and hauled off the field by members of Sale Rugby Club, hired as a precaution. Lancashire's chief executive, John Bower, demanded afterwards that Parliament should declare such disruptions a criminal offence. – *Tony Becca.*

Man of the Match: D. G. Cork. *Attendance:* 76,464; *receipts* £1,373,092.

Close of play: First day, England 65-2 (M. A. Atherton 15*); Second day, England 347-7 (M. Watkinson 25*, D. G. Cork 3*); Third day, West Indies 159-3 (B. C. Lara 59*, R. B. Richardson 21*).

West Indies

C. L. Hooper c Crawley b Cork	16 – (7) lbw b Cork	0
S. L. Campbell c Russell b Fraser	10 – (1) c Russell b Watkinson	44
B. C. Lara lbw b Cork	87 – c Knight b Fraser	145
J. C. Adams c Knight b Fraser	24 – c and b Watkinson	1
*R. B. Richardson c Thorpe b Fraser	2 – b Cork	22
K. L. T. Arthurton c Cork b Watkinson	17 – (2) run out	17
†J. R. Murray b Emburey b Watkinson	13 – (6) lbw b Cork	0
I. R. Bishop c Russell b Cork	9 – c Crawley b Watkinson	9
C. E. L. Ambrose not out	7 – (10) not out	23
K. C. G. Benjamin b Cork	14 – (9) c Knight b Fraser	15
C. A. Walsh c Knight b Fraser	11 – b Cork	16
L-b 1, n-b 5	6 B 5, l-b 9, n-b 8	22

1/21 (2) 2/35 (1) 3/86 (4) 4/94 (5) 216 1/36 (2) 2/93 (1) 3/97 (4) 314
5/150 (6) 6/166 (3) 7/184 (7) 4/161 (5) 5/161 (6) 6/161 (7)
8/185 (8) 9/205 (10) 10/216 (11) 7/191 (8) 8/234 (9)
9/283 (3) 10/314 (11)

Bowling: *First Innings*—Fraser 16.2–5–45–4; Cork 20–1–86–4; White 5–0–23–0; Emburey 10–2–33–0; Watkinson 9–2–28–2. *Second Innings*—Fraser 19–5–53–2; Cork 23.5–2–111–4; Emburey 20–5–49–0; White 6–0–23–0; Watkinson 23–4–64–3.

England

N. V. Knight b Walsh	17	– c sub (S. Chanderpaul) b Bishop	13
*M. A. Atherton c Murray b Ambrose	47	– run out	22
J. P. Crawley b Walsh	8	– not out	15
G. P. Thorpe c Murray b Bishop	94	– c Ambrose b Benjamin	0
R. A. Smith c sub (S. C. Williams) b Ambrose	44	– retired hurt	1
C. White c Murray b Benjamin	23	– c sub (S. Chanderpaul) b Benjamin	1
†R. C. Russell run out	35	– not out	31
M. Watkinson c sub (S. C. Williams) b Walsh	37		
D. G. Cork not out	56		
J. E. Emburey b Bishop	8		
A. R. C. Fraser c Adams b Walsh	4		
B 18, l-b 11, w 1, n-b 34	64	L-b 2, w 1, n-b 8	11

1/45 (1) 2/65 (3) 3/122 (2) 4/226 (5)　　　　437　1/39 (2) 2/41 (1)　　　(4 wkts) 94
5/264 (4) 6/293 (6) 7/337 (7)　　　　　　　　3/45 (4) 4/48 (6)
8/378 (8) 9/418 (10) 10/437 (11)

In the second innings R. A. Smith retired hurt at 47.

Bowling: *First Innings*—Ambrose 24–2–91–2; Walsh 38–5–92–4; Bishop 29–3–103–2; Benjamin 28–4–83–1; Adams 8–1–21–0; Arthurton 9–2–18–0. *Second Innings*—Ambrose 5–1–16–0; Walsh 5–0–17–0; Bishop 12–6–18–1; Benjamin 9–1–29–2; Arthurton 2.5–1–5–0; Adams 2–0–7–0.

Umpires: C. J. Mitchley (South Africa) and H. D. Bird.
Referee: J. R. Reid (New Zealand).

SOMERSET v WEST INDIANS

At Taunton, August 2, 3, 4. West Indians won by 155 runs. Toss: West Indians.

Because their original opponents were engaged in the NatWest Trophy, the West Indians met Somerset again. A stunning performance by Gibson brought them victory on a firm pitch in blistering heat. When the last day began they were 132 ahead and effectively seven down. But Gibson hit a maiden century from 69 balls, with seven sixes and eight fours, and then reduced Somerset to 33 for four. On the opening day, Chanderpaul made a beautiful hundred from 104 balls, with 20 fours, to rescue the tourists from 71 for five; Kerr gathered a career-best five for 82 and Turner took six catches, equalling the county record. Somerset also collapsed before the later order built a sturdy lead of 144, led by Turner and Kerr, whose 80 was another career-best, and helped by 69 extras. The match swung again when Williams and Richardson put on 206, before van Troost's spell of four for 12, during which Adams ducked into his first ball and fractured his cheekbone, an injury which ended his tour. But the final twist was provided by Gibson's last-day heroics.

Close of play: First day, Somerset 162-6 (R. J. Turner 25*, J. I. D. Kerr 4*); Second day, West Indians 276-6 (S. Chanderpaul 16*, O. D. Gibson 32*).

West Indians

S. C. Williams c and b Kerr................	0	– c Ecclestone b van Troost......	119
J. R. Murray c Turner b Ecclestone..........	19	– lbw b Ecclestone............	6
*R. B. Richardson c Turner b Kerr..........	33	– b van Troost................	88
J. C. Adams c Turner b van Troost..........	7	– retired hurt..................	0
K. L. T. Arthurton c Batty b Kerr..........	0	– c Turner b van Troost.........	1
S. Chanderpaul lbw b Ecclestone............	100	– c Turner b van Troost........	26
†C. O. Browne c Turner b Kerr.............	19	– c Bowler b Trump	1
V. C. Drakes c Turner b Kerr.............	0	– c Holloway b van Troost.......	4
O. D. Gibson c Turner b van Troost........	17	– not out.....................	101
I. R. Bishop b Trump	5	– c Parsons b Trump	25
R. Dhanraj not out	13	– c Lathwell b Batty...........	1
B 4, l-b 2, w 5, n-b 6	17	L-b 5, w 3, n-b 6........	14

1/7 2/43 3/58 4/60 5/71	230	1/12 2/218 3/219 4/224 5/231 386
6/138 7/138 8/184 9/211		6/237 7/292 8/347 9/386

In the second innings J. C. Adams retired hurt at 218.

Bowling: *First Innings*—van Troost 19–5–53–2; Kerr 14–1–82–5; Ecclestone 14–4–31–2; Parsons 3–2–8–0; Trump 11.4–3–38–1; Hayhurst 2–1–12–0. *Second Innings*—van Troost 19–1–120–5; Ecclestone 3–0–17–1; Trump 34–10–95–2; Kerr 6–0–45–0; Batty 17–2–104–1.

Somerset

M. N. Lathwell b Drakes	23	– c Browne b Gibson	17
P. D. Bowler c Bishop b Gibson	19	– c Murray b Gibson	1
*A. N. Hayhurst c Adams b Gibson	10	– c Browne b Gibson	5
P. C. L. Holloway c Bishop b Drakes	5	– not out.....................	16
K. A. Parsons c Browne b Dhanraj	1	– c Williams b Gibson	6
S. C. Ecclestone c Williams b Dhanraj	37	– run out	12
†R. J. Turner c Browne b Bishop..........	72	– b Bishop	0
J. I. D. Kerr b Arthurton	80	– c sub (B. C. Lara) b Drakes	2
J. D. Batty not out......................	45	– c Drakes b Dhanraj...........	13
H. R. J. Trump lbw b Arthurton	4	– c Chanderpaul b Dhanraj	5
A. P. van Troost c Bishop b Drakes	9	– st Browne b Dhanraj	0
B 1, l-b 10, w 1, n-b 57	69	B 2, l-b 4, n-b 4	10

1/48 2/58 3/65 4/81 5/83	374	1/12 2/23 3/24 4/33 5/45 87
6/149 7/285 8/347 9/363		6/45 7/58 8/81 9/87

Bowling: *First Innings*—Bishop 16–2–86–1; Gibson 19–0–100–2; Drakes 16.2–0–75–3; Dhanraj 20–3–83–2; Arthurton 5–0–19–2. *Second Innings*—Bishop 10–2–24–1; Gibson 11–2–32–4; Drakes 9–3–23–1; Dhanraj 3–1–2–3.

Umpires: V. A. Holder and A. G. T. Whitehead.

GLOUCESTERSHIRE v WEST INDIANS

At Bristol, August 5, 6, 7. West Indians won by 74 runs. Toss: West Indians.

This match again suggested how difficult the tourists find it to motivate themselves against the counties. Even allowing for a depleted attack, the West Indians seemed to flirt with defeat. Eventually, after leaving Gloucestershire a modest target of 197, they rediscovered their purpose and bowled out the county for 122, even though Benjamin, who took five wickets (nine in the match) had to open the attack with Hooper bowling gentle seam; Ambrose and Drakes had minor injuries and a suspect finger ruled out Hooper's usual off-spin. In both innings the West Indians played loose, careless shots. But Williams and Campbell had set off like express trains on the first day, while Chanderpaul showed the greatest disinclination to give his wicket away on the second. A liberal contingent of West Indian supporters must still have been disconcerted at the way their team disintegrated twice. Sheeraz, 21 and making his fourth first-class appearance, emerged with 11 wickets to cherish for a lifetime. Of Gloucestershire's batsmen, Wright and Symonds had both hinted that the tourists could be challenged and even beaten.

Close of play: First day, Gloucestershire 137-2 (A. J. Wright 57*, R. I. Dawson 30*); Second day, West Indians 186-9 (C. E. L. Ambrose 8*).

West Indians

S. C. Williams c R. C. J. Williams b Smith	48 – c R. C. J. Williams b Sheeraz ..	56
S. L. Campbell c Ball b Smith	27 – lbw b Sheeraz...............	0
B. C. Lara c R. C. J. Williams b Sheeraz	30 – (5) lbw b Sheeraz...........	0
C. L. Hooper lbw b Smith	7 – (8) c Dawson b Ball..........	4
*R. B. Richardson c R. C. J. Williams b Sheeraz	26 – (6) c R. C. J. Williams b Alleyne	18
S. Chanderpaul lbw b R. C. Williams	10 – (4) lbw b Symonds	53
†C. O. Browne c R. C. J. Williams b Sheeraz ..	22 – (3) c Wright b Alleyne......	25
V. C. Drakes c Hancock b Sheeraz	17 – (7) c Alleyne b Sheeraz	7
C. E. L. Ambrose c R. C. J. Williams b Sheeraz	1 – not out....................	10
K. C. G. Benjamin b Sheeraz	5 – lbw b Sheeraz	0
R. Dhanraj not out	0 – c R. C. Williams b Ball.......	5
B 1, l-b 9, w 3, n-b 36	49 B 1, l-b 10, w 2, n-b 2 ...	15
	242	193

1/79 2/94 3/143 4/177 5/185
6/189 7/234 8/236 9/237

1/10 2/71 3/110 4/110 5/142
6/167 7/178 8/178 9/186

In the first innings C. L. Hooper, when 5, retired hurt at 126 and resumed at 177.

Bowling: *First Innings*—Smith 11.2-1-57-3; Sheeraz 16.1-3-67-6; R. C. Williams 10-1-68-1; Alleyne 11-2-40-0. *Second Innings*—Sheeraz 20-5-44-5; Alleyne 16-3-64-2; Ball 30.4-10-61-2; Symonds 3-0-13-1.

Gloucestershire

A. J. Wright c Lara b Ambrose	73 – c Ambrose b Hooper	7
M. G. N. Windows lbw b Ambrose..........	13 – c Browne b Benjamin	5
T. H. C. Hancock lbw b Dhanraj	24 – lbw b Benjamin	0
R. I. Dawson c Browne b Dhanraj	43 – b Hooper..................	0
*M. W. Alleyne c Ambrose b Dhanraj	0 – b Hooper	9
A. Symonds c Browne b Benjamin	51 – b Dhanraj	41
R. C. Williams st Browne b Dhanraj	1 – c Williams b Benjamin	17
†R. C. J. Williams c Browne b Benjamin	7 – c Ambrose b Benjamin	19
M. C. J. Ball not out....................	0 – c Campbell b Dhanraj	4
K. P. Sheeraz b Benjamin	0 – not out	1
A. M. Smith c Browne b Benjamin	0 – c Chanderpaul b Benjamin	0
B 4, l-b 1, n-b 22..................	27 B 9, l-b 6, n-b 4	19
	239	122

1/27 2/78 3/166 4/170 5/178
6/198 7/234 8/239 9/239

1/13 2/13 3/13 4/18 5/29
6/72 7/112 8/117 9/121

Bowling: *First Innings*—Ambrose 20-5-52-2; Benjamin 22-8-53-4; Drakes 4-0-17-0; Dhanraj 30-7-110-4; Williams 1-0-2-0. *Second Innings*—Benjamin 16.3-4-52-5; Hooper 19-7-34-3; Dhanraj 11-4-21-2.

Umpires: M. K. Reed and R. A. White.

ENGLAND v WEST INDIES

Fifth Cornhill Test

At Nottingham, August 10, 11, 12, 13, 14. Drawn. Toss: England.

Bat finally dominated ball often enough to bring the first draw of the series. But even though the last Test pitch produced by retiring groundsman Ron Allsopp was, by his own admission, a little too slow and lacking in bounce to be ideal, a fifth positive outcome appeared likely when a crucial catch was offered midway through the final afternoon.

England were only 214 ahead and nine wickets down in their second innings as Watkinson clipped Walsh straight to Campbell at mid-wicket. A fielder who had built a reputation for making difficult catches look easy spilled a relatively simple, two-handed chance and a heroic rescue act was allowed to develop. West Indies would have been left with 42 overs to chase victory and the contest could have gone either way. Instead, Watkinson – then 22 – went on to score 82 not out, his maiden Test half-century, while Illingworth defied a broken right index finger and medical advice to keep him company for 90 painful minutes. The last pair added 80 runs, 78 of them after Watkinson's escape, to steer England out of harm's way.

The first note of drama came on the eve of the match when both Atherton and Hick, who was restored to the team after Smith's accident, complained of stiff backs. England were sufficiently concerned to summon Yorkshire's David Byas to Trent Bridge and Russell contemplated the unexpected challenge of Test captaincy. But, next morning, the casualties declared themselves fit. Both went on to score centuries. An England batsman with a broken leg might have tried to drag himself into this Test: a docile pitch was welcoming enough but a West Indian attack forced to replace Ambrose – victim of his own back injury – with an internationally inexperienced leg-spinner, Dhanraj, was not to be missed. Three other West Indians made their first appearances of the series; Williams and Chanderpaul replaced the injured Hooper and Adams while Browne, who was born in London, was given a chance to demonstrate his qualifications to be first-choice wicket-keeper. For England, Illingworth returned in place of Embury, having recovered from a blow to his left hand.

Atherton and Knight made such smooth progress up to tea it looked as though they might become the first England openers to bat through a full day's play since Hobbs and Sutcliffe, on the third day of the Melbourne Test in 1924-25. But then Knight offered no shot to Benjamin, Crawley edged the same bowler to a lone slip fielder, Atherton called for a single and was run out by Dhanraj's direct hit from mid-on and Thorpe snicked a ball angled across him by Bishop. From 148 for nought, England slipped to 227 for four by the close. Atherton had registered his country's first hundred of the series, but England needed another if their fine start was not to be wasted. It came from Hick (his third in 36 Tests) and was all the sweeter following the selectors' decision to drop him at Old Trafford. Uncharacteristically, he had made a public challenge to chairman Ray Illingworth to restore him, two days before this match. Smith's fractured cheekbone had provided a way back and the benign pitch offered every encouragement, but an undefeated 118 proved, on this occasion at least, that Hick could handle real pressure. With all but White helping out, England registered a solid 440 despite Benjamin's five-wicket haul.

The third day belonged to Lara. An exquisite 152 off 182 balls with 28 fours, his second century in successive Test innings, inevitably overshadowed important contributions from openers Williams and Campbell. Lara scored 104 out of a 140-run stand with Campbell – though he then took the back seat to Richardson, who smashed 40 out of 56. It was a real surprise to see Lara helping a leg-side delivery from Cork into Russell's gloves five overs from the close.

When West Indies were dismissed midway through day four, just 23 behind, stalemate seemed assured. Illingworth, his non-bowling hand heavily strapped after being hit while acting as night-watchman on the first evening, had claimed Test-best figures of four for 96, but most thoughts were with Knight, detained in hospital after a frightening blow to the back of his helmetless head. The ball had struck him behind the right ear while he was fielding three or four yards from Benjamin's swinging bat. Happily, Knight returned to Trent Bridge next morning. But, despite batting at No. 7, he was dismissed before lunch as England lurched into danger on the final day. Bishop and Walsh were both struggling with injuries and Dhanraj posed little threat, but Benjamin – superbly supported by keeper Browne – reduced the home team to 189 for nine. Benjamin finished with his first ten-wicket Test haul, an outstanding effort on an unhelpful pitch, while Browne held nine catches in the match, equalling the West Indian Test record. In the end, however, Watkinson and Illingworth made sure a 2-2 scoreline was transferred to The Oval . . . with Campbell's helping hands. – David Lloyd.

Man of the Match: K. C. G. Benjamin.   *Attendance:* 52,199; *receipts* £946,688.

Close of play: First day, England 227-4 (R. K. Illingworth 8*, G. A. Hick 6*); Second day, West Indies 25-0 (S. C. Williams 16*, S. L. Campbell 8*); Third day, West Indies 334-5 (R. Dhanraj 3*, S. Chanderpaul 8*); Fourth day, England 111-2 (M. A. Atherton 38*, G. P. Thorpe 47*).

England

N. V. Knight lbw b Benjamin	57	– (7) c Browne b Benjamin	2
*M. A. Atherton run out	113	– (1) c Browne b Bishop	43
J. P. Crawley c Williams b Benjamin	14	– (2) b Walsh	11
G. P. Thorpe c Browne b Bishop	19	– c Browne b Walsh	76
R. K. Illingworth retired hurt	8	– (11) not out	14
G. A. Hick not out	118	– (3) b Benjamin	7
C. White c Browne b Bishop	1	– (5) c Campbell b Bishop	1
†R. C. Russell c Browne b Bishop	35	– (6) c Browne b Benjamin	7
M. Watkinson lbw b Benjamin	24	– (8) not out	82
D. G. Cork c Browne b Benjamin	31	– (9) c Browne b Benjamin	4
A. R. C. Fraser b Benjamin	0	– (10) c Arthurton b Benjamin	4
B 4, l-b 8, n-b 8	20	L-b 4, n-b 14	18

1/148 (1) 2/179 (3) 3/206 (2)　　　　　440　　1/17 (2) 2/36 (3)　　(9 wkts dec.) 269
4/211 (4) 5/239 (7) 6/323 (8)　　　　　　　　3/117 (1) 4/125 (5)
7/380 (9) 8/440 (10) 9/440 (11)　　　　　　　5/139 (6) 6/148 (7)
　　　　　　　　　　　　　　　　　　　　　7/171 (4) 8/176 (9)
　　　　　　　　　　　　　　　　　　　　　9/189 (10)

In the first innings R. K. Illingworth retired hurt at 227.

Bowling: *First Innings*—Walsh 39–5–93–0; Bishop 30.1–6–62–3; Benjamin 34.3–7–105–5; Dhanraj 40–7–137–0; Arthurton 9–0–31–0. *Second Innings*—Walsh 30–6–70–2; Bishop 21–8–50–2; Benjamin 25–8–69–5; Dhanraj 15–1–54–0; Arthurton 13–3–22–0.

West Indies

S. C. Williams c Atherton b Illingworth	62		
S. L. Campbell c Crawley b Watkinson	47	– c Russell b Cork	16
B. C. Lara c Russell b Cork	152	– (1) c Russell b Fraser	20
*R. B. Richardson c Hick b Illingworth	40		
K. L. T. Arthurton b Illingworth	13		
R. Dhanraj c Knight b Cork	3		
S. Chanderpaul c Crawley b Watkinson	18	– (3) not out	5
†C. O. Browne st Russell b Illingworth	34	– (4) not out	1
I. R. Bishop c Hick b Watkinson	4		
K. C. G. Benjamin not out	14		
C. A. Walsh b Fraser	19		
B 2, l-b 7, n-b 2	11		

1/77 (1) 2/217 (2) 3/273 (4) 4/319 (5)　　　417　　1/36 (1) 2/36 (2)　　(2 wkts) 42
5/323 (3) 6/338 (6) 7/366 (7)
8/374 (9) 9/384 (8) 10/417 (11)

Bowling: *First Innings*—Fraser 17.3–6–77–1; Cork 36–9–110–2; Watkinson 35–12–84–3; Illingworth 51–21–96–4; Hick 4–1–11–0; White 5–0–30–0. *Second Innings*—Fraser 6–1–17–1; Cork 5–1–25–1.

Umpires: C. J. Mitchley (South Africa) and N. T. Plews.
Referee: J. R. Reid (New Zealand).

HAMPSHIRE v WEST INDIANS

At Southampton, August 16, 17, 18. Drawn. Toss: Hampshire.

　　Hampshire had beaten the West Indians in a one-day match in May, but there was no chance of a repeat. The West Indians made their second-highest total as a touring team, passed only by their 730 for three at Cambridge in 1950. Hampshire scored a modest 192 – their only half-century coming from Extras – as they fell to the pace of Anderson Cummins, whistled up from league cricket in Kent to cover the party's injury crisis. Though Phil Simmons, another understudy, went early, bowling soon became a chore on a bland pitch. Campbell batted fluently for 172, becoming the first of the West Indians to reach 1,000 on the tour, but it was the destructive brilliance of Hooper, returning after injury, which enthralled a surprisingly small crowd. He fell just short of a double-hundred, hitting ten sixes and 20 fours in just under four hours. Richardson declared at their overnight 696 for six – the biggest total conceded by Hampshire since the 1921 Australians' 708 for seven. The tourists had scored 561 in a day; responding, Hampshire avoided a second collapse and were 302 for five when a halt was called.

Close of play: First day, West Indians 135-1 (S. L. Campbell 76*, K. L. T. Arthurton 34*); Second day, West Indians 696-6 (C. O. Browne 74*, J. R. Murray 44*).

Hampshire

V. P. Terry b Gibson	4	– c Browne b Dhanraj	60
J. S. Laney c Murray b Cummins	8	– c Chanderpaul b Cummins	29
*J. P. Stephenson c Browne b Simmons	35	– c Browne b Dhanraj	49
T. C. Middleton c Murray b Cummins	10	– c sub (C. E. L. Ambrose) b Dhanraj	31
M. Keech c Browne b Cummins	2	– c Richardson b Arthurton	41
K. D. James c Chanderpaul b Cummins	3	– not out	28
†A. N. Aymes c Arthurton b Cummins	12	– not out	37
M. J. Thursfield c Richardson b Dhanraj	30		
H. H. Streak b Gibson	4		
C. A. Connor not out	24		
R. R. Dibden c Gibson b Dhanraj	0		
B 8, l-b 12, n-b 40	60	L-b 1, n-b 26	27

1/4 2/16 3/55 4/61 5/67   192   1/61 2/153 3/154   (5 wkts) 302
6/117 7/117 8/142 9/192   4/228 5/230

Bowling: *First Innings*—Gibson 15-6-48-2; Cummins 17-3-60-5; Simmons 15-5-30-1; Hooper 12-2-34-0; Dhanraj 2.3-2-0-2. *Second Innings*—Gibson 9-0-43-0; Cummins 10-0-49-1; Simmons 11-0-55-0; Hooper 24-3-72-0; Dhanraj 28-8-68-3; Arthurton 10-6-11-1; Chanderpaul 4-3-3-0.

West Indians

P. V. Simmons c Keech b Thursfield	10	C. O. Browne not out	74
S. L. Campbell c Laney b Thursfield	172	†J. R. Murray not out	44
K. L. T. Arthurton c Aymes b Connor	59	B 11, l-b 14, n-b 16	41
C. L. Hooper c Aymes b James	195		
S. Chanderpaul c Keech b Thursfield	18	1/45 2/209 3/296	(6 wkts dec.) 696
*R. B. Richardson c Connor b Keech	83	4/374 5/532 6/625	

O. D. Gibson, A. C. Cummins and R. Dhanraj did not bat.

Bowling: Streak 18-4-53-0; Connor 18-0-116-1; Thursfield 26-2-108-3; James 26-1-137-1; Dibden 12-0-95-0; Stephenson 20-0-107-0; Keech 10-0-55-1.

Umpires: K. E. Palmer and G. Sharp.

ESSEX v WEST INDIANS

At Chelmsford, August 19, 20, 21. Drawn. Toss: West Indians.

Left a target of 327 in a minimum of 60 overs, Essex set off with 73 in 15 overs but abandoned their attempt after Gooch departed for an entertaining 50 from 68 deliveries. In the first innings, Gooch had contributed his third hundred in successive first-class matches before retiring, citing a migraine, at tea. This may or may not have been connected with his new and much publicised hair transplant. But the chief beneficiary of a pitch unfriendly to bowlers was Simmons. Having joined the West Indians because of their injury problems, he scored a century in each innings, hitting out with great power and freedom. On the first day, he struck 15 fours and a six in 156 balls, while his unbeaten 139 came from 153 and included 18 fours and three sixes. With Chanderpaul, he shared an unbroken opening stand of 260 in 50 overs.

Close of play: First day, Essex 4-0 (G. A. Gooch 2*, D. D. J. Robinson 0*); Second day, West Indians 106-0 (S. Chanderpaul 23*, P. V. Simmons 76*).

West Indians

S. C. Williams c Rollins b Ilott	25		
P. V. Simmons b Irani	112 – not out	139	
K. L. T. Arthurton c Rollins b Such	49		
S. Chanderpaul lbw b Irani	14 – (1) not out	103	
*C. L. Hooper c Ilott b Such	0		
†C. O. Browne c Rollins b Cousins	30		
O. D. Gibson c Robinson b Pearson	49		
A. C. Cummins b Cousins	16		
C. E. L. Ambrose not out	27		
V. C. Drakes lbw b Gooch	11		
R. Dhanraj lbw b Gooch	22		
B 5, l-b 6	11	B 6, l-b 9, w 3	18

1/48 2/138 3/179 4/190 5/209   366   (no wkt dec.) 260
6/280 7/294 8/304 9/334

Bowling: *First Innings*—Ilott 9-1-56-1; Cousins 13-1-63-2; Irani 18-1-88-2; Such 24-6-48-2; Pearson 21-2-78-1; Gooch 4.4-0-22-2. *Second Innings*—Ilott 3-1-21-0; Cousins 4-0-30-0; Such 16-2-76-0; Pearson 20.3-1-89-0; Gooch 5-0-22-0; Robinson 1-0-7-0.

Essex

G. A. Gooch retired ill	109 – c Hooper b Dhanraj	50	
D. D. J. Robinson b Cummins	6 – lbw b Drakes	17	
J. B. Lewis b Ambrose	37 – c Ambrose b Drakes	13	
N. Hussain b Dhanraj	56 – not out	42	
*P. J. Prichard not out	32 – b Dhanraj	1	
R. C. Irani st Browne b Arthurton	8 – c Dhanraj b Chanderpaul	22	
†R. J. Rollins not out	5 – c sub (J. R. Murray)		
		b Chanderpaul	28
M. C. Ilott (did not bat)	– not out	2	
B 3, l-b 7, w 1, n-b 36	47	B 4, l-b 6, n-b 17	27

1/13 2/113 3/247 4/277   (4 wkts dec.) 300   1/73 2/95 3/109   (6 wkts) 202
                                                4/115 5/152 6/198

R. M. Pearson, D. M. Cousins and P. M. Such did not bat.

In the first innings G. A. Gooch retired ill at 250.

Bowling: *First Innings*—Cummins 10-1-45-1; Gibson 5-1-16-0; Ambrose 11-5-24-1; Drakes 10-1-52-0; Dhanraj 19-0-89-1; Simmons 11-3-35-0; Chanderpaul 1-0-1-0; Hooper 5-1-15-0; Arthurton 7-1-13-1. *Second Innings*—Cummins 5-0-26-0; Gibson 6-1-30-0; Drakes 8-0-30-2; Dhanraj 21-2-64-2; Simmons 2-1-1-0; Chanderpaul 12-1-41-2.

Umpires: B. Dudleston and P. B. Wight.

ENGLAND v WEST INDIES

Sixth Cornhill Test

At The Oval, August 24, 25, 26, 27, 28. Drawn. Toss: England. Test debut: A. P. Wells.

Not for many years had a Test in England received such advance attention; in the circumstances, the draw was a deflating anticlimax. The cricket was conditioned by a pitch that had been anaesthetised for the occasion and was lifted above the humdrum only by several fine innings and the peerless fast bowling of Ambrose, on what appeared to be his final Test appearance in England. It left the series drawn, justly and honourably – but, as four helter-skelter matches, packed with drama, had been sedately followed by two tamer draws, it also left both sides sensing a missed opportunity.

Only 22 wickets fell in five full days of cricket and the body language of many a bowler told of the bias of the conditions. Paul Brind was making his Test debut as head groundsman, but the challenging pace and bounce that characterised his father Harry's recent Test pitches had been replaced by something unfailingly true but far more sluggish. As there was no help for spin either, the batsmen held sway virtually undisturbed. It was only the speed with which West Indies, in particular Lara, scored runs that imposed pressure on England to bat out time on the last day. This they achieved through the latest demonstration of Atherton's technique and stoicism.

England had caused surprise by recalling Tufnell to their squad but caused more by then omitting him from the eventual eleven; they also brought back Malcolm, dropped after the First Test, to the scene of his triumph against South Africa. Alan Wells was given a belated and, as it transpired, unfortunate debut. Gallian joined his three Lancashire team-mates at the last minute because Knight was assaulting a finger. Hooper and Ambrose returned after injury for West Indies, who dropped Arthurton and Dhanraj. Atherton won the toss for the fourth time in five Tests and might have been revising his views on the pitch when Ambrose's second ball struck him in the ribcage. The first hour was difficult, the bounce of the new ball a shade uneven, but the pitch was never again to betray itself. England were uneasy at the end of the first day, having lost the assertive Thorpe and Wells in successive balls from Ambrose. Wells had played 15 seasons of county cricket before this moment – he played his first delivery off his chest to short leg. Hick and Russell then put on 144 for the sixth wicket. Both fell in the nineties and, in between, Watkinson became Walsh's 300th Test victim. After more than 11 hours in the field, West Indies' out-cricket bore signs of fatigue and resentment. But patriotic belief that their batting would disintegrate proved fanciful in the extreme: for the ensuing two days, they dwarfed England's once-imposing 454 to lead by 238.

England paid dearly for some missed opportunities on the third morning. Benjamin, the night-watchman, ought to have been caught at slip off the first ball he received from

Malcolm and instead occupied 80 minutes; then Lara, habitually a chancer in his early overs, could have been run out just before lunch. He did not err again, his majestic 179 coming from only 206 balls and containing 110 in boundaries: 26 fours and a six. Atherton dispensed with all close catchers long before the end of Lara's innings, his third century in consecutive Tests, lifting his aggregate to 765 runs in the series. There was general sympathy for the popular Richardson, out seven short of his hundred, but the weary England bowlers may not have shared it. Hooper, back in the middle order, did complete his first century of the series and Chanderpaul, so long in the wings of his team, made a cultured 80. He became the third victim of Cork, who bowled with heart despite being restricted by a groin strain.

West Indies' total of 692 for eight was their biggest against England and the tenth-highest in Test cricket; five of the ten have been achieved at The Oval. England did not help themselves – Hooper was dropped by Malcolm, off his own bowling, when on one – but it was a tiresomely one-sided contest, called off in time for England to face 19 overs before the close of the fourth day. These were safely negotiated but Ambrose, bowling with withering speed, dismissed Gallian and Crawley in quick succession on Monday morning. When Walsh removed Thorpe just after lunch, England were still 106 behind and defeat remained possible. Atherton stood firm with Hick, however, and when finally he fell after six hours, the fourth man in the match to be out in the nineties, Wells had time to register three Test runs.

The first four days of the game had been sold out for several months and all tickets could easily have been sold twice over. It was an occasion to savour, at the end of a compelling series, but it was not a good cricket match, because neither side ever really looked likely to win it. – Alan Lee.

Man of the Match: B. C. Lara.　　　*Attendance:* 71,301; *receipts* £1,511,379.

Men of the Series: England – M. A. Atherton; West Indies – B. C. Lara.

Close of play: First day, England 233-5 (G. A. Hick 43*, R. C. Russell 9*); Second day, West Indies 50-1 (S. L. Campbell 17*, K. C. G. Benjamin 2*); Third day, West Indies 424-4 (R. B. Richardson 87*, C. L. Hooper 5*); Fourth day, England 39-0 (J. E. R. Gallian 22*, M. A. Atherton 17*).

England

*M. A. Atherton c Williams b Benjamin	36	– (2) c Browne b Bishop	95
J. E. R. Gallian c Hooper b Ambrose	0	– (1) c Williams b Ambrose	25
J. P. Crawley c Richardson b Hooper	50	– c Browne b Ambrose	2
G. P. Thorpe c Browne b Ambrose	74	– c Williams b Walsh	38
G. A. Hick c Williams b Benjamin	96	– not out	51
A. P. Wells c Campbell b Ambrose	0	– not out	3
†R. C. Russell b Ambrose	91		
M. Watkinson c Browne b Walsh	13		
D. G. Cork b Ambrose	33		
A. R. C. Fraser not out	10		
D. E. Malcolm c Lara b Benjamin	10		
B 15, l-b 11, n-b 15	41	L-b 4, n-b 5	9

1/9 (2) 2/60 (1) 3/149 (3) 4/192 (4) 　454　　1/60 (1) 2/64 (3) 　　(4 wkts) 223
5/192 (6) 6/336 (5) 7/372 (8) 　　　　　　　3/132 (4) 4/212 (2)
8/419 (7) 9/443 (9) 10/454 (11)

Bowling: *First Innings*—Ambrose 42–10–96–5; Walsh 32–6–84–1; Benjamin 27–6–81–3; Bishop 35–5–111–0; Hooper 23–7–56–1. *Second Innings*—Walsh 28–7–80–1; Ambrose 19–8–35–2; Hooper 22–11–26–0; Chanderpaul 6–0–22–0; Bishop 22–4–56–1; Lara 1–1–0–0.

West Indies

S. C. Williams c Russell b Malcolm	30	I. R. Bishop run out	10
S. L. Campbell c Russell b Fraser	89	C. E. L. Ambrose not out	5
K. C. G. Benjamin c Atherton b Cork	20		
B. C. Lara c Fraser b Malcolm	179	B 5, l-b 20, w 5, n-b 2	32
*R. B. Richardson c Hick b Cork	93		
C. L. Hooper c Russell b Malcolm	127	1/40 (1) 2/94 (3) 3/202 (2) (8 wkts dec.) 692	
S. Chanderpaul c Gallian b Cork	80	4/390 (4) 5/435 (5) 6/631 (7)	
†C. O. Browne not out	27	7/653 (6) 8/686 (9)	
C. A. Walsh did not bat.			

YOUNG AUSTRALIA IN ENGLAND, 1995

In 1992-93, England A had visited Australia on one of their least rewarding tours. They were hardly noticed as they travelled around the country and the closest thing on offer to a representative match, a four-day game against the Australian Cricket Academy, was even denied first-class status. But the Young Australia team – originally billed as Australia A – which toured England in 1995 were not given a noticeably warm welcome either. Despite some rampaging performances with the bat, they received little publicity and their representative match, against a TCCB XI, proved to be a damp squib. It was treated as a side-show not merely to the County Championship – only players whose counties had a week off were selected – but, in one case, to the Second Eleven knockout competition. Moreover, the teams had to play on an Edgbaston pitch so unpredictable that the match was over by tea on the second of its scheduled four days (England and West Indies had a similar experience in their Test at the same venue).

The change of name to Young Australia was a confusing one, especially with a South African Under-19 team touring England at the same time. Nor was the label entirely truthful. Four of the 14-man party were over 25 and Peter McIntyre, their only specialist spinner, was 29. Jo Angel, Matthew Hayden, Justin Langer and McIntyre had all appeared in Test cricket, Stuart Law and Ricky Ponting in limited-overs internationals. Manager Dave Gilbert expected several members of the squad to return to England for the next Ashes series in 1997 – Hayden had already toured with the senior team in 1993, when he scored 1,150 without playing a Test.

The team's strength was its batting, and the speed at which they could score runs. Twice they passed 500 in their first innings. Six batsmen averaged over 40 and a seventh was just short, while Hayden, Langer and Martin Love all passed 500. But perhaps the most successful was Adam Gilchrist, the Western Australian wicket-keeper/batsman, who scored 495 runs at 61.87 and made 38 dismissals. The bowling was not so widely admired. The leading wicket-takers included the two oldest tourists, leg-spinner McIntyre, who bowled by far the most overs, 297, for 34 wickets at 29.94, and 27-year-old pace bowler Angel, with 27 at 26.25. Mike Kasprowicz, who had played for Essex in 1994, also took 27 and headed the averages at 22.18. But they rarely dominated games in quite the way that their batting colleagues did.

It was ironic, then, that their final victory, over the TCCB XI, should have come in such a low-scoring match. But that was on a freak pitch, and the difference between the sides was not the bowling but a decisive innings of 70 – the only half-century of the game – from the Australian captain, Law of Queensland. It enabled them to go out on the winning note that had prevailed for most of the tour. Their only first-class defeat came in two days at Leicester, though their last pair had to scrape a draw against Worcestershire, and there were five wins. Whether it was noticed by the public or not, the trip succeeded in giving some Australian hopefuls experience of English conditions – and confidence that they could thrive in them.

YOUNG AUSTRALIA TOURING PARTY

S. G. Law (Queensland) (*captain*), J. L. Langer (Western Australia) (*vice-captain*), J. Angel (Western Australia), M. T. G. Elliott (Victoria), S. P. George (South Australia), A. C. Gilchrist (Western Australia), M. A. Harrity (South Australia), M. L. Hayden (Queensland), M. S. Kasprowicz (Queensland), M. L. Love (Queensland), P. E. McIntyre (South Australia), R. T. Ponting (Tasmania), B. A. Williams (Victoria), S. Young (Tasmania).

B. P. Julian (Western Australia), originally named, was replaced by George after being called up for Australia's tour of the West Indies.

Manager: D. R. Gilbert.   *Coach:* W. L. Stillman.

YOUNG AUSTRALIA TOUR RESULTS

First-class matches – Played 8: Won 5, Lost 1, Drawn 2.
Wins - Somerset, Derbyshire, Hampshire, Sussex, TCCB XI.
Loss – Leicestershire.
Draws – Glamorgan, Worcestershire.
Non-first-class matches – Played 6: Won 4, Lost 2. *Wins* – England NCA, Minor Counties, Leicestershire, Surrey. *Losses* – Yorkshire, Gloucestershire.

YOUNG AUSTRALIA TOUR AVERAGES – FIRST-CLASS MATCHES

BATTING

	M	I	NO	R	HS	100s	Avge	Ct/St
A. C. Gilchrist	8	11	3	495	122	2	61.87	33/5
J. L. Langer	7	12	3	516	149	2	57.33	5
M. L. Love	7	13	2	510	181	2	46.36	10
R. T. Ponting	7	12	2	460	103*	1	46.00	7
M. L. Hayden	7	14	2	551	178	2	45.91	3
S. G. Law	7	11	2	397	134	1	44.11	13
M. T. G. Elliott	6	12	3	357	89*	0	39.66	5
J. Angel	6	7	4	103	29*	0	34.33	6
S. Young	7	10	0	228	110	1	22.80	4
M. S. Kasprowicz	5	6	2	65	43*	0	16.25	0
B. A. Williams	5	6	1	72	28	0	14.40	0
P. E. McIntyre	8	8	1	26	13	0	3.71	4

Played in five matches: M. A. Harrity 18, 0, 0 (2 ct). Played in three matches: S. P. George 10, 7, 29 (1 ct).

* *Signifies not out.*

BOWLING

	O	M	R	W	BB	5W/i	Avge
M. S. Kasprowicz	175.1	42	599	27	5-19	1	22.18
S. Young	128	36	359	16	3-23	0	22.43
J. Angel	179.5	39	709	27	4-31	0	26.25
P. E. McIntyre	297	70	1,018	34	5-38	1	29.94
B. A. Williams	134.3	26	443	14	4-79	0	31.64
M. A. Harrity	135.2	33	497	13	4-37	0	38.23
S. P. George	72	6	422	7	3-91	0	60.28

Also bowled: M. T. G. Elliott 7-2-23-1; R. T. Ponting 10-1-36-0.

Note: Matches in this section which were not first-class are signified by a dagger.

†At Trowbridge, July 3. Young Australia won by 63 runs. Toss: Young Australia. Young Australia 328 for five (55 overs) (M. L. Hayden 159, M. T. G. Elliott 30, S. G. Law 61, Extras 32; K. A. Arnold three for 46); England NCA 265 for eight (55 overs) (S. J. Dean 146 not out, Extras 43; P. E. McIntyre three for 39).

SOMERSET v YOUNG AUSTRALIA

At Taunton, July 5, 6, 7. Young Australia won by 30 runs. Toss: Young Australia.

A suitably thrilling finish to a remarkable match ended with Somerset, chasing hard throughout, just failing to reach a target of 461 in 97 overs. Lathwell and Parsons, who scored a maiden hundred, set the innings up but the loss of Rose proved fatal. Rose had started a sparkling match of 1,502 runs in three days on a firm, true pitch by dismissing Hayden first ball. Young and Gilchrist rescued the Australians from a faltering 156 for five by adding 195 at more than a run a ball until Young became Trescothick's first first-class wicket. Trescothick, brought on in desperation to bowl his innocuous seamers, immediately followed up with a hat-trick, beginning with Gilchrist, for a 101-ball century including eight sixes and 13 fours. Somerset replied at the same high speed, the ball racing across the lightning-fast outfield and declared 74 behind. This time the Australian top order all fired, especially Love and Hayden, who opened with a stand of 169. Love set up the final equation by hitting three sixes and 24 fours in 181 from 190 balls, the biggest score of a marvellous game.

Close of play: First day, Somerset 176-4 (P. C. L. Holloway 5*); Second day, Young Australia 386-3 (R. T. Ponting 52*, S. G. Law 47*).

Young Australia

M. L. Hayden c Harden b Rose	0	– (2) st Turner b Trump		67
J. L. Langer c Turner b Rose	4	– (3) c Parsons b Trump		31
R. T. Ponting c and b Rose	54	– (4) not out		52
*S. G. Law lbw b Rose	20	– (5) not out		47
M. L. Love c Trescothick b Kerr	32	– (1) c Batty b Trescothick		181
S. Young c Rose b Trescothick	110			
†A. C. Gilchrist c Rose b Trescothick	122			
J. Angel lbw b Trescothick	4			
B. A. Williams not out	0			
P. E. McIntyre c Turner b Trescothick	0			
S. P. George st Turner b Batty	10			
L-b 6, n-b 18	24	L-b 3, w 1, n-b 4		8

1/0 2/24 3/62 4/93 5/156   380   1/169 2/251 3/288   (3 wkts dec.) 386
6/351 7/369 8/369 9/369

Bowling: *First Innings*—Rose 15-4-50-4; Kerr 15-2-83-1; Trump 22-7-85-0; Parsons 6-1-51-0; Batty 6-0-69-1; Trescothick 4-1-36-4. *Second Innings*—Rose 10-0-45-0; Kerr 4-0-26-0; Trump 27-5-109-2; Parsons 9-0-58-0; Batty 25-1-128-0; Trescothick 4-1-11-1; Lathwell 1-0-6-0.

Somerset

M. N. Lathwell c Hayden b McIntyre	89	– c McIntyre b Angel	84
*P. D. Bowler c Young b Williams	0	– c sub (M. T. G. Elliott) b Young	32
R. J. Harden b George	30	– c sub (M. T. G. Elliott) b George	2
K. A. Parsons b Williams	40	– c Law b Angel	105
P. C. L. Holloway not out	59	– c Langer b George	25
M. E. Trescothick c Gilchrist b Angel	19	– b McIntyre	1
G. D. Rose c and b George	27	– c Love b George	71
†R. J. Turner b George	8	– c Ponting b Angel	16
J. I. D. Kerr c Gilchrist b Williams	0	– c Gilchrist b Young	15
J. D. Batty b Williams	0	– c Angel b Young	21
H. R. J. Trump (did not bat)	–	– not out	0
L-b 6, n-b 28	34	B 4, l-b 3, w 3, n-b 48	58

1/4 2/77 3/165 4/176 5/223   (9 wkts dec.) 306   1/60 2/95 3/174 4/247 5/258   430
6/280 7/302 8/306 9/306   6/301 7/345 8/406 9/416

Bowling: First Innings—Angel 13–1–79–1; Williams 15.3–2–79–4; McIntyre 14–2–49–1; George 10–0–93–3. *Second Innings*—Angel 24–2–160–3; Williams 5–1–16–0; Young 14–3–60–3; George 16–2–91–3; McIntyre 31–5–96–1.

Umpires: J. H. Hampshire and A. A. Jones.

GLAMORGAN v YOUNG AUSTRALIA

At Neath, July 8, 9, 10. Drawn. Toss: Glamorgan.

A thunderstorm ended play at 3.40 p.m. on the final afternoon with the tourists 208 behind and five wickets down to Croft and Kendrick on a spinner's pitch. Glamorgan had held the advantage from the opening day, when they ran up 362. Acting-captain Maynard put on 137 with Cottey, who scored his fifth century of the season, after Hemp marked his recall to the first team by rediscovering his confidence and form. Langer struck an unbeaten 111 in reply but, with none of his colleagues reaching 40, Young Australia were 101 runs adrift. A century from James helped to set them a final target of 388; despite an attacking innings from Elliott, Glamorgan had the better chance of victory when rain washed out the final session.

Close of play: First day, Young Australia 22-1 (M. T. G. Elliott 15*, J. L. Langer 0*); Second day, Glamorgan 195-2 (S. P. James 86*, A. D. Shaw 4*).

Glamorgan

S. P. James b Harrity	4	– c Langer b McIntyre	116
A. Dale c Gilchrist b Kasprowicz	15	– b Young	43
D. L. Hemp lbw b Young	88	– (5) b McIntyre	1
A. J. Dalton c Law b McIntyre	29	– (3) lbw b McIntyre	43
P. A. Cottey not out	123	– (9) c Elliott b Kasprowicz	8
*M. P. Maynard c Ponting b Kasprowicz	56	– (8) run out	7
R. D. B. Croft c Gilchrist b Kasprowicz	0	– (6) c Gilchrist b Kasprowicz	14
†A. D. Shaw not out	4	– (4) c Law b Kasprowicz	14
S. D. Thomas (did not bat)	–	(7) not out	18
N. M. Kendrick (did not bat)	–	– c Gilchrist b McIntyre	0
S. R. Barwick (did not bat)	–	– absent hurt	
B 5, l-b 3, w 2, n-b 33	43	L-b 8, w 4, n-b 10	22

1/12 2/54 3/125 4/206   (6 wkts dec.) 362   1/89 2/176 3/223 4/226 5/251   286
5/343 6/343   6/257 7/264 8/285 9/286

Bowling: First Innings—Harrity 20–5–100–1; Kasprowicz 24–7–63–3; George 13–1–82–0; Young 13–8–15–1; McIntyre 22–4–94–1. *Second Innings*—Harrity 6–1–36–0; Kasprowicz 17–2–96–3; Young 7–1–38–1; McIntyre 20.3–1–75–4; George 7–0–33–0.

Young Australia

M. T. G. Elliott run out	32 – not out.	89
M. L. Love c Cottey b Croft	6 – b Croft	13
J. L. Langer not out	111 – st Shaw b Croft	10
R. T. Ponting lbw b Dale	4 – c Dalton b Kendrick	31
*S. G. Law c Dale b Barwick	17 – c Croft b Kendrick	5
S. Young c and b Croft	0 – c Dale b Kendrick	15
†A. C. Gilchrist c Shaw b Thomas	36 – not out.	7
M. S. Kasprowicz lbw b Thomas	11	
S. P. George b Barwick	7	
P. E. McIntyre c Dalton b Croft	13	
M. A. Harrity st Shaw b Croft	18	
B 4, 1-b 1, w 1	6 B 4, 1-b 2, w 1, n-b 2	9

1/22 2/47 3/53 4/81 5/81   261   1/41 2/71 3/118   (5 wkts) 179
6/140 7/162 8/188 9/233   4/124 5/156

Bowling: *First Innings*—Thomas 13–1–74–2; Barwick 20–6–62–2; Croft 23.4–11–45–4; Dale 7–0–14–1; Kendrick 11–1–61–0. *Second Innings*—Thomas 5–0–25–0; Dale 2–0–19–0; Croft 19–3–56–2; Kendrick 18.4–3–73–3.

Umpires: G. I. Burgess and M. J. Harris.

†At Reading, July 12. Young Australia won by 71 runs. Toss: Young Australia. Young Australia 316 for five (55 overs) (M. T. G. Elliott 62, R. T. Ponting 120, S. G. Law 66, J. L. Langer 40); Minor Counties 245 for eight (55 overs) (S. J. Dean 36, S. V. Laudat 33, S. D. Myles 50 not out, Extras 41).

†At Leeds, July 18. Yorkshire won by 68 runs. Toss: Yorkshire. Yorkshire 224 for six (55 overs) (M. P. Vaughan 76, D. Byas 73, A. McGrath 41); Young Australia 156 (45.5 overs) (M. L. Hayden 31, A. C. Gilchrist 51; A. C. Morris five for 32).

DERBYSHIRE v YOUNG AUSTRALIA

At Chesterfield, July 19, 20, 21. Young Australia won by four wickets. Toss: Derbyshire.
Cork, one of only three capped players in the team, led Derbyshire for the first time in an excellent match settled in the final over. A heavy atmosphere and reckless batting produced 17 wickets on the first day, though Owen rescued Derbyshire with a vivid fifty and Gilchrist batted as well as he had kept wicket. Gilchrist reached his century with his fourth six and also hit 14 fours from 107 balls. Derbyshire batted more consistently the second time. Owen was again impressive, as was Cassar until he fell to a marvellous outfield catch by Ponting. After a blank third morning, Young Australia were set 274 in 51 overs and won with five balls to spare. Love, who completed a fine century in 99 balls, and Ponting added 137 in 23 mostly erratic overs, with Malcolm particularly expensive.
Close of play: First day, Young Australia 171-7 (A. C. Gilchrist 61*, B. A. Williams 18*); Second day, Derbyshire 290-8 (D. G. Cork 32*, A. J. Harris 8*).

Derbyshire

A. S. Rollins c Love b Harrity	8	– c Gilchrist b Harrity	12
W. A. Dessaur b Angel	0	– c Love b Harrity	46
C. J. Adams b Angel	7	– c Love b Angel	5
T. A. Tweats c Angel b Harrity	3	– c Love b Williams	58
J. E. Owen b Williams	65	– c Gilchrist b Angel	45
*D. G. Cork c Gilchrist b McIntyre	22	– (8) not out	50
M. E. Cassar c Hayden b Harrity	32	– c Ponting b McIntyre	29
†A. D. Bairstow st Gilchrist b McIntyre	26	– (6) c Elliott b McIntyre	22
P. Aldred c sub (M. S. Kasprowicz) b Harrity	0	– lbw b Angel	7
A. J. Harris c Ponting b McIntyre	8	– not out	14
D. E. Malcolm not out	4		
B 4, l-b 10, n-b 2	16	B 9, l-b 10, w 5, n-b 4	28

1/4 2/8 3/16 4/40 5/105   191   1/14 2/19 3/109   (8 wkts dec.) 316
6/112 7/157 8/164 9/187   4/176 5/189 6/231
                                             7/250 8/261

Bowling: *First Innings*—Harrity 12.1–2–37–4; Angel 17–5–62–2; Williams 11–3–33–1; Young 6–1–20–0; McIntyre 10–4–25–3. *Second Innings*—Harrity 16–3–64–2; Angel 16.1–3–82–3; Williams 21–7–44–1; McIntyre 27–11–76–2; Young 11–1–24–0; Ponting 2–0–7–0.

Young Australia

M. T. G. Elliott run out	37	– c Rollins b Malcolm	4
R. T. Ponting c Cork b Malcolm	6	– (4) c Adams b Tweats	64
*S. G. Law c Bairstow b Malcolm	6	– (7) not out	34
M. L. Hayden c Tweats b Harris	12	– (2) c Adams b Cork	6
S. Young lbw b Harris	7	– st Bairstow b Dessaur	19
M. L. Love c Adams b Aldred	12	– (3) c and b Cassar	108
†A. C. Gilchrist not out	105	– (6) run out	11
J. Angel c Bairstow b Aldred	1	– not out	16
B. A. Williams c sub (A. C. Cottam) b Harris	28		
P. E. McIntyre b Malcolm	8		
M. A. Harrity b Aldred	0		
B 6, l-b 1, w 1, n-b 4	12	B 9, l-b 3, n-b 2	14

1/11 2/23 3/59 4/68 5/71   234   1/4 2/48 3/185   (6 wkts) 276
6/91 7/107 8/183 9/225   4/202 5/215 6/240

Bowling: *First Innings*—Malcolm 19–1–77–3; Harris 19–4–83–3; Cassar 0.2–0–1–0; Cork 5.4–1–19–0; Aldred 11.5–2–47–3. *Second Innings*—Malcolm 10–1–62–1; Cork 10.4–4–36–1; Aldred 5–2–27–0; Harris 7.1–1–50–0; Cassar 6–0–36–1; Tweats 9–0–45–1; Dessaur 3–0–8–1.

Umpires: H. D. Bird and J. F. Steele.

WORCESTERSHIRE v YOUNG AUSTRALIA

At Worcester, July 22, 23, 24. Drawn. Toss: Worcestershire.

After the tourists' top order put on a first-innings batting exhibition, last man McIntyre had to hold out with Langer for the last 8.2 overs of the match to deny Worcestershire. On the first day, the county subsided to 160 for six before Rhodes made a career-best 122 not out. The Australian batsmen responded powerfully. Ponting scored 103 in 136 balls, sharing century stands with Langer and Love. It must have seemed all too familiar to Moody; back at home, he had seen the Tasmanian Ponting take five hundreds off his native Western Australia in three seasons. The tourists declared 65 ahead and reduced Worcestershire to 139 for six before Moody steadied the ship and set a target of 264 in 45 overs. Langer raised Australian hopes but was forced to abandon his aggressive stance after a collapse and settled for survival.

Close of play: First day, Worcestershire 397; Second day, Worcestershire 62-1 (T. S. Curtis 21*, G. R. Haynes 9*).

Worcestershire

T. S. Curtis c Love b Williams	14	– run out	25
W. P. C. Weston c Gilchrist b Kasprowicz	62	– c Gilchrist b Young	24
G. R. Haynes run out	36	– b Young	31
M. J. Church c Gilchrist b Young	0	– b McIntyre	31
S. R. Lampitt c Ponting b Young	2	– c and b McIntyre	13
K. R. Spiring c Gilchrist b Young	1	– c Love b George	3
*T. M. Moody run out	38	– not out	44
†S. J. Rhodes not out	122	– not out	10
N. V. Radford c Hayden b Kasprowicz	50		
P. Mirza c Gilchrist b Williams	2		
P. A. Thomas b McIntyre	8		
B 4, l-b 12, n-b 46	62	L-b 8, w 3, n-b 6	17

1/32 2/142 3/143 4/145 5/145   397   1/42 2/86 3/102   (6 wkts dec.) 198
6/160 7/220 8/338 9/349   4/128 5/139 6/139

Bowling: *First Innings*—Williams 19–1–73–2; Kasprowicz 29–5–89–2; George 11–1–63–0;
McIntyre 21.3–4–103–1; Young 22–7–53–3; Ponting 1–1–0–0. *Second Innings*—Williams
10–1–29–0; George 15–2–60–1; Kasprowicz 13–4–46–0; Young 15–5–25–2; McIntyre
11–4–30–2.

Young Australia

M. L. Hayden c Rhodes b Radford	7	– (2) b Thomas	7
M. T. G. Elliott b Thomas	48	– (1) c Rhodes b Radford	7
*J. L. Langer lbw b Mirza	88	– (5) not out	72
R. T. Ponting not out	103	– c Moody b Lampitt	30
M. L. Love not out	53	– (3) lbw b Radford	21
S. Young (did not bat)		– run out	4
†A. C. Gilchrist (did not bat)		– c Rhodes b Lampitt	6
M. S. Kasprowicz (did not bat)		– c Haynes b Lampitt	0
B. A. Williams (did not bat)		– c Spiring b Thomas	23
S. P. George (did not bat)		– lbw b Radford	29
P. E. McIntyre (did not bat)		– not out	2
L-b 9, n-b 24	33	L-b 7, n-b 12	19

1/26 2/111 3/221   (3 wkts dec.) 332   1/8 2/20 3/38   (9 wkts) 220
                                      4/106 5/116 6/128
                                      7/128 8/163 9/203

Bowling: *First Innings*—Radford 19.5–5–81–1; Thomas 16–3–57–1; Lampitt 12–1–48–0;
Mirza 16–3–63–1; Haynes 10–1–45–0; Weston 5–0–29–0. *Second Innings*—Radford
12–2–45–3; Thomas 11–0–75–2; Mirza 10–2–41–0; Lampitt 11–3–52–3; Moody 1–1–0–0.

Umpires: P. Adams and A. G. T. Whitehead.

†At Cheltenham, July 26. Gloucestershire won by two wickets. Toss: Young Australia.
Young Australia 262 for four (48 overs) (M. T. G. Elliott 51, M. L. Hayden 46, S. G. Law
76 not out, M. L. Love 49); Gloucestershire 265 for eight (47.3 overs) (M. W. Alleyne 102
not out, A. Symonds 50, R. I. Dawson 39; B. A. Williams three for 57).

HAMPSHIRE v YOUNG AUSTRALIA

At Southampton, July 28, 29, 30. Young Australia won by ten wickets. Toss: Young
Australia.
The TCCB had allowed four days for this match, but the fourth was redundant: Hampshire were outclassed, and only greater resolve in their second innings averted utter
humiliation. Though they extracted Elliott without a run on the board, their attack was
taken apart by Hayden and Law, who shared a brilliant partnership of 239. Law scored

particularly quickly, with 134 from 158 balls, and declared on the second morning at 527. But Hampshire's response was pitiful. From 51 for one, they just scraped into three figures and needed 427 to avoid an innings defeat. Terry batted doggedly for three and a half hours, with solid support from Stephenson, and Streak made a forceful 69 in 76 balls to avert that ignominy. But Young Australia needed only 20 for victory and a day off.

Close of play: First day, Young Australia 408-4 (J. L. Langer 31*, R. T. Ponting 33*); Second day, Hampshire 126-1 (V. P. Terry 61*, J. P. Stephenson 47*).

Young Australia

M. T. G. Elliott lbw b Connor	0	– (2) not out	3
M. L. Hayden c James b Connor	146	– (1) not out	18
M. L. Love c Stephenson b Udal	42		
*S. G. Law lbw b Dibden	134		
J. L. Langer c Connor b Streak	32		
R. T. Ponting lbw b Udal	87		
†A. C. Gilchrist c Whitaker b Dibden	62		
M. S. Kasprowicz not out	0		
B 7, l-b 8, w 3, n-b 6	24		

1/0 2/71 3/310 4/367 5/418 (7 wkts dec.) 527	(no wkt) 21
6/521 7/527	

J. Angel, P. E. McIntyre and M. A. Harrity did not bat.

Bowling: First Innings—Connor 23-3-121-2; Streak 22-1-70-1; Udal 26-3-116-2; Stephenson 12-1-45-0; Dibden 25.3-10-62-2; James 20-3-98-0. *Second Innings*—Udal 3-2-5-0; Dibden 2.4-0-16-0.

Hampshire

V. P. Terry c Ponting b Angel	26	– c McIntyre b Elliott	104
J. S. Laney lbw b Harrity	5	– c Law b Angel	5
J. P. Stephenson c Gilchrist b Harrity	30	– lbw b McIntyre	89
P. R. Whitaker c Elliott b Kasprowicz	6	– c Gilchrist b Kasprowicz	24
†A. N. Aymes b Angel	1	– (7) c Gilchrist b Kasprowicz	61
K. D. James c Gilchrist b Kasprowicz	2	– c Gilchrist b Angel	34
S. D. Udal c Angel b Kasprowicz	8	– (8) c Harrity b Kasprowicz	1
*M. C. J. Nicholas st Gilchrist b McIntyre	7	– (5) c Law b McIntyre	6
H. H. Streak not out	4	– b McIntyre	69
C. A. Connor lbw b Kasprowicz	5	– c Langer b Angel	32
R. R. Dibden c Gilchrist b Kasprowicz	0	– not out	0
B 1, l-b 1, n-b 4	6	B 1, l-b 9, w 3, n-b 8	21

1/7 2/51 3/71 4/71 5/74 100	1/8 2/207 3/221 4/241 5/245 446
6/74 7/91 8/91 9/96	6/312 7/314 8/388 9/446

Bowling: First Innings—Harrity 10-3-27-2; Angel 13-3-36-2; McIntyre 5-0-16-1; Kasprowicz 8.1-4-19-5. *Second Innings*—Harrity 15-5-35-0; Angel 23-8-54-3; Kasprowicz 34-9-120-3; McIntyre 43.1-11-175-3; Ponting 7-0-29-0; Elliott 7-2-23-1.

Umpires: R. Palmer and P. Willey.

LEICESTERSHIRE v YOUNG AUSTRALIA

At Leicester, August 3, 4. Leicestershire won by four wickets. Toss: Young Australia.

Young Australia arrived at Grace Road with an unbeaten first-class record and a reputation for big scores. Both looked shaky after they were bowled out on a good pitch for 220, their lowest completed total of the tour so far, on the first day, and they were blown away on the second. Leicestershire's hero was 21-year-old left-arm pace bowler Sheriyar, who had been plagued by no-ball trouble for most of the season. He took ten wickets in the match, including a career-best six for 30 in the second innings, when he started with four for eight in 16 balls. The Australians staggered from 20 for five to 146 all out, leaving a target of only 44. But Kasprowicz and Williams nearly turned the match on its head, reducing Leicestershire to 36 for six, before a no-ball in the 15th over ended the tension. The county had flourished in their first innings, especially Whitaker, who returned after an ankle injury to score his third century of 1995.

Close of play: First day, Leicestershire 196-3 (B. F. Smith 16*, A. R. K. Pierson 2*).

Young Australia

M. T. G. Elliott lbw b Mullally	7	– (2) c Nixon b Sheriyar	50
M. L. Hayden c and b Pierson	49	– (1) c Whitaker b Sheriyar	4
J. L. Langer lbw b Mullally	7	– lbw b Sheriyar	0
R. T. Ponting c Sutcliffe b Sheriyar	4	– c Nixon b Sheriyar	1
*S. G. Law c Sheriyar b Cronje	36	– c Nixon b Sheriyar	3
S. Young lbw b Brimson	62	– c Whitaker b Mullally	2
†A. C. Gilchrist c Nixon b Sheriyar	29	– b Mullally	48
B. A. Williams b Sheriyar	2	– c sub (V. P. Clarke) b Mullally	0
M. S. Kasprowicz c and b Brimson	7	– c Whitaker b Mullally	4
J. Angel not out	1	– not out	24
P. E. McIntyre b Sheriyar	0	– c Nixon b Sheriyar	1
B 8, n-b 8	16	L-b 5, n-b 4	9

1/10 2/18 3/43 4/107 5/111　　　　　　220　　1/7 2/7 3/11 4/17 5/20　　　　146
6/184 7/208 8/212 9/218　　　　　　　　　　 6/106 7/106 8/110 9/130

Bowling: First Innings—Mullally 14-2-61-2; Sheriyar 11-2-55-4; Wells 5-1-25-0; Cronje 4-0-10-1; Pierson 13-2-47-1; Brimson 5-1-14-2. *Second Innings*—Mullally 13-2-51-4; Sheriyar 11.3-3-30-6; Wells 3-0-20-0; Pierson 4-0-26-0; Cronje 4-2-2-0; Brimson 2-0-12-0.

Leicestershire

*J. J. Whitaker b Angel	103	– (6) b Kasprowicz	4
I. J. Sutcliffe c Young b Kasprowicz	0		
W. J. Cronje b Angel	53	– b Kasprowicz	8
B. F. Smith c Elliott b Angel	44	– c Gilchrist b Kasprowicz	6
A. R. K. Pierson c Gilchrist b Williams	38	– (7) not out	9
V. J. Wells c and b Angel	1	– (1) c Langer b Williams	4
A. Habib b Law b McIntyre	48	– (2) not out	4
†P. A. Nixon lbw b McIntyre	1	– (5) c Elliott b Williams	1
A. D. Mullally lbw b Kasprowicz	0	– (8) c Angel b Kasprowicz	0
M. T. Brimson not out	0		
A. Sheriyar c Law b McIntyre	2		
B 12, l-b 10, w 1, n-b 10	33	L-b 1, n-b 4	5

1/4 2/137 3/192 4/238 5/242　　　　323　　1/12 2/22 3/25　　(6 wkts) 45
6/311 7/318 8/321 9/321　　　　　　　　　　 4/30 5/36 6/36

In the second innings A. Habib, when 0, retired hurt at 1 and resumed at 36-6.

Bowling: First Innings—Williams 17-4-51-1; Kasprowicz 16-4-57-2; Angel 19-4-93-4; Young 9-1-42-0; McIntyre 20.3-6-58-3. *Second Innings*—Williams 7-1-27-2; Kasprowicz 7-1-17-4.

Umpires: J. D. Bond and P. B. Wight.

†At Leicester, August 5. Young Australia won by 57 runs. Toss: Young Australia. Young Australia 236 for six (38 overs) (M. L. Hayden 103, R. T. Ponting 63; A. R. K. Pierson three for 41); Leicestershire 179 for nine (38 overs) (P. E. Robinson 75, J. J. Whitaker 40; M. S. Kasprowicz three for 27).

†At The Oval, August 8. Young Australia won by 179 runs. Toss: Young Australia. Young Australia 322 for six (55 overs) (M. L. Love 30, S. G. Law 163, R. T. Ponting 71); Surrey 143 (29 overs) (N. Shahid 63; S. Young five for 39).

SUSSEX v YOUNG AUSTRALIA

At Hove, August 11, 12, 13. Young Australia won by nine wickets. Toss: Young Australia.

Sussex had sensationally beaten the West Indians by an innings in July but, four Championship defeats later, they were no match for the well-drilled Australians. Two 20-year-old Sussex players could look back proudly, though: Danny Law completed a maiden century in 89 balls and Alex Edwards, on his first-class debut for the county, was the most successful home bowler. The bowling was too wayward, too often, however, as Young Australia rattled up 580 on a Hove shirtfront. Hayden batted throughout the first day and added 261 with fellow left-hander Langer. With Wells resting, Sussex collapsed horribly and followed on 471 behind. But they did better at their second attempt. Lenham hit 94 and then Law tore into the Australian attack, reaching fifty in just 40 balls and thumping three sixes and 18 fours, while Phillips joined in the fun with 53. At least they made the tourists bat again – and Law dismissed Hayden in the first over.

Close of play: First day, Young Australia 421-3 (M. L. Hayden 178*, J. L. Langer 113*); Second day, Sussex 74-0 (C. W. J. Athey 34*, M. T. E. Peirce 33*).

Young Australia

M. T. G. Elliott c Moores b Edwards	79	– (2) not out	1
M. L. Hayden lbw b Lewry	178	– (1) lbw b Law	0
M. L. Love c Moores b Edwards	9	– not out	5
*S. G. Law c Lewry b Giddins	25		
J. L. Langer b Phillips	149		
S. Young b Lewry	8		
†A. C. Gilchrist not out	64		
P. E. McIntyre c Moores b Edwards	0		
B. A. Williams c Phillips b Lewry	19		
J. Angel not out	29		
B 4, l-b 5, w 3, n-b 8	20	L-b 1, n-b 2	3

1/117 2/137 3/173 4/434 5/442   (8 wkts dec.) 580 1/0   (1 wkt) 9
6/471 7/472 8/510

M. A. Harrity did not bat.

Bowling: First Innings—Lewry 31–4–139–3; Giddins 22–6–75–1; Law 13–0–73–0; Edwards 22–4–83–3; Phillips 40–11–157–1; Lenham 4–0–17–0; Peirce 3–0–16–0; Greenfield 4–0–11–0. *Second Innings*—Law 1.3–0–4–1; Edwards 1–0–4–0.

Sussex

C. W. J. Athey lbw b Angel	20	– c Gilchrist b Williams	40
M. T. E. Peirce c Young b Williams	1	– lbw b McIntyre	44
N. J. Lenham lbw b McIntyre	21	– c Love b Angel	94
J. W. Hall c Angel b Young	7	– b Harrity	26
K. Greenfield c Gilchrist b Harrity	24	– c Young b Angel	6
*†P. Moores b Williams	4	– c Love b Young	41
D. R. Law run out	8	– c Gilchrist b Angel	115
A. D. Edwards c Love b McIntyre	1	– c Law b Young	22
N. C. Phillips b Harrity	0	– b Harrity	53
J. D. Lewry c Law b McIntyre	5	– b Angel	6
E. S. H. Giddins not out	10	– not out	0
B 1, l-b 3, n-b 4	8	B 9, l-b 14, w 3, n-b 6	32

1/5 2/26 3/49 4/54 5/67   109   1/82 2/98 3/160 4/179 5/257   479
6/89 7/92 8/94 9/99   6/302 7/389 8/469 9/477

Bowling: First Innings—Williams 10–4–21–2; Harrity 12.1–3–33–2; Angel 8–4–13–1; Young 5–0–15–1; McIntyre 11–6–23–3. *Second Innings*—Williams 19–2–70–1; Harrity 29–7–131–2; McIntyre 38–4–143–1; Angel 25.4–5–68–4; Young 16–5–44–2.

Umpires: B. J. Meyer and K. E. Palmer.

TCCB XI v YOUNG AUSTRALIA

At Birmingham, August 17, 18. Young Australia won by nine wickets. Toss: TCCB XI.

The planned climax of the tour was an embarrassing disappointment. Like the Edgbaston Test in July, the match finished with more than two days to spare and, again, the pitch took the blame. Dry, dusty and unpredictable, it was reported by the umpires after 16 wickets fell on the first day. The tourists already had reason to feel deprived of the contest they deserved. The supposedly representative TCCB XI drew only from counties without a Championship fixture. Surrey withdrew bowler Alex Tudor for a Second Eleven game and Paul Taylor of Northamptonshire preferred to play in a benefit match; he was later fined by his county. Morris chose to bat but was forced off in Young's first over when he was struck on the left thumb. Young then took three wickets in 18 balls and, though Morris returned to hit 47, steering the innings close to 200, leg-spinner McIntyre wrapped it up. The Australians also struggled against Capel's seam and Croft's off-spin. But their captain, Law, batted two hours for a match-winning 70, with unexpected support from Kasprowicz, who hit an unbeaten 43 in 46 balls. When the TCCB XI resumed, 67 behind, Angel had two men caught behind in his first three balls and a third in his second over. Gilchrist eventually completed ten dismissals in the match, the best wicket-keeping performance of the summer. Again, Morris led the resistance, holding out for 66 minutes. But the Australians knocked off 35 by tea. Their reward was two free days in Birmingham.

Close of play: First day, Young Australia 158-6 (S. G. Law 33*, J. Angel 12*).

TCCB XI

*H. Morris not out.	47	– (7) st Gilchrist b McIntyre	29
M. A. Butcher c Gilchrist b Young	25	– (1) c Gilchrist b Angel.	0
M. P. Maynard c Law b Young	21	– c Gilchrist b Angel	0
A. J. Hollioake c Gilchrist b Young	0	– c Gilchrist b Angel	5
P. A. Cottey lbw b Kasprowicz	12	– c Gilchrist b Kasprowicz	8
D. J. Capel c Gilchrist b Kasprowicz	23	– c Harrity b Kasprowicz	6
R. D. B. Croft st Gilchrist b McIntyre	13	– (8) c Ponting b Kasprowicz	19
†P. A. Nixon c Langer b McIntyre	20	– (2) c McIntyre b Angel	14
A. R. K. Pierson c Law b McIntyre	1	– not out.	9
A. D. Mullally lbw b McIntyre	0	– c Law b McIntyre	0
A. Sheriyar c Law b McIntyre	0	– st Gilchrist b McIntyre	0
B 7, l-b 13, w 1, n-b 8	29	B 2, l-b 4, w 3, n-b 2	11

1/58 2/62 3/75 4/94 5/121   191   1/0 2/0 3/11 4/33 5/33   101
6/131 7/132 8/173 9/173   6/50 7/71 8/101 9/101

In the first innings H. Morris, when 11, retired hurt at 45 and resumed at 132.

Bowling: *First Innings*—Angel 10–2–31–0; Kasprowicz 20–3–63–2; Harrity 9–4–16–0; Young 10–4–23–3; McIntyre 18.2–8–38–5. *Second Innings*—Angel 11–2–31–4; Harrity 6–0–18–0; Kasprowicz 7–3–29–3; McIntyre 4–0–17–3.

Young Australia

M. L. Hayden c and b Capel	33	– (2) not out.	24
M. L. Love lbw b Capel	28	– (1) c Maynard b Mullally	0
J. L. Langer c Butcher b Capel	4	– not out.	8
R. T. Ponting b Croft	24		
*S. G. Law st Nixon b Croft	70		
S. Young lbw b Croft	1		
†A. C. Gilchrist c and b Pierson	5		
J. Angel lbw b Pierson	28		
M. S. Kasprowicz not out	43		
P. E. McIntyre c Capel b Croft	2		
M. A. Harrity lbw b Croft	0		
B 4, l-b 12, n-b 4.	20	L-b 2, w 1	3

1/66 2/72 3/91 4/121 5/129   258   1/0   (1 wkt) 35
6/136 7/194 8/252 9/258

Bowling: *First Innings*—Mullally 12–1–45–0; Sheriyar 4–0–24–0; Capel 9–1–40–3; Croft 16.5–3–58–5; Pierson 15–1–75–2. *Second Innings*—Mullally 4.4–2–9–1; Sheriyar 3–0–18–0; Croft 1–0–6–0.

Umpires: B. Leadbeater and R. A. White.

BRITANNIC ASSURANCE
COUNTY CHAMPIONSHIP, 1995

Of its nature, the County Championship is largely routine. In 1995 it came as near as it can ever get to being an epic. It ended with Warwickshire retaining the title they won in 1994 and thus becoming champions for the fifth time, which is what the bookmakers and many pundits expected. However, they secured the Championship only on the penultimate day of the season, having been harried to the end by Middlesex and Northamptonshire, who both had summers that would normally have made them winners and, very likely, easy winners.

It was an exceptionally hot and dry summer; the four-day matches were often played on three-day wickets; and there was no incentive – and not much evidence of ability or inclination – for teams who were losing a game to attempt to hold out. This meant an unprecedented proportion of games were played to a finish. Only 29 of the 153 Championship matches were drawn – less than 19 per cent, easily the lowest in any post-war season.

More often than not, between 1967 and the tentative introduction of four-day cricket in 1988, more than half were drawn. Two counties, Essex and Durham, went through the season without a single draw, a feat last achieved – with more dramatic effect – by Surrey when they were champions in 1955. Of the 124 matches that did produce a result, 48 finished inside three days (five of these in two). Hampshire did not stretch a game until the Monday, win or lose, until the second half of June.

Warwickshire drew only one of their games, and they won 14, giving them a win percentage of 82.35 per cent, which is the best ever. Surrey in 1955, when they won 23 and lost five, held the previous record of 82.14 per cent. But their two main rivals both had records above 70 per cent.

BRITANNIC ASSURANCE CHAMPIONSHIP

Win = 16 pts	Played	Won	Lost	Drawn	Bonus points Batting	Bowling	Points
1 – Warwickshire (1)....	17	14	2	1	49	64	337
2 – Middlesex (4).......	17	12	2	3	51	62	305
3 – Northamptonshire (5)	17	12	2	3	41	57	290
4 – Lancashire (10)	17	10	4	3	48	61	269
5 – Essex (6)	17	8	9	0	42	58	228
6 – Gloucestershire (12) .	17	8	4	5	45	50	223
7 – Leicestershire (2)....	17	7	8	2	41	61	214
8 – Yorkshire (13)	17	7	8	2	39	55	206
9 – Somerset (11).......	17	7	5	5	40	49	201
10 – Worcestershire (15)..	17	6	7	4	29	57	182
11 – Nottinghamshire (3) .	17	5	9	3	41	54	175
12 – Surrey (7).........	17	5	8	4	34	55	169
13 – Hampshire (13)	17	5	8	4	32	56	168
14 – Derbyshire (17).....	17	4	10	3	39	64	167
15 – Sussex (8)..........	17	4	7	6	37	51	152
16 – Glamorgan (18).....	17	3	8	6	40	57	145
17 – Durham (16)	17	4	13	0	20	53	137
18 – Kent (9)..........	17	3	10	4	40	44	132

1994 positions are shown in brackets.

The champions were comparatively rusty early on. But they still won four of their first five matches. And from late June onwards they won every match – and all by huge margins – except one. That was the confrontation against Northamptonshire at Edgbaston, universally regarded as one of the greatest of all Championship matches, which shifted from one side to the other until Northamptonshire eventually scrambled home by seven runs. This meant that Warwickshire started August with a lead of two points rather than 34, and kept the door ajar until the very last match.

The team pushing longest were Middlesex, who in mid-June were lying in eighth place but won their next eight matches, a feat last achieved – once again – by Surrey in 1955. As with Warwickshire, the margins varied from the convincing to the overwhelming.

Northamptonshire also kept in the hunt but their wins looked altogether less pre-ordained. They conjured up a succession of victories, some of which surpassed the improbable and became almost unbelievable. They were bowled out for the two lowest scores of the season, 46 against Essex and 59 against Surrey, but won both matches. And they won an even more amazing game against Nottinghamshire, when they conceded 527 then rattled up 781 for seven before declaring and rolling over the opposition to win by an innings.

However, they then had to play Middlesex at Uxbridge and the two teams, overwhelmed by the pressure, fought each other to a standstill and allowed Warwickshire to go clear. Middlesex secured a one-run win over Leicestershire which forced the planned celebrations at Edgbaston to be postponed, but Warwickshire's three-day win at Canterbury in the last match finally settled matters.

Lancashire had the satisfaction of beating all the top three counties and early on, when they were in blistering form, they looked very probable champions. But they were not quite consistent enough in such a season, and crucial defeats against Gloucestershire and Yorkshire prevented them getting into the shake-up. They were, however, a very clear fourth, well ahead of Essex, who won their last five matches to race into fifth place, and Gloucestershire, whose reshaped squad played with great spirit to become the surprise team of the season.

Leicestershire often looked bad in defeat but produced enough victories to come seventh, ahead of Yorkshire, where the pre-season optimism lasted longer than normal – they won their first three matches – but evaporated in the end. Somerset started badly then won four matches in June before settling in mid-table. Worcestershire were even more extreme: all their six wins came in June and July. Nottinghamshire, widely tipped as possible champions, never threatened and lost their last six matches. Surrey, wracked by internal turmoil, were bottom until beating Nottinghamshire at Guildford in July and quite relieved to finish 12th.

Hampshire lost their first three matches, won their next three, and achieved little after that. The five teams below them all flirted with the wooden spoon. Derbyshire had big wins to begin and end the season but long, arid stretches in between. Sussex went three months without a win between late May and late August, almost as long as Glamorgan's blank run – they won their two opening matches to lead the table then fell steadily to earth until they had the good fortune to meet Nottinghamshire in their penultimate match.

The same luck with the fixtures saved Durham from last place. Their innings win over Nottinghamshire in the final round of matches lifted them ahead of Kent, who came last for the first time in exactly 100 years. But their more blinkered supporters were so busy celebrating success in the Sunday League they hardly even noticed.

Under the TCCB playing conditions, two extras were scored for every no-ball bowled whether scored off or not. Any runs scored off the bat were credited to the batsman, while byes and leg-byes were counted as no-balls, in accordance with Law 24.9, in addition to the initial penalty.

Pre-season betting (William Hill): 9-2 WARWICKSHIRE; 6-1 Middlesex; 13-2 Lancashire; 15-2 Essex; 8-1 Surrey; 9-1 Nottinghamshire; 11-1 Northamptonshire; 12-1 Kent and Worcestershire; 16-1 Leicestershire; 18-1 Yorkshire; 22-1 Sussex; 28-1 Somerset; 33-1 Derbyshire and Hampshire; 40-1 Glamorgan; 50-1 Gloucestershire; 80-1 Durham.

Leaders: from May 8 Glamorgan; May 15 Northamptonshire; July 10 Northamptonshire and Warwickshire; July 24 Warwickshire; August 7 Northamptonshire; August 21 Middlesex; September 1 onwards Warwickshire. Warwickshire became champions on September 16.

Bottom place: from May 8 Worcestershire; May 15 Hampshire; May 22 Worcestershire; June 12 Durham; June 26 Derbyshire; July 3 Surrey; July 24 Sussex; August 21 Durham; September 18 Kent.

Prize money

First (Warwickshire)	£55,000
Second (Middlesex)	£27,500
Third (Northamptonshire)	£15,000
Fourth (Lancashire)	£7,750
Fifth (Essex)	£4,000
Winner of each match	£750

Scoring of Points

(*a*) For a win, 16 points plus any points scored in the first innings.

(*b*) In a tie, each side scores eight points, plus any points scored in the first innings.

(*c*) If the scores are equal in a drawn match, the side batting in the fourth innings scores eight points, plus any points scored in the first innings.

(*d*) First-innings points (awarded only for performances in the first 120 overs of each first innings and retained whatever the result of the match).

   (i) A maximum of four batting points to be available: 200 to 249 runs – 1 point; 250 to 299 runs – 2 points; 300 to 349 – 3 points; 350 runs or over – 4 points.

   (ii) A maximum of four bowling points to be available: 3 or 4 wickets taken – 1 point; 5 or 6 wickets taken – 2 points; 7 or 8 wickets taken – 3 points; 9 or 10 wickets taken – 4 points.

(*e*) If play starts when less than eight hours' playing time remains and a one-innings match is played, no first-innings points shall be scored. The side winning on the one innings scores 12 points. In a tie, each side scores six points. If the scores are equal in a drawn match, the side batting in the second innings scores six points.

(*f*) A county which is adjudged to have prepared a pitch unsuitable for first-class cricket shall be liable to have 25 points deducted. In addition, a penalty of ten or 15 points may in certain circumstances be imposed on a county in respect of a poor pitch.

(*g*) The side which has the highest aggregate of points shall be the Champion County. Should any sides in the Championship table be equal on points the side with most wins will have priority.

CHAMPION COUNTY SINCE 1864

Note: The earliest county champions were decided usually by the fewest matches lost, but in 1888 an unofficial points system was introduced. In 1890, the Championship was constituted officially. From 1977 to 1983 it was sponsored by Schweppes, and since 1984 by Britannic Assurance.

Unofficial champions

1864	Surrey	·1901	Yorkshire	1953	Surrey
1865	Nottinghamshire	1902	Yorkshire	1954	Surrey
1866	Middlesex	1903	Middlesex	1955	Surrey
1867	Yorkshire	1904	Lancashire	1956	Surrey
1868	Nottinghamshire	1905	Yorkshire	1957	Surrey
1869 {	Nottinghamshire / Yorkshire	1906	Kent	1958	Surrey
		1907	Nottinghamshire	1959	Yorkshire
1870	Yorkshire	1908	Yorkshire	1960	Yorkshire
1871	Nottinghamshire	1909	Kent	1961	Hampshire
1872	Nottinghamshire	1910	Kent	1962	Yorkshire
1873 {	Gloucestershire / Nottinghamshire	1911	Warwickshire	1963	Yorkshire
		1912	Yorkshire	1964	Worcestershire
1874	Gloucestershire	1913	Kent	1965	Worcestershire
1875	Nottinghamshire	1914	Surrey	1966	Yorkshire
1876	Gloucestershire	1919	Yorkshire	1967	Yorkshire
1877	Gloucestershire	1920	Middlesex	1968	Yorkshire
1878	Undecided	1921	Middlesex	1969	Glamorgan
1879 {	Nottinghamshire / Lancashire	1922	Yorkshire	1970	Kent
		1923	Yorkshire	1971	Surrey
1880	Nottinghamshire	1924	Yorkshire	1972	Warwickshire
1881	Lancashire	1925	Yorkshire	1973	Hampshire
1882 {	Nottinghamshire / Lancashire	1926	Lancashire	1974	Worcestershire
		1927	Lancashire	1975	Leicestershire
1883	Nottinghamshire	1928	Lancashire	1976	Middlesex
1884	Nottinghamshire	1929	Nottinghamshire	1977 {	Middlesex / Kent
1885	Nottinghamshire	1930	Lancashire		
1886	Nottinghamshire	1931	Yorkshire	1978	Kent
1887	Surrey	1932	Yorkshire	1979	Essex
1888	Surrey	1933	Yorkshire	1980	Middlesex
1889 {	Surrey / Lancashire / Nottinghamshire	1934	Lancashire	1981	Nottinghamshire
		1935	Yorkshire	1982	Middlesex
		1936	Derbyshire	1983	Essex
Official champions		1937	Yorkshire	1984	Essex
1890	Surrey	1938	Yorkshire	1985	Middlesex
1891	Surrey	1939	Yorkshire	1986	Essex
1892	Surrey	1946	Yorkshire	1987	Nottinghamshire
1893	Yorkshire	1947	Middlesex	1988	Worcestershire
1894	Surrey	1948	Glamorgan	1989	Worcestershire
1895	Surrey	1949 {	Middlesex / Yorkshire	1990	Middlesex
1896	Yorkshire			1991	Essex
1897	Lancashire	1950 {	Lancashire / Surrey	1992	Essex
1898	Yorkshire			1993	Middlesex
1899	Surrey	1951	Warwickshire	1994	Warwickshire
1900	Yorkshire	1952	Surrey	1995	Warwickshire

Notes: The title has been won outright as follows: Yorkshire 31 times, Surrey 18, Nottinghamshire 14, Middlesex 11, Lancashire 8, Essex and Kent 6, Warwickshire and Worcestershire 5, Gloucestershire 3, Glamorgan and Hampshire 2, Derbyshire and Leicestershire 1.

Since the championship was constituted officially in 1890 it has been won outright as follows: Yorkshire 29 times, Surrey 15, Middlesex 10, Lancashire 7, Essex and Kent 6, Warwickshire and Worcestershire 5, Nottinghamshire 4, Glamorgan and Hampshire 2, Derbyshire and Leicestershire 1.

The title has been shared eight times as follows: Nottinghamshire 5, Lancashire 4, Middlesex, Surrey and Yorkshire 2, Gloucestershire and Kent 1. Only three of these instances have occurred since 1890, involving Middlesex twice, Kent, Lancashire, Surrey and Yorkshire.

Wooden Spoons: Since the major expansion of the Championship from nine teams to 14 in 1895, the counties have finished outright bottom as follows: Derbyshire, Northamptonshire and Somerset 11; Glamorgan 9; Nottinghamshire 8; Leicestershire 7; Gloucestershire, Sussex and Worcestershire 6; Hampshire 5; Warwickshire 3; Durham and Kent 2; Essex and Yorkshire 1. Lancashire, Middlesex and Surrey have never finished bottom. Leicestershire have also shared bottom place twice, once with Hampshire and once with Somerset.

BRITANNIC ASSURANCE CHAMPIONSHIP
STATISTICS FOR 1995

County	Runs	For Wickets	Avge	Runs	Against Wickets	Avge
Derbyshire	8,598	294	29.24	8,147	285	28.58
Durham	7,233	299	24.19	8,877	228	38.93
Essex	9,784	308	31.76	9,047	291	31.08
Glamorgan	9,112	272	33.50	9,236	249	37.09
Gloucestershire	8,541	254	33.62	8,109	268	30.25
Hampshire	7,957	275	28.93	8,340	264	31.59
Kent	8,977	284	31.60	9,336	241	38.73
Lancashire	8,700	254	34.25	8,150	284	28.69
Leicestershire	8,163	273	29.90	8,266	252	32.80
Middlesex	8,657	214	40.45	8,047	308	26.12
Northamptonshire	8,605	241	35.70	8,678	312	27.81
Nottinghamshire	8,580	291	29.48	9,701	244	39.75
Somerset	9,797	263	37.25	9,142	248	36.86
Surrey	9,588	297	32.28	9,514	286	33.26
Sussex	7,855	278	28.25	8,109	242	33.50
Warwickshire	8,279	212	39.05	7,228	312	23.16
Worcestershire	8,721	260	33.54	8,991	251	35.82
Yorkshire	8,137	254	32.03	8,366	258	32.42
	155,284	4,823	32.19	155,284	4,823	32.19

COUNTY CHAMPIONSHIP – MATCH RESULTS, 1864-1995

County	Years of Play	Played	Won	Lost	Tied	Drawn
Derbyshire	1871-87; 1895-1995	2,207	545	806	1	855
Durham	1992-1995	73	12	43	0	18
Essex	1895-1995	2,169	626	627	5	911
Glamorgan	1921-1995	1,704	370	584	0	750
Gloucestershire	1870-1995	2,443	721	905	2	815
Hampshire	1864-85; 1895-1995	2,279	594	785	4	896
Kent	1864-1995	2,567	925	778	5	859
Lancashire	1865-1995	2,645	983	550	3	1,109
Leicestershire	1895-1995	2,137	472	796	1	868
Middlesex	1864-1995	2,347	880	588	5	874
Northamptonshire	1905-1995	1,904	470	663	3	768
Nottinghamshire	1864-1995	2,476	756	653	1	1,066
Somerset	1882-85; 1891-1995	2,177	514	879	3	781
Surrey	1864-1995	2,724	1,073	608	4	1,039
Sussex	1864-1995	2,616	728	899	6	983
Warwickshire	1895-1995	2,150	581	626	1	942
Worcestershire	1899-1995	2,091	521	728	2	840
Yorkshire	1864-1995	2,744	1,218	471	2	1,053
Cambridgeshire	1864-69; 1871	19	8	8	0	3
		19,736	11,997	11,997	24	7,715

Notes: Matches abandoned without a ball bowled are wholly excluded.

Counties participated in the years shown, except that there were no matches in the years 1915-18 and 1940-45; Hampshire did not play inter-county matches in 1868-69, 1871-74 and 1879; Worcestershire did not take part in the Championship in 1919.

OVERS BOWLED AND RUNS SCORED IN THE BRITANNIC ASSURANCE CHAMPIONSHIP, 1995

County	Over-rate per hour	Run-rate/ 100 balls
Derbyshire (14)	18.67	55.23
Durham (17)	17.92†	50.33
Essex (5)	18.34*	55.60
Glamorgan (16)	18.94	57.42
Gloucestershire (6)	18.04*	55.34
Hampshire (13)	17.55†	50.13
Kent (18)	18.18*	55.17
Lancashire (4)	18.61	54.14
Leicestershire (7)	17.65†	52.98
Middlesex (2)	19.22	59.08
Northamptonshire (3)	18.26*	55.72
Nottinghamshire (11)	18.51	49.00
Somerset (9)	18.59	52.75
Surrey (12)	17.06‡	54.41
Sussex (15)	18.04*	54.61
Warwickshire (1)	18.05*	52.51
Worcestershire (10)	18.04*	52.29
Yorkshire (8)	17.70†	52.05
1995 average rate	18.19	53.82

1995 Championship positions are shown in brackets.

* £4,000 fine.
† £6,000 fine.
‡ £8,000 fine.

SUMMARY OF RESULTS, 1995

	Derbyshire	Durham	Essex	Glamorgan	Gloucestershire	Hampshire	Kent	Lancashire	Leicestershire	Middlesex	Northamptonshire	Nottinghamshire	Somerset	Surrey	Sussex	Warwickshire	Worcestershire	Yorkshire
Derbyshire	—	L	L	W	L	W	D	W	L	D	L	L	L	L	W	L	D	L
Durham	W	—	L	W	L	W	L	L	L	L	L	W	L	L	L	L	L	L
Essex	W	W	—	W	L	W	L	L	L	L	L	L	L	L	L	W	L	W
Glamorgan	L	L	L	—	D	L	D	D	L	L	W	W	W	D	D	L	D	L
Gloucestershire	W	W	W	D	—	D	W	W	D	L	L	W	D	L	D	L	W	W
Hampshire	L	L	L	W	D	—	L	L	W	L	L	W	D	W	L	W	L	L
Kent	D	W	L	D	L	W	—	D	W	L	L	L	L	D	L	L	L	L
Lancashire	L	W	W	D	L	W	D	—	W	W	W	D	W	W	W	L	L	L
Leicestershire	W	W	W	W	D	L	L	L	—	L	L	D	W	W	W	L	W	W
Middlesex	D	W	W	W	W	W	W	L	W	—	D	W	D	W	W	L	W	W
Northamptonshire	W	W	W	L	D	W	L	W	D	—	W	W	W	D	W	W	W	W
Nottinghamshire	W	L	W	L	L	L	W	L	D	D	L	—	D	L	W	L	L	W
Somerset	W	W	W	L	D	D	W	D	L	L	L	D	L	—	D	L	W	D
Surrey	W	W	L	D	W	D	D	L	L	L	L	W	L	—	D	L	W	D
Sussex	L	W	W	D	D	L	W	L	L	L	D	L	L	D	—	D	W	D
Warwickshire	W	W	W	W	W	W	W	L	W	W	W	W	D	L	D	—	W	W
Worcestershire	D	W	L	D	L	L	W	W	W	L	L	W	D	W	L	L	—	D
Yorkshire	W	W	L	W	L	W	W	W	W	L	L	L	L	L	L	D	L	—

Home games in bold, away games in italics. W = Won, L = Lost, D = Drawn.

COUNTY CHAMPIONSHIP – FINAL POSITIONS, 1890-1995

	Derbyshire	Essex	Glamorgan	Gloucestershire	Hampshire	Kent	Lancashire	Leicestershire	Middlesex	Northamptonshire	Nottinghamshire	Somerset	Surrey	Sussex	Warwickshire	Worcestershire	Yorkshire
1890	—	—	—	6	—	3	2	—	7	—	5	—	1	8	—	—	3
1891	—	—	—	9	—	5	2	—	3	—	4	5	1	7	—	—	8
1892	—	—	—	7	—	7	4	—	5	—	2	3	1	9	—	—	6
1893	—	—	—	9	—	4	2	—	3	—	6	8	5	7	—	—	1
1894	—	—	—	9	—	4	4	—	3	—	7	6	1	8	—	—	2
1895	5	9	—	4	10	14	2	12	6	—	12	8	1	11	6	—	3
1896	7	5	—	10	8	9	2	13	3	—	6	11	4	14	12	—	1
1897	14	3	—	5	9	12	1	13	8	—	10	11	2	6	7	—	4
1898	9	5	—	3	12	7	6	13	2	—	8	13	4	9	9	—	1
1899	15	6	—	9	10	8	4	13	2	—	10	13	1	5	7	12	3
1900	13	10	—	7	15	3	2	14	7	—	5	11	7	3	6	12	1
1901	15	10	—	14	7	7	3	12	2	—	9	12	6	4	5	11	1
1902	10	13	—	14	15	7	5	11	12	—	3	7	4	2	6	9	1
1903	12	8	—	13	14	8	4	14	1	—	5	10	11	2	7	6	3
1904	10	14	—	9	15	3	1	7	4	—	5	12	11	6	7	13	2
1905	14	12	—	8	16	6	2	5	11	13	10	15	4	3	7	8	1
1906	16	7	—	9	8	1	4	15	11	11	5	11	3	10	6	14	2
1907	16	7	—	10	12	8	6	11	5	15	1	14	4	13	9	2	2
1908	14	11	—	10	9	2	7	13	4	15	8	16	3	5	12	6	1
1909	15	14	—	16	8	1	2	13	6	7	10	11	5	4	12	8	3
1910	15	11	—	12	6	1	4	10	3	9	5	16	2	7	14	13	8
1911	14	6	—	12	11	2	4	15	3	10	8	16	5	13	1	9	7
1912	12	15	—	11	6	3	4	13	5	2	8	14	7	10	9	16	1
1913	13	15	—	9	10	1	8	14	6	4	5	16	3	7	11	12	2
1914	12	8	—	16	5	3	11	13	2	9	10	15	1	6	7	14	4
1919	9	14	—	8	7	2	5	9	13	12	3	5	4	11	15	—	1
1920	16	9	—	8	11	5	2	13	1	14	7	10	3	6	12	15	4
1921	12	15	17	7	6	4	5	11	1	13	8	10	2	9	16	14	3
1922	11	8	16	13	6	4	5	14	7	15	2	10	3	9	12	17	1
1923	10	13	16	11	7	5	3	14	8	17	2	9	4	6	12	15	1
1924	17	15	13	6	12	5	4	11	2	16	6	8	3	10	9	14	1
1925	14	7	17	10	9	5	3	12	6	11	4	15	2	13	8	16	1
1926	11	9	8	15	7	3	1	13	6	16	4	14	5	10	12	17	2
1927	5	8	15	12	13	4	1	7	9	16	2	14	6	10	11	17	3
1928	10	16	15	5	12	2	1	9	8	13	3	14	6	7	11	17	4
1929	7	12	17	4	11	8	2	9	6	13	1	15	10	4	14	16	2
1930	9	6	11	2	13	5	1	12	16	17	4	13	8	7	15	10	3
1931	7	10	15	2	12	3	6	16	11	17	5	13	8	4	9	14	1
1932	10	14	15	13	8	3	6	12	10	16	4	7	5	2	9	17	1
1933	6	4	16	10	14	3	5	17	12	13	8	11	9	2	7	15	1
1934	3	8	13	7	14	5	1	12	10	17	9	15	11	2	4	16	5
1935	2	9	13	15	16	10	4	6	3	17	5	14	11	7	8	12	1
1936	1	9	16	4	10	8	11	15	2	17	5	7	6	14	13	12	3
1937	3	6	7	4	14	12	9	16	2	17	10	13	8	5	11	15	1
1938	5	6	16	10	14	9	4	15	2	17	12	7	3	8	13	11	1
1939	9	4	13	3	15	5	6	17	2	16	12	14	8	10	11	7	1
1946	15	8	6	5	10	6	3	11	2	16	13	4	11	17	14	8	1
1947	5	11	9	2	16	4	3	14	1	17	11	11	6	9	15	7	7
1948	6	13	1	8	9	15	5	11	3	17	14	12	2	16	7	10	4
1949	15	9	8	7	16	13	11	17	1	6	11	9	5	13	4	3	1

	Derbyshire	Durham	Essex	Glamorgan	Gloucestershire	Hampshire	Kent	Lancashire	Leicestershire	Middlesex	Northamptonshire	Nottinghamshire	Somerset	Surrey	Sussex	Warwickshire	Worcestershire	Yorkshire
1950	5	—	17	11	7	12	9	1	16	14	10	15	7	1	13	4	6	3
1951	11	—	8	5	12	9	16	3	15	7	13	17	14	6	10	1	4	2
1952	4	—	10	7	9	12	15	3	6	5	8	16	17	1	13	10	14	2
1953	6	—	12	10	6	14	16	3	3	5	11	8	17	1	2	9	15	12
1954	3	—	15	4	13	14	11	10	16	7	7	5	17	1	9	6	11	2
1955	8	—	14	16	12	3	13	9	6	5	7	11	17	1	4	9	15	2
1956	12	—	11	13	3	6	16	2	17	5	4	8	15	1	9	14	9	3
1957	4	—	5	9	12	13	14	6	17	7	2	15	8	1	9	11	16	3
1958	5	—	6	15	14	2	8	7	12	10	4	17	3	1	13	16	9	11
1959	7	—	9	6	2	8	13	5	16	10	11	17	12	3	15	4	14	1
1960	5	—	6	11	8	12	10	2	17	3	9	16	14	7	4	15	13	1
1961	7	—	6	14	5	1	11	13	9	3	16	17	10	15	8	12	4	2
1962	7	—	9	14	4	10	11	16	17	13	8	15	6	5	12	3	2	1
1963	7	—	17	12	2	8	10	13	15	6	6	9	3	11	4	4	14	1
1964	12	—	10	11	17	12	7	14	16	6	3	15	8	4	9	2	1	5
1965	9	—	15	3	10	12	5	13	14	6	2	17	7	8	16	11	1	4
1966	9	—	16	14	14	15	11	4	12	8	12	5	17	3	7	6	2	1
1967	6	—	15	14	17	12	2	11	2	7	9	15	8	4	13	10	5	1
1968	8	—	14	3	16	5	2	6	9	13	4	12	15	17	7	4	12	1
1969	16	—	6	1	2	5	10	15	14	11	9	8	17	3	7	4	12	13
1970	7	—	12	2	17	10	1	3	15	16	14	11	13	5	9	7	6	4
1971	17	—	10	16	8	9	4	3	5	6	14	12	7	1	11	2	15	13
1972	17	—	5	13	3	9	2	15	6	8	4	14	11	12	16	1	7	10
1973	16	—	8	11	5	1	4	9	13	3	17	10	2	15	7	6	14	11
1974	17	—	12	6	14	2	10	8	4	6	3	15	5	7	13	9	1	11
1975	15	—	7	9	16	3	5	4	1	11	8	13	12	6	17	14	10	2
1976	15	—	6	17	3	12	14	16	4	1	9	13	7	9	10	5	11	8
1977	7	—	6	14	3	11	1	16	5	1	9	17	4	14	8	10	13	12
1978	14	—	2	13	10	8	1	12	6	3	17	7	5	16	9	11	15	4
1979	16	—	1	17	10	12	5	13	6	14	11	9	8	3	4	15	2	7
1980	9	—	8	13	7	17	16	15	10	1	12	3	5	2	4	14	11	6
1981	12	—	5	14	13	7	9	16	8	4	15	1	3	6	2	17	11	10
1982	11	—	7	16	15	3	13	12	2	1	9	4	6	5	8	17	14	10
1983	9	—	1	15	12	3	7	12	4	2	6	14	10	8	11	5	16	17
1984	12	—	1	13	17	15	5	16	4	3	11	2	7	8	6	9	10	14
1985	13	—	4	12	3	2	9	14	16	1	10	8	17	6	7	15	5	11
1986	11	—	1	17	2	6	8	15	7	12	9	4	16	3	14	12	5	10
1987	6	—	12	13	10	5	14	2	3	16	7	1	11	4	17	15	9	8
1988	14	—	3	17	10	15	2	9	8	7	12	5	11	4	16	6	1	13
1989	6	—	2	17	9	6	15	4	13	3	5	11	14	12	10	8	1	16
1990	12	—	2	8	13	3	16	6	7	1	11	13	15	9	17	5	4	10
1991	3	—	1	12	13	9	6	8	16	15	10	4	17	5	11	2	6	14
1992	5	18	1	14	10	15	2	12	8	11	3	4	9	13	7	6	17	16
1993	15	18	11	3	17	13	8	13	9	1	4	7	5	6	10	16	2	12
1994	17	16	6	18	12	13	9	10	2	4	5	3	11	7	8	1	15	13
1995	14	17	5	16	6	13	18	4	7	2	3	11	9	12	15	1	10	8

Note: From 1969 onwards, positions have been given in accordance with the Championship regulations which state that "Should *any* sides in the table be equal on points the side with most wins will have priority".

TCCB COUNTY PITCHES TABLE OF MERIT

First-Class Matches

		Points	Matches	Average in 1995	Average in 1994
1	Gloucestershire (15)	100	10	5.00	4.29
1	Hampshire (5)	100	10	5.00	4.70
3	Sussex (5)	98	10	4.90	4.70
4	Lancashire (14)	96	10	4.80	4.30
5	Surrey (2)	105	11	4.77	4.80
6	Yorkshire (7)	104	11	4.73	4.68
7	Essex (16)	94	10	4.70	4.11
8	Leicestershire (12)	100	11	4.55	4.39
8	Somerset (1)	100	11	4.55	4.90
10	Derbyshire (2)	81	9	4.50	4.80
11	Kent (18)	89	10	4.45	3.90
12	Glamorgan (11)	88	10	4.40	4.45
12	Northamptonshire (9)	88	10	4.40	4.56
14	Nottinghamshire (8)	77	9	4.28	4.64
15	Worcestershire (17)	82	10	4.10	4.09
16	Durham (9)	80	10	4.00	4.56
17	Middlesex (13)	95	12	3.96	4.56
17	Warwickshire (4)	95	12	3.96	4.75
	Oxford University	89	9	4.94	4.64
	Cambridge University	52	6	4.33	3.56

One-Day Matches

		Points	Matches	Average in 1995	Average in 1994
1	Sussex (10)	122	12	5.08	4.36
2	Surrey (3)	140	14	5.00	4.90
3	Nottinghamshire (1)	129	13	4.96	4.95
4	Hampshire (5)	108	11	4.91	4.59
5	Derbyshire (11)	97	10	4.85	4.32
6	Kent (8)	116	12	4.83	4.40
7	Essex (6)	125	13	4.81	4.56
8	Lancashire (4)	142	15	4.73	4.64
9	Warwickshire (12)	118	13	4.54	4.27
10	Somerset (1)	90	10	4.50	4.95
11	Yorkshire (13)	142	16	4.44	4.22
12	Gloucestershire (8)	115	13	4.42	4.40
13	Glamorgan (15)	121	14	4.32	4.05
14	Northamptonshire (16)	102	12	4.25	3.90
15	Middlesex (17)	106	13	4.08	3.88
16	Leicestershire (14)	97	12	4.04	4.14
17	Durham (7)	88	12	3.67	4.44
18	Worcestershire (18)	94	13	3.62	3.82
	Oxford University	10	1	5.00	4.00
	Cambridge University	19	2	4.75	—

In both tables 1994 positions are shown in brackets. Each umpire in a game marks the pitch on the following scale of merit: 6 – very good; 5 – good; 4 – above average; 3 – below average; 2 – poor; 1 – unfit.

The tables, provided by the TCCB, cover all major matches, including Tests etc., played on grounds under the county's jurisdiction. Middlesex pitches at Lord's are the responsibility of MCC.

DERBYSHIRE

President: G. L. Willatt
Chairman: M. A. Horton
Chairman, Cricket Committee: B. Holling
Secretary/General Manager: R. G. Taylor
Captain: 1995 – K. J. Barnett
        1996 – D. M. Jones
Coach: W. L. Stillman
Head Groundsman: S. Birks
Scorer: S. W. Tacey

Derbyshire won their first and last Championship matches so easily as to make their performances in the intervening months the more irritating. There was high individual achievement in Kim Barnett's last season as captain, most notably from Dominic Cork, but a lack of corporate effectiveness did not give the impression of a happy summer, despite perfect playing conditions for weeks on end. Cork's best bowling figures, nine for 43 on a swinging day against Northamptonshire, were soon followed by a Test debut at Lord's. Derbyshire players, as well as spectators, believed it to be overdue and Cork immediately gave substance to that theory. He was at home in the international game but, because he is such an intense cricketer, was often drained when he returned to the county and, for that reason, sometimes had to be rested.

Cork's arrival in Test cricket was at the expense of Phillip DeFreitas who, despite frequent recalls over the years, began to feel that his England career was at an end. DeFreitas bowled exceptionally well, often better than reflected in his figures, but it was late in the summer when his batting flourished. He withdrew briefly from cricket because his daughter Alex was severely scalded in a domestic accident. Devon Malcolm, awarded a benefit in 1997, also lost his England place before his inevitable return at The Oval. As in the previous year, when the selectors' policy followed a similar pattern, Malcolm responded by taking more wickets for the county – 60 – than ever before. The unassuming Allan Warner ended his benefit season on a high note, with a career-best six for 21 against Lancashire. These four leading bowlers took 209 Championship wickets between them at a cost of less than 24. On that basis, more should have been achieved, even if the absence of spin was keenly felt in a dry summer. Barnett was the only spinner remotely capable of taking wickets and Derbyshire were weakened by Matthew Vandrau's decision to become a home-based player in South Africa.

Four batsmen passed 1,000 runs in the Championship, a mark no one reached in 1994, and Colin Wells was close in all first-class cricket – his recovery from a difficult first season with Derbyshire afforded much pleasure. Chris Adams, too, made progress – although first wicket down is not the ideal position for him – and was seen at his best when scoring 216 at Maidstone, an innings of elegant power.

The South African Daryll Cullinan began magnificently, with centuries in his first two Championship innings, but suffered a setback when he broke a finger on a difficult pitch at Chesterfield. One side effect was that he did not field in the slips again. Although he played several more innings of high quality, he began to appear an isolated figure, not finding all the ways of English cricket in accord with his serious approach. Barnett passed 1,000 for the 12th time and became only the second player, following Denis Smith, to complete 20,000 runs for the county. Given all their assets, including capable wicket-keepers in Karl Krikken and Steven Griffiths, Derbyshire should have been higher than 14th in the Championship. It was a slight improvement on the two previous seasons but they showed an inability to grasp good situations, allowing at least four games to drift away from them. Nor was there any compensation in the one-day competitions. Derbyshire did not survive their Benson and Hedges Cup group and, after a good victory over Sussex, were routed by Warwickshire in the NatWest Trophy. Mixed form in the Sunday League brought a mid-table position but no genuine challenge.

In retrospect, it was a mistake for Barnett to announce in the previous winter that 1995 would be his final year as captain: there was a sense of drift. He led Derbyshire for longer, 13 seasons, and in more first-class matches, 271, than anybody in the club's history. Barnett emerged heavily in credit, with two one-day trophies and the highest Championship placing, third in 1991, since the Second World War. He was central to building a new team after replacing Barry Wood a few weeks into the 1983 season, when he was not quite 23. But the final phase of his command was marked by friction. John Morris and Peter Bowler went to other counties, Adams asked to be released before and after the 1995 season and, when playing standards dipped, there were rumours that a move might suit Barnett too.

There was a desire for a fresh start and, within 48 hours of the season ending, Derbyshire announced the appointment of Dean Jones as captain and overseas player. He has played in 52 Tests for Australia, leads Victoria and will be accompanied by the state's coach, Les Stillman, with Alan Hill reverting to the Second Eleven and cricket development. Durham, for whom Jones played in 1992, their inaugural first-class season, had hoped he would return to them, but the chance to lead a county swayed the issue. Barnett decided to stay on under the new regime. Jones will find Derbyshire in a healthier financial position than ever before because of the expertise of chairman Mike Horton and his staff. Inside two years, Derbyshire reduced their overdraft from £480,000 to nothing, cleared £175,000 in loans and declared two record profits. In 1995, they made £123,532, twice as much as the previous best 12 months earlier. Horton acknowledges that a legacy of £235,000 from the estate of Frank Stretton, a Derbyshire farmer, speeded the recovery by 18 months and the generosity will be commemorated in planned new development. – Gerald Mortimer.

DERBYSHIRE 1995

[Bill Smith]

Back row: F. A. Griffith, A. C. Cottam, A. Richardson, A. S. Rollins, T. A. Tweats, T. W. Harrison, S. J. Base, A. J. Harris, P. Aldred.
Middle row: K. M. Krikken, C. J. Adams, T. J. G. O'Gorman, D. G. Cork, J. E. Owen, M. Taylor, M. E. Cassar, A. Brentnall (physiotherapist).
Front row: D. E. Malcolm, A. E. Warner, A. Hill (coach), K. J. Barnett (captain), B. J. M. Maher, P. A. J. DeFreitas, C. M. Wells.
Insets: D. J. Cullinan, A. D. Bairstow.

DERBYSHIRE RESULTS

All first-class matches – Played 19 : Won 5, Lost 11, Drawn 3.

County Championship matches – Played 17 : Won 4, Lost 10, Drawn 3.

Bonus points – Batting 39, Bowling 64.

*Competition placings – Britannic Assurance County Championship, 14th ;
NatWest Bank Trophy, q-f ; Benson and Hedges Cup, 3rd in Group B ;
AXA Equity & Law League, 8th.*

BRITANNIC ASSURANCE CHAMPIONSHIP AVERAGES

BATTING

	Birthplace	M	I	NO	R	HS	Avge
D. J. Cullinan§	Kimberley, SA	14	26	4	1,003	161	45.59
‡K. J. Barnett	Stoke-on-Trent	16	31	3	1,251	169	44.67
‡C. J. Adams	Whitwell	13	25	0	1,084	216	43.36
‡A. S. Rollins	Barking	16	31	1	1,075	200*	35.83
‡C. M. Wells	Newhaven	15	29	3	861	106	33.11
W. A. Dessaur	Nottingham	6	12	1	311	84*	28.27
F. A. Griffith	Walthamstow	8	13	4	240	53	26.66
‡K. M. Krikken	Bolton	10	14	3	271	61	24.63
‡P. A. J. DeFreitas . .	Scotts Head, Dominica	15	24	3	450	94*	21.42
T. A. Tweats	Stoke-on-Trent	7	14	1	247	78*	19.00
‡A. E. Warner	Birmingham	14	22	8	265	43	18.92
‡D. G. Cork	Newcastle-under-Lyme	11	20	2	311	84*	17.27
‡T. J. G. O'Gorman . .	Woking	4	7	0	108	39	15.42
J. E. Owen	Derby	3	6	0	90	50	15.00
A. C. Cottam	Northampton	4	5	0	59	32	11.80
T. W. Harrison	Peterborough	5	10	1	102	61*	11.33
P. Aldred	Chellaston	5	9	0	77	33	8.55
S. P. Griffiths	Hereford	5	9	0	75	20	8.33
‡D. E. Malcolm	Kingston, Jamaica	11	17	3	106	25*	7.57
A. D. Bairstow	Dewsbury	2	4	0	25	16	6.25

Also batted: ‡S. J. Base (*Maidstone*) (1 match) 7*, 10; A. J. Harris (*Ashton-under-Lyne*)
(2 matches) 5*, 5, 2.

* Signifies not out.   ‡ *Denotes county cap.*   § *Overseas player.*

The following played a total of 13 three-figure innings for Derbyshire in County
Championship matches – D. J. Cullinan 5, C. J. Adams 3, K. J. Barnett 2, A. S. Rollins 2,
C. M. Wells 1.

BOWLING

	O	M	R	W	BB	5W/i	Avge
D. G. Cork	348	69	965	56	9-43	3	17.23
D. E. Malcolm	382.1	73	1,333	56	6-61	3	23.80
A. E. Warner	375.1	90	1,050	39	6-21	3	26.92
P. A. J. DeFreitas	564.1	124	1,636	58	6-35	2	28.20
C. M. Wells	110	25	326	10	4-29	0	32.60
F. A. Griffith	190.4	42	614	17	4-89	0	36.11
K. J. Barnett	193.2	32	572	15	3-51	0	38.13

Also bowled: C. J. Adams 15-3-47-0; P. Aldred 67-10-241-9; S. J. Base 17-2-99-1;
A. C. Cottam 56-8-257-1; W. A. Dessaur 4-1-16-0; A. J. Harris 31.4-3-152-6; T. W.
Harrison 77-19-282-5; A. S. Rollins 3-1-19-1; T. A. Tweats 34.4-3-149-3.

Wicket-keepers: K. M. Krikken 34 ct, 1 st; S. P. Griffiths 14 ct; A. D. Bairstow 5 ct; A. S.
Rollins 4 ct.

Leading Fielder: C. M. Wells 16.

DERBYSHIRE v SUSSEX

At Derby, April 27, 28, 29. Derbyshire won by an innings and 379 runs. Derbyshire 24 pts, Sussex 1 pt. Toss: Derbyshire. Championship debut: D. J. Cullinan.

Derbyshire took an instant grip, never relinquished it and, inside seven sessions, completed the most decisive victory in their history. The previous best winning margins were both against Warwickshire at Derby, by an innings and 317 in 1933 and by an innings and 250 runs in 1902. They also passed 600 for only the second time – following 645 against Hampshire at Derby in 1898 – and established their biggest ever first-innings lead, 492. Sussex were hurried out for 111, with Malcolm, at his best, claiming six, and Derbyshire were ahead by tea with all wickets standing. Jarvis had broken down in his third over, and Sussex's twelfth man, Hemmings, faced a harder time than he envisaged. Barnett shared an opening stand of 189 with Rollins and made the first of three centuries in the innings. Adams batted coolly and the South African, Daryll Cullinan, became the first player to score a hundred on debut for Derbyshire in a Championship match. DeFreitas completed the rout with six for 35, his best figures for the county.

Close of play: First day, Derbyshire 262-1 (K. J. Barnett 152*, C. J. Adams 39*); Second day, Sussex 68-4 (A. P. Wells 21*, I. D. K. Salisbury 2*).

Sussex

N. J. Lenham c O'Gorman b Malcolm	45	– lbw b DeFreitas		27
C. W. J. Athey c Cullinan b Cork	0	– c sub b Malcolm		0
J. W. Hall b Malcolm	0	– lbw b DeFreitas		9
*A. P. Wells c Krikken b Cork	10	– not out		46
K. Greenfield c Krikken b Malcolm	7	– lbw b Cork		5
†P. Moores c Krikken b Malcolm	0	– (7) b Malcolm		1
F. D. Stephenson c Krikken b Malcolm	19	– (8) b DeFreitas		10
C. C. Remy c Rollins b Warner	4	– (9) b DeFreitas		1
I. D. K. Salisbury c Adams b Malcolm	4	– (6) lbw b DeFreitas		8
P. W. Jarvis not out	4	– b Malcolm		0
E. S. H. Giddins lbw b Warner	5	– lbw b DeFreitas		1
L-b 8, w 1, n-b 4	13	B 1, l-b 2, n-b 2		5
	111			**113**

1/8 2/9 3/34 4/65 5/65
6/74 7/80 8/99 9/104

1/5 2/26 3/55 4/66 5/89
6/94 7/107 8/111 9/112

Bonus points – Derbyshire 4.

Bowling: *First Innings*—Malcolm 16-2-61-6; Cork 9-4-12-2; DeFreitas 5-2-13-0; Warner 8.4-1-17-2. *Second Innings*—Malcolm 15-0-56-3; Cork 7-2-19-1; DeFreitas 18-5-35-6.

Derbyshire

*K. J. Barnett c Greenfield b Stephenson	.164	P. A. J. DeFreitas c Lenham b Giddins	4
A. S. Rollins c Greenfield b Giddins	. . . 52	C. M. Wells not out	2
C. J. Adams run out	111		
D. J. Cullinan c sub b Giddins	134	B 4, l-b 22, w 1, n-b 8	35
T. J. G. O'Gorman lbw b Stephenson	. . 17	1/189 2/281 3/425	(6 wkts dec.) 603
D. G. Cork not out	 84	4/454 5/586 6/590	

A. E. Warner, †K. M. Krikken and D. E. Malcolm did not bat.

Bonus points – Derbyshire 4, Sussex 1 (Score at 120 overs: 475-4).

Bowling: Stephenson 29-3-117-2; Jarvis 2.3-0-11-0; Remy 22.3-2-114-0; Giddins 41-2-157-3; Salisbury 41-13-118-0; Athey 2-0-15-0; Greenfield 13.1-1-45-0.

Umpires: K. E. Palmer and P. Willey.

At Nottingham, May 4, 5, 6, 8. DERBYSHIRE lost to NOTTINGHAMSHIRE by 114 runs.

DERBYSHIRE v YORKSHIRE

At Chesterfield, May 11, 12, 13. Yorkshire won by seven runs. Yorkshire 20 pts, Derbyshire 4 pts. Toss: Derbyshire. First-class debut: A. D. Bairstow.

Only three men reached 30 in an exciting but unsatisfactory match. Despite rain on the second day, it was completed in 172.2 overs. Hartley's disciplined bowling was decisive. His nine for 41 in the final innings, the best analysis of his career, was the reward for putting the ball on the spot more consistently than the four international bowlers. The unreliable bounce of the pitch was illustrated on the first day, when Moxon broke his right thumb and Cullinan his right index finger. Moxon came in at No. 10 in the second innings and added 14 with Stemp, which later proved invaluable. Derbyshire, needing 142, reached 76 for two but were wrecked as Hartley grabbed five wickets in nine balls, including his first hat-trick (DeFreitas, Harrison and Cork). But Warner and Malcolm took them to 120 and Malcolm, batting one-handed, helped them to within eight of victory before Hartley bowled Warner. Derbyshire introduced wicket-keeper Andrew Bairstow, son of David, the former Yorkshire and England keeper; Krikken, the regular incumbent, had chicken-pox.

Close of play: First day, Derbyshire 122-7 (A. D. Bairstow 15*, A. E. Warner 2*); Second day, Yorkshire 90-8 (R. D. Stemp 2*).

Yorkshire

*M. D. Moxon retired hurt	2	– (10) not out		6
M. P. Vaughan b Cork	28	– c Adams b DeFreitas		0
D. Byas c Adams b DeFreitas	17	– (1) b Malcolm		4
M. G. Bevan b Cork	0	– (3) lbw b Warner		28
C. White c Cork b Warner	28	– c sub b Malcolm		15
†R. J. Blakey b Malcolm	45	– (5) c Bairstow b Malcolm		4
A. P. Grayson c Barnett b Malcolm	5	– (6) c Barnett b DeFreitas		9
D. Gough not out	18	– (7) b Cork		17
P. J. Hartley b Malcolm	0	– (8) c Bairstow b Cork		9
R. D. Stemp c Bairstow b DeFreitas	13	– (9) b DeFreitas		7
M. A. Robinson b DeFreitas	0	– lbw b DeFreitas		0
L-b 12, w 5, n-b 4	21	L-b 2, w 1, n-b 2		5

1/43 2/52 3/65 4/136 5/142   177   1/4 2/5 3/30 4/34 5/49   104
6/146 7/146 8/177 9/177   6/76 7/85 8/90 9/104

Bonus points – Derbyshire 4.

In the first innings M. D. Moxon retired hurt at 11.

Bowling: *First Innings*—Malcolm 18-3-69-3; Cork 14-3-40-2; DeFreitas 12.5-3-24-3; Warner 11-3-32-1. *Second Innings*—Malcolm 11-3-41-3; DeFreitas 14.5-2-30-4; Cork 7-1-23-2; Warner 3-0-8-1.

Derbyshire

*K. J. Barnett c Byas b Gough	6	– c Byas b Hartley		3
A. S. Rollins c Byas b Hartley	38	– (7) c Grayson b Hartley		3
C. J. Adams c Byas b Robinson	0	– (2) c Bevan b Gough		24
D. J. Cullinan retired hurt	1	– (11) not out		1
T. J. G. O'Gorman c Byas b Gough	13	– (3) c Blakey b Hartley		24
D. G. Cork c Blakey b Gough	9	– (4) c Byas b Hartley		24
P. A. J. DeFreitas b Hartley	25	– (5) lbw b Hartley		0
T. W. Harrison c Blakey b Robinson	9	– (6) lbw b Hartley		0
†A. D. Bairstow b Robinson	16	– (8) c Vaughan b Hartley		0
A. E. Warner not out	9	– (9) b Hartley		33
D. E. Malcolm c Bevan b Robinson	8	– (10) c Gough b Hartley		18
L-b 2, n-b 4	6	L-b 4		4

1/12 2/15 3/35 4/46 5/80   140   1/5 2/29 3/76 4/76 5/76   134
6/105 7/117 8/130 9/140   6/77 7/77 8/94 9/120

Bonus points – Yorkshire 4.

In the first innings A. S. Rollins, when 8, retired hurt at 14 and resumed at 35; D. J. Cullinan retired hurt at 20.

Bowling: *First Innings*—Gough 17-3-38-3; Hartley 9-0-27-2; Robinson 17-6-58-4; White 3-0-15-0. *Second Innings*—Gough 14-2-72-1; Hartley 16.4-4-41-9; Robinson 4-0-17-0.

Umpires: R. Palmer and P. B. Wight.

At Leicester, May 18, 19, 20. DERBYSHIRE lost to LEICESTERSHIRE by nine wickets.

At Oxford, May 25, 26, 27. DERBYSHIRE beat OXFORD UNIVERSITY by five wickets.

At Lord's, June 1, 2, 3, 5. DERBYSHIRE drew with MIDDLESEX.

DERBYSHIRE v NORTHAMPTONSHIRE

At Derby, June 8, 9. Northamptonshire won by four wickets. Northamptonshire 20 pts, Derbyshire 4 pts. Toss: Derbyshire.

Twenty-three wickets fell on the first day and the match was over by tea on Friday. Northamptonshire's middle order saw them to victory despite a remarkable sustained effort from Cork, who bowled without relief through both innings to take 13 of Northamptonshire's 16 wickets for 93. The victorious captain, Lamb, condemned the pitch but Barnett defended it and the umpires made no complaint; it was grassy, but first-day totals of 113 and 120 owed as much to swing as to seam. Derbyshire collapsed after winning the toss, with Barnett on the way to the first pair of his career, but Cork put them back in the game, taking a career-best nine for 43. He would have become the first to take all ten for Derbyshire since T. B. Mitchell in 1935 had Wells held Warren at slip on 109 for nine, and his high-class performance helped to elevate him to England's team at Lord's. Derbyshire lost three more important wickets before the close, however, which shifted the balance. Set a target of 133, Bailey, Lamb and Warren gave Northamptonshire enough substance to extend their Championship lead.

Close of play: First day, Derbyshire 59-3 (W. A. Dessaur 22*, A. J. Harris 0*).

Derbyshire

*K. J. Barnett c Warren b Taylor	0	– c Warren b Taylor	0
W. A. Dessaur b Mallender	0	– lbw b Taylor	40
A. S. Rollins lbw b Penberthy	42	– c Warren b Taylor	8
D. J. Cullinan b Curran	23	– b Capel	25
C. M. Wells c Fordham b Curran	7	– (6) c Fordham b Capel	2
D. G. Cork b Penberthy b Taylor	10	– (8) not out	16
†K. M. Krikken b Taylor	0	– lbw b Mallender	17
P. Aldred c Curran b Penberthy	0	– (9) lbw b Mallender	0
A. E. Warner c Mallender b Curran	11	– (10) b Kumble	8
A. C. Cottam b Taylor	7	– (11) c Curran b Taylor	2
A. J. Harris not out	5	– (5) c Fordham b Kumble	5
L-b 7, w 1	8	B 1, l-b 12, w 1, n-b 2	16
	113		**139**

1/0 2/1 3/52 4/60 5/86   113   1/0 2/18 3/59 4/68 5/71   139
6/86 7/86 8/86 9/101   6/100 7/112 8/116 9/132

Bonus points – Northamptonshire 4.

Bowling: *First Innings*—Taylor 13-6-23-4; Mallender 5-0-22-1; Capel 5-0-19-0; Curran 10.3-1-36-3; Penberthy 6-3-6-2. *Second Innings*—Taylor 13.5-1-44-4; Mallender 10-2-33-2; Capel 10-4-18-2; Penberthy 1-0-5-0; Kumble 12-4-26-2.

Northamptonshire

R. R. Montgomerie c Dessaur b Cork	0	– lbw b Cork	8
A. Fordham lbw b Cork	0	– lbw b Cork	7
R. J. Bailey c Wells b Cork	7	– c Wells b Aldred	32
*A. J. Lamb lbw b Cork	37	– c Krikken b Cork	27
†R. J. Warren not out	42	– c Krikken b Cork	29
K. M. Curran c Warner b Cork	4	– c Wells b Aldred	0
D. J. Capel c Aldred b Cork	0	– not out	17
A. L. Penberthy c Rollins b Cork	1	– not out	0
A. Kumble c Aldred b Cork	0		
N. A. Mallender lbw b Cork	11		
J. P. Taylor b Aldred	2		
L-b 8, n-b 8	16	L-b 15	15

1/0 2/3 3/34 4/57 5/61   120   1/15 2/24 3/80   (6 wkts) 135
6/61 7/65 8/65 9/101   4/92 5/96 6/130

Bonus points – Derbyshire 4.

Bowling: *First Innings*—Cork 22–5–43–9; Warner 16–2–57–0; Aldred 5.3–0–12–1. *Second Innings*—Cork 20.3–5–50–4; Warner 5–2–15–0; Harris 7–0–18–0; Aldred 8–0–37–2.

Umpires: J. H. Harris and M. J. Kitchen.

DERBYSHIRE v SOMERSET

At Derby, June 15, 16, 17, 19. Somerset won by 79 runs. Somerset 20 pts, Derbyshire 8 pts.
Toss: Somerset.

Derbyshire's cricket committee held an emergency meeting after their defeat. It was the first time the county had lost after enforcing the follow-on since 1882, at Hove. Cullinan's third century for Derbyshire had put them in a good position, on a pitch at the other end of the spectrum from that in the Northamptonshire game. Driving cleanly on both sides of the wicket, he hit 30 fours, backed up in a stand of 134 by Wells, who had just been capped. Excellent seam bowling confirmed Derbyshire's control but Somerset gradually stole the initiative after following on 187 behind. Bowler, who left Derbyshire in 1994, with dislike unconcealed on either side, launched the revival with a composed 138, but the decider was Turner's fine unbeaten 106, his highest score. The last three wickets added 132 and Hayhurst returned with a broken hand to help Turner past 100. Derbyshire finished the third day at 28 for four and, despite aggressive batting from Wells, slipped to a humiliating defeat.

Close of play: First day, Derbyshire 376; Second day, Somerset 123-2 (P. D. Bowler 57*, R. J. Harden 47*); Third day, Derbyshire 28-4 (T. A. Tweats 7*, C. M. Wells 6*).

Derbyshire

*K. J. Barnett c Lathwell b Rose	0	– (7) not out	16
W. A. Dessaur b Mushtaq Ahmed	28	– c Turner b Rose	0
A. S. Rollins lbw b Mushtaq Ahmed	56	– (1) lbw b Mushtaq Ahmed	11
D. J. Cullinan c Turner b Kerr	161	– lbw b Rose	1
C. M. Wells c Trescothick b Parsons	47	– (6) b Mushtaq Ahmed	98
T. A. Tweats lbw b Mushtaq Ahmed	7	– (3) c Parsons b Dimond	17
D. G. Cork b Mushtaq Ahmed	3	– (8) c Trescothick b Parsons	2
P. A. J. DeFreitas c Turner b Rose	4	– (9) c Kerr b Parsons	0
†K. M. Krikken b Kerr	27	– (5) b Rose	0
A. E. Warner not out	28	– b Mushtaq Ahmed	5
D. E. Malcolm lbw b Mushtaq Ahmed	1	– c Bowler b Rose	0
L-b 6, n-b 8	14	B 4, l-b 8, w 2, n-b 4	18

1/0 2/82 3/99 4/233 5/260   376   1/3 2/16 3/21 4/21 5/117   168
6/278 7/287 8/332 9/375   6/151 7/156 8/156 9/165

Bonus points – Derbyshire 4, Somerset 4.

Bowling: *First Innings*—Rose 21–5–76–2; Kerr 20–2–87–2; Dimond 10–1–54–0; Mushtaq Ahmed 42.1–13–107–5; Parsons 10–4–28–1; Trescothick 3–0–18–0. *Second Innings*—Rose 16–5–27–4; Kerr 5–0–38–0; Mushtaq Ahmed 23–10–64–3; Dimond 4–1–16–1; Parsons 4–1–11–2.

Somerset

M. N. Lathwell lbw b DeFreitas	1	– c Krikken b DeFreitas	8
M. E. Trescothick c Wells b Malcolm	22	– lbw b Cork	0
P. D. Bowler c Wells b Malcolm	0	– c Wells b Malcolm	138
R. J. Harden c Tweats b Malcolm	33	– c Krikken b Malcolm	63
*A. N. Hayhurst b Warner	16	– run out	0
K. A. Parsons b Cork	43	– c Krikken b Barnett	29
G. D. Rose lbw b Cork	28	– c Krikken b Cork	11
†R. J. Turner lbw b Cork	1	– not out	106
Mushtaq Ahmed not out	10	– c sub b Barnett	1
J. I. D. Kerr b Cork	2	– b Malcolm	13
M. Dimond c Krikken b DeFreitas	7	– c Wells b Barnett	26
B 1, l-b 12, w 1, n-b 12	26	B 6, l-b 19, w 2, n-b 12	39

1/12 2/25 3/34 4/81 5/109	189	1/0 2/20 3/160 4/229 5/258	434
6/157 7/167 8/168 9/174		6/301 7/302 8/339 9/422	

Bonus points – Derbyshire 4.

In the second innings A. N. Hayhurst, when 0, retired hurt at 164 and resumed at 422.

Bowling: *First Innings*—Malcolm 18–3–76–3; DeFreitas 12–5–16–2; Warner 12–3–44–1; Cork 15–0–40–4. *Second Innings*—DeFreitas 31–5–84–1; Cork 22–2–73–2; Warner 29–6–74–0; Malcolm 25–1–127–3; Barnett 24–4–51–3.

Umpires: N. T. Plews and P. B. Wight.

At Chester-le-Street, June 22, 23, 24. DERBYSHIRE lost to DURHAM by eight wickets.

DERBYSHIRE v HAMPSHIRE

At Derby, June 29, 30, July 1. Derbyshire won by six wickets. Derbyshire 22 pts, Hampshire 6 pts. Toss: Hampshire.

Derbyshire clambered off the foot of the table on a pitch that rewarded quality in all departments. Malcolm and DeFreitas bowled well and would have dismissed Hampshire more cheaply but for Stephenson, who made his highest score since leaving Essex, and six dropped catches. Adams launched a blitz – 60 out of 64 in boundaries – but the home lead was restricted to 11 by James, who returned six for 38, the best Championship figures of his career. Hampshire lost three wickets before the end of the second day and Nicholas to the first ball of the third. After that, only White stood in Derbyshire's way as Wells took four wickets in six overs, recording his best figures for the county, and DeFreitas again bowled exceptionally well. Derbyshire's progress to their first Championship victory since April, with a day to spare, was interrupted only by the loss of three wickets in two overs from James and Stephenson.

Close of play: First day, Derbyshire 14-0 (A. S. Rollins 6*, W. A. Dessaur 4*); Second day, Hampshire 69-3 (R. A. Smith 31*, M. C. J. Nicholas 19*).

Hampshire

V. P. Terry c Rollins b Malcolm	1	– (2) b DeFreitas	6
J. P. Stephenson c Krikken b Malcolm	93	– (1) c Adams b DeFreitas	6
P. R. Whitaker c Krikken b Griffith	19	– lbw b Malcolm	1
R. A. Smith b Wells	20	– c Krikken b Griffith	39
*M. C. J. Nicholas c Krikken b DeFreitas	34	– c Krikken b DeFreitas	19
G. W. White lbw b DeFreitas	8	– c Krikken b DeFreitas	62
K. D. James run out	14	– c DeFreitas b Wells	13
†A. N. Aymes not out	40	– c Griffith b Wells	4
S. D. Udal c Wells b Griffith	13	– c DeFreitas b Wells	5
M. J. Thursfield c and b Wells	16	– c and b Wells	0
C. A. Connor b DeFreitas	2	– not out	1
B 7, l-b 11, w 2, n-b 4	24	B 8, l-b 1, w 2	11

1/6 2/41 3/78 4/149 5/171   284   1/12 2/13 3/17 4/69 5/89   167
6/199 7/208 8/231 9/281   6/125 7/139 8/151 9/155

Bonus points – Hampshire 2, Derbyshire 4.

Bowling: *First Innings*—Malcolm 22–5–58–2; DeFreitas 26.4–7–60–3; Griffith 24–5–66–2; Wells 13–2–43–2; Adams 6–3–8–0; Cottam 8–3–31–0. *Second Innings*—Malcolm 20–6–40–1; DeFreitas 26.4–10–63–4; Griffith 10–2–26–1; Wells 11–5–29–4; Barnett 1–1–0–0.

Derbyshire

A. S. Rollins c Terry b Connor	6	– b Stephenson	43
W. A. Dessaur c Terry b Connor	67	– c Aymes b Stephenson	37
C. J. Adams b James	64	– c Whitaker b James	13
D. J. Cullinan b James	0	– not out	34
C. M. Wells c Aymes b James	10	– lbw b Stephenson	0
*K. J. Barnett c Aymes b James	76	– not out	22
P. A. J. DeFreitas c Aymes b Stephenson	8		
†K. M. Krikken not out	23		
F. A. Griffith c Terry b Thursfield	14		
A. C. Cottam c Aymes b James	5		
D. E. Malcolm c and b James	2		
B 4, l-b 3, w 1, n-b 12	20	L-b 4, n-b 4	8

1/14 2/113 3/121 4/131 5/211   295   1/82 2/95 3/95 4/95   (4 wkts) 157
6/224 7/263 8/284 9/289

Bonus points – Derbyshire 2, Hampshire 4.

Bowling: *First Innings*—Connor 19–4–89–2; Thursfield 19–5–59–1; Udal 18–4–36–0; Stephenson 13–0–66–1; James 15.1–2–38–6. *Second Innings*—Connor 13–1–54–0; Thursfield 6–0–23–0; James 14–6–20–1; Stephenson 12–2–51–3; Udal 0.3–0–5–0.

Umpires: J. D. Bond and J. W. Holder.

At Maidstone, July 5, 6, 7, 8. DERBYSHIRE drew with KENT.

At Chesterfield, July 19, 20, 21. DERBYSHIRE lost to YOUNG AUSTRALIA by four wickets (See Young Australia tour section).

DERBYSHIRE v GLAMORGAN

At Derby, July 27, 28, 29, 31. Derbyshire won by 195 runs. Derbyshire 24 pts, Glamorgan 5 pts. Toss: Derbyshire.

Wells scored his first Championship century for Derbyshire and shared a stand of 140 with Krikken, the county's best for the seventh wicket against Glamorgan. Adams had launched the innings forcefully but Anthony took two wickets in an over, and Derbyshire were faltering until Wells revived them, reaching a powerful hundred with his 16th four. Croft, bowling with good control, earned his six wickets but his colleagues struggled to 90 for six against DeFreitas and Warner on an overcast second morning. Only the tail averted the follow-on. Rollins then scored his maiden century, a fortnight before his brother did the same for Essex, also against Glamorgan; he was the 100th batsman to register a hundred for Derbyshire. Set 517 to win, Glamorgan reached a sound 156 for one by stumps. Conditions were perfect for batting on the final morning, but DeFreitas bowled splendidly. He was unlucky to take only two wickets – the vital ones of James and Maynard – but undermined the innings enough to help Harris take career-best figures as Glamorgan subsided.

Close of play: First day, Glamorgan 13-0 (S. P. James 1*, H. Morris 5*); Second day, Derbyshire 166-2 (A. S. Rollins 43*, D. J. Cullinan 36*); Third day, Glamorgan 156-1 (S. P. James 77*, D. L. Hemp 35*).

Derbyshire

*K. J. Barnett c Cottey b Croft	25	– run out	46
A. S. Rollins c Hemp b Watkin	10	– c Croft b Anthony	118
C. J. Adams c Metson b Anthony	83	– c Metson b Anthony	27
D. J. Cullinan c Metson b Croft	0	– b Watkin	41
T. A. Tweats c Maynard b Anthony	17	– c James b Anthony	40
C. M. Wells c Metson b Croft	106	– b Thomas	51
P. A. J. DeFreitas c Maynard b Anthony	4	– c Metson b Anthony	0
†K. M. Krikken c James b Croft	61	– b Thomas	25
F. A. Griffith not out	40	– not out	0
A. E. Warner lbw b Croft	7		
A. J. Harris c and b Croft	2		
L-b 11, w 4, n-b 22	37	B 5, l-b 11, w 6, n-b 2	24
	392	(8 wkts dec.)	**372**

1/24 2/90 3/90 4/146 5/173 6/177 7/317 8/362 9/386

1/73 2/103 3/172 4/284 5/297 6/297 7/371 8/372

Bonus points – Derbyshire 4, Glamorgan 4.

Bowling: *First Innings*—Watkin 25-4-100-1; Anthony 16-3-63-3; Croft 43.3-9-120-6; Thomas 16-4-77-0; Hemp 2-0-21-0. *Second Innings*—Watkin 26-9-70-1; Anthony 17-0-97-4; Thomas 18.5-2-98-2; Croft 47-20-77-0; Hemp 2-1-14-0.

Glamorgan

S. P. James c Adams b Warner	32	– c Krikken b DeFreitas	96
*H. Morris c Adams b Warner	13	– lbw b Wells	25
D. L. Hemp c Barnett b Warner	2	– b Griffith	47
M. P. Maynard b DeFreitas	0	– lbw b DeFreitas	10
P. A. Cottey b DeFreitas	19	– c Krikken b Harris	34
A. J. Dalton c Krikken b Harris	46	– lbw b Barnett	11
R. D. B. Croft b DeFreitas	1	– c DeFreitas b Harris	13
H. A. G. Anthony c Krikken b Harris	33	– c Wells b Barnett	13
S. D. Thomas not out	51	– c Rollins b Harris	13
†C. P. Metson c Krikken b Wells	19	– not out	10
S. L. Watkin c DeFreitas b Wells	3	– c Griffith b Harris	4
L-b 6, w 3, n-b 20	29	B 8, l-b 8, w 3, n-b 26	45
	248		**321**

1/35 2/45 3/46 4/74 5/80 6/90 7/146 8/193 9/240

1/76 2/194 3/194 4/211 5/231 6/262 7/277 8/303 9/303

Bonus points – Glamorgan 1, Derbyshire 4.

Bowling: *First Innings*—DeFreitas 21-2-84-3; Griffith 14-1-60-0; Warner 15-5-44-3; Harris 10-2-50-2; Wells 2-1-4-2. *Second Innings*—DeFreitas 26-8-74-2; Harris 14.4-1-84-4; Griffith 19-10-30-1; Warner 12-6-27-0; Wells 10-5-22-1; Barnett 19-4-68-2.

Umpires: M. J. Kitchen and D. R. Shepherd.

At Kidderminster, August 10, 11, 12, 14. DERBYSHIRE drew with WORCESTERSHIRE.

At Bristol, August 17, 18, 19, 21. DERBYSHIRE lost to GLOUCESTERSHIRE by three wickets.

DERBYSHIRE v SURREY

At Derby, August 24, 25, 26. Surrey won by seven wickets. Surrey 24 pts, Derbyshire 4 pts. Toss: Derbyshire.

Derbyshire had a wretched match, bowling poorly on a weather-disrupted first day and batting ineptly on the second. The absence of Cullinan, Cork and Malcolm was no excuse. Surrey did not take full advantage of an easy pitch, although they were eventually awarded a fourth batting point, the scorers having initially missed the single Butcher scored before he was run out trying for a second. When they came to bowl, Barnett was a solitary figure as Derbyshire collapsed around him. Tudor confirmed his promise, taking five wickets for the first time, but the batting was deplorable. Following on 169 behind, Adams hit his third Championship century of the season, from 120 balls, and Harrison, soon to be released, his only fifty. But their efforts could not change the match. Chasing 165, Surrey's openers put on 132 and, by claiming the extra half-hour on the third day, the visitors won with two balls and three sessions to spare.

Close of play: First day, Surrey 269-6 (A. W. Smith 13*, G. J. Kersey 7*); Second day, Derbyshire 91-2 (C. J. Adams 30*, S. P. Griffiths 4*).

Surrey

D. J. Bicknell c Adams b DeFreitas	36	– run out	50
J. D. Ratcliffe c Griffiths b Barnett	68	– c Harrison b Tweats	65
M. A. Butcher run out	12	– b Harrison	4
A. D. Brown c DeFreitas b Aldred	4	– not out	14
N. Shahid b Aldred	74	– not out	8
*A. J. Hollioake lbw b Aldred	47		
A. W. Smith b DeFreitas	38		
†G. J. Kersey c Tweats b Griffith	18		
M. P. Bicknell not out	27		
A. J. Tudor lbw b DeFreitas	12		
C. G. Rackemann lbw b DeFreitas	0		
L-b 6, n-b 8	14	B 5, l-b 12, w 1, n-b 8	26

1/76 2/106 3/113 4/160 5/249	350	1/132 2/136 3/153 (3 wkts) 167
6/250 7/295 8/318 9/350		

Bonus points – Surrey 4, Derbyshire 4.

Bowling: *First Innings*—DeFreitas 31.5–5–104–4; Warner 15–5–32–0; Griffith 19–6–53–1; Aldred 21–3–89–3; Barnett 17–6–30–1; Wells 7–2–36–0. *Second Innings*—DeFreitas 13–2–38–0; Aldred 8–3–11–0; Wells 5–0–20–0; Griffith 6–2–23–0; Harrison 12–4–35–1; Tweats 6.4–1–23–1.

Derbyshire

*K. J. Barnett b Hollioake	72	– c Hollioake b Rackemann	14
A. S. Rollins c Kersey b M. P. Bicknell	4	– lbw b Shahid	32
C. J. Adams c Brown b Tudor	10	– c Kersey b Butcher	101
T. A. Tweats c Kersey b Tudor	0	– (5) c Kersey b Tudor	0
C. M. Wells c Brown b M. P. Bicknell	2	– (6) c Holliaoke b Butcher	23
T. W. Harrison b M. P. Bicknell	19	– (7) not out	61
P. A. J. DeFreitas c Butcher b M. P. Bicknell	2	– (8) lbw b Shahid	11
F. A. Griffith lbw b Tudor	33	– (9) c Kersey b M. P. Bicknell	12
P. Aldred c Kersey b Tudor	17	– (10) c Holliaoke b M. P. Bicknell	22
†S. P. Griffiths b Tudor	3	– (4) c Kersey b Tudor	20
A. E. Warner not out	4	– c Rackemann b M. P. Bicknell	11
B 1, l-b 5, w 1, n-b 8	15	B 4, l-b 5, w 1, n-b 16	26

1/20 2/33 3/47 4/62 5/114   181   1/30 2/83 3/119 4/119 5/199   333
6/116 7/116 8/150 9/158   6/208 7/230 8/271 9/313

Bonus points – Surrey 4.

Bowling: *First Innings*—Rackemann 12-1-58-0; M. P. Bicknell 17-6-48-4; Tudor 9.4-2-32-5; Butcher 4-0-20-0; Holliaoke 6-2-17-1. *Second Innings*—M. P. Bicknell 26.5-4-99-3; Tudor 12-0-70-2; Rackemann 20-6-74-1; Butcher 12-5-47-2; Smith 3-1-5-0; Shahid 10-3-29-2.

Umpires: R. Julian and R. A. White.

At Chelmsford, August 29, 30, 31, September 1. DERBYSHIRE lost to ESSEX by 256 runs.

At Birmingham, September 7, 8, 9, 11. DERBYSHIRE lost to WARWICKSHIRE by ten wickets.

DERBYSHIRE v LANCASHIRE

At Derby, September 14, 15, 16, 18. Derbyshire won by 282 runs. Derbyshire 22 pts, Lancashire 4 pts. Toss: Derbyshire.

Derbyshire's season ended as it began, with a victory substantial enough to make their otherwise wasted summer even more frustrating. The first day brought 401 runs and 18 wickets. On a receptive pitch, Derbyshire had a flying start against poorly directed bowling. Barnett, in his final game as captain, became the second player to complete 20,000 runs for the county, following Denis Smith, and Cork ripped through Lancashire's top order; they were 51 for seven when Austin came in and averted the follow-on, with 80 not out from 51 balls. Cork's seven for 61 gave him 90 wickets for the season. Derbyshire were 112 ahead and Barnett led the way as they extended it to 437. Lancashire, who had played feebly throughout, showed no interest in defence and were routed by Warner's career-best six for 21. Rollins was capped on the first day, when Derbyshire turned down Adams's request to be released.

Close of play: First day, Lancashire 134-8 (I. D. Austin 59*, G. Chapple 7*); Second day, Derbyshire 161-2 (K. J. Barnett 80*, D. J. Cullinan 10*); Third day, Lancashire 19-0 (J. E. R. Gallian 3*, S. P. Titchard 12*).

Derbyshire

*K. J. Barnett b Austin	42	– c Hegg b Martin	88
A. S. Rollins c Fairbrother b Chapple	17	– lbw b Chapple	24
C. J. Adams c Hegg b Martin	21	– c Fairbrother b Austin	38
D. J. Cullinan c Hegg b Martin	7	– b Martin	15
C. M. Wells b Chapple	45	– b Austin	14
J. E. Owen c Gallian b Watkinson	5	– c Crawley b Gallian	14
D. G. Cork c Hegg b Austin	4	– c Crawley b Watkinson	29
P. A. J. DeFreitas not out	94	– b Gallian	39
†K. M. Krikken c Hegg b Gallian	20	– not out	24
P. Aldred c Hegg b Gallian	0	– lbw b Gallian	0
A. E. Warner c Hegg b Gallian	1	– c Atherton b Watkinson	20
L-b 6, w 1, n-b 4	11	B 5, l-b 13, n-b 2	20

1/26 2/83 3/83 4/90 5/108   267   1/73 2/146 3/174 4/175 5/203   325
6/124 7/197 8/261 9/265   6/226 7/280 8/280 9/280

Bonus points – Derbyshire 2, Lancashire 4.

Bowling: *First Innings*—Martin 19–5–76–2; Chapple 15–0–93–2; Austin 14–4–48–2; Watkinson 9–1–30–1; Gallian 5–1–14–3. *Second Innings*—Martin 19–5–47–2; Austin 25–5–82–2; Chapple 14–2–80–1; Watkinson 10.4–3–33–2; Fairbrother 1–1–0–0; Gallian 11–0–65–3.

Lancashire

S. P. Titchard b Cork	2	– (2) retired hurt	12
J. E. R. Gallian b Cork	6	– (1) lbw b DeFreitas	5
J. P. Crawley lbw b Cork	4	– c Krikken b Warner	52
N. H. Fairbrother c Cork b DeFreitas	4	– c Krikken b DeFreitas	0
M. A. Atherton c Krikken b Cork	10	– b Warner	27
N. J. Speak lbw b Warner	27	– b Warner	12
*M. Watkinson lbw b Cork	0	– b Aldred	4
†W. K. Hegg lbw b Warner	2	– c Cork b Warner	0
I. D. Austin not out	80	– not out	2
G. Chapple lbw b Cork	7	– (11) c Aldred b Warner	23
P. J. Martin lbw b Cork	0	– (10) c Cork b Warner	13
L-b 2, w 1, n-b 10	13	L-b 5	5

1/4 2/12 3/19 4/19 5/40   155   1/25 2/25 3/83 4/108 5/117   155
6/40 7/51 8/90 9/137   6/117 7/117 8/130 9/155

Bonus points – Derbyshire 4.

In the second innings S. P. Titchard retired hurt at 21.

Bowling: *First Innings*—DeFreitas 10–3–35–1; Cork 18.1–3–61–7; Warner 9–2–56–2; Wells 1–0–1–0. *Second Innings*—Cork 9–1–43–0; DeFreitas 14–2–59–2; Warner 7.5–3–21–6; Aldred 2–0–27–1.

Umpires: B. Dudleston and T. E. Jesty.

CHAMPIONSHIP SEASONS WITHOUT DRAWN GAMES

	Season	Played	Won	Lost
Sussex	1890	12	1	11
Surrey	1894	16*	13	2
Leicestershire	1910	17	6	11
Somerset	1914	19†	3	16
Derbyshire	1920	18‡	0	17
Gloucestershire	1921	24	12	12
Surrey	1955	28	23	5
Essex	1995	17	8	9
Durham	1995	17	4	13

  * *One match tied.*
  † *Another fixture was abandoned owing to war.*
  ‡ *One match abandoned without a ball bowled.*

DURHAM

Patrons: Sir Donald Bradman and A. W. Austin
President: G. W. Midgley
Chairman: J. D. Robson
Director of Cricket: G. Cook
Coach: N. Gifford.
Captain: M. A. Roseberry
Head Groundsman: T. Flintoft
Scorer: B. Hunt

A season which began full of hope for Durham reached its zenith in early July with a second successive Championship win. The downward spiral which followed brought a run of seven heavy defeats before they won the last game. Without that, they would have finished bottom for the third time in four years.

The arrival of Mike Roseberry from Middlesex to captain his native county coincided perfectly with the move into the new Riverside ground at Chester-le-Street. But this was a marriage without a honeymoon. Nothing would go right for Roseberry. In the Championship, he averaged 20 and lost the toss 11 successive times, and he was among a host of players troubled by injury. Steve Lugsden missed the entire season with a recurrence of the stress fracture of the back which kept him out of the England Under-19 tour of the West Indies, and fellow pace bowler John Wood suffered a similar injury after an excellent start to the season.

Another player of whom big things were expected, Jimmy Daley, topped the batting averages, despite also having his season wrecked by injury. He was the most serious victim of the uneven bounce of the newly-laid Riverside pitches, which gradually undermined the batsmen's confidence. Daley was developing into a batsman of solid dependability when he suffered a chipped knuckle in the first Sunday game at the ground. Shortly after his return from an eight-week lay-off, a broken finger ruled him out until the last match. He was sorely missed as Durham accrued a mere 20 batting points, gaining the maximum of four for the first time in the final match, against Nottinghamshire. From a team which began the season with a top six of Roseberry, Larkins, Morris, Daley, Prabhakar and Saxelby, this was a severe let-down. Saxelby had scored 1,102 runs at 34.43 as an opening batsman in his first season with Durham, but Roseberry's arrival forced him down the order, where his failures led to the early announcement of his release.

Larkins, who was almost 42, was also released. He batted magnificently on his return to his old stamping ground at Northampton, completing his full set of centuries against the other 17 counties, and bowed out with his 59th first-class hundred, his tenth for Durham, in the last match. It was a sad farewell for Larkins, who had hoped to go on for two more years. During his four seasons with Durham, he remained one of the game's great entertainers; his exit left only Phil Bainbridge of the original seasoned recruits still on the staff. Bainbridge's role was largely that of captaining the Second Eleven, who came third in their own championship, their best showing yet.

In so far as he took 51 wickets and scored 896 runs, the Indian Test all-rounder Manoj Prabhakar was a steady contributor. But with the bat he dealt more in brief cameos than match-winning marathons and did not do full justice to his obvious talent. John Morris, with 1,297, was the only player to top 1,000 runs. He scored three glorious centuries but, under the pressure of trying to bat more responsibly in a flimsy line-up, he was again inconsistent.

Progress, such as it was, came from the fact that Durham introduced several more youngsters to Championship cricket, among them Darren Blenkiron, who provided the highlight of the season when his maiden century won the match at Swansea. He made 145 and his stand of 177 with Stewart Hutton was the stuff of dreams for the Durham pioneers. Unfortunately, it was nearly all downhill after that. Simon Brown took 40 wickets at 21.87 in his opening nine first-class games and 12 at 80.41 in the next eight as the burden of carrying the attack took its toll. The off-spinner James Boiling had a disappointing first season after moving from Surrey, although he finished with a season's-best five for 73 to wrap up victory over Nottinghamshire. There was a moment of glory for Alan Walker, whose whole-hearted efforts earned a popular reward when he had a 14-wicket haul at Chelmsford. Injury-prone himself, he might never have played a first-class game but for other players' wounds; in fact, he became a fixture in the second half of the season and had his contract extended. At one stage Durham had seven unfit seamers and they were grateful to be able to call on 19-year-old Neil Killeen, a student who made pleasing progress when selected for the last six games. Another young pace bowler, Melvyn Betts, also made encouraging strides.

The long, hot summer meant there was no hiding place when the going got tough. With not a draw in sight, Durham suffered 13 defeats, three more than in each of their first three seasons. They were also heavily beaten at home by Gloucestershire in the second round of the NatWest Trophy and finished 16th in the Sunday League, never having finished lower than ninth before.

Contracts were awarded at the end of the season to three more locals – wicket-keeper/batsman Neil Pratt, all-rounder Paul Collingwood and pace bowler Colin Campbell. But the signing the members wanted – that of Dean Jones, their original overseas player in 1992 – fell through at the last minute when the Australian decided to accept Derbyshire's offer of the captaincy. It was the final straw for some fans, who were not appeased by the last-match victory against a dispirited Nottinghamshire. The club hoped to improve their standing when they signed Barbadian opening batsman Sherwin Campbell, who had just had a successful tour of England with the West Indian Test team, and the experienced Norman Gifford as first-team coach. But the departure of chief executive Alan Wright at the end of October, two years into a three-year contract, did nothing to disperse an atmosphere of uncertainty. Considering the level of expectation in April, this was Durham's most disappointing season to date. – Tim Wellock.

DURHAM 1995

Back row: D. G. C. Ligertwood, S. D. Birbeck, M. M. Betts, R. M. S. Weston, M. Saxelby, P. J. Wilcock, S. Lugsden, S. Hutton, J. A. Daley, J. I. Longley. *Front row*: D. A. Blenkiron, J. Boiling, C. W. Scott, P. Bainbridge, W. Larkins, M. A. Roseberry (*captain*), J. E. Morris, A. Walker, S. J. E. Brown, J. Wood, D. M. Cox.

DURHAM RESULTS

All first-class matches – Played 19: Won 4, Lost 13, Drawn 2.

County Championship matches – Played 17: Won 4, Lost 13.

Bonus points – Batting 20, Bowling 53.

Competition placings – Britannic Assurance County Championship, 17th;
NatWest Bank Trophy, 2nd round; Benson and Hedges Cup, 4th in Group A;
AXA Equity & Law League, 16th.

BRITANNIC ASSURANCE CHAMPIONSHIP AVERAGES

BATTING

	Birthplace	M	I	NO	R	HS	Avge
J. A. Daley	Sunderland	6	10	1	362	55	40.22
J. E. Morris	Crewe	17	32	1	1,123	169	36.22
W. Larkins	Roxton	13	23	0	737	121	32.04
M. Prabhakar§	Ghaziabad, India	17	31	3	896	101	32.00
S. Hutton	Stockton-on-Tees	10	19	1	551	98	30.61
D. A. Blenkiron	Solihull	8	15	1	413	145	29.50
J. I. Longley	New Brunswick, USA	7	14	1	365	58	28.07
S. D. Birbeck	Sunderland	4	6	2	106	75*	26.50
C. W. Scott	Thorpe-on-the-Hill	6	11	0	270	56	24.54
M. A. Roseberry	Sunderland	14	26	2	480	56	20.00
M. Saxelby	Worksop	5	10	0	194	68	19.40
J. Wood	Crofton	3	6	1	67	40*	13.40
D. G. C. Ligertwood	Oxford	11	19	2	225	40	13.23
N. Killeen	Shotley Bridge	6	11	3	100	48	12.50
S. J. E. Brown	Cleadon	17	29	5	262	36	10.91
J. Boiling	New Delhi, India	16	29	6	235	24	10.21
A. Walker	Emley	9	13	2	72	19	6.54
D. M. Cox	Southall	3	5	0	23	17	4.60
M. M. Betts	Sacriston	8	14	4	44	14	4.40
R. M. S. Weston	Durham	3	6	0	15	9	2.50

Also batted: P. Bainbridge (*Stoke-on-Trent*) (2 matches) 0, 4, 0; J. R. G. Lawrence (*Portsmouth*) (1 match), 0, 7*; J. P. Searle (*Bath*) (1 match) 2*, 0.

* *Signifies not out.*   § *Overseas player.*   *Durham have awarded all playing staff county caps.*

The following played a total of seven three-figure innings for Durham in County Championship matches – J. E. Morris 3, W. Larkins 2, D. A. Blenkiron 1, M. Prabhakar 1.

BOWLING

	O	M	R	W	BB	5W/i	Avge
J. Wood	74.4	16	255	12	4-54	0	21.25
A. Walker	242.3	42	769	29	8-118	2	26.51
M. Prabhakar	579.1	163	1,439	51	7-65	1	28.21
S. J. E. Brown	557.3	107	1,890	52	6-69	4	36.34
D. M. Cox	129.5	28	422	11	4-141	0	38.36
N. Killeen	175.3	28	658	16	5-118	1	41.12
M. M. Betts	175.5	29	733	13	3-35	0	56.38
J. Boiling	541	123	1,575	25	5-73	2	63.00

Also bowled: P. Bainbridge 15-2-55-1; S. D. Birbeck 64-8-271-4; D. A. Blenkiron 16-1-64-1; S. Hutton 2-0-13-0; J. R. G. Lawrence 40-8-123-3; J. I. Longley 4-0-47-0; M. A. Roseberry 2.4-0-14-0; M. Saxelby 13.4-0-60-1; C. W. Scott 3.2-0-30-0; J. P. Searle 36-3-126-2; R. M. S. Weston 22.1-2-70-1.

Wicket-keepers: D. G. C. Ligertwood 33 ct, 3 st; C. W. Scott 14 ct.

Leading Fielder: M. A. Roseberry 15.

At Oxford, April 13, 14, 15. DURHAM drew with OXFORD UNIVERSITY.

DURHAM v HAMPSHIRE

At Stockton-on-Tees, April 27, 28, 29. Durham won by 26 runs. Durham 20 pts, Hampshire 4 pts. Toss: Durham. Championship debuts: M. Prabhakar; H. H. Streak.

Durham opened their fourth Championship campaign with a three-day win, despite the efforts of former Durham University seamer James Bovill, now with Hampshire. In his eighth first-class match, he improved on his career-best return in both innings and had match figures of 12 for 68 on a slow pitch offering some assistance. Though not consistently accurate, Bovill benefited from the element of surprise in his better deliveries. Larkins was the only batsman to rise above the general mediocrity on the first day, when 17 wickets fell. But Udal and the Zimbabwean Streak took their overnight stand to 72 to set up Hampshire's 17-run lead. Prabhakar, like Streak a distinguished newcomer to county cricket, and Smith both played handsomely in the second innings. Smith seemed certain to win the game as he raced to 50 off 51 balls. But his stand of 95 with Terry was ended by Brown, who finished with five for 49. Hampshire's last six fell for 33.

Close of play: First day, Hampshire 126-7 (S. D. Udal 17*, H. H. Streak 0*); Second day, Hampshire 1-1 (V. P. Terry 1*, C. A. Connor 0*).

Durham

*M. A. Roseberry c Terry b Bovill	19	– c Aymes b Streak		0
W. Larkins lbw b Bovill	47	– c Terry b Bovill		31
J. E. Morris c Udal b Bovill	4	– c Morris b Bovill		28
J. A. Daley c Aymes b Bovill	25	– lbw b Bovill		33
M. Prabhakar b Stephenson	7	– lbw b Connor		84
M. Saxelby c Terry b Streak	4	– c Streak b Connor		18
†C. W. Scott run out	20	– b Connor		1
J. Wood c Aymes b Connor	2	– b Bovill		8
J. Boiling not out	14	– lbw b Bovill		0
S. J. E. Brown c White b Bovill	0	– not out		8
M. M. Betts c Smith b Bovill	8	– c White b Bovill		6
B 1, l-b 7, w 5, n-b 14	27	L-b 8, w 4, n-b 19		31
	177			**248**

1/76 2/80 3/81 4/92 5/101   1/0 2/64 3/71 4/150 5/199
6/131 7/143 8/143 9/147   6/213 7/224 8/226 9/236

Bonus points – Hampshire 4.

Bowling: *First Innings*—Connor 15-3-39-1; Streak 15-4-45-1; Bovill 15.2-8-39-6; Udal 7-3-19-0; Stephenson 9-2-27-1. *Second Innings*—Streak 16-2-46-1; Connor 17-2-66-3; Udal 22-3-68-0; Bovill 16.5-8-29-6; Stephenson 9-2-31-0.

Hampshire

J. P. Stephenson lbw b Prabhakar	8	– lbw b Brown		0
V. P. Terry lbw b Brown	11	– lbw b Brown		49
R. S. M. Morris lbw b Wood	10	– (4) lbw b Wood		10
R. A. Smith c Saxelby b Wood	12	– (5) c Scott b Brown		77
*M. C. J. Nicholas lbw b Betts	15	– (6) c Scott b Brown		14
G. W. White lbw b Prabhakar	16	– (7) not out		16
†A. N. Aymes lbw b Prabhakar	0	– (8) b Prabhakar		3
S. D. Udal b Betts	42	– (9) lbw b Brown		4
H. H. Streak c Morris b Wood	32	– (10) c Boiling b Wood		2
C. A. Connor b Betts	0	– (3) c Daley b Betts		5
J. N. B. Bovill not out	6	– lbw b Brown		7
L-b 16, w 1, n-b 25	42	L-b 8, n-b 10		18
	194			**205**

1/17 2/25 3/46 4/51 5/89   1/0 2/13 3/52 4/147 5/172
6/102 7/113 8/185 9/185   6/175 7/178 8/182 9/185

Bonus points – Durham 4.

Bowling: *First Innings*—Brown 21–6–50–1; Prabhakar 22–9–36–3; Wood 12–1–57–3; Betts 8.2–3–35–3. *Second Innings*—Brown 21.3–8–49–5; Betts 11–2–51–1; Prabhakar 22–8–50–2; Wood 9–2–31–2; Boiling 6–3–13–0; Saxelby 1–0–3–0.

Umpires: B. Dudleston and A. G. T. Whitehead.

At Manchester, May 4, 5, 6, 8. DURHAM lost to LANCASHIRE by eight wickets.

At The Oval, May 11, 12, 13, 15. DURHAM lost to SURREY by an innings and 159 runs.

DURHAM v WARWICKSHIRE

At Chester-le-Street (Riverside), May 18, 19, 20, 22. Warwickshire won by 111 runs. Warwickshire 22 pts, Durham 5 pts. Toss: Warwickshire.

First-class cricket arrived at Durham's new headquarters, the Riverside Ground. But in bitter weather the great day attracted fewer than 4,000 spectators and they had to endure some dismal cricket, far less memorable than the teams' 1994 Championship match. On the first day, Warwickshire ground their way to 240 for two off 96 overs – Moles occupying 291 balls for his 90 – before bad light intervened. Doubting that the pitch would last four days, they ploughed on to 424 at 2.62 an over. The champions' attack, missing Donald, Munton and Small, was held up in turn by Morris, who became Riverside's first century-maker, reaching 100 off 200 balls in a highly disciplined display. Durham saved the follow-on with only four wickets down, but threw the rest away for 38 more runs. Brown reduced Warwickshire to 39 for four that evening, passing 200 wickets for Durham, and finished with 11 for 192, the county's best match analysis. But a first-innings lead of 111 enabled Reeve to set a testing target of 257 and only Prabhakar resisted long.

Close of play: First day, Warwickshire 240-2 (T. L. Penney 40*, D. P. Ostler 9*); Second day, Durham 105-2 (J. E. Morris 15*, J. A. Daley 7*); Third day, Warwickshire 76-4 (T. L. Penney 7*, D. A. Reeve 32*).

Warwickshire

A. J. Moles c Larkins b Brown	90	– b Brown			22
N. V. Knight c Roseberry b Wood	89	– lbw b Brown			4
T. L. Penney lbw b Brown	48	– (5) c Prabhakar b Brown			8
D. P. Ostler c Ligertwood b Brown	18	– c Saxelby b Brown			7
R. G. Twose c Ligertwood b Betts	51	– (3) c Ligertwood b Brown			2
*D. A. Reeve c Saxelby b Prabhakar	4	– c Boiling b Betts			47
D. R. Brown c Roseberry b Betts	33	– c Ligertwood b Prabhakar			8
P. A. Smith c Prabhakar b Brown	44	– lbw b Brown			3
†K. J. Piper c Morris b Prabhakar	24	– not out			30
R. P. Davis c Daley b Brown	6	– not out			11
M. A. V. Bell not out	0				
L-b 13, n-b 4	17	L-b 2, w 1			3

1/172 2/223 3/258 4/259 5/270   424   1/20 2/29 3/30   (8 wkts dec.) 145
6/339 7/362 8/403 9/423   4/39 5/77 6/92
                                             7/101 8/119

Bonus points – Warwickshire 2, Durham 2 (Score at 120 overs: 287-5).

Bowling: *First Innings*—Brown 41–11–123–5; Wood 14–6–25–1; Prabhakar 38.4–13–62–2; Betts 27–6–103–2; Boiling 37–6–86–0; Saxelby 4–0–12–0. *Second Innings*—Brown 25–3–69–6; Prabhakar 15–6–38–1; Betts 8–3–21–1; Boiling 2–0–15–0.

Durham

*M. A. Roseberry b Brown	25	– lbw b Bell	2
W. Larkins c Piper b Reeve	58	– lbw b Brown	0
J. E. Morris c and b Twose	128	– c Davis b Reeve	25
J. A. Daley c Twose b Brown	31	– absent hurt	
M. Saxelby lbw b Smith	16	– (4) c Piper b Brown	9
M. Prabhakar c Piper b Twose	27	– (5) c Piper b Reeve	66
†D. G. C. Ligertwood lbw b Twose	2	– (6) c Piper b Smith	2
J. Wood c Davis b Reeve	5	– (7) c Reeve b Smith	8
J. Boiling not out	14	– (8) c Piper b Reeve	11
S. J. E. Brown c Knight b Bell	1	– (9) b Brown	15
M. M. Betts lbw b Brown	2	– (10) not out	0
L-b 2, n-b 2	4	L-b 3, w 4	7

1/83 2/83 3/165 4/204 5/282   313   1/1 2/3 3/16 4/79 5/94   145
6/289 7/294 8/296 9/303   6/104 7/122 8/137 9/145

Bonus points – Durham 3, Warwickshire 4 (Score at 120 overs: 305-9).

Bowling: *First Innings*—Brown 24.2-7-65-3; Bell 29-10-77-1; Reeve 28-11-59-2; Smith 18-5-45-1; Twose 20-6-51-3; Davis 2-1-14-0. *Second Innings*—Brown 12.3-1-62-3; Bell 9-1-34-1; Reeve 15-7-24-3; Smith 6-1-22-2.

Umpires: J. C. Balderstone and J. H. Hampshire.

At Leicester, May 25, 26, 27. DURHAM lost to LEICESTERSHIRE by an innings and 91 runs.

DURHAM v KENT

At Chester-le-Street, June 1, 2, 3, 5. Kent won by 115 runs. Kent 18 pts, Durham 4 pts. Toss: Kent.

With only 67.5 overs possible on the first three days, intense negotiations were necessary on Monday morning. The pitch had sweated under covers since Friday and Durham refused to chase more than 200. This target was duly set by feeding Roseberry and Longley 23 donkey drops, after which Kent forfeited their second innings. But when serious cricket resumed, Longley shouldered arms to McCague's opening delivery and lost his off stump, and Headley and McCague skittled Durham for 85 and their fifth consecutive defeat. Far from farming the strike, Prabhakar accepted the singles offered and faced only 12 balls in the last 12 overs. Only 115 overs were bowled in the entire match. On the first day, de Silva raced to the fastest first-class fifty scored against Durham, off 33 deliveries. He was cut short by a hail-storm at 79 off 68 and lasted only three balls in the morning.

Close of play: First day, Kent 144-4 (P. A. de Silva 79*, G. R. Cowdrey 18*); Second day, Kent 272-9 (M. J. McCague 15*, D. W. Headley 0*); Third day, No play.

Kent

T. R. Ward c Ligertwood b Prabhakar	4	M. M. Patel c Prabhakar b Walker	32
*M. R. Benson c Ligertwood b Brown	10	M. J. McCague not out	15
M. A. Ealham c Larkins b Walker	21	D. W. Headley not out	0
P. A. de Silva c Ligertwood b Brown	83	L-b 7, w 4, n-b 2	13
M. J. Walker c Longley b Betts	6		
G. R. Cowdrey lbw b Brown	19	1/15 2/15 3/90	(9 wkts dec.) 272
M. V. Fleming b Prabhakar	22	4/103 5/148 6/167	
†S. A. Marsh c and b Prabhakar	47	7/175 8/237 9/272	

Bonus points – Kent 2, Durham 4.

Bowling: Brown 17-4-69-3; Prabhakar 23.5-2-83-3; Walker 17-4-52-2; Betts 10-0-61-1.

Kent forfeited their second innings.

Durham

J. I. Longley not out	31 – b McCague	0
*M. A. Roseberry not out	41 – c Marsh b McCague	6
J. E. Morris (did not bat)....................	– lbw b Headley	4
D. A. Blenkiron (did not bat)....................	– c Ward b McCague	4
W. Larkins (did not bat)....................	– lbw b Ealham	4
M. Prabhakar (did not bat)....................	– not out	35
†D. G. C. Ligertwood (did not bat)....................	– run out	3
J. Boiling (did not bat)	– lbw b Headley	10
A. Walker (did not bat)....................	– c Ward b Headley	4
S. J. E. Brown (did not bat)	– c Ward b Headley	1
M. M. Betts (did not bat)	– c Ward b Headley	0
	B 4, l-b 4, w 2, n-b 4 ..	14

(no wkt dec.) 72   1/0 2/9 3/15 4/15 5/37   85
6/46 7/65 8/77 9/85

Bowling: *First Innings*—Cowdrey 2–0–36–0; Ward 1.5–0–36–0. *Second Innings*—McCague 16–4–29–3; Headley 19.2–4–32–5; Ealham 8–1–16–1.

Umpires: R. A. White and P. Willey.

At Chelmsford, June 8, 9, 10, 12. DURHAM lost to ESSEX by 179 runs.

At Chester-le-Street, June 17, 18, 19. DURHAM drew with WEST INDIANS (See West Indian tour section).

DURHAM v DERBYSHIRE

At Chester-le-Street, June 22, 23, 24. Durham won by eight wickets. Durham 22 pts, Derbyshire 4 pts. Toss: Derbyshire.

Durham ended a run of six Championship defeats and swapped places with Derbyshire at the foot of the table. Again, there was some variable bounce in the Riverside pitch and some undistinguished batting. Derbyshire were 66 for seven at lunch on the first day when DeFreitas flew in from London, having been omitted by England. He made 49 not out off 50 balls and quickly trapped opener Longley. Griffith followed up with three wickets in ten balls, leaving Durham 75 for five. They were rescued by Morris, with a fine 99 against his old county, and Birbeck, with a dogged, unbeaten 75 – his previous best in five first-class innings was ten. Derbyshire lost six wickets clearing arrears of 79, but were saved from a two-day defeat by Barnett's second accomplished half-century. Brown finished with nine for 81 and Durham needed only 117. DeFreitas's final contribution was a sad come-down: he conceded 40 in six overs on the final morning as Durham sped to victory.

Close of play: First day, Durham 156-5 (J. E. Morris 65*, S. D. Birbeck 27*); Second day, Durham 10-0 (J. I. Longley 5*, M. A. Roseberry 3*).

Derbyshire

A. S. Rollins b Prabhakar	6 – c Bainbridge b Prabhakar	6
W. A. Dessaur b Brown	1 – run out	21
C. J. Adams c Morris b Betts	9 – lbw b Brown	1
D. J. Cullinan lbw b Walker	10 – b Brown	0
C. M. Wells c Roseberry b Brown	15 – c Roseberry b Brown	4
*K. J. Barnett c Ligertwood b Birbeck	58 – c Ligertwood b Bainbridge	74
†K. M. Krikken c Ligertwood b Brown	3 – lbw b Betts	0
F. A. Griffith c Ligertwood b Brown	0 – (9) c and b Brown	53
A. E. Warner b Walker	22 – (10) not out	2
P. A. J. DeFreitas not out....................	49 – (8) c Ligertwood b Walker	24
D. E. Malcolm run out	14 – b Brown	0
L-b 4, w 1, n-b 2	7	B 1, l-b 7, w 2	10

1/3 2/15 3/28 4/28 5/56   194   1/12 2/13 3/17 4/25 5/42   195
6/64 7/64 8/110 9/165   6/52 7/87 8/189 9/195

Bonus points – Durham 4.

Bowling: *First Innings*—Brown 16–5–39–4; Prabhakar 14–0–45–1; Betts 10–2–44–1; Walker 14.5–2–42–2; Birbeck 6–1–20–1. *Second Innings*—Brown 16.4–4–42–5; Prabhakar 21–4–53–1; Walker 10–3–22–1; Betts 8–2–37–1; Birbeck 6–2–28–0; Bainbridge 5–2–5–1.

Durham

J. I. Longley lbw b DeFreitas	7	– lbw b Warner	50
*M. A. Roseberry c Griffith b Malcolm	10	– not out	36
J. E. Morris lbw b Malcolm	99	– c Wells b Griffith	3
S. Hutton c Krikken b Griffith	18	– not out	19
M. Prabhakar c and b Griffith	2		
P. Bainbridge lbw b Griffith	0		
S. D. Birbeck not out	75		
†D. G. C. Ligertwood c and b DeFreitas	1		
A. Walker lbw b Warner	6		
S. J. E. Brown c Adams b Malcolm	6		
M. M. Betts c Krikken b Malcolm	1		
B 13, l-b 5, w 4, n-b 26	48	L-b 2, n-b 8	10

1/23 2/25 3/73 4/75 5/75   273   1/90 2/93   (2 wkts) 118
6/200 7/215 8/243 9/267

Bonus points – Durham 2, Derbyshire 4.

Bowling: *First Innings*—Malcolm 27.1–4–91–4; DeFreitas 23–3–77–2; Warner 24–5–61–1; Griffith 8–2–26–3. *Second Innings*—DeFreitas 8–1–46–0; Malcolm 4–1–15–0; Warner 10.2–1–33–1; Griffith 6–0–22–1.

Umpires: G. I. Burgess and B. Leadbeater.

At Swansea, June 29, 30, July 1, 3. DURHAM beat GLAMORGAN by six wickets.

DURHAM v WORCESTERSHIRE

At Darlington, July 6, 7, 8. Worcestershire won by ten wickets. Worcestershire 23 pts, Durham 2 pts. Toss: Worcestershire.

Durham lost the toss for the seventh successive Championship match and were ground down by Worcestershire's attrition on an easy-paced pitch. The visitors made 424 for eight in 156 overs, only Leatherdale playing with any fluency. Boiling, who entered the match with nine first-class wickets at 97.11, became the first Durham spinner to take a wicket at home since August 1, 1994. Despite the absence of turn, he took five for 119 as the seamers toiled in vain. However, Newport proved the pitch was not that lifeless: he finished the innings with a spell of three for one in 25 balls, and Durham had to follow on. Prabhakar, who made 59 in each innings, briefly threatened to turn the game, adding 119 with Blenkiron. But Lampitt removed them and Newport again finished off Durham, this time with a burst of four for six.

Close of play: First day, Worcestershire 248-5 (D. A. Leatherdale 44*, S. J. Rhodes 0*); Second day, Durham 157-6 (M. Prabhakar 51*, J. Boiling 2*).

Worcestershire

T. S. Curtis lbw b Betts	28 – not out	23
W. P. C. Weston c and b Boiling	80 – not out	0
G. R. Haynes c Prabhakar b Boiling	11	
*T. M. Moody c Betts b Boiling	38	
D. A. Leatherdale c Hutton b Prabhakar	93	
S. R. Lampitt c Morris b Boiling	36	
†S. J. Rhodes not out	70	
V. S. Solanki c Brown b Betts	14	
P. J. Newport c Prabhakar b Boiling	30	
P. Mirza not out	8	
B 2, l-b 10, w 2, n-b 2	16	W 2 2

1/65 2/100 3/163 4/172 5/248　(8 wkts dec.) 424　(no wkt) 25
6/318 7/348 8/407

P. A. Thomas did not bat.

Bonus points – Worcestershire 3, Durham 2 (Score at 120 overs: 316-5).

Bowling: *First Innings*—Brown 27–5–88–0; Prabhakar 27–7–52–1; Walker 27–4–79–0; Betts 23–1–74–2; Boiling 52–14–119–5. *Second Innings*—Brown 1–0–13–0; Betts 0.3–0–12–0.

Durham

J. I. Longley c Lampitt b Newport	9 – c Moody b Mirza	32
*M. A. Roseberry lbw b Lampitt	22 – (7) c Lampitt b Mirza	5
J. E. Morris c Solanki b Newport	13 – c Haynes b Mirza	37
S. Hutton c Rhodes b Mirza	7 – (2) c Curtis b Lampitt	0
M. Prabhakar c Weston b Newport	59 – c Moody b Lampitt	59
D. A. Blenkiron c Moody b Haynes	19 – (4) b Lampitt	34
†D. G. C. Ligertwood lbw b Haynes	19 – (6) c Weston b Newport	7
J. Boiling not out	17 – c Lampitt b Newport	0
A. Walker c Rhodes b Newport	4 – c Leatherdale b Newport	19
S. J. E. Brown c Rhodes b Newport	0 – b Newport	5
M. M. Betts run out	0 – not out	1
L-b 5, w 1, n-b 16	22	B 8, l-b 13, w 1, n-b 34 .. 56

1/14 2/36 3/53 4/68 5/109　191　1/4 2/73 3/85 4/204 5/211　255
6/145 7/174 8/182 9/186　6/224 7/224 8/230 9/254

Bonus points – Worcestershire 4.

Bowling: *First Innings*—Newport 22.4–9–45–5; Thomas 10–2–32–0; Lampitt 9–1–19–1; Mirza 17–3–51–1; Haynes 8–2–21–2; Solanki 4–1–18–0. *Second Innings*—Thomas 5–2–9–0; Lampitt 21–8–56–3; Newport 11–3–27–4; Mirza 14–2–79–3; Haynes 11–0–39–0; Solanki 12–4–20–0; Moody 1–0–4–0.

Umpires: H. D. Bird and N. T. Plews.

At Harrogate, July 20, 21, 22, 24. DURHAM lost to YORKSHIRE by 211 runs.

At Northampton, August 3, 4, 5. DURHAM lost to NORTHAMPTONSHIRE by an innings and 76 runs.

DURHAM v MIDDLESEX

At Chester-le-Street, August 10, 11, 12, 14. Middlesex won by 386 runs. Middlesex 23 pts, Durham 5 pts. Toss: Middlesex.

Middlesex captain Gatting sympathised with Durham for having to bat on a pitch that was at its most venomous on the final morning, when they lost their last seven for 32 inside an hour. The wicket offered such steep bounce that Pooley took six catches at short leg during the match, and Johnson and Nash took full advantage in those closing minutes. Gatting himself suffered on the first day, when a ball from Killeen hit his recently-broken finger. He thought the pitch had eased on the Saturday, when he delayed declaring until mid-afternoon to set Durham 501, only for the first rain for weeks to wipe out 32 overs. Ramprakash countered the variable bounce with an immaculately straight bat in a superb 155, while Carr scored two eighties. Middlesex had hopes of a fifth successive innings win when Roseberry and Morris fell in Johnson's first over. Larkins and Prabhakar avoided that, but could not stave off Durham's biggest defeat by a margin of runs.

Close of play: First day, Durham 17-2 (S. Hutton 7*, J. Boiling 8*); Second day, Middlesex 202-2 (M. R. Ramprakash 100*, M. A. Feltham 25*); Third day, Durham 82-2 (M. A. Roseberry 26*, W. Larkins 28*).

Middlesex

P. N. Weekes c Hutton b Prabhakar	48	– c Ligertwood b Brown	12
J. C. Pooley c Roseberry b Prabhakar	17	– c Prabhakar b Boiling	64
M. R. Ramprakash c Ligertwood b Walker	6	– c and b Boiling	155
*M. W. Gatting lbw b Boiling	29		
J. D. Carr b Blenkiron b Walker	89	– not out	81
†K. R. Brown c Roseberry b Walker	6	– c Roseberry b Prabhakar	39
D. J. Nash c Ligertwood b Brown	20	– not out	7
R. L. Johnson c Ligertwood b Brown	25		
M. A. Feltham c Walker b Boiling	3	– (4) c Boiling b Prabhakar	25
J. E. Emburey c Morris b Killeen	33		
P. C. R. Tufnell not out	22		
L-b 2, w 5, n-b 2	9	B 8, l-b 1, w 3, n-b 2	14

1/32 2/44 3/100 4/118 5/167   307   1/24 2/125 3/204   (5 wkts dec.) 397
6/207 7/227 8/253 9/258   4/303 5/383

Bonus points – Middlesex 3, Durham 4.

In the first innings M. W. Gatting, when 27, retired hurt at 112 and resumed at 253.

Bowling: *First Innings*—Brown 27-4-103-2; Prabhakar 23-8-61-2; Killeen 17.2-6-47-1; Walker 17-4-65-3; Boiling 12-4-29-2. *Second Innings*—Brown 13-2-66-1; Killeen 20-2-83-0; Prabhakar 20-6-71-2; Boiling 26-1-114-2; Walker 14-3-36-0; Roseberry 1-0-7-0; Blenkiron 2-0-11-0.

Durham

*M. A. Roseberry c Feltham b Johnson	0	– c Brown b Johnson	28
S. Hutton hit wkt b Nash	9	– c Carr b Feltham	14
J. E. Morris c Ramprakash b Johnson	2	– c Pooley b Johnson	0
J. Boiling c Pooley b Johnson	10	– (8) b Nash	2
W. Larkins lbw b Johnson	41	– (4) c Weekes b Johnson	33
M. Prabhakar b Emburey b Johnson	86	– (5) c Pooley b Johnson	8
D. A. Blenkiron not out	26	– (6) b Nash	0
†D. G. C. Ligertwood c Brown b Nash	9	– (7) c Pooley b Johnson	3
N. Killeen c Pooley b Nash	2	– not out	0
A. Walker lbw b Nash	0	– absent hurt	
S. J. E. Brown c Pooley b Nash	0	– (10) c Carr b Nash	5
B 1, l-b 8, n-b 10	19	B 4, w 9, n-b 8	21

1/0 2/2 3/29 4/29 5/153   204   1/32 2/35 3/94 4/97 5/100   114
6/174 7/198 8/200 9/204   6/104 7/109 8/109 9/114

Bonus points – Durham 1, Middlesex 4.

Bowling: *First Innings*—Johnson 18-4-50-5; Nash 20.5-6-47-5; Emburey 5-0-25-0; Feltham 9-1-41-0; Tufnell 15-7-32-0. *Second Innings*—Johnson 17-3-48-5; Nash 10.1-4-29-3; Feltham 12-3-33-1.

Umpires: B. Leadbeater and A. G. T. Whitehead.

DURHAM v SOMERSET

At Chester-le-Street, August 17, 18, 19. Somerset won by 286 runs. Somerset 23 pts, Durham 5 pts. Toss: Somerset. First-class debuts: J. R. G. Lawrence, R. M. S. Weston.

This was almost an action replay of Durham's previous match: they recovered sufficiently to avoid the follow-on, only to be set a target of over 500 and lose by a crushing margin, this time with a day to spare. With several bowlers injured, they rushed through the registration of James Lawrence, a left-arm pace bowler from Darlington, and he made his debut the day he received his A-level results; he had the unusual experience of hearing his exam successes being announced over the loudspeakers and applauded by the crowd. On a pitch marked "poor" by the umpires, because of its uneven bounce, Somerset's Caddick thrived. Returning after time off with sore shins, he followed a career-best 61 by becoming the first bowler to take eight wickets in an innings against Durham. One of the two he missed was Robin Weston, brother of Worcestershire's Philip, out first ball on his debut, to Kerr. Scott and Killeen rescued them from 98 for seven, but Durham's problems heightened. Brown and Prabhakar both suffered ankle injuries, leaving Hayhurst and Harden – who resumed after a blow to his hand – to plunder centuries off a threadbare attack.

Close of play: First day, Durham 34-2 (J. E. Morris 23*, J. Boiling 4*); Second day, Somerset 214-3 (A. N. Hayhurst 86*, G. D. Rose 0*).

Somerset

M. N. Lathwell c Scott b Prabhakar	16	– lbw b Prabhakar	4
P. D. Bowler c Larkins b Lawrence	10	– c Larkins b Prabhakar	24
*A. N. Hayhurst c Brown b Killeen	25	– c Larkins b Lawrence	107
R. J. Harden c Larkins b Boiling	18	– not out	100
K. A. Parsons c Scott b Brown	8	– c and b Weston	69
G. D. Rose c Larkins b Lawrence	48	– c Larkins b Killeen	1
†R. J. Turner c Weston b Killeen	65	– not out	71
J. I. D. Kerr c Larkins b Prabhakar	6		
Mushtaq Ahmed c Scott b Prabhakar	0		
A. R. Caddick c Roseberry b Killeen	61		
A. P. van Troost not out	28		
B 2, l-b 21, w 3, n-b 2	28	B 4, l-b 6, w 2, n-b 2	14

1/27 2/48 3/82 4/100 5/114   333   1/15 2/32 3/213   (5 wkts dec.) 390
6/194 7/212 8/212 9/271   4/219 5/267

Bonus points – Somerset 3, Durham 4.

In the second innings R. J. Harden, when 26, retired hurt at 70 and resumed at 219.

Bowling: *First Innings*—Brown 28-2-107-1; Prabhakar 23-6-59-3; Lawrence 16-5-44-2; Killeen 19-3-83-3; Boiling 11-5-17-1. *Second Innings*—Brown 9-1-31-0; Prabhakar 17-3-40-2; Killeen 21-2-96-1; Lawrence 24-3-79-1; Boiling 28-7-80-0; Weston 15.1-2-41-1; Hutton 2-0-13-0.

Durham

*M. A. Roseberry c Turner b Caddick	0	– c Harden b Caddick	4
S. Hutton b Caddick	4	– b Mushtaq Ahmed	34
J. E. Morris c Turner b Caddick	38	– c Harden b Kerr	50
J. Boiling c Turner b Kerr	12	– (8) c Turner b van Troost	13
W. Larkins c Turner b Caddick	14	– (4) c Caddick b Mushtaq Ahmed	20
R. M. S. Weston lbw b Kerr	0	– (5) c Turner b Caddick	4
M. Prabhakar c Harden b Caddick	9	– run out	45
†C. W. Scott c Harden b Caddick	55	– (6) st Turner b Mushtaq Ahmed	1
N. Killeen b Caddick	48	– c Rose b Mushtaq Ahmed	19
S. J. E. Brown not out	14	– st Turner b Mushtaq Ahmed	2
J. R. G. Lawrence c Bowler b Caddick	0	– not out	7
B 16, l-b 5, n-b 6	27	B 4, l-b 7, w 6	17

1/0 2/25 3/64 4/64 5/64   221   1/4 2/72 3/106 4/121 5/125   216
6/95 7/98 8/200 9/221   6/125 7/187 8/188 9/193

Bonus points – Durham 1, Somerset 4.

Bowling: *First Innings*—Caddick 19.4–1–69–8; Rose 5–2–11–0; van Troost 5–0–33–0; Kerr 9–0–51–2; Mushtaq Ahmed 10–1–36–0. *Second Innings*—Caddick 21–4–62–2; van Troost 12–0–45–1; Kerr 9–1–29–1; Mushtaq Ahmed 17.4–8–60–5; Rose 2–0–9–0.

Umpires: J. D. Bond and D. J. Constant.

DURHAM v SUSSEX

At Hartlepool, August 24, 25, 26, 28. Sussex won by an innings and 50 runs. Sussex 24 pts, Durham 2 pts. Toss: Durham.

A match between two of the Championship's bottom three was no contest from the moment Jarvis destroyed Durham's middle order on a blameless pitch. He took four wickets in 26 balls and later Giddins completed the first ten-wicket match haul of his career to consign Durham to their sixth successive heavy defeat. Each of Sussex's first three wickets put on more than a hundred; Athey, Hall and Lenham scored centuries, Athey for the third season running against Durham. The home side's only encouraging performance came from Killeen, who took five wickets in his fifth first-class match. Rain gave Durham a faint chance of a draw; they resumed on 170 for two on the final day, but only Hutton, with 98, offered prolonged resistance. Giddins and Jarvis bowled unchanged to complete the task in the over before lunch; after a team meeting, Durham admitted their confidence was shattered.

Close of play: First day, Sussex 60-0 (C. W. J. Athey 24*, M. T. E. Peirce 26*); Second day, Sussex 436-6 (K. Greenfield 25*, I. D. K. Salisbury 9*); Third day, Durham 170-2 (S. Hutton 65*, J. E. Morris 13*).

Durham

W. Larkins c Jarvis b Kirtley	19	– (2) c Kirtley b Giddins	43
S. Hutton lbw b Giddins	0	– (1) c Kirtley b Giddins	98
J. I. Longley c Athey b Jarvis	34	– b Jarvis	35
*J. E. Morris c Salisbury b Jarvis	25	– b Jarvis	21
R. M. S. Weston c Greenfield b Jarvis	0	– b Giddins	0
M. Prabhakar c Salisbury b Jarvis	11	– b Giddins	0
†C. W. Scott c Moores b Giddins	31	– b Jarvis	24
J. Boiling c Moores b Giddins	18	– c and b Giddins	18
N. Killeen not out	19	– c Salisbury b Jarvis	4
S. J. E. Brown run out	1	– b Giddins	1
A. Walker b Giddins	1	– not out	4
L-b 9, w 3, n-b 6	18	L-b 10, w 5, n-b 8	23
	177		**271**

1/5 2/51 3/67 4/67 5/83
6/125 7/142 8/170 9/173

1/68 2/134 3/188 4/189 5/189
6/234 7/245 8/262 9/266

Bonus points – Sussex 4.

Bowling: *First Innings*—Giddins 19.1–5–57–4; Jarvis 21–6–46–4; Kirtley 18–6–42–1; Salisbury 6–0–23–0. *Second Innings*—Giddins 26.4–6–87–6; Jarvis 29–5–104–4; Kirtley 8–2–29–0; Salisbury 11–3–28–0; Law 2–0–13–0.

Sussex

C. W. J. Athey b Killeen	108
M. T. E. Peirce c Weston b Walker	44
J. W. Hall c Walker b Killeen	100
N. J. Lenham b Killeen	104
K. Greenfield b Prabhakar	45
D. R. Law lbw b Killeen	2
†P. Moores c Scott b Prabhakar	6
*I. D. K. Salisbury not out	29

P. W. Jarvis c and b Killeen	18
R. J. Kirtley not out	1
L-b 14, w 9, n-b 18	41

1/114 2/234 3/371   (8 wkts dec.) **498**
4/398 5/404 6/419
7/470 8/497

E. S. H. Giddins did not bat.

Bonus points – Sussex 4, Durham 2 (Score at 120 overs: 415-5).

Bowling: Brown 29–5–111–0; Prabhakar 29–5–85–2; Killeen 29–4–118–5; Walker 17–2–85–1; Boiling 31–9–56–0; Weston 7–0–29–0.

Umpires: T. E. Jesty and A. A. Jones.

At Bristol, September 7, 8, 9, 11. DURHAM lost to GLOUCESTERSHIRE by 19 runs.

DURHAM v NOTTINGHAMSHIRE

At Chester-le-Street, September 14, 15, 16. Durham won by an innings and 14 runs. Durham 24 pts, Nottinghamshire 3 pts. Toss: Nottinghamshire.

After a run of seven defeats, Durham had to win to avoid the wooden spoon. They found ideal opponents in Nottinghamshire, who raised barely a whimper in what was their sixth successive defeat. Rain had drawn the pitch's sting, undermining Johnson's decision to field. With Cairns unable to bowl because of a bad knee, Durham achieved maximum batting points for the first time in 1995. Larkins, in what proved to be his final innings before his release was announced, scored 121, his tenth hundred for Durham, and put on 180 with Morris, who made a century off 131 balls. Daley and Roseberry, both returning from injury, added fifties. Off-spinner Bates did take five wickets for the first time, but Nottinghamshire's only other consolation was a maiden fifty for No. 11 Pennett. He put on 85 with Pick after excellent seam bowling from Walker had wrecked the top order at 29 for five. Walker too injured his knee but, when Nottinghamshire followed on, Boiling found turn where previously none had existed to record a season's-best five for 73. Durham won on Saturday afternoon, the first result of the Championship's concluding round.

Close of play: First day, Durham 258-2 (W. Larkins 113*, J. A. Daley 15*); Second day, Nottinghamshire 159-9 (R. A. Pick 38*, D. B. Pennett 28*).

Durham

W. Larkins c Noon b Bates 121	N. Killeen lbw b Archer	0
S. Hutton c Bates b Wileman 10	S. J. E. Brown c Noon b Archer	17
J. E. Morris c Noon b Bates 109	A. Walker not out	2
J. A. Daley run out 50		
*M. A. Roseberry b Bates 53	B 5, l-b 11, n-b 12	28
M. Prabhakar c Pennett b Bates 2		
†C. W. Scott c and b Archer 32	1/39 2/219 3/293 4/315 5/322	424
J. Boiling b Bates 0	6/378 7/379 8/380 9/402	

Bonus points – Durham 4, Nottinghamshire 3 (Score at 120 overs: 381-8).

Bowling: Pennett 23–4–75–0; Pick 27–8–70–0; Wileman 18–3–50–1; Chapman 15–0–75–0; Bates 33.1–11–88–5; Archer 17–2–50–3.

Nottinghamshire

R. T. Robinson c Scott b Walker	5 – lbw b Boiling	39
J. R. Wileman lbw b Walker	0 – b Brown	0
G. F. Archer c Brown b Killeen	37 – c Scott b Boiling	35
*P. Johnson b Walker	0 – b Boiling	4
N. A. Gie b Prabhakar	4 – c Killeen b Boiling	27
C. L. Cairns b Walker	8 – c Roseberry b Brown	17
†W. M. Noon b Brown	8 – not out	52
R. T. Bates c Roseberry b Prabhakar	11 – lbw b Brown	0
R. A. Pick not out	46 – c Killeen b Boiling	14
R. J. Chapman lbw b Prabhakar	0 – c Scott b Brown	22
D. B. Pennett c Roseberry b Killeen	50 – c Hutton b Prabhakar	1
B 8, l-b 13	21	L-b 8, w 1	9

1/4 2/5 3/5 4/16 5/29	190	1/13 2/73 3/79 4/84 5/120	220
6/50 7/76 8/85 9/105		6/134 7/136 8/163 9/208	

Bonus points – Durham 4.

Bowling: *First Innings*—Prabhakar 17–4–38–3; Walker 12–2–29–4; Brown 10–1–50–1; Killeen 6.1–0–20–2; Boiling 8–2–32–0. *Second Innings*—Brown 22–5–61–4; Killeen 14–0–54–0; Prabhakar 9.4–2–24–1; Boiling 29–6–73–5.

Umpires: G. Sharp and P. Willey.

ESSEX

ESSEX

President: D. J. Insole
Chairman: D. L. Acfield
Chairman, Cricket Committee: G. J. Saville
Secretary/General Manager: P. J. Edwards
Captain: P. J. Prichard
Head Groundsman: S. Kerrison
Scorer: C. F. Driver

Paul Prichard never expected his first season as captain to be easy and he was not disappointed. Last summer confirmed that he faces a huge task to weld Essex into a team capable of lifting as many honours as they did in the 1980s. Prichard will no doubt draw comfort from the final weeks of the season, when Essex won their last five Championship matches to finish in fifth place, the same position attained in the Sunday League. However, the teams occupying the four top places in both competitions all beat Essex. That fact alone indicated Essex had some way to go before regaining the summit. When one also reflects that they made little progress in the one-day knockouts, last summer's deeds can only be termed as mediocre by the standards Essex have set.

Yet there were encouraging signs. Wicket-keeper Robert Rollins, preferred at the start to Mike Garnham, who announced his retirement, looked destined for bigger things. He did suffer an indifferent spell in mid-season, when his concentration tended to waver in the heat, but either side of that confirmed his promise with many stunning catches and superb athleticism. His batting, too, blossomed in the latter stages: 469 of his 809 runs arrived from the final six first-class games and he was awarded his county cap in September. Ronnie Irani also made good progress. Although he struggled for consistency with the ball, his stature as a hard-hitting middle-order batsman grew as he passed 1,000 runs in a season for the first time in his career, and deservedly won a place on England A's winter tour to Pakistan. In the Sunday League match against Gloucestershire at Cheltenham, he scored a century from 47 balls, the fastest by an Essex player in the competition.

Mark Ilott can look back on 1995 with satisfaction. Displaying greater zest and consistency, he had a haul of 78 first-class wickets, which included nine for 19 against Northamptonshire – the third best return by an Essex bowler ever, and containing a hat-trick of lbws. Ilott's whole-hearted efforts were rewarded with selection for England's tour of South Africa. Unfortunately – and this is where Essex's biggest problem surfaced – he lacked quality support with the new ball. Neil Williams, recruited from Middlesex, made a minimal contribution. He spent much of the summer on the injury list and when he did play took only 21 wickets from eight Championship matches. That left Darren Cousins to form the main spearhead with Ilott. Though a willing and enthusiastic performer, his inability to get movement through the air or off the pitch hardly made him a potent threat, as a dozen wickets at 53.33 illustrated. At various times, Irani, Mark Waugh and Steve Andrew were also thrust into action with the new ball, but none came close to matching Ilott's menace.

Once his left-arm seam was withdrawn from the attack Essex were usually left relying on spinners John Childs and Peter Such to make an impact. Between them they claimed 145 wickets and with the 59th of his 68 victims, Childs captured the 1,000th of his career, shortly after his 44th birthday. One of cricket's gentlemen, Childs is now the game's elder statesman, following the retirement of Eddie Hemmings. Twice, Such captured more than ten wickets in a match, against Worcestershire and Hampshire, on his way to a total of 77 and was unlucky to be ignored by England.

Graham Gooch turned 42 but continued to be an enormous force. He helped himself to seven centuries while accumulating 1,669 runs at an average of just over 50. Lack of mobility rather than a declining ability to score runs is likely to determine when he calls it a day. But it was Nasser Hussain who emerged as the county's most productive and consistent batsman. He had never played better, scoring 1,854 first-class runs at an average of 54.52, recording six centuries, and 634 runs in the Sunday League. Statistics, however, do not tell the whole story. Greater concentration allied to a steely resolve proved his growing maturity as a batsman, without curbing his natural instinct to attack and entertain. His form failed to win him a Test recall against West Indies or a tour of South Africa, but Hussain will have been honoured by his appointment as captain of England A on their tour of Pakistan.

Waugh reached Essex in May, looking tired after Australia's epic series in the West Indies and anything but a world-class player. One half-century in his first 12 innings mocked his natural talent before he discovered his form to score five hundreds, including two in the match against Derbyshire, while amassing 1,347 at 51 for the county. Prichard was the fifth batsman to pass 1,000 runs. He adopted a low-key style of leadership but his batting lacked his usual confidence – an indication that the burden of captaincy was bigger than he might care to admit. Nick Knight's decision to join Warwickshire provided Darren Robinson with an opportunity to open the innings. Centuries against Durham and Gloucestershire suggested promise, but too often he flattered to deceive; it will need a great deal of application and hard work for him to establish himself on the county circuit. The same can be said of Jonathan Lewis, who failed to make the most of his opportunities in the top order during the early part of the season and spent most of the summer performing twelfth man duties. Lewis was one of the players to benefit from advice from Keith Fletcher who, after his dismissal as England manager, returned to the club as cricket consultant, and concentrated on helping the youngsters. At least the Essex tradition of continuity is still alive. – Nigel Fuller.

ESSEX 1995

[*Bill Smith*

Back row: A. J. E. Hibbert, R. J. Rollins, D. D. J. Robinson, C. I. O. Ricketts, N. A. Derbyshire, N. F. Williams, S. D. Peters.
Middle row: J. S. W. Davis (*physiotherapist*), D. M. Cousins, R. C. Irani, S. J. W. Andrew, R. M. Pearson, A. P. Cowan, D. W. Ayres, A. R. Butcher. *Front row:* M. A. Garnham, J. H. Childs, N. Hussain, P. J. Prichard (*captain*), G. A. Gooch, P. M. Such, J. J. B. Lewis.

ESSEX RESULTS

All first-class matches – Played 19: Won 8, Lost 9, Drawn 2.

County Championship matches – Played 17: Won 8, Lost 9.

Bonus points – Batting 42, Bowling 58.

*Competition placings – Britannic Assurance County Championship, 5th;
NatWest Bank Trophy, 2nd round; Benson and Hedges Cup, 4th in Group C;
AXA Equity & Law League, 5th.*

BRITANNIC ASSURANCE CHAMPIONSHIP AVERAGES

BATTING

	Birthplace	*M*	*I*	*NO*	*R*	*HS*	*Avge*
‡N. Hussain	*Madras, India*	17	32	0	1,688	186	52.75
‡M. E. Waugh§	*Sydney, Australia*	15	28	2	1,347	173	51.80
‡G. A. Gooch	*Leytonstone*	17	32	0	1,510	165	47.18
‡R. C. Irani	*Leigh*	17	32	2	1,135	108	37.83
‡P. J. Prichard	*Billericay*	17	31	0	1,047	109	33.77
‡R. J. Rollins	*Plaistow*	17	31	2	727	133*	25.06
D. D. J. Robinson ..	*Braintree*	15	28	0	665	123	23.75
A. P. Cowan	*Hitchin*	2	4	1	47	22	15.66
‡J. J. B. Lewis	*Isleworth*	5	10	0	141	75	14.10
‡M. C. Ilott	*Watford*	15	27	3	288	37	12.00
‡P. M. Such	*Helensburgh*	17	30	8	214	32	9.72
D. M. Cousins	*Cambridge*	7	14	3	99	18*	9.00
N. F. Williams	*Hope Well, St Vincent*	8	12	2	90	17	9.00
‡J. H. Childs	*Plymouth*	16	27	11	112	18	7.00

Also batted: S. J. W. Andrew (*London*) (1 match) 0, 4; N. A. Derbyshire (*Ramsbottom*) (1 match) 9, 17.

* *Signifies not out.*   ‡ *Denotes county cap.*   § *Overseas player.*

The following played a total of 23 three-figure innings for Essex in County Championship matches – G. A. Gooch 6, N. Hussain 6, M. E. Waugh 5, P. J. Prichard 2, D. D. J. Robinson 2, R. C. Irani 1, R. J. Rollins 1.

BOWLING

	O	*M*	*R*	*W*	*BB*	*5W/i*	*Avge*
M. C. Ilott	539.4	115	1,684	76	9-19	6	22.15
P. M. Such	708.4	166	1,940	75	8-93	6	25.86
J. H. Childs	648.3	171	1,690	62	6-36	2	27.25
N. F. Williams	188.4	31	743	21	5-93	1	35.38
R. C. Irani	343.5	70	1,134	25	5-62	1	45.36
M. E. Waugh	256	45	789	17	4-76	0	46.41

Also bowled: S. J. W. Andrew 19–2–70–0; D. M. Cousins 138–18–491–8; A. P. Cowan 24–2–113–1; N. A. Derbyshire 5–1–20–1; G. A. Gooch 20–4–68–4.

Wicket-keeper: R. J. Rollins 48 ct, 9 st.

Leading Fielders: N. Hussain 33, D. D. J. Robinson 22, M. E. Waugh 19.

ESSEX v LEICESTERSHIRE

At Chelmsford, April 27, 28, 29, 30. Leicestershire won by 102 runs. Leicestershire 21 pts, Essex 8 pts. Toss: Essex. Championship debut: W. J. Cronje.

A painful accident brought Whitticase's 114-run partnership with Millns to an abrupt end on Saturday evening. In poor light (four warning lamps were showing), he lost sight of a ball from Williams and had seven teeth knocked out. Jack Birkenshaw, Leicestershire's cricket manager, said the umpires should have offered the light to the batsmen, and Whitticase was later reported to be seeking legal advice to recover the cost of his treatment. He was making his first Championship appearance since 1992 because first-choice keeper Nixon had broken a finger. He resumed batting briefly on Sunday, but Robinson kept wicket. Whitticase and Millns, who made a career-best 70, had given Leicestershire a solid advantage, but their victory owed most to Briers, who failed by just five runs to complete a century in each innings. Gooch failed by eight to perform the feat for a sixth time and his dismissal signalled the capitulation of Essex, who had been in the ascendency for the first two days. Ilott and Williams, who claimed eight wickets in his first Championship game since leaving Middlesex, ran through Leicestershire's batting, while centuries from Gooch and Hussain established a first-innings lead of 151.

Close of play: First day, Essex 150-2 (G. A. Gooch 80*, D. M. Cousins 3*); Second day, Leicestershire 76-1 (N. E. Briers 23*, W. J. Cronje 38*); Third day, Leicestershire 414-8 (D. J. Millns 61*, A. R. K. Pierson 2*).

Leicestershire

T. J. Boon c Rollins b Williams	5	– c Hussain b Williams	15
*N. E. Briers c Rollins b Williams	114	– c Such b Ilott	95
W. J. Cronje c Rollins b Williams	34	– c Such b Ilott	38
J. J. Whitaker b Ilott	14	– b Cousins	48
P. E. Robinson c Gooch b Ilott	0	– c Lewis b Such	5
V. J. Wells c Rollins b Williams	0	– c Rollins b Such	31
G. J. Parsons lbw b Ilott	7	– b Cousins	26
†P. Whitticase b Ilott	22	– not out	62
A. R. K. Pierson b Cousins	26	– (11) lbw b Williams	7
D. J. Millns c Rollins b Williams	7	– (9) c Rollins b Williams	70
A. D. Mullally not out	2	– (10) c Williams b Cousins	13
L-b 4, n-b 18	22	B 1, l-b 11, n-b 10	22
	253		**432**

1/5 2/67 3/86 4/86 5/87   1/29 2/76 3/182 4/195 5/231
6/94 7/132 8/232 9/250   6/273 7/275 8/408 9/423

Bonus points – Leicestershire 2, Essex 4.

In the second innings P. Whitticase, when 60, retired hurt at 389 and resumed at 423.

Bowling: *First Innings*—Ilott 23–2–78–4; Williams 18.3–3–93–5; Irani 6–0–38–0; Cousins 8–0–26–1; Such 6–1–14–0. *Second Innings*—Ilott 28–5–104–2; Williams 25.2–3–93–3; Irani 15–4–60–0; Such 44–13–90–2; Cousins 29–3–73–3.

Essex

G. A. Gooch c Whitticase b Wells	139	– b Mullally	92
*P. J. Prichard c Millns b Cronje	63	– lbw b Millns	16
J. J. B. Lewis run out	2	– c Robinson b Mullally	4
D. M. Cousins c Wells b Mullally	13	– (1) b Mullally	0
N. Hussain c Robinson b Millns	100	– (4) lbw b Cronje	11
D. D. J. Robinson run out	24	– (5) c sub b Parsons	9
R. C. Irani lbw b Parsons	17	– (6) c sub b Wells	11
†R. J. Rollins b Millns	11	– (7) b Wells	0
M. C. Ilott c Boon b Wells	5	– (8) c sub b Millns	10
N. F. Williams c Whitticase b Wells	12	– (9) lbw b Millns	0
P. M. Such not out	6	– (10) not out	6
L-b 9, w 1, n-b 2	12	B 13, l-b 6, w 1	20
	404		**179**

1/138 2/146 3/194 4/233 5/300   1/36 2/43 3/61 4/76 5/102
6/342 7/374 8/379 9/385   6/102 7/117 8/117 9/179

Bonus points – Essex 4, Leicestershire 3 (Score at 120 overs: 379-7).

Bowling: *First Innings*—Millns 31–6–120–2; Mullally 32–7–93–1; Parsons 31–9–84–1; Wells 20.2–5–60–3; Cronje 13–4–29–1; Pierson 1–0–9–0. *Second Innings*—Mullally 13.4–2–33–3; Millns 15–3–47–3; Parsons 19–6–34–1; Cronje 12–3–20–1; Wells 9–0–26–2.

Umpires: D. J. Constant and M. J. Kitchen (R. Julian deputised for M. J. Kitchen after 1st day).

ESSEX v WORCESTERSHIRE

At Chelmsford, May 4, 5, 6, 8. Essex won by 208 runs. Essex 24 pts, Worcestershire 6 pts. Toss: Essex.

Career-best match figures of 12 for 178 from Such carried Essex to victory on a pitch which provided generous bounce for his off-spin. On the batting side, Gooch, who scored 101 and 205 when the counties met in 1994, played two more innings of authority. In the second, he hit 165, including 21 fours and two sixes, from 189 balls in 233 minutes. This took his total in his last five Championship innings against Worcestershire to 716. By comparison Curtis, coming in at No. 4 after splitting his finger, batted 259 balls and 282 minutes for his 76, to hold Worcestershire's first innings together. He, like so many others, was undone by Such, though in the second he was the only man to fall to seam as his team failed to rise to a challenge of 446.

Close of play: First day, Essex 361-7 (R. C. Irani 61*, P. M. Such 16*); Second day, Worcestershire 240-8 (T. S. Curtis 65*, N. V. Radford 0*); Third day, Worcestershire 40-1 (T. S. Curtis 22*).

Essex

G. A. Gooch b Haynes	86	– c Moody b Radford	165
*P. J. Prichard lbw b Radford	30	– c Rhodes b Haynes	45
J. J. B. Lewis lbw b Radford	75	– c Rhodes b Haynes	0
N. Hussain c sub b Leatherdale	33	– c Moody b Leatherdale	47
D. D. J. Robinson lbw b Leatherdale	29	– c Illingworth b Leatherdale	16
R. C. Irani lbw b Illingworth	63	– c Weston b Radford	11
†R. J. Rollins c Leatherdale b Illingworth	3	– c Leatherdale b Illingworth	21
M. C. Ilott b Illingworth	0	– c Illingworth b Radford	0
P. M. Such c Haynes b Illingworth	19	– b Illingworth	7
D. M. Cousins not out	15	– lbw b Radford	1
J. H. Childs b Newport	7	– not out	0
B 7, l-b 17, w 1, n-b 4	29	L-b 7, w 6, n-b 6	19
	389		**332**

1/86 2/196 3/220 4/266 5/286
6/307 7/323 8/366 9/371

1/106 2/112 3/235 4/266 5/299
6/305 7/309 8/331 9/332

Bonus points – Essex 4, Worcestershire 4 (Score at 120 overs: 372-9).

Bowling: *First Innings*—Newport 27.5–5–83–1; Wylie 12–1–51–0; Illingworth 47–20–80–4; Radford 20–3–82–2; Haynes 10–6–26–1; Leatherdale 10–2–43–2. *Second Innings*—Wylie 5–0–27–0; Radford 11.1–1–50–4; Illingworth 24–3–93–2; Newport 8–0–48–0; Hick 8–0–40–0; Haynes 7–2–31–2; Leatherdale 8–1–36–2.

Worcestershire

W. P. C. Weston c Lewis b Such	25	– lbw b Such	18
T. M. Moody b Ilott	17	– (4) lbw b Childs	79
G. A. Hick c Rollins b Such	37	– b Such	14
*T. S. Curtis c Hussain b Such	76	– (2) c Cousins b Ilott	22
G. R. Haynes lbw b Childs	11	– st Rollins b Such	41
D. A. Leatherdale b Childs	2	– c Hussain b Such	0
†S. J. Rhodes c Hussain b Childs	54	– st Rollins b Such	21
P. J. Newport c Hussain b Such	17	– not out	10
R. K. Illingworth c Rollins b Such	0	– c Robinson b Childs	5
N. V. Radford c Childs b Such	17	– lbw b Such	17
A. Wylie not out	3	– c Ilott b Childs	4
B 8, l-b 6, w 3	17	B 1, l-b 5	6
	276		**237**

1/31 2/72 3/89 4/127 5/133
6/211 7/240 8/240 9/271

1/40 2/40 3/66 4/122 5/136
6/198 7/202 8/209 9/232

Bonus points – Worcestershire 2, Essex 4.

Bowling: *First Innings*—Ilott 8–1–32–1; Cousins 7–2–34–0; Irani 11–0–35–0; Such 38.4–9–84–6; Childs 36–10–77–3. *Second Innings*—Ilott 11–2–32–1; Irani 4–0–18–0; Such 33–9–94–6; Childs 22.3–9–60–3; Cousins 3–0–27–0.

Umpires: R. Julian and A. G. T. Whitehead.

At Cambridge, May 11, 12 13. ESSEX drew with CAMBRIDGE UNIVERSITY.

At Hove, May 18, 19, 20, 22. ESSEX lost to SUSSEX by 278 runs.

ESSEX v MIDDLESEX

At Chelmsford, May 25, 26, 27, 29. Middlesex won by ten wickets. Middlesex 24 pts, Essex 3 pts. Toss: Middlesex. Championship debut: T. A. Radford.

Middlesex achieved their first Championship win at Chelmsford since 1976 just after lunch on the final day, when Emburey took three wickets in 11 balls. He finished with eight for 125 in the match. Essex were totally outplayed but were spared a three-day defeat by Irani, who scored two battling fifties on Saturday. A series of rash strokes, rather than the vagaries of the pitch, contributed to their downfall. Gooch failed to score a half-century for a second successive Championship match – the first time he had suffered such a barren patch for exactly four years. By contrast, five Middlesex batsmen passed 50 in their first innings. Radford performed well on his Championship debut, adding 146 with Gatting; later Nash made a career-best 67 and even Tufnell helped Emburey put on 56 for the last wicket.

Close of play: First day, Middlesex 329-6 (D. J. Nash 23*, J. E. Emburey 21*); Second day, Essex 135-6 (R. C. Irani 15*, M. C. Ilott 4*); Third day, Essex 257-6 (R. C. Irani 62*, M. C. Ilott 34*).

Middlesex

T. A. Radford c Such b Cousins	69	– not out	9
J. C. Pooley c Waugh b Irani	19	– not out	16
*M. W. Gatting b Such	94		
J. D. Carr lbw b Ilott	1		
P. N. Weekes c Childs b Such	17		
†K. R. Brown c Rollins b Ilott	57		
D. J. Nash lbw b Childs	67		
J. E. Emburey b Waugh	87		
M. A. Feltham c Cousins	2		
R. L. Johnson c Rollins b Childs	0		
P. C. R. Tufnell not out	23		
B 2, l-b 10, w 1, n-b 24	37		

1/40 2/186 3/202 4/202 5/255   473   (no wkt) 25
6/287 7/411 8/416 9/417

Bonus points – Middlesex 4, Essex 2 (Score at 120 overs: 353-6).

Bowling: *First Innings*—Ilott 34.1–7–95–2; Cousins 33–6–90–2; Irani 17–3–53–1; Such 37–9–72–2; Childs 24–0–99–2; Waugh 14.2–3–52–1. *Second Innings*—Such 5.1–2–8–0; Childs 5–1–17–0.

Essex

G. A. Gooch b Nash	17	– b Tufnell	17
*P. J. Prichard lbw b Weekes	32	– c Brown b Weekes	69
M. E. Waugh b Johnson	5	– c Feltham b Johnson	1
N. Hussain c Radford b Emburey	34	– run out	9
J. J. B. Lewis c Radford b Emburey	15	– lbw b Emburey	9
R. C. Irani c Radford b Johnson	69	– b Emburey	82
†R. J. Rollins c Carr b Tufnell	4	– c Johnson b Tufnell	32
M. C. Ilott c Johnson b Emburey	6	– c Carr b Tufnell	37
P. M. Such c Weekes b Emburey	2	– not out	6
D. M. Cousins c Brown b Tufnell	10	– c Gatting b Emburey	0
J. H. Childs not out	2	– c Weekes b Emburey	4
L-b 3, n-b 8	11	B 1, l-b 11, n-b 12	24

1/34 2/46 3/76 4/105 5/114   207   1/57 2/78 3/103 4/119 5/119   290
6/129 7/140 8/148 9/202   6/177 7/270 8/282 9/282

Bonus points – Essex 1, Middlesex 4.

Bowling: First Innings—Nash 12–4–35–1; Feltham 9–2–30–0; Johnson 13–4–41–2; Tufnell 20.1–9–33–2; Emburey 26–6–53–4; Weekes 10–4–12–1. *Second Innings*—Nash 17–5–49–0; Feltham 3–0–10–0; Weekes 20–4–43–1; Johnson 12–1–38–1; Tufnell 22–5–66–3; Emburey 30–8–72–4.

Umpires: B. Dudleston and B. Leadbeater.

At Nottingham, June 1, 2, 3, 5. ESSEX lost to NOTTINGHAMSHIRE by 16 runs.

ESSEX v DURHAM

At Chelmsford, June 8, 9, 10, 12. Essex won by 179 runs. Essex 24 pts, Durham 6 pts. Toss: Essex.

Even a match haul of 14 for 177 by Walker, during which he achieved a career-best eight for 118, failed to spare Durham their sixth successive Championship defeat. Both analyses were Durham's best in first-class cricket and they were the best match figures at Chelmsford. Essex's first innings had reached 202 for one before he dismissed Gooch and Waugh but, from 315 for three, seven wickets fell for 58. Walker added six more in the second innings, which was held together by the 22-year-old Robinson. He scored a maiden century, including 12 fours and a six, while only one other batsman got to 20. Another young player, the 21-year-old Blenkiron, ran up an attacking 94 from 99 balls in his fourth first-class innings for Durham (following scores of three, nought and four). But Durham made no impression on a target of 329 in 92 overs. Only Prabhakar and Longley resisted for long. Larkins could not bat after breaking a thumb in the Sunday League game.

Close of play: First day, Essex 339-8 (N. A. Derbyshire 5*, D. M. Cousins 4*); Second day, Durham 246-9 (J. Boiling 11*, S. J. E. Brown 4*); Third day, Essex 224-8 (D. M. Cousins 1*, N. A. Derbyshire 9*).

Essex

G. A. Gooch c Longley b Walker	97	– c Ligertwood b Prabhakar	11
D. D. J. Robinson c Ligertwood b Brown	4	– st Ligertwood b Cox	110
M. E. Waugh c Ligertwood b Walker	95	– lbw b Walker	12
N. Hussain lbw b Walker	6	– b Cox	23
*P. J. Prichard c Boiling b Walker	47	– b Morris b Prabhakar	16
R. C. Irani c Morris b Blenkiron	6	– b Walker	11
†R. J. Rollins lbw b Walker	1	– c Blenkiron b Walker	15
P. M. Such c Ligertwood b Walker	2	– c Blenkiron b Walker	13
N. A. Derbyshire c Roseberry b Walker	9	– (10) b Walker	17
D. M. Cousins not out	18	– (9) b Walker	3
J. H. Childs c Ligertwood b Walker	15	– not out	9
B 2, l-b 4, w 1, n-b 6	13	L-b 3	3

1/11 2/202 3/217 4/315 5/322   373   1/44 2/73 3/122 4/155 5/180   243
6/326 7/328 8/331 9/345   6/184 7/212 8/212 9/232

Bonus points – Essex 4, Durham 4 (Score at 120 overs: 361-9).

Bowling: *First Innings*—Brown 33–6–87–1; Prabhakar 21–4–40–0; Walker 39.2–8–118–8; Cox 12–3–46–0; Boiling 18–4–66–0; Blenkiron 4–1–10–1. *Second Innings*—Brown 14–4–27–0; Prabhakar 18–3–56–2; Walker 23.1–5–59–6; Cox 27–7–72–2; Boiling 7–1–26–0.

Durham

J. I. Longley b Irani	21	– lbw b Waugh		35
*M. A. Roseberry lbw b Irani	23	– (6) c Waugh b Childs		18
J. E. Morris c Hussain b Waugh	4	– c Gooch b Waugh		7
M. Prabhakar c Hussain b Waugh	4	– not out		46
W. Larkins c Gooch b Derbyshire	22	– absent hurt		
D. A. Blenkiron c Irani b Cousins	94	– (5) c Rollins b Waugh		0
†D. G. C. Ligertwood c Rollins b Childs	25	– (2) lbw b Irani		17
J. Boiling c Gooch b Waugh	24	– (7) c Rollins b Childs		1
D. M. Cox b Rollins b Such	5	– b Such		0
A. Walker b Childs	5	– st Rollins b Such		8
S. J. E. Brown not out	32	– (8) st Rollins b Childs		7
B 7, l-b 3, w 3, n-b 16	29	L-b 4, n-b 6		10

1/43 2/50 3/54 4/67 5/116   288   1/28 2/63 3/76 4/80 5/120   149
6/199 7/219 8/227 9/238   6/122 7/138 8/139 9/149

Bonus points – Durham 2, Essex 4.

Bowling: *First Innings*—Cousins 14–2–41–1; Waugh 22.5–5–65–3; Irani 25–6–86–2; Derbyshire 5–1–20–1; Childs 22–8–32–2; Gooch 4–1–17–0; Such 10–4–17–1. *Second Innings*—Cousins 6–1–29–0; Irani 12–4–35–1; Waugh 13–6–18–3; Such 12.2–2–44–2; Childs 6–0–19–3.

Umpires: A. A. Jones and K. J. Lyons.

At Luton, June 15, 16. ESSEX lost to NORTHAMPTONSHIRE by two wickets.

At Manchester, June 22, 23, 24, 26. ESSEX lost to LANCASHIRE by ten wickets.

ESSEX v WARWICKSHIRE

At Ilford, June 29, 30, July 1. Warwickshire won by ten wickets. Warwickshire 24 pts, Essex 6 pts. Toss: Essex.

Warwickshire celebrated their first Championship victory in seven attempts at Valentine's Park with a day to spare. They claimed the extra half-hour on the third day and knocked off a target of 35 inside five overs. Essex may have regretted their decision to bat when their openers departed for two runs; though Hussain and Waugh revived them with an entertaining stand of 152 in 47 overs, the innings gradually subsided once they were separated. Warwickshire's own third-wicket pair, Ostler and Penney, put on 151 in 36 overs. Both were dropped reaching 50 and took full advantage, making centuries and pointing the way to a substantial first-innings lead. The home side's lack of penetration was further highlighted when Brown and Donald reached Championship-best scores, gathered 90 for the ninth wicket and pushed Warwickshire's total past the ground record. Essex then capitulated against the spin of Smith, although he discovered no extravagant turn, after Donald had inflicted early damage.

Close of play: First day, Essex 318-9 (R. C. Irani 53*, J. H. Childs 2*); Second day, Warwickshire 346-6 (T. L. Penney 114*).

Essex

G. A. Gooch c Khan b Donald	0	– c Reeve b Donald	8
D. D. J. Robinson lbw b Munton	2	– c Knight b Donald	16
N. Hussain c Piper b Reeve	94	– b Munton	59
M. E. Waugh run out	80	– c Knight b Smith	48
*P. J. Prichard c Brown b Smith	40	– c Khan b Smith	4
R. C. Irani c Reeve b Donald	63	– c Reeve b Munton	22
†R. J. Rollins lbw b Donald	8	– lbw b Smith	1
M. C. Ilott lbw b Smith	11	– c Ostler b Donald	21
N. F. Williams b Reeve	7	– lbw b Smith	17
P. M. Such lbw b Reeve	0	– c Penney b Smith	11
J. H. Childs not out	2	– not out	0
L-b 2, w 1, n-b 18	21	B 4, l-b 8	12

1/2 2/2 3/154 4/207 5/233   328   1/16 2/27 3/108 4/120 5/167   219
6/254 7/300 8/311 9/311   6/168 7/170 8/193 9/219

Bonus points – Essex 3, Warwickshire 4.

Bowling: *First Innings*—Donald 25.4–5–70–3; Munton 27–7–66–1; Brown 13–0–52–0; Reeve 16–4–37–3; Twose 2–0–14–0; Smith 31–10–87–2. *Second Innings*—Donald 17–3–49–3; Munton 16–7–47–2; Brown 4–0–23–0; Smith 23.1–4–67–5; Reeve 7–1–21–0.

Warwickshire

N. V. Knight lbw b Childs	40	– not out	21
W. G. Khan c Robinson b Williams	3	– not out	6
D. P. Ostler lbw b Irani	116		
T. L. Penney c Such b Williams	141		
R. G. Twose lbw b Gooch	24		
†K. J. Piper c Hussain b Childs	0		
*D. A. Reeve c Hussain b Such	9		
D. R. Brown c Robinson b Such	85		
N. M. K. Smith c Hussain b Ilott	0		
A. A. Donald c Prichard b Waugh	44		
T. A. Munton not out	0		
B 15, l-b 18, n-b 18	51	L-b 5, w 1, n-b 2	8

1/10 2/88 3/239 4/323 5/333   513   (no wkt) 35
6/346 7/407 8/415 9/505

Bonus points – Warwickshire 4, Essex 3 (Score at 120 overs: 410-7).

Bowling: *First Innings*—Ilott 23–7–78–1; Williams 15–1–66–2; Irani 15–4–48–1; Waugh 15.4–3–45–1; Such 45–5–122–2; Childs 28–3–104–2; Gooch 3–0–17–1. *Second Innings*—Ilott 2.4–0–18–0; Williams 2–0–12–0.

Umpires: R. Julian and P. B. Wight.

At The Oval, July 6, 7, 8, 10. ESSEX beat SURREY by seven wickets.

ESSEX v SOMERSET

At Southend, July 20, 21, 22, 24. Somerset won by seven wickets. Somerset 23 pts. Toss: Somerset.

Mushtaq Ahmed, who was promoted to No. 5 when the top order faltered against the spinners, struck 62 from 42 deliveries, including three sixes off Such, to carry Somerset to their first Championship victory in Essex since 1975. Mushtaq had also bowled 82.4 overs in the match for eight wickets. This was the first time since the system of bonus points was introduced that Essex had failed to gain a point in a match uninterrupted by the weather – the consequence of an opening day which saw only two wickets fall and a second day which featured 18. Bowler's fifth and highest century of the season dominated Somerset's first innings. He batted for eight hours, hit 23 fours and added 202 for the second wicket with Hayhurst. Apart from Waugh and Prichard, Essex's response was feeble and they followed on 235 behind. They struggled against the spin of Mushtaq and Trump, although the ball turned only slowly. Only the magnificence of Waugh, who batted five and half hours for 173, carried the match into a final day.

Close of play: First day, Somerset 304-2 (P. D. Bowler 159*, R. J. Harden 11*); Second day, Essex 186; Third day, Essex 360-8 (M. C. Ilott 17*, P. M. Such 0*).

Somerset

M. N. Lathwell c Robinson b Irani	42	– b Such	17
P. D. Bowler st Rollins b Such	196	– c Rollins b Childs	4
*A. N. Hayhurst c Childs b Ilott	78	– not out	40
R. J. Harden c Rollins b Ilott	29	– c Prichard b Such	12
P. C. L. Holloway c Waugh b Ilott	4		
K. A. Parsons c Rollins b Childs	6		
G. D. Rose lbw b Ilott	3		
†R. J. Turner c Hussain b Such	30		
Mushtaq Ahmed lbw b Childs	6	– (5) not out	62
A. R. Caddick b Childs	0		
H. R. J. Trump not out	4		
B 4, l-b 11, n-b 8	23	L-b 2, n-b 2	4
	421	(3 wkts)	139

1/71 2/273 3/356 4/368 5/368   1/21 2/25 3/54
6/372 7/391 8/405 9/405

Bonus points – Somerset 3 (Score at 120 overs: 332-2).

Bowling: *First Innings*—Ilott 31–9–84–4; Williams 26–6–94–0; Such 34.1–9–75–2; Irani 15–5–31–1; Childs 37–10–84–3; Waugh 18–6–38–0. *Second Innings*—Ilott 3–0–8–0; Williams 2–0–10–0; Such 16–2–60–2; Childs 17.4–3–54–1; Waugh 2–0–5–0.

Essex

G. A. Gooch b Rose	10	– c Turner b Caddick	18
D. D. J. Robinson lbw b Rose	2	– lbw b Rose	0
N. Hussain b Rose	0	– b Mushtaq Ahmed	25
M. E. Waugh c Rose b Trump	56	– c Harden b Caddick	173
*P. J. Prichard c Parsons b Trump	71	– b Mushtaq Ahmed	47
R. C. Irani lbw b Mushtaq Ahmed	13	– lbw b Trump	38
†R. J. Rollins c Mushtaq Ahmed	6	– lbw b Mushtaq Ahmed	10
M. C. Ilott b Mushtaq Ahmed	0	– not out	22
N. F. Williams c Parsons b Trump	10	– lbw b Caddick	5
P. M. Such b Mushtaq Ahmed	4	– b Mushtaq Ahmed	3
J. H. Childs not out	2	– c Turner b Trump	0
B 8, l-b 2, n-b 2	12	B 11, l-b 18, n-b 2	31
	186		372

1/7 2/7 3/28 4/129 5/150   1/3 2/30 3/48 4/142 5/247
6/160 7/170 8/170 9/180   6/278 7/336 8/348 9/371

Bonus points – Somerset 4.

Bowling: *First Innings*—Rose 9–2–37–3; Caddick 6–0–35–0; Mushtaq Ahmed 26.4–9–74–4; Trump 16–7–30–3. *Second Innings*—Rose 4–0–14–1; Caddick 27–7–94–3; Mushtaq Ahmed 56–16–142–4; Trump 32.2–8–88–2; Parsons 1–0–5–0.

Umpires: J. D. Bond and D. R. Shepherd.

At Cheltenham, July 27, 28, 29, 31. ESSEX lost to GLOUCESTERSHIRE by three wickets.

ESSEX v HAMPSHIRE

At Colchester, August 3, 4, 5, 7. Essex won by an innings and 254 runs. Essex 24 pts, Hampshire 3 pts. Toss: Essex.

Gooch led Essex out of a lean patch in which he had scored a mere 92 in nine Championship innings and the team had lost five matches out of six. Their 662 for seven was the highest total of the summer to date and the best ever at Colchester. Gooch hit 23 fours and a six in his 142, and completed 1,000 runs for the 19th time in an English season; a little later Irani, in nappies when Gooch made his debut, did it for the first time. Hussain and Waugh also scored fluent centuries, and Rollins inflicted further punishment. Such then took centre stage, undermining Hampshire with a career-best eight for 93. Fellow-spinner Childs took over when Hampshire followed on 407 behind. Deliveries turning out of the footholds undid many batsmen. But Stephenson batted with great determination against his old county in both innings. Hampshire's last pair survived the extra half-hour on Saturday but Such separated them in the third over of the final day.

Close of play: First day, Essex 452-4 (M. E. Waugh 114*); Second day, Hampshire 148-3 (J. P. Stephenson 71*, M. C. J. Nicholas 9*); Third day, Hampshire 150-9 (S. D. Udal 18*, R. R. Dibden 0*).

Essex

G. A. Gooch lbw b Dibden	142	M. C. Ilott not out.................	18
D. D. J. Robinson c Udal b Stephenson	12		
N. Hussain c Nicholas b Udal	145	B 4, l-b 10, w 2, n-b 12	 28
M. E. Waugh b Udal	136		—
*P. J. Prichard c Laney b Dibden	 18	1/49 2/225 3/411 (7 wkts dec.)	662
R. C. Irani c Nicholas b Connor	 78	4/452 5/489	
†R. J. Rollins lbw b Whitaker	 85	6/583 7/662	

N. F. Williams, P. M. Such and J. H. Childs did not bat.

Bonus points – Essex 4, Hampshire 1 (Score at 120 overs: 484-4).

Bowling: Streak 27–5–88–0; Connor 28–5–124–1; Stephenson 16–2–68–1; James 15–4–49–0; Udal 55–8–183–2; Dibden 23–0–132–2; Whitaker 1–0–4–1.

Hampshire

V. P. Terry c Robinson b Such	 29	– b Irani...............	1
J. S. Laney c Prichard b Such	 10	– c Waugh b Such...........	11
J. P. Stephenson b Such	 94	– c Waugh b Childs	63
P. R. Whitaker lbw b Such	 26	– c Hussain b Childs........	6
*M. C. J. Nicholas c Hussain b Such	 22	– b Such..............	28
K. D. James not out	 41	– c Ilott b Childs..........	1
†A. N. Aymes c and b Childs	 0	– c Rollins b Childs	3
S. D. Udal c Robinson b Such	 8	– not out..............	18
H. H. Streak c Waugh b Childs	 5	– c Hussain b Childs........	0
C. A. Connor c Robinson b Such	 3	– c Prichard b Childs	8
R. R. Dibden c sub b Such	 0	– c Robinson b Such........	0
B 12, l-b 4, w 1	 17	L-b 13, w 1	14

1/29 2/72 3/122 4/172 5/185	255	1/6 2/37 3/48 4/107 5/108 153
6/186 7/213 8/234 9/241		6/113 7/114 8/114 9/142

Bonus points – Hampshire 2, Essex 4.

Bowling: *First Innings*—Ilott 15–8–31–0; Williams 4–1–14–0; Such 49.1–18–93–8; Childs 39–9–101–2. *Second Innings*—Ilott 4–0–23–0; Irani 3–0–14–1; Such 28.5–9–67–3; Childs 28–15–36–6.

Umpires: J. C. Balderstone and G. I. Burgess.

At Swansea, August 10, 11, 12, 14. ESSEX beat GLAMORGAN by 147 runs.

At Chelmsford, August 19, 20, 21. ESSEX drew with WEST INDIANS (See West Indian tour section).

At Canterbury, August 24, 25, 26. ESSEX beat KENT by an innings and 12 runs.

ESSEX v DERBYSHIRE

At Chelmsford, August 29, 30, 31, September 1. Essex won by 256 runs. Essex 23 pts, Derbyshire 6 pts. Toss: Essex. First-class debut: A. P. Cowan.

The fact that Derbyshire lasted into the fourth afternoon was an achievement considering their catalogue of misfortunes. Barnett pulled out on the morning of the match because of a stomach bug; DeFreitas responded to the sudden challenge of captaincy with five wickets and a dashing 91 – but, after two days, had to rush to his five-year-old daughter's hospital bedside after she was scalded in the bath. Griffith could not bowl at all, having pulled a thigh muscle on the opening day, while Malcolm was hampered by a leg injury and Adams by illness. Tweats retired briefly after being struck by a fielder's throw-in. Waugh took full advantage of Derbyshire's weakness to plunder two hundreds – two 121s, in fact – sharing successive century partnerships with Gooch and Prichard in the second innings and leaving Derbyshire a target of 423. Spinners Childs, who had claimed his 1,000th first-class wicket on the second day, and Such hastened the visitors' demise; between them, they took 17 of the 19 wickets.

Close of play: First day, Essex 315-9 (M. E. Waugh 113*, J. H. Childs 2*); Second day, Essex 40-1 (G. A. Gooch 16*, N. Hussain 11*); Third day, Derbyshire 38-3 (T. W. Harrison 3*).

Essex

G. A. Gooch c Harrison b DeFreitas	68	– c Griffiths b Rollins 94
D. D. J. Robinson c Cullinan b DeFreitas	19	– c Rollins b Cork 9
N. Hussain c Griffiths b Cork	33	– c Rollins b Malcolm 17
M. E. Waugh not out	121	– b Harrison 121
*P. J. Prichard c Adams b Malcolm	6	– c sub b Tweats 93
R. C. Irani b Malcolm	15	– c and b Harrison 6
†R. J. Rollins c Tweats b Cork	18	– b Harrison 15
M. C. Ilott c Wells b DeFreitas	1	– c sub b Harrison 8
A. P. Cowan c Tweats b DeFreitas	19	– not out. 0
P. M. Such b DeFreitas	0	– not out. 0
J. H. Childs c Griffiths b Malcolm	3	
B 1, l-b 4, w 8, n-b 10	23	B 8, l-b 3, w 2, n-b 10 ... 23

1/53 2/123 3/137 4/148 5/172   326   1/15 2/63 3/184   (8 wkts dec.) 386
6/219 7/226 8/283 9/291   4/329 5/339 6/363
                                    7/386 8/386

Bonus points – Essex 3, Derbyshire 4.

Bowling: *First Innings*—Cork 21-3-68-2; Malcolm 23-4-107-3; DeFreitas 22-3-66-5; Wells 7-0-39-0; Harrison 10-3-22-0; Tweats 6-0-19-0. *Second Innings*—Cork 19-2-71-1; DeFreitas 4-0-16-0; Harrison 30-7-153-4; Malcolm 6-0-19-1; Wells 17-2-40-0; Tweats 13-1-57-1; Rollins 3-1-19-1.

Derbyshire

A. S. Rollins c Rollins b Such	48	– c Robinson b Such 13
T. A. Tweats c Childs b Ilott	20	– c Childs b Ilott 33
C. J. Adams c Waugh b Such	12	– (6) c Waugh b Childs 61
D. J. Cullinan b Irani c Childs	30	– c Hussain b Childs. 0
C. M. Wells c Robinson b Such	19	– (3) c Waugh b Childs 8
T. W. Harrison c Gooch b Such	0	– (5) b Childs. 4
*P. A. J. DeFreitas c Robinson b Childs	91	– absent
D. G. Cork c Rollins b Childs	31	– (7) c Waugh b Such 5
F. A. Griffith c Gooch b Such	12	– (8) not out. 6
†S. P. Griffiths c Cowan b Childs	16	– (9) c Robinson b Such 0
D. E. Malcolm not out	2	– (10) c Robinson b Such 18
L-b 5, n-b 4	9	B 4, l-b 11, w 1, n-b 2 ... 18

1/33 2/72 3/93 4/129 5/131   290   1/30 2/30 3/38 4/43 5/130   166
6/137 7/246 8/259 9/284   6/134 7/146 8/146 9/166

Bonus points – Derbyshire 2, Essex 4.

In the second innings T. A. Tweats, when 7, retired hurt at 20 and resumed at 38.

Bowling: *First Innings*—Ilott 12-2-71-1; Cowan 6-0-29-0; Such 26.5-6-86-5; Irani 2-1-3-0; Childs 25-6-81-4; Gooch 4-0-15-0. *Second Innings*—Ilott 8-0-14-1; Cowan 2-1-5-0; Such 28.3-7-93-4; Childs 30-18-39-4.

Umpires: V. A. Holder and K. J. Lyons.

ESSEX v YORKSHIRE

At Chelmsford, September 14, 15, 16, 18. Essex won by 89 runs. Essex 23 pts, Yorkshire 7 pts. Toss: Essex.

Essex staged a fine recovery, completing the season with their fifth successive Championship victory to finish fifth in the table. After leading by just four runs on first innings, Essex collapsed to 41 for five in their second – almost for six, when Prichard was dropped at slip by McGrath before he had scored. Reprieved, he scored a hundred from 107 balls and, with Rollins, put on 157 in only 25 overs; because of bad weather, though, the partnership spread over three days. Yorkshire never threatened to score the 275 needed for victory, and spinners Such and Childs reaped the rewards of their suicidal "hit out or get out" policy. There were several attractive performances in Essex's first innings, but Byas and Kettleborough, with a maiden fifty, had kept Yorkshire on level terms, enabling their seamers to make what looked like being the decisive intervention.

Close of play: First day, Yorkshire 53-1 (M. D. Moxon 15*, D. Byas 29*); Second day, Essex 62-5 (P. J. Prichard 9*, R. J. Rollins 12*); Third day, Essex 88-5 (P. J. Prichard 27*, R. J. Rollins 20*).

Essex

G. A. Gooch c Hartley b Gough	2	– c Gough b Silverwood	14
D. D. J. Robinson c McGrath b Gough	7	– c Blakey b Gough	0
N. Hussain c Blakey b Hartley	58	– b Hartley	17
M. E. Waugh lbw b Silverwood	20	– c Byas b Silverwood	2
*P. J. Prichard c Byas b Bevan	54	– b Gough	104
R. C. Irani c Silverwood b Stemp	40	– b Hartley	3
†R. J. Rollins b Stemp	63	– c Blakey b Gough	77
M. C. Ilott c Blakey b Silverwood	8	– b Hartley	16
A. P. Cowan b Hartley	22	– lbw b Hartley	6
P. M. Such not out	9	– lbw b Gough	13
J. H. Childs c Bevan b Hartley	0	– not out	8
B 4, l-b 6, n-b 20	30	L-b 2, n-b 8	10

1/2 2/11 3/61 4/157 5/193   313   1/9 2/30 3/38 4/38 5/41   270
6/221 7/267 8/302 9/313   6/198 7/235 8/249 9/249

Bonus points – Essex 3, Yorkshire 4.

In the first innings P. J. Prichard, when 32, retired hurt at 126 and resumed at 267.

Bowling: *First Innings*—Gough 16-1-80-2; Hartley 16-1-80-3; Silverwood 12-0-73-2; Stemp 24-9-56-2; Bevan 4-0-14-1. *Second Innings*—Gough 18.5-1-94-4; Hartley 20-5-105-4; Silverwood 10-2-36-2; Stemp 8-1-33-0.

Yorkshire

*M. D. Moxon lbw b Ilott	15	– b Irani	8
M. P. Vaughan b Ilott	5	– c Irani b Childs	20
D. Byas b Irani	98	– c Gooch b Ilott	4
M. G. Bevan c Rollins b Ilott	9	– c and b Such	27
A. McGrath st Rollins b Childs	38	– b Such	38
R. A. Kettleborough c Rollins b Ilott	55	– lbw b Childs	4
†R. J. Blakey c Ilott b Such	9	– c Rollins b Such	9
D. Gough c Prichard b Cowan	20	– c Hussain b Such	29
P. J. Hartley c Hussain b Such	24	– b Childs	18
C. E. W. Silverwood not out	10	– not out	6
R. D. Stemp c Hussain b Such	15	– c Hussain b Such	13
L-b 8, w 1, n-b 2	11	B 4, l-b 2, n-b 3	9

1/13 2/57 3/77 4/151 5/197   309   1/27 2/32 3/91 4/100 5/104   185
6/224 7/251 8/282 9/284   6/114 7/129 8/159 9/169

Bonus points – Yorkshire 3, Essex 4.

In the second innings M. P. Vaughan, when 20, retired hurt at 43 and resumed at 100.

Bowling: *First Innings*—Ilott 26-7-97-4; Cowan 11-1-53-1; Irani 16-6-36-1; Such 17.5-3-54-3; Waugh 8-2-25-0; Childs 14-3-36-1. *Second Innings*—Ilott 11-2-27-1; Cowan 5-0-26-0; Irani 5-2-6-1; Such 17.5-4-89-5; Childs 13-3-31-3.

Umpires: J. D. Bond and K. E. Palmer.

GLAMORGAN

Patron: HRH The Prince of Wales
President: W. Wooller
Chairman: F. D. Morgan
Chairman, Cricket Committee: H. D. Davies
Secretary: G. R. Stone
Cricket Secretary: M. J. Fatkin
Captain: 1995 – H. Morris
      1996 – M. P. Maynard
Director of Coaching: A. Jones
Grounds Supervisor: L. A. Smith
Scorer: B. T. Denning

Glamorgan had expected an improvement in 1995 but, after showing encouraging early season form with six straight wins in all competitions, including two successive Championship victories, they did not win another first-class match until the penultimate game in early September. And in the end they finished 16th in the County Championship, only two places higher than the bottom spot they occupied the previous year. They also fell away in the Sunday League, finishing sixth after winning seven of their first eight games, and the possible consolation of a Lord's final was destroyed by Warwickshire in the NatWest semi-final.

On the first day of the final home game against Nottinghamshire, Hugh Morris announced he would not seek re-appointment as captain for 1996. Morris, who led the team for four years before his previous resignation in 1989, and another three in the 1990s, said he was anxious to concentrate on his batting and to spend more time with his young family. He was also disillusioned with the team's unfulfilled potential and their failure, apart from one notable exception against Kent at Tunbridge Wells, to contribute collectively. Matthew Maynard, Morris's vice-captain for the past three years, succeeded him, despite rumours that the club had considered appointing a player from outside the county.

Although four batsmen exceeded 1,000 runs, the batting could not be relied on under pressure, lacking the necessary technique and application on pitches which assisted opposing bowlers. They were twice exposed within a month by the Warwickshire seam attack at Sophia Gardens. Glamorgan slumped to 26 for seven on the first morning of a Championship match which they lost in a day and a half, then suffered humiliation in the NatWest semi-final, losing by eight wickets. With the prospect of a Lord's final for the first time since 1977, Glamorgan supporters were at the ground hours before the start. By lunch, many were on their way home after seeing their side capitulate to 77 for eight, and at 3.30 p.m. the game was over.

Unfortunately, Glamorgan's season was assessed on that dismal performance. Earlier successes in the competition, against Leicestershire and Middlesex, were quickly forgotten. There were also three near misses in the Championship which, had they gone Glamorgan's way, would have ensured a mid-table position. They were two runs short of beating Kent, who had set them a stiff target; then 22 overs were lost to bad light on the third evening at The Oval, where Surrey held out on the final day with one wicket left; Gloucestershire's final pair denied Glamorgan a win at Abergavenny.

Maynard emerged as the leading run-maker, with 1,569, a little ahead of Morris and Tony Cottey. Morris, who struck six centuries, passed 15,000 runs for the county and requires ten more hundreds to equal Alan Jones's record of 52. Cottey, the county's Player of the Year in 1994, again made a significant contribution. His aggregate of 1,445 runs at 51.60 was his best in first-class cricket and once again he was unfortunate to miss out on the England A tour. Steve James had a splendid one-day season, creating a Glamorgan record with 815 runs in the Sunday League – 1,263 in all limited-overs games. Although inconsistent in the Championship, he flourished at the end of the season, hitting a career-best 230 not out at Leicester. David Hemp's slump in form was a major disappointment; yet he is not the first young batsman to falter following an outstanding first full season, as opposing bowlers discover the flaws. Adrian Dale, with 622 runs, experienced another miserable year, although batting anywhere between No. 1 and 6 could not have helped his confidence.

Of the bowlers, Steve Watkin and Robert Croft were the most impressive, with first-class hauls of 65 and 63 respectively. Watkin was also the country's leading Sunday League wicket-taker, with 32, and Croft supplemented his wickets with 684 first-class runs. Antiguan Hamish Anthony – returning to Glamorgan at the last minute when West Indies picked Ottis Gibson for their touring squad – ended with 44 wickets but rarely threatened to win a game or dismiss the opposition cheaply. Neil Kendrick's left-arm spin claimed 27 victims at the high average of 46.48, while Darren Thomas produced some quick spells but continued to bowl too many loose deliveries.

The Second Eleven finished at the bottom of their championship but there were encouraging performances from Gareth Edwards, an 18-year-old off-spinner who toured Kenya and Zimbabwe with the England Under-19 squad during the winter, and Dean Cosker, a left-arm spinner in his final year at Millfield School.

After 74 years as a first-class county, Glamorgan completed negotiations for the purchase of their own ground at Sophia Gardens for £2.5 million. Another £4.5 million will be spent to provide a headquarters that might serve the club for the next hundred years and eventually provide an arena equipped to stage international cricket. West Wales members were worried by the scheme, fearing that the St Helen's ground in Swansea would lose its first-class status. Petitions were signed and meetings convened, but in September members were assured that Swansea would host at least 12 days' cricket in 1996. The other outgrounds, at Colwyn Bay and Abergavenny, may now be used in alternate years; yet these games are very popular – one being by the seaside, the other in an idyllic setting. Progress can never please everyone. – *Edward Bevan.*

GLAMORGAN 1995

Aiming to ?

ANDERSEN CONSULTING

[*Bill Smith*]

Back row: B. S. Phelps, A. Roseberry, A. P. Davies, G. J. M. Edwards, A. D. Shaw, P. S. Jones, B. M. Morgan, D. A. Cosker, A. J. Dalton. *Middle row:* G. N. Lewis (*Second Eleven scorer*), G. R. Stone (*secretary*), A. Jones (*director of coaching*), R. P. Lefebvre, G. P. Butcher, N. M. Kendrick, S. D. Thomas, D. L. Hemp, J. Derrick (*Second Eleven captain and coach*), D. O. Conway (*physiotherapist*), B. T. Denning (*First Eleven scorer*). *Front row:* P. A. Cottey, S. P. James, S. R. Barwick, C. P. Metson, H. Morris (*captain*), M. P. Maynard, S. L. Watkin, R. D. B. Croft, A. Dale.

GLAMORGAN RESULTS

All first-class matches – Played 19: Won 3, Lost 8, Drawn 8.

County Championship matches – Played 17: Won 3, Lost 8, Drawn 6.

Bonus points – Batting 40, Bowling 57.

Competition placings – Britannic Assurance County Championship, 16th; NatWest Bank Trophy, s-f; Benson and Hedges Cup, 3rd in Group C; AXA Equity & Law League, 6th.

BRITANNIC ASSURANCE CHAMPIONSHIP AVERAGES

BATTING

	Birthplace	M	I	NO	R	HS	Avge
‡P. A. Cottey	Swansea	16	27	2	1,237	130	49.48
‡H. Morris	Cardiff	16	30	2	1,373	166*	49.03
‡M. P. Maynard	Oldham	17	31	1	1,420	164	47.33
‡S. P. James	Lydney	13	24	3	842	230*	40.09
S. D. Thomas	Morriston	10	14	3	313	78*	28.45
‡D. L. Hemp	Bermuda	16	29	0	776	157	26.75
‡A. Dale	Germiston, SA	10	19	2	420	133	24.70
‡R. D. B. Croft	Morriston	17	30	3	612	143	22.66
A. J. Dalton	Bridgend	4	8	1	129	46	18.42
N. M. Kendrick	Bromley	13	20	4	291	59	18.18
‡C. P. Metson	Goffs Oak	16	23	9	253	26*	18.07
H. A. G. Anthony§ .	Urlings Village, Antigua	14	25	1	433	91	18.04
‡S. L. Watkin	Maesteg	15	23	9	174	30	12.42
‡S. R. Barwick	Neath	6	6	2	19	14	4.75

Also batted: ‡R. P. Lefebvre (*Rotterdam, Netherlands*) (2 matches) 13, 18, 24; A. D. Shaw (*Neath*) (1 match) 0, 2. A. P. Davies (*Neath*) (1 match) did not bat.

* *Signifies not out.* ‡ *Denotes county cap.* § *Overseas player.*

The following played a total of 17 three-figure innings for Glamorgan in County Championship matches – H. Morris 5, P. A. Cottey 4, M. P. Maynard 3, S. P. James 2, R. D. B. Croft 1, A. Dale 1, D. L. Hemp 1.

BOWLING

	O	M	R	W	BB	5W/i	Avge
S. L. Watkin	561.4	135	1,685	62	7-49	2	27.17
H. A. G. Anthony.....	397.5	70	1,402	44	6-77	2	31.86
R. D. B. Croft	774.3	184	2,180	56	6-104	3	38.92
N. M. Kendrick	334.1	85	1,088	24	4-70	0	45.33
S. D. Thomas	285.3	50	1,257	26	5-99	1	48.34
S. R. Barwick	213.4	52	619	12	4-116	0	51.58

Also bowled: P. A. Cottey 17.1–0–80–0; A. Dale 124.5–26–419–8; A. P. Davies 3–0–17–0; D. L. Hemp 22–2–110–3; R. P. Lefebvre 67–22–134–0.

Wicket-keepers: C. P. Metson 45 ct, 6 st; A. D. Shaw 2 ct.

Leading Fielder: M. P. Maynard 22.

At Oxford, April 18, 19, 20. GLAMORGAN drew with OXFORD UNIVERSITY.

At Taunton, April 27, 28, 29, 30. GLAMORGAN beat SOMERSET by eight wickets.

GLAMORGAN v NORTHAMPTONSHIRE

At Cardiff, May 4, 5, 6, 8. Glamorgan won by three wickets. Glamorgan 23 pts, Northamptonshire 8 pts. Toss: Northamptonshire.

Glamorgan pulled off their sixth straight win in competitive matches to head the early Championship table. Needing 287, they were taken most of the way by Morris, who scored 109 in his first Championship game of 1995. But at 229, Capel had Maynard caught behind by stand-in wicket-keeper Loye. He followed up with three wickets in four balls, including Morris, another Loye victim, leaving Glamorgan 242 for six. Cottey steered them out of trouble, as he had done in the first innings, when he came in at 19 for three and made 116. Glamorgan were 43 behind a Northamptonshire first-innings total dominated by Lamb's 87th century. But he batted at No. 11 in the second innings because of a damaged wrist. By the end, Ripley and Montgomerie had broken fingers and second-choice keeper Fordham a bad back. Northamptonshire used their coach, their physiotherapist and a Cardiff club player as substitutes.

Close of play: First day, Northamptonshire 359-9 (A. Kumble 6*, J. P. Taylor 15*); Second day, Northamptonshire 34-2 (R. J. Bailey 17*, D. Ripley 3*); Third day, Glamorgan 47-0 (S. P. James 20*, H. Morris 21*).

Northamptonshire

R. R. Montgomerie c Hemp b Dale	25	– lbw b Watkin	0
A. Fordham c Metson b Kendrick	57	– lbw b Watkin	11
R. J. Bailey c Maynard b Kendrick	27	– lbw b Watkin	31
M. B. Loye c Maynard b Croft	0	– (5) c Thomas b Croft	5
*A. J. Lamb st Metson b Kendrick	124	– (11) not out	24
K. M. Curran c Dale b Kendrick	23	– c and b Kendrick	46
D. J. Capel lbw b Watkin	0	– b Thomas	23
J. N. Snape lbw b Croft	55	– c Metson b Croft	15
†D. Ripley b Watkin	15	– (4) b Kendrick	40
A. Kumble c Metson b Watkin	18	– (9) c Hemp b Kendrick	21
J. P. Taylor not out	21	– (10) c Metson b Watkin	19
L-b 7, w 1, n-b 4	12	B 4, l-b 1, w 1, n-b 2	8

1/70 2/91 3/98 4/146 5/180   377   1/0 2/27 3/52 4/57 5/112   243
6/195 7/287 8/337 9/337   6/161 7/170 8/192 9/200

Bonus points – Northamptonshire 4, Glamorgan 4.

Bowling: *First Innings*—Watkin 23.1–5–74–3; Thomas 13–2–66–0; Dale 15–2–54–1; Croft 34–11–78–2; Kendrick 33–11–98–4. *Second Innings*—Watkin 23.2–5–55–4; Thomas 17–4–56–1; Kendrick 33–13–62–3; Croft 32–9–60–2; Cottey 1–0–5–0.

Glamorgan

S. P. James lbw b Taylor	1	– run out	23
*H. Morris lbw b Taylor	17	– c Loye b Capel	109
D. L. Hemp c Snape b Capel	1	– c and b Kumble	58
M. P. Maynard lbw b Kumble	30	– c Loye b Capel	32
P. A. Cottey c Montgomerie b Kumble	116	– not out	29
A. Dale c Curran b Kumble	61	– (7) c sub b Capel	0
R. D. B. Croft c Montgomerie b Kumble	9	– (6) lbw b Capel	0
S. D. Thomas c Montgomerie b Kumble	0	– c Curran b Kumble	14
N. M. Kendrick c Curran b Bailey	16	– not out	2
†C. P. Metson not out	26		
S. L. Watkin c and b Taylor	23		
B 12, l-b 13, w 1, n-b 8	34	B 9, l-b 10, n-b 4	23

1/4 2/15 3/19 4/79 5/240   334   1/57 2/166 3/229 4/242   (7 wkts) 290
6/254 7/257 8/262 9/288   5/242 6/242 7/270

Bonus points – Glamorgan 3, Northamptonshire 4.

Bowling: *First Innings*—Taylor 13.3–0–51–3; Capel 15–2–63–1; Curran 13–4–40–0; Kumble 32–9–65–5; Snape 8–0–45–0; Bailey 19–6–45–1. *Second Innings*—Taylor 22.3–5–63–0; Capel 11–3–36–4; Kumble 41–9–94–2; Bailey 7–0–25–0; Snape 14–2–32–0; Curran 5–0–21–0.

Umpires: J. H. Hampshire and P. B. Wight.

GLAMORGAN v SUSSEX

At Swansea, May 11, 12, 13, 15. Drawn. Glamorgan 5 pts, Sussex 4 pts. Toss: Sussex. First-class debuts: R. J. Kirtley, K. Newell.

Sussex failed to pursue the challenge of scoring 287 from 64 overs to the end, although Athey and Hall laid the foundation with an opening partnership of 165. The dismissal of Stephenson, fifth man out, discouraged them and they opted for the draw when 51 runs were required from seven overs. A total of 159 overs were lost to rain during the first two days but a green pitch offered plenty of encouragement to the seamers. Giddins produced a career-best six for 87 in Glamorgan's first innings, while Anthony, returning to Wales because Gibson was needed by West Indies, recorded his best Championship figures. Among his victims was Wells, who had struck three centuries in his previous five first-class innings. In this game he bagged a pair – out second ball both times – but Newell scored 63 on first-class debut. On the final day, Maynard and Croft set up Glamorgan's declaration with a stand of 101 in 18 overs.

Close of play: First day, Glamorgan 7-1 (H. Morris 3*, D. L. Hemp 1*); Second day, Glamorgan 173-8 (N. M. Kendrick 9*, C. P. Metson 15*); Third day, Glamorgan 115-2 (H. Morris 44*, M. P. Maynard 25*).

Glamorgan

S. P. James lbw b Lewry	0 – c Athey b Stephenson	6
*H. Morris c Moores b Giddins	9 – lbw b Stephenson	61
D. L. Hemp c Greenfield b Giddins	3 – c Wells b Salisbury	28
M. P. Maynard b Lewry	32 – b Stephenson	74
P. A. Cottey c Salisbury b Kirtley	17 – c Moores b Stephenson	1
A. Dale c Greenfield b Giddins	20 – lbw b Giddins	0
R. D. B. Croft c Moores b Giddins	28 – not out	52
H. A. G. Anthony b Giddins	12 – b Stephenson	0
N. M. Kendrick not out	35 – not out	8
†C. P. Metson c Hall b Giddins	19	
S. L. Watkin c Salisbury b Stephenson	8	
B 5, l-b 16, w 4, n-b 4	29	B 4, l-b 20, w 6, n-b 10 .. 40

1/0 2/10 3/23 4/64 5/79　　　　　212　　1/9 2/74 3/140　　　(7 wkts dec.) 270
6/118 7/134 8/144 9/187　　　　　　　　4/146 5/155
　　　　　　　　　　　　　　　　　　　6/256 7/256

Bonus points – Glamorgan 1, Sussex 4.

Bowling: *First Innings*—Lewry 17–6–31–2; Stephenson 12.5–2–42–1; Giddins 28–7–87–6; Kirtley 11–3–28–1; Salisbury 2–0–3–0. *Second Innings*—Stephenson 17–4–64–5; Kirtley 1–0–4–0; Lewry 11–1–46–0; Giddins 23–1–74–1; Salisbury 11–1–58–1.

Sussex

C. W. J. Athey c Metson b Anthony	17	– c and b Watkin	92
J. W. Hall c Metson b Watkin	5	– run out	85
K. Newell c Watkin b Hemp	63	– (5) not out	34
*A. P. Wells c Maynard b Anthony	0	– (3) c Maynard b Dale	0
K. Greenfield c Cottey b Anthony	2	– (4) c Metson b Watkin	8
†P. Moores c Morris b Anthony	12	– (7) not out	16
F. D. Stephenson b Kendrick	30	– (6) b Anthony	16
I. D. K. Salisbury c Watkin b Croft	33		
J. D. Lewry c James b Croft	9		
R. J. Kirtley not out	2		
E. S. H. Giddins c James b Croft	20		
B 1, n-b 2	3	L-b 5	5

1/13 2/27 3/27 4/53 5/71   196   1/165 2/167 3/187   (5 wkts) 256
6/112 7/158 8/174 9/175   4/190 5/216

Bonus points – Glamorgan 4.

Bowling: *First Innings*—Watkin 19–3–45–1; Anthony 19–4–47–4; Kendrick 20–8–56–1; Croft 8.3–0–37–3; Hemp 2–0–10–1. *Second Innings*—Watkin 17–2–49–2; Anthony 12–0–57–1; Dale 15–4–60–1; Kendrick 10–1–48–0; Croft 9.2–2–37–0.

Umpires: A. A. Jones and G. Sharp.

At Bradford, May 18, 19, 20. GLAMORGAN lost to YORKSHIRE by seven wickets.

At Tunbridge Wells, May 24, 25, 26, 27. GLAMORGAN drew with KENT.

GLAMORGAN v HAMPSHIRE

At Cardiff, June 1, 2, 3. Hampshire won by eight wickets. Hampshire 23 pts, Glamorgan 4 pts. Toss: Hampshire.

Glamorgan were outplayed and beaten with a day and a half to spare because Hampshire adapted far better to a pitch of variable bounce which assisted the quicker bowlers. The home team failed by one run to avoid the follow-on, despite a stand of 61 between Thomas and Anthony for the ninth wicket, and lost six more wickets by the close. Cottey denied Hampshire for three hours, interrupted by a wet Saturday morning, but he was dismissed at 192 and the last three all fell at 204, leaving a simple target of 55. Hampshire's openers were removed by Watkin, but Smith, whose return to England's squad was announced next day, led them to victory before tea. Earlier in the game, Nicholas and Stephenson scored their first Championship fifties of the season while Anthony, with six for 77, achieved career-best figures for Glamorgan. Bovill helped to enforce the follow-on with three wickets in four balls on his 24th birthday.

Close of play: First day, Glamorgan 12-1 (H. Morris 5*, C. P. Metson 0*); Second day, Glamorgan 155-6 (P. A. Cottey 40*, N. M. Kendrick 0*).

Hampshire

V. P. Terry lbw b Watkin	24	– (2) b Watkin	3
R. S. M. Morris c Hemp b Thomas	33	– (1) c Metson b Watkin	4
J. P. Stephenson c Metson b Anthony	65	– not out	14
R. A. Smith c Maynard b Anthony	36	– not out	30
*M. C. J. Nicholas lbw b Anthony	75		
G. W. White run out	10		
†A. N. Aymes c Thomas b Anthony	32		
S. D. Udal b Anthony	0		
H. H. Streak b Anthony	20		
C. A. Connor b Watkin	13		
J. N. B. Bovill not out	1		
B 7, l-b 2, n-b 6	15	N-b 4	4

1/46 2/96 3/164 4/171 5/186   324   1/4 2/17   (2 wkts) 55
6/282 7/282 8/299 9/314

Bonus points – Hampshire 3, Glamorgan 4.

Bowling: *First Innings*—Watkin 19–5–44–2; Anthony 23.3–3–77–6; Thomas 16–3–61–1; Dale 6–0–28–0; Croft 24–3–60–0; Kendrick 14–3–45–0. *Second Innings*—Watkin 5–0–14–2; Anthony 3–0–17–0; Thomas 3–1–8–0; Dale 1.5–0–16–0.

Glamorgan

A. Dale c Stephenson b Connor	5	– c Aymes b Udal ... 12
*H. Morris c Morris b Stephenson	33	– c Aymes b Connor ... 23
†C. P. Metson c Aymes b Streak	6	– (10) not out ... 0
M. P. Maynard c White b Connor	31	– lbw b Connor ... 5
P. A. Cottey c White b Streak	1	– c Morris b Streak ... 62
R. D. B. Croft b Bovill	18	– c Morris b Stephenson ... 20
D. L. Hemp b Bovill	1	– (3) c Stephenson b Bovill ... 34
S. D. Thomas c Aymes b Stephenson	41	– (7) c Udal b Stephenson ... 7
N. M. Kendrick lbw b Bovill	0	– (8) c Terry b Udal ... 17
H. A. G. Anthony c Morris b Streak	16	– (9) c Connor b Streak ... 3
S. L. Watkin not out	4	– c Terry b Streak ... 0
L-b 2, n-b 16	18	B 1, l-b 5, w 1, n-b 14 ... 21

1/12 2/35 3/65 4/66 5/93   174   1/40 2/48 3/56 4/86 5/110   204
6/104 7/105 8/105 9/166   6/140 7/192 8/204 9/204

Bonus points – Hampshire 4.

Bowling: *First Innings*—Connor 12–2–60–2; Bovill 18–6–51–3; Streak 13–5–29–3; Stephenson 8.4–1–27–2; Udal 3–1–5–0. *Second Innings*—Streak 14.1–4–41–3; Connor 17–4–65–2; Udal 21–8–41–2; Bovill 10–4–24–1; Stephenson 12–5–27–2.

Umpires: J. H. Harris and B. Leadbeater.

At Manchester, June 8, 9, 10, 12. GLAMORGAN drew with LANCASHIRE.

GLAMORGAN v MIDDLESEX

At Colwyn Bay, June 15, 16, 17, 19. Middlesex won by eight wickets. Middlesex 24 pts, Glamorgan 4 pts. Toss: Glamorgan.

Glamorgan's failure to consolidate after winning the toss for the first time in the 1995 Championship enabled Middlesex to gain a 254-run first-innings lead and capitalise on a turning pitch towards the end of the game. A home total of 276 was inadequate and would have been worse without Anthony's maiden fifty for the county. Centuries from three Middlesex players emphasised the point. Pooley hit 14 fours and five sixes – one smashing twelfth man Farbrace's car windscreen – in a career-best 125. He added 193 for the second wicket with Ramprakash, while Carr and Brown put on 209 for the fifth wicket, denying Glamorgan maximum bowling points for the first time in the season. Though James and Morris opened with 147 in the second innings, the return of the spinners left Middlesex only 79 to win. Appropriately, Pooley completed an unbeaten fifty with the winning boundary. Barwick, who took four wickets in Middlesex's first innings and five in the Sunday League game, was rewarded with a collection of £850 towards his benefit fund.

Close of play: First day, Middlesex 43-1 (J. C. Pooley 33*, M. R. Ramprakash 5*); Second day, Middlesex 459-6 (K. R. Brown 104*, J. E. Emburey 0*); Third day, Glamorgan 258-5 (P. A. Cottey 20*, N. M. Kendrick 4*).

Glamorgan

S. P. James b Emburey	6	– c Pooley b Emburey	84
*H. Morris c Emburey b Johnson	53	– c Brown b Nash	66
D. L. Hemp c Nash b Emburey	6	– b Emburey	26
M. P. Maynard c Nash b Fraser	47	– b Tufnell	14
P. A. Cottey run out	23	– c Emburey b Nash	36
R. D. B. Croft c Pooley b Emburey	13	– b Emburey	2
H. A. G. Anthony c Gatting b Johnson	58	– c Brown b Nash	6
N. M. Kendrick b Tufnell	34	– c sub b Emburey	11
†C. P. Metson b Tufnell	16	– lbw b Tufnell	17
S. L. Watkin not out	4	– c Ramprakash b Tufnell	30
S. R. Barwick lbw b Tufnell	0	– not out	0
L-b 10, n-b 6	16	B 12, l-b 12, n-b 16	40

1/23 2/37 3/112 4/126 5/147   276   1/147 2/187 3/214 4/240 5/244   332
6/166 7/237 8/259 9/276   6/274 7/279 8/288 9/323

Bonus points – Glamorgan 2, Middlesex 4.

In the second innings H. A. G. Anthony, when 4, retired hurt at 249 and resumed at 274.

Bowling: *First Innings*—Fraser 16–5–33–1; Nash 13–4–46–0; Emburey 32–11–79–3; Tufnell 25.5–10–61–3; Johnson 14–3–47–2. *Second Innings*—Fraser 14–6–19–0; Johnson 8–3–17–0; Tufnell 36.3–10–105–3; Emburey 48–17–97–4; Weekes 14–4–29–0; Nash 14–2–41–3.

Middlesex

P. N. Weekes c Maynard b Anthony	1	– b Watkin	0
J. C. Pooley c Cottey b Barwick	125	– not out	50
M. R. Ramprakash c Cottey b Watkin	69	– b Kendrick	19
J. D. Carr c Barwick b Croft	129	– not out	2
*M. W. Gatting run out	7		
†K. R. Brown not out	147		
D. J. Nash c Metson b Croft	8		
J. E. Emburey run out	17		
R. L. Johnson c Hemp b Barwick	3		
A. R. C. Fraser b Barwick	3		
P. C. R. Tufnell c James b Barwick	0		
B 9, l-b 6, n-b 6	21	L-b 8	8

1/5 2/198 3/206 4/217 5/426   530   1/10 2/58   (2 wkts) 79
6/458 7/514 8/522 9/530

Bonus points – Middlesex 4, Glamorgan 2 (Score at 120 overs: 430-5).

Bowling: *First Innings*—Watkin 33–11–87–1; Anthony 13–2–56–1; Croft 38–5–135–2; Kendrick 15–1–82–0; Barwick 40.5–6–116–4; Hemp 7–0–26–0; Cottey 3–0–13–0. *Second Innings*—Watkin 6–1–22–1; Anthony 3–0–10–0; Croft 6–1–18–0; Kendrick 4–0–21–1.

Umpires: G. I. Burgess and K. J. Lyons.

At The Oval, June 22, 23, 24, 26. GLAMORGAN drew with SURREY.

GLAMORGAN v DURHAM

At Swansea, June 29, 30, July 1, 3. Durham won by six wickets. Durham 23 pts, Glamorgan 7 pts. Toss: Glamorgan.

Both counties were seeking a third Championship win, but Durham got it, thanks to left-handers Blenkiron and Hutton. When Watkin dismissed Longley in the first over, becoming the second bowler to reach 50 wickets for the season, and then bowled Roseberry, Durham were 37 for two, a long way from a target of 341. But Blenkiron, with 145 from 204 balls, a maiden century, including 18 fours and four sixes, and Hutton added 177. John Morris continued the assault, achieving victory with nearly 18 overs to spare. The pitch had been expected to turn but remained as easy-paced as on the first day, when Hugh Morris scored his fourth hundred of 1995. Prabhakar made his first century for Durham, after Longley and Roseberry compiled the county's first 100-run opening partnership for 13 months. There were more landmarks on Saturday, when Maynard and Cottey, who also made his fourth century of the season, passed 1,000 first-class runs, two days after Byas of Yorkshire had won that race.

Close of play: First day, Glamorgan 310-8 (A. J. Dalton 26*, S. L. Watkin 0*); Second day, Durham 318-6 (S. D. Birbeck 6*, S. J. E. Brown 0*); Third day, Glamorgan 304-8 (P. A. Cottey 113*, S. L. Watkin 0*).

Glamorgan

S. P. James c Ligertwood b Brown	11	– lbw b Cox 36
*H. Morris c Prabhakar b Boiling	106	– lbw b Prabhakar 28
A. Dale c Birbeck b Brown	11	– run out 2
M. P. Maynard b Prabhakar	59	– b Prabhakar 67
P. A. Cottey b Boiling	60	– st Ligertwood b Cox 130
A. J. Dalton not out	34	– c Ligertwood b Cox 9
R. D. B. Croft c Ligertwood b Cox	1	– c sub b Cox 13
H. A. G. Anthony c Ligertwood b Cox	6	– lbw b Boiling 6
†C. P. Metson b Prabhakar	10	– run out 8
S. L. Watkin b Prabhakar	1	– not out 15
S. R. Barwick c Boiling b Prabhakar	14	
L-b 10, w 6, n-b 6	22	B 9, l-b 12, w 1 22

1/22 2/46 3/152 4/264 5/269   **335**   1/49 2/61 3/77   (9 wkts dec.) **336**
6/270 7/278 8/309 9/316   4/184 5/212 6/254
                                                          7/265 8/302 9/336

Bonus points – Glamorgan 3, Durham 4.

Bowling: *First Innings*—Brown 25-3-97-2; Prabhakar 22.1-12-47-4; Birbeck 14-1-49-0; Cox 26-8-54-2; Boiling 24-10-51-2; Blenkiron 6-0-27-0. *Second Innings*—Brown 13-2-49-0; Cox 38.5-6-141-4; Boiling 34-7-102-1; Prabhakar 15-6-23-2.

Durham

J. I. Longley c Anthony b Croft	58	– lbw b Watkin 4
*M. A. Roseberry c Cottey b Watkin	56	– b Watkin 18
J. E. Morris lbw b Watkin	7	– (5) not out 45
S. Hutton c Anthony b Barwick	26	– (3) lbw b Croft 91
M. Prabhakar c Dale b Croft	101	– (6) not out 24
D. A. Blenkiron c Maynard b Barwick	53	– (4) c Morris b Anthony 145
S. D. Birbeck not out	16	
S. J. E. Brown lbw b Watkin	0	
†D. G. C. Ligertwood lbw b Anthony	2	
J. Boiling lbw b Anthony	0	
D. M. Cox b Anthony	1	
B 4, l-b 1, n-b 6	11	B 4, l-b 8, n-b 4 16

1/100 2/108 3/124 4/208 5/302   **331**   1/4 2/37 3/214 4/300   (4 wkts) **343**
6/318 7/318 8/323 9/323

Bonus points – Durham 3, Glamorgan 4.

Bowling: *First Innings*—Watkin 23-9-44-3; Anthony 21.2-5-65-3; Dale 7-1-33-0; Barwick 27-7-74-2; Cottey 1-0-2-0; Croft 30-6-108-2. *Second Innings*—Watkin 17-2-78-2; Anthony 14-2-75-1; Croft 28-5-94-1; Barwick 23-8-74-0; Cottey 2.1-0-10-0.

Umpires: T. E. Jesty and B. J. Meyer.

At Neath, July 8, 9, 10. GLAMORGAN drew with YOUNG AUSTRALIA (See Young Australia tour section).

GLAMORGAN v WARWICKSHIRE

At Cardiff, July 20, 21. Warwickshire won by nine wickets. Warwickshire 21 pts, Glamorgan 4 pts. Toss: Glamorgan.

Munton's swing and Donald's speed devastated Glamorgan and set up Warwickshire's second successive two-day win. Glamorgan had elected to bat but slumped to 26 for seven in the first 67 minutes. Munton exploited the overcast conditions to take five for 11 in 35 deliveries of outstanding swing and seam and Glamorgan averted complete humiliation only through a 66-run stand between Anthony and Kendrick. Anthony was back in action as he and Watkin took Warwickshire's first three wickets for 34. But the innings was rescued by Brown, with a pugnacious fifty. Glamorgan were relieved to trail by only 86, but Donald soon wrecked their second innings with his exceptional pace. Before lunch, he had a spell of three for nought from nine balls. With Cottey absent, having twisted his ankle while jogging, they were all out for 122 again; Warwickshire needed just 37 to win and achieved victory shortly after tea, to take the outright lead in the Championship for the first time in 1995.

Close of play: First day, Warwickshire 169-7 (D. A. Reeve 31*, A. F. Giles 0*).

Glamorgan

S. P. James lbw b Donald	0	– c Piper b Donald 1
*H. Morris c Smith b Munton	0	– b Donald 9
D. L. Hemp c Reeve b Munton	2	– c Donald b Munton 26
M. P. Maynard lbw b Munton	12	– c Piper b Donald 0
P. A. Cottey c Ostler b Munton	6	– absent hurt
A. Dale c Knight b Munton	0	– (5) c Ostler b Donald 1
R. D. B. Croft c Twose b Reeve	1	– (6) lbw b Giles 31
H. A. G. Anthony b Munton	38	– (7) run out 23
N. M. Kendrick c Penney b Donald	16	– (8) lbw b Smith 3
†C. P. Metson not out	10	– (9) run out 11
S. L. Watkin b Smith	9	– (10) not out 3
L-b 16, n-b 12	28	B 1, l-b 7, n-b 6 14

1/0 2/2 3/7 4/17 5/19   122   1/2 2/23 3/27 4/29 5/67   122
6/24 7/26 8/92 9/92   6/103 7/106 8/109 9/122

Bonus points – Warwickshire 4.

Bowling: *First Innings*—Donald 15-4-49-2; Munton 13-3-42-5; Reeve 6-5-1-1; Giles 8-4-13-1; Smith 0.4-0-1-1. *Second Innings*—Donald 10-3-25-4; Munton 12-2-46-1; Smith 10-2-23-1; Giles 9.3-3-14-1; Reeve 3-1-6-0.

Warwickshire

R. G. Twose b Anthony	4	– run out 0
N. V. Knight c James b Watkin	5	– not out 13
D. P. Ostler c Metson b Anthony	20	– not out 20
T. L. Penney c Metson b Watkin	14	
D. R. Brown run out	52	
*D. A. Reeve c Metson b Kendrick	36	
N. M. K. Smith b Anthony	0	
†K. J. Piper c Maynard b Watkin	28	
A. F. Giles c Dale b Kendrick	24	
A. A. Donald run out	2	
T. A. Munton not out	2	
B 4, l-b 2, w 1, n-b 14	21	N-b 4 4

1/9 2/23 3/34 4/84 5/123   208   1/0   (1 wkt) 37
6/123 7/165 8/187 9/203

Bonus points – Warwickshire 1, Glamorgan 4.

Bowling: *First Innings*—Watkin 18-6-59-3; Anthony 21-2-62-3; Croft 21-4-44-0; Dale 8-1-19-0; Kendrick 12.1-4-18-2. *Second Innings*—Croft 6.1-0-26-0; Kendrick 6-1-11-0.

Umpires: B. Dudleston and N. T. Plews.

At Derby, July 27, 28, 29, 31. GLAMORGAN lost to DERBYSHIRE by 195 runs.

GLAMORGAN v ESSEX

At Swansea, August 10, 11, 12, 14. Essex won by 147 runs. Essex 23 pts, Glamorgan 6 pts. Toss: Essex.

The day before his 44th birthday, Childs exploited a wearing pitch to send Glamorgan to their fourth successive Championship defeat. He took five for 60 with his left-arm spin, although Glamorgan's batsmen, with their abysmal lack of technique and application, contributed to the rout; only Cottey, with his second fifty of the game, resisted. On the first day, Gooch and Hussain both scored hundreds for the second successive innings. But when their 189-run stand ended, Croft instigated a mid-order collapse, until Robert Rollins emulated his older brother Adrian, a fortnight earlier at Derby, by making Glamorgan victims of his maiden century. Despite some solid middle-order contributions, Glamorgan conceded a lead of 83; Ilott, a late arrival after being left out of the Test team at Trent Bridge, took five wickets before Hussain, played another commanding innings, leaving Glamorgan a target of 328 from 95 overs. Off-spinner Croft's match figures of ten for 191 merely heralded Childs's triumph.

Close of play: First day, Essex 330-7 (R. J. Rollins 74*, N. F. Williams 0*); Second day, Glamorgan 264-4 (M. P. Maynard 52*, C. P. Metson 0*); Third day, Essex 227-7 (R. J. Rollins 36*).

Essex

G. A. Gooch st Metson b Croft	102	– b Watkin	0
D. D. J. Robinson b Anthony	5	– c Maynard b Anthony	11
N. Hussain c Metson b Anthony	103	– c Metson b Kendrick	80
M. E. Waugh b Croft	10	– c Metson b Kendrick	16
*P. J. Prichard b Croft	7	– st Metson b Kendrick	31
R. C. Irani c Morris b Croft	4	– c James b Kendrick	38
†R. J. Rollins not out	133	– lbw b Croft	41
M. C. Ilott c Hemp b Watkin	18	– c Maynard b Croft	7
N. F. Williams c James b Croft	16	– not out	0
P. M. Such c Metson b Anthony	11	– c Kendrick b Croft	8
J. H. Childs st Metson b Croft	4	– c James b Croft	4
B 4, l-b 5	9	B 2, l-b 1, w 1, n-b 4	8

1/10 2/199 3/221 4/224 5/228　　　　422　　1/0 2/13 3/98 4/127 5/170　　　244
6/255 7/328 8/373 9/405　　　　　　　　　6/203 7/227 8/232 9/240

Bonus points – Essex 3, Glamorgan 3 (Score at 120 overs: 344-7).

Bowling: *First Innings*—Watkin 30–4–111–1; Anthony 29–6–79–3; Kendrick 24–2–100–0; Barwick 11–6–19–0; Croft 41.3–7–104–6. *Second Innings*—Watkin 10–5–26–1; Anthony 11–2–49–1; Croft 26.5–8–87–4; Kendrick 24–4–79–4.

Glamorgan

S. P. James b Ilott	0	– c Rollins b Williams	1
*H. Morris c Rollins b Such	47	– c Rollins b Ilott	17
D. L. Hemp c Hussain b Childs	66	– b Such	31
M. P. Maynard b Ilott	61	– c Robinson b Childs	21
P. A. Cottey c Prichard b Gooch	76	– c Robinson b Childs	53
†C. P. Metson c Hussain b Ilott	11	– (9) st Rollins b Childs	4
R. D. B. Croft lbw b Ilott	28	– (6) c Hussain b Childs	28
H. A. G. Anthony c Hussain b Such	0	– (7) b Childs	0
N. M. Kendrick lbw b Such	11	– (8) lbw b Such	1
S. L. Watkin not out	6	– c Robinson b Ilott	9
S. R. Barwick c Such b Ilott	4	– not out	0
B 4, l-b 7, n-b 18	29	B 8, l-b 1, w 2, n-b 4	15

1/0 2/129 3/129 4/260 5/275　　　　339　　1/1 2/31 3/81 4/81 5/123　　　180
6/290 7/291 8/311 9/329　　　　　　　　　6/123 7/132 8/143 9/180

Bonus points – Glamorgan 3, Essex 4.

Bowling: *First Innings*—Ilott 25.5–7–53–5; Williams 9–1–23–0; Such 37–9–100–3; Childs 26–8–103–1; Irani 9–2–32–0; Waugh 4–1–13–0; Gooch 3–2–4–1. *Second Innings*—Ilott 10–2–18–2; Williams 4–1–14–1; Such 24–2–79–2; Childs 22.1–2–60–5.

Umpires: J. H. Harris and V. A. Holder.

GLAMORGAN v GLOUCESTERSHIRE

At Abergavenny, August 23, 24, 25, 26. Drawn. Glamorgan 7 pts, Gloucestershire 8 pts. Toss: Glamorgan.

At 11.55 on the third morning Gloucestershire's 20-year-old Anglo-Australian batsman Andrew Symonds hit the 16th six of his innings off Watkin just right of the sightscreen. It landed on a tennis court about 20 feet over the boundary and gave Symonds a world record, beating the 15 by John Reid for Wellington v Northern Districts in 1962-63. Symonds went on to hit four more sixes in the second innings, surpassing the world match record of 17, by Jim Stewart for Warwickshire v Lancashire in 1959. The 16 sixes came in an unbeaten 254 from only 206 balls; there were also 22 fours. Symonds became the youngest player to score a double-century for Gloucestershire and, though he was undoubtedly helped by the short boundaries, it would have been a hugely effective innings on any ground in the world. Even without Symonds, this contest would have maintained the reputation of Pen-y-Pound for producing extraordinary county matches. Glamorgan collapsed from 145 for one to 203 for eight, before recovering to 334. Then Gloucestershire slumped to 79 for five before Symonds began his assault. They eventually led by 127 before Glamorgan hit back, beginning the final day in sight of records of their own – the third-wicket stand between Hemp and Maynard was then worth 302. However, Srinath broke the partnership four runs later and, working up remarkable pace from his gentle run, tore through the batting for career-best figures of nine for 76. That left Gloucestershire to score 345 in at least 77 overs. Symonds's four sixes came in a score of 76 and at 204 for three Gloucestershire were favourites. But rain hit their chances and this switchback game had one final twist: Watkin and Thomas broke through and Gloucestershire finished defending desperately with last man Pike in for the concluding 20 balls.

Close of play: First day, Glamorgan 249-8 (S. D. Thomas 37*, N. M. Kendrick 9*); Second day, Gloucestershire 373-7 (A. Symonds 197*, J. Srinath 33*); Third day, Glamorgan 420-2 (D. L. Hemp 151*, M. P. Maynard 160*).

Glamorgan

A. J. Dalton lbw b Srinath	0	– lbw b Srinath	12
*H. Morris lbw b Ball	67	– c Windows b Srinath	62
D. L. Hemp c Symonds b Ball	71	– lbw b Sheeraz	157
M. P. Maynard lbw b Ball	10	– b Srinath	164
P. A. Cottey b Srinath	7	– c Williams b Srinath	10
†A. D. Shaw b Srinath	0	– c Wright b Srinath	2
R. D. B. Croft c Williams b Srinath	2	– c Alleyne b Srinath	8
H. A. G. Anthony c Wright b Ball	4	– b Srinath	0
S. D. Thomas not out	78	– c Williams b Srinath	3
N. M. Kendrick b Sheeraz	21	– c Hancock b Srinath	10
S. L. Watkin b Pike	24	– not out	6
L-b 13, w 7, n-b 30	50	B 13, l-b 13, w 5, n-b 6	37
	334		**471**

1/0 2/145 3/166 4/189 5/189   6/191 7/198 8/203 9/276

1/41 2/118 3/424 4/440 5/440   6/448 7/448 8/455 9/458

Bonus points – Glamorgan 3, Gloucestershire 4.

Bowling: *First Innings*—Srinath 20–6–74–4; Sheeraz 23–3–103–1; Alleyne 17–5–59–0; Ball 33–9–54–4; Pike 9.3–1–31–1. *Second Innings*—Srinath 21–3–76–9; Sheeraz 14–3–72–1; Ball 26–8–74–0; Pike 31–6–97–0; Symonds 15–1–52–0; Alleyne 12–3–59–0; Hancock 2–0–15–0.

Gloucestershire

A. J. Wright c Hemp b Watkin	31	– c Anthony b Thomas	23
M. G. N. Windows lbw b Watkin	0	– b Thomas	24
T. H. C. Hancock b Anthony	12	– c Shaw b Croft	14
M. A. Lynch lbw b Anthony	32	– (7) not out	56
*M. W. Alleyne b Thomas	2	– (4) c Dalton b Thomas	64
A. Symonds not out	254	– (5) lbw b Watkin	76
†R. C. J. Williams c Kendrick b Croft	52	– (6) c Shaw b Thomas	17
M. C. J. Ball lbw b Kendrick	2	– c sub b Thomas	2
J. Srinath c Morris b Croft	39	– c and b Watkin	1
K. P. Sheeraz b Watkin	3	– c Maynard b Watkin	0
V. J. Pike c sub b Croft	22	– not out	0
L-b 2, n-b 10	12	B 3, l-b 5, n-b 8	16

1/11 2/36 3/72 4/79 5/79   461   1/43 2/58 3/83   (9 wkts) 293
6/292 7/295 8/379 9/394   4/204 5/229 6/236
                            7/249 8/263 9/277

Bonus points – Gloucestershire 4, Glamorgan 4.

Bowling: *First Innings*—Watkin 24-3-122-3; Anthony 18-3-81-2; Thomas 18-3-100-1; Croft 26.5-6-90-3; Kendrick 10-0-66-1. *Second Innings*—Watkin 16-3-51-3; Anthony 10-1-45-0; Croft 19-5-70-1; Thomas 17-0-99-5; Kendrick 4-0-20-0.

Umpires: J. W. Holder and P. B. Wight.

At Leicester, August 29, 30, 31, September 1. GLAMORGAN lost to LEICESTERSHIRE by six wickets.

GLAMORGAN v NOTTINGHAMSHIRE

At Cardiff, September 7, 8, 9, 11. Glamorgan won by 189 runs. Glamorgan 22 pts, Nottinghamshire 5 pts. Toss: Nottinghamshire.

On the washed-out first day, Morris announced that he would relinquish the captaincy at the end of the season. But unlike Robinson, who had already handed the command of Nottinghamshire to Johnson, he remained in charge, struck two unbeaten centuries – the first, 166, beat his own highest score – and secured Glamorgan's first Championship win since May 8. He was on the field throughout, and became the first player ever to score two centuries in a match against the same opposition three times. He led his county to 417 for six in the first innings and shared an unbroken opening stand of 213 with James in the second, before his declaration, the third of the match, set a target of 312. With Pollard absent, having been stretchered off with a serious groin injury on the third morning, Nottinghamshire put up no fight. Croft removed their top four and, after Thomas bowled a hostile second spell of 5-4-4-3, completed Nottinghamshire's fifth successive defeat.

Close of play: First day, No play; Second day, Glamorgan 344-5 (H. Morris 144*, S. D. Thomas 4*); Third day, Glamorgan 8-0 (S. P. James 5*, H. Morris 3*).

Glamorgan

S. P. James c Archer b Bates	35	– not out	101
*H. Morris not out	166	– not out	104
D. L. Hemp b Bates	5		
M. P. Maynard b Pennett	45		
P. A. Cottey c Pollard b Bates	57		
R. D. B. Croft st Noon b Hindson	26		
S. D. Thomas b Bates	37		
H. A. G. Anthony not out	18		
B 18, l-b 3, w 1, n-b 6	28	B 5, l-b 3	8

1/57 2/89 3/182 4/295 5/340   (6 wkts dec.) 417   (no wkt dec.) 213
6/391

N. M. Kendrick, †C. P. Metson and S. R. Barwick did not bat.

Bonus points – Glamorgan 4, Nottinghamshire 2.

Bowling: *First Innings*—Cairns 13–3–39–0; Pick 13.4–4–47–0; Archer 6–0–29–0; Bates 34–9–138–4; Hindson 17–3–73–1; Pennett 18–4–70–1. *Second Innings*—Pennett 7.3–1–28–0; Archer 1–0–4–0; Hindson 19–1–84–0; Bates 24–2–89–0.

Nottinghamshire

P. R. Pollard retired hurt	7	– absent hurt	
R. T. Robinson c Cottey b Thomas	21	– (1) lbw b Croft	36
G. F. Archer b Kendrick	110	– c Metson b Croft	21
*P. Johnson lbw b Croft	46	– c Maynard b Croft	0
N. A. Gie c Croft b Barwick	34	– (2) c Anthony b Croft	18
C. L. Cairns b Anthony	43	– (5) st Metson b Kendrick	8
†W. M. Noon not out	37	– (6) b Thomas	14
R. T. Bates c sub b Kendrick	0	– (7) c Metson b Thomas	10
J. E. Hindson not out	12	– (8) b Thomas	4
R. A. Pick (did not bat)		– (9) c Metson b Croft	4
D. B. Pennett (did not bat)		– (10) not out	0
L-b 9	9	B 4, l-b 3	7

1/59 2/145 3/218 4/244 5/272   (6 wkts dec.) 319   1/44 2/56 3/60 4/71 5/95   122
6/277   6/110 7/113 8/122 9/122

Bonus points – Nottinghamshire 3, Glamorgan 2.

In the first innings P. R. Pollard retired hurt at 14.

Bowling: *First Innings*—Anthony 15–3–45–1; Thomas 19–7–62–1; Croft 18–3–62–1; Barwick 16–2–46–1; Kendrick 21–4–92–2; Hemp 1–0–3–0. *Second Innings*—Anthony 4–0–14–0; Thomas 13–7–28–3; Croft 23.1–6–47–5; Kendrick 11–3–26–1.

Umpires: J. C. Balderstone and R. Julian.

At Worcester, September 14, 15, 16, 18. GLAMORGAN drew with WORCESTERSHIRE.

UMPIRES FOR 1996

FIRST-CLASS UMPIRES

J. C. Balderstone, H. D. Bird, J. D. Bond, G. I. Burgess, A. Clarkson, D. J. Constant, B. Dudleston, J. H. Hampshire, J. H. Harris, J. W. Holder, V. A. Holder, T. E. Jesty, A. A. Jones, R. Julian, M. J. Kitchen, B. Leadbeater, K. J. Lyons, B. J. Meyer, K. E. Palmer, R. Palmer, N. T. Plews, G. Sharp, D. R. Shepherd, R. A. White, A. G. T. Whitehead and P. Willey. *Reserves:* P. Adams, M. J. Harris, M. K. Reed and J. F. Steele.

MINOR COUNTIES UMPIRES

P. Adams, K. Bray, P. Brown, A. R. Bundy, D. L. Burden, D. J. Halfyard, M. A. Johnson, C. S. Kelly, S. W. Kuhlmann, D. Lea, G. I. McLean, M. P. Moran, D. Norton, C. T. Puckett, G. P. Randall-Johnson, J. G. Reed, M. K. Reed, K. S. Shenton, W. E. Smith, C. T. Spencer, C. Stone, J. M. Tythcott, G. Williams, T. G. Wilson and R. Wood. *Reserves:* N. Bainton, S. F. Bishopp, A. Carter, S. P. Chitty, A. R. Clark, P. D. Clubb, K. Coburn, D. R. M. Crowson, C. J. Edwards, J. H. Evans, A. J. Hardy, J. Ilott, P. W. Kingston-Davey, R. E. Lawson, G. Lowden, G. Ripley, K. Sutherland and B. H. Willey.

GLOUCESTERSHIRE

Patron: HRH The Princess of Wales
President: J. A. Horne
Chairman: R. W. Rossiter
Chief Executive: P. G. M. August
Captain: 1995 – R. C. Russell
1996 – C. A. Walsh
Coach: A. W. Stovold
Assistant Coach: P. W. Romaines
Head Groundsman: D. Bridle
Scorer: B. H. Jenkins

There is a West Country characteristic of cussedness which surfaces when a team is given little chance. The pre-season forecasts of gloom enveloping Nevil Road in Bristol may have been excessive but they still seemed to carry an element of logic. Gloucestershire's captain and renowned match-winner, Courtney Walsh, was missing; a relatively unknown Indian fast bowler, who had not been their first choice, was being brought over as the short-term overseas player; the county were to be led by a virtually novice captain; and the overall look of the team, however promising in parts, conveyed fragility and inexperience.

Walsh, due back in 1996 – though for how much longer is uncertain – was of course engaged with the West Indian tourists. But he remained close to his county in spirit. He phoned regularly for progress reports and occasionally he watched. It must have been gratifying to him to note how well, and often how competitively, they sustained the season. Gloucestershire climbed to sixth position in the Championship, with eight wins, and were one of the shock sides. Once, not so long ago, they had been a pushover. Now they offered sturdy opposition, with an unlikely combative glint in the eyes at times. Never once were they taken lightly. They played, for the most part, a hard, efficient game and were disappointed not to end even higher in the table.

Javagal Srinath, signed after Australian batsman David Boon withdrew, did not remain unknown for long. He became Gloucestershire's golden bowler, eventually robbed of his 100 wickets only by sheer fatigue and a virus. He was quiet, popular and immensely talented. He bowled straight with some exquisite changes of pace, finishing third in the national averages with 87 wickets at 19.09. With him at one end and Mike Smith at the other, Gloucestershire possessed an enviable new-ball attack. Smith, a short, skidding left-arm bowler of natural in-swing, was restricted by injury but deservedly earned a place on the England A tour. In several matches, Srinath and Smith complemented each other to exceptional effect, as Lancashire would no doubt reluctantly confirm. And at Abergavenny, in a match yielding 1,559 runs, the silky Indian took nine for 76 in 21 overs.

If Srinath elevated Gloucestershire hopes and morale, so did Andrew Symonds. The interminable polemics about his registration, the administrative confusion and what was seen at Bristol as undue mean-spiritedness in some quarters, appeared to leave him blissfully unmoved when he reached the crease. Not yet fully recognised back in Australia, he went after the bowling here like a veteran in a hurry. He occasionally veered from the orthodox but his skills, incorporating an innate sense of enterprise and even daring, could be exceptional. This he demonstrated with his world record 20 sixes, against Glamorgan at Abergavenny.

A third significant influence on the county's success rate was Jack Russell. Maybe against his nature, he was consciously more gregarious. The responsibilities and demands of captaincy helped him, he believed, to come "out of his shell". He demonstrated a strict sense of what he wanted from his players, was never seriously at fault with his tactics, and did quite enough to ensure his skipper's role, if he wishes, as Walsh's successor. Russell led with apposite determination. He kept wicket as well as ever; he batted resolutely, with a personalised style that so nearly brought him 1,000 runs for the first time. And he won back his England place.

Tony Wright failed by seven runs to reach a double-hundred against Nottinghamshire. There was much evidence that he had rediscovered the technical assurance that once deserted him and caused him to give up the captaincy. Monte Lynch, with five centuries, mocked Surrey's latter disinclination to use him. He made, as ever, a few rash, untimely shots. But he also produced some delightful strokes, took his slip catches as adeptly as he did 15 years ago at The Oval, and passed on plenty of cricketing wisdom to his younger team-mates. In the tradition of recent years, Mark Alleyne saved his best cricket for Cheltenham. Here, against Essex, he captained the county for the first time in the Championship; here he fashioned the most attractive hundred of his career. He squeezed past 1,000 runs and every Gloucestershire supporter knew it should have been more. He is numbered with the West Country's enigmas.

It proved an indeterminate summer for batsmen like Bobby Dawson – despite a maiden Championship century against Worcestershire – Matt Windows and Tim Hancock, whose battling 79 was crucial to the win over Derbyshire. Rob Cunliffe, restricted by injury, appeared to make the most obvious progress. At Cheltenham, his dour, disciplined 92 not out was a most commendable ingredient in Lancashire's defeat. He would appear to be an ideal opening partner for Wright in the future. Among the emerging bowlers, Kamran Sheeraz snatched at his chance against the West Indians in August. He captured 11 wickets in the match but never quite lived up to that in the fixtures that followed. Seam bowler Jon Lewis arrived towards the end of the season and made a striking impression in the brief time allowed. He turned up at Edgbaston to take four wickets in the first innings – and then he took another eight in the following match with Durham. He seemed to be staking his claim for 1996.

Gloucestershire did win five Sunday League games but their final position – 15th – again suggested a deficient technique in that competition. It could have been different in the NatWest – and the pedestrian scoring by the early batsmen in the quarter-finals against Northamptonshire continued to haunt the county for weeks. The hapless Dean Hodgson was the main offender. His recent lack of match practice was embarrassingly apparent and maybe he should not have been risked. Unsentimentally, he was not easily forgiven and, after he was dropped, his contract – with a year to go – was terminated, to his disappointment. Another player to leave, more abruptly, was Ricardo Williams, the fast bowler. Explanations were briefly discreet and mentioned only "disciplinary reasons". One or two umpires, it seems, had been less than pleased at his reactions on the field. – David Foot.

GLOUCESTERSHIRE 1995

[*Bill Smith*]

Back row: D. R. Hewson, R. J. Cunliffe, R. C. J. Williams, D. J. P. Boden, M. J. Cawdron, R. C. Williams. *Middle row*: K. P. Sheeraz, V. J. Pike, A. M. Smith, R. I. Dawson, M. C. J. Ball, T. H. C. Hancock, M. Davies, M. G. N. Windows, B. H. Jenkins (*scorer*). *Front row*: P. W. Romaines (*assistant coach*), A. J. Wright, A. W. Stovold (*coach*), R. C. Russell (*captain*), R. W. Rossiter (*chairman*), M. W. Alleyne, M. A. Lynch, G. D. Hodgson, K. E. Cooper. *Inset*: A. Symonds.

GLOUCESTERSHIRE RESULTS

All first-class matches – Played 19: Won 9, Lost 5, Drawn 5.

County Championship matches – Played 17: Won 8, Lost 4, Drawn 5.

Bonus points – Batting 45, Bowling 50.

*Competition placings – Britannic Assurance County Championship, 6th;
NatWest Bank Trophy, q-f; Benson and Hedges Cup, q-f;
AXA Equity & Law League, 15th.*

BRITANNIC ASSURANCE CHAMPIONSHIP AVERAGES

BATTING

	Birthplace	M	I	NO	R	HS	Avge
A. Symonds........	Birmingham	17	29	5	1,346	254*	56.08
‡A. J. Wright	Stevenage	17	32	4	1,321	193	47.17
R. J. Cunliffe	Oxford	6	7	2	222	92*	44.40
‡R. C. Russell......	Stroud	14	21	3	778	87	43.22
‡M. A. Lynch.......	Georgetown, BG	17	29	2	1,026	114	38.00
‡M. W. Alleyne	Tottenham	17	29	2	988	141	36.59
‡G. D. Hodgson	Carlisle	9	17	0	524	148	30.82
R. I. Dawson	Exmouth	7	13	1	312	101	26.00
T. H. C. Hancock .	Reading	6	10	1	214	79*	23.77
M. C. J. Ball	Bristol	16	25	8	395	48	23.23
M. G. N. Windows .	Bristol	6	12	1	230	56	20.90
M. Davies	Neath	5	6	3	62	22	20.66
R. C. J. Williams ..	Bristol	3	6	0	107	52	17.83
‡J. Srinath§........	Mysore, India	15	24	4	314	44	15.70
R. C. Williams	Camberwell	2	4	0	41	22	10.25
‡K. E. Cooper	Hucknall	3	5	1	36	32	9.00
V. J. Pike	Taunton	5	8	3	42	22	8.40
‡A. M. Smith	Dewsbury	10	9	2	37	11	5.28
K. P. Sheeraz	Wellington	8	9	3	7	3	1.16

Also batted: D. J. P. Boden (*Eccleshall*) (1 match) 2; J. Lewis (*Aylesbury*) (3 matches) 0, 0, 3.

* Signifies not out. ‡ Denotes county cap. § Overseas player.

The following played a total of 16 three-figure innings for Gloucestershire in County Championship matches – M. A. Lynch 5, A. Symonds 4, A. J. Wright 4, M. W. Alleyne 1, R. I. Dawson 1, G. D. Hodgson 1.

BOWLING

	O	M	R	W	BB	5W/i	Avge
J. Lewis	67.4	12	209	12	4-34	0	17.41
J. Srinath	568.4	147	1,661	87	9-76	5	19.09
A. M. Smith	404.1	103	1,218	56	7-70	4	21.75
M. C. J. Ball	521.5	129	1,373	38	5-49	2	36.13
M. W. Alleyne........	380.5	116	1,093	25	3-59	0	43.72
V. J. Pike...........	195.3	39	592	11	3-72	0	53.81
K. P. Sheeraz	189	27	777	13	3-89	0	59.76

Also bowled: D. J. P. Boden 34–4–123–3; K. E. Cooper 77–20–188–6; M. Davies 88–20–252–6; R. I. Dawson 15–6–28–0; T. H. C. Hancock 5–1–20–0; M. A. Lynch 2–0–3–0; A. Symonds 35–9–87–0; R. C. Williams 61–9–223–1.

Wicket-keepers: R. C. Russell 41 ct, 1 st; R. C. J. Williams 13 ct.

Leading Fielder: M. A. Lynch 25.

At The Oval, April 27, 28, 29, 30. GLOUCESTERSHIRE lost to SURREY by 93 runs.

At Taunton, May 4, 5, 6, 8. GLOUCESTERSHIRE drew with SOMERSET.

GLOUCESTERSHIRE v NOTTINGHAMSHIRE

At Bristol, May 11, 12, 13, 15. Gloucestershire won by 134 runs. Gloucestershire 23 pts, Nottinghamshire 4 pts. Toss: Gloucestershire.

This was a statement of intent from Gloucestershire, generally given no chance of achieving anything this season. There was no play on the first day; then Wright and Hodgson attractively created a new record opening stand for their county in the Championship. Their 362, occupying six hours, beat 315 by Arthur Milton and David Green at Hove 27 years before. The Nottinghamshire attack was denuded by Cairns's side strain, though that should not excuse their overall aura of gloom and the five catches they put down. Their bowling also lacked variety and accuracy. None of this should detract from the openers' vibrant batting, however. Wright, pulling and driving with some freedom, hit four sixes and 17 fours in a career-best 193; Hodgson struck 15 boundaries. Gloucestershire declared twice and left Nottinghamshire to score 277 in 54 overs. They were bowled out, by the unpretentious swing of Smith and the off-spin of Ball, with 28 deliveries remaining. Evans and Pennett almost alone offered resistance.

Close of play: First day, No play; Second day, Gloucestershire 389-3 (M. A. Lynch 12*, M. W. Alleyne 7*); Third day, Nottinghamshire 300-8 dec.

Gloucestershire

A. J. Wright c Archer b Pick 193	– c French b Evans	4
G. D. Hodgson c Afford b Evans 148	– c Afford b Evans	15
R. I. Dawson c Evans b Pick 0	– (4) not out	53
M. A. Lynch not out 12	– (3) lbw b Pennett	32
M. W. Alleyne not out 7	– c Johnson b Afford	40
A. Symonds (did not bat)	– not out	29
B 8, l-b 9, n-b 12 29	L-b 12, n-b 2	14

1/362 2/364 3/371   (3 wkts dec.) 389   1/5 2/40   (4 wkts dec.) 187
                                       3/59 4/144

*†R. C. Russell, J. Srinath, M. C. J. Ball, K. P. Sheeraz and A. M. Smith did not bat.

Bonus points – Gloucestershire 4, Nottinghamshire 1.

Bowling: *First Innings*—Pick 19–1–76–2; Evans 20–5–39–1; Pennett 17–1–92–0; Mike 19–2–72–0; Afford 31–5–84–0; Archer 4–0–9–0. *Second Innings*—Pick 11–2–41–0; Evans 8–1–22–2; Mike 7–3–21–0; Pennett 8–1–36–1; Afford 11–3–55–1.

Nottinghamshire

M. P. Dowman lbw b Ball 63	– (2) lbw b Smith	18
P. Johnson b Smith 0	– (4) st Russell b Ball	19
G. F. Archer c Lynch b Srinath 62	– c Lynch b Smith	3
*R. T. Robinson b Srinath 18	– (1) lbw b Smith	1
C. L. Cairns b Smith 24	– c Lynch b Ball	0
K. P. Evans not out 78	– lbw b Ball	41
G. W. Mike c Lynch b Srinath 4	– run out	0
†B. N. French b Srinath 2	– b Ball	16
R. A. Pick c Russell b Ball 34	– lbw b Ball	0
D. B. Pennett not out 6	– not out	25
J. A. Afford (did not bat)	– lbw b Smith	6
L-b 5, n-b 4 9	B 4, l-b 1, n-b 8	13

1/2 2/125 3/137 4/168 5/195   (8 wkts dec.) 300   1/1 2/17 3/36 4/36 5/54   142
6/219 7/221 8/285   6/66 7/98 8/98 9/117

Bonus points – Nottinghamshire 3, Gloucestershire 3.

Bowling: *First Innings*—Srinath 22–8–34–4; Smith 25–7–72–2; Sheeraz 13–2–52–0; Alleyne 12–2–40–0; Ball 38.1–11–97–2. *Second Innings*—Srinath 14–3–37–0; Smith 16.2–6–51–4; Ball 19–7–49–5.

Umpires: J. D. Bond and B. Dudleston.

GLOUCESTERSHIRE v WORCESTERSHIRE

At Gloucester, May 25, 26, 27. Gloucestershire won by an innings and 73 runs. Gloucestershire 24 pts, Worcestershire 4 pts. Toss: Worcestershire. Championship debut: P. A. Thomas.

It was all over well before lunch on the third day. Worcestershire's resounding defeat was largely self-induced and could not be blamed on the pitch. But there was also some excellent bowling by Gloucestershire, especially from Smith. He returned his best figures so far – six for 57 – in the second innings and finished with ten altogether. The challenge of Srinath and accurate medium-pace of Alleyne, which helped to dismiss Worcestershire inside 75 overs on the first day, also made crucial contributions. Dawson's first Championship hundred, backed by fifties from Symonds and Russell, ensured a lead of 203 on first innings. Worcestershire looked a thoroughly dispirited side, and dogged batting by Curtis was little more than a gesture. Nothing went their way; Lampitt, after claiming three wickets, was taken off in mid-over for persistently running on the pitch.

Close of play: First day, Gloucestershire 122-2 (G. D. Hodgson 35*, R. I. Dawson 4*); Second day, Worcestershire 49-3 (T. S. Curtis 16*, R. K. Illingworth 0*).

Worcestershire

W. P. C. Weston c Lynch b Srinath	14	– c Hodgson b Srinath	22
*T. S. Curtis lbw b Srinath	44	– b Smith	24
T. M. Moody lbw b Smith	2	– lbw b Ball	0
G. R. Haynes lbw b Alleyne	0	– b Smith	9
D. A. Leatherdale c Russell b Srinath	18	– (6) lbw b Ball	19
†S. J. Rhodes lbw b Smith	34	– (7) c and b Smith	1
S. R. Lampitt b Alleyne	3	– (8) c Russell b Smith	11
P. J. Newport not out	22	– (9) not out	25
R. K. Illingworth c Russell b Smith	4	– (5) c Dawson b Srinath	5
N. V. Radford lbw b Srinath	12	– c Srinath b Smith	1
P. A. Thomas b Smith	1	– c Lynch b Smith	0
B 6, l-b 8, n-b 4	18	B 1, l-b 3, w 5, n-b 4	13

1/34 2/38 3/39 4/76 5/107   172   1/37 2/38 3/49 4/58 5/78   130
6/122 7/142 8/146 9/165   6/86 7/90 8/122 9/130

Bonus points – Gloucestershire 4.

Bowling: *First Innings*—Srinath 21–9–35–4; Smith 21.1–6–68–4; Alleyne 25–16–36–2; Dawson 6–2–18–0; Ball 1–0–1–0. *Second Innings*—Smith 18.2–5–57–6; Alleyne 4–1–11–0; Srinath 13–4–35–2; Ball 16–10–23–2; Davies 1–1–0–0.

Gloucestershire

A. J. Wright c Rhodes b Radford	29	M. C. J. Ball lbw b Illingworth	7
G. D. Hodgson b Lampitt	42	M. Davies lbw b Radford	1
M. A. Lynch b Weston b Illingworth	40	A. M. Smith not out	4
R. I. Dawson c Leatherdale b Radford	101		
M. W. Alleyne lbw b Lampitt	9	B 1, l-b 1, w 2, n-b 30	34
A. Symonds b Lampitt	52		
*†R. C. Russell c Illingworth b Radford	56	1/39 2/110 3/129 4/153 5/255	375
J. Srinath c Moody b Radford	0	6/330 7/336 8/351 9/362	

Bonus points – Gloucestershire 4, Worcestershire 4.

Bowling: Radford 16.1–4–45–5; Haynes 10–2–33–0; Thomas 15–0–78–0; Newport 17–2–72–0; Lampitt 24.3–5–80–3; Illingworth 22.3–5–63–2; Leatherdale 1–0–2–0.

Umpires: J. W. Holder and B. J. Meyer.

At Hove, June 1, 2, 3, 5. GLOUCESTERSHIRE drew with SUSSEX.

At Canterbury, June 8, 9, 10, 12. GLOUCESTERSHIRE beat KENT by 104 runs.

GLOUCESTERSHIRE v HAMPSHIRE

At Bristol, June 15, 16, 17, 19. Drawn. Gloucestershire 6 pts, Hampshire 7 pts. Toss: Hampshire.

Playing at all on a Monday was a novelty for Hampshire: their six previous Championship matches had all finished in three days. However, most of the third day was lost to rain and the fourth was played sensibly, without connivance. Nicholas astutely set a target of 251 and the result might have gone either way. Gloucestershire ran out of strokemakers, were still 100 short with ten overs left, and then blocked for a draw – apart from the newly capped Srinath, who swung Udal for three sixes, failing, to the small crowd's amusement, to heed words of caution from Alleyne. It was a game of individual merits. Robin Smith's 136, after Hampshire were 16 for three, was powerful, selective and technically sound; James followed it with a determined fifty. In different circumstances, Russell's fighting, undefeated 82 was as valuable as Smith's century. He ensured there would be no follow-on, and then declared 75 behind. The best of the bowling came from Udal, whose six for 65 was a demonstration of thoughtful off-spin. Pike, the Gloucestershire leg-spinner, was rushed into service after Ball hurt his back picking up his baby, and took four.

Close of play: First day, Hampshire 323-9 (K. D. James 51*, C. A. Connor 10*); Second day, Gloucestershire 266-9 (R. C. Russell 82*, V. J. Pike 12*); Third day, Hampshire 16-0 (R. S. M. Morris 11*, V. P. Terry 5*).

Hampshire

V. P. Terry b Smith	12	– (2) retired hurt	5
R. S. M. Morris b Smith	0	– (1) b Srinath	21
J. P. Stephenson c Lynch b Boden	4		
R. A. Smith lbw b Smith	136	– b Pike	20
*M. C. J. Nicholas c Russell b Srinath	6	– c sub b Srinath	5
G. W. White lbw b Pike	34	– c Srinath b Boden	39
K. D. James c Russell b Boden	53	– (3) c Dawson b Smith	8
†A. N. Aymes run out	18	– (7) not out	32
S. D. Udal b Pike	32	– (8) c Srinath b Pike	13
H. H. Streak c Russell b Smith	8	– (9) not out	13
C. A. Connor not out	20		
B 4, l-b 3, w 1, n-b 10	18	L-b 6, n-b 13	19

1/1 2/12 3/16 4/52 5/169   341   1/38 2/38 3/48   (6 wkts dec.) 175
6/209 7/243 8/285 9/303   4/109 5/127 6/145

Bonus points – Hampshire 3, Gloucestershire 4.

In the second innings V. P. Terry retired hurt at 16.

Bowling: *First Innings*—Smith 27–6–76–4; Boden 22–2–73–2; Srinath 18–4–50–1; Alleyne 19–7–41–0; Pike 28–2–94–2. *Second Innings*—Srinath 15–8–22–2; Smith 14–4–45–1; Boden 12–2–50–1; Pike 12–1–52–2.

Gloucestershire

A. J. Wright c and b Udal	50	– lbw b Streak	47
G. D. Hodgson lbw b Udal	27	– lbw b Connor	4
M. A. Lynch b Streak	14	– (4) c Connor b Streak	26
R. I. Dawson c White b Udal	12	– (3) b James	18
M. W. Alleyne b Udal	25	– not out	24
*†R. C. Russell not out	82	– (7) c Terry b Udal	8
A. Symonds c Streak b Udal	2	– (6) lbw b Udal	10
J. Srinath c Smith b Udal	10	– not out	33
D. J. P. Boden lbw b Stephenson	2		
A. M. Smith c Stephenson b Connor	10		
V. J. Pike not out	12		
B 2, l-b 4, n-b 14	20	B 4, l-b 2, w 1, n-b 2	9

1/83 2/100 3/106 4/121 5/162   (9 wkts dec.) 266   1/7 2/50 3/97   (6 wkts) 180
6/168 7/191 8/202 9/229   4/100 5/115 6/137

Bonus points – Gloucestershire 2, Hampshire 4.

Bowling: *First Innings*—Connor 15–3–42–1; Streak 24–6–58–1; Stephenson 18–5–44–1; James 12–1–51–0; Udal 34–10–65–6. *Second Innings*—Streak 13–2–44–2; Connor 13–2–26–1; Udal 18.3–1–66–2; James 4–0–28–1; Stephenson 3–0–10–0; White 1–1–0–0.

Umpires: J. C. Balderstone and P. Willey.

GLOUCESTERSHIRE v OXFORD UNIVERSITY

At Bristol, June 23, 24, 25. Gloucestershire won by an innings and 62 runs. Toss: Oxford University.

Oxford were not happy about the pitch prepared for them and a new one was hurriedly made available. They then surveyed its greenish appearance, put the county in and reduced them to 144 for six. By the close, however, Gloucestershire had reached 321, a total made possible by the seventh-wicket stand by the promising opener Cunliffe and reserve wicket-keeper Williams, which reached 184 next day. Cunliffe went on to a career-best 190, while Williams was out for 90, again his highest. Oxford's batting showed frailties, especially against the control and movement of Cooper, making his return after a stomach strain. He had one spell of four for seven in the University's first innings, and followed up with three more cheap wickets in the second, when he conceded only six runs in 11 overs. Sutcliffe and Ridley at least displayed obduracy.

Close of play: First day, Gloucestershire 321-6 (R. J. Cunliffe 155*, R. C. J. Williams 87*); Second day, Oxford University 78-1 (I. J. Sutcliffe 46*, A. C. Ridley 18*).

Gloucestershire

R. J. Cunliffe not out	190	†R. C. J. Williams run out	90
M. G. N. Windows c Townsend b MacRobert	8	M. Davies not out	15
R. I. Dawson run out	0	B 3, l-b 3, w 1, n-b 2	9
*M. W. Alleyne c Macmillan b Kendall	10		
T. H. C. Hancock c Kendall b Malik	37	1/17 2/17 3/43 (7 wkts dec.) 378	
R. C. Williams c Sutcliffe b Malik	5	4/104 5/109	
M. C. J. Ball lbw b Ricketts	18	6/144 7/328	

K. E. Cooper and D. J. P. Boden did not bat.

Bowling: MacRobert 15–3–50–1; Kendall 12–3–35–1; Yeabsley 11–0–68–0; Malik 28–5–85–2; Ricketts 25–7–60–1; Attfield 3–0–15–0; Macmillan 13–0–59–0.

Oxford University

J. M. Attfield lbw b Boden	12	– b Boden	7
I. J. Sutcliffe c R. C. J. Williams b Boden	6	– c Hancock b Cooper	53
A. C. Ridley c Alleyne b Boden	18	– c Hancock b Alleyne	45
W. S. Kendall c Alleyne b Cooper	22	– c Ball b Cooper	0
M. E. D. Jarrett c R. C. J. Williams b R. C. Williams	3	– c Windows b R. C. Williams	3
H. S. Malik run out	28	– c Boden b R. C. Williams	14
*G. I. Macmillan c R. C. J. Williams b Cooper	0	– (9) lbw b Cooper	6
R. S. Yeabsley c Boden b Cooper	4	– (10) c Windows b Ball	2
J. D. Ricketts c R. C. J. Williams b Cooper	4	– (7) lbw b Alleyne	1
A. D. MacRobert lbw b Ball	12	– (11) not out	8
†C. J. Townsend not out	3	– (8) c Cunliffe b R. C. Williams	27
L-b 9, n-b 4	13	B 8, l-b 11, w 2, n-b 4	25

1/16 2/34 3/57 4/66 5/76   125   1/11 2/93 3/93 4/101 5/129   191
6/80 7/84 8/92 9/113   6/130 7/161 8/176 9/183

Bowling: *First Innings*—Cooper 15–5–34–4; Boden 12–1–38–3; R. C. Williams 12–3–26–1; Alleyne 2–1–4–0; Ball 4.5–1–14–1. *Second Innings*—Boden 13.4–5–26–1; R. C. Williams 20.3–7–44–3; Davies 19.2–8–36–0; Ball 20–4–33–1; Alleyne 12–3–27–2; Cooper 11–7–6–3.

Umpires: J. H. Harris and T. E. Jesty.

At Middlesbrough, June 29, 30, July 1. GLOUCESTERSHIRE beat YORKSHIRE by nine wickets.

GLOUCESTERSHIRE v MIDDLESEX

At Bristol, July 6, 7, 8. Middlesex won by an innings and 11 runs. Middlesex 24 pts, Gloucestershire 1 pt. Toss: Middlesex.

Middlesex completed their sixth Championship win of the season with all-round efficiency and a day to spare, causing Northamptonshire and Warwickshire to look anxiously over their shoulders. There seemed an impatience in the manner they had Gloucestershire in visible discomfort at 94 for six before lunch. By Bristol standards it was quite a pacy wicket, as Johnson discovered. He and Emburey took four each; the only significant resistance came from Wright and Russell, with an admirably cussed 69. Middlesex built their remorseless reply through a trio of centuries, Pooley, with a career-best 136, Ramprakash and Gatting. Their work was done by Saturday morning, when a golden spell of intelligence and fluctuating pace from Srinath claimed six for eight inside nine overs. But it had no effect on the match. Again, Gloucestershire failed against an attack of enviable balance, Alleyne alone prolonging the innings. Cynics might say Gloucestershire got too many things wrong, including a mysterious but erroneous mention on the scorecards that Horfield Prison was among the sponsors.

Close of play: First day, Middlesex 34-0 (P. N. Weekes 16*, J. C. Pooley 18*); Second day, Middlesex 410-2 (M. R. Ramprakash 123*, M. W. Gatting 103*).

Gloucestershire

A. J. Wright b Emburey	54	– c Tufnell b Johnson	25
G. D. Hodgson c Ramprakash b Feltham	8	– c Brown b Feltham	13
R. J. Cunliffe c Carr b Johnson	11	– b Nash	5
M. A. Lynch c Weekes b Johnson	0	– lbw b Feltham	15
M. W. Alleyne c Brown b Johnson	0	– c Johnson b Weekes	69
A. Symonds lbw b Emburey	12	– lbw b Tufnell	6
*†R. C. Russell not out	69	– c Brown b Johnson	29
R. C. Williams c Brown b Johnson	22	– lbw b Johnson	0
J. Srinath c Weekes b Feltham	11	– b Tufnell	17
M. C. J. Ball c Gatting b Emburey	13	– c Johnson b Weekes	24
K. E. Cooper b Emburey	0	– not out	2
L-b 4, n-b 4	8	B 6, l-b 9, n-b 2	17

1/32 2/77 3/77 4/79 5/91   208   1/44 2/52 3/70 4/80 5/96   222
6/94 7/165 8/183 9/208   6/131 7/131 8/164 9/216

Bonus points – Gloucestershire 1, Middlesex 4.

Bowling: *First Innings*—Nash 17–5–35–0; Johnson 21–6–53–4; Feltham 20–8–46–2; Emburey 27.1–12–33–4; Tufnell 10–7–16–0; Weekes 4–0–21–0. *Second Innings*—Nash 14–0–49–1; Johnson 16–4–34–3; Emburey 22–9–46–0; Tufnell 11–2–26–2; Feltham 11–2–32–2; Weekes 9.1–1–20–2.

Middlesex

P. N. Weekes c Lynch b Alleyne	33	R. L. Johnson c Symonds b Cooper	5
J. C. Pooley c Symonds b Cooper	136	M. A. Feltham not out	0
M. R. Ramprakash c Russell b Cooper	133	P. C. R. Tufnell b Srinath	0
*M. W. Gatting c Cunliffe b Srinath	108		
J. D. Carr lbw b Srinath	2	B 1, l-b 4, n-b 10	15
†K. R. Brown c Russell b Srinath	0		
D. J. Nash lbw b Srinath	4	1/81 2/223 3/419 4/421 5/421	441
J. E. Emburey c Russell b Srinath	5	6/431 7/431 8/439 9/441	

Bonus points – Middlesex 4 (Score at 120 overs: 419-2).

Bowling: Srinath 34.4–14–78–6; Cooper 28–7–92–3; Ball 27–5–95–0; Alleyne 23–5–88–1; Williams 22–2–83–0.

Umpires: D. R. Shepherd and R. A. White.

GLOUCESTERSHIRE v LANCASHIRE

At Cheltenham, July 20, 21, 22. Gloucestershire won by ten wickets. Gloucestershire 22 pts, Lancashire 5 pts. Toss: Lancashire.

Fifteen wickets fell on the first day and Gloucestershire, 44 for five in reply to 231, appeared to be facing the follow-on when Symonds fell first ball next morning. But Cunliffe and Russell added 125, preparing the way for a first-innings lead, and Gloucestershire won just after lunch on the third day. It was gratifying for the home supporters, but a fine Festival crowd did feel somewhat short-changed. There were absorbing elements to compensate – and unlikely heroes. Lancashire's best batting came from the eighth-wicket pair, Hegg and Austin. Gloucestershire, in turn, leaned on the calm and wisdom of the inexperienced Cunliffe, who was stranded eight away from a maiden Championship hundred. It was a fastish, bouncy wicket, with enticing short boundaries. That big totals never materialised was due in part to nondescript batting, in part to fine bowling by Wasim Akram and Austin, who started with four for six in eight overs, and then Srinath and Smith. Among those present was Ray Illingworth, chairman of the selectors, who included Russell and Watkinson in the Test squad announced on the Sunday.

Close of play: First day, Gloucestershire 44-5 (R. J. Cunliffe 10*); Second day, Lancashire 87-8 (W. K. Hegg 14*, G. Chapple 2*).

Lancashire

M. A. Atherton lbw b Smith	10	– c Windows b Srinath	21
S. P. Titchard c Lynch b Pike	42	– b Smith	10
J. P. Crawley c Ball b Alleyne	21	– lbw b Srinath	0
N. H. Fairbrother run out	0	– c Russell b Srinath	20
G. D. Lloyd c Cunliffe b Alleyne	4	– c Lynch b Smith	4
*M. Watkinson lbw b Smith	7	– c Symonds b Srinath	4
Wasim Akram run out	0	– (8) c Wright b Srinath	0
I. D. Austin c Cunliffe b Ball	43	– (9) c Ball b Smith	2
†W. K. Hegg b Srinath	61	– (7) c Russell b Smith	14
G. Chapple run out	17	– b Smith	27
G. Keedy not out	11	– not out	4
B 4, l-b 4, w 1, n-b 6	15	B 4, w 1, n-b 6	11

1/13 2/46 3/52 4/57 5/86	231	1/20 2/31 3/46 4/57 5/57	117
6/86 7/92 8/194 9/206		6/65 7/65 8/74 9/87	

Bonus points – Lancashire 1, Gloucestershire 4.

Bowling: *First Innings*—Srinath 20–4–62–1; Smith 22.1–6–66–2; Alleyne 17–8–31–2; Pike
19–7–49–1; Ball 7–1–15–1. *Second Innings*—Srinath 22–4–53–5; Smith 22.3–6–60–5; Pike
1–1–0–0.

Gloucestershire

A. J. Wright c Hegg b Wasim Akram	4	– not out	30
M. G. N. Windows c Crawley b Wasim Akram	16	– not out	51
R. J. Cunliffe not out	92		
M. A. Lynch lbw b Austin	0		
M. W. Alleyne b Austin	10		
V. J. Pike b Austin	4		
A. Symonds b Austin	0		
*†R. C. Russell c Atherton b Watkinson	83		
J. Srinath c Hegg b Wasim Akram	19		
M. C. J. Ball c Lloyd b Wasim Akram	34		
A. M. Smith c Hegg b Wasim Akram	0		
L-b 1, n-b 2	3	L-b 3	3

1/8 2/25 3/26 4/40 5/44   265   (no wkt) 84
6/44 7/169 8/196 9/265

Bonus points – Gloucestershire 2, Lancashire 4.

Bowling: *First Innings*—Wasim Akram 23.5–6–58–5; Chapple 14–5–31–0; Austin
26–10–50–4; Watkinson 19–3–64–1; Keedy 18–4–61–0. *Second Innings*—Chapple 7–3–12–0;
Austin 5–0–19–0; Keedy 6–2–16–0; Watkinson 5–1–20–0; Fairbrother 0.5–0–14–0.

Umpires: D. J. Constant and R. Julian.

At Cheltenham, July 26. GLOUCESTERSHIRE beat YOUNG AUSTRALIA by two
wickets (See Young Australia tour section).

GLOUCESTERSHIRE v ESSEX

At Cheltenham, July 27, 28, 29, 31. Gloucestershire won by three wickets. Gloucestershire
24 pts, Essex 5 pts. Toss: Gloucestershire.
A Festival which brought large crowds, record receipts and eloquent arguments that, in
such a setting, there could not be too much wrong with county cricket, produced an
apposite finish of excitement and native reward. Gloucestershire started the last day – with
four wickets gone and Cunliffe's thumb broken – still needing 220. Alleyne, captaining
the county for the first time in the Championship, rose sublimely to the occasion with a
controlled innings of 141, backed by well-advised restraint from Symonds. On the first day,
after Essex had been put in, Hussain and Irani gave a teetering innings some substance
against the excellent in-swing of Smith, who took seven for the first time. In the second
innings, a career-best 123 by Robinson and an assertive 80 by Waugh hauled their county
back into the game, after highly entertaining hundreds by Lynch and Symonds had given
Gloucestershire a formidable lead of 156. Essex lacked some of their traditional sparkle but
it remained an engrossing match, if bucking the Cheltenham tradition by rewarding seam
far more than spin.
Close of play: First day, Gloucestershire 115-3 (M. A. Lynch 54*, M. W. Alleyne 10*);
Second day, Essex 148-1 (D. D. J. Robinson 77*, N. Hussain 35*); Third day,
Gloucestershire 62-4 (M. W. Alleyne 22*, A. Symonds 7*).

Essex

G. A. Gooch c R. C. J. Williams b Srinath	....	8	– c sub b Ball	22
D. D. J. Robinson lbw b Smith	....	28	– b Srinath	123
N. Hussain b Smith	....	85	– c Windows b Ball	65
M. E. Waugh c Cunliffe b Smith	......	5	– c Windows b R. C. Williams	80
*P. J. Prichard c Ball b Alleyne	....	3	– c R. C. J. Williams b Alleyne	19
R. C. Irani c Symonds b Ball	......	54	– c R. C. J. Williams b Srinath	68
†R. J. Rollins c Lynch b Smith	......	4	– c R. C. J. Williams b Smith	1
M. C. Ilott b Smith	......	12	– c Lynch b Ball	4
N. F. Williams not out	......	6	– c Symonds b Srinath	12
P. M. Such b Smith	......	2	– not out	1
J. H. Childs c R. C. J. Williams b Smith	......	0	– b Srinath	0
B 4, l-b 3, n-b 30	......	37	B 4, l-b 7, w 5, n-b 26	42

1/12 2/59 3/85 4/88 5/210   244   1/79 2/205 3/297 4/334 5/371   437
6/212 7/221 8/238 9/242   6/374 7/392 8/436 9/437

Bonus points – Essex 1, Gloucestershire 4.

Bowling: *First Innings*—Srinath 13–4–60–1; Smith 23.4–7–70–7; R. C. Williams 16–4–46–0; Alleyne 10–2–30–1; Ball 12–2–31–1. *Second Innings*—Smith 21–2–55–1; R. C. Williams 23–3–94–1; Ball 39–8–129–3; Alleyne 22–2–82–1; Symonds 10–5–13–0; Srinath 17.5–2–53–4.

Gloucestershire

A. J. Wright b Williams	......	2	– c Robinson b Ilott	20
M. G. N. Windows lbw b Irani	......	20	– c Such b Irani	13
R. C. Williams lbw b Irani	......	19	– c Rollins b Ilott	0
M. A. Lynch c Such b Waugh	......	111	– c Waugh b Ilott	0
*M. W. Alleyne c Rollins b Ilott	......	77	– c Such b Irani	141
A. Symonds not out	......	123	– c Rollins b Williams	57
†R. C. J. Williams c Rollins b Ilott	......	0	– c Waugh b Ilott	12
M. C. J. Ball c Such b Williams	......	27	– not out	6
A. M. Smith b Williams	......	0		
J. Srinath run out	......	0	– (9) not out	18
R. J. Cunliffe absent hurt				
L-b 7, n-b 14	......	21	B 2, n-b 16	18

1/3 2/48 3/89 4/216 5/304   400   1/22 2/30 3/30 4/42   (7 wkts) 285
6/314 7/400 8/400 9/400   5/183 6/241 7/265

Bonus points – Gloucestershire 4, Essex 4.

Bowling: *First Innings*—Ilott 24–7–92–2; Williams 18.4–1–105–3; Irani 17–0–75–2; Waugh 20–5–85–1; Such 2–1–5–0; Childs 5–1–31–0. *Second Innings*—Ilott 28–6–81–4; Williams 18–2–73–1; Irani 17–5–46–2; Such 10–1–54–0; Childs 6.5–0–29–0.

Umpires: T. E. Jesty and G. Sharp.

At Bristol, August 5, 6, 7. GLOUCESTERSHIRE lost to WEST INDIANS by 74 runs (See West Indian tour section).

At Northampton, August 10, 11, 12, 14. GLOUCESTERSHIRE lost to NORTHAMPTONSHIRE by 209 runs.

GLOUCESTERSHIRE v DERBYSHIRE

At Bristol, August 17, 18, 19, 21. Gloucestershire won by three wickets. Gloucestershire 21 pts, Derbyshire 8 pts. Toss: Derbyshire.

Derbyshire were left wondering how they had failed to capitalise after taking a first-innings lead of 112 and then having Gloucestershire in trouble on 78 for four at the third-day close. A target of 217 seemed beyond the home side's grasp as Warner's deceptive swing gave him four for 15 in 21 balls. But Hancock became the match-winner, surviving four chances – some difficult – in a dogged stay of three and a half hours, while Russell, at the other end, chipped away to orchestrate victory. Derbyshire had piled up 463, with Rollins carrying his bat for his first double-century after nine hours of intense application. He shared hundred stands with Barnett, who reached 1,000 runs for the 12th time, equalling Denis Smith's county record, and Adams, who was in forceful form at the expense of Srinath, who seemed to be feeling the effects of an arduous season. That notion was discounted as he took five cheap wickets in the second innings to topple Derbyshire for 104.

Close of play: First day, Derbyshire 336-4 (A. S. Rollins 129*, D. G. Cork 17*); Second day, Gloucestershire 248-5 (R. C. Russell 0*); Third day, Gloucestershire 78-4 (T. H. C. Hancock 12*, M. W. Alleyne 1*).

Derbyshire

*K. J. Barnett c Lynch b Alleyne	68	– (8) b Ball	16
A. S. Rollins not out	200	– (1) b Srinath	0
C. J. Adams c Sheeraz b Ball	68	– c Alleyne b Srinath	12
T. A. Tweats c Windows b Alleyne	24	– (2) c Lynch b Srinath	4
C. M. Wells b Sheeraz	5	– (4) b Ball	0
D. G. Cork c Russell b Sheeraz	29	– (5) lbw b Srinath	0
P. A. J. DeFreitas c Lynch b Sheeraz	5	– (6) b Srinath	25
F. A. Griffith lbw b Srinath	11	– (7) c Sheeraz b Pike	23
†S. P. Griffiths c Russell b Srinath	9	– run out	2
A. E. Warner retired hurt	6	– not out	16
D. E. Malcolm b Srinath	0	– b Ball	0
B 14, l-b 5, w 3, n-b 16	38	L-b 6	6

1/106 2/213 3/287 4/306 5/373   463   1/2 2/11 3/16 4/20 5/28   104
6/395 7/429 8/455 9/463   6/65 7/76 8/78 9/104

Bonus points – Derbyshire 4, Gloucestershire 1 (Score at 120 overs: 363-4).

In the first innings A. E. Warner retired hurt at 463-8.

Bowling: *First Innings*—Srinath 31-5-120-3; Sheeraz 22-6-89-3; Pike 49-16-107-0; Alleyne 23-5-81-2; Ball 23-10-35-1; Symonds 5-3-12-0. *Second Innings*—Srinath 15-9-25-5; Ball 22.2-5-52-3; Pike 8-1-21-1.

Gloucestershire

A. J. Wright not out	56	– c Adams b Warner	25
M. G. N. Windows c Griffiths b Griffith	56	– c DeFreitas b Warner	15
T. H. C. Hancock b Cork	26	– not out	79
M. A. Lynch c DeFreitas b Griffith	27	– (5) c Griffiths b Warner	6
M. W. Alleyne c Tweats b Malcolm	28	– (6) lbw b Warner	21
A. Symonds lbw b Barnett	71	– (7) c Rollins b Cork	8
*†R. C. Russell b Malcolm	12	– (8) c Griffith b DeFreitas	34
M. C. J. Ball lbw b DeFreitas	28	– (9) not out	2
J. Srinath c Adams b DeFreitas	13		
K. P. Sheeraz run out	1		
V. J. Pike c and b DeFreitas	0	– (4) c Tweats b Warner	4
B 10, l-b 2, w 3, n-b 18	33	B 1, l-b 7, w 1, n-b 14	23

1/64 2/123 3/155 4/248 5/248   351   1/43 2/56 3/66 4/72   (7 wkts) 217
6/264 7/300 8/328 9/345   5/108 6/130 7/215

Bonus points – Gloucestershire 4, Derbyshire 4.

In the first innings A. J. Wright, when 10, retired hurt at 12 and resumed at 248-5.

Bowling: *First Innings*—Malcolm 22–6–86–2; DeFreitas 28.2–8–72–3; Cork 11–1–36–1; Barnett 21.1–3–66–1; Griffith 17–3–79–2. *Second Innings*—Malcolm 8–1–31–0; Cork 12–2–40–1; Warner 21–6–62–5; DeFreitas 29.5–11–68–1; Griffith 1–0–8–0.

Umpires: A. A. Jones and B. J. Meyer.

At Abergavenny, August 23, 24, 25, 26. GLOUCESTERSHIRE drew with GLAMORGAN.

At Birmingham, August 29, 30, 31. GLOUCESTERSHIRE lost to WARWICKSHIRE by ten wickets.

GLOUCESTERSHIRE v DURHAM

At Bristol, September 7, 8, 9, 11. Gloucestershire won by 19 runs. Gloucestershire 23 pts, Durham 2 pts. Toss: Durham.

Durham had appeared to be having the best of the negotiated last-day challenge, but they caved in from 127 for one to 179 for seven and Gloucestershire won with ten balls left. Rain had restricted the first two days to 53 overs, and Gloucestershire had scored 77 in donated runs in their second innings, leaving Durham a target of 256 in 65 overs. It looked well within reach with Hutton and acting-captain Morris at the crease. Then came a mid-order collapse, and fading hopes rested on some adventurous shots from Brown. Ball's off-spinners brought him five wickets; Lewis, in only his second Championship match, took four in each innings. A first-innings century from Wright, backed by 84 from Alleyne and a punchy 66 from Russell to ensure full batting points, had sustained Gloucestershire's interest amid gloomy conditions.

Close of play: First day, No play; Second day, Gloucestershire 160-3 (A. J. Wright 71*, M. W. Alleyne 32*); Third day, Durham 172-7 (J. Boiling 3*, N. Killeen 5*).

Gloucestershire

A. J. Wright c Scott b Boiling	117	– (2) not out	22	
R. J. Cunliffe b Killeen	16			
T. H. C. Hancock c Scott b Walker	4			
M. A. Lynch c Weston b Killeen	28			
M. W. Alleyne b Killeen	84			
A. Symonds c Weston b Boiling	6	– (1) not out	54	
*†R. C. Russell not out	66			
M. C. J. Ball not out	11			
B 2, l-b 9, w 1, n-b 6	18	W 1	1	

1/28 2/44 3/96 4/240   (6 wkts dec.) 350   (no wkt dec.) 77
5/252 6/285

A. M. Smith, J. Lewis and K. P. Sheeraz did not bat.

Bonus points – Gloucestershire 4, Durham 2.

Bowling: *First Innings*—Brown 24.3–6–79–0; Killeen 28–8–85–3; Walker 19–2–72–1; Prabhakar 15–4–33–0; Boiling 16–0–70–2. *Second Innings*—Longley 4–0–47–0; Scott 3.2–0–30–0.

Durham

W. Larkins lbw b Smith	1	– c Russell b Sheeraz	28
S. Hutton c Russell b Alleyne	60	– c Russell b Lewis	44
J. I. Longley c Lynch b Lewis	48	– (5) c Sheeraz b Ball	1
*J. E. Morris c Russell b Lewis	3	– (3) b Ball	70
R. M. S. Weston b Sheeraz	2	– (6) b Ball	9
M. Prabhakar c Symonds b Lewis	15	– (4) c Hancock b Lewis	9
†C. W. Scott c Ball b Lewis	0	– c Russell b Ball	28
J. Boiling not out	3	– (11) not out	0
N. Killeen not out	5	– (8) c Russell b Lewis	0
S. J. E. Brown (did not bat)		– (9) c Sheeraz b Ball	36
A. Walker (did not bat)		– (10) c Hancock b Lewis	5
L-b 1, w 8, n-b 26	35	W 2, n-b 4	6

1/13 2/113 3/120 4/147 5/148   (7 wkts dec.) 172   1/43 2/127 3/145 4/148 5/159   236
6/148 7/151   6/174 7/179 8/217 9/234

Bonus points – Gloucestershire 3.

Bowling: *First Innings*—Smith 11–4–24–1; Sheeraz 12–1–76–1; Lewis 15–4–34–4; Ball 4–0–9–0; Alleyne 12.5–5–28–1. *Second Innings*—Smith 2–0–12–0; Sheeraz 9–1–47–1; Lewis 24–1–87–4; Alleyne 5–0–20–0; Ball 20.2–0–65–5; Hancock 3–1–5–0.

Umpires: K. J. Lyons and A. G. T. Whitehead.

At Leicester, September 14, 15, 16, 18. GLOUCESTERSHIRE drew with LEICESTER-SHIRE.

YOUNG CRICKETER OF THE YEAR

(Elected by the Cricket Writers' Club)

1950	R. Tattersall	1974	P. H. Edmonds
1951	P. B. H. May	1975	A. Kennedy
1952	F. S. Trueman	1976	G. Miller
1953	M. C. Cowdrey	1977	I. T. Botham
1954	P. J. Loader	1978	D. I. Gower
1955	K. F. Barrington	1979	P. W. G. Parker
1956	B. Taylor	1980	G. R. Dilley
1957	M. J. Stewart	1981	M. W. Gatting
1958	A. C. D. Ingleby-Mackenzie	1982	N. G. Cowans
1959	G. Pullar	1983	N. A. Foster
1960	D. A. Allen	1984	R. J. Bailey
1961	P. H. Parfitt	1985	D. V. Lawrence
1962	P. J. Sharpe	1986 {	A. A. Metcalfe
1963	G. Boycott		J. J. Whitaker
1964	J. M. Brearley	1987	R. J. Blakey
1965	A. P. E. Knott	1988	M. P. Maynard
1966	D. L. Underwood	1989	N. Hussain
1967	A. W. Greig	1990	M. A. Atherton
1968	R. M. H. Cottam	1991	M. R. Ramprakash
1969	A. Ward	1992	I. D. K. Salisbury
1970	C. M. Old	1993	M. N. Lathwell
1971	J. Whitehouse	1994	J. P. Crawley
1972	D. R. Owen-Thomas	1995	A. Symonds
1973	M. Hendrick		

An additional award, in memory of Norman Preston, Editor of *Wisden* from 1951 to 1980, was made to C. W. J. Athey in 1980.

HAMPSHIRE

President: W. J. Weld
Chairman: B. G. Ford
Chairman, Cricket Committee: J. R. Gray
Chief Executive: A. F. Baker
Captain: 1995 – M. C. J. Nicholas
1996 – J. P. Stephenson
Coach: T. M. Tremlett
Head Groundsman: N. Gray
Scorer: V. H Isaacs

Optimism is a wonderful thing; it is also a fragile thread. So Hampshire discovered in the long hot days of 1995. Mark Nicholas had preached a message of optimism when he addressed the county members' annual meeting in the run-up to what became his farewell season, after a decade in which he had become, on some reckonings, the most successful captain in their history, seeing them to four one-day titles. He was confident that the transitional phase following the retirement of David Gower, Malcolm Marshall and Jon Ayling was past. While not forecasting a sensational rise, he expected Hampshire to be a major force. Eight weeks later, Nicholas delivered another homily of a very different tone, to the players on whom he had based his upbeat prediction. This time, his message was more blunt – something like "Get your fingers out."

By May 21, Hampshire had been bounced out of the Benson and Hedges Cup, and beaten in three Championship matches and in two Sunday League games. They had won twice – although won was something of a misnomer in one case. In the Benson and Hedges Cup, they had seen off the youthful enthusiasm of Combined Universities by dint of losing one wicket fewer when the scores were tied. Other than that, they had inflicted a one-day defeat on a West Indian party still adjusting to the chill of an early English summer. Throw in a largely meaningless meeting with Oxford University, in which the undergraduate batsmen hit his bowlers for 317 for a single wicket, and the reason for Nicholas's blunt dressing-room message was clear.

But it worked. Sussex came to Portsmouth for the next match and, with Robin Smith responding to the presence of an England talent-spotter to play a century of majestic technique and awesome concentration, and Paul Terry shedding his diffidence to hit 170, his highest score of an under-achieving summer, they were seen off by an innings. In the next fortnight, first Glamorgan, then Leicestershire were put to the sword. After a weather-spoiled draw in Bristol, Worcestershire also fell victims to a suddenly resurgent side.

Sadly, that flush of mid-season victories, which lifted Hampshire to joint third place, was illusory. Soon they had slipped back to their earlier ineffectiveness and five emphatic defeats in their next six matches pushed them down the table again. They won just once more – a handsome innings victory at Trent Bridge, just after Nicholas had handed the reins to his successor, John Stephenson.

The Sunday League remained a no-go area for Hampshire – their first victory came in their fifth match, when they reached a rain-revised target against Leicestershire. They won only twice more, though they tied with Worcestershire, and Nicholas, who had lifted the title in 1986, bowed out with the wooden spoon. The NatWest Trophy offered the last chance of success. Hampshire drew the short straw in the first round – one of only two all-first-class ties. They seemed to have the match won when they prised out Leicestershire's ninth wicket, 33 runs in arrears. But, as so often, Hampshire could not get ten and jack out. Alan Mullally and Adrian Pierson hung in there, levelled the scores, and Leicestershire won through having been ahead at the 30-overs mark. Hampshire's depression hit a new low and was never really thrown off.

Corporately, it was a summer best forgotten and there were few individuals who could look back with full satisfaction either. Luck was unkind. Losing Robin Smith to Ian Bishop's bouncer in the Fourth Test was a cruel blow – he remained Hampshire's star batting act. Another great loss was that of young pace bowler Jim Bovill. He played only seven Championship matches before a serious back injury forced him out, but had taken 29 wickets, including 12 in the opening game with Durham, and shown high promise.

The leading bowlers were two seamers, Cardigan Connor and the Zimbabwean, Heath Streak, and off-spinner Shaun Udal. All took over 50 first-class wickets and Streak was more successful than the previous year's overseas player, West Indian Winston Benjamin. Still, he never managed five in an innings. Hampshire's most successful overseas fast bowler, Malcolm Marshall, was to return in 1996, but only to join the coaching staff. Benjamin is coming back to play, and one of Marshall's major tasks will be maintaining his enthusiasm.

Batsman Tony Middleton was appointed cricket development officer, and Norman Cowans, who joined from Middlesex the previous year, was forced into retirement by injury early in the season. But the most notable departure was that of Nicholas. He, at least, switched from full-time cricket to full-time journalism with a sense of personal achievement. He was understandably disappointed that his 11th year as captain had produced so little. But he was the only batsman to reach 1,000 Championship runs – Terry was the one other to pass four figures in all first-class matches for Hampshire. Stephenson, newly arrived from Essex, took a while to find his form at first-class level, and finished with 892.

Towards the end of the season, a powerful opening batsman, Jason Laney, suggested that his may become a familiar name. The other encouraging newcomer was 20-year-old locally raised off-spinner Richard Dibden. He played only four matches, took six wickets, and his final average of 71.33 was no great shakes. But not every novice comes up against Carl Hooper, bent on revenge for the West Indians' earlier defeat at Southampton. Dibden's figures of nought for 95 off 12 overs were painful – but the lad kept coming back and trying to find a way past the Hooper bat.

Laney and Dibden have much to prove; so too do the others on whom the new era depends. Batsmen like Sean Morris, Giles White and Paul Whitaker have demonstrated their batting quality, but must now add the resilience to fill out their promise. Nicholas is lucky when he succeeded Nick Pocock – he inherited Terry, Chris and Robin Smith, Marshall and Gordon Greenidge. Nicholas's legacy is largely one of unproven potential: helping it to be fulfilled is the major challenge facing Stephenson. As he admits, "Mark will be a hard act to follow." – Mike Neasom.

HAMPSHIRE 1995

Back row: L. Savident, M. Keech, J. N. B. Bovill, G. W. White, J. S. Laney, M. J. Thursfield, L. J. Botham, R. R. Dibden. *Middle row*: H. H. Streak, G. R. Treagus, A. N. Aymes, R. S. M. Morris, K. D. James, S. D. Udal, D. B. Goldstraw, D. P. J. Flint, P. R. Whitaker, N. G. Cowans, T. C. Middleton, T. M. Tremlett (*coach*). *Front row*: D. M. Thomas, R. J. Maru, C. A. Connor, M. C. J. Nicholas (*captain*), J. P. Stephenson, V. P. Terry, R. A. Smith, M. Garaway.

HAMPSHIRE RESULTS

All first-class matches – Played 20: Won 5, Lost 9, Drawn 6.

County Championship matches – Played 17: Won 5, Lost 8, Drawn 4.

Bonus points – Batting 32, Bowling 56.

*Competition placings – Britannic Assurance County Championship, 13th;
NatWest Bank Trophy, 1st round; Benson and Hedges Cup, 5th in Group C;
AXA Equity & Law League, 18th.*

BRITANNIC ASSURANCE CHAMPIONSHIP AVERAGES

BATTING

	Birthplace	M	I	NO	R	HS	Avge
‡R. A. Smith	Durban, SA	8	15	1	812	172	58.00
‡M. C. J. Nicholas...	London	17	30	3	1,077	147	39.88
J. S. Laney	Winchester	7	13	1	423	73	35.25
P. R. Whitaker....	Keighley	11	18	0	566	119	31.44
‡J. P. Stephenson	Stebbing	15	26	4	689	127	31.31
‡V. P. Terry	Osnabruck, W. Germany	17	30	2	796	170	28.42
‡A. N. Aymes	Southampton	17	28	7	547	60*	26.04
G. W. White	Barnstaple	14	23	2	497	62	23.66
‡S. D. Udal........	Farnborough, Hants	16	26	4	477	85	21.68
R. S. M. Morris	Great Horwood	9	17	0	354	47	20.82
‡K. D. James	Lambeth	10	17	2	274	53	18.26
J. N. B. Bovill	High Wycombe	7	10	5	90	31	18.00
‡C. A. Connor	The Valley, Anguilla	15	24	5	275	33	14.47
H. H. Streak§	Bulawayo, Rhodesia	16	25	2	301	38	13.08
R. R. Dibden	Southampton	2	4	1	0	0*	0.00

Also batted: D. P. J. Flint (*Basingstoke*) (1 match) 17*; M. Keech (*Hampstead*) (1 match) 35, 22; ‡R. J. Maru (*Nairobi, Kenya*) (2 matches) 1, 0*, 7; ‡T. C. Middleton (*Winchester*) (1 match) 7, 0; M. J. Thursfield (*South Shields*) (1 match) 16, 0.

* Signifies not out. ‡ Denotes county cap. § Overseas player.

The following played a total of nine three-figure innings for Hampshire in County Championship matches – M. C. J. Nicholas 3, R. A. Smith 3, J. P. Stephenson 1, V. P. Terry 1, P. R. Whitaker 1.

BOWLING

	O	M	R	W	BB	5W/i	Avge
J. N. B. Bovill	231.3	61	741	29	6-29	2	25.55
H. H. Streak	459.4	109	1,448	52	4-40	0	27.84
C. A. Connor.........	513.2	112	1,707	54	6-44	3	31.61
S. D. Udal..........	570.2	126	1,692	53	6-65	5	31.92
J. P. Stephenson	326	61	1,164	36	7-51	1	32.33
K. D. James	189.2	43	632	18	6-38	1	35.11

Also bowled: R. R. Dibden 63-10-255-4; D. P. J. Flint 32-11-64-2; M. Keech 10.3-0-43-1; R. J. Maru 105.5-47-199-9; M. C. J. Nicholas 7-0-26-0; M. J. Thursfield 25-5-82-1; P. R. Whitaker 4-0-15-1; G. W. White 4-1-22-0.

Wicket-keeper: A. N. Aymes 51 ct, 3 st.

Leading Fielder: V. P. Terry 30.

At Stockton-on-Tees, April 27, 28, 29. HAMPSHIRE lost to DURHAM by 26 runs.

At Lord's, May 4, 5, 6. HAMPSHIRE lost to MIDDLESEX by 205 runs.

At Oxford, May 11, 12, 13. HAMPSHIRE drew with OXFORD UNIVERSITY.

At Southampton, May 14. HAMPSHIRE beat WEST INDIANS by 43 runs (See West Indian tour section).

HAMPSHIRE v KENT

At Southampton, May 18, 19, 20. Kent won by 39 runs. Kent 21 pts, Hampshire 4 pts. Toss: Kent. Championship debut: S. C. Willis.

Three successive defeats – all in three days – represented Hampshire's worst start to a Championship season since 1906. The third defeat was almost inevitable from the second morning, when they lost their last six first-innings wickets for 22 in 10.2 overs. McCague took four for eight in 23 deliveries and presented Kent with a lead of 70, on a pitch offering enough movement to induce uncertainty in every batsman's mind. Kent stretched their advantage to 358 through a solid fourth-wicket partnership of 115 between Taylor and Walker, the only batsmen who played Udal with confidence. Udal, just called up for England's one-day squad, collected five for 81. With 30 wickets down inside two days, Hampshire resumed on Friday evening. Their second-innings batting showed greater application but, after another solid start from Terry and Morris, the middle order struggled. Nicholas was forced off after being hit on the head by McCague, though he made a brief return. The late defiance of Aymes, with an unbeaten 60, threatened to avert defeat. But Headley sealed Kent's victory by dismissing Connor and Bovill in the last over on the Saturday.

Close of play: First day, Hampshire 115-4 (C. A. Connor 4*, M. C. J. Nicholas 1*); Second day, Hampshire 47-0 (V. P. Terry 31*, R. S. M. Morris 11*).

Kent

T. R. Ward b Connor	0	– c Aymes b Bovill	8
*M. R. Benson c Aymes b Udal	13	– lbw b Stephenson	47
N. R. Taylor c Terry b Udal	24	– c Terry b Udal	87
P. A. de Silva c Connor b Streak	28	– lbw b Stephenson	0
M. J. Walker c Streak b Stephenson	9	– c Stephenson b Bovill	53
M. A. Ealham c Aymes b Streak	23	– c Stephenson b Udal	8
†S. C. Willis run out	17	– lbw b Udal	1
M. M. Patel c Morris b Bovill	17	– c and b Udal	28
M. J. McCague not out	36	– b Udal	17
D. W. Headley c Aymes b Stephenson	5	– c Aymes b Connor	5
A. P. Igglesden b Connor	18	– not out	15
L-b 4, n-b 18	22	L-b 5, n-b 14	19

1/0 2/41 3/48 4/61 5/107   207   1/17 2/80 3/80 4/195 5/208   288
6/123 7/140 8/157 9/172   6/213 7/224 8/257 9/268

Bonus points – Kent 1, Hampshire 4.

Bowling: First Innings—Connor 13.3–3–52–2; Bovill 12–2–62–1; Udal 14–7–21–2; Streak 10–3–31–2; Stephenson 13–4–37–2. *Second Innings*—Connor 13.2–2–42–1; Bovill 15–2–59–2; Streak 14–3–46–0; Udal 19–2–81–5; Stephenson 15–1–55–2.

Hampshire

V. P. Terry lbw b McCague	37	– lbw b Igglesden	48
R. S. M. Morris c McCague b Ealham	47	– lbw b Igglesden	40
G. W. White c Willis b Headley	0	– (6) lbw b McCague	25
R. A. Smith run out	20	– c de Silva b Patel	22
C. A. Connor not out	14	– (10) lbw b Headley	19
*M. C. J. Nicholas c Patel b McCague	7	– (5) c McCague b Patel	37
J. P. Stephenson c Willis b McCague	2	– (3) c Ward b de Silva	8
†A. N. Aymes c Willis b Igglesden	1	– (7) not out	60
S. D. Udal lbw b McCague	1	– (8) c Willis b Headley	5
H. H. Streak lbw b McCague	1	– (9) c Headley b McCague	30
J. N. B. Bovill c Ealham b Igglesden	1	– b Headley	0
B 1, w 1, n-b 4	6	B 5, l-b 9, w 1, n-b 10	25

1/78 2/79 3/103 4/108 5/122   137   1/85 2/96 3/129 4/129 5/193   319
6/128 7/133 8/134 9/136   6/206 7/250 8/281 9/319

Bonus points – Kent 4.

In the second innings M. C. J. Nicholas, when 30, retired hurt at 186 and resumed at 250.

Bowling: *First Innings*—McCague 16–4–47–5; Igglesden 11.2–2–40–2; Ealham 10–4–15–1; Headley 10–2–34–1. *Second Innings*—McCague 31–8–70–2; Headley 22.4–3–64–3; Igglesden 14–3–47–2; Patel 30–9–62–2; Ealham 14–5–20–0; de Silva 16–5–42–1.

Umpires: N. T. Plews and G. Sharp.

HAMPSHIRE v SUSSEX

At Portsmouth, May 25, 26, 27. Hampshire won by an innings and 106 runs. Hampshire 24 pts, Sussex 1 pt. Toss: Hampshire.

Hampshire, who had held a dressing-room crisis meeting after their disastrous start to 1995, responded spectacularly. Inspired by a third-wicket partnership of 259 in 74 overs between Terry and Smith – which earned their first batting points of the season – they cruised to victory with a day to spare. Smith's watchful innings, with 15 fours, was witnessed by England talent-spotter Brian Bolus and helped to clinch his Test return, announced a week later. Terry was more belligerent, hitting one six and 18 fours, and, once the Sussex bowling was softened up, the later batsmen, led by Aymes, drove Hampshire to a massive 534. On a pitch favouring the quicker bowlers, Sussex never threatened to avoid the follow-on, nor did they look capable of taking the match into the fourth day against Hampshire's all-seam attack. After 70 successive Championship matches, Wells was absent from the Sussex team because he was making his England one-day debut.

Close of play: First day, Hampshire 356-3 (V. P. Terry 162*, P. R. Whitaker 15*); Second day, Sussex 143-7 (I. D. K. Salisbury 7*, P. W. Jarvis 13*).

Hampshire

R. S. M. Morris c Moores b Giddins	23	H. H. Streak lbw b Hemmings	11
V. P. Terry c Moores b Giddins	170	C. A. Connor c Athey b Salisbury	10
J. P. Stephenson lbw b Jarvis	8	J. N. B. Bovill not out	8
R. A. Smith c Jarvis b Stephenson	120		
P. R. Whitaker c Moores b Jarvis	46	B 12, l-b 10, w 3, n-b 14	39
*M. C. J. Nicholas c Moores b Giddins	1		
G. W. White lbw b Hemmings	38	1/58 2/70 3/329 4/381 5/397	534
†A. N. Aymes run out	60	6/400 7/479 8/501 9/516	

Bonus points – Hampshire 4, Sussex 1 (Score at 120 overs: 383-4).

Bowling: Stephenson 27–7–62–1; Jarvis 28–3–111–2; Hemmings 25.4–4–81–2; Giddins 33–7–91–3; Salisbury 31–2–123–1; Newell 15–3–35–0; Athey 3–1–9–0.

Sussex

C. W. J. Athey c Stephenson b Bovill	7	– b Connor		17
J. W. Hall c Aymes b Streak	30	– c Aymes b Streak		32
K. Newell c Streak b Stephenson	24	– c Aymes b Streak		35
N. J. Lenham c Aymes b Bovill	7	– c Aymes b Stephenson		28
K. Greenfield lbw b Stephenson	0	– b Connor		15
†P. Moores c Whitaker b Bovill	23	– c Morris b Stephenson		8
F. D. Stephenson c Aymes b Connor	19	– c Aymes b Streak		17
*I. D. K. Salisbury c Morris b Stephenson	38	– c Bovill b Stephenson		20
P. W. Jarvis lbw b Stephenson	28	– c Stephenson b Connor		38
E. S. H. Giddins c Morris b Streak	1	– c White b Streak		9
E. E. Hemmings not out	0	– not out		3
B 1, l-b 4, n-b 14	19	L-b 1, n-b 9		10

1/23 2/61 3/67 4/67 5/102   196   1/37 2/58 3/103 4/117 5/139   232
6/107 7/127 8/195 9/196   6/143 7/170 8/176 9/189

Bonus points – Hampshire 4.

Bowling: *First Innings*—Connor 25–6–64–1; Bovill 21–5–60–3; Stephenson 14–3–45–4; Streak 10.3–3–22–2. *Second Innings*—Connor 15.5–3–43–3; Bovill 13–3–43–0; Stephenson 19–3–64–3; Streak 17–4–81–4.

Umpires: V. A. Holder and P. B. Wight.

At Cardiff, June 1, 2, 3. HAMPSHIRE beat GLAMORGAN by eight wickets.

HAMPSHIRE v LEICESTERSHIRE

At Basingstoke, June 7, 8, 9. Hampshire won by nine wickets. Hampshire 23 pts, Leicestershire 4 pts. Toss: Hampshire.

Quality pace bowling by Connor and Streak swept Hampshire to a third successive victory. Like the previous two and the three defeats that preceded them, it came inside three days; the players were getting accustomed to free Mondays. Connor claimed ten for 127, while the Zimbabwean Streak showed he was adjusting to English conditions with four in each innings. His first three Championship games had brought five wickets, the next three 20. Hampshire's batting was fitful. Stephenson rallied them from a poor start and then Nicholas and White took control, adding 110 in 35 overs for the fifth wicket. There was a sensational start to the Leicestershire innings: they collapsed to 26 for six, all six falling to Connor, four of them in 13 balls on the second morning, when his late movement caused considerable problems. Streak struck twice on 59 and, though Smith and Millns shared a ninth-wicket partnership of 73, Leicestershire followed on 165 behind. The second innings was slightly better, with Smith again looking impressive, but Streak demolished the tail with four wickets in seven balls and Hampshire required only 89 for victory.

Close of play: First day, Leicestershire 7-2 (A. R. K. Pierson 2*, W. J. Cronje 1*); Second day, Leicestershire 196-6 (P. A. Nixon 8*, G. J. Parsons 7*).

Hampshire

R. S. M. Morris c Wells b Mullally	5	– c Cronje b Pierson		29
V. P. Terry lbw b Parsons	11	– not out		45
J. P. Stephenson c Nixon b Parsons	55	– not out		11
P. R. Whitaker c Nixon b Pierson	21			
*M. C. J. Nicholas c Pierson b Mullally	50			
G. W. White c Parsons b Pierson	62			
†A. N. Aymes c Nixon b Millns	20			
S. D. Udal c Nixon b Mullally	6			
H. H. Streak c Nixon b Parsons	7			
C. A. Connor b Parsons	32			
J. N. B. Bovill not out	12			
B 12, l-b 13, w 3, n-b 10	38	L-b 5, n-b 2		7

1/6 2/35 3/91 4/114 5/224   319   1/67   (1 wkt) 92
6/244 7/255 8/268 9/278

Bonus points – Hampshire 3, Leicestershire 4.

Bowling: *First Innings*—Mullally 22–8–43–3; Millns 21–0–95–1; Cronje 17–6–48–0; Parsons 24.4–9–58–4; Pierson 15–1–50–2. *Second Innings*—Mullally 8–5–5–0; Parsons 7–2–32–0; Millns 5–0–14–0; Cronje 4–1–10–0; Pierson 5–0–26–1.

Leicestershire

D. L. Maddy lbw b Connor	0	– lbw b Connor	14
*N. E. Briers c Aymes b Connor	1	– c Udal b Connor	5
A. R. K. Pierson b Connor	4	– (10) b Streak	0
W. J. Cronje c Aymes b Connor	9	– (3) b Connor	66
J. J. Whitaker b Connor	0	– (4) b Udal	11
V. J. Wells c Terry b Connor	0	– (5) b Udal	0
B. F. Smith not out	57	– (6) lbw b Connor	67
†P. A. Nixon lbw b Streak	17	– (7) not out	44
G. J. Parsons b Streak	0	– (8) c Terry b Streak	20
D. J. Millns lbw b Streak	30	– (9) c White b Streak	0
A. D. Mullally c Aymes b Streak	14	– c Aymes b Streak	2
L-b 6, w 1, n-b 15	22	B 1, l-b 7, n-b 16	24

1/1 2/2 3/11 4/11 5/17   154   1/11 2/50 3/75 4/75 5/180   253
6/26 7/59 8/59 9/132   6/185 7/251 8/251 9/251

Bonus points – Hampshire 4.

Bowling: *First Innings*—Connor 13–2–44–6; Bovill 14–3–48–0; Streak 9.3–1–44–4; Udal 6–3–5–0; Stephenson 6–2–7–0. *Second Innings*—Connor 25–9–83–4; Bovill 26–8–57–0; Udal 15–1–46–2; Streak 13–5–40–4; Stephenson 4–1–19–0.

Umpires: G. Sharp and D. R. Shepherd.

At Bristol, June 15, 16, 17, 19. HAMPSHIRE drew with GLOUCESTERSHIRE.

HAMPSHIRE v WORCESTERSHIRE

At Southampton, June 22, 23, 24, 26. Hampshire won by 70 runs. Hampshire 24 pts, Worcestershire 5 pts. Toss: Hampshire. First-class debut: V. S. Solanki.

A record-breaking match – the aggregate of 1,474 runs was the highest in Hampshire's Championship history – reached a dramatic conclusion. With three overs remaining, Worcestershire, who had been challenged to score 484, were 411 for seven. Though Lampitt had retired, struck on the fingers, they seemed in little danger. Then newcomer Solanki, tempted by a short ball from left-arm spinner Flint, was caught on the mid-wicket boundary. The over ended with Flint bowling Thomas. Lampitt returned but never took guard as, three balls later, Newport was caught off bat and pad, to give Hampshire an improbable victory with nine balls to spare. The tail had given Hampshire their initial advantage, adding 176 for the last four wickets, which almost enabled them to enforce the follow-on. They declared their second innings on the back of a 199-run partnership between Nicholas and Whitaker. Both hit hundreds, for the left-handed Whitaker it was the first of his career. Worcestershire made a spirited response but, once Moody fell cheaply, the odds were on the draw. After tea on the first day the umpires forgot to bring the ball out; each thought the other had it.

Close of play: First day, Hampshire 314-6 (A. N. Aymes 24*, S. D. Udal 35*); Second day, Worcestershire 289; Third day, Worcestershire 41-0 (T. S. Curtis 20*, W. P. C. Weston 18*).

Hampshire

R. S. M. Morris c Weston b Haynes	27	– c Lampitt b Thomas	1
V. P. Terry c Leatherdale b Solanki	73	– lbw b Lampitt	11
P. R. Whitaker c Moody b Lampitt	4	– c and b Solanki	119
*M. C. J. Nicholas lbw b Newport	73	– not out	138
G. W. White c Rhodes b Lampitt	33	– c and b Moody	21
K. D. James b Thomas	17	– c Rhodes b Haynes	10
†A. N. Aymes c Rhodes b Newport	26	– not out	36
S. D. Udal lbw b Thomas	56		
H. H. Streak b Haynes	38		
J. N. B. Bovill c and b Lampitt	31		
D. P. J. Flint not out	17		
L-b 17, n-b 16	33	N-b 8	8

1/60 2/69 3/169 4/210 5/242   428   1/5 2/31 3/230   (5 wkts dec.) 344
6/252 7/339 8/339 9/390   4/270 5/293

Bonus points – Hampshire 4, Worcestershire 3 (Score at 120 overs: 355-8).

Bowling: *First Innings*—Newport 31-8-95-2; Thomas 30-5-98-2; Haynes 25-8-68-2; Lampitt 29.4-10-73-3; Solanki 19-4-76-1; Weston 1-0-1-0. *Second Innings*—Newport 10-4-23-0; Thomas 11-3-37-1; Lampitt 17.4-4-66-1; Haynes 17-2-56-1; Solanki 18-3-70-1; Tolley 4-0-23-0; Weston 4-0-24-0; Moody 8-0-45-1.

Worcestershire

T. S. Curtis lbw b Bovill	0	– lbw b Streak	40
W. P. C. Weston c and b Streak	33	– c Udal b James	57
C. M. Tolley b Bovill	20	– c James b Udal	24
*T. M. Moody c Terry b James	41	– c Terry b Udal	8
G. R. Haynes lbw b James	32	– c Aymes b Udal	78
D. A. Leatherdale c Morris b Bovill	83	– lbw b Udal	69
†S. J. Rhodes c White b Udal	5	– lbw b Bovill	43
S. R. Lampitt lbw b Udal	18	– not out	22
V. S. Solanki c Nicholas b Bovill	30	– c Streak b Flint	31
P. J. Newport not out	9	– c White b Udal	13
P. A. Thomas b Streak	1	– b Flint	0
L-b 7, n-b 10	17	B 7, l-b 9, w 4, n-b 8	28

1/0 2/32 3/84 4/104 5/149   289   1/105 2/105 3/130 4/147 5/272   413
6/163 7/214 8/271 9/288   6/313 7/347 8/411 9/411

Bonus points – Worcestershire 2, Hampshire 4.

In the second innings S. R. Lampitt, when 22, retired hurt at 388 and resumed at 411-9.

Bowling: *First Innings*—Bovill 15-2-66-4; Streak 18-2-74-2; Udal 19-3-70-2; James 17-2-60-2; Flint 9-4-12-0. *Second Innings*—Bovill 25-6-99-1; Streak 14-2-61-1; Udal 46.3-13-144-5; Flint 23-7-52-2; James 15-4-35-1; Whitaker 2-0-6-0.

Umpires: B. Dudleston and R. Julian.

At Derby, June 29, 30, July 1. HAMPSHIRE lost to DERBYSHIRE by six wickets.

HAMPSHIRE v YORKSHIRE

At Southampton, July 6, 7, 8, 10. Yorkshire won by three wickets. Yorkshire 22 pts, Hampshire 5 pts. Toss: Hampshire. First-class debuts: R. R. Dibden; A. C. Morris.

The match sprang to life only on the final day, which Hampshire entered with a lead of 164 and three wickets down. Far from setting a daunting target, their fragile batting collapsed. Stephenson had broken a finger and the last seven fell for 65, leaving Yorkshire to score 264 from 64 overs. Bevan, supported by Vaughan, led the chase. There was a late wobble when Bevan and Parker succumbed to debutant off-spinner Richard Dibden. Hartley hit Dibden for two sixes, however, and they eased home with five balls to spare. For the first three days, it was largely a tactical exercise. On a bland pitch, Hampshire built a formidable 429 around a watchful seven-hour 147 by Nicholas, with 23 fours and a six, and a late violent flurry from Udal, who hit two sixes and 11 fours. Yorkshire batted with equal caution, their dominant figure being the Australian Bevan, whose 247-minute century was his second in successive matches.

Close of play: First day, Hampshire 346-6 (M. C. J. Nicholas 90*, H. H. Streak 4*); Second day, Yorkshire 225-2 (D. Byas 31*, M. G. Bevan 26*); Third day, Hampshire 166-3 (V. P. Terry 76*, C. A. Connor 0*).

Hampshire

V. P. Terry c Blakey b Hartley	1	– c Blakey b Stemp	94
R. S. M. Morris c Kellett b Hartley	46	– c Byas b Hartley	1
J. P. Stephenson retired hurt	0	– (11) not out	0
P. R. Whitaker c Morris b Robinson	72	– (3) c Blakey b White	28
*M. C. J. Nicholas c Stemp b Hartley	147	– (4) c White b Hartley	36
G. W. White c Blakey b Hartley	4	– c Parker b Hartley	12
†A. N. Aymes c Vaughan b White	22	– (8) c Byas b Hartley	17
S. D. Udal c Parker b Robinson	85	– (7) c Blakey b Hartley	1
H. H. Streak c Byas b Robinson	4	– lbw b Stemp	4
C. A. Connor c Byas b Robinson	19	– (5) c Blakey b Stemp	33
R. R. Dibden not out	0	– (10) lbw b Stemp	0
L-b 3, w 2, n-b 24	29	B 10, l-b 7, n-b 22	39

1/10 2/121 3/139 4/160 5/206   429 1/13 2/85 3/157 4/200 5/237   265
6/340 7/354 8/386 9/429   6/239 7/244 8/263 9/265

Bonus points – Hampshire 4, Yorkshire 3 (Score at 120 overs: 369-7).

In the first innings J. P. Stephenson retired hurt at 10-1.

Bowling: *First Innings*—Hartley 35.1-7-109-4; Robinson 36-15-72-4; White 20-3-78-1; Stemp 16-1-83-0; Morris 13-4-51-0; Bevan 10-5-21-0; Vaughan 4-1-12-0. *Second Innings*—Hartley 19.5-5-56-5; Robinson 16-2-60-0; Stemp 25.1-6-68-4; White 13-3-34-1; Vaughan 5-0-19-0; Morris 4-1-11-0.

Yorkshire

S. A. Kellett run out	86	– c Morris b Udal	27
M. P. Vaughan c Morris b Udal	66	– b Connor	70
*D. Byas c White b Connor	62	– c Aymes b Udal	1
M. G. Bevan b Connor	107	– c Terry b Dibden	56
C. White lbw b Stephenson	20	– c Aymes b Udal	36
B. Parker c Nicholas b Streak	40	– c Terry b Dibden	6
†R. J. Blakey lbw b Streak	3	– not out	27
A. C. Morris c Terry b Streak	1	– (9) not out	0
P. J. Hartley not out	7	– (8) c Aymes b Streak	14
B 9, l-b 9, w 7, n-b 14	39	B 1, l-b 10, w 1, n-b 16	28

1/135 2/179 3/298 4/349 5/411   (8 wkts dec.) 431   1/74 2/76 3/142 4/203   (7 wkts) 265
6/423 7/424 8/431   5/216 6/225 7/261

R. D. Stemp and M. A. Robinson did not bat.

Bonus points – Yorkshire 3, Hampshire 1 (Score at 120 overs: 349-4).

Bowling: *First Innings*—Connor 36-9-107-2; Streak 24.2-7-57-3; Udal 36-8-96-1; Stephenson 17-0-66-1; Dibden 32-9-87-0. *Second Innings*—Streak 9-2-43-1; Connor 15.1-1-52-1; Stephenson 10-2-44-0; Udal 21-1-79-3; Dibden 8-1-36-2.

Umpires: B. J. Meyer and A. G. T. Whitehead.

At Northampton, July 20, 21, 22, 24. HAMPSHIRE drew with NORTHAMPTONSHIRE.

At Southampton, July 28, 29, 30. HAMPSHIRE lost to YOUNG AUSTRALIA by ten wickets (See Young Australia tour section).

At Colchester, August 3, 4, 5, 7. HAMPSHIRE lost to ESSEX by an innings and 254 runs.

HAMPSHIRE v WARWICKSHIRE

At Southampton, August 10, 11, 12. Warwickshire won by an innings and 89 runs. Warwickshire 24 pts, Hampshire 3 pts. Toss: Hampshire.

Hampshire suffered another crushing defeat inside three days. Their fragile batting was initially exposed by Donald's pace on a bland pitch; only Nicholas's 162 minutes of defiance averted complete disaster. Warwickshire then turned the screw ruthlessly, with Khan grinding out a five-hour maiden century. Seizing his chance while Knight was in the Test team, he advanced to 181 in almost eight hours of solid application, hitting 27 fours and sharing stands of 148 with Piper and 208 with Penney. A late, typically improvised flourish by Reeve salted Hampshire's wounds, although Connor's perseverance was rewarded with five wickets. Facing a 310-run deficit, Terry and the impressive Laney, with a maiden fifty, offered the promise of a fight. They put together Hampshire's only century opening partnership in 1995. But they were parted just before tea on Saturday, and the last nine wickets subsided gently, mostly to Smith's off-spin, in the final session.

Close of play: First day, Warwickshire 65-2 (W. G. Khan 24*, K. J. Piper 27*); Second day, Warwickshire 429-6 (D. A. Reeve 13*, N. M. K. Smith 16*).

Hampshire

V. P. Terry c Piper b Munton	14	– c Piper b Smith	46
J. S. Laney c Piper b Donald	42	– c Piper b Donald	61
J. P. Stephenson c Piper b Munton	36	– c Piper b Donald	5
T. C. Middleton lbw b Reeve	7	– c and b Smith	0
*M. C. J. Nicholas not out	45	– c Khan b Smith	15
M. Keech c Piper b Donald	35	– c Khan b Munton	22
K. D. James st Piper b Giles	2	– c Piper b Smith	18
†A. N. Aymes lbw b Giles	0	– c Donald b Smith	13
S. D. Udal run out	0	– b Smith	0
H. H. Streak c Munton b Donald	20	– b Giles	11
C. A. Connor c Donald b Smith	0	– not out	0
B 12, l-b 6, w 2, n-b 4	24	B 9, l-b 11, n-b 10	30
	225		**221**

1/48 2/81 3/114 4/118 5/163 6/174 7/174 8/174 9/224

1/111 2/120 3/123 4/147 5/147 6/190 7/196 8/196 9/221

Bonus points – Hampshire 1, Warwickshire 4.

Bowling: *First Innings*—Donald 21-8-48-3; Munton 27-8-61-2; Brown 4-0-16-0; Reeve 18-9-23-1; Twose 4-2-12-0; Giles 11-2-32-2; Smith 3-0-15-1. *Second Innings*—Donald 19-7-50-2; Munton 16-5-43-1; Reeve 6-4-6-0; Smith 33.2-10-72-6; Giles 15-5-30-1.

Warwickshire

R. G. Twose c Middleton b Connor	12	A. F. Giles c Terry b Keech	32
W. G. Khan b Connor	181	A. A. Donald not out	4
D. P. Ostler lbw b Connor	0		
†K. J. Piper b Udal	99	B 1, l-b 8, w 4, n-b 10	23
T. L. Penney lbw b Connor	85		
D. R. Brown c Aymes b Connor	1	1/31 2/31 3/179	(8 wkts dec.) 535
*D. A. Reeve not out	77	4/387 5/389 6/406	
N. M. K. Smith c sub b Streak	21	7/435 8/525	

T. A. Munton did not bat.

Bonus points – Warwickshire 4, Hampshire 2 (Score at 120 overs: 403-5).

Bowling: Streak 35-12-98-1; Connor 40-10-121-5; Udal 26-4-83-1; James 16-1-72-0; Stephenson 23-4-99-0; Keech 10.3-0-43-1; Nicholas 2-0-10-0.

Umpires: J. H. Hampshire and D. R. Shepherd.

At Southampton, August 16, 17, 18. HAMPSHIRE drew with WEST INDIANS (See West Indian tour section).

HAMPSHIRE v LANCASHIRE

At Portsmouth, August 24, 25, 26, 28. Lancashire won by five wickets. Lancashire 22 pts, Hampshire 4 pts. Toss: Hampshire. First-class debut: A. Flintoff.

Wasim Akram kept up his unbeaten record as Lancashire's stand-in captain with a third win, and led from the front. His masterly demonstration of the fast bowler's art wrecked Hampshire in the first two sessions. Moving the ball both ways at speed, Wasim was almost unplayable, collecting seven for 52 as Hampshire folded in less than 48 overs. Lancashire did not find batting too easy, either, but a solid 77 from Titchard held them together and they recovered from 196 for six to lead by 139. Hampshire needed a major innings to head off another three-day defeat and Stephenson produced it. He scored his first century for his new county, batting five hours, with obdurate support from Aymes. But even so, Lancashire needed only 214. Although they wobbled – when Streak hit Hegg on the finger, they were effectively 111 for five – Lloyd met the crisis with his best Championship innings of the summer. He finished unbeaten on 97 from 89 balls as Lancashire cruised home before lunch.

Close of play: First day, Lancashire 172-4 (S. P. Titchard 55*, W. K. Hegg 34*); Second day, Hampshire 159-4 (J. P. Stephenson 61*, G. W. White 13*); Third day, Lancashire 77-2 (N. J. Speak 39*, G. D. Lloyd 14*).

Hampshire

V. P. Terry b Wasim Akram	2	– c Martin b Chapple	15
J. S. Laney c Hegg b Chapple	21	– c Hegg b Austin	33
J. P. Stephenson lbw b Wasim Akram	6	– c Chapple b Austin	127
P. R. Whitaker c Fairbrother b Wasim Akram . .	41	– b Flintoff b Chapple	4
*M. C. J. Nicholas c Hegg b Austin	11	– c Flintoff b Wasim Akram	24
G. W. White b Wasim Akram	9	– c Hegg b Martin	16
K. D. James c Hegg b Wasim Akram	0	– lbw b Chapple	3
†A. N. Aymes not out	16	– c Hegg b Martin	60
S. D. Udal c Austin b Wasim Akram	6	– not out	8
H. H. Streak b Wasim Akram	0	– lbw b Wasim Akram	14
C. A. Connor c Fairbrother b Chapple	19	– b Wasim Akram	20
L-b 3, w 3, n-b 10	23	B 1, l-b 10, w 1, n-b 16	28

1/2 2/8 3/50 4/77 5/99   154
6/99 7/122 8/132 9/132

1/39 2/73 3/82 4/122 5/175   352
6/180 7/304 8/304 9/329

Bonus points – Lancashire 4.

In the second innings S. D. Udal, when 2, retired hurt at 309 and resumed at 329.

Bowling: *First Innings*—Wasim Akram 16-4-52-7; Martin 5-2-10-0; Chapple 6.2-0-22-2; Austin 16-7-45-1; Flintoff 4-0-15-0. *Second Innings*—Wasim Akram 27.1-4-104-3; Martin 28-12-43-2; Austin 29-8-51-2; Chapple 22-4-73-3; Keedy 14-3-46-0; Flintoff 7-0-24-0.

Lancashire

S. P. Titchard c Laney b Udal	77	– c Aymes b Streak	4
N. J. Speak b Connor	7	– b Stephenson	43
N. H. Fairbrother c Terry b Stephenson	41	– c Aymes b James	16
G. D. Lloyd c Aymes b Streak	17	– not out	97
A. Flintoff c Terry b Streak	7	– b Streak	0
†W. K. Hegg lbw b James	42	– retired hurt	2
*Wasim Akram c Nicholas b James	4	– (8) not out	3
I. D. Austin lbw b Udal	45	– (7) c White b James	37
P. J. Martin c Terry b Udal	5		
G. Chapple c Terry b Streak	24		
G. Keedy not out	3		
L-b 9, n-b 12	21	B 1, l-b 9, w 2	12

1/10 2/65 3/94 4/106 5/190   293
6/196 7/250 8/264 9/264

1/10 2/42 3/99   (5 wkts) 214
4/100 5/198

Bonus points – Lancashire 2, Hampshire 4.

In the second innings W. K. Hegg retired hurt at 111.

Bowling: *First Innings*—Streak 25.2–4–77–3; Connor 25–10–58–1; Stephenson 19–5–48–1; James 17–4–55–2; Udal 22–9–46–3. *Second Innings*—Streak 13–5–36–2; Connor 11–3–32–0; Stephenson 14–5–57–1; James 6.1–1–28–2; Udal 7–0–51–0.

Umpires: M. J. Kitchen and K. J. Lyons.

At Nottingham, August 29, 30, 31. HAMPSHIRE beat NOTTINGHAMSHIRE by an innings and seven runs.

HAMPSHIRE v SOMERSET

At Southampton, September 7, 8, 9, 11. Drawn. Hampshire 4 pts, Somerset 3 pts. Toss: Somerset.

Rain claimed the first two days to wreck Nicholas's farewell performance at Northlands Road. He had handed over the captaincy to Stephenson at Nottingham and confirmed that he was retiring just before this game. When play began, it merely provided Hampshire with the stage to demonstrate their inconsistency again. They reduced Somerset to 195 for seven but failed to finish them off and allowed the last pair, Turner and Trump, to put on 94. Stephenson sent Nicholas in as opener, to take his final bow to a decent Saturday afternoon audience. On the last morning, Hampshire declared and, after Somerset forfeited, they set out to chase 298 in a minimum of 70 overs. With Mushtaq Ahmed finding considerable turn on a damp surface, an away win seemed more likely. But Laney scored a handsome 73 before becoming Mushtaq's fourth victim and then White and James frustrated the bowlers for 24 overs.

Close of play: First day, No play; Second day, No play; Third day, Hampshire 19-0 (J. S. Laney 8*, M. C. J. Nicholas 10*).

Somerset

M. E. Trescothick lbw b Streak	0	J. I. D. Kerr c Aymes b Streak	14
P. D. Bowler c White b Connor	5	Mushtaq Ahmed c Terry b Stephenson	16
P. C. L. Holloway c Aymes b Connor	65	H. R. J. Trump c and b Connor	47
R. J. Harden b Connor	4		
*A. N. Hayhurst c Udal b Connor	38	B 4, l-b 9, n-b 14	27
K. A. Parsons lbw b Stephenson	42		
G. D. Rose lbw b Stephenson	9	1/0 2/20 3/28 4/112 5/141	333
†R. J. Turner not out	66	6/156 7/195 8/220 9/239	

Bonus points – Somerset 3, Hampshire 4.

Bowling: Streak 22.4–4–76–2; Connor 23.3–4–79–5; Udal 7–1–30–0; James 15–1–61–0; Stephenson 24–6–74–3.

Somerset forfeited their second innings.

Hampshire

J. S. Laney not out	8	– c Trump b Mushtaq Ahmed	73
M. C. J. Nicholas not out	27	– (5) lbw b Mushtaq Ahmed	0
V. P. Terry (did not bat)		– (2) run out	1
*J. P. Stephenson (did not bat)		– (3) b Mushtaq Ahmed	29
P. R. Whitaker (did not bat)		– (4) c Trump b Mushtaq Ahmed	6
G. W. White (did not bat)		– not out	40
K. D. James (did not bat)		– not out	16
L-b 1	1	B 1, l-b 14, n-b 10	25

(no wkt dec.) 36   1/3 2/60 3/76   (5 wkts) 190
4/76 5/145

†A. N. Aymes, S. D. Udal, H. H. Streak and C. A. Connor did not bat.

Bowling: *First Innings*—Rose 4–3–3–0; Kerr 5–0–10–0; Parsons 1–0–5–0; Harden 1–0–17–0. *Second Innings*—Kerr 8–0–51–0; Rose 12–2–43–0; Mushtaq Ahmed 31–14–57–4; Trump 12–7–13–0; Hayhurst 6–2–11–0.

Umpires: V. A. Holder and A. A. Jones.

At The Oval, September 14, 15, 16, 18. HAMPSHIRE drew with SURREY.

KENT

Patron: HRH The Duke of Kent
President: N. Heroys
Chairman: D. S. Kemp
Chairman, Cricket Committee: D. G. Ufton
Secretary: S. T. W. Anderson
Captain: M. R. Benson
Cricket Administrator: Ms D. F. Potter
Coach: D. H. Foster
Head Groundsman: B. A. Fitch
Scorer: J. C. Foley

Kent's recent history has been full of near-misses. They have finished as beaten finalists or runners-up nine times in the 17 seasons since their days of regular trophy-collecting came to an end in 1978. When they lost their fifth successive Lord's final, to Lancashire in the Benson and Hedges in July, the sequence looked set to continue indefinitely. September 17, 1995 was the day they finally came good, becoming Sunday League champions and bringing home a piece of silverware at last. It may be a turning point.

The last match, against Warwickshire, was lost, and Kent won the title because Worcestershire's match was rained off. And the Sunday League went together with bottom place in the Championship, a bizarre double previously completed by Yorkshire in 1983. Kent, who last came bottom in 1895, failed to win a single Championship match after June 5.

As a result, some Kent members were not inclined to join in the general celebrations and one wrote to all the papers in the county trying to drum up support for an extraordinary meeting. The necessary numbers appeared not to be forthcoming and the committee rejected the idea of calling such a meeting itself. However, the club chairman, David Kemp, insisted in the autumn newsletter: "There is absolutely no complacency about our performances in the Championship. How could there be?"

Everyone did agree that Aravinda de Silva was a huge success as the county's one-season overseas replacement for Carl Hooper. Full credit was due to Mark Benson, whose decision to bring de Silva to Canterbury was entirely justified after a few eyebrows were raised. He made a slow start – with the dramatic change of climate and temperature he had experienced in coming to England, he was often to be seen with hands dug firmly into his trousers. Once the weather warmed up, though, de Silva blossomed. Double-centuries off Nottinghamshire and Derbyshire, record-breaking partnerships with Mark Ealham and Graham Cowdrey, and winning the race to 1,000 runs in the Championship made him a very popular performer. Then came Lord's and the biggest stage. Kent went into the Benson and Hedges final as underdogs, but anyone liking exhilarating strokeplay would have been privileged to witness arguably the best innings of the whole summer.

That innings and impressive Championship statistics made certain de Silva was Kent's Player of the Year. Sadly, he was unable to collect the award in person, as he had already left for Pakistan where he helped Sri Lanka to a historic Test series win. He scored 1,781 first-class runs at

59.36 – all but 120 of them being made in the Championship – and seven centuries. No other Kent batsman passed 1,000. Trevor Ward and Cowdrey were close, with 932 and 930 respectively, but once again the batting lacked the consistency to mount a sustained four-day challenge. The third and last victory, over Durham, was a reward for Benson's boldness in getting a result out of a game badly affected by rain.

The winless sequence that followed reached 11 games, concluding with a final defeat by Warwickshire. Difficulties in building a big first-innings score were a major frailty, but Kent also struggled to bowl the opposition out twice. Martin McCague's threat was diluted by the frequent absence of his partner Alan Igglesden, who sent down just over 170 overs but still managed to finish top of Kent's first-class averages. Min Patel was the county's leading wicket-taker, with 61, but did not live up to the form that attracted the selectors in 1994. Instead, it was Dean Headley who was called up for England A in Pakistan – after Peter Martin was promoted to tour South Africa – and his batting showed real signs of developing in the right direction late in the season. Ealham went in as high as No. 3 for a while in June, and earned compliments for his development as an all-rounder. His record Sunday hundred off just 44 balls against Derbyshire was an impressive display of controlled hitting.

Matthew Walker and David Fulton were both given extended chances to stake a regular place in the side, and sometimes kept out the experienced Neil Taylor. These two, together with Nigel Llong, must contribute more in 1996 when and wherever their opportunities come. Fulton's season was delayed by a broken leg, sustained playing soccer, but his big chance came when Benson was injured just before the most important week of Kent's season: the NatWest Trophy tie against Warwickshire at Edgbaston, followed by the Benson and Hedges Cup showpiece. Fulton stood in as opener in both and surprised many observers by facing Wasim Akram and company at Lord's wearing a sunhat rather than a helmet. His explanation was a noble one: "I wanted to be seen on the biggest day of my career, and didn't want to be anonymous."

Benson had broken his finger while fielding in a Sunday League game at Maidstone. He admitted he cried when the specialist told him he must miss Lord's but 1,358 runs at 38.80 in all competitions proved his worth to the team – an amazing run of century opening partnerships with Ward had been the key to the Benson and Hedges campaign – and he was re-appointed captain in mid-October. The 1995 season saw the retirement of popular all-rounder Chris Penn, unable to shake off a persistent shoulder injury. The county had already recognised his long service with a testimonial for 1996. Steve Herzberg was released after one year on the staff, but Kent retained the registration of another Anglo-Australian, Duncan Spencer, who spent the summer rehabilitating in Australia after back trouble.

After earlier doubts, the continuation of the Maidstone festival was assured and Tunbridge Wells was granted a second week in 1996, with the penultimate home game, against Nottinghamshire, earmarked for the picturesque surroundings of the Nevill Ground. – *Andrew Gidley.*

KENT 1995

[*Bill Smith*]

Back row: N. W. Preston, S. Herzberg, J. B. D. Thompson, B. J. Phillips, E. J. Stanford, S. C. Willis. *Middle row*: M. A. Ealham, N. J. Llong, D. P. Fulton, D. W. Headley, M. J. McCague, T. N. Wren, M. J. Walker. *Front row*: T. R. Ward, C. Penn, N. R. Taylor, M. R. Benson (*captain*), S. A. Marsh, G. R. Cowdrey, A. P. Igglesden, M. V. Fleming.

KENT RESULTS

All first-class matches – Played 19: Won 4, Lost 11, Drawn 4.

County Championship matches – Played 17: Won 3, Lost 10, Drawn 4.

Bonus points – Batting 40, Bowling 44.

*Competition placings – Britannic Assurance County Championship, 18th;
NatWest Bank Trophy, 2nd round; Benson and Hedges Cup, finalists;
AXA Equity & Law League, winners.*

BRITANNIC ASSURANCE CHAMPIONSHIP AVERAGES

BATTING

	Birthplace	M	I	NO	R	HS	Avge
‡P. A. de Silva§	Colombo, Sri Lanka	15	28	0	1,661	255	59.32
‡G. R. Cowdrey	Farnborough, Kent	11	18	1	778	137	45.76
‡N. R. Taylor......	Orpington	7	12	2	421	127	42.10
‡N. J. Llong	Ashford, Kent	8	14	0	516	118	36.85
‡M. R. Benson	Shoreham	13	21	0	702	192	33.42
‡T. R. Ward	Farningham	17	30	1	929	114*	32.03
‡M. A. Ealham......	Willesborough	17	29	1	860	121	30.71
‡S. A. Marsh	London	15	26	3	673	67*	29.26
‡M. V. Fleming	Macclesfield	8	13	1	335	61	27.91
D. P. Fulton	Lewisham	6	12	0	284	59	23.66
‡M. J. McCague.....	Larne	13	23	5	327	59	18.16
‡M. M. Patel.......	Bombay, India	15	24	5	294	56	15.47
‡D. W. Headley	Stourbridge	14	24	6	253	54	14.05
M. J. Walker	Gravesend	8	12	0	160	53	13.33
‡A. P. Igglesden	Farnborough, Kent	6	9	4	62	18	12.40
T. N. Wren	Folkestone	5	9	4	56	23	11.20
S. Herzberg........	Carshalton	5	9	2	61	18	8.71

Also batted: E. J. Stanford (*Dartford*) (1 match) 0*, 4; J. B. D. Thompson (*Cape Town, SA*) (1 match) 17, 4; S. C. Willis (*Greenwich*) (2 matches) 17, 1, 53.

* Signifies not out.   ‡ Denotes county cap.   § Overseas player.

The following played a total of 16 three-figure innings for Kent in County Championship matches – P. A. de Silva 6, M. R. Benson 2, G. R. Cowdrey 2, N. J. Llong 2, T. R. Ward 2, M. A. Ealham 1, N. R. Taylor 1.

BOWLING

	O	M	R	W	BB	5W/i	Avge
D. W. Headley	430.5	101	1,276	44	7-58	3	29.00
M. J. McCague	401.4	71	1,364	47	5-47	2	29.02
A. P. Igglesden	142.2	26	501	17	5-92	1	29.47
T. N. Wren	172.4	23	675	18	5-148	1	37.50
M. M. Patel..........	669.3	149	2,095	51	6-206	2	41.07
M. A. Ealham	367.2	91	1,114	27	3-45	0	41.25

Also bowled: G. R. Cowdrey 3-0-46-0; P. A. de Silva 213-36-634-5; M. V. Fleming 112-19-395-5; S. Herzberg 115.4-21-401-9; N. J. Llong 62.4-11-232-3; S. A. Marsh 2-1-8-0; E. J. Stanford 51-12-145-2; J. B. D. Thompson 12-1-52-0; T. R. Ward 3.5-0-43-0.

Wicket-keepers: S. A. Marsh 27 ct, 2 st; S. C. Willis 6 ct.

Leading Fielder: T. R. Ward 23.

KENT v NORTHAMPTONSHIRE

At Canterbury, April 27, 28, 29, 30. Northamptonshire won by nine wickets. Northamptonshire 24 pts, Kent 6 pts. Toss: Northamptonshire. Championship debuts: P. A. de Silva; A. Kumble.

Kent's downfall was completed just after noon on the final day. This was the 22nd consecutive year they failed to win their opening Championship match of the season. It was Northamptonshire's first win at Canterbury; they had played only five Championship matches there before. Their batting looked shaky until mid-way through the first afternoon. Then Montgomerie and Capel began a sixth-wicket partnership of 337, the eighth-highest ever, which continued until just after lunch the following day. Montgomerie batted 582 minutes, the sixth-longest innings in Championship history and 52 minutes longer than any previous score below 200. Both registered career-bests and Capel recorded his first hundred since July 1992, putting behind him two miserable, injury-dogged seasons. Another man with an unhappy medical history, McCague, retired on the second morning with a side strain, leaving his colleagues to concede 561 before Lamb declared. Kent failed to save the follow-on by 60 runs and, despite Ward, who carried his bat for a hundred, only just avoided an innings defeat. Northamptonshire faced a target of just seven; they lost Fordham before completing an emphatic victory.

Close of play: First day, Northamptonshire 343-5 (R. R. Montgomerie 113*, D. J. Capel 85*); Second day, Kent 257-5 (M. V. Fleming 41*); Third day, Kent 192-7 (T. R. Ward 100*, M. M. Patel 0*).

Northamptonshire

R. R. Montgomerie c Marsh b Patel	192	– not out	5
A. Fordham b Ealham	36	– c Marsh b Patel	1
R. J. Bailey c Marsh b McCague	3	– not out	1
M. B. Loye b Patel b McCague	3		
*A. J. Lamb b Ealham	54		
K. M. Curran c Walker b Ealham	11		
D. J. Capel c Ward b Patel	167		
A. Kumble not out	35		
J. G. Hughes c Ward b Headley	7		
B 11, l-b 10, w 18, n-b 14	53		

1/62 2/80 3/86 4/156 5/172   (8 wkts dec.) 561   1/4   (1 wkt) 7
6/509 7/542 8/561

†D. Ripley and J. P. Taylor did not bat.

Bonus points – Northamptonshire 4, Kent 2 (Score at 120 overs: 382-5).

Bowling: *First Innings*—McCague 22-2-105-2; Headley 37.5-9-112-1; Fleming 23-5-87-0; Ealham 33-10-114-3; Patel 43-6-122-2. *Second Innings*—de Silva 3-0-4-0; Patel 2.3-1-3-1.

Kent

T. R. Ward lbw b Kumble	76	– not out	114
*M. R. Benson b Capel	42	– c Lamb b Taylor	13
M. J. Walker b Curran	34	– c and b Kumble	13
P. A. de Silva c and b Curran	2	– lbw b Capel	13
N. R. Taylor c Bailey b Kumble	30	– c Ripley b Capel	6
M. V. Fleming c Montgomerie b Hughes	61	– c Fordham b Taylor	5
M. A. Ealham lbw b Capel	28	– lbw b Kumble	3
†S. A. Marsh c Bailey b Capel	37	– lbw b Hughes	23
M. M. Patel c Lamb b Capel	3	– c Lamb b Taylor	2
D. W. Headley c Curran b Capel	1	– lbw b Taylor	0
M. J. McCague not out	0	– c Lamb b Taylor	7
B 8, l-b 16, n-b 14	38	B 4, l-b 11, w 1	16

1/90 2/174 3/176 4/176 5/257   352   1/38 2/68 3/117 4/125 5/137   215
6/293 7/331 8/338 9/349   6/140 7/191 8/197 9/201

Bonus points – Kent 4, Northamptonshire 4.

Bowling: *First Innings*—Taylor 20–2–82–1; Hughes 17–1–72–1; Capel 12.2–1–50–4; Kumble 33–11–74–2; Curran 9–2–50–2. *Second Innings*—Taylor 21.2–7–49–5; Hughes 9–1–31–1; Curran 11–3–30–0; Kumble 27–4–60–2; Capel 5–0–30–2.

Umpires: V. A. Holder and B. Leadbeater.

At Hove, May 4, 5, 6, 8. KENT lost to SUSSEX by 75 runs.

KENT v LEICESTERSHIRE

At Canterbury, May 11, 12, 13. Kent won by an innings and 121 runs. Kent 24 pts, Leicestershire 5 pts. Toss: Kent. Championship debut: S. Herzberg.

Kent's first Championship win of the season was built around their highest ever total at Canterbury. They dominated almost from the start, when Ward's departure in the first over heralded a 192-run stand from Benson and Taylor. Taylor's excellent hundred was scored in uncharacteristically quick time; he took 119 balls and hit 19 fours, becoming the first Kent player to reach 100 before lunch at Canterbury since 1964, when Peter Richardson did it on the first day and Colin Cowdrey on the third against Hampshire. After he went, Benson added another 134 with de Silva, but his dismissal for 192 signalled a mini-collapse, before Nos 9 and 10, Patel and McCague, regained the momentum with a stand of 95. Leicestershire needed 426 to avoid the follow-on and Cronje's maiden Championship hundred held them together until the close. He departed early on the third morning, however, and Robinson soon ran out of partners. McCague immediately struck again, removing Briers, and then Cronje for the second time in the session. Kent's two spinners, the newcomer Steve Herzberg, Surrey-born and Australian-bred, and Patel took the last eight wickets with more than a day to spare.

Close of play: First day, Kent 397-4 (M. R. Benson 159*, M. A. Ealham 32*); Second day, Leicestershire 227-4 (W. J. Cronje 120*, P. E. Robinson 25*).

Kent

T. R. Ward lbw b Millns	0	M. M. Patel st Whitticase b Pierson	56
*M. R. Benson run out	192	M. J. McCague c Wells b Pierson	35
N. R. Taylor c Whitticase b Mullally	127	D. W. Headley not out	1
P. A. de Silva c Boon b Pierson	57		
M. J. Walker lbw b Millns	5	L-b 11, w 4, n-b 8	23
M. A. Ealham c Pierson b Mullally	38		
†S. A. Marsh c Pierson b Parsons	41	1/0 2/192 3/326 4/331 5/411	575
S. Herzberg c Whitticase b Pierson	0	6/479 7/479 8/479 9/574	

Bonus points – Kent 4, Leicestershire 2 (Score at 120 overs: 428-5).

Bowling: Millns 25–3–123–2; Mullally 36–7–113–2; Parsons 28–6–96–1; Pierson 47.5–11–141–4; Cronje 9–2–47–0; Wells 15–4–44–0.

Leicestershire

T. J. Boon c Benson b McCague	16	c McCague b Herzberg	14
*N. E. Briers b McCague	7	c Headley b McCague	0
W. J. Cronje c Ward b McCague	124	b McCague	8
J. J. Whitaker c and b Headley	34	c Walker b Patel	34
V. J. Wells c Walker b Patel	12	b Herzberg	40
P. E. Robinson not out	60	c McCague b Herzberg	12
G. J. Parsons c Marsh b McCague	3	st Marsh b Patel	1
†P. Whitticase lbw b Headley	5	c sub b Herzberg	10
A. R. K. Pierson run out	12	lbw b Herzberg	8
D. J. Millns b Headley	13	b Patel	3
A. D. Mullally run out	0	not out	13
B 3, l-b 10, n-b 4	17	L-b 6, n-b 2	8

1/21 2/24 3/102 4/157 5/235	303	1/0 2/8 3/57 4/61 5/77	151
6/243 7/248 8/265 9/303		6/90 7/118 8/123 9/133	

Bonus points – Leicestershire 3, Kent 4.

Bowling: *First Innings*—McCague 20–3–80–4; Headley 20–5–65–2; Ealham 6–1–21–0; Patel 22.5–3–79–1; Herzberg 13–2–45–1. *Second Innings*—Headley 9–2–28–0; McCague 7–0–22–2; Ealham 5–3–3–0; Patel 19–3–59–3; Herzberg 15.4–4–33–5.

Umpires: K. J. Lyons and A. G. T. Whitehead.

At Southampton, May 18, 19, 20. KENT beat HAMPSHIRE by 39 runs.

KENT v GLAMORGAN

At Tunbridge Wells, May 24, 25, 26, 27. Drawn. Kent 7 pts, Glamorgan 8 pts. Toss: Kent.
    The annual match at the Nevill Ground produced a thrilling finish. Glamorgan needed five from Patel's final over, having taken 14 off his previous one. But Cottey was caught on the boundary with two required from two balls, and the non-striker, Metson, was run out trying for a last-ball bye. The rain-shortened first day saw 98 from Ward and next day de Silva advanced to his second hundred of the season, striking 23 fours in 228 balls, before Kent lost their last six for 55. Morris and Dale gave Glamorgan a perfect start of 238. Dale reached his century first, from 139 balls, while Morris went on to the 40th of his career. Kent began the final day 150 ahead, and extended their lead until Benson declared after lunch. At first a challenge of 271 from a minimum 44 overs – which became 50 – looked too stiff. But Maynard, with 73 off 68 balls, and Cottey, making the most of being dropped on 33, kept Glamorgan's hopes alive to the end.
    Close of play: First day, Kent 164-3 (P. A. de Silva 32*, M. A. Ealham 0*); Second day, Glamorgan 155-0 (A. Dale 74*, H. Morris 72*); Third day, Kent 133-5 (M. A. Ealham 36*, S. A. Marsh 0*).

Kent

T. R. Ward run out	98	– b Kendrick	31
*M. R. Benson c Croft b Dale	14	– c Cottey b Croft	31
N. R. Taylor retired hurt	13		
P. A. de Silva lbw b Anthony	135	– c Anthony b Kendrick	5
M. J. Walker c Metson b Anthony	6	– c Hemp b Kendrick	24
M. A. Ealham lbw b Watkin	58	– (3) c Metson b Thomas	72
†S. A. Marsh c Maynard b Watkin	13	– c Hemp b Croft	24
M. M. Patel not out	21	– (6) c Maynard b Anthony	0
M. J. McCague c and b Anthony	1	– (8) c Watkin b Kendrick	23
D. W. Headley c sub b Anthony	2	– (9) not out	29
A. P. Igglesden c Cottey b Anthony	2	– (10) not out	5
L-b 1, w 1, n-b 4	6	B 3, l-b 4, n-b 2	9

1/50 2/148 3/163 4/314 5/342 6/350 7/351 8/361 9/369   **369**   1/57 2/85 3/99 4/130 5/133 6/194 7/194 8/231   (8 wkts dec.) **253**

Bonus points – Kent 4, Glamorgan 4.

In the first innings N. R. Taylor retired hurt at 88.

Bowling: *First Innings*—Watkin 30–5–98–2; Anthony 24.1–6–70–5; Thomas 13–0–61–0; Dale 10–4–31–1; Croft 25–8–63–0; Kendrick 13–2–37–0; Hemp 2–1–8–0. *Second Innings*—Watkin 15–2–40–0; Anthony 16–6–36–1; Thomas 12.4–0–53–1; Kendrick 37–17–70–4; Croft 23–7–47–2.

Glamorgan

A. Dale c Marsh b McCague	133	– c Ward b Patel	32
*H. Morris lbw b Patel	114	– c Marsh b Headley	3
D. L. Hemp c Headley b Igglesden	9	– lbw b Patel	20
M. P. Maynard b Igglesden	1	– b Patel	73
P. A. Cottey not out	37	– c Headley b Patel	85
R. D. B. Croft b de Silva	15	– (7) c and b Patel	7
S. D. Thomas b McCague	0	– (8) not out	7
N. M. Kendrick c Ward b Patel	2		
H. A. G. Anthony c sub b Patel	0	– (6) run out	23
†C. P. Metson not out	14	– (9) run out	0
B 5, l-b 17, w 1, n-b 4	27	B 4, l-b 11, n-b 4	19

1/238 2/275 3/275 4/276 5/304   (8 wkts dec.) 352   1/4 2/42 3/81 4/170   (8 wkts) 269
6/308 7/325 8/325   5/223 6/242 7/269 8/269

S. L. Watkin did not bat.

Bonus points – Glamorgan 4, Kent 3.

Bowling: *First Innings*—McCague 20–2–64–2; Igglesden 16–2–67–2; Headley 21.3–4–85–0; Ealham 5–1–15–0; Patel 37–9–94–3; de Silva 4–1–5–1. *Second Innings*—McCague 16–1–83–0; Headley 9–0–44–1; Patel 21–2–99–5; de Silva 1–0–6–0; Igglesden 3–0–22–0.

Umpires: D. J. Constant and A. A. Jones.

At Chester-le-Street, June 1, 2, 3, 5. KENT beat DURHAM by 115 runs.

KENT v GLOUCESTERSHIRE

At Canterbury, June 8, 9, 10, 12. Gloucestershire won by 104 runs. Gloucestershire 23 pts, Kent 4 pts. Toss: Gloucestershire.

Unfancied Gloucestershire's third Championship win carried them to fourth place, one behind Kent, who paid the price for a disappointing first innings. Russell's enthusiasm seemed to have rubbed off on his entire side, who produced a confident all-round display. The visitors took the upper hand on the rain-affected second day, as Kent struggled from 13 for one to 98 for seven and subsequently 137 all out in the morning. Left-armer Smith took six for 66. Gloucestershire waived the follow-on, allowing Lynch to score hundreds in both innings for the first time in a 19-year career. On the first day, he and Symonds batted them out of a poor start with a stand of 114 in 26 overs; on the third, he and Dawson compounded Kent's problems by adding 136 in 36. The declaration set Kent 451 to win but, once Benson was out for 102, having batted 324 minutes, there was little doubt that Gloucestershire would wrap up victory.

Close of play: First day, Kent 13-1 (M. R. Benson 0*, M. M. Patel 1*); Second day, Kent 98-7 (M. V. Fleming 3*, S. A. Marsh 5*); Third day, Kent 73-1 (M. R. Benson 24*, M. A. Ealham 27*).

Gloucestershire

A. J. Wright b Headley	4	– b Headley	5
G. D. Hodgson b McCague	4	– c Patel b McCague	4
M. A. Lynch c Marsh b Headley	108	– lbw b Patel	114
R. I. Dawson c Cowdrey b Headley	8	– lbw b Fleming	58
M. W. Alleyne c Marsh b McCague	4	– b Ealham	20
A. Symonds b McCague	52	– c Patel b Ealham	19
*†R. C. Russell b McCague	46	– c and b Patel	34
J. Srinath b Headley	44	– b Ealham	0
M. C. J. Ball c Benson b McCague	16	– not out	5
M. Davies not out	8		
A. M. Smith b Headley	11		
B 6, l-b 8, n-b 2	16	L-b 3, w 2, n-b 2	7

1/13 2/13 3/29 4/42 5/156   321   1/9 2/11 3/147   (8 wkts dec.) 266
6/198 7/276 8/297 9/302   4/205 5/205 6/228
                                                          7/228 8/266

Bonus points – Gloucestershire 3, Kent 4.

Bowling: *First Innings*—McCague 25-5-68-5; Headley 25.1-8-68-5; Ealham 10-3-30-0; Patel 27-3-100-0; Herzberg 8-0-31-0; Fleming 4-1-10-0. *Second Innings*—McCague 8-3-26-1; Headley 10-2-26-1; Ealham 12-2-45-3; Patel 26-7-71-2; Herzberg 7-1-56-0; Fleming 9-0-39-1.

Kent

T. R. Ward lbw b Srinath	6	– b Smith	17
*M. R. Benson c Russell b Smith	0	– b Ball	102
M. M. Patel c Russell b Alleyne	26	– (9) lbw b Alleyne	0
M. A. Ealham c Russell b Srinath	33	– (3) c Ball b Smith	27
P. A. de Silva lbw b Smith	3	– (4) c Ball b Smith	4
G. R. Cowdrey lbw b Smith	2	– (5) lbw b Srinath	71
M. J. McCague c Russell b Smith	4	– (10) c Russell b Srinath	18
M. V. Fleming not out	36	– (6) c Wright b Ball	14
†S. A. Marsh c and b Srinath	8	– (7) b Alleyne	40
S. Herzberg lbw b Smith	0	– (8) c Ball b Srinath	17
D. W. Headley c Russell b Smith	0	– not out	0
B 1, l-b 6, n-b 12	19	B 4, l-b 2, w 1, n-b 29	36

1/8 2/14 3/69 4/72 5/84   137   1/26 2/83 3/87 4/213 5/238   346
6/90 7/90 8/136 9/137   6/293 7/316 8/316 9/341

Bonus points – Gloucestershire 4.

Bowling: *First Innings*—Srinath 19-9-35-3; Smith 26-11-66-6; Alleyne 10-2-25-1; Ball 1-1-0-0; Davies 1-0-4-0. *Second Innings*—Srinath 28.1-4-109-3; Smith 25-5-72-3; Ball 33-9-72-2; Davies 14-1-51-0; Alleyne 7-0-36-2.

Umpires: B. Leadbeater and K. E. Palmer.

At Leeds, June 15, 16, 17, 19. KENT lost to YORKSHIRE by eight wickets.

At Nottingham, June 22, 23, 24, 26. KENT lost to NOTTINGHAMSHIRE by three wickets.

KENT v CAMBRIDGE UNIVERSITY

At Folkestone, July 1, 2, 3. Kent won by 168 runs. Toss: Cambridge University. First-class debut: E. J. Stanford.

Kent, the last first-class county to lose to the University, in 1992, continued their revenge by crushing them for the third year running, this time at Cheriton Road, which was hosting first-class cricket for the first time since 1991. Just as at Cambridge the previous season, Fulton scored a century and Patel took ten wickets. Fulton hit 16 fours from 172 balls and put on 173 with his acting-captain Fleming, who set a brisker tempo in a 99-ball hundred. Fleming's first scoring stroke was a six that cleared the 85-yard leg-side boundary and he added 16 fours. Battye rescued Cambridge from 40 for six and, after Kent put on more quick runs, Ragnauth made 82, his highest score, enabling the students to take the game into its final session. But they stood little chance against Patel on a wearing pitch.

Close of play: First day, Cambridge University 23-1 (D. R. H. Churton 15*, J. Ratledge 4*); Second day, Kent 108-3 (J. B. D. Thompson 13*, D. P. Fulton 8*).

Kent

D. P. Fulton c Ragnauth b Whittall	116	– (6) not out	8
M. J. Walker c and b Haste	2	– retired hurt	0
G. R. Cowdrey c Ragnauth b Janisch	41	– (1) c Carroll b Janisch	48
*M. V. Fleming c Cake b Whittall	100		
N. J. Llong c Ragnauth b Haste	3	– (3) c Battye b Whittall	19
M. M. Patel c Churton b Haste	4	– (4) c How b Janisch	6
†S. C. Willis st Churton b Ratledge	82		
J. B. D. Thompson not out	40	– (5) not out	13
B 6, l-b 7, w 2, n-b 6	21	B 3, w 7, n-b 4	14

1/5 2/79 3/252 4/274 5/274   (7 wkts dec.) 409   1/67 2/86 3/95   (3 wkts dec.) 108
6/279 7/409

A. P. Igglesden, E. J. Stanford and T. N. Wren did not bat.

In the second innings M. J. Walker retired hurt at 13.

Bowling: *First Innings*—Haste 18–2–74–3; How 15–3–75–0; Whittall 20–3–104–2; Janisch 11–2–43–1; Freeth 18–1–84–0; Ratledge 1.4–0–16–1. *Second Innings*—Haste 5–1–19–0; How 6–0–44–0; Whittall 8–3–17–1; Janisch 8–1–24–2; Freeth 1–0–1–0.

Cambridge University

R. T. Ragnauth c Fulton b Igglesden	0	– c Fulton b Patel	82
†D. R. H. Churton b Wren	20	– c Willis b Thompson	0
J. Ratledge c Willis b Igglesden	6	– b Thompson	1
R. Q. Cake c Willis b Igglesden	1	– c Fulton b Patel	49
J. P. Carroll c Fulton b Wren	4	– lbw b Igglesden	24
R. A. Battye b Stanford	63	– c Thompson b Patel	17
*A. R. Whittall c Fulton b Patel	1	– (8) lbw b Patel	7
N. J. Haste b Patel	11	– (7) b Patel	16
J. W. O. Freeth c Llong b Patel	18	– (10) c Walker b Wren	1
A. N. Janisch c Willis b Patel	6	– (9) c Walker b Patel	4
E. J. How not out	0	– not out	0
B 1, l-b 11	12	B 3, l-b 3	6

1/0 2/27 3/31 4/31 5/39   142   1/5 2/19 3/119 4/150 5/174   207
6/40 7/72 8/106 9/124   6/182 7/192 8/198 9/203

Bowling: *First Innings*—Igglesden 18–9–27–3; Wren 10–4–23–2; Patel 25–14–43–4; Llong 1–0–4–0; Stanford 10.5–2–33–1. *Second Innings*—Thompson 8–3–10–2; Patel 36.2–14–74–6; Igglesden 11–2–35–1; Llong 8–0–37–0; Stanford 16–5–42–0; Wren 4–3–3–1.

Umpires: A. Clarkson and A. A. Jones.

KENT v DERBYSHIRE

At Maidstone, July 5, 6, 7, 8. Drawn. Kent 6 pts, Derbyshire 5 pts. Toss: Kent.

A shirt-front pitch at The Mote produced 1,587 runs and some sensational batting by de Silva, but no definite result. Kent were faltering at 54 for three when Cowdrey joined de Silva. They shared an all-wicket county record of 368 in 80 overs, passing 366 for the second wicket by Neil Taylor and Simon Hinks against Middlesex at Canterbury in 1990. De Silva made his second double-hundred in successive games in 227 deliveries. He went on to 255, only five short of Percy Chapman's ground record in 1927, and faced 313 balls in 352 minutes, hitting a six and 36 fours. On the way, he won the race to 1,000 Championship runs and in the second innings he became the fourth Kent player (after Hardinge, Fagg and Taylor) to score a double-hundred and hundred in one match. In reply, Adams also made a double-century, his first; his 216 took 256 balls with 38 fours and three sixes. Derbyshire took a 12-run lead. But the game petered out after Benson's declaration left them needing 328 from 48 overs.

Close of play: First day, Kent 486-4 (P. A. de Silva 243*, M. A. Ealham 31*); Second day, Derbyshire 322-3 (C. J. Adams 130*, C. M. Wells 41*); Third day, Kent 215-4 (P. A. de Silva 88*, M. J. McCague 2*).

Kent

T. R. Ward lbw b Warner	21	– c Griffith b Warner	19
*M. R. Benson c Cullinan b Warner	19	– c Rollins b Warner	92
N. R. Taylor lbw b Griffith	5	– c Krikken b DeFreitas	8
P. A. de Silva c Krikken b Warner	255	– b DeFreitas	116
G. R. Cowdrey c Griffith b Cottam	137	– c Wells b Barnett	0
M. A. Ealham c Griffith b Warner	35	– (7) c Wells b Warner	1
†S. A. Marsh c Griffith b Warner	3	– (8) not out	57
M. M. Patel c Cullinan b Griffith	8	– (9) c Krikken b DeFreitas	13
M. J. McCague c Rollins b Griffith	7	– (6) lbw b Barnett	15
A. P. Igglesden b Griffith	10	– st Krikken b Barnett	6
T. N. Wren not out	0	– not out	3
B 15, l-b 3, w 6, n-b 10	34	L-b 3, w 2, n-b 4	9

1/45 2/51 3/54 4/422 5/502   534   1/33 2/48 3/200   (9 wkts dec.) 339
6/503 7/512 8/524 9/530   4/205 5/231 6/242
                                      7/271 8/297 9/310

Bonus points – Kent 4, Derbyshire 1 (Score at 120 overs: 478-4).

Bowling: *First Innings*—DeFreitas 20-0-88-0; Warner 38-10-75-5; Griffith 25.4-3-89-4; Wells 17-4-50-0; Cottam 21-1-103-1; Adams 9-0-39-0; Barnett 10-0-56-0; Dessaur 4-1-16-0. *Second Innings*—DeFreitas 26-1-95-3; Warner 28-7-65-3; Cottam 15-2-73-0; Griffith 11-1-28-0; Barnett 28-3-75-3.

Derbyshire

A. S. Rollins c Ealham b de Silva	82	– b Wren	29
W. A. Dessaur c Benson b Wren	29	– c Patel b McCague	0
C. J. Adams c Wren b McCague	216	– lbw b Wren	43
D. J. Cullinan c Cowdrey b Wren	35	– c Ward b Patel	20
C. M. Wells c Marsh b Igglesden	98	– not out	45
*K. J. Barnett c Marsh b Wren	23	– not out	16
†K. M. Krikken c Marsh b Ealham	11		
P. A. J. DeFreitas lbw b Wren	20		
F. A. Griffith not out	10		
A. E. Warner c McCague b Wren	5		
B 2, l-b 14, w 1	17	B 6, l-b 4, w 1, n-b 4	15

1/69 2/178 3/241 4/465 5/481   (9 wkts dec.) 546   1/5 2/66 3/97 4/115   (4 wkts) 168
6/501 7/523 8/537 9/546

A. C. Cottam did not bat.

Bonus points – Derbyshire 4, Kent 2 (Score at 120 overs: 482-5).

Bowling: *First Innings*—McCague 17-2-80-1; Igglesden 22-6-80-1; Wren 29.4-4-148-5; Patel 27-6-84-0; Ealham 21-5-70-1; de Silva 20-3-68-1. *Second Innings*—McCague 8-0-50-1; Igglesden 6-0-24-0; Ealham 3-0-4-0; Wren 7-0-24-2; de Silva 6-2-9-0; Patel 12-4-22-1; Ward 2-0-7-0; Marsh 2-1-8-0; Cowdrey 1-0-10-0.

Umpires: G. Sharp and P. Willey.

At Canterbury, July 19, 20, 21. KENT lost to WEST INDIANS by six wickets (See West Indian tour section).

At Worcester, July 27, 28, 29, 31. KENT lost to WORCESTERSHIRE by 61 runs.

KENT v SURREY

At Canterbury, August 3, 4, 5, 7. Drawn. Kent 5 pts, Surrey 8 pts. Toss: Surrey. Championship debut: G. J. Kennis.

Kent, chasing 402 in 78 overs, went very close. Llong's highest score and first hundred since May 1993 was the ideal platform; he and de Silva added 173, with de Silva striking 89 from 91 balls, and Cowdrey maintained the attacking tempo with an 87-ball 98. But all three fell to the occasional slowish left-arm bowling of Darren Bicknell, the best return of his career. Bicknell and Thorpe had led Surrey's first-innings run-spree, with 260 for the second wicket, breaking a 108-year-old county record against Kent, and Hollioake maintained the momentum. Patel collected six wickets, but at a cost – he was the first Kent bowler to concede 200 in an innings since 1897. He and Headley then saved the follow-on by one run, with a last-wicket stand of 74 in 11 overs. Kent had started disastrously, losing three for five, though Ward revived them with a hundred, and Surrey's second innings looked equally unstable at nought for two after two balls. But Brown hit an unbeaten century and Kent supporters were chafing at the delay when Hollioake finally declared. The match aggregate of 1,601 was the highest ever in Kent.

Close of play: First day, Surrey 345-2 (G. P. Thorpe 152*, A. D. Brown 3*); Second day, Kent 154-4 (T. R. Ward 79*, N. J. Llong 22*); Third day, Surrey 151-5 (A. D. Brown 70*).

Surrey

D. J. Bicknell c Fulton b Herzberg	146	– b Headley	0
M. A. Butcher c Herzberg b Patel	34	– c de Silva b Herzberg	52
G. P. Thorpe lbw b Ealham	152	– b Headley	0
A. D. Brown c Marsh b Patel	14	– not out	124
N. Shahid c and b Patel	9	– b Patel	14
*A. J. Hollioake c Patel b Ealham	90	– run out	2
†G. J. Kersey c Fulton b Patel	1	– b Patel	21
G. J. Kennis c Fulton b Patel	29	– c Ward b Patel	18
M. P. Bicknell c and b Patel	61	– not out	5
R. W. Nowell lbw b Herzberg	5		
J. M. de la Pena not out	0		
L-b 14, n-b 4	18	B 4, l-b 1, n-b 11	16

1/72 2/332 3/347 4/365 5/370   559   1/0 2/0 3/119   (7 wkts dec.) 252
6/374 7/472 8/518 9/557   4/144 5/151
                            6/207 7/243

Bonus points – Surrey 4, Kent 1 (Score at 120 overs: 351-3).

Bowling: *First Innings*—Headley 26–6–76–0; Ealham 32–9–71–2; Patel 59.5–10–206–6; Herzberg 30–6–92–2; de Silva 27–1–71–0; Llong 11–3–29–0. *Second Innings*—Headley 14–2–63–2; Ealham 5–0–28–0; Patel 31–8–93–3; Herzberg 8–0–32–1; de Silva 11–1–31–0.

Kent

D. P. Fulton c Kersey b M. P. Bicknell	0	– c Shahid b M. P. Bicknell	19
*M. R. Benson b de la Pena	2	– (8) st Kersey b Nowell	18
T. R. Ward b de la Pena	101	– (2) c Brown b Nowell	16
P. A. de Silva c Kersey b M. P. Bicknell	0	– b D. J. Bicknell	89
G. R. Cowdrey c and b Butcher	28	– st Kersey b D. J. Bicknell	98
N. J. Llong c Nowell b de la Pena	59	– (3) b D. J. Bicknell	118
M. A. Ealham st Kersey b Nowell	47	– (6) b Nowell	0
†S. A. Marsh st Kersey b Nowell	57	– (7) c Kersey b Nowell	6
S. Herzberg c Shahid b Nowell	5	– (10) not out	4
D. W. Headley not out	47	– (9) not out	1
M. M. Patel c Brown b Nowell	26		
B 5, l-b 5, w 4, n-b 24	38	B 3, l-b 4, n-b 4	11

1/4 2/4 3/5 4/69 5/190   410   1/29 2/49 3/222 4/293   (8 wkts) 380
6/256 7/289 8/328 9/336   5/298 6/308 7/366 8/376

Bonus points – Kent 4, Surrey 4.

Bowling: *First Innings*—M. P. Bicknell 26–4–98–2; de la Pena 19–2–112–3; Butcher 9–3–32–1; Nowell 28.1–6–105–4; Shahid 7–0–36–0; Kennis 3–3–0–0; D. J. Bicknell 6–4–2–0; Hollioake 3–0–15–0. *Second Innings*—M. P. Bicknell 15–2–74–1; de la Pena 4–1–20–0; Nowell 35–6–144–4; Shahid 8–1–47–0; D. J. Bicknell 16–0–88–3.

Umpires: M. J. Kitchen and K. E. Palmer.

At Taunton, August 10, 11, 12. KENT lost to SOMERSET by eight wickets.

At Lord's, August 17, 18, 19, 21. KENT lost to MIDDLESEX by 140 runs.

KENT v ESSEX

At Canterbury, August 24, 25, 26. Essex won by an innings and 12 runs. Essex 24 pts, Kent 1 pt. Toss: Essex.

Another poor first-innings batting display by Kent condemned them to an innings defeat with a day to spare. Ilott and Williams had reduced them to 35 for five – four caught behind by Rollins – before de Silva and Fleming shared a sixth-wicket stand of 93. But Essex enforced the follow-on after taking a first-innings advantage of 294. Gooch had scored his 120th first-class century and his fourth in four games, Hussain made 186 and there was a stylish fifty by Waugh. De Silva once again rose above Kent's batting frailties as he hit a run-a-ball 95, including 16 fours and a six, in less than two hours at the crease. But after he was trapped lbw by Gooch and Irani took five wickets in an innings for the first time, Essex completed victory just in time for tea on Saturday.

Close of play: First day, Essex 375-4 (N. Hussain 128*, R. C. Irani 14*); Second day, Kent 29-1 (T. R. Ward 16*, D. W. Headley 0*).

Essex

G. A. Gooch st Marsh b Patel	106	N. F. Williams c Llong b Patel		5
D. D. J. Robinson run out	40	P. M. Such c Marsh b Headley		6
N. Hussain lbw b McCague	186	J. H. Childs not out		5
M. E. Waugh c Marsh b McCague	58			
*P. J. Prichard c Marsh b Fleming	15	B 4, l-b 3, w 1, n-b 14		22
R. C. Irani c Cowdrey b Headley	17			
†R. J. Rollins c Marsh b Fleming	4	1/101 2/187 3/304 4/336 5/401		472
M. C. Ilott b Fleming	8	6/408 7/420 8/425 9/449		

Bonus points – Essex 4, Kent 1 (Score at 120 overs: 395-4).

Bowling: McCague 31.4–8–91–2; Headley 35–10–95–2; Ealham 14–2–43–0; Fleming 26–5–93–3; Patel 37–11–113–2; de Silva 5–0–30–0.

Kent

T. R. Ward c Rollins b Ilott	8	– (2) c Rollins b Childs	64
*M. R. Benson c Rollins b Williams	0	– (1) c Waugh b Irani	12
N. J. Llong c Rollins b Ilott	4	– (4) c Waugh b Irani	43
P. A. de Silva c Rollins b Ilott	45	– (5) lbw b Gooch	95
G. R. Cowdrey b Robinson b Williams	0	– (6) c Such b Irani	8
M. A. Ealham c Rollins b Ilott	4	– (7) c and b Irani	30
M. V. Fleming c Prichard b Williams	61	– (8) st Rollins b Gooch	3
†S. A. Marsh not out	36	– (9) lbw b Waugh	12
D. W. Headley c Gooch b Williams	6	– (3) b Ilott	12
M. J. McCague c Waugh b Ilott	6	– b Irani	0
M. M. Patel c Waugh b Ilott	2	– not out	0
B 4, l-b 1, w 1	6	B 1, l-b 2	3

1/8 2/10 3/21 4/30 5/35	178	1/28 2/56 3/114 4/190 5/210	282
6/128 7/128 8/151 9/158		6/252 7/258 8/282 9/282

Bonus points – Essex 4.

Bowling: *First Innings*—Ilott 21.3–5–58–6; Williams 13.1–4–38–4; Irani 11.5–1–53–0; Waugh 4–0–24–0. *Second Innings*—Ilott 21–3–81–1; Waugh 20.1–8–55–1; Irani 20–6–62–5; Childs 18–2–66–1; Gooch 6–1–15–2.

Umpires: H. D. Bird and J. D. Bond.

At Manchester, September 7, 8, 9, 11. KENT drew with LANCASHIRE.

KENT v WARWICKSHIRE

At Canterbury, September 14, 15, 16. Warwickshire won by an innings and 105 runs. Warwickshire 24 pts, Kent 3 pts. Toss: Warwickshire.

Donald polished off Kent's last three wickets just after 5 p.m. on the third afternoon and sank to his knees in triumph; Warwickshire's 14th victory ensured that they would retain the County Championship, with a day to spare. But defeat fulfilled the fears of Kent's most pessimistic supporters; they finished bottom of the Championship for the first time in 100 years. Reeve won the toss and his batsmen immediately grabbed the initiative against a poor Kent attack, spurred on by news that rain had held up Middlesex's tilt at the title down in Somerset. Knight batted superbly for a career-best 174, his maiden first-class hundred for Warwickshire at the very end of his debut season for them, while Twose marked his final match before departing for New Zealand with his first Championship hundred away from Edgbaston. They had 300 up before losing their third wicket, whereas Kent's top order slumped to 20 for four. It was left to Cowdrey to shore up the innings with a 148-ball hundred. He was then out straight away, nursing a badly bruised finger, but last man Igglesden fared worse, suffering a triple fracture of the thumb. Neither batted in the second innings, delayed by rain on Saturday. Donald and Giles swept through the remaining batting, taking seven of the eight wickets. Former Kent captain Mike Denness presented the Championship trophy to Reeve. Durham's victory over Nottinghamshire meant the Kent crowd had to watch knowing their team had finished last of all.

Close of play: First day, Warwickshire 309-3 (R. G. Twose 54*, T. L. Penney 5*); Second day, Kent 18-0 (M. R. Benson 8*, T. R. Ward 9*).

Warwickshire

N. V. Knight c Walker b Ealham	174	N. M. K. Smith c Cowdrey b Patel	54
W. G. Khan run out	51		
D. P. Ostler c Llong b McCague	8	B 11, l-b 9, w 1, n-b 4	25
R. G. Twose not out	109		
T. L. Penney b Igglesden	47	1/148 2/166 3/300 (6 wkts dec.)	468
*D. A. Reeve b Igglesden	0	4/372 5/372 6/468	

M. A. V. Bell, †K. J. Piper, A. F. Giles and A. A. Donald did not bat.

Bonus points – Warwickshire 4, Kent 2 (Score at 120 overs: 459-5).

Bowling: Igglesden 27-5-78-2; McCague 18-2-74-1; Ealham 20-4-63-1; Fleming 13-2-63-0; Patel 29-7-95-1; Llong 14-2-75-0.

Kent

*M. R. Benson c Piper b Reeve	2	– c Piper b Giles	15
T. R. Ward b Bell	8	– c Piper b Giles	13
N. J. Llong c Piper b Donald	2	– b Giles	1
M. J. Walker c Knight b Reeve	7	– c Piper b Donald	2
G. R. Cowdrey c Ostler b Reeve	103	– absent hurt	
M. A. Ealham c Donald b Giles	36	– (5) c and b Bell	33
M. V. Fleming c Ostler b Bell	37	– (6) c Piper b Donald	35
†S. A. Marsh c Knight b Reeve	15	– (7) c Piper b Donald	15
M. J. McCague b Donald	12	– (8) not out	0
M. M. Patel not out	0	– (9) c Smith b Donald	0
A. P. Igglesden c Ostler b Reeve	0	– absent hurt	
B 8, l-b 2, w 1, n-b 6	17	B 1, l-b 6, w 1, n-b 2	10
1/4 2/7 3/16 4/20 5/92	239	1/31 2/32 3/33 4/41 5/83	124
6/177 7/218 8/235 9/239		6/113 7/124 8/124	

Bonus points – Kent 1, Warwickshire 4.

Bowling: *First Innings*—Donald 17-3-48-2; Reeve 18-7-30-5; Bell 16-5-68-2; Giles 11-1-64-1; Smith 4-1-19-0. *Second Innings*—Donald 15-0-43-4; Reeve 4-2-3-0; Smith 2-1-3-0; Giles 20-10-41-3; Bell 8-2-27-1.

Umpires: A. A. Jones and D. R. Shepherd.

LANCASHIRE

Patron: HM The Queen
President: Sir Bernard Lovell
Chairman: R. Bennett
Chairman, Cricket Committee: G. Ogden
Chief Executive: J. M. Bower
Cricket Secretary: Miss R. B. FitzGibbon
Captain: M. Watkinson
Head Coach: D. Lloyd
Head Groundsman: P. Marron
Scorer: W. Davies

When Lancashire won the Benson and Hedges Cup on July 15, many observers felt sure there would be other trophies to follow. They were lying fourth in the Championship and in the Sunday League, and were due to meet Yorkshire in the quarter-final of the NatWest Trophy. Disappointingly, that was as far as they got, losing to Yorkshire in the NatWest and remaining fourth in both the other two competitions, after sitting on the shirt-tails of the leaders all summer. Their unquestioned ability was shown in their victories over the other four teams in the top five of the Championship, Warwickshire, Middlesex, Northamptonshire and Essex. Yet they continued to lose crucial games.

Lancashire started the season in fine fettle, winning the first three Championship matches, including victories by an innings and 175 runs against Middlesex and by six wickets over Warwickshire, who, it must be said, were without key players in Allan Donald, Dermot Reeve and Tim Munton. They also won nine of their first ten limited-overs games – the other was washed out after 18 overs – and broke several batting records in the Benson and Hedges Cup. One report of their quarter-final win over Nottinghamshire began: "The Lancashire juggernaut keeps thundering along, apparently unstoppable." It was heady stuff, but it was the Championship and perhaps the end of a 61-year wait since their last outright victory that was uppermost in everybody's minds at Old Trafford. But the stirring start of three wins had been followed by two draws and an innings defeat by Worcestershire, which pushed Lancashire down to the middle of the table.

Lancashire pulled themselves together with five wins in the next six matches, including an important 233-run win over the leaders, Northamptonshire. By August 14, with only five games remaining, they were 27 points behind the leaders with a game in hand. Now, it seemed, was the time for the push. But in the following match, against Yorkshire at Old Trafford, Lancashire put together what was probably their sloppiest first-innings performance of the summer, meekly surrendering a 267-run advantage before losing by nine wickets. Although they beat Hampshire and Surrey in the next two games, that defeat by Yorkshire had killed off their title hopes. Lancashire also tended to fail in critical games on Sundays, losing their 100 per cent record when they were unable to overtake Glamorgan's modest total of 162, and missing the opportunity to return to the top of the table when beaten by Northamptonshire, whose success was their first in eight Sunday matches. The third defeat at Old Trafford, against the leaders Kent in the penultimate match, proved decisive and enabled Kent to go on and become Sunday champions.

Before the season started David Lloyd, the head coach, said he had only one worry – that there could be too many Test calls in a summer when every England match coincided with Lancashire fixtures. In the event, six players represented England, with Mike Atherton missing seven rounds of county games because of international duties, Peter Martin four, Mike Watkinson and John Crawley three each, Jason Gallian two and Neil Fairbrother one. Yet, ironically, the loss of players did not prove a handicap in the Championship where Lancashire won five and drew two without their Test representatives. On Sundays, the score was four wins, three defeats.

Wasim Akram was in inspirational form throughout the season until he had to return home for Pakistan's Test series against Sri Lanka. In 14 games he took 81 wickets, far and away his best performance for Lancashire and the highest number of wickets for the county since Peter Lee took 112 in 1975. He was fourth in the national bowling averages at 19.72. His replacement in 1996, the South African Steve Elworthy, will have a very hard act to follow. Martin's sound start, on the heels of his encouraging form in 1994, earned him an England call-up for the one-day internationals and the first three Tests. Unfortunately, when the Edgbaston Test finished inside three days, he got home in time to play in a Sunday match, tore his ankle ligaments and was out for a month. Glen Chapple, on the other hand, had a lean season, all the more disappointing following the immense promise he showed in 1994, and on his subsequent tour of India with England A. In 14 Championship matches he claimed only 33 wickets, one step backward following two forward the previous year.

The only bowler other than Wasim to take more than 50 wickets was the captain, Watkinson, with 57 wickets for Lancashire as well as 731 runs. He delighted everybody at Old Trafford by making his debut for England, on his home ground, just before his 34th birthday. Lancashire showed their belief in new left-arm spinner Gary Keedy, from Yorkshire, by giving him a good run in the first team; although his 33 wickets in 12 Championship games were costly, at 38.63, there were signs of better things to come.

Only two batsmen, Crawley and Gallian, reached 1,000 runs in the Championship, although Atherton, his stature growing with every game as England captain, joined them in all first-class matches. Atherton, as in 1994, found runs difficult to come by when opening for Lancashire between England engagements. In three Championship matches leading up to the one-day internationals, he scored 268 runs from four completed innings. In the next 12 weeks, he played only three games for Lancashire for 50 runs in five innings and for the remainder of the season batted at No. 5, scoring 341 runs in six innings. The middle order was a problem, with Nick Speak, Graham Lloyd and Fairbrother, dogged by hamstring trouble in his benefit year, having moderate seasons and giving Steve Titchard the opportunity to earn his county cap. Warren Hegg was in ebullient but consistent wicket-keeping form, while the phlegmatic Ian Austin once more proved his worth as a tidy medium-paced bowler and aggressive batsman who never lets Lancashire down. – Brian Bearshaw.

LANCASHIRE 1995

Back row: N. T. Wood, R. J. Green, P. C. McKeown, D. J. Shadford, A. Flintoff, D. J. Thompson, C. Brown, P. J. Seal, L. J. Marland, N. P. Harvey. *Middle row:* R. Spriggs (*dressing-room attendant*), P. R. Sleep (*Second Eleven coach*), G. Chapple, G. Yates, S. P. Titchard, P. J. Martin, A. A. Barnett, G. Keedy, D. Lloyd (*coach*), W. Davies (*scorer*), L. Brown (*physiotherapist*). *Front row:* N. J. Speak, W. K. Hegg, I. D. Austin, N. H. Fairbrother, G. Ogden (*chairman of cricket*), M. Watkinson (*captain*), M. A. Atherton, J. E. R. Gallian, G. D. Lloyd, J. P. Crawley. *Inset:* Wasim Akram.

LANCASHIRE RESULTS

All first-class matches – Played 19: Won 10, Lost 5, Drawn 4.

County Championship matches – Played 17: Won 10, Lost 4, Drawn 3.

Bonus points – Batting 48, Bowling 61.

*Competition placings – Britannic Assurance County Championship, 4th;
NatWest Bank Trophy, q-f; Benson and Hedges Cup, winners;
AXA Equity & Law League, 4th.*

BRITANNIC ASSURANCE CHAMPIONSHIP AVERAGES

BATTING

	Birthplace	*M*	*I*	*NO*	*R*	*HS*	*Avge*
‡J. P. Crawley	*Maldon*	14	24	1	1,203	182	52.30
‡J. E. R. Gallian	*Sydney, Australia*	14	26	3	1,044	158	45.39
‡M. A. Atherton	*Manchester*	10	16	1	659	155*	43.93
‡S. P. Titchard	*Warrington*	12	22	2	689	130	34.45
‡M. Watkinson	*Westhoughton*	13	21	1	672	161	33.60
‡N. J. Speak	*Manchester*	15	27	2	795	83	31.80
‡N. H. Fairbrother ..	*Warrington*	13	22	2	578	132	28.90
‡W. K. Hegg	*Whitefield*	16	25	4	556	101	26.47
‡P. J. Martin	*Accrington*	8	9	1	210	71	26.25
‡G. D. Lloyd	*Accrington*	12	19	2	439	97*	25.82
‡I. D. Austin	*Haslingden*	11	19	4	348	80*	23.20
‡Wasim Akram§...	*Lahore, Pakistan*	14	22	3	423	61	22.26
‡G. Chapple	*Skipton*	14	20	6	275	58	19.64
G. Keedy	*Wakefield*	12	15	11	73	15*	18.25
‡G. Yates	*Ashton-under-Lyne*	5	6	0	98	41	16.33

Also batted: A. Flintoff (*Preston*) (1 match) 7, 0; R. J. Green (*Warrington*) (1 match) 1;
D. J. Shadford (*Oldham*) (2 matches) 1, 0*.

* *Signifies not out.*   ‡ *Denotes county cap.*   § *Overseas player.*

The following played a total of 13 three-figure innings for Lancashire in County
Championship matches – J. P. Crawley 3, M. A. Atherton 2, N. H. Fairbrother 2, J. E. R.
Gallian 2, M. Watkinson 2, W. K. Hegg 1, S. P. Titchard 1.

BOWLING

	O	*M*	*R*	*W*	*BB*	*5W/i*	*Avge*
Wasim Akram	518.1	108	1,598	81	7-52	7	19.72
P. J. Martin	211.5	65	547	27	4-51	0	20.25
I. D. Austin	314.4	93	781	33	4-50	0	23.66
M. Watkinson	466.4	119	1,439	51	7-140	2	28.21
J. E. R. Gallian	98.5	11	374	13	3-14	0	28.76
G. Chapple	361.1	75	1,188	33	4-44	0	36.00
G. Keedy	438.5	115	1,275	33	4-35	0	38.63

Also bowled: M. A. Atherton 1-0-1-0; N. H. Fairbrother 1.5-1-14-0; A. Flintoff
11-0-39-0; R. J. Green 20-2-87-3; D. J. Shadford 29.5-4-107-3; N. J. Speak 1-0-6-0;
G. Yates 68-15-269-6.

Wicket-keepers: W. K. Hegg 53 ct, 7 st; J. P. Crawley 5 ct.

Leading Fielder: N. H. Fairbrother 16.

At Cambridge, April 18, 19, 20. LANCASHIRE drew with CAMBRIDGE UNIVERSITY.

At Leeds, April 27, 28, 29, May 1. LANCASHIRE lost to YORKSHIRE by 219 runs (Non-Championship fixture).

LANCASHIRE v DURHAM

At Manchester, May 4, 5, 6, 8. Lancashire won by eight wickets. Lancashire 24 pts, Durham 5 pts. Toss: Durham.

The last day was the 50th anniversary of VE Day and, before the cricket, dressing-room attendant Ron Spriggs played the Lancashire team extracts from Churchill's speeches and Vera Lynn's songs. They responded by taking Durham's final wicket with the first ball before making light of a target of 312 in 99 overs. Atherton batted five hours for his fourth century in all cricket in 11 days – though his first in the Championship since June 1993. He shared a stand of 179 with Crawley, who was dropped on nought. Durham disappointed with a first-innings 249 on a good pitch but had regained ground when Lancashire were 105 for five. The next five added 265, however. Watkinson hit 16 fours and four sixes in his 108 before last-wicket pair Martin and Keedy put on 89. A three-day defeat loomed over Durham at 51 for three, until Morris, in commanding form, revived them. He batted almost all day, facing 257 balls to steer them to 432, their best-ever second-innings total. But Lancashire were to make it four wins out of four against Durham.

Close of play: First day, Lancashire 37-1 (M. A. Atherton 16*, G. Chapple 10*); Second day, Durham 47-1 (W. Larkins 19*, J. Boiling 1*); Third day, Durham 432-9 (J. Wood 40*).

Durham

*M. A. Roseberry c Hegg b Keedy	44 –	b Wasim Akram 13
W. Larkins b Martin	23 –	c Gallian b Watkinson 19
J. E. Morris c Atherton b Chapple	68 –	(4) c sub b Watkinson 169
J. A. Daley b Wasim Akram	27 –	(5) c Crawley b Watkinson .. 55
M. Prabhakar c Chapple b Martin	21 –	(6) c Speak b Watkinson...... 1
M. Saxelby c Crawley b Watkinson	19 –	(7) lbw b Keedy 31
†C. W. Scott c Hegg b Wasim Akram	22 –	(8) c Hegg b Gallian 56
J. Wood b Wasim Akram	4 –	(9) not out 40
J. Boiling not out	6 –	(3) b Wasim Akram.......... 1
S. J. E. Brown c Hegg b Wasim Akram	2 –	(11) b Chapple 0
M. M. Betts b Wasim Akram	0 –	(10) lbw b Chapple 5
L-b 7, n-b 6	13	B 7, l-b 18, w 1, n-b 16 .. 42

1/44 2/103 3/169 4/180 5/210   249   1/39 2/47 3/51 4/201 5/219   432
6/217 7/232 8/247 9/249   6/278 7/362 8/413 9/432

Bonus points – Durham 1, Lancashire 4.

Bowling: *First Innings*—Wasim Akram 20.3-8-40-5; Martin 18-6-47-2; Chapple 19-6-43-1; Watkinson 17-2-70-1; Keedy 15-3-41-1; Gallian 1-0-1-0. *Second Innings*—Wasim Akram 32-6-112-2; Chapple 24.4-8-68-2; Watkinson 36-6-115-4; Keedy 25-2-85-1; Gallian 7-1-27-1.

Lancashire

M. A. Atherton lbw b Brown	29	– not out	155
J. E. R. Gallian c Boiling b Brown	6	– c Scott b Wood	43
G. Chapple c Scott b Brown	58		
J. P. Crawley c Betts b Prabhakar	3	– (3) c Morris b Wood	81
N. H. Fairbrother c Boiling b Wood	13	– (4) not out	13
N. J. Speak c Daley b Betts	13		
*M. Watkinson c Saxelby b Boiling	108		
Wasim Akram c Scott b Wood	10		
†W. K. Hegg c Roseberry b Wood	11		
P. J. Martin c Boiling b Wood	71		
G. Keedy not out	15		
B 12, l-b 3, w 2, n-b 16	33	B 3, l-b 4, w 3, n-b 12	22

1/14 2/62 3/67 4/81 5/105   370   1/94 2/273   (2 wkts) 314
6/190 7/222 8/246 9/281

Bonus points – Lancashire 4, Durham 4.

Bowling: *First Innings*—Brown 25-6-72-3; Wood 18.4-4-54-4; Betts 20-1-103-1; Prabhakar 23-8-49-1; Boiling 18-4-61-1; Saxelby 3-0-16-0. *Second Innings*—Wood 21-3-88-2; Betts 12-1-75-0; Boiling 34-6-99-0; Prabhakar 14-4-38-0; Roseberry 1.4-0-7-0.

Umpires: B. J. Meyer and K. E. Palmer.

LANCASHIRE v WARWICKSHIRE

At Manchester, May 11, 12, 13, 15. Lancashire won by six wickets. Lancashire 23 pts, Warwickshire 5 pts. Toss: Warwickshire.

Lancashire's strong batting array again proved decisive in a wintry match, enabling them to take a first-innings lead of 148 despite the loss of Atherton and Crawley on the first evening. After injuring a calf early in his innings, Fairbrother had to make 103 of his 129 runs, scored in five and a half hours, with the aid of a succession of runners (Atherton, Crawley and Speak). He shared a lively partnership of 136 with Watkinson, who followed his century against Durham with 91. An opening stand of 168 from Moles and Khan, who made 78 in his second first-class match, rallied Warwickshire and they looked safe at 266 for three – 118 ahead – on the final morning. But the last seven fell for 31 in 15 overs from Martin and Chapple with the new ball. Needing 150, Lancashire were led by the secure hand of Crawley to their third win of the month over the champions, who were severely handicapped by the absence of Donald, Reeve and Munton, all injured.

Close of play: First day, Lancashire 16-2 (J. E. R. Gallian 3*, N. H. Fairbrother 2*); Second day, Lancashire 352-7 (W. K. Hegg 35*, P. J. Martin 8*); Third day, Warwickshire 194-3 (D. P. Ostler 10*, R. P. Davis 6*).

Warwickshire

*A. J. Moles c Atherton b Keedy	51	– lbw b Watkinson	66
W. G. Khan b Wasim Akram	38	– lbw b Keedy	78
R. G. Twose c Speak b Keedy	0	– c Speak b Keedy	4
D. P. Ostler lbw b Wasim Akram	11	– b Chapple	50
T. L. Penney b Watkinson	25	– (6) c Crawley b Martin	0
P. A. Smith b Martin	13	– (7) c Hegg b Martin	7
D. R. Brown lbw b Keedy	47	– (8) c Hegg b Martin	7
†M. Burns lbw b Martin	28	– (9) lbw b Chapple	6
N. M. K. Smith c Gallian b Martin	21	– (10) b Chapple	0
R. P. Davis c Hegg b Martin	0	– (5) b Martin	30
G. C. Small not out	6	– not out	6
L-b 6, n-b 16	22	B 15, l-b 11, w 1, n-b 16	43

1/96 2/96 3/102 4/111 5/147   262   1/168 2/168 3/178 4/266 5/266   297
6/165 7/230 8/236 9/239   6/278 7/278 8/287 9/287

Bonus points – Warwickshire 2, Lancashire 4.

Bowling: *First Innings*—Wasim Akram 16–3–47–2; Martin 17.5–3–68–4; Chapple 11–0–31–0; Watkinson 21–9–45–1; Keedy 28–11–65–3. *Second Innings*—Wasim Akram 20–7–65–0; Chapple 18–3–46–3; Watkinson 32–10–55–1; Martin 19.3–4–51–4; Keedy 24–7–53–2; Atherton 1–0–1–0.

Lancashire

M. A. Atherton lbw b Brown	4	– c Burns b Brown	26
J. E. R. Gallian lbw b Davis	44	– c Burns b P. A. Smith	18
J. P. Crawley c Davis b Small	5	– not out	56
N. H. Fairbrother b Brown	129		
N. J. Speak b Davis	15	– (4) c P. A. Smith b Davis	9
*M. Watkinson c Brown b Davis	91	– not out	29
Wasim Akram c Penney b Small	10		
†W. K. Hegg c Brown b Small	44		
P. J. Martin c and b Davis	40		
G. Chapple b Davis	0	– (5) c Ostler b Small	4
G. Keedy not out	15		
B 5, l-b 8	13	B 1, l-b 4, w 1, n-b 2	8

1/5 2/10 3/101 4/147 5/283   410   1/30 2/56 3/87 4/100   (4 wkts) 150
6/300 7/334 8/367 9/367

Bonus points – Lancashire 3, Warwickshire 3 (Score at 120 overs: 341-7).

Bowling: *First Innings*—Small 27–7–76–3; Brown 22–4–63–2; N. M. K. Smith 42–11–112–0; Davis 53.2–13–118–5; Twose 1–1–0–0; P. A. Smith 8–2–28–0. *Second Innings*—Small 11.4–2–32–1; Brown 11.2–0–47–1; P. A. Smith 3–0–12–1; Davis 15.1–2–40–1; N. M. K. Smith 2–0–14–0.

Umpires: J. W. Holder and R. A. White.

At Lord's, May 18, 19, 20. LANCASHIRE beat MIDDLESEX by an innings and 175 runs.

LANCASHIRE v NOTTINGHAMSHIRE

At Liverpool, May 25, 26, 27, 29. Drawn. Lancashire 7 pts, Nottinghamshire 6 pts. Toss: Lancashire. Championship debut: J. R. Wileman.

Victory proved to be beyond the reach of both teams in a game which lost over five hours to rain. Nottinghamshire, pursuing 256 in what became 61 overs, reached the last 20 at 111 for two, but gave up after losing three more wickets. Lancashire kept going and Keedy enlivened the end with two wickets in the last over, but they never quite had a realistic chance of winning. Cairns had bowled splendidly on the first day and Robinson then held his team's batting together with his 53rd century. Gallian and Titchard opened Lancashire's second innings with a century partnership, though a series of sacrifices in the quest for quick runs enabled Hindson to pick up five wickets. Titchard, like Austin, made the most of his first Championship appearance of the season, while Atherton, Fairbrother and Martin were playing in the one-day series with West Indies.

Close of play: First day, Lancashire 277-8 (W. K. Hegg 4*, G. Chapple 0*); Second day, Nottinghamshire 244-5 (R. T. Robinson 130*, K. P. Evans 11*); Third day, Lancashire 110-0 (S. P. Titchard 56*, J. E. R. Gallian 50*).

Lancashire

J. E. R. Gallian b Cairns	9	– (2) c sub b Afford	52
S. P. Titchard c Evans b Cairns	57	– (1) st Noon b Afford	81
J. P. Crawley lbw b Cairns	49	– run out	18
N. J. Speak lbw b Cairns	50	– c Wileman b Hindson	21
G. D. Lloyd lbw b Evans	15	– c Archer b Hindson	17
*M. Watkinson c and b Evans	21	– (7) b Hindson	7
Wasim Akram c Archer b Afford	47	– (6) c Cairns b Hindson	0
I. D. Austin lbw b Pick	2	– not out	25
†W. K. Hegg c Noon b Cairns	22	– c Evans b Hindson	0
G. Chapple c Noon b Pick	12	– not out	8
G. Keedy not out	0		
L-b 8, w 1, n-b 16	25	L-b 3, n-b 6	9

1/37 2/127 3/128 4/152 5/190   309   1/116 2/140 3/178   (8 wkts dec.) 238
6/269 7/273 8/273 9/309   4/183 5/184 6/202
                                    7/205 8/205

Bonus points – Lancashire 3, Nottinghamshire 4.

Bowling: *First Innings*—Cairns 24.4–2–64–5; Pick 21–9–50–2; Evans 24–5–55–2; Afford 34–9–83–1; Hindson 9–0–49–0. *Second Innings*—Cairns 12–2–30–0; Pick 8–2–20–0; Evans 6–0–15–0; Afford 25–3–99–2; Hindson 16–5–71–5.

Nottinghamshire

M. P. Dowman b Wasim Akram	0	– lbw b Chapple	2
*R. T. Robinson lbw b Austin	136	– st Hegg b Keedy	63
G. F. Archer b Austin	50	– (10) not out	0
J. R. Wileman c Titchard b Keedy	12	– (3) lbw b Austin	37
C. L. Cairns c Gallian b Keedy	13	– c Watkinson b Austin	23
P. Johnson c Hegg b Watkinson	15	– (4) b Austin	2
K. P. Evans c Hegg b Austin	12	– (6) not out	13
†W. M. Noon lbw b Wasim Akram	5	– (7) lbw b Watkinson	10
J. E. Hindson not out	24	– (8) c Hegg b Keedy	0
R. A. Pick b Wasim Akram	7	– (9) b Keedy	4
J. A. Afford run out	2		
L-b 2, w 2, n-b 12	16	B 8, l-b 4, n-b 6	18

1/0 2/117 3/152 4/166 5/216   292   1/5 2/107 3/115 4/131   (8 wkts) 172
6/247 7/252 8/262 9/280   5/141 6/161 7/168 8/172

Bonus points – Nottinghamshire 2, Lancashire 4.

Bowling: *First Innings*—Wasim Akram 26–6–74–3; Chapple 12–1–35–0; Austin 29–9–63–3; Keedy 27–9–52–2; Watkinson 15–3–55–1; Gallian 3–0–11–0. *Second Innings*—Wasim Akram 9–1–24–0; Chapple 8–3–25–1; Austin 11–3–23–3; Keedy 19.5–5–61–3; Watkinson 13–5–27–1.

Umpires: G. I. Burgess and K. E. Palmer.

LANCASHIRE v GLAMORGAN

At Manchester, June 8, 9, 10, 12. Drawn. Lancashire 6 pts, Glamorgan 8 pts. Toss: Lancashire.

A slow pitch made for batsmen, on which Crawley scored two centuries, ensured that neither team's attack was strong enough to force victory. Glamorgan were presented with a target of 281 in 61 overs, an objective they turned their backs on after Croft, Cottey and Anthony were all stumped in successive overs of Watkinson's off-spin. There were 1,463 runs and five centuries in the match, and not for the first time, Crawley highlighted his absence from England's Test team with some impressive run-scoring. His first-innings 182 lasted five and a quarter hours and included 25 fours; in the second innings he hit a three-hour 108 out of a 196-run partnership with Gallian. The last Lancashire player to make twin centuries at Old Trafford was Harry Pilling in 1970. Glamorgan had taken a first-innings lead through Maynard and Cottey, who put together 237, a county third-wicket record against Lancashire. Dale broke a thumb batting against Wasim Akram, which kept him out for three weeks.

Close of play: First day, Lancashire 378-8 (W. K. Hegg 5*, G. Chapple 11*); Second day, Glamorgan 338-2 (M. P. Maynard 119*, P. A. Cottey 105*); Third day, Lancashire 140-1 (J. E. R. Gallian 64*, J. P. Crawley 49*).

Lancashire

J. E. R. Gallian c Kendrick b Barwick	36	– c Cottey b Hemp	158
N. J. Speak run out	7	– lbw b Croft	26
J. P. Crawley c sub b Croft	182	– c Cottey b Croft	108
N. H. Fairbrother c Watkin b Barwick	14	– not out	28
G. D. Lloyd lbw b Croft	50	– not out	1
*M. Watkinson c sub b Croft	44		
Wasim Akram c Cottey b Dale	10		
I. D. Austin run out	8		
†W. K. Hegg not out	35		
G. Chapple c Kendrick b Watkin	16		
G. Keedy c and b Watkin	4		
B 5, l-b 4, n-b 2	11	L-b 9, n-b 8	17

1/17 2/84 3/132 4/226 5/316   417   1/65 2/261 3/330   (3 wkts dec.) 338
6/350 7/350 8/363 9/397

Bonus points – Lancashire 4, Glamorgan 4 (Score at 120 overs: 408-9).

Bowling: *First Innings*—Watkin 23.4-4-67-2; Anthony 15-2-62-0; Barwick 30-8-78-2; Croft 29-4-93-3; Dale 16-2-50-1; Kendrick 9-0-58-0. *Second Innings*—Watkin 11-5-24-0; Anthony 21-6-57-0; Barwick 14-1-47-0; Croft 40-3-132-2; Cottey 10-0-50-0; Hemp 3-0-19-1.

Glamorgan

A. Dale retired hurt	31		
*H. Morris c Crawley b Keedy	67	– c Hegg b Austin	31
D. L. Hemp c Hegg b Wasim Akram	11	– b Keedy	25
M. P. Maynard c Crawley b Austin	138	– lbw b Keedy	67
P. A. Cottey c Hegg b Wasim Akram	124	– st Hegg b Watkinson	45
R. D. B. Croft c and b Watkinson	32	– st Hegg b Watkinson	12
H. A. G. Anthony lbw b Wasim Akram	0	– not out	6
N. M. Kendrick b Watkinson	20	– not out	9
†C. P. Metson c Hegg b Wasim Akram	19	– (1) c Keedy b Watkinson	8
S. L. Watkin not out	15	– (9) not out	0
S. R. Barwick b Watkinson	1		
B 4, l-b 3, n-b 10	17	B 14, l-b 10, n-b 6	30

1/82 2/140 3/377 4/381 5/383   475   1/40 2/44 3/119 4/174   (7 wkts) 233
6/435 7/442 8/462 9/475   5/209 6/218 7/227

Bonus points – Glamorgan 4, Lancashire 2 (Score at 120 overs: 435-5).

In the first innings A. Dale retired hurt at 50.

Bowling: *First Innings*—Wasim Akram 25-6-77-4; Chapple 18-3-85-0; Austin 26-3-81-1; Watkinson 31.1-7-103-3; Keedy 28-6-106-1; Gallian 5-1-16-0. *Second Innings*—Wasim Akram 13.4-2-42-0; Chapple 12-4-35-0; Watkinson 18-4-51-4; Austin 5-3-7-1; Keedy 12-0-74-2.

Umpires: J. C. Balderstone and B. Dudleston.

At Worcester, June 15, 16, 17. LANCASHIRE lost to WORCESTERSHIRE by an innings and 50 runs.

LANCASHIRE v ESSEX

At Manchester, June 22, 23, 24, 26. Lancashire won by ten wickets. Lancashire 24 pts, Essex 2 pts. Toss: Lancashire. First-class debut: D. J. Shadford.

This game was a personal triumph for Watkinson, who followed a career-best innings of 161 with match figures of nine for 130. Lancashire were in control from the first session, when opening batsmen Gallian and Speak put on 123. Watkinson and Titchard, who had been recalled from a second-team match when Fairbrother was taken ill, followed up with a fifth-wicket stand of 225. Titchard's century was only his second in 46 first-class matches since 1990 and he was awarded his cap before the Sunday game. Gooch retorted with his 116th first-class century in a lone but unsuccessful attempt to save Essex from following on. But they went in again, 248 behind, and Gooch was out for the second time in an hour, this time for nought to debutant seamer Darren Shadford. The other Essex batsmen performed more solidly in the second innings but Lancashire needed only 103 to win and Gallian and Speak completed their second century opening partnership of the match. Essex sustained their sixth defeat in eight games soon after lunch on the final day.

Close of play: First day, Lancashire 322-4 (S. P. Titchard 96*, M. Watkinson 64*); Second day, Essex 190-4 (G. A. Gooch 115*, M. C. Ilott 1*); Third day, Essex 320-7 (M. C. Ilott 34*, P. M. Such 26*).

Lancashire

J. E. R. Gallian lbw b Childs	43	– not out	40
N. J. Speak b Ilott	83	– not out	64
J. P. Crawley b Childs	1		
S. P. Titchard b Robinson b Irani	130		
G. D. Lloyd b Irani	13		
*M. Watkinson b Ilott	161		
Wasim Akram c Rollins b Ilott	20		
†W. K. Hegg b Childs	5		
G. Yates lbw b Ilott	1		
D. J. Shadford c Rollins b Ilott	1		
G. Keedy not out	6		
B 10, l-b 14, w 6, n-b 2	32	L-b 2	2

1/123 2/125 3/137 4/171 5/396   **496**   (no wkt) **106**
6/436 7/469 8/470 9/485

Bonus points – Lancashire 4, Essex 1 (Score at 120 overs: 367-4).

Bowling: *First Innings*—Ilott 31.2-4-86-5; Andrew 18-2-67-0; Irani 28-4-85-2; Waugh 20-1-63-0; Such 24.5-5-83-0; Childs 36-10-88-3. *Second Innings*—Ilott 5-0-16-0; Andrew 1-0-3-0; Childs 9.2-1-48-0; Such 8-0-31-0; Waugh 2-0-6-0.

Essex

G. A. Gooch c Hegg b Watkinson	123	– c Gallian b Shadford	0
D. D. J. Robinson b Gallian	43	– c Crawley b Wasim Akram	86
M. E. Waugh st Hegg b Keedy	1	– b Watkinson	26
N. Hussain lbw b Wasim Akram	5	– b Watkinson	0
*P. J. Prichard b Watkinson	1	– lbw b Watkinson	35
M. C. Ilott c Gallian b Wasim Akram	3	– (8) not out	36
R. C. Irani st Hegg b Keedy	28	– (6) c Speak b Yates	45
†R. J. Rollins b Watkinson	0	– (7) c Hegg b Watkinson	29
P. M. Such b Wasim Akram	0	– b Wasim Akram	32
S. J. W. Andrew b Wasim Akram	0	– b Watkinson	4
J. H. Childs not out	2	– c Crawley b Watkinson	6
B 18, l-b 2, n-b 22	42	B 16, l-b 10, w 5, n-b 20	51

1/129 2/136 3/173 4/187 5/192   **248**   1/0 2/56 3/60 4/118 5/193   **350**
6/228 7/228 8/237 9/237   6/219 7/264 8/335 9/344

Bonus points – Essex 1, Lancashire 4.

Bowling: *First Innings*—Wasim Akram 25-5-86-4; Shadford 7-1-19-0; Watkinson 19-6-39-3; Yates 8-2-36-0; Gallian 8-1-24-1; Keedy 13-5-24-2. *Second Innings*—Shadford 11-1-36-1; Gallian 4-0-12-0; Keedy 26-3-82-0; Watkinson 28.5-13-91-6; Wasim Akram 22-4-79-2; Yates 6-0-24-1.

Umpires: H. D. Bird and P. Willey.

LANCASHIRE v NORTHAMPTONSHIRE

At Manchester, July 6, 7, 8, 10. Lancashire won by 233 runs. Lancashire 24 pts, Northamptonshire 4 pts. Toss: Lancashire.

A partnership of 237 between Crawley and Hegg, which lasted from the 27th to the 104th over of the opening day, proved decisive. Crawley, who had won the toss in Watkinson's absence, batted for seven and a half hours for his 173. Hegg's century was only his third in ten seasons. He was promoted to No. 6 to allow Watkinson a little rest after he had driven up the motorway from Birmingham, having been released from the Test squad. Northamptonshire's wicket-keeper also batted well: Warren stayed more than three and a half hours for his 90, and the last pair squeezed their team past the follow-on target. But there was no escape. Lancashire set them 428, which proved academic as Wasim Akram took seven for 73, his best analysis of the season to date, for a match return of ten for 172 and Lancashire's first win over Northamptonshire since 1979. Northamptonshire's defeat was their first in the Championship for two months, after six successive wins, and they failed to take full bowling points for the first time, enabling Warwickshire to join them at the head of the table.

Close of play: First day, Lancashire 346-6 (J. P. Crawley 153*, Wasim Akram 5*); Second day, Northamptonshire 212-5 (R. J. Warren 60*, D. J. Capel 11*); Third day, Northamptonshire 29-1 (A. Fordham 8*, A. R. Roberts 10*).

Lancashire

S. P. Titchard c Bailey b Capel	14	– run out	53
N. J. Speak c Bailey b Taylor	34	– c Warren b Taylor	9
J. P. Crawley lbw b Kumble	173	– st Warren b Bailey	64
N. H. Fairbrother c Capel b Taylor	0	– run out	32
G. D. Lloyd c Taylor b Curran	2	– b Bailey	23
†W. K. Hegg c Curran b Taylor	101	– (7) b Kumble	26
*M. Watkinson b Mallender	9	– (6) c Bailey b Taylor	0
Wasim Akram c Fordham b Mallender	50	– (9) not out	39
I. D. Austin c Montgomerie b Mallender	0	– (8) lbw b Bailey	13
G. Chapple not out	20	– c Curran b Bailey	4
G. Keedy b Curran	2		
B 14, l-b 12, n-b 6	32	B 7, l-b 10	17
	437	(9 wkts dec.)	**280**

1/34 2/74 3/74 4/85 5/322 6/341 7/401 8/408 9/415

1/13 2/130 3/155 4/166 5/171 6/205 7/219 8/260 9/280

Bonus points – Lancashire 4, Northamptonshire 2 (Score at 120 overs: 390-6).

Bowling: *First Innings*—Taylor 28-4-97-3; Mallender 23-5-63-3; Capel 15-1-65-1; Curran 19.3-7-49-2; Kumble 38-14-70-1; Roberts 11-2-45-0; Bailey 4-1-22-0. *Second Innings*—Taylor 11-1-42-2; Mallender 3-1-8-0; Capel 7-2-26-0; Kumble 23-3-95-1; Curran 5-0-26-0; Bailey 16.3-4-66-4.

Northamptonshire

R. R. Montgomerie c Austin b Wasim Akram	12	– c Hegg b Wasim Akram	2
A. Fordham b Watkinson	62	– c Hegg b Wasim Akram	13
*R. J. Bailey c Hegg b Austin	16	– (4) lbw b Wasim Akram	49
M. B. Loye b Watkinson	20	– (5) c Hegg b Keedy	20
†R. J. Warren b Wasim Akram	90	– (6) c Lloyd b Keedy	0
K. M. Curran c Lloyd b Keedy	2	– (7) lbw b Watkinson	14
D. J. Capel c Hegg b Wasim Akram	11	– (8) c Titchard b Watkinson	17
A. R. Roberts b Watkinson	11	– (3) c Austin b Wasim Akram	10
A. Kumble b Watkinson	14	– c Hegg b Wasim Akram	26
N. A. Mallender lbw b Austin	6	– not out	6
J. P. Taylor not out	0	– b Wasim Akram	0
B 13, l-b 5, n-b 28	46	B 8, l-b 15, n-b 14	37
	290		**194**

1/22 2/85 3/113 4/142 5/151 6/216 7/251 8/276 9/284

1/14 2/36 3/63 4/102 5/116 6/134 7/151 8/171 9/192

Bonus points – Northamptonshire 2, Lancashire 4.

Bowling: *First Innings*—Wasim Akram 26–4–99–3; Chapple 9–2–26–0; Austin 18.4–5–50–2; Watkinson 34–13–62–4; Keedy 18–6–35–1. *Second Innings*—Wasim Akram 22.5–7–73–7; Chapple 10–4–18–0; Watkinson 18–3–60–1; Keedy 10–4–20–2.

Umpires: T. E. Jesty and P. B. Wight.

At Cheltenham, July 20, 21, 22. LANCASHIRE lost to GLOUCESTERSHIRE by ten wickets.

At Taunton, July 27, 28, 29. LANCASHIRE beat SOMERSET by ten wickets.

LANCASHIRE v SUSSEX

At Lytham, August 3, 4, 5, 7. Lancashire won by 60 runs. Lancashire 24 pts, Sussex 7 pts. Toss: Lancashire. Championship debut: M. T. E. Peirce.

The pitch, shaved of grass and bone dry, prompted the umpires to phone Lord's; they thought it too helpful to spin. The TCCB said that no action was necessary, but this match may be best remembered for the intervention from even higher authority. The opening over on Friday was twice interrupted by snatches of Holy Communion from the nearby church of St Cuthbert, mysteriously transmitted to the public address speakers. Otherwise, the spinners were dominant, though never quite in control, taking 16 wickets in the first two innings. Salisbury took four as Lancashire made an uneasy 147 for five, before Titchard and Watkinson launched the recovery which added another 208. A splendid century by Wells, his sixth of the season, pegged the Sussex deficit back to 38. Surprisingly, it was Jarvis's seam which discomfited Lancashire on the third day, when he took five before lunch. But Crawley played a decisive innings after being dropped when three and a target of 254 proved too much for Sussex. They lost their last wickets in eight overs on the final morning and Watkinson's tenth wicket sealed their fifth successive Championship defeat.

Close of play: First day, Sussex 16-1 (C. W. J. Athey 8*, N. C. Phillips 3*); Second day, Lancashire 38-2 (J. E. R. Gallian 21*, J. P. Crawley 0*); Third day, Sussex 145-6 (P. Moores 7*, I. D. K. Salisbury 1*).

Lancashire

J. E. R. Gallian c Wells b Salisbury	53	– (2) c Moores b Phillips	42
M. A. Atherton b Jarvis	5	– (1) b Salisbury	14
J. P. Crawley c Moores b Salisbury	34	– (4) c and b Jarvis	70
N. H. Fairbrother b Salisbury	0	– (5) b Salisbury	11
S. P. Titchard c Athey b Salisbury	60	– (6) lbw b Phillips	0
N. J. Speak b Salisbury	25	– (7) c Moores b Jarvis	11
*M. Watkinson b Giddins	58	– (8) lbw b Jarvis	0
Wasim Akram c and b Phillips	52	– (9) c Peirce b Jarvis	11
†W. K. Hegg c Moores b Salisbury	0	– (10) c Peirce b Phillips	27
I. D. Austin c Wells b Phillips	36	– (3) c Peirce b Salisbury	0
G. Keedy not out	1	– not out	8
B 5, l-b 18, n-b 8	31	B 13, l-b 6, n-b 2	21

1/10 2/90 3/90 4/105 5/147   355   1/30 2/38 3/84 4/133 5/134   215
6/245 7/277 8/277 9/354   6/155 7/155 8/170 9/181

Bonus points – Lancashire 4, Sussex 4.

Bowling: *First Innings*—Giddins 16–4–49–1; Jarvis 19–4–56–1; Phillips 20.3–2–106–2; Salisbury 33–5–107–6; Peirce 6–1–14–0. *Second Innings*—Giddins 5–1–10–0; Jarvis 14–2–55–5; Phillips 21.2–3–78–3; Salisbury 23–7–53–2.

Sussex

C. W. J. Athey b Watkinson	57	– b Watkinson	40
M. T. E. Peirce b Keedy	3	– lbw b Austin	15
N. C. Phillips b Austin	52	– (9) b Wasim Akram	1
N. J. Lenham c Speak b Watkinson	8	– (3) c Crawley b Keedy	24
*A. P. Wells c Fairbrother b Watkinson	105	– (4) c Fairbrother b Keedy	36
K. Greenfield lbw b Watkinson	0	– (5) c Titchard b Austin	7
†P. Moores c Hegg b Watkinson	10	– (6) b Wasim Akram	7
D. R. Law c Wasim Akram b Watkinson	17	– (7) lbw b Watkinson	0
I. D. K. Salisbury c Hegg b Watkinson	26	– (8) c Hegg b Wasim Akram	16
P. W. Jarvis c Fairbrother b Wasim Akram	11	– hit wkt b Watkinson	24
E. S. H. Giddins not out	1	– not out	0
B 12, l-b 15	27	B 8, l-b 11, n-b 4	23

1/13 2/112 3/130 4/135 5/135   317   1/26 2/83 3/111 4/135 5/137   193
6/159 7/209 8/297 9/316   6/142 7/146 8/162 9/179

Bonus points – Sussex 3, Lancashire 4.

Bowling: *First Innings*—Wasim Akram 14–4–26–1; Austin 15–7–16–1; Watkinson 40.2–10–140–7; Keedy 35–5–102–1; Speak 1–0–6–0. *Second Innings*—Wasim Akram 16–3–34–3; Austin 13–9–13–2; Watkinson 24–5–82–3; Keedy 16–4–45–2.

Umpires: K. J. Lyons and R. Palmer.

At Leicester, August 10, 11, 12. LANCASHIRE beat LEICESTERSHIRE by four wickets.

LANCASHIRE v YORKSHIRE

At Manchester, August 17, 18, 19, 21. Yorkshire won by nine wickets. Yorkshire 24 pts, Lancashire 4 pts. Toss: Yorkshire.

A fine team effort by Yorkshire virtually ended Lancastrian thoughts of the Championship. The only highlight for home supporters came from England captain Atherton, who had intended resting but was recruited when Fairbrother cried off with a strained hamstring. Batting in the middle order, he scored 61 and 100, his sixth century against Yorkshire, to equal Clive Lloyd's record for Lancashire in Roses games. But it was to no avail. Lancashire batted and bowled poorly in the first innings, surrendering a lead of 267 and following on – even though Yorkshire's usual opening bowlers, Gough and Hartley, were injured. Metcalfe, in his first first-class match of the season, had played his biggest Championship innings for four years; Silverwood struck a maiden 50 off 46 balls and was last out attempting a third successive six. Lancashire showed more grit in their second innings and Crawley scored his second fifty of the game. But they were all out in the fifth over of the final morning and Yorkshire knocked off a target of 96 before lunch. For the first time in many years the match was televised, on satellite TV.

Close of play: First day, Yorkshire 393-6 (A. A. Metcalfe 55*, G. M. Hamilton 23*); Second day, Lancashire 3-0 (J. E. R. Gallian 0*, S. P. Titchard 1*); Third day, Lancashire 346-7 (M. A. Atherton 93*, I. D. Austin 2*).

Yorkshire

*M. D. Moxon c Hegg b Wasim Akram	47	– not out	50
M. P. Vaughan c and b Chapple	32	– c Watkinson b Gallian	28
D. Byas st Hegg b Keedy	76	– not out	13
M. G. Bevan c Hegg b Watkinson	95		
C. White c Hegg b Watkinson	11		
A. A. Metcalfe c Titchard b Wasim Akram	79		
†R. J. Blakey b Watkinson	2		
G. M. Hamilton c Hegg b Wasim Akram	29		
C. E. W. Silverwood c Chapple b Keedy	50		
R. D. Stemp b Keedy	19		
M. A. Robinson not out	1		
B 8, l-b 22, w 2, n-b 32	64	B 4, l-b 1	5

1/67 2/129 3/239 4/303 5/308   505   1/62   (1 wkt) 96
6/332 7/406 8/451 9/492

Bonus points – Yorkshire 4, Lancashire 3 (Score at 120 overs: 424-7).

Bowling: *First Innings*—Wasim Akram 32-3-104-3; Chapple 27-5-87-1; Austin 17-3-60-0; Watkinson 30-7-117-3; Keedy 24-7-90-3; Gallian 4-0-17-0. *Second Innings*—Chapple 7-1-32-0; Austin 4-0-9-0; Watkinson 4-0-17-0; Gallian 4-0-11-1; Keedy 3.5-1-22-0.

Lancashire

J. E. R. Gallian st Blakey b Stemp	34	– c Byas b Vaughan	33
S. P. Titchard c White b Hamilton	2	– c Byas b Silverwood	16
J. P. Crawley b Stemp	83	– c Hamilton b Vaughan	58
N. J. Speak lbw b Robinson	2	– b Silverwood	28
M. A. Atherton c Metcalfe b Hamilton	61	– c Byas b Stemp	100
*M. Watkinson lbw b Stemp	2	– c Hamilton b Stemp	40
†W. K. Hegg c Byas b Vaughan	3	– (8) b White	38
Wasim Akram c and b Vaughan	4	– (7) st Blakey b Bevan	5
I. D. Austin b Robinson	11	– c Blakey b White	11
G. Chapple not out	6	– not out	0
G. Keedy c Metcalfe b Robinson	1	– c Vaughan b White	0
B 12, l-b 7, n-b 10	29	B 4, l-b 13, n-b 16	33

1/9 2/104 3/119 4/137 5/143   238   1/18 2/118 3/122 4/188 5/275   362
6/199 7/211 8/211 9/236   6/286 7/334 8/358 9/362

Bonus points – Lancashire 1, Yorkshire 4.

Bowling: *First Innings*—Hamilton 13-5-25-2; Silverwood 8-1-40-0; Stemp 24-8-50-3; Vaughan 8-3-22-2; Robinson 9.2-2-23-3; White 5-1-22-0; Bevan 10-0-37-0. *Second Innings*—Robinson 13-4-40-0; Stemp 36-11-58-2; White 15.1-2-52-3; Silverwood 12-3-42-2; Hamilton 12-3-43-0; Bevan 12-1-52-1; Vaughan 16-3-58-2.

Umpires: J. C. Balderstone and V. A. Holder.

At Portsmouth, August 24, 25, 26, 28. LANCASHIRE beat HAMPSHIRE by five wickets.

At The Oval, August 29, 30, 31, September 1. LANCASHIRE beat SURREY by nine wickets.

LANCASHIRE v KENT

At Manchester, September 7, 8, 9, 11. Drawn. Lancashire 2 pts, Kent 3 pts. Toss: Lancashire.

Rain prevented play except on the third day, when Fairbrother reached 50 for only the third time in this, his benefit season. On the other occasions – against Warwickshire and Somerset – he went on to centuries. Atherton continued to show a liking for batting at No. 5, adding 82 to previous innings of 61, 100 and 61. The draw finally extinguished Lancashire's last, mathematical, hope of becoming champions, while Kent had now gone ten games, since June 5, without a Championship win.

Close of play: First day, No play; Second day, No play; Third day, Lancashire 269-8 (W. K. Hegg 9*, P. J. Martin 2*).

Lancashire

J. E. R. Gallian lbw b Igglesden	6	†W. K. Hegg not out 9
S. P. Titchard c Igglesden b Patel	33	I. D. Austin c and b Patel 4
J. P. Crawley c Walker b Ealham	13	P. J. Martin not out 2
N. H. Fairbrother c Ward b Llong	52	B 10, l-b 6, w 3, n-b 8 27
M. A. Atherton b Patel	82	
G. D. Lloyd b Llong	16	1/16 2/47 3/72 4/165 5/203 (8 wkts) 269
*M. Watkinson c Llong b Patel	25	6/238 7/249 8/259

G. Chapple did not bat.

Bonus points – Lancashire 2, Kent 3.

Bowling: Headley 13–3–32–0; Igglesden 13–2–30–1; Ealham 11–5–23–1; Patel 39–10–109–4; Fleming 4–0–12–0; Llong 20–5–47–2.

Kent

*M. R. Benson, T. R. Ward, N. J. Llong, M. J. Walker, G. R. Cowdrey, M. A. Ealham, M. V. Fleming, †S. A. Marsh, D. W. Headley, M. M. Patel and A. P. Igglesden.

Umpires: R. Palmer and G. Sharp.

At Derby, September 14, 15, 16, 18. LANCASHIRE lost to DERBYSHIRE by 282 runs.

COUNTY CAPS AWARDED IN 1995

Derbyshire	A. S. Rollins, C. M. Wells.
Essex	R. J. Rollins.
Gloucestershire	K. E. Cooper, M. A. Lynch, A. M. Smith, J. Srinath.
Hampshire	J. P. Stephenson.
Kent	P. A. de Silva.
Lancashire	S. P. Titchard.
Leicestershire	W. J. Cronje, A. R. K. Pierson, B. F. Smith.
Middlesex	M. A. Feltham, R. L. Johnson, D. J. Nash, J. C. Pooley.
Northamptonshire ..	A. Kumble, R. R. Montgomerie, R. J. Warren.
Nottinghamshire ...	G. F. Archer, W. M. Noon.
Somerset	P. D. Bowler.
Surrey	A. J. Hollioake, A. C. S. Pigott.
Warwickshire	D. R. Brown, N. V. Knight.
Worcestershire	W. P. C. Weston.
Yorkshire	M. G. Bevan, M. P. Vaughan.

No caps were awarded by Glamorgan or Sussex. Durham give caps to all their playing staff.

LEICESTERSHIRE

President: B. A. F. Smith
Chairman: J. M. Josephs
Chairman, Cricket Committee: P. R. Haywood
Chief Executive: A. O. Norman
Captain: 1995 – N. E. Briers
        1996 – J. J. Whitaker
Cricket Manager: J. Birkenshaw
Head Groundsman: L. Spence
Scorer: G. A. York

While Leicestershire do not have the resources to compete for long with the biggest guns in cricket, they have spiked several in the last couple of years and will probably continue to do so. Finishing seventh in the Championship proved, to some extent, that their position of runners-up in 1994 was not a fluke. Seventh may not sound too special but, with a bit more calm and good fortune, Leicestershire, a solid, hard-working rather than spectacular side, could have finished fifth or even higher.

Losing the penultimate game to Middlesex when it was seemingly in the bag – needing two to win off nine balls, last man Alan Mullally was caught going for the big heave and glory – and having the last game against Gloucestershire washed out did them no favours. Neither did an injury crisis in mid-season when, following a decent start, they crashed to four defeats and a draw in five matches.

Injuries are part and parcel of cricket, but the loss of Hansie Cronje, James Whitaker and Vince Wells ripped the heart out of the middle order, and the way Whitaker tore his ankle ligaments – landing on the boundary rope during the warm-up at Worcester – just about summed up the bizarre situation. To make matters worse, David Millns was sidelined from mid-June by an Achilles tendon problem, which later needed an operation. With Mullally at half his usual speed because of a side strain, the pace attack had all the threat of a pea-shooter.

That Leicestershire came through the crisis, winning four and drawing one of their last seven games, as well as hammering the Young Australians inside two days – their only first-class defeat – owed much to a resilience and competitiveness instilled in them by captain Nigel Briers. Briers resigned at the end of the season after six years, having steered Leicestershire through a transitional period following the loss of several stars at the end of the 1980s. He said he would stay on as a batsman but believed it was time for a fresh voice. It had been clear from the close season, when James Whitaker was persuaded not to join Somerset, that he was earmarked to take over. And so he did.

Injuries were not the only problem at Grace Road in 1995. It became clear that some players were unhappy with Jack Birkenshaw's role, their preference being for a coach rather than a manager. But the biggest threat to the future seemed to be outside interest being shown in three of their pace attack. At the end of the season, Mullally, Alamgir Sheriyar and Gordon Parsons were all said to be targets for other clubs. Parsons rejected an offer from Somerset and signed a new contract but Sheriyar chose to leave.

One player who would not be back was Cronje, as West Indian Phil Simmons was due to complete his two-year contract. Cronje enjoyed his stay so much, however, that he did not rule out a return in the future. After a poor start the South African captain, Parsons's brother-in-law, came good, easily heading the county averages with 1,301 Championship runs at an average of 52.04, including four centuries, one a double against Somerset. Cronje, like Simmons, was a popular figure. His positive attitude and encouragement helped young batsman Ben Smith blossom towards the end of the season, when he received his cap. Even an old hand like Whitaker found inspiration in him.

If anything, the batting was slightly more consistent than the previous year – even though six out of nine Championship games finished inside three days at Grace Road. Only two batsmen, Cronje and Briers, passed 1,000 Championship runs; Whitaker did it in all first-class matches.

Off-spinner Adrian Pierson, who was also capped after ten years in the game, was a plus, finishing as leading Championship wicket-taker with 65 at 28.80. But that was offset by Mullally's continuing failure to achieve his full potential. Losing his strike partner, Millns, was a blow but while his total of 52 wickets was nearly twice his figure in 1994, he did not do his ambitions to play for England any good. Nor did wicket-keeper Paul Nixon, who started the season as an England possible but finished it looking at a winter of thumb-twiddling after missing out on the England A tour to Pakistan. It was his hand, broken by Allan Donald in the season's opening game between England A and Warwickshire, which kept him out for the first month. He never fully recovered and, after passing 1,000 in 1994, scored just 461 runs at 18.44 in all first-class cricket.

Leicestershire then lost Nixon's deputy as well when Phil Whitticase was hit in the mouth while batting during the opening Championship match against Essex, which cost him several teeth; he needed £2,000 worth of dental treatment. Birkenshaw claimed the umpires should have taken the teams off because the light was so bad.

Perhaps the biggest disappointment of 1995 was Leicestershire's failures in one-day cricket. They made a pig's ear of the Benson and Hedges Cup, losing the first two games to Durham and Lancashire after, as Birkenshaw quipped, being 4-0 up at half-time: Durham were 39 for six and, against Lancashire, Leicestershire scored 312. They went on to lose to Minor Counties and were bottom of their group. In the NatWest Trophy, they squeezed through the first round against Hampshire, thanks to a better run-rate in the first 30 overs after finishing with identical scores, but crashed out of the second, losing a low-scoring match to Glamorgan at home.

With talented young players like Darren Maddy and Jon Dakin coming through, Leicestershire had fancied their chances in the Sunday League. Seventh was an improvement of three places on 1994, but they lost matches they should have won, against Kent and Somerset, and a controversial end to a rain-affected match against Essex, which they lost on scoring-rate by 0.06, added to their sense of injustice.

Leicestershire released opening batsman Tim Boon after 16 years at the club but, with Oxford University pair Gregor Macmillan and the highly rated Iain Sutcliffe making their mark when they arrived in July, there were signs that Leicestershire had the makings of a decent side – assuming it is kept together. – *Chris Goddard.*

LEICESTERSHIRE 1995

[*Bill Smith*

Back row: D. L. Maddy, M. T. Brimson, W. J. Cronje, A. R. K. Pierson, J. M. Dakin, V. J. Wells, A. Sheriyar, B. F. Smith. *Front row*: P. A. Nixon, J. J. Whitaker, N. E. Briers (*captain*), G. J. Parsons, A. D. Mullally. *Insets*: G. I. Macmillan, D. J. Millns.

LEICESTERSHIRE RESULTS

All first-class matches – Played 20: Won 9, Lost 9, Drawn 2.

County Championship matches – Played 17: Won 7, Lost 8, Drawn 2.

Bonus points – Batting 41, Bowling 61.

*Competition placings – Britannic Assurance County Championship, 7th;
NatWest Bank Trophy, 2nd round; Benson and Hedges Cup, 6th in Group A;
AXA Equity & Law League, 7th.*

BRITANNIC ASSURANCE CHAMPIONSHIP AVERAGES

BATTING

	Birthplace	M	I	NO	R	HS	Avge
‡W. J. Cronje§	Bloemfontein, SA	15	26	1	1,301	213	52.04
G. I. Macmillan	Guildford	6	10	1	389	122	43.22
‡N. E. Briers	Leicester	15	27	2	1,046	175*	41.84
‡J. J. Whitaker.	Skipton	13	21	0	869	127	41.38
J. M. Dakin	Hitchin	6	10	2	306	101*	38.25
‡P. Whitticase	Solihull	3	5	1	150	62*	37.50
‡B. F. Smith	Corby	15	25	4	698	112	33.23
‡V. J. Wells	Dartford	13	22	1	645	124	30.71
‡D. J. Millns	Clipstone	7	12	2	259	70	25.90
M. T. Brimson	Plumstead	5	4	0	40	25	20.00
P. E. Robinson	Keighley	3	6	1	99	60*	19.80
‡P. A. Nixon	Carlisle	13	22	4	356	79	19.77
‡G. J. Parsons	Slough	17	26	2	472	73	19.66
‡A. R. K. Pierson	Enfield	17	26	6	316	50	15.80
‡T. J. Boon	Doncaster	6	12	0	177	38	14.75
D. L. Maddy.	Leicester	7	13	0	121	24	9.30
V. P. Clarke	Liverpool	2	4	0	35	29	8.75
‡A. D. Mullally	Southend-on-Sea	17	26	6	150	22	7.50
A. Sheriyar	Birmingham	4	7	1	38	18	6.33

Also batted: C. D. Crowe (*Leicester*) (1 match) 1, 9; I. J. Sutcliffe (*Leeds*) (2 matches) 21, 34, 8.

* Signifies not out.   *‡ Denotes county cap.*   *§ Overseas player.*

The following played a total of 14 three-figure innings for Leicestershire in County Championship matches – W. J. Cronje 4, N. E. Briers 3, G. I. Macmillan 2, J. J. Whitaker 2, J. M. Dakin 1, B. F. Smith 1, V. J. Wells 1.

BOWLING

	O	M	R	W	BB	5W/i	Avge
V. J. Wells.	131.3	32	393	19	3-28	0	20.68
A. R. K. Pierson	583.1	124	1,872	65	5-48	2	28.80
A. D. Mullally	540	165	1,534	52	6-50	2	29.50
G. J. Parsons	549.2	167	1,527	50	4-46	0	30.54
A. Sheriyar.	106.4	15	424	11	3-46	0	38.54
D. J. Millns	187.2	25	725	18	3-47	0	40.27
W. J. Cronje	248.2	80	676	14	3-42	0	48.28

Also bowled: M. T. Brimson 89–20–243–9; V. P. Clarke 44.2–6–155–4; C. D. Crowe 3–2–4–0; J. M. Dakin 54–9–194–2; D. L. Maddy 6–0–41–0; B. F. Smith 11.3–2–69–1.

Wicket-keepers: P. A. Nixon 34 ct; P. Whitticase 7 ct, 1 st; P. E. Robinson 4 ct; D. L. Maddy 3 ct.

Leading Fielder: G. J. Parsons 14.

At Chelmsford, April 27, 28, 29, 30. LEICESTERSHIRE beat ESSEX by 102 runs.

LEICESTERSHIRE v YORKSHIRE

At Leicester, May 4, 5, 6. Yorkshire won by nine wickets. Yorkshire 23 pts, Leicestershire 4 pts. Toss: Yorkshire. Championship debut: M. G. Bevan.

Leicestershire's early-season optimism was savaged as Yorkshire wiped the floor with them, winning by nine wickets in three days. Though there was intense interest in England's winter hero, Gough, and the new overseas players on both sides, Bevan and Cronje, the key figure was the less glamorous 35-year-old seamer Hartley. Yorkshire's first-innings 332 was inspired by White, who hit three sixes in an over off Pierson to make sure of his century with nine wickets down. Hartley, bowling straight and hitting the seam, then took five for 19 to help skittle Leicestershire for 147. Only Millns showed any resistance, with his second successive half-century. He was promoted to open in the follow-on but scored only seven. Despite a fighting 75 from Wells, who retired briefly after Gough hit him on the head, Leicestershire were bowled out again for 221, leaving a simple target of 37. It was an unconvincing home start for Leicestershire's new overseas player, Cronje. He made nought and five – 256 less than his predecessor Simmons on his Grace Road debut a year earlier. During tea on the first day a spectator fell asleep on the outfield, having apparently enjoyed himself too much; the Leicestershire fielders had to carry him off.

Close of play: First day, Leicestershire 1-2 (T. J. Boon 1*, W. J. Cronje 0*); Second day, Leicestershire 102-5 (V. J. Wells 22*, P. E. Robinson 12*).

Yorkshire

*M. D. Moxon c Maddy b Mullally	9	– not out	9
M. P. Vaughan c Robinson b Millns	49	– c Millns b Mullally	23
D. Byas run out	26	– not out	2
M. G. Bevan c Robinson b Millns	13		
C. White c Robinson b Mullally	107		
†R. J. Blakey b Pierson	11		
A. P. Grayson b Mullally	73		
D. Gough c Cronje b Mullally	5		
P. J. Hartley b Pierson	6		
R. D. Stemp c Cronje b Pierson	2		
M. A. Robinson not out	7		
B 8, l-b 6, w 6, n-b 4	24	L-b 3	3

1/40 2/87 3/105 4/110 5/133   332   1/35   (1 wkt) 37
6/252 7/272 8/289 9/301

Bonus points – Yorkshire 3, Leicestershire 4.

Bowling: *First Innings*—Millns 27-3-90-2; Mullally 24.1-9-62-4; Parsons 15-5-31-0; Cronje 12-3-33-0; Pierson 16-1-77-3; Wells 7-1-25-0. *Second Innings*—Mullally 4.1-0-21-1; Pierson 4-1-13-0.

Leicestershire

T. J. Boon lbw b Hartley	12	– (3) b Stemp	38
*N. E. Briers c Byas b Hartley	0	– c White b Gough	6
A. R. K. Pierson c Vaughan b Gough	0	– (10) b Gough	0
W. J. Cronje c Vaughan b Gough	0	– c Bevan b Stemp	5
B. F. Smith c Vaughan b Hartley	25	– c Stemp b Robinson	11
V. J. Wells c Stemp b Hartley	0	– b Vaughan	75
†P. E. Robinson c Bevan b Hartley	3	– c Byas b Stemp	19
D. L. Maddy c Hartley b White	24	– c Moxon b Vaughan	20
G. J. Parsons c Blakey b Gough	20	– c Moxon b Hartley	34
D. J. Millns not out	50	– (1) c Byas b Hartley	7
A. D. Mullally lbw b Robinson	1	– not out	2
L-b 4, w 8	12	B 1, l-b 3	4

1/0 2/1 3/5 4/43 5/43   147   1/7 2/24 3/43 4/66 5/76   221
6/44 7/47 8/75 9/144   6/112 7/160 8/218 9/219

Bonus points – Yorkshire 4.

In the second innings V. J. Wells, when 30, retired hurt at 118 and resumed at 160.

Bowling: *First Innings*—Gough 18–7–46–3; Hartley 20–12–19–5; Robinson 11.4–3–42–1; Stemp 13–5–34–0; White 1–0–2–1. *Second Innings*—Gough 23–5–67–2; Robinson 8–3–15–1; Stemp 28–12–49–3; Vaughan 16.1–5–32–3; Hartley 10–2–38–1; White 6–1–16–0.

Umpires: D. J. Constant and D. R. Shepherd.

At Canterbury, May 11, 12, 13. LEICESTERSHIRE lost to KENT by an innings and 121 runs.

LEICESTERSHIRE v DERBYSHIRE

At Leicester, May 18, 19, 20. Leicestershire won by nine wickets. Leicestershire 24 pts, Derbyshire 6 pts. Toss: Leicestershire.

Leicestershire played Jekyll and Hyde, bouncing back from two successive three-day defeats to win by nine wickets – also in three days. They bowled Derbyshire out for 256, Parsons taking four for 55, and 173, when left-armer Mullally did the damage. His six for 50 suggested he had woken from the previous season's nightmare, when he took just 28 Championship wickets. Derbyshire owed both their batting points to a last-wicket stand of 58 from Warner and Malcolm, after Owen scored a maiden half-century in his second Championship match. Their second innings owed much to Colin Wells, who finally reached fifty for the first time in any competition since joining Derbyshire in 1994. Another player back in form was Whitaker with 120, the backbone of Leicestershire's 357. Leicestershire knocked off 73 to win for the loss of Maddy, who was picked ahead of Boon after scoring nearly 1,500 for the Seconds in 1994. He also acted as emergency wicket-keeper when Whitticase was taken ill, making three catches.

Close of play: First day, Leicestershire 73-3 (J. J. Whitaker 5*); Second day, Derbyshire 121-2 (K. J. Barnett 63*, C. M. Wells 37*).

Derbyshire

*K. J. Barnett b Parsons	11	– c Millns b Mullally	71
C. J. Adams c Pierson b Parsons	44	– lbw b Parsons	17
T. J. G. O'Gorman b Mullally	11	– c Whitticase b Parsons	0
J. E. Owen b Wells	50	– (8) c Maddy b Wells	11
D. G. Cork c Maddy b Wells	5	– (6) lbw b Mullally	1
C. M. Wells c Wells b Cronje	8	– (4) b Mullally	61
P. A. J. DeFreitas c Whitticase b Millns	28	– c Maddy b Mullally	3
T. W. Harrison c Whitticase b Parsons	2	– (5) lbw b Mullally	0
†A. D. Bairstow b Millns	5	– b Mullally	4
A. E. Warner b Parsons	43	– c Maddy b Wells	0
D. E. Malcolm not out	25	– not out	0
B 4, l-b 4, n-b 16	24	L-b 3, n-b 2	5

1/39 2/70 3/70 4/81 5/99   256   1/36 2/36 3/134 4/134 5/142   173
6/140 7/155 8/166 9/198   6/152 7/169 8/173 9/173

Bonus points – Derbyshire 2, Leicestershire 4.

Bowling: *First Innings*—Millns 13–0–66–2; Mullally 20–3–81–1; Parsons 19.2–5–55–4; Wells 11–3–31–2; Cronje 9–6–15–1. *Second Innings*—Millns 1.1–0–15–0; Mullally 23–10–50–6; Wells 6.3–3–12–2; Parsons 22–6–64–2; Pierson 5–1–15–0; Cronje 4–1–14–0.

Leicestershire

*N. E. Briers c Wells b Cork	32	– (2) not out	34
D. L. Maddy lbw b Malcolm	2	– (1) c O'Gorman b Barnett	24
W. J. Cronje c DeFreitas b Cork	27	– not out	6
J. J. Whitaker c Bairstow b Cork	120		
V. J. Wells lbw b DeFreitas	30		
B. F. Smith c sub b Warner	17		
G. J. Parsons b Malcolm	27		
†P. Whitticase c Bairstow b Cork	51		
A. R. K. Pierson b Cork	0		
D. J. Millns not out	8		
A. D. Mullally lbw b DeFreitas	3		
B 9, l-b 17, w 4, n-b 10	40	L-b 7, n-b 2	9

1/13 2/56 3/73 4/175 5/203   357   1/61   (1 wkt) 73
6/244 7/342 8/343 9/344

Bonus points – Leicestershire 4, Derbyshire 4.

Bowling: *First Innings*—Malcolm 24–4–100–2; DeFreitas 25.1–9–64–2; Cork 26–3–74–5; Warner 21–3–57–1; Wells 7–1–13–0; Harrison 8–2–23–0. *Second Innings*—Cork 11–6–18–0; DeFreitas 13–3–27–0; Warner 5–0–15–0; Barnett 2.1–1–6–1.

Umpires: D. J. Constant and V. A. Holder.

LEICESTERSHIRE v DURHAM

At Leicester, May 25, 26, 27. Leicestershire won by an innings and 91 runs. Leicestershire 24 pts, Durham 3 pts. Toss: Leicestershire.

Off-spinner Pierson ended a ten-year wait for a county cap as he led Leicestershire to an easy win, maintaining their 100 per cent record against Durham, after five matches. Pierson, who spent seven years at Warwickshire before moving via Cambridgeshire to Grace Road in 1993, was capped after claiming five for 48 in Durham's first innings. Durham were bowled out for 138 and 151, two thoroughly sub-standard batting performances. Leicestershire's innings was also flawed. Despite 92 from Whitaker and 58 from Wells, they had slumped to 245 for seven, with Prabhakar taking six on his way to seven for 65. But Parsons and Millns put on 98; an eventual total of 380 set up Leicestershire's second three-day win in succession.

Close of play: First day, Leicestershire 349-8 (G. J. Parsons 60*, A. R. K. Pierson 1*); Second day, Durham 100-4 (M. Saxelby 15*, J. Boiling 4*).

Leicestershire

D. L. Maddy lbw b Prabhakar	0	D. J. Millns c Ligertwood b Prabhakar	40
*N. E. Briers lbw b Prabhakar	41	A. R. K. Pierson c and b Brown	15
W. J. Cronje b Prabhakar	8	A. D. Mullally not out	0
J. J. Whitaker b Prabhakar	92		
V. J. Wells b Prabhakar	58	L-b 8, n-b 12	20
B. F. Smith lbw b Prabhakar	33		
†P. A. Nixon lbw b Boiling	0	1/1 2/15 3/121 4/158 5/242	380
G. J. Parsons c Ligertwood b Brown	73	6/245 7/245 8/343 9/377	

Bonus points – Leicestershire 4, Durham 3 (Score at 120 overs: 362-8).

Bowling: Brown 21.5–2–85–2; Prabhakar 30–7–65–7; Betts 27–8–73–0; Birbeck 16–1–55–0; Boiling 26–6–78–1; Blenkiron 4–0–16–0.

Durham

*M. A. Roseberry c Maddy b Pierson	25	– b Parsons	4
W. Larkins c Nixon b Millns	27	– c Cronje b Wells	26
J. E. Morris c Parsons b Pierson	38	– c Millns b Cronje	41
M. Saxelby c Parsons b Pierson	2	– c Nixon b Pierson	22
D. A. Blenkiron lbw b Millns	3	– (7) lbw b Pierson	0
M. Prabhakar c Parsons b Mullally	18	– (5) c Parsons b Mullally	7
S. D. Birbeck c Nixon b Mullally	4	– (8) c Parsons b Mullally	1
†D. G. C. Ligertwood c Maddy b Pierson	3	– (9) not out	26
J. Boiling b Mullally	0	– (6) c Parsons b Pierson	4
S. J. E. Brown c Smith b Pierson	6	– b Millns	13
M. M. Betts not out	0	– b Millns	0
B 1, l-b 10, w 1	12	L-b 3, w 4	7

1/58 2/60 3/91 4/106 5/106   138   1/5 2/61 3/74 4/93 5/100   151
6/126 7/129 8/129 9/137   6/100 7/107 8/111 9/137

Bonus points – Leicestershire 4.

Bowling: *First Innings*—Mullally 17–6–32–3; Parsons 7–4–18–0; Millns 12–3–29–2; Pierson 21.3–8–48–5. *Second Innings*—Mullally 18–9–24–2; Parsons 7–1–20–1; Millns 8.2–0–29–2; Pierson 26–8–63–3; Wells 0.4–0–2–1; Cronje 6.2–1–10–1.

Umpires: J. D. Bond and R. Julian.

At Leicester, May 30, 31, June 1. LEICESTERSHIRE lost to WEST INDIANS by 287 runs (See West Indian tour section).

At Oxford, June 2, 3, 5. LEICESTERSHIRE beat OXFORD UNIVERSITY by five wickets.

At Basingstoke, June 7, 8, 9. LEICESTERSHIRE lost to HAMPSHIRE by nine wickets.

LEICESTERSHIRE v NOTTINGHAMSHIRE

At Leicester, June 15, 16, 17, 19. Drawn. Leicestershire 8 pts, Nottinghamshire 8 pts. Toss: Nottinghamshire.

This match produced four centuries and 1,348 runs, partly because both teams' bowlers were carrying an assortment of injuries. In the end, the loss of their two strike bowlers, Millns, whose Achilles tendon gave way, and Mullally, who could manage only slow left-arm, cost Leicestershire a third successive home Championship win. Set 375 in what became 102 overs, Nottinghamshire fell to 99 for four, but held out thanks to an unbeaten 122 from Archer. Whitaker and Cronje scored hundreds for Leicestershire – Cronje's nearly doubled his home aggregate of 61 in six innings. But the plaudits went to 22-year-old left-hander Jonathan Dakin, playing his second Championship match, who reached his century on the second morning and later topped 66. Johnson and Cairns added 150 in 29 overs in Nottinghamshire's first innings, which was boosted by 64 extras, but only a marvellous bowling performance by Pick kept the visitors in the game. Despite a knee injury, Pick took five for 82 in 30 overs.

Close of play: First day, Leicestershire 356-8 (J. M. Dakin 87*, A. D. Mullally 0*); Second day, Nottinghamshire 364; Third day, Leicestershire 335-9 (J. M. Dakin 56*, A. R. K. Pierson 2*).

Leicestershire

D. L. Maddy c Archer b Pick	1	– lbw b Pick	20
*N. E. Briers lbw b Chapman	20	– lbw b Hindson	46
W. J. Cronje lbw b Evans	15	– c Noon b Pick	113
J. J. Whitaker c Noon b Hindson	127	– c sub b Hindson	7
B. F. Smith c Hindson b Chapman	4	– lbw b Pick	0
†P. A. Nixon c Archer b Evans	39	– c Archer b Pick	3
J. M. Dakin not out	101	– b Chapman	66
G. J. Parsons c Johnson b Hindson	12	– b Pick	28
D. J. Millns c Archer b Pick	20	– c Evans b Chapman	11
A. D. Mullally c Pick b Evans	1	– c Cairns b Evans	14
A. R. K. Pierson b Pick	8	– not out	13
B 5, l-b 9, w 1, n-b 18	33	B 6, l-b 17, w 1, n-b 12	36

1/2 2/32 3/42 4/60 5/173   381   1/32 2/176 3/198 4/198 5/202   357
6/261 7/295 8/351 9/368   6/203 7/255 8/285 9/320

Bonus points – Leicestershire 4, Nottinghamshire 4.

Bowling: *First Innings*—Pick 21.5–3–81–3; Mike 23–6–62–0; Evans 27–9–66–3; Chapman 14–2–78–2; Hindson 33–9–80–2. *Second Innings*—Pick 30–4–82–5; Evans 32–7–78–1; Hindson 36–11–111–2; Chapman 13.2–3–63–2.

Nottinghamshire

M. P. Dowman b Mullally	0	– c Nixon b Pierson	27
*R. T. Robinson b Millns	4	– c Smith b Dakin	9
G. F. Archer b Parsons	24	– not out	122
P. Johnson b Mullally	70	– c Cronje b Pierson	0
C. L. Cairns c and b Parsons	99	– c Nixon b Parsons	18
†W. M. Noon b Pierson	45	– c Parsons b Pierson	28
K. P. Evans c Dakin b Pierson	22	– lbw b Dakin	3
J. E. Hindson b Maddy b Pierson	7	– lbw b Parsons	7
G. W. Mike run out	8	– not out	9
R. A. Pick b Millns	18		
R. J. Chapman not out	3		
B 10, l-b 14, w 2, n-b 38	64	B 10, l-b 3, w 6, n-b 4	23

1/9 2/26 3/59 4/209 5/274   364   1/22 2/75 3/75 4/99   (7 wkts) 246
6/309 7/328 8/337 9/348   5/209 6/220 7/235

Bonus points – Nottinghamshire 4, Leicestershire 4.

Bowling: *First Innings*—Mullally 13–0–90–2; Millns 20.5–4–75–2; Parsons 26–8–75–2; Dakin 3–1–14–0; Cronje 5–1–25–0; Pierson 29–8–61–3. *Second Innings*—Millns 8–3–22–0; Parsons 20.4–6–49–2; Dakin 9–2–20–2; Pierson 40–12–104–3; Smith 1–1–0–0; Cronje 9–6–8–0; Maddy 2–0–5–0; Mullally 12–3–25–0.

Umpires: A. A. Jones and M. J. Kitchen.

At Northampton, June 22, 23, 24, 26. LEICESTERSHIRE lost to NORTHAMPTON-SHIRE by an innings and 37 runs.

At Worcester, June 29, 30, July 1, 3. LEICESTERSHIRE lost to WORCESTERSHIRE by 134 runs.

LEICESTERSHIRE v WARWICKSHIRE

At Leicester, July 6, 7. Warwickshire won by an innings and 89 runs. Warwickshire 23 pts, Leicestershire 4 pts. Toss: Leicestershire. First-class debut: C. D. Crowe.

Champions Warwickshire went top of the table, level with Northamptonshire, and gave themselves two days off, after completing victory inside two days. It was Leicestershire's third successive defeat and the nadir of their season. Fielding one of their most inexperienced line-ups because of a worsening injury crisis – Whitaker, Cronje and Millns were all sidelined and they introduced 19-year-old all-rounder Carl Crowe – Leicestershire were skittled twice for next to nothing. Their second-innings 67 was the performance of a demoralised team. Warwickshire captain Reeve was the destroyer in the first innings, with a spell of four for seven in 12 overs of his medium-pace swing. In the second it was Munton with four for 14. Leicestershire's predicament was summed up by their failure to deliver a telling blow when their opponents were on the ropes. At 211 for eight, Warwickshire led by only 60. But a 51-ball 67 by Neil Smith, assisted by Donald in a stand of 92, swung the game inexorably away from them.

Close of play: First day, Warwickshire 102-3 (D. P. Ostler 45*, R. G. Twose 12*).

Leicestershire

T. J. Boon lbw b Donald	6	– b Brown		12
*N. E. Briers c Piper b Donald	7	– lbw b Reeve		13
V. J. Wells b Brown	17	– c Knight b Munton		10
B. F. Smith c Ostler b Reeve	0	– absent hurt		
D. L. Maddy c Ostler b Reeve	0	– (4) run out		0
C. D. Crowe lbw b Reeve	1	– b Munton		9
†P. A. Nixon not out	37	– (5) run out		13
V. P. Clarke b Brown	0	– (7) c Knight b Munton		0
G. J. Parsons b Donald	42	– (8) c Knight b Munton		0
A. R. K. Pierson c Piper b Donald	0	– (9) not out		6
A. D. Mullally c Khan b Munton	5	– (10) c Penney b Reeve		0
B 2, l-b 12, n-b 12	26	B 1, l-b 1, n-b 2		4

1/8 2/24 3/44 4/44 5/52
6/52 7/56 8/142 9/142   151

1/26 2/30 3/32 4/47 5/53
6/53 7/53 8/66 9/67   67

Bonus points – Warwickshire 4.

Bowling: *First Innings*—Donald 21–9–38–3; Munton 11.5–5–25–1; Reeve 23–13–30–4; Brown 14–8–22–2; Smith 8–1–22–0. *Second Innings*—Donald 6–3–15–0; Munton 10–4–14–4; Reeve 10.4–4–17–2; Brown 8–2–16–1; Smith 3–1–3–0.

Warwickshire

N. V. Knight b Mullally	21	N. M. K. Smith not out	67
W. G. Khan b Parsons	1	A. A. Donald c Crowe b Pierson	24
D. P. Ostler c Nixon b Mullally	59	T. A. Munton b Pierson	4
T. L. Penney b Pierson	14		
R. G. Twose lbw b Parsons	33	B 8, l-b 7, n-b 6	21
*D. A. Reeve c Maddy b Parsons	14		
D. R. Brown c Wells b Pierson	44	1/26 2/26 3/65 4/117 5/146	307
†K. J. Piper b Parsons	5	6/197 7/206 8/211 9/303	

Bonus points – Warwickshire 3, Leicestershire 4.

Bowling: Mullally 27–11–76–2; Parsons 23–7–70–4; Pierson 34.4–10–107–4; Clarke 7–0–35–0; Crowe 3–2–4–0.

Umpires: V. A. Holder and B. Leadbeater.

At Hove, July 20, 21, 22, 24. LEICESTERSHIRE beat SUSSEX by 63 runs.

LEICESTERSHIRE v SURREY

At Leicester, July 27, 28, 29. Leicestershire won by an innings and 37 runs. Leicestershire 24 pts, Surrey 4 pts. Toss: Leicestershire.

Despite rumblings of dressing-room discontent about manager Jack Birkenshaw's role, Leicestershire romped to a second successive win, before tea on the third day. The pairing of Cronje, back after injury, and Macmillan, arrived from Oxford, had lifted their confidence. At Hove, they had added 137 together; here they set up a match-winning total of 503. Cronje's 163 was his third and highest Championship hundred, but it was the flamboyant, unorthodox Macmillan who dominated a third-wicket stand of 195. His career-best 122 was his third century in successive games, starting with the University Match at Lord's. Off-spinner Pierson then destroyed Surrey on a turning pitch. He claimed five wickets in the first innings to make them follow on, and another four took him to 50 in a season for the first time in his 11-year career. He and Mullally had reduced Surrey to 126 for eight second time round when Tudor came in – he hit a maiden fifty and almost doubled the total with Kersey and Rackemann.

Close of play: First day, Leicestershire 431-7 (G. J. Parsons 22*, A. R. K. Pierson 2*); Second day, Surrey 202-9 (G. J. Kersey 8*, C. G. Rackemann 8*).

Leicestershire

*N. E. Briers c Kersey b Tudor	37	A. R. K. Pierson c Kersey	
I. J. Sutcliffe c Kersey b M. P. Bicknell	8	b M. P. Bicknell	18
G. I. Macmillan c Nowell b Smith	122	A. D. Mullally b M. P. Bicknell	0
W. J. Cronje c Kersey b Smith	163	M. T. Brimson c Rackemann b Nowell	25
B. F. Smith lbw b M. P. Bicknell	51	L-b 4, w 2, n-b 18	24
V. J. Wells b M. P. Bicknell	8		
†P. A. Nixon c Kersey b Smith	2	1/16 2/64 3/259 4/358 5/370	503
G. J. Parsons not out	45	6/373 7/426 8/463 9/467	

Bonus points – Leicestershire 4, Surrey 3 (Score at 120 overs: 458-7).

Bowling: Rackemann 22-3-55-0; M. P. Bicknell 34-3-117-5; Tudor 15-1-57-1; Hol lioake 13-2-55-0; Nowell 19.3-2-93-1; Smith 24-1-112-3; Shahid 4-1-10-0.

Surrey

D. J. Bicknell c Cronje b Pierson	6	– c Cronje b Pierson	18
M. A. Butcher c Parsons b Pierson	65	– lbw b Mullally	19
A. W. Smith lbw b Parsons	15	– c Nixon b Mullally	0
A. D. Brown b Pierson	5	– b Pierson	4
N. Shahid c Nixon b Pierson	51	– c Macmillan b Mullally	48
*A. J. Hollioake lbw b Parsons	7	– lbw b Pierson	4
†G. J. Kersey not out	18	– c Nixon b Mullally	54
M. P. Bicknell b Wells	4	– c Macmillan b Pierson	13
R. W. Nowell c Parsons b Pierson	4	– b Mullally	0
A. J. Tudor c Nixon b Wells	15	– c Pierson b Brimson	56
C. G. Rackemann c Wells b Pierson	12	– not out	20
B 3, l-b 7, w 2, n-b 4	16	B 7, l-b 3, n-b 2	12
1/14 2/33 3/46 4/151 5/159	218	1/23 2/27 3/32 4/79 5/87	248
6/159 7/167 8/176 9/191		6/107 7/126 8/126 9/191	

Bonus points – Surrey 1, Leicestershire 4.

Bowling: *First Innings*—Mullally 14.5-5-35-0; Parsons 20-10-46-3; Pierson 38.1-10-80-5; Cronje 4-1-17-0; Brimson 6-2-7-0; Wells 7-2-23-2. *Second Innings*—Mullally 18-9-47-5; Parsons 8-2-27-0; Pierson 25.4-4-133-4; Brimson 5.2-2-31-1.

Umpires: B. Dudleston and J. W. Holder.

At Leicester, August 3, 4. LEICESTERSHIRE beat YOUNG AUSTRALIA by four wickets (See Young Australia tour section).

LEICESTERSHIRE v LANCASHIRE

At Leicester, August 10, 11, 12. Lancashire won by four wickets. Lancashire 23 pts, Leicestershire 5 pts. Toss: Leicestershire.

Leicestershire's mini-revival was brought to a shuddering halt by a superb one-man show from Pakistani all-rounder Wasim Akram. Captaining Lancashire for only the second time, in the absence of England trio Watkinson, Atherton and Crawley, he took 12 wickets and hit a match-winning unbeaten half-century. He came in when his team, chasing 215, were struggling at 143 for five, and hit 50 off just 35 balls, including 11 fours. Despite fine fifties from Whitaker – whose toe was broken by a yorker from Wasim – Cronje and Wells, Leicestershire's first-innings 235 was well below par after they elected to bat. But it was not until a ninth-wicket stand of 61 in 11 overs between Martin and Yates that Lancashire took the lead. Another half-century from Wells helped Leicestershire to 282 at their second attempt, giving them something to bowl at, but Wasim rose to the challenge. This was the sixth Championship match at Grace Road in 1995 to end inside three days.

Close of play: First day, Lancashire 46-1 (J. E. R. Gallian 18*); Second day, Leicestershire 157-4 (V. J. Wells 63*, A. R. K. Pierson 7*).

Leicestershire

G. I. Macmillan lbw b Wasim Akram	2	– lbw b Wasim Akram	0
*N. E. Briers c Fairbrother b Wasim Akram	12	– c Lloyd b Wasim Akram	1
J. J. Whitaker c Martin b Wasim Akram	63	– (7) b Martin	26
W. J. Cronje lbw b Keedy	55	– b Wasim Akram	13
B. F. Smith lbw b Wasim Akram	1	– lbw b Wasim Akram	53
V. J. Wells c Fairbrother b Austin	78	– (3) c Hegg b Austin	78
†P. A. Nixon lbw b Wasim Akram	0	– (8) lbw b Wasim Akram	4
G. J. Parsons b Yates	11	– (9) not out	32
A. R. K. Pierson not out	24	– (6) c Hegg b Martin	24
A. D. Mullally b Austin	0	– b Wasim Akram	4
A. Sheriyar b Wasim Akram	1	– c Fairbrother b Austin	9
B 2, l-b 6, w 1, n-b 8	17	B 1, l-b 19, n-b 18	38
	235		**282**

1/2 2/23 3/127 4/138 5/145
6/148 7/171 8/226 9/226

1/0 2/17 3/45 4/148 5/188
6/221 7/232 8/236 9/253

Bonus points – Leicestershire 1, Lancashire 4.

Bowling: *First Innings*—Wasim Akram 20-4-72-6; Martin 11-3-34-0; Austin 17-7-39-2; Gallian 3-0-13-0; Yates 17-9-33-1; Keedy 19-8-36-1. *Second Innings*—Wasim Akram 27-5-93-6; Martin 15-4-47-2; Austin 21-1-79-2; Keedy 18-8-43-0; Gallian 2-2-0-0.

Lancashire

J. E. R. Gallian lbw b Mullally	76	– c Macmillan b Parsons	47
S. P. Titchard lbw b Pierson	21	– b Sheriyar	5
N. J. Speak c Macmillan b Mullally	4	– lbw b Pierson	64
N. H. Fairbrother c Nixon b Mullally	13	– c Macmillan b Pierson	8
G. D. Lloyd lbw b Wells	35	– b Wells	8
†W. K. Hegg b Pierson	26	– c and b Pierson	7
*Wasim Akram c Sheriyar b Mullally	7	– not out	50
I. D. Austin b Sheriyar	10	– not out	13
P. J. Martin c Nixon b Wells	41		
G. Yates c Pierson b Wells	41		
G. Keedy not out	3		
B 1, l-b 8, w 5, n-b 12	26	B 15, l-b 1	16
	303	(6 wkts)	**218**

1/46 2/51 3/73 4/148 5/168
6/183 7/207 8/225 9/286

1/19 2/101 3/120
4/139 5/143 6/162

Bonus points – Lancashire 3, Leicestershire 4.

Bowling: *First Innings*—Mullally 24-6-64-4; Sheriyar 17-3-50-1; Parsons 3-0-5-0; Pierson 22-2-110-2; Cronje 15-6-37-0; Wells 7.1-2-28-3. *Second Innings*—Mullally 8-5-12-0; Sheriyar 7-1-15-1; Cronje 5-1-16-0; Pierson 21.4-3-99-3; Parsons 14-4-41-1; Wells 5-1-19-1.

Umpires: G. I. Burgess and R. A. White.

At Weston-super-Mare, August 24, 25, 26, 28. LEICESTERSHIRE beat SOMERSET by two wickets.

LEICESTERSHIRE v GLAMORGAN

At Leicester, August 29, 30, 31, September 1. Leicestershire won by six wickets. Leicestershire 22 pts, Glamorgan 6 pts. Toss: Glamorgan.

Leicestershire, hardly renowned as run-chasers, probably surprised even themselves with some spectacular hitting. After a washed-out first day, three declarations created a cracking finale. Morris set Leicestershire 283 off what became 69 overs – a tempting target on a flat pitch. But they were in a rut at 138 for three against some tight bowling. Then Cronje and Smith took Glamorgan's attack apart, smashing 130 off 15 overs, and Leicestershire eased to victory with more than seven overs to spare. Cronje, trying out a new heavy bat, hit eight fours and four sixes in a 96-ball 99. Though he fell just short of a fifth hundred, he received a standing ovation for what turned out to be the final innings of his season at Grace Road. Batsmen prospered from the start: for Glamorgan, James batted throughout the second day for 230 from 328 balls, his maiden double-hundred. He added 242 in 54 overs with Maynard, and later Macmillan and Briers shared Leicestershire's only century opening partnership of the season.

Close of play: First day, No play; Second day, Glamorgan 439-5 (S. P. James 230*, R. D. B. Croft 43*); Third day, Glamorgan 22-0 (S. P. James 12*, H. Morris 9*).

Glamorgan

S. P. James not out	230	– b Pierson	22
*H. Morris c Macmillan b Parsons	9	– c Cronje b Pierson	61
D. L. Hemp b Mullally	9	– c Cronje b Pierson	8
M. P. Maynard b Brimson	103	– c and b Parsons	53
A. J. Dalton b Mullally	9	– b Pierson	8
A. Dale c Nixon b Cronje	8	– not out	30
R. D. B. Croft not out	43	– not out	5
B 12, l-b 8, n-b 8	28	B 5, l-b 2	7

1/24 2/60 3/302 4/350 5/367 (5 wkts dec.) 439   1/38 2/52 3/131 (5 wkts dec.) 194
4/144 5/177

†C. P. Metson, S. L. Watkin, S. R. Barwick and S. D. Thomas did not bat.

Bonus points – Glamorgan 4, Leicestershire 2.

Bowling: *First Innings*—Mullally 30-7-132-2; Parsons 23-5-99-1; Cronje 25-8-56-1; Pierson 11-1-53-0; Dakin 3-0-23-0; Brimson 18-2-56-1. *Second Innings*—Mullally 2-1-2-0; Parsons 22-5-97-1; Dakin 2-0-8-0; Pierson 19-2-80-4.

Leicestershire

G. I. Macmillan c Watkin b Croft	85	– c Maynard b Watkin	10
*N. E. Briers b Dale	73		
J. J. Whitaker c Dalton b Barwick	29	– b Croft	65
W. J. Cronje c Hemp b Thomas	47	– c Thomas b Croft	99
B. F. Smith b Barwick	94	– not out	62
J. M. Dakin lbw b Barwick	5	– not out	7
†P. A. Nixon not out	5	– (2) c James b Thomas	26
L-b 5, n-b 8	13	B 4, l-b 10, n-b 2	16

1/153 2/195 3/197 4/298 (6 wkts dec.) 351   1/16 2/91 (4 wkts) 285
5/328 6/351   3/138 4/268

G. J. Parsons, A. R. K. Pierson, A. D. Mullally and M. T. Brimson did not bat.

Bonus points – Leicestershire 4, Glamorgan 2.

Bowling: *First Innings*—Watkin 7–1–34–0; Thomas 21–5–83–1; Barwick 26.5–7–78–3; Croft 37–5–131–1; Dale 7–0–20–1. *Second Innings*—Watkin 10–2–49–1; Barwick 25–7–87–0; Croft 18.3–1–96–2; Thomas 8–1–39–1.

Umpires: H. D. Bird and R. A. White.

At Uxbridge, September 7, 8, 9, 11. LEICESTERSHIRE lost to MIDDLESEX by one run.

LEICESTERSHIRE v GLOUCESTERSHIRE

At Leicester, September 14, 15, 16, 18. Drawn. Leicestershire 4 pts. Toss: Gloucestershire.
Leicestershire had to settle for seventh place after losing this match to the weather. Victory would have meant leapfrogging Gloucestershire into fifth place and £4,000 prize money, to cushion the £6,000 fine they were due to receive for a slow over-rate. They held the advantage at the end of the first day. Led by Whitaker, just appointed captain to succeed Briers, who was standing down after six years, Leicestershire bowled out Glamorgan for 196 – a collapse from 94 without loss – and then reached 57 for one, before rain intervened, terminally.

Close of play: First day, Leicestershire 57-1 (G. I. Macmillan 19*, B. F. Smith 9*); Second day, No play; Third day, No play.

Gloucestershire

A. J. Wright lbw b Parsons	40	J. Lewis c Dakin b Brimson	3
R. J. Cunliffe c Parsons b Pierson	42	K. E. Cooper lbw b Parsons	2
T. H. C. Hancock c Cronje b Mullally	29	K. P. Sheeraz not out	0
M. A. Lynch lbw b Pierson	3		
M. W. Alleyne c Smith b Pierson	10	B 4, l-b 3, w 3, n-b 4	14
A. Symonds lbw b Mullally	13		
*†R. C. Russell c Cronje b Parsons	30	1/94 2/104 3/132 4/133 5/150	196
M. C. J. Ball c Dakin b Brimson	10	6/168 7/191 8/194 9/194	

Bonus points – Leicestershire 4.

A. J. Wright, when 39, retired hurt at 74 and resumed at 150.

Bowling: Mullally 15–2–53–2; Parsons 20.3–7–44–3; Cronje 5–1–10–0; Dakin 5–1–13–0; Brimson 9–5–11–2; Wells 4–0–8–0; Pierson 20–6–50–3.

Leicestershire

V. J. Wells b Cooper	22
G. I. Macmillan not out	19
B. F. Smith not out	9
L-b 3, n-b 4	7

1/38   (1 wkt) 57

*J. J. Whitaker, W. J. Cronje, J. M. Dakin, †P. A. Nixon, G. J. Parsons, A. R. K. Pierson, M. T. Brimson and A. D. Mullally did not bat.

Bowling: Lewis 9–1–17–0; Sheeraz 4–0–28–0; Cooper 5–2–9–1.

Umpires: H. D. Bird and J. H. Harris.

MIDDLESEX

Patron: HRH The Duke of Edinburgh
President: D. C. S. Compton
Chairman: R. V. C. Robins
Chairman, Cricket Committee: R. A. Gale
Secretary: J. Hardstaff
Captain: M. W. Gatting
Coach: D. Bennett
Scorer: M. J. Smith

Middlesex came desperately close to winning their eighth Championship in 20 years in 1995 and they made Warwickshire wait until the very last round to be sure of retaining their title. Warwickshire had struck the first blow, back in April, beating them heavily at Edgbaston. But after a moderate start – they were halfway down the table after four matches – Middlesex gained such momentum that, from mid-June, they recorded eight successive wins, the best sequence by any county in 40 years.

That run was checked by a draw with Northamptonshire, when two contenders effectively fought each other to a standstill. Just as Warwickshire were uncorking the champagne, however, Middlesex conjured a thrilling one-run win over Leicestershire. They travelled to Taunton for the last game 15 points adrift. But rain in Somerset and Kent's feeble performance against Warwickshire kept them in second place – their fifth finish in the top four in seven years.

The Somerset match was John Emburey's last for the county he joined in 1973. He began a new career in coaching by taking England A to Pakistan and it was soon confirmed that he would become Northamptonshire's chief coach in 1996. In 23 seasons, he had taken 1,250 first-class wickets at 24.06 for Middlesex. He was still their most successful bowler in 1995, with 74 wickets. His departure seemed likely to turn the following season into a watershed year and give some younger players a chance to show their worth.

The county had already had the difficult task of replacing openers Desmond Haynes and Mike Roseberry. The initial experiment of Mike Gatting opening with Jason Pooley did not work. Gatting never looked happy and his elevation deprived the upper-middle order of its solidity. After their erratic early form, Middlesex's season took a turn for the better at Chelmsford, when Toby Radford opened successfully and Gatting seemed more comfortable at No. 3. Then came the run of eight victories. There were two apparent reasons for this turnaround: the promotion of Paul Weekes to open with Pooley and the astonishing form of Mark Ramprakash after his pair against West Indies in the Lord's Test. In his next match, he scored 214 against Surrey and embarked on a remarkable sequence of nine centuries in 14 Championship innings. He passed 2,000 runs for the first time, finished top of the national averages, and was included in the England party to tour South Africa.

Not surprisingly, Ramprakash was named Middlesex's Player of the Year. But for him, though, Pooley might have been in contention. He made nearly 1,200 Championship runs and four centuries, and his years of patient waiting were rewarded with a call-up for the England A tour. His partnership with Weekes gave the team some excellent starts. Impetuosity sometimes proved their downfall, but they were seen at their best against Northamptonshire, when they made a superb assault on an unlikely – and ultimately unattainable – target.

Spin continued to dominate the Middlesex attack. Emburey and Philip Tufnell were the leading wicket-takers, with a combined total of 142 at only 22.12 in the Championship. Emburey was even picked for the Fourth Test, at the age of 42, though Tufnell was still out of favour; he was summoned for the Oval Test but sent away again. With Emburey gone, it would be helpful if Weekes could take more responsibility as an off-spinner, but so far his wickets have proved costly.

Angus Fraser remained his reliable self between Test calls and, when he played, Richard Johnson confirmed the promise of 1994. But injury restricted him to nine Championship appearances and forced him out of England's tour, for which he was a surprise selection. It must be hoped that a winter's rest will bring a complete recovery. Chas Taylor had to retire, having failed to recover fully from a freak accident the previous season, and Kevin Shine was released.

Perhaps too much was expected of him, but New Zealander Dion Nash was a disappointment. He started well, with nine wickets in his second game, against Hampshire, but his next nine first-class matches brought him only 16 wickets at 48 apiece. His bowling looked up in August, when he took eight against Durham, but his batting was even more disappointing: some wondered whether he would have retained his place had he not been the overseas player. What must be borne in mind is that Nash has had very limited experience for a 23-year-old. In England, cricketers have a chance to play professionally from their teens. Before joining Middlesex, Nash had made ten Test appearances, but only 37 in first-class matches. By comparison, Dominic Cork of Derbyshire, three months older and a not dissimilar player, had 83 games under his belt. Middlesex showed faith in Nash and renewed his contract, hoping he would have learned from his first county season.

Keith Brown contributed usefully in the middle order, while his wicket-keeping was adequate. For a side that relies so much on spin, a specialist keeper might seem a better idea but, for all his lack of style, Brown misses very few chances. Cover was available from Paul Farbrace and, for the future, 17-year-old David Nash, whom coach Don Bennett has described as "a rare wicket-keeping talent". He played promisingly for England Under-19. Mark Feltham once again proved to be a useful "bits and pieces" cricketer but he is another who should score more runs. John Carr, following his storming end to 1994, just scraped past 1,000 in all first-class cricket but played several significant innings and took 39 excellent catches. Meanwhile, Gatting passed 1,000 runs for the 17th time in an English season, at an average of 54.23. In September, he was confirmed as captain for a 14th year.

It was difficult to explain how a team which played such good Championship cricket could play with such embarrassing ineptitude on Sundays. Only a win at Taunton on the last day enabled Middlesex to escape bottom place. The county did take the opportunity to blood young players: wicket-keeper Nash, Owais Shah, aged 16, Umer Rashid (19), James Hewitt (19) and Ricky Fay (21), all of whom gave cause for optimism. Form in the knockouts was little better. Middlesex reached both quarter-finals, but their batting performances at Canterbury in the Benson and Hedges Cup and at Cardiff in the NatWest Trophy were bitterly disappointing, when they fell some way short of apparently straightforward targets. – *Norman de Mesquita.*

MIDDLESEX 1995

[*Bill Smith*]

Back row: K. P. Dutch, A. A. Khan, D. Follett, J. C. Pooley, P. N. Weekes, T. A. Radford. *Middle row*: D. Bennett (*coach*), M. A. Feltham, R. L. Johnson, D. J. Nash, C. W. Taylor, K. Marc, K. J. Shine, J. C. Harrison, P. Farbrace, A. Jones (*Second Eleven scorer*), I. J. Gould (*assistant coach*). *Front row*: M. R. Ramprakash, J. E. Emburey, M. W. Gatting (*captain*), J. D. Carr, A. R. C. Fraser, K. R. Brown. *Insets*: M. J. Smith (*First Eleven scorer*), P. C. R. Tufnell, U. B. A. Rashid, D. C. Nash.

MIDDLESEX RESULTS

All first-class matches – Played 20: Won 12, Lost 2, Drawn 6.

County Championship matches – Played 17: Won 12, Lost 2, Drawn 3.

Bonus points – Batting 51, Bowling 62.

*Competition placings – Britannic Assurance County Championship, 2nd;
NatWest Bank Trophy, q-f; Benson and Hedges Cup, q-f;
AXA Equity & Law League, 17th.*

BRITANNIC ASSURANCE CHAMPIONSHIP AVERAGES
BATTING

	Birthplace	M	I	NO	R	HS	Avge
‡M. R. Ramprakash .	Bushey	16	26	3	2,147	235	93.34
‡M. W. Gatting	Kingsbury	16	22	1	1,139	148	54.23
‡J. C. Pooley	Hammersmith	16	27	3	1,181	136	49.20
‡K. R. Brown	Edmonton	17	25	4	894	147*	42.57
‡J. D. Carr	St John's Wood	17	26	5	830	129	39.52
T. A. Radford	Caerphilly	3	5	1	122	69	30.50
‡P. N. Weekes......	Hackney	17	27	1	771	127*	29.65
‡J. E. Emburey......	Peckham	16	19	1	379	87	21.05
‡D. J. Nash§	Auckland, NZ	17	22	3	351	67	18.47
‡M. A. Feltham	St John's Wood	12	13	4	97	25	10.77
‡R. L. Johnson......	Chertsey	9	10	0	92	25	9.20
‡P. C. R. Tufnell...	Barnet	16	14	6	65	23*	8.12
‡A. R. C. Fraser	Billinge	12	13	4	73	20	8.11

Also batted: R. A. Fay (*Kilburn*) (1 match) 1*; D. Follett (*Newcastle-under-Lyme*)
(1 match) 1, 4*. A. A. Khan (*Lahore, Pakistan*) (1 match) did not bat.

* Signifies not out. ‡ *Denotes county cap.* § *Overseas player.*

The following played a total of 23 three-figure innings for Middlesex in County
Championship matches – M. R. Ramprakash 10, M. W. Gatting 5, J. C. Pooley 4, J. D.
Carr 2, K. R. Brown 1, P. N. Weekes 1.

BOWLING

	O	M	R	W	BB	5W/i	Avge
R. L. Johnson	222.5	58	596	36	5-48	2	16.55
J. E. Emburey	678.4	191	1,619	74	7-82	5	21.87
P. C. R. Tufnell	638.1	199	1,523	68	5-74	4	22.39
A. R. C. Fraser	404.2	104	1,069	40	5-56	1	26.72
D. J. Nash	424.2	85	1,388	51	5-35	2	27.21
M. A. Feltham	229.3	58	675	21	4-55	0	32.14
P. N. Weekes	172.4	36	449	10	3-26	0	44.90

Also bowled: K. R. Brown 15-0-114-1; R. A. Fay 3-0-25-0; D. Follett 30-6-95-1;
M. W. Gatting 5-0-31-0; A. A. Khan 2-2-0-0; J. C. Pooley 4-0-15-0; M. R. Ramprakash
20-3-91-3.

Wicket-keepers: K. R. Brown 43 ct, 5 st; M. W. Gatting 1 ct.

Leading Fielders: J. D. Carr 32, J. C. Pooley 25, J. E. Emburey 17, P. N. Weekes 15.

At Birmingham, April 27, 28, 29, 30. MIDDLESEX lost to WARWICKSHIRE by 215 runs.

MIDDLESEX v HAMPSHIRE

At Lord's, May 4, 5, 6. Middlesex won by 205 runs. Middlesex 20 pts, Hampshire 4 pts. Toss: Middlesex.

Except on the second afternoon, when Ramprakash and Carr added 253 at more than four an over, the bowlers held sway in this match. The umpires saw fit to report the pitch, which was judged "poor", carrying the suspended threat of a ten-point penalty even though MCC rather than Middlesex are in charge of preparation. But the batsmen's difficulties owed more to the heavy, humid atmosphere. Stephenson's swing earned a career-best analysis; his seven wickets all came for 17 runs in 52 balls as Middlesex collapsed from 153 for two to 189 all out. Nash and Feltham also benefited from the overcast conditions and six Hampshire wickets fell by the close. Next morning, Tufnell mopped up the tail to give Middlesex a first-innings lead of 20; neither side gained a batting point. Batting was easier when Middlesex resumed and Hampshire's attack looked inept with Ramprakash in such fine form. Gatting left a target of 448; Terry and Morris opened well and Smith scored 75, but Nash took his match haul to nine as Middlesex won inside three days.

Close of play: First day, Hampshire 105-6 (A. N. Aymes 15*, S. D. Udal 13*); Second day, Middlesex 342-3 (M. R. Ramprakash 128*, P. N. Weekes 6*).

Middlesex

*M. W. Gatting c Aymes b Connor	27	– b Bovill	33
J. C. Pooley c Udal b Connor	11	– c Aymes b Streak	30
M. R. Ramprakash c Terry b Stephenson	71	– not out	163
J. D. Carr b Stephenson	29	– c and b Connor	129
P. N. Weekes c Aymes b Stephenson	7	– c and b Stephenson	24
†K. R. Brown c Aymes b Stephenson	3	– lbw b Bovill	14
D. J. Nash lbw b Stephenson	2	– b Connor	0
M. A. Feltham c Terry b Connor	12	– not out	10
J. E. Emburey c White b Stephenson	2		
A. R. C. Fraser c Aymes b Stephenson	0		
P. C. R. Tufnell not out	7		
L-b 9, w 3, n-b 6	18	B 7, l-b 10, w 1, n-b 6	24

1/29 2/62 3/153 4/158 5/164   189   1/65 2/69 3/322   (6 wkts dec.) 427
6/166 7/167 8/173 9/181   4/365 5/400 6/413

Bonus points – Hampshire 4.

Bowling: *First Innings*—Connor 22-8-44-3; Streak 7-0-37-0; Bovill 10-1-40-0; Stephenson 18-4-51-7; Udal 4-1-8-0. *Second Innings*—Connor 30-3-113-2; Streak 26-6-80-1; Bovill 20.2-3-64-2; Stephenson 19-1-90-1; Udal 6-1-25-0; White 3-0-22-0; Nicholas 5-0-16-0.

Hampshire

V. P. Terry c Gatting b Feltham	14	– (2) lbw b Nash	30
R. S. M. Morris c Brown b Feltham	16	– (1) lbw b Nash	41
G. W. White c Brown b Nash	15	– lbw b Nash	6
R. A. Smith c Emburey b Nash	15	– b Fraser	75
*M. C. J. Nicholas c Gatting b Nash	6	– c Pooley b Fraser	5
†A. N. Aymes not out	35	– (7) c Pooley b Nash	2
J. P. Stephenson c and b Emburey	7	– (6) st Brown b Emburey	25
S. D. Udal c Emburey b Nash	30	– c Brown b Nash	0
H. H. Streak c Weekes b Tufnell	10	– b Fraser	9
C. A. Connor b Nash	0	– c Feltham b Tufnell	22
J. N. B. Bovill lbw b Tufnell	15	– not out	9
L-b 4, n-b 2	6	B 5, l-b 3, n-b 10	18

1/29 2/34 3/55 4/66 5/69   169   1/72 2/79 3/100 4/114 5/168   242
6/86 7/129 8/147 9/147   6/201 7/201 8/201 9/226

Bonus points – Middlesex 4.

Bowling: *First Innings*—Fraser 20–6–46–0; Nash 20–6–61–4; Emburey 11–4–17–1; Feltham 14–6–25–2; Tufnell 5.2–1–16–3. *Second Innings*—Fraser 19–3–60–3; Nash 13–4–35–5; Emburey 13–2–44–1; Tufnell 17–4–55–1; Weekes 1–0–4–0; Feltham 5–1–36–0.

Umpires: J. H. Harris and R. Palmer.

At Worcester, May 11, 12, 13, 15. MIDDLESEX beat WORCESTERSHIRE by an innings and 30 runs.

MIDDLESEX v LANCASHIRE

At Lord's, May 18, 19, 20. Lancashire won by an innings and 175 runs. Lancashire 24 pts, Middlesex 4 pts. Toss: Lancashire.

This match was reminiscent of Lancashire's last Championship victory at Lord's, in 1989, when DeFreitas and Patterson destroyed Middlesex for 96 and 43. A similar demolition was carried out by Wasim Akram, with nine for 63 in the match, supported by Martin, just named in England's one-day squad, and Chapple. Despite losing Gallian in the second over, Atherton, acting captain for the injured Watkinson, and Crawley put on 114 for Lancashire by lunch and, despite a wobble in the afternoon, Lloyd helped the last five wickets more than double the total to 375. But Middlesex batted dreadfully, with only three players reaching double figures. They were following on less than half an hour into the third day and – even allowing for good bowling – were almost as bad the second time. Only a few lusty blows by Emburey prevented the Lancashire players watching Manchester United and Everton kick off in the FA Cup final. But they were in front of their television, having completed their third straight Championship win, by five past three.

Close of play: First day, Lancashire 338-9 (G. Chapple 17*, G. Yates 7*); Second day, Middlesex 78-7 (K. R. Brown 10*).

Lancashire

*M. A. Atherton c Brown b Nash	54	P. J. Martin b Emburey		35
J. E. R. Gallian c Emburey b Nash	0	G. Chapple not out		40
J. P. Crawley c Brown b Nash	55	G. Yates c Brown b Johnson		21
N. H. Fairbrother c Nash b Feltham	31			
N. J. Speak c Brown b Johnson	16	B 4, l-b 5, n-b 8		17
G. D. Lloyd c Ramprakash b Emburey	75			
Wasim Akram lbw b Emburey	11	1/2 2/114 3/121 4/155 5/184		375
†W. K. Hegg c Brown b Johnson	20	6/235 7/258 8/282 9/330		

Bonus points – Lancashire 4, Middlesex 4.

Bowling: Fraser 24–7–85–0; Nash 23–4–85–3; Johnson 22.3–3–67–3; Feltham 17–3–62–1; Weekes 8–2–16–0; Emburey 17–5–51–3.

Middlesex

*M. W. Gatting lbw b Wasim Akram	3	– c Martin b Wasim Akram	0
J. C. Pooley b Chapple	7	– c Speak b Wasim Akram	2
M. R. Ramprakash c Atherton b Wasim Akram	0	– c Crawley b Martin	1
J. D. Carr lbw b Wasim Akram	8	– c and b Gallian	12
P. N. Weekes b Martin	27	– b Chapple	16
†K. R. Brown c Gallian b Wasim Akram	19	– c Crawley b Chapple	18
D. J. Nash c Yates b Gallian	15	– c Gallian b Chapple	6
R. L. Johnson b Wasim Akram	1	– c Chapple b Wasim Akram	4
J. E. Emburey c Hegg b Wasim Akram	0	– c sub b Martin	25
M. A. Feltham not out	1	– not out	13
A. R. C. Fraser c Atherton b Gallian	0	– lbw b Martin	0
L-b 5, n-b 2	7	B 2, l-b 4, w 1, n-b 8	15
1/6 2/6 3/18 4/34 5/51	88	1/0 2/3 3/3 4/26 5/40	112
6/77 7/78 8/78 9/87		6/56 7/68 8/68 9/112	

Bonus points – Lancashire 4.

Bowling: *First Innings*—Wasim Akram 19–4–35–6; Martin 16–9–10–1; Chapple 8–4–14–1; Gallian 10.5–3–24–2. *Second Innings*—Wasim Akram 12–4–28–3; Martin 9.3–3–31–3; Chapple 13–4–27–3; Gallian 7–1–20–1.

Umpires: J. D. Bond and A. A. Jones.

At Chelmsford, May 25, 26, 27, 29. MIDDLESEX beat ESSEX by ten wickets.

MIDDLESEX v DERBYSHIRE

At Lord's, June 1, 2, 3, 5. Drawn. Middlesex 4 pts, Derbyshire 6 pts. Toss: Derbyshire.

Derbyshire's slow scoring on the first day and the loss of the third to rain made a result unlikely. Barnett's lunchtime declaration on Monday set a target of 303 in 71 overs, but that did not appeal to Middlesex and time was called with 14 overs unbowled. Derbyshire might still have won had Cullinan run out Ramprakash on 22, but he survived and batted through to the end. The opening day belonged to Wells, who put a dreadful 1994 behind him with 81, his third score over fifty in successive matches. He helped Derbyshire to 267, though it took them nearly 119 overs. Middlesex scored more quickly, but lost wickets at frequent intervals, conceded a first-innings deficit of 93 and failed to gain a batting point for the third successive home game. Only Pooley stood firm, becoming the first man to carry his bat for Middlesex since Wilf Slack, at Headingley in 1986.

Close of play: First day, Derbyshire 258-6 (D. G. Cork 28*, K. M. Krikken 20*); Second day, Derbyshire 83-1 (W. A. Dessaur 35*, A. S. Rollins 29*); Third day, No play.

Derbyshire

*K. J. Barnett c Carr b Feltham	30	– c Brown b Fraser	14
W. A. Dessaur b Fraser	4	– not out	84
A. S. Rollins b Emburey	61	– b Nash	72
D. J. Cullinan lbw b Feltham	10		
C. M. Wells lbw b Fraser	81	– (4) lbw b Fraser	22
D. G. Cork c Ramprakash b Fraser	28		
P. A. J. DeFreitas lbw b Emburey	2		
†K. M. Krikken b Fraser	24		
P. Aldred c Carr b Nash	5		
A. E. Warner not out	0		
D. E. Malcolm c Emburey b Nash	0		
L-b 8, n-b 14	22	B 1, l-b 8, w 4, n-b 4	17
	267	(3 wkts dec.)	**209**

1/5 2/69 3/89 4/199 5/207 6/214 7/262 8/263 9/267

1/26 2/151 3/209

Bonus points – Derbyshire 2, Middlesex 4.

Bowling: *First Innings*—Fraser 24–10–39–4; Nash 21.2–5–50–2; Feltham 16–4–44–2; Emburey 28–10–52–2; Tufnell 23–10–54–0; Weekes 6–0–20–0. *Second Innings*—Fraser 20.1–1–64–2; Nash 15–1–46–1; Emburey 13–4–30–0; Tufnell 11–5–13–0; Feltham 10–2–26–0; Weekes 10–3–21–0.

Middlesex

T. A. Radford c Rollins b DeFreitas	1	– c Krikken b Warner	10
J. C. Pooley not out	85	– lbw b DeFreitas	3
M. R. Ramprakash c Rollins b Cork	23	– not out	75
*J. D. Carr c Rollins b Warner	8	– c Krikken b Cork	7
P. N. Weekes c Rollins b Warner	3	– run out	11
†K. R. Brown c Barnett b Warner	3	– not out	1
D. J. Nash c Krikken b Cork	1		
J. E. Emburey b Malcolm	10		
M. A. Feltham lbw b DeFreitas	2		
A. R. C. Fraser b Malcolm	8		
P. C. R. Tufnell c Krikken b Malcolm	0		
L-b 14, n-b 16	30	L-b 6, w 1, n-b 16	23
	174	(4 wkts)	**130**

1/3 2/42 3/71 4/99 5/103 6/106 7/146 8/155 9/174

1/11 2/41 3/56 4/128

Bonus points – Derbyshire 4.

Bowling: *First Innings*—Malcolm 11.5–3–37–3; DeFreitas 13–4–37–2; Cork 15–4–49–2; Warner 13–3–37–3. *Second Innings*—Malcolm 15–4–30–0; DeFreitas 11–3–20–1; Cork 15–3–39–1; Warner 9–4–15–1; Aldred 6–1–16–0; Barnett 1–0–4–0.

Umpires: K. E. Palmer and R. Palmer.

At Cambridge, June 9, 10, 11. MIDDLESEX drew with CAMBRIDGE UNIVERSITY.

At Colwyn Bay, June 15, 16, 17, 19. MIDDLESEX beat GLAMORGAN by eight wickets.

At Oxford, June 20, 21, 22. MIDDLESEX drew with OXFORD UNIVERSITY.

MIDDLESEX v SURREY

At Lord's, June 29, 30, July 1. Middlesex won by an innings and 76 runs. Middlesex 24 pts, Surrey 2 pts. Toss: Middlesex. First-class debut: A. J. Tudor.

An outstanding double-century from Ramprakash – his second against Surrey – gained Middlesex their first home batting points of 1995. Emburey, with ten for 98, and Tufnell then exploited a deteriorating pitch to dismiss Surrey twice before tea on the third day, pushing them to the bottom of the Championship table. Ramprakash hit 37 fours in 337 balls, adding 104 with Weekes, who scored 62 in his new role as opener, and 217 with Brown, who made a determined 86; the next best was 16 from Gatting. Surrey's attack was far from menacing, although 17-year-old debutant Alex Tudor looked extremely promising as he claimed Pooley, Weekes and, eventually, Ramprakash. Surrey had responded to the team's poor form by dropping both Brown and Darren Bicknell, but the rejigged line-up performed woefully: too many fell to poor shots and they were following on early on the third day. Stewart was soon hit by Johnson on his vulnerable, twice-broken finger but batted on for 15 minutes before retiring. His team-mates showed little sign of lasting into the fourth day so, with the Third Test imminent, he did not risk himself again.

Close of play: First day, Middlesex 356-4 (M. R. Ramprakash 185*, K. R. Brown 65*); Second day, Surrey 180-9 (J. E. Benjamin 3*, C. G. Rackemann 2*).

Middlesex

P. N. Weekes c Kersey b Tudor	62	R. L. Johnson b Hollioake	9
J. C. Pooley lbw b Tudor	6	A. R. C. Fraser not out	9
M. R. Ramprakash c Shahid b Tudor	214	P. C. R. Tufnell c and b Hollioake	0
*M. W. Gatting b Rackemann	16		
J. D. Carr c Smith b Butcher	1	L-b 11, w 5, n-b 6	22
†K. R. Brown c Thorpe b Benjamin	86		
D. J. Nash c Kersey b Rackemann	0	1/24 2/128 3/165 4/174 5/391	425
J. E. Emburey c Butcher b Benjamin	0	6/392 7/396 8/411 9/421	

Bonus points – Middlesex 4, Surrey 1 (Score at 120 overs: 389-4).

Bowling: Rackemann 28–9–73–2; Benjamin 30–8–66–2; Tudor 19–1–63–3; Smith 9–2–47–0; Butcher 16–1–56–1; Hollioake 26.3–7–77–2; Shahid 3–0–15–0; Thorpe 6–2–17–0.

Surrey

J. D. Ratcliffe c Pooley b Fraser	10	– lbw b Johnson	8
*A. J. Stewart b Nash	2	– retired hurt	12
M. A. Butcher st Brown b Emburey	32	– c Pooley b Emburey	32
G. P. Thorpe c Carr b Tufnell	15	– c Carr b Tufnell	41
N. Shahid c Ramprakash b Emburey	76	– c Gatting b Emburey	3
A. J. Hollioake c Gatting b Emburey	0	– c Brown b Emburey	1
A. W. Smith c Emburey b Fraser	22	– c Fraser b Tufnell	0
†G. J. Kersey c Johnson b Emburey	6	– not out	33
A. J. Tudor lbw b Tufnell	2	– c Gatting b Tufnell	1
J. E. Benjamin c Tufnell b Emburey	23	– c Nash b Emburey	1
C. G. Rackemann not out	11	– b Emburey	1
B 2, l-b 7, w 1	10	L-b 7	7
	209		**140**

1/8 2/25 3/49 4/85 5/85
6/148 7/170 8/175 9/175

1/20 2/96 3/98 4/100 5/101
6/105 7/125 8/132 9/140

Bonus points – Surrey 1, Middlesex 4.

In the second innings A. J. Stewart retired hurt at 25.

Bowling: *First Innings*—Fraser 17–3–50–2; Nash 7–2–24–1; Tufnell 22–10–32–2; Emburey 27–3–9–64–5; Weekes 9–2–12–0; Johnson 5–1–18–0. *Second Innings*—Nash 5–0–35–0; Fraser 10–3–22–0; Johnson 4–2–12–1; Emburey 16.4–5–34–5; Tufnell 19–8–30–3.

Umpires: J. C. Balderstone and G. Sharp.

At Bristol, July 6, 7, 8. MIDDLESEX beat GLOUCESTERSHIRE by an innings and 11 runs.

At Lord's, July 22, 23, 24. MIDDLESEX drew with WEST INDIANS (See West Indian tour section).

MIDDLESEX v SUSSEX

At Lord's, July 27, 28, 29. Middlesex won by an innings and 286 runs. Middlesex 24 pts, Sussex 2 pts. Toss: Sussex. Championship debut: A. A. Khan.

A day after their coach, Norman Gifford, resigned, bottom-of-the-table Sussex arrived at Lord's to find themselves on the wrong end of Middlesex's third successive Championship innings victory. In 1993, they lost by an innings after Wells elected to bat; this time he put Middlesex in on a dreary morning and they reached 415 for two by the close. Weekes showed that opening suited him and Ramprakash completed his third hundred in consecutive Championship innings. Next day he converted it into a second double; since his pair in the Lord's Test he had scored 552 Championship runs. In all, he made 205 from 295 balls, with 34 fours. Gatting joined him with a second successive century; they added a merciless 242 and Middlesex declared at 602 for seven. A Sussex defeat seemed inevitable from their first over, when Nash dismissed Athey and Newell. Only Wells and Stephenson, who needed a runner after twisting his ankle while bowling, delayed Middlesex long in the first innings; following on, nobody delayed them at all. Again, Nash struck twice in his first over and they were all out seven minutes after lunch on Saturday.

Close of play: First day, Middlesex 415-2 (M. R. Ramprakash 185*, M. W. Gatting 92*); Second day, Sussex 13-0 (C. W. J. Athey 9*, J. W. Hall 4*).

Middlesex

P. N. Weekes c Law b Salisbury	80	D. J. Nash not out	50
T. A. Radford c Moores b Law	33	M. A. Feltham lbw b Lewry	1
M. R. Ramprakash b Lewry	205	B 7, l-b 5, n-b 22	34
*M. W. Gatting lbw b Lewry	101		—
J. D. Carr c Newell b Law	78	1/74 2/193 3/435 4/458 (7 wkts dec.) 602
†K. R. Brown st Moores b Salisbury	20	5/523 6/596 7/602

A. A. Khan, R. L. Johnson and P. C. R. Tufnell did not bat.

Bonus points – Middlesex 4, Sussex 1 (Score at 120 overs: 483-4).

Bowling: Stephenson 12.5–1–48–0; Giddins 28.1–2–121–0; Lewry 33–8–116–3; Law 21–4–115–2; Salisbury 37–7–129–2; Greenfield 4–0–26–0; Newell 9–1–35–0.

Sussex

C. W. J. Athey lbw b Nash	0	– c Feltham b Johnson	16
J. W. Hall c Brown b Johnson	17	– c Weekes b Nash	4
K. Newell b Nash	0	– c Brown b Nash	0
K. Greenfield b Johnson	4	– (5) not out	24
*A. P. Wells b Nash	61	– (4) c and b Tufnell	9
†P. Moores c Carr b Johnson	4	– c Ramprakash b Johnson	0
F. D. Stephenson c Johnson b Weekes	55	– c Brown b Nash	13
D. R. Law c Johnson b Tufnell	16	– c Brown b Weekes	19
I. D. K. Salisbury not out	22	– c Brown b Weekes	16
J. D. Lewry c and b Tufnell	10	– st Brown b Weekes	2
E. S. H. Giddins c Radford b Tufnell	0	– c Ramprakash b Tufnell	1
L-b 6, n-b 6	12	L-b 1, n-b 10	11

1/0 2/2 3/9 4/39 5/53	201	1/13 2/15 3/33 4/35 5/36 115
6/130 7/169 8/169 9/189		6/56 7/90 8/112 9/114

Bonus points – Sussex 1, Middlesex 4.

Bowling: *First Innings*—Nash 11–0–47–3; Johnson 14–1–64–3; Feltham 4–0–16–0; Tufnell 17–2–47–3; Khan 1–1–0–0; Weekes 3–0–21–1. *Second Innings*—Feltham 3–1–6–0; Johnson 13–7–15–2; Tufnell 18.2–8–30–2; Khan 1–1–0–0; Nash 7–0–37–3; Weekes 6–0–26–3.

Umpires: J. D. Bond and A. A. Jones.

MIDDLESEX v NOTTINGHAMSHIRE

At Lord's, August 3, 4, 5. Middlesex won by an innings and 186 runs. Middlesex 24 pts, Nottinghamshire 5 pts. Toss: Middlesex.

Yet another Middlesex innings win followed the pattern of the previous two at Lord's: a large first-innings score proved too daunting for the opposition, who followed on and were dismissed twice by tea on the third day. Nottinghamshire at least showed some appetite for a contest; Cairns scored a career-best 115, becoming the first batsman to take a Championship hundred off Middlesex in 1995. They still trailed by 302 and their second innings was all over in 50 overs, with only Pollard passing 20. Pooley and Weekes had given Middlesex the perfect start with 157 in 36 overs; Pooley reached his first hundred at Lord's just before lunch, off 94 balls. Gatting then made his third century in as many innings, 148 from 182 balls, and added 213 with Brown, so that Middlesex scored 500 on the opening day. Tufnell was fined £250 for making a gesture at spectators in the Mound Stand on Friday.

Close of play: First day, Middlesex 500-6 (D. J. Nash 4*, R. L. Johnson 1*); Second day, Nottinghamshire 263-8 (C. L. Cairns 106*, R. A. Pick 2*).

Middlesex

P. N. Weekes lbw b Cairns	50	J. E. Emburey c and b Pennett	43
J. C. Pooley c Pollard b Pick	133	A. R. C. Fraser c Pick b Pennett	7
M. R. Ramprakash c Johnson b Pick	62	P. C. R. Tufnell not out	0
*M. W. Gatting b Cairns	148		
J. D. Carr lbw b Pick	0	L-b 8, w 2, n-b 12	22
†K. R. Brown c Hindson b Pick	83		
D. J. Nash c Archer b Pick	23	1/157 2/224 3/272 4/280 5/493	587
R. L. Johnson c and b Cairns	16	6/493 7/520 8/546 9/577	

Bonus points – Middlesex 4, Nottinghamshire 3 (Score at 120 overs: 544-7).

Bowling: Pick 28–3–119–5; Cairns 31–4–103–3; Pennett 27.4–5–119–2; Hindson 18–0–121–0; Afzaal 10–0–64–0; Archer 11–1–41–0; Banton 3–1–12–0.

Nottinghamshire

P. R. Pollard c Emburey b Johnson	0	lbw b Nash	23
*R. T. Robinson b Emburey	25	b Emburey	13
G. F. Archer c Carr b Tufnell	39	c Carr b Fraser	20
P. Johnson c Brown b Nash	1	lbw b Nash	0
C. Banton c Weekes b Johnson	28	lbw b Tufnell	12
C. L. Cairns c Emburey b Tufnell	115	c Gatting b Fraser	4
†W. M. Noon lbw b Nash	16	c Nash b Fraser	8
U. Afzaal c Carr b Tufnell	1	c Emburey b Fraser	0
J. E. Hindson lbw b Tufnell	2	c and b Johnson	6
R. A. Pick c Weekes b Tufnell	13	b Tufnell	17
D. B. Pennett not out	0	not out	1
B 9, l-b 14, n-b 22	45	B 6, l-b 2, n-b 4	12

1/19 2/34 3/41 4/83 5/152	285	1/36 2/38 3/38 4/70 5/74	116
6/218 7/234 8/248 9/277		6/88 7/88 8/88 9/108	

Bonus points – Nottinghamshire 2, Middlesex 4.

Bowling: *First Innings*—Fraser 14–3–54–0; Johnson 15–4–48–2; Emburey 24–8–59–1; Tufnell 26.2–5–74–5; Nash 11–3–20–2; Weekes 4–1–7–0. *Second Innings*—Fraser 15–6–41–4; Johnson 7.2–4–3–1; Nash 7–2–20–2; Emburey 7–2–15–1; Tufnell 13–6–29–2.

Umpires: J. W. Holder and B. Leadbeater.

At Chester-le-Street, August 10, 11, 12, 14. MIDDLESEX beat DURHAM by 386 runs.

MIDDLESEX v KENT

At Lord's, August 17, 18, 19, 21. Middlesex won by 140 runs. Middlesex 24 pts, Kent 4 pts.
Toss: Middlesex.

For only the second time in 1995, a Championship match at Lord's went into the fourth day, but the result was the same as in Middlesex's previous six matches: an emphatic win, which took them to the top of the Championship table. Another enormous total seemed likely, with Gatting making his fourth century in five innings - 136 in 140 minutes, despite a broken finger. Kent lost the use of Headley after tea, when umpire Jesty had him taken off for running on the pitch. The tail failed to capitalise, however, and a second-innings total of 201 was Middlesex's lowest since early June, as they forgot discretion in the search for quick runs. But it proved more than enough. For Kent, de Silva showed his abundant class in a four-hour 88, hitting Emburey into the pavilion twice. That enabled them to save the follow-on and he added another half-century in the second innings. But Kent fell well short of the 347 needed; Tufnell took five of the last six wickets in a 13-over spell.

Close of play: First day, Middlesex 362-5 (K. R. Brown 36*, D. J. Nash 29*); Second day, Kent 205-5 (P. A. de Silva 69*, S. A. Marsh 18*); Third day, Kent 37-2 (N. J. Llong 16*, P. A. de Silva 16*).

Middlesex

P. N. Weekes lbw b Headley	0	– lbw b Headley	8
J. C. Pooley run out	95	– c Llong b Headley	3
M. R. Ramprakash c Fulton b McCague	8	– c Ward b Ealham	34
*M. W. Gatting lbw b McCague	136	– c Cowdrey b Patel	42
J. D. Carr lbw b Headley	39	– b Patel	30
†K. R. Brown c Marsh b McCague	53	– c Fulton b Llong	17
D. J. Nash lbw b Ealham	29	– c Llong b Patel	4
R. L. Johnson c Llong b Patel	18	– (9) c Ealham b Patel	11
J. E. Emburey c Headley b McCague	6	– (8) c Patel b Headley	24
A. R. C. Fraser not out	3	– c Ward b Headley	20
P. C. R. Tufnell c Marsh b Patel	1	– not out	1
B 3, l-b 6, w 3, n-b 10	22	B 2, l-b 2, w 1, n-b 2	7

1/7 2/26 3/215 4/288 5/298	410	1/4 2/26 3/71 4/108 5/135	201
6/362 7/386 8/396 9/406		6/145 7/151 8/177 9/200	

Bonus points – Middlesex 4, Kent 2 (Score at 120 overs: 378-6).

Bowling: *First Innings*—McCague 32–8–81–4; Headley 20–5–74–2; Ealham 23–5–63–1; Patel 29.5–9–87–2; Herzberg 16–3–61–0; de Silva 13–2–35–0. *Second Innings*—McCague 7–1–17–0; Headley 11.4–3–32–4; Patel 21–2–78–4; Ealham 5–2–13–1; Llong 12–0–57–1.

Kent

D. P. Fulton c Brown b Fraser	16	– c Brown b Fraser	5
T. R. Ward lbw b Tufnell	59	– b Johnson	0
N. J. Llong c Carr b Tufnell	14	– lbw b Fraser	38
P. A. de Silva lbw b Nash	88	– c Pooley b Tufnell	60
G. R. Cowdrey c Brown b Tufnell	14	– b Emburey	13
M. A. Ealham c Brown b Fraser	4	– c Nash b Tufnell	13
*†S. A. Marsh b Emburey	24	– lbw b Tufnell	0
D. W. Headley lbw b Tufnell	10	– st Brown b Emburey	37
M. J. McCague b Nash	11	– b Tufnell	19
S. Herzberg c Carr b Johnson	3	– not out	11
M. M. Patel not out	0	– lbw b Tufnell	3
B 6, l-b 13, w 1, n-b 2	22	L-b 5, n-b 2	7

1/35 2/65 3/114 4/146 5/154	265	1/2 2/8 3/77 4/105 5/130	206
6/224 7/236 8/258 9/261		6/130 7/135 8/163 9/201	

Bonus points – Kent 2, Middlesex 4.

Bowling: *First Innings*—Johnson 19–8–28–1; Fraser 20–7–24–2; Tufnell 34.2–6–73–4; Emburey 19–2–71–1; Nash 19–5–50–2. *Second Innings*—Fraser 14–4–37–2; Johnson 4–0–13–1; Tufnell 28.4–5–76–5; Emburey 21–3–63–2; Nash 4–0–10–0; Weekes 2–1–2–0.

Umpires: T. E. Jesty and R. Julian.

At Leeds, August 24, 25, 26, 28. MIDDLESEX beat YORKSHIRE by an innings and 25 runs.

MIDDLESEX v NORTHAMPTONSHIRE

At Uxbridge, August 29, 30, 31, September 1. Drawn. Middlesex 5 pts, Northamptonshire 5 pts. Toss: Northamptonshire.

In contrast to Lord's, the Park Road outfield was completely parched after the dry summer and, but for the roar of traffic, the match might have been taking place in the desert. With Middlesex heading the table and Northamptonshire lying third, this match was vital to the Championship run-in. But the draw helped hand the title to Warwickshire. Two factors worked against a result: the pitch offered little to any bowler and both sides seemed inhibited by the game's importance. Northamptonshire showed a surprising lack of confidence in asking Middlesex to score 367 in 55 overs – at 6.67. They themselves had failed to achieve three an over in their first innings, on a fast-scoring ground. They deprived Middlesex of maximum bowling points for the first time in 1995, but failed to force the pace and did not help by coming off for bad light on the third evening, when Bailey was 98 not out and Warren looked comfortable. Middlesex declared their first innings as soon as they had four batting points, conceding a lead of 128. Once again, Ramprakash batted superbly, completing his sixth century in eight Championship matches. Before Lamb's delayed declaration, Bailey scored his second hundred of the game, and in the final stages Weekes made an unbeaten 127, which started by giving Middlesex an outside chance of victory and ended with a good defensive display.

Close of play: First day, Northamptonshire 237-3 (R. J. Bailey 98*, R. J. Warren 8*); Second day, Middlesex 57-1 (P. N. Weekes 25*, M. R. Ramprakash 16*); Third day, Northamptonshire 13-1 (R. R. Montgomerie 8*, R. J. Bailey 3*).

Northamptonshire

R. R. Montgomerie c Emburey b Nash	50	– c Carr b Emburey	17
A. Fordham c Brown b Feltham	22	– c Brown b Emburey	2
R. J. Bailey c Carr b Nash	157	– c Feltham b Emburey	119
*A. J. Lamb c Tufnell b Fraser	36	– c Pooley b Emburey	5
R. J. Warren c Brown b Emburey	79	– b Emburey	22
K. M. Curran c Pooley b Feltham	7	– not out	38
D. J. Capel b Emburey	21	– c Ramprakash b Feltham	6
J. N. Snape c Weekes b Fraser	12	– not out	16
†D. Ripley c Brown b Fraser	4		
A. Kumble c Weekes b Emburey	38		
J. P. Taylor not out	4		
L-b 25, n-b 24	49	B 4, l-b 3, n-b 6	13

1/46 2/143 3/205 4/363 5/382   479   1/4 2/43 3/57   (6 wkts dec.) 238
6/395 7/408 8/416 9/462   4/107 5/200 6/212

Bonus points – Northamptonshire 4, Middlesex 1 (Score at 120 overs: 362-3).

Bowling: *First Innings*—Fraser 37-7-106-3; Nash 27-6-90-2; Feltham 31-7-72-2; Emburey 46.2-9-124-3; Tufnell 18-3-56-0; Weekes 1-0-6-0. *Second Innings*—Feltham 5.3-0-31-1; Gatting 4.2-0-23-0; Emburey 25-7-101-5; Weekes 5-3-6-0; Fraser 9-1-36-0; Tufnell 8.4-2-34-0.

Middlesex

P. N. Weekes c Capel b Kumble	43	– not out	127
J. C. Pooley c Bailey b Taylor	11	– c Ripley b Kumble	74
M. R. Ramprakash st Ripley b Snape	111	– run out	8
*M. W. Gatting c Warren b Snape	83	– run out	27
J. D. Carr not out	49	– c Lamb b Snape	1
†K. R. Brown not out	42	– c Ripley b Snape	16
J. E. Emburey (did not bat)		– c Montgomerie b Kumble	1
D. J. Nash (did not bat)		– not out	8
L-b 6, n-b 6	12	B 7, l-b 2, n-b 6	15

1/22 2/104 3/241 4/268   (4 wkts dec.) 351   1/126 2/141 3/201   (6 wkts) 277
                                  4/207 5/237 6/240

M. A. Feltham, A. R. C. Fraser and P. C. R. Tufnell did not bat.

Bonus points – Middlesex 4, Northamptonshire 1.

Bowling: *First Innings*—Kumble 39–5–127–1; Taylor 20.3–3–78–1; Curran 19–5–47–0; Capel 11–2–38–0; Snape 18–3–48–2; Bailey 1–0–7–0. *Second Innings*—Taylor 3–1–17–0; Curran 4–1–24–0; Kumble 23.3–2–111–2; Capel 5–0–30–0; Snape 18–4–82–2; Bailey 1–0–4–0.

Umpires: G. Sharp and A. G. T. Whitehead.
I. J. Gould deputised for A. G. T. Whitehead on the 1st day.

MIDDLESEX v LEICESTERSHIRE

At Uxbridge, September 7, 8, 9, 11. Middlesex won by one run. Middlesex 21 pts, Leicestershire 7 pts. Toss: Middlesex.

A cliff-hanging denouement brought Middlesex the closest possible victory and took the race for the Championship into the final round. Though leaders Warwickshire had beaten Derbyshire in the morning, this result meant that Middlesex were still hanging on, 15 points behind. Leicestershire were favourites until the very last moment, when Mullally, seeking two to win, holed out to Emburey at deep mid-wicket with nine balls to go. He was Tufnell's tenth victim of the match. It had taken enterprise from both captains – Leicestershire were still competing for place money – to set up the enthralling conclusion. Rain allowed only three balls on the first day, when all other matches were washed out, and prevented further play until after lunch on the second. On the final morning, Leicestershire declared on gaining their third batting point – earned mainly by Wells, who scored his first hundred of the year – and then some undemanding bowling helped Middlesex to 212 runs in 100 minutes. Ramprakash struck the ball so beautifully that his second century of the match and his eighth in 13 Championship innings seemed inevitable, whatever the conditions. He took 69 balls and 58 minutes to reach his hundred, well before lunch, and coasted past 2,000 runs for the season. Leicestershire were left to score 251 in the last two sessions, which the spinners made into 74 overs, and looked like winning at 131 for two, with Whitaker and Cronje going strong. Emburey and Tufnell took the next six wickets for 73, but Pierson batted responsibly to stay on target. His disgust at Mullally's fatal lapse was hardly surprising.

Close of play: First day, Middlesex 0-0 (P. N. Weekes 0*, J. C. Pooley 0*); Second day, Middlesex 239-4 (M. R. Ramprakash 124*, K. R. Brown 37*); Third day, Leicestershire 284-4 (B. F. Smith 2*).

Middlesex

P. N. Weekes c Nixon b Parsons	1	– c Maddy b Brimson	30
J. C. Pooley b Parsons	0	– c Whitaker b Smith	18
M. R. Ramprakash b Brimson	158	– not out	111
*M. W. Gatting c Maddy b Mullally	28		
J. D. Carr lbw b Parsons	38		
†K. R. Brown c Maddy b Pierson	38	– (4) not out	48
D. J. Nash lbw b Pierson	39		
J. E. Emburey run out	4		
M. A. Feltham c Wells b Brimson	15		
A. R. C. Fraser b Pierson	0		
P. C. R. Tufnell not out	1		
B 8, l-b 5, w 1, n-b 2	16	B 1, l-b 3, w 1	5

1/7 2/12 3/72 4/144 5/241   338   1/38 2/55   (2 wkts dec.) 212
6/305 7/318 8/324 9/324

Bonus points – Middlesex 3, Leicestershire 4.

Bowling: *First Innings*—Mullally 8–0–32–1; Parsons 19–5–40–3; Cronje 11–2–42–0; Dakin 8–2–35–0; Pierson 28–4–116–3; Brimson 25.4–3–60–2. *Second Innings*—Parsons 4–1–17–0; Dakin 4–1–11–0; Brimson 3–0–20–1; Pierson 2–1–1–0; Cronje 8–0–54–0; Smith 10.3–1–69–1; Maddy 4–0–36–0.

Leicestershire

V. J. Wells c Carr b Tufnell	124	– b Fraser	17
D. L. Maddy c Pooley b Tufnell	5	– c Carr b Emburey	11
*J. J. Whitaker c Weekes b Tufnell	39	– c Pooley b Emburey	51
W. J. Cronje c Gatting b Tufnell	84	– b Tufnell	53
B. F. Smith not out	12	– c Gatting b Tufnell	0
J. M. Dakin b Tufnell	6	– lbw b Emburey	19
†P. A. Nixon not out	0	– c Brown b Emburey	7
G. J. Parsons (did not bat)		– b Tufnell	19
A. R. K. Pierson (did not bat)		– not out	20
M. T. Brimson (did not bat)		– b Tufnell	9
A. D. Mullally (did not bat)		– c Emburey b Tufnell	2
B 12, l-b 8, n-b 10	30	B 12, l-b 11, n-b 18	41

1/14 2/96 3/281 4/284 5/292   (5 wkts dec.) 300   1/32 2/36 3/131 4/139 5/161   249
6/174 7/200 8/204 9/237

Bonus points – Leicestershire 3, Middlesex 2.

Bowling: *First Innings*—Fraser 14–1–35–0; Nash 4–0–16–0; Tufnell 37–7–102–5; Emburey 19–2–54–0; Weekes 14–1–57–0; Feltham 2–0–8–0; Gatting 0.4–0–8–0. *Second Innings*—Fraser 10–1–40–1; Nash 2–1–4–0; Emburey 32–7–81–4; Tufnell 26.3–5–100–5; Weekes 2–1–1–0.

Umpires: B. J. Meyer and N. T. Plews.

At Taunton, September 14, 15, 16, 18. MIDDLESEX drew with SOMERSET.

FIELDING IN 1995

(Qualification: 20 dismissals)

65	G. J. Kersey (60 ct, 5 st)	31	T. M. Moody
64	R. J. Turner (54 ct, 10 st)	30	*J. R. Murray (27 ct, 3 st)
63	R. J. Blakey (59 ct, 4 st)	30	V. P. Terry
62	W. K. Hegg (53 ct, 9 st)	28	*R. J. Warren (27 ct, 1 st)
62	R. J. Rollins (53 ct, 9 st)	27	R. R. Montgomerie
61	K. J. Piper (59 ct, 2 st)	26	N. V. Knight
58	S. J. Rhodes (51 ct, 7 st)	25	M. A. Lynch
56	A. N. Aymes (53 ct, 3 st)	25	D. P. Ostler
54	*C. O. Browne (47 ct, 7 st)	25	J. C. Pooley
54	C. P. Metson (47 ct, 7 st)	25	D. D. J. Robinson
52	R. C. Russell (50 ct, 2 st)	24	R. C. J. Williams
51	K. R. Brown (45 ct, 6 st)	23	G. I. Macmillan
48	P. A. Nixon (46 ct, 2 st)	23	M. P. Maynard
46	P. Moores (44 ct, 2 st)	23	†A. J. Stewart
43	K. M. Krikken (42 ct, 1 st)	23	T. R. Ward
42	D. Byas	22	K. M. Curran
39	J. D. Carr	22	G. A. Hick
38	A. C. Gilchrist (33 ct, 5 st)	21	R. J. Bailey
37	W. M. Noon (32 ct, 5 st)	21	†J. P. Crawley
36	D. G. C. Ligertwood (33 ct, 3 st)	20	A. D. Brown
34	N. Hussain	20	P. N. Weekes
34	S. A. Marsh (32 ct, 2 st)		

* *C. O. Browne, J. R. Murray and R. J. Warren each took one catch in the field.*
† *A. J. Stewart took nine catches as wicket-keeper and J. P. Crawley took five.*

NORTHAMPTONSHIRE

Patrons: The Earl of Dalkeith and
The Earl Spencer
President: W. R. F. Chamberlain
Chairman: L. A. Wilson
Chairman, Cricket Committee: R. Wills
Chief Executive: S. P. Coverdale
Captain: 1995 – A. J. Lamb
1996 – R. J. Bailey
Coach: J. E. Emburey
Cricket Development Officer: B. L. Reynolds
Head Groundsman: R. R. Bailey
Scorer: A. C. Kingston

Northamptonshire failed to lift a trophy in 1995, but if that suggests business as usual at Wantage Road, nothing could be further from the truth. Victory over Leicestershire on June 26 – their sixth successive Championship win, equalling the county's best-ever sequence – left Allan Lamb's side 43 points clear at the top of the table. A month later, they defeated Warwickshire by seven runs in an unforgettable contest at Edgbaston. Even Northamptonshire's traditionally sceptical supporters began to believe that a first Championship title, the club's holy grail, was within reach.

It was not to be, however. Despite winning 12 matches, more than any champion county since 1989, they had to settle for third place. Defeat in the NatWest Trophy final – another triumph for Warwickshire – denied them a consolation prize, and ensured that one topic dominated the conversation whenever two or more followers were gathered together in the weeks following the game; the leg-before decision given in Dermot Reeve's favour during the tense closing stages. Reeve's speech at Northamptonshire's end-of-season dinner drew plenty of laughs, but there were not too many on that Sunday afternoon at Lord's.

No one could deny, though, the team's contribution to the season as a whole. Conventional cricketing wisdom was undermined time and again as a burgeoning sense of self-belief helped to secure a string of triumphs that ranged from the unlikely to the almost impossible. Northamptonshire were dismissed for the two lowest totals of the summer – 46 against Essex at Luton and 59 against Surrey at Northampton – but went on to win both matches. They also built up the season's biggest score, 781 for seven declared, to set up an innings victory after Nottinghamshire had made 527.

These results reflected clearly Lamb's style of captaincy: a blend of confidence, arrogance, enterprise and sheer willpower. Relishing his additional responsibilities – he took charge of first-team affairs following the departure of the former director of cricket, Phil Neale – Lamb led by example and, at 41, batted as commandingly as he has ever done. Conscious that this was his last year in charge, he never gave up hope of some silverware until it became a mathematical impossibility.

To Lamb, too, went the credit for the decision to bring the Indian leg-spinner Anil Kumble to Northampton. It was an inspired move. He captured 105 first-class wickets, becoming the first bowler to reach three figures since Neil Foster – Northamptonshire's newly appointed development coach – and

Waqar Younis in 1991, and the first to achieve the feat for the county since another Indian, Bishan Bedi, in 1973. Kumble's variations of pace and spin were intriguing for spectators, and unnerving even for some of the circuit's most experienced and accomplished batsmen. Nor should his success be measured solely in terms of wickets taken. He proved popular with team-mates and was a model professional, courteous towards all those eager to claim a slice of his time. Not many cricketers of his international stature would have been found, within half an hour of reaching the 100-wicket milestone, chatting to a couple of aspiring leg-spinners from his county's under-12 squad.

If Kumble was unquestionably the Player of the Year, Russell Warren was equally deserving of the accolade of Northamptonshire's top young cricketer. Pressed into service as a wicket-keeper, initially through an injury to David Ripley and subsequently to maintain the captain's preferred balance within the Championship side, he showed commendable application in the unfamiliar role. His batting also blossomed and, after a number of near misses, he scored his maiden century against Nottinghamshire in August.

Others deserved their moments in the spotlight. Rob Bailey enjoyed an outstanding NatWest Trophy campaign, taking three consecutive match awards; Alan Fordham lost form, and his place, early on but bounced back to score four Championship hundreds; David Capel, after two nightmare seasons, stayed fit and came into contention for an England recall; and Paul Taylor had a productive start to the summer, picking up 40 wickets in the first seven Championship games. Taylor, Capel, Bailey, Kumble and Kevin Curran were ever-present in the Championship team.

Richard Montgomerie failed to build on his confidence-boosting 192 in the opening match at Canterbury, but had an important part to play as a close catcher. He held 17 chances off Kumble's bowling, mostly at short leg, which Lamb had identified as a key position. The club's handling of Mal Loye, who endured a bitterly frustrating year, lacked sensitivity at times, but he still showed glimpses of his talent on Sundays. Another of the younger players, Jeremy Snape, had far more opportunities and performed usefully, but has yet to prove himself as an off-spinner capable of bowling sides out.

The NatWest aside, Northamptonshire were not much of a one-day team: it was July 9 before they beat another county. But the strength in depth of the playing staff was underlined by their Second Eleven, who finished runners-up in their Championship, losing the title to Hampshire on the final day of the season. Just as Kumble dominated in the first team, another leg-spinner, Andy Roberts, was the outstanding figure in the seconds. His return of 791 runs and 73 wickets made him the competition's Player of the Year. Fast bowler Scott Boswell and batsmen David Sales and David Roberts continued to make encouraging progress.

The close season brought major changes, with John Emburey arriving from Middlesex to become the club's new chief coach, to replace Bob Carter, who had emigrated to New Zealand, and vice-captain Bailey, after much internal debate about Fordham as an alternative, stepping up to succeed Lamb. With Kumble on tour, Curtly Ambrose will return for one last year as overseas player. Chief executive Steve Coverdale said that, after such a season, new leadership was a good thing to prevent a sense of anticlimax in 1996. Northamptonshire have the makings of an exciting side to carry them into the next century. The hope is that, having missed one surging tide, they will not have to wait too long before it runs in their favour again. – Andrew Radd.

NORTHAMPTONSHIRE 1995

[Bill Smith

Back row: J. N. Snape, K. J. Innes, J. F. Brown, A. J. Swann, S. A. J. Boswell, J. G. Hughes, M. J. Foster, D. J. Roberts, C. S. Atkins, A. R. Roberts. *Middle row*: K. Russell (*physiotherapist*), T. C. Walton, M. N. Bowen, M. B. Loye, R. J. Warren, J. P. Taylor, A. L. Penberthy, R. R. Montgomerie, R. M. Carter (*coach*). *Front row*: D. Ripley, D. J. Capel, R. J. Bailey, A. J. Lamb (*captain*), N. G. B. Cook, A. Fordham, N. A. Mallender, K. M. Curran. *Insets*: D. J. Sales, M. V. Steele, A. Kumble.

NORTHAMPTONSHIRE RESULTS

All first-class matches – Played 18: Won 12, Lost 2, Drawn 4.

County Championship matches – Played 17: Won 12, Lost 2, Drawn 3.

Bonus points – Batting 41, Bowling 57.

Competition placings – Britannic Assurance County Championship, 3rd;
NatWest Bank Trophy, finalists; Benson and Hedges Cup, 4th in Group B;
AXA Equity & Law League, 13th.

BRITANNIC ASSURANCE CHAMPIONSHIP AVERAGES

BATTING

	Birthplace	M	I	NO	R	HS	Avge
‡A. J. Lamb	*Langebaanweg, SA*	16	26	4	1,237	166	56.22
‡R. J. Warren	*Northampton*	15	26	5	877	154	41.76
‡R. J. Bailey	*Biddulph*	17	29	3	1,008	157	38.76
‡D. J. Capel	*Northampton*	17	26	3	885	175	38.47
‡A. Fordham	*Bedford*	15	28	1	1,025	130	37.96
‡K. M. Curran	*Rusape, S. Rhodesia*	17	27	3	863	117	35.95
‡D. Ripley	*Leeds*	5	4	1	87	40	29.00
J. N. Snape	*Stoke-on-Trent*	12	15	3	344	55	28.66
‡R. R. Montgomerie .	*Rugby*	13	23	1	605	192	27.50
‡J. P. Taylor	*Ashby-de-la-Zouch*	17	20	8	277	86	23.08
T. C. Walton	*Low Head*	3	6	1	104	71	20.80
‡A. Kumble§	*Bangalore, India*	17	21	5	321	40*	20.06
‡M. B. Loye	*Northampton*	7	10	1	134	51*	14.88
‡A. L. Penberthy	*Troon, Cornwall*	3	5	1	42	35	10.50
‡N. A. Mallender	*Kirk Sandall*	6	9	2	72	18	10.28
J. G. Hughes	*Wellingborough*	5	6	1	32	16	6.40

Also batted: C. S. Atkins (*Melbourne, Australia*) (1 match) 5, 8*; A. R. Roberts (*Kettering*) (1 match) 11, 10.

* *Signifies not out.* ‡ *Denotes county cap.* § *Overseas player.*

The following played a total of 17 three-figure innings for Northamptonshire in County Championship matches – R. J. Bailey 4, A. Fordham 4, D. J. Capel 3, A. J. Lamb 3, K. M. Curran 1, R. R. Montgomerie 1, R. J. Warren 1.

BOWLING

	O	M	R	W	BB	5W/i	Avge
A. Kumble	899.4	265	2,143	105	7-82	8	20.40
N. A. Mallender	130.2	29	382	17	4-49	0	22.47
D. J. Capel	338.2	68	1,129	47	7-44	2	24.02
J. P. Taylor	558.4	118	1,685	57	7-50	2	29.56
K. M. Curran	357.1	84	1,202	37	4-78	0	32.48
J. N. Snape	212	47	681	19	5-65	1	35.84

Also bowled: C. S. Atkins 11–4–46–1; R. J. Bailey 106.3–20–376–7; A. Fordham 6–0–51–0; J. G. Hughes 90–15–320–7; A. L. Penberthy 41–6–141–4; A. R. Roberts 11–2–45–0.

Wicket-keepers: R. J. Warren 27 ct, 1 st; D. Ripley 7 ct, 2 st; M. B. Loye 2 ct.

Leading Fielders: R. R. Montgomerie 27, K. M. Curran 22, R. J. Bailey 20, J. N. Snape 16, A. J. Lamb 15.

At Canterbury, April 27, 28, 29, 30. NORTHAMPTONSHIRE beat KENT by nine wickets.

At Cardiff, May 4, 5, 6, 8. NORTHAMPTONSHIRE lost to GLAMORGAN by three wickets.

NORTHAMPTONSHIRE v SOMERSET

At Northampton, May 11, 12, 13, 15. Northamptonshire won by seven wickets. Northamptonshire 22 pts, Somerset 5 pts. Toss: Somerset.

Lamb unleashed a ferocious assault to give his team victory 45 minutes into the final day's play, which began at 10 a.m. because Somerset were travelling to Ireland for the following day's Benson and Hedges Cup fixture. He hit an unbeaten 85 off 68 balls, including two sixes off Mushtaq Ahmed to pass the target. Both sides recovered from poor starts. Somerset rallied from 68 for six on the first day, with Rose and Ecclestone adding 153 in 42 overs. In turn, Curran, Capel and Snape engineered Northamptonshire's fightback from 112 for five. Trescothick then wrested the initiative with a superb display of powerful driving, making 151 – his third and biggest century – out of 229, in three and a half hours, with a six and 25 fours. Needing 289, Northamptonshire lost both openers at 55. But Bailey and Walton, after a maiden half-century, retrieved the situation with a stand of 121, setting the stage for Lamb's pyrotechnics.

Close of play: First day, Northamptonshire 75-3 (R. J. Bailey 28*, A. J. Lamb 13*); Second day, Somerset 123-3 (M. E. Trescothick 83*, K. A. Parsons 0*); Third day, Northamptonshire 206-3 (R. J. Bailey 47*, A. J. Lamb 19*).

Somerset

M. N. Lathwell lbw b Hughes	17	– c Snape b Kumble	18
M. E. Trescothick c Warren b Taylor	11	– lbw b Capel	151
P. D. Bowler c and b Taylor	5	– lbw b Kumble	11
R. J. Harden c Snape b Hughes	0	– lbw b Taylor	1
*A. N. Hayhurst c Taylor b Curran	17	– (6) not out	58
K. A. Parsons c Bailey b Curran	13	– (5) c Curran b Taylor	1
G. D. Rose lbw b Hughes	84	– c Curran b Capel	0
S. C. Ecclestone lbw b Snape	81	– c Warren b Curran	50
†R. J. Turner lbw b Kumble	5	– b Curran	0
Mushtaq Ahmed c Fordham b Snape	3	– c Lamb b Kumble	20
H. R. J. Trump not out	0	– c Bailey b Kumble	0
L-b 4, n-b 2	6	B 13, l-b 16, n-b 4	33

1/17 2/31 3/32 4/35 5/61   242   1/39 2/117 3/122 4/152 5/229   343
6/68 7/221 8/239 9/239   6/229 7/299 8/299 9/342

Bonus points – Somerset 1, Northamptonshire 4.

Bowling: *First Innings*—Taylor 17–7–37–2; Hughes 18–4–69–3; Capel 11–4–27–0; Curran 13–1–48–2; Kumble 14–2–45–1; Snape 8.2–3–12–2. *Second Innings*—Taylor 24–7–71–2; Capel 14–2–49–2; Kumble 30–9–87–4; Curran 15–0–61–2; Snape 9–1–46–0.

Northamptonshire

†R. J. Warren c Turner b Rose	15	– b Trump	24
A. Fordham b Hayhurst	4	– c Trescothick b Mushtaq Ahmed	29
R. J. Bailey lbw b Rose	45	– b Rose	66
T. C. Walton c Turner b Rose	9	– lbw b Ecclestone	71
*A. J. Lamb c Trescothick b Hayhurst	13	– not out	85
K. M. Curran b Mushtaq Ahmed	96		
D. J. Capel lbw b Parsons	30		
J. N. Snape not out	54		
A. Kumble c Trump b Mushtaq Ahmed	0		
J. G. Hughes lbw b Mushtaq Ahmed	0		
J. P. Taylor b Trump	8		
B 4, l-b 15, w 2, n-b 2	23	B 10, l-b 6	16

1/16 2/30 3/40 4/75 5/112   297   1/55 2/55 3/176   (3 wkts) 291
6/204 7/263 8/273 9/273

Bonus points – Northamptonshire 2, Somerset 4.

Bowling: *First Innings*—Rose 23–7–67–3; Ecclestone 9–2–32–0; Hayhurst 12–2–39–2; Mushtaq Ahmed 26–6–77–3; Parsons 4–0–25–1; Trump 19.3–8–38–1. *Second Innings*—Rose 16–5–65–0; Hayhurst 4–0–16–0; Trump 14–4–46–1; Mushtaq Ahmed 22.4–3–110–1; Ecclestone 9–1–38–1.

Umpires: G. I. Burgess and B. J. Meyer.

NORTHAMPTONSHIRE v SURREY

At Northampton, May 18, 19, 20. Northamptonshire won by nine runs. Northamptonshire 24 pts, Surrey 5 pts. Toss: Northamptonshire. First-class debut: C. S. Atkins.

Northamptonshire consolidated their position as early-season leaders after the first of several extraordinary days' cricket they were to produce during the season. Resuming 140 ahead, they were dismissed for 59 in less than two hours by Pigott and Benjamin who, maintaining an almost faultless line and length, skilfully exploited a wearing pitch. Pigott finished with 11 wickets in the match, Benjamin with eight. Surrey, left five sessions to score 200, started confidently as Bicknell and Stewart put on 66 in 12 overs. But Stewart's departure sowed the seeds of doubt, and Kumble's accuracy prompted a succession of risky shots against the seamers at the other end. Holliaoke demonstrated a sound technique and excellent temperament in his two-and-a-half-hour fifty before he ran out of partners, and Northamptonshire triumphed in a tense finish on Saturday evening. Lamb, with 166 in five and a half hours, and Curran, whose 117 was his best score for the county, had earned their first-innings advantage, adding 282 in 80 overs. Surrey then toiled against Kumble, who foreshadowed his third-day exploits with a miserly performance. He bowled 51.5 overs in the match, and took seven for 76.

Close of play: First day, Northamptonshire 363-4 (A. J. Lamb 150*, K. M. Curran 111*); Second day, Surrey 261-9 (J. E. Benjamin 3*, S. G. Kenlock 10*).

Northamptonshire

†R. J. Warren c Kersey b Pigott	39	– c Bicknell b Benjamin	0
A. Fordham c Kersey b Benjamin	8	– c Kersey b Benjamin	1
R. J. Bailey c Kersey b Kenlock	23	– b Pigott	13
T. C. Walton lbw b Pigott	5	– c Kersey b Pigott	2
*A. J. Lamb lbw b Pigott	166	– c Thorpe b Benjamin	4
K. M. Curran c Butcher b Pigott	117	– c Stewart b Benjamin	9
D. J. Capel c Kenlock b Pigott	2	– c Nowell b Pigott	4
A. L. Penberthy c Stewart b Benjamin	1	– b Benjamin	5
A. Kumble c Stewart b Pigott	2	– b Pigott	1
C. S. Atkins b Benjamin	5	– not out	8
J. P. Taylor not out	4	– b Pigott	6
B 4, l-b 11, w 2, n-b 14	31	B 1, l-b 1, n-b 4	6

1/41 2/80 3/86 4/101 5/383   403   1/0 2/1 3/4 4/11 5/27   59
6/391 7/392 8/392 9/397   6/33 7/42 8/43 9/43

Bonus points – Northamptonshire 4, Surrey 3 (Score at 120 overs: 394-8).

Bowling: *First Innings*—Benjamin 24.3–2–79–3; Pigott 31–7–91–6; Kenlock 16–0–67–1; Butcher 16–4–53–0; Nowell 21–3–62–0; Hollioake 13–1–36–0. *Second Innings*—Benjamin 12–3–37–5; Pigott 11.3–4–20–5.

Surrey

D. J. Bicknell c Capel b Taylor	0	– c Lamb b Kumble	33
*A. J. Stewart b Capel	9	– c Curran b Capel	39
M. A. Butcher c Curran b Atkins	52	– c Warren b Capel	8
G. P. Thorpe c Curran b Kumble	42	– lbw b Kumble	0
A. D. Brown b Penberthy	7	– c and b Capel	3
A. J. Hollioake lbw b Kumble	47	– not out	54
†G. J. Kersey lbw b Kumble	64	– c Curran b Taylor	3
A. C. S. Pigott c Fordham b Kumble	5	– b Capel	19
R. W. Nowell c Taylor b Penberthy	9	– b Taylor	8
J. E. Benjamin not out	3	– b Taylor	8
S. G. Kenlock lbw b Taylor	12	– b Kumble	0
L-b 11, n-b 2	13	B 8, l-b 5, n-b 2	15

1/0 2/14 3/86 4/101 5/142   263   1/66 2/80 3/80 4/83 5/83   190
6/178 7/194 8/248 9/250   6/116 7/153 8/177 9/189

Bonus points – Surrey 2, Northamptonshire 4.

Bowling: *First Innings*—Taylor 17.4–4–53–2; Capel 5–2–22–1; Kumble 30–12–47–4; Bailey 2–2–0–0; Penberthy 15–1–56–2; Curran 12–4–28–0; Atkins 11–4–46–1. *Second Innings*—Taylor 13–1–42–3; Curran 3–0–29–0; Capel 18–3–62–4; Penberthy 5–1–15–0; Kumble 21.5–5–29–3.

Umpires: B. Leadbeater and K. J. Lyons.

At Sheffield, May 25, 26, 27, 29. NORTHAMPTONSHIRE beat YORKSHIRE by seven wickets.

At Northampton, June 3, 4, 5. NORTHAMPTONSHIRE drew with WEST INDIANS (See West Indian tour section).

At Derby, June 8, 9. NORTHAMPTONSHIRE beat DERBYSHIRE by four wickets.

NORTHAMPTONSHIRE v ESSEX

At Luton, June 15, 16. Northamptonshire won by two wickets. Northamptonshire 20 pts, Essex 4 pts. Toss: Northamptonshire.

Bowled out for 59 before winning their previous home match, Northamptonshire made that seem commonplace. They recovered and won after being dismissed for 46, their lowest Championship total since 1946. The first day was breathtaking, with 30 wickets falling, the most in a Championship day since 1960. Yet the umpires did not report the pitch. It contained some residual moisture but they did not regard it as unfit. The hazy day, which helped the ball swing prodigiously and, when Ilott was bowling, unplayably, was probably more significant. Essex struggled against Capel, apart from Rollins, with an unbeaten maiden fifty. But Ilott then destroyed Northamptonshire with a spell of nine for 11 in 36 balls, finishing with a hat-trick of lbws – only the sixth known instance in first-class cricket. Umpire White judged these three and, in all, 14 of the 17 lbws given in the match. Essex failed to build substantially on their 81-run lead, most of their batsmen falling to Taylor, whose seven for 50 received little attention amidst all the activity. Northamptonshire were batting again before the close. Overnight, Lamb said the pitch was drying out and batting should become easier. His assessment proved correct, though his chances looked slim at 161 for eight chasing 189. It took a half-century of great determination by Lamb himself to ensure that Ilott, despite match figures of 14 for 105, finished on the losing side. The game was won after an unbroken stand of 31 with Kumble who told Lamb: "Don't worry, skipper, I'll get the runs." No winning team had won from a score as low as 46 in the Championship since 1934, when Warwickshire beat Yorkshire by one wicket at Scarborough, having been all out for 45 in the first innings.

Close of play: First day, Northamptonshire 1-0 (N. A. Mallender 1*, R. R. Montgomerie 0*).

Essex

G. A. Gooch b Taylor	4	– lbw b Mallender	20
D. D. J. Robinson b Mallender	8	– lbw b Mallender	3
M. E. Waugh lbw b Taylor	12	– lbw b Taylor	9
N. Hussain b Kumble	27	– c Capel b Taylor	0
*P. J. Prichard c Montgomerie b Capel	11	– lbw b Taylor	0
R. C. Irani lbw b Capel	0	– c Montgomerie b Taylor	26
†R. J. Rollins not out	52	– c Warren b Taylor	4
M. C. Ilott lbw b Capel	1	– c Bailey b Taylor	0
D. M. Cousins b Capel	0	– b Taylor	17
P. M. Such b Kumble	2	– run out	19
J. H. Childs c Warren b Capel	4	– not out	3
L-b 4, n-b 2	6	L-b 6	6

1/6 2/22 3/24 4/44 5/44   127   1/16 2/33 3/35 4/35 5/35   107
6/78 7/79 8/79 9/88   6/63 7/63 8/68 9/103

Bonus points – Northamptonshire 4.

Bowling: *First Innings*—Taylor 10–1–18–2; Mallender 8–0–22–1; Curran 6–1–15–0; Capel 14.1–3–29–5; Kumble 10–2–39–2. *Second Innings*—Taylor 14.1–2–50–7; Mallender 8–3–22–2; Curran 4–0–22–0; Kumble 2–0–7–0.

Northamptonshire

R. R. Montgomerie b Ilott	18	– (2) c Hussain b Ilott	18
M. B. Loye lbw b Ilott	3	– (3) lbw b Irani	14
R. J. Bailey lbw b Ilott	0	– (4) lbw b Ilott	1
*A. J. Lamb c Rollins b Ilott	19	– (5) not out	50
†R. J. Warren b Ilott	0	– (6) c Hussain b Waugh	25
K. M. Curran lbw b Ilott	6	– (7) c Prichard b Waugh	24
D. J. Capel c Rollins b Irani	0	– (8) c Robinson b Ilott	6
J. N. Snape lbw b Ilott	0	– (9) lbw b Ilott	14
A. Kumble lbw b Ilott	0	– (10) not out	17
N. A. Mallender lbw b Ilott	0	– (1) lbw b Ilott	8
J. P. Taylor not out	0		
		B 4, l-b 2, w 1, n-b 8	15

1/17 2/17 3/39 4/39 5/45   46   1/24 2/49 3/53 4/56   (8 wkts) 192
6/46 7/46 8/46 9/46   5/94 6/131 7/142 8/161

Bonus points – Essex 4.

Bowling: *First Innings*—Ilott 10.1–2–19–9; Cousins 4–0–9–0; Irani 6–2–18–1. *Second Innings*—Ilott 22–0–86–5; Irani 17–7–53–1; Waugh 17–4–47–2.

Umpires: D. J. Constant and R. A. White.

NORTHAMPTONSHIRE v LEICESTERSHIRE

At Northampton, June 22, 23, 24, 26. Northamptonshire won by an innings and 37 runs. Northamptonshire 24 pts, Leicestershire 6 pts. Toss: Northamptonshire.

Northamptonshire went 43 points clear after they equalled their best-ever winning Championship sequence of six, previously achieved in 1909, 1955 and 1958. Leicestershire capitulated in abject fashion on the final afternoon, losing their last seven for 46 in 15 overs. The home side improved on their third-highest Championship total and Capel on his career-best score, both for the second time in the season. He batted more than six hours, hitting two sixes and 27 fours, after Lamb retired with his right thumb cracked, courtesy of a lifting ball from Sheriyar. Loye was also interrupted when Parsons struck him on the wrist, but returned to complete a spectacular 49-ball fifty. Leicestershire made a spirited if unsuccessful attempt to avoid the follow-on, Smith reaching his second first-class century, while Dakin drove handsomely. Bad light and drizzle docked 45 overs from the third day, making Northamptonshire's task more difficult, but in the event they were assisted by the visitors' spineless second effort. Cronje joined the injury list when his finger was broken by Taylor.

Close of play: First day, Northamptonshire 385-4 (D. J. Capel 71*, J. N. Snape 20*); Second day, Leicestershire 185-4 (B. F. Smith 80*, A. D. Mullally 0*); Third day, Leicestershire 18-0 (T. J. Boon 1*, N. E. Briers 17*).

Northamptonshire

R. R. Montgomerie c and b Sheriyar	49	A. Kumble c Smith b Parsons		6
M. B. Loye not out	51	N. A. Mallender b Pierson		13
R. J. Bailey c Parsons b Pierson	15	J. P. Taylor c Dakin b Sheriyar		15
*A. J. Lamb retired hurt	55			
K. M. Curran c Nixon b Parsons	53	B 8, l-b 17, n-b 12		37
†R. J. Warren b Cronje	75			
D. J. Capel b Pierson	175	1/58 2/148 3/221 4/343 5/386		564
J. N. Snape c Nixon b Sheriyar	20	6/395 7/467 8/500 9/564		

Bonus points – Northamptonshire 4, Leicestershire 2 (Score at 120 overs: 406-6).

M. B. Loye, when 19, retired hurt at 22 and resumed at 500. A. J. Lamb retired hurt at 148-2.

Bowling: Mullally 23–6–63–0; Parsons 38–12–106–2; Sheriyar 32–3–152–3; Pierson 44.2–7–141–3; Dakin 13–2–51–0; Cronje 11–3–26–1.

Leicestershire

T. J. Boon run out	11	– c Warren b Curran		6
*N. E. Briers lbw b Bailey	68	– c Snape b Taylor		35
W. J. Cronje c Montgomerie b Curran	6	– b Curran		18
J. J. Whitaker b Kumble	0	– c Montgomerie b Kumble		22
B. F. Smith b Snape	112	– c Curran b Kumble		25
A. D. Mullally b Kumble	20	– (9) not out		9
†P. A. Nixon c Montgomerie b Kumble	19	– (6) c Bailey b Mallender		1
J. M. Dakin c Snape b Taylor	77	– (7) c Snape b Mallender		14
G. J. Parsons c Warren b Mallender	4	– (8) c Kumble b Mallender		0
A. Sheriyar b Mallender	5	– b Kumble		18
A. R. K. Pierson not out	4	– c Warren b Mallender		1
B 14, l-b 27	41	B 4, l-b 1, n-b 6		11

1/24 2/43 3/48 4/185 5/230   367   1/25 2/65 3/67 4/114 5/115   160
6/264 7/295 8/355 9/361   6/125 7/128 8/131 9/159

Bonus points – Leicestershire 4, Northamptonshire 4.

Bowling: *First Innings*—Taylor 23–3–86–1; Mallender 16–3–59–2; Curran 6–1–24–1; Kumble 36–12–83–3; Capel 6–0–24–0; Snape 16–8–34–1; Bailey 8–2–16–1. *Second Innings*—Taylor 11–1–51–1; Mallender 14.2–3–49–4; Curran 10–3–32–2; Kumble 9–2–23–3.

Umpires: J. C. Balderstone and R. Palmer.

At Manchester, July 6, 7, 8, 10. NORTHAMPTONSHIRE lost to LANCASHIRE by 233 runs.

NORTHAMPTONSHIRE v HAMPSHIRE

At Northampton, July 20, 21, 22, 24. Drawn. Northamptonshire 4 pts, Hampshire 8 pts. Toss: Hampshire. First-class debut: J. S. Laney.

Hampshire, left to score 127 in 22 overs, squandered their chance and almost presented Northamptonshire with another unlikely triumph. They were 76 for one in the 16th over, thanks largely to Jason Laney, in his first Championship match, before Kumble destroyed the middle order, aided by some fine catching in the deep. Lamb did his best to keep Hampshire interested but, although two wickets fell in the final over – giving Kumble 13 in the match – there was not quite time for either side to force a win. Hampshire had looked impregnable, making Northamptonshire follow on after Smith, who hit 33 fours, and Nicholas, with 18 plus two sixes, had added 249 to set up the highest-ever total in matches between these two counties. Lamb and night-watchman Taylor provided the home resistance in the first innings. Then Fordham, with his first century of the season, gave Northamptonshire what initially appeared to be only an escape route; it nearly paved the way for victory.

Close of play: First day, Hampshire 353-3 (R. A. Smith 156*, M. C. J. Nicholas 80*); Second day, Northamptonshire 152-3 (R. J. Bailey 55*, J. P. Taylor 0*); Third day, Northamptonshire 140-2 (A. Fordham 72*, A. J. Lamb 6*).

Hampshire

V. P. Terry c Warren b Mallender	4	– c Lamb b Kumble 16
J. S. Laney lbw b Kumble	38	– c Kumble b Curran 42
P. R. Whitaker c Snape b Kumble	57	– (4) c Montgomerie b Curran 3
R. A. Smith lbw b Capel	172	– (3) c Fordham b Kumble 18
*M. C. J. Nicholas b Kumble	120	– (6) b Kumble 9
K. D. James c Capel b Kumble	12	
†A. N. Aymes lbw b Curran	18	– (8) not out 10
S. D. Udal not out	62	– (7) c and b Kumble 5
H. H. Streak lbw b Kumble	25	– (5) c Montgomerie b Kumble 1
R. J. Maru c Bailey b Kumble	1	– not out 0
C. A. Connor c Montgomerie b Kumble	18	– (9) c Lamb b Kumble 2
B 16, l-b 6, w 1, n-b 10	33	B 4, l-b 4, n-b 4 12

1/16 2/79 3/130 4/379 5/420   560   1/47 2/76 3/86 4/89 5/93 (8 wkts) 118
6/421 7/449 8/520 9/524   6/101 7/114 8/116

Bonus points – Hampshire 4, Northamptonshire 1 (Score at 120 overs: 374-3).

Bowling: *First Innings*—Taylor 25-7-79-0; Mallender 11-4-37-1; Curran 24-7-91-1; Kumble 57.5-21-131-7; Capel 12-3-59-1; Snape 18-4-53-0; Bailey 21-1-88-0. *Second Innings*—Taylor 7-0-25-0; Kumble 10.5-1-61-6; Curran 3-0-14-2; Bailey 1-0-10-0.

Northamptonshire

R. R. Montgomerie b Streak	1	– c Terry b James 6
A. Fordham c Aymes b Connor	7	– c Aymes b Connor 120
R. J. Bailey b Udal	55	– b Maru 49
*A. J. Lamb c Udal b Maru	88	– c Terry b Streak 13
J. P. Taylor c Smith b Udal	58	– (11) not out 11
D. J. Capel c Aymes b James	9	– (7) c James b Streak 32
K. M. Curran c Aymes b Streak	39	– (6) b Connor 45
†R. J. Warren lbw b Connor	1	– (5) b Udal 28
J. N. Snape c Maru b James	32	– (8) st Aymes b Udal 26
A. Kumble c Laney b Udal	27	– (9) b Udal 0
N. A. Mallender not out	0	– (10) st Aymes b Maru 18
L-b 3, w 1	4	B 9, l-b 4, n-b 4 17

1/5 2/13 3/146 4/152 5/161   321   1/35 2/124 3/167 4/217 5/273   365
6/220 7/221 8/280 9/307   6/274 7/309 8/309 9/345

Bonus points – Northamptonshire 3, Hampshire 4.

Bowling: *First Innings*—Connor 13-3-47-2; Streak 13-3-55-2; James 20-7-68-2; Maru 18-6-41-1; Udal 31-6-107-3. *Second Innings*—Streak 21-7-47-2; Connor 26-8-74-2; Udal 44-13-127-3; James 9-3-25-1; Maru 31.5-14-74-2; Whitaker 1-0-5-0.

Umpires: A. A. Jones and R. A. White.

At Birmingham, July 27, 28, 29, 31. NORTHAMPTONSHIRE beat WARWICKSHIRE by seven runs.

NORTHAMPTONSHIRE v DURHAM

At Northampton, August 3, 4, 5. Northamptonshire won by an innings and 76 runs. Northamptonshire 24 pts, Durham 1 pt. Toss: Durham.

Not even a magnificent century from Larkins could save Durham from heavy defeat with a day to spare. Larkins responded gloriously after they resumed 344 behind, hitting a six and 17 fours in three and a half hours. He earned a warm ovation as a hundred off his old team completed his "set" against the other 17 counties – he never played Durham. But once he had gone, it was a familiar scenario. From an opening stand of 181, Durham collapsed abjectly, losing five for 11 and allowing off-spinner Snape to claim five wickets for the first time. Kumble's nine in the match took him to 32 in three games. Like Montgomerie and Warren, he was awarded his county cap on the opening day, which Northamptonshire dominated completely. They dismissed Durham inside 64 overs and closed just one run behind with eight wickets standing, and pressed on through Bailey, Taylor – who holed out in sight of a maiden hundred – and, most spectacularly, Lamb, with 97 from 93 balls. Victory took Northamptonshire back to the top of the table.

Close of play: First day, Northamptonshire 147-2 (R. J. Bailey 18*, J. P. Taylor 0*); Second day, Durham 68-0 (W. Larkins 35*, S. Hutton 27*).

Durham

W. Larkins c Warren b Curran	18	– c and b Kumble	112
S. Hutton c Taylor b Curran	13	– c Bailey b Snape	57
D. A. Blenkiron c Warren b Kumble	15	– (4) run out	5
M. Prabhakar c Warren b Capel	1	– (5) c Bailey b Kumble	46
*J. E. Morris c Montgomerie b Kumble	21	– (3) c and b Snape	0
P. Bainbridge c Montgomerie b Taylor	4	– c and b Snape	0
†D. G. C. Ligertwood run out	23	– b Kumble	2
J. Boiling c Montgomerie b Kumble	2	– c Curran b Kumble	14
N. Killeen lbw b Kumble	0	– c Montgomerie b Snape	3
S. J. E. Brown not out	21	– not out	0
D. M. Cox b Kumble	17	– b Snape	0
L-b 3, n-b 10	13	B 10, l-b 17, n-b 2	29
	148		268

1/40 2/51 3/52 4/66 5/78 6/90 7/102 8/102 9/116

1/181 2/181 3/191 4/192 5/192 6/227 7/263 8/268 9/268

Bonus points – Northamptonshire 4.

Bowling: *First Innings*—Taylor 11–0–27–1; Hughes 11–2–29–0; Curran 12–4–40–2; Capel 13–4–23–1; Kumble 16.5–6–26–5. *Second Innings*—Taylor 13–6–32–0; Hughes 4–0–19–0; Kumble 41–14–75–4; Snape 27.4–5–65–5; Curran 11–4–20–0; Capel 7–0–30–0.

Northamptonshire

R. R. Montgomerie c Ligertwood b Cox	46	K. M. Curran not out	21
A. Fordham c Larkins b Cox	79		
R. J. Bailey c Larkins b Prabhakar	132	B 2, l-b 6, w 1, n-b 2	11
J. P. Taylor c Prabhakar b Cox	86		
*A. J. Lamb lbw b Killeen	97	1/107 2/142 3/288 (5 wkts dec.)	492
†R. J. Warren not out	20	4/443 5/453	

D. J. Capel, J. N. Snape, A. Kumble and J. G. Hughes did not bat.

Bonus points – Northamptonshire 4, Durham 1 (Score at 120 overs: 420-3).

Bowling: Brown 22–4–96–0; Prabhakar 26–8–73–1; Killeen 21–3–72–1; Boiling 29–6–84–0; Cox 26–4–109–3; Bainbridge 10–0–50–0.

Umpires: B. Dudleston and D. R. Shepherd.

NORTHAMPTONSHIRE v GLOUCESTERSHIRE

At Northampton, August 10, 11, 12, 14. Northamptonshire won by 209 runs. Northamptonshire 23 pts, Gloucestershire 6 pts. Toss: Northamptonshire.

Northamptonshire failed to tidy up the match in the extra ten overs on Saturday evening, but needed just 12 minutes on Monday morning. Once Taylor had removed the dangerous Symonds second ball, to leave Gloucestershire 75 for five, a target of 341 was beyond them. On the first day Northamptonshire missed out on maximum batting points. And they were restricted to a 28-run lead after Gloucestershire recovered from 22 for three, inspired by Lynch. He made the most of an escape on four to complete his fifth century of the season, hitting one six and 17 fours in 121 balls. Lynch added 99 with Symonds in 21 overs of powerful strokeplay, and 62 with Srinath for the ninth wicket. It was then Northamptonshire's turn to struggle; at the second-day close they were only 148 ahead with five down. But Curran batted with admirable restraint against his former county and Gloucestershire never regained the initiative.

Close of play: First day, Gloucestershire 22-3 (R. C. J. Williams 0*, T. H. C. Hancock 0*); Second day, Northamptonshire 120-5 (K. M. Curran 4*, J. P. Taylor 0*); Third day, Gloucestershire 127-8 (M. C. J. Ball 4*, K. P. Sheeraz 1*).

Northamptonshire

R. R. Montgomerie c Windows b Srinath	5	– c and b Srinath 24
A. Fordham c Ball b Sheeraz	82	– c Pike b Sheeraz 43
R. J. Bailey c and b Pike	7	– c Williams b Sheeraz 8
*A. J. Lamb b Srinath	36	– c and b Alleyne 24
†R. J. Warren c Williams b Srinath	8	– c Williams b Alleyne 9
D. J. Capel c Pike b Sheeraz	58	– (8) b Pike 9
K. M. Curran c Williams b Ball.............	14	– (6) lbw b Srinath 84
J. N. Snape c Windows b Ball	45	– (9) c Lynch b Pike 10
A. Kumble not out	29	– (10) not out 40
J. P. Taylor c Lynch b Ball...............	1	– (7) b Pike 31
J. G. Hughes lbw b Alleyne	16	– c Williams b Snape 5
B 7, l-b 10, w 1, n-b 2	20	B 8, l-b 13, w 2, n-b 2 ... 25

1/8 2/40 3/109 4/135 5/178   321   1/45 2/78 3/79 4/108 5/119   312
6/205 7/268 8/275 9/281   6/194 7/218 8/246 9/268

Bonus points – Northamptonshire 3, Gloucestershire 4.

Bowling: *First Innings*—Srinath 25-5-81-3; Sheeraz 22-3-63-2; Alleyne 13.5-3-42-1; Pike 20-1-69-1; Ball 16-5-49-3. *Second Innings*—Srinath 26.3-6-61-3; Sheeraz 17-2-59-2; Alleyne 15-3-41-2; Ball 25-10-56-0; Pike 18-3-72-3; Symonds 1-0-2-0.

Gloucestershire

A. J. Wright c Warren b Taylor.............	8	– c Warren b Taylor 37
M. G. N. Windows lbw b Kumble	13	– c Snape b Hughes 0
K. P. Sheeraz lbw b Kumble	0	– (10) c Snape b Taylor 1
†R. C. J. Williams b Curran	6	– (7) b Snape 20
T. H. C. Hancock c Fordham b Kumble	23	– (3) lbw b Capel 18
M. A. Lynch lbw b Kumble	104	– c Bailey b Curran 3
*M. W. Alleyne c Lamb b Curran	21	– (5) b Kumble 33
A. Symonds lbw b Snape	56	– (6) c Warren b Taylor 0
M. C. J. Ball c Warren b Kumble	20	– (8) not out 8
J. Srinath c Fordham b Kumble.............	29	– (9) c Fordham b Snape 2
V. J. Pike not out	0	– c Warren b Snape 0
B 1, l-b 6, n-b 6	13	B 4, l-b 4, w 1 9

1/22 2/22 3/22 4/57 5/61   293   1/3 2/43 3/46 4/75 5/75   131
6/98 7/197 8/226 9/288   6/102 7/122 8/126 9/131

Bonus points – Gloucestershire 2, Northamptonshire 4.

Bowling: *First Innings*—Taylor 15-6-33-1; Hughes 8-2-25-0; Kumble 24.2-7-76-6; Curran 12-1-82-2; Capel 3-0-22-0; Snape 11-0-48-1. *Second Innings*—Taylor 13-7-17-4; Hughes 4-0-14-1; Kumble 21-6-53-1; Snape 12-5-14-2; Capel 7-2-18-1; Curran 6-3-7-1.

Umpires: D. J. Constant and R. Palmer.

NORTHAMPTONSHIRE v NOTTINGHAMSHIRE

At Northampton, August 24, 25, 26, 28. Northamptonshire won by an innings and 97 runs. Northamptonshire 21 pts, Nottinghamshire 5 pts. Toss: Nottinghamshire.

Northamptonshire's victory, achieved with 17 balls to spare, went beyond the merely extraordinary into the realms of the apparently impossible. Nottinghamshire scored 527, 61 more than any team in history had ever made in a match they lost by an innings. They were 353 for one after the first day and next morning Robinson and Archer took their stand to 294: Robinson scored 209 in 334 balls with 29 fours and a six. The later batting was less successful; even so Nottinghamshire's total was enough to make most teams hope, at best, that they might avoid the follow-on and then get a kindly declaration. However, Nottinghamshire are not famous for kindly declarations and, having won several improbable games already in 1995, Lamb decided to go for the jackpot. Northamptonshire raced to the seventh-highest total in Championship history. The pitch offered the bowlers nothing but, even allowing for that, the Nottinghamshire spinners were particularly poor. Four men made hundreds, including Lamb, who became the fifth man to pass 20,000 runs for Northamptonshire in the course of his 121-ball innings, and Warren, who batted with great fluency for his maiden century. The third day saw 560 runs in 109.3 overs. Nottinghamshire went in again on the final morning 254 behind and at 72 for one the match was apparently heading for a draw. Then three wickets fell in eight balls and Northamptonshire picked up the scent of victory. Kumble was again outstanding, with five wickets at barely a run an over giving him 48 in his last five games. In a final twist Noon, once Northamptonshire's reserve wicket-keeper, threatened to deny them. Overcoming discomfort from a bruised jaw, he held out for a gallant 47 overs before he was dropped by Kumble off Taylor. But Kumble trapped last man Afford next ball. Northamptonshire cricket's elder statesman, Dennis Brookes, was among the spectators. "I've never seen anything like it," he said.

HIGHEST TOTALS IN THE COUNTY CHAMPIONSHIP

887	Yorkshire v Warwickshire at Birmingham	1896
863	Lancashire v Surrey at The Oval	1990
811	Surrey v Somerset at Taunton	1899
810-4 dec.	Warwickshire v Durham at Birmingham	1994
803-4 dec.	Kent v Essex at Brentwood	1934
801	Lancashire v Somerset at Taunton	1895
781-7 dec.	**Northamptonshire v Nottinghamshire at Northampton**	**1995**
761-6 dec.	Essex v Leicestershire at Chelmsford	1990
742	Surrey v Hampshire at The Oval	1909
739-7 dec.	Nottinghamshire v Leicestershire at Nottingham	1903
726	Nottinghamshire v Sussex at Nottingham	1895
707-9 dec.	Surrey v Lancashire at The Oval	1990
706-4 dec.	Surrey v Nottinghamshire at Nottingham	1947
705-8 dec.	Sussex v Surrey at Hastings	1902
704	Yorkshire v Surrey at The Oval	1899
701-4 dec.	Leicestershire v Worcestershire at Worcester	1906

HIGHEST SCORES BY A TEAM LOSING BY AN INNINGS

527	**Notts. (527 and 157) v Northants (781-7 dec.) at Northampton**	**1995**
466	Jamaica (466 and 95) v Barbados (664) at Georgetown	1961-62
461	Trinidad† (131 and 461) v Barbados (623-5 dec.) at Bridgetown	1919-20
439	Sussex (439 and 131) v Gloucestershire (586) at Eastbourne	1936
432	New South Wales (432 and 209) v A. C. MacLaren's XI (769) at Sydney .	1901-02
431	Indians (64 and 431) v Somerset (506-6 dec.) at Taunton	1946
413	Victoria (413 and 130) v New South Wales (705) at Melbourne	1925-26
407	Queensland† (189 and 407) v Victoria (793) at Melbourne	1927-28
405	England (405 and 251) v Australia (695) at The Oval	1930

† *Batted second and followed on.*

Note: The previous highest score by a team losing by an innings in the County Championship was 385 by Surrey (150 and 385) v Hampshire (603-7 dec.) at Southampton, 1994.

Close of play: First day, Nottinghamshire 353-1 (R. T. Robinson 204*, G. F. Archer 93*); Second day, Northamptonshire 149-0 (R. R. Montgomerie 59*, A. Fordham 74*); Third day, Northamptonshire 709-7 (D. J. Capel 74*).

Nottinghamshire

P. R. Pollard c Capel b Kumble	30	– b Curran	16
*R. T. Robinson lbw b Curran	209	– b Kumble	31
G. F. Archer lbw b Capel	158	– lbw b Capel	17
P. Johnson c Lamb b Curran	4	– c and b Kumble	0
C. L. Cairns c Lamb b Taylor	0	– (6) c Montgomerie b Kumble	11
M. P. Dowman c Capel b Kumble	8	– (5) c Snape b Curran	2
†W. M. Noon c Montgomerie b Kumble	33	– (8) not out	25
J. E. Hindson lbw b Capel	9	– (7) c Warren b Curran	4
R. A. Pick lbw b Kumble	11	– c Montgomerie b Kumble	23
R. J. Chapman not out	11	– c Fordham b Taylor	5
J. A. Afford lbw b Curran	12	– lbw b Kumble	0
B 9, l-b 15, n-b 18	42	B 6, l-b 8, w 1, n-b 8	23

1/68 2/362 3/372 4/373 5/419   527   1/24 2/72 3/72 4/72 5/85   157
6/457 7/475 8/487 9/502   6/85 7/90 8/133 9/150

Bonus points – Nottinghamshire 4, Northamptonshire 1 (Score at 120 overs: 403-4).

Bowling: *First Innings*—Taylor 27-8-59-1; Curran 29.1-5-97-3; Capel 23-1-84-2; Penberthy 14-1-59-0; Kumble 50-15-118-4; Snape 14-2-59-0; Bailey 8-0-27-0. *Second Innings*—Taylor 15-3-40-1; Curran 19-7-39-3; Kumble 39.1-21-43-5; Snape 4-3-1-0; Capel 8-3-16-1; Bailey 3-2-4-0.

Northamptonshire

R. R. Montgomerie c Pollard b Cairns	69	A. L. Penberthy c Robinson b Hindson . 35
A. Fordham c Noon b Pick	130	J. N. Snape not out 27
R. J. Bailey c Pollard b Afford	3	B 9, l-b 21, w 10, n-b 24 64
*A. J. Lamb c Johnson b Hindson	115	
†R. J. Warren lbw b Afford	154	1/188 2/205 3/253 (7 wkts dec.) 781
K. M. Curran c Noon b Afford	70	4/412 5/567
D. J. Capel not out	114	6/609 7/709

A. Kumble and J. P. Taylor did not bat.

Bonus points – Northamptonshire 4, Nottinghamshire 1 (Score at 120 overs: 504-4).

Bowling: Cairns 26-4-65-1; Pick 24-3-119-1; Chapman 21-1-109-0; Hindson 33-4-160-2; Afford 41-4-223-3; Archer 12-3-45-0; Dowman 5-0-30-0.

Umpires: J. H. Harris and N. T. Plews.

At Uxbridge, August 29, 30, 31, September 1. NORTHAMPTONSHIRE drew with MIDDLESEX.

NORTHAMPTONSHIRE v WORCESTERSHIRE

At Northampton, September 7, 8, 9, 11. Northamptonshire won by five wickets. Northamptonshire 20 pts, Worcestershire 4 pts. Toss: Worcestershire.

The first Championship fixture to begin at Northampton in September, a novelty made possible by the football club's departure, produced Northamptonshire's 12th win of the season. But the last hope that 1995 would bring their long-awaited maiden Championship had vanished on the final morning, with the news that Warwickshire had beaten Derbyshire; only Middlesex could now catch up. With second place still available, Northamptonshire gratefully accepted Moody's challenge of 260 in 60 overs and sailed past with 40 balls to spare; Capel hit two straight sixes off Lampitt after Fordham and Lamb had added 127 in 24 overs. For home supporters the match was most memorable for the achievement of Anil Kumble in becoming the first bowler since 1991 to claim 100 first-class wickets in a season, and the first to do it for Northamptonshire since another Indian spinner, Bishan Bedi, in 1973. Kumble reached the milestone just before lunch on the third day – the first day and a half were lost to rain – when Solanki drove to extra cover.

Close of play: First day, No play; Second day, Worcestershire 124-5 (S. R. Lampitt 0*, G. R. Haynes 11*); Third day, Worcestershire 54-1 (W. P. C. Weston 22*, T. M. Moody 7*).

Worcestershire

T. S. Curtis c Montgomerie b Curran	20	– lbw b Kumble 20
W. P. C. Weston c Capel b Snape	44	– c Montgomerie b Kumble 89
*T. M. Moody c Snape b Kumble	41	– b Curran 42
D. A. Leatherdale b Kumble	3	– c Ripley b Curran 5
†S. J. Rhodes c Montgomerie b Kumble	1	– c Montgomerie b Curran 32
S. R. Lampitt c Kumble b Curran	2	– not out 17
G. R. Haynes lbw b Kumble	12	– c Ripley b Curran 0
V. S. Solanki c Snape b Kumble	36	– not out 16
P. J. Newport b Taylor	20	
N. V. Radford b Kumble	3	
P. A. Thomas not out	0	
B 1, l-b 11, n-b 2	14	B 7, l-b 7, n-b 2 16

1/35 2/102 3/112 4/112 5/113   196   1/42 2/116 3/144   (6 wkts dec.) 237
6/127 7/131 8/166 9/187   4/174 5/208 6/208

Bonus points – Northamptonshire 4.

Bowling: *First Innings*—Taylor 15–0–50–1; Curran 14–3–45–2; Kumble 31.2–12–63–6; Capel 7–1–21–0; Snape 5–3–5–1. *Second Innings*—Taylor 8–0–32–0; Curran 18–3–78–4; Kumble 21–3–70–2; Snape 5–2–4–0; Capel 9–0–39–0.

Northamptonshire

R. R. Montgomerie c Rhodes b Newport	10	– b Lampitt 13
A. Fordham c Rhodes b Thomas	16	– c Rhodes b Newport 126
R. J. Bailey c Rhodes b Thomas	10	– b Radford 1
*A. J. Lamb c Moody b Newport	2	– c Rhodes b Lampitt 40
R. J. Warren c Solanki b Lampitt	64	– not out 37
K. M. Curran c Rhodes b Lampitt	19	– lbw b Lampitt 0
D. J. Capel c Weston b Lampitt	1	– not out 24
J. N. Snape b Solanki	1	
†D. Ripley not out	28	
A. Kumble lbw b Lampitt	0	
J. P. Taylor not out	0	
B 2, l-b 7, n-b 14	23	B 4, l-b 2, n-b 18 24

1/24 2/41 3/46 4/48 5/94   (9 wkts dec.) 174   1/63 2/70 3/197   (5 wkts) 265
6/106 7/117 8/159 9/159   4/231 5/241

Bonus points – Worcestershire 4.

Bowling: *First Innings*—Newport 10–3–32–2; Thomas 14–2–50–2; Radford 14–3–39–0; Lampitt 12–4–34–4; Solanki 2–0–10–1. *Second Innings*—Newport 15–2–63–1; Thomas 6–1–26–0; Radford 10–4–41–1; Lampitt 11.2–2–70–3; Haynes 4–0–20–0; Moody 5–0–27–0; Solanki 2–0–12–0.

Umpires: J. W. Holder and M. J. Kitchen.

At Hove, September 14, 15, 16, 18. NORTHAMPTONSHIRE drew with SUSSEX.

NOTTINGHAMSHIRE

President: 1995 – C. W. Gillott
Chairman: A. Wheelhouse
Chairman, Cricket Committee: A. Wheelhouse
Secretary/General Manager: B. Robson
Captain: 1995 – R. T. Robinson
1996 – P. Johnson
Cricket Manager: J. A. Ormrod
Head Groundsman: F. Dalling
Scorer: G. Stringfellow

A depressing finish of six successive Championship defeats reduced what was already a bitterly disappointing season for Nottinghamshire to one bordering on total disaster. Four of those last six defeats were by an innings, one by ten wickets, the other by 189 runs. It meant they finished 11th, out of the top five, and thus the prize money, for only the sixth time since the club's upturn in fortunes in 1980.

Their one-day record was no better. Out of Sunday League contention from an early stage – they were 11th there, too – they fell well short of Lord's in the knockout competitions. All of that brought Tim Robinson's turbulent eight-year term as captain to a miserable end, leaving successor Paul Johnson with an unenviable task.

Robinson had predicted that Nottinghamshire would end his reign on a high note, believing the squad was as strong as it had ever been in his time at Trent Bridge, especially with the Test all-rounders, Chris Cairns and Chris Lewis, linking up again. In reality, it proved to be a lack of strength in depth which was the county's undoing. Things started to go wrong as early as the curtain-raising victory over Warwickshire in the Benson and Hedges Cup, on the face of it a win that seemed to justify the pre-season optimism. Lewis was clearly in discomfort with a hip injury that not only wrecked his season, but also brought things to a head so far as his future was concerned; his six-year contract was terminated in July.

Nottinghamshire always knew that refusing Lewis's earlier request to leave, in 1994, was probably only delaying the inevitable. By April, he was citing the alleged firebombing of his mother's flat in London as a further reason for wanting to move closer to his family. The club's patience ran out after Lewis publicly stated he wanted to play for Surrey or Middlesex, thus breaching TCCB regulations; within days his departure was agreed. Whether Nottinghamshire would have been so receptive had he been fit and reproducing his outstanding late-summer form of 1994 is debatable, but news of his release was greeted with cheers around Trent Bridge. This was a sorry end to a stay that promised great things when he arrived in 1992; it was particularly disappointing that his pairing with Cairns never really produced any fireworks.

While Lewis's departure was no surprise, the battle to hold on to the New Zealander Cairns was not something Nottinghamshire had expected. Cairns originally rejected a contract for 1996, saying he was worried about the physical strain of playing all year round; he feared it would disrupt his attempts to revive his stop-start international career after major knee surgery. Subsequently, he agreed to return for at least one more season. The county have already become far too dependent on him producing something spectacular. This was not wholly surprising. Cairns batted with great style and consistency, while his bowling benefited from a Richard Hadlee-style cut in his run-up as he worked his way back to full fitness. His bowling was most effective at Arundel, where he demolished Sussex with 15 for 83, the best match figures of the season and the best for Nottinghamshire for over 40 years. But injuries to other seamers meant he was overworked, rather than used in short, sharp bursts.

When it came to reliability, nobody performed better than Robinson, who carried the side a number of times when injuries hit hard and enjoyed one particularly prolific spell when he hit four centuries and amassed 870 runs in six Championship matches, passing 20,000 first-class runs for Nottinghamshire. Graeme Archer was rewarded for another season of steady improvement with his county cap but, those two and Cairns apart, only one other batsman averaged above 30 in the Championship. That was Johnson, who performed well in one-day cricket but was generally disappointing. In mitigation, he had the added concerns of his daughter's ill-health, his benefit and the imminent captaincy. Of the other batsmen, Paul Pollard overcame injury early in the season with some prolific one-day form, but he could not reproduce that in the Championship either. Mathew Dowman did not make the progress expected of him, while Championship newcomers Jon Wileman and Colin Banton, both already in their mid-twenties, struggled to adjust.

The lack of strength in Nottinghamshire's bowling was even more apparent, especially with all-rounders Kevin Evans and Greg Mike, as well as Lewis, being long-term absentees. Andy Pick provided admirable front-line support for Cairns, while left-arm spinner Jimmy Hindson emerged as the county's leading wicket-taker and a match-winning bowler in helpful conditions, producing ten-wicket hauls in the Essex and Somerset matches. For a while, he seemed a strong candidate for the England A tour, but his confidence suffered badly in the general decline. The responsibility and workload Cairns, Pick and Hindson had to shoulder can be gauged from the fact that no other bowler managed 20 Championship wickets.

With Bruce French announcing his retirement early in the season, Wayne Noon was left unchallenged as wicket-keeper. While there is room for improvement in his glovework, he again proved to be a capable middle-order batsman, and earned his cap. There were also encouraging performances from two youngsters, batsman Noel Gie and left-arm spinner Usman Afzaal; both were picked for the England Under-19 tour of Zimbabwe.

Consequently, it was not all gloom and despondency. But Johnson and Alan Ormrod, who was promoted from senior coach to cricket manager in August, recognised that a lot of work needed doing to pull things round again and they quickly moved to strengthen the squad by signing the Yorkshire batsman Ashley Metcalfe and the Worcestershire seamer Chris Tolley.

One Trent Bridge institution will be missing in 1996. Ron Allsopp has retired as head groundsman after 21 years. However, tradition will be maintained in a remarkable way. He will be succeeded by his assistant Frank Dalling, whose father was Allsopp's predecessor. Four Dallings from three generations have served almost 150 years at Trent Bridge between them. – Nick Lucy.

NOTTINGHAMSHIRE 1995

[*Bill Smith*]

Back row: I. Riches, C. Banton, R. J. Chapman, R. T. Bates, J. R. Wileman, M. Broadhurst, U. Afzaal, M. P. Dowman, L. N. Walker.
Middle row: M. G. Field-Buss, G. F. Archer, G. W. Mike, C. C. Lewis, C. L. Cairns, D. B. Pennett, J. E. Hindson, W. M. Noon.
Front row: P. R. Pollard, J. A. Afford, K. P. Evans, R. T. Robinson (*captain*), J. A. Ormrod (*coach*), P. Johnson, B. N. French, R. A. Pick, M. Newell.

NOTTINGHAMSHIRE RESULTS

All first-class matches – Played 19: Won 5, Lost 9, Drawn 5.

County Championship matches – Played 17: Won 5, Lost 9, Drawn 3.

Bonus points – Batting 41, Bowling 54.

Competition placings – Britannic Assurance County Championship, 11th;
NatWest Bank Trophy, 2nd round; Benson and Hedges Cup, q-f;
AXA Equity & Law League, 11th.

BRITANNIC ASSURANCE CHAMPIONSHIP AVERAGES

BATTING

	Birthplace	*M*	*I*	*NO*	*R*	*HS*	*Avge*
‡R. T. Robinson.....	Sutton-in-Ashfield	17	31	0	1,627	209	52.48
‡G. F. Archer	Carlisle	17	32	3	1,171	158	40.37
‡C. L. Cairns§	Picton, NZ	16	29	1	1,061	115	37.89
‡P. Johnson	Newark	16	29	1	923	120*	32.96
‡P. R. Pollard......	Nottingham	11	19	2	506	120	29.76
‡W. M. Noon	Grimsby	16	29	6	672	64*	29.21
D. B. Pennett	Leeds	7	12	8	89	50	22.25
M. P. Dowman	Grantham	7	14	1	278	73	21.38
‡K. P. Evans	Calverton	6	12	2	207	78*	20.70
‡R. A. Pick........	Nottingham	16	26	4	395	50	17.95
N. A. Gie	Pretoria, SA	3	6	0	98	34	16.33
J. R. Wileman	Sheffield	7	14	3	160	37	14.54
C. Banton	Fish Hoek, SA	5	10	2	114	37	14.25
U. Afzaal	Rawalpindi, Pakistan	7	12	2	134	37	13.40
J. E. Hindson	Huddersfield	15	26	4	251	47	11.40
R. J. Chapman	Nottingham	7	11	3	78	22	9.75
‡J. A. Afford	Crowland	6	9	3	57	15*	9.50
R. T. Bates	Stamford	3	6	0	41	11	6.83
G. W. Mike	Nottingham	3	6	1	23	9*	4.60

Also batted: M. G. Field-Buss (*Mtarfa, Malta*) (1 match) 2, 2; ‡B. N. French (*Warsop*) (1 match) 2, 16.

* Signifies not out.   ‡ Denotes county cap.   § Overseas player.

The following played a total of 12 three-figure innings for Nottinghamshire in County Championship matches – R. T. Robinson 6, G. F. Archer 3, C. L. Cairns 1, P. Johnson 1, P. R. Pollard 1.

BOWLING

	O	*M*	*R*	*W*	*BB*	*5W/i*	*Avge*
C. L. Cairns..........	363.5	84	1,022	49	8-47	3	20.85
R. A. Pick	462.4	95	1,554	45	5-82	2	34.53
J. E. Hindson	628	147	2,059	59	5-67	5	34.89
R. T. Bates	112.1	30	367	10	5-88	1	36.70
K. P. Evans	213.1	55	514	14	3-66	0	36.71
J. A. Afford	276.5	50	921	18	4-58	0	51.16
R. J. Chapman	164.2	22	719	10	3-119	0	71.90

Also bowled: U. Afzaal 182–42–582–5; G. F. Archer 79–11–261–6; C. Banton 3–1–12–0; M. P. Dowman 5–0–30–0; M. G. Field-Buss 32–7–95–0; G. W. Mike 67.5–15–242–4; D. B. Pennett 191.1–33–730–9; J. R. Wileman 89–33–214–4.

Wicket-keepers: W. M. Noon 32 ct, 5 st; B. N. French 1 ct.

Leading Fielder: G. F. Archer 16.

At Cambridge, April 27, 28, 29. NOTTINGHAMSHIRE drew with CAMBRIDGE UNIVERSITY.

NOTTINGHAMSHIRE v DERBYSHIRE

At Nottingham, May 4, 5, 6, 8. Nottinghamshire won by 114 runs. Nottinghamshire 21 pts, Derbyshire 7 pts. Toss: Nottinghamshire. First-class debuts: T. W. Harrison, J. E. Owen. County debut: A. C. Cottam.

Despite Nottinghamshire's margin of victory, this was a closely fought contest until the final morning. Derbyshire resumed on 24 for one, chasing 235 for victory. But only Barnett and night-watchman Cottam – now with his third county – survived for long. Slow left-armers Hindson and Afford exploited helpful conditions and poor batting to finish with four wickets apiece. Lacking Krikken, who had chicken-pox, the visitors were dismissed 45 minutes after lunch. They had held the advantage from the first afternoon, when Nottinghamshire let slip their promising position of 163 for two. Cork took three for 23 in a nine-over burst, backed up by Malcolm. Then Cullinan, who had already scored two centuries in his three previous innings for Derbyshire, struck 131, including 17 fours, to give them a useful first-innings lead of 68. But the determination of Pollard, who overcame a rib muscle injury, and later Johnson and Cairns, who hit two sixes and four fours, enabled Nottinghamshire to leave what proved an awkward target.

Close of play: First day, Derbyshire 43-0 (K. J. Barnett 28*, A. S. Rollins 14*); Second day, Nottinghamshire 31-0 (P. R. Pollard 15*, R. T. Robinson 14*); Third day, Derbyshire 24-1 (K. J. Barnett 17*, A. C. Cottam 0*).

Nottinghamshire

P. R. Pollard lbw b Malcolm	17	– c Cork b DeFreitas		85
*R. T. Robinson b Malcolm	15	– lbw b Barnett		18
G. F. Archer lbw b Barnett	61	– lbw b Cork		9
P. Johnson lbw b Cork	65	– b DeFreitas		47
C. L. Cairns c Cullinan b Cork	18	– b Cork		64
M. P. Dowman not out	23	– c Rollins b Cork		17
†W. M. Noon lbw b Cork	2	– c O'Gorman b Cork		0
K. P. Evans lbw b DeFreitas	18	– c Harrison b Malcolm		4
G. W. Mike c Cullinan b Malcolm	2	– c Barnett b Malcolm		0
J. E. Hindson b Malcolm	3	– c Rollins b Malcolm		9
J. A. Afford c Cullinan b Cork	0	– not out		10
B 2, l-b 7, n-b 11	20	B 20, l-b 10, w 3, n-b 6		39
	244			**302**

1/29 2/50 3/163 4/183 5/189   244   1/38 2/73 3/169 4/196 5/260   302
6/192 7/224 8/227 9/241   6/260 7/279 8/279 9/279

Bonus points – Nottinghamshire 1, Derbyshire 4.

Bowling: First Innings—Malcolm 21-7-53-4; Cork 21.2-4-51-4; DeFreitas 19-4-49-1; Cottam 6-1-30-0; Barnett 20-6-52-1. *Second Innings*—Malcolm 21.1-2-57-3; Cork 31-11-65-4; DeFreitas 26-11-43-2; Barnett 11-0-38-1; Cottam 6-1-20-0; Harrison 17-3-49-0.

Derbyshire

*K. J. Barnett c Noon b Cairns	28	– c Pollard b Hindson		37
A. S. Rollins lbw b Cairns	15	– c Noon b Evans		5
D. J. Cullinan b Hindson	131	– (4) b Hindson		0
T. J. G. O'Gorman c Evans b Cairns	39	– (5) b Hindson		4
J. E. Owen c Pollard b Afford	4	– (6) b Afford		6
D. G. Cork c and b Mike	8	– (7) lbw b Hindson		2
P. A. J. DeFreitas lbw b Mike	0	– (8) not out		11
T. W. Harrison c Noon b Mike	1	– (9) c Dowman b Afford		6
†K. M. Krikken not out	36	– absent ill		
D. E. Malcolm c Afford b Cairns	13	– c Dowman b Afford		5
A. C. Cottam c Noon b Mike	13	– (3) b Afford		32
B 5, l-b 1, n-b 18	24	B 4, l-b 5, w 1, n-b 2		12
	312			**120**

1/43 2/44 3/139 4/165 5/186   312   1/24 2/56 3/60 4/77 5/89   120
6/186 7/196 8/270 9/292   6/96 7/108 8/114 9/120

Bonus points – Derbyshire 3, Nottinghamshire 4.

Bowling: *First Innings*—Cairns 26–6–83–4; Evans 24–7–43–0; Afford 27–5–57–1; Hindson 10–0–36–1; Mike 18.5–4–87–4. *Second Innings*—Cairns 4–0–17–0; Evans 7–4–6–1; Afford 27.5–8–58–4; Hindson 25–11–30–4.

Umpires: J. D. Bond and N. T. Plews.

At Bristol, May 11, 12, 13, 15. NOTTINGHAMSHIRE lost to GLOUCESTERSHIRE by 134 runs.

At Oxford, May 18, 19, 20. NOTTINGHAMSHIRE drew with OXFORD UNIVERSITY.

At Liverpool, May 25, 26, 27, 29. NOTTINGHAMSHIRE drew with LANCASHIRE.

NOTTINGHAMSHIRE v ESSEX

At Nottingham, June 1, 2, 3, 5. Nottinghamshire won by 16 runs. Nottinghamshire 23 pts, Essex 7 pts. Toss: Nottinghamshire. Championship debut: C. Banton.

The first ten-wicket haul of Hindson's career saw Nottinghamshire to a thrilling victory off the penultimate ball. They took the last five wickets for three runs in 14 balls after Essex entered the final 20 overs needing 119 with seven wickets in hand. Spin played a major role from the first day and claimed 26 of the 36 wickets. But batsmen also prospered. Tim Robinson and Dowman shared century opening stands in both innings and Robinson became the tenth man to pass 20,000 runs for Nottinghamshire on the rain-shortened third day. Their first innings collapsed after that solid start, before Noon and Pick led a recovery. Prichard dropped down the order and provided Essex's backbone with his first hundred of the season. His team looked to be on top when Nottinghamshire's middle order crumbled again to Such's spin. But once again Noon rallied them, this time in an unbroken stand of 103 with Cairns. Set 288 for victory in what became 66 overs, Hussain kept Essex on course with a two-and-a-half-hour century, before three run-outs and Hindson's cool nerve conspired to bring about their dramatic downfall.

Close of play: First day, Essex 0-0 (G. A. Gooch 0*, D. D. J. Robinson 0*); Second day, Nottinghamshire 50-0 (M. P. Dowman 23*, R. T. Robinson 23*); Third day, Nottinghamshire 114-1 (M. P. Dowman 56*, G. F. Archer 6*).

Nottinghamshire

M. P. Dowman c Hussain b Childs	29	– c Cousins b Childs 73
*R. T. Robinson b Irani	101	– lbw b Such 48
C. Banton b Such	1	– (4) b Childs 0
C. L. Cairns c Hussain b Childs	50	– (8) not out 68
J. R. Wileman c Lewis b Such	12	– lbw b Such 1
G. F. Archer b Such	13	– (3) c Lewis b Such 36
K. P. Evans lbw b Childs	2	– (6) c Hussain b Such 8
†W. M. Noon not out	63	– (7) not out 35
J. E. Hindson b Childs	0	
R. A. Pick b Waugh	29	
J. A. Afford b Cousins	1	
L-b 11, n-b 2	13	B 1, l-b 2, n-b 2 5

1/107 2/108 3/181 4/191 5/209   314   1/103 2/153 3/157   (6 wkts dec.) 274
6/218 7/218 8/218 9/278   4/161 5/164 6/171

Bonus points – Nottinghamshire 3, Essex 4.

Bowling: *First Innings*—Cousins 6–1–31–1; Waugh 22–7–40–1; Irani 23–5–64–1; Such 26–5–94–3; Childs 36–10–74–4. *Second Innings*—Waugh 14–2–58–0; Cousins 2–0–11–0; Childs 39–6–115–2; Such 35–10–87–4.

Essex

G. A. Gooch c Evans b Hindson	45	– b Hindson	37
D. D. J. Robinson c Dowman b Cairns	8	– lbw b Hindson	31
M. E. Waugh c Hindson b Cairns	7	– lbw b Afford	2
N. Hussain c Evans b Hindson	32	– run out	106
*P. J. Prichard c Banton b Hindson	109	– lbw b Afford	39
R. C. Irani lbw b Afford	36	– run out	30
J. J. B. Lewis lbw b Pick	1	– st Noon b Hindson	14
†R. J. Rollins c Cairns b Pick	16	– c Dowman b Hindson	0
P. M. Such c Pick b Hindson	1	– not out	2
D. M. Cousins not out	17	– (11) c Robinson b Hindson	0
J. H. Childs c Cairns b Hindson	18	– (10) run out	0
B 1, l-b 6, n-b 4	11	B 4, l-b 6	10

1/23 2/33 3/77 4/116 5/198	301	1/54 2/67 3/77 4/185 5/242	271
6/201 7/237 8/238 9/269		6/268 7/268 8/271 9/271	

Bonus points – Essex 3, Nottinghamshire 4.

Bowling: *First Innings*—Hindson 31.1–4–92–5; Pick 20–4–64–2; Cairns 11–1–40–2; Afford 17–5–52–1; Evans 20–7–46–0. *Second Innings*—Pick 8–0–33–0; Evans 12–1–37–0; Hindson 27.5–1–105–5; Afford 18–0–86–2.

Umpires: J. H. Hampshire and G. Sharp.

NOTTINGHAMSHIRE v WORCESTERSHIRE

At Nottingham, June 8, 9, 10, 12. Worcestershire won by three wickets. Worcestershire 23 pts, Nottinghamshire 5 pts. Toss: Nottinghamshire.

Umpires Whitehead and White summoned TCCB officials to look at the pitch, which looked roughed-up, and turned from the start. But the match produced 1,243 runs and a lot of fascinating cricket, and Nottinghamshire were exonerated, though they were warned that they had "sailed close to the wind" in their method of preparation. An outstanding performance from Moody, who scored two hundreds in the match, enabled Worcestershire to triumph, despite having only one spinner – D'Oliveira, recalled from the second team because Illingworth and Hick were on Test duty – to Nottinghamshire's three. In fact, Moody was particularly severe on the slower bowlers. He hit 17 fours and three sixes in his 306-ball 157, putting on 227 with Weston first time round, and then hammered 15 fours in 106 off 115 balls in the second. He paved Worcestershire's way to a tricky target of 261 in 60 overs, coming in at six for two, which soon deteriorated to 11 for three. But he and Haynes added 151 in 31 overs, and Worcestershire eventually won with five balls to spare. Moody also made five slip catches, including Johnson – Nottinghamshire's top batsman in both innings – twice.

Close of play: First day, Nottinghamshire 277-9 (W. M. Noon 42*, J. A. Afford 10*); Second day, Worcestershire 279-3 (T. M. Moody 132*, N. V. Radford 1*); Third day, Nottinghamshire 200-3 (P. Johnson 62*, C. L. Cairns 9*).

Nottinghamshire

M. P. Dowman c Moody b Haynes	9	– c Moody b Haynes	7
*R. T. Robinson c and b Newport	40	– c Rhodes b Lampitt	51
G. F. Archer c Moody b Lampitt	9	– b Newport	61
P. Johnson c Moody b Lampitt	96	– c Moody b Newport	73
C. L. Cairns st Rhodes b D'Oliveira	26	– c D'Oliveira b Lampitt	42
K. P. Evans b D'Oliveira	6	– lbw b Newport	0
†W. M. Noon b Newport	59	– c Curtis b Lampitt	45
J. E. Hindson c Weston b D'Oliveira	1	– lbw b Lampitt	6
R. A. Pick lbw b Newport	15	– st Rhodes b D'Oliveira	2
M. G. Field-Buss lbw b Newport	2	– c sub b D'Oliveira	2
J. A. Afford not out	15	– not out	11
L-b 7, n-b 16	23	L-b 3, n-b 16	19

1/21 2/44 3/101 4/160 5/172	301	1/21 2/87 3/168 4/221 5/221	319
6/212 7/215 8/232 9/236		6/282 7/292 8/295 9/299	

Bonus points – Nottinghamshire 3, Worcestershire 4.

Bowling: *First Innings*—Newport 26.4–5–61–4; Haynes 12–3–31–1; Lampitt 22–6–59–2; D'Oliveira 28–4–88–3; Leatherdale 1–0–10–0; Radford 10–2–38–0; Moody 3–0–7–0. *Second Innings*—Newport 20–8–61–3; D'Oliveira 37–3–122–2; Haynes 6–1–15–1; Radford 9–1–40–0; Lampitt 23.1–7–71–4; Weston 1–0–7–0.

Worcestershire

*T. S. Curtis lbw b Pick	0 – lbw b Evans	3
W. P. C. Weston c Noon b Hindson	105 – c Evans b Pick	3
M. J. Church lbw b Hindson	25 – b Pick	0
T. M. Moody c Robinson b Evans	157 – b Hindson	106
N. V. Radford c Johnson b Evans	1 – (9) not out	4
G. R. Haynes c Dowman b Pick	7 – (5) c Dowman b Hindson	55
†S. J. Rhodes c Archer b Afford	22 – (6) b Evans	27
S. R. Lampitt c Cairns b Hindson	15 – (7) not out	32
D. B. D'Oliveira b Afford	0 – (8) run out	16
P. J. Newport c Dowman b Afford	1	
D. A. Leatherdale not out	5	
B 4, l-b 13, w 1, n-b 4	22	B 7, l-b 7, w 1, n-b 2 17

1/5 2/48 3/275 4/279 5/294   360   1/6 2/6 3/11 4/162   (7 wkts) 263
6/318 7/352 8/352 9/354   5/189 6/227 7/250

Bonus points – Worcestershire 3, Nottinghamshire 2 (Score at 120 overs: 334-6).

Bowling: *First Innings*—Pick 18–4–60–2; Evans 19–7–61–2; Hindson 35.1–9–85–3; Field-Buss 28–7–66–0; Afford 35–8–71–3. *Second Innings*—Evans 14.1–2–46–2; Pick 8–2–35–2; Hindson 23–4–86–2; Afford 10–0–53–0; Field-Buss 4–0–29–0.

Umpires: R. A. White and A. G. T. Whitehead.

At Leicester, June 15, 16, 17, 19. NOTTINGHAMSHIRE drew with LEICESTERSHIRE.

NOTTINGHAMSHIRE v KENT

At Nottingham, June 22, 23, 24, 26. Nottinghamshire won by three wickets. Nottinghamshire 23 pts, Kent 6 pts. Toss: Kent. First-class debut: U. Afzaal.

Evidently mindful of the umpires' suspicions of their previous pitch, Trent Bridge prepared a batsman's paradise. It yielded 1,642 runs, the third-highest aggregate in Championship history, and 535 on the final day, when Nottinghamshire did well to meet a stiff target of 330 in 51 overs. Yet such riches were unimaginable after 80 minutes' play, when Kent were 68 for five. De Silva responded magnificently. For the second time in a week, he scored a century between lunch and tea. He batted for 317 minutes, hitting 35 fours and two sixes in 225 from 273 balls and put on 315 with maiden centurion Ealham, a Kent sixth-wicket record. Kent passed their highest total against Nottinghamshire, and the run-glut continued when Robinson scored 196 in seven and a half hours in Nottinghamshire's solid reply. Then Kent ran up 287 before Benson declared, ruthlessly stranding Taylor on 99. At first the challenge looked too steep, but Nottinghamshire got there with three balls to spare, scoring at seven and a half an over after tea. Robinson uncharacteristically blasted six sixes and four fours and put on 164 in 29 overs with Pollard.

Close of play: First day, Kent 398-6 (M. A. Ealham 114*, S. C. Willis 2*); Second day, Nottinghamshire 201-2 (R. T. Robinson 92*, P. Johnson 57*); Third day, Kent 83-0 (D. P. Fulton 22*, T. R. Ward 57*).

Kent

D. P. Fulton lbw b Pennett	2	– c Noon b Pennett	52
*M. R. Benson b Cairns	16		
T. R. Ward c Pick b Pennett	23	– (2) run out	59
P. A. de Silva c Wileman b Pennett	225	– c and b Pick	16
N. R. Taylor c Noon b Cairns	4	– (3) not out	99
G. R. Cowdrey lbw b Pick	0	– (5) not out	53
M. A. Ealham c Johnson b Pick	121		
†S. C. Willis b Pick	53		
M. M. Patel b Cairns	13		
M. J. McCague b Hindson	59		
T. N. Wren not out	4		
L-b 7, n-b 6	13	L-b 7, w 1	8

1/3 2/41 3/43 4/65 5/68   533   1/89 2/138 3/170   (3 wkts dec.) 287
6/383 7/405 8/443 9/523

Bonus points – Kent 4, Nottinghamshire 3 (Score at 120 overs: 416-7).

Bowling: *First Innings*—Pick 27.1-6-75-3; Pennett 35-5-136-3; Cairns 26-9-71-3; Wileman 20-4-59-0; Hindson 18-3-85-1; Afzaal 26-4-91-0; Archer 3-0-9-0. *Second Innings*—Pick 15-1-53-1; Pennett 13-3-56-1; Hindson 23-5-72-0; Afzaal 19-4-73-0; Wileman 6-1-26-0.

Nottinghamshire

P. R. Pollard b Patel	25	– c McCague b Ealham	75
*R. T. Robinson b Patel	196	– b Ealham	88
G. F. Archer b Patel	16	– (5) c McCague b Patel	22
P. Johnson b McCague	68	– (3) run out	45
C. L. Cairns c Cowdrey b Ealham	30	– (4) c Willis b McCague	41
J. R. Wileman c Ward b Wren	16	– (7) not out	17
†W. M. Noon b Ealham	16	– (6) c and b McCague	6
U. Afzaal lbw b Ealham	2		
J. E. Hindson c Willis b McCague	47	– not out	2
R. A. Pick not out	50	– (8) run out	0
D. B. Pennett not out	1		
B 4, l-b 16, w 4	24	B 14, l-b 9, w 12	35

1/71 2/103 3/224 4/275 5/323   (9 wkts dec.) 491   1/164 2/205 3/249 4/295 (7 wkts) 331
6/381 7/384 8/391 9/488   5/307 6/316 7/322

Bonus points – Nottinghamshire 4, Kent 2 (Score at 120 overs: 359-5).

Bowling: *First Innings*—McCague 30-3-122-2; Wren 27-4-75-1; Ealham 22-6-78-3; Patel 48.3-14-137-3; de Silva 27-7-59-0. *Second Innings*—McCague 10-0-53-2; Wren 12-1-67-0; Patel 16.3-0-107-1; de Silva 4-0-30-0; Ealham 8-0-51-2.

Umpires: K. J. Lyons and B. J. Meyer.

NOTTINGHAMSHIRE v SOMERSET

At Nottingham, June 29, 30, July 1, 3. Drawn. Nottinghamshire 8 pts, Somerset 6 pts. Toss: Nottinghamshire.

The game petered out into a draw noteworthy only for personal landmarks: Hindson took ten wickets for the second time in the season; Robinson became the second man to reach 1,000 runs, a day after Byas of Yorkshire; and Bowler followed him on the Monday. Almost two years to the day since his Test debut on this ground, Lathwell showed glimpses of the form that earned his call-up, hitting 23 fours in a three-and-a-half-hour century. But Nottinghamshire's two left-arm spinners, Hindson and Afzaal, pegged Somerset back in the afternoon. Robinson continued his prolific June form with his third hundred in four home games, while Pollard scored his first of the season; they opened with a stand of 233 in 67 overs. At 332 for two, Nottinghamshire had their sights set on a massive lead. But once Mushtaq Ahmed overcame a virus and returned to take three wickets, they fell short of expectations. Although they pushed hard for victory on the final day, Somerset stood firm. Bowler battled for 311 minutes and 91 runs to lead the rearguard action, with Ecclestone providing worthy support.

Close of play: First day, Somerset 320-8 (J. I. D. Kerr 10*, Mushtaq Ahmed 10*); Second day, Nottinghamshire 342-3 (P. Johnson 21*, C. L. Cairns 4*); Third day, Somerset 105-3 (P. D. Bowler 46*, H. R. J. Trump 1*).

Somerset

M. N. Lathwell b Hindson	110	– b Chapman	11
P. D. Bowler c Pollard b Hindson	35	– c Pollard b Hindson	91
†R. J. Turner b Cairns	12	– (8) c Noon b Pick	5
R. J. Harden c Hindson b Chapman	66	– c Noon b Hindson	18
P. C. L. Holloway hit wkt b Cairns	19	– (3) c Noon b Hindson	19
K. A. Parsons c Archer b Hindson	1	– c Noon b Hindson	61
S. C. Ecclestone c Archer b Afzaal	38	– c Noon b Archer	67
*A. N. Hayhurst c Pollard b Afzaal	0	– (9) not out	25
J. I. D. Kerr st Noon b Hindson	37	– (10) c Pollard b Wileman	25
Mushtaq Ahmed b Hindson	20	– (11) c Johnson b Archer	9
H. R. J. Trump not out	4	– (5) b Hindson	1
L-b 18, n-b 6	24	B 6, l-b 11, n-b 12	29

1/98 2/152 3/176 4/227 5/234   366   1/19 2/47 3/101 4/105 5/206   361
6/289 7/289 8/305 9/353   6/239 7/268 8/337 9/355

Bonus points – Somerset 4, Nottinghamshire 4.

In the second innings A. N. Hayhurst, when 25, retired hurt at 313 and resumed at 355.

Bowling: *First Innings*—Pick 9–1–46–0; Cairns 27–6–73–2; Wileman 10–5–25–0; Hindson 25.3–6–67–5; Afzaal 29–8–73–2; Chapman 18–4–64–1. *Second Innings*—Cairns 27–10–55–0; Chapman 15–2–63–1; Hindson 44–20–78–5; Afzaal 28–11–63–0; Pick 12–1–54–1; Wileman 8–4–21–1; Archer 2–0–10–2.

Nottinghamshire

P. R. Pollard c and b Trump	120		
*R. T. Robinson c Trump b Lathwell	134		
G. F. Archer b Ecclestone	39		
P. Johnson c Harden b Trump	21		
C. L. Cairns c Lathwell b Mushtaq Ahmed	35		
J. R. Wileman c Turner b Mushtaq Ahmed	3	– (1) not out	4
†W. M. Noon lbw b Kerr	20		
U. Afzaal c Turner b Kerr	34	– (2) not out	0
J. E. Hindson not out	27		
R. A. Pick lbw b Mushtaq Ahmed	18		
R. J. Chapman c Turner b Ecclestone	1		
B 2, l-b 14, w 9, n-b 2	27	N-b 4	4

1/233 2/293 3/332 4/344 5/375   479   (no wkt) 8
6/376 7/410 8/447 9/468

Bonus points – Nottinghamshire 4, Somerset 2 (Score at 120 overs: 375-5).

Bowling: *First Innings*—Kerr 20–3–98–2; Ecclestone 20.3–6–48–2; Mushtaq Ahmed 43–18–81–3; Parsons 9–1–35–0; Hayhurst 11–0–44–0; Trump 41–16–75–2; Bowler 6–0–30–0; Lathwell 12–2–52–1. *Second Innings*—Mushtaq Ahmed 1–0–8–0.

Umpires: H. D. Bird and R. Palmer.

At Arundel, July 6, 7. NOTTINGHAMSHIRE beat SUSSEX by ten wickets.

At Guildford, July 20, 21, 22, 24. NOTTINGHAMSHIRE lost to SURREY by 171 runs.

NOTTINGHAMSHIRE v YORKSHIRE

At Nottingham, July 27, 28, 29. Nottinghamshire won by eight wickets. Nottinghamshire 23 pts, Yorkshire 5 pts. Toss: Yorkshire.

Yorkshire lost in three days after collapsing twice. They had started solidly, reaching a comfortable 154 for two, but lost their next eight for 102. Ironically, their decline followed the clearing of seating behind the bowler's arm at the pavilion end, which they requested at lunch. Robinson's fifth Championship hundred of the season, a five-hour 124 containing 17 fours, provided the rock on which Nottinghamshire built a lead of 147. There was no way back for Yorkshire. Only a second stylish contribution from Vaughan, and a late flourish from Hartley, ensured Nottinghamshire would bat again; Cairns, with a burst of three for one in nine deliveries, and Hindson picked up four wickets each. Nottinghamshire needed only 17, but the game ended farcically with two tailenders sacrificing their wickets as two Yorkshire batsmen bowled in caps. Trent Bridge paid its tribute to Harold Larwood with a minute's silence. However, when Nottinghamshire announced the release of Chris Lewis, in the fourth year of a six-year contract, the crowd cheered.

Close of play: First day, Nottinghamshire 75-0 (P. R. Pollard 34*, R. T. Robinson 41*); Second day, Nottinghamshire 366-8 (U. Afzaal 14*, R. A. Pick 6*).

Yorkshire

S. A. Kellett c Archer b Cairns	4	– run out	0
M. P. Vaughan c and b Hindson	61	– c and b Hindson	42
*D. Byas c Hindson b Cairns	60	– c Noon b Cairns	1
M. G. Bevan c Pollard b Hindson	33	– lbw b Hindson	21
A. McGrath lbw b Pick	23	– lbw b Pick	1
B. Parker lbw b Pick	1	– b Hindson	12
†R. J. Blakey st Noon b Afzaal	15	– c Noon b Cairns	9
P. J. Hartley c Afzaal b Pick	10	– c Noon b Cairns	27
C. E. W. Silverwood c Noon b Afzaal	6	– c Robinson b Hindson	8
R. D. Stemp not out	22	– c Archer b Cairns	5
M. A. Robinson c Noon b Hindson	8	– not out	4
L-b 10, w 1, n-b 2	13	B 10, l-b 11, w 2, n-b 10	33
	256		**163**

1/11 2/106 3/154 4/164 5/167 6/200 7/216 8/223 9/224

1/16 2/18 3/52 4/53 5/86 6/98 7/134 8/147 9/153

Bonus points – Yorkshire 2, Nottinghamshire 4.

Bowling: *First Innings*—Pick 18–2–66–3; Cairns 17–4–36–2; Chapman 8–0–36–0; Hindson 21.2–7–67–3; Afzaal 19–5–41–2. *Second Innings*—Cairns 13–5–32–4; Chapman 4–0–19–0; Hindson 22.3–10–65–4; Pick 6–1–12–1; Afzaal 8–1–14–0.

Nottinghamshire

P. R. Pollard lbw b Stemp	35		
*R. T. Robinson c Parker b Robinson	124		
G. F. Archer b Stemp	1	– (4) not out	4
P. Johnson c Bevan b Stemp	65		
C. Banton b Silverwood	37	– (3) not out	5
C. L. Cairns c Byas b Bevan	41		
†W. M. Noon lbw b Silverwood	17		
U. Afzaal c Byas b Vaughan	37	– (2) c Stemp b Vaughan	0
J. E. Hindson b Vaughan	7		
R. A. Pick b Stemp	16		
R. J. Chapman not out	0	– (1) c Kellett b Vaughan	9
B 9, l-b 6, n-b 8	23		
	403	1/5 2/10 (2 wkts)	**18**

1/79 2/81 3/209 4/247 5/296 6/324 7/341 8/360 9/391

Bonus points – Nottinghamshire 3, Yorkshire 3 (Score at 120 overs: 343-7).

Bowling: *First Innings*—Hartley 30–8–75–0; Silverwood 17–2–72–2; Robinson 22–8–54–1; Stemp 57–20–108–4; Vaughan 21.5–4–64–2; Bevan 7–2–15–1. *Second Innings*—Vaughan 4.4–1–10–2; Bevan 4–2–8–0.

Umpires: D. J. Constant and K. J. Lyons.

At Lord's, August 3, 4, 5. NOTTINGHAMSHIRE lost to MIDDLESEX by an innings and 186 runs.

NOTTINGHAMSHIRE v WARWICKSHIRE

At Nottingham, August 17, 18, 19. Warwickshire won by ten wickets. Warwickshire 24 pts, Nottinghamshire 4 pts. Toss: Nottinghamshire.

Losing the toss for the seventh Championship match running was no handicap for the champions. Cairns and Johnson rescued Nottinghamshire from humiliation twice, but could not prevent Warwickshire completing their tenth win, on the third day. In the first innings they combined at 44 for four and put on 84 in 21 overs, before Munton dismissed both in six deliveries; he took four for 16 in an 11-over spell in the afternoon heat. In the second, an innings defeat was on the cards as Nottinghamshire slumped to 66 for four and lost Banton when Donald hit him, breaking a bone just above his left wrist. This time Johnson and Cairns shared an entertaining stand of 151; Cairns blasted five sixes and eight fours, and Johnson scored his first Championship hundred of the season, ensuring that Warwickshire had to bat again briefly. Munton swept away the last four wickets in 24 balls, for match figures of ten for 116. Penney had set up Warwickshire's first-innings lead of 248 with a stunning four-hour 144, striking three sixes and 23 fours.

Close of play: First day, Warwickshire 139-2 (W. G. Khan 62*, K. J. Piper 10*); Second day, Nottinghamshire 66-4 (P. Johnson 25*).

Nottinghamshire

P. R. Pollard c Knight b Donald	6	– b Donald	14
*R. T. Robinson lbw b Donald	6	– c Piper b Reeve	14
G. F. Archer lbw b Munton	9	– c Reeve b Munton	10
P. Johnson c Knight b Munton	44	– not out	120
C. Banton c Piper b Giles	5	– (6) retired hurt	0
C. L. Cairns lbw b Munton	52	– (7) b Donald	83
†W. M. Noon b Munton	5	– (8) b Munton	2
U. Afzaal c Piper b Munton	11	– (9) c Piper b Munton	0
J. E. Hindson b Donald	10	– (10) c Knight b Munton	8
R. A. Pick c Ostler b Reeve	9	– (11) c Ostler b Munton	9
D. B. Pennett not out	0	– (5) b Donald	0
B 2, l-b 5, n-b 2	9	B 4, l-b 4, n-b 4	12

1/8 2/17 3/25 4/44 5/128   166   1/14 2/29 3/64 4/66 5/223   272
6/133 7/142 8/151 9/166   6/238 7/242 8/262 9/272

Bonus points – Warwickshire 4.

In the second innings C. Banton retired hurt at 72.

Bowling: *First Innings*—Donald 17–4–52–3; Munton 23–10–37–5; Giles 16–3–52–1; Reeve 8.3–5–9–1; Twose 4–2–9–0. *Second Innings*—Donald 26.6–6–78–3; Munton 27.5–9–79–5; Reeve 15–2–48–1; Smith 14–5–49–0; Twose 1–1–0–0; Giles 1–0–10–0.

Warwickshire

N. V. Knight b Pick	6	– not out	18
W. G. Khan b Cairns	68	– not out	10
D. P. Ostler c Pennett b Hindson	47		
†K. J. Piper c Noon b Cairns	18		
R. G. Twose lbw b Afzaal	44		
T. L. Penney b Cairns	144		
*D. A. Reeve lbw b Pick	1		
N. M. K. Smith b Cairns	14		
A. F. Giles c Banton b Archer	10		
A. A. Donald c Hindson b Pick	3		
T. A. Munton not out	19		
B 13, l-b 8, w 4, n-b 15	40		

1/12 2/126 3/160 4/176 5/240   414   (no wkt) 28
6/255 7/279 8/324 9/341

Bonus points – Warwickshire 4, Nottinghamshire 4.

Bowling: *First Innings*—Pick 27–10–65–3; Cairns 24.1–7–81–4; Pennett 20–5–61–0; Hindson 26–5–105–1; Afzaal 11–2–52–1; Archer 9–2–29–1. *Second Innings*—Pick 4.4–0–20–0; Archer 4–2–8–0.

Umpires: G. I. Burgess and P. Willey.

At Northampton, August 24, 25, 26, 28. NOTTINGHAMSHIRE lost to NORTHAMPTON-SHIRE by an innings and 97 runs.

NOTTINGHAMSHIRE v HAMPSHIRE

At Nottingham, August 29, 30, 31. Hampshire won by an innings and seven runs. Hampshire 22 pts, Nottinghamshire 3 pts. Toss: Hampshire. First-class debut: N. A. Gie.

History repeated itself for Udal, who had taken ten for 171 on Hampshire's previous visit to Trent Bridge in 1993. He went one better this time, with 11 for 170, as Nottinghamshire suffered their fourth successive Championship defeat to complete a miserable August. They had lost three of those matches by an innings and the other by ten wickets. It was an encouraging start for Stephenson, who had just taken over the captaincy from Nicholas; Hampshire had not won since June 26. A battling 264-minute innings of 88 by Whitaker helped Hampshire build up a strong position on a pitch already assisting the slower bowlers and Udal chipped in with a breezy 45 not out. Maru, called up for his second Championship appearance of the season, took his 500th first-class wicket, providing good support for Udal; Nottinghamshire followed on and subsided again without much of a fight on the third day.

Close of play: First day, Hampshire 198-4 (P. R. Whitaker 66*, G. W. White 5*); Second day, Nottinghamshire 142-9 (W. M. Noon 37*, D. B. Pennett 0*).

Hampshire

V. P. Terry lbw b Wileman	14	S. D. Udal not out		45
J. S. Laney b Pennett	44	H. H. Streak c Noon b Hindson		0
*J. P. Stephenson c Pick b Wileman	11	R. J. Maru b Hindson		7
P. R. Whitaker lbw b Pick	88			
M. C. J. Nicholas c Wileman b Bates	49	B 13, l-b 5, w 1, n-b 4		23
G. W. White c Robinson b Pick	25			
K. D. James c Pick b Hindson	20	1/22 2/38 3/85 4/184 5/236		333
†A. N. Aymes lbw b Pick	7	6/245 7/257 8/305 9/305		

Bonus points – Hampshire 2, Nottinghamshire 3 (Score at 120 overs: 279-7).

Bowling: Pick 24–6–72–3; Pennett 22–4–57–1; Wileman 27–16–33–2; Archer 4–0–11–0; Hindson 38.3–13–90–3; Bates 21–8–52–1.

Nottinghamshire

P. R. Pollard lbw b Streak	0	– c Maru b Udal	29
*R. T. Robinson c Maru b Udal	37	– c Terry b Udal	18
G. F. Archer c Maru b Udal	16	– c Aymes b Maru	47
P. Johnson c Aymes b Maru	13	– c Laney b Udal	0
N. A. Gie lbw b Udal	0	– lbw b Udal	15
J. R. Wileman c Laney b Udal	26	– c Terry b Maru	22
†W. M. Noon st Aymes b Maru	43	– c Aymes b Maru	0
R. T. Bates run out	9	– lbw b Streak	11
J. E. Hindson b Udal	0	– c and b Udal	11
R. A. Pick c Laney b Maru	2	– not out	8
D. B. Pennett not out	1	– c and b Udal	4
L-b 5, n-b 2	7	B 4, l-b 3	7
1/0 2/50 3/61 4/61 5/75	154	1/46 2/67 3/67 4/97 5/113	172
6/118 7/136 8/136 9/141		6/123 7/145 8/145 9/168	

Bonus points – Hampshire 4.

Bowling: *First Innings*—Streak 6–3–9–1; James 7–5–16–0; Udal 34–10–85–5; Maru 33–19–38–3; Stephenson 1–0–1–0. *Second Innings*—Streak 12–4–25–1; James 4–1–9–0; Udal 28.5–5–85–6; Maru 23–8–46–3.

Umpires: B. Dudleston and B. J. Meyer.

At Cardiff, September 7, 8, 9, 11. NOTTINGHAMSHIRE lost to GLAMORGAN by 189 runs.

At Chester-le-Street, September 14, 15, 16. NOTTINGHAMSHIRE lost to DURHAM by an innings and 14 runs.

SOMERSET

President: J. Luff
Chairman: R. Parsons
Chairman, Cricket Committee: B. C. Rose
Chief Executive: P. W. Anderson
Captain: A. N. Hayhurst
Director of Cricket: R. M. H. Cottam
Coach: P. J. Robinson
Head Groundsman: P. Frost
Scorer: D. A. Oldam

Somerset's advances in 1995 were slight. They rose two places in both the Championship and the Sunday League – to ninth and 14th respectively. They reached the Benson and Hedges semi-final, albeit slightly freakishly, having beaten only two first-class counties on the way, but succumbed after giving Kent a fair run at Canterbury. In the NatWest Trophy they went out in the first round, though it was a noble failure, as they were drawn against eventual winners Warwickshire, conceded 357 and lost by only 18 runs.

Supporters will remember with relish the week in which Somerset beat Gloucestershire, in the Benson and Hedges quarter-final, and Yorkshire, for the first time in the Championship since 1981, and also in the Sunday League. That began a triumphant June, which featured four consecutive Championship victories. In the next match, they beat Surrey by scoring the highest fourth-innings winning total in their history; a week later, against Derbyshire, they won after following on, for the first time since 1905; and victory against Sussex lifted them to joint fifth in the Championship, four weeks after they had been next to bottom. There was another encouraging run of three wins in four games a little later, but they finally settled in the middle of the table.

Somerset's two greatest handicaps were the injuries which restricted strike bowlers Andrew Caddick and Andre van Troost to six Championship matches each and the poor form of their two young openers, Mark Lathwell and Marcus Trescothick. The shin troubles which had previously bedevilled Caddick flared up again, while van Troost, still fast and wayward, suffered a back injury which prevented any real development of his undoubted attributes. A string of injuries to various support players made life even more difficult for captain Andy Hayhurst, who was briefly out of action himself. Meanwhile, the failure to get the innings off to a good start thrust a huge responsibility on the rest of the batting. Lathwell, who played reasonably well in the first two months, fell away, just squeezing past 1,000 first-class runs before he was dropped for the final three games. Trescothick scored 151 at Northampton but reached 30 on only two more occasions in his 22 visits to the crease. What made this more disappointing was the stark contrast with his batting successes for England Under-19; he averaged over 70 in the unofficial Tests against South Africa in July and August.

Peter Bowler, a winter acquisition from Derbyshire, rose magnificently to the resulting challenge, even though he just missed scoring a century on county debut for a record third time in his peripatetic career. He scored 1,619 first-class runs at 53.96, with six hundreds, while Richard Harden, happy at No. 4, had one of his most productive years, passing 1,400 and making five centuries. No one else reached four figures, though Hayhurst performed a lot of useful repair jobs when the batting faltered, as did wicket-keeper Rob Turner, notably at Derby, where his hundred helped to turn the match. In addition, three young batsmen gave promising signs for the future. Piran Holloway, a gritty left-hander who always improves the running between the wickets, did well in all forms of cricket, earned a regular place and made a match-winning century against Sussex at Bath. A good run in the side gave the batting of Keith Parsons a new poise and confidence, and his bowling might be more often used on Sundays. Though beset by injuries, Simon Ecclestone, another left-hander, demonstrated the desire and ability to hit the ball hard and regularly; his bowling, too, could develop. Jeremy Hallett showed considerable batting skill in both innings of the final Championship match, against Middlesex, even if his hundred came against declaration bowling.

While Bowler and Harden were at the heart of many of Somerset's successes, it was Mushtaq Ahmed, the Pakistani leg-spinner, who made the indispensable contribution. In the county's seven wins, he took 58 of his 95 first-class wickets for the season. His enthusiasm never diminished, through 952 overs – more than anyone else bowled in England in 1995 – and he often looked the only bowler likely to take a wicket. Shane Lee, the New South Wales pace bowler, has been signed as the overseas player for 1996, when Mushtaq is expected to be touring England with Pakistan. Caddick played a decisive part in one victory, with ten wickets against Durham, and Graham Rose did some noble work in propping up a thin seam department; he took 39 wickets and scored 771 runs in another satisfactory season. Harvey Trump took more wickets than in 1994 – 40, up from 26, in two more games – at a higher cost. His fellow off-spinner, Jeremy Batty, had one great day in the Benson and Hedges quarter-final against Gloucestershire, when he had figures of 11–5–13–2, and Jason Kerr occasionally looked a prospective all-rounder. Fielding was poor.

The County Ground's attractions were further enhanced by two new buildings. The opulent Ondaatjie Pavilion, built for £800,000 of private and public cash, contains a six-lane cricket school, while the excellent new Press Box was opened in August. There was plenty of interesting cricket for Taunton enthusiasts outside the county's competitive programme. Two matches against the West Indies, in which Somerset more than held their own for the first two days of the second game, until Ottis Gibson turned it upside down, one against Young Australia, which produced 1,502 runs in three days and a close finish, and the first Under-19 Test between England and South Africa all varied the diet. The year was remarkable for good weather and much entertaining cricket, which also blessed the festivals at Bath and Weston-super-Mare. These attracted decent crowds, though they ran at a slight financial loss. As usual, the committee asked themselves whether the festival weeks were worth the cost and effort, when they could be ruined by a bout of bad weather, and the old argument of the county's obligation to take cricket to the people runs a little thin in days of almost universal private transport. But some of the huge handouts from Test match profits could be set aside to maintain these historic and well-loved festivals. – Eric Hill.

579

SOMERSET 1995

[Bill Smith]

Back row: P. C. L. Holloway, J. C. Hallett, S. C. Ecclestone, J. I. D. Kerr, K. A. Parsons, M. Dimond. *Middle row*: J. D. Batty, H. R. J. Trump,
A. P. van Troost, A. R. Caddick, M. E. Trescothick, R. J. Harden, R. J. Turner. *Front row*: G. D. Rose, P. D. Bowler, A. N. Hayhurst (*captain*),
R. Parsons (*chairman*), R. M. H. Cottam (*director of cricket*), M. N. Lathwell, P. J. Robinson (*coach*). *Inset*: Mushtaq Ahmed.

SOMERSET RESULTS

All first-class matches – Played 20 : Won 7, Lost 7, Drawn 6.

County Championship matches – Played 17 : Won 7, Lost 5, Drawn 5.

Bonus points – Batting 40, Bowling 49.

Competition placings – Britannic Assurance County Championship, 9th ;
NatWest Bank Trophy, 1st round ; Benson and Hedges Cup, s-f ;
AXA Equity & Law League, 14th.

BRITANNIC ASSURANCE CHAMPIONSHIP AVERAGES

BATTING

	Birthplace	M	I	NO	R	HS	Avge
J. C. Hallett	Yeovil	2	4	1	229	111*	76.33
S. C. Ecclestone	Great Dunmow	5	9	2	417	81	59.57
‡P. D. Bowler	Plymouth	16	28	3	1,483	196	59.32
P. C. L. Holloway	Helston	10	18	4	758	129*	54.14
‡R. J. Harden	Bridgwater	17	32	6	1,319	129*	50.73
‡A. N. Hayhurst	Manchester	15	26	5	803	107	38.23
‡A. R. Caddick	Christchurch, NZ	6	7	0	237	92	33.85
‡R. J. Turner	Malvern	16	24	5	594	106*	31.26
‡G. D. Rose	Tottenham	14	22	0	658	84	29.90
K. A. Parsons	Taunton	13	22	1	617	78	29.38
‡M. N. Lathwell	Bletchley	14	27	0	737	111	27.29
M. E. Trescothick	Keynsham	10	18	0	373	151	20.72
‡H. R. J. Trump	Taunton	13	18	8	197	47	19.70
J. I. D. Kerr	Bolton	11	15	2	252	42	19.38
‡Mushtaq Ahmed§	Sahiwal, Pakistan	16	22	2	299	62*	14.95
A. P. van Troost	Schiedam, Netherlands	6	9	3	73	34	12.16

Also batted: J. D. Batty (*Bradford*) (2 matches) 35, 11 ; M. Dimond (*Taunton*) (1 match) 7, 26.

* *Signifies not out.*   ‡ *Denotes county cap.*   § *Overseas player.*

The following played a total of 19 three-figure innings for Somerset in County Championship matches – P. D. Bowler 6, R. J. Harden 5, P. C. L. Holloway 2, M. N. Lathwell 2, J. C. Hallett 1, A. N. Hayhurst 1, M. E. Trescothick 1, R. J. Turner 1.

BOWLING

	O	M	R	W	BB	5W/i	Avge
A. R. Caddick	183.1	34	613	24	8-69	1	25.54
Mushtaq Ahmed	928	281	2,716	92	6-38	7	29.52
G. D. Rose	376	82	1,217	34	5-78	1	35.79
J. I. D. Kerr	241.1	50	898	22	4-68	0	40.81
H. R. J. Trump	470	141	1,316	32	5-85	1	41.12

Also bowled: J. D. Batty 63.4–10–282–5; P. D. Bowler 16.2–3–68–1; M. Dimond 14–2–70–1; S. C. Ecclestone 66–14–222–7; J. C. Hallett 14–1–86–2; R. J. Harden 1–0–17–0; A. N. Hayhurst 120.2–20–405–8; P. C. L. Holloway 2–1–12–0; M. N. Lathwell 24–5–76–2; K. A. Parsons 66–10–270–5; M. E. Trescothick 15–1–63–0; A. P. van Troost 107.3–17–451–9.

Wicket-keepers: R. J. Turner 42 ct, 7 st; P. C. L. Holloway 1 ct.

Leading Fielders: R. J. Harden 12, M. E. Trescothick 12.

SOMERSET v GLAMORGAN

At Taunton, April 27, 28, 29, 30. Glamorgan won by eight wickets. Glamorgan 24 pts, Somerset 6 pts. Toss: Somerset.

Glamorgan's all-round superiority, exemplified in an exhilarating century by Croft and ten wickets from Watkin, brought a comfortable victory despite the loss of the third day to rain. On the first day, the ball swung and seamed; Somerset struggled and owed much to a devoted hundred from Harden. Batting conditions were much easier for Glamorgan, who scored 405 inside 94 overs. Croft raced to 143, his maiden Championship century, in 147 balls, with two sixes and 23 fours. After spending Saturday under the covers, the pitch offered Watkin sharp encouragement on the last day: he took four wickets in his first nine-over spell, and a run-out left Somerset 59 for five. Bowler and Rose rallied, adding 129, before Watkin broke the stand and finished with seven for 49; Bowler, the only player to score a century on first-class debut for two counties, was stranded on 84 in his first Championship game for Somerset. Glamorgan needed 87 in 22 overs and James made short work of the task.

Close of play: First day, Somerset 247-8 (R. J. Harden 101*, H. R. J. Trump 1*); Second day, Somerset 5-0 (M. N. Lathwell 3*, M. E. Trescothick 2*); Third day, No play.

Somerset

M. N. Lathwell run out	21	– b Watkin		6
M. E. Trescothick c Metson b Thomas	0	– c Dale b Watkin		16
P. D. Bowler lbw b Watkin	10	– not out		84
R. J. Harden b Thomas	113	– c Metson b Watkin		8
*A. N. Hayhurst c and b Croft	24	– c Metson b Watkin		2
†R. J. Turner b Kendrick	20	– run out		1
G. D. Rose c Metson b Thomas	18	– c Metson b Watkin		84
Mushtaq Ahmed c Metson b Dale	4	– c Maynard b Hemp		0
A. R. Caddick lbw b Watkin	31	– c Thomas b Watkin		7
H. R. J. Trump not out	13	– c Kendrick b Watkin		0
A. P. van Troost c Metson b Watkin	6	– run out		0
B 4, l-b 4, w 9	17	B 1, l-b 1, n-b 4		6

1/2 2/28 3/43 4/88 5/134   277   1/16 2/25 3/50 4/54 5/59   214
6/166 7/171 8/246 9/266   6/188 7/189 8/206 9/210

Bonus points – Somerset 2, Glamorgan 4 (Score at 120 overs: 277-9).

Bowling: *First Innings*—Watkin 28.1–6–55–3; Thomas 26–5–98–3; Lefebvre 22–7–36–0; Dale 16–5–37–1; Croft 21–13–26–1; Kendrick 7–3–17–1. *Second Innings*—Watkin 24.2–9–49–7; Croft 14–3–36–0; Thomas 13–0–51–0; Lefebvre 16–5–34–0; Kendrick 10–4–21–0; Dale 4–2–12–0; Hemp 3–0–9–1.

Glamorgan

S. P. James c Turner b van Troost	36	– not out		47
A. Dale b Rose	60	– c Turner b Caddick		6
D. L. Hemp c Harden b Rose	46	– b van Troost		17
*M. P. Maynard c Trump b Rose	62	– not out		11
P. A. Cottey lbw b Mushtaq Ahmed	12			
R. D. B. Croft c Bowler b Rose	143			
S. D. Thomas run out	9			
N. M. Kendrick c Turner b Rose	0			
R. P. Lefebvre b van Troost	13			
†C. P. Metson not out	8			
S. L. Watkin c Bowler b van Troost	0			
L-b 3, w 3, n-b 10	16	L-b 1, n-b 7		8

1/82 2/145 3/160 4/183 5/304   405   1/35 2/63   (2 wkts) 89
6/378 7/378 8/397 9/397

Bonus points – Glamorgan 4, Somerset 4.

Bowling: *First Innings*—Caddick 14–3–60–0; van Troost 15.5–3–72–3; Mushtaq Ahmed 35–4–135–1; Trump 10–1–57–0; Rose 19.2–2–78–5. *Second Innings*—Caddick 4–0–17–1; Mushtaq Ahmed 6.2–1–47–0; van Troost 3–0–24–1.

Umpires: T. E. Jesty and R. A. White.

SOMERSET v GLOUCESTERSHIRE

At Taunton, May 4, 5, 6, 8. Drawn. Somerset 6 pts, Gloucestershire 5 pts. Toss: Somerset.

A placid pitch defeated all the bowlers. The only slight chance of a result appeared on the final afternoon: Gloucestershire were 129 for four, only 75 ahead with nearly four hours remaining. But Hodgson and Symonds, who hit his second hundred in two Championship matches, snuffed out the danger. Gloucestershire, astonished when Hayhurst put them in, batted steadily throughout the first day. Lynch scored a maiden century for his new county, and his first since August 1992, and next day Ball struck 48 from 47 balls. Srinath removed both Somerset openers cheaply and Harden was missed on 22 and 42. But he and Bowler shared a dogged stand of 193 and Hayhurst and Rose ensured a 54-run lead. Caddick had Wright dropped in the first over of the second innings and then limped off with a shin injury; Somerset's other opening bowler, van Troost, had already left the field with a back strain on the first morning.

Close of play: First day, Gloucestershire 326-5 (M. W. Alleyne 58*, R. C. Russell 5*); Second day, Somerset 218-2 (P. D. Bowler 78*, R. J. Harden 92*); Third day, Gloucestershire 47-0 (A. J. Wright 33*, G. D. Hodgson 11*).

Gloucestershire

A. J. Wright c Turner b Caddick	75	– lbw b Hayhurst	47
G. D. Hodgson c Trescothick b Hayhurst	44	– c Trescothick b Mushtaq Ahmed	81
M. A. Lynch c sub b Mushtaq Ahmed	105	– c sub b Trump	10
R. I. Dawson c Hayhurst b Caddick	3	– c Trescothick b Mushtaq Ahmed	0
M. W. Alleyne b Mushtaq Ahmed	71	– c Lathwell b Trump	5
A. Symonds lbw b Mushtaq Ahmed	8	– c Turner b Trump	102
*†R. C. Russell lbw b Rose	17	– c Mushtaq Ahmed b Trump	35
J. Srinath c Bowler b Rose	13	– c Turner b Trump	0
M. C. J. Ball c Trescothick b Caddick	48	– not out	41
M. Davies c Harden b Caddick	11	– not out	9
K. P. Sheeraz not out	1		
B 1, l-b 13, w 6, n-b 8	28	B 7, l-b 7, w 1, n-b 2	17

1/113 2/173 3/195 4/295 5/309　　　　424　　1/77 2/93 3/100 4/129　　(8 wkts) 347
6/351 7/351 8/379 9/409　　　　　　　　　　5/187 6/287 7/287 8/316

Bonus points – Gloucestershire 4, Somerset 3 (Score at 120 overs: 355-7).

Bowling: *First Innings*—Caddick 28.3–4–65–4; van Troost 4–0–21–0; Rose 26–4–93–2; Mushtaq Ahmed 46–12–141–3; Hayhurst 10–1–31–1; Trump 21–3–56–0; Trescothick 1–0–3–0. *Second Innings*—Caddick 1–0–4–0; Mushtaq Ahmed 37–16–115–2; Rose 12–2–49–0; Trump 40–16–85–5; Hayhurst 13–6–26–1; Bowler 5–2–9–0; Trescothick 10–1–37–0; Lathwell 8–2–8–0.

Somerset

M. N. Lathwell lbw b Srinath	15	A. R. Caddick lbw b Davies	16
M. E. Trescothick c Russell b Srinath	14	H. R. J. Trump not out	0
P. D. Bowler c Ball b Davies	136	A. P. van Troost c Russell b Srinath	0
R. J. Harden b Davies	103		
*A. N. Hayhurst c Russell b Alleyne	76	B 3, l-b 12, w 1, n-b 12	28
G. D. Rose c Hodgson b Sheeraz	53		
†R. J. Turner run out	0	1/35 2/42 3/235 4/358 5/401	478
Mushtaq Ahmed c Wright b Davies	37	6/406 7/442 8/473 9/478	

Bonus points – Somerset 3, Gloucestershire 1 (Score at 120 overs: 310-3).

Bowling: Srinath 26.3–3–81–3; Sheeraz 33–3–107–1; Ball 38–6–87–0; Alleyne 33–9–89–1; Dawson 7–4–5–0; Davies 30–10–86–4; Symonds 4–0–8–0.

Umpires: A. A. Jones and G. Sharp.

At Northampton, May 11, 12, 13, 15. SOMERSET lost to NORTHAMPTONSHIRE by seven wickets.

At Taunton, May 19, 20, 21. SOMERSET drew with WEST INDIANS (See West Indian tour section).

At Birmingham, May 25, 26, 27, 29. SOMERSET lost to WARWICKSHIRE by three wickets.

SOMERSET v YORKSHIRE

At Taunton, June 1, 2, 3, 5. Somerset won by seven wickets. Somerset 22 pts, Yorkshire 4 pts. Toss: Yorkshire.

Two declarations, after rain washed out half the third day, left Somerset to score 260 in what became 58 overs. A stand of 145 in 29 overs between Lathwell, who made his first century of the season, and Harden turned the game. It gave Somerset their first Championship win of 1995, and their first over Yorkshire since 1981, with 13 balls to spare. A slow, slightly turning pitch produced a batsman's match. Yorkshire's youngest-ever opening pair, 19-year-old McGrath and 20-year-old Vaughan, put on 115, with McGrath proceeding to a maiden half-century; Byas and the tail provided a suitable follow-up to reach 413. Somerset's reply was led by Harden, who scored his third Championship hundred in three matches at Taunton. The spinners reduced Yorkshire's second innings to 33 for three, but Byas and Bevan retrieved the situation and allowed them to declare. Mushtaq Ahmed took nine of the 16 Yorkshire wickets to fall.

Close of play: First day, Yorkshire 269-6 (A. P. Grayson 6*, D. Gough 4*); Second day, Somerset 248-4 (R. J. Harden 65*, S. C. Ecclestone 35*); Third day, Yorkshire 32-2 (R. D. Stemp 0*, D. Byas 0*).

Yorkshire

A. McGrath b Mushtaq Ahmed	84	– b Mushtaq Ahmed	18
M. P. Vaughan c Trump b Ecclestone	46	– b Batty	10
*D. Byas b Mushtaq Ahmed	66	– (4) b Mushtaq Ahmed	49
M. G. Bevan lbw b Mushtaq Ahmed	32	– (5) c Bowler b Trump	79
C. White b Trump	18	– (6) lbw b Mushtaq Ahmed	0
†R. J. Blakey b Trump	3	– (7) not out	7
A. P. Grayson c Turner b Kerr	37	– (8) not out	24
D. Gough b Mushtaq Ahmed	49		
P. J. Hartley c Turner b Mushtaq Ahmed	38		
R. D. Stemp c Trescothick b Ecclestone	18	– (3) c Bowler b Mushtaq Ahmed	1
M. A. Robinson not out	4		
B 5, l-b 13	18	B 7, l-b 2	9

1/115 2/155 3/235 4/246 5/258   413   1/32 2/32 3/33   (6 wkts dec.) 197
6/261 7/340 8/356 9/409   4/122 5/132 6/168

Bonus points – Yorkshire 2, Somerset 2 (Score at 120 overs: 275-6).

Bowling: *First Innings*—Kerr 23–6–71–1; Ecclestone 16.3–3–53–2; Hayhurst 4–2–11–0; Mushtaq Ahmed 51–16–126–5; Trump 35–8–77–2; Batty 21–5–57–0. *Second Innings*—Kerr 2–0–4–0; Ecclestone 3–0–10–0; Mushtaq Ahmed 29.3–7–86–4; Batty 9–2–20–1; Trump 11–6–68–1.

Somerset

M. N. Lathwell c Bevan b Hartley	61	— c Blakey b Stemp 111
M. E. Trescothick c Blakey b Stemp	28	— c Blakey b Hartley 0
P. D. Bowler c Blakey b Vaughan	48	— c Byas b Stemp 26
R. J. Harden not out	129	— not out 80
*A. N. Hayhurst c Hartley b Stemp	6	
S. C. Ecclestone lbw b Robinson	44	— (5) not out 29
†R. J. Turner not out	19	
B 4, l-b 5, w 1, n-b 6	16	B 11, l-b 2, n-b 2 15

1/56 2/116 3/161 4/180 5/273   (5 wkts dec.) 351   1/4 2/67 3/212   (3 wkts) 261

J. D. Batty, Mushtaq Ahmed, J. I. D. Kerr and H. R. J. Trump did not bat.

Bonus points – Somerset 4, Yorkshire 2.

Bowling: *First Innings*—Gough 16.3–5–72–0; Hartley 12–3–49–1; Robinson 18–5–57–1; Stemp 27–7–77–2; Vaughan 17–4–52–1; Grayson 6–4–5–0; Bevan 3–1–5–0; White 5–0–25–0. *Second Innings*—Gough 10–1–40–0; Hartley 5.5–0–33–1; Stemp 19–2–69–2; Robinson 2–0–16–0; Vaughan 11–1–57–0; Grayson 8–1–33–0.

Umpires: R. Julian and M. J. Kitchen.

At The Oval, June 8, 9, 10, 12. SOMERSET beat SURREY by five wickets.

At Derby, June 15, 16, 17, 19. SOMERSET beat DERBYSHIRE by 79 runs.

SOMERSET v SUSSEX

At Bath, June 22, 23, 24, 26. Somerset won by 124 runs. Somerset 20 pts, Sussex 5 pts. Toss: Somerset.

A disciplined, fighting 129 not out from Holloway, his first century for Somerset, averted a two-day defeat and then set up a fourth successive win. Soon after he came in, they were five down and only 58 ahead in their second innings. But his perseverance was matched by Rose, Turner and Kerr, who all shared vital stands, and established a lead of 296. Sussex collapsed and even the diligence of their captain, Wells, who had to bat at No. 6 after a trip home to see his newborn son, only prolonged the game into Monday, when the last two wickets went in 14 balls. The pitch rewarded both seam and spin: Giddins took a career-best six for 73 and Mushtaq Ahmed ten in the match. Somerset were out by tea on the first day, with acting-captain Bowler – capped beforehand – out first ball. Mushtaq, with four wickets, restored the balance. But Wells scored a lovely hundred to gain a first-innings lead and his spinners then seemed to have given Sussex control.

Close of play: First day, Sussex 102-4 (A. P. Wells 34*, E. E. Hemmings 6*); Second day, Somerset 200-5 (P. C. L. Holloway 59*, G. D. Rose 49*); Third day, Sussex 156-8 (J. D. Lewry 2*, E. E. Hemmings 8*).

Somerset

M. N. Lathwell lbw b Giddins	18	— b Salisbury 45
M. E. Trescothick c Moores b Lewry	1	— (6) lbw b Salisbury 12
*P. D. Bowler lbw b Lewry	0	— (2) c Lenham b Hemmings 13
R. J. Harden b Giddins	21	— (3) lbw b Hemmings 0
P. C. L. Holloway lbw b Salisbury	10	— (4) not out 129
K. A. Parsons c Moores b Giddins	59	— (5) lbw b Hemmings 1
G. D. Rose b Salisbury	7	— lbw b Giddins 49
†R. J. Turner c Law b Giddins	23	— lbw b Lewry 25
Mushtaq Ahmed c Moores b Giddins	25	— c Law b Stephenson 1
J. I. D. Kerr b Giddins	0	— b Hemmings 22
H. R. J. Trump not out	4	— c Greenfield b Giddins 18
L-b 5, w 1, n-b 4	10	B 4, l-b 16, n-b 10 30

1/4 2/4 3/40 4/41 5/72   178   1/39 2/47 3/75 4/84 5/107   345
6/86 7/140 8/167 9/167   6/201 7/261 8/264 9/318

Bonus points – Sussex 4.

Bowling: *First Innings*—Stephenson 15–2–48–0; Lewry 12–2–27–2; Giddins 21.5–2–73–6; Salisbury 8–2–16–2; Hemmings 5–3–9–0. *Second Innings*—Stephenson 24–6–72–1; Lewry 13–0–53–1; Giddins 20–3–67–2; Hemmings 43–18–57–4; Salisbury 28–6–76–2.

Sussex

N. J. Lenham c Trescothick b Mushtaq Ahmed	32	– b Kerr	8
K. Newell c Kerr b Mushtaq Ahmed	10	– lbw b Rose	9
K. Greenfield lbw b Mushtaq Ahmed	6	– lbw b Mushtaq Ahmed	20
*A. P. Wells lbw b Kerr	106	– (6) st Turner b Mushtaq Ahmed.	43
D. R. Law c Trescothick b Mushtaq Ahmed	8	– (4) c Turner b Rose	4
E. E. Hemmings lbw b Kerr	18	– (10) b Rose	12
†P. Moores lbw b Kerr	0	– (5) b Trump	9
F. D. Stephenson c Turner b Kerr	9	– (7) c Parsons b Trump	21
I. D. K. Salisbury st Turner b Mushtaq Ahmed	4	– (8) b Mushtaq Ahmed	23
J. D. Lewry c Turner b Mushtaq Ahmed	11	– (9) st Turner b Mushtaq Ahmed.	13
E. S. H. Giddins not out	8	– not out	1
B 2, l-b 5, n-b 8	15	B 4, l-b 5	9

1/32 2/46 3/66 4/84 5/127   227   1/17 2/21 3/32 4/45 5/87   172
6/127 7/148 8/153 9/196   6/110 7/132 8/148 9/170

Bonus points – Sussex 1, Somerset 4.

Bowling: *First Innings*—Rose 25–4–74–0; Kerr 20.1–6–68–4; Mushtaq Ahmed 31–13–54–6; Parsons 5–1–14–0; Trump 1–0–10–0. *Second Innings*—Rose 13–1–47–3; Kerr 10–6–16–1; Mushtaq Ahmed 27.2–10–62–4; Trump 19–6–38–2.

Umpires: M. J. Kitchen and R. A. White.

At Nottingham, June 29, 30, July 1, 3. SOMERSET drew with NOTTINGHAMSHIRE.

At Taunton, July 5, 6, 7. SOMERSET lost to YOUNG AUSTRALIANS by 30 runs (See Young Australia tour section).

At Southend, July 20, 21, 22, 24. SOMERSET beat ESSEX by seven wickets.

SOMERSET v LANCASHIRE

At Taunton, July 27, 28, 29. Lancashire won by ten wickets. Lancashire 24 pts, Somerset 4 pts. Toss: Lancashire.

With Watkinson, Atherton and Crawley all playing for England, Wasim Akram led Lancashire for the first time; they won before lunch on the third day. The foundations were laid by Fairbrother and Speak, who added 177 in 44 overs, on a dry pitch in hot, humid weather. Let off on 42 and 79, Fairbrother led a swashbuckling 132 from 149 balls, with six sixes and 17 fours. Somerset needed 280 to avoid the follow-on but Keedy took a career-best four for 35, including three in 12 balls either side of lunch, and only Bowler held out for long. Resuming, Somerset were soon 29 for three. Hayhurst arrested the collapse until he received a blow amidships from Austin; Holloway kept up the work and, on the third morning, Parsons and Kerr defied the seamers for an hour. But once Keedy broke through, he and Yates completed matters as the tail swung hopefully at the spinners: Trump hit 32 from 12 balls. Lancashire reached their six-run target when Gallian hit Bowler's first delivery, a no-ball, for four, to give him a baffling bowling analysis.

Close of play: First day, Lancashire 399-7 (Wasim Akram 50*, G. Yates 6*); Second day, Somerset 152-4 (K. A. Parsons 16*, J. I. D. Kerr 4*).

Lancashire

S. P. Titchard b van Troost	35	– not out	0
J. E. R. Gallian c Parsons b Trump	43	– not out	4
N. J. Speak c Hayhurst b Parsons	76		
N. H. Fairbrother st Turner b Trump	132		
G. D. Lloyd c Parsons b van Troost	3		
†W. K. Hegg st Turner b Mushtaq Ahmed	16		
*Wasim Akram lbw b Mushtaq Ahmed	61		
I. D. Austin b van Troost	6		
G. Yates lbw b Mushtaq Ahmed	19		
G. Chapple c Harden b van Troost	4		
G. Keedy not out	0		
B 12, l-b 8, w 4, n-b 10	34	N-b 2	2

1/79 2/115 3/292 4/313 5/317   429   (no wkt) 6
6/344 7/359 8/415 9/420

Bonus points – Lancashire 4, Somerset 4 (Score at 120 overs: 421-9).

Bowling: *First Innings*—van Troost 28–6–87–3; Kerr 9–1–44–0; Mushtaq Ahmed 45.2–16–127–4; Trump 33–10–113–2; Hayhurst 4–0–15–0; Parsons 3–0–23–1. *Second Innings*—Holloway 1–1–0–0; Bowler 0–0–6–0.

Somerset

M. N. Lathwell c and b Chapple	19	– b Chapple	1
P. D. Bowler lbw b Austin	57	– lbw b Austin	5
*A. N. Hayhurst b Keedy	21	– not out	70
R. J. Harden c Fairbrother b Keedy	4	– c Keedy b Austin	8
P. C. L. Holloway lbw b Keedy	0	– c Titchard b Yates	48
K. A. Parsons b Wasim Akram	15	– c Speak b Yates	36
†R. J. Turner c Hegg b Wasim Akram	4	– (8) c Speak b Yates	18
Mushtaq Ahmed c Speak b Keedy	16	– (9) c Fairbrother b Keedy	6
J. I. D. Kerr c Hegg b Austin	0	– (7) c Fairbrother b Keedy	16
H. R. J. Trump b Austin	0	– c Gallian b Yates	32
A. P. van Troost not out	0	– b Wasim Akram	4
B 1, l-b 4, n-b 20	25	B 2, l-b 8, w 1, n-b 18	29

1/40 2/83 3/97 4/97 5/130   161   1/6 2/6 3/29 4/114 5/187   273
6/134 7/155 8/155 9/161   6/199 7/217 8/228 9/261

Bonus points – Lancashire 4.

In the second innings A. N. Hayhurst, when 53, retired hurt at 140 and resumed at 187.

Bowling: *First Innings*—Wasim Akram 14–1–58–2; Chapple 7–1–25–1; Austin 7–3–14–3; Yates 8–0–24–0; Keedy 17.1–6–35–4. *Second Innings*—Chapple 12–2–46–1; Austin 16–6–32–2; Keedy 22–6–81–2; Wasim Akram 9.1–0–37–1; Yates 14–3–67–4.

Umpires: N. T. Plews and A. G. T. Whitehead.

At Taunton, August 2, 3, 4. SOMERSET lost to WEST INDIANS by 155 runs (See West Indian touring section).

SOMERSET v KENT

At Taunton, August 10, 11, 12. Somerset won by eight wickets. Somerset 23 pts, Kent 6 pts. Toss: Kent.

Beautiful leg-spin from Mushtaq Ahmed, whose final spell of five for 16 in 41 balls gave him match figures of 11 for 144, brought this game to an unexpectedly early conclusion at 2.35 p.m. on Saturday. An hour before lunch, Kent were 84 for two, and night-watchman Herzberg had survived 23 overs on a slightly wearing pitch. But the last eight fell for 35 in

13 overs. On the first day, Kent relied on a solid century from Llong, his second in successive innings. Van Troost was ordered out of the attack by umpire Dudleston after a high full toss at Cowdrey, following three bouncers at Llong in his previous over. Bowler anchored Somerset's reply, but they struggled against Igglesden before the later order set up a 67-run lead. It looked slight – until Mushtaq changed everything. Somerset needed only ten overs to score 53.

Close of play: First day, Somerset 77-1 (P. D. Bowler 35*, A. N. Hayhurst 33*); Second day, Kent 41-1 (T. R. Ward 25*, S. Herzberg 0*).

Kent

D. P. Fulton c Turner b van Troost	16	– c Turner b Mushtaq Ahmed 14
T. R. Ward lbw b Rose	5	– c Turner b Rose 33
N. J. Llong b Mushtaq Ahmed	100	– (4) lbw b Mushtaq Ahmed 24
P. A. de Silva c Parsons b Mushtaq Ahmed	42	– (5) c Trump b Mushtaq Ahmed . 0
G. R. Cowdrey b Trump	52	– (6) c Rose b Trump 9
M. A. Ealham lbw b Trump	5	– (7) c Holloway b Trump 7
*†S. A. Marsh lbw b Rose	10	– (8) c Trump b Mushtaq Ahmed . 3
D. W. Headley c and b Mushtaq Ahmed	3	– (9) b Trump 0
J. B. D. Thompson c Turner b Mushtaq Ahmed	17	– (10) lbw b Mushtaq Ahmed 4
S. Herzberg c Harden b Mushtaq Ahmed	3	– (3) c Turner b Mushtaq Ahmed . 18
A. P. Igglesden not out	6	– not out..................... 0
L-b 2, w 2, n-b 8	12	B 4, l-b 3 7

1/12 2/22 3/89 4/174 5/192   271   1/41 2/52 3/84 4/84 5/105   119
6/220 7/235 8/250 9/262   6/109 7/113 8/114 9/119

Bonus points – Kent 2, Somerset 4.

Bowling: *First Innings*—Rose 17–4–43–2; van Troost 10.4–4–35–1; Mushtaq Ahmed 30.3–9–106–5; Trump 22–4–69–2; Hayhurst 4.2–0–16–0. *Second Innings*—van Troost 10–2–23–0; Rose 9–1–34–1; Mushtaq Ahmed 19–8–38–6; Hayhurst 3–2–2–0; Trump 8.2–3–15–3.

Somerset

M. N. Lathwell c Ward b Headley	2	– c Marsh b Igglesden 0
P. D. Bowler c Marsh b Igglesden	85	– c de Silva b Igglesden 13
*A. N. Hayhurst c Llong b Igglesden	33	
R. J. Harden c Ward b Igglesden	37	– not out..................... 8
P. C. L. Holloway c Ward b Headley	14	– (3) not out.................. 30
K. A. Parsons lbw b Ealham	44	
G. D. Rose c and b Ealham	36	
†R. J. Turner not out	37	
Mushtaq Ahmed c Llong b Igglesden	21	
H. R. J. Trump c Ealham b Igglesden	12	
A. P. van Troost run out	1	
B 1, l-b 3, w 4, n-b 8	16	N-b 2 2

1/13 2/78 3/150 4/178 5/193   338   1/0 2/15   (2 wkts) 53
6/262 7/267 8/305 9/331

Bonus points – Somerset 3, Kent 4.

Bowling: *First Innings*—Igglesden 26–6–92–5; Headley 26–7–67–2; Thompson 12–1–52–0; de Silva 16–4–40–0; Herzberg 18–5–51–0; Ealham 15–6–32–2. *Second Innings*—Igglesden 4–0–21–2; Headley 3–0–12–0; Llong 1.4–0–12–0; de Silva 1–0–8–0.

Umpires: B. Dudleston and M. J. Kitchen.

At Chester-le-Street, August 17, 18, 19. SOMERSET beat DURHAM by 286 runs.

SOMERSET v LEICESTERSHIRE

At Weston-super-Mare, August 24, 25, 26, 28. Leicestershire won by two wickets. Leicestershire 24 pts, Somerset 6 pts. Toss: Leicestershire.

Leicestershire's well-planned chase for 312 in 83 overs was anchored by emergency opener Pierson. Last man in the first innings, he was promoted because Briers had been off the field injured, and defended splendidly for a 245-minute half-century, while his partners provided the necessary impetus. Four quick wickets brought Somerset back into the game, but Mullally was dropped at 295 and Wells hit the winning runs with five overs left. A greenish pitch, some cloudy weather and several missed catches helped create an interesting match. Somerset started poorly, but Holloway survived two chances to make a three-and-a-half-hour maiden century. Leicestershire took a 57-run lead, due entirely to Cronje, who was dropped three times on the way to his fourth hundred for Leicestershire, but went on to 213 from 242 balls, with six sixes and 28 fours, out of 335 while he was at the crease. The game turned again as Harden and Parsons put on 198 for Somerset's third wicket, enabling Hayhurst to set up the final equation.

Close of play: First day, Somerset 246-8 (J. I. D. Kerr 8*); Second day, Leicestershire 341-9 (A. Sheriyar 0*); Third day, Somerset 299-5 (P. C. L. Holloway 12*, J. I. D. Kerr 1*).

Somerset

M. N. Lathwell c Briers b Cronje	27	– b Mullally 43
*A. N. Hayhurst c Macmillan b Parsons	0	– (8) not out 20
P. C. L. Holloway c Nixon b Cronje	117	– (5) not out 51
R. J. Harden c Nixon b Mullally	4	– (3) c and b Cronje 124
K. A. Parsons c Nixon b Sheriyar	0	– (4) c Pierson b Parsons 78
S. C. Ecclestone c Macmillan b Pierson	42	
G. D. Rose c Nixon b Sheriyar	21	– (6) c Nixon b Cronje 0
†R. J. Turner c Macmillan b Wells	19	– (2) c Cronje b Mullally 10
J. I. D. Kerr not out	23	– (7) c Nixon b Cronje 10
A. R. Caddick c sub b Sheriyar	30	
Mushtaq Ahmed run out	1	
B 3, l-b 2, w 4	9	B 14, l-b 9, w 7, n-b 2 ... 32

1/0 2/71 3/86 4/93 5/197   293   1/21 2/80 3/278   (6 wkts dec.) 368
6/197 7/224 8/246 9/292   4/282 5/289 6/311

Bonus points – Somerset 2, Leicestershire 4.

Bowling: *First Innings*—Mullally 17–8–50–1; Parsons 18–4–82–1; Sheriyar 12.4–4–46–3; Cronje 16–8–33–2; Pierson 6–1–27–1; Wells 14–4–50–1. *Second Innings*—Mullally 24–7–100–2; Parsons 20–7–47–1; Sheriyar 10–1–60–0; Cronje 19–6–42–3; Wells 7.1–1–29–0; Pierson 27.5–6–67–0.

Leicestershire

G. I. Macmillan c Turner b Caddick	4	– c Turner b Mushtaq Ahmed 44
*N. E. Briers c Turner b Mushtaq Ahmed	49	– (7) lbw b Rose 9
J. J. Whitaker c Turner b Caddick	0	– c Turner b Rose 46
W. J. Cronje b Caddick	213	– c Turner b Caddick 21
B. F. Smith b Kerr	6	– c Turner b Lathwell 26
V. J. Wells c Lathwell b Kerr	3	– (8) not out 14
†P. A. Nixon c Harden b Kerr	11	– (6) b Mushtaq Ahmed 79
G. J. Parsons b Caddick	39	– (9) c Lathwell b Mushtaq Ahmed .. 6
A. D. Mullally c Lathwell b Mushtaq Ahmed	0	– (10) not out 6
A. Sheriyar not out	0	
A. R. K. Pierson b Mushtaq Ahmed	9	– (2) b Mushtaq Ahmed 50
B 4, l-b 3, w 3, n-b 6	16	B 4, l-b 7, w 1 12

1/6 2/6 3/123 4/138 5/183   350   1/52 2/107 3/133 4/165   (8 wkts) 313
6/229 7/332 8/341 9/341   5/261 6/286 7/288 8/294

Bonus points – Leicestershire 4, Somerset 4.

Bowling: *First Innings*—Caddick 23–3–90–4; Kerr 16–3–58–3; Mushtaq Ahmed 30.5–5–122–3; Rose 13–2–59–0; Parsons 4–0–13–0; Lathwell 1–0–1–0. *Second Innings*—Caddick 19–5–65–1; Kerr 7–0–33–0; Mushtaq Ahmed 32.5–5–150–4; Rose 16–1–39–2; Lathwell 3–1–15–1.

Umpires: J. C. Balderstone and K. E. Palmer.

At Worcester, August 29, 30, 31, September 1. SOMERSET drew with WORCESTERSHIRE.

At Southampton, September 7, 8, 9, 11. SOMERSET drew with HAMPSHIRE.

SOMERSET v MIDDLESEX

At Taunton, September 14, 15, 16, 18. Drawn. Somerset 4 pts, Middlesex 7 pts. Toss: Somerset.

Still chasing the Championship, Middlesex had to go for victory. Despite a first-day washout, their batsmen put on a tremendous performance, scoring 350 at more than six an over before declaring 26 behind. Shortly afterwards, news came of Warwickshire's victory at Canterbury, and when their nearest rivals, Northamptonshire, were rained off on Monday, Middlesex were certain to be runners-up. But they still set up a target by feeding Somerset runs, and Hallett scored a maiden first-class century. The pursuit of 350 in what would have been 63 overs was on while Weekes and Ramprakash were adding 145 in 26. But spinners Batty and Trump – Mushtaq Ahmed was ill – then took five wickets in ten overs. Carr and Emburey put on another 60 in eight before rain set in. Though Fraser had worked his way through the Somerset first innings between absences with back pains, Middlesex failed to take the tail-end wicket they needed for full bowling points. Their batting lived up to form, however: Pooley smashed 90 in 80 balls, Ramprakash 115 in 134 – his third consecutive hundred, his fifth in six innings and his tenth of the season – and Gatting 122 in 104. John Emburey was playing his 377th and final match for Middlesex; it was also the last match for Peter Wight, once a Somerset player, who was retiring after 30 years as a first-class umpire.

Close of play: First day, No play; Second day, Somerset 306-8 (J. C. Hallett 12*, J. D. Batty 5*); Third day, Somerset 102-2 (J. C. Hallett 22*, J. D. Batty 5*).

Somerset

M. E. Trescothick c Brown b Fraser	3	– c Carr b Emburey	59
P. D. Bowler b Fraser	14		
P. C. L. Holloway lbw b Fraser	15	– b Emburey	10
R. J. Harden c Weekes b Feltham	63	– (5) c sub b Ramprakash	19
*A. N. Hayhurst b Nash	71	– (8) run out	36
K. A. Parsons lbw b Fraser	62	– (9) not out	22
G. D. Rose c Gatting b Weekes	24	– c sub b Brown	12
†R. J. Turner b Fraser	23		
J. C. Hallett c Pooley b Emburey	47	– (2) not out	111
J. D. Batty c Feltham b Tufnell	35	– (4) b Ramprakash	11
H. R. J. Trump not out	2	– (6) c Gatting b Ramprakash	36
B 1, l-b 4, w 4, n-b 8	17	B 4, l-b 1, n-b 2	7

1/8 2/25 3/42 4/151 5/188   376   1/71 2/91 3/113   (7 wkts dec.) 323
6/251 7/285 8/298 9/364   4/159 5/209
                                  6/224 7/278

Bonus points – Somerset 3, Middlesex 3 (Score at 120 overs: 343-8).

Bowling: *First Innings*—Fraser 23–5–56–5; Nash 23–4–78–1; Feltham 19–6–69–1; Emburey 30.1–6–76–1; Tufnell 24–7–57–1; Weekes 10–0–35–1. *Second Innings*—Fraser 5–1–31–0; Nash 4–1–28–0; Emburey 12–4–27–2; Tufnell 7–5–8–0; Weekes 5–2–4–0; Ramprakash 20–3–91–3; Brown 15–0–114–1; Pooley 4–0–15–0.

Middlesex

P. N. Weekes c Hallett b Rose	0	– c and b Batty	79
J. C. Pooley lbw b Trump	90	– c Turner b Rose	22
M. R. Ramprakash c Parsons b Hayhurst	115	– b Trump	73
*M. W. Gatting not out	122	– c Rose b Batty	2
J. D. Carr not out	1	– not out	42
†K. R. Brown (did not bat)		– lbw b Batty	4
D. J. Nash (did not bat)		– c Bowler b Batty	7
J. E. Emburey (did not bat)		– not out	27
B 2, l-b 8, n-b 12	22	B 2, n-b 4	6

1/16 2/148 3/324 (3 wkts dec.) 350   1/33 2/178 3/180   (6 wkts) 262
4/180 5/184 6/202

M. A. Feltham, A. R. C. Fraser and P. C. R. Tufnell did not bat.

Bonus points – Middlesex 4, Somerset 1.

Bowling: *First Innings*—Rose 13–5–42–1; Hallett 4–0–52–0; Trump 12–1–79–1; Batty 18.4–0–135–0; Hayhurst 7–0–27–1; Trescothick 1–0–5–0. *Second Innings*—Rose 7–1–30–1; Hayhurst 3–0–12–0; Trump 23–3–127–1; Parsons 5–1–21–0; Batty 15–3–70–4.

Umpires: M. J. Kitchen and P. B. Wight.

COUNTY MEMBERSHIP

	1985	*1994*	*1995*
Derbyshire	1,666	2,216	2,580
Durham	—	5,448	5,795
Essex	7,971	8,120	7,502
Glamorgan	3,103	13,382	11,893
Gloucestershire	3,962	4,354	4,672
Hampshire	4,368	4,950	4,790
Kent	5,273	5,416	5,657
Lancashire	9,758	13,237	13,638
Leicestershire	3,641	4,654	4,878
Middlesex	8,187	8,474	8,581
Northamptonshire	1,952	2,526	2,296
Nottinghamshire	3,832	4,362	4,861
Somerset	5,609	5,732	5,517
Surrey	5,994	5,996	6,588
Sussex	4,740	5,421	5,243
Warwickshire	8,866	13,543	14,441
Worcestershire	3,113	4,921	5,141
Yorkshire	10,600	8,184	9,190
MCC	18,121	19,812	19,808
Total	110,756	140,748	143,071

Note: The methods of recording these figures vary from county to county; e.g. corporate membership may be regarded as representing one person or more than one. Since 1994, Warwickshire's figures have been adjusted retrospectively to include all joint members.

SURREY

Patron: HM The Queen
President: J. P. Getty
Chairman: M. Soper
Chief Executive: P. Sheldon
Captain: A. J. Stewart
Coach: D. R. Gilbert
Director of Cricket: M. J. Edwards
Head Groundsman: P. D. Brind
Scorer: K. R. Booth

Surrey are nothing if not consistent in their inability to win something. They have brought only three trophies home since their great Championship sequence ended in 1958 and, far from inspiring an improvement, their 150th anniversary year showed a marked decline. Grandiose schemes for rebuilding the Vauxhall End to take The Oval into the 21st century are all very well, but on current form it is unlikely they will have a team to match. By mid-July, they had gone seven Championship games without winning and were bottom of the table – and out of both knockouts. In the end, 12th in the Championship and ninth in the Sunday League seemed some kind of triumph.

Things got to such a pitch that a large group of members called for a special general meeting, held in early October. The motion to be heard was sent to the membership, together with the committee's arguments against it, but they did not see fit to include anything in its support. Since one of the motion's demands was a more democratically-run organisation, the irony was not lost on the so-called rebels. They won the vote in the hall but lost on the postal ballot. However, Mike Soper, who had taken over as chairman following the resignation of Brian Downing, handled the meeting well and professed himself "staggered" by the depth of feeling.

His promise to listen sympathetically to their views did not sound like empty rhetoric and, two months later, the rebels achieved what looked like victory when Glyn Woodman, Surrey's controversial chief executive, resigned. The club had asked Sir Peter Imbert, the former Metropolitan Police commissioner, to lead a review into management. His report's 44 recommendations included a suggested cutback in Woodman's authority, especially over cricketing matters. The committee supported this, and Woodman said his position had become untenable.

This does not necessarily mean that Surrey's attempts to turn themselves into something more like a business enterprise than a traditional county cricket club have come to an end. However, future steps may be taken in a more diplomatic and sensitive fashion. "I just want to bring the fun back for everyone in the club and make us the acceptable face of cricket," Soper said. Paul Sheldon was immediately named as Woodman's successor, suggesting that the resignation did not come as a surprise to everyone. Sheldon was the organiser of the club's anniversary celebrations.

The Surrey coach Grahame Clinton had already left, and the Australian fast bowler Dave Gilbert was hired from the Australian Cricket Academy to replace him. Graham Dilley's future was unclear; having been employed as bowling coach, he had found himself rapidly reduced to Second Eleven nursemaid. Mike Edwards, the director of cricket, kept his job title but his remit shifted towards development. It was understandable that the captaincy should also be linked to the vortex of rumours. Alec Stewart, on international duty or injured for much of the season, could not be held directly responsible for a lot of what went wrong. But the leadership of Adam Hollioake, which produced three victories, including unlikely wins over Nottinghamshire and Yorkshire, and hauled Surrey off the bottom of the Championship table, prompted speculation about the long-term future of both men. The official title of vice-captain is an honour rarely bestowed at Surrey, but Hollioake has been given it.

Surrey were not helped by a veritable parade of casualties from the start of the season. Martin Bicknell broke down three times in the first seven weeks, Stewart managed just seven Championship matches and Joey Benjamin missed a chunk of the second half of the campaign – but still finished as the county's leading wicket-taker, with 53 in 12 first-class games. Despite Surrey's care in giving 17-year-old fast bowler Alex Tudor a gentle introduction into the hard grind of real cricket life, he broke down in his fifth Championship match. By then he had done enough to suggest that here was the genuine article: a home-grown out-and-out speed merchant who can also bat a bit; he scored a maiden fifty at Leicester. A last-minute replacement for the injured Waqar Younis, Queenslander Carl Rackemann was reliability itself and his 47 Championship wickets were a valuable contribution, but the attack still lacked penetration. Replacing Waqar remains a priority.

The batting again disappointed. On paper it is a seriously talented line-up, but only three men – Hollioake, Alistair Brown and Mark Butcher – passed 1,000 runs for Surrey, though Darren Bicknell, who scored an unbeaten double-hundred against Nottinghamshire, and Nadeem Shahid were close. A glance at the Championship statistics reveals that Surrey batsmen reached half-centuries 66 times, but converted only 14 of them into hundreds. Even some of the heroes of the summer were culpable. Butcher is an opener of outstanding ability and, if he works on his bowling, could become something of an all-rounder, but he scored only two hundreds. Brown passed 1,000 runs for the third consecutive season, but ought to collect a few more centuries on the way. Nevertheless, his career-best 187 in the opening match against Gloucestershire revealed a marked improvement in temperament. That he was blamed for everyone else's shortcomings after an innings of 92 against Glamorgan was crass. Trying to teach a lesson to the one player doing all he could for the cause was possibly one of the coaching department's worst mistakes. Dropped for the match with Middlesex (which was lost), Brown returned against Essex with another hundred. But, when he was omitted again, shortly before the end of the season – and missed another defeat – outsiders began to wonder if the club had something against one of the most prodigious talents Surrey have produced in a long while.

There were other pluses, notably Shahid, who made himself an indispensable team member with 900 runs. Graham Kersey, until he broke his thumb, finally established himself in the role the county wanted – that of wicketkeeper/batsman. Tudor and slow left-armer Richard Nowell are rich with promise and Jason Ratcliffe, like Shahid, seemed to be a shrewd winter signing. Surrey hoped the same would be true of enigmatic England all-rounder Chris Lewis. He joined the club on a two-year contract and will be looking to resuscitate his Test career, while Surrey will be looking to him to revive their fortunes. – *David Llewellyn.*

593

SURREY 1995

[Bill Smith]

Back row: N. Shahid, B. C. Hollioake, G. J. Kennis, A. J. Tudor, J. M. de la Pena, J. D. Ratcliffe, O. M. Slipper, R. W. Nowell, S. G. Kenlock.
Middle row: G. R. Dilley (*assistant coach*), G. J. Kersey, A. W. Smith, M. A. Butcher, A. J. Hollioake, N. F. Sargeant, M. R. Bainbridge,
G. S. Clinton (*coach*). *Front row:* J. E. Benjamin, G. P. Thorpe, M. P. Bicknell, A. J. Stewart (*captain*), D. M. Ward, D. J. Bicknell, A. D. Brown,
A. C. S. Pigott. *Inset:* J. A. Knott, C. G. Rackemann.

SURREY RESULTS

All first-class matches – Played 18: Won 5, Lost 8, Drawn 5.

County Championship matches – Played 17: Won 5, Lost 8, Drawn 4.

Bonus points – Batting 34, Bowling 55.

*Competition placings – Britannic Assurance County Championship, 12th;
NatWest Bank Trophy, 2nd round; Benson and Hedges Cup, 3rd in Group D;
AXA Equity & Law League, 9th.*

BRITANNIC ASSURANCE CHAMPIONSHIP AVERAGES

BATTING

	Birthplace	M	I	NO	R	HS	Avge
‡A. J. Stewart.......	Merton	7	13	1	534	151	44.50
‡A. D. Brown	Beckenham	15	29	4	1,054	187	42.16
‡G. P. Thorpe	Farnham	10	18	0	717	152	39.83
‡D. J. Bicknell	Guildford	14	27	2	981	228*	39.24
N. Shahid	Karachi, Pakistan	13	25	2	900	139	39.13
‡A. J. Hollioake	Melbourne, Australia	17	30	2	1,094	117*	39.07
M. A. Butcher	Croydon	16	31	0	1,175	167	37.90
J. D. Ratcliffe	Solihull	8	16	0	536	75	33.50
G. J. Kersey	Plumstead	15	28	4	708	83	29.50
‡M. P. Bicknell	Guildford	8	12	3	213	61	23.66
A. W. Smith	Sutton	8	13	0	272	88	20.92
‡D. M. Ward	Croydon	2	4	0	66	51	16.50
C. G. Rackemann§ .	Wondai, Australia	12	20	12	120	20*	15.00
A. J. Tudor	London	5	9	0	123	56	13.66
‡J. E. Benjamin	Christ Church, St Kitts	11	18	4	174	49	12.42
S. G. Kenlock......	Portland, Jamaica	4	8	2	50	12	8.33
‡A. C. S. Pigott	London	6	11	1	76	19	7.60
R. W. Nowell......	Croydon	11	20	2	134	27	7.44

Also batted: J. M. de la Pena (*London*) (2 matches) 0*, 0*, 2*; G. J. Kennis (*Yokohama, Japan*) (1 match) 29, 18; N. F. Sargeant (*Hammersmith*) (2 matches) 6, 2.

* *Signifies not out.* ‡ *Denotes county cap.* § *Overseas player.*

The following played a total of 14 three-figure innings for Surrey in County Championship matches – A. D. Brown 3, D. J. Bicknell 2, M. A. Butcher 2, N. Shahid 2, A. J. Stewart 2, G. P. Thorpe 2, A. J. Hollioake 1.

BOWLING

	O	M	R	W	BB	5W/i	Avge
M. P. Bicknell	272	64	899	41	5-61	3	21.92
A. J. Tudor	83.3	7	320	14	5-32	1	22.85
J. E. Benjamin........	401.4	84	1,244	51	5-37	3	24.39
C. G. Rackemann	445	111	1,394	47	6-60	1	29.65
A. C. S. Pigott........	209.3	50	667	22	6-91	2	30.31
A. J. Hollioake	230.3	46	721	21	4-22	0	34.33
R. W. Nowell.........	424.5	117	1,264	32	4-43	0	39.50
M. A. Butcher	226.5	37	865	21	4-72	0	41.19

Also bowled: D. J. Bicknell 24.3–5–96–3; J. M. de la Pena 44–8–208–6; S. G. Kenlock 119–20–440–8; G. J. Kennis 3–3–0–0; N. Shahid 114–14–524–7; A. W. Smith 144–25–543–8; A. J. Stewart 3–0–18–0; G. P. Thorpe 23.4–4–59–2.

Wicket-keepers: G. J. Kersey 60 ct, 5 st; N. F. Sargeant 11 ct.

Leading Fielder: A. D. Brown 19.

SURREY v GLOUCESTERSHIRE

At The Oval, April 27, 28, 29, 30. Surrey won by 93 runs. Surrey 21 pts, Gloucestershire 8 pts. Toss: Gloucestershire. First-class debut: R. W. Nowell. Championship debuts: J. Srinath, A. Symonds.

Surrey pulled off a rare feat by winning after following on 175 behind. But the opening stages were dominated by Andrew Symonds, Gloucestershire's Birmingham-born, Queensland-bred 19-year-old. His clinical dismantling of the Surrey attack – which lost Martin Bicknell early on – prompted calls for him to be named in England's one-day international squad to prevent Australia laying claim to the prodigy. Having spent 21 deliveries over his first nine circumspect runs, Symonds launched a withering attack, taking a further 73 balls to reach an unbeaten century on his Championship debut (despite a chance on 98). Gloucestershire's official overseas player, Srinath, then helped to bowl Surrey out for 217. But Brown then played a mature, career-best innings, uncharacteristically taking 156 balls to reach three figures. His four sixes were his only boundaries in a period of 40 overs, the first bringing up his hundred, the third his 150. Chasing 301, Gloucestershire were bowled out by the ever-dangerous Benjamin with seven overs to spare.

Close of play: First day, Surrey 17-0 (D. J. Bicknell 6*, M. A. Butcher 11*); Second day, Surrey 74-0 (D. J. Bicknell 33*, M. A. Butcher 39*); Third day, Surrey 431-7 (A. D. Brown 167*, R. W. Nowell 4*).

Gloucestershire

A. J. Wright lbw b Benjamin	0	– b Kenlock	27
G. D. Hodgson c Shahid b Kenlock	22	– c Kersey b Kenlock	1
M. A. Lynch c Kenlock b Hollioake	46	– b Benjamin	4
R. I. Dawson hit wkt b Benjamin	51	– lbw b Benjamin	0
M. W. Alleyne c Stewart b Benjamin	32	– b Shahid	60
A. Symonds not out	161	– c Shahid b Benjamin	1
*†R. C. Russell lbw b Benjamin	1	– st Kersey b Nowell	56
J. Srinath run out	16	– c Butcher b Shahid	7
M. C. J. Ball b Hollioake	18	– not out	37
K. E. Cooper b Kenlock	32	– c D. J. Bicknell b Nowell	0
A. M. Smith c Butcher b Nowell	0	– c Kersey b Nowell	2
L-b 7, n-b 6	13	B 2, l-b 1, w 1, n-b 8	12

1/1 2/69 3/85 4/157 5/166   **392**   1/16 2/21 3/21 4/43 5/44   **207**
6/184 7/278 8/318 9/371   6/107 7/117 8/186 9/186

Bonus points – Gloucestershire 4, Surrey 4.

Bowling: First Innings—M. P. Bicknell 6.3-3-17-0; Benjamin 24-5-77-4; Kenlock 26-3-105-2; Hollioake 19.3-2-84-2; Nowell 19-5-73-1; Shahid 5-0-29-0. *Second Innings*—Benjamin 24-8-68-4; Kenlock 19-2-71-2; Nowell 20-11-24-2; Hollioake 9-2-11-0; Shahid 7-0-30-2.

Surrey

D. J. Bicknell c Wright b Alleyne	42	– lbw b Smith	45
M. A. Butcher c Russell b Cooper	71	– c Russell b Srinath	51
*A. J. Stewart lbw b Srinath	2	– c Cooper b Ball	65
A. D. Brown c Hodgson b Cooper	16	– c Lynch b Smith	187
A. J. Hollioake lbw b Smith	27	– c Lynch b Smith	32
N. Shahid run out	6	– lbw b Ball	11
†G. J. Kersey c Russell b Srinath	12	– c Russell b Srinath	13
M. P. Bicknell c Russell b Smith	9	– lbw b Srinath	17
R. W. Nowell c Russell b Srinath	0	– run out	13
S. G. Kenlock not out	4	– not out	9
J. E. Benjamin lbw b Smith	0	– c Alleyne b Srinath	2
B 1, l-b 7, n-b 20	28	B 1, l-b 9, w 2, n-b 18	30

1/96 2/103 3/151 4/153 5/160   **217**   1/96 2/124 3/223 4/292 5/339   **475**
6/196 7/202 8/205 9/217   6/374 7/414 8/464 9/464

Bonus points – Surrey 1, Gloucestershire 4.

Bowling: *First Innings*—Srinath 26–5–83–3; Smith 26.4–11–60–3; Ball 5–1–9–0; Cooper 20–7–22–2; Alleyne 13–4–35–1. *Second Innings*—Smith 31–6–90–3; Cooper 24–4–65–0; Alleyne 13–2–42–0; Ball 42–6–128–2; Lynch 2–0–3–0; Srinath 33.3–4–137–4.

Umpires: J. C. Balderstone and B. J. Meyer.

At Birmingham, May 4, 5, 6, 8. SURREY lost to WARWICKSHIRE by 91 runs.

SURREY v DURHAM

At The Oval, May 11, 12, 13, 15. Surrey won by an innings and 159 runs. Surrey 24 pts, Durham 3 pts. Toss: Durham. Championship debut: S. D. Birbeck. County debut: D. G. C. Ligertwood.

Surrey's sixth-highest total ever ensured their fourth win in four Championship encounters with Durham. It owed much to Butcher's career-best 167 and Stewart's 151, his 32nd century. They added 193 for the second wicket, one of four century partnerships in the innings. A largely ineffectual attack, in which five bowlers conceded more than 100, compounded Durham's shortcomings with the bat. It was an unhappy return to The Oval for Boiling, whose former team-mates knocked him about for 150 in 36 overs, though he also batted for two hours with Ligertwood in a first-innings recovery from 45 for four. Ligertwood, Surrey's reserve wicket-keeper in 1992, had to be whisked to London from a Second XI fixture at Derby after Scott suffered a back spasm, but provided much of the resistance in both innings. Benjamin took his 200th wicket for Surrey – Boiling – near the end of Durham's second innings, in which slow left-arm bowler Nowell proved a model of economy and Martin Bicknell left the field with another strain.

Close of play: First day, Durham 235-8 (D. G. C. Ligertwood 38*, S. J. E. Brown 5*); Second day, Surrey 288-1 (A. J. Stewart 147*, M. A. Butcher 89*); Third day, Durham 56-2 (W. Larkins 18*, J. A. Daley 19*).

Durham

*M. A. Roseberry c D. J. Bicknell			
b M. P. Bicknell	5	– c Kersey b M. P. Bicknell	7
W. Larkins c Stewart b Benjamin	2	– c Kersey b M. P. Bicknell	28
J. E. Morris c Stewart b Benjamin	5	– c Kersey b Benjamin	9
J. A. Daley c Thorpe b M. P. Bicknell	55	– c Stewart b Nowell	49
M. Prabhakar c Nowell b Butcher	23	– lbw b Nowell	41
M. Saxelby c Kersey b Nowell	68	– c Kersey b M. P. Bicknell	5
S. D. Birbeck lbw b M. P. Bicknell	0	– c Kersey b Nowell	10
†D. G. C. Ligertwood c Kersey b M. P. Bicknell	40	– not out	28
J. Boiling c Kersey b Pigott	1	– lbw b Benjamin	1
S. J. E. Brown c Pigott b Benjamin	33	– lbw b Hollioake	26
J. P. Searle not out	2	– b Hollioake	0
L-b 3, w 3, n-b 12	18	L-b 3, w 3, n-b 14	20

1/7 2/15 3/15 4/45 5/128   269   1/7 2/22 3/78 4/121 5/149   224
6/142 7/166 8/210 9/243   6/154 7/163 8/174 9/224

Bonus points – Durham 2, Surrey 4.

Bowling: *First Innings*—Benjamin 22.1–3–57–3; M. P. Bicknell 26–12–81–4; Butcher 13–3–32–1; Pigott 20–6–46–1; Nowell 16–7–38–1; Hollioake 5–1–12–0. *Second Innings*—Benjamin 20–3–64–2; M. P. Bicknell 18–8–32–3; Nowell 32–9–71–3; Pigott 11–2–26–0; Hollioake 4–1–7–2; Butcher 3–0–21–0.

Surrey

D. J. Bicknell st Ligertwood b Boiling	47	A. C. S. Pigott c Roseberry b Saxelby	9
*A. J. Stewart b Searle	151	R. W. Nowell run out	1
M. A. Butcher c Daley b Birbeck	167		
G. P. Thorpe c Ligertwood b Birbeck	62	B 4, l-b 6, n-b 8	18
A. D. Brown lbw b Birbeck	44		
A. J. Hollioake c Roseberry b Boiling	83	1/103 2/296 3/417 (9 wkts dec.) 652	
†G. J. Kersey b Searle	55	4/456 5/511 6/620	
M. P. Bicknell not out	15	7/625 8/646 9/652	

J. E. Benjamin did not bat.

Bonus points – Surrey 4, Durham 1 (Score at 120 overs: 471-4).

Bowling: Brown 17-0-102-0; Prabhakar 32-8-116-0; Birbeck 22-3-119-3; Boiling 36-7-150-2; Searle 36-3-126-2; Saxelby 5.4-0-29-1.

Umpires: J. H. Harris and V. A. Holder.

At Northampton, May 18, 19, 20. SURREY lost to NORTHAMPTONSHIRE by nine runs.

At Worcester, June 1, 2, 3, 5. SURREY lost to WORCESTERSHIRE by 134 runs.

SURREY v SOMERSET

At The Oval, June 8, 9, 10, 12. Somerset won by five wickets. Somerset 22 pts, Surrey 5 pts. Toss: Surrey.

Surrey's batting, missing Stewart and Thorpe, on Test duty, and Darren Bicknell, forced out by a back strain after 87 consecutive Championship appearances, looked inadequate in the first innings, in which they were bemused by Mushtaq Ahmed. They did atone by keeping Somerset's lead to 39, with Martin Bicknell claiming five, and then topping 400 second time round, when Butcher hammered a hundred. Ward and Smith, fighting for their places in the side, added welcome half-centuries and Somerset were set to chase 381 on the final day. But once Bicknell hobbled off with a knee injury – the third time in three Championship matches he had failed to stay the course – a fragile attack was torn to shreds. Bowler and Lathwell gave Somerset a fine start, with Bowler scoring his third century for his new county and hitting 15 fours and two sixes: he was still there at the end as Somerset, making light of the loss of six overs to rain, won with nine balls to spare.

Close of play: First day, Somerset 74-3 (R. J. Harden 36*, A. N. Hayhurst 8*); Second day, Surrey 70-0 (J. D. Ratcliffe 35*, M. A. Butcher 33*); Third day, Surrey 419-9 (A. C. S. Pigott 13*, C. G. Rackemann 1*).

Surrey

J. D. Ratcliffe lbw b Mushtaq Ahmed	70	– lbw b Kerr	48
M. A. Butcher c Turner b Ecclestone	29	– c Kerr b Ecclestone	102
N. Shahid lbw b Mushtaq Ahmed	26	– c Hayhurst b Mushtaq Ahmed	17
A. J. Hollioake b Rose	36	– lbw b Trump	0
A. D. Brown run out	12	– b Mushtaq Ahmed	31
D. M. Ward c Lathwell b Mushtaq Ahmed	13	– b Trump	51
A. W. Smith lbw b Kerr	9	– c and b Kerr	88
†G. J. Kersey b Kerr	2	– lbw b Rose	13
M. P. Bicknell lbw b Mushtaq Ahmed	5	– c Mushtaq Ahmed b Hayhurst	31
*A. C. S. Pigott b Mushtaq Ahmed	8	– not out	13
C. G. Rackemann not out	1	– not out	1
B 1, l-b 5, n-b 4	10	B 5, l-b 11, n-b 8	24

1/66 2/130 3/135 4/159 5/189	221	1/111 2/162 3/163 (9 wkts dec.) 419
6/203 7/205 8/208 9/212		4/189 5/218 6/286
		7/320 8/404 9/410

Bonus points – Surrey 1, Somerset 4.

Bowling: *First Innings*—Rose 14–1–44–1; Kerr 16–5–47–2; Ecclestone 5–1–29–1; Hayhurst 8–3–15–0; Mushtaq Ahmed 32.1–16–54–5; Trump 8–2–26–0. *Second Innings*—Rose 24–4–101–1; Kerr 16–4–64–2; Mushtaq Ahmed 42–7–140–2; Trump 39–21–67–2; Ecclestone 3–1–12–1; Hayhurst 4–0–19–1.

Somerset

M. N. Lathwell lbw b Rackemann	2	– hit wkt b Rackemann	75
M. E. Trescothick c Brown b Bicknell	0	– c Bicknell b Smith	34
P. D. Bowler c Kersey b Pigott	25	– not out	132
R. J. Harden c Brown b Bicknell	90	– c Kersey b Rackemann	41
*A. N. Hayhurst c Kersey b Rackemann	9	– c Brown b Pigott	0
G. D. Rose b Smith	33	– b Smith	51
S. C. Ecclestone b Bicknell	41	– not out	25
†R. J. Turner lbw b Bicknell	0		
Mushtaq Ahmed c Ward b Bicknell	1		
J. I. D. Kerr not out	26		
H. R. J. Trump c Brown b Pigott	17		
B 3, l-b 2, w 1, n-b 10	16	B 2, l-b 11, n-b 12	25

1/2 2/4 3/50 4/80 5/152   260   1/70 2/156 3/257   (5 wkts) 383
6/210 7/210 8/214 9/214   4/257 5/326

Bonus points – Somerset 2, Surrey 4.

Bowling: *First Innings*—Rackemann 21–5–58–2; Bicknell 19–8–61–5; Pigott 15.5–4–36–2; Shahid 5–1–18–0; Smith 15–3–51–1; Hollioake 1–0–5–0; Butcher 4–0–26–0. *Second Innings*—Rackemann 18–6–63–2; Bicknell 7.2–1–31–0; Pigott 16.1–3–79–1; Butcher 11–1–51–0; Smith 36–7–123–2; Hollioake 6–0–23–0.

Umpires: J. W. Holder and T. E. Jesty.

At Horsham, June 15, 16, 17, 19. SURREY drew with SUSSEX.

SURREY v GLAMORGAN

At The Oval, June 22, 23, 24, 26. Drawn. Surrey 7 pts, Glamorgan 8 pts. Toss: Glamorgan.
A high-scoring match had a breathless start and a tense finish, when Rackemann had to keep out Watkin's final over. Surrey looked capable of victory while Brown was scoring an explosive 92. But from 259 for three the wickets fell steadily. It was Kersey who earned the draw, spending 75 minutes at the crease for six runs. Throughout the first innings there appeared to be runs for the taking. Glamorgan openers James and Morris had 60 on the board within ten overs, Cottey made his third hundred of the season and Thomas registered a maiden fifty. When Surrey replied, Shahid scored his first century for the county, but Glamorgan took a lead of 53 and extended it with the help of career-best scores from Anthony and Kendrick, another Surrey exile, before leaving the home team just over a day to score 383.
Close of play: First day, Glamorgan 422-7 (S. D. Thomas 50*, N. M. Kendrick 3*); Second day, Surrey 391-9 (J. E. Benjamin 1*, C. G. Rackemann 1*); Third day, Surrey 5-0 (D. J. Bicknell 4*, J. D. Ratcliffe 1*).

Glamorgan

S. P. James c Brown b Rackemann	28	– lbw b Pigott	9
*H. Morris b Butcher	51	– c Kersey b Rackemann	10
D. L. Hemp c Brown b Rackemann	2	– c Hollioake b Rackemann	15
M. P. Maynard lbw b Shahid	63	– c Rackemann b Butcher	97
P. A. Cottey lbw b Hollioake	125	– c Hollioake b Butcher	16
R. D. B. Croft lbw b Pigott	41	– c Kersey b Pigott	4
H. A. G. Anthony c Shahid b Benjamin	36	– lbw b Butcher	91
S. D. Thomas c Benjamin b Rackemann	51	– c Butcher b Rackemann	2
N. M. Kendrick c Brown b Hollioake	16	– c Ratcliffe b Butcher	59
†C. P. Metson not out	13	– not out	6
S. L. Watkin c Ward b Hollioake	0	– c Shahid b Rackemann	0
L-b 8, n-b 16	24	B 6, l-b 5, w 3, n-b 6	20

1/60 2/70 3/102 4/189 5/321	**450**	1/19 2/25 3/76 4/160 5/164	**329**
6/341 7/403 8/427 9/442		6/174 7/189 8/310 9/324	

Bonus points – Glamorgan 4, Surrey 3 (Score at 120 overs: 433-8).

Bowling: *First Innings*—Rackemann 29–6–102–3; Benjamin 36–10–108–1; Butcher 15–3–54–1; Pigott 22–3–84–1; Hollioake 16.2–6–40–3; Shahid 10–1–54–1. *Second Innings*—Rackemann 21.4–6–70–4; Benjamin 8.5–1–27–0; Pigott 14–2–70–2; Butcher 16–1–72–4; Hollioake 7.1–1–34–0; Shahid 9–1–45–0.

Surrey

D. J. Bicknell c Metson b Watkin	11	– c Maynard b Croft	53
J. D. Ratcliffe c Metson b Anthony	56	– c Metson b Anthony	75
M. A. Butcher b Thomas	25	– c Metson b Thomas	16
A. D. Brown b Thomas	15	– c James b Croft	92
N. Shahid lbw b Croft	125	– c Croft b Watkin	22
D. M. Ward c Metson b Thomas	1	– c Metson b Croft	1
A. J. Hollioake b Thomas	88	– c Hemp b Anthony	3
†G. J. Kersey c Metson b Anthony	54	– not out	6
*A. C. S. Pigott c Hemp b Watkin	0	– b Watkin	3
J. E. Benjamin c Metson b Anthony	3	– c Metson b Watkin	0
C. G. Rackemann not out	5	– not out	0
B 2, l-b 12	14	B 20, l-b 9, n-b 2	31

1/30 2/60 3/98 4/118 5/121	**397**	1/137 2/153 3/173	**(9 wkts) 302**
6/270 7/384 8/384 9/386		4/259 5/262 6/277	
		7/293 8/298 9/302	

Bonus points – Surrey 4, Glamorgan 4.

Bowling: *First Innings*—Watkin 20–6–82–3; Anthony 15.5–2–75–2; Thomas 19–3–95–4; Croft 22–4–72–1; Kendrick 13–1–59–0. *Second Innings*—Watkin 23.9–9–43–3; Anthony 24–7–55–2; Croft 41–18–94–3; Thomas 14–2–79–1; Kendrick 4–3–2–0.

Umpires: J. D. Bond and J. H. Hampshire.

At Lord's, June 29, 30, July 1. SURREY lost to MIDDLESEX by an innings and 76 runs.

SURREY v ESSEX

At The Oval, July 6, 7, 8, 10. Essex won by seven wickets. Essex 24 pts, Surrey 6 pts. Toss: Essex.

The crisis at Surrey, already bottom of the table, deepened as Such and Childs sent them spinning to their sixth defeat. Their second innings slid quickly from 118 for one to 203 all out. A target of 148 gave the bowlers no room for manoeuvre, though Nowell delivered three short, sharp shocks in 14 balls before Waugh and Irani steered Essex to victory. Their unbeaten fifties complemented hundreds in the first innings, when Hussain also reached a century, his third of the summer. Surrey found some bright spots during the first two days: Brown, dropped at Lord's for repeated batting profligacy, returned with a hundred as responsible as they come; wicket-keeper Kersey, under instructions to aim for an average of 25 throughout the season, touched 30 after his fourth half-century, and 17-year-old Tudor, though used sparingly by Surrey's stand-in captain, Hollioake, bowled effectively.

Close of play: First day, Surrey 342-8 (G. J. Kersey 37*); Second day, Essex 311-4 (N. Hussain 120*, R. C. Irani 7*); Third day, Surrey 123-2 (D. J. Bicknell 50*, A. D. Brown 0*).

Surrey

D. J. Bicknell c Waugh b Ilott	2	– c Hussain b Childs	50
J. D. Ratcliffe c Rollins b Williams	45	– c Rollins b Childs	10
M. A. Butcher c Rollins b Williams	59	– c Robinson b Ilott	59
A. D. Brown c Prichard b Such	103	– b Such	18
N. Shahid c Hussain b Such	39	– (6) b Such	4
*A. J. Hollioake c Rollins b Childs	25	– (7) st Rollins b Childs	30
†G. J. Kersey c Gooch b Ilott	64	– (8) c sub b Such	8
R. W. Nowell b Ilott	8	– (4) lbw b Childs	2
A. J. Tudor lbw b Ilott	2	– c Gooch b Such	3
J. E. Benjamin c Robinson b Such	49	– not out	2
C. G. Rackemann not out	13	– b Such	5
B 9, l-b 8, w 1, n-b 10	28	B 8, l-b 4	12

1/10 2/100 3/129 4/239 5/284   437   1/118 2/123 3/124 4/130 5/145   203
6/302 7/331 8/342 9/379   6/160 7/178 8/190 9/192

Bonus points – Surrey 4, Essex 4 (Score at 120 overs: 389-9).

In the second innings J. D. Ratcliffe, when 5, retired hurt at 11 and resumed at 124.

Bowling: *First Innings*—Ilott 29-7-101-4; Williams 28-6-96-2; Irani 13-2-52-0; Waugh 10-1-40-0; Childs 27-6-80-1; Such 22.4-3-51-3. *Second Innings*—Ilott 19-7-44-1; Williams 5-2-12-0; Such 36.4-12-79-5; Childs 44-19-55-4; Waugh 3-2-1-0.

Essex

G. A. Gooch c Kersey b Tudor	21	– b Nowell	5
D. D. J. Robinson c Kersey b Benjamin	10	– c Tudor b Nowell	10
N. Hussain c Kersey b Rackemann	137	– b Nowell	5
M. E. Waugh c Shahid b Tudor	126	– not out	59
*P. J. Prichard c Butcher b Nowell	9		
R. C. Irani c Shahid b Nowell	108	– (5) not out	61
†R. J. Rollins c Butcher b Rackemann	30		
M. C. Ilott b Rackemann	2		
N. F. Williams c Kersey b Rackemann	0		
P. M. Such not out	4		
J. H. Childs b Tudor	4		
B 12, l-b 8, w 2, n-b 20	42	B 3, l-b 4, n-b 4	11

1/40 2/44 3/252 4/277 5/408   493   1/13 2/25 3/26   (3 wkts) 151
6/470 7/475 8/485 9/485

Bonus points – Essex 4, Surrey 2 (Score at 120 overs: 435-5).

Bowling: *First Innings*—Rackemann 34-10-99-4; Benjamin 25-3-120-1; Tudor 18-2-77-3; Butcher 11-1-38-0; Nowell 40-10-103-2; Hollioake 5-0-23-0; Shahid 3-0-13-0. *Second Innings*—Rackemann 10-3-36-0; Nowell 20-1-71-3; Benjamin 4-1-13-0; Tudor 4-0-9-0; Shahid 4-0-15-0.

Umpires: K. J. Lyons and R. Palmer.

SURREY v NOTTINGHAMSHIRE

At Guildford, July 20, 21, 22, 24. Surrey won by 171 runs. Surrey 21 pts, Nottinghamshire 7 pts. Toss: Nottinghamshire.

Surrey's first win since May 15 dragged them off the bottom of the table, after an unbeaten 228 from Darren Bicknell. It was the second double-hundred of his career, exactly 12 months after the first, also against Nottinghamshire, which was the longest innings in Championship history. This effort was 46 minutes shorter, at 592 minutes, and included 34 fours and a six. It was all the sweeter at Guildford, his home club ground. Acting-captain Holliake set a target of 444 and winkled out Nottinghamshire with a session to spare. The ever-improving slow left-armer, Nowell, took a career-best four for 43 – beginning when Robinson was caught off Shahid's heel. Surrey's first innings had declined after the first of two dazzling half-centuries from Thorpe. They conceded a lead of 85 and then lost Benjamin, who had just taken five wickets, when he turned an ankle, but Bicknell inspired them to rise to the task. A minute's silence was observed on Saturday to mark the death of Harold Larwood.

Close of play: First day, Nottinghamshire 144-5 (G. F. Archer 39*); Second day, Surrey 194-3 (D. J. Bicknell 65*, N. Shahid 21*); Third day, Nottinghamshire 37-2 (R. T. Robinson 14*, P. Johnson 5*).

Surrey

D. J. Bicknell b Cairns	6	– not out	228
M. A. Butcher c Hindson b Pick	2	– b Chapman	15
G. P. Thorpe run out	72	– c Afzaal b Hindson	63
A. D. Brown b Cairns	55	– c sub b Chapman	20
N. Shahid c Johnson b Chapman	4	– b Chapman	57
*A. J. Holliake run out	48	– lbw b Cairns	56
†G. J. Kersey lbw b Cairns	1	– lbw b Hindson	27
R. W. Nowell c Pollard b Pick	12	– lbw b Hindson	0
J. E. Benjamin b Hindson	4	– (11) not out	15
S. G. Kenlock c Robinson b Pick	8	– (9) c Noon b Hindson	2
C. G. Rackemann not out	10	– (10) run out	10
L-b 10, w 3, n-b 4	17	B 9, l-b 12, w 5, n-b 9	35

1/5 2/18 3/33 4/143 5/144   239   1/26 2/113 3/162   (9 wkts dec.) 528
6/148 7/180 8/185 9/196   4/265 5/341 6/400
                             7/400 8/408 9/505

Bonus points – Surrey 1, Nottinghamshire 4.

In the first innings A. D. Brown, when 0, retired hurt at 18-2 and resumed at 144.

Bowling: *First Innings*—Cairns 17.1-3-53-3; Pick 15-2-40-3; Chapman 7-0-27-1; Archer 6-1-16-0; Hindson 10-0-53-1; Afzaal 7-0-40-0. *Second Innings*—Cairns 30-11-97-1; Chapman 30-6-119-3; Pick 21-7-76-0; Hindson 54-12-162-4; Afzaal 21-7-53-0.

Nottinghamshire

P. R. Pollard lbw b Rackemann	1	– b Rackemann	0
R. T. Robinson b Benjamin	3	– c Thorpe b Nowell	52
C. Banton lbw b Benjamin	14	– c Kersey b Rackemann	12
*P. Johnson c Brown b Kenlock	16	– st Kersey b Shahid	57
G. F. Archer b Kenlock	43	– lbw b Shahid	46
C. L. Cairns b Benjamin	50	– lbw b Holliake	48
†W. M. Noon not out	64	– b Rackemann	1
U. Afzaal c Brown b Benjamin	6	– c Brown b Nowell	20
J. E. Hindson lbw b Benjamin	33	– c Kenlock b Nowell	8
R. A. Pick c and b Rackemann	37	– not out	1
R. J. Chapman c Holliake b Nowell	6	– lbw b Nowell	2
B 3, l-b 15, w 8, n-b 25	51	B 5, l-b 7, w 1, n-b 12	25

1/13 2/19 3/38 4/55 5/144   324   1/0 2/16 3/105 4/155 5/204   272
6/160 7/181 8/243 9/316   6/205 7/253 8/261 9/265

Bonus points – Nottinghamshire 3, Surrey 4.

Bowling: *First Innings*—Benjamin 20.1–4–53–5; Rackemann 25–2–98–1; Kenlock 24–5–88–2; Butcher 5–1–10–0; Nowell 12.1–4–35–2; Hollioake 5–0–22–0. *Second Innings*—Rackemann 20–6–73–3; Kenlock 12–3–45–0; Nowell 22–10–43–4; Shahid 19–4–87–2; Hollioake 7–4–12–1.

Umpires: V. A. Holder and T. E. Jesty.

At Leicester, July 27, 28, 29. SURREY lost to LEICESTERSHIRE by an innings and 37 runs.

At Canterbury, August 3, 4, 5, 7. SURREY drew with KENT.

At The Oval, August 8. SURREY lost to YOUNG AUSTRALIA by 179 runs (See Young Australia tour section).

SURREY v YORKSHIRE

At The Oval, August 10, 11, 12, 14. Surrey won by one run. Surrey 24 pts, Yorkshire 8 pts. Toss: Surrey.

This was Surrey's second one-run win in their history (the other being against Lancashire in 1948). The conclusion was bizarre as well as desperate. Hollioake rapped last man Robinson on the pad and appealed for lbw, while the ball carried on to be well taken by Butcher at slip. Robinson indicated he had got some bat on it and the bowler was turned down, only for Butcher to appeal successfully for the catch. Hollioake had dismissed Yorkshire's last three for one run in 12 balls, for his best-ever figures. Yorkshire, needing a modest 219, began the final morning just 145 from victory, with nine wickets in hand. But they obligingly folded after lunch, losing their last seven in 20 overs for just 32 runs. On the first day, Shahid and Kersey made career-best scores, which lifted Surrey past 400. For Yorkshire, Bevan made his fifth and biggest century of the summer, and Silverwood took five wickets for the first time in a feeble Surrey second innings.

Close of play: First day, Surrey 383-6 (G. J. Kersey 71*, R. W. Nowell 9*); Second day, Yorkshire 294-4 (M. G. Bevan 109*, R. J. Blakey 25*); Third day, Yorkshire 74-1 (M. D. Moxon 35*, S. M. Milburn 0*).

Surrey

D. J. Bicknell c Blakey b Hamilton	0	– c Blakey b Silverwood	5
M. A. Butcher lbw b Stemp	57	– c Blakey b Stemp	62
N. Shahid c Blakey b Robinson	139	– c Moxon b Milburn	15
A. D. Brown b Milburn	48	– b Silverwood	5
*A. J. Hollioake c Blakey b Silverwood	40	– b Hamilton	38
A. W. Smith c Byas b Robinson	0	– lbw b Silverwood	3
†G. J. Kersey c Byas b Silverwood	83	– st Blakey b Stemp	20
R. W. Nowell c Blakey b Robinson	10	– b Stemp	6
C. G. Rackemann c Bevan b Silverwood	0	– b Silverwood	5
S. G. Kenlock c Moxon b Robinson	7	– c Byas b Silverwood	8
J. M. de la Pena not out	0	– not out	2
L-b 10, w 3, n-b 12	25	L-b 4, n-b 2	6

1/1 2/137 3/224 4/279 5/283   409 1/36 2/72 3/92 4/96 5/117 175
6/328 7/390 8/400 9/401   6/138 7/160 8/165 9/169

Bonus points – Surrey 4, Yorkshire 4 (Score at 120 overs: 401-9).

Bowling: *First Innings*—Silverwood 22–3–94–3; Hamilton 14–2–72–1; Milburn 10–2–39–1; Robinson 24.4–8–64–4; Stemp 41–12–103–1; Vaughan 11–3–27–0. *Second Innings*—Silverwood 16.1–2–62–5; Robinson 12–4–22–0; Stemp 18–6–37–3; Milburn 6–0–21–1; Hamilton 8–1–29–1.

Yorkshire

*M. D. Moxon b Holhoake	63	– c Shahid b Nowell	90
M. P. Vaughan c Kersey b de la Pena	19	– c and b Smith	38
D. Byas c Hollioake b Rackemann	30	– (4) c Brown b Hollioake	15
M. G. Bevan not out	153	– (5) c Shahid b Nowell	29
S. A. Kellett c Kersey b Kenlock	28	– (6) lbw b Rackemann	4
†R. J. Blakey c Hollioake b Butcher	26	– (7) c Kersey b Rackemann	0
G. M. Hamilton b Rackemann	9	– (8) not out	12
S. M. Milburn c Kersey b Rackemann	2	– (3) c Shahid b Smith	0
C. E. W. Silverwood b de la Pena	10	– c Brown b Hollioake	9
R. D. Stemp b de la Pena	0	– c Shahid b Hollioake	0
M. A. Robinson b Rackemann	0	– c Butcher b Hollioake	0
B 3, l-b 6, w 1, n-b 16	26	B 4, l-b 2, w 2, n-b 12	20

1/39 2/105 3/129 4/187 5/299   366   1/73 2/77 3/126 4/185 5/194   217
6/312 7/324 8/355 9/355   6/194 7/197 8/215 9/215

Bonus points – Yorkshire 4, Surrey 4.

Bowling: *First Innings*—Rackemann 26.3–9–64–4; Kenlock 20–7–50–1; de la Pena 19–5–53–3; Smith 7–0–43–0; Nowell 23–6–66–0; Hollioake 12–1–49–1; Butcher 9–4–32–1. *Second Innings*—Rackemann 26–8–63–2; de la Pena 2–0–23–0; Nowell 17–7–41–2; Kenlock 2–0–14–0; Smith 19–6–47–2; Shahid 2–1–1–0; Hollioake 10–2–22–4.

Umpires: P. B. Wight and P. Willey.

At Derby, August 24, 25, 26. SURREY beat DERBYSHIRE by seven wickets.

SURREY v LANCASHIRE

At The Oval, August 29, 30, 31, September 1. Lancashire won by nine wickets. Lancashire 24 pts, Surrey 3 pts. Toss: Lancashire. First-class debut: R. J. Green.

Another hefty defeat was typical of Surrey's dismal summer. They slumped to 44 for four on the first morning and Hollioake and Thorpe did only half the job of reviving them, falling shortly after reaching fifties; Hollioake was bowled by Richard Green from Warrington, an eager Championship debutant. Gallian demonstrated the application they lacked in a five-hour 110, which gave Lancashire a winning platform. Martin Bicknell, in only his seventh first-class match of the summer, did pick up his third five-wicket haul, and Sargeant, recalled because Kersey had a broken thumb, took five catches. But Surrey soon suffered another injury: Tudor succumbed to a side strain after six overs of high-class fast bowling. Though Wasim Akram was injured, Martin and Chapple fulfilled the strike bowlers' roles admirably. Lancashire needed only 69 to win, and took only 45 minutes on the last morning.

Close of play: First day, Lancashire 39-0 (S. P. Titchard 9*, J. E. R. Gallian 21*); Second day, Lancashire 343-5 (G. D. Lloyd 0*, M. Watkinson 0*); Third day, Lancashire 19-1 (J. E. R. Gallian 15*, N. J. Speak 0*).

Surrey

D. J. Bicknell c Atherton b Chapple	16	– c Crawley b Martin 26
J. D. Ratcliffe c Watkinson b Chapple	11	– lbw b Watkinson 20
M. A. Butcher c Crawley b Martin	5	– b Watkinson 9
N. Shahid lbw b Martin	7	– c Titchard b Chapple. 32
G. P. Thorpe lbw b Chapple	61	– b Green..................... 22
*A. J. Hollioake b Green	51	– c Gallian b Martin 40
A. W. Smith c Speak b Chapple	1	– c Crawley b Watkinson 51
†N. F. Sargeant b Green	6	– lbw b Martin 2
M. P. Bicknell c Crawley b Shadford	20	– c Atherton b Chapple 6
A. J. Tudor c Watkinson b Shadford	30	– c Atherton b Chapple 2
C. G. Rackemann not out	3	– not out..................... 6
B 4, l-b 6	10	B 5, l-b 10, w 2, n-b 6 ... 23

1/22 2/31 3/43 4/44 5/157   221   1/27 2/41 3/101 4/106 5/144   239
6/157 7/164 8/170 9/200   6/184 7/192 8/227 9/233

Bonus points – Surrey 1, Lancashire 4.

Bowling: *First Innings*—Martin 20–3–59–2; Chapple 16–4–44–4; Shadford 7.5–1–40–2; Gallian 4–0–28–0; Green 10–1–40–2. *Second Innings*—Chapple 19.1–4–66–3; Green 10–1–47–1; Watkinson 18–6–61–3; Martin 14–6–24–3; Gallian 3–0–14–0; Shadford 4–1–12–0.

Lancashire

S. P. Titchard c Sargeant b Thorpe	33	– (2) c Sargeant b M. P. Bicknell . 2
J. E. R. Gallian c Sargeant b Thorpe	110	– (1) not out.................. 48
†J. P. Crawley c Sargeant b Rackemann	26	
N. J. Speak b Rackemann	72	– (3) not out................. 13
M. A. Atherton c Sargeant b M. P. Bicknell	61	
G. D. Lloyd b M. P. Bicknell	20	
*M. Watkinson lbw b M. P. Bicknell	20	
R. J. Green c Sargeant b M. P. Bicknell	1	
G. Chapple c and b Butcher	1	
D. J. Shadford not out	0	
P. J. Martin c D. J. Bicknell b M. P. Bicknell	3	
L-b 7, w 4, n-b 34	45	N-b 8 8

1/98 2/163 3/224 4/343 5/343   392   1/10   (1 wkt) 71
6/375 7/388 8/389 9/389

Bonus points – Lancashire 4, Surrey 2 (Score at 120 overs: 362-5).

Bowling: *First Innings*—Tudor 5.5–1–12–0; M. P. Bicknell 36.2–7–107–5; Rackemann 24.1–4–77–2; Butcher 22–4–60–1; Thorpe 17–2–42–2; Smith 16–3–53–0; Shahid 9–1–34–0. *Second Innings*—Rackemann 7–1–25–0; M. P. Bicknell 6–1–9–1; Shahid 3–0–12–0; Smith 5–0–19–0; D. J. Bicknell 2.3–1–6–0.

Umpires: D. J. Constant and N. T. Plews.

SURREY v NEW SOUTH WALES

Peter May Memorial Cup

At The Oval, September 6, 7, 8. Drawn. Toss: New South Wales. First-class debut: J. A. Knott.

A match intended to mark both Surrey's 150th anniversary and the twinning of The Oval with Sydney Cricket Ground ended as a damp squib, with rain on the last two days. At least Taylor and Slater, the Australian Test openers, entertained the few who braved the inclement weather with a stand of 133. Roberts also helped himself to a belligerent fifty, before becoming the first victim of wicket-keeper Jamie Knott, son of Alan. Overthrows set up two unusual moments: a five for Roberts and a seven for Emery. The Peter May Memorial Cup remained in London; Surrey are due to take it to Australia to resume this series in 1997 and the sides will play for it every two years. A one-day match scheduled for September 10 was rained off.

Close of play: First day, Surrey 57-1 (D. J. Bicknell 16*, M. A. Butcher 10*); Second day, No play.

New South Wales

*M. A. Taylor c Brown b Butcher	61	†P. A. Emery not out	10
M. J. Slater c Ratcliffe b Benjamin	69		
K. J. Roberts c Knott b Rackemann	53	L-b 4, w 2, n-b 38	44
M. W. Patterson c Butcher b Shahid	46		—
M. E. Waugh lbw b Benjamin	45	1/133 2/185 3/230 (7 wkts dec.) 398	
G. R. J. Matthews c Shahid b Smith	40	4/261 5/332	
S. Lee b Smith	30	6/380 7/398	

A. M. Stuart, D. A. Freedman and G. D. McGrath did not bat.

Bowling: M. P. Bicknell 13–1–79–0; Rackemann 12–3–36–1; Benjamin 19–1–82–2; Butcher 8–0–70–1; Smith 21.3–2–104–2; Shahid 6–2–23–1.

Surrey

D. J. Bicknell not out	16
J. D. Ratcliffe run out	14
M. A. Butcher not out	10
B 4, l-b 3, n-b 10	17
	—
1/40 (1 wkt)	57

A. D. Brown, N. Shahid, D. M. Ward, A. W. Smith, *M. P. Bicknell, †J. A. Knott, J. E. Benjamin and C. G. Rackemann did not bat.

Bowling: McGrath 7–1–21–0; Stuart 5–0–29–0; Matthews 2–2–0–0.

Umpires: B. Dudleston and P. Willey.

SURREY v HAMPSHIRE

At The Oval, September 14, 15, 16, 18. Drawn. Surrey 4 pts. Toss: Hampshire.

Hampshire's long-time leader Mark Nicholas marked his retirement with the 117th fifty of his first-class career (36 of them were hundreds). The grinning Surrey players had formed a guard of honour, more tongue in cheek than bat in air, when he marched out to make half a dozen on the first day. The weather robbed everyone of the next two days but Nicholas seized his chance in an otherwise woeful Hampshire second innings. His team-mates were undone by Martin Bicknell, who took eight in the match and bowled Surrey to the brink of a welcome victory. They needed 267 in 60 overs and Bicknell's brother, Darren, shared an enterprising stand of 135 in 27 with Shahid. But not long after he was out, three short of 1,000 runs for the season, the game was washed away.

Close of play: First day, Surrey 71-2 (D. J. Bicknell 21*, A. D. Brown 23*); Second day, No play; Third day, No play.

Hampshire

V. P. Terry c Thorpe b M. P. Bicknell	9	– absent hurt	
J. S. Laney c Sargeant b Benjamin	17	– b Benjamin	23
*J. P. Stephenson c Sargeant b M. P. Bicknell..	7	– (1) lbw b Benjamin	5
P. R. Whitaker c Ratcliffe b M. P. Bicknell ...	17	– (3) c Brown b M. P. Bicknell ...	8
M. C. J. Nicholas c Sargeant b Rackemann	6	– c D. J. Bicknell b Rackemann ..	53
G. W. White c Thorpe b Rackemann	3	– (4) c Sargeant b M. P. Bicknell .	3
K. D. James c Brown b Benjamin	36	– (6) lbw b M. P. Bicknell	10
†A. N. Aymes lbw b Benjamin	6	– (7) lbw b M. P. Bicknell	6
S. D. Udal lbw b Rackemann	19	– (8) b Rackemann	13
H. H. Streak c Hollioake b M. P. Bicknell	25	– (9) not out.................	11
C. A. Connor not out	6	– (10) c Sargeant b Benjamin ...	9
N-b 34	34	L-b 2, w 1, n-b 8.......	11
	185		**152**

1/28 2/28 3/50 4/57 5/63   1/5 2/36 3/36 4/47 5/86
6/70 7/79 8/116 9/163   6/102 7/128 8/135 9/152

Bonus points – Surrey 4.

Bowling: *First Innings*—M. P. Bicknell 19-3-65-4; Benjamin 10.1-1-62-3; Rackemann 16-4-58-3. *Second Innings*—M. P. Bicknell 15-2-60-4; Benjamin 13.2-3-32-3; Rackemann 11-0-58-2.

Surrey

D. J. Bicknell not out	21	– c sub b Streak	75
J. D. Ratcliffe c Aymes b Streak	14	– c White b Connor	10
G. P. Thorpe c James b Streak	4		
A. D. Brown not out	23	– not out	7
N. Shahid (did not bat)...................		– (3) not out	77
B 3, l-b 5, w 1	9	B 3, l-b 2, w 1	6

1/33 2/44   (2 wkts dec.) 71   1/18 2/153   (2 wkts) 175

*A. J. Hollioake, A. W. Smith, M. P. Bicknell, †N. F. Sargeant, J. E. Benjamin and C. G. Rackemann did not bat.

Bowling: *First Innings*—Streak 8.1-0-28-2; Connor 8-1-35-0. *Second Innings*—Streak 9-1-30-1; Connor 9-1-52-1; James 3-1-17-0; Stephenson 9.2-1-56-0; Udal 5-0-15-0.

Umpires: D. J. Constant and A. G. T. Whitehead.

COUNTY BENEFITS AWARDED FOR 1996

Derbyshire	... Derbyshire CCC.	Northamptonshire .	A. J. Lamb
Durham	..... P. Bainbridge (testimonial).		(testimonial).
Essex	.... P. J. Prichard.	Nottinghamshire ..	R. A. Pick.
Glamorgan	... M. P. Maynard.	Somerset	.... R. J. Harden.
Gloucestershire	A. J. Wright.	Surrey	.... D. M. Ward.
Hampshire	... R. A. Smith.	Sussex	.... A. P. Wells.
Kent	.... C. Penn.	Warwickshire	.... D. A. Reeve.
Lancashire	.... M. Watkinson.	Worcestershire	... S. J. Rhodes.
Middlesex	.... M. W. Gatting.	Yorkshire	.... P. J. Hartley.

No benefit was awarded by Leicestershire.

SUSSEX

President: The Duke of Richmond and Gordon
Chairman: A. M. Caffyn
Secretary: N. Bett
Captain: A. P. Wells
Coach: D. L. Haynes
Head Groundsman: P. Eaton
Scorer: L. V. Chandler

Sussex firmly believed they could lay their hands on some much-needed silverware in 1995: a top four finish in the Championship and a major challenge for one of the limited-overs competitions were said to be realistic objectives. Yet hopes of landing their first trophy for nine years evaporated into all-too-familiar disappointment. Some consolation for Sussex supporters came from captain Alan Wells's long-awaited England call-up, but that turned into a personal disaster; in any case, after his best season with the bat for four years, he said he would have happily swapped all his runs for a trophy.

As in 1994, the batting was inadequate. "A number of the batsmen went in with a bit more pressure on them, following on from the last season, and when you're lacking in confidence it's very difficult to score runs," said Wells, the only one to reach four figures. "We batted indifferently and, although we have the ability, everyone is only too aware that we have not come up with the goods consistently enough."

Sussex managed only four Championship victories in slipping down seven places to 15th, and made no impact on any of the one-day competitions. Events in July best summed up their summer. Sussex began the month with a historic innings win against the West Indians. It was the first time they had beaten them for 29 years and the defeat was the heaviest inflicted on the West Indians by any county. But they were then routed by ten wickets in two days by Nottinghamshire at Arundel before a poor home performance saw them crash out of the NatWest Trophy against Derbyshire. Another Championship defeat against Leicestershire a fortnight later pushed them to bottom of the table and they rounded off the month with a fourth consecutive failure, to Middlesex by an innings and 286 runs.

Before that match cricket manager Norman Gifford resigned after seven seasons, in a manner that bore more resemblance to football than cricket. Gifford admitted the team's performances had been extremely disappointing and said he had to accept the ultimate responsibility. However, he thought the future looked healthy, with a number of promising young players coming through. Chairman Alan Caffyn believed Gifford had made a "tremendous contribution", but the club refused to expand on the reasons for his departure or its timing.

The parting of the ways prompted a fundamental overhaul of the county's cricket structure. Sussex decided to appoint a first-team coach and create the new position of director of cricket and coaching. Both are included in a ten-man cricket management group, chaired by former Sussex captain John Barclay, which will also contain a full-time vice-captain and a senior player to skipper the Second Eleven. Sussex wasted no time in filling the first position: in October, West Indies opening batsman Desmond Haynes was named coach on a three-year contract. Haynes, left out of the West Indian touring squad, turned down playing offers from other English counties in favour of the challenge of reviving Sussex's fortunes.

It was hoped that Haynes's experience and knowledge would have a highly beneficial effect on the players. The batting department needs to be the first to profit. Wells bounced back after 1994, his leanest season for seven years, to score 1,343 for the county. But apart from Bill Athey and Neil Lenham, who were both restricted by injury, no one else even threatened to hit the thousand mark. The loss of potential match-winner Martin Speight for the entire season, to a virus affecting his muscles and joints, was described by Wells as a "massive blow". Such was the debilitating effect of the illness, picked up on the pre-season trip to Malaga, that it quickly became obvious Speight would not be fit enough to play. He lost a stone in weight and his only appearance was for the Second Eleven in May, when he made a typically swashbuckling 92 but then spent three days in bed recovering.

The bowling gave more cause for satisfaction, especially pace bowler Ed Giddins and leg-spinner Ian Salisbury, the leading wicket-takers with 68 and 54 respectively. Both were picked to tour Pakistan with England A. The fast left-armer Jason Lewry also performed very well in his first full summer. Only two years earlier Lewry was playing for Goring in the Sussex Invitation League while working with a firm of electrical wholesalers in Chichester, but he claimed 47 first-class wickets at an average of 26.53. A succession of injuries limited Paul Jarvis to only nine appearances while Franklyn Stephenson, who is giving way to fellow West Indian Vasbert Drakes, sat out the final five Championship matches and finished with 690 runs and 35 wickets from 13 games. Former England off-spinner Eddie Hemmings finally called it a day in July, aged 46, after 30 seasons on the circuit and 1,515 first-class wickets at 29.30.

The vacancies thus created allowed youngsters to be blooded and several responded with eye-catching performances. Openers Keith Newell and Toby Peirce stepped up after impressing in the Second Eleven and both batted with determination and promise, all-rounder Danny Law continued to make progress and off-spinner Nicky Phillips was also given a run in the side. Fast bowler James Kirtley proved himself a fine prospect with 58 wickets at 22.43 in the Second Eleven Championship and all-rounder Robin Martin-Jenkins is another player thought to have a bright future.

Sussex released all-rounders John North and Carlos Remy, while David Smith, who helped to coach the first team after Gifford's departure, also left the club after six years. Smith, who was registered for first-class cricket but not called upon, stressed he wanted to remain in the game in some capacity. Opener Jamie Hall, capped in 1992 two years after making his debut, requested a move and Sussex agreed to it, but said they would honour his contract if he failed to find another county. – Jack Arlidge.

609

SUSSEX 1995

[Bill Smith]

Back row: S. M. B. Robertson (physiotherapist), J. A. North, J. J. Bates, A. D. Edwards, S. Humphries, N. C. Phillips. Middle row: L. V. Chandler (First Eleven scorer), E. E. Hemmings, M. T. E. Peirce, C. C. Remy, R. J. Kirtley, K. Greenfield, J. D. Lewry, D. R. Law, M. Newell, K. Newell, I. C. Waring (youth development officer), J. F. Hartridge (Second Eleven scorer), C. E. Waller (Second Eleven coach), J. W. Hall, E. S. H. Giddins, N. J. Lenham, N. Gifford (cricket manager), A. P. Wells (captain), D. M. Smith, P. Moores, C. W. J. Athey. Insets: P. W. Jarvis, M. P. Speight, I. D. K. Salisbury. F. D. Stephenson, R. S. C. Martin-Jenkins.

SUSSEX RESULTS

All first-class matches – Played 19: Won 5, Lost 8, Drawn 6.

County Championship matches – Played 17: Won 4, Lost 7, Drawn 6.

Bonus points – Batting 37, Bowling 51.

Competition placings – Britannic Assurance County Championship; 15th;
NatWest Bank Trophy, 2nd round; Benson and Hedges Cup, 4th in Group D;
AXA Equity & Law League, 10th.

BRITANNIC ASSURANCE CHAMPIONSHIP AVERAGES

BATTING

	Birthplace	M	I	NO	R	HS	Avge
‡A. P. Wells	Newhaven	15	26	1	1,322	142	52.88
‡C. W. J. Athey	Middlesbrough	14	25	1	869	163*	36.20
‡N. J. Lenham	Worthing	13	22	3	624	104	32.84
‡F. D. Stephenson§	St James, Barbados	12	22	0	658	106	29.90
K. Greenfield	Brighton	17	29	1	794	121	28.35
‡J. W. Hall	Chichester	11	20	0	504	100	25.20
‡I. D. K. Salisbury	Northampton	17	29	3	599	74	23.03
K. Newell	Crawley	9	18	2	365	63	22.81
M. T. E. Peirce	Maidenhead	5	8	0	174	60	21.75
‡P. Moores	Macclesfield	17	29	2	570	94	21.11
N. C. Phillips	Pembury	5	8	1	130	52	18.57
P. W. Jarvis	Redcar	8	12	2	177	38	17.70
‡E. E. Hemmings	Leamington Spa	6	12	7	70	18	14.00
J. D. Lewry	Worthing	10	16	3	139	34	10.69
‡E. S. H. Giddins	Eastbourne	17	25	10	127	34	8.46
D. R. Law	London	6	10	0	82	19	8.20

Also batted: R. J. Kirtley (*Eastbourne*) (2 matches) 2*, 1*; R. S. C. Martin-Jenkins (*Guildford*) (2 matches) 0*, 50; C. C. Remy (*Castries, St Lucia*) (1 match) 4, 1.

* Signifies not out.   ‡ Denotes county cap.   § Overseas player.

The following played a total of 12 three-figure innings for Sussex in County Championship matches – A. P. Wells 6, C. W. J. Athey 2, K. Greenfield 1, J. W. Hall 1, N. J. Lenham 1, F. D. Stephenson 1.

BOWLING

	O	M	R	W	BB	5W/i	Avge
J. D. Lewry	287.4	50	1,008	38	6-43	3	26.52
P. W. Jarvis	202.4	39	629	23	5-55	1	27.34
E. S. H. Giddins	583.4	104	1,929	67	6-73	4	28.79
I. D. K. Salisbury	550.2	128	1,649	52	7-72	5	31.71
F. D. Stephenson	346.2	71	1,069	31	5-64	1	34.48
E. E. Hemmings	159.5	46	402	11	4-57	0	36.54

Also bowled: C. W. J. Athey 7-1-35-0; K. Greenfield 17.1-1-71-0; R. J. Kirtley 38-11-103-2; D. R. Law 45-6-215-4; N. J. Lenham 2-0-10-1; R. S. C. Martin-Jenkins 3-1-11-0; K. Newell 40-8-127-0; M. T. E. Peirce 6-1-14-0; N. C. Phillips 114.5-23-364-7; C. C. Remy 22.3-2-114-0.

Wicket-keeper: P. Moores 38 ct, 2 st.

Leading Fielder: I. D. K. Salisbury 16.

At Derby, April 27, 28, 29. SUSSEX lost to DERBYSHIRE by an innings and 379 runs.

SUSSEX v KENT

At Hove, May 4, 5, 6, 8. Sussex won by 75 runs. Sussex 23 pts, Kent 8 pts. Toss: Sussex.

Glorious weather saw cricket to match, with Wells leading from the front, and veteran off-spinner Hemmings ending obdurate Kent resistance on the final afternoon. Wells became the first Sussex batsman to score centuries in both innings at Hove since C. B. Fry, also against Kent, in 1903. They were his first Championship hundreds since September 1993. De Silva matched him with some gloriously fluent strokes in his maiden century for Kent and Ealham followed up with 88, his highest first-class score, establishing a first-innings lead of 38. But Wells was soon back at the crease, unveiling his trademark straight drives and square cuts as he shared century stands with Athey and Greenfield. He was finally bowled by Headley, who took a career-best seven for 58. Chasing 306 in 98 overs on a pitch taking spin, Kent slumped to 68 for six, with left-armer Lewry, in his fourth Championship match, claiming three. Ealham and Marsh revived their hopes, adding 126, before Hemmings took three for one in 16 balls to guarantee victory.

Close of play: First day, Kent 18-0 (T. R. Ward 7*, M. R. Benson 10*); Second day, Sussex 6-1 (C. W. J. Athey 6*, E. S. H. Giddins 0*); Third day, Sussex 341-9 (J. D. Lewry 3*).

Sussex

N. J. Lenham c Marsh b Headley	11	– (8) b Headley 0
C. W. J. Athey lbw b Ealham	62	– (1) lbw b Headley 72
J. W. Hall b Ealham	19	– (2) lbw b Headley 0
*A. P. Wells c Ward b Wren	107	– (5) b Headley 136
K. Greenfield b Fleming	1	– (6) c Fleming b Headley .. 68
†P. Moores lbw b Headley	0	– (4) c Fleming b Wren 5
F. D. Stephenson b Patel	48	– c Ward b Patel 29
I. D. K. Salisbury c Ward b Wren	9	– (9) lbw b Headley 0
J. D. Lewry b Patel	34	– (10) c Benson b Headley ... 3
E. S. H. Giddins lbw b Patel	9	– (3) lbw b Wren 5
E. E. Hemmings not out	0	– not out 0
B 5, l-b 15, w 1, n-b 2	23	B 6, l-b 8, w 1, n-b 10 ... 25

1/30 2/70 3/163 4/172 5/173   323   1/1 2/14 3/42 4/145 5/306   343
6/235 7/247 8/297 9/320   6/317 7/319 8/319 9/341

Bonus points – Sussex 3, Kent 4.

Bowling: *First Innings*—Headley 25-4-69-2; Wren 15-1-62-2; Patel 29.2-7-79-3; Ealham 21-4-58-2; Fleming 7-1-23-1; de Silva 2-0-12-0. *Second Innings*—Headley 26.4-9-58-7; Patel 34-10-102-1; Wren 22-3-68-2; Ealham 4-0-16-0; Fleming 10-2-23-0; de Silva 16-1-62-0.

Kent

T. R. Ward c Moores b Stephenson	13	– c Moores b Stephenson .. 8
*M. R. Benson c Moores b Stephenson	45	– c Moores b Lewry 17
M. J. Walker run out	0	– lbw b Lewry 1
P. A. de Silva lbw b Lewry	117	– run out 0
N. R. Taylor c Wells b Giddins	13	– lbw b Lewry 5
M. V. Fleming b Salisbury	9	– c Greenfield b Salisbury .. 27
M. A. Ealham c Moores b Salisbury	88	– not out 77
†S. A. Marsh c Athey b Stephenson	24	– b Hemmings 59
M. M. Patel c Salisbury b Lewry	10	– c Greenfield b Hemmings .. 1
D. W. Headley b Stephenson	19	– st Moores b Hemmings ... 0
T. N. Wren not out	8	– c Wells b Hemmings 23
B 1, l-b 8, w 2, n-b 4	15	L-b 1, w 5, n-b 6 12

1/31 2/36 3/130 4/157 5/172   361   1/15 2/23 3/24 4/31 5/42   230
6/218 7/255 8/292 9/343   6/68 7/194 8/196 9/198

Bonus points – Kent 4, Sussex 4.

Bowling: *First Innings*—Stephenson 31–9–86–4; Giddins 27–3–94–1; Salisbury 21.3–2–76–2; Lewry 21–3–73–2; Hemmings 11–3–23–0. *Second Innings*—Stephenson 13–4–49–1; Hemmings 19.1–4–63–4; Lewry 13–1–54–3; Salisbury 20–5–63–1.

Umpires: G. I. Burgess and R. A. White.

At Swansea, May 11, 12, 13, 15. SUSSEX drew with GLAMORGAN.

SUSSEX v ESSEX

At Hove, May 18, 19, 20, 22. Sussex won by 278 runs. Sussex 23 pts, Essex 4 pts. Toss: Sussex.

Greenfield, often a peripheral figure at Hove, and Moores put together two century partnerships, one to rescue Sussex and the second to set up a resounding win on the final morning. They first combined at 82 for four and added 161, Moores leading the way with his best first-class score for nearly three years. An unorthodox cameo innings from Giddins added to Essex's frustration, though Ilott bowled well to take a career-best seven for 82. Giddins then put the Essex batsmen on the back foot with a burst of three for 15 and, though Irani made an intelligent half-century, Sussex led by 141, which became a healthy 310 going into the third day. Wells scored a dominant 69 on the day of his call-up into the England one-day squad, Greenfield reached a Championship-best 121, of crisply struck shots on both sides of the wicket, while Moores played pugnaciously for 94. A target of 532 was quite beyond Essex, though Waugh, just arrived in England, and Hussain offered some resistance. Salisbury took seven wickets, which might have been eight had Moores not missed a chance to stump Ilott.

Close of play: First day, Essex 50-3 (N. Hussain 18*); Second day, Sussex 169-4 (K. Greenfield 26*, P. Moores 23*); Third day, Essex 202-6 (R. J. Rollins 32*, M. C. Ilott 0*).

Sussex

C. W. J. Athey c Rollins b Ilott	8	– b Ilott	21
J. W. Hall lbw b Ilott	10	– b Ilott	15
K. Newell c Waugh b Irani	33	– c Waugh b Irani	10
*A. P. Wells c Gooch b Ilott	4	– b Childs	69
K. Greenfield c Rollins b Such	51	– c Rollins b Waugh	121
†P. Moores c Hussain b Such	86	– lbw b Childs	94
F. D. Stephenson c Irani b Ilott	10	– c Hussain b Waugh	18
I. D. K. Salisbury c Irani b Ilott	25	– c Hussain b Ilott	18
J. D. Lewry c Prichard b Ilott	4	– c Lewis b Waugh	1
E. S. H. Giddins c Irani b Ilott	34	– c Gooch b Waugh	0
E. E. Hemmings not out	7	– not out	7
L-b 6, w 4, n-b 44	54	B 4, l-b 3, w 3, n-b 6	16

1/20 2/49 3/53 4/82 5/243   326   1/29 2/42 3/49 4/137 5/285   390
6/250 7/254 8/262 9/301   6/310 7/360 8/361 9/361

Bonus points – Sussex 3, Essex 4.

Bowling: *First Innings*—Ilott 26–7–82–7; Cousins 13–2–73–0; Irani 23–0–71–1; Waugh 9–2–33–0; Such 12–2–43–2; Childs 7–2–18–0. *Second Innings*—Ilott 27–6–75–3; Cousins 13–1–47–0; Such 21–4–72–0; Irani 13–1–60–1; Waugh 17–3–76–4; Childs 25–6–53–2.

Essex

G. A. Gooch lbw b Lewry	1	– b Salisbury	36
*P. J. Prichard c Salisbury b Stephenson	4	– c Salisbury b Stephenson	9
M. E. Waugh lbw b Giddins	27	– lbw b Salisbury	39
N. Hussain c Moores b Giddins	26	– c Athey b Salisbury	60
J. J. B. Lewis lbw b Giddins	21	– lbw b Giddins	0
R. C. Irani not out	57	– c Lewry b Salisbury	15
†R. J. Rollins lbw b Giddins	5	– lbw b Salisbury	38
M. C. Ilott lbw b Salisbury	17	– c and b Hemmings	17
P. M. Such b Stephenson	8	– c and b Salisbury	17
D. M. Cousins c and b Salisbury	5	– c Newell b Salisbury	0
J. H. Childs c Salisbury b Giddins	2	– not out	8
B 2, l-b 3, w 1, n-b 6	12	B 4, l-b 10	14

1/5 2/7 3/50 4/79 5/88   185   1/21 2/84 3/99 4/100 5/143   253
6/100 7/139 8/164 9/177   6/198 7/211 8/235 9/239

Bonus points – Sussex 4.

Bowling: *First Innings*—Stephenson 23–6–66–2; Lewry 6–1–21–1; Salisbury 13–5–23–2; Giddins 13.1–2–48–5; Newell 10–3–22–0. *Second Innings*—Stephenson 6–1–24–1; Lewry 7–0–33–0; Salisbury 27–7–72–7; Giddins 6–0–33–1; Hemmings 20–4–77–1.

Umpires: J. H. Harris and T. E. Jesty.

At Portsmouth, May 25, 26, 27. SUSSEX lost to HAMPSHIRE by an innings and 106 runs.

SUSSEX v GLOUCESTERSHIRE

At Hove, June 1, 2, 3, 5. Drawn. Sussex 8 pts, Gloucestershire 3 pts. Toss: Gloucestershire. Championship debut: N. C. Phillips.

Rain, which washed out all but the final, dimly lit half-hour of the third day, and some obdurate batting from Wright denied Sussex victory. Russell chose to bat on what looked a good pitch, but sullen skies suited Sussex's swing bowlers perfectly and Lewry took a career-best six for 45. They suited Alleyne, too, and Sussex were four down overnight. Athey then dropped anchor, batting throughout the second day for his 50th first-class hundred. Stephenson, with a sparkling century, Salisbury and off-spinner Phillips, with fifty on his Championship debut, all helped Athey bat his old county out of contention. The pitch remained true on the final day to frustrate Sussex, despite some intelligent bowling changes. Wright's four-and-a-half-hour vigil was ended by Lenham's third ball of the season. During his first-innings 83, shots from Symonds twice hit the same spectator, a woman from Bristol. Having been struck in the face by a four, she returned from treatment only to be hit on the leg by a six.

Close of play: First day, Sussex 113-4 (C. W. J. Athey 48*, P. Moores 25*); Second day, Sussex 482-7 (C. W. J. Athey 163*, N. C. Phillips 50*); Third day, Gloucestershire 20-0 (A. J. Wright 6*, G. D. Hodgson 10*).

Gloucestershire

A. J. Wright c Salisbury b Giddins	10	– b Lenham	139
G. D. Hodgson lbw b Lewry	12	– c Lenham b Salisbury	52
M. A. Lynch c Lenham b Giddins	12	– lbw b Salisbury	17
R. I. Dawson c Stephenson b Lewry	0	– c Lenham b Salisbury	8
M. W. Alleyne lbw b Giddins	11	– c Lenham b Stephenson	91
A. Symonds c Giddins b Lewry	83	– c Moores b Giddins	11
*†R. C. Russell b Salisbury	27	– b Giddins	1
J. Srinath lbw b Lewry	7	– not out	21
M. C. J. Ball c Lenham b Lewry	12	– not out	16
M. Davies not out	11		
A. M. Smith b Lewry	9		
B 1, l-b 5, n-b 2	8	B 5, l-b 11, n-b 8	24

1/19 2/35 3/35 4/46 5/54   202   1/132 2/166 3/176 (7 wkts dec.) 380
6/135 7/156 8/177 9/182   4/272 5/295
                                  6/319 7/362

Bonus points – Gloucestershire 1, Sussex 4.

Bowling: *First Innings*—Stephenson 16–4–39–0; Lewry 17.2–3–45–6; Giddins 17–2–79–3; Salisbury 8–1–33–1. *Second Innings*—Giddins 29–7–96–2; Lewry 19–2–72–0; Salisbury 34–7–85–3; Phillips 18–2–67–0; Stephenson 11–2–34–1; Lenham 2–0–10–1.

Sussex

C. W. J. Athey not out	163	I. D. K. Salisbury b Ball	74
J. W. Hall c Lynch b Alleyne	15	N. C. Phillips not out	50
N. J. Lenham c Russell b Alleyne	0	L-b 10, n-b 26	36
*A. P. Wells lbw b Alleyne	8		
K. Greenfield c and b Smith	4	1/34 2/34 3/56	(7 wkts dec.) 482
†P. Moores c Russell b Srinath	26	4/61 5/118	
F. D. Stephenson c Russell b Davies	106	6/280 7/407	

J. D. Lewry and E. S. H. Giddins did not bat.

Bonus points – Sussex 4, Gloucestershire 2 (Score at 120 overs: 361-6).

Bowling: Srinath 34–9–113–1; Smith 35–6–142–1; Alleyne 33–17–59–3; Ball 24–5–74–1; Dawson 2–0–5–0; Davies 30–2–79–1.

Umpires: K. J. Lyons and N. T. Plews.

At Birmingham, June 8, 9, 10, 12. SUSSEX drew with WARWICKSHIRE.

SUSSEX v SURREY

At Horsham, June 15, 16, 17, 19. Drawn. Sussex 7 pts, Surrey 4 pts. Toss: Surrey.

Despite another wet Saturday, these old rivals provided marvellous entertainment for the festival crowd, with Giddins and Lewry surviving 21 balls at the end to deny Surrey. Sussex were in the box seat on the first day, when Lewry swung the ball prodigiously to take four for 77, including three in four balls, and Giddins chipped in with another four. Then Newell and Wells defied some penetrative bowling, especially from Benjamin, to take a lead of 117. The sun shone on the second day and so did Surrey's batsmen. Thorpe and Stewart flayed the attack to all parts of this small ground, adding 243 in 51 overs: Stewart smashed 23 fours and a six, with some textbook shots, and Thorpe scored his first hundred of the season. Sussex needed 385 in 79 overs. Hall and Lenham opened with 128 but, after tea, Rackemann bent his back to rip through the middle order. Suddenly Sussex's only thought was survival; Lewry batted sensibly for 24 overs to meet that objective.

Close of play: First day, Sussex 209-5 (K. Greenfield 9*, F. D. Stephenson 4*); Second day, Surrey 394-5 (A. J. Hollioake 32*, A. W. Smith 10*); Third day, No play.

Surrey

J. D. Ratcliffe lbw b Giddins	17	– c Salisbury b Lewry	9
*A. J. Stewart lbw b Lewry	6	– c Greenfield b Lewry	150
M. A. Butcher c Lenham b Stephenson	40	– lbw b Giddins	5
G. P. Thorpe c Salisbury b Giddins	30	– b Lewry	110
A. D. Brown b Lewry	14	– c Wells b Salisbury	42
A. J. Hollioake b Lewry	0	– c and b Giddins	51
A. W. Smith b Lewry	0	– b Lewry	45
†G. J. Kersey b Stephenson	44	– not out	34
R. W. Nowell c Moores b Giddins	6	– lbw b Lewry	1
J. E. Benjamin lbw b Giddins	0	– not out	10
C. G. Rackemann not out	12		
B 1, l-b 3, w 4, n-b 10	18	B 12, l-b 21, w 1, n-b 10	44

1/10 2/48 3/84 4/116 5/116	187	1/39 2/54 3/297 (8 wkts dec.) 501
6/116 7/116 8/137 9/139		4/304 5/382 6/430
		7/468 8/476

Bonus points – Sussex 4.

Bowling: *First Innings*—Stephenson 11.3-1-46-2; Lewry 16-3-77-4; Giddins 11-0-54-4; Hemmings 4-1-6-0. *Second Innings*—Giddins 32-4-129-2; Lewry 19.2-0-110-5; Hemmings 23-5-63-0; Salisbury 24-4-106-1; Stephenson 9-0-60-0.

Sussex

N. J. Lenham lbw b Butcher	21	– b Rackemann		72
J. W. Hall lbw b Benjamin	41	– c Hollioake b Nowell		54
K. Newell c Kersey b Hollioake	53	– c Kersey b Rackemann		9
*A. P. Wells c Kersey b Benjamin	47	– lbw b Rackemann		21
K. Greenfield c Stewart b Benjamin	29	– (6) c Brown b Benjamin		26
†P. Moores c Kersey b Benjamin	0	– (7) c Kersey b Rackemann		1
F. D. Stephenson c Kersey b Benjamin	25	– (5) lbw b Rackemann		0
I. D. K. Salisbury lbw b Butcher	11	– c Stewart b Rackemann		0
J. D. Lewry not out	31	– not out		11
E. S. H. Giddins c Stewart b Butcher	0	– (11) not out		6
E. E. Hemmings c Stewart b Rackemann	4	– (10) hit wkt b Benjamin		2
B 9, l-b 2, w 3, n-b 28	42	L-b 8, n-b 20		28

1/70 2/88 3/193 4/193 5/195	304	1/128 2/144 3/161
6/250 7/257 8/275 9/275		4/161 5/182 6/184 (9 wkts) 230
		7/184 8/218 9/224

Bonus points – Sussex 3, Surrey 4.

Bowling: *First Innings*—Rackemann 10.5-3-40-1; Benjamin 26-6-94-5; Butcher 15-1-71-3; Nowell 14-8-24-0; Smith 5-0-36-0; Hollioake 12-3-28-1. *Second Innings*—Rackemann 27-8-60-6; Benjamin 17-3-60-2; Nowell 16-4-56-1; Hollioake 10-4-21-0; Butcher 4-1-18-0; Smith 5-2-7-0.

Umpires: B. Leadbeater and A. G. T. Whitehead.

At Bath, June 22, 23, 24, 26. SUSSEX lost to SOMERSET by 124 runs.

At Hove, July 1, 2, 3. SUSSEX beat WEST INDIANS by an innings and 121 runs (See West Indian tour section).

SUSSEX v NOTTINGHAMSHIRE

At Arundel, July 6, 7. Nottinghamshire won by ten wickets. Nottinghamshire 22 pts, Sussex 4 pts. Toss: Sussex.

Sussex were routed inside two days after a career-best performance from New Zealander Cairns, whose match figures of 15 for 83 were the best of the season and the best for Nottinghamshire since Bruce Dooland's 16 for 83 against Essex in 1954. Wells was quickly made to regret his decision to bat. On an Arundel pitch with more grass than usual, under cloudy skies, Cairns ran amok, taking four for seven in 23 balls after breaking Lenham's left index finger. Stephenson and Salisbury staged a rapid recovery from 14 for five, but Cairns finished Sussex off for an inadequate 134. In sunshine, the pitch lost much of its venom and Robinson scored a patient 72, while Nottinghamshire's last pair, Chapman and Afzaal, took their lead to 121. Cairns then produced another inspired spell to destroy Sussex's top order again. They were six down before they ensured that Nottinghamshire would bat again; only Greenfield and Stephenson applied themselves before Cairns dismissed them in successive overs. Nottinghamshire captain Robinson spent part of his unscheduled Saturday off umpiring a local league match.

Close of play: First day, Nottinghamshire 161-5 (C. L. Cairns 9*, J. E. Hindson 0*).

Sussex

N. J. Lenham retired hurt	0 – absent hurt			
K. Newell c Pollard b Cairns	0 – b Cairns			11
K. Greenfield c Afzaal b Cairns	0 – b Cairns			46
*A. P. Wells lbw b Cairns	7 – b Cairns			2
C. W. J. Athey c Noon b Cairns	4 – (1) c Noon b Cairns			4
†P. Moores lbw b Pick	0 – (5) c and b Pick			9
F. D. Stephenson c Johnson b Cairns	68 – (6) c Noon b Cairns			40
I. D. K. Salisbury b Cairns	38 – (7) b Cairns			11
J. D. Lewry b Cairns	4 – (8) b Cairns			5
E. S. H. Giddins c Archer b Cairns	1 – not out			0
E. E. Hemmings not out	4 – (9) c and b Pick			13
L-b 3, w 1, n-b 4	8	B 3, w 3, n-b 2		8

1/2 2/5 3/9 4/14 5/14   134   1/12 2/27 3/31 4/52 5/115   149
6/99 7/123 8/127 9/134   6/120 7/126 8/149 9/149

Bonus points – Nottinghamshire 4.

In the first innings N. J. Lenham retired hurt at 0.

Bowling: *First Innings*—Cairns 16.5–4–47–8; Pick 13–6–37–1; Chapman 6–1–30–0; Hindson 9–3–17–0. *Second Innings*—Cairns 18–3–36–7; Pick 13.2–3–41–2; Chapman 13–3–36–0; Hindson 3–1–15–0; Afzaal 4–0–18–0.

Nottinghamshire

P. R. Pollard c Salisbury b Giddins	7 – not out			16
*R. T. Robinson c Moores b Salisbury	72			
G. F. Archer b Stephenson	31			
P. Johnson b Salisbury	32			
J. R. Wileman lbw b Giddins	1 – (2) not out			9
C. L. Cairns c Moores b Giddins	30			
J. E. Hindson c sub b Stephenson	4			
†W. M. Noon c Moores b Stephenson	13			
U. Afzaal not out	23			
R. A. Pick b Lewry	8			
R. J. Chapman c Moores b Salisbury	19			
B 2, l-b 7, w 2, n-b 4	15	L-b 4		4

1/19 2/92 3/147 4/148 5/156   255   (no wkt) 29
6/182 7/196 8/204 9/217

Bonus points – Nottinghamshire 2, Sussex 4.

Bowling: *First Innings*—Stephenson 19–3–33–3; Lewry 15–3–45–1; Giddins 27–7–76–3; Hemmings 9–4–23–0; Salisbury 24–9–69–3. *Second Innings*—Giddins 4–0–16–0; Lewry 3.2–0–9–0.

Umpires: J. H. Harris and R. Julian.

SUSSEX v LEICESTERSHIRE

At Hove, July 20, 21, 22, 24. Leicestershire won by 63 runs. Leicestershire 21 pts, Sussex 5 pts. Toss: Leicestershire. Championship debuts: G. I. Macmillan, I. J. Sutcliffe.

Defeat forced Sussex to the foot of the Championship and coach Norman Gifford resigned two days later. Alan Wells had led the chase for 357 with a brilliant century, his fifth of 1995, and was finally ninth out, but received little support. Sussex self-destructed either side of lunch: Greenfield followed a lifter from Cronje, then Moores and Stephenson played ugly strokes against Pierson's off-spin. Earlier, Salisbury had also benefited from a slow bowler's pitch. He took five for nine in six overs as Leicestershire struggled to 90 for six. But Briers organised some tail-end resistance with a patient century. Wells, Moores and Stephenson revived Sussex from 40 for five. But on Saturday, the sun-drenched crowd was treated to some marvellous strokeplay. Macmillan raced to 100 in 108 balls, with 13 fours and three sixes, becoming the fifth player to score a century on first-class debut for Leicestershire. He put on 137 with Cronje, and Vince Wells added a rapid fifty. Salisbury then ripped through the tail, finishing with 11 wickets and giving Sussex a short-lived glimmer of hope.

Close of play: First day, Sussex 33-2 (K. Newell 6*, N. C. Phillips 4*); Second day, Leicestershire 59-1 (I. J. Sutcliffe 32*, A. R. K. Pierson 5*); Third day, Sussex 73-2 (K. Newell 28*, A. P. Wells 16*).

Leicestershire

*N. E. Briers c and b Stephenson	125	– c Newell b Salisbury	17
I. J. Sutcliffe c Hall b Salisbury	21	– b Stephenson	34
G. I. Macmillan lbw b Salisbury	0	– (4) lbw b Jarvis	103
W. J. Cronje b Salisbury	7	– (5) c Jarvis b Salisbury	69
V. J. Wells c Greenfield b Salisbury	0	– (6) c Wells b Salisbury	55
B. F. Smith b Salisbury	11	– (7) c Wells b Salisbury	11
†P. A. Nixon lbw b Jarvis	6	– (8) lbw b Jarvis	18
G. J. Parsons b Giddins	19	– (9) b Salisbury	0
A. R. K. Pierson b Stephenson	9	– (3) b Giddins	20
A. D. Mullally c Moores b Jarvis	22	– c Hall b Salisbury	7
M. T. Brimson not out	1	– not out	5
B 8, l-b 6, w 1, n-b 6	21	B 4, l-b 3, w 1	8

1/51 2/51 3/67 4/67 5/83   242   1/54 2/63 3/96 4/233 5/296   347
6/90 7/138 8/151 9/215   6/317 7/317 8/327 9/339

Bonus points – Leicestershire 1, Sussex 4.

Bowling: *First Innings*—Stephenson 15.1–4–32–2; Jarvis 18–6–59–2; Salisbury 28–9–70–5; Giddins 26–7–60–1; Phillips 3–0–7–0. *Second Innings*—Stephenson 15.2–4–44–1; Jarvis 21.1–1–63–2; Giddins 15–3–72–1; Salisbury 33–5–101–6; Phillips 15–8–38–0; Newell 4–1–11–0; Athey 2–0–11–0.

Sussex

C. W. J. Athey c Smith b Cronje	18	– b Parsons	21
J. W. Hall lbw b Parsons	0	– b Mullally	5
K. Newell b Mullally	7	– b Parsons	28
N. C. Phillips c Nixon b Parsons	4	– (10) c Smith b Pierson	5
*A. P. Wells lbw b Parsons	35	– (4) c Pierson b Brimson	142
K. Greenfield b Mullally	0	– (5) c Nixon b Cronje	24
†P. Moores c Nixon b Brimson	58	– (6) b Pierson	8
F. D. Stephenson lbw b Wells	80	– (7) c Nixon b Pierson	13
I. D. K. Salisbury c Nixon b Cronje	9	– (8) c Wells b Parsons	5
P. W. Jarvis c Smith b Wells	5	– (9) b Pierson	6
E. S. H. Giddins not out	0	– not out	0
B 2, l-b 9, n-b 6	17	B 17, l-b 10, w 1, n-b 8	36

1/10 2/28 3/34 4/34 5/40   233   1/12 2/49 3/73 4/152 5/181   293
6/101 7/173 8/219 9/231   6/237 7/252 8/287 9/293

Bonus points – Sussex 1, Leicestershire 4.

Bowling: *First Innings*—Mullally 17–3–53–2; Parsons 20–8–29–3; Cronje 16–7–40–2; Wells 13.4–5–24–2; Brimson 19–4–52–1; Pierson 6–0–24–0. *Second Innings*—Mullally 17–5–50–1; Parsons 23–11–58–3; Cronje 13–3–44–1; Pierson 29.1–5–96–4; Wells 4–1–12–0; Brimson 3–2–6–1.

Umpires: J. H. Hampshire and P. B. Wight.

At Lord's, July 27, 28, 29. SUSSEX lost to MIDDLESEX by an innings and 286 runs.

At Lytham, August 3, 4, 5, 7. SUSSEX lost to LANCASHIRE by 60 runs.

At Hove, August 11, 12, 13. SUSSEX lost to YOUNG AUSTRALIA by nine wickets (See Young Australia section).

SUSSEX v WORCESTERSHIRE

At Eastbourne, August 17, 18, 19, 21. Sussex won by 75 runs. Sussex 23 pts, Worcestershire 4 pts. Toss: Sussex.

Sussex ended a three-month run without a Championship win, and escaped the bottom of the table, through some fine bowling on a Saffrons pitch that was perfect for four-day cricket. For once, there was some application in the batting: Peirce, in only his second Championship match, and Wells, with his seventh century of the season, led them to 326. Left-arm Lewry then claimed a career-best six for 43 as Worcestershire lost their last seven for 28 runs. Though Sussex led by 156, they waived the follow-on, and, by the second-day close, extended their advantage to 355 as Lenham returned to form. Their last six tumbled for 68 next day, however, as Newport grabbed three for ten. Worcestershire wanted 424 in just over five sessions. With Lewry forced off by a hip injury, they had a chance. They began the final day 177 short with six wickets in hand. But Giddins quickly snared centurion Weston, off-spinner Phillips produced his best showing yet, and Salisbury took his fifth wicket shortly after lunch. On the second day, lunch was delayed 15 minutes so the Red Arrows could stage a fly-past.

Close of play: First day, Worcestershire 54-0 (T. S. Curtis 29*, W. P. C. Weston 9*); Second day, Sussex 199-4 (N. J. Lenham 77*, N. C. Phillips 5*); Third day, Worcestershire 247-4 (W. P. C. Weston 111*, V. S. Solanki 17*).

Sussex

C. W. J. Athey c Hick b Newport	3	– c Newport b Mirza 33
M. T. E. Peirce c Curtis b Newport	60	– run out 12
N. J. Lenham c Hick b Newport	0	– c Solanki b Newport 84
*A. P. Wells c Leatherdale b Lampitt	108	– c Rhodes b Thomas 55
K. Greenfield c Hick b Lampitt	99	– b Thomas 3
D. R. Law c Solanki b Newport	16	– (7) lbw b Newport 0
†P. Moores lbw b Newport	5	– (8) c Curtis b Lampitt 30
I. D. K. Salisbury c Hick b Thomas	12	– (9) c Moody b Thomas 18
N. C. Phillips c Leatherdale b Lampitt	9	– (6) c Hick b Newport 7
J. D. Lewry c Moody b Thomas	0	– c Solanki b Thomas 0
E. S. H. Giddins not out	0	– not out 5
L-b 4, n-b 10	14	B 8, l-b 4, n-b 8 20

1/22 2/22 3/133 4/214 5/280	326	1/28 2/72 3/182 4/190 5/204 267
6/290 7/308 8/318 9/318		6/204 7/211 8/253 9/258

Bonus points – Sussex 3, Worcestershire 4.

Bowling: *First Innings*—Newport 22-6-66-5; Thomas 14-2-67-2; Mirza 16-6-47-0; Lampitt 20-5-78-3; Hick 15-1-50-0; Solanki 3-1-14-0. *Second Innings*—Newport 18-8-32-3; Thomas 18.3-4-78-4; Lampitt 12-5-23-1; Mirza 14-2-44-1; Hick 18-5-45-0; Solanki 8-1-33-0.

Worcestershire

T. S. Curtis lbw b Lewry	38	– c Moores b Salisbury	31
W. P. C. Weston c Peirce b Lewry	17	– lbw b Giddins	111
G. A. Hick c Greenfield b Giddins	40	– c Moores b Law	19
*T. M. Moody lbw b Lewry	0	– c Moores b Giddins	18
D. A. Leatherdale b Law	26	– c and b Salisbury	38
V. S. Solanki c Moores b Giddins	4	– lbw b Salisbury	18
†S. J. Rhodes c Moores b Lewry	7	– not out	51
S. R. Lampitt lbw b Lewry	3	– b Salisbury	15
P. J. Newport not out	4	– b Phillips	25
P. Mirza lbw b Giddins	2	– c and b Phillips	3
P. A. Thomas b Lewry	0	– b Salisbury	0
B 4, l-b 2, w 1, n-b 22	29	B 8, l-b 3, w 2, n-b 6	19

1/67 2/78 3/78 4/142 5/151   170   1/41 2/86 3/142 4/219 5/248   348
6/158 7/162 8/162 9/167   6/248 7/289 8/339 9/347

Bonus points – Sussex 4.

Bowling: *First Innings*—Giddins 20–1–55–3; Lewry 19.4–7–43–6; Salisbury 10–3–20–0; Law 10–1–46–1. *Second Innings*—Giddins 34–9–84–2; Lewry 2–0–9–0; Phillips 36–8–64–2; Salisbury 51.5–19–139–5; Law 12–1–41–1.

Umpires: J. H. Hampshire and J. W. Holder.

At Hartlepool, August 24, 25, 26, 28. SUSSEX beat DURHAM by an innings and 50 runs.

At Scarborough, September 7, 8, 9, 11. SUSSEX drew with YORKSHIRE.

SUSSEX v NORTHAMPTONSHIRE

At Hove, September 14, 15, 16, 18. Drawn. Sussex 3 pts, Northamptonshire 4 pts. Toss: Sussex.

A dismal season for Sussex ended on a downbeat note: rain washed out the final day after the captains tried to contrive a finish. Northamptonshire were the more frustrated, however, as they were still bidding to secure runners-up spot. Sussex's first innings lasted into the third afternoon because of interruptions from the weather. They were indebted to Moores and Martin-Jenkins, who added 94 in 22 overs for the ninth wicket, after Capel threatened to run through the side. Martin-Jenkins, on his second first-class appearance, played some textbook cover drives in a maiden fifty. Reciprocal declarations and some joke bowling left Northamptonshire a target of 423. But their chances of pursuing it were ruined by rain.

Close of play: First day, Sussex 104-2 (C. W. J. Athey 42*, A. P. Wells 10*); Second day, Sussex 111-2 (C. W. J. Athey 45*, A. P. Wells 14*); Third day, Northamptonshire 36-0 (A. Fordham 25*, R. J. Warren 11*).

Sussex

C. W. J. Athey run out	56	– st Ripley b Snape	41
M. T. E. Peirce lbw b Capel	20	– c Ripley b Bailey	14
N. J. Lenham c Bailey b Snape	28	– (4) not out	6
*A. P. Wells b Kumble	40		
K. Greenfield c Bailey b Kumble	10		
†P. Moores not out	89		
I. D. K. Salisbury lbw b Capel	10	– (3) not out	67
P. W. Jarvis c Ripley b Capel	1		
N. C. Phillips c Snape b Capel	2		
R. S. C. Martin-Jenkins b Kumble	50		
E. S. H. Giddins run out	20		
L-b 6	6	L-b 3, w 1	4

1/50 2/86 3/143 4/149 5/176   331   1/38 2/96   (2 wkts dec.) 132
6/201 7/201 8/207 9/301

Bonus points – Sussex 3, Northamptonshire 4.

Bowling: *First Innings*—Taylor 17.2–6–52–0; Curran 10–4–20–0; Capel 25–4–102–4; Kumble 35–13–68–3; Snape 15–2–83–1. *Second Innings*—Bailey 10–1–42–1; Fordham 6–0–51–0; Snape 4–0–36–1.

Northamptonshire

A. Fordham b Giddins	6	– not out....................	25
R. J. Warren not out	7	– not out....................	11
R. J. Bailey not out	18		
B 1, l-b 3, n-b 6	10		

1/18   (1 wkt dec.) 41   (no wkt) 36

*A. J. Lamb, M. B. Loye, K. M. Curran, D. J. Capel, J. N. Snape, †D. Ripley, A. Kumble and J. P. Taylor did not bat.

Bowling: *First Innings*—Giddins 5–2–22–1; Jarvis 2–1–4–0; Martin-Jenkins 3–1–11–0. *Second Innings*—Giddins 4–0–26–0; Jarvis 2–0–6–0; Phillips 1–0–4–0.

Umpires: J. C. Balderstone and B. J. Meyer.

HIGHEST PERCENTAGE OF WINS IN A CHAMPIONSHIP SEASON

	Season	Played	Won	%
Warwickshire	1995	17	14	82.35
Surrey	1955	28	23	82.14
Surrey	1894	16*	13	81.25
Surrey	1892	16	13	81.25
Yorkshire	1894	15	12	80.00
Nottinghamshire ...	1907	19	15	78.95
Yorkshire	1923	32	25	78.13
Kent	1910	25	19	76.00
Yorkshire	1955	28	21	75.00
Surrey	1957	28	21	75.00
Middlesex	1920	20	15	75.00
Middlesex	1921	20	15	75.00
Surrey	1891	16	12	75.00
Yorkshire	1893	16	12	75.00

* *Includes one tied match.*
Despite their record, Yorkshire failed to win the Championship in 1894 and 1955.

WARWICKSHIRE

President: The Earl of Aylesford
Chairman: M. J. K. Smith
Chairman, Cricket Committee: J. Whitehouse
Chief Executive: D. L. Amiss
Captain: D. A. Reeve
Director of Coaching: P. A. Neale
Head Groundsman: S. J. Rouse
Scorer: A. E. Davis

Warwickshire almost repeated their unique treble of 1994, winning the County Championship and the NatWest Trophy and finishing second to Kent in the Sunday League – beaten only on run-rate. If anything, Warwickshire's performances in the Championship were even more remarkable than before. Their 14 wins in 17 matches constituted the highest percentage of wins in Championship history, shading the 23 out of 28 by Surrey in 1955. The good summer helped. But the margins of their victories and the fact they were equally divided home and away were testimony to the county's all-round strengths.

In 1994 Brian Lara had provided a rare batting impetus. This time, Allan Donald produced the best and most consistent fast bowling seen in county cricket for years. His strike-rate was over six wickets in each Championship match and he headed the national bowling averages with 89 at 16.07. The captain, Dermot Reeve, and his deputy, Tim Munton, joined him in the top five.

Criticism of the help Donald obtained from Edgbaston pitches was put into perspective by the margins of Warwickshire's victories away from home, usually on wickets more conducive to spin than pace. There were three wins by an innings, two by ten wickets, one by nine wickets and one by 111 runs. Away from Edgbaston, they lost only to Lancashire, when Warwickshire were without five key players. At home, they won one innings victory, three by ten wickets, one each by 215 and 91 runs and one, against Somerset, by three wickets – the only match where the opposition declared to set a target. Northamptonshire beat them by seven runs, in one of the best four-day games ever seen, and the rain-affected game with Sussex was drawn.

That was the only Championship match in which Donald, Munton and Gladstone Small played together. Munton missed the first five games after a back operation and Small played only five times, which is why Donald's contribution was crucial. In 121 games for Warwickshire, Donald has taken 456 wickets at 20.95; if he plays no more county cricket, he will remember his last delivery, at Canterbury, which clinched the Championship.

There were many other contributions to a triumphant season, not least the brilliant leadership of Reeve. Long acknowledged as the best one-day captain, he orchestrated the four-day campaign – half of which he missed in 1994 – wonderfully well. He inspired a self-belief among his players, which paid rich dividends when games were apparently running against them, and was never afraid to back a hunch. After taking five for 30 against Kent and enforcing the follow-on, he surprisingly opened the bowling on the fourth day with Donald and Ashley Giles, a 22-year-old left-arm spinner. Giles repaid him with three wickets in eight deliveries.

After Lara, there was always a question of whether Warwickshire could score enough runs. But the arrival of Nick Knight, whose form earned him a Test place, from Essex, together with outstanding performances from Trevor Penney and Roger Twose, who both passed 1,000 runs at an average over 45, ensured they were never short. Andy Moles was averaging more than 40 when he suffered an Achilles tendon injury which prevented him playing after June. Another youngster, Wasim Khan, seized his chance and scored 740 Championship runs at 46.25 in his debut season, including a hundred. A left-hander, like Knight, he showed a pleasing technique and temperament. Dominic Ostler scored a maiden double-century against Surrey and got over a disappointing period mid-season to score 909 at 43.28.

That only two batsmen topped 1,000 runs is explained by the fact that many of them were rarely required to bat a second time. Nobody played more than 27 Championship innings, yet six batsmen averaged over 40. Dougie Brown, Neil Smith, Keith Piper and Reeve also made crucial runs as well. Brown, a naturally clean hitter, made such an all-round impact that he was capped after only 18 first-class matches for Warwickshire. But Paul Smith played mostly one-day games in his benefit year, and suffered several injuries.

Neil Smith's all-round form earned recognition when he was added to the preliminary squad for the World Cup, along with Reeve. Knight toured Pakistan with England A, as did Ostler and Piper, with Munton a late reinforcement. Add Donald for South Africa and Twose, who made his Test debut for New Zealand, thus ending his career as an Englishman, and eight of the team were picked for international duty in 1995-96, compared with two the previous year – Lara and Piper.

Before the Championship campaign began, Warwickshire started poorly with defeats by England A and in the opening Benson and Hedges Cup game, which cost them a place in the quarter-final. They also lost their first three Sunday League matches but recovered with ten successive wins, until a stumble against Worcestershire finally prevented them from retaining one of their three 1994 titles. But they secured the one which had escaped them – the NatWest Trophy – in thrilling style against Northamptonshire. Reeve won his third match award in a NatWest final, another first, after Munton won successive awards in the previous rounds: he had bowled two unbroken spells of 12 overs each for a combined return of three for 31.

That NatWest victory meant Warwickshire had won five trophies in two seasons and six in 24 months. The smooth replacement of Bob Woolmer as director of coaching with Phil Neale, who moved from Northamptonshire, and the way that Reeve adjusted his tactics to maximise Donald's performances suggested that this was not a glorious fluke. Nevertheless, there was the odd cloud on the horizon. In August, Lara asked to be excused in 1996, the first season of a three-year contract, because his international duties were exhausting him. Many supporters believed the wrong decision had been made in preferring Lara to Donald, with commercial considerations perhaps blurring the issue. But Donald, also in need of a rest, had accepted a coaching job at Edgbaston and was now unwilling to play. All the club's administrative expertise could not break the deadlock and, in November, Warwickshire agreed to release Lara. Efforts were soon concentrated on securing one of Donald's South African pace colleagues, Shaun Pollock. Reeve, too, indicated that his future plans were uncertain; he accepted another two-year contract, but asked for the option of a release after one. – *Jack Bannister.*

623

WARWICKSHIRE 1995

[*Bill Smith*]

Back row: T. Frost, A. Singh, A. F. Giles, M. J. Powell, D. A. Altree. *Middle row*: D. L. Amiss (*chief executive*), T. L. Penney, W. G. Khan, M. A. V. Bell, N. V. Knight, R. G. Twose, R. P. Davis, M. Burns, G. Welch, K. J. Piper, S. Nottingham (*physiotherapist*). *Front row*: R. N. Abberley (*coach and youth cricket organiser*), N. M. K. Smith, A. J. Moles, D. P. Ostler, T. A. Munton, M. J. K. Smith (*chairman*), D. A. Reeve (*captain*), P. A. Neale (*director of coaching*), G. C. Small, P. A. Smith, Asif Din. *Insets*: A. A. Donald, D. R. Brown.

WARWICKSHIRE RESULTS

All first-class matches – Played 19: Won 14, Lost 3, Drawn 2.

County Championship matches – Played 17: Won 14, Lost 2, Drawn 1.

Bonus points – Batting 49, Bowling 64.

*Competition placings – Britannic Assurance County Championship, winners;
NatWest Bank Trophy, winners; Benson and Hedges Cup, 3rd in Group A;
AXA Equity & Law League, 2nd.*

BRITANNIC ASSURANCE CHAMPIONSHIP AVERAGES

BATTING

	Birthplace	M	I	NO	R	HS	Avge
‡N. V. Knight	Watford	11	19	5	798	174	57.00
‡T. L. Penney	Salisbury, Rhodesia	17	24	2	1,133	144	51.50
W. G. Khan	Birmingham	12	21	5	740	181	46.25
‡R. G. Twose	Torquay	17	27	4	1,036	191	45.04
‡D. P. Ostler.......	Solihull	16	23	2	909	208	43.28
‡A. J. Moles	Solihull	7	13	0	532	131	40.92
‡D. A. Reeve	Kowloon, Hong Kong	15	20	3	575	77*	33.82
‡D. R. Brown	Stirling	13	17	2	441	85	29.40
‡K. J. Piper	Leicester	14	16	2	388	99	27.71
‡N. M. K. Smith	Birmingham	16	20	1	413	75	21.73
A. F. Giles	Chertsey	6	5	0	84	32	16.80
‡P. A. Smith........	Jesmond	2	4	0	67	44	16.75
‡G. C. Small.......	St George, Barbados	5	7	4	50	15	16.66
‡T. A. Munton	Melton Mowbray	10	10	6	66	19*	16.50
‡A. A. Donald§	Bloemfontein, SA	14	14	5	145	44	16.11
M. Burns..........	Barrow-in-Furness	3	5	0	78	35	15.60
‡R. P. Davis	Margate	5	7	1	79	30	13.16

Also batted: M. A. V. Bell (*Birmingham*) (3 matches) 0*; A. Singh (*Kanpur, India*) (1 match) 5, 7.

* Signifies not out. ‡ Denotes county cap. § Overseas player.

The following played a total of 13 three-figure innings for Warwickshire in County Championship matches – T. L. Penney 4, R. G. Twose 4, D. P. Ostler 2, W. G. Khan 1, N. V. Knight 1, A. J. Moles 1.

BOWLING

	O	M	R	W	BB	5W/i	Avge
A. A. Donald.........	511.3	128	1,363	88	6-56	6	15.48
D. A. Reeve..........	293.4	112	620	36	5-30	1	17.22
T. A. Munton	353.5	104	900	46	5-37	3	19.56
A. F. Giles...........	146.5	46	354	16	5-23	1	22.12
D. R. Brown	268.4	62	842	34	4-24	0	24.76
G. C. Small	159.5	41	444	17	5-71	1	26.11
N. M. K. Smith	400	88	1,190	36	6-72	3	33.05
R. P. Davis	187.2	48	495	12	5-118	1	41.25

Also bowled: M. A. V. Bell 80–25–265–7; W. G. Khan 7–1–22–0; A. J. Moles 7–0–22–0; P. A. Smith 35–8–107–4; R. G. Twose 96–28–261–8.

Wicket-keepers: K. J. Piper 55 ct, 1 st; M. Burns 9 ct, 1 st.

Leading Fielders: D. P. Ostler 25, N. V. Knight 21, W. G. Khan 16, D. A. Reeve 16.

WARWICKSHIRE v ENGLAND A

At Birmingham, April 18, 19, 20, 21. England A won by an innings and 58 runs. Toss: Warwickshire.

Triple champions Warwickshire were brought down to earth with a jolt by an England A team fresh from their successes in India. It was a disappointing end to Bob Woolmer's career as Warwickshire's director of coaching. Now employed by South Africa, he took charge one last time because his successor Phil Neale was coach to England A. Play was delayed by a hailstorm and later punctuated by rain, snow – and some bright sunshine. Except for Moles, Warwickshire looked uncomfortable against the lively pace of Cork and Chapple. Only Smith's aggression – seven fours and two sixes in an entertaining 42-ball 55 – lifted them to 240. Ramprakash and Wells survived a rapid opening spell from Donald and then cut loose, plundering 152. Wells reached his first century since January 1994 – also for England A – and struck 26 fours and five sixes in 209 balls. After Nixon retired, his finger broken by Donald, an eighth-wicket stand of 113 between Ilott and Patel, who both made career-best scores, increased Warwickshire's frustration and Patel and Cork ripped through their second attempt. The belated resistance of Reeve and Donald prevented a three-day finish. But Stemp required only six balls to take the last wicket on the fourth day. Before this passage of play, there was a minute's silence to mark the death of R. E. S. Wyatt, the former Warwickshire and England captain.

Close of play: First day, England A 6-0 (J. E. R. Gallian 2*, M. P. Vaughan 0*); Second day, England A 390-7 (P. A. Nixon 51*, M. C. Ilott 4*); Third day, Warwickshire 205-9 (D. A. Reeve 77*, A. A. Donald 33*).

Warwickshire

A. J. Moles c Nixon b Stemp	67	– c Gallian b Ilott 13
R. G. Twose c Ramprakash b Cork	29	– c Ramprakash b Patel 25
T. L. Penney c Wells b Stemp	14	– lbw b Patel 14
D. P. Ostler c Gallian b Chapple	26	– c Gallian b Patel 2
G. Welch c Ramprakash b Chapple	0	– b Cork 2
*D. A. Reeve c Nixon b Chapple	0	– not out 77
†K. J. Piper lbw b Stemp	8	– c Cork b Patel 0
D. R. Brown b Cork	9	– c sub b Cork 3
N. M. K. Smith not out	55	– b Cork 18
G. C. Small c Patel b Cork	10	– c Gallian b Cork 12
A. A. Donald lbw b Patel	16	– c and b Stemp 33
L-b 4	6	L-b 6 6
	240	**205**

1/58 2/101 3/116 4/123 5/131   **240**   1/16 2/52 3/54 4/57 5/59   **205**
6/142 7/153 8/163 9/197   6/61 7/74 8/94 9/130

Bowling: *First Innings*—Ilott 14-4-68-0; Chapple 17-6-35-3; Cork 18-2-56-3; Stemp 24-7-65-3; Patel 2.4-0-10-1. *Second Innings*—Ilott 17-5-68-1; Chapple 2-0-6-0; Patel 32-12-58-4; Cork 21-5-63-4; Stemp 7-5-4-1.

England A

J. E. R. Gallian lbw b Donald	2	M. C. Ilott c and b Reeve	60
M. P. Vaughan c Piper b Welch	9	M. M. Patel c Penney b Smith	55
M. R. Ramprakash lbw b Welch	79	R. D. Stemp not out	0
*A. P. Wells st Piper b Smith	178		
D. L. Hemp c Piper b Reeve	7	B 5, l-b 14, w 3, n-b 14	36
D. G. Cork c Piper b Brown	9		
†P. A. Nixon retired hurt	51	1/6 2/49 3/201 4/228 5/244	**503**
G. Chapple c Piper b Brown	17	6/331 7/379 8/503 9/503	

P. A. Nixon retired hurt at 390.

Bowling: Donald 24-6-68-1; Small 23-7-63-0; Welch 17-1-80-2; Brown 26-4-121-2; Smith 24-4-111-2; Reeve 18.2-5-41-2.

Umpires: D. J. Constant and J. W. Holder.

WARWICKSHIRE v MIDDLESEX

At Birmingham, April 27, 28, 29, 30. Warwickshire won by 215 runs. Warwickshire 22 pts, Middlesex 5 pts. Toss: Middlesex. First-class debut: D. Follett.

Warwickshire started their defence of the County Championship with an emphatic win shortly after lunch on the fourth day over the team who would eventually come close to unseating them. Gatting may have misread a green-tinged pitch when he put them in: Knight, a winter recruit from Essex, made an immediate impression, sweeping and pulling the spinners and adding 126 with fellow left-hander Twose. But Tufnell and Emburey then worked through the middle order, with Carr taking three brilliant low slip catches off Emburey and equalling the county record of six in an innings. Warwickshire were grateful for Ostler's belligerence, which took them to 282. It was Donald who put them ahead next day, marking his first Championship appearance since July 1993 with six wickets in three hostile spells. Only Ramprakash got to grips with him. Resuming, Knight completed his second half-century and Penney played enterprisingly to leave Middlesex a target of 353. But Ramprakash was run out in the first over of the final day and Small, displaying superb control, accounted for Carr and Gatting. Donald's pace and Smith's spin did the rest as Middlesex's last nine fell for 77.

Close of play: First day, Middlesex 14-0 (M. W. Gatting 8*, J. C. Pooley 4*); Second day, Warwickshire 133-4 (T. L. Penney 20*, R. P. Davis 0*); Third day, Middlesex 60-1 (M. W. Gatting 20*, M. R. Ramprakash 10*).

Warwickshire

A. J. Moles c Carr b Nash	31	– b Fraser	0
N. V. Knight c Pooley b Tufnell	85	– c Brown b Nash	72
R. G. Twose c Carr b Tufnell	66	– c Ramprakash b Nash	26
D. P. Ostler c Carr b Emburey	12	– lbw b Tufnell	12
T. L. Penney lbw b Follett	0	– c Carr b Tufnell	88
*D. A. Reeve c Weekes b Tufnell	7	– (7) c Carr b Tufnell	10
†M. Burns c Carr b Emburey	1	– (8) b Fraser	35
N. M. K. Smith c Pooley b Tufnell	4	– (9) c Follett b Emburey	11
R. P. Davis c Carr b Emburey	13	– (6) c Brown b Fraser	9
A. A. Donald c Carr b Emburey	3	– not out	1
G. C. Small not out	6	– b Emburey	4
L-b 7, n-b 2	9	B 11, l-b 8, w 1, n-b 6	26

1/58 2/184 3/185 4/186 5/209   282   1/0 2/45 3/67 4/133 5/148   294
6/219 7/224 8/268 9/273   6/201 7/265 8/289 9/289

Bonus points – Warwickshire 2, Middlesex 4.

Bowling: *First Innings*—Fraser 17–6–49–0; Nash 12–0–60–1; Follett 17–4–61–1; Emburey 20.1–9–31–4; Tufnell 31.3–13–55–4; Weekes 5.3–2–19–0. *Second Innings*—Fraser 22–5–50–3; Nash 17–5–51–2; Tufnell 28–9–91–3; Emburey 22.1–7–49–2; Follett 13–2–34–0.

Middlesex

*M. W. Gatting c Burns b Donald	8	– b Small	25
J. C. Pooley c Burns b Donald	8	– c Reeve b Small	19
M. R. Ramprakash lbw b Small	85	– run out	10
J. D. Carr c Knight b Donald	11	– b Small	1
P. N. Weekes c Knight b Donald	36	– c and b Donald	1
†K. R. Brown lbw b Donald	1	– lbw b Davis	13
D. J. Nash b Donald	33	– c Ostler b Smith	22
J. E. Emburey b Small	4	– c Knight b Donald	23
A. R. C. Fraser not out	15	– c Burns b Smith	0
D. Follett c Ostler b Smith	1	– not out	4
P. C. R. Tufnell lbw b Reeve	0	– st Burns b Smith	6
B 5, l-b 8, n-b 9	22	B 2, l-b 4, w 1, n-b 6	13

1/14 2/25 3/53 4/119 5/123   224   1/31 2/60 3/61 4/66 5/68   137
6/186 7/198 8/202 9/223   6/92 7/127 8/127 9/129

Bonus points – Middlesex 1, Warwickshire 4.

In the second innings D. J. Nash, when 1, retired hurt at 71 and resumed at 92.

Bowling: *First Innings*—Donald 22–3–56–6; Small 20–2–52–2; Davis 15–4–60–0; Smith 5–1–18–1; Reeve 7.2–1–25–1. *Second Innings*—Donald 17–3–48–2; Small 12–4–25–3; Smith 15–3–44–3; Reeve 2–1–4–0; Davis 7–3–10–1.

Umpires: G. I. Burgess and J. H. Hampshire.

WARWICKSHIRE v SURREY

At Birmingham, May 4, 5, 6, 8. Warwickshire won by 91 runs. Warwickshire 24 pts, Surrey 3 pts. Toss: Surrey. First-class debut: W. G. Khan.

Another visiting captain was left regretting his decision to field when a grassy pitch played better than Stewart expected. Ostler, at his fluent best, reached his eighth first-class century but his first on his home ground, and next day converted it into a maiden double-hundred. His powerful pulling and cutting took him to 208 in 340 balls, with 33 fours and two sixes. Surrey had a solid start before Donald claimed his second six-wicket haul in successive matches, with another display of controlled aggression. He dismissed Surrey 33 short of saving the follow-on, but Reeve, mindful of a wearing pitch, batted again, giving Ostler another chance to punish the bowlers, while Khan, in his fifth season on Warwickshire's staff, made a promising first-class debut. Surrey were set an unlikely 393. Though a damaged foot kept Donald off, Small offered no respite and by lunch Surrey were 116 for eight. Hollioake fought on almost to tea, with Nowell and Benjamin helping him to add 186 and complete an entertaining century. The Zimbabwe Test player Grant Flower, playing league cricket nearby, was one of three Warwickshire substitutes.

Close of play: First day, Warwickshire 344-4 (D. P. Ostler 181*, D. A. Reeve 34*); Second day, Surrey 168-5 (A. C. S. Pigott 2*, A. J. Hollioake 2*); Third day, Surrey 7-1 (M. A. Butcher 0*, G. J. Kersey 1*).

Warwickshire

A. J. Moles run out	2	– c Thorpe b Butcher	35
W. G. Khan b Pigott	19	– lbw b Nowell	25
R. G. Twose c Stewart b Benjamin	26	– c Kersey b Butcher	7
D. P. Ostler lbw b Pigott	208	– not out	66
T. L. Penney c Thorpe b Nowell	38	– c Thorpe b Hollioake	26
*D. A. Reeve c Kersey b Benjamin	53	– not out	20
†M. Burns run out	8		
N. M. K. Smith b Hollioake	40		
R. P. Davis lbw b Hollioake	10		
A. A. Donald not out	4		
G. C. Small c Shahid b Pigott	3		
B 8, l-b 3, w 2, n-b 46	59	B 6, l-b 6, w 1, n-b 18 ...	31

1/23 2/54 3/75 4/198 5/391   470   1/62 2/77   (4 wkts dec.) 210
6/404 7/412 8/449 9/463   3/80 4/148

Bonus points – Warwickshire 4, Surrey 1 (Score at 120 overs: 381-4).

Bowling: *First Innings*—Benjamin 31–5–82–2; Pigott 34–12–92–3; Butcher 16–2–62–0; Nowell 46–13–119–1; Shahid 6–0–49–0; Hollioake 16–3–55–2. *Second Innings*—Benjamin 12–2–33–0; Pigott 4–0–19–0; Hollioake 13–2–42–1; Butcher 9–1–35–2; Nowell 12–1–51–1; Stewart 3–0–18–0.

Surrey

D. J. Bicknell lbw b Reeve	43	– lbw b Donald	0
M. A. Butcher c Burns b Donald	54	– lbw b Small	4
*A. J. Stewart b Donald	10	– (4) lbw b Twose	33
G. P. Thorpe c Burns b Donald	0	– (5) lbw b Small	15
A. D. Brown b Small	42	– (6) c Burns b Twose	36
A. C. S. Pigott c Penney b Smith	12	– (9) c Khan b Twose	0
A. J. Holliake lbw b Reeve	53	– not out	117
N. Shahid b Donald	34	– run out	2
†G. J. Kersey c Khan b Donald	6	– (3) c Burns b Small	11
R. W. Nowell not out	6	– c Davis b Small	27
J. E. Benjamin b Donald	0	– b Small	32
B 10, l-b 5, w 3, n-b 10	28	B 4, l-b 6, n-b 14	24

1/76 2/98 3/98 4/163 5/166   288   1/0 2/11 3/36 4/56 5/104   301
6/200 7/256 8/275 9/286   6/105 7/114 8/115 9/201

Bonus points – Surrey 2, Warwickshire 4.

Bowling: *First Innings*—Donald 25.5–3–64–6; Small 20–9–38–1; Davis 25–7–58–0; Smith 27–6–76–1; Reeve 15–5–37–2. *Second Innings*—Donald 2.4–0–13–1; Small 19.3–7–71–5; Reeve 0.2–0–1–0; Davis 31–8–93–0; Smith 12–0–63–0; Twose 11–0–50–3.

Umpires: B. Dudleston and P. Willey.

At Manchester, May 11, 12, 13, 15. WARWICKSHIRE lost to LANCASHIRE by six wickets.

At Chester-le-Street, May 18, 19, 20, 22. WARWICKSHIRE beat DURHAM by 111 runs.

WARWICKSHIRE v SOMERSET

At Birmingham, May 25, 26, 27, 29. Warwickshire won by three wickets. Warwickshire 20 pts, Somerset 4 pts. Toss: Warwickshire.

Bowler's challenge to Warwickshire to score 301 in 80 overs brought a moribund contest to life: Moles, defying a leg injury, set up an improbable win with seven balls to spare. Reeve fell into exactly the same trap as Gatting and Stewart before him, inserting the opposition on a pitch which turned out to offer little help to the bowlers. His team was made to pay heavily by Bowler, leading Somerset because Hayhurst had dislocated a finger. He batted until just before lunch next day, putting on 187 with Holloway, once Warwickshire's reserve wicket-keeper. The total of 495 was Somerset's best at Edgbaston. The reply was painstaking, although Khan advanced his first-class best for the fifth successive innings and Penney defended stoutly. The captains then broke the stalemate: Reeve declared 181 behind and Bowler waived the follow-on, to set up a run chase. Moles needed some luck on a turning pitch against Mushtaq Ahmed, who had countless appeals rejected. But he paced his century to perfection, with the aid of a runner, only to be dismissed with the scores level. Brown hit the next ball for four.

Close of play: First day, Somerset 298-4 (P. D. Bowler 122*, P. C. L. Holloway 39*); Second day, Warwickshire 96-1 (N. V. Knight 48*, W. G. Khan 28*); Third day, Somerset 66-3 (R. J. Harden 13*, J. C. Hallett 37*).

Somerset

M. N. Lathwell lbw b Twose	47	– b Brown	0
M. E. Trescothick c Piper b Small	14	– c Reeve b Davis	8
*P. D. Bowler b Davis	176		
R. J. Harden lbw b Brown	32	– not out	43
K. A. Parsons c Piper b Small	21	– (3) c Khan b Davis	5
†P. C. L. Holloway lbw b Smith	61	– not out	12
G. D. Rose lbw b Brown	33		
J. C. Hallett c Piper b Twose	29	– (5) c Khan b Brown	42
J. I. D. Kerr b Davis	16		
Mushtaq Ahmed c Twose b Davis	27		
H. R. J. Trump not out	7		
B 7, l-b 9, w 2, n-b 14	32	B 4, l-b 5	9

1/35 2/76 3/137 4/175 5/362   495   1/0 2/12   (4 wkts dec.) 119
6/390 7/418 8/459 9/467   3/19 4/92

Bonus points – Somerset 3, Warwickshire 1 (Score at 120 overs: 321-4).

Bowling: *First Innings*—Small 29-9-74-2; Brown 40-7-140-2; Reeve 31-9-69-0; Twose 22-5-67-2; Smith 27-6-52-1; Davis 28.5-8-77-3. *Second Innings*—Brown 11-4-27-2; Twose 4-3-2-0; Smith 3.1-0-12-0; Davis 10-2-25-2; Moles 7-0-22-0; Khan 7-1-22-0.

Warwickshire

A. J. Moles b Kerr	16	– c Parsons b Trump	131
N. V. Knight b Mushtaq Ahmed	58	– b Mushtaq Ahmed	18
W. G. Khan lbw b Hallett	89	– b Trump	23
T. L. Penney not out	101	– lbw b Mushtaq Ahmed	12
R. G. Twose c Holloway b Hallett	5	– c Trescothick b Rose	39
*D. A. Reeve not out	23	– lbw b Kerr	19
N. M. K. Smith (did not bat)		– c Trump b Mushtaq Ahmed	5
D. R. Brown (did not bat)		– not out	36
†K. J. Piper (did not bat)		– not out	0
B 10, l-b 10, w 2	22	B 12, l-b 6, w 1, n-b 2	21

1/30 2/126 3/225 4/235   (4 wkts dec.) 314   1/24 2/88 3/111 4/187   (7 wkts) 304
                                           5/214 6/219 7/300

G. C. Small and R. P. Davis did not bat.

Bonus points – Warwickshire 3, Somerset 1 (Score at 120 overs: 305-4).

Bowling: *First Innings*—Rose 22-12-29-0; Kerr 21-7-44-1; Mushtaq Ahmed 38-14-89-1; Trump 27-4-87-0; Hallett 8-1-22-2; Bowler 2.2-1-10-0; Parsons 3-0-13-0. *Second Innings*—Rose 15-0-56-1; Kerr 11-2-50-1; Mushtaq Ahmed 35-7-116-3; Hallett 2-0-12-0; Trump 15.5-3-52-2.

Umpires: J. H. Harris and K. J. Lyons.

WARWICKSHIRE v SUSSEX

At Birmingham, June 8, 9, 10, 12. Drawn. Warwickshire 5 pts, Sussex 8 pts. Toss: Warwickshire.

Rain, which washed out half the third day, condemned the game to a tame end. Warwickshire had wiped out first-innings arrears of 113 and were pressing on quickly in hope of setting a target when the weather closed in, leaving them little alternative but to bat for a draw. Moles, with his fifth half-century in seven innings, gave Warwickshire an excellent start on the first morning, but they lost their way against the hostile Stephenson and persistent Giddins. Their last six went for only 40 in 16 overs, while Sussex batted solidly down the order. Greenfield and Moores provided the backbone, adding 105, after Wells followed his century for England A on the same ground with an aggressive 49 from 58 balls. Despite losing Moles for nought, Warwickshire fared better second time around. Twose and Knight put on 154 and, though Knight pulled out after being concussed in the Sunday game, Twose bravely took body blows from Stephenson and Jarvis in completing his first century of the summer, before the token declaration.

Close of play: First day, Sussex 41-1 (J. W. Hall 10*, P. W. Jarvis 11*); Second day, Sussex 360-9 (J. D. Lewry 0*, E. S. H. Giddins 0*); Third day, Warwickshire 154-1 (N. V. Knight 74*, R. G. Twose 68*).

Warwickshire

A. J. Moles c Moores b Stephenson	66	– c Jarvis b Stephenson	0
N. V. Knight b Stephenson	4	– retired hurt	74
R. G. Twose b Stephenson	27	– not out	131
D. P. Ostler lbw b Giddins	31	– c Moores b Jarvis	7
T. L. Penney lbw b Giddins	51	– c Jarvis b Giddins	16
D. R. Brown c Moores b Lewry	13	– b Jarvis	50
†K. J. Piper c Jarvis b Lewry	3	– c Lenham b Jarvis	4
N. M. K. Smith b Giddins	3	– c Hall b Giddins	11
G. C. Small c Hall b Giddins	15	– not out	10
A. A. Donald run out	6		
*T. A. Munton not out	1		
B 4, l-b 10, n-b 14	28	B 5, l-b 6, w 2, n-b 16	29

1/19 2/99 3/114 4/167 5/208   248   1/0 2/163 3/202   (6 wkts dec.) 332
6/210 7/219 8/223 9/241   4/273 5/281 6/318

Bonus points – Warwickshire 1, Sussex 4.

In the second innings N. V. Knight retired hurt at 154.

Bowling: *First Innings*—Stephenson 15-6-35-3; Lewry 20-5-63-2; Giddins 26.4-7-59-4; Jarvis 16-3-47-0; Salisbury 13-4-30-0. *Second Innings*—Stephenson 24-4-68-1; Lewry 23-5-81-0; Jarvis 30-8-67-3; Giddins 25-10-53-2; Salisbury 12-2-28-0; Newell 2-0-24-0.

Sussex

N. J. Lenham lbw b Donald	13	– not out	20
J. W. Hall c Moles b Brown	42	– c Moles b Smith	21
P. W. Jarvis c Knight b Munton	20		
K. Newell c Ostler b Munton	39	– (3) not out	0
*A. P. Wells c sub b Donald	49		
K. Greenfield c Smith b Donald	84		
†P. Moores c Piper b Munton	56		
F. D. Stephenson c Smith b Donald	12		
I. D. K. Salisbury c Moles b Brown	10		
J. D. Lewry not out	1		
E. S. H. Giddins c Knight b Brown	0		
B 2, l-b 15, n-b 18	35	B 4, l-b 2	6

1/26 2/53 3/108 4/154 5/195   361   1/42   (1 wkt) 47
6/300 7/313 8/350 9/360

Bonus points – Sussex 4, Warwickshire 4.

Bowling: *First Innings*—Donald 29-3-112-4; Small 18-0-74-0; Munton 28-7-59-3; Brown 21.5-6-55-3; Smith 7-4-15-0; Twose 14-5-29-0. *Second Innings*—Donald 5-0-23-0; Munton 5-1-15-0; Small 2.4-1-2-0; Smith 2-1-1-1.

Umpires: J. D. Bond and R. Palmer.

At Cambridge, June 16, 17, 18. **WARWICKSHIRE** drew with **CAMBRIDGE UNIVERSITY**.

WARWICKSHIRE v YORKSHIRE

At Birmingham, June 22, 23, 24. Warwickshire won by an innings and 168 runs. Warwickshire 24 pts, Yorkshire 2 pts. Toss: Yorkshire.

Feeble batting hastened Warwickshire to an emphatic win on the third day, when Yorkshire lost their last seven wickets for six runs in five overs. Munton, playing only his second Championship game of the season after a back operation, was denied a hat-trick when Brown bowled Robinson for a career-best return. Yorkshire had already crashed once, for 96 on the first day. Donald took five wickets on a pitch offering little assistance, with Brown contributing four. Warwickshire were batting 45 minutes after lunch and Knight and Ostler tightened their grip with a stand of 147 – although Knight fell nine short of a maiden century for his new county. Night-watchman Piper increased Yorkshire's frustration, continuing into the afternoon shift and scoring 90, adding 137 with Penney. Amid some dispirited bowling, only Hartley emerged with credit. Despite trailing by 353, Moxon and Vaughan revived Yorkshire's hopes of saving the game with a century opening partnership, although another hostile spell from Donald broke Moxon's thumb – the same digit that had been broken the previous month. Donald took only one wicket, but Moxon did not resume on Saturday morning, when Warwickshire wrapped up their sixth successive victory over Yorkshire after the sensational collapse.

Close of play: First day, Warwickshire 209-4 (K. J. Piper 5*, T. L. Penney 1*); Second day, Yorkshire 115-0 (M. D. Moxon 36*, M. P. Vaughan 56*).

Yorkshire

*M. D. Moxon c Ostler b Donald	3	– retired hurt ... 36
M. P. Vaughan b Munton	14	– b Munton ... 65
D. Byas c Brown b Donald	7	– c Ostler b Donald ... 24
M. G. Bevan c Piper b Brown	2	– b Brown ... 22
C. White c Moles b Brown	13	– lbw b Munton ... 5
†R. J. Blakey lbw b Brown	18	– c Ostler b Brown ... 5
A. P. Grayson c Donald b Brown	4	– lbw b Brown ... 1
P. J. Hartley c Ostler b Donald	9	– c Brown b Munton ... 0
S. M. Milburn c Reeve b Donald	7	– c Piper b Munton ... 0
R. D. Stemp c Knight b Donald	5	– not out ... 0
M. A. Robinson not out	5	– b Brown ... 0
B 1, l-b 5, w 1, n-b 2	9	B 5, l-b 6, n-b 16 ... 27

1/19 2/29 3/33 4/37 5/61   96   1/126 2/158 3/179 4/179 5/184   185
6/65 7/76 8/82 9/91   6/185 7/185 8/185 9/185

Bonus points – Warwickshire 4.

In the second innings M. D. Moxon retired hurt at 115.

Bowling: *First Innings*—Donald 12.1–3–21–5; Munton 9–2–26–1; Brown 12–2–35–4; Reeve 4–2–8–0. *Second Innings*—Donald 20–4–55–1; Munton 22–6–63–4; Brown 8.4–4–24–4; Smith 6–1–20–0; Reeve 2–1–7–0; Twose 2–0–5–0.

Warwickshire

A. J. Moles b Hartley	22	N. M. K. Smith b Hartley	32
N. V. Knight c Byas b Hartley	91	A. A. Donald not out	0
R. G. Twose c Bevan b Milburn	7	T. A. Munton c Blakey b Hartley	13
D. P. Ostler b Vaughan	57		
†K. J. Piper c Bevan b Robinson	90	L-b 5, n-b 34	39
T. L. Penney c Moxon b Milburn	50		
*D. A. Reeve c Grayson b Milburn	21	1/34 2/56 3/203 4/203 5/340	449
D. R. Brown c Vaughan b Stemp	27	6/366 7/383 8/435 9/435	

Bonus points – Warwickshire 4, Yorkshire 2 (Score at 120 overs: 360-5).

Bowling: Hartley 26.3–6–109–4; Milburn 22–5–50–3; Robinson 26–7–74–1; White 23–4–53–0; Stemp 33–7–120–1; Vaughan 11–3–29–1; Grayson 1–0–9–0.

Umpires: A. A. Jones and K. E. Palmer.

At Ilford, June 29, 30, July 1. WARWICKSHIRE beat ESSEX by ten wickets.

At Leicester, July 6, 7. WARWICKSHIRE beat LEICESTERSHIRE by an innings and 89 runs.

At Cardiff, July 20, 21. WARWICKSHIRE beat GLAMORGAN by nine wickets.

WARWICKSHIRE v NORTHAMPTONSHIRE

At Birmingham, July 27, 28, 29, 31. Northamptonshire won by seven runs. Northamptonshire 20 pts, Warwickshire 5 pts. Toss: Northamptonshire. First-class debut: A. Singh.

This nerve-shredding encounter was described by both captains as the best Championship game they had ever played in. It was probably one of the best of all time. Northamptonshire won at 2.45 p.m. on the final day. Had they lost, Warwickshire would have been near-certain champions already; victory reduced the gap between them to two points. A match of dramatic twists was exemplified in the final innings. Chasing 275, Warwickshire slumped to 53 for six against Kumble, recovered to 201 for six, thanks to Reeve and Smith, lost their ninth wicket with 47 required and still fell only eight short. There was a succession of heroic performances: from Capel, who scored a crucial fifty followed up with a career-best seven for 44; from Twose, who batted throughout Warwickshire's first innings and scored 62.5 per cent of their total; from Fordham and Warren, whose determined batting set up the final challenge; but most of all from Donald and Kumble. The South African pace bowler and Indian leg-spinner bowled long spells in exhausting heat and each took ten wickets, Donald for the first time in the season, Kumble for the second match running. On the first morning, Donald and Munton reduced Northamptonshire to a disastrous 69 for six, and even after Capel's efforts, 152 all out. Capel bounced back with three wickets in four overs, but a patient century from Twose took Warwickshire to a 72-run lead before he was last out, hooking to fine leg. The next-highest scorer was Extras. Back in the field, Warwickshire paid heavily for dropped catches. Fordham reached a century after nearly six hours and Warren struck an aggressive 70. Donald endured wretched luck and almost bowled himself into the ground for his six wickets. But his role was not over. After Warwickshire had collapsed to a magical spell from Kumble – four for 32 in 16 teasing overs – the application of Reeve and Smith prevented a three-day defeat and then took Warwickshire to within 74 of victory. When Kumble took another three wickets, however, the job was left to Donald and Munton. Combining luck with sensible placement, they scraped together 39 runs before Capel trapped Munton lbw. The players were still drained an hour later. "It was like a little bit of a war out there," said Lamb, "but that's the way county cricket should be played."

Close of play: First day, Warwickshire 159-6 (R. G. Twose 98*, N. M. K. Smith 6*); Second day, Northamptonshire 254-6 (A. Fordham 100*, R. J. Warren 25*); Third day, Warwickshire 161-6 (D. A. Reeve 56*, N. M. K. Smith 45*).

Northamptonshire

R. R. Montgomerie b Donald	6	– c Ostler b Munton	29
A. Fordham b Donald	8	– c Piper b Donald	101
R. J. Bailey lbw b Munton	7	– c Piper b Brown	2
M. B. Loye c Smith b Munton	12	– c Piper b Munton	6
*A. J. Lamb c Piper b Reeve	22	– b Donald	22
K. M. Curran b Brown	10	– c Brown b Donald	30
D. J. Capel c Ostler b Munton	50	– c Singh b Donald	17
†R. J. Warren c Ostler b Donald	20	– c Reeve b Donald	70
A. Kumble c Piper b Donald	0	– c Ostler b Brown	21
J. G. Hughes c Reeve b Munton	0	– (11) not out	4
J. P. Taylor not out	4	– (10) c Piper b Donald	3
B 4, l-b 3, n-b 6	13	B 9, l-b 11, w 1, n-b 20	41

1/14 2/23 3/23 4/45 5/69   152   1/57 2/60 3/71 4/124 5/182   346
6/69 7/120 8/120 9/125   6/202 7/278 8/337 9/339

Bonus points – Warwickshire 4.

Bowling: *First Innings*—Donald 16–8–41–4; Munton 20.3–6–47–4; Reeve 12–4–26–1; Brown 7–0–31–1. *Second Innings*—Donald 39.1–10–95–6; Munton 29–8–83–2; Brown 23–9–51–2; Reeve 6–1–25–0; Smith 21–4–72–0.

Warwickshire

R. G. Twose c Kumble b Capel	140	– b Capel	16
W. G. Khan b Capel	17	– lbw b Hughes	3
D. P. Ostler lbw b Capel	0	– c Lamb b Kumble	14
T. L. Penney c Curran b Capel	1	– c Bailey b Kumble	0
A. Singh b Kumble	5	– c Montgomerie b Kumble	7
D. R. Brown b Kumble	0	– c Warren b Kumble	4
*D. A. Reeve c Bailey b Capel	14	– c Bailey b Kumble	74
N. M. K. Smith b Capel	18	– b Kumble	75
†K. J. Piper c Curran b Capel	1	– b Kumble	10
A. A. Donald c Montgomerie b Kumble	9	– not out	27
T. A. Munton not out	0	– lbw b Capel	10
L-b 12, n-b 8	20	B 8, l-b 11, n-b 8	27
	224		**267**

1/67 2/67 3/79 4/108 5/108   1/14 2/32 3/37 4/42 5/52
6/145 7/181 8/181 9/218   6/53 7/201 8/225 9/228

Bonus points – Warwickshire 1, Northamptonshire 4.

Bowling: *First Innings*—Taylor 17–3–41–0; Curran 7–0–26–0; Kumble 29–7–69–3; Hughes 7–2–32–0; Capel 18.5–3–44–7. *Second Innings*—Taylor 31–6–78–0; Hughes 12–3–29–1; Kumble 42–16–82–7; Capel 19–9–26–2; Curran 5–1–17–0; Bailey 4–1–16–0.

Umpires: R. Julian and K. E. Palmer.

At Southampton, August 10, 11, 12. WARWICKSHIRE beat HAMPSHIRE by an innings and 89 runs.

At Nottingham, August 17, 18, 19. WARWICKSHIRE beat NOTTINGHAMSHIRE by ten wickets.

WARWICKSHIRE v WORCESTERSHIRE

At Birmingham, August 24, 25, 26, 28. Warwickshire won by ten wickets. Warwickshire 24 pts, Worcestershire 4 pts. Toss: Warwickshire.

Twose's third century of the season laid the foundations for another crushing Warwickshire win. After Reeve won the toss for the first time in eight Championship matches, Worcestershire assisted Warwickshire with some dreadful bowling. Twose needed no second invitation. He made smooth progress to his century, from 197 deliveries, and needed only 57 more to reach 150, but fell nine short of his double-century to Newport, the pick of a poor attack which contributed 71 extras, 45 from no-balls. Worcestershire's batsmen showed little more application. Curtis carried his bat but, apart from Moody, no one else reached double figures as Giles, the slow left-armer, exploited a gently turning pitch to take his first five-wicket haul with intelligent variations of pace. Following on, Moody scored a second half-century, but only Rhodes's belligerence and rain prevented a three-day defeat as Warwickshire's other spinner, Smith, worked through the batting. Victory came quickly on the final morning.

Close of play: First day, Warwickshire 403-6 (R. G. Twose 179*, K. J. Piper 40*); Second day, Worcestershire 16-1 (T. S. Curtis 5*, S. R. Lampitt 10*); Third day, Worcestershire 325-9 (S. J. Rhodes 70*, P. A. Thomas 13*).

Warwickshire

R. G. Twose b Newport	191	– not out	37
W. G. Khan lbw b Newport	21	– not out	26
D. P. Ostler c Solanki b Newport	9		
T. L. Penney c Tolley b Lampitt	44		
D. R. Brown c Mirza b Moody	5		
*D. A. Reeve c Solanki b Thomas	44		
N. M. K. Smith run out	0		
†K. J. Piper c and b Moody	40		
A. F. Giles c Lampitt b Newport	2		
A. A. Donald b Mirza	18		
T. A. Munton not out	17		
B 8, l-b 18, n-b 45	71	N-b 6	6

1/78 2/108 3/197 4/202 5/339   462   (no wkt) 69
6/340 7/409 8/423 9/424

Bonus points – Warwickshire 4, Worcestershire 4 (Score at 120 overs: 460-9).

Bowling: *First Innings*—Newport 29-8-98-4; Thomas 17-2-64-1; Lampitt 26-6-76-1; Mirza 18.2-3-95-1; Solanki 16-1-80-0; Moody 14-6-23-2. *Second Innings*—Newport 6-1-17-0; Thomas 5-1-20-0; Solanki 4-0-26-0; Moody 3.1-1-6-0.

Worcestershire

T. S. Curtis not out	75	– c Khan b Smith	25
W. P. C. Weston c Reeve b Munton	8	– c Twose b Reeve	0
C. M. Tolley lbw b Munton	3	– (4) c Khan b Smith	0
*T. M. Moody lbw b Giles	62	– (5) b Smith	78
D. A. Leatherdale c Piper b Donald	1	– (6) b Donald	40
V. S. Solanki lbw b Donald	0	– (7) c Reeve b Smith	1
†S. J. Rhodes c Khan b Donald	1	– (8) not out	81
S. R. Lampitt b Giles	0	– (3) lbw b Munton	31
P. J. Newport c Piper b Giles	8	– c Penney b Smith	47
P. Mirza b Giles	2	– c Munton b Donald	4
P. A. Thomas b Giles	0	– c Reeve b Munton	25
B 7, l-b 6, n-b 4	17	L-b 16, n-b 2	18

1/34 2/40 3/146 4/149 5/149   177   1/4 2/49 3/51 4/77 5/173   350
6/155 7/155 8/171 9/175   6/176 7/205 8/271 9/310

Bonus points – Warwickshire 4.

Bowling: *First Innings*—Donald 25-7-57-3; Munton 13-4-32-2; Brown 8-2-25-0; Smith 8-2-27-0; Giles 15.2-7-23-5. *Second Innings*—Donald 24.2-11-47-2; Munton 27.3-7-67-2; Reeve 4-2-6-1; Giles 27-6-52-0; Smith 40-5-162-5.

Umpires: R. Palmer and G. Sharp.

WARWICKSHIRE v GLOUCESTERSHIRE

At Birmingham, August 29, 30, 31. Warwickshire won by ten wickets. Warwickshire 22 pts, Gloucestershire 4 pts. Toss: Warwickshire. First-class debut: J. Lewis.

Warwickshire required only two days to complete their third successive ten-wicket win, which put them 12 points clear at the top of the table. The first day was rained off, but they soon made up for lost time. Khan was the only player to reach 50 in the match as Warwickshire, in pursuit of quick runs, became careless; Jonathan Lewis, a 20-year-old medium-fast bowler making his Championship debut, profited with four for 64. But apart from the Anglo-Australian Symonds, who returned to the city of his birth after 18 years and hit 41 in 48 balls, Gloucestershire's batsmen showed little fight against the menacing Donald. Following on, Wright grafted for 59 overs, but his team-mates perished to a sequence of poor strokes. Twose and Khan needed only 20 balls to secure victory. Warwickshire's one blemish was that Munton pulled up with a side strain after his first ball in Gloucestershire's second innings and was ruled out of the NatWest final two days later. Despite mutterings from elsewhere, those present – including the umpires – thought the two-tone pitch played acceptably.

Close of play: First day, No play; Second day, Gloucestershire 54-4 (M. A. Lynch 7*, M. C. J. Ball 1*).

Warwickshire

R. G. Twose b Sheeraz	10	– not out	1
W. G. Khan b Lewis	68	– not out	9
D. P. Ostler b Alleyne	30		
T. L. Penney b Srinath	43		
D. R. Brown not out	29		
*D. A. Reeve lbw b Srinath	35		
N. M. K. Smith c Lynch b Alleyne	8		
†K. J. Piper c Lynch b Lewis	17		
A. F. Giles c Windows b Lewis	16		
A. A. Donald b Srinath	0		
T. A. Munton c Alleyne b Lewis	0		
B 6, l-b 6, n-b 10	22	W 1	1

1/23 2/75 3/161 4/179 5/221   278   (no wkt) 11
6/258 7/262 8/278 9/278

Bonus points – Warwickshire 2, Gloucestershire 4.

In the first innings D. R. Brown, when 29, retired hurt at 213 and resumed at 278.

Bowling: *First Innings*—Srinath 19–6–50–3; Sheeraz 18–3–77–1; Alleyne 18–7–51–2; Lewis 18.2–6–64–4; Ball 5–0–24–0. *Second Innings*—Sheeraz 2–0–4–0; Lewis 1.2–0–7–0.

Gloucestershire

A. J. Wright c Piper b Munton	10	– b Donald	47
M. G. N. Windows c Piper b Donald	12	– c Piper b Brown	10
T. H. C. Hancock c Piper b Reeve	9	– lbw b Donald	0
M. A. Lynch c Piper b Reeve	24	– b Brown	9
M. W. Alleyne b Smith	5	– lbw b Reeve	22
M. C. J. Ball lbw b Reeve	1	– (9) c Khan b Smith	7
A. Symonds c Reeve b Donald	41	– (6) b Giles	35
*†R. C. Russell b Donald	2	– (7) c Reeve b Smith	3
J. Srinath not out	7	– (8) c Khan b Smith	7
J. Lewis c Piper b Donald	0	– b Donald	0
K. P. Sheeraz c Piper b Donald	1	– not out	0
B 1, l-b 1, n-b 10	12	B 3, l-b 1, n-b 18	22

1/27 2/41 3/41 4/49 5/55   124   1/20 2/23 3/42 4/72 5/119   162
6/86 7/107 8/116 9/120   6/132 7/142 8/162 9/162

Bonus points – Warwickshire 4.

Bowling: *First Innings*—Donald 12.4–1–37–5; Munton 16–3–48–1; Reeve 14–5–27–3; Giles 4–2–3–0; Smith 3–0–7–1. *Second Innings*—Donald 16.2–8–22–3; Munton 0.1–0–0–0; Reeve 7.5–2–51–1; Brown 9–3–27–2; Twose 8–1–20–0; Giles 9–3–20–1; Smith 10–4–18–3.

Umpires: T. E. Jesty and P. Willey.

WARWICKSHIRE v DERBYSHIRE

At Birmingham, September 7, 8, 9, 11. Warwickshire won by ten wickets. Warwickshire 24 pts, Derbyshire 5 pts. Toss: Warwickshire.

Warwickshire completed their 13th win – and their fourth in a row by ten wickets – at 12.10 on the final day and thought it might be enough to secure the Championship. The players – along with some of the members and the sponsors' representatives who had the cheque and the trophy – hung about all day, following Middlesex's game against Leicestershire by radio and teletext. But when Middlesex won off the final ball, celebrations were postponed. Rain wiped out the first day and an hour of the second, but Warwickshire quickly reduced Derbyshire to 86 for four. Cullinan survived some testing bowling by his fellow-South African Donald to reach his fifth century of the summer, including 20 fours, a six and a seven, with excellent timing and powerful off-driving. Poor light finally forced Donald out of the attack and Bell, abandoning pace, took two wickets with spin. Warwickshire also struggled, despite Ostler's first fifty in any cricket since July 9, until an entertaining stand of 168 between Penney and Reeve. Dropping Penney on 41 proved costly, as he went on to a hundred and Warwickshire led by 119. Donald took three wickets in eight balls on the third evening and Reeve whipped through the innings with three for nought in six in the morning. Warwickshire needed only four to win, and they left the field to a standing ovation.

Close of play: First day, No play; Second day, Warwickshire 19-1 (W. G. Khan 4*, D. P. Ostler 12*); Third day, Derbyshire 31-3 (C. J. Adams 0*, S. J. Base 10*).

Derbyshire

*K. J. Barnett c Piper b Brown	15	– b Donald	4
A. S. Rollins c Khan b Donald	14	– c Twose b Donald	11
C. J. Adams c Piper b Donald	1	– (4) c Ostler b Smith	28
D. J. Cullinan c Knight b Reeve	121	– (6) c Piper b Reeve	37
T. A. Tweats c Donald b Smith	3	– (7) b Donald	2
C. M. Wells c Knight b Brown	9	– (8) c Ostler b Reeve	9
D. G. Cork c Piper b Donald	21	– (9) lbw b Reeve	0
P. Aldred c Khan b Bell	33	– (10) b Donald	0
†S. P. Griffiths c Knight b Smith	17	– (3) c Ostler b Donald	0
A. E. Warner c and b Bell	7	– (11) not out	4
S. J. Base not out	7	– (5) c Penney b Smith	10
B 6, l-b 8, w 1	15	B 4, l-b 7, n-b 6	17
	268		**122**

1/15 2/18 3/35 4/86 5/125   268   1/12 2/12 3/15 4/32 5/80   122
6/186 7/192 8/246 9/258   6/93 7/113 8/113 9/114

Bonus points – Derbyshire 2, Warwickshire 4.

Bowling: *First Innings*—Donald 18-5-42-3; Brown 12-2-52-2; Reeve 8-3-16-1; Bell 18-7-59-2; Smith 26.4-4-83-2; Twose 3-2-2-0. *Second Innings*—Donald 16.4-4-65-5; Brown 3-1-9-0; Smith 11-1-33-2; Reeve 2-1-4-3.

Warwickshire

N. V. Knight lbw b Cork	0	– not out	5
W. G. Khan lbw b Warner	4	– not out	0
D. P. Ostler lbw b Aldred	62		
R. G. Twose c Griffiths b Cork	24		
T. L. Penney not out	137		
D. R. Brown c Adams b Aldred	0		
*D. A. Reeve c Adams b Wells	67		
N. M. K. Smith c Warner b Tweats	29		
†K. J. Piper b Base	20		
B 7, l-b 10, w 5, n-b 22	44		
	387		**5**

1/0 2/19 3/67 4/120 5/124   (8 wkts dec.) 387   (no wkt) 5
6/292 7/341 8/387

M. A. V. Bell and A. A. Donald did not bat.

Bonus points – Warwickshire 4, Derbyshire 3.

Bowling: *First Innings*—Cork 21-4-49-2; Warner 22-3-81-1; Base 17-2-99-1; Aldred 16-3-45-2; Barnett 3-0-17-0; Wells 13-3-29-1; Tweats 9-1-50-1. *Second Innings*—Cork 1-0-1-0; Aldred 0.3-0-4-0.

Umpires: D. J. Constant and B. Leadbeater.

At Canterbury, September 14, 15, 16. **WARWICKSHIRE** beat **KENT** by an innings and 105 runs.

WORCESTERSHIRE

Patron: The Duke of Westminster
President: T. W. Graveney
Chairman: C. D. Fearnley
Chairman, Cricket Committee: J. E. Chadd
Secretary: The Rev. Michael Vockins
Captain: 1995 – T. S. Curtis
    1996 – T. M. Moody
Coach: D. L. Houghton
Head Groundsman: R. McLaren
Scorer: J. W. Sewter

Events in a transitional period at New Road were overshadowed by the sudden death of the 24-year-old fast bowler Parvaz Mirza, less than a week after the season had ended. Mirza had been earmarked to play an important part in Worcestershire's future following his emergence, alongside Paul Thomas, in bolstering an aging attack. But Mirza's death, by natural causes at his Birmingham home, left a void that will be hard to fill. One suspects the loss of someone so young will not hit home fully until the squad reports back for pre-season training in April.

It was a year of change for Worcestershire, with a new coach in Zimbabwean Test batsman David Houghton, a new assistant coach and Second Eleven captain in Damian D'Oliveira, and a new cricket committee chairman in John Chadd, who had two years on the staff in the 1950s. However, there was one change in mid-stream which had not been envisaged: the resignation of Tim Curtis, the county's captain for three and a half years. Only nine playing weeks earlier, Curtis had held aloft the NatWest Trophy at Lord's, after Worcestershire had halted Warwickshire's 1994 attempt on the Grand Slam. But in mid-June, he stood down – 48 hours after a Benson and Hedges Cup semi-final with Lancashire which Worcestershire had controlled completely until the final hour. Though Curtis stressed the setback did not influence his decision, it became evident that this pleasant, shy man had lost the confidence of his team-mates when it came to decision-making.

The reins were handed to Tom Moody – a man whose friendly exterior masks a typically Australian determination to succeed – for the remainder of the season. He was then confirmed as captain for 1996, ending months of speculation about his future at New Road by signing a new contract.

On the field, events followed a similar pattern to 1994, with Worcestershire maintaining their position as a potent force in one-day cricket. But they also showed an improvement in the Championship, climbing from 15th to tenth. Their Championship performance can be split into three precise sections. They made their worst start to a season for 67 years in losing their opening three matches. Then came a run of six victories in the next seven matches, during which they briefly touched fifth place in the table. At the start of August, they were only 40 points behind leaders Warwickshire with a match in hand. But there were to be no more tangible successes. During the scorching heat of August, Moody lost five tosses on the trot on a series of batsman-friendly wickets. His bowlers – and the Championship challenge – ran out of steam.

It was a case of what might have been in one-day cricket. Worcestershire looked to be heading for their third successive Lord's final after taking control of that Benson and Hedges game with Lancashire at New Road. One local journalist was even heard to ask for his "usual seat" in the Lord's press box. But Wasim Akram's 64 off 47 balls ended that fantasy. In the Sunday League, Worcestershire, who were runners-up in 1994, finished level on points with champions Kent and Warwickshire. But an inferior run-rate consigned them to third spot. They could only look on in frustration as rain ended their last two Sunday matches before they could achieve results.

The arrival of Birmingham-born Thomas, who previously had trials with Warwickshire, was a major plus factor and he marked his debut with five for 70 against the West Indians. He became a virtual regular in the Championship side and his natural pace caused batsmen to duck and dive in a way not seen at New Road since the days of Graham Dilley. Equally important, he had the desire – and strength – to bowl with almost as much fire in his belly at the end of the day as at the beginning. At 32, Phil Newport showed that his potency as a class swing bowler remained undiminished and his 69 first-class wickets earned him the supporters' Player of the Year award. Left-arm spinner Richard Illingworth shrugged off his "one-day expert" tag and displayed sufficient extra guile and flight to resurrect his England Test career after four years in the wilderness.

On the batting front, Worcestershire obtained a greater degree of consistency. Four players achieved 1,000 first-class runs for the county, and David Leatherdale fell only seven short. Moody led from the front, with 1,600 runs scored in powerful style, and was also the second-highest Sunday League scorer in the country with 797, 18 behind Glamorgan's Steve James. Curtis shook off his traumas about the captaincy to put together a solid second half of the season and his opening partner, former England Under-19 captain Phil Weston, passed 1,000 runs for the first time to earn his cap. Wicket-keeper Steve Rhodes's initial poor form with the bat helped Jack Russell to leapfrog over him back into the England team. But he recovered and also scored 1,000 runs for the first time – no mean feat given that he usually comes in at No. 7.

The major disappointments were Gavin Haynes's failures with the bat in the Championship and the fact that pace bowler Neal Radford was unable to reach his 1,000 first-class wickets before being released after 11 years' sterling service. Worcestershire showed that there is still room for sentiment by recalling him in the closing stages to help him towards that milestone, but almost continual rain in the final game meant he finished six wickets short. – *John Curtis.*

WORCESTERSHIRE 1995

[Bill Smith]

Back row: T. Edwards, P. Mirza, C. J. Eyers, M. J. Church, B. E. A. Preece, P. A. Thomas. Middle row: J. E. Brinkley, D. A. Leatherdale, S. R. Lampitt, P. J. Newport, C. M. Tolley, G. R. Haynes, W. P. C. Weston, A. Wylie. Front row: D. B. D'Oliveira (Second Eleven captain and assistant coach), R. K. Illingworth, N. V. Radford, T. S. Curtis (captain), S. J. Rhodes, G. A. Hick, T. M. Moody, D. L. Houghton (coach).

WORCESTERSHIRE RESULTS

All first-class matches – Played 20: Won 6, Lost 7, Drawn 7.

County Championship matches – Played 17: Won 6, Lost 7, Drawn 4.

Bonus points – Batting 29, Bowling 57.

Competition placings – Britannic Assurance County Championship, 10th;
NatWest Bank Trophy, 2nd round; Benson and Hedges Cup, s-f;
AXA Equity & Law League, 3rd.

BRITANNIC ASSURANCE CHAMPIONSHIP AVERAGES

BATTING

	Birthplace	M	I	NO	R	HS	Avge
‡T. M. Moody§	Adelaide, Australia	17	29	1	1,518	168	54.21
‡G. A. Hick	Salisbury, Rhodesia	10	16	1	768	152	51.20
‡T. S. Curtis	Chislehurst	17	31	4	1,064	169*	39.40
‡S. J. Rhodes	Bradford	17	29	6	867	81*	37.69
‡D. A. Leatherdale ..	Bradford	16	27	3	866	93	36.08
‡W. P. C. Weston ...	Durham	17	31	1	1,020	111	34.00
‡P. J. Newport	High Wycombe	16	22	7	401	50	26.73
‡S. R. Lampitt	Wolverhampton	14	21	4	454	97	26.70
‡G. R. Haynes	Stourbridge	15	25	0	586	78	23.44
V. S. Solanki	Udaipur, India	6	9	1	150	36	18.75
‡D. B. D'Oliveira ..	Cape Town, SA	2	4	0	59	25	14.75
‡R. K. Illingworth ...	Bradford	8	11	4	91	23*	13.00
‡C. M. Tolley	Kidderminster	3	5	0	62	24	12.40
‡N. V. Radford	Luanshya, N. Rhodesia	8	10	2	80	22	10.00
M. J. Church	Guildford	2	4	0	26	25	6.50
P. Mirza	Birmingham	5	9	2	37	18*	5.28
P. A. Thomas	Birmingham	12	14	4	49	25	4.90
A. Wylie	Tamworth	2	4	1	14	7	4.66

* Signifies not out.   ‡ Denotes county cap.   § Overseas player.

The following played a total of 12 three-figure innings for Worcestershire in County Championship matches – T. M. Moody 5, G. A. Hick 3, T. S. Curtis 2, W. P. C. Weston 2.

BOWLING

	O	M	R	W	BB	5W/i	Avge
P. J. Newport	508	134	1,445	63	5-45	4	22.93
R. K. Illingworth	371.5	115	899	33	4-30	0	27.24
S. R. Lampitt	430.1	113	1,302	46	4-34	0	28.30
N. V. Radford	181.2	40	626	18	5-45	1	34.77
G. R. Haynes	244	68	761	20	4-33	0	38.05
P. Mirza.............	149.1	35	557	13	5-110	1	42.84
P. A. Thomas	343.4	60	1,352	25	4-78	0	54.08

Also bowled: T. S. Curtis 1-0-5-0; D. B. D'Oliveira 113.5-15-369-5; G. A. Hick 156-35-462-8; D. A. Leatherdale 28-3-123-4; T. M. Moody 71.1-19-209-5; V. S. Solanki 88-15-359-3; C. M. Tolley 4-0-23-0; W. P. C. Weston 13.4-0-58-0; A. Wylie 35-7-143-1.

Wicket-keeper: S. J. Rhodes 43 ct, 4 st.

Leading Fielders: T. M. Moody 30, G. A. Hick 16.

At Oxford, April 27, 28, 29. WORCESTERSHIRE drew with OXFORD UNIVERSITY.

At Chelmsford, May 4, 5, 6, 8. WORCESTERSHIRE lost to ESSEX by 208 runs.

WORCESTERSHIRE v MIDDLESEX

At Worcester, May 11, 12, 13, 15. Middlesex won by an innings and 30 runs. Middlesex 24 pts, Worcestershire 4 pts. Toss: Middlesex.

Worcestershire were threatened with a suspended ten-point penalty by the TCCB pitches committee for a wicket of variable bounce and lateral movement. Preparations had been hindered by flooding from the Severn. The only injury sustained was in the field – Hick cracked a finger while catching Carr at slip. Fraser expertly exploited the conditions to obtain steepling bounce and match figures of eight for 92. In contrast, Worcestershire's bowling, apart from Newport, was short and erratic. Middlesex opener Pooley completed a maiden first-class century, sharing two stands of 120, with Gatting and Brown, whose gutsy 99 held the second half of their innings together. With Hick, who had shone on the rain-shortened opening day, unable to bat, the visiting seamers effectively reduced the contest when Worcestershire were reduced to 55 for five. A sixth-wicket stand of 87 between Moody and Lampitt helped to extend the game into the fourth day, but only for 40 deliveries.

Close of play: First day, Worcestershire 78-3 (G. A. Hick 50*, G. R. Haynes 20*); Second day, Middlesex 230-4 (J. C. Pooley 100*, K. R. Brown 26*); Third day, Worcestershire 161-7 (T. M. Moody 82*, R. K. Illingworth 7*).

Worcestershire

W. P. C. Weston c Brown b Fraser	2	– c Brown b Tufnell	14
*T. S. Curtis lbw b Fraser	1	– lbw b Fraser	8
G. A. Hick b Fraser	59	– absent hurt	
T. M. Moody lbw b Feltham	5	– (3) not out	90
G. R. Haynes lbw b Feltham	38	– (4) lbw b Fraser	1
D. A. Leatherdale c Brown b Nash	32	– (5) lbw b Feltham	7
†S. J. Rhodes c Emburey b Feltham	1	– (6) c Brown b Nash	7
S. R. Lampitt lbw b Nash	14	– (7) lbw b Feltham	31
P. J. Newport c Pooley b Feltham	13	– (8) c Pooley b Feltham	6
R. K. Illingworth not out	14	– (9) c Emburey b Fraser	7
A. Wylie c Brown b Fraser	7	– (10) c Brown b Fraser	0
L-b 7	7	L-b 1, w 1, n-b 2	4

1/2 2/3 3/18 4/106 5/110 **193** 1/22 2/25 3/33 4/48 5/55 **170**
6/118 7/157 8/172 9/172 6/142 7/152 8/165 9/170

Bonus points – Middlesex 4.

Bowling: *First Innings*—Fraser 20.3–9–40–4; Nash 23–3–88–2; Feltham 22–5–55–4; Emburey 1–0–3–0. *Second Innings*—Fraser 19.4–4–52–4; Nash 17–1–64–1; Tufnell 3–1–15–1; Feltham 13–5–27–3; Emburey 2–0–11–0.

Middlesex

*M. W. Gatting b Illingworth	70	J. E. Emburey c Leatherdale b Wylie	31
J. C. Pooley st Rhodes b Illingworth	121	A. R. C. Fraser not out	8
M. R. Ramprakash c Weston b Moody	3	P. C. R. Tufnell b Lampitt	4
J. D. Carr c Hick b Newport	1		
P. N. Weekes lbw b Newport	2	B 4, l-b 28, w 1, n-b 13	46
†K. R. Brown c Rhodes b Newport	99		
D. J. Nash c Moody b Newport	0	1/120 2/134 3/149 4/155 5/275	**393**
M. A. Feltham lbw b Newport	8	6/276 7/300 8/374 9/380	

Bonus points – Middlesex 4, Worcestershire 4.

Bowling: Newport 29–4–83–5; Wylie 18–6–65–1; Lampitt 28.3–4–87–1; Haynes 11–2–36–0; Illingworth 19–5–46–2; Moody 5–3–12–1; Leatherdale 8–0–32–0.

Umpires: D. J. Constant and P. Willey.

At Worcester, May 16, 17, 18. WORCESTERSHIRE drew with WEST INDIANS (See West Indian tour section).

At Gloucester, May 25, 26, 27. WORCESTERSHIRE lost to GLOUCESTERSHIRE by an innings and 73 runs.

WORCESTERSHIRE v SURREY

At Worcester, June 1, 2, 3, 5. Worcestershire won by 134 runs. Worcestershire 21 pts, Surrey 4 pts. Toss: Worcestershire. Championship debut: C. G. Rackemann.

After losing their three opening games, for the first time since 1928, Worcestershire recorded their first Championship win by taking eight wickets in the final session. The third day was washed out and Curtis set a tempting target of 287 in 74 overs. Surrey were 100 for two at tea. But the dismissal of Stewart proved crucial: Illingworth, just recalled by England, and Lampitt bowled them out with 6.5 overs remaining. Ultimately Hick's century – then the fastest of the Championship season, off 76 balls – proved the difference on another fickle New Road pitch. Before his entrance, 21 wickets had fallen for 413. Hick batted on another plane, scoring 120 in all from 98 balls with three sixes and 19 fours. Curtis contributed just 23 to a stand of 151. Australian Carl Rackemann marked his first day with Surrey by claiming four victims, while Benjamin removed three in 12 balls. But the home attack was equally effective, taking six Surrey wickets for 60, though Brown's aggressive 58, with five sixes, kept the deficit to 21.

Close of play: First day, Surrey 34-2 (D. J. Bicknell 18*, A. C. S. Pigott 1*); Second day, Worcestershire 178-3 (T. S. Curtis 44*, G. R. Haynes 0*); Third day, No play.

Worcestershire

*T. S. Curtis b Rackemann	40	– b Pigott	52
W. P. C. Weston b Rackemann	4	– lbw b Benjamin	2
G. A. Hick c Hollioake b Butcher	16	– c Stewart b Rackemann	120
T. M. Moody c Stewart b Benjamin	40	– c Kersey b Butcher	1
G. R. Haynes c Butcher b Benjamin	32	– c Kersey b Benjamin	0
D. A. Leatherdale c Kersey b Benjamin	0	– not out	42
†S. J. Rhodes lbw b Benjamin	34	– c Kersey b Butcher	21
S. R. Lampitt c Kersey b Hollioake	19	– c and b Butcher	12
P. J. Newport c Thorpe b Rackemann	2		
R. K. Illingworth not out	4		
N. V. Radford c Thorpe b Rackemann	0		
B 4, l-b 1, n-b 8	13	B 1, l-b 6, w 2, n-b 6	15
	204	(7 wkts dec.)	**265**

1/7 2/59 3/76 4/138 5/138
6/143 7/194 8/200 9/200

1/26 2/177 3/178 (7 wkts dec.) 265
4/180 5/206
6/231 7/265

Bonus points – Worcestershire 1, Surrey 4.

Bowling: *First Innings*—Rackemann 18.5–5–56–4; Benjamin 19.3–7–47–4; Butcher 9–0–32–1; Pigott 17–5–36–0; Nowell 7–4–17–0; Hollioake 4–0–11–1. *Second Innings*—Rackemann 17–6–34–1; Benjamin 22–6–65–2; Butcher 7.5–1–43–3; Pigott 13–2–68–1; Nowell 5–0–28–0; Hollioake 7–2–20–0.

Surrey

D. J. Bicknell c Rhodes b Haynes	21	– c Moody b Newport	1
*A. J. Stewart b Haynes	5	– c Moody b Illingworth	50
M. A. Butcher c Rhodes b Lampitt	7	– lbw b Lampitt	26
A. C. S. Pigott c Rhodes b Lampitt	5	– (8) c Lampitt b Hick	2
G. P. Thorpe c Hick b Newport	10	– (4) lbw b Newport	18
A. D. Brown c Leatherdale b Illingworth	58	– (5) c Lampitt b Illingworth	11
A. J. Hollioake c Rhodes b Newport	0	– (6) b Lampitt	24
†G. J. Kersey c Moody b Lampitt	35	– (7) lbw b Radford	2
R. W. Nowell not out	16	– lbw b Lampitt	0
J. E. Benjamin c Moody b Newport	16	– c Hick b Illingworth	6
C. G. Rackemann b Illingworth	1	– not out	4
B 3, l-b 3, w 1, n-b 2	9	L-b 8	8

1/22 2/31 3/37 4/45 5/60   183   1/2 2/64 3/102 4/108 5/115   152
6/60 7/130 8/151 9/179   6/128 7/141 8/141 9/141

Bonus points – Worcestershire 4.

Bowling: *First Innings*—Newport 16–7–37–3; Haynes 14–7–31–2; Lampitt 20–5–58–3; Illingworth 15.3–4–51–2. *Second Innings*—Newport 14–6–29–2; Haynes 8–5–13–0; Lampitt 14–4–43–3; Radford 11–2–33–1; Illingworth 16.1–7–23–3; Hick 4–2–3–1.

Umpires: G. I. Burgess and D. R. Shepherd.

At Nottingham, June 8, 9, 10, 12. WORCESTERSHIRE beat NOTTINGHAMSHIRE by three wickets.

WORCESTERSHIRE v LANCASHIRE

At Worcester, June 15, 16, 17. Worcestershire won by an innings and 50 runs. Worcestershire 24 pts, Lancashire 5 pts. Toss: Lancashire.

Moody led Worcestershire to a third successive Championship win, beating the only undefeated county. He had been appointed captain for the rest of 1995 after Curtis resigned just before the game. Moody registered his third century in consecutive Championship innings and added 250 in 53 overs with Hick. They staged a savage display on the second morning, when Hick scored 117 and Moody 94 before lunch. Lampitt, who made 97, and the lower order pressed home the advantage. Despite a delayed start, Worcestershire avenged their Benson and Hedges semi-final defeat with a day to spare, Thomas bowling with sustained aggression. Lancashire were in trouble from the first innings when they were undone by quality swing and spin. Only Speak, with 51 in four hours, suggested any permanence, while Atherton was prevented from batting until No. 8 by his recurrent back complaint. He lasted six balls and took no further part; Moody did not allow a substitute, as Atherton entered the match unfit.

Close of play: First day, Worcestershire 74-2 (G. A. Hick 27*, T. M. Moody 16*); Second day, Lancashire 32-1 (J. E. R. Gallian 11*, G. Yates 4*).

Lancashire

J. E. R. Gallian c Curtis b Illingworth	29	– c Rhodes b Thomas	59
N. J. Speak c Hick b Newport	51	– b Newport	13
J. P. Crawley c Rhodes b Newport	22	– (4) c Rhodes b Lampitt	25
N. H. Fairbrother c Rhodes b Lampitt	7	– (5) c Lampitt b Illingworth	14
G. D. Lloyd b Thomas	4	– (6) c Rhodes b Thomas	35
*M. Watkinson b Illingworth	26	– (7) c Rhodes b Newport	16
Wasim Akram c Rhodes b Haynes	19	– (8) c Weston b Lampitt	10
M. A. Atherton lbw b Illingworth	0	– absent	
†W. K. Hegg not out	14	– c Rhodes b Lampitt	31
G. Yates c Moody b Illingworth	12	– (3) c Hick b Thomas	4
G. Chapple c Haynes b Lampitt	4	– (10) not out	0
B 1, l-b 6, w 1, n-b 10	18	L-b 2, w 4, n-b 18	24

1/36 2/71 3/89 4/94 5/142   206   1/17 2/38 3/86 4/107 5/148   231
6/168 7/170 8/170 9/201   6/178 7/194 8/230 9/231

Bonus points – Lancashire 1, Worcestershire 4.

Bowling: *First Innings*—Newport 18–8–35–2; Thomas 17–5–47–1; Lampitt 16.4–6–44–2; Illingworth 26–11–63–4; Haynes 4–0–10–1. *Second Innings*—Newport 21–7–48–2; Thomas 21–3–103–3; Illingworth 18–6–36–1; Lampitt 11.4–1–42–3.

Worcestershire

T. S. Curtis c Fairbrother b Chapple	16		S. R. Lampitt c Speak b Watkinson	97
W. P. C. Weston lbw b Chapple	11		P. J. Newport c Hegg b Wasim Akram	20
G. A. Hick c Hegg b Chapple	152		R. K. Illingworth not out	23
*T. M. Moody c Hegg b Wasim Akram	110		B 5, l-b 16, w 1, n-b 4	25
G. R. Haynes c Fairbrother				
b Wasim Akram	2		1/25 2/30 3/280	(9 wkts dec.) 487
C. M. Tolley c Gallian b Chapple	15		4/290 5/314 6/315	
†S. J. Rhodes c Fairbrother b Gallian	16		7/372 8/424 9/487	

P. A. Thomas did not bat.

Bonus points – Worcestershire 4, Lancashire 4.

Bowling: Wasim Akram 30–7–79–3; Chapple 32–2–124–4; Gallian 17–1–77–1; Watkinson 23.4–2–102–1; Yates 15–1–85–0.

Umpires: V. A. Holder and G. Sharp.

At Southampton, June 22, 23, 24, 26. WORCESTERSHIRE lost to HAMPSHIRE by 70 runs.

WORCESTERSHIRE v LEICESTERSHIRE

At Worcester, June 29, 30, July 1, 3. Worcestershire won by 134 runs. Worcestershire 22 pts, Leicestershire 7 pts. Toss: Worcestershire.

A collapse of nine wickets for 24 runs against the spin of Hick and Illingworth settled an intriguing contest. Leicestershire had reached 59 without loss in pursuit of 218. Nineteen overs later, they had been dismissed for 83, with Hick achieving a career-best five for 18. Whitaker was absent, having torn his ankle ligaments tripping over a boundary rope before play. Until the final afternoon, the match was finely balanced, though Worcestershire might have struggled but for the gift of 91 extras. The dominant figure was Leicestershire captain Briers, who carried his bat for the fourth time in his career after a seven-hour innings. His last-wicket stand of 122 with Pierson looked like being decisive when the home team lost their fourth wicket only nine runs after clearing first-innings arrears of 80. But Worcestershire's lower order came to their rescue, with Newport compiling a first-class fifty after a gap of almost two years.

Close of play: First day, Leicestershire 17-0 (T. J. Boon 9*, N. E. Briers 8*); Second day, Leicestershire 334-9 (N. E. Briers 161*, A. R. K. Pierson 30*); Third day, Worcestershire 281-7 (P. J. Newport 34*, R. K. Illingworth 8*).

Worcestershire

T. S. Curtis c Sheriyar	45	– lbw b Parsons	9
W. P. C. Weston b Sheriyar	29	– c Nixon b Sheriyar	19
G. A. Hick b Clarke	8	– lbw b Clarke	27
*T. M. Moody c Nixon b Parsons	51	– c sub b Clarke	15
G. R. Haynes b Mullally	55	– lbw b Parsons	37
D. A. Leatherdale b Parsons	3	– c sub b Mullally	51
†S. J. Rhodes c Clarke b Pierson	9	– c Smith b Pierson	45
P. J. Newport c Boon b Parsons	2	– c Dakin b Clarke	50
R. K. Illingworth not out	17	– lbw b Pierson	8
P. Mirza c Boon b Pierson	0	– c Boon b Pierson	0
P. A. Thomas b Pierson	5	– not out	0
B 9, l-b 14, w 4, n-b 28	55	B 15, l-b 21	36

1/91 2/108 3/108 4/190 5/204   279   1/29 2/39 3/82 4/89 5/155   297
6/244 7/247 8/265 9/265   6/210 7/258 8/285 9/285

Bonus points – Worcestershire 2, Leicestershire 4.

Bowling: *First Innings*—Sheriyar 13–1–62–2; Parsons 24.1–6–46–4; Mullally 28–14–47–1; Pierson 15–6–34–2; Dakin 7–0–19–0; Clarke 15–3–48–1. *Second Innings*—Mullally 25–7–46–1; Parsons 23.6–57–2; Sheriyar 15–2–39–1; Clarke 22.2–3–72–3; Pierson 23–5–47–3.

Leicestershire

T. J. Boon lbw b Thomas	13	– c Mirza b Hick 29
*N. E. Briers not out	175	– c Weston b Illingworth 24
J. J. Whitaker c and b Mirza	41	– absent hurt
B. F. Smith c Leatherdale b Illingworth	1	– (3) c Haynes b Hick 0
J. M. Dakin run out	10	– (4) c Leatherdale b Hick 1
†P. A. Nixon c Haynes b Illingworth	18	– c Leatherdale b Illingworth 7
V. P. Clarke c Rhodes b Newport	29	– (5) c Moody b Illingworth 6
G. J. Parsons c Rhodes b Newport	0	– (7) c Mirza b Illingworth 4
A. D. Mullally c Hick b Illingworth	10	– (8) b Hick 0
A. Sheriyar c Weston b Mirza	5	– (9) c Rhodes b Hick 0
A. R. K. Pierson c Haynes b Thomas	40	– (10) not out 0
B 6, l-b 9, w 2	17	B 8, l-b 1, w 3 12

1/23 2/89 3/96 4/115 5/150   359   1/59 2/59 3/61 4/61 5/75   83
6/211 7/211 8/228 9/237   6/83 7/83 8/83 9/83

Bonus points – Leicestershire 3, Worcestershire 4 (Score at 120 overs: 341-9).

Bowling: *First Innings*—Newport 23–4–72–2; Thomas 17.1–3–62–2; Illingworth 43–13–89–3; Mirza 18–5–68–2; Hick 21–4–47–0; Haynes 3–1–6–0. *Second Innings*—Newport 6–2–12–0; Thomas 4–0–7–0; Mirza 5–2–7–0; Illingworth 16.5–8–30–4; Hick 13–6–18–5.

Umpires: J. H. Hampshire and K. E. Palmer.

At Darlington, July 6, 7, 8. WORCESTERSHIRE beat DURHAM by ten wickets.

At Worcester, July 22, 23, 24. WORCESTERSHIRE drew with YOUNG AUSTRALIA
(See Young Australia tour section).

WORCESTERSHIRE v KENT

At Worcester, July 27, 28, 29, 31. Worcestershire won by 61 runs. Worcestershire 23 pts, Kent 7 pts. Toss: Worcestershire. Championship debut: E. J. Stanford.

With Hick released from England duty at Old Trafford, Worcestershire fielded a full-strength side for the first time in two months and achieved the peak of their Championship season with a sixth win in seven games. They scored a solid 332 on the first day, built round Moody's 87, and then reduced Kent to 193 for seven. But Cowdrey, who made 94 out of 132 added while he was in, put on 84 with Headley, eventually limiting their first-innings deficit to 12. Headley's fifty was his first for Kent. When Worcestershire resumed, most of their batsmen contributed, and Hick played with carefree abandon in a run-a-ball 64, before providing slow left-armer Eddie Stanford with his first Championship wicket. Moody's declaration set Kent a 348-run target in 109 overs. The ball did not turn as expected, although Illingworth's perseverance earned him four wickets. The run-out of Cowdrey by Leatherdale from cover was the turning point, but Marsh's defiance kept Worcestershire waiting until the final hour.

Close of play: First day, Kent 30-2 (D. P. Fulton 4*, N. J. Llong 0*); Second day, Worcestershire 14-1 (W. P. C. Weston 4*, S. R. Lampitt 0*); Third day, Kent 30-0 (T. R. Ward 9*, N. J. Llong 17*).

Worcestershire

T. S. Curtis c Ealham b McCague	16	– c Marsh b McCague	2
W. P. C. Weston c Ealham b Headley	36	– c Ward b Stanford	35
G. R. Haynes c Fulton b McCague	8	– (6) c Llong b Wren	47
*T. M. Moody c McCague b de Silva	87	– (5) b de Silva	34
D. A. Leatherdale b McCague	15	– (7) lbw b Headley	41
G. A. Hick c Stanford b Headley	34	– (4) c Wren b Stanford	64
†S. J. Rhodes c Cowdrey b Headley	48	– (8) not out	54
S. R. Lampitt b Ealham	41	– (3) c Headley b McCague	0
P. J. Newport c Marsh b Ealham	20	– not out	25
R. K. Illingworth b Ealham	4		
P. A. Thomas not out	4		
L-b 7, n-b 12	19	B 19, l-b 7, w 3, n-b 4	33

1/34 2/54 3/77 4/105 5/153	332	1/10 2/14 3/93 (7 wkts dec.) 335
6/235 7/297 8/310 9/325		4/150 5/154
		6/221 7/274

Bonus points – Worcestershire 3, Kent 4.

Bowling: First Innings—McCague 19–4–74–3; Wren 13–2–57–0; Ealham 18.2–5–48–3; Headley 20–5–53–3; Stanford 14–2–49–0; de Silva 12–1–44–1. *Second Innings*—McCague 7–2–24–2; Headley 18–7–51–1; Wren 10–1–44–1; Stanford 37–10–96–2; Ealham 12–0–43–0; de Silva 16–5–39–1; Llong 4–1–12–0.

Kent

D. P. Fulton b Haynes	59	– (3) c Moody b Lampitt	21
T. R. Ward c Hick b Newport	12	– (1) c Rhodes b Newport	19
M. J. McCague c Hick b Newport	8	– (8) c Rhodes b Lampitt	23
N. J. Llong c Hick b Haynes	44	– (2) c Hick b Newport	20
P. A. de Silva c Curtis b Haynes	11	– (4) c Haynes b Illingworth	5
G. R. Cowdrey st Rhodes b Illingworth	94	– (5) run out	77
M. A. Ealham c Rhodes b Illingworth	0	– (6) b Illingworth	10
*†S. A. Marsh run out	1	– (7) not out	67
D. W. Headley b Newport	54	– c Moody b Illingworth	8
T. N. Wren c Moody b Haynes	13	– c Curtis b Newport	5
E. J. Stanford not out	0	– c Leatherdale b Illingworth	4
B 2, l-b 3, w 1, n-b 18	24	B 5, l-b 2, n-b 20	27

1/13 2/27 3/136 4/145 5/156	320	1/38 2/62 3/69 4/105 5/136	286
6/159 7/193 8/277 9/320		6/173 7/207 8/230 9/251

Bonus points – Kent 3, Worcestershire 4.

Bowling: First Innings—Newport 17.3–5–46–3; Thomas 22–7–66–0; Illingworth 39–12–92–2; Lampitt 17–4–52–0; Haynes 14–6–33–4; Hick 3–0–26–0. *Second Innings*—Newport 20–4–64–3; Thomas 13–2–45–0; Illingworth 34.5–7–89–4; Hick 7–1–26–0; Lampitt 18–4–53–2; Haynes 2–1–2–0.

Umpires: G. I. Burgess and P. B. Wight.

At Scarborough, August 3, 4, 5, 7. WORCESTERSHIRE drew with YORKSHIRE.

WORCESTERSHIRE v DERBYSHIRE

At Kidderminster, August 10, 11, 12, 14. Drawn. Worcestershire 3 pts, Derbyshire 8 pts. Toss: Derbyshire. First-class debut: S. P. Griffiths.

Worcestershire's last pair, Thomas and Mirza, held out for nine overs to preserve the county's unbeaten record at Chester Road since first-class cricket returned there in 1987. It was a thrilling finale to a gripping last day; at one stage Worcestershire harboured visions of reaching a massive target of 517. Malcolm's second five-wicket haul of the match was a splendid effort on a flat pitch. A week earlier, Worcestershire had conceded a combined total of 831 for seven at Scarborough; here, their weakened attack was hit for 750. Barnett dominated a first-innings 471, achieving his 150th score of 50 or more for Derbyshire and advancing to his 46th county hundred. Mirza persevered to take five in the innings. Malcolm then pressed home the advantage, dismissing Worcestershire for less than half their total. But Barnett opted not to enforce the follow-on and Worcestershire were a different proposition on the final day. Moody led their ambitious assault with 168 from 183 balls. They had never passed 400 in the fourth innings before, but finally closed on 467 for nine.

Close of play: First day, Derbyshire 355-4 (T. A. Tweats 33*, S. P. Griffiths 7*); Second day, Worcestershire 180-5 (D. A. Leatherdale 44*, S. J. Rhodes 9*); Third day, Worcestershire 27-1 (W. P. C. Weston 4*, G. R. Haynes 8*).

Derbyshire

*K. J. Barnett c Rhodes b Thomas	169	– c Rhodes b Thomas	43
A. S. Rollins lbw b Mirza	43	– c Rhodes b Thomas	6
C. J. Adams b Radford	26	– c Mirza b Radford	54
D. J. Cullinan c Weston b Mirza	65	– not out	101
T. A. Tweats not out	78	– c Rhodes b Haynes	2
†S. P. Griffiths c Curtis b Radford	8		
C. M. Wells b Mirza	10	– (6) not out	55
P. A. J. DeFreitas b Mirza	1		
F. A. Griffith run out	26		
A. E. Warner c D'Oliveira b Thomas	23		
D. E. Malcolm b Mirza	0		
L-b 4, w 2, n-b 16	22	B 4, l-b 8, n-b 6	18

1/116 2/157 3/288 4/341 5/358   471   1/23 2/68   (4 wkts dec.) 279
6/382 7/392 8/434 9/467   3/136 4/151

Bonus points – Derbyshire 4, Worcestershire 2 (Score at 120 overs: 360-5).

Bowling: *First Innings*—Thomas 29-1-116-2; Radford 32-8-92-2; Haynes 23-11-50-0; Moody 6-2-10-0; Mirza 32.5-10-110-5; D'Oliveira 34-7-89-0. *Second Innings*—Thomas 18-4-69-2; Radford 14.5-5-32-1; Mirza 14-2-56-0; Haynes 9-0-40-1; D'Oliveira 14.5-1-70-0.

Worcestershire

T. S. Curtis c Griffiths b Malcolm	70	– c Adams b Warner	15
W. P. C. Weston run out	14	– c sub b DeFreitas	32
G. R. Haynes lbw b Barnett	29	– c Griffith b Malcolm	21
*T. M. Moody c Griffiths b Griffith	4	– b Barnett	168
D. A. Leatherdale run out	44	– b Malcolm	66
M. J. Church c Cullinan b Malcolm	0	– b Malcolm	1
†S. J. Rhodes c Griffiths b Malcolm	20	– c Griffiths b Malcolm	71
D. B. D'Oliveira c Griffiths b Malcolm	25	– c Malcolm b Griffith	18
N. V. Radford not out	3	– lbw b Malcolm	22
P. Mirza b Malcolm	0	– not out	18
P. A. Thomas c Griffiths b Warner	5	– not out	1
B 7, l-b 13	20	B 8, l-b 10, w 3, n-b 6	27

1/49 2/98 3/103 4/146 5/152   234   1/15 2/54 3/82   (9 wkts) 467
6/180 7/214 8/227 9/229   4/241 5/243 6/345
    7/376 8/423 9/440

Bonus points – Worcestershire 1, Derbyshire 4.

Bowling: *First Innings*—Malcolm 24-8-65-5; DeFreitas 10-1-47-0; Warner 19.2-8-42-1; Barnett 20-2-40-1; Griffith 10-2-20-1. *Second Innings*—Malcolm 30-6-114-5; Warner 21-2-80-1; DeFreitas 23-1-102-1; Griffith 20-5-84-1; Barnett 16-2-69-1.

Umpires: J. C. Balderstone and J. D. Bond.

At Eastbourne, August 17, 18, 19, 21. WORCESTERSHIRE lost to SUSSEX by 75 runs.

At Birmingham, August 24, 25, 26, 28. WORCESTERSHIRE lost to WARWICKSHIRE by ten wickets.

WORCESTERSHIRE v SOMERSET

At Worcester, August 29, 30, 31, September 1. Drawn. Worcestershire 7 pts, Somerset 4 pts. Toss: Somerset.

Worcestershire captain Moody accepted a new three-year contract but lost the toss for the fifth time running and saw his weary bowlers concede 400 in the first innings for the fourth time in those five matches. Once the home batsmen responded with their highest-ever total, however, the only winner could be the lifeless pitch. It yielded 1,370 runs for the loss of only 20 wickets. No one managed a hundred in Somerset's first innings, though tailender Caddick fell only eight short. But Worcestershire's 670 for seven included three century-makers in Curtis, Hick and Moody, who scored 155 in only 156 balls. One casualty – apart from Somerset's nine bowlers – was a spectator struck on the head by one of Hick's three sixes. He left for a hospital check-up, but returned soon after. Worcestershire led by 245, but Somerset encountered little difficulty in batting through for a draw, thanks to Bowler's accomplished hundred, his sixth of the season.

Close of play: First day, Somerset 267-6 (R. J. Turner 27*, J. I. D. Kerr 11*); Second day, Worcestershire 121-1 (T. S. Curtis 46*, G. A. Hick 3*); Third day, Worcestershire 574-4 (D. A. Leatherdale 72*, S. J. Rhodes 3*).

Somerset

*A. N. Hayhurst c Hick b Thomas	31	– c Rhodes b Thomas	0
P. D. Bowler lbw b Newport	10	– not out	130
P. C. L. Holloway c Rhodes b Thomas	74	– c Rhodes b Hick	80
R. J. Harden c Lampitt b Radford	23	– (5) not out	5
K. A. Parsons lbw b Lampitt	1		
G. D. Rose c Moody b Newport	53		
†R. J. Turner lbw b Lampitt	34		
J. I. D. Kerr c Leatherdale b Newport	42		
A. R. Caddick c sub b Newport	92		
Mushtaq Ahmed c sub b Newport	13		
A. P. van Troost not out	0	– (4) c Thomas b Radford	34
L-b 6, n-b 46	52	B 6, l-b 14, n-b 6	26

1/18 2/71 3/137 4/138 5/206   425   1/1 2/191 3/244   (3 wkts) 275
6/233 7/283 8/400 9/420

Bonus points – Somerset 4, Worcestershire 3 (Score at 120 overs: 389-7).

Bowling: *First Innings*—Newport 33.2-7-105-5; Radford 20-5-70-1; Thomas 17-3-84-2; Hick 9-3-23-0; Lampitt 36-15-74-2; Haynes 13-2-49-0; Moody 5-2-14-0. *Second Innings*—Newport 9-4-11-0; Thomas 9-4-29-1; Moody 17-5-48-0; Radford 14-2-64-1; Lampitt 7-3-17-0; Haynes 3-0-15-0; Hick 16-2-66-1; Curtis 1-0-5-0.

Worcestershire

T. S. Curtis c Parsons b Mushtaq Ahmed	129	G. R. Haynes lbw b Mushtaq Ahmed	11
W. P. C. Weston c Turner b Caddick	60	P. J. Newport not out	32
G. A. Hick c and b Rose	128		
*T. M. Moody c Parsons b Bowler	155	B 4, l-b 6, w 7, n-b 14	31
D. A. Leatherdale c Harden b Hayhurst	81		
†S. J. Rhodes lbw b Hayhurst	8		
S. R. Lampitt not out	35		

1/111 2/322 3/382   (7 wkts dec.) 670
4/568 5/588
6/589 7/608

N. V. Radford and P. A. Thomas did not bat.

Bonus points – Worcestershire 4 (Score at 120 overs: 371-2).

Bowling: Caddick 20–7–52–1; van Troost 19–2–111–0; Kerr 14–4–35–0; Rose 19–7–47–1; Mushtaq Ahmed 60–17–192–2; Hayhurst 27–2–121–2; Parsons 17–2–77–0; Holloway 1–0–12–0; Bowler 3–0–13–1.

Umpires: R. Julian and M. J. Kitchen.

At Northampton, September 7, 8, 9, 11. WORCESTERSHIRE lost to NORTHAMPTON-SHIRE by five wickets.

WORCESTERSHIRE v GLAMORGAN

At Worcester, September 14, 15, 16, 18. Drawn. Toss: Glamorgan.

Only 18 overs and 69 minutes' play were possible – on the third day, when the match had already been reduced by the weather to a one-innings contest with no bonus points. The real blow for Worcestershire came on the Sunday, when their hopes of becoming 40-overs champions were washed away.

Close of play: First day, No play; Second day, No play; Third day, Worcestershire 79-1 (T. S. Curtis 23*, G. A. Hick 36*).

Worcestershire

T. S. Curtis not out	. . . .	23
W. P. C. Weston c Metson b Thomas	. .	16
G. A. Hick not out	. . . .	36
N-b 4	. . . .	4

1/29   (1 wkt) 79

*T. M. Moody, D. A. Leatherdale, S. R. Lampitt, †S. J. Rhodes, G. R. Haynes, P. J. Newport, N. V. Radford and V. S. Solanki did not bat.

Bowling: Thomas 8–1–43–1; Anthony 5–0–19–0; Davies 3–0–17–0; Croft 2–2–0–0.

Glamorgan

S. P. James, *H. Morris, D. L. Hemp, M. P. Maynard, P. A. Cottey, R. D. B. Croft, S. D. Thomas, H. A. G. Anthony, N. M. Kendrick, †C. P. Metson and A. P. Davies.

Umpires: B. Leadbeater and R. Palmer.

THE WHYTE & MACKAY RANKINGS

Mark Ramprakash of Middlesex and Dominic Cork of Derbyshire won £10,000 each after finishing top of the inaugural Whyte & Mackay Rankings, a domestic version of the Coopers & Lybrand Ratings for Test cricket.

Players were given a computerised mark for their performance in each match, adjusted to take account of the strength of the opposition and the nature of the pitch. Prizes down to £1,000 were given to the top 20 in both batting and bowling. Only England-qualified players were eligible but special £1,000 awards were made to the leading overseas batsman and bowler.

Batting: 1 M. R. Ramprakash 710 pts; **2** N. Hussain 673; **3** G. A. Hick 626; **4=** M. A. Atherton, G. P. Thorpe 594; **6** D. Byas 584; **7** A. J. Wright 583; **8** G. A. Gooch 582; **9** R. T. Robinson 567; **10** M. P. Maynard 537. **Overseas award:** T. M. Moody 634.

Bowling: 1 D. G. Cork 637 pts; **2** A. R. C. Fraser 604; **3** P. J. Newport 554; **4** M. C. Ilott 537; **5** P. J. Hartley 525; **6** S. L. Watkin 523; **7** J. E. Emburey 517; **8** P. A. J. DeFreitas 509; **9** P. M. Such 503; **10** R. D. B. Croft 499. **Overseas award:** A. Kumble 665.

YORKSHIRE

Patron: HRH The Duchess of Kent
President and Chairman: Sir Lawrence Byford
Chairman of Cricket: R. K. Platt
Chief Executive: C. D. Hassell
Captain: 1995 – M. D. Moxon
        1996 – D. Byas
Head Groundsman: A. W. Fogarty
Scorer: J. T. Potter

Needing, no doubt, to look on the bright side, Yorkshire were eager to claim some improvement in 1995. They did climb from joint 13th to eighth in the Championship. Additionally, they reached the quarter-finals of the Benson and Hedges Cup and the semi-finals of the NatWest Trophy, although they also endured some embarrassing experiences in the Sunday League.

Realistically, however, the team proved as vulnerable as ever to pressure. Martyn Moxon reflected widespread disappointment when, after six years in charge, he stood down as captain, being replaced by David Byas. Steve Oldham's position as director of cricket was abolished and he is destined to concentrate on the second team, while former seam bowler Bob Platt took over from Brian Close as cricket chairman. The committee announced it would search the world for a major figure who could fill the post of team manager.

The batting failed far too often for comfort. Indeed, defeats at all levels generally reflected a shortage of runs, together with an inability to make the most of promising situations. Too often, Yorkshire appeared to believe that the job had been done when they gained an advantage. The top four of Moxon, Michael Vaughan, Byas and Michael Bevan contributed their runs consistently enough, but a series of major collapses in the bottom half of the order brought some disappointing results.

Interestingly, eight players – Richard Blakey, Paul Grayson, Craig White, Richard Stemp, Bradley Parker, Simon Kellett, Ashley Metcalfe and Richard Kettleborough – occupied the No. 6 position and collectively averaged 19.78, while Grayson, Darren Gough, Parker, Blakey and Gavin Hamilton managed only 12.13 at No. 7. Kellett, Parker and Grayson were all released. Subsequently, Metcalfe declined the offer of another two-year engagement at the end of his benefit season and joined Nottinghamshire, a decision which left the senior squad somewhat short of experience. Blakey had a miserable time, although he kept wicket well enough, losing confidence with the bat to such an extent that his place was in doubt during the second half of the campaign. As Yorkshire's new captain, Byas must have pondered the batting order throughout the ensuing long winter nights.

The one bonus was the development of Anthony McGrath into a player of obvious class. Moxon, Vaughan, who achieved consistency without making enough big scores, and McGrath are all specialist openers, but one of them will have to operate in the middle order in the new season. McGrath was required for all the England Under-19 internationals during the summer, but he made the most of his first-team opportunities and marked his Sunday League debut by taking 72 off the Sussex attack at Scarborough.

Australian left-hander Bevan established himself as Yorkshire's most successful overseas recruit yet, earning a return engagement – and the vice-captaincy. After a dazzling start, with hundreds in friendlies against Cambridge and Lancashire, he entered an uncertain spell, in which he found himself on several unreliable pitches while trying to come to terms with English conditions. But he emerged to score heavily at all levels. He amassed 704 in the Sunday League, beating Byas's county record of 702 in 1994. Moxon stood second in the national batting averages with 1,145 at 76.33, despite missing seven Championship games after further injuries to his fragile hands. Byas had easily his best season. He was the first man in the country to 1,000 runs, finished with 1,913 at 56.26, was the country's leading fielder with 42 catches, and came close to England honours.

Unfortunately, White, who did pick up two Test caps, met with mixed fortunes and never lived up to expectations as a match-winning all-rounder. He managed three centuries, but, more significantly, failed to reach 30 in 18 out of 23 Championship innings, while his bowling lacked the bite which first brought him to the attention of the chairman of selectors. Among the bowlers, Peter Hartley enjoyed an outstanding campaign, with a career-best nine for 41 against Derbyshire. He defied a painful ankle to sustain the attack almost single-handedly at times, although the drier pitches created by the long hot summer eventually took their toll; he was restricted to 13 wickets in Yorkshire's last seven Championship matches, two of which he missed through injury. Nevertheless, his first-class haul of 81 was the best for Yorkshire since 1976, when Geoff Cope claimed 87 victims. Gough was a notable absentee, appearing in only nine Championship games because of, firstly, international calls and, later, an inflamed left foot. All in all, he fell some way short of the high standards he set in 1994, although he gave 100 per cent effort on every occasion.

Mark Robinson bowled steadily without threatening to exert a decisive influence, failing to take five wickets in any match, so the decision to part company with Stuart Milburn, a promising seamer, came as something of a surprise. The left-arm spinner, Stemp, of whom much was expected following his success with England A in India, made very little contribution. He found control elusive and, despite the helpful presence of former Australian leg-spinner Peter Philpott as a coach, claimed four wickets in an innings only twice. Indeed, Vaughan, gradually feeling his way as an off-spinner, compared favourably with Stemp in the slow bowling department. Chris Silverwood and Hamilton showed considerable promise as quicker bowlers and left-hand batsman Kettleborough grasped his moment at the end of the campaign to advertise his potential in the middle order. But Yorkshire will have to work much harder at their collective game if they are to mount a genuine challenge for honours.

During the winter, the difficulties that afflict any club which does not own its own home re-surfaced, and led Yorkshire to investigate the possibility of building a new HQ – perhaps in Wakefield – or buying the cricket side of Headingley from the landlords, the Leeds Cricket, Football and Athletic Club. There will be one definite change at Headingley in 1996: groundsman Keith Boyce is to concentrate on the rugby pitch, and will be replaced on cricket by Andy Fogarty from Old Trafford. – *John Callaghan.*

652

YORKSHIRE 1995

[*Bill Smith*]

Back row: C. A. Chapman, R. A. Kettleborough, G. M. Hamilton, A. G. Wharf, A. C. Morris, A. McGrath, S. M. Milburn, C. J. Schofield. *Middle row*: W. P. Morton (*physiotherapist*), B. Parker, C. E. W. Silverwood, S. A. Kellett, M. A. Robinson, M. P. Vaughan, A. P. Grayson, R. D. Stemp, C. White. *Front row*: D. Byas, M. G. Bevan, A. A. Metcalfe, S. Oldham (*director of cricket*), M. D. Moxon (*captain*), P. J. Hartley, R. J. Blakey, D. Gough, D. E. V. Padgett (*coach*).

YORKSHIRE RESULTS

All first-class matches – Played 20: Won 8, Lost 8, Drawn 4.

County Championship matches – Played 17: Won 7, Lost 8, Drawn 2.

Bonus points – Batting 39, Bowling 55.

Competition placings – Britannic Assurance County Championship, 8th;
NatWest Bank Trophy, s-f; Benson and Hedges Cup, q-f;
AXA Equity & Law League, 12th.

BRITANNIC ASSURANCE CHAMPIONSHIP AVERAGES

BATTING

	Birthplace	M	I	NO	R	HS	Avge
‡M. D. Moxon	Barnsley	10	18	7	839	203*	76.27
‡D. Byas	Kilham	17	32	3	1,476	213	50.89
‡M. G. Bevan§	Belconnen, Australia	17	29	4	1,249	153*	49.96
‡M. P. Vaughan	Manchester	17	32	0	1,151	88	35.96
‡C. White	Morley	14	23	3	627	110	31.35
A. McGrath	Bradford	5	10	0	280	84	28.00
‡D. Gough	Barnsley	9	11	1	235	60	23.50
B. Parker	Mirfield	4	8	1	161	40	23.00
‡S. A. Kellett	Mirfield	6	11	1	228	86	22.80
A. P. Grayson	Ripon	7	11	1	160	73	16.00
C. E. W. Silverwood . .	Pontefract	7	9	2	106	50	15.14
‡P. J. Hartley	Keighley	15	20	2	235	38	13.05
‡R. J. Blakey	Huddersfield	17	25	3	284	45	12.90
R. D. Stemp	Birmingham	17	23	3	178	22*	8.90
‡M. A. Robinson	Hull	15	19	8	70	23	6.36
S. M. Milburn	Harrogate	3	6	1	15	7	3.00

Also batted: G. M. Hamilton (*Broxburn*) (2 matches) 9, 12*, 29; R. A. Kettleborough (*Sheffield*) (1 match) 55, 4; ‡A. A. Metcalfe (*Horsforth*) (3 matches) 79, 1, 20*; A. C. Morris (*Barnsley*) (1 match) 1, 0*.

* Signifies not out.   ‡ Denotes county cap.   § Overseas player.

The following played a total of ten three-figure innings for Yorkshire in County Championship matches – M. G. Bevan 3, C. White 3, D. Byas 2, M. D. Moxon 2.

BOWLING

	O	M	R	W	BB	5W/i	Avge
S. M. Milburn	69	15	204	10	4-68	0	20.40
P. J. Hartley	470.2	107	1,556	71	9-41	4	21.91
D. Gough	283.5	68	895	32	4-34	0	27.96
M. A. Robinson	413.1	117	1,158	38	4-46	0	30.47
C. White	216.1	39	687	20	4-40	0	34.35
C. E. W. Silverwood . . .	147.1	23	630	18	5-62	1	35.00
M. P. Vaughan	238.4	57	744	19	3-32	0	39.15
R. D. Stemp	610.1	193	1,628	36	4-68	0	45.22

Also bowled: M. G. Bevan 85–20–292–6; A. P. Grayson 24–7–75–0; G. M. Hamilton 47–11–169–4; A. C. Morris 17–5–62–0.

Wicket-keeper: R. J. Blakey 51 ct, 3 st.

Leading Fielders: D. Byas 39, M. G. Bevan 15.

At Cambridge, April 13, 14, 15. YORKSHIRE drew with CAMBRIDGE UNIVERSITY.

YORKSHIRE v LANCASHIRE

Non-Championship Match

At Leeds, April 27, 28, 29, May 1. Yorkshire won by 219 runs. Toss: Yorkshire.

A full-strength Yorkshire side proved too strong for Lancashire, already weakened by injuries and soon deprived of Martin, who was taken ill, and Austin, who damaged a shoulder. Byas and Gough made the most of the situation, each producing a career-best performance – one with the bat, the other making 435 to win. Byas broke Lancashire's spirit with 193 from 250 balls, hitting one six and 34 fours and setting up a total of 417. Not even a well-organised century by the stylish Atherton – his fifth in Roses games, but his first in Yorkshire – could turn the tide. They just avoided following on. Bevan also scored a purposeful hundred as Moxon kept control. Lancashire never had any realistic hopes of making 435 to win. Gough, with seven for 28 in the second innings and ten for 80 in the match, proved irresistible, although a determined 93-run stand between Hegg and Yates delayed the end.

Close of play: First day, Yorkshire 386-7 (R. J. Blakey 65*, P. J. Hartley 2*); Second day, Yorkshire 45-1 (M. D. Moxon 29*, M. G. Bevan 16*); Third day, Lancashire 70-3 (N. J. Speak 0*).

Yorkshire

*M. D. Moxon lbw b Watkinson	18	– c Atherton b Gallian	84
M. P. Vaughan b Martin	0	– lbw b Watkinson	0
D. Byas lbw b Yates	193	– (5) b Keedy	26
M. G. Bevan b Watkinson	0	– (3) b Yates	108
C. White b Gallian	72	– (6) c Gallian b Keedy	50
†R. J. Blakey not out	77	– (7) not out	14
A. P. Grayson c Atherton b Yates	15	– (4) lbw b Gallian	1
D. Gough lbw b Austin	11		
P. J. Hartley not out	21		
L-b 2, w 2, n-b 6	10	B 1, l-b 4	5

1/2 2/57 3/65 4/216 5/316 (7 wkts dec.) 417 1/3 2/189 3/198 (6 wkts dec.) 288
6/352 7/375   4/198 5/251 6/288

R. D. Stemp and M. A. Robinson did not bat.

Bowling: *First Innings*—Martin 22-5-75-1; Austin 27-7-70-1; Watkinson 20-5-86-2; Gallian 10-3-47-1; Yates 20-2-81-2; Keedy 13-2-56-0. *Second Innings*—Watkinson 17-3-50-1; Gallian 9-2-56-2; Yates 18-4-88-1; Keedy 21.1-1-89-2.

Lancashire

M. A. Atherton c Bevan b Robinson	129	– (2) b Gough	27
J. E. R. Gallian lbw b Hartley	8	– (1) c Blakey b Gough	36
N. J. Speak b Hartley	0	– lbw b Hartley	8
G. D. Lloyd c Byas b Gough	19	– c Stemp b Gough	0
S. P. Titchard b Gough	2	– lbw b Gough	6
*M. Watkinson b White	23	– c Vaughan b Gough	13
I. D. Austin c Grayson b Robinson	49	– c and b Gough	5
†W. K. Hegg c White b Robinson	6	– b Hartley	64
G. Yates c Grayson b Gough	11	– (10) not out	42
G. Keedy not out	0	– (11) c Byas b Hartley	0
P. J. Martin absent ill		– (9) c Robinson b Gough	4
L-b 8, w 2, n-b 14	24	B 1, l-b 3, n-b 6	10

1/37 2/43 3/76 4/98 5/140   271   1/67 2/70 3/70 4/80 5/94   215
6/242 7/254 8/259 9/271   6/101 7/108 8/122 9/215

Bowling: *First Innings*—Gough 17–4–52–3; Robinson 19–9–47–3; Hartley 16–2–56–2; Stemp 7–1–23–0; White 8–0–38–1; Bevan 2–0–16–0; Vaughan 7–2–31–0. *Second Innings*—Gough 17–7–28–7; Hartley 16.4–2–74–3; Robinson 10–2–33–0; Stemp 12–3–44–0; White 7–0–32–0.

Umpires: J. H. Harris and G. Sharp.

At Leicester, May 4, 5, 6. YORKSHIRE beat LEICESTERSHIRE by nine wickets.

At Chesterfield, May 11, 12, 13. YORKSHIRE beat DERBYSHIRE by seven runs.

YORKSHIRE v GLAMORGAN

At Bradford, May 18, 19, 20. Yorkshire won by seven wickets. Yorkshire 20 pts, Glamorgan 4 pts. Toss: Yorkshire. First-class debut: A. McGrath.

Batsmen struggled to cope throughout with a pitch which the umpires reported on the second day for offering excessive bounce. No further action was taken after a visit from TCCB inspector Harry Brind. In the end, Yorkshire won because they applied themselves with rather more determination. Some fine catching further assisted the bowlers and Vaughan played the decisive innings as he negotiated his way skilfully through 144 balls for 74. Watkin found some movement, and his persistence eventually brought about a collapse in which Yorkshire lost their last eight for 47 in 18 overs. Nevertheless, they led by 54, an important psychological advantage. Hartley took the first six wickets in Glamorgan's second innings, raising the prospect of a two-day finish until Cottey and the robust Anthony brought some respectability. Pursuing 159, McGrath marked his debut with a solid 36, while Byas and Bevan put the conditions into perspective by adding 69 in 30 overs.

Close of play: First day, Yorkshire 142-4 (R. D. Stemp 0*, C. White 0*); Second day, Yorkshire 72-2 (D. Byas 26*, M. G. Bevan 5*).

Glamorgan

S. P. James run out		9	– lbw b Hartley	28
*H. Morris c Byas b Gough		8	– c Gough b Hartley	4
D. L. Hemp c Byas b Robinson		25	– c Blakey b Hartley	25
M. P. Maynard lbw b Robinson		19	– c Bevan b Hartley	19
P. A. Cottey c Blakey b Stemp		5	– lbw b Robinson	51
A. Dale c Blakey b Gough		8	– c Blakey b Hartley	0
R. D. B. Croft b White		12	– c Bevan b Hartley	4
H. A. G. Anthony c Blakey b White		4	– c Blakey b Gough	37
R. P. Lefebvre c McGrath b Hartley		18	– run out	24
†C. P. Metson not out		16	– c Bevan b Robinson	2
S. L. Watkin c Stemp b Hartley		0	– not out	10
L-b 2, w 1, n-b 8		11	B 5, l-b 3	8

1/17 2/19 3/56 4/75 5/75 135 1/14 2/52 3/70 4/83 5/85 212
6/89 7/99 8/108 9/129   6/101 7/149 8/186 9/198

Bonus points – Yorkshire 4.

Bowling: *First Innings*—Gough 16–6–32–2; Hartley 11.1–2–45–2; Robinson 17–6–37–2; Stemp 3–0–7–1; White 7–3–12–2. *Second Innings*—Gough 11–1–44–1; Hartley 18–3–64–6; White 7–0–35–0; Robinson 11.5–2–40–2; Stemp 8–6–13–0; Vaughan 3–1–8–0.

Yorkshire

A. McGrath c Maynard b Watkin	0	– c Cottey b Croft	36
M. P. Vaughan c James b Watkin	74	– lbw b Watkin	3
*D. Byas c Hemp b Watkin	45	– st Metson b Croft	57
M. G. Bevan c Metson b Croft	22	– not out	51
R. D. Stemp c Morris b Dale	8		
C. White b Dale	0	– (5) not out	8
†R. J. Blakey c Cottey b Watkin	4		
A. P. Grayson c Maynard b Watkin	6		
D. Gough c Maynard b Anthony	8		
P. J. Hartley not out	10		
M. A. Robinson c Hemp b Watkin	7		
L-b 5	5	L-b 4, n-b 2	6

1/4 2/96 3/142 4/142 5/142   189   1/29 2/61 3/130   (3 wkts) 161
6/155 7/163 8/168 9/172

Bonus points – Glamorgan 4.

Bowling: *First Innings*—Watkin 23–6–55–6; Anthony 16–4–49–1; Dale 13–3–38–2; Lefebvre 12–4–34–0; Croft 4–2–8–1. *Second Innings*—Watkin 12–3–38–1; Anthony 11–1–40–0; Lefebvre 17–6–30–0; Croft 15.1–4–28–2; Dale 6–2–21–0.

Umpires: J. W. Holder and P. Willey.

YORKSHIRE v NORTHAMPTONSHIRE

At Sheffield, May 25, 26, 27, 29. Northamptonshire won by seven wickets. Northamptonshire 23 pts, Yorkshire 5 pts. Toss: Northamptonshire.

Northamptonshire maintained their early Championship lead when they scrambled to victory by running a bye to the wicket-keeper from each of the last two possible deliveries. Rain throughout the last afternoon left them only 23 overs to score 146. They achieved it largely thanks to Lamb, with 49 from 39 balls, and Curran, unbeaten on 42 from 38. Yorkshire, however, did not help themselves by bowling too wide and too short to confused field placings. Northamptonshire had the advantage of bowling first, when the ball was moving off the seam, and consolidated their position through a century from Bailey, who used up 332 balls and hit only 11 boundaries. Despite a splendid opening spell of 10–5–6–2 from Milburn, on his first home Championship appearance, Yorkshire trailed by 107. They had retrieved some of the ground lost, however, in reaching 147 for two, when Bevan surrendered his wicket to a careless stroke. Kumble exploited that error by taking three for one in five balls, breaking the back of Yorkshire's second innings.

Close of play: First day, Yorkshire 229-7 (C. White 106*, R. D. Stemp 9*); Second day, Northamptonshire 262-5 (R. J. Bailey 95*, J. N. Snape 13*); Third day, Yorkshire 174-6 (D. Byas 57*, B. Parker 0*).

Yorkshire

A. McGrath c Lamb b Taylor	12	– lbw b Curran	30
M. P. Vaughan c Warren b Capel	25	– c Fordham b Curran	11
*D. Byas b Mallender	31	– c Lamb b Taylor	88
M. G. Bevan b Capel	9	– c Fordham b Snape	50
C. White c Curran b Kumble	110	– c Snape b Kumble	14
†R. J. Blakey c Capel b Curran	16	– (7) c and b Kumble	0
B. Parker c Curran b Kumble	4	– (8) lbw b Taylor	32
P. J. Hartley lbw b Kumble	4	– (9) c Warren b Kumble	0
R. D. Stemp c Curran b Kumble	14	– (6) c Capel b Kumble	0
S. M. Milburn b Taylor	4	– not out	2
M. A. Robinson not out	6	– c Warren b Taylor	2
B 4, l-b 7, n-b 4	15	B 3, l-b 10, n-b 10	23

1/34 2/38 3/68 4/103 5/167   250   1/49 2/54 3/147 4/168 5/170   252
6/182 7/196 8/237 9/242   6/174 7/245 8/246 9/250

Bonus points – Yorkshire 2, Northamptonshire 4.

Bowling: *First Innings*—Taylor 27.2–6–92–2; Mallender 17–4–38–1; Capel 15–8–25–2; Kumble 28–6–63–4; Curran 12–4–21–1. *Second Innings*—Taylor 20.3–4–74–3; Mallender 15–4–29–0; Curran 10–5–23–2; Capel 7–1–32–0; Kumble 31–12–63–4; Snape 5–0–14–1; Bailey 1–0–4–0.

Northamptonshire

†R. J. Warren c Blakey b Milburn	8	
A. Fordham c Blakey b Milburn	6 – c Byas b Hartley	23
R. J. Bailey lbw b Robinson	111	
T. C. Walton c Blakey b Hartley	10 – (5) not out	7
K. M. Curran c Byas b Milburn	39 – (4) not out	42
D. J. Capel c Robinson b Hartley	72 – (1) c Stemp b Milburn	20
J. N. Snape c Bevan b Robinson	17	
*A. J. Lamb c Byas b Milburn	30 – (3) c McGrath b Robinson	49
A. Kumble not out	26	
N. A. Mallender c Vaughan b White	10	
J. P. Taylor b Hartley	4	
L-b 3, w 1, n-b 20	24	B 2, l-b 3	5

1/12 2/17 3/47 4/121 5/232   357   1/41 2/46 3/121   (3 wkts) 146
6/266 7/309 8/313 9/336

Bonus points – Northamptonshire 3, Yorkshire 3 (Score at 120 overs: 336-8).

Bowling: *First Innings*—Hartley 32–7–87–3; Milburn 26–8–68–4; Robinson 29–6–86–2; Stemp 18–7–34–0; White 15–5–41–1; Vaughan 5–1–20–0; Bevan 5–2–18–0. *Second Innings*—Hartley 10–0–61–1; Milburn 5–0–26–1; White 4–0–34–0; Robinson 4–0–20–1.

Umpires: T. E. Jesty and A. G. T. Whitehead.

At Taunton, June 1, 2, 3, 5. YORKSHIRE lost to SOMERSET by seven wickets.

YORKSHIRE v KENT

At Leeds, June 15, 16, 17, 19. Yorkshire won by eight wickets. Yorkshire 24 pts, Kent 3 pts. Toss: Kent.

Moxon dominated the contest, being on the field throughout and scoring 268 runs in the match without being out. A weakened Kent paid dearly for fielding first on an easy-paced pitch. The last-minute withdrawal of the injured Benson and Cowdrey forced them to start with only ten men as they awaited the arrival of Fulton. Headley then strained his side muscles and Patel bowled with a painful right shoulder. Moxon, himself just recovered from injury, scored his fourth double-century but his first in Yorkshire. He hit 31 boundaries in only four and a half hours as his side surpassed their previous best home total against Kent: 459 in 1896. Gough ripped through the visitors' lower order, with four wickets in five balls, including his first hat-trick, but de Silva batted superbly in the follow-on, driving and cutting to reach 115 from only 151 balls. White polished off the resistance, leaving Moxon and Byas to complete the triumph before lunch on the fourth day, with an unbroken partnership worth 125 from 32 overs.

Close of play: First day, Yorkshire 346-3 (M. D. Moxon 158*, C. White 17*); Second day, Kent 12-0 (D. P. Fulton 3*, T. R. Ward 9*); Third day, Yorkshire 15-2 (M. D. Moxon 9*, D. Byas 0*).

Yorkshire

*M. D. Moxon not out	203 – not out	65
M. P. Vaughan c Marsh b McCague	71 – lbw b McCague	5
D. Byas c Llong b McCague	47 – (4) not out	58
M. G. Bevan lbw b Wren	29	
C. White b Wren	17	
†R. J. Blakey lbw b Wren	3	
A. P. Grayson b Wren	0	
D. Gough c Marsh b Patel	60	
R. D. Stemp (did not bat)	– (3) c Marsh b Wren	0
B 6, l-b 9, w 9, n-b 8	32	B 6, l-b 2, w 2, n-b 2	12

1/132 2/238 3/298 4/362 5/378   (7 wkts dec.) 462   1/13 2/15   (2 wkts) 140
6/378 7/462

P. J. Hartley and M. A. Robinson did not bat.

Bonus points – Yorkshire 4, Kent 2 (Score at 120 overs: 378-6).

Bowling: *First Innings*—McCague 32-7-77-2; Wren 28-5-93-4; Headley 8-1-36-0; Patel 18.5-6-63-1; Ealham 26-7-109-0; Fleming 16-3-45-0; de Silva 8-2-24-0. *Second Innings*—McCague 9-2-27-1; Wren 9-2-37-1; Ealham 4-1-22-0; Patel 8.2-3-31-0; de Silva 5-1-15-0.

Kent

D. P. Fulton c Stemp b Hartley	21 – lbw b White	59
T. R. Ward c Blakey b Stemp	65 – run out	29
M. A. Ealham c Blakey b Hartley	2 – c and b Robinson	36
P. A. de Silva c Blakey b Robinson	52 – c Robinson b Hartley	115
N. J. Llong b Gough	19 – c Byas b Hartley	30
M. V. Fleming lbw b Stemp	10 – c Moxon b Stemp	15
*†S. A. Marsh c Blakey b Gough	22 – c Byas b White	29
M. M. Patel not out	14 – lbw b Robinson	19
M. J. McCague lbw b Gough	0 – not out	11
T. N. Wren lbw b Gough	0 – lbw b White	0
D. W. Headley b Robinson	13 – c Blakey b White	5
L-b 4, n-b 12	16	B 4, l-b 7, n-b 6	17

1/40 2/52 3/148 4/152 5/171   234   1/78 2/111 3/237 4/266 5/296   365
6/193 7/206 8/206 9/206   6/308 7/345 8/351 9/351

Bonus points – Kent 1, Yorkshire 4.

Bowling: *First Innings*—Gough 19-8-34-4; Hartley 10-2-35-2; Robinson 17.3-3-68-2; White 8-1-24-0; Stemp 17-4-69-2; Vaughan 1-1-0-0. *Second Innings*—Gough 17-1-56-0; Robinson 21-3-57-2; Hartley 20-5-68-2; Stemp 23-10-93-1; White 14.4-2-40-4; Vaughan 4-0-18-0; Grayson 6-1-22-0.

Umpires: J. D. Bond and J. H. Harris.

At Birmingham, June 22, 23, 24. YORKSHIRE lost to WARWICKSHIRE by an innings and 168 runs.

YORKSHIRE v GLOUCESTERSHIRE

At Middlesbrough, June 29, 30, July 1. Gloucestershire won by nine wickets. Gloucestershire 22 pts, Yorkshire 7 pts. Toss: Yorkshire.

Yorkshire surrendered the match with two inexcusable collapses on an excellent pitch. From 275 for three in the first innings, they lost seven for 65 in 18 overs, and in their second, the last eight went for 57 in 25. Byas, whose century made him the first man to reach 1,000 runs for the season, and Bevan had created the illusion of confidence while adding 190 in 61 overs. But Srinath's persistence in extreme heat turned the game on its head. He claimed six for 63, going on to ten for the first time in his career. Yorkshire's 340 was boosted by a career-best 23 from Robinson, a notoriously unsuccessful No. 11. But Gloucestershire also fell into trouble, with five down for 96. Lynch and Russell rallied the innings, punishing Gough for bowling much too short, but Yorkshire still had a 64-run lead, before keen fielding and accurate bowling threw them into total confusion. A measured hundred from Wright completed Gloucestershire's victory by 5 p.m. on the third day, bringing relief to local residents who had complained about the volume and frequency of the loudspeaker announcements.

Close of play: First day, Gloucestershire 19-0 (A. J. Wright 6*, G. D. Hodgson 7*); Second day, Yorkshire 125-8 (P. J. Hartley 21*, R. D. Stemp 2*).

Yorkshire

S. A. Kellett c Wright b Smith	6	– b Srinath	9
M. P. Vaughan c Ball b Srinath	9	– c Russell b Srinath	12
*D. Byas b Srinath	108	– c and b Ball	36
M. G. Bevan c Russell b Smith	102	– c and b Ball	28
C. White c Russell b Srinath	28	– run out	1
†R. J. Blakey not out	17	– c Lynch b Davies	8
A. P. Grayson b Srinath	0	– lbw b Alleyne	1
D. Gough c Symonds b Srinath	7	– lbw b Alleyne	0
P. J. Hartley c Lynch b Srinath	0	– c Alleyne b Srinath	31
R. D. Stemp c and b Ball	8	– b Smith	6
M. A. Robinson b Smith	23	– not out	2
B 4, l-b 7, w 1, n-b 20	32	L-b 1, n-b 10	11

1/7 2/29 3/219 4/275 5/276	340	1/18 2/35 3/88 4/93 5/94	145
6/276 7/284 8/286 9/305		6/96 7/96 8/113 9/132	

Bonus points – Yorkshire 3, Gloucestershire 4.

Bowling: First Innings—Srinath 24–5–63–6; Smith 24.2–4–80–3; Alleyne 13–2–46–0; Ball 32–7–112–1; Davies 8–3–28–0. *Second Innings*—Srinath 9.3–4–34–4; Smith 12–1–52–0; Alleyne 11–6–21–2; Ball 13–3–33–2; Davies 4–3–4–1.

Gloucestershire

A. J. Wright c Hartley b Gough	33	– not out	107
G. D. Hodgson b Hartley	13	– c Kellett b Vaughan	34
R. J. Cunliffe lbw b Robinson	5	– not out	51
M. A. Lynch c White b Hartley	68		
M. W. Alleyne c Blakey b Gough	1		
A. Symonds lbw b Robinson	4		
*†R. C. Russell b Byas b White	87		
J. Srinath c Kellett b Robinson	0		
M. C. J. Ball c Kellett b Robinson	0		
M. Davies c Blakey b Gough	22		
A. M. Smith not out	1		
B 4, l-b 16, n-b 22	42	B 2, l-b 4, n-b 12	18

1/40 2/47 3/71 4/81 5/96	276	1/96	(1 wkt) 210
6/181 7/185 8/188 9/256			

Bonus points – Gloucestershire 2, Yorkshire 4.

In the first innings M. A. Lynch, when 68, retired hurt at 181-5 and resumed at 185.

Bowling: First Innings—Gough 20–5–76–3; Hartley 17–4–71–2; Robinson 17–4–46–4; White 7.5–0–33–1; Stemp 4–2–9–0; Vaughan 5–2–21–0. *Second Innings*—Gough 9–4–17–0; Hartley 10–0–39–0; Stemp 26–13–65–0; Robinson 12.1–5–32–0; Vaughan 12–4–31–1; Grayson 3–1–6–0; White 5–2–14–0.

Umpires: V. A. Holder and N. T. Plews.

At Southampton, July 6, 7, 8, 10. YORKSHIRE beat HAMPSHIRE by three wickets.

At Leeds, July 18. YORKSHIRE beat YOUNG AUSTRALIA by 68 runs (See Young Australia tour section).

YORKSHIRE v DURHAM

At Harrogate, July 20, 21, 22, 24. Yorkshire won by 211 runs. Yorkshire 23 pts, Durham 5 pts. Toss: Yorkshire.

Yorkshire controlled the game throughout, although they failed to capitalise on a sound start on a pitch which offered extra bounce from just short of a length. Byas, missed by wicket-keeper Ligertwood before scoring, put his side in a strong position at 175 for one, despite some hostile bowling by Walker. But Yorkshire's seamers bowled a length better suited to the conditions, with Hartley, in particular, a dangerous proposition – quite literally for Durham's captain, Roseberry, whose right hand he struck twice. Roseberry retired with a chipped knuckle; he bravely returned to help avert the follow-on, but sensibly did not risk himself in the second-innings collapse. Some punishing strokeplay by Bevan had enabled Byas to set a target of 337 in just over a day's play and Durham folded, their batsmen showing little resolve against the lifting ball. The game attracted very large crowds, with receipts of more than £8,000.

Close of play: First day, Yorkshire 296-7 (D. Gough 22*, P. J. Hartley 3*); Second day, Durham 113-3 (M. Prabhakar 21*, D. A. Blenkiron 6*); Third day, Durham 4-1 (S. Hutton 1*, A. Walker 2*).

Yorkshire

S. A. Kellett c Ligertwood b Walker	27	– lbw b Brown 31
M. P. Vaughan c Ligertwood b Brown	87	– c Ligertwood b Brown 40
*D. Byas c Daley b Brown	64	– run out 28
M. G. Bevan c Hutton b Boiling	13	– not out 64
C. White c Walker b Brown	10	– c Boiling b Prabhakar 0
B. Parker c Ligertwood b Brown	29	– not out 37
†R. J. Blakey c Brown b Prabhakar	37	
D. Gough b Prabhakar	22	
P. J. Hartley c Hutton b Prabhakar	23	
R. D. Stemp c Hutton b Prabhakar	19	
M. A. Robinson not out	1	
B 1, l-b 3, n-b 2	6	L-b 3, w 1 4
	338	**(4 wkts dec.) 204**

1/67 2/175 3/182 4/197 5/207   338   1/68 2/77   (4 wkts dec.) 204
6/265 7/292 8/300 9/321   3/122 4/122

Bonus points – Yorkshire 3, Durham 4.

Bowling: *First Innings*—Brown 27–7–90–4; Prabhakar 27.5–9–87–4; Betts 9–0–35–0; Walker 18.1–3–42–1; Boiling 38–13–80–1. *Second Innings*—Brown 11–1–35–2; Prabhakar 13–7–15–1; Walker 14–0–68–0; Betts 2–0–9–0; Boiling 19–2–74–0.

Durham

*M. A. Roseberry c Byas b Hartley	16	– absent hurt	
S. Hutton c Byas b Gough	21	– c Blakey b White	26
J. E. Morris c Byas b Hartley	46	– (4) lbw b Hartley	4
J. A. Daley c Byas b Gough	0	– (5) not out	37
M. Prabhakar c Blakey b White	35	– (6) c Byas b White	8
D. A. Blenkiron b Hartley	7	– (7) c Blakey b Robinson	8
†D. G. C. Ligertwood c Byas b Robinson	13	– (1) lbw b Hartley	0
J. Boiling c Blakey b Gough	18	– b Hartley	4
A. Walker b Hartley	12	– (3) c Blakey b Gough	2
S. J. E. Brown b Gough	5	– (9) c sub b Hartley	5
M. M. Betts not out	7	– (10) c sub b Gough	14
B 12, l-b 7, w 1, n-b 6	26	L-b 13, n-b 8	21

1/63 2/69 3/87 4/117 5/135   206   1/1 2/32 3/41 4/56 5/60   125
6/154 7/182 8/182 9/190   6/77 7/88 8/98 9/125

Bonus points – Durham 1, Yorkshire 4.

In the first innings M. A. Roseberry, when 5, retired hurt at 9 and resumed at 154.

Bowling: *First Innings*—Gough 26·7-7-57–4; Hartley 26-6-65–4; Robinson 11-3-22–1; White 16-3-30–1; Stemp 7-3-13–0. *Second Innings*—Gough 15.3-7-28–2; Hartley 20-6-51–4; Robinson 9-4-17–1; White 4-2-16–2.

Umpires: M. J. Kitchen and R. Palmer.

At Nottingham, July 27, 28, 29. YORKSHIRE lost to NOTTINGHAMSHIRE by eight wickets.

YORKSHIRE v WORCESTERSHIRE

At Scarborough, August 3, 4, 5, 7. Drawn. Yorkshire 6 pts, Worcestershire 5 pts. Toss: Yorkshire.

A pitch offering no hint of assistance to the bowlers produced nothing but records. The aggregate of 1,473 runs was the biggest for any match involving Yorkshire, whose 600 for four was the highest total at Scarborough. Worcestershire endured this innings without taking the new ball, in 167 overs; Byas scored a maiden double-century, hitting 27 fours in 376 balls, and added 180 with Bevan and 207 with White. White had two lives, when Illingworth and Lampitt missed return catches, though in general the bowling was tidy. White in turn gave Moody a second chance when he failed to hold a drive against Stemp at cover. Worcestershire batted slowly, with Curtis occupying 458 balls and eight hours, and then sat back to wait for the declaration. With little chance of victory, Moxon set a target of 379 in 71 overs. Worcestershire lost four for 31 in a careless first hour, before playing out an almost unchallenged draw.

Close of play: First day, Yorkshire 379-3 (D. Byas 113*, C. White 1*); Second day, Worcestershire 188-2 (T. S. Curtis 51*, T. M. Moody 63*); Third day, Yorkshire 80-1 (M. P. Vaughan 35*, D. Byas 37*).

Yorkshire

*M. D. Moxon lbw b Haynes	51	– b Newport	0
M. P. Vaughan c Moody b Newport	88	– c Moody b Haynes	61
D. Byas b Moody	213	– c Haynes b Hick	69
M. G. Bevan b Lampitt	89	– not out	44
C. White not out	107	– not out	41
S. A. Kellett not out	6		
B 8, l-b 9, w 1, n-b 28	46	L-b 5, w 1, n-b 10	16

1/118 2/193 3/373 4/580   (4 wkts. dec.) 600   1/0 2/145 3/145   (3 wkts. dec.) 231

†R. J. Blakey, P. J. Hartley, C. E. W. Silverwood, R. D. Stemp and M. A. Robinson did not bat.

Bonus points – Yorkshire 4, Worcestershire 1 (Score at 120 overs: 409-3).

Bowling: First Innings—Newport 21–2–70–1; Thomas 18–2–86–0; Haynes 22–6–91–1; Lampitt 26–4–92–1; Illingworth 38–9–112–0; Hick 30–6–93–0; Weston 7.4–0–26–0; Moody 4–0–13–1. *Second Innings*—Newport 6–2–10–1; Thomas 13–2–79–0; Lampitt 7–0–35–0; Illingworth 12–5–32–0; Hick 12–5–25–1; Haynes 8–1–45–1.

Worcestershire

T. S. Curtis not out	169	– lbw b Hartley		0
W. P. C. Weston b Stemp	52	– lbw b Vaughan		68
G. A. Hick c White b Vaughan	7	– lbw b Silverwood		7
*T. M. Moody c Blakey b Hartley	64	– run out		5
G. R. Haynes b Vaughan	41	– b Hartley		8
D. A. Leatherdale c White b Stemp	15	– not out		67
†S. J. Rhodes not out	72	– not out		16
B 2, l-b 6, w 1, n-b 24	33	B 4, l-b 2, n-b 12		18

1/92 2/103 3/203 4/281 5/298   (5 wkts dec.) 453   1/0 2/11 3/21   (5 wkts) 189
4/31 5/147

P. J. Newport, S. R. Lampitt, R. K. Illingworth and P. A. Thomas did not bat.

Bonus points – Worcestershire 4, Yorkshire 2 (Score at 120 overs: 371-5).

Bowling: First Innings—Hartley 11–2–49–1; Silverwood 9–2–49–0; Robinson 22–9–50–0; White 6–0–24–0; Stemp 57.5–24–128–2; Vaughan 37–10–114–2; Bevan 7–1–31–0. *Second Innings*—Hartley 14–1–53–2; Silverwood 11–3–33–1; Robinson 5–1–15–0; Stemp 17–7–39–0; Vaughan 12–4–33–1; Bevan 2–1–5–0; White 4–3–5–0.

Umpires: T. E. Jesty and N. T. Plews.

At The Oval, August 10, 11, 12, 14. YORKSHIRE lost to SURREY by one run.

At Manchester, August 17, 18, 19, 21. YORKSHIRE beat LANCASHIRE by nine wickets.

YORKSHIRE v MIDDLESEX

At Leeds, August 24, 25, 26, 28. Middlesex won by an innings and 25 runs. Middlesex 24 pts, Yorkshire 3 pts. Toss: Middlesex. First-class debut: R. A. Fay.

On a pitch allowing some turn from the first day, Championship leaders Middlesex's match-winner was Emburey, who took 12 for 157. The stage was set, however, by a high-class innings from Ramprakash. His third double-hundred of the season, a career-best 235, equalled Allan Lamb's 1990 record for the highest score against Yorkshire at Headingley. He faced 426 balls and hit one six and 31 fours. Yorkshire's left-arm spinner, Stemp, bowled too short too often, assisting Middlesex's rapid progress, although White eventually hastened the declaration with three wickets in 11 deliveries. Moxon played two innings of genuine quality, completing 1,000 runs in the tenth match of his interrupted season, but, with no support, Yorkshire collapsed badly twice. They reached 210 for three in both innings, only to lose their last seven for 40 the first time and for 31 in the follow-on. Emburey's nagging accuracy and some variable bounce on the last pitch prepared by groundsman Keith Boyce meant the game was over before lunch on the fourth day.

Close of play: First day, Middlesex 346-4 (M. R. Ramprakash 141*, K. R. Brown 49*); Second day, Yorkshire 202-3 (M. D. Moxon 86*, C. White 22*); Third day, Yorkshire 179-2 (D. Byas 33*, M. G. Bevan 5*).

Middlesex

P. N. Weekes lbw b Vaughan	53	M. A. Feltham b White	5
J. C. Pooley c Blakey b Silverwood	16	R. A. Fay not out	1
M. R. Ramprakash c Blakey b White	235		
*M. W. Gatting c Vaughan b Stemp	30	B 2, l-b 15, n-b 8	25
J. D. Carr b Stemp	41		
†K. R. Brown lbw b Robinson	67	1/24 2/116 3/178 (9 wkts dec.)	516
D. J. Nash c Vaughan b Stemp	6	4/241 5/411 6/422	
J. E. Emburey b White	37	7/506 8/513 9/516	

P. C. R. Tufnell did not bat.

Bonus points – Middlesex 4, Yorkshire 1 (Score at 120 overs: 396-4).

Bowling: Hartley 28-7-57-0; Silverwood 24-4-85-1; Robinson 17-4-54-1; White 25.4-4-80-3; Stemp 39-3-140-3; Vaughan 12-1-52-1; Bevan 6-0-31-0.

Yorkshire

*M. D. Moxon b Tufnell	104	– c Carr b Tufnell	78
M. P. Vaughan c and b Nash	0	– lbw b Tufnell	49
D. Byas b Emburey	28	– st Brown b Emburey	49
M. G. Bevan c Pooley b Weekes	37	– c Pooley b Emburey	5
C. White lbw b Emburey	27	– b Tufnell	11
A. A. Metcalfe lbw b Tufnell	1	– not out	20
†R. J. Blakey c Emburey b Tufnell	6	– c Pooley b Emburey	0
P. J. Hartley c Feltham b Emburey	5	– c Nash b Emburey	0
C. E. W. Silverwood c Weekes b Emburey	3	– c Nash b Emburey	4
R. D. Stemp not out	3	– b Emburey	0
M. A. Robinson lbw b Emburey	0	– c Carr b Emburey	0
B 14, l-b 10, n-b 12	36	B 10, l-b 7, n-b 8	25

1/1 2/71 3/132 4/210 5/215	250	1/95 2/160 3/179 4/210 5/210	241
6/230 7/241 8/243 9/248		6/219 7/221 8/239 9/239	

Bonus points – Yorkshire 2, Middlesex 4.

Bowling: *First Innings*—Nash 6-0-22-1; Fay 3-0-25-0; Tufnell 38-10-68-3; Emburey 36.5-10-75-5; Weekes 14-2-36-1. *Second Innings*—Nash 8-2-36-0; Emburey 44.4-13-82-7; Feltham 4-2-6-0; Tufnell 41-17-69-3; Weekes 10-3-31-0.

Umpires: G. I. Burgess and B. Dudleston.

At Scarborough, August 30, 31, September 1. YORKSHIRE drew with WEST INDIANS (See West Indian tour section).

At Scarborough, September 3. YORKSHIRE beat WEST INDIANS by 11 runs.

YORKSHIRE v SUSSEX

At Scarborough, September 7, 8, 9, 11. Drawn. Yorkshire 3 pts, Sussex 4 pts. Toss: Yorkshire. First-class debut: R. S. C. Martin-Jenkins.

Play was possible only on the third day, because of heavy rain. Sussex scored steadily, aided by poor fielding Wells was badly missed when ten, by Byas at slip off Hartley; he went on to add 163 in 40 overs with Lenham before Greenfield took over as the dominant force. There was just time for Robin Martin-Jenkins, son of the BBC commentator Christopher, to make a first, brief, appearance in first-class cricket.

Close of play: First day, No play; Second day, No play; Third day, Sussex 357-8 (P. W. Jarvis 23*, R. S. C. Martin-Jenkins 0*).

Sussex

C. W. J. Athey c Bevan b Hartley	9	I. D. K. Salisbury b Hartley	43
M. T. E. Peirce c Metcalfe b Hartley	6	P. W. Jarvis not out	23
N. J. Lenham b Bevan	86	R. S. C. Martin-Jenkins not out	0
*A. P. Wells b Bevan	76	L-b 6, n-b 16	22
K. Greenfield b Gough	85		
D. R. Law c Metcalfe b Vaughan	0	1/14 2/21 3/184 4/193 (8 wkts) 357
†P. Moores lbw b Bevan	7	5/206 6/217 7/293 8/346

E. S. H. Giddins did not bat.

Bonus points – Sussex 4, Yorkshire 3.

Bowling: Gough 17–4–42–1; Hartley 23–9–70–3; Silverwood 6–1–44–0; White 0.5–0–2–0; Stemp 21.1–7–73–0; Vaughan 22–5–65–1; Bevan 15–5–55–3.

Yorkshire

*M. D. Moxon, M. P. Vaughan, D. Byas, M. G. Bevan, C. White, A. A. Metcalfe, †R. J. Blakey, D. Gough, P. J. Hartley, C. E. W. Silverwood and R. D. Stemp.

Umpires: D. R. Shepherd and R. A. White.

At Chelmsford, September 14, 15, 16, 18. YORKSHIRE lost to ESSEX by 89 runs.

I ZINGARI RESULTS, 1995

Matches 23: Won 8, Lost 4, Drawn 11. Abandoned 1.

April 25	Eton College	Lost by six wickets
May 14	Hampshire Hogs	Won by 73 runs
May 20	Eton Ramblers	Drawn
May 21	Staff College	Won by 101 runs
June 1	Harrow School	Lost by 34 runs
June 3	Royal Armoured Corps	Abandoned
June 11	Earl of Carnarvon's XI	Drawn
June 17	Charterhouse School	Won by six wickets
June 18	Sandhurst Wanderers	Drawn
June 24	Guards CC	Won by four wickets
July 2	J. Paul Getty's XI	Drawn
July 4	Winchester College	Drawn
July 9	Hagley CC	Lost by six wickets
July 15	Green Jackets Club	Drawn
July 16	Rickling Green CC	Won by 142 runs
July 23	Lavinia, Duchess of Norfolk's XI	Drawn
July 23	Sir John Starkey's XI	Drawn
July 29	Hurlingham CC	Drawn
July 30	Royal Artillery	Won by six wickets
August 6	Band of Brothers	Won by 18 runs
August 12	South Wales Hunts XI	Drawn
August 13	South Wales Hunts XI	Lost by 121 runs
August 20	Willow Warblers	Won by 42 runs
September 10	J. H. Pawle's XI	Drawn

NATWEST BANK TROPHY, 1995

The one competition that eluded Warwickshire in 1994 came safely home a year later when they beat Northamptonshire in a rain-affected but tense final by four wickets. Dermot Reeve, their captain, collected both the Man of the Match award and the trophy. It was Warwickshire's fifth victory in a September cup final, equalling Lancashire's record, and they also became only the second team to reach the final three years running, matching Lancashire's sequences from 1970 to 1972 and 1974 to 1976.

Warwickshire got there the hard way: they had to overcome first-class opposition in every round and only just overcame a determined Somerset assault on a target of 358 in their opening match. Most of the other counties, meanwhile, were going through the traditional first-round ritual of beating lesser opposition by margins that ranged from the comfortable to the brutal. The minor teams' task was made harder than ever before because only four out of 14 were drawn at home. However, newcomers Holland, barred from home fixtures because of the absence of grass wickets, batted extremely well before going down to Northamptonshire.

There was a fight for Warwickshire in the second round as well, but they overcame Kent by ten runs. Otherwise, there were very few close matches before the final. The exception was at a packed Headingley, when the quarter-final draw pitted the Roses counties against each other – and Yorkshire, the underdogs, were steered to a thrilling two-wicket win by their Australian batsman Michael Bevan.

Yorkshire were easily beaten by Northamptonshire in their semi-final, in which Rob Bailey won his third consecutive match award; he was his team's top scorer again in the final. Glamorgan, aiming for their first Lord's final since 1977, collapsed even more dramatically in the other semi. They were bowled out for 86 and Tim Munton, the Warwickshire seamer, had combined figures in that match and the previous round at Derby of 24–13–31–3. He missed Lord's because of injury, but Warwickshire proved unstoppable anyway.

Prize money

£35,000 for winners: WARWICKSHIRE.
£17,500 for runners-up: NORTHAMPTONSHIRE.
£8,750 for losing semi-finalists: GLAMORGAN and YORKSHIRE.
£4,375 for losing quarter-finalists: DERBYSHIRE, GLOUCESTERSHIRE, LANCASHIRE and MIDDLESEX.

Man of the Match award winners received £750 in the final, £350 in the semi-finals, £300 in the quarter-finals, £250 in the second round and £200 in the first round. The prize money was increased from £83,530 in the 1994 tournament to £95,350.

FIRST ROUND

CAMBRIDGESHIRE v DERBYSHIRE

At March, June 27. Derbyshire won by 157 runs. Toss: Derbyshire.

Cambridgeshire's batsmen survived the opening blast from Malcolm, though he yielded only nine in eight overs, and Cork, the hero of the Lord's Test the previous day, who was hampered by a blistered foot. DeFreitas took five, however, as they lost eight for 44. Derbyshire's day began in dismay, when Rollins was bowled by Akhtar's second ball. But Cullinan scored an unbeaten 119 on his NatWest debut, adding 169 in 41 overs with Dessaur.

Man of the Match: D. J. Cullinan.

Derbyshire

A. S. Rollins b Akhtar	0	C. M. Wells not out	51
W. A. Dessaur b Donelan	85	B 2, l-b 4, w 6	12
C. J. Adams c Donelan b Ralfs	22		
D. J. Cullinan not out	119	1/1 2/35 3/204 (3 wkts, 60 overs)	289

*K. J. Barnett, D. G. Cork, †K. M. Krikken, P. A. J. DeFreitas, F. A. Griffith and D. E. Malcolm did not bat.

Bowling: Akhtar 11–2–53–1; Ralfs 12–3–45–1; Toogood 12–0–66–0; Burton 10–2–51–0; Donelan 11–0–52–1; S. Mohammed 4–1–16–0.

Cambridgeshire

*N. T. Gadsby b DeFreitas	17	B. T. P. Donelan c DeFreitas b Wells	32
Salim Mohammed lbw b Griffith	11	A. Akhtar c Cullinan b Barnett	13
D. P. Norman lbw b DeFreitas	8	D. F. Ralfs not out	5
G. W. Ecclestone lbw b Barnett	8		
Nadeem Mohammed c Krikken b DeFreitas	7	B 4, l-b 6, w 6, n-b 2	18
M. A. Burton c Krikken b DeFreitas	0	1/31 2/40 3/55 (49.2 overs)	132
†S. L. Williams b Barnett	13	4/55 5/58 6/67	
G. J. Toogood lbw b DeFreitas	0	7/67 8/75 9/100	

Bowling: Malcolm 8–3–9–0; Cork 5–0–12–0; Griffith 11–3–33–1; DeFreitas 12–3–28–5; Barnett 12–3–40–3; Wells 1.2–1–0–1.

Umpires: J. C. Balderstone and J. H. Hampshire.

CHESHIRE v ESSEX

At Chester, June 27. Essex won by 64 runs. Toss: Cheshire.

Former Surrey seamer Murphy grabbed three early wickets and Essex were 156 for seven soon after lunch. But Prichard finally found a partner in Ilott, whose unbeaten 54 came at a run a ball. Spinners Such and Childs tied down Cheshire, and their fight was ended by Gooch. His five for eight in 16 balls were his best limited-overs figures.

Man of the Match: P. J. Prichard.

Essex

G. A. Gooch c Bryson b Murphy	17	M. C. Ilott not out	54
D. D. J. Robinson c Gray b Murphy	10	P. M. Such not out	8
N. Hussain c Bramhall b Murphy	4		
M. E. Waugh b Hignett	38	L-b 8, w 15, n-b 6	29
*P. J. Prichard c Bean b Hignett	81		
R. C. Irani c Gray b Hignett	0	1/34 2/38 3/57 (8 wkts, 60 overs)	265
J. J. B. Lewis b Greasley	16	4/113 5/120 6/146	
†R. J. Rollins c Bramhall b Murphy	8	7/156 8/234	

J. H. Childs did not bat.

Bowling: Murphy 12–1–48–4; Peel 12–0–57–0; O'Brien 12–5–46–0; Greasley 12–2–31–1; Hignett 12–0–75–3.

Cheshire

T. J. Bostock c Hussain b Childs	42	A. D. Greasley c and b Gooch	2
P. R. J. Bryson c Hussain b Ilott	15	A. J. Murphy not out	3
*I. Cockbain c Prichard b Such	29	N. D. Peel st Rollins b Gooch	0
J. D. Bean b Such	2	B 8, l-b 4, w 8, n-b 4	24
J. D. Gray b Gooch	27		
R. G. Hignett b Gooch	55	1/22 2/84 3/92 (57.4 overs)	201
†S. Bramhall b Gooch	1	4/96 5/185 6/188	
J. F. M. O'Brien b Waugh	1	7/191 8/192 9/197	

Bowling: Irani 10–0–50–0; Ilott 10–1–24–1; Waugh 11–1–45–1; Childs 12–3–26–1; Such 12–5–36–2; Gooch 2.4–0–8–5.

Umpires: J. W. Holder and V. A. Holder.

CORNWALL v MIDDLESEX

At St Austell, June 27. Middlesex won by 104 runs. Toss: Middlesex.

One-day opener Weekes remained undefeated on 143 from 181 balls, with 23 fours and a six, as Middlesex passed 300 for the first time in 60-overs cricket. Feltham, Emburey and Johnson – who hit 30 in 15 balls – helped him add 167 after they had been 130 for five. Fraser flat-batted the final delivery for six and then bowled five overs for two Cornish wickets and only two runs. Cornwall's captain, Godfrey Furse, and his girlfriend were both seriously injured next day after his hot dog van exploded when he returned to the ground to collect it.

Man of the Match: P. N. Weekes.

Middlesex

P. N. Weekes not out	143	R. L. Johnson c Walton b Berryman ... 30
J. C. Pooley c Snell b Lovell	1	A. R. C. Fraser not out	6
M. R. Ramprakash c Walton b Kent	25	
*J. D. Carr run out	27	L-b 8, w 5, n-b 14	27
†K. R. Brown c Seymour b Willcock	2	
D. J. Nash c Snell b Furse	4	1/12 2/52 3/103 (8 wkts, 60 overs) 304
M. A. Feltham c Seymour b Kent	30	4/111 5/130 6/192
J. E. Emburey run out	9	7/255 8/297

P. C. R. Tufnell did not bat.

Bowling: Lovell 12–0–74–1; Berryman 10–0–77–1; Willcock 12–3–52–1; Kent 12–1–41–2; Seymour 12–0–35–0; Furse 2–0–17–1.

Cornwall

S. M. Williams c Brown b Emburey ...	48	K. J. Willcock c Fraser b Ramprakash .	1
G. M. Thomas c Carr b Fraser	6	†A. M. Snell not out	3
A. C. H. Seymour c Emburey b Fraser .	0	K. P. Berryman lbw b Emburey	6
J. E. M. Nicolson c Brown b Feltham..	38	B 9, l-b 6, w 4, n-b 4	23
R. T. Walton st Brown b Ramprakash .	39	
J. P. Kent st Brown b Weekes	27	1/7 2/12 3/95 (59.2 overs) 200
*G. R. Furse run out	2	4/133 5/165 6/177
C. C. Lovell c Feltham b Emburey	7	7/183 8/186 9/193

Bowling: Fraser 5–3–2–2; Nash 5–0–23–0; Johnson 5–1–8–0; Emburey 10.2–3–18–3; Tufnell 12–3–56–0; Weekes 12–2–45–1; Feltham 6–3–9–1; Ramprakash 4–0–24–2.

Umpires: J. H. Harris and M. A. Johnson.

DURHAM v HEREFORDSHIRE

At Chester-le-Street, June 27. Durham won by 207 runs. Toss: Herefordshire.

Durham ravaged NatWest newcomers Herefordshire for 326, their biggest one-day total, at nearly five and a half an over. Roseberry and Hutton opened with 255 – a first-wicket record for any county in any of the three limited-overs competitions – and both reached their highest one-day scores. Walker bowled especially economically and Boiling wound up Herefordshire's tail with almost 15 overs in hand.

Man of the Match: M. A. Roseberry.

Durham

*M. A. Roseberry c Skyrme b Fowles	121	P. Bainbridge not out	10
S. Hutton c and b Fowles	125	L-b 4, w 14, n-b 10	28
J. E. Morris c and b Jarvis	29	
M. Prabhakar c and b Jarvis	4	1/255 2/288 (4 wkts, 60 overs) 326
D. A. Blenkiron not out	9	3/305 4/307

S. D. Birbeck, †D. G. C. Ligertwood, J. Boiling, A. Walker and S. J. E. Brown did not bat.

Bowling: Jarvis 11–0–45–2; Weston 12–4–40–0; Fowles 12–1–73–2; Harding 10–0–56–0; Bailey 7–0–35–0; Robinson 8–0–73–0.

Herefordshire

H. V. Patel c Roseberry b Brown	1	M. G. Fowles not out	2
M. J. Weston c Ligertwood b Walker	9	R. J. Harding c Walker b Boiling	10
S. M. Brogan c Ligertwood b Walker	10	K. B. S. Jarvis c Morris b Boiling	4
J. P. Wright c Prabhakar b Birbeck	20	L-b 2, w 10	12
M. F. Robinson lbw b Birbeck	15		
*R. P. Skyrme c Roseberry b Boiling	10	1/7 2/24 3/26	(45.4 overs) 119
†S. R. Bevins lbw b Brown	26	4/51 5/63 6/93	
M. J. Bailey b Boiling	0	7/93 8/103 9/115	

Bowling: Brown 9-1-22-2; Walker 8-4-13-2; Prabhakar 6-1-23-0; Birbeck 8-0-27-2; Boiling 9.4-5-22-4; Bainbridge 5-1-10-0.

Umpires: A. Clarkson and N. T. Plews.

GLAMORGAN v DORSET

At Cardiff, June 27. Glamorgan won by ten wickets. Toss: Dorset.

Glamorgan needed barely two-thirds of their allocated 60 overs to complete victory. Morris, with a 112-ball hundred, his fourth in the competition, and James scored the runs without being parted. Earlier, Dorset's batsmen preserved their pride by losing only four wickets; Hardy, who played for three first-class counties, scored 90 not out.

Man of the Match: H. Morris.

Dorset

T. W. Richings b Anthony	32	S. W. D. Rintoul not out	16
J. Cassell c James b Watkin	5	L-b 13, w 10	23
J. J. E. Hardy not out	90		
R. J. Scott c Hemp b Cottey	14	1/8 2/78	(4 wkts, 60 overs) 191
*†G. D. Reynolds lbw b Lefebvre	11	3/105 4/128	

A. Willows, R. A. Pyman, J. H. Shackleton, S. R. Walbridge and P. L. Garlick did not bat.

Bowling: Watkin 12-2-29-1; Lefebvre 12-3-32-1; Croft 12-2-27-0; Barwick 12-4-38-0; Anthony 8-0-41-1; Cottey 4-0-11-1.

Glamorgan

S. P. James not out	74
*H. Morris not out	105
B 2, l-b 1, w 2, n-b 8	13
	(no wkt, 40.5 overs) 192

M. P. Maynard, P. A. Cottey, D. L. Hemp, R. D. B. Croft, H. A. G. Anthony, R. P. Lefebvre, †C. P. Metson, S. L. Watkin and S. R. Barwick did not bat.

Bowling: Garlick 8.5-2-44-0; Shackleton 8-1-23-0; Scott 4-0-24-0; Walbridge 12-0-47-0; Pyman 7-0-49-0; Willows 1-0-2-0.

Umpires: D. J. Dennis and R. A. White.

GLOUCESTERSHIRE v SUFFOLK

At Bristol, June 27. Gloucestershire won by 124 runs. Toss: Suffolk.

Wright's highest one-day innings saw Gloucestershire to 301 after Carter claimed three early wickets. He put on 114 with Alleyne and 107 with Russell. Suffolk had to play without former Test batsman Derek Randall, who was held up in traffic. Peck and Caley shared a stand of 77, but then six wickets fell for 18, five of them to Boden.

Man of the Match: A. J. Wright.

Gloucestershire

A. J. Wright not out	142	*†R. C. Russell not out	59
G. D. Hodgson c Clinch b Carter	16		
R. J. Cunliffe b Carter	0	L-b 10, w 3, n-b 14	27
M. A. Lynch c Peck b Carter	0		—
M. W. Alleyne c Carter b Miller	43	1/41 2/51 3/51 (5 wkts, 60 overs) 301	
A. Symonds c Caley b Miller	14	4/165 5/194	

J. Srinath, M. C. J. Ball, D. J. P. Boden and A. M. Smith did not bat.

Bowling: Carter 12–4–31–3; Graham 5–1–27–0; Golding 12–0–43–0; Caley 12–0–53–0; Gofton 7–0–60–0; Miller 12–0–77–2.

Suffolk

S. M. Clements run out	15	A. K. Golding b Lynch	15
S. J. Halliday c Lynch b Smith	2	†A. D. Brown c Russell b Boden	0
J. L. Clinch c Cunliffe b Boden	18	D. M. Carter not out	3
M. J. Peck c Wright b Boden	49	L-b 5, w 8, n-b 12	25
*P. J. Caley c Wright b Boden	41		—
R. P. Gofton lbw b Boden	6	1/4 2/36 3/60 (58.4 overs) 177	
I. D. Graham c Russell b Srinath	0	4/137 5/149 6/151	
C. A. Miller c Wright b Boden	3	7/151 8/155 9/155	

Bowling: Srinath 8–1–16–1; Smith 9–1–28–1; Alleyne 12–1–40–0; Boden 12–2–26–6; Ball 12–1–39–0; Lynch 3.4–0–11–1; Symonds 2–0–12–0.

Umpires: D. J. Halfyard and M. J. Kitchen.

LANCASHIRE v NORFOLK

At Manchester, June 27. Lancashire won by eight wickets. Toss: Lancashire.
Rogers was run out without a run on the board, and Wasim then struck twice to leave Norfolk 11 for three. But Goldsmith, former Test player Neil Foster and Harvey weighed in, lifting them to 188. That scarcely troubled Lancashire, however. Gallian reached his century with a boundary as they overtook Norfolk in the 41st over.
Man of the Match: J. E. R. Gallian.

Norfolk

C. J. Rogers run out	0	N. Fox c Wasim Akram b Watkinson	20
S. G. Plumb b Wasim Akram	5	R. A. Bunting b Austin	9
S. C. Goldsmith lbw b Watkinson	47	†S. C. Crowley not out	2
C. Amos b Wasim Akram	4	B 1, l-b 2, w 2, n-b 14	19
*D. R. Thomas c Hegg b Austin	6		—
N. A. Foster c Hegg b Martin	36	1/0 2/5 3/11 (59.2 overs) 188	
S. R. Harvey lbw b Watkinson	39	4/36 5/96 6/122	
M. G. Powell lbw b Martin	1	7/126 8/169 9/182	

Bowling: Wasim Akram 12–1–46–2; Martin 10–4–25–2; Austin 11.2–3–24–2; Watkinson 11–3–41–3; Gallian 3–0–19–0; Yates 12–0–30–0.

Lancashire

J. E. R. Gallian not out	101
M. A. Atherton c Powell b Bunting	17
J. P. Crawley st Crowley b Powell	22
N. H. Fairbrother not out	34
B 1, l-b 6, w 7, n-b 2	16

1/40 2/122   (2 wkts, 40.4 overs) 190

G. D. Lloyd, *M. Watkinson, Wasim Akram, †W. K. Hegg, I. D. Austin, G. Yates and P. J. Martin did not bat.

Bowling: Foster 6–0–37–0; Bunting 6–1–18–1; Powell 12–0–60–1; Plumb 3–0–23–0; Thomas 8–0–25–0; Goldsmith 5.4–0–20–0.

Umpires: M. J. Harris and B. Leadbeater.

LEICESTERSHIRE v HAMPSHIRE

At Leicester, June 27. Leicestershire won by virtue of their higher score after 30 overs. Toss: Hampshire.

Hampshire's victory seemed assured when Leicestershire were nine down in the 55th over, still 33 behind, but they were squeezed out on a technical knockout. Both teams finished on 204 for nine, but Leicestershire had scored 101 for four from their first 30 overs to Hampshire's 91 for three. This was the first time the arbitrary 30-over rule had had to be invoked. It would have been irrelevant without last man Pierson. Despite a broken finger, he and Mullally plundered 32 off Connor and Stephenson before left-armer Maru bowled the final over. Mullally was beaten, then nearly stumped, then managed a single to draw level. Having checked the position with the umpires, Pierson coolly blocked the last three balls. On a slow pitch, Hampshire just passed 200 after a mid-innings stutter, with Pierson taking three for 36.

Man of the Match: A. R. K. Pierson.

Hampshire

R. S. M. Morris c Mason b Pierson	23	S. D. Udal not out	14
V. P. Terry c Mason b Pierson	34	R. J. Maru run out	1
R. A. Smith c Robinson b Maddy	45	C. A. Connor not out	1
*M. C. J. Nicholas c Robinson			
b Pierson	0	B 2, l-b 5, w 5	12
P. R. Whitaker run out	13		—
J. P. Stephenson b Parsons	34	1/53 2/89 3/89 (9 wkts, 60 overs)	204
K. D. James b Maddy	9	4/116 5/125 6/151	
†A. N. Aymes b Parsons	18	7/179 8/193 9/198	

Bowling: Parsons 12–2–46–2; Mullally 10–2–32–0; Dakin 3–0–15–0; Pierson 12–0–36–3; Mason 12–1–30–0; Maddy 11–1–38–2.

Leicestershire

†P. A. Nixon c Aymes b Connor	5	T. J. Mason run out	5
*N. E. Briers lbw b Connor	15	A. D. Mullally not out	10
J. J. Whitaker b Connor	0	A. R. K. Pierson not out	20
B. F. Smith c Aymes b Udal	27	L-b 14, w 2, n-b 2	18
P. E. Robinson c and b Maru	40		—
J. M. Dakin c Stephenson b James	26	1/10 2/16 3/31 (9 wkts, 60 overs)	204
D. L. Maddy c Terry b Connor	34	4/80 5/110 6/142	
G. J. Parsons b Stephenson	4	7/159 8/167 9/171	

Bowling: Connor 12–4–41–4; James 10–3–21–1; Udal 12–1–33–1; Maru 10–0–39–1; Stephenson 10–0–39–1; Whitaker 6–0–17–0.

Umpires: K. J. Lyons and G. Sharp.

NORTHAMPTONSHIRE v HOLLAND

At Northampton, June 27. Northamptonshire won by seven wickets. Toss: Holland.

Holland had a good debut in British competitive cricket, scoring 267 against the Championship leaders, Northamptonshire – who had, however, played 11 one-day games in 1995 and beaten only Scotland. Though the Dutch were more used to matting pitches than grass, Clarke, the 46-year-old Barbadian, and the Australian Cantrell opened with a stand of 88 in 19 overs; Holland were 150 for one halfway through the innings. Kumble's unfamiliar leg-spin stifled the later order, and an inexperienced attack, missing the injured Bakker as well as those Dutch bowlers signed up with English counties, had a stiff task.

Montgomerie and Fordham put on 124 but Northamptonshire took nearly 57 overs, and three big sixes from Loye, to finish the match. Dutch manager John Wories wrote in the programme that he hoped his country would now be famous for cricket – as well as "dykes, tulips, windmills, cigars, cheese, drugs and free sex".

Man of the Match: N. E. Clarke.

Holland

N. E. Clarke c Penberthy b Capel	86	E. Gouka not out	8
P. E. Cantrell c Warren b Curran	47	H. Boerstra b Kumble	6
G. J. A. F. Aponso c Curran b Capel	23	F. Jansen not out	5
T. B. M. de Leede run out	8	B 3, l-b 19, w 5, n-b 2	29
R. R. A. Bradley b Kumble	13		—
*S. W. Lubbers b Kumble	34	1/88 2/152 3/170 (9 wkts, 60 overs)	267
†R. H. Scholte lbw b Kumble	2	4/186 5/205 6/213	
W. F. Stelling c Warren b Curran	6	7/236 8/251 9/261	

Bowling: Taylor 4–1–26–0; Mallender 6–1–24–0; Curran 11–0–44–2; Kumble 12–0–50–4; Penberthy 4–0–30–0; Bailey 12–2–28–0; Capel 11–0–43–2.

Northamptonshire

R. R. Montgomerie c and b Gouka	69	K. M. Curran not out	21
A. Fordham c and b Lubbers	99	W 4, n-b 2	6
*R. J. Bailey b Lubbers	25		
M. B. Loye not out	49	1/124 2/180 3/205 (3 wkts, 56.5 overs)	269

†R. J. Warren, D. J. Capel, A. L. Penberthy, A. Kumble, N. A. Mallender and J. P. Taylor did not bat.

Bowling: Stelling 10–2–45–0; Boerstra 4–0–14–0; Aponso 12–0–52–0; Jansen 11.5–1–68–0; Lubbers 12–0–58–2; de Leede 5–0–22–0; Gouka 2–0–10–1.

Umpires: J. D. Bond and A. G. T. Whitehead.

NOTTINGHAMSHIRE v SCOTLAND

At Nottingham, June 27. Nottinghamshire won by eight wickets. Toss: Nottinghamshire.

Scotland were eight for three after Pick claimed a hat-trick of lbws, only the eighth hat-trick in the competition, and the first for seven years. Storie, batting 59 overs for his 56, and West Indian Test star Malcolm Marshall added 80 for the next wicket. But it was still nowhere near enough. Pollard's unbeaten 83 was his sixth in successive one-day innings, three each side of a month's lay-off.

Man of the Match: R. A. Pick.

Scotland

B. M. W. Patterson lbw b Pick	2	†D. A. Orr b Cairns	9
*A. C. Storie lbw b Pick	56	I. M. Stanger not out	12
G. B. J. McGurk lbw b Pick	0	K. L. P. Sheridan not out	1
G. Salmond lbw b Pick	0	L-b 12, w 16, n-b 4	32
M. D. Marshall c Archer b Wileman	45		—
J. G. Williamson lbw b Pennett	1	1/6 2/8 3/8 (9 wkts, 60 overs)	171
M. J. D. Allingham b Cairns	13	4/88 5/101 6/130	
J. W. Govan b Pick	0	7/131 8/146 9/164	

Bowling: Pick 11–0–23–5; Pennett 12–4–22–1; Cairns 12–1–39–2; Hindson 11–1–26–0; Chapman 12–1–40–0; Wileman 2–0–9–1.

Nottinghamshire

P. R. Pollard not out	....	83
*R. T. Robinson c and b Sheridan	.....	28
P. Johnson c Salmond b Govan	....	0
C. L. Cairns not out	....	48
L-b 1, w 10, n-b 2	....	13

1/82 2/91   (2 wkts, 36.3 overs) 172

G. F. Archer, R. J. Chapman, J. R. Wileman, †W. M. Noon, R. A. Pick, J. E. Hindson and D. B. Pennett did not bat.

Bowling: Marshall 9–0–32–0; Stanger 6–0–35–0; Sheridan 7–0–39–1; Allingham 3.3–0–24–0; Govan 7–0–24–1; Williamson 4–0–17–0.

Umpires: K. E. Palmer and P. B. Wight.

STAFFORDSHIRE v KENT

At Stone, June 27. Kent won by 91 runs. Toss: Kent.

Potter – on Kent's books ten years earlier – reached a century with his third six, to help Staffordshire to a highly respectable 258. The initial momentum came from Dean and Cartledge, who ran up 57 in nine overs. But Kent had already scored 349, the second-biggest total of the day. Taylor and Cowdrey put on 100 and there were short blasts from de Silva, Fleming and McCague.

Man of the Match: L. Potter.

Kent

D. P. Fulton c and b Ridgway	....	19	M. M. Patel c Dean b Heap	 4
T. R. Ward c Humphries b Potter	.....	53	M. J. McCague not out	 31
N. R. Taylor b Heap	....	86		
*P. A. de Silva c Shaw b Brown	....	24	L-b 2, w 4, n-b 2	 8
G. R. Cowdrey b Ridgway	....	65		
M. A. Ealham c Potter b Ridgway	...	5	1/38 2/94 3/126	(8 wkts, 60 overs) 349
M. V. Fleming c Humphries b Ridgway	35	4/226 5/257 6/293	
†S. C. Willis not out	....	19	7/298 8/306	

A. P. Igglesden did not bat.

Bowling: Newman 12–2–76–0; Heap 12–1–58–2; Ridgway 12–1–62–4; Potter 12–0–79–1; Brown 12–1–72–1.

Staffordshire

S. J. Dean c McCague b Ealham	......	29	†M. I. Humphries b de Silva	 21
D. Cartledge c Willis b Ealham	......	26	P. G. Newman not out	 28
K. N. Patel run out	....	1	B 4, l-b 9, w 12	 25
L. Potter not out	....	105		
P. F. Shaw c Cowdrey b Patel	....	9	1/57 2/62 3/63	(6 wkts, 60 overs) 258
*N. J. Archer c Ward b Patel	....	14	4/117 5/148 6/197	

P. F. Ridgway, T. M. Heap and J. F. Brown did not bat.

Bowling: McCague 6–0–34–0; Igglesden 7–0–22–0; Ealham 5–0–17–2; Patel 12–1–40–2; Fleming 12–0–43–0; de Silva 12–0–45–1; Ward 3–0–14–0; Cowdrey 2–0–21–0; Fulton 1–0–9–0.

Umpires: P. Adams and R. Palmer.

SURREY v BERKSHIRE

At The Oval, June 27. Surrey won by nine wickets. Toss: Berkshire. First-team debut: A. J. Tudor.

Surrey won the shortest encounter of the day, bowling out Berkshire inside 52 overs and needing less than half that to pass a target of 149. Only wicket-keeper Horner reached 30 for Berkshire, with Benjamin, bowling tightly for four wickets, and Stewart, taking six catches, sharing the honours. Bicknell and Butcher saw Surrey into the second round by tea-time.

Man of the Match: J. E. Benjamin.

Berkshire

G. E. Loveday c Stewart b Tudor	.....	15
A. Habib lbw b Rackemann	....	3
J. R. Wood c Stewart b Rackemann	..	10
S. D. Myles lbw b Benjamin	....	2
*M. L. Simmons c Stewart b Butcher	..	15
D. A. Shaw c Stewart b Hollioake	.....	9
†R. W. Horner c Stewart b Benjamin	..	32
P. J. Oxley b Benjamin	....	7

R. J. Pitcher not out	....	16
D. J. B. Hartley c Stewart b Benjamin	.	0
D. J. Foster c Shahid b Rackemann	..	21
L-b 1, w 15, n-b 2	....	18

1/13 2/24 3/31   (51.1 overs) 148
4/34 5/56 6/65
7/95 8/109 9/109

Bowling: Benjamin 12–2–20–4; Rackemann 9.1–1–40–3; Tudor 10–0–27–1; Pigott 10–1–33–0; Hollioake 6–2–22–1; Butcher 4–2–5–1.

Surrey

D. J. Bicknell not out	....	52
J. D. Ratcliffe c Simmons b Oxley	.....	4
M. A. Butcher not out	....	79
L-b 2, w 2, n-b 12	....	16

1/11   (1 wkt, 24.2 overs) 151

*†A. J. Stewart, A. D. Brown, A. J. Hollioake, N. Shahid, A. J. Tudor, A. C. S. Pigott, J. E. Benjamin and C. G. Rackemann did not bat.

Bowling: Foster 4–0–31–0; Oxley 5–0–22–1; Hartley 7–0–55–0; Pitcher 6.2–0–32–0; Myles 1–0–6–0; Shaw 1–0–3–0.

Umpires: R. Julian and M. K. Reed.

SUSSEX v DEVON

At Hove, June 27. Sussex won by seven wickets. Toss: Devon.

Devon, the reigning minor champions, edged out Holland for the best non-first-class total of the day, 267 for four. Folland, who had scored a Benson and Hedges century for the Minor Counties and a Sunday League one for Somerset, added one in this tournament, putting on 157 with Gaywood. But Lenham replied with his maiden one-day hundred, sharing large stands with Newell and Greenfield.

Man of the Match: N. J. Lenham.

Devon

N. R. Gaywood b Lewry	....	69
J. G. Wyatt lbw b Lewry	....	0
N. A. Folland c Hemmings b Stephenson	.	104
*P. M. Roebuck not out	....	46
G. T. J. Townsend b Lewry	....	6

A. J. Pugh not out	....	18
B 1, l-b 15, w 2, n-b 6	....	24

1/2 2/159   (4 wkts, 60 overs) 267
3/222 4/236

†C. M. W. Read, K. Donohue, J. Rhodes, M. C. Woodman and A. W. Allin did not bat.

Bowling: Stephenson 12–0–66–1; Lewry 12–1–63–3; Hemmings 12–1–32–0; Giddins 11–1–41–0; Salisbury 12–0–44–0; Greenfield 1–0–5–0.

Sussex

N. J. Lenham not out	129	F. D. Stephenson not out	37
K. Newell c Townsend b Wyatt	48	L-b 3, w 9, n-b 4	16
K. Greenfield run out	40		
*A. P. Wells b Allin	1	1/92 2/207 3/209 (3 wkts, 55.2 overs) 271	

D. R. Law, †P. Moores, I. D. K. Salisbury, J. D. Lewry, E. E. Hemmings and E. S. H. Giddins did not bat.

Bowling: Donohue 10–1–58–0; Woodman 9–1–40–0; Allin 12–0–56–1; Roebuck 11–1–39–0; Rhodes 9–0–45–0; Wyatt 4–0–25–1; Gaywood 0.2–0–5–0.

Umpires: D. J. Constant and B. Dudleston.

WARWICKSHIRE v SOMERSET

At Birmingham, June 27. Warwickshire won by 18 runs. Toss: Warwickshire.

A flat pitch produced 696 runs in one of the round's two all-first-class matches. Set to score 358 – more than any side had made batting second in this competition – Somerset were well up with the rate until the last few overs, helped by Warwickshire's extravagance with extras. But they had been losing batsmen steadily since Harden and Parsons, who added 134 in 22 overs, were parted, and Reeve's fourth wicket effectively halted their charge. Knight's 151, his maiden one-day hundred, was the solid base of Warwickshire's massive 357. He hit 14 fours and three sixes before falling in the final over, having put on 178 with Moles and 146 in 20 overs with Ostler, whose 76 took just 59 balls.

Man of the Match: N. V. Knight.

Warwickshire

A. J. Moles lbw b Mushtaq Ahmed	90	P. A. Smith not out	4
N. V. Knight c Trump b Kerr	151	B 10, l-b 7, w 7, n-b 6	30
D. P. Ostler c Harden b Kerr	76		
N. M. K. Smith not out	6	1/178 2/324 3/348 (3 wkts, 60 overs) 357	

R. G. Twose, T. L. Penney, *D. A. Reeve, †K. J. Piper, A. A. Donald and T. A. Munton did not bat.

Bowling: Rose 11–0–91–0; Kerr 11–0–74–2; Trump 10–0–44–0; Parsons 8–1–44–0; Mushtaq Ahmed 12–1–56–1; Ecclestone 8–0–31–0.

Somerset

M. N. Lathwell c Donald b Reeve	15	Mushtaq Ahmed c Twose b Reeve	28
*P. D. Bowler c Penney b Munton	8	J. I. D. Kerr c Munton b Reeve	3
R. J. Harden b N. M. K. Smith	104	H. R. J. Trump not out	10
G. D. Rose c Donald b Reeve	30	B 5, l-b 15, w 12, n-b 8	40
K. A. Parsons c Twose b Munton	48		
S. C. Ecclestone lbw b N. M. K. Smith	0	1/25 2/32 3/93 (9 wkts, 60 overs) 339	
†P. C. L. Holloway not out	50	4/227 5/227 6/231	
R. J. Turner run out	3	7/235 8/292 9/305	

Bowling: Donald 12–0–67–0; Munton 12–0–40–2; Reeve 12–0–54–4; P. A. Smith 4–0–43–0; Twose 10–0–55–0; N. M. K. Smith 10–0–60–2.

Umpires: T. E. Jesty and P. Willey.

WORCESTERSHIRE v CUMBERLAND

At Worcester, June 27. Worcestershire won by 65 runs. Toss: Cumberland.

Only two batsmen reached 30 in the match. Both Worcestershire openers were caught behind at seven and Cumberland were delighted when Hick and Moody were gone by 81. But Haynes added 102 with Solanki and went on to a maiden one-day century. Cumberland started as badly as Worcestershire had done. Their 192 owed everything to Berry, who made 81 before being caught in the deep.

Man of the Match: G. R. Haynes.

Worcestershire

T. S. Curtis c Dutton b Scothern	4	P. J. Newport run out	0
W. P. C. Weston c Dutton b Sharp	1	N. V. Radford not out	19
G. A. Hick c Kippax b O'Shaughnessy	25		
*T. M. Moody c Dutton b Makinson	27	B 1, l-b 3, w 8, n-b 6	18
G. R. Haynes not out	116		
V. S. Solanki c Berry b Kippax	29	1/7 2/7 3/52 (8 wkts, 60 overs)	257
†S. J. Rhodes c Dutton b Makinson	7	4/81 5/183 6/205	
R. K. Illingworth run out	11	7/226 8/226	

P. A. Thomas did not bat.

Bowling: Sharp 12–1–37–1; Scothern 12–2–53–1; Makinson 11–1–44–2; O'Shaughnessy 11–1–49–1; Kippax 7–1–35–1; Ellwood 7–1–35–0.

Cumberland

G. J. Clarke c Rhodes b Thomas	3	M. G. Scothern c Rhodes b Hick	18
D. J. Pearson c Rhodes b Radford	9	R. Ellwood not out	24
D. Patel c Hick b Newport	0	M. A. Sharp not out	1
P. J. Berry c Radford b Hick	81	B 3, l-b 9, w 12, n-b 6	30
S. J. O'Shaughnessy b Haynes	10		
D. J. Makinson c Rhodes b Illingworth	0	1/4 2/4 3/42 (9 wkts, 60 overs)	192
*†S. M. Dutton b Moody b Thomas	6	4/74 5/75 6/101	
S. A. J. Kippax c Haynes b Solanki	10	7/128 8/147 9/183	

Bowling: Newport 7–2–19–1; Thomas 10–2–30–2; Illingworth 12–2–25–1; Radford 6–2–10–1; Haynes 6–0–17–1; Solanki 11–0–48–1; Hick 6–1–15–2; Curtis 2–0–16–0.

Umpires: A. A. Jones and B. J. Meyer.

YORKSHIRE v IRELAND

At Leeds, June 27. Yorkshire won by 71 runs. Toss: Ireland.
Ireland were celebrating when Eagleson and Patterson reduced Yorkshire to 31 for three. But Kellett and White scored centuries while adding 207 in 44 overs. White later took three wickets, ran out Rea and caught Smyth. Warke and Rea had an opening partnership of 92, enabling Ireland to reach 200 for the first time in their 16th game in the tournament.
Man of the Match: S. A. Kellett.

Yorkshire

S. A. Kellett run out	107	P. J. Hartley not out	4
M. P. Vaughan c Smyth b Eagleson	4	A. C. Morris not out	1
*D. Byas c and b Eagleson	4	B 1, l-b 4, w 12, n-b 10	27
M. G. Bevan c Smyth b Patterson	6		
C. White c Rea b Patterson	113	1/14 2/18 3/31 (6 wkts, 60 overs)	299
D. Gough b Patterson	33	4/238 5/277 6/297	

†C. A. Chapman, R. D. Stemp and M. A. Robinson did not bat.

Bowling: Eagleson 12–1–65–2; Patterson 12–2–66–3; Harrison 12–0–35–0; Graham 9–0–41–0; Gillespie 1–0–10–0; Doak 9–0–44–0; Lewis 5–0–33–0.

Ireland

S. J. S. Warke c Kellett b Morris	82	P. G. Gillespie c Kellett b White	5
M. P. Rea run out	48	R. L. Eagleson not out	0
S. G. Smyth c White b Hartley	26	B 4, l-b 13, w 4, n-b 2	23
*D. A. Lewis lbw b Hartley	0		
N. G. Doak lbw b White	1	1/92 2/140 3/140 (7 wkts, 60 overs)	228
G. D. Harrison c Chapman b White	23	4/149 5/194	
S. Graham not out	23	6/208 7/228	

M. W. Patterson and †S. Ogilby did not bat.

Bowling: Gough 9–1–27–0; Hartley 12–2–35–2; Robinson 12–0–37–0; Stemp 7–0–31–0; White 12–2–38–3; Morris 8–0–43–1.

Umpires: H. D. Bird and C. T. Spencer.

SECOND ROUND

DURHAM v GLOUCESTERSHIRE

At Chester-le-Street, July 12. Gloucestershire won by 159 runs. Toss: Durham.

With Prabhakar absent because of flu, Durham failed to exploit steamy conditions and uneven bounce, and Gloucestershire's total of 276 for six was well above par. Wright was quick to spot the difficulties and eliminated risk in making 84 off 172 balls, which earned him his second successive match award, while Lynch provided timely acceleration with 58 off 55 balls. Both Durham openers, Roseberry and Larkins, quickly fell lbw to Srinath. With figures of two for nine in six overs, Srinath could afford to drop two sitters at mid-on as the hosts made a complete hash of their reply. They could not manage even half their target and were all out in 42 overs.

Man of the Match: A. J. Wright.

Gloucestershire

A. J. Wright c Walker b Brown	84	*†R. C. Russell not out	14
M. G. N. Windows lbw b Walker	0	J. Srinath not out	11
R. J. Cunliffe b Saxelby	40	B 1, l-b 11, w 11	23
M. A. Lynch b Betts	58		—
M. W. Alleyne c Blenkiron b Brown	29	1/2 2/77 3/183　　(6 wkts, 60 overs) 276	
A. Symonds c Morris b Brown	17	4/230 5/249 6/251	

M. C. J. Ball, K. E. Cooper and A. M. Smith did not bat.

Bowling: Brown 12–1–64–3; Walker 12–2–49–1; Betts 12–0–47–1; Bainbridge 12–0–46–0; Saxelby 9–0–44–1; Blenkiron 3–0–14–0.

Durham

*M. A. Roseberry lbw b Srinath	1	A. Walker lbw b Cooper	12
W. Larkins lbw b Srinath	9	S. J. E. Brown not out	1
J. E. Morris c Russell b Cooper	10	M. M. Betts b Ball	9
S. Hutton c Wright b Alleyne	20	L-b 1, w 6	7
D. A. Blenkiron c and b Cooper	29		—
P. Bainbridge run out	10	1/9 2/16 3/38　　(42 overs) 117	
M. Saxelby run out	4	4/48 5/69 6/80	
†D. G. C. Ligertwood st Russell b Ball	5	7/92 8/106 9/107	

Bowling: Srinath 6–1–9–2; Smith 7–1–26–0; Cooper 8–1–15–3; Alleyne 10–3–21–1; Ball 11–0–45–2.

Umpires: K. J. Lyons and G. Sharp.

ESSEX v YORKSHIRE

At Chelmsford, July 12. Yorkshire won by 97 runs. Toss: Yorkshire.

An unbroken stand of 120 in 11 overs between Bevan and White hurried Yorkshire past 300. Though Ilott and Cousins initially tied down the openers, Kellett scored a solid 92 and then Bevan and White accelerated. The principal casualty was Waugh, Bevan's team-mate from New South Wales. He went for eight an over and his analysis was the most expensive ever for a first-class county in this competition. Hussain and Robinson had put on 100 for Essex's second wicket when Hussain's foot slipped as he set off for a run and hit his stumps. That unlucky dismissal started a collapse and Essex were bowled out with nearly 12 overs to spare.

Man of the Match: M. G. Bevan.

Yorkshire

S. A. Kellett c Robinson b Ilott	92	C. White not out	51
M. P. Vaughan c Hussain b Such	5	B 4, l-b 3, w 1, n-b 10	18
*D. Byas run out	50		
M. G. Bevan not out	91	1/29 2/114 3/187 (3 wkts, 60 overs)	307

B. Parker, †R. J. Blakey, A. P. Grayson, D. Gough, P. J. Hartley and M. A. Robinson did not bat.

Bowling: Ilott 12–4–52–1; Cousins 12–1–60–0; Irani 12–1–56–0; Such 12–2–36–1; Waugh 12–1–96–0.

Essex

G. A. Gooch run out	17	M. C. Ilott run out	4
D. D. J. Robinson b Hartley	55	P. M. Such lbw b Hartley	0
N. Hussain hit wkt b Robinson	48	D. M. Cousins run out	0
M. E. Waugh c Kellett b Robinson	2	L-b 12, w 3	15
*P. J. Prichard not out	35		
R. C. Irani c Grayson b White	12	1/28 2/128 3/132 (48.2 overs)	210
J. J. B. Lewis c Blakey b Gough	1	4/145 5/166 6/167	
†R. J. Rollins lbw b White	21	7/202 8/207 9/207	

Bowling: Gough 9–1–46–1; Hartley 10–1–34–2; Robinson 9.2–1–36–2; White 8–0–24–2; Grayson 12–0–58–0.

Umpires: G. I. Burgess and K. E. Palmer.

LANCASHIRE v WORCESTERSHIRE

At Manchester, July 12. Lancashire won by four wickets. Toss: Worcestershire.

With Fairbrother dropping out because of a hamstring strain, Titchard came into the side and responded with 92 crucial runs. He shared in Lancashire's best opening partnership in this competition, 167 in 40 overs, with Atherton. Home nerves were tested when they lost five wickets in seven overs but Wasim Akram brought up victory with an over to spare. Only Hick, who played beautifully for his 87 in 78 balls, and Curtis, who batted through for an unbeaten 106, passed 30 for Worcestershire. Moody became uncharacteristically bogged down, struggling to ten in 14 overs, and they fell well short of the 300 needed on a good pitch.

Man of the Match: S. P. Titchard.

Worcestershire

T. S. Curtis not out	106	S. R. Lampitt b Wasim Akram	29
W. P. C. Weston run out	0	†S. J. Rhodes not out	2
G. A. Hick c Titchard b Austin	87		
*T. M. Moody c Wasim Akram b Chapple	10	B 1, l-b 7, w 9, n-b 4	21
G. R. Haynes c and b Watkinson	2	1/0 2/143 3/181 (6 wkts, 60 overs)	271
D. A. Leatherdale c Atherton b Yates	14	4/187 5/221 6/265	

V. S. Solanki, P. J. Newport and P. Mirza did not bat.

Bowling: Wasim Akram 12–3–45–1; Chapple 12–0–69–1; Austin 12–0–50–1; Yates 12–1–50–1; Watkinson 12–1–49–1.

Lancashire

M. A. Atherton c Moody b Newport	70	Wasim Akram not out	13
S. P. Titchard st Rhodes b Hick	92	I. D. Austin not out	7
J. P. Crawley c Hick b Newport	31	B 3, l-b 3, w 9, n-b 10	25
N. J. Speak run out	20		
G. D. Lloyd run out	16	1/167 2/210 3/211 (6 wkts, 59 overs)	275
*M. Watkinson b Mirza	1	4/236 5/245 6/260	

†W. K. Hegg, G. Chapple and G. Yates did not bat.

Bowling: Haynes 8–1–26–0; Solanki 9–0–43–0; Newport 12–1–53–2; Lampitt 7–1–36–0; Hick 12–0–50–1; Mirza 11–0–61–1.

Umpires: J. H. Harris and D. R. Shepherd.

LEICESTERSHIRE v GLAMORGAN

At Leicester, July 12. Glamorgan won by six wickets. Toss: Leicestershire. County debut: I. J. Sutcliffe.

The NatWest represented Leicestershire's last hope of salvaging something from what was turning into a rough season. With their injury crisis unresolved, the arrival of Sutcliffe and Macmillan, two in-form Oxford University batsmen, was a bit like the cavalry coming over the hill. Both were thrown into action and Sutcliffe scored a splendid 68. Despite his efforts, however, Leicestershire scored only 197 for seven on a slow, low pitch. Though Mullally and Pierson reduced Glamorgan to 32 for three in 15 overs, a fourth-wicket stand of 161 between Cottey and Hemp, who made his first half-century in the competition, saw them home with more than five overs to spare.

Man of the Match: D. L. Hemp.

Leicestershire

*N. E. Briers run out	8	A. R. K. Pierson run out	10
I. J. Sutcliffe lbw b Watkin	68	G. J. Parsons not out	25
G. I. Macmillan c Anthony b Croft	9	B 4, l-b 6, w 3	13
V. J. Wells b Dale	23		
P. E. Robinson run out	5	1/29 2/55 3/92 (7 wkts, 60 overs) 197	
J. M. Dakin c Metson b Dale	5	4/98 5/107	
†P. A. Nixon not out	31	6/139 7/163	

T. J. Mason and A. D. Mullally did not bat.

Bowling: Watkin 12–3–39–1; Anthony 11–1–36–0; Thomas 9–1–36–0; Croft 12–2–30–1; Dale 9–1–28–2; Cottey 7–0–18–0.

Glamorgan

S. P. James c Sutcliffe b Mullally	12	A. Dale not out	2
*H. Morris c Parsons b Pierson	19	B 12, l-b 11, w 3	26
M. P. Maynard c Nixon b Mullally	0		
P. A. Cottey not out	61	1/26 2/30 (4 wkts, 54.2 overs) 198	
D. L. Hemp c Mason b Macmillan	78	3/32 4/193	

R. D. B. Croft, H. A. G. Anthony, †C. P. Metson, S. L. Watkin and S. D. Thomas did not bat.

Bowling: Mullally 9–3–27–2; Parsons 12–2–37–0; Pierson 9.2–3–34–1; Dakin 9–3–22–0; Mason 12–0–42–0; Macmillan 3–0–13–1.

Umpires: D. J. Constant and R. Palmer.

NOTTINGHAMSHIRE v NORTHAMPTONSHIRE

At Nottingham, July 12. Northamptonshire won by 38 runs. Toss: Northamptonshire.

Fordham and Montgomerie gave Northamptonshire the launch pad to their highest total in the competition against first-class opposition, with 232 in 43 overs, a county record for any wicket in the NatWest. Fordham hit 11 fours and four sixes in his 132, from 142 balls, while Montgomerie reached a maiden NatWest hundred. Bailey kept that momentum going and then turned in a crucial spell of off-spin. Until that point, Nottinghamshire had been scenting an unlikely win. Pollard, with a run-a-ball 96, his eighth half-century in nine one-day innings, had raised their hopes during an opening stand of 180 in 33 overs with Robinson. But Nottinghamshire fell away after Bailey dismissed Robinson and Johnson in one over.

Man of the Match: R. J. Bailey.

Northamptonshire

R. R. Montgomerie st Noon b Hindson	109	A. L. Penberthy run out	1
A. Fordham lbw b Evans	132	J. N. Snape not out	2
*R. J. Bailey c Robinson b Hindson	48	B 2, l-b 6, w 10, n-b 2	20
M. B. Loye b Wileman	7		
K. M. Curran c Evans b Cairns	18	1/232 2/305 3/312 (8 wkts, 60 overs) 352
D. J. Capel c Pollard b Pick	11	4/322 5/343 6/348
†R. J. Warren c and b Cairns	4	7/348 8/352

A. Kumble and J. P. Taylor did not bat.

Bowling: Pick 10–1–79–1; Cairns 12–1–41–2; Evans 12–1–64–1; Afzaal 11–0–57–0; Hindson 9–0–57–2; Wileman 6–0–46–1.

Nottinghamshire

P. R. Pollard b Kumble	96	K. P. Evans lbw b Taylor	14
*R. T. Robinson b Bailey	73	J. E. Hindson not out	16
P. Johnson c Snape b Bailey	3		
C. L. Cairns b Snape	27	B 4, l-b 11, w 8, n-b 2	25
G. F. Archer c Warren b Taylor	15		
J. R. Wileman c Penberthy b Snape	12	1/180 2/189 3/190 (8 wkts, 60 overs) 314
†W. M. Noon c Bailey b Kumble	7	4/227 5/235 6/252
U. Afzaal not out	26	7/253 8/296

R. A. Pick did not bat.

Bowling: Taylor 12–1–49–2; Capel 7–0–41–0; Kumble 12–0–49–2; Penberthy 3–0–26–0; Snape 12–0–67–2; Curran 4–0–25–0; Bailey 10–0–42–2.

Umpires: H. D. Bird and B. Leadbeater.

SURREY v MIDDLESEX

At The Oval, July 12. Middlesex won by 79 runs. Toss: Middlesex.

In another of the Cup collapses which Surrey have made a speciality, they lost six wickets for 25 in fewer than eight overs. Only Bicknell applied himself, until he was bowled by the wily Emburey, who conceded only 23 in 11 overs. But Johnson deserved credit for ripping out the heart of the innings, just when Surrey threatened to get going. Middlesex scored 304 for the second time running in this tournament, and Radford marked his NatWest debut with a solid 82 in a valuable opening stand of 165 at four an over with Weekes. The middle order increased even that tempo and the last 16 overs brought 139. When 36, Gatting joined Gooch as the only batsmen to have scored 2,000 runs in this competition.

Man of the Match: J. E. Emburey.

Middlesex

P. N. Weekes c Pigott b Holloake	72	M. A. Feltham b Holloake	0
T. A. Radford c Nowell b Benjamin	82	R. L. Johnson not out	1
M. R. Ramprakash c Pigott b Benjamin	40	B 2, l-b 4, w 11, n-b 12	29
*M. W. Gatting c Shahid b Holloake	40		
†K. R. Brown c Butcher b Rackemann	34	1/165 2/189 3/230 (7 wkts, 60 overs) 304
J. D. Carr not out	5	4/284 5/298
D. J. Nash c Thorpe b Holloake	1	6/303 7/303

J. E. Emburey and A. R. C. Fraser did not bat.

Bowling: Rackemann 11–1–69–1; Benjamin 12–5–47–2; Butcher 8–0–29–0; Pigott 12–1–65–0; Nowell 5–0–35–0; Holloake 12–1–53–4.

Surrey

D. J. Bicknell b Emburey	77	J. E. Benjamin lbw b Johnson	7
M. A. Butcher st Brown b Emburey	26	R. W. Nowell not out	2
†G. J. Kersey c Brown b Fraser	21	C. G. Rackemann c Weekes b Feltham	6
G. P. Thorpe c Nash b Weekes	32	L-b 7, w 4	11
A. D. Brown b Johnson	24		
N. Shahid b Johnson	11	1/48 2/84 3/159	(55.5 overs) 225
*A. J. Hollioake st Brown b Feltham	5	4/174 5/200 6/201	
A. C. S. Pigott run out	3	7/207 8/215 9/218	

Bowling: Fraser 10–1–39–1; Johnson 12–1–41–3; Emburey 11–1–23–2; Nash 7–0–34–0; Weekes 10–0–57–1; Feltham 5.5–0–24–2.

Umpires: B. J. Meyer and P. B. Wight.

SUSSEX v DERBYSHIRE

At Hove, July 12. Derbyshire won by eight wickets. Toss: Sussex.

Sussex coach Norman Gifford laid into his side after this defeat, accusing them of taking their responsibilities too lightly. On a belter of a pitch, a total of 222 set no serious challenge to Derbyshire, with Adams in punishing form. He won the match by hitting Giddins for three successive fours, the first of which brought up his hundred. Earlier, he had added 100 in 24 overs with Rollins. In the home innings, Derbyshire's bowlers maintained an unyielding line and length. Barnett and Colin Wells, returning to face his old county and his brother Alan, conceded only 67 in their 24 overs; Hall and Newell batted solidly, but could not score quickly enough.

Man of the Match: C. J. Adams.

Sussex

C. W. J. Athey c Krikken b DeFreitas	20	J. D. Lewry not out	2
J. W. Hall c Malcolm b Cork	70	E. E. Hemmings not out	1
K. Greenfield c DeFreitas b Malcolm	2		
*A. P. Wells c Griffith b Barnett	15	L-b 11, w 9	20
K. Newell c Rollins b Cork	52		
F. D. Stephenson c Barnett b Cork	28	1/46 2/49 3/101	(8 wkts, 60 overs) 222
†P. Moores b Cork	8	4/160 5/206 6/206	
I. D. K. Salisbury run out	4	7/219 8/220	

E. S. H. Giddins did not bat.

Bowling: DeFreitas 12–2–24–1; Cork 11–0–50–4; Malcolm 9–0–45–1; Barnett 12–0–36–1; Wells 12–3–31–0; Griffith 4–0–25–0.

Derbyshire

*K. J. Barnett c Moores b Giddins	17
A. S. Rollins c Moores b Stephenson	56
C. J. Adams not out	109
D. J. Cullinan not out	29
B 4, l-b 2, w 2, n-b 6	14

1/45 2/145   (2 wkts, 53.5 overs) 225

W. A. Dessaur, C. M. Wells, D. G. Cork, P. A. J. DeFreitas, †K. M. Krikken, F. A. Griffith and D. E. Malcolm did not bat.

Bowling: Stephenson 10–1–48–1; Lewry 6–0–32–0; Giddins 10.5–0–49–1; Hemmings 12–1–31–0; Salisbury 12–1–39–0; Greenfield 1–0–8–0; Athey 2–0–12–0.

Umpires: V. A. Holder and A. G. T. Whitehead.

WARWICKSHIRE v KENT

At Birmingham, July 12. Warwickshire won by ten runs. Toss: Kent.

Warwickshire knocked Kent out of the NatWest Trophy at Edgbaston for the fourth year running. Kent hoped their luck had changed when Warwickshire were a jittery 11 for two, with the ball wobbling around on a slow pitch. But Smith and Brown took the attack to them. Smith went on to 65 and Twose added a responsible 93 not out. Ward gave Kent an excellent start in pursuit of a challenging 263, but he fell trying to force the pace. There was an element of panic as Kent's middle order played themselves in and got themselves out. Marsh, dropped when 18 on the mid-wicket boundary, batted sensibly enough to take Kent into the final over needing 14, but he was bowled by Reeve.

Man of the Match: R. G. Twose.

Warwickshire

N. V. Knight lbw b Wren	0	
N. M. K. Smith b de Silva	65	
D. P. Ostler c Marsh b McCague	5	
D. R. Brown c de Silva b McCague	21	
R. G. Twose not out	93	
*D. A. Reeve c Ealham b de Silva	6	
T. L. Penney b Headley	25	

P. A. Smith c Marsh b Fleming 7
†K. J. Piper not out 11
  L-b 11, w 12, n-b 6 29

1/0 2/11 3/80   (7 wkts, 60 overs) 262
4/133 5/155
6/209 7/244

A. A. Donald and T. A. Munton did not bat.

Bowling: Wren 10–1–51–1; McCague 10–1–42–2; Headley 12–0–40–1; Ealham 9–2–29–0; de Silva 12–0–45–2; Fleming 7–0–44–1.

Kent

D. P. Fulton lbw b Donald	4	
T. R. Ward c Knight b Munton	68	
N. R. Taylor lbw b P. A. Smith	2	
P. A. de Silva c Piper b Reeve	22	
G. R. Cowdrey b Reeve	19	
M. V. Fleming b Donald	12	
M. A. Ealham c Knight b P. A. Smith	18	
*†S. A. Marsh b Reeve	55	

M. J. McCague b Brown 3
D. W. Headley not out 24
T. N. Wren not out 1
  L-b 9, w 5, n-b 10 24

1/35 2/56 3/90   (9 wkts, 60 overs) 252
4/127 5/142 6/144
7/182 8/200 9/249

Bowling: Donald 12–1–51–2; Munton 12–0–47–1; N. M. K. Smith 5–0–16–0; P. A. Smith 12–1–47–2; Reeve 12–0–41–3; Brown 7–0–41–1.

Umpires: J. W. Holder and R. A. White.

QUARTER-FINALS

DERBYSHIRE v WARWICKSHIRE

At Derby, August 1. Warwickshire won by 116 runs. Toss: Warwickshire.

After losing Smith in the first over of the day, Warwickshire completely outplayed Derbyshire before a 6,000-strong crowd. Krikken broke a finger, so Rollins had to keep wicket, and DeFreitas and Cork suffered injuries as Warwickshire attacked freely. As so often, there was plenty of support throughout the order to go with fifties from Knight, Brown and Twose. At least two of Derbyshire's major batsmen had to succeed. But they were pinned down by Munton, who bowled through from the start and conceded only 13, rightly earning the match award, although Donald took five wickets. Once Barnett, who completed 1,000 runs in the competition, and Wells went, Warwickshire were assured of their fifth consecutive NatWest semi-final.

Man of the Match: T. A. Munton.

Warwickshire

N. V. Knight run out	71		T. L. Penney not out		22
N. M. K. Smith c Krikken b Malcolm	0		A. F. Giles not out		21
D. P. Ostler c Tweats b Cork	23		B 2, l-b 7, w 9		18
D. R. Brown c Cullinan b Barnett	58				
R. G. Twose c DeFreitas b Malcolm	51		1/1 2/40 3/138	(6 wkts, 60 overs)	290
*D. A. Reeve c Adams b DeFreitas	26		4/174 5/230 6/249		

†K. J. Piper, A. A. Donald and T. A. Munton did not bat.

Bowling: Malcolm 12–0–53–2; DeFreitas 12–4–27–1; Wells 6–0–30–0; Cork 10–0–57–1; Warner 12–0–63–0; Barnett 8–0–51–1.

Derbyshire

*K. J. Barnett c Piper b Smith	53		†K. M. Krikken not out		7
A. S. Rollins b Donald	2		A. E. Warner b Donald		0
C. J. Adams c Piper b Munton	10		D. E. Malcolm b Donald		8
D. J. Cullinan c Penney b Reeve	0		B 1, l-b 3, w 1		5
C. M. Wells c Penney b Smith	48				
T. A. Tweats c Reeve b Smith	16		1/11 2/28 3/29	(46.5 overs)	174
D. G. Cork c Knight b Donald	21		4/108 5/113 6/148		
P. A. J. DeFreitas b Donald	4		7/155 8/161 9/161		

Bowling: Donald 10.5–1–41–5; Munton 12–6–13–1; Reeve 6–0–27–1; Giles 4–0–25–0; Smith 10–1–36–3; Brown 4–0–28–0.

Umpires: J. D. Bond and G. I. Burgess.

GLAMORGAN v MIDDLESEX

At Cardiff, August 1. Glamorgan won by 66 runs. Toss: Glamorgan.

Glamorgan qualified for the semi-finals for only the third time – following 1977 and 1993 – after reducing Middlesex to 16 for four in the 14th over. A total of 242 was 30 short of what they had hoped for, but it ceased to matter when Ramprakash was out third ball and Gatting for two. A thunder-storm interrupted play but when it restarted at 7.30 p.m. Anthony immediately claimed the final two wickets, finishing, like Watkin, with four. But the match award went to Metson, who took an astonishing reflex catch as Brown attempted a reverse sweep. When Glamorgan had batted, James completed his 12th one-day fifty of the season, making the most of a pitch that got progressively slower.

Man of the Match: C. P. Metson.

Glamorgan

S. P. James c Carr b Emburey	56		†C. P. Metson b Johnson		20
*H. Morris c Emburey b Johnson	31		S. L. Watkin lbw b Nash		2
M. P. Maynard c Ramprakash			S. R. Barwick not out		1
b Johnson	0				
P. A. Cottey run out	19		L-b 11, w 4, n-b 4		19
D. L. Hemp b Weekes	37				
A. Dale run out	30		1/71 2/73 3/115	(9 wkts, 60 overs)	242
R. D. B. Croft not out	23		4/117 5/173 6/201		
H. A. G. Anthony lbw b Weekes	4		7/205 8/234 9/241		

Bowling: Fraser 12–2–36–0; Nash 8–0–36–1; Feltham 7–1–22–0; Johnson 9–2–33–3; Emburey 12–0–49–1; Weekes 12–0–55–2.

Middlesex

P. N. Weekes c Maynard b Watkin	2	M. A. Feltham b Anthony	37
J. C. Pooley c Metson b Anthony	8	J. E. Emburey lbw b Anthony	6
M. R. Ramprakash lbw b Watkin	0	A. R. C. Fraser not out	2
*M. W. Gatting lbw b Anthony	2	L-b 4, n-b 2	6
J. D. Carr c Croft b Watkin	62		
†K. R. Brown c Metson b Croft	17	1/4 2/4 3/11	(51.5 overs) 176
D. J. Nash lbw b Croft	1	4/16 5/54 6/56	
R. L. Johnson c James b Watkin	33	7/123 8/139 9/165	

Bowling: Watkin 11–4–26–4; Anthony 9.5–3–25–4; Dale 10–0–34–0; Croft 12–1–53–2; Barwick 9–0–34–0.

Umpires: T. E. Jesty and R. Julian.

GLOUCESTERSHIRE v NORTHAMPTONSHIRE

At Bristol, August 1. Northamptonshire won by 24 runs. Toss: Gloucestershire.

A crowd of 5,000 was left groaning as Gloucestershire badly mismanaged their reply. Far too much was asked of their later batsmen after the most pedestrian of starts. Hodgson, controversially selected after injury, took 22 overs to score eight singles and Wright could not compensate. Lynch, Symonds and Russell did their best; the rampaging Symonds scored 48 in 40 balls before he was bowled leaning back to cut Bailey's off-spin. That key success followed Bailey's earlier, oddly circumspect, 52. Yet, in this low-scoring, frustrating match, his calculated approach proved correct. Lamb was run out when beginning to chase and the late runs were left to Warren. Of the bowlers, Taylor and Srinath were the most successful, Cooper the most economical.

Man of the Match: R. J. Bailey.

Northamptonshire

R. R. Montgomerie c Russell b Srinath	18	J. N. Snape b Srinath	12
A. Fordham c Russell b Srinath	11	A. Kumble not out	6
R. J. Bailey c Srinath b Alleyne	52	J. P. Taylor b Srinath	0
*A. J. Lamb run out	40	L-b 7, w 6, n-b 12	25
K. M. Curran lbw b Ball	15		
D. J. Capel c Wright b Ball	0	1/29 2/41 3/103	(58.2 overs) 226
†R. J. Warren c Ball b Alleyne	44	4/129 5/129 6/195	
A. L. Penberthy c Russell b Cooper	3	7/203 8/207 9/226	

Bowling: Smith 11–0–56–0; Cooper 9–3–17–1; Srinath 11.2–1–38–4; Alleyne 8–0–35–2; Ball 12–2–40–2; Symonds 7–0–33–0.

Gloucestershire

A. J. Wright c Snape b Penberthy	36	K. E. Cooper b Taylor	5
M. G. N. Windows c Warren b Taylor	9	J. Srinath c Curran b Taylor	0
G. D. Hodgson c Kumble b Snape	8	A. M. Smith not out	0
M. A. Lynch c Warren b Snape	29	B 4, l-b 4, w 1	9
M. W. Alleyne c Bailey b Kumble	19		
A. Symonds b Bailey	48	1/21 2/52 3/66	(57.4 overs) 202
*†R. C. Russell c Curran b Taylor	27	4/110 5/110 6/183	
M. C. J. Ball c Lamb b Curran	12	7/197 8/199 9/199	

Bowling: Taylor 9.4–2–34–4; Curran 10–3–22–1; Penberthy 8–2–24–1; Capel 2.5–0–16–0; Snape 11.1–0–43–2; Kumble 12–3–34–1; Bailey 4–0–21–1.

Umpires: A. A. Jones and N. T. Plews.

YORKSHIRE v LANCASHIRE

At Leeds, August 1. Yorkshire won by two wickets. Toss: Lancashire.

A poor batting performance brought Lancashire's downfall on a good pitch with reasonable pace and bounce. Gough, playing against the wishes of the England selectors, who wanted him to rest an inflamed left foot, produced a hostile new-ball spell and Lancashire's top half got out to a series of unforced errors. A partnership of 70 from 21 overs between Fairbrother and Watkinson was not enough to rescue them; they were all out for 169 in the 54th over. But Yorkshire struggled in turn, particularly against the very accurate off-spin of Yates. Bevan worked his way carefully through 126 balls for a decisive unbeaten 60, while Metcalfe provided the necessary aggression as Yorkshire scrambled through with three balls to spare and eight wickets down. The gates were closed in the morning, with 18,900 inside and some 2,000 locked out.

Man of the Match: M. G. Bevan.

Lancashire

M. A. Atherton c Blakey b Gough	5	I. D. Austin not out 15
J. E. R. Gallian lbw b Robinson	7	G. Yates run out 9
J. P. Crawley lbw b White	13	G. Chapple lbw b Robinson 0
N. H. Fairbrother st Blakey b Grayson	46	L-b 2, w 2, n-b 8 12
G. D. Lloyd c Blakey b White	0	
*M. Watkinson c White b Robinson	55	(53.3 overs) 169
Wasim Akram c Byas b Bevan	0	1/8 2/14 3/47
†W. K. Hegg c Blakey b Hartley	7	4/47 5/117 6/118
		7/136 8/149 9/169

Bowling: Gough 9–2–18–1; Hartley 12–0–50–1; Robinson 10.3–2–21–3; White 9–0–28–2; Grayson 9–0–36–1; Bevan 4–0–14–1.

Yorkshire

S. A. Kellett c Hegg b Austin	6	A. P. Grayson c Hegg b Chapple	7
M. P. Vaughan c Fairbrother b Austin	14	D. Gough b Austin	10
*D. Byas c Hegg b Yates	31	P. J. Hartley not out	3
M. G. Bevan not out	60	W 3, n-b 2	5
C. White c Crawley b Watkinson	0	
A. A. Metcalfe c Fairbrother		1/20 2/29 3/66 (8 wkts, 59.3 overs) 170
b Watkinson	33	4/69 5/121 6/123
†R. J. Blakey run out	1	7/132 8/155

M. A. Robinson did not bat.

Bowling: Wasim Akram 12–1–38–0; Chapple 11.3–1–47–1; Austin 12–2–32–3; Watkinson 12–0–36–2; Yates 12–2–17–1.

Umpires: B. Dudleston and D. R. Shepherd.

SEMI-FINALS

GLAMORGAN v WARWICKSHIRE

At Cardiff, August 15. Warwickshire won by eight wickets. Toss: Glamorgan.

Glamorgan's hopes of qualifying for a Lord's final for the first time in 18 years were effectively over at lunch, when Warwickshire's accurate attack had reduced them to 77 for eight. A capacity crowd in glorious sunshine was stunned as the home batsmen surrendered with injudicious strokeplay and two needless run-outs on a slow, easy-paced pitch. Both Maynard and Hemp underestimated Penney's fielding skills: Maynard was run out by a direct hit while Hemp was dismissed by two yards attempting an impossible single. Munton was again Warwickshire's most effective bowler, dismissing Morris in his first over and returning outstanding figures of two for 18 from an unchanged 12-over spell. Barwick took two wickets as the pitch began to turn and bounce, but by 3.30 p.m. the game was over and Warwickshire had qualified for their third successive NatWest final.

Man of the Match: T. A. Munton.

Glamorgan

S. P. James c Piper b Donald	5	†C. P. Metson c Reeve b Giles	0
*H. Morris c Piper b Munton	0	S. L. Watkin b Giles	0
D. L. Hemp run out	28	S. R. Barwick b Smith	0
M. P. Maynard run out	11	L-b 1, w 3, n-b 4	8
P. A. Cottey c Piper b Munton	5		
A. Dale c and b Smith	5	1/4 2/12 3/34	(47 overs) 86
R. D. B. Croft not out	16	4/52 5/52 6/62	
H. A. G. Anthony b Giles	8	7/77 8/77 9/81	

Bowling: Donald 11–5–23–1; Munton 12–7–18–2; Reeve 4–1–15–0; Smith 9–2–15–2; Giles 11–3–14–3.

Warwickshire

N. V. Knight c Dale b Barwick	14
N. M. K. Smith c Morris b Barwick	32
D. P. Ostler not out	22
D. R. Brown not out	14
L-b 4, n-b 2	6

1/38 2/52   (2 wkts, 24.1 overs) 88

R. G. Twose, *D. A. Reeve, T. L. Penney, A. F. Giles, †K. J. Piper, A. A. Donald and T. A. Munton did not bat.

Bowling: Watkin 5–0–27–0; Anthony 4–2–9–0; Barwick 8.1–4–15–2; Croft 7–0–33–0.

Umpires: D. J. Constant and P. Willey.

YORKSHIRE v NORTHAMPTONSHIRE

At Leeds, August 15. Northamptonshire won by 87 runs. Toss: Northamptonshire.

A brilliant partnership of 131 in 22 overs between Bailey and Lamb crushed Yorkshire's spirit and punished too much short-pitched bowling. Lamb raised the tempo with some bold hitting in a 67-ball 63; Bailey faced 103 deliveries for his unbeaten 93, which brought him a third successive NatWest award. In contrast, Northamptonshire's attack operated to a full length, putting the batsmen under pressure. Nervous Yorkshire fell steadily behind; the normally forceful Byas managed only 19 from 71 balls. Northamptonshire could afford to ignore some late blows by Blakey and Gough. There were five run-outs in the match and the umpires referred nine decisions to TV replay, eventually trying the patience of the crowd. That was probably not the reason, however, for brawling on the Western Terrace; 15 were arrested, and six charged with public order offences next day.

Man of the Match: R. J. Bailey.

Northamptonshire

R. R. Montgomerie run out	26	†R. J. Warren not out	8
A. Fordham run out	48		
R. J. Bailey not out	93	B 1, l-b 5, n-b 4	10
*A. J. Lamb c and b Grayson	63		
K. M. Curran b Gough	29	1/75 2/79 3/210	(5 wkts, 60 overs) 286
D. J. Capel lbw b Hartley	9	4/263 5/272	

A. L. Penberthy, J. N. Snape, A. Kumble and J. P. Taylor did not bat.

Bowling: Gough 12–1–39–1; Hartley 12–3–37–1; White 12–1–62–0; Robinson 8–0–48–0; Grayson 11–1–66–1; Bevan 5–0–28–0.

Yorkshire

*M. D. Moxon c Warren b Curran	15	D. Gough c Curran b Kumble	22
M. P. Vaughan run out	34	P. J. Hartley b Kumble	16
D. Byas c Capel b Penberthy	19	M. A. Robinson not out	0
M. G. Bevan run out	9	L-b 12, w 9	21
C. White run out	4		
A. A. Metcalfe lbw b Kumble	0	1/26 2/76 3/91	(54.3 overs) 199
†R. J. Blakey c Warren b Capel	39	4/97 5/97 6/99	
A. P. Grayson c Lamb b Penberthy	20	7/154 8/161 9/199	

Bowling: Taylor 10–3–23–0; Curran 10–2–22–1; Penberthy 11–0–42–2; Capel 12–1–59–1; Kumble 11.3–0–41–3.

Umpires: J. C. Balderstone and J. H. Hampshire.

FINAL

NORTHAMPTONSHIRE v WARWICKSHIRE

At Lord's, September 2, 3. Warwickshire won by four wickets. Toss: Northamptonshire.

Allan Lamb spat in the face of cricketing history when he chose to bat; history exacted the customary penalty. For the tenth year running, the NatWest final went to the team batting second and for the second year out of three that team was Warwickshire. Lamb's decision was quite logical and legitimate: rain delayed the start until 3 p.m. on the Saturday thus, in effect, reversing the normal sequence – the team batting second could expect to have to contend with any morning juice in the wicket. However, except that it added further to the superstitions surrounding this extraordinary sequence, the toss itself made no difference. Warwickshire won a tight, low-scoring contest primarily because, as in the 1987 final, Northamptonshire wilted when the heat was on. Having sustained their form brilliantly during a long, tough season, their fielding came unstuck at the crucial moment.

Warwickshire were theoretically hampered by the absence of Munton, whose bowling had been virtually unplayable in their previous two matches. But Brown proved an able back-up to Donald, and the Northamptonshire batting was in trouble from the start. There was no obvious reason – the pitch was dry and apparently sound. But none of the batsmen seemed comfortable for long. Lamb, their best hope, in what might have been his last big match, appeared in manic mood from his first delivery: he faced three in all before edging a drive to first slip. Only Bailey, maintaining the form he had shown throughout the tournament, and Warren, who scored a bonny 41, kept Northamptonshire in the game. Penney's fielding was probably the highlight of the afternoon.

Bad light halted play at 197 for eight with nine balls remaining, and it was assumed the contest was over. When Sunday dawned bright and clear, with no sign of moisture in the air, Lord's was only a third full for what most people presumed would be the formality of Warwickshire's victory.

It did not work out like that. Once again, the batsmen were unable to establish any dominance: Brown was third out in the 17th over, with only 28 on the board. Then Kumble began to assert something of the mastery he had shown all season and, once he flipped one through Ostler's defence, the advantage began to shift. However, the more wickets the opposition take, the more dangerous Warwickshire become. And when Reeve strode to the wicket at 122 for five, Northamptonshire's nemesis had arrived. He put on 54 with Twose in the next 12 overs. Twose was dropped twice, arguably three times, as the batsmen applied pressure with which fielders less accustomed to major occasions could not cope. Even so, Northamptonshire would probably have won if umpire Bird had shared the majority opinion that Reeve was out lbw to Kumble in the 52nd over. Reeve survived and Warwickshire began an unstoppable surge towards victory. It was a worthy contest between two in-form teams and the tension of the closing stages redeemed the disappointment of the first rainy Saturday in months. – *Matthew Engel.*

Man of the Match: D. A. Reeve.　　　*Attendance:* 24,855; receipts £695,520.

Close of play: Northamptonshire 197-8 (58.3 overs) (R. J. Warren 41*, A. Kumble 0*).

Northamptonshire

R. R. Montgomerie b Donald	1	A. Kumble c Twose b Bell	2
A. Fordham b Brown	20	J. P. Taylor not out	0
R. J. Bailey b N. M. K. Smith	44		
*A. J. Lamb c Ostler b Brown	0	B 4, l-b 9, w 11	24
K. M. Curran b Donald	30		
D. J. Capel c Piper b Reeve	12	1/4 (1) 2/39 (2) 3/39 (4) (59.5 overs) 200
†R. J. Warren b Bell	41	4/89 (3) 5/110 (6) 6/128 (5)
A. L. Penberthy run out	5	7/158 (8) 8/197 (9)
J. N. Snape c Piper b Donald	21	9/200 (10) 10/200 (7)

Bowling: Donald 12–1–33–3; Brown 10–2–35–2; Bell 8.5–1–41–2; N. M. K. Smith 12–1–23–1; Reeve 12–1–31–1; P. A. Smith 5–0–24–0.

Warwickshire

N. V. Knight c Bailey b Taylor	2	*D. A. Reeve not out	37
N. M. K. Smith c Warren b Taylor	2	P. A. Smith not out	4
D. P. Ostler b Kumble	45		
D. R. Brown c Warren b Penberthy	8	B 2, l-b 14, w 1	17
R. G. Twose run out	68	1/5 (2) 2/14 (1) (6 wkts, 58.5 overs) 203
T. L. Penney c Montgomerie		3/28 (4) 4/74 (3)
b Penberthy	20	5/122 (6) 6/176 (5)

†K. J. Piper, A. A. Donald and M. A. V. Bell did not bat.

Bowling: Taylor 11.5–4–37–2; Curran 11–3–31–0; Penberthy 11–1–44–2; Kumble 12–0–29–1; Capel 12–0–40–0; Snape 1–0–6–0.

Umpires: H. D. Bird and M. J. Kitchen.

NATWEST BANK TROPHY RECORDS

(Including Gillette Cup, 1963-80)

Batting

Highest individual scores: 206, A. I. Kallicharran, Warwickshire v Oxfordshire, Birmingham, 1984; 180*, T. M. Moody, Worcestershire v Surrey, The Oval, 1994; 177, C. G. Greenidge, Hampshire v Glamorgan, Southampton, 1975; 172*, G. A. Hick, Worcestershire v Devon, Worcester, 1987; 165*, V. P. Terry, Hampshire v Berkshire, Southampton, 1985; 162*, I. V. A. Richards, Glamorgan v Oxfordshire, Swansea, 1993; 162*, C. J. Tavaré, Somerset v Devon, Torquay, 1990; 159, C. L. Smith, Hampshire v Cheshire, Chester, 1989; 158, G. D. Barlow, Middlesex v Lancashire, Lord's, 1984; 158, Zaheer Abbas, Gloucestershire v Leicestershire, Leicester, 1983; 156, D. I. Gower, Leicestershire v Derbyshire, Leicester, 1984; 155, J. J. Whitaker, Leicestershire v Wiltshire, Swindon, 1984; 154*, H. Morris, Glamorgan v Staffordshire, Cardiff, 1989; 154, P. Willey, Leicestershire v Hampshire, Leicester, 1987; 153, A. Hill, Derbyshire v Cornwall, Derby, 1986; 151*, M. P. Maynard, Glamorgan v Durham, Darlington, 1991; 151, N. V. Knight, Warwickshire v Somerset, Birmingham, 1995. (93 hundreds were scored in the Gillette Cup; 173 hundreds have been scored in the NatWest Bank Trophy.)

Most runs: 2,417, G. A. Gooch; 2,006, M. W. Gatting; 1,998, A. J. Lamb; 1,950, D. L. Amiss.

Fastest hundred: G. D. Rose off 36 balls, Somerset v Devon, Torquay, 1990.

Most hundreds: 7, C. L. Smith; 6, G. A. Gooch; 5, D. I. Gower, I. V. A. Richards and G. M. Turner.

Highest totals (off 60 overs): 413 for four, Somerset v Devon, Torquay, 1990; 404 for three, Worcestershire v Devon, Worcester, 1987; 392 for five, Warwickshire v Oxfordshire, Birmingham, 1984; 386 for five, Essex v Wiltshire, Chelmsford, 1988; 384 for six, Kent v Berkshire, Finchampstead, 1994; 372 for five, Lancashire v Gloucestershire, Manchester, 1990; 371 for four, Hampshire v Glamorgan, Southampton, 1975; 365 for three, Derbyshire v Cornwall, Derby, 1986; 361 for eight, Essex v Cumberland, Chelmsford, 1992; 361 for eight, Warwickshire v Bedfordshire, Birmingham, 1994; 360 for two, Northamptonshire v Staffordshire, Northampton, 1990; 359 for four, Kent v Dorset, Canterbury, 1989; 357 for two, Worcestershire v Surrey, The Oval, 1994; 357 for three, Warwickshire v Somerset, Birmingham, 1995; 354 for seven, Leicestershire v Wiltshire, Swindon, 1984; 352 for eight, Northamptonshire v Nottinghamshire, Nottingham, 1995; 350, Surrey v Worcestershire, The Oval, 1994. *In the final:* 322 for five, Warwickshire v Sussex, Lord's, 1993.

Highest total by a minor county: 305 for nine, Durham v Glamorgan, Darlington, 1991.

Highest total by a side batting first and losing: 321 for six (60 overs), Sussex v Warwickshire, Lord's, 1993 (*in the final*).

Highest totals by a side batting second: 350 (59.5 overs), Surrey lost to Worcestershire, The Oval, 1994; 339 for nine (60 overs), Somerset lost to Warwickshire, Birmingham, 1995; 326 for nine (60 overs), Hampshire lost to Leicestershire, Leicester, 1987; 322 for five (60 overs), Warwickshire beat Sussex, Lord's, 1993 (*in the final*); 319 for nine (59.5 overs), Essex beat Lancashire, Chelmsford, 1992; 314 for eight (60 overs), Nottinghamshire lost to Northamptonshire, Nottingham, 1995; 307 for five (60 overs), Hampshire beat Essex, Chelmsford, 1990; 305 for six (59.3 overs), Gloucestershire beat Leicestershire, Leicester, 1983; 305 for nine (60 overs), Durham lost to Glamorgan, Darlington, 1991.

Lowest completed totals: 39 (26.4 overs), Ireland v Sussex, Hove, 1985; 41 (20 overs), Cambridgeshire v Buckinghamshire, Cambridge, 1972; 41 (19.4 overs), Middlesex v Essex, Westcliff, 1972; 41 (36.1 overs), Shropshire v Essex, Wellington, 1974. *In the final:* 118 (60 overs), Lancashire v Kent, 1974.

Lowest total by a side batting first and winning: 98 (56.2 overs), Worcestershire v Durham, Chester-le-Street, 1968.

Shortest innings: 10.1 overs (60 for one), Worcestershire v Lancashire, Worcester, 1963.

Matches re-arranged on a reduced number of overs are excluded from the above.

Record partnerships for each wicket

255 for 1st	M. A. Roseberry and S. Hutton, Durham v Herefordshire at Chester-le-Street		1995
286 for 2nd	I. S. Anderson and A. Hill, Derbyshire v Cornwall at Derby		1986
309* for 3rd	T. S. Curtis and T. M. Moody, Worcestershire v Surrey at The Oval		1994
234* for 4th	D. Lloyd and C. H. Lloyd, Lancashire v Gloucestershire at Manchester		1978
166 for 5th	M. A. Lynch and G. R. J. Roope, Surrey v Durham at The Oval		1982
123 for 6th	D. A. Reeve and T. L. Penney, Warwickshire v Leicestershire at Leicester		1994
160* for 7th	C. J. Richards and I. R. Payne, Surrey v Lincolnshire at Sleaford		1983
83 for 8th	S. N. V. Waterton and D. A. Hale, Oxfordshire v Gloucestershire at Oxford		1989
87 for 9th	M. A. Nash and A. E. Cordle, Glamorgan v Lincolnshire at Swansea		1974
81 for 10th	S. Turner and R. E. East, Essex v Yorkshire at Leeds		1982

Bowling

Most wickets: 81, G. G. Arnold; 79, J. Simmons.

Best bowling (12 overs unless stated): eight for 21 (10.1 overs), M. A. Holding, Derbyshire v Sussex, Hove, 1988; eight for 31 (11.1 overs), D. L. Underwood, Kent v Scotland, Edinburgh, 1987; seven for 15, A. L. Dixon, Kent v Surrey, The Oval, 1967; seven for 15 (9.3 overs), R. P. Lefebvre, Somerset v Devon, Torquay, 1990; seven for 19, N. V. Radford, Worcestershire v Bedfordshire, Bedford, 1991; seven for 30, P. J. Sainsbury, Hampshire v Norfolk, Southampton, 1965; seven for 32, S. P. Davis, Durham v Lancashire, Chester-le-Street, 1983; seven for 33, R. D. Jackman, Surrey v Yorkshire, Harrogate, 1970; seven for 37, N. A. Mallender, Northamptonshire v Worcestershire, Northampton, 1984.

Most economical analysis: 12–9–3–1, J. Simmons, Lancashire v Suffolk, Bury St Edmunds, 1985.

Most expensive analysis: 12–0–106–2, D. A. Gallop, Oxfordshire v Warwickshire, Birmingham, 1984.

Hat-tricks (8): J. D. F. Larter, Northamptonshire v Sussex, Northampton, 1963; D. A. D. Sydenham, Surrey v Cheshire, Hoylake, 1964; R. N. S. Hobbs, Essex v Middlesex, Lord's, 1968; N. M. McVicker, Warwickshire v Lincolnshire, Birmingham, 1971; G. S. le Roux, Sussex v Ireland, Hove, 1985; M. Jean-Jacques, Derbyshire v Nottinghamshire, Derby, 1987; J. F. M. O'Brien, Cheshire v Derbyshire, Chester, 1988; R. A. Pick, Nottinghamshire v Scotland, Nottingham, 1995.

Four wickets in five balls: D. A. D. Sydenham, Surrey v Cheshire, Hoylake, 1964.

Wicket-keeping and Fielding

Most dismissals: 66 (58 ct, 8 st), R. W. Taylor; 65 (59 ct, 6 st), A. P. E. Knott.

Most dismissals in an innings: 7 (all ct), A. J. Stewart, Surrey v Glamorgan, Swansea, 1994.

Most catches by a fielder: 26, J. Simmons; 25, G. Cook and G. A. Gooch; 24, P. J. Sharpe.

Most catches by a fielder in an innings: 4 – A. S. Brown, Gloucestershire v Middlesex, Bristol, 1963; G. Cook, Northamptonshire v Glamorgan, Northampton, 1972; C. G. Greenidge, Hampshire v Cheshire, Southampton, 1981; D. C. Jackson, Durham v Northamptonshire, Darlington, 1984; T. S. Smith, Hertfordshire v Somerset, St Albans, 1984; H. Morris, Glamorgan v Scotland, Edinburgh, 1988; C. C. Lewis, Nottinghamshire v Worcestershire, Nottingham, 1992.

Results

Largest victories in runs: Somerset by 346 runs v Devon, Torquay, 1990; Worcestershire by 299 runs v Devon, Worcester, 1987; Essex by 291 runs v Wiltshire, Chelmsford, 1988; Sussex by 244 runs v Ireland, Hove, 1985; Lancashire by 241 runs v Gloucestershire, Manchester, 1990; Nottinghamshire by 228 runs v Northumberland, Jesmond, 1994; Warwickshire by 227 runs v Oxfordshire, Birmingham, 1984; Essex by 226 runs v Oxfordshire, Chelmsford, 1985; Durham by 207 runs v Herefordshire, Chester-le-Street, 1995.

Victories by ten wickets (13): By Glamorgan, Hampshire (twice), Middlesex, Northamptonshire, Surrey, Sussex, Warwickshire (twice), Yorkshire (four times).

Earliest finishes: both at 2.20 p.m. Worcestershire beat Lancashire by nine wickets at Worcester, 1963; Essex beat Middlesex by eight wickets at Westcliff, 1972.

Scores level (10): Nottinghamshire 215, Somerset 215 for nine at Taunton, 1964; Surrey 196, Sussex 196 for eight at The Oval, 1970; Somerset 287 for six, Essex 287 at Taunton, 1978; Surrey 195 for seven, Essex 195 at Chelmsford, 1980; Essex 149, Derbyshire 149 for eight at Derby, 1981; Northamptonshire 235 for nine, Derbyshire 235 for six at Lord's, 1981 (*in the final*); Middlesex 222 for nine, Somerset 222 for eight at Lord's, 1983; Hampshire 224 for eight, Essex 224 for seven at Southampton, 1985; Essex 307 for six, Hampshire 307 for five at Chelmsford, 1990; Hampshire 204 for nine, Leicestershire 204 for nine at Leicester, 1995. Under the rules the side which lost fewer wickets won; at Leicester in 1995, Leicestershire won by virtue of their higher total after 30 overs.

Match Awards

Most awards: 9, G. A. Gooch; 8, C. H. Lloyd and C. L. Smith.

WINNERS

Gillette Cup

1963 SUSSEX beat Worcestershire by 14 runs.
1964 SUSSEX beat Warwickshire by eight wickets.
1965 YORKSHIRE beat Surrey by 175 runs.
1966 WARWICKSHIRE beat Worcestershire by five wickets.
1967 KENT beat Somerset by 32 runs.
1968 WARWICKSHIRE beat Sussex by four wickets.
1969 YORKSHIRE beat Derbyshire by 69 runs.
1970 LANCASHIRE beat Sussex by six wickets.
1971 LANCASHIRE beat Kent by 24 runs.
1972 LANCASHIRE beat Warwickshire by four wickets.
1973 GLOUCESTERSHIRE beat Sussex by 40 runs.
1974 KENT beat Lancashire by four wickets.
1975 LANCASHIRE beat Middlesex by seven wickets.
1976 NORTHAMPTONSHIRE beat Lancashire by four wickets.
1977 MIDDLESEX beat Glamorgan by five wickets.
1978 SUSSEX beat Somerset by five wickets.
1979 SOMERSET beat Northamptonshire by 45 runs.
1980 MIDDLESEX beat Surrey by seven wickets.

NatWest Bank Trophy

1981 DERBYSHIRE beat Northamptonshire by losing fewer wickets with the scores level.
1982 SURREY beat Warwickshire by nine wickets.
1983 SOMERSET beat Kent by 24 runs.
1984 MIDDLESEX beat Kent by four wickets.
1985 ESSEX beat Nottinghamshire by one run.
1986 SUSSEX beat Lancashire by seven wickets.
1987 NOTTINGHAMSHIRE beat Northamptonshire by three wickets.
1988 MIDDLESEX beat Worcestershire by three wickets.
1989 WARWICKSHIRE beat Middlesex by four wickets.
1990 LANCASHIRE beat Northamptonshire by seven wickets.
1991 HAMPSHIRE beat Surrey by four wickets.
1992 NORTHAMPTONSHIRE beat Leicestershire by eight wickets.
1993 WARWICKSHIRE beat Sussex by five wickets.
1994 WORCESTERSHIRE beat Warwickshire by eight wickets.
1995 WARWICKSHIRE beat Northamptonshire by four wickets.

TEAM RECORDS 1963-95

| | Rounds reached | | | | Matches | | |
	W	F	SF	QF	P	W	L
Derbyshire	1	2	3	10	64*	32	32
Durham	0	0	0	1	36	11	25
Essex	1	1	4	13	69	37	32
Glamorgan.	0	1	3	13	69	36	33
Gloucestershire	1	1	5	14	68	36	32
Hampshire	1	1	8	19	83	51	32
Kent	2	5	7	14	77	46	31
Lancashire	5	8	13	18	91	63	28
Leicestershire	0	1	3	14	67	34	33
Middlesex	4	6	13	18	90	61	29
Northamptonshire	2	7	10	19	86	55	31
Nottinghamshire	1	2	3	11	69	37	32
Somerset	2	4	9	16	79	48	31

		Rounds reached				Matches	
	W	F	SF	QF	P	W	L
Surrey.............	1	4	9	19	82*	50	32
Sussex	4	8	12	17	85	56	29
Warwickshire	5	9	15	19	94	66	28
Worcestershire......	1	4	10	14	76	44	32
Yorkshire...........	2	2	5	14	68	37	31

* Derbyshire and Surrey totals each include a bowling contest after their first-round matches were abandoned in 1991; Derbyshire lost to Hertfordshire and Surrey beat Oxfordshire.

MINOR COUNTY RECORDS

From 1964 to 1979 the previous season's top five Minor Counties were invited to take part in the competition. In 1980 these were joined by Ireland, and in 1983 the competition was expanded to embrace 13 Minor Counties, Ireland and Scotland. The number of Minor Counties dropped to 12 in 1992 when Durham attained first-class status, and 11 in 1995 when Holland were admitted to the competition.

Between 1964 and 1991 Durham qualified 21 times, including 15 years in succession from 1977-91. They reached the second round a record six times.

Including the 1996 tournament, Hertfordshire, Oxfordshire and Staffordshire have qualified most among the other Minor Counties, 18 times, followed by Devon 17, Berkshire, Cambridgeshire, Cheshire and Suffolk 16, Buckinghamshire and Norfolk 15, Shropshire and Wiltshire 12, Dorset and Lincolnshire 11, Bedfordshire and Cumberland 10, Northumberland 8, Cornwall 7, Wales Minor Counties twice and Herefordshire once.

Only Hertfordshire have reached the quarter-finals, beating Berkshire and then Essex in 1976.

Wins by a minor county over a first-class county (8): Durham v Yorkshire (by five wickets), Harrogate, 1973; Lincolnshire v Glamorgan (by six wickets), Swansea, 1974; Hertfordshire v Essex (by 33 runs), 2nd round, Hitchin, 1976; Shropshire v Yorkshire (by 37 runs), Telford, 1984; Durham v Derbyshire (by seven wickets), Derby, 1985; Buckinghamshire v Somerset (by seven runs), High Wycombe, 1987; Cheshire v Northamptonshire (by one wicket), Chester, 1988; Hertfordshire v Derbyshire (2-1 in a bowling contest after the match was abandoned), Bishop's Stortford, 1991.

BENSON AND HEDGES CUP, 1995

Lancashire hit a run of early-season form to take the Benson and Hedges Cup in tremendous style, striking temporary fear into the hearts of both rivals and bookmakers about the possibility of them surpassing Warwickshire in 1994 and winning all four competitions.

They were the tournament's dominant team from the start, passing 300 against other first-class counties in three successive zonal matches. After a comfortable win over Nottinghamshire in the quarter-finals, they proved their resilience by coming back from an apparently impossible position at Worcester in the semi-finals, thanks to an inspired batting performance by Wasim Akram.

In the final, led by the England players, Mike Atherton and John Crawley, they again out-batted the opposition and won by 35 runs. Their opponents were Kent, who went through to their 12th semi-final in the tournament's 24 years and seventh final (both records) on the back of a remarkable series of opening partnerships by their captain, Mark Benson, and Trevor Ward. However, Benson was injured for the final. Kent provided the day's outstanding performance, a thrilling century by Aravinda de Silva, but he had insufficient support to give them a chance of victory.

After two years as a pure knockout, the tournament reverted to a zonal qualifying system. This gave all the teams, especially the four non-Championship ones, more chance to do themselves justice. But with 22 sides involved, it meant that 57 matches had to be played early in the season, when many critics believe players should be concentrating on honing their skills in the first-class game. The news that Benson and Hedges had renewed their sponsorship for five more years, agreeing to put in £4 million between 1996 and 2000, was thus not greeted with universal approval.

Prize money

£35,000 for winners: LANCASHIRE.
£17,500 for runners-up: KENT.
£8,750 for losing semi-finalists: SOMERSET and WORCESTERSHIRE.
£4,375 for losing quarter-finalists: GLOUCESTERSHIRE, MIDDLESEX, NOTTING-
HAMSHIRE and YORKSHIRE.

There was also £750 each for the winners of group matches. Gold Award winners received £750 in the final, £350 in the semi-finals, £300 in the quarter-finals, £200 in the group matches. £1,000 was awarded to the first batsman to score 400 runs, T. R. Ward of Kent on May 30, but no bowler took 20 wickets or wicket-keeper made eight dismissals in an innings to collect an equivalent bonus. The prize money was increased from £97,680 in the 1994 tournament to £137,650; the total sponsorship rose from £622,629 to £641,307.

FINAL GROUP TABLE

	Played	Won	Lost	No result	Points	Net run-rate
Group A						
LANCASHIRE	5	4	0	1	9	22.56
NOTTINGHAMSHIRE	5	3	1	1	7	0.70
Warwickshire	5	2	2	1	5	4.68
Durham	5	2	2	1	5	− 3.17
Minor Counties	5	1	3	1	3	− 11.76
Leicestershire	5	0	4	1	1	− 7.58

	Played	Won	Lost	No result	Points	Net run-rate
Group B						
YORKSHIRE	4	3	0	1	7	17.34
WORCESTERSHIRE	4	3	1	0	6	26.02
Derbyshire	4	2	1	1	5	−3.11
Northamptonshire	4	1	3	0	2	−1.49
Scotland	4	0	4	0	0	−37.35
Group C						
GLOUCESTERSHIRE	5	5	0	0	10	9.99
MIDDLESEX	5	4	1	0	8	7.69
Glamorgan	5	3	2	0	6	16.45
Essex	5	1	3	1	3	−2.48
Hampshire	5	1	3	1	3	−6.09
Combined Universities	5	0	5	0	0	−28.04
Group D						
KENT	4	4	0	0	8	27.13
SOMERSET	4	2	2	0	4	12.17
Surrey	4	2	2	0	4	4.66
Sussex	4	2	2	0	4	0.46
Ireland	4	0	4	0	0	−46.00

Net run-rate was calculated by subtracting runs conceded per 100 balls from runs scored per 100 balls, discounting those matches not played to a result.

GROUP A

The Minor Counties' squad for the competition was: I. Cockbain (Cheshire) (*captain*), K. A. Arnold (Oxfordshire), S. J. Dean (Staffordshire), R. A. Evans (Oxfordshire), R. J. Evans (Lincolnshire), S. C. Goldsmith (Norfolk), R. G. Hignett (Cheshire), M. I. Humphries (Staffordshire), K. Jahangir (Hertfordshire), S. D. Myles (Berkshire), P. G. Newman (Staffordshire), L. Potter (Staffordshire), M. J. Roberts (Buckinghamshire), M. G. Scothern (Cumberland), M. A. Sharp (Cumberland), D. R. Thomas (Norfolk).

DURHAM v LEICESTERSHIRE

At Stockton-on-Tees, April 23. Durham won by 50 runs. Toss: Leicestershire. County debuts: M. Prabhakar; W. J. Cronje.

Durham's win was unimaginable at 39 for six. Briers put them in after 300 gallons of water had been removed from the outfield: Millns bowled straight through for his best one-day figures and Cronje dismissed Morris with his first ball for Leicestershire. But Saxelby put on 52 with Wood and 69 with last man Brown, who held out for 21 overs and scored eight. Leicestershire collapsed from 53 for one to 115 all out once Cronje fell just before tea.

Gold Award: M. Saxelby.

Durham

*M. A. Roseberry c and b Millns......	6	J. Boiling c Pierson b Wells	0
W. Larkins b Millns	2	A. Walker c Wells b Parsons	0
M. Prabhakar c Smith b Millns	7	S. J. E. Brown run out	8
J. E. Morris c Robinson b Cronje	6	B 1, l-b 10, w 15	26
J. I. Longley c Wells b Cronje	3		
M. Saxelby not out	80	1/6 2/14 3/29	(54.2 overs) 165
†C. W. Scott lbw b Millns	0	4/35 5/37 6/39	
J. Wood b Parsons	27	7/91 8/94 9/96	

Bowling: Mullally 10-0-30-0; Millns 11-3-26-4; Cronje 11-0-26-2; Parsons 11-2-38-2; Wells 3-0-9-1; Pierson 8.2-1-25-0.

Leicestershire

V. J. Wells run out	26		A. R. K. Pierson not out	10	
*N. E. Briers b Prabhakar	13		D. J. Millns lbw b Walker	1	
W. J. Cronje lbw b Wood	22		A. D. Mullally lbw b Walker	0	
J. J. Whitaker c Larkins b Walker	2		L-b 5, w 5	10	
P. E. Robinson b Prabhakar	13				
B. F. Smith c Scott b Brown	14		1/18 2/53 3/56	(44.4 overs) 115	
†P. Whitticase lbw b Brown	0		4/79 5/85 6/92		
G. J. Parsons c Prabhakar b Boiling	4		7/99 8/114 9/115		

Bowling: Prabhakar 11–2–36–2; Brown 9–3–23–2; Walker 7.4–0–22–3; Wood 11–2–20–1; Saxelby 2–0–3–0; Boiling 4–1–6–1.

Umpires: B. Dudleston and A. G. T. Whitehead.

MINOR COUNTIES v LANCASHIRE

At Leek, April 23. Lancashire won by nine wickets. Toss: Lancashire. First-team debut: A. Flintoff.

Austin bowled a spell of nine overs for eight runs to leave Minor Counties at 29 for four and Gallian finished them off with five for 15. Only Roberts and Humphries reached double figures as they were bowled out for their lowest total in the competition. Lancashire knocked off the runs without breaking sweat.

Gold Award: I. D. Austin.

Minor Counties

S. J. Dean lbw b Austin	6		R. A. Evans c Austin b Gallian	0	
R. J. Evans lbw b Austin	0		K. A. Arnold b Gallian	0	
M. J. Roberts c Watkinson b Flintoff	20		M. A. Sharp not out	0	
*I. Cockbain c Hegg b Austin	8		L-b 8, w 10	18	
S. D. Myles lbw b Austin	0				
D. R. Thomas c Hegg b Gallian	2		1/2 2/11 3/25	(35.5 overs) 70	
†M. I. Humphries b Gallian	14		4/29 5/37 6/53		
P. G. Newman c Hegg b Gallian	2		7/61 8/64 9/64		

Bowling: Martin 6–2–12–0; Austin 9–6–8–4; Watkinson 6–1–17–0; Gallian 8.5–3–15–5; Flintoff 6–2–10–1.

Lancashire

M. A. Atherton not out	24		
J. E. R. Gallian c Humphries b Arnold	9		
J. P. Crawley not out	31		
W 5, n-b 2	7		
1/24	(1 wkt, 24.1 overs) 71		

N. H. Fairbrother, A. Flintoff, G. D. Lloyd, *M. Watkinson, †W. K. Hegg, I. D. Austin, G. Yates and P. J. Martin did not bat.

Bowling: Newman 7–2–11–0; Sharp 6–1–18–0; Arnold 8–1–18–1; Thomas 2–0–22–0; R. A. Evans 1.1–0–2–0.

Umpires: G. I. Burgess and V. A. Holder.

NOTTINGHAMSHIRE v WARWICKSHIRE

At Nottingham, April 23. Nottinghamshire won by six runs. Toss: Warwickshire. County debut: N. V. Knight.

Holders Warwickshire needed 13 from the final over, but lost their last three wickets on 224, a startling collapse from 172 for two. Once Evans dismissed Ostler, no one else passed eight. Johnson dominated Nottinghamshire's innings, though he might have been run out on 42 if the fielder, Twose, had not knocked over umpire Kitchen, obstructing his view.

Gold Award: K. P. Evans.

Nottinghamshire

P. R. Pollard run out	18	†W. M. Noon b Welch		23
*R. T. Robinson c Twose b Reeve	21	K. P. Evans not out		5
G. F. Archer c Twose b Smith	37	L-b 8, w 19, n-b 4		31
P. Johnson not out	70			
C. L. Cairns c Moles b Donald	17	1/39 2/50 3/118	(6 wkts, 55 overs)	230
C. C. Lewis c Twose b Donald	8	4/149 5/165 6/224		

G. W. Mike, R. A. Pick and J. A. Afford did not bat.

Bowling: Donald 11–2–39–2; Small 11–1–21–0; Reeve 11–2–34–1; Welch 10–0–66–1; Smith 9–0–42–1; Twose 3–0–20–0.

Warwickshire

A. J. Moles b Cairns	51	†K. J. Piper run out		6
N. V. Knight lbw b Lewis	3	G. C. Small not out		0
D. P. Ostler c sub b Evans	87	A. A. Donald c Lewis b Cairns		0
R. G. Twose b Cairns	54	L-b 2, w 11		13
T. L. Penney run out	8			
*D. A. Reeve b Evans	0	1/9 2/122 3/172	(54.5 overs)	224
G. Welch c sub b Lewis	1	4/198 5/198 6/202		
N. M. K. Smith b Evans	1	7/203 8/224 9/224		

Bowling: Lewis 11–2–38–2; Evans 10–1–35–3; Pick 7–0–36–0; Mike 10–2–41–0; Afford 10–1–42–0; Cairns 6.5–0–30–3.

Umpires: M. J. Kitchen and B. J. Meyer.

LANCASHIRE v LEICESTERSHIRE

At Manchester, April 25. Lancashire won by five wickets. Toss: Leicestershire.

Cronje batted brilliantly to equal Brian Davison's 23-year-old county record in the tournament. He faced only 156 balls for his 158 and hit 13 fours and four sixes, sharing stands of 92 with Briers and 175 in 22 overs with Whitaker. Lancashire needed 313, the highest second-innings total in the competition's history. But they pursued it with systematic determination. Atherton and Crawley put on 124 in 21 overs; Fairbrother defied a bruised finger to add 61 in nine with Lloyd, who struck the winning six with three balls left. The match aggregate of 630 was also a tournament record.

Gold Award: W. J. Cronje.

Leicestershire

V. J. Wells c Hegg b Austin	7	G. J. Parsons not out		1
*N. E. Briers c Fairbrother b Yates	28			
W. J. Cronje c Fairbrother b Martin	158	L-b 7, w 3		10
J. J. Whitaker c Gallian b Austin	88			
P. E. Robinson not out	17	1/11 2/103 3/278	(5 wkts, 55 overs)	312
B. F. Smith c Watkinson b Martin	3	4/303 5/310		

†P. Whitticase, A. R. K. Pierson, A. D. Mullally and D. J. Millns did not bat.

Bowling: Martin 11–2–48–2; Austin 11–1–49–2; Chapple 11–0–72–0; Watkinson 9–0–55–0; Yates 9–0–44–1; Gallian 4–0–37–0.

Lancashire

M. A. Atherton b Cronje	71	I. D. Austin not out		16
J. E. R. Gallian c Whitticase b Millns	11			
J. P. Crawley c Robinson b Wells	89	L-b 5, w 1		6
N. H. Fairbrother c Smith b Cronje	44			
G. D. Lloyd not out	81	1/25 2/149 3/200	(5 wkts, 54.3 overs)	318
*M. Watkinson c Cronje b Parsons	0	4/201 5/262		

†W. K. Hegg, G. Chapple, G. Yates and P. J. Martin did not bat.

N. H. Fairbrother, when 6, retired hurt at 155 and resumed at 201.

Bowling: Mullally 11–1–45–0; Millns 9–0–46–1; Cronje 11–0–63–2; Parsons 10.3–0–65–1; Wells 10–0–75–1; Pierson 3–0–19–0.

Umpires: J. D. Bond and K. J. Lyons.

MINOR COUNTIES v NOTTINGHAMSHIRE

At Leek, April 25. Nottinghamshire won by nine wickets. Toss: Nottinghamshire.

Lewis reduced Minor Counties to 20 for three and, though Potter and Cockbain rallied, Kevin Evans earned his second Gold Award in three days with four for 19. His younger brother and former Nottinghamshire team-mate, Russell, was opening for the opposition; the third Evans, off-spinner Rupert, was no relation.

Gold Award: K. P. Evans.

Minor Counties

S. J. Dean b Lewis	0		R. A. Evans c French b Evans	0
R. J. Evans c French b Lewis	8		K. A. Arnold b Evans	0
M. J. Roberts c French b Lewis	0		M. A. Sharp not out	1
L. Potter c Dowman b Mike	28		L-b 2, w 4, n-b 4	10
*I. Cockbain lbw b Cairns	34			
S. D. Myles run out	7		1/2 2/4 3/20	(53.2 overs) 114
†M. I. Humphries lbw b Evans	13		4/49 5/84 6/86	
P. G. Newman b Evans	13		7/107 8/107 9/111	

Bowling: Lewis 6–1–11–3; Evans 9.2–2–19–4; Cairns 10–1–26–1; Pick 6–1–11–0; Mike 11–6–18–1; Afford 11–3–27–0.

Nottinghamshire

P. R. Pollard b Potter	52
*R. T. Robinson not out	52
P. Johnson not out	4
L-b 2, w 5	7
1/92 (1 wkt, 38.5 overs)	115

M. P. Dowman, C. L. Cairns, C. C. Lewis, †B. N. French, K. P. Evans, G. W. Mike, R. A. Pick and J. A. Afford did not bat.

Bowling: Newman 9–0–34–0; Arnold 6–1–30–0; R. A. Evans 9–2–22–0; Sharp 7–2–11–0; Potter 7.5–2–16–1.

Umpires: J. H. Harris and P. Willey.

WARWICKSHIRE v DURHAM

At Birmingham, April 25. Warwickshire won by 91 runs. Toss: Warwickshire.

Warwickshire secured their first win of the season as Durham took another battering from their left-handers. On their last visit to Edgbaston, Lara scored his 501 not out; this time Knight and Twose narrowly missed centuries, adding 127 in 20 overs. Reeve gave the innings a final boost with 28 from 31 balls and then collected a tournament-best four for 37.

Gold Award: N. V. Knight.

Warwickshire

A. J. Moles lbw b Brown	18		†M. Burns c Scott b Brown	0
N. V. Knight c Scott b Wood	91		N. M. K. Smith not out	10
D. P. Ostler c Longley b Wood	13		B 1, l-b 4, w 7, n-b 6	18
R. G. Twose c Larkins b Prabhakar	90			
T. L. Penney c Scott b Wood	9		1/31 2/55 3/182	(7 wkts, 55 overs) 285
*D. A. Reeve not out	28		4/207 5/253	
G. Welch lbw b Prabhakar	8		6/267 7/268	

G. C. Small and A. A. Donald did not bat.

Bowling: Brown 11–2–46–2; Prabhakar 11–0–62–2; Walker 11–1–51–0; Wood 11–0–50–3; Boiling 6–0–46–0; Saxelby 5–0–25–0.

Durham

*M. A. Roseberry lbw b Small	5	J. Boiling c Smith b Reeve	2
W. Larkins run out	27	S. J. E. Brown c Burns b Reeve	12
M. Prabhakar c Ostler b Reeve	8	A. Walker not out	4
J. E. Morris c and b Reeve	62	B 3, l-b 5, w 13, n-b 6	27
J. I. Longley hit wkt b Twose	35		
M. Saxelby c Burns b Welch	2	1/40 2/48 3/60	(47.3 overs) 194
†C. W. Scott c Reeve b Small	6	4/131 5/141 6/157	
J. Wood c Twose b Donald	4	7/175 8/176 9/189	

Bowling: Donald 9–0–45–1; Small 11–1–24–2; Reeve 9.3–1–37–4; Smith 6–0–33–0; Welch 9–1–24–1; Twose 3–0–23–1.

Umpires: T. E. Jesty and G. Sharp.

DURHAM v NOTTINGHAMSHIRE

At Stockton-on-Tees, May 2. Nottinghamshire won by five wickets. Toss: Durham.
Larkins and Prabhakar put on 119 and Morris added a 34-ball fifty but, from a promising 262 for three, Durham lost seven for six in 13 balls. Nottinghamshire still needed 100 with 13 overs to go; Johnson and Cairns provided the momentum. Cairns hit 46 from 33 balls, his highest score in the competition, to complement his best bowling.
Gold Award: C. L. Cairns.

Durham

*M. A. Roseberry lbw b Pick	16	A. Walker b Cairns	0
W. Larkins lbw b Evans	80	J. Boiling not out	1
M. Prabhakar c and b Mike	69	S. J. E. Brown run out	2
J. E. Morris b Cairns	51	B 1, l-b 9, w 13, n-b 4	27
J. I. Longley c Pollard b Evans	20		
M. Saxelby b Evans	0	1/32 2/151 3/204	(55 overs) 268
J. Wood b Cairns	1	4/262 5/262 6/262	
†C. W. Scott c Dowman b Cairns	1	7/265 8/265 9/266	

Bowling: Pick 11–3–48–1; Evans 11–2–56–3; Cairns 11–0–47–4; Mike 11–0–58–1; Afford 11–0–49–0.

Nottinghamshire

P. R. Pollard c Larkins b Boiling	56	M. P. Dowman not out	0
*R. T. Robinson c Prabhakar b Brown	84		
G. F. Archer c Scott b Brown	14	L-b 4, w 6	10
P. Johnson not out	56		
C. L. Cairns c Prabhakar b Walker	46	1/103 2/142 3/169	(5 wkts, 53.5 overs) 271
K. P. Evans c Prabhakar b Brown	5	4/250 5/263	

G. W. Mike, †B. N. French, R. A. Pick and J. A. Afford did not bat.

Bowling: Wood 11–1–58–0; Brown 10.5–1–39–3; Walker 11–0–53–1; Prabhakar 10–0–54–0; Boiling 11–0–63–1.

Umpires: J. C. Balderstone and B. Leadbeater.

LEICESTERSHIRE v MINOR COUNTIES

At Leicester, May 2. Minor Counties won by 26 runs. Toss: Minor Counties.
Leicestershire's nightmare continued. After improbable defeats at Stockton and Old Trafford, they surrendered to Minor Counties. To make it worse, Laurie Potter, whom they let go in 1993, won the Gold Award, scoring 32 and taking four wickets with his left-arm

spin. There were no worries as openers Boon and Wells reached 70, but Leicestershire then lost four wickets for six runs to Potter and Newman; two more mini-collapses gave the part-timers their sixth Benson and Hedges win, with 27 balls to spare.

Gold Award: L. Potter.

Minor Counties

S. J. Dean c Cronje b Wells	44	P. G. Newman lbw b Parsons	1
R. J. Evans c Maddy b Mason	25	R. A. Evans run out	0
L. Potter lbw b Parsons	32	K. A. Arnold b Mullally	0
*I. Cockbain not out	65	L-b 17, w 6, n-b 2	25
S. C. Goldsmith b Mullally	17		
†M. I. Humphries b Wells	9	1/77 2/85 3/143 (54.4 overs)	224
K. Jahangir c Robinson b Parsons	0	4/172 5/191 6/201	
D. R. Thomas lbw b Mullally	6	7/213 8/214 9/214	

Bowling: Mullally 10.4–2–39–3; Millns 3–0–13–0; Parsons 11–0–46–3; Cronje 11–2–41–0; Wells 8–0–34–2; Mason 11–2–34–1.

Leicestershire

T. J. Boon c Humphries b Arnold	54	D. J. Millns b Newman	6
V. J. Wells lbw b Potter	39	A. D. Mullally c Thomas b Potter	3
W. J. Cronje c Jahangir b Potter	0	T. J. Mason not out	5
*J. J. Whitaker b Newman	2	L-b 8, w 2, n-b 2	12
†P. E. Robinson b Newman	1		
B. F. Smith c and b Potter	21	1/70 2/70 3/72 (50.3 overs)	198
D. L. Maddy b Goldsmith	27	4/76 5/126 6/126	
G. J. Parsons c Humphries b Newman	28	7/183 8/187 9/191	

Bowling: Newman 10–1–29–4; Arnold 10–2–33–1; R. A. Evans 10–1–42–0; Potter 10.3–2–23–4; Thomas 3–0–31–0; Goldsmith 7–0–32–1.

Umpires: B. Dudleston and B. J. Meyer.

WARWICKSHIRE v LANCASHIRE

At Birmingham, May 2. Lancashire won by 40 runs. Toss: Lancashire.

Lancashire cruised past 300; this was thanks to Atherton, who reached his century before lunch, Gallian, who helped him add 210 in 43 overs, and Fairbrother, who smashed 60 in 34 deliveries after being dropped second ball. Welch became the first bowler to concede a century in the Benson and Hedges Cup. Warwickshire's hopes perished when a 160-run stand between Moles and Ostler was ended by Yates.

Gold Award: M. A. Atherton.

Lancashire

M. A. Atherton c Reeve b Smith	114
J. E. R. Gallian not out	116
J. P. Crawley c Small b Smith	2
N. H. Fairbrother not out	60
L-b 3, n-b 10	13
1/210 2/214 (2 wkts, 55 overs)	305

G. D. Lloyd, *M. Watkinson, Wasim Akram, †W. K. Hegg, I. D. Austin, P. J. Martin and G. Yates did not bat.

Bowling: Donald 11–0–47–0; Small 11–2–25–0; Reeve 11–0–50–0; Welch 11–0–103–0; Smith 11–0–77–2.

Warwickshire

A. J. Moles c and b Yates	89	G. Welch not out	27
N. V. Knight b Austin	3	G. C. Small b Martin	3
D. P. Ostler c Watkinson b Yates	73	A. A. Donald c Watkinson	
R. G. Twose c Hegg b Martin	0	b Wasim Akram	2
T. L. Penney c Hegg b Yates	1	L-b 14, w 6, n-b 13	33
*D. A. Reeve b Austin	20		
N. M. K. Smith c Atherton		1/20 2/180 3/181	(51.1 overs) 265
b Wasim Akram	2	4/184 5/211 6/216	
†M. Burns b Watkinson	12	7/220 8/259 9/262	

Bowling: Wasim Akram 9.1–0–58–2; Martin 10–1–35–2; Austin 11–2–65–2; Watkinson 10–1–41–1; Yates 11–0–52–3.

Umpires: A. G. T. Whitehead and P. B. Wight.

LANCASHIRE v NOTTINGHAMSHIRE

At Manchester, May 9. Lancashire won by 77 runs. Toss: Lancashire.

Lancashire passed 300 for the third time in the qualifying rounds and went on to their highest total in the competition, a record for matches between first-class counties, and the third highest in 24 years of the tournament. Though Atherton was caught behind fourth ball, Gallian and Crawley added 250 in 41 overs, an all-wicket record for Lancashire in one-day cricket. Gallian scored 134 from 137 balls, his second successive Benson and Hedges century, and Crawley made his first, 114 from 120. Cairns had been unfit to bowl (spinner Afford shared the new ball) and a side strain later prevented Pollard batting. Though Nottinghamshire could not approach the asking-rate, the aggregate of 629 was only one below the record set by Lancashire and Leicestershire two weeks earlier.

Gold Award: J. E. R. Gallian.

Lancashire

M. A. Atherton c French b Evans	0	I. D. Austin b Evans	6
J. E. R. Gallian st French b Hindson	134	†W. K. Hegg not out	4
J. P. Crawley b Afford	114	L-b 5, w 10	15
N. H. Fairbrother c Cairns b Mike	37		
G. D. Lloyd c Pick b Mike	7	1/0 2/250 3/277	(7 wkts, 55 overs) 353
*M. Watkinson not out	34	4/301 5/312	
Wasim Akram c sub b Pick	2	6/322 7/348	

G. Chapple and G. Yates did not bat.

Bowling: Evans 9–1–59–2; Afford 10–0–38–1; Pick 9–0–65–1; Hindson 10–0–69–1; Mike 11–0–73–2; Archer 6–0–44–0.

Nottinghamshire

*R. T. Robinson c Fairbrother		†B. N. French c Chapple b Fairbrother	9
b Wasim Akram	36	R. A. Pick not out	21
P. Johnson c Yates b Wasim Akram	12		
G. F. Archer c Austin b Gallian	74	B 1, l-b 6, w 5, n-b 6	18
C. L. Cairns c Fairbrother b Yates	9		
K. P. Evans b Watkinson	47	1/15 2/89 3/112	(7 wkts, 55 overs) 276
G. W. Mike c Lloyd b Watkinson	9	4/169 5/191	
J. E. Hindson not out	41	6/201 7/246	

P. R. Pollard and J. A. Afford did not bat.

Bowling: Wasim Akram 7–0–20–2; Austin 8–2–20–0; Chapple 6–0–28–0; Watkinson 11–0–44–2; Yates 11–0–53–1; Gallian 6–0–45–1; Lloyd 3–0–42–0; Fairbrother 3–0–17–1.

Umpires: D. R. Shepherd and P. Willey.

LEICESTERSHIRE v WARWICKSHIRE

At Leicester, May 9. Warwickshire won by eight wickets. Toss: Leicestershire.

Leicestershire were already out of the competition but Warwickshire's comfortable victory kept them in with a chance. Moles put on 88 with Ostler, who scored 52 from 55 balls despite a knee injury, and 120 with Twose.

Gold Award: A. J. Moles.

Leicestershire

V. J. Wells b Brown	17		G. J. Parsons not out		21
*N. E. Briers lbw b Brown	0		A. R. K. Pierson not out		9
W. J. Cronje run out	34				
J. J. Whitaker c Davis b P. A. Smith	50		L-b 8, w 7		15
B. F. Smith run out	12				—
†P. E. Robinson c Twose b P. A. Smith	54		1/14 2/20 3/105	(8 wkts, 55 overs)	224
D. L. Maddy st Burns b N. M. K. Smith	4		4/109 5/132 6/145		
J. M. Dakin b Brown	8		7/174 8/199		

A. D. Mullally did not bat.

Bowling: Small 6–1–18–0; Brown 11–2–43–3; Davis 7–0–30–0; Welch 11–0–49–0; P. A. Smith 11–1–49–2; N. M. K. Smith 9–1–27–1.

Warwickshire

*A. J. Moles c Wells b Parsons	78	
D. P. Ostler b Parsons	52	
R. G. Twose not out	62	
T. L. Penney not out	12	
L-b 4, w 19	23	
1/88 2/208	(2 wkts, 52 overs)	227

P. A. Smith, G. Welch, †M. Burns, D. R. Brown, N. M. K. Smith, G. C. Small and R. P. Davis did not bat.

Bowling: Mullally 11–1–46–0; Parsons 11–2–36–2; Cronje 11–0–35–0; Dakin 2–0–27–0; Pierson 11–0–52–0; Wells 6–0–27–0.

Umpires: J. H. Harris and R. Julian.

MINOR COUNTIES v DURHAM

At Jesmond, May 9. Durham won by seven runs. Toss: Minor Counties.

At 133 for one from 36 overs, Minor Counties might just have pulled off a second win. But Birbeck and Walker saw off the threat. Earlier, Larkins faced 20 balls before managing a scoring stroke, in the ninth over, but scored a hundred off his next 88. He hit 15 fours and three sixes and added 163 with Prabhakar.

Gold Award: W. Larkins.

Durham

*M. A. Roseberry b Sharp	7		†C. W. Scott c Potter b Hignett		1
W. Larkins c Thomas b Sharp	123		J. Boiling not out		5
M. Prabhakar c Arnold b Potter	58		A. Walker not out		1
J. A. Daley c Dean b Arnold	17		L-b 4, w 5		9
M. Saxelby c Hignett b Thomas	20				
J. I. Longley c Arnold b Thomas	4		1/7 2/170 3/202	(9 wkts, 55 overs)	250
S. D. Birbeck run out	1		4/219 5/225 6/227		
J. Wood c Scothern b Thomas	4		7/238 8/240 9/246		

Bowling: Arnold 11–4–23–1; Sharp 11–4–36–2; Thomas 7–0–34–3; Scothern 6–0–51–0; Goldsmith 3–0–28–0; Potter 11–0–48–1; Hignett 6–0–26–1.

Minor Counties

S. J. Dean b Birbeck	40	M. G. Scothern run out	1
R. J. Evans b Walker	56	M. A. Sharp b Walker	0
L. Potter c Scott b Prabhakar	34	K. A. Arnold not out	2
*I. Cockbain c Scott b Birbeck	15	B 1, l-b 6, w 11	18
S. C. Goldsmith c Birbeck b Walker	10		
†M. I. Humphries b Walker	26	1/75 2/133 3/139 (9 wkts, 55 overs) 243	
R. G. Hignett c Walker b Birbeck	23	4/151 5/165 6/204	
D. R. Thomas not out	18	7/227 8/229 9/230	

Bowling: Wood 11–1–54–0; Prabhakar 11–1–35–1; Walker 11–0–42–4; Boiling 11–0–41–0; Birbeck 11–0–64–3.

Umpires: J. W. Holder and K. E. Palmer.

LANCASHIRE v DURHAM

At Manchester, May 16, 17. No result. Toss: Lancashire.

Only 18 overs were possible after a 2.45 p.m. start on the first day. Wasim Akram had just dismissed the Durham openers, in his first two overs, when rain returned, ending Durham's last chance of qualifying.

Durham

*M. A. Roseberry c Fairbrother b Wasim Akram	27	J. E. Morris not out	1
W. Larkins lbw b Wasim Akram	19	L-b 2, w 2	4
M. Prabhakar not out	6	1/46 2/49 (2 wkts, 18 overs) 57	

J. A. Daley, M. Saxelby, S. D. Birbeck, †D. G. C. Ligertwood, J. Boiling, A. Walker and J. P. Searle did not bat.

Bowling: Chapple 6–1–24–0; Martin 3–1–9–0; Austin 6–1–17–0; Wasim Akram 3–1–5–2.

Lancashire

*M. A. Atherton, J. E. R. Gallian, J. P. Crawley, N. H. Fairbrother, G. D. Lloyd, Wasim Akram, I. D. Austin, †W. K. Hegg, P. J. Martin, G. Chapple and G. Yates.

Umpires: P. B. Wight and P. Willey.

NOTTINGHAMSHIRE v LEICESTERSHIRE

At Nottingham, May 16, 17. No result. Toss: Leicestershire.

A flooded outfield prevented any resumption on the second day, and one point was enough to safeguard Nottinghamshire's second place in the group table.

Leicestershire

D. L. Maddy c French b Afford	50	G. J. Parsons not out	1
*N. E. Briers lbw b Pick	5	†P. Whitticase not out	0
W. J. Cronje c French b Cairns	14	B 2, l-b 2, w 3, n-b 4	11
J. J. Whitaker run out	72		
V. J. Wells c and b Afford	31	1/14 2/57 3/88 (6 wkts, 49.3 overs) 211	
B. F. Smith c Robinson b Mike	27	4/138 5/207 6/211	

A. R. K. Pierson, A. D. Mullally and D. J. Millns did not bat.

Bowling: Evans 9–1–30–0; Pick 10–1–40–1; Mike 9.3–1–44–1; Cairns 8–0–34–1; Afford 10–0–44–2; Wileman 3–0–15–0.

Nottinghamshire

*R. T. Robinson, M. P. Dowman, G. F. Archer, P. Johnson, C. L. Cairns, J. R. Wileman, †B. N. French, K. P. Evans, G. W. Mike, R. A. Pick and J. A. Afford.

Umpires: J. C. Balderstone and J. W. Holder.

WARWICKSHIRE v MINOR COUNTIES

At Birmingham, May 16, 17. No result. Toss: Minor Counties.

Rain here and at Nottingham ended Warwickshire's defence of their title. Moles fell to Sharp's first ball but Knight and Ostler added 99 before play was called off.

Warwickshire

A. J. Moles lbw b Sharp	1
N. V. Knight not out	42
D. P. Ostler not out	54
W 3	3

1/1   (1 wkt, 23 overs) 100

R. G. Twose, *D. A. Reeve, P. A. Smith, N. M. K. Smith, †M. Burns, D. R. Brown, R. P. Davis and M. A. V. Bell did not bat.

Bowling: Arnold 3.3–1–7–0; Sharp 7–0–29–1; Myles 3.3–0–12–0; Potter 5–0–25–0; R. A. Evans 4–0–27–0.

Minor Counties

S. J. Dean, R. J. Evans, L. Potter, *I. Cockbain, S. D. Myles, S. C. Goldsmith, M. A. Sharp, R. G. Hignett, †M. I. Humphries, R. A. Evans and K. A. Arnold.

Umpires: T. E. Jesty and R. Palmer.

GROUP B

DERBYSHIRE v NORTHAMPTONSHIRE

At Derby, April 23. Derbyshire won by eight wickets. Toss: Derbyshire. County debuts: D. J. Cullinan; A. Kumble.

Northamptonshire lost both openers for ten, and only Lamb passed 25; Wells was especially unhittable. In contrast, Barnett and Adams added 160 for the second wicket in 36 overs. Adams hit 14 fours in 101 balls and was out six short of victory.

Gold Award: C. J. Adams.

Northamptonshire

A. Fordham b Malcolm	0	A. Kumble c DeFreitas b Malcolm	3
M. B. Loye c Krikken b Warner	2	J. G. Hughes c Krikken b Malcolm	2
R. J. Bailey c Cork b DeFreitas	10	J. P. Taylor not out	4
*A. J. Lamb c Barnett b Wells	41	L-b 12, w 8, n-b 4	24
K. M. Curran c Barnett b Cork	22		
†R. J. Warren run out	23	1/2 2/10 3/46 (53.1 overs) 179
D. J. Capel lbw b Malcolm	23	4/86 5/93 6/129
A. L. Penberthy lbw b DeFreitas	25	7/145 8/159 9/164

Bowling: Malcolm 11–1–50–4; Warner 11–1–31–1; DeFreitas 10.1–0–28–2; Cork 11–0–40–1; Wells 10–1–18–1.

Derbyshire

*K. J. Barnett not out	58
A. S. Rollins lbw b Hughes	4
C. J. Adams c Fordham b Hughes	94
D. J. Cullinan not out	1
B 1, l-b 7, w 9, n-b 6	23

1/14 2/174   (2 wkts, 39.5 overs) 180

T. J. G. O'Gorman, D. G. Cork, P. A. J. DeFreitas, C. M. Wells, †K. M. Krikken, A. E. Warner and D. E. Malcolm did not bat.

Bowling: Taylor 5–0–24–0; Hughes 7.5–1–47–2; Penberthy 9–3–17–0; Capel 5–0–18–0; Kumble 9–0–40–0; Curran 4–0–26–0.

Umpires: J. D. Bond and K. J. Lyons.

WORCESTERSHIRE v SCOTLAND

At Worcester, April 23. Worcestershire won by ten wickets. Toss: Worcestershire.

Scotland's last pair, Haggo and Thomson, put on 35 to take them into three figures from 83 for nine. Their new professional, West Indian Test star Malcolm Marshall, made only two and later had three catches dropped as Weston and Curtis eased home without loss in less than half their allotted 55 overs.

Gold Award: N. V. Radford.

Scotland

S. T. Crawley c Radford b Moody	1	†D. J. Haggo not out		20
*A. C. Storie c Moody b Lampitt	12	P. D. Steindl b Lampitt		2
G. N. Reifer c Rhodes b Newport	4	K. Thomson b Illingworth		17
M. J. Smith c Rhodes b Radford	23	B 1, l-b 6, w 2, n-b 6		15
G. B. J. McGurk c Haynes b Lampitt	11			
M. D. Marshall b Radford	2	1/3 2/16 3/30	(53.1 overs)	118
J. G. Williamson lbw b Radford	0	4/48 5/54 6/56		
I. M. Stanger c Rhodes b Lampitt	11	7/73 8/78 9/83		

Bowling: Newport 11–2–27–1; Moody 7–3–10–0; Radford 11–3–23–3; Lampitt 11–3–24–4; Illingworth 10.1–3–19–1; Haynes 3–0–8–0.

Worcestershire

W. P. C. Weston not out	54
*T. S. Curtis not out	54
L-b 2, w 1, n-b 8	11

(no wkt, 27.1 overs) 119

T. M. Moody, G. A. Hick, G. R. Haynes, M. J. Church, †S. J. Rhodes, S. R. Lampitt, P. J. Newport, R. K. Illingworth and N. V. Radford did not bat.

Bowling: Marshall 7–1–19–0; Stanger 6.1–0–22–0; Steindl 4–0–17–0; Thomson 5–0–32–0; Reifer 3–0–13–0; Williamson 2–0–14–0.

Umpires: J. C. Balderstone and J. H. Harris.

SCOTLAND v DERBYSHIRE

At Titwood, Glasgow, April 25. Derbyshire won by 46 runs. Toss: Derbyshire.

Cullinan made an unbeaten century on a slow pitch after being dropped off Marshall on 13. Scotland's prospects disappeared after a fifth-wicket stand of 54 between Love and Marshall was broken.

Gold Award: D. J. Cullinan.

Derbyshire

*K. J. Barnett c Love b Thomson	40	P. A. J. DeFreitas c Stanger b Marshall		0
A. S. Rollins c Haggo b Steindl	9	C. M. Wells not out		3
C. J. Adams c Haggo b Steindl	12	L-b 8, w 11, n-b 8		27
D. J. Cullinan not out	101			
T. J. G. O'Gorman lbw b Steindl	16	1/33 2/52 3/94	(6 wkts, 55 overs)	220
D. G. Cork b Marshall	12	4/166 5/190 6/190		

†K. M. Krikken, A. E. Warner and D. E. Malcolm did not bat.

Bowling: Marshall 11–2–35–2; Stanger 11–1–64–0; Steindl 11–0–43–3; Thomson 11–0–32–1; Govan 11–0–38–0.

Scotland

S. T. Crawley c DeFreitas b Malcolm . .	34	†D. J. Haggo lbw b Malcolm	2
A. C. Storie b Warner	2	P. D. Steindl not out	14
G. N. Reifer lbw b Warner	10	K. Thomson b DeFreitas	0
M. J. Smith lbw b Cork	0	L-b 6, w 4, n-b 2	12
*J. D. Love lbw b DeFreitas	35		
M. D. Marshall c O'Gorman b Malcolm	36	1/6 2/29 3/38	(53 overs) 174
I. M. Stanger c Rollins b Malcolm	27	4/59 5/113 6/137	
J. W. Govan c Krikken b Cork	2	7/143 8/146 9/172	

Bowling: DeFreitas 10–2–22–2; Warner 11–4–26–2; Cork 11–0–43–2; Barnett 6–2–21–0; Wells 5–0–22–0; Malcolm 10–0–34–4.

Umpires: B. Dudleston and A. G. T. Whitehead.

YORKSHIRE v WORCESTERSHIRE

At Leeds, April 25. Yorkshire won by six wickets. Toss: Yorkshire.

Australian Michael Bevan achieved victory by hitting Illingworth for six, reaching an unbeaten 83 on his first home appearance for Yorkshire. Earlier, Hick scored a hundred, but without his usual fluency; like Gough and White, it was his first competitive appearance after injury on the Ashes tour. Hartley might have had him caught on 16 and 78.

Gold Award: M. G. Bevan.

Worcestershire

W. P. C. Weston c Grayson b Robinson	0	†S. J. Rhodes c Moxon b Gough	12
*T. S. Curtis lbw b White	35	S. R. Lampitt not out	1
G. A. Hick run out	109	B 8, l-b 9, w 7	24
T. M. Moody b Hartley	10		
G. R. Haynes lbw b Gough	12	1/2 2/88 3/149	(6 wkts, 55 overs) 208
D. A. Leatherdale not out	5	4/181 5/190 6/204	

P. J. Newport, R. K. Illingworth and N. V. Radford did not bat.

Bowling: Gough 11–2–27–2; Robinson 11–1–23–1; Hartley 11–3–35–1; White 11–0–68–1; Stemp 11–2–38–0.

Yorkshire

*M. D. Moxon b Newport	7	†R. J. Blakey not out	19
M. P. Vaughan c Illingworth b Lampitt	14	L-b 2, w 1, n-b 14	17
D. Byas run out	29		
M. G. Bevan not out	83	1/17 2/31	(4 wkts, 51.4 overs) 212
C. White c Rhodes b Radford	43	3/66 4/165	

A. P. Grayson, D. Gough, P. J. Hartley, R. D. Stemp and M. A. Robinson did not bat.

Bowling: Newport 10–0–49–1; Moody 3–1–9–0; Lampitt 11–2–28–1; Radford 11–0–42–1; Illingworth 9.4–1–37–0; Haynes 7–0–45–0.

Umpires: G. I. Burgess and D. J. Constant.

NORTHAMPTONSHIRE v WORCESTERSHIRE

At Northampton, May 2. Worcestershire won by 103 runs. Toss: Northamptonshire.

Northamptonshire disappointed in their first home match since the removal of the football terraces; they were bowled out in 47 overs for 137, which owed everything to Curran's fifty. Illingworth took four for 27 and Newport's 11 overs cost just 13. Hick looked more confident than at Leeds, as he and Moody added 91 in 21 overs. Again, Curran provided Northamptonshire's sole highlight, with four for 38.

Gold Award: G. A. Hick.

Worcestershire

W. P. C. Weston c Penberthy b Taylor	3
*T. S. Curtis c Warren b Curran	30
G. A. Hick c and b Curran	94
T. M. Moody c and b Bailey	41
G. R. Haynes run out	27
D. A. Leatherdale c Warren b Curran	2
†S. J. Rhodes c Kumble b Curran	6
N. V. Radford not out	12
R. K. Illingworth not out	4
B 4, l-b 9, w 8	21

P. Mirza and P. J. Newport did not bat.

1/5 2/69 3/160   (7 wkts, 55 overs) 240
4/201 5/207
6/215 7/219

Bowling: Taylor 8–1–29–1; Hughes 4–1–15–0; Penberthy 7–0–39–0; Curran 11–3–38–4; Kumble 11–0–40–0; Capel 10–0–37–0; Bailey 4–0–29–1.

Northamptonshire

R. R. Montgomerie run out	5
A. Fordham c Rhodes b Haynes	20
R. J. Bailey c Rhodes b Newport	0
*A. J. Lamb b Haynes	16
K. M. Curran b Illingworth	50
†R. J. Warren c and b Illingworth	8
D. J. Capel b Illingworth	6
A. L. Penberthy c Rhodes b Haynes	17
A. Kumble b Newport	2
J. G. Hughes st Rhodes b Illingworth	0
J. P. Taylor not out	7
L-b 5, w 1	6

1/12 2/12 3/37   (46.5 overs) 137
4/58 5/76 6/88
7/117 8/120 9/123

Bowling: Newport 11–3–13–2; Mirza 9–0–40–0; Haynes 6.5–1–21–3; Radford 9–1–31–0; Illingworth 11–1–27–4.

Umpires: A. A. Jones and D. R. Shepherd.

SCOTLAND v YORKSHIRE

At Titwood, Glasgow, May 2. Yorkshire won by ten wickets. Toss: Yorkshire.
    Yorkshire became the first team to win three Benson and Hedges fixtures by ten wickets as Moxon and Vaughan swept past their small target with 32.3 overs in hand. Scotland were 31 for five before Love, the former Yorkshire player, fought his way to 54. Robinson bowled 11 overs for only eight runs.
    Gold Award: P. J. Hartley.

Scotland

S. T. Crawley c White b Robinson	14
G. N. Reifer b Gough	0
G. B. J. McGurk b Hartley	7
M. J. Smith b Stemp	2
*J. D. Love c Blakey b Hartley	54
M. D. Marshall c Blakey b Hartley	0
J. G. Williamson b Stemp	19
I. M. Stanger c White b Gough	3
J. W. Govan c Blakey b Hartley	14
†D. J. Haggo c Blakey b White	6
P. D. Steindl not out	2
B 1, l-b 4, w 3	8

1/1 2/21 3/24   (51.1 overs) 129
4/24 5/31 6/70
7/87 8/116 9/123

Bowling: Gough 9–1–21–2; Robinson 11–6–8–1; Hartley 11–4–21–4; Stemp 11–1–28–2; White 6.1–0–26–1; Grayson 3–0–20–0.

Yorkshire

*M. D. Moxon not out	66
M. P. Vaughan not out	50
L-b 7, w 3, n-b 4	14

(no wkt, 22.3 overs) 130

D. Byas, M. G. Bevan, C. White, †R. J. Blakey, A. P. Grayson, D. Gough, P. J. Hartley, R. D. Stemp and M. A. Robinson did not bat.

Bowling: Marshall 5–0–24–0; Stanger 6–1–23–0; Steindl 4–0–32–0; Williamson 5–0–17–0; Govan 2.3–0–27–0.

Umpires: J. D. Bond and J. W. Holder.

WORCESTERSHIRE v DERBYSHIRE

At Worcester, May 9. Worcestershire won by 132 runs. Toss: Worcestershire.

Hick scored an undefeated 127 from 124 balls, with 13 fours and a six. It was his sixth and biggest century in the competition. In reply, Derbyshire collapsed to 34 for five. Haynes took three for six in his first seven overs; Lampitt also bowled with great economy.

Gold Award: G. A. Hick.

Worcestershire

W. P. C. Weston run out	13	S. R. Lampitt c Rollins b Malcolm	13
*T. S. Curtis b Warner	6	L-b 6, w 7, n-b 2	15
G. A. Hick not out	127		
T. M. Moody c Cullinan b Harris	51		
G. R. Haynes c DeFreitas b Malcolm ..	11	1/18 2/25 3/114 (7 wkts, 55 overs)	267
D. A. Leatherdale c Malcolm b Warner	29	4/139 5/224	
†S. J. Rhodes c O'Gorman b Malcolm .	2	6/234 7/267	

P. J. Newport, R. K. Illingworth and N. V. Radford did not bat.

Bowling: DeFreitas 11–2–24–0; Warner 11–0–54–2; Cork 11–0–59–0; Malcolm 11–0–70–3; Harris 11–0–54–1.

Derbyshire

*K. J. Barnett lbw b Haynes	0	A. J. Harris lbw b Lampitt	5
†A. S. Rollins c Rhodes b Lampitt ...	15	A. E. Warner not out	2
C. J. Adams b Haynes	5	D. E. Malcolm c Hick b Lampitt	4
D. J. Cullinan b Newport	4	B 2, l-b 1, w 6, n-b 2	11
T. J. G. O'Gorman lbw b Haynes	1		
D. G. Cork c Rhodes b Illingworth ...	26	1/0 2/9 3/14 (41 overs)	135
P. A. J. DeFreitas c Rhodes b Newport	37	4/17 5/34 6/77	
T. W. Harrison c Lampitt b Illingworth	25	7/101 8/127 9/131	

Bowling: Haynes 8–2–17–3; Newport 11–1–41–2; Lampitt 7–2–19–3; Radford 8–0–34–0; Illingworth 7–0–21–2.

Umpires: J. D. Bond and B. J. Meyer.

YORKSHIRE v NORTHAMPTONSHIRE

At Leeds, May 9. Yorkshire won by ten runs. Toss: Northamptonshire.

Bevan scored another half-century for Yorkshire, who were 143 for two before their last eight went for 80. But with three front-line batsmen injured, Northamptonshire depended heavily on Bailey and Curran. Their 88-run partnership ended when Bevan ran out Bailey with a direct hit.

Gold Award: M. G. Bevan.

Yorkshire

*M. D. Moxon c Bailey b Penberthy ...	24	P. J. Hartley not out	8
M. P. Vaughan b Capel	23	R. D. Stemp b Kumble	0
D. Byas b Snape	35	M. A. Robinson lbw b Kumble	1
M. G. Bevan c and b Taylor	64	L-b 4, w 6, n-b 4	14
C. White c Walton b Penberthy	9		
†R. J. Blakey c Warren b Penberthy ...	13	1/53 2/56 3/143 (53.4 overs)	223
A. P. Grayson run out	18	4/154 5/178 6/193	
D. Gough c Hughes b Snape	14	7/213 8/215 9/215	

Bowling: Taylor 10–1–39–1; Hughes 3–0–17–0; Capel 7–1–21–1; Penberthy 11–1–39–3; Curran 6–0–35–0; Kumble 10.4–0–40–2; Snape 6–0–28–2.

Northamptonshire

†R. J. Warren c Vaughan b Robinson..	22	A. Kumble b Grayson	0
M. B. Loye lbw b Gough	0	J. G. Hughes b Hartley	9
*R. J. Bailey run out	61	J. P. Taylor not out	1
T. C. Walton c and b Hartley	6	L-b 8, w 4	12
K. M. Curran lbw b Stemp...........	53		
D. J. Capel b Stemp	0	1/7 2/41 3/50	(54.4 overs) 213
A. L. Penberthy st Blakey b Grayson ..	26	4/138 5/138 6/171	
J. N. Snape c Grayson b Hartley	23	7/188 8/188 9/211	

Bowling: Gough 11–2–39–1; Robinson 9–3–22–1; Hartley 9.4–2–37–3; White 7–1–32–0; Stemp 11–1–39–2; Grayson 7–0–36–2.

Umpires: N. T. Plews and R. A. White.

DERBYSHIRE v YORKSHIRE

At Chesterfield, May 16, 17. No result (abandoned).

A washout ended Derbyshire's chances of reaching the quarter-finals, which depended on their winning; Yorkshire made sure of heading the group.

NORTHAMPTONSHIRE v SCOTLAND

At Northampton, May 16. Northamptonshire won by 153 runs. Toss: Scotland. First-team debut: S. A. J. Boswell.

Northamptonshire's highest Benson and Hedges total brought their first win in one-day competitions in 1995. Fordham scored his second hundred in the tournament – the first was also against Scotland – and added 164 with Bailey. Scotland's openers failed to score and they reached only half their target. Newcomer Scott Boswell bowled five overs for six runs.

Gold Award: R. J. Bailey.

Northamptonshire

†R. J. Warren c Stanger b Marshall ...	0	A. L. Penberthy c Stanger b Cowan ...	8
A. Fordham c Love b Williamson	108	J. N. Snape not out	1
R. J. Bailey not out	93	B 6, l-b 12, w 17, n-b 6	41
T. C. Walton c Stanger b Cowan	29		
*A. J. Lamb c Crawley b Cowan	22	1/1 2/165 3/224	(6 wkts, 55 overs) 304
K. M. Curran b Stanger	2	4/265 5/270 6/294	

A. Kumble, J. P. Taylor and S. A. J. Boswell did not bat.

Bowling: Marshall 11–1–47–1; Cowan 11–0–64–3; Williamson 9–0–65–1; Stanger 11–1–55–1; Govan 11–0–46–0; Reifer 2–0–9–0.

Scotland

S. T. Crawley lbw b Taylor..........	0	*J. D. Love not out	14
A. C. Storie c Warren b Boswell	0		
G. N. Reifer not out	57	L-b 6, w 9, n-b 4	19
M. J. Smith c Penberthy b Snape	35		
J. G. Williamson c Lamb b Kumble	24	1/0 2/20 3/70	(5 wkts, 55 overs) 151
M. D. Marshall c Warren b Walton ...	2	4/119 5/123	

D. Cowan, J. W. Govan, I. M. Stanger and †D. J. Haggo did not bat.

Bowling: Taylor 5–3–15–1; Boswell 5–2–6–1; Curran 5–0–22–0; Penberthy 5–1–16–0; Bailey 11–2–21–0; Snape 11–3–23–1; Kumble 7–1–15–1; Walton 6–0–27–1.

Umpires: G. Sharp and A. G. T. Whitehead.

GROUP C

The Combined Universities' squad for the competition was: G. I. Macmillan (Oxford) (*captain*), J. N. Batty (Durham), A. D. Edwards (Loughborough), S. W. K. Ellis (Warwick), C. M. Gupte (Oxford), M. E. Harvey (Loughborough), W. S. Kendall (Oxford), G. A. Khan (Swansea), N. Killeen (Teesside), A. D. MacRobert (Oxford), M. T. E. Peirce (Durham), U. B. A. Rashid (South Bank), S. J. Renshaw (Leeds), K. R. Spiring (Durham), I. G. S. Steer (Cheltenham & Gloucester CHE), I. J. Sutcliffe (Oxford), A. R. Whittall (Cambridge).

ESSEX v GLAMORGAN

At Chelmsford, April 23. Glamorgan won by 28 runs. Toss: Essex. County debut: N. F. Williams.

James, called up because Morris had a back injury, set up Glamorgan's total while Croft, scoring fifty in 42 balls, pushed them past five an over. For Essex, Prichard reached 92 from 108 balls, but once he went at 207 the rest soon followed, giving Glamorgan their first Benson and Hedges win in Essex.

Gold Award: S. P. James.

Glamorgan

S. P. James lbw b Irani	82	R. P. Lefebvre run out	4
D. L. Hemp lbw b Irani	29	†C. P. Metson not out	10
*M. P. Maynard c Williams b Such	25	L-b 19, w 6, n-b 10	35
P. A. Cottey c Such b Irani	25		
A. Dale c Cousins b Such	17	1/58 2/98 3/189 (7 wkts, 55 overs) 277	
R. D. B. Croft not out	50	4/194 5/229	
G. P. Butcher lbw b Such	0	6/229 7/243	

S. L. Watkin and S. R. Barwick did not bat.

Bowling: Ilott 11–0–62–0; Williams 6–0–44–0; Irani 11–2–48–3; Such 11–2–27–3; Cousins 7–0–44–0; Gooch 9–0–33–0.

Essex

G. A. Gooch b Watkin	21	N. F. Williams c Croft b Watkin	3
*P. J. Prichard c Maynard b Croft	92	P. M. Such c and b Dale	0
J. J. B. Lewis b Lefebvre	10	D. M. Cousins not out	12
N. Hussain c Metson b Lefebvre	10	B 1, l-b 6, w 7, n-b 2	16
R. C. Irani lbw b Dale	26		
D. D. J. Robinson lbw b Dale	14	1/42 2/62 3/82 (52.2 overs) 249	
†M. A. Garnham c Metson b Watkin	24	4/145 5/167 6/207	
M. C. Ilott b Dale	21	7/211 8/221 9/221	

Bowling: Watkin 11–0–56–3; Lefebvre 9.2–0–42–3; Croft 11–0–53–1; Barwick 10–1–43–0; Dale 11–1–48–3.

Umpires: R. A. White and P. B. Wight.

GLOUCESTERSHIRE v COMBINED UNIVERSITIES

At Bristol, April 23. Gloucestershire won by 126 runs. Toss: Combined Universities. County debuts: M. A. Lynch, J. Srinath, A. Symonds.

Symonds, the 19-year-old dual national born in Birmingham but brought up in Australia, had a stunning English debut, striking 95·from 70 balls with 12 fours and a six. He and Alleyne put on 108 after Gloucestershire were 86 for four. The county's new overseas player, Srinath, also flourished, with four wickets.

Gold Award: A. Symonds.

Gloucestershire

A. J. Wright c Spiring b MacRobert	... 13		M. C. J. Ball c Edwards b Killeen	.....	2
T. H. C. Hancock c Peirce b MacRobert	32		K. E. Cooper c MacRobert b Killeen	..	6
M. A. Lynch c Edwards b Whittall	... 28		A. M. Smith not out	....	1
R. I. Dawson c Batty b Whittall	 9		L-b 1, w 2, n-b 6	....	9
M. W. Alleyne c Killeen b Renshaw	... 34				
A. Symonds c Renshaw b Edwards	95		1/29 2/54 3/83	(9 wkts, 55 overs)	259
*†R. C. Russell not out	 29		4/86 5/194 6/237		
J. Srinath c Whittall b MacRobert	 1		7/239 8/245 9/257		

Bowling: Renshaw 11–3–43–1; Edwards 11–2–65–1; MacRobert 11–2–51–3; Killeen 11–0–50–2; Whittall 11–1–49–2.

Combined Universities

*G. I. Macmillan b Alleyne	 36		A. D. Edwards not out	....	7
M. T. E. Peirce lbw b Cooper	 19		A. R. Whittall c and b Srinath	.....	21
I. G. S. Steer lbw b Ball	 3		S. J. Renshaw lbw b Srinath	....	0
K. R. Spiring b Srinath	 2		B 3, l-b 8, w 5, n-b 8	......	24
M. E. Harvey lbw b Srinath	 0				
†J. N. Batty b Ball	 11		1/50 2/74 3/75	(43.3 overs)	133
A. D. MacRobert c Alleyne b Ball	 6		4/76 5/79 6/96		
N. Killeen b Smith	 4		7/96 8/103 9/133		

Bowling: Srinath 10.3–2–33–4; Smith 11–2–26–1; Cooper 5–1–20–1; Alleyne 6–0–17–1; Ball 11–4–26–3.

Umpires: T. E. Jesty and R. Julian.

MIDDLESEX v HAMPSHIRE

At Lord's, April 23. Middlesex won by six wickets. Toss: Middlesex. First-team debut: D. Follett. County debuts: D. J. Nash; J. P. Stephenson, H. H. Streak.

Stephenson, newly arrived from Essex, collected 82 runs, the wickets of Gatting and Carr in one over and the Gold Award, but still could not bring Hampshire victory. They fell away after he and Terry opened with 94. Ramprakash and Weekes, who scored 46 in 52 balls, took Middlesex most of the way with 80 in 17 overs.

Gold Award: J. P. Stephenson.

Hampshire

V. P. Terry b Emburey	 43		S. D. Udal not out	....	6
J. P. Stephenson c Feltham b Weekes	.. 82		M. J. Thursfield not out	....	0
R. A. Smith c Brown b Fraser	 17				
*M. C. J. Nicholas lbw b Weekes	 3		L-b 14, w 4, n-b 2	.....	20
P. R. Whitaker b Nash	 5				
†A. N. Aymes c Brown b Follett	 12		1/94 2/118 3/131	(8 wkts, 55 overs)	208
H. H. Streak run out	 18		4/141 5/172 6/174		
K. D. James b Follett	 2		7/199 8/203		

C. A. Connor did not bat.

Bowling: Fraser 9–1–21–1; Feltham 5–1–18–0; Weekes 10–0–39–2; Nash 11–2–43–1; Follett 11–1–44–2; Emburey 9–2–29–1.

Middlesex

*M. W. Gatting lbw b Stephenson	 38		†K. R. Brown not out	....	8
J. C. Pooley c Terry b James	 42		B 5, l-b 4, w 15, n-b 2	......	26
M. R. Ramprakash not out	 52				
J. D. Carr lbw b Stephenson	 0		1/73 2/113	(4 wkts, 51.3 overs)	212
P. N. Weekes c and b Streak	 46		3/113 4/193		

D. J. Nash, J. E. Emburey, M. A. Feltham, A. R. C. Fraser and D. Follett did not bat.

Bowling: Streak 11–0–41–1; Connor 8–2–26–0; Udal 11–0–38–0; Thursfield 6–1–25–0; James 5–1–23–1; Stephenson 9–1–33–2; Whitaker 1–0–13–0; Nicholas 0.3–0–4–0.

Umpires: B. Leadbeater and K. E. Palmer.

ESSEX v MIDDLESEX

At Chelmsford, April 25. Middlesex won by seven wickets. Toss: Middlesex.

Weekes figured in another match-winning stand, adding 167, a county fourth-wicket record in this competition, in 30 overs with Gatting. He also dismissed Prichard and Hussain, the only significant contributors for Essex until Robinson took 21 off the final over from Fraser.

Gold Award: P. N. Weekes.

Essex

G. A. Gooch lbw b Feltham	5	M. C. Ilott b Fraser		13
*P. J. Prichard b Weekes	65	N. F. Williams lbw b Fraser		0
J. J. B. Lewis lbw b Follett	6	P. M. Such not out		5
N. Hussain c Pooley b Weekes	65	L-b 1, w 2, n-b 2		5
R. C. Irani run out	25			
D. D. J. Robinson not out	35	1/16 2/53 3/118	(8 wkts, 55 overs)	225
†M. A. Garnham c Ramprakash		4/164 5/175 6/178		
b Fraser	1	7/197 8/197		

D. M. Cousins did not bat.

Bowling: Fraser 10–1–43–3; Feltham 7–1–28–1; Nash 10–1–50–0; Follett 6–0–24–1; Emburey 11–0–36–0; Weekes 11–0–43–2.

Middlesex

*M. W. Gatting not out	93	P. N. Weekes not out		67
J. C. Pooley lbw b Irani	15	B 9, l-b 7, w 4, n-b 6		26
M. R. Ramprakash lbw b Ilott	1			
J. D. Carr lbw b Williams	26	1/20 2/21 3/61	(3 wkts, 50.1 overs)	228

†K. R. Brown, D. J. Nash, J. E. Emburey, M. A. Feltham, A. R. C. Fraser and D. Follett did not bat.

Bowling: Ilott 11–0–37–1; Irani 11–3–36–1; Williams 9–0–49–1; Cousins 7.1–0–40–0; Such 10–0–42–0; Gooch 2–0–8–0.

Umpires: V. A. Holder and M. J. Kitchen.

GLAMORGAN v COMBINED UNIVERSITIES

At Cardiff, April 25. Glamorgan won by 217 runs. Toss: Glamorgan.

A maiden one-day century by Hemp saw Glamorgan to their highest Benson and Hedges total (beating 302 against the same opponents at the same venue in 1988). Thomas followed up with six for 20, equalling the county's best limited-overs bowling figures, by Croft in the Sunday League the previous season; and Glamorgan completed what was then the second biggest win by runs in the tournament's history. Hemp put on 164 with James and 85 with Maynard. For the students, only Spiring passed 15.

Gold Award: D. L. Hemp.

Glamorgan

S. P. James c and b Edwards	75	A. Dale not out		37
D. L. Hemp c Edwards b Killeen	121	B 5, l-b 4, w 4, n-b 4		17
*M. P. Maynard c Whittall b Killeen	41			
P. A. Cottey not out	27	1/164 2/249 3/262	(3 wkts, 55 overs)	318

R. D. B. Croft, G. P. Butcher, S. L. Watkin, R. P. Lefebvre, †C. P. Metson and S. D. Thomas did not bat.

Bowling: Renshaw 10–1–52–0; Edwards 11–3–45–1; Killeen 11–0–53–2; Whittall 11–0–65–0; MacRobert 8–0–67–0; Macmillan 4–0–27–0.

Combined Universities

*G. I. Macmillan lbw b Watkin	13	A. R. Whittall c and b Thomas	15
M. T. E. Peirce lbw b Lefebvre	15	A. D. Edwards c Cottey b Thomas	7
C. M. Gupte c Metson b Lefebvre	2	S. J. Renshaw not out	0
K. R. Spiring b Thomas	23	L-b 4, w 2, n-b 2	8
W. S. Kendall c Metson b Thomas	14		
†I. G. S. Steer c Metson b Thomas	4	1/20 2/30 3/33 (34.2 overs)	101
A. D. MacRobert c Metson b Thomas	0	4/62 5/71 6/71	
N. Killeen c Lefebvre b Croft	0	7/72 8/76 9/100	

Bowling: Watkin 8–2–28–1; Lefebvre 9–0–33–2; Thomas 9.2–3–20–6; Croft 8–2–16–1.

Umpires: J. C. Balderstone and A. A. Jones.

HAMPSHIRE v GLOUCESTERSHIRE

At Southampton, April 25. Gloucestershire won by four wickets. Toss: Gloucestershire.

Smith, returning his best bowling figures in senior competition, helped to reduce Hampshire to 78 for five. Gloucestershire's reply started disastrously, when Streak removed Hancock and Lynch for two, but Wright and Dawson saw them into three figures and Symonds tugged victory into sight with 33 in 25 balls.

Gold Award: A. M. Smith.

Hampshire

V. P. Terry c Russell b Smith	13	H. H. Streak b Smith	3
J. P. Stephenson lbw b Smith	11	M. J. Thursfield not out	4
R. A. Smith run out	28	C. A. Connor c Lynch b Smith	11
*M. C. J. Nicholas c Russell b Smith	1	B 1, l-b 8, w 6, n-b 5	20
P. R. Whitaker c Lynch b Alleyne	42		
†A. N. Aymes lbw b Ball	2	1/23 2/46 3/57 (55 overs)	162
K. D. James c Russell b Smith	15	4/66 5/78 6/110	
S. D. Udal c Dawson b Srinath	12	7/141 8/145 9/148	

Bowling: Srinath 11–0–36–1; Cooper 11–1–22–0; Smith 11–0–39–6; Alleyne 9–1–27–1; Ball 10–0–17–1; Dawson 3–0–12–0.

Gloucestershire

A. J. Wright c Aymes b Thursfield	51	*†R. C. Russell not out	8
T. H. C. Hancock c and b Streak	1	J. Srinath not out	0
M. A. Lynch c Terry b Streak	0	B 2, l-b 9, w 7	18
R. I. Dawson c Aymes b Thursfield	34		
M. W. Alleyne lbw b Udal	21	1/2 2/2 3/100 (6 wkts, 50.1 overs)	166
A. Symonds c James b Streak	33	4/115 5/139 6/162	

M. C. J. Ball, A. M. Smith and K. E. Cooper did not bat.

Bowling: Connor 10.1–5–23–0; Streak 9–3–28–3; Thursfield 8–1–40–2; James 6–2–14–0; Udal 11–3–22–1; Stephenson 6–0–28–0.

Umpires: J. H. Hampshire and R. Julian.

COMBINED UNIVERSITIES v ESSEX

At Cambridge, May 2. Essex won by eight wickets. Toss: Combined Universities.

Gooch expanded his record collection of Benson and Hedges hundreds and awards to 13 and 22 respectively. His unbeaten 115 took 140 balls and included 15 fours; he and Hussain put on 189 to give Essex victory after an edgy start. Gooch was in action in the seventh over of the match, which he completed when Williams pulled a hamstring.

Gold Award: G. A. Gooch.

Combined Universities

*G. I. Macmillan c Robinson b Such	.. 54	N. Killeen not out	2
I. J. Sutcliffe c Ilott b Irani	39	U. B. A. Rashid not out	6
M. T. E. Peirce c Pearson b Such	26	B 4, l-b 5, w 4, n-b 4	17
K. R. Spiring c Lewis b Irani	35		
W. S. Kendall run out	17	1/87 2/112 3/147 (7 wkts, 55 overs) 209	
A. R. Whittall c Rollins b Ilott	12	4/176 5/197	
A. D. Edwards b Irani	1	6/198 7/202	

†J. N. Batty and S. J. Renshaw did not bat.

Bowling: Williams 3.3–0–14–0; Ilott 11–0–39–1; Gooch 10.3–1–36–0; Irani 9–0–40–3; Pearson 11–0–43–0; Such 10–0–28–2.

Essex

G. A. Gooch not out	115
*P. J. Prichard run out	0
J. J. B. Lewis c Batty b Renshaw	11
N. Hussain not out	81
L-b 4, w 2	6

1/2 2/24 (2 wkts, 50.4 overs) 213

D. D. J. Robinson, R. C. Irani, M. C. Ilott, N. F. Williams, P. M. Such, †R. J. Rollins and R. M. Pearson did not bat.

Bowling: Renshaw 9–1–34–1; Edwards 10–1–40–0; Killeen 11–2–40–0; Rashid 11–0–46–0; Whittall 7–0–33–0; Macmillan 2.4–0–16–0.

Umpires: D. J. Constant and K. E. Palmer.

GLOUCESTERSHIRE v MIDDLESEX

At Bristol, May 2. Gloucestershire won by five runs. Toss: Middlesex.

Gloucestershire secured a third successive win when Follett was run out in the final over, bowled by Srinath, who had earlier taken the vital wickets of Gatting and Ramprakash. The home team's 186 had not looked enough to defend, but the pitch was sluggish and no one reached 50.

Gold Award: J. Srinath.

Gloucestershire

A. J. Wright b Follett	24	M. C. J. Ball lbw b Fraser	1
T. H. C. Hancock c Brown b Feltham	8	K. E. Cooper not out	16
M. A. Lynch run out	11		
R. I. Dawson c Nash b Emburey	38	L-b 6, w 3	9
M. W. Alleyne c Brown b Nash	42		
A. Symonds c Pooley b Emburey	1	1/14 2/35 3/68 (8 wkts, 55 overs) 186	
*†R. C. Russell not out	34	4/96 5/100 6/151	
J. Srinath b Nash	2	7/155 8/158	

A. M. Smith did not bat.

Bowling: Fraser 10–0–43–1; Feltham 7–1–24–1; Nash 11–2–31–2; Follett 7–0–32–1; Emburey 11–3–23–2; Weekes 9–0–27–0.

Middlesex

*M. W. Gatting c Lynch b Srinath	11	J. E. Emburey lbw b Srinath	0
J. C. Pooley c Russell b Alleyne	47	A. R. C. Fraser c Wright b Smith	1
M. R. Ramprakash lbw b Srinath	0	D. Follett run out	4
J. D. Carr c and b Ball	40	L-b 7, w 3	10
P. N. Weekes lbw b Ball	15		
†K. R. Brown run out	23	1/18 2/18 3/82 (54.4 overs) 181	
D. J. Nash b Alleyne	16	4/113 5/120 6/146	
M. A. Feltham not out	14	7/167 8/171 9/176	

Bowling: Srinath 10.4–4–26–3; Cooper 11–2–29–0; Smith 11–0–44–1; Ball 11–2–32–2; Alleyne 11–3–43–2.

Umpires: J. H. Hampshire and T. E. Jesty.

HAMPSHIRE v GLAMORGAN

At Southampton, May 2. Glamorgan won by seven wickets. Toss: Glamorgan.

James's third consecutive fifty and second successive century opening partnership with Hemp ensured that Glamorgan secured their third straight win in the tournament. For Hampshire, Stephenson and Smith added 125 for the second wicket, but both fell to Dale.

Gold Award: A. Dale.

Hampshire

J. P. Stephenson b Dale	55		H. H. Streak not out	3
V. P. Terry lbw b Watkin	17		†A. N. Aymes not out	4
R. A. Smith c Hemp b Dale	83		L-b 3, w 4, n-b 2	9
*M. C. J. Nicholas c Watkin b Dale	8			—
G. W. White run out	37		1/25 2/150 3/168	(6 wkts, 55 overs) 225
S. D. Udal c Dale b Barwick	9		4/175 5/209 6/220	

K. D. James, C. A. Connor and J. N. B. Bovill did not bat.

Bowling: Watkin 11–1–51–1; Lefebvre 11–2–35–0; Croft 11–1–34–0; Barwick 11–0–48–1; Dale 9–0–42–3; Butcher 2–0–12–0.

Glamorgan

S. P. James b Stephenson	54		A. Dale not out	19
D. L. Hemp lbw b Stephenson	52		B 4, l-b 6, w 9, n-b 8	27
*M. P. Maynard c Aymes b James	37			—
P. A. Cottey not out	38		1/116 2/121 3/188	(3 wkts, 46.1 overs) 227

R. D. B. Croft, G. P. Butcher, R. P. Lefebvre, †C. P. Metson, S. L. Watkin and S. R. Barwick did not bat.

Bowling: Streak 3–0–28–0; Connor 7–1–30–0; Bovill 8.1–0–50–0; Udal 11–1–37–0; Stephenson 10–1–35–2; James 7–0–37–1.

Umpires: G. I. Burgess and P. Willey.

COMBINED UNIVERSITIES v HAMPSHIRE

At Oxford, May 9. Hampshire won by virtue of losing fewer wickets. Toss: Combined Universities.

After six defeats in 1995, Hampshire won at the seventh attempt when Connor levelled the scores off the final ball; they had eight wickets down to the Universities' nine. They entered the final over looking for ten, and Killeen removed Aymes and Maru. Such a scrape had seemed unlikely as Stephenson and Terry opened with a stand of 145. The students also started well as the captain, Macmillan, helped each of the first three wickets to put on more than 50. A blow to his knee prevented him from fielding.

Gold Award: J. P. Stephenson.

Combined Universities

*G. I. Macmillan c Terry b Streak	77		N. Killeen c Connor b Udal	8
I. J. Sutcliffe lbw b Maru	28		†J. N. Batty not out	1
M. T. E. Peirce c Aymes b Stephenson	30			
K. R. Spiring c Aymes b Connor	27		B 1, l-b 6, w 4, n-b 8	19
W. S. Kendall run out	23			—
A. R. Whittall c Aymes b Connor	0		1/62 2/118 3/175	(9 wkts, 55 overs) 228
A. D. Edwards lbw b Connor	6		4/177 5/182 6/194	
U. B. A. Rashid b Bovill	9		7/213 8/226 9/228	

S. J. Renshaw did not bat.

Bowling: Connor 11–0–36–3; Bovill 8–1–37–1; Maru 6–0–24–1; Streak 11–2–35–1; Udal 11–0–49–1; Stephenson 7–1–33–1; Nicholas 1–0–7–0.

Hampshire

J. P. Stephenson c Whittall b Rashid	98	R. J. Maru b Killeen		0
V. P. Terry lbw b Renshaw	68	C. A. Connor not out		2
R. A. Smith run out	1			
G. W. White b Renshaw	0	L-b 2, w 4, n-b 6		12
*M. C. J. Nicholas c and b Whittall	3			
†A. N. Aymes c sub b Killeen	29	1/145 2/149 3/152	(8 wkts, 55 overs)	228
S. D. Udal b Edwards	7	4/164 5/184 6/217		
H. H. Streak not out	8	7/219 8/226		

J. N. B. Bovill did not bat.

Bowling: Renshaw 11–2–34–2; Edwards 11–0–31–1; Rashid 11–0–56–1; Killeen 11–2–43–2; Whittall 11–0–62–1.

Umpires: A. G. T. Whitehead and P. B. Wight.

ESSEX v GLOUCESTERSHIRE

At Chelmsford, May 9. Gloucestershire won by two wickets. Toss: Gloucestershire.

Russell struck the final ball to the third-man boundary to preserve Gloucestershire's unbeaten one-day record, under threat when off-spinner Pearson removed three of their top four. Only Gooch managed 50 on a slow pitch.

Gold Award: R. C. Russell.

Essex

G. A. Gooch c Cooper b Ball	69	M. C. Ilott c Alleyne b Smith		0
*P. J. Prichard lbw b Srinath	6	P. M. Such not out		1
D. D. J. Robinson lbw b Ball	32	B 1, l-b 7, w 6		14
N. Hussain c Symonds b Alleyne	27			
R. C. Irani c Ball b Srinath	40	1/11 2/96 3/118	(8 wkts, 55 overs)	208
J. J. B. Lewis b Smith	19	4/157 5/203 6/207		
†R. J. Rollins c Wright b Smith	0	7/207 8/208		

R. M. Pearson and D. M. Cousins did not bat.

Bowling: Srinath 11–3–30–2; Cooper 11–2–25–0; Smith 11–0–43–3; Ball 11–0–47–2; Alleyne 11–1–55–1.

Gloucestershire

A. J. Wright lbw b Irani	27	M. C. J. Ball run out		5
T. H. C. Hancock c Hussain b Pearson	36	K. E. Cooper not out		3
M. A. Lynch c Irani b Pearson	30	B 1, l-b 7, w 8		16
R. I. Dawson c Lewis b Pearson	20			
M. W. Alleyne c Rollins b Ilott	2	1/50 2/99 3/106	(8 wkts, 55 overs)	211
A. Symonds c Rollins b Such	24	4/125 5/125 6/171		
*†R. C. Russell not out	42	7/181 8/198		
J. Srinath c Gooch b Cousins	6			

A. M. Smith did not bat.

Bowling: Ilott 11–3–22–1; Cousins 11–1–46–1; Irani 11–0–44–1; Such 11–1–45–1; Pearson 11–2–46–3.

Umpires: G. I. Burgess and R. Palmer.

GLAMORGAN v MIDDLESEX

At Cardiff, May 9. Middlesex won by five wickets. Toss: Glamorgan.

Though Morris was fit, he stood aside for an extra bowler, while James passed his fifth half-century in five one-day games. But the Middlesex spinners confined Glamorgan to 209 and their run of six wins in all competitions ended when another in-form batsman, Ramprakash, hit seven fours and a six in his unbeaten 91.

Gold Award: M. R. Ramprakash.

Glamorgan

S. P. James c Fraser b Weekes	90	†C. P. Metson c Brown b Weekes		0
D. L. Hemp c Carr b Fraser	0	S. L. Watkin not out		7
*M. P. Maynard c Nash b Fraser	27	S. R. Barwick not out		10
P. A. Cottey run out	14	L-b 3, w 3, n-b 2		8
A. Dale run out	7			—
R. D. B. Croft c Carr b Weekes	28	1/1 2/42 3/77	(9 wkts, 55 overs)	209
H. A. G. Anthony c Carr b Emburey	2	4/100 5/167 6/170		
R. P. Lefebvre lbw b Fraser	16	7/184 8/184 9/196		

Bowling: Fraser 9-1-30-3; Nash 4-0-21-0; Feltham 3-1-17-0; Tufnell 11-0-39-0; Emburey 11-1-37-1; Weekes 11-0-33-3; Ramprakash 6-0-29-0.

Middlesex

J. C. Pooley lbw b Watkin	5	D. J. Nash not out		21
J. D. Carr b Lefebvre	22			
M. R. Ramprakash not out	91			
*M. W. Gatting c Dale b Anthony	7	B 4, l-b 2, w 4, n-b 2		12
P. N. Weekes c Metson b Anthony	51			—
†K. R. Brown lbw b Anthony	1	1/16 2/36 3/50	(5 wkts, 53.3 overs)	210
		4/159 5/163		

J. E. Emburey, M. A. Feltham, A. R. C. Fraser and P. C. R. Tufnell did not bat.

Bowling: Watkin 11-1-45-1; Lefebvre 10.3-0-34-1; Croft 9-0-35-0; Anthony 11-1-40-3; Dale 2-0-10-0; Barwick 10-0-40-0.

Umpires: B. Dudleston and A. A. Jones.

GLAMORGAN v GLOUCESTERSHIRE

At Swansea, May 16, 17. Gloucestershire won by nine runs. Toss: Glamorgan.

Rain interrupted Gloucestershire in the 37th over, at 95 for four; resuming at 7 p.m., they lost another four, leaving Glamorgan to score 177 next day. Though they lost their openers in seven balls and subsided to 68 for five, the home team were only ten short when Metson was bowled. Gloucestershire finished their group matches unbeaten; Srinath took the award for his three for 16 in 11 overs.

Gold Award: J. Srinath.

Close of play: Gloucestershire 176-8 (55 overs).

Gloucestershire

A. J. Wright lbw b Croft	40	J. Srinath c and b Watkin		1
G. D. Hodgson c Lefebvre b Barwick	31	M. C. J. Ball b Barwick		12
M. A. Lynch c Watkin b Croft	5	B 5, l-b 9, w 11		25
R. I. Dawson c Maynard b Croft	8			—
M. W. Alleyne run out	23	1/76 2/77 3/88	(8 wkts, 55 overs)	176
A. Symonds run out	4	4/95 5/104 6/145		
*†R. C. Russell not out	27	7/148 8/176		

K. E. Cooper and A. M. Smith did not bat.

Bowling: Lefebvre 11-3-39-0; Watkin 11-3-23-1; Barwick 11-0-36-2; Croft 11-1-33-3; Dale 11-1-31-0.

Glamorgan

S. P. James c Russell b Srinath	0	†C. P. Metson b Smith	22
D. L. Hemp lbw b Cooper	0	S. L. Watkin b Srinath	4
M. P. Maynard c Lynch b Smith	40	S. R. Barwick not out	0
P. A. Cottey b Cooper	15	L-b 9, w 8	17
*H. Morris c Lynch b Alleyne	9		
A. Dale c Lynch b Alleyne	28	1/0 2/4 3/45	(53.1 overs) 167
R. D. B. Croft c Russell b Srinath	22	4/61 5/68 6/122	
R. P. Lefebvre run out	10	7/124 8/152 9/167	

Bowling: Srinath 11–6–16–3; Cooper 11–1–41–2; Smith 10.1–2–44–2; Alleyne 11–1–30–2; Ball 10–0–27–0.

Umpires: G. I. Burgess and D. J. Constant.

HAMPSHIRE v ESSEX

At Southampton, May 16, 17. No result. Toss: Hampshire.

Both teams were out of the tournament, so the abandonment had little significance. Gooch, however, scored his 14th century in the competition, hitting 12 fours in 144 balls.

Essex

G. A. Gooch not out	117	J. J. B. Lewis not out	6
*P. J. Prichard b Cowans	4	L-b 16, w 3	19
D. D. J. Robinson b Streak	18		
N. Hussain lbw b Streak	46	1/22 2/87	(4 wkts, 49 overs) 211
R. C. Irani c Smith b Streak	1	3/189 4/197	

†R. J. Rollins, M. C. Ilott, N. A. Derbyshire, P. M. Such and D. M. Cousins did not bat.

Bowling: Connor 8–2–21–0; Cowans 11–1–41–1; Streak 10–1–39–3; Thursfield 10–0–54–0; Udal 10–0–40–0.

Hampshire

V. P. Terry, R. A. Smith, *M. C. J. Nicholas, G. W. White, R. S. M. Morris, †A. N. Aymes, S. D. Udal, H. H. Streak, C. A. Connor, M. J. Thursfield and N. G. Cowans.

Umpires: J. D. Bond and B. J. Meyer.

MIDDLESEX v COMBINED UNIVERSITIES

At Lord's, May 16, 17. Middlesex won on scoring-rate. Toss: Middlesex.

Play was halted in the Universities' 36th over. They were unable to continue next day, and Middlesex won on scoring-rate. Their innings took off when Brown and Nash combined to add 119 in 16 overs, a one-day sixth-wicket record for the county.

Gold Award: K. R. Brown.

Middlesex

*M. W. Gatting c MacRobert b Renshaw	19	M. A. Feltham c Harvey b MacRobert	1
J. C. Pooley c Macmillan b MacRobert	25	J. E. Emburey not out	0
M. R. Ramprakash c Harvey b Edwards	36	L-b 3, w 4	7
J. D. Carr b Rashid	47		
P. N. Weekes c Batty b Edwards	12	1/39 2/50 3/115	(8 wkts, 55 overs) 276
†K. R. Brown run out	75	4/143 5/143 6/262	
D. J. Nash c Edwards b Macmillan	54	7/264 8/276	

A. R. C. Fraser and P. C. R. Tufnell did not bat.

Bowling: Renshaw 8–0–47–1; Edwards 11–0–51–2; Killeen 11–1–48–0; MacRobert 11–2–55–2; Rashid 11–0–52–1; Macmillan 3–0–20–1.

Combined Universities

C. M. Gupte run out	19	†J. N. Batty not out	10	
I. J. Sutcliffe c Brown b Fraser	3	W 5, n-b 2	7	
M. T. E. Peirce lbw b Tufnell	44			
*G. I. Macmillan not out	34	1/11 2/34	(4 wkts, 35.2 overs) 120	
M. E. Harvey lbw b Nash	3	3/90 4/93		

A. D. Edwards, U. B. A. Rashid, A. D. MacRobert, N. Killeen and S. J. Renshaw did not bat.

Bowling: Fraser 7.2–3–12–1; Nash 9–1–28–1; Feltham 7–0–32–0; Emburey 5–1–20–0; Tufnell 7–0–28–1.

Umpires: J. H. Harris and K. J. Lyons.

GROUP D

SOMERSET v SUSSEX

At Taunton, April 23. Somerset won by 54 runs. Toss: Sussex. County debut: P. D. Bowler. Mushtaq Ahmed wrecked Sussex, taking three for six in 22 balls as five wickets fell for 24. Stephenson was dropped by Trump and then hit him for two sixes before another skier landed in Harden's grasp. Earlier, Lathwell and Bowler, making his debut for his third county, added 111 for Somerset's second wicket.

Gold Award: Mushtaq Ahmed.

Somerset

M. N. Lathwell b Salisbury	74	†R. J. Turner not out	11	
M. E. Trescothick c Moores b Giddins	0	A. R. Caddick not out	10	
P. D. Bowler run out	52			
R. J. Harden run out	50	L-b 2, w 10, n-b 2	14	
*A. N. Hayhurst b Stephenson	25			
G. D. Rose c Lenham b Giddins	1	1/9 2/120 3/139	(7 wkts, 55 overs) 241	
Mushtaq Ahmed c Greenfield		4/196 5/199		
b Stephenson	4	6/206 7/229		

J. I. D. Kerr and H. R. J. Trump did not bat.

Bowling: Giddins 9–3–30–2; Stephenson 10–0–47–2; Remy 5–0–21–0; Jarvis 10–0–66–0; Salisbury 11–1–35–1; Greenfield 10–0–40–0.

Sussex

C. W. J. Athey c Trescothick		I. D. K. Salisbury b Kerr	17	
b Mushtaq Ahmed	38	P. W. Jarvis c Lathwell b Kerr	2	
J. W. Hall c Turner b Caddick	30	E. S. H. Giddins not out	0	
K. Greenfield c Harden b Trump	9			
*A. P. Wells lbw b Mushtaq Ahmed	0	L-b 8, w 15, n-b 6	29	
N. J. Lenham b Mushtaq Ahmed	11			
F. D. Stephenson c Harden b Rose	45	1/62 2/93 3/93	(46 overs) 187	
†P. Moores c Turner b Trump	3	4/93 5/107 6/117		
C. C. Remy lbw b Mushtaq Ahmed	3	7/137 8/172 9/186		

Bowling: Caddick 8–1–27–1; Rose 8–1–35–1; Kerr 8–0–35–2; Mushtaq Ahmed 11–4–29–4; Trump 11–1–53–2.

Umpires: G. Sharp and P. Willey.

SURREY v IRELAND

At The Oval, April 23. Surrey won by eight wickets. Toss: Ireland. First-team debut: R. W. Nowell. County debuts: J. D. Ratcliffe, N. Shahid.

Ireland's second Benson and Hedges match took less than 50 overs for both innings. Kenlock wiped out their last four for one run in 11 balls, three lbw and one caught behind by Stewart – his fourth dismissal of the innings.

Gold Award: S. G. Kenlock.

Ireland

S. J. S. Warke c Stewart	
b M. P. Bicknell . 3	
M. V. Narasimha Rao lbw b Pigott.... 14	
*D. A. Lewis c Stewart b Kenlock..... 1	
J. D. R. Benson lbw b Hollioake...... 10	
G. D. Harrison c Stewart b Hollioake.. 17	
S. Graham run out.................. 14	
J. D. Curry not out 11	
G. Cooke lbw b Kenlock 0	

†R. B. Millar lbw b Kenlock 0
C. J. Hoey c Stewart b Kenlock....... 0
O. F. X. Butler lbw b Kenlock........ 0

L-b 4, w 4, n-b 2.......... 10

1/10 2/11 3/29   (32 overs) 80
4/35 5/66 6/70
7/76 8/76 9/80

Bowling: M. P. Bicknell 7–2–14–1; Kenlock 8–3–15–5; Hollioake 8–0–30–2; Pigott 6–2–5–1; Nowell 3–0–12–0.

Surrey

D. J. Bicknell c and b Cooke 10
J. D. Ratcliffe b Hoey.............. 14
*†A. J. Stewart not out 26
A. D. Brown not out 6
        B 5, l-b 4, w 12, n-b 4 25

1/15 2/51   (2 wkts, 17.1 overs) 81

D. M. Ward, A. J. Hollioake, N. Shahid, R. W. Nowell, M. P. Bicknell, A. C. S. Pigott and S. G. Kenlock did not bat.

Bowling: Butler 7–1–27–0; Cooke 5–0–21–1; Hoey 3.1–1–8–1; Narasimha Rao 2–0–16–0.

Umpires: A. A. Jones and N. T. Plews.

KENT v SURREY

At Canterbury, April 25. Kent won by 93 runs. Toss: Kent. County debut: P. A. de Silva.
    Trevor Ward, whose maiden century in the tournament lasted 140 balls and featured 14 fours and two sixes, and Benson opened with 229 in 40 overs, an all-wicket record for Kent in one-day cricket. They fell one short of their highest Cup total, 319, but that mattered little once Surrey were reduced to 12 for three.
    Gold Award: T. R. Ward.

Kent

T. R. Ward c Benjamin b Kenlock 125
*M. R. Benson b Shahid 85
M. V. Fleming b Kenlock............ 5
M. J. Walker run out 15
P. A. de Silva c D. J. Bicknell
        b M. P. Bicknell . 16
G. R. Cowdrey run out 28
M. A. Ealham st Stewart b Pigott 6

†S. A. Marsh b Pigott 1
M. M. Patel not out................ 0

        B 1, l-b 21, w 11, n-b 4 37

1/229 2/237 3/241   (8 wkts, 55 overs) 318
4/269 5/300 6/316
7/317 8/318

M. J. McCague and D. W. Headley did not bat.

Bowling: M. P. Bicknell 11–1–56–1; Benjamin 9–0–37–0; Kenlock 10–0–69–2; Pigott 11–0–52–2; Hollioake 3–0–23–0; Shahid 11–0–59–1.

Surrey

D. J. Bicknell run out 0
*†A. J. Stewart c Marsh b Ealham 45
G. P. Thorpe b Headley 5
D. M. Ward lbw b Headley 0
A. D. Brown b Fleming 29
A. J. Hollioake lbw b Ealham 23
N. Shahid not out 65

M. P. Bicknell c McCague b Ealham .. 43
A. C. S. Pigott not out 5
        L-b 2, w 1, n-b 7............ 10

1/0 2/6 3/12   (7 wkts, 55 overs) 225
4/68 5/112
6/113 7/202

J. E. Benjamin and S. G. Kenlock did not bat.

Bowling: McCague 9–1–31–0; Headley 11–1–45–2; Fleming 11–0–41–1; Ealham 11–1–55–3; Patel 11–1–38–0; de Silva 2–0–13–0.

Umpires: R. Palmer and N. T. Plews.

SUSSEX v IRELAND

At Hove, April 25. Sussex won by 63 runs. Toss: Ireland.

Sussex benefited substantially from the gift of 40 extras, including 26 wides, mostly from Ireland's enthusiastic opening bowlers. Michael Rea celebrated his 50th cap for Ireland with the highest innings of the match, 73.

Gold Award: M. P. Rea.

Sussex

†C. W. J. Athey lbw b Harrison	42	P. W. Jarvis c Benson b Patterson	8
J. W. Hall c Graham b Butler	59	J. D. Lewry not out	14
K. Greenfield c Curry b Harrison	21		
*A. P. Wells lbw b Hoey	15	L-b 8, w 26, n-b 6	40
N. J. Lenham not out	49		
F. D. Stephenson c Warke b Butler	5	1/84 2/120 3/146 (8 wkts, 55 overs) 261
C. C. Remy c Lewis b Butler	7	4/174 5/185 6/208
I. D. K. Salisbury c Rea b Patterson	1	7/214 8/228

E. S. H. Giddins did not bat.

Bowling: Butler 11–0–53–3; Patterson 10–1–51–2; Graham 11–1–44–0; Harrison 11–0–34–2; Hoey 10–1–59–1; Curry 2–0–12–0.

Ireland

S. J. S. Warke b Jarvis	29	†R. B. Millar lbw b Stephenson	0
M. P. Rea c Hall b Giddins	73	C. J. Hoey not out	4
*D. A. Lewis lbw b Jarvis	0	O. F. X. Butler not out	3
J. D. R. Benson lbw b Salisbury	26	B 1, l-b 8, w 16, n-b 2	27
J. D. Curry lbw b Jarvis	20		
G. D. Harrison b Stephenson	7	1/57 2/58 3/123 (9 wkts, 55 overs) 198
S. Graham b Stephenson	0	4/151 5/169 6/172
M. W. Patterson st Athey b Salisbury	9	7/177 8/177 9/192

Bowling: Giddins 11–0–32–1; Stephenson 11–2–29–3; Jarvis 11–2–39–3; Remy 5–0–16–0; Lewry 5–0–25–0; Salisbury 9–0–40–2; Greenfield 3–0–8–0.

Umpires: B. Leadbeater and P. B. Wight.

KENT v SOMERSET

At Canterbury, May 2. Kent won by 119 runs. Toss: Kent.

Wren, playing because Igglesden and McCague were unfit, returned six for 41, Kent's best figures in the competition, including five for nine in 17 balls. He had also taken six when Somerset visited Canterbury in the Championship in 1994. Earlier, Ward made his third century in three county matches and shared another three-figure stand with Benson.

Gold Award: T. N. Wren.

Kent

T. R. Ward b Trump	113	M. A. Ealham b Caddick	14
*M. R. Benson b Trump	36	†S. A. Marsh not out	2
M. J. Walker lbw b Rose	34	B 1, l-b 12, w 13	26
P. A. de Silva run out	10		
G. R. Cowdrey c Turner b van Troost	1	1/117 2/199 3/209 (6 wkts, 55 overs) 280
M. V. Fleming not out	44	4/216 5/216 6/260

T. N. Wren, M. M. Patel and D. W. Headley did not bat.

Bowling: Rose 11–2–50–1; van Troost 9–0–70–1; Caddick 11–1–42–1; Mushtaq Ahmed 11–0–41–0; Trump 11–1–46–2; Hayhurst 2–0–18–0.

Somerset

M. N. Lathwell lbw b Wren	10	A. R. Caddick c Wren b Patel	28
M. E. Trescothick c Ward b Wren	9	H. R. J. Trump c Marsh b Wren	11
P. D. Bowler c Cowdrey b Wren	0	A. P. van Troost c Cowdrey b Ealham	5
R. J. Harden c Marsh b Wren	0	L-b 10, w 9, n-b 2	21
*A. N. Hayhurst b Wren	4		
G. D. Rose c de Silva b Patel	36	1/17 2/17 3/18 (52.5 overs) 161	
†R. J. Turner not out	37	4/22 5/31 6/79	
Mushtaq Ahmed c and b de Silva	0	7/80 8/125 9/142	

Bowling: Headley 11–4–18–0; Wren 11–0–41–6; Ealham 4.5–0–27–1; Fleming 4–0–15–0; Patel 11–1–29–2; de Silva 11–0–21–1.

Umpires: V. A. Holder and R. Julian.

SURREY v SUSSEX

At The Oval, May 2. Sussex won by eight wickets. Toss: Surrey.

Though his maiden Benson and Hedges century narrowly eluded Athey, he did enough to earn his county victory. He put on 81 with Hall and 117 with Lenham. For Surrey, Brown's dismissal just after lunch sparked a collapse of three wickets for nine runs.

Gold Award: C. W. J. Athey.

Surrey

D. J. Bicknell b Stephenson	14	A. C. S. Pigott b Giddins	8
M. A. Butcher lbw b Giddins	5	R. W. Nowell not out	15
*†A. J. Stewart c and b Salisbury	29	L-b 13, w 4, n-b 6	23
A. D. Brown lbw b Stephenson	82		
D. M. Ward not out	60	1/17 2/27 3/107 (7 wkts, 55 overs) 239	
A. J. Hollioake lbw b Giddins	3	4/167 5/176	
N. Shahid run out	0	6/176 7/195	

S. G. Kenlock and J. E. Benjamin did not bat.

Bowling: Giddins 11–2–28–3; Stephenson 11–2–35–2; Salisbury 11–1–40–1; Lewry 11–0–71–0; Greenfield 7–0–31–0; North 4–0–21–0.

Sussex

C. W. J. Athey c Hollioake b Pigott	97		
J. W. Hall c and b Nowell	29		
N. J. Lenham not out	73		
*A. P. Wells not out	23		
L-b 6, w 4, n-b 8	18		

1/81 2/198   (2 wkts, 52.1 overs) 240

K. Greenfield, J. A. North, F. D. Stephenson, †P. Moores, I. D. K. Salisbury, J. D. Lewry and E. S. H. Giddins did not bat.

Bowling: Benjamin 11–0–33–0; Kenlock 6–1–35–0; Nowell 11–1–35–1; Pigott 9.1–0–55–1; Hollioake 8–0–36–0; Shahid 7–0–40–0.

Umpires: J. H. Harris and R. A. White.

IRELAND v KENT

At Comber, May 9. Kent won by ten wickets. Toss: Ireland.

Ireland's top three departed for 21 in 11 overs before Lewis scored an unbeaten 67, which earned him the match award. Ward and Benson needed less than 33 overs to overtake a target of 147, however, sharing their fourth century opening partnership in four one-day games.

Gold Award: D. A. Lewis.

Ireland

S. J. S. Warke lbw b Wren	8	M. W. Patterson run out	3
A. R. Dunlop c Ward b Ealham	7	C. J. Hoey c Benson b de Silva	0
J. D. R. Benson c Benson b Wren	1	†R. B. Millar b Fleming	4
*D. A. Lewis not out	67	L-b 11, w 5	16
G. D. Harrison b Ealham	14		
S. Graham c Walker b Fleming	25		(54 overs) 146
J. D. Curry b Fleming	1	1/12 2/14 3/21	
G. Cooke c and b de Silva	0	4/61 5/122 6/127	
		7/128 8/134 9/137	

Bowling: Headley 9–2–17–0; Wren 11–2–29–2; Ealham 11–2–24–2; Patel 11–3–35–0; de Silva 7–1–12–2; Fleming 5–0–18–3.

Kent

T. R. Ward not out	62		
*M. R. Benson not out	76		
B 1, l-b 2, w 4, n-b 4	11		

(no wkt, 32.1 overs) 149

M. J. Walker, P. A. de Silva, G. R. Cowdrey, M. V. Fleming, M. A. Ealham, †S. A. Marsh, D. W. Headley, M. M. Patel and T. N. Wren did not bat.

Bowling: Patterson 6–2–23–0; Cooke 6–0–41–0; Hoey 6–0–30–0; Harrison 5–0–28–0; Graham 9.1–1–24–0.

Umpires: J. C. Balderstone and T. E. Jesty.

SOMERSET v SURREY

At Taunton, May 9. Surrey won by seven wickets. Toss: Somerset. County debut: J. D. Batty.

Somerset lost six for 44 as Benjamin, with three for 12 in eight overs, made a mockery of their decision to bat. Only Rose and Ecclestone saved them from humiliation. Despite two quick wickets from Batty, newly arrived from Yorkshire, Surrey won with 11 balls to spare.

Gold Award: J. E. Benjamin.

Somerset

M. N. Lathwell c Stewart b Benjamin	0	Mushtaq Ahmed c Hollioake b Pigott	21
M. E. Trescothick b Kenlock	26	J. D. Batty not out	19
P. D. Bowler c Hollioake b Benjamin	0	H. R. J. Trump b Kenlock	0
R. J. Harden c D. J. Bicknell			
b M. P. Bicknell	6	L-b 12, w 5	17
*A. N. Hayhurst c Brown b Benjamin	1		
†R. J. Turner lbw b Kenlock	3	1/0 2/0 3/17	(54 overs) 202
G. D. Rose c Ward b Kenlock	79	4/26 5/34 6/44	
S. C. Ecclestone c Stewart b Benjamin	30	7/145 8/181 9/188	

Bowling: Benjamin 11–6–27–4; M. P. Bicknell 11–2–33–1; Kenlock 11–0–52–4; Pigott 10–0–27–1; Hollioake 4–0–19–0; Shahid 7–0–32–0.

Surrey

D. J. Bicknell not out	81	D. M. Ward not out	28
*†A. J. Stewart c sub b Mushtaq Ahmed	52	B 4, l-b 8, w 4	16
G. P. Thorpe b Batty	25		
A. D. Brown c Ecclestone b Batty	1	1/98 2/140 3/142	(3 wkts, 53.1 overs) 203

A. J. Hollioake, N. Shahid, M. P. Bicknell, A. C. S. Pigott, S. G. Kenlock and J. E. Benjamin did not bat.

Bowling: Rose 10–4–33–0; Ecclestone 3–0–18–0; Hayhurst 3–0–8–0; Trump 11–1–37–0; Batty 11–0–36–2; Mushtaq Ahmed 11–0–29–1; Bowler 4–0–29–0; Lathwell 0.1–0–1–0.

Umpires: D. J. Constant and J. H. Hampshire.

IRELAND v SOMERSET

At Eglinton, May 16. Somerset won by 233 runs. Toss: Ireland.

The second most crushing victory in the tournament's history secured Somerset a quarter-final place on net run-rate. Trescothick hit 122 from 112 balls, with 15 fours and a six; his 163-run partnership with Bowler was a Somerset second-wicket record in the 55-overs game. Rose added a run-a-ball 47 and then reduced Ireland to 37 for four. Their last five failed to score, as Hayhurst bowled 6.2 overs for two runs.

Gold Award: G. D. Rose.

Somerset

M. N. Lathwell c Curry b Patterson ...	16	*A. N. Hayhurst not out..............	15
M. E. Trescothick c Ogilby b Butler ...	122		
P. D. Bowler c Dunlop b Patterson	54	L-b 10, w 10, n-b 4.........	24
R. J. Harden lbw b Patterson.........	10		—
G. D. Rose not out	47	1/39 2/202 3/216 (5 wkts, 55 overs)	316
S. C. Ecclestone b Butler.............	28	4/232 5/279	

†R. J. Turner, Mushtaq Ahmed, H. R. J. Trump and J. D. Batty did not bat.

Bowling: Butler 11–1–69–2; Patterson 11–0–48–3; Graham 9–0–43–0; Harrison 9–1–52–0; Lewis 11–0–65–0; Dunlop 4–0–29–0.

Ireland

S. J. S. Warke lbw b Rose	19	M. W. Patterson c Turner b Hayhurst..	0
A. R. Dunlop lbw b Rose	1	†S. Ogilby c Trescothick b Trump	0
S. G. Smyth c Trescothick b Rose	11	O. F. X. Butler not out	0
*D. A. Lewis b Trump	23		
J. D. R. Benson c Trescothick b Rose ..	4	L-b 4, w 3	7
G. D. Harrison c Trescothick			—
b Hayhurst .	18	1/12 2/32 3/33 (39.2 overs)	83
J. D. Curry b Trump	0	4/37 5/73 6/75	
S. Graham lbw b Hayhurst...........	0	7/80 8/80 9/81	

Bowling: Rose 11–3–21–4; Ecclestone 5–0–19–0; Mushtaq Ahmed 6–1–10–0; Trump 9–1–17–3; Batty 2–1–10–0; Hayhurst 6.2–4–2–3.

Umpires: R. Julian and K. E. Palmer.

SUSSEX v KENT

At Hove, May 16, 17. Kent won by eight wickets. Toss: Kent.

Sussex piled on the runs even though Kent, unusually, had both their England bowlers, Igglesden and McCague, fit; Athey finally scored a century in his 75th Benson and Hedges match in 20 years. Kent needed 304, the second-highest winning total after Lancashire's 318 in April. But, on the second day, Ward and Benson scored their fourth century opening partnership in four group games; Benson also put on a hundred with Walker. Sussex would have qualified with a no-result or under the different run-rate system used up to 1992 when the competition last had qualifying groups.

Gold Award: M. J. Walker.

Close of play: Kent 31-0 (7 overs) (T. R. Ward 17*, M. R. Benson 11*).

Sussex

C. W. J. Athey b McCague	118	F. D. Stephenson not out	18
J. W. Hall b Llong.................	67	†P. Moores not out	6
K. Newell c Fleming b Igglesden.......	35	B 3, l-b 14, w 11, n-b 4	32
*A. P. Wells c Fleming b Wren.......	4		—
K. Greenfield b Fleming	13	1/145 2/209 3/220 (6 wkts, 55 overs)	303
J. A. North c Cowdrey b Fleming	10	4/259 5/265 6/291	

I. D. K. Salisbury, E. S. H. Giddins and J. D. Lewry did not bat.

Bowling: Wren 11–0–78–1; Igglesden 11–0–45–1; McCague 11–0–62–1; Fleming 11–0–42–2; de Silva 6–0–28–0; Llong 5–0–31–1.

Kent

T. R. Ward c Giddins b Stephenson ... 76
*M. R. Benson c and b Salisbury......119
M. J. Walker not out 69
P. A. de Silva not out 18
     L-b 8, w 9, n-b 8............ 25

1/147 2/285   (2 wkts, 52.1 overs) 307

G. R. Cowdrey, N. J. Llong, M. V. Fleming, †S. C. Willis, T. N. Wren, A. P. Igglesden and M. J. McCague did not bat.

Bowling: Giddins 9–0–47–0; Stephenson 10.1–1–65–1; Lewry 10–0–56–0; Greenfield 9–0–59–0; North 3–0–24–0; Salisbury 11–0–48–1.

Umpires: B. Dudleston and V. A. Holder.

QUARTER-FINALS

GLOUCESTERSHIRE v SOMERSET

At Bristol, May 30, 31. Somerset won by six wickets. Toss: Gloucestershire.

Gloucestershire were all out by the 50th over, leaving a packed house to ruminate on whether Russell had been wise to bat first. Injuries forced Somerset to field three spinners and he was influenced by their apparently weakened pace attack. In fact, the spinners collected seven wickets very cheaply – Batty bowled 11 overs for 13 runs – and the only worthwhile home stand was 33 between Dawson and Symonds, who was out to a spectacular boundary catch by Bowler. Both wicket-keepers also made fine leg-side catches to lift a drab match. Lack of imagination and flexibility over meal-times meant the game, restricted by rain, ran into 40 minutes of the second day. Trescothick, in trouble against Srinath early on, survived for the only half-century.

Gold Award: J. D. Batty.

Close of play: Somerset 63-2 (25 overs) (M. E. Trescothick 35*, R. J. Harden 9*).

Gloucestershire

A. J. Wright b Mushtaq Ahmed	13	M. C. J. Ball c Bowler b Trump	11
G. D. Hodgson lbw b Rose...........	0	K. E. Cooper not out................	0
M. A. Lynch c Trump b Ecclestone....	2	A. M. Smith lbw b Mushtaq Ahmed ...	0
R. I. Dawson c and b Batty	38	L-b 2, w 5	7
M. W. Alleyne c Turner b Hayhurst ...	10		
A. Symonds c Bowler b Trump	23	1/3 2/8 3/36	(49.4 overs) 113
*†R. C. Russell c Ecclestone b Batty ..	7	4/57 5/90 6/96	
J. Srinath c Turner b Mushtaq Ahmed .	2	7/99 8/113 9/113	

Bowling: Rose 8–3–13–1; Ecclestone 8–0–27–1; Mushtaq Ahmed 10.4–4–23–3; Hayhurst 3–0–20–1; Batty 11–5–13–2; Trump 9–3–15–2.

Somerset

M. N. Lathwell c Russell b Cooper	7	S. C. Ecclestone not out	4
M. E. Trescothick lbw b Smith	52	W 2, n-b 2................	4
P. D. Bowler c Russell b Srinath	10		
R. J. Harden not out	30	1/11 2/28	(4 wkts, 35.1 overs) 114
G. D. Rose c Alleyne b Srinath	7	3/97 4/104	

*A. N. Hayhurst, †R. J. Turner, Mushtaq Ahmed, H. R. J. Trump and J. D. Batty did not bat.

Bowling: Srinath 10.1–3–35–2; Cooper 8–0–21–1; Smith 10–1–37–1; Alleyne 2–0–7–0; Ball 5–1–14–0.

Umpires: V. A. Holder and B. Leadbeater.

KENT v MIDDLESEX

At Canterbury, May 30. Kent won by 26 runs. Toss: Kent.

Kent triumphed after Benson and Ward continued their extraordinary run of a century opening stand in every match of this tournament. When they were both dismissed by Feltham, shortly after a rain interruption, Kent's innings subsided quickly. But Ealham provided a late flurry with 30 off 26 balls and then stopped Middlesex in their tracks by removing Pooley and Ramprakash after they looked well set at 120 for one. With Gatting forced to use a runner because of a groin problem, their progress was hampered as the asking-rate climbed. And late wickets for Fleming and Headley, against his former county, helped Kent into the semi-finals. Ealham's all-round performance, which also took in a crucial catch, won him his first Gold Award.

Gold Award: M. A. Ealham.

Kent

T. R. Ward c Nash b Feltham	64	M. M. Patel c and b Fraser	1
*M. R. Benson c Pooley b Feltham	56	M. J. McCague not out	5
M. J. Walker c Brown b Fraser	19	D. W. Headley not out	7
P. A. de Silva c Brown b Nash	8	L-b 12, w 9, n-b 4	25
G. R. Cowdrey c Brown b Fraser	14		
M. V. Fleming lbw b Emburey	11	1/132 2/132 3/146 (9 wkts, 55 overs) 250
M. A. Ealham run out	30	4/179 5/182 6/198
†S. A. Marsh c Brown b Fraser	10	7/235 8/237 9/239

Bowling: Fraser 11–0–49–4; Nash 11–1–50–1; Emburey 11–0–52–1; Feltham 11–0–42–2; Weekes 11–0–45–0.

Middlesex

M. A. Feltham c Patel b de Silva	37	R. L. Johnson c Marsh b Headley	0
J. C. Pooley c Walker b Ealham	47	J. E. Emburey not out	3
M. R. Ramprakash b Ealham	34	A. R. C. Fraser b Fleming	1
*M. W. Gatting b Headley	30	L-b 13, w 4	17
J. D. Carr c Walker b Fleming	16		
†K. R. Brown c Ealham b McCague	16	1/70 2/120 3/133 (54.4 overs) 224
P. N. Weekes b Headley	17	4/167 5/183 6/208
D. J. Nash c Marsh b Fleming	6	7/220 8/220 9/221

Bowling: McCague 11–1–40–1; Headley 11–1–47–3; Ealham 11–2–38–2; Fleming 10.4–1–41–3; de Silva 4–0–18–1; Patel 7–0–27–0.

Umpires: H. D. Bird and M. J. Kitchen.

LANCASHIRE v NOTTINGHAMSHIRE

At Manchester, May 30. Lancashire won by six wickets. Toss: Lancashire.

This comfortable win, with 32 balls in hand, was Lancashire's third in three weeks over Nottinghamshire and their ninth in nine completed games in one-day competitions in 1995. Lloyd followed his Sunday half-century against the same team two days earlier with a match-winning unbeaten 72 from 68 balls. His stand of 70 in 15 overs with Fairbrother put the result beyond doubt. Lewis, in only his third game of the season because of injury, played purely as a batsman; his 48 was responsible for Nottinghamshire at least reaching 200 after being 65 for three in the 23rd over.

Gold Award: G. D. Lloyd.

Nottinghamshire

J. R. Wileman c Atherton b Wasim Akram .	0	†W. M. Noon not out	17
*R. T. Robinson c Crawley b Austin . .	32	G. W. Mike b Wasim Akram	9
C. Banton b Yates	40	R. A. Pick not out	10
C. L. Cairns c Atherton b Austin	1		
C. C. Lewis run out	48	B 3, l-b 13, w 4, n-b 6	26
M. P. Dowman c Fairbrother b Watkinson .	6	(8 wkts, 55 overs)	201
K. P. Evans c Wasim Akram b Austin	12		

1/0 2/60 3/65 4/99 5/122 6/140 7/162 8/185

J. A. Afford did not bat.

Bowling: Wasim Akram 11-3-40-2; Chapple 11-0-38-0; Watkinson 11-0-31-1; Austin 11-0-45-3; Yates 11-1-31-1.

Lancashire

M. A. Atherton c Noon b Cairns	21	*M. Watkinson not out	6
J. E. R. Gallian c Wileman b Evans . . .	5	B 2, l-b 2, w 4, n-b 4	12
J. P. Crawley lbw b Afford	48		
N. H. Fairbrother c Cairns b Evans	41	(4 wkts, 49.4 overs)	205
G. D. Lloyd not out	72		

1/9 2/66 3/90 4/160

Wasim Akram, I. D. Austin, †W. K. Hegg, G. Chapple and G. Yates did not bat.

Bowling: Evans 9-2-28-2; Pick 10.4-1-57-0; Mike 8-1-31-0; Cairns 11-0-49-1; Afford 11-1-36-1.

Umpires: J. W. Holder and B. J. Meyer.

YORKSHIRE v WORCESTERSHIRE

At Leeds, May 30. Worcestershire won by seven wickets. Toss: Worcestershire.

The toss was decisive on a pitch offering exceptional movement and bounce. The whole square had been flooded following a cloudburst only 48 hours before the tie which caught the groundstaff unawares; head groundsman Keith Boyce was unable to attend the final preparations because of the death of his wife. Yorkshire never recovered from losing four wickets for ten runs in eight overs and were all out for 88. The Worcestershire bowlers maintained the essential full length and Lampitt claimed four for two in 16 deliveries; only Byas, who faced 121 balls for his 47, threatened any serious resistance. Yorkshire then bowled too short as Worcestershire strolled to victory in the 23rd over, with Moody in robust mood.

Gold Award: S. R. Lampitt.

Yorkshire

S. A. Kellett c Rhodes b Newport	6	P. J. Hartley b Lampitt	0
A. McGrath c Moody b Newport	2	R. D. Stemp not out	0
*D. Byas c and b Lampitt	47	M. A. Robinson c Hick b Lampitt	0
M. G. Bevan c Rhodes b Haynes	0	B 1, l-b 5, w 4	10
C. White c Moody b Haynes	0		
†R. J. Blakey st Rhodes b Illingworth . .	6	(48.5 overs)	88
A. P. Grayson c Rhodes b Lampitt	14		
D. Gough b Radford	3		

1/8 2/9 3/10 4/10 5/44 6/81 7/86 8/88 9/88

Bowling: Newport 8-4-9-2; Haynes 7-2-10-2; Lampitt 7.5-2-16-4; Radford 8-3-10-1; Illingworth 11-2-21-1; Hick 7-0-16-0.

Worcestershire

W. P. C. Weston lbw b Hartley	4	G. R. Haynes not out	12
*T. S. Curtis c Byas b Robinson	8	L-b 1, w 1, n-b 4	6
G. A. Hick c Bevan b Robinson	27		
T. M. Moody not out	32	(3 wkts, 22.5 overs)	89

1/5 2/35 3/40

D. A. Leatherdale, S. R. Lampitt, †S. J. Rhodes, P. J. Newport, R. K. Illingworth and N. V. Radford did not bat.

Bowling: Gough 8–2–33–0; Hartley 4–0–14–1; Robinson 6–3–15–2; White 2.5–0–9–0; Stemp 2–0–17–0.

Umpires: J. H. Harris and K. E. Palmer.

SEMI-FINALS

KENT v SOMERSET

At Canterbury, June 13, 14. Kent won by 31 runs. Toss: Somerset.

Again, Ealham proved the inspiration behind Kent's victory, as they reached a record seventh Benson and Hedges Cup final. Persistent rain delayed proceedings until mid-afternoon, when Ward and Benson opened with 53, a disappointment for a pair averaging 193.5. Mushtaq Ahmed's leg-spin then gave Somerset control in damp conditions; Kent were 98 for five when Ealham arrived, to add 51 in ten overs with de Silva and 60 in ten with Marsh. Ealham scored 52 off 61 balls and McCague's 24 in 11 ensured a final flourish. Bad light delayed Somerset's reply until the following morning, when Trescothick was bowled in Wren's first over. Wren, who took six on Somerset's previous visit, also removed Lathwell, after an 86-run stand with Bowler, and Harden one later. Hayhurst kept Somerset in the contest, but Kent's impressive out-cricket helped to tie them down.

Gold Award: M. A. Ealham.
Close of play: Kent 250-9 (55 overs).

Kent

T. R. Ward c Turner b Trump	22		M. J. McCague b Ecclestone		24
*M. R. Benson run out	29		D. W. Headley not out		4
M. V. Fleming b Mushtaq Ahmed	5		T. N. Wren not out		4
P. A. de Silva b Mushtaq Ahmed	39		B 5, l-b 10, w 6		21
G. R. Cowdrey c Lathwell b Batty	22				
N. J. Llong run out	1		1/53 2/59 3/59	(9 wkts, 55 overs)	250
M. A. Ealham c Harden b Hayhurst	52		4/96 5/98 6/149		
†S. A. Marsh b Ecclestone	27		7/209 8/219 9/238		

Bowling: Rose 11–2–33–0; Ecclestone 7–1–44–2; Mushtaq Ahmed 11–2–28–2; Trump 6–0–32–1; Hayhurst 11–0–46–1; Batty 9–0–52–1.

Somerset

M. N. Lathwell c McCague b Wren	38		Mushtaq Ahmed c Benson b Headley		11
M. E. Trescothick b Wren	0		J. D. Batty not out		0
P. D. Bowler b Fleming	53				
R. J. Harden c Marsh b Wren	0		L-b 8, w 6		14
*A. N. Hayhurst not out	69				
G. D. Rose c Headley b Fleming	15		1/2 2/88 3/89	(8 wkts, 55 overs)	219
S. C. Ecclestone b Fleming	3		4/110 5/143 6/150		
†R. J. Turner c Headley b Ealham	16		7/183 8/214		

H. R. J. Trump did not bat.

Bowling: Headley 11–1–42–1; Wren 11–1–34–3; Ealham 11–1–33–1; McCague 11–0–51–0; Fleming 11–0–51–3.

Umpires: J. W. Holder and G. Sharp.

WORCESTERSHIRE v LANCASHIRE

At Worcester, June 13. Lancashire won by two wickets. Toss: Worcestershire.

A ferocious innings from Wasim Akram revived a seemingly hopeless cause and secured Lancashire's fifth Lord's final in six seasons. Lancashire had struggled to 169 for seven, still needing 93 off the final 11 overs, but Wasim emphasised the depth of his side's batting by plundering 64, off 47 balls, with six fours and two sixes. His dismissal left 24 needed off four overs but Hegg, who had accompanied Wasim in a stand of 69 in seven, and Yates completed the task with four balls remaining. Worcestershire could only shake their heads in disbelief after being in control of proceedings for nine-tenths of the game. Hick scored his third Benson and Hedges century in 1995, adding 120 in 21 overs with Moody. Later, Hick dismissed Fairbrother and Lloyd in what seemed like a match-winning performance until Wasim's intervention. Curtis resigned the Worcestershire captaincy two days later, though he said this defeat was not his reason.

Gold Award: Wasim Akram.

Worcestershire

*T. S. Curtis c Hegg b Yates	50	†S. J. Rhodes not out	4
W. P. C. Weston c Atherton b Chapple	7		
G. A. Hick b Wasim Akram	109	L-b 6, n-b 4	10
T. M. Moody not out	75		
G. R. Haynes b Wasim Akram	6	1/18 2/113 3/233 (5 wkts, 55 overs)	261
C. M. Tolley b Wasim Akram	0	4/255 5/255	

S. R. Lampitt, R. K. Illingworth, P. J. Newport and N. V. Radford did not bat.

Bowling: Wasim Akram 11-1-59-3; Chapple 10-1-58-1; Austin 11-1-34-0; Watkinson 11-1-52-0; Yates 9-0-42-1; Gallian 3-0-10-0.

Lancashire

M. A. Atherton lbw b Lampitt	24	†W. K. Hegg not out	31
J. E. R. Gallian lbw b Radford	24	G. Yates not out	19
J. P. Crawley b Haynes	18		
N. H. Fairbrother b Hick	30	L-b 11, w 2	13
G. D. Lloyd c Weston b Hick	24		
*M. Watkinson c Curtis b Illingworth	2	1/54 2/56 3/88 (8 wkts, 54.2 overs)	264
Wasim Akram b Newport	64	4/126 5/129 6/135	
I. D. Austin b Lampitt	15	7/169 8/238	

G. Chapple did not bat.

Bowling: Newport 11-3-43-1; Haynes 10-0-43-1; Lampitt 11-0-54-2; Radford 7-0-41-1; Illingworth 10.2-0-42-1; Hick 5-0-30-2.

Umpires: R. Palmer and A. G. T. Whitehead.

FINAL

KENT v LANCASHIRE

At Lord's, July 15. Lancashire won by 35 runs. Toss: Kent.

Lancashire, still hoping to equal or even better Warwickshire's triple success of 1994, took the first of the season's domestic trophies and a cheque for £35,000 back to Old Trafford. But Kent's overseas player, Aravinda de Silva, claimed the Gold Award and the headlines with a dazzling century.

On a changeable day – the start was delayed by ten minutes and rain caused a 34-minute stoppage shortly after tea – Lancashire were sent in and ran up a total which has been exceeded only once in the final (Essex's 290 for six in 1979). Openers Atherton and Gallian ensured there would be no early collapse, and scored at four an over before Gallian, who played despite a broken finger suffered during his Test debut the previous week, was bowled by Ealham, the most impressive of Kent's bowlers on the day. Atherton, whose nine fours included some luscious cover-drives, and Crawley then added 121 before Atherton was well caught at wide mid-on for 93 from 141 balls. Crawley scored 83 in 89 balls, with a six off McCague, who dismissed him soon afterwards. With two catches, two run-outs and this wicket, McCague was prominent in the final flurry, which saw Lancashire reach 274, setting Kent exactly five an over to win.

In the lead-up to the final, Kent had been sent on their way by openers Benson and Ward, with stands of 229, 117, 149, 147, 132 and 53. Now, however, Kent's captain Benson was on the sidelines, nursing a finger broken the previous Sunday. Although his replacement as opener, Fulton, looked both promising and audacious – spurning a helmet for a sunhat, and receiving a blow on the shoulder from Wasim Akram for his cheek – he and Ward had departed by the time 37 was on the board.

The remainder of the reply was carried by de Silva, who had scored double-centuries in his last two Championship matches but, surprisingly, averaged under 19, with no fifties, in his previous 15 one-day innings for the county. He soon swung Austin into the Mound Stand for two sixes on his way to 50 from as many balls, and not long afterwards added another six, off Chapple, and a cover-driven four, his tenth, to take him past his hundred. He added one more boundary before holing out at deep mid-wicket. De Silva's memorable 112, made from 95 balls, was only the third century in a Benson and Hedges final (following Graham Gooch's 120 in 1979 and Viv Richards's 132 not out in 1981), and the first not to bring about victory.

Apart from Cowdrey, with 25, none of the other batsmen was able to stay with him for long and, with Yates and Watkinson both taking three wickets, Kent subsided with 17 balls unbowled. The final act saw last man Wren slogging high to long-on, but the game might have ended a few balls earlier, when umpire Plews referred a run-out appeal to his colleague in the pavilion, John Hampshire. Wren survived his trial by TV. – Steven Lynch.

Gold Award: P. A. de Silva. *Attendance:* 25,083; receipts £696,509.

Lancashire

M. A. Atherton c Fulton b Headley	93	I. D. Austin not out	5
J. E. R. Gallian b Ealham	36	L-b 2, w 10, n-b 7	19
J. P. Crawley c Taylor b McCague	83		
N. H. Fairbrother c McCague b Headley	16	1/80 (2) 2/201 (1) (7 wkts, 55 overs)	274
G. D. Lloyd run out	12	3/236 (4) 4/258 (3)	
Wasim Akram run out	10	5/259 (5) 6/266 (7)	
*M. Watkinson c McCague b Fleming	0	7/274 (6)	

†W. K. Hegg, G. Chapple and G. Yates did not bat.

Bowling: Wren 5–0–21–0; Headley 11–0–57–2; McCague 11–0–65–1; Ealham 11–0–33–1; de Silva 8–0–36–0; Fleming 9–0–60–1.

Kent

D. P. Fulton lbw b Chapple	25	D. W. Headley c Chapple b Watkinson	5
T. R. Ward c Hegg b Chapple	7	T. N. Wren c Austin b Watkinson	7
N. R. Taylor b Yates	14	L-b 7, w 2, n-b 6	15
P. A. de Silva c Lloyd b Austin	112		
G. R. Cowdrey lbw b Yates	25	1/28 (2) 2/37 (1) (52.1 overs)	239
M. V. Fleming b Yates	11	3/81 (3) 4/142 (5)	
M. A. Ealham lbw b Watkinson	3	5/162 (6) 6/180 (7)	
*†S. A. Marsh c Crawley b Austin	4	7/214 (4) 8/214 (8)	
M. J. McCague not out	11	9/219 (10) 10/239 (11)	

Bowling: Wasim Akram 10–0–57–0; Chapple 10–1–55–2; Austin 11–4–36–2; Watkinson 10.1–0–42–3; Yates 11–0–42–3.

Umpires: N. T. Plews and D. R. Shepherd.

BENSON AND HEDGES CUP RECORDS

Batting

Highest individual scores: 198*, G. A. Gooch, Essex v Sussex, Hove, 1982; 177, S. J. Cook, Somerset v Sussex, Hove, 1990; 173*, C. G. Greenidge, Hampshire v Minor Counties (South), Amersham, 1973; 167*, A. J. Stewart, Surrey v Somerset, The Oval, 1994; 158*, B. F. Davison, Leicestershire v Warwickshire, Coventry, 1972; 158, W. J. Cronje, Leicestershire v Lancashire, Manchester, 1995; 155*, M. D. Crowe, Somerset v Hampshire, Southampton, 1987; 155*, R. A. Smith, Hampshire v Glamorgan, Southampton, 1989; 154*, M. J. Procter, Gloucestershire v Somerset, Taunton, 1972; 154*, C. L. Smith, Hampshire v Combined Universities, Southampton, 1990. *In the final:* 132*, I. V. A. Richards, Somerset v Surrey, 1981. (257 hundreds have been scored in the competition. The most hundreds in one season is 24 in 1991.)

Most runs: 4,934, G. A. Gooch; 2,776, M. W. Gatting; 2,761, C. J. Tavaré; 2,663, D. W. Randall; 2,660, W. Larkins; 2,636, A. J. Lamb.

Fastest hundred: M. A. Nash in 62 minutes, Glamorgan v Hampshire at Swansea, 1976.

Most hundreds: 14, G. A. Gooch; 7, G. A. Hick and W. Larkins; 5, C. G. Greenidge, A. J. Lamb and N. R. Taylor.

Highest totals: 388 for seven, Essex v Scotland, Chelmsford, 1992; 366 for four, Derbyshire v Combined Universities, Oxford, 1991; 353 for seven, Lancashire v Nottinghamshire, Manchester, 1995; 350 for three, Essex v Oxford & Cambridge Univs, Chelmsford, 1979; 333 for four, Essex v Oxford & Cambridge Univs, Chelmsford, 1985; 331 for five, Surrey v Hampshire, The Oval, 1990; 330 for four, Lancashire v Sussex, Manchester, 1991; 327 for four, Leicestershire v Warwickshire, Coventry, 1972; 327 for two, Essex v Sussex, Hove, 1982; 325 for five, Middlesex v Leicestershire, Leicester, 1992; 321 for one, Hampshire v Minor Counties (South), Amersham, 1973; 321 for five, Somerset v Sussex, Hove, 1990. *In the final:* 290 for six, Essex v Surrey, 1979.

Highest total by a side batting second and winning: 318 for five (54.3 overs), Lancashire v Leicestershire (312 for five), Manchester, 1995. *In the final:* 244 for six (55 overs), Yorkshire v Northamptonshire (244 for seven), 1987; 244 for seven (55 overs), Nottinghamshire v Essex (243 for seven), 1989.

Highest total by a side batting second and losing: 303 for seven (55 overs), Derbyshire v Somerset (310 for three), Taunton, 1990. *In the final:* 255 (51.4 overs), Surrey v Essex (290 for six), 1979.

Highest match aggregates: 630 for ten wickets, Leicestershire (312 for five) v Lancashire (318 for five), Manchester, 1995; 629 for 14 wickets, Lancashire (353 for seven) v Nottinghamshire (276 for seven), Manchester, 1995; 613 for ten wickets, Somerset (310 for three) v Derbyshire (303 for seven), Taunton, 1990; 610 for eight wickets, Sussex (303 for six) v Kent (307 for two), Hove, 1995; 602 runs for 14 wickets, Essex (307 for four) v Warwickshire (295), Birmingham, 1991; 601 runs for 13 wickets, Somerset (307 for six) v Gloucestershire (294 for seven), Taunton, 1982; 600 runs for 16 wickets, Derbyshire (300 for six) v Northamptonshire (300), Derby, 1987.

Lowest totals: 50 in 27.2 overs, Hampshire v Yorkshire, Leeds, 1991; 56 in 26.2 overs, Leicestershire v Minor Counties, Wellington, 1982; 59 in 34 overs, Oxford & Cambridge Univs v Glamorgan, Cambridge, 1983; 61 in 26 overs, Sussex v Middlesex, Hove, 1978; 61 in 25.3 overs, Essex v Lancashire, Chelmsford, 1992; 62 in 26.5 overs, Gloucestershire v Hampshire, Bristol, 1975. *In the final:* 117 in 46.3 overs, Derbyshire v Hampshire, 1988.

Shortest completed innings: 21.4 overs (156), Surrey v Sussex, Hove, 1988.

Record partnership for each wicket

252	for 1st	V. P. Terry and C. L. Smith, Hampshire v Combined Universities at Southampton	1990
285*	for 2nd	C. G. Greenidge and D. R. Turner, Hampshire v Minor Counties (South) at Amersham	1973
269*	for 3rd	P. M. Roebuck and M. D. Crowe, Somerset v Hampshire at Southampton	1987
184*	for 4th	D. Lloyd and B. W. Reidy, Lancashire v Derbyshire at Chesterfield	1980
160	for 5th	A. J. Lamb and D. J. Capel, Northamptonshire v Leicestershire at Northampton	1986
121	for 6th	P. A. Neale and S. J. Rhodes, Worcestershire v Yorkshire at Worcester	1988
149*	for 7th	J. D. Love and C. M. Old, Yorkshire v Scotland at Bradford	1981
109	for 8th	R. E. East and N. Smith, Essex v Northamptonshire at Chelmsford	1977
83	for 9th	P. G. Newman and M. A. Holding, Derbyshire v Nottinghamshire at Nottingham	1985
80*	for 10th	D. L. Bairstow and M. Johnson, Yorkshire v Derbyshire at Derby ..	1981

Bowling

Most wickets: 147, J. K. Lever; 132, I. T. Botham.

Best bowling: seven for 12, W. W. Daniel, Middlesex v Minor Counties (East), Ipswich, 1978; seven for 22, J. R. Thomson, Middlesex v Hampshire, Lord's, 1981; seven for 32, R. G. D. Willis, Warwickshire v Yorkshire, Birmingham, 1981. *In the final:* five for 13, S. T. Jefferies, Hampshire v Derbyshire, 1988.

Hat-tricks (10): G. D. McKenzie, Leicestershire v Worcestershire, Worcester, 1972; K. Higgs, Leicestershire v Surrey in the final, Lord's, 1974; A. A. Jones, Middlesex v Essex, Lord's, 1977; M. J. Procter, Gloucestershire v Hampshire, Southampton, 1977; W. Larkins, Northamptonshire v Oxford & Cambridge Univs, Northampton, 1980; E. A. Moseley, Glamorgan v Kent, Cardiff, 1981; G. C. Small, Warwickshire v Leicestershire, Leicester, 1984; N. A. Mallender, Somerset v Combined Universities, Taunton, 1987; W. K. M. Benjamin, Leicestershire v Nottinghamshire, Leicester, 1987; A. R. C. Fraser, Middlesex v Sussex, Lord's, 1988.

Wicket-keeping and Fielding

Most dismissals: 122 (117 ct, 5 st), D. L. Bairstow.

Most dismissals in an innings: 8 (all ct), D. J. S. Taylor, Somerset v Oxford & Cambridge Univs, Taunton, 1982.

Most catches by a fielder: 63, G. A. Gooch; 54, C. J. Tavaré; 53, I. T. Botham.

Most catches by a fielder in an innings: 5, V. J. Marks, Oxford & Cambridge Univs v Kent, Oxford, 1976.

Results

Largest victories in runs: Essex by 272 runs v Scotland, Chelmsford, 1992; Somerset by 233 runs v Ireland, Eglinton, 1995; Glamorgan by 217 runs v Combined Universities, Cardiff, 1995; Essex by 214 runs v Oxford & Cambridge Univs, Chelmsford, 1979; Derbyshire by 206 runs v Combined Universities, Oxford, 1991; Yorkshire by 189 runs v Hampshire, Leeds, 1991; Sussex by 186 runs v Cambridge University, Hove, 1974.

Victories by ten wickets (19): By Derbyshire, Essex (twice), Glamorgan, Hampshire, Kent (twice), Lancashire, Leicestershire (twice), Middlesex, Northamptonshire, Somerset, Warwickshire, Worcestershire (twice), Yorkshire (three times).

Gold Awards

Most awards: 22, G. A. Gooch; 11, M. W. Gatting, T. E. Jesty and B. Wood.

WINNERS 1972-95

1972 LEICESTERSHIRE beat Yorkshire by five wickets.
1973 KENT beat Worcestershire by 39 runs.
1974 SURREY beat Leicestershire by 27 runs.
1975 LEICESTERSHIRE beat Middlesex by five wickets.
1976 KENT beat Worcestershire by 43 runs.
1977 GLOUCESTERSHIRE beat Kent by 64 runs.
1978 KENT beat Derbyshire by six wickets.
1979 ESSEX beat Surrey by 35 runs.
1980 NORTHAMPTONSHIRE beat Essex by six runs.
1981 SOMERSET beat Surrey by seven wickets.
1982 SOMERSET beat Nottinghamshire by nine wickets.
1983 MIDDLESEX beat Essex by four runs.
1984 LANCASHIRE beat Warwickshire by six wickets.
1985 LEICESTERSHIRE beat Essex by five wickets.
1986 MIDDLESEX beat Kent by two runs.
1987 YORKSHIRE beat Northamptonshire, having taken more wickets with the scores tied.
1988 HAMPSHIRE beat Derbyshire by seven wickets.
1989 NOTTINGHAMSHIRE beat Essex by three wickets.

1990 LANCASHIRE beat Worcestershire by 69 runs.
1991 WORCESTERSHIRE beat Lancashire by 65 runs.
1992 HAMPSHIRE beat Kent by 41 runs.
1993 DERBYSHIRE beat Lancashire by six runs.
1994 WARWICKSHIRE beat Worcestershire by six wickets.
1995 LANCASHIRE beat Kent by 35 runs.

WINS BY NON-CHAMPIONSHIP TEAMS

1973 OXFORD beat Northamptonshire at Northampton by two wickets.
1975 { OXFORD & CAMBRIDGE beat Worcestershire at Cambridge by 66 runs.
       OXFORD & CAMBRIDGE beat Northamptonshire at Oxford by three wickets.
1976 OXFORD & CAMBRIDGE beat Yorkshire at Barnsley by seven wickets.
1980 MINOR COUNTIES beat Gloucestershire at Chippenham by three runs.
1981 MINOR COUNTIES beat Hampshire at Southampton by three runs.
1982 MINOR COUNTIES beat Leicestershire at Wellington by 131 runs.
1984 OXFORD & CAMBRIDGE beat Gloucestershire at Bristol by 27 runs.
1986 SCOTLAND beat Lancashire at Perth by three runs.
1987 MINOR COUNTIES beat Glamorgan at Oxford (Christ Church) by seven wickets.
1989 { COMBINED UNIVERSITIES beat Surrey at Cambridge by nine runs.
       COMBINED UNIVERSITIES beat Worcestershire at Worcester by five wickets.
1990 { COMBINED UNIVERSITIES beat Yorkshire at Leeds by two wickets.
       SCOTLAND beat Northamptonshire at Northampton by two runs.
1992 MINOR COUNTIES beat Sussex at Marlow by 19 runs.
1995 MINOR COUNTIES beat Leicestershire at Leicester by 26 runs.

TEAM RECORDS 1972-95

| | Rounds reached | | | | | Matches | | |
	W	F	SF	QF	P	W	L	NR
Derbyshire	1	3	4	9	107	57	42	8
Durham	0	0	0	0	12	5	6	1
Essex	1	5	8	14	119	73	44	2
Glamorgan	0	0	1	7	100	43	53	4
Gloucestershire	1	1	2	6	101	49	49	3
Hampshire	2	2	5	12	111	58	48	5
Kent	3	7	12	16	125	80	43	2
Lancashire	3	5	9	15	121	75	39	7
Leicestershire	3	4	6	9	112	60	45	7
Middlesex	2	3	5	14	115	62	45	8
Northamptonshire	1	2	4	9	105	47	50	8
Nottinghamshire	1	2	5	13	112	66	40	6
Somerset	2	2	8	12	112	61	49	2
Surrey	1	3	7	10	112	60	48	4
Sussex	0	1	1	9	102	51	50	1
Warwickshire	1	2	6	12	111	61	44	6
Worcestershire	1	5	8	15	118	63	51	4
Yorkshire	1	2	5	9	106	55	44	7
Cambridge University	0	0	0	0	8	0	8	0
Oxford University	0	0	0	0	4	1	3	0
Oxford & Cambridge Universities	0	0	0	0	48	4	42	2
Combined Universities	0	0	0	1	32	3	28	1
Minor Counties	0	0	0	0	60	6	50	4
Minor Counties (North)	0	0	0	0	20	0	20	0
Minor Counties (South)	0	0	0	0	20	0	19	1
Minor Counties (East)	0	0	0	0	12	0	12	0
Minor Counties (West)	0	0	0	0	12	0	12	0
Scotland	0	0	0	0	58	2	53	3
Ireland	0	0	0	0	5	0	5	0

Middlesex beat Gloucestershire on the toss of a coin in their quarter-final in 1983. Derbyshire, Kent, Somerset and Warwickshire totals each include a bowling contest; Derbyshire beat Somerset and Warwickshire beat Kent when their quarter-finals, in 1993 and 1994 respectively, were abandoned.

AXA EQUITY & LAW LEAGUE, 1995

Kent became the first team to win the Sunday League four times when they took the 1995 competition, one of the most closely contested in the League's 27-year history.

After the early pacesetters, Glamorgan, fell away at the end of July, five counties were still in with a serious chance, and three of them – Kent, Warwickshire and Worcestershire – eventually finished level on points, with Kent winning on run-rate.

Their success caused rapture in Canterbury: the county had not won a trophy since their great decade ended in 1978. It might have been modified by the knowledge that, in contrast, they had finished bottom of the Championship for the first time this century, and by the circumstances: rain in Worcester threw the title to Kent even as they were losing particularly ineptly to Warwickshire. However, they showed consistent mastery of Sunday cricket's particular skills throughout the season, and the triumph was a reward for near-misses the two previous years: this was the third season running in which Kent had won 12 of their 17 matches.

The 1994 champions Warwickshire lost their first three matches, then accelerated like a Derby winner emerging from Tattenham Corner, giving

Continued overleaf

AXA EQUITY & LAW LEAGUE

	M	W	L	T	NR	Pts	Run-Rate
1 – Kent (3)	17	12	4	0	1	50	93.49
2 – Warwickshire (1)	17	12	4	0	1	50	84.40
3 – Worcestershire (2)	17	11	3	1	2	50	84.22
4 – Lancashire (4)	17	11	5	0	1	46	82.86
5 – Essex (17)	17	10	6	1	0	42	90.73
6 – Glamorgan (7)	17	8	6	0	3	38	89.17
7 – Leicestershire (10)	17	8	7	0	2	36	89.47
8 – Derbyshire (8)	17	7	6	1	3	36	80.54
9 – Surrey (6)	17	7	8	0	2	32	91.79
10 – Sussex (15)	17	7	8	0	2	32	82.85
11 – Nottinghamshire (11)	17	7	9	0	1	30	91.01
12 – Yorkshire (5)	17	7	9	0	1	30	76.20
13 – Northamptonshire (13)	17	6	8	1	2	30	84.94
14 – Somerset (16)	17	5	9	0	3	26	82.45
15 – Gloucestershire (18)	17	5	10	0	2	24	81.41
16 – Durham (9)	17	4	9	1	3	24	73.48
17 – Middlesex (14)	17	4	11	0	2	20	76.86
18 – Hampshire (12)	17	3	12	1	1	16	82.89

1994 positions are shown in brackets.

When two or more counties finish with an equal number of points, the positions are decided by a) most wins, b) runs per 100 balls.

No play was possible in the following seven matches: June 4 – Durham v Kent at Chester-le-Street; June 11 – Surrey v Somerset at The Oval; September 10 – Glamorgan v Nottinghamshire at Cardiff, Gloucestershire v Durham at Bristol, Hampshire v Somerset at Southampton, Middlesex v Leicestershire at Uxbridge; September 17 – Leicestershire v Gloucestershire at Leicester.

the impression that the early sluggishness was all part of their masterplan. They won their next ten matches, and would have been champions again had they not gone down to a two-run defeat at Worcester on August 27.

That kept Worcestershire in contention, and the following week they joined Kent at the top of the table. However, they were undone when the weather broke and their last two matches were washed away. Lancashire, made hot favourites after winning their first four games, might have proved the bookmakers right had they not lost controversially at Leicester in a game restarted because the original pitch was deemed unsafe.

Essex, who have not won a one-day trophy since 1985, were leaders for much of August. But they were beaten at Pontypridd in Glamorgan's solitary win after June and then faded away. Glamorgan undoubtedly had the individuals of the year in the three Steves: James the opener, apparently flourishing in the absence of close fielders, was the League's leading scorer with 815, while the opening bowlers, Watkin and Barwick, were the only men anywhere to reach 30 wickets. All might have broken League records had their last two matches not been rained off. The same went for their team-mate Colin Metson, who was only two short of Steve Rhodes's wicket-keeping record of 29 dismissals.

On the opening day of the season 17 players new to the competition took the field, the most since the Sunday League's very first day in 1969. And, as the season wore on, several counties not in contention – especially those chasing hard for the Championship – continued the long-standing tradition of resting their leading players, to the benefit of both the weary stars and the youngsters who replace them, if not necessarily to the benefit of spectators who still regard the competition seriously. After two years the counties changed their costumes for the League, the coloured designs being mixed with more white. Some observers thought they did look a little less like pyjamas – but only to look more like tracksuits.

Leading run-scorers: S. P. James 815 (£3,000 individual award), T. M. Moody 797 (£1,500), M. G. Bevan 704, N. Hussain 634, P. Johnson 617, C. L. Cairns 615, M. E. Waugh 608, G. R. Cowdrey 593, P. R. Pollard 577, G. A. Hick 551.

Leading wicket-takers: S. L. Watkin 32 (£3,000 individual award), S. R. Barwick 30 (£1,500), Wasim Akram 29, D. W. Headley 24, H. H. Streak, R. C. Irani and M. C. Ilott 22, M. J. McCague and S. R. Lampitt 21.

Most economical bowlers (runs per over, minimum 100 overs) Wasim Akram 3.68, P. J. Newport 3.85, G. R. Haynes 4.01, S. L. Watkin 4.06, G. J. Parsons 4.14, I. D. Austin 4.26, M. A. Ealham 4.41, R. D. B. Croft 4.48.

Leading wicket-keepers: C. P. Metson 27 (20 ct, 7 st) (£3,000 individual award), A. N. Aymes 26 (23 ct, 3 st), K. J. Piper 26 (24 ct, 2 st), S. A. Marsh 24 (23 ct, 1 st), S. J. Rhodes 24 (17 ct, 7 st).

Leading fielders: J. Boiling 12, D. L. Hemp 11, G. F. Archer, K. Greenfield and J. R. Wileman 9.

Prize money

£35,000 for winners: KENT.
£17,500 for runners-up: WARWICKSHIRE
£8,750 for third place: WORCESTERSHIRE.
£4,375 for fourth place: LANCASHIRE.
£400 for the winners of each match, shared if tied or no result.

SUMMARY OF RESULTS, 1995

	Derbyshire	Durham	Essex	Glamorgan	Gloucestershire	Hampshire	Kent	Lancashire	Leicestershire	Middlesex	Northamptonshire	Nottinghamshire	Somerset	Surrey	Sussex	Warwickshire	Worcestershire	Yorkshire
Derbyshire	—	W	L	W	W	W	L	N	L	W	T	W	L	W	N	N	L	L
Durham	L	—	T	W	N	L	N	L	L	L	W	L	L	L	N	W	L	W
Essex	W	T	—	L	W	L	L	W	W	W	W	W	W	W	L	L	L	L
Glamorgan	L	L	W	—	L	W	L	W	L	W	N	N	W	L	L	L	L	L
Gloucestershire	L	N	L	W	—	W	L	W	N	W	L	L	W	L	L	L	T	L
Hampshire	L	W	L	L	L	—	L	L	W	L	L	W	N	L	L	L	W	W
Kent	W	N	W	L	W	W	—	W	W	L	L	W	W	W	W	W	W	W
Lancashire	N	W	W	L	L	W	L	—	L	W	L	W	W	W	W	W	W	W
Leicestershire	W	W	L	W	N	L	L	W	—	N	W	W	L	W	L	L	L	W
Middlesex	L	W	L	L	W	W	L	L	N	—	L	W	W	N	L	L	N	N
Northamptonshire	T	L	L	L	W	W	W	W	L	W	—	L	L	L	W	L	N	N
Nottinghamshire	L	W	L	N	W	L	W	L	L	L	W	—	W	L	L	L	L	W
Somerset	W	W	N	L	N	L	N	L	L	W	L	L	—	N	L	L	L	L
Surrey	L	W	L	L	W	W	L	L	L	N	W	W	N	—	L	W	L	W
Sussex	N	N	L	L	W	W	L	L	W	L	W	L	W	W	—	L	L	L
Warwickshire	N	L	W	W	W	W	W	L	W	W	W	W	L	W	W	—	L	W
Worcestershire	W	W	W	N	W	T	L	W	W	N	L	W	W	L	W	W	—	W
Yorkshire	W	L	W	W	W	W	L	L	L	W	N	L	L	L	L	W	L	—

Home games in bold, away games in italics. W = Won, L = Lost, T = Tied, N = No result.

DERBYSHIRE

At Nottingham, May 7. DERBYSHIRE beat NOTTINGHAMSHIRE by 21 runs.

DERBYSHIRE v YORKSHIRE

At Chesterfield, May 14. Yorkshire won by 59 runs. Toss: Derbyshire.

Derbyshire's fourth defeat in all competitions in the space of a week came after their batting collapsed in the face of an apparently modest Yorkshire total. Warner had kept the visitors in check but then Hartley, who had claimed nine for 41 in the Championship contest the previous day, shone again for Yorkshire.

Yorkshire

*D. Byas c Wells b Malcolm	19	D. Gough run out	24
M. P. Vaughan c Bairstow b Warner	17		
M. G. Bevan c Bairstow b Warner	19	L-b 16, w 21	37
C. White c Bairstow b Warner	0		
†R. J. Blakey not out	38	1/27 2/63 3/63 (7 wkts, 40 overs)	167
A. P. Grayson c Adams b Warner	4	4/66 5/83	
B. Parker c DeFreitas b Harris	9	6/104 7/167	

P. J. Hartley, S. M. Milburn and M. A. Robinson did not bat.

Bowling: Malcolm 7-1-21-1; DeFreitas 8-0-38-0; Cork 8-0-37-0; Warner 8-3-14-4; Wells 3-0-14-0; Harris 6-0-27-1.

Derbyshire

D. G. Cork c Parker b Robinson	2	A. J. Harris c and b Grayson	2
C. J. Adams c Grayson b Hartley	35	A. E. Warner b White	9
T. J. G. O'Gorman c Blakey b Hartley	6	D. E. Malcolm not out	0
*K. J. Barnett run out	5	L-b 2, w 12	14
P. A. J. DeFreitas c Blakey b Gough	18		
C. M. Wells st Blakey b Grayson	8	1/21 2/37 3/54	(32.4 overs) 108
T. W. Harrison run out	9	4/59 5/84 6/88	
†A. D. Bairstow run out	1	7/96 8/96 9/102	

Bowling: Robinson 6–0–25–1; Gough 5–1–18–1; Hartley 6–2–7–2; White 5.4–1–20–1; Milburn 5–0–27–0; Grayson 5–1–9–2.

Umpires: R. Palmer and P. B. Wight.

At Leicester, May 21. DERBYSHIRE lost to LEICESTERSHIRE by 23 runs.

At Lord's, June 4. DERBYSHIRE beat MIDDLESEX by 24 runs.

DERBYSHIRE v NORTHAMPTONSHIRE

At Derby, June 11. Tied. Toss: Derbyshire.

Needing 14 from the final over, bowled by Taylor, Derbyshire scored 12 off the first five balls, but could only scramble a bye from the last. Kumble had pegged them back after Wells, with 73 off as many balls, had put them in charge.

Northamptonshire

M. B. Loye c Krikken b Harris	34	†R. J. Warren not out	4
D. J. Capel b Warner	18	A. L. Penberthy not out	3
K. M. Curran c Krikken b Warner	60	L-b 9, w 5	14
T. C. Walton b Harris	4		
*R. J. Bailey c Harris b Warner	58	1/33 2/75 3/81	(6 wkts, 40 overs) 200
D. J. Sales lbw b Cork	5	4/177 5/186 6/194	

A. Kumble, N. A. Mallender and J. P. Taylor did not bat.

Bowling: Warner 8–1–38–3; Cork 8–0–50–1; Wells 8–1–29–0; Harris 7–0–28–2; Griffith 4–0–16–0; Aldred 5–0–30–0.

Derbyshire

*K. J. Barnett c Warren b Mallender	9	A. E. Warner b Capel	5
D. G. Cork c Warren b Mallender	23	P. Aldred not out	11
D. J. Cullinan b Penberthy	20	A. J. Harris not out	1
C. M. Wells b Kumble	73	B 2, l-b 11, w 13	26
A. S. Rollins c Warren b Capel	26		
W. A. Dessaur c Capel b Kumble	5	1/30 2/39 3/85	(9 wkts, 40 overs) 200
†K. M. Krikken run out	1	4/161 5/175 6/179	
F. A. Griffith c and b Kumble	0	7/179 8/184 9/186	

Bowling: Taylor 8–0–43–0; Mallender 8–1–21–2; Penberthy 8–1–32–1; Capel 8–0–55–2; Kumble 7–1–25–3; Walton 1–0–11–0.

Umpires: J. H. Harris and M. J. Kitchen.

DERBYSHIRE v SOMERSET

At Derby, June 18. Somerset won by 19 runs. Toss: Somerset.

A tidy spell from Trump restricted Derbyshire's progress, and Cullinan's efforts proved in vain. Somerset were boosted by Parsons, whose maiden one-day fifty came off just 35 balls.

Somerset

M. N. Lathwell c and b Aldred	55	Mushtaq Ahmed c Adams b DeFreitas		1
M. E. Trescothick lbw b Cork	13	†R. J. Turner not out		1
*P. D. Bowler lbw b Cork	7	B 4, l-b 4, w 5, n-b 4		17
R. J. Harden b Malcolm	31			
G. D. Rose b Malcolm	7	1/18 2/32 3/97	(7 wkts, 40 overs)	212
P. C. L. Holloway b DeFreitas	28	4/119 5/129		
K. A. Parsons not out	52	6/209 7/211		

J. I. D. Kerr and H. R. J. Trump did not bat.

Bowling: DeFreitas 8-0-37-2; Cork 8-0-27-2; Harris 8-0-64-0; Malcolm 8-0-30-2; Aldred 8-0-46-1.

Derbyshire

D. G. Cork st Turner b Trump	36	P. A. J. DeFreitas c Rose b Kerr		0
*K. J. Barnett b Kerr	30	F. A. Griffith not out		5
C. J. Adams b Parsons	1			
D. J. Cullinan not out	76	L-b 3, w 7		10
A. S. Rollins st Turner				
b Mushtaq Ahmed	6	1/63 2/64 3/77	(6 wkts, 40 overs)	193
†K. M. Krikken b Rose	29	4/105 5/170 6/173		

A. J. Harris, P. Aldred and D. E. Malcolm did not bat.

Bowling: Rose 8-0-46-1; Parsons 8-1-32-1; Kerr 8-0-33-2; Trump 8-0-28-1; Mushtaq Ahmed 8-0-51-1.

Umpires: N. T. Plews and P. B. Wight.

At Chester-le-Street, June 25. DERBYSHIRE beat DURHAM by five wickets.

DERBYSHIRE v HAMPSHIRE

At Derby, July 2. Derbyshire won by five wickets. Toss: Derbyshire.

Cork turned in a decisive all-round performance. Despite delivering ten wides, he played his part in containing Hampshire and then led the chase with a 62-ball half-century.

Hampshire

J. P. Stephenson c Krikken b Cork	25	†A. N. Aymes c Rollins b Warner		13
R. S. M. Morris c Wells b Griffith	23	S. D. Udal run out		9
M. Keech lbw b Griffith	11	L-b 12, w 20		32
R. A. Smith c Wells b Harris	4			
G. W. White lbw b Cork	11	1/47 2/71 3/76	(8 wkts, 40 overs)	154
*M. C. J. Nicholas c Wells b Harris	2	4/76 5/80 6/105		
K. D. James not out	27	7/141 8/154		

M. J. Thursfield and C. A. Connor did not bat.

Bowling: Warner 8-0-31-1; DeFreitas 8-0-36-0; Cork 8-0-34-2; Griffith 8-1-22-2; Harris 8-1-19-2.

Derbyshire

D. G. Cork c Aymes b Thursfield	57	†K. M. Krikken not out		15
C. J. Adams lbw b Stephenson	22			
A. S. Rollins lbw b Udal	8	L-b 3, w 1, n-b 2		6
D. J. Cullinan not out	46			
C. M. Wells c Aymes b Thursfield	1	1/52 2/83 3/93	(5 wkts, 37.3 overs)	159
*K. J. Barnett c and b James	4	4/97 5/104		

P. A. J. DeFreitas, F. A. Griffith, A. J. Harris and A. E. Warner did not bat.

Bowling: Thursfield 8–1–26–2; James 8–0–31–1; Stephenson 7.3–0–41–1; Connor 7–0–32–0; Udal 5–0–14–1; Keech 2–0–12–0.

Umpires: J. D. Bond and J. W. Holder.

At Maidstone, July 9. DERBYSHIRE lost to KENT by four runs.

DERBYSHIRE v SUSSEX

At Derby, July 16. No result. Toss: Derbyshire.

When rain halted play, Giddins was left on a hat-trick, having dismissed Cork and Rollins with successive balls.

Sussex

K. Greenfield c Krikken b Cork	0	P. W. Jarvis lbw b Cork 4
*A. P. Wells lbw b Cork	85	R. S. C. Martin-Jenkins b Malcolm 1
F. D. Stephenson c Tweats b Wells	20	E. S. H. Giddins c Cork b Harris ... 0
C. W. J. Athey st Krikken b Wells	5	B 4, l-b 13, w 10 27
K. Newell c and b Griffith	5	
†P. Moores b Griffith	3	1/2 2/84 3/98 (39.4 overs) 198
D. R. Law not out	41	4/109 5/121 6/163
I. D. K. Salisbury c Adams b Malcolm	7	7/188 8/194 9/195

Bowling: Malcolm 8–1–25–2; Cork 8–0–38–3; Harris 5.4–0–36–1; Griffith 8–1–29–2; Wells 8–0–38–2; Barnett 2–0–15–0.

Derbyshire

D. G. Cork b Giddins	0
C. J. Adams not out	0
A. S. Rollins lbw b Giddins	0
W 1	1

1/1 2/1   (2 wkts, 0.3 overs) 1

D. J. Cullinan, C. M. Wells, *K. J. Barnett, T. A. Tweats, †K. M. Krikken, F. A. Griffith, A. J. Harris and D. E. Malcolm did not bat.

Bowling: Giddins 0.3–0–1–2.

Umpires: G. I. Burgess and D. J. Constant.

DERBYSHIRE v GLAMORGAN

At Derby, July 30. Derbyshire won by one wicket. Toss: Glamorgan.

Malcolm was Derbyshire's batting hero in an exciting finish, making amends for an expensive bowling stint. Coming in after Derbyshire had lost five wickets for 22, and with three balls left, he hit his first, from Barwick, for six to level the scores, and then clinched victory with a four off the final delivery. Earlier, James had passed 1,000 one-day runs in the season for Glamorgan.

Glamorgan

S. P. James run out	60	R. D. B. Croft not out 66
*H. Morris lbw b DeFreitas	2	H. A. G. Anthony not out 2
M. P. Maynard c Krikken b DeFreitas	0	L-b 2, w 13 15
P. A. Cottey c Tweats b Barnett	56	
D. L. Hemp b Barnett	3	1/12 2/12 3/121 (6 wkts, 40 overs) 247
A. Dale c Wells b Malcolm	43	4/131 5/133 6/219

†C. P. Metson, S. L. Watkin and S. R. Barwick did not bat.

Bowling: Warner 6–0–43–0; DeFreitas 8–1–26–2; Wells 2–0–17–0; Malcolm 8–0–73–1; Griffith 8–0–54–0; Barnett 8–0–32–2.

Derbyshire

*K. J. Barnett c Metson b Anthony ...	2
C. J. Adams c Cottey b Watkin	67
A. S. Rollins lbw b Watkin	8
D. J. Cullinan c James b Croft	43
C. M. Wells c James b Watkin	67
T. A. Tweats b Watkin	19
P. A. J. DeFreitas c Cottey b Barwick .	8
†K. M. Krikken not out	9

F. A. Griffith c Watkin b Dale	0
A. E. Warner b Barwick	1
D. E. Malcolm not out	10
L-b 5, w 8, n-b 4	17
1/7 2/24 3/103 (9 wkts, 40 overs) 251	
4/174 5/219 6/220	
7/235 8/237 9/241	

Bowling: Watkin 8–0–38–4; Anthony 8–0–49–1; Barwick 8–0–40–2; Croft 8–0–50–1; Dale 8–0–69–1.

Umpires: M. J. Kitchen and D. R. Shepherd.

At Worcester, August 13. DERBYSHIRE lost to WORCESTERSHIRE by ten wickets.

At Bristol, August 20. DERBYSHIRE beat GLOUCESTERSHIRE by eight wickets.

DERBYSHIRE v SURREY

At Derby, August 27. Derbyshire won by three wickets. Toss: Derbyshire.
 A high-scoring match included two maiden one-day centuries. Having been set a revised target of 249 in 37 overs, Derbyshire raced home, thanks to Rollins; he reached a hundred from only 68 balls, facing 87 in all and hitting 17 fours. Surrey's total was built round a stand of 190 in 25 overs between Darren Bicknell and Shahid, whose century took 84 balls, with three sixes and ten fours.

Surrey

D. J. Bicknell c Harrison b Griffith	91
A. D. Brown c Griffith b Harris	26
N. Shahid c Tweats b Griffith	101
*A. J. Hollioake c Harrison b Griffith..	9
A. W. Smith c Tweats b Griffith	3
M. A. Butcher c Adams b DeFreitas...	8
†N. F. Sargeant b DeFreitas	3

M. P. Bicknell not out	3
J. E. Benjamin not out	0
B 1, l-b 12, w 8, n-b 4	25
1/44 2/234 3/242 (7 wkts, 40 overs) 269	
4/250 5/260	
6/266 7/267	

S. G. Kenlock and C. G. Rackemann did not bat.

Bowling: Aldred 6–0–41–0; DeFreitas 8–1–30–2; Griffith 8–0–56–4; Harris 6–0–39–1; Richardson 6–0–41–0; Tweats 4–0–27–0; Harrison 2–0–22–0.

Derbyshire

T. J. G. O'Gorman lbw b Benjamin ...	8
C. J. Adams c Kenlock b M. P. Bicknell .	13
†A. S. Rollins not out	126
J. E. Owen c D. J. Bicknell b Smith ...	45
T. A. Tweats lbw b Kenlock	6
T. W. Harrison b Kenlock	8
*P. A. J. DeFreitas c Sargeant b Rackemann .	19

F. A. Griffith run out	12
P. Aldred not out	5
B 4, l-b 2, w 3	9
1/13 2/28 3/131 (7 wkts, 34.5 overs) 251	
4/176 5/192	
6/223 7/245	

A. J. Harris and A. Richardson did not bat.

Bowling: M. P. Bicknell 6.5–0–28–1; Benjamin 8–0–40–1; Rackemann 8–0–67–1; Smith 5–0–52–1; Kenlock 6–0–49–2; Hollioake 1–0–9–0.

Umpires: R. Julian and R. A. White.

At Chelmsford, September 3. DERBYSHIRE lost to ESSEX by 24 runs.

At Birmingham, September 10. WARWICKSHIRE v DERBYSHIRE. No result.

DERBYSHIRE v LANCASHIRE

At Derby, September 17. No result. Toss: Lancashire.

Lancashire, put in, had reached 12 for no wicket when that first match was abandoned after 3.3 overs. When a new match of ten overs a side was started, Wells launched a violent assault, hitting 66 from 26 balls including six sixes and three fours. But his efforts came to nothing as another storm prevented Lancashire replying.

Derbyshire

D. G. Cork c Chapple b Martin	7	*K. J. Barnett not out	5
C. M. Wells c Fairbrother b Chapple	66	L-b 3, w 4	7
C. J. Adams c Fairbrother b Watkinson	9		
D. J. Cullinan c Hegg b Chapple	6	1/12 2/20	(4 wkts, 10 overs) 119
J. E. Owen not out	19	3/49 4/109	

A. S. Rollins, T. A. Tweats, †K. M. Krikken, P. Aldred and A. E. Warner did not bat.

Bowling: Austin 2–0–15–0; Martin 2–0–18–1; Watkinson 2–0–32–1; Chapple 2–0–21–2; Yates 2–0–30–0.

Lancashire

M. A. Atherton, J. E. R. Gallian, J. P. Crawley, N. H. Fairbrother, G. D. Lloyd, *M. Watkinson, †W. K. Hegg, I. D. Austin, P. J. Martin, G. Yates and G. Chapple.

Umpires: B. Dudleston and T. E. Jesty.

DURHAM

At Manchester, May 7. DURHAM lost to LANCASHIRE by 84 runs.

At The Oval, May 14. DURHAM lost to SURREY by seven wickets.

DURHAM v WARWICKSHIRE

At Chester-le-Street, May 21. Durham won by two runs. Toss: Durham.

A crowd of more than 6,000 for the first Sunday League match at the Riverside ground saw the home side inflict Warwickshire's third successive Sunday defeat. Small and Paul Smith conceded only 36 runs in 16 overs – 14 of those in wides – as Durham struggled on a bouncy pitch, but Warwickshire were then undone by the medium-pace of Saxelby. Having already claimed three wickets, he returned to the attack when 13 runs were needed from three overs and conceded only four in the last to earn Durham an unexpected win.

Durham

*M. A. Roseberry b Brown	14	S. J. E. Brown c Piper b Bell		4
W. Larkins c Knight b Reeve	0	A. Walker not out		15
M. Prabhakar c Piper b Small	32	M. M. Betts not out		5
J. E. Morris b Brown	1			
J. A. Daley c and b Small	18	L-b 5, w 19, n-b 2		26
M. Saxelby c Piper b Small	4			
†D. G. C. Ligertwood c Knight		1/5 2/25 3/29	(9 wkts, 38 overs)	132
b P. A. Smith	0	4/71 5/83 6/85		
J. Boiling c Piper b Reeve	13	7/85 8/92 9/127		

Bowling: Reeve 7–0–16–2; Brown 8–0–42–2; Small 8–2–23–3; P. A. Smith 8–1–13–1; Bell 4–0–20–1; Twose 3–0–13–0.

Warwickshire

N. V. Knight c Ligertwood b Saxelby	44	†K. J. Piper c Larkins b Prabhakar		6
N. M. K. Smith b Prabhakar	9	G. C. Small not out		7
A. J. Moles b Brown	11	M. A. V. Bell not out		8
R. G. Twose c Roseberry b Brown	0	L-b 2, w 8		10
*D. A. Reeve c Ligertwood b Betts	0			
P. A. Smith c Boiling b Saxelby	15	1/13 2/44 3/44	(9 wkts, 38 overs)	130
T. L. Penney c Ligertwood b Saxelby	0	4/51 5/81 6/82		
D. R. Brown c Ligertwood b Brown	20	7/97 8/115 9/117		

Bowling: Prabhakar 8–1–26–2; Walker 8–0–36–0; Brown 8–1–26–3; Betts 8–0–22–1; Saxelby 6–0–18–3.

Umpires: J. C. Balderstone and J. H. Hampshire.

At Leicester, May 28. DURHAM lost to LEICESTERSHIRE on scoring-rate.

DURHAM v KENT

At Chester-le-Street, June 4. No result (abandoned).

At Chelmsford, June 11. DURHAM tied with ESSEX.

DURHAM v DERBYSHIRE

At Chester-le-Street, June 25. Derbyshire won by five wickets. Toss: Derbyshire.

Batting proved difficult for both sides on a pitch of uneven bounce that had already been used for the Championship contest between the two teams. Despite an economical spell from Prabhakar, Cullinan and Barnett settled the issue with a stand of 62.

Durham

J. E. Morris c Rollins b Warner	2	A. Walker c Griffith b Harris		8
*M. A. Roseberry c Krikken b Warner	0	S. J. E. Brown b Harris		2
M. Prabhakar b Malcolm	20	M. M. Betts not out		14
J. I. Longley lbw b Warner	4	L-b 7, w 2		9
D. A. Blenkiron b DeFreitas	2			
S. Hutton b Harris	30	1/1 2/6 3/14	(39 overs)	113
S. D. Birbeck c Harris b Malcolm	9	4/24 5/36 6/53		
†D. G. C. Ligertwood b Wells	13	7/82 8/86 9/94		

Bowling: Warner 8–2–14–3; DeFreitas 8–2–13–1; Griffith 8–1–21–0; Malcolm 7–0–23–2; Wells 3–0–20–1; Harris 5–1–15–3.

Derbyshire

A. S. Rollins c and b Brown	3	P. A. J. DeFreitas st Ligertwood		
C. J. Adams c Roseberry b Brown	0		b Birbeck	8
D. J. Cullinan not out	52	†K. M. Krikken not out		3
C. M. Wells c Brown b Walker	6	L-b 2, w 2		4
*K. J. Barnett c Ligertwood				—
b Prabhakar	38	1/1 2/5 3/21 4/83 5/92 (5 wkts, 37 overs)		114

F. A. Griffith, A. J. Harris, A. E. Warner and D. E. Malcolm did not bat.

Bowling: Brown 7-0-22-2; Prabhakar 8-2-12-1; Walker 8-0-21-1; Betts 6-0-31-0; Birbeck 8-1-26-1.

Umpires: G. I. Burgess and B. Leadbeater.

At Swansea, July 2. DURHAM beat GLAMORGAN by five wickets.

DURHAM v WORCESTERSHIRE

At Darlington, July 9. Worcestershire won by 79 runs. Toss: Durham.

Hick bounced back in his customary fashion after his Test failure at Edgbaston and made his highest Sunday League score off 81 balls with six sixes – two of them into the neighbouring football ground – and 12 fours. After Worcestershire piled on 185 in the last 20 overs, Durham finished well short with Hick claiming the final two wickets. Hick passed 5,000 runs in the League, the youngest to reach that landmark. When Rhodes stumped Hutton, he became the first player to complete League stumpings against every other county.

Worcestershire

*T. M. Moody c Prabhakar		S. R. Lampitt not out		10
b Bainbridge	28	W. P. C. Weston not out		0
T. S. Curtis c Ligertwood b Walker	10			
G. A. Hick c Boiling b Bainbridge	130	L-b 11, w 2, n-b 4		17
G. R. Haynes c Brown b Prabhakar	30			—
D. A. Leatherdale c Roseberry		1/44 2/44 3/162 (5 wkts, 40 overs)		272
b Bainbridge	47	4/261 5/262		

V. S. Solanki, †S. J. Rhodes, P. J. Newport and P. Mirza did not bat.

Bowling: Brown 8-0-41-0; Prabhakar 8-0-46-1; Bainbridge 8-0-56-3; Walker 8-0-51-1; Boiling 4-0-30-0; Blenkiron 4-0-37-0.

Durham

*M. A. Roseberry c Curtis b Haynes	16	J. Boiling b Mirza		12
W. Larkins c Rhodes b Haynes	17	A. Walker c Curtis b Hick		1
M. Prabhakar c Leatherdale b Haynes	16	S. J. E. Brown not out		0
J. E. Morris c Solanki b Lampitt	74	L-b 5, w 6		11
S. Hutton st Rhodes b Hick	9			—
D. A. Blenkiron run out	6	1/26 2/45 3/60 (36 overs)		193
P. Bainbridge run out	0	4/78 5/104 6/104		
†D. G. C. Ligertwood st Rhodes b Hick	31	7/156 8/188 9/193		

Bowling: Newport 8-2-22-0; Haynes 8-0-38-3; Lampitt 6-0-43-1; Hick 8-0-51-3; Mirza 6-0-34-1.

Umpires: H. D. Bird and N. T. Plews.

DURHAM v HAMPSHIRE

At Chester-le-Street, July 16. Hampshire won by four wickets. Toss: Durham.

Hampshire's victory, gained with four balls to spare, was made possible by James and Aymes, whose stand of 109 rallied their side from 61 for five.

Durham

J. E. Morris c Aymes b Connor	0	†D. G. C. Ligertwood not out	4
*M. A. Roseberry b Udal	31		
M. Prabhakar c Aymes b Streak	7	B 1, l-b 9, w 5, n-b 4	19
S. Hutton c Udal b James	33		
J. A. Daley not out	53	1/0 2/16 3/68 (5 wkts, 40 overs) 170	
D. A. Blenkiron b Connor	23	4/97 5/154	

J. Boiling, N. Killeen, A. Walker and M. M. Betts did not bat.

Bowling: Connor 8–3–23–2; James 8–2–26–1; Streak 8–0–40–1; Thursfield 8–1–38–0; Udal 8–1–33–1.

Hampshire

R. S. M. Morris lbw b Prabhakar	4	†A. N. Aymes b Prabhakar	41
P. R. Whitaker c Ligertwood b Betts	19	S. D. Udal not out	0
M. Keech c Walker b Killeen	31	L-b 8, w 7	15
V. P. Terry c Boiling b Killeen	2		
*M. C. J. Nicholas b Betts	0	1/4 2/51 3/59 (6 wkts, 39.2 overs) 174	
K. D. James not out	62	4/61 5/61 6/170	

H. H. Streak, C. A. Connor and M. J. Thursfield did not bat.

Bowling: Prabhakar 8–0–43–2; Walker 7.2–0–34–0; Killeen 8–0–37–2; Betts 8–0–26–2; Boiling 8–0–26–0.

Umpires: V. A. Holder and P. Willey.

At Leeds, July 23. DURHAM beat YORKSHIRE by seven wickets.

At Northampton, August 6. DURHAM beat NORTHAMPTONSHIRE by 28 runs.

DURHAM v MIDDLESEX

At Chester-le-Street, August 13. Middlesex won by seven wickets. Toss: Middlesex.
Middlesex collected only their third Sunday League win of the season with 25 balls to spare. Weekes and Pooley set them on course with an opening stand of 87 before Ramprakash finished Durham off.

Durham

W. Larkins c Brown b Fay	9	S. J. E. Brown c Brown b Feltham	7
S. Hutton c Brown b Nash	13	N. Killeen b Nash	2
M. Prabhakar c and b Feltham	7	J. Boiling not out	0
J. I. Longley c Brown b Fay	25	B 1, l-b 11, w 7, n-b 12	31
*J. E. Morris c Yeabsley b Tufnell	51		
D. A. Blenkiron c Feltham b Yeabsley	0	1/21 2/33 3/39 (9 wkts, 40 overs) 180	
P. Bainbridge c Carr b Feltham	24	4/99 5/106 6/150	
†D. G. C. Ligertwood not out	11	7/162 8/177 9/180	

Bowling: Nash 8–0–35–2; Fay 8–0–32–2; Tufnell 8–0–32–1; Feltham 8–0–28–3; Weekes 5–0–28–0; Yeabsley 3–0–13–1.

Middlesex

P. N. Weekes c Ligertwood		O. A. Shah not out	2
b Prabhakar	47		
J. C. Pooley c Blenkiron b Prabhakar	41	B 4, w 4, n-b 4	12
M. R. Ramprakash not out	54		
*J. D. Carr c Ligertwood b Brown	25	1/87 2/103 3/167 (3 wkts, 35.5 overs) 181	

†K. R. Brown, D. J. Nash, M. A. Feltham, R. S. Yeabsley, R. A. Fay and P. C. R. Tufnell did not bat.

Bowling: Killeen 8–0–36–0; Brown 7.5–0–33–1; Boiling 4–0–29–0; Bainbridge 5–0–32–0; Prabhakar 6–0–25–2; Blenkiron 5–0–22–0.

Umpires: B. Leadbeater and A. G. T. Whitehead.

DURHAM v SOMERSET

At Chester-le-Street, August 20. Somerset won by five wickets. Toss: Somerset. First-team debut: P. D. Collingwood.

Harden's second century in two days guided Somerset to victory with four balls remaining. Durham were so badly hit by injuries that they hurried through the registration of the 19-year-old seam bowler, Paul Collingwood. They were well-placed when Blenkiron and Longley put on 104, but Harden and Rose timed Somerset's acceleration to perfection. It was their first League win for nine weeks.

Durham

S. Hutton b Caddick	9	†C. W. Scott not out	1
D. A. Blenkiron c Lathwell b Trump	56	N. Killeen not out	0
J. I. Longley b Hayhurst	92	B 5, l-b 5, w 2, n-b 2	14
W. Larkins b Caddick	23		
*P. Bainbridge c Parsons b Caddick	3	1/18 2/122 3/185 (6 wkts, 40 overs) 202
P. D. Collingwood b Hayhurst	4	4/193 5/199 6/202

J. Boiling, M. M. Betts and J. P. Searle did not bat.

Bowling: Caddick 8–0–41–3; Kerr 8–2–21–0; Rose 6–1–28–0; Trump 8–1–51–1; Ecclestone 6–0–34–0; Hayhurst 4–0–17–2.

Somerset

M. N. Lathwell b Boiling	23	*A. N. Hayhurst not out	1
S. C. Ecclestone c Blenkiron b Killeen	1		
R. J. Harden not out	100	B 2, l-b 7, w 4	13
K. A. Parsons c Larkins b Boiling	12		
P. D. Bowler c Boiling b Betts	10	1/2 2/50 3/77 (5 wkts, 39.2 overs) 205
G. D. Rose c Boiling b Betts	45	4/110 5/195

†R. J. Turner, J. I. D. Kerr, H. R. J. Trump and A. R. Caddick did not bat.

Bowling: Betts 8–0–38–2; Killeen 7.2–0–34–1; Collingwood 3–0–16–0; Boiling 8–1–22–2; Bainbridge 7–0–40–0; Searle 2–0–19–0; Blenkiron 4–0–27–0.

Umpires: J. D. Bond and D. J. Constant.

DURHAM v SUSSEX

At Hartlepool, August 27. No result. Toss: Durham.

Only three brief sessions were possible as rain reduced the match to 37 overs a side, then 24, and finally ended play altogether.

Sussex

K. Greenfield c Scott b Killeen	10	†P. Moores not out	4
J. W. Hall b Betts	7	L-b 1, w 5, n-b 2	8
F. D. Stephenson not out	34		
N. J. Lenham c Scott b Brown	26	1/17 2/17 3/84 (3 wkts, 14.2 overs) 89

C. W. J. Athey, D. R. Law, *I. D. K. Salisbury, P. W. Jarvis, R. J. Kirtley and E. S. H. Giddins did not bat.

Bowling: Betts 7–1–35–1; Killeen 4.2–0–33–1; Brown 3–0–20–1.

Durham

S. Hutton, W. Larkins, J. I. Longley, *J. E. Morris, P. Bainbridge, S. D. Birbeck, †C. W. Scott, J. Boiling, N. Killeen, S. J. E. Brown and M. M. Betts.

Umpires: T. E. Jesty and A. A. Jones.

At Bristol, September 10. GLOUCESTERSHIRE v DURHAM. No result (abandoned).

DURHAM v NOTTINGHAMSHIRE

At Chester-le-Street, September 17. Nottinghamshire won by two wickets. Toss: Nottinghamshire. First-team debut: I. Riches.

Cairns maintained his rush of one-day form, driving the last ball of the match, from Brown, to the extra-cover boundary to win the contest. His unbeaten 75 came off 59 deliveries.

Durham

J. I. Longley lbw b Cairns	12	N. Killeen c Archer b Wileman	20
S. Hutton c Johnson b Pennett	34	S. J. E. Brown not out	4
J. E. Morris c Wileman b Archer	52	L-b 5, w 10	15
J. A. Daley lbw b Hindson	15		
*M. A. Roseberry c Robinson b Archer	9	1/25 2/71 3/116 (7 wkts, 40 overs) 203	
P. D. Collingwood not out	33	4/134 5/142	
†C. W. Scott b Pennett	9	6/166 7/192	

J. Boiling and M. M. Betts did not bat.

Bowling: Cairns 4-0-20-1; Pick 8-0-29-0; Riches 3-0-21-0; Pennett 6-0-38-2; Wileman 8-0-44-1; Archer 6-0-19-2; Hindson 5-0-27-1.

Nottinghamshire

R. T. Robinson c Longley b Betts	37	D. B. Pennett run out	2
G. F. Archer c Morris b Betts	12	R. J. Chapman not out	4
*P. Johnson c Brown b Betts	11		
C. L. Cairns not out	75	L-b 5, w 7, n-b 2	14
†W. M. Noon c Daley b Brown	38		
J. R. Wileman c Hutton b Boiling	9	1/39 2/61 3/69 (8 wkts, 40 overs) 206	
J. E. Hindson run out	3	4/159 5/179 6/190	
R. A. Pick b Killeen	1	7/192 8/194	

I. Riches did not bat.

Bowling: Killeen 8-0-37-1; Brown 8-0-43-1; Betts 8-1-39-3; Collingwood 8-0-37-0; Boiling 8-0-45-1.

Umpires: G. Sharp and P. Willey.

ESSEX

ESSEX v WORCESTERSHIRE

At Chelmsford, May 7. Worcestershire won by 178 runs. Toss: Worcestershire.

Essex suffered their heaviest ever Sunday League defeat. Moody hit four sixes and seven fours in a run-a-ball 106, putting on 160 in 21 overs with Hick. Then Newport claimed Sunday-best figures of five for 32 in an unbroken eight-over stint.

Worcestershire

W. P. C. Weston b Cousins	21	*†S. J. Rhodes not out	8
T. M. Moody c Hussain b Such	106	S. R. Lampitt not out	10
G. A. Hick c Ilott b Pearson	80	L-b 6, w 3, n-b 4	13
G. R. Haynes c and b Pearson	2		
D. A. Leatherdale c Hussain b Such	11	1/40 2/200 3/209 (6 wkts, 40 overs) 253
M. J. Church b Such	2	4/233 5/233 6/235

N. V. Radford, P. J. Newport and R. K. Illingworth did not bat.

Bowling: Cousins 8–1–32–1; Ilott 8–0–33–0; Pearson 8–0–67–2; Irani 8–1–46–0; Such 8–0–69–3.

Essex

G. A. Gooch run out	2	P. M. Such c Moody b Illingworth	0
*P. J. Prichard c Haynes b Newport	7	R. M. Pearson st Rhodes b Illingworth	7
N. Hussain b Newport	18	D. M. Cousins not out	2
R. C. Irani lbw b Haynes	1	B 1, l-b 9, w 3	13
D. D. J. Robinson c Church b Lampitt	11		
†M. A. Garnham b Newport	0	1/6 2/32 3/35 (25.5 overs) 75
J. J. B. Lewis lbw b Newport	0	4/35 5/35 6/35
M. C. Ilott c Illingworth b Newport	14	7/55 8/57 9/63

Bowling: Haynes 8–2–19–1; Newport 8–1–32–5; Lampitt 5–1–11–1; Illingworth 4.5–2–3–2.

Umpires: R. Julian and A. G. T. Whitehead.

At Hove, May 21. ESSEX beat SUSSEX by 13 runs.

ESSEX v MIDDLESEX

At Chelmsford, May 28. Essex won by two runs. Toss: Middlesex.

Rain in the 35th over reduced the match to 37 a side, and Essex shaded victory despite Gatting's all-round contribution. He picked up four for 44 with his gentle seamers – including Gooch for a 36-ball fifty – and then top-scored for his side with 46; but when he was out in the penultimate over, Middlesex were unable to score 12 from the last.

Essex

*P. J. Prichard c and b Gatting	54	J. J. B. Lewis c Weekes b Gatting	5
M. E. Waugh c Brown b Feltham	19		
N. Hussain st Brown b Gatting	13	L-b 8, w 10, n-b 2	20
G. A. Gooch c Feltham b Gatting	50		
R. C. Irani lbw b Tufnell	4	1/49 2/99 3/106 (6 wkts, 37 overs) 178
D. D. J. Robinson not out	13	4/121 5/171 6/178

†R. J. Rollins, S. J. W. Andrew, P. M. Such and D. M. Cousins did not bat.

Bowling: Johnson 7–0–50–0; Nash 6–0–18–0; Feltham 8–0–25–1; Tufnell 8–0–33–1; Gatting 8–0–44–4.

Middlesex

M. A. Feltham b Cousins	23	R. L. Johnson b Andrew	8
J. C. Pooley c Rollins b Irani	10	T. A. Radford not out	2
P. N. Weekes run out	7	P. C. R. Tufnell not out	1
J. D. Carr b Irani	10	B 1, l-b 12, w 10	23
*M. W. Gatting c Prichard b Andrew	46		
†K. R. Brown lbw b Irani	10	1/43 2/48 3/60 (9 wkts, 37 overs) 176
P. Farbrace b Waugh	26	4/64 5/95 6/142
D. J. Nash run out	10	7/158 8/167 9/174

Bowling: Cousins 8-1-29-1; Andrew 7-0-49-2; Waugh 8-0-30-1; Such 6-1-23-0; Irani 8-0-32-3.

Umpires: B. Dudleston and B. Leadbeater.

At Nottingham, June 4. ESSEX beat NOTTINGHAMSHIRE by 112 runs.

ESSEX v DURHAM

At Chelmsford, June 11. Tied. Toss: Essex.

Lewis was run out by Walker's throw, attempting a second run that would have given Essex victory. They had embarked on the final over from Prabhakar needing nine to win. Only Morris passed 20 in a game reduced to 26 overs a side, and steady bowling from Brown and Prabhakar enabled Durham to defend their modest total.

Durham

*J. E. Morris c Hussain b Waugh	37	†D. G. C. Ligertwood not out	7
W. Larkins retired hurt	2	S. J. E. Brown not out	4
M. Prabhakar c Waugh b Andrew	6		
J. I. Longley lbw b Irani	0	B 1, l-b 6, w 10	17
D. A. Blenkiron b Waugh	19		
S. Hutton c Robinson b Cousins	18	1/29 2/30 3/69 (6 wkts, 26 overs) 116
S. D. Birbeck b Waugh	6	4/90 5/94 6/105	

J. Boiling and A. Walker did not bat.

W. Larkins retired hurt at 4.

Bowling: Andrew 8-0-23-1; Cousins 8-1-31-1; Irani 5-0-35-1; Waugh 5-0-20-3.

Essex

*P. J. Prichard c Morris b Brown	0	P. M. Such b Prabhakar	1
M. E. Waugh b Prabhakar	19	S. J. W. Andrew run out	7
N. Hussain b Brown	1	D. M. Cousins not out	4
G. A. Gooch c Prabhakar b Birbeck	13		
R. C. Irani c Morris b Walker	18	L-b 7, w 5	12
D. D. J. Robinson c Ligertwood			
b Brown	16	1/6 2/11 3/39 (26 overs) 116
J. J. B. Lewis run out	18	4/45 5/76 6/76	
†R. J. Rollins lbw b Prabhakar	7	7/95 8/97 9/105	

Bowling: Brown 8-0-32-3; Prabhakar 8-0-30-3; Birbeck 4-0-14-1; Walker 6-0-33-1.

Umpires: A. A. Jones and K. J. Lyons.

At Luton, June 18. ESSEX beat NORTHAMPTONSHIRE by 105 runs.

At Manchester, June 25. ESSEX lost to LANCASHIRE by three wickets.

ESSEX v WARWICKSHIRE

At Ilford, July 2. Warwickshire won by three wickets. Toss: Essex.

Warwickshire won with eight balls to spare, after their target had been revised to 160 in 31 overs, thanks to Twose's unbeaten 47 from 61 deliveries. Essex had been given a chance by Ilott and Rollins, who shared a roistering unbroken eighth-wicket stand of 58 in their last five overs.

Essex

M. E. Waugh c Piper b Brown	1	M. C. Ilott not out	25
*P. J. Prichard c Penney b Reeve	26	†R. J. Rollins not out	28
N. Hussain b Donald	55	B 4, l-b 3, w 9, n-b 2	18
G. A. Gooch c Piper b Donald	3		
R. C. Irani lbw b N. M. K. Smith	37	1/6 2/68 3/74 (7 wkts, 39 overs) 201	
D. D. J. Robinson b P. A. Smith	7	4/120 5/140	
J. J. B. Lewis c Twose b P. A. Smith	1	6/142 7/143	

P. M. Such and D. M. Cousins did not bat.

Bowling: Munton 8–0–25–0; Brown 8–0–29–1; Reeve 6–0–38–1; Donald 8–0–31–2; P. A. Smith 3–0–34–2; N. M. K. Smith 6–0–37–1.

Warwickshire

N. V. Knight b Cousins	23	D. R. Brown lbw b Ilott	4
N. M. K. Smith c Such b Ilott	17	†K. J. Piper not out	1
D. P. Ostler c Ilott b Irani	25	L-b 10, w 5	15
P. A. Smith c Rollins b Ilott	1		
R. G. Twose not out	47	1/39 2/42 3/45 (7 wkts, 29.4 overs) 160	
T. L. Penney lbw b Such	26	4/91 5/149	
*D. A. Reeve c Rollins b Waugh	1	6/152 7/157	

T. A. Munton and A. A. Donald did not bat.

Bowling: Ilott 7.4–0–27–4; Cousins 8–1–36–1; Irani 7–0–45–1; Waugh 6–0–36–1; Such 1–0–6–0.

Umpires: R. Julian and P. B. Wight.

At The Oval, July 9. ESSEX beat SURREY by 61 runs.

ESSEX v LEICESTERSHIRE

At Chelmsford, July 16. Essex won on scoring-rate. Toss: Essex.
Essex were 0.06 of a run ahead on scoring-rate when rain ended play; had Leicestershire scored just three more, they would have won.

Essex

M. E. Waugh b Cronje	19	†R. J. Rollins not out	0
*P. J. Prichard c Nixon b Parsons	36	M. C. Ilott not out	0
N. Hussain c Maddy b Mullally	58	B 3, l-b 9, w 12	24
G. A. Gooch c Briers b Parsons	1		
R. C. Irani b Maddy	50	1/58 2/58 3/62 (6 wkts, 40 overs) 211	
D. D. J. Robinson c Mason b Mullally	23	4/152 5/210 6/210	

R. M. Pearson, P. M. Such and D. M. Cousins did not bat.

Bowling: Mullally 8–0–39–2; Parsons 6–1–26–2; Cronje 6–1–30–1; Dakin 6–0–33–0; Mason 8–0–43–0; Maddy 6–0–28–1.

Leicestershire

V. J. Wells b Irani	42	J. M. Dakin c Prichard b Waugh	14
*N. E. Briers run out	37	L-b 11, w 10	21
G. I. Macmillan b sub b Such	38		
W. J. Cronje c Waugh b Such	12	1/89 2/101 3/122 (5 wkts, 35.4 overs) 186	
B. F. Smith not out	33	4/161 5/186	

†P. A. Nixon, D. L. Maddy, T. J. Mason, G. J. Parsons and A. D. Mullally did not bat.

Bowling: Ilott 6–0–24–0; Cousins 6–1–13–0; Such 8–0–47–2; Irani 8–0–37–1; Pearson 4–0–28–0; Waugh 3.4–0–26–1.

Umpires: B. J. Meyer and R. A. White.

ESSEX v SOMERSET

At Southend, July 23. Essex won by four wickets. Toss: Somerset.

Essex joined Glamorgan at the top of the table after Hussain scored his fifth successive half-century in the competition. Irani and Ilott added an unbroken 51 to see their side home with three balls to spare.

Somerset

M. N. Lathwell run out	12	P. C. L. Holloway not out	26
P. D. Bowler c Rollins b Irani	17	L-b 12, w 6, n-b 2	20
R. J. Harden b Cousins	60		
K. A. Parsons c Hussain b Irani	12	1/25 2/34	(4 wkts, 40 overs) 211
*A. N. Hayhurst not out	64	3/73 4/174	

A. P. van Troost, †R. J. Turner, Mushtaq Ahmed, A. R. Caddick and H. R. J. Trump did not bat.

Bowling: Ilott 8–0–46–0; Cousins 8–1–33–1; Irani 8–2–25–2; Waugh 8–0–44–0; Such 5–0–32–0; Pearson 3–0–19–0.

Essex

*P. J. Prichard c Hayhurst b Parsons	0	†R. J. Rollins lbw b Trump	4
M. E. Waugh b Parsons	40	M. C. Ilott not out	20
N. Hussain c van Troost b Caddick	57	B 1, l-b 6, w 6, n-b 2	15
G. A. Gooch c Trump b van Troost	36		
R. C. Irani not out	39	1/0 2/76 3/139	(6 wkts, 39.3 overs) 212
D. D. J. Robinson st Turner b Trump	1	4/148 5/153 6/161	

R. M. Pearson, P. M. Such and D. M. Cousins did not bat.

Bowling: Parsons 8–0–37–2; van Troost 6–0–41–1; Mushtaq Ahmed 8–1–38–0; Caddick 8–0–45–1; Trump 8–0–32–2; Hayhurst 1.3–0–12–0.

Umpires: J. D. Bond and D. R. Shepherd.

At Cheltenham, July 30. ESSEX beat GLOUCESTERSHIRE by 68 runs.

ESSEX v HAMPSHIRE

At Colchester, August 6. Essex won by 36 runs. Toss: Hampshire.

Essex registered a comfortable victory – their fifth in a row – to stay top of the table. They scored freely before a tight opening spell by Andrew kept Hampshire in check, although Nicholas did his best to wrest the initiative with two successive sixes off Such.

Essex

*P. J. Prichard c James b Streak	22	M. C. Ilott not out	4
M. E. Waugh run out	55		
N. Hussain c Aymes b Streak	66	B 1, l-b 13, w 6	20
G. A. Gooch c Aymes b Connor	16		
R. C. Irani lbw b Streak	22	1/52 2/122 3/150	(5 wkts, 39 overs) 235
D. D. J. Robinson not out	30	4/179 5/222	

†R. J. Rollins, S. J. W. Andrew, P. M. Such and D. M. Cousins did not bat.

Bowling: Connor 8–0–42–1; James 8–0–28–0; Streak 8–0–45–3; Thursfield 8–0–50–0; Udal 3–0–27–0; Stephenson 4–0–29–0.

Hampshire

R. S. M. Morris b Irani	36	†A. N. Aymes not out	20
P. R. Whitaker b Andrew	7	M. J. Thursfield c Cousins b Gooch	5
M. Keech c Robinson b Such	27		
*M. C. J. Nicholas c Waugh b Gooch	43	L-b 12, w 12, n-b 8	32
J. P. Stephenson c Hussain b Cousins	9		
K. D. James c Irani b Ilott	0	1/14 2/68 3/104 (9 wkts, 39 overs) 199
H. H. Streak c Irani b Ilott	20	4/139 5/139 6/152
S. D. Udal lbw b Ilott	0	7/160 8/181 9/199

C. A. Connor did not bat.

Bowling: Cousins 5–0–29–1; Andrew 8–0–24–1; Ilott 8–0–42–3; Such 6–0–37–1; Irani 7–0–28–1; Gooch 5–0–27–2.

Umpires: J. C. Balderstone and G. I. Burgess.

At Pontypridd, August 13. ESSEX lost to GLAMORGAN by four wickets.

At Canterbury, August 27. ESSEX lost to KENT by 21 runs.

ESSEX v DERBYSHIRE

At Chelmsford, September 3. Essex won by 24 runs. Toss: Essex.

Derbyshire wasted a strong position: Adams and Barnett compiled a century opening stand in 24 overs; then they lost all ten wickets for 71. Gooch was the key man for Essex: he top-scored with 63 from 53 balls and then held three catches, including an outstanding one off his own bowling to dismiss Wells.

Essex

M. E. Waugh c Cork b Aldred	17	M. C. Ilott run out	12
*P. J. Prichard c Rollins b Wells	48	A. P. Cowan not out	0
N. Hussain b Wells	5	L-b 6, w 8, n-b 8	22
G. A. Gooch not out	63		
R. C. Irani c Tweats b Base	3	1/62 2/72 3/81 (7 wkts, 40 overs) 196
D. D. J. Robinson c Cork b Base	1	4/99 5/107
†R. J. Rollins c Cork	25	6/148 7/186

P. M. Such and D. M. Cousins did not bat.

Bowling: Barnett 8–0–25–0; Cork 8–0–43–1; Wells 8–0–22–2; Aldred 8–0–45–1; Base 8–0–55–2.

Derbyshire

*K. J. Barnett c Rollins b Ilott	46	T. W. Harrison c Gooch b Ilott	0
C. J. Adams c Irani b Such	54	P. Aldred lbw b Cousins	2
†A. S. Rollins lbw b Gooch	3	S. J. Base not out	5
D. J. Cullinan c Rollins b Cousins	9	B 6, l-b 8, w 2	16
J. E. Owen c Gooch b Irani	17		
C. M. Wells c and b Gooch	0	1/101 2/109 3/111 (38.2 overs) 172
D. G. Cork c Waugh b Cousins	7	4/132 5/133 6/144
T. A. Tweats b Ilott	13	7/145 8/148 9/152

Bowling: Ilott 7.2–0–32–3; Cowan 4–0–20–0; Irani 6–0–24–1; Such 8–1–19–1; Gooch 8–0–43–2; Cousins 5–0–20–3.

Umpires: G. Sharp and P. Willey.

ESSEX v YORKSHIRE

At Chelmsford, September 17. Yorkshire won by nine wickets. Toss: Essex.

Byas hit Ilott three successive fours to earn Yorkshire victory in a match cut to ten overs a side. He put on 74 with Bevan, whose final tally of 704 runs was the best by a Yorkshire player and by any player in his first Sunday League season.

Essex

*P. J. Prichard c Hartley b Silverwood .	13	†R. J. Rollins not out	3
M. E. Waugh b Silverwood	15		
G. A. Gooch c McGrath b Bevan	2	B 1, l-b 1	2
R. C. Irani run out	15		
N. Hussain b Hartley	29	1/13 2/29 3/35 (6 wkts, 10 overs) 82	
D. D. J. Robinson run out	3	4/74 5/78 6/82	

S. J. W. Andrew, M. C. Ilott, D. M. Cousins and J. J. B. Lewis did not bat.

Bowling: Robinson 2–0–18–0; Silverwood 2–0–12–2; Bevan 1–0–5–1; Morris 1–0–13–0; Gough 2–0–16–0; Hartley 2–0–16–1.

Yorkshire

*D. Byas not out	36
M. G. Bevan c Rollins b Cousins	42
M. P. Vaughan not out	0
L-b 3, w 5	8
1/74 (1 wkt, 9.4 overs) 86	

A. McGrath, R. A. Kettleborough, A. C. Morris, †R. J. Blakey, D. Gough, P. J. Hartley, C. E. W. Silverwood and M. A. Robinson did not bat.

Bowling: Irani 2–0–14–0; Andrew 1–0–15–0; Waugh 2–0–16–0; Gooch 1–0–11–0; Cousins 2–0–8–1; Ilott 1.4–0–19–0.

Umpires: J. D. Bond and K. E. Palmer.

GLAMORGAN

GLAMORGAN v NORTHAMPTONSHIRE

At Cardiff, May 7. Glamorgan won by four wickets. Toss: Northamptonshire.

James anchored Glamorgan's reply after Northamptonshire had failed to capitalise on a 90-run partnership between Montgomerie and Curran. Anthony bowled effectively in his first match for Glamorgan since 1990.

Northamptonshire

R. R. Montgomerie st Metson b Dale . .	49	J. N. Snape not out	4
*R. J. Bailey c Maynard b Watkin	0	A. Kumble not out	2
K. M. Curran b Croft	50		
T. C. Walton c Morris b Dale	56	B 1, l-b 6, w 5	12
M. B. Loye c Cottey b Anthony	8		
D. J. Capel c Metson b Anthony	5	1/1 2/91 3/114 (8 wkts, 40 overs) 194	
†R. J. Warren c Metson b Anthony	4	4/149 5/168 6/178	
A. L. Penberthy b Lefebvre	4	7/187 8/191	

J. P. Taylor did not bat.

Bowling: Watkin 8–1–41–1; Lefebvre 8–0–37–1; Croft 8–0–32–1; Dale 8–0–37–2; Anthony 8–0–40–3.

Glamorgan

S. P. James not out	93	R. D. B. Croft b Taylor		5
D. L. Hemp run out	18	H. A. G. Anthony not out		3
M. P. Maynard c Warren b Taylor	3	L-b 7, w 1		8
P. A. Cottey lbw b Kumble	26			
*H. Morris c Walton b Curran	20	1/38 2/43 3/102	(6 wkts, 39.3 overs)	195
A. Dale c Montgomerie b Taylor	19	4/149 5/178 6/187		

R. P. Lefebvre, †C. P. Metson and S. L. Watkin did not bat.

Bowling: Taylor 7–0–23–3; Curran 7–0–40–1; Penberthy 7.3–0–35–0; Capel 8–1–28–0; Kumble 8–0–46–1; Bailey 2–0–16–0.

Umpires: J. H. Hampshire and P. B. Wight.

GLAMORGAN v SUSSEX

At Swansea, May 14. Glamorgan won by nine wickets. Toss: Glamorgan.

Sussex struggled against miserly bowling, especially from Croft and Barwick, and only Salisbury's fighting innings down the order made the total respectable. Glamorgan duly coasted in with James and Maynard sharing an unbroken partnership of 124.

Sussex

C. W. J. Athey c Metson b Watkin	5	J. D. Lewry b Lefebvre		3
J. A. North c Metson b Lefebvre	2	R. J. Kirtley c Cottey b Barwick		2
*A. P. Wells c and b Croft	14	E. S. H. Giddins c Lefebvre b Barwick		1
K. Greenfield c Hemp b Barwick	37	L-b 7, w 3		10
K. Newell c Maynard b Croft	6			
F. D. Stephenson run out	1	1/3 2/9 3/32	(39.2 overs)	132
†P. Moores b Anthony	3	4/38 5/40 6/46		
I. D. K. Salisbury not out	48	7/95 8/117 9/122		

Bowling: Lefebvre 8–1–27–2; Watkin 8–2–21–1; Barwick 7.2–1–16–3; Croft 8–2–13–2; Anthony 5–0–30–1; Cottey 3–0–18–0.

Glamorgan

S. P. James not out	44			
D. L. Hemp c Moores b Giddins	6			
M. P. Maynard not out	69			
L-b 11, w 3	14			
1/9		(1 wkt, 23.4 overs)	133	

P. A. Cottey, *H. Morris, R. D. B. Croft, H. A. G. Anthony, R. P. Lefebvre, †C. P. Metson, S. L. Watkin and S. R. Barwick did not bat.

Bowling: Giddins 4–0–21–1; Stephenson 5–1–12–0; Lewry 5–0–32–0; Salisbury 3–0–22–0; Greenfield 3.4–0–15–0; Kirtley 3–0–20–0.

Umpires: A. A. Jones and G. Sharp.

At Leeds, May 21. GLAMORGAN lost to YORKSHIRE by two runs.

At Tunbridge Wells, May 28. GLAMORGAN beat KENT by 11 runs.

GLAMORGAN v HAMPSHIRE

At Cardiff, June 4. Glamorgan won by 113 runs. Toss: Hampshire.

James again led the Glamorgan batting before Watkin and Lefebvre reduced Hampshire to 20 for four on their way to their fourth League defeat out of four. Metson's four catches and two stumpings – both off wides – matched the county record set by Eifion Jones in 1978.

Glamorgan

S. P. James lbw b Udal	87
*H. Morris run out	42
M. P. Maynard not out	58
P. A. Cottey not out	20
B 1, l-b 11, w 13, n-b 6	31

1/106 2/181   (2 wkts, 40 overs) 238

D. L. Hemp, A. Dale, R. D. B. Croft, R. P. Lefebvre, †C. P. Metson, S. L. Watkin and S. R. Barwick did not bat.

Bowling: Bovill 5–0–30–0; James 8–0–47–0; Connor 8–0–53–0; Streak 8–1–31–0; Udal 8–0–38–1; Nicholas 3–0–27–0.

Hampshire

V. P. Terry c Metson b Lefebvre	4	S. D. Udal b Dale	1
R. S. M. Morris b Watkin	8	C. A. Connor c Metson b Barwick	8
R. A. Smith c Metson b Watkin	7	J. N. B. Bovill run out	0
G. W. White c Metson b Lefebvre	0	L-b 6, w 4	10
*M. C. J. Nicholas c Dale b Croft	8		
K. D. James st Metson b Dale	30	1/4 2/15 3/18 (32.1 overs) 125	
†A. N. Aymes st Metson b Barwick	25	4/20 5/41 6/75	
H. H. Streak not out	24	7/104 8/114 9/123	

Bowling: Lefebvre 6–1–17–2; Watkin 6–2–11–2; Barwick 6–0–21–2; Croft 8–0–34–1; Dale 6.1–0–36–2.

Umpires: J. H. Harris and B. Leadbeater.

At Manchester, June 11. GLAMORGAN beat LANCASHIRE by nine runs.

GLAMORGAN v MIDDLESEX

At Colwyn Bay, June 18. Glamorgan won by 29 runs. Toss: Glamorgan.

Morris's 100 off 118 balls, with two sixes and 11 fours, took him past Alan Jones's record League aggregate for the county of 4,702 runs, and helped to keep Glamorgan top of the table. Middlesex were in contention as Gatting, using Ramprakash as a runner, and Brown added 88 for the fifth wicket. But once that stand had been broken, Glamorgan regained control, thanks largely to Barwick's five for 30.

Glamorgan

S. P. James c Brown b Fraser	31	H. A. G. Anthony b Nash	7
*H. Morris c Ramprakash b Nash	100		
M. P. Maynard c Brown b Fraser	12	B 5, l-b 19, w 8	32
P. A. Cottey b Johnson	35		
D. L. Hemp c Johnson b Emburey	12	1/92 2/123 3/183 (6 wkts, 40 overs) 249	
R. D. B. Croft not out	20	4/216 5/218 6/249	

R. P. Lefebvre, †C. P. Metson, S. L. Watkin and S. R. Barwick did not bat.

Bowling: Johnson 8–0–51–1; Nash 8–0–44–2; Emburey 6–0–48–1; Weekes 4–0–16–0; Feltham 6–0–38–0; Fraser 8–1–28–2.

Middlesex

P. N. Weekes c James b Barwick	27	J. E. Emburey c James b Barwick	2
J. C. Pooley b Barwick	26	R. L. Johnson b Lefebvre	1
M. R. Ramprakash c Lefebvre b Croft	8	A. R. C. Fraser not out	0
J. D. Carr c James b Croft	11	L-b 12, w 5, n-b 2	19
†K. R. Brown b Anthony	47		—
*M. W. Gatting c Croft b Watkin	50	1/47 2/66 3/70 (39.1 overs) 220
M. A. Feltham b Barwick	16	4/89 5/177 6/192
D. J. Nash c Lefebvre b Barwick	13	7/217 8/218 9/220

Bowling: Lefebvre 8-0-27-1; Watkin 8-0-40-1; Barwick 7.1-0-30-5; Croft 8-0-53-2; Anthony 8-0-58-1.

Umpires: G. I. Burgess and K. J. Lyons.

At The Oval, June 25. GLAMORGAN beat SURREY by nine wickets.

GLAMORGAN v DURHAM

At Swansea, July 2. Durham won by five wickets. Toss: Glamorgan.

Durham ended Glamorgan's run of five successive wins, off the last ball. Needing two to win, they reached their target off an overthrow, when Maynard missed the stumps as the batsmen attempted a leg-bye. For Glamorgan, James passed 50 for the ninth time in one-day cricket during the season, before Roseberry, who hit five sixes, and Prabhakar led the reply. The stand was broken by Lefebvre, who managed to complete his spell before being stretchered off with a groin injury.

Glamorgan

S. P. James b Prabhakar	87	H. A. G. Anthony b Brown	2
*H. Morris run out	35	R. P. Lefebvre not out	4
M. P. Maynard run out	8	L-b 1, w 3, n-b 2	6
P. A. Cottey b Boiling	2		—
A. Dale st Ligertwood b Blenkiron	25	1/68 2/81 3/84 (6 wkts, 40 overs) 212
R. D. B. Croft not out	43	4/134 5/191 6/194

†C. P. Metson, S. L. Watkin and S. R. Barwick did not bat.

Bowling: Brown 6-0-39-1; Prabhakar 8-0-51-1; Boiling 8-1-22-1; Walker 8-0-44-0; Bainbridge 6-0-30-0; Blenkiron 4-0-25-1.

Durham

J. E. Morris lbw b Watkin	27	P. Bainbridge not out	4
*M. A. Roseberry b Lefebvre	94	L-b 4, w 3	7
M. Prabhakar st Metson b Lefebvre	69		—
J. I. Longley st Metson b Barwick	6	1/42 2/194 3/199 (5 wkts, 40 overs) 213
S. Hutton lbw b Lefebvre	4	4/205 5/207
D. A. Blenkiron not out	2	

†D. G. C. Ligertwood, J. Boiling, A. Walker and S. J. E. Brown did not bat.

Bowling: Lefebvre 8-0-29-3; Watkin 8-2-39-1; Barwick 8-0-39-1; Croft 8-0-47-0; Anthony 4-0-26-0; Dale 4-0-29-0.

Umpires: T. E. Jesty and B. J. Meyer.

At Taunton, July 16. SOMERSET v GLAMORGAN. No result.

GLAMORGAN v WARWICKSHIRE

At Cardiff, July 23. Warwickshire won by eight runs. Toss: Glamorgan.

Knight celebrated his England call-up with a solid 80 from 100 balls – comfortably the highest score of the match – and held the innings together after a collapse from 85 for one to 108 for six. Glamorgan appeared in good shape at 162 for four, but they too slumped, losing their last six wickets for 20 – and the outright lead in the League.

Warwickshire

N. V. Knight c Hemp b Barwick	80	†K. J. Piper not out	13
N. M. K. Smith b Watkin	23	A. A. Donald not out	5
D. P. Ostler c Metson b Barwick	19		
T. L. Penney c Hemp b Croft	2	L-b 6, w 4, n-b 6	16
D. R. Brown c Maynard b Barwick	1		
R. G. Twose b Croft	7	1/40 2/85 3/90 (8 wkts, 39 overs) 190	
*D. A. Reeve b Croft	1	4/93 5/106 6/108	
P. A. Smith lbw b Anthony	23	7/152 8/173	

T. A. Munton did not bat.

Bowling: Anthony 8–0–51–1; Watkin 8–0–29–1; Barwick 7–0–41–3; Croft 8–0–28–3; Dale 8–2–35–0.

Glamorgan

S. P. James c Reeve b Munton	50	†C. P. Metson run out	2
*H. Morris c Piper b Brown	9	S. L. Watkin b N. M. K. Smith	4
M. P. Maynard b Donald	33	S. R. Barwick not out	2
P. A. Cottey c Piper b Donald	12		
D. L. Hemp c Knight b Twose	39	L-b 6, n-b 6	12
A. Dale c N. M. K. Smith b Reeve	12		
R. D. B. Croft st Piper		1/17 2/63 3/87 (39 overs) 182	
b N. M. K. Smith	4	4/146 5/162 6/171	
H. A. G. Anthony b Reeve	3	7/173 8/176 9/176	

Bowling: Brown 5–0–22–1; Munton 8–0–35–1; Donald 8–0–35–2; Reeve 8–1–35–2; N. M. K. Smith 8–0–35–2; Twose 2–0–14–1.

Umpires: B. Dudleston and N. T. Plews.

At Derby, July 30. GLAMORGAN lost to DERBYSHIRE by one wicket.

GLAMORGAN v ESSEX

At Pontypridd, August 13. Glamorgan won by four wickets. Toss: Essex.

Glamorgan triumphed off the penultimate ball when Croft, with two runs needed, pushed Waugh to mid-wicket and Gooch's shy at the stumps resulted in an overthrow. Earlier, Gooch had top-scored for Essex, but Glamorgan replied strongly with Morris and James putting on 133. Five wickets then fell for 34, before Maynard and Dale came to the rescue. Ten were needed off the last over.

Essex

M. E. Waugh c Metson b Thomas	32	N. F. Williams lbw b Watkin	0
*P. J. Prichard c Morris b Croft	39	S. J. W. Andrew c Hemp b Anthony	5
N. Hussain c Maynard b Croft	7		
G. A. Gooch b Thomas	65	B 4, l-b 3, w 7	14
R. C. Irani c Morris b Dale	26		
D. D. J. Robinson c Metson b Thomas	36	1/59 2/69 3/88 (9 wkts, 40 overs) 236	
†R. J. Rollins c Croft b Anthony	9	4/154 5/217 6/218	
M. C. Ilott not out	3	7/226 8/226 9/236	

P. M. Such did not bat.

Bowling: Watkin 8–0–39–1; Anthony 8–0–45–2; Croft 8–0–42–2; Thomas 8–0–44–3; Dale 5–0–34–1; Cottey 3–0–25–0.

Glamorgan

S. P. James c Robinson b Irani	40	A. Dale not out	24
*H. Morris c Rollins b Irani	80	R. D. B. Croft not out	6
M. P. Maynard c Such b Ilott	54	L-b 13, w 12, n-b 4	29
H. A. G. Anthony lbw b Ilott	3		
P. A. Cottey lbw b Irani	0	1/133 2/143 3/156 (6 wkts, 39.5 overs) 237	
D. L. Hemp run out	1	4/161 5/167 6/226	

†C. P. Metson, S. L. Watkin and S. D. Thomas did not bat.

Bowling: Ilott 8–0–24–2; Andrew 5–0–26–0; Irani 8–0–39–3; Williams 4–0–25–0; Such 5–0–36–0; Waugh 7.5–0–62–0; Gooch 2–0–12–0.

Umpires: J. H. Harris and V. A. Holder.

GLAMORGAN v GLOUCESTERSHIRE

At Ebbw Vale, August 27. Gloucestershire won by six wickets. Toss: Glamorgan.

Symonds settled a low-scoring contest with a savage 69 from 35 balls, including seven sixes – five of them off Barwick and four in one over. This followed his world record 20 sixes in the Championship game which finished at Abergavenny the previous day. Of the Glamorgan batsmen, only James came to terms with the visitors' attack, Alleyne's seamers proving particularly successful. Gloucestershire slipped to 23 for two but Symonds was again unstoppable.

Glamorgan

S. P. James c Williams b Alleyne	78	†C. P. Metson c Symonds b Lewis	3
*H. Morris lbw b Sheeraz	16	S. L. Watkin b Alleyne	0
M. P. Maynard lbw b Alleyne	17	S. R. Barwick not out	0
D. L. Hemp c Windows b Alleyne	3	B 1, l-b 2, w 4, n-b 2	9
A. Dale lbw b Ball	1		
R. D. B. Croft c Symonds b Alleyne	6	1/38 2/66 3/74 (39.1 overs) 153	
S. D. Thomas run out	19	4/75 5/84 6/119	
H. A. G. Anthony lbw b Ball	1	7/132 8/153 9/153	

Bowling: Sheeraz 8–0–24–1; Cawdron 8–1–25–0; Lewis 7.1–0–36–1; Alleyne 8–2–28–5; Ball 8–0–37–2.

Gloucestershire

T. H. C. Hancock c Hemp b Croft	32	R. I. Dawson not out	11
M. G. N. Windows c Hemp b Watkin	0	L-b 3, w 6	9
*M. W. Alleyne c Metson b Watkin	5		
A. Symonds lbw b Dale	69	1/7 2/23 (4 wkts, 29.1 overs) 154	
A. J. Wright not out	28	3/69 4/133	

M. J. Cawdron, J. Lewis, M. C. J. Ball, †R. C. J. Williams and K. P. Sheeraz did not bat.

Bowling: Watkin 8–0–23–2; Anthony 5–0–22–0; Barwick 4–0–49–0; Croft 3–0–19–1; Thomas 5–0–20–0; Dale 4.1–1–18–1.

Umpires: J. W. Holder and P. B. Wight.

At Leicester, September 3. GLAMORGAN lost to LEICESTERSHIRE by four wickets.

GLAMORGAN v NOTTINGHAMSHIRE

At Cardiff, September 10. No result (abandoned).

At Worcester, September 17. WORCESTERSHIRE v GLAMORGAN. No result.

GLOUCESTERSHIRE

At Taunton, May 7. GLOUCESTERSHIRE beat SOMERSET by six wickets.

GLOUCESTERSHIRE v NOTTINGHAMSHIRE

At Bristol, May 14. Nottinghamshire won by four wickets. Toss: Nottinghamshire.

Rain reduced the match to 33 overs a side but Gloucestershire could not even last that long, Wileman proving their principal tormentor. Nottinghamshire in turn had to work hard for victory but Cairns led them to their target, which they reached with four balls remaining.

Gloucestershire

A. J. Wright lbw b Pick	1	M. C. J. Ball b Wileman		5
G. D. Hodgson c Johnson b Wileman	29	K. P. Sheeraz lbw b Mike		1
M. A. Lynch c Archer b Pick	5	A. M. Smith not out		1
A. Symonds c Archer b Evans	7	L-b 12, w 11, n-b 2		25
R. I. Dawson lbw b Mike	1			
M. W. Alleyne run out	9	1/3 2/14 3/23	(30.2 overs)	115
*†R. C. Russell c and b Wileman	20	4/36 5/67 6/80		
J. Srinath c Mike b Wileman	11	7/101 8/109 9/112		

Bowling: Evans 5–0–9–1; Pick 5–1–21–2; Mike 6–1–21–2; Hindson 8–0–31–0; Wileman 6.2–0–21–4.

Nottinghamshire

*R. T. Robinson c Alleyne b Srinath	16	K. P. Evans not out		13
M. P. Dowman c Hodgson b Srinath	2	G. W. Mike not out		1
P. Johnson c Dawson b Alleyne	15	L-b 4, w 2		6
C. L. Cairns c Alleyne b Smith	45			
G. F. Archer lbw b Alleyne	8	1/19 2/24 3/48	(6 wkts, 32.2 overs)	116
J. R. Wileman run out	10	4/83 5/92 6/108		

†B. N. French, J. E. Hindson and R. A. Pick did not bat.

Bowling: Srinath 7.2–1–23–2; Smith 8–1–36–1; Sheeraz 6–0–22–0; Alleyne 8–1–24–2; Ball 3–0–7–0.

Umpires: J. D. Bond and B. Dudleston.

GLOUCESTERSHIRE v WORCESTERSHIRE

At Gloucester, May 28. Worcestershire won on scoring-rate. Toss: Gloucestershire.

Pursuing a revised target of 181 in 32 overs, Gloucestershire required three to win off the last delivery. Ball skied it to long-on where Moody held a brilliant catch, rounding off a fine match in which he had earlier hit nine fours in making a rapid 65. The home side appeared out of contention at 91 for five, but Russell clubbed an unbeaten 56 in 36 balls to keep the contest alive. Rhodes completed 200 dismissals in the League.

Worcestershire

*T. S. Curtis not out	82	D. A. Leatherdale not out		8
M. J. Church c Dawson b Cooper	17	L-b 1, w 4, n-b 8		13
T. M. Moody st Russell b Ball	65			
G. R. Haynes c and b Srinath	40	1/35 2/145 3/208	(3 wkts, 40 overs)	225

†S. J. Rhodes, S. R. Lampitt, V. S. Solanki, P. J. Newport, R. K. Illingworth and N. V. Radford did not bat.

Bowling: Srinath 8–1–44–1; Cooper 8–1–35–1; Smith 7.4–1–40–0; Ball 8–0–44–1; Dawson 2–0–2–0; Alleyne 8–0–59–0.

Gloucestershire

A. J. Wright b Illingworth	39	J. Srinath c Moody b Radford		1
G. D. Hodgson lbw b Haynes	4	M. C. J. Ball c Moody b Radford		15
M. A. Lynch b Lampitt	21	B 2, l-b 2, w 3, n-b 6		13
R. I. Dawson c Rhodes b Radford	15			
M. W. Alleyne c and b Radford	3	1/17 2/63 3/79	(8 wkts, 32 overs)	178
A. Symonds b Radford	11	4/89 5/91 6/122		
*†R. C. Russell not out	56	7/130 8/178		

K. E. Cooper and A. M. Smith did not bat.

Bowling: Newport 8–0–41–0; Haynes 4–0–13–1; Lampitt 6–0–31–1; Illingworth 8–0–32–1; Radford 6–0–57–5.

Umpires: J. W. Holder and B. J. Meyer.

At Hove, June 4. GLOUCESTERSHIRE lost to SUSSEX by six wickets.

At Canterbury, June 11. GLOUCESTERSHIRE lost to KENT by five wickets.

GLOUCESTERSHIRE v HAMPSHIRE

At Bristol, June 18. Gloucestershire won by four runs. Toss: Hampshire.

A stand of 119 in 22 overs between Morris and Smith was not enough to deny Gloucestershire a narrow win. Boden turned the match back Gloucestershire's way with three important wickets in two overs. Alleyne had hit three sixes in his 70. Hampshire became the first county to have scored 70,000 runs in the competition.

Gloucestershire

A. Symonds c Aymes b Streak	34	R. C. Williams not out		2
A. J. Wright c White b James	10	D. J. P. Boden run out		0
M. A. Lynch c Aymes b Whitaker	46	L-b 7, w 10, n-b 2		19
R. I. Dawson c Aymes b Whitaker	16			
M. W. Alleyne c Nicholas b Udal	70	1/44 2/44 3/105	(7 wkts, 40 overs)	223
*†R. C. Russell c Whitaker		4/133 5/207		
b Stephenson	26	6/223 7/223		

K. P. Sheeraz, M. Davies and A. M. Smith did not bat.

Bowling: Stephenson 8–0–47–1; James 8–1–37–1; Streak 8–1–36–1; Udal 7–0–43–1; Keech 2–0–21–0; Whitaker 7–0–32–2.

Hampshire

R. S. M. Morris b Boden	87	H. H. Streak not out		0
P. R. Whitaker b Sheeraz	22			
R. A. Smith c Lynch b Boden	55	L-b 14, w 4, n-b 4		22
*M. C. J. Nicholas c Lynch b Boden	0			
G. W. White not out	12	1/60 2/179 3/179	(5 wkts, 40 overs)	219
M. Keech run out	21	4/188 5/218		

J. P. Stephenson, K. D. James, †A. N. Aymes and S. D. Udal did not bat.

Bowling: Boden 8–2–34–3; Smith 8–0–50–0; Sheeraz 8–3–24–1; Williams 4–0–27–0; Davies 8–0–35–0; Alleyne 4–0–35–0.

Umpires: J. C. Balderstone and P. Willey.

At Middlesbrough, July 2. GLOUCESTERSHIRE lost to YORKSHIRE by 93 runs.

GLOUCESTERSHIRE v MIDDLESEX

At Bristol, July 9. Gloucestershire won by six wickets. Toss: Gloucestershire.

Alleyne, making his 100th consecutive Sunday League appearance, guided Gloucestershire to victory with an unbeaten 60 from 78 balls. Gatting's breezy 63 off only 42 deliveries carried him past 6,000 runs in the competition.

Middlesex

P. N. Weekes b Sheeraz	8	J. E. Emburey c Russell b Sheeraz		2
J. D. Carr b Smith	3	T. A. Radford b Smith		3
M. R. Ramprakash c Russell		A. R. C. Fraser not out		8
b Williams	24			
†K. R. Brown c Symonds b Williams	36	L-b 8, w 10		18
*M. W. Gatting b Williams	63			
M. A. Feltham c Symonds b Williams	1	1/13 2/13 3/59	(40 overs)	200
D. J. Nash run out	32	4/124 5/129 6/152		
R. L. Johnson b Ball	2	7/155 8/166 9/173		

Bowling: Smith 8-1-26-2; Sheeraz 7-1-20-2; Alleyne 7-0-36-0; Williams 8-0-51-4; Windows 3-0-17-0; Ball 7-0-42-1.

Gloucestershire

A. J. Wright c Brown b Nash	22	*†R. C. Russell not out		14
M. G. N. Windows c Weekes b Nash	8	L-b 9, w 17, n-b 2		28
M. W. Alleyne not out	60			
M. A. Lynch c Fraser b Johnson	41	1/36 2/46	(4 wkts, 38.5 overs)	203
A. Symonds lbw b Nash	30	3/130 4/174		

R. I. Dawson, R. C. Williams, M. C. J. Ball, K. P. Sheeraz and A. M. Smith did not bat.

Bowling: Johnson 8-0-38-1; Feltham 7.5-0-47-0; Nash 8-0-34-3; Fraser 8-0-21-0; Emburey 7-0-54-0.

Umpires: D. R. Shepherd and R. A. White.

At The Oval, July 16. GLOUCESTERSHIRE lost to SURREY by 19 runs.

GLOUCESTERSHIRE v LANCASHIRE

At Cheltenham, July 23. Gloucestershire won by five wickets. Toss: Gloucestershire.

Lancashire's visit to Cheltenham was disastrous for their hopes in two competitions and Gloucestershire followed up their ten-wicket Championship win the day before with a Sunday success, achieved with 13 balls to spare. Lancashire were contained by Smith – until Austin hit his last two balls for six and four – and Symonds in reply provided vital acceleration, hammering 47 from 34 balls, including two sixes.

Lancashire

M. A. Atherton c Russell b Smith	8	†W. K. Hegg run out		5
S. P. Titchard lbw b Smith	6	G. Yates c Symonds b Sheeraz		5
J. P. Crawley c Russell b Williams	28	G. Chapple not out		2
N. H. Fairbrother c Ball b Alleyne	17	L-b 7, w 10, n-b 2		19
G. D. Lloyd c Windows b Williams	29			
*M. Watkinson c Williams b Dawson	17	1/10 2/20 3/66	(9 wkts, 40 overs)	182
Wasim Akram c Alleyne b Ball	21	4/66 5/106 6/139		
I. D. Austin not out	25	7/150 8/159 9/167		

Bowling: Sheeraz 8-0-41-1; Smith 8-1-23-2; Alleyne 8-0-30-1; Williams 8-1-34-2; Ball 4-0-19-1; Windows 2-0-9-0; Dawson 2-0-19-1.

Gloucestershire

A. J. Wright b Watkinson	39	R. I. Dawson not out		4
M. G. N. Windows c and b Yates	29			
M. W. Alleyne c and b Yates	10	B 1, l-b 8, w 5, n-b 6		20
M. A. Lynch lbw b Wasim Akram	13			
A. Symonds c Hegg b Watkinson	47	1/50 2/75 3/91	(5 wkts, 37.5 overs)	183
*†R. C. Russell not out	21	4/126 5/157		

R. C. Williams, M. C. J. Ball, K. P. Sheeraz and A. M. Smith did not bat.

Bowling: Chapple 7–0–34–0; Wasim Akram 8–2–21–1; Watkinson 7.5–0–43–2; Austin 8–1–32–0; Yates 7–0–44–2.

Umpires: D. J. Constant and R. Julian.

GLOUCESTERSHIRE v ESSEX

At Cheltenham, July 30. Essex won by 68 runs. Toss: Essex. First-team debut: M. J. Cawdron. Irani powered Essex to a formidable total with a remarkable maiden one-day century, which included eight sixes and five fours. He faced only 47 balls, his second fifty coming from just 16. Gloucestershire were well adrift at the end and newcomer Michael Cawdron scored 50 on his old school ground, without being forced to try for victory.

Essex

M. E. Waugh run out	78	M. C. Ilott st R. C. J. Williams		
*P. J. Prichard c R. C. J. Williams		b R. C. Williams		4
b Alleyne	28	†R. J. Rollins c Lynch		
N. Hussain c R. C. J. Williams		b R. C. Williams		0
b R. C. Williams	13	L-b 5, w 7, n-b 6		18
G. A. Gooch c Sheeraz b				
R. C. Williams	51	1/75 2/110 3/145	(7 wkts, 40 overs)	303
R. C. Irani not out	101	4/236 5/299		
D. D. J. Robinson c Cawdron b Ball	10	6/303 7/303		

S. J. W. Andrew, P. M. Such and D. M. Cousins did not bat.

Bowling: Sheeraz 7–0–75–0; Cawdron 8–0–35–0; Alleyne 8–0–53–1; R. C. Williams 8–1–57–4; Ball 8–0–48–1; Dawson 3–0–30–0.

Gloucestershire

A. J. Wright c Rollins b Cousins	0	M. J. Cawdron b Ilott		50
M. G. N. Windows c Rollins b Andrew	10	†R. C. J. Williams lbw b Ilott		19
*M. W. Alleyne c Rollins b Irani	58	K. P. Sheeraz not out		5
M. A. Lynch c Rollins b Andrew	5	B 2, l-b 4, w 5, n-b 20		31
A. Symonds c Gooch b Andrew	11			
R. I. Dawson c Rollins b Andrew	5	1/3 2/27 3/39	(36.1 overs)	235
R. C. Williams c Prichard b Irani	31	4/55 5/63 6/141		
M. C. J. Ball c and b Irani	10	7/154 8/158 9/226		

Bowling: Andrew 8–0–40–4; Cousins 7–0–69–1; Such 8–0–54–0; Irani 8–0–33–3; Ilott 5.1–0–33–2.

Umpires: T. E. Jesty and G. Sharp.

At Northampton, August 13. GLOUCESTERSHIRE lost to NORTHAMPTONSHIRE by 52 runs.

GLOUCESTERSHIRE v DERBYSHIRE

At Bristol, August 20. Derbyshire won by eight wickets. Toss: Gloucestershire. First-team debut: J. Lewis.

Gloucestershire's meagre total was boosted by 20 wides. Derbyshire's fielders executed three direct-hit run-outs before their batsmen eased home after an 85-run start from Barnett and Adams.

Gloucestershire

A. J. Wright c Barnett b Griffith	24	M. C. J. Ball not out 6
M. G. N. Windows c Adams b Warner	1	J. Lewis run out 5
M. W. Alleyne c Adams b DeFreitas	4	K. P. Sheeraz run out 0
M. A. Lynch c Adams b Griffith	19	L-b 8, w 20 28
A. Symonds c Tweats b Aldred	28	
*†R. C. Russell b Aldred	7	1/15 2/31 3/43 (38 overs) 138
R. I. Dawson run out	12	4/70 5/93 6/103
M. J. Cawdron b Aldred	4	7/112 8/126 9/138

Bowling: DeFreitas 8–1–16–1; Warner 8–1–20–1; Cork 7–0–17–0; Griffith 4–0–29–2; Aldred 7–1–28–3; Barnett 4–0–20–0.

Derbyshire

*K. J. Barnett not out	53
C. J. Adams c Lynch b Alleyne	42
†A. S. Rollins b Symonds	9
D. G. Cork not out	22
L-b 10, w 3	13

1/85 2/98   (2 wkts, 37.2 overs) 139

T. A. Tweats, T. J. G. O'Gorman, P. A. J. DeFreitas, T. W. Harrison, F. A. Griffith, A. E. Warner and P. Aldred did not bat.

Bowling: Sheeraz 3–0–15–0; Cawdron 5–1–14–0; Lewis 7.2–0–31–0; Ball 8–1–28–0; Alleyne 8–0–18–1; Symonds 6–1–23–1.

Umpires: A. A. Jones and B. J. Meyer.

At Ebbw Vale, August 27. GLOUCESTERSHIRE beat GLAMORGAN by six wickets.

At Birmingham, September 5. GLOUCESTERSHIRE lost to WARWICKSHIRE by four wickets.

GLOUCESTERSHIRE v DURHAM

At Bristol, September 10. No result (abandoned).

At Leicester, September 17. LEICESTERSHIRE v GLOUCESTERSHIRE. No result (abandoned).

HAMPSHIRE

At Lord's, May 7. HAMPSHIRE lost to MIDDLESEX by 37 runs.

HAMPSHIRE v KENT

At Southampton, May 21. Kent won by 66 runs. Toss: Hampshire.

A superb unbeaten 105 by Cowdrey, off 62 balls with three sixes – all at Udal's expense – and 12 fours, left Kent in a virtually unassailable position. They were 84 for three at the halfway mark, but Cowdrey's fourth-wicket partnership with Benson realised 145 in 16 overs, and thereafter Hampshire, captained by Stephenson for the first time, were never in the hunt.

Kent

T. R. Ward b Connor 10	M. A. Ealham not out.............	8
*M. R. Benson run out 92		
M. J. Walker c Aymes b Stephenson ... 15	B 1, l-b 6, w 10, n-b 10	27
P. A. de Silva c Aymes b Stephenson . 3		
G. R. Cowdrey not out 105	1/30 2/67 3/80 (5 wkts, 40 overs) 276	
M. V. Fleming c Stephenson b Connor . 16	4/225 5/242	

†S. A. Marsh, M. J. McCague, D. W. Headley and A. P. Igglesden did not bat.

Bowling: Connor 8–0–43–2; Cowans 8–0–51–0; Udal 8–0–77–0; Stephenson 8–1–56–2; Streak 8–0–42–0.

Hampshire

*J. P. Stephenson c Cowdrey	†A. N. Aymes not out.............	23
b McCague . 37	S. D. Udal not out...............	15
R. S. M. Morris run out 46		
R. A. Smith b Headley 17	L-b 9, w 10	19
G. W. White b McCague 34		
V. P. Terry lbw b Headley 4	1/67 2/105 3/116 (6 wkts, 40 overs) 210	
P. R. Whitaker b Fleming 15	4/124 5/146 6/178	

H. H. Streak, C. A. Connor and N. G. Cowans did not bat.

Bowling: Igglesden 4–0–24–0; Ealham 6–0–27–0; McCague 8–0–41–2; Headley 8–0–34–2; de Silva 8–0–39–0; Fleming 5–0–29–1; Cowdrey 1–0–7–0.

Umpires: N. T. Plews and G. Sharp.

HAMPSHIRE v SUSSEX

At Portsmouth, May 28. Sussex won by eight runs. Toss: Hampshire.

A battling 66 off 82 balls by Nicholas failed to swing the match Hampshire's way as Franklyn Stephenson returned to the attack near the end with good effect. Earlier, Sussex had recovered after James made early inroads with a spell of three for five in 15 balls.

Sussex

K. Greenfield c Nicholas b James 11	*I. D. K. Salisbury b Connor 22	
J. W. Hall b James 8	P. W. Jarvis not out 1	
F. D. Stephenson c Aymes b James 6	L-b 5, w 9, n-b 2........... 16	
N. J. Lenham c Maru b Connor 39		
J. A. North c Aymes b Stephenson ... 32	1/18 2/26 3/34 (7 wkts, 40 overs) 206	
K. Newell c Nicholas b James 37	4/91 5/141	
†P. Moores not out 34	6/152 7/202	

J. D. Lewry and E. S. H. Giddins did not bat.

Bowling: Connor 8–0–47–2; James 8–0–35–4; Streak 8–0–36–0; Maru 8–0–27–0; Stephenson 8–0–56–1.

Hampshire

J. P. Stephenson c Moores b Lewry	12	K. D. James not out	18
R. S. M. Morris c Moores b Stephenson	35	C. A. Connor c Greenfield b Stephenson	2
R. A. Smith b Lewry	2		
V. P. Terry c Moores b Giddins	3	L-b 8, w 11	19
G. W. White c Moores b Giddins	3		
*M. C. J. Nicholas b Stephenson	66	1/17 2/45 3/62 (9 wkts, 40 overs) 198	
†A. N. Aymes b Lewry	19	4/66 5/80 6/129	
H. H. Streak c Salisbury b Stephenson	19	7/165 8/196 9/198	

R. J. Maru did not bat.

Bowling: Newell 4-0-21-0; Lewry 8-0-44-3; Giddins 8-1-35-2; Stephenson 8-0-37-4; Salisbury 5-0-24-0; Jarvis 5-0-16-0; Greenfield 2-0-13-0.

Umpires: V. A. Holder and P. B. Wight.

At Cardiff, June 4. HAMPSHIRE lost to GLAMORGAN by 113 runs.

HAMPSHIRE v LEICESTERSHIRE

At Basingstoke, June 11. Hampshire won by seven wickets. Toss: Hampshire.
   Hampshire gained their first Sunday League win of the season, reaching a revised target of 123 in 24 overs with seven balls to spare.

Leicestershire

V. J. Wells c White b Streak	30	G. J. Parsons c White b Bovill	12
*N. E. Briers c Terry b James	1	A. R. K. Pierson b Streak	6
W. J. Cronje c James b Maru	26		
J. J. Whitaker c Morris b Stephenson	37	L-b 7, w 7	14
B. F. Smith c Aymes b James	32		
†P. A. Nixon c Bovill b James	13	1/5 2/51 3/76 (9 wkts, 40 overs) 204	
D. L. Maddy c sub b Streak	6	4/123 5/146 6/153	
J. M. Dakin not out	27	7/157 8/196 9/204	

A. D. Mullally did not bat.

Bowling: Bovill 6-0-36-1; James 8-0-32-3; Streak 7-0-48-3; Udal 8-0-31-0; Maru 8-0-31-1; Stephenson 3-0-19-1.

Hampshire

J. P. Stephenson c Maddy b Cronje	9	G. W. White not out	6
R. S. M. Morris c Wells b Cronje	38	L-b 3, w 8	11
*M. C. J. Nicholas not out	42		
V. P. Terry c Dakin b Cronje	17	1/46 2/57 3/105 (3 wkts, 22.5 overs) 123	

K. D. James, †A. N. Aymes, S. D. Udal, H. H. Streak, R. J. Maru and J. N. B. Bovill did not bat.

Bowling: Mullally 7.5-0-42-0; Parsons 8-0-41-0; Cronje 7-0-37-3.

Umpires: D. R. Shepherd and P. B. Wight.

At Bristol, June 18. HAMPSHIRE lost to GLOUCESTERSHIRE by four runs.

HAMPSHIRE v WORCESTERSHIRE

At Southampton, June 25. Tied. Toss: Worcestershire.

Moody, Worcestershire's newly appointed captain, hit a spectacular 108 from 76 balls, including five sixes and seven fours, but his side just failed to overhaul Hampshire's total. They had needed nine off Streak's last over and two off the last ball with the last pair together. At 216 for one, Hampshire had looked on course for an even bigger score, but Lampitt undermined the middle order with four for nine in 20 balls. The match was the highest-scoring tie in the competition's history.

Hampshire

R. S. M. Morris c Rhodes b Radford . .	21	†A. N. Aymes not out	2
P. R. Whitaker b Lampitt	97	R. J. Maru c Rhodes b Mirza	0
M. Keech b Lampitt	98	M. J. Thursfield not out	0
*M. C. J. Nicholas c Rhodes b Lampitt	2	L-b 10, w 2	12
G. W. White run out	11		
S. D. Udal c Rhodes b Lampitt	0	1/58 2/216 3/220 (9 wkts, 39 overs) 275
K. D. James b Mirza	21	4/237 5/237 6/240
H. H. Streak c Solanki b Newport	11	7/270 8/273 9/273

Bowling: Newport 7–0–41–1; Haynes 6–0–46–0; Lampitt 8–1–43–4; Radford 8–0–70–1; Mirza 7–0–33–2; Solanki 3–0–32–0.

Worcestershire

*T. M. Moody c Streak b Maru	108	N. V. Radford b Streak	21
T. S. Curtis b James	3	P. J. Newport not out	15
G. R. Haynes c Keech b James	6	P. Mirza not out	0
C. M. Tolley c Aymes b Streak	30		
W. P. C. Weston c Nicholas		L-b 9, w 12	21
b Thursfield	25		
S. R. Lampitt st Aymes b Udal	29	1/8 2/44 3/148 (9 wkts, 39 overs) 275
†S. J. Rhodes c Aymes b Streak	5	4/163 5/210 6/218
V. S. Solanki c Thursfield b Streak . .	12	7/225 8/251 9/274

Bowling: James 8–1–52–2; Thursfield 7–0–42–1; Udal 8–0–55–1; Maru 8–0–61–1; Streak 8–0–56–4.

Umpires: B. Dudleston and R. Julian.

At Derby, July 2. HAMPSHIRE lost to DERBYSHIRE by five wickets.

HAMPSHIRE v YORKSHIRE

At Southampton, July 9. Yorkshire won by 19 runs. Toss: Yorkshire.

Inspired by a brilliant 115 off 105 balls by Smith, Hampshire made a brave effort to reach their target, but his departure to Hamilton ended their hopes. After Byas and Bevan had put on 118, Bevan and White blasted 91 from the last seven overs, including 24 off the last, bowled by Maru. White's 50 came off only 24 balls.

Yorkshire

*D. Byas st Aymes b Udal	78
S. A. Kellett c Smith b Streak	13
M. G. Bevan not out	97
C. White not out	50
L-b 11, w 12, n-b 3	26

1/55 2/173   (2 wkts, 40 overs) 264

B. Parker, A. A. Metcalfe, †R. J. Blakey, A. P. Grayson, D. Gough, G. M. Hamilton and M. A. Robinson did not bat.

Bowling: James 8–1–37–0; Thursfield 8–1–34–0; Maru 8–0–53–0; Streak 7–0–57–1; Udal 8–0–61–1; Whitaker 1–0–11–0.

Hampshire

R. S. M. Morris c Blakey b Hamilton ..	0	H. H. Streak not out	32
P. R. Whitaker c Kellett b Hamilton...	6	†A. N. Aymes not out	15
R. A. Smith c Blakey b Hamilton 115		L-b 1, w 8, n-b 6	15
M. Keech b Hamilton	2		
*M. C. J. Nicholas c Hamilton b Bevan	44	1/0 2/11 3/32 (7 wkts, 40 overs) 245	
K. D. James c Blakey b Robinson ...	5	4/127 5/160	
S. D. Udal c Gough b White	11	6/180 7/200	

R. J. Maru and M. J. Thursfield did not bat.

Bowling: Hamilton 7–0–38–4; Gough 8–0–55–0; Grayson 8–0–55–0; White 7–1–36–1; Robinson 7–0–41–1; Bevan 3–0–19–1.

Umpires: B. J. Meyer and A. G. T. Whitehead.

At Chester-le-Street, July 16. HAMPSHIRE beat DURHAM by four wickets.

At Northampton, July 23. HAMPSHIRE lost to NORTHAMPTONSHIRE by seven wickets.

At Colchester, August 6. HAMPSHIRE lost to ESSEX by 36 runs.

HAMPSHIRE v WARWICKSHIRE

At Southampton, August 13. Warwickshire won by 67 runs. Toss: Warwickshire.

Warwickshire's ninth successive Sunday League win owed much to Reeve, whose 50 off 59 balls was vital as he led a fightback from 133 for five, adding 82 with Penney. He then snapped up three top-order wickets as Hampshire squandered a positive start of 64 in ten overs from Laney and Terry. With Donald, the fifth bowler, conceding only 11 runs, Warwickshire's total was never threatened.

Warwickshire

W. G. Khan c Aymes b James	1	†K. J. Piper not out	1
N. M. K. Smith b Maru	55		
D. P. Ostler c Stephenson b Connor ...	48	B 1, l-b 8, w 9, n-b 2	20
D. R. Brown c Terry b Maru	12		
R. G. Twose c Aymes b Streak	2	1/4 2/102 3/120 (7 wkts, 40 overs) 226	
*D. A. Reeve c Stephenson b Streak...	50	4/124 5/133	
T. L. Penney c Aymes b Connor	37	6/215 7/226	

A. A. Donald, T. A. Munton and M. A. V. Bell did not bat.

Bowling: Connor 8–0–42–2; James 8–1–44–1; Maru 8–0–33–2; Thursfield 5–0–34–0; Streak 8–0–47–2; Stephenson 3–0–17–0.

Hampshire

V. P. Terry run out	33	M. J. Thursfield c Ostler b Smith	7
J. S. Laney c Bell b Reeve	49	R. J. Maru not out	9
M. Keech c Twose b Reeve	7	C. A. Connor not out	7
*J. P. Stephenson c Khan b Reeve	4	L-b 10, w 7	17
P. R. Whitaker b Donald	3		
H. H. Streak b Smith	2	1/64 2/81 3/95 (9 wkts, 40 overs) 159	
K. D. James run out	10	4/103 5/105 6/107	
†A. N. Aymes c Brown b Smith	11	7/129 8/140 9/144	

AXA Equity & Law League, 1995

Bowling: Munton 6–0–29–0; Brown 6–0–35–0; Smith 8–0–29–3; Reeve 8–0–30–3; Donald 8–2–11–1; Bell 4–0–15–0.

Umpires: J. H. Hampshire and D. R. Shepherd.

HAMPSHIRE v LANCASHIRE

At Portsmouth, August 27. Lancashire won by 15 runs. Toss: Lancashire.

Martin tilted the balance in Lancashire's favour, after Hampshire had apparently played themselves into a winning position, needing 90 from 18 overs with only two wickets down. He claimed three wickets in four overs, finishing with four for 29 and leaving the home side still rooted to the foot of the table.

Lancashire

S. P. Titchard b Stephenson	47	I. D. Austin not out	10
A. Flintoff st Aymes b Maru	22	P. J. Martin run out	0
N. H. Fairbrother c Udal b Streak	28	B 1, l-b 3, w 6	10
G. D. Lloyd c White b Maru	8		
N. J. Speak c Whitaker b Connor	27	1/47 2/85 3/96	(8 wkts, 40 overs) 196
*Wasim Akram c Terry b Connor	29	4/127 5/168 6/168	
†W. K. Hegg c Connor b Streak	15	7/191 8/196	

G. Chapple and G. Keedy did not bat.

Bowling: Connor 8–0–37–2; Stephenson 8–0–30–1; Maru 8–0–31–2; Streak 8–0–50–2; Udal 8–0–44–0.

Hampshire

V. P. Terry c Fairbrother b Martin	2	S. D. Udal c and b Wasim Akram	6
J. S. Laney b Martin	47	H. H. Streak not out	17
M. Keech lbw b Austin	33	B 1, l-b 11, w 5	17
G. W. White b Wasim Akram	32		
P. R. Whitaker c Hegg b Martin	8	1/4 2/70 3/107	(7 wkts, 40 overs) 181
*J. P. Stephenson lbw b Martin	2	4/125 5/129	
†A. N. Aymes not out	17	6/144 7/152	

R. J. Maru and C. A. Connor did not bat.

Bowling: Chapple 8–0–32–0; Martin 8–2–29–4; Wasim Akram 8–0–29–2; Austin 8–0–44–1; Keedy 8–0–35–0.

Umpires: M. J. Kitchen and K. J. Lyons.

At Nottingham, September 3. HAMPSHIRE beat NOTTINGHAMSHIRE by five wickets.

HAMPSHIRE v SOMERSET

At Southampton, September 10. No result (abandoned).

At The Oval, September 17. HAMPSHIRE lost to SURREY by six wickets.

KENT

At Hove, May 7. KENT beat SUSSEX by seven runs.

KENT v LEICESTERSHIRE

At Canterbury, May 14. Kent won by four wickets. Toss: Leicestershire.

Cowdrey clinched an exciting victory with his 11th four off the last possible ball. He and de Silva had laid the foundations with a stand of 110 in 16 overs, after Kent ran into trouble at 70 for three. Leicestershire's total was built around Briers, who batted through the innings for a fifth Sunday League century, equalling David Gower's county record.

Leicestershire

V. J. Wells c Marsh b McCague	17	D. L. Maddy not out	16
*N. E. Briers not out	108		
W. J. Cronje c de Silva b Headley	13	L-b 9, w 9, n-b 4	22
J. J. Whitaker lbw b McCague	1		
B. F. Smith c Marsh b Fleming	30	1/50 2/79 3/82 (5 wkts, 40 overs)	235
P. E. Robinson b McCague	28	4/148 5/202	

G. J. Parsons, A. R. K. Pierson, †P. Whitticase and A. D. Mullally did not bat.

Bowling: Wren 5–0–23–0; de Silva 8–0–44–0; McCague 8–0–41–3; Headley 8–0–40–1; Fleming 8–0–56–1; Llong 3–0–22–0.

Kent

T. R. Ward run out	29	N. J. Llong b Parsons	7
*M. R. Benson c Cronje b Parsons	4	†S. A. Marsh not out	1
M. J. Walker run out	14	L-b 9, w 16	25
P. A. de Silva b Pierson	42		
G. R. Cowdrey not out	92	1/36 2/46 3/70 (6 wkts, 40 overs)	239
M. V. Fleming c Robinson b Pierson	25	4/180 5/217 6/232	

T. N. Wren, M. J. McCague and D. W. Headley did not bat.

Bowling: Mullally 8–0–50–0; Parsons 7–0–24–2; Cronje 8–0–42–0; Pierson 8–0–50–2; Wells 6–0–42–0; Maddy 3–0–22–0.

Umpires: K. J. Lyons and A. G. T. Whitehead.

At Southampton, May 21. KENT beat HAMPSHIRE by 66 runs.

KENT v GLAMORGAN

At Tunbridge Wells, May 28. Glamorgan won by 11 runs. Toss: Kent.

Kent suffered their first one-day defeat of the season in a match reduced to 23 overs a side. A 33-ball half-century from Cottey gave momentum to Glamorgan's innings, which had been interrupted by rain after eight overs. In reply, Fleming raced to 36 off 19 balls and Ealham blazed 47 from 24, including four sixes. But Barwick dashed Kent's hopes by removing these two, plus Marsh and Headley – the last three in his final over – to finish with six wickets.

Glamorgan

S. P. James b Headley	29	R. D. B. Croft not out	7
*H. Morris c Cowdrey b Headley	38		
M. P. Maynard b Headley	8	B 1, l-b 4, w 4	9
P. A. Cottey b Headley	52		
D. L. Hemp c Igglesden b McCague	1	1/61 2/76 3/107 (6 wkts, 23 overs)	180
A. Dale run out	36	4/112 5/165 6/180	

R. P. Lefebvre, †C. P. Metson, S. L. Watkin and S. R. Barwick did not bat.

Bowling: Igglesden 4–0–32–0; Ealham 3–0–14–0; Headley 8–0–59–4; McCague 6–0–48–1; Fleming 2–0–22–0.

Kent

T. R. Ward c Metson b Barwick	32	M. J. McCague run out	1
*M. R. Benson c Morris b Lefebvre	6	D. W. Headley c Lefebvre b Barwick	0
M. J. Walker lbw b Lefebvre	13	A. P. Igglesden not out	1
P. A. de Silva c Lefebvre b Watkin	4	L-b 12, w 1	13
G. R. Cowdrey c Hemp b Barwick	0		
M. V. Fleming c Dale b Barwick	36	1/18 2/45 3/54	(22.3 overs) 169
M. A. Ealham c Maynard b Barwick	47	4/63 5/64 6/105	
†S. A. Marsh c Lefebvre b Barwick	16	7/164 8/166 9/167	

Bowling: Watkin 8–0–58–1; Lefebvre 7.3–0–50–2; Barwick 7–0–49–6.

Umpires: H. D. Bird and N. T. Plews.

At Chester-le-Street, June 4. DURHAM v KENT. No result (abandoned).

KENT v GLOUCESTERSHIRE

At Canterbury, June 11. Kent won by five wickets. Toss: Kent. County debut: D. J. P. Boden.
  Fleming spearheaded Kent's victory charge, reaching 50 from 39 balls and virtually settling the result in a partnership of 81 with Benson in 12 overs. Gloucestershire never recovered from losing Lynch to the first ball of the match.

Gloucestershire

M. A. Lynch c Llong b Wren	0	M. C. J. Ball c Marsh b Fleming	7
A. J. Wright lbw b Wren	9	D. J. P. Boden b Fleming	5
A. Symonds c Marsh b Headley	16	A. M. Smith not out	6
R. I. Dawson b Headley	2	L-b 8, w 13, n-b 2	23
M. W. Alleyne c Marsh b McCague	16		
*†R. C. Russell b McCague	18	1/0 2/27 3/29	(8 wkts, 37 overs) 136
J. Srinath retired hurt	1	4/37 5/68 6/80	
R. C. Williams not out	33	7/110 8/122	

J. Srinath retired hurt at 72.

Bowling: Wren 8–0–26–2; Headley 8–0–33–2; Ealham 6–0–15–0; McCague 8–0–22–2; Fleming 7–0–32–2.

Kent

T. R. Ward c Russell b Srinath	13	M. A. Ealham not out	4
*M. R. Benson c and b Srinath	36		
M. V. Fleming c Russell b Alleyne	55	L-b 4, w 4, n-b 10	18
P. A. de Silva c Russell b Srinath	0		
G. R. Cowdrey b Alleyne	9	1/28 2/109 3/109	(5 wkts, 27.1 overs) 140
N. J. Llong not out	5	4/127 5/136	

T. N. Wren, †S. A. Marsh, M. J. McCague and D. W. Headley did not bat.

Bowling: Srinath 8–2–27–3; Smith 8–0–38–0; Williams 3–0–29–0; Boden 5.1–1–36–0; Alleyne 3–2–6–2.

Umpires: B. Leadbeater and K. E. Palmer.

At Leeds, June 18. KENT beat YORKSHIRE by 86 runs.

At Nottingham, June 25. KENT lost to NOTTINGHAMSHIRE by nine wickets.

KENT v DERBYSHIRE

At Maidstone, July 9. Kent won by four runs. Toss: Kent.

A superb display of cultured, belligerent strokeplay by Ealham set a new Sunday League record: he hit a 44-ball hundred, two balls faster than Graham Rose of Somerset, against Glamorgan at Neath in 1990. Ealham faced 51 balls in all and struck nine fours and seven sixes, although he was dropped three times, all by Adams. He added two more sixes before being last man out to a standing ovation from the 6,000 crowd at The Mote. Adams atoned for his earlier errors with a stylish 79, but Derbyshire, needing six off the last ball, only managed a single. Kent's victory was marred by a broken finger suffered by Benson, which forced him out of the Benson and Hedges final.

Kent

T. R. Ward c Cullinan b Warner	5	†S. A. Marsh not out	22
*M. R. Benson c DeFreitas b Warner	16	M. J. McCague not out	0
N. R. Taylor c Krikken b DeFreitas	13	B 1, l-b 4, w 1, n-b 2	8
P. A. de Silva c Cullinan b Griffith	43		
G. R. Cowdrey c Barnett b Harris	20	1/7 2/34 3/38	(7 wkts, 40 overs) 253
M. V. Fleming c Cullinan b Cork	14	4/102 5/105	
M. A. Ealham c Warner b Griffith	112	6/171 7/247	

D. W. Headley and T. N. Wren did not bat.

Bowling: Warner 8-1-24-2; DeFreitas 8-1-26-1; Wells 6-0-45-0; Cork 8-0-65-1; Griffith 6-0-60-2; Harris 4-0-28-1.

Derbyshire

D. G. Cork c Cowdrey b McCague	3	†K. M. Krikken not out	28
C. J. Adams b Headley	79	A. E. Warner not out	0
A. S. Rollins c and b de Silva	35	B 1, l-b 13, w 9	23
D. J. Cullinan b Fleming	25		
P. A. J. DeFreitas lbw b Fleming	28	1/15 2/101 3/134	(7 wkts, 40 overs) 249
*K. J. Barnett lbw b Headley	2	4/180 5/192	
C. M. Wells c Headley b McCague	26	6/192 7/247	

F. A. Griffith and A. J. Harris did not bat.

Bowling: Wren 5-0-34-0; McCague 8-1-44-2; Headley 8-0-37-2; Ealham 4-0-30-0; de Silva 7-0-42-1; Fleming 8-0-48-2.

Umpires: J. C. Balderstone and P. Willey.

KENT v NORTHAMPTONSHIRE

At Canterbury, July 18 (Tuesday). Northamptonshire won by eight wickets. Toss: Kent.

Having lost a cup final three days earlier, Kent had their hopes of this title dented by Curran, who scored a hard-hitting, unbeaten 119 from 101 balls, including two sixes and 15 fours. It earned Northamptonshire victory with 19 deliveries to spare. He added 138 in 23 overs with Montgomerie – who was dropped three times. Ealham's robust 89 not out came from 79 balls with three sixes and nine fours.

Kent

D. P. Fulton c Snape b Curran	3	*†S. A. Marsh c Bowen b Curran	4
T. R. Ward c Warren b Bowen	26	M. J. McCague not out	8
P. A. de Silva c Bowen b Penberthy	33	B 1, l-b 5, w 8	14
G. R. Cowdrey b Kumble	43		
N. J. Llong b Penberthy	1	1/10 2/38 3/79	(7 wkts, 40 overs) 235
M. A. Ealham not out	89	4/81 5/147	
M. V. Fleming c Kumble b Curran	14	6/181 7/217	

A. P. Igglesden and D. W. Headley did not bat.

Bowling: Curran 8-0-49-3; Bowen 7-0-41-1; Penberthy 7-1-24-2; Capel 7-0-38-0; Snape 3-0-24-0; Kumble 8-0-53-1.

Northamptonshire

R. R. Montgomerie c Marsh b Ealham . 60
A. Fordham c Marsh b McCague 1
K. M. Curran not out 119
M. B. Loye not out 39
    L-b 11, w 4, n-b 4 19

1/20 2/158   (2 wkts, 36.5 overs) 238

D. J. Capel, *R. J. Bailey, †R. J. Warren, A. L. Penberthy, J. N. Snape, A. Kumble and M. N. Bowen did not bat.

Bowling: Igglesden 8-0-28-0; McCague 6-0-28-1; Headley 8-0-63-0; Ealham 6-0-40-1; Fleming 6.5-0-53-0; de Silva 2-0-15-0.

Umpires: J. H. Harris and J. W. Holder.

At Worcester, July 30. KENT beat WORCESTERSHIRE by four wickets.

KENT v SURREY

At Canterbury, August 6. Kent won by 55 runs. Toss: Kent.
    Ward and de Silva punished the Surrey attack with a second-wicket stand of 241 in 34 overs, a Kent record for any wicket in the competition, while the eventual total of 301 was a county record in 40-overs cricket. De Silva, whose hundred came off 83 balls, hit three sixes and 11 fours, while Ward's second century against Surrey in two days took 102 balls. One of their sixes broke a spectator's nose. Surrey's reply got off to a dismal start when Brown and Thorpe departed in the first four overs, but Hollioake's 93 off 74 deliveries salvaged some pride before Headley demolished the tail.

Kent

M. V. Fleming c Kersey	*†S. A. Marsh c Hollioake	
b M. P. Bicknell . 11	b M. P. Bicknell . 0	
T. R. Ward c Shahid b D. J. Bicknell ..123	J. B. D. Thompson not out 0	
P. A. de Silva b M. P. Bicknell 124	L-b 4, w 13, n-b 10 27	
G. R. Cowdrey c Brown b Butcher .. 3		
M. A. Ealham st Kersey b Hollioake . 8	1/20 2/261 3/270 (7 wkts, 40 overs) 301	
N. J. Llong c Kersey b Hollioake 5	4/295 5/295	
M. J. Walker not out 5	6/299 7/299	

A. P. Igglesden and D. W. Headley did not bat.

Bowling: Ratcliffe 7-0-77-0; M. P. Bicknell 8-0-43-3; Butcher 8-0-73-1; Smith 8-0-56-0; Hollioake 7-0-37-2; D. J. Bicknell 2-0-11-1.

Surrey

D. J. Bicknell c Cowdrey b Headley ... 39	G. J. Kennis c Fleming b Headley 5	
A. D. Brown c Ward b Ealham 1	M. P. Bicknell c Marsh b Headley ... 11	
G. P. Thorpe c Walker b Ealham 1	M. A. Butcher not out 1	
*A. J. Hollioake c Thompson b de Silva 93	B 7, l-b 10, w 11 28	
J. D. Ratcliffe c Llong b Fleming 2		
N. Shahid c Igglesden b Headley 12	1/4 2/10 3/102 (39 overs) 246	
A. W. Smith b Headley 42	4/106 5/125 6/196	
†G. J. Kersey c and b Headley 11	7/220 8/230 9/245	

Bowling: Igglesden 8-0-28-0; Ealham 8-0-39-2; Thompson 4-0-52-0; Headley 8-0-42-6; Fleming 7-0-37-1; de Silva 2-0-12-1; Llong 2-0-19-0.

Umpires: M. J. Kitchen and K. E. Palmer.

At Taunton, August 13. KENT beat SOMERSET by nine wickets.

At Lord's, August 20. KENT beat MIDDLESEX by 46 runs.

KENT v ESSEX

At Canterbury, August 27. Kent won by 21 runs. Toss: Kent.

McCague's best bowling in the competition inspired a crucial victory for Kent, who would have found themselves joined at the top of the table by their visitors had they lost. Kent's innings lacked momentum until Ealham and Llong added 61 for the sixth wicket and it looked inadequate as Essex swept to 175 for three, with Hussain hitting his seventh fifty in nine Sunday League innings. However, McCague initiated a collapse in which the last seven wickets fell for 25 runs in less than five overs and effectively ended Essex's bid for the title.

Kent

T. R. Ward lbw b Such	38	N. J. Llong not out		37
*M. R. Benson c Rollins b Cousins	15	†S. A. Marsh not out		13
P. A. de Silva c Lewis b Irani	8	L-b 13, w 10		23
G. R. Cowdrey lbw b Such	29			
M. V. Fleming c Lewis b Waugh	16	1/43 2/64 3/74	(6 wkts, 39 overs)	221
M. A. Ealham b Waugh	42	4/115 5/141 6/202		

M. J. McCague, A. P. Igglesden and D. W. Headley did not bat.

Bowling: Ilott 8-0-42-0; Cousins 8-0-31-1; Irani 8-0-46-1; Such 8-0-33-2; Waugh 7-0-56-2.

Essex

*P. J. Prichard c and b Igglesden	2	M. C. Ilott lbw b Fleming		0
M. E. Waugh c Fleming b McCague	51	P. M. Such not out		2
N. Hussain b Ealham	83	D. M. Cousins b McCague		0
G. A. Gooch c Marsh b McCague	1			
R. C. Irani c Ealham b Headley	30	L-b 4, w 4, n-b 2		10
D. D. J. Robinson c Cowdrey b McCague	11	1/9 2/99 3/102	(37.4 overs)	200
†R. J. Rollins c Marsh b McCague	8	4/175 5/175 6/194		
J. J. B. Lewis run out	2	7/194 8/197 9/200		

Bowling: Igglesden 8-1-27-1; Headley 8-0-44-1; McCague 7.4-0-40-5; Fleming 6-0-43-1; Ealham 8-1-42-1.

Umpires: H. D. Bird and J. D. Bond.

At Manchester, September 10. KENT beat LANCASHIRE by seven wickets.

KENT v WARWICKSHIRE

At Canterbury, September 17. Warwickshire won by five wickets. Toss: Warwickshire.

Kent claimed their first trophy for 17 years, despite losing to the 1994 League champions in their final, rain-delayed match. The celebrations began at the start of the 18th over of Warwickshire's innings, when supporters heard via their radios that Worcestershire's game had been abandoned. The cheer that went up halted Fleming in his run-up and told the players that they were assured of the title – on points if they won the match, on run-rate if they lost. In the event, Kent performed very poorly and Warwickshire won with ten balls to spare, in a match reduced to 35 overs. Twose marking his last appearance before emigrating to New Zealand by steering his side to victory and second place in the table. It completed a weekend of contrasts for Kent, who finished bottom of the Championship one day and won the Sunday League the next.

Kent

*M. R. Benson c Giles b Twose	26	†S. A. Marsh c N. M. K. Smith		
M. V. Fleming b Bell	6	b Brown	.	9
T. R. Ward lbw b Reeve	3	M. J. McCague b Reeve		2
G. R. Cowdrey c Ostler		D. W. Headley lbw b Reeve		4
b N. M. K. Smith.	24	T. N. Wren not out		4
M. A. Ealham c Ostler		L-b 21, w 3, n-b 2		26
b N. M. K. Smith.	5			
N. J. Llong c Knight b Reeve	51	1/16 2/27 3/58	(34.5 overs)	166
D. P. Fulton c Penney		4/77 5/95 6/110		
b N. M. K. Smith.	6	7/139 8/143 9/161		

Bowling: Reeve 6.5–0–22–4; Bell 7–0–31–1; Twose 6–0–24–1; P. A. Smith 3–0–23–0; N. M. K. Smith 7–0–23–3; Brown 5–1–22–1.

Warwickshire

N. V. Knight c Fulton b Ealham	35	*D. A. Reeve not out	15
N. M. K. Smith c Marsh b McCague	55		
D. P. Ostler c Cowdrey b McCague	2		
D. R. Brown b Fleming	3	B 2, l-b 4, w 3, n-b 4	13
R. G. Twose not out	35		
T. L. Penney c Marsh b McCague	9	1/81 2/89 3/94 (5 wkts, 33.2 overs)	167
		4/104 5/127	

P. A. Smith, †K. J. Piper, A. F. Giles and M. A. V. Bell did not bat.

Bowling: Ealham 6–0–32–1; Wren 6–0–39–0; Headley 7–0–22–0; McCague 7–1–34–3; Fleming 6.2–0–27–1; Llong 1–0–7–0.

Umpires: A. A. Jones and D. R. Shepherd.

LANCASHIRE

LANCASHIRE v DURHAM

At Manchester, May 7. Lancashire won by 84 runs. Toss: Durham. First-team debut: R. J. Green.

After slipping to 63 for three, Lancashire rallied through Atherton, who completed his century from 94 balls. He added 140 with Lloyd and the last 20 overs of Lancashire's innings yielded 168. Durham never threatened to get close, with only Roseberry looking settled. Richard Green, from Warrington, made a useful debut for Lancashire with three wickets.

Lancashire

M. A. Atherton c Larkins b Prabhakar	.103	†W. K. Hegg not out		22
J. E. R. Gallian c Scott b Betts	28	G. Yates not out		1
J. P. Crawley b Birbeck	4			
N. H. Fairbrother c Larkins		B 1, l-b 2, w 3, n-b 2		8
b Prabhakar	1			
G. D. Lloyd run out	63	1/55 2/62 3/63	(7 wkts, 40 overs)	249
*M. Watkinson run out	18	4/203 5/203		
Wasim Akram b Prabhakar	1	6/207 7/235		

G. Chapple and R. J. Green did not bat.

Bowling: Betts 7–0–38–1; Walker 8–0–66–0; Birbeck 8–1–38–1; Prabhakar 8–0–44–3; Boiling 6–0–37–0; Saxelby 3–0–23–0.

Durham

*M. A. Roseberry c Lloyd b Green	54
W. Larkins run out	2
M. Prabhakar b Yates	19
J. E. Morris c Hegg b Wasim Akram ..	0
M. Saxelby b Yates	23
J. A. Daley c Hegg b Green	4
S. D. Birbeck b Green...............	10
†C. W. Scott c Atherton b Watkinson..	14

J. Boiling b Watkinson	6
A. Walker b Gallian	10
M. M. Betts not out.................	14
B 3, l-b 3, w 3.............	9
1/11 2/54 3/56　　　(38.5 overs)	165
4/99 5/109 6/114	
7/128 8/139 9/142	

Bowling: Watkinson 8-1-31-2; Chapple 6-0-32-0; Yates 8-1-24-2; Wasim Akram 6-0-15-1; Green 8-0-38-3; Gallian 2.5-0-19-1.

Umpires: B. J. Meyer and K. E. Palmer.

LANCASHIRE v WARWICKSHIRE

At Manchester, May 14. Lancashire won by five wickets. Toss: Warwickshire.

Warwickshire's defence of the League title suffered a second setback as Lancashire won with 15 balls to spare. Lloyd hit a six to finish the match and reach his fifty off as many deliveries. Neil Smith's catch on the mid-wicket boundary to dismiss Crawley was allowed after discussion, when the umpires ruled that the fielder's heel was raised and not touching the rope as the ball was taken.

Warwickshire

A. J. Moles c Hegg b Chapple	10
N. M. K. Smith lbw b Yates	47
R. G. Twose lbw b Yates	30
*D. A. Reeve c Hegg b Austin........	23
T. L. Penney run out	15
P. A. Smith c sub b Wasim Akram ...	30
G. Welch b Martin	24
†M. Burns b Wasim Akram	1

D. R. Brown not out	2
R. P. Davis not out	3
L-b 5, w 1, n-b 2.............	8
1/29 2/81 3/96　　(8 wkts, 40 overs)	193
4/129 5/143 6/168	
7/176 8/190	

M. A. V. Bell did not bat.

Bowling: Martin 8-0-38-1; Chapple 8-0-47-1; Austin 8-0-31-1; Wasim Akram 8-0-31-2; Yates 8-0-41-2.

Lancashire

*M. A. Atherton b Brown............	21
J. E. R. Gallian b Davis............	31
J. P. Crawley c N. M. K. Smith b Davis	40
N. J. Speak b P. A. Smith	25
G. D. Lloyd not out................	50
Wasim Akram b Bell	11

I. D. Austin not out................	6
L-b 3, w 7, n-b 2 ...	12
1/39 2/66 3/109　(5 wkts, 37.3 overs)	196
4/147 5/169	

P. J. Martin, †W. K. Hegg, G. Chapple and G. Yates did not bat.

Bowling: Brown 7-0-32-1; Welch 3-0-19-0; Reeve 2-0-11-0; Davis 8-0-30-2; N. M. K. Smith 4.3-0-34-0; Bell 8-0-43-1; P. A. Smith 5-0-24-1.

Umpires: J. W. Holder and R. A. White.

At Lord's, May 21. LANCASHIRE beat MIDDLESEX by eight wickets.

LANCASHIRE v NOTTINGHAMSHIRE

At Manchester, May 28. Lancashire won by four wickets. Toss: Lancashire.

Lloyd and Austin conjured up a match-winning stand of 79 in 12 overs after Lancashire had slipped to 94 for six in pursuit of 173. The victory came when the first ball of Evans's last over was called a wide.

Nottinghamshire

M. P. Dowman c Hegg b Wasim Akram 13	K. P. Evans run out		7
*R. T. Robinson c Watkinson b Yates . 63	L-b 5, w 2		7
P. Johnson b Austin 28			
C. L. Cairns c Watkinson b Yates 27	1/44 2/103 3/113	(5 wkts, 39 overs)	172
G. F. Archer not out 27	4/157 5/172		

J. R. Wileman, G. W. Mike, †W. M. Noon, J. E. Hindson and R. A. Pick did not bat.

Bowling: Austin 8–1–38–1; Chapple 7–0–26–0; Watkinson 8–0–32–0; Wasim Akram 8–0–33–1; Yates 8–1–38–2.

Lancashire

J. E. R. Gallian c Archer b Evans 0	Wasim Akram run out		4
S. P. Titchard c Hindson b Cairns 14	I. D. Austin not out		36
J. P. Crawley b Evans 7	L-b 3, w 5, n-b 4		12
N. J. Speak c Noon b Cairns 22			
G. D. Lloyd not out 59	1/0 2/12 3/48	(6 wkts, 38 overs)	173
*M. Watkinson st Noon b Hindson 19	4/49 5/79 6/94		

†W. K. Hegg, G. Chapple and G. Yates did not bat.

Bowling: Evans 7–2–26–2; Pick 8–1–17–0; Mike 8–0–44–0; Cairns 8–0–37–2; Hindson 6–0–35–1; Wileman 1–0–11–0.

Umpires: G. I. Burgess and K. E. Palmer.

LANCASHIRE v GLAMORGAN

At Manchester, June 11. Glamorgan won by nine runs. Toss: Glamorgan.

Glamorgan successfully defended a modest total to inflict Lancashire's first defeat of the season in any competition. Glamorgan had stands of 47 for the first wicket and 21 for the last with little in between. However, they then fielded brilliantly and bowled tidily to reduce Lancashire to 58 for five, and then 153 all out.

Glamorgan

S. P. James b Yates 29	R. P. Lefebvre run out		8
*H. Morris c Hegg b Yates 19	S. L. Watkin not out		13
M. P. Maynard c and b Austin 5	S. R. Barwick c Watkinson b Chapple .		9
P. A. Cottey c Wasim Akram b Yates . 35			
D. L. Hemp run out 6	L-b 6, w 2		8
R. D. B. Croft c Gallian			
b Wasim Akram . 27	1/47 2/54 3/56	(39.2 overs)	162
H. A. G. Anthony b Yates 1	4/79 5/114 6/119		
†C. P. Metson b Chapple 2	7/122 8/133 9/141		

Bowling: Chapple 7.2–0–34–2; Wasim Akram 8–2–27–1; Austin 8–0–27–1; Yates 8–0–40–4; Watkinson 8–1–28–0.

Lancashire

J. E. R. Gallian c and b Watkin	. . . . .	10
N. J. Speak b Barwick	. . . .	19
J. P. Crawley b Lefebvre	. . . .	0
N. H. Fairbrother run out	. . . .	16
G. D. Lloyd b Croft	. . . .	11
*M. Watkinson c and b Cottey	. . . . . .	22
Wasim Akram c Metson b Anthony	. . .	15
I. D. Austin c Metson b Watkin	. . . . .	8

†W. K. Hegg not out	. . . .	27
G. Yates c Maynard b Watkin	. . . .	7
G. Chapple c Hemp b Barwick	. . . . . .	8
L-b 5, w 5	. . . .	10

1/19 2/20 3/36   (39.1 overs) 153
4/53 5/58 6/97
7/103 8/118 9/129

Bowling: Lefebvre 8-1-31-1; Watkin 8-0-28-3; Barwick 7.1-1-16-2; Croft 8-0-31-1; Anthony 6-0-34-1; Cottey 2-0-8-1.

Umpires: J. C. Balderstone and B. Dudleston.

At Worcester, June 18. LANCASHIRE beat WORCESTERSHIRE by seven wickets.

LANCASHIRE v ESSEX

At Manchester, June 25. Lancashire won by three wickets. Toss: Essex.
Wasim Akram played a key role, claiming three for 25 as Essex slumped from 141 for one and then steering Lancashire home with an unbeaten 22 from 17 balls. Titchard celebrated the award of his county cap before the match with a half-century.

Essex

*P. J. Prichard c Gallian b Austin	. . . . .	17
M. E. Waugh c Crawley		
	b Wasim Akram	83
N. Hussain run out	. . . .	73
G. A. Gooch run out	. . . .	10
R. C. Irani lbw b Austin	. . . .	4
D. D. J. Robinson b Wasim Akram	. . .	0
J. J. B. Lewis run out	. . . .	1
M. C. Ilott b Wasim Akram	. . . .	0

†R. J. Rollins run out	. . . .	0
P. M. Such b Watkinson	. . . .	2
D. M. Cousins not out	. . . .	1
L-b 4, w 1, n-b 4	. . . .	9

1/22 2/141 3/176   (40 overs) 200
4/186 5/187 6/188
7/189 8/190 9/198

Bowling: Austin 8-0-33-2; Watkinson 8-0-39-1; Wasim Akram 8-0-25-3; Gallian 5-0-35-0; Keedy 3-0-19-0; Yates 8-0-45-0.

Lancashire

J. E. R. Gallian c Such b Waugh	. . . . .	39
S. P. Titchard c Such b Waugh	. . . . .	53
J. P. Crawley c Waugh b Such	. . . . .	5
N. J. Speak c Waugh b Such	. . . .	1
G. D. Lloyd run out	. . . .	22
*M. Watkinson c Cousins	. . . .	26
Wasim Akram not out	. . . .	22

I. D. Austin c Waugh b Ilott	. . . .	2
†W. K. Hegg not out	. . . .	4
B 9, l-b 3, w 7, n-b 8	. . . .	27

1/87 2/97 3/103   (7 wkts, 39 overs) 201
4/105 5/163
6/179 7/186

G. Keedy and G. Yates did not bat.

Bowling: Ilott 7-0-29-1; Cousins 8-0-35-1; Irani 8-0-62-0; Such 8-1-25-2; Waugh 8-0-38-2.

Umpires: H. D. Bird and P. Willey.

LANCASHIRE v NORTHAMPTONSHIRE

At Manchester, July 9. Northamptonshire won by one run. Toss: Lancashire.
Northamptonshire's first Sunday League victory of the season, in their eighth game, denied Lancashire the chance to go top of the table. The home side needed only four runs from the final over, and three from the last ball, but Bailey restricted Yates to just a single. After Martin was carried off with damaged ankle ligaments, Fairbrother – who had previously sent down just two overs in 161 League appearances – had to bowl, and dismissed Fordham. Martin was only playing because the Edgbaston Test had finished on the Saturday.

Northamptonshire

R. R. Montgomerie	J. N. Snape lbw b Austin 0
lbw b Wasim Akram . 11	A. Kumble c Speak b Wasim Akram .. 1
A. Fordham c Lloyd b Fairbrother 26	M. N. Bowen lbw b Wasim Akram.... 6
K. M. Curran c and b Watkinson 34	
M. B. Loye c Austin b Yates 11	
D. J. Capel not out 57	L-b 11, w 2, n-b 2 15
*R. J. Bailey b Wasim Akram 24	1/25 2/58 3/87 (39.5 overs) 201
†R. J. Warren c Atherton b Austin ... 13	4/98 5/140 6/173
A. L. Penberthy lbw b Austin 3	7/186 8/186 9/187

Bowling: Austin 8-0-30-3; Martin 2-0-8-0; Wasim Akram 7.5-1-29-4; Fairbrother 6-0-33-1; Watkinson 8-0-41-1; Yates 8-0-49-1.

Lancashire

M. A. Atherton c Warren b Penberthy . 17	I. D. Austin not out 14
N. J. Speak c Capel b Penberthy 36	G. Yates not out 1
J. P. Crawley c Snape b Bailey 53	
N. H. Fairbrother run out 34	B 2, l-b 12, w 2 16
G. D. Lloyd b Kumble 20	
*M. Watkinson b Kumble 6	1/60 2/69 3/136 (8 wkts, 40 overs) 200
Wasim Akram st Warren b Kumble ... 1	4/167 5/173 6/175
†W. K. Hegg b Bailey 2	7/180 8/199

P. J. Martin did not bat.

Bowling: Curran 7-0-34-0; Bowen 4-0-17-0; Capel 5-0-32-0; Penberthy 4-0-21-2; Snape 8-0-38-0; Kumble 8-0-30-3; Bailey 4-0-14-2.

Umpires: T. E. Jesty and P. B. Wight.

At Cheltenham, July 23. LANCASHIRE lost to GLOUCESTERSHIRE by five wickets.

At Taunton, July 30. LANCASHIRE beat SOMERSET by 87 runs.

LANCASHIRE v SUSSEX

At Manchester, August 6. Lancashire won by 22 runs. Toss: Lancashire.

Lancashire suffered a mid-innings collapse, losing seven wickets for 31 in 14 overs, but Sussex in turn declined from 56 for one, with Wasim Akram shattering the tail to claim four for 16.

Lancashire

M. A. Atherton st Moores b Salisbury . 46	I. D. Austin b Lewry 5
J. E. R. Gallian b Stephenson 19	G. Yates not out 24
J. P. Crawley c Lenham b Salisbury ... 20	
N. H. Fairbrother c Moores b Jarvis .. 1	L-b 10, w 2 12
G. D. Lloyd c Stephenson b Giddins .. 6	
*M. Watkinson b Giddins 4	1/42 2/90 3/92 (8 wkts, 40 overs) 166
Wasim Akram b Giddins 0	4/96 5/106 6/106
†W. K. Hegg not out 29	7/110 8/121

P. J. Martin did not bat.

Bowling: Lewry 8-1-41-1; Giddins 8-0-44-2; Stephenson 8-2-24-1; Salisbury 8-0-30-2; Jarvis 8-1-17-2.

Sussex

K. Greenfield b Austin	0	P. W. Jarvis b Wasim Akram	10
*A. P. Wells lbw b Wasim Akram	17	J. D. Lewry b Austin	3
F. D. Stephenson c Crawley b Yates	39	E. S. H. Giddins not out	1
C. W. J. Athey c and b Yates	17	L-b 6, w 1	7
N. J. Lenham c Gallian b Martin	25		
†P. Moores b Wasim Akram	8	1/0 2/56 3/56	(38 overs) 144
D. R. Law c Hegg b Wasim Akram	8	4/86 5/108 6/117	
I. D. K. Salisbury run out	9	7/118 8/130 9/140	

Bowling: Austin 7–1–25–2; Martin 8–0–44–1; Wasim Akram 7–1–16–4; Yates 8–1–23–2; Watkinson 8–1–30–0.

Umpires: K. J. Lyons and R. Palmer.

At Leicester, August 13. LANCASHIRE lost to LEICESTERSHIRE by six wickets.

LANCASHIRE v YORKSHIRE

At Manchester, August 20. Lancashire won by 36 runs. Toss: Yorkshire.

Despite Blakey's unbeaten 53 from 57 balls, Yorkshire never fully recovered after Chapple had reduced them to 41 for three. In front of a crowd of more than 11,000, Fairbrother provided the backbone of Lancashire's innings with 60 off 58 balls.

Lancashire

J. E. R. Gallian c Blakey b White	40	†W. K. Hegg c Blakey b Hartley	1
A. Flintoff c Byas b Silverwood	12	I. D. Austin not out	14
J. P. Crawley b Hamilton	35	L-b 4, w 3, n-b 8	15
N. H. Fairbrother not out	60		
G. D. Lloyd b Grayson	7	1/34 2/79 3/114	(7 wkts, 40 overs) 210
*M. Watkinson c Bevan b Silverwood	14	4/131 5/156	
Wasim Akram b White	12	6/185 7/186	

G. Chapple and P. J. Martin did not bat.

Bowling: Silverwood 8–1–38–2; Hartley 8–0–55–1; Hamilton 8–0–33–1; White 8–0–49–2; Grayson 8–1–31–1.

Yorkshire

*M. D. Moxon c Crawley b Chapple	7	P. J. Hartley c Hegg b Martin	10
D. Byas b Chapple	1	G. M. Hamilton b Wasim Akram	1
M. P. Vaughan lbw b Chapple	16		
M. G. Bevan c Watkinson b Austin	16	L-b 7, w 6, n-b 4	17
C. White b Watkinson	13		
A. A. Metcalfe b Watkinson	29	1/4 2/9 3/41	(9 wkts, 40 overs) 174
†R. J. Blakey not out	53	4/47 5/76 6/103	
A. P. Grayson c Hegg b Austin	11	7/142 8/168 9/174	

C. E. W. Silverwood did not bat.

Bowling: Martin 8–1–33–1; Chapple 8–0–36–3; Austin 8–0–37–2; Wasim Akram 8–0–32–1; Watkinson 8–0–29–2.

Umpires: J. C. Balderstone and V. A. Holder.

At Portsmouth, August 27. LANCASHIRE beat HAMPSHIRE by 15 runs.

At The Oval, September 3. LANCASHIRE beat SURREY by six wickets.

LANCASHIRE v KENT

At Manchester, September 10. Kent won by seven wickets. Toss: Lancashire.

Kent secured a vital win, their sixth in succession, in their penultimate match, to take the outright lead in the table. They removed Lancashire's three Test batsmen of 1995 in the space of nine balls. The innings disintegrated after that, and Kent cruised in, thanks to a third-wicket stand of 76 between Cowdrey and de Silva, who was making his final appearance for the county before flying back to join the Sri Lankan national side. Marsh held five catches for the second time in the Sunday League.

Lancashire

M. A. Atherton c Benson b Igglesden ..	19	G. Yates run out	2
J. E. R. Gallian c Marsh b Igglesden ..	23	P. J. Martin lbw b Headley	2
J. P. Crawley c Marsh b Headley	1	G. Chapple c de Silva b McCague	4
N. H. Fairbrother c Marsh b Ealham ..	27	L-b 2, w 4, n-b 2	8
G. D. Lloyd c Marsh b Headley	8		
*M. Watkinson c Marsh b Fleming	19	1/45 2/46 3/46	(36.5 overs) 126
†W. K. Hegg lbw b Fleming	1	4/60 5/100 6/105	
I. D. Austin not out	12	7/107 8/111 9/119	

Bowling: Igglesden 8–1–23–2; Ealham 8–1–24–1; Headley 8–3–19–3; McCague 5.5–0–35–1; de Silva 1–0–9–0; Fleming 6–3–14–2.

Kent

T. R. Ward b Martin	13	M. V. Fleming not out	9
*M. R. Benson run out	7	B 4, l-b 3, w 6, n-b 2	15
P. A. de Silva b Martin	40		
G. R. Cowdrey c Lloyd b Watkinson ..	44	1/17 2/22 3/98	(3 wkts, 31.2 overs) 128

M. A. Ealham, N. J. Llong, †S. A. Marsh, M. J. McCague, A. P. Igglesden and D. W. Headley did not bat.

Bowling: Martin 8–2–10–1; Chapple 4–0–22–0; Austin 6–0–35–0; Watkinson 8–1–29–1; Yates 5.2–0–25–0.

Umpires: R. Palmer and G. Sharp.

At Derby, September 17. DERBYSHIRE v LANCASHIRE. No result.

LEICESTERSHIRE

LEICESTERSHIRE v YORKSHIRE

At Leicester, May 7. Leicestershire won by 30 runs. Toss: Yorkshire.

Leicestershire failed to build on a good start, in which Wells and Briers put on 90 in 19 overs, and they suffered five run-outs in an attempt to accelerate. After Yorkshire had slipped to 65 for five, Blakey's defiance was not enough to deny the home side victory.

Leicestershire

V. J. Wells run out	79	G. J. Parsons run out	2
*N. E. Briers run out...............	44	A. R. K. Pierson not out	8
W. J. Cronje b Stemp	5	B 2, l-b 4, w 3.............	9
B. F. Smith run out	37		
†P. E. Robinson c Blakey b Gough ..	2	1/90 2/104 3/167	(7 wkts, 40 overs) 200
D. L. Maddy run out	6	4/171 5/178	
J. M. Dakin not out	8	6/185 7/190	

T. J. Mason and A. D. Mullally did not bat.

Bowling: Hartley 8–0–36–0; Gough 8–0–32–1; Robinson 8–1–20–0; White 5–0–36–0; Stemp 8–0–47–1; Vaughan 2–0–18–0; Grayson 1–0–5–0.

Yorkshire

*M. D. Moxon c Pierson b Mullally	...	3	P. J. Hartley b Wells	7
D. Byas b Parsons		14	R. D. Stemp c Pierson b Mullally	11
M. P. Vaughan c Robinson b Dakin	...	28	M. A. Robinson not out	0
M. G. Bevan c Robinson b Cronje	....	7	B 2, l-b 4, w 6	12
C. White b Wells		11		
†R. J. Blakey run out		61	1/6 2/24 3/40	(38.3 overs) 170
A. P. Grayson c Robinson b Dakin	....	4	4/63 5/65 6/80	
D. Gough lbw b Dakin		12	7/114 8/134 9/170	

Bowling: Mullally 7.3–1–23–2; Parsons 8–0–20–1; Cronje 8–0–34–1; Dakin 8–0–32–3; Wells 7–0–55–2.

Umpires: D. J. Constant and D. R. Shepherd.

At Canterbury, May 14. LEICESTERSHIRE lost to KENT by four wickets.

LEICESTERSHIRE v DERBYSHIRE

At Leicester, May 21. Leicestershire won by 23 runs. Toss: Derbyshire.

Pierson won the match with five for 36, twice taking two wickets with successive balls. The first instance turned the match as it removed the second-wicket pair, Cork and O'Gorman, after a stand of 118. Wells and Briers again gave Leicestershire a solid platform with 69 in 12 overs.

Leicestershire

V. J. Wells c Krikken b Malcolm	.....	50	G. J. Parsons not out	9
*N. E. Briers b Malcolm		19	A. R. K. Pierson c Krikken b Warner	1
W. J. Cronje c Harris b Wells		32	A. D. Mullally c Cork b Warner	1
J. J. Whitaker c Tweats b Harris	.....	31	B 4, l-b 6, w 4, n-b 4	18
B. F. Smith lbw b Cork		7		
P. E. Robinson c DeFreitas b Wells	...	3	1/69 2/80 3/128	(39 overs) 217
D. L. Maddy c DeFreitas b Wells	.....	20	4/145 5/151 6/158	
†P. A. Nixon b Warner		26	7/200 8/204 9/214	

Bowling: Cork 8–1–41–1; DeFreitas 6–0–39–0; Warner 8–0–31–3; Malcolm 7–0–39–2; Harris 4–0–26–1; Wells 6–1–31–3.

Derbyshire

D. G. Cork c Smith b Pierson	....	47	†K. M. Krikken not out	14
C. J. Adams c Nixon b Parsons	....	0	T. A. Tweats not out	15
T. J. G. O'Gorman c Nixon b Pierson	.	57		
*K. J. Barnett c Robinson b Cronje	...	7	B 3, l-b 8, w 3, n-b 6	20
P. A. J. DeFreitas c Mullally b Pierson.		10		
C. M. Wells c Cronje b Pierson	....	13	1/1 2/119 3/119	(8 wkts, 40 overs) 194
A. E. Warner b Parsons	....	11	4/131 5/138 6/156	
D. E. Malcolm b Pierson	....	0	7/156 8/166	

A. J. Harris did not bat.

Bowling: Parsons 8–3–23–2; Mullally 8–1–35–0; Wells 6–0–36–0; Cronje 8–0–38–1; Pierson 8–0–36–5; Maddy 2–0–15–0.

Umpires: D. J. Constant and V. A. Holder.

LEICESTERSHIRE v DURHAM

At Leicester, May 28. Leicestershire won on scoring-rate. Toss: Durham.

Leicestershire's target had been revised twice as rain interrupted the match, and by the time it finally ended play, Wells had ensured that Leicestershire were well ahead of the required rate. Larkins made 42 off 48 balls, but Durham struggled, especially against Maddy's medium-pace.

Durham

*M. A. Roseberry c Pierson b Parsons .	11	N. Killeen st Nixon b Pierson	5
W. Larkins c Maddy b Cronje	42	S. J. E. Brown b Mullally	6
M. Prabhakar c Whitaker b Pierson	28	M. M. Betts not out	0
M. Saxelby c Maddy b Cronje	0		
J. E. Morris lbw b Maddy	15	L-b 7, w 12	19
J. I. Longley c Nixon b Maddy	26		
†D. G. C. Ligertwood c Pierson		1/29 2/75 3/76　　(9 wkts, 40 overs) 160	
b Maddy .	3	4/88 5/120 6/135	
J. Boiling not out	5	7/144 8/150 9/160	

Bowling: Parsons 5–0–20–1; Mullally 8–0–22–1; Millns 4–0–27–0; Cronje 8–1–19–2; Pierson 8–0–34–2; Maddy 7–1–31–3.

Leicestershire

V. J. Wells not out	66
*N. E. Briers c Boiling b Killeen	22
W. J. Cronje not out	30
L-b 3, w 3, n-b 2	8
1/43　　　　(1 wkt, 25 overs) 126	

D. L. Maddy, J. J. Whitaker, B. F. Smith, †P. A. Nixon, D. J. Millns, G. J. Parsons, A. R. K. Pierson and A. D. Mullally did not bat.

Bowling: Prabhakar 4–1–11–0; Brown 5–0–22–0; Killeen 5–1–31–1; Betts 5–0–21–0; Saxelby 4–0–20–0; Boiling 2–0–18–0.

Umpires: J. D. Bond and R. Julian.

At Basingstoke, June 11. LEICESTERSHIRE lost to HAMPSHIRE by seven wickets.

LEICESTERSHIRE v NOTTINGHAMSHIRE

At Leicester, June 18. Leicestershire won by ten runs. Toss: Leicestershire.
A high-scoring contest ended with Nottinghamshire failing to score 20 off Parsons's final over, despite Wileman hitting the first ball for six. Dakin and Maddy forced the pace in the later stages of Leicestershire's innings, Maddy taking 22 off the last over from Wileman.

Leicestershire

†P. A. Nixon c Wileman b Cairns	15	D. L. Maddy c Cairns b Wileman	48
*N. E. Briers c Robinson b Cairns	54	G. J. Parsons not out	7
W. J. Cronje c Robinson b Cairns	29	L-b 12, w 9, n-b 10	31
J. J. Whitaker c Pollard b Chapman	23		
J. M. Dakin c Pennett b Wileman	45	1/59 2/113 3/114　(8 wkts, 40 overs) 285	
B. F. Smith c Cairns b Wileman	11	4/187 5/188 6/214	
P. E. Robinson c Cairns b Wileman	22	7/251 8/285	

T. J. Mason and J. Ormond did not bat.

Bowling: Pennett 7–0–48–0; Chapman 8–0–51–1; Cairns 8–0–34–3; Archer 5–0–42–0; Hindson 4–1–27–0; Wileman 8–0–71–4.

Nottinghamshire

P. R. Pollard st Nixon b Mason	74	†W. M. Noon c and b Parsons	33
*R. T. Robinson c Nixon b Parsons	4	J. E. Hindson not out	3
P. Johnson c Smith b Dakin	35	L-b 10, w 7	17
C. L. Cairns c Briers b Maddy	48		
C. C. Lewis c Cronje b Mason	14	1/16 2/97 3/166　(7 wkts, 40 overs) 275	
G. F. Archer run out	2	4/181 5/185	
J. R. Wileman not out	45	6/191 7/259	

R. J. Chapman and D. B. Pennett did not bat.

Bowling: Parsons 8–1–30–2; Ormond 6–0–41–0; Cronje 5–0–57–0; Dakin 6–0–49–1; Mason 8–0–53–2; Maddy 7–0–35–1.

Umpires: A. A. Jones and M. J. Kitchen.

At Northampton, June 25. LEICESTERSHIRE beat NORTHAMPTONSHIRE by 41 runs.

At Worcester, July 2. LEICESTERSHIRE lost to WORCESTERSHIRE by 28 runs.

LEICESTERSHIRE v WARWICKSHIRE

At Leicester, July 9. Warwickshire won by 112 runs. Toss: Warwickshire.

Warwickshire's batsmen encountered few problems against a weakened Leicestershire attack. Twose and Reeve hammered 83 in eight overs after a solid start. The end was hastened by Reeve, who took three wickets in four balls.

Warwickshire

N. V. Knight c Pierson b Mason	30	*D. A. Reeve not out	39
N. M. K. Smith c Mullally b Parsons	57	B 5, l-b 5, w 10, n-b 2	22
D. P. Ostler c Mullally b Pierson	58		
D. R. Brown b Mason	7	1/90 2/95 (4 wkts, 40 overs)	277
R. G. Twose not out	64	3/112 4/194	

P. A. Smith, T. L. Penney, †K. J. Piper, T. A. Munton and A. A. Donald did not bat.

Bowling: Mullally 8–1–42–0; Parsons 8–0–43–1; Maddy 8–0–62–0; Pierson 8–0–79–1; Mason 8–0–41–2.

Leicestershire

V. J. Wells c Donald b Munton	20	G. J. Parsons c Twose b P. A. Smith	5
*N. E. Briers c Piper b Munton	27	A. R. K. Pierson not out	21
†P. A. Nixon c Penney b Donald	23	A. D. Mullally c Reeve b P. A. Smith	8
A. Habib c Piper b Donald	15	B 1, l-b 5, w 3	9
P. E. Robinson c Munton b Reeve	26		
D. L. Maddy c Brown b Donald	10	1/41 2/67 3/90 (38.2 overs)	165
V. P. Clarke c Knight b Reeve	1	4/102 5/128 6/131	
T. J. Mason c Munton b Reeve	0	7/131 8/131 9/149	

Bowling: Munton 8–0–28–2; Brown 7–0–35–0; N. M. K. Smith 7–0–29–0; Donald 8–0–40–3; Reeve 5–0–18–3; P. A. Smith 3.2–0–9–2.

Umpires: V. A. Holder and B. Leadbeater.

At Chelmsford, July 16. LEICESTERSHIRE lost to ESSEX on scoring-rate.

At Hove, July 23. LEICESTERSHIRE lost to SUSSEX by seven wickets.

LEICESTERSHIRE v SURREY

At Leicester, July 30. Leicestershire won by five wickets. Toss: Surrey.

Hollioake and Brown contributed usefully for Surrey, but a stand of 96 between Whitaker and Smith settled matters for Leicestershire with 17 balls to spare.

Surrey

D. J. Bicknell c and b Parsons	7	A. J. Tudor lbw b Parsons	11	
J. D. Ratcliffe c Smith b Mullally	11	R. W. Nowell lbw b Maddy	0	
*A. J. Holliokae c Nixon b Cronje	43	J. M. de la Pena not out	2	
A. D. Brown c Smith b Mason	43	L-b 7, w 8, n-b 2	17	
N. Shahid c and b Maddy	7			
A. W. Smith c Nixon b Maddy	1	1/17 2/21 3/94	(38.2 overs) 180	
†G. J. Kersey run out	24	4/101 5/103 6/146		
M. P. Bicknell run out	14	7/161 8/169 9/169		

Bowling: Mullally 6–0–36–1; Parsons 7.2–1–28–2; Cronje 8–0–33–1; Wells 2–0–24–0; Mason 8–1–23–1; Maddy 7–2–29–3.

Leicestershire

V. J. Wells b Tudor	0	†P. A. Nixon not out	6	
*N. E. Briers run out	9			
W. J. Cronje c D. J. Bicknell b Smith	32	B 8, l-b 9, w 4, n-b 5	26	
J. J. Whitaker not out	65			
J. M. Dakin c Tudor b Smith	1	1/3 2/52 3/52	(5 wkts, 37.1 overs) 181	
B. F. Smith c Tudor b M. P. Bicknell	42	4/54 5/150		

D. L. Maddy, G. J. Parsons, T. J. Mason and A. D. Mullally did not bat.

Bowling: de la Pena 4–0–27–0; Tudor 4–0–19–1; Smith 8–1–21–2; M. P. Bicknell 6.1–0–30–1; Nowell 8–0–31–0; Holliokae 3–0–18–0; Ratcliffe 4–0–18–0.

Umpires: B. Dudleston and J. W. Holder.

LEICESTERSHIRE v LANCASHIRE

At Leicester, August 13. Leicestershire won by six wickets. Toss: Lancashire.

For the second time in three years a Sunday League match at Grace Road had to be abandoned because of a dangerous pitch. When Wells was struck by a ball from Martin, with Leicestershire 35 for one from 7.2 overs, the umpires and captains agreed to start a new game on the adjacent strip, used for the Championship contest which had ended the previous day. Leicestershire went on to win thanks to Cronje, whose undefeated 93 came off 89 balls. The result infuriated Lancashire, whose chances of winning the League were severely damaged; some players and supporters thought they should have been awarded the match.

Lancashire

J. E. R. Gallian c Cronje b Wells	51	I. D. Austin not out	5	
S. P. Titchard c and b Wells	11	P. J. Martin not out	1	
N. H. Fairbrother st Nixon b Pierson	29	B 4, l-b 8, w 7	19	
G. D. Lloyd b Wells	12			
N. J. Speak c Smith b Maddy	21	1/68 2/73 3/90	(7 wkts, 40 overs) 198	
*Wasim Akram c Briers b Maddy	32	4/139 5/165		
†W. K. Hegg c Pierson b Maddy	17	6/165 7/195		

G. Chapple and G. Keedy did not bat.

Bowling: Mullally 5–0–25–0; Cronje 8–0–38–0; Mason 8–2–24–0; Wells 8–1–32–3; Pierson 5–1–36–1; Maddy 6–0–31–3.

Leicestershire

V. J. Wells b Martin	40	J. M. Dakin not out	4	
*N. E. Briers run out	12	L-b 5, w 9, n-b 4	18	
G. I. Macmillan b Chapple	0			
W. J. Cronje not out	93	1/32 2/32	(4 wkts, 35.3 overs) 202	
B. F. Smith c Hegg b Chapple	35	3/121 4/192		

D. L. Maddy, †P. A. Nixon, A. R. K. Pierson, T. J. Mason and A. D. Mullally did not bat.

Bowling: Chapple 8–0–34–2; Austin 7.3–0–31–0; Keedy 5–0–34–0; Wasim Akram 6–0–36–0; Martin 7–0–48–1; Gallian 2–0–14–0.

Umpires: G. I. Burgess and R. A. White.

At Weston-super-Mare, August 27. LEICESTERSHIRE lost to SOMERSET by four wickets.

LEICESTERSHIRE v GLAMORGAN

At Leicester, September 3. Leicestershire won by four wickets. Toss: Leicestershire.

An unbeaten 78 not out from 59 balls by Smith steered Leicestershire to a comfortable victory. When five, James had passed Hugh Morris's Glamorgan record of 737 runs in a Sunday League season.

Glamorgan

S. P. James lbw b Dakin	80	R. D. B. Croft not out	10
*H. Morris b Parsons	12	R. P. Lefebvre not out	10
M. P. Maynard st Nixon b Parsons	1	L-b 6, w 3	9
P. A. Cottey b Maddy	12		
D. L. Hemp c and b Maddy	74	1/42 2/46 3/70 (6 wkts, 40 overs) 212	
A. Dale c Wells b Mullally	4	4/158 5/184 6/196	

†C. P. Metson, S. L. Watkin and S. R. Barwick did not bat.

Bowling: Parsons 8–2–25–2; Mullally 8–1–37–1; Cronje 8–0–42–0; Maddy 8–0–46–2; Mason 4–0–30–0; Dakin 4–0–26–1.

Leicestershire

V. J. Wells b Croft	50	†P. A. Nixon run out	7
G. I. Macmillan c Metson b Watkin	3	D. L. Maddy not out	18
W. J. Cronje c Croft b Lefebvre	5	L-b 8, w 7	15
*J. J. Whitaker c Cottey b Croft	37		
B. F. Smith not out	78	1/17 2/24 3/86 (6 wkts, 38.3 overs) 215	
J. M. Dakin run out	2	4/126 5/132 6/149	

G. J. Parsons, T. J. Mason and A. D. Mullally did not bat.

Bowling: Lefebvre 8–0–31–1; Watkin 8–0–29–1; Barwick 7.3–0–50–0; Croft 8–1–41–2; Dale 7–0–56–0.

Umpires: T. E. Jesty and A. G. T. Whitehead.

At Uxbridge, September 10. MIDDLESEX v LEICESTERSHIRE. No result (abandoned).

LEICESTERSHIRE v GLOUCESTERSHIRE

At Leicester, September 17. No result (abandoned).

MIDDLESEX

MIDDLESEX v HAMPSHIRE

At Lord's, May 7. Middlesex won by 37 runs. Toss: Middlesex.

Middlesex owed their winning total to partnerships of 97 for the third wicket between Ramprakash and Carr and 113 unbroken for the fourth between Weekes and Brown. White made his first one-day fifty for Hampshire, who went down to their sixth defeat out of six in all competitions in 1995.

Middlesex

*M. W. Gatting c Aymes b Connor....	5	†K. R. Brown not out	54
J. C. Pooley c Aymes b Connor......	24	L-b 8, w 9, n-b 6..............	23
M. R. Ramprakash lbw b Streak	64		
J. D. Carr lbw b Streak	24	1/26 2/33	(4 wkts, 40 overs) 244
P. N. Weekes not out	50	3/130 4/131	

D. J. Nash, M. A. Feltham, J. E. Emburey, A. R. C. Fraser and R. L. Johnson did not bat.

Bowling: Cowans 6-0-25-0; Connor 8-1-42-2; Udal 8-0-22-0; Stephenson 6-0-57-0; Streak 8-0-69-2; Nicholas 4-0-21-0.

Hampshire

R. A. Smith c Nash b Johnson	10	S. D. Udal not out.............	2
J. P. Stephenson c Carr b Fraser	14	C. A. Connor c Nash b Feltham	0
M. Keech c Carr b Johnson	9	N. G. Cowans not out..........	2
V. P. Terry b Feltham..........	30		
G. W. White c Nash b Feltham......	59	B 2, l-b 4, w 9, n-b 12	27
*M. C. J. Nicholas c Emburey			
b Feltham .	47	1/24 2/30 3/68	(9 wkts, 40 overs) 207
H. H. Streak run out	0	4/111 5/171 6/177	
†A. N. Aymes b Feltham	7	7/203 8/203 9/203	

Bowling: Fraser 5-0-10-1; Nash 4-0-14-0; Weekes 8-0-26-0; Johnson 7-0-54-2; Feltham 8-0-51-5; Emburey 8-0-46-0.

Umpires: J. H. Harris and R. Palmer.

At Worcester, May 14. MIDDLESEX lost to WORCESTERSHIRE by 77 runs.

MIDDLESEX v LANCASHIRE

At Lord's, May 21. Lancashire won by eight wickets. Toss: Middlesex.
   Lancashire ran out easy winners, containing Middlesex effectively and reaching their target with 9.2 overs to spare. Crawley, who had earlier held two catches as wicket-keeper, took them most of the way in a second-wicket partnership of 122 with Gallian.

Middlesex

*M. W. Gatting c Crawley b Austin ...	23	J. E. Emburey lbw b Martin.........	11
J. C. Pooley c Atherton b Wasim Akram	2	R. L. Johnson not out	18
J. D. Carr c Crawley b Chapple.....	4	A. R. C. Fraser not out...........	7
P. N. Weekes c Austin b Gallian.....	45	B 1, l-b 10, w 11, n-b 2	24
†K. R. Brown c Gallian b Watkinson ...	1		
P. Farbrace c Martin b Watkinson ...	1	1/4 2/27 3/46	(9 wkts, 40 overs) 155
D. J. Nash c Watkinson b Gallian	5	4/63 5/84 6/95	
M. A. Feltham c Yates b Martin	14	7/95 8/120 9/124	

Bowling: Martin 8-0-25-2; Wasim Akram 8-0-29-1; Austin 8-2-24-1; Chapple 8-0-26-1; Watkinson 5-0-29-2; Gallian 3-0-11-2.

Lancashire

M. A. Atherton lbw b Fraser	18
J. E. R. Gallian not out	51
†J. P. Crawley c Pooley b Johnson	75
N. H. Fairbrother not out	7
L-b 3, w 2, n-b 2	7

1/20 2/142   (2 wkts, 30.4 overs) 158

I. D. Austin, G. D. Lloyd, Wasim Akram, *M. Watkinson, P. J. Martin, G. Chapple and G. Yates did not bat.

Bowling: Feltham 4-0-32-0; Fraser 6-2-13-1; Johnson 8-0-38-1; Emburey 5-0-30-0; Nash 6-0-33-0; Gatting 1.4-0-9-0.

Umpires: J. D. Bond and A. A. Jones.

At Chelmsford, May 28. MIDDLESEX lost to ESSEX by two runs.

MIDDLESEX v DERBYSHIRE

At Lord's, June 4. Derbyshire won by 24 runs. Toss: Middlesex.

Bowlers dominated a match reduced to 31 overs a side. Fraser, with his best one-day figures, made life difficult for Derbyshire – before his own side crumbled to 83 for eight. Although Emburey and Feltham brought some respectability, they could not prevent Middlesex slipping to their fourth successive Sunday defeat.

Derbyshire

*K. J. Barnett c Feltham b Emburey...	17	A. E. Warner c Feltham b Fraser	0
D. G. Cork b Nash	22	D. E. Malcolm c Ramprakash b Fraser.	0
D. J. Cullinan st Brown b Weekes.....	15		
C. M. Wells c Carr b Emburey	6	L-b 8, w 3, n-b 4............	15
P. A. J. DeFreitas b Fraser	23		
A. S. Rollins b Fraser	11	1/37 2/47 3/58 (9 wkts, 31 overs) 152	
†K. M. Krikken not out	25	4/87 5/92 6/106	
W. A. Dessaur c Weekes b Fraser.....	18	7/145 8/147 9/152	

P. Aldred did not bat.

Bowling: Fraser 6-0-32-5; Nash 6-0-33-1; Emburey 7-0-15-2; Johnson 6-0-32-0; Weekes 6-0-32-1.

Middlesex

P. N. Weekes b Malcolm	17	R. L. Johnson c Warner b Aldred	0
J. C. Pooley lbw b Warner	4	J. E. Emburey c Rollins b Cork.......	11
M. R. Ramprakash lbw b DeFreitas ...	8	A. R. C. Fraser c Cullinan b Aldred ...	2
†K. R. Brown c Malcolm b DeFreitas..	5	B 6, l-b 5, w 7, n-b 4	22
P. Farbrace b Aldred...............	12		
*J. D. Carr b Cork	12	1/25 2/33 3/37 (28.4 overs) 128	
D. J. Nash run out	2	4/40 5/68 6/73	
M. A. Feltham not out	33	7/78 8/83 9/125	

Bowling: Malcolm 6-0-27-1; DeFreitas 7-1-15-2; Warner 5-0-13-1; Aldred 5.4-0-47-3; Cork 5-0-15-2.

Umpires: K. E. Palmer and R. Palmer.

At Colwyn Bay, June 18. MIDDLESEX lost to GLAMORGAN by 29 runs.

MIDDLESEX v SURREY

At Lord's, July 2. No result. Toss: Middlesex.

Ramprakash, dropped by England for the Edgbaston Test, began his response with an unbeaten 85 from 99 balls before rain intervened. Surrey, left facing a revised target of 165 in 32 overs, were in trouble when the weather closed in again.

Middlesex

P. N. Weekes c sub b Butcher	34	†K. R. Brown not out		24
J. C. Pooley lbw b Benjamin	0	B 1, l-b 9		10
M. R. Ramprakash not out	85			
J. D. Carr c Kenlock b Pigott	27	1/1 2/65 3/129	(3 wkts, 35 overs)	180

D. J. Nash, M. A. Feltham, *J. E. Emburey, R. L. Johnson, A. R. C. Fraser and J. C.
Harrison did not bat.

Bowling: Benjamin 8–2–26–1; Pigott 8–0–42–1; Butcher 5–0–25–1; Rackemann
6–0–34–0; Kenlock 8–0–43–0.

Surrey

M. A. Butcher c Brown b Fraser	7	*A. J. Hollioake not out		1
A. D. Brown c Pooley b Fraser	6	L-b 2, w 1		3
G. P. Thorpe c Pooley b Nash	0			
D. M. Ward run out	10	1/14 2/14	(4 wkts, 15 overs)	40
N. Shahid not out	13	3/18 4/37		

†G. J. Kersey, A. C. S. Pigott, S. G. Kenlock, J. E. Benjamin and C. G. Rackemann
did not bat.

Bowling: Fraser 8–1–23–2; Nash 4–0–6–1; Emburey 3–0–9–0.

Umpires: J. C. Balderstone and G. Sharp.

At Bristol, July 9. MIDDLESEX lost to GLOUCESTERSHIRE by six wickets.

At Birmingham, July 16. MIDDLESEX lost to WARWICKSHIRE by eight wickets.

MIDDLESEX v SUSSEX

At Lord's, July 30. Sussex won by seven wickets. Toss: Middlesex. First-team debuts: R. A.
Fay, U. B. A. Rashid.

Another poor Sunday batting performance by Middlesex, who were well below strength,
allowed Sussex a straightforward win, thanks to Greenfield and Athey, who put on 117 for
the third wicket.

Middlesex

P. N. Weekes lbw b Martin-Jenkins	48	K. P. Dutch not out		21
J. C. Pooley c Greenfield b Lewry	0	U. B. A. Rashid lbw b Lewry		1
M. R. Ramprakash b Salisbury	25	R. A. Fay not out		12
†K. R. Brown c Moores b Giddins	21			
*J. D. Carr c Greenfield b Martin-Jenkins	0	L-b 7, w 13		20
J. C. Harrison lbw b Salisbury	2	1/2 2/83 3/96	(9 wkts, 40 overs)	163
M. A. Feltham b Lewry	11	4/96 5/105 6/126		
R. L. Johnson run out	2	7/126 8/133 9/141		

Bowling: Lewry 8–1–23–3; Giddins 8–1–27–1; Martin-Jenkins 7–0–41–2; Stephenson
8–0–29–0; Newell 1–0–14–0; Salisbury 8–1–22–2.

Sussex

K. Greenfield c Brown b Harrison	77	†P. Moores not out		1
*A. P. Wells b Feltham	15	B 2, l-b 7, w 18		27
F. D. Stephenson b Feltham	2			
C. W. J. Athey not out	42	1/39 2/46 3/163	(3 wkts, 38 overs)	164

R. S. C. Martin-Jenkins, K. Newell, D. R. Law, I. D. K. Salisbury, J. D. Lewry and
E. S. H. Giddins did not bat.

Bowling: Johnson 5–0–31–0; Fay 6–0–25–0; Feltham 6–0–23–2; Weekes 4–0–13–0; Rashid 8–0–23–0; Dutch 8–0–37–0; Harrison 1–0–3–1.

Umpires: J. D. Bond and A. A. Jones.

MIDDLESEX v NOTTINGHAMSHIRE

At Lord's, August 6. Middlesex won by one run. Toss: Middlesex. First-team debut: O. A. Shah.

Middlesex recorded their first Sunday League win since May 7. Tufnell's well-controlled left-arm spin applied the brakes as Nottinghamshire declined from 88 for two in pursuit of a modest total and they found themselves needing 15 off the last over, bowled by Nash. They managed 13, including a six over long-off by Pick.

Middlesex

P. N. Weekes lbw b Pennett	2	R. A. Fay b Pick	8
J. C. Pooley run out	5	A. R. C. Fraser not out	2
M. R. Ramprakash st Noon b Wileman	28	P. C. R. Tufnell not out	1
*J. D. Carr lbw b Cairns	6	B 1, l-b 6, w 3	10
†K. R. Brown c Pollard b Afzaal	26		
O. A. Shah c and b Wileman	14	1/3 2/18 3/42　(9 wkts, 40 overs) 149	
D. J. Nash b Pick	35	4/50 5/72 6/109	
K. P. Dutch b Cairns	12	7/130 8/144 9/146	

Bowling: Pick 7–1–13–2; Pennett 5–0–32–1; Wileman 8–0–27–2; Cairns 7–0–25–2; Hindson 8–1–20–0; Afzaal 5–0–25–1.

Nottinghamshire

P. R. Pollard c Brown b Fraser	39	J. E. Hindson c Brown b Nash	14
*R. T. Robinson c Dutch b Tufnell	24	R. A. Pick b Nash	8
P. Johnson c Carr b Weekes	0	D. B. Pennett not out	0
C. L. Cairns c Pooley b Fay	27	B 1, l-b 10, w 5	16
G. F. Archer run out	4		
J. R. Wileman run out	0	1/38 2/39 3/88　(9 wkts, 40 overs) 148	
†W. M. Noon not out	14	4/103 5/103 6/105	
U. Afzaal b Weekes	2	7/122 8/139 9/147	

Bowling: Fraser 8–3–24–1; Nash 8–1–41–2; Tufnell 8–3–13–1; Weekes 8–0–21–2; Dutch 3–0–18–0; Fay 5–0–20–1.

Umpires: J. W. Holder and B. Leadbeater.

At Chester-le-Street, August 13. MIDDLESEX beat DURHAM by seven wickets.

MIDDLESEX v KENT

At Lord's, August 20. Kent won by 46 runs. Toss: Middlesex.

Kent's tenth win was inspired by Cowdrey's second Sunday League century of the season. He faced 81 balls, his second fifty coming off 25, and hit seven fours and five sixes – including three in an over off Rashid. Fraser caused a mid-innings hiccup with three wickets in one over. But Kent's total was always enough, as de Silva – following centuries on the two previous Sundays – caused problems with his bowling, and the last seven Middlesex wickets tumbled in nine overs.

Kent

T. R. Ward b Fraser	1	*†S. A. Marsh c Pooley b Tufnell	19
M. V. Fleming lbw b Tufnell	30	M. J. McCague run out	9
P. A. de Silva c Nash b Tufnell	26	L-b 10, w 2	12
G. R. Cowdrey not out	101		
M. A. Ealham b Fraser	21	1/2 2/59 3/63	(8 wkts, 40 overs) 219
N. J. Llong c Brown b Fraser	0	4/124 5/124 6/124	
M. J. Walker c Brown b Fraser	0	7/199 8/219	

A. P. Igglesden and D. W. Headley did not bat.

Bowling: Fraser 8-1-18-4; Nash 8-1-50-0; Fay 6-0-28-0; Tufnell 8-0-43-3; Rashid 2-0-23-0; Weekes 8-0-47-0.

Middlesex

P. N. Weekes c Marsh b de Silva	32	R. A. Fay c Marsh b Ealham	8
J. C. Pooley lbw b de Silva	51	A. R. C. Fraser not out	12
M. R. Ramprakash c Walker b de Silva	14	P. C. R. Tufnell lbw b Ealham	0
*J. D. Carr lbw b Igglesden	12	B 4, l-b 9, w 13, n-b 2	28
†K. R. Brown b de Silva	5		
O. A. Shah c Fleming b Igglesden	0	1/81 2/108 3/118	(37 overs) 173
D. J. Nash run out	3	4/132 5/132 6/135	
U. B. A. Rashid lbw b Headley	8	7/137 8/157 9/173	

Bowling: Igglesden 8-0-26-2; Ealham 7-0-34-2; McCague 4-0-17-0; Headley 7-0-36-1; de Silva 8-0-28-4; Llong 3-0-19-0.

Umpires: T. E. Jesty and R. Julian.

At Leeds, August 27. MIDDLESEX lost to YORKSHIRE by 18 runs.

MIDDLESEX v NORTHAMPTONSHIRE

At Uxbridge, September 5 (Tuesday). Northamptonshire won by six wickets. Toss: Middlesex.

An inconsequential match was enlivened by Ramprakash, who celebrated his 26th birthday with a fine century, hitting three sixes and four fours, off 118 deliveries. He added 117 with Gatting to rescue Middlesex from 37 for four. However, rain reduced Northamptonshire's target to 158 in 27 overs, and they reached it thanks to Loye, whose three sixes included one off Weekes to open his scoring.

Middlesex

P. N. Weekes run out	13	†K. R. Brown not out	29
J. C. Pooley hit wkt b Boswell	7	J. P. Hewitt not out	0
M. R. Ramprakash c Sales b Snape	103	L-b 2, w 3, n-b 2	7
J. D. Carr c Warren b Penberthy	0		
O. A. Shah c Warren b Penberthy	6	1/13 2/29 3/29	(6 wkts, 40 overs) 233
*M. W. Gatting c Warren b Snape	68	4/37 5/154 6/232	

A. R. C. Fraser, P. C. R. Tufnell and R. A. Fay did not bat.

Bowling: Boswell 6-0-21-1; Penberthy 6-0-26-2; Innes 6-0-29-0; Foster 6-0-26-0; Bailey 8-0-70-0; Snape 8-0-59-2.

Northamptonshire

R. R. Montgomerie c Gatting b Weekes	25	*R. J. Bailey not out	13
A. Fordham c Hewitt b Weekes	41	B 1, l-b 1, w 8, n-b 4	23
†R. J. Warren b Weekes	7		
M. B. Loye not out	41	1/55 2/84	(4 wkts, 26.2 overs) 158
D. J. Sales c Shah b Weekes	8	3/103 4/116	

A. L. Penberthy, J. N. Snape, K. J. Innes, M. J. Foster and S. A. J. Boswell did not bat.

Bowling: Fay 4–0–23–0; Hewitt 4–0–22–0; Weekes 8–0–41–4; Tufnell 6–0–37–0; Fraser 4–0–22–0; Ramprakash 0.2–0–2–0.

Umpires: J. W. Holder and V. A. Holder.

MIDDLESEX v LEICESTERSHIRE

At Uxbridge, September 10. No result (abandoned).

At Taunton, September 17. MIDDLESEX beat SOMERSET by seven wickets.

NORTHAMPTONSHIRE

At Cardiff, May 7. NORTHAMPTONSHIRE lost to GLAMORGAN by four wickets.

NORTHAMPTONSHIRE v SOMERSET

At Northampton, May 14. Somerset won by two wickets. Toss: Somerset.

Mushtaq Ahmed's 23 from 18 balls decided the match, and he hit the final delivery from Kumble, his fellow leg-spinner, to the extra-cover boundary. Northamptonshire had stayed in the game thanks to Capel and Snape, who added 47 in the last five overs of the innings.

Northamptonshire

R. J. Bailey c Turner b Ecclestone	12	A. L. Penberthy lbw b Trump	10
A. Fordham b Mushtaq Ahmed	39	J. N. Snape not out	15
K. M. Curran b Ecclestone	2		
*A. J. Lamb b Trump	34	L-b 8, w 15	23
T. C. Walton c Harden b Mushtaq Ahmed	2	1/27 2/41 3/84 (7 wkts, 40 overs) 195	
†R. J. Warren lbw b Trump	10	4/103 5/113	
D. J. Capel not out	48	6/130 7/148	

A. Kumble and J. P. Taylor did not bat.

Bowling: Rose 7–1–38–0; Ecclestone 8–1–21–2; Batty 8–1–42–0; Mushtaq Ahmed 8–0–36–2; Trump 8–0–42–3; Hayhurst 1–0–8–0.

Somerset

M. N. Lathwell st Warren b Kumble	41	J. D. Batty run out	3
M. E. Trescothick c Lamb b Capel	3	†R. J. Turner not out	11
P. D. Bowler c and b Penberthy	57		
R. J. Harden b Kumble	2	L-b 8, w 8	16
G. D. Rose c Snape b Bailey	36	1/10 2/83 3/91 (8 wkts, 40 overs) 198	
*A. N. Hayhurst c Taylor b Bailey	3	4/118 5/136 6/141	
S. C. Ecclestone run out	3	7/156 8/179	
Mushtaq Ahmed not out	23		

H. R. J. Trump did not bat.

Bowling: Taylor 8–0–41–0; Capel 7–1–18–1; Curran 8–0–46–0; Kumble 8–0–31–2; Penberthy 6–0–32–1; Bailey 3–0–22–2.

Umpires: G. I. Burgess and B. J. Meyer.

NORTHAMPTONSHIRE v SURREY

At Northampton, May 21. Surrey won by 14 runs. Toss: Surrey.

Hollioake gave a superb exhibition of controlled, powerful hitting. He scored 49 off 20 balls with four sixes and accounted for 26 of the 27 runs taken off Penberthy in the 38th over. Northamptonshire made a spirited response, giving Surrey a few anxious moments as Warren scored 44 from 38 balls before victory was secured.

Surrey

D. J. Bicknell c Curran b Penberthy	76	N. Shahid not out	11
A. D. Brown c Capel b Curran	39		
*†A. J. Stewart b Penberthy	17	B 2, l-b 4, w 6, n-b 2	14
G. P. Thorpe c Warren b Snape	1		
D. M. Ward b Curran	49	1/81 2/118 3/119 (5 wkts, 40 overs) 256	
A. J. Hollioake not out	49	4/168 5/206	

M. A. Butcher, J. E. Benjamin, A. C. S. Pigott and S. G. Kenlock did not bat.

Bowling: Taylor 8–0–55–0; Capel 3–0–21–0; Kumble 8–1–33–0; Curran 8–0–41–2; Snape 5–0–31–1; Penberthy 8–0–69–2.

Northamptonshire

A. Fordham c Brown b Pigott	18	A. L. Penberthy c Stewart b Benjamin	15
D. J. Capel run out	38	J. N. Snape not out	17
K. M. Curran c Stewart b Butcher	33	B 1, l-b 10, w 4	15
*A. J. Lamb b Pigott	48		
T. C. Walton lbw b Benjamin	12	1/32 2/84 3/94 (7 wkts, 40 overs) 242	
R. J. Bailey b Benjamin	2	4/128 5/136	
†R. J. Warren not out	44	6/163 7/202	

A. Kumble and J. P. Taylor did not bat.

Bowling: Benjamin 8–0–51–3; Pigott 8–0–31–2; Butcher 8–1–56–1; Shahid 2–0–14–0; Hollioake 8–0–47–0; Kenlock 6–0–32–0.

Umpires: B. Leadbeater and K. J. Lyons.

At Sheffield, May 28. YORKSHIRE v NORTHAMPTONSHIRE. No result.

At Derby, June 11. NORTHAMPTONSHIRE tied with DERBYSHIRE.

NORTHAMPTONSHIRE v ESSEX

At Luton, June 18. Essex won by 105 runs. Toss: Northamptonshire.

This match belonged to Irani, who struck 50 from 26 balls, taking 24 off an over from Capel as Essex smashed 62 in the last four overs. Northamptonshire's batting fell apart when Irani came on second change. He removed both openers and the team slumped from 41 for nought to 111 all out.

Essex

M. E. Waugh lbw b Mallender	21	J. J. B. Lewis not out	0
*P. J. Prichard c Taylor b Kumble	81		
N. Hussain c Warren b Penberthy	7	L-b 4, w 3, n-b 6	13
G. A. Gooch c Montgomerie b Taylor	42		
R. C. Irani c Taylor b Kumble	50	1/46 2/57 3/131 (6 wkts, 40 overs) 216	
D. D. J. Robinson lbw b Kumble	2	4/206 5/214 6/216	

†R. J. Rollins, P. M. Such, M. C. Ilott and D. M. Cousins did not bat.

Bowling: Taylor 8–0–41–1; Mallender 8–0–19–1; Penberthy 8–0–28–1; Capel 8–0–59–0; Kumble 8–0–65–3.

Northamptonshire

R. R. Montgomerie b Irani	18	A. Kumble c Prichard b Ilott		8
D. J. Capel c Rollins b Irani	18	J. P. Taylor not out		6
K. M. Curran c Rollins b Such	1	N. A. Mallender absent ill		
M. B. Loye c Gooch b Such	3	L-b 12, w 5		17
*R. J. Bailey b Waugh	11			
†R. J. Warren c Rollins b Ilott	29	1/41 2/42 3/48	(30.3 overs)	111
A. L. Penberthy c Such b Cousins	0	4/49 5/83 6/92		
J. N. Snape b Ilott	0	7/94 8/99 9/111		

Bowling: Ilott 5.3–0–21–3; Cousins 7–0–33–1; Such 8–0–23–2; Irani 5–2–4–2; Waugh 5–1–18–1.

Umpires: D. J. Constant and R. A. White.

NORTHAMPTONSHIRE v LEICESTERSHIRE

At Northampton, June 25. Leicestershire won by 41 runs. Toss: Leicestershire.

Leicestershire never looked back after a county record opening partnership of 144 in 25 overs from Nixon and Briers. Cronje pressed home the advantage with a forceful 48-ball innings, and Northamptonshire were unable to mount a serious challenge. Maddy pulled off a breathtaking catch to dismiss Fordham – holding the ball one-handed at full stretch after running round the cover boundary.

Leicestershire

†P. A. Nixon b Bailey	53	P. E. Robinson not out		5
*N. E. Briers run out	82			
W. J. Cronje not out	67	L-b 11, w 3		14
J. M. Dakin lbw b Kumble	6			
J. J. Whitaker b Mallender	5	1/144 2/144 3/152	(5 wkts, 40 overs)	246
B. F. Smith c Snape b Curran	14	4/170 5/208		

D. L. Maddy, G. J. Parsons, T. J. Mason and A. D. Mullally did not bat.

Bowling: Mallender 7–0–35–1; Capel 4–0–27–0; Curran 7–0–48–1; Penberthy 4–0–25–0; Snape 4–0–32–0; Kumble 8–0–40–1; Bailey 6–0–28–1.

Northamptonshire

A. Fordham c Maddy b Cronje	53	A. L. Penberthy run out		7
D. J. Capel c Whitaker b Mullally	0	J. N. Snape not out		10
K. M. Curran run out	19	L-b 9, w 4		13
M. B. Loye run out	16			
†R. J. Warren c Robinson b Maddy	2	1/0 2/35 3/72	(7 wkts, 40 overs)	205
*R. J. Bailey not out	61	4/77 5/106		
T. C. Walton c Whitaker b Cronje	24	6/145 7/158		

N. A. Mallender and A. Kumble did not bat.

Bowling: Parsons 6–1–22–0; Mullally 6–1–25–1; Cronje 8–0–36–2; Dakin 6–0–51–0; Mason 8–0–36–0; Maddy 6–0–26–1.

Umpires: J. C. Balderstone and R. Palmer.

At Manchester, July 9. NORTHAMPTONSHIRE beat LANCASHIRE by one run.

At Canterbury, July 18. NORTHAMPTONSHIRE beat KENT by eight wickets.

NORTHAMPTONSHIRE v HAMPSHIRE

At Northampton, July 23. Northamptonshire won by seven wickets. Toss: Hampshire.
Montgomerie, with 58 from 75 balls, ushered Northamptonshire to a bloodless victory with nearly ten overs to spare.

Hampshire

R. S. M. Morris c Montgomerie b Curran . 36	C. A. Connor b Kumble	1
P. R. Whitaker c Capel b Bowen	2	R. J. Maru not out	7
R. A. Smith b Bowen	4	K. D. James not out	0
M. Keech b Snape	25		
*M. C. J. Nicholas c Warren b Snape	10	L-b 7, w 4, n-b 2	13
†A. N. Aymes c Montgomerie b Bailey	23		
S. D. Udal c Kumble b Bailey	6	1/12 2/31 3/69 (9 wkts, 40 overs) 155	
H. H. Streak b Kumble	28	4/78 5/92 6/103	
		7/144 8/147 9/151	

Bowling: Taylor 6–0–32–0; Bowen 6–0–11–2; Kumble 6–0–24–2; Curran 6–1–20–1; Snape 8–0–25–2; Bailey 8–0–36–2.

Northamptonshire

R. R. Montgomerie c Morris b Udal	58	D. J. Capel not out	24
A. Fordham c Smith b Connor	9	L-b 8, w 7	15
K. M. Curran lbw b Udal	24		
M. B. Loye not out	31	1/23 2/66 3/121 (3 wkts, 30.3 overs) 161	

*R. J. Bailey, †R. J. Warren, M. N. Bowen, J. N. Snape, A. Kumble and J. P. Taylor did not bat.

Bowling: James 4–0–11–0; Connor 4–0–19–1; Morris 7.3–0–44–0; Udal 8–1–31–2; Whitaker 2–0–16–0; Streak 2–0–16–0; Nicholas 3–0–16–0.

Umpires: A. A. Jones and R. A. White.

At Birmingham, July 30. NORTHAMPTONSHIRE lost to WARWICKSHIRE by 24 runs.

NORTHAMPTONSHIRE v DURHAM

At Northampton, August 6. Durham won by 28 runs. Toss: Northamptonshire. County debut: M. J. Foster.
With six regular first-team players either injured or resting after their emphatic Championship victory over their visitors on Saturday, Northamptonshire contained Durham well. However, they then struggled against their former team-mate Walker and, particularly, Killeen, who returned the best figures by a Durham bowler in the competition; only Loye offered much resistance, improvising brilliantly for 48 off 45 balls.

Durham

*J. E. Morris c Penberthy b Foster	36	S. J. E. Brown lbw b Hughes	0
S. Hutton lbw b Bowen	1	J. Boiling not out	5
M. Prabhakar lbw b Foster	37		
J. I. Longley b Hughes	38	L-b 7, w 11	18
D. A. Blenkiron c Loye b Bowen	23		
P. Bainbridge not out	31	1/12 2/79 3/92 (7 wkts, 39 overs) 191	
†D. G. C. Ligertwood c Fordham b Penberthy . 2	4/136 5/156	
		6/167 7/169	

A. Walker and N. Killeen did not bat.

Bowling: Bowen 8–0–27–2; Hughes 8–0–39–2; Penberthy 7–1–35–1; Foster 6–0–30–2; Snape 8–0–38–0; Walton 2–0–15–0.

Northamptonshire

R. R. Montgomerie c and b Killeen	10	M. J. Foster c Boiling b Killeen	9
*A. Fordham c Boiling b Walker	29	M. N. Bowen lbw b Killeen	1
R. J. Warren c Ligertwood b Killeen	3	J. G. Hughes not out	0
M. B. Loye c Bainbridge b Prabhakar	48	L-b 13, w 7, n-b 2	22
T. C. Walton c Bainbridge b Walker	23		
A. L. Penberthy c Boiling b Walker	6	1/34 2/38 3/57	(36 overs) 163
J. N. Snape c Boiling b Brown	3	4/128 5/133 6/140	
†D. Ripley c Ligertwood b Killeen	9	7/142 8/158 9/161	

Bowling: Brown 8–2–23–1; Killeen 8–0–26–5; Boiling 8–0–43–0; Walker 6–0–34–3; Prabhakar 6–0–24–1.

Umpires: B. Dudleston and D. R. Shepherd.

NORTHAMPTONSHIRE v GLOUCESTERSHIRE

At Northampton, August 13. Northamptonshire won by 52 runs. Toss: Northamptonshire.
Two home players shared the honours: Walton provided vital late impetus with an entertaining 44 from 22 deliveries, before Penberthy tore through Gloucestershire's middle order with four prime wickets, including Symonds and Lynch with consecutive balls.

Northamptonshire

R. R. Montgomerie c Windows b Sheeraz	1	A. L. Penberthy c R. C. J. Williams b Lynch	14
A. Fordham c Hancock b Symonds	57	M. J. Foster not out	1
K. M. Curran c Alleyne b Symonds	34	J. N. Snape not out	7
M. B. Loye st R. C. J. Williams b Ball	38	B 1, l-b 8, w 11	20
†R. J. Warren c Hancock b Symonds	4		
*R. J. Bailey c R. C. J. Williams b R. C. Williams	7	1/2 2/89 3/132	(8 wkts, 40 overs) 227
T. C. Walton run out	44	4/141 5/154 6/162	
		7/210 8/218	

S. A. J. Boswell did not bat.

Bowling: Sheeraz 7–0–30–1; Cawdron 7–1–37–0; R. C. Williams 7–0–51–1; Ball 8–0–39–1; Symonds 8–0–38–3; Lynch 3–0–23–1.

Gloucestershire

A. J. Wright st Warren b Snape	22	M. C. J. Ball c Walton b Foster	20
M. G. N. Windows c Montgomerie b Boswell	6	†R. C. J. Williams not out	14
*M. W. Alleyne c Bailey b Penberthy	25	K. P. Sheeraz not out	6
M. A. Lynch c Warren b Penberthy	23	B 6, l-b 4, w 3	13
A. Symonds c Walton b Penberthy	9		
T. H. C. Hancock c Warren b Snape	1	1/11 2/49 3/67	(9 wkts, 40 overs) 175
R. C. Williams c Loye b Bailey	32	4/87 5/87 6/91	
M. J. Cawdron b Penberthy	4	7/96 8/137 9/164	

Bowling: Curran 5–0–13–0; Boswell 7–1–29–1; Snape 8–1–36–2; Penberthy 8–0–29–4; Bailey 7–0–30–1; Foster 5–0–28–1.

Umpires: D. J. Constant and R. Palmer.

NORTHAMPTONSHIRE v NOTTINGHAMSHIRE

At Northampton, August 27. Nottinghamshire won by seven wickets. Toss: Northamptonshire.
Johnson and Cairns laid about Northamptonshire's weak attack with gusto, hitting five sixes each and adding 158 in 16 overs to take Nottinghamshire to their target with almost contemptuous ease. For Northamptonshire, Loye, who faced 45 deliveries, showed a good deal of flair.

Northamptonshire

R. R. Montgomerie b Pennett	60	M. J. Foster hit wkt b Cairns	4
A. Fordham lbw b Pick	20		
*R. J. Bailey b Pennett	52	L-b 8, w 13, n-b 2	23
M. B. Loye not out	57		
D. J. Capel b Hindson	9	1/45 2/139 3/150	(6 wkts, 40 overs) 249
†R. J. Warren c Noon b Cairns	24	4/193 5/245 6/249	

D. J. Sales, J. N. Snape, A. L. Penberthy and C. S. Atkins did not bat.

Bowling: Pennett 8–0–55–2; Pick 8–0–54–1; Chapman 4–0–30–0; Cairns 8–0–44–2; Wileman 4–0–21–0; Hindson 8–1–37–1.

Nottinghamshire

P. R. Pollard c Foster b Snape	18	G. F. Archer not out	4
*R. T. Robinson c Warren b Penberthy	10	L-b 3, w 5, n-b 4	12
P. Johnson not out	136		
C. L. Cairns b Snape	70	1/22 2/71 3/229	(3 wkts, 33.2 overs) 250

J. R. Wileman, †W. M. Noon, J. E. Hindson, R. J. Chapman, R. A. Pick and D. B. Pennett did not bat.

Bowling: Penberthy 7–1–31–1; Capel 6–0–57–0; Snape 8–0–35–2; Foster 4–0–40–0; Bailey 4–0–46–0; Atkins 4.2–0–38–0.

Umpires: J. H. Harris and N. T. Plews.

At Uxbridge, September 5. NORTHAMPTONSHIRE beat MIDDLESEX by six wickets.

NORTHAMPTONSHIRE v WORCESTERSHIRE

At Northampton, September 10. No result. Toss: Northamptonshire.
Worcestershire, eager for a win to keep up the pressure on their rivals for the title, were frustrated by the weather after establishing a strong position in a match originally reduced to 33 overs a side. Curtis and Moody passed 6,000 and 3,000 runs in the competition respectively during their innings. Moody's 3,000 came from only 72 innings, four fewer than the previous best by Geoff Boycott in 1976.

Worcestershire

*T. M. Moody c Loye b Curran	56
T. S. Curtis not out	41
G. A. Hick not out	14
L-b 2, w 5	7
1/84	(1 wkt, 22.1 overs) 118

D. A. Leatherdale, W. P. C. Weston, S. R. Lampitt, G. R. Haynes, †S. J. Rhodes, N. V. Radford, P. J. Newport and P. Mirza did not bat.

Bowling: Taylor 6.1–0–24–0; Boswell 6–0–34–0; Curran 5–0–23–1; Penberthy 5–0–35–0.

Northamptonshire

R. R. Montgomerie, A. Fordham, *R. J. Bailey, M. B. Loye, D. J. Capel, K. M. Curran, S. A. J. Boswell, J. N. Snape, †D. Ripley, A. L. Penberthy and J. P. Taylor.

Umpires: J. W. Holder and M. J. Kitchen.

At Hove, September 17. NORTHAMPTONSHIRE beat SUSSEX by 13 runs.

NOTTINGHAMSHIRE

NOTTINGHAMSHIRE v DERBYSHIRE

At Nottingham, May 7. Derbyshire won by 21 runs. Toss: Nottinghamshire.
Nottinghamshire squandered a promising position, losing their last seven wickets for 40, after Pollard had given them an ideal start with a 49-ball half-century.

Derbyshire

*K. J. Barnett c Robinson b Hindson	51	†A. S. Rollins run out		4
C. J. Adams run out	34	T. W. Harrison not out		8
D. J. Cullinan b Archer	64	B 2, l-b 8, w 7, n-b 2		19
D. G. Cork lbw b Hindson	1			
P. A. J. DeFreitas c Archer b Hindson	28	1/87 2/103 3/112	(6 wkts, 39 overs)	219
T. J. G. O'Gorman not out	10	4/182 5/198 6/206		

A. J. Harris, A. E. Warner and D. E. Malcolm did not bat.

Bowling: Evans 7–0–48–0; Pick 7–0–29–0; Mike 7–0–42–0; Wileman 4–0–13–0; Archer 6–0–30–1; Hindson 8–0–47–3.

Nottinghamshire

P. R. Pollard c Harrison b Cork	57	G. W. Mike c Rollins b Warner		9
*R. T. Robinson b Cork	18	J. E. Hindson not out		9
P. Johnson run out	44	R. A. Pick run out		2
C. L. Cairns c DeFreitas b Harris	30	B 1, l-b 2, w 4, n-b 2		9
G. F. Archer run out	9			
J. R. Wileman c Rollins b Warner	6	1/64 2/89 3/147	(36.1 overs)	198
†W. M. Noon c Adams b Malcolm	3	4/158 5/170 6/171		
K. P. Evans run out	2	7/174 8/178 9/189		

Bowling: DeFreitas 6.1–0–50–0; Warner 8–0–47–2; Cork 8–1–25–2; Malcolm 7–0–34–1; Harris 7–0–39–1.

Umpires: J. D. Bond and N. T. Plews.

At Bristol, May 14. NOTTINGHAMSHIRE beat GLOUCESTERSHIRE by four wickets.

At Manchester, May 28. NOTTINGHAMSHIRE lost to LANCASHIRE by four wickets.

NOTTINGHAMSHIRE v ESSEX

At Nottingham, June 4. Essex won by 112 runs. Toss: Nottinghamshire.
When 16, Gooch became the first batsman to reach 8,000 runs in the Sunday League in his 248th innings – a rapid 55 from 37 balls. He built on the foundations laid by Waugh, who shared a stand of 126 with Prichard. A depleted Nottinghamshire slid to 29 for five and 71 for eight, but their ninth-wicket pair, Wileman and Pick, more than doubled the total before the overs ran out.

Essex

M. E. Waugh c Noon b Mike	89	D. D. J. Robinson not out		8
*P. J. Prichard c Harrison b Wileman	57	L-b 6, w 10, n-b 4		20
N. Hussain c Robinson b Mike	33			
G. A. Gooch not out	55	1/126 2/186	(4 wkts, 40 overs)	267
R. C. Irani run out	5	3/217 4/242		

R. M. Pearson, †R. J. Rollins, S. J. W. Andrew, P. M. Such and D. M. Cousins did not bat.

Bowling: Mike 8–0–56–2; Evans 8–0–62–0; Pick 8–0–39–0; Pennett 6–0–44–0; Hindson 5–0–33–0; Wileman 5–0–27–1.

Nottinghamshire

M. P. Dowman b Cousins	0	J. E. Hindson c Rollins b Such	5
*R. T. Robinson b Hussain b Cousins	7	R. A. Pick not out	58
G. F. Archer run out	14		
†W. M. Noon c Such b Cousins	5	L-b 2, w 5, n-b 2	9
C. Banton c Rollins b Andrew	1		
J. R. Wileman not out	42	1/0 2/18 3/28 (8 wkts, 40 overs) 155
K. P. Evans b Such	14	4/29 5/29 6/55
G. W. Mike c Such b Waugh	0	7/58 8/71

D. B. Pennett did not bat.

Bowling: Cousins 8–1–36–3; Andrew 8–2–26–1; Waugh 8–0–31–1; Such 8–0–20–2; Pearson 6–0–21–0; Robinson 2–0–19–0.

Umpires: J. H. Hampshire and G. Sharp.

NOTTINGHAMSHIRE v WORCESTERSHIRE

At Nottingham, June 11. Nottinghamshire won by 61 runs. Toss: Worcestershire.

Nottinghamshire's winning total was built around a solid 82 from Robinson and 47 off 32 balls from Johnson. In reply, Worcestershire were reduced to 40 for three by Pennett's opening burst and, unable to recover, lost their unbeaten League record. An outburst from Cairns at Haynes's dismissal was reported by the umpires as a breach of the TCCB's code of conduct and earned him a fine and severe reprimand from Nottinghamshire.

Nottinghamshire

*R. T. Robinson c Rhodes b Radford	82	K. P. Evans not out	26
J. R. Wileman c Rhodes b Haynes	14		
P. Johnson b Lampitt	47	L-b 6, w 3, n-b 4	13
C. L. Cairns c Church b Lampitt	13		
G. F. Archer c Rhodes b Lampitt	4	1/38 2/105 3/123 (5 wkts, 38 overs) 216
†W. M. Noon not out	17	4/132 5/177

G. W. Mike, J. E. Hindson, R. A. Pick and D. B. Pennett did not bat.

Bowling: Newport 8–0–39–0; Haynes 8–0–33–1; Radford 8–1–40–1; Mirza 6–0–49–0; Lampitt 8–0–49–3.

Worcestershire

*T. S. Curtis lbw b Hindson	54	N. V. Radford run out	0
M. J. Church b Pennett	0	P. J. Newport run out	0
T. M. Moody c Hindson b Pennett	6	P. Mirza not out	2
G. R. Haynes c Archer b Pennett	8	L-b 8, w 20, n-b 5	33
V. S. Solanki c Cairns b Hindson	12		
W. P. C. Weston c Noon b Mike	27	1/6 2/24 3/40 (32.2 overs) 155
†S. J. Rhodes c Wileman b Mike	2	4/67 5/125 6/130
S. R. Lampitt c and b Evans	11	7/150 8/151 9/151

Bowling: Pennett 6–0–27–3; Pick 6–0–26–0; Mike 8–0–32–2; Evans 4.2–0–18–1; Hindson 7–0–32–2; Wileman 1–0–12–0.

Umpires: R. A. White and A. G. T. Whitehead.

At Leicester, June 18. NOTTINGHAMSHIRE lost to LEICESTERSHIRE by ten runs.

NOTTINGHAMSHIRE v KENT

At Nottingham, June 25. Nottinghamshire won by nine wickets. Toss: Kent.

History repeated itself as Johnson – whose unbeaten 167 had damaged Kent's title challenge in 1993 – hit an unbeaten 104 in 85 balls, to inflict a heavy defeat. Kent's innings was a disappointment, only Cowdrey making an impression.

Kent

D. P. Fulton c Wileman b Mike	4		M. J. McCague run out	14
T. R. Ward run out	5		A. P. Igglesden run out	13
*P. A. de Silva c Noon b Chapman	18		T. N. Wren not out	3
M. V. Fleming c Noon b Mike	0		L-b 1, w 7, n-b 2	10
G. R. Cowdrey b Pennett	80			
N. R. Taylor c Pollard b Cairns	34		1/5 2/22 3/23	(40 overs) 194
M. A. Ealham lbw b Cairns	0		4/38 5/91 6/91	
†S. C. Willis c Wileman b Chapman	13		7/150 8/170 9/184	

Bowling: Mike 8–1–39–2; Chapman 6–0–36–2; Pennett 8–0–33–1; Cairns 8–2–27–2; Wileman 2–0–15–0; Hindson 8–0–43–0.

Nottinghamshire

P. R. Pollard not out	81
*R. T. Robinson c Willis b McCague	3
P. Johnson not out	104
B 1, l-b 1, w 5	7
1/8	(1 wkt, 34.3 overs) 195

G. F. Archer, C. L. Cairns, J. R. Wileman, †W. M. Noon, G. W. Mike, J. E. Hindson, R. J. Chapman and D. B. Pennett did not bat.

Bowling: McCague 6–0–33–1; Wren 6–0–36–0; Igglesden 7–0–38–0; Ealham 7.3–0–41–0; de Silva 5–0–26–0; Fleming 3–0–19–0.

Umpires: K. J. Lyons and B. J. Meyer.

NOTTINGHAMSHIRE v SOMERSET

At Nottingham, July 2. Nottinghamshire won by six wickets. Toss: Nottinghamshire. First-team debut: J. P. Hart.

Half-centuries from Lathwell and Harden helped Somerset to an apparently sound total against a weakened attack. But then Pollard took over, passing 50 for the seventh time in successive one-day innings as he blazed 132 off 120 balls, with a six and 14 fours – the last of which won the match with seven balls to spare. Nottinghamshire's two opening bowlers, Bobby Chapman and Jamie Hart, both had fathers who played football for Nottingham Forest: Sammy Chapman and Paul Hart.

Somerset

M. N. Lathwell c Afzaal b Wileman	53		Mushtaq Ahmed not out	20
*P. D. Bowler c Noon b Afzaal	34		P. C. L. Holloway not out	4
R. J. Harden b Cairns	61		L-b 7, w 1	8
G. D. Rose c Wileman b Chapman	45			
K. A. Parsons c Afzaal b Cairns	15		1/69 2/103 3/193	(6 wkts, 40 overs) 253
S. C. Ecclestone c Johnson b Hart	13		4/195 5/216 6/225	

†R. J. Turner, J. I. D. Kerr and H. R. J. Trump did not bat.

Bowling: Chapman 7–0–43–1; Hart 8–1–48–1; Afzaal 8–0–38–1; Cairns 8–0–57–2; Hindson 4–0–23–0; Wileman 5–0–37–1.

Nottinghamshire

P. R. Pollard not out	132		J. R. Wileman not out	0
*R. T. Robinson c Lathwell b Kerr	15		B 2, l-b 5, w 12	19
P. Johnson c Turner b Trump	37			
C. L. Cairns b Ecclestone	40		1/44 2/113	(4 wkts, 38.5 overs) 257
G. F. Archer c Turner b Kerr	14		3/190 4/247	

†W. M. Noon, J. E. Hindson, J. P. Hart, U. Afzaal and R. J. Chapman did not bat.

Bowling: Rose 7.5–0–41–0; Parsons 8–0–37–0; Kerr 5–0–42–2; Trump 6–0–64–1; Ecclestone 4–0–27–1; Mushtaq Ahmed 8–1–39–0.

Umpires: H. D. Bird and R. Palmer.

At Arundel, July 9. NOTTINGHAMSHIRE lost to SUSSEX by 12 runs.

At Guildford, July 23. NOTTINGHAMSHIRE lost to SURREY by one run.

NOTTINGHAMSHIRE v YORKSHIRE

At Cleethorpes, July 30. Nottinghamshire won by five wickets. Toss: Yorkshire.

Pollard continued his prolific one-day form, helping Nottinghamshire to victory with seven balls to spare, and passing 500 Sunday League runs for the season in only his seventh innings. Yorkshire had looked to be on course for a big total when Vaughan and Bevan were adding 85 in 14 overs, but the spinners applied the brakes.

Yorkshire

*D. Byas run out	1	C. E. W. Silverwood c Hindson		
M. P. Vaughan c Pollard b Hindson	46		b Wileman	7
M. G. Bevan c Noon b Hindson	56	M. A. Robinson c Afzaal b Pick		4
B. Parker c Noon b Afzaal	1			
A. A. Metcalfe b Afzaal	8	L-b 7, w 7		14
†R. J. Blakey c and b Pick	17			
A. P. Grayson not out	33	1/2 2/87 3/88		(40 overs) 194
A. C. Morris c Noon b Pennett	7	4/104 5/122 6/150		
G. M. Hamilton b Pennett	0	7/168 8/168 9/188		

Bowling: Pennett 8–0–34–2; Pick 8–0–34–2; Cairns 3–0–20–0; Wileman 5–0–39–1; Hindson 8–0–35–2; Afzaal 8–1–25–2.

Nottinghamshire

P. R. Pollard c Vaughan b Silverwood	95	†W. M. Noon not out		3
*R. T. Robinson b Silverwood	9			
P. Johnson c Blakey b Silverwood	1	L-b 6, w 9		15
C. L. Cairns b Morris	54			
G. F. Archer b Robinson	15	1/18 2/22 3/135	(5 wkts, 38.5 overs)	197
J. R. Wileman not out	5	4/186 5/190		

U. Afzaal, J. E. Hindson, R. A. Pick and D. B. Pennett did not bat.

Bowling: Hamilton 6–0–27–0; Silverwood 7–1–31–3; Vaughan 4–1–13–0; Robinson 6.5–0–42–1; Grayson 4–0–22–0; Morris 7–0–34–1; Bevan 4–0–22–0.

Umpires: D. J. Constant and K. J. Lyons.

At Lord's, August 6. NOTTINGHAMSHIRE lost to MIDDLESEX by one run.

NOTTINGHAMSHIRE v WARWICKSHIRE

At Nottingham, August 20. Warwickshire won by four wickets. Toss: Nottinghamshire.

An unbeaten 78 off 67 balls by Brown ushered Warwickshire to their tenth successive Sunday League win in the final over. Johnson, in his benefit match, provided the backbone of the home side's innings, making 82 from 77 deliveries with three sixes and seven fours.

Nottinghamshire

*R. T. Robinson c Ostler b Bell	67	J. R. Wileman not out		12
M. P. Dowman c Reeve		†W. M. Noon not out		5
	b N. M. K. Smith	22	L-b 3, w 14, n-b 6	23
P. Johnson c P. A. Smith b Bell	82			
C. L. Cairns c P. A. Smith b Munton	8	1/56 2/146 3/173	(5 wkts, 38 overs)	219
G. F. Archer c Piper b Munton	0	4/178 5/201		

J. E. Hindson, U. Afzaal, R. A. Pick and D. B. Pennett did not bat.

Bowling: Munton 8–1–47–2; Brown 1–0–11–0; Reeve 7–0–46–0; Donald 8–0–32–0; N. M. K. Smith 6–1–27–1; Bell 8–0–53–2.

Warwickshire

N. V. Knight c Hindson b Cairns 11	P. A. Smith b Pick 8
N. M. K. Smith c Archer b Hindson .. 42	†K. J. Piper not out 16
D. P. Ostler c Dowman b Wileman 32	L-b 6, w 7, n-b 5 18
D. R. Brown not out 78	
R. G. Twose c Noon b Archer 4	1/52 2/88 3/107 (6 wkts, 37.3 overs) 222
*D. A. Reeve c Dowman b Pennett ... 13	4/112 5/176 6/196

A. A. Donald, T. A. Munton and M. A. V. Bell did not bat.

Bowling: Pick 8–1–33–1; Pennett 5–0–37–1; Cairns 7.3–0–50–1; Hindson 7–0–37–1; Wileman 6–0–39–1; Archer 4–0–20–1.

Umpires: G. I. Burgess and P. Willey.

At Northampton, August 27. NOTTINGHAMSHIRE beat NORTHAMPTONSHIRE by seven wickets.

NOTTINGHAMSHIRE v HAMPSHIRE

At Nottingham, September 3. Hampshire won by five wickets. Toss: Hampshire.
Cairns hit a 75-ball century, including six sixes, but the home total was not enough. Hampshire's chase began strongly with Laney and Morris posting 119 in 20 overs before Whitaker finished the job.

Nottinghamshire

P. R. Pollard b Stephenson 8	J. R. Wileman not out 2
*R. T. Robinson c Whitaker b Udal ... 39	L-b 4, w 4 8
P. Johnson c Stephenson b Maru 29	
C. L. Cairns c White b Connor 101	1/11 2/52 3/104 (5 wkts, 40 overs) 240
G. F. Archer c Aymes b Connor 53	4/219 5/240

†W. M. Noon, J. E. Hindson, R. A. Pick, U. Afzaal and D. B. Pennett did not bat.

Bowling: Stephenson 8–0–39–1; Connor 8–0–42–2; Maru 8–0–52–1; Streak 8–0–42–0; Udal 8–0–61–1.

Hampshire

R. S. M. Morris c Pick b Afzaal 64	†A. N. Aymes not out 5
J. S. Laney c Johnson b Afzaal 53	
M. Keech b Cairns 14	B 3, l-b 8, w 3, n-b 2 16
G. W. White run out 24	
P. R. Whitaker not out 41	1/119 2/133 3/158 (5 wkts, 38.5 overs) 244
*J. P. Stephenson c Johnson b Pennett . 27	4/171 5/214

S. D. Udal, H. H. Streak, R. J. Maru and C. A. Connor did not bat.

Bowling: Pennett 7–1–30–1; Pick 7–0–50–0; Hindson 5–0–34–0; Cairns 6.5–1–40–1; Wileman 8–0–43–0; Afzaal 5–0–36–2.

Umpires: K. E. Palmer and D. R. Shepherd.

At Cardiff, September 10. GLAMORGAN v NOTTINGHAMSHIRE. No result (abandoned).

At Chester-le-Street, September 17. NOTTINGHAMSHIRE beat DURHAM by two wickets.

SOMERSET

SOMERSET v GLOUCESTERSHIRE

At Taunton, May 7. Gloucestershire won by six wickets. Toss: Gloucestershire.

Somerset's total was easily overhauled, thanks to two significant Gloucestershire partnerships. Wright and Lynch gave the team a start and Alleyne and Symonds put on 72 in seven overs.

Somerset

M. N. Lathwell lbw b Smith	0	Mushtaq Ahmed c Ball b Smith 14
M. E. Trescothick b Srinath	27	J. I. D. Kerr b Srinath	6
P. D. Bowler b Ball	17	H. R. J. Trump not out 3
R. J. Harden c Russell b Sheeraz	46	L-b 8, w 7, n-b 4 19
*A. N. Hayhurst c Russell b Srinath	20	
G. D. Rose c Srinath b Ball	7	1/6 2/46 3/71 (9 wkts, 40 overs) 217
S. C. Ecclestone not out	45	4/116 5/122 6/151
†R. J. Turner c Wright b Sheeraz	13	7/177 8/199 9/213

Bowling: Smith 8–1–47–2; Sheeraz 8–0–37–2; Srinath 8–0–35–3; Alleyne 8–0–39–0; Ball 8–0–51–2.

Gloucestershire

A. J. Wright c Trump		M. W. Alleyne not out 35
b Mushtaq Ahmed	63	A. Symonds not out 42
T. H. C. Hancock c Ecclestone b Kerr	1	B 1, l-b 4, w 2, n-b 2 9
M. A. Lynch c Ecclestone		
b Mushtaq Ahmed	50	1/5 2/109 (4 wkts, 36 overs) 219
R. I. Dawson c Kerr b Trump	19	3/136 4/147

*†R. C. Russell, J. Srinath, M. C. J. Ball, K. P. Sheeraz and A. M. Smith did not bat.

Bowling: Rose 6–0–32–0; Kerr 4–0–27–1; Ecclestone 7–0–59–0; Hayhurst 4–0–20–0; Mushtaq Ahmed 7–0–49–2; Trump 8–0–27–1.

Umpires: A. A. Jones and G. Sharp.

At Northampton, May 14. SOMERSET beat NORTHAMPTONSHIRE by two wickets.

At Birmingham, May 28. SOMERSET lost to WARWICKSHIRE on scoring-rate.

SOMERSET v YORKSHIRE

At Taunton, June 4. Somerset won by three wickets. Toss: Yorkshire.

Rose's innings was decisive. Coming in at 64 for four, he hit an undefeated 60 from 56 balls, and put Somerset back on course. Yorkshire's innings was dominated by 80 from Bevan.

Yorkshire

*D. Byas c Turner b Ecclestone	39	D. Gough lbw b Hayhurst 1
M. P. Vaughan c Mushtaq Ahmed		P. J. Hartley not out 15
b Trump	3	
M. G. Bevan run out	80	L-b 11, w 2 13
C. White c Bowler b Mushtaq Ahmed	29	
†R. J. Blakey c Lathwell b Ecclestone	16	1/19 2/84 3/136 (6 wkts, 40 overs) 213
B. Parker not out	17	4/178 5/181 6/197

R. D. Stemp, A. P. Grayson and M. A. Robinson did not bat.

Bowling: Rose 8–0–35–0; Trump 8–0–41–1; Mushtaq Ahmed 8–1–23–1; Ecclestone 8–0–58–2; Batty 5–1–28–0; Hayhurst 3–0–17–1.

Somerset

M. N. Lathwell c Bevan b Hartley	19	†R. J. Turner b Gough		16
M. E. Trescothick lbw b Stemp	21	Mushtaq Ahmed not out		4
P. D. Bowler lbw b Robinson	7	B 2, l-b 3, w 2, n-b 2		9
R. J. Harden b Robinson	42			
*A. N. Hayhurst run out	2	1/34 2/50 3/60	(7 wkts, 38.2 overs)	215
G. D. Rose not out	60	4/64 5/120		
S. C. Ecclestone b Hartley	35	6/178 7/203		

J. D. Batty and H. R. J. Trump did not bat.

Bowling: Hartley 8-0-45-2; Gough 7-0-36-1; Stemp 8-0-29-1; Robinson 5-0-29-2; Grayson 6-0-33-0; White 3.2-0-25-0; Bevan 1-0-13-0.

Umpires: R. Julian and M. J. Kitchen.

At The Oval, June 11. SURREY v SOMERSET. No result (abandoned).

At Derby, June 18. SOMERSET beat DERBYSHIRE by 19 runs.

SOMERSET v SUSSEX

At Bath, June 25. Sussex won by 16 runs. Toss: Sussex.

Batsmen struggled on an unpredictable pitch. Somerset's response faltered once Harden and Parsons were parted, having added 89, and Lewry ran through the tail to finish with four for 29.

Sussex

K. Greenfield c Bowler b Rose	1	R. S. C. Martin-Jenkins		
*A. P. Wells c Trump b Ecclestone	48	b Mushtaq Ahmed		0
F. D. Stephenson lbw b Parsons	13	J. D. Lewry not out		7
N. J. Lenham b Parsons	4			
K. Newell lbw b Trump	35	B 1, l-b 5, w 14		20
†P. Moores not out	45			
D. R. Law c Bowler b Mushtaq Ahmed	6	1/13 2/30 3/37	(8 wkts, 40 overs)	197
I. D. K. Salisbury c Bowler		4/106 5/121 6/128		
b Mushtaq Ahmed	18	7/163 8/163		

E. S. H. Giddins did not bat.

Bowling: Rose 8-0-39-1; Parsons 8-0-26-2; Kerr 7-1-30-0; Trump 7-0-41-1; Mushtaq Ahmed 8-1-40-3; Ecclestone 2-0-15-1.

Somerset

M. N. Lathwell c Moores b Stephenson	11	Mushtaq Ahmed b Lewry		12
*P. D. Bowler b Lewry	9	J. I. D. Kerr b Lewry		1
P. C. L. Holloway c Law b Giddins	5	H. R. J. Trump not out		3
R. J. Harden c Moores b Stephenson	69	L-b 6, w 5		11
K. A. Parsons c Moores b Stephenson	46			
G. D. Rose st Moores b Salisbury	0	1/18 2/24 3/50	(39.1 overs)	181
S. C. Ecclestone run out	3	4/139 5/140 6/145		
†R. J. Turner b Lewry	11	7/158 8/172 9/176		

Bowling: Stephenson 8-1-37-3; Lewry 7.1-0-29-4; Giddins 8-0-50-1; Martin-Jenkins 8-2-26-0; Salisbury 8-0-33-1.

Umpires: M. J. Kitchen and R. A. White.

At Nottingham, July 2. SOMERSET lost to NOTTINGHAMSHIRE by six wickets.

SOMERSET v GLAMORGAN

At Taunton, July 16. No result. Toss: Glamorgan.

Caddick was making his first appearance for Somerset since May 8, but was prevented from bowling when rain ended play early in Glamorgan's innings.

Somerset

M. N. Lathwell lbw b Watkin	0	Mushtaq Ahmed c and b Barwick	2
P. D. Bowler c Morris b Watkin	65	A. R. Caddick not out	1
R. J. Harden b Anthony	10	H. R. J. Trump not out	2
K. A. Parsons c Maynard b Croft	29	L-b 2, w 10	12
G. D. Rose c Cottey b Watkin	22		
*A. N. Hayhurst run out	39	1/0 2/30 3/83	(9 wkts, 40 overs) 196
M. E. Trescothick c Metson b Watkin	3	4/134 5/142 6/148	
†P. C. L. Holloway lbw b Barwick	11	7/187 8/193 9/194	

Bowling: Watkin 8–0–42–4; Anthony 8–1–24–1; Barwick 8–1–31–2; Croft 8–0–51–1; Dale 8–0–46–0.

Glamorgan

S. P. James not out	8
*H. Morris not out	7
W 1	1

(no wkt, 3 overs) 16

M. P. Maynard, P. A. Cottey, A. Dale, R. D. B. Croft, H. A. G. Anthony, D. L. Hemp, †C. P. Metson, S. L. Watkin and S. R. Barwick did not bat.

Bowling: Rose 2–0–5–0; Parsons 1–0–11–0.

Umpires: T. E. Jesty and K. E. Palmer.

At Southend, July 23. SOMERSET lost to ESSEX by four wickets.

SOMERSET v LANCASHIRE

At Taunton, July 30. Lancashire won by 87 runs. Toss: Lancashire.

Lancashire were indebted for their impressive total to Fairbrother and Lloyd, who piled on an unbroken 179 for the third wicket in 19 overs. Somerset were never serious contenders, despite a defiant effort from Hayhurst against his former county.

Lancashire

J. E. R. Gallian st Holloway b Mushtaq Ahmed	28	G. D. Lloyd not out	88
S. P. Titchard c Parsons b Trump	37	B 8, l-b 5, w 10, n-b 6	29
N. H. Fairbrother not out	86	1/60 2/89	(2 wkts, 40 overs) 268

N. J. Speak, *Wasim Akram, †W. K. Hegg, I. D. Austin, G. Chapple, G. Yates and G. Keedy did not bat.

Bowling: Parsons 8–1–37–0; van Troost 5–1–39–0; Mushtaq Ahmed 8–2–17–1; Trump 8–0–52–1; Kerr 5–0–42–0; Ecclestone 4–0–56–0; Hayhurst 2–0–12–0.

Somerset

M. N. Lathwell run out	22	J. I. D. Kerr b Wasim Akram	8
M. E. Trescothick c and b Austin	3	H. R. J. Trump b Wasim Akram	5
P. D. Bowler c Fairbrother b Chapple	1	A. P. van Troost c and b Austin	9
K. A. Parsons c Hegg b Chapple	18	L-b 3, w 10, n-b 6	19
*A. N. Hayhurst not out	70		
S. C. Ecclestone st Hegg b Keedy	24	1/7 2/8 3/43	(36 overs) 181
†P. C. L. Holloway c Hegg b Gallian	2	4/48 5/109 6/117	
Mushtaq Ahmed c Hegg b Gallian	0	7/117 8/144 9/162	

Bowling: Chapple 8–1–27–2; Austin 6–0–22–2; Keedy 8–0–40–1; Wasim Akram 6–0–38–2; Yates 5–0–34–0; Gallian 3–0–17–2.

Umpires: N. T. Plews and A. G. T. Whitehead.

SOMERSET v KENT

At Taunton, August 13. Kent won by nine wickets. Toss: Somerset.

Somerset recovered bravely from 18 for five through Rose and Ecclestone, whose 106 for the sixth wicket was a county record for the competition. However, Ward and de Silva powered Kent to victory with an unbroken partnership of 169 after Fleming had fallen in the first over. It was a second successive Sunday League century for de Silva, who hit five sixes and 16 fours from 81 balls.

Somerset

M. N. Lathwell c Marsh b Ealham	8	†R. J. Turner not out	14
P. D. Bowler c Headley b Ealham	1	A. R. Caddick not out	22
R. J. Harden c Marsh b Igglesden	2	L-b 5, w 6, n-b 2	13
K. A. Parsons c Ward b Igglesden	4		
*A. N. Hayhurst c Marsh b Ealham	2	1/5 2/12 3/16	(7 wkts, 40 overs) 166
G. D. Rose c McCague b Ealham	59	4/18 5/18	
S. C. Ecclestone b Fleming	41	6/124 7/129	

Mushtaq Ahmed and H. R. J. Trump did not bat.

Bowling: Igglesden 8–4–12–2; Ealham 8–2–21–4; Headley 8–0–34–0; McCague 8–0–50–0; Fleming 8–0–44–1.

Kent

T. R. Ward not out	52
M. V. Fleming c Harden b Rose	0
P. A. de Silva not out	105
W 7, n-b 6	13
1/1	(1 wkt, 29.1 overs) 170

G. R. Cowdrey, M. A. Ealham, N. J. Llong, M. J. Walker, *†S. A. Marsh, M. J. McCague, D. W. Headley and A. P. Igglesden did not bat.

Bowling: Rose 8–0–52–1; Caddick 8–0–30–0; Ecclestone 2–0–17–0; Mushtaq Ahmed 6.1–0–61–0; Trump 5–0–10–0.

Umpires: B. Dudleston and M. J. Kitchen.

At Chester-le-Street, August 20. SOMERSET beat DURHAM by five wickets.

SOMERSET v LEICESTERSHIRE

At Weston-super-Mare, August 27. Somerset won by four wickets. Toss: Somerset.

A maiden one-day century from Smith, whose 115 came off 95 balls, enabled Leicestershire to rally strongly from seven for three. But he still finished on the losing side when Somerset reached their target with two deliveries to spare, Bowler and Holloway having set up the win with 124 for the third wicket.

Leicestershire

G. I. Macmillan c Bowler b Kerr	5	G. J. Parsons not out		26
D. L. Maddy c Harden b Caddick	0	T. J. Mason not out		17
W. J. Cronje c Turner b Kerr	0	L-b 3, w 2		5
*J. J. Whitaker c and b Parsons	22			
B. F. Smith c sub b Trump	115	1/5 2/5 3/7	(7 wkts, 40 overs)	232
J. M. Dakin c Harden b Parsons	13	4/71 5/107		
†P. A. Nixon run out	29	6/183 7/191		

A. R. K. Pierson and A. D. Mullally did not bat.

Bowling: Caddick 4-0-11-1; Kerr 8-1-44-2; Rose 8-0-64-0; Parsons 4-0-16-2; Trump 8-0-46-1; Mushtaq Ahmed 8-0-48-0.

Somerset

M. N. Lathwell b Mullally	29	Mushtaq Ahmed not out		22
*P. D. Bowler c Nixon b Dakin	76	†R. J. Turner not out		4
R. J. Harden c Parsons b Mullally	0	B 4, l-b 12, w 4, n-b 2		22
P. C. L. Holloway c Whitaker b Dakin	66			
G. D. Rose b Dakin	0	1/54 2/54 3/178	(6 wkts, 39.4 overs)	236
K. A. Parsons c Pierson b Parsons	17	4/188 5/193 6/227		

A. R. Caddick, J. I. D. Kerr and H. R. J. Trump did not bat.

Bowling: Mullally 8-0-44-2; Parsons 7.4-0-49-1; Cronje 8-1-23-0; Mason 5-0-36-0; Maddy 7-0-45-0; Dakin 4-0-23-3.

Umpires: J. C. Balderstone and K. E. Palmer.

At Worcester, September 3. SOMERSET lost to WORCESTERSHIRE by 68 runs.

At Southampton, September 10. HAMPSHIRE v SOMERSET. No result (abandoned).

SOMERSET v MIDDLESEX

At Taunton, September 17. Middlesex won by seven wickets. Toss: Somerset. First-team debut: D. C. Nash.

Somerset were dismissed cheaply after rain had initially reduced the match to 37 overs a side. A further shower then left Middlesex to score 111 in 31 overs, a task they accomplished with ten to spare, thus avoiding the wooden spoon.

Somerset

M. N. Lathwell lbw b D. J. Nash	1	†R. J. Turner c Ramprakash b Fraser		19
M. E. Trescothick c Brown b Follett	5	J. I. D. Kerr c Gatting b Fraser		6
P. C. L. Holloway b Follett	3	H. R. J. Trump not out		6
R. J. Harden c D. C. Nash b D. J. Nash	4			
K. A. Parsons c D. C. Nash b Fraser	25	B 1, l-b 5, w 12, n-b 4		22
G. D. Rose c Weekes b Rashid	28			
Mushtaq Ahmed st D. C. Nash b Rashid	5	1/1 2/14 3/19	(36.4 overs)	132
*A. N. Hayhurst c Follett b Weekes	8	4/20 5/72 6/86		
		7/89 8/114 9/116		

Bowling: Follett 7-1-27-2; D. J. Nash 6-0-13-2; Weekes 8-1-21-1; Rashid 8-1-38-2; Fraser 7.4-0-27-3.

Middlesex

P. N. Weekes c Parsons b Kerr	23	M. R. Ramprakash not out	23
K. R. Brown c Turner b Rose	12	L-b 6, w 7	13
*J. D. Carr c Trump b Rose	3		
J. C. Pooley not out	40	1/26 2/34 3/65 (3 wkts, 21 overs)	114

M. W. Gatting, D. J. Nash, †D. C. Nash, D. Follett, A. R. C. Fraser and U. B. A. Rashid did not bat.

Bowling: Rose 7–1–28–2; Mushtaq Ahmed 6–0–20–0; Trump 4–0–16–0; Kerr 4–0–44–1.

Umpires: M. J. Kitchen and P. B. Wight.

SURREY

At Birmingham, May 7. SURREY beat WARWICKSHIRE by 47 runs.

SURREY v DURHAM

At The Oval, May 14. Surrey won by seven wickets. Toss: Durham.

Surrey ran out comfortable winners; after their bowlers had contained Durham, their innings was given impetus by Brown, who blitzed the Durham attack with a 39-ball half-century.

Durham

*M. A. Roseberry b Pigott	8	J. Boiling not out	21
W. Larkins b Pigott	10	A. Walker not out	14
M. Prabhakar c Smith b Butcher	28		
J. E. Morris c Butcher b Kenlock	19		
J. A. Daley b Butcher	14	L-b 9, w 11, n-b 2	22
M. Saxelby run out	17		
S. D. Birbeck c Stewart b Pigott	23	1/11 2/22 3/59 (8 wkts, 40 overs)	189
†D. G. C. Ligertwood c Stewart		4/79 5/99 6/115	
b M. P. Bicknell	13	7/151 8/153	

M. M. Betts did not bat.

Bowling: M. P. Bicknell 8–0–29–1; Pigott 8–1–34–3; Butcher 8–0–35–2; Kenlock 5–0–26–1; Hollioake 8–0–43–0; Smith 3–0–13–0.

Surrey

D. J. Bicknell c Ligertwood b Betts	19	D. M. Ward not out	32
A. D. Brown c Betts b Boiling	79	L-b 3, w 4	7
*†A. J. Stewart not out	44		
G. P. Thorpe c Larkins b Boiling	9	1/56 2/122 3/137 (3 wkts, 35.1 overs)	190

A. J. Hollioake, A. W. Smith, M. A. Butcher, M. P. Bicknell, A. C. S. Pigott and S. G. Kenlock did not bat.

Bowling: Prabhakar 7–1–22–0; Walker 8–0–44–0; Betts 7.1–0–52–1; Birbeck 5–0–31–0; Boiling 8–0–38–2.

Umpires: J. H. Harris and V. A. Holder.

At Northampton, May 21. SURREY beat NORTHAMPTONSHIRE by 14 runs.

At Worcester, June 4. SURREY lost to WORCESTERSHIRE by nine wickets.

SURREY v SOMERSET

At The Oval, June 11. No result (abandoned).

At Horsham, June 18. SURREY lost to SUSSEX by ten runs.

SURREY v GLAMORGAN

At The Oval, June 25. Glamorgan won by nine wickets. Toss: Glamorgan.

The League leaders inflicted a crushing defeat on Surrey, whose batting fell away after Brown and Ratcliffe had scored 38 in the first five overs. James set the tone for Glamorgan's reply and they won with nearly half their overs remaining.

Surrey

J. D. Ratcliffe c Hemp b Watkin	19	*A. C. S. Pigott not out	8
A. D. Brown b Watkin	21	S. G. Kenlock b Lefebvre	0
M. A. Butcher lbw b Croft	9	C. G. Rackemann c Lefebvre b Barwick	0
A. J. Hollioake c Morris b Watkin	9	L-b 4, w 6	10
N. Shahid lbw b Watkin	0		
D. M. Ward b Lefebvre	37	1/38 2/47 3/59	(38.5 overs) 152
†G. J. Kersey lbw b Croft	14	4/59 5/73 6/93	
M. P. Bicknell run out	25	7/137 8/147 9/151	

Bowling: Lefebvre 7–0–34–2; Watkin 8–0–40–4; Barwick 7.5–1–13–1; Croft 8–0–22–2; Anthony 7–0–25–0; Cottey 1–0–14–0.

Glamorgan

S. P. James not out	80
*H. Morris lbw b Butcher	14
M. P. Maynard not out	42
L-b 11, w 5, n-b 2	18

1/74   (1 wkt, 20.1 overs) 154

P. A. Cottey, D. L. Hemp, R. D. B. Croft, H. A. G. Anthony, R. P. Lefebvre, †C. P. Metson, S. L. Watkin and S. R. Barwick did not bat.

Bowling: Rackemann 3–0–23–0; Bicknell 4–0–21–0; Pigott 2–0–23–0; Butcher 3–0–24–1; Hollioake 5.1–0–42–0; Kenlock 3–0–10–0.

Umpires: J. D. Bond and J. H. Hampshire.

At Lord's, July 2. MIDDLESEX v SURREY. No result.

SURREY v ESSEX

At The Oval, July 9. Essex won by 61 runs. Toss: Surrey.

Any hopes Surrey may have had of passing Essex's substantial total were wiped out by Ilott, in a destructive spell of four wickets in 13 balls.

Essex

*P. J. Prichard c Bicknell b Hollioake	78	M. C. Ilott run out	0
M. E. Waugh b Kersey b Hollioake	48	J. J. B. Lewis not out	0
N. Hussain not out	68	B 1, l-b 6, w 5	12
G. A. Gooch b Kenlock	17		
R. C. Irani b Benjamin	10	1/123 2/144 3/186	(6 wkts, 38 overs) 271
D. D. J. Robinson c Brown b Hollioake	38	4/202 5/266 6/270	

†R. J. Rollins, P. M. Such and D. M. Cousins did not bat.

Bowling: Benjamin 8–0–71–1; Tudor 3–0–29–0; Rackemann 8–0–35–0; Kenlock 8–0–46–1; Hollioake 8–0–58–3; Butcher 3–0–25–0.

Surrey

D. J. Bicknell run out	11	J. E. Benjamin c Rollins b Ilott	2
A. D. Brown b Irani	48	S. G. Kenlock c Robinson b Cousins	9
M. A. Butcher c Ilott b Such	5	C. G. Rackemann not out	15
D. M. Ward c Rollins b Waugh	19	B 1, l-b 7, w 6, n-b 2	16
N. Shahid c Such b Ilott	34		
*A. J. Hollioake c and b Ilott	22	1/40 2/70 3/70 (9 wkts, 38 overs)	210
†G. J. Kersey c Rollins b Ilott	0	4/105 5/146 6/147	
A. J. Tudor not out	29	7/152 8/159 9/183	

Bowling: Cousins 8–0–42–1; Ilott 8–1–30–4; Irani 8–1–44–1; Such 5–0–26–1; Waugh 8–0–52–1; Gooch 1–0–8–0.

Umpires: K. J. Lyons and R. Palmer.

SURREY v GLOUCESTERSHIRE

At The Oval, July 16. Surrey won by 19 runs. Toss: Gloucestershire.

Bicknell joined forces with Thorpe in a county second-wicket record for the competition of 203 in 32 overs. Thorpe hit six sixes. The second half of Surrey's innings yielded 179 runs, and at 90 for five in reply Gloucestershire looked out of it. They were revived by Russell, but victory was beyond them.

Surrey

D. J. Bicknell not out	102
A. D. Brown lbw b Smith	1
G. P. Thorpe c Windows b Williams	112
*A. J. Hollioake not out	32
L-b 6, w 8, n-b 4	18

1/4 2/207 (2 wkts, 40 overs) 265

A. W. Smith, N. Shahid, M. A. Butcher, †G. J. Kersey, S. G. Kenlock, J. E. Benjamin and C. G. Rackemann did not bat.

Bowling: Smith 8–2–24–1; Sheeraz 7–0–58–0; Williams 8–0–69–1; Alleyne 8–0–46–0; Ball 6–1–39–0; Windows 3–0–23–0.

Gloucestershire

A. J. Wright c Smith b Kenlock	17	M. C. J. Ball run out	4
M. G. N. Windows c Hollioake b Smith	13	K. P. Sheeraz not out	14
M. W. Alleyne c Kersey b Rackemann	17		
M. A. Lynch c Brown b Smith	17	B 6, l-b 7, w 7, n-b 8	28
A. Symonds lbw b Smith	5		
R. I. Dawson c Smith b Benjamin	45	1/35 2/58 3/58 (8 wkts, 40 overs)	246
*†R. C. Russell not out	76	4/69 5/90 6/170	
R. C. Williams b Kenlock	10	7/187 8/195	

A. M. Smith did not bat.

Bowling: Benjamin 8–0–35–1; Kenlock 8–0–51–2; Smith 8–0–36–3; Rackemann 8–0–41–1; Butcher 4–0–30–0; Hollioake 3–0–26–0; Thorpe 1–0–14–0.

Umpires: A. A. Jones and P. B. Wight.

SURREY v NOTTINGHAMSHIRE

At Guildford, July 23. Surrey won by one run. Toss: Nottinghamshire.

Hollioake, Surrey's acting-captain, denied Nottinghamshire the 11 runs they needed from his final over, although Wileman hit the last ball for six. Surrey's innings was given substance by Darren Bicknell and Thorpe, who shared a second successive century partnership in the competition. Pollard and Robinson hit back by putting on 111, and Cairns set up the finale with 69 from 39 balls.

Surrey

D. J. Bicknell c Wileman b Archer	58	M. P. Bicknell b Cairns	8
A. D. Brown c Robinson b Pick	32	S. G. Kenlock not out	3
G. P. Thorpe c Pollard b Archer	66		
*A. J. Hollioake c Noon b Wileman	13	B 2, l-b 2, w 8, n-b 2	14
N. Shahid not out	46		
A. W. Smith c Cairns b Wileman	19	1/45 2/157 3/170 (8 wkts, 40 overs) 268
†G. J. Kersey c Robinson b Pennett	4	4/174 5/205 6/220
M. A. Butcher b Pennett	5	7/230 8/247

C. G. Rackemann did not bat.

Bowling: Pick 8–0–44–1; Pennett 8–1–42–2; Hindson 3–0–31–0; Chapman 7–0–52–0; Cairns 6–0–44–1; Wileman 6–0–35–2; Archer 2–0–16–2.

Nottinghamshire

P. R. Pollard c Hollioake b Rackemann	43	†W. M. Noon run out	2
*R. T. Robinson b Hollioake	70	R. A. Pick not out	7
P. Johnson c Brown b Butcher	25	L-b 8, w 10, n-b 2	20
C. L. Cairns c Brown b Hollioake	69		
G. F. Archer lbw b Rackemann	1	1/111 2/142 3/166 (6 wkts, 40 overs) 267
J. R. Wileman not out	30	4/169 5/249 6/252

D. B. Pennett, J. E. Hindson and R. J. Chapman did not bat.

Bowling: M. P. Bicknell 8–0–46–0; Kenlock 8–0–59–0; Smith 2–0–14–0; Butcher 6–0–48–1; Hollioake 8–0–55–2; Rackemann 8–0–37–2.

Umpires: V. A. Holder and T. E. Jesty.

At Leicester, July 30. SURREY lost to LEICESTERSHIRE by five wickets.

At Canterbury, August 6. SURREY lost to KENT by 55 runs.

SURREY v YORKSHIRE

At The Oval, August 13. Surrey won by 12 runs. Toss: Surrey.

Surrey only just managed to defend an imposing total, which was founded on an opening stand of 184 between Bicknell and Brown, who made a brilliant 74-ball century. Yorkshire also galloped towards 300 but Surrey kept their nerve to win.

Surrey

D. J. Bicknell b Kettleborough	68	†G. J. Kersey lbw b Robinson	1
A. D. Brown c Vaughan b Bevan	100	M. A. Butcher not out	25
J. D. Ratcliffe lbw b Silverwood	31	L-b 12, w 9	21
*A. J. Hollioake b Kettleborough	8		
N. Shahid c Metcalfe b Silverwood	25	1/184 2/188 3/200 (6 wkts, 40 overs) 308
A. W. Smith not out	29	4/248 5/262 6/275

M. P. Bicknell, C. G. Rackemann and R. W. Nowell did not bat.

Bowling: Hamilton 3–0–34–0; Silverwood 8–1–50–2; Milburn 3–0–29–0; Robinson 7–0–52–1; Grayson 5–0–33–0; Bevan 8–0–55–1; Kettleborough 6–0–43–2.

Yorkshire

*D. Byas b Smith	59	G. M. Hamilton b Hollioake	1
M. P. Vaughan run out	33	S. M. Milburn not out	13
†R. J. Blakey lbw b Ratcliffe	36	C. E. W. Silverwood not out	3
M. G. Bevan c Shahid b M. P. Bicknell	60	L-b 11, w 3, n-b 10	24
A. A. Metcalfe c Brown b Butcher	50		
A. P. Grayson b Hollioake	10	1/72 2/119 3/146 (8 wkts, 40 overs) 296
R. A. Kettleborough c Nowell		4/249 5/263 6/267
b Hollioake	7	7/280 8/285

M. A. Robinson did not bat.

Bowling: M. P. Bicknell 8–0–51–1; Butcher 8–0–62–1; Rackemann 8–0–51–0; Smith 6–0–44–1; Hollioake 8–0–62–3; Ratcliffe 2–0–15–1.

Umpires: P. B. Wight and P. Willey.

At Derby, August 27. SURREY lost to DERBYSHIRE by three wickets.

SURREY v LANCASHIRE

At The Oval, September 3. Lancashire won by six wickets. Toss: Surrey.
In his last appearance for Lancashire before returning to Pakistan for the Test series against Sri Lanka, Wasim Akram took his season's tally of League wickets to a county record 29. He pegged Surrey back after a bright start and was also there at the end, partnering Lloyd as Lancashire won with 15 balls to spare.

Surrey

D. J. Bicknell c Hegg b Watkinson	33	M. P. Bicknell not out	18
A. D. Brown b Austin	12	J. E. Benjamin b Austin	4
N. Shahid c Hegg b Wasim Akram	18	C. G. Rackemann not out	4
*G. P. Thorpe c Hegg b Gallian	25	L-b 2, w 13, n-b 4	19
M. A. Butcher b Watkinson	15		
J. D. Ratcliffe c and b Gallian	2	1/17 2/58 3/92 (9 wkts, 40 overs) 189
A. W. Smith b Wasim Akram	34	4/116 5/120 6/135
†N. F. Sargeant c and b Wasim Akram	5	7/161 8/165 9/176

Bowling: Austin 8–1–38–2; Martin 7–0–26–0; Wasim Akram 8–1–30–3; Green 5–0–24–0; Watkinson 8–0–52–2; Gallian 4–1–17–2.

Lancashire

M. A. Atherton c Shahid b Benjamin	13	Wasim Akram not out	11
J. E. R. Gallian run out	62		
J. P. Crawley run out	40	B 2, l-b 3, w 6, n-b 8	19
N. H. Fairbrother c Shahid			
b D. J. Bicknell	7	1/23 2/99 (4 wkts, 37.3 overs) 190
G. D. Lloyd not out	38	3/116 4/156

*M. Watkinson, †W. K. Hegg, I. D. Austin, R. J. Green and P. J. Martin did not bat.
Bowling: M. P. Bicknell 7–0–23–0; Benjamin 8–0–39–1; Smith 8–0–46–0; Rackemann 8–0–27–0; D. J. Bicknell 4–0–28–1; Butcher 2.3–0–22–0.

Umpires: J. H. Harris and B. J. Meyer.

SURREY v HAMPSHIRE

At The Oval, September 17. Surrey won by six wickets. Toss: Surrey.
Hampshire were condemned to the wooden spoon after Surrey reached their rain-revised target of 108 in 20 overs. Shahid's 37-ball innings secured the win.

Hampshire

J. S. Laney c Sargeant b M. P. Bicknell	12	S. D. Udal not out	9
R. S. M. Morris c Sargeant b Benjamin	24	H. H. Streak not out	1
M. Keech run out	70	L-b 7, n-b 8	15
G. W. White c Sargeant b Holioake	30		
P. R. Whitaker b Kenlock	4	1/30 2/52 3/142 (6 wkts, 31 overs) 166
*J. P. Stephenson b Holioake	1	4/147 5/148 6/165

†A. N. Aymes, K. D. James and C. A. Connor did not bat.

Bowling: M. P. Bicknell 6–1–25–1; Benjamin 8–0–35–1; Rackemann 8–0–45–0; Kenlock 6–0–39–1; Holioake 3–0–15–2.

Surrey

D. J. Bicknell run out	20	J. D. Ratcliffe not out	7
A. D. Brown c Morris b Streak	0	B 1, l-b 6, w 2, n-b 2	11
*A. J. Holioake c Aymes b Streak	17		
D. M. Ward b Streak	5	1/2 2/31 (4 wkts, 19 overs) 109
N. Shahid not out	49	3/37 4/55

†N. F. Sargeant, M. P. Bicknell, S. G. Kenlock, J. E. Benjamin and C. G. Rackemann did not bat.

Bowling: Streak 8–0–41–3; Connor 7–0–41–0; James 2–0–13–0; Stephenson 2–1–7–0.

Umpires: D. J. Constant and A. G. T. Whitehead.

SUSSEX

SUSSEX v KENT

At Hove, May 7. Kent won by seven runs. Toss: Sussex. First-team debut: R. J. Kirtley.

Kent, given a 136-run start by Ward and Benson, found their total further boosted by 27 wides – six of them in a 13-ball opening over from Giddins.

Kent

T. R. Ward b Giddins	70	†S. A. Marsh b Kirtley	5
*M. R. Benson b Salisbury	53	M. J. McCague not out	7
P. A. de Silva c Athey b North	1	D. W. Headley not out	6
M. J. Walker c and b Salisbury	1	L-b 12, w 27, n-b 4	43
M. V. Fleming c and b Salisbury	0		
G. R. Cowdrey c Hall b Greenfield	24	1/136 2/137 3/140 (9 wkts, 40 overs) 225
M. A. Ealham run out	4	4/140 5/184 6/187
N. J. Llong c Moores b Stephenson	11	7/200 8/211 9/211

Bowling: Stephenson 8–2–22–1; Giddins 7–0–56–1; North 7–1–39–1; Kirtley 8–0–49–1; Salisbury 8–0–34–3; Greenfield 2–0–13–1.

Sussex

C. W. J. Athey c Marsh b Ealham	40	J. A. North not out	3
J. W. Hall c Ward b Headley	8		
K. Newell not out	76	L-b 4, w 5, n-b 2	11
*A. P. Wells c Fleming b Ealham	14		
K. Greenfield c Benson b Fleming	44	1/24 2/84 3/106 (5 wkts, 40 overs) 218
F. D. Stephenson run out	22	4/182 5/213

†P. Moores, I. D. K. Salisbury, R. J. Kirtley and E. S. H. Giddins did not bat.

Bowling: Headley 8–0–49–1; Ealham 8–2–28–2; de Silva 8–1–44–0; McCague 8–1–42–0; Fleming 8–0–51–1.

Umpires: G. I. Burgess and R. A. White.

At Swansea, May 14. SUSSEX lost to GLAMORGAN by nine wickets.

SUSSEX v ESSEX

At Hove, May 21. Essex won by 13 runs. Toss: Essex.

Essex recovered from 134 for six, thanks to a late flourish from Ilott and Robinson, who added 57 in eight overs. Such put Sussex in trouble with three important wickets.

Essex

*P. J. Prichard c Moores b Giddins ...	5	M. C. Ilott not out	56
M. E. Waugh b Salisbury	21	P. M. Such run out	6
N. Hussain b Salisbury	48	R. M. Pearson not out	4
G. A. Gooch b Jarvis	26	B 1, l-b 4, w 7, n-b 2	14
R. C. Irani b Jarvis	4		
D. D. J. Robinson c Salisbury		(8 wkts, 40 overs) 217	
b Stephenson .	29	1/13 2/39 3/104	
†R. J. Rollins b Jarvis	4	4/113 5/119 6/134	
		7/191 8/208	

D. M. Cousins did not bat.

Bowling: Giddins 8–0–46–1; Newell 3–0–15–0; Stephenson 8–1–46–1; Salisbury 8–0–47–2; Greenfield 1–0–5–0; Jarvis 8–0–31–3; North 4–0–22–0.

Sussex

C. W. J. Athey c Robinson b Pearson..	12	I. D. K. Salisbury b Waugh	23
J. W. Hall lbw b Irani	47	P. W. Jarvis not out	13
J. A. North lbw b Irani.............	16	E. S. H. Giddins not out...........	0
*A. P. Wells c Waugh b Such	19	L-b 5, w 16	21
K. Greenfield run out	32		
F. D. Stephenson c Prichard b Such ...	6	1/44 2/85 3/92 (9 wkts, 40 overs) 204	
†P. Moores lbw b Such	1	4/123 5/139 6/143	
K. Newell c Robinson b Waugh	14	7/150 8/184 9/204	

Bowling: Ilott 8–0–40–0; Cousins 8–0–29–0; Pearson 4–0–27–1; Such 8–1–41–3; Irani 8–0–29–2; Waugh 4–0–33–2.

Umpires: J. H. Harris and T. E. Jesty.

At Portsmouth, May 28. SUSSEX beat HAMPSHIRE by eight runs.

SUSSEX v GLOUCESTERSHIRE

At Hove, June 4. Sussex won by six wickets. Toss: Sussex.

After rain had restricted the match to 21 overs a side, Gloucestershire made rapid progress, with Lynch and Symonds boosting the total by 80 in ten overs. But Sussex had the advantage of being able to pace their reply and won comfortably.

Gloucestershire

A. J. Wright b Lewry	13	G. D. Hodgson not out	11
M. A. Lynch st Moores b Salisbury	58	L-b 4, w 3, n-b 2	9
A. Symonds lbw b Jarvis	37		
R. I. Dawson c Lewry b Salisbury	5	1/21 2/101 (4 wkts, 21 overs) 166	
M. W. Alleyne not out	33	3/119 4/120	

*†R. C. Russell, J. Srinath, M. C. J. Ball, K. E. Cooper and A. M. Smith did not bat.

Bowling: Stephenson 4–0–28–0; Lewry 4–0–21–1; Giddins 5–0–43–0; Jarvis 4–0–36–1; Salisbury 4–0–34–2.

Sussex

K. Greenfield run out	0	†P. Moores not out	24
J. A. North b Srinath	6	B 2, l-b 2, w 4, n-b 2	10
F. D. Stephenson b Srinath	54		
*A. P. Wells not out	70	1/7 2/23	(4 wkts, 19.3 overs) 168
N. J. Lenham run out	4	3/107 4/120	

P. W. Jarvis, I. D. K. Salisbury, J. D. Lewry, E. S. H. Giddins and N. C. Phillips did not bat.

Bowling: Srinath 4.3–0–33–2; Smith 3–0–14–0; Cooper 4–0–31–0; Alleyne 4–0–38–0; Ball 4–0–48–0.

Umpires: K. J. Lyons and N. T. Plews.

At Birmingham, June 11. SUSSEX lost to WARWICKSHIRE by 14 runs.

SUSSEX v SURREY

At Horsham, June 18. Sussex won by ten runs. Toss: Surrey. First-team debut: R. S. C. Martin-Jenkins.

Extras proved to be top scorer in Sussex's total, despite good scoring from Law and Moores. Surrey rallied from a bad start but Salisbury destroyed the tail to clinch victory for Sussex.

Sussex

K. Greenfield run out	26	I. D. K. Salisbury c Pigott b Rackemann	0
J. W. Hall c Stewart b Hollioake	18	R. S. C. Martin-Jenkins not out	0
F. D. Stephenson c Hollioake b Rackemann	35	B 5, l-b 21, w 12, n-b 10	48
*A. P. Wells run out	0		
K. Newell b Pigott	31	1/65 2/75 3/80	(7 wkts, 37 overs) 222
D. R. Law not out	39	4/134 5/142	
†P. Moores c Thorpe b Rackemann	25	6/221 7/221	

J. D. Lewry and E. S. H. Giddins did not bat.

Bowling: Rackemann 8–0–36–3; Benjamin 8–0–31–0; Pigott 7–0–42–1; Kenlock 8–0–46–0; Hollioake 5–0–25–1; Butcher 1–0–16–0.

Surrey

M. A. Butcher c Salisbury b Stephenson	4	S. G. Kenlock b Salisbury	0
A. D. Brown c Law b Giddins	20	J. E. Benjamin c Lewry b Salisbury	13
*†A. J. Stewart c Greenfield b Martin-Jenkins	17	C. G. Rackemann run out	12
G. P. Thorpe lbw b Lewry	53	L-b 10, w 19, n-b 6	35
D. M. Ward lbw b Giddins	2		
A. J. Hollioake c Moores b Salisbury	36	1/18 2/54 3/62	(36.4 overs) 212
A. W. Smith c Law b Salisbury	1	4/65 5/154 6/162	
A. C. S. Pigott not out	19	7/164 8/164 9/186	

Bowling: Stephenson 8–0–45–1; Lewry 7–0–41–1; Martin-Jenkins 7–0–35–1; Giddins 7.4–0–42–2; Salisbury 7–0–39–4.

Umpires: B. Leadbeater and A. G. T. Whitehead.

At Bath, June 25. SUSSEX beat SOMERSET by 16 runs.

SUSSEX v NOTTINGHAMSHIRE

At Arundel, July 9. Sussex won by 12 runs. Toss: Sussex.

Sussex's fifth win in six matches was achieved through a maiden Sunday League century by Greenfield and a solid innings from Athey, who passed 7,000 runs in the competition. Archer and Wileman fought hard to get Nottinghamshire close, but 16 off Lewry's last over proved too great a task.

Sussex

K. Greenfield b Afzaal	102	D. R. Law run out	9
*A. P. Wells c and b Cairns	10		
F. D. Stephenson c Robinson b Cairns	5	B 1, l-b 6, w 12, n-b 2	21
C. W. J. Athey c Archer b Afzaal	52		
†P. Moores not out	39	1/35 2/43 3/156　(6 wkts, 40 overs)	241
K. Newell b Cairns	3	4/185 5/193 6/241	

I. D. K. Salisbury, P. W. Jarvis, R. S. C. Martin-Jenkins and J. D. Lewry did not bat.

Bowling: Hart 4–0–39–0; Pick 8–0–45–0; Cairns 8–1–53–3; Hindson 8–1–35–0; Afzaal 8–0–41–2; Wileman 4–0–21–0.

Nottinghamshire

P. R. Pollard b Salisbury	30	†W. M. Noon c Stephenson b Lewry	34
*R. T. Robinson c Greenfield b Jarvis	24	U. Afzaal not out	0
P. Johnson lbw b Martin-Jenkins	23	L-b 4, w 5, n-b 4	13
C. L. Cairns c Newell b Salisbury	8		
G. F. Archer run out	46	1/55 2/61 3/88　(6 wkts, 40 overs)	229
J. R. Wileman not out	51	4/102 5/163 6/226	

J. E. Hindson, R. A. Pick and J. P. Hart did not bat.

Bowling: Stephenson 8–0–50–0; Lewry 6–0–44–1; Martin-Jenkins 8–0–36–1; Jarvis 7–0–34–1; Salisbury 8–1–39–2; Greenfield 3–0–22–0.

Umpires: J. H. Harris and R. Julian.

At Derby, July 16. DERBYSHIRE v SUSSEX. No result.

SUSSEX v LEICESTERSHIRE

At Hove, July 23. Sussex won by seven wickets. Toss: Sussex.

Athey and Moores were the architects of victory, adding an unbeaten 152 in 19 overs as Sussex won with 28 balls to spare. Moores batted brilliantly, making his highest one-day score off 58 deliveries with two sixes and 13 fours. Leicestershire had earlier recovered from the depths of 40 for four, thanks to a partnership of 136 in 16 overs between Nixon and Maddy, a sixth-wicket record for any team in the competition.

Leicestershire

V. J. Wells b Giddins	2	A. D. Mullally not out	10
*N. E. Briers b Stephenson	1	G. J. Parsons not out	4
W. J. Cronje c Newell b Stephenson	13		
J. M. Dakin run out	21	B 1, l-b 1, w 5, n-b 2	9
B. F. Smith c Stephenson b Salisbury	35		
†P. A. Nixon lbw b Jarvis	84	1/4 2/6 3/39　(8 wkts, 40 overs)	262
D. L. Maddy c Law b Jarvis	69	4/40 5/89 6/225	
I. J. Sutcliffe run out	14	7/240 8/257	

T. J. Mason did not bat.

Bowling: Giddins 8–0–49–1; Stephenson 8–0–35–2; Martin-Jenkins 8–1–54–0; Jarvis 8–0–67–2; Salisbury 7–0–47–1; Newell 1–0–8–0.

Sussex

K. Greenfield c Sutcliffe b Wells 56	†P. Moores not out 89	
*A. P. Wells c Sutcliffe b Parsons 2	B 1, l-b 2, w 2 5	
F. D. Stephenson b Wells 50		
C. W. J. Athey not out 61	1/4 2/108 3/111 (3 wkts, 35.2 overs) 263	

K. Newell, D. R. Law, I. D. K. Salisbury, P. W. Jarvis, R. S. C. Martin-Jenkins and E. S. H. Giddins did not bat.

Bowling: Mullally 5–0–46–0; Parsons 6–0–46–1; Maddy 3–0–33–0; Cronje 8–0–37–0; Wells 8–0–45–2; Mason 4–0–34–0; Dakin 1.2–0–19–0.

Umpires: J. H. Hampshire and P. B. Wight.

At Lord's, July 30. SUSSEX beat MIDDLESEX by seven wickets.

At Manchester, August 6. SUSSEX lost to LANCASHIRE by 22 runs.

SUSSEX v WORCESTERSHIRE

At Eastbourne, August 20. Worcestershire won by 80 runs. Toss: Worcestershire.

Weston and Newport starred in Worcestershire's straightforward victory. Weston's 80 from 92 balls led a recovery from 26 for four and Newport then made early inroads to leave Sussex in trouble. Hick tidied up with three late wickets in 15 balls.

Worcestershire

*T. M. Moody c Wells b Stephenson . . . 8	†S. J. Rhodes not out 31	
T. S. Curtis c Stephenson b Giddins . . . 9	P. J. Newport run out 0	
G. A. Hick c Greenfield b Jarvis 3	P. Mirza not out 0	
G. R. Haynes c Moores b Salisbury . . . 34	L-b 8, w 10, n-b 2 20	
D. A. Leatherdale c Moores b Jarvis . . . 0		
W. P. C. Weston c Greenfield b Jarvis . 80	1/12 2/20 3/26 (9 wkts, 40 overs) 197	
V. S. Solanki st Moores b Greenfield . . 2	4/26 5/93 6/108	
S. R. Lampitt c Moores b Stephenson . . 10	7/136 8/194 9/195	

Bowling: Giddins 8–2–48–1; Stephenson 8–0–31–2; Jarvis 8–1–33–3; Martin-Jenkins 5–0–27–0; Salisbury 7–0–36–1; Greenfield 4–0–14–1.

Sussex

N. J. Lenham c Hick b Newport 5	P. W. Jarvis c Haynes b Mirza 1	
K. Greenfield c Rhodes b Lampitt 38	R. S. C. Martin-Jenkins c Curtis b Hick 1	
F. D. Stephenson lbw b Newport 4	E. S. H. Giddins c Weston b Hick 0	
*A. P. Wells lbw b Newport 2	L-b 9, w 6, n-b 2 17	
M. T. E. Peirce c Rhodes b Lampitt . . . 7		
†P. Moores not out 36	1/14 2/46 3/48 (32.3 overs) 117	
D. R. Law c Weston b Mirza 0	4/64 5/87 6/88	
I. D. K. Salisbury c Haynes b Hick 6	7/102 8/105 9/116	

Bowling: Newport 8–1–24–3; Haynes 6–1–25–0; Moody 4–0–15–0; Lampitt 6–0–14–2; Mirza 6–0–26–2; Hick 2.3–0–4–3.

Umpires: J. H. Hampshire and J. W. Holder.

At Hartlepool, August 27. DURHAM v SUSSEX. No result.

At Scarborough, September 10. SUSSEX lost to YORKSHIRE by seven wickets.

SUSSEX v NORTHAMPTONSHIRE

At Hove, September 17. Northamptonshire won by 13 runs. Toss: Sussex.

Sussex, chasing 194 to win, crumbled from 155 for four with 14 overs remaining to throw away a likely victory. Jarvis had earlier kept the visitors in check with his best Sunday League figures for Sussex.

Northamptonshire

R. R. Montgomerie c Wells b Jarvis	25	A. R. Roberts b Jarvis		4
A. Fordham c Lenham b Jarvis	31	J. P. Taylor not out		9
*R. J. Bailey c Phillips b Greenfield	35	S. A. J. Boswell b Jarvis		2
K. M. Curran c Moores b Phillips	0	B 1, l-b 10, w 8, n-b 2		21
D. J. Capel b Greenfield	28			
T. C. Walton lbw b Jarvis	20	1/49 2/70 3/82	(38.5 overs)	193
J. N. Snape b Jarvis	17	4/128 5/142 6/175		
†D. Ripley b Greenfield	1	7/176 8/177 9/191		

Bowling: Martin-Jenkins 6–0–43–0; Giddins 4–1–9–0; Phillips 8–0–35–1; Jarvis 7.5–0–29–6; Salisbury 6–0–32–0; Greenfield 7–0–34–3.

Sussex

K. Greenfield b Boswell	0	N. C. Phillips run out		0
C. W. J. Athey c Capel b Taylor	6	R. S. C. Martin-Jenkins b Curran		10
*A. P. Wells c Fordham b Curran	56	E. S. H. Giddins c Fordham b Roberts		0
N. J. Lenham lbw b Capel	15	L-b 3, w 4, n-b 2		9
†P. Moores c Walton b Taylor	63			
D. R. Law c Taylor b Snape	9	1/0 2/32 3/77	(37.5 overs)	180
I. D. K. Salisbury run out	0	4/89 5/155 6/155		
P. W. Jarvis not out	12	7/157 8/157 9/173		

Bowling: Boswell 4–0–20–1; Taylor 8–1–16–2; Curran 8–0–53–2; Capel 6–0–32–1; Roberts 3.5–0–33–1; Snape 8–1–23–1.

Umpires: J. C. Balderstone and B. J. Meyer.

WARWICKSHIRE

WARWICKSHIRE v SURREY

At Birmingham, May 7. Surrey won by 47 runs. Toss: Surrey.

A telling all-round performance by Hollioake sent the 1994 champions to defeat. He put on 105 with Thorpe to repair a bad start and then took four wickets. Warwickshire were hampered by the absence of Reeve, who had to go off in mid-over after damaging his back.

Surrey

D. J. Bicknell run out	20	A. J. Hollioake not out		54
A. D. Brown c Burns b Brown	6	N. Shahid not out		6
*†A. J. Stewart c N. M. K. Smith		B 5, l-b 2, w 3		10
b Brown	35			
G. P. Thorpe c sub b P. A. Smith	60	1/6 2/59 3/72	(5 wkts, 39 overs)	192
D. M. Ward b N. M. K. Smith	1	4/76 5/181		

M. P. Bicknell, A. C. S. Pigott, M. A. Butcher and S. G. Kenlock did not bat.

Bowling: Reeve 2.5–1–9–0; Brown 8–0–41–2; Twose 1.1–0–6–0; Small 8–0–38–0; N. M. K. Smith 8–1–37–1; Davis 8–0–34–0; P. A. Smith 3–0–20–1.

Warwickshire

D. P. Ostler c Pigott b Kenlock	41	G. C. Small c Shahid b Hollioake	9
N. M. K. Smith c Stewart b Pigott	0	R. P. Davis not out	2
A. J. Moles c D. J. Bicknell b Hollioake	46	*D. A. Reeve absent hurt	
P. A. Smith lbw b Kenlock	0	L-b 1, w 1, n-b 2	4
R. G. Twose c Stewart b Pigott	25		
T. L. Penney c Kenlock b Hollioake	3	1/2 2/75 3/75	(35 overs) 145
†M. Burns b Hollioake	7	4/99 5/115 6/121	
D. R. Brown lbw b Pigott	8	7/134 8/134 9/145	

Bowling: M. P. Bicknell 6-0-16-0; Pigott 8-0-31-3; Kenlock 8-0-36-2; Butcher 6-0-39-0; Hollioake 7-0-22-4.

Umpires: B. Dudleston and P. Willey.

At Manchester, May 14. WARWICKSHIRE lost to LANCASHIRE by five wickets.

At Chester-le-Street, May 21. WARWICKSHIRE lost to DURHAM by two runs.

WARWICKSHIRE v SOMERSET

At Birmingham, May 28. Warwickshire won on scoring-rate. Toss: Somerset.

Warwickshire stopped the rot after three defeats as Somerset fell short of their revised target of 189 in 29 overs, following two interruptions by rain. Neil Smith launched the home innings on a positive note, hitting 71 from 55 balls, and Twose maintained the momentum. Somerset were left with too much to do once Munton had celebrated his return after a back operation with three wickets.

Warwickshire

N. V. Knight c Trescothick b Trump	23	D. R. Brown b Kerr	0
N. M. K. Smith lbw b Trump	71	†K. J. Piper not out	2
A. J. Moles c Harden b Trump	32	B 8, l-b 14, w 6	28
R. G. Twose c Trescothick b Hallett	58		
*D. A. Reeve not out	17	1/68 2/128 3/147	(7 wkts, 40 overs) 260
P. A. Smith b Kerr	20	4/213 5/245	
T. L. Penney c Holloway b Kerr	9	6/258 7/258	

G. C. Small and T. A. Munton did not bat.

Bowling: Rose 8-0-45-0; Ecclestone 4-1-19-0; Hallett 4-0-47-1; Kerr 8-0-52-3; Trump 8-1-37-3; Mushtaq Ahmed 8-1-38-0.

Somerset

M. E. Trescothick c Piper b Munton	7	S. C. Ecclestone not out	31
M. N. Lathwell c Piper b Munton	5	Mushtaq Ahmed not out	4
*P. D. Bowler c Piper b P. A. Smith	34	L-b 6, w 6, n-b 4	16
R. J. Harden c N. M. K. Smith b P. A. Smith	31		
G. D. Rose c Penney b Munton	49	1/10 2/18 3/84	(5 wkts, 29 overs) 177
		4/85 5/171	

J. C. Hallett, †P. C. L. Holloway, J. I. D. Kerr and H. R. J. Trump did not bat.

Bowling: Reeve 7-0-35-0; Munton 6-0-45-3; Small 8-2-31-0; P. A. Smith 8-0-60-2.

Umpires: J. H. Harris and K. J. Lyons.

WARWICKSHIRE v SUSSEX

At Birmingham, June 11. Warwickshire won by 14 runs. Toss: Sussex.

The Smiths shared all the Sussex wickets to earn Warwickshire victory in a match reduced by rain to 34 overs a side. Paul Smith scored 85 from 86 balls, and then claimed three wickets in 11 balls. Neil Smith completed the damage with his best one-day return of six for 33 as Sussex lost their last seven men for 42. Knight, stretchered off the pitch unconscious, was taken to hospital with concussion after colliding with Penney as they both tried to catch Salisbury.

Warwickshire

N. V. Knight run out	59	†K. J. Piper c Lenham b Giddins	0
N. M. K. Smith c Hall b Stephenson	0	A. A. Donald not out	4
D. P. Ostler lbw b Stephenson	3		
P. A. Smith run out	85	L-b 4, w 6, n-b 2	12
R. G. Twose lbw b Stephenson	1		
A. J. Moles c North b Stephenson	4		
T. L. Penney b Stephenson	0		(8 wkts, 34 overs) 180
D. R. Brown not out	12		

*T. A. Munton did not bat.

1/0 2/10 3/139 4/143 5/156 6/156 7/166 8/166

Bowling: Lewry 8–3–15–0; Stephenson 8–0–38–5; Giddins 8–0–50–1; Jarvis 5–0–45–0; Salisbury 3–0–11–0; Greenfield 2–0–17–0.

Sussex

K. Greenfield c Piper b P. A. Smith	43	P. W. Jarvis not out	7
J. W. Hall b P. A. Smith	40	J. D. Lewry b N. M. K. Smith	4
F. D. Stephenson c Piper b P. A. Smith	1	E. S. H. Giddins b N. M. K. Smith	0
*A. P. Wells b N. M. K. Smith	31		
N. J. Lenham b N. M. K. Smith	19	B 1, l-b 5, w 2, n-b 2	10
J. A. North c Munton b P. A. Smith	1		
†P. Moores b N. M. K. Smith	4		(32.3 overs) 166
I. D. K. Salisbury c Penney b N. M. K. Smith	6		

1/83 2/85 3/93 4/124 5/125 6/134 7/154 8/154 9/166

Bowling: Donald 7–1–24–0; Munton 7–0–36–0; Brown 4–0–28–0; P. A. Smith 8–1–39–4; N. M. K. Smith 6.3–0–33–6.

Umpires: J. D. Bond and R. Palmer.

WARWICKSHIRE v YORKSHIRE

At Birmingham, June 25. Warwickshire won by 119 runs. Toss: Warwickshire. First-team debut: A. C. Morris.

Yorkshire were destroyed by the pace of Donald, whose figures were the best by a Warwickshire bowler in the competition. Following their collapse in the Championship on Saturday, Yorkshire lost all their wickets for 20 runs, including seven in 50 balls, to record their lowest total in the competition – 18 fewer than their previous worst, also against Warwickshire, in 1972. The home side had looked unlikely winners at 46 for four, but Twose's 93-ball innings held them together.

Warwickshire

N. V. Knight c Byas b Hamilton	4	D. R. Brown c Robinson b Hamilton	9
N. M. K. Smith c Milburn b Robinson	33	T. L. Penney not out	10
D. P. Ostler c Bevan b Hamilton	0	B 6, l-b 3, w 11	20
P. A. Smith lbw b Hamilton	0		
R. G. Twose not out	69		(6 wkts, 38 overs) 175
*D. A. Reeve b Robinson	30		

1/26 2/34 3/34 4/46 5/130 6/150

†K. J. Piper, T. A. Munton and A. A. Donald did not bat.

Bowling: Hamilton 8–0–27–4; Milburn 8–0–33–0; Robinson 8–0–48–2; Morris 8–3–17–0; Stemp 4–0–33–0; Bevan 2–0–8–0.

Yorkshire

*D. Byas c Reeve b Munton	17	R. D. Stemp b P. A. Smith	0
M. P. Vaughan lbw b Donald	17	M. A. Robinson b Donald	0
M. G. Bevan c Piper b Donald	9	†R. J. Blakey absent ill	
B. Parker c and b Munton	2	L-b 1, w 3, n-b 2	6
A. P. Grayson not out	4		
A. C. Morris c Piper b Donald	0	1/36 2/44 3/48	(18.4 overs) 56
G. M. Hamilton b Donald	0	4/48 5/49 6/51	
S. M. Milburn c Munton b Donald	1	7/55 8/55 9/56	

Bowling: Reeve 3–0–19–0; Munton 8–4–21–2; Donald 6.4–1–15–6; P. A. Smith 1–1–0–1.

Umpires: A. A. Jones and K. E. Palmer.

At Ilford, July 2. WARWICKSHIRE beat ESSEX by three wickets.

At Leicester, July 9. WARWICKSHIRE beat LEICESTERSHIRE by 112 runs.

WARWICKSHIRE v MIDDLESEX

At Birmingham, July 16. Warwickshire won by eight wickets. Toss: Warwickshire.
   The match was originally reduced to 33 overs a side after a delayed start and, when further rain curtailed Middlesex's innings, Warwickshire were left to score 82 in only 20 overs. Ostler eased them home.

Middlesex

P. N. Weekes c Penney b Munton	19	†P. Farbrace not out	7
T. A. Radford c Munton b Reeve	30	B 1, l-b 3, w 3, n-b 6	13
J. D. Carr c Piper b Donald	0		
*M. W. Gatting b Donald	18	1/30 2/32	(4 wkts, 24.3 overs) 100
J. C. Harrison not out	13	3/71 4/83	

M. A. Feltham, D. J. Nash, R. L. Johnson, K. P. Dutch and A. R. C. Fraser did not bat.

Bowling: Munton 7–0–22–1; Brown 5–0–17–0; Donald 7–0–28–2; Smith 4–0–19–0; Reeve 1.3–0–10–1.

Warwickshire

D. P. Ostler not out	46
N. M. K. Smith b Nash	0
D. R. Brown b Weekes	17
*D. A. Reeve not out	6
B 3, l-b 4, w 2, n-b 4	13

1/5 2/49   (2 wkts, 16.1 overs) 82

N. V. Knight, R. G. Twose, T. L. Penney, Asif Din, †K. J. Piper, A. A. Donald and T. A. Munton did not bat.

Bowling: Nash 5–2–11–1; Johnson 3–0–18–0; Fraser 4–1–28–0; Weekes 3.1–0–16–1; Dutch 1–0–2–0.

Umpires: H. D. Bird and J. D. Bond.

At Cardiff, July 23. WARWICKSHIRE beat GLAMORGAN by eight runs.

WARWICKSHIRE v NORTHAMPTONSHIRE

At Birmingham, July 30. Warwickshire won by 24 runs. Toss: Warwickshire.

Warwickshire won the Sunday fixture – contested in the middle of the epic Championship match between the sides – after Neil Smith and Twose had built a strong position with 97 for the third wicket. Northamptonshire slipped to 114 for six in reply and, although Warren and Penberthy added 69, it was too little, too late.

Warwickshire

D. P. Ostler lbw b Hughes	0	T. L. Penney not out	42
N. M. K. Smith c Montgomerie b Bailey	60	P. A. Smith not out	10
D. R. Brown c Capel b Penberthy	23	L-b 4, w 1, n-b 2	7
R. G. Twose c Fordham b Bailey	62		
Asif Din b Bailey	4	**(6 wkts, 40 overs)**	**222**
*D. A. Reeve c Capel b Bowen	14		

1/1 2/39 3/136 4/154 5/157 6/188

†K. J. Piper, A. A. Donald and T. A. Munton did not bat.

Bowling: Hughes 6–0–32–1; Bowen 7–1–52–1; Penberthy 8–0–33–1; Snape 8–0–40–0; Curran 6–0–33–0; Bailey 5–0–28–3.

Northamptonshire

R. R. Montgomerie b Munton	12	J. N. Snape not out	3
A. Fordham c Piper b Brown	5	J. G. Hughes c Asif Din b Reeve	0
K. M. Curran c N. M. K. Smith b Donald	44	M. N. Bowen not out	7
M. B. Loye run out	6	L-b 6, w 4, n-b 2	12
D. J. Capel lbw b Munton	1		
*R. J. Bailey c and b Donald	22	**(9 wkts, 40 overs)**	**198**
†R. J. Warren b N. M. K. Smith	42		
A. L. Penberthy c Piper b Reeve	44		

1/13 2/30 3/38 4/52 5/94 6/114 7/183 8/189 9/189

Bowling: Munton 8–0–20–2; Brown 4–0–21–1; Donald 8–0–40–2; N. M. K. Smith 8–1–47–1; Reeve 8–0–33–2; P. A. Smith 0.2–0–2–0; Twose 3.4–0–29–0.

Umpires: R. Julian and K. E. Palmer.

At Southampton, August 13. WARWICKSHIRE beat HAMPSHIRE by 67 runs.

At Nottingham, August 20. WARWICKSHIRE beat NOTTINGHAMSHIRE by four wickets.

At Worcester, August 27. WARWICKSHIRE lost to WORCESTERSHIRE by two runs.

WARWICKSHIRE v GLOUCESTERSHIRE

At Birmingham, September 5 (Tuesday). Warwickshire won by four wickets. Toss: Warwickshire.

Rain ended Gloucestershire's innings, with Symonds in full flow, on 38 from 26 balls. Warwickshire, fresh from their NatWest Trophy victory, were left to score 110 in 32 overs and immediately collapsed to 13 for three. They were still in trouble at 72 for six before Piper joined Knight to finish the job with an unbroken 40-run stand.

Gloucestershire

T. H. C. Hancock b Bell	24	R. I. Dawson run out	1
A. J. Wright c Penney b Brown	9	M. C. J. Ball not out	17
M. W. Alleyne b P. A. Smith	7	L-b 7, w 2, n-b 2	11
M. A. Lynch b Bell	4		
A. Symonds not out	38	1/24 2/42 3/50	(6 wkts, 32.2 overs) 111
*†R. C. Russell b Bell	0	4/50 5/50 6/66	

K. P. Sheeraz, M. J. Cawdron and J. Lewis did not bat.

Bowling: Donald 8-1-17-0; Brown 8-1-18-1; Bell 8-0-25-3; P. A. Smith 6.2-0-31-1; Twose 1-0-4-0; N. M. K. Smith 1-0-9-0.

Warwickshire

N. V. Knight not out	36	P. A. Smith c Russell b Alleyne	0
N. M. K. Smith b Lewis	3	†K. J. Piper not out	27
D. P. Ostler b Lewis	1	L-b 9, w 5, n-b 2	16
D. R. Brown b Sheeraz	0		
*R. G. Twose c Lynch b Lewis	8	1/10 2/12 3/13	(6 wkts, 28.1 overs) 112
T. L. Penney c Alleyne b Cawdron	21	4/36 5/67 6/72	

A. F. Giles, A. A. Donald and M. A. V. Bell did not bat.

Bowling: Lewis 8-0-27-3; Sheeraz 7-0-23-1; Cawdron 7-0-23-1; Alleyne 6.1-0-30-1.

Umpires: B. Dudleston and N. T. Plews.

WARWICKSHIRE v DERBYSHIRE

At Birmingham, September 10. No result. Toss: Warwickshire.

Warwickshire effectively lost their chance of a second successive treble when rain ended play with Derbyshire already in crisis at 81 for five. Two points left them four behind Kent, who had an unassailably superior run-rate.

Derbyshire

*K. J. Barnett not out	37	D. G. Cork not out	5
C. J. Adams c Piper b Bell	0		
†A. S. Rollins run out	2	L-b 4, w 6	10
D. J. Cullinan lbw b Bell	9		
J. E. Owen c Giles b P. A. Smith	10	1/3 2/9 3/32	(5 wkts, 25 overs) 81
C. M. Wells lbw b P. A. Smith	8	4/60 5/75	

T. A. Tweats, A. E. Warner, S. J. Base and P. Aldred did not bat.

Bowling: Reeve 6-1-13-0; Bell 8-1-19-2; Twose 6-0-22-0; P. A. Smith 4-0-21-2; Brown 1-0-2-0.

Warwickshire

N. V. Knight, N. M. K. Smith, D. P. Ostler, R. G. Twose, T. L. Penney, D. R. Brown, *D. A. Reeve, A. F. Giles, P. A. Smith, †K. J. Piper and M. A. V. Bell.

Umpires: D. J. Constant and B. Leadbeater.

At Canterbury, September 17. WARWICKSHIRE beat KENT by five wickets.

WORCESTERSHIRE

At Chelmsford, May 7. WORCESTERSHIRE beat ESSEX by 178 runs.

WORCESTERSHIRE v MIDDLESEX

At Worcester, May 14. Worcestershire won by 77 runs. Toss: Worcestershire.

Moody's 57 from 74 balls was the highlight for Worcestershire before Middlesex's top-order collapse made the result a formality.

Worcestershire

*T. S. Curtis run out	25	S. R. Lampitt not out	6
M. J. Church st Brown b Emburey	0	V. S. Solanki not out	0
T. M. Moody st Brown b Tufnell	57		
G. R. Haynes b Nash	41	B 5, l-b 24, w 8	37
D. A. Leatherdale c Ramprakash			
b Nash	32	1/12 2/85 3/125　　(6 wkts, 40 overs) 199	
†S. J. Rhodes c Weekes b Emburey	1	4/184 5/189 6/196	

P. J. Newport, R. K. Illingworth and N. V. Radford did not bat.

Bowling: Fraser 8–1–21–0; Emburey 7–1–21–2; Weekes 8–0–37–0; Nash 8–0–33–2; Feltham 4–0–24–0; Tufnell 5–0–34–1.

Middlesex

*M. W. Gatting b Newport	15	J. E. Emburey not out	14
J. C. Pooley c Leatherdale b Newport	4	A. R. C. Fraser lbw b Illingworth	3
M. R. Ramprakash c Leatherdale		P. C. R. Tufnell b Lampitt	5
b Haynes	23		
J. D. Carr lbw b Radford	7	L-b 4, w 1, n-b 4	9
P. N. Weekes run out	23		
†K. R. Brown c Rhodes b Lampitt	8	1/15 2/35 3/47　　(33.3 overs) 122	
D. J. Nash run out	9	4/59 5/87 6/92	
M. A. Feltham lbw b Illingworth	2	7/96 8/103 9/111	

Bowling: Newport 6–0–20–2; Haynes 8–0–26–1; Radford 8–0–37–1; Lampitt 4.3–0–21–2; Illingworth 7–3–14–2.

Umpires: D. J. Constant and P. Willey.

At Gloucester, May 28. WORCESTERSHIRE beat GLOUCESTERSHIRE on scoring-rate.

WORCESTERSHIRE v SURREY

At Worcester, June 4. Worcestershire won by nine wickets. Toss: Surrey.

Surrey were totally outplayed. First, their top batsmen fell to the medium-pace of Haynes, who recorded his best one-day figures before Mirza finished off the tail, and then their bowlers were unable to contain Moody and Hick, whose unbroken stand of 128 in 24 overs ensured an early finish.

Surrey

D. J. Bicknell c Rhodes b Haynes	1	A. C. S. Pigott b Mirza	8
A. D. Brown lbw b Haynes	28	S. G. Kenlock b Mirza	1
*†A. J. Stewart c Rhodes b Haynes	1	C. G. Rackemann not out	0
G. P. Thorpe c Rhodes b Haynes	15	L-b 3	3
D. M. Ward b Mirza	7		—
A. J. Hollioake run out	26	1/9 2/11 3/45	(39.3 overs) 126
M. A. Butcher st Rhodes b Illingworth	29	4/48 5/55 6/99	
M. P. Bicknell c Curtis b Lampitt	7	7/111 8/120 9/125	

Bowling: Newport 8–0–20–0; Haynes 8–1–21–4; Lampitt 8–0–28–1; Mirza 7.3–0–24–3; Illingworth 8–0–30–1.

Worcestershire

T. M. Moody not out	73		
*T. S. Curtis lbw b Rackemann	0		
G. A. Hick not out	51		
B 1, l-b 1, w 1, n-b 2	5		

1/1				(1 wkt, 24.4 overs) 129

V. S. Solanki, G. R. Haynes, D. A. Leatherdale, †S. J. Rhodes, S. R. Lampitt, P. J. Newport, P. Mirza and R. K. Illingworth did not bat.

Bowling: Rackemann 6–2–8–1; M. P. Bicknell 6–0–37–0; Pigott 5.4–0–40–0; Kenlock 4–0–18–0; Hollioake 3–0–24–0.

Umpires: G. I. Burgess and D. R. Shepherd.

At Nottingham, June 11. WORCESTERSHIRE lost to NOTTINGHAMSHIRE by 61 runs.

WORCESTERSHIRE v LANCASHIRE

At Worcester, June 18. Lancashire won by seven wickets. Toss: Worcestershire.

Lancashire put behind them their crushing Championship defeat the day before and repeated their victory in the Benson and Hedges Cup semi-final at the same venue five days earlier. Hick's eighth half-century in 11 one-day innings held Worcestershire together, but otherwise only Weston and Extras passed 12. Fairbrother, who struck a six and 12 fours in 90 balls, was 99 and on strike as the 33rd over began – but was denied a century when Hick delivered a no-ball to end the match.

Worcestershire

*T. M. Moody c Hegg b Chapple	11	V. S. Solanki b Gallian	5
T. S. Curtis lbw b Chapple	12	N. V. Radford b Wasim Akram	12
G. A. Hick not out	80	R. K. Illingworth not out	0
G. R. Haynes c Hegg b Wasim Akram	10	L-b 8, w 4, n-b 2	14
W. P. C. Weston c Fairbrother			—
b Wasim Akram	37	1/23 2/28 3/61	(8 wkts, 40 overs) 189
S. R. Lampitt lbw b Watkinson	7	4/122 5/136 6/138	
†S. J. Rhodes c and b Watkinson	1	7/143 8/186	

P. J. Newport did not bat.

Bowling: Chapple 6–1–29–2; Martin 8–1–35–0; Wasim Akram 8–0–24–3; Watkinson 8–0–34–2; Yates 4–0–22–0; Gallian 6–0–37–1.

Lancashire

J. E. R. Gallian lbw b Haynes	3	G. D. Lloyd not out	11
N. J. Speak run out	8	B 3, l-b 6, w 2, n-b 4	15
J. P. Crawley c Illingworth b Lampitt	54		
N. H. Fairbrother not out	99	1/5 2/24 3/139 (3 wkts, 32 overs)	190

*M. Watkinson, Wasim Akram, P. J. Martin, †W. K. Hegg, G. Yates and G. Chapple did not bat.

Bowling: Newport 8–0–32–0; Haynes 8–0–37–1; Radford 3–0–15–0; Lampitt 6–0–29–1; Illingworth 6–0–52–0; Hick 1–0–16–0.

Umpires: V. A. Holder and G. Sharp.

At Southampton, June 25. WORCESTERSHIRE tied with HAMPSHIRE.

WORCESTERSHIRE v LEICESTERSHIRE

At Worcester, July 2. Worcestershire won by 28 runs. Toss: Worcestershire.

Worcestershire revived their title challenge with a win that had looked unlikely as only Moody made much headway in a disappointing batting effort. However, Leicestershire capitulated in the face of some tight bowling, first from Radford and then from Hick, who hastened the end with three wickets in five balls. Top scorer was Briers, who became the first Leicestershire batsman to reach 6,000 runs in the competition.

Worcestershire

*T. M. Moody c Robinson b Dakin	52	N. V. Radford not out	9
T. S. Curtis run out	2	P. J. Newport not out	3
G. A. Hick c Nixon b Parsons	1		
G. R. Haynes lbw b Parsons	8	L-b 7, w 4	11
W. P. C. Weston c Nixon b Maddy	14		
C. M. Tolley b Dakin	14	1/2 2/3 3/27 (8 wkts, 40 overs)	142
†S. J. Rhodes c Dakin b Mason	12	4/61 5/94 6/97	
S. R. Lampitt b Parsons	16	7/121 8/134	

P. Mirza did not bat.

Bowling: Mullally 8–1–20–0; Parsons 8–1–22–3; Dakin 8–0–22–2; Maddy 8–0–32–1; Mason 8–0–39–1.

Leicestershire

†P. A. Nixon c Moody b Haynes	4	G. J. Parsons not out	0
*N. E. Briers b Lampitt	30	A. D. Mullally b Hick	0
V. J. Wells b Mirza	22	T. J. Mason run out	5
B. F. Smith c Tolley b Radford	21	L-b 4, w 3	7
P. E. Robinson b Radford	0		
J. M. Dakin c Lampitt b Radford	16	(36.4 overs)	114
D. L. Maddy b Hick	4	1/13 2/51 3/63	
V. P. Clarke c Mirza b Hick	5	4/70 5/97 6/100	
		7/108 8/109 9/109	

Bowling: Newport 6–1–13–0; Haynes 8–2–20–1; Lampitt 6–1–23–1; Mirza 5.4–1–15–1; Radford 5–0–22–3; Hick 6–1–17–3.

Umpires: J. H. Hampshire and K. E. Palmer.

At Darlington, July 9. WORCESTERSHIRE beat DURHAM by 79 runs.

WORCESTERSHIRE v KENT

At Worcester, July 30. Kent won by four wickets. Toss: Worcestershire.

Curtis anchored Worcestershire's batting through 38 overs, but could not accelerate as the accurate Kent bowlers conceded only ten boundaries in all. Fleming did better with a six and ten fours in a characteristic 70 off 44 balls as he set up an important win.

Worcestershire

*T. M. Moody b Thompson	44	P. J. Newport st Marsh b Llong	0
T. S. Curtis c Cowdrey b Llong	68	R. K. Illingworth not out	0
G. A. Hick c Ward b Thompson	1		
G. R. Haynes b Headley	15	L-b 5, w 1	6
D. A. Leatherdale b de Silva	14		
W. P. C. Weston b de Silva	1	1/80 2/82 3/110 (8 wkts, 40 overs)	164
†S. J. Rhodes c Ward b Fleming	13	4/139 5/144 6/155	
S. R. Lampitt not out	2	7/160 8/161	

P. Mirza did not bat.

Bowling: Igglesden 5-0-21-0; Ealham 8-1-31-0; Thompson 8-1-27-2; Headley 5-0-21-1; de Silva 8-0-38-2; Fleming 4-0-14-1; Llong 2-0-7-2.

Kent

T. R. Ward b Haynes	0	M. J. Walker not out	24
M. V. Fleming c Weston b Mirza	70	*†S. A. Marsh not out	3
P. A. de Silva b Mirza	11	L-b 3, w 9, n-b 6	18
G. R. Cowdrey b Newport	19		
M. A. Ealham c Lampitt b Newport	16	1/1 2/83 3/92 (6 wkts, 37.2 overs)	168
N. J. Llong lbw b Illingworth	7	4/124 5/127 6/141	

J. B. D. Thompson, A. P. Igglesden and D. W. Headley did not bat.

Bowling: Newport 8-2-35-2; Haynes 3-0-32-1; Illingworth 8-1-22-1; Mirza 7-0-37-2; Lampitt 7.2-0-23-0; Hick 4-0-16-0.

Umpires: G. I. Burgess and P. B. Wight.

At Scarborough, August 6. WORCESTERSHIRE beat YORKSHIRE by 33 runs.

WORCESTERSHIRE v DERBYSHIRE

At Worcester, August 13. Worcestershire won by ten wickets. Toss: Derbyshire.

Derbyshire were overwhelmed as Moody and Curtis cruised past their inadequate total without being separated. The early damage had been done by D'Oliveira and Mirza, whose four for 27 was his best one-day return, and Worcestershire were never challenged.

Derbyshire

*K. J. Barnett run out	7	F. A. Griffith b Mirza	6
C. J. Adams st Rhodes b Mirza	31	A. E. Warner c Haynes b Mirza	0
†A. S. Rollins c Haynes b Mirza	30	D. E. Malcolm not out	1
C. M. Wells c Weston b D'Oliveira	21		
T. A. Tweats c Haynes b D'Oliveira	7	L-b 12	12
T. J. G. O'Gorman c Church b D'Oliveira	8	1/11 2/77 3/88 (39.5 overs)	163
P. A. J. DeFreitas c Weston b Haynes	25	4/101 5/115 6/116	
T. W. Harrison c Church b Haynes	15	7/145 8/161 9/161	

Bowling: Radford 8-2-20-0; Haynes 8-0-35-2; Brinkley 8 0 24 0; Mirza 7.5-1-27-4; D'Oliveira 8-0-45-3.

Worcestershire

*T. M. Moody not out	98
T. S. Curtis not out	58
L-b 3, w 3, n-b 2	8

(no wkt, 35 overs) 164

G. R. Haynes, D. A. Leatherdale, W. P. C. Weston, M. J. Church, †S. J. Rhodes, D. B. D'Oliveira, P. Mirza, N. V. Radford and J. E. Brinkley did not bat.

Bowling: DeFreitas 8–0–23–0; Warner 7–0–25–0; Malcolm 8–0–45–0; Wells 4–0–20–0; Griffith 6–0–29–0; Harrison 2–0–19–0.

Umpires: J. C. Balderstone and J. D. Bond.

At Eastbourne, August 20. WORCESTERSHIRE beat SUSSEX by 80 runs.

WORCESTERSHIRE v WARWICKSHIRE

At Worcester, August 27. Worcestershire won by two runs. Toss: Warwickshire.

Worcestershire ended Warwickshire's run of 14 consecutive one-day victories and edged two points ahead to take second place in the table. Batsmen struggled on a slow pitch and Worcestershire's meagre total owed much to Curtis, who battled for 99 balls to reach 62. It proved adequate when Warwickshire lost their way against Moody after a promising start. They required only 25 from six overs and eight off the last, but Newport kept it tight to earn his side a tense win.

Worcestershire

*T. M. Moody b Munton	26	V. S. Solanki not out	2
T. S. Curtis c Piper b Donald	62	N. V. Radford not out	1
G. R. Haynes c N. M. K. Smith			
b Small	9	L-b 3, w 5	8
D. A. Leatherdale b P. A. Smith	33		
S. R. Lampitt c Munton b P. A. Smith	9	1/42 2/70 3/127 (7 wkts, 39 overs) 157	
M. J. Church st Piper b Reeve	6	4/142 5/153	
†S. J. Rhodes c Piper b P. A. Smith	1	6/153 7/156	

P. J. Newport and P. Mirza did not bat.

Bowling: Donald 8–0–38–1; Munton 8–2–16–1; Small 8–0–34–1; Reeve 4–0–20–1; N. M. K. Smith 4–0–27–0; P. A. Smith 7–0–19–3.

Warwickshire

D. P. Ostler c Radford b Moody	15	A. A. Donald not out	5
N. M. K. Smith lbw b Moody	32	G. C. Small not out	1
D. R. Brown c Radford b Moody	16		
R. G. Twose b Mirza	24	L-b 6, w 5, n-b 2	13
T. L. Penney run out	2		
*D. A. Reeve b Newport	21	1/41 2/63 3/70 (8 wkts, 39 overs) 155	
P. A. Smith c Moody b Newport	19	4/72 5/110 6/137	
†K. J. Piper b Newport	7	7/144 8/153	

T. A. Munton did not bat.

Bowling: Newport 8–1–25–3; Haynes 5–1–22–0; Lampitt 8–0–22–0; Moody 8–0–25–3; Radford 6–0–25–0; Mirza 4–0–30–1.

Umpires: R. Palmer and G. Sharp.

WORCESTERSHIRE v SOMERSET

At Worcester, September 3. Worcestershire won by 68 runs. Toss: Worcestershire.

Worcestershire's fifth consecutive Sunday League victory took them level with Kent at the top of the table. Hick dominated the match with bat and ball, making 72 from 87 balls and then claiming his best one-day figures as Somerset folded.

Worcestershire

*T. M. Moody c Turner b Hallett	22	N. V. Radford not out	16
T. S. Curtis c Turner b Hallett	18	†S. J. Rhodes not out	1
G. A. Hick run out	72	L-b 8, n-b 2	10
D. A. Leatherdale c Parsons b Hallett	2		
W. P. C. Weston st Turner b Trump	11	1/28 2/49 3/53 (7 wkts, 40 overs) 174
S. R. Lampitt c Rose b Parsons	14	4/76 5/131
G. R. Haynes b Rose	8	6/152 7/165

P. J. Newport and P. Mirza did not bat.

Bowling: Rose 8–1–34–1; Hallett 8–2–33–3; Trump 8–0–24–1; Mushtaq Ahmed 8–0–32–0; Hayhurst 6–1–26–0; Parsons 2–0–17–1.

Somerset

M. N. Lathwell lbw b Haynes	5	J. C. Hallett c Newport b Hick	2
P. D. Bowler c Lampitt b Newport	14	Mushtaq Ahmed c Moody b Radford	11
R. J. Harden c Rhodes b Hick	33	H. R. J. Trump not out	2
P. C. L. Holloway c Rhodes b Lampitt	0	B 2, l-b 5, w 1, n-b 4	12
G. D. Rose b Lampitt	7		
K. A. Parsons b Radford	12	1/5 2/30 3/34 (33.5 overs) 106
*A. N. Hayhurst c Newport b Hick	1	4/48 5/79 6/81
†R. J. Turner st Rhodes b Hick	7	7/87 8/93 9/96

Bowling: Newport 6–2–9–1; Haynes 4–0–17–1; Moody 7–0–29–0; Lampitt 4–0–8–2; Hick 7–0–21–4; Radford 5.5–1–15–2.

Umpires: D. J. Constant and P. B. Wight.

At Northampton, September 10. NORTHAMPTONSHIRE v WORCESTERSHIRE. No result.

WORCESTERSHIRE v GLAMORGAN

At Worcester, September 17. No result. Toss: Glamorgan.

Two washouts on successive Sundays scuppered Worcestershire's title hopes, and Warwickshire's win over Kent at Canterbury meant they had to settle for third place. Victory over Glamorgan was essential if they were to have any chance of taking the trophy, but rain halted play after Weston – awarded his county cap before the match – had laid the foundations for a useful total. The recalculation left the visitors to make 118 from 30 overs but another storm ended the contest just ten balls into their reply.

Worcestershire

*T. M. Moody b Thomas	4	N. V. Radford st Metson b Barwick	1
T. S. Curtis c Morris b Watkin	12	G. R. Haynes not out	2
G. A. Hick run out	6	B 2, l-b 6, w 6	14
D. A. Leatherdale b Cottey	14		
W. P. C. Weston c Dale b Watkin	63	1/8 2/28 3/28 (6 wkts, 37.1 overs) 145
S. R. Lampitt not out	29	4/69 5/132 6/142

†S. J. Rhodes, P. J. Newport and P. Mirza did not bat.

Bowling: Watkin 7.1–2–14–2; Thomas 6–0–30–1; Barwick 7–0–20–1; Croft 8–2–23–0; Cottey 4–0–19–1; Dale 5–0–31–0.

Glamorgan

S. P. James not out 2
*H. Morris not out 1

(no wkt, 1.4 overs) 3

M. P. Maynard, P. A. Cottey, D. L. Hemp, A. Dale, R. D. B. Croft, S. D. Thomas, †C. P. Metson, S. L. Watkin and S. R. Barwick did not bat.

Bowling: Newport 1–0–2–0; Haynes 0.4–0–1–0.

Umpires: B. Leadbeater and R. Palmer.

YORKSHIRE

At Leicester, May 7. YORKSHIRE lost to LEICESTERSHIRE by 30 runs.

At Chesterfield, May 14. YORKSHIRE beat DERBYSHIRE by 59 runs.

YORKSHIRE v GLAMORGAN

At Leeds, May 21. Yorkshire won by two runs. Toss: Glamorgan.
Gough yorked Dale with the final ball of the match after Glamorgan had embarked on the last over needing six to win with four wickets in hand. Dale had given his side a fighting chance with 48 from 39 balls in a low-scoring contest. Only Byas passed 20 for Yorkshire, whose last seven wickets fell for 46 in ten overs.

Yorkshire

*D. Byas c Croft b Watkin	54	P. J. Hartley not out	3
M. P. Vaughan c Hemp b Watkin	7	R. D. Stemp b Lefebvre	0
M. G. Bevan c and b Croft	15	M. A. Robinson lbw b Barwick	2
C. White c Metson b Dale	18	L-b 8, w 4	12
†R. J. Blakey st Metson b Dale	14		
A. P. Grayson c Metson b Watkin	13	1/17 2/54 3/90	(39.4 overs) 157
B. Parker run out	13	4/111 5/125 6/131	
D. Gough c Hemp b Barwick	6	7/146 8/153 9/153	

Bowling: Watkin 8–1–16–3; Lefebvre 8–0–30–1; Croft 8–0–30–1; Barwick 7.4–0–36–2; Dale 6–0–30–2; Cottey 2–0–7–0.

Glamorgan

S. P. James st Blakey b Robinson	17	R. P. Lefebvre run out	1
*H. Morris b Grayson	39	†C. P. Metson not out	0
M. P. Maynard c Parker b Stemp	5	B 1, l-b 2, w 2	5
P. A. Cottey b White	37		
D. L. Hemp b Grayson	1	1/30 2/41 3/80	(8 wkts, 40 overs) 155
A. Dale b Gough	48	4/88 5/122 6/136	
R. D. B. Croft b White	2	7/153 8/155	

S. L. Watkin and S. R. Barwick did not bat.

Bowling: Gough 8–1–24–1; Hartley 7–3–17–0; Robinson 8–2–19–1; Stemp 8–0–40–1; Grayson 4–0–21–2; White 5–1–31–2.

Umpires: J. W. Holder and P. Willey.

YORKSHIRE v NORTHAMPTONSHIRE

At Sheffield, May 28. No result. Toss: Yorkshire.
Bailey and 17-year-old Sales had added 58 in nine overs before the weather closed in, giving Northamptonshire their first Sunday League points of the season.

Northamptonshire

A. Fordham lbw b Hartley	7	D. J. Sales not out		27
D. J. Capel c Stemp b Milburn	18	B 2, l-b 4, w 1		7
K. M. Curran c Vaughan b Milburn	4			
T. C. Walton b Bevan	39	1/13 2/18	(4 wkts, 31.4 overs)	145
*R. J. Bailey not out	43	3/41 4/87		

†R. J. Warren, N. A. Mallender, J. N. Snape, A. Kumble and J. P. Taylor did not bat.

Bowling: Milburn 8–1–29–2; Hartley 6.4–0–29–1; Robinson 6–1–23–0; Stemp 3–0–19–0; White 6–0–32–0; Bevan 2–0–7–1.

Yorkshire

*D. Byas, M. P. Vaughan, M. G. Bevan, C. White, †R. J. Blakey, A. A. Metcalfe, B. Parker, P. J. Hartley, R. D. Stemp, S. M. Milburn and M. A. Robinson.

Umpires: T. E. Jesty and A. G. T. Whitehead.

At Taunton, June 4. YORKSHIRE lost to SOMERSET by three wickets.

YORKSHIRE v KENT

At Leeds, June 18. Kent won by 86 runs. Toss: Kent.
Ward's well-organised 63 from 71 balls was easily the highest individual score of the match. Igglesden had figures of 8–3–11–3 as Yorkshire were dismissed less than halfway to a modest target.

Kent

D. P. Fulton c Gough b Hartley	11	M. J. McCague b Robinson		10
T. R. Ward b Gough	63	A. P. Igglesden run out		2
M. J. Walker lbw b Hartley	5	T. N. Wren not out		3
*P. A. de Silva lbw b White	15	L-b 6, w 3, n-b 2		11
M. V. Fleming run out	3			
M. A. Ealham b Stemp	13	1/25 2/34 3/58	(38.1 overs)	161
N. J. Llong lbw b Grayson	13	4/69 5/109 6/126		
†S. C. Willis b Grayson	12	7/140 8/149 9/152		

Bowling: Hartley 4–0–25–2; Gough 7–0–31–1; Robinson 7.1–0–30–1; White 8–1–30–1; Stemp 8–0–25–1; Grayson 4–0–14–2.

Yorkshire

*M. D. Moxon b Igglesden	8	P. J. Hartley b Ealham		4
D. Byas c McCague b Wren	7	R. D. Stemp b Ealham		10
M. G. Bevan c Willis b Wren	0	M. A. Robinson b Fleming		7
C. White lbw b Igglesden	6	L-b 4, w 2		6
†R. J. Blakey c Willis b Wren	2			
A. P. Grayson b Igglesden	4	1/15 2/15 3/24	(30.5 overs)	75
B. Parker not out	20	4/25 5/31 6/31		
D. Gough b Ealham	1	7/38 8/54 9/66		

Bowling: McCague 5–2–8–0; Wren 8–1–20–3; Igglesden 8–3–11–3; Ealham 7–0–25–3; Fleming 2.5–0–7–1.

Umpires: J. D. Bond and J. H. Harris.

At Birmingham, June 25. YORKSHIRE lost to WARWICKSHIRE by 119 runs.

YORKSHIRE v GLOUCESTERSHIRE

At Middlesbrough, July 2. Yorkshire won by 93 runs. Toss: Gloucestershire.

Bevan propelled Yorkshire to an impressive total with his first one-day century for the county, scored off 108 balls. He then wrapped up Gloucestershire's innings after they had lost half their wickets for 54.

Yorkshire

*D. Byas b Ball	19	A. A. Metcalfe not out 10
S. A. Kellett run out	17	L-b 4, w 10, n-b 6 20
M. G. Bevan not out	103	
C. White c Ball b Alleyne	40	1/28 2/54 (4 wkts, 40 overs) 235
B. Parker c Symonds b Smith	26	3/151 4/202

†R. J. Blakey, A. P. Grayson, P. J. Hartley, G. M. Hamilton and M. A. Robinson did not bat.

Bowling: Ball 8–1–22–1; Srinath 8–0–51–0; Boden 5–0–33–0; Smith 8–0–49–1; Williams 7–0–43–0; Alleyne 4–0–33–1.

Gloucestershire

A. Symonds c White b Hamilton	7	M. C. J. Ball b Bevan 0
A. J. Wright c Blakey b Hartley	14	D. J. P. Boden c Hamilton b Bevan ... 1
R. J. Cunliffe c and b Grayson	10	A. M. Smith not out 5
M. A. Lynch c Blakey b White	18	L-b 3, w 2 5
M. W. Alleyne c Metcalfe b White	0	
*†R. C. Russell c Byas b Robinson	42	1/7 2/32 3/34 (37.1 overs) 142
R. C. Williams c and b Bevan	4	4/35 5/54 6/119
J. Srinath c Hartley b Robinson	0	7/124 8/126 9/132

Bowling: Hartley 6–0–16–1; Hamilton 5–0–28–1; Grayson 8–0–32–1; White 5–0–15–2; Robinson 8–1–27–2; Bevan 5.1–0–21–3.

Umpires: V. A. Holder and N. T. Plews.

At Southampton, July 9. YORKSHIRE beat HAMPSHIRE by 19 runs.

YORKSHIRE v DURHAM

At Leeds, July 23. Durham won by seven wickets. Toss: Durham.

Brown demolished Yorkshire's middle order with a burst of three wickets for one run in four balls and, although Gough tried to engineer a late-order recovery, Durham were left with a modest target, which they reached with nearly seven overs to spare.

Yorkshire

*D. Byas c Hutton b Killeen	6	P. J. Hartley c Brown b Prabhakar ... 3
M. P. Vaughan c Ligertwood b Walker	13	G. M. Hamilton run out 3
M. G. Bevan c Ligertwood b Brown	4	M. A. Robinson not out 0
C. White b Walker	7	L-b 10, w 2 12
B. Parker lbw b Brown	28	
†R. J. Blakey c Boiling b Brown	24	1/9 2/20 3/30 (39.1 overs) 133
A. P. Grayson c Boiling b Brown	3	4/33 5/93 6/94
D. Gough b Walker	30	7/97 8/122 9/133

Bowling: Brown 8–1–20–4; Killeen 8–2–14–1; Walker 7.1–1–23–3; Prabhakar 8–1–43–1; Boiling 8–1–23–0.

Durham

W. Larkins c Parker b Hamilton	16	*J. E. Morris not out	28
S. Hutton c Blakey b Gough	5	L-b 4, w 2, n-b 2	8
M. Prabhakar c sub b Hartley	55		
J. A. Daley not out	25	1/7 2/39 3/106 (3 wkts, 33.1 overs) 137	

D. A. Blenkiron, †D. G. C. Ligertwood, J. Boiling, S. J. E. Brown, A. Walker and N. Killeen did not bat.

Bowling: Gough 6–1–14–1; Hartley 8–3–35–1; White 7–0–26–0; Hamilton 3–0–11–1; Robinson 6.1–0–36–0; Grayson 3–0–11–0.

Umpires: M. J. Kitchen and R. Palmer.

At Cleethorpes, July 30. YORKSHIRE lost to NOTTINGHAMSHIRE by five wickets.

YORKSHIRE v WORCESTERSHIRE

At Scarborough, August 6. Worcestershire won by 33 runs. Toss: Worcestershire.

Hick made his second Sunday League century of the season, off 83 balls. Yorkshire never completely recovered from a slide to 45 for three, but they gained respectability from Bevan's 92-ball innings, in which he reached his second hundred with a six out of the ground.

Worcestershire

*T. M. Moody st Blakey b Robinson	33	S. R. Lampitt not out	15
T. S. Curtis b Grayson	24	L-b 7, w 3, n-b 2	12
G. A. Hick not out	113		
G. R. Haynes lbw b Grayson	16	1/64 2/76 (4 wkts, 40 overs) 251	
D. A. Leatherdale c White b Robinson	38	3/102 4/216	

W. P. C. Weston, †S. J. Rhodes, P. J. Newport, R. K. Illingworth and P. Mirza did not bat.

Bowling: Silverwood 8–2–41–0; Hamilton 8–0–51–0; Robinson 8–0–47–2; White 8–0–50–0; Grayson 6–0–39–2; Bevan 2–0–16–0.

Yorkshire

*D. Byas c Mirza b Haynes	17	G. M. Hamilton run out	0
M. P. Vaughan c and b Haynes	23	C. E. W. Silverwood not out	4
†R. J. Blakey run out	4	M. A. Robinson not out	2
M. G. Bevan b Mirza	101	L-b 4, w 3	7
C. White st Rhodes b Illingworth	32		
A. A. Metcalfe c Leatherdale b Lampitt	25	1/28 2/45 3/45 (9 wkts, 40 overs) 218	
B. Parker lbw b Lampitt	2	4/102 5/160 6/196	
A. P. Grayson run out	1	7/205 8/212 9/212	

Bowling: Newport 8–0–54–0; Haynes 8–1–18–2; Lampitt 8–0–37–2; Illingworth 8–0–43–1; Mirza 8–0–62–1.

Umpires: T. E. Jesty and N. T. Plews.

At The Oval, August 13. YORKSHIRE lost to SURREY by 12 runs.

At Manchester, August 20. YORKSHIRE lost to LANCASHIRE by 36 runs.

YORKSHIRE v MIDDLESEX

At Leeds, August 27. Yorkshire won by 18 runs. Toss: Yorkshire. First-team debut: J. P. Hewitt.

Another notable all-round contribution from Bevan secured victory for Yorkshire. He accounted for half his side's runs and then captured three wickets to restrict Middlesex, for whom Owais Shah, Karachi-born, locally bred, and still two months from his 17th birthday, top-scored.

Yorkshire

*M. D. Moxon b Feltham	5	†R. J. Blakey not out 11
D. Byas b Rashid	20	P. J. Hartley c Weekes b Hewitt .. 1
M. P. Vaughan c Brown b Feltham....	1	L-b 8, w 2 10
M. G. Bevan c Pooley b Ramprakash ..	81	
C. White c Carr b Rashid	29	1/10 2/20 3/43 (8 wkts, 37 overs) 161
A. A. Metcalfe c Gatting b Weekes	1	4/95 5/98 6/113
D. Gough b Hewitt	2	7/156 8/161

A. P. Grayson and C. E. W. Silverwood did not bat.

Bowling: Feltham 6–1–10–2; Fay 8–0–27–0; Rashid 8–1–34–2; Weekes 8–0–33–1; Hewitt 5–0–31–2; Ramprakash 2–0–18–1.

Middlesex

P. N. Weekes lbw b Gough	10	U. B. A. Rashid c Byas b Gough 5
J. C. Pooley b Silverwood	1	J. P. Hewitt b Gough 3
M. R. Ramprakash c Moxon b Bevan ..	26	R. A. Fay not out 6
J. D. Carr lbw b Hartley	5	B 2, l-b 3, w 3, n-b 2 10
O. A. Shah c White b Gough..........	64	
†K. R. Brown c Blakey b Grayson	1	1/6 2/12 3/26 (36.4 overs) 143
*M. W. Gatting c White b Bevan	10	4/65 5/70 6/93
M. A. Feltham c Blakey b Bevan	2	7/107 8/123 9/132

Bowling: Gough 7.4–0–35–4; Silverwood 5–2–10–1; Hartley 6–0–23–1; White 4–1–11–0; Grayson 6–0–24–1; Bevan 8–0–35–3.

Umpires: G. I. Burgess and B. Dudleston.

YORKSHIRE v SUSSEX

At Scarborough, September 10. Yorkshire won by seven wickets. Toss: Sussex.

Sussex's meagre total was overhauled with just one ball to spare after Yorkshire's opening pair, Vaughan and McGrath, had put together a stand of 114 in 27 overs. McGrath was particularly impressive, making 72 from 93 balls on his League debut.

Sussex

K. Greenfield b Hartley	11	P. W. Jarvis b Hartley 9
C. W. J. Athey c Blakey b Bevan	39	N. C. Phillips c Bevan b Gough 2
*A. P. Wells c McGrath b Morris	20	B 1, l-b 6, w 1, n-b 4 12
N. J. Lenham not out	56	
†P. Moores c Byas b Stemp	3	1/26 2/67 3/89 (8 wkts, 40 overs) 164
D. R. Law c Byas b Stemp	0	4/108 5/108 6/128
I. D. K. Salisbury c Metcalfe b Bevan .	12	7/157 8/164

R. S. C. Martin-Jenkins and E. S. H. Giddins did not bat.

Bowling: Hartley 8–1–23–2; Gough 7–0–31–1; Robinson 7–0–21–0; Stemp 8–0–41–2; Morris 3–0–8–1; Bevan 7–0–33–2.

Yorkshire

M. P. Vaughan c Greenfield b Martin-Jenkins . 39	A. A. Metcalfe not out 8
A. McGrath c Athey b Greenfield 72	L-b 11, w 9 20
*D. Byas c and b Greenfield 12	
M. G. Bevan not out 14	1/114 2/136 3/145 (3 wkts, 39.5 overs) 165

A. C. Morris, †R. J. Blakey, D. Gough, P. J. Hartley, R. D. Stemp and M. A. Robinson did not bat.

Bowling: Giddins 8–0–27–0; Phillips 8–1–34–0; Salisbury 8–0–28–0; Jarvis 7.5–1–28–0; Martin-Jenkins 4–0–24–1; Greenfield 4–0–13–2.

Umpires: D. R. Shepherd and R. A. White.

At Chelmsford, September 17. YORKSHIRE beat ESSEX by nine wickets.

SUNDAY LEAGUE RECORDS

Batting

Highest individual score: 176, G. A. Gooch, Essex v Glamorgan, Southend, 1983.

Most runs: 8,359, G. A. Gooch; 7,499, W. Larkins; 7,214, C. W. J. Athey; 7,062, D. W. Randall; 7,040, D. L. Amiss; 6,650, C. T. Radley; 6,639, D. R. Turner; 6,506, P. Willey; 6,443, K. J. Barnett; 6,344, C. G. Greenidge; 6,265, C. E. B. Rice; 6,144, G. M. Turner; 6,132, M. W. Gatting; 6,121, C. J. Tavaré; 6,096, N. E. Briers; 6,031, T. S. Curtis. **In a season:** 917, T. M. Moody, Worcestershire, 1991.

Most hundreds: 14, W. Larkins; 12, G. A. Gooch; 11, C. G. Greenidge; 9, K. S. McEwan and B. A. Richards. 516 hundreds have been scored in the League. The most in one season is 40 in 1990.

Most sixes in an innings: 13, I. T. Botham, Somerset v Northamptonshire, Wellingborough School, 1986. **By a team in an innings:** 18, Derbyshire v Worcestershire, Knypersley, 1985 and Surrey v Yorkshire, Scarborough, 1994. **In a season:** 26, I. V. A. Richards, Somerset, 1977.

Highest total: 375 for four, Surrey v Yorkshire, Scarborough, 1994. **By a side batting second:** 317 for six, Surrey v Nottinghamshire, The Oval, 1993 (50-overs match).

Highest match aggregate: 631 for 13 wickets, Nottinghamshire (314 for seven) v Surrey (317 for six), The Oval, 1993 (50-overs match).

Lowest total: 23 (19.4 overs), Middlesex v Yorkshire, Leeds, 1974.

Shortest completed innings: 16 overs (59), Northamptonshire v Middlesex, Tring, 1974.

Record partnerships for each wicket

239	for 1st	G. A. Gooch and B. R. Hardie, Essex v Nottinghamshire at Nottingham	1985
273	for 2nd	G. A. Gooch and K. S. McEwan, Essex v Nottinghamshire at Nottingham	1983
223	for 3rd	S. J. Cook and G. D. Rose, Somerset v Glamorgan at Neath	1990
219	for 4th	C. G. Greenidge and C. L. Smith, Hampshire v Surrey at Southampton	1987
190	for 5th	R. J. Blakey and M. J. Foster, Yorkshire v Leicestershire at Leicester	1993
136	for 6th	P. A. Nixon and D. L. Maddy, Leicestershire v Sussex at Hove	1995
132	for 7th	K. R. Brown and N. F. Williams, Middlesex v Somerset at Lord's . .	1988
110*	for 8th	C. L. Cairns and B. N. French, Nottinghamshire v Surrey at The Oval	1993
105	for 9th	D. G. Moir and R. W. Taylor, Derbyshire v Kent at Derby	1984
57	for 10th	D. A. Graveney and J. B. Mortimore, Gloucestershire v Lancashire at Tewkesbury	1973

Bowling

Most wickets: 386, J. K. Lever; 346, D. L. Underwood; 338, J. E. Emburey; 307, J. Simmons; 303, S. Turner; 284, N. Gifford; 281, E. E. Hemmings; 267, J. N. Shepherd; 260, A. C. S. Pigott; 256, I. T. Botham; 249, T. E. Jesty; 234, R. D. Jackman and P. Willey. **In a season:** 34, R. J. Clapp, Somerset, 1974, and C. E. B. Rice, Nottinghamshire, 1986.

Best bowling: eight for 26, K. D. Boyce, Essex v Lancashire, Manchester, 1971; seven for 15, R. A. Hutton, Yorkshire v Worcestershire, Leeds, 1969; seven for 39, A. Hodgson, Northamptonshire v Somerset, Northampton, 1976; seven for 41, A. N. Jones, Sussex v Nottinghamshire, Nottingham, 1986; six for six, R. W. Hooker, Middlesex v Surrey, Lord's, 1969; six for seven, M. Hendrick, Derbyshire v Nottinghamshire, Nottingham, 1972; six for nine, N. G. Cowans, Middlesex v Lancashire, Lord's, 1991.

Most economical analysis: 8–8–0–0, B. A. Langford, Somerset v Essex, Yeovil, 1969.

Most expensive analyses: 8–0–96–1, D. G. Cork, Derbyshire v Nottinghamshire, Nottingham, 1993; 8–0–94–2, P. N. Weekes, Middlesex v Leicestershire, Leicester, 1994; 7.5–0–89–3, G. Miller, Derbyshire v Gloucestershire, Gloucester, 1984; 8–0–88–1, E. E. Hemmings, Nottinghamshire v Somerset, Nottingham, 1983.

Hat-tricks: There have been 24 hat-tricks, four of them for Glamorgan.

Four wickets in four balls: A. Ward, Derbyshire v Sussex, Derby, 1970.

Wicket-keeping and Fielding

Most dismissals: 257 (234 ct, 23 st), D. L. Bairstow; 236 (187 ct, 49 st), R. W. Taylor; 223 (184 ct, 39 st), E. W. Jones; 221 (172 ct, 49 st), S. J. Rhodes. **In a season:** 29 (26 ct, 3 st), S. J. Rhodes, Worcestershire, 1988. **In an innings:** 7 (6 ct, 1 st), R. W. Taylor, Derbyshire v Lancashire, Manchester, 1975.

Most catches in an innings: 6, K. Goodwin, Lancashire v Worcestershire, Worcester, 1969; R. W. Taylor, Derbyshire v Lancashire, Manchester, 1975; K. M. Krikken, Derbyshire v Hampshire, Southampton, 1994; and P. A. Nixon, Leicestershire v Essex, Leicester, 1994.

Most stumpings in an innings: 4, S. J. Rhodes, Worcestershire v Warwickshire, Birmingham, 1986 and N. D. Burns, Somerset v Kent, Taunton, 1991.

Most catches by a fielder: 103, V. P. Terry; 101, J. F. Steele; 97, D. P. Hughes; 96, G. A. Gooch; 95, C. W. J. Athey†; 94, G. Cook and P. W. G. Parker. **In a season:** 16, J. M. Rice, Hampshire, 1978. **In an innings:** 5, J. M. Rice, Hampshire v Warwickshire, Southampton, 1978.

† C. W. J. Athey has also taken two catches as a wicket-keeper.

Results

Largest victory in runs: Somerset by 220 runs v Glamorgan, Neath, 1990.

Victories by ten wickets (28): By Derbyshire, Durham, Essex (three times), Glamorgan (twice), Hampshire (twice), Leicestershire (twice), Middlesex (twice), Northamptonshire, Nottinghamshire, Somerset (twice), Surrey (twice), Warwickshire, Worcestershire (five times) and Yorkshire (three times). This does not include those matches in which the side batting second was set a reduced target but does include matches where both sides faced a reduced number of overs.

Ties: There have been 42 tied matches. Worcestershire have tied nine times.

Shortest match: 2 hr 13 min (40.3 overs), Essex v Northamptonshire, Ilford, 1971.

CHAMPIONS 1969-95

John Player's County League		*John Player Special League*	
1969	Lancashire	1984	Essex
John Player League		1985	Essex
1970	Lancashire	1986	Hampshire
1971	Worcestershire	*Refuge Assurance League*	
1972	Kent	1987	Worcestershire
1973	Kent	1988	Worcestershire
1974	Leicestershire	1989	Lancashire
1975	Hampshire	1990	Derbyshire
1976	Kent	1991	Nottinghamshire
1977	Leicestershire	*Sunday League*	
1978	Hampshire	1992	Middlesex
1979	Somerset	*AXA Equity & Law League*	
1980	Warwickshire	1993	Glamorgan
1981	Essex	1994	Warwickshire
1982	Sussex	1995	Kent
1983	Yorkshire		

MATCH RESULTS 1969-95

			Matches			*League positions*		
	P	*W*	*L*	*T*	*NR*	*1st*	*2nd*	*3rd*
Derbyshire	436	187	203	3	43	1	0	1
Durham	68	25	30	2	11	0	0	0
Essex	436	230	162	7	37	3	5*	3
Glamorgan	436	154	231	4	47	1	0	0
Gloucestershire	436	150	232	4	50	0	1	1
Hampshire	436	214	179	7	36	3	1	3
Kent	436	236	153	5	42	4	3	4
Lancashire	436	220	159	8	49	3	2	2
Leicestershire	436	186	194	2	54	2	2*	2
Middlesex	436	198	186	6	46	1	1	3
Northamptonshire	436	166	220	5	45	0	0	1
Nottinghamshire	436	180	214	3	39	1	2	1
Somerset	436	203	187	2	44	1	6*	0
Surrey	436	191	194	4	47	0	0	1
Sussex	436	190	195	5	46	1	2*	1
Warwickshire	436	179	203	6	48	2	1	1
Worcestershire	436	214	176	9	37	3	3	2
Yorkshire	436	191	196	4	47	1	1	0

* *Includes one shared 2nd place in 1976.*

THE UNIVERSITIES IN 1995

OXFORD

President: C. A. Fry (Trinity)
Hon. Treasurer: Dr S. R. Porter (Nuffield College)

Captain: G. I. Macmillan (Guildford CS, Charterhouse, University of Southampton and Keble)
Secretary: W. S. Kendall (Bradfield College and Keble)

Captain for 1996: C. M. Gupte (John Lyon and Pembroke)
Secretary: D. P. Mather (Wirral GS and St Hugh's)

Though the Varsity Match provided Oxford's sole first-class victory, the only real disappointment of their short season was the weather, most of which was cold and miserable. The sun did shine in the opening game against Durham and for the visit of the West Indians to play Combined Universities, but, for the remainder, it did not encourage spectators. That was unfortunate, because the eight home matches against first-class counties – two lost and the others drawn – produced a veritable feast of runs, with Oxford often equal contributors. But their best moments came against Cambridge, whom they beat not only in the 150th University Match but also in an inaugural 55-overs game at Fenner's.

As in 1994, batting was the University's main strength. Gregor Macmillan, the new captain, was lucky to have the nucleus of the previous year's side available for most matches. He himself dropped down the order after a knee injury. But that resulted in Chinmay Gupte's promotion to open with Iain Sutcliffe, a move which was spectacularly successful. In one week of May, Gupte and Sutcliffe put on 283 against Hampshire, 204 in the one-day match with Cambridge, and 90 against Nottinghamshire. They also shared opening stands of 92 and 73 for Combined Universities against the West Indians, and Sutcliffe made a major contribution to beating Cambridge at Lord's. Macmillan began the season opening well with Sutcliffe and provided the backbone of the Combined Universities batting in the Benson and Hedges Cup. He returned to opening in Oxford's final first-class innings in the Varsity Match, when his unbeaten 113 saw them to victory. It was his maiden first-class hundred. Sutcliffe and Gupte were Oxford's other century-makers. Lower down the order, Andrew Ridley, the second Bradman Scholar, and Will Kendall were models of consistency. Kendall added 139 with Gupte against Leicestershire, when Oxford scored 320, their best total of the season, only to lose after a series of contrived declarations.

The bowling could not match the batting, though there were encouraging signs. With Richard Yeabsley, the only seamer available from 1994, missing the start – he had broken his finger in a rugby match – Macmillan had to rely on South African Angus MacRobert and left-armer David Mather, a medical student expected to be at Oxford for six years. They began promisingly, with four wickets each in Durham's first innings, but they found it a hard season and injuries took their toll. Yeabsley returned for the last home match, with Middlesex, and claimed four wickets in Cambridge's

OXFORD UNIVERSITY 1995

[Bill Smith]

Back row: L. J. Jarrett (*coach*), J. M. Attfield, A. C. Ridley, D. P. Mather, J. D. Ricketts, I. J. Sutcliffe, A. D. MacRobert, H. S. Malik, M. E. D. Jarrett, G. S. Gordon (*scorer*). *Front row*: C. M. Gupte, R. S. Yeabsley, G. I. Macmillan (*captain*), W. S. Kendall, C. J. Townsend.

second innings at Lord's – after Kendall dismissed both openers. It was ample reward for the experiment of grooming Kendall as a fourth seamer. The slow bowling was shared by off-spinners Jeremy Attfield, Hasnain Malik and Macmillan, and leg-spinner Justin Ricketts, who emerged as the most successful; as his batting improved, he developed into a promising all-rounder.

Another pleasing aspect of Oxford's cricket was the high standard of fielding, maintained from the previous year, for which much credit was due to coach Les Lenham. Head groundsman Richard Sula also contributed to the run-glut with his usual excellent pitches. – Paton Fenton.

Paton Fenton has retired after 27 years as Wisden's Oxford *correspondent. Successive editors have all been very grateful for his efforts.*

OXFORD UNIVERSITY RESULTS

First-class matches – Played 10: Won 1, Lost 3, Drawn 6.

FIRST-CLASS AVERAGES
BATTING AND FIELDING

	Birthplace	*M*	*I*	*NO*	*R*	*HS*	*Avge*	*Ct/St*
I. J. Sutcliffe.......	Leeds	10	18	3	673	163*	44.86	8
W. S. Kendall	Wimbledon	10	15	2	442	94	34.00	5
C. M. Gupte	Poona, India	9	16	2	472	119	33.71	1
G. I. Macmillan....	Guildford	10	15	2	357	113*	27.46	11
A. C. Ridley.......	Sydney, Australia	10	16	1	375	71	25.00	4
C. J. Townsend	Wokingham	6	7	4	72	27	24.00	11/1
M. E. D. Jarrett...	London	7	11	4	137	40	19.57	8/1
H. S. Malik	Sargodha, Pakistan	8	10	1	160	64	17.77	8
J. D. Ricketts......	Salisbury	10	11	1	148	63	14.80	3
J. M. Attfield	Kettering	6	8	2	76	23*	12.66	2
A. D. MacRobert ..	Pretoria, SA	9	9	2	80	29	11.42	3
D. P. Mather	Bebington	8	6	3	19	8*	6.33	2
R. S. Yeabsley	St Albans	3	4	0	13	4	3.25	1

Also batted: N. F. C. Martin (*Birmingham*) (2 matches) 3, 7; J. M. Windsor (*Chesterfield*) (2 matches) 6*, 14, 8.

* Signifies not out.

The following played a total of three three-figure innings for Oxford University – C. M. Gupte 1, G. I. Macmillan 1, I. J. Sutcliffe 1.

BOWLING

	O	*M*	*R*	*W*	*BB*	*5W/i*	*Avge*
W. S. Kendall	76	13	233	8	3-37	0	29.12
R. S. Yeabsley	85	16	277	8	4-34	0	34.62
D. P. Mather	227.1	49	710	18	4-65	0	39.44
J. D. Ricketts......	224.5	35	732	17	3-30	0	43.05
A. D. MacRobert ..	264	37	843	18	4-41	0	46.83
H. S. Malik	152	22	539	6	2-55	0	89.83
G. I. Macmillan....	129.3	13	460	5	1-53	0	92.00

Also bowled: J. M. Attfield 87.3–12–310–3; N. F. C. Martin 23–2–123–1; I. J. Sutcliffe 9–1–31–1; J. M. Windsor 41.4–12–93–3.

Note: Matches in this section which were not first-class were signified by a dagger.

†At Oxford, April 12. Gloucestershire won by seven wickets. Toss: Oxford University. Oxford University 152 (53.3 overs) (I. J. Sutcliffe 59, C. M. Gupte 45; A. M. Smith five for 17); Gloucestershire 155 for three (28.4 overs) (M. A. Lynch 38, T. H. C. Hancock 63 not out).

OXFORD UNIVERSITY v DURHAM

At Oxford, April 13, 14, 15. Drawn. Toss: Durham. First-class debuts: A. D. MacRobert, D. P. Mather, J. D. Ricketts. County debuts: J. Boiling, M. A. Roseberry.

Roseberry nearly marked his official debut as Durham's captain with a century, batting 260 minutes for 90. Morris came even closer, falling for 99, including three sixes and 11 fours, after dominating their second-wicket stand of 163. The remainder of the county's batting was uninspiring, while the students' bowling was tidy; MacRobert and Mather claimed four wickets each on debut. Oxford's new captain, Macmillan, then hit his way from ten to 46 in 30 balls and Sutcliffe and Gupte were equally entertaining as they reached 124 for one. But an alarming collapse saw the last seven wickets fall for 17 in 14 overs, and Oxford avoided following on by just ten runs. Durham set a target of 277 in three hours, but bad light prevented a finish.

Close of play: First day, Durham 272-4 (J. I. Longley 37*, S. Hutton 3*); Second day, Durham 5-0 (M. Saxelby 3*, S. Hutton 2*).

Durham

*M. A. Roseberry c Townsend b Mather	90	
M. Saxelby c Macmillan b MacRobert	16 – (1) lbw b Mather	5
J. E. Morris c Ricketts b Macmillan	99	
J. A. Daley b Mather	20 – not out	53
J. I. Longley c Macmillan b Mather	37 – (3) b MacRobert	11
S. Hutton c Macmillan b MacRobert	15 – (2) c Ridley b Mather	21
†C. W. Scott b MacRobert	0 – (5) not out	41
J. Boiling c Townsend b MacRobert	0	
J. Wood not out	19	
A. Walker c Macmillan b Mather	0	
S. J. E. Brown not out	16	
L-b 5, w 1, n-b 4	10	L-b 6	6

1/29 2/192 3/211 4/254 5/273 (9 wkts dec.) 322   1/7 2/18 3/58 (3 wkts dec.) 137
6/274 7/274 8/287 9/288

Bowling: *First Innings*—MacRobert 28–2–93–4; Martin 4–0–22–0; Mather 27–5–65–4; Ricketts 12–3–43–0; Macmillan 24–5–53–1; Malik 16–6–35–0; Kendall 1–0–6–0. *Second Innings*—MacRobert 21–4–52–1; Mather 19–5–55–2; Macmillan 3.1–0–17–0; Malik 2–0–7–0.

Oxford University

*G. I. Macmillan b Wood	46 – c Scott b Wood	1
I. J. Sutcliffe c Scott b Saxelby	38 – not out	20
C. M. Gupte c Roseberry b Brown	48 – lbw b Brown	2
A. C. Ridley run out	6 – c Longley b Walker	21
W. S. Kendall c Scott b Brown	17 – not out	34
H. S. Malik c Roseberry b Boiling	0	
N. F. C. Martin c Scott b Brown	3	
A. D. MacRobert c Saxelby b Boiling	0	
J. D. Ricketts b Brown	0	
†C. J. Townsend not out	7	
D. P. Mather run out	1	
L-b 5, n-b 12	17	L-b 5, n-b 10	15

1/58 2/124 3/133 4/166 5/167 183   1/1 2/8 3/41 (3 wkts) 93
6/173 7/174 8/174 9/174

Bowling: *First Innings*—Brown 23.4-8-54-4; Wood 15-5-37-1; Boiling 25-13-29-2; Walker 8-2-43-0; Saxelby 5-2-15-1. *Second Innings*—Brown 8.2-2-7-1; Wood 8-4-11-1; Boiling 12-7-7-0; Saxelby 6-0-25-0; Walker 8-1-38-1.

Umpires: J. W. Holder and M. J. Kitchen.

OXFORD UNIVERSITY v GLAMORGAN

At Oxford, April 18, 19, 20. Drawn. Toss: Oxford University.

Macmillan's decision to bowl on a slow pitch did not pay off: Morris and Maynard put on 162 in 42 overs. Macmillan himself finally separated them, but Morris batted on, reaching 125 in five hours, despite a troublesome back. He returned to Cardiff for X-rays on the second day – which was interrupted by snow. Glamorgan had declared overnight and Oxford's reply was feeble. They lost their first four for 64 and, after 79 runs from Kendall and Malik, their last six for 14. Lefebvre, with three wickets in five balls, took a career-best six for 45. Maynard did not enforce the follow-on, allowing Dale to hit a century. A target of 433 was purely theoretical, though Macmillan and Sutcliffe ensured the draw.

Close of play: First day, Glamorgan 360-5 (R. D. B. Croft 31*, G. P. Butcher 4*); Second day, Glamorgan 41-0 (S. P. James 19*, A. Dale 15*).

Glamorgan

A. Dale c MacRobert b Martin	23	– (2) c Macmillan b Ricketts	121
*H. Morris c Townsend b Ricketts	125		
M. P. Maynard c Townsend b Macmillan	86		
P. A. Cottey c Macmillan b Ricketts	37	– (3) c Kendall b Ricketts	40
S. P. James run out	28	– (1) lbw b MacRobert	21
R. D. B. Croft not out	31	– (4) c Mather b Ricketts	27
G. P. Butcher not out	4	– (5) not out	3
L-b 8, w 2, n-b 16	26	B 4, l-b 8, w 1, n-b 4	17

1/36 2/198 3/291 4/307 5/354   (5 wkts dec.) 360   1/46 2/144   (4 wkts dec.) 229
3/205 4/229

N. M. Kendrick, R. P. Lefebvre, †C. P. Metson and S. L. Watkin did not bat.

Bowling: *First Innings*—MacRobert 18-1-64-0; Mather 14-2-50-0; Martin 14-2-61-1; Malik 24-3-78-0; Macmillan 15-1-53-1; Ricketts 11-2-46-2. *Second Innings*—MacRobert 15-2-48-1; Mather 18-5-64-0; Malik 6-0-35-0; Ricketts 8.5-0-30-3; Martin 5-0-40-0.

Oxford University

*G. I. Macmillan b Lefebvre	6	– not out	53
I. J. Sutcliffe b Lefebvre	1	– lbw b Cottey	44
C. M. Gupte c Metson b Watkin	13	– not out	3
A. C. Ridley st Metson b Croft	34		
W. S. Kendall lbw b Lefebvre	52		
H. S. Malik c Dale b Watkin	27		
N. F. C. Martin c Metson b Watkin	7		
A. D. MacRobert b Lefebvre	7		
J. D. Ricketts lbw b Lefebvre	0		
†C. J. Townsend b Lefebvre	0		
D. P. Mather not out	0		
B 4, l-b 5	9	B 3, n-b 2	5

1/7 2/8 3/44 4/64 5/143   157   1/92   (1 wkt) 105
6/147 7/151 8/152 9/152

Bowling: *First Innings*—Watkin 21-6-59-3; Lefebvre 18.3-6-45-6; Dale 7-2-8-0; Croft 7-5-3-1; Kendrick 11-8-10-0; Butcher 7-2-23-0. *Second Innings*—Watkin 8-3-11-0; Butcher 9-3-22-0; Dale 4-0-12-0; Croft 5-4-5-0; Kendrick 15-5-23-0; Cottey 15-2-29-1.

Umpires: P. Adams and N. T. Plews.

†At Oxford, April 24. Midlands Club Cricket Conference won by seven wickets. Toss: Oxford University. Oxford University 143 for six (45 overs) (J. M. Attfield 58); Midlands Club Cricket Conference 147 for three (44 overs) (D. Smithson 38, D. Banks 56 not out).

OXFORD UNIVERSITY v WORCESTERSHIRE

At Oxford, April 27, 28, 29. Drawn. Toss: Worcestershire. First-class debut: J. M. Attfield. Oxford debut: M. E. D. Jarrett.

Worcestershire openers Curtis and Weston put on 163 and Weston proceeded to a century before Oxford hit back, capturing four wickets after tea. Gupte led their reply and Ridley completed a maiden fifty. But the usual collapse followed Gupte's dismissal: a slump from 136 for two to 198 for nine. The makeshift county opening pair of Leatherdale and Haynes raised another century stand and Oxford were set 282 in four hours. They lost Macmillan and Gupte without a run scored, before Sutcliffe – with his own maiden half-century – and Ridley steadied them. Nevertheless, they faced defeat at 106 for six with 22 overs left until Attfield and Jarrett, a Cambridge Blue in 1992 and 1993, negotiated 12 of them and Curtis settled for the draw.

Close of play: First day, Oxford University 10-0 (G. I. Macmillan 2*, I. J. Sutcliffe 3*); Second day, Worcestershire 29-0 (D. A. Leatherdale 13*, G. R. Haynes 15*).

Worcestershire

W. P. C. Weston c Kendall b Malik	100		
*T. S. Curtis c Kendall b Macmillan	81		
G. A. Hick c and b Malik	22		
G. R. Haynes run out	17	– (2) b Ricketts	55
D. A. Leatherdale b MacRobert	34	– (1) c Jarrett b Ricketts	92
M. J. Church lbw b Mather	35	– (3) not out	29
†S. J. Rhodes c Malik b Mather	6		
S. R. Lampitt not out	14		
P. J. Newport not out	3		
J. E. Brinkley (did not bat)		– (4) not out	5
L-b 5, w 3	8	B 2, l-b 3	5

1/163 2/204 3/210 4/250 5/293 (7 wkts. dec.) 320   1/136 2/175 (2 wkts. dec.) 186
6/299 7/309

R. K. Illingworth did not bat.

Bowling: *First Innings*—MacRobert 18-1-69-1; Mather 23-3-68-2; Kendall 3-0-15-0; Macmillan 17-2-59-1; Ricketts 7-0-35-0; Attfield 4-1-14-0; Malik 16-1-55-2. *Second Innings*—MacRobert 16-0-56-0; Mather 3-1-13-0; Attfield 9-1-35-0; Ricketts 9-0-38-2; Malik 5-0-39-0.

Oxford University

*G. I. Macmillan st Rhodes b Illingworth	32	– c Rhodes b Newport	0
I. J. Sutcliffe c Rhodes b Newport	3	– lbw b Brinkley	57
C. M. Gupte lbw b Haynes	60	– c Lampitt b Newport	0
A. C. Ridley c Rhodes b Lampitt	50	– lbw b Lampitt	22
W. S. Kendall lbw b Newport	11	– c Rhodes b Illingworth	9
H. S. Malik c Church b Newport	6	– c Rhodes b Lampitt	2
J. M. Attfield b Newport	0	– not out	15
†M. E. D. Jarrett lbw b Lampitt	4	– not out	1
A. D. MacRobert c Hick b Lampitt	0		
J. D. Ricketts not out	22		
D. P. Mather b Illingworth	6		
L-b 6, w 1, n-b 24	31	L-b 3, n-b 14	17

1/14 2/88 3/136 4/170 5/180   225   1/0 2/0 3/73 (6 wkts) 123
6/180 7/185 8/185 9/198   4/90 5/95 6/106

Bowling: *First Innings*—Newport 21–7–51–4; Brinkley 14–3–49–0; Lampitt 17–6–49–3; Illingworth 21.4–7–47–2; Weston 1–0–4–0; Haynes 10–3–19–1. *Second Innings*—Newport 7–5–7–2; Brinkley 12–2–50–1; Haynes 8–4–15–0; Illingworth 16–6–21–1; Lampitt 8–0–24–2; Weston 2–2–0–0; Curtis 2–1–3–0.

Umpires: J. W. Holder and N. T. Plews.

†At Oxford, May 3. Oxford University won by 133 runs. Toss: Oxford University. Oxford University 273 for nine dec. (C. M. Gupte 80, I. J. Sutcliffe 36, M. E. D. Jarrett 67, J. D. Ricketts 30; C. K. Bullen four for 101, A. J. Trott four for 66); Bedfordshire 140 (A. J. Trott 43; J. M. Attfield five for 51, J. D. Ricketts four for 67).

†At Oxford, May 4. Oxford University won by two wickets. Toss: Oxfordshire. Oxfordshire 218 for five (55 overs) (A. G. Sabin 44, D. A. J. Wise 74, A. P. White 33); Oxford University 219 for eight (53.5 overs) (C. M. Gupte 65, Extras 46).

†At Oxford, May 5. Tied. Toss: Oxford University. Oxford University 231 (53 overs) (J. M. Attfield 36, A. C. Ridley 87, W. S. Kendall 33, R. S. Yeabsley 34; R. S. Jerome five for 33); Hertfordshire 231 (54.3 overs) (S. March 54, N. Gilbert 37, R. S. Jerome 37; R. S. Yeabsley four for 37).

OXFORD UNIVERSITY v HAMPSHIRE

At Oxford, May 11, 12, 13. Drawn. Toss: Hampshire.

Rain cut the first day to 66 minutes and there was no proper contest, but Sutcliffe and Gupte, promoted to open, performed wonders. After batting for 18 overs on the second evening, next day they took their partnership to 283, easily beating the highest stand for any Oxford wicket against Hampshire: 209 by G. R. R. Colman and I. P. F. Campbell at Southampton in 1913. The partnership finally ended when Gupte was caught for 119. Sutcliffe advanced from his maiden first-class century to 163 not out, bettering the highest Oxford score against Hampshire: M. B. Hofmeyr's 154 in 1949. Earlier, Nicholas won the toss for the first time in eight matches in 1995 – he had lost the seventh to Macmillan two days earlier, when they captained Hampshire and Combined Universities on the same ground. He elected to bat and made the most of it, passing 1,000 runs against Oxford during his 120.

Close of play: First day, Hampshire 35–1 (V. P. Terry 17*, G. W. White 4*); Second day, Oxford University 55–0 (C. M. Gupte 27*, I. J. Sutcliffe 22*).

Hampshire

V. P. Terry b Mather 22	†A. N. Aymes not out 62
R. S. M. Morris c Malik b Mather 14	S. D. Udal c Jarrett b Attfield 26
G. W. White c Malik b Kendall 57	B 1, w 1 2
*M. C. J. Nicholas c Sutcliffe	
b Ricketts .120	1/22 2/41 3/134 (6 wkts. dec.) 331
P. R. Whitaker c Attfield b MacRobert. 28	4/184 5/292 6/331

D. P. J. Flint, H. H. Streak, J. N. B. Bovill and M. J. Thursfield did not bat.

Bowling: MacRobert 22–5–57–1; Mather 27–7–81–2; Ricketts 21–3–66–1; Attfield 13.3–1–62–1; Kendall 3–0–12–1; Malik 10–0–41–0; Sutcliffe 1–0–6–0; Macmillan 1–0–5–0.

Oxford University

C. M. Gupte c Morris b Bovill 119	
I. J. Sutcliffe not out 163	
†M. E. D. Jarrett not out 16	
L-b 13, n-b 6 19	
1/283 (1 wkt. dec.) 317	

*G. I. Macmillan, A. C. Ridley, W. S. Kendall, H. S. Malik, J. M. Attfield, A. D. MacRobert, J. D. Ricketts and D. P. Mather did not bat.

Bowling: Bovill 20–1–73–1; Streak 16.4–1–58–0; Thursfield 21–6–48–0; Udal 29–6–51–0; Flint 18–5–59–0; Whitaker 6–2–15–0.

Umpires: J. H. Hampshire and R. Julian.

At Cambridge, May 14. OXFORD UNIVERSITY beat CAMBRIDGE UNIVERSITY by 112 runs.

†At Oxford, May 15. Drawn. Toss: Oxford University. Oxford University 314 for nine dec. (A. D. MacRobert 114, G. Morgan 75; P. Lambsdale four for 68, R. Pack three for 83); Berkshire 210 for four (R. W. Horner 67, J. R. Wood 101).

†At Oxford, May 16. Drawn. Toss: Oxford University. Oxford University 132 for one (D. Amm 44 not out, J. D. Ricketts 61 not out) v Royal Navy.

OXFORD UNIVERSITY v NOTTINGHAMSHIRE

At Oxford, May 18, 19, 20. Drawn. Toss: Nottinghamshire.

Neither a young county side – without a single capped player – nor the University could control a game which featured three declarations and only 17 wickets. Oxford's bowling contained the Nottinghamshire batting for much of the first day. After tea, however, Mike and Hindson, who hit a maiden fifty, knocked 80 off ten overs. Acting-captain Noon declared overnight and Oxford made a spirited reply, Gupte and Sutcliffe continuing their fine form with a stand of 90. Ridley and Kendall put on 126 before Macmillan declared 23 behind. Another big stand, 168 from Noon and Dowman, who added 107 to his 102 against Cambridge in April, challenged Oxford to score 267 from 51 overs. Their hopes were soon deflated when Gupte failed.

Close of play: First day, Nottinghamshire 303-6 (G. W. Mike 66*, J. E. Hindson 53*); Second day, Nottinghamshire 34-0 (M. P. Dowman 21*, W. M. Noon 11*).

Nottinghamshire

M. P. Dowman c Sutcliffe b Attfield 18	– c and b Macmillan	107
C. Banton c Jarrett b Mather 63	– (5) not out	17
J. R. Wileman c Gupte b Mather 43	– (4) not out	27
G. W. Mike not out 66		
*W. M. Noon c Malik b Attfield 7	– (2) c Kendall b Mather	66
†L. N. Walker st Jarrett b Ricketts 24	– (3) c Sutcliffe b Mather	18
R. T. Bates c Jarrett b Malik 9		
J. E. Hindson not out 53		
B 2, l-b 8, n-b 10.................. 20	B 2, l-b 4, n-b 2	8

1/56 2/132 3/133 4/148   (6 wkts dec.) 303   1/168 2/192 3/203   (3 wkts dec.) 243
5/195 6/223

M. G. Field-Buss, D. B. Pennett and R. J. Chapman did not bat.

Bowling: *First Innings*—MacRobert 9-0-52-0; Mather 26-8-75-2; Attfield 36-8-76-2; Ricketts 8-1-34-1; Malik 11-3-56-1. *Second Innings*—MacRobert 6-2-13-0; Mather 20-1-62-2; Malik 2-1-1-0; Macmillan 19-1-88-1; Sutcliffe 1-0-1-0; Ricketts 12-0-34-0; Attfield 9-0-38-0.

Oxford University

C. M. Gupte c Banton b Mike 44	– c Field-Buss b Mike	13
I. J. Sutcliffe b Hindson 39	– not out	44
A. C. Ridley c Chapman b Pennett 71	– st Walker b Field-Buss	30
W. S. Kendall c Walker b Mike 74	– (5) not out	1
J. M. Attfield not out 23		
H. S. Malik b Hindson 5		
*G. I. Macmillan (did not bat)	– (4) c Walker b Chapman	15
B 1, l-b 9, n-b 14................. 24	B 5	5

1/90 2/96 3/222 4/263 5/280   (5 wkts dec.) 280   1/16 2/85 3/106   (3 wkts) 108

†M. E. D. Jarrett, A. D. MacRobert, J. D. Ricketts and D. P. Mather did not bat.

Bowling: *First Innings*—Pennett 13-1-69-1; Chapman 12-1-47-0; Mike 12-1-32-2; Hindson 25-6-70-2; Field-Buss 12-2-49-0; Wileman 6-3-3-0. *Second Innings*—Mike 6-0-19-1; Pennett 4-1-12-0; Field-Buss 13-5-28-1; Hindson 11-3-31-0; Chapman 3-0-11-1; Bates 3-2-2-0.

Umpires: M. K. Reed and A. G. T. Whitehead.

†At Arundel, May 23. Drawn. Toss: Oxford University. Oxford University 282 for six dec. (C. M. Gupte 55, M. E. D. Jarrett 45, I. J. Sutcliffe 64, W. S. Kendall 44, J. D. Ricketts 32 not out; I. J. Curtis four for 73); Lavinia, Duchess of Norfolk's XI 279 for eight (K. Greenfield 53, T. J. G. O'Gorman 52, K. G. Sedgbeer 52, P. Moores 41; A. D. MacRobert three for 38, J. M. Attfield three for 75).

OXFORD UNIVERSITY v DERBYSHIRE

At Oxford, May 25, 26, 27. Derbyshire won by five wickets. Toss: Oxford University. First-class debuts: J. M. Windsor; P. Aldred, A. Richardson. County debut: W. A. Dessaur.

Oxford suffered their first defeat of 1995, though they recovered their dignity on the final day. They resumed only ten ahead, with six second-innings wickets down, but Jarrett, Ricketts and MacRobert all turned in their highest scores for Oxford. The last five wickets had taken the University from 109 to 258. Then Derbyshire lost five wickets in reaching 95. The students had paid heavily for choosing to field; Dessaur, formerly with Nottinghamshire, became the fourth player to score a century on debut for Derbyshire and added 204 with Wells, who made his first hundred since leaving Sussex. Another first-class debutant, Richardson, removed both Oxford openers that evening; next day, they were all out for 97 and followed on 164 behind.

Close of play: First day, Oxford University 15-2 (J. M. Attfield 6*, M. E. D. Jarrett 4*); Second day, Oxford University 174-6 (M. E. D. Jarrett 33*, J. D. Ricketts 13*).

Derbyshire

W. A. Dessaur not out 119	– c Jarrett b Kendall...........	2
T. J. G. O'Gorman c Jarrett b Mather 17		
C. M. Wells c Sutcliffe b Ricketts 115		
†K. M. Krikken not out 2	– (6) not out	15
P. Aldred (did not bat)	– (2) c Ridley b Kendall	13
M. E. Cassar (did not bat)	– (4) c Attfield b MacRobert	7
A. J. Harris (did not bat)	– not out	13
A. Richardson (did not bat)	– (5) c MacRobert b Kendall.....	4
A. C. Cottam (did not bat).................	– (3) c Jarrett b MacRobert	36
L-b 6, n-b 2 8	L-b 4, w 1	5

1/48 2/252   (2 wkts dec.) 261   1/10 2/27 3/58   (5 wkts) 95
                                                                    4/62 5/73

*K. J. Barnett and C. J. Adams did not bat.

Bowling: *First Innings*—Mather 19-6-37-1; MacRobert 20-1-75-0; Windsor 12-2-24-0; Attfield 7-1-37-0; Ricketts 8-1-26-1; Macmillan 11-1-37-0; Kendall 1-0-6-0; Sutcliffe 3-0-13-0. *Second Innings*—Kendall 12-0-37-3; Ricketts 15-1-47-0; MacRobert 4-2-7-2.

Oxford University

C. M. Gupte c Krikken b Richardson	2	– run out	37
I. J. Sutcliffe lbw b Richardson	3	– c Krikken b Cassar	23
J. M. Attfield b Harris	6	– (6) lbw b Cottam	11
†M. E. D. Jarrett lbw b Aldred	16	– (7) c Aldred b Cassar	40
A. C. Ridley b Richardson	12	– (3) c Krikken b Barnett	1
W. S. Kendall lbw b Cottam	31	– (4) c Krikken b Harris	19
*G. I. Macmillan lbw b Aldred	0	– (5) b Barnett	22
J. D. Ricketts c Krikken b Harris	11	– c Krikken b Cassar	31
A. D. MacRobert lbw b Harris	0	– c Krikken b Harris	29
J. M. Windsor not out	6	– c Krikken b Aldred	14
D. P. Mather c Cassar b Cottam	0	– not out	4
L-b 2, n-b 8	10	B 6, l-b 7, n-b 14	27

1/4 2/11 3/15 4/42 5/42   97   1/58 2/66 3/72 4/109 5/109   258
6/42 7/59 8/63 9/95   6/152 7/194 8/206 9/241

Bowling: *First Innings*—Harris 16-3-36-3; Richardson 10-2-27-3; Aldred 10-4-24-2; Cottam 6.3-2-5-2; Barnett 4-1-3-0. *Second Innings*—Cassar 24-9-54-4; Richardson 9-1-33-0; Aldred 14.3-4-36-1; Barnett 21-9-60-1; Harris 12-5-33-2; Cottam 17-6-29-1.

Umpires: J. H. Hampshire and M. K. Reed.

OXFORD UNIVERSITY v LEICESTERSHIRE

At Oxford, June 2, 3, 5. Leicestershire won by five wickets. Toss: Oxford University. First-class debuts: S. Bartle, J. Ormond.

Oxford lost their second match running, but only after reciprocal declarations and a remarkable run-chase. Chasing 404 in 83 overs, Maddy and Habib scored maiden first-class centuries, putting on 192 in 39 overs, and Habib saw Leicestershire home with four balls remaining. He hit 21 fours in an unbeaten 174 from 203 balls. Oxford's decision to bat seemed to have backfired at 11 for two, but Gupte shared successive century stands to take them to 252 for three. Though the innings faltered after tea, the students declared on 320, their best total of the season. Sheriyar took a career-best five for 61. Leicestershire declared after a second-day washout; Oxford scored 83 in 16 overs before setting their challenge.

Close of play: First day, Leicestershire 0-0 (D. L. Maddy 0*, B. F. Smith 0*); Second day, No play.

Oxford University

C. M. Gupte c Nixon b Sheriyar	97		
I. J. Sutcliffe c Maddy b Sheriyar	7		
A. C. Ridley b Sheriyar	0	– (2) not out	20
*G. I. Macmillan c Ormond b Sheriyar	37		
W. S. Kendall c Bartle b Dakin	94		
M. E. D. Jarrett c Mason b Ormond	15	– (3) not out	39
J. M. Attfield b Sheriyar	2		
J. D. Ricketts b Brimson	6	– (1) c Nixon b Dakin	0
A. D. MacRobert not out	17		
†C. J. Townsend b Ormond	5		
D. P. Mather not out	8		
L-b 14, w 6, n-b 12	32	L-b 1, w 1, n-b 22	24

1/11 2/11 3/113 4/252 5/267   (9 wkts dec.) 320   1/0   (1 wkt dec.) 83
6/267 7/279 8/284 9/289

Bowling: *First Innings*—Sheriyar 21.5-6-61-5; Ormond 17-6-65-2; Dakin 17-2-54-1; Mason 19-4-57-0; Brimson 14-3-41-1; Clarke 8-2-28-0. *Second Innings*—Dakin 2-1-1-1; Bartle 2-0-42-0; Clarke 6-2-17-0; Mason 6-0-22-0.

Leicestershire

D. L. Maddy not out	0	c Sutcliffe b Ricketts	131
B. F. Smith not out	0	lbw b Mather	30
A. Habib (did not bat)	–	not out	174
*†P. A. Nixon (did not bat)	–	c Macmillan b Ricketts	1
S. Bartle (did not bat)	–	b MacRobert	32
J. M. Dakin (did not bat)	–	c and b Macmillan	19
V. P. Clarke (did not bat)	–	not out	5
L-b 6, w 2, n-b 4			12

(no wkt dec.) 0   1/65 2/257 3/275   (5 wkts) 404
4/344 5/381

A. Sheriyar, M. T. Brimson, T. J. Mason and J. Ormond did not bat.

Bowling: First Innings—Kendall 1–1–0–0. *Second Innings*—Kendall 2–0–13–0; Mather 14–3–70–1; MacRobert 26–1–111–1; Ricketts 21–1–108–2; Macmillan 13.2–0–63–1; Attfield 6–0–33–0.

Umpires: A. Clarkson and A. G. T. Whitehead.

†At Oxford, June 6. Oxford University won by 60 runs. Toss: Oxford University. Oxford University 224 (49.2 overs) (C. M. Gupte 33, A. C. Ridley 50, G. I. Macmillan 64; E. A. Upashantha three for 51, M. Muralitharan five for 23); Sri Lankan Cavaliers 164 (40.4 overs) (R. S. Kaluwitharana 64; J. M. Attfield three for 44).

†At Oxford, June 7, 8, 9. Drawn. Toss: MCC. MCC 167 (R. P. Gofton 44; R. S. Yeabsley five for 23) and 380 for nine (A. J. T. Miller 48, A. M. Brown 114, D. P. Hughes 52, P. A. W. Heseltine 64 not out; A. D. MacRobert three for 82); Oxford University 342 for nine dec. (C. M. Gupte 84, J. M. Attfield 42, M. E. D. Jarrett 36, W. S. Kendall 37, A. C. Ridley 81 not out; P. A. Waterman three for 36, D. P. Hughes three for 69).

†At Oxford, June 10. Free Foresters won by two wickets. Toss: Oxford University. Oxford University 247 for eight dec. (C. J. Townsend 96, J. M. Attfield 74; P. Krasinski four for 85); Free Foresters 250 for eight (W. Holland 30, Hon. P. Fitzherbert 61, I. Barnes 37, N. Hadcock 42).

†At Oxford, June 12, 13. Drawn. Toss: Oxford University. Oxford University 262 for three dec. (C. M. Gupte 34, I. J. Sutcliffe 113, J. M. Attfield 68); Harlequins 243 for seven (R. D. Oliphant-Callum 38, N. F. C. Martin 41, B. C. A. Ellison 79, M. P. W. Jeh 40).

†At Oxford, June 14, 15, 16. Oxford University won by ten wickets. Toss: Combined Services. Combined Services 145 (Flt Lt A. W. J. Spiller 30; R. S. Yeabsley three for nine) and 223 (SAC J. T. A. Bibby 96; W. S. Kendall three for 34, R. S. Yeabsley three for 33); Oxford University 215 (J. M. Attfield 92, R. S. Yeabsley 35; Flt Lt P. R. Singleton three for 35, Capt. P. D. O. Logan three for 64, Pte D. Matthews three for 46) and 157 for no wkt (J. M. Attfield 87 not out, A. C. Ridley 60 not out).

†At Oxford, June 17. Drawn. Toss: Oxford University. Oxford University 322 for six dec. (C. M. Gupte 71, A. C. Ridley 127, W. S. Kendall 35); Durham University 33 for two.

OXFORD UNIVERSITY v MIDDLESEX

At Oxford, June 20, 21, 22. Drawn. Toss: Middlesex.

Weekes batted for all but 20 minutes of the opening day, ending a lean first-class run with a career-best 143. He and Brown put on 154 against an Oxford attack missing seamers MacRobert and Mather and off-spinner Attfield – though Yeabsley, also on Middlesex's books, was back from his exams. He and Windsor, in his second first-class match, snapped up five wickets after tea. Next day, Oxford were 70 for seven, four of them falling to Taylor, playing his first match after being injured in 1994. Ricketts led a late recovery with his maiden half-century. Already 101 ahead, Middlesex declared again as soon as Pooley reached his third hundred of the season and Nash his fifty. They set the students 269 in 67 overs, but the shutters went up once Sutcliffe and Gupte fell.

Close of play: First day, Middlesex 303-7 (R. L. Johnson 29*, T. A. Radford 1*); Second day, Middlesex 50-0 (T. A. Radford 13*, J. C. Pooley 36*).

Middlesex

P. N. Weekes c Townsend b Windsor	143	
J. C. Pooley b Kendall	6	– not out 100
*J. D. Carr b Windsor	37	
†K. R. Brown c Sutcliffe b Yeabsley	70	
D. J. Nash c Townsend b Yeabsley	3	– (3) not out 50
M. A. Feltham c Malik b Yeabsley	8	
R. L. Johnson not out	29	
P. Farbrace c Jarrett b Windsor	1	
T. A. Radford not out	1	– (1) st Townsend b Malik 14
L-b 4, w 1	5	B 2, l-b 1 3

1/27 2/82 3/236 4/246 5/260 (7 wkts dec.) 303   1/53 (1 wkt dec.) 167
6/287 7/293

A. A. Khan and C. W. Taylor did not bat.

Bowling: *First Innings*—Kendall 22–4–66–1; Yeabsley 22–2–87–3; Windsor 26–10–51–3; Malik 10–0–38–0; Ricketts 16–1–57–0. *Second Innings*—Kendall 6–1–23–0; Yeabsley 15–1–43–0; Windsor 3.4–0–18–0; Malik 17–2–45–1; Ricketts 10–2–35–0.

Oxford University

C. M. Gupte b Johnson	4	– c Carr b Khan 12
I. J. Sutcliffe c Farbrace b Khan	27	– run out 21
A. C. Ridley c Radford b Feltham	25	– c Brown b Weekes 18
W. S. Kendall lbw b Taylor	3	– c Brown b Radford 34
*G. I. Macmillan lbw b Khan	24	
M. E. D. Jarrett c Khan b Taylor	0	– not out 0
H. S. Malik lbw b Taylor	2	– (5) not out 12
R. S. Yeabsley lbw b Taylor	4	
J. D. Ricketts c Carr b Khan	63	
†C. J. Townsend not out	21	
J. M. Windsor b Feltham	8	
B 1, l-b 9, w 3, n-b 8	21	

1/13 2/51 3/57 4/61 5/62 202   1/32 2/34 3/76 4/97 (4 wkts) 97
6/66 7/70 8/117 9/175

Bowling: *First Innings*—Nash 11–1–31–0; Johnson 17–2–51–1; Khan 29–9–56–3; Feltham 14.4–5–39–2; Taylor 8–4–15–4. *Second Innings*—Johnson 7–3–14–0; Feltham 5–3–6–0; Weekes 22–10–38–1; Taylor 3–0–11–0; Khan 18–8–28–1; Radford 1–1–0–1; Farbrace 1–1–0–0.

Umpires: V. A. Holder and P. B. Wight.

At Bristol, June 23, 24, 25. OXFORD UNIVERSITY lost to GLOUCESTERSHIRE by an innings and 62 runs.

†At Oxford, June 26. Oxford University won by three wickets. Toss: Wiltshire. Wiltshire 250 (S. M. Perrin 64, A. Muggleton 33, K. J. Parsons 52; D. P. Mather three for 34, J. D. Ricketts three for 32); Oxford University 251 for seven (C. M. Gupte 86, W. S. Kendall 63, J. D. Ricketts 30 not out).

†At Oxford, July 3. Drawn. Toss: Oxford University. Oxford University 306 for eight dec. (C. M. Gupte 131, W. S. Kendall 103; M. G. Lickley five for 84); Berkshire 167 for seven (T. L. Hall 65, M. Lane 46 not out; R. S. Yeabsley three for 15).

At Lord's, July 5, 6, 7. OXFORD UNIVERSITY beat CAMBRIDGE UNIVERSITY by nine wickets.

†At Wormsley, July 23. Drawn. Toss: J. Paul Getty's XI. Oxford University 231 for five dec. (J. M. Attfield 90 not out, R. S. Yeabsley 62); J. Paul Getty's XI 191 for eight (C. T. Radley 74, R. D. V. Knight 44).

CAMBRIDGE

President: Professor A. D. Buckingham (Pembroke)

Captain: A. R. Whittall (Falcon College, Zimbabwe, and Trinity)
Secretary: R. Q. Cake (KCS, Wimbledon, and St John's)

Captain for 1996: R. Q. Cake (KCS, Wimbledon, and St John's)
Secretary: D. R. H. Churton (Wellington College and St Catharine's)

Until the final day against Oxford, Cambridge won nothing but praise for the way they played their cricket. In the words of skipper Andy Whittall, his team had constantly surprised by performing above the level expected.

At the start of the term, there had been an air of resignation, with no outstanding new recruits and perceived weaknesses in both batting and bowling. There were to be only six home games, partly because pitches were being re-laid and partly because of the timing of the university term and examinations. Long-serving groundsman Tony Pocock had been absent all winter with the illness that forced him to resign during the season.

But things only got better. Improving pitches reflected the work put in by Pocock's deputy, John Moden, and the cricket played by the students was equally encouraging. There were five century partnerships during the season, four against counties. The university was only bowled out twice at Fenner's, where all six matches were drawn, and twice in a match only at Folkestone and Lord's – their two defeats.

The 150th Varsity Match was one of the best of recent years – helped considerably by the efforts of MCC and the two universities to encourage support. After holding a slight edge for much of the first two days, Cambridge subsided on the final day, when Oxford exposed their limitations – as in the first one-day Varsity Match between the two, which Oxford won by 112 runs at Fenner's.

Inevitably, Russell Cake, who achieved a starred first in his final engineering exams, headed the batting averages, scoring the team's only century, at Lord's. It was little surprise that, when Whittall decided not to stand for a third year as captain, Cake was elected for 1996. But the relative success of this side perhaps owed most to the emergence of several seniors. Richard Battye, a Yorkshireman who did not appear at all while he was completing a first in mathematics, became an overnight sensation when, in his seventh year at the university, he scored five half-centuries against the counties to average 32.58. Reimell Ragnauth, a second-year

848

CAMBRIDGE UNIVERSITY 1995

[Bill Smith]

Back row: G. J. Saville (*coach*), D. R. H. Churton, E. J. How, R. A. Battye, J. P. Carroll, A. N. Janisch, J. W. O. Freeth, A. R. May (*scorer*).
Front row: R. T. Ragnauth, R. Q. Cake, A. R. Whittall (*captain*), N. J. Haste, J. Ratledge.

student, opened and scored three half-centuries, as did John Ratledge. The bowling was more of a struggle. Nick Haste and Whittall bore the main burden, claiming 47 wickets – nearly twice as many as the other nine bowlers put together. Whittall had the heaviest workload, bowling 328 overs in eight matches. He took career-best figures of six for 46 against Essex and 11 for 113 in the match.

As performances improved, optimism broke through. A good deal of money was being spent on re-laying the Fenner's square, with financial and practical help from the TCCB. There were also rumours, and later concrete evidence, that cricketers were again being encouraged to win places at the university. Although this is outside the hands of the club, it is essential to the first-class status of Oxbridge cricket that talent is introduced – and that they are given the best pitches to play on. – David Hallett.

CAMBRIDGE UNIVERSITY RESULTS

First-class matches – Played 8: Lost 2, Drawn 6.

FIRST-CLASS AVERAGES

BATTING AND FIELDING

	Birthplace	M	I	NO	R	HS	Avge	Ct/St
R. Q. Cake	Chertsey	7	14	3	511	101	46.45	4
R. A. Battye	Huddersfield	8	14	2	391	70*	32.58	3
J. P. Carroll......	Bebington	8	15	2	292	42	22.46	4
J. Ratledge	Preston	8	16	0	358	67	22.37	4
R. T. Ragnauth ...	Cambridge	8	16	1	335	82	22.33	10
A. R. Whittall	Mutare, Zimbabwe	8	13	2	185	81*	16.81	6
N. J. Haste	Northampton	7	10	4	83	16	13.83	1
D. R. H. Churton ..	Salisbury	6	10	0	118	39	11.80	7/3
A. N. Janisch	Hammersmith	7	8	4	38	18*	9.50	2
J. W. O. Freeth....	Bournemouth	7	6	1	35	18	7.00	2
D. E. Stanley......	Bromley	2	4	0	10	6	2.50	0
M. I. Yeabsley ...	St Albans	2	4	0	2	2	0.50	0
E. J. How	Amersham	4	4	2	0	0*	0.00	1

Also batted: M. J. Birks (*Keighley*) (2 matches) 18*, 2, 23* (2 ct); L. P. Clarke (*Sheffield*) (2 matches) 14, 3, 0 (1 ct); E. R. Hughes (*Ipswich*) (2 matches) 0.

* Signifies not out.

R. Q. Cake scored the only three-figure innings for Cambridge University.

BOWLING

	O	M	R	W	BB	5W/i	Avge
N. J. Haste	197	41	655	18	5-73	1	36.38
A. R. Whittall....	328.4	85	1,064	29	6-46	2	36.68
A. N. Janisch	185	21	723	10	3-38	0	72.30
J. W. O. Freeth ..	210.3	33	721	8	2-62	0	90.12

Also bowled: R. A. Battye 0.4-0-14-0; J. P. Carroll 26-3-98-0; L. P. Clarke 7-0-55-1; E. J. How 75-9-299-1; E. R. Hughes 54-5-234-2; J. Ratledge 4.4-0-42-1; M. I. Yeabsley 18-3-84-2.

Note: Matches in this section which were not first-class are signified by a dagger.

†At Cambridge, April 10. Loughborough Students won by six wickets. Toss: Loughborough Students. Cambridge University 177 for five (50 overs) (R. Q. Cake 51, J. Ratledge 42; R. R. Dibden three for 53); Loughborough Students 178 for four (49 overs) (R. M. S. Weston 109).

†At Cambridge, April 11. Cambridge University won by five wickets. Toss: Loughborough Students. Loughborough Students 239 for eight (50 overs) (M. E. Harvey 84, W. J. Hearsey 54); Cambridge University 240 for five (43.1 overs) (R. Q. Cake 91, R. A. Battye 55, Extras 30).

CAMBRIDGE UNIVERSITY v YORKSHIRE

At Cambridge, April 13, 14, 15. Drawn. Toss: Cambridge University. First-class debuts: R. A. Battye, D. R. H. Churton, L. P. Clarke, J. W. O. Freeth, A. N. Janisch, R. T. Ragnauth. County debut: M. G. Bevan.

Moxon beat Byas to the first hundred of the season by 25 minutes, as they added 235 for the second wicket, and there was no respite when Australian Michael Bevan, Yorkshire's new overseas player, arrived. His hundred was the fastest of the three, taking 100 minutes and 125 balls, and he put on 132 with Byas and 106 with White. Cambridge struggled in reply, though Ratledge scored 56 despite a badly bruised thumb. Clarke and Churton had broken bones, however, and the umpires allowed substitute Malcolm Birks to keep wicket in Yorkshire's second innings. Declining to enforce the follow-on, Yorkshire extended their lead to 470 before a token declaration. Umpire Bird was another casualty on the final day, when he pulled out with a bad knee; Peter Chismon, a shotgun salesman, took over.

Close of play: First day, Cambridge University 12-0 (R. T. Ragnauth 2*, R. Q. Cake 10*); Second day, Yorkshire 3-0 (A. P. Grayson 3*, M. P. Vaughan 0*).

Yorkshire

*M. D. Moxon c Carroll b Clarke	130		
M. P. Vaughan b Haste	1	– retired hurt	52
D. Byas c and b Freeth	181		
M. G. Bevan not out	113		
C. White not out	50	– (4) b Whittall	32
A. P. Grayson (did not bat)	–	(1) st sub b Whittall	59
†R. J. Blakey (did not bat)	–	(3) st sub b Whittall	9
P. J. Hartley (did not bat)	–	(5) not out	0
G. M. Hamilton (did not bat)	–	(6) not out	9
B 1, w 1, n-b 2	4	L-b 3, w 1	4

1/6 2/241 3/373   (3 wkts dec.) 479   1/112 2/153 3/154   (3 wkts dec.) 165

R. D. Stemp and M. A. Robinson did not bat.

In the second innings M. P. Vaughan retired hurt at 112-1.

Bowling: *First Innings*—Haste 12–2–58–1; Clarke 7–0–55–1; Janisch 23–2–112–0; Whittall 25.3–7–116–0; Freeth 26–3–111–1; Ratledge 3–0–26–0. *Second Innings*—Haste 15–3–47–0; Whittall 21–7–46–3; Janisch 12–1–48–0; Freeth 6–1–21–0.

Cambridge University

R. T. Ragnauth lbw b Hamilton	12	– c Blakey b Robinson	1
R. Q. Cake c Bevan b Hamilton	19	– not out	25
J. P. Carroll run out	28	– (4) lbw b Grayson	0
R. A. Battye lbw b Robinson	1	– (5) lbw b Grayson	1
†D. R. H. Churton lbw b Stemp	14		
J. Ratledge lbw b White	56	– (3) st Blakey b Vaughan	17
L. P. Clarke c Blakey b Hartley	14		
*A. R. Whittall c Byas b Hartley	7	– (6) not out	4
N. J. Haste not out	15		
A. N. Janisch lbw b White	0		
J. W. O. Freeth c Blakey b Hamilton	2		
L-b 6	6	N-b 4	4

1/29 2/36 3/41 4/74 5/78   174   1/6 2/43 3/44 4/48   (4 wkts) 52
6/106 7/116 8/171 9/171

Bowling: *First Innings*—Hartley 20–6–36–2; Hamilton 22.2–9–41–3; Robinson 14–2–32–1; White 16–7–31–2; Stemp 18–8–23–1; Vaughan 3–1–5–0. *Second Innings*—Robinson 5–2–4–1; Hamilton 6–4–14–0; Stemp 9–2–11–0; Vaughan 9–2–14–1; Grayson 8–6–5–2; Bevan 6–4–4–0.

Umpires: H. D. Bird and R. Julian. P. Chismon deputised for H. D. Bird on the 3rd day.

CAMBRIDGE UNIVERSITY v LANCASHIRE

At Cambridge, April 18, 19, 20. Drawn. Toss: Lancashire. First-class debut: M. J. Birks. County debut: G. Keedy.

Neither Atherton nor Crawley scored a century against their old university, though Crawley reached 74. However, Speak, whose careful effort took three and a half hours, did get there; he and Crawley put on 146 in 36 overs. Showers cut the opening day to 79 overs and Lancashire declared overnight. They reduced Cambridge to 76 for six, but Battye scored 65, enabling Whittall to declare 77 behind. With the county reshuffling their batting order, Lloyd was promoted to open and scored a three-hour hundred before Watkinson invited the students to score 321 in 200 minutes. Ragnauth easily batted out time, reaching an unbeaten 65 and sharing an unbroken century stand with Cake. Lloyd's father David, the county coach, took the field after Crawley was hit on the ankle.

Close of play: First day, Lancashire 245-4 (N. H. Fairbrother 24*, M. Watkinson 0*); Second day, Lancashire 44-1 (G. D. Lloyd 22*, W. K. Hegg 12*).

Lancashire

M. A. Atherton c Janisch b Whittall	20			
N. J. Speak c Carroll b Haste	116			
J. P. Crawley b Janisch	74			
N. H. Fairbrother not out	24			
G. D. Lloyd lbw b Haste	9	– (1) c Whittall b Janisch	117
*M. Watkinson not out	0	– (4) c Ragnauth b Freeth	23
I. D. Austin (did not bat)		– (2) c Battye b Haste	10
†W. K. Hegg (did not bat)		– (3) c Ratledge b Freeth	43
P. J. Martin (did not bat)		– (5) not out	34
G. Yates (did not bat)		– (6) not out	11
B 1, l-b 1	2	L-b 3, n-b 2	5

1/46 2/192 3/225 4/245   (4 wkts dec.) 245   1/13 2/121   (4 wkts dec.) 243
                                                          3/167 4/208

G. Keedy did not bat.

Bowling: First Innings—Haste 21-9-30-2; Janisch 17-1-69-1; Whittall 26-6-83-1; Freeth 15-5-61-0. *Second Innings*—Haste 15-2-58-1; Janisch 18-5-44-1; Whittall 16-2-76-0; Freeth 10-0-62-2.

Cambridge University

R. T. Ragnauth lbw b Martin	0	– not out	65
D. E. Stanley c Watkinson b Austin	6	– b Martin	0
J. Ratledge b Watkinson	13	– st Hegg b Keedy	28
R. Q. Cake b Yates	27	– not out	47
J. P. Carroll lbw b Watkinson	0		
R. A. Battye b Yates	65		
*A. R. Whittall st Hegg b Keedy	9		
N. J. Haste c Fairbrother b Watkinson	15		
†M. J. Birks not out	18		
A. N. Janisch not out	0		
B 5, l-b 6, n-b 4	15	B 3, l-b 1	4

1/0 2/6 3/38 4/38 5/51   (8 wkts dec.) 168   1/3 2/43   (2 wkts) 144
6/76 7/106 8/158

J. W. O. Freeth did not bat.

Bowling: First Innings—Martin 14-5-36-1; Austin 17-8-36-1; Watkinson 16-6-27-3; Keedy 16-7-21-1; Yates 20-9-37-2. *Second Innings*—Martin 7-0-23-1; Austin 5-3-2-0; Yates 10-3-19-0; Keedy 16-3-57-1; Watkinson 10-4-19-0; Speak 3-0-20-0.

Umpires: B. Leadbeater and B. J. Meyer.

CAMBRIDGE UNIVERSITY v NOTTINGHAMSHIRE

At Cambridge, April 27, 28, 29. Drawn. Toss: Nottinghamshire. First-class debuts: E. R. Hughes, M. I. Yeabsley; C. Banton.

Cairns scored 100 in 65 balls and 76 minutes, which was to remain the fastest century of the season. He smashed seven fours and seven sixes and went on to 110, his highest score for Nottinghamshire, before falling to Whittall, who took a career-best four for 131. Robinson's hundred was more sedate, taking 164 balls and three hours. Cambridge were bowled out for 91, 322 behind, with Afford taking three for four in ten overs. But the county preferred batting practice to victory. Dowman scored a maiden century before retiring overnight with a back injury and Nottinghamshire took their advantage to 567 without losing a wicket. Ratledge staved off defeat but Cambridge's best batting came in the final 90 minutes, when Whittall and Birks put on 110 for the seventh wicket.

Close of play: First day, Cambridge University 11-2 (J. Ratledge 5*, M. J. Birks 0*); Second day, Nottinghamshire 161-0 (M. P. Dowman 102*, C. Banton 55*).

Nottinghamshire

M. P. Dowman c Birks b Hughes	43	– retired hurt	102
*R. T. Robinson c Ragnauth b Yeabsley	101		
P. Johnson c Carroll b Janisch	73		
C. L. Cairns c Janisch b Whittall	110		
C. Banton b Whittall	18	– (2) not out	80
K. P. Evans c and b Whittall	53		
G. W. Mike b Whittall	0	– (3) not out	54
J. E. Hindson c Birks b Janisch	5		
†B. N. French not out	1		
B 1, l-b 6, n-b 2	9	B 2, l-b 5, n-b 2	9

1/84 2/189 3/258 4/341 5/364   (8 wkts dec.) 413   (no wkt dec.) 245
6/374 7/405 8/413

R. A. Pick and J. A. Afford did not bat.

In the second innings M. P. Dowman retired hurt at 161.

Bowling: *First Innings*—Janisch 19-2-91-2; Carroll 12-1-43-0; Whittall 32.3-8-131-4; Hughes 13-1-62-1; Freeth 7-0-47-0; Yeabsley 4-0-32-1. *Second Innings*—Janisch 17-0-64-0; Whittall 27-11-50-0; Carroll 5-1-29-0; Hughes 13-2-48-0; Freeth 10-1-23-0; Yeabsley 5-0-24-0.

Cambridge University

R. T. Ragnauth c Cairns b Afford	4	– (4) lbw b Hindson	1
D. E. Stanley b Cairns	2	– (1) c French b Cairns	2
J. Ratledge b Afford	23	– (2) lbw b Pick	65
†M. J. Birks c Banton b Cairns	2	– (8) not out	23
J. P. Carroll lbw b Hindson	17	– (3) c and b Hindson	13
R. A. Battye b Pick	22	– (5) lbw b Pick	22
M. I. Yeabsley c Robinson b Hindson	0	– (6) lbw b Pick	0
*A. R. Whittall c French b Afford	11	– (7) not out	81
A. N. Janisch lbw b Pick	4		
E. R. Hughes lbw b Pick	0		
J. W. O. Freeth not out	0		
B 1, l-b 5	6	B 1, l-b 10	11

1/3 2/11 3/14 4/40 5/48   91   1/8 2/65 3/69   (6 wkts) 218
6/48 7/59 8/86 9/86   4/101 5/103 6/108

Bowling: *First Innings*—Cairns 8–4–7–2; Pick 16.4–6–22–3; Mike 3–2–1–0; Afford 19–12–23–3; Hindson 9–4–15–2; Evans 7–2–17–0. *Second Innings*—Cairns 4–1–6–1; Pick 11–4–26–3; Evans 18–3–59–0; Afford 19–7–47–0; Hindson 19–5–44–2; Banton 5–0–25–0.

Umpires: K. J. Lyons and P. B. Wight.

†At Cambridge, May 4, 5, 6. Drawn. Toss: Cambridge University. Cambridge University 196 (R. T. Ragnauth 45, M. J. Birks 32 not out; G. M. Charlesworth three for 25) and 293 for seven dec. (J. Ratledge 120, R. A. Battye 45, M. J. Birks 58 not out; G. J. Toogood three for 74); MCC 308 for eight dec. (J. R. Prentis 34, D. P. Hughes 134 not out, Extras 35; A. N. Janisch three for 52, J. P. Carroll three for 62) and nine for no wkt.

†At Cambridge, May 8. Club Cricket Conference Under-25 won by 38 runs. Toss: Cambridge University. Club Cricket Conference Under-25 228 for nine (55 overs) (C. Hollins 91); Cambridge University 190 (54.1 overs) (R. T. Ragnauth 54, L. P. Clarke 36, M. I. Yeabsley 31 not out; C. Hollins four for 33).

CAMBRIDGE UNIVERSITY v ESSEX

At Cambridge, May 11, 12, 13. Drawn. Toss: Cambridge University. First-class debut: A. J. E. Hibbert. County debut: N. A. Derbyshire.

Cambridge chased an unlikely victory after their captain, the off-spinner Whittall, improved on his career-best analysis in both innings to finish with 11 for 113. The pitch turned from the start and only Essex's acting-captain, Hussain, looked totally comfortable as the University bowled out a first-class team for the first time since May 1993. They then lost three for 39 but Cake led a spirited rally. Whittall declared 85 in arrears and claimed six more wickets – including five for eight in 22 balls. Hussain's declaration set Cambridge 250 in 192 minutes. Needing 130 from the last 20 overs with six wickets in hand, they had high hopes. A shower cost four overs, but it was the loss of four wickets, especially Battye, for four runs that finally forced discretion on them.

Close of play: First day, Cambridge University 15-1 (R. T. Ragnauth 3*, D. R. H. Churton 2*); Second day, Essex 27-2 (J. J. B. Lewis 4*, R. J. Rollins 0*).

Essex

*N. Hussain c Ragnauth b Whittall	68		
D. D. J. Robinson c Whittall b Haste	11	– (1) lbw b Whittall	13
J. J. B. Lewis b Haste	48	– b Whittall	60
A. J. E. Hibbert c Ratledge b Haste	24	– (2) c Churton b Haste	7
M. A. Garnham c Ragnauth b Whittall	7	– c Battye b Whittall	41
†R. J. Rollins b Whittall	36	– (4) b Freeth	13
R. M. Pearson c Clarke b Whittall	27	– lbw b Whittall	0
N. A. Derbyshire c Ratledge b Freeth	12	– not out	9
S. J. W. Andrew st Churton b Whittall	0	– c Cake b Whittall	3
D. M. Cousins not out	11	– (6) c Cake b Whittall	11
J. H. Childs b Freeth	1		
B 2, l-b 7, n-b 6	15	B 1, l-b 6	7

1/29 2/127 3/138 4/162 5/179   260   1/15 2/24 3/45   (8 wkts dec.) 164
6/225 7/246 8/246 9/250   4/140 5/140 6/140
                                                   7/153 8/164

Bowling: *First Innings*—Haste 18–4–56–3; Janisch 14–3–42–0; Whittall 27–9–67–5; Carroll 6–1–22–0; Freeth 28.3–6–64–2. *Second Innings*—Haste 10–1–22–1; Janisch 11–1–48–0; Freeth 16–5–41–1; Whittall 17.4–8–46–6.

Cambridge University

R. T. Ragnauth c Rollins b Derbyshire	6	– c Cousins b Childs	17
J. Ratledge c Lewis b Childs	9	– c Rollins b Cousins	7
†D. R. H. Churton b Childs	10	– (8) c Hussain b Childs	3
R. Q. Cake c Lewis b Childs	61	– (3) c Lewis b Cousins	0
J. P. Carroll b Pearson	38	– (4) b Pearson	42
R. A. Battye c Lewis b Andrew	3	– (5) c Robinson b Childs	64
L. P. Clarke b Pearson	3	– c Robinson b Pearson	0
*A. R. Whittall c Garnham b Pearson	28	– (6) b Pearson	7
N. J. Haste not out	2	– not out	10
A. N. Janisch (did not bat)		– not out	2
B 2, l-b 7, n-b 6	15	B 4, l-b 3, w 1, n-b 4	12

1/13 2/22 3/39 4/128 5/141   (8 wkts dec.) 175   1/9 2/13 3/39 4/119   (8 wkts) 164
6/141 7/158 8/175   5/149 6/149 7/152 8/153

J. W. O. Freeth did not bat.

Bowling: First Innings—Cousins 15–2–38–0; Andrew 15–6–24–1; Childs 14–6–28–3; Pearson 19.3–5–58–3; Derbyshire 11–4–18–1. *Second Innings*—Cousins 6–2–18–2; Derbyshire 5–0–10–0; Pearson 20–5–77–3; Childs 15.5–7–39–3; Andrew 4–1–13–0.

Umpires: B. Leadbeater and D. R. Shepherd.

†At Cambridge, May 14. Oxford University won by 112 runs. Toss: Oxford University. Oxford University 329 for six (55 overs) (C. M. Gupte 90, I. J. Sutcliffe 101, G. I. Macmillan 63, R. S. Yeabsley 32); Cambridge University 217 (49.2 overs) (J. Ratledge 65, D. R. H. Churton 34; G. I. Macmillan three for 28, H. S. Malik three for 44).

The first limited-overs Varsity Match. Gupte and Sutcliffe opened with 204 for Oxford and Macmillan hit 63 from 27 balls, including seven fours and two sixes.

†At Cambridge, May 18. Cambridgeshire won by seven runs. Toss: Cambridgeshire. Cambridgeshire 233 for four (55 overs) (N. T. Gadsby 55, N. J. Adams 36, M. A. Burton 66 not out, B. T. P. Donelan 37); Cambridge University 226 (54.3 overs) (R. A. Battye 63, L. P. Clarke 33, J. P. Carroll 35, N. J. Haste 30; B. T. P. Donelan three for 54).

CAMBRIDGE UNIVERSITY v MIDDLESEX

At Cambridge, June 9, 10, 11. Drawn. Toss: Cambridge University. First-class debuts: E. J. How; A. A. Khan.

Carr dominated the first day, with an unbeaten 116, after Haste ended a century opening stand by bowling both Weekes and Pooley. Middlesex declared overnight and Cambridge's innings followed a familiar pattern: an early wicket, some solid middle-order batting led by Battye, and a declaration in arrears. The students' total of 230 for eight was their best of the season to date. Rain on the final day prevented much meaningful cricket, though Shine, with four wickets in his first seven overs, briefly threatened Cambridge's unbeaten first-class record after what had seemed a token declaration at tea. They batted out time without further loss.

Close of play: First day, Middlesex 327-5 (J. D. Carr 116*, R. L. Johnson 14*); Second day, Middlesex 23-0 (T. A. Radford 7*, J. C. Harrison 15*).

Middlesex

P. N. Weekes b Haste	58		
J. C. Pooley b Haste	48		
*J. D. Carr not out	116		
T. A. Radford c Churton b Yeabsley	18	– (1) not out	51
J. C. Harrison c Churton b Whittall	44	– (2) not out	46
†P. Farbrace c Churton b Hughes	16		
R. L. Johnson not out	14		
B 4, l-b 6, w 1, n-b 2	13	B 5, l-b 2	7

1/113 2/118 3/181 4/269 5/292   (5 wkts dec.) 327   (no wkt dec.) 104

K. J. Shine, A. A. Khan, K. P. Dutch and K. Marc did not bat.

Bowling: *First Innings*—Haste 24–6–67–2; How 13–3–28–0; Whittall 25–6–92–1; Hughes 24–2–98–1; Carroll 3–0–4–0; Yeabsley 9–3–28–1. *Second Innings*—Haste 11–3–28–0; Whittall 5–0–14–0; How 7–1–29–0; Hughes 4–0–26–0.

Cambridge University

R. T. Ragnauth c Weekes b Khan	52	– c Farbrace b Shine	13
J. Ratledge c Radford b Johnson	2	– (3) c Farbrace b Shine	9
R. Q. Cake c Dutch b Johnson	43	– (4) c Dutch b Shine	0
J. P. Carroll c Carr b Khan	38	– (5) not out	11
R. A. Battye not out	70	– (6) not out	6
M. I. Yeabsley c Carr b Weekes	0	– (2) c Weekes b Shine	2
*A. R. Whittall c Carr b Khan	6		
†D. R. H. Churton lbw b Khan	0		
N. J. Haste b Johnson	8		
L-b 9, n-b 2	11	B 4, n-b 4	8

1/5 2/82 3/114 4/176 5/177   (8 wkts dec.) 230   1/8 2/23 3/25 4/30   (4 wkts) 49
6/192 7/192 8/230

E. R. Hughes and E. J. How did not bat.

Bowling: *First Innings*—Johnson 16.5–9–24–3; Shine 13–1–43–0; Marc 9–0–37–0; Khan 23–5–51–4; Weekes 19–3–42–1; Dutch 12–5–24–0. *Second Innings*—Johnson 6–2–10–0; Shine 10–4–23–4; Khan 4–0–7–0; Dutch 2–2–0–0; Weekes 2–0–5–0.

Umpires: D. J. Constant and V. A. Holder.

†At Cambridge, June 13. Cambridge University won by seven wickets. Toss: Middlesex League Select XI. Middlesex League Select XI 170 for nine (50 overs) (B. Watson 30, B. Yock 56; A. R. Whittall three for 51); Cambridge University 175 for three (38 overs) (J. Ratledge 44, R. Q. Cake 76 not out).

†At Arundel, June 15. Drawn. Toss: Lavinia, Duchess of Norfolk's XI. Lavinia, Duchess of Norfolk's XI 236 for seven dec. (A. Tarrant 66, A. Dunlop 77, J. Arscott 34); Cambridge University 127 for eight (R. A. Battye 81; S. Johnson five for 29).

CAMBRIDGE UNIVERSITY v WARWICKSHIRE

At Cambridge, June 16, 17, 18. Drawn. Toss: Cambridge University.

Three Warwickshire openers were left kicking themselves after getting out in the nineties. Moles and Twose had shared 193 for the first wicket when Whittall dismissed both of them and, in the second innings, Khan was run out nine short of what would have been his maiden first-class hundred. Cambridge's own openers started less well, going for nine runs, but a stand of 119 between the night-watchman, Churton, and Cake plus another fifty from

Battye carried the University to a confident 220 for seven. Whittall then invited Warwick-shire to bat again and in turn was offered a target of 289 in 53 overs. The students opted for safety and their sixth draw of the season at Fenner's.

Close of play: First day, Cambridge University 9-1 (J. Ratledge 8*, D. R. H. Churton 0*); Second day, Warwickshire 22-0 (W. G. Khan 12*, D. R. Brown 10*).

Warwickshire

A. J. Moles b Whittall	98				
R. G. Twose c and b Whittall	96				
D. P. Ostler b Freeth	46				
T. L. Penney not out	37				
W. G. Khan not out	16	– (1) run out	91
D. R. Brown (did not bat)		– (2) b Whittall	53
P. A. Smith (did not bat)		– (3) c and b Freeth	57
†K. J. Piper (did not bat)		– (4) st Churton b Whittall	2
N. M. K. Smith (did not bat)		– (5) b Whittall	0
R. P. Davis (did not bat)		– (6) not out	0
B 2, l-b 4, w 1	7	B 2, l-b 1, n-b 2	5

1/193 2/208 3/260	(3 wkts dec.) 300	1/93 2/196 3/205 (5 wkts dec.) 208
		4/205 5/208

*T. A. Munton did not bat.

Bowling: *First Innings*—Haste 11–2–41–0; How 14–0–39–0; Whittall 30–4–108–2; Janisch 10–1–23–0; Freeth 29.4–7–83–1. *Second Innings*—Haste 9–2–31–0; How 8–0–28–0; Janisch 7–0–55–0; Whittall 16–1–48–3; Freeth 17.2–2–43–1.

Cambridge University

R. T. Ragnauth lbw b Munton	0	– lbw b Twose	33
J. Ratledge c Khan b Munton	8	– (3) c Munton b Davis	39
†D. R. H. Churton b N. M. K. Smith	39	– (2) b Brown	0
R. Q. Cake c Penney b Davis	75	– not out	20
J. P. Carroll c Brown b Twose	26	– not out	21
R. A. Battye c Moles b Davis	50		
*A. R. Whittall lbw b Twose	5		
N. J. Haste not out	4		
B 7, l-b 4, n-b 6	17	L-b 4, n-b 2	6

1/0 2/9 3/128 4/130 5/214	(7 wkts dec.) 220	1/3 2/52 3/86 (3 wkts) 119
6/220 7/220		

E. J. How, A. N. Janisch and J. W. O. Freeth did not bat.

Bowling: *First Innings*—Munton 15–4–46–2; Brown 10–4–25–0; Twose 5–1–14–2; P. A. Smith 8–2–29–0; N. M. K. Smith 20–7–33–1; Davis 21.2–6–62–2. *Second Innings*—Brown 7–1–23–1; Munton 5–3–6–0; N. M. K. Smith 16–6–41–0; Twose 7–0–26–1; Davis 8–4–19–1.

Umpires: H. D. Bird and B. J. Meyer.

†At Cambridge, June 20, 21, 22. Combined Services won by 109 runs. Toss: Cambridge University. Combined Services 298 for eight dec. (Sgt G. S. Lumb 150 not out, Lt C. H. C. St George 53; E. J. How three for 33) and 205 for six dec. (Sgt G. S. Lumb 65, Lt C. H. C. St George 42, Pte D. Matthews 39 not out); Cambridge University 248 for seven dec. (L. P. Clarke 36, J. P. Carroll 64, R. Q. Cake 88) and 146 (M. J. Birks 41, J. Ratledge 51; Capt. P. D. O. Logan four for 46, Flt Lt P. R. Singleton five for 53).

†At Cambridge, June 24. Cambridge University won by 53 runs. Toss: Cambridge University. Cambridge University 226 for six dec. (M. J. Birks 37, R. Q. Cake 93; R. A. Pyman three for 55); Quidnuncs 173 (R. I. Clitheroe 43, J. C. Hammill 38, T. A. Bristowe 44; J. W. O. Freeth three for 33).

†At Cambridge, June 25. Drawn. Toss: Free Foresters. Cambridge University 186 (D. E. Stanley 42, J. P. Carroll 30, M. I. Yeabsley 56; R. A. Pyman four for 37); Free Foresters 184 for nine (G. B. A. Dyer 61, M. Semmence 31; A. H. Rose three for 31, M. I. Yeabsley four for 42).

At Folkestone, July 1, 2, 3. CAMBRIDGE UNIVERSITY lost to KENT by 168 runs.

THE UNIVERSITY MATCH, 1995

OXFORD UNIVERSITY v CAMBRIDGE UNIVERSITY

At Lord's, July 5, 6, 7. Oxford University won by nine wickets. Toss: Cambridge University.

Oxford captain Macmillan completed victory with seven overs to spare by smashing two sixes into the Mound Stand. His century was the 100th in Varsity Matches – in the 150th encounter. Though favourites, Oxford had trailed for most of the first two days. Cambridge gratefully exploited a true pitch to reach their best total of the season, built around a century from Cake. He hit five sixes and ten fours and added 102 with Ratledge, who had 11 fours after a sound start from openers Ragnauth and Churton. From a powerful 267 for four, however, the last six wickets fell for 28 runs. That seemed a trifle when Whittall, opening the bowling with his off-spin, and Haste reduced Oxford to 15 for three. But Sutcliffe batted patiently for three and a half hours, putting on 74 with Kendall and 85 with Malik. After Haste took a career-best five for 73, Macmillan declared 62 behind, gave the new ball to medium-pacer Kendall and was rewarded when he dismissed both openers. Yeabsley followed up with two more wickets before the close. With Cambridge 40 for four from 21 overs, Oxford were in the driving seat at last. It took another 42 anxious overs to see off the next six; Cake survived two and a half hours. But Cambridge's second-lowest total of the season left a target of just 189 from 54 overs. Macmillan resumed the opener's role for the first time since May and raised 143 with Sutcliffe, who made his second fifty of the game. Macmillan advanced to his maiden hundred, knocking off 113 in 150 balls. He hit 11 fours as well as the final, conclusive, sixes.

Close of play: First day, Cambridge University 284-8 (A. N. Janisch 2*, J. W. O. Freeth 5*); Second day, Cambridge University 40-4 (R. Q. Cake 9*, J. P. Carroll 6*).

Cambridge University

R. T. Ragnauth (*The Perse and Trinity Hall*) c Ricketts b MacRobert .	35	– c Ridley b Kendall............	14
†D. R. H. Churton (*Wellington C. and St Catharine's*) c Sutcliffe b Ricketts .	31	– c Townsend b Kendall.........	1
J. Ratledge (*Bolton School and St John's*) c Ridley b Mather .	67	– c MacRobert b Yeabsley.......	8
R. Q. Cake (*KCS, Wimbledon, and St John's*) c Ricketts b Sutcliffe .	101	– b MacRobert	43
J. P. Carroll (*Rendcomb and Homerton*) c Townsend b Ricketts .	17	– (6) lbw b Yeabsley	13
R. A. Battye (*Salendine Nook HS, Huddersfield, New C. and Trinity*) c Townsend b Ricketts .	6	– (7) c Macmillan b MacRobert ..	1
*A. R. Whittall (*Falcon, Zimbabwe, and Trinity*) lbw b MacRobert .	2	– (8) c and b Yeabsley	17
N. J. Haste (*Wellingborough and Pembroke*) c Townsend b Yeabsley .	6	– (5) c Malik b Yeabsley	0
A. N. Janisch (*Abingdon and Trinity*) not out .	4	– not out....................	18
J. W. O. Freeth (*Sherborne and Pembroke*) c Malik b MacRobert .	13	– c Mather b Ricketts..........	1
E. J. How (*Dr Challoner's GS and Gonville & Caius*) lbw b MacRobert .	0	– b Mather	0
B 5, l-b 7, w 1	13	B 4, l-b 6	10

1/57 2/83 3/185 4/215 5/267   295   1/14 2/19 3/30 4/33 5/55   126
6/267 7/276 8/276 9/295   6/60 7/81 8/103 9/106

Bowling: *First Innings*—MacRobert 23–8–41–4; Mather 17–3–70–1; Yeabsley 18–6–45–1; Ricketts 29–8–59–3; Kendall 5–2–7–0; Malik 5–1–24–0; Macmillan 13–3–26–0; Sutcliffe 4–1–11–1. *Second Innings*—MacRobert 23–5–55–2; Kendall 8–2–13–2; Yeabsley 19–7–34–4; Ricketts 12–5–14–1; Mather 0.1–0–0–1.

Oxford University

C. M. Gupte (*John Lyon and Pembroke*)			
	c Ragnauth b Whittall	5	– (3) not out 13
I. J. Sutcliffe (*Leeds GS and Queen's*)			
	c Ragnauth b Janisch	71	– c Churton b How 52
A. C. Ridley (*St Aloysius C., Sydney, Sydney U. and Exeter*) c Churton b Haste		2	
*G. I. Macmillan (*Charterhouse, Soton U. and Keble*) lbw b Haste		2	– (1) not out 113
W. S. Kendall (*Bradfield C. and Keble*)			
	c Whittall b Haste	41	
H. S. Malik (*KCS, Wimbledon, and Keble*)			
	c Whittall b Haste	64	
R. S. Yeabsley (*Haberdashers' Aske's, Elstree, and Keble*) c Ragnauth b Haste		3	
J. D. Ricketts (*Sherborne and Balliol*) c Cake b Janisch		10	
A. D. MacRobert (*Grey HS, Port Elizabeth, Cape Town U. and Keble*) c Ratledge b Janisch		7	
†C. J. Townsend (*Dean Close and Brasenose*) not out		9	
B 4, l-b 11, w 2, n-b 2		19	B 6, l-b 2, w 2, n-b 2 12

1/10 2/13 3/15 4/89 5/174   (9 wkts dec.) 233   1/143   (1 wkt) 190
6/183 7/196 8/215 9/233

D. P. Mather (*Wirral GS and St Hugh's*) did not bat.

Bowling: *First Innings*—Whittall 19–7–47–1; Haste 19–4–73–5; How 8–2–32–0; Janisch 12–2–38–3; Freeth 12–1–28–0. *Second Innings*—Whittall 13–3–19–0; Haste 9–0–51–0; Freeth 14–1–52–0; Janisch 6–0–22–0; How 4–0–24–1; Battye 0.4–0–14–0.

Umpires: B. Dudleston and K. E. Palmer.

OXFORD v CAMBRIDGE, NOTES

The University Match dates back to 1827. Altogether there have been 150 official matches, Cambridge winning 55 and Oxford 48, with 47 drawn. Since the war Cambridge have won nine times (1949, 1953, 1957, 1958, 1972, 1979, 1982, 1986 and 1992) and Oxford nine (1946, 1948, 1951, 1959, 1966, 1976, 1984, 1993 and 1995). All other matches have been drawn; the 1988 fixture was abandoned without a ball being bowled.

One hundred three-figure innings have been played in the University matches, 53 for Oxford and 47 for Cambridge. For the fullest lists see the 1940 and 1993 *Wisdens*. There have been three double-centuries for Cambridge (211 by G. Goonesena in 1957, 201 by A. Ratcliffe in 1931 and 200 by Majid Khan in 1970) and two for Oxford (238* by Nawab of Pataudi, sen. in 1931 and 201* by M. J. K. Smith in 1954). Ratcliffe's score was a record for the match for only one day, before being beaten by Pataudi's. M. J. K. Smith and R. J. Boyd-Moss (Cambridge) are the only players to score three hundreds.

The highest totals in the fixture are 503 in 1900, 457 in 1947, 453 for eight in 1931 and 453 for nine in 1994, all by Oxford. Cambridge's highest is 432 for nine in 1936. The lowest totals are 32 by Oxford in 1878 and 39 by Cambridge in 1858.

F. C. Cobden, in the Oxford v Cambridge match in 1870, performed the hat-trick by taking the last three wickets and won an extraordinary game for Cambridge by two runs. Other hat-tricks, all for Cambridge, have been achieved by A. G. Steel (1879), P. H. Morton (1880), J. F. Ireland (1911) and R. G. H. Lowe (1926). S. E. Butler, in the 1871 match, took all ten wickets in the Cambridge first innings.

D. W. Jarrett (Oxford 1975, Cambridge 1976), S. M. Wookey (Cambridge 1975-76, Oxford 1978) and G. Pathmanathan (Oxford 1975-78, Cambridge 1983) gained Blues for both Universities.

A full list of Blues from 1837 may be found in Wisdens *published between 1923 and 1939. The lists thereafter were curtailed:* Wisdens *from 1948 to 1972 list Blues since 1880; from 1973 to 1983 since 1919; from 1984 to 1992 since 1946.*

THE LUCOZADE SPORT BUSA CHAMPIONSHIP, 1995

By GRENVILLE HOLLAND

For the first time, the university championship was conducted under the aegis of the British Universities Sports Association (BUSA), which had succeeded the Universities Athletic Union. But the winners, for the seventh time in ten years, were Durham. They are the most conspicuous of a well-defined group of universities whose consistent success over the past decade ought to elevate them to a higher level of competition. This they deserve, and a premier league of ten universities, including Oxford and Cambridge, would provide it. A post-examination festival in June, with a final at Lord's or The Oval, would be a true test for the champion university. Senior and junior divisions could be organised along regional lines as at present, promotion and relegation offering fluidity and incentive.

Competition has to be the key. Too often, unequal matches played in the spirit of fraternity use up precious time and resources. A restructuring would give more universities the chance to compete at their natural level and achieve success, however modest: any side will strive to win through to an attainable target but enthusiasm for a hopeless task swiftly evaporates. BUSA has already streamlined the competition slightly, by limiting the senior division to those universities strong enough to run two teams. This reduced the top level of the tournament to 86 sides, down from 105. But the challenge facing BUSA is to design a competition that encompasses the abilities and aspirations of players in the broad spread of university institutions while lifting the standards of student cricket across the country.

Durham finally claimed their 14th title with a crushing 239-run win over Exeter. But they had several tight squeezes along the way, and might not have reached the knockout stage but for a hair's-breadth victory over Northumbria. Having won their previous league games, they relaxed; and 154 was barely adequate on a good Racecourse pitch. Lee Marland led Northumbria's steady reply, with 67, and by tea they needed 35 with only two down. Suddenly it dawned on Durham that defeat would see them eliminated on bonus points. From then on, every run was contested, and Robin Jones was superbly economical. He finished with six for 21 – in a one-run victory. In the challenge rounds, Durham beat Hull and St Andrews easily enough; Matt Windows scored 218 not out against Hull, believed to be the first double-hundred in the competition. But their quarter-final against Newcastle went to the final over. They were restricted to 213 for eight by some fine spin bowling from Massoud Mirza, and Newcastle made good headway; however, twelfth man Gavin Moffat took four catches and then secured the final wicket with a rifling throw from the boundary, when Durham's lead was down to five. Newcastle had already visited the Racecourse ground, when Durham inflicted their only league defeat, but Mirza was in match-winning form in the challenge rounds. His low flighted off-breaks claimed five wickets against Leeds Metropolitan, to which he added an unbeaten fifty, and he took another five on Newcastle's trip to Edinburgh.

Durham's semi-final opponents were Loughborough, who looked strong contenders for the title, even though Nottingham Trent had sprung a surprise by bowling them out for 115 to defeat them in the league section. But three conclusive wins had taken them into the challenge round, where they played Manchester. Mark Harvey led Loughborough to 203 to set up a 104-run win. In the next game, against Chester, he was stumped on 99 in a score of 244; seamer Matthew Evans dismissed Chester for just 69. In the quarter-final, Warwick, previously unbeaten in four league and two knockout games, fared even worse: Evans bowled them out for 62 after Loughborough's steady batting scored 246.

The third quarter-final was between Exeter and Brighton. Both had beaten second-string Blues teams in the challenge rounds. Exeter went to the very last ball against Oxford, who finished two runs short, with three wickets in hand, after Tom Newman scored an unbeaten 123 out of Exeter's 226 for four. Brighton's impressive all-round strength claimed several scalps on the way to the quarter-finals, and they lost only to Kent in the south-eastern division. They sailed through a one-sided challenge game against Essex, whom they dismissed for 65 in 37 overs, with Ben Kempster taking five for 20, before coasting to a ten-wicket victory. Then they met Cambridge, who, despite fielding several first-class players, were no match for Neil Fergus. He scored a commanding 123 not out, while off-spinner Glyn Treagus captured seven Cambridge wickets for 33. Brighton struck disaster, however, when they travelled to Exeter for the quarter-final. Replying to 217 for nine, they collapsed abjectly for 81 in just 28 overs; right-arm seamer Christopher Allbut took seven for 42.

Exeter's only league defeat had been inflicted by Bristol, who overwhelmed all their other opponents until the second knockout round. They finally found serious opposition in Cheltenham & Gloucester, who restricted them to a modest 115 for nine – before being held to an even more modest 95 for nine. Bristol went through to the last eight to play Swansea, the 1994 UAU champions. Swansea had ambled through the southern Welsh league and overcame a poor pitch at Chichester – for whom Colin Broughton took seven for 78 – in the knockout round. They brushed aside ten men from Brunel by 216 runs to reach the quarter-final at Bristol. There, the home team struggled to 138 on a disappointing pitch, with Scott Moffat taking five for 24, and Andrew Varley steered Swansea to a five-wicket victory.

Swansea found their semi-final against Exeter less straightforward. On an excellent Southgate pitch, in fine, sunny conditions, David Bowen and Jerome Connor helped Swansea to 210 for five with ten overs to go. But Jeremy Preston engineered a collapse which saw their last five fall for 16. Andrew Jones and Newman opened Exeter's innings with 125 and Adrian Small completed a comfortable eight-wicket win. Durham had another close contest when they met Loughborough on a worn pitch at Chesterfield. Loughborough's batsmen began briskly enough until the introduction of Jones slowed the run-rate to a trickle. In reply, Windows and Toby Peirce rattled the score along until a hat-trick by Evans left Durham reeling at 88 for six. It was their last-wicket pair, Jim Kendall and Chris Chandler, who saw them home with six overs to spare.

SEMI-FINALS

At Southgate, June 19. Exeter won by eight wickets. Toss: Swansea. Swansea 226 (57.3 overs) (D. M. Bowen 86, J. M. Connor 52; J. R. Preston four for 43); Exeter 227 for two (48.4 overs) (A. J. Jones 95, T. P. Newman 55, A. M. Small 64 not out).

At Chesterfield, June 19. Durham won by one wicket. Toss: Loughborough. Loughborough 163 (58.1 overs) (R. M. S. Weston 35, M. Fletcher 40; R. O. Jones five for 41, M. J. Semmence four for 65); Durham 165 for nine (53.4 overs) (M. T. E. Peirce 65, M. G. N. Windows 40; M. R. Evans six for 39, including a hat-trick).

FINAL

DURHAM v EXETER

At Wardown Park, Luton, June 26. Durham won by 239 runs. Toss: Exeter.

The morning mists had hardly risen from the neighbouring rooftops when Exeter's captain, Andrew Jones, invited Durham to bat first. He probably had in mind the recent Championship game between Northamptonshire and Essex at the same venue, when 30 wickets fell on the first day. But the sun broke through, the pitch was fast and true and Windows was in belligerent mood. Too often, Exeter's bowlers pitched short and Windows, sure-footed and powerful, pulled the ball dismissively. When the bowlers pitched it up, there was little movement and he simply punched it to the off-side boundary. Ably supported by Peirce, he led Durham to a daunting 215 for one by lunch and they took their partnership for 275, a record in university finals, before Peirce was caught in the deep. Windows was finally out for a brilliant 198 off 185 balls, and Durham finished on 388 for four – almost six and a half an over and a record for the final. Exeter faced an impossible task. Newman made an impressive fifty, while Small and Jones tried to keep up. But no one else passed six against tight bowling from Robin Jones and Mark Semmence. Exeter succumbed for 149, with nearly 15 overs to spare. After so many tribulations on their way to their 12th successive final, Durham's winning margin of 239 runs, yet another record for the final, represented a stunning performance.

Durham

*J. R. A. Williams b Preston	3	†J. N. Batty not out	4
M. G. N. Windows lbw b Allbut	198	B 9, w 1, n-b 10	20
M. T. E. Peirce c Newman b Gibney	115		
T. Hodgson not out	44	1/16 2/291 (4 wkts, 60 overs) 388	
R. O. Jones c Jones b Preston	4	3/354 4/359	

P. J. Deakin, D. E. Atkin, M. J. Semmence, J. A. Kendall and C. J. Chandler did not bat.

Bowling: Allbut 14–1–81–1; Preston 11–0–70–2; Greenhill 13–0–71–0; Gibney 19–0–134–1; Small 3–0–23–0.

Exeter

*A. J. Jones c Batty b Chandler	20	J. R. Preston b Jones	3
T. P. Newman b Jones	58	C. S. Allbut not out	5
A. M. Small c Batty b Kendall	31	D. G. B. Gibney lbw b Jones	0
T. P. J. Caston c and b Semmence	3	L-b 1, n-b 5	6
J. S. Czerpak c Batty b Semmence	6		
D. F. Kings b Semmence	5	1/35 2/95 3/110	(45.2 overs) 149
C. S. Greenhill b Jones	6	4/121 5/123 6/133	
†J. C. Bobby lbw b Semmence	6	7/133 8/143 9/146	

Bowling: Atkin 7–0–30–0; Chandler 5–0–27–1; Jones 17.2–1–50–4; Kendall 8–2–20–1; Semmence 8–2–21–4.

Umpires: D. Bushell and K. Hopley.

WINNERS 1927-95

The UAU Championship was replaced by the BUSA Championship after 1994.

1927 Manchester	1955 Birmingham	1975 Loughborough Colls.
1928 Manchester	1956 Null and void	1976 Loughborough
1929 Nottingham	1957 Loughborough Colls.	1977 Durham
1930 Sheffield	1958 Null and void	1978 Manchester
1931 Liverpool	1959 Liverpool	1979 Manchester
1932 Manchester	1960 Loughborough Colls.	1980 Exeter
1933 Manchester	1961 Loughborough Colls.	1981 Durham
1934 Leeds	1962 Manchester	1982 Exeter
1935 Sheffield	1963 Loughborough Colls.	1983 Exeter
1936 Sheffield	1964 Loughborough Colls.	1984 Bristol
1937 Nottingham	1965 Hull	1985 Birmingham
1938 Durham	1966 { Newcastle	1986 Durham
1939 Durham	{ Southampton	1987 Durham
1946 Not completed	1967 Manchester	1988 Swansea
1947 Sheffield	1968 Southampton	1989 Loughborough
1948 Leeds	1969 Southampton	1990 Durham
1949 Leeds	1970 Southampton	1991 Durham
1950 Manchester	1971 Loughborough Colls.	1992 Durham
1951 Manchester	1972 Durham	1993 Durham
1952 Loughborough Colls.	1973 { Leicester	1994 Swansea
1953 Durham	{ Loughborough Colls.	1995 Durham
1954 Manchester	1974 Durham	

MCC MATCHES IN 1995

In a year when English cricket had very few problems with the weather, it was unfortunate that two of MCC's celebratory matches were hit by rain. The drought of 1995 broke just before Lord's hosted a match to mark the centenary of the Minor Counties Cricket Association. An unbeaten 133 from David Ward of Surrey enabled the club to declare, setting the Minor Counties 301 to win – then the heavens opened.

Early in the season the club had sent a team down to Cornwall for a two-day match to mark the county club's centenary. The match will be best remembered for magnificent hundreds from John Meadows and the Zimbabwean Test captain Andy Flower, and the statement from Flower's compatriot Bryan Strang that it was like bowling in a big fridge – just before a cold rain came and put him out of his misery.

There was better weather for Wales Minor Counties' first match at Lord's, a two-day game in which Flower, with 92, again starred, and his brother Grant eventually bowled MCC to an eight-run win with his left-arm spinners.

MCC played 220 schools, the same number as in 1994. It is heartening to report that the policy of encouraging schools cricket will be continued, despite the ever-increasing demands placed on students by a shortened summer term and the exam timetables. Of their 350 scheduled matches against all teams, MCC won 142, lost 61, drew 124 and tied two. Twenty-one were abandoned, compared to 37 in 1994. – John Jameson.

Note: Matches in this section were not first-class.

At Lord's, May 3. MCC Young Cricketers won by seven wickets. Toss: MCC. MCC 195 for four dec. (Mudassar Nazar 70 not out, S. J. Cooper 46 not out); MCC Young Cricketers 198 for three (J. A. Knott 94 not out, D. T. Wyrill 52 not out).

At Cambridge, May 4, 5, 6. MCC drew with CAMBRIDGE UNIVERSITY (See The Universities in 1995).

At Boscawen Park, Truro, May 10, 11. Drawn. Toss: MCC. MCC 251 for six dec. (A. Flower 53, J. L. P. Meadows 115, R. M. Cox 30, P. J. Mir 30 not out; C. Libby three for 75) and 221 for four dec. (B. C. Strang 38, A. Flower 108 not out, S. J. Young 46 not out); Cornwall 214 for six dec. (G. M. Thomas 31, C. P. Lello 44, J. P. Kent 74) and 43 for three.

At Winchmore Hill CC, May 17. Club Cricket Conference v MCC. Abandoned.

At Marlow, June 2. Drawn. Toss: National Association of Young Cricketers (South). MCC 246 for seven dec. (A. Fordham 120, J. E. M. Nicolson 55; J. P. Hart three for 59); National Association of Young Cricketers (South) 221 for six (R. W. J. Howitt 67, C. D. Crowe 60, W. J. House 33).

At Wormsley, June 4. MCC won by 40 runs. Toss: MCC. MCC 225 for six dec. (N. E. Briers 54, P. W. G. Parker 44, K. G. Sedgbeer 36 not out; D. R. Doshi three for 71); J. Paul Getty's XI 185 (I. J. F. Hutchinson 30, D. W. Randall 71, J. K. Lever 31; P. D. McKeown five for 58).

At Lord's, June 7, 8. Drawn. Toss: MCC. MCC 259 for three dec. (D. C. Briance 59, J. D. Robinson 100 not out, A. Flower 53 not out) and 222 for nine dec. (K. C. Williams 52, J. D. Robinson 41, R. J. Parks 42; M. W. Patterson three for 73, R. Eagleson three for 33); Ireland 212 for three dec. (S. J. S. Warke 41, S. G. Smyth 66, D. A. Lewis 74 not out) and 264 for eight (A. R. Dunlop 44, D. A. Lewis 72, S. Graham 40; K. C. Williams three for 68, K. Staple four for 55).

At Oxford, June 7, 8, 9. MCC drew with OXFORD UNIVERSITY (See The Universities in 1995).

At Durham, June 12, 13. Durham University won by four wickets. Toss: MCC. MCC 195 for six dec. (D. A. Banks 67 not out, J. N. Batty 52; C. J. Chandler three for 45) and 237 for one dec. (J. P. Stephenson 112 not out, M. S. Ahluwalia 70, Mudassar Nazar 50 not out); Durham University 167 for seven dec. (T. Hodgson 50, R. O. Jones 63; G. H. Dean three for 52) and 266 for six (J. R. A. Williams 47, M. T. E. Peirce 95, D. Lockhart 38, P. J. Deakin 34).

At Arundel, June 18. Drawn. Toss: MCC. MCC 282 for four dec. (L. Potter 123, N. J. L. Trestrail 106 not out); Lavinia, Duchess of Norfolk's XI 252 for seven (M. H. Richardson 38, A. R. Roberts 79, K. J. Innes 46, G. Toyana 49; L. Potter three for 40).

At Dean Park, Bournemouth, July 14. Dorset won by four wickets. Toss: Dorset. MCC 299 for three dec. (T. J. G. O'Gorman 117, N. Gilbert 31, A. Flower 126); Dorset 301 for six (T. W. Richings 159 not out, M. Miller 40, S. W. D. Rintoul 31; C. M. Pitcher three for 56).

At Lord's, August 9, 10. MCC won by eight runs. Toss: MCC. MCC 216 for six dec. (A. Flower 92, Mudassar Nazar 37; M. Walton three for 48) and 243 for six dec. (D. A. Thorne 87, K. D. Young 42, A. J. Mackay 45; J. P. J. Sylvester four for 55); Wales 188 for eight dec. (M. J. Newbold 39, K. M. Bell 51) and 263 (J. P. J. Sylvester 35, A. W. Harris 50, M. J. Newbold 40, A. Jones 41, M. Leaf 32; G. W. Flower five for 62).

At Portsmouth, August 10. Combined Services won by three wickets. Toss: MCC. MCC 218 for six dec. (N. G. Folland 78, W. S. Kendall 47); Combined Services 222 for seven (Sgt N. Palmer 106, Fg Off. G. Cartmell 38; J. D. Robinson three for 19).

At Kenilworth Wardens CC, August 16. Midlands Club Cricket Conference won by three wickets. Toss: MCC. MCC 258 for eight dec. (D. M. Bowen 118, E. L. Home 40; B. Byrne five for 60); Midlands Club Cricket Conference 262 for seven (S. J. Dean 88, S. Mohammed 32, A. Farooque 65; I. M. Henderson five for 59).

At Southport, August 17. MCC won by five wickets. Toss: National Association of Young Cricketers (North). National Association of Young Cricketers (North) 143 for eight dec. (M. J. Chilton 33, N. M. Ellsmore 35 not out; J. Simmons three for 18); MCC 146 for five (P. Bedford 74).

At Aberdeen, August 23, 24, 25. Drawn. Toss: Scotland. Scotland 281 (I. L. Philip 44, G. N. Reifer 58, D. R. Lockhart 31, J. G. Williamson 30, A. G. Davies 44, J. W. Govan 30 not out; K. C. Williams four for 56, P. N. Hepworth three for 46) and 107 for two dec. (N. J. McRae 42 not out, G. N. Reifer 42); MCC 133 for three dec. (A. Flower 69) and 213 for nine (C. J. Rogers 117, D. A. Lewis 37; J. W. Govan four for 74).

At Lord's, September 5. Drawn. Toss: MCC. MCC 300 for three dec. (A. Flower 36, G. W. Flower 81, D. M. Ward 133 not out); Minor Counties 105 for two (S. J. Dean 37, L. Potter 36).

OTHER MATCHES, 1995

Note: Matches in this section were not first-class.

At Taunton, April 18, 19, 20. England Under-19 won by 309 runs. Toss: England Under-19. England Under-19 371 (A. McGrath 88, D. J. Sales 49, A. Singh 59; Mushtaq Ahmed six for 88) and 352 (A. McGrath 70, A. Singh 71; M. Amjad three for 88, Mushtaq Ahmed three for 85); Somerset Second XI 197 (A. R. Caddick 75; M. Dimond five for 58, A. C. Morris three for 38) and 217 (K. A. Parsons 61; J. P. Searle four for 21).

At Oxford, April 21. Northamptonshire won by six runs. Toss: Northamptonshire. Northamptonshire 269 for seven (55 overs) (R. J. Bailey 85, A. J. Lamb 101 retired out); Combined Universities 263 for eight (55 overs) (M. T. E. Peirce 40, I. G. S. Steer 40, K. R. Spiring 37, M. E. Harvey 69, Extras 31; J. G. Hughes three for 51).

At Leeds, April 30. Yorkshire won by 91 runs. Toss: Lancashire. Yorkshire 221 for four (40 overs) (M. P. Vaughan 71, A. P. Grayson 82 not out); Lancashire 130 (27 overs) (C. White three for 30, S. M. Milburn three for 32).

At Horsham, May 8, 9, 10. Sussex Second XI won by 108 runs. Toss: Sussex Second XI. Sussex Second XI 225 (D. R. Law 32, M. Newell 52, R. S. C. Martin-Jenkins 48; K. J. Innes three for 50, A. C. Morris three for 30) and 289 for nine dec. (K. Newell 46, C. C. Remy 34, D. R. Law 80, R. S. C. Martin-Jenkins 73; R. J. Green three for 76); England Under-19 180 (A. Flintoff 43, I. Dawood 37; R. J. Kirtley three for 55, D. R. Law three for 25) and 226 (K. J. Innes 35, R. J. Green 42, I. Dawood 36 not out; N. C. Phillips four for 73, J. J. Bates three for 92).

At Birmingham, June 4. Rest of the World XI won by three runs. Toss: Warwickshire. Rest of the World XI 235 for eight (50 overs) (W. J. Cronje 51, S. R. Waugh 52; N. M. K. Smith three for 45); Warwickshire 232 for six (50 overs) (N. M. K. Smith 51, P. A. Smith 37, R. G. Twose 48).

At Bradford, June 26, 27. England Under-19 won by five wickets. Toss: England Under-19. Yorkshire Second XI 335 (M. J. Wood 53, J. W. Hood 84, L. C. Weekes 77); England Under-19 339 for five (A. Flintoff 31 retired hurt, N. Killeen 34, C. J. Schofield 91, A. Singh 78 not out, Extras 56).

At Bradford, June 28. Yorkshire Second XI won by six wickets. Toss: England Under-19. England Under-19 202 (53.4 overs) (D. J. Sales 64, A. C. Morris 49; P. M. Hutchison five for 24); Yorkshire Second XI 203 for four (52.5 overs) (M. J. Wood 62, A. A. Metcalfe 33, R. A. Kettleborough 33).

COSTCUTTER CUP

A 55-over competition contested by Yorkshire and three other invited counties.

At Harrogate, July 17. Nottinghamshire won by 28 runs. Toss: Yorkshire. Nottinghamshire 215 for six (37 overs) (P. R. Pollard 101, C. L. Cairns 34; S. M. Milburn three for 46); Yorkshire 187 for eight (37 overs) (S. A. Kellett 30, M. P. Vaughan 46, B. Parker 35, A. C. Morris 32; C. L. Cairns three for 27).

At Harrogate, July 18. Gloucestershire won by five wickets. Toss: Gloucestershire. Essex 185 for seven (31 overs) (M. A. Garnham 46 not out; K. P. Sheeraz three for 21); Gloucestershire 187 for five (30.3 overs) (M. A. Lynch 62).

At Harrogate, July 19. **Final:** Gloucestershire won by four wickets. Toss: Nottinghamshire. Nottinghamshire 181 (47.4 overs) (P. R. Pollard 36, G. F. Archer 41; M. Davies five for 22); Gloucestershire 182 for six (47 overs) (M. A. Lynch 31, A. Symonds 39, R. C. Williams 39 not out, Extras 34).

PETER MAY MEMORIAL MATCH

At Arundel, July 18. P. B. H. May's XI won by five wickets. Surrey 206 for eight (G. J. Kersey 52, A. D. Brown 50); P. B. H. May's XI 209 for five (M. A. Atherton 31, A. P. Wells 63).

IRELAND v SCOTLAND

At Rathmines, August 13. Scotland won by eight runs. Toss: Scotland. Scotland 234 for seven (55 overs) (B. M. W. Patterson 58, I. L. Philip 33, M. J. Smith 65; S. Graham three for 50); Ireland 226 (54.2 overs) (S. J. S. Warke 41, J. D. R. Benson 40, G. D. Harrison 37, N. G. Doak 43; J. G. Williamson three for 54).

The annual first-class match was cancelled, because Hugh Stevenson, chairman of the Scottish selectors, suffered a heart attack as he arrived at the ground. He died later in hospital. The teams agreed to play two one-day games instead. Caps were not awarded for the second match, also won by Scotland, who scored 154 for nine from 40 overs and dismissed Ireland for 98.

NORTHERN ELECTRIC TROPHY

At Scarborough, September 2. Yorkshire v Durham. No result (abandoned).

TETLEY BITTER FESTIVAL TROPHY

A 50-over competition contested by Yorkshire and three other invited counties.

At Scarborough, September 4. Nottinghamshire won by 121 runs. Toss: Nottinghamshire. Nottinghamshire 298 for six (50 overs) (G. F. Archer 41 retired hurt, R. T. Robinson 76 not out, C. L. Cairns 62, Extras 31); Yorkshire 177 (41.2 overs) (S. A. Kellett 64; D. B. Pennett three for 32, R. J. Chapman four for 41).

At Scarborough, September 5. Kent won by 52 runs. Toss: Durham. Kent 328 for seven (50 overs) (M. R. Benson 94, G. R. Cowdrey 145, M. A. Ealham 33); Durham 276 (48.1 overs) (S. Hutton 53, P. D. Collingwood 74, C. W. Scott 41; N. J. Llong three for 62).

At Scarborough, September 6. **Final:** Nottinghamshire won by 60 runs. Toss: Nottinghamshire. Nottinghamshire 197 for nine (40 overs) (N. A. Gie 34, C. L. Cairns 62 not out, R. T. Bates 36; M. V. Fleming three for 63); Kent 137 (33.2 overs) (M. V. Fleming 33, G. R. Cowdrey 39; R. A. Pick three for 17).

THE MINOR COUNTIES IN 1995

By MICHAEL BERRY and ROBERT BROOKE

The centenary season of Minor Counties cricket was a memorable one, in which the representative side defeated Leicestershire in the Benson and Hedges Cup in May, and recorded a famous four-wicket victory over the West Indian tourists at Reading in July. The newly formed Under-25 team also held their own in the Bain Hogg Trophy, winning three of their eight fixtures. However, the 100-year milestone was tarnished by uncertainty behind the scenes over the role of Minor Counties cricket under the umbrella of the new English Cricket Board. The domestic titles were won by Devon, who beat Lincolnshire in a rain-affected Championship final, and Cambridgeshire, who overcame Herefordshire at Lord's.

Devon's achievement in retaining the Championship made it four trophies in four years. Peter Roebuck's side, which accumulated a record-breaking 135 points, won five of their nine divisional matches, and might have defeated chief rivals Cheshire as well had rain not intervened. Nick Folland, back after two years with Somerset, piled up 963 runs, and although his unavailability for the final denied him his 1,000, his average of 96.30 won him the Wilfred Rhodes Trophy for the second time in four years. Nick Gaywood (801), Julian Wyatt (641) and Gareth Townsend (518) all scored freely, and Wiltshire were blitzed for 333 for four off only 49.3 overs at Swindon, a feat that prompted Roebuck to report the wicket for being "too good for two-day cricket". Roebuck was Devon's key bowler with 38 wickets, and slow left-armer Ryan Horrell performed the hat-trick against Herefordshire.

Cheshire's hopes of taking the regional crown collapsed when they slumped from 131 for two to 205 all out in their penultimate fixture against Dorset. Chasing 224, the long-time leaders lost their last three wickets for no score, with last man Tony Murphy given out handled the ball. Cheshire had performed a similar act of batting subsidence against both Herefordshire and Berkshire earlier in the season. John Bean (597 runs) registered his maiden county century against Dorset, while Ian Cockbain (463), Jon Gray (456) and Paul Bryson (445) did their best to shore up some brittle batting. Phil Carrick, the former Yorkshire captain, struggled to fill the boots of the retired Geoff Miller, but Tony Murphy's return after ten years on the first-class circuit was a boost. Murphy took 42 wickets, and his presence helped his new-ball partner, Nigel Peel, to a best-ever return of 34. Off-spinner Andrew Greasley also reappeared to claim 21 victims in only four games.

Aftab Habib, Simon Myles and Rob Pitcher, a trio of newcomers to the **Berkshire** ranks, all performed with great distinction. Habib, released by Middlesex and courted by Leicestershire during the season, was a classy addition to the batting, and his 805 Championship runs – including three centuries – were augmented by a brilliant 158 not out in the MCC Trophy win over Oxfordshire. Myles, formerly of Staffordshire, scored 697, while Julian Wood (507) compiled the third-highest innings for the county when he made 220 not out in the mammoth 446 for five against Dorset. The reliable Gary Loveday made 561 and slow left-armer Pitcher was the most successful bowler with 32 victims. At the end of the season, Mark Simmons stood down as captain after nine years in charge, and will be succeeded by Loveday.

Cornwall's season was marred by a horrific accident to their captain, Godfrey Furse, and his girlfriend, Valerie Stow, who were both badly burned when one of Furse's hot-dog vans exploded as they were clearing up the day after the NatWest Trophy tie with Middlesex at St Austell. Newcomer Adam Seymour, previously of Essex and Worcestershire, amassed 798 runs, while Gary Thomas had 712 and Steve Williams 586. Chris Lovell and David Angove, a promising 21-year-old pace bowler, claimed 20 wickets apiece, Lovell's coming in just four matches at a cost of 13.10 each to win him the Frank Edwards Bowling Trophy. Paul Berryman's burst of five for seven in 18 balls was the key to the five-wicket victory over Devon in the MCC Trophy, and Cornwall picked up a NatWest Trophy place on the strength of winning their last three Championship matches, knocking off a 308 target in 73 overs with eight balls to spare against Oxfordshire.

Oxfordshire recovered some of their lost pride after a miserable 1994 and won their first two matches. Although they lost the services of Tim Lester (who had emigrated) and long-serving former captain Phil Garner (retired), they had three of the Championship's top up-and-coming players in Stewart Laudat (492 runs), Bruce Ellison (419) and wicket-keeper Jon Batty, and their blend of youth and experience was well served by the bowling of old hands Rupert Evans (34 wickets), Ian Curtis (27) and Keith Arnold (26).

Although David Lawrence, the former England Test bowler, had signed for **Herefordshire**, a broken finger suffered in a club game ruled him out all season. They narrowly failed to qualify for the NatWest Trophy. However, Herefordshire were still a major force, whose potent batting hit top form in the MCC Trophy. Batting second, they amassed 328 for six to beat Norfolk and 302 without loss off 47.1 overs to see off Suffolk, Martin Weston scoring 157 not out and Harshad Patel 126 not out. Patel's season spectacularly gathered momentum as he scored centuries in both innings against Dorset, and with 97 in the penultimate fixture with Devon at Torquay, he became the first batsman to pass 1,000 Championship runs in a season since Timur Mohamed for Suffolk in 1979. He finished with 1,093, the fourth-best in the history of the Championship. Steve Brogan made 535 runs and Mike Bailey, an off-spinner, took 23 wickets.

Kevin Sharp was within touching distance of 1,000 Championship runs for **Shropshire**. The former Yorkshire left-hander, playing as an amateur after a couple of years as the county's professional, finished with 925, and was backed up by Tony Parton (586) and Mark Davies, the captain, who made 416. The loss of paceman Paul Thomas to Worcestershire exaggerated the lack of bowling penetration, although Andy Barnard took 20 wickets. A late surge brought victory in their last two matches, but it was too little too late, and they just missed a place in the NatWest Trophy.

Giles Reynolds quit as captain of **Dorset** at the end of the season, bowing out with 682 runs, a tally bettered only by Tim Richings's 737. Another campaign of highs and lows saw Dorset bowled out by Buckinghamshire for just 49 – a record low in the knockout cup – but then beat title-chasing Cheshire in their end-of-season run-in. Matthew Swarbrick was an impressive newcomer with the bat, while Julian Shackleton again shouldered the bulk of the bowling responsibility with 26 wickets and Shaun Walbridge finished with 22.

Wiltshire also lost their captain when Kevin Foyle stood down, due to a new work commitment, on the eve of the season and was replaced by David Mercer, who had rejoined the county after an acrimonious split with Berkshire. Wiltshire were woefully short of quality bowling and struggled for points: only a remarkable win over Cornwall prevented them finishing bottom. Dwain Winter's maiden century was behind the nine-wicket triumph after Cornwall had dominated the opening day, declaring their first innings on 236 without loss. Mercer (531 runs) and Winter (472) both did themselves justice with the bat and Jamie Glasson scored his first Championship century as Wiltshire, chasing 317 to beat Dorset, were dismissed just 15 short.

Wales, who had undertaken a brief tour to the West Indies in March, had a new captain in Barry Lloyd, replacing Andy Puddle. The only side without a Championship win, they finished bottom of the Western Division and made an early exit from the MCC Trophy. Individually, Jamie Sylvester (773 runs), Andrew Harris (558) and Mike Newbold (493) all shone with the bat, while Adrian Griffiths took 22 wickets and opening bowler Mark Walton, the former Norwich City goalkeeper, also performed well, as did the new wicket-keeper James Langworth.

Lincolnshire's triumph as Eastern Division winners was the reward for their positive outlook under captain Mark Fell. David Storer's spectacular return to form was significant, his tally of 716 runs being inspired by scores of 99, 150 not out, 102 and 132 not out in his first four Championship innings. Russell Evans (534) and Fell (526) provided solid support in the absence of Jonathan Wileman, who had returned to Nottinghamshire, while slow left-armer Steve Bradford's 47 victims took his tally in the Championship to 102 in the last two seasons. Despite early-season washouts in both the Championship and MCC Trophy – in which they lost to Hertfordshire in a bowling contest – they achieved victory in four of their other eight Championship fixtures.

Norfolk were another county who parted company with their captain in 1995. David Thomas announced his retirement midway through the annual Lakenham festival, to be replaced in 1996 by Paul Newman, recruited from Staffordshire. Norfolk's major signing was Neil Foster, who finished as the county's leading wicket-taker with 29 scalps, the first two of which came against Hertfordshire in his first over in Minor Counties cricket. Mark Powell (25) and Rodney Bunting (24) were close behind. Steve Goldsmith (816 runs) again starred with the bat and Stephen Plumb – a professional with Norfolk for 18 years who will play for Lincolnshire in 1996 – scored 684 runs to pass 10,000 runs for the county. Norfolk almost came from nowhere to take the regional title, winning three of their last five fixtures and claiming an extra eight points for batting last when the scores finished level in a thriller against Buckinghamshire at Lakenham.

Suffolk were prevented from overhauling Lincolnshire at the top of the table by their close East Anglian rivals Norfolk. Again fuelled by the runs of Derek Randall and the wickets of Andrew Golding, Suffolk could have leap-frogged Lincolnshire had they beaten Norfolk in their final fixture at North Runcton, but in the event lost by four wickets. Randall was unavailable early in the season, but still managed to finish with 727 runs, while Simon Clements (500) and Phil Caley (465) also weighed in. Golding, the slow left-armer, wrote a new chapter in the Suffolk history books with 66 wickets, which bettered the county's previous best of 63 by Wally Duckham in 1946 and included a match return of 12 for 59 in the comprehensive victory over Cumberland.

Cumberland's season was a roller-coaster ride of fluctuating fortunes, in which a good day was often followed by a bad day, or vice-versa – most notably when beating Buckinghamshire by six wickets at Slough. After trailing by 106 runs on first innings, they knocked off a target of 271 in 99 overs for the loss of only four wickets with more than 20 overs to spare. Their summer was summed up by the contrast of beating Bedfordshire by an innings and 69 runs but losing to Suffolk by an innings and 15 runs. The leading performers were David Pearson, with 505 runs, and Marcus Sharp and Mike Scothern, who both collected 22 wickets.

Nigel Gadsby, the **Cambridgeshire** captain, finally got his hands on some Minor Counties silverware. Having led Cambridgeshire to five previous finals in the Championship and knockout cup since 1987 – all of which ended in defeat – he deserved the honour of captaining his side to victory over Herefordshire in the MCC Trophy final at Lord's. With Bruce Roberts failing to return from South Africa, Cambridgeshire employed the services of Brad Donelan, who finished with 472 runs and 27 wickets. Gadsby (429) and Salim Mohammed (411) also made vital contributions and Ajaz Akhtar also took 27 wickets.

Staffordshire, winners of a hat-trick of Championship titles and two knockout cups between 1991 and 1993, reached the end of an era when Nick Archer, their long-serving captain, announced his retirement after 11 years at the helm – on the day his side suffered a ten-wicket defeat by Norfolk at Lakenham. The arrival of Laurie Potter from Cornwall was a big success. His 441 runs and 42 wickets were augmented by 669 runs from Steve Dean and 36 wickets from Paul Newman, while Paul Humphries, formerly of Herefordshire, packed a penetrative punch with 20 wickets in four matches. Newman, who was named Norfolk's captain for 1996, ended his five-year Staffordshire career with match figures of 13 for 81 in a remarkable win over Cumberland. Their collapse from 93 for three to 108 all out, in pursuit of 128, enabled Staffordshire to scrape into the 1996 NatWest Trophy.

Buckinghamshire's prolific opening batsman, Malcolm Roberts, reached 5,000 Championship runs for the county during 1995; both he and Bruce Percy scored 484 runs, while Tim Scriven, the captain, followed with 427. Scriven also took 32 wickets, bettered only by leg-spinner Andrew Clarke's 33, which included a match return of nine for 136 in the win over Bedfordshire. Simon Stanway, a pace bowler, had his best season to date with 27 victims and newcomer Charles Jaggard showed promise.

Two new faces provided the major highlights of **Hertfordshire's** season. Opening batsman Rob Smith hit 645 runs, while Cliff Spinks, a slow left-arm bowler, scored 392 runs and took 27 wickets. However, the side were handicapped by a shoulder injury to their captain, David Surridge. Alan Garofall made a surprise return to Minor Counties cricket at the age of 49, but it was Ian Fletcher, back from Somerset, who supplied a champagne moment when he smashed 32 runs, including five sixes, off a single over from Norfolk's debutant slow left-armer, Shaun White.

Chris Pickles, previously with Yorkshire, scored 495 runs in his first season with **Northumberland**, and Graeme Morris led from the front with 557. However, their biggest individual success was David Borthwick, the wicket-keeper, whose 30 victims in seven games (27 caught, three stumped) was only one short of the county record of Harry Henderson, achieved in a 12-match campaign in 1955. While no bowler took 20 wickets, six claimed 12 or more and Northumberland finished the season with 70 points, which would have been enough for a far higher final placing in previous seasons. Instead they finished one off the bottom.

For **Bedfordshire**, the Eastern Division wooden-spoonists, Chris Bullen made 517 runs, Ray Swann hit 467 and Bobby Sher reappeared with great effect to collect 276 runs and 28 wickets in six appearances. They were bowled out for 75 and 65 in losing by an innings and 69 runs to Cumberland, but there was consolation in a second successive victory over Staffordshire, achieved by 17 runs off the last ball at Wardown Park.

LEADING AVERAGES, 1995

BATTING

(Qualification: 8 innings, average 30.00)

	M	I	NO	R	HS	100s	Avge
N. A. Folland (*Devon*)	9	16	6	963	151*	3	96.30
P. M. Roebuck (*Devon*)	10	9	5	297	88*	0	74.25
H. V. Patel (*Herefordshire*)	9	16	1	1,093	135*	4	72.86
B. S. Percy (*Buckinghamshire*)	7	13	6	484	89*	0	69.14
R. J. Evans (*Lincolnshire*)	6	10	2	534	114*	1	66.75
K. Sharp (*Shropshire*)	9	17	3	925	146*	3	66.07
D. B. Storer (*Lincolnshire*)	8	14	2	716	150*	3	59.66
Nadeem Mohammed (*Cambridgeshire*)	5	10	4	358	118*	1	59.66
S. M. Brogan (*Herefordshire*)	7	12	3	535	105*	1	59.44
S. C. Goldsmith (*Norfolk*)	9	17	3	816	156*	3	58.28
J. G. Wyatt (*Devon*)	8	13	2	641	112*	2	58.27
A. Habib (*Berkshire*)	8	16	2	805	146*	3	57.50
N. R. Gaywood (*Devon*)	9	16	2	801	138*	2	57.21
D. W. Randall (*Suffolk*)	7	13	0	727	118	3	55.92
J. P. J. Sylvester (*Wales*)	9	16	2	773	138	3	55.21
S. V. Laudat (*Oxfordshire*)	6	10	1	492	104*	1	54.66
J. N. Batty (*Oxfordshire*)	6	9	2	376	102*	1	53.71
A. C. H. Seymour (*Cornwall*)	9	17	2	798	111	1	53.20
S. G. Plumb (*Norfolk*)	9	18	5	684	109*	3	52.61
A. W. Jones (*Wales*)	4	8	1	359	94*	0	51.28
J. R. Wood (*Berkshire*)	6	11	1	507	220*	1	50.70
J. Hodgson (*Berkshire*)	5	10	3	346	101*	1	49.42
J. J. E. Hardy (*Dorset*)	6	12	2	493	86	0	49.30
G. T. J. Townsend (*Devon*)	9	14	3	518	123	2	47.09
P. J. Caley (*Suffolk*)	9	15	5	465	114*	1	46.50
M. P. Briers (*Cornwall*)	7	13	3	462	111*	1	46.20
R. S. Jerome (*Hertfordshire*)	8	14	5	413	73*	0	45.88
K. J. Parsons (*Wiltshire*)	6	11	2	412	87	0	45.77
G. D. Reynolds (*Dorset*)	8	16	1	682	106*	1	45.46
A. N. Johnson (*Shropshire*)	5	10	4	269	63	0	44.83
G. M. Thomas (*Cornwall*)	9	18	2	712	148*	3	44.50
M. A. Fell (*Lincolnshire*)	9	16	4	526	91	0	43.83

	M	I	NO	R	HS	100s	Avge
M. R. Evans (*Hertfordshire*)	5	8	4	175	82	0	43.75
M. C. G. Wright (*Hertfordshire*)	5	10	3	303	74*	0	43.28
G. R. Morris (*Northumberland*)	7	14	1	557	70	0	42.84
J. D. Bean (*Cheshire*)	8	16	2	597	136	1	42.64
N. D. Burns (*Buckinghamshire*)	5	10	2	341	88	0	42.62
R. Swann (*Bedfordshire*)	6	12	1	467	96*	0	42.45
M. R. Davies (*Shropshire*)	9	15	5	416	78	0	41.60
M. J. Newbold (*Wales*)	9	14	2	493	119*	1	41.08
S. D. Myles (*Berkshire*)	9	17	0	697	122	1	41.00
T. W. Richings (*Dorset*)	9	18	0	737	127	2	40.94
A. W. Harris (*Wales*)	8	15	1	558	105	1	39.85
B. T. P. Donelan (*Cambridgeshire*)	9	15	3	472	100*	1	39.33
P. J. Heseltine (*Lincolnshire*)	5	8	0	314	74	0	39.25
A. J. Pugh (*Devon*)	10	13	2	429	80	0	39.00
M. I. Humphries (*Staffordshire*)	9	12	6	234	41*	0	39.00
D. J. M. Mercer (*Wiltshire*)	9	17	3	531	86*	0	37.92
C. J. Rogers (*Norfolk*)	7	14	1	491	119*	1	37.76
J. Langworth (*Wales*)	7	12	4	302	81*	0	37.75
S. J. Dean (*Staffordshire*)	9	18	0	669	90	0	37.16
L. Potter (*Staffordshire*)	8	16	4	441	65	0	36.75
P. A. Rawden (*Lincolnshire*)	7	10	1	328	66	0	36.44
R. S. Smith (*Hertfordshire*)	9	18	0	645	67	0	35.83
C. N. Spinks (*Hertfordshire*)	9	16	5	392	58*	0	35.63
I. Cockbain (*Cheshire*)	8	16	3	463	87	0	35.61
R. G. Hignett (*Cheshire*)	6	10	1	320	74	0	35.55
C. S. Pickles (*Northumberland*)	7	14	0	495	109	1	35.35
D. P. Norman (*Cambridgeshire*)	6	12	2	352	56	0	35.20
G. E. Loveday (*Berkshire*)	9	17	1	561	100*	1	35.06
B. C. A. Ellison (*Oxfordshire*)	9	16	4	419	64*	0	34.91
M. J. Roberts (*Buckinghamshire*)	7	14	0	484	140	1	34.57
Z. A. Sher (*Bedfordshire*)	6	10	2	276	66*	0	34.50
T. Parton (*Shropshire*)	9	17	0	586	110	1	34.47
S. M. Williams (*Cornwall*)	9	18	1	586	126*	1	34.47
S. M. Clements (*Suffolk*)	8	15	0	500	96	0	33.33
A. J. Hall (*Cheshire*)	4	8	2	198	58*	0	33.00
C. K. Bullen (*Bedfordshire*)	9	18	2	517	106*	1	32.31
P. R. J. Bryson (*Cheshire*)	8	16	2	445	100*	1	31.78
K. M. Wijesuriya (*Suffolk*)	7	13	2	349	99	0	31.72
R. Hall (*Herefordshire*)	6	11	1	317	131	1	31.70
D. J. Pearson (*Cumberland*)	9	17	1	505	79	0	31.56
T. J. A. Scriven (*Buckinghamshire*)	9	16	2	427	74*	0	30.50
S. Bramhall (*Cheshire*)	9	12	6	183	35*	0	30.50
D. Cartledge (*Staffordshire*)	7	14	0	424	106	1	30.28

* *Signifies not out.*

BOWLING

(Qualification: 10 wickets, average 30.00)

	O	M	R	W	BB	5W/i	Avge
S. J. O'Shaughnessy (*Cumberland*) ...	65.2	14	190	15	5-10	1	12.66
C. C. Lovell (*Cornwall*)	88.1	20	262	20	6-52	3	13.10
J. H. Shackleton (*Dorset*)	155.2	53	401	26	6-24	1	15.42
A. O. F. Le Fleming (*Devon*)	90.3	28	232	14	5-17	1	16.57
L. Potter (*Staffordshire*)	319	112	697	42	6-36	3	16.59
A. K. Golding (*Suffolk*)	379	86	1,150	66	6-24	7	17.42
P. C. Graham (*Northumberland*)	119.2	33	300	17	4-47	0	17.64
P. J. Humphries (*Staffordshire*)	103	16	355	20	5-47	1	17.75
A. Jones (*Oxfordshire*)	88.4	22	262	14	5-70	1	18.71
P. M. Roebuck (*Devon*)	339.1	111	724	38	5-38	2	19.05

	O	M	R	W	BB	5W/i	Avge
P. G. Newman (*Staffordshire*)	268.3	72	706	36	7-40	3	19.61
R. M. Horrell (*Devon*)	127	39	366	18	4-52	0	20.33
N. D. Peel (*Cheshire*)	200.2	43	697	34	5-50	1	20.50
A. D. Greasley (*Cheshire*)	137.4	37	434	21	6-47	2	20.66
R. A. Bunting (*Norfolk*)	180.1	54	500	24	5-53	2	20.83
M. G. Scothern (*Cumberland*)	140.1	30	459	22	6-60	2	20.86
R. A. Evans (*Oxfordshire*)	257	60	732	34	6-40	1	21.52
D. M. Owen (*Buckinghamshire*)	130.4	24	410	19	4-47	0	21.57
I. J. Curtis (*Oxfordshire*)	190.1	42	583	27	8-39	1	21.59
N. A. Foster (*Norfolk*)	203	48	637	29	4-22	0	21.96
M. A. Sharp (*Cumberland*)	156.1	47	490	22	5-28	2	22.27
S. Turner (*Cambridgeshire*)	94	16	274	12	3-54	0	22.83
A. J. Murphy (*Cheshire*)	264.5	50	970	42	6-50	3	23.09
R. J. Harding (*Herefordshire*)	90.4	28	278	12	3-23	0	23.16
S. C. Goldsmith (*Norfolk*)	83	15	302	13	4-22	0	23.23
C. A. Miller (*Suffolk*)	94.2	17	373	16	4-51	0	23.31
J. Rhodes (*Devon*)	123.5	27	420	17	4-16	0	24.70
S. F. Stanway (*Buckinghamshire*) . . .	208.1	32	678	27	4-39	0	25.11
Z. A. Sher (*Bedfordshire*)	172.5	27	705	28	8-74	1	25.17
R. G. Pitcher (*Berkshire*)	269.3	54	843	32	5-91	1	26.34
A. J. Trott (*Bedfordshire*)	119.5	14	506	19	5-71	1	26.63
I. D. Graham (*Suffolk*)	89.1	14	320	12	3-54	0	26.66
M. G. Powell (*Norfolk*)	211.5	49	668	25	6-69	1	26.72
K. Donohue (*Devon*)	190	37	540	20	5-45	1	27.00
S. A. J. Kippax (*Cumberland*)	75.1	9	325	12	5-76	1	27.08
T. J. A. Scriven (*Buckinghamshire*) . . .	254.1	62	871	32	5-92	1	27.21
A. R. Wilson (*Cumberland*)	99.5	20	409	15	4-56	0	27.26
D. Surridge (*Hertfordshire*)	132.4	28	356	13	4-30	0	27.38
D. J. Angove (*Cornwall*)	153.2	35	548	20	6-25	1	27.40
M. J. Bailey (*Herefordshire*)	217.2	48	631	23	4-28	0	27.43
M. R. Evans (*Hertfordshire*)	107	16	414	15	5-69	1	27.60
S. A. Bradford (*Lincolnshire*)	351.5	81	1,322	47	6-24	3	28.12
A. Akhtar (*Cambridgeshire*)	227.4	57	771	27	6-56	1	28.55
C. Stanley (*Northumberland*)	136.2	20	516	18	6-73	1	28.66
A. S. Barnard (*Shropshire*)	192.5	44	577	20	3-28	0	28.85
M. R. White (*Bedfordshire*)	121.4	22	440	15	3-48	0	29.33
A. R. Clarke (*Buckinghamshire*) . . .	282.4	53	969	33	7-80	2	29.36
K. A. Arnold (*Oxfordshire*)	254	58	774	26	5-49	1	29.76
S. D. Myles (*Berkshire*)	139.3	28	510	17	3-31	0	30.00

MINOR COUNTIES CHAMPIONSHIP, 1995

Champions: Devon.

Eastern Division	M	W	L	D	NR	Bonus Points Batting	Bonus Points Bowling	Total Points
Lincolnshire[NW]	9	4	0	4	1	23	17	109
Norfolk[NW]	9	3	1	5	0	25	26	107
Suffolk[NW]	9	3	1	5	0	23	24	95
Cumberland[NW]	9	3	4	2	0	11	28	87
Cambridgeshire[NW]	9	3	2	4	0	13	24	85
Staffordshire[NW]	9	2	2	5	0	23	29	84
Buckinghamshire	9	2	3	4	0	24	22	78
Hertfordshire	9	2	3	4	0	25	20	77
Northumberland	9	2	3	3	1	15	18	70
Bedfordshire	9	1	6	2	0	15	22	53

Western Division	M	W	L	D	NR	*Bonus Points* Batting	*Bonus Points* Bowling	Total Points
Devon[NW]	9	5	0	4	0	29	26	135
Cheshire[NW]	9	4	3	2	0	26	28	118
Berkshire[NW]	9	3	2	4	0	18	25	91
Cornwall[NW]	9	3	3	3	0	19	20	87
Oxfordshire[NW]	9	3	2	4	0	15	23	86
Herefordshire	9	2	1	6	0	25	23	80
Shropshire	9	2	3	4	0	22	19	73
Dorset	9	2	3	4	0	18	18	68
Wiltshire	9	1	4	4	0	14	12	42
Wales	9	0	4	5	0	24	18	42

The total for Norfolk includes 8 points for batting second in a match drawn with the scores level.

Win = 16 pts. No result = 5 pts.

[NW] *Denotes qualified for NatWest Bank Trophy in 1996.*

Eastern Division

At Sleaford, May 28, 29. Lincolnshire won by two wickets. Hertfordshire 230 for seven dec. and 262 for seven dec.; Lincolnshire 231 for four dec. and 265 for eight. *Lincolnshire 23 pts, Hertfordshire 5 pts.*

At Mildenhall, May 30, 31. Drawn. Hertfordshire 192 for eight dec. and 248 for seven dec. (S. J. Page 101; A. K. Golding five for 99); Suffolk 184 for seven dec. and 107 for three. *Suffolk 3 pts, Hertfordshire 5 pts.*

At Hitchin, June 4, 5. Drawn. Hertfordshire 262 for six dec. (I. Fletcher 115) and 259 for eight dec.; Norfolk 258 for eight dec. and 147 for nine (C. N. Spinks five for 38). *Hertfordshire 7 pts, Norfolk 5 pts.*

At Jesmond, June 4, 5. Abandoned, owing to rain. *Northumberland 5 pts, Lincolnshire 5 pts.*

At High Wycombe, June 6, 7. Drawn. Buckinghamshire 205 for nine dec. and 193 (L. Potter six for 36); Staffordshire 186 for eight dec. and 116 for five. *Buckinghamshire 3 pts, Staffordshire 6 pts.*

At Wisbech, June 6, 7. Drawn. Cambridgeshire 160 and 222; Norfolk 188 for eight dec. (S. C. Goldsmith 112) and 33 for no wkt. *Cambridgeshire 3 pts, Norfolk 6 pts.*

At Leek, June 14, 15. Drawn. Staffordshire 253 and 182 for four dec. (D. Cartledge 106); Cambridgeshire 174 and 257 for five. *Staffordshire 6 pts, Cambridgeshire 3 pts.*

At Bedford, June 18, 19. Drawn. Suffolk 189 for seven dec. and 187 for six dec.; Bedfordshire 140 (A. K. Golding five for 41) and 234 for eight. *Bedfordshire 3 pts, Suffolk 6 pts.*

At Askam, June 18, 19. Drawn. Cumberland 197 for eight dec. (S. A. Bradford five for 65) and 100 for three; Lincolnshire 231 for six dec. (S. A. J. Kippax five for 76). *Cumberland 4 pts, Lincolnshire 6 pts.*

At Radlett, June 18, 19. Hertfordshire won by 80 runs. Hertfordshire 199 for eight dec. and 232 for eight dec.; Northumberland 197 for six dec. and 154. *Hertfordshire 20 pts, Northumberland 5 pts.*

At Beaconsfield, June 20, 21. Buckinghamshire won by 79 runs. Buckinghamshire 280 for five dec. (M. J. Roberts 140) and 146 for six dec.; Northumberland 182 for eight dec. and 165. *Buckinghamshire 23 pts, Northumberland 2 pts.*

At Ransome's, Ipswich, June 21, 22. Suffolk won by 148 runs. Suffolk 205 for four dec. and 258 for six dec.; Cambridgeshire 177 for four dec. and 138 (A. K. Golding five for 27). *Suffolk 20 pts, Cambridgeshire 3 pts.*

At Cleethorpes, June 25, 26. Lincolnshire won by 160 runs. Lincolnshire 249 for two dec. (D. B. Storer 150*) and 310 for three dec. (D. B. Storer 102); Buckinghamshire 234 for three dec. and 165 (S. A. Bradford six for 24). *Lincolnshire 21 pts, Buckinghamshire 4 pts.*

At Wolverhampton, July 4, 5. Drawn. Staffordshire 281 for three dec. and 203 for three dec.; Northumberland 171 for six dec. and 262 for eight. *Staffordshire 6 pts, Northumberland 1 pt.*

At Marlow, July 5, 6. Drawn. Buckinghamshire 196 and 191 for eight dec.; Cambridgeshire 179 and 182 for seven. *Buckinghamshire 4 pts, Cambridgeshire 6 pts.*

At Slough, July 9, 10. Cumberland won by six wickets. Buckinghamshire 212 for five dec. and 164 for seven dec.; Cumberland 106 and 274 for four. *Cumberland 18 pts, Buckinghamshire 7 pts.*

At Bourne, July 9, 10. Drawn. Norfolk 197 and 258 for four dec. (S. G. Plumb 109*); Lincolnshire 220 for seven dec. (D. B. Storer 132*; R. A. Bunting five for 53) and 109 for six. *Lincolnshire 6 pts, Norfolk 5 pts.*

At St Albans, July 11, 12. Hertfordshire won by six wickets. Cumberland 180 for three dec. and 158; Hertfordshire 220 for seven dec. and 119 for four. *Hertfordshire 20 pts, Cumberland 4 pts.*

At Netherfield, July 16, 17. Cambridgeshire won by six wickets. Cumberland 268 for five dec. and 124 for eight dec. (A. Akhtar six for 56); Cambridgeshire 176 and 221 for four. *Cambridgeshire 18 pts, Cumberland 7 pts.*

At Jesmond, July 16, 17. Northumberland won by seven wickets. Bedfordshire 225 for three dec. and 182 (C. Stanley six for 73); Northumberland 209 for seven dec. and 199 for three (C. S. Pickles 109). *Northumberland 20 pts, Bedfordshire 7 pts.*

At Shenley Park, July 17, 18. Staffordshire won by five wickets. Hertfordshire 140 and 249 (P. J. Humphries five for 47); Staffordshire 223 for eight dec. (M. R. Evans five for 69) and 170 for five. *Staffordshire 23 pts, Hertfordshire 3 pts.*

At Barrow, July 18, 19. Cumberland won by an innings and 69 runs. Cumberland 209 for eight dec. (A. J. Trott five for 71); Bedfordshire 75 (M. G. Scothern five for 41) and 65 (S. J. O'Shaughnessy five for ten). *Cumberland 23 pts, Bedfordshire 3 pts.*

At Jesmond, July 18, 19. Drawn. Cambridgeshire 218 and 278 for five dec. (Nadeem Mohammed 118*); Northumberland 178 for six dec. and 257 for six. *Northumberland 6 pts, Cambridgeshire 3 pts.*

At Lakenham, July 25, 26. Drawn. Norfolk 225 for seven dec. and 244 for one dec. (S. G. Plumb 103*); Cumberland 166 and 248 for seven. *Norfolk 8 pts, Cumberland 3 pts.*

At Longton, July 25, 26. Drawn. Staffordshire 281 for three dec. and 216 for six dec.; Lincolnshire 217 (L. Potter five for 41) and 145 for seven. *Staffordshire 8 pts, Lincolnshire 2 pts.*

At Lakenham, July 27, 28. Norfolk won by four wickets. Bedfordshire 240 for nine dec. and 117; Norfolk 187 (Z. A. Sher eight for 74) and 172 for six. *Norfolk 22 pts, Bedfordshire 5 pts.*

At Ipswich School, July 27, 28. Suffolk won by an innings and 15 runs. Suffolk 198 for seven dec. (D. M. Wheatman five for 54); Cumberland 80 (A. K. Golding six for 24) and 103 (A. K. Golding six for 35). *Suffolk 21 pts, Cumberland 3 pts.*

At Lakenham, July 31, August 1. Drawn with the scores level. Buckinghamshire 253 for four dec. and 284 for seven dec.; Norfolk 245 for seven dec. (S. G. Plumb 104) and 292 for nine (S. C. Goldsmith 118; T. J. A. Scriven five for 92). *Norfolk 12 pts, Buckinghamshire 7 pts.*

At Copdock, July 31, August 1. Drawn. Suffolk 274 for five dec. (D. W. Randall 103) and 212; Staffordshire 266 for eight dec. (A. K. Golding five for 88) and 26 for two. *Suffolk 6 pts, Staffordshire 5 pts.*

At March, August 2, 3. Lincolnshire won by 90 runs. Lincolnshire 282 for seven dec. and 268 for six dec.; Cambridgeshire 275 for three dec. (N. T. Gadsby 116) and 185. *Lincolnshire 21 pts, Cambridgeshire 7 pts.*

At Lakenham, August 2, 3. Norfolk won by ten wickets. Staffordshire 207 for eight dec. and 203 (M. G. Powell six for 69); Norfolk 181 (L. Potter five for 61) and 234 for no wkt (C. J. Rogers 119*). *Norfolk 20 pts, Staffordshire 5 pts.*

At Bury St Edmunds, August 2, 3. Suffolk won by 77 runs. Suffolk 227 for four dec. (P. J. Caley 114*) and 246 (A. R. Clarke seven for 80); Buckinghamshire 202 for six dec. and 194. *Suffolk 22 pts, Buckinghamshire 4 pts.*

At Dunstable, August 6, 7. Buckinghamshire won by 75 runs. Buckinghamshire 230 for five dec. and 179; Bedfordshire 203 for eight dec. and 131 (A. R. Clarke five for 50). *Buckinghamshire 23 pts, Bedfordshire 3 pts.*

At Luton, August 8, 9. Bedfordshire won by 17 runs. Bedfordshire 211 for four dec. and 196 (P. G. Newman five for 33); Staffordshire 233 for four dec. (J. A. Waterhouse 102*) and 157. *Bedfordshire 19 pts, Staffordshire 5 pts.*

At March, August 10, 11. Cambridgeshire won by eight wickets. Hertfordshire 249 for six dec. and 172; Cambridgeshire 215 for eight dec. and 209 for two. *Cambridgeshire 19 pts, Hertfordshire 6 pts.*

At Hertford, August 13, 14. Drawn. Hertfordshire 206 for six dec. and 278 for nine dec; Bedfordshire 226 for four dec. and 181 for six. *Hertfordshire 4 pts, Bedfordshire 6 pts.*

At Lincoln (Lindum), August 13, 14. Drawn. Lincolnshire 190 (A. K. Golding five for 66) and 278 for eight dec; Suffolk 212 for six dec. (D. W. Randall 111; S. A. Bradford five for 90) and 218 for seven. *Lincolnshire 3 pts, Suffolk 6 pts.*

At Jesmond, August 13, 14. Northumberland won by 52 runs. Northumberland 235 for seven dec. and 277 for eight dec.; Norfolk 225 for eight dec. and 235. *Northumberland 21 pts, Norfolk 7 pts.*

At Brewood, August 14, 15. Staffordshire won by 19 runs. Staffordshire 100 (M. A. Sharp five for 28) and 188 (M. G. Scothern six for 60); Cumberland 161 (P. G. Newman six for 41) and 108 (P. G. Newman seven for 40). *Staffordshire 20 pts, Cumberland 5 pts.*

At Jesmond, August 15, 16. Drawn. Suffolk 264 for three dec. (D. W. Randall 118) and 234 (B. Leech six for 92); Northumberland 225 for four dec. and 204 for five. *Northumberland 5 pts, Suffolk 5 pts.*

At Southill Park, August 20, 21. Lincolnshire won by four wickets. Bedfordshire 223 for six dec. and 299 (N. A. Stanley 102); Lincolnshire 242 for four dec. (R. J. Evans 114*) and 282 for six. *Lincolnshire 22 pts, Bedfordshire 4 pts.*

At Carlisle, August 20, 21. Cumberland won by four wickets. Northumberland 198 for seven dec. and 207 (M. A. Sharp five for 45); Cumberland 167 for eight dec. and 241 for six. *Cumberland 20 pts, Northumberland 5 pts.*

At Amersham, August 27, 28. Drawn. Hertfordshire 231 for three dec. and 224 for seven dec.; Buckinghamshire 175 for eight dec. and 161 for four. *Buckinghamshire 3 pts, Hertfordshire 7 pts.*

At North Runcton, August 27, 28. Norfolk won by four wickets. Suffolk 233 for five dec. (R. A. Bunting five for 65) and 160; Norfolk 225 for six dec. (S. C. Goldsmith 156*) and 170 for six. *Norfolk 22 pts, Suffolk 6 pts.*

At Saffron Walden, August 30, 31. Cambridgeshire won by four wickets. Bedfordshire 174 for eight dec. and 241 for four dec. (C. K. Bullen 106*); Cambridgeshire 191 for seven dec. (B. T. P. Donelan 100*) and 225 for six. *Cambridgeshire 21 pts, Bedfordshire 3 pts.*

Western Division

At Kidmore End, May 28, 29. Drawn. Shropshire 182 for five dec. and 196 for eight dec.; Berkshire 137 (M. J. Marvell six for 13) and 149 for six. *Berkshire 2 pts, Shropshire 4 pts.*

At Colwyn Bay, May 28, 29. Drawn. Herefordshire 157 for six dec. and 330 for eight dec. (R. Hall 131); Wales 255 for three dec. and 154 for one. *Wales 6 pts, Herefordshire 2 pts.*

At Swindon, May 28, 29. Drawn. Devon 333 for four dec. (J. G. Wyatt 112) and 184 for five dec.; Wiltshire 182 for six dec. and 30 for one. *Wiltshire 1 pt, Devon 6 pts.*

At Thame, May 30, 31. Oxfordshire won by eight wickets under one-day rules after rain had washed out the first day. Shropshire 220 for eight dec.; Oxfordshire 222 for two. *Oxfordshire 16 pts.*

At Exmouth, June 4, 5. Drawn. Devon 283 for four dec. (N. A. Folland 151*) and 219 for seven dec.; Cornwall 261 for six dec. and 203 for six. *Devon 6 pts, Cornwall 3 pts.*

At Challow and Childrey, June 4, 5. Oxfordshire won by 74 runs. Oxfordshire 203 for five dec. and 215; Wiltshire 199 for seven dec. and 145 (I. J. Curtis eight for 39). *Oxfordshire 20 pts, Wiltshire 4 pts.*

At Pontarddulais, June 4, 5. Cheshire won by six wickets. Wales 210 and 128 for nine dec. (A. J. Murphy five for 62); Cheshire 181 for eight dec. and 158 for four. *Cheshire 22 pts, Wales 4 pts.*

At Leominster, June 6, 7. Herefordshire won by 49 runs. Herefordshire 244 for eight dec. (N. D. Peel five for 50) and 220; Cheshire 226 for four dec. and 189. *Herefordshire 19 pts, Cheshire 7 pts.*

At Shifnal, June 12, 13. Drawn. Cornwall 196 and 286 for three dec. (G. M. Thomas 148*); Shropshire 228 for three dec. and 164 for eight. *Shropshire 8 pts, Cornwall 3 pts.*

At Toft, June 14, 15. Cheshire won by 107 runs. Cheshire 226 for four dec. and 182 for six dec.; Cornwall 121 (A. J. Murphy six for 50) and 180 (R. G. Hignett five for 21). *Cheshire 24 pts, Cornwall 1 pt.*

At Colwall, June 18, 19. Drawn. Berkshire 159 and 228 for seven; Herefordshire 334 for nine dec. *Herefordshire 7 pts, Berkshire 4 pts.*

At Rover, Cowley, June 18, 19. Drawn. Dorset 126 and 338 for four dec.; Oxfordshire 244 for six dec. and 152 for five (S. V. Laudat 104*). *Oxfordshire 8 pts, Dorset 2 pts.*

At Marchwiel, June 18, 19. Drawn. Wiltshire 197 for seven dec. and 294 for seven dec.; Wales 284 for two dec. (J. P. J. Sylvester 138, M. J. Newbold 119*) and 62 for one. *Wales 7 pts, Wiltshire 2 pts.*

At Weymouth, July 5, 6. Drawn. Herefordshire 248 for one dec. (H. V. Patel 135*, S. M. Brogan 105*) and 264 for eight dec. (H. V. Patel 105; S. R. Walbridge five for 98); Dorset 240 for seven dec. and 214 for six. *Dorset 4 pts, Herefordshire 7 pts.*

At Falkland CC, July 9, 10. Drawn. Dorset 245 for eight dec. (R. G. Pitcher five for 91) and 243 for five; Berkshire 446 for five dec. (J. R. Wood 220*). *Berkshire 7 pts, Dorset 3 pts.*

At Wellington, July 9, 10. Devon won by six wickets. Shropshire 261 for five dec. (K. Sharp 145*) and 160; Devon 242 for one dec. (N. R. Gaywood 122*) and 182 for four. *Devon 22 pts, Shropshire 3 pts.*

At Pontypridd, July 9, 10. Drawn. Oxfordshire 234 for two dec. (S. N. V. Waterton 126*) and 216 for five dec.; Wales 198 for six dec. and 134 for seven. *Wales 2 pts, Oxfordshire 6 pts.*

At Marlborough, July 9, 10. Herefordshire won by nine wickets. Herefordshire 260 for two dec. (H. V. Patel 129) and 80 for one; Wiltshire 139 and 200. *Herefordshire 24 pts.*

At Bowdon, July 11, 12. Drawn. Cheshire 143 and 160 for six (K. Donohue five for 45); Devon 331 for four dec. (N. A. Folland 146). *Cheshire 1 pt, Devon 8 pts.*

At Bournemouth, July 16, 17. Drawn. Wales 250 for two dec. (J. P. J. Sylvester 128*, A. W. Harris 105) and 256 for five dec. (J. P. J. Sylvester 114*); Dorset 225 for four dec. and 273 for seven. *Dorset 4 pts, Wales 5 pts.*

At Brockhampton, July 16, 17. Drawn. Herefordshire 222 for six dec. and 235 for seven (A. Jones five for 70); Oxfordshire 164 for nine dec. (E. P. M. Holland five for 41). *Herefordshire 7 pts, Oxfordshire 2 pts.*

At Shrewsbury, July 16, 17. Cheshire won by nine wickets. Shropshire 234 for five dec. and 105; Cheshire 255 for six dec. and 87 for one. *Cheshire 22 pts, Shropshire 5 pts.*

At Truro, July 24, 25. Berkshire won by four wickets. Cornwall 245 for eight dec. (M. P. Briers 111*) and 260 for four dec; Berkshire 232 for seven dec. and 274 for six. *Berkshire 22 pts, Cornwall 7 pts.*

At Sidmouth, July 26, 27. Devon won by six wickets. Berkshire 204 for six dec. and 249 (A. Habib 138; A. M. Small six for 37); Devon 200 for seven dec. and 257 for four. *Devon 21 pts, Berkshire 3 pts.*

At Camborne, July 30, 31. Drawn. Cornwall 207 and 220 for five dec.; Wales 132 and 137 for eight (C. C. Lovell five for 42). *Cornwall 6 pts, Wales 4 pts.*

At Sherborne School, July 30, 31. Devon won by eight wickets. Dorset 199 for five dec. (G. D. Reynolds 106*) and 115; Devon 147 (J. H. Shackleton six for 24) and 168 for two (G. T. J. Townsend 102). *Devon 18 pts, Dorset 6 pts.*

At Christ Church, Oxford, July 30, 31. Drawn. Cheshire 158 (R. A. Evans six for 40) and 209 for eight dec.; Oxfordshire 180 and 117 for two. *Oxfordshire 4 pts, Cheshire 5 pts.*

At Trowbridge, July 30, 31. Drawn. Wiltshire 220 for eight dec. and 254 for eight dec.; Shropshire 222 for five dec. (I. R. Payne 106) and 123 for four. *Wiltshire 4 pts, Shropshire 6 pts.*

At Finchampstead, August 1, 2. Berkshire won by 31 runs. Berkshire 249 for seven dec. (T. L. Hall 137*) and 245 for six dec. (A. Habib 115); Cheshire 201 for seven dec. and 262. *Berkshire 21 pts, Cheshire 6 pts.*

At Hereford, August 1, 2. Drawn. Shropshire 225 for four dec. and 260 for six dec.; Herefordshire 205 for four dec. and 246 for eight (H. V. Patel 103). *Herefordshire 4 pts, Shropshire 3 pts.*

At Usk, August 6, 7. Berkshire won by 176 runs. Berkshire 289 for eight dec. and 261 for two dec. (A. Habib 146*); Wales 221 for four dec. and 153. *Berkshire 21 pts, Wales 6 pts.*

At Westbury, August 6, 7. Wiltshire won by nine wickets. Cornwall 236 for no wkt dec. (G. M. Thomas 100*, S. M. Williams 126*) and 206; Wiltshire 225 for three dec. and 221 for one (D. A. Winter 109*). *Wiltshire 20 pts, Cornwall 5 pts.*

At Dorchester, August 8, 9. Cornwall won by seven wickets. Cornwall 287 for nine dec. and 104 for three; Dorset 113 (D. J. Angove six for 25) and 277 (C. C. Lovell six for 52). *Cornwall 21 pts, Dorset 4 pts.*

At Reading, August 13, 14. Drawn. Berkshire 277 for three dec. (S. D. Myles 122, J. Hodgson 101*) and 184 for four dec.; Wiltshire 165 and 228 for six. *Berkshire 8 pts, Wiltshire 2 pts.*

At Oxton, August 13, 14. Dorset won by 18 runs. Dorset 254 for nine dec. (T. W. Richings 118) and 195 (A. D. Greasley six for 47); Cheshire 226 for four dec. (J. D. Bean 136) and 205 (R. A. Pyman five for 38). *Dorset 19 pts, Cheshire 8 pts.*

At St Austell, August 13, 14. Cornwall won by two wickets. Oxfordshire 223 for four dec. and 232 for four dec. (J. N. Batty 102*); Cornwall 148 and 313 for eight. *Cornwall 17 pts, Oxfordshire 7 pts.*

At Mount Wise, Plymouth, August 15, 16. Devon won by 126 runs. Devon 224 for seven dec. and 124 for six dec.; Oxfordshire 136 (P. M. Roebuck five for 38) and 86 (A. O. F. Le Fleming five for 17). *Devon 22 pts, Oxfordshire 3 pts.*

At Bridgnorth, August 15, 16. Shropshire won by four wickets. Dorset 245 for three dec. (T. W. Richings 127) and 267 for eight dec.; Shropshire 207 for five dec. and 309 for six (K. Sharp 146*). *Shropshire 20 pts, Dorset 5 pts.*

At New Brighton, August 20, 21. Cheshire won by nine wickets. Wiltshire 220 for eight dec. (A. D. Greasley five for 95) and 236 (A. J. Murphy five for 101); Cheshire 230 for six dec. (I. G. Osborne five for 62) and 229 for one (P. R. J. Bryson 100*). *Cheshire 23 pts, Wiltshire 5 pts.*

At Torquay, August 20, 21. Drawn. Devon 265 for three dec. and 211 for six dec.; Herefordshire 206 for nine dec. and 206 for seven. *Devon 8 pts, Herefordshire 2 pts.*

At Oswestry, August 20, 21. Shropshire won by three wickets. Wales 224 (J. A. L. Henderson five for 47) and 298 for three dec.; Shropshire 256 for six dec. (K. Sharp 113) and 267 for seven. (T. Parton 110). *Shropshire 24 pts, Wales 5 pts.*

At Bovey Tracey, August 27, 28. Devon won by eight runs. Devon 301 for one dec. (J. G. Wyatt 112*, N. A. Folland 111*) and 266 for four dec. (G. T. J. Townsend 123); Wales 275 for nine dec. (P. M. Roebuck five for 53) and 284. *Devon 24 pts, Wales 3 pts.*

At Bournemouth, August 27, 28. Dorset won by 14 runs. Dorset 245 and 193 for two dec.; Wiltshire 122 for eight dec. and 302 (J. M. Glasson 100). *Dorset 21 pts, Wiltshire 4 pts.*

At Banbury, August 27, 28. Oxfordshire won by 132 runs. Oxfordshire 244 for six dec. and 247 for five dec. (D. A. J. Wise 100*); Berkshire 262 for four dec. (G. E. Loveday 100*) and 97 (K. A. Arnold five for 49). *Oxfordshire 20 pts, Berkshire 3 pts.*

At Falmouth, August 29, 30. Cornwall won by 96 runs. Cornwall 262 for nine dec. and 275 for three dec. (G. M. Thomas 137, A. C. H. Seymour 111); Herefordshire 264 for nine dec. (M. P. Briers five for 81) and 177 (C. C. Lovell five for 49). *Cornwall 24 pts, Herefordshire 8 pts.*

FINAL

DEVON v LINCOLNSHIRE

At Worcester, September 10, 11. Devon won by 57 runs. Toss: Lincolnshire.

Rain again disrupted the two-day final, which was played under a new ruling: each first innings was restricted to 50 overs, with no bonus points, and in the event of a draw, overall run-rate during the whole game was to determine the winner. However, when the weather turned nasty on Sunday, the two captains were authorised further to amend the match to a straight one-innings contest. Rather than start a new game, though, Devon were surprisingly allowed to continue from an already formidable 170 for one off 36 overs and added a further 93 runs. Gaywood completed his second showpiece century against Lincolnshire in consecutive seasons. Lincolnshire's brave run-chase always lagged behind the asking-rate, despite the occasional lusty burst.

Devon

N. R. Gaywood not out	....	138
J. G. Wyatt c Fell b Bradford	....	50
*P. M. Roebuck lbw b Towse	....	33
G. T. J. Townsend not out	....	35
B 3, l-b 2, n-b 2	....	7

1/133 2/177   (2 wkts, 50 overs) 263

A. J. Pugh, A. M. Small, A. O. F. Le Fleming, K. Donohue, †D. K. Boase, M. C. Woodman and A. W. Allin did not bat.

Bowling: French 7–2–35–0; Towse 16–2–75–1; Bradford 17–2–101–1; Christmas 4–0–26–0; Fell 6–0–21–0.

Lincolnshire

D. B. Storer lbw b Le Fleming	....	25
G. M. Evison c Boase b Allin	....	7
D. E. Gillett b Le Fleming	....	31
R. J. Evans b Le Fleming	....	42
*M. A. Fell b Allin	....	32
D. A. Christmas b Roebuck	....	12
A. D. Towse c Woodman b Roebuck	..	10
N. French run out	....	2
S. N. Warman not out	....	21
S. A. Bradford not out	....	10
B 1, l-b 13	....	14

1/15 2/58 3/79   (8 wkts, 50 overs) 206
4/149 5/162 6/162
7/164 8/179

†G. B. Wilson did not bat.

Bowling: Donohue 6–2–19–0; Woodman 10–1–42–0; Allin 9–1–45–2; Le Fleming 10–0–33–3; Roebuck 14–3–42–2; Gaywood 1–0–11–0.

Umpires: P. Adams and T. G. Wilson.

THE MINOR COUNTIES CHAMPIONS

	Norfolk	1902	Wiltshire	1914	Staffordshire†
1895	Durham	1903	Northamptonshire	1920	Staffordshire
	Worcestershire	1904	Northamptonshire	1921	Staffordshire
1896	Worcestershire	1905	Norfolk	1922	Buckinghamshire
1897	Worcestershire	1906	Staffordshire	1923	Buckinghamshire
1898	Worcestershire	1907	Lancashire II	1924	Berkshire
1899	Northamptonshire	1908	Staffordshire	1925	Buckinghamshire
	Buckinghamshire	1909	Wiltshire	1926	Durham
	Glamorgan	1910	Norfolk	1927	Staffordshire
1900	Durham	1911	Staffordshire	1928	Berkshire
	Northamptonshire	1912	In abeyance	1929	Oxfordshire
1901	Durham	1913	Norfolk	1930	Durham

1931	Leicestershire II	1957	Yorkshire II	1977	Suffolk
1932	Buckinghamshire	1958	Yorkshire II	1978	Devon
1933	Undecided†	1959	Warwickshire II	1979	Suffolk
1934	Lancashire II	1960	Lancashire II	1980	Durham
1935	Middlesex II	1961	Somerset II	1981	Durham
1936	Hertfordshire	1962	Warwickshire II	1982	Oxfordshire
1937	Lancashire II	1963	Cambridgeshire	1983	Hertfordshire
1938	Buckinghamshire	1964	Lancashire II	1984	Durham
1939	Surrey II	1965	Somerset II	1985	Cheshire
1946	Suffolk	1966	Lincolnshire	1986	Cumberland
1947	Yorkshire II	1967	Cheshire	1987	Buckinghamshire
1948	Lancashire II	1968	Yorkshire II	1988	Cheshire
1949	Lancashire II	1969	Buckinghamshire	1989	Oxfordshire
1950	Surrey II	1970	Bedfordshire	1990	Hertfordshire
1951	Kent II	1971	Yorkshire II	1991	Staffordshire
1952	Buckinghamshire	1972	Bedfordshire	1992	Staffordshire
1953	Berkshire	1973	Shropshire	1993	Staffordshire
1954	Surrey II	1974	Oxfordshire	1994	Devon
1955	Surrey II	1975	Hertfordshire	1995	Devon
1956	Kent II	1976	Durham		

† Disputed. Some sources claim the Championship was never decided.

MCC TROPHY FINAL

CAMBRIDGESHIRE v HEREFORDSHIRE

At Lord's, August 23. Cambridgeshire won by two wickets. Toss: Cambridgeshire.

An enthralling finish saw Cambridgeshire win a Minor Counties final at the sixth attempt since 1987. Herefordshire, unable to accelerate from their lunch-time 126 for one off 37 overs, managed only 64 in boundaries, despite the usual short hit on the Tavern side. They were always struggling to defend their modest total, although Cambridgeshire did their best to foul things up. Having recovered from 81 for three to 160 for three, they then stuttered to 182 for seven when Adams and Turner fell to successive balls in the 50th over. Needing 19 off the last two overs, they took 15 off the penultimate one, bowled by Jarvis, including a six over mid-wicket from Ajaz Akhtar.

Herefordshire

H. V. Patel lbw b Donelan	35	R. Hall not out	1
M. J. Weston c Adams b Masters	86	B 1, l-b 8, w 11, n-b 2	22
S. M. Brogan not out	60		
J. P. Wright c Williams b Turner	7	1/86 2/160 (4 wkts, 55 overs)	226
*R. P. Skyrme b Akhtar	15	3/174 4/223	

K. B. S. Jarvis, †S. R. Bevins, M. G. Fowles, E. P. M. Holland and R. J. Harding did not bat.

Bowling: Masters 11–1–52–1; Akhtar 11–1–48–1; Ralfs 11–3–32–0; Turner 11–1–53–1; Donelan 11–0–32–1.

Cambridgeshire

*N. T. Gadsby c Bevins b Weston	42	A. Akhtar not out	18
Salim Mohammed c Bevins b Holland	9	D. F. Ralfs not out	12
G. W. Ecclestone c and b Fowles	23		
N. J. Adams c Jarvis b Weston	48	B 4, l-b 12, w 5	21
Nadeem Mohammed c Bevins b Holland	38		
B. T. P. Donelan c Weston b Harding	2	1/32 2/81 3/81 (8 wkts, 54.3 overs)	227
†S. L. Williams c Skyrme b Jarvis	14	4/160 5/169 6/182	
S. Turner run out	0	7/182 8/195	

K. D. Masters did not bat.

Bowling: Jarvis 11–1–53–1; Holland 11–3–39–2; Harding 11–1–38–1; Weston 11–1–40–2; Fowles 10.3–1–41–1.

Umpires: K. Bray and C. Stone.

SECOND ELEVEN CHAMPIONSHIP, 1995

The Second Eleven Championship was won by Hampshire, whose title was their fourth in all and their first since 1981, when Chris and Robin Smith featured prominently in the side. Victorious in ten matches, they were just six points ahead of the runners-up Northamptonshire, who won nine but had more bonus points than any other county. These two were well ahead of the rest, with a gap of 29 points separating them from third-placed Durham. None of the front-runners fared well in the Bain Hogg Trophy, which was won by Leicestershire, finalists in 1994 and winners in 1993, who managed only 12th place in the Championship.

Seven batsmen passed 1,000 runs, the most prolific being Muneeb Diwan, who scored 1,084 while playing in every Worcestershire match, but also managed to play three early-season matches for Derbyshire, taking his total for both counties to 1,357. Anthony McGrath of Yorkshire had the best average of the seven, 67.29. Of the players who scored more than 500 runs, Nadeem Shahid of Surrey was alone in achieving a three-figure average, scoring his 660 runs at 110. Both Tim O'Gorman of Derbyshire and Richard Kettleborough of Yorkshire scored five centuries. The highest of nine double-centuries was 258 by Gregor Kennis for Surrey against Leicestershire, while 250s also came from Asif Din (253 not out for Warwickshire against Middlesex) and Matthew Keech (251 for Hampshire against Glamorgan). Tim Hancock's 233 for Gloucestershire against Nottinghamshire at Bristol contributed to a Championship sixth-wicket record of 304 with Reggie Williams.

The leading bowler was the Northamptonshire leg-spinner, Andy Roberts, who took 73 wickets at 24.53. No one else passed 60, the next being the Sussex fast bowler James Kirtley with 58 at 22.43. Roberts, one of eight players who appeared in all their county's matches, bowled 658.1 overs. Only two others bowled more than 500: Keith Dutch of Middlesex and Richard Pearson of Essex. Roberts, the leading all-rounder, also scored 791 runs at 43.94 and was named Second Eleven Player of the Year, for which he received £700. The leading wicket-keeper was Simon Willis of Kent, who caught 45 and stumped six.

Continued over

SECOND ELEVEN CHAMPIONSHIP, 1995

					Bonus points		
Win = 16 points	M	W	L	D	Batting	Bowling	Points
1 – Hampshire (13)	17	10	2	5	56	62	278
2 – Northamptonshire (5) ..	17	9	3	5	66	62	272
3 – Durham (7)............	17	8	3	6	58	57	243
4 – Kent (3)	17	8	4	5	52	59	239
5 – Yorkshire (2)	17	7	1	9	55	53	220
6 – Warwickshire (14)	17	7	2	8*	54	50	216
7 – Surrey (11)	17	5	5	7	56	52	188
8 – Worcestershire (8)	17	5	7	5	46	56	182
9 – Sussex (9)	17	5	5	7	46	46	172
10 – Middlesex (10)	17	4	8	5	48	53	165
11 – Nottinghamshire (18)...	17	4	8	5	37	54	163
12 – Leicestershire (4)	17	4	5	8	48	47	159
13 – Lancashire (15).......	17	4	10	3	37	53	154
14 – Gloucestershire (6).....	17	4	6	7*	35	47	146
15 – Somerset (1)	17	3	7	7	40	51	139
16 – Derbyshire (16)	17	3	7	7	43	47	138
17 – Essex (12)	17	3	6	8	38	51	137
18 – Glamorgan (17)	17	3	7	7	38	49	135

1994 positions are shown in brackets.
The total for Nottinghamshire includes 8 points for batting second in a match drawn with the scores level.

* *Indicates one match abandoned without a ball bowled.*

Derbyshire were unable to improve on 16th place, but O'Gorman's 1,155 runs were a county record, comfortably passing Gary Steer's 1,057 in 1992. Tom Harrison was also prolific with 840 runs, including 149 not out against Kent and five fifties, while Andrew Bairstow had four fifties in his 727. Michael May's maiden century was an impressive 173 not out against Yorkshire. Simon Base and the ever-present Alan Richardson took 30 wickets each, but at significant cost.

In contrast to their first team, **Durham** were again successful, thanks to some consistent performances. Jon Longley and Phil Bainbridge both passed 700 runs, Longley's 880 being a county record. Robin Weston, with 669, was rewarded with a first-team call after making three centuries in successive matches. Longley also had three hundreds, the biggest of which – 166 against Yorkshire – was followed in the second innings by 96. Jimmy Daley's 173 against Glamorgan was the highest innings yet for the county and three bowling records also tumbled. Left-arm spinner David Cox broke his own record with 51 wickets; the England Under-19 representative Colin Campbell had a new innings-best with seven for 32 against Kent, and Paul Collingwood's nine for 39 against Leicestershire was the best match return to date. Off-spinner Jason Searle shared the main burden of the attack with Cox and finished with 40 wickets.

The **Essex** batting was headed by two experienced players, Mike Garnham and Jonathan Lewis. Garnham, an inspirational leader, was just 12 short of 1,000 runs in his last season, while Lewis scored 820 in 11 innings, his three late-season hundreds including 225 against Worcestershire. That match also featured a maiden century from Tim Hodgson, a left-handed opener who joined the staff after coming down from Durham University, and a return of ten for 92 by the off-spinner, Pearson. Hodgson passed 500 runs, as did Andrew Hibbert and Paul Shaw, in his first season. The leading fast bowlers were Steve Andrew and Neil Williams, who took six for 34 against his old county, Middlesex. However, lack of penetration was blamed for the county's poor placing.

Glamorgan's performance was very much like their first team's. They had a bright start, with victory in their first match against Middlesex, but won only twice more and sank back to the bottom of the table. Alistair Dalton was the pick of the batsmen, and was well supported by Andrew Roseberry and Adrian Shaw, who also kept wicket tidily and was named the club's Young Player of the Year. These three all scored centuries in a total of 427 for two against Lancashire, when the left-arm spinner, Stuart Phelps, took six for 87. Gary Butcher's all-round ability was highlighted in his seven for 59 against Leicestershire and his century against Nottinghamshire.

Gloucestershire won as many matches as they had in each of the last two years, when they finished in the top third of the table, but, managing fewer bonus points than any other county, they dropped to 14th. There was consolation, though, in reaching the final of the Bain Hogg Trophy. Their batting was mostly disappointing, despite Hancock's county record of 233 in 230 balls against Nottinghamshire. Victory was sealed by a return of nine for 78 from fast bowler David Boden, who finished with match figures of 13 for 153. Other significant innings were Dean Hodgson's 193 against Middlesex and Bobby Dawson's 171 not out against Yorkshire. Maiden centuries were scored against Kent by Chris Taylor, a promising newcomer, and, in a first-ever victory over Lancashire, by wicket-keeper Philip Nicholson.

Hampshire's meteoric rise of 12 places to their first title since 1981 was the result of fine contributions throughout the team. Both Tony Middleton and Keech passed 1,000 runs, five others passed 500, four averaged more than 60 and eight batsmen shared 15 centuries, including two double-centuries. The biggest was Keech's county record 251 in 256 balls against Glamorgan, while Giles White made 229 not out against Surrey. Paul Whitaker and Middleton had three hundreds each – and Middleton might have had a fourth had he not declared when he was 99 not out against Gloucestershire, having made 100 in the first innings. Glyn Treagus confirmed his promise with a maiden century against Derbyshire. Off-spinner Richard Dibden, whose 39 wickets cost only 19.61 apiece, took ten in his first match of the season after coming down from Loughborough University and had five in an innings five times, including seven for 55 against Lancashire. The mainstays of the attack were the experienced left-arm spinner Raj Maru and Martin Thursfield, at fast-medium, with significant all-round contributions from Kevan James. Mark Garaway, ever-present, as he was in 1994, effected 48 dismissals.

Kent's blend of youth and experience was reflected in a fine team effort. Two young newcomers, Chris Walsh and Jamie Ford, both passed 600 runs with three centuries apiece, including 212 from Ford against Derbyshire. David Fulton and the left-handed Nigel Llong, also prolific, featured in a county record first-wicket partnership of 329 against Somerset at Maidstone. There were maiden centuries for Nick Preston against Worcestershire and for the South African-born doctor, Julian Thompson, against Glamorgan. Despite missing part of the season through injury, Steve Herzberg was another to confirm his all-round ability with 29 economical wickets, while the left-arm spinner Eddie Stanford again took the most with 49. Seam bowler Ben Phillips made good progress in his first full season and Darren Scott, an off-spinner, impressed in his four matches.

The overall team performances for **Lancashire** were disappointing and only Gloucestershire earned fewer batting points. The 38-year-old Australian Test player Peter Sleep captained the side and topped both averages. However, Richard Green and Nathan Wood, a left-hander, scored the most runs, closely followed by 17-year-old Andrew Flintoff and Patrick McKeown, who compiled a maiden century against Gloucestershire, while Mark Chilton made an impressive debut with 262 in two matches. Green and Darren Shadford bowled effectively at medium pace and acquitted themselves well when they found their way into the first team during the season.

Winners of the Bain Hogg Trophy, **Leicestershire** were disappointing in the Championship and dropped eight places. Phil Robinson scored four hundreds, but Aftab Habib, formerly with Middlesex, was the most prolific runmaker. Four others passed 600 runs: Darren Maddy, who played the highest innings of 182 against Surrey, Steve Bartle, Vince Clarke and Jonathan Dakin. Clarke, who joined the county from Somerset, had a particularly good all-round match against Derbyshire, when he scored a century and took five for 81. That match was also significant for a maiden century from Carl Crowe, an off-spinning all-rounder in his first season on the staff. Left-arm spinner Matthew Brimson was the leading wicket-taker with 43, including seven for 74 against Sussex. James Ormond looked a fine prospect and had match figures of 12 for 84 against Nottinghamshire.

Progress was patchy for **Middlesex**, whose resources were strained by the loss from the first team of Mike Roseberry and Desmond Haynes. Toby Radford passed 1,000 runs for the first time, with Paul Farbrace close behind. The only others to pass 500 were Jason Harrison, whose 225 against Northamptonshire was a county record, and Dutch, who played in all the matches and showed a welcome return to form. He particularly excelled with the ball, taking 54 wickets. David Goodchild and David Nash both scored maiden centuries, while Nash's England Under-19 colleague, 16-year-old Owais Shah, looked a precocious talent and made his first-team debut. The attack was hampered by injury, although the spin department, when at full strength, was well balanced, featuring Amer Khan's leg-breaks, Dutch's off-breaks and Umer Rashid bowling slow left-arm. However, the seam attack lacked bite, Kevin Shine and Kervin Marc proving particularly expensive, although Rickie Fay showed more penetration later in the season.

But for some last-over defeats, **Northamptonshire** might easily have won the title. The batting was strong, with young players to the fore: 17-year-old David Sales scored over 900, while 18-year-old David Roberts followed his maiden century – against Yorkshire – with two more. The off-spinner Jason Brown and Scott Boswell, a young seam bowler, both had excellent seasons.

Nottinghamshire moved up seven places from the bottom of the table and reached the one-day semi-finals. Although six batsmen passed 500 runs, only Colin Banton made 600. At the top of the averages was Noel Gie, son of Clive Gie of Western Province and Natal and, like Banton, born in South Africa. Most of the wickets fell to the spinners, Andy Afford, Usman Afzaal – both left-armers – plus off-spinners Michael Field-Buss and Richard Bates.

With only 17 full-time professionals on the staff at the start of the season, **Somerset** often struggled to raise a team and in all called on 59 players, two-thirds of them newcomers. Champions in 1994, they crashed down to 15th place. With injuries to senior players, Jeremy Batty was often the only staff bowler in the side, but he coped well with the task, bowling tirelessly for his 45 wickets. No one else took 20, although Ian Bishop, a young seam bowler from Taunton, looked promising when he appeared in the last few matches. Keith Parsons and Piran Holloway held the side together when they played and headed the batting averages. Holloway, Sam Trego and Jeremy Hallett were the only players to pass 500 runs, although Brett Crosdale scored 377 in his four matches, including a maiden century against Worcestershire. In the same match, Andy Caddick scored his first century in any type of cricket on his way back from injury.

Surrey began well, heading the table at one stage until first-team injuries depleted their resources in July and August. However, their seventh place was an improvement on their performance in 1994 and they were also semi-finalists in the Bain Hogg Trophy. The stylish opener Kennis followed his maiden century against Sussex with 258 against Leicestershire a week later. It equalled the fourth-highest by any player in the Championship and included 41 fours. It was followed by a return of eight for 56 from Jason de la Pena. Shahid, recruited from Essex, made a century in each of his four matches, before being promoted to the first team. Jamie Knott, son of Alan and also a wicket-keeper, scored six fifties and Oliver Slipper recorded his maiden century against Glamorgan. Richard Nowell, a left-arm spinner, and the England Under-19 fast bowler Alex Tudor both had ten-wicket returns: Nowell took seven for 29 and five for 46 against Derbyshire and Tudor collected 11 for 93 against Essex. Ben Holloioake, at medium pace, took the most wickets.

Like many other counties, **Sussex** could not always field a full-strength side. However, they always played positively and maintained their position in the middle of the table, despite recording the fewest bowling points. The innings of the season was played by Danny Law, whose maiden century against Lancashire at Hove developed into 229 not out, with 12 sixes and 28 fours. Having honed his batting skills during the winter in Australia, he returned as a valuable all-rounder, despite being restricted in his bowling by injury. Robin Martin-Jenkins also made great strides, following his maiden century against Worcester with another against Glamorgan a week later to finish with 603 runs and 27 wickets. Kirtley's whole-hearted fast bowling earned him 58 economical wickets, and there was useful support from two off-spinners, Justin Bates and Nick Phillips.

Although **Warwickshire's** early hopes of adding this title to all the others were dashed by a couple of bad results in August, they still finished well up the table. They were the most settled side, calling on only 25 players all season. The experienced Asif Din played in all the matches and was the leading run-scorer, well supported by Wasim Khan, Ashley Giles, Anurag Singh and Michael Powell. They scored attractively and set up many winning positions. In his last season, Asif Din hit a county record 253 not out against Middlesex. Left-arm pace bowler Darren Altree returned career-best figures of seven for 19 as Glamorgan were dismissed for 83, and Dougie Brown took six for 16 as Worcestershire were dismissed for 76.

Worcestershire's batting was dominated by Chris Tolley and Diwan, both of whom passed 1,000 runs. Tolley, who asked to be released at the end of the season, hit four hundreds; Diwan, who joined the county from Essex, had one hundred plus six fifties. Against Leicestershire, Parvaz Mirza had match figures of ten for 197, and came top of the averages with 52 wickets from 11 games, before his tragic death a week after the season ended.

Yorkshire were beaten only by Gloucestershire but drew more games than any other county and finished fifth. McGrath and Kettleborough dominated the batting. Alex Morris, a talented all-rounder, followed his maiden century – 172 against Lancashire – with another against Durham. There were also maiden centuries for James Hood, who hit 102 against Worcestershire, and the promising opener Matthew Wood, who scored 137 against Northamptonshire. The left-arm spinner, Ian Fisher, bowled nearly twice as many overs as anyone else and was rewarded with 42 wickets. Gavin Hamilton, who like Morris bats left-handed but bowls right-arm medium, took seven for 39 against Sussex and six for 75 against Worcestershire. The strength of the club's Cricket Academy was reflected in the fact that half the side were often under 19, although McGrath, Morris and Chris Schofield were often on England Under-19 duty.

DERBYSHIRE SECOND ELEVEN

Matches 17: Won – Essex, Glamorgan, Lancashire. Lost – Hampshire, Kent, Northamptonshire, Surrey, Sussex, Warwickshire, Worcestershire. Drawn – Durham, Gloucestershire, Leicestershire, Middlesex, Nottinghamshire, Somerset, Yorkshire.

Batting Averages

	M	I	NO	R	HS	100s	Avge
M. Diwan............	3	5	1	273	107*	1	68.25
T. A. Tweats	3	6	1	258	108*	1	51.60
*T. J. G. O'Gorman ..	13	25	2	1,155	140	5	50.21
M. R. May	8	14	2	520	173*	1	43.33
A. J. Harris	3	4	2	79	35	0	39.50
T. W. Harrison	13	25	3	840	149*	1	38.18
†A. J. Thompson	2	3	1	73	72*	0	36.50
J. E. Owen	10	19	0	684	147	1	36.00
†A. D. Bairstow......	13	23	1	727	91	0	33.04
W. A. Dessaur	10	18	1	534	101	1	31.41
F. A. Griffith	4	8	1	183	49	0	26.14
M. E. Cassar	12	20	6	358	53	0	25.57
A. C. Cottam	12	14	3	279	72	0	25.36
P. Aldred	6	9	2	163	78	0	23.28
†S. Griffiths	5	8	2	115	52*	0	19.16
J. D. Cokayne	2	4	0	55	24	0	13.75
*S. J. Base	14	20	5	193	32*	0	12.86
S. O. Moore	3	3	0	37	29	0	12.33
M. Taylor..........	13	18	5	147	42	0	11.30
I. G. S. Steer	3	6	0	65	40	0	10.83
†P. G. T. Davies	3	4	0	27	14	0	6.75
A. Richardson	17	17	6	52	15	0	4.72

Played in two matches: †K. M. Krikken 33, 0; †B. J. M. Maher 1*. Played in one match: N. D. R. Bannister 9, 34; P. S. Carter 4; †I. Dawood 13, 3*; J. J. Greaves 29*, 17; T. W. Hancock 1; M. J. Marvell 20*; P. K. May 1; I. C. Parkin 8*; A. S. Rollins 0, 0; C. M. Wells 68, 3; I. S. Thompson did not bat.

Bowling Averages

	O	M	R	W	BB	Avge
F. A. Griffith	118	36	305	18	5-24	16.94
M. E. Cassar	236	45	829	27	6-57	30.70
A. C. Cottam	308.3	86	840	26	5-80	32.30
P. Aldred	144.2	29	510	15	5-146	34.00
A. Richardson	351.3	58	1,257	35	5-52	35.91
M. Taylor..........	272.3	61	930	24	4-66	38.75
S. J. Base	342.4	58	1,326	30	5-69	44.20
A. J. Harris	52.4	11	213	4	2-31	53.25
T. W. Harrison	161.1	47	521	8	1-10	65.12

Also bowled: N. D. R. Bannister 11-0-55-0; P. S. Carter 11-0-55-0; W. A. Dessaur 37-4-148-0; J. J. Greaves 5-0-29-0; T. W. Hancock 21-2-61-1; M. J. Marvell 5-1-13-0; S. O. Moore 50-7-194-3; I. C. Parkin 9-1-33-0; I. G. S. Steer 2-0-19-0; T. A. Tweats 2-0-10-0; C. M. Wells 9-1-43-0.

DURHAM SECOND ELEVEN

Matches 17: Won – Essex, Glamorgan, Kent, Lancashire, Leicestershire, Middlesex, Northamptonshire, Nottinghamshire. Lost – Hampshire, Surrey, Worcestershire. Drawn – Derbyshire, Gloucestershire, Somerset, Sussex, Warwickshire, Yorkshire.

Batting Averages

	M	I	NO	R	HS	100s	Avge
J. A. Daley............	4	7	1	469	173	1	78.16
J. I. Longley.........	8	13	0	880	166	3	67.69
R. M. S. Weston.....	7	12	1	669	135*	3	60.81
S. Hutton...........	7	11	2	487	103*	1	54.11
*P. Bainbridge.......	12	18	3	796	154	1	53.06
†D. G. C. Ligertwood..	5	7	2	252	74*	0	50.40
W. Larkins.........	2	3	0	141	122	1	47.00
†C. W. Scott.........	10	16	3	588	111	1	45.23
I. M. Stanger........	5	5	1	170	85	0	42.50
M. Saxelby.........	5	9	2	282	83	0	40.28
N. Killeen.........	3	5	2	108	69	0	36.00
S. D. Birbeck.......	5	7	0	250	80	0	35.71
D. A. Blenkiron.....	8	12	1	315	122*	1	28.63
C. Clark...........	6	9	0	228	72	0	25.33
R. A. Hawthorne....	2	3	1	49	44	0	24.50
P. J. Wilcock.......	10	18	2	337	67	0	21.06
D. Williamson......	6	8	3	95	32	0	19.00
Q. J. Hughes.......	3	6	0	107	42	0	17.83
P. D. Collingwood....	11	17	1	278	52*	0	17.37
D. M. Cox.........	14	16	2	223	50	0	15.92
I. Jones...........	12	12	4	123	38	0	15.37
C. L. Campbell......	6	3	2	12	7	0	12.00
B. C. Usher........	3	5	0	45	24	0	9.00
M. J. Robinson.....	2	3	0	21	10	0	7.00
J. P. Searle........	10	10	3	34	18	0	4.85

Played in four matches: M. M. Betts 28, 11*; H. Hubber 3*. Played in two matches: J. R. G. Lawrence 0; †A. Pratt 44*, 21. Played in one match: G. Angus 8; P. L. Carlin 40; D. M. Lane 19*, 6*; M. A. Roseberry 12; D. J. Rutherford 24; N. J. Trainor 21, 7; A. Walker 6, 2; J. B. Windows 55*; A. Robson and C. Stanley did not bat.

Note: In the match v Sussex at Horsham M. Saxelby, called up for a first-team match, was replaced by R. A. Hawthorne.

Bowling Averages

	O	M	R	W	BB	Avge
P. D. Collingwood....	147.5	34	400	20	5-20	20.00
C. L. Campbell......	152	33	400	20	7-32	20.00
D. M. Cox.........	475.5	161	1,158	51	6-51	22.70
J. R. G. Lawrence....	65	22	139	6	2-38	23.16
B. C. Usher........	55	10	192	8	4-57	24.00
I. M. Stanger........	102.1	25	302	12	4-24	25.16
M. M. Betts........	78	12	264	10	3-39	26.40
S. D. Birbeck.......	83.2	13	324	12	5-57	27.00
J. P. Searle.........	329	83	1,105	40	4-32	27.62
D. Williamson......	114.5	19	402	14	5-53	28.71
P. Bainbridge......	48	13	133	4	4-57	33.25
N. Killeen.........	77.3	19	233	7	4-56	33.28
H. Hubber.........	51.4	9	168	5	1-6	33.60
I. Jones...........	193	33	728	20	4-32	36.40
D. A. Blenkiron.....	44	0	177	4	1-12	44.25

Also bowled: G. Angus 42–13–105–2; C. Clark 53–9–184–2; D. M. Lane 15–4–44–1; J. I. Longley 0.5–0–8–0; A. Robson 22–4–75–2; D. J. Rutherford 9.1–1–45–0; M. Saxelby 5–1–9–0; C. Stanley 26–8–64–1; A. Walker 32–5–93–2; R. M. S. Weston 24.5–2–128–0; J. B. Windows 18–4–36–3.

ESSEX SECOND ELEVEN

Matches 17: Won – Middlesex, Nottinghamshire, Worcestershire. Lost – Derbyshire, Durham, Hampshire, Kent, Surrey, Yorkshire. Drawn – Glamorgan, Gloucestershire, Lancashire, Leicestershire, Northamptonshire, Somerset, Sussex, Warwickshire.

Batting Averages

	M	I	NO	R	HS	100s	Avge
J. J. B. Lewis........	7	11	1	820	225	3	82.00
*†M. A. Garnham....	15	27	4	988	141*	3	42.95
T. P. Hodgson	8	15	3	504	139	1	42.00
C. J. Rogers	3	6	0	202	72	0	33.66
G. A. Khan	9	16	1	459	107	2	30.60
R. G. Hignett........	5	9	2	213	68	0	30.42
A. J. E. Hibbert......	12	23	1	622	122	2	28.27
P. R. Shaw	10	19	0	515	93	0	27.10
P. Ayres	7	14	3	293	64*	0	26.63
C. I. O. Ricketts	14	23	1	447	81	0	20.31
A. P. Cowan	11	14	6	160	40*	0	20.00
R. M. Pearson	13	20	5	286	48	0	19.06
A. Habib	2	4	0	74	34	0	18.50
N. F. Williams.......	4	5	0	80	26	0	16.00
S. D. Peters	5	9	1	127	53	0	15.87
S. J. W. Andrew	11	15	3	184	66	0	15.33
N. Macrae	2	4	0	60	30	0	15.00
S. Ahmed	3	6	0	85	29	0	14.16
G. J. A. Goodwin	5	5	0	58	23	0	11.60
*A. R. Butcher......	4	7	0	79	36	0	11.28
D. W. Ayres	6	11	2	65	21	0	7.22
N. A. Derbyshire....	13	19	3	107	23	0	6.68
D. M. Cousins	6	8	1	29	15	0	4.14

Played in two matches: A. Clark 1, 2, 22, 43*; B. J. Hyam 23, 0, 27, 43*. Played in one match: J. H. Childs 2*, 1*; S. Renshaw 2*, 0*; D. D. J. Robinson 74, 2; J. R. M. Runciman 0*; M. Saggers 9, 5; A. C. H. Seymour 19, 4; M. Sheikh 31, 0; E. J. Wilson 0, 3.

Bowling Averages

	O	M	R	W	BB	Avge
N. F. Williams.......	87.5	18	267	17	6-34	15.70
R. M. Pearson	503.5	105	1,387	56	6-97	24.76
S. J. W. Andrew	242.2	49	723	26	5-24	27.80
R. G. Hignett........	80.3	16	236	8	4-44	29.50
J. H. Childs	49	20	120	4	2-41	30.00
D. W. Ayres	100.4	22	362	11	5-68	32.90
D. M. Cousins	124.2	24	419	10	2-28	41.90
G. J. A. Goodwin	116.2	32	341	8	2-25	42.62
A. P. Cowan	199.4	35	754	17	3-115	44.35
N. A. Derbyshire....	268	23	1,088	21	4-87	51.80
C. I. O. Ricketts	392.1	107	1,099	20	3-74	54.95

Also bowled: S. Ahmed 12-2-52-2; A. R. Butcher 2-0-3-0; A. Clark 18.2-4-92-2; A. J. E. Hibbert 7.3-0-44-1; G. A. Khan 13.5-0-61-3; J. J. B. Lewis 8-0-31-0; S. Renshaw 9-1-33-2; J. R. M. Runciman 3-0-9-0; M. Saggers 15-0-74-1; M. Sheikh 4-0-35-1.

GLAMORGAN SECOND ELEVEN

Matches 17: Won – Lancashire, Middlesex, Nottinghamshire. Lost – Derbyshire, Durham, Hampshire, Kent, Leicestershire, Northamptonshire, Warwickshire. Drawn – Essex, Gloucester-shire, Somerset, Surrey, Sussex, Worcestershire, Yorkshire.

Batting Averages

	M	I	NO	R	HS	100s	Avge
S. P. James.........	2	4	1	168	130*	1	56.00
*A. Dale.............	3	4	0	197	122	1	49.25
*D. L. Hemp.........	3	5	0	191	105	1	38.20
R. P. Lefebvre.......	6	8	1	259	89	0	37.00
A. J. Dalton.........	13	23	0	849	129	3	36.91
*J. Derrick..........	11	15	6	331	70*	0	36.77
A. Roseberry	13	24	1	804	153*	1	34.95
†A. D. Shaw	15	26	5	722	110	1	34.38
W. L. Law	3	4	1	99	43	0	33.00
G. P. Butcher.......	15	26	2	680	104	1	28.33
N. Pratt	5	9	1	220	38	0	27.50
C. E. Mulraine......	3	6	0	162	70	0	27.00
J. R. A. Williams	8	13	0	338	119	1	26.00
P. S. Jones	8	10	5	126	54*	0	25.20
G. H. J. Rees........	8	14	1	281	68	0	21.61
S. D. Thomas	8	13	0	273	73	0	21.00
I. P. Gompertz.......	7	12	1	202	43	0	18.36
A. P. Davies	7	8	1	94	37	0	13.42
M. D. O'Leary	3	5	2	37	22	0	12.33
B. S. Phelps	16	21	4	166	33	0	9.76
N. M. Kendrick......	2	4	0	21	11	0	5.25
A. D. Rowlands......	2	4	2	9	5*	0	4.50
G. J. M. Edwards	11	11	5	20	8	0	3.33

Played in two matches: S. R. Barwick 6*, 4, 0*; I. J. Capon 17, 3; J. D. Chaminda 15, 4, 0; D. A. Cosker 1; A. W. Evans 43, 26, 45; †R. E. Evans 24, 0, 1. Played in one match: A. Majeed 10, 3*; J. D. J. Manville 0, 0; M. F. Robinson 5.

Bowling Averages

	O	M	R	W	BB	Avge
S. R. Barwick.......	71	32	122	5	3-60	24.40
S. D. Thomas.......	225.1	58	639	23	7-29	27.78
A. P. Davies	135	28	468	15	3-39	31.20
A. D. Rowlands......	38	13	126	4	2-44	31.50
D. A. Cosker	96.3	26	253	8	6-58	31.62
G. J. M. Edwards	303.5	74	990	31	7-29	31.93
G. P. Butcher.......	201.5	35	794	23	7-59	34.52
B. S. Phelps	359.5	82	1,210	31	6-87	39.03
J. Derrick..........	87.5	24	279	7	2-33	39.85
R. P. Lefebvre	110	32	253	6	2-20	42.16
I. P. Gompertz.......	36.2	4	177	4	2-33	44.25
P. S. Jones	127	23	468	8	2-45	58.50
N. Pratt	103.2	23	365	5	1-29	73.00

Also bowled: I. J. Capon 16–0–117–1; A. Dale 13–2–56–0; A. J. Dalton 22.2–1–105–0; D. L. Hemp 1–0–3–0; N. M. Kendrick 71.2–21–243–2; A. Majeed 23.1–1–126–1; M. D. O'Leary 30–2–154–1; M. F. Robinson 12–4–29–1.

GLOUCESTERSHIRE SECOND ELEVEN

Matches 16: Won – Lancashire, Nottinghamshire, Worcestershire, Yorkshire. Lost – Hampshire, Kent, Middlesex, Northamptonshire, Somerset, Sussex. Drawn – Derbyshire, Durham, Essex, Glamorgan, Leicestershire, Surrey. Abandoned – Warwickshire.

Batting Averages

	M	I	NO	R	HS	100s	Avge
R. J. Cunliffe	5	8	2	470	142	2	78.33
G. D. Hodgson	5	7	0	412	193	1	58.85
R. I. Dawson	8	15	3	506	171*	2	42.16
*T. H. C. Hancock ...	10	16	1	625	233	1	41.66
†R. C. J. Williams	12	19	3	628	110	1	39.25
K. P. Sheeraz	6	8	5	96	26	0	32.00
D. R. Hewson	4	7	1	173	61*	0	28.83
*M. Davies	10	15	5	274	67*	0	27.40
†P. J. Nicholson	4	7	0	187	100	1	26.71
J. Lewis	8	11	2	233	52	0	25.88
C. G. Taylor.........	5	8	0	195	110	1	24.37
M. J. Cawdron	15	23	2	470	83*	0	22.38
†C. S. Knightley	3	5	0	97	40	0	19.40
I. M. Collins	7	13	0	247	88	0	19.00
R. C. Williams.......	11	17	0	279	64	0	16.41
D. J. P. Boden	9	12	4	125	33*	0	15.62
*V. J. Pike	12	11	4	100	23	0	14.28
*K. E. Cooper	4	6	1	51	21*	0	10.20
B. L. Worrad	4	8	0	81	32	0	10.12
J. G. Whitby-Coles ...	6	9	4	21	8*	0	4.20

Played in three matches: Muhammad Akram 1, 32. Played in two matches: P. S. Lazenbury 52, 36, 0, 17; P. W. Romaines 91*, 14*; P. A. Spence 0, 31*; U. D. Valjee 0, 24, 7, 13; M. J. Whitney 0, 12, 13; M. G. N. Windows 35, 4, 21, 50. Played in one match: *M. W. Alleyne 27, 8; C. R. J. Budd 0, 0; D. A. T. Dalton 14, 55; B. C. A. Ellison 21, 13; Imran Mohammad 8, 29; D. E. A. Lawrence 0, 6; M. A. Lynch 26, 20; †C. M. W. Read 1, 36; A. M. Smith 3; A. Symonds 80, 31*; D. K. Taylor 0, 7; J. L. Taylor 3; R. J. Williams 7.

Bowling Averages

	O	M	R	W	BB	Avge
K. E. Cooper	144	41	358	17	5-26	21.05
D. J. P. Boden	254.5	53	912	40	9-78	22.80
M. J. Cawdron	273.1	74	851	28	5-43	30.39
K. P. Sheeraz	142.4	31	437	14	5-65	31.21
J. Lewis	210	44	656	19	3-50	34.52
R. C. Williams	186.2	35	694	19	4-80	36.52
M. Davies...........	284.2	76	821	22	5-76	37.31
V. J. Pike..........	354	69	1,201	28	3-86	42.89

Also bowled: M. W. Alleyne 16–2–66–0; C. R. J. Budd 11–1–60–0; R. I. Dawson 40–11–128–3; B. C. A. Ellison 18–3–92–1; T. H. C. Hancock 29–4–76–1; Muhammad Akram 75–15–244–6; A. M. Smith 30–5–83–5; P. A. Spence 37–12–106–1; A. Symonds 5–0–33–0; J. G. Whitby-Coles 77–22–247–5.

HAMPSHIRE SECOND ELEVEN

Matches 17: Won – Derbyshire, Durham, Essex, Glamorgan, Gloucestershire, Kent, Lancashire, Leicestershire, Somerset, Worcestershire. Lost – Sussex, Yorkshire. Drawn – Middlesex, Northamptonshire, Nottinghamshire, Surrey, Warwickshire.

Batting Averages

	M	I	NO	R	HS	100s	Avge
G. W. White	6	7	2	377	229*	1	75.40
K. D. James.........	5	7	2	339	114*	2	67.80
P. R. Whitaker	7	12	3	596	144	3	66.22
T. C. Middleton	15	24	7	1,070	119	3	62.94

	M	I	NO	R	HS	100s	Avge
W. S. Kendall	8	11	3	421	79*	0	52.62
M. Keech	14	22	0	1,054	251	2	47.90
R. S. M. Morris	9	13	1	555	133	1	46.25
G. R. Treagus	11	14	1	549	117	1	42.23
J. S. Laney	11	17	0	696	109	2	40.94
†M. Garaway	17	21	7	532	76*	0	38.00
R. J. Maru	13	10	4	194	74	0	32.33
M. J. Thursfield	13	15	2	378	67	0	29.07
D. B. Goldstraw......	9	6	1	55	30	0	11.00
D. P. J. Flint	12	6	1	34	16	0	6.80

Played in seven matches: R. R. Dibden 23*, 17, 0; S. J. Renshaw 2, 5, 16*. Played in five matches: N. G. Cowans 2*, 4*. Played in four matches: L. J. Botham 56, 2, 0, 0. Played in three matches: D. N. Blackwood 19*, 1; C. E. Sketchley 6, 1, 15, 19. Played in two matches: J. N. B. Bovill 37*; W. F. Stelling 28, 57*. Played in one match: D. Chisholm 15*; D. M. Thomas 0; J. E. Allen, H. Barton and P. A. Spence did not bat.

Note: In the match v Gloucestershire at Southampton M. J. Thursfield, called up for a first-team match, was replaced by R. J. Maru.

Bowling Averages

	O	M	R	W	BB	Avge
K. D. James........	121.2	27	350	24	6-48	14.58
J. N. B. Bovill	46.2	16	129	7	3-47	18.42
N. G. Cowans	78.5	24	192	10	2-17	19.20
R. R. Dibden	272.1	76	765	39	7-55	19.61
R. J. Maru	479.3	192	883	39	4-23	22.64
M. J. Thursfield	310.3	77	892	38	6-76	23.47
M. Keech	140	32	394	15	5-33	26.26
D. N. Blackwood	71.5	17	226	8	4-67	28.25
S. J. Renshaw	145	35	494	16	3-28	30.87
P. R. Whitaker	62.5	14	166	5	2-26	33.20
D. P. J. Flint	271.4	76	774	22	6-37	35.18
D. B. Goldstraw.....	178	33	667	12	3-34	55.58

Also bowled: J. E. Allen 6–1–31–0; L. J. Botham 14–0–76–0; W. S. Kendall 8–2–34–0; J. S. Laney 4–1–16–0; T. C. Middleton 3–0–44–0; C. E. Sketchley 45–8–153–2; P. A. Spence 12–3–48–1; W. F. Stelling 48.2–13–149–3; D. M. Thomas 23.4–7–66–3; G. R. Treagus 1–0–4–0; G. W. White 19.5–4–75–2.

KENT SECOND ELEVEN

Matches 17: Won – Derbyshire, Essex, Glamorgan, Gloucestershire, Middlesex, Northamptonshire, Somerset, Worcestershire. Lost – Durham, Hampshire, Lancashire, Nottinghamshire. Drawn – Leicestershire, Surrey, Sussex, Warwickshire, Yorkshire.

Batting Averages

	M	I	NO	R	HS	100s	Avge
*N. R. Taylor	8	11	4	552	141*	1	78.85
N. J. Llong	6	10	0	655	159	2	65.50
D. P. Fulton.........	7	11	1	514	178	1	51.40
C. D. Walsh.........	10	14	0	618	142	3	44.14
J. A. Ford	10	16	0	616	212	3	38.50
*C. Penn............	3	4	0	150	112	1	37.50
S. Herzberg	10	16	2	506	87	0	36.14
M. V. Fleming.......	4	7	0	247	91	0	35.28
J. B. D. Thompson ...	11	16	3	440	108	1	33.84
M. R. Fletcher.......	7	10	1	264	80*	0	29.33

	M	I	NO	R	HS	100s	Avge
M. J. Walker	10	19	2	480	157	1	28.23
N. W. Preston	15	23	3	469	103	1	23.45
W. J. House	10	17	0	271	36	0	15.94
†S. C. Willis.........	14	21	1	307	72	0	15.35
B. J. Phillips	14	19	6	163	30*	0	12.53
T. N. Wren	6	7	1	71	47	0	11.83
A. P. Igglesden	4	4	1	25	16	0	8.33
E. J. Stanford	15	17	7	70	15	0	7.00

Played in four matches: D. A. Scott 0, 0*, 1*, 1*. Played in two matches: D. M. Cook 0, 10*; C. E. Dagnall 25*, 4, 21, 13; M. Featherstone 32, 137, 27, 61. Played in one match: G. R. Cowdrey 58, 72; A. G. E. Ealham 29, 24; J. M. Golding 1*; R. Key 23, 13; S. Luckhurst 1, 35; M. J. McCague 68*; †P. J. Nicholson 3, 10; †N. C. Price 29; P. D. Scott 9, 9; G. J. J. Sheen 47, 1; L. Stone 4, 4; S. J. Taylor 0, 16; †R. E. White 7, 0.

Bowling Averages

	O	M	R	W	BB	Avge
M. J. McCague	20.4	3	57	6	3-26	9.50
J. A. Ford...........	42.2	14	96	10	3-13	9.60
S. Herzberg	210.5	52	510	29	4-27	17.58
A. P. Igglesden	107.3	22	295	16	5-97	18.43
C. Penn	41	6	114	6	3-22	19.00
J. B. D. Thompson ...	258.2	58	773	37	6-36	20.89
D. A. Scott	142.3	35	366	17	4-55	21.52
M. V. Fleming	77	8	259	12	3-50	21.58
E. J. Stanford	405.5	116	1,141	49	6-76	23.28
B. J. Phillips	201	39	643	26	4-36	24.73
N. W. Preston	429.4	105	1,213	45	5-62	26.95
C. E. Dagnall.......	40	8	156	4	2-54	39.00
T. N. Wren	87	2	376	6	2-73	62.66

Also bowled: D. M. Cook 27–5–95–3; M. R. Fletcher 3–0–22–0; J. M. Golding 6–1–29–1; W. J. House 43–7–153–1; N. J. Llong 36.4–12–93–0; P. D. Scott 7–1–33–0; L. Stone 15.3–0–76–1; S. J. Taylor 5–0–48–0; M. J. Walker 2–0–4–0; C. D. Walsh 2–0–8–0.

LANCASHIRE SECOND ELEVEN

Matches 17: Won – Kent, Middlesex, Nottinghamshire, Surrey. Lost – Derbyshire, Durham, Glamorgan, Gloucestershire, Hampshire, Leicestershire, Northamptonshire, Sussex, Worcestershire, Yorkshire. Drawn – Essex, Somerset, Warwickshire.

Batting Averages

	M	I	NO	R	HS	100s	Avge
*P. R. Sleep	9	14	8	530	112*	2	88.33
M. J. Chilton	2	4	1	262	95	0	87.33
S. P. Titchard.......	5	10	2	336	115	1	42.00
A. Flintoff	10	20	2	668	145*	2	37.11
G. A. Knowles......	4	8	0	271	59	0	33.87
S. I. Dublin	2	4	0	128	62	0	32.00
R. J. Green	13	25	2	702	113	2	30.52
P. C. McKeown.....	12	23	0	679	116	1	29.52
N. T. Wood	15	30	0	728	135	1	24.26
D. J. Shadford	15	28	3	589	99	0	23.56
M. E. Harvey	8	16	1	352	72	0	23.46
L. J. Marland	9	17	0	303	75	0	17.82
A. A. Barnett.......	12	22	1	363	46*	0	17.28
G. Yates	4	7	0	101	58	0	14.42

	M	I	NO	R	HS	100s	Avge
C. Brown	15	21	5	177	35*	0	11.06
D. J. Thompson	14	23	2	209	39	0	9.95
†N. P. Harvey	16	28	4	214	35	0	8.91
P. J. Seal	10	13	7	12	5	0	2.00

Played in one match: I. D. Austin 24; A. D. Bairstow 85, 26; C. E. Dagnall 11*, 1*; N. A. Din 67*, 9; †J. J. Haynes 43, 26; G. Keedy 5, 2*; B. A. Knowles 4, 0; D. Leather 0; G. D. Lloyd 47, 34; P. J. Martin 1; P. Ridgeway 0*, 0; N. J. Speak 109, 0.

Bowling Averages

	O	M	R	W	BB	Avge
P. R. Sleep	53	19	107	9	4-26	11.88
R. J. Green	238.2	53	789	31	4-55	25.45
A. A. Barnett	430.1	123	1,236	45	9-79	27.46
A. Flintoff	47.1	11	156	5	3-57	31.20
C. Brown	444.2	96	1,616	44	6-129	36.72
D. J. Shadford	264	32	1,115	30	5-42	37.16
D. J. Thompson	311	37	1,218	29	5-46	42.00
G. Yates	115.5	24	371	7	4-42	53.00
P. J. Seal	188	34	738	12	3-111	61.50

Also bowled: I. D. Austin 13-3-36-2; C. E. Dagnall 2-0-24-0; N. A. Din 30-2-124-2; S. I. Dublin 32-12-104-3; G. Keedy 34-5-98-2; B. A. Knowles 15-2-110-1; D. Leather 18-2-86-3; P. J. Martin 24-3-84-0; P. Ridgeway 16-7-43-1; S. P. Titchard 6-1-13-0; N. T. Wood 2-0-10-0.

LEICESTERSHIRE SECOND ELEVEN

Matches 17: Won – Glamorgan, Lancashire, Nottinghamshire, Sussex. Lost – Durham, Hampshire, Northamptonshire, Warwickshire, Yorkshire. Drawn – Derbyshire, Essex, Gloucestershire, Kent, Middlesex, Somerset, Surrey, Worcestershire.

Batting Averages

	M	I	NO	R	HS	100s	Avge
A. Habib	9	16	3	865	128	2	66.53
T. J. Boon	7	12	2	480	108	1	48.00
D. L. Maddy	7	14	0	649	182	1	46.35
J. M. Dakin	10	17	4	600	110	2	46.15
*†P. E. Robinson.....	14	17	1	718	136	4	44.87
S. Bartle	11	19	1	658	77	0	36.55
†M. D. R. Sutliff.....	3	6	0	202	81	0	33.66
V. P. Clarke	14	22	3	626	105*	1	32.94
C. D. Crowe	13	21	6	491	134*	1	32.73
D. Stevens	9	16	3	417	79	0	32.07
T. J. Mason	10	14	3	314	72	0	28.54
S. Ahmed	6	12	1	311	81	0	28.27
†J. J. Haynes	4	7	3	95	35*	0	23.75
M. T. Brimson	13	14	4	221	60*	0	22.10
†C. D. Durant	11	12	5	98	21*	0	14.00
A. Sheriyar	8	6	4	26	10*	0	13.00
J. Ormond	9	10	0	126	48	0	12.60
S. Kirby	2	3	1	10	9*	0	5.00

Played in two matches: D. J. Millns 53*; F. Patel 1, 1; A. R. K. Pierson 1*, 19; V. J. Wells 70, 16; N. R. Widdowson 0; D. Williamson 12. Played in one match: J. J. Bull 18, 18; A. S. Christmas 30, 4; P. Khakhar 11, 7; S. T. Knox 2, 19; G. I. Macmillan 75, 40; R. A. E. Martin 22, 9; N. Patel 15*, 0; †N. J. Pullen 0, 16; C. C. Remy 12*; M. J. Saggers 3*; B. F. Smith 52, 29; K. B. Smith 9*; A. G. Statham 0, 0*; D. A. Walker 0; †F. O. Walker 8*, 22; J. J. Whitaker 51*, 12; P. M. Ridgeway and K. G. Sedgbeer did not bat.

Note: Owing to first-team calls, T. J. Boon was replaced by P. Khakhar in the match v Yorkshire at Oakham, J. M. Dakin was replaced by N. Patel in the match v Nottinghamshire at Barwell and P. E. Robinson was replaced by V. J. Wells in the match v Derbyshire at Rocester.

Bowling Averages

	O	M	R	W	BB	Avge
S. Kirby	31.3	2	128	8	6-63	16.00
D. J. Millns	47	10	187	10	3-21	18.70
N. R. Widdowson	39	6	105	5	2-19	21.00
C. D. Crowe........	237.2	65	582	26	5-81	22.38
J. Ormond	213.1	44	717	27	6-41	26.55
M. T. Brimson	469.3	131	1,146	43	7-74	26.65
J. M. Dakin	104	20	349	13	3-35	26.84
A. R. K. Pierson	54.2	11	169	5	2-36	33.80
V. P. Clarke	378.1	61	1,428	35	6-35	40.80
S. Bartle	44.2	4	232	5	2-37	46.40
A. Sheriyar	214.5	34	836	16	3-48	52.25
T. J. Mason	182	37	541	5	3-65	108.20

Also bowled: S. Ahmed 70–10–307–3; T. J. Boon 20–3–64–2; A. S. Christmas 8–0–55–1; A. Habib 7–2–19–1; P. Khakhar 3–0–10–0; D. L. Maddy 52–14–133–3; F. Patel 31–4–145–1; C. C. Remy 12–0–69–0; P. M. Ridgeway 14–2–69–0; P. E. Robinson 2–0–6–1; M. J. Saggers 19–1–88–1; K. G. Sedgbeer 11–2–38–0; B. F. Smith 7–0–57–0; K. B. Smith 19–1–64–1; D. Stevens 1–0–9–0; D. A. Walker 16–2–84–0; V. J. Wells 2–0–8–0; D. Williamson 26–7–62–2.

MIDDLESEX SECOND ELEVEN

Matches 17: Won – Gloucestershire, Nottinghamshire, Somerset, Sussex. Lost – Durham, Essex, Glamorgan, Kent, Lancashire, Surrey, Warwickshire, Worcestershire. Drawn – Derbyshire, Hampshire, Leicestershire, Northamptonshire, Yorkshire.

Batting Averages

	M	I	NO	R	HS	100s	Avge
C. M. Gupte	2	4	1	205	74	0	68.33
U. B. A. Rashid ...	5	5	3	117	80*	0	58.50
T. A. Radford	11	21	3	1,041	160*	2	57.83
*†P. Farbrace........	15	27	2	933	131	3	37.32
J. C. Harrison	10	18	2	542	225	2	33.87
†D. C. Nash.........	5	9	2	237	105*	1	33.85
†M. J. Marvell......	5	10	1	303	109*	1	33.66
O. A. Shah	8	16	2	456	96	0	32.57
*†K. P. Dutch	17	29	6	725	104	1	31.52
J. P. Hewitt	7	12	3	283	65	0	31.44
D. J. Goodchild.....	7	14	1	393	121	1	30.23
R. L. Johnson	4	7	0	208	50	0	29.71
C. W. Taylor	5	6	3	87	22	0	29.00
R. P. Lane	2	4	0	105	58	0	26.25
S. Patel	7	12	1	278	62	0	25.27
R. S. Yeabsley	5	9	1	153	77*	0	19.12
K. Marc	8	9	5	67	21	0	16.75
*I. J. Gould	8	6	2	64	24	0	16.00
P. A. Sogbodjor	2	3	0	48	23	0	16.00
A. A. Khan	12	17	2	236	42	0	15.73
G. J. J. Sheen	2	4	0	57	26	0	14.25
R. A. Fay..........	5	5	1	53	42	0	13.25

	M	I	NO	R	HS	100s	Avge
P. A. R. de Silva	2	4	0	47	17	0	11.75
C. E. Dagnall	2	3	1	23	18*	0	11.50
B. Gannon	4	5	2	32	28	0	10.66
K. J. Shine	10	12	3	34	18	0	3.77

Played in two matches: A. K. Durgacharan 39, 13; M. R. Evans 14, 14*. Played in one match: †J. Bahl 28*; †J. N. Batty 0; A. W. Evans 0, 63; M. A. Feltham 41; R. J. Greatorex 4, 3; R. A. Hawthorne 0; R. J. Hodges 0; C. J. Hollins 18, 8; A. W. Laraman 7, 9; S. P. Moffat 5, 78; A. N. Muggleton 17, 2; J. C. Pooley 15, 108*; R. Rao 12, 0; P. E. Wellings 14; D. A. Horsley did not bat.

Note: Owing to first-team calls, T. A. Radford and K. P. Dutch were replaced by S. Patel and R. S. Yeabsley in the match v Gloucestershire at Harrow.

Bowling Averages

	O	M	R	W	BB	Avge
M. R. Evans	40	12	121	7	2-22	17.28
R. A. Fay	100.4	25	279	16	3-33	17.43
M. J. Marvell	82	24	210	10	5-34	21.00
S. Patel	42.4	8	159	7	4-40	22.71
D. J. Goodchild	53	13	166	6	3-10	27.66
U. B. A. Rashid	121.1	31	307	11	3-12	27.90
K. P. Dutch	514.2	109	1,614	54	7-99	29.88
A. A. Khan	375	98	1,088	33	4-87	32.96
R. L. Johnson	102.3	17	333	10	4-90	33.30
D. A. Horsley	45	11	149	4	3-69	37.25
C. W. Taylor	97	15	354	9	4-74	39.33
K. J. Shine	221.1	40	824	19	6-49	43.36
B. Gannon	77	10	271	5	3-48	54.20
J. P. Hewitt	109.2	19	393	7	2-29	56.14
K. Marc	143	19	668	10	2-29	66.80

Also bowled: C. E. Dagnall 26–2–135–3; M. A. Feltham 19.4–6–77–3; I. J. Gould 3.3–0–13–1; J. C. Harrison 2–0–2–0; C. J. Hollins 4–1–18–2; R. P. Lane 17–6–37–2; A. N. Muggleton 10–3–22–2; O. A. Shah 2.2–0–14–0; P. E. Wellings 2–0–19–0; R. S. Yeabsley 27–1–115–2.

NORTHAMPTONSHIRE SECOND ELEVEN

Matches 17: Won – Derbyshire, Glamorgan, Gloucestershire, Lancashire, Leicestershire, Nottinghamshire, Surrey, Sussex, Worcestershire. Lost – Durham, Kent, Somerset. Drawn – Essex, Hampshire, Middlesex, Warwickshire, Yorkshire.

Batting Averages

	M	I	NO	R	HS	100s	Avge
A. Fordham	3	5	0	329	91	0	65.80
*†D. Ripley	12	21	9	728	96	0	60.66
A. L. Penberthy	8	15	4	631	105*	2	57.36
M. J. Foster	13	20	6	790	114*	1	56.42
M. B. Loye	9	18	0	966	146	3	53.66
D. J. Roberts	12	21	3	852	114	3	47.33
A. R. Roberts	17	25	7	791	91	0	43.94
A. J. Swann	5	10	0	429	98	0	42.90
D. J. Sales	13	24	0	935	131	2	38.95
J. N. Snape	6	10	1	333	84	0	37.00
T. C. Walton	12	23	0	826	139	2	35.91
R. R. Montgomerie . . .	4	7	0	237	74	0	33.85

	M	I	NO	R	HS	100s	Avge
M. N. Bowen	9	8	3	129	56	0	25.80
C. S. Atkins	10	11	4	159	42	0	22.71
K. J. Innes	11	14	4	169	54*	0	16.90
S. A. J. Boswell	15	11	2	76	27	0	8.44

Played in 11 matches: J. F. Brown 9*, 0*, 0*, 0*, 0*, 0*, 4*. Played in four matches: J. G. Hughes 17, 5, 4. Played in two matches: †T. M. B. Bailey 32; N. G. B. Cook 0, 0, 14; †G. D. Herbert 13, 28, 7, 2. Played in one match: J. M. Attfield 0, 32; R. M. Carter 0; P. Clitheroe 1, 8; †I. Dawood 6*, 46; S. A. Pearce 5, 4; M. V. Steele 9; G. Swann 14; R. J. Warren 2, 6; N. A. Mallender did not bat.

Note: Owing to first-team calls, M. N. Bowen was replaced by A. R. Roberts in the match v Nottinghamshire at Northampton and T. C. Walton was replaced by A. J. Swann in the match v Gloucestershire at Bristol.

Bowling Averages

	O	M	R	W	BB	Avge
T. C. Walton	130	28	345	16	3-17	21.56
J. F. Brown	386	110	953	42	8-57	22.69
A. R. Roberts	658.1	188	1,791	73	8-125	24.53
A. L. Penberthy......	115.4	26	350	13	4-53	26.92
M. N. Bowen	274.2	60	834	29	4-22	28.75
S. A. J. Boswell	401	74	1,358	47	5-72	28.89
C. S. Atkins	263.5	91	669	23	2-18	29.08
J. N. Snape	175.4	39	569	17	6-69	33.47
K. J. Innes	173	36	553	11	3-7	50.27
J. G. Hughes	86.3	21	298	5	2-29	59.60
M. J. Foster	166	33	488	8	2-47	61.00

Also bowled: P. Clitheroe 22–5–74–2; M. B. Loye 1–0–19–0; N. A. Mallender 24–5–56–1; R. R. Montgomerie 5–0–26–0; M. V. Steele 5–1–22–0.

NOTTINGHAMSHIRE SECOND ELEVEN

Matches 17: Won – Kent, Somerset, Surrey, Warwickshire. Lost – Durham, Essex, Glamorgan, Gloucestershire, Lancashire, Leicestershire, Middlesex, Northamptonshire. Drawn – Derbyshire, Hampshire, Sussex, Worcestershire, Yorkshire.

Batting Averages

	M	I	NO	R	HS	100s	Avge
N. A. Gie...........	6	12	1	399	129	1	36.27
C. Banton...........	11	19	1	601	110*	1	33.38
G. W. Mike	2	3	0	97	51	0	32.33
†L. N. Walker	12	20	3	515	60*	0	30.29
J. R. Wileman	10	19	2	503	92	0	29.58
*M. Newell	14	21	1	561	80	0	28.05
U. Afzaal	11	19	1	501	95	0	27.83
K. Afzaal	4	7	2	133	80*	0	26.60
M. G. Field-Buss.....	13	22	4	432	86	0	24.00
R. W. J. Howitt......	3	5	1	92	44*	0	23.00
R. J. Chapman	12	15	8	158	45	0	22.57
R. T. Bates.........	14	25	0	540	61	0	21.60
M. P. Dowman	10	19	0	406	121	1	21.36
S. J. Musgrove	7	11	0	225	58	0	20.45
P. R. Pollard	2	3	0	49	26	0	16.33
J. P. Hart..........	9	14	1	207	34	0	15.92
M. R. Evans........	2	3	1	29	16*	0	14.50
N. J. Armstrong	4	4	0	51	21	0	12.75

	M	I	NO	R	HS	100s	Avge
J. A. Afford	12	18	7	130	27*	0	11.81
D. B. Pennett	8	12	2	87	17	0	8.70
M. Broadhurst	5	6	2	25	17	0	6.25
J. N. Batty	2	4	0	23	13	0	5.75
I. Riches	4	6	4	3	1*	0	1.50

Played in two matches: T. E. Hemmings 8, 3; G. E. Welton 49, 2. Played in one match: G. F. Archer 72, 43; K. P. Evans 22; P. Franks 21, 1; B. N. French 4*; P. Johnson 31, 5; K. J. Murden 8, 2; J. A. Quereshi 12, 9; D. Smit 54, 38; P. A. Spence 6, 2; N. Spencer 6, 3.

Note: Owing to first-team calls, D. B. Pennett was replaced by U. Afzaal in the match v Somerset at Nottingham, R. J. Chapman was replaced by S. J. Musgrove in the match v Durham at South Shields, M. Newell was replaced by R. J. Chapman in the match v Northamptonshire at Northampton and C. Banton was replaced by S. J. Musgrove in the match v Leicestershire at Barwell.

Bowling Averages

	O	M	R	W	BB	Avge
G. W. Mike	52	14	133	11	5-32	12.09
J. R. Wileman	39.2	7	137	7	3-33	19.57
M. R. Evans.	30	2	156	7	4-75	22.28
P. Franks	28	5	105	4	3-61	26.25
R. T. Bates.	148.2	31	517	19	4-59	27.21
T. E. Hemmings	39	7	147	5	3-83	29.40
U. Afzaal	287.4	77	859	27	6-27	31.81
J. A. Afford	288.1	88	851	26	6-48	32.73
J. P. Hart	162	25	532	16	7-94	33.25
D. B. Pennett	173.3	36	604	17	4-54	35.52
I. Riches	84.3	18	256	7	6-44	36.57
M. G. Field-Buss	334.5	89	988	25	5-75	39.52
R. J. Chapman	208	30	783	19	3-49	41.21
M. Broadhurst	73	10	316	7	2-56	45.14

Also bowled: G. F. Archer 11–3–27–0; N. J. Armstrong 47.3–8–181–2; M. P. Dowman 5–3–6–0; K. P. Evans 16–4–47–0; S. J. Musgrove 12–2–40–0; M. Newell 1–1–0–0; P. A. Spence 19–2–93–1.

SOMERSET SECOND ELEVEN

Matches 17: Won – Gloucestershire, Northamptonshire, Warwickshire. Lost – Hampshire, Kent, Middlesex, Nottinghamshire, Surrey, Worcestershire, Yorkshire. Drawn – Derbyshire, Durham, Essex, Glamorgan, Lancashire, Leicestershire, Sussex.

Batting Averages

	M	I	NO	R	HS	100s	Avge
K. A. Parsons	5	9	2	422	134	1	60.28
†P. C. L. Holloway ...	8	12	1	638	132	2	58.00
B. L. Crosdale	4	8	1	377	136	1	53.85
M. E. Trescothick	3	5	0	240	122	1	48.00
S. C. Ecclestone	4	7	1	250	95	0	41.66
H. J. Morgan	3	5	1	153	84*	0	38.25
J. I. D. Kerr.	3	5	2	111	73	0	37.00
S. M. Trego	15	22	6	590	71*	0	36.87
A. R. Caddick	5	10	0	292	102	1	29.20
*J. C. Hallett	14	23	1	607	80	0	27.59
J. D. Batty	12	19	3	338	53*	0	21.12
A. O. F. Le Fleming ..	8	13	0	255	74	0	19.61
J. M. Smallridge	7	14	1	243	78	0	18.69

	M	I	NO	R	HS	100s	Avge
J. Burke	4	7	4	50	16*	0	16.66
L. Sutton	6	11	0	180	54	0	16.36
D. F. Lye	6	12	2	163	44	0	16.30
G. R. Swinney	6	10	0	162	54	0	16.20
M. Dimond	7	9	4	79	33	0	15.80
M. J. Gear	3	3	0	43	31	0	14.33
L. D. W. Trumper ...	3	5	2	42	16*	0	14.00
A. P. van Troost ...	5	6	2	50	35	0	12.50
P. J. Robinson	3	4	1	15	10	0	5.00
P. C. Turner	5	3	1	1	1	0	0.50

Played in three matches: I. E. Bishop 5, 0; M. R. Liddle 3, 3. Played in two matches: M. Amjad 0, 0*; G. G. Angus 6, 0; C. J. Barker 6, 30, 2, 26; G. Brown 7, 46; M. J. Crook 6, 6; S. P. Griffiths 9, 106, 2, 1; R. Horrell 18*, 14; M. N. Lathwell 33, 0, 19; R. J. Turner 9, 73, 129, 33. Played in one match: N. F. Anson 0; K. A. Barrett 43*, 39; P. J. Bassingthwaighte 0, 2; D. J. Bostock 6, 7*; N. R. Boulton 27, 0; G. A. Bucknell 37, 12; B. T. Collins 26, 7; J. R. Dalwood 34*, 11; A. Dart 1, 0; A. N. Hayhurst 80, 42; M. P. Hunt 1, 49; S. P. Jenkins 6*, 0; J. M. Kerslake 6, 2; R. J. Pannell 9, 0; K. J. Parsons 0, 9; G. D. Rose 44, 103*; G. R. Tucker 2, 41; J. Tucker 2, 22*; P. J. Witherly 0; O. Youll 34, 2; A. Ahmed, R. E. Berry, T. W. J. Farley, P. M. Lacy and C. Stanley did not bat.

Note: In the match v Nottinghamshire at Nottingham, K. A. Parsons, called up for a first-team match, was replaced by J. D. Batty.

Bowling Averages

	O	M	R	W	BB	Avge
I. E. Bishop	54.4	9	171	13	5-58	13.15
K. A. Parsons	60.3	19	192	12	5-43	16.00
M. E. Trescothick ...	31	6	98	5	3-54	19.60
P. C. Turner	60.4	14	161	8	3-29	20.12
A. R. Caddick	47	10	162	6	5-55	27.00
R. Horrell	63.2	17	163	6	2-48	27.16
J. C. Hallett	116.1	15	372	13	4-36	28.61
J. I. D. Kerr	71.2	15	220	7	3-59	31.42
S. C. Ecclestone	69	15	224	7	3-66	32.00
J. D. Batty	496.5	109	1,606	45	7-83	35.68
A. O. F. Le Fleming ..	148	30	529	14	3-76	37.78
J. C. Smallridge	49.3	8	234	6	3-44	39.00
M. Dimond	91	19	323	8	3-36	40.37
A. P. van Troost	82	15	300	7	2-29	42.85
L. D. W. Trumper ...	59.5	8	253	5	2-65	50.60
G. R. Swinney	100.5	17	391	6	4-81	65.16
S. M. Trego	147.1	22	550	6	2-101	91.66

Also bowled: A. Ahmed 8-0-42-0; M. Amjad 17-4-55-1; G. G. Angus 28-5-98-2; D. J. Bostock 16-4-60-1; J. Burke 40-7-164-3; M. J. Crook 24.1-7-99-3; B. L. Crosdale 36-4-148-3; T. W. J. Farley 9-2-34-1; A. N. Hayhurst 15-1-55-1; M. P. Hunt 15-1-83-0; P. M. Lacy 12-1-40-1; M. N. Lathwell 30.3-3-109-3; D. F. Lye 8-1-29-0; H. J. Morgan 3-0-9-0; R. J. Pannell 9-0-57-0; P. J. Robinson 9-3-19-0; G. D. Rose 10-2-32-0; C. Stanley 17-3-83-2; G. R. Tucker 21-2-79-0; J. Tucker 6-0-41-0; P. J. Witherly 17-2-65-0.

SURREY SECOND ELEVEN

Matches 17: Won – Derbyshire, Durham, Essex, Middlesex, Somerset. Lost – Lancashire, Northamptonshire, Nottinghamshire, Sussex, Warwickshire. Drawn – Glamorgan, Gloucestershire, Hampshire, Kent, Leicestershire, Worcestershire, Yorkshire.

Batting Averages

	M	I	NO	R	HS	100s	Avge
N. Shahid	4	7	1	660	141	4	110.00
†J. A. Knott	10	17	5	645	86*	0	53.75
G. J. Kennis	13	21	1	783	258	2	39.15
A. J. Tudor	9	12	4	304	57*	0	38.00
D. M. Ward	10	18	3	572	118	1	33.64
J. D. Ratcliffe	9	16	1	495	96	0	33.00
A. W. Smith	9	12	1	353	92	0	32.09
D. J. Bicknell	3	6	2	116	53	0	29.00
R. W. Nowell	6	10	1	248	64	0	27.55
M. R. Bainbridge	11	18	3	404	81*	0	26.93
†N. F. Sargeant	13	21	0	470	80	0	22.38
S. G. Kenlock	11	13	3	220	57	0	22.00
B. C. Hollioake	16	27	2	540	70	0	21.60
O. M. Slipper	14	23	0	464	112	1	20.17
J. M. de la Pena	12	14	9	38	15*	0	7.60
J. Powell	6	10	2	40	10	0	5.00

Played in three matches: P. Bainbridge 9, 4, 29; R. Rao 54, 34*, 56, 22. Played in two matches: N. A. Brett 16, 24, 4*, 3*; P. Dickinson 19, 9, 4; †G. J. Kersey 25, 15, 35; J. A. North 8, 12, 6; A. C. S. Pigott 0, 3, 6; M. R. Powell 39, 2; I. Thompson 0, 2, 0*. Played in one match: M. P. Bicknell 46, 18*; A. D. Brown 19; S. P. Byrne 0; D. G. J. Carson 1, 11; D. M. Carter 35, 0; L. Clarke 28; N. Cross 12, 39; D. R. Drepaul 0*, 5; B. W. Meaney 10; K. T. Medlycott 9; N. Mughal 0*; R. Sladden 23; M. A. Butcher did not bat.

Note: Owing to first team calls, M. A. Butcher was replaced by B. W. Meaney in the match v Middlesex at Cheam and D. J. Bicknell was replaced by P. Bainbridge in the match v Sussex at Hove.

Bowling Averages

	O	M	R	W	BB	Avge
L. Clarke	8.4	0	48	4	4-42	12.00
A. J. Tudor	149.4	31	526	30	6-43	17.53
R. W. Nowell	191	56	534	26	7-29	20.53
M. P. Bicknell	37	8	88	4	3-61	22.00
J. Powell	28	8	93	4	2-19	23.25
G. J. Kennis	238.2	65	685	24	5-70	28.54
B. C. Hollioake	272	42	1,055	33	4-38	31.96
A. W. Smith	196.2	55	568	17	3-23	33.41
R. Rao	36	5	134	4	1-0	33.50
N. Shahid	69	12	216	6	2-19	36.00
S. G. Kenlock	253.3	59	765	21	5-49	36.42
J. M. de la Pena	246.5	44	1,130	28	8-56	40.35
N. A. Brett	48.2	7	214	4	2-43	53.50

Also bowled: M. R. Bainbridge 64-8-282-2; D. J. Bicknell 7.3-0-42-1; S. P. Byrne 11-4-45-0; D. M. Carter 19-6-56-0; P. Dickinson 20.3-4-65-2; J. A. Knott 27.4-7-149-1; K. T. Medlycott 8-5-8-0; N. Mughal 3-1-10-0; J. A. North 5-0-23-0; A. C. S. Pigott 19-4-60-1; M. R. Powell 35-5-117-2; J. D. Ratcliffe 59.3-19-179-2; R. Sladden 43-14-98-0; O. M. Slipper 38-5-151-3.

SUSSEX SECOND ELEVEN

Matches 17: Won – Derbyshire, Gloucestershire, Hampshire, Lancashire, Surrey. *Lost –* Leicestershire, Middlesex, Northamptonshire, Warwickshire, Yorkshire. *Drawn –* Durham, Essex, Glamorgan, Kent, Nottinghamshire, Somerset, Worcestershire.

Batting Averages

	M	I	NO	R	HS	100s	Avge
J. W. Hall	5	8	1	525	168	3	75.00
J. A. North	6	11	3	436	100*	1	54.50
M. T. E. Peirce	5	9	1	334	132	1	41.75
D. R. Law	12	20	1	765	229*	1	40.26
R. S. C. Martin-Jenkins	12	17	2	603	133*	2	40.20
M. Newell	16	26	5	786	113*	1	37.42
J. D. Chaplin	3	4	1	97	44*	0	32.33
*K. Newell	10	18	1	541	100*	1	31.82
C. C. Remy	14	24	3	642	139	1	30.57
G. B. Horan	5	8	1	177	55*	0	25.28
†S. Humphries	17	25	7	443	70	0	24.61
A. J. Law	3	4	1	57	43	0	19.00
J. J. Bates	15	21	3	288	108*	1	16.00
*D. M. Smith	6	7	3	57	13*	0	14.25
N. C. Phillips	10	15	1	187	39*	0	13.35
R. J. Kirtley	15	11	7	53	18	0	13.25
A. D. Edwards	5	5	1	43	25*	0	10.75
P. G. Hudson	3	6	0	42	13	0	7.00
G. R. Haywood	3	5	0	25	14	0	5.00
R. C. Thelwell	5	5	1	9	9*	0	2.25

Played in two matches: D. A. Alderman 0, 6*, 21; N. J. Lenham 21, 97, 66; J. D. Lewry 8. Played in one match: J. J. B. Freeland 19, 7; K. Greenfield 36, 17; T. E. Hemmings 3, 0*; P. W. Jarvis 4; C. G. Mason 26, 0; C. M. Mole 19, 2; J. M. Palmer 1, 0; R. Rao 34, 0; C. E. Waller 4, 1; J. P. Whittaker 13*; E. E. Hemmings did not bat.

Bowling Averages

	O	M	R	W	BB	Avge
J. D. Lewry	29.3	9	120	10	6-53	12.00
R. S. C. Martin-Jenkins	210.4	52	579	27	4-13	21.44
R. J. Kirtley	408.1	87	1,301	58	5-31	22.43
C. C. Remy	172.4	47	526	18	5-74	29.22
D. R. Law	252.2	46	804	27	4-43	29.77
M. T. E. Peirce	89.4	31	234	7	2-37	33.42
J. J. Bates	363.1	91	1,178	32	4-95	36.81
N. C. Phillips	371.1	120	872	21	5-75	41.52
J. A. North	67	7	259	6	2-40	43.16
J. D. Chaplin	64	9	195	4	1-25	48.75
A. D. Edwards	75.4	14	226	4	2-27	56.50

Also bowled: D. A. Alderman 15-4-50-0; J. J. B. Freeland 4-0-22-0; K. Greenfield 23-3-89-2; E. E. Hemmings 18-7-75-2; T. E. Hemmings 11-0-87-0; G. B. Horan 33-10-108-3; P. G. Hudson 20-3-94-0; P. W. Jarvis 21-2-63-2; N. J. Lenham 3-1-7-0; C. G. Mason 13-3-30-1; K. Newell 48-10-203-3; J. M. Palmer 9-0-21-0; R. Rao 6-0-40-1; J. P. Whittaker 11-3-44-0.

WARWICKSHIRE SECOND ELEVEN

Matches 16: Won – Derbyshire, Glamorgan, Leicestershire, Middlesex, Surrey, Sussex, Worcestershire. Lost – Nottinghamshire, Somerset. Drawn – Durham, Essex, Hampshire, Kent, Lancashire, Northamptonshire, Yorkshire. Abandoned: Gloucestershire.

Batting Averages

	M	I	NO	R	HS	100s	Avge
W. G. Khan.........	8	15	1	845	150	4	60.35
A. Singh	11	18	3	699	117*	1	46.60
A. F. Giles	12	16	2	646	129	1	46.14
P. A. Smith	3	3	0	134	111	1	44.66
Asif Din	16	25	3	929	253*	2	42.22
D. R. Brown	3	5	0	202	92	0	40.40
M. J. Powell	15	25	1	869	110	1	36.20
M. A. Wagh	4	6	1	150	80	0	30.00
†T. Frost..........	14	21	3	530	70	0	29.44
M. A. Sheikh	4	7	0	204	92	0	29.14
G. Welch	14	22	2	564	120	1	28.20
M. A. V. Bell	15	19	7	334	56*	0	27.83
†M. Burns	12	20	1	453	82*	0	23.84
S. McDonald	5	5	4	22	9*	0	22.00
C. R. Howell	2	3	1	41	26	0	20.50
R. P. Davis	11	15	2	250	49	0	19.23
T. A. Munton	3	3	0	52	31	0	17.33
S. Vestergaard	5	5	2	51	14*	0	17.00
D. A. Alltree	13	9	6	19	9	0	6.33

Played in two matches: N. M. K. Smith 11, 111. Played in one match: D. P. Ostler 4;
†K. J. Piper 22; G. C. Small 19*, 4*; G. D. Yates 0, 34; M. J. Rawnsley did not bat.

Note: In the match against Durham at Coventry M. A. V. Bell, called up for a first-team
match, was replaced by M. J. Rawnsley.

Bowling Averages

	O	M	R	W	BB	Avge
Asif Din	92.4	26	309	16	5-39	19.31
D. A. Altree	230.3	56	742	37	7-19	20.05
M. Burns	34	11	87	4	4-31	21.75
D. R. Brown	67.1	16	274	12	6-16	22.83
R. P. Davis	342.2	99	971	40	5-68	24.27
M. A. V. Bell	354.3	88	1,123	45	4-33	24.95
T. A. Munton	82	21	189	7	4-21	27.00
S. Vestergaard	79.4	19	264	9	2-21	29.33
A. F. Giles	259.2	72	712	21	5-39	33.90
G. Welch	305.3	50	1,134	33	4-89	34.36
N. M. K. Smith	63.5	16	182	5	3-64	36.40

Also bowled: T. Frost 2-0-18-1; C. R. Howell 8-1-31-0; M. J. Powell 20-5-82-1; M. A.
Sheikh 27-3-145-1; A. Singh 8-1-73-1; G. C. Small 24-5-74-2; P. A. Smith 31-3-139-0;
M. A. Wagh 8-0-49-0; G. D. Yates 9-0-38-0.

WORCESTERSHIRE SECOND ELEVEN

*Matches 17: Won – Derbyshire, Durham, Lancashire, Middlesex, Somerset. Lost – Essex,
Gloucestershire, Hampshire, Kent, Northamptonshire, Warwickshire, Yorkshire. Drawn –
Glamorgan, Leicestershire, Nottinghamshire, Surrey, Sussex.*

Batting Averages

	M	I	NO	R	HS	100s	Avge
C. M. Tolley.........	15	26	2	1,140	183	4	47.50
W. P. C. Weston	2	4	0	177	124	1	44.25
V. S. Solanki	2	4	0	158	85	0	39.50
M. Diwan...........	17	31	2	1,084	115	1	37.37
K. R. Spiring	10	18	4	499	95	0	35.64
M. J. Church	13	23	0	704	127	3	30.60

	M	I	NO	R	HS	100s	Avge
D. B. D'Oliveira	13	17	2	454	150	1	30.26
†T. Edwards...........	15	22	3	536	101*	1	28.21
C. E. Mulraine........	5	8	0	182	110	1	22.75
I. J. Ward...........	3	5	1	79	37*	0	19.75
C. J. Eyers...........	14	22	2	392	79	0	19.60
A. R. Whittall	3	5	1	78	31	0	19.50
J. E. Brinkley........	11	14	4	184	39*	0	18.40
C. R. Wardle	4	8	0	145	46	0	18.12
P. A. Thomas.........	5	8	5	51	20*	0	17.00
S. W. K. Ellis........	10	13	1	150	36	0	12.50
P. Mirza	11	16	3	90	45	0	6.92
B. E. A. Preece	12	16	6	64	33	0	6.40
A. Wylie............	4	4	1	14	8	0	4.66

Played in three matches: G. M. Roberts 8, 0. Played in two matches: C. E. Dagnall 6*, 0*; G. R. Haynes 49*, 30. Played in one match: S. E. Brinkley 7, 0; B. T. P. Donelan 13, 14; A. Flower 112, 47; M. P. D. Isaacs 2, 4; D. A. Leatherdale 134, 108; C. G. Mason 38; S. J. Price 25*, 34*; M. J. Rawnsley 2; M. A. Sheikh 5, 12; J. P. J. Sylvester 42, 84; D. Wesson 4; I. Dawood did not bat.

Note: In the match against Northamptonshire at Oundle C. M. Tolley, called up for a first-team match, was replaced by D. B. D'Oliveira.

Bowling Averages

	O	M	R	W	BB	Avge
P. Mirza	309.3	59	1,053	52	6-89	20.25
W. P. C. Weston	34	8	103	5	3-69	20.60
I. J. Ward	20	5	96	4	4-58	24.00
B. E. A. Preece	313.5	54	1,157	47	5-40	24.61
V. S. Solanki	42	5	175	6	3-59	29.16
C. M. Tolley.........	256.2	56	887	30	5-35	29.56
C. E. Dagnall	41.1	6	155	5	3-48	31.00
A. Wylie............	85	13	311	10	4-28	31.10
C. J. Eyers	141.3	21	603	16	2-1	37.68
S. W. K. Ellis	145	20	610	16	5-66	38.12
G. M. Roberts	56.3	13	154	4	3-8	38.50
J. E. Brinkley	236	57	781	18	4-42	43.38
P. A. Thomas	120.3	26	456	9	2-29	50.66
D. B. D'Oliveira	77.5	21	280	5	3-59	56.00

Also bowled: M. J. Church 14–2–68–2; M. Diwan 6–0–22–2; B. T. P. Donelan 26–2–132–2; G. R. Haynes 26–3–67–2; D. A. Leatherdale 14–6–27–0; C. G. Mason 12–4–23–1; M. J. Rawnsley 22–4–85–2; J. P. J. Sylvester 23.4–3–104–3; C. R. Wardle 19–1–66–0; D. Wesson 8.2–0–38–1; A. R. Whittall 46.2–9–175–3.

YORKSHIRE SECOND ELEVEN

Matches 17: Won – Essex, Hampshire, Lancashire, Leicestershire, Somerset, Sussex, Worcestershire. Lost – Gloucestershire. Drawn – Derbyshire, Durham, Glamorgan, Kent, Middlesex, Northamptonshire, Nottinghamshire, Surrey, Warwickshire.

Batting Averages

	M	I	NO	R	HS	100s	Avge
†R. J. Blakey	2	3	0	251	144	1	83.66
A. McGrath	13	22	5	1,144	151	4	67.29
A. C. Morris	12	12	3	565	172	2	62.77
M. J. Wood	7	10	2	468	137	1	58.50
R. A. Kettleborough ..	17	24	7	969	130	5	57.00
A. P. Grayson	5	8	3	267	79	0	53.40

	M	I	NO	R	HS	100s	Avge
S. A. Kellett	9	17	3	737	136	2	52.64
*A. A. Metcalfe	7	10	3	338	153*	1	48.28
B. Parker	10	17	2	666	120*	1	44.40
J. W. Hood	4	4	0	149	102	1	37.25
†C. A. Chapman	14	15	5	328	64*	0	32.80
C. J. Schofield	15	21	1	631	140	1	31.55
G. M. Hamilton	8	9	4	125	29*	0	25.00
J. D. Middlebrook	6	6	1	101	51	0	20.20
A. G. Wharf	5	4	0	64	34	0	16.00
I. D. Fisher	14	9	4	45	25	0	9.00
C. E. W. Silverwood . .	7	3	0	26	23	0	8.66
S. M. Milburn	9	5	2	6	6	0	2.00

Played in six matches: M. J. Hoggard 2*, 0*. Played in four matches: R. J. Sidebottom 0*, 0. Played in three matches: G. J. Batty 1*, 1*. Played in two matches: †D. J. Pipe 17*, 6; R. Robinson 14, 8; R. D. Stemp 10; L. C. Weekes 0, 0; P. M. Hutchison did not bat. Played in one match: M. P. Vaughan 52, 11.

Note: In the match against Worcestershire at Bradford A. A. Metcalfe, called up for a first-team match, was replaced by R. Robinson.

Bowling Averages

	O	M	R	W	BB	Avge
P. M. Hutchison	69	25	155	8	3-39	19.37
M. P. Vaughan	28	4	85	4	2-15	21.25
R. D. Stemp	69.3	35	107	5	2-23	21.40
A. C. Morris	173	35	588	26	3-12	22.61
G. M. Hamilton	170	29	664	27	7-39	24.59
R. A. Kettleborough . .	96.1	21	367	14	3-27	26.21
M. J. Hoggard	141.2	29	562	20	4-51	28.10
C. E. W. Silverwood . .	190.4	34	640	22	6-34	29.09
A. G. Wharf	115.5	24	430	14	5-36	30.71
R. J. Sidebottom	83	17	323	10	4-22	32.30
I. D. Fisher	497.4	137	1,361	42	4-26	32.40
S. M. Milburn	270	55	944	28	4-41	33.71
A. McGrath	114.4	25	356	9	3-9	39.55
J. D. Middlebrook	137	28	518	10	4-86	51.80
A. P. Grayson	88.1	23	247	4	2-34	61.75

Also bowled: G. J. Batty 55.2–12–206–3; R. Robinson 3–0–17–0; L. C. Weekes 61–9–241–2.

SECOND ELEVEN CHAMPIONS

1959	Gloucestershire	1972	Nottinghamshire	1985	Nottinghamshire
1960	Northamptonshire	1973	Essex	1986	Lancashire
1961	Kent	1974	Middlesex	1987 {	Kent
1962	Worcestershire	1975	Surrey		Yorkshire
1963	Worcestershire	1976	Kent	1988	Surrey
1964	Lancashire	1977	Yorkshire	1989	Middlesex
1965	Glamorgan	1978	Sussex	1990	Sussex
1966	Surrey	1979	Warwickshire	1991	Yorkshire
1967	Hampshire	1980	Glamorgan	1992	Surrey
1968	Surrey	1981	Hampshire	1993	Middlesex
1969	Kent	1982	Worcestershire	1994	Somerset
1970	Kent	1983	Leicestershire	1995	Hampshire
1971	Hampshire	1984	Yorkshire		

BAIN HOGG TROPHY, 1995

Counties are restricted to players qualified for England and for competitive county cricket, only two of whom may be capped players. The matches are of 55 overs per side.

North Zone	*P*	*W*	*L*	*NR*	*Points*	*Net run-rate*
Nottinghamshire	8	6	2	0	12	11.58
Durham	8	5	3	0	10	7.68
Yorkshire	8	5	3	0	10	4.83
Lancashire	8	3	5	0	6	−9.70
Derbyshire	8	1	7	0	2	−14.57

Central Zone	*P*	*W*	*L*	*NR*	*Points*	*Net run-rate*
Leicestershire	8	7	1	0	14	20.40
Northamptonshire	8	6	2	0	12	16.80
Minor Counties	8	3	5	0	6	−9.57
Warwickshire	8	3	5	0	6	−9.59
Middlesex	8	1	7	0	2	−16.20

South-West Zone	*P*	*W*	*L*	*NR*	*Points*	*Net run-rate*
Gloucestershire	8	6	2	0	12	−6.79
Worcestershire	8	5	3	0	10	7.65
Hampshire	8	4	4	0	8	3.33
Glamorgan	8	3	4	1	7	7.15
Somerset	8	1	6	1	3	−12.18

South-East Zone	*P*	*W*	*L*	*NR*	*Points*	*Net run-rate*
Surrey	8	5	3	0	10	−7.45
Kent	8	4	3	1	9	0.30
Essex	8	4	4	0	8	−0.01
Sussex	8	3	4	1	7	4.64
MCC Young Cricketers	8	3	5	0	6	1.91

SEMI-FINALS

At Worksop, August 17. Gloucestershire won by 73 runs. Toss: Gloucestershire. Gloucestershire 267 for eight (55 overs) (G. D. Hodgson 65, C. G. Taylor 33, C. S. Knightley 59; J. A. Afford three for 35); Nottinghamshire 194 (49.2 overs) (S. J. Musgrove 53, N. A. Gie 31; K. E. Cooper three for 38).

At Cheam, August 18. Leicestershire won by six wickets. Toss: Surrey. Surrey 197 (53.4 overs) (J. D. Ratcliffe 68, A. W. Smith 48; J. Ormond three for 30, M. T. Brimson three for 37); Leicestershire 198 for four (32.4 overs) (D. L. Maddy 38, A. Habib 52, B. F. Smith 47, J. M. Dakin 34).

FINAL

GLOUCESTERSHIRE v LEICESTERSHIRE

At Bristol, September 4. Leicestershire won by five wickets. Toss: Leicestershire.
Man of the Match: G. I. Macmillan.

Gloucestershire

R. J. Cunliffe c Smith b Ormond	79	M. J. Cawdron c Habib b Maddy	8
C. G. Taylor lbw b Dakin	6	M. Davies not out	9
R. I. Dawson c Haynes b Ormond	70	J. Lewis not out	4
*T. H. C. Hancock c Haynes b Ormond	0	L-b 14, w 14, n-b 2	30
C. S. Knightley c Haynes b Ormond	11		
R. C. Williams c Haynes b Maddy	3	1/13 2/162 3/162 (8 wkts, 55 overs) 224	
†R. C. J. Williams c Macmillan		4/171 5/184 6/190	
b Maddy	4	7/199 8/214	

K. E. Cooper did not bat.

Bowling: Ormond 11–0–53–4; Dakin 11–3–36–1; Maddy 11–1–45–3; Brimson 11–1–42–0; Mason 11–1–34–0.

Leicestershire

D. L. Maddy c R. C. J. Williams		*P. E. Robinson not out	35
b Cawdron	51	V. P. Clarke not out	6
A. Habib c Dawson b Cawdron	17	L-b 6, n-b 12	18
G. I. Macmillan c Hancock b Lewis	76		
B. F. Smith run out	16	1/56 2/95 3/116 (5 wkts, 45.3 overs) 227	
J. M. Dakin c Cooper b Cawdron	8	4/131 5/216	

†J. J. Haynes, T. J. Mason, M. T. Brimson and J. Ormond did not bat.

Bowling: Cooper 7–0–32–0; Lewis 8–0–31–1; R. C. Williams 7–0–56–0; Cawdron 11–0–45–3; Davies 11–0–39–0; Hancock 1–0–7–0; Dawson 0.3–0–11–0.

Umpires: J. D. Bond and R. Julian.

WINNERS 1986-95

TCCB SECOND ELEVEN REGIONAL CHALLENGE

SEMI-FINALS

At Leicester, August 24, 25, 26, 27. Central won by 127 runs. Toss: Central. Central 580 for nine dec. (T. A. Radford 133, M. J. Powell 43, A. Singh 101, S. Bartle 83, V. P. Clarke 59, K. P. Dutch 75; S. M. Milburn three for 114) and 233 for five dec. (M. J. Powell 57, M. V. Steele 35, A. Singh 40, S. Bartle 45); North 321 (A. McGrath 70, D. A. Blenkiron 33, A. C. Morris 33, A. A. Barnett 98; K. J. Innes three for 29, K. P. Dutch four for 110) and 365 (D. J. Thompson 34, D. A. Blenkiron 43, B. Parker 81, N. A. Gie 69, A. C. Morris 44; K. J. Innes three for 70, V. P. Clarke three for 98, K. P. Dutch four for 119).

At Chelmsford, August 24, 25, 26, 27. South-East won by four wickets. Toss: South-West. South-West 357 (M. E. Trescothick 36, M. J. Church 101, J. C. Hallett 45, J. D. Batty 67, Extras 45) and 184 (M. E. Trescothick 52, R. I. Dawson 46; J. M. de la Pena three for 27, G. J. Kennis four for 51); South-East 333 (K. Newell 54, G. J. Kennis 73, M. Newell 61, Extras 50; J. D. Batty five for 135) and 211 for six (A. W. Evans 65, G. A. Khan 38 not out; J. C. Hallett three for 60).

FINAL

At Birmingham, September 14, 15, 16, 17. Drawn. Toss: Central. Central 199 for six (A. Habib 30, D. J. Sales 65) v South-East. There was no play after the first day.

CAREER FIGURES

Players not expected to appear in county cricket in 1996.

BATTING

	M	I	NO	R	HS	100s	Avge	1,000r/ season
Asif Din	210	341	45	9,058	217	9	30.60	2
C. S. Atkins	1	2	1	13	8*	0	13.00	0
A. D. Bairstow	3	6	0	73	26	0	12.16	0
A. A. Barnett	50	48	20	263	38	0	9.39	0
T. J. Boon	248	419	42	11,821	144	14	31.35	7
M. N. Bowen	13	14	4	116	23*	0	11.60	0
N. G. B. Cook	356	365	96	3,137	75	0	11.66	0
N. G. Cowans	239	248	68	1,605	66	0	8.91	0
M. Davies	45	64	22	632	54	0	15.04	0
W. A. Dessaur	22	38	3	1,121	148	3	32.02	0
T. Edwards	10	11	7	116	47	0	29.00	0
M. G. Field-Buss	38	43	14	311	34*	0	10.72	0
M. J. Foster	5	7	1	165	63*	0	27.50	0
B. N. French	360	471	92	7,160	123	2	18.89	0
M. A. Garnham	207	282	55	6,240	123	5	27.48	0
T. W. Harrison	5	10	1	102	61*	0	11.33	0
E. E. Hemmings.....	518	683	169	9,533	127*	1	18.54	0
G. D. Hodgson	103	179	10	5,675	166	9	33.57	4
S. A. Kellett	87	149	10	4,234	125*	2	30.46	2
W. Larkins	482	842	54	27,143	252	59	34.44	13
B. J. M. Maher	133	205	36	3,689	126	4	21.82	0
T. C. Middleton	109	187	16	5,753	221	13	33.64	2
P. Mirza	9	15	3	86	40	0	7.16	0
M. C. J. Nicholas ...	377	620	89	18,262	206*	36	34.39	10
B. Parker..........	15	28	3	776	127	1	31.04	0
C. Penn	128	146	36	2,048	115	1	18.61	0
B. S. Phelps	3	4	1	18	11	0	6.00	0
N. V. Radford	296	298	73	3,537	76*	0	15.72	0
C. C. Remy	21	29	3	480	60	0	18.46	0
A. Richardson	1	1	0	4	4	0	4.00	0
A. Roseberry........	7	10	1	263	94	0	29.22	0
M. Saxelby	60	104	7	2,893	181	2	29.82	1
K. J. Shine	69	56	26	303	26*	0	10.10	0
I. G. S. Steer	7	10	3	299	67	0	42.71	0
C. W. Taylor	33	25	9	175	28*	0	10.93	0
M. Taylor	4	5	2	25	14*	0	8.33	0
R. C. Williams	26	41	6	453	44	0	12.94	0
A. Wylie	3	5	1	14	7	0	3.50	0

* *Signifies not out.*

BOWLING AND FIELDING

	R	W	BB	Avge	5W/i	10W/m	Ct/St
Asif Din	4,393	79	5-61	55.60	2	0	114
C. S. Atkins	46	1	1-46	46.00	—	—	0
A. D. Bairstow ...	—	—	—	—	—	—	7/1
A. A. Barnett	5,191	113	5-36	45.93	5	0	14
T. J. Boon	563	11	3-40	51.18	—	—	124
M. N. Bowen	1,196	30	4-124	39.86	—	—	3
N. G. B. Cook ...	25,507	879	7-34	29.01	31	4	197

	R	W	BB	Avge	5W/i	10W/m	Ct/St
N. G. Cowans	16,461	662	6-31	24.86	23	1	63
M. Davies	3,878	110	5-57	35.25	3	1	19
W. A. Dessaur	118	1	1-8	118.00	—	—	6
T. Edwards	—	—	—	—	—	—	21
M. G. Field-Buss ...	2,464	63	6-42	39.11	1	0	13
M. J. Foster	150	6	3-39	25.00	—	—	6
B. N. French	70	1	1-37	70.00	—	—	817/100
M. A. Garnham	39	0	—	—	—	—	429/41
T. W. Harrison	282	5	4-153	56.40	0	0	3
E. E. Hemmings	44,403	1,515	10-175	29.30	70	15	212
G. D. Hodgson......	65	0	—	—	—	—	45
S. A. Kellett	19	0	—	—	—	—	77
W. Larkins	1,915	42	5-59	45.59	1	0	306
B. J. M. Maher	234	4	2-69	58.50	—	—	289/14
T. C. Middleton	241	5	2-41	48.20	—	—	79
P. Mirza	854	23	5-110	37.13	1	0	6
M. C. J. Nicholas ...	3,245	72	6-37	45.06	2	—	215
B. Parker..........	—	—	—	—	—	—	10
C. Penn...........	9,840	296	7-70	33.24	12	0	56
B. S. Phelps	363	5	2-70	72.60	—	—	0
N. V. Radford	26,707	994	9-70	26.86	48	7	130
C. C. Remy	1,051	19	4-63	55.31	—	—	7
A. Richardson	60	3	3-27	20.00	—	—	0
A. Roseberry........	—	—	—	—	—	—	3
M. Saxelby	903	11	3-41	82.09	—	—	18
K. J. Shine	5,885	155	8-47	37.96	7	1	11
I. G. S. Steer	46	3	3-23	15.33	—	—	4
C. W. Taylor	2,421	72	5-33	33.62	1	0	6
M. Taylor	205	7	3-25	29.28	—	—	0
R. C. Williams	1,960	44	4-28	44.54	—	—	6
A. Wylie	216	2	1-50	108.00	—	—	0

Note: N. V. Radford, who did so twice, was the only bowler from this list to take 100 wickets in a season.

HONOURS' LIST, 1995-96

In 1995-96, the following were decorated for their services to cricket:

Queen's Birthday Honours, 1995: N. J. Izard (England women's manager) OBE, E. D. Weekes (West Indies – services to cricket and public service) KCMG.

Queen's Birthday Honours (Australia), 1995: R. G. Archer (Australia) AM, G. Noblet (Australia) OAM, S. Brogden (author of *The First Test Match* – services to journalism) OAM.

Jamaican Independence Day Honours, 1995: S. A. Bucknor (Test umpire) OD.

New Year's Honours, 1996: Dr J. H. Heslop (former New Zealand Board delegate – services to medicine, sport and community) CBE, D. A. Reeve (England) OBE, A. C. Smith (England; TCCB chief executive) CBE, J. C. Woodcock (former cricket correspondent of *The Times* and editor of *Wisden* – services to sports journalism) OBE.

THE LANCASHIRE LEAGUES, 1995

By CHRIS ASPIN

League cricket in Lancashire was thrown into turmoil when Lancashire County Cricket Club came up with a plan for a super league, picking off the best dozen clubs to act primarily as a feeder for the first-class side. Initial reaction was very unfavourable. The idea of dispensing with professionals was contrary to tradition, and there was concern about the loss of local derbies and the whole social side of League cricket. Since Lancashire had drawn up their plan with no consultation whatever, there was also a powerful feeling that they had been high-handed. The subject looked unlikely to go away, however.

The 1995 season itself produced a rich crop of records and one surprise: the decline of Haslingden, Lancashire League champions seven times since 1983. In mid-season, with the Australian Test bowler Paul Reiffel in deadly form, Haslingden headed the table and had reached the Jennings Worsley Cup final. Then Reiffel injured a foot; Haslingden lost the final to Nelson and won only one more league game. They finished seventh.

Another Australian, Peter Sleep, stood in for Reiffel at the end of the season, which he had started as Rishton's professional. However, Sleep was injured early on and it was West Indian Phil Simmons who helped Rishton clinch their first championship for 40 years, with two wins on the final weekend of the season. The crucial victory was over Ramsbottom, on Saturday. They finished runners-up after their professional, New Zealander Chris Harris, became only the fourth player in league history to complete the season's double of 1,000 runs and 100 wickets. Remarkably, Harris and two other pros, Joe Scuderi of Nelson and Roger Harper of Bacup, occupied the first three places in both the batting and bowling averages.

Rishton amateur Russell Whalley played one of two swashbuckling innings against Enfield in 1995. A former Enfield player himself, Whalley hit 142 – with 19 fours and seven sixes – off 72 balls. The same attack also felt the restless bat of Trevor Kegg, a Nelson bowler with no reputation for batting. He went in at No. 9 and last man Michael Warburton joined him at 79 for nine. They added 98; Kegg reached his maiden century off 75 deliveries with a six and was out next ball. Warburton had contributed five. Nelson won and Kegg earned over £100 in a collection.

The best all-round performance of the season came from Colne's Australian professional, Scott Williams, who followed a century against Haslingden with a return of eight for 58 – though Todmorden wicket-keeper David Whitehead ran him close, hitting 82 and claiming seven victims against East Lancashire. Another wicket-keeper, Jack Simpson of Ramsbottom, had a record 56 dismissals. Jonathan Harvey became the first amateur to score 1,000 league runs in a season for Burnley.

Rochdale rolled up their old Dane Street square, re-laid it on their new ground, at Redbrook – and then won their fourth Central Lancashire League championship in six years. The club's South African professional, Dave Callaghan, scored 1,375 runs and took 52 wickets, the Australian amateur Ryan Campbell contributed 1,338, and Mo Bux picked up 64 wickets. Walsden regained the Lees Wood Cup after 20 years when they beat Ashton by seven wickets in the final.

Littleborough scored a record 310 for one against Norden, thanks to an unbroken second-wicket stand of 285 between professional Dexter Fitton and Chris Dearden. The Norden bowlers were also punished by Oldham pro John Sylvester, whose unbeaten 165 was the season's highest innings. These humiliations for Norden were offset by the fine form of Gus Logie, the former West Indian Test player, who hit six centuries.

For once, the leading run-maker was an amateur, Dean Temple, who amassed 1,659, a league record, for Stand. Temple was one of several Australians playing in the Central Lancs., apart from the professionals; such players are barred in the Lancashire League. Temple's fellow Queenslander, Michael Warden, the Stand professional, took 123 wickets to top the league averages. Werneth all-rounder John Punchard picked up 95 at 16.29 and enjoyed a memorable afternoon against Heywood, taking seven for 65 and passing 10,000 league runs. There was a special cheer for the Crompton skipper, Alan Whiston, when he scored his maiden century – an unbeaten 102 against Milnrow – in his 31st season.

MARSDEN LANCASHIRE LEAGUE

	P	W	L	NR	Bonus Pts	Pts	Professional	Runs	Avge	Wkts	Avge
Rishton	26	21	3	2	10	96	*P. V. Simmons ...	746	53.28	63	15.04
Ramsbottom	26	20	6	0	12	92	C. Z. Harris	1,231	87.92	112	12.46
Nelson	26	18	7	1	12	85	J. C. Scuderi	1,263	63.15	84	12.57
Bacup	26	15	8	3	9	72	R. A. Harper	1,071	53.55	87	13.10
Church	26	15	9	2	9	71	*N. Johnson	531	48.27	27	20.92
Lowerhouse	26	14	12	0	14	70	S. Flegler	962	45.80	74	19.01
Haslingden	26	13	12	1	6	59	*P. R. Reiffel	260	37.14	45	13.84
East Lancs.	26	12	11	3	7	58	A. C. Dawson.....	885	49.16	49	13.53
Burnley	26	11	13	2	6	52	R. P. Singh	730	40.55	64	20.70
Colne	26	9	15	2	11	49	S. B. Williams	803	32.12	92	14.29
Todmorden	26	9	15	2	9	47	A. J. Gale	390	20.52	53	18.37
Enfield	26	6	19	1	7	32	F. A. Rose	696	30.26	91	16.76
Rawtenstall	26	5	20	1	3	24	*R. E. Veenstra ...	391	30.07	38	21.18
Accrington	26	4	22	0	4	20	*C. R. Miller	625	32.89	68	15.73

Note: Four points awarded for a win; one point for a no-result; one point for bowling out the opposition.

* Did not play full season.

CENTRAL LANCASHIRE LEAGUE

	P	OW	LW	L	D	Pts	Professional	Runs	Avge	Wkts	Avge
Rochdale ...	30	9	12	3	6	105	D. J. Callaghan ...	1,375	72.36	52	16.80
Middleton ..	30	10	9	8	3	92	K. C. Williams....	1,093	37.68	72	18.80
Littleborough	30	8	10	6	6	92	J. D. Fitton	1,514	65.82	48	22.18
Stand	30	9	9	7	5	91	M. Warden	870	36.25	123	12.76
Werneth	30	7	8	9	6	80*	S. J. O'Shaughnessy	903	37.62	38	22.10
Walsden	30	9	6	11	4	77	J. Bakker	1,594	66.41	85	15.94
Heywood ...	30	5	7	12	6	65	A. Badenhorst	547	21.88	79	19.65
Norden	30	5	6	13	6	61	A. L. Logie......	1,623	57.96	57	24.68
Unsworth ..	30	6	5	14	5	60	A. Payne	289	17.00	38	26.89
Royton	30	6	4	14	6	58	J. Grant	501	26.36	75	20.14
Radcliffe ..	30	5	5	14	6	57	P. Skuse	1,278	45.64	36	29.11
Crompton...	30	4	6	15	5	54	Zafar Iqbal	742	29.68	78	21.97
Ashton	30	7	2	16	5	53	D. Hodgson	950	35.18	45	22.53
Oldham ...	30	3	4	16	7	46*	J. Sylvester	1,143	45.72	41	30.00
Milnrow ...	30	5	2	19	4	41	J. A. Ehrke......	725	26.85	77	25.80
Stockport ..	30	2	4	22	2	30	Qaifer Rasheed....	799	36.31	27	23.40

Notes: Five points awarded for an outright win; four points for a limited win; two points for a draw. A team achieves an outright win by bowling out the opposition. Averages include cup games.

* Includes three points for a tie.

LEAGUE CRICKET IN ENGLAND AND WALES, 1995

By GEOFFREY DEAN

For the second year running, the Birmingham League – always one of the most competitive in the country – produced an extraordinary finish to the season, and this time it was spiced with controversy. In 1994, four teams were chasing the title down to the last afternoon. On the final day of the 1995 season Walsall, needing 15 runs off the last 16 balls with five wickets in hand to retain the Championship, were forced off the field at 7.40 p.m., owing to bad light.

Both captains had wanted to play on. The Walsall captain Nick Archer said afterwards: "This game is for the players not the umpires, yet those two have decided the destination of this year's Championship." However, conditions, after a dank and miserable day, were atrocious: the scorers had to keep flicking cigarette lighters in order to see their books, and the League supported the umpires' view that there was a risk of serious injury. The row has had one effect: in future September games will start early.

Walsall's failure to win threw the Championship, by one point, to Barnt Green who were in their first season after moving up from the Midland Club Championship to replace the collapsed M & B club. Barnt Green's star batsman was the Zimbabwean Test player Grant Flower, who became the tenth man in the League's history to pass 1,000 runs in a season. The ninth, one week earlier, was his brother and Test captain Andy, who was playing for West Bromwich Dartmouth.

Batting feats of this sort were far more common across the country in the hot, dry summer of 1995 than arguments about bad light. The most remarkable of all was performed in Wales, by the Indian Test player Aashish Kapoor, who hammered 300 out of a 50-over total of 375 for six for Abergavenny against Swansea.

The Pen-y-Pound ground is known for fast scoring: Andrew Symonds broke the first-class six-hit record there a few weeks later. And this innings came in the Welsh Championship, a Sunday competition, against an attack short of full strength. It was none the less a phenomenal exhibition of hitting. Kapoor batted through 45 overs of a 50-over match, striking 42 fours and four sixes. The previous week he had beaten the Three Counties League individual record by scoring 179, and he finished the League season with an aggregate of 1,416 runs at 67.42 – plus 70 wickets. But he still could not win Abergavenny the title: it went to Usk for the first time.

Kapoor's feat was the most extreme example. But up and down the country batsmen – not all of them from overseas – scored large quantities of runs, often without getting their teams anywhere near their League titles. The Tasmanian batsman Bruce Cruse scored 2,126 runs for Shaw in the Saddleworth league. But this was not a League record: Hylton Ackerman once scored 2,591. Further south, though, smaller totals were easily enough to break records: for instance the 1,106 scored by Simon Luckhurst, son of the former England batsman Brian, was 104 more than the old mark in the Kent League, set by the Australian Test player Justin Langer. Luckhurst, who plays for St Lawrence, missed the 1994 season due to business commitments. And the Langley Mill captain Andrew Brown scored 1,278 to beat the Derbyshire League record.

Individual record scores also kept tumbling. In the Kent League it happened twice. James Barr, at 23 The Mote's youngest ever captain, led his team to the title for the first time since 1980 and scored 178 against Dover in July. That stood as a League record for just two months. Then in the last game of the season Ed Smith of Sevenoaks Vine smashed the same, hapless, Dover attack for 183 not out, off just 139 balls.

In the Northants County League, Ed Turnham of Wellingborough Town hit 198 not out against Old Northamptonians, 17 better than the old Premier Division record held by his own captain, Richard Dalton. But in a Second Division match Steve Wharton of Stony Stratford hit 203 not out against Weekley and Warkton, the best ever in the whole League. His team still lost: Nick Dalziel scored an unbeaten 182 for the opposition and they successfully chased a target of 281. The most ferocious hitting of the year came in the Bolton League from the Kearsley professional Steve Dublin, who made a hundred against Heaton off 35 balls, 48 of the runs in one over that included three no-balls.

Some bowlers, understandably, wanted a piece of the action for themselves: the former Yorkshire seamer Chris Pickles scored more than 1,300 runs for Spen Victoria in the Bradford League. But some non-batsmen did manage to ply their craft successfully. The 81 wickets taken by John Carruthers were crucial to Hanging Heaton's triumph in the Bradford League, in which the Pakistani professional, Iqbal Sikandar, took 133 wickets for Tonge, breaking a record set by Fred Hartley in 1941.

Winchester won all their matches on their way to becoming champions of the Southern League, a feat achieved twice before since the League began in 1969. Morecambe won 15 out of 22 on their way to winning the Northern League, largely due to their West Indian professional Robert Haynes. This League, involving 12 clubs and centred on North Lancashire, was preening itself on its successes in inter-League competitions, headed by Chorley's triumph at Lord's in the National Clubs final, and it now believes itself more than a match for the better-known Lancashire leagues.

Some Leagues threw up champions in circumstances almost as impossible as Barnt Green's title. Knypersley of the North Staffs. and South Cheshire avoided relegation in 1994 only because Nantwich had been docked points for fielding an ineligible player; in 1995 they took the title. And Methley won the Central Yorkshire League after having their square vandalised in April and being forced to play their first few home games away.

Some champions were novel. Teddington won the Middlesex League for the first time in ten years to end Finchley's three-year run. And Newport defied all their English rivals to win the Western League for the first time. Some were very familiar: Exmouth won the Devon League for the sixth successive year, and Marchwiel won the North Wales League for the umpteenth time and promptly resigned from it. In 1996 they will play in the Liverpool & District.

The Essex League threw up one of the season's more bizarre controversies, when John Lever of Ilford – *the* John Lever – was given out handled the ball when he picked it up after a defensive shot and threw it back to the bowler. Gary Neicho, the South Woodford captain, appealed from mid-off and Lever was given out. He was disgusted and Neicho was criticised in both the local and national press; he insisted the ball was still rolling towards the stumps when Lever picked it up.

LEAGUE WINNERS, 1995

League	Winners	League	Winners
Airedale & Wharfedale	Beckwithshaw	**Norfolk Alliance**	Swardeston
Bassetlaw	Farnsfield	**Northants County**	County Colts
Birmingham	Barnt Green	**Northern**	Morecambe
Bolton	Little Lever	**North Staffs. & South Cheshire**	Knypersley
Bradford	Hanging Heaton	**Northumberland County**	Ashington
Central	Lutterworth	**North Wales**	Marchwiel
Central Yorkshire	Methley	**North Yorks. & South Durham**	Richmondshire
Cheshire County	Poynton	**Notts. Alliance**	Sandiacre Town
Cornwall	Troon	**Ribblesdale**	Padiham
Derbyshire County	Ockbrook & Borrowash	**Saddleworth**	Heyside
Devon	Exmouth	**Shropshire**	Wroxeter
Durham County	Tudhoe	**Somerset**	Bridgwater
Durham Senior	Horden	**Southern**	Winchester
Essex	Saffron Walden	**South Thames**	Orpington
Hertfordshire	Radlett	**South Wales Association**	Swansea
Huddersfield	Elland	**Surrey Championship**	Wimbledon
Kent	The Mote	**Sussex**	Eastbourne
Lancashire County	Denton	**Thames Valley**	Ickenham
Leeds	Woodhouse	**Three Counties**	Usk
Lincolnshire	Messingham	**Two Counties (Suffolk/Essex)**	Clacton
Liverpool Competition	Bootle	**Tyneside Senior**	Blaydon
Manchester Association	Leigh	**Western**	Newport
Middlesex	Teddington	**West Wales Club Conference**	Lampeter
Midland Club Championship	Knowle & Dorridge	**Yorkshire**	Sheffield Collegiate
Midland Combined Counties	Highway		

Note: To avoid confusion traditional League names have been given in this list and sponsors' names omitted.

SOWETO TOUR OF BRITISH ISLES, 1995

Though their share of the headlines was minor compared to the West Indian tourists, the young players from Soweto Cricket Club – the first black township side ever to visit the British Isles – turned heads and won friends wherever they played in July 1995.

Soweto's 14-match tour was not merely a success on the field, where they won six, drew two, tied one and lost five against a mixture of strong club sides and representative XIs. Off it, they experienced a liberating taste of life away from home, and showed such enthusiasm for a game they were only recently encouraged to play that many of their opponents found their own love of the sport reinvigorated. Along the way, not least during their tied match against the Neath club Ynysygerwyn – where the local MP and long-time anti-apartheid activist Peter Hain met and made up with his former adversary Ali Bacher – tears of genuine happiness were shed.

To mount such a tour was an inspirational feat in itself for a club that has experienced many low ebbs and has twice lain dormant since it was founded in the mid-1960s. Two years of money-raising and sponsor-hunting generated £50,000 to send the squad of 17 players and six officials around England, Wales and Ireland.

Several of Soweto's star players were missing, including the left-arm spinner Jacob Malao, who was with MCC Young Cricketers in 1994, Geoffrey Toyana, who replaced Malao at Lord's in 1995 but found time to score 90 in Soweto's last game against Shepherd's Bush, and the fast-medium bowler Walter Masemula, who was with the South African Under-19 team.

There were other names to conjure with though, like the three young brothers, Peace, Justice and Harmony Nkutha, the whole-hearted opening bowler Piet Lephoi and the 21-year-old spinner Moses Mphela, who recorded the tour's best bowling figures of five for 18 against Chagford. But most impressive of all, perhaps, was Solomon Ndima, an 18-year-old batsman of great promise, who scored a superb century – the only one of the tour – at Ynysygerwyn.

The collective achievements of the Soweto players were, however, more important. Well-schooled, well-disciplined and supremely self-confident, they played with undisguised enjoyment and commitment, which, despite the obstacles, have brought them a long way in a short space of time. – *Peter Mason.*

NATIONAL CLUB CHAMPIONSHIP, 1995

The Northern League club Chorley emulated the feat achieved by both Scarborough and Old Hill in the 1980s when they won the National Club Championship for the second year running. They took the Abbot Ale Cup by beating Clifton Flax Bourton from Bristol by 12 runs.

It was a slightly muted triumph because the competition took place with virtually no representation from the south-east. The Club Cricket Conference carried out its threat to boycott the competition in response to a change of rules allowing semi-professionals to play. A total of 148 clubs pulled out, including all the representatives of the Surrey, Middlesex, Essex, Kent and Sussex Leagues.

The dispute was resolved in August and the tournament will be back to full strength in 1996: the Conference accepted a slight change of wording in the new rule, but clubs from leagues which allow semi-pros will continue to be able to field them; full professionals remain banned.

The boycott had some strange effects and Rottingdean were able to reach the last eight without playing a match. Competition in other parts of the country remained as tough as ever: Chorley had to defeat three former finalists, including Old Hill, four times winners. They beat them by four wickets in the quarter-finals, then went on to an easy win over Gateshead Fell. In the other semi-final, Long Eaton were bowled out for 83 and lost by seven wickets.

An emergency Club Cricket Conference Challenge Trophy was staged with a final at Radlett. Eastbourne beat Finchley by one run.

FINAL

CHORLEY v CLIFTON FLAX BOURTON

At Lord's, August 25. Chorley won by 12 runs. Toss: Clifton Flax Bourton.
Clifton Flax Bourton collapsed within sight of victory. They lost five wickets for 14 runs after Oliver Smith, their captain, and John Meadows had put on 140 for the second wicket. Seamer Gordon Lee took three wickets in his second spell and this, combined with a couple of run-outs, transformed the game. Chorley had lost opener James Fazackerley without scoring, but their captain Richard Horridge shared big stands with the team's two Neils, Bannister and Senior, to set up a formidable 45-over total.

Chorley

N. Bannister c Brooks b Holdsworth ... 64
J. Fazackerley c Scott b Costeloe 0
*R. Horridge not out 95
†N. Senior not out 61
B 2, l-b 10, w 3, n-b 4 19

1/6 2/149   (2 wkts, 45 overs) 239

N. J. Heaton, G. Lee, P. Deakin, R. Purnell, M. Critchley, R. Demming and K. Eccleshare did not bat.

Bowling: Watkinson 9-1-80-0; Costeloe 9-1-20-1; Holdsworth 9-1-44-1; Meadows 9-0-48-0; Howarth 9-0-35-0.

Clifton Flax Bourton

*O. C. K. Smith b Demming	90	R. J. W. Holdsworth run out		0
A. J. T. Halliday st Senior b Purnell	7	F. M. J. Costeloe not out		3
J. L. P. Meadows lbw b Lee	73			
D. P. Simkins c Lee b Purnell	14	L-b 9, w 5, n-b 1		15
†J. S. L. Brooks lbw b Lee	14			
M. D. J. Ingram run out	9	1/18 2/158 3/179	(8 wkts, 45 overs)	227
H. C. Watkinson b Lee	0	4/207 5/216 6/216		
S. J. Y. Scott not out	2	7/221 8/221		

R. I. Howarth did not bat.

Bowling: Lee 9–0–38–3; Purnell 9–1–27–2; Demming 9–0–41–1; Eccleshare 9–0–38–0; Deakin 5–0–31–0; Critchley 4–0–43–0.

Umpires: B. Flute and R. Holland.

WINNERS 1969-95

1969	Hampstead	1978	Cheltenham	1987	Old Hill
1970	Cheltenham	1979	Scarborough	1988	Enfield
1971	Blackheath	1980	Moseley	1989	Teddington
1972	Scarborough	1981	Scarborough	1990	Blackpool
1973	Wolverhampton	1982	Scarborough	1991	Teddington
1974	Sunbury	1983	Shrewsbury	1992	Optimists
1975	York	1984	Old Hill	1993	Old Hill
1976	Scarborough	1985	Old Hill	1994	Chorley
1977	Southgate	1986	Stourbridge	1995	Chorley

NATIONAL VILLAGE CRICKET CHAMPIONSHIP, 1995

None of the last four in the 24th National Village Championship had reached the final before, ensuring that a new name would appear on the trophy in its first year under new sponsors, Alliance & Leicester Giro. Woodhouse Grange, a village near York too small to appear on many maps, eventually won a low-scoring final against Tiddington, from Oxfordshire. The winners knocked out 1985 champions Freuchie when they travelled to Scotland for the quarter-finals, and then dismissed Caldy, from Merseyside, for 74 in their semi. Caldy had beaten the reigning champions Elvaston. Tiddington got to Lord's after a three-run win over Horndon on the Hill, a powerful batting side from Essex.

In the first round, St Mary Bourne from Hampshire lost to Dogmersfield by two wickets, only to be reinstated: a player from the winning side exposed himself as a ringer by asking them which team was which on arrival. Applecross Allsorts from the coast of Wester Ross made it to round three courtesy of two byes, after four years without a win. They have to play their home matches 80 miles away from their village – and even then their groundsman has to cut back the Highland heather, chase off the cattle, shovel away the sheep dung and make stumps out of broom handles. The club dog set a record for Slad Exiles of Gloucestershire, in the fourth round, by recovering no fewer than six lost balls. – Amanda Ripley.

FINAL

TIDDINGTON v WOODHOUSE GRANGE

At Lord's, August 27. Woodhouse Grange won by 14 runs. Toss: Tiddington.

Tiddington's decision to field on a cool, overcast morning looked right when Woodhouse's top three were back in the pavilion by the 18th over. Two had fallen to Stephen Robins, who bowled with great accuracy and conceded only ten runs. Mark Burton and Mike Burdett steadied the innings, adding 47, but three quick wickets left them 89 for six with eight overs left. Steve Young came to the rescue with 24 from 27 balls, mostly in the air towards the short Tavern boundary, and 17 wides boosted the total. Woodhouse Grange's last five overs brought 45 runs; Tiddington entered their last five needing exactly the same. They, too, had struggled after Brian Stow removed both Manger brothers, Adrian and Philip, early on. John Hurley contributed 30, the highest score of the match, but Peter Head took Tiddington's eighth wicket with 32 still required and maintained a good line to leave the tail 15 short of their target.

Woodhouse Grange

S. Craven c Manning b Smith	2	S. Johnson run out	5
J. E. Bean c Anderson b Robins	11	P. W. Head not out	10
*S. H. W. Gill c and b Robins	9	B. Stow not out	3
M. A. Burton lbw b A. S. W. Manger	23	B 2, l-b 9, w 17, n-b 3	31
†M. N. Burdett c Edmondson b Pykett	26		
S. J. Young b A. S. W. Manger	24	1/8 2/30 3/40 (9 wkts, 40 overs) 151
D. Gilbertson b A. S. W. Manger	0	4/87 5/89 6/89
R. W. Bilton b Smith	7	7/124 8/128 9/147

Bowling: Smith 9-0-46-2; Robins 9-4-10-2; Pykett 9-3-16-1; Anderson 5-1-25-0; A. S. W. Manger 6-0-34-3; P. J. Manger 2-0-9-0.

Tiddington

P. J. Manger b Stow	9	†P. G. Manning b Head	3
A. S. W. Manger c Burdett b Stow	0	S. Robins not out	4
P. E. Clarke c Young b Gill	12	B 1, l-b 13, w 9, n-b 1	24
P. C. Green b Johnson	23		
J. C. Hurley c Stow b Gill	30	1/8 2/17 3/38 (8 wkts, 40 overs) 137
N. M. Edmondson c Johnson b Head	5	4/67 5/92 6/92
N. ·C. Smith b Head	7	7/107 8/120
R. Anderson not out	20		

*R. J. Pykett did not bat.

Bowling: Stow 9-1-28-2; Head 9-1-31-3; Gill 9-0-26-2; Bilton 9-1-22-0; Johnson 4-0-16-1.

Umpires: M. A. Johnson and W. D. Jones.

WINNERS 1972-95

IRISH CRICKET IN 1995

By DEREK SCOTT

The Irish team had more games than ever in 1995, mainly because the Benson and Hedges Cup expanded to include a zonal phase for the first time since Ireland joined in.

They failed to win a match, and did not expect to do so, especially so early in the season against professionals. It is difficult for players to get enough time off to fulfil such a programme, but the experience of playing – and talking to – county cricketers should be invaluable when the next ICC Trophy comes round in 1997.

The worst day was in the very first match when they went to The Oval to face a Surrey team fresh from a pre-season visit to Western Australia. The weather at home had been so bad that Ireland had not even been able to practise on grass, never mind play a match. Under the circumstances, it might have been wiser not to bat first: Ireland were bowled out for 80.

However, subsequent performances were far more respectable and Ireland had a good day at Hove and in the NatWest Trophy at Headingley. They were helped by having a professional national coach, Mike Hendrick, in place in 1995 for the first time. He did a great deal of work, was much respected and has been appointed for a further two seasons.

The actual amount of cricket played was no greater than many years ago, because all but two of the matches were one-dayers, and the first-class fixture against Scotland was abandoned in tragic circumstances (See page 866). It was, overall, a curate's egg season and only two of the 12 games were won: against Wales in the Triple Crown and at Arundel against Lavinia, Duchess of Norfolk's XI. Twenty-two players had to be used because of injury; but the good news was that six of them were 21 or under, and two young opening bowlers, Ryan Eagleson and Mark Patterson, were among those who made their mark.

The Interprovincial Tournament was rather undistinguished, partly due to poor weather during a three-day, nine-match Festival. It was won by South Leinster after a hat-trick of wins by North-West. The format will change for 1996: there will be one team from each Provincial Union plus a Development XI who will have first call on good young players throughout the country.

The Royal Liver Irish Senior Cup went to North Down for the third time, equalling Lurgan's record. The final was marvellous. Bready, from the North-West, lost by one run after looking well beaten five overs before the end with eight wickets down. In Munster, Cork County did a League/Cup double.

There was great excitement in the Northern Union, where Cliftonville beat Lisburn in the final match, climbed above them and won the title for the first time since 1938. This famous old club was forced to leave its ground, in a front-line area of Belfast, in the early years of the Troubles. The team struggled for many years and this was only their second year back in the top section after a long absence. The Touche Ross Cup was easily won by Waringstown who beat Lurgan to give them 18 wins in 31 seasons.

In Dublin, Clontarf completed a double, the Belvedere Bond League and Conqueror Cup, having achieved this previously in 1992. Limavady retained the Lion Sport League in the North-West – just. A revitalised Sion Mills team were ahead going into the last match, but a century by Desmond Curry saw Limavady home.

SCOTTISH CRICKET IN 1995

By J. WATSON BLAIR

Assisted by a glorious summer, Scotland could feel some satisfaction at their progress as newly-accepted associate members of ICC. Visits to Ireland brought Scotland their greatest success of the season – when they retained the Triple Crown in July – and, a few weeks later, their saddest moment, when the chairman of selectors, Hugh Stevenson, suffered a heart attack before the annual first-class match with Ireland. He collapsed as the team bus arrived at Rathmines and died soon afterwards. The match was abandoned; Scotland won limited-overs games arranged for the following two days.

On their previous trip to Ireland, Scotland had successfully defended the Triple Crown under the captaincy of George Salmond. Victory over England NCA gave them a head start, they defeated Ireland in a bowl-out and beating Wales gave them a clean sweep. Also in July, it was Scotland's turn to host the quadrangular competition involving Denmark, Holland and the home nation's second team. Both visiting countries made a favourable impression and Denmark emerged as narrow winners. Earlier, Scotland's youth team were placed third in a six-nation tournament in the Netherlands.

In June, Raeburn Place in Edinburgh had staged an electrifying match against the West Indians, watched by a large and enthusiastic crowd. The Scots refused to be daunted when Stuart Williams led the tourists to 305 in 55 overs; Salmond and Greig Williamson rattled up 117 in 54 minutes for the fifth wicket and Scotland were 258 in the final over when the crowd surged on to the pitch. MCC's trip to Aberdeen in August, though disrupted by rain and bad light, provided Scotland with a moral victory; the visitors were set 256 to win and were 43 short with only one wicket standing at the close.

The most disappointing results came in the English limited-overs competitions. The Benson and Hedges Cup, in April and May, arrives too early for Scotland's amateur cricketers. They lost all four group matches and did themselves justice only against Derbyshire, who might have been in difficulty had Daryll Cullinan not been dropped on 13. He went on to a century, despite some fine bowling by Scotland's new pro, West Indian Malcolm Marshall. In the NatWest Trophy, Scotland succumbed to a hat-trick by Nottinghamshire's Andy Pick.

At the domestic level, Drumpellier took the Whyte and Mackay Scottish Cup after an enthralling game with West of Scotland went to the final over, while Arbroath triumphed over Fifeshire in the SCU Trophy. The Royal Bank Axa Championship, which had to be scaled down because of the heavy league, cup and representative programme, went to Edinburgh. West Lothian won the Caledonian 80/- County Championship after Aberdeenshire lost 25 points for failing to fulfil a fixture; Heriot's Former Pupils won the Ryden East League for the second year running and Progress Software Clydesdale took the D. M. Hall Western Union.

Winners of other Scottish Leagues and Cups:

Duke's Strathmore Union: Dundee HSFP; **North of Scotland CA:** Buckie (third successive year); **Intersport Border League:** St Michael's; **3D Sports Glasgow and District League:** Glasgow High/Kelvinside; **Small Clubs' Cup:** Buckie; **Masterton Trophy:** Carlton; **Rowan Cup:** Clydesdale; **West League Cup:** Clydesdale.

THE TRIPLE CROWN TOURNAMENT, 1995

By GARETH A. DAVIES

Scotland, the only undefeated side, retained the Triple Crown title in 1995 after a wet week in Ireland and a tournament dominated by the bowlers. Two of the six matches had to be decided by bowl-outs, but the surprise of the real cricket was a comfortable Scottish victory over England on the opening day.

England were called the England NCA XI instead of the England Amateur XI to allow for the inclusion of semi-professionals from the leagues. It was no help. They were bowled out at Comber for 127 despite batting more than 54 overs. The left-arm seamer George Reifer and the former Northamptonshire off-spinner Jimmy Govan both bowled 11 overs each: Reifer took one for 11 and Govan two for 18.

The Scots proceeded to win their bowl-out against Ireland, and then had a six-wicket win over Wales. They were only five short of victory with nine wickets standing before Tim Hemp, brother of Glamorgan player David and an occasional bowler, recorded the competition's first-ever hat-trick.

At Comber, July 19. Scotland won by six wickets. Toss: England NCA XI. England NCA XI 127 (54.1 overs) (M. J. Roberts 32); Scotland 128 for four (53.1 overs) (G. N. Reifer 49).

At Downpatrick, July 19. Ireland won by six wickets. Toss: Wales. Wales 176 for eight (55 overs) (K. M. Bell 50; R. L. Eagleson three for 40); Ireland 179 for four (45.4 overs) (S. G. Smyth 30, D. A. Lewis 37, J. D. R. Benson 38 not out).

At Ormeau, July 20. Scotland won 4-2 in a bowl-out after the match was abandoned. Toss: Ireland. Scotland 69 for two (25.1 overs).

At Downpatrick, July 20. England NCA XI won 4-0 in a bowl-out after the match was abandoned. Toss: England NCA XI. Wales 129 for eight (40 overs) (T. Hemp 36).

At Comber, July 21. England NCA XI won by one run. Toss: Ireland. England NCA XI 173 for nine (50 overs) (D. Clarke 62); Ireland 172 for seven (50 overs) (S. G. Smyth 61; I. R. J. McLaren three for 34).

At Ormeau, Belfast, July 21. Scotland won by six wickets. Toss: Scotland. Wales 148 (54.5 overs) (J. Langworth 32, G. Lewis 39; K. Thomson three for 24); Scotland 149 for four (I. L. Philip 55, B. M. W. Patterson 40 not out; T. Hemp three for six).

FINAL TABLE

	Played	Won	Lost	Points
Scotland	3	3	0	6
England NCA XI	3	2	1	4
Ireland	3	1	2	2
Wales	3	0	3	0

SOUTH AFRICA UNDER-19 IN ENGLAND, 1995

By GERALD HOWAT

Hardly any of the South African Under-19 party which toured England in 1995 had experience of first-class cricket, although several had played internationally at Under-15 or Under-17 level. Unlike in other Test-playing countries, cricket at this level in South Africa is school-based. Chairman of selectors was the former South African captain, Jackie McGlew, who was also involved in the selection of the South African schoolboy side, featuring Barry Richards and Mike Procter, which toured England 32 years earlier. The multiracial basis of South African cricket was reflected in the composition of the side, which included six players from the South African Development Programme. The unity created within the team – with the breaking down of barriers of race, language and background – boded well for the future, and inspired the manager, Morgan Pilay, to describe the side as "a role model for a whole new generation of Test cricketers".

The youngsters found the tour very challenging, especially as it coincided with one of England's hottest spells, which took its toll of players who had virtually no experience of three-day – let alone four-day – matches. The South Africans began badly with four consecutive defeats, being completely overwhelmed in the two one-day internationals. Meeting young English professionals for the first time, they were initially overawed by the media coverage. However, three successive wins against regional Development of Excellence sides did much for their morale, so that by the First Test all the leading batsmen had played at least one substantial innings and the bowlers had begun to take wickets.

In all three Tests, the South Africans played well up to a point, but only in the First Test did they look possible winners, before poor fielding let them down. The difference between the two sides lay in the professionalism of the England batting right down the order. While the South African bowlers made immense strides as the tour progressed, the batsmen too often lost their wickets through impatience or lack of concentration.

The most successful batsmen were Hendrik Dippenaar and Ashwell Prince, with over 600 runs and a century apiece. Dippenaar was a stylish and accomplished player, while Prince, a left-hander, should have a promising future once he masters the discipline required of an opening batsman. Mark Boucher, with 582 runs at 34.23, was a reliable opener in most of his Test innings. Although Ahmed Omar showed his talent with a sparkling century in the First Unofficial Test, he failed too often, largely through hitting the ball in the air and playing his shots too soon. Neil McKenzie was a good leader both on and off the field, and his approach to field-setting improved as the matches went by. He struggled to find form, but scored half-centuries in each of the last two Tests.

The tourists lacked a genuine all-rounder, with only Bruce Stigant and Pierre Joubert looking likely contenders. Stigant rose to the major occasions with some solid batting and economical spin bowling; Joubert, a medium-pace bowler capable of bursts of speed, had few opportunities to bat but made the most of his chance at Worcester. Fast bowling was expected to be the side's strength, so when early injuries deprived them of both David Terbrugge and Chrisjan Vorster, an additional burden fell on Joubert,

Walter Masemula and the deceptively quick Makhaya Ntini. Showing determination, especially in the hot weather, Ntini secured 25 wickets; Masemula took only 14 but looked potentially formidable. Sixteen-year-old Tulani Ngxoweni, a left-arm spinner who achieved considerable control of direction and flight, took 20 at 23.75.

As expected, the experienced England players outclassed their visitors. Marcus Trescothick finished his Under-19 career as the second-highest scorer at this level, his 1,028 runs leaving him 25 behind John Crawley. He led his side aggressively, benefiting from strong contributions from the whole team, particularly Anthony McGrath with the bat, all-rounder Vikram Solanki and Umer Rashid with the ball.

TOUR PARTY

N. D. McKenzie (Transvaal) (*captain*), M. V. Boucher (Border), B. W. Clark (Western Province), H. H. Dippenaar (Orange Free State), B. K. Hughes (Natal), P. Joubert (Northern Transvaal), W. S. Masemula (Transvaal), M. Morkel (Transvaal), T. Ngxoweni (Border), M. Ntini (Border), A. M. Omar (Transvaal), A. G. Prince (Eastern Province), J. September (Eastern Province), B. G. Stigant (Eastern Province), D. J. Terbrugge (Transvaal), C. J. Vorster (Boland), L. Zondi (Natal).

Manager: M. Pilay.   *Cricket manager:* A. M. Griffiths.   *Coach:* S. A. Jones.

RESULTS

Matches – Played 12: Won 3, Lost 7, Drawn 2.

Note: Matches in this section were not first-class.

At Wellington College, June 26. Hampshire Second XI won by four wickets. Toss: South Africa Under-19. South Africa Under-19 229 for seven (55 overs) (A. M. Omar 39, H. H. Dippenaar 39, N. D. McKenzie 54); Hampshire Second XI 230 for six (53.4 overs) (G. R. Treagus 49, M. J. Thursfield 58).

At Finchampstead, June 28. National Cricket Association XI won by 84 runs. Toss: National Cricket Association XI. National Cricket Association XI 265 for five (55 overs) (S. Foster 103, M. J. Roberts 60); South Africa Under-19 181 (53 overs) (N. D. McKenzie 41; R. J. Pack five for 24).

At Canterbury, July 1. First unofficial one-day international: England Under-19 won by ten wickets. Toss: South Africa Under-19. South Africa Under-19 182 (51.3 overs) (M. V. Boucher 45, B. K. Hughes 34; A. C. Morris four for 34); England Under-19 183 for no wkt (37.3 overs) (M. E. Trescothick 84 not out, A. McGrath 89 not out).

At Chelmsford, July 4. Second unofficial one-day international: England Under-19 won by nine wickets. Toss: England Under-19. South Africa Under-19 232 for five (55 overs) (M. V. Boucher 38, A. G. Prince 52, H. H. Dippenaar 38, B. K. Hughes 59, A. M. Omar 30 not out); England Under-19 236 for one (45 overs) (M. E. Trescothick 111, A. McGrath 106 not out).

At Ipswich, July 6, 7, 8. South Africa Under-19 won by seven wickets. Toss: Southern Development of Excellence XI. Southern Development of Excellence XI 211 (W. L. Law 36, L. J. Botham 59; P. Joubert four for 39) and 254 (O. A. Shah 103, W. J. House 59 not out; P. Joubert three for 40); South Africa Under-19 270 (A. G. Prince 114, L. Zondi 61; D. W. Ayres four for 62) and 197 for three (A. G. Prince 65, H. H. Dippenaar 60 not out).

At Sleaford, July 10, 11, 12. South Africa Under-19 won by 37 runs. Toss: South Africa Under-19. South Africa Under-19 207 (B. K. Hughes 47, M. Ntini 35; C. L. Campbell five for 58) and 295 for five dec. (M. V. Boucher 143, A. G. Prince 41); Northern Development of Excellence XI 89 (M. Morkel three for 13) and 376 (L. J. Marland 104, D. Williamson 119; W. S. Masemula four for 74, M. Morkel three for 28).

At Oundle, July 15, 16, 17. South Africa Under-19 won by six wickets. Toss: Midlands Development of Excellence XI. Midlands Development of Excellence XI 218 (M. V. Steele 62, D. J. Roberts 46; M. Ntini four for 58) and 198 (U. Afzaal 75; T. Ngxoweni four for 45); South Africa Under-19 264 (B. K. Hughes 102, A. M. Omar 70; J. Ormond three for 57, U. Afzaal three for 69) and 153 for four (M. V. Boucher 54, H. H. Dippenaar 71).

ENGLAND UNDER-19 v SOUTH AFRICA UNDER-19

First Unofficial Test

At Taunton, July 20, 21, 22, 23. Drawn. Toss: England Under-19.

A target of 406 in a maximum of 109 overs proved beyond the South Africans, who had earlier looked likely winners. Putting their poor one-day internationals behind them, they began in spectacular fashion by reducing England to 115 for nine, before a record last-wicket partnership of 108 between Nash and Rashid almost doubled England's score. South Africa still gained a substantial first-innings lead, which owed most to Omar's positive play in a partnership with Stigant. England's opening pair then batted as they had at Canterbury and at Chelmsford, passing by 39 the previous best first-wicket stand in England Under-19 Tests, set by Mike Atherton and Mark Ramprakash against Sri Lanka in 1987. Trescothick's century came in 96 deliveries, while the more cautious McGrath ensured that England would be able to set the South Africans a stiff target.

Close of play: First day, South Africa Under-19 76-3 (H. H. Dippenaar 9*, B. K. Hughes 8*); Second day, England Under-19 99-0 (M. E. Trescothick 63*, A. McGrath 34*); Third day, South Africa Under-19 5-0 (M. V. Boucher 0*, A. G. Prince 2*).

England Under-19

*M. E. Trescothick c Omar b Masemula	23	– lbw b Stigant	136
A. McGrath b Ntini	13	– c Prince b Masemula	187
A. Singh c Omar b Masemula	6	– lbw b Ntini	21
V. S. Solanki c Omar b Joubert	0	– b Stigant	60
D. J. Sales c and b Stigant	7	– run out	48
A. C. Morris c McKenzie b Stigant	31	– b Stigant	8
A. Flintoff c Omar b Ntini	4	– c Boucher b Masemula	2
†D. C. Nash not out	56	– not out	25
A. J. Tudor c Boucher b Ntini	4	– not out	14
J. Ormond c Ntini b Stigant	2		
U. B. A. Rashid c Boucher b Joubert	64		
B 6, l-b 2, w 1, n-b 4	13	B 4, l-b 16, w 7	27
	223	(7 wkts dec.)	528

1/21 2/43 3/44 4/44 5/65 6/86 7/86 8/102 9/115   223

1/247 2/298 3/423 4/437 5/445 6/456 7/498   (7 wkts dec.) 528

Bowling: *First Innings*—Ntini 19–3–82–3; Morkel 3–0–11–0; Masemula 14–6–20–2; Joubert 14.4–5–40–2; Stigant 21–7–45–3; McKenzie 1–0–7–0; Boucher 2–0–10–0. *Second Innings*—Ntini 25–3–120–1; Joubert 24.2–111–0; Masemula 23–2–124–2; Stigant 32–8–115–3; McKenzie 7–1–17–0; Boucher 5–1–21–0.

South Africa Under-19

M. V. Boucher c Morris b Flintoff	21	– b Rashid	39
A. G. Prince lbw b Flintoff	25	– c Trescothick b Morris	16
H. H. Dippenaar c Nash b Tudor	23	– c Nash b Solanki	84
*N. D. McKenzie lbw b Morris	4	– lbw b Trescothick	28
B. K. Hughes lbw b Flintoff	30	– not out	51
†A. M. Omar c Sales b Ormond	123	– c and b Morris	15
B. G. Stigant c Trescothick b Tudor	40	– c Morris b Ormond	8
P. Joubert c Morris b Ormond	0		
M. Ntini c Trescothick b Flintoff	13		
M. Morkel not out	13	– (8) not out	7
W. S. Masemula lbw b Morris	9		
B 6, l-b 14, w 7, n-b 18	45	L-b 11, w 2, n-b 8	21

1/55 2/56 3/61 4/114 5/118   346   1/33 2/102 3/162   (6 wkts) 269
6/293 7/294 8/303 9/337   4/195 5/219 6/251

Bowling: First Innings—Tudor 21–5–57–2; Ormond 14–3–47–2; Flintoff 21–5–63–4; Morris 15.4–2–49–2; Rashid 15–3–46–0; Solanki 9–1–46–0; Trescothick 7–1–18–0. *Second Innings*—Tudor 18–10–22–0; Ormond 13–7–19–1; Rashid 27–16–28–1; Morris 15–3–83–2; Flintoff 12–1–49–0; Solanki 9–0–36–1; Trescothick 10–5–15–1; McGrath 1–0–6–0.

Umpires: J. C. Balderstone and G. I. Burgess.

At Old Hill, July 25, 26, 27. England Under-18 won by 196 runs. Toss: England Under-18. England Under-18 355 for eight dec. (D. J. Roberts 79, M. A. Wagh 65, S. M. Trego 57) and 205 for two dec. (M. J. Wood 94 not out, M. A. Wagh 53 not out); South Africa Under-19 195 (A. G. Prince 74; P. M. Hutchison five for 65) and 169 (M. V. Boucher 60; S. M. Trego four for 56).

At Shrewsbury, July 29, 30, 31. Drawn. Toss: A Development of Excellence XI. A Development of Excellence XI 248 (T. Roberts 58, S. Widdup 56; T. Ngxoweni five for 22) and 252 for eight (A. J. Swann 85 not out; T. Ngxoweni three for 65); South Africa Under-19 347 for seven dec. (A. M. Omar 38, A. G. Prince 53, H. H. Dippenaar 66, N. D. McKenzie 63, B. K. Hughes 42, P. Joubert 44).

ENGLAND UNDER-19 v SOUTH AFRICA UNDER-19

Second Unofficial Test

At Worcester, August 3, 4, 5, 6. England Under-19 won by seven wickets. Toss: South Africa Under-19.

In blistering heat, both sides used their spinners extensively, Rashid getting some turn on the first day, when McKenzie finally found form to score 88. Another century opening stand from Trescothick and McGrath appeared to have set England on their way to a significant lead, before Stigant, bowling three overs consecutively, inspired the loss of four middle-order wickets for nine runs. At that point the match looked evenly poised, but the South African bowlers could not press home their advantage and were demoralised on the third morning, when Nash and Rashid extended their eighth-wicket partnership to 146 – another record for the Middlesex pair – and Tudor took the England total past 500. After Prince was out quickly, Boucher and Dippenaar put on 111. Three more wickets fell before the close. England were frustrated by an attacking 90 from the night-watchman Joubert, but it was not enough.

Close of play: First day, South Africa Under-19 280-7 (N. D. McKenzie 77*, P. Joubert 37*); Second day, England Under-19 324-7 (D. C. Nash 18*, U. B. A. Rashid 18*); Third day, South Africa Under-19 133-4 (P. Joubert 8*, B. K. Hughes 0*).

South Africa Under-19

M. V. Boucher c Nash b Solanki	67	– b Searle	66
A. G. Prince b Searle	27	– c Nash b Flintoff	0
H. H. Dippenaar c Flintoff b Solanki	31	– b Morris	35
*N. D. McKenzie c Solanki b Searle	88	– c Nash b Searle	4
†B. K. Hughes b Tudor	1	– (6) c Sales b Tudor	0
B. G. Stigant c Trescothick b Rashid	16	– (8) b Morris	6
M. Morkel c and b Rashid	3	– (9) c Nash b Flintoff	26
A. M. Omar lbw b Rashid	0	– (7) c Sales b Tudor	0
P. Joubert run out	40	– (5) lbw b Flintoff	90
M. Ntini not out	8	– c Nash b Flintoff	2
W. S. Masemula lbw b Searle	5	– not out	5
B 8, l-b 13, n-b 4	25	B 4, l-b 15, w 1, n-b 26	46

1/79 2/143 3/143 4/152 5/196   311   1/0 2/111 3/120 4/133 5/140   280
6/200 7/200 8/293 9/295   6/140 7/182 8/263 9/273

Bowling: *First Innings*—Tudor 14–3–45–1; Flintoff 11–3–29–0; Trescothick 6–2–16–0; Morris 11–3–31–0; Searle 35–14–62–3; Rashid 36–14–73–3; Solanki 13–3–34–2. *Second Innings*—Tudor 17–4–72–2; Flintoff 20.1–4–62–4; Rashid 17–9–35–0; Searle 23–10–34–2; Morris 15–2–37–2; Solanki 9–2–21–0.

England Under-19

*M. E. Trescothick c Boucher b Stigant	88	– c Hughes b Joubert	9
A. McGrath run out	75	– c Dippenaar b Joubert	29
A. Singh c Morkel b Ntini	60	– c Masemula b Morkel	22
V. S. Solanki c Stigant b Dippenaar	22	– not out	15
D. J. Sales c Prince b Stigant	25	– not out	10
A. C. Morris c McKenzie b Stigant	2		
A. Flintoff lbw b Ntini	0		
†D. C. Nash c Hughes b Joubert	69		
U. B. A. Rashid not out	97		
A. J. Tudor c Prince b Stigant	32		
J. P. Searle c Hughes b Morkel	2		
B 18, l-b 7, w 2, n-b 8	35	L-b 1	1

1/166 2/171 3/215 4/284 5/288   507   1/25 2/46 3/70   (3 wkts) 86
6/288 7/293 8/439 9/504

Bowling: *First Innings*—Ntini 20–5–72–2; Joubert 20–3–70–1; Morkel 17–0–62–1; Masemula 10–2–52–0; Stigant 52–10–132–4; Dippenaar 24–3–83–1; McKenzie 6–2–11–0. *Second Innings*—Ntini 4–0–22–0; Joubert 6.5–0–51–2; Morkel 3–0–12–1.

Umpires: J. H. Hampshire and G. Sharp.

ENGLAND UNDER-19 v SOUTH AFRICA UNDER-19

Third Unofficial Test

At Leeds, August 10, 11, 12, 13. England Under-19 won by ten wickets. Toss: South Africa Under-19.

As in the earlier matches, the South Africans began well, before showing the strains of a demanding tour against more experienced opponents. Dippenaar made a splendid century, well supported by McKenzie, with 95 runs coming in an hour on the first afternoon. England's reply began with an opening partnership of 51 in 5.4 overs, which took Trescothick and McGrath's total of runs against the tourists to 1,074. Trescothick was out for 98 to the spinner Ngxoweni immediately he came on to bowl. Nash was left stranded on the same score, as the middle and late order again demonstrated its strength. On the final morning, South Africa collapsed terribly to 88 all out, with Rashid taking six for 15. A boundary by Trescothick gave England a 2-0 win in the series before lunch.

Close of play: First day, South Africa Under-19 364-8 (M. Morkel 10*, M. Ntini 15*); Second day, England Under-19 306-6 (A. C. Morris 44*); Third day, South Africa Under-19 72-4 (A. G. Prince 14*, A. M. Omar 1*).

South Africa Under-19

M. V. Boucher b Flintoff	9	– lbw b Morris	17
A. G. Prince b Morris	38	– c Morris b Solanki	20
H. H. Dippenaar c sub (P. M. Hutchison)			
b Rashid	.133	– b Tudor	17
*N. D. McKenzie c Singh b Solanki	73	– c McGrath b Rashid	12
B. K. Hughes c Tudor b Solanki	15	– c Nash b Rashid	0
†A. M. Omar st Nash b Rashid	9	– c Sales b Rashid	2
B. G. Stigant b Morris	20	– b Rashid	5
P. Joubert c Nash b Morris	11	– c Trescothick b Rashid	2
M. Morkel b Rashid	16	– lbw b Rashid	0
M. Ntini c sub (P. M. Hutchison) b Rashid	31	– not out	0
T. Ngxoweni not out	0	– c McGrath b Solanki	2
B 11, l-b 5, w 1, n-b 14	31	B 1, n-b 10	11

1/23 2/93 3/257 4/276 5/293   386   1/21 2/40 3/71 4/71 5/75   88
6/313 7/334 8/337 9/386   6/80 7/82 8/86 9/86

Bowling: *First Innings*—Tudor 15–3–69–0; Flintoff 10–2–42–1; Morris 23–6–73–3; Trescothick 4–0–20–0; Searle 21–8–67–0; Rashid 28.5–12–56–4; Solanki 15–6–43–2. *Second Innings*—Tudor 10–2–36–1; Morris 6–0–23–1; Rashid 21–13–15–6; Searle 14–7–12–0; Solanki 3.5–2–1–2.

England Under-19

*M. E. Trescothick st Omar b Ngxoweni	98	– not out	4
A. McGrath b Ntini	22	– not out	0
A. Singh b Ntini	1		
V. S. Solanki b Stigant	66		
D. J. Sales c Stigant b Ngxoweni	0		
A. C. Morris c Morkel b Ngxoweni	72		
A. Flintoff lbw b Ntini	54		
†D. C. Nash not out	98		
U. B. A. Rashid b Joubert	6		
A. J. Tudor c Prince b Stigant	17		
J. P. Searle b Stigant	2		
B 10, l-b 5, w 2, n-b 18	35		

1/51 2/53 3/196 4/196 5/196   471   (no wkt) 4
6/306 7/391 8/422 9/468

Bowling: *First Innings*—Ntini 22–2–112–3; Joubert 29.1–3–112–1; Morkel 16.5–3–58–0; Stigant 40–11–88–3; Ngxoweni 34–11–76–3; McKenzie 5–2–10–0. *Second Innings*—Boucher 0.3–0–4–0.

Umpires: H. D. Bird and J. W. Holder.

SIR GARFIELD SOBERS SCHOOLS CRICKET FESTIVAL, 1995

The ninth Sir Garfield Sobers Schools Cricket Festival, held in Barbados in July and August, was contested by ten schools: Canford, Clifton College and Mill Hill from Britain; The Lodge School, Princess Margaret School, Ellerslie School and Samuel Taylor Jackman Polytechnic from Barbados; St Vincent's School from St Vincent; Presentation College from Trinidad; and Dominican Schools. The tournament was won by Canford – semi-finalists in 1990 – who won seven of their nine round-robin matches before beating Clifton in the semi-finals and Dominican Schools in the final at the Carlton Club. Bowled out for 111, they looked beaten, but became the first British school to win the tournament when Dominican Schools crumpled for 67 in the face of a spirited performance in the field, led by Toby Cutler, who was named Man of the Match in the final and All-rounder of the Tournament.

NAYC UNDER-19 COUNTY FESTIVALS, 1995

By PHILIP HOARE

Kent were the National Association of Young Cricketers' double champions, winning both the grand final of the Under-19s festival, at Oxford in August, and the season-long Hilda Overy Championship, which embraces the festival and other games. Having won the Oxford area final, Kent went on to defeat Cambridge champions Durham, who remained frustratingly consistent – it was their third year running as beaten finalists. This time, Durham may have been exhausted by a hard-fought area final against Leicestershire in Cambridge the previous day.

Paul Collingwood and Richard Hawthorne scored freely on a shirtfront of a pitch and, after both were run out, the hard-hitting Dominic Williamson carried Durham to 236 for six. But Michael Sutliff and James Bull opened with 143 for Leicestershire before leg-spinner Harry Hubber and a series of run-outs gave Durham victory by just eight runs. In contrast, Kent could rest after an easy win over Shropshire in Oxford. James Golding and Alastair Ramsey bowled Shropshire out in 41 overs and openers Chris Walsh and James Baldock raced to their target in less than 12.

Other players who distinguished themselves at Oxford included Charles Hodgson of Berkshire, with 138 against Devon, the highest innings of the week, and five for 46 against Worcestershire, Kevin Dean, who took eight for 26 for Derbyshire against Shropshire and Tom Sharp, whose seven for 58 for Cornwall against Buckinghamshire included a hat-trick and four wickets in five balls. At Cambridge, Anthony Crozier of Lancashire made two centuries, against Suffolk and Cumbria, while Durham's Collingwood scored 106 against Sussex and took six wickets against West of Scotland and five against Huntingdonshire.

The two festivals attracted 32 of the NAYC's 40 members. Five – Essex, Gloucestershire, Hampshire, Middlesex and Surrey – had withdrawn in order to concentrate on two-day cricket and played in the breakaway Reader League, together with Kent and Sussex. Several other counties played two-day fixtures, which were originally intended to count towards the Hilda Overy Championship. But, as some of these games were used to assess triallists, the NAYC decided to ignore them. The two-day experience evidently boosted Kent. They won all seven of their one-day matches and bowled out the opposition six times; Oxfordshire were second, with Cheshire and Leicestershire third and fourth on run-rate, having tied on points average with Lancashire.

After the season ended, the NAYC held talks with the Reader League, whose aim was to provide greater continuity between youth cricket and county second elevens by introducing players to the longer game. The seven counties involved had played a round-robin tournament of one-innings 110-overs-a-side matches, which Middlesex won on the very last day. They planned to repeat the competition in 1996 but the negotiations with the NAYC produced a plan to reunite these branches of Under-19 cricket by 1997, with a two-day league and a one-day cup.

AREA FINALS

At Clare College, Cambridge, August 11. Durham won by eight runs. Toss: Durham. Durham 236 for six (55 overs) (P. D. Collingwood 91, R. A. Hawthorne 41, D. Williamson 47 not out); Leicestershire 228 for nine (55 overs) (M. D. R. Sutliff 71, J. J. Bull 58; H. Hubber four for 60).

At Jesus College, Oxford, August 11. Kent won by ten wickets. Toss: Shropshire. Shropshire 79 (40.3 overs) (J. M. Golding four for 22, A. Ramsey four for nine); Kent 80 for no wkt (11.2 overs) (C. D. Walsh 39 not out, J. Baldock 37 not out).

FINAL

DURHAM v KENT

At Christ Church, Oxford, August 12. Kent won by 65 runs. Toss: Kent.

Tight Kent bowling and fielding prevented Durham from making it third time lucky; they had lost the previous two NAYC finals to Lancashire and Yorkshire. Kent chose to bat on a hard-baked pitch taking spin, and leg-spinner Harry Hubber, who finished with four wickets, had reduced them to 50 for three when Ed Smith came in. He hit ten fours in a stylish 83, which enabled Kent to reach 200. It did not seem a demanding target – until James Golding removed Durham captain Wayne Ritzema with the first ball of the innings. From then on, it was an uphill struggle. Paul Collingwood made 33 in a lengthy stay at the crease but only two more batsmen reached double figures. Opening bowler Grant Stephens had the excellent figures of three for 15 in ten overs while slow left-armer Jamie Ford controlled his line and length to good effect to apply the brakes. Durham were dismissed with six overs to spare.

Kent

C. D. Walsh b Williamson	8	N. Taylor not out		8
J. Baldock lbw b Hubber	24	G. Stephens not out		1
J. A. Ford c Clark b Hubber	32	L-b 15, w 3, n-b 1		19
W. J. House lbw b Hubber	0			
E. T. Smith c McDonald b Lawrence	83	1/19 2/50 3/50	(7 wkts, 55 overs)	200
N. Gowers c and b Hubber	16	4/75 5/138		
*A. Ramsey b Lawrence	9	6/167 7/196		

J. M. Golding and †J. Bond did not bat.

Bowling: Lawrence 13–3–45–2; Williamson 8–4–22–1; Collingwood 7–2–15–0; Hubber 17–3–59–4; Clark 8–0–30–0; Hawthorne 2–0–14–0.

Durham

*†W. Ritzema c Smith b Golding	0	I. Jones b Ford		2
C. Clark c Ford b Stephens	8	D. Beall b Stephens		5
P. D. Collingwood c and b Ramsey	33	J. R. G. Lawrence not out		3
R. A. Hawthorne run out	2	B 4, l-b 5, w 5		14
D. Williamson b House	5			
S. Naylor run out	29	1/0 2/15 3/21	(49 overs)	135
A. McDonald c House b Ford	7	4/39 5/66 6/88		
H. Hubber c Walsh b Stephens	27	7/95 8/107 9/122		

Bowling: Golding 6–1–15–1; Stephens 10–2–15–3; Ramsey 15–3–37–1; House 5–0–18–1; Ford 13–0–41–2.

Umpires: R. Julian and K. J. Lyons.

PAST WINNERS

1986	Lancashire	1990	Essex	1994	Yorkshire
1987	Yorkshire	1991	Middlesex	1995	Kent
1988	Warwickshire	1992	Yorkshire		
1989	Warwickshire	1993	Lancashire		

SCHOOLS CRICKET IN 1995

The MCC Oxford Festival again benefited from the fine July weather. Forty-four of the most talented young players were selected to participate by the Headmasters' Conference (HMC) and English Schools Cricket Association (ESCA). It was unfortunate that some of the players were below their best, owing to the amount of cricket they had played in the preceding two weeks: three of the seam bowlers broke down through injury on the first two days of the Festival and other players were unavailable for the final game at Lord's owing to exhaustion or injuries.

At the end of the four days at Oxford, the following 13 players were selected to play at Lord's: Toby Bailey, Paul Bainbridge, Andrew Birley, Anthony Crozier, Sam Diment, Noel Gie, Giles Goodwin, Tim Lamb, James Lawrence, David Lewis, Luke Sutton, Chris Taylor and Mark Wagh.

HMC SOUTHERN SCHOOLS v HMC NORTHERN SCHOOLS

At Wadham College, Oxford, July 14, 15. Drawn.

On an excellent pitch, batsmen and bowlers alike were able to demonstrate their skills in a tense and well-fought match. South had the better of the first day, with all their batsmen chipping in and the bowlers restricting North to 183 for seven. A highlight was the wicket-keeping of Bailey, who executed two very sharp leg-side stumpings, while Birley thoroughly deserved his six wickets and Fulton batted thoughtfully. Taylor and Strauss showed their class with the bat on the second day, enabling Sutton to set a target of 269 in four hours. After the usually prolific Chilton and Lowe had gone cheaply, North only just managed to stave off some spirited bowling and salvage a draw, thanks to a sensible half-century from Bailey.

HMC Southern Schools

C. G. Taylor (*Colston's*) lbw b Birley	11 – retired hurt	80
E. J. Wilson (*Felsted*) lbw b Birley	15 – (4) not out	32
A. J. Strauss (*Radley*) st Bailey b Birley	30 – retired ill	72
T. C. Z. Lamb (*Bryanston*) c Hancock b Palmer	17 – (2) c Diment b Palmer	17
*†L. D. Sutton (*Millfield*) b Birley	32 – b Birley	8
R. E. Arthur (*Epsom*) st Bailey b Birley	29 – run out	5
I. J. W. McCarter (*Shrewsbury*) c Birley b Palmer	5	
G. C. Mason (*Oundle*) c Hancock b Birley	21	
G. J. A. Goodwin (*Felsted*) not out	32	
M. R. Bellhouse (*Radley*) not out	13	
Extras	17	Extras 15

1/20 2/46 3/58 4/97 5/138   (8 wkts. dec.) 222   1/29 2/201 3/229   (3 wkts. dec.) 229
6/143 7/159 8/170

S. H. L. Diment (*King's, Taunton*) did not bat.

Bowling: *First Innings*—Deane 5–3–6–0; Birley 20–4–62–6; Feather 13–4–36–0; Hancock 10–4–26–0; Palmer 12–1–75–2. *Second Innings*—Birley 8–3–14–1; Feather 15–1–70–0; Hancock 18.4–8–46–0; Palmer 11–1–55–1; Chilton 10–1–29–0.

HMC Northern Schools

*M. Bishop (*St Ambrose*) lbw b Goodwin	22	– c Arthur b McCarter 21
N. A. Gie (*Trent*) c Sutton b Diment.........	39	– lbw b McCarter 18
J. A. G. Fulton (*Eton*) run out	59	– c Mason b Goodwin 20
E. J. Lowe (*Rugby*) c Sutton b Diment	2	– c Arthur b Diment........... 2
†T. M. B. Bailey (*Bedford*) c Taylor b Bellhouse	26	– not out.................... 56
M. J. Chilton (*Manchester GS*) c Sutton b Mason	8	– c Taylor b Diment 16
Z. R. Feather (*Birkenhead*) not out	12	– c Bellhouse b Diment 8
J. M. Palmer (*Lord Wandsworth*) c Sutton		
b Diment .	4	– c Lamb b Bellhouse 4
T. W. Hancock (*Trent*) not out..............	2	– c Wilson b Bellhouse 0
M. Deane (*Abbotsholme*) (did not bat)	–	– not out 18
Extras.....................	9	Extras 5

1/64 2/64 3/74 4/120 5/141   (7 wkts dec.) 183   1/28 2/53 3/57 4/91   (8 wkts) 168
6/173 7/177   5/109 6/117 7/125 8/127

A. B. Birley (*Birkenhead*) did not bat.

Bowling: First Innings—Bellhouse 11–2–45–1; McCarter 10–2–28–0; Mason 19–2–27–1; Goodwin 19–5–48–1; Diment 11–2–30–3. *Second Innings*—Bellhouse 10–2–24–2; McCarter 16–4–41–2; Mason 7–3–15–0; Goodwin 17–2–41–1; Diment 16–3–37–3; Taylor 3–2–7–0.

ESCA NORTH v ESCA SOUTH

At St Edward's School, Oxford, July 14, 15. ESCA North won by nine wickets.

In a one-sided match, the North dominated throughout. Their bowlers always had the better of things, the left-armer Lawrence looking the quickest and most impressive, while Smart also looked promising until he was injured. Only Howell made fifty for the South, while Crozier, Clark and Bolton all contributed for the North, who lost only four wickets in the two innings.

ESCA South

*M. A. Wagh (*King Edward's, Birmingham; Warwicks.*) c Chronnell b Smart .	7	– c Jeffrey b Smart 6
C. Howell (*Bishop Walsh; Warwicks.*) b Lawrence	6	– c Jeffrey b Clark 63
P. C. Bainbridge (*Richmond C.; Surrey*) c Crozier b Lewis .	34	– c Chronnell b Collins.......... 18
G. Swann (*Sponne; Northants.*) c Jeffrey b Smart	1	– c Clark b Collins 7
M. Swarbrick (*Claysmore; Dorset*) c Jeffrey b Lawrence .	13	– run out 9
R. Nagra (*King Edward VI, Stourbridge; Worcs.*) c Chronnell b Bourke	17	– c Lewis b Chronnell........... 15
L. R. J. List (*Abingdon; Oxon.*) c Bolton b Lewis	4	– c and b Chronnell 23
M. Mohammed (*Bournville C.; Warwicks.*) run out .	23	– b Clark 0
†J. Dhillon (*Highfield; Staffs.*) not out	29	– st Jeffrey b Collins........... 10
R. L. Dredge (*Cheltenham C.; Glos.*) c Staunton b Bourke .	16	– not out 2
D. J. Lewis (*Shrewsbury SFC; Salop.*) c Lewis b Bourke .	0	– c Lewis b Chronnell........... 12
Extras.........................	4	Extras 17

1/15 2/15 3/16 4/39 5/64   154   1/7 2/46 3/58 4/88 5/119   182
6/84 7/84 8/131 9/149   6/127 7/133 8/163 9/167

Bowling: First Innings—Lawrence 12–4–24–2; Smart 14–4–34–2; Collins 6–0–26–0; Lewis 6–1–25–2; Bourke 8–4–9–3; Chronnell 10–3–36–0. *Second Innings*—Lawrence 10–3–21–0; Smart 6–2–22–1; Collins 12–1–35–3; Lewis 5–0–22–0; Bourke 7–3–11–0; Chronnell 23–7–41–3; Clark 9–2–20–2.

ESCA North

*C. Clark (*Newcastle C.; *Durham*) b Swann	46	– retired	35
A. Bourke (*New C.; *Yorks.*) b Dredge	8		
A. J. Crozier (*Bridgewater County HS; *Cheshire*) retired .	54	– (2) c Wagh b List	40
P. Bolton (*Clitheroe RGS; *Lancs.*) retired .... c Dhillon b List	61 6	– (3) not out	26
B. R. F. Staunton (*Beechen Cliff; *Somerset*)			
G. Lewis (*Embley Park; *Hants*) not out	20		
†J. Jeffrey (*Benton Park; *Yorks.*) not out	4	– (4) not out	10
Extras	22	Extras	6

1/16 2/112 3/134   (3 wkts dec.) 221   1/63   (1 wkt) 117

L. Chronnell (*Poynton County HS; *Cheshire*), L. Collins (*Cheltenham SFC; *Glos.*), J. R. G. Lawrence (*Queen Elizabeth SFC; *Durham*) and R. Smart (*Ripon GS; *Yorks.*) did not bat.

Bowling: *First Innings*—Dredge 5–0–23–1; Mohammed 7–2–18–0; Howell 5–1–16–0; Lewis 10–2–30–0; Nagra 11–1–35–0; Swann 13–1–49–1; List 6–0–38–1; Wagh 3–1–6–0. *Second Innings*—Mohammed 8–1–30–0; Howell 1–0–4–0; Lewis 5–0–20–0; Nagra 5–0–17–0; Swann 8–1–22–0; List 5–0–18–1.

At St Edward's School, Oxford, July 16. L. D. Sutton's XI won by seven wickets. C. Clark's XI 147 (T. C. Z. Lamb 30; P. C. Bainbridge three for 33); L. D. Sutton's XI 148 for three (P. C. Bainbridge 79 not out).
L. D. Sutton held seven catches behind the stumps.

At St John's College, Oxford, July 16. Drawn. M. A. Wagh's XI 195 for seven dec. (A. J. Crozier 51, B. R. F. Staunton 45; D. J. Lewis three for 62); M. Bishop's XI 162 for eight (N. A. Gie 44, E. J. Lowe 30; T. W. Hancock three for 55, M. A. Wagh three for 21).

At Christ Church, Oxford, July 17. MCC Schools West won by 14 runs. MCC Schools West 170 (C. G. Taylor 34, M. A. Wagh 43, T. C. Z. Lamb 48; L. R. J. List three for 17, P. C. Bainbridge three for 18); MCC Schools East 156 (N. A. Gie 32, M. J. Chilton 38; D. J. Lewis four for 20, S. H. L. Diment three for 36).

MCC v MCC SCHOOLS

At Lord's, July 18. MCC won by 71 runs. Toss: MCC.
A well-judged declaration made for an interesting match, and although MCC Schools were always struggling after the early loss of Taylor, they never gave up. Clements was the mainstay of the MCC innings, in which Lawrence bowled particularly well and was unlucky not to have a wicket. Wagh provided the backbone of the Schools' innings, keeping one end going in a competent display and dominating a last-wicket partnership of 21 with Birley.

MCC

R. A. McGregor c Taylor b Diment ...	35	R. P. Gofton not out	15
M. Bell c Gie b Birley	7		
C. M. Gupte hit wicket b Goodwin....	59	B 2, l-b 3, w 2, n-b 1	8
S. M. Clements not out 111			
Mushtaq Mohammad c Lawrence b Wagh .	10	1/29 2/50 (4 wkts dec.) 245 3/192 4/203	

*G. J. Toogood, †J. S. Brooks, S. McDonald, M. G. Stear and C. M. Pitcher did not bat.

Bowling: Lawrence 13–2–31–0; Birley 13–3–49–1; Bainbridge 5–2–10–0; Diment 7–1–35–1; Goodwin 14–2–74–1; Wagh 11–2–41–1.

MCC Schools

C. G. Taylor lbw b Pitcher	0	S. H. L. Diment c Brooks b Pitcher	...	2
P. C. Bainbridge c Mushtaq b Stear	15	J. R. G. Lawrence b Stear	...	0
A. J. Crozier c Bell b Gofton	28	A. B. Birley c Brooks b Mushtaq	...	1
M. A. Wagh not out	87			
N. A. Gie st Brooks b Mushtaq	10	B 6, l-b 6, w 4		16
*L. D. Sutton lbw b Mushtaq	7			
†T. M. B. Bailey lbw b Pitcher	8	1/0 2/37 3/54 4/88 5/104		174
G. J. A. Goodwin c Pitcher b McDonald	0	6/136 7/137 8/148 9/153		

Bowling: Pitcher 12–1–60–3; Stear 10–3–16–2; Toogood 3–1–2–0; Gofton 7–2–22–1; Mushtaq 11.3–2–36–3; McDonald 9–3–26–1.

Umpires: R. H. Duckett and K. F. Forsyth.

MCC SCHOOLS v NATIONAL ASSOCIATION OF YOUNG CRICKETERS

At Lord's, July 19. NAYC won by two wickets. Toss: NAYC.

Hart's six off the fourth ball of the last over ended an exciting match in favour of NAYC. Gie dominated the Schools' innings, missing out on a century when he was run out as the non-striker out of his crease when the ball was deflected. The Schools bowlers then picked up wickets regularly until Bailey led the chase for 127 off the last 20 overs, with Ellsmore hitting two sixes and Hart settling matters.

MCC Schools

P. C. Bainbridge b Hart	22	T. M. B. Bailey not out		3
C. G. Taylor c Davies b Ellsmore	43			
N. A. Gie run out	99	B 4, l-b 3, w 3		10
M. A. Wagh run out	11			
T. C. Z. Lamb c Davies b Carey	6	1/34 2/98 3/123		(6 wkts dec.) 213
*†L. D. Sutton run out	19	4/129 5/192 6/213		

G. J. A. Goodwin, D. J. Lewis, J. R. G. Lawrence and A. B. Birley did not bat.

Bowling: Hart 14–4–55–1; Bellew 8–2–20–0; Hudson 10.4–3–47–0; Ellsmore 4–0–22–1; Bailey 3–1–6–0; Brett 12–4–30–0; Carey 8–3–26–1.

National Association of Young Cricketers

*M. D. R. Sutliff c Wagh b Goodwin	16	N. A. Brett not out		8
P. G. Hudson b Goodwin	34	S. D. Bellew run out		1
C. D. J. Bailey b Bainbridge	78	J. P. Hart not out		8
I. D. Cheeseright c Lawrence b Goodwin	9	L-b 9, w 1		10
I. J. O'Sullivan c Sutton b Bainbridge	22	1/36 2/59 3/85		(8 wkts) 214
†P. G. T. Davies c Lewis b Bainbridge	7	4/144 5/168 6/173		
N. M. Ellsmore c Lawrence b Birley	21	7/201 8/206		

M. Carey did not bat.

Bowling: Lawrence 8–2–14–0; Birley 9–3–29–1; Goodwin 18–5–61–3; Lewis 12–2–43–0; Bainbridge 7.4–0–58–3.

Umpires: K. Bray and R. H. Duckett.

The National Cricket Association selected the following to play for NCA Young Cricketers against Combined Services: T. M. B. Bailey (Northants), S. D. Bellew (Bucks.), A. B. Birley (Cheshire), N. A. Brett (Surrey), N. M. Ellsmore (Staffs.), G. J. A. Goodwin (Essex), J. P. Hart (Notts.), P. G. Hudson (Sussex), T. C. Z. Lamb (Dorset), M. D. R. Sutliff (Leics.), M. A. Wagh (Warwicks.).

At Lord's, July 20. NCA Young Cricketers won by six wickets. Toss: NCA Young Cricketers. Combined Services 225 for four dec. (Capt. R. J. Greatorex 35, Sgt G. S. Lumb

62, Cpl A. Jones 58, Sgt N. Palmer 34 not out; N. M. Ellsmore three for 16); NCA Young
Cricketers 228 for four (P. G. Hudson 67, M. D. R. Sutliff 41, M. A. Wagh 43).

ETON v HARROW

At Lord's, June 27. Drawn. Toss: Harrow.

Harrow had the satisfaction of bowling Eton out, thanks to the swing of Leathes, whose
six for 19 included a spell of five for three in 23 balls. It was the first time since 1991 that
either side had been dismissed. But the breakthrough came too late to make a match of it.
Dixon had batted four hours for Eton's third century in successive years, hitting 13 fours
and adding 110 in even time with Lea. It was Lea's removal, by Nicol, which signalled a
falling-away for Eton: their last seven fell for 54, with Dixon reaching three figures just
before he became Leathes's fifth victim. Harrow had to chase 220 in what became 45 overs
and, after a slow start – 12 for two in the 12th over – they never looked like getting there.
Cox was their leading batsman, with 45, and though Spry lived up to his name with seven
fours in 31, wickets fell at regular intervals and it was left to Gillions to ensure safety. Two
male streakers, carrying blue shirts, loped across the outfield in the evening sunshine.

Eton

H. H. Dixon c MacAndrew b Leathes. .100		R. W. J. Bruce c Gillions b Leathes ...	7
H. J. H. Loudon c MacAndrew		A. F. Jafri c Nicol b Leathes	19
	b Leathes.	R. J. Dunlop not out	1
	5	†A. R. Lewis b Parker	1
*J. A. G. Fulton c MacAndrew			
	b Engelen . 16	B 4, l-b 9, w 6, n-b 1	20
N. A. Bailey b Parker	0		───
A. M. Lea c MacAndrew b Nicol	48		219
S. K. Patel c sub b Leathes	2	1/14 2/50 3/55 4/165 5/173	
O. L. Barnett c MacAndrew b Leathes.	0	6/173 7/191 8/202 9/215	

Bowling: Parker 18.2–2–52–2; Leathes 16–9–19–6; Titchener-Barrett 11–1–45–0; Engelen
15–8–26–1; Nicol 14–0–64–1.

Harrow

*S. D. G. Engelen c Lewis b Dunlop ...	2	C. R. C. Parker c Lewis b Barnett....	8
J. R. W. Norris c Lewis b Bruce	2	E. W. Nicol not out	0
†R. G. MacAndrew c Fulton b Patel...	12	B 6, l-b 4, w 6, n-b 13	29
A. N. L. Cox c Lewis b Bruce	45		───
E. G. L. Maydon c Bailey b Jafri	14	(7 wkts) 176	
W. A. T. Gillions not out	33	1/7 2/12 3/52	
O. C. P. Spry c Dixon b Dunlop	31	4/95 5/100	
		6/153 7/175	

D. C. A. Titchener-Barrett and T. D. de M. Leathes did not bat.

Bowling: Barnett 10–2–25–1; Bruce 14.5–5–26–2; Dunlop 9–0–45–2; Patel 6–1–28–1; Jafri
6–0–42–1.

Umpires: K. T. Bailey and T. H. Duckett.

*Of the 160 matches played between the two schools since 1805, Eton have won 52, Harrow 44
and 64 have been drawn. Matches during the two world wars are excluded from the reckoning.
The fixture was reduced from a two-day, two-innings-a-side match to one day in 1982. Forty-
nine centuries have been scored, the highest being 183 by D. C. Boles of Eton in 1904; M. C.
Bird of Harrow is the only batsman to have made two hundreds in a match, in 1907. The highest
score since the First World War is 161 not out by M. K. Fosh of Harrow in 1975, Harrow's last
victory. Since then Eton have won in 1977, 1985, 1990 and 1991; all other games have been
drawn. A full list of centuries since 1918 and results from 1950 can be found in* Wisdens *prior
to 1994.*

International matches

At Trinity College, Dublin, July 9, 10, 11. Drawn. Irish Schools 228 (R. O'Reilly 63,
D. McCann 42, B. Cunningham 35; Adrian Harries four for 38, Andrew Harries three for

69) and 158 for nine dec. (P. Lee 37; Andrew Harries four for 54); Welsh Schools 218 (E. M. G. Britton 39, S. Givlin 43 not out; D. McCann three for 37, R. Beattie three for 43) and 78 for no wkt (M. Powell 52 not out).

At Abergavenny, July 25, 26, 27. Drawn. Welsh Schools 362 for nine dec. (E. M. G. Britton 38, M. Powell 55, S. C. B. Tomlinson 70, M. Leaf 60) and 238 (E. M. G. Britton 37, A. P. Davies 67, M. Leaf 37; K. A. Stott three for 78); Scotland Young Cricketers 314 for five dec. (D. R. Lockhart 111, J. S. D. Moffatt 106) and 117 for four.

At Neston, July 31, August 1. English Schools won by 170 runs. English Schools 268 for seven dec. (C. G. Taylor 50, P. C. Bainbridge 119, L. D. Sutton 32; Andrew Harries four for 80) and 202 for five dec. (C. G. Taylor 59, P. C. Bainbridge 84); Welsh Schools 221 for seven dec. (E. M. G. Britton 83, Adrian Harries 32, Andrew Harries 32, A. P. Davies 37 not out; M. A. Wagh three for 23) and 79 (J. R. G. Lawrence four for 27, G. J. A. Goodwin three for nine).

At Edinburgh, August 3, 4. English Schools won by eight wickets. Scottish Young Cricketers 142 for seven dec. (D. G. O. Fergusson 35 not out) and 133 (D. G. O. Fergusson 37; G. J. A. Goodwin four for 53, M. A. Wagh six for 50); English Schools 205 (L. D. Sutton 56; R. Mitchinson three for 62, K. A. Stott three for 60) and 71 for two (C. G. Taylor 39).

HIGHLIGHTS FROM THE SCHOOLS

Once the pitches dried out and many became a batsman's paradise, batting records tumbled. From the schools reviewed here, 16 batsmen scored 1,000 runs, five more than the previous best of 11 in 1990 and 1993.

Eight of these played fewer than 20 innings and the most prolific, C. G. Taylor of Colston's, made his 1,597 in only 18, at an average of 106.46. He also took 31 wickets at 18.87 and won the Cricket Society's Wetherall Award. Others to pass 1,300 runs were S. E. P. Davies of Bradford Grammar School, D. Grundy of Merchant Taylors', Northwood and M. J. Chilton of Manchester Grammar, who scored 1,361 at 104.69 in only 16 innings. Four batsmen recorded four-figure aggregates with three-figure averages; in addition to Taylor and Chilton, E. J. Wilson of Felsted made 1,202 at the season's highest average of 120.20 and R. W. J. Howitt of Denstone scored 1,016 at 101.60, while D. Young of Warwick was close with 923 at 102.55 from just 12 innings.

Of the five double-centuries reported, Taylor had two: 278 not out, which equalled the highest for an English public school by J. L. Guise in 1921, and 201. Other double-centuries came from N. A. Gie of Trent, S. C. B. Tomlinson of Oratory and R. G. H. Widdowson of Loughborough Grammar. There were hundreds galore, with nine batsmen scoring five or more. Taylor topped this list too, his eight coming at the rate of one every 2.25 innings, while Chilton and M. Swarbrick of Clayesmore had seven at a similar rate.

As might be expected, the bowling figures were less spectacular, although some bowlers were surprisingly economical. No one took 60 wickets, but four had 50 — one more than in 1994. T. Slade of Caterham was the most successful with 57 at 11.75, followed by N. Sapra of Merchant Taylors', Northwood (53 at 12.69), B. W. O'Connell of Tiffin (50 at 19.50) and A. T. J. Clark of Trinity, who bowled the most, with 50 at 18.30 off 341 overs. O'Connell also scored 635 runs and Clark 501. There were five single-figure averages recorded by bowlers with more than 30 wickets. The most economical was M. Breetzke of Stonyhurst, whose 42 cost just 7.42 apiece, followed by E. Lamb of Merchant Taylors', Northwood (39 at 8.64), A. B. Birley of Birkenhead (33 at 9.78), S. S. Nanji of Gordonstoun (36 at 9.88) and M. J. Williamson of Bangor Grammar (38 at 9.97). Exeter's A. O. F. Le Fleming had the best analysis with nine for 26, while other nine-wicket returns were achieved by A. Herman of Portsmouth Grammar (nine for 29), J. A. S. Pye of Solihull (nine for 40) and L. J. Ratcliffe of Marlborough (nine for 62). Hat-tricks abounded. Eight were reported from M. Attwood of Wrekin, B. Barton and Slade both of Caterham, S. D. G. Engelen and D. de Jager of Harrow, M. Joel of St Edward's, Oxford, M. Klein of Kimbolton and D. Walder of Oundle.

In terms of quantity, the leading all-rounders were M. A. Wagh of King Edward's, Birmingham with 1,062 runs at 53.10 and 40 wickets at 12.87, J. M. Palmer of Lord Wandsworth (742 runs and 48 wickets), J. Gibson of The Edinburgh Academy (724 runs and 46 wickets) and P. R. Mouncey of Pocklington (721 runs and 41 wickets). In terms of averages, four players with 500 runs and 30 wickets averaged 50 with the bat and 14 with the ball – Palmer, Wagh, Gibson and J. W. Hatch of Barnard Castle, while Le Fleming, although ten runs short of the criterion, had the best averages with 490 runs at 61.25 and 35 runs at 10.48.

Of the 35 schools who won more than half their matches, Oratory had the most impressive record with 76 per cent won, followed by Canford with 72 per cent. Oratory were one of five unbeaten sides, the others being Forest, Malvern, Plymouth and Radley. Of these, Radley and Forest won more than they drew and Malvern won half their games, but Plymouth had only three wins to offset as many as 11 draws. Although several sides won only once, Sutton Valence were alone in managing none. The experiment with limited-overs games often proved popular and, following the MCC initiative at the beginning of the season, there were fewer complaints of negative play. Despite the increasing influence of examinations during the season, many schools played more than 20 matches.

Details of records broken, other outstanding performances and interesting features of the season may be found in the returns from the schools which follow.

THE SCHOOLS

(Qualification: Batting 150 runs; Bowling 15 wickets)

* On name indicates captain.   * On figures indicates not out.

Note: The line for batting reads Innings–Not Outs–Runs–Highest Score–100s–Average; that for bowling reads Overs–Maidens–Runs–Wickets–Best Bowling–Average.

ABINGDON SCHOOL   *Played 16: W 4, L 5, D 7. A 1*

Master i/c: A. M. Broadbent

Luke List, an all-rounder who could bowl fast, played for Oxfordshire.

Batting—H. R. W. Whalen 14–2–426–81–0–35.50; *L. R. J. List 13–0–341–56–0–26.23; R. J. Finch 13–1–270–63–0–22.50; J. R. V. Dolleymore 13–2–234–74–0–21.27; J. R. C. Horton 12–0–230–76–0–19.16.

Bowling—S. E. Watts 175.5–40–659–30–4/49–21.96; L. R. J. List 160–39–510–22–4/53–23.18.

ALLEYN'S SCHOOL   *Played 14: W 4, L 6, D 4*

Master i/c: D. Tickner   Cricket professional: P. Edwards

M. A. R. Bennett's 160 not out was the highest innings for 40 years. The side included twins Thomas and James Allen.

Batting—M. A. R. Bennett 13–3–617–160*–2–61.70; *M. H. Berglund 14–2–344–62*–0–28.66; S. Z. Tabassum 12–1–289–58–0–26.27; T. J. Allen 11–1–248–69*–0–24.80; S. Payne 13–0–291–59–0–22.38.

Bowling—S. Payne 71.4–6–274–15–5/49–18.26; J. L. Allen 116.2–10–459–22–4/41–20.86.

AMPLEFORTH COLLEGE   *Played 15: W 9, L 3, D 3. A 3*

Master i/c: G. D. Thurman   Cricket professional: D. Wilson

Batting—H. R. P. Lucas 15–1–554–80–0–39.57; R. J. Simpson 15–1–495–92–0–35.35; T. E. L. Walsh 10–2–190–33–0–23.75; P. Field 14–0–322–72–0–23.00; P. Wilkie 13–2–218–64*–0–19.81.

Bowling—T. E. Pinsent 132–29–419–22–5/63–19.04; D. A. H. Johnston Stewart 113–16–489–19–4/44–25.73; P. Wilkie 189–37–651–25–6/72–26.04; C. G. Shillington 83.5–9–422–16–5/32–26.37.

ARDINGLY COLLEGE   *Played 22: W 7, L 9, D 6. A 1*

Master i/c: R. A. King   Cricket professional: S. Sawant

Batting—G. M. Turner 22–4–982–172*–2–54.55; *G. I. Best 13–1–504–122*–2–42.00; N. Strugnell 12–2–227–108–1–22.70; J. R. Andrews 18–2–358–96–0–22.37; M. F. Lacey 9–0–187–97–0–20.77; J. C. M. Lindsten 10–1–162–49–0–18.00; R. J. Willis 13–0–186–43–0–14.30; A. D. H. Spencer 20–0–239–32–0–11.95.

Bowling—G. I. Best 115.2–15–483–23–5/38–21.00; J. K. Dower 154.2–41–579–23–5/26–25.17; A. D. H. Spencer 103–10–513–20–4/12–25.65; G. M. Turner 130.3–10–541–18–4/49–30.05; A. J. Toomey 130.4–12–692–21–5/40–32.95.

ARNOLD SCHOOL   *Played 13: W 5, L 7, D 1. A 4*

Master i/c: D. Grimshaw   Cricket professional: J. Simmons

Led by David Fielding, who represented the XI for a record fourth season, the side fielded enthusiastically and played positively. A highlight was an unbroken partnership of 143 in 18 overs against Old Arnoldians between Fielding and Martin Wallwork.

Batting—*D. Fielding 12–3–518–105–1–57.55; M. Wallwork 13–2–451–92*–0–41.00; J. Ashworth 8–1–156–51–0–22.28; A. Pickup 10–0–150–45–0–15.00; T. Lyles 13–0–192–69–0–14.76.

Bowling—M. Wallwork 62.3–13–214–15–3/27–14.26; J. Ashworth 108–18–356–19–3/39–18.73.

ASHVILLE COLLEGE   *Played 18: W 2, L 3, D 13. A 1*

Master i/c: S. Herrington

The season was dominated by fifth-formers Richard Rawlings, whose 850 runs beat by three the previous record, and Ben Quick, who would have done better than his 37 wickets had more catches been held.

Batting—R. Rawlings 16–1–850–116*–3–56.66; J. Cartwright 16–0–460–78–0–28.75; B. Quick 13–2–309–66–0–28.09; J. Cousen 16–0–358–57–0–22.37.

Bowling—J. Cartwright 87–5–255–17–5/31–15.00; B. Quick 177–28–674–37–6/16–18.21.

BABLAKE SCHOOL   *Played 14: W 4, L 5, D 5. A 1*

Master i/c: B. J. Sutton

Stephen Byng and Adam Smyth, younger brother of the captain, both played for Warwickshire Under-14, while Hedley Ayres represented Warwickshire Under-16.

Batting—M. Wisdish 13–1–331–58–0–27.58; S. D. Byng 9–1–220–61*–0–27.50; C. J. Gardiner 10–0–271–67–0–27.10; A. C. Smyth 11–3–162–41*–0–20.25; *S. N. Smyth 12–0–218–68–0–18.16.

Bowling—H. Ayres 112–22–405–25–6/40–16.20; A. C. Smyth 92.4–21–302–17–4/18–17.76.

BANCROFT'S SCHOOL   *Played 21: W 12, L 5, D 4*

Master i/c: J. G. Bromfield   Cricket professional: J. K. Lever

One of the side's most successful seasons, with a record number of victories, owed much to Philip Baker, who led from the front. His 1,100 runs were a school record, as were his four centuries. The highest of these was 140 not out in an unbroken opening partnership of 204 with David Hurd against Colfe's. He also took 31 wickets with his lively medium-pace and held ten catches, being well supported with both bat and ball by Stuart Greenhill and Philip Eacott.

Batting—*P. D. Baker 21–7–1,100–140*–4–78.57; P. M. Eacott 18–6–524–113*–1–43.66; S. M. Greenhill 18–3–561–98–0–37.40; D. M. Hurd 21–3–605–82*–0–33.61; J. R. Davey 18–0–372–72–0–20.66.

Bowling—P. D. Baker 226.3–45–792–31–4/23–25.54; P. M. Eacott 166–24–629–23–5/19–27.34; S. M. Greenhill 208.3–26–710–25–3/46–28.40.

BANGOR GRAMMAR SCHOOL   *Played 23: W 13, L 4, D 6. A 3*

Master i/c: C. C. J. Harte

Another successful season culminated in a tour of north-west England. A more ambitious tour was planned for December, to the Sydney Youth Cricket Festival.

Batting—B. J. Cunningham 19–3–778–116–3–48.62; M. T. C. English 20–3–556–103*–1–32.70; M. J. Williamson 18–4–374–52–0–26.71; N. M. Scott 20–1–387–69–0–20.36; J. C. W. Harte 13–4–177–35–0–19.66; M. K. Hutchinson 14–4–168–76*–0–16.80; A. E. Magowan 18–1–280–55*–0–16.47; M. McBride 21–3–254–44–0–14.11.

Bowling—P. B. Neill 50.3–12–165–17–4/3–9.70; M. J. Williamson 147–46–379–38–5/17–9.97; J. C. W. Harte 142.5–34–375–35–5/23–10.71; M. R. Cheevers 151.4–35–457–33–4/20–13.84; M. K. Hutchinson 121.2–19–471–27–5/33–17.44.

BARNARD CASTLE SCHOOL   *Played 18: W 9, L 3, D 6. A 1*

Master i/c: C. P. Johnson

Jodie Hatch was again to the fore, taking his tally in two years to 1,700 runs and 80 wickets. However, the side's success owed as much to a fine team effort, in which Hatch was well supported by Martin Walker, Simon Whitehead and his own brother, Nick – with whom he put on 172 for the first wicket against the touring Antipodeans.

Batting—J. W. Hatch 18–2–802–149–2–50.12; S. N. Whitehead 17–5–417–105–1–34.75; M. G. J. Walker 18–3–354–50–0–23.60; N. G. Hatch 17–1–254–46–0–15.87; P. Martin 12–1–62–54–0–14.72; L. A. J. Haslam 18–3–172–30–0–11.46.

Bowling—J. W. Hatch 140.3–23–419–33–5/19–12.69; D. M. Cook 112–26–339–23–4/15–14.73; N. G. Hatch 219.3–47–666–42–6/54–15.85; M. G. J. Walker 221–59–668–40–7/27–16.70.

BEDFORD SCHOOL   *Played 18: W 12, L 2, D 4*

Master i/c: D. W. Jarrett   Cricket professional: R. G. Caple

In a climax to their best ever season, Bedford again won all three games at the Stowe Festival. They owed much to Toby Bailey, who collected 894 runs and 42 dismissals, going on to play for MCC Schools and NCA Young Cricketers and join Northamptonshire on a summer contract. He was well supported by the batting of Marc Snell, who returned to form, and the bowling of Amir Gulzar.

Batting—*T. M. B. Bailey 20–6–894–120*–3–63.85; M. E. Snell 19–2–731–125–1–43.00; B. J. Smith 16–2–310–79–0–22.14; S. S. H. Amerasekera 16–5–194–52–0–17.63; B. S. Cheema 19–2–291–46–0–17.11; M. J. Oliver 14–0–168–42–0–12.00.

Bowling—A. Gulzar 235–52–615–44–6/60–13.97; T. W. J. Chapman 205–40–657–30–5/25–21.90; T. B. J. Beagent 274–62–794–34–7/36–23.35; M. J. Oliver 163–22–615–22–5/50–27.95; B. J. Smith 209–54–603–20–4/43–30.15.

BEDFORD MODERN SCHOOL   *Played 20: W 7, L 1, D 12. A 2*

Master i/c: N. J. Chinneck

Highlights were a return of seven for 11 against The Leys by Ashley Sharp, bowling fast-medium, and the batting of Ivan Chadwick, who scored 106 against Highgate plus seven fifties.

Batting—R. D. T. Barcock 8–6–153–66*–0–76.50; I. R. Chadwick 19–0–825–106–1–43.42; K. P. Harris 15–6–318–66–0–35.33; O. J. Clayson 14–3–379–69*–0–34.45; P. E. Timewell 18–2–449–68–0–28.06; K. Patel 13–1–332–70–0–27.66; *A. G. Brown 18–3–358–66–0–23.86.

Bowling—A. L. Sharp 139.5–39–446–23–7/11–19.39; P. E. Timewell 94.3–14–418–16–4/43–26.12.

BEECHEN CLIFF SCHOOL   *Played 10: W 6, L 3, D 1. A 2*

Master i/c: K. J. L. Mabe   Cricket professional: P. J. Colbourne

Inspired by a five-wicket victory over MCC, the team put behind them an indifferent start to the season and went on to win their last four matches, a particular highlight being the defeat of a strong Colston's Collegiate side. Ben Staunton, who was available for only three matches, passed 1,000 runs for the XI and played for Somerset Second XI.

Batting—B. R. F. Staunton 3–2–197–108*–1–197.00; N. G. Priscott 8–1–270–93–0–38.57; S. L. Kembery 8–1–189–52–0–27.00; J. E. Brunt 9–0–150–63–0–16.66.

Bowling—M. Thorburn 137.2–40–379–22–5/26–17.22.

BERKHAMSTED SCHOOL *Played 17: W 3, L 10, D 4*

Master i/c: J. G. Tolchard   Cricket professional: M. Herring

The side was captained by Edward Tolchard, son of Jeff Tolchard, who played for Leicestershire.

Batting—G. A. S. McHugh 17–0–501–81–0–29.47; *E. N. Tolchard 17–3–407–61*–0–29.07; M. D. Pullen 16–1–336–55*–0–22.40; C. M. Aitken 15–1–288–66–0–20.57.

Bowling—L. J. Honour 89–12–377–18–5/14–20.94; E. N. Clark 144–21–565–18–3/4–31.38.

BIRKENHEAD SCHOOL *Played 15: W 6, L 3, D 6*

Master i/c: P. A. Whittel

Andrew Birley, who headed the bowling, played for MCC Schools, NCA Young Cricketers and English Schools. The XI was coached by Hartley Alleyne.

Batting—Z. R. Feather 12–4–475–116*–1–59.37; O. J. Rule 8–0–209–74–0–26.12; R. N. Cross 14–5–205–44*–0–22.77; W. P. L. Roberts 14–0–299–74–0–21.35; *A. B. Birley 9–1–152–55–0–19.00; S. J. Carpenter 14–1–230–40–0–17.69; R. J. Whalley 12–0–206–47–0–17.16.

Bowling—A. B. Birley 140–48–323–33–7/6–9.78; Z. R. Feather 116–36–355–21–3/25–16.90; B. C. Attwood 124–27–480–22–5/78–21.81.

BISHOP'S STORTFORD COLLEGE *Played 20: W 7, L 3, D 9, T 1*

Master i/c: D. A. Hopper   Cricket professional: R. J. Pithey

A strong batting line-up compiled six totals of 200 or more, including a record 301 for nine against Stamford. The ground fielding was superb, but the slip catching was less reliable and the attack depended too heavily on Andrew Bruce. Two sets of brothers played in the XI: Sam Fishpool, who was an aggressive and positive captain, and his younger brother Paul, plus James and Andrew Hill, both excellent fielders.

Batting—*S. J. C. Fishpool 20–1–631–87–0–33.21; P. J. H. Fishpool 19–3–480–76–0–30.00; D. O'Donnell 20–0–587–88–0–29.35; J. J. Mew 18–3–404–102*–1–26.93; N. T. McEwan 11–2–232–60–0–25.77; L. P. Westell 16–3–244–66–0–18.76; S. F. Shearing 14–3–190–62*–0–17.27; T. N. Bunbury 15–3–163–23*–0–13.58.

Bowling—A. J. Bruce 244.1–41–794–42–6/51–18.90; S. J. C. Fishpool 174.1–45–495–25–3/16–19.80; J. F. Beatty 122–20–466–19–4/53–24.52; L. P. Westell 202–45–712–24–6/65–29.66.

BLOXHAM SCHOOL *Played 14: W 4, L 3, D 7. A 3*

Master i/c: C. N. Boyns

Batting—I. de Weymarn 14–5–616–100*–1–68.44; M. Palmer 14–3–543–111*–2–49.36; R. Tarrant 10–1–275–92–0–30.55; *M. Hicks 12–2–266–45*–0–26.60.

Bowling—P. Thompson 62–9–259–16–4/23–16.18; R. Moore 129–36–381–22–6/27–17.31; S. Covington 160–35–493–26–4/45–18.96.

BLUNDELL'S SCHOOL *Played 15: W 2, L 11, D 2. A 1*

Master i/c: N. A. Folland   Cricket professional: R. H. Harriott

In a season of rebuilding, Paul Warren made a useful all-round contribution, his seam bowling particularly impressive at times, while Mark Vaughan scored the side's only century to bring victory over Clifton. However, they were too often let down by fragile batting.

Batting—M. Vaughan 15–3–464–115*–1–38.66; J. Francis 15–0–422–98–0–28.13; P. Warren 13–2–292–51–0–26.54; E. Hulme 9–0–193–49–0–21.44; Q. Miller 15–0–281–66–0–18.73; *J. Goode 14–1–167–45–0–12.84.

Bowling—P. Warren 198–33–646–28–4/22–23.07; Q. Miller 121–14–558–17–4/33–32.82; P. Stormonth 194–29–793–15–4/23–52.86.

BRADFIELD COLLEGE   Played 15: W 3, L 4, D 8. A 1

Master i/c: D. R. Evans   Cricket professional: J. F. Harvey

Although they won only three matches, the wins were against strong opposition: the Old Boys, MCC and the touring Hamilton Boys HS from New Zealand. Brothers Russell and Jonathan Perkins both played for the side.

Batting—R. J. Holland 13–2–415–95–0–37.72; J. R. Perkins 14–1–399–75–0–30.69; H. G. Austen-Brown 13–3–277–54*–0–27.70; W. M. Robinson 14–6–208–55*–0–26.00; *R. D. Perkins 15–1–353–68–0–25.21; R. S. Walker 9–1–180–36–0–22.50; B. C. Petter 15–0–335–72–0–22.33.

Bowling—N. A. Denning 140.4–35–366–19–6/37–19.26; W. J. N. Gemmel 113–20–343–17–5/51–20.17; R. D. Perkins 95.3–15–349–17–3/25–20.52; W. M. Robinson 149.3–28–586–16–3/18–36.62.

BRADFORD GRAMMAR SCHOOL   Played 27: W 7, L 11, D 9. A 2

Master i/c: A. G. Smith

An exciting season culminated in an enjoyable and stimulating tour of Kenya. Simon Davies, with 1,050 runs in the school season and 374 on tour, became the first to make 1,000 for the school. His four centuries were also a record, as was his career aggregate of 3,047 runs. He was well supported by the wicket-keeper David Greaves, most notably in a record partnership of 230 against Manchester GS. The bowling lacked penetration, although the discovery of the young opening bowler Karl Howes was a bonus.

Batting—*S. E. P. Davies 26–3–1,424–143*–4–61.91; D. J. Greaves 27–2–755–137–1–30.20; A. J. Myers 25–2–515–79–0–22.39; M. R. Snow 22–3–392–65–0–20.63; J. R. Cockcroft 18–3–246–43–0–16.40; A. J. Modgill 24–4–294–31–0–16.33; P. J. Bates 13–1–180–27–0–15.00; C. H. Harper 13–0–159–41–0–12.23.

Bowling—K. D. A. Howes 93.4–21–272–20–4/22–13.60; A. C. Jackson 87.1–14–372–15–3/28–24.80; G. R. Saxton 120–14–554–22–4/45–25.18; G. S. Kinvig 128–19–555–22–5/33–25.22; J. R. Cockcroft 156.2–18–672–22–5/47–30.54; I. M. Elson 182.1–24–812–25–3/17–32.48; A. J. Myers 166.3–26–671–18–4/42–37.27.

BRENTWOOD SCHOOL   Played 13: W 3, L 4, D 6

Master i/c: B. R. Hardie

Batting—N. D. E. Boyce 6–1–165–67–0–33.00; E. J. Hearn 12–2–283–56–0–28.30; J. R. Stanton 11–1–324–69*–0–27.00; P. D. A. Jones 12–1–232–60–0–21.09; J. E. P. Crapnell 12–0–229–56–0–19.08.

Bowling—A. W. Pratt 129–27–490–20–5/15–24.50; R. A. J. Wybrow 92–6–380–15–4/52–25.33.

BRIGHTON COLLEGE   Played 20: W 4, L 7, D 9. A 1

Master i/c: J. Spencer   Cricket professional: J. D. Morley

Following a winter tour of Zimbabwe, Brighton College celebrated their 150th anniversary by holding a successful and enjoyable International Cricket Festival in July, with Prince Edward School from Harare, Hamilton Boys' High from New Zealand and Newington College from Sydney.

Batting—G. B. F. Hudson 19–3–659–106*–2–41.18; S. E. Green 16–0–487–75–0–30.43; R. Shepley-Smith 20–1–479–114–1–25.21; J. B. James 10–2–187–47*–0–23.37; J. B. Holt 10–1–186–84–0–20.66; R. W. Ainsworth 10–1–157–69*–0–17.44; T. P. Gayton 15–1–235–57–0–16.78; R. J. Watkins 16–4–177–56*–0–14.75.

Bowling—A. J. Pope 152.2–27–494–28–6/31–17.64; R. Shepley-Smith 141.3–28–476–19–4/11–25.05; G. B. F. Hudson 190.3–30–747–25–4/71–29.88.

BRISTOL GRAMMAR SCHOOL   Played 18: W 5, L 11, D 2. A 2

Masters i/c: K. R. Blackburn and D. M. Crawford

A highlight was a first win over Richard Huish, thanks to a magnificent unbeaten century from Mike Sutherland.

Batting—A. M. Richardson 15-2-388-72-0-29.84; J. A. Tyler 18-2-468-97-0-29.25; M. D. Sutherland 17-2-431-111*-1-28.73; M. N. Bolton 9-3-155-37-0-25.83; J. P. Barnes 9-1-195-56-0-24.37; R. M. Dallimore 15-2-261-82*-0-20.07; *A. J. Mitchell 12-2-164-33-0-16.40; J. A. Reed 16-3-165-39-0-12.69.

Bowling—G. J. Moore 104-8-465-20-3/13-23.25; A. J. Mitchell 156-39-540-22-4/83-24.54.

BROMSGROVE SCHOOL   *Played 16: W 6, L 3, D 7. A 3*

Master i/c: P. Newman

Batting—E. P. Sawtell 15-3-534-103*-1-44.50; A. D. Langlands 10-4-201-55-0-33.50; *W. Glover 12-1-335-73-0-30.45; P. Goodrem 13-2-327-101-1-29.72; R. Meese 15-1-320-63*-0-22.85; R. Gough 12-1-250-75*-0-22.72; E. Binham 11-2-201-43-0-22.33.

Bowling—J. Robertson 151.1-32-440-28-7/40-15.71; R. Howell 157-23-521-22-4/26-23.68; A. D. Langlands 136.5-19-547-21-4/30-26.04.

BRYANSTON SCHOOL   *Played 16: W 8, L 4, D 4. A 1*

Master i/c: T. J. Hill

Tim Lamb, who scored hundreds against Monkton Combe (136) and King's, Bruton (100 not out), played for English Schools, MCC Schools and NCA Young Cricketers. Tom Brunner took his 100th wicket in his fourth season.

Batting—*T. C. Z. Lamb 15-2-804-136-2-61.84; P. J. Brenchley 16-2-659-94-0-47.07; T. P. W. Brunner 10-4-179-49-0-29.83; P. G. P. Chapman 11-4-176-40*-0-25.14; B. E. Leigh 15-2-215-45-0-16.53; E. O. G. Hunt 15-0-198-44-0-13.20.

Bowling—T. P. W. Brunner 198-49-510-36-6/21-14.16; T. C. Z. Lamb 92-17-358-18-3/32-19.88; T. H. Jenkins 116.1-34-372-16-2/15-23.25; S. J. Denning 131.3-11-477-17-5/79-28.05.

CAMPBELL COLLEGE   *Played 12: W 6, L 4, D 2*

Master i/c: E. T. Cooke   Cricket professional: S. Walker

Batting—*J. H. S. Montgomery 10-3-415-93-0-59.28.

Bowling—J. H. S. Montgomery 63-11-191-16-4/33-11.93; R. K. Long 84-7-271-15-5/58-18.06.

CANFORD SCHOOL   *Played 25: W 18, L 6, D 1. A 3*

Master i/c: A. Hobbs   Cricket professional: J. J. E. Hardy

A highlight was the tour to Barbados, where Canford won the Sir Garfield Sobers Schools Cricket Festival, thanks to a strong batting line-up and the presence of three good off-spinners in Toby Cutler, Jon Druitt and Peter Young, plus leg-spinner Andrew Major.

Batting—A. Major 20-4-658-119-1-41.12; T. Cutler 25-2-844-115-1-36.69; *S. Neal 23-2-746-116-1-35.52; R. Lawson 17-4-411-91-0-31.61; N. Makin 24-3-663-83-0-31.57; N. Lebas 22-5-360-58-0-21.17; P. Stapleton 16-0-232-68-0-14.50.

Bowling—P. Young 60.2-3-228-19-3/10-12.00; J. Druitt 139-16-580-35-4/27-16.57; T. Cutler 201.1-44-621-37-4/10-16.78; N. Makin 191.1-32-614-33-3/21-18.60; A. Major 134.4-19-542-26-3/12-20.84; S. Neal 112.5-22-378-17-2/10-22.23.

CATERHAM SCHOOL   *Played 16: W 9, L 3, D 4. A 1*

Master i/c: A. G. Tapp   Cricket professional: W. Raja

Tim Slade was an outstanding seam bowler, whose 57 wickets included eight for 46 against Hampton School and a hat-trick against the Old Caterhamians. B. Barton also performed the feat against the touring New Forest High School from Durban.

Batting—M. Miller 14-4-272-44-0-27.20; G. Goodwin 14-5-241-50*-0-26.77; R. Jackson 16-1-380-69*-0-25.33; N. Alexander 11-4-153-34-0-21.85; A. Patel 15-3-230-40-0-19.16; B. Barton 13-0-172-54-0-13.23.

Bowling—T. Slade 270-74-670-57-8/46-11.75; B. Barton 161-34-482-37-6/36-13.02; R. Jackson 95.5-25-284-17-7/24-16.70; M. Miller 137-15-434-19-4/56-22.84.

CHARTERHOUSE   *Played 23: W 3, L 9, D 11*

Master i/c: J. M. Knight   Cricket professional: R. V. Lewis

It was a season of rebuilding after the departure of what was probably the best side for some years. Without the prolific L. J. Webb and G. H. Tassell, who had scored 762 and 604 runs respectively in 1994, the batting relied on S. D. Brazier and T. J. W. Dawes, who made 1,260 runs between them. Slow left-armer C. J. Allen confirmed his promise of the previous year by taking his wickets.

Batting—S. D. Brazier 17-1-658-99*-0-41.12; T. J. W. Dawes 21-2-602-111*-2-31.68; A. J. M. Burrows 21-0-492-69-0-23.42; J. R. C. Hamblin 18-3-345-64*-0-23.00; W. J. McKeran 14-2-274-80-0-22.83; B. M. J. Warburton 16-2-256-48-0-18.28; *M. W. R. Bowes 9-0-152-38-0-16.88; N. A. Hare 10-0-153-45-0-15.30; J. R. Dyson 13-1-161-28-0-13.41; W. J. S. Evans 16-4-154-34-0-12.83.

Bowling—W. J. S. Evans 102.3-11-393-19-3/54-20.68; B. M. J. Warburton 143.2-26-592-27-5/13-21.92; C. J. Allen 270.5-72-788-28-5/60-28.14; W. J. McKeran 148-24-593-17-4/34-34.88; J. R. C. Hamblin 192.3-34-714-16-3/33-44.62.

CHELTENHAM COLLEGE   *Played 15: W 2, L 1, D 12. A 1*

Master i/c: M. W. Stovold   Cricket professional: M. Briers

Batting—W. F. A. Chambers 10-4-370-71*-0-61.66; S. T. J. Cowley 14-3-387-89-0-35.18; T. D. A. Arengo-Jones 9-1-206-66-0-25.75; *M. S. Inglis 10-1-221-69*-0-24.55; R. A. Harding 8-0-186-57-0-23.25; T. R. Allen 13-0-242-66-0-18.61.

Bowling—R. L. Dredge 170.2-22-460-24-4/25-19.16; D. J. E. Brown 210.4-31-854-39-5/52-21.89.

CHIGWELL SCHOOL   *Played 15: W 6, L 7, D 2. A 2*

Master i/c: D. N. Morrison   Cricket professional: F. A. Griffith

The victory over Highams Park School was memorable for the season's best batting and bowling performances: 143 from M. Ali and six for 30 from N. J. Timpson. Ali also shared a partnership of 118 with G. Calder against Magdalen College School at the Wellingborough Festival.

Batting—M. Ali 15-3-598-143-3-49.83; G. Calder 13-2-258-58-0-23.45; *T. J. Jolly 15-1-320-54-0-22.85; K. S. Choudhry 12-2-190-79*-0-19.00; R. Chauhan 14-0-225-46-0-16.07; S. Spindlow 11-0-153-26-0-13.90.

Bowling—D. Sharma 144-33-481-28-4/36-17.17; M. Ali 89-27-292-16-5/21-18.25; R. Chauhan 173.1-34-552-29-5/43-19.03; O. Mahmood 71.4-8-288-15-4/23-19.20.

CHRIST COLLEGE, BRECON   *Played 15: W 3, L 2, D 10. A 2*

Master i/c: C. W. Kleiser   Cricket professional: R. P. Lefebvre

Cricket is blossoming at the College, for whom a highlight was the defeat of Royal GS, Worcester. Andrew Davies, who headed both sets of averages, joined Glamorgan on a full contract and played for Welsh Schools.

Batting—*A. P. Davies 9-1-369-101-1-46.12; T. D. T. Harbottle 13-1-288-84*-0-24.00; B. G. John 11-2-173-41-0-19.22; R. J. W. Fish 11-1-171-50-0-17.10; R. J. Chilman 13-0-216-50-0-16.61.

Bowling—A. P. Davies 73.2-14-246-16-5/25-15.37; C. M. P. Davenport 144.4-25-455-29-5/28-15.68; G. E. Colville 128-28-462-22-4/29-21.00; R. H. Jones 133.1-19-423-19-4/19-22.26.

CHRIST'S COLLEGE, FINCHLEY   *Played 20: W 6, L 9, D 5*

Master i/c: S. S. Goldsmith

Batting—M. H. Cable 11-1-412-106-1-41.20; C. Depala 9-0-156-44-0-17.33; R. R. Persad 18-1-229-45-0-13.47.

Bowling—A. Bijlani 96.4-14-383-26-5/11-14.73; R. Depala 79.4-11-283-16-5/30-17.68.

CHRIST'S HOSPITAL   *Played 15: W 5, L 2, D 8. A 2*

Master i/c: H. P. Holdsworth   Cricket professionals: K. G. Suttle and P. J. Graves

Batting—*A. M. Buset 13–3–401–86–0–40.10; P. J. Wilkins 14–2–336–91–0–28.00; J. J. Kingsbury 14–3–253–55*–0–23.00; R. J. Pannell 10–2–151–28–0–18.87; J. R. Berressem 14–1–221–40–0–17.00; N. J. Codd 13–0–216–50–0–16.61; J. A. Cordery 15–1–215–52*–0–15.35; P. N. E Hughes 12–1–154–32–0–14.00.

Bowling—J. R. Berressem 126.1–26–443–29–4/14–15.27; B. M. H. Bystry 174–32–560–33–5/25–16.96; A. H. Meredith-Jones 177.1–21–571–33–6/53–17.30.

CLAYESMORE SCHOOL   *Played 16: W 7, L 6, D 3*

Masters i/c: R. J. Hammond and R. J. Denning

Opening batsman Matthew Swarbrick was outstanding. He became the first to score 1,000 in a season – including seven centuries, with three in successive matches – broke his own innings record with 152 not out against Milton Abbey and in the same match set a new record partnership for any wicket when he put on 217 with his opening partner, Tom Hicks, who also headed the bowling. Swarbrick, who has represented Dorset and Wiltshire at rugby and Dorset at swimming, played cricket for Dorset and Hampshire Second XI.

Batting—*M. Swarbrick 15–2–1,251–152*–7–96.23; A. M. Philp 13–4–444–82*–0–49.33; T. C. Hicks 15–3–505–105*–2–42.08; R. J. Wyatt 10–3–259–96–0–37.00.

Bowling—T. C. Hicks 216–43–713–32–6/32–22.28; A. M. Philp 186–26–628–26–5/42–24.15.

CLIFTON COLLEGE   *Played 16: W 5, L 6, D 5. A 3*

Master i/c: D. C. Henderson   Cricket professional: F. J. Andrew

June was a prolific month for David England, who scored 359 in four innings. In July the side toured Barbados, where they reached the semi-finals of the Sir Garfield Sobers Schools Cricket Festival.

Batting—*D. J. R. England 16–1–663–112*–2–44.20; G. J. Corrigan 10–2–285–87–0–35.62; R. W. Swetman 12–0–386–72–0–32.16; B. Lockwood 13–3–253–60–0–25.30; D. R. Grewcock 15–1–335–57–0–23.92; D. A. Kirtley 14–1–251–76–0–19.30; J. D. Walters 10–0–181–43–0–18.10; J. Kitchen 12–3–154–40*–0–17.11.

Bowling—B. Lockwood 199.2–31–745–34–6/59–21.91; B. A. Love 178–26–602–27–6/48–22.29.

COLSTON'S COLLEGIATE SCHOOL   *Played 18: W 11, L 3, D 4. A 1*

Master i/c: M. P. B. Tayler

In the school's most successful season, Christopher Taylor was outstanding. His 1,597 runs at 106.46 took his tally for three years to 3,414 and included 809 in ten days. He has scored 14 hundreds in all, the eight in 1995 including 210 against the XL Club and 278 not out against Hutton GS, which equalled the record for an English public school – J. L. Guise's 278 for Winchester against Eton in 1921. He also took 31 wickets with his off-spin, being well supported in both departments by Alistair Bell, whose 652 runs and 34 wickets would have been more prominent in any other XI. Taylor went on to play for Gloucestershire Second XI, NAYC, MCC Schools and English schools.

Batting—*C. G. Taylor 18–3–1,597–278*–8–106.46; A. J. Bell 17–4–652–94*–0–50.15; R. M. Bryan 17–6–515–109*–1–46.81; J. A. Ewens 15–2–471–67–0–36.23; B. S. Tarasiuk 13–2–281–77*–0–25.54.

Bowling—A. J. Bell 131.5–19–487–34–6/46–14.32; C. G. Taylor 165.1–39–585–31–5/61–18.87; B. S. Tarasiuk 87.2–5–471–23–4/20–20.47.

CRANBROOK SCHOOL   *Played 19: W 7, L 5, D 7. A 1*

Master i/c: A. J. Presnell

A highlight was a first win for 26 years over Sutton Valence, featuring a first-wicket stand of 168 in 18 overs between Dan Furnival and Nick Pink.

Batting—N. Byrom 15–1–398–70–0–28.42; D. Furnival 19–0–537–90–0–28.26; P. Wicken 8–2–154–58*–0–25.66; J. Harfoot 11–3–190–37–0–23.75; N. Pink 18–2–334–100*–1–20.87.

Bowling—W. Chuter 45.3–9–104–15–5/17–6.93; B. Cowan 168.4–54–411–24–4/27–17.12; H. Trollope 167–21–536–30–8/18–17.86; P. Wicken 123.3–19–364–18–6/10–20.22; D. Guy 116.5–21–381–15–3/29–25.40.

CRANLEIGH SCHOOL   *Played 17: W 4, L 4, D 9. A 2*

Master i/c: D. C. Williams

The side played positively and attractively, the preponderance of draws reflecting their lack of a strike bowler to finish off the opposition in several close finishes. Ben Wright and the Hillier brothers were the mainstays of the attack, while the batting was stronger than in the previous season with the consistent Graeme Brown and D. E. M. G. Copleston both passing 500 runs.

Batting—*G. A. M. Brown 17–2–533–76*–0–35.53; D. E. M. G. Copleston 17–1–533–103*–1–33.31; J. Bennett 9–2–195–50–0–27.85; N. S. Shepherd 10–3–184–80–0–26.28; L. E. Moorby 15–4–215–63*–0–19.54; J. C. D. Wright 12–2–187–45–0–18.70; M. D. Colgate 14–1–172–37–0–13.23.

Bowling—B. J. Wright 163–26–638–30–6/50–21.26; A. G. Hillier 144.1–21–483–22–8/44–21.95; M. J. Hillier 172–36–538–19–5/60–28.31.

CULFORD SCHOOL   *Played 16: W 4, L 4, D 8*

Master i/c: R. P. Shepperson

The season featured some close finishes: Wisbech GS and St Joseph's, Ipswich, were beaten in exciting run-chases and MCC took the last wicket with three balls remaining. Another highlight was the two-day, two-innings Centenary match against the Old Culfordians. Matthew Grinham's aggregate of 598 runs was a school record, while George Ornbo led his young side and the attack excellently, taking 42 wickets with his fast left-arm deliveries, as well as playing some crucial middle-order innings.

Batting—M. J. L. Grinham 17–2–598–87–0–39.86; *G. A. Ornbo 17–5–285–52*–0–23.75; D. S. Holliday 15–1–282–61–0–20.14; B. Backhouse 15–0–301–70–0–20.06; G. N. Lindley 13–0–244–58–0–18.76; S. F. Ornbo 17–1–260–42–0–16.25.

Bowling—M. J. L. Grinham 143–32–360–27–5/16–13.33; G. A. Ornbo 203–44–630–42–8/39–15.00; P. R. Hamshere 130–30–393–16–2/21–24.56; B. J. Unwin 149–29–510–16–3/39–31.87.

DARTFORD GRAMMAR SCHOOL   *Played 16: W 3, L 5, D 7, T 1. A 2*

Masters i/c: C. J. Plummer and G. T. Prout

In the tied match against Bishop's Stortford, both sides were dismissed for 130.

Batting—M. J. L. Pask 16–0–491–98–0–30.68; E. C. Tyler 10–0–262–49–0–26.20; K. C. Newman 14–0–266–50–0–19.00; D. J. Hills 16–1–277–69*–0–18.46.

Bowling—D. W. Ring 104.1–18–372–26–6/17–14.30; M. J. L. Pask 139.3–33–440–30–6/41–14.66.

DAUNTSEY'S SCHOOL   *Played 15: W 9, L 2, D 4*

Master i/c: D. C. R. Baker   Cricket professional: P. Knowles

Batting—O. Lawson 15–1–475–117*–1–33.92; M. Gauguier 13–3–322–51–0–32.20; D. Hagelthorn 10–5–159–69*–0–31.80; *S. Gaiger 15.4–286–65–0–26.00; D. Bell 15–1–323–75–0–23.07; N. Paget 13–4–197–51–0–21.88; J. Hope 15–0–298–70–0–19.86.

Bowling—D. Hagelthorn 159.1–28–552–28–4/18–19.71; D. Bell 122–35–395–20–3/19–19.75; A. Houchin 88–18–365–18–4/5–20.27; O. Lawson 150–32–546–20–3/46–27.30.

DEAN CLOSE SCHOOL   *Played 18: W 7, L 2, D 9. A 2*

Master i/c: C. M. Kenyon   Cricket professional: S. Hansford

The excellent results owed much to the captain and fast bowler, Mpumelelo Mbangwa from Zimbabwe, who set high standards and often proved too good for the opposition. Opening batsman Anthony Thompson, who was also a useful fast bowler, set three new batting records with 746 runs, three centuries and his innings of 155 not out against King's, Worcester.

Batting—A. J. Thompson 17–1–746–155*–3–46.62; *M. Mbangwa 17–3–446–72*–0–31.85; D. T. Gilroy 17–1–445–69–0–27.81; N. G. A. Miller 15–2–297–83–0–22.84; J. Mears 11–1–152–40–0–15.20.

Bowling—M. Mbangwa 199–41–576–36–5/35–16.00; A. J. Thompson 145–19–606–21–5/33–28.85.

DENSTONE COLLEGE *Played 19: W 9, L 1, D 9. A 4*

Master i/c: A. N. James

In the best season for more than 20 years, Richard Howitt was outstanding. He broke his own aggregate record with 1,016 runs at a record average of 101.60, overtaking Alistair Hignell's career record for the school with 3,006 runs at 46.24. He went on to play for Nottinghamshire Second XI.

Batting—*R. W. J. Howitt 16–6–1,016–113*–3–101.60; A. T. Griffin 14–1–507–150*–1–39.00; P. R. Davies 14–2–408–64–0–34.00; A. I. Foyers 10–4–200–53–0–33.33; M. P. Tweddle 16–3–284–43–0–21.84.

Bowling—A. T. Griffin 144.4–20–482–32–7/34–15.06; B. S. Johal 118.3–34–337–20–5/24–16.85; J. A. J. Cure 205.1–40–625–35–7/46–17.85.

DOUAI SCHOOL *Played 8: W 1, L 4, D 3*

Master i/c: G. Jones   Cricket professional: M. O'Connor

Batting—S. Wicks 7–0–158–79–0–22.57.

Bowling—J. Midmore 111–20–376–20–3/37–18.80; B. Briggs 87–13–307–15–4/37–20.46.

DOVER COLLEGE *Played 15: W 4, L 7, D 4*

Master i/c: D. C. Butler

In a strong attack, which featured four bowlers averaging under 20 for the first time in many years, the left-arm spinner Ashley Couchman took five in an innings four times. The Telford brothers, Matthew and James, showed good all-round form with the former extending his record in four seasons to 937 runs and 52 wickets in 51 appearances.

Batting—*M. T. Telford 14–2–403–83*–0–33.58; J. R. Telford 14–1–288–54–0–22.15; M. J. Brooke 14–2–207–67–0–17.25; C. D. G. Crofton-Martin 14–2–178–37*–0–14.83; S. C. Hooper 14–3–154–56*–0–14.00.

Bowling—J. R. Telford 91.3–21–280–21–5/24–13.33; A. W. Barrow 65.1–5–227–17–3/22–13.35; M. T. Telford 141.2–41–363–27–3/14–13.44; A. A. H. Couchman 237–45–808–44–7/62–18.36.

DOWNSIDE SCHOOL *Played 14: W 4, L 8, D 2. A 2*

Master i/c: K. J. Burke   Cricket professional: J. Bird

Christopher Reid's 46 wickets included eight for 68 against Downside Wanderers.

Batting—J. P. Taylor 12–1–357–74–0–32.45; H. D. Vyvyan 12–0–273–89–0–22.75; E. J. T. Mellish 14–3–202–48*–0–18.36; *C. P. Reid 11–2–157–39–0–17.44.

Bowling—C. P. Reid 186.2–40–538–46–8/68–11.69; B. W. Pountney 101.4–19–294–15–5/24–19.60; I. W. Kirkpatrick 122.1–14–481–16–4/49–30.06.

DUKE OF YORK'S ROYAL MILITARY SCHOOL *Played 14: W 1, L 4, D 9. A 2*

Master i/c: S. Salisbury   Cricket professionals: C. R. Penn and S. J. Milton

Batting—H. P. Jellard 10–3–228–54*–0–32.57.

Bowling—N. I. Barrow 99–25–287–19–5/9–15.10; M. Hayward 94–16–329–18–3/30–18.27; J. D. Budd 89–18–309–16–5/48–19.31.

DULWICH COLLEGE *Played 15: W 6, L 7, D 2*

Master i/c: S. Northcote-Green   Cricket professional: A. Ransom

After a mid-season slump, the XI finished on a high note at the Downside Festival, where the hosts, Strathallan and Royal GS, Lancaster were all beaten. Nateel Bhatti was a prominent all-rounder.

Batting—N. J. Lloyd 14–1–492–109*–1–37.84; N. Bhatti 15–2–480–88–0–36.92; *S. M. Blythe 14–0–300–65–0–21.42; F. Hutton-Mills 12–4–171–38*–0–21.37; A. M. Patel 11–1–172–40–0–17.20.

Bowling—N. J. Easter 103–23–337–17–3/12–19.82; N. Bhatti 146–25–520–21–3/22–24.76; F. Hutton-Mills 151–27–480–17–3/20–28.23.

DURHAM SCHOOL   Played 17: W 11, L 3, D 3. A 4

Master i/c: N. J. Willings   Cricket professional: M. Hirsch

Another fine season began with seven successive victories. Of the seven centuries scored by five batsmen, the most spectacular came from the Moroccan, Omar Jaber, against Ampleforth: he faced 51 balls in 60 minutes, hitting five sixes and 15 fours in 28 scoring shots. Michael Coates and Fraser Diver were both genuine all-rounders with 1,438 runs and 58 wickets between them.

Batting—S. Birtwisle 13–2–572–117–2–52.00; *M. Coates 18–0–820–115–2–45.55; F. Diver 16–2–618–110–1–44.14; W. Halford 20–5–526–101–1–35.06; O. Jaber 18–3–484–100–1–32.26; R. McLaren 18–3–344–57–0–22.93; R. Windows 16–4–196–34–0–16.33.

Bowling—M. Coates 152–48–430–26–5/12–16.53; F. Diver 177–27–566–32–6/9–17.68; O. Jaber 93–8–377–16–3/34–23.56; R. McLaren 175–30–705–25–4/22–28.20; R. Windows 173–27–751–24–4/32–31.29.

EASTBOURNE COLLEGE   Played 18: W 7, L 7, D 4. A 3

Master i/c: N. L. Wheeler   Cricket professional: J. N. Shepherd

A highlight in a mixed season was winning the Langdale Cup. With 15-year-olds A. D. Simcox and M. J. Lock heading the batting and bowling averages respectively, there was optimism for the future.

Batting—A. D. Simcox 16–4–489–75–0–40.75; M. J. Lock 15–2–457–67–0–35.15; *R. F. Marchant 18–2–481–58–0–30.06; M. S. M. Justice 17–0–470–86–0–27.64; S. J. W. Whitton 12–5–176–50*–0–25.14; D. J. M. Garner 13–2–231–58–0–21.00.

Bowling—M. J. Lock 130–32–346–20–3/4–17.30; R. F. S. Hill 85–15–283–16–5/28–17.68; I. E. MacLean 112–22–403–15–4/14–26.86; S. J. W. Whitton 214.2–56–725–25–5/84–29.00.

THE EDINBURGH ACADEMY   Played 18: W 8, L 5, D 5. A 1

Master i/c: P. J. Rodgers

A strong batting side were bowled out only three times, reached 190 nine times and had 12 partnerships of 75 or more. James Gibson, a New Zealander, was outstanding with 46 wickets and 724 runs, including 113 not out against Fettes in a partnership of 177 with Jamie Boyd. Stuart Moffat passed 600 runs for the second successive season and played with distinction for Scotland under-19.

Batting—J. Gibson 18–7–724–113*–1–65.81; *J. S. D. Moffat 17–4–672–104*–1–51.69; P. A. T. G. Rutherford 18–1–425–85–0–25.00; I. A. Hathorn 16–0–374–97–0–23.37; J. P. L. Boyd 15–2–279–91–0–21.46; G. B. Macleod 16–3–161–27–0–12.38.

Bowling—J. Gibson 250–73–634–46–6/37–13.78; I. A. Hathorn 133–24–523–24–5/63–21.79; J. S. D. Moffat 133–39–384–15–2/7–25.60.

ELIZABETH COLLEGE, GUERNSEY   Played 22: W 6, L 7, D 9. A 2

Master i/c: M. E. Kinder

The season was badly affected by rain and the withdrawal of visiting sides to the Island. However, the cricket was positive, and while success came at home against adult club sides, the opposition on a tour to England proved more challenging. Matthew Brehaut was the leading all-rounder, opening the batting and bowling off-spin.

Batting—M. Brehaut 15–3–396–85*–0–33.00; K. R. Graham 16–1–333–69*–0–22.20; O. T. Brock 15–1–297–55–0–21.21; *S. J. Fooks 20–4–329–30–0–20.56; N. J. Bachmann 10–0–196–58–0–19.60; J. M. Arnold 17–2–233–55–0–15.53; M. C. Stokes 17–0–224–85–0–13.17.

Bowling—M. O. Walker 141.1–34–371–22–7/20–16.86; R. A. Collenette 158.4–40–502–27–4/12–18.59; M. Brehaut 139–11–549–26–5/48–21.11.

ELLESMERE COLLEGE   *Played 16: W 3, L 8, D 5*

Master i/c: E. Marsh

Cricket professional: R. G. Mapp

Batting—C. N. C. Hill 11–1–281–56–0–28.10; O. M. Dunk 13–2–281–65–0–25.54; *T. F. Stewart 13–0–328–79–0–25.23; J. P. Terry 12–0–275–46–0–22.91; O. J. Pughe 14–1–230–71*–0–17.69; P. Bisht 15–2–170–41–0–13.07.

Bowling—J. P. Terry 98–18–318–17–7/27–18.70.

ELTHAM COLLEGE   *Played 21: W 7, L 5, D 9*

Masters i/c: P. C. McCartney and B. M. Withecombe   Cricket professionals: R. W. Hills and R. Winup

A strong batting side won the Lemon Cup for the fourth time and against St Dunstan's compiled a record score of 300 for six dec. However, the bowlers struggled on the excellent home wickets.

Batting—B. P. Dell 19–2–686–104–1–40.35; T. W. Barwick 20–2–639–109*–1–35.50; M. Roche 14–3–282–50*–0–25.63; P. S. Pay 19–4–378–66–0–25.20; T. B. Beames 17–3–334–100*–1–23.85; *J. M. Bensted 20–0–401–83–0–20.05; D. J. Hadley 19–1–329–74–0–18.27.

Bowling—P. Fenn 137–31–442–20–5/39–22.10; J. M. Bensted 161.2–33–636–28–3/22–22.71; T. B. Beames 170.3–25–662–24–5/27–27.58.

ENFIELD GRAMMAR SCHOOL   *Played 21: W 4, L 8, D 9. A 2*

Master i/c: M. Alder

Aaron Laraman, who was by far the outstanding batsman, played for Middlesex Second XI and England Under-17.

Batting—A. Laraman 11–3–697–154*–1–87.12; M. Bowen 16–1–383–102*–1–25.53; M. Kapadia 6–0–150–70–0–25.00; M. Marston 14–4–233–52–0–23.30; M. Wright 8–1–157–50*–0–22.42; M. Nicholls 13–3–184–51–0–18.40; A. Atkins 16–1–239–62–0–15.93; D. Grace 13–1–178–59–0–14.83.

Bowling—M. Nicholls 163–15–617–36–5/53–17.13; M. Bowen 102–10–430–19–3/42–22.63; J. Marston 138–22–536–20–4/77–26.80.

EPSOM COLLEGE   *Played 16: W 7, L 1, D 8. A 2*

Master i/c: G. A. Jones

Cricket professional: J. W. Lloyds

Batting—R. E. Arthur 12–2–463–102*–1–46.30; A. Nicol 10–5–228–73–0–45.60; N. Harris 16–3–552–103*–3–42.46; N. Wherry 13–2–431–96–0–39.18; G. Fowler 15–0–604–78–0–37.75; M. Snow 14–1–395–87–0–30.38; J. Felton 11–5–168–53–0–28.00; A. Baird 10–3–181–50–0–25.85; C. Valentine 13–0–216–54–0–16.61.

Bowling—C. Richards 68–11–234–15–4/25–15.60; N. Harris 200–45–639–29–5/30–22.03; N. Wherry 112–17–365–16–5/23–22.81; L. Webster 158–29–638–25–5/62–25.52.

ETON COLLEGE   *Played 17: W 7, L 1, D 9. A 1*

Master i/c: J. A. Claughton

Cricket professional: J. M. Rice

Eton won the Silk Trophy at Shrewsbury by beating the hosts, Radley (the only side to have beaten them earlier), and Guildford GS from Perth. Henry Dixon was the most consistent player, with two hundreds and five fifties, although James Fulton came into his own at the Festival, where latecomer Charles Jowett took ten wickets for 89 runs. The fathers of all the top four batsmen had also played for the Eton XI.

Batting—*J. A. G. Fulton 15–2–709–100*–1–54.53; H. H. Dixon 17–1–783–100–2–48.93; A. M. Lea 15–4–488–40–0–32.36; H. J. H. Loudon 15–1–395–62–0–28.21; N. A. Bailey 16–3–349–72–0–26.84.

Bowling—S. K. Patel 146.3–34–351–20–4/29–17.55; O. R. A. Shuttleworth 111–20–361–16–3/28–22.56; R. W. J. Bruce 148.5–36–464–16–3/36–29.00; A. F. Jafri 149–40–479–16–4/79–29.93.

EXETER SCHOOL   *Played 16: W 6, L 4, D 6. A 3*

Master i/c: M. C. Wilcock

Although the side failed to reach their potential as a unit, they had two talented all-rounders in Mark Price (off-spin) and Orlando Le Fleming (fast-medium). A highlight was Le Fleming's return of nine for 26 against Wellington School – seven bowled, two lbw. Price was selected for Welsh Schools and Le Fleming played for Somerset and Devon before taking up a place at the Royal Academy of Music.

Batting—M. H. Price 16–5–702–118*–1–63.81; *A. O. F. Le Fleming 11–3–490–96*–0–61.25; W. C. Cruft 15–2–392–89–0–30.15; R. J. Smith 13–1–251–49–0–20.91; T. A. Sowman 11–2–176–68–0–19.55; M. J. Porter 12–2–179–71–0–17.90.

Bowling—A. O. F. Le Fleming 126.5–24–367–35–9/26–10.48; M. H. Price 141.1–13–459–23–4/20–19.95.

FELSTED SCHOOL   *Played 16: W 5, L 5, D 6. A 1*

Master i/c: F. C. Hayes   Cricket professional: G. Barker

Two England players' records fell as Elliott Wilson and Giles Goodwin both completed their school careers in tremendous style. Wilson's 1,202 runs at 120.20, with five hundreds and a 99, surpassed Nick Knight's record of 1,027 in 1987. Goodwin dominated the attack with 47 economical wickets – including a return of seven for 12 in 19 overs – and his career tally of 184 wickets was 20 more than Derek Pringle's. Both Wilson and Goodwin played for Essex Second XI and the club have awarded Goodwin a contract. He also played for England Under-19, MCC Schools and NAYC, while Timothy Phillips, a young bowler introduced towards the end of the season, played for England Under-14 and won the *Daily Telegraph* Under-14 bowling award.

Batting—E. J. Wilson 16–6–1,202–128*–5–120.20; *G. J. A. Goodwin 13–5–372–78–0–46.50; R. F. C. Hayes 15–0–379–50–0–25.26; M. G. Alston 11–3–181–37–0–22.62; B. J. Tabor 12–0–204–54–0–17.00.

Bowling—G. J. A. Goodwin 237–102–561–47–7/12–11.93; M. E. Bundy 78–13–291–16–4/17–18.18.

FETTES COLLEGE   *Played 14: W 3, L 9, D 2*

Master i/c: J. G. A. Frost   Cricket professional: J. van Geloven

Although the first team had a moderate season, some notable performances for the Junior Colts promised well for the future.

Batting—S. A. Morrison 14–0–275–74–0–19.64; R. C. Graham-Brown 10–0–179–48–0–17.90; O. A. Morse 13–2–156–56–0–14.18; C. D. Stevens 12–0–170–47–0–14.16; C. R. Dennis 11–0–152–32–0–13.81.

Bowling—S. A. Morrison 171–24–599–31–6/53–19.32; F. M. Mair 111–16–373–18–3/14–20.72.

FOREST SCHOOL   *Played 17: W 9, L 0, D 8*

Master i/c: S. Turner

Everyone in the side contributed to an excellent, unbeaten season. C. White, a 15-year-old, generated a lively pace and led the bowling averages.

Batting—*R. Rogers 15–5–474–84*–0–47.40; J. McKay 17–1–538–111–1–33.62; S. Kuru 15–2–335–59–0–25.76; S. Blockley 11–3–178–33*–0–22.25; S. Woolmer 13–2–211–39–0–19.18; J. Banks 17–2–285–45–0–19.00.

Bowling—C. White 131.1–31–397–30–6/35–13.23; W. Rogers 159–24–452–31–5/25–14.58; J. McKay 178–28–617–34–4/16–20.56.

FOYLE AND LONDONDERRY COLLEGE   *Played 17: W 10, L 7*

Masters i/c: G. R. McCarter and I. McCracken

Batting—*R. S. Dougherty 15–2–357–82–0–27.46; S. R. Hanna 10–1–175–50–0–19.44; G. King 15–4–195–53–0–17.72; S. A. McLean 13–0–213–41–0–16.38; R. K. Dunn 16–2–217–32–0–15.50; A. R. Fleming 16–1–223–48–0–14.86.

Bowling—G. Moore 77.3–17–231–20–3/8–11.55; R. S. Dougherty 67.3–11–231–18–3/10–12.83; G. King 75–14–260–16–5/16–16.25; A. R. Fleming 119.4–27–384–22–7/26–17.45.

FRAMLINGHAM COLLEGE   *Played 15: W 8, L 2, D 5. A 2*

Master i/c: P. J. Hayes

Cricket professional: C. Rutterford

Jonathan Phillips was the leading batsman, with two hundreds and five fifties in his 810 runs. In the last match of the season, against Kimbolton, the final two wickets were taken by two different bowlers, each with his first ball in first-team cricket.

Batting—*J. H. Phillips 15–2–810–137–2–62.30; J. A. Misick 10–2–240–58*–0–30.00; C. J. Clementson 11–0–315–71–0–28.63; C. J. Goodfellow 14–1–349–71–0–26.84; M. A. H. Rodwell 12–4–179–49–0–22.37.

Bowling—P. J. Pineo 180.2–28–566–36–5/20–15.72; P. R. Elsley 117.5–38–301–16–5/37–18.81; W. D. Buck 146–40–415–20–5/38–20.75.

GIGGLESWICK SCHOOL   *Played 14: W 2, L 4, D 8. A 1*

Master i/c: C. Green

Batting—*J. A. E. Caton 13–0–399–89–0–30.69; C. R. Woolsey 9–2–159–49–0–22.71; C. J. Shorrock 9–0–198–59–0–22.00; O. R. J. Cruse 13–0–273–68–0–21.00; E. W. M. Smith 12–1–151–38–0–13.72; K. A. H. Robertson 13–1–152–39–0–12.66.

Bowling—E. W. M. Smith 87–20–312–19–4/23–16.42; J. B. Savage 169–34–566–19–4/40–29.78.

GLENALMOND   *Played 13: W 6, L 1, D 6. A 1*

Master i/c: J. D. Bassett

The side's only defeat came at the hands of Sedbergh in a two-day game. Tom Stevenson was the most reliable batsman in a generally solid line-up, with strong support from Andrew Gully, a left-arm seamer, who also headed the bowling. The second-wicket partnership of 175 between these two, who made 69 not out and 98 respectively against the Edinburgh Academy, was a school record for any wicket.

Batting—T. M. Stevenson 15–3–549–89*–0–45.75; A. D. M. Gully 14–0–326–99–0–23.28; G. Christie 11–4–162–34*–0–23.14; A. Sim 9–1–154–44–0–19.25; E. L. M. Massie 15–3–226–69*–0–18.83; A. R. Croall 15–1–243–49–0–17.35.

Bowling—A. D. M. Gully 231.1–60–657–36–6/60–18.25; R. Trantor 73–16–274–15–4/32–18.26; E. L. M. Massie 122.3–39–304–16–3/26–19.00; H. Monro 147.1–36–390–20–4/11–19.50.

GORDONSTOUN SCHOOL   *Played 9: W 5, L 2, D 2. A 2*

Master i/c: C. J. Barton

In a particularly wet season – the fine weather did not reach Morayshire until after the end of term – a highlight was the bowling of Samir Nanji, a Kenyan off-spinner whose 36 wickets cost less than ten apiece. He went on to tour South Africa with Kenya Under-21.

Batting—M. C. Hepburn 7–2–189–54–0–37.80; *A. H. B. Fraser-Tytler 8–2–199–80*–0–33.16; J. L. Shrago 9–1–260–117*–1–32.50.

Bowling—S. S. Nanji 117.2–26–356–36–8/58–9.88; J. L. Shrago 91.4–18–283–16–6/24–17.68.

GRENVILLE COLLEGE   *Played 9: W 1, L 3, D 5. A 1*

Master i/c: C. R. Beechey

Batting—*J. Morris 8–0–336–105–1–42.00; J. Kirkham-Brown 8–1–227–100*–1–32.42; B. C. Moore 8–2–164–58–0–27.33; A. Bott 9–1–151–112*–1–18.87.

Bowling—D. Gunion 70–14–194–18–4/6–10.77; J. Kirkham-Brown 47.2–8–227–15–3/4–15.13.

GRESHAM'S SCHOOL   *Played 17: W 9, L 6, D 2. A 2*

Master i/c: A. M. Ponder

The brothers Nick and Tom Hood scored 109 and 110 not out respectively in compiling a record opening partnership of 229 against Wymondham College, against whom their father had also made a century when a schoolboy.

Batting—J. Wyatt 15–3–567–116–1–47.25; J. Cuff 7–2–199–51–0–39.80; O. Morgan 12–1–324–80–0–29.45; *N. Hood 15–2–362–109–1–27.84; M. Burman 11–2–229–73–0–25.44; D. Copas 12–2–253–59–0–25.30; T. Hood 17–3–351–110*–1–25.07.

Bowling—J. Worby 152.3–28–502–30–6/47–16.73; J. Woodwark 162.3–31–482–24–5/51–20.08; J. Hughes 118.3–20–440–20–3/12–22.00.

HABERDASHERS' ASKE'S SCHOOL   *Played 19: W 4, L 5, D 10. A 2*

Masters i/c: S. D. Charlwood and D. I. Yeabsley

Although it was a disappointing season in terms of results, there were encouraging individual performances, notably from Jason Bilimoria with the bat and Matthew Spiro with the ball. A winter tour to Hong Kong, Singapore and Malaysia was planned in conjunction with the school's hockey and rugby clubs.

Batting—*J. Bilimoria 18–2–576–107*–1–36.00; R. Allen 15–2–383–59*–0–29.46; S. Shah 18–1–334–73*–0–19.64; C. C. Brown 14–2–215–49–0–17.91; S. L. Bloom 15–0–256–77–0–17.06; H. Saegusa 15–1–217–53–0–15.50.

Bowling—M. G. Spiro 185–39–671–30–4/48–22.36; H. Saegusa 197.5–33–662–26–4/35–25.46; P. R. Samuels 181.3–43–666–18–4/39–37.00.

HAILEYBURY   *Played 18: W 5, L 5, D 8. A 1*

Master i/c: M. S. Seymour   Cricket professionals: P. M. Ellis and G. D. Barlow

Batting—N. D. Hughes 19–2–848–98–0–49.88; J. E. L. Dahl 12–2–468–120*–1–46.80; S. M. Osman 17–0–389–65–0–22.88; M. O. Elmes 13–1–230–70–0–19.16; E. P. C. Mitchell 17–3–249–60–0–17.78; T. J. Pearman 14–3–156–40*–0–14.18; J. E. Collyer 17–4–182–34–0–14.00.

Bowling—*D. W. Stahl 211–60–626–42–6/47–14.90; N. D. Hughes 280–30–591–27–4/25–21.88; P. A. C. Mansfield 217–43–710–29–5/50–24.48.

HAMPTON SCHOOL   *Played 20: W 4, L 5, D 11. A 2*

Master i/c: A. J. Cook   Cricket professional: P. Farbrace

The youngest side in living memory performed creditably and gave encouragement for the future.

Batting—B. C. A. Mott 20–3–940–165–2–55.29; *T. J. Green 18–3–705–104–3–47.00; P. J. Frost 17–0–436–76–0–25.64; S. B. Powell 18–0–390–70–0–21.66; M. J. Templeman 18–0–384–82–0–21.33.

Bowling—N. Critchley 100.5–14–445–18–4/43–24.72; P. J. Frost 191–48–582–23–7/27–25.30; A. J. Evans 145.4–25–592–22–6/50–26.90.

HARROW SCHOOL   *Played 21: W 8, L 2, D 11. A 1*

Master i/c: C. M. B. Williams   Cricket professional: R. K. Sethi

In a strong batting side Robin MacAndrew, a left-handed batsman and wicket-keeper, achieved the highest aggregate for some years and effected 30 dismissals, including five at Lord's. There were two hat-tricks: from Simon Engelen, who bowls left-arm in-swing, against Felsted, and from Douglas de Jager against Upper Canada College. Although Tim Leathes (fast-medium) was also effective with 34 wickets, the attack often lacked penetration. The side attended a festival at Rossall for the first time and were encouraged to find throughout the season that, as a result of the MCC initiative, all but three of their matches were played positively, with a sensible overs split.

Batting—R. G. MacAndrew 20–3–775–85–0–45.58; E. G. L. Maydon 21–7–473–105*–1–33.78; *S. D. G. Engelen 18–2–462–113*–1–28.87; A. N. L. Cox 20–1–538–108–2–28.31; J. R. W. Norris 16–0–326–74–0–20.37; W. A. T. Gillions 19–4–301–76–0–20.06; O. C. P. Spry 15–0–151–42–0–10.06.

Bowling—S. D. G. Engelen 240.3–68–662–43–6/24–15.39; T. D. de M. Leathes 173–40–588–34–6/19–17.29; R. D. C. R. Pollock-Hill 95–14–318–15–4/45–21.20; W. A. T. Gillions 131–37–368–17–2/5–21.64; C. R. C. Parker 187.2–39–512–19–2/23–26.94.

THE HARVEY GRAMMAR SCHOOL   *Played 18: W 5, L 6, D 7. A 1*

Master i/c: P. J. Harding

Batting—*M. C. Bristow 11–1–357–86*–0–35.70; L. Fletcher 18–2–369–52–0–23.06; K. Temple 18–2–309–75*–0–19.31; T. Timmins 17–3–236–59*–0–16.85; N. G. Brandon 14–0–234–101–1–16.71; S. Patel 10–0–158–35–0–15.80; N. Jackson 17–0–248–46–0–14.58.

Bowling—T. Timmins 86.4–10–391–25–6/38–15.64; M. Ritchie 87.4–8–401–18–3/23–22.27; L. Fletcher 142.4–21–500–22–5/33–22.72.

HEREFORD CATHEDRAL SCHOOL   *Played 19: W 10, L 4, D 5. A 1*

Master i/c: A. Connop

Batting—S. J. Price 17–4–684–90*–0–52.61; T. I. Hall 13–5–356–77*–0–44.50; *B. J. Albright 19–5–589–71–0–42.07; A. Johnson 12–3–260–50–0–28.88; M. D. Price 13–3–258–56–0–25.80; M. Tomlinson 8–1–156–53–0–22.28.

Bowling—J. E. A. Layton 221.1–44–649–38–7/53–17.07; D. Jennings 105.2–27–301–17–3/5–17.70; M. Tomlinson 180.1–32–583–24–4/35–24.29; N. Brown 118–16–415–16–3/19–25.93.

HIGHGATE SCHOOL   *Played 14: W 1, L 5, D 7, T 1*

Master i/c: R. G. W. Marsh

Batting—M. A. P. O'Brien 12–4–630–163*–3–78.75; C. J. P. Thomas 7–4–162–55*–0–54.00; R. A. Swann 11–0–465–151–1–42.27; D. C. Cohen 11–4–281–126–1–40.14; *S. M. Khan 13–1–285–90*–0–23.75; R. H. Beenstock 11–0–186–45–0–16.90.

Bowling—C. J. P. Thomas 146–29–523–25–6/61–20.92; D. C. Cohen 136.3–14–580–18–4/88–32.22.

HURSTPIERPOINT COLLEGE   *Played 16: W 6, L 3, D 7. A 2*

Master i/c: M. J. Mance   Cricket professional: D. J. Semmence

Despite slightly disappointing results, it was an enjoyable season in which Simon May set a fine example behind the stumps and led from the front when batting; his 150 against Cranleigh was an excellent innings. He and Lee Atkins, the leading bowler, played for Sussex Under-19.

Batting—*S. P. May 17–3–757–150–2–54.07; R. K. H. Redford 13–2–373–58*–0–33.90; N. J. Jenkin 16–3–430–80–0–33.07; A. C. Scoones 13–5–209–52*–0–26.12; L. J. Atkins 13–5–204–40–0–25.50; J. E. Riddy 17–1–329–61–0–20.56; T. J. W. Larman 14–2–231–76–0–19.25.

Bowling—L. J. Atkins 188.3–37–567–29–7/18–19.55; J. C. A. Catterall 148–22–538–27–5/59–19.92; A. C. Scoones 158.1–29–623–22–7/69–28.31.

IPSWICH SCHOOL   *Played 16: W 11, L 1, D 4. A 1*

Master i/c: A. K. Golding   Cricket professional: R. E. East

The 11 wins were a school record.

Batting—D. R. Sim 10–4–343–79–0–57.16; J. P. East 16–3–529–121–1–40.69; G. J. McCartney 16–3–525–101*–1–40.38; C. Robinson 15–3–401–62*–0–33.41; S. Henwood 16–0–459–86–0–28.68; M. Laws 10–0–243–68–0–24.30; J. F. Collins 12–2–218–67–0–21.80.

Bowling—J. P. East 198–40–586–35–5/8–16.74; J. Druitt 143–27–520–21–4/37–24.76; C. Robinson 210.4–42–681–22–5/19–30.95.

ISLEWORTH & SYON SCHOOL   *Played 16: W 8, L 3, D 5*

Master i/c: B. A. Goldsby

The side were runners-up in the County Cup, losing a close final to Mill Hill. Owais Shah, still only 16, played for Middlesex and the Southern Development of Excellence XI and was selected for the England Under-19 tour to Zimbabwe. B. M. Goldsby completed four seasons in the eleven with more than 1,000 runs and 75 wickets.

Batting—O. A. Shah 5–1–333–149–2–83.25; T. P. McLoughlin 10–4–336–76–0–56.00; *B. M. Goldsby 14–4–396–71*–0–39.60; K. H. Bokhari 12–3–207–43–0–23.00; N. Ahmed 14–0–297–57–0–21.21.

Bowling—B. M. Goldsby 138.5–17–559–35–5/26–15.97; E. W. Harding 81.5–11–347–16–5/30–21.68.

THE JOHN LYON SCHOOL   *Played 16: W 6, L 5, D 5. A 1*

Master i/c: I. Parker

A young side did better than expected, with K. Merali heading both averages.

Batting—*K. Merali 13–3–403–108*–1–40.30; M. Navratnarajah 14–3–297–66*–0–27.00; N. Goh 15–2–336–67*–0–25.84; S. Choudhary 13–3–169–48*–0–16.90; J. Leach 13–3–158–34–0–15.80.

Bowling—K. Merali 109.3–19–398–17–3/8–23.41; N. Goh 151.3–28–463–19–3/25–24.36.

KELLY COLLEGE   *Played 12: W 3, L 2, D 7*

Master i/c: G. C. L. Cooper

Katy Roué, a fifth-former whose brother James was team captain, played once for the XI. An off-break bowler, she also plays for the West of England Ladies Under-20s.

Batting—*J. L. Roué 12–1–412–119–1–37.45; R. G. Goldring 10–0–219–81–0–21.90; R. H. Harrison 11–2–196–77*–0–21.77; A. M. Hurst 10–0–207–66–0–20.70; A. R. Gander 11–0–171–88–0–15.54.

Bowling—R. B. Koshoni 87–24–283–20–5/9–14.15.

KIMBOLTON SCHOOL   *Played 18: W 1, L 11, D 6. A 2*

Master i/c: R. P. Merriman   Cricket professional: M. E. Latham

Although results were poor in a season of rebuilding, there was encouragement from some individual performances. Against Leicestershire Gentlemen, Paul Pippard set new records with his innings of 134 and his eighth-wicket partnership of 104 with Jeremy Follett. Mark Klein took a hat-trick (all bowled) in the same match and in the victory over Berkhamsted took six for 51 and scored his second century of the season.

Batting—P. S. Pippard 18–0–657–134–2–36.50; M. D. Klein 18–2–442–108–2–27.62; W. J. T. Follett 18–0–390–92–0–21.66; O. Bailey 18–2–206–36–0–12.87.

Bowling—M. D. Klein 126.4–13–457–22–6/51–20.77; J. C. R. Follett 181.5–36–672–27–6/21–24.88.

KING EDWARD VI COLLEGE, STOURBRIDGE   *Played 14: W 2, L 9, D 3. A 1*

Master i/c: R. A. Williams

Batting—R. Nagra 10–0–357–103–1–35.70; *R. J. Crowley 12–0–262–44–0–21.83; R. Bhogal 14–2–227–63–0–18.91.

Bowling—R. Bhogal 76.2–11–310–17–5/22–18.23; R. Nagra 124–24–429–22–6/47–19.50.

KING EDWARD VI SCHOOL, SOUTHAMPTON   *Played 19: W 10, L 4, D 5. A 5*

Master i/c: R. J. Putt

In a successful season, the school retained the Altham Trophy for local sixth forms. John Claughton again headed the batting. Simon Francis played for England Under-17 and his brother John played for England Under-14.

Batting—J. A. Claughton 16–1–746–101–1–49.73; A. J. Hart 14–2–523–106*–2–43.58; W. H. Baker 6–1–194–100*–1–38.80; A. M. Dyke 7–2–152–60*–0–30.40; C. F. Craft 17–2–446–104–1–29.73; L. D. Sully 12–3–193–49–0–21.44; *D. R. Baxendale 13–5–170–40–0–21.25; M. H. Tarry 13–0–235–46–0–18.07.

Bowling—S. R. G. Francis 173–40–540–36–7/42–15.00; D. R. Baxendale 193.2–35–648–34–6/35–19.05; S. J. Andrews 160.1–26–591–24–7/26–24.62; L. D. Sully 108–20–384–15–3/20–25.60.

KING EDWARD VII SCHOOL, LYTHAM *Played 17: W 4, L 10, D 3. A 2*

Master i/c: S. T. Godfrey

A highlight was Michael Moore's innings of 173 against Manchester GS, which came off 157 balls, with two sixes and 28 fours.

Batting—*R. M. Moore 16-0-663-173-1-41.43; G. Evans 12-1-203-55-0-18.45; J. Kok 14-0-238-52-0-17.00; L. Hilton 17-1-189-45-0-11.81; J. Kok 14-0-238-52-0-17.00; L. Hilton 17-1-189-45-0-11.81; T. T. Godfrey 14-1-151-30*-0-11.61; S. Long 15-0-152-31-0-10.13.

Bowling—R. M. Moore 148.2-35-405-28-5/53-14.46; G. Evans 96.1-26-311-20-4/26-15.55; T. Brown 160-37-461-26-5/12-17.73.

KING EDWARD'S SCHOOL, BIRMINGHAM *Played 25: W 7, L 5, D 12, T 1. A 1*

Master i/c: M. D. Stead   Cricket professional: J. Huband

Mark Wagh was again outstanding, with 1,062 runs, including five centuries, and 40 wickets with his off-breaks. He made his first-team debut for Warwickshire and played for England Under-18, English Schools, MCC Schools and NCA Young Cricketers.

Batting—*M. A. Wagh 21-1-1,062-145-5-53.10; A. J. Martin 12-4-212-47-0-26.50; A. P. Blaikley 22-2-473-84*-0-23.65; R. J. McGuire 19-4-267-37-0-17.80; A. M. Purdon 18-3-262-43*-0-17.46; B. J. Tier 21-5-264-43-0-16.50; A. R. Chitre 23-0-357-46-0-15.52.

Bowling—M. A. Wagh 242.5-74-515-40-6/38-12.87; J. S. Ross 223-36-787-34-4/39-23.14; A. P. Blaikley 181.3-20-735-29-3/28-25.34; S. A. McCrory 153-22-420-16-6/33-26.25.

KING WILLIAM'S COLLEGE *Played 10: W 4, L 3, D 3*

Master i/c: A. A. Maree   Cricket professional: D. Mark

Batting—R. Hendry 8-0-316-98-0-39.50; J. Manuja 9-1-196-59-0-24.50; E. Zuiderent 10-2-178-101*-1-22.25; R. Cowley 9-0-161-37-0-17.88.

Bowling—N. Gawne 67.4-14-249-19-5/41-13.10; R. Hendry 97-13-341-26-8/43-13.11; R. Cowley 86.2-23-234-15-4/36-15.60.

KING'S COLLEGE, TAUNTON *Played 14: W 8, L 3, D 3*

Master i/c: R. T. R. Yeates   Cricket professional: D. Breakwell

It was agreed that the introduction of some limited-overs games proved a positive influence throughout, with the cricket generally exciting and rewarding. Nicholas Boulton, a fourth-former who made five centuries, set new records with his innings of 187, his aggregate of 899 and his average of 74.91. Sam Diment had a steady but unspectacular season, going on to play for MCC Schools.

Batting—N. R. Boulton 14-2-899-187-5-74.91; J. H. Duder 13-2-457-103-1-41.54; S. H. L. Diment 12-3-365-67-0-40.55; N. J. Raymond 11-2-302-100*-1-33.55; P. J. R. Chappell 13-3-306-96-0-30.60; D. J. Bostock 12-1-182-48-0-16.54.

Bowling—S. H. L. Diment 126.2-19-473-16-2/29-29.56; D. J. Bostock 151.3-26-544-17-3/20-32.00.

KING'S COLLEGE SCHOOL, WIMBLEDON *Played 23: W 7, L 6, D 10*

Master i/c: G. C. McGinn   Cricket professional: L. J. Moody

In a season of rebuilding, much depended on the batting of the Sleigh brothers – Richard, the captain, and Andrew, in his first season – who scored almost 2,000 runs between them. The attack, spearheaded by Samir Sheikh and Jacques Rossouw, lacked the guile of a slow bowler.

Batting—A. Sleigh 24-6-1,014-91*-0-56.33; *R. Sleigh 22-3-974-120*-1-51.26; D. Bowen 4-1-151-100*-1-50.33; S. Pervez 18-6-412-92*-0-34.33; L. Whitaker 20-5-514-67-0-34.26; S. Sheikh 14-2-308-79-0-25.66; B. Moir 16-1-302-100*-1-20.13.

Bowling—S. Sheikh 181-28-605-34-6/37-17.79; J. Rossouw 205.2-33-755-35-6/30-21.57; C. Elliot 62-3-344-15-3/24-22.93; J. Walsh 165.3-17-648-19-4/37-34.10.

KING'S SCHOOL, BRUTON   *Played 13: W 7, L 3, D 3. A 1*

Master i/c: P. Platts-Martin   Cricket professional: N. J. Lockhart

Batting—J. E. K. Rooke 12–0–421–86–0–35.08; J. P. Thomas 12–1–277–61–0–25.18; L. Kemp 13–1–281–63–0–23.41; C. B. Higgins 13–0–296–64–0–22.76; K. J. Pike 12–2–156–28*–0–15.60; S. R. Pollok 11–1–152–39–0–15.20.

Bowling—J. P. Thomas 137.1–30–410–29–5/28–14.13; D. G. Wyatt 101.1–21–308–21–4/40–14.66; N. A. B. Price 94.4–15–336–22–4/18–15.27; *L. C. Crofts 92–27–270–16–3/14–16.87.

THE KING'S SCHOOL, CANTERBURY   *Played 14: W 2, L 4, D 8*

Master i/c: A. W. Dyer   Cricket professional: A. G. E. Ealham

A highlight was William Bax's century against Sutton Valence – the first by a fifth-former against another school since the war.

Batting—Q. Wiseman 15–2–441–106–1–33.92; C. M. North 11–1–279–67–0–27.90; W. R. Bax 13–3–231–123–1–23.10; T. W. Stazicker 14–2–274–51–0–22.83; M. J. A. Pyke 14–1–245–45–0–18.84; T. J. Palmer 14–1–206–44–0–15.84; M. J. Davies 13–0–203–47–0–15.61.

Bowling—C. M. Mounsey-Thear 179–36–546–25–5/19–21.84; C. M. North 141.4–33–493–22–4/60–22.40; *W. J. G. Finch 144–28–477–16–3/80–29.81.

THE KING'S SCHOOL, CHESTER   *Played 18: W 9, L 6, D 3. A 2*

Master i/c: S. Neal

Robert Falconer shared in two significant partnerships. He scored 90 in a first-wicket stand of 131 with Kieron Ollier (75) to set up a second successive victory over MCC, and made 96 in a second-wicket stand of 216 with Scott McCormick (113 not out) against a strong Old King's Scholars XI.

Batting—R. J. Falconer 18–1–585–96–0–34.41; K. J. Ollier 15–1–464–97–0–33.14; *S. J. McCormick 17–2–421–113*–1–28.06; R. L. Owen 13–3–234–65*–0–23.40; B. K. Smith 13–1–180–45–0–15.00; A. C. Lamond 12–0–179–44–0–14.91.

Bowling—A. J. Douglas 164–35–494–33–4/18–14.96; R. J. Falconer 136–31–407–26–5/25–15.65; J. N. A. Cornelius 108–18–371–21–5/23–17.66.

THE KING'S SCHOOL, ELY   *Played 19: W 9, L 1, D 9. A 1*

Masters i/c: C. J. Limb and W. J. Marshall

The success of the side, who won the Cambridgeshire Schools Cup for the third year running, owed much to the consistent batting of Chris Marshall, Ian Haigh and Matthew Parker, who scored seven centuries between them. Another batting highlight was a record total of 319 for five against Newport Free GS. Wickets were shared between eight members of a strong attack, assisted by some excellent catches by Matthew Setchell behind the stumps.

Batting—*C. D. Marshall 18–3–682–152*–2–45.46; I. P. N. Haigh 13–0–584–106–2–44.92; M. C. Parker 18–1–660–113–3–38.82; C. W. Kisby 17–3–373–98–0–26.64; D. M. Donaldson 15–6–161–36*–0–17.88; T. J. N. Shanassy 15–3–157–32–0–13.08.

Bowling—C. W. Kisby 54.5–6–221–17–4/10–13.00; M. C. Parker 179.1–45–547–36–4/14–15.19; C. J. Douglass 90–9–408–23–4/53–17.73; A. R. Cable 106–26–423–23–4/40–18.39.

THE KING'S SCHOOL, MACCLESFIELD   *Played 18: W 3, L 5, D 10. A 3*

Master i/c: D. M. Harbord   Cricket professional: S. Moores

Batting—A. S. Bones 17–1–606–100–1–37.87; S. D. Gatie 18–2–392–71–0–24.50; M. J. Patterson 17–2–344–58*–0–22.93; N. M. Mason 16–0–347–82–0–21.68; C. J. Buckley 17–2–297–82–0–19.80; A. D. Emslie 15–2–232–65–0–17.84; J. Farshchi 14–2–179–54*–0–14.91.

Bowling—G. A. Emmett 164–24–550–35–7/35–15.71; *P. M. Daniels 123–22–452–18–3/22–25.11; A. J. Wheeler 150–25–538–21–5/29–25.61.

KING'S SCHOOL, ROCHESTER   *Played 18: W 3, L 7, D 8*

Master i/c: G. R. Williams

The results were disappointing, although most of the defeats were by a small margin. The bowling was rarely accurate enough to dismiss sides cheaply, and the senior batsmen often failed to do themselves justice when chasing runs. Both batting and bowling averages were headed by Glynn Davies and Simon Nicholls, son of the former Kent player, David Nicholls.

Batting—G. E. Davies 18-3-593-89-0-39.53; S. P. A. Nicholls 18-1-414-78-0-24.35; R. A. Batchelor 18-1-321-52-0-18.88; D. N. Philp 11-1-162-91*-0-16.20; O. T. Davies 16-2-218-61-0-15.57.

Bowling—G. E. Davies 155-31-460-28-4/31-16.42; S. P. A. Nicholls 93-14-363-17-5/86-21.35; D. N. Philp 182-31-583-25-4/27-23.32.

KING'S SCHOOL, WORCESTER   *Played 20: W 11, L 4, D 5. A 1*

Master i/c: D. P. Iddon

A successful season began with a flourish as five of the first six games were won. Artisham Fiaz and Max Rowan excelled throughout, and with three Under-15 players figuring prominently in the averages, there is promise for the future.

Batting—*A. Fiaz 19-2-904-107*-2-53.17; S. R. Thomas 18-5-564-100-1-43.38; E. M. Oliver 16-2-413-51*-0-29.50; R. E. Haines 12-2-243-70-0-24.30; D. A. Cullen 15-6-152-31-0-16.88; T. A. Morris 16-0-191-36-0-11.93.

Bowling—M. Rowan 245.5-62-697-46-5/48-15.15; D. J. Kendrick 147.3-30-566-31-4/47-18.25; J. Riaz 151.2-38-461-22-4/51-20.95; A. Fiaz 157-36-530-23-3/54-23.04; T. S. Heyes 187-38-644-27-4/39-23.85.

KINGSTON GRAMMAR SCHOOL   *Played 19: W 10, L 5, D 4*

Master i/c: J. A. Royce   Cricket professional: C. Mutucumarana

A well-balanced and varied attack earned some excellent results, including victory in the Alexander Cup (Surrey Under-19).

Batting—L. D. Garrard 18-1-583-101*-1-34.29; P. W. Anderson 16-3-384-77-0-29.53; J. A. Smith 6-0-161-67-0-26.83; J. R. J. Ebsworth 17-2-285-40-0-19.00; G. Narinesingh 18-1-280-75-0-16.47; M. J. Newport 13-1-170-33-0-14.16; L. R. E. Mallett 18-3-207-37-0-13.80; A. D. Evans 17-3-179-36-0-12.78; N. Patel 19-2-193-51*-0-11.35.

Bowling—D. J. Spenceley 135.2-28-415-27-4/6-15.37; *G. R. Spenceley 110.2-15-425-25-5/21-17.00; N. Patel 123.4-16-566-29-5/62-19.51; P. W. Anderson 163.2-46-559-28-6/9-19.96.

KINGSWOOD SCHOOL   *Played 9: W 3, L 5, D 1*

Master i/c: T. P. A. Reeman

Batting—D. P. L. Willis 8-1-191-59*-0-27.28.

Bowling—No bowler took 15 wickets. The leading bowler was U. J. A. Warmann 68.3-12-231-12-6/44-19.25.

LANCING COLLEGE   *Played 18: W 6, L 4, D 8. A 1*

Master i/c: M. P. Bentley   Cricket professional: R. Davies

The season was memorable for some notable partnerships: George Campbell and Nick Hayday compiled 212 for the first wicket against the XL Club and 159 for the second against Rugby, while Dominic Clapp and Giles Haywood put on 140 for the third against Christ's Hospital. Hayday completed his fifth season in the XI, having played every game for them in five years since he was 14.

Batting—G. Campbell 19-3-950-128*-2-59.37; D. Clapp 20-2-592-74-0-32.88; *N. Hayday 20-0-571-88-0-28.55; G. Haywood 15-0-356-118-1-23.73; G. Price 15-2-272-87*-0-20.92; W. Monson 14-1-214-78-0-16.46.

Bowling—G. Haywood 119-29-686-30-5/45-22.86.

LANGLEY PARK SCHOOL   *Played 15: W 6, L 2, D 7*

Master i/c: C. H. Williams

Batting—S. Evans 14–3–724–137*–4–65.81; B. Simpson 10–3–322–86*–0–46.00; J. Roberts 8–1–195–62*–0–27.85; R. Wakeman 9–2–184–71–0–26.28; T. Summerfield 12–1–157–37*–0–15.70.

Bowling—N. Codling 64.4–10–210–16–4/8–13.12; *J. Rayfield 102–18–246–18–6/14–13.66; D. Montefusco 97–22–291–18–6/22–16.16; A. Shepherd 99–11–514–20–8/61–25.70.

LEEDS GRAMMAR SCHOOL   *Played 15: W 1, L 5, D 9*

Master i/c: R. Hill

Batting—M. N. Richmond 15–1–517–100*–1–36.92; T. J. N. Golby 14–1–441–62–0–33.92; A. R. Brown 10–2–244–56–0–30.50; L. W. B. Kendall 11–4–207–57*–0–29.57; J. R. Wyn-Griffiths 12–0–231–113–1–19.25.

Bowling—*P. J. Miller 92–17–406–17–3/66–23.88; D. H. Butler 109.1–24–606–18–7/62–33.66.

THE LEYS SCHOOL   *Played 15: W 4, L 9, D 2. A 2*

Master i/c: T. Firth   Cricket professional: D. Gibson

Batting—R. Pallister 15–2–305–80–0–23.46; N. Barber 15–1–264–55–0–18.85; R. Bentley 14–0–238–47–0–17.00; *C. Parnell 14–1–173–62–0–13.30.

Bowling—N. Romans 114.1–23–399–24–6/47–16.62; T. Biddle 76–11–259–15–4/37–17.26; S. Graham 177–34–485–27–4/47–17.96.

LLANDOVERY COLLEGE   *Played 13: W 1, L 6, D 6. A 2*

Master i/c: T. G. Marks

Batting—I. E. Jones 9–3–181–44*–0–30.16; M. Venables 8–2–153–57*–0–25.50; H. Lock 8–0–186–57–0–23.25.

Bowling—No bowler took 15 wickets. The leading bowler was C. Rees 63–3–291–13–3/27–22.38.

LORD WANDSWORTH COLLEGE   *Played 15: W 4, L 2, D 9. A 2*

Master i/c: M. C. Russell

The record of four wins and nine draws does not reflect the positive cricket played under the inspired captaincy of Jon Palmer, who played for Sussex Second XI and was named the 1996 Arundel Scholar. He dominated both batting and bowling (slow left-arm), his 48 wickets being 12 more than the previous best. Jon Wilkinson also bowled well at fast-medium, in his first full season. Inconsistency in the middle order proved a handicap in the first part of the season. The catching was impressive, with a record 71 held, including nine against Portsmouth GS.

Batting—*J. M. Palmer 15–1–742–105–1–53.00; S. J. Butler 14–2–329–65*–0–27.41; C. J. Walker 14–2–310–54–0–25.83; D. I. Holman 13–2–206–110–1–18.72.

Bowling—J. M. Palmer 231.3–71–556–48–7/28–11.58; J. P. Wilkinson 203.1–48–552–34–5/44–16.23.

LORD WILLIAMS'S SCHOOL, THAME   *Played 13: W 2, L 5, D 6*

Master i/c: J. E. Fulkes

Batting—M. Costar 13–3–402–100*–1–40.20; D. Bennett 13–0–469–113–1–36.07; M. Kelloway 11–1–253–87*–0–25.30; S. Whittam 8–1–168–56–0–24.00; A. Cawston 9–0–195–56–0–21.66; A. Wilson 11–0–179–55–0–16.27.

Bowling—S. Whittam 91.4–19–343–20–5/37–17.15.

LORETTO SCHOOL   *Played 18: W 9, L 4, D 5*

Master i/c: R. P. Whait

Batting—*R. A. G. Grant 16–3–502–102*–1–38.61; W. A. Nicholson 12–1–262–49–0–23.81; A. G. Fleming-Brown 14–0–315–66–0–22.50; J. T. Boon 16–4–235–34–0–19.58; M. J. Ritchie 14–2–183–37–0–15.25.

Bowling—J. T. Boon 133.5–35–390–24–4/14–16.25; M. B. McCreath 244.1–64–607–37–5/25–16.40; R. A. G. Grant 169.3–49–511–31–6/46–16.48.

LOUGHBOROUGH GRAMMAR SCHOOL　　*Played 16: W 8, L 2, D 6. A 2*

Master i/c: J. S. Weitzel　　　　　　　　　　Cricket professional: H. T. Tunnicliffe

It was a season for batsmen. In an opening partnership of 278 against King Henry VIII, Coventry, Richard Widdowson scored 200 off 162 balls with 41 fours and Stewart Morgan hit 68 not out, while in the high-scoring two-day game against Manchester GS, Morgan and Ben Keast put on 201 unbroken for the second wicket. A record total of 302 for five was amassed against the XL Club and MCC were beaten for the second successive season.

Batting—C. B. Keast 14–7–493–107*–1–70.42; R. G. H. Widdowson 16–0–809–200–2–50.56; S. Morgan 18–3–599–79*–0–39.93; R. J. Peregrine 15–4–433–70–0–39.36; M. J. Simpson 9–3–188–86–0–31.33; *D. P. Reddyhough 5–0–378–64–0–25.20; E. O. Woodcock 11–2–170–37–0–18.88.

Bowling—D. P. Hemmings 172–20–700–27–5/26–25.92; C. B. Keast 146.1–21–674–24–6/90–28.08.

MAGDALEN COLLEGE SCHOOL　　*Played 18: W 3, L 8, D 7*

Master i/c: P. Askew　　　　　　　　　　Cricket professional: R. A. Winstone

Batting—P. J. Denning 18–2–548–109*–1–34.25; B. J. Thompson 15–2–426–80–0–32.76; C. J. Rees-Gay 16–4–338–79–0–28.16; S. M. Ison 14–1–400–89*–0–26.66; *A. Booth 18–1–439–106*–1–25.82; D. D. Harris 16–3–261–77*–0–20.07; S. R. Sharpe 17–3–213–55*–0–15.21; N. J. Carlsen 15–1–150–38–0–10.71.

Bowling—S. R. Sharpe 227.5–46–746–30–4/24–24.86; B. Bradshaw 132.5–28–441–15–4/17–29.40; A. Booth 190.5–20–840–21–3/42–40.00.

MALVERN COLLEGE　　*Played 18: W 9, L 0, D 9*

Master i/c: A. J. Murtagh　　　　　　　　　　Cricket professional: R. W. Tolchard

With the best results since the war, Malvern were unbeaten. The side featured the England Under-19 wicket-keeper, David Nash, who also played for Middlesex, and Dan Walker, son of Peter, formerly of Glamorgan and England.

Batting—D. C. Nash 15–4–687–101*–1–62.45; M. A. Hardinges 17–4–690–128*–2–53.07; S. J. Varney 9–5–212–59*–0–53.00; J. B. Horton 12–2–351–80–0–35.10; *G. D. Franklin 15–4–360–107*–1–32.72; N. D. Harrison 13–0–150–65*–0–21.42; D. G. Walker 13–1–168–55–0–14.00.

Bowling—G. D. Franklin 243.1–65–612–41–7/45–14.92; S. J. Varney 88–25–266–15–6/42–17.73; M. A. Hardinges 162–29–560–30–4/28–18.66; N. W. S. Beard 144.1–42–456–23–6/50–19.82.

MANCHESTER GRAMMAR SCHOOL　　*Played 18: W 6, L 4, D 8*

Master i/c: D. Moss

Mark Chilton was outstanding. His aggregate of 1,361 runs at 104.69 was easily a record; he passed 50 in 13 of his 16 innings and scored seven hundreds, finishing the season with two, both unbeaten, in the two-day game against Loughborough GS. Jonathan Lee also passed 500 runs and at 14 became the youngest to score a hundred for the first team. Neil Lomax always bowled accurately in an attack that otherwise tended to be wayward.

Batting—*M. J. Chilton 16–3–1,361–143–7–104.69; N. D. Garner 14–7–311–82*–0–44.42; J. R. Lee 16–3–568–110*–1–43.69; S. A. Richardson 11–1–374–98–0–37.40; R. J. Salisbury 13–1–278–58–0–23.16; R. P. J. Seddon 13–1–260–66–0–21.66; A. Malhotra 13–1–230–58–0–19.16.

Bowling—N. R. Lomax 216.5–55–582–35–6/51–16.62; M. J. Chilton 131.3–21–439–16–3/7–27.43.

MARLBOROUGH COLLEGE　　*Played 13: W 2, L 8, D 3. A 1*

Master i/c: R. B. Pick　　　　　　　　　　Cricket professional: R. M. Ratcliffe

Much depended on Lee Ratcliffe, who was below his best until after the A-levels, when he made an unbeaten 122 against Winchester and finished with 45 wickets.

Batting—*L. J. Ratcliffe 11–1–364–122*–1–36.40; P. S. E. Tuggey 10–2–183–48–0–22.87; M. E. Hopper 13–2–220–54–0–20.00; W. O. Caldwell 13–0–252–63–0–19.38; C. M. Cannon 12–0–186–78–0–15.50.

Bowling—L. J. Ratcliffe 220.1–51–598–45–9/62–13.28.

MERCHANT TAYLORS' SCHOOL, CROSBY   *Played 15: W 8, L 4, D 3*

Master i/c: Rev. D. A. Smith   Cricket professional: S. Prescott

A highlight was the first ever defeat of Royal GS, Lancaster, in which Colin Inkson took seven for 69. Guy Edwards completed his career in the eleven with 1,823 runs, the fourth-highest aggregate for the school.

Batting—C. J. Cheetham 12–5–280–67*–0–40.00; S. B. Howard 14–2–469–74*–0–39.08; *G. A. Edwards 14–1–379–71–0–29.15; G. R. Ball 14–2–344–71–0–28.66; N. M. Delaney 13–2–218–41–0–19.81.

Bowling—G. R. Ball 94–23–339–20–5/8–16.95; N. M. Shaw 88–12–351–17–4/11–20.64; C. D. Inkson 125–23–445–19–7/69–23.42; N. M. Delaney 134–25–466–19–4/28–24.52.

MERCHANT TAYLORS' SCHOOL, NORTHWOOD   *Played 29: W 19, L 3, D 7. A 2*

Master i/c: H. C. Latchman

The 16-year-old opening batsman Daniel Grundy's 1,419 runs beat the 94-year-old record by 22. Andrew Thorpe was also prolific, while Neeraj Sapra, a medium-pace bowler capable of long, accurate spells, took 53 wickets. The season was followed by a successful tour of Malaysia and Singapore.

Batting—D. Grundy 26–9–1,419–158*–3–83.47; A. Thorpe 25–6–849–178–2–44.68; E. Lamb 19–8–412–98–0–37.45; A. Latchman 13–4–300–74–0–33.33; P. Wise 26–4–678–77–0–30.81; J. Rasheed 13–2–195–76–0–17.72.

Bowling—E. Lamb 144–46–337–39–6/16–8.64; N. Sapra 298.1–84–673–53–5/11–12.69; J. Rasheed 227–45–639–41–5/44–15.58.

MERCHISTON CASTLE SCHOOL   *Played 18: W 6, L 4, D 8. A 1*

Master i/c: C. W. Swan

The strongest batting side for ten years recorded two centuries and a wealth of runs in June. The first fixture against MCC since 1971 was drawn, as were seven other games, owing mainly to a lack of a penetrative attack.

Batting—G. M. English 17–1–500–87–0–31.25; J. N. Mackley 19–3–498–115*–1–31.12; A. P. Paterson 13–5–246–62*–0–30.75; A. J. Scott 17–0–510–99–0–30.00; C. M. R. Tulloch 19–3–478–109*–1–29.87; M. J. M. Mayer 15–3–252–45–0–21.00.

Bowling—A. J. Scott 166–28–373–30–7/49–12.43; A. P. Paterson 180–40–522–36–5/33–14.50; S. J. Whitmee 75–15–247–15–4/21–16.46; C. M. R. Tulloch 199–41–611–19–3/51–32.15.

MILLFIELD SCHOOL   *Played 13: W 6, L 2, D 5. A 3*

Master i/c: R. M. Ellison   Cricket professional: G. C. Wilson

Inspired by the captaincy of Luke Sutton, the side produced disciplined performances coupled with a sense of enjoyment. A highlight was the three-day match against Durban HS, which Millfield won by three wickets after being set 239 runs in 63 overs. Sutton captained MCC Schools and played for English Schools, while Dean Cosker played for England Under-17 and Glamorgan Second XI – not Somerset, as incorrectly stated in the 1995 edition of *Wisden*.

Batting—A. N. Edwards 11–1–459–92–0–45.90; *L. D. Sutton 11–1–378–89–0–37.80; M. T. Byrne 13–2–373–122*–1–33.90; W. T. Simmons 11–4–225–47–0–32.14; C. P. Curtis 7–2–152–63*–0–30.40.

Bowling—D. A. Cosker 192.2–75–390–25–5/48–15.60; B. M. McCorkill 168.2–46–460–25–7/42–18.40; E. J. S. Newton 88–21–373–15–5/58–24.86.

MILTON ABBEY SCHOOL   *Played 13: W 3, L 8, D 2. A 2*

Master i/c: P. Wood

The Gold brothers, C. M. and J. E., headed the batting and bowling averages respectively.

Batting—C. M. Gold 11–1–300–62–0–30.00; F. Gibson 13–1–346–87–0–28.83; T. D. G. Ellis-Jones 13–0–219–58–0–16.84.

Bowling—*J. E. Gold 114.2–26–359–21–5/19–17.09; C. M. Gold 101.4–17–381–21–7/32–18.14; F. Gibson 92–14–333–17–6/32–19.58; T. H. Godsal 144.3–30–486–21–6/26–23.14.

MONKTON COMBE SCHOOL   *Played 13: W 4, L 7, D 2*

Master i/c: N. D. Botton

Batting—*M. D. Beeby 14–3–364–100*–1–33.09; J. S. Wheeler 14–0–283–68–0–20.21; R. D. Heathcote 13–1–226–73*–0–18.83; D. P. W. Smith 13–2–157–38–0–14.27; R. J. Clifford 13–1–160–31–0–13.33.

Bowling—M. E. K. Rooke 125–27–382–26–6/25–14.69; M. Teli 117.4–22–342–20–6/47–17.10; D. P. W. Smith 138–23–505–26–5/28–19.42.

MONMOUTH SCHOOL   *Played 19: W 6, L 11, D 2. A 3*

Master i/c: D. H. Messenger   Cricket professional: G. I. Burgess

An excellent start, with five of the first six matches won, could not be maintained, and there was only one more victory. A combination of positive declarations and more limited-overs matches resulted in only two drawn games. Tom Allan and Nils Jorgensen, who made their debuts for the XI, played for Wales Under-14 and Under-15 respectively.

Batting—*J. T. Goodwin 15–3–370–86–0–30.83; M. M. Brogan 19–1–523–73–0–29.05; N. Jorgensen 15–2–314–51–0–24.15; J. N. Hern 16–0–323–55–0–20.18; A. S. Narula 18–1–279–37–0–16.41.

Bowling—B. M. Morgan 81.4–25–191–15–5/24–12.73; G. J. Curtis 158.3–26–639–17–4/63–37.58.

NEWCASTLE-UNDER-LYME SCHOOL   *Played 16: W 5, L 4, D 7*

Master i/c: S. A. Robson   Cricket professional: T. Fielding

A difficult season finished on a high note when the last three matches were won. Although seven totals of 200 or more were conceded, two batting records were broken: C. D. Moss (44) and R. T. Howell (66) put on 103 for the fourth wicket against Bishop Vesey's GS and R. M. Wheat (40 not out) and I. S. Roberts (12 not out) added 53 unbroken for the ninth wicket against Bromsgrove.

Batting—V. K. Khunger 11–2–228–64*–0–25.33; N. R. Allchin 14–2–262–83–0–21.83; B. R. Oakden 15–0–284–65–0–18.93; R. T. Howell 15–0–266–66–0–17.73; *P. D. A. Turner 16–1–264–89–0–17.60.

Bowling—T. A. Barlow 50–8–188–16–5/34–11.75; A. D. Sims 125.5–33–414–27–5/24–15.33; I. S. Roberts 81.4–10–318–17–6/65–18.70; R. M. Wheat 115–19–471–16–5/51–29.43.

NOTTINGHAM HIGH SCHOOL   *Played 18: W 5, L 3, D 10. A 1*

Master i/c: J. Lamb   Cricket professional: K. Poole

Batting—R. A. Nicholson 14–5–545–129*–2–60.55; K. S. Tate 15–5–493–77–0–49.30; A. J. Hunt 17–3–497–84–0–35.50; J. L. Rayner 10–3–214–43–0–30.57; M. A. Fletcher 10–3–194–100*–1–27.71; *P. M. Dunn 8–0–206–52–0–25.75; C. J. Freeston 10–0–336–66–0–21.00.

Bowling—G. S. McNaughton 131.1–31–462–28–6/28–16.50; N. J. Ferguson 139.1–23–508–24–7/90–21.16; A. A. Phillips 159.5–46–555–24–6/78–23.12.

OAKHAM SCHOOL   *Played 20: W 9, L 5, D 6. A 1*

Master i/c: J. Wills   Cricket professional: D. S. Steele

The batting was headed by Robert Duck, the England Schools golf captain, who recorded three centuries.

Batting—*R. M. Duck 14–3–586–103–3–53.27; O. J. C. Marshall 12–3–411–84–0–45.66; R. A. E. Martin 12–1–502–90–0–45.63; M. R. K. Bailey 14–1–319–88*–0–24.53; C. Ward 10–2–184–42*–0–23.00; L. R. S. Condon 12–2–215–45*–0–21.50; W. H. J. M. Greaves 15–0–240–67–0–16.00; A. M. James 15–2–164–25–0–12.61.

Bowling—A. M. James 244.1–61–677–47–6/48–14.40; O. J. C. Marshall 141.1–29–451–18–4/59–25.05.

THE ORATORY SCHOOL   *Played 17: W 13, L 0, D 4. A 5*

Master i/c: P. L. Tomlinson   Cricket professional: J. B. K. Howell

In a superb, unbeaten season, 16-year-old Steven Tomlinson was outstanding. He broke the school batting record with 971 runs at 97.10 and scored 200 not out in a fourth-wicket partnership of 289 with Dominic Orchard (103 not out) in the last match of the season. He then declared, just 29 short of his thousand runs. He also headed the bowling averages and went on to play for Wales Under-19. The leading wicket-taker was James Urquhart (left-arm fast), whose 43 included eight for 39 against Royal GS, High Wycombe.

Batting—S. C. B. Tomlinson 17–7–971–200*–3–97.10; D. H. Orchard 11–2–364–103*–1–40.44; *J. P. C. Stebbings 12–2–392–79–0–39.20; C. Clayton 7–2–172–32*–0–34.40; J. A. D. Urquhart 11–1–342–122–1–34.20; D. P. J. Allaway 17–0–385–58–0–22.64.

Bowling—S. C. B. Tomlinson 95–23–289–24–5/23–12.04; J. A. D. Urquhart 152–14–608–43–8/39–14.13; E. W. Orchard 83–4–334–22–4/47–15.18; T. G. Limburn 122–10–512–28–6/51–18.28.

OUNDLE SCHOOL   *Played 21: W 13, L 3, D 5. A 1*

Master i/c: J. R. Wake   Cricket professional: T. Howorth

Attacking play was the feature of a season, in which victories over Durban High School and Wesley College, Melbourne, at their International Festival took Oundle to a record 13 wins and extended their tally over three seasons to 35 won and five lost. Jeremy Pilch broke the 11-year-old batting record with 1,091 runs, including four centuries. Although the left-arm spin bowler, Henry Bryers, headed the averages, David Walder was the leading wicket-taker and took the first hat-trick on the ground since the war. A tour of South Africa was planned for December, to coincide with the Test series against England.

Batting—J. Pilch 19–3–1,091–128–4–68.18; *E. Reynolds 17–1–626–88–0–39.12; C. Wilson 18–2–603–69*–0–37.68; M. Mountain 20–3–550–60–0–32.35; D. Walder 17–1–393–59–0–24.56; J. Thomas 15–1–323–59*–0–23.07; J. Milton 17–2–324–61–0–21.60.

Bowling—H. Bryers 134–39–365–24–4/44–15.20; D. Walder 193–43–631–37–5/17–17.05; W. Jefferson 139.1–26–414–22–6/60–18.81; J. Milton 205.5–37–744–34–6/34–21.88; G. C. Mason 138.1–27–497–21–5/19–23.66; C. Daniels 230–55–764–31–4/29–24.64.

THE PERSE SCHOOL   *Played 17: W 6, L 9, D 2*

Master i/c: A. C. Porter   Cricket professional: D. C. Collard

Batting—P. Siddle 18–0–535–97–0–29.72; R. Horsley 12–3–207–39*–0–23.00; D. P. Colquhoun 16–2–308–74–0–22.00; *J. R. Mayer 15–2–283–67–0–21.76; J. C. Salmon 17–1–315–54–0–19.68; M. G. Lorimer 15–0–213–51–0–14.20.

Bowling—M. Vincze 66–8–254–20–5/18–12.70; J. Garner 66.4–10–256–15–4/11–17.06; M. Brittain 162.4–38–472–20–4/11–23.60; J. R. Mayer 198–41–587–24–4/40–24.45.

PLYMOUTH COLLEGE   *Played 14: W 3, L 0, D 10, T 1. A 4*

Master i/c: T. J. Stevens

The outstanding player was John Fabian, who headed both averages, hit four centuries in 13 innings and achieved the school's second-best batting average.

Batting—*J. Fabian 13–4–764–132*–4–84.88; N. Pope 10–1–245–74–0–27.22; J. Conaghan 9–0–213–102–1–23.66; R. Moist 14–1–287–78–0–22.07; D. Saunders 12–1–236–40–0–21.45.

Bowling—J. Fabian 84–10–308–18–3/24–17.11; D. Mellor 84–20–272–15–5/45–18.13; N. Pope 137–28–466–24–5/36–19.41.

POCKLINGTON SCHOOL   *Played 24: W 12, L 7, D 5*

Master i/c: D. Nuttall

A strong batting side, in which nine players scored fifties, was headed by Matthew Stacey and the England Under-15 representative Paul Mouncey, who had 721 runs and 41 wickets. Although the attack tended to lack penetration, they achieved 12 victories.

Batting—P. R. Mouncey 21–4–721–101–1–42.41; *M. B. Stacey 24–1–956–95–0–41.56; N. G. Hadfield 15–5–220–64*–0–27.50; R. S. Milne 17–2–407–74*–0–27.13; G. J. T. Stewart 21–0–506–74–0–24.09; C. R. Wood 22–1–453–60–0–21.57; C. R. Rook 12–1–186–61–0–16.90; G. Johnson 18–2–261–51*–0–16.31; R. J. R. Poskitt 15–3–177–50*–0–14.75; S. D. Mouncey 15–1–194–39–0–13.85.

Bowling—P. R. Mouncey 203.3–41–701–41–5/42–17.09; M. B. Stacey 123–22–391–21–3/33–18.61; S. D. Mouncey 207.2–25–777–27–4/41–28.77; G. J. T. Stewart 258.5–47–821–26–4/51–31.57.

PORTSMOUTH GRAMMAR SCHOOL   *Played 13: W 6, L 4, D 3*

Master i/c: G. D. Payne   Cricket professional: R. J. Parks

A highlight was Alexander Herman's nine for 29, which brought victory over Seaford College. The brothers James and Christopher Moon played together in ten matches. The school's first overseas tour – to Cape Town – was planned for October.

Batting—*J. C. E. Moon 13–5–528–104*–1–66.00; N. E. Taylor 11–3–398–102*–1–49.75; S. A. Bell 11–1–413–80–0–41.30; R. G. Burgess 9–4–205–61*–0–41.00; S. A. Hamilton 12–0–234–67–0–19.50; J. E. Gannon 8–0–156–68–0–19.50; C. P. Moon 9–1–153–39*–0–19.12.

Bowling—A. Herman 75–17–220–22–9/29–10.00; J. R. Scott 142–31–459–27–4/19–17.00; M. Bulbeck 106–15–451–15–3/36–30.06.

PRIOR PARK COLLEGE   *Played 15: W 6, L 5, D 4. A 2*

Master i/c: D. R. Holland

Batting—S. Phillips 9–5–187–102*–1–46.75; L. Dokic 15–1–420–100*–1–30.00; A. Atkins 15–1–281–54–0–20.07; P. O'Dea 15–1–242–54–0–17.28; *J. Etheridge 15–0–239–61–0–15.93; D. Ash 14–1–151–50–0–11.61.

Bowling—S. Phillips 54–13–267–20–4/38–13.35; L. Doric 158–31–514–30–6/28–17.13.

QUEEN ELIZABETH'S HOSPITAL   *Played 14: W 5, L 5, D 4*

Masters i/c: M. S. E. Broadley and P. J. Kirby

All-rounder Peter Ross made an impact in his first full season, while his opening partner, Neil Varshney, scored the first century at this level for at least a decade. Adam Brenner captained Somerset Under-17, for whom Varshney also played.

Batting—N. Varshney 14–1–542–119–1–41.69; A. J. Brenner 14–2–435–89*–0–36.25; R. D. Cale 9–2–190–61–0–27.14; *N. Patel 13–2–270–60*–0–24.54; P. A. Ross 14–1–314–77–0–24.15.

Bowling—P. A. Ross 133.5–27–535–29–5/42–18.44.

QUEEN'S COLLEGE, TAUNTON   *Played 12: W 5, L 5, D 2. A 3*

Master i/c: A. S. Free

The team developed well during the season and won four of the last five games. While Paul Burke emerged as a useful all-rounder, the batting was bolstered by the brothers Grant and Alex Bailey, whose younger brother Oliver averaged 111 for the Under-13s.

Batting—P. M. Burke 11–2–280–77–0–31.11; G. C. Bailey 11–1–276–57–0–27.60; A. W. Bailey 12–3–245–63*–0–27.22; W. R. Handel 9–2–185–58–0–26.42; *H. L. Bowden 10–1–219–58–0–24.33.

Bowling—S. J. Pratt 109–26–376–21–7/21–17.90; P. M. Burke 94–13–362–15–3/15–24.13.

RADLEY COLLEGE   *Played 13: W 8, L 0, D 5. A 1*

Master i/c: W. J. Wesson   Cricket professionals: A. G. Robinson and A. R. Wagner

In an unbeaten season of positive cricket, the left-handed Ben Hutton (grandson of Sir Leonard, son of Richard) opened both batting and bowling. He and his first-wicket partner Andrew Strauss were the mainstays of the batting, with Malcolm Borwick – a semi-professional polo player in Argentina – whose 163 against Cheltenham was the highest innings by a Radleian for more than 50 years. Opening bowler Michael Bellhouse took the most wickets, followed by Charles Goldsmith, with his steady, accurate away swing.

Batting—M. P. Borwick 12–6–439–163–1–73.16; *A. J. Strauss 12–2–614–134*–2–61.40; B. L. Hutton 11–0–360–76–0–32.72; M. R. Bellhouse 8–2–150–53–0–25.00.

Bowling—C. R. N. Jennings 66.2–17–132–15–5/32–8.80; B. L. Hutton 72.2–15–171–15–5/35–11.40; M. R. Bellhouse 139.3–26–372–30–6/29–12.40; C. W. G. Goldsmith 111–38–288–20–5/70–14.40; B. C. A. Hawkins 89–26–232–16–5/23–14.50.

REIGATE GRAMMAR SCHOOL   *Played 18: W 2, L 6, D 10*

Master i/c: D. C. R. Jones   Cricket professional: H. Newton

Again no school was beaten, although there was encouragement from eight totals of more than 200 and record partnerships of 94 unbroken for the sixth wicket between Robbie Young and Toby Briggs and 78 for the eighth from David O'Hanlon and James Hylton. Fifteen-year-old Young looked a fine prospect, able to play long innings and bowling his off-spin tidily. However, off-spinning all-rounder Hylton was outstanding with 904 runs and 31 wickets, to become only the second player to pass 1,000 runs and 50 wickets for the XI, with a year to go.

Batting—*J. J. Hylton 17–0–904–117–1–53.17; M. R. Bowden 16–3–483–93–0–37.15; R. C. G. Young 17–3–375–68*–0–26.78; T. W. Briggs 14–1–319–69–0–24.53.

Bowling—J. J. Hylton 208–32–763–31–5/31–24.61; T. W. Briggs 155.5–24–580–19–3/67–30.52; R. C. G. Young 140.5–23–465–15–4/65–31.00.

RENDCOMB COLLEGE   *Played 13: W 3, L 4, D 6*

Master i/c: J. P. Watson   Cricket professional: D. Essenhigh

Batting—F. W. Newcombe 13–0–402–74–0–30.92; H. E. J. Davies 10–1–271–70*–0–30.11; F. G. E. Barton 12–3–244–58*–0–27.11; *C. E. Jarrett 9–0–192–60–0–21.33.

Bowling—P. D. Boydell 140.5–29–423–29–7/28–14.58; S. J. Roney 123.5–21–490–15–4/39–32.66.

REPTON SCHOOL   *Played 14: W 2, L 7, D 5*

Master i/c: M. Stones   Cricket professional: M. K. Kettle

Batting—M. W. S. Waine 12–2–378–76*–0–37.80; P. R. Abson 13–0–342–66–0–26.30; D. J. O'Gram 12–0–258–82–0–21.50; J. G. R. Cook 12–0–233–57–0–19.41; A. E. Kington 13–2–153–28–0–13.90.

Bowling—J. R. Webster 126–20–452–25–5/27–18.08.

RICHARD HUISH COLLEGE   *Played 12: W 6, L 4, D 2*

Master i/c: J. L. N. Grace

A highlight was the record return of eight for 34 by Nick Taylor. The side was captained by James Breakwell, son of Dennis, formerly of Northamptonshire and Somerset, while Steven Jenkins and Peter Lacy both went on to play for Somerset Second XI.

Batting—A. Warren 12–4–523–112*–1–65.37; S. Jenkins 12–3–426–105–1–47.33.

Bowling—N. J. Taylor 111.1–35–291–29–8/34–10.03; E. Warren 76.3–14–331–18–3/13–18.38; P. Lacy 85–13–369–15–4/61–24.60; *J. Breakwell 84–14–376–15–5/25–25.06.

ROSSALL SCHOOL   *Played 15: W 7, L 5, D 3. A 4*

Master i/c: P. Philpott

Liam Botham, son of Ian, was again the leading all-rounder, although his contribution was less spectacular than in 1994. He played for Hampshire Second XI and the Southern Development of Excellence XI.

Batting—*L. J. Botham 10–1–342–80*–0–38.00; J. R. Atkins 13–1–370–78–0–30.83; M. J. Dewhurst 8–1–160–69*–0–22.85; N. Roberts 14–3–212–49*–0–19.27.

Bowling—C. Simpson 70.5–19–189–17–4/20–11.11; L. J. Botham 144.1–30–428–27–5/15–15.85; M. J. Dewhurst 185.4–37–620–27–6/22–22.96.

THE ROYAL GRAMMAR SCHOOL, GUILDFORD *Played 18 : W 8, L 3, D 7. A 1*

Master i/c: S. B. R. Shore

Notable batting performances during the season included Andrew Hemingway's record aggregate of 811 runs, his opening stand of 177 against Reigate with Rupert Kitzinger and a century in 69 balls against Kingston GS by Chris Adams. The attack was dominated by Tom Grafton, whose 48 wickets included 24 from four consecutive matches.

Batting—A. R. Hemingway 18–1–811–127–2–47.70; Rupert C. Kitzinger 18–3–646–107*–2–43.06; D. L. Tompsett 18–2–574–150*–1–35.87; T. W. Grafton 18–5–416–72–0–32.00; *H. T. Stephens 15.4–309–78*–0–28.09; C. B. Adams 15.1–355–100*–1–25.35.

Bowling—T. W. Grafton 241.4–46–956–48–7/61–19.91; C. A. G. Cooper 74.2–7–351–15–3/17–23.40; P. T. Griffiths 141.3–15–627–16–3/33–39.18.

THE ROYAL GRAMMAR SCHOOL, NEWCASTLE *Played 18 : W 12, L 4, D 2*

Master i/c: D. W. Smith   Cricket professional: C. Craven

Ben Jones-Lee, with 787 runs, broke both the season and career aggregate records, while M. J. Smalley led by example with 524 runs and 46 wickets.

Batting—B. A. Jones-Lee 18–5–787–123*–2–60.53; *M. J. Smalley 17–6–524–85*–0–47.63; I. B. Park 17–2–501–71*–0–33.40; S. M. Stoker 13–1–267–60*–0–22.25; A. W. Tyson 18–0–330–70–0–18.33; C. P. Mordue 12–2–167–56–0–16.70.

Bowling—M. J. Smalley 219.1–51–557–46–5/63–12.10; C. B. E. Robson 137–36–403–31–5/42–13.00.

THE ROYAL GRAMMAR SCHOOL, WORCESTER *Played 22 : W 13, L 5, D 4. A 1*

Master i/c: B. M. Rees   Cricket professional: M. J. Horton

In a successful season, two of the seven fifth-formers in the side scored centuries. Mark Sellek was too quick for many batsmen, but unfortunately the edges were often too quick for the slip fielders.

Batting—E. Sellwood 20–1–748–95–0–39.36; J. E. K. Schofield 21–4–612–119*–2–36.00; M. W. J. Wilkinson 23–3–624–108–1–31.20; J. R. J. Cockrell 20–4–458–64*–0–28.62; R. J. Hall 22–1–517–70–0–24.61; M. J. Sellek 18–3–307–45–0–20.46; J. A. Leach 18–2–240–62–0–15.00.

Bowling—J. E. K. Schofield 74.4–8–289–20–3/11–14.45; M. J. Sellek 184.5–39–493–34–7/21–14.50; J. H. Parsons 107.2–21–305–16–4/33–19.06; E. Sellwood 203.2–37–644–33–7/79–19.51; *M. J. McNelis 145–27–416–21–3/23–19.80.

RUGBY SCHOOL   *Played 16 : W 5, L 5, D 6*

Master i/c: P. J. Rosser   Cricket professional: L. Tennant

Ed Lowe reached 1,000 runs for the season in his 13th innings and finished with a school record of more than 2,500 in four years.

Batting—E. J. Lowe 17–2–1,046–168*–5–69.73; R. D. Carter 17–2–509–88–0–33.93; J. A. Roper 16–1–445–112*–1–29.66; M. J. Howe 16–1–375–60*–0–25.00; S. Fawkes-Underwood 15–5–240–50*–0–24.00; *J. D. B. Lloyd 17–0–294–59–0–17.29.

Bowling—J. A. Froome 195–55–662–32–5/31–20.68; M. J. Howe 225.3–48–665–30–5/62–22.16; A. R. Davies 117.1–19–554–19–3/14–29.15; C. R. Steel 136–23–456–15–4/17–30.40.

ST ALBANS SCHOOL   *Played 22: W 9, L 8, D 5. A 1*

Master i/c: I. P. Jordan

Records tumbled in a successful season. These included B. J. Collins's unbeaten 141 against Dr Challoner's GS, the school's highest score, and a fifth century by J. A. Freedman. For the first time four players passed 300 runs. After 54 games, J. A. Mote finished with a bowling average of 15.31. The post-season tour to Barbados, Grenada and St Vincent was a tremendous experience.

Batting—J. A. Freedman 21-5-815-124-2-50.93; B. J. Collins 12-2-324-141*-1-32.40; S. J. Wood 15-1-396-118-1-28.28; R. J. Bee 17-2-368-55-0-24.53; J. D. Jacobs 12-3-176-44-0-19.55; *J. A. Mote 17-4-162-37-0-12.46.

Bowling—J. A. Mote 143.3-20-497-36-5/30-13.80; D. C. Jacobs 84.3-13-304-18-5/18-16.88; D. S. Curtis 182-34-594-35-7/31-16.97; T. C. Shuttleworth 157.2-22-645-15-2/19-43.00.

ST DUNSTAN'S COLLEGE   *Played 15: W 3, L 5, D 7. A 1*

Master i/c: O. T. Price   Cricket professionals: M. M. Patel and M. J. Walker

Winter coaching from Kent players Min Patel and Matthew Walker paid dividends in fine performances from young players. Nick Kirby made an excellent hundred against St Paul's, while Luke Speed overcame difficult conditions on a poor wicket to record 127 not out against Colfe's. David Farley bowled ever better as the season progressed, while John Welch was a promising all-rounder.

Batting—J. M. Scott 10-5-217-38*-0-43.40; N. V. Kirby 15-1-474-104-1-33.85; D. G. Darroch 12-1-264-51-0-24.00; *L. J. Speed 12-1-260-127*-1-23.63; I. A. Stewart 12-3-174-38*-0-19.33; J. C. Welch 14-1-177-36-0-13.61.

Bowling—D. K. Farley 156.5-35-556-31-6/60-17.93; J. C. Welch 143-28-518-26-5/38-19.92; M. Z. Chowdhry 127.5-30-475-19-5/72-25.00.

ST EDWARD'S SCHOOL, OXFORD   *Played 14: W 5, L 2, D 7*

Master i/c: D. Drake-Brockman   Cricket professional: G. V. Palmer

Highlights of an enjoyable season were a century from left-hander Robin Matthews against Bradfield, Matthew Joel's four wickets in five balls – including a hat-trick – against Marlborough, and the draw with Eton, in which St Edward's finished on 218 for five in reply to Eton's 218 for four declared.

Batting—G. S. Peddy 14-3-373-73*-0-33.90; R. P. Matthews 14-2-394-104*-1-32.83; M. J. Glover 12-2-323-85*-0-32.30; R. W. Tootill 13-1-351-86-0-29.25; M. R. Locker-Marsh 10-2-202-50-0-25.25; R. P. Pillai 12-1-192-50-0-17.45.

Bowling—J. N. St J. Blythe 163-42-483-24-4/18-20.12; *N. G. L. Prior 187-43-552-23-6/28-24.00.

ST GEORGE'S COLLEGE, WEYBRIDGE   *Played 17: W 2, L 11, D 4*

Master i/c: D. G. Ottley

Batting—C. Fletcher 16-0-618-100-1-38.62; R. Wilson 15-2-343-63-0-26.38; A. Allen 13-0-325-94-0-25.00; A. Neill 12-0-240-68-0-20.00; *J. Turner 16-0-310-82-0-19.37; M. Lawson 14-0-211-36-0-15.07.

Bowling—J. Knox 98-3-383-17-4/50-22.52; C. Fletcher 231-30-902-40-7/28-22.55.

ST JOHN'S SCHOOL, LEATHERHEAD   *Played 17: W 1, L 5, D 11*

Master i/c: A. B. Gale   Cricket professional: E. Shepperd

Batting—*T. E. Goodyer 17-1-601-125*-1-37.56; R. B. Vosser 16-1-367-121*-1-24.46; N. Keeley 14-0-300-51-0-21.42; R. D. Harradine 16-1-266-55*-0-17.73; J. M. A. Cook 16-0-280-67-0-17.50; N. B. Diacon 15-1-217-43*-0-15.50; J. J. Porter 14-2-181-52*-0-15.08.

Bowling—N. B. Diacon 145.3-21-534-19-3/21-28.10; H. C. R. Harris 145.1-15-587-19-8/40-30.89; J. S. Harvey 193-33-605-18-4/46-33.61.

ST JOSEPH'S COLLEGE, IPSWICH   *Played 18: W 7, L 7, D 4*

Master i/c: A. C. Rutherford   Cricket professional: K. Brooks

Batting—P. King 14–3–499–84–0–45.36; D. Potter 16–3–571–106–1–43.92; N. Rider 17–2–467–82–0–31.13; R. Daynes 13–3–300–68–0–30.00; J. Debenham 12–3–194–50*–0–21.55; *J. Townrow 17–1–281–48–0–17.56; C. Townrow 13–2–154–38–0–14.00.

Bowling—C. Jack 134.2–29–377–25–6/34–15.08; J. Regan 120–20–397–20–5/39–19.85; J. Townrow 188.5–45–701–33–4/9–21.24.

ST LAWRENCE COLLEGE, RAMSGATE   *Played 15: W 8, L 2, D 5. A 1*

Master i/c: N. O. S. Jones   Cricket professional: A. P. E. Knott

A highlight of another successful season was the win over MCC, thanks to a second-wicket stand of 183 between N. G. Morris and B. C. Swindells. The team generally relied on the first five batsmen.

Batting—*B. C. Swindells 15–4–723–113*–2–65.72; N. G. Morris 15–1–579–143–2–41.35; A. J. Boaler 15–0–561–84–0–37.40; B. J. Cotterell 14–5–316–62*–0–35.11; A. J. Snell 12–4–197–41–0–24.62.

Bowling—J. E. Langman 72.4–20–267–19–6/33–14.05; A. J. Boaler 110.5–28–362–19–4/31–19.05; R. A. Hicks 127.5–19–449–17–6/29–26.41.

ST PAUL'S SCHOOL   *Played 18: W 8, L 1, D 9*

Master i/c: G. Hughes   Cricket professional: M. Heath

The school enjoyed the best season since 1970. Fahad Badat completed four seasons in the eleven with 1,886 runs at 44.90.

Batting—*F. A. Badat 16–2–662–89–0–47.28; D. S. Hyman 15–5–450–57*–0–45.00; C. S. H. Bond 16–0–428–68–0–26.75; S. W. Peters 10–3–170–63–0–24.28; J. S. Grant 9–1–187–50–0–23.37; C. W. Miller 15–1–325–78–0–23.21.

Bowling—R. W. S. Carroll 114.2–24–397–25–5/6–15.88; D. J. McGaughey 189–67–565–30–5/52–18.83; J. S. Grant 189.4–40–654–30–4/33–21.80; J. A. C. Matthews 133.5–29–432–15–4/45–28.80; P. de Villiers 151–30–522–15–3/68–34.80.

ST PETER'S SCHOOL, YORK   *Played 19: W 3, L 8, D 8. A 2*

Master i/c: D. Kirby   Cricket professional: K. F. Mohan

Batting—N. J. Ogden 19–2–632–118–1–37.17; N. J. C. Kay 17–1–477–76–0–29.81; *T. J. Archer 19–2–465–68–0–27.35; S. P. Bradley 8–0–216–64–0–27.00; A. L. T. Kay 16–0–375–100–1–23.43; M. C. Dodgson 10–1–192–40*–0–21.33; J. E. Reynolds 12–1–166–40–0–15.09.

Bowling—T. J. Archer 132.2–29–434–19–4/32–22.84; D. Joshi 139.1–24–553–24–4/54–23.04; N. J. Ogden 218.1–51–755–26–4/37–29.03; P. T. Batty 174.5–38–576–16–4/47–36.00.

SEDBERGH SCHOOL   *Played 11: W 5, L 3, D 3. A 2*

Master i/c: N. A. Rollings

Batting—M. B. Crookes 11–2–411–108–1–45.66; P. J. Jameson 13–2–444–101–1–40.36; D. R. Scargill 9–3–189–98–0–31.50; J. C. M. Lofthouse 12–1–287–86–0–26.09; C. E. Heap 13–1–305–77*–0–25.41; C. P. Simpson-Daniel 12–2–254–42–0–25.40.

Bowling—J. M. Chapman 180.3–39–633–35–7/39–18.08; B. R. Biker 157.5–24–601–16–4/32–37.56.

SEVENOAKS SCHOOL   *Played 18: W 4, L 8, D 6*

Masters i/c: I. J. B. Walker and C. J. Tavaré

Batting—*N. Shirreff 18–5–839–137*–2–64.53; H. Snuggs 13–1–340–73–0–28.33; C. Young-Wootton 14–2–263–66–0–21.91; M. Wesley 17–0–342–77–0–20.11; M. Wilson 15–2–183–35–0–14.07.

Bowling—P. Amin 128.4–20–454–26–5/15–17.46; C. Young-Wootton 144.1–26–551–26–5/25–21.19; S. Shirreff 98.4–14–380–16–4/15–23.75.

SHEBBEAR COLLEGE   *Played 14: W 5, L 1, D 7, T 1*

Master i/c: A. Bryan

Chris Knapman compiled a record aggregate of 533 runs, while his brother Russell made an impact in his first season and was selected for England Under-14.

Batting—C. Knapman 14–1–533–79*–0–41.00; *P. Lockyer 13–1–444–102–1–37.00; G. Spencer 11–4–206–38–0–29.42; W. Coates 13–2–195–48–0–17.72.

Bowling—P. Lockyer 109–28–268–26–5/18–10.30; R. Knapman 83–19–242–17–5/36–14.23; N. Laws 102–25–376–22–6/12–17.09.

SHERBORNE SCHOOL   *Played 15: W 4, L 5, D 5, T 1*

Masters i/c: M. Nurton and G. Reynolds   Cricket professional: A. Willows

Overcoming a poor start, the side improved to play competitively in the last week of term and at the Haileybury Festival.

Batting—W. Bristow 11–5–284–56*–0–47.33; A. Nurton 14–5–273–53*–0–30.33; T. Ambrose 15–0–452–138–1–30.13; A. Searson 15–0–419–59–0–27.93.

Bowling—A. Nurton 174.1–32–526–30–7/44–17.53; J. Harris-Bass 94–22–300–17–4/25–17.64; W. Sanderson 118–22–372–18–3/15–20.66; J. Ambrose 101.3–24–346–16–4/29–21.62.

SHREWSBURY SCHOOL   *Played 20: W 11, L 6, D 3*

Master i/c: S. M. Holroyd   Cricket professional: A. P. Pridgeon

In a successful season, much was owed to Ian McCarter, a fifth-former. He carried the attack with 44 wickets and scored 567 runs, including 194 not out against Guildford GS from Perth, Australia, in the Silk Trophy.

Batting—*D. J. Umpleby 16–5–390–53*–0–35.45; J. D. W. Cox 21–3–618–113*–1–34.33; I. J. W. McCarter 21–4–567–194*–1–33.35; B. J. Chesters 19–4–497–101–1–33.13; K. M. Cornwall-Legh 19–2–407–65–0–23.94; N. J. B. Green 16–1–334–108–1–22.26.

Bowling—I. J. W. McCarter 264–54–734–44–6/33–16.68; K. M. Cornwall-Legh 105–18–387–18–3/25–21.50; B. J. Chesters 134–14–470–19–3/14–24.73; R. A. Carloss 145–26–438–17–3/26–25.76; J. P. Elcock 208.3–40–589–16–2/12–36.81.

SIMON LANGTON GRAMMAR SCHOOL   *Played 16: W 9, L 4, D 3. A 1*

Master i/c: R. H. Green

Batting—E. Roberts 15–3–687–116*–3–57.25; J. Cattell 8–2–225–101*–1–37.50; D. Patching 13–4–276–66*–0–30.66; S. Fletcher 16–0–487–100–1–30.43; *R. Marsh 16–3–388–48–0–29.84.

Bowling—R. Murray 65.2–22–152–16–6/18–9.50; O. Lloyd-James 92–9–394–26–5/18–15.15; R. Marsh 127–34–404–21–4/65–19.23; M. Bridger 98.4–10–425–21–6/45–20.23.

SOLIHULL SCHOOL   *Played 15: W 3, L 9, D 3. A 1*

Master i/c: S. A. Morgan   Cricket professional: K. Patel

The inexperienced side developed in confidence to achieve three wins late in the season. Highlights were James Pye's return of nine for 40 against Newcastle-under-Lyme School and a century against Loughborough GS from James Parks.

Batting—J. A. Spires 9–3–162–72–0–27.00; J. C. Parks 15–0–376–107–1–25.06; T. E. Whitelock 15–0–344–67–0–22.93; L. O. R. Davis 13–3–229–73–0–22.90; *W. L. W. Speer 15–1–307–47–0–21.92; T. M. Stretton 15–0–222–58–0–14.80.

Bowling—P. O. Cox 68–15–301–15–3/31–20.06; J. A. S. Pye 98–17–425–18–9/40–23.61; W. L. W. Speer 140–25–558–20–4/16–27.90.

SOUTH CRAVEN SCHOOL   *Played 10: W 4, L 3, D 3. A 2*

Master i/c: D. M. Birks

Andrew Waggett and Lee Gordon broke the record for any wicket with a stand of 157 in 23 overs against Grange School. The Army Apprentices College were dismissed for 36, with Neil Spragg returning figures of 5–5–0–5 and Adrian Emmott 5–2–4–4.

Batting—M. Ellison 7–1–233–82–0–38.83; A. Emmott 9–4–183–44*–0–36.60; *N. Spragg 7–0–217–82–0–31.00.

Bowling—A. Emmott 79.5–20–251–21–6/28–11.95.

STAMFORD SCHOOL   *Played 17: W 7, L 4, D 6*

Master i/c: P. D. McKeown

Luke Jackson's 791 runs were the best for the school since the war and second only to C. L. Edgson's 1,125 in 1934.

Batting—*L. H. Jackson 17–2–791–144–3–52.73; R. J. H. Thorley 17–3–610–93*–0–43.57; T. E. Smith 16–2–427–69–0–30.50; D. J. Scott 16–0–300–55–0–18.75; E. J. Taylor 14–4–183–42–0–18.30.

Bowling—R. J. H. Thorley 149.1–34–578–27–6/27–21.40; S. E. G. Fuller 154.4–32–583–26–5/101–22.42; L. H. Jackson 211.2–33–849–25–4/39–33.96.

STOCKPORT GRAMMAR SCHOOL   *Played 15: W 8, L 2, D 5. A 2*

Master i/c: S. Teasdale   Cricket professional: D. J. Makinson

Batting—*N. S. Thompson 14–2–565–77*–0–47.08; B. Wren 8–1–158–40–0–22.57; T. Pritchard 11–1–200–48–0–20.00; C. Pimlott 11–0–194–51–0–17.63; T. W. Clarke 14–1–170–39–0–13.07.

Bowling—C. Pimlott 163–42–397–33–6/8–12.03; N. S. Thompson 190.3–47–475–36–5/32–13.19.

STONYHURST COLLEGE   *Played 12: W 6, L 1, D 5*

Master i/c: C. E. Foulds   Cricket professional: R. A. Harper

In the match against Giggleswick, Michael Breetzke and Oliver Gregory both made unbeaten centuries, Gregory having also scored a century in the same fixture in 1994. Breetzke, who joined the sixth form from South Africa, also made an impact with the ball, taking 42 economical wickets.

Batting—P. Dineen 3–1–157–103–1–78.50; *M. Bradbury 7–4–178–80*–0–59.33; M. Breetzke 10–2–330–106*–1–41.25; I. Balshaw 5–1–150–83*–0–37.50; O. Gregory 12–3–281–104*–1–31.22.

Bowling—M. Breetzke 126.3–36–312–42–7/17–7.42; P. Broatch 114.3–23–304–19–3/16–16.00.

STOWE SCHOOL   *Played 14: W 2, L 5, D 7. A 2*

Master i/c: M. J. Harris

The side included R. A. Harris, son of M. J. Harris, formerly of Middlesex and Nottinghamshire.

Batting—J. W. R. McDonagh 9–1–234–63–0–29.25; R. A. White 13–0–306–98–0–23.53; R. A. Harris 13–1–259–79*–0–21.58; M. M. G. Smith 12–0–154–54–0–12.83.

Bowling—W. A. G. Milling 90–11–352–15–3/33–23.46; S. J. Branch 118–26–386–16–4/17–24.12; *M. J. M. Konig 142–26–444–15–5/65–29.60; R. A. Harris 144–23–511–16–3/20–31.93.

STRATHALLAN SCHOOL   *Played 17: W 5, L 7, D 5. A 1*

Master i/c: R. J. W. Proctor

Batting—R. J. D. Barr 16–5–462–79*–0–42.00; *D. G. O. Fergusson 15–1–450–68–0–32.14; A. J. MacDonell 13–2–329–52–0–29.90; D. G. Forbes 15–2–360–79–0–27.69; B. S. Ward 14–2–223–50–0–18.58.

Bowling—D. R. G. Elder 221.2–37–694–35–7/47–19.82; P. J. Watson 214–37–678–29–5/77–23.37; D. M. A. Camilleri 88–7–432–15–4/56–28.80.

SUTTON VALENCE SCHOOL   *Played 11: W 0, L 10, D 1*

Master i/c: J. Kittermaster   Cricket professional: A. R. Day

Batting—*M. J. Sands 8–0–152–34–0–19.00; J. Milsted 11–0–151–37–0–13.72.

Bowling—No bowler took 15 wickets.

TAUNTON SCHOOL   *Played 12: W 5, L 2, D 5*

Master i/c: D. Baty   Cricket professional: A. Kennedy

Batting—D. Law 9–3–228–108*–1–38.00; H. Tarr 6–0–191–91–0–31.83; R. Selway 13–0–383–72–0–29.46; S. Rose 11–2–258–66–0–28.66; T. Phillips 11–2–231–78*–0–25.66; T. Bradnock 10–2–205–36–0–25.62; *D. Cooper 11–1–224–45*–0–22.40.

Bowling—T. Bradnock 105.1–23–341–17–4/30–20.05; R. Selway 115–22–322–16–4/20–20.12; J. Ord 148.5–31–517–19–6/35–27.21.

TIFFIN SCHOOL   *Played 19: W 6, L 5, D 8*

Master i/c: M. J. Williams

Of the four batsmen who passed 400 runs, the most prolific was Brendan O'Connell, who headed both batting and bowling and shared 87 wickets with his brothers Tim (31) and Chris (6), who also played for the XI.

Batting—B. W. O'Connell 18–2–635–87*–0–39.68; A. D. Nutt 17–3–497–73*–0–35.50; J. T. Lynch 17–1–484–102*–1–30.25; R. C. Ward 18–1–470–118*–1–27.64; M. C. Anstey 15–2–339–95–0–26.07; S. M. Pashley 17–2–309–68–0–20.60; *M. J. Hooke 14–2–160–30–0–13.33.

Bowling—B. W. O'Connell 310–95–975–50–7/25–19.50; T. J. O'Connell 219–47–716–31–4/62–23.09; M. C. Anstey 130–30–462–20–6/39–23.10; M. J. Hooke 133–21–526–22–4/37–23.90.

TONBRIDGE SCHOOL   *Played 18: W 12, L 2, D 4*

Master i/c: P. B. Taylor   Cricket professional: C. Stone

A fine fielding side achieved 15 run-outs. They were inspired by Jonathan Bond, an outstanding wicket-keeper who held 19 catches and made six stumpings. Seven centuries were scored by three batsmen, three coming from James McCulley, a colt, while Edward Smith took his total for two seasons to 1,704 runs at 77.45.

Batting—E. T. Smith 17–3–984–149–2–70.28; J. J. McCulley 16–4–638–128*–3–53.16; J. P. Pyemont 19–3–716–111–2–44.75; A. D. Boldt 14–2–402–77–0–33.50; J. G. C. Rowe 13–7–201–39*–0–33.50; *W. M. Fyfe 11–2–298–81*–0–33.11.

Bowling—J. G. C. Rowe 66.2–17–221–17–5/21–13.00; T. E. Goodworth 153.4–28–405–22–4/20–18.40; W. M. Fyfe 151.4–27–478–23–5/43–20.78; M. J. Bluett 182.4–38–536–24–4/20–22.33; J. E. Davis 217.5–43–654–25–4/47–26.16; A. D. Boldt 105–18–420–16–3/53–26.25.

TRENT COLLEGE   *Played 20: W 12, L 5, D 3*

Master i/c: T. P. Woods   Cricket professional: G. Miller

In a superb season, with no matches lost to the weather, the 12 wins surpassed the previous best of nine in 1903. Noel Gie scored five hundreds and took his career aggregate to 3,153 with ten hundreds. He played for MCC Schools, made his first-class debut for Nottinghamshire in August and was selected to tour Zimbabwe with England Under-19, while Ben Spendlove played for England Under-17.

Batting—N. A. Gie 17–4–1,153–204*–5–88.69; B. L. Spendlove 18–3–782–105*–1–52.13; A. C. Garratt 10–2–365–82–0–45.62; F. L. Larke 4–0–155–61–0–38.75; K. G. Reesby 7–2–161–56*–0–32.20; M. L. White 11–3–229–49–0–28.62; D. I. Jordison 16–4–240–52–0–20.00; T. W. Hancock 18–1–332–68–0–19.52; N. J. Brown 14–1–232–67–0–17.84.

Bowling—D. I. Jordison 143–29–441–25–4/48–17.64; M. L. White 215.5–44–664–34–6/31–19.52; N. C. M. Owen 202.2–31–680–33–5/41–20.60; B. S. Morrison 177.4–23–623–28–4/18–22.25; T. W. Hancock 197.5–54–551–22–4/44–25.04.

TRINITY SCHOOL   *Played 20: W 11, L 2, D 7. A 1*

Masters i/c: I. W. Cheyne and B. Widger

An uneven start was followed by a run of 12 matches unbeaten, with seven victories. Shehan De Silva's 1,261 runs were second only to R. W. Nowell's 1,505 in 1993, while the England Under-15 player Scott Newman had 968, including a record 181 against St George's, Weybridge. Of the record 12 centuries scored by the side, these two made six and four respectively and shared in three double-century opening partnerships. The school made seven totals over 275, including a record 315 for four against Royal GS, Guildford. Opening bowler Andrew Clark confirmed his all-round prowess with 501 runs and 50 wickets from 341 overs.

Batting—*S. N. De Silva 20-5-1,261-156*-6-84.06; S. A. Newman 16-1-968-181-4-64.53; A. T. J. Clark 17-2-501-100*-1-33.40; R. J. Duke 10-4-194-85-0-32.33; M. G. Macaskill 18-8-295-60*-0-29.50; D. O. Robinson 20-2-523-120-1-29.05; A. J. C. Mutucumarana 11-4-179-61-0-25.57.

Bowling—A. T. J. Clark 341-83-915-50-5/19-18.30; P. A. R. D. Frost 122.3-17-442-23-5/36-19.21; R. J. Duke 133.2-22-436-17-4/52-25.64; D. Tanner 124.3-17-477-16-4/48-29.81; A. J. C. Mutucumarana 206.2-41-901-18-4/42-50.05.

TRURO SCHOOL   *Played 13: W 3, L 6, D 4*

Master i/c: D. M. Phillips

Despite losing all three of their limited-overs matches, the side did themselves justice in the other encounters, winning three and being on top in all the draws, when crucial catches were dropped. Tom Sharp, the captain, went on to play for Cornwall.

Batting—*T. Sharp 10-1-378-73-0-42.00; R. Harmer 11-3-262-75-0-32.75; T. Hick 11-0-315-85-0-28.63; C. Penhaligon 9-3-157-47*-0-26.16; C. Shreck 8-1-172-50-0-24.57; J. Price 11-1-220-60-0-22.00.

Bowling—C. Shreck 121.3-26-319-16-6/29-19.93.

UNIVERSITY COLLEGE SCHOOL   *Played 18: W 6, L 5, D 7*

Master i/c: S. M. Bloomfield   Cricket professional: W. G. Jones

A talented side boasted greater depth in batting than in bowling. The three top batsmen performed consistently well, with P. J. Durban and T. S. R. Gladstone compiling three century opening partnerships and D. Beary proving a fluent left-hander. A varied attack featured three seam bowlers and three spinners.

Batting—T. S. R. Gladstone 17-4-674-100*-2-51.84; D. Beary 15-0-452-58-0-30.13; P. J. Durban 17-2-392-100*-1-26.13; *J. D. Buck 14-2-177-45-0-14.75; B. J. Marshall 15-2-182-46-0-14.00.

Bowling—N. B. Hastings 154-22-499-24-3/11-20.79; S. Lawrence 177-13-646-29-6/65-22.27; A. J. Renton 222-48-625-25-3/14-25.00; D. L. Sanders 113-20-382-15-5/25-25.46; D. J. Krikler 145-16-465-15-4/67-31.00.

UPPINGHAM SCHOOL   *Played 18: W 4, L 6, D 7, T 1*

Master i/c: J. Lickess   Cricket professional: M. R. Hallam

Batting—C. D. Gent 19-1-592-73-0-32.88; J. M. T. Hunter 17-1-461-97-0-28.81; S. C. Debenham 18-3-369-81-0-24.60; *A. D. J. Dawe 18-0-418-64-0-23.22; R. E. C. Watts 16-0-327-81-0-20.43; A. D. A. Hunter Smart 19-4-305-100-1-20.33; C. R. Battle 16-1-301-58-0-20.06; R. R. J. Buchanan 13-3-192-66*-0-19.20.

Bowling—A. T. Menzies 125.5-30-406-27-6/41-15.03; R. R. J. Buchanan 181.4-44-532-32-4/47-16.62; C. A. P. Freestone 153.1-27-501-22-3/33-22.77; C. D. Dent 168-34-619-23-4/18-26.91; S. C. Debenham 188-51-528-16-3/39-33.00.

VICTORIA COLLEGE, JERSEY   *Played 17: W 4, L 8, D 5*

Master i/c: D. A. R. Ferguson

Batting—C. N. A. Gothard 16-0-444-76-0-27.75; I. J. A. MacEachern 14-3-286-66*-0-26.00; J. R. Cartmell 10-2-193-50*-0-24.12; R. D. Minty 9-0-157-71-0-17.44; R. A. Skilton 16-1-240-39-0-16.00; C. D. Mullin 17-4-204-64-0-15.69.

Bowling—C. N. A. Gothard 163–31–581–31–5/55–18.74; S. P. O'Flaherty 95–12–492–20–4/37–24.60.

WARWICK SCHOOL   *Played 13: W 5, L 5, D 3. A 1*

Master i/c: G. A. Tedstone

David Young was outstanding with a record aggregate of 923 runs at 102.55, his four centuries including 187 not out against MCC. He played for England Under-17 and Somerset Second XI.

Batting—*D. Young 12–3–923–187*–4–102.55; E. Dorr 6–1–181–83–0–36.20; A. Hume 10–1–255–101*–1–28.33; D. Daniel 11–3–221–85*–0–27.62; W. Evans 13–0–265–56–0–20.38.

Bowling—D. Young 108–26–338–15–4/28–22.53; D. Daniel 94.2–19–429–15–3/16–28.60.

WATFORD GRAMMAR SCHOOL   *Played 15: W 1, L 6, D 8*

Master i/c: W. E. Miller

An inexperienced side lacked bowling support for Farouk Khan (left-arm medium), who took half the wickets to fall. James Phang was distracted by the burden of captaincy, but younger batsmen shaped encouragingly.

Batting—*J. C. K. Phang 15–0–346–55–0–23.06; K. T. Farrell 13–0–280–62–0–21.53; B. J. Chandler 13–2–189–44*–0–17.18; J. A. Rylett 14–0–222–63–0–15.85; J. B. Millman 14–0–179–55–0–12.78; K. Elampooranar 15–2–164–47–0–12.61.

Bowling—F. M. Khan 223.4–45–704–44–8/48–16.00.

WELLINGBOROUGH SCHOOL   *Played 18: W 5, L 7, D 6*

Master i/c: M. H. Askham   Cricket professional: J. C. J. Dye

In a season of mixed results, Keith Potter proved the outstanding all-rounder. He was supported by Andy Taylor, who topped the batting averages, and left-arm spinner Kris Saville.

Batting—A. L. Taylor 17–5–444–80*–0–37.00; *K. G. Potter 18–0–659–123–1–36.61; J. J. Lower 13–1–239–53–0–19.91; T. N. Mason 12–0–190–37–0–15.83.

Bowling—K. G. Potter 205.4–31–689–29–4/48–23.75; R. Johnson 157.5–31–562–19–4/49–29.57; K. Saville 219.2–25–923–30–5/58–30.76.

WELLINGTON COLLEGE   *Played 18: W 5, L 6, D 7. A 2*

Masters i/c: C. M. St G. Potter and R. I. H. B. Dyer   Cricket professional: P. J. Lewington

Charles Hodgson scored 1,025 runs, breaking the 19-year-old record of 948, set by Robin Dyer, formerly of Warwickshire and now one of the school's cricket masters. Hodgson, whose six centuries were also a record, followed his three brothers into the XI. Edward Britton, who also scored a century, played for Wales Under-19.

Batting—C. P. R. Hodgson 20–3–1,025–137*–6–60.29; A. C. Northey 20–2–554–71–0–30.77; E. M. G. Britton 20–1–556–104*–1–29.26; E. J. Bennett 12–5–155–32*–0–22.14; A. J. Ash 19–1–358–72*–0–19.88; H. E. Johnson 11–2–172–74–0–19.11; *J. D. J. Brownrigg 15–3–205–51–0–17.08; M. P. Chicken 14–1–189–53–0–14.53.

Bowling—T. H. Wheeler 189.3–26–620–40–5/41–15.50; C. P. R. Hodgson 256–70–676–23–6/64–29.39; E. J. Bennett 137.2–30–513–15–2/17–34.20; R. A. R. Ritchie 167–24–575–16–3/27–35.93; J. D. J. Brownrigg 196.1–24–781–15–3/54–52.06.

WELLINGTON SCHOOL   *Played 18: W 7, L 8, D 3*

Master i/c: P. M. Pearce

Batting—J. P. Derbyshire 16–3–403–62–0–31.00; *A. J. Fulker 17–2–364–74–0–24.26; R. J. Urwin 17–2–343–85*–0–22.86; H. T. Spotswood 18–3–331–92*–0–22.06; M. A. Colman 18–0–331–82–0–18.38; A. D. J. Reid 9–0–156–76–0–17.33; S. A. Sheldon 15–2–200–50–0–15.38.

Bowling—A. J. Fulker 179.1–14–725–37–6/58–19.59; H. T. Spotswood 129–14–602–25–5/17–24.08; S. Cooper 159–25–606–25–4/8–24.24; M. A. Colman 176–43–756–18–3/21–42.00.

WELLS CATHEDRAL SCHOOL   *Played 14: W 6, L 8*

Master i/c: M. Stringer

Batting—J. Pym 13–1–465–71–0–38.75; J. Stone 11–0–295–110–1–26.81; B. Clements 14–3–210–28–0–19.09.

Bowling—B. Clements 107–20–385–23–4/45–16.73; M. Ferguson 76.2–7–268–16–4/14–16.75.

WESTMINSTER SCHOOL   *Played 12: W 2, L 2, D 8*

Master i/c: D. Cook   Cricket professional: R. O. Butcher

The excellent wickets at Vincent Square tended to make for high-scoring draws, the best of which was against the touring side from St Peter's, Adelaide. The one limited-overs match ended in ignominious defeat.

Batting—H. Stevenson 10–0–418–108–1–41.80; R. Korgaonkar 8–0–262–105–1–32.75; A. Jones 8–0–169–48–0–21.12; *C. Miller 9–0–189–57–0–21.00; T. Munro 10–0–179–40–0–17.90; J. Bentham 9–0–154–42–0–17.11; K. Raghuveer 12–0–205–64–0–17.08.

Bowling—B. Gordon 74.4–16–248–15–6/62–16.53; G. Zitko 63–4–339–15–5/37–22.60; K. Raghuveer 125–18–474–18–5/39–26.33; H. Hameed 136–20–540–16–3/56–33.75.

WHITGIFT SCHOOL   *Played 18: W 8, L 3, D 7*

Master i/c: P. C. Fladgate   Cricket professional: G. Durose

After a disappointing start, eight sides were beaten in nine games, including MCC. Moez Dungarwalla was the leading batsman, although it was James Furner who scored the only hundred – against Honesti – and the under-15 player Nishal Patel made a promising start. Gareth Tucker's off-spin brought him 41 wickets – the most for at least 20 years – while wicket-keeper Darren Blake effected 26 dismissals (18 caught, 8 stumped) and Stephen Lampkin shone with bat and ball.

Batting—S. P. O. Lampkin 16–4–442–72–0–36.83; N. A. Patel 5–0–177–55–0–35.40; N. D. A. Jarvis 7–1–186–76–0–31.00; M. Dungarwalla 19–2–494–86*–0–29.05; M. D. Dawton 16–4–312–60–0–26.00; J. P. Furner 17–1–415–104*–1–25.93; D. A. Blake 16–1–359–92–0–23.93; A. E. Courtenay 10–1–213–75–0–23.66.

Bowling—G. A. J. Tucker 249–59–662–41–6/48–16.14; A. A. Chmielowski 196.5–48–589–30–5/49–19.63; S. P. O. Lampkin 199.5–50–587–19–5/80–30.89; *G. R. Weale 139–18–571–15–5/28–38.06.

WINCHESTER COLLEGE   *Played 20: W 9, L 2, D 9. A 2*

Master i/c: C. J. Good   Cricket professional: I. C. D. Stuart

Edward Craig confirmed his promise with 1,033 runs, including three centuries.

Batting—E. D. C. Craig 21–2–1,033–126*–3–54.36; T. J. Powell-Jackson 9–2–263–58*–0–37.57; S. J. Hollis 20–4–430–67–0–26.87; J. D. Adams 17–4–327–45*–0–25.15; S. C. Kent 21–1–441–69–0–22.05; M. H. Whitcomb 12–3–155–50*–0–17.22; *G. C. Close-Brooks 17–2–230–50–0–15.33; T. O. V. Hanson 15–4–168–24–0–15.27; J. E. H. Sorrell 15–4–160–41–0–14.54.

Bowling—T. J. Powell-Jackson 49.3–11–145–15–5/40–9.66; G. C. Close-Brooks 238.5–53–687–45–7/23–15.26; M. H. Witcomb 200.4–43–581–33–5/42–17.60; E. D. C. Craig 129–23–423–19–3/25–22.26; R. C. J. Grisedale 167–40–459–15–3/27–30.60.

WOODBRIDGE SCHOOL   *Played 15: W 1, L 4, D 10*

Master i/c: Rev. M. E. Percival

Batting—*T. E. Percival 16–0–552–81–0–34.50; M. Johnston 12–3–283–100*–1–31.44; S. Tollit 14–3–209–58–0–19.00; R. Sledmere 13–1–151–65–0–12.58.

Bowling—T. E. Percival 111–21–423–29–5/36–14.58; M. Johnston 119.3–16–438–18–4/35–24.33.

WOODHOUSE GROVE SCHOOL   *Played 16: W 3, L 3, D 9, T 1*

Master i/c: R. I. Frost   Cricket professional: F. H. Tyson

A highlight was an unbeaten century by Duncan Sayers against the XL Club. Andrew Brimacombe, a fourth-former, displayed a sound technique with the bat, while leg-spinner Guy Bennett took 29 wickets and Nick Verity (medium-fast) took 19. Both Bennett and Verity played at Under-14 level for Yorkshire and the North of England. Frank Tyson came over from Australia and coached the players.

Batting—D. Sayers 16–2–453–102*–1–32.35; A. Peel 12–0–373–93–0–31.08; *D. T. Brier 16–2–419–69–0–29.92; A. Brimacombe 15–2–346–70–0–26.61; M. Gullick 13–1–244–45–0–20.33; A. Rowan 13–3–167–41–0–16.70; C. Dibb 14–2–157–27–0–13.08.

Bowling—B. Rhodes 97.5–16–336–23–4/22–14.60; G. Bennett 144.4–32–490–29–6/11–16.89; N. Verity 122–23–413–19–4/20–21.73.

WREKIN COLLEGE   *Played 14: W 5, L 5, D 4. A 3*

Master i/c: M. de Weymarn   Cricket professional: D. A. Banks

Highlights were an unbeaten hundred, out of 160, by Iain McArthur against Denstone and a hat-trick in the victory over Ellesmere College by Matthew Attwood. The side participated in the highly successful inaugural international tournament at St Columba's, Dublin.

Batting—V. S. Padhaal 13–4–386–61*–0–42.88; I. W. McArthur 13–2–288–100*–1–26.18; *S. A. Ingram 13–2–285–54*–0–25.90; R. M. A. Boyes 10–2–153–63–0–19.12; A. P. Rickard 13–1–228–60*–0–19.00.

Bowling—V. S. Padhaal 131–32–355–20–8/26–17.75.

WYCLIFFE COLLEGE   *Played 13: W 3, L 7, D 3*

Master i/c: C. R. C. Tetley

Batting—J. Skinner 10–2–263–58–0–32.87; *D. G. Singer 13–2–355–63–0–32.27; L. J. Bowery 11–3–225–66–0–28.12; M. Arnold 13–0–279–53–0–21.46.

Bowling—D. G. Singer 103–18–386–19–4/39–20.31; J. Skinner 115–18–457–18–5/37–25.38; L. J. Bowery 104–6–486–18–4/33–27.00.

WYGGESTON & QUEEN ELIZABETH I SIXTH FORM COLLEGE

Played 10: W 5, L 1, D 4. A 2

Master i/c: G. G. Wells

The County Under-19 Cup was retained in a thrilling last-ball victory over Lutterworth GS.

Batting—*S. Patel 9–1–348–77–0–43.50; M. J. C. Sutliff 9–2–249–93–0–35.57; J. Mason 9–0–251–64–0–27.88.

Bowling—S. Patel 52.2–12–153–21–4/12–7.28.

GIRLS' SCHOOLS

DENSTONE COLLEGE   *Played 12: W 9, L 3*

Mistress i/c: J. Morris

The side featured 16-year-old twins, Elizabeth and Mary Pattison, plus Caroline Chell, who was selected to keep wicket for West Midlands Ladies' Under-24.

Batting—*C. H. Chell 11–2–280–57*–0–31.11; E. C. Pattison 12–1–232–42–0–21.09.

Bowling—E. C. Pattison 73.2–16–193–32–4/6–6.03; M. H. Pattison 57.3–22–150–22–7/20–6.81.

ROEDEAN SCHOOL   *Played 14: W 6, L 8*

Staff i/c: A. S. England and A. F. Romanov

Against Newlands Manor, Sadia Halim achieved the best return since the war when she took eight for 16 in 4.4 overs, including the last four wickets in four balls.

Batting—G. M. Baker 12–2–230–48*–0–23.00.

Bowling—G. M. Baker 61–11–210–21–4/32–10.00; *S. Halim 45.1–4–200–16–8/16–12.50; E. L. Hamilton 30.5–0–202–15–5/19–13.46.

YOUTH CRICKET, 1995

UNDER-15 CRICKET

The North won the Bunbury ESCA Festival for four English regional under-15 teams, staged in the Bournemouth area from July 24–26. They beat the South and the West and drew with the Midlands. John Inglis of Yorkshire won the Neil Lloyd Trophy as best batsman of the week.

After the annual match against the ESCA President's Headmasters' Conference XI was drawn, ESCA then selected a squad from the two sides for the international matches against Wales, who were beaten by 140 runs, and Scotland, who drew. The party comprised Richard Dawson (Yorkshire) (*captain*), Jamie Bruce (Hampshire), Michael Dobson (Humberside), Michael Gough (Cleveland), Chris Hellings (Hampshire), Chris Hewison (Durham), John Inglis (Yorkshire), Richard Logan (Nottinghamshire), Paul Mouncey (Humberside), Graham Napier (Essex), Scott Newman (Surrey) and Jamie Rendell (Avon).

Pudsey St Lawrence of Yorkshire, Sir Len Hutton's club, won the Sun Life of Canada Under-15 Club Championship, beating Ilford by 11 runs in the final at Basingstoke. Trowbridge of Wiltshire and Horsford (Norfolk) were the beaten semi-finalists. A total of 1,300 clubs took part in the competition.

Millfield won the Lord's Taverners/Cricketer Colts Trophy for Schools for the sixth time in ten years, beating Birkenhead School by 128 runs in the final at Trent Bridge. The Millfield captain Danny White scored 76. Yorkshire won the final of the Army Careers/ESCA Under-15 County Championship at Sandhurst, beating Kent by 159 runs. Richard Dawson of Batley Grammar School scored 64 not out and took five for 20 as Kent were bowled out for 93.

UNDER-13 CRICKET

Cheltenham won the Ken Barrington Trophy in 1995 for the second time in three years when they took the NatWest Under-13 Club Championship, held from August 7–11 at Sherborne School. They lost only one match out of seven in the round-robin finals, being beaten by Tynemouth, the runners-up.

Other finalists, in order of finishing, were St Lawrence & Highland Court (Canterbury), Bournemouth, Wolverhampton, Kimberley Institute (Notts.), Ilkley and Bury St Edmunds, who lost all seven of their matches but won the Bill Ainsworth Fair Play Award.

The games are eight a side and Cheltenham's squad was: Richard Howell (captain), Phillip Arnold, Luke Bishop, Tom Donkin, Chris Downes, Nic Dymock, Charles Langton, Will Radcliffe and Edward Shaw.

UNDER-11 CRICKET

For the second year running, Headfield Junior School from Dewsbury, Yorkshire, won the Wrigley Softball Cricket Tournament, held at Edgbaston on July 17. It was Headfield's third consecutive year in the finals, which bring 16 primary schools together for a day out at Edgbaston, and their captain, Akber Valli, who had played all three years, received a special award from the tournament founder Trevor Bailey, who said that the whole team had played with "a maturity and discipline which was very refreshing". Other members of the winning squad, all Yorkshire-born, were: Zahir Asmal, Nabeel Hafeez, Zakaria Hughes, Murtaza Hussain, Nasir Hussain, Suhail Ibrahim, Zubair Ibrahim, Zuber Patel and Fida Zafir.

The beaten finalists, Crynallt School of Neath, also reached the last 16 in 1994. Headfield beat Green Mount County Primary of Bury in their semi-final, while Crynallt beat Hillside Avenue Primary, from Norwich. The margins in both games were very tight – 11 and four runs respectively – but in the final Headfield sailed away to win by 46 runs.

Each team has eight players and 12 overs per innings – they start with 200 runs and forfeit six every time a wicket falls; pairs of batsmen stay in for three overs, regardless of how many times they are out.

Other finalists were: Galmpton Primary School (Devon), Oakridge Primary (Stafford), Bigyn Primary (Llanelli), Butlers Court Primary (Beaconsfield), Stivichall Primary (Coventry), South Morningside Primary (Edinburgh), Ingrave Johnstone Primary (Brentwood), Dale Primary (Derby), Crook County Primary (Durham), Fircroft Primary (Tooting), St Mary's Primary (Timsbury, Bath) and Chantry Middle School (Morpeth). Ian and Kathy Botham were guests of honour for the day. Ian was said to have "signed his arm off".

WOMEN'S CRICKET, 1995

By CAROL SALMON

The Women's Cricket Association took some encouraging steps forward, particularly at grassroots level, in 1995. The number of affiliated clubs continued to grow: 62 were registered, up from just 39 in 1992. A reduction in affiliation fees has helped considerably, with a separate payment for entering the national league and cup competitions working well. The decision to appoint development officers in Hampshire and Derbyshire has paid off, with ever-expanding numbers playing the game in these previously barren counties. The WCA will now expand this scheme into other areas which have struggled in recent years.

Building on the growing interest of young people in cricket, special attention has been paid to establishing age group competitions. Following on from the Under-15 indoor six-a-side schools tournament, there is an eight-a-side festival, and a territorial tournament at Under-17 level and an Under-20 championship, won by Sussex in 1995. An England Under-21 side is expected to tour Australia in 1996-97. Standards at this level are particularly high: two of the present squad, left-arm seam bowler Suzanne Redfern and all-rounder Clare Connor, earned selection for the senior England team that retained the European Cup in Dublin in July and for the subsequent Test tour of India in November and December.

For the first time the county championship, held annually in Cambridge, was split into two divisions, with promotion and relegation. Yorkshire won the championship for the fourth year in a row; Kent, like their male counterparts, came bottom and were the first team to be relegated. The West were second division champions; their talented youngsters are reaching maturity and have been supplemented by international Janet Godman, formerly with Thames Valley. Like Yorkshire, the West won all their five matches and were promoted. The development of women's cricket in Hampshire and Derbyshire prompted calls for a third division, which would also allow more county Second Elevens to take part. At present Surrey and Yorkshire Seconds play off annually for a place at Cambridge. The territorial tournament, usually held in late August, was replaced by a four-day representative match, to assist the selectors in considering their options for the tour of India.

After the long and glorious summer, September was a dismal month on and off the field. Firstly, holders Newark & Sherwood won a disappointing National Knockout final against Invicta of Kent by nine wickets. Then the National League final, between the northern and southern winners Wakefield and Redoubtables, was abandoned without a ball bowled. Overshadowing these matches, however, was the death of Molly Hide, one of the legends of the game.

After relatively little international action following the 1993 World Cup, England could stage three successive home series after returning from India. New Zealand, whom they beat in the World Cup final, are due to play three Tests and three one-day internationals in a six-week tour during 1996; officials were considering an invitation to South Africa for a one-day series in 1997, in the run-up to the 1997-98 World Cup in India; and Australia have expressed interest in touring in 1998. In 1995 the England team's only competition before going to India was the European Cup against Ireland, Holland and Denmark, held round Dublin in July. They won their three qualifying matches comfortably, despite including six new caps (under a new coach, John Bown) and looking a little rusty. In the final a run-a-ball 47 from Barbara Daniels gave them victory over the Irish and the European title for the fourth time in succession.

Note: Matches in this section were not first-class.

AREA CHAMPIONSHIP

Division One

	Played	Won	Lost	Tied	Points
Yorkshire	5	5	0	0	91.5
East Midlands	5	4	1	0	85.5
Surrey	5	3	2	0	72
West Midlands	5	2	3	0	52.5
East Anglia	5	0	4	1	31
Kent	5	0	4	1	30.5

Division Two

	Played	Won	Lost	Tied	Points
The West	5	5	0	0	100.5
Middlesex	5	3	2	0	72.5
Surrey Second XI	5	3	2	0	70.5
Thames Valley	5	2	3	0	57
Sussex	5	1	4	0	47
Lancashire & Cheshire	5	1	4	0	46.5

ENGLAND REPRESENTATIVE MATCH

At Oundle School, August 25, 26, 27, 28. Drawn. Toss: Barbara Daniels's XI. Barbara Daniels's XI 295 (B. A. Daniels 82, S. Redfern 44) and 292 for six (H. C. Plimmer 124, B. A. Daniels 46, R. Lupton 44); Karen Smithies's XI 448 for eight dec. (S. Metcalfe 137, J. Godman 72, J. Smit 45, K. Leng 40).

NATIONAL CLUB KNOCKOUT FINAL

At Norbury, September 2. Newark & Sherwood won by nine wickets. Toss: Newark & Sherwood. Invicta 61 (32.2 overs) (K. Smithies five for six); Newark & Sherwood 62 for one (20.3 overs) (J. Smit 31).

PREMIER LEAGUE FINAL

At Norbury, September 10. Redoubtables v Wakefield. Abandoned.

EUROPEAN CUP

Final: At Clontarf, Dublin, July 22. England won by seven wickets. Toss: Ireland. Ireland 150 for eight (50 overs) (E. Owens 37, M. Grealey 46); England 153 for three (40.3 overs) (J. Smit 40 not out, B. A. Daniels 47, K. Smithies 34 not out).

PART FOUR: OVERSEAS CRICKET IN 1994-95

FEATURES OF 1994-95

Double-Hundreds (51)

324*	D. M. Jones	Victoria v South Australia at Melbourne.
312‡	R. Lamba	Delhi v Himachal Pradesh at Delhi.
300	Ramiz Raja	Allied Bank v Habib Bank at Lahore.
297‡	Bhupinder Singh, jun.	Punjab v Delhi at Delhi.
292	S. S. Bhave	West Zone v South Zone at Rourkela.
272	T. M. Moody	Western Australia v Tasmania at Hobart.
266†	D. L. Houghton	Zimbabwe v Sri Lanka (Second Test) at Bulawayo.
250*	W. V. Raman	South Zone v West Zone at Rourkela.
249	Manzoor Akhtar	Karachi Blues v Faisalabad at Karachi.
247	J. Jaymon	Burgher RC v Galle CC at Colombo.
241*	J. L. Langer	Western Australia v New South Wales at Perth.
240	Ajay Sharma§	Delhi v Punjab at Delhi.
237*	G. K. Khoda	Rajasthan v Uttar Pradesh at Kanpur.
237	Salim Malik	Pakistan v Australia (Second Test) at Rawalpindi.
233	C. Grainger	Transvaal B v Orange Free State B at Johannesburg.
226	S. I. de Saram	Western Province (North) v North-Western Province at Colombo.
224‡	Ghulam Ali	Karachi Blues v Sargodha at Karachi.
224	S. V. Manjrekar	Bombay v Punjab at Bombay.
220	A. A. Muzumdar	Bombay v Maharashtra at Solapur.
216‡	R. Sehgal	Delhi v Himachal Pradesh at Delhi.
214	Bantoo Singh	North Zone v East Zone at Calcutta.
212*	S. Jayantha	Singha SC v Antonians SC at Colombo.
211	R. T. Ponting	Tasmania v Western Australia at Hobart.
210*	A. Gupta	Jammu and Kashmir v Himachal Pradesh at Una.
209*	A. Ranatunga	Sinhalese SC v Kurunegala Youth CC at Colombo.
209	R. P. A. H. Wickremaratne	Western Province (North) v Western Province (South) at Panadura.
208*	P. Krishnakumar	Rajasthan v Assam at Udaipur.
208‡	Asif Mujtaba	Karachi Blues v Lahore City at Peshawar.
208‡	Mahmood Hamid	Karachi Blues v Lahore City at Peshawar.
206*	Tariq Mahmood	Lahore City v Faisalabad at Lahore.
206	S. R. Waugh§	New South Wales v Tasmania at Hobart.
204	V. S. K. Waragoda	Colombo CC v Colts CC at Colombo.
203*	D. M. Benkenstein	Natal B v Northern Transvaal B at Durban.
203*	M. W. Gatting	England XI v Queensland at Toowoomba.
203*	Mohammad Ramzan	Faisalabad v Karachi Whites at Faisalabad.
202*‡	P. Dharmani	Punjab v Delhi at Delhi.
202*	Ijaz Ahmed, jun.	Faisalabad v Sargodha at Sargodha.
202*	D. S. Lehmann	South Australia v Victoria at Melbourne.
202*	Mohammad Nawaz	Sargodha v Faisalabad at Sargodha.
202	P. A. de Silva	Sri Lankans v Mashonaland Country Districts at Harare.
202	R. A. Harper	Guyana v Windward Islands at Georgetown.
202	Ajay Sharma§	North Zone v Central Zone at Gauhati.
201*	G. W. Flower	Zimbabwe v Pakistan (First Test) at Harare.
201*	M. L. Hayden	Queensland v Victoria at Brisbane.
201*	D. L. Haynes	Barbados v Windward Islands at Arnos Vale.
201*	Mazhar Qayyum	Peshawar v Sargodha at Peshawar.
201*‡	Shoaib Mohammad	Karachi Blues v Sargodha at Karachi.
200*	Saurav C. Ganguly	Bengal v Bihar at Calcutta.

200*	A. H. Shah	Mashonaland v Mashonaland Under-24 at Harare.
200	Atif Rauf	ADBP v Railways at Sialkot.
200	S. R. Waugh§	Australia v West Indies (Fourth Test) at Kingston.

† *National record.* ‡ *R. Lamba and R. Sehgal scored double-hundreds in the same innings, as did Bhupinder Singh, jun. and P. Dharmani, Ghulam Ali and Shoaib Mohammad, and Asif Mujtaba and Mahmood Hamid.* § *Ajay Sharma and S. R. Waugh both scored two double-hundreds.*

Hundred on First-Class Debut

122*	J. M. Henderson	Boland B v Orange Free State B at Bloemfontein.
106	Jyoti P. Yadav	Uttar Pradesh v Kerala at Lucknow.
103	B. S. Naik	Andhra v Karnataka at Bangalore.
102	D. Bora	Assam v Tripura at Agartala.
101	Iftikhar Hussain	Lahore City v Sargodha at Sargodha.
101	C. R. Wilson	Border B v Eastern Transvaal at Springs.

Four Hundreds in Successive Innings

Ijaz Ahmed, jun. (Faisalabad) .... 202* v Sargodha at Sargodha, 119 v Rawalpindi B at Faisalabad, 194 v Karachi Blues at Karachi, 168 v Lahore City at Rawalpindi.

S. R. Tendulkar (Bombay) .... 166 v Tamil Nadu at Bombay, 109 v Uttar Pradesh at Bombay, 140 and 139 v Punjab at Bombay.

Three Hundreds in Successive Innings

Mohammad Nawaz (Sargodha) ... 135 and 100* v Karachi Whites at Sargodha, 202* v Faisalabad at Sargodha.

Ten Fifties in Successive Innings

R. S. Kaluwitharana (Galle CC/Western Province (South))† .... 54*, 55, 52, 65, 71, 67, 72, 92*, 142, 70.

† *Equals world record.*

Hundred in Each Innings of a Match

Atif Rauf	121	100*	ADBP v PNSC at Peshawar.
W. R. James	107	127	Matabeleland Select XI v South Africa A at Bulawayo.
S. G. Law	102	138	Queensland v Tasmania at Hobart.
M. L. Love	187	116	Queensland v Tasmania at Brisbane.
Mohammad Nawaz	135	100*	Sargodha v Karachi Whites at Sargodha.
M. H. Parmar	109	155*	Gujarat v Baroda at Vallabh Vidyanagar.
M. V. Sridhar	107	102*	Hyderabad v Goa at Secunderabad.
S. R. Tendulkar	140	139	Bombay v Punjab at Bombay.

Hundred Before Lunch

| S. R. Tendulkar | 35* to 158* | Bombay v Tamil Nadu at Bombay (2nd day). |
| S. R. Tendulkar | 100* | Bombay v Punjab at Bombay (5th day). |

Carrying Bat Through Completed Innings

Z. Bharucha	164*	Bombay (424) v Rest of India at Bombay.
P. W. Dobbs	81*	Otago (177) v Canterbury at Oamaru.
G. W. Flower	145*	Mashonaland Under-24 (283) v Mashonaland at Harare.
W. A. M. P. Perera	79*	Antonians SC (242) v Bloomfield C and AC at Colombo.
M. Rajapakse	87*	Burgher RC (181) v Colombo CC at Colombo.
D. Ranatunga	166*	Western Province (North) (389) v Central Province at Katunayake.
C. D. Thomson	26*	Services (71) v Delhi at Delhi.

Unusual Dismissals

Obstructing the field	S. J. Kalyani, Bengal v Orissa at Calcutta.
Handled the ball	A. C. Waller, Mashonaland v Mashonaland Under-24 at Harare.

Notable Partnerships

First Wicket
464‡ R. Sehgal/R. Lamba, Delhi v Himachal Pradesh at Delhi.
287 B. R. Hartland/G. R. Stead, Canterbury v Wellington at Christchurch.

Second Wicket
324 R. Kalsi/Bhupinder Singh, jun., Punjab v Himachal Pradesh at Mandi.
290 Ghulam Ali/Shoaib Mohammad, Karachi Blues v Sargodha at Karachi.
286 S. S. Dighe/S. V. Manjrekar, Bombay v Punjab at Bombay.

Third Wicket
326 M. L. Love/S. G. Law, Queensland v Tasmania at Brisbane.
304 Vikram Rathore/Ajay Sharma, North Zone v Central Zone at Gauhati.
299‡ S. Ranatunga/P. A. de Silva, Sri Lankans v Mashonaland CD at Harare.
290 S. S. More/A. A. Muzumdar, Bombay v Maharashtra at Solapur.

Fourth Wicket
279 A. Gupta/V. Bhaskar, Jammu and Kashmir v Himachal Pradesh at Una.
279 D. R. Martyn/T. M. Moody, Western Australia v Tasmania at Hobart.
278† R. P. A. H. Wickremaratne/M. S. Atapattu, Sinhalese SC v Tamil Union at Colombo.
269§ G. W. Flower/A. Flower, Zimbabwe v Pakistan (First Test) at Harare.

Fifth Wicket
319 R. T. Ponting/R. J. Tucker, Tasmania v Western Australia at Hobart.
285 D. N. Nadarajah/U. U. Chandana, Tamil Union v Kurunegala Youth at Colombo.
270 D. S. Lehmann/J. A. Brayshaw, South Australia v Victoria at Melbourne.
233*‡§ G. W. Flower/G. J. Whittall, Zimbabwe v Pakistan (First Test) at Harare.

Seventh Wicket
460† Bhupinder Singh, jun./P. Dharmani, Punjab v Delhi at Delhi.
283‡ Bantoo Singh/A. R. Kapoor, North Zone v East Zone at Calcutta.

Eighth Wicket
215 J. R. Murray/A. C. Cummins, West Indians v Otago at Dunedin.
211 Ijaz Ahmed, jun./Nadeem Afzal, Faisalabad v Karachi Blues at Karachi.

Ninth Wicket
268‡ J. B. Commins/N. Boje, South Africa A v Mashonaland at Harare.

Tenth Wicket
117*‡ E. A. Brandes/D. J. Rowett, Zimbabwe Board XI v Griqualand West at Kimberley.
108 P. S. de Villiers/R. E. Bryson, Northern Transvaal v Border at Verwoerdburg.
101 N. J. Astle/M. B. Owens, Canterbury v Northern Districts at Hamilton.
100 C. D. Lee/C. M. Brown, Auckland v Otago at Dunedin.

* *Unbroken partnership.* † *World record for that wicket.*
‡ *National record for that wicket.* § *Same innings.*

Most Wickets in a Match

16-99	A. Kumble	Karnataka v Kerala at Tellicherry.
14-152	K. G. Perera	Western Province (South) v North-Western Province at Moratuwa.
13-55	C. A. Walsh	West Indies v New Zealand (Second Test) at Wellington.
13-123	W. D. Phillip	Leeward Islands v Jamaica at Grove Park, Nevis.
13-124	K. V. P. Rao	Bihar v Tripura at Jamshedpur.
13-125	O. D. Gibson	Border v Natal at Durban.
13-141	Sajid Shah	Peshawar v Rawalpindi A at Rawalpindi.

Eight or More Wickets in an Innings

9-35	Naved Anjum	Lahore City v Islamabad at Lahore.
8-8	M. Muralitharan	Tamil Union C and AC v Burgher RC at Colombo.
8-37	M. J. G. Davis	Northern Transvaal B v Western Transvaal at Potchefstroom.
8-41	A. Kumble	Karnataka v Kerala at Tellicherry (2nd innings)
8-58	A. Kumble	Karnataka v Kerala at Tellicherry (1st innings)
8-60	K. G. Perera	Western Province (South) v North-Western Province at Moratuwa.
8-65	Athar Laeeq	Karachi Blues v Rawalpindi A at Karachi.
8-71	S. K. Warne	Australia v England (First Test) at Brisbane.
8-72	Masood Anwar	Faisalabad v Islamabad at Faisalabad.
8-79	N. N. Amerasinghe	Burgher RC v Galle CC at Colombo.
8-90	S. D. Anurasiri	Western Province (South) v Central Province at Moratuwa.
8-92	W. D. Phillip	Leeward Islands v Jamaica at Grove Park, Nevis.
8-97	Tariq Hussain	Karachi v United Bank at Peshawar.
8-101	D. Kolugala	Moors SC v Nondescripts CC at Colombo.
8-111†	Shafiq Ahmed	Bahawalpur v Karachi Blues at Karachi.
8-114	D. Vasu	Tamil Nadu v Karnataka at Madras.
8-115	Arshad Khan	Peshawar v Islamabad at Peshawar.
8-130	Suranjith Silva	Western Province (South) v Southern Province at Moratuwa.

† *On debut in first-class cricket.*

Hat-Tricks

‡Ali Gauhar†	Karachi Blues v United Bank at Peshawar.
F. Davids	Western Province B v Zimbabwe Board XI at Cape Town.
§D. W. Fleming	Australia v Pakistan (Second Test) at Rawalpindi.
C. Z. Harris	New Zealanders v Orange Free State at Bloemfontein.
C. W. Henderson	Boland v Warwickshire at Paarl.
Suranjith Silva	Sinhalese SC v Tamil Union C and AC at Colombo.
‡Tauseef Ahmed	United Bank v Karachi Blues at Peshawar.
R. E. Veenstra	Natal v Transvaal at Johannesburg.
S. K. Warne	Australia v England (Second Test) at Melbourne.

† *Also four wickets in four balls.*   ‡ *In the same match.*   § *On Test debut.*

Most Runs Conceded in an Innings

68-5-234-2	Shahid Mahmood	Habib Bank v United Bank at Karachi.
72.2-14-231-4	Mohammad Hussain	Lahore City v Karachi Blues at Karachi.

Most Runs Conceded in a Match

55.4-3-308-1	A. R. Kapoor	Punjab v Bombay at Bombay.

Most Overs Bowled in an Innings

78–18–176–4	...... U. Chatterjee	East Zone v North Zone at Calcutta.
75–20–197–1	...... Mohammad Asif	Lahore City v Karachi Blues at Peshawar.

Nine Wicket-Keeping Dismissals in a Match

6 ct, 3 st	.... S. S. Dighe	Bombay v Baroda at Bombay.
9 ct	.... I. A. Healy	Australia v England (First Test) at Brisbane.
9 ct	.... S. J. Palframan	Border v Natal at Durban.

Six Wicket-Keeping Dismissals in an Innings

5 ct, 1 st	.... Ahsan Raza	Sargodha v Islamabad at Islamabad.
6 ct	.... M. N. Atkinson	Tasmania v Western Australia at Perth.
4 ct, 2 st	.... S. S. Dighe	Bombay v Baroda at Bombay.
6 ct	.... L-M. Germishuys	Boland v Western Province at Cape Town.
6 ct	.... A. C. Gilchrist	Western Australia v Victoria at Perth.
5 ct, 1 st	.... R. G. Hart	Northern Districts v Canterbury at Hamilton.
6 ct	.... R. S. Kaluwitharana	Galle CC v Colombo CC at Colombo.
5 ct, 1 st	.... K. J. Rule	Northern Transvaal v Orange Free State at Verwoerdburg.
4 ct, 2 st	.... W. A. Seccombe	Queensland v New South Wales at Sydney.
6 ct	.... Z. Zuffri	Assam v Orissa at Guwahati.

Seven Catches in a Match in the Field

C. B. Lambert ...... Northern Transvaal v Boland at Paarl.

Five Catches in an Innings in the Field

C. P. Mapatuna .... Nondescripts CC v Panadura SC at Panadura.

Match Double (100 Runs and 10 Wickets)

R. B. Biswal	.... 126; 5-33, 7-38	Orissa v Tripura at Agartala.
M. J. G. Davis	..... 60, 46; 8-37, 4-47	N. Transvaal B v W. Transvaal at Potchefstroom.
P. Krishnakumar	... 12, 106*; 6-63, 5-101	Rajasthan v Vidarbha at Nagpur.

No Byes Conceded in Total of 500 or More

M. N. Atkinson	.... Tasmania v Western Australia (502-6) at Hobart.
D. S. Berry	.... Victoria v South Australia (524-8 dec.) at Adelaide.
P. B. Dassanayake	.. Bloomfield C and AC v Sinhalese SC (509-8 dec.) at Colombo.
A. C. Parore	.... New Zealand v West Indies (Second Test) (660-5 dec.) at Wellington.
Pathik Patel	.... Gujarat v Maharashtra (544-8 dec.) at Pune.

Highest Innings Totals

802-8 dec.......... Karachi Blues v Lahore City at Peshawar.
780-8 .... Punjab v Delhi at Delhi.
716 .... North Zone v East Zone at Calcutta.
690-6 dec.......... Bombay v Punjab at Bombay.
664 .... Queensland v South Australia at Brisbane.
660-5 dec.......... West Indies v New Zealand (Second Test) at Wellington.
637-3 dec.......... Delhi v Himachal Pradesh at Delhi.
600-6 dec.†........ Sri Lankans v Mashonaland Country Districts at Harare.

   † *National record.*

Highest Fourth-Innings Totals

475-4 .... Wellington v Canterbury at Christchurch (set 475).
417-4 .... Mashonaland v Northamptonshire at Harare (set 417).
406-5 .... Leeward Islands v Barbados at Anguilla (set 481).

Lowest Innings Totals

52 .... Saurashtra v Bihar at Rajkot.
62 .... Lahore City v United Bank at Peshawar.
65 .... PIA v United Bank at Karachi.
69 .... Islamabad v Lahore City at Lahore.
71 .... Sri Lanka v Pakistan (Third Test) at Kandy.
71 .... Services v Delhi at Delhi.
74 .... North-Western Province v Western Province (City) at Colombo.

Match Aggregates of 1,500 Runs

Runs-Wkts
1,945-18 .... Canterbury v Wellington at Christchurch.
1,716-24 .... Bombay v Punjab at Bombay.
1,547-23 .... Orange Free State v New Zealanders at Bloemfontein.

Four Hundreds in an Innings

Sri Lankans (502-3 dec.) v ZCU President's XI at Harare:
   R. S. Mahanama 105*, A. P. Gurusinha 141, H. P. Tillekeratne 105*, A. Ranatunga 100*.
South Australia (524-8 dec.) v Victoria at Adelaide:
   G. S. Blewett 112, P. C. Nobes 110, D. S. Lehmann 100, J. A. Brayshaw 134*.
Karachi Blues (802-8 dec.) v Lahore City at Peshawar:
   Shoaib Mohammad 100, Asif Mujtaba 208, Mahmood Hamid 208, Moin Khan 107.
Bombay (690-6 dec.) v Punjab at Bombay.
   S. S. Dighe 137, S. V. Manjrekar 224, S. R. Tendulkar 140, V. G. Kambli 107*.

Most Extras in an Innings

	b	l-b	w	n-b	
65	10	18	1	36	Zimbabwe (319-8) v Sri Lanka (First Test) at Harare.
64	4	18	6	36	South Africa (460) v Pakistan (Only Test) at Johannesburg.
63†	5	11	1	46	New South Wales (469) v Queensland at Sydney.
63	16	8	1	38	Bloomfield C and AC (400-8 dec.) v Nondescripts CC at Colombo.

   † *Under Australian Cricket Board regulations two extras were scored for every no-ball, excluding runs scored off the delivery.*

ENGLAND IN AUSTRALIA, 1994-95

By JOHN THICKNESSE

England's tour of Australia resembled its predecessor in that a key player suffered severe damage to a finger within a week of arrival, in each case with far-reaching consequences. In 1990-91, Graham Gooch, the captain, was kept out of the First Test, which England duly lost inside three days. In 1994-95, Alec Stewart's broken index finger mended in time for him to play in Brisbane. But when he broke it again in the Second Test in Melbourne, and sustained a further blow to it as soon as he was passed fit to reappear – against Victoria just before the Fourth Test – Mike Atherton was deprived of his regular opening partner in all the last three Tests.

In a series in which it was clear from the start that England needed luck to smile on them, the handicap of Stewart's absence might alone have ensured that Australia kept the Ashes. In the event, England's misfortune with illness and injuries was so uniformly foul that the vice-captain's was merely the first item on a list so long that six replacements were required. Granted Australia's known superiority, especially in bowling through Shane Warne's devastating leg-spin and Craig McDermott's fire and pace, it was no disgrace in the circumstances that, after being two down with three to play, England held the margin to 3-1. The Executive Committee of the Test and County Cricket Board took a different view, however. Within a month of the tour ending, Keith Fletcher was told by A. C. Smith, the TCCB's chief executive, that his contract as team manager had been terminated midway through its five-year course. Two days later, Smith announced that Ray Illingworth, the chairman of selectors, was in addition to take on Fletcher's duties, and stressed that the county chairmen and secretaries had pledged their full support. He appeared to find no irony in the fact that the self-same functionaries had just granted Benson and Hedges a five-year extension to a competition that was probably the most disruptive on the fixture-list from the selectors' point of view.

The longer the tour lasted, the more obvious it became that in the small print of the game – fielding, running between wickets, practice techniques, plus attitude to practice – England were running second not only to Australia, but to state and colts teams too: successive defeats by Cricket Academy XIs at North Sydney Oval on a weekend in December ranked among their worst humiliations. In mitigation, though, better teams than Atherton's might have been demoralised by the spate of injuries.

Darren Gough, the find of the tour with 20 wickets in three Tests and some carefree batting down the order, and Graeme Hick, who averaged 41.60 at No. 3, both missed the last two Tests, suffering respectively from a broken foot and a slipped disc. But the most damaging setback to morale probably came when the attacking spearhead, Devon Malcolm, went down with chicken-pox 48 hours before the First Test. Inconsistent though he had always been, Malcolm's nine for 57 had shattered South Africa in England's most recent Test and he had also played a significant role in their only win over Australia in 1993, where he removed all of the top six batsmen. His physical presence, as well as his pace, meant a lot to England psychologically, so that when Mark Taylor won the toss and, with Michael

Slater, hammered Phil DeFreitas and Martin McCague for 26 in the first four overs, the whole team's confidence was in tatters.

Slater went on to score 176, the first of his three hundreds in the series, with Mark Waugh contributing a classical 140 to Australia's 426. When England, batting feebly, permitted McDermott to rout them for 167, Australia might have won by an innings had Taylor enforced the follow-on. To give an exceptionally dry pitch its best chance of breaking up, however, he decided to bat again. Despite Australia's massive victory – 184 runs – and the fact that Warne took eight for 71 in the second innings, Taylor's decision seemed mistaken; Hick and Graham Thorpe went some of the way towards restoring England's self-esteem in a stand of 160. But a month later Australia won the Second Test by an even wider margin, and it was clear the captain's apparent generosity had done their cause no lasting harm.

In addition to Gough and Hick, McCague, the Kent fast bowler, who had a stress fracture of the shin, Yorkshire all-rounder Craig White and Hampshire off-spinner Shaun Udal, both with torn side muscles, also flew home early. Stewart would have joined them if his wife and small son had not been holidaying in Perth. His Surrey team-mate Joey Benjamin, whose chicken-pox was wrongly diagnosed as shingles, went four weeks without a game mid-tour; like Udal, he was never in serious contention for a Test place. There were lesser injuries for Atherton (back), Thorpe (adductor), DeFreitas (groin and hamstring) and John Crawley (calf). Even physio David Roberts broke a finger in fielding practice.

Hollow laughter was afforded by the fact that the oldest players, 41-year-old Graham Gooch and 37-year-old Mike Gatting, were available for every match, a distinction shared only by Steve Rhodes and Phil Tufnell among the original 16. In order of call-up, England were reinforced by Angus Fraser, Mark Ilott, Jack Russell, Neil Fairbrother, Chris Lewis and Mark Ramprakash. After a brief stay without playing, Ilott joined the A team in India; Russell's only appearance was as a substitute in Bendigo; while Fairbrother failed to see the tour out after falling awkwardly on his right shoulder in a World Series game.

England's many injuries and the high standard of batting and fielding in Australia (Warne and McDermott excepted, they were not overstocked with bowlers) were not the only reasons the tourists were so consistently outclassed, however. Two ill-judged pieces of selection by Illingworth's panel – the original omission of Fraser and the inclusion of both Gooch *and* Gatting – also played their part, as did Atherton's lack of drive and urgency as captain. M. J. K. Smith's narrow interpretation of his duties as manager and distant treatment of the media, to the disadvantage of both parties, were also sadly unenlightened.

The only criticism that could be levelled at Atherton's batting was that he passed 40 in ten of his 20 first-class innings without going on to make a hundred. Atherton's resolution and commitment were unquestioned. As captain, however, he was unable to communicate his aggression to the players. On a personal level, he created temporary disunity within the team when he deprived Hick of a virtually certain hundred by declaring in the Sydney Test.

As Fraser was to prove when he replaced McCague, he should have been an automatic choice in the original 16. At 29, he had lost some of the explosiveness he possessed before his hip and back injuries on England's previous tour Down Under, but he was still far the best and most accurate bowler of his type. Having captained England in Australia, Illingworth should have known how valuable it would be to Atherton to have a seamer who could shut a game down, especially with the unreliable Malcolm as his likely partner. The other mistake lay in backing experience to the extent of picking two old stagers, Gooch and Gatting, in a country whose conditions so much favoured youth. Not since Jack Hobbs in 1928-29 had an English batsman in his 40s enjoyed a successful series in Australia and Gooch's record in the last five Tests of 1994 – 152 runs at 16.88 – hardly suggested he could reverse the trend. Gatting was actually the sounder choice, despite having lost his place after the Lord's Test of 1993, and the fact that he owed his recall to the hope, optimistic as it turned out, that his belligerence against spin might unsettle Warne. In the event, though they trained and practised hard together – and England would not have won the Adelaide Test without Gatting's battling hundred – neither was able, overall, to justify selection. They were not blessed by luck in the Tests, Gooch getting the sticky end of an lbw decision in Sydney when he was shaping to play his best innings of the series, and Gatting being out to three balls from McDermott he would have been relieved to survive in his prime. But Gooch's aggregate of 245 from ten innings and Gatting's of 182 from nine were a fair reflection of their impact. Both announced their retirement from Test cricket as the tour was drawing to a close.

When naming the 16, Illingworth made a point of saying the selectors' priority had been to pick a team capable of winning back the Ashes. But their failure even to reach the finals of the one-day World Series ahead of Australia's second string highlighted their poor standards of fielding. These were typified by Crawley, who, though only 23, was omitted in favour of Gooch for the opening World Series game. Once Stewart and White were injured, Gooch held his place for all six qualifiers. But his and others' lack of mobility was a severe handicap. Irrespective of whether they were engaged in a five-day Test or a 50-overs game, England's fielding and running between wickets were conceding half a run an over against Australia and Australia A, and little less against the state teams. Before cricket writers wearied of the topic, England's practice sessions were derided in Australian newspapers. When Greg Baum of *The Age* began his preview to the Melbourne Test by writing: "England trained and grass grew at the MCG yesterday, two activities virtually indistinguishable from one another in tempo, but each with its own fascination," he was considered to be in greater peril of being sued for libel by the grass.

Of those still present when the series ended with Australia's crushing win in Perth, only Thorpe enhanced his stature: had he scored six instead of nought in his final innings, he would have averaged 50. Of his nine dismissals, Warne was responsible for five, the last with the help of an expert stumping by Ian Healy when Thorpe, with 123, had completed only the second hundred of the series for England. By scoring 444, though – all but 200 more than anyone but Atherton – Thorpe substantiated the belief that Warne's threat decreased when he was bowling to left-handers. Apart from a hot-headed attempt to take the initiative in the second innings in Melbourne, when conservation of wickets was clearly the order of the day, Thorpe appeared to have the temperament, as well as the technique, to be a fixture in the team for several years.

Gough, whose high-spirited delight in taking part made him a favourite both with spectators and his team-mates, was the other great success. His bowling had lacked discipline in the last two Tests against South Africa, but here he responded to Atherton's warning that, if he placed too much reliance on his bouncer, yorker and slower ball, they would lose the value of surprise. Consequently, he put more work into improving his stock ball and was rewarded when it earned more than half his 20 Test wickets. In Sydney, where he followed a breezy 56-ball 51 by taking six for 49, he had the pleasure of receiving a note from Ray Lindwall. It read: "Well batted, well bowled. Great effort. You will remember this match for ever. Keep up the great work and best wishes for the future." Gough showed his own respect for history by going to visit 90-year-old Harold Larwood in his Sydney bungalow.

Not even Malcolm's chicken-pox deflated the tourists more than Gough's injury, which came a week after the Sydney Test as he jumped into his delivery stride in a day/night match at Melbourne, shortly after he had completed a match-winning 45. Contrarily, England's record improved following his departure, thanks to Australia's random batting in the second innings in Adelaide. But there was as little doubt that Gough belonged in the side as that vigorous rebuilding was required.

Allowances had to be made for Tufnell, in that he was often obliged to bowl over the wicket to a leg-side field, which did not suit his temperament or style; the mercurial Lewis took 11 wickets in the last two Tests, and sharpened up the fielding; and Ramprakash advanced his claims by scoring 72 and 42 in Perth. Crawley's moderate fielding detracted from the composure of his batting; Rhodes had a patchy tour as wicket-keeper and failed with the bat; while DeFreitas and Malcolm each paid more than 40 for his Test wickets. It was no surprise that the team had been turned upside down again midway through the home series that followed.

Australia looked unbeatable in the first two Tests, when it seemed Taylor had only to throw Warne the ball for wickets to start tumbling. His figures in Brisbane and Melbourne were 112.2–43–190–20, including, in the Second Test, his first hat-trick. In the New Year, however, his workload increased when off-spinner Tim May was dropped, and inevitably it took its toll: in the last three Tests Warne's seven wickets cost 51.28 apiece. By Perth, rather than touring New Zealand and the Caribbean, Warne looked in need of a holiday to rest his bowling shoulder.

Even so, it was a tribute to McDermott's strength that, at 29, he outlasted a spinner four years his junior, taking 32 wickets to Warne's 27. That eight supporting bowlers had to be content with 30 wickets, though, showed how much Australia relied on their big two. Damien Fleming, fast-medium swing and seam, was the most successful of the rest, with ten. Glenn McGrath's sharp form in Perth suggested England were lucky he bowled so untidily in Brisbane – he was left out of the following three Tests. Had Merv Hughes been even four-fifths the force he was in England in 1993, he might have opened the bowling with McDermott. But his legs were spluttering SOS signals about the increasing bulk they had to carry, and six games for Australia A were the closest he came to an international recall.

That the batting was less effective than in any Ashes series since 1986-87 could be explained on two counts. David Boon, at No. 3, suffered such a loss of confidence, passing 50 only once, in his century at Melbourne, that in the final Test Taylor sent in a night-watchman an unAustralian 25 minutes before the close to protect him. The second cause was Allan

Border's retirement. On paper, Australia's top seven still looked as strong as any in the world. But without the reassuring presence of their unflappable ex-captain in the middle of the order, they were edgy under pressure. It was hard to imagine England bowling Australia out in four and a half hours in Adelaide, on a flat pitch, had Border been in charge. With Taylor as captain, however, the series was played in a better spirit than in Border's latter days.

Seeking to maintain the right-hand/left-hand balance, the selectors turned first to New South Wales left-hander Michael Bevan to fill the gap at No. 5. England discovered how good he was when his century for Australia A at Sydney in the World Series ensured that England would not reach the finals. In three Tests, though, he played without conviction, and was dropped. Such were Australia's resources that any one of three middle-order batsmen could have been chosen to replace him: Justin Langer, a dogged left-hander in the Border mould, his Western Australian captain Damien Martyn, or another outstanding strokeplayer, 20-year-old Ricky Ponting of Tasmania. Instead, because the dislocated shoulder Steve Waugh sustained in Pakistan still prevented him from bowling, the panel chose South Australia's Greg Blewett, a young opener cum medium-pacer, who vindicated their judgment by making hundreds in both his first two Tests, though he failed to take a wicket. With Border gone, though, and Boon out of sorts, there was a brittleness about the batting England had not experienced in three series.

The change was reflected by Australia's average partnership – 33.94 per wicket, compared with 57.86 in 1989, 38.57 in 1990-91 and 51.28 in 1993. One thing, regrettably, was incontestable: neither England's batting, bowling, nor fielding, nor organisation was improving. Of the 22 Tests played over the four series, Australia had won 14 compared with England's two – both of them achieved when the battle for the Ashes was already decided.

ENGLAND TOURING PARTY

M. A. Atherton (Lancashire) *(captain)*, A. J. Stewart (Surrey) *(vice-captain)*, J. E. Benjamin (Surrey), J. P. Crawley (Lancashire), P. A. J. DeFreitas (Derbyshire), M. W. Gatting (Middlesex), G. A. Gooch (Essex), D. Gough (Yorkshire), G. A. Hick (Worcestershire), M. J. McCague (Kent), D. E. Malcolm (Derbyshire), S. J. Rhodes (Worcestershire), G. P. Thorpe (Surrey), P. C. R. Tufnell (Middlesex), S. D. Udal (Hampshire), C. White (Yorkshire).

McCague, White, Gough, Stewart, Udal and Hick were all forced out of the tour by injury. At various times the party was reinforced by N. H. Fairbrother (Lancashire) – who also withdrew through injury – A. R. C. Fraser (Middlesex), M. C. Ilott (Essex), C. C. Lewis (Nottinghamshire), M. R. Ramprakash (Middlesex) and R. C. Russell (Gloucestershire).

Tour manager: M. J. K. Smith (Warwickshire). *Team manager:* K. W. R. Fletcher. *Scorer:* A. E. Davis (Warwickshire). *Physiotherapist:* D. G. Roberts (Worcestershire).

ENGLAND TOUR RESULTS

Test matches – Played 5: Won 1, Lost 3, Drawn 1.
First-class matches – Played 11: Won 3, Lost 4, Drawn 4.
Wins – Australia, South Australia, Queensland.
Losses – Australia (3), New South Wales.
Draws – Australia, Western Australia, Australian XI, Victoria.
One-day internationals – Played 4: Won 2, Lost 2. *Wins* – Australia, Zimbabwe. *Losses* – Australia, Zimbabwe. *Note:* Matches against Australia A did not have international status.
Other non-first-class matches – Played 9: Won 4, Lost 5. *Wins* – ACB Chairman's XI, Bradman XI, Australian Capital Territory, Australia A. *Losses* – Western Australia, Prime Minister's XI, Australian Cricket Academy (2), Australia A.

TEST MATCH AVERAGES

AUSTRALIA – BATTING

	T	I	NO	R	HS	100s	Avge	Ct/St
G. S. Blewett	2	4	1	249	115	2	83.00	3
M. J. Slater	5	10	0	623	176	3	62.30	0
S. R. Waugh	5	10	3	345	99*	0	49.28	3
M. A. Taylor	5	10	0	471	113	1	47.10	7
M. E. Waugh.	5	10	0	435	140	1	43.50	8
I. A. Healy.	5	10	3	249	74	0	35.57	23/2
D. C. Boon	5	10	0	246	131	1	24.60	2
T. B. A. May	3	5	3	31	10*	0	15.50	0
M. G. Bevan	3	6	0	81	35	0	13.50	0
D. W. Fleming	3	4	0	40	24	0	10.00	2
C. J. McDermott. . . .	5	8	2	42	21*	0	7.00	3
S. K. Warne	5	10	1	60	36*	0	6.66	5

Played in two Tests: G. D. McGrath 0, 0. Played in one Test: J. Angel 11, 0; P. E. McIntyre 0, 0.

* Signifies not out.

BOWLING

	O	M	R	W	BB	5W/i	Avge
M. E. Waugh.	53	11	157	8	5-40	1	19.62
S. K. Warne	256.1	84	549	27	8-71	2	20.33
C. J. McDermott. . . .	232.5	56	675	32	6-38	4	21.09
D. W. Fleming	102.2	30	274	10	3-52	0	27.40
G. D. McGrath	67	16	229	6	3-40	0	38.16

Also bowled: J. Angel 25.3–7–85–3; M. G. Bevan 7–1–19–0; G. S. Blewett 24–5–91–0; P. E. McIntyre 27.3–3–87–2; T. B. A. May 101–30–219–1.

ENGLAND – BATTING

	T	I	NO	R	HS	100s	Avge	Ct/St
G. P. Thorpe	5	10	1	444	123	1	49.33	5
G. A. Hick	3	6	1	208	98*	0	41.60	9
M. A. Atherton	5	10	0	407	88	0	40.70	4
J. P. Crawley	3	5	0	171	72	0	34.20	1
G. A. Gooch	5	10	0	245	56	0	24.50	0
D. Gough.	3	5	1	98	51	0	24.50	4
A. J. Stewart	2	4	1	73	33	0	24.33	2
M. W. Gatting	5	9	0	182	117	1	20.22	3
P. A. J. DeFreitas. . . .	4	8	0	141	88	0	17.62	2
C. C. Lewis	2	4	0	68	40	0	17.00	1
D. E. Malcolm	4	7	3	50	29	0	12.50	1
A. R. C. Fraser	3	5	0	53	27	0	10.60	0
S. J. Rhodes.	5	9	1	72	39*	0	9.00	20/1
P. C. R. Tufnell	4	7	3	6	4*	0	1.50	2

Played in one Test: M. J. McCague 1, 0; M. R. Ramprakash 72, 42 (2 ct).

* Signifies not out.

BOWLING

	O	M	R	W	BB	5W/i	Avge
D. Gough............	152.5	33	425	20	6-49	1	21.25
C. C. Lewis.........	78.5	14	249	11	4-24	0	22.63
A. R. C. Fraser....	129.5	25	389	14	5-73	1	27.78
P. A. J. DeFreitas....	184	39	558	13	3-91	0	42.92
P. C. R. Tufnell.....	207.4	45	442	10	4-79	0	44.20
D. E. Malcolm	181.1	32	588	13	4-39	0	45.23

Also bowled: G. A. Gooch 25–6–74–1; G. A. Hick 16–3–58–0; M. J. McCague 19.2–4–96–2; M. R. Ramprakash 19–1–74–0.

ENGLAND TOUR AVERAGES – FIRST-CLASS MATCHES

BATTING

	M	I	NO	R	HS	100s	Avge	Ct/St
G. A. Hick	8	15	1	877	172	3	62.64	16
A. J. Stewart	5	9	4	291	101*	1	58.20	2
G. P. Thorpe........	10	20	3	756	123	1	44.47	9
J. P. Crawley.......	9	15	2	563	91	0	43.30	3
M. A. Atherton......	10	20	1	755	88	0	39.73	8
G. A. Gooch	10	19	0	685	101	2	36.05	3
M. W. Gatting	9	16	1	532	203*	2	35.46	5
C. White	3	5	0	125	46	0	25.00	2
D. Gough...........	5	8	2	114	51	0	19.00	5
C. C. Lewis	2	4	0	68	40	0	17.00	3
P. A. J. DeFreitas....	7	13	1	190	88	0	15.83	2
S. J. Rhodes........	11	19	2	240	50	0	14.11	40/6
A. R. C. Fraser.....	4	6	1	60	27	0	12.00	1
D. E. Malcolm	8	12	4	91	29	0	11.37	1
S. D. Udal	2	4	0	30	16	0	7.50	1
M. J. McCague	4	5	1	29	16	0	7.25	3
J. E. Benjamin	4	4	0	11	7	0	2.75	1
P. C. R. Tufnell	9	13	7	12	4*	0	2.00	6

Played in one match: M. R. Ramprakash 72, 42 (2 ct).

Signifies not out.

BOWLING

	O	M	R	W	BB	5W/i	Avge
C. C. Lewis	78.5	14	249	11	4-24	0	22.63
D. Gough...........	222.5	44	688	26	6-49	2	26.46
C. White	60.5	10	195	7	3-13	0	27.85
D. E. Malcolm	340.3	55	1,133	34	6-70	1	33.32
M. J. McCague	125.2	21	487	14	5-31	1	34.78
P. A. J. DeFreitas....	299.1	67	852	24	4-60	0	35.50
A. R. C. Fraser.....	157.5	30	504	14	5-73	1	36.00
P. C. R. Tufnell	384.2	70	1,018	27	5-71	1	37.70
J. E. Benjamin	105.5	22	341	6	2-36	0	56.83
S. D. Udal	81.5	4	345	5	2-95	0	69.00

Also bowled: M. A. Atherton 2–0–6–0; G. A. Gooch 27–7–79–2; G. A. Hick 61–8–224–2; M. R. Ramprakash 19–1–74–0; G. P. Thorpe 2–1–6–0.

Note: Matches in this section which were not first-class are signified by a dagger.

†At Lilac Hill, October 25. England XI won by seven wickets. Toss: ACB Chairman's XI. ACB Chairman's XI 232 (49.4 overs) (G. R. Marsh 46, R. T. Ponting 82, D. R. Martyn 36, G. B. Hogg 33; D. Gough five for 32): England XI 236 for three (47.2 overs) (G. A. Gooch 129, G. P. Thorpe 61 not out).

†At Perth, October 27 (day/night). Western Australia won by 51 runs. Toss: England XI. Western Australia 248 for five (50 overs) (M. P. Lavender 83, D. R. Martyn 51, G. B. Hogg 34, M. R. J. Veletta 35 not out): England XI 197 (45.5 overs) (G. P. Thorpe 35, C. White 35; C. E. Coulson three for 31).

In a "quartered" match, each team faced 25 overs in daylight and then resumed for another 25 under floodlights. Western Australia were 90 for one after their first half-innings and England XI were 83 for four.

WESTERN AUSTRALIA v ENGLAND XI

At Perth, October 29, 30, 31, November 1. Drawn. Toss: England XI.

Murray Goodwin, a stocky 21-year-old making his debut, denied England a win in their first-class opener by adding 77 to his first-innings 91; he batted more than eight hours in all. After Atherton chose to bat and, with Gooch, luckily survived some skilful out-swing from Coulson, England should have done better than 245. On the second day, however, Malcolm, near his fastest, recaptured the initiative, taking five for 23 in 46 balls after Western Australia reached 178 for two. The remaining wickets went down for 60. England's second innings was dominated by Hick, whose first 19 runs were spread over 26 overs, but went on to drive and pull with great power. His second 50 came off 62 balls and his third off 25; he struck 28 fours in nearly five hours. Declaring overnight, England's chances of victory looked good when a full-length leg-side catch by Rhodes dislodged the left-handed Hogg in the opening over. But on a pitch now short of pace, Goodwin and Lavender added 119 and, with false strokes reluctant to go to hand, the game drifted to an early close.

Close of play: First day, England XI 241-9 (J. P. Crawley 36*); Second day, England XI 37-0 (G. A. Gooch 29*, M. A. Atherton 6*); Third day, England XI 393-6 (J. P. Crawley 67*, P. A. J. DeFreitas 4*).

England XI

G. A. Gooch c Lavender b Reid	38	– c Gilchrist b Stewart	68
*M. A. Atherton c Coulson b Cary	68	– c Lavender b Moody	35
G. A. Hick c Lavender b Moody	41	– c Gilchrist b Cary	172
G. P. Thorpe c Gilchrist b Cary	4	– c sub (R. C. Kelly) b Cary	14
M. W. Gatting c Goodwin b Reid	7	– c Moody b Stewart	6
J. P. Crawley not out	40	– not out	67
†S. J. Rhodes c Gilchrist b Cary	13	– c Martyn b Cary	16
P. A. J. DeFreitas c Hogg b Reid	20	– not out	4
M. J. McCague c Veletta b Coulson	1		
J. E. Benjamin b Reid	1		
D. E. Malcolm run out	0		
B 1, l-b 1, n-b 10	12	L-b 2, w 1, n-b 8	11

1/77 2/149 3/153 4/157 5/171   245   1/80 2/129 3/174   (6 wkts dec.) 393
6/199 7/239 8/240 9/241   4/203 5/354 6/388

Bowling: *First Innings*—Reid 25-7-71-4; Coulson 24.4-6-87-1; Cary 24-11-55-3; Moody 15-5-28-1; Stewart 7-5-2-0. *Second Innings*—Reid 29-8-82-0; Coulson 18-4-83-0; Moody 17-6-23-1; Cary 22-3-114-3; Stewart 22-4-89-2.

Western Australia

M. P. Lavender c Hick b Malcolm	1	– (2) lbw b DeFreitas	51
M. R. J. Veletta c Rhodes b Benjamin	67		
M. W. Goodwin c Rhodes b Malcolm	91	– c sub (C. White) b DeFreitas	77
*D. R. Martyn c Thorpe b Malcolm	31	– c Rhodes b McCague	36
T. M. Moody b McCague	0	– c Rhodes b DeFreitas	19
G. B. Hogg c Rhodes b McCague	4	– (1) c Rhodes b DeFreitas	0
†A. C. Gilchrist c Thorpe b Malcolm	0	– (6) not out	40
C. E. Coulson not out	16	– (7) not out	32
J. Stewart c Rhodes b Malcolm	0		
S. R. Cary b Malcolm	7		
B. A. Reid b DeFreitas	4		
L-b 9, n-b 8	17	L-b 15, n-b 2	17

1/1 2/124 3/178 4/179 5/189   238 1/0 2/119 3/167   (5 wkts) 272
6/190 7/211 8/215 9/233   4/186 5/217

Bowling: *First Innings*—DeFreitas 15-3-41-1; Malcolm 21-6-70-6; McCague 16-1-64-2; Benjamin 12-5-34-1; Hick 5-0-20-0. *Second Innings*—DeFreitas 21-4-60-4; Malcolm 18-4-42-0; Benjamin 6-1-32-0; McCague 19-2-57-1; Hick 14-3-60-0; Atherton 2-0-6-0.

Umpires: S. J. Davis and T. A. Prue.

SOUTH AUSTRALIA v ENGLAND XI

At Adelaide, November 4, 5, 6, 7. England XI won by four wickets. Toss: England XI.

A well-paced hundred by Gooch enabled England to squeeze home with two overs to spare. But only South Australia's determination in their second innings had made a close call of a game that had the makings of a rout. Two cold and rainy days beforehand prevented the pitch from drying; when acting-captain Gatting put them in, the state collapsed in 74 minutes to 21 for six against McCague's lively lift and movement. When England reached 114 for two, a 12-run lead, that evening, South Australia looked beyond redemption. Next day, however, after Hick's second successive century, England's last seven wickets went for 52. Facing a deficit of 221, South Australia lost Blewett fifth ball but recovered to 116 for one, which they advanced to 415 for five in a strong, cold crosswind on the third day. But Siddons swept at Tufnell 41 minutes into the final morning, the first of five wickets to fall for 25, leaving England to score 260 at well under four an over. Gooch's 101 took 171 balls; Hick and Brayshaw made the same score in 123 and 192 balls respectively, while Siddons ran up 121 in 182.

Close of play: First day, England XI 114-2 (G. A. Hick 52*, G. P. Thorpe 6*); Second day, South Australia 116-1 (M. P. Faull 41*, P. C. Nobes 68*); Third day, South Australia 415-5 (J. D. Siddons 100*, T. J. Nielsen 33*).

South Australia

G. S. Blewett c Tufnell b Benjamin	9	– c Rhodes b Gough	0
P. C. Nobes c White b McCague	0	– (3) c Rhodes b McCague	72
J. A. Brayshaw c Hick b McCague	0	– (5) c Hick b White	101
D. S. Webber c Hick b McCague	2	– lbw b Benjamin	49
M. P. Faull c Hick b Benjamin	5	– (2) c McCague b Gough	47
*J. D. Siddons b McCague	31	– lbw b Tufnell	121
†T. J. Nielsen c Crawley b McCague	2	– c Gooch b Gough	52
P. E. McIntyre c McCague b White	16	– c Rhodes b Gough	15
S. P. George c Gough b White	3	– st Rhodes b Tufnell	4
D. J. Hickey not out	16	– b Gough	0
M. J. Minagall c Thorpe b White	5	– not out	1
L-b 3, n-b 10	13	L-b 10, n-b 8	18

1/0 2/0 3/10 4/17 5/18   102 1/0 2/126 3/126 4/214 5/316   480
6/21 7/78 8/81 9/86   6/455 7/455 8/478 9/478

Bowling: *First Innings*—Gough 9–5–19–0; McCague 15–3–31–5; Benjamin 8–1–36–2; White 4.5–2–13–3. *Second Innings*—Gough 38–4–143–5; McCague 32–10–124–1; Benjamin 26–3–76–1; Tufnell 25.1–6–68–2; White 17–1–52–1; Hick 2–0–7–0.

England XI

G. A. Gooch lbw b Blewett	50	– c Nielsen b Blewett	101
J. P. Crawley c Siddons b George	0	– c Nielsen b George	0
G. A. Hick hit wkt b Hickey	101	– lbw b McIntyre	32
G. P. Thorpe b McIntyre	80	– c Faull b Minagall	8
*M. W. Gatting c Nielsen b George	45	– b Hickey	56
C. White c Siddons b George	2	– c Nielsen b McIntyre	31
†S. J. Rhodes c Nielsen b George	0	– not out	12
D. Gough c Webber b McIntyre	5	– not out	7
M. J. McCague not out	11		
J. E. Benjamin c Brayshaw b McIntyre	7		
P. C. R. Tufnell c Webber b McIntyre	4		
L-b 8, n-b 10	18	B 6, l-b 4, w 1, n-b 4	15

1/11 2/97 3/186 4/271 5/281	323	1/11 2/75 3/94 (6 wkts) 262
6/281 7/292 8/299 9/315		4/186 5/228 6/248

Bowling: *First Innings*—George 29–5–114–4; Hickey 21–2–83–1; Blewett 6–0–31–1; Minagall 11–3–39–0; McIntyre 18.4–3–48–4. *Second Innings*—George 8–1–45–1; Hickey 20–2–74–1; McIntyre 26–3–89–2; Minagall 12–3–24–1; Blewett 8–0–20–1.

Umpires: D. J. Harper and C. D. Timmins.

†At Canberra, November 9. Prime Minister's XI won by two wickets. Toss: Prime Minister's XI. England XI 143 (46.3 overs) (M. A. Atherton 31, Extras 31; S. H. Cook three for 24, B. P. Julian three for 28); Prime Minister's XI 144 for eight (47.4 overs) (D. S. Lehmann 43; D. Gough three for 27, P. C. R. Tufnell three for 30).

NEW SOUTH WALES v ENGLAND XI

At Newcastle, November 12, 13, 14, 15. New South Wales won by four wickets. Toss: England XI.

Wasting a good opening, England lost the initiative on the first evening and never recaptured it. With Hick, Thorpe and Crawley all getting two-thirds of the way to centuries in helpful conditions, 328 was a good hundred short of par. New South Wales also failed to capitalise fully after Taylor and Waugh added 163 in 141 minutes for the second wicket; Taylor's fluent 150 contained 17 fours. But from 302 for four, they lost their remaining wickets for 63, Malcolm taking four for 11 in six overs. England were not without hope when they resumed only 37 behind. But Atherton was out freakishly, caught in the covers off a rebound from silly point's boot, and the innings always lacked conviction, though at 200 for five, Gatting having survived an uncomfortable 138 minutes, they had the means to escape. Bad batting on the final morning allowed New South Wales 70 overs to make 208. Slater and Taylor, putting on 94 in 22 overs through superb running between wickets, made the task straightforward, despite the fall of four wickets shortly after tea.

Close of play: First day, England XI 318-9 (D. E. Malcolm 3*, P. C. R. Tufnell 0*); Second day, New South Wales 314-5 (S. Lee 15*, N. D. Maxwell 6*); Third day, England XI 200-5 (M. W. Gatting 33*, C. White 31*).

England XI

*M. A. Atherton c Kershler b Maxwell	43	– (2) c Taylor b Robertson	37
†S. J. Rhodes c Glassock b Lee	4	– (1) lbw b Lee	16
G. A. Hick c Robertson b Kershler	73	– b Holdsworth	12
G. P. Thorpe b McNamara	67	– c Lee b Kershler	27
M. W. Gatting c Waugh b Kershler	0	– st Glassock b Kershler	33
J. P. Crawley c Waugh b Holdsworth	71	– c and b Kershler	14
C. White hit wkt b Holdsworth	28	– b Holdsworth	46
P. A. J. DeFreitas c Lee b McNamara	13	– c Waugh b Robertson	11
S. D. Udal b McNamara	1	– c Kershler b Holdsworth	9
D. E. Malcolm b McNamara	11	– b McNamara	5
P. C. R. Tufnell not out	0	– not out	0
B 1, l-b 5, w 1, n-b 10	17	B 8, l-b 11, w 1, n-b 14	34
	328		**244**

1/25 2/80 3/163 4/163 5/251   328   1/20 2/48 3/102 4/125 5/149   244
6/294 7/309 8/313 9/313   6/200 7/215 8/237 9/244

Bowling: First Innings—Holdsworth 15.2–5–69–2; Lee 11.2–2–57–1; McNamara 23.1–9–50–4; Maxwell 17–4–47–1; Robertson 19–0–51–0; Waugh 6–0–21–0; Kershler 8–2–27–2. *Second Innings*—Holdsworth 15.4–4–40–3; Lee 11–3–50–1; McNamara 10.2–5–18–1; Robertson 23–13–53–2; Waugh 6–1–15–0; Kershler 20–9–41–3; Bevan 1–1–0–0; Maxwell 10–4–8–0.

New South Wales

*M. A. Taylor c Gatting b White	150	– (2) c Rhodes b Tufnell	47
M. J. Slater c Atherton b DeFreitas	18	– (1) c and b Tufnell	94
M. E. Waugh c Tufnell b Hick	80	– c and b Udal	0
M. G. Bevan c Gatting b Tufnell	20	– lbw b Tufnell	20
B. E. McNamara c sub (M. J. McCague) b White	11	– lbw b Malcolm	0
S. Lee lbw b DeFreitas	45	– b Malcolm	9
N. D. Maxwell b Rhodes b Malcolm	18	– not out	21
†C. A. Glassock c Thorpe b Malcolm	0	– not out	15
G. R. Robertson lbw b Malcolm	4		
A. J. Kershler not out	4		
W. J. Holdsworth b Malcolm	0		
L-b 10, w 1, n-b 4	15	L-b 3, n-b 2	5
	365	(6 wkts)	**211**

1/54 2/217 3/266 4/280 5/302   365   1/94 2/97 3/162   (6 wkts) 211
6/331 7/335 8/356 9/362   4/165 5/169 6/184

Bowling: First Innings—DeFreitas 26–9–63–2; Malcolm 20.4–3–81–4; White 17–4–60–2; Udal 19–1–73–0; Tufnell 18–2–67–1; Hick 3–0–11–1. *Second Innings*—DeFreitas 8–2–14–0; Malcolm 9–1–34–2; White 4–0–14–0; Udal 14.5–0–69–1; Tufnell 23–5–67–3; Hick 4–1–10–0.

Umpires: D. B. Hair and W. P. Sheahan.

AUSTRALIAN XI v ENGLAND XI

At Hobart, November 18, 19, 20, 21. Drawn. Toss: Australian XI.

Steady rain on the third day, which restricted play to 15 minutes, denied the Australian XI the chance of pressing home a well-earned advantage. Though Martyn optimistically enforced the follow-on when Rhodes mis-hit to mid-off early on the final day, a good batting pitch had by then lost all its pace, and Stewart made the most of it. In his first appearance of the tour, after his index finger was broken in a practice game, he scored 101 not out with ten fours, timing the ball flawlessly on both sides of the wicket. Other omens were less favourable for the tourists in their final game before the Brisbane Test. Martyn, Ponting and Law all batted in commanding style; Martyn hit 14 fours from a wide variety of strokes in a dashing three-hour hundred. England's bowlers had begun well, but lost their line and bowled too short: 150 runs came on the leg side. Against batting described by Keith Fletcher as "pathetic", Hughes, Reiffel and Angel demonstrated the rewards of bowling a full length, and at the stumps.

Close of play: First day, Australian XI 328-5 (S. G. Law 54*, M. N. Atkinson 25*); Second day, England XI 200-9 (S. J. Rhodes 41*, P. C. R. Tufnell 0*); Third day, England XI 205-9 (S. J. Rhodes 46*, P. C. R. Tufnell 0*).

Australian XI

M. L. Hayden c White b McCague	8	G. R. Robertson c Rhodes b Benjamin	18
G. S. Blewett b McCague	53		
J. L. Langer c Rhodes b White	10	L-b 1, w 1, n-b 2	4
*D. R. Martyn b Tufnell...........	103		
R. T. Ponting c Rhodes b McCague ...	71	1/9 2/40 3/99	(7 wkts dec.) 386
S. G. Law c McCague b Gough	68	4/232 5/268	
†M. N. Atkinson not out	51	6/347 7/386	

M. G. Hughes, P. R. Reiffel and J. Angel did not bat.

Bowling: Gough 23-2-101-1; McCague 24-1-115-3; Benjamin 15.5-2-51-1; White 18-3-56-1; Tufnell 23-3-62-1.

England XI

*M. A. Atherton c Reiffel b Hughes	2	– c Hughes b Blewett	49
A. J. Stewart c Langer b Reiffel...........	27	– not out...........	101
G. P. Thorpe b Angel	19	– not out...........	48
G. A. Gooch b Reiffel...........	50		
J. P. Crawley st Atkinson b Robertson	14		
C. White lbw b Angel	18		
†S. J. Rhodes c Reiffel b Hughes	50		
D. Gough c Blewett b Angel	4		
M. J. McCague c Atkinson b Hughes	16		
J. E. Benjamin lbw b Hughes	1		
P. C. R. Tufnell not out	0		
B 4, l-b 2, n-b 2	8	B 3, l-b 2, n-b 4	9

1/18 2/36 3/92 4/117 5/117   209   1/131   (1 wkt) 207
6/152 7/156 8/194 9/200

Bowling: First Innings—Hughes 17.4-4-51-4; Reiffel 19-8-41-2; Robertson 26-7-72-1; Angel 12-2-36-3; Blewett 4-2-3-0. *Second Innings*—Hughes 10-2-43-0; Reiffel 16-6-33-0; Angel 12-3-30-0; Robertson 18-3-68-0; Blewett 6-0-28-1.

Umpires: P. D. Parker and S. G. Randell.

AUSTRALIA v ENGLAND

First Test Match

At Brisbane, November 25, 26, 27, 28, 29. Australia won by 184 runs. Toss: Australia.

Yet another display of exceptional all-round cricket took Australia to victory by the now-familiar crushing margin. Warne, who had held England's batsmen spellbound from the moment he bowled Gatting at Old Trafford in 1993, was again the executioner, taking three for 39 and eight for 71 – his best analysis in first-class cricket. It was not until the final innings, though, that he commandeered the spotlight. During the first three days, it was the combined efforts of Slater, Taylor, Mark Waugh, McDermott and Healy which forced the tourists into a position from which there was little prospect of escape.

England suffered a severe setback when Malcolm went down with chicken-pox three days before the game, and one of even greater significance when Atherton lost the toss on Brisbane's driest and most closely shaven pitch for an Ashes Test in more than 20 years. It was a formality that Australia would bat. Indeed, it was so obvious that there would be more help for spinners the longer the game lasted that Taylor chose to bat again with a lead of 259, rather than enforce the follow-on, after England, through pitiful batting against McDermott, were dismissed for 167 on the third day. It was a mistake because it allowed England the opportunity to regain a little self-respect, but it did no lasting damage.

The ball swung on the first morning. But when an erratic start by DeFreitas and McCague allowed Slater and Taylor to score 26 off four overs by doing nothing more than punish leg-side balls and off-side long-hops, the initiative was won and lost in 20 minutes. In the 33rd over Slater was responsible for Taylor's run-out, failing to respond to a call for a sharp single to mid-off. But the mistake increased his resolution. He scored a dashing 112 out of 182 with Mark Waugh, and was on course to pass 200 in the day when, 36 minutes from the close, he failed to clear mid-off against Gooch. Slater faced 244 balls and scored a hundred in fours.

Australia lost six for 97 on the second day; Mark Waugh, who faced 215 balls as he completed his third century against England, was ninth out when a ball from Gough inexplicably reared shoulder-high and carried to the covers from a fend-off. But then England's disintegration began: Stewart was caught at the wicket off a wide out-swinger in what might otherwise have been the last over of McDermott's new-ball spell; Hick soon followed, caught behind, mis-hooking; only while Atherton and Thorpe were adding 47 did England briefly promise to recover. All that subsequently redeemed a supine effort were 234 minutes of orthodox defence by Atherton and a huge swept six by Gooch off Warne, during a calculated attempt to hit the spinners off their length. But Gooch perished after half an hour, another catch for Healy, off a soaring top edge when May's drift from round the wicket undermined a sweep.

Batting again before lunch on the third day, Australia began their second innings with a stand of 109 in 28 overs from Taylor and Slater. But frustrated by Tufnell's accuracy over the wicket, into the rough, they lost eight for 92 before Healy pushed the lead beyond 500. Taylor's declaration left his bowlers 11 hours to win the match and England, improbably, 508 runs.

There was a possibility of Australia winning inside four days when, in Warne's second and third overs, Stewart was bowled by an undetected flipper midway through a pull and Atherton played back to a full-length leg-break and was lbw. Hick and Thorpe spared England that embarrassment, doggedly adding 152 in four hours to the close. On the last day, however, Warne was irresistible. In action from the start with May and - in contrast to the fourth day - bowling mainly round the wicket, he pinned Thorpe to defence for half an hour before beating him with a yorker. The 160 Thorpe added with Hick in 275 minutes was England's highest stand in eight Ashes Tests. England's chance of survival ended there, however: in Warne's next over, Hick was caught at the wicket via pad, chest and back of bat. Gooch hit ten fours in scoring 56, but he became the last of Healy's nine victims (equalling the Australian Test record) and the first wicket of Warne's final spell, in which he captured the last four wickets to bring his figures on the final day to six for 27 off 25.2 overs. They truly told the story of Warne's brilliance.

Man of the Match: S. K. Warne.   *Attendance:* 46,022.

Close of play: First day, Australia 329-4 (M. E. Waugh 82*, S. K. Warne 0*); Second day, England 133-6 (M. A. Atherton 49*); Third day, Australia 194-7 (I. A. Healy 7*, C. J. McDermott 0*); Fourth day, England 211-2 (G. A. Hick 72*, G. P. Thorpe 66*).

Australia

M. J. Slater c Gatting b Gooch	176	– (2) lbw b Gough 45
*M. A. Taylor run out	59	– (1) c Stewart b Tufnell 58
D. C. Boon b Gough	3	– b Tufnell 28
M. E. Waugh c Stewart b Gough	140	– b Tufnell 15
M. G. Bevan c Hick b Gough	7	– c Rhodes b DeFreitas 21
S. K. Warne c Rhodes b Gough........	2	– (8) sub (C. White) b DeFreitas 0
S. R. Waugh c Hick b DeFreitas	19	– (6) sub (C. White) b Tufnell . 7
†I. A. Healy c Hick b DeFreitas	7	– (7) not out 45
C. J. McDermott c Gough b McCague ...	2	– c Rhodes b Gough 6
T. B. A. May not out	3	– not out 9
G. D. McGrath c Gough b McCague	0	
B 5, l-b 2, n-b 1	8	B 2, l-b 9, w 2, n-b 1 14

1/99 (2) 2/126 (3) 3/308 (1) 4/326 (5)   426   1/109 (2) 2/117 (1)   (8 wkts dec.) 248
5/352 (6) 6/379 (7) 7/407 (8)   3/139 (4) 4/174 (5)
8/419 (9) 9/425 (4) 10/426 (11)   5/183 (6) 6/190 (3)
                                                        7/191 (8) 8/201 (9)

Bowling: *First Innings*—DeFreitas 31–8–102–2; McCague 19.2–4–96–2; Gough 32–7–107–4; Tufnell 25–3–72–0; Hick 4–0–22–0; Gooch 9–2–20–1. *Second Innings*—DeFreitas 22–1–74–2; Gough 23–3–78–2; Tufnell 38–10–79–4; Gooch 3–2–5–0; Hick 2–1–1–0.

England

*M. A. Atherton c Healy b McDermott	54	– lbw b Warne	23
A. J. Stewart c Healy b McDermott	16	– b Warne	33
G. A. Hick c Healy b McDermott	3	– c Healy b Warne	80
G. P. Thorpe c and b Warne	28	– b Warne	67
G. A. Gooch c Healy b May	20	– b Warne	56
M. W. Gatting lbw b McDermott	10	– c Healy b McDermott	13
M. J. McCague b McDermott	1	– (10) lbw b Warne	0
†S. J. Rhodes lbw b McDermott	4	– (7) c Healy b McDermott	2
P. A. J. DeFreitas c Healy b Warne	7	– (8) b Warne	11
D. Gough not out	17	– (9) c M. E. Waugh b Warne	10
P. C. R. Tufnell c Taylor b Warne	0	– not out	2
L-b 1, n-b 6	7	B 9, l-b 5, n-b 12	26
	167		**323**

1/22 (2) 2/35 (3) 3/82 (4) 4/105 (5) 5/131 (6) 6/133 (7) 7/140 (1) 8/147 (9) 9/151 (8) 10/167 (11)

1/50 (2) 2/59 (1) 3/219 (4) 4/220 (3) 5/250 (6) 6/280 (7) 7/309 (5) 8/310 (8) 9/310 (10) 10/323 (9)

Bowling: *First Innings*—McDermott 19–3–53–6; McGrath 10–2–40–0; May 17–3–34–1; Warne 21.2–7–39–3. *Second Innings*—McDermott 23–4–90–2; McGrath 19–4–61–0; Warne 50.2–22–71–8; May 35–16–59–0; M. E. Waugh 7–1–17–0; Bevan 3–0–11–0.

Umpires: C. J. Mitchley (South Africa) and S. G. Randell.
Referee: J. R. Reid (New Zealand).

†At Bowral, December 2. England XI won by four wickets. Toss: Bradman XI. Bradman XI 205 for four (50 overs) (J. L. Arnberger 79, J. Cox 42); England XI 208 for six (48.5 overs) (J. P. Crawley 91 not out).

†At Canberra, December 4. England XI won by 100 runs. Toss: England XI. England XI 253 for four (50 overs) (M. A. Atherton retired hurt 53, A. J. Stewart 53, G. A. Hick 50, G. P. Thorpe 38, G. A. Gooch 40 not out); Australian Capital Territory 153 (42.2 overs) (P. L. Evans 37, J. H. Bull 32; D. Gough four for 19).

England's matches v Australia, Australia A and Zimbabwe in the Benson and Hedges World Series (December 6–December 15) may be found in that section.

†At North Sydney Oval, December 10. Australian Cricket Academy won by five wickets. Toss: Australian Cricket Academy. England XI 231 for four (50 overs) (G. A. Hick 118, G. P. Thorpe 62; M. A. Harrity three for 44); Australian Cricket Academy 234 for five (48.2 overs) (R. J. Baker 57, I. J. Harvey 80, R. A. Allanby 46 not out).

†At North Sydney Oval, December 11. Australian Cricket Academy won by six wickets. Toss: England XI. England XI 245 for seven (50 overs) (M. A. Atherton 95, M. W. Gatting 62; I. J. Harvey three for 40); Australian Cricket Academy 249 for four (43.1 overs) (N. W. Ashley 30, R. M. Campbell 57, B. J. Hodge 96 not out, D. J. Marsh 46 not out).

QUEENSLAND v ENGLAND XI

At Toowoomba, December 17, 18, 19, 20. England XI won by 37 runs. Toss: England XI.

After looking likely losers while Barsby and Hayden put on 231, in pursuit of 352 from 70 overs, England had victory thrust upon them with 5.3 overs remaining. A leaping left-handed catch by Atherton at mid-wicket to dismiss Hayden proved the turning point; in the next over a 25-yard direct hit by Fraser ran out Barsby. When Healy, Law and Love swiftly followed, Queensland might have drawn in their horns had it been a Sheffield Shield match. Instead, Healy decided his team needed the experience of a run-chase under pressure. All ten wickets fell for 83 runs in 18.2 overs, Tufnell emerging with five for 71 despite a battering by the openers. On a picturesque, fast-scoring ground, cut into the Darling Downs, the Barsby-Hayden stand was one of two double-century partnerships for Queensland. Maher, 20, and Symonds, 19, who had recently signed for Gloucestershire, both scored hundreds in the first innings and added an unbroken 205 for the fifth wicket. A chanceless 203 not out from Gatting, in 344 balls, with 30 fours, provided the meat of England's 507 for six, before he cut his mouth in the second over of Queensland's first innings, when a ball for which he was diving hopped over his hands. He took no further part, and thus missed the chance to field for 95 overs and 436 runs between the fall of wickets. Gatting's attempt to convince his team-mates of his disappointment was only partially successful. England were forced to use a local university cricketer, Paul Farmer, as substitute.

Close of play: First day, England XI 355-5 (M. W. Gatting 114*, S. D. Udal 14*); Second day, Queensland 197-4 (J. P. Maher 22*, A. Symonds 4*); Third day, England XI 188-3 (J. P. Crawley 45*, S. J. Rhodes 26*).

England XI

G. A. Gooch c Rowell b McDermott	50	– lbw b Tazelaar	7
*M. A. Atherton b Tazelaar	6	– c Rowell b Symonds	49
G. A. Hick c Love b Rowell	49	– c Law b McDermott	46
M. W. Gatting not out	203	– absent hurt	
J. P. Crawley c Law b Kasprowicz	91	– (4) lbw b Kasprowicz	63
†S. J. Rhodes lbw b Kasprowicz	0	– (5) c Love b Kasprowicz	26
S. D. Udal b Tazelaar	16	– c Healy b Tazelaar	4
A. J. Stewart not out	53	– (6) c Healy b Tazelaar	0
A. R. C. Fraser (did not bat)		– (8) not out	7
P. C. R. Tufnell (did not bat)		– (9) c Law b Tazelaar	2
D. E. Malcolm (did not bat)		– (10) not out	14
B 4, l-b 12, w 3, n-b 20	39	B 5, l-b 5, n-b 8	18

1/16 2/106 3/118 4/320 5/330 (6 wkts dec.) 507 1/19 2/93 3/153 (8 wkts dec.) 236
6/362 4/198 5/201 6/207
7/215 8/219

Bowling: *First Innings*—McDermott 26-5-98-1; Tazelaar 25-6-72-2; Symonds 10-2-51-0; Rowell 33-7-116-1; Kasprowicz 22-3-89-2; Maher 7-1-25-0; Hayden 7.1-0-40-0. *Second Innings*—McDermott 12-5-33-1; Tazelaar 20-5-56-4; Rowell 6-2-20-0; Kasprowicz 17-2-85-2; Symonds 4-0-31-1.

Queensland

T. J. Barsby c Rhodes b Malcolm	15	– run out	101
M. L. Hayden c Rhodes b Malcolm	8	– c Atherton b Malcolm	119
M. L. Love st Rhodes b Udal	47	– (4) c sub (P. Farmer) b Tufnell	24
S. G. Law c Fraser b Udal	91	– (5) c Crawley b Udal	7
J. P. Maher not out	100	– (6) b Udal	15
A. Symonds not out	108	– (7) c Gooch b Tufnell	7
*†I. A. Healy (did not bat)		– (3) c Gooch b Tufnell	8
C. J. McDermott (did not bat)		– st Rhodes b Tufnell	7
G. J. Rowell (did not bat)		– not out	1
M. S. Kasprowicz (did not bat)		– run out	8
D. Tazelaar (did not bat)		– b Tufnell	0
L-b 10, w 1, n-b 12	23	B 1, l-b 10, n-b 6	17

1/11 2/66 3/116 4/187 (4 wkts dec.) 392 1/231 2/237 3/248 4/269 5/279 314
6/290 7/304 8/306 9/314

Bowling: *First Innings*—Malcolm 20–1–97–2; Fraser 17–4–65–0; Tufnell 23–1–89–0; Udal 28–2–108–2; Hick 6–0–23–0. *Second Innings*—Malcolm 16–1–66–1; Fraser 11–1–50–0; Tufnell 13.3–0–71–5; Udal 20–1–95–2; Hick 4–0–21–0.

Umpires: D. W. Holt and P. D. Parker.

AUSTRALIA v ENGLAND

Second Test Match

At Melbourne, December 24, 26, 27, 28, 29. Australia won by 295 runs. Toss: England.

The first ball of the third day, a full toss which Gooch drove back to McDermott, marked the moment when England lost their chance of cancelling out their defeat in Brisbane. From then on McDermott sealed Australia's victory, two days later, what was left of England's resolve and fighting spirit disappeared. It was almost a relief when a hat-trick by Warne, the first in an Ashes Test since 1903-04, hurried Australia to within a wicket of a 2-0 lead on the final morning. Tufnell fell in McDermott's next over and Australia completed their 14th Ashes victory in 21 starts since the Fifth Test of 1986-87.

From Gooch's dismissal in the first innings, which pulled England back to 148 for five from what had been a promising 119 for one, the only redeeming features of England's cricket were Atherton's determination, Gough's buoyancy and Tufnell's discipline in bowling defensively against his inclinations in Australia's second innings. Ray Illingworth, the chairman of selectors, who had arrived 36 hours before the game, commented that, without dramatic improvements, the tour was in danger of ending in a "shambles".

Crushing as the defeat was, however, it was an unlucky match for England. If Australia's first-innings 279 was at least 80 more than Atherton would have hoped for, having let his bowlers loose on a damp first-day pitch, England might still have overtaken it with several wickets standing. But the first ball after lunch broke Stewart's right index finger, for the second time on tour, and close decisions went against the other three of the top four batsmen. England had scored ten when Stewart, defending a length ball from McDermott on the back foot, was unable to adjust to its lift. Though he returned next morning and batted at No. 7 in the second innings, his scores had no bearing on the match.

Forty minutes later, Hick was given out by umpire Randell after a breakback appeared to deflect to Healy off his thigh. Warne came on next over. Through sensible and watchful cricket, however, Atherton and Thorpe re-established the innings, adding 79 off 33 overs, only for both to fall to Warne, leaving England 124 for three. Atherton was out lbw to a leg-break that turned at least an inch before hitting his pad; umpire Bucknor declined to give him the benefit of the doubt. Thorpe, like Atherton defending on the front foot, fell bat-pad to Mark Waugh at silly point. The appeal, from all four close fielders, was instantaneous but Thorpe clearly believed the deflection came off pad alone. Taken in conjunction with Steve Waugh's narrow lbw escape off his first ball, from Gough, two crucial wickets in seven overs meant a reverse England could not withstand.

Australia exploited the opening with the efficiency of a team who knew they had the edge. Handed Gatting's wicket 23 minutes later, when Steve Waugh, 30 yards from the bat behind square leg, acrobatically pulled down an ill-judged sweep, Warne and McDermott finished England off in 15.4 overs on the third morning, following Gooch's crestfallen departure.

Batting again with a lead of 67, Australia had Boon to thank for keeping them in control. Using every time-wasting device, Atherton saw to it that England bowled no more than 124 overs in 533 minutes – 13.95 per hour – despite Tufnell bowling 48 of them. Through the ICC's inflated allowances (four minutes per drinks break, two minutes per wicket), plus the fact that over-rates were being calculated over the whole match, no fine could be levied. But if, as some believed, the torpor induced in the players was a factor in their subsequent collapse, Atherton and England got what they deserved. Boon's patience was inexhaustible as he completed his first Test hundred at Melbourne, and his 20th in all. On an uneven, two-paced pitch, he was sustained for 378 minutes by his on-drive and square-cut.

England's remote chance of holding out for 120 overs vanished when Fleming, playing his second Test, had Gooch caught behind and Hick bowled with textbook out-swingers in his first two overs. When Thorpe succumbed to a loose stroke and Atherton, after an untroubled 73 minutes, received a second dubious decision from umpire Bucknor, England closed at 79 for four. The remaining batsmen fell in 12.5 overs on the final day, McDermott and Warne – who had passed the milestones of 250 and 150 Test wickets respectively – taking three each. DeFreitas, Gough and Malcolm formed Warne's hat-trick, his first in any cricket. All were victims of leg-breaks, DeFreitas lbw on the back foot to one that skidded through, Gough well taken at the wicket off one that turned and bounced and Malcolm brilliantly caught off his gloves by Boon, who dived two feet to his right to scoop up a fast low half-chance.

Man of the Match: C. J. McDermott. *Attendance*: 144,492.

Close of play: First day, Australia 220-7 (S. R. Waugh 61*); Second day, England 148-4 (G. A. Gooch 15*, D. Gough 1*); Third day, Australia 170-3 (D. C. Boon 64*, M. G. Bevan 3*); Fourth day, England 79-4 (M. W. Gatting 23*, S. J. Rhodes 13*).

Australia

M. J. Slater run out	3	– (2) st Rhodes b Tufnell	44
*M. A. Taylor lbw b DeFreitas	9	– (1) lbw b Gough	19
D. C. Boon c Hick b Tufnell	41	– lbw b DeFreitas	131
M. E. Waugh c Thorpe b DeFreitas	71	– c and b Gough	29
M. G. Bevan c Atherton b Gough	3	– c sub (J. P. Crawley) b Tufnell	35
S. R. Waugh not out	94	– not out	26
†I. A. Healy c Rhodes b Tufnell	17	– c Thorpe b Tufnell	17
S. K. Warne c Hick b Gough	6	– c DeFreitas b Gough	0
T. B. A. May lbw b Gough	9		
C. J. McDermott b Gough	0	– (9) not out	2
D. W. Fleming c Hick b Malcolm	16		
L-b 7, n-b 3	10	B 1, l-b 9, w 1, n-b 6	17
	279	(7 wkts dec.)	320

1/10 (1) 2/39 (2) 3/91 (3) 4/100 (5)
5/171 (4) 6/208 (7) 7/220 (8)
8/242 (9) 9/242 (10) 10/279 (11)

1/61 (1) 2/81 (2) (7 wkts dec.)
3/157 (4) 4/269 (5)
5/275 (3) 6/316 (7)
7/317 (8)

Bowling: *First Innings*—Malcolm 28.3-4-78-1; DeFreitas 23-4-66-2; Gough 26-9-60-4; Tufnell 28-7-59-2; Hick 2-0-9-0. *Second Innings*—Malcolm 22-3-86-0; DeFreitas 26-2-70-1; Tufnell 48-8-90-3; Gough 25-6-59-3; Hick 3-2-5-0.

England

*M. A. Atherton lbw b Warne	44	– (2) c Healy b McDermott	25
A. J. Stewart c and b Warne	16	– (7) not out	8
G. A. Hick c Healy b McDermott	23	– b Fleming	2
G. P. Thorpe c M. E. Waugh b Warne	51	– c Healy b McDermott	9
G. A. Gooch c and b McDermott	15	– (1) c Healy b Fleming	2
M. W. Gatting c S. R. Waugh b Warne	9	– (5) c Taylor b McDermott	25
D. Gough c Healy b McDermott	20	– (9) c Healy b Warne	0
†S. J. Rhodes c M. E. Waugh b Warne	0	– (6) c M. E. Waugh b McDermott	16
P. A. J. DeFreitas st Healy b Warne	14	– (8) lbw b Warne	0
D. E. Malcolm not out	11	– c Boon b Warne	0
P. C. R. Tufnell run out	0	– c Healy b McDermott	0
L-b 7, n-b 2	9	L-b 2, n-b 3	5
	212		92

1/40 (3) 2/119 (1) 3/124 (4) 4/140 (6)
5/148 (5) 6/151 (8) 7/185 (2)
8/189 (7) 9/207 (9) 10/212 (11)

1/3 (1) 2/10 (3) 3/23 (4)
4/43 (2) 5/81 (5) 6/88 (6)
7/91 (8) 8/91 (9)
9/91 (10) 10/92 (11)

In the first innings A. J. Stewart, when 1, retired hurt at 10 and resumed at 151.

Bowling: *First Innings*—McDermott 24-6-72-3; Fleming 11-5-30-0; M. E. Waugh 3-1-11-0; Warne 27.4-8-64-6; May 18-5-28-0. *Second Innings*—McDermott 16.5-5-42-5; Fleming 9-1-24-2; Warne 13-6-16-3; May 4-1-8-0.

Umpires: S. A. Bucknor (West Indies) and S. G. Randell.
Referee: J. R. Reid (New Zealand).

AUSTRALIA v ENGLAND

Third Test Match

At Sydney, January 1, 2, 3, 4, 5. Drawn. Toss: England.

An eighth-wicket stand between Warne and May, lasting 77 minutes, saved Australia from an astonishing defeat in a game that had seemed dead two and a half hours earlier. Australia, who abandoned a bold pursuit of 449 only when rain intervened, were then 239 for two. An hour and a quarter later, however, they were 292 for seven; in three overs Fraser scythed down their middle order with a spell of four for four. With play continuing until 7.26, England were handicapped in their final thrust by fading light, which forced Atherton to stop using his pace bowlers. But, with up to eight fielders round the bat, it was a gritty achievement by the tailenders to survive, thus ensuring Australia would hold the Ashes for a fourth successive term.

It was a match of startling fluctuations and surprises, not least the fact that Warne bowled 52 overs for a solitary wicket – Malcolm's! On every day except the fourth, when only one wicket fell for 304 runs, as England constructed a cautious declaration and Taylor and Slater aggressively replied, the faster bowlers took charge. Of 29 wickets to fall, they claimed 27. The pitch had pace and regular bounce but, before Australia's brief first innings, sweated under its ground-level covers. In humid and frequently overcast conditions, the ball often swung.

Atherton had to bat first. But, with McDermott and Fleming exploiting the humidity, England were 20 for three inside an hour; Gooch, opening in Stewart's absence, fell in the second over. Their luck turned when umpire Bucknor denied Fleming a convincing lbw appeal against Atherton. Reprieved, the captain put the innings on its feet, adding 174 with Crawley, who played with composure in his first Ashes Test. It looked like England's day, before McDermott darted an off-cutter with the new ball between bat and pad to bowl Atherton for 88, and four balls later had a hapless Gatting caught behind. Before the close, Crawley edged Fleming to second slip and Rhodes was run out attempting a run off a misfield; Australia had the initiative again.

It was recaptured, however, by Gough with a jaunty innings of village-green innocence and charm. Throwing his bat at anything pitched up and hooking or pulling vigorously when it was short, he cracked 51 in 56 balls, before he mishooked McDermott to deep fine leg. Malcolm followed Gough's example, needing only 18 balls to make 29, his highest Test score. He was bowled whirling at a leg-break after straight-driving Warne for his second six. When Fraser, the night-watchman turned anchor-man, was caught off a skier, Gough's joyous thrash had inspired the addition of 111 runs in even time that morning.

Those extra runs completely changed the picture. For when rain allowed only 3.3 overs after lunch and a downpour next morning forced groundstaff to replace the covers in the hour before play restarted, Slater and Taylor found themselves resuming in ideal conditions for the seamers. Not helped by Boon and Steve Waugh, who shouldered arms to Gough and were bowled, Australia collapsed to 65 for eight, needing another 45 to save the follow-on. Though Taylor was still in, there might have been no escape had Malcolm, at mid-on, run to catch a mis-hit off Gough by McDermott, instead of leaving it to Gooch, more distant at mid-off. When Malcolm came on to bowl, Taylor and McDermott counter-attacked, taking 17 off his first three overs. Then, at 107 for eight, an inept Malcolm bouncer sailed high over Rhodes for four byes and the follow-on was saved. Almost immediately, Gough took a return catch from Taylor off his slower ball, and next ball yorked Fleming, to return six for 49, his first haul of five or more in Test cricket. But England's best chance of victory had gone.

Atherton's respect for the Australian batting was implicit in the tempo of England's second innings. Despite a lead of 193, they took 72 overs scoring 255 for two, and it was not until Thorpe joined Hick that they stepped up to four an over. In what was thought to be the last-but-one over of the innings, Hick, on 98, blocked three successive balls, and Atherton lost patience and ungenerously declared; he had batted far more slowly himself.

No team had ever made as much as 449 to win a Test. But Taylor and Slater set out with such a will that Australia might have had a real chance had the weather held. Overnight, they needed another 310 off 90 overs. Atherton was concerned enough to instruct Tufnell to bowl over the wicket to a five-man leg-side field. But though that held Australia to 67 off 31 overs up to lunch, the openers were still together, despite a run-out appeal which Taylor might not have survived had umpire Hair called for the replay. It was only when rain prolonged lunch long enough to embrace an early tea interval that Taylor decided that chasing 243, at 4.67 an over, was too risky. Officially, only seven overs were lost, because of the additional hour, but the conditions had also turned against Australia.

Both men reached hundreds. Slater was superbly caught by Tufnell, running diagonally backwards at deep square leg, and at 239 Taylor was bowled by Malcolm with the new ball. But it was not until Boon, Bevan, Steve Waugh, Mark Waugh and Healy were swept aside in nine overs by Gough and Fraser that England – too late – began running between overs. Thanks to their earlier slow over-rate, it was 6.25 when the umpires signalled the start of the last hour. Seven wickets were down, but Fraser and Gough managed only three more overs before the darkness impelled Atherton to take them off. Warne and May handled what followed so calmly that when Warne was put down at mid-off by Malcolm off Gooch, off the final ball of the minimum 15 overs, there was very little chance that it affected the result.

In the event, a great Test ended bizarrely when, with the batsmen almost through the players' gate and tractors circling the infield, Atherton pointed out to the umpires that the clock indicated 7.24, leaving time for a 16th over. May negotiated four balls from Tufnell safely.

Man of the Match: D. Gough.   *Attendance:* 126,485.

Close of play: First day, England 198-7 (A. R. C. Fraser 3*, D. Gough 0*); Second day, Australia 4-0 (M. J. Slater 4*, M. A. Taylor 0*); Third day, England 90-1 (M. A. Atherton 32*, G. A. Hick 22*); Fourth day, Australia 139-0 (M. A. Taylor 64*, M. J. Slater 65*).

England

G. A. Gooch c Healy b Fleming	1	– lbw b Fleming	29
*M. A. Atherton b McDermott	88	– c Taylor b Fleming	67
G. A. Hick b McDermott	2	– not out	98
G. P. Thorpe lbw b McDermott	10	– not out	47
J. P. Crawley c M. E. Waugh b Fleming	72		
M. W. Gatting c Healy b McDermott	0		
A. R. C. Fraser c Healy b Fleming	27		
†S. J. Rhodes run out	1		
D. Gough c Fleming b McDermott	51		
D. E. Malcolm b Warne	29		
P. C. R. Tufnell not out	4		
B 8, l-b 7, n-b 9	24	L-b 6, w 1, n-b 7	14
	309	(2 wkts dec.)	**255**

1/1 (1) 2/10 (3) 3/20 (4) 4/194 (2)   1/54 (1) 2/158 (2)   (2 wkts dec.) 255
5/194 (6) 6/196 (5) 7/197 (8)
8/255 (9) 9/295 (10) 10/309 (7)

Bowling: *First Innings*—McDermott 30-7-101-5; Fleming 26.2-12-52-3; Warne 36-10-88-1; May 17-4-35-0; M. E. Waugh 6-1-10-0; Bevan 4-1-8-0. *Second Innings*—McDermott 24-2-76-0; Fleming 20-3-66-2; M. E. Waugh 2-1-4-0; Warne 16-2-48-0; May 10-1-55-0.

Australia

M. J. Slater b Malcolm	11	– (2) c Tufnell b Fraser	103
*M. A. Taylor c and b Gough	49	– (1) b Malcolm	113
D. C. Boon b Gough	3	– c Hick b Gough	17
M. E. Waugh c Rhodes b Malcolm	3	– lbw b Fraser	25
M. G. Bevan c Thorpe b Fraser	8	– c Rhodes b Fraser	7
S. R. Waugh b Gough	1	– c Rhodes b Fraser	0
†I. A. Healy c Hick b Gough	10	– c Rhodes b Fraser	5
S. K. Warne c Gatting b Fraser	0	– not out	36
T. B. A. May c Hick b Gough	0	– not out	10
C. J. McDermott not out	21		
D. W. Fleming b Gough	0		
B 6, l-b 1, n-b 3	10	B 12, l-b 3, w 1, n-b 12	28
	116	(7 wkts)	**344**

1/12 (1) 2/15 (3) 3/18 (4) 4/38 (5)   116   1/208 (2) 2/239 (1)   (7 wkts) 344
5/39 (6) 6/57 (7) 7/62 (8)   3/265 (3) 4/282 (5)
8/65 (9) 9/116 (2) 10/116 (11)   5/286 (6) 6/289 (4)
                                               7/292 (7)

Bowling: *First Innings*—Malcolm 13–4–34–2; Gough 18.5–4–49–6; Fraser 11–1–26–2. *Second Innings*—Malcolm 21–4–75–1; Gough 28–4–72–1; Fraser 25–3–73–5; Tufnell 35.4–9–61–0; Hick 5–0–21–0; Gooch 7–1–27–0.

Umpires: S. A. Bucknor (West Indies) and D. B. Hair. Referee: J. R. Reid (New Zealand).

England's matches v Australia, Australia A and Zimbabwe in the Benson and Hedges World Series (January 7–January 12) may be found in that section.

VICTORIA v ENGLAND XI

At Bendigo, January 20, 21, 22, 23. Drawn. Toss: England XI.

A week after being knocked out of the World Series, England returned to action, presumably refreshed, though their performance did not show it. Nor did their luck change: injuries to Stewart's finger and Hick's back ruled them out of the last two Tests. Stewart, in his first game since his index finger was broken on Boxing Day, was hit on it again. Ironically, he was batting in the middle order to avoid the new ball – only to be at the wicket when the second one was claimed. He might have escaped had Cook not had him dropped in the gully off the previous delivery. Hick, missed first ball and again at 13, made his 80th first-class hundred, but his four-hour innings aggravated his back strain. There were other disappointments for England. They failed to exploit good bowling conditions on the first day, and missed five chances in Victoria's second innings, among them a sharp one at point to Russell, Stewart's substitute, when Hodge was 23; he survived to score 104 with impressive timing. England proved unable to take up a fair challenge of 252 at 4.58 an over, not least because Cook and Reiffel stretched Atherton to the limit to avoid a pair. The innings was in its eighth over when Atherton got off the mark. He went on to make 59 not out.

Close of play: First day, Victoria 222-8 (D. S. Berry 30*, S. H. Cook 7*); Second day, England XI 288-5 (A. J. Stewart 24*, S. J. Rhodes 18*); Third day, Victoria 228-5 (B. J. Hodge 63*, D. A. Emerson 12*).

Victoria

M. T. G. Elliott st Rhodes b Tufnell	10	– (2) st Rhodes b Tufnell 73
R. P. Larkin c Benjamin b Malcolm	49	– (1) c Atherton b DeFreitas 27
*D. M. Jones lbw b DeFreitas	4	– c Rhodes b Malcolm 31
B. J. Hodge c Atherton b Malcolm	10	– c Rhodes b DeFreitas 104
G. B. Gardiner c Hick b Tufnell	5	– b Malcolm 0
I. J. Harvey c and b Hick	41	– c sub (R. C. Russell) b Tufnell .. 2
D. A. Emerson b Tufnell	3	– b DeFreitas 23
P. R. Reiffel lbw b Gooch	34	– not out 22
†D. S. Berry not out	47	– c Rhodes b Malcolm 8
S. H. Cook c Tufnell b Benjamin	13	– not out................................... 13
T. F. Corbett b Malcolm	0	
B 1, l-b 7, n-b 16	24	B 2, l-b 10, w 1, n-b 18 .. 31

1/43 2/52 3/72 4/87 5/96　　　　　　246　　1/73 2/127 3/151　　(8 wkts dec.) 334
6/106 7/165 8/210 9/246　　　　　　　　　　4/152 5/172 6/286
　　　　　　　　　　　　　　　　　　　　　　　7/289 8/308

Bowling: *First Innings*—Malcolm 25.4–2–67–3; Benjamin 21–6–45–1; DeFreitas 21–7–42–1; Tufnell 20–2–59–3; Hick 7–1–14–1; Thorpe 2–1–6–0; Gooch 2–1–5–1. *Second Innings*—Malcolm 29–5–88–3; DeFreitas 24.1–3–74–3; Tufnell 31–6–93–2; Benjamin 17–4–67–0.

England XI

G. A. Gooch c Berry b Corbett	28	– c Berry b Harvey	48
*M. A. Atherton c Jones b Reiffel	0	– not out	59
G. A. Hick lbw b Reiffel	143		
G. P. Thorpe b Emerson	22	– (3) not out	23
J. P. Crawley c Corbett b Cook	32		
A. J. Stewart retired hurt	37		
†S. J. Rhodes c Larkin b Cook	31		
P. A. J. DeFreitas c Berry b Reiffel	1		
D. E. Malcolm c Gardiner b Reiffel	11		
J. E. Benjamin lbw b Cook	2		
P. C. R. Tufnell not out	0		
B 5, l-b 10, w 1, n-b 6	22	L-b 6, w 1, n-b 2	9

1/2 2/48 3/105 4/216 5/243   329   1/94   (1 wkt) 139
6/316 7/316 8/321 9/329

In the first innings A. J. Stewart retired hurt at 316-6.

Bowling: *First Innings*—Cook 17-3-64-3; Reiffel 23.3-7-63-4; Corbett 19-4-58-1; Harvey 15-6-56-0; Emerson 17-4-73-1. *Second Innings*—Cook 11-4-32-0; Reiffel 14-3-35-0; Corbett 9-1-37-0; Harvey 10-4-24-1; Emerson 4-3-4-0; Gardiner 2-1-1-0.

Umpires: R. A. Emerson and D. W. Holt.

AUSTRALIA v ENGLAND

Fourth Test Match

At Adelaide, January 26, 27, 28, 29, 30. England won by 106 runs. Toss: England. Test debuts: G. S. Blewett, P. E. McIntyre.

An over-confident and ill-paced attempt by Australia to score 263 in 67 overs led to England's first Test win in Australia for eight years, a further example of the ability of Atherton's England to win occasional Tests when the odds were most stacked against them. Handicapped by injury and illness as England had been in Brisbane and Sydney, here they were reduced to five fit batsmen, injuries to Hick (prolapsed disc), Stewart (index finger – for the third time) and Fairbrother (shoulder) having forced them out of the tour. Additionally, Gough had flown home with a foot in plaster. Lewis, who had been playing sub-district cricket in Melbourne, joined the party, while Ramprakash, vice-captain of the England A team, was summoned from India as the tourists' sixth and final reinforcement.

In keeping with this disordered background, Gatting, who thought he had played his final game on tour, made the top score of the match: a laborious 410-minute 117 which ensured England did not wholly waste an opening stand of 93 after winning a useful toss. It was Gatting's first Test hundred since 1987, tenth in all, and one that he will never forget. Taylor made him fight for every run, with Warne and McDermott helping to hold him for 77 minutes in the 90s – an agonising 31 minutes on 99. It was almost as much a relief to the 16,000 crowd as it was to Gatting when, in the 11th over of McDermott's mighty spell, a crooked throw by Steve Waugh enabled DeFreitas to complete a jumpy single after a stop-go in mid-pitch. Gatting was last out, caught at short third man mistiming a leg-break from Peter McIntyre, one of two new caps. The other, 23-year-old Greg Blewett, became the 16th Australian to score a hundred on Test debut.

Slater and Taylor opened with a commanding 128 on an even-bouncing pitch with no extra pace. Some rebuilding was needed when Taylor was removed by a questionable lbw and Mark Waugh was beaten by Fraser's late movement next over. But Blewett and Healy advanced to 394 for five by the close and a match-winning lead seemed likely. Instead, the five outstanding wickets fell in 50 minutes, Blewett needing the support of McIntyre at No. 10 to see him past his hundred – just as last man McDermott returned from hospital after suffering stomach cramps. More used to opening for South Australia, Blewett, lightly and athletically built, gave no chance in 261 minutes, handsomely cover-driving boundaries off balls most batsmen would have pushed for ones and twos.

England resumed only 46 adrift, and Thorpe scored a dashing 83 after lunch on the fourth day. Despite Warne's waning influence, however, England appeared to be heading for a third defeat when Lewis was bowled at 181 for six. Crawley and DeFreitas steadied the ship, but England's lead was only 154, with four wickets standing, at the close. Next day, however, with nine overs to bowl before the new ball, no established third seamer, and Fleming troubled by a hamstring, Taylor chose to open with McDermott. The move misfired. From the moment the new ball was taken DeFreitas saw it like a football – and a flagging McDermott was hammered for 41 in three overs. Mark Waugh, *en route* to a Test-best five for 40, ended a run-a-minute stand of 89 with a return catch off Crawley. DeFreitas, though, hitting classically through the off side, proceeded to plunder 22 off McDermott's third over – four fours and a six. He was deprived of a deserved maiden Test hundred when he was caught at the wicket pulling Waugh. Orthodox but aggressive, without a single ugly stroke, he scored 68 of England's 108 in 18.5 overs on the final morning. In all DeFreitas batted exactly two hours, hitting two sixes and nine fours off 95 balls.

On a pitch still favouring the England bat, it was hard to see beyond a draw or a third home win when Australia were 16 for no wicket at lunch. But just afterwards, Taylor was caught at first slip, whereupon three more fell in 16 balls. Steve Waugh was beaten by Malcolm's pace and bowled between bat and pad, but Boon and Slater – mis-hooking – made presents of their wickets. Australia were unlucky when a deflection from Gatting's toecap at short leg bounced into his hands, dislodging Mark Waugh who was batting easily. But the damage was done: when Lewis dismissed Warne and McDermott in the over spanning tea, Australia were 83 for eight. Fleming stayed with Healy nearly two hours but, with eight overs to go, a short ball from Lewis slewed down, trapping him lbw as he tried to pull. Finally Malcolm, replacing Tufnell, won an unconvincing lbw against McIntyre with his range-finder. England won with 35 balls remaining. Healy, with a second disciplined fifty, showed how easily the match could have been saved.

Referee John Reid later fined Lewis 30 per cent of his fee for pointing McDermott to the dressing-room. Reid also punished the entire England team for their slow over-rate, levying a fine of 15 per cent and reprimanding Atherton.

Man of the Match: P. A. J. DeFreitas.   *Attendance:* 89,448.

Close of play: First day, England 196-2 (M. W. Gatting 50*, G. P. Thorpe 16*); Second day, Australia 81-0 (M. J. Slater 36*, M. A. Taylor 43*); Third day, Australia 394-5 (G. S. Blewett 91*, I. A. Healy 72*); Fourth day, England 220-6 (J. P. Crawley 49*, P. A. J. DeFreitas 20*).

England

G. A. Gooch c M. E. Waugh b Fleming	47	– c Healy b McDermott	34
*M. A. Atherton c Boon b Fleming	80	– lbw b M. E. Waugh	14
M. W. Gatting c S. R. Waugh b McIntyre	117	– b M. E. Waugh	0
G. P. Thorpe c Taylor b Warne	26	– c Warne b McDermott	83
J. P. Crawley b Warne	28	– c and b M. E. Waugh	71
†S. J. Rhodes c Taylor b McDermott	6	– c Fleming b Warne	2
C. C. Lewis c Blewett b McDermott	10	– b Fleming	7
P. A. J. DeFreitas c Blewett b McIntyre	21	– c Healy b M. E. Waugh	88
A. R. C. Fraser run out	7	– c McDermott b M. E. Waugh	5
D. E. Malcolm b McDermott	0	– not out	10
P. C. R. Tufnell not out	0	– lbw b Warne	0
B 2, l-b 5, w 2, n-b 2	11	B 6, l-b 8	14
	353		328

1/93 (1) 2/175 (2) 3/211 (4) 4/286 (5) 5/293 (6) 6/307 (7) 7/334 (8) 8/353 (9) 9/353 (10) 10/353 (3)

1/26 (2) 2/30 (3) 3/83 (1) 4/154 (4) 5/169 (6) 6/181 (7) 7/270 (5) 8/317 (9) 9/317 (8) 10/328 (11)

Bowling: First Innings—McDermott 41–15–66–3; Fleming 16–4–59–0; Warne 31–9–72–2; McIntyre 19.3–3–51–2; M. E. Waugh 9–1–33–0. *Second Innings*—McDermott 27–5–96–2; Fleming 11–3–37–1; Warne 30.5–9–82–2; M. E. Waugh 14–4–40–5; McIntyre 8–0–36–0; Blewett 4–0–23–0.

Australia

M. J. Slater c Atherton b DeFreitas	67 – (2) c Tufnell b Malcolm	5
*M. A. Taylor lbw b Lewis	90 – (1) c Thorpe b Malcolm	13
D. C. Boon c Rhodes b DeFreitas	0 – c Rhodes b Fraser	4
M. E. Waugh c Rhodes b Fraser	39 – c Gatting b Tufnell	24
S. R. Waugh c Atherton b Lewis	19 – b Malcolm	0
G. S. Blewett not out	102 – c Rhodes b Lewis	12
†I. A. Healy c Rhodes b Malcolm	74 – not out	51
S. K. Warne c Thorpe b Fraser	7 – lbw b Lewis	2
D. W. Fleming c Rhodes b Malcolm	0 – (10) lbw b Lewis	24
P. E. McIntyre b Malcolm	0 – (11) lbw b Malcolm	0
C. J. McDermott c Crawley b Fraser	5 – (9) c Rhodes b Lewis	0
B 2, l-b 7, n-b 7	16	B 3, l-b 5, n-b 13	21

1/128 (1) 2/130 (3) 3/202 (2) 4/207 (4)   419   1/17 (1) 2/22 (1) 3/22 (2)   156
5/232 (5) 6/396 (7) 7/405 (8)   4/23 (5) 5/64 (4) 6/75 (6)
8/406 (9) 9/414 (10) 10/419 (11)   7/83 (8) 8/83 (9)
                                           9/152 (10) 10/156 (11)

Bowling: *First Innings*—Malcolm 26–5–78–3; Fraser 28.5–6–95–3; Tufnell 24.5–6–64–0; DeFreitas 20–3–70–2; Lewis 18–1–81–2; Gooch 5–0–22–0. *Second Innings*—Malcolm 16.1–3–39–4; Fraser 12–1–37–1; DeFreitas 11–3–31–0; Lewis 13–4–24–4; Tufnell 9–3–17–1.

Umpires: S. Venkataraghavan (India) and P. D. Parker.
Referee: J. R. Reid (New Zealand).

AUSTRALIA v ENGLAND

Fifth Test Match

At Perth, February 3, 4, 5, 6, 7. Australia won by 329 runs. Toss: Australia.

Chastened by losing in Adelaide, Australia hit back with their biggest win of the rubber. Blewett became their third player, after Bill Ponsford (1924-25) and Doug Walters (1965-66), to score hundreds in his first two Tests; Slater made his fourth in 11 Tests against England and McDermott ended proceedings before lunch on the last day by taking six for 38.

A vigorous hundred by Thorpe and two calm innings from Ramprakash, who displaced Tufnell from the winning team of Adelaide, were England's only gains. Things started going wrong from the moment Gooch, at third slip, missed Slater off Malcolm's fourth ball – the first of seven missed catches in the innings, and ten by England in the match. Gooch had announced that his 118th Test, breaking David Gower's England record, would be his last, and Gatting followed suit. Though Gooch finished with 8,900 Test runs – behind only Border and Gavaskar – scores of 37 and four for him, and nought and eight for Gatting, were an inappropriate end to distinguished Test careers.

Winning a good toss and scoring 402, Australia lost command only while Thorpe and Ramprakash were adding 158 in England's first innings. Thrown together at 77 for four on the second evening, they were still there 40 minutes into the third afternoon. Then, at 235, Thorpe jumped down the pitch to off-drive Warne, and was expertly stumped by Healy off a top-spinner that reached him shoulder-high.

But England might have seized the initiative several times. After Lewis, in a fast spell, dismissed Taylor and Boon in successive overs, he had Mark Waugh dropped at 18 by Crawley in the gully. Then Malcolm missed Slater at 59 off an undemanding caught and bowled and gave him a third life, at 87, when he misjudged a hook off DeFreitas. After Slater and Waugh had added 183, Lewis and DeFreitas traded catches off each other's bowling to remove them at last. England made a lucky start to the second day when Blewett was given out caught from a deflection off his thigh, but their catching soon redressed the balance. The most expensive miss came when Steve Waugh, on 35, slashed DeFreitas shoulder-high between two motionless slips, Thorpe and Atherton. Angel, who helped Waugh add 58, was also dropped, twice, by Rhodes and Atherton. Waugh was finally stranded on 99 when his twin Mark, McDermott's runner, attempted an improbable single and was thrown out at the bowler's end by Gooch. Steve, frequently beaten in his first 50, had dug in for 289 minutes, sealing Australia's advantage.

The temporary absence of McDermott, who had strained his back, provided little relief. After three Tests as 12th man, McGrath, in his first over, had Atherton caught down the leg side off a glove and next ball bowled Gatting via an inside edge. Ninety minutes later, Mark Waugh's first over saw off Gooch and Crawley.

Thorpe, hitting confidently through the line of his off and straight drives, needed only 218 balls to score 123 and struck 19 fours. Most of Ramprakash's 11 fours were sturdily driven between mid-off and mid-on, but his encouraging innings ended when he attempted to ward off a huge leg-break from Warne. Lewis, missed off a sharp caught-and-bowled chance by Angel before scoring, hit eight fours in an hour. Nevertheless, from Thorpe's dismissal, England lost six for 60 to be 107 behind.

Despite having his right thumb broken in Malcolm's third over, Slater gave Australia a flying start, scoring 45 off 55 balls before Atherton took a lovely diving catch at second slip. Even after protecting Boon by using a night-watchman uncharacteristically early – 25 minutes from the close – Australia were forced to consolidate when they slipped to 123 for five. But Blewett, off-driving as handsomely as in Adelaide and this time scoring as smoothly off his legs, removed all danger of Australia losing. Outscoring Waugh by 114 to 77 in a stand of 203, he faced only 158 balls, hitting 19 fours.

Left 104 overs to hold out for a draw after Taylor's declaration – a target of 453 was well out of range – England's hopes were shattered when McDermott and McGrath ripped five out for 27 in 14 overs before the close. Menacingly as they bowled to a catching ring of seven, it was feeble batting on a pitch still full of runs. Atherton's dismissal to the 12th ball of the final morning, again caught down the leg side off McGrath, made Australia's third win a certainty. Ramprakash and Rhodes, adding 68, threatened to take the game into the afternoon, until Mark Waugh cramped Ramprakash with unexpected bounce; unable to get on top of it, he cut to gully. McDermott saw the tail off in four overs, claiming his 32nd wicket of the series by cartwheeling Malcolm's middle stump with a dramatic yorker.

Man of the Match: S. R. Waugh.   *Man of the Series:* C. J. McDermott.
Attendance: 71,679.

Close of play: First day, Australia 283-4 (S. R. Waugh 23*, G. S. Blewett 17*); Second day, England 110-4 (G. P. Thorpe 54*, M. R. Ramprakash 14*); Third day, Australia 87-2 (M. A. Taylor 32*, D. C. Boon 6*); Fourth day, England 27-5 (M. A. Atherton 8*, M. R. Ramprakash 0*).

Australia

M. J. Slater c Lewis b DeFreitas		124	– (2) c Atherton b Fraser	45
*M. A. Taylor c Rhodes b Lewis		9	– (1) b Fraser	52
D. C. Boon c Ramprakash b Lewis		1	– (4) c Rhodes b Malcolm	18
M. E. Waugh c DeFreitas b Lewis		88	– (5) c Rhodes b DeFreitas	1
S. R. Waugh not out		99	– (6) c Ramprakash b Lewis	80
G. S. Blewett c Rhodes b Fraser		20	– (7) c Malcolm b Lewis	115
†I. A. Healy c Lewis b DeFreitas		12	– (8) not out	11
S. K. Warne c Rhodes b DeFreitas		1	– (9) c Lewis b Malcolm	6
J. Angel run out		11	– (3) run out	0
G. D. McGrath run out		0		
C. J. McDermott run out		6		
B 14, l-b 4, w 4, n-b 9		31	B 1, l-b 9, n-b 7	17

1/47 (2) 2/55 (3) 3/238 (1) 4/247 (4)   402   1/75 (2) 2/79 (3)   (8 wkts dec.) 345
5/287 (6) 6/320 (7) 7/328 (8)   3/102 (4) 4/115 (5)
8/386 (9) 9/388 (10) 10/402 (11)   5/123 (1) 6/326 (6)
                                                 7/333 (7) 8/345 (9)

Bowling: First Innings—Malcolm 31–6–93–0; DeFreitas 29–8–91–3; Fraser 32–11–84–1; Lewis 31.5–8–73–3; Gooch 1–1–0–0; Ramprakash 11–0–43–0. *Second Innings*—Malcolm 23.3–3–105–2; Fraser 21–3–74–2; Lewis 16–1–71–2; DeFreitas 22–10–54–1; Ramprakash 8–1–31–0.

England

G. A. Gooch lbw b M. E. Waugh	37	– c and b McDermott	4
*M. A. Atherton c Healy b McGrath	4	– c Healy b McGrath	8
M. W. Gatting b McGrath	0	– b McDermott	8
G. P. Thorpe st Healy b Warne	123	– (5) c Taylor b McGrath	0
J. P. Crawley c Warne b M. E. Waugh	0	– (6) c M. E. Waugh b McDermott	0
M. R. Ramprakash b Warne	72	– (7) c S. R. Waugh b M. E. Waugh	42
†S. J. Rhodes b Angel	2	– (8) not out	39
C. C. Lewis c Blewett b McGrath	40	– (9) lbw b McDermott	11
P. A. J. DeFreitas b Angel	0	– (10) c Taylor b McDermott	0
A. R. C. Fraser c Warne b Angel	9	– (4) lbw b McGrath	5
D. E. Malcolm not out	0	– b McDermott	0
B 4, l-b 1, n-b 3	8	L-b 1, w 1, n-b 4	6
	295		**123**

1/5 (2) 2/5 (3) 3/77 (1) 4/77 (5)
5/235 (4) 6/246 (7) 7/246 (6)
8/247 (9) 9/293 (8) 10/295 (10)

1/4 (1) 2/17 (3) 3/26 (4)
4/26 (5) 5/27 (6) 6/27 (2)
7/95 (7) 8/121 (9)
9/123 (10) 10/123 (11)

Bowling: First Innings—Angel 22.3–7–65–3; McGrath 25–6–88–3; Blewett 4–1–9–0; M. E. Waugh 9–2–29–2; Warne 23–8–58–2; McDermott 13–5–41–0. *Second Innings*—McDermott 15–4–38–6; McGrath 13–4–40–3; Angel 3–0–20–0; Warne 7–3–11–0; M. E. Waugh 3–0–13–1.

Umpires: K. E. Liebenberg (South Africa) and S. G. Randell.
Referee: J. R. Reid (New Zealand).

THE ASHES

"In affectionate remembrance of English cricket which died at The Oval, 29th August, 1882. Deeply lamented by a large circle of sorrowing friends and acquaintances, R.I.P. N.B. The body will be cremated and the Ashes taken to Australia."

Australia's first victory on English soil over the full strength of England, on August 29, 1882, inspired a young London journalist, Reginald Shirley Brooks, to write this mock "obituary". It appeared in the *Sporting Times*.

Before England's defeat at The Oval, by seven runs, arrangements had already been made for the Hon. Ivo Bligh, afterwards Lord Darnley, to lead a team to Australia. Three weeks later they set out, now with the popular objective of recovering the Ashes. In the event, Australia won the First Test by nine wickets, but with England winning the next two it became generally accepted that they brought back the Ashes.

It was long accepted that the real Ashes – a small urn believed to contain the ashes of a bail used in the third match – were presented to Bligh by a group of Melbourne women. At the time of the 1982 centenary of The Oval Test match, however, evidence was produced which suggested that these ashes were the remains of a ball and that they were given to the England captain by Sir William Clarke, the presentation taking place before the Test matches in Australia in 1883. The certain origin of the Ashes, therefore, is the subject of some dispute.

After Lord Darnley's death in 1927, the urn was given to MCC by Lord Darnley's Australian-born widow, Florence. It can be seen in the cricket museum at Lord's, together with a red and gold velvet bag, made specially for it, and the scorecard of the 1882 match.

ENGLAND A IN INDIA AND BANGLADESH, 1994-95

By MARK BALDWIN

A new era for English cricket may have begun in India early in 1995 – and not just because a hugely successful tour, in which England A thrashed their Indian counterparts, threw up a clutch of young players bursting with talent, character and naked ambition. The achievements of Alan Wells's party ran in parallel with the failure of an aging senior team to wrest the Ashes from Australia. Similarly, their proud collection of victories – they beat India A 3-0 in the unofficial Tests and 2-1 in the one-day series – contrasted sharply with the miseries suffered by the full England side who had toured India just two years earlier. That team, led by Graham Gooch, lost the Test series 3-0. It never came to terms with Indian spinners, Indian conditions, or India itself.

How refreshing, then, to see a young side beating the Indians at their own game, adapting quickly to the unique demands of cricket on the subcontinent and positively relishing the chance to learn new skills. Off the field, too, England's youngsters set out to enjoy the whole Indian experience. There was no "done the poverty, done the elephants, what else is there?" mentality and, because of that, the battle was often half won. India, cricket-wise and otherwise, can test a player's character to the limit. The key to success on the field and enjoyment off it is flexibility, maturity, adaptability and a kind of smiling determination to get a job done. In this, the management team of John Barclay, Phil Neale and captain Wells provided a perfect example – yet their task was undoubtedly made easier by the intelligence of their young charges and the way in which the group gelled together.

"They quickly developed a strong collective belief in each other's ability," said Barclay. "In each Test, the Indians won the toss, a massive advantage, because to bat first on those types of pitches is to have by far the best of the conditions over five days. But, each time, the team fought until it had overturned that advantage." Barclay said the players genuinely enjoyed the tour. "They ate the food, they went out into the streets, they met the people and they haggled in the marketplaces. There has been a vibrant spirit which I applaud."

England's selectors had done their job well by picking a balanced and predominantly youthful squad – only Wells, at 33, and Stemp, 27, were over 25. That suited the trip's purpose admirably. The previous winter's A tour, to South Africa, had provided a finishing school for the likes of Darren Gough, John Crawley and Steve Rhodes. This time even more players seemed ready for Test cricket. Mark Ramprakash made the jump during the tour, leaving India temporarily when England recalled him to replace the injured Hick; he played two convincing innings in the Perth Test. Glen Chapple, Jason Gallian, Richard Stemp and Min Patel were the other most notable performers, but Nick Knight, Dominic Cork, David Hemp, Paul Nixon and Keith Piper all displayed international potential. Paul Weekes's all-round abilities marked him out as a World Cup possible, while Wells's batting illustrated why his peers rated him the best current English batsman never to have played a Test. Leg-spinner Ian Salisbury enjoyed a brilliant start at Bombay, with nine wickets against a Youth team, but then lost confidence – though he did deliver the spell which swung the Calcutta match England's way. Richard Johnson and Michael Vaughan, the youngest members of the squad at 20, had less opportunity than most but will have learned much. Johnson, too, earned reward for his patience and good humour when his gutsy, forthright 33 not out helped settle the dogfight in Chandigarh, which England won by one wicket.

Ramprakash was the outstanding batsman, proving himself good enough to play the Indian spinners with his bat from the start, whereas the other players – Gallian especially – first learned the art of pad-play before working out ways to attack. Ramprakash also thrived in the position of vice-captain. New-ball bowlers Chapple and Cork quickly realised that to waste the shine is almost a capital offence in India. Chapple grew into a high-class purveyor of seam and swing. Strong and athletic, with an enviable temperament, he combined control with sustained menace in largely unhelpful conditions to finish with 19 wickets in the unofficial Tests at only 15.57 runs apiece. Cork was the ideal foil and also fielded brilliantly, but needed to improve his batting to become a true Test all-rounder. Left-arm spinners Stemp and Patel were the other successful bowlers, as different in character as in bowling style, complementing each other well. Both added strength to a combative fielding side – Patel in the outfield, Salisbury at slip, Knight at bat-pad and Ramprakash at cover were all of the highest class. The only criticism of the team was that too many of them were inclined to get involved in on-field exchanges with the opposition, both in India and during the short "goodwill" visit to Bangladesh which followed.

The Indians had come late to the idea of A team cricket and picked essentially a second team, including several players in their late twenties and early thirties. The team managers, Sandeep Patil and Syed Kirmani (who took over when Patil left to manage the Under-19s in Australia), were impressed with England's policy of concentrating on youngsters. None the less, they had several players young enough and good enough to be likely Test cricketers, most obviously the outstanding 20-year-old Amol Muzumdar, but also the left-hander Saurav Ganguly, the lively medium-pacer Paras Mhambre and the leg-spinning all-rounder Sairaj Bahutule. The pitches, perfect for five-day cricket, helped make India an ideal environment for this tour.

ENGLAND A TOURING PARTY

A. P. Wells (Sussex) (*captain*), M. R. Ramprakash (Middlesex) (*vice-captain*), G. Chapple (Lancashire), D. G. Cork (Derbyshire), J. E. R. Gallian (Lancashire), D. L. Hemp (Glamorgan), M. C. Ilott (Essex), R. L. Johnson (Middlesex), N. V. Knight (Essex), P. A. Nixon (Leicestershire), M. M. Patel (Kent), K. J. Piper (Warwickshire), I. D. K. Salisbury (Sussex), R. D. Stemp (Yorkshire), M. P. Vaughan (Yorkshire), P. N. Weekes (Middlesex).

Ilott returned home injured. Ramprakash briefly left the tour to join England in Australia but then returned.

Tour manager: J. R. T. Barclay. *Team manager*: P. A. Neale (Northamptonshire). *Physiotherapist*: W. P. Morton (Yorkshire).

ENGLAND A TOUR RESULTS

First-class matches – Played 5: Won 4, Drawn 1.
Wins – Indian Youth XI, India XI (3).
Draw – Indian Board President's XI.
Non-first-class matches – Played 8: Won 5, Lost 2, Drawn 1. *Wins* – Combined Indian
    Universities (four days), India A (2), Bangladesh XI (2). *Losses* – Cricket Club of India
    XI, India A. *Draw* – Bangladesh XI (three days).

ENGLAND A AVERAGES – FIRST-CLASS MATCHES

BATTING

	M	I	NO	R	HS	100s	Avge	Ct/St
M. R. Ramprakash....	2	4	1	210	99	0	70.00	4
A. P. Wells	5	10	0	363	93	0	36.30	6
J. E. R. Gallian	5	10	0	327	79	0	32.70	0
D. L. Hemp........	4	8	1	208	99*	0	29.71	1
N. V. Knight........	5	10	0	286	50	0	28.60	9
M. M. Patel	3	6	2	86	35	0	21.50	0
R. L. Johnson	2	4	1	64	33*	0	21.33	2
P. N. Weekes	3	6	0	114	38	0	19.00	0
D. G. Cork	5	10	1	154	69	0	17.11	5
R. D. Stemp	4	6	4	32	11*	0	16.00	2
P. A. Nixon	3	5	1	60	23	0	15.00	11/2
I. D. K. Salisbury	4	6	1	62	21	0	12.40	5
G. Chapple	4	6	1	60	26	0	12.00	1
K. J. Piper..........	2	4	0	40	30	0	10.00	7
M. P. Vaughan	3	6	0	50	17	0	8.33	0

Played in one match: M. C. Ilott 2, 0*.

* *Signifies not out.*

BOWLING

	O	M	R	W	BB	5W/i	Avge
G. Chapple	155.2	48	337	20	5-32	2	16.85
D. G. Cork	175.3	46	406	19	4-46	0	21.36
R. D. Stemp	198.5	58	384	17	6-83	1	22.58
I. D. K. Salisbury....	119	19	421	15	6-48	1	28.06
M. M. Patel	152.3	50	297	10	3-43	0	29.70

Also bowled: J. E. R. Gallian 12–1–61–0; M. C. Ilott 12–3–27–1; R. L. Johnson
40.3–4–110–1; M. P. Vaughan 8–2–27–1; P. N. Weekes 48–6–131–2.

Note: Matches in this section which were not first-class are signified by a dagger.

†At Brabourne Stadium, Bombay, January 2. Cricket Club of India XI won by one run.
Toss: England A. Cricket Club of India XI 209 for six (50 overs) (S. S. Dighe 55, A. A.
Muzumdar 49 not out; R. D. Stemp three for 44); England A 208 for eight (50 overs) (A. P.
Wells 44, D. L. Hemp 43; S. V. Bahutule five for 41).

INDIAN YOUTH XI v ENGLAND A

At Wankhede Stadium, Bombay, January 3, 4, 5, 6. England A won by 96 runs. Toss: England A.

England A began their first-class programme with a good win. Their key players were Salisbury – with nine wickets – and Cork, who batted and bowled with gusto. Ramprakash, with a three-hour fifty, held together the top order on the first day, but the innings looked wobbly at 125 for five. That was doubled while Cork was in; he hit ten fours in his 69. The Indian Youth reply was wrecked by Salisbury, who, though not introduced until the 49th over, gained immediate reward for hard tour preparation, finishing with six for 48. He was at times unplayable on a turning pitch; the talented Muzumdar did very well to edge the brute of a delivery which accounted for him. Resuming, England A batted positively to extend their lead to 288 before Cork's swing, in a mid-afternoon spell of three for six, opened the door to victory. It was completed by the spinners: Stemp was miserly, Salisbury expansive, as he tried out all his variations – but they shared five wickets.

Close of play: First day, England A 221-6 (D. G. Cork 52*, I. D. K. Salisbury 0*); Second day, Indian Youth XI 152-5 (S. S. Dighe 16*, Obaid Kamal 15*); Third day, Indian Youth XI 21-1 (Jitender Singh 13*, A. A. Muzumdar 7*).

England A

J. E. R. Gallian b Mhambre	4	– (2) c Muzumdar b Balaji Rao	25
N. V. Knight c Dighe b Obaid Kamal	16	– (1) b Vij	23
M. R. Ramprakash lbw b Iqbal Siddiqui	59	– c Muzumdar b Balaji Rao	16
*A. P. Wells c Dighe b Balaji Rao	21	– c Dighe b Balaji Rao	36
D. L. Hemp lbw b Mhambre	7	– c and b Balaji Rao	24
P. N. Weekes c Laxman b Obaid Kamal	33	– lbw b Mhambre	25
D. G. Cork c Dighe b Vij	69	– lbw b Vij	0
I. D. K. Salisbury c Dighe b Obaid Kamal	18	– (10) not out	8
†P. A. Nixon run out	6	– (8) lbw b Balaji Rao	23
G. Chapple c Jitender Singh b Balaji Rao	8	– (9) lbw b Mhambre	5
R. D. Stemp not out	7	– b Mhambre	7
B 7, l-b 15, w 3, n-b 10	35	B 1, l-b 5, w 1, n-b 5	12
	283		**204**

1/15 2/49 3/108 4/125 5/125   1/48 2/65 3/72 4/129 5/131
6/217 7/251 8/268 9/268   6/132 7/177 8/187 9/190

Bowling: *First Innings*—Mhambre 24-9-46-2; Iqbal Siddiqui 21-3-46-1; Obaid Kamal 22-3-56-3; Balaji Rao 20.4-6-49-2; Vij 26-9-64-1. *Second Innings*—Mhambre 11.2-3-26-3; Iqbal Siddiqui 4-0-24-0; Vij 18-4-75-2; Obaid Kamal 6-1-17-0; Balaji Rao 18-4-56-5.

Indian Youth XI

Z. Bharucha c and b Cork	5	– lbw b Chapple	1
Jitender Singh c Ramprakash b Weekes	12	– c Nixon b Cork	63
A. A. Muzumdar c Wells b Salisbury	68	– c Knight b Cork	8
V. V. S. Laxman lbw b Stemp	10	– c Nixon b Stemp	3
S. Sharath c Knight b Salisbury	17	– st Nixon b Salisbury	59
*†S. S. Dighe c Wells b Stemp	26	– c Nixon b Cork	17
Obaid Kamal c Stemp b Salisbury	36	– lbw b Cork	0
P. L. Mhambre b Salisbury	1	– (9) c Knight b Salisbury	1
Iqbal Siddiqui c Knight b Salisbury	0	– (8) c Chapple b Stemp	9
B. Vij c Ramprakash b Salisbury	9	– lbw b Salisbury	14
W. D. Balaji Rao not out	6	– not out	9
B 1, l-b 4, n-b 4	9	L-b 2, n-b 6	8
	199		**192**

1/14 2/42 3/75 4/119 5/120   1/9 2/23 3/33 4/136 5/158
6/183 7/183 8/183 9/192   6/158 7/158 8/165 9/175

Bowling: *First Innings*—Cork 6–2–23–1; Chapple 14–6–23–0; Stemp 26–6–49–2; Weekes 21–3–51–1; Salisbury 18.1–6–48–6. *Second Innings*—Cork 24–10–46–4; Chapple 8–4–18–1; Stemp 17–6–19–2; Salisbury 21.5–2–93–3; Weekes 2–0–14–0.

Umpires: Jasbir Singh and A. V. Jayaprakash.

INDIAN BOARD PRESIDENT'S XI v ENGLAND A

At Madras, January 8, 9, 10, 11. Drawn. Toss: Indian Board President's XI.

A side injury to Ilott on the first afternoon, which eventually forced him home, did not help England A's cause. He never bowled again though, as last man, he joined Patel to bat out the final 22 deliveries of the match and save his team from defeat. After Ilott dismissed Mehra early on the first day, the English bowling was steady but managed little more than a holding operation. Rathore and Ganguly both batted attractively and Dravid and Shamshad then piled on the runs. Top-class spin left England A struggling, though Gallian batted well over five hours and displayed technique and temperament. Set 291 to win in 78 overs, they did well to survive after slipping to 48 for three. They hung on through a brave 44-minute ninth-wicket stand between Patel and Johnson, who faced 55 balls for one run, before Ilott was required to make his final appearance.

Close of play: First day, Indian Board President's XI 255-3 (R. S. Dravid 72*, Rizwan Shamshad 31*); Second day, England A 131-4 (J. E. R. Gallian 36*, D. G. Cork 17*); Third day, Indian Board President's XI 151-2 (Saurav C. Ganguly 54*, R. S. Dravid 34*).

Indian Board President's XI

*Vikram Rathore c Johnson b Salisbury	59	– c Wells b Salisbury	42
Ajay Mehra lbw b Ilott	8	– b Patel	18
Saurav C. Ganguly c and b Salisbury	65	– c Hemp b Cork	65
R. S. Dravid lbw b Cork	84	– c Wells b Patel	49
Rizwan Shamshad c Cork b Patel	78	– (6) not out	9
S. V. Bahutule c Piper b Vaughan	4	– (5) not out	16
†A. Vaidya not out	10		
B 8, l-b 3, w 1, n-b 9	21	B 1, l-b 3, n-b 1	5

1/25 2/117 3/160 4/278　　　(6 wkts dec.) 333　　1/41 2/93　　　(4 wkts dec.) 204
5/285 6/333　　　　　　　　　　　　　　　　　　3/169 4/193

S. A. Ankola, A. Kuruvilla, U. Chatterjee and Kanwaljit Singh did not bat.

Bowling: *First Innings*—Ilott 12–3–27–1; Johnson 15–1–42–0; Gallian 8–1–44–0; Cork 22–5–51–1; Salisbury 34–8–77–2; Patel 32.3–10–61–1; Vaughan 5–1–20–1. *Second Innings*—Cork 20–3–59–1; Johnson 8–2–17–0; Patel 23–6–67–2; Salisbury 7–0–57–1.

England A

N. V. Knight c Bahutule b Kanwaljit Singh	41	– lbw b Kuruvilla	4
M. P. Vaughan b Kuruvilla	14	– lbw b Kanwaljit Singh	17
J. E. R. Gallian st Vaidya b Bahutule	79	– c Vaidya b Kuruvilla	2
*A. P. Wells c Vikram Rathore b Chatterjee	5	– c Ajay Mehra b Chatterjee	43
D. L. Hemp lbw b Kanwaljit Singh	5	– lbw b Kanwaljit Singh	31
D. G. Cork c Ajay Mehra b Chatterjee	27	– c Rizwan Shamshad b Bahutule	24
†K. J. Piper c Dravid b Chatterjee	5	– c Rizwan Shamshad b Bahutule	4
I. D. K. Salisbury c Ganguly b Kanwaljit Singh	21	– c Vikram Rathore b Kanwaljit Singh	10
R. L. Johnson c Ganguly b Kanwaljit Singh	26	– c Ajay Mehra b Kanwaljit Singh	1
M. C. Ilott c Vikram Rathore b Bahutule	2	– (11) not out	0
M. M. Patel not out	1	– (10) not out	25
B 6, l-b 5, n-b 10	21	B 4, l-b 2, n-b 1	7

1/33 2/80 3/95 4/106 5/159　　　　　247　1/5 2/11 3/48　　　(9 wkts) 168
6/171 7/203 8/240 9/246　　　　　　　　4/88 5/124 6/124
　　　　　　　　　　　　　　　　　　　7/138 8/138 9/168

Bowling: *First Innings*—Ankola 10–2–36–0; Kuruvilla 8–1–23–1; Kanwaljit Singh 32–10–56–4; Bahutule 29.5–6–65–2; Chatterjee 29–10–56–3. *Second Innings*—Ankola 4–1–12–0; Kuruvilla 7–2–15–2; Chatterjee 22–11–38–1; Bahutule 23–13–30–2; Kanwaljit Singh 22–7–67–4.

Umpires: S. Choudhury and N. Menon.

INDIA A v ENGLAND A

First Unofficial Test

At Bangalore, January 14, 15, 16, 17. England A won by four wickets. Toss: India A.

England A took the opening five-day international with a day to spare. Appropriately, Ramprakash was at the crease; his technique had put him a notch above any other batsman in the match and earned him a call-up to Australia before the series resumed in Calcutta. However, the game was all but decided by a remarkable final session on the third day: a pumped-up England A, spearheaded by quality seam and swing bowling from Chapple and Cork and backed up by some superb catching, reduced the Indians from 21 for one to 83 for seven at the close. Only Muzumdar resisted and his skilful fifty was ended by Chapple early next morning. A target of 116 was low enough for England A to be able to afford some nerve-wracking moments on a wearing pitch. The tourists slipped to 89 for six, with Test spinner Chauhan claiming three, but Ramprakash held firm for the second time.

On the first day, Indian opener Vikram Rathore made a high-class 90, with 11 fours, before Salisbury picked up a brilliant caught-and-bowled from a full-blooded straight drive. Early on the second morning India A were 252 for four and apparently on course for an impregnable total. However, a spell of four for 27 from 15.2 overs by Stemp dramatically altered the state of the game. He thoroughly deserved figures of six for 83 for his sustained control and menace. Ramprakash led England A's reply in some style, just missing his hundred, after Knight and Gallian produced gritty half-centuries.

Close of play: First day, India A 236-4 (R. S. Dravid 50*, V. S. Yadav 14*); Second day, England A 153-3 (M. R. Ramprakash 30*, A. P. Wells 6*); Third day, India A 83-7 (A. A. Muzumdar 48*, R. K. Chauhan 0*).

India A

Jitender Singh c Knight b Stemp	32	– c Ramprakash b Chapple 5
Vikram Rathore c and b Salisbury	90	– c Nixon b Chapple 10
A. A. Muzumdar c Wells b Stemp	1	– lbw b Chapple 51
*P. K. Amre c Nixon b Chapple	38	– c Cork b Chapple 12
R. S. Dravid lbw b Stemp	60	– b Cork 1
†V. S. Yadav c Knight b Chapple	19	– (7) c Salisbury b Weekes 5
S. V. Bahutule lbw b Stemp	3	– (6) c Salisbury b Cork 1
U. Chatterjee c Nixon b Cork	24	– c Ramprakash b Stemp 0
R. K. Chauhan c Knight b Stemp	3	– run out 11
P. L. Mhambre not out	6	– c Cork b Chapple 6
A. Kuruvilla b Stemp	9	– not out 1
B 7, l-b 7, n-b 1	15	L-b 1 1
	300	**104**

1/99 (1) 2/101 (3) 3/157 (2) 4/207 (4)   300   1/5 (1) 2/21 (2) 3/43 (4)   104
5/252 (5) 6/254 (6) 7/258 (7)   4/44 (5) 5/46 (6) 6/77 (7)
8/270 (9) 9/285 (8) 10/300 (11)   7/80 (8) 8/86 (3)
                                    9/102 (10) 10/104 (9)

Bowling: *First Innings*—Cork 22–6–37–1; Chapple 31–8–82–2; Stemp 46.2–16–83–6; Salisbury 9–1–42–1; Weekes 11–1–42–0. *Second Innings*—Cork 11–3–31–2; Chapple 17–3–32–5; Stemp 16–5–22–1; Salisbury 5–2–16–0; Weekes 3–1–2–1.

England A

N. V. Knight c Yadav b Chatterjee	50	– c Yadav b Chauhan ... 20
M. P. Vaughan lbw b Mhambre	1	– c Rathore b Mhambre ... 2
J. E. R. Gallian c Vikram Rathore b Bahutule	58	– lbw b Chauhan ... 25
M. R. Ramprakash c Yadav b Chauhan	99	– not out ... 36
*A. P. Wells c Muzumdar b Chatterjee	20	– c Dravid b Chatterjee ... 15
P. N. Weekes lbw b Bahutule	3	– c Bahutule b Chauhan ... 0
D. G. Cork c and b Bahutule	6	– st Yadav b Chatterjee ... 0
†P. A. Nixon c sub (Rizwan Shamshad)		
b Bahutule	0	– not out ... 9
G. Chapple c Chatterjee b Mhambre	26	
I. D. K. Salisbury c Muzumdar b Mhambre	5	
R. D. Stemp not out	2	
B 8, n-b 11	19	B 4, l-b 2, n-b 4 ... 10

1/2 (2) 2/97 (3) 3/136 (1) 4/191 (5)	**289**	1/10 (2) 2/43 (1)	(6 wkts) 117
5/207 (6) 6/213 (7) 7/213 (8)		3/50 (3) 4/83 (5)	
8/265 (4) 9/283 (10) 10/289 (9)		5/88 (6) 6/89 (7)	

Bowling: *First Innings*—Mhambre 14.3–3–42–3; Kuruvilla 7–0–23–0; Chauhan 28–7–67–1; Chatterjee 26–6–53–2; Bahutule 37–10–96–4. *Second Innings*—Mhambre 6–1–14–1; Kuruvilla 2–0–3–0; Chauhan 19.2–7–43–3; Chatterjee 13–3–25–2; Bahutule 6–1–26–0.

Umpires: Jasbir Singh and V. K. Ramaswamy.

†At Delhi, January 21, 22, 23, 24. England A won by 439 runs. Toss: England A. England A 553 (M. R. Ramprakash 124, A. P. Wells 51, P. N. Weekes 93, J. E. R. Gallian 100 retired out, G. Chapple 35, R. L. Johnson 30 not out, Extras 39; A. Tandon three for 142, P. Khole three for 87) and 214 for five dec. (M. P. Vaughan 87, K. J. Piper 48, M. M. Patel 56); Combined Universities 165 (S. Pathak 47; R. L. Johnson three for 43) and 163 (C. Vasant Kumar 46, S. Pathak 58; M. M. Patel six for 35).

Ruled not first-class by the BCCI as only one of the Combined Universities team had previously played first-class cricket.

INDIA A v ENGLAND A

Second Unofficial Test

At Calcutta, January 27, 28, 29, 30, 31. England A won by five wickets. Toss: India A.

England A made sure of the series with a second victory, reasserting their superiority after letting their advantage slip more than once. Their hero on the final day was Hemp, whose unbeaten 99 suggested the arrival of an exciting batting talent. Hemp might not have played but for Ramprakash's departure; he had been out first ball against the Combined Universities and was still more embarrassed on visiting a Calcutta orphanage, where he was bowled by a nine-year-old. The first day began well for the tourists. Cork, with a determined new-ball burst of three for 22 from 11 overs, wrecked the Indian top order and Chapple kept up the pressure, until a spirited unbeaten 72 from Chatterjee, who came in at 95 for seven, took the score over 200. England A almost passed them with only two wickets down, after a stand of 154 between Gallian and Wells. But they collapsed, and led by only 100. India A depended as much on the whippy fast-medium pace of Mhambre, who removed Wells after four hours, as on their highly rated spin trio of Chauhan, Chatterjee and Bahutule.

A brilliant century from Vikram Rathore, the tall, elegant Punjabi opener, swung the match back the Indians' way, before Salisbury took two key wickets in quick succession, instigating the loss of the last six for 53. England A needed 254 to win and were 82 for four when Knight charged wildly at Chauhan. But with Wells grimly determined in the anchor role, they were propelled to victory by Hemp. The Indian spinners looked shocked as he struck them cleanly to all parts. He went from 50 to 99 in 55 balls and thought he had completed his century. But he had run three when only two were needed to win. The umpires had to remind players and scorers that, under Law 21, the third run should not count.

Close of play: First day, India A 216; Second day, England A 275-6 (P. A. Nixon 7*, M. M. Patel 2*); Third day, India A 204-2 (Vikram Rathore 113*, R. S. Dravid 48*); Fourth day, England A 80-2 (N. V. Knight 39*, M. M. Patel 0*).

India A

Vikram Rathore c Nixon b Cork	4	– (2) c Nixon b Cork	127
Jitender Singh lbw b Chapple	4	– (1) c Cork b Stemp	13
A. A. Muzumdar b Cork	7	– c Knight b Patel	23
R. S. Dravid run out	25	– c Nixon b Cork	52
*P. K. Amre c Nixon b Cork	5	– c Wells b Salisbury	43
Saurav C. Ganguly c Salisbury b Chapple	24	– b Salisbury	25
†V. S. Yadav st Nixon b Stemp	0	– (8) c Knight b Patel	4
S. V. Bahutule b Patel	21	– (7) run out	15
U. Chatterjee not out	72	– c Nixon b Stemp	10
R. K. Chauhan lbw b Chapple	19	– lbw b Cork	11
P. L. Mhambre lbw b Stemp	12	– not out	11
L-b 19, n-b 4	23	B 11, l-b 5, n-b 3	19

1/4 (1) 2/8 (2) 3/26 (3) 4/47 (5)   216   1/54 (1) 2/103 (3) 3/222 (4)   353
5/68 (4) 6/68 (7) 7/95 (6)   4/239 (2) 5/300 (6) 6/301 (5)
8/123 (8) 9/194 (10) 10/216 (11)   7/319 (8) 8/326 (7)
                                          9/331 (9) 10/353 (10)

Bowling: *First Innings*—Cork 25-5-48-3; Chapple 20-9-37-3; Gallian 4-0-17-0; Stemp 12.3-4-33-2; Patel 13-5-24-1; Salisbury 10-0-31-0; Vaughan 3-1-7-0. *Second Innings*—Cork 19.3-1-53-3; Chapple 21-8-47-0; Stemp 42-12-104-2; Salisbury 14-0-57-2; Patel 33-7-76-2.

England A

N. V. Knight c Yadav b Mhambre	31	– st Yadav b Chauhan	40
M. P. Vaughan c Ganguly b Mhambre	15	– lbw b Ganguly	1
J. E. R. Gallian c Yadav b Chatterjee	77	– st Yadav b Chauhan	37
*A. P. Wells c Yadav b Mhambre	93	– (5) c Chauhan b Chatterjee	65
D. L. Hemp lbw b Mhambre	18	– (6) not out	99
D. G. Cork lbw b Chauhan	12	– (7) not out	0
†P. A. Nixon c Yadav b Chauhan	22		
M. M. Patel lbw b Chatterjee	9	– (4) lbw b Bahutule	1
G. Chapple not out	9		
I. D. K. Salisbury c Mhambre b Chatterjee	0		
R. D. Stemp c Bahutule b Chauhan	5		
B 5, l-b 17, n-b 3	25	L-b 9, n-b 2	11

1/38 (2) 2/55 (1) 3/209 (3) 4/243 (5)   316   1/4 (2) 2/77 (3)   (5 wkts) 254
5/250 (4) 6/270 (6) 7/301 (7)   3/82 (4) 4/82 (1)
8/303 (8) 9/303 (10) 10/316 (11)   5/237 (5)

Bowling: *First Innings*—Mhambre 24-4-63-4; Ganguly 5-1-21-0; Chauhan 36.4-6-95-3; Chatterjee 31-8-76-3; Bahutule 13-2-36-0; Dravid 1-0-3-0. *Second Innings*—Mhambre 11-0-33-0; Ganguly 3-0-13-1; Chatterjee 16-1-42-1; Chauhan 29-7-87-2; Bahutule 30-11-69-1; Dravid 1-0-1-0.

Umpires: S. K. Bansal and A. V. Jayaprakash.

INDIA A v ENGLAND A

Third Unofficial Test

At Chandigarh, February 4, 5, 6, 7, 8. England A won by one wicket. Toss: India A.

A low-scoring scrap on a crumbling surface reached its climax ten overs into the final morning. Chasing 177, England A had 168, thanks to a heroic ninth-wicket stand of 41 from Johnson and Patel, when Chatterjee trapped Patel. Last man Stemp strode out, blocked his first ball, swept his second for six, took a single off the third and drove the next, from Mhambre, over extra cover for the winning boundary. England's players celebrated their clean sweep by dancing a lap of honour round the near-deserted Sector 16 Stadium.

India's selectors had reacted to losing the series by dropping five players – including the captain, Amre – for the final match. The new captain, Vikram Rathore, was bowled third ball and by the sixth over India A were ten for three. But Dravid and tailender Mhambre batted particularly well as they fought back to a total of 229 and, with England A also struggling, only a ninth-wicket stand of 56 between Piper and Patel hauled them up within sight of that. The second day was soured by verbal clashes on the field; the umpires, having spoken to Rathore about constant appealing, and to England A opener Knight, lectured both captains and team managers at the close. Resuming, India A's openers failed again, but Dravid and Muzumdar added 81 for the fourth wicket before the innings was dismantled by Chapple. He bowled with great heart, skill and sense for five wickets, his line and length faultless throughout three spells. A target of 177, however, was never easy on a sub-standard surface, especially against two experienced spinners in left-armer Chatterjee and off-spinner Kanwaljit Singh. Several English batsmen all threatened to play match-winning innings but, when Weekes was stumped, England A were 108 for seven. It was left to the tail to provide a hard-fought series with a thrilling finish.

Close of play: First day, India A 183-8 (P. L. Mhambre 17*, Kanwaljit Singh 16*); Second day, England A 145-7 (K. J. Piper 7*, R. L. Johnson 0*); Third day, India A 136-8 (A. A. Muzumdar 41*, Kanwaljit Singh 2*); Fourth day, England A 146-8 (R. L. Johnson 18*, M. M. Patel 8*).

India A

*Vikram Rathore b Cork	0	– (2) lbw b Patel	18
G. K. Khoda lbw b Chapple	7	– (1) lbw b Chapple	0
Saurav C. Ganguly c Piper b Chapple	0	– c Piper b Cork	8
R. S. Dravid b Cork	59	– lbw b Chapple	47
A. A. Muzumdar b Chapple	31	– b Chapple	55
Rizwan Shamshad b Patel	22	– c Piper b Chapple	4
†A. Vaidya c Piper b Stemp	4	– c Piper b Chapple	0
U. Chatterjee b Chapple	20	– run out	6
P. L. Mhambre not out	42	– b Patel	4
Kanwaljit Singh c Johnson b Stemp	20	– c Stemp b Patel	2
K. N. A. Padmanabhan c Piper b Johnson	13	– not out	6
B 2, l-b 7, w 1, n-b 1	11	B 3, l-b 1, w 1, n-b 1	6

1/0 (1) 2/3 (3) 3/10 (2) 4/56 (5)	229	1/1 (1) 2/23 (3) 3/33 (2)	156
5/93 (6) 6/102 (7) 7/144 (4)		4/114 (4) 5/120 (6) 6/120 (7)
8/156 (8) 9/193 (10) 10/229 (11)		7/126 (8) 8/132 (9)
		9/136 (10) 10/156 (5)

Bowling: *First Innings*—Cork 16-8-32-2; Chapple 25-7-60-4; Stemp 31-8-51-2; Johnson 9.3-1-29-1; Patel 20-10-26-1; Weekes 11-1-22-0. *Second Innings*—Cork 10.4-4-26-1; Chapple 19.2-3-38-5; Patel 31-12-43-3; Johnson 8-0-22-0; Stemp 8-1-23-0.

England A

N. V. Knight b Kanwaljit Singh	40	– (2) c Rizwan Shamshad b Kanwaljit Singh .	21
J. E. R. Gallian c Vaidya b Ganguly	11	– (1) c Ganguly b Chatterjee	9
D. L. Hemp c Dravid b Kanwaljit Singh	19	– c Dravid b Kanwaljit Singh	5
*A. P. Wells c Rizwan Shamshad b Chatterjee	42	– b Kanwaljit Singh	23
P. N. Weekes c Rizwan Shamshad b Chatterjee	15	– st Vaidya b Kanwaljit Singh	38
D. G. Cork b Mhambre	9	– lbw b Chatterjee	7
†K. J. Piper lbw b Ganguly	30	– c Vaidya b Chatterjee	1
G. Chapple c Vaidya b Mhambre	0	– c Rizwan Shamshad b Mhambre	12
R. L. Johnson lbw b Mhambre	4	– not out	33
M. M. Patel c Muzumdar b Mhambre	35	– lbw b Chatterjee	15
R. D. Stemp not out	0	– not out	11
L-b 2, n-b 2	4	L-b 3, n-b 1	4
	209	**(9 wkts)**	**179**

1/18 (2) 2/47 (3) 3/103 (4) 4/119 (5) 209
5/138 (1) 6/143 (6) 7/143 (8)
8/153 (9) 9/209 (7) 10/209 (10)

1/20 (1) 2/37 (3) (9 wkts) 179
3/38 (2) 4/81 (4)
5/92 (6) 6/108 (7)
7/108 (5) 8/127 (8)
9/168 (10)

Bowling: *First Innings*—Mhambre 20.1–6–63–4; Ganguly 10–0–32–2; Padmanabhan 10–3–40–0; Kanwaljit Singh 20–10–35–2; Chatterjee 22–9–37–2. *Second Innings*—Mhambre 15.1–5–34–1; Ganguly 5–2–9–0; Chatterjee 33–12–71–4; Kanwaljit Singh 29–14–49–4; Padmanabhan 4–0–13–0.

Umpires: S. Choudhury and K. A. Parthasarathy.

†At Indore, February 11. First unofficial one-day international: India A won by six runs. Toss: England A. India A 201 for seven (50 overs) (A. A. Muzumdar 79); England A 195 (49 overs) (M. R. Ramprakash 36, P. N. Weekes 33; A. S. Wassan three for 47, U. Chatterjee four for 32).
England A were penalised one over in their reply because of their slow over-rate.

†At Ahmedabad, February 14. Second unofficial one-day international: England A won by three wickets. Toss: India A. India A 207 for eight (50 overs) (A. A. Muzumdar 69, R. S. Dravid 57; P. N. Weekes three for 35); England A 208 for seven (48.4 overs) (D. L. Hemp 41, M. R. Ramprakash 70, J. E. R. Gallian 46; U. Chatterjee three for 42).

†At Hyderabad, February 16 (day/night). Third unofficial one-day international: England A won by 98 runs. Toss: India A. England A 254 for six (50 overs) (N. V. Knight 114 not out, M. R. Ramprakash 57); India A 156 (46 overs) (P. N. Weekes three for 40).
England A took the series 2-1.

†At Dhaka, February 20. England A won by 58 runs. Toss: England A. England A 203 for eight (50 overs) (J. E. R. Gallian 58, A. P. Wells 47, P. N. Weekes 36 not out); Bangladesh XI 145 for eight (50 overs) (Minhaz-ul-Abedin 34, Mohammad Rafiq 30).

†At Dhaka, February 22. England A won by 20 runs. Toss: Bangladesh XI. England A 235 for eight (50 overs) (N. V. Knight 117, D. L. Hemp 52; Anis-ur-Rahman three for 54, Ather Ali Khan three for 30); Bangladesh XI 215 (48.3 overs) (Javed Belim 36, Ather Ali Khan 46, Amin-ul-Islam 52, Mohammad Rafiq 43 not out).

†At Dhaka, February 24, 25, 26. Drawn. Toss: Bangladesh XI. Bangladesh XI 365 for six dec. (Javed Belim 39, Amin-ul-Islam 121, Minhaz-ul-Abedin 81, Naim-ur-Rahman 34 not out, Extras 32); England A 421 for seven (N. V. Knight 150, D. L. Hemp 190).
Knight and Hemp added 283 for England A's third wicket.

THE PAKISTANIS IN SRI LANKA, 1994-95

By WAHEED KHAN

The Pakistanis arrived in Colombo in July expecting a demanding tour. Their previous visit in 1985-86, when the Sri Lankans' uncompromising play had earned their first Test victory over Pakistan, had been soured by their suspicions of the local umpiring. Moreover, it was only six months since Salim Malik had inherited the captaincy, after a player-mutiny displaced his predecessor.

But the trip was to be a triumph for Malik and his new-look Pakistan team. It did indeed turn out to be a tough one, but only off the field, as political unrest over Sri Lanka's general election disrupted the itinerary and caused several anxious moments for the visitors. By winning both the Tests played and taking the one-day series – extended to five matches – 4-1, Pakistan became the first team for ten years to return from Sri Lanka as complete victors.

The Second Test, due to begin a few days after the election, was called off by the Sri Lankan board, which said a curfew made the match impossible; they added two extra one-day internationals to the programme instead. The change of plan was not announced until what should have been the first morning of the match, and annoyed those who thought that, in view of Sri Lanka's need for Test experience, preserving the five-day fixture should have been the board's priority. The home team's limited-overs record was less of a worry, it was argued: they had not lost one of the six limited-overs series played on the island in the previous two seasons.

Wasim Akram, at least, benefited from the altered programme – in the fifth one-day match he overtook Kapil Dev's record of 251 wickets in limited-overs internationals. He and Waqar Younis were the main difference between the two sides, taking a combined total of 27 wickets in the Tests. In the First Test at the P. Saravanamuttu Stadium, they exposed Sri Lanka's fallibility against top-class pace bowling, even though the pitch had been prepared for the home attack of three spinners and only one fast bowler. Though Waqar was recovering from an appendix operation in the early part of the tour, he found his rhythm to destroy the Sri Lankans in the final Test at Kandy with 11 wickets for 119. For Sri Lanka, the young off-spinner, Kumara Dharmasena, was the most successful bowler, with 12 wickets in the two Tests, but he never really looked capable of running through the strong Pakistani batting line-up. Malik had a wonderful series, not only as captain but also finding fine form with the bat, especially in the one-day games. Saeed Anwar batted with consistent excellence, compared with the erratic brilliance of Aravinda de Silva for Sri Lanka.

The hosts had hoped the series would provide a chance for Sri Lankan cricket to redeem itself after a string of defeats and controversies. After a 3-0 thrashing in India in January and February, the Sri Lankan board received an adverse report on captain Arjuna Ranatunga's conduct of the tour, and there were stories of a rift between Ranatunga and other senior players, notably Asanka Gurusinha. Worse was to follow: days before the Austral-Asia Cup in Sharjah, Ranatunga and several others pulled out. They objected to new and rigorous fitness tests and rebelled against the decision to drop leading batsman de Silva, who had failed them. Opener

Roshan Mahanama was appointed captain but the team fared badly. Sri Lanka still required the experience of Ranatunga and de Silva; after much persuasion and some arm-twisting, both were recalled and Ranatunga was reinstated as captain.

Pakistan had faced similar controversy earlier in the year, centring on the omission of Javed Miandad for the tours of New Zealand and Sharjah and the continuing intrigue over the captaincy. A rebellion against Wasim resulted in his replacement by Malik; meanwhile, Miandad announced his retirement, was persuaded to rescind it by prime minister Benazir Bhutto, scored a hundred in a trial match for the Sri Lankan tour and then withdrew because of a knee injury.

Despite the troubled background on both sides, the tour ended without any official reprimands by the ICC referee, West Indian Cammie Smith, though some thought he had taken a lenient view of several incidents, especially at Kandy.

PAKISTANI TOURING PARTY

Salim Malik (Lahore/Habib Bank) *(captain)*, Asif Mujtaba (Karachi/PIA) *(vice-captain)*, Aamir Sohail (Lahore/Habib Bank), Akram Raza (Sargodha/Habib Bank), Ashfaq Ahmed (Lahore/PIA), Basit Ali (Karachi/United Bank), Inzamam-ul-Haq (Multan/United Bank), Kabir Khan (Peshawar/HBFC), Mushtaq Ahmed (Multan/United Bank), Ramiz Raja (Lahore/Allied Bank), Rashid Latif (Karachi/United Bank), Saeed Anwar (Karachi/ADBP), Waqar Younis (Multan/United Bank), Wasim Akram (Lahore/PIA), Zahid Fazal (Lahore/PIA).

Javed Miandad (Karachi/Habib Bank) withdrew through injury before the start of the tour.
Tour manager: Intikhab Alam.

PAKISTANI TOUR RESULTS

Test matches – Played 2: Won 2. Cancelled 1.
First-class matches – Played 4: Won 2, Drawn 2. Cancelled 1.
Wins – Sri Lanka (2).
Draws – Sri Lankan Board President's XI (2).
One-day internationals – Played 5: Won 4, Lost 1.
Other non-first-class match – Lost v Sri Lankan Board President's XI.

TEST MATCH AVERAGES

SRI LANKA – BATTING

	T	I	NO	R	HS	100s	Avge	Ct
H. P. Tillekeratne	2	4	1	134	83*	0	44.66	4
P. A. de Silva	2	4	0	144	127	1	36.00	1
A. Ranatunga	2	4	0	84	41	0	21.00	0
R. S. Mahanama	2	4	0	70	37	0	17.50	0
P. B. Dassanayake	2	4	1	47	24	0	15.66	6
H. D. P. K. Dharmasena	2	4	0	34	30	0	8.50	1

Played in one Test: A. P. Gurusinha 11, 8 (1 ct); S. T. Jayasuriya 9, 1 (3 ct); R. S. Kalpage 6, 62 (1 ct); M. Muralitharan 0, 20* (1 ct); K. R. Pushpakumara 6, 0; S. Ranatunga 5, 4; D. P. Samaraweera 6, 13 (1 ct); W. P. U. J. C. Vaas 0, 4; K. P. J. Warnaweera 4, 0; G. P. Wickremasinghe 0*, 4.

* *Signifies not out.*

BOWLING

	O	M	R	W	BB	5W/i	Avge
H. D. P. K. Dharmasena	105.1	22	258	12	6-99	1	21.50
K. P. J. Warnaweera	59	6	171	5	3-63	0	34.20
K. R. Pushpakumara	26	3	145	4	4-145	0	36.25

Also bowled: P. A. de Silva 1–0–5–0; A. P. Gurusinha 4–1–24–0; S. T. Jayasuriya 13–0–53–0; R. S. Kalpage 11–0–50–0; M. Muralitharan 47–6–165–1; W. P. U. J. C. Vaas 22–2–80–0; G. P. Wickremasinghe 17–0–84–0.

PAKISTAN – BATTING

	T	I	NO	R	HS	100s	Avge	Ct
Inzamam-ul-Haq....	2	3	2	188	100*	1	188.00	1
Saeed Anwar.......	2	3	0	261	136	1	87.00	1
Aamir Sohail.......	2	3	0	180	74	0	60.00	5
Salim Malik	2	3	1	73	50*	0	36.50	0
Asif Mujtaba.......	2	3	0	92	44	0	30.66	2
Basit Ali	2	3	0	91	53	0	30.33	4

Played in two Tests: Mushtaq Ahmed 5*, 0 (1 ct); Rashid Latif 0, 7 (8 ct, 1 st); Waqar Younis 2, 20 (1 ct); Wasim Akram 37, 12 (2 ct). Played in one Test: Akram Raza 25 (2 ct); Kabir Khan did not bat.

* Signifies not out.

BOWLING

	O	M	R	W	BB	5W/i	Avge
Wasim Akram	75.2	24	175	13	5-43	1	13.46
Waqar Younis......	55	6	231	14	6-34	2	16.50
Mushtaq Ahmed....	27.3	4	116	6	3-34	0	19.33
Akram Raza	35	10	129	6	3-46	0	21.50

Also bowled: Aamir Sohail 2–0–3–0; Kabir Khan 10–1–39–1.

Note: Matches in this section which were not first-class are signified by a dagger.

SRI LANKAN BOARD PRESIDENT'S XI v PAKISTANIS

At Matara, July 23, 24, 25. Drawn. Toss: Pakistanis.

Rain washed out the first five sessions of the tour opener, against a strong Board President's XI. They fielded six Test players, including off-spinner Warnaweera, whose action was questioned by Salim Malik. Interestingly, Warnaweera did not take a wicket.

The Pakistani batsmen got some valuable practice on an easy-paced pitch, where the ball seamed around a bit. Saeed Anwar and Aamir Sohail, settling down into a reliable opening pair, put on 111 in 157 minutes; Malik also made the most of his time, scoring 77 before declaring, though the rest of the batting struggled and two young fast bowlers, Vaas and Pushpakumara, looked promising. In the Board President's XI's brief innings, medium-pacer Ashfaq Ahmed, bidding for a Test place, gave the home batsmen some anxious moments.

Close of play: First day, No play; Second day, Pakistanis 118-1 (Saeed Anwar 63*, Asif Mujtaba 1*).

Pakistanis

Saeed Anwar c Anurasiri b Kalpage ...	95	†Rashid Latif st Fernando b Jayasuriya	2
Aamir Sohail c and b Anurasiri	49	Akram Raza not out	0
Asif Mujtaba b Vaas	1	B 4, l-b 1, w 4, n-b 2	11
*Salim Malik not out...............	77		
Basit Ali c Atapattu b Kalpage	0	1/111 2/118 3/185 (6 wkts dec.)	250
Inzamam-ul-Haq c Vaas b Anurasiri ...	15	4/194 5/225 6/248	

Mushtaq Ahmed, Waqar Younis and Ashfaq Ahmed did not bat.

Bowling: Pushpakumara 11-1-36-0; Vaas 17-3-50-1; Kalpage 18-3-69-2; Warnaweera 14-3-34-0; Anurasiri 15-4-40-2; Jayasuriya 4-0-16-1.

Sri Lankan Board President's XI

M. A. R. Samarasekera		*S. T. Jayasuriya not out.............	18
b Mushtaq Ahmed .	14	R. S. Kalpage not out	0
A. A. W. Gunawardene			
b Ashfaq Ahmed .	4	L-b 2, n-b 6	8
M. S. Atapattu c Basit Ali			
b Ashfaq Ahmed .	2	1/16 2/20 3/46 (3 wkts)	46

†U. N. K. Fernando, U. U. Chandana, S. D. Anurasiri, W. P. U. J. C. Vaas, K. R. Pushpakumara and K. P. J. Warnaweera did not bat.

Bowling: Waqar Younis 5-1-7-0; Ashfaq Ahmed 7-1-18-2; Mushtaq Ahmed 6-3-17-1; Akram Raza 3-2-2-0.

Umpires: M. M. Mendis and D. N. Pathirana.

SRI LANKAN BOARD PRESIDENT'S XI v PAKISTANIS

At Kurunegala, July 28, 29, 30. Drawn. Toss: Sri Lankan Board President's XI.

Medium-paced off-spinner Dharmasena's splendid bowling earned him figures of seven for 111 and a place in the First Test. But none of his colleagues made much impression as the Pakistanis piled up 492, opting for batting practice rather than trying to force a win. The home team showed no interest in a result either, spending the first day compiling 280 for five; Sanjeeva Ranatunga, brother of the Test captain, batted almost throughout for 93. Wasim Akram and Waqar Younis proved expensive on a soft pitch, with Waqar conceding 62 in 14 overs. But next morning Wasim and Ashfaq Ahmed claimed the last five for 46 with the new ball. Aamir Sohail led the tourists' reply, scoring a swashbuckling 146 after being dropped on four and 96. He faced 170 balls and hit 23 fours and two sixes. Salim Malik and Saeed Anwar followed up with half-centuries; Anwar, batting down the order after being indisposed, hit four sixes and six fours in 69 balls.

Close of play: First day, Sri Lankan Board President's XI 280-5 (S. Ranatunga 93*, H. D. P. K. Dharmasena 21*); Second day, Pakistanis 276-4 (Salim Malik 13*, Saeed Anwar 9*).

Sri Lankan Board President's XI

D. P. Samaraweera c Saeed Anwar		
b Wasim Akram . 28	– (2) st Rashid Latif	
	b Mushtaq Ahmed . 10	
U. C. Hathurusinghe c Rashid Latif	– (1) c Mushtaq Ahmed	
b Ashfaq Ahmed . 0	b Wasim Akram . 1	
S. Ranatunga c Aamir Sohail b Wasim Akram . 97	– not out 24	
*H. P. Tillekeratne lbw b Ashfaq Ahmed 34	– not out 20	
R. P. A. H. Wickremaratne		
lbw b Ashfaq Ahmed . 69		
†R. S. Kaluwitharana lbw b Mushtaq Ahmed . . 15		
H. D. P. K. Dharmasena b Wasim Akram 23		
E. A. Upashantha c Inzamam-ul-Haq		
b Wasim Akram . 6		
M. Munasinghe not out 17		
Suranjith Silva c Rashid Latif b Wasim Akram 12		
A. W. Ekanayake c Inzamam-ul-Haq		
b Ashfaq Ahmed . 2		
L-b 4, n-b 19 23	B 2, w 1, n-b 6 9	

1/3 2/80 3/130 4/226 5/246   326   1/3 2/22   (2 wkts) 64
6/283 7/293 8/294 9/316

In the first innings S. Ranatunga, when 52, retired hurt at 123 and resumed at 130.

Bowling: *First Innings*—Wasim Akram 23–6–76–5; Ashfaq Ahmed 16.1–6–47–4; Waqar Younis 14–0–62–0; Mushtaq Ahmed 25–3–105–1; Aamir Sohail 4–0–14–0; Basit Ali 2–0–9–0; Salim Malik 1–0–9–0. *Second Innings*—Wasim Akram 4–0–8–1; Waqar Younis 8–4–18–0; Mushtaq Ahmed 9–3–26–1; Ashfaq Ahmed 4–2–10–0.

Pakistanis

Aamir Sohail c Tillekeratne	Wasim Akram c Kaluwitharana	
b Dharmasena . 146	b Dharmasena . 29	
Asif Mujtaba c Hathurusinghe	Mushtaq Ahmed run out 7	
b Dharmasena . 30	Waqar Younis c Munasinghe	
Inzamam-ul-Haq c Hathurusinghe	b Dharmasena . 31	
b Dharmasena . 47	Ashfaq Ahmed not out 0	
*Salim Malik st Kaluwitharana		
b Ekanayake . 62		
Basit Ali c Munasinghe b Dharmasena 16	N-b 18 18	
Saeed Anwar c Munasinghe		
b Ekanayake . 66	1/120 2/231 3/238 4/262 492	
†Rashid Latif c Kaluwitharana	5/369 6/388 7/428	
b Dharmasena . 40	8/440 9/474	

Bowling: Munasinghe 12–0–85–0; Upashantha 16–1–65–0; Dharmasena 38.2–7–111–7; Ekanayake 31–1–156–2; Silva 13–1–75–0.

Umpires: S. Ponnadurai and E. K. G. Wijedasa.

†At P. Saravanamuttu Stadium, Colombo, August 1. Sri Lankan Board President's XI won by two wickets. Toss: Sri Lankan Board President's XI. Pakistanis 195 for eight (47 overs) (Aamir Sohail 45, Salim Malik 62; K. R. Pushpakumara three for 26); Sri Lankan Board President's XI 198 for eight (46.3 overs) (S. Ranatunga 41; Waqar Younis three for 48).

†SRI LANKA v PAKISTAN

First One-Day International

At R. Premadasa (formerly Khettarama) Stadium, Colombo, August 3 (day/night). Pakistan won by nine wickets, their target having been revised to 169 from 42 overs. Toss: Sri Lanka. International debut: S. Ranatunga.

Opener Saeed Anwar hit an explosive 70 off 83 balls as Pakistan raced home. He might have made his fifth one-day hundred against Sri Lanka if rain had not cut eight overs from Pakistan's innings and reduced their target to 169 – which they achieved with nearly 12 overs in hand. Anwar began with a mixture of aggression and caution, but he and Inzamam-ul-Haq ploughed into the bowling, knocking off 98 in 17 overs after Aamir Sohail had fallen to Muralitharan's off-spin for a rapid 38. The only other highlight for a partisan crowd of 40,000 was a one-day international career-best 77 from makeshift opener Jayasuriya, who put on 86 with debutant Sanjeeva Ranatunga.

Man of the Match: Saeed Anwar.

Sri Lanka

S. T. Jayasuriya c Akram Raza		H. P. Tillekeratne run out	13
b Salim Malik	77	R. S. Kalpage not out	7
S. Ranatunga st Rashid Latif		†P. B. Dassanayake not out	5
b Salim Malik	31	L-b 4, w 6, n-b 4	14
A. P. Gurusinha b Akram Raza	5		
P. A. de Silva run out	15	1/86 2/97 3/133 (6 wkts, 50 overs)	200
*A. Ranatunga run out	33	4/143 5/186 6/194	

C. P. H. Ramanayake, G. P. Wickremasinghe and M. Muralitharan did not bat.

Bowling: Wasim Akram 10–0–38–0; Waqar Younis 8–2–38–0; Ashfaq Ahmed 8–1–33–0; Akram Raza 10–1–27–1; Salim Malik 10–0–44–2; Aamir Sohail 4–0–16–0.

Pakistan

Saeed Anwar not out		70
Aamir Sohail c Tillekeratne		
b Muralitharan		38
Inzamam-ul-Haq not out		53
B 3, l-b 5		8

1/71 (1 wkt, 30.2 overs) 169

*Salim Malik, Asif Mujtaba, Zahid Fazal, †Rashid Latif, Wasim Akram, Waqar Younis, Akram Raza and Ashfaq Ahmed did not bat.

Bowling: Wickremasinghe 7–0–43–0; Ramanayake 7.2–0–38–0; Kalpage 9–1–34–0; Gurusinha 1–0–10–0; Muralitharan 4–1–21–1; Jayasuriya 2–0–15–0.

Umpires: K. T. Francis and W. A. U. Wickremasinghe.

†SRI LANKA v PAKISTAN

Second One-Day International

At R. Premadasa Stadium, Colombo, August 6. Sri Lanka won by seven wickets. Toss: Sri Lanka.

Sri Lanka pulled level in the series after the left-handers Jayasuriya and Sanjeeva Ranatunga, the captain's younger brother, raised their country's first century opening stand against Pakistan in limited-overs cricket. Ranatunga struck a composed 70 in his second international. Earlier, Pakistan had to bat in overcast conditions with the ball moving around; Saeed Anwar was dismissed by the second ball of the match and, by the 13th over, Aamir Sohail and Inzamam-ul-Haq were also gone. Salim Malik and Basit Ali revived the innings with a stand of 74, but off-spinner Kalpage dismissed both and added two more wickets with his final two deliveries.

Man of the Match: S. Ranatunga.

Pakistan

Saeed Anwar c and b Wickremasinghe	0	Asif Mujtaba not out	12
Aamir Sohail b Vaas	11	Waqar Younis c and b Kalpage	0
Inzamam-ul-Haq c de Silva		Akram Raza not out	9
b A. Ranatunga	14		
*Salim Malik c Wickremasinghe			
b Kalpage	61	L-b 2, w 3, n-b 1	6
Basit Ali b Kalpage	40		
†Rashid Latif c Jayasuriya b Kalpage	27		
Wasim Akram c Dassanayake		1/0 2/21 3/39 (8 wkts, 50 overs) 180	
b Muralitharan	0	4/113 5/142 6/145	
		7/163 8/163	

Ashfaq Ahmed did not bat.

Bowling: Wickremasinghe 7-1-25-1; Vaas 7-0-20-1; A. Ranatunga 10-0-35-1; Muralitharan 10-1-36-1; Kalpage 10-1-36-4; Jayasuriya 6-0-26-0.

Sri Lanka

S. T. Jayasuriya st Rashid Latif		*A. Ranatunga not out	15
b Akram Raza	54	A. P. Gurusinha not out	10
S. Ranatunga lbw b Aamir Sohail	70	L-b 5, w 3, n-b 2	10
P. A. de Silva c Rashid Latif			
b Waqar Younis	22	1/104 2/153 3/153 (3 wkts, 47.2 overs) 181	

H. P. Tillekeratne, R. S. Kalpage, †P. B. Dassanayake, G. P. Wickremasinghe, W. P. U. J. C. Vaas and M. Muralitharan did not bat.

Bowling: Wasim Akram 10-2-34-0; Waqar Younis 9-0-43-1; Ashfaq Ahmed 5-1-20-0; Akram Raza 10-0-27-1; Salim Malik 6-0-26-0; Aamir Sohail 7.2-0-26-1.

Umpires: I. Anandappa and T. M. Samarasinghe.

†SRI LANKA v PAKISTAN

Third One-Day International

At Sinhalese Sports Club, Colombo, August 7. Pakistan won by 19 runs. Toss: Sri Lanka.

Salim Malik scored an unbeaten 93 from 94 balls to set up the victory which apparently ended Sri Lanka's unbeaten record in their last six home limited-overs series, dating back to 1985-86. Reviving memories of his 72 in 35 balls in Calcutta in 1986-87, he took Pakistan to 237 from a modest 45-over score of 166 for five. He turned the tide with a sustained display of big hitting, clobbering Muralitharan for three sixes and a four in one over, which yielded 27 runs. When Sri Lanka replied, Wasim Akram took two wickets in his third over. The home team never really recovered, though Jayasuriya made his third successive fifty and Kalpage and Vaas kept faint hope alive with a ninth-wicket stand of 76.

Man of the Match: Salim Malik.

Pakistan

Saeed Anwar c Dassanayake		Wasim Akram st Dassanayake	
b A. Ranatunga	33	b Kalpage	23
Aamir Sohail c Jayasuriya		Asif Mujtaba c Mahanama	
b Wickremasinghe	4	b Wickremasinghe	6
Inzamam-ul-Haq c Mahanama		Waqar Younis not out	4
b Kalpage	10	L-b 6, w 5, n-b 1	12
*Salim Malik not out	93		
Basit Ali c Gurusinha b Jayasuriya	50	1/7 2/50 3/58 4/154 (7 wkts, 50 overs) 237	
†Rashid Latif c Gurusinha b Jayasuriya	2	5/161 6/193 7/222	

Akram Raza and Ashfaq Ahmed did not bat.

Bowling: Wickremasinghe 8-1-26-2; Vaas 7-1-22-0; A. Ranatunga 10-0-44-1; Kalpage 10-0-48-2; Muralitharan 8-1-53-0; Jayasuriya 7-0-38-2.

Sri Lanka

S. T. Jayasuriya c Inzamam-ul-Haq		
b Akram Raza .	50	
S. Ranatunga c Rashid Latif		
b Wasim Akram .	2	
A. P. Gurusinha lbw b Wasim Akram .	0	
P. A. de Silva c Salim Malik		
b Waqar Younis .	21	
R. S. Mahanama lbw b Salim Malik ...	32	
*A. Ranatunga b Aamir Sohail	19	
†P. B. Dassanayake st Rashid Latif		
b Aamir Sohail .	1	

R. S. Kalpage not out 44
G. P. Wickremasinghe c Saeed Anwar
b Salim Malik . 0
W. P. U. J. C. Vaas b Wasim Akram .. 33
M. Muralitharan b Waqar Younis 1

L-b 6, w 7, n-b 2 15

1/13 2/13 3/51 (49 overs) 218
4/97 5/118 6/121
7/132 8/133 9/209

Bowling: Wasim Akram 9–0–24–3; Waqar Younis 10–0–57–2; Ashfaq Ahmed 4–0–31–0; Akram Raza 10–2–31–1; Salim Malik 10–1–45–2; Aamir Sohail 6–0–24–2.

Umpires: B. C. Cooray and P. Manuel.

SRI LANKA v PAKISTAN

First Test Match

At P. Saravanamuttu Stadium, Colombo, August 9, 10, 11, 13. Pakistan won by 301 runs. Toss: Pakistan.

Sri Lanka's mistaken approach to Test cricket was epitomised by their leading batsman, de Silva, in their first innings of this match. He batted as if in a hurry to catch a plane, smashing 127 runs from 156 balls. It was quality entertainment for a sparse crowd, as he brought up his century with a six – for the third time in Tests – and struck 19 fours. But in the final count he only hastened defeat for his team. In contrast, Pakistan chose to graft on a pitch which got progressively slower and developed an uneven bounce, making stroke-making hazardous. Their professionalism was embodied by Saeed Anwar, the left-handed opener, who scored 94 and 136.

Sri Lanka selected three off-spinners, Dharmasena, Warnaweera and Muralitharan – but not Kalpage, who had troubled Pakistan in the one-day series – and only one specialist fast bowler, Wickremasinghe. Though the hard-working Dharmasena took eight wickets in his third Test, he and Warnaweera, who continued to be dogged by complaints about the legality of his action, tended to hurry the ball off the pitch, instead of giving it the air it needed to turn. In fact, the Pakistani spinners proved more effective. Mushtaq Ahmed took three wickets before tea on the second day and off-spinner Aamir Raza claimed six in the match. The pace bowling of Wasim Akram and Waqar Younis was too good for Sri Lanka on any pitch. Wasim picked up eight wickets and though Waqar, returning after an appendicitis operation in April, was savaged by de Silva in the first innings, he had the last laugh on the fourth day, when he caught and bowled him with a slower ball.

On the first day, Pakistan reached 297 for six; Anwar narrowly missed his century before falling to Warnaweera, who shared most of the wickets with Dharmasena. Next day some ragged fielding helped the tourists advance to 390 after Inzamam-ul-Haq and Wasim, with a belligerent 37, added 37, took their stand to 85. At tea, Sri Lanka were 60 for four. Wasim removed Jayasuriya, who retained the opener's spot after his success in the one-day series, in his third over and then Mushtaq sparked a mini-collapse. But de Silva, in spanking form, and Tillekeratne halted the rout. De Silva punished Waqar persistently for bowling short on a slow pitch and reached his seventh Test century in the morning, though Raza subsequently dismissed him and the last two batsmen in one over. By the close, Pakistan had extended their lead by 238 and Anwar had completed his second Test hundred. After the rest day, he went on to 136 from 218 balls and Salim Malik contributed an unbeaten fifty, passing 4,000 Test runs, before declaring. Needing 483 for victory, Sri Lanka were 75 for five at tea, with Gurusinha and de Silva falling to Waqar. They folded for 181 with 42 minutes of the day left; Ranatunga, in his 50th Test, delayed the inevitable with a lone hand of 41 from 43 balls, but Wasim polished off the tail with three wickets in ten deliveries.

Man of the Match: Saeed Anwar.

Close of play: First day, Pakistan 297-6 (Inzamam-ul-Haq 46*, Wasim Akram 22*); Second day, Sri Lanka 152-4 (P. A. de Silva 74*, H. P. Tillekeratne 25*); Third day, Pakistan 238-2 (Saeed Anwar 110*, Salim Malik 15*).

Pakistan

Saeed Anwar c Jayasuriya b Warnaweera	94	c Dassanayake b Warnaweera	136
Aamir Sohail b Dharmasena	41	c Jayasuriya b Dharmasena	65
Asif Mujtaba c Dassanayake b Dharmasena	44	c Dassanayake b Warnaweera	31
*Salim Malik c Tillekeratne b Dharmasena	1	not out	50
Basit Ali lbw b Warnaweera	27	b Dharmasena	11
Inzamam-ul-Haq c Tillekeratne b Dharmasena	81	not out	7
†Rashid Latif c Dassanayake b Muralitharan	0		
Wasim Akram c Jayasuriya b Dharmasena	37		
Akram Raza c Tillekeratne b Warnaweera	25		
Mushtaq Ahmed not out	5		
Waqar Younis c Gurusinha b Dharmasena	2		
B 11, l-b 6, n-b 16	33	L-b 6, n-b 12	18

1/65 (2) 2/180 (1) 3/181 (4) 4/221 (3)   390   1/128 (2) 2/202 (3) (4 wkts dec.) 318
5/247 (5) 6/260 (7) 7/345 (8)   3/273 (1) 4/298 (5)
8/354 (6) 9/387 (9) 10/390 (11)

Bowling: *First Innings*—Wickremasinghe 12-0-59-0; Gurusinha 4-1-24-0; Dharmasena 45.2-13-99-6; Muralitharan 36-6-123-1; Warnaweera 28-5-63-3; de Silva 1-0-5-0. *Second Innings*—Wickremasinghe 5-0-25-0; Dharmasena 31-2-84-2; Warnaweera 31-1-108-2; Muralitharan 11-0-42-0; Jayasuriya 13-0-53-0.

Sri Lanka

R. S. Mahanama b Mushtaq Ahmed	21	c sub (Zahid Fazal) b Akram Raza	37
S. T. Jayasuriya c Aamir Sohail b Wasim Akram	9	c Rashid Latif b Wasim Akram	1
A. P. Gurusinha c Rashid Latif b Mushtaq Ahmed	11	c Asif Mujtaba b Waqar Younis	8
P. A. de Silva c Aamir Sohail b Akram Raza	127	c and b Waqar Younis	5
*A. Ranatunga c and b Mushtaq Ahmed	9	(6) st Rashid Latif b Akram Raza	41
H. P. Tillekeratne lbw b Waqar Younis	34	(5) c and b Akram Raza	8
†P. B. Dassanayake c Rashid Latif b Wasim Akram	3	b Wasim Akram	24
H. D. P. K. Dharmasena c Aamir Sohail b Wasim Akram	1	lbw b Wasim Akram	30
G. P. Wickremasinghe not out	0	b Wasim Akram	4
M. Muralitharan c Asif Mujtaba b Akram Raza	0	not out	20
K. P. J. Warnaweera c and b Akram Raza	4	b Wasim Akram	0
B 1, l-b 5, n-b 1	7	L-b 2, n-b 1	3

1/13 (2) 2/41 (1) 3/42 (3) 4/60 (5)   226   1/1 (2) 2/30 (3) 3/38 (4)   181
5/179 (6) 6/215 (7) 7/218 (8)   4/52 (5) 5/59 (1) 6/118 (7)
8/222 (4) 9/222 (10) 10/226 (11)   7/135 (6) 8/160 (9)
                                                         9/181 (8) 10/181 (11)

Bowling: *First Innings*—Wasim Akram 17-4-30-3; Waqar Younis 16-1-84-1; Mushtaq Ahmed 14-2-57-3; Akram Raza 19-7-46-3; Aamir Sohail 2-0-3-0. *Second Innings*—Wasim Akram 18-4-43-5; Waqar Younis 7-0-28-2; Akram Raza 16-3-83-3; Mushtaq Ahmed 6-1-25-0.

Umpires: I. D. Robinson (Zimbabwe) and K. T. Francis.
Referee: C. W. Smith (West Indies).

SRI LANKA v PAKISTAN

Second Test Match

At Sinhalese Sports Club, Colombo, August 19, 20, 21, 23, 24. Cancelled without a ball bowled because of the curfew following the general election.

The Sri Lankan board's decision to cancel was not universally approved. The local press protested that Sri Lanka desperately needed more Test exposure and had had plenty of limited-overs cricket. The argument was that the Test could have been staged a day later. It seemed to be going ahead as normal when the two teams arrived at the ground and held nets on what should have been the first morning; the umpires walked on to the field and, after inspecting the pitch, which was still wet after overnight rain, decided that play should begin 40 minutes late. It was shortly after they returned to the pavilion that the board secretary, former captain Anura Tennekoon, circulated a press release announcing the change of plan. Pakistani manager Intikhab Alam supported the decision – he did not think the atmosphere in Colombo was right for Test cricket. But it was a disappointment for the players, who had already been holed up in their hotel for almost a week since wrapping up the First Test in four days.

†SRI LANKA v PAKISTAN

Fourth One-Day International

At Sinhalese Sports Club, Colombo, August 22. Pakistan won by five wickets. Toss: Pakistan.

Two additional one-day games were arranged in place of the Test and gave Sri Lanka a chance to recover their unbeaten record in home limited-overs series, though the Pakistan camp argued that they were not part of the rubber which they had already won 2-1. But another comfortable victory for Pakistan, who seemed untroubled by an eight-day lay-off during the curfew, made the question irrelevant. Sri Lanka lost five for 55 in the first 19 overs, with Akram Raza having a hand in three of the dismissals. They might have been in even worse straits but for a superb 74 from captain Arjuna Ranatunga. A target of 175 hardly tested Pakistan. Several of their main batsmen got out after making good starts, before Salim Malik saw them home, despite fading light and humid conditions, with his third straight fifty of the series.

Man of the Match: Akram Raza.

Sri Lanka

R. S. Mahanama c Akram Raza b Waqar Younis .	11	†P. B. Dassanayake b Wasim Akram . .	13	
S. T. Jayasuriya lbw b Wasim Akram . .	2	W. P. U. J. C. Vaas not out	7	
S. Ranatunga c and b Akram Raza	14	G. P. Wickremasinghe b Waqar Younis	11	
P. A. de Silva c Aamir Sohail b Akram Raza .	5			
*A. Ranatunga run out	74	L-b 5, w 6, n-b 2	13	
H. P. Tillekeratne run out	0	1/5 2/23 3/29 (9 wkts, 50 overs)	174	
R. S. Kalpage c Salim Malik b Aamir Sohail .	24	4/55 5/55 6/102		
		7/155 8/157 9/174		

K. R. Pushpakumara did not bat.

Bowling: Wasim Akram 10-1-35-2; Waqar Younis 10-1-35-2; Akram Raza 10-1-26-2; Mushtaq Ahmed 10-1-28-0; Aamir Sohail 5-0-17-1; Salim Malik 5-0-28-0.

Pakistan

Saeed Anwar c Dassanayake b Pushpakumara .	9	Asif Mujtaba b de Silva	3	
Aamir Sohail c S. Ranatunga b Kalpage	35	Akram Raza not out	8	
Inzamam-ul-Haq c and b Jayasuriya . . .	33	L-b 2, w 3, n-b 6	11	
*Salim Malik not out	50	1/20 2/61 3/114 (5 wkts, 41.4 overs)	175	
Basit Ali st Dassanayake b Jayasuriya . .	26	4/160 5/165		

Wasim Akram, †Rashid Latif, Waqar Younis and Mushtaq Ahmed did not bat.

Bowling: Vaas 6-1-23-0; Pushpakumara 7-0-50-1; Wickremasinghe 5.4-1-26-0; Kalpage 10-0-39-1; Jayasuriya 10-0-28-2; de Silva 3-0-7-1.

Umpires: I. Anandappa and T. M. Samarasinghe.

†SRI LANKA v PAKISTAN

Fifth One-Day International

At R. Premadasa Stadium, Colombo, August 24. Pakistan won by 27 runs. Toss: Sri Lanka.

Wasim Akram, who equalled Kapil Dev's record of 251 wickets in limited-overs internationals in the previous game, passed it when he trapped Jayasuriya leg-before in his first over. He needed only 174 matches to Kapil's 220. Meanwhile, Waqar Younis returned to his best form since an operation for appendicitis. Together they halted a brave victory charge by Sri Lanka, who required 66 from the last ten overs with six wickets in hand. In two overs, Waqar bowled Tillekeratne and Arjuna Ranatunga with swinging yorkers and dismissed Mahanama, who had resumed with a runner after suffering cramps, despite a protest from Salim Malik that he should have been consulted. Pakistan's own innings never gained momentum; most of the top-order batsmen got settled but threw away their wickets.

Man of the Match: Waqar Younis.

Pakistan

Saeed Anwar c and b Wickremasinghe	0	†Rashid Latif b Kalpage	0
Aamir Sohail run out	25	Waqar Younis b Kalpage	13
Inzamam-ul-Haq lbw b A. Ranatunga	25	Mushtaq Ahmed b Vaas	1
*Salim Malik run out	19		
Basit Ali c Vaas b Dharmasena	31	L-b 5, w 3, n-b 4	12
Asif Mujtaba c Mahanama			
b Dharmasena	28	1/1 2/54 3/59	(49.5 overs) 187
Wasim Akram run out	0	4/92 5/130 6/130	
Akram Raza not out	33	7/160 8/162 9/184	

Bowling: Wickremasinghe 3–0–9–1; Vaas 7.5–1–39–1; A. Ranatunga 10–0–23–1; Kalpage 10–1–38–2; Jayasuriya 10–0–39–0; Dharmasena 9–0–34–2.

Sri Lanka

R. S. Mahanama c Asif Mujtaba		R. S. Kalpage c Salim Malik	
b Waqar Younis	52	b Wasim Akram	4
S. T. Jayasuriya lbw b Wasim Akram	0	H. D. P. K. Dharmasena not out	3
S. Ranatunga run out	23	W. P. U. J. C. Vaas run out	1
P. A. de Silva c Rashid Latif		G. P. Wickremasinghe c Rashid Latif	
b Aamir Sohail	6	b Wasim Akram	1
*A. Ranatunga b Waqar Younis	32	B 2, l-b 6, w 10, n-b 1	19
†R. S. Kaluwitharana			
lbw b Akram Raza	4	1/4 2/58 3/73 4/102 5/139	(48.1 overs) 160
H. P. Tillekeratne b Waqar Younis	15	6/140 7/151 8/151 9/157	

R. S. Mahanama, when 44, retired hurt at 93 and resumed at 139.

Bowling: Wasim Akram 9.1–2–20–3; Waqar Younis 8–0–33–3; Akram Raza 10–0–25–1; Mushtaq Ahmed 10–0–27–0; Aamir Sohail 10–0–41–1; Salim Malik 1–0–6–0.

Umpires: P. Manuel and W. A. U. Wickremasinghe.

SRI LANKA v PAKISTAN

Third Test Match

At Kandy, August 26, 27, 28. Pakistan won by an innings and 52 runs. Toss: Pakistan. Test debuts: K. R. Pushpakumara, S. Ranatunga, W. P. U. J. C. Vaas; Kabir Khan.

Caught on a green-top pitch with plenty of moisture in it, while clouds hovered persistently over the stadium, Sri Lanka crumbled for 71 – their lowest Test score – in two hours 25 minutes and were finally brushed aside with more than two days remaining.

Hoping to square the series, the hosts made five changes, bringing in Sanjeeva Ranatunga, the third Ranatunga brother to play Test cricket, and pace bowlers Chaminda Vaas and Ravindra Pushpakumara. Opener Samaraweera and off-spinner Kalpage also returned while batsmen Gurusinha and Jayasuriya and spinners Warnaweera and Muralitharan were dropped; seamer Wickremasinghe was injured. Pakistan blooded left-arm pace bowler Kabir Khan in place of spinner Akram Raza, though he did not get a chance to bowl until the 24th over of Sri Lanka's second innings. Until then, Wasim Akram and Waqar Younis had bowled unchanged for 51.2 overs. Waqar took centre stage with 11 for 119; Wasim had to be content with five wickets in the match, though he bowled eight consecutive maidens at the start of the second innings. The pair were all smiles on seeing the pitch and Sri Lankan captain Arjuna Ranatunga tried to postpone the start after losing the toss, claiming that the bowler's run up was slippery after overnight rain. The umpires allowed only ten minutes' delay, however, though a further break extended lunch. The ball moved and fizzed around, but it was a gutless display by the Sri Lankan batsmen. Ranatunga's dismissal was typical. Waqar peppered him with short-pitched deliveries and then forced him to glove one to slip. Sri Lanka would have gone for 56 if Kabir had not dropped last man Pushpakumara in the covers; he put on 25 valuable runs with Dassanayake.

When Pakistan batted, Pushpakumara's hostile bowling made the openers play and miss repeatedly, but they got off to a fighting start with 94 in 23 overs. Aamir Sohail was in swashbuckling form, despite a temperature, playing some handsome drives and passing 50 with a six. By the close, Pakistan already led by 38, with eight wickets in hand. They consolidated their advantage next day, when Inzamam-ul-Haq scored an unbeaten 100 from 125 balls, adding 98 in even time with Basit Ali, whose fifty featured some exquisite shots on the off side. That evening Sri Lanka lost another three wickets inside ten overs, all to Waqar. When they were reduced to 78 for six, only a hard-hitting stand of 131 between Tillekeratne, who finished undefeated on 83, and Kalpage saved the home team from complete embarrassment. They gave the 15,000 Sunday crowd something to cheer as Kalpage reached his fifty in 49 balls and slammed Wasim for three boundaries in an over. But Kabir ended the fun when he had Kalpage caught and Mushtaq Ahmed wiped out the tail with three wickets in 15 balls.

Man of the Match: Waqar Younis.

Close of play: First day, Pakistan 109-2 (Aamir Sohail 68*, Asif Mujtaba 1*); Second day, Sri Lanka 17-3 (D. P. Samaraweera 2*).

Sri Lanka

R. S. Mahanama c Rashid Latif b Waqar Younis	2	– c Inzamam-ul-Haq b Waqar Younis . 10
D. P. Samaraweera c Rashid Latif b Wasim Akram	6	– lbw b Waqar Younis 13
S. Ranatunga c Rashid Latif b Waqar Younis . .	5	– (4) c Wasim Akram b Waqar Younis . 4
P. A. de Silva lbw b Wasim Akram	7	– (5) c Rashid Latif b Wasim Akram . 5
*A. Ranatunga c Saeed Anwar b Waqar Younis	0	– (6) c Rashid Latif b Waqar Younis . 34
H. P. Tillekeratne b Waqar Younis	9	– (7) not out 83
R. S. Kalpage c Aamir Sohail b Wasim Akram	6	– (8) c sub (Ramiz Raja) b Kabir Khan . 62
†P. B. Dassanayake not out	19	– (3) lbw b Waqar Younis 1
H. D. P. K. Dharmasena lbw b Waqar Younis .	0	– c sub (Zahid Fazal) b Mushtaq Ahmed . 3
W. P. U. J. C. Vaas c Wasim Akram b Waqar Younis	0	– lbw b Mushtaq Ahmed 4
K. R. Pushpakumara c Aamir Sohail b Wasim Akram .	6	– lbw b Mushtaq Ahmed 0
B 1, l-b 4, w 5, n-b 1	11	L-b 6, n-b 9 15
	71	**234**

1/12 (1) 2/20 (2) 3/22 (3) 4/28 (5) 5/28 (4) 6/43 (6) 7/45 (7) 8/46 (9) 9/46 (10) 10/71 (11) **71**

1/11 (1) 2/13 (3) 3/17 (4) 4/22 (5) 5/42 (2) 6/78 (6) 7/209 (8) 8/221 (9) 9/234 (10) 10/234 (11) **234**

Bowling: *First Innings*—Wasim Akram 14.2–4–32–4; Waqar Younis 14–4–34–6. *Second Innings*—Wasim Akram 26–12–70–1; Waqar Younis 18–1–85–5; Kabir Khan 10–1–39–1; Mushtaq Ahmed 7.3–1–34–3.

Pakistan

Saeed Anwar lbw b Pushpakumara	31	Wasim Akram c de Silva	
Aamir Sohail c Tilakeratne		b Pushpakumara	12
b Pushpakumara	74	Waqar Younis c Kalpage	
Mushtaq Ahmed run out	0	b Dharmasena	20
Asif Mujtaba c Dassanayake			
b Pushpakumara	17		
*Salim Malik c Dassanayake		B 4, l-b 3, w 1, n-b 13	21
b Dharmasena	22		
Basit Ali c and b Dharmasena	53	1/94 (1) 2/94 (3) 3/117 (2) (9 wkts dec.)	357
Inzamam-ul-Haq not out	100	4/158 (4) 5/158 (5)	
†Rashid Latif c Samaraweera		6/256 (6) 7/264 (8)	
b Dharmasena	7	8/297 (9) 9/357 (10)	

Kabir Khan did not bat.

Bowling: Vaas 22-2-80-0; Pushpakumara 26-3-145-4; Dharmasena 28.5-7-75-4; Kalpage 11-0-50-0.

Umpires: I. D. Robinson (Zimbabwe) and B. C. Cooray.
Referee: C. W. Smith (West Indies).

ONE HUNDRED YEARS AGO

From JOHN WISDEN'S CRICKETERS' ALMANACK FOR 1896

W. G. GRACE By A. G. Steel: "Yielding to none in admiration of the 'hero' of a hundred centuries, and to none in love for the game in which he is so proficient, I am bound to say I was not altogether pleased with the *Daily Telegraph* testimonial. A national testimonial in honour of the greatest cricketer the world has ever seen, on his completion of a performance which may be a 'record' for all time, was indeed fitting. Surely the greatest cricket club in the world – the M.C.C. – was the proper initiator of the testimonial to the greatest cricketer. Day after day, as one read of the flood of shillings pouring in, accompanied by such varied correspondence, one could not but feel a little alarm for the dignity of our great game. But whether the means adopted for raising the testimonial were the right ones or not, the fact remains that it was an enormous success, and showed that the personality of W. G. Grace had taken a deep hold upon all classes of the English people. The enthusiasm was such as has probably never before been kindled concerning the exponent of any modern form of athletics."

PUBLIC SCHOOL CRICKET IN 1895 By W. G. Ford: "Nothing would be more delightful or more interesting to cricketers than an arrangement by which the leading public schools could meet each other in a series of matches conducted on the league principle. Unfortunately, nothing is more impossible, though something approaching to it was realised when Eton, Harrow, and Winchester played a week's cricket against each other in turns at Lord's. Unhappily, that week has long since been abolished and the difficulty of classification – apart from scholastic reasons – would make an attempt at such organisation hopeless. Consequently, the question as to the best public school of the year is only to be decided by individual judgment, and not by points or proportional parts."

THE UNIVERSITIES – OXFORD: "It is likely enough that if the Oxford eleven could have fulfilled their own expectations and beaten Cambridge at Lord's, they would have been referred to as the best team the Dark Blues had had since Mr. M. C. Kemp's famous side in 1884. As everyone knows, however, they met with a startling reverse in the big match, Cambridge winning by a majority of 134 runs. This unexpected defeat in the all-important game of the season naturally damaged their reputation a great deal, but though they failed when most was demanded of them, it is certain that, allowing for some weakness in bowling, they were a capital eleven."

THE AUSTRALIANS IN PAKISTAN, 1994-95

By MIKE COWARD

It has long been the view of the vast majority of Australian cricketers that a tour of Pakistan is both exhausting and unrewarding. Yet more often than not they have exaggerated the difficulty of the exercise. This was again the case in 1994-95, when they squandered precious opportunities to win their first Test match in Pakistan since 1959-60.

Despite being the most relaxed, focused and aware Australian team to visit Pakistan – they were even briefed on how to answer awkward questions – new captain Mark Taylor and his team were beset by the same problem that plagued their predecessors: dropped catches. They put down 13 in the three Tests; the last three Australian teams to Pakistan are estimated to have put down 48 in nine Tests. Allan Border's petulant party of 1988-89 dropped 14, while Kim Hughes's team of 1982-83 dropped 21. Yet, in spite of these lapses and a sequence of serious injuries to their most influential players, the Australians earned a substantial first-innings advantage in all three Tests and had legitimate winning chances in each of them. They even forced the follow-on in Rawalpindi.

But they were thwarted at every turn, principally by Pakistan captain Salim Malik, who proved a formidable opponent. He batted for 21 hours in the series, amassing 557 runs at 92.83, beating Graham Yallop's record for Australian and Pakistan Tests of 554 at 92.33 in 1983-84. In Rawalpindi and Lahore he composed match-saving, series-winning hundreds. Despite Malik's impressive batting performance, which seemed to strengthen his grip on the captaincy he had acquired as a compromise candidate, the series was to lead to his downfall a few months later. While Pakistan were touring Zimbabwe in February, an Australian newspaper alleged that he had offered Shane Warne, Tim May and Mark Waugh bribes to throw the Karachi Test; the Australian players later made written statements to ICC. Malik denied the reports, but he was sacked on his return home.

Though leg-spinner Warne equalled Richie Benaud's record 18 wickets for an Australian in Pakistan, the bowlers struggled at crucial moments. To be fair, Taylor never had all his new-ball bowlers available for the same match. "We just couldn't get the big wicket," he said. "It started with Karachi: we needed one wicket, couldn't do it. The morning of the fourth day at Rawalpindi we needed a wicket, couldn't get it. And on the final morning in Lahore we needed one wicket, couldn't do it. You look back on the tour and say it was pretty good. But you've got to look at results. That's what's going to be there for everyone to see in years to come, and we lost 1-0."

The tenor of an absorbing series was set in Karachi in the First Test, when Pakistan won a thrilling match by one wicket and Warne, Wasim Akram and Waqar Younis, the world's three most destructive bowlers at the time, took 23 wickets between them. Yet, with the exception of the dramatic final day in Karachi, the crowds stayed away, preferring matches in the limited-overs competition which also included South Africa. Australia won that, having played indifferently in a four-way tournament in Sri Lanka before their arrival.

Anxious to make reparation for an acrimonious visit in 1988-89, the Australians – particularly Warne – were popular everywhere they travelled. And, while Taylor had a frustrating introduction to the demands and challenges of captaincy, he none the less acquitted himself impressively. It was clear he had immeasurably more support inside and outside the dressing-room than did his counterpart Malik.

AUSTRALIAN TOURING PARTY

M. A. Taylor (New South Wales) (*captain*), I. A. Healy (Queensland) (*vice-captain*), J. Angel (Western Australia), M. G. Bevan (New South Wales), D. C. Boon (Tasmania), D. W. Fleming (Victoria), J. L. Langer (Western Australia), C. J. McDermott (Queensland), G. D. McGrath (New South Wales), T. B. A. May (South Australia), G. R. Robertson (New South Wales), M. J. Slater (New South Wales), S. K. Warne (Victoria), M. E. Waugh (New South Wales), S. R. Waugh (New South Wales).

P. A. Emery (New South Wales) joined the party as a replacement for the injured Healy. *Manager:* C. Egar. *Coach:* R. B. Simpson.

AUSTRALIAN TOURING RESULTS

Test matches – Played 3: Lost 1, Drawn 2.
First-class matches – Played 4: Lost 1, Drawn 3.
Loss – Pakistan.
Draws – Pakistan (2), President's XI.
One-day internationals – Played 7: Won 5, Lost 1, No result 1. *Wins* – Pakistan (2), South Africa (3). *Loss* – Pakistan. *No result* – Pakistan.

TEST MATCH AVERAGES

PAKISTAN – BATTING

	T	I	NO	R	HS	100s	Avge	Ct
Salim Malik	3	6	0	557	237	2	92.83	0
Aamir Sohail.......	3	6	0	328	105	1	54.66	3
Saeed Anwar.......	3	6	0	314	85	0	52.33	1
Wasim Akram	2	4	1	93	45*	0	31.00	1
Inzamam-ul-Haq....	3	6	1	150	66	0	30.00	1
Rashid Latif	2	4	0	93	38	0	23.25	5
Mushtaq Ahmed....	3	6	2	63	27	0	15.75	1
Akram Raza	2	4	0	47	32	0	11.75	0
Zahid Fazal........	2	4	0	41	27	0	10.25	1
Waqar Younis......	2	4	0	36	13	0	9.00	0
Basit Ali	2	4	0	14	12	0	3.50	0
Mohsin Kamal	2	4	2	6	4	0	3.00	2

Played in one Test: Aamer Malik 11, 65; Aqib Javed 2, 2; Ijaz Ahmed 48, 6 (1 ct); Moin Khan 115*, 16 (4 ct).

* Signifies not out.

BOWLING

	O	M	R	W	BB	5W/i	Avge
Wasim Akram	70.5	10	200	9	5-63	1	22.22
Waqar Younis......	74.2	13	258	10	4-69	0	25.80
Mohsin Kamal	54	6	225	7	4-116	0	32.14
Mushtaq Ahmed....	127.1	13	415	9	4-121	0	46.11

Also bowled: Aamer Malik 5-2-16-0; Aamir Sohail 33-3-105-3; Akram Raza 69-11-192-2; Aqib Javed 31-9-75-0; Rashid Latif 2-0-10-0; Saeed Anwar 2-2-0-0; Salim Malik 2-0-11-0.

AUSTRALIA – BATTING

	T	I	NO	R	HS	100s	Avge	Ct
M. G. Bevan	3	4	0	243	91	0	60.75	5
S. R. Waugh	2	3	0	171	98	0	57.00	2
M. E. Waugh	3	4	0	220	71	0	55.00	3
D. C. Boon	3	5	2	149	114*	1	49.66	3
M. J. Slater	3	5	0	244	110	1	48.80	1
I. A. Healy	2	3	0	123	58	0	41.00	8
M. A. Taylor	3	5	1	106	69	0	26.50	3
S. K. Warne	3	4	0	69	33	0	17.25	2
J. Angel	2	3	0	20	8	0	6.66	1
T. B. A. May......	2	3	1	12	10	0	6.00	0
G. D. McGrath....	2	3	0	4	3	0	1.33	0

Played in two Tests: C. J. McDermott 9*, 29 (1 ct). Played in one Test: P. A. Emery 8* (5 ct, 1 st); J. L. Langer 69; D. W. Fleming did not bat.

* Signifies not out.

BOWLING

	O	M	R	W	BB	5W/i	Avge
D. W. Fleming	48	5	161	7	4-75	0	23.00
S. K. Warne	181.4	50	504	18	6-136	2	28.00
G. D. McGrath.....	80.1	15	245	7	4-92	0	35.00
T. B. A. May......	92	20	251	6	3-69	0	41.83
C. J. McDermott....	98	17	328	7	4-74	0	46.85
J. Angel	80.1	13	306	6	3-54	0	51.00

Also bowled: M. G. Bevan 8-0-48-1; D. C. Boon 3-1-9-0; M. J. Slater 1.1-0-4-1; M. A. Taylor 3-1-11-1; M. E. Waugh 27-2-93-2; S. R. Waugh 30-5-78-1.

PRESIDENT'S XI v AUSTRALIANS

At Rawalpindi, September 23, 24. 25. Drawn. Toss: President's XI.

The Australians emerged confidently from the southern winter and finished only one wicket short of their first first-class victory in Pakistan for 35 years. Last-wicket pair Moin Khan and Ashfaq Ahmed held out for half an hour to deny them. Boon scored a chanceless century, and Steve Waugh began to make amends for an unproductive tour in 1988-89 with an unbeaten fifty. Bevan also struck a half-century on the second day, while pace bowler McGrath quickly adapted to unfamiliar conditions and took ten wickets for 81 in the match. Zahid Fazal, with a competent 91, and Mohsin Kamal, who returned match figures of six for 96, were the only home players to demand further attention from the selectors.

Close of play: First day, President's XI 3-0 (Shakeel Ahmed 1*, Shoaib Mohammad 0*); Second day, Australians 134-2 (M. G. Bevan 62*, I. A. Healy 40*).

Australians

M. J. Slater c Moin Khan b Mohsin Kamal....	20	– (2) c sub (Atif Rauf)	
		b Mohsin Kamal .	21
*M. A. Taylor c Moin Khan b Mohsin Kamal..	4	– (1) lbw b Mohsin Kamal.......	1
D. C. Boon b Mohsin Kamal.................	101		
M. E. Waugh b Manzoor Akhtar.............	57		
M. G. Bevan run out......................	38	– (3) not out...................	62
S. R. Waugh not out......................	53		
†I. A. Healy c Moin Khan b Ata-ur-Rehman...	20	– (4) not out...................	40
S. K. Warne lbw b Manzoor Akhtar.........	4		
C. J. McDermott lbw b Ata-ur-Rehman......	12		
T. B. A. May lbw b Ata-ur-Rehman.........	0		
G. D. McGrath b Mohsin Kamal............	0		
B 8, l-b 6, n-b 15.............	29	B 4, l-b 2, n-b 4........	10

1/14 2/49 3/153 4/219 5/266   338   1/18 2/33   (2 wkts dec.) 134
6/298 7/321 8/336 9/336

Bowling: *First Innings*—Mohsin Kamal 14.1–0–74–4; Ata-ur-Rehman 16–0–74–3; Ashfaq Ahmed 13–1–78–0; Haaris Khan 15–1–57–0; Manzoor Akhtar 10–2–41–2. *Second Innings*—Mohsin Kamal 8–3–22–2; Ata-ur-Rehman 3–0–16–0; Ashfaq Ahmed 8–1–18–0; Haaris Khan 5–1–21–0; Manzoor Akhtar 6–0–32–0; Shoaib Mohammad 4–0–19–0.

President's XI

Shakeel Ahmed c Healy b McGrath...........	10	– c Healy b McGrath...........	29
Shoaib Mohammad c Boon b McDermott......	10	– lbw b McGrath...........	55
*Ramiz Raja c S. R. Waugh b McDermott	0	– lbw b McGrath...........	2
Zahid Fazal lbw b McGrath.................	6	– b McGrath...........	91
Ijaz Ahmed c Boon b Warne................	38	– c S. R. Waugh b Warne........	9
Manzoor Akhtar c McDermott b McGrath.....	0	– lbw b Warne...........	11
†Moin Khan b McDermott...........	11	– not out...........	49
Haaris Khan c Healy b McGrath.............	30	– c Taylor b May...........	0
Mohsin Kamal c Healy b Warne.............	10	– c Healy b McGrath...........	4
Ata-ur-Rehman c Healy b Warne............	11	– c Healy b McGrath...........	0
Ashfaq Ahmed not out	3	– not out...........	0
B 5, l-b 7, n-b 4	16	B 6, l-b 12, n-b 2...........	20

1/17 2/17 3/31 4/44 5/51   145   1/64 2/70 3/117   (9 wkts) 270
6/88 7/88 8/103 9/133   4/137 5/177 6/231
                                               7/234 8/245 9/245

Bowling: *First Innings*—McDermott 15–2–56–3; McGrath 11.2–4–32–4; S. R. Waugh 4–2–2–0; Warne 10–3–42–3; May 1–0–1–0. *Second Innings*—McDermott 16–1–74–0; McGrath 20–5–49–6; S. R. Waugh 4–1–10–0; May 18–9–42–1; Warne 19–6–52–2; M. E. Waugh 3–1–13–0; Bevan 2–0–12–0.

Umpires: Javed Akhtar and Riazuddin.

PAKISTAN v AUSTRALIA

First Test Match

At National Stadium, Karachi, September 28, 29, 30, October 1, 2. Pakistan won by one wicket. Toss: Australia. Test debut: M. G. Bevan.

Australia's new era, after the end of Allan Border's decade of captaincy, began with an epic encounter. What looked like their first Test victory in Pakistan for 35 years was turned into a home triumph by the bold batting of Inzamam-ul-Haq and Mushtaq Ahmed on a slow, low pitch. Coming together at 258 for nine with the awesome task of averting Pakistan's first ever defeat at the National Stadium, Inzamam and Mushtaq added 57 on a worn pitch against the redoubtable leg-spin of Warne. To the unrestrained delight of a crowd which steadily grew in number and chanted Allah-O-Akbar (God is great), they accomplished their goal in 8.1 overs, against an attack weakened by the withdrawal of McDermott, with an infected toe, and then by injuries to McGrath and May. In the end, Warne and Angel, in his second Test, were the only front-line bowlers still standing. Pakistan had never scored as much as 314 in a fourth innings to win; coach Intikhab Alam described the victory as the country's finest ever. Observers hoped it might revive interest in Test cricket in Pakistan.

It was especially deflating for Taylor, the first man to score a pair of spectacles in his first Test as captain. He had decided to take the new ball at 229 for seven, when Warne was in full cry. The final result was disappointing for both Warne, who gave another command performance – eight for 150 from 63.1 overs – and Michael Bevan, who announced his arrival in the Test arena with a composed 82. It was especially dispiriting for the vice-captain and wicket-keeper, Healy, who blamed himself for the defeat: Pakistan gained the winning runs from four leg-byes when Inzamam was out of his ground attacking Warne.

The Australians had converted a useful first-innings lead of 81 into a handsome overall advantage of 313, thanks principally to Boon, who scored his 19th century in 90 Tests, and added 122 in 174 minutes with Mark Waugh. Waugh's dismissal precipitated a collapse of eight wickets for 61 runs, the last five for just 19 in 9.2 overs, against the irresistible fast bowling of Wasim Akram and Waqar Younis. Wasim finished with a match analysis of eight for 138 and Waqar seven for 144. They were responsible for six ducks over Australia's two innings. Flamboyant opener Saeed Anwar was inspired to play two wonderfully expressive hands of 85 and 77.

Just when it seemed Australia's ensign might finally be raised again in Pakistan, his efforts were backed up by Inzamam, who was undefeated over two hours and 35 minutes, Rashid Latif, with a daring 35 from 56 balls at No. 9, and Mushtaq. Pakistan's famous victory was only the seventh by one wicket in Tests. It was Australia's third wafer-thin failure in successive seasons, following the defeat by one run against West Indies at Adelaide in 1992-93 and by five runs against South Africa at Sydney in 1993-94.

Man of the Match: S. K. Warne.

Close of play: First day, Australia 325-7 (I. A. Healy 54*); Second day, Pakistan 209-7 (Wasim Akram 12*, Akram Raza 1*); Third day, Australia 181-5 (D. C. Boon 85*, I. A. Healy 3*); Fourth day, Pakistan 155-3 (Saeed Anwar 67*, Akram Raza 1*).

Australia

M. J. Slater lbw b Wasim Akram	36	– (2) lbw b Mushtaq Ahmed	23
*M. A. Taylor c and b Wasim Akram	0	– (1) c Rashid Latif b Waqar Younis	0
D. C. Boon b Mushtaq Ahmed	19	– not out	114
M. E. Waugh c Zahid Fazal b Mushtaq Ahmed	20	– b Waqar Younis	61
M. G. Bevan c Aamir Sohail b Mushtaq Ahmed	82	– b Wasim Akram	0
S. R. Waugh b Waqar Younis	73	– lbw b Wasim Akram	0
†I. A. Healy c Rashid Latif b Waqar Younis	57	– c Rashid Latif b Wasim Akram	8
S. K. Warne c Rashid Latif b Aamir Sohail	22	– lbw b Waqar Younis	8
J. Angel b Wasim Akram	5	– c Rashid Latif b Wasim Akram	8
T. B. A. May not out	1	– b Wasim Akram	1
G. D. McGrath b Waqar Younis	0	– b Waqar Younis	1
B 2, l-b 12, n-b 8	22	B 7, l-b 4, n-b 5	16
	337		**232**

1/12 (2) 2/41 (3) 3/75 (4) 4/95 (1)   337
5/216 (6) 6/281 (5) 7/325 (8)
8/335 (7) 9/335 (9) 10/337 (11)

1/1 (1) 2/49 (2) 3/171 (4)   232
4/174 (5) 5/174 (6) 6/213 (7)
7/218 (8) 8/227 (9)
9/229 (10) 10/232 (11)

Bowling: *First Innings*—Wasim Akram 25-4-75-3; Waqar Younis 19.2-2-75-3; Mushtaq Ahmed 24-2-97-3; Akram Raza 14-1-50-0; Aamir Sohail 5-0-19-1; Salim Malik 1-0-7-0. *Second Innings*—Wasim Akram 22-3-63-5; Waqar Younis 18-2-69-4; Mushtaq Ahmed 21-3-51-1; Akram Raza 10-1-19-0; Aamir Sohail 7-0-19-0.

Pakistan

Saeed Anwar c M. E. Waugh b May	85	– c and b Angel	77
Aamir Sohail c Bevan b Warne	36	– run out	34
Zahid Fazal c Boon b May	27	– c Boon b Warne	3
*Salim Malik lbw b Angel	26	– c Taylor b Angel	43
Basit Ali c Bevan b McGrath	0	– (6) lbw b Warne	12
Inzamam-ul-Haq c Taylor b Warne	9	– (8) not out	58
†Rashid Latif c Taylor b Warne	2	– (9) lbw b S. R. Waugh	35
Wasim Akram c Healy b Angel	39	– (7) c and b Warne	4
Akram Raza b McGrath	13	– (5) lbw b Warne	2
Waqar Younis c Healy b Angel	6	– c Healy b Warne	7
Mushtaq Ahmed not out	2	– not out	20
L-b 7, n-b 4	11	B 4, l-b 13, n-b 3	20
	256	(9 wkts)	**315**

1/90 (2) 2/153 (1) 3/154 (3) 4/157 (5)   256   1/45 (2) 2/64 (3)   (9 wkts) 315
5/175 (6) 6/181 (7) 7/200 (4)   3/148 (4) 4/157 (5)
8/234 (9) 9/253 (10) 10/256 (8)   5/174 (1) 6/179 (7)
                                                 7/184 (6) 8/236 (9)
                                                 9/258 (10)

Bowling: *First Innings*—McGrath 25–6–70–2; Angel 13.1–0–54–3; May 20–5–55–2; Warne 27–10–61–3; S. R. Waugh 2–0–9–0. *Second Innings*—McGrath 6–2–18–0; Angel 28–10–92–2; S. R. Waugh 15–3–28–1; Warne 36.1–12–89–5; May 18–4–67–0; M. E. Waugh 3–1–4–0.

Umpires: H. D. Bird (England) and Khizar Hayat.   Referee: J. R. Reid (New Zealand).

PAKISTAN v AUSTRALIA

Second Test Match

At Rawalpindi, October 5, 6, 7, 8, 9. Drawn. Toss: Pakistan. Test debut: D. W. Fleming.

For the second week running, the Australians forfeited a priceless opportunity to win. This time it literally slipped through their hands. Having compelled Pakistan to follow on, for only the second time in a home Test, they paid dearly for dropping catches offered by Salim Malik and Aamir Sohail. Malik, reprieved by Taylor on 20, batted for seven hours and 23 minutes before falling to the hat-trick ball from Test newcomer Damien Fleming. By then, Malik had changed the course of the series with 237 runs, including 34 boundaries, the highest score for Pakistan against Australia. Sohail, put down by Warne on nine and briefly retiring for stitches in a cut lip, helped him add 109 in just 99 minutes. Malik also shared century partnerships with Saeed Anwar and Aamer Malik. Having collapsed in five hours and 39 minutes to McDermott and Fleming in the first innings, Pakistan stubbornly resisted for ten and a half hours to ensure a draw.

Regrettably, a match of memorable drama ended in farce with non-bowlers Taylor and Slater taking wickets and Mushtaq Ahmed giving a convincing impression of Malcolm Marshall. Such levity was a far cry from the ebullient strokeplay of Slater and the enthralling duel between Wasim Akram and Steve Waugh as Australia amassed an imposing first-innings 521 for nine declared. Slater scored his third Test hundred and shared his fourth century opening stand with his mentor Taylor in 16 Tests. Given that the Australians had been sent in just three days after their profound disappointment at Karachi, it was a stirring performance. Intent on exposing Steve Waugh's well-documented vulnerability against the steepling delivery, Wasim defied a back injury to bowl with great hostility on a well-grassed bouncy pitch. Some observers, but not the umpires, considered Wasim had intimidated Waugh, but Waugh came through the crisis magnificently, and was cruelly deprived of his century when he played on to Waqar Younis for 98.

When Pakistan replied, the Australian new-ball bowlers carried all before them – McDermott and Fleming each took four wickets. Only the daring Sohail, striking 80 from 83 balls, offered any significant resistance. Apart from Wasim, with a controlled, undefeated 45, the Pakistanis endeavoured to emulate Sohail – but their cavalier approach handed the bowlers the initiative for the only time until the final day, by which time it was too late.

Then, 24-year-old Fleming became only the third bowler to take a hat-trick on Test debut, after Maurice Allom of England in 1929-30 and Peter Petherick of New Zealand in 1976-77. That it was Malik's wicket which gave him the hat-trick heightened the achievement. "I felt a Sarfraz spell coming on, but unfortunately it stopped at three," said Fleming, referring to Sarfraz Nawaz's extraordinary burst of seven for one at Melbourne in 1978-79.

Man of the Match: Salim Malik.

Close of play: First day, Australia 305-3 (M. E. Waugh 61*, M. G. Bevan 52*); Second day, Pakistan 48-1 (Aamir Sohail 28*, Zahid Fazal 4*); Third day, Pakistan 28-0 (Saeed Anwar 11*, Aamir Sohail 9*); Fourth day, Pakistan 324-2 (Aamir Sohail 72*, Salim Malik 155*).

Australia

*M. A. Taylor lbw b Mohsin Kamal	69	– (2) not out		5
M. J. Slater c Inzamam-ul-Haq b Mohsin Kamal	110	– (1) b Waqar Younis		1
D. C. Boon b Mushtaq Ahmed	4	– not out		7
M. E. Waugh c Aamir Sohail b Mohsin Kamal	68			
M. G. Bevan lbw b Waqar Younis	70			
S. R. Waugh b Waqar Younis	98			
†I. A. Healy c Mohsin Kamal b Aamir Sohail	58			
S. K. Warne c and b Aamir Sohail	14			
J. Angel b Wasim Akram	7			
C. J. McDermott not out	9			
B 3, l-b 3, w 3, n-b 5	14	L-b 1		1

1/176 (1) 2/181 (3) 3/198 (2)   (9 wkts dec.) 521   1/2 (1)   (1 wkt) 14
4/323 (4) 5/347 (5) 6/456 (7)
7/501 (8) 8/511 (6) 9/521 (9)

D. W. Fleming did not bat.

Bowling: First Innings—Wasim Akram 23.5–3–62–1; Waqar Younis 32–6–112–2; Mohsin Kamal 26–3–109–3; Mushtaq Ahmed 36–2–145–1; Aamir Sohail 21–3–67–2; Aamer Malik 5–2–16–0; Salim Malik 1–0–4–0. *Second Innings*—Waqar Younis 5–3–2–1; Rashid Latif 2–0–10–0; Saeed Anwar 2–2–0–0; Mushtaq Ahmed 1–0–1–0.

Pakistan

Saeed Anwar c S. R. Waugh b McDermott	15	– c Healy b M. E. Waugh		75
Aamir Sohail b Fleming	80	– c Healy b McDermott		72
Zahid Fazal b Fleming	10	– c Healy b M. E. Waugh		1
*Salim Malik b McDermott	33	– c Healy b Fleming		237
Aamer Malik lbw b McDermott	11	– c Bevan b Fleming		65
Inzamam-ul-Haq lbw b Warne	14	– lbw b Fleming		0
†Rashid Latif c Slater b Fleming	18	– c Bevan b Taylor		38
Wasim Akram not out	45	– c Healy b Angel		5
Mushtaq Ahmed c Warne b McDermott	0	– c S. R. Waugh b McDermott		0
Waqar Younis lbw b Fleming	13	– lbw b Slater		10
Mohsin Kamal run out	2	– not out		0
B 10, l-b 7, n-b 2	19	B 17, l-b 13, n-b 3		34

1/28 (1) 2/90 (3) 3/119 (2) 4/152 (4)   260   1/79 (2) 2/227 (1) 3/336 (2)   537
5/155 (5) 6/189 (7) 7/189 (6)   4/469 (5) 5/469 (6) 6/478 (4)
8/198 (9) 9/253 (10) 10/260 (11)   7/495 (8) 8/496 (9)
                                 9/537 (7) 10/537 (10)

In the second innings Aamir Sohail, when 30, retired hurt at 65 and resumed at 227.

Bowling: First Innings—McDermott 22–8–74–4; Fleming 22–3–75–4; Warne 21.4–8–58–1; Angel 11–2–36–0. *Second Innings*—McDermott 33–3–86–2; Fleming 26–2–86–3; Angel 28–1–124–1; M. E. Waugh 16–1–63–2; Warne 25–6–56–0; Bevan 4–0–27–0; S. R. Waugh 3–2–41–0; Slater 1.1–0–4–1; Boon 3–1–9–0; Taylor 3–1–11–1.

Umpires: K. E. Liebenberg (South Africa) and Mahboob Shah.
Referee: J. R. Reid (New Zealand).

Australia's matches v Pakistan and South Africa in the Wills Triangular Series (October 12–October 30) may be found in that section.

PAKISTAN v AUSTRALIA

Third Test Match

At Lahore, November 1, 2, 3, 4, 5. Drawn. Toss: Pakistan. Test debut: P. A. Emery.

Again, Salim Malik led from the front to extricate Pakistan from the mire while Australia won everywhere but on the scoreboard. And they had no-one but themselves to blame after dropping another five catches, four of them in the first innings after Malik chose to bat on a pitch which was soft on top and slower than expected. Malik's choice was effectively made for him when Wasim Akram and Waqar Younis withdrew at the last minute, officially after failing fitness tests but prompting speculation of dressing-room conflict. This left the attack in the hands of Aqib Javed and Mohsin Kamal – playing his second Test after a seven-year gap. The Australians also had their troubles – Healy had fractured his left thumb and Steve Waugh damaged his shoulder in the triangular one-day tournament. Phil Emery flew out to make his debut, but he too had his thumb badly bruised.

Given their delight at beating Pakistan in the limited-overs final two days earlier, the Australians made an untidy and unconvincing start to their bid to square the series and never recovered from the lapses on the first two days. Inzamam-ul-Haq, missed on one, finished with 66, Ijaz Ahmed, controversially recalled after some limited-overs successes, was also reprieved at one on his way to 48, while Moin Khan, replacing the injured Rashid Latif, was put down on 51 and 70. He eventually scored his first Test century – an undefeated 115 with 13 fours and three sixes as Pakistan reached a healthy 373. Nevertheless, Australia still managed their third solid first-innings lead of the series – this time 82, through half-centuries from Slater, Mark Waugh, the remarkably consistent Bevan and – despite having played so little cricket on the tour – Langer.

A rejuvenated McGrath then cut a swathe through Pakistan's brittle top order to provide Australia with another chance of a famous victory. Indeed, Pakistan entered the final day only 55 ahead with five wickets standing. But again the belligerent Malik matched his wits with the bowlers, for a further three hours and ten minutes – after two hours' stubborn resistance on the fourth day – and scored another hundred. Along the way he cajoled Sohail into forgetting the stiff neck which forced him to wear a brace the previous afternoon, so persuasively that Sohail completed a century at No. 7, adding 196 in 215 minutes with Malik to dash Australian hopes. Not even Warne could break through, although he battled manfully for three for 104 and match figures of nine for 240, from a colossal 71.5 overs; fears were expressed for his right shoulder under such a heavy workload.

Man of the Match: Salim Malik.

Men of the Series: Pakistan – Salim Malik; Australia – S. K. Warne.

Close of play: First day, Pakistan 255-5 (Ijaz Ahmed 35*, Moin Khan 39*); Second day, Australia 107-2 (M. J. Slater 60*, P. A. Emery 0*); Third day, Australia 344-5 (J. L. Langer 38*, S. K. Warne 7*); Fourth day, Pakistan 137-5 (Salim Malik 59*, Aamir Sohail 4*).

Pakistan

Saeed Anwar b Warne	30	– (2) c Emery b McGrath	32
Aamir Sohail c Emery b McGrath	1	– (7) st Emery b Warne	105
Inzamam-ul-Haq lbw b May	66	– c Emery b McDermott	3
*Salim Malik c Bevan b May	75	– b Bevan	143
Ijaz Ahmed c Boon b Warne	48	– lbw b McGrath	6
Basit Ali c Waugh b Warne	0	– (1) c Emery b McGrath	2
†Moin Khan not out	115	– (6) c McDermott b May	16
Akram Raza b Warne	0	– lbw b Warne	32
Mushtaq Ahmed b May	14	– c Emery b McGrath	27
Aqib Javed c Waugh b Warne	2	– b Warne	2
Mohsin Kamal lbw b Warne	4	– not out	0
B 5, l-b 7, n-b 6	18	B 8, l-b 16, w 4, n-b 8	36
	373		404

1/8 (2) 2/34 (1) 3/157 (3) 4/204 (4) 373
5/209 (6) 6/294 (5) 7/294 (8)
8/346 (9) 9/355 (10) 10/373 (11)

1/20 (1) 2/28 (3) 3/60 (2) 404
4/74 (5) 5/107 (6) 6/303 (4)
7/363 (7) 8/384 (8)
9/394 (10) 10/404 (9)

Bowling: *First Innings*—McDermott 24–4–87–0; McGrath 24–6–65–1; Warne 41.5–12–136–6; May 29–7–69–3; Waugh 2–0–4–0. *Second Innings*—McDermott 19–2–81–1; McGrath 25.1–1–92–4; Warne 30–2–104–3; May 25–4–60–1; Bevan 4–0–21–1; Waugh 6–0–22–0.

Australia

M. J. Slater c Moin Khan	
b Mohsin Kamal . 74	
*M. A. Taylor c Saeed Anwar	
b Mushtaq Ahmed . 32	
D. C. Boon c Moin Khan b Akram Raza 5	
†P. A. Emery not out 8	
M. E. Waugh c Moin Khan	
b Mohsin Kamal . 71	
M. G. Bevan c sub (Nadeem Khan)	
b Mushtaq Ahmed . 91	
J. L. Langer c Ijaz Ahmed	
b Mohsin Kamal . 69	

S. K. Warne c and b Mohsin Kamal . . . 33
C. J. McDermott
      c and b Mushtaq Ahmed . 29
T. B. A. May c Moin Khan
        b Akram Raza . 10
G. D. McGrath b Mushtaq Ahmed 3

    B 3, l-b 17, w 2, n-b 8 30

1/97 (2) 2/106 (3) 3/126 (1) 4/248 (5)   455
5/318 (6) 6/402 (8) 7/406 (7)
8/443 (9) 9/450 (10) 10/455 (11)

P. A. Emery, when 2, retired hurt at 119 and resumed at 443.

Bowling: Aqib Javed 31–9–75–0; Mohsin Kamal 28–3–116–4; Mushtaq Ahmed 45.1–6–121–4; Akram Raza 45–9–123–2.

Umpires: C. J. Mitchley (South Africa) and Riazuddin.   Referee: J. R. Reid (New Zealand).

MEN WHO UMPIRED AND PLAYED IN TEST CRICKET

Peter Willey, the former England all-rounder, was promoted to the international umpires' panel in 1996. He is due to stand in a Test match this summer and will become the 34th person both to play and umpire Test cricket. The other 33 are:

	Tests Played	Tests Umpired		Tests Played	Tests Umpired
England			**Australia**		
James Lillywhite, jun.	2	6	G. Coulthard	1	2
A. Hill	2	1	P. G. McShane	3	1
A. M. Miller	1	2	C. Bannerman	3	12
R. G. Barlow	17	1	A. J. Richardson	9	2
M. Sherwin	3	1	**South Africa**		
H. R. Butt	3	6	F. Hearne	6*	6
G. J. Tompson	6	2	W. W. Wade	11	1
H. I. Young	2	3	**West Indies**		
L. C. Braund	23	3	E. Achong	6	1
J. Hardstaff, sen.	5	21	G. E. Gomez	29	1
A. Dolphin	1	6	**New Zealand**		
E. J. Smith	11	8	J. Cowie	9	3
J. W. Hitch	7	4	E. W. T. Tindill	5	1
N. Oldfield	1	2	**India**		
J. F. Crapp	7	4	S. Venkataraghavan .	57	11†
W. F. F. Price	1	8	**Pakistan**		
A. E. Fagg	5	18	Mohammad Aslam . .	1	3
K. E. Palmer	1	22	Javed Akhtar	1	12
J. Birkenshaw	5	2			
J. H. Hampshire	8	11			

* Played two Tests for England and four for South Africa.
† Up to September 1995.

THE SRI LANKANS IN ZIMBABWE AND SOUTH AFRICA, 1994-95

By GEOFFREY DEAN

The Sri Lankans arrived in Zimbabwe in October 1994 having lost their previous five Tests, four by an innings. They achieved what they then set out to do – avoid defeat. All three Tests were drawn and the tone was set on the opening day of the series, when Sri Lanka crawled to 157 for one from 90 overs on the flattest of pitches. Despite possessing several natural strokeplayers, they maintained this negative approach throughout. Indeed, the two sides rarely lifted their scoring-rate as high as two and a half an over in any innings. Sri Lanka never had a sniff of their first Test victory overseas, though Zimbabwe were not far off their first win in the Second Test at Bulawayo, where they enforced the follow-on for the first time.

Had they played on the livelier seamers' pitches which were prepared for the subsequent encounters with Pakistan, the Zimbabweans might well have won. But, to coach John Hampshire's disappointment, all the Tests were played on shirtfronts offering minimal turn. Zimbabwe were dismissed in only one of their three Test innings and had to be satisfied with claiming victory on points. The series confirmed that they were making steady progress as a Test nation and it was a personal triumph for David Houghton, still a world-class batsman at 37 and one of the best players of spin. He became the first Zimbabwean to score a double-hundred in Tests and followed it up with another century in his next innings to amass 466 at 155.33. Alistair Campbell was the only other home batsman with an aggregate in three figures. The Sri Lankans' leading scorer was Sanjeeva Ranatunga, younger brother of the captain, Arjuna. He made 273 at 68.25, including two hundreds, with Asanka Gurusinha not far behind. Aravinda de Silva, the batsman Zimbabwe feared most, had a disappointing series, totalling only 112 at 28.00.

Each side could boast a young pace bowler of great promise, in Heath Streak and Chaminda Vaas, both aged 20. Streak took 13 wickets and Vaas ten, both at an average of just over 23. Vaas, a left-armer, swung the ball back into the right-hander and demonstrated excellent control; like Ravindra Pushpakumara, who took seven in Zimbabwe's only innings of the Third Test, he had been coached by Dennis Lillee at his fast bowling academy in Madras. Streak, strong as an ox, also swung the ball out and bowled some long spells in great heat.

The unexciting pace of the Tests was reflected in the low attendances – the biggest crowd for any day was 1,000, on the Sunday at Bulawayo. The one-day games, won 2-1 by Sri Lanka, did attract more, with 3,000 watching the decider at Harare Sports Club. The same number attended some three months later on the day Zimbabwe completed their first Test victory, over Pakistan, which was encouraging for the hard-up Zimbabwe Cricket Union. But where was their financial acumen when they scheduled the rest day of the Third Test against Sri Lanka on a Saturday?

In December, Sri Lanka went to South Africa for a quadrangular one-day tournament. They had victories over their hosts and New Zealand, but could not reach the final. They also played two first-class matches against provincial sides, both of which were drawn.

SRI LANKAN TOURING PARTY

A. Ranatunga (Sinhalese SC) (*captain*), P. B. Dassanayake (Bloomfield C and AC), P. A. de Silva (Nondescripts CC), H. D. P. K. Dharmasena (Bloomfield C and AC), A. P. Gurusinha (Sinhalese SC), S. T. Jayasuriya (Bloomfield C and AC), R. S. Kalpage (Bloomfield C and AC), R. S. Mahanama (Bloomfield C and AC), M. Muralitharan (Tamil Union), K. R. Pushpakumara (Nondescripts CC), S. Ranatunga (Nondescripts CC), D. P. Samaraweera (Colts CC), H. P. Tillekeratne (Nondescripts CC), W. P. U. J. C. Vaas (Colts CC), G. P. Wickremasinghe (Sinhalese SC).

E. A. Upashantha (Colts CC) was included in the party for South Africa.

Coach: E. R. Fernando.

SRI LANKAN TOUR RESULTS

Test matches – Played 3: Drawn 3.

First-class matches – Played 7: Won 1, Drawn 6.

Win – Mashonaland Country Districts XI.

Draws – Zimbabwe (3), ZCU President's XI, Eastern Province, Border.

One-day internationals – Played 9: Won 4, Lost 4, No result 1. *Wins* – Zimbabwe (2), New Zealand, South Africa. *Losses* – Zimbabwe, Pakistan (2), South Africa. *No result* – New Zealand.

Other non-first-class matches – Played 4: Won 3, Lost 1. *Wins* – Griqualand West, Orange Free State, Eastern Province Invitation XI. *Loss* – Natal.

TEST MATCH AVERAGES

ZIMBABWE – BATTING

	T	I	NO	R	HS	100s	Avge	Ct
D. L. Houghton....	3	3	0	466	266	2	155.33	0
A. D. R. Campbell .	3	3	0	161	99	0	53.66	0
G. J. Whittall	3	3	1	77	61*	0	38.50	3
A. Flower.........	3	3	0	86	50	0	28.66	5
M. H. Dekker	3	3	0	54	40	0	18.00	7
W. R. James	3	3	0	53	33	0	17.66	13
G. W. Flower	3	3	0	47	41	0	15.66	0
H. H. Streak	3	3	0	28	20	0	9.33	1

Played in three Tests: M. P. Jarvis 2 (1 ct). Played in two Tests: D. H. Brain 6*, 0; S. G. Peall 9*, 30. Played in one Test: J. A. Rennie 19*; P. A. Strang 6.

* *Signifies not out.*

BOWLING

	O	M	R	W	BB	5W/i	Avge
H. H. Streak....	134.5	40	304	13	4-79	0	23.38
M. P. Jarvis	137	67	195	7	3-30	0	27.85
G. J. Whittall	95.1	26	208	7	4-70	0	29.71
D. H. Brain	50	7	147	4	2-48	0	36.75

Also bowled: A. D. R. Campbell 2-1-1-0; M. H. Dekker 6-3-5-0; G. W. Flower 14-5-29-0; S. G. Peall 93-28-192-2; J. A. Rennie 50-20-85-0; P. A. Strang 25-6-65-3.

SRI LANKA – BATTING

	T	I	NO	R	HS	100s	Avge	Ct
S. Ranatunga..............	3	5	1	273	118	2	68.25	0
A. P. Gurusinha	3	5	0	268	128	1	53.60	1
A. Ranatunga..............	3	4	1	157	62	0	52.33	0
H. P. Tillekeratne.........	3	4	1	133	116	1	44.33	6
H. D. P. K. Dharmasena....	2	3	0	93	54	0	31.00	1
P. A. de Silva	3	5	1	112	41*	0	28.00	0
W. P. U. J. C. Vaas........	3	3	1	33	16*	0	16.50	0
R. S. Mahanama...........	3	5	0	37	24	0	7.40	2

Played in two Tests: P. B. Dassanayake 0, 8 (7 ct, 1 st); M. Muralitharan 0, 15* (1 ct); K. R. Pushpakumara 6*, 8; G. P. Wickremasinghe 15, 7. Played in one Test: S. T. Jayasuriya 10; R. S. Kalpage 14.

* *Signifies not out.*

BOWLING

	O	M	R	W	BB	5W/i	Avge
K. R. Pushpakumara	55.4	7	184	8	7-116	1	23.00
W. P. U. J. C. Vaas........	125.3	37	235	10	4-74	0	23.50
M. Muralitharan	87	28	168	3	2-60	0	56.00
H. D. P. K. Dharmasena....	80	20	180	3	2-109	0	60.00
G. P. Wickremasinghe......	65	11	185	3	2-125	0	61.66

Also bowled: P. A. de Silva 7-0-24-0; A. P. Gurusinha 17-3-54-0; S. T. Jayasuriya 2-0-12-0; R. S. Kalpage 12-5-31-0; A. Ranatunga 11-1-31-0.

Note: Matches in this section which were not first-class are signified by a dagger.

MASHONALAND COUNTRY DISTRICTS XI v SRI LANKANS

At Harare South Country Club, October 3, 4, 5. Sri Lankans won by an innings and 298 runs. Toss: Mashonaland Country Districts XI.

Sri Lanka's only first-class win of the tour was robbed of meaning by Mashonaland Country Districts' failure to field anything like a regular team. Only Peall, the Test off-spinner, had bowled seriously in first-class cricket before: his 44 overs represented a third of the Sri Lankan innings, and nearly a third of their 600 runs. De Silva and Sanjeeva Ranatunga put on 299 for the third wicket, with de Silva retiring after a double-century which included 33 fours and a six. Country Districts' combined aggregate for the match was barely half the tourists' one innings, with Glamorgan batsman Steve James their highest scorer.

Close of play: First day, Sri Lankans 135-1 (A. P. Gurusinha 73*, S. Ranatunga 2*); Second day, Mashonaland Country Districts XI 54-1 (S. P. James 42*, M. P. Stannard 4*).

Mashonaland Country Districts XI

M. P. Stannard c Kalpage b Pushpakumara	34	– (3) c A. Ranatunga b de Silva	4
T. G. Bartlett c Dassanayake b Pushpakumara	5	– run out	4
S. P. James lbw b Pushpakumara	0	– (1) c Dassanayake b Wickremasinghe	44
*†R. D. Brown b Muralitharan	13	– c Dassanayake b Wickremasinghe	3
C. B. Wishart run out	41	– c Dassanayake b Wickremasinghe	0
K. G. B. Ziehl c Samaraweera b Muralitharan	1	– c Wickremasinghe b Kalpage	15
R. J. Becks b Muralitharan	0	– c Gurusinha b Wickremasinghe	2
S. G. Peall c Kalpage b Muralitharan	12	– b Kalpage	2
T. B. Stead b Muralitharan	15	– not out	16
G. V. Steyn not out	21	– b Muralitharan	10
J. D. Gibson c Gurusinha b Muralitharan	22	– c Gurusinha b Muralitharan	4
B 3, l-b 5, w 2, n-b 3	13	B 2, w 1, n-b 18	21

1/9 2/9 3/33 4/93 5/96   177   1/9 2/55 3/57 4/57 5/68   125
6/96 7/108 8/119 9/134   6/74 7/89 8/91 9/121

Bowling: First Innings—Wickremasinghe 10–2–27–0; Pushpakumara 16–5–37–3; Gurusinha 4–1–9–0; Muralitharan 24.5–8–55–6; Jayasuriya 4–1–13–0; Kalpage 8–0–28–0. *Second Innings*—Wickremasinghe 12–2–20–4; Pushpakumara 10–0–47–0; Muralitharan 4.1–1–25–2; de Silva 6–1–7–1; Kalpage 10–4–24–2.

Sri Lankans

A. P. Gurusinha c and b Peall	82	R. S. Kalpage not out	21
D. P. Samaraweera lbw b Stannard	53	†P. B. Dassanayake not out	13
S. Ranatunga c Ziehl b Stannard	119	B 9, l-b 7, n-b 5	21
P. A. de Silva retired out	202		
*A. Ranatunga c Wishart b Ziehl	31	1/133 2/157 3/456 (6 wkts dec.) 600	
S. T. Jayasuriya c Stead b Peall	58	4/475 5/539 6/567	

G. P. Wickremasinghe, M. Muralitharan and K. R. Pushpakumara did not bat.

Bowling: Gibson 21–3–109–0; Stead 25–5–100–0; Peall 44–3–189–2; Steyn 7–0–48–0; Ziehl 13–6–29–1; Stannard 7–1–26–2; Wishart 12–1–71–0; Brown 1–0–12–0.

Umpires: Q. J. Goosen and R. Strang.

ZCU PRESIDENT'S XI v SRI LANKANS

At Old Hararians, Harare, October 7, 8, 9. Drawn. Toss: Sri Lankans.

Last-wicket pair Ranchod and Everton Matambanadzo survived the final ten minutes of the game to draw, though Ranchod was dropped at slip in the penultimate over. Everton's brother, Darlington, had been the eighth man out when he was caught by Dassanayake, the substitute, who was allowed to keep wicket despite the prohibitions of Law 2.2. Mahanama and Gurusinha opened with 204 and Tillekeratne and Arjuna Ranatunga also reached three figures; it was the first time any Sri Lankan team had registered four individual hundreds in an innings. The home team were all out for 96, with extras the biggest contributor, and followed on 406 behind.

Close of play: First day, Sri Lankans 295-2 (H. P. Tillekeratne 25*, D. P. Samaraweera 13*); Second day, ZCU President's XI 68-6 (U. Ranchod 15*, B. D. Moore-Gordon 3*).

Sri Lankans

R. S. Mahanama retired hurt 105	D. P. Samaraweera	
A. P. Gurusinha c Ranchod	lbw b D. Matambanadzo .	33
b D. Matambanadzo .141	*A. Ranatunga not out	100
S. Ranatunga c E. Matambanadzo	B 5, l-b 12, n-b 1	18
b Rennie . 0		
†H. P. Tillekeratne not out 105	1/213 2/273 3/342	(3 wkts dec.) 502

S. T. Jayasuriya, R. S. Kalpage, H. D. P. K. Dharmasena, W. P. U. J. C. Vaas and K. R. Pushpakumara did not bat.

R. S. Mahanama retired hurt at 204.

Bowling: Jarvis 28–10–67–0; E. Matambanadzo 24–6–58–0; Martin 29–7–81–0; D. Matambanadzo 19–1–81–2; Ranchod 53–16–141–0; Abrams 6–0–38–0; Rennie 5–2–19–1.

ZCU President's XI

G. J. Rennie b Vaas	13 – sub (P. B. Dassanayake) b Vaas	5
P. M. Mitchell c Mahanama b Pushpakumara ..	6 – b Dharmasena	30
G. C. Martin c Tillekeratne b Pushpakumara ..	2 – c S. Ranatunga b Dharmasena ..	31
D. N. Erasmus lbw b Vaas	0 – b Pushpakumara	42
C. B. Wishart c Tillekeratne b Pushpakumara .	13 – c S. Ranatunga b Kalpage	31
M. D. Abrams c Mahanama b Vaas	0 – b Jayasuriya	0
U. Ranchod c Gurusinha b Pushpakumara ..	16 – not out	14
†B. D. Moore-Gordon c Tillekeratne b Vaas	12 – b Kalpage	3
D. Matambanadzo c Samaraweera b Vaas	5 – c sub (P. B. Dassanayake)	
	b Pushpakumara .	8
*M. P. Jarvis c S. Ranatunga b Pushpakumara .	10 – c Samaraweera b Pushpakumara.	0
E. Matambanadzo not out	0 – not out	1
B 1, l-b 6, n-b 12	19	L-b 10, n-b 13 23

1/16 2/30 3/30 4/39 5/39	96	1/5 2/68 3/86 (9 wkts) 188
6/53 7/69 8/85 9/92		4/147 5/160 6/160
		7/166 8/186 9/186

Bowling: *First Innings*—Pushpakumara 18.3–6–38–5; Vaas 20–6–41–5; Dharmasena 6–2–9–0; Jayasuriya 2–1–1–0. *Second Innings*—Pushpakumara 11–3–20–2; Vaas 10–4–27–1; Dharmasena 35–18–51–3; Gurusinha 4–0–8–0; Jayasuriya 9–3–24–1; Kalpage 22–10–48–2.

Umpires: G. C. Batte and N. Fleming.

ZIMBABWE v SRI LANKA

First Test Match

At Harare, October 11, 12, 13, 15, 16. Drawn. Toss: Sri Lanka.

The inaugural Test between these two countries never looked like producing a result after a terrible first day, on which Sri Lanka laboured for 90 overs to score 157 runs. When they finally took the field, they found prising out batsmen as difficult as the Zimbabweans had done. The unusually early rains which interrupted the third and fourth days and washed out the last only hastened the inevitable conclusion.

The match featured the third-slowest century in Test cricket, made by Gurusinha in 535 minutes. Only Mudassar Nazar (557 minutes, for Pakistan against England in 1977-78) and Jackie McGlew (545 minutes, for South Africa against Australia in 1957-58) had taken longer. Gurusinha used up 405 balls and his 128 lasted just over ten hours, until a rare lapse in concentration when he drove a half-volley straight to short extra cover.

Having removed Mahanama after an hour, Zimbabwe had to wait another 115 overs for their next wicket. During that time, Gurusinha and Sanjeeva Ranatunga, the captain's younger brother, ground out 217 on a slow pitch that neither seamed nor turned. Ranatunga reached his maiden Test century, on his second appearance, before he was finally caught behind for 118 from 348 balls. His brother, Arjuna, produced by far the most positive batting of the match, with 62 off 102 balls. Without him, the Sri Lankans would have scored at under two an over – it was still an abysmal 2.12, clearly a result of their paranoia about losing.

The Zimbabweans were only a little quicker, at 2.59. But, as they had no hope of winning once Sri Lanka had used up two days over 383, it was understandable that crease occupation was their first objective. Grant Flower scored one run in his first 75 minutes, but went on to help Dekker construct Zimbabwe's highest opening partnership in their eight Tests – 113 in 44 overs. The top four all made useful contributions, with Houghton's four-and-a-half-hour 58 the precursor of better and longer innings to come. The biggest score, however, was 65 from extras, the third-highest figure ever conceded in a Test innings.

Despite the preponderance of bat over ball, several bowlers put in excellent performances. Zimbabwe were reduced to three seamers when Brain broke down after bowling five overs, but Whittall rose to the occasion with four for 70 and Jarvis fulfilled the role of stock bowler admirably. He gave away just 33 in 24 overs on the first day and later took an outstanding diving return catch to dismiss de Silva. For Sri Lanka, Vaas displayed impressive accuracy and swing.

Whittall became the first Zimbabwean to be fined in a Test, for dissent after umpire Ian Robinson gave him out caught behind. Whittall gestured that the ball had struck him on the forearm rather than the glove, for which referee Peter van der Merwe deducted 25 per cent of his match fee – about £25.

Close of play: First day, Sri Lanka 157-1 (A. P. Gurusinha 67*, S. Ranatunga 65*); Second day, Sri Lanka 383; Third day, Zimbabwe 172-2 (A. D. R. Campbell 27*, D. L. Houghton 22*); Fourth day, Zimbabwe 319-8 (S. G. Peall 9*, D. H. Brain 6*).

Sri Lanka

R. S. Mahanama c James b Jarvis	8
A. P. Gurusinha c A. Flower b Whittall	128
S. Ranatunga c James b Whittall	118
P. A. de Silva c and b Jarvis	19
*A. Ranatunga c sub (C. B. Wishart) b Streak	62
H. P. Tillekeratne c James b Whittall . .	1
†P. B. Dassanayake lbw b Whittall	0
W. P. U. J. C. Vaas lbw b Streak	3
G. P. Wickremasinghe c James b Streak	15
M. Muralitharan c and b Streak	0
K. R. Pushpakumara not out	6
L-b 19, w 1, n-b 3	23

1/28 (1) 2/245 (3) 3/281 (4) 4/318 (2)   383
5/322 (6) 6/330 (7) 7/361 (8)
8/376 (5) 9/376 (10) 10/383 (9)

Bowling: Brain 5–2–9–0; Streak 42.5–14–79–4; Jarvis 41–18–76–2; Whittall 33–8–70–4; Peall 50–11–114–0; G. W. Flower 8–2–16–0.

Zimbabwe

G. W. Flower c Dassanayake b Vaas . .	41
M. H. Dekker c sub (D. P. Samaraweera) b Muralitharan	40
A. D. R. Campbell c Tillekeratne b Wickremasinghe	44
D. L. Houghton c Dassanayake b Vaas	58
*A. Flower c Dassanayake b Vaas	26
G. J. Whittall c Dassanayake b Pushpakumara	4
†W. R. James c Dassanayake b Vaas . .	18
H. H. Streak c Gurusinha b Muralitharan	8
S. G. Peall not out	9
D. H. Brain not out	6
B 10, l-b 18, w 1, n-b 36	65

1/113 (1) 2/115 (2) 3/202 (3)   (8 wkts) 319
4/259 (5) 5/264 (6) 6/274 (4)
7/294 (7) 8/307 (8)

M. P. Jarvis did not bat.

Bowling: Wickremasinghe 26–4–60–1; Vaas 37–11–74–4; Pushpakumara 20–0–68–1; de Silva 6–0–20–0; Muralitharan 32–7–60–2; A. Ranatunga 2–0–9–0.

Umpires: L. H. Barker (West Indies) and I. D. Robinson.
Referee: P. L. van der Merwe (South Africa).

ZIMBABWE v SRI LANKA

Second Test Match

At Queens Sports Club, Bulawayo, October 20, 21, 22, 23, 24. Drawn. Toss: Zimbabwe.

Zimbabwe enforced the follow-on for the first time in Tests, but several factors conspired against a maiden victory. First, they did not score quickly enough – 2.45 an over – delaying the declaration until the third morning; secondly, Sri Lanka's tail used up valuable time on the fourth day, when it took 76 overs to remove their last four; thirdly, the Sri Lankan top order could not possibly bat as badly again as they had in their first innings, when four of them were caught behind down the leg side; and finally, the pitch was another slow, flat wicket, which gave the tiring Zimbabweans no assistance whatever. Thanks to their success in making Sri Lanka follow on, and to an accident of the weather, they spent three successive days out under a hot sun. Torrential rain had caused the entire match to be put back 48 hours and the rest day, which would have provided a break, was scrapped.

Queens became Test cricket's 73rd venue and the second in Bulawayo. It was instantly graced by an outstanding innings from Houghton. His 266 was not only a career-best but the first Test double-hundred for Zimbabwe – whose previous highest was his own 121 against India in 1992-93. Houghton came in at five for two and was almost run out soon after, but he batted for eleven and a quarter hours and faced 541 balls, hitting 35 fours and three sixes, until Muralitharan, again Sri Lanka's best bowler, took the third new ball and immediately had him lbw with an in-swinger. He added 121 in 39 overs with Andy Flower for the fourth wicket and 100 in 38 with James for the sixth. The most impressive feature of his batting was his shot selection; he played only a handful of false strokes, yet showed both enterprise and cheek, reaching both 150 and 200 with reverse-swept fours.

After nearly 13 hours in the field, the Sri Lankans batted like tired men. Streak and Jarvis reduced them to 96 for six by tea. Crucially, however, rain washed out the final session; it was not until after tea the next day that they were finally bowled out, Gurusinha having orchestrated the resistance for five and a half hours. That left Zimbabwe what proved 115 overs to dismiss them again. Despite taking two wickets that night, they never looked like making serious inroads on the final day. The night-watchman, Dharmasena, who had survived for nearly five hours in the first innings, held out again for 99 minutes. The main obstacle, however, was Sanjeeva Ranatunga, who completed his second hundred in successive Tests off the very last ball. Much to the home side's irritation, Sri Lanka had taken the optional last half-hour of a dead match to allow him to reach his century. Jarvis finished with the remarkable match figures of 58–36–54–4.

A minute's silence was observed before play on the final day in memory of Sri Lankan board president Gamini Dissanayake, who was killed in Colombo by a suicide bomber the night before.

Close of play: First day, Zimbabwe 213-4 (D. L. Houghton 116*, G. J. Whittall 10*); Second day, Zimbabwe 427-8 (J. A. Rennie 15*, S. G. Peall 5*); Third day, Sri Lanka 96-6 (A. P. Gurusinha 39*, H. D. P. K. Dharmasena 0*); Fourth day, Sri Lanka 30-2 (S. Ranatunga 13*, H. D. P. K. Dharmasena 0*).

Zimbabwe

G. W. Flower c Dassanayake		†W. R. James c Dassanayake b Vaas ..	33
b Wickremasinghe .	1	H. H. Streak c Dharmasena b Vaas....	0
M. H. Dekker st Mahanama		J. A. Rennie not out	19
b Dharmasena .	0	S. G. Peall b Vaas	30
A. D. R. Campbell st Dassanayake			
b Muralitharan .	18	B 5, l-b 11, w 2, n-b 15	33
D. L. Houghton lbw b Vaas	266		
*A. Flower c Muralitharan		1/3 (1) 2/5 (2) 3/65 (3) (9 wkts dec.)	462
b Dharmasena .	50	4/186 (5) 5/223 (6)	
G. J. Whittall c Tillekeratne		6/323 (7) 7/335 (8)	
b Wickremasinghe .	12	8/419 (4) 9/462 (10)	

M. P. Jarvis did not bat.

Bowling: Wickremasinghe 39–7–125–2; Vaas 44.3–14–85–4; Dharmasena 45–11–109–2; Muralitharan 55–21–108–1; de Silva 1–0–4–0; Gurusinha 4–0–15–0.

Sri Lanka

R. S. Mahanama c James b Streak	1	– c A. Flower b Streak	4
A. P. Gurusinha c Dekker b Peall	63	– c James b Jarvis	10
S. Ranatunga c James b Jarvis	4	– not out	.100
P. A. de Silva c James b Streak	0	– (5) b Peall	27
*A. Ranatunga c James b Jarvis	34		
H. P. Tillekeratne c Dekker b Jarvis	1	– not out	15
†P. B. Dassanayake c James b Streak	8		
H. D. P. K. Dharmasena run out	54	– (4) c James b Whittall	18
W. P. U. J. C. Vaas c Dekker b Whittall	14		
G. P. Wickremasinghe b Whittall	7		
M. Muralitharan not out	15		
L-b 4, w 1, n-b 12	17	B 5, l-b 6, w 4, n-b 4	19

1/4 (1) 2/22 (3) 3/23 (4) 4/77 (5)   218   1/4 (1) 2/30 (2)   (4 wkts) 193
5/79 (6) 6/91 (7) 7/142 (2)   3/80 (4) 4/164 (5)
8/171 (9) 9/193 (10) 10/218 (8)

Bowling: *First Innings*—Streak 28–10–68–3; Jarvis 34–22–30–3; Rennie 29–10–46–0; Peall 17–7–35–1; Whittall 17.1–6–35–2; G. W. Flower 1–1–0–0. *Second Innings*—Streak 14–4–28–1; Rennie 21–10–39–0; Whittall 17–7–29–1; Jarvis 24–14–24–1; Peall 26–10–43–1; G. W. Flower 5–2–13–0; Dekker 6–3–5–0; Campbell 2–1–1–0.

Umpires: B. L. Aldridge (New Zealand) and I. D. Robinson.
Referee: P. L. van der Merwe (South Africa).

ZIMBABWE v SRI LANKA

Third Test Match

At Harare, October 26, 27, 28, 30, 31. Drawn. Toss: Sri Lanka. Test debut: P. A. Strang.

Two days after Bulawayo, the teams returned to Harare Sports Club, which offered a pitch as benign as the one prepared for the First Test. This virtually ensured that the match, and the series, would end in stalemate. Neither side was going to bowl the other out twice, even without the loss of 33 overs to bad light on the fourth afternoon and 76 overs to rain on the final day. Indeed, it was the first time Sri Lanka had bowled Zimbabwe out once. But their bowlers took so long – nearly 151 overs – that the first-innings lead was only 27 and they had no chance to get the Zimbabweans in again.

Winning the toss, Arjuna Ranatunga condemned the home players to a fourth day fielding, after only one day off between Tests. Considering that Sri Lanka batted for another five hours next day, Zimbabwe spent the equivalent of almost an entire Test in the field. The Sri Lankans, who had picked seven left-handers, exploited this weariness with their most positive batting of the series: they scored at three an over for most of the first day. On the second day, Tillekeratne reached a maiden Test hundred, from 243 balls, in his 28th match, before hitting a full toss from debutant leg-spinner Paul Strang to short leg, where Dekker held a freakish one-handed catch.

When Zimbabwe finally batted, Houghton played a pugnacious innings of 142 from 268 balls, his second successive hundred and his third in Tests. His partnership of 194 in 70 overs with Campbell was a Zimbabwean all-wicket Test record until the Flowers improved on it three months later against Pakistan. Campbell almost scored his own maiden international century but was caught behind after 15 minutes on 99. He was one of seven victims for Pushpakumara, who bowled with pace and aggression to return the second-best figures in Tests for Sri Lanka, after Ravi Ratnayeke's eight for 83 against Pakistan in 1985-86. Whittall stood firm for four hours to score his first fifty at this level. Sri Lanka resumed for ten overs on the fourth day and another 14 on the fifth; Arjuna Ranatunga hit the last ball permitted by the weather, bowled by Jarvis, for six.

Close of play: First day, Sri Lanka 248-4 (H. P. Tillekeratne 63*, A. Ranatunga 25*); Second day, Zimbabwe 10-1 (M. H. Dekker 5*); Third day, Zimbabwe 276-4 (D. L. Houghton 125*, G. J. Whittall 10*); Fourth day, Sri Lanka 20-1 (A. P. Gurusinha 13*, S. Ranatunga 4*).

Sri Lanka

R. S. Mahanama c Dekker b Streak	24	– (2) lbw b Brain	0
A. P. Gurusinha c A. Flower b Brain	54	– (1) c Whittall b Brain	13
S. Ranatunga c Whittall b Strang	43	– c Whittall b Streak	8
†H. P. Tillekeratne c Dekker b Strang	116		
P. A. de Silva c Dekker b Streak	25	– (4) not out	41
*A. Ranatunga c Dekker b Streak	39	– (5) not out	22
S. T. Jayasuriya c James b Streak	10		
R. S. Kalpage c James b Brain	14		
H. D. P. K. Dharmasena c A. Flower b Strang	21		
W. P. U. J. C. Vaas not out	16		
K. R. Pushpakumara c A. Flower b Jarvis	8		
B 7, l-b 11, w 4, n-b 10	32	L-b 2, n-b 3	5
	402	(3 wkts)	**89**

1/64 (1) 2/100 (2) 3/149 (3) 4/192 (5)   1/5 (2) 2/24 (1)   (3 wkts) 89
5/267 (6) 6/280 (7) 7/329 (8)   3/36 (3)
8/366 (4) 9/380 (9) 10/402 (11)

Bowling: *First Innings*—Brain 34–4–90–2; Streak 38–8–97–4; Jarvis 37–13–58–1; Whittall 28–5–74–0; Strang 25–6–65–3. *Second Innings*—Streak 12–4–32–1; Brain 11–1–48–2; Jarvis 1–0–7–0.

Zimbabwe

G. W. Flower c Tillekeratne b Pushpakumara	5	H. H. Streak c Tillekeratne b Pushpakumara	20
M. H. Dekker lbw b Pushpakumara	14	D. H. Brain lbw b Pushpakumara	0
A. D. R. Campbell c Tillekeratne b Pushpakumara	99	P. A. Strang b Dharmasena	6
D. L. Houghton b Vaas	142	M. P. Jarvis b Pushpakumara	2
*A. Flower c Tillekeratne b Vaas	10	L-b 8, n-b 6	14
G. J. Whittall not out	61		**375**
†W. R. James c Mahanama b Pushpakumara	2		

1/10 (1) 2/25 (2) 3/219 (3) 4/235 (5)   375
5/297 (4) 6/305 (7) 7/363 (8)
8/363 (9) 9/372 (10) 10/375 (11)

Bowling: Vaas 44–12–76–2; Pushpakumara 35.4–7–116–7; Dharmasena 35–9–71–1; Gurusinha 13–3–39–0; Kalpage 12–5–31–0; Jayasuriya 2–0–12–0; A. Ranatunga 9–1–22–0.

Umpires: Mahboob Shah (Pakistan) and K. Kanjee.
Referee: P. L. van der Merwe (South Africa).

†ZIMBABWE v SRI LANKA

First One-Day International

At Harare, November 3. Sri Lanka won by 56 runs. Toss: Zimbabwe. International debut: G. C. Martin.

After a miserable lack of runs in the Tests – where he scored 37 in five innings – Mahanama set up Sri Lanka's victory with an undefeated 119 from 142 balls. He added 119 for the second wicket with Sanjeeva Ranatunga, and in the closing overs de Silva scored a brilliant 35 from 24 balls. Zimbabwe's interest in the match was effectively ended when they slipped to 20 for three by the eighth over; they got to 200 only thanks to Andy Flower, who made 61. Vaas took four cheap wickets.

Sri Lanka

R. S. Mahanama not out	119	R. S. Kalpage not out	0
A. P. Gurusinha c Dekker b Whittall	20		
S. Ranatunga c Houghton b Dekker	51	L-b 6, w 10	16
*A. Ranatunga b Peall	14		
P. A. de Silva c Waller b Whittall	35	1/40 2/159 3/198 (5 wkts, 50 overs) 256	
S. T. Jayasuriya c Waller b Whittall	1	4/252 5/255	

†H. P. Tillekeratne, G. P. Wickremasinghe, W. P. U. J. C. Vaas and K. R. Pushpakumara did not bat.

Bowling: Streak 9-1-50-0; Brain 7-1-31-0; Whittall 10-1-58-3; Martin 10-1-39-0; Peall 7-0-36-1; G. W. Flower 2-0-12-0; Dekker 5-0-24-1.

Zimbabwe

G. W. Flower c Tillekeratne b Pushpakumara	0	M. H. Dekker c Vaas b Kalpage	20
A. C. Waller c sub (D. P. Samaraweera) b Wickremasinghe	40	G. C. Martin c de Silva b Kalpage	7
		D. H. Brain b Pushpakumara	10
A. D. R. Campbell c A. Ranatunga b Vaas	5	H. H. Streak not out	18
		S. G. Peall b Vaas	21
D. L. Houghton c Jayasuriya b Vaas	1	B 1, l-b 8, w 7, n-b 1	17
*†A. Flower b Vaas	61		
G. J. Whittall c Tillekeratne b Wickremasinghe	0	1/0 2/12 3/20 (48.1 overs) 200	
		4/66 5/71 6/129	
		7/145 8/149 9/167	

Bowling: Pushpakumara 10-0-51-2; Vaas 9.1-1-20-4; Wickremasinghe 8-0-42-2; A. Ranatunga 10-1-38-0; Kalpage 10-1-27-2; Jayasuriya 1-0-13-0.

Umpires: Q. J. Goosen and I. D. Robinson.

†ZIMBABWE v SRI LANKA

Second One-Day International

At Harare, November 5. Zimbabwe won by two runs. Toss: Zimbabwe.

A superlative innings from Campbell, his first hundred at this level, helped Zimbabwe to their first international win on home turf. He scored 131 not out from 115 balls, including four sixes and 11 fours. Campbell's furious assault enabled his team to plunder 138 from the last 17 overs. Sri Lanka were well placed at 233 for two in the 43rd over, but then lost Mahanama for his second consecutive hundred; three more wickets fell within three overs. Some excellent improvisation from de Silva, whose 97 came off 89 balls, kept the target in sight. He thought he needed six off the last ball; in fact, owing to a mistake on the scoreboard, it was seven, and he only managed four anyway. As he returned to the pavilion, a spectator who thought de Silva had earlier obstructed the field attempted to punch him.

Zimbabwe

*†A. Flower b Vaas	76	M. H. Dekker b Vaas	9
G. W. Flower run out	21	G. J. Whittall not out	15
A. D. R. Campbell not out	131	B 1, l-b 8, w 3, n-b 1	13
D. L. Houghton c Kalpage b Pushpakumara	22	1/60 2/152 3/228 (5 wkts, 50 overs) 290	
A. C. Waller c Tillekeratne b Vaas	3	4/235 5/250	

G. C. Martin, H. H. Streak, S. G. Peall and J. A. Rennie did not bat.

Bowling: Vaas 10-0-59-3; Pushpakumara 10-1-43-1; Wickremasinghe 10-0-55-0; A. Ranatunga 5-0-38-0; Kalpage 10-0-53-0; Gurusinha 5-0-33-0.

Sri Lanka

R. S. Mahanama c G. W. Flower		†H. P. Tillekeratne run out	7
b Streak	.108	G. P. Wickremasinghe b Whittall	1
S. T. Jayasuriya c Waller b Streak	37	W. P. U. J. C. Vaas not out	0
S. Ranatunga run out	15		
P. A. de Silva not out	97	B 3, l-b 3, w 10, n-b 2	18
*A. Ranatunga c Waller b Whittall	1		
A. P. Gurusinha c G. W. Flower		1/66 2/111 3/233 (8 wkts, 50 overs) 288	
b Streak	. 4	4/234 5/245 6/245	
R. S. Kalpage lbw b Streak	0	7/276 8/278	

K. R. Pushpakumara did not bat.

Bowling: Streak 10-0-44-4; Rennie 8-0-54-0; Whittall 8-0-57-2; Martin 2-0-24-0; Peall 10-0-52-0; G. W. Flower 7-0-28-0; Dekker 5-0-23-0.

Umpires: N. Fleming and K. Kanjee.

†ZIMBABWE v SRI LANKA

Third One-Day International

At Harare, November 6. Sri Lanka won by 191 runs. Toss: Zimbabwe.
More wonderful batting from de Silva, whose unbeaten 107 came off 100 balls, and a hard-hit 85 from 83 by Ranatunga swept Sri Lanka to a total of 296, which proved way out of Zimbabwe's reach. The Sri Lankans added 143 for the fourth wicket in just 24 overs and de Silva brought up his hundred with a six. The series decider ceased to be a contest when Zimbabwe were four down in their first five overs. They made no attempt thereafter to meet an asking-rate of six an over and were bowled out for a mere 105 (Dekker having retired with a cut finger) in front of a disappointed 3,000-strong crowd.

Sri Lanka

R. S. Mahanama lbw b Brain	40	R. S. Kalpage not out	12
S. T. Jayasuriya c A. Flower b Brain	11	L-b 6, w 10	16
A. P. Gurusinha c A. Flower b Whittall	25		
P. A. de Silva not out	107	1/18 2/76 (4 wkts, 50 overs) 296	
*A. Ranatunga c G. W. Flower b Brain	85	3/106 4/249	

†H. P. Tillekeratne, M. Muralitharan, G. P. Wickremasinghe, W. P. U. J. C. Vaas and K. R. Pushpakumara did not bat.

Bowling: Streak 10-1-40-0; Brain 10-0-67-3; Rennie 7-0-60-0; Whittall 7-0-43-1; Peall 8-0-41-0; G. W. Flower 3-0-13-0; Campbell 3-0-14-0; Dekker 2-0-12-0.

Zimbabwe

*A. Flower c Muralitharan		H. H. Streak run out	8
b Pushpakumara	. 8	D. H. Brain b Muralitharan	0
G. W. Flower c Tillekeratne b Vaas	0	J. A. Rennie not out	20
A. D. R. Campbell c Mahanama b Vaas	2	S. G. Peall b Wickremasinghe	2
D. L. Houghton lbw b Pushpakumara	0	L-b 3, w 1, n-b 2	6
M. H. Dekker retired hurt	23		
G. J. Whittall c Gurusinha		1/1 2/9 3/9 (48.1 overs) 105	
b Pushpakumara	7	4/11 5/22 6/69	
†W. R. James run out	29	7/70 8/86 9/93	

M. H. Dekker, when 18, retired hurt at 51, resumed at 93 and retired again at 105.

Bowling: Vaas 7-2-12-2; Pushpakumara 9-1-25-3; Wickremasinghe 9-1-17-1; Muralitharan 10-0-21-1; Kalpage 10-1-21-0; Jayasuriya 2-1-2-0; Tillekeratne 1-0-1-0; Mahanama 0.1-0-3-0.

Umpires: I. D. Robinson and R. Strang.

†At Pietermaritzburg, November 30. Natal won by six wickets. Toss: Sri Lankans. Sri Lankans 200 for eight (50 overs) (P. A. de Silva 63); Natal 204 for four (47.3 overs) (N. C. Johnson 58 not out, E. L. R. Stewart 79 not out).

Sri Lanka's matches v South Africa, New Zealand and Pakistan in the Mandela Trophy (December 2–December 21) may be found in that section.

†At Kimberley, December 10. Sri Lankans won by 45 runs. Toss: Sri Lankans. Sri Lankans 229 for seven (50 overs) (R. S. Mahanama 76, S. Ranatunga 33, R. S. Kalpage 34); Griqualand West 184 for seven (50 overs) (M. Michau 56, H. A. Page 34).

†At Virginia, December 13 (day/night). Sri Lankans won by five wickets. Toss: Orange Free State. Orange Free State 221 (50 overs) (F. D. Stephenson 99, J. F. Venter 43; G. P. Wickremasinghe four for 42, M. Muralitharan three for 41); Sri Lankans 222 for five (47.4 overs) (A. P. Gurusinha 45, P. A. de Silva 71 not out, H. P. Tillekeratne 30).

†At Zwide, December 22. Sri Lankans won by 36 runs. Toss: Eastern Province Invitation XI. Sri Lankans 202 (49.4 overs) (S. Clay three for 32, C. du Plessis three for 50, R. Qeqe three for 40); Eastern Province Invitation XI 166 (47.2 overs) (L. Masikazana 35, L. Coetzee 32).

EASTERN PROVINCE v SRI LANKANS

At Port Elizabeth, December 26, 27, 28, 29. Drawn. Toss: Sri Lankans.

Most of the match was lost to weather, with no play from lunch on the first day until the start of the final morning. Wessels, who had just announced his international retirement, was the province's highest scorer with 48, but he fell early on the resumption, one of three wickets for Vaas, while Muralitharan's off-spin accounted for six of the rest. Gurusinha and Sanjeeva Ranatunga took the tourists' total to 107 for one before spinners Huckle and Abrahams instigated a mini-collapse of four for 15.

Close of play: First day, Eastern Province 93-1 (G. Morgan 30*, K. C. Wessels 48*); Second day, No play; Third day, No play.

Eastern Province

P. G. Amm b Vaas	7	G. A. Roe not out		14
†G. Morgan c Gurusinha b Vaas	31	A. G. Huckle st Dassanayake		
*K. C. Wessels b Vaas	48		b Muralitharan	16
D. J. Callaghan c Vaas b Pushpakumara	18	Q. E. de Bruin b Muralitharan		2
L. J. Koen b Muralitharan	23	L-b 4, n-b 8		12
G. K. Miller b Muralitharan	25			
E. A. E. Baptiste b Muralitharan	2	1/7 2/93 3/100 4/120 5/150		198
S. Abrahams hit wkt b Muralitharan	0	6/154 7/163 8/169 9/192		

Bowling: Pushpakumara 22.4–6–70–1; Vaas 15–4–32–3; Upashantha 11–2–43–0; Muralitharan 19.4–8–42–6; Dharmasena 4.2–1–7–0.

Sri Lankans

A. P. Gurusinha c Baptiste b Abrahams	48	P. A. de Silva not out		7
†P. B. Dassanayake c Miller b de Bruin	13	E. A. Upashantha not out		2
S. Ranatunga b Huckle	44	B 2, l-b 2, w 1, n-b 1		6
S. T. Jayasuriya c Baptiste b Huckle	0			
H. D. P. K. Dharmasena c de Bruin		1/38 2/107 3/107	(5 wkts)	125
b Abrahams	5	4/116 5/122		

*A. Ranatunga, W. P. U. J. C. Vaas, K. R. Pushpakumara and M. Muralitharan did not bat.

Bowling: Baptiste 6–2–10–0; de Bruin 7–1–29–1; Roe 7–2–25–0; Abrahams 13–1–34–2; Huckle 8–0–23–2.

Umpires: W. Diedricks and R. E. Koertzen.

BORDER v SRI LANKANS

At East London, January 1, 2, 3, 4. Drawn. Toss: Border.

The Sri Lankans scored 454 to establish a first-innings lead of 231 but were unable to bowl out Border on the final day. Their massive total was built on two partnerships: 166 from openers Gurusinha, who hit 16 fours and a six in his century, and Dassanayake, and 168 for the seventh wicket from Arjuna Ranatunga, who also reached his hundred, and Upashantha. Border threw away a promising start in their first innings, losing seven men to Muralitharan, but Lawson and Cronje saw them to 204 for one in their second. They were still six behind when play ended.

Close of play: First day, Border 218-9 (P. A. N. Emslie 18*, J. A. Ehrke 14*); Second day, Sri Lankans 249-6 (A. Ranatunga 11*, E. A. Upashantha 0*); Third day, Border 79-0 (M. P. Stonier 41*, A. G. Lawson 30*).

Border

M. P. Stonier c Upashantha b Muralitharan	60	– c Dassanayake b Wickremasinghe	46
A. G. Lawson c Jayasuriya b Kalpage	25	– c Dassanayake b Muralitharan	77
F. J. C. Cronje lbw b Wickremasinghe	51	– lbw b Kalpage	70
*P. N. Kirsten b Muralitharan	24	– not out	12
P. C. Strydom b Muralitharan	0	– not out	3
P. J. Botha b Muralitharan	1		
†S. J. Palframan c Upashantha b Muralitharan	2		
I. L. Howell run out	0		
B. C. Fourie b Muralitharan	8		
P. A. N. Emslie not out	20		
J. A. Ehrke c Gurusinha b Muralitharan	17		
L-b 8, n-b 7	15	B 7, l-b 8, n-b 2	17
	223	(3 wkts)	**225**

1/78 2/98 3/138 4/138 5/142 6/146 7/146 8/163 9/202

1/85 2/204 3/210

Bowling: *First Innings*—Wickremasinghe 24-7-36-1; Vaas 24-5-47-0; Upashantha 6-1-31-0; Muralitharan 35.4-13-57-7; Kalpage 18-5-33-1; de Silva 4-0-11-0. *Second Innings*—Wickremasinghe 13-1-33-1; Vaas 13-5-17-0; Kalpage 30-9-63-1; Muralitharan 35-15-53-1; Jayasuriya 8-3-15-0; de Silva 6-3-12-0; Upashantha 4-1-12-0; S. Ranatunga 3-1-5-0.

Sri Lankans

A. P. Gurusinha c Strydom b Emslie	117	W. P. U. J. C. Vaas b Emslie	6
†P. B. Dassanayake c Cronje b Howell	40	G. P. Wickremasinghe b Fourie	0
S. Ranatunga c Botha b Emslie	34	M. Muralitharan not out	31
S. T. Jayasuriya lbw b Emslie	10		
R. S. Kalpage b Ehrke	0		
P. A. de Silva c Palframan b Ehrke	21	B 5, l-b 14, w 1, n-b 2	22
*A. Ranatunga b Ehrke	116		
E. A. Upashantha c sub (C. R. Wilson) b Ehrke	57		**454**

1/166 2/180 3/211 4/212 5/228 6/241 7/409 8/415 9/416

Bowling: Fourie 31-6-66-1; Ehrke 27-6-85-4; Botha 20-7-39-0; Howell 26-2-100-1; Emslie 43.3-9-85-4; Cronje 3-0-27-0; Kirsten 11-1-33-0.

Umpires: S. F. Marais and R. A. Noble.

THE WEST INDIANS IN INDIA, 1994-95

By R. MOHAN

An outbreak of pneumonic plague in the western state of Gujarat raised doubts about whether this tour would take place at all. Eventually, the West Indians arrived a week late – and they left the preservation of their reputation very late too. Having gone one down in the First Test at Bombay and drawn at Nagpur, they waited until the last day of the tour to hit back and level the series. West Indies had not lost a Test series since their 1-0 defeat in New Zealand in March 1980; the turnaround at Mohali, near Chandigarh, was a great escape for Courtney Walsh and his party on a tour when little went right.

The West Indians found India a difficult experience. It was easy to sympathise with their lot in having to criss-cross the country on a hectic schedule to play on grossly under-prepared Test wickets. They were impoverished by the absence of regular captain Richie Richardson, who was suffering from exhaustion, and Curtly Ambrose, with a shoulder injury. In addition, opener Desmond Haynes had chosen to play in South Africa, after a misunderstanding over the captaincy, and all-rounder Winston Benjamin had been suspended over an off-the-field incident in April. Nevertheless, West Indies also seemed to suffer from an attitude problem. Their professionalism was in question before the Tests began, when they lost a one-day series to India for the first time – and again, in the final of a triangular tournament involving New Zealand.

The hastily rearranged itinerary was heavily loaded with one-day cricket. Though West Indies began the bilateral series (reduced from six games to five) with an emphatic win, India made sure of it by winning the next four. And the Indians also dominated the fortnight of the triangular competition, which interrupted the main programme. Star batsman Brian Lara had problems adjusting to the conditions, and the inexperience of the middle order and the support pace bowling was harshly exposed. The rub of the green did not favour the West Indians, either; several umpiring decisions went against them at a time when the officials were still unclear when and how to resort to the television replay.

West Indies thus reached Bombay for the Test series in a downbeat mood. Still, they had every chance to win there, especially when Kenneth Benjamin had India on the run at 11 for three in the second innings. But a couple of vital chances went begging and Sachin Tendulkar – unexpectedly backed up by tailender Javagal Srinath – set up India's tenth successive home victory, which was also the tenth Test win for captain Mohammad Azharuddin, an Indian record. Bombay was the worst pitch of the tour, but a slow surface at Nagpur did not suit the West Indians either. As India ran up a total of 546 for nine, thanks to centuries from Sidhu and Tendulkar – who scored his eighth Test hundred, while still only 21 – West Indies were in danger of losing their unbeaten series record. Here, however, they began to turn the tide, when the dogged persistence of Jimmy Adams and the classy strokeplay of Carl Hooper just about saved them. Adams scored an undefeated 125, demonstrating the value of concentration and studious pad-play, while Hooper, the outstanding batsman of the one-day matches, found his somewhat suspect Test temperament in the nick of time, and also picked up seven wickets with his off-spin. Their ability to keep out the spinners, who had led India's triumphal progress of recent seasons, was a heartening sign; it was noteworthy that the touring batsmen could pick leg-spinner Anil Kumble, who had been destroyer-in-chief. Adams made a far more positive hundred at Mohali, where he took his series aggregate to 520 at a phenomenal 173.33. But Walsh was also at his best in Mohali, as captain and bowler. A normal Test pitch must have come as a sight for sore eyes, and the bracing winter weather also seemed to perk up the West Indians' attitude. Walsh deserved credit, though, first for his courage in defying a neck injury to play, and then for planning and carrying out his winning strategy to the last detail. Promoting Lara to open the second innings, when quick runs were essential, was a master stroke, giving the world record-holder one last chance on a forgettable tour, and on the final day Benjamin and Walsh swept aside the Indian batting. The pair had had to carry the pace attack throughout the series and finished it with 17 wickets apiece. Bouncing back to win by 243 runs did Walsh and his team great credit, and earned them the newly-constituted Fatesinhrao Gaekwad Trophy (on the strength of their 3-0 series win the previous time the teams met). Meanwhile, India had to accept their first defeat in 15 Tests since they lost in South Africa in December 1992.

WEST INDIAN TOURING PARTY

C. A. Walsh (Jamaica) (*captain*), B. C. Lara (Trinidad & Tobago) (*vice-captain*), J. C. Adams (Jamaica), K. L. T. Arthurton (Leeward Islands), K. C. G. Benjamin (Leeward Islands), B. St A. Browne (Guyana), S. L. Campbell (Barbados), S. Chanderpaul (Guyana), C. E. Cuffy (Windward Islands), A. C. Cummins (Barbados), R. Dhanraj (Trinidad & Tobago), R. I. C. Holder (Barbados), C. L. Hooper (Guyana), J. R. Murray (Windward Islands), P. V. Simmons (Trinidad & Tobago), S. C. Williams (Leeward Islands).

Manager: D. A. J. Holford.   *Cricket manager:* R. B. Kanhai.

WEST INDIAN TOUR RESULTS

Test matches – Played 3: Won 1, Lost 1, Drawn 1.
First-class matches – Played 5: Won 1, Lost 1, Drawn 3.
Win – India.
Loss – India.
Draws – India, Indian Board President's XI, Bombay.
One-day internationals – Played 10: Won 3, Lost 6, No result 1. *Wins* – India (2), New Zealand. *Losses* – India (6). *No result* – New Zealand.
Other non-first-class match – Lost v Chandigarh Administrator's XI.

TEST MATCH AVERAGES

INDIA – BATTING

	T	I	NO	R	HS	100s	Avge	Ct
S. R. Tendulkar	3	6	0	402	179	1	67.00	5
J. Srinath	3	6	3	136	60	0	45.33	2
N. S. Sidhu	3	6	0	224	107	1	37.33	1
M. Azharuddin	3	6	1	178	97	0	35.60	7
N. R. Mongia	3	6	0	183	80	0	30.50	6

	T	I	NO	R	HS	100s	Avge	Ct/St
M. Prabhakar	3	6	1	152	120	1	30.40	1
S. V. Manjrekar....	3	6	0	179	66	0	29.83	3/1
A. Kumble........	3	6	2	117	52*	0	29.25	1
V. G. Kambli	3	6	0	64	40	0	10.66	1
S. L. V. Raju	3	5	1	40	16	0	10.00	1
R. K. Chauhan	2	3	1	6	4	0	3.00	0

Played in one Test: A. R. Kapoor 15, 1 (1 ct).

* Signifies not out.

BOWLING

	O	M	R	W	BB	5W/i	Avge
S. L. V. Raju	172.5	33	463	20	5-60	2	23.15
A. Kumble	145.5	33	409	13	4-90	0	31.46
J. Srinath	106	19	337	8	4-48	0	42.12
R. K. Chauhan....	75	22	214	3	1-45	0	71.33

Also bowled: A. R. Kapoor 37–5–122–1; M. Prabhakar 38–5–149–2; S. R. Tendulkar 4–0–19–0.

WEST INDIES – BATTING

	T	I	NO	R	HS	100s	Avge	Ct/St
J. C. Adams	3	6	3	520	174*	2	173.33	3
J. R. Murray.........	3	4	0	193	85	0	48.25	11/1
C. L. Hooper.........	3	6	0	262	81	0	43.66	7
K. L. T. Arthurton....	3	6	2	164	70*	0	41.00	3
B. C. Lara	3	6	0	198	91	0	33.00	3
S. C. Williams........	3	5	0	114	49	0	22.80	6
P. V. Simmons	3	6	0	112	50	0	18.66	6
C. A. Walsh	3	4	1	18	11	0	6.00	0
K. C. G. Benjamin....	3	4	0	2	2	0	0.50	0
C. E. Cuffy	2	3	1	1	1	0	0.50	0

Played in two Tests: A. C. Cummins 17, 50 (1 ct). Played in one Test: S. Chanderpaul 4, 11* (1 ct); R. Dhanraj 1, 4.

* Signifies not out.

BOWLING

	O	M	R	W	BB	5W/i	Avge
C. A. Walsh	140.5	31	361	17	6-79	1	21.23
K. C. G. Benjamin....	137.4	27	490	17	5-65	1	28.82
C. L. Hooper.........	115.1	19	320	9	5-116	1	35.55
C. E. Cuffy	52.2	10	190	5	3-80	0	38.00
A. C. Cummins	58	3	198	3	2-45	0	66.00

Also bowled: J. C. Adams 17–5–56–0; S. Chanderpaul 20–4–63–1; R. Dhanraj 25.1–1–93–2.

Note: Matches in this section which were not first-class are signified by a dagger.

†At Chandigarh, October 14. Chandigarh Administrator's XI won by five wickets. Toss: Chandigarh Administrator's XI. West Indians 245 for eight (50 overs) (S. C. Williams 45, C. L. Hooper 61, K. L. T. Arthurton 50); Chandigarh Administrator's XI 246 for five (49.1 overs) (A. D. Jadeja 85, Rajesh Puri 33, Ajay Sharma 65, R. R. Singh 38 not out).

†INDIA v WEST INDIES

First One-Day International

At Faridabad, October 17. West Indies won by 96 runs. Toss: West Indies. International debut: C. E. Cuffy.

A century opening stand between Simmons and Williams, in his first one-day international, gave the tourists an ideal start. Though Lara went cheaply, Hooper reached 50 in just 47 balls, and the 90 he added with Arthurton took West Indies to a fine 273. That was out of India's range after ten overs, in which Walsh and Cuffy reduced them to 21 for four. Though Sidhu and Bedade then contributed half-centuries, their significance was academic. Kapil Dev had a sad match, which turned out to be his final international appearance; he damaged his hamstring in regaining the crease, after being mauled by Simmons while bowling, when he conceded 37 runs in five wicketless overs.

Man of the Match: P. V. Simmons.

West Indies

P. V. Simmons c Mongia b Chauhan .. 76	†J. C. Adams not out 1	
S. C. Williams c Kumble b Srinath 61		
B. C. Lara c Azharuddin b Kumble.... 10	B 6, l-b 12, w 5, n-b 2 25	
C. L. Hooper not out................ 61		
K. L. T. Arthurton hit wkt b Srinath .. 39	1/132 2/148 3/164 (5 wkts, 50 overs) 273	
A. C. Cummins c Bedade b Srinath.... 0	4/254 5/254	

S. Chanderpaul, K. C. G. Benjamin, *C. A. Walsh and C. E. Cuffy did not bat.

Bowling: Prabhakar 10–1–45–0; Srinath 10–2–42–3; Kapil Dev 5–0–37–0; Kumble 10–0–54–1; Tendulkar 5–0–32–0; Chauhan 10–1–45–1.

India

M. Prabhakar b Walsh 3	A. Kumble c Simmons b Hooper 4	
S. R. Tendulkar c Lara b Walsh 0	R. K. Chauhan c Adams b Arthurton .. 20	
N. S. Sidhu c Cummins b Benjamin 52	J. Srinath c Simmons b Hooper 0	
*M. Azharuddin c Lara b Cuffy....... 1	L-b 2, w 2, n-b 9............. 13	
V. G. Kambli c Adams b Cuffy 5		
A. C. Bedade c Adams b Benjamin 51	1/2 2/5 3/12 (45 overs) 177	
Kapil Dev c Walsh b Simmons 12	4/21 5/117 6/129	
†N. R. Mongia not out 16	7/135 8/149 9/176	

Bowling: Walsh 5–0–11–2; Cuffy 7–2–19–2; Cummins 7–0–27–0; Benjamin 8–0–48–2; Simmons 10–1–38–1; Hooper 6–0–23–2; Arthurton 2–0–9–1.

Umpires: S. K. Sharma and I. Shivaram.

†INDIA v WEST INDIES

Second One-Day International

At Bombay, October 20. India won on scoring-rate when rain stopped play. Toss: India. International debut: B. St A. Browne.

India won thanks to Sidhu, whose six off Cummins lifted their run-rate above the West Indians' just before the gathering clouds burst; their requirement at 33 overs was calculated as 127. Had the match been played out, India would have been penalised two overs for failing to complete their 50 on time. They had put West Indies in and had them tottering at 51 for five, Srinath and Prasad exploiting a seamer's pitch. Hooper came to the rescue with a classy 70 off 86 balls, despite a controversial end to a fine stand of 60 in 12 overs with Chanderpaul, who was given run out by the third umpire, although everyone else interpreted the TV replay differently. Later, India lost both openers for two runs – Tendulkar made his second successive duck. But Sidhu, supported by Azharuddin, kept them in the chase; he hit two sixes and four fours in his unbeaten 65.

Man of the Match: N. S. Sidhu.

West Indies

P. V. Simmons lbw b Prasad	24	*C. A. Walsh c Bedade b Prasad	3
S. C. Williams c Kambli b Srinath	0	B. St A. Browne not out	8
B. C. Lara c Prasad b Srinath	6	C. E. Cuffy not out	1
C. L. Hooper c Mongia b Srinath	70		
K. L. T. Arthurton c Mongia b Kumble	2	L-b 3, w 13, n-b 4	20
†J. C. Adams c Mongia b Prasad	2		
S. Chanderpaul run out	22	1/3 2/17 3/33 (9 wkts, 50 overs) 192	
A. C. Cummins c Tendulkar		4/48 5/51 6/111	
b Prabhakar	34	7/154 8/167 9/182	

Bowling: Prabhakar 10-2-34-1; Srinath 10-2-34-3; Prasad 10-1-36-3; Kumble 10-0-42-1; Chauhan 10-1-43-0.

India

M. Prabhakar c Lara b Walsh	0	A. C. Bedade not out	11
S. R. Tendulkar c Hooper b Cuffy	0	L-b 1, w 4, n-b 3	8
N. S. Sidhu not out	65		
*M. Azharuddin c Chanderpaul b Cuffy	34	1/0 2/2 (4 wkts, 33.1 overs) 135	
V. G. Kambli c Arthurton b Cummins	17	3/63 4/111	

†N. R. Mongia, A. Kumble, J. Srinath, R. K. Chauhan and B. K. V. Prasad did not bat.

Bowling: Walsh 7-1-15-1; Cuffy 8.1-1-29-2; Cummins 6-0-34-1; Browne 7-0-27-0; Hooper 5-0-29-0.

Umpires: N. Menon and R. T. Ramachandran.

West Indies' matches v India and New Zealand in the Wills World Series (October 23–November 5) may be found in that section.

†INDIA v WEST INDIES

Third One-Day International

At Vishakhapatnam, November 7. India won by four runs. Toss: India.

Returning to the bilateral Pepsi series two days after the Wills final, the tourists found most of their kit had been flown on to Madras by mistake. By the time it was retrieved, there was time for only 44 overs a side, and West Indies' slow over-rate cut their own innings to 43. In excellent conditions, Sidhu saw his team to a fine 260 with his fifth century in one-day internationals, an Indian record. Simmons and Williams began the chase soundly, but the latter stages were sustained almost single-handedly by Hooper, who smashed 74 not out off a mere 47 balls, with seven fours and two sixes. He needed to hit Prabhakar's final ball for six to tie; but he managed only two.

Man of the Match: N. S. Sidhu.

India

A. D. Jadeja c Murray b Cummins	 38	M. Prabhakar not out	 1
S. R. Tendulkar c Cummins b Hooper	. 54	L-b 2, w 4, n-b 2	 8
N. S. Sidhu not out	114		
*M. Azharuddin c Walsh b Arthurton	.. 45	1/64 2/137	(4 wkts, 44 overs) 260
V. G. Kambli c Arthurton b Walsh	 0	3/250 4/258	

†N. R. Mongia, A. Kumble, J. Srinath, B. K. V. Prasad and S. L. V. Raju did not bat.

Bowling: Browne 5-0-41-0; Walsh 9-0-50-1; Cuffy 9-0-41-0; Cummins 7-0-43-1; Simmons 5-0-23-0; Hooper 7-0-46-1; Arthurton 2-0-14-1.

West Indies

P. V. Simmons b Tendulkar	 51	*C. A. Walsh b Kumble	 3
S. C. Williams run out	 49	†J. R. Murray not out	 3
B. C. Lara c Raju b Prabhakar	 39		
C. L. Hooper not out	 74	B 2, l-b 15, w 5	 22
K. L. T. Arthurton c Azharuddin b Kumble	. 13	1/86 2/145	(7 wkts, 43 overs) 256
A. C. Cummins run out	 2	3/178 4/202	
R. I. C. Holder c Azharuddin b Prabhakar	. 0	5/215 6/220 7/230	

C. E. Cuffy and B. St A. Browne did not bat.

Bowling: Prabhakar 9-1-61-2; Srinath 8-1-31-0; Prasad 3-0-26-0; Kumble 7-0-41-2; Tendulkar 9-0-39-1; Raju 7-0-41-0.

Umpires: H. S. Sekhon and R. C. Sharma.

†INDIA v WEST INDIES

Fourth One-Day International

At Cuttack, November 9. India won by eight wickets. Toss: West Indies.

Though India had won limited-overs championships in which West Indies were one of several competing teams, they had never beaten them in a one-to-one contest before. This win gave them a 3-1 lead with one to play; it came with only four balls to spare but it had seemed inevitable after Jadeja and Tendulkar opened the innings with 176 in little more than 35 overs. Jadeja scored his maiden international century, 104 from 126 balls, and later Kambli kept India up with the asking-rate through an undefeated 40 from 35 balls. For West Indies, Lara made 89 from 106 balls, his highest score yet on Indian soil, but a total of 251 appeared inadequate on a slow pitch.

Man of the Match: A. D. Jadeja.

West Indies

P. V. Simmons run out	 32	A. C. Cummins lbw b Kumble	 8
S. C. Williams c Prabhakar b Chetan Sharma	. 15	*C. A. Walsh b Kumble	 0
B. C. Lara st Mongia b Kumble	 89	C. E. Cuffy not out	 17
C. L. Hooper run out	 2	L-b 3, w 7, n-b 12	 22
K. L. T. Arthurton c Mongia b Raju	... 27		
R. I. C. Holder c Mongia b Kumble	... 36	1/47 2/67 3/77	(9 wkts, 50 overs) 251
S. Chanderpaul lbw b Jadeja	 0	4/168 5/191 6/192	
†J. R. Murray c Prabhakar b Jadeja	... 3	7/202 8/228 9/228	

Bowling: Prabhakar 8-0-36-0; Srinath 7-0-32-0; Chetan Sharma 7-1-31-1; Kumble 10-0-43-3; Tendulkar 2-0-20-0; Raju 6-0-31-1; Jadeja 10-0-55-2.

India

A. D. Jadeja c Cuffy b Walsh	104
S. R. Tendulkar b Simmons	88
V. G. Kambli not out	40
*M. Azharuddin not out	17
L-b 1, w 5, n-b 1	7

1/176 2/222   (2 wkts, 49.2 overs) 256

A. C. Bedade, M. Prabhakar, †N. R. Mongia, Chetan Sharma, A. Kumble, S. L. V. Raju and J. Srinath did not bat.

Bowling: Walsh 10-1-29-1; Cuffy 10-1-36-0; Cummins 9.2-0-58-0; Hooper 4-0-34-0; Arthurton 3-0-28-0; Simmons 8-0-46-1; Chanderpaul 5-0-24-0.

Umpires: A. V. Jayaprakash and J. Kurishinkal.

†INDIA v WEST INDIES

Fifth One-Day International

At Jaipur, November 11. India won by five runs. Toss: India.

Tendulkar scored his third limited-overs century in two months, following his 115 against New Zealand a fortnight earlier and 110 against Australia in September. He was named Man of the Series, in which he amassed 246, despite two noughts. Tendulkar put on 95 with Jadeja and 117 with Kambli and India raced to 212 for one after Lara, leading West Indies as Walsh rested, put them in. The middle order lost momentum, however, and the tourists' target was a reachable 260. Despite losing the openers cheaply, Lara, Hooper and Adams gave them a chance. But once Adams and Hooper – who scored 84 from 88 balls – fell in successive overs, no-one could get Raju's left-arm spin away on a helpful pitch.

Man of the Match: C. L. Hooper.   *Man of the Series:* S. R. Tendulkar.

India

A. D. Jadeja c and b Hooper	31	M. Prabhakar not out	4
S. R. Tendulkar c Adams b Browne	105		
V. G. Kambli c Lara b Cummins	66	B 6, l-b 11, w 9, n-b 9	35
A. C. Bedade not out	15		
*M. Azharuddin c Simmons b Cummins	2	1/95 2/212 3/239 (5 wkts, 50 overs) 259
Chetan Sharma c Cuffy b Browne	1	4/245 5/252	

†N. R. Mongia, A. Kumble, J. Srinath and S. L. V. Raju did not bat.

Bowling: Cummins 10-0-49-2; Cuffy 10-0-40-0; Browne 10-1-50-2; Hooper 10-1-35-1; Simmons 5-0-25-0; Chanderpaul 5-0-43-0.

West Indies

P. V. Simmons c Azharuddin b Srinath	2	S. Chanderpaul c Bedade b Prabhakar	8
S. C. Williams c Mongia		A. C. Cummins b Raju	1
b Chetan Sharma	13	C. E. Cuffy b Raju	2
*B. C. Lara lbw b Raju	47	B. St A. Browne not out	0
C. L. Hooper lbw b Raju	84	B 1, l-b 16, w 5, n-b 3	25
†J. C. Adams c Kambli b Kumble	50		
K. L. T. Arthurton c Azharuddin		1/3 2/50 3/90 (49 overs) 254
b Kumble	14	4/215 5/218 6/238	
R. I. C. Holder run out	8	7/247 8/251 9/252	

Bowling: Prabhakar 9-1-35-1; Srinath 7-1-42-1; Chetan Sharma 10-0-39-1; Kumble 10-1-44-2; Raju 9-0-46-4; Tendulkar 4-0-31-0.

Umpires: S. Chowdhury and S. Porel.

INDIAN BOARD PRESIDENT'S XI v WEST INDIANS

At Bangalore, November 13, 14, 15. Drawn. Toss: Indian Board President's XI.

After two consecutive one-day internationals, the tourists had a single first-class match in which to adjust their game for the Test series. They put in some serious practice, especially the bowlers competing for the right to support Walsh, who continued his rest. Leg-spinners Dhanraj and Chanderpaul looked good with three wickets apiece in the first innings, when only Punjab opener Vikram Rathore reached 50; Cuffy's pace claimed three too. Then several West Indian batsmen spent time in the middle, with Arthurton running up a century and Simmons and Adams just missing the mark. Young off-spinner Kapoor took six wickets to catch the selectors' eye. But the West Indians had a first-innings lead of 165, though Amre baulked them of a possible win with a gritty 90.

Close of play: First day, West Indians 2-0 (P. V. Simmons 1*, S. C. Williams 0*); Second day, West Indians 371-4 (J. C. Adams 78*, K. L. T. Arthurton 99*).

Indian Board President's XI

Vikram Rathore c Cuffy b Dhanraj	64	– lbw b Benjamin	27
*S. V. Manjrekar c Murray b Cuffy	4	– lbw b Benjamin	14
R. S. Dravid c Lara b Benjamin	13	– c Adams b Benjamin	1
P. K. Amre c Benjamin b Dhanraj	0	– c Benjamin b Dhanraj	90
Rizwan Shamshad c sub (R. I. C. Holder) b Cuffy	9	– c Benjamin b Dhanraj	9
†A. Vaidya lbw b Chanderpaul	25	– c Adams b Dhanraj	25
A. R. Kapoor c sub (S. L. Campbell) b Cuffy	42	– c Lara b Benjamin	19
U. Chatterjee c Adams b Chanderpaul	2	– (9) not out	8
S. V. Bahutule c Adams b Dhanraj	31	– (8) not out	8
Iqbal Siddiqui b Chanderpaul	4		
P. S. Vaidya not out	22		
B 1, l-b 1, n-b 20	22	B 14, l-b 6, n-b 13	33

1/37 2/96 3/96 4/106 5/115   238   1/39 2/48 3/63   (7 wkts) 234
6/159 7/177 8/179 9/183   4/110 5/170
                                                        6/202 7/212

Bowling: *First Innings*—Benjamin 12-3-39-1; Cuffy 20-5-55-3; Browne 13-4-44-0; Dhanraj 24.3-12-52-3; Chanderpaul 11-2-46-3. *Second Innings*—Cuffy 4-0-16-0; Benjamin 18-6-49-4; Dhanraj 21-2-93-3; Browne 4-0-38-0; Chanderpaul 6-1-18-0.

West Indians

P. V. Simmons b Bahutule	91	C. E. Cuffy c Rathore b Iqbal Siddiqui	0
S. C. Williams b Kapoor	46	K. C. G. Benjamin st A. Vaidya b Kapoor	0
S. Chanderpaul c Dravid b Kapoor	7		
*B. C. Lara b Kapoor	22	B. St A. Browne not out	1
J. C. Adams c Dravid b Iqbal Siddiqui	95		
K. L. T. Arthurton c A. Vaidya b P. S. Vaidya	104	B 5, l-b 7, w 2, n-b 18	32
†J. R. Murray st A. Vaidya b Kapoor	0		
R. Dhanraj c Bahutule b Kapoor	5	1/93 2/107 3/143 4/196 5/384	403
		6/389 7/396 8/396 9/397	

Bowling: Iqbal Siddiqui 16-5-67-2; P. S. Vaidya 24-6-62-1; Chatterjee 22-2-88-0; Kapoor 41.2-11-102-6; Bahutule 22-3-72-1.

Umpires: V. Srinivasan and C. R. Vijayaraghavan.

INDIA v WEST INDIES

First Test Match

At Bombay, November 18, 19, 20, 21, 22. India won by 96 runs. Toss: India. Test debuts: C. E. Cuffy, R. Dhanraj.

India began life after Kapil Dev with their tenth successive home Test victory, which was also Azharuddin's tenth win as captain, beating the nine of the Nawab of Pataudi junior and Sunil Gavaskar. But the advantage swung between the teams, and between bat and ball, until well into the fourth day.

With the pitch an underprepared horror, Azharuddin won an important toss. But Walsh had Prabhakar caught at short leg off his second ball, and took three more as India slid to 99 for five. Manjrekar and Mongia built some late-order resistance in a stand of 136, finally broken by Rajindra Dhanraj, the first specialist leg-spinner to play a Test for West Indies since David Holford, now the tour manager, in April 1977. He and fellow-debutant Cameron Cuffy had few successes but Walsh finished with six, for the first time in India. West Indies, too, were in danger of folding at 120 for four. However, an aggressive innings from Arthurton and deadpan defence from Adams kept them in the game. Raju, bowling with flight and intelligence, finally removed them both. Despite the spin attack, the pitch's brutality was clear when Arthurton called for a chest guard.

India's lead of 29 seemed worthless when Benjamin had them reeling at 11 for three at the second-day close. But there was an odd twist in the morning: the bowlers' footholes had not dried out properly near the stumps at the pavilion end. Dickie Bird, the first umpire from ICC's international panel to stand in an Indian Test, ordered a 45-minute delay, which meant the West Indian bowlers lost their chance to exploit the early moisture. As the pitch developed into a slow turner, Tendulkar improved India's fortunes, batting nearly three hours for 85, with ten fours and a six. Still, India were only 191 ahead when he fell. Their position brightened dramatically when first Kumble and then Srinath joined Manjrekar, who notched up a second half-century. Kumble hit 42 and Srinath, in his first home Test, a rousing 60, including a six out of the ground off Hooper.

When Srinath was last out, West Indies' target was 363, more than they had ever made to win in the fourth innings. Their hopes took an immediate blow when Prabhakar dismissed Simmons and Lara in his first over and, with Srinath following up, half the side went for 82. Adams and Murray restored West Indian pride with a stand of 162 in three hours. The Indians fumed because it began with Bird rejecting a slip catch against Murray, but Hooper and Arthurton had suffered harsh decisions earlier. (By now, there was no third umpire to rule on video replays, as television company TWI had pulled out after the first day.) Relief came at last when off-spinner Chauhan turned one off Murray's bat to dislodge a bail, and next over Srinath had Adams leg-before. West Indies were eight down by the close, and India completed victory 22 minutes into the final morning.

Man of the Match: J. Srinath.

Close of play: First day, India 272; Second day, India 11-3 (N. S. Sidhu 0*); Third day, India 287-8 (J. Srinath 20*, R. K. Chauhan 2*); Fourth day, West Indies 252-8 (R. Dhanraj 3*).

India

M. Prabhakar c Adams b Walsh	0	– c Hooper b Benjamin	7
N. S. Sidhu lbw b Walsh	18	– lbw b Benjamin	12
V. G. Kambli c Murray b Walsh	40	– (4) c Hooper b Benjamin	0
S. R. Tendulkar lbw b Walsh	34	– (5) c Murray b Hooper	85
*M. Azharuddin c Simmons b Benjamin	0	– (6) c Arthurton b Hooper	17
S. V. Manjrekar c Lara b Dhanraj	51	– (7) c Cuffy b Walsh	66
†N. R. Mongia c Murray b Benjamin	80	– (3) c Adams b Benjamin	0
A. Kumble c Hooper b Walsh	19	– c Hooper b Cuffy	42
S. L. V. Raju c Hooper b Walsh	4	– (11) not out	3
R. K. Chauhan c Williams b Benjamin	1	– c Murray b Walsh	4
J. Srinath not out	0	– (9) st Murray b Dhanraj	60
B 5, l-b 7, n-b 13	25	B 12, l-b 14, n-b 11	37

1/0 (1) 2/49 (3) 3/96 (4) 4/99 (5)   272   1/8 (1) 2/10 (3) 3/11 (4)   333
5/99 (2) 6/235 (6) 7/265 (7)   4/43 (2) 5/88 (6) 6/162 (5)
8/271 (9) 9/272 (8) 10/272 (10)   7/237 (8) 8/265 (7)
                                         9/309 (10) 10/333 (9)

Bowling: *First Innings*—Walsh 22-4-79-6; Benjamin 21.3-8-48-3; Cuffy 18-4-63-0; Hooper 9-0-23-0; Dhanraj 15-1-47-1. *Second Innings*—Walsh 28-6-64-2; Benjamin 24-3-82-4; Dhanraj 10.1-0-46-1; Hooper 24-4-69-2; Cuffy 12-2-46-1.

West Indies

P. V. Simmons c Manjrekar b Srinath	19	– c Mongia b Prabhakar	0
S. C. Williams c Azharuddin b Chauhan	49	– lbw b Srinath	11
B. C. Lara b Raju	14	– b Prabhakar	0
C. L. Hooper c Tendulkar b Raju	28	– c Mongia b Srinath	23
K. L. T. Arthurton c Tendulkar b Raju	42	– c Azharuddin b Raju	20
J. C. Adams c Kambli b Raju	39	– lbw b Srinath	81
†J. R. Murray lbw b Raju	23	– b Chauhan	85
R. Dhanraj c Mongia b Kumble	1	– c Tendulkar b Raju	4
K. C. G. Benjamin c Srinath b Kumble	0	– c Azharuddin b Raju	2
*C. A. Walsh not out	2	– c and b Srinath	11
C. E. Cuffy c and b Kumble	0	– not out	0
B 11, l-b 12, n-b 3	26	B 13, l-b 10, n-b 6	29

1/34 (1) 2/82 (3) 3/120 (4) 4/120 (2)   243   1/1 (1) 2/2 (3) 3/26 (2)   266
5/194 (5) 6/230 (7) 7/241 (8)   4/48 (4) 5/82 (5) 6/244 (7)
8/241 (9) 9/242 (6) 10/243 (11)   7/246 (6) 8/252 (9)
                                                9/266 (10) 10/266 (8)

Bowling: *First Innings*—Prabhakar 4–0–18–0; Srinath 13–5–37–1; Kumble 23.5–7–48–3; Chauhan 21–7–57–1; Raju 21–7–60–5. *Second Innings*—Prabhakar 3–0–17–2; Srinath 20–8–48–4; Raju 28.4–6–85–3; Kumble 12–1–39–0; Chauhan 15–3–45–1; Tendulkar 3–0–9–0.

Umpires: H. D. Bird (England) and S. K. Bansal.   Referee: R. Subba Row (England).

BOMBAY v WEST INDIANS

At Kozikhode, November 25, 26, 27. Drawn. Toss: Bombay.

There was only one day's play in Kozikhode, formerly Calicut. The match was caught up in a political maelstrom in the state of Kerala; the second day was abandoned because the opposition called a "bandh" or total stoppage, after police had shot seven demonstrators dead. And West Indian manager David Holford announced that his players were "in no mental state to resume" on the last day after witnessing some violent incidents near their hotel. He had also criticised the uneven pitch, laid out in a football stadium, and a few cynics suggested that he was wary of further blows to cricketing morale. Bombay had dismissed the tourists for 176, a recovery from 77 for five, with only Chanderpaul reaching fifty. Abey Kuruvilla, a pupil of Frank Tyson, took five wickets on a seaming surface.

Close of play: First day, Bombay 53-2 (J. V. Paranjpe 20*, A. A. Muzumdar 14*); Second day, No play.

West Indians

P. V. Simmons c and b Ankola	5	R. Dhanraj b Kuruvilla	4
S. L. Campbell c Dighe b Kuruvilla	26	C. E. Cuffy st Dighe b N. M. Kulkarni	0
*B. C. Lara c Dighe b Kuruvilla	29	B. St A. Browne not out	0
R. I. C. Holder b Kuruvilla	3		
S. Chanderpaul c and b N. M. Kulkarni	56	L-b 7, n-b 9	16
C. L. Hooper lbw b Kuruvilla	4		
†J. R. Murray c Bharucha b Bahutule	27		176
A. C. Cummins run out	6		

1/11 2/66 3/67 4/70 5/77
6/118 7/139 8/176 9/176

Bowling: Ankola 8–3–27–1; Mhambre 14–3–32–0; Kuruvilla 13.1–0–42–5; Bahutule 21–4–44–1; N. M. Kulkarni 13–4–24–2.

Bombay

Z. Bharucha c Murray b Cummins 4
S. S. More b Cummins 0
J. V. Paranjpe not out 20
A. A. Muzumdar not out 14
     B 6, l-b 2, n-b 7 15

1/10 2/16   (2 wkts) 53

S. K. Kulkarni, *†S. S. Dighe, S. V. Bahutule, P. L. Mhambre, A. Kuruvilla, S. A. Ankola and N. M. Kulkarni did not bat

Bowling: Cummins 7–2–16–2; Cuffy 5–2–8–0; Browne 4–0–14–0; Dhanraj 2–0–7–0.

Umpires: S. Balachandran and V. Chopra.

INDIA v WEST INDIES

Second Test Match

At Nagpur, December 1, 2, 3, 4, 5. Drawn. Toss: India.

India's winning streak was finally halted by the determined resistance of Hooper and Adams. But some critics felt Azharuddin had let West Indies off the hook. In the first innings, the Indian batsmen piled up 546, but in the second, when quick runs were needed, they batted circumspectly, delaying the declaration until late on the fifth morning.

The home team was unchanged, while West Indies strengthened their batting, bringing in Chanderpaul and Cummins for Dhanraj and Cuffy. But India claimed first use of a decidedly slow pitch and flourished from the start. It was only the fourth time they had scored 500 against West Indies in 64 encounters. Sidhu made his second Test hundred against the West Indians, Tendulkar his first and Azharuddin was only three short when he flicked to backward short leg. Tendulkar's century was the most remarkable. It was the highest of his eight Test hundreds and he reached three figures by hooking Walsh for six. He also hit 24 fours in nearly seven hours. The innings was interrupted twice on the first day: Walsh pulled his team off after a hail of missiles at the deep fielders, culminating in a large guava fruit. After an hour was lost, policemen were stationed facing the crowds at ten-yard intervals and there were no further incidents.

India were well-placed to exert pressure on a slow turner and, despite patient fifties from Simmons and Lara, West Indies were well short of the follow-on mark when they lost four for 155. But then Hooper joined the left-hander Adams, who was promoted to break up the spinners' line while Hooper rested after bowling 40 overs for five wickets. Adams used his pads freely as Hooper shrugged off a nervous start to play some sumptuous shots. Their stand raised 133 before three quick wickets fell. The tourists were still 27 from safety when Murray combined with Adams to add 97 in two hours. Adams remained undefeated on 125 after 406 minutes, after Raju picked up his fourth bag of five wickets in three home Tests.

Walsh removed Prabhakar and Kambli before his recurring neck injury forced him off, leaving an inexperienced attack to cope with Sidhu and Tendulkar. They had put on 177 on the first day, and added 128 now, but batted with unaccustomed caution. The innings dragged on until just before lunch on the final day. The declaration set West Indies 327 in a minimum of 65 overs and they were in trouble when the spinners removed the openers and Lara for 22. But once again Adams provided stability and Hooper lashed out, with 67 off 89 balls, to break the bowlers' grip. Both fell just before the final 15 overs began but Adams's 162 minutes of stoic defence that killed off the Indians' ambitions and the teams agreed on an early finish.

Man of the Match: C. L. Hooper.

Close of play: First day, India 230-4 (S. R. Tendulkar 81*); Second day, West Indies 15-1 (P. V. Simmons 1*, A. C. Cummins 0*); Third day, West Indies 302-5 (J. C. Adams 68*, K. L. T. Arthurton 5*); Fourth day, India 95-2 (N. S. Sidhu 44*, S. R. Tendulkar 29*).

India

M. Prabhakar c Williams b Hooper	19	– c Lara b Walsh	6
N. S. Sidhu c Murray b Hooper	107	– c Simmons b Hooper	76
V. G. Kambli c Williams b Hooper	0	– b Walsh	6
S. R. Tendulkar c Lara b Walsh	179	– c Arthurton b Benjamin	54
S. L. V. Raju c Adams b Walsh	2		
*M. Azharuddin c Simmons b Hooper	97	– (5) not out	32
S. V. Manjrekar c Simmons b Hooper	0	– (6) c Murray b Benjamin	5
†N. R. Mongia c Hooper b Cummins	44	– run out	11
A. Kumble not out	52	– not out	3
J. Srinath c and b Chanderpaul	6	– (7) lbw b Hooper	1
R. K. Chauhan not out	1		
B 12, l-b 9, n-b 18	39	B 3, l-b 5, n-b 6	14

1/48 (1) 2/49 (3) 3/226 (2)   (9 wkts dec.) 546   1/9 (1) 2/24 (3)   (7 wkts dec.) 208
4/230 (5) 5/432 (6) 6/434 (7)   3/152 (4) 4/157 (2)
7/444 (4) 8/537 (8) 9/543 (10)   5/163 (6) 6/174 (7)
                                                           7/193 (8)

Bowling: *First Innings*—Walsh 32–7–93–2; Benjamin 26–4–120–0; Cummins 27–1–96–1; Hooper 40–8–116–5; Chanderpaul 20–4–63–1; Adams 10–2–37–0. *Second Innings*—Walsh 5.5–3–2–2; Benjamin 13.4–1–69–2; Hooper 25.1–6–62–2; Adams 4–2–10–0; Cummins 15–0–57–0.

West Indies

P. V. Simmons c Manjrekar b Kumble	50	– c Sidhu b Kumble	8
S. C. Williams c Azharuddin b Chauhan	12	– b Raju	8
A. C. Cummins c Manjrekar b Raju	17		
B. C. Lara c Mongia b Raju	50	– (3) c Tendulkar b Raju	3
J. C. Adams not out	125	– (4) c Tendulkar b Kumble	23
C. L. Hooper c Prabhakar b Srinath	81	– (5) c Azharuddin b Kumble	67
K. L. T. Arthurton c Azharuddin b Raju	7	– (6) not out	7
S. Chanderpaul c Azharuddin b Raju	4	– (7) not out	11
†J. R. Murray lbw b Raju	54		
K. C. G. Benjamin lbw b Kumble	0		
*C. A. Walsh b Kumble	1		
B 5, l-b 14, n-b 8	27	B 2, n-b 3	5

1/15 (2) 2/61 (3) 3/98 (1) 4/155 (4)   428   1/18 (2) 2/18 (1)   (5 wkts) 132
5/288 (6) 6/306 (7) 7/320 (8)   3/22 (3) 4/112 (5)
8/417 (9) 9/422 (10) 10/428 (11)   5/115 (4)

Bowling: *First Innings*—Prabhakar 4–1–15–0; Srinath 14–2–39–1; Chauhan 34–9–97–1; Raju 50–11–127–5; Kumble 51–15–131–3. *Second Innings*—Srinath 7–2–12–0; Kumble 23–7–45–3; Raju 27–4–58–2; Chauhan 5–3–15–0.

Umpires: N. T. Plews (England) and V. K. Ramaswamy.
Referee: R. Subba Row (England).

INDIA v WEST INDIES

Third Test Match

At Mohali, December 10, 11, 12, 13, 14. West Indies won by 243 runs. Toss: West Indies. Test debut: A. R. Kapoor.

West Indies levelled the series to remain unbeaten since March 1980, while India went down to their first home defeat since November 1988. The outcome was uncertain when West Indies led by only 56 on first innings. But Walsh then got exactly what he wanted from his batsmen and swept India away in a striking burst from Benjamin on the fifth morning. Walsh had been a doubtful starter, because of a recurring whiplash injury to his neck. He discarded his neck brace the day before the match – and did himself a favour by winning the toss. West Indies batted and he had another day's rest.

The first Test in Mohali, a suburb of Chandigarh, was played on the truest pitch of the series, prompting the West Indians to revert to their standard four quick bowlers. Cuffy replaced Chanderpaul, while India introduced off-spinner Aashish Kapoor. But West Indies almost tossed away the advantage of batting first when Hooper – stumped by Manjrekar, as wicket-keeper Mongia was off with a stomach bug – and Arthurton played careless shots just after tea. Once again, Adams played with patient determination, and this time used his bat more than his pads. His third Test hundred was a career-best 174 not out in seven and a half hours. Though Kumble was still largely blunted, he picked up four wickets to reach 99 in his 20th Test. After Sidhu was bowled off his helmet by Walsh, Prabhakar batted 405 minutes for an equally patient century, his first in his 36 Tests. Later, Srinath put on 64 with Raju, a tenth-wicket record for India against West Indies, as they inched towards the tourists' 443.

But then West Indies seized the initiative, scoring 301 inside 57 overs. Promoted to open, Lara played his best innings of the tour, 91 from 104 balls. It ended when he walked after tickling a catch to the wicket-keeper. However, Adams and Arthurton kept up the pace with an unbroken stand of 145 in 106 minutes. Walsh was able to declare 357 ahead and have an hour's bowling at India on the fourth evening. Only Sidhu was out, but Prabhakar was led off after one over, his nose broken by a ball from Walsh that burst through his helmet grille. That made the Indian batsmen uneasy, especially on a pitch which continued to play true; it retained some bounce to the end and the ball moved in the morning. Benjamin and Walsh dismissed Tendulkar and Manjrekar in the day's third and fourth overs and bowled unchanged as they reduced India to 68 for eight. The assault was planned to a nicety, short-pitched enough to cause grave discomfort to the batsmen yet not enough to test the two-bouncer-per-over law. Finally meeting some resistance – another last-wicket stand between Srinath and Raju – Walsh turned to Cuffy, who had Raju glove a catch to Murray in his first over, the 21st of the morning.

Man of the Match: J. C. Adams.   *Man of the Series:* J. C. Adams.

Close of play: First day, West Indies 296-6 (J. C. Adams 84*, A. C. Cummins 11*); Second day, India 95-1 (M. Prabhakar 55*, S. V. Manjrekar 33*); Third day, India 379-9 (J. Srinath 47*, S. L. V. Raju 12*); Fourth day, India 37-1 (S. V. Manjrekar 14*, S. R. Tendulkar 6*).

West Indies

P. V. Simmons c Mongia b Srinath	10	– run out	25
S. C. Williams lbw b Kumble	34		
B. C. Lara lbw b Srinath	40	– (2) c Mongia b Raju	91
J. C. Adams not out	174	– not out	78
C. L. Hooper st Manjrekar b Kapoor	43	– (3) lbw b Raju	20
K. L. T. Arthurton c Kapoor b Raju	18	– (5) not out	70
†J. R. Murray lbw b Kumble	31		
A. C. Cummins lbw b Raju	50		
*C. A. Walsh lbw b Kumble	4		
K. C. G. Benjamin lbw b Kumble	0		
C. E. Cuffy b Raju	1		
B 6, l-b 13, w 5, n-b 14	38	B 10, l-b 4, n-b 3	17

1/36 (1) 2/93 (2) 3/103 (3) 4/195 (5)   443   1/85 (1) 2/135 (3)   (3 wkts dec.) 301
5/220 (6) 6/269 (7) 7/368 (8)   3/156 (2)
8/406 (9) 9/422 (10) 10/443 (11)

Bowling: *First Innings*—Prabhakar 18-3-65-0; Srinath 32-2-106-2; Raju 33.4-5-73-3; Kapoor 30-4-90-1; Kumble 29-3-90-4. *Second Innings*—Prabhakar 9-1-34-0; Srinath 20-0-95-0; Kumble 7-0-56-0; Raju 12.3-0-60-2; Kapoor 7-1-32-0; Tendulkar 1-0-10-0.

India

M. Prabhakar c Murray b Walsh . . . . .120 – retired hurt 0
N. S. Sidhu b Walsh . . . . 0 – lbw b Benjamin 11
S. V. Manjrekar lbw b Benjamin . . . . 40 – c Murray b Walsh 17
S. R. Tendulkar c Williams b Cuffy . . . . 40 – c Arthurton b Benjamin 10
*M. Azharuddin c Williams b Cummins . . . . 27 – c Cummins b Benjamin 5
V. G. Kambli c Simmons b Benjamin . . . . 18 – c sub (S. L. Campbell)
                                                                    b Benjamin . 0
†N. R. Mongia hit wkt b Cummins . . . . 34 – c Williams b Walsh 14
A. R. Kapoor c Simmons b Cuffy . . . . 15 – c Murray b Walsh 1
A. Kumble c Hooper b Cuffy . . . . 0 – b Benjamin 1
J. Srinath not out . . . . 52 – not out 17
S. L. V. Raju c Murray b Benjamin . . . . 15 – c Murray b Cuffy 16
        B 5, l-b 3, w 1, n-b 17 26   B 1, l-b 13, n-b 8 22
                                                              ———   ———
                                                              387   114

1/1 (2) 2/104 (3) 3/168 (4) 4/228 (5)   1/17 (2) 2/44 (4) 3/46 (3)
5/262 (6) 6/265 (1) 7/305 (8)   4/48 (6) 5/66 (7) 6/66 (5)
8/310 (9) 9/323 (7) 10/387 (11)   7/68 (8) 8/68 (9) 9/114 (11)

In the second innings M. Prabhakar retired hurt at 0.

Bowling: *First Innings*—Walsh 35–4–89–2; Benjamin 35.3–8–106–3; Cuffy 22–4–80–3;
Cummins 16–2–45–2; Hooper 17–1–50–0; Adams 3–1–9–0. *Second Innings*—Walsh
18–7–34–3; Benjamin 17–3–65–5; Cuffy 0.2–0–1–1.

Umpires: R. S. Dunne (New Zealand) and S. Venkataraghavan.
Referee: R. Subba Row (England).

FUTURE TOURS

1996	Indians to England	1997	Australians to England
	Pakistanis to England		
		1997-98	New Zealanders to Sri Lanka*
1996-97	Australians to Sri Lanka*		South Africans to Pakistan
	Australians to India		West Indians to Pakistan
	West Indians to Australia		New Zealanders to Australia
	England to Zimbabwe		South Africans to Australia
	Pakistanis to Australia		
	England to New Zealand	1998	South Africans to England*
	Indians to South Africa		
	Australians to South Africa	1999	WORLD CUP in England
	Indians to the West Indies		
	Australians to Zimbabwe*		

* *Signifies unconfirmed. The New Zealanders are expected to tour England after the World
Cup in 1999 and the West Indians in 2000.*

THE NEW ZEALANDERS IN SOUTH AFRICA, 1994-95

By JACK BANNISTER

New Zealand's third tour of South Africa, and first for 33 years, began promisingly, with a well-crafted win in the First Test at Johannesburg, but ended with their squad in disarray. They lost the next two Tests to become the first side since Australia against England in 1888 to lose a three-match series after being ahead. They also failed to win one of their six one-day internationals in the quadrangular Mandela Trophy, and returned to New Zealand to face a barrage of criticism.

The recriminations intensified when Matthew Hart, Dion Nash, Stephen Fleming and Chris Pringle were all suspended – the first three for smoking cannabis, Pringle for unspecified misbehaviour. Manager Michael Sandlant and coach Geoff Howarth resigned in mid-January. Captain Ken Rutherford, who twice fell foul of ICC referee Peter Burge, was sacked after the home season degenerated into a series of traumas. Leading the critics in this series was Sir Richard Hadlee, who was commentating for New Zealand television and attacked the team's lack of discipline. The criticism was difficult to refute: the performances in the Durban and Cape Town Tests bordered on the suicidal.

Senior players were not exempt: Martin Crowe and Rutherford set the tone with six dismissals from short deliveries between them, in situations which cried out for applied defence. Adam Parore, Bryan Young, Shane Thomson and the promising Fleming also perished to injudicious hooks and pulls fed by intelligent bowling from the home pace attack, well instructed by new coach Bob Woolmer.

Thomson was the only New Zealander to average over 40 in the series. Fleming was just short but every other batsman, including Crowe and Rutherford, was below 30. Those two aggregated only 290 in their 12 Test innings; one major performance from each would have prevented one, if not both Test defeats. It has to be said that Crowe was carrying a knee injury so inhibiting that he was an embarrassment in the field. As for batting, he could venture only the safest of singles. Apart from his opening innings of 83, he never threatened to score the century he needed to become the first batsman to reach a hundred against the other eight Test-playing countries.

Young was obdurate, particularly at Kingsmead when his 51, the third-slowest half-century ever made in Test cricket, deserved to save the game. Parore contrived to run himself out twice in bizarre circumstances, but still advanced his claims as a genuine top-order Test batsman. Fleming was one of the few to improve throughout the tour; these players, together with Thomson, pace bowler Nash and left-arm spinner Hart offered a nucleus for the future.

New Zealand were not helped by injuries nor by crucial decisions which went against them. The overseas independent umpires did not inspire confidence; three different visiting members of the panel stood in the series, which spoiled the continuity, as well as wasting money.

South Africa were playing their first home Tests since readmission to world cricket without Kepler Wessels. He had resigned the captaincy in early November to concentrate on his batting, but a recurring knee injury kept him out of the team and he announced his retirement from the international game before the Second Test. His successor, Hansie Cronje, was the most consistent batsman in the top half of the order and proved himself as a leader by presiding over the recovery after Johannesburg. The bowling continued to depend on pace, despite the absence of Allan Donald with a foot injury; Fanie de Villiers, South Africa's most successful bowler of 1994, put in some outstanding spells for 20 wickets at 20.05. But the player of the series was the wicket-keeper, Dave Richardson. With Donald missing, he became South Africa's only ever-present in their 20 Tests since readmission and reinforced his claims to be considered the world's foremost wicket-keeper/batsman with 247 runs at 82.33, including his maiden Test hundred, as well as 16 catches. His batting was the more creditable in that he usually came in at No. 7 or 8 with his side in trouble.

The United Cricket Board of South Africa triumphed on three fronts. An astute marketing policy, involving a gradual reduction of admission prices throughout each day's play, attracted healthy crowds; over 150,000 watched the three Tests. The large proportion of youngsters, previously strangers to five-day cricket, was particularly encouraging to the Board, who had been criticised for undue devotion to one-day cricket. Secondly, the technological assistance available via the third umpire was improved. There were four cameras, rather than two, bolted to brackets and operated automatically as for a racing photo-finish. With one camera square to each batting crease on either side, the chance of a fielder masking the action was mostly eliminated. The system could break down a replay to half a frame – one-fiftieth part of a second. The Board also equipped umpires with walkie-talkies.

Most important of all was the enterprise shown by both countries' administrators, in agreeing that the ICC mandatory minimum of 90 overs per day meant just that and could not be reduced by recalculating the overs after a change of innings. That removed the incentive for the side at a disadvantage on the fourth day to slow down play.

Another small piece of cricket history came when referee Burge, on instructions from ICC, began supervising each Test match toss. This edict followed an apparent linguistic misunderstanding between Rutherford and Salim Malik in Auckland in February 1994.

NEW ZEALAND TOURING PARTY

K. R. Rutherford (Otago) (*captain*), M. D. Crowe (Wellington) (*vice-captain*), R. P. de Groen (Northern Districts), S. B. Doull (Northern Districts), S. P. Fleming (Canterbury), L. K. Germon (Canterbury), C. Z. Harris (Canterbury), M. N. Hart (Northern Districts), B. R. Hartland (Canterbury), D. J. Murray (Canterbury), D. J. Nash (Northern Districts), A. C. Parore (Auckland), C. Pringle (Auckland), M. L. Su'a (Auckland), S. A. Thomson (Northern Districts), B. A. Young (Northern Districts).

M. W. Priest (Canterbury) joined the party for the Mandela Trophy and D. K. Morrison (Auckland), originally omitted because of injury, replaced the injured Nash.

Manager: M. Sandlant. *Coach:* G. P. Howarth.

NEW ZEALAND TOUR RESULTS

Test matches – Played 3: Won 1, Lost 2.
First-class matches – Played 7: Won 2, Lost 3, Drawn 2.
Wins – South Africa, Griqualand West.
Losses – South Africa (2), Orange Free State.
Draws – Northern Transvaal, Boland.
One-day internationals – Played 6: Lost 5, No result 1. *Losses* – South Africa (2), Pakistan (2), Sri Lanka. *No result* – Sri Lanka.
Other non-first-class matches – Played 3: Won 1, Lost 1, Drawn 1. *Win* – Transvaal Invitation XI. *Loss* – Transvaal. *Draw* – N. F. Oppenheimer's XI.

TEST MATCH AVERAGES

SOUTH AFRICA – BATTING

	T	I	NO	R	HS	100s	Avge	Ct
D. J. Richardson	3	4	1	247	109	1	82.33	16
W. J. Cronje	3	5	1	227	112	1	56.75	3
G. Kirsten	3	6	1	226	66*	0	45.20	6
J. B. Commins	2	4	1	112	45	0	37.33	2
P. S. de Villiers ..	3	4	3	36	28	0	36.00	2
D. J. Cullinan	3	6	1	162	58	0	32.40	1
B. M. McMillan	3	4	0	82	42	0	20.50	4
J. N. Rhodes	3	4	0	56	37	0	14.00	1
C. E. Eksteen	2	3	0	31	22	0	10.33	1
A. C. Hudson	2	4	0	26	10	0	6.50	1
C. R. Matthews	2	3	0	17	7	0	5.66	0

Played in two Tests: S. D. Jack 0, 7 (1 ct). Played in one Test: R. P. Snell 16, 1; P. J. R. Steyn 38, 12.

* *Signifies not out.*

BOWLING

	O	M	R	W	BB	5W/i	Avge
P. S. de Villiers	169.2	50	401	20	5-61	2	20.05
B. M. McMillan ...	126	39	267	13	4-65	0	20.53
C. R. Matthews ...	78	26	194	8	5-42	1	24.25
S. D. Jack	77	24	196	8	4-69	0	24.50
R. P. Snell	49.5	14	166	4	3-112	0	41.50

Also bowled: W. J. Cronje 30–14–54–1; C. E. Eksteen 94–41–163–2; G. Kirsten 5–2–11–1.

NEW ZEALAND – BATTING

	T	I	NO	R	HS	100s	Avge	Ct
S. A. Thomson	3	6	0	246	84	0	41.00	1
S. P. Fleming	3	6	0	230	79	0	38.33	3
B. A. Young	3	6	0	174	51	0	29.00	3
K. R. Rutherford	3	6	0	156	68	0	26.00	1
S. B. Doull	3	6	2	95	31*	0	23.75	2
M. D. Crowe	3	6	0	134	83	0	22.33	6

	T	I	NO	R	HS	100s	Avge	Ct
D. K. Morrison	2	4	2	37	24*	0	18.50	0
C. Pringle	2	4	2	36	30	0	18.00	1
A. C. Parore	3	6	0	104	49	0	17.33	6
M. N. Hart	3	6	0	76	34	0	12.66	2
D. J. Murray	3	6	0	71	38	0	11.83	2

Played in one Test: R. P. de Groen 26, 0; D. J. Nash 18, 20.

* Signifies not out.

BOWLING

	O	M	R	W	BB	5W/i	Avge
S. B. Doull	115.1	37	257	14	5-73	1	18.35
R. P. de Groen	33	5	80	3	2-59	0	26.66
M. N. Hart	158.4	28	432	15	5-77	1	28.80
S. A. Thomson	56	17	126	4	3-65	0	31.50
D. J. Nash	32	8	98	3	3-81	0	32.66
D. K. Morrison ...	78	13	231	5	4-70	0	46.20

Also bowled: C. Pringle 43–10–92–1.

Note: Matches in this section which were not first-class are signified by a dagger.

†At Randjesfontein, November 9. Drawn. New Zealanders batted first by mutual agreement. New Zealanders 232 for five dec. (D. J. Murray 57, M. D. Crowe 74; C. E. B. Rice three for 23); N. F. Oppenheimer's XI 231 for nine (M. W. Rushmere 47, J. A. Teeger 34, W. J. Cronje 34, H. A. Page 59 not out).

NORTHERN TRANSVAAL v NEW ZEALANDERS

At Verwoerdburg, November 11, 12, 13. Drawn. Toss: Northern Transvaal.

The New Zealanders' opening first-class fixture, on the delightful Centurion Park ground, provided a satisfactory work-out. Despite the ominous twin failure with the bat of their two old hands, Rutherford and Crowe, the young side flourished. Fleming scored 114 off 117 deliveries, including 15 fours and three sixes, one of which took him to his hundred. Young and Murray opened with 114 to set up a total of 356, from 102.2 overs, in answer to Northern Transvaal's 292, in which Rindel made 91 in 98 balls. But rain interrupted play for over five hours in the first two days, causing the New Zealanders to settle for practice, rather than contriving a declaration.

Close of play: First day, Northern Transvaal 260-7 (S. Elworthy 2*, M. J. G. Davis 1*); Second day, New Zealanders 145-1 (D. J. Murray 60*, S. P. Fleming 21*).

Northern Transvaal

B. J. Sommerville b Nash	0 –	not out 23
C. B. Lambert c Hart b Su'a	8 –	not out 52
R. F. Pienaar b Su'a	0	
L. P. Vorster b Doull	38	
M. J. R. Rindel lbw b Doull	91	
*J. J. Strydom c Parore b Hart	50	
†K. J. Rule c Parore b Hart	50	
S. Elworthy c Young b Doull	25	
M. J. G. Davis c Crowe b Hart	6	
R. E. Bryson c Fleming b Nash	0	
G. J. Smith not out	4	
B 1, l-b 8, n-b 11	20	B 1, l-b 6, n-b 2 9

1/4 2/6 3/21 4/124 5/173   292   (no wkt) 84
6/246 7/257 8/287 9/288

Bowling: *First Innings*—Nash 20-6-69-2; Su'a 10-0-62-2; Doull 21.5-6-64-3; Hart 25-6-65-3; Thomson 11-3-23-0. *Second Innings*—Nash 5-1-14-0; Su'a 9-2-30-0; Doull 6-1-19-0; Hart 2-0-14-0.

New Zealanders

B. A. Young b Elworthy	45	D. J. Nash b Davis	6
D. J. Murray lbw b Smith	72	M. L. Su'a not out	12
S. P. Fleming c Lambert b Davis	114		
M. D. Crowe c Sommerville b Smith	3	L-b 15, w 1, n-b 15	31
*K. R. Rutherford c Pienaar b Bryson	12		
S. A. Thomson c Smith b Davis	18	1/114 2/183 3/199	(9 wkts. dec.) 356
†A. C. Parore b Davis	23	4/232 5/281 6/299	
M. N. Hart run out	20	7/333 8/339 9/356	

S. B. Doull did not bat.

Bowling: Elworthy 25-4-96-1; Smith 19-1-90-2; Rindel 4-0-19-0; Bryson 12-4-46-1; Davis 28.2-8-53-4; Sommerville 14-5-37-0.

Umpires: S. B. Lambson and D. L. Orchard.

GRIQUALAND WEST v NEW ZEALANDERS

At Kimberley, November 15, 16, 17. New Zealanders won by 23 runs. Toss: New Zealanders.

The tourists' first win was achieved against Bowl opposition, thanks to positive batting and Griqualand West's ready acceptance of a challenging declaration. The New Zealanders scored a match aggregate of 565 from 154.5 overs, thanks to hundreds from Harris and Murray and a brilliant 96 from Parore. De Groen advanced his claim to be the support seamer in the Test team with seven wickets in the match, and young spinners Hart and Thomson took eight between them on the final day, to hold off a home charge which fell only 24 short of a target of 348 in less than five hours.

Close of play: First day, Griqualand West 41-2 (M. I. Gidley 9*, M. Michau 0*); Second day, New Zealanders 173-1 (D. J. Murray 91*, A. C. Parore 38*).

New Zealanders

D. J. Murray run out	63	– c Burger b Page	109
B. R. Hartland c Koster b McLaren	14	– c Burger b McLaren	32
A. C. Parore c Michau b McLaren	8	– st Burger b Viljoen	96
C. Z. Harris not out	110		
*K. R. Rutherford c McLaren b Page	50		
S. A. Thomson run out	20	– (4) not out	30
†L. K. Germen not out	1		
B 6, l-b 1, n-b 12	19	B 6, l-b 2, w 1, n-b 4	13
1/58 2/70 3/130	(5 wkts. dec.) 285	1/85 2/204	(3 wkts. dec.) 280
4/203 5/256		3/280	

M. N. Hart, M. L. Su'a, C. Pringle and R. P. de Groen did not bat.

Bowling: *First Innings*—van Troost 9-0-29-0; Swanepoel 16-4-58-0; Page 16-6-33-1; McLaren 11-4-43-2; Gidley 22-5-66-0; Michau 8-0-49-0. *Second Innings*—van Troost 8-2-11-0; Swanepoel 15-0-77-0; Page 11-3-38-1; McLaren 10-1-42-1; Gidley 24-4-72-0; Viljoen 4.5-0-32-1.

Griqualand West

W. E. Schonegevel lbw b Su'a	2	– b Thomson	32
M. I. Gidley lbw b Su'a	9	– c Rutherford b Hart	34
F. C. Brooker lbw b de Groen	23	– c and b Hart	27
M. Michau c Hartland b de Groen	3	– c Su'a b Thomson	95
R. A. Koster c Hart b de Groen	19	– lbw b Thomson	21
*H. A. Page c Germon b de Groen	85	– c Harris b de Groen	72
F. J. J. Viljoen c Parore b Thomson	40	– not out	26
P. McLaren c Parore b de Groen	5	– c and b Thomson	9
†J. Burger lbw b Thomson	3	– (10) lbw b de Groen	1
A. J. Swanepoel not out	2	– (11) b Hart	0
A. P. van Troost st Germon b Thomson	13	– (9) b Thomson	0
B 4, l-b 7, w 1, n-b 2	14	L-b 4, w 1, n-b 2	7

1/2 2/41 3/41 4/51 5/64   218   1/47 2/88 3/99 4/131 5/278   324
6/172 7/190 8/199 9/203   6/295 7/311 8/311 9/314

Bowling: *First Innings*—Su'a 16-5-43-2; Pringle 6-4-6-0; Hart 12-1-64-0; de Groen 21-10-34-5; Thomson 14.1-2-60-3. *Second Innings*—Su'a 9-3-35-0; de Groen 16-1-68-2; Harris 8-0-25-0; Thomson 25-3-101-5; Hart 19.3-2-91-3.

Umpires: R. E. Koertzen and C. J. Mitchley.

ORANGE FREE STATE v NEW ZEALANDERS

At Bloemfontein, November 19, 20, 21, 22. Orange Free State won by two wickets. Toss: New Zealanders.

A benign pitch at Springbok Park yielded 1,547 runs, 23 wickets, three declarations and a thrilling finish, with Free State racing to 383 inside 84 overs. Crowe batted brilliantly for 213 runs in the match, including his 68th first-class hundred. In the first innings, he put on 172 with Young, who hit a solid 111; Parore, with a spectacular unbeaten 127, and Harris then added 201 on the way to New Zealand's biggest ever total on South African soil. Their bowling was less satisfactory; though Harris had a hat-trick in the first innings, the score was 325 for two beforehand and Steyn had scored 157. Pace bowler Su'a conceded 108 twice and only Nash stood up to Wilkinson and Boje on the last day. Still, at 252 for six, Free State looked beaten. But Cronje, from No. 8, steered them home with five balls to spare.

Close of play: First day, New Zealanders 409-5 (C. Z. Harris 50*, A. C. Parore 50*); Second day, Orange Free State 184-0 (J. M. Arthur 81*, P. J. R. Steyn 92*); Third day, New Zealanders 140-3 (M. D. Crowe 66*, C. Z. Harris 28*).

New Zealanders

B. R. Hartland lbw b Parsons	28	– c Liebenberg b Pretorius	5
B. A. Young c Radley b Pretorius	111		
S. P. Fleming c Parsons b Pretorius	10	– c Parsons b Pretorius	17
M. D. Crowe c Cronje b Pretorius	89	– (2) not out	124
*K. R. Rutherford c Craven b Pretorius	59	– (4) c Venter b Boje	7
C. Z. Harris run out	95	– (5) not out	62
†A. C. Parore not out	127		
D. J. Nash b Pretorius	0		
B 5, l-b 7, n-b 7	19	B 8, l-b 5, n-b 6	19

1/50 2/77 3/249 4/254 5/331   (7 wkts dec.) 538   1/19 2/46 3/68   (3 wkts dec.) 234
6/532 7/538

R. P. de Groen, S. B. Doull and M. L. Su'a did not bat.

Bowling: *First Innings*—Pretorius 38.1-4-182-5; Parsons 28-10-74-1; Cronje 25-8-73-0; Boje 34-6-96-0; Venter 17-0-101-0. *Second Innings*—Pretorius 15-1-56-2; Parsons 5-1-17-0; Boje 24-9-99-1; Venter 13-3-47-0; Cronje 1-0-2-0.

Orange Free State

J. M. Arthur lbw b Doull	83	– lbw b Nash	85
P. J. R. Steyn c and b Harris	157	– run out	28
*W. J. Cronje lbw b Doull	56	– (8) not out	44
J. F. Venter not out	55	– (5) c Parore b Nash	13
L. J. Wilkinson c Rutherford b Harris	0	– (4) lbw b Su'a	89
G. F. J. Liebenberg c Fleming b Harris	0	– (3) c Hartland b Su'a	9
C. F. Craven not out	12	– (6) c Fleming b Nash	10
N. Boje (did not bat)		– (7) c Fleming b Nash	66
†P. J. L. Radley (did not bat)		– b Harris	4
G. J. Parsons (did not bat)		– not out	8
B 12, l-b 10, n-b 7	29	B 7, l-b 17, w 1, n-b 2	27

1/190 2/309 3/325 4/325 5/325   (5 wkts. dec.) 392   1/39 2/56 3/202 4/229   (8 wkts) 383
                                                         5/249 6/252 7/355 8/360

N. W. Pretorius did not bat.

Bowling: *First Innings*—Nash 26–11–51–0; Doull 24–9–64–2; de Groen 29–7–76–0; Su'a 21–3–108–0; Crowe 4–1–16–0; Harris 25–5–55–3. *Second Innings*—Nash 21–5–83–4; Doull 15.1–1–56–0; Su'a 18–1–108–2; de Groen 11–2–41–0; Harris 18–1–71–1.

Umpires: K. E. Liebenberg and W. J. Wilson.

SOUTH AFRICA v NEW ZEALAND

First Test Match

At Johannesburg, November 25, 26, 27, 28, 29. New Zealand won by 137 runs. Toss: New Zealand. Test debut: D. J. Murray.

New Zealand's convincing win stunned South Africa, who were playing their first home Test without Kepler Wessels since their readmission to world cricket. His successor as captain, Cronje, led the pursuit of 327 in four and a half sessions, with 62, but had minimal support from the middle order. The South Africans crumbled on the final morning on a worn pitch. The game was full of twists and turns, with New Zealand's first-innings 411 eventually decisive. Both sides distrusted the pitch but it played well enough until the fourth day, when the cracks visible from the start had widened enough to help the faster bowlers.

New Zealand could have lost several wickets on the first morning, with de Villiers particularly unlucky. Fleming, who batted frenetically, was dropped at fine leg and played and missed many times before de Villiers finally bowled him after lunch. Crowe, displaying his class, and Rutherford took the innings to a healthy 218 for three. Rutherford had just hit Eksteen for six, but the next ball was bravely tossed up and was well held by Cronje at mid-off. Early next day, Crowe was lbw to Snell for 83 and Parore and Hart soon followed; 280 for seven looked like a waste of batting first, especially as South Africa were without the injured Donald. But Thomson held the tail together in a combative 84 with 15 fours, mostly off the back foot, and Doull and de Groen shared a tenth-wicket stand of 57. That gave New Zealand a commanding 411.

South Africa were 38 for three within an hour, with Hudson first to go. Controversially, he walked for a catch by Parore which, television showed, had bounced. Cullinan's 58 started a recovery which Richardson continued. Batting with a guard on his broken right thumb, he scored 93 out of 132 added in his three hours at the wicket, and South Africa avoided the follow-on. Crowe had some consolation for missing his hundred when he caught Snell and surpassed Jeremy Coney's New Zealand record of 64 Test catches.

De Villiers bowled brilliantly when New Zealand resumed, 132 ahead. He trapped debutant Darrin Murray first ball, then, after changing ends, dismissed Crowe, Rutherford and Young in nine balls, reducing them to 34 for five. Thomson and Parore held firm and on the fourth day extended their partnership to 69. With useful contributions from Hart and Nash, a total of 194 left South Africa needing 327 on a wearing pitch.

Even though New Zealand's strike bowler, Nash, suffered a side strain which was to end his tour, Doull took four wickets and left-arm spinner Hart shrewdly used the rough from over the wicket to gain a Test-best five for 77. South Africa, who began the final day 198 behind with eight wickets standing, lost their last seven for 39 before lunch. Doull's match figures of six for 103, plus 45 runs without being dismissed, earned him the match award.

Man of the Match: S. B. Doull.

Close of play: First day, New Zealand 242-4 (M. D. Crowe 81*, S. A. Thomson 5*); Second day, South Africa 109-4 (D. J. Cullinan 35*, J. N. Rhodes 23*); Third day, New Zealand 81-5 (S. A. Thomson 14*, A. C. Parore 32*); Fourth day, South Africa 128-2 (B. M. McMillan 42*, W. J. Cronje 34*).

New Zealand

B. A. Young c McMillan b Snell	7	– (2) c Richardson b de Villiers	18
D. J. Murray c Richardson b de Villiers	25	– (1) lbw b de Villiers	0
S. P. Fleming b de Villiers	48	– c Richardson b Matthews	15
M. D. Crowe lbw b Snell	83	– b de Villiers	0
*K. R. Rutherford c Cronje b Eksteen	68	– c McMillan b de Villiers	0
S. A. Thomson c Matthews	84	– b Snell	29
†A. C. Parore c McMillan b Matthews	13	– c Richardson b Matthews	49
M. N. Hart c Richardson b Matthews	0	– b Matthews	34
D. J. Nash c Hudson b Eksteen	18	– c Richardson b Matthews	20
S. B. Doull not out	31	– not out	14
R. P. de Groen b Snell	26	– b Matthews	0
L-b 5, w 2, n-b 1	8	B 9, l-b 4, w 1	15
	411		**194**

1/7 (1) 2/79 (3) 3/92 (2) 4/218 (5)   1/0 (1) 2/32 (3) 3/33 (4)
5/249 (4) 6/280 (7) 7/280 (8)   4/33 (5) 5/34 (2) 6/103 (7)
8/354 (6) 9/354 (9) 10/411 (11)   7/130 (6) 8/168 (8)
                                          9/190 (9) 10/194 (11)

Bowling: *First Innings*—de Villiers 34-8-78-2; Snell 33.5-9-112-3; Matthews 28-3-98-3; McMillan 24-8-56-0; Eksteen 23.10-49-2; Cronje 3-0-13-0. *Second Innings*—de Villiers 23.9-52-4; Snell 16-5-54-1; Matthews 19-9-42-5; Eksteen 14-5-32-0; McMillan 2-1-1-0; Cronje 1-1-0-0.

South Africa

A. C. Hudson c Parore b Nash	10	– lbw b Doull	2
G. Kirsten c Crowe b de Groen	9	– lbw b Hart	33
B. M. McMillan c Murray b Nash	5	– lbw b Doull	42
*W. J. Cronje lbw b de Groen	20	– c Parore b de Groen	62
D. J. Cullinan c Parore b Doull	58	– c Crowe b Doull	12
J. N. Rhodes lbw b Doull	37	– lbw b Doull	0
†D. J. Richardson lbw b Nash	93	– c and b Hart	6
R. P. Snell c Crowe b Hart	16	– c Doull b Hart	1
C. R. Matthews c Crowe b Hart	4	– b Hart	6
C. E. Eksteen c Fleming b Hart	9	– b Hart	0
P. S. de Villiers not out	6	– not out	1
B 6, l-b 6	12	B 17, l-b 6, w 1	24
	279		**189**

1/20 (1) 2/28 (2) 3/38 (3) 4/73 (4)   1/9 (1) 2/70 (2) 3/130 (3)
5/147 (5) 6/148 (6) 7/173 (8)   4/150 (5) 5/150 (6) 6/167 (7)
8/197 (9) 9/254 (10) 10/279 (7)   7/175 (8) 8/180 (4)
                                          9/184 (9) 10/189 (10)

Bowling: *First Innings*—Nash 24-6-81-3; Doull 21-6-70-2; de Groen 21-2-59-2; Hart 26-7-57-3. *Second Innings*—Nash 8-2-17-0; Doull 15-5-33-4; Hart 32.4-7-77-5; de Groen 12-4-21-1; Thomson 11-6-18-0.

Umpires: I. D. Robinson (Zimbabwe) and K. E. Liebenberg.
Referee: P. J. P. Burge (Australia).

†At Soweto, December 1. New Zealanders won by nine runs. Toss: New Zealanders. New Zealanders 252 for six (50 overs) (B. R. Hartland 81, B. A. Young 54, M. D. Crowe 50 not out, S. A. Thomson 33); Transvaal Invitation XI 243 for eight (50 overs) (M. W. Rushmere 80, S. D. Jack 54; C. Pringle three for 52).

†At Johannesburg, December 3. Transvaal won by eight wickets. Toss: Transvaal. New Zealanders 214 (49.1 overs) (A. C. Parore 36, K. R. Rutherford 39, C. Z. Harris 33; D. R. Laing three for 36); Transvaal 216 for two (41 overs) (S. D. Jack 107, M. W. Rushmere 47).

New Zealand's matches v South Africa, Pakistan and Sri Lanka in the Mandela Trophy (December 6–December 19) may be found in that section.

BOLAND v NEW ZEALANDERS

At Paarl, December 21, 22. Drawn. Toss: Boland.

After 22 wickets fell on the first day, the umpires abandoned the match after one over, bowled by Doull, next morning when opener Wylie was struck on the helmet before being caught. They said the pitch's "excessive and unpredictable bounce" posed a danger to the players. Only Fleming and Young reached double figures for the tourists, whose first-innings total of 86 was still three more than Boland managed. After the Mandela Trophy, the New Zealanders badly needed first-class practice before the Second Test and their management lodged an official protest to the United Cricket Board. They, in turn, warned the provincial authorities that, unless the Boland Park pitches improved, future fixtures would be taken away.

Close of play: First day, Boland 31-2 (A. R. Wylie 11*, J. B. Commins 15*).

Boland

L. D. Ferreira c Young b Morrison	0	– lbw b Nash	2
A. R. Wylie c Germon b Pringle	8	– c Germon b Doull	11
M. S. Nackerdien b Morrison	0	– c Murray b Pringle	1
*J. B. Commins lbw b Doull	11	– not out	15
K. M. Curran b Morrison	21	– not out	0
W. S. Truter c Germon b Pringle	20		
M. S. Bredell b Nash	5		
†L-M. Germishuys not out	3		
M. Erasmus c sub (C. Z. Harris) b Pringle	0		
H. S. Williams b Nash	4		
C. M. Willoughby run out	0		
L-b 11	11	L-b 2	2
	83	**(3 wkts)**	**31**

1/0 2/0 3/22 4/22 5/58   1/2 2/3 3/31
6/71 7/73 8/77 9/83

Bowling: *First Innings*—Morrison 10–3–21–3; Nash 13.2–8–16–2; Doull 6–0–18–1; Pringle 12–5–17–3. *Second Innings*—Nash 5–1–6–1; Pringle 5–2–12–1; Doull 3–2–5–1; Hart 2–1–6–0.

New Zealanders

B. A. Young c Wylie b Erasmus	10	D. J. Nash c Germishuys b Curran	0
D. J. Murray c Germishuys b Willoughby	4	S. B. Doull c Truter b Erasmus	5
S. P. Fleming b Erasmus	30	D. K. Morrison not out	2
B. R. Hartland lbw b Erasmus	0	C. Pringle b Curran	0
†L. K. Germon lbw b Erasmus	0	B 11, l-b 8, w 1, n-b 1	21
*K. R. Rutherford c and b Curran	5		
M. N. Hart c and b Erasmus	9	1/23 2/41 3/51 4/53 5/64	**86**
		6/76 7/79 8/84 9/86	

Bowling: Willoughby 8–4–20–1; Williams 11–3–17–0; Erasmus 9–2–22–6; Curran 4.5–0–8–3.

Umpires: B. G. Jerling and C. J. Mitchley.

SOUTH AFRICA v NEW ZEALAND

Second Test Match

At Durban, December 26, 27, 28, 29, 30. South Africa won by eight wickets. Toss: New Zealand. Test debuts: J. B. Commins, S. D. Jack.

South Africa squared the series in a low-scoring match through superior application in all departments, while New Zealand's irresponsible batting cost them dear. The first three innings totalled only 603, South Africa securing a priceless first-innings lead of 41, but too many tourists played injudicious shots, with Crowe and Rutherford most culpable.

Fast bowler Steven Jack and Boland captain John Commins supplanted Snell and Eksteen; Morrison, recently flown in, and Pringle replaced de Groen and the injured Nash. Jack made a fine debut, bowling Young for two and catching Fleming at long leg off de Villiers, when he attempted the first ill-advised hook of the game. De Villiers returned the favour when Crowe fell into the leg-side trap, hooking Jack. When Rutherford pulled a short delivery to mid-wicket and Murray was caught behind, New Zealand were 66 for five. Again, Thomson counter-attacked; he punished anything short and his first seven scoring

SLOWEST FIFTIES IN TEST CRICKET

Minutes	Balls		
357	350	T. E. Bailey, England v Australia at Brisbane	1958-59
350	236	C. J. Tavaré, England v Pakistan at Lord's	1982
333	**229**	**B. A. Young, New Zealand v South Africa at Durban**	**1994-95**
326		S. M. Gavaskar, India v Sri Lanka at Colombo (SSC)	1985-86
318	209	Ramiz Raja, Pakistan v West Indies at Karachi	1986-87
316		C. P. S. Chauhan, India v Pakistan at Kanpur	1979-80
315		Shoaib Mohammad, Pakistan v Zimbabwe at Lahore	1993-94
313		D. J. McGlew, South Africa v Australia at Johannesburg ..	1957-58
312	212	J. J. Crowe, New Zealand v Sri Lanka at Colombo (CCC) ..	1986-87

strokes included five fours and a six. But he could not break the pace attack's grip and a burst from McMillan – three wickets in 19 balls – made it 114 for eight. Morrison defended stoutly for 140 minutes and 66 was added before Thomson was brilliantly caught by Kirsten, off another mis-hook, for 82.

The unfortunate Hudson edged to slip but South Africa then batted solidly until Doull had Cullinan lbw and Commins out hooking. This prompted a collapse from 110 for two to 182 for nine. Morrison took three in five overs and worried everyone with his movement off the pitch from an impeccable off-stump line. But Richardson remained unbeaten for two and a half hours and, with de Villiers's support in a last-wicket stand of 44, put South Africa in the lead.

New Zealand's second innings started disastrously, with Murray lbw and Rutherford pulling to mid-wicket – just as he had in the first innings. They never recovered, despite an heroic 51 from Young. Crowe became New Zealand's leading Test scorer, passing John Wright's 5,334 when four, but he added only six more. Young's half-century was the third-slowest in Test history at 333 minutes, behind Chris Tavaré's 350 against Pakistan in 1982, and Trevor Bailey's 357 at Brisbane in 1958-59. But once McMillan had him caught at gully and Cronje bowled Thomson with a break break-back off a crack, the last six went for 18. Parore's run-out was bizarre. After a defensive stroke, he remained a yard out of his crease; Cronje made a token throw at the stumps and television showed that Parore failed to ground his bat in time.

Chasing 152, South Africa shrugged off the loss of Hudson, whose run of 56 in eight Test innings cost him his place, and Kirsten led them to victory with an unbeaten 66. De Villiers was the home team's hero, with match figures of 55.2–17–120–8, but their collective spirit and aggression had been too much for New Zealand, whose decline now looked terminal.

Man of the Match: P. S. de Villiers.

Close of play: First day, New Zealand 130-8 (S. A. Thomson 53*, D. K. Morrison 0*); Second day, South Africa 122-5 (W. J. Cronje 10*, B. M. McMillan 0*); Third day, New Zealand 48-3 (B. A. Young 18*, S. P. Fleming 10*); Fourth day, South Africa 41-1 (G. Kirsten 19*, J. B. Commins 10*).

New Zealand

B. A. Young b Jack	2	– (2) c Cullinan b McMillan	51
D. J. Murray b Richardson b de Villiers	38	– (1) lbw b de Villiers	0
S. P. Fleming c Jack b de Villiers	4	– (5) c Richardson b Jack	31
M. D. Crowe c de Villiers b Jack	18	– c Richardson b McMillan	10
*K. R. Rutherford c Commins b de Villiers	0	– (3) c Commins b McMillan	6
S. A. Thomson c Kirsten b de Villiers	82	– b Cronje	35
†A. C. Parore c Kirsten b McMillan	5	– run out	1
M. N. Hart c Cronje b McMillan	6	– c Richardson b Kirsten	6
S. B. Doull c Richardson b McMillan	0	– c Richardson b de Villiers	19
D. K. Morrison not out	24	– c McMillan b de Villiers	12
C. Pringle c Kirsten b de Villiers	0	– not out	6
L-b 4, n-b 3	7	L-b 11, n-b 4	15
	185		**192**

1/9 (1) 2/19 (3) 3/62 (4) 4/65 (5)   185
5/66 (2) 6/102 (7) 7/114 (8)
8/114 (9) 9/180 (6) 10/185 (11)

1/2 (1) 2/11 (3) 3/28 (4)   192
4/81 (5) 5/144 (2) 6/144 (6)
7/153 (7) 8/153 (8)
9/179 (9) 10/192 (10)

Bowling: First Innings—de Villiers 24-7-64-5; Jack 16-7-32-2; Matthews 19-11-37-0; McMillan 19-8-40-3; Cronje 4-1-8-0. *Second Innings*—de Villiers 31.2-10-56-3; Jack 15-3-45-1; McMillan 30-8-53-3; Matthews 12-3-17-0; Cronje 10-6-10-1; Kirsten 2-2-0-1.

South Africa

A. C. Hudson c Young b Morrison	8	– c Parore b Doull	6
G. Kirsten c Parore b Doull	29	– not out	66
J. B. Commins c Hart b Doull	30	– c Young b Hart	45
D. J. Cullinan lbw b Doull	34	– not out	25
*W. J. Cronje c Thomson b Morrison	19		
J. N. Rhodes c Fleming b Hart	1		
B. M. McMillan b Doull	17		
†D. J. Richardson not out	39		
C. R. Matthews c Parore b Morrison	7		
S. D. Jack c Crowe b Morrison	0		
P. S. de Villiers c Fleming b Doull	28		
L-b 6, n-b 8	14	L-b 9, n-b 2	11
	226		**153**

1/13 (1) 2/61 (2) 3/110 (4) 4/111 (3)   226
5/122 (6) 6/141 (5) 7/168 (7)
8/182 (9) 9/182 (10) 10/226 (11)

1/20 (1) 2/117 (3)   (2 wkts) 153

Bowling: First Innings—Morrison 25-4-70-4; Doull 29.5-9-73-5; Pringle 15-5-23-0; Hart 17-2-54-1. *Second Innings*—Doull 15-5-26-1; Morrison 15-1-56-0; Hart 13.4-2-52-1; Thomson 2-1-10-0.

Umpires: Khizar Hayat (Pakistan) and C. J. Mitchley. Referee: P. J. P. Burge (Australia).

SOUTH AFRICA v NEW ZEALAND

Third Test Match

At Cape Town, January 2, 3, 4, 5, 6. South Africa won by seven wickets. Toss: New Zealand. Test debut: P. J. R. Steyn.

Cronje became the second Test captain, after W. G. Grace in the 1888 Ashes, to win a three-match series after going one down. Another aggressive South African performance exposed the frailties of their dispirited opponents. On a newly relaid pitch, unusually pacy for Newlands, the fast bowlers overwhelmed New Zealand, but they helped with their own destruction: Crowe, Rutherford, Parore, Young and Fleming all perished to rash hooks and pulls. That they came within 45 minutes of the draw, despite squandering at least six wickets, illustrates their careless approach throughout the later stages of a tour which started so well. Fleming, with two half-centuries at No. 7, seemed to be one of the few still competing.

On the first day, in front of over 17,000 spectators, the fiery Jack and McMillan reduced New Zealand to 96 for five. Parore fell to a second bizarre run-out: he had taken two off his second ball when his call of "wait" was blown away from Young by a cross-wind. Rutherford led the fight-back, with 56, until he pulled recklessly to mid-wicket - his most culpable dismissal of a disappointing series. Fleming and Hart kept at the task, but an eventual 288 included 30 from last man Pringle.

South Africa's debutant opener, Rudolf Steyn, played pleasantly for 38 before three wickets for off-spinner Thomson brought New Zealand back into the game. Cronje, however, survived a confident appeal and another simple chance, and completed his fourth Test century, a patient 112. He was seventh out at 325, but South Africa pushed onwards, with Richardson scoring his maiden Test hundred, batting five hours and earning a lead of 152. Though the pitch offered turn, Thomson and Hart showed their inexperience. Too often, Hart bowled negatively over the wicket into the rough outside leg stump.

New Zealand had five sessions to save the game and needed to bat for four - not impossible in still favourable conditions. Murray was unlucky to be judged lbw, another victim of variable umpiring, though Fleming was later reprieved on nine when Lambson recalled him after initially approving a catch to silly point. At 63 for one in the afternoon, the tourists were fighting back - only for Parore and Crowe to go hooking. Rutherford was then given lbw and his reactions brought a fine and a suspended two-match ban from referee Burge, for dissent both on the field and in the pavilion, in what Burge judged to be earshot of the umpires. Again, Young held the innings together, and he and Thomson were still there at the close.

But their dismissals typified New Zealand's attitude. Young's admirable resistance ended after 278 minutes in another mis-hook, falling into an obvious trap, and Thomson was run out when he posed for ten seconds outside his crease, holding a forward defensive stroke. Five minutes after lunch, they were seven down and only 21 ahead. Fleming and Doull showed much-needed application, adding 51 before de Villiers took the last three wickets in 12 deliveries. But South Africa needed a mere 88 in 42 overs; Cronje hit the winning boundary with nearly 11 overs to spare.

Man of the Match: D. J. Richardson.   *Man of the Series:* D. J. Richardson.

Close of play: First day, New Zealand 211-6 (S. P. Fleming 58*, M. N. Hart 8*); Second day, South Africa 152-3 (J. B. Commins 22*, W. J. Cronje 11*); Third day, South Africa 381-7 (D. J. Richardson 70*, C. E. Eksteen 10*); Fourth day, New Zealand 121-4 (B. A. Young 42*, S. A. Thomson 1*).

New Zealand

B. A. Young lbw b McMillan	45	- c Kirsten b McMillan	51
D. J. Murray c Kirsten b McMillan	5	- lbw b de Villiers	3
†A. C. Parore run out	2	- c Eksteen b de Villiers	34
M. D. Crowe c Richardson b Jack	18	- c Richardson b McMillan	5
*K. R. Rutherford c Kirsten b McMillan	56	- lbw b McMillan	26
S. A. Thomson b McMillan	0	- run out	16
S. P. Fleming b Jack	79	- c Richardson b de Villiers	53
M. N. Hart c Richardson b Jack	24	- c de Villiers b Jack	7
S. B. Doull c Cronje b Jack	6	- c Rhodes b de Villiers	25
D. K. Morrison not out	0	- lbw b de Villiers	1
C. Pringle b de Villiers	30	- not out	0
L-b 13, n-b 10	23	B 5, l-b 6, w 1, n-b 6	18
	288		**239**

1/17 (2) 2/19 (3) 3/61 (4) 4/95 (1)							288
5/96 (6) 6/179 (5) 7/245 (7)
8/255 (9) 9/255 (8) 10/288 (11)

1/19 (2) 2/63 (3) 3/73 (4)							239
4/115 (5) 5/131 (1) 6/154 (6)
7/173 (8) 8/224 (9)
9/230 (10) 10/239 (7)

Bowling: *First Innings*—de Villiers 28.5–7–90–1; Jack 27–7–69–4; McMillan 26–5–65–4; Cronje 5–3–8–0; Eksteen 26–10–36–0; Kirsten 2–0–7–0. *Second Innings*—de Villiers 28.1–9–61–5; Jack 19–7–50–1; McMillan 25–9–52–3; Cronje 7–3–15–0; Eksteen 31–16–46–0; Kirsten 1–0–4–0.

South Africa

G. Kirsten b Thomson	64	– lbw b Hart	25
P. J. R. Steyn lbw b Thomson	38	– c Doull b Thomson	12
J. B. Commins c Rutherford b Hart	27	– not out	10
D. J. Cullinan c Young b Thomson	5	– hit wkt b Hart	28
*W. J. Cronje c Pringle b Hart	112	– not out	14
J. N. Rhodes b Doull	18		
B. M. McMillan lbw b Pringle	18		
†D. J. Richardson c Crowe b Doull	109		
C. E. Eksteen b Hart	22		
S. D. Jack c Murray b Morrison	7		
P. S. de Villiers not out	1		
B 7, l-b 3, w 1, n-b 8	19		

1/106 (2) 2/119 (1) 3/125 (4) 4/161 (3)   **440**   1/37 (2) 2/37 (1)   (3 wkts) **89**
5/225 (6) 6/271 (7) 7/325 (5)   3/69 (4)
8/410 (9) 9/429 (10) 10/440 (8)

Bowling: *First Innings*—Morrison 34–7–100–1; Doull 34.2–12–55–2; Pringle 28–5–69–1; Hart 54–8–141–3; Thomson 31–7–65–3. *Second Innings*—Morrison 4–1–5–0; Hart 15.2–5–51–2; Thomson 12–3–33–1.

Umpires: K. T. Francis (Sri Lanka) and S. B. Lambson.
Referee: P. J. P. Burge (Australia).

CRICKETERS IN ICC ASSOCIATE MEMBER COUNTRIES

	Clubs	Players		Clubs	Players
Bangladesh	1,588	93,000	Singapore	36	1,200
Canada	502	23,904	Namibia	16	1,154
Scotland	319	17,500	Kenya	46	900
Ireland	198	9,043	East Africa	42	645
United States	410	7,130	Israel	23	600
Holland	71	6,818	Bermuda	34	530
Papua New Guinea	144	3,500	Argentina	14	500
Denmark	51	3,327	Hong Kong	37	450
United Arab Emirates	176	3,168	Malaysia	63	370
Fiji	90	1,300	Gibraltar	22	330

Figures, supplied by ICC, refer to 1994 and include both seniors and juniors. West Africa failed to provide a return.

THE ZIMBABWEANS IN AUSTRALIA, 1994-95

The Zimbabweans were invited to Australia in 1994-95 as the fourth team in the World Series tournament, which also featured England and the controversial Australia A side. As on their previous visit, for the World Cup in early 1992, the highlight was Zimbabwe's limited-overs victory over England. For three weeks, their international record against England was "played two, won two", though the return game in January made it 2-1.

The trip also featured Zimbabwe's first first-class matches in Australia, though one was lost and the other wrecked by rain. They were more successful in their one-day games, winning more than half their encounters with states and country elevens. The leading players, in both first-class and World Series programmes, were Andy Flower and his younger brother, Grant.

ZIMBABWEAN TOURING PARTY

A. Flower (Mashonaland) (*captain*), D. L. Houghton (Mashonaland) (*vice-captain*), D. H. Brain (Mashonaland), E. A. Brandes (Mashonaland Country Districts), A. D. R. Campbell (Mashonaland Country Districts), M. H. Dekker (Matabeleland), G. W. Flower (Mashonaland Under-24), W. R. James (Matabeleland), G. C. Martin (Mashonaland), S. G. Peall (Mashonaland Country Districts), D. J. Rowett (Mashonaland Under-24), P. A. Strang (Mashonaland Country Districts), H. H. Streak (Matabeleland), G. J. Whittall (Matabeleland).

I. P. Butchart (Mashonaland Country Districts) joined the party after Brandes returned home injured and Houghton for family reasons.

Coach: J. H. Hampshire.

ZIMBABWEAN TOUR RESULTS

First-class matches – Played 2: Lost 1, Drawn 1.
Loss – Queensland.
Draw – Tasmania.
One-day internationals – Played 4: Won 1, Lost 3. *Win* – England. *Losses* – Australia (2), England. *Note:* Matches against Australia A did not have international status.
Other non-first-class matches – Played 12: Won 6, Lost 6. *Wins* – Australian Cricket Academy, Western Australian Country XI, Western Australia, Victorian Country XI, New South Wales Country XI, Queensland Chairman's XI. *Losses* – Western Australian XI, South Australia, Tasmania, Australia A (2), Queensland.

Note: Matches in this section which were not first-class are signified by a dagger.

†At Kalgoorlie, November 20. Western Australian XI won by 30 runs. Toss: Western Australian XI. Western Australian XI 266 for five (50 overs) (M. R. J. Veletta 34, M. P. Lavender 74, M. W. Goodwin 52, A. C. Gilchrist 41 not out); Zimbabweans 236 (47.3 overs) (G. J. Whittall 38, E. A. Brandes 38, P. A. Strang 43; B. A. Reid three for 19).

†At Adelaide, November 23, 24, 25. Zimbabweans won by three wickets. Toss: Australian Cricket Academy. Australian Cricket Academy 271 for seven dec. (C. J. Richards 60, D. J. Marsh 100 not out, M. J. Nicholson 42) and 189 (C. J. Richards 38, I. J. Harvey 36, C. A. Glassock 48; E. A. Brandes four for 49); Zimbabweans 245 for nine dec. (A. Flower 70, G. J. Whittall 30, W. R. James 59, P. A. Strang 57; S. Lee three for 45) and 220 for seven (G. W. Flower 46, A. D. R. Campbell 32, A. Flower 78 not out; D. J. Marsh three for 72).

†At Adelaide, November 27. South Australia won by seven wickets. Toss: Zimbabweans. Zimbabweans 186 (47.5 overs) (A. D. R. Campbell 66; J. N. Gillespie four for 30); South Australia 187 for three (38.3 overs) (D. S. Lehmann 59, G. S. Blewett 56 not out).

†At Busselton, November 29. Zimbabweans won by 152 runs. Toss: Zimbabweans. Zimbabweans 269 for seven (50 overs) (A. Flower 88, A. D. R. Campbell 65, M. H. Dekker 42); Western Australian Country XI 117 (46.4 overs).

†At Perth, November 30 (day/night). Zimbabweans won by five runs. Toss: Zimbabweans. Zimbabweans 207 for nine (50 overs) (D. L. Houghton 78); Western Australia 202 for seven (50 overs) (M. P. Lavender 58, J. L. Langer 40, T. M. Moody 36; H. H. Streak three for 48).

Zimbabwe's matches v Australia, Australia A and England in the Benson and Hedges World Series (December 2–January 7) may be found in that section.

†At Launceston, December 17. Tasmania won by seven wickets. Toss: Zimbabweans. Zimbabweans 159 (49.5 overs) (G. J. Whittall 62); Tasmania 162 for three (36 overs) (J. Cox 57, M. J. Di Venuto 36, D. C. Boon 31 not out).

TASMANIA v ZIMBABWEANS

At Devonport, December 18, 19, 20. Drawn. Toss: Zimbabweans.

The youngest Sheffield Shield state hosted the youngest Test nation for Zimbabwe's first-class debut in Australia. But the match was ruined by rain, which ended the second day at 2.15 p.m. and permitted no play before lunch on the final day. Reciprocal declarations left the Zimbabweans a target of 253 in 49 overs. There was little prospect of a result, though the Flower brothers had time to make half-centuries. On the first day, the tourists' seamers reduced Tasmania to 122 for five before Tucker and Young shared an unbeaten stand of 135.

Close of play: First day, Zimbabweans 30-0 (G. W. Flower 11*, M. H. Dekker 9*); Second day, Zimbabweans 141-3 (A. D. R. Campbell 0*, A. Flower 0*).

Tasmania

D. F. Hills c Dekker b Brain	50	– (2) c Whittall b Streak	4
J. Cox c Dekker b Brain	18	– (1) not out	63
M. J. Di Venuto c A. Flower b Martin	16	– c Campbell b Whittall	21
*D. C. Boon c A. Flower b Streak	11		
R. T. Ponting c Butchart b Streak	2	– (4) st A. Flower b Peall	18
R. J. Tucker not out	78		
S. Young not out	41		
†M. N. Atkinson (did not bat)	– (5) not out		16
L-b 7, w 2, n-b 32	41	B 1, l-b 3, w 2, n-b 8	14

1/46 2/85 3/105 4/109 5/122   (5 wkts dec.) 257   1/12 2/65 3/96   (3 wkts dec.) 136

C. R. Miller, C. D. Matthews and B. A. Robinson did not bat.

Bowling: *First Innings*—Brain 20-7-49-2; Streak 17-2-55-2; Martin 14-3-50-1; Whittall 13-2-48-0; Peall 5-0-15-0; Butchart 2-0-14-0; Strang 3-1-19-0. *Second Innings*—Brain 5-1-20-0; Streak 7-3-11-1; Martin 6-2-20-0; Whittall 5-0-37-1; Peall 4-0-22-1; Butchart 4-0-22-0.

Zimbabweans

G. W. Flower c Young b Robinson	59	– (2) c and b Miller	63
M. H. Dekker c Tucker b Miller	41	– (1) b Miller	22
G. J. Whittall lbw b Boon	24	– c Matthews b Robinson	6
A. D. R. Campbell not out	0	– c Tucker b Miller	1
*†A. Flower not out	0	– not out	53
I. P. Butchart (did not bat)		– b Miller	2
P. A. Strang (did not bat)		– not out	1
B 1, l-b 5, w 1, n-b 10	17	L-b 4, w 2, n-b 2	8

1/79 2/134 3/141   (3 wkts dec.) 141   1/49 2/60 3/61   (5 wkts) 156
                                                     4/146 5/148

G. C. Martin, H. H. Streak, S. G. Peall and D. H. Brain did not bat.

Bowling: *First Innings*—Matthews 10-3-23-0; Miller 14-2-32-1; Young 10-2-25-0; Robinson 9-2-30-1; Tucker 4-0-9-0; Boon 6.4-1-16-1. *Second Innings*—Matthews 3-1-11-0; Miller 14-5-35-4; Robinson 10-1-51-1; Young 7-0-24-0; Tucker 8-1-31-0.

Umpires: S. A. Bucknor (West Indies) and T. R. Hogarth.

†At Yea, December 22. Zimbabweans won by 61 runs. Toss: Victorian Country XI. Zimbabweans 228 for five (50 overs) (G. W. Flower 83, G. J. Whittall 33); Victorian Country XI 167 for five (50 overs) (D. Smith 36, B. Heath 40).

†At Dubbo, December 26 (day/night). Zimbabweans won by 82 runs. Toss: Zimbabweans. Zimbabweans 277 for five (50 overs) (G. W. Flower 91, A. Flower 114); New South Wales Country XI 195 for nine (50 overs) (P. Stanbridge 42, M. Garoni 38; P. A. Strang three for 25).

QUEENSLAND v ZIMBABWEANS

At Maryborough, December 29, 30, 31. Queensland won by four wickets. Toss: Zimbabweans.

The Zimbabweans effectively lost the game in the first over of their second innings, when Kasprowicz sent back Dekker, Whittall and Campbell for ducks. They struggled into three figures but Queensland knocked off 201 without trouble. Acting-captain Hayden played another dominant innings, with an unbeaten 90, to follow 64, with ten fours and a six, first time round. Streak, with a strained thigh muscle, did not bowl on the final day. The match had started well for the tourists, when Andy Flower elected to bat and scored a career-best 139, with 23 fours and a six. This match made Newtown Oval the 39th first-class venue in Australia.

Close of play: First day, Queensland 33-1 (M. P. Mott 10*, M. L. Love 2*); Second day, Zimbabweans 73-6 (A. Flower 24*, P. A. Strang 7*).

Zimbabweans

M. H. Dekker c Mott b Rackemann	52	– b Kasprowicz	0
G. W. Flower b Jackson	38	– c Symonds b Jackson	19
G. J. Whittall b Rackemann	0	– c Love b Kasprowicz	0
A. D. R. Campbell b Kasprowicz	9	– lbw b Kasprowicz	0
*A. Flower not out	139	– (7) c Love b Kasprowicz	31
†W. R. James c Seccombe b Kasprowicz	4	– (5) lbw b Tazelaar	14
G. C. Martin c Tazelaar b Jackson	11	– (6) lbw b Tazelaar	4
P. A. Strang not out	37	– not out	29
H. H. Streak (did not bat)		– b Tazelaar	6
S. G. Peall (did not bat)		– b Rackemann	11
D. H. Brain (did not bat)		– c Hayden b Rackemann	0
L-b 1, w 1, n-b 2	4	L-b 9, n-b 6	15

1/82 2/90 3/90 4/114   (6 wkts dec.) 294   1/0 2/0 3/0 4/23 5/27   129
5/122 6/144   6/56 7/85 8/98 9/121

Bowling: *First Innings*—Kasprowicz 19.2-8-54-2; Tazelaar 16-3-67-0; Rackemann 11-1-34-2; Jackson 22-4-84-2; Symonds 4-0-24-0; Maher 4-0-30-0. *Second Innings*—Kasprowicz 17-10-27-4; Tazelaar 16-6-36-3; Jackson 11-5-16-1; Rackemann 9.1-3-32-2; Hayden 3-1-9-0.

Queensland

T. J. Barsby run out	18 – c Martin b Brain	13
M. P. Mott c Dekker b Strang	55 – c A. Flower b Whittall	11
M. L. Love c Dekker b Brain.................	9 – c and b Peall	55
*M. L. Hayden c James b Whittall	64 – not out........................	90
J. P. Maher not out......................	37 – st James b Peall	7
A. Symonds c Dekker b Brain	35 – (7) c James b Peall.............	3
†W. A. Seccombe (did not bat)	– (6) c James b Peall.............	7
M. S. Kasprowicz (did not bat)	– not out..........................	6
L-b 1, n-b 4	5	L-b 4, w 1, n-b 4........ 9

1/19 2/46 3/145   (5 wkts dec.) 223   1/16 2/42 3/131   (6 wkts) 201
4/161 5/223   4/158 5/186 6/194

D. Tazelaar, C. G. Rackemann and P. W. Jackson did not bat.

Bowling: *First Innings*—Brain 8.5-2-45-2; Streak 9-2-32-0; Strang 11-2-45-1; Peall 10-0-44-0; Martin 8-4-19-0; Whittall 9-2-37-1. *Second Innings*—Brain 5-2-22-1; Martin 4-1-9-0; Peall 19-4-52-4; Strang 18.4-0-73-0; Whittall 8-1-20-1; Dekker 4-0-21-0.

Umpires: D. J. Harper and A. J. McQuillan.

†At Bundaberg, January 1. Zimbabweans won by one wicket. Toss: Queensland Chairman's XI. Queensland Chairman's XI 245 for seven (50 overs) (M. P. Mott 45, M. L. Love 79, M. L. Hayden 52); Zimbabweans 246 for nine (49.2 overs) (A. D. R. Campbell 129 not out, I. P. Butchart 87; M. S. Kasprowicz three for 46, D. Tazelaar three for 23).

†At Beenleigh, January 4. Queensland won by four wickets. Toss: Queensland. Zimbabweans 165 (47.5 overs) (A. Flower 45; G. J. Rowell three for 31, M. S. Kasprowicz four for 34, S. G. Law three for 33); Queensland 166 for six (42 overs) (M. L. Hayden 51, M. L. Love 48).

THE PAKISTANIS IN SOUTH AFRICA
AND ZIMBABWE, 1994-95

By QAMAR AHMED

Pakistan will not remember their three-month tour of South Africa and Zimbabwe fondly. They arrived with good reason to be confident, after winning a gruelling Test series against a strong Australian side and beating South Africa three times out of three in a one-day triangular series. At first, that form carried over into the four-nation limited-overs Mandela Trophy, in which they won five of their six qualifying matches. But as the tour progressed, they declined not only in form, but in their overall make-up, their discipline and their disposition. They were heavily beaten in two first-class games against Western Province and Natal, lost both legs of the one-day final and then went down to a crushing 324-run defeat in their inaugural Test with South Africa. Hansie Cronje led his team to their third successive Test win, Fanie de Villiers took ten wickets and scored fifty, while Brian McMillan made a maiden Test century.

Pakistan's embarrassment continued on arrival in Zimbabwe. They were beaten by an innings inside four days, the first ever Test victory for the newest cricket nation, after the Flower brothers shared a stand of 269 for the fourth wicket and Heath Streak took nine for 105 in the match. Though Pakistan came back to win the three-Test series 2-1, only the third such recovery in history, off the field the tour had descended into controversy and chaos. There were persistent rumours that some of the party were being paid by bookmakers to throw matches and the players were reported to have sworn their innocence on the Koran. During the Zimbabwean leg of the tour, it was revealed that Australians Shane Warne and Tim May had alleged that Pakistan captain Salim Malik offered them huge sums of money to throw their Test in Karachi. Malik continued to court controversy by accusing Zimbabwean umpire Ian Robinson of applying sweat to one side of the ball during the Third Test in Harare. On his return to Pakistan, he was sacked as captain and suspended from the game while the board asked him to answer the charges of bribery.

Meanwhile, during the one-day series with Zimbabwe, which was shared 1-1 after the first match was tied, the vice-captain and wicket-keeper Rashid Latif and batsman Basit Ali pulled out, announcing their retirement from international cricket. They said they no longer enjoyed playing. Though they recanted three months later, their move seemed to confirm persistent rumours of rifts inside the squad, especially after Malik's unexpected decision to field first in both legs of the Mandela Trophy final, when the dressing-room consensus was believed to favour batting.

The atmosphere of the Zimbabwean tour turned sour, in marked contrast to their series in Pakistan the previous year, and referee Jackie Hendriks was kept busy. The ill feeling began in the first game, with a President's XI, when openers Aamir Sohail and Saeed Anwar accused fast bowler Henry Olonga of throwing, and he was no-balled by local umpire Ahmed Esat. Olonga, who was born in Zambia to a Kenyan father and a Zimbabwean mother, subsequently made history as the first non-white player to appear for Zimbabwe. But he made more history when he was no-balled again for throwing in the First Test and had to withdraw from the rest of the series with a side strain. In the Second Test, the Zimbabweans accused the Pakistanis of ball-tampering and sledging; Wasim Akram was reprimanded for snatching his cap from umpire Quentin Goosen after an lbw appeal was turned down, and David Houghton was later fined for saying the umpiring was weak. Malik was fined half his match fee and given a suspended ban while Aamir Sohail was reprimanded for their allegations against umpire Robinson in the Third Test. In the one-day series, Bryan Strang was cautioned for pointing a batsman back to the pavilion.

Not all Pakistan's troubles were of their own making. Their two main strike bowlers, Waqar Younis and Wasim Akram, were in harness together for only a few days. Wasim arrived in South Africa just before the final, having needed medical treatment for a sinus problem in England. Waqar withdrew from the Test in Johannesburg shortly before the start, with back pains that were eventually diagnosed as a stress fracture. He was replaced by Aamir Nazir, who arrived in the country an hour before the match started. Latif also withdrew from the Test complaining of back trouble. There was some dissatisfaction with their South African itinerary, which took up nearly 60 days, though they played on only 24, including one-day games against Nicky Oppenheimer's XI and in the townships, as part of the United Cricket Board's development programme. In Zimbabwe, local umpires lacked experience at top level and did make mistakes.

Pakistan's most encouraging performances came from Inzamam-ul-Haq, who repeatedly rallied their batting after frequent collapses. He was only five short of a deserved century in the second innings at Johannesburg, when they were all out for 165 half an hour into the final day. He did score 101 in Harare and averaged 73.40 in the Zimbabwean Tests and 60.33 in all first-class matches. His most consistent batting support came from Ijaz Ahmed. Malik reached 99 in the Johannesburg Test but it was his only half-century of the tour. Wasim bowled Pakistan to victory in Bulawayo, and Nazir and Aqib Javed played an important role in winning the decisive Third Test. Rightly, however, Inzamam was named as Man of the Series in Zimbabwe, along with Streak, the home team's most consistent player, who took 22 wickets at 13.54.

PAKISTANI TOURING PARTY

Salim Malik (Lahore/Habib Bank) (*captain*), Rashid Latif (Karachi/United Bank) (*vice-captain*), Aamir Sohail (Lahore/Habib Bank), Akram Raza (Sargodha/Habib Bank), Aqib Javed (Islamabad/Allied Bank), Asif Mujtaba (Karachi/PIA), Ata-ur-Rehman (Lahore), Basit Ali (Karachi/United Bank), Ijaz Ahmed (Lahore), Inzamam-ul-Haq (Multan/United Bank), Kabir Khan (Peshawar), Manzoor Elahi (ADBP), Moin Khan (Karachi/PIA), Saeed Anwar (Karachi/ADBP), Shakeel Ahmed (Islamabad/Habib Bank), Waqar Younis (Multan/United Bank), Wasim Akram (Lahore/PIA).

Wasim missed the first leg of the South African tour with sinus trouble. Aamir Nazir (Islamabad/Allied Bank) joined the tour party when Waqar Younis returned home injured.

Tour manager: Intikhab Alam.

PAKISTANI TOURING RESULTS

Test matches – Played 4: Won 2, Lost 2.
First-class matches – Played 7: Won 3, Lost 4.
Wins – Zimbabwe (2), ZCU President's XI.
Losses – South Africa, Zimbabwe, Western Province, Natal.
One-day internationals – Played 11: Won 6, Lost 4, Tied 1. *Wins* – Sri Lanka (2), New Zealand (2), South Africa, Zimbabwe. *Losses* – South Africa (3), Zimbabwe. *Tie* – Zimbabwe.
Other non-first-class matches – Played 3: Won 2, Drawn 1. *Wins* – Transvaal Invitation XI, Eastern Cape Invitation XI. *Draw* – N. F. Oppenheimer's XI.

TEST MATCH AVERAGES – ZIMBABWE v PAKISTAN

ZIMBABWE – BATTING

	T	I	NO	R	HS	100s	Avge	Ct
G. W. Flower	3	5	1	237	201*	1	59.25	5
A. Flower	3	5	0	250	156	1	50.00	10
G. J. Whittall	3	5	1	161	113*	1	40.25	2
S. V. Carlisle	3	4	1	78	46*	0	26.00	5
A. D. R. Campbell....	3	5	0	93	60	0	18.60	4
H. H. Streak	3	4	1	54	30*	0	18.00	1
P. A. Strang	3	4	0	68	32	0	17.00	3
D. L. Houghton	3	5	0	83	25	0	16.60	2
D. H. Brain..........	3	4	1	35	22*	0	11.66	1
M. H. Dekker	2	3	0	11	9	0	3.66	2
B. C. Strang	2	4	1	6	6	0	2.00	1

Played in one Test: I. P. Butchart 15, 8 (1 ct); H. R. Olonga did not bat.

* *Signifies not out.*

BOWLING

	O	M	R	W	BB	5W/i	Avge
B. C. Strang	84.4	43	120	9	3-43	0	13.33
H. H. Streak.....	118	30	298	22	6-90	2	13.54
G. J. Whittall....	100	22	288	10	3-58	0	28.80
D. H. Brain	88.4	15	337	8	3-50	0	42.12

Also bowled: I. P. Butchart 3–0–11–0; M. H. Dekker 4–0–10–0; H. R. Olonga 10–0–27–1; P. A. Strang 62–15–169–1.

PAKISTAN – BATTING

	T	I	NO	R	HS	100s	Avge	Ct/St
Inzamam-ul-Haq....	3	5	0	367	101	1	73.40	3
Ijaz Ahmed........	3	5	0	239	76	0	47.80	3
Aamir Sohail	3	6	0	178	61	0	29.66	5
Salim Malik	3	5	0	107	44	0	21.40	1
Shakeel Ahmed.....	2	4	0	74	33	0	18.50	4
Rashid Latif	3	6	1	74	38	0	14.80	5/1
Saeed Anwar.......	2	4	0	45	26	0	11.25	1
Wasim Akram	3	5	0	51	27	0	10.20	1

	T	I	NO	R	HS	100s	Avge	Ct/St
Kabir Khan	2	3	2	10	8*	0	10.00	1
Aamir Nazir	2	3	2	7	7	0	7.00	2
Manzoor Elahi	2	4	1	14	13	0	4.66	2
Aqib Javed	2	4	0	5	3	0	1.25	1

Played in one Test: Akram Raza 19, 2*; Asif Mujtaba 2, 4; Basit Ali 0.

* Signifies not out.

BOWLING

	O	M	R	W	BB	5W/i	Avge
Aamir Nazir	61	11	171	11	5-46	1	15.54
Aqib Javed	76.5	16	163	8	4-64	0	20.37
Manzoor Elahi ..	48	17	110	5	2-38	0	22.00
Wasim Akram ..	132.2	31	313	13	5-43	1	24.07
Kabir Khan	62	10	213	5	3-26	0	42.60

Also bowled: Aamir Sohail 10.1–2–39–2; Akram Raza 34–6–112–0; Asif Mujtaba 7–0–30–0; Salim Malik 9–0–42–0.

Note: Matches in this section which were not first-class are signified by a dagger.

†At Randjesfontein, November 30. Drawn. Pakistanis batted first by mutual agreement. Pakistanis 349 for seven dec. (Saeed Anwar 37, Salim Malik 135 retired out, Basit Ali 41, Rashid Latif 50 not out); N. F. Oppenheimer's XI 168 for five (J. A. Teeger 30, M. J. R. Rindel 100 not out).

Pakistan's matches v South Africa, New Zealand and Sri Lanka in the Mandela Trophy (December 2–January 12) may be found in that section.

†At Lenasia, December 7. Pakistanis won by 51 runs. Toss: Pakistanis. Pakistanis 262 for seven (50 overs) (Shakeel Ahmed 58, Ijaz Ahmed 112, Asif Mujtaba 32); Transvaal Invitation XI 211 (49.4 overs) (D. R. Laing 40, M. W. Rushmere 55; Akram Raza three for 33).

†At Alice, December 20. Pakistanis won by 143 runs. Toss: Eastern Cape Invitation XI. Pakistanis 260 for seven (50 overs) (Asif Mujtaba 101, Shakeel Ahmed 31, Manzoor Elahi 45 not out); Eastern Cape Invitation XI 117 (33 overs) (S. Abrahams 77 not out; Ata-ur-Rehman five for 18).

WESTERN PROVINCE v PAKISTANIS

At Cape Town, December 26, 27, 28, 29. Western Province won by 192 runs. Toss: Western Province.

Western Province's first victory over a touring Test team was a convincing one. Taking first use of the pitch and full advantage of the absence of Waqar Younis, who was rested, they embarked on a run spree. Ackerman reached his hundred in 147 balls and next day Simons added his own century before retiring with an ankle injury. Three Pakistanis scored fifties but no-one played the big innings required and they trailed by 128. Western Province set about extending that, and 19-year-old Kallis scored his second half-century of the match. Simons's declaration left a target of 399. They got to 168 for three, but the last seven fell for 38. Off-spinner Rundle claimed six for 51.

Close of play: First day, Western Province 330-6 (E. O. Simons 40*, D. B. Rundle 26*); Second day, Pakistanis 232-5 (Asif Mujtaba 45*, Manzoor Elahi 6*); Third day, Western Province 196-4 (J. H. Kallis 57*, A. C. Dawson 24*).

Western Province

S. G. Koenig c Asif Mujtaba b Kabir Khan	11	– c Manzoor Elahi		
		b Ata-ur-Rehman	26	
D. L. Haynes b Manzoor Elahi	44	– c and b Kabir Khan	6	
H. H. Gibbs b Kabir Khan	12	– c Manzoor Elahi b Aamir Sohail	35	
H. D. Ackerman c Shakeel Ahmed				
b Akram Raza	118	– c and b Akram Raza	32	
J. H. Kallis c Shakeel Ahmed b Manzoor Elahi	53	– lbw b Kabir Khan	74	
*E. O. Simons retired hurt	102	– (9) not out	9	
†R. J. Ryall c Akram Raza b Ata-ur-Rehman	4	– b Aqib Javed	0	
D. B. Rundle lbw b Ata-ur-Rehman	50	– b Kabir Khan	18	
A. C. Dawson c Shakeel Ahmed				
b Manzoor Elahi	1	– (6) b Kabir Khan	51	
C. V. English c Aamir Sohail b Ata-ur-Rehman	1			
D. G. Payne not out	12			
B 4, l-b 7, w 3, n-b 14	28	B 7, l-b 8, w 1, n-b 3	19	

1/25 2/38 3/108 4/248 5/276   436   1/22 2/55 3/91   (8 wkts dec.) 270
6/287 7/386 8/387 9/388   4/127 5/226 6/229
                                               7/258 8/270

In the first innings E. O. Simons retired hurt at 436-9.

Bowling: *First Innings*—Aqib Javed 30-6-82-0; Kabir Khan 20-6-70-2; Ata-ur-Rehman 27.2-3-101-3; Manzoor Elahi 20-1-81-3; Akram Raza 19-3-55-1; Aamir Sohail 13-2-36-0. *Second Innings*—Aqib Javed 19-3-49-1; Kabir Khan 16.3-1-45-4; Ata-ur-Rehman 11-2-37-1; Manzoor Elahi 5-0-14-0; Akram Raza 26-9-71-1; Aamir Sohail 18-6-39-1.

Pakistanis

Saeed Anwar c Dawson b Rundle	51	– b Rundle	14	
Aamir Sohail lbw b Payne	4	– (6) b Rundle	0	
†Shakeel Ahmed c Kallis b Dawson	43	– (2) c Koenig b Payne	13	
*Asif Mujtaba b Payne	55	– (3) b Kallis	65	
Basit Ali lbw b English	53	– (4) b Rundle	14	
Inzamam-ul-Haq c Ackerman b Dawson	18	– (5) c Kallis b Rundle	57	
Manzoor Elahi run out	9	– c Simons b Payne	1	
Akram Raza c Ryall b Payne	11	– c Haynes b Rundle	20	
Kabir Khan not out	26	– lbw b English	11	
Ata-ur-Rehman c Ryall b English	10	– (11) not out	3	
Aqib Javed c Simons b English	13	– (10) lbw b Rundle	2	
B 1, l-b 9, w 1, n-b 4	15	L-b 4, w 1, n-b 1	6	

1/9 2/102 3/106 4/194 5/226   308   1/21 2/53 3/83 4/168 5/168   206
6/240 7/256 8/257 9/272   6/168 7/180 8/196 9/198

Bowling: *First Innings*—Payne 21-6-62-3; English 17-2-70-3; Dawson 20-3-49-2; Rundle 36-8-102-1; Kallis 4-1-15-0. *Second Innings*—Payne 13-3-55-2; English 9-1-50-1; Rundle 13-2-51-6; Dawson 7-1-21-0; Kallis 11-3-25-1.

Umpires: M. Bagus and R. Brooks.

NATAL v PAKISTANIS

At Durban, January 4, 5, 6, 7. Natal won by 232 runs. Toss: Pakistanis.

The tourists suffered another massive defeat, with half a day to spare, in a virtual reprise of the Western Province game. They chose to bowl but, after losing three for 81, Natal hit an ill-directed attack for 391 in 98 overs. Benkenstein, the 20-year-old acting-captain, played an exhilarating innings of 76. In reply, a hurricane run-a-ball 55 from Waqar Younis just averted the follow-on, before a century from Johnson set up an unlikely challenge of 492. Though Inzamam-ul-Haq made a powerful 77 and Ijaz Ahmed hit 53 in 45 balls, defeat always looked inevitable. As at Newlands, the leading wicket-taker was an off-spinner, this time Crookes.

Close of play: First day, Pakistanis 2-0 (Saeed Anwar 2*, Aamir Sohail 0*); Second day, Natal 73-1 (A. C. Hudson 36*, N. E. Wright 35*); Third day, Pakistanis 81-3 (Inzamam-ul-Haq 16*, Shakeel Ahmed 0*).

Natal

A. C. Hudson c Aamir Sohail b Kabir Khan	14	– c and b Manzoor Elahi	57
D. J. Watson c Rashid Latif b Kabir Khan	31	– c Saeed Anwar b Waqar Younis	0
N. E. Wright b Waqar Younis	57	– c Rashid Latif b Manzoor Elahi	36
N. C. Johnson c Inzamam-ul-Haq b Kabir Khan	4	– c Shakeel Ahmed b Asif Mujtaba	114
†M. L. Bruyns c Saeed Anwar b Aamir Sohail	46	– st Rashid Latif b Asif Mujtaba	49
*D. M. Benkenstein c Aqib Javed b Asif Mujtaba	76	– st Rashid Latif b Asif Mujtaba	8
D. N. Crookes c Saeed Anwar b Kabir Khan	83	– c Aamir Sohail b Asif Mujtaba	68
L. Klusener b Aamir Sohail	46	– not out	4
R. E. Veenstra run out	0		
S. M. Pollock b Aamir Sohail	6		
T. Bosch not out	3		
L-b 5, w 1, n-b 6	12	B 1, l-b 5, w 1, n-b 4	11

1/30 2/49 3/81 4/154 5/174   391   1/1 2/74 3/126   (7 wkts dec.) 347
6/312 7/368 8/368 9/382   4/198 5/220
                                     6/336 7/347

Bowling: First Innings—Waqar Younis 15.4–3–49–1; Aqib Javed 17.2–4–84–0; Manzoor Elahi 15–3–61–0; Kabir Khan 18–4–70–4; Aamir Sohail 25.4–1–106–3; Asif Mujtaba 6–0–16–1. *Second Innings*—Waqar Younis 10-0–28–1; Aqib Javed 19-3–64–0; Kabir Khan 21–3–68–0; Manzoor Elahi 19–3–76–2; Asif Mujtaba 22.2–1–74–4; Inzamam-ul-Haq 3–0–17–0; Saeed Anwar 1–0–14–0.

Pakistanis

Saeed Anwar c Wright b Veenstra	2	– c Wright b Crookes	7
Aamir Sohail b Pollock	43	– c Bosch b Pollock	48
Inzamam-ul-Haq c Pollock b Klusener	28	– c Benkenstein b Crookes	77
Ijaz Ahmed c Veenstra b Klusener	6	– (9) lbw b Crookes	53
Asif Mujtaba c Klusener b Veenstra	5	– (4) run out	8
Shakeel Ahmed b Johnson	31	– (5) c Veenstra b Crookes	18
*†Rashid Latif c Bruyns b Klusener	26	– (6) c Wright b Veenstra	10
Manzoor Elahi c Wright b Johnson	37	– (7) c Bruyns b Veenstra	12
Kabir Khan lbw b Klusener	1	– (8) c Bruyns b Klusener	8
Waqar Younis c Bruyns b Veenstra	55	– c Bruyns b Pollock	9
Aqib Javed not out	0	– not out	0
L-b 6, n-b 7	13	B 1, n-b 8	9

1/17 2/78 3/84 4/84 5/91   247   1/23 2/65 3/77 4/139 5/168   259
6/144 7/157 8/159 9/247   6/172 7/186 8/212 9/226

Bowling: First Innings—Bosch 10–1–36–0; Veenstra 14.4–6–39–3; Pollock 15–2–47–1; Klusener 15–2–63–4; Johnson 11–3–23–2; Crookes 5–0–33–0. *Second Innings*—Bosch 7–1–25–0; Veenstra 14–5–54–2; Pollock 15–3–57–2; Crookes 13.1–2–40–4; Klusener 16–1–67–1; Johnson 3–1–15–0.

Umpires: W. Diedricks and D. L. Orchard.

SOUTH AFRICA v PAKISTAN

Inaugural Test Match

At Johannesburg, January 19, 20, 21, 22, 23. South Africa won by 324 runs. Toss: South Africa.

Cronje led South Africa to their biggest ever home victory, while Pakistan surrendered their record of at least one Test victory in their inaugural series against each of their opponents.

Waqar Younis and Rashid Latif were declared unfit; rather than replacing Waqar with one of the bowlers to hand, the tour management selected Aamir Nazir, who was still on a 14-hour journey from Pakistan. He landed at Johannesburg an hour before play and entered the field 35 minutes late. Nazir broke down with cramp in his seventh over, but returned after tea, had Rhodes caught at slip to end a 157-run partnership, bowled Richardson next ball, broke down again and returned next day.

South Africa had lost three men in the first 75 minutes. But Kirsten and Cronje repaired the damage before Rhodes and McMillan shared South Africa's biggest partnership since their return to international cricket. They put on 157 in 39 overs, Rhodes reaching his first Test fifty since March and McMillan completing a maiden Test hundred from 146 balls. He was then bowled by a no-ball from Wasim: no-balls contributed 36 to the innings. McMillan hit 15 fours and helped South Africa to almost four an over on the first day. After his departure next morning, de Villiers raced to a maiden Test half-century, with nine fours and three sixes in 68 balls; he added 71 in 35 minutes.

De Villiers continued to dominate play, removing Pakistan's top three as they reached 44 and bowling Ijaz Ahmed round his legs after tea. The tourists were 177 for six at stumps, with only Salim Malik standing firm. In the morning, he got within one run of a third hundred in successive Tests, but Eksteen held a hard catch at gully to deny him. He had struck 16 fours in 154 balls. Pakistan were bowled out for exactly half South Africa's total and faced following on.

Cronje, however, preferred to establish a huge lead rather than bat last on a deteriorating pitch. The openers set off at a run a minute until Steyn received his second doubtful caught-behind decision of the Test. When the batsmen accepted an offer of bad light on the third evening, the advantage was 391, which South Africa extended by 98 before declaring at lunch. The morning saw two first-ball dismissals: Commins, who had a groin strain, forgot he had a runner and ran himself out, while Richardson completed a king duck.

Pakistan needed 490 from five sessions, but the home crowd of 28,000 were already celebrating by the close, with seven down for 149. De Villiers and Donald had grabbed three as the score reached five; Asif Mujtaba survived for nearly three hours, the first 45 minutes on nought, but his dismissal triggered another collapse. Pakistan's only comfort was a battling 95 from Inzamam-ul-Haq. They lost their last three wickets in 6.3 overs on the final morning, when de Villiers became the first South African to take ten wickets and score fifty in a Test. Pakistan manager Intikhab Alam afterwards described their batting as "unprofessional", but Salim Malik denied reports of rifts within the team. "All rumours," he insisted.

Man of the Match: P. S. de Villiers.

Close of play: First day, South Africa 354-7 (B. M. McMillan 106*, C. E. Eksteen 1*); Second day, Pakistan 177-6 (Salim Malik 86*, Wasim Akram 10*); Third day, South Africa 161-3 (D. J. Cullinan 23*, J. N. Rhodes 2*); Fourth day, Pakistan 149-7 (Inzamam-ul-Haq 86*, Kabir Khan 4*).

South Africa

G. Kirsten c Aamir Sohail b Kabir Khan	62	– b Wasim Akram	42
P. J. R. Steyn c Moin Khan b Wasim Akram	1	– c Moin Khan b Aamir Nazir	17
J. B. Commins b Aqib Javed	13	– (6) run out	0
D. J. Cullinan c Moin Khan b Aqib Javed	0	– not out	69
*W. J. Cronje c Asif Mujtaba b Kabir Khan	41	– (3) c Aamir Sohail b Aqib Javed	48
J. N. Rhodes c Inzamam-ul-Haq b Aamir Nazir	72	– (5) c Moin Khan b Wasim Akram	16
B. M. McMillan c Moin Khan b Aqib Javed	113	– c Salim Malik b Kabir Khan	33
†D. J. Richardson b Aamir Nazir	0	– lbw b Aqib Javed	0
C. E. Eksteen c Moin Khan b Wasim Akram	13	– not out	2
P. S. de Villiers not out	66		
A. A. Donald c Inzamam-ul-Haq b Aamir Sohail	15		
B 4, l-b 18, w 6, n-b 36	64	B 6, l-b 5, w 15, n-b 6	32

1/1 (2) 2/55 (3) 3/59 (4) 4/138 (5)   460   1/69 (2) 2/96 (1)   (7 wkts dec.) 259
5/168 (1) 6/325 (6) 7/325 (8)   3/155 (3) 4/185 (5)
8/367 (7) 9/389 (9) 10/460 (11)   5/185 (6) 6/251 (7)
                                                   7/255 (8)

Bowling: *First Innings*—Wasim Akram 36–11–113–2; Aqib Javed 29.4–6–102–3; Kabir Khan 19.1–4–60–2; Aamir Nazir 13.1–1–67–2; Aamir Sohail 14.2–2–47–1; Salim Malik 8–0–49–0. *Second Innings*—Wasim Akram 23–5–53–2; Aqib Javed 26–2–82–2; Aamir Nazir 13–1–55–1; Kabir Khan 18–0–58–1.

Pakistan

Aamir Sohail c Richardson b de Villiers	23	– c McMillan b de Villiers	0
Saeed Anwar c Cullinan b de Villiers	2	– c de Villiers b Donald	1
Asif Mujtaba c Richardson b de Villiers	0	– c Richardson b McMillan	26
*Salim Malik b Eksteen b Donald	99	– lbw b de Villiers	1
Ijaz Ahmed b de Villiers	19	– (6) c Richardson b McMillan	1
Inzamam-ul-Haq b McMillan	19	– (5) c Richardson b de Villiers	95
†Moin Khan c de Villiers b McMillan	9	– c Rhodes b Eksteen	0
Wasim Akram b de Villiers	41	– c Kirsten b Eksteen	11
Kabir Khan c Richardson b Donald	4	– c Eksteen b Donald	10
Aqib Javed not out	0	– c Richardson b de Villiers	0
Aamir Nazir b de Villiers	0	– not out	1
L-b 5, n-b 9	14	B 8, l-b 7, w 1, n-b 3	19
	230		**165**

1/20 (2) 2/20 (3) 3/44 (1) 4/106 (5)
5/134 (6) 6/158 (7) 7/193 (4)
8/207 (9) 9/230 (8) 10/230 (11)

1/3 (1) 2/3 (2) 3/5 (4)
4/98 (3) 5/100 (6) 6/101 (7)
7/124 (8) 8/164 (9)
9/164 (5) 10/165 (10)

Bowling: *First Innings*—Donald 17–2–63–2; de Villiers 20.5–4–81–6; McMillan 12–3–46–2; Eksteen 7–1–16–0; Cronje 9–5–19–0. *Second Innings*—Donald 15–3–53–2; de Villiers 19.3–11–27–4; McMillan 11–1–33–2; Eksteen 19–7–34–2; Cronje 5–2–3–0.

Umpires: M. J. Kitchen (England) and C. J. Mitchley. Referee: P. J. P. Burge (Australia).

ZCU PRESIDENT'S XI v PAKISTANIS

At Harare South Country Club, January 27, 28, 29. Pakistanis won by seven wickets. Toss: ZCU President's XI.

The match was marred by acrimonious exchanges on the first evening, after the Pakistani openers complained about fast bowler Olonga's action and the umpires responded by calling Olonga for throwing four times. The slip fielders jeered Aamir Sohail when Olonga dismissed him; he turned back towards them, raising his bat, before the umpires intervened. Earlier, a stand of 215 between Flower and Whittall enabled Essop-Adam to declare at a powerful 301 for four. The tourists then batted until tea on the second day, taking a 26-run lead as Asif Mujtaba reached an unbeaten 113. The President's XI were 97 for two by the close, but were routed by Wasim Akram and Akram Raza next morning, adding only 46 more runs. A target of 118 took the Pakistanis less than 25 overs.

Close of play: First day, Pakistanis 76-2 (Asif Mujtaba 12*); Second day, ZCU President's XI 97-2 (H. J. Hira 1*, A. D. R. Campbell 1*).

ZCU President's XI

M. H. Dekker c sub (Moin Khan) b Akram Raza	28	– b Wasim Akram	26
G. W. Flower c Rashid Latif b Asif Mujtaba	137	– (7) c Akram Raza b Wasim Akram	13
G. J. Whittall c Wasim Akram b Aqib Javed	104	– (8) b Akram Raza	0
†A. D. R. Campbell c Rashid Latif b Wasim Akram	12	– c Asif Mujtaba b Akram Raza	1
*E. A. Essop-Adam not out	10	– lbw b Wasim Akram	0
M. G. Burmester (did not bat)		– (2) c Akram Raza b Wasim Akram	67
H. J. Hira (did not bat)		– (3) c sub (Moin Khan) b Akram Raza	6
G. A. Briant (did not bat)		– (6) c sub (Moin Khan) b Akram Raza	11
J. E. Bourdillon (did not bat)		– c Rashid Latif b Asif Mujtaba	5
B. W. Pswarayi (did not bat)		– b Akram Raza	0
H. K. Olonga (did not bat)		– not out	0
B 2, l-b 2, n-b 6	10	B 4, l-b 3, w 5, n-b 2	14
	(4 wkts dec.) 301		**143**

1/45 2/260 3/285 4/301

1/95 2/96 3/97 4/100 5/117
6/120 7/129 8/143 9/143

Bowling: *First Innings*—Wasim Akram 15–4–41–1; Aqib Javed 21.1–3–63–1; Akram Raza 19–4–62–1; Kabir Khan 7–0–38–0; Aamir Sohail 10–2–30–0; Salim Malik 15–1–54–0; Asif Mujtaba 5–1–9–1. *Second Innings*—Wasim Akram 21–11–26–4; Aqib Javed 5–0–21–0; Kabir Khan 9–4–23–0; Akram Raza 26.4–10–52–5; Asif Mujtaba 6–3–12–1; Salim Malik 2–0–2–0.

Pakistanis

Aamir Sohail c Burmester b Olonga	23	– c Pswarayi b Flower	56
Saeed Anwar c Whittall b Bourdillon	26		
Asif Mujtaba not out	113	– (2) c and b Bourdillon	8
*Salim Malik c Flower b Whittall	27		
Ijaz Ahmed c Flower b Whittall	47	– (3) c Burmester b Whittall	5
Inzamam-ul-Haq c Pswarayi b Essop-Adam	25	– (4) not out	38
†Rashid Latif c Olonga b Flower	32	– (5) not out	7
Akram Raza not out	6		
B 11, l-b 9, w 1, n-b 7	28	B 3, w 2	5

1/39 2/76 3/115 4/218 (6 wkts. dec.) 327   1/28 2/33 3/94 (3 wkts) 119
5/264 6/311

Wasim Akram, Kabir Khan and Aqib Javed did not bat.

Bowling: *First Innings*—Olonga 17–1–72–1; Pswarayi 12–4–33–0; Hira 9–2–14–0; Whittall 13–4–44–2; Bourdillon 12–4–36–1; Burmester 9–2–25–0; Flower 8–0–41–1; Dekker 5–0–16–0; Essop-Adam 6–0–26–1. *Second Innings*—Olonga 5–1–16–0; Pswarayi 5–1–7–0; Whittall 5–0–21–1; Bourdillon 5–0–46–1; Flower 2.2–0–8–1; Hira 2–0–18–0.

Umpires: A. Esat and Q. J. Goosen.

ZIMBABWE v PAKISTAN

First Test Match

At Harare, January 31, February 1, 2, 4. Zimbabwe won by an innings and 64 runs. Toss: Zimbabwe. Test debuts: S. V. Carlisle, H. K. Olonga.

Zimbabwe not only created history with their first victory in their 11th Test, but did it with style, by an innings inside four days. The Flowers took control on the first afternoon in a record-breaking fourth-wicket partnership, and Pakistan never got back into the game. Streak forced them to follow on and they folded in 62 overs on their second attempt.

The match had a farcical start when the referee, Jackie Hendriks, demanded a second toss. Salim Malik had called "Bird", the national symbol on one side of the Zimbabwean coin, instead of "Heads"; Andy Flower congratulated him on winning but Hendriks said he had not heard the call. Flower won at the second attempt and chose to bat. Until lunch, Pakistan seemed to shrug off their frustration. Aqib Javed and Wasim Akram dismissed Dekker, Campbell and Houghton as Zimbabwe reached 42. After the interval, Wasim bowled seven maiden overs in succession. But from then on, the Flowers flourished.

Andy, the elder brother, was the dominant partner, reaching his second Test century in three and a half hours. The brothers' stand passed 194, Zimbabwe's all-wicket record set by Campbell and Houghton against Sri Lanka three months earlier, and was 247 at the close, with Andy on 142 and Grant on 88. Next day they took it to 269, overtaking the fraternal Test record of 264 shared by Greg and Ian Chappell for Australia's third wicket against New Zealand in 1973-74, before Andy was out. But there was no relief for the bowlers. Whittall joined Grant in another double-hundred partnership. Both completed maiden Test centuries; Grant, who had been dropped at 24 and 98, took 343 balls to reach his hundred but then speeded up to convert it to a double in another 177. He had batted for 11 hours and hit only ten fours in a marathon display of discipline and concentration. His brother declared at 544 for four, Zimbabwe's highest Test total, beating their 462 for nine against Sri Lanka in October.

Pakistan lost one wicket on the second evening, to Henry Olonga, the first non-white player to appear for Zimbabwe. His first delivery went for four wides, his second was a bouncer, and Andy Flower caught Saeed Anwar down the leg side off the third. But Olonga's debut ended in disaster next day. As in the previous tour match, he was no-balled for throwing, by umpire Robinson – the first recognised bowler to be called in a Test since Ian Meckiff for Australia against South Africa in Brisbane in 1963-64 – and later retired with a side strain. But accurate medium-pace bowling by Streak, with six for 90, brilliant fielding and some careless shots by the batsmen finished off Pakistan 222 in arrears. Aamir Sohail, Salim Malik and Ijaz Ahmed all made a start before getting themselves out; Inzamam-ul-Haq, batting at No. 8 after damaging his shoulder in the slips, showed more authority in making 71. Inzamam was also the principal source of resistance when Pakistan followed on and collapsed to 35 for five. He and Rashid Latif added 96 but, apart from them and Wasim, no-one else reached double figures. There were three wickets each for seamers Streak, who returned the best Test analysis yet for Zimbabwe, Brain and Whittall, as Pakistan were all out for an ignominious 158.

Men of the Match: A. Flower and G. W. Flower.

Close of play: First day, Zimbabwe 289-3 (G. W. Flower 88*, A. Flower 142*); Second day, Pakistan 51-1 (Aamir Sohail 28*, Akram Raza 8*); Third day, Pakistan 271-7 (Inzamam-ul-Haq 53*).

Zimbabwe

M. H. Dekker c Rashid Latif b Aqib Javed	2	G. J. Whittall not out	113
G. W. Flower not out	201		
A. D. R. Campbell lbw b Wasim Akram	1	B 4, l-b 19, w 3, n-b 22	48
D. L. Houghton c Aamir Sohail b Aqib Javed	23		
*†A. Flower c Wasim Akram b Kabir Khan	156	1/4 (1) 2/9 (3) (4 wkts dec.) 544	
		3/42 (4) 4/311 (5)	

S. V. Carlisle, P. A. Strang, H. H. Streak, D. H. Brain and H. K. Olonga did not bat.

Bowling: Wasim Akram 39.5-12-95-1; Aqib Javed 34.1-8-73-2; Kabir Khan 35-5-142-1; Salim Malik 9-0-42-0; Akram Raza 34-6-112-0; Asif Mujtaba 7-0-30-0; Aamir Sohail 6-1-27-0.

Pakistan

Aamir Sohail c Houghton b Brain	61	– c Campbell b Brain	5
Saeed Anwar c A. Flower b Olonga	8	– lbw b Whittall	7
Akram Raza c Whittall b Streak	19	– (9) not out	2
Asif Mujtaba c Carlisle b Streak	2	– (3) b Brain	4
*Salim Malik c Carlisle b Whittall	32	– (4) c A. Flower b Brain	6
Ijaz Ahmed c G. W. Flower b Streak	65	– (5) c Brain b Streak	2
†Rashid Latif c Campbell b Whittall	6	– c Houghton b Whittall	38
Inzamam-ul-Haq c G. W. Flower b Streak	71	– (6) c A. Flower b Whittall	65
Wasim Akram c Carlisle b Streak	27	– (8) c Dekker b Strang	19
Kabir Khan not out	2	– b Streak	0
Aqib Javed lbw b Streak	0	– b Streak	2
B 3, l-b 4, w 9, n-b 13	29	W 2, n-b 6	8

1/36 (2) 2/82 (3) 3/88 (4) 4/131 (1)	322	1/13 (2) 2/16 (1) 3/26 (3)	158
5/135 (5) 6/151 (7) 7/271 (6)		4/29 (4) 5/35 (5) 6/131 (6)	
8/317 (9) 9/322 (8) 10/322 (11)		7/142 (7) 8/156 (8)	
		9/156 (10) 10/158 (11)	

Bowling: *First Innings*—Streak 39-11-90-6; Brain 27-4-94-1; Olonga 10-0-27-1; Whittall 29-10-49-2; Strang 15-5-45-0; Dekker 4-1-10-0. *Second Innings*—Brain 16-4-50-3; Streak 11-5-13-3; Strang 19-3-35-1; Whittall 16-3-58-3.

Umpires: M. J. Kitchen (England) and I. D. Robinson.

Referee: J. L. Hendriks (West Indies).

ZIMBABWE v PAKISTAN

Second Test Match

At Queens Sports Club, Bulawayo, February 7, 8, 9. Pakistan won by eight wickets. Toss: Zimbabwe. Test debut: B. C. Strang.

Pakistan struck back with a vengeance at Bulawayo, levelling the series with a three-day victory. Wasim Akram was to the fore on a substandard pitch, taking eight for 83 as

Zimbabwe subsided for 174 and 146 – less than the two Flowers made in the First Test. Though Streak wrecked Pakistan's top order, Ijaz Ahmed played solidly to set up a total of 260, which proved adequate insurance against a repeat of their embarrassment at Harare.

Pakistan made four changes, while Zimbabwe replaced the injured Olonga with Bryan Strang, a left-arm seamer in his first first-class season. He joined his brother Paul, a leg-spinner, in a rare double alongside the Flowers, while Pakistan fielded brothers-in-law Salim Malik and Ijaz.

Again, Zimbabwe won the toss but lost early wickets; this time there was no record-breaking recovery. Grant Flower, the double-centurion of Harare, was bowled for 16, giving Wasim his 250th wicket in his 60th Test. When Carlisle, who had not batted on his debut, scored his first Test run after 24 balls and fell to Wasim immediately afterwards, Zimbabwe were 86 for six. Campbell batted patiently for nearly four hours and 60 runs, but his only effective partner was Paul Strang.

Streak might have had both openers out that evening had Whittall held a simple chance at mid-off from Aamir Sohail. But Streak made up for the error, dismissing all of Pakistan's top four for 63. The arrival of Ijaz steadied the innings. He added 70 with Malik and 79 with Inzamam-ul-Haq, who hit a breezy 47. Ijaz himself batted for nearly four hours, striking 12 fours and a six, to establish a lead of 86. Streak finished with his third five-wicket haul in Tests, all against Pakistan.

The pitch was developing awkward bounce and next day Wasim played havoc as Zimbabwe collapsed inside 59 overs. He took five wickets for the 18th time in Tests and also broke Houghton's thumb in two places, while Aamir Nazir broke Dekker's finger. Only Carlisle, undefeated after an hour and 37 minutes, showed any defiance. Pakistan's target was 61. They needed barely 12 overs to achieve it, thanks to Aamir Sohail's onslaught on Brain, who went for 22 runs in his first over. Sohail smashed 46 from 26 balls before falling to Bryan Strang when the scores were level.

Relations between the teams deteriorated badly. The Zimbabweans raised the state of the ball with referee Hendriks on the first day, and the umpires subsequently spoke to Malik about marks on it. The home team also accused the Pakistanis of persistent sledging; Houghton was subsequently fined ten per cent of his match fee after reportedly saying that "the umpires must have been deaf not to have heard it". Wasim was reprimanded for snatching his cap from umpire Goosen after an lbw appeal was rejected.

Man of the Match: Wasim Akram.

Close of play: First day, Pakistan 11-1 (Aamir Sohail 5*, Rashid Latif 1*); Second day, Pakistan 260.

Zimbabwe

M. H. Dekker c Shakeel Ahmed b Aamir Nazir	0	– c Aamir Sohail b Wasim Akram	9
G. W. Flower b Wasim Akram	6	– b Manzoor Elahi	22
A. D. R. Campbell c Ijaz Ahmed b Manzoor Elahi	60	– c Shakeel Ahmed b Wasim Akram	0
D. L. Houghton b Wasim Akram	11	– lbw b Wasim Akram	25
*†A. Flower c Ijaz Ahmed b Kabir Khan	14	– lbw b Wasim Akram	8
G. J. Whittall c Aamir Sohail b Manzoor Elahi	7	– c sub (Moin Khan) b Aamir Nazir	5
S. V. Carlisle c Kabir Khan b Wasim Akram	1	– not out	46
P. A. Strang b Aamir Nazir	32	– c Aamir Sohail b Kabir Khan	3
H. H. Streak st Rashid Latif b Aamir Sohail	13	– c Manzoor Elahi b Kabir Khan	11
D. H. Brain c Rashid Latif b Aamir Sohail	5	– b Kabir Khan	0
B. C. Strang not out	0	– lbw b Wasim Akram	0
B 1, l-b 9, n-b 15	25	L-b 6, n-b 11	17
	174		**146**

1/3 (1) 2/7 (2) 3/23 (4) 4/56 (5)
5/73 (6) 6/86 (7) 7/134 (3)
8/167 (9) 9/174 (8) 10/174 (10)

1/14 (1) 2/16 (3) 3/58 (2) 4/73 (4)
5/77 (5) 6/93 (6) 7/106 (8)
8/145 (9) 9/145 (10) 10/146 (11)

Bowling: *First Innings*—Wasim Akram 22–9–40–3; Aamir Nazir 18–4–36–2; Kabir Khan 16–2–45–1; Manzoor Elahi 21–8–38–2; Aamir Sohail 2.1–1–5–2. *Second Innings*—Wasim Akram 22.3–7–43–5; Aamir Nazir 11–1–39–1; Manzoor Elahi 14–6–32–1; Kabir Khan 11–3–26–3.

Pakistan

Aamir Sohail lbw b Streak	26	– c Campbell b B. C. Strang 46
Shakeel Ahmed lbw b Streak	5	– lbw b B. C. Strang 7
†Rashid Latif c A. Flower b Streak	17	– not out 1
Basit Ali c B. C. Strang b Streak	0	
*Salim Malik b Streak	44	
Ijaz Ahmed b B. C. Strang	76	
Inzamam-ul-Haq lbw b Whittall	47	
Wasim Akram c Dekker b B. C. Strang	1	
Manzoor Elahi c A. Flower b B. C. Strang	13	– (4) not out 1
Kabir Khan not out	8	
Aamir Nazir b Brain	7	
B 2, l-b 5, w 2, n-b 7	16	L-b 2, w 1, n-b 3 6
	260	(2 wkts) **61**

1/9 (2) 2/47 (3) 3/52 (1) 4/63 (4)
5/133 (5) 6/212 (7) 7/226 (8)
8/231 (6) 9/246 (9) 10/260 (11)

1/56 (2) 2/60 (1)   (2 wkts) 61

Bowling: *First Innings*—Streak 26–5–70–5; Brain 15–4–49–1; B. C. Strang 23–10–44–3; Whittall 15–3–42–1; P. A. Strang 15–4–48–0. *Second Innings*—Streak 6–1–18–0; Brain 2–0–35–0; B. C. Strang 3.4–2–6–2.

Umpires: B. C. Cooray (Sri Lanka) and Q. J. Goosen.
Referee: J. L. Hendriks (West Indies).

ZIMBABWE v PAKISTAN

Third Test Match

At Harare, February 15, 16, 18, 19. Pakistan won by 99 runs. Toss: Pakistan. Test debut: I. P. Butchart.

Pakistan joined England (against Australia in 1888) and South Africa (against New Zealand in January 1995) as the third team to come from behind to win a three-Test series; they were the first such winners away from home. But Salim Malik's triumph was clouded. On the first day, he had to deny allegations that he tried to bribe Australian players to throw the Karachi Test. Afterwards, he was fined half his fee and given a suspended two-Test ban, while Aamir Sohail was severely reprimanded, for accusing umpire Robinson of wetting one side of the ball. The entire team lost a quarter of their fee for a slow over-rate, despite winning in four days.

Though the final result was decisive, the advantage had swung from one side to another. Once again, Streak knocked down Pakistan's top order, reducing them to 83 for four, before Ijaz Ahmed and Inzamam-ul-Haq launched a stand of 76. Streak finally removed Ijaz, before departing with a side strain, and Bryan Strang then took three quick wickets. Inzamam was fast running out of partners but Aamir Nazir hung on as a few hefty blows brought up Inzamam's fourth Test hundred. He was last out after three and a half hours, having struck 12 fours and two sixes.

Zimbabwe's performance next day was disappointing: 69 for two at lunch, 146 for five at tea, 243 all out, a slender lead of 12. Carlisle, opening in place of the injured Dekker, battled almost three hours for 31, but there was no major innings. Only a ninth-wicket stand of 40 from Paul Strang and Brain pushed them past Pakistan.

Seam continued to hold sway on the third day, with Pakistan indebted again to Inzamam and Ijaz. This time they combined at 88 for three and put on 116; Inzamam scored 83 in four hours, while Ijaz made 55. But after they were parted, the last six fell for 20. Another four for Streak, who needed cortisone injections before he could return to the game, took his series aggregate to 22, while Bryan Strang bowled 26 overs for only 27 runs.

Zimbabwe had nearly two days to score 239 for their first series win in Test cricket. They were in immediate trouble when Nazir bowled both openers as the score reached 12. He went on to devastate the innings, taking five wickets for the first time in his fifth Test. With eight down at tea, Zimbabwe were dead and buried. The last two wickets did put on

44. The Pakistanis believed Saeed Anwar had caught Streak at first slip to win the game and were leaving the field when Robinson disallowed it. Dismayed, Anwar dropped another catch three balls later, but the real end was not delayed for long.

Man of the Match: Inzamam-ul-Haq.

Men of the Series: Zimbabwe – H. H. Streak; Pakistan – Inzamam-ul-Haq.

Close of play: First day, Zimbabwe 4-0 (G. W. Flower 0*, S. V. Carlisle 3*); Second day, Zimbabwe 243; Third day, Pakistan 235-6 (Rashid Latif 1*, Wasim Akram 0*).

Pakistan

Aamir Sohail c P. A. Strang b Streak	21	– (6) c G. W. Flower b Whittall	19
Shakeel Ahmed c A. Flower b Whittall	29	– c A. Flower b B. C. Strang	33
Saeed Anwar c Butchart b Streak	4	– (1) c Carlisle b Streak	26
*Salim Malik c G. W. Flower b Streak	20	– c Carlisle b Whittall	5
Ijaz Ahmed lbw b Streak	41	– c Whittall b Streak	55
Inzamam-ul-Haq c P. A. Strang b Brain	101	– (3) c G. W. Flower b Whittall	83
†Rashid Latif c P. A. Strang b B. C. Strang	6	– c A. Flower b Streak	6
Wasim Akram b B. C. Strang	0	– c Campbell b Brain	4
Manzoor Elahi c Streak b B. C. Strang	0	– c A. Flower b Streak	0
Aqib Javed run out	0	– c A. Flower b Brain	3
Aamir Nazir not out	0	– not out	0
L-b 3, w 3, n-b 3	9	L-b 3, w 3, n-b 10	16
	231		**250**

1/42 (1) 2/46 (3) 3/64 (2) 4/83 (4)
5/159 (5) 6/180 (7) 7/180 (8)
8/183 (9) 9/204 (10) 10/231 (6)

1/58 (2) 2/72 (1) 3/88 (4)
4/204 (3) 5/230 (6) 6/233 (5)
7/246 (8) 8/247 (9)
9/250 (7) 10/250 (10)

Bowling: First Innings—Streak 18–4–53–4; Brain 12.3–1–48–1; B. C. Strang 32–15–43–3; Whittall 18–3–73–1; Butchart 3–0–11–0. *Second Innings*—Streak 18.4–4–52–4; Brain 16.1–2–61–2; Whittall 22–3–66–3; B. C. Strang 26–16–27–1; P. A. Strang 13–3–41–0.

Zimbabwe

G. W. Flower b Aamir Nazir	6	– b Aamir Nazir	2
S. V. Carlisle c Salim Malik b Aqib Javed	31	– b Aamir Nazir	0
A. D. R. Campbell c Manzoor Elahi b Aamir Nazir	14	– c Rashid Latif b Aamir Nazir	18
D. L. Houghton c Rashid Latif b Wasim Akram	19	– (6) c Rashid Latif b Aamir Nazir	5
*†A. Flower c Aqib Javed b Manzoor Elahi	37	– (4) c Aamir Nazir b Manzoor Elahi	35
G. J. Whittall b Aqib Javed	34	– (5) c Shakeel Ahmed b Wasim Akram	2
I. P. Butchart c Inzamam-ul-Haq b Wasim Akram	15	– c and b Aamir Nazir	8
P. A. Strang c Aamir Sohail b Aamir Nazir	28	– c Ijaz Ahmed b Aqib Javed	5
H. H. Streak lbw b Aqib Javed	0	– not out	30
D. H. Brain not out	22	– c Inzamam-ul-Haq b Wasim Akram	8
B. C. Strang c Inzamam-ul-Haq b Aqib Javed	6	– c Shakeel Ahmed b Aqib Javed	0
L-b 4, w 1, n-b 26	31	B 5, l-b 5, n-b 16	26
	243		**139**

1/20 (1) 2/51 (3) 3/79 (4) 4/94 (2)
5/145 (5) 6/175 (7) 7/193 (6)
8/193 (9) 9/233 (8) 10/243 (11)

1/2 (2) 2/12 (1) 3/37 (3)
4/68 (4) 5/72 (5) 6/85 (6)
7/95 (7) 8/95 (8)
9/122 (10) 10/139 (11)

Bowling: First Innings—Wasim Akram 28–2–90–2; Aqib Javed 25–5–64–4; Aamir Nazir 13–3–50–3; Manzoor Elahi 10–3–28–1; Aamir Sohail 2–0–7–0. *Second Innings*—Wasim Akram 20–1–45–2; Aamir Nazir 19–3–46–5; Aqib Javed 17.4–3–26–2; Manzoor Elahi 3–0–12–1.

Umpires: S. G. Randell (Australia) and I. D. Robinson.
Referee: J. L. Hendriks (West Indies).

†ZIMBABWE v PAKISTAN

First One-Day International

At Harare, February 22. Tied. Toss: Zimbabwe.

Wasim Akram, batting No. 11 and with one hand after he needed six stitches in the other one, could only hit the penultimate ball back to the bowler, Whittall, and the match was tied. He had split the webbing in his right hand attempting a return catch off Peall. Pakistan required 51 from the last ten overs, but faltered after two run-outs, while Bryan Strang, who had claimed two early wickets, added two more. Aamir Nazir holed out at the start of the final over; Saeed Anwar reached his eighth one-day international century with a four off the third ball, but the leg-bye which levelled the scores left Wasim in the firing line. Whittall himself hit 14 in the final over of Zimbabwe's innings, before being caught off Aqib Javed's final ball.

Men of the Match: Saeed Anwar and B. C. Strang.

Zimbabwe

*A. Flower b Aamir Nazir	25		S. V. Carlisle run out			0
G. W. Flower c Rashid Latif			P. A. Strang c Rashid Latif			
b Aamir Sohail	41		b Wasim Akram			9
M. G. Burmester b Aamir Sohail	25		S. G. Peall b Aqib Javed			1
†A. D. R. Campbell c Ijaz Ahmed			B. C. Strang not out			4
b Aamir Sohail	21		L-b 19, w 4, n-b 5			28
D. L. Houghton c Rashid Latif						
b Wasim Akram	32		1/45 2/105 3/108		(9 wkts, 50 overs)	219
G. J. Whittall c Inzamam-ul-Haq			4/159 5/168 6/170			
b Aqib Javed	33		7/188 8/189 9/219			

M. P. Jarvis did not bat.

Bowling: Wasim Akram 8.5-0-24-2; Aqib Javed 10-1-43-2; Aamir Nazir 10-0-52-1; Manzoor Elahi 8-0-36-0; Aamir Sohail 10-0-33-3; Salim Malik 3.1-0-12-0.

Pakistan

Aamir Sohail c and b B. C. Strang	7		Aqib Javed c A. Flower b B. C. Strang			0
Saeed Anwar not out	103		Aamir Nazir c Carlisle b Whittall			3
Inzamam-ul-Haq c Campbell			Wasim Akram c and b Whittall			0
b B. C. Strang	0					
*Salim Malik c Campbell b Whittall	22		B 4, l-b 5, w 3			12
Ijaz Ahmed c B. C. Strang b Peall	25					
Shakeel Ahmed run out	25		1/9 2/13 3/68		(49.5 overs)	219
†Rashid Latif run out	1		4/107 5/172 6/175			
Manzoor Elahi c P. A. Strang			7/209 8/210 9/213			
b B. C. Strang	21					

Bowling: Jarvis 7-0-30-0; B. C. Strang 11-0-36-4; Whittall 9.5-0-46-3; Burmester 3-0-16-0; Peall 6-0-27-1; P. A. Strang 10-0-41-0; A. Flower 4-0-14-0.

Umpires: A. Esat and I. D. Robinson.

†ZIMBABWE v PAKISTAN

Second One-Day International

At Harare, February 25. Pakistan won by four wickets. Toss: Pakistan.

Pakistan were in dire trouble when Streak and Bryan Strang had down for 23, but Inzamam-ul-Haq and Ijaz Ahmed regained the initiative with a stand of 152. Though Strang earned figures of three for 22 – and a caution from referee Hendriks for pointing Ijaz back to the pavilion – Inzamam steered Pakistan to victory with nine wickets to spare, finishing on 116. Houghton dominated Zimbabwe's innings, striking a fluent 73 not out from 77 balls. He helped to put on 75 in the final ten overs after the tourists tied down the earlier batsmen. After the match, a handful of opposing supporters clashed with each other; the disturbance was promptly quelled by the police.

Man of the Match: Inzamam-ul-Haq.

Zimbabwe

*†A. Flower c Moin Khan	D. L. Houghton not out 73
b Wasim Akram . 9	G. J. Whittall c Ijaz Ahmed
G. W. Flower c Moin Khan	b Wasim Akram . 13
b Manzoor Elahi . 32	S. V. Carlisle not out 9
M. G. Burmester c Aamir Sohail	L-b 13, w 11, n-b 5 29
b Manzoor Elahi . 17	
A. D. R. Campbell c Aamir Sohail	1/26 2/70 3/74 (5 wkts, 50 overs) 209
b Salim Malik . 27	4/130 5/185

S. G. Peall, P. A. Strang, H. H. Streak and B. C. Strang did not bat.

Bowling: Wasim Akram 10-0-40-2; Aqib Javed 10-1-41-0; Manzoor Elahi 10-0-36-2; Akram Raza 10-0-27-0; Aamir Sohail 6-0-30-0; Salim Malik 4-0-22-1.

Pakistan

Aamir Sohail c Whittall b Streak 7	†Moin Khan c Houghton b P. A. Strang 19
Saeed Anwar c Burmester b B. C. Strang 0	Manzoor Elahi not out 3
Inzamam-ul-Haq not out 116	L-b 2, w 8, n-b 1 11
Asif Mujtaba c A. Flower b B. C. Strang 0	
*Salim Malik c A. Flower b Streak 0	1/9 2/17 3/19 (6 wkts, 48.3 overs) 210
Ijaz Ahmed b B. C. Strang 54	4/23 5/175 6/206

Wasim Akram, Akram Raza and Aqib Javed did not bat.

Bowling: Streak 9-1-50-2; B. C. Strang 10-0-22-3; Whittall 7-0-33-0; Burmester 4-0-21-0; P. A. Strang 8-0-33-1; Peall 8-0-35-0; G. W. Flower 2-0-13-0; Campbell 0.3-0-1-0.

Umpires: A. Esat and Q. J. Goosen.

†ZIMBABWE v PAKISTAN

Third One-Day International

At Harare, February 26. Zimbabwe won by 74 runs. Toss: Pakistan.

Pakistan's controversial tour ended in their first one-day defeat by Zimbabwe in nine meetings, when they were bowled out with 39 balls to spare. Chasing 223, they were flustered by Malcolm Jarvis, the 39-year-old medium-pacer, who dismissed both openers. Again, Inzamam-ul-Haq repaired the damage, scoring 45 in 54 balls. But the last six wickets fell for 42, with Aamir Sohail unable to bat because of a back injury. As Zimbabwe celebrated levelling the series, Jarvis announced his retirement. Andy Flower was the pick of the home batsmen, with 73; wicket-keeper Moin Khan, included after what turned out to be the temporary retirement of Rashid Latif and Basit Ali, took five catches in Zimbabwe's innings, equalling the limited-overs record.

Man of the Match: A. Flower.

Zimbabwe

*†A. Flower c Moin Khan	S. V. Carlisle c Moin Khan
b Manzoor Elahi . 73	b Wasim Akram . 4
G. W. Flower c Moin Khan	P. A. Strang c Moin Khan b Aqib Javed 4
b Wasim Akram . 6	H. H. Streak c Manzoor Elahi
M. G. Burmester c Ijaz Ahmed	b Aqib Javed . 18
b Akram Raza . 39	B. C. Strang not out 0
D. L. Houghton c Aqib Javed	
b Salim Malik . 34	L-b 16, w 9 25
A. D. R. Campbell c Inzamam-ul-Haq	
b Aqib Javed . 18	1/15 2/119 3/171 (9 wkts, 50 overs) 222
G. J. Whittall c Moin Khan	4/171 5/175 6/187
b Manzoor Elahi . 1	7/194 8/222 9/222

M. P. Jarvis did not bat.

Bowling: Wasim Akram 10-1-33-2; Aqib Javed 10-1-46-3; Manzoor Elahi 10-0-41-2; Akram Raza 10-0-45-1; Aamir Sohail 6.5-0-31-0; Salim Malik 3.1-0-10-1.

Pakistan

Shakeel Ahmed c A. Flower b Jarvis	36	Aqib Javed not out	2
†Moin Khan c Whittall b Jarvis	8	Wasim Akram st A. Flower	
Inzamam-ul-Haq c sub (D. N. Erasmus)		b G. W. Flower	3
b P. A. Strang	45	Aamir Sohail absent hurt	
*Salim Malik c Whittall b P. A. Strang	3		
Ijaz Ahmed c B. C. Strang		L-b 3, w 4	7
b P. A. Strang	12		
Asif Mujtaba run out	20	1/26 2/73 3/80	(43.3 overs) 148
Manzoor Elahi c Carlisle b Whittall	10	4/106 5/112 6/138	
Akram Raza c A. Flower b Whittall	2	7/143 8/143 9/148	

Bowling: Streak 6–2–7–0; B. C. Strang 6–1–15–0; Whittall 6–0–24–2; Jarvis 10–1–37–2; P. A. Strang 10–0–42–3; G. W. Flower 5.3–0–20–1.

Umpires: Q. J. Goosen and I. D. Robinson.

FIFTY YEARS AGO

From WISDEN CRICKETERS' ALMANACK 1946

CRICKET UNDER THE JAPS By Major E. W. Swanton R.A.: "It is strange, perhaps, but true, how many of us agreed on this: That we were never so thankful for having been cricketers as we were when we were guests of the Japanese. There were periods when we could play 'cricket' if our antics do not desecrate the word. There were occasions when we could lecture, and be lectured to, about it. It was a subject that filled countless hours in pitch-dark huts between sundown and the moment that continued to be euphemistically known as lights-out. And it inspired many a daydream, contrived often in the most gruesome setting, whereby one combated the present by living either in the future or the past."

THE SERVICES IN 1945 – Central Mediterranean Force: "When the end of hostilities in Europe appeared in sight, the thoughts of all cricketers serving in the Italian war theatre turned to the game for which few of them for so long had found either the time or opportunity. Some of the more ardent enthusiasts decided to embark on a programme of ground preparation to be completed in time for the forthcoming season. The story of their work is one of successful perseverance over difficulties. Firm, flat meadows did not exist. The problem was to find flat surfaces of any kind. Appeals to various departments of the Services brought willing and excellent assistance, and in a comparatively short time grounds of first-class order sprang up all over the country. That at Bari, in its perfect Adriatic setting, was particularly good. The plain earth outfield of this large enclosure responded so well to treatment from the "Bulldozer" and heavy roller that it soon became a true surface. Matting was stretched over the concrete wicket, sight screens and score boxes were erected, the arena roped off, seating accommodation provided for hundreds of people, refreshment tents and marquees put up, score cards – with the fall of the last wicket – given away and loudspeakers provided a running commentary all through the game."

THE PUBLIC SCHOOLS, 1945 By E. M. Wellings: "Nobody would claim that 1945 was a vintage year for Public School cricket. The effects of six years of war were felt more than in the previous five, and those effects, which are common to all schoolboy cricket, are going to be felt in English cricket as a whole for some time to come. We should not delude ourselves with the thought that junior cricket will immediately return to its former standard now that the war is at a fighting end. The return to normal can take place only gradually.

Among the greatest handicaps imposed on the Schools were the absence of the younger masters, from whose ranks come many of the cricket teachers, and weaker opposition from club sides than during ordinary times. The first of these handicaps probably has been the greater, and, as shortage of masters able to instruct in cricket has been apparent at preparatory as well as Public Schools, it is obvious that the effects must linger."

THE WEST INDIANS IN NEW ZEALAND, 1994-95

By TERRY POWER

The first team from the Caribbean to win a Test series in New Zealand since 1955-56 had a much more pleasant visit than either of the last two – the umpire-barging, stumps-kicking brigade of 1979-80, when the West Indians suffered their most recent series defeat, and the 1986-87 party, whose captain Viv Richards had equally sulphurous if less spectacular exchanges with anyone who did not do his bidding. Success and good humour, of course, often go together, and Courtney Walsh, a less famous leader than either Clive Lloyd or Richards, showed himself better equipped to get along harmoniously in New Zealand, with the wry smile regularly half-forming from the left side of his mouth by no means his smallest qualification.

On paper, and at times on the field, the West Indians looked less formidable than their recent predecessors. Ambrose, recovering from injury, was rarely at full blast; the back-up pace bowlers did not complete the lethal four-man barrages of the 1970s and 1980s; Richie Richardson had not yet returned after exhaustion forced him to leave Yorkshire the previous year; with Desmond Haynes absent, the new opening combination of Sherwin Campbell and Stuart Williams looked tentative early in the tour, as did wicket-keeper Junior Murray. Walsh himself bowled magnificently to take 16 of the 30 New Zealand wickets to fall in the two Tests, especially at Wellington, where he won the series. Brian Lara, if less consistent, also reached his high point when most needed. The less elegant left-hander, Jimmy Adams, was just as effective.

This time it was the home team, not the visitors, who were the source of the turmoil. The tour was accompanied by what started as noises off but soon threatened to take centre stage. The New Zealand manager, coach and four suspended players all made dramatic exits. Three re-entered just in time for the Tests – Dion Nash for the briefest of cameos before he broke a finger. A wide assortment of other injuries, and the use by New Zealand in the disastrous Second Test of two players who had been suspended by their provinces, added to their growing disarray. In Christchurch, they were rescued by the lower middle order, led by Adam Parore, but the team fell to pieces in considerably easier batting conditions at the Basin Reserve and went down to their heaviest defeat in any Test. Andrew Jones's international comeback, welcomed in the spring, ended with a double failure. He had no success in five matches, and even after he was dropped New Zealand Cricket still had to fulfil their side of the contract they had given him. The home authority did deserve credit for improved tour planning. After years of pitting overseas teams against meaningless conglomerations of players, with misleading titles like New Zealand Second XI and U-Bix XI, outside the Tests, this time it gave matches to Auckland, Northern Districts and Otago. That revived some competitive interest and there were markedly better crowds.

WEST INDIAN TOURING PARTY

C. A. Walsh (Jamaica) (*captain*), B. C. Lara (Trinidad & Tobago) (*vice-captain*), J. C. Adams (Jamaica), C. E. L. Ambrose (Leeward Islands), K. L. T. Arthurton (Leeward Islands), K. C. G. Benjamin (Leeward Islands), W. K. M. Benjamin (Leeward Islands), S. L. Campbell (Barbados), S. Chanderpaul (Guyana), A. C. Cummins (Barbados), R. Dhanraj (Trinidad & Tobago), R. I. C. Holder (Barbados), J. R. Murray (Windward Islands), S. C. Williams (Leeward Islands).

C. L. Hooper (Guyana) was selected but missed the tour due to malaria.

Manager: D. A. J. Holford.   *Cricket manager:* R. B. Kanhai.

WEST INDIAN TOUR RESULTS

Test matches – Played 2: Won 1, Drawn 1.
First-class matches – Played 3: Won 1, Drawn 2.
Win – New Zealand.
Draws – New Zealand, Otago.
One-day internationals – Played 3: Won 3.
Other non-first-class matches: Played 2: Won 2. Abandoned 1. *Wins* – Sir Ron Brierley's XI, Auckland. *Abandoned* – Northern Districts.

TEST MATCH AVERAGES

NEW ZEALAND – BATTING

	T	I	NO	R	HS	100s	Avge	Ct
A. C. Parore	2	3	2	137	100*	1	137.00	3
S. P. Fleming	2	3	0	133	56	0	44.33	1
D. J. Murray	2	4	0	146	52	0	36.50	1
K. R. Rutherford....	2	4	1	54	22	0	18.00	0
B. A. Young........	2	4	0	69	29	0	17.25	0
M. N. Hart	2	3	0	46	45	0	15.33	0
S. A. Thomson......	2	3	0	34	20	0	11.33	0
A. H. Jones	2	4	1	24	12	0	8.00	0

Played in two Tests: S. B. Doull 0, 0 (1 ct); D. K. Morrison 0*, 14. Played in one Test: D. J. Nash 3; M. L. Su'a 6, 8 (2 ct).

* *Signifies not out.*

BOWLING

	O	M	R	W	BB	5W/i	Avge
D. K. Morrison	55.2	14	151	8	6-69	1	18.87
S. A. Thomson	18	3	61	2	2-61	0	30.50
S. B. Doull........	59.2	10	247	3	2-162	0	82.33

Also bowled: M. N. Hart 71–6–256–0; A. H. Jones 13–2–50–0; D. J. Nash 5–2–11–0; M. L. Su'a 44–4–179–0.

WEST INDIES – BATTING

	T	I	NO	R	HS	100s	Avge	Ct
S. Chanderpaul	2	2	1	130	69	0	130.00	0
J. R. Murray	2	2	1	129	101*	1	129.00	7
J. C. Adams	2	2	0	164	151	1	82.00	1
B. C. Lara	2	2	0	149	147	1	74.50	3
S. L. Campbell	2	2	0	139	88	0	69.50	2
K. L. T. Arthurton	2	2	0	71	70	0	35.50	1
S. C. Williams	2	2	0	36	26	0	18.00	1

Played in two Tests: C. E. L. Ambrose 33 (1 ct); K. C. G. Benjamin 5; C. A. Walsh 0*.
Played in one Test: W. K. M. Benjamin 85 (2 ct); R. Dhanraj did not bat.

* Signifies not out.

BOWLING

	O	M	R	W	BB	5W/i	Avge
C. A. Walsh	70	21	132	16	7-37	2	8.25
C. E. L. Ambrose	58.1	22	113	5	3-57	0	22.60
R. Dhanraj	45	8	146	4	2-49	0	36.50
K. C. G. Benjamin	51	8	174	4	2-91	0	43.50

Also bowled: J. C. Adams 3-1-4-0; K. L. T. Arthurton 7-1-12-0; W. K. M. Benjamin 38-5-106-1; S. Chanderpaul 5-3-10-0; B. C. Lara 4-0-8-0.

Note: Matches in this section which were not first-class are signified by a dagger.

†At Hamilton, January 15. West Indians won by 41 runs. Toss: West Indians. West Indians 273 for three (50 overs) (S. C. Williams 121, S. L. Campbell 108); Sir Ron Brierley's XI 232 for six (50 overs) (J. G. Wright 34, M. D. Bailey 31, G. E. Bradburn 39, N. J. Astle 59 not out; R. Dhanraj three for 35).

†At Auckland, January 17. West Indians won by 105 runs. Toss: West Indians. West Indians 206 for nine (50 overs) (B. C. Lara 38, W. K. M. Benjamin 74); Auckland 101 (35.2 overs) (J. T. C. Vaughan 33; W. K. M. Benjamin four for ten, K. L. T. Arthurton four for 26).

†At Whangarei, January 19. Northern Districts v West Indians. No result (abandoned).

†NEW ZEALAND v WEST INDIES

First One-Day International

At Auckland, January 22. West Indies won on scoring-rate. Toss: New Zealand. International debut: N. J. Astle.

Lara and Williams added 88 from 59 deliveries to make sure that West Indies were well ahead of an asking-rate of four and a half an over when a third burst of rain terminated their innings. They were some way behind, with 61 from 18 overs, when Lara arrived, but he scored 55 from only 32 balls. After a sedate start, Williams finished with 73 from 80. Rutherford had chosen to bat on a showery day, which damaged New Zealand's prospects; they were interrupted at 65 for two off 21 overs and their innings reduced first to 43 overs, then to 37. Astle – making his debut after four players were suspended – Thomson and Vaughan added 98 in their last 15 overs.

Man of the Match: B. C. Lara.

New Zealand

B. A. Young b Arthurton	42	J. T. C. Vaughan not out 21
A. H. Jones c Lara b Walsh	10	S. B. Doull not out 6
†A. C. Parore c Adams b Walsh	1	L-b 4, w 1, n-b 3........... 8
*K. R. Rutherford c Adams b Arthurton	17	
S. A. Thomson run out	37	1/31 2/35 3/67 (6 wkts, 37 overs) 167
N. J. Astle c Cummins b Dhanraj	25	4/80 5/123 6/146

D. N. Patel, G. R. Larsen and D. K. Morrison did not bat.

Bowling: Ambrose 8-1-34-0; Walsh 8-1-26-2; Cummins 7-1-25-0; Benjamin 6-0-32-0; Arthurton 4-0-25-2; Dhanraj 4-0-21-1.

West Indies

S. C. Williams not out...........	73
S. L. Campbell b Larsen	17
B. C. Lara not out	55
L-b 3, n-b 1	4
1/61 (1 wkt, 27.4 overs)	149

K. L. T. Arthurton, R. I. C. Holder, †J. C. Adams, A. C. Cummins, C. E. L. Ambrose, K. C. G. Benjamin, *C. A. Walsh and R. Dhanraj did not bat.

Bowling: Morrison 5-0-19-0; Doull 6.4-1-32-0; Vaughan 4-0-14-0; Larsen 7-0-35-1; Patel 1-0-8-0; Astle 3-0-27-0; Thomson 1-0-11-0.

Umpires: B. L. Aldridge and D. B. Cowie.

---

†NEW ZEALAND v WEST INDIES

Second One-Day International

At Wellington, January 25. West Indies won by 41 runs. Toss: New Zealand.

Young and Jones raced to 50 in the 11th over, with Young's square drives recapturing the aggression of his middle-order play for Northern Districts rather than his recent efforts as a Test opener. But once the openers left, New Zealand slipped behind the required rate of five an over. West Indies had responded to a deep-set field by running 105 singles; Rutherford estimated his team's poor fielding gave away 20 runs. Lara reached 3,000 runs in his 79th one-day international, hitting 72 off 85 balls after the openers were skittled early on, and Cummins whacked 44 off 38 at the end.

The Basin Reserve square was vandalised the previous day, though the match was not held up. This incident followed the occupation of TVNZ studios by Maoris protesting that cricket telecasts were being given preference over the daily news in Maori.

Man of the Match: B. C. Lara.

West Indies

S. C. Williams b Doull	8	†J. C. Adams c Parore b Morrison	8
S. L. Campbell b Morrison	7	C. E. L. Ambrose not out	8
B. C. Lara run out	72	L-b 22, w 7 29
K. L. T. Arthurton run out	30	
R. I. C. Holder c Morrison b Thomson	35	1/15 2/15 3/95 (7 wkts, 50 overs) 246
W. K. M. Benjamin b Astle	5	4/163 5/173
A. C. Cummins not out	44	6/187 7/223

*C. A. Walsh and R. Dhanraj did not bat.

Bowling: Morrison 8-1-32-2; Doull 7-0-37-1; Larsen 10-1-30-0; Vaughan 6-0-30-0; Patel 5-0-28-0; Astle 8-0-46-1; Thomson 6-0-21-1.

New Zealand

B. A. Young c Benjamin b Cummins . .	39	G. R. Larsen c Ambrose b Arthurton . .	15	
A. H. Jones c and b Dhanraj	26	S. B. Doull not out.	9	
†A. C. Parore lbw b Walsh	18	D. K. Morrison st Adams b Arthurton .	2	
*K. R. Rutherford c Adams b Dhanraj .	16	L-b 3, w 5, n-b 5	13	
S. A. Thomson c Adams b Ambrose . . .	22			
N. J. Astle c Adams b Benjamin	11	1/54 2/81 3/103	(48.5 overs) 205	
J. T. C. Vaughan run out	9	4/109 5/137 6/151		
D. N. Patel b Walsh	25	7/151 8/193 9/194		

Bowling: Walsh 9–1–42–2; Ambrose 8–0–29–1; Cummins 5–0–34–1; Dhanraj 10–0–31–2; Benjamin 9–2–29–1; Arthurton 7.5–0–37–2.

Umpires: R. S. Dunne and C. E. King.

---

†NEW ZEALAND v WEST INDIES

Third One-Day International

At Christchurch, January 28. West Indies won by nine wickets. Toss: West Indies. International debut: R. L. Hayes.

West Indies casually completed a clean sweep with 12.2 overs in hand, while New Zealand completed 16 limited-overs internationals without a win. Ambrose was unlucky to finish wicketless after he exerted the early pressure, bowling with three slips and a gully on a hard pitch. Others reaped the benefit: Arthurton, Dhanraj and Benjamin were introduced with immediate success. When West Indies replied, chasing 147, Lara earned the biggest cheer of the day from a subdued 12,000-strong crowd, took his series aggregate to 161 for once out and struck the winning four. Fast bowler Roydon Hayes was a startling choice – Northern Districts had dropped him from the one-day Shell Cup because his bowling was so expensive.

Man of the Match: W. K. M. Benjamin.

New Zealand

B. A. Young c Adams b Arthurton	13	G. R. Larsen b Adams	12	
A. H. Jones c Murray b Arthurton	9	D. K. Morrison not out	14	
†A. C. Parore c Holder b Dhanraj	9	R. L. Hayes c Holder b Arthurton	13	
*K. R. Rutherford b Benjamin	30	B 1, l-b 3, w 6, n-b 3	13	
M. W. Douglas c Ambrose b Benjamin .	12			
S. A. Thomson c Murray b Benjamin . .	3	1/17 2/24 3/53	(49 overs) 146	
N. J. Astle c Holder b Cummins	9	4/69 5/73 6/85		
J. T. C. Vaughan run out	9	7/99 8/109 9/123		

Bowling: Ambrose 7–2–15–0; Benjamin 8–1–12–3; Arthurton 10–0–31–3; Cummins 8–1–23–1; Dhanraj 10–0–37–1; Adams 6–0–24–1.

West Indies

S. C. Williams not out	69
S. L. Campbell b Larsen	36
*B. C. Lara not out	34
L-b 1, w 1, n-b 2	10

1/98   (1 wkt, 37.4 overs) 149

K. L. T. Arthurton, R. I. C. Holder, J. C. Adams, †J. R. Murray, A. C. Cummins, W. K. M. Benjamin, C. E. L. Ambrose and R. Dhanraj did not bat.

Bowling: Morrison 10–1–29–0; Hayes 7–0–31–0; Larsen 10–4–39–1; Vaughan 3–0–16–0; Thomson 5–1–19–0; Astle 2.4–0–14–0.

Umpires: C. E. King and D. M. Quested.

OTAGO v WEST INDIANS

At Dunedin, January 29, 30, 31. Drawn. Toss: West Indians.

The tourists were 222 for seven when Marshall bowled acting-captain Lara for 19. But Cummins, in his only first-class innings of the tour, added 215 with Murray, reaching a maiden century. Off-spinner Wiseman was the pick of the home bowlers, with four wickets at barely two and a half an over. Lara's brief innings was marked by a burst of bad feeling: Richardson, at slip, called out "C'mon, Zoe" to the bowler, Finch, referring to the Australian woman who had recently dismissed Lara. The batsman took it personally and a sharp exchange followed. Richardson later scored a century to avert the follow-on. Campbell used the final afternoon to prepare for his Test debut by scoring the game's fourth hundred.

Close of play: First day, West Indians 295-7 (J. R. Murray 74*, A. C. Cummins 34*); Second day, Otago 173-5 (M. H. Richardson 8*, C. J. W. Finch 5*).

West Indians

S. C. Williams run out	54			
S. L. Campbell lbw b Gale	0	– (1) not out		108
R. I. C. Holder b Finch	25	– (2) c Rutherford b Marshall		3
J. C. Adams b Wiseman	59			
S. Chanderpaul c sub (R. P. Wixon) b Gale	10	– (3) not out		50
K. L. T. Arthurton c Rutherford b Wiseman	20			
†J. R. Murray not out	141			
*B. C. Lara b Marshall	19			
A. C. Cummins c Kennedy b Wiseman	107			
K. C. G. Benjamin lbw b Wiseman	0			
R. Dhanraj not out	3			
B 1, l-b 10, w 1	12	L-b 5, n-b 1		6

1/4 2/65 3/94 4/125 5/168 (9 wkts dec.) 450   1/13 (1 wkt) 167
6/179 7/222 8/437 9/437

Bowling: *First Innings*—Kennedy 23-1-87-0; Gale 24-4-60-2; Marshall 24-2-72-1; Finch 22-2-89-1; Wiseman 48-14-122-4; Richardson 3-0-9-0. *Second Innings*—Kennedy 10-2-38-0; Gale 8-4-15-0; Marshall 10-0-43-1; Finch 6-0-32-0; Wiseman 11-2-30-0; Billcliff 0.4-0-4-0.

Otago

*P. W. Dobbs c Murray b Dhanraj	34	A. J. Gale b Benjamin	9
J. M. Allan c Murray b Benjamin	39	P. J. Wiseman lbw b Cummins	25
†M. G. Croy b Dhanraj	16	E. J. Marshall c Murray b Benjamin	0
K. R. Rutherford c Campbell b Dhanraj	36	R. J. Kennedy not out	0
I. S. Billcliff b Benjamin	20	B 4, l-b 5, w 2, n-b 10	21
M. H. Richardson c Arthurton b Benjamin	103		
C. J. W. Finch c Campbell b Dhanraj	6		309

1/62 2/90 3/107 4/159 5/159 6/175 7/208 8/290 9/309

Bowling: Benjamin 26.4-4-97-5; Cummins 19-5-46-1; Dhanraj 37-7-123-4; Arthurton 4-1-9-0; Chanderpaul 3-0-6-0; Adams 4-1-19-0.

Umpires: R. S. Dunne and C. E. King.

NEW ZEALAND v WEST INDIES

First Test Match

At Christchurch, February 3, 4, 5, 6, 7. Drawn. Toss: West Indies. Test debut: S. L. Campbell.

New Zealand had the better of a Test heavily abbreviated by rain, though they depended too much on Parore and Morrison. Parore rescued them from a precarious 128 for five, with a brave maiden Test hundred; Morrison cleaned out West Indies' top four and might have made them follow on.

The pitch helped the quicker bowlers by taking a long time to dry out under heavy cloud cover. Walsh put New Zealand in, but only 11.4 overs were possible on the first day. Murray batted doggedly for three hours, until Ambrose, returning after a shoulder injury but still the most awkward of the attack, dismissed him and Rutherford after lunch on the second. Thomson lasted an hour, but Fleming found his best ally in Parore. Seeing the ball earlier than other batsmen, Fleming stroked some stylish boundaries while maintaining the evasion necessary for survival. Meanwhile Parore, consistently right in behind the ball, collected several bruises but began to hook as he gained confidence. Walsh, surprisingly, often left the third-man boundary vacant, which provided a useful source of runs. Though he lost Fleming, Parore was joined by Hart, a youth international opener, who looked the part as they took the seventh-wicket stand to 118 after the third day was washed out. On Waitangi Day, Parore became the first Maori to score a Test century; he batted for five hours and hit nine fours in 249 balls.

Rutherford immediately declared and Morrison raced in against the West Indian batsmen. He looked the best bowler in the match, fast and mostly on-target; he bowled Lara with his slower ball, had Williams and Adams caught hooking and, after Rutherford threw out Arthurton, trapped the debutant Campbell for fifty. At 98 for five, West Indies were still in danger of the follow-on. But Nash's return after his suspension ended when he broke a finger fielding, and Chanderpaul, who played the best-timed strokes in the innings, and Murray vigorously eliminated that risk on the final morning. With the pressure off, the last five wickets added 214, reducing New Zealand's lead to 29 and giving the match a misleadingly even look. Winston Benjamin hit 85 from 87 balls and Ambrose also laid about him. When Morrison returned to finish off the innings, his sixth wicket took him past Lance Cairns to be New Zealand's second-highest wicket-taker with 131 – a mere 300 behind Sir Richard Hadlee. There was time for New Zealand to play a nominal second innings, in which Murray was controversially given out by ICC umpire Nigel Plews, caught behind off his glove. Television suggested that Murray's hand was not on the bat when the ball made contact.

Man of the Match: A. C. Parore.

Close of play: First day, New Zealand 24-0 (B. A. Young 16*, D. J. Murray 4*); Second day, New Zealand 221-6 (A. C. Parore 34*, M. N. Hart 2*); Third day, No play; Fourth day, West Indies 102-5 (S. Chanderpaul 18*, J. R. Murray 3*).

New Zealand

B. A. Young c Murray b Walsh	19	– c Murray b K. C. G. Benjamin . 21
D. J. Murray c Campbell b Ambrose	43	– c Murray b Walsh 8
A. H. Jones c Williams b K. C. G. Benjamin	12	– not out..................... 10
*K. R. Rutherford c Murray b Ambrose	11	– not out..................... 16
S. P. Fleming c Lara b Walsh	56	
S. A. Thomson c W. K. M. Benjamin b K. C. G. Benjamin	20	
†A. C. Parore not out	100	
M. N. Hart c and b W. K. M. Benjamin	45	
D. J. Nash c Campbell b Ambrose	3	
B 12, l-b 5, n-b 15	32	L-b 1, n-b 5 6

1/32 (1) 2/63 (3) 3/92 (4)   (8 wkts dec.) 341 1/33 (2) 2/33 (1)   (2 wkts) 61
4/97 (2) 5/128 (6) 6/210 (5)
7/328 (8) 8/341 (9)

S. B. Doull and D. K. Morrison did not bat.

Bowling: *First Innings*—Ambrose 31.1–12–57–3; Walsh 30–5–69–2; W. K. M. Benjamin 33–4–94–1; K. C. G. Benjamin 25–7–91–2; Chanderpaul 3–1–10–0; Arthurton 2–0–3–0. *Second Innings*—Ambrose 3–0–7–0; W. K. M. Benjamin 5–1–12–0; K. C. G. Benjamin 6–0–12–1; Walsh 4–1–8–1; Arthurton 5–1–9–0; Adams 3–1–4–0; Lara 4–0–8–0; Chanderpaul 2–2–0–0.

West Indies

S. C. Williams c Parore b Morrison	10	C. E. L. Ambrose b Morrison	33
S. L. Campbell lbw b Morrison	51	*C. A. Walsh not out	0
B. C. Lara b Morrison	0	K. C. G. Benjamin c Parore b Morrison	5
J. C. Adams c Doull b Morrison	13	L-b 11, n-b 4	15
K. L. T. Arthurton run out	1		
S. Chanderpaul b Thomson	69	1/10 (1) 2/21 (3) 3/49 (4) 4/54 (5)	312
†J. R. Murray c Murray b Thomson	28	5/98 (2) 6/155 (7) 7/232 (6)	
W. K. M. Benjamin b Doull	85	8/299 (9) 9/307 (8) 10/312 (11)	

Bowling: Morrison 26.2–9–69–6; Nash 5–2–11–0; Doull 22–5–85–1; Hart 25–2–75–0; Thomson 18–3–61–2.

Umpires: N. T. Plews (England) and B. L. Aldridge.
Referee: P. L. van der Merwe (South Africa).

NEW ZEALAND v WEST INDIES

Second Test Match

At Wellington, February 10, 11, 12, 13. West Indies won by an innings and 322 runs. Toss: West Indies.

Outstanding bowling by Walsh secured West Indies the fourth-biggest victory in Test history and New Zealand's heaviest defeat, despite a Basin Reserve pitch made for batsmen. With awkward bounce unobtainable, Walsh concentrated on an immaculate line and length. He was at his best bowling across the left-handers; one over in which he repeatedly flummoxed Fleming, apparently well-set on 47, and finally had him caught was worthy of inclusion in any coaching video. His match figures were 13 for 55, bettered for West Indies only by Michael Holding's 14 for 149 at The Oval in 1976, and he conceded just 1.52 an over. He beat his previous best Test return of six for 62 in both innings and, when he dismissed Young for the second time, reached 250 wickets in his 70th Test.

There were no excuses for the home batting, on a pitch Adams rated "nine point plenty" out of ten. Darrin Murray, who batted nearly five hours over two innings, and Young got New Zealand through a tricky 12 overs on the second evening, and next morning Murray went to fifty. But, as so often in New Zealand's centenary season, the batsmen failed to dig in; there were too many dashers when grafters were required.

Their double batting failure followed West Indies' innings of 660 for five, their fourth-highest total in Tests and the biggest ever conceded by New Zealand. It included three centuries, which could have been four if Campbell had not slowed down after damaging a hamstring. Lara, after some early false shots, upheld his reputation with a glorious array of strokes all around the wicket before being given lbw to the slower ball which Morrison calls his "soft pie". He had made 147 from 181 balls, with 23 fours, and added 221 with Adams, a West Indian third-wicket record against New Zealand. Adams was a little slower, but advanced to 151 from 226 balls, primarily through drives and pushes; his first hook came on 80. The punchline was Murray's maiden Test hundred, from 88 balls, scored overwhelmingly on the under-populated leg side. He was almost cut short by Hart and Parore on 98, when he was not given caught behind, and next ball offered a straightforward leg-side stumping chance.

That was the major blemish in what was generally efficient, dedicated New Zealand fielding in trying conditions. But they had handicapped themselves from the start. Thomson needed eight stitches below the knee after falling over an advertising hoarding at fielding practice. He was mistakenly passed fit to play next day but had to stand in the unaccustomed position of first slip, did not bowl an over and batted without freedom. Doull and Rutherford also carried injuries. Su'a was a dubious selection for other reasons; he had been suspended by Auckland for abusing an umpire in a club match, but he played for New Zealand until a later hearing suspended him afresh. New Zealand also used Stephen Mather as a substitute; he was on hand only because he had been suspended by Wellington for off-field misconduct, and he earned more than he would have done playing in their Shell Trophy game.

Man of the Match: C. A. Walsh.

Close of play: First day, West Indies 356-3 (J. C. Adams 87*, K. L. T. Arthurton 0*); Second day, New Zealand 23-0 (B. A. Young 12*, D. J. Murray 7*); Third day, New Zealand 52-3 (D. J. Murray 13*, S. P. Fleming 28*).

West Indies

S. C. Williams c Parore b Doull	26	†J. R. Murray not out	101
S. L. Campbell c Su'a b Morrison	88	L-b 6, n-b 10	16
B. C. Lara lbw b Morrison	147		
J. C. Adams c Su'a b Doull	151	1/85 (1) 2/134 (2)	(5 wkts dec.) 660
K. L. T. Arthurton run out	70	3/355 (3) 4/449 (4)	
S. Chanderpaul not out	61	5/521 (5)	

C. E. L. Ambrose, *C. A. Walsh, K. C. G. Benjamin and R. Dhanraj did not bat.

Bowling: Morrison 29–5–82–2; Su'a 44–4–179–0; Doull 37.2–5–162–2; Hart 46–4–181–0; Jones 13–2–50–0.

New Zealand

B. A. Young lbw b Walsh	29	– b Walsh	0
D. J. Murray lbw b Ambrose	52	– b Walsh	43
A. H. Jones c Murray b Walsh	0	– lbw b Benjamin	2
*K. R. Rutherford lbw b Dhanraj	22	– lbw b Ambrose	5
S. P. Fleming c Lara b Walsh	47	– b Walsh	30
S. A. Thomson b Walsh	6	– b Dhanraj	8
†A. C. Parore c Adams b Walsh	32	– not out	5
M. N. Hart c Lara b Dhanraj	0	– c Ambrose b Dhanraj	1
M. L. Su'a c Murray b Walsh	6	– c Arthurton b Walsh	8
S. B. Doull b Walsh	0	– lbw b Walsh	0
D. K. Morrison not out	0	– c Murray b Walsh	14
B 1, l-b 14, n-b 7	22	L-b 2, n-b 4	6

1/50 (1) 2/52 (3) 3/108 (4) 4/135 (2)	216	1/0 (1) 2/3 (3) 3/15 (4)	122
5/160 (6) 6/196 (5) 7/197 (8)		4/70 (5) 5/93 (2) 6/93 (6)
8/207 (9) 9/211 (10) 10/216 (7)		7/97 (8) 8/106 (9)
		9/106 (10) 10/122 (11)

Bowling: *First Innings*—Ambrose 19–9–32–1; Walsh 20.4–7–37–7; Dhanraj 33–6–97–2; Benjamin 12–1–35–0. *Second Innings*—Walsh 15.2–8–18–6; Benjamin 8–0–36–1; Ambrose 5–1–17–1; Dhanraj 12–2–49–2.

Umpires: V. K. Ramaswamy (India) and R. S. Dunne.   Referee: B. N. Jarman (Australia).

THE SOUTH AFRICANS IN NEW ZEALAND, 1994-95

By PETER ROBINSON

South Africa's first tour of New Zealand for 31 years was either a limited success or a partial failure, depending on how it was viewed. They were one of five Test teams to visit during the centenary of New Zealand cricket. With the 1996 World Cup in mind, Hansie Cronje's party included a number of one-day specialists, but South Africa fared poorly in the quadrangular limited-overs tournament, losing to Australia and the hosts, and failing to reach the final. This placed additional pressure on them to maintain the superiority established over New Zealand on their recent tour of South Africa in the one-off Centenary Test, the official highlight of New Zealand's season. With Cronje leading from the front, victory at Eden Park was achieved on a remarkable last day. Cronje, who made his fifth Test century in his 21st Test, continued to progress as a captain. He was building on foundations laid by his predecessor, Kepler Wessels, but where Wessels's instincts might have urged caution, Cronje opted for adventure.

The tour revealed little that was not previously known about the players. South Africa's strength remained the quality of their fast and medium-pace bowling, particularly from Fanie de Villiers and Craig Matthews, but the batting was still brittle and prone to sudden collapse. The notable exception was Gary Kirsten, who enhanced his reputation as an opener. Kirsten reached 50 in four of his six innings, though a Test century still eluded him. Daryll Cullinan, too, provided glimpses of his rare talent with an intelligent one-day 65 against India and a cultured 96 in the Test. These innings were all the more impressive after a nightmare start, when he was tormented and then dismissed for nought by Shane Warne in a one-day international in Wellington.

SOUTH AFRICAN TOURING PARTY

W. J. Cronje (Orange Free State) (*captain*), D. J. Callaghan (Eastern Province), D. J. Cullinan (Border), P. S. de Villiers (Northern Transvaal), A. A. Donald (Orange Free State), C. E. Eksteen (Transvaal), A. C. Hudson (Natal), S. D. Jack (Transvaal), G. Kirsten (Western Province), B. M. McMillan (Western Province), C. R. Matthews (Western Province), J. N. Rhodes (Natal), D. J. Richardson (Eastern Province), M. J. R. Rindel (Northern Transvaal), E. O. Simons (Western Province), R. P. Snell (Transvaal), P. J. R. Steyn (Orange Free State), P. L. Symcox (Natal).

Manager: C. Docrat. *Coach*: R. A. Woolmer.

SOUTH AFRICAN TOUR RESULTS

Test match – Played 1: Won 1.
First-class matches – Played 2: Won 2.
Wins – New Zealand, New Zealand Academy XI.
One-day internationals – Played 3: Won 1, Lost 2. *Win* – India. *Losses* – Australia, New Zealand.
Other non-first-class match – Tied v Wellington.

Note: Matches in this section which were not first-class were signified by a dagger.

South Africa's matches v New Zealand, Australia and India in the Centenary Tournament (February 15–February 24) may be found in that section.

†At Wellington, February 20. Tied. Toss: South Africans. Wellington 234 for six (50 overs) (M. W. Douglas 100, J. M. Aiken 47 not out); South Africans 234 for seven (50 overs) (A. C. Hudson 37, G. Kirsten 85, D. J. Callaghan 42; L. J. Doull three for 34).
    The umpires raised Douglas's score from 96 to 100 between innings, ruling that a ball which crossed the boundary after a misfield was not dead.

NEW ZEALAND ACADEMY XI v SOUTH AFRICANS

At Nelson, February 27, 28, March 1. South Africans won by eight wickets. Toss: New Zealand Academy XI.
    The South Africans won a low-scoring match, dominated by the seamers, early on the third day. They were already 33 ahead by the first-day close, after Donald and Jack bowled out the Academy inside 43 overs. Cullinan hit an attractive 51 as Kerry Walmsley bowled himself into the New Zealand selectors' sights with five for 73. The home batsmen collapsed again in their second innings against the South African pace attack and a target of 82 allowed just enough time for Hudson to play himself into form with an unbeaten 52.
    Close of play: First day, South Africans 153-7 (S. D. Jack 20*, C. R. Matthews 4*); Second day, South Africans 13-1 (A. C. Hudson 5*, C. E. Eksteen 0*).

New Zealand Academy XI

M. E. Parlane run out	35	– b Symcox	7
J. M. Aiken c Rhodes b Jack	2	– c Eksteen b Jack	1
*L. G. Howell c Symcox b Jack	0	– c Donald b Jack	8
M. H. Richardson c Richardson b Matthews	7	– c Richardson b Matthews	12
N. J. Astle c Eksteen b Donald	49	– c Rhodes b Matthews	12
R. A. Jones c Matthews b Donald	4	– lbw b Matthews	30
†M. G. Croy lbw b Jack	1	– c Rhodes b Donald	5
P. J. Wiseman c Richardson b Donald	11	– c Cullinan b Jack	6
A. J. Gale c Eksteen b Jack	2	– c Steyn b Donald	20
G. R. Jonas b Donald	1	– c Eksteen b Matthews	1
K. P. Walmsley not out	2	– not out	14
B 1, l-b 1, n-b 4	6	L-b 5, n-b 5	10

1/5 2/5 3/40 4/51 5/65   120   1/2 2/15 3/24 4/32 5/43   126
6/67 7/108 8/117 9/117   6/58 7/68 8/101 9/105

Bowling: First Innings—Donald 13.2–3–39–4; Jack 14.4–4–47–4; Cronje 5–1–13–0; Matthews 6–2–16–1; Symcox 2–1–1–0; Eksteen 2–1–2–0. *Second Innings*—Donald 15.5–3–52–2; Jack 10–0–28–3; Matthews 16–6–23–4; Symcox 12–6–11–1; Eksteen 6–4–7–0.

South Africans

A. C. Hudson b Walmsley	0	– not out	52
P. J. R. Steyn c Croy b Gale	32	– c Aiken b Walmsley	0
*W. J. Cronje lbw b Jonas	6	– (4) not out	6
D. J. Cullinan c Astle b Wiseman	51		
J. N. Rhodes c Aiken b Gale	0		
†D. J. Richardson c Aiken b Walmsley	33		
P. L. Symcox c Parlane b Wiseman	0		
S. D. Jack not out	28		
C. R. Matthews b Walmsley	4		
C. E. Eksteen c Aiken b Walmsley	0	– (3) c and b Wiseman	18
A. A. Donald c Howell b Walmsley	4		
L-b 6, n-b 1	7	B 8, n-b 1	9

1/0 2/27 3/61 4/61 5/110   165   1/13 2/79   (2 wkts) 85
6/110 7/148 8/153 9/153

Bowling: *First Innings*—Walmsley 16.3–3–73–5; Jonas 14–5–38–1; Gale 12·5–5–23–2; Wiseman 12–3–25–2; Richardson 1–1–0–0. *Second Innings*—Walmsley 8–3–20–1; Jonas 5–2–19–0; Wiseman 5.5–0–29–1; Gale 3–0–9–0.

Umpires: C. E. King and D. M. Quested.

NEW ZEALAND v SOUTH AFRICA

Centenary Test Match

At Auckland, March 4, 5, 6, 7, 8. South Africa won by 93 runs. Toss: South Africa.

Cronje's tempting declaration 15 minutes before lunch on the fifth day left New Zealand 275 to win in 63 overs and enough time to get themselves out. The hosts, in the middle of what was proving to be a disastrous centenary season, duly obliged, losing their last seven wickets after tea in less than 28 overs.

The first session of the match was lost to rain, but Cullinan celebrated his 28th birthday by scoring 82 by the close as South Africa recovered from the loss of two early wickets to reach 153 for three. Cullinan was unable to push on to his second Test century, however, and was out early on the second morning as the seamers began to work their way through the middle order. New Zealand had brought in Patel to replace the injured Thomson on the eve of the match, but neither his off-spin nor Hart's slow left-arm gained a wicket as the pitch became progressively more placid, rewarding only line and length. The South African batsmen, however, failed to capitalise and only a brisk 41 from Cronje interrupted the steadiness of the bowling.

A cautious 74 from Young and a more flamboyant 89 from Parore took New Zealand to stumps on the third day with a lead of 22 and three first-innings wickets intact, but in the morning South Africa began what was to be a match-winning innings. Donald and de Villiers snipped off the New Zealand tail for the addition of only 12 more runs and then Kirsten and Hudson paved the way for Cronje's fifth Test century. He had also scored a hundred in the team's last Test encounter, two months earlier. Cronje launched into the attack, striking three sixes as he galloped to 50 off 67 balls, and reached three figures on the fifth morning, before calling the innings to a close. Initially, New Zealand picked up the challenge. At tea, with seven wickets standing and 161 needed off 35 overs, the chase was still on. But Fleming went to the third ball after the interval, and, when Rutherford pulled de Villiers to mid-on for 56, New Zealand had shot their bolt. De Villiers, coming to the end of an exhausting summer, was so anxious to complete one more five-wicket haul that he protested when Cronje wanted to replace him with Donald. But it was the equally indefatigable Matthews who trapped Nash leg-before to end the match with 7.1 overs remaining.

Man of the Match: W. J. Cronje.

Close of play: First day, South Africa 153-3 (D. J. Cullinan 82*, C. E. Eksteen 0*); Second day, New Zealand 94-1 (B. A. Young 62*, M. D. Crowe 1*); Third day, New Zealand 316-7 (G. R. Larsen 20*, D. N. Patel 11*); Fourth day, South Africa 232-4 (W. J. Cronje 58*, J. N. Rhodes 7*).

South Africa

G. Kirsten b Larsen	16	– c Parore b Nash	76
P. J. R. Steyn c Patel b Morrison	46	– c Rutherford b Patel	13
A. C. Hudson c Parore b Nash	1	– c Young b Patel	64
D. J. Cullinan c Murray b Morrison	96	– c Parore b Hart	12
C. E. Eksteen c Fleming b Nash	21		
*W. J. Cronje c Crowe b Morrison	41	– (5) c Hart b Larsen	101
J. N. Rhodes c Parore b Nash	0	– (6) b Larsen	28
†D. J. Richardson c Parore b Nash	18	– (7) not out	8
C. R. Matthews c Parore b Larsen	26	– (8) not out	4
P. S. de Villiers c Hart b Larsen	12		
A. A. Donald not out	4		
L-b 13	13	L-b 1, n-b 1	2
	294	**(6 wkts dec.)**	**308**

1/41 (1) 2/42 (3) 3/145 (2) 4/168 (4)
5/230 (5) 6/230 (6) 7/230 (7)
8/276 (9) 9/276 (8) 10/294 (10)

1/41 (2) 2/123 (1) (6 wkts dec.) 308
3/135 (4) 4/218 (3)
5/277 (6) 6/300 (5)

Bowling: First Innings—Morrison 26–9–53–3; Nash 27–13–72–4; Larsen 24.3–7–57–3; Hart 11–3–45–0; Patel 17–2–54–0. *Second Innings*—Morrison 23–6–78–0; Nash 22–3–67–1; Patel 30–9–81–2; Larsen 18–6–31–2; Hart 12–3–50–1.

New Zealand

B. A. Young c Richardson b Donald	74	– c Cullinan b de Villiers	4
D. J. Murray c Kirsten b Cronje	25	– c Matthews b de Villiers	24
M. D. Crowe c Hudson b de Villiers	16	– c Cullinan b Matthews	14
S. P. Fleming b Matthews	17	– c Richardson b Matthews	27
*K. R. Rutherford c Richardson b Cronje	28	– c Hudson b de Villiers	56
†A. C. Parore c Richardson b Donald	89	– c Cullinan b Eksteen	24
M. N. Hart lbw b Matthews	28	– (8) c Richardson b de Villiers	6
G. R. Larsen not out	26	– (9) c Richardson b Donald	1
D. N. Patel c Richardson b Donald	15	– (7) run out	12
D. J. Nash lbw b de Villiers	1	– lbw b Matthews	6
D. K. Morrison c Cullinan b Donald	0	– not out	0
L-b 4, w 1, n-b 3	9	B 1, l-b 4, n-b 2	7

1/86 (2) 2/108 (1) 3/137 (4) 4/144 (3)   328   1/11 (1) 2/42 (3) 3/50 (2)   181
5/226 (5) 6/268 (6) 7/303 (7)   4/114 (4) 5/145 (5) 6/167 (7)
8/321 (9) 9/322 (10) 10/328 (11)   7/174 (6) 8/174 (8)
                                                         9/179 (9) 10/181 (10)

Bowling: First Innings—Donald 32.4–11–88–4; de Villiers 36–13–78–2; Matthews 32–11–66–2; Cronje 17–3–48–2; Eksteen 23–9–43–0. *Second Innings*—Eksteen 14–5–25–1; de Villiers 18–6–42–4; Donald 8–2–44–1; Matthews 12.5–3–47–3; Cronje 3–1–18–0.

Umpires: D. B. Hair (Australia) and R. S. Dunne.   Referee: B. N. Jarman (Australia).

ERRATA

WISDEN, 1985

Page 1027   In Tasmania's match with Western Australia on February 17-20, 1984, K. H. MacLeay of Western Australia was c Allen b Clough 0.

WISDEN, 1995

Page 392   R. J. Evans of Lincolnshire, not R. A. Evans of Oxfordshire, represented Minor Counties against the South Africans.

Page 644   In Gloucestershire's first innings, R. C. Russell was caught by S. J. Rhodes, not P. J. Newport, and the falls of wicket should read 6/289 7/305 8/326.

Page 957   Dean Cosker of Millfield played for Glamorgan Second XI, not Somerset.

Page 1067   In Pakistan's second innings, H. H. Streak's figures were 16–4–25–0.

THE SRI LANKANS IN NEW ZEALAND, 1994-95

By D. J. CAMERON

For Sri Lanka, triumph. For New Zealand, more agony. By winning the First Test at Napier by 241 runs, Sri Lanka gained their first overseas win in 32 attempts since entering Test cricket in 1981-82. By working comfortably to a draw in the Second Test at Dunedin, they completed their first series win outside Sri Lanka. As they grew in style and confidence, the tour became a landmark in their history and they left trailing clouds of glory.

In total contrast, for New Zealand this was the final act of a season that had degenerated into the script of a horror film. The Sri Lankan tour should have been a pleasant way to round off a celebratory centenary programme. Instead, after months of indiscipline, resignations, defeats and injuries, New Zealand cricket was in crisis even before this. (A full account of the troubles appears in the Cricket in New Zealand section.) The effect of the injuries was to force the selectors into hasty and ill-considered changes.

The Sri Lankans had been disconcerted to arrive at the Napier ground to find a green pitch prepared, so the gossip had it, for New Zealand's medium-fast bowlers, especially 22-year-old Kerry Walmsley, who had only three first-class games behind him. The New Zealanders rubbed their hands when Sri Lanka had to bat first and were out for 183. But from that point onward they were wringing their hands in despair. The pitch lent itself just as well to the left-arm seam of Chaminda Vaas, who took ten wickets in the match to set up a crushing victory. Even allegations from the New Zealand camp about the action of off-spinner Muttiah Muralitharan, who claimed five in the second innings, could not obscure the brilliance of Vaas's bowling, sharp Sri Lankan catching, and the ability of their batsmen to fight their way out of trouble. Chamara Dunusinghe, Sri Lanka's new wicket-keeper, also emerged as a hero at Napier. His keeping was speculative, but he fought hard as a No. 7 batsman; his second-innings 91 played a major part in securing victory.

On a steadier pitch at Dunedin, Vaas shone again, with a maiden fifty and six more wickets. Despite a 74-run lead, New Zealand's prospects of forcing a win to draw the series disappeared as Asanka Gurusinha and Hashan Tillekeratne scored centuries. The home team were more cheerful when the one-day internationals began, taking the first two high-scoring games, but Sri Lanka finished their tour with a flourish by winning the third at Eden Park.

Although Roshan Mahanama missed the tour, Sri Lanka proved to have a solid batting line-up, despite the lack of any substantial help from the explosive Aravinda de Silva. As for the bowling, the arrival of Vaas, the steadiness of Pramodya Wickremasinghe and the perplexing spin of Muralitharan – plus the versatility of Sanath Jayasuriya and Ruwan Kalpage in the one-day game – gave Sri Lanka an effective all-round attack. Though their opponents were not in good form or humour, the Sri Lankans improved with every passing day; even in top form, New Zealand would have had trouble avoiding defeat by what became known as Ranatunga's Raiders.

SRI LANKAN TOURING PARTY

A. Ranatunga (Sinhalese SC) (*captain*), P. A. de Silva (Nondescripts CC), C. I. Dunusinghe (Antonians SC), J. C. Gamage (Galle CC), A. P. Gurusinha (Sinhalese SC), S. T. Jayasuriya (Bloomfield C and AC), R. S. Kalpage (Bloomfield C and AC), C. Mendis (Colts CC), M. Muralitharan (Tamil Union), K. R. Pushpakumara (Nondescripts CC), S. Ranatunga (Nondescripts CC), D. P. Samaraweera (Colts CC), K. J. Silva (Bloomfield C and AC), H. P. Tillekeratne (Nondescripts CC), W. P. U. J. C. Vaas (Colts CC), G. P. Wickremasinghe (Sinhalese SC).

Tour manager: N. Perera.　　　*Cricket manager:* T. B. Kehelgamuwa.

SRI LANKAN TOUR RESULTS

Test matches – Played 2: Won 1, Drawn 1.
First-class matches – Played 4: Won 2, Drawn 2.
Wins – New Zealand, New Zealand Academy XI.
Draws – New Zealand, New Zealand XI.
One-day internationals – Played 3: Won 1, Lost 2.
Other non-first-class matches – Played 2: Won 1, No result 1. *Win* – Canterbury. *No result* – New Zealand Academy XI.

TEST MATCH AVERAGES

NEW ZEALAND – BATTING

	T	I	NO	R	HS	100s	Avge	Ct
S. P. Fleming.......	2	3	0	101	66	0	33.66	4
B. A. Young.......	2	4	1	100	84	0	33.33	6
G. R. Larsen	2	3	1	37	21*	0	18.50	3
M. J. Greatbatch....	2	3	0	47	46	0	15.66	0
A. C. Parore	2	3	0	43	19	0	14.33	7
D. J. Murray	2	4	1	37	36	0	12.33	2
K. P. Walmsley	2	3	0	8	4	0	2.66	0

Played in two Tests: K. R. Rutherford 32, 20 (1 ct). Played in one Test: D. K. Morrison 7*, 0; D. J. Nash 0, 0 (1 ct); D. N. Patel 52 (2 ct); C. Pringle 4; M. L. Su'a 20*; S. A. Thomson 8, 4.

* Signifies not out.

BOWLING

	O	M	R	W	BB	5W/i	Avge
D. K. Morrison	44.3	10	101	7	4-61	0	14.42
D. N. Patel	78	23	158	7	4-96	0	22.57
G. R. Larsen	94.4	35	173	7	3-73	0	24.71
M. L. Su'a	46.5	8	140	4	2-43	0	35.00
C. Pringle	37	9	106	3	3-51	0	35.33
D. J. Nash........	52	16	115	3	2-28	0	38.33
K. P. Walmsley	111	22	344	7	3-70	0	49.14

Also bowled: S. A. Thomson 6–3–10–0.

SRI LANKA – BATTING

	T	I	NO	R	HS	100s	Avge	Ct
H. P. Tillekeratne........	2	4	0	227	108	1	56.75	4
A. Ranatunga	2	4	0	173	90	0	43.25	0
A. P. Gurusinha	2	4	0	165	127	1	41.25	4
W. P. U. J. C. Vaas	2	4	1	123	51	0	41.00	0
C. I. Dunusinghe	2	4	0	113	91	0	28.25	8
P. A. de Silva	2	4	0	93	62	0	23.25	1
D. P. Samaraweera.......	2	4	0	77	33	0	19.25	1
S. Ranatunga	2	4	0	64	23	0	16.00	2
G. P. Wickremasinghe....	2	4	0	48	16	0	12.00	0
M. Muralitharan.........	2	4	1	33	10*	0	11.00	1
K. R. Pushpakumara	2	4	2	19	17*	0	9.50	0

* Signifies not out.

BOWLING

	O	M	R	W	BB	5W/i	Avge
W. P. U. J. C. Vaas	85.4	22	177	16	6-87	3	11.06
M. Muralitharan.........	86	35	141	7	5-64	1	20.14
G. P. Wickremasinghe....	58	15	124	3	3-33	0	41.33

Also bowled: P. A. de Silva 1-0-11-0; A. P. Gurusinha 6-2-10-0; K. R. Pushpakumara 30-6-84-2.

Note: Matches in this section which were not first-class are signified by a dagger.

†At New Plymouth, February 24. No result. Toss: Sri Lanka. New Zealand Academy XI 101 for five (27.1 overs) (L. G. Howell 31; J. C. Gamage four for 22) v Sri Lankans.

NEW ZEALAND XI v SRI LANKANS

At Wanganui, February 26, 27, 28, March 1. Drawn. Toss: New Zealand XI.

Though Vaas reduced the home team to 76 for five on the first day, opener Murray reclaimed the initiative with an eight-hour innings of 182, and the Sri Lankans were never on top again. Murray was ninth out, in the 112th over, after striking 24 fours. His one ally was Germon, in a 157-run stand for the sixth wicket. The Sri Lankan batsmen were unconvincing, with too many edges to the wicket-keeper and slips, and only Jayasuriya reached 50. Despite bowling 16 no-balls, Davis wound up the innings with five for 46 from 20 overs. Already 135 ahead, the New Zealand XI extended their lead to 355 before declaring. The tourists made no attempt on the target, but Samaraweera and Tillekeratne ensured they were safe from defeat.

Close of play: First day, New Zealand XI 268-7 (D. J. Murray 150*); Second day, Sri Lankans 170-6 (S. T. Jayasuriya 51*, W. P. U. J. C. Vaas 0*); Third day, New Zealand XI 197-5 (W. A. Wisneski 24*, C. Z. Harris 0*).

New Zealand XI

D. J. Murray b Pushpakumara	182	
C. M. Spearman c Samaraweera b Vaas	11	– (1) lbw b Silva 47
A. H. Jones lbw b Vaas	0	– c Dunusinghe b Pushpakumara . 66
R. G. Twose c Dunusinghe b Vaas	7	– b Silva 9
S. R. Mather b Pushpakumara	0	– c Samaraweera b de Silva 15
C. Z. Harris c Dunusinghe b Vaas	10	– (7) not out 4
*†L. K. Germon c Gamage b Pushpakumara	64	– (8) not out 13
M. N. Hart c Dunusinghe b Gurusinha	9	– (2) lbw b Vaas 19
W. A. Wisneski c Dunusinghe b Gamage	1	– (6) c Jayasuriya b Pushpakumara 25
A. L. Penn not out	12	
H. T. Davis lbw b Vaas	4	
B 4, l-b 9, n-b 14	27	B 4, l-b 12, n-b 6 22
	327	**220**

1/16 2/16 3/38 4/48 5/76　　　　　327　　1/74 2/74 3/107　(6 wkts dec.) 220
6/233 7/268 8/275 9/319　　　　　　　　4/146 5/196 6/197

Bowling: First Innings—Vaas 34.1–13–87–5; Pushpakumara 23–4–71–3; Gamage 30–11–81–1; de Silva 7–3–15–0; Silva 9–1–33–0; Jayasuriya 5–0–19–0; Gurusinha 6–2–8–1. *Second Innings*—Vaas 21–4–47–1; Pushpakumara 18.5–4–53–2; Gamage 10.1–1–39–0; Gurusinha 2–1–4–0; Silva 28–13–47–2; de Silva 7–1–14–1.

Sri Lankans

A. P. Gurusinha c Twose b Mather	36	– c Germon b Penn 1
D. P. Samaraweera lbw b Wisneski	9	– c Murray b Hart 46
S. Ranatunga c Harris b Hart	10	– c Hart b Davis 21
*P. A. de Silva c Germon b Davis	21	– c Germon b Penn 5
H. P. Tillekeratne b Davis	2	– not out 68
S. T. Jayasuriya c Spearman b Penn	51	– c Wisneski b Jones 5
†C. I. Dunusinghe c Harris b Wisneski	20	– not out 5
W. P. U. J. C. Vaas c Germon b Davis	0	
K. R. Pushpakumara b Davis	17	
J. C. Gamage not out	4	
K. J. Silva c Harris b Davis	0	
L-b 4, w 1, n-b 17	22	W 2, n-b 2 4
	192	**155**

1/38 2/61 3/90 4/94 5/97　　　　　192　　1/3 2/64 3/74　(5 wkts) 155
6/166 7/170 8/172 9/191　　　　　　　　4/87 5/99

Bowling: First Innings—Davis 19.5–5–46–5; Penn 17–2–50–1; Wisneski 14–6–31–2; Mather 3–0–20–1; Hart 16–8–41–1. *Second Innings*—Davis 17–10–31–1; Penn 11–2–33–2; Wisneski 7–2–16–0; Hart 23–7–56–1; Jones 1–1–0–1; Harris 3–2–3–0; Mather 3–0–14–0; Twose 3–2–2–0.

Umpires: D. B. Cowie and E. A. Watkin.

NEW ZEALAND ACADEMY XI v SRI LANKANS

At Palmerston North, March 4, 5, 6, 7. Sri Lankans won by 242 runs. Toss: Sri Lankans.

A crushing victory put the Sri Lankans in the right mood for the First Test. Nearly all the top order had struck form, and the spinners wrecked the Academy: slow left-armer Jayantha Silva took seven wickets - but still did not play at Napier - and off-spinner Muralitharan nine. The tourists had not looked so confident on the first day, leaning heavily on 75 from Mendis. But Silva and Muralitharan were soon among the wickets, taking the Academy's last nine for 90. The Sri Lankan openers more than doubled a first-innings lead of 124 and the Ranatunga brothers put on 150 in 130 minutes for the fourth wicket. Arjuna hit 107 from 130 balls, with 14 fours and two sixes, before declaring at tea, setting a target of 448 in four sessions. His spinners bowled out the Academy again in five hours; only Astle, who held out for 213 minutes, detained them past lunch on the final day.

Close of play: First day, New Zealand Academy XI 12-1 (J. M. Aiken 5*, L. G. Howell 0*); Second day, Sri Lankans 94-0 (A. P. Gurusinha 54*, D. P. Samaraweera 36*); Third day, New Zealand Academy XI 110-4 (N. J. Astle 14*, R. A. Jones 3*).

Sri Lankans

A. P. Gurusinha c Croy b Jonas	49	– c Jones b Jonas	63
D. P. Samaraweera c Jones b Jonas	3	– c Jones b Astle	78
S. Ranatunga c Croy b Kennedy	36	– st Croy b Astle	46
P. A. de Silva b Kennedy	30	– lbw b Wiseman	0
*A. Ranatunga c Parlane b Haslam	6	– c Parlane b Wiseman	107
C. Mendis c Croy b Jonas	75	– (7) not out	0
†C. I. Dunusinghe lbw b Kennedy	12	– (6) not out	2
G. P. Wickremasinghe b Jonas	17		
M. Muralitharan c Astle b Haslam	8		
J. C. Gamage c Howell b Haslam	13		
K. J. Silva not out	0		
B 1, l-b 4, n-b 3	8	B 4, l-b 21, n-b 2	27

1/8 2/82 3/121 4/127 5/131   257   1/128 2/167 3/168   (5 wkts dec.) 323
6/162 7/222 8/233 9/253   4/318 5/323

Bowling: *First Innings*—Kennedy 17–6–40–3; Jonas 25–7–67–4; Astle 6–0–19–0; Haslam 30.3–2–110–3; Wiseman 3–1–16–0. *Second Innings*—Kennedy 17–5–56–0; Jonas 19.4–61–1; Wiseman 36–13–80–2; Haslam 13–5–38–0; Richardson 5–1–14–0; Astle 20–4–49–2.

New Zealand Academy XI

M. E. Parlane c Dunusinghe b Wickremasinghe	6	– b Silva	27
J. M. Aiken c Samaraweera b Muralitharan	20	– c sub (S. T. Jayasuriya) b Muralitharan	39
*L. G. Howell st Dunusinghe b Silva	43	– b Muralitharan	4
M. H. Richardson c Dunusinghe b Muralitharan	18	– b Muralitharan	18
N. J. Astle c Gurusinha b Silva	9	– c Mendis b Silva	80
R. A. Jones lbw b Silva	0	– c de Silva b Silva	9
†M. G. Croy c A. Ranatunga b Silva	14	– b Silva	1
P. J. Wiseman b Muralitharan	4	– c Gurusinha b Muralitharan	1
M. J. Haslam b Silva	3	– c Samaraweera b Muralitharan	2
G. R. Jonas c de Silva b Muralitharan	7	– not out	9
R. J. Kennedy not out	1	– b Silva	0
B 10, l-b 3, n-b 5	18	B 7, n-b 8	15

1/11 2/43 3/78 4/88 5/88   133   1/45 2/70 3/83 4/100 5/126   205
6/104 7/112 8/118 9/132   6/131 7/136 8/177 9/205

Bowling: *First Innings*—Wickremasinghe 18–9–25–1; Gamage 8–3–21–0; Muralitharan 34–19–45–4; Silva 25.5–12–29–5. *Second Innings*—Wickremasinghe 8–1–35–0; Gamage 3–1–19–0; Silva 34.4–14–77–5; Muralitharan 39–16–56–5; S. Ranatunga 2–1–1–0; Mendis 2–0–10–0.

Umpires: B. L. Aldridge and B. F. Bowden.

NEW ZEALAND v SRI LANKA

First Test Match

At Napier, March 11, 12, 13, 14, 15. Sri Lanka won by 241 runs. Toss: New Zealand. Test debuts: K. P. Walmsley; C. I. Dunusinghe.

After their initial batting torment, Sri Lanka steadily took command and finished off New Zealand before lunch on the fifth day – their first Test win overseas. The triumph gained lustre from the fact that the pitch was tailored for the New Zealand medium-fast bowlers, Morrison, Nash and the 6ft 8in 22-year-old Kerry Walmsley. Napier pitches are usually hard and true, offering bowlers little help. This one had a solid covering of grass and 13 wickets fell on the first day.

After sending Sri Lanka in, New Zealand scented a morale-building win when Walmsley, despite being erratic, and Nash claimed three wickets for 40. Sri Lanka struggled to 88 for six, but were sustained for a while by a 49-run stand between Arjuna Ranatunga and Vaas. Ranatunga became the first Sri Lankan to score 3,000 Test runs when 39.

Their recovery to 183 suggested the pitch was losing its sting. But Wickremasinghe and Vaas gained sharp movement off the pitch and through the air as they captured three wickets for six in 20 balls. New Zealand were lucky not to be five down by stumps, as Fleming was dropped and Rutherford might have been lbw. On a misty second morning, they offered only brief resistance to more sharp medium-fast bowling and improved catching. Rutherford toiled for three hours, but Sri Lanka brushed New Zealand aside for 109 inside 43 overs, with left-armer Vaas taking five for 47.

Sri Lanka seemed to have wasted a 74-run lead at 22 for three. Samaraweera was given run out at 14 – although he had gained his ground and then jumped in the air to avoid a throw, an action allowed under Law 38.1 – and, when Larsen had Gurusinha and Sanjeeva Ranatunga lbw, the match was swinging back to New Zealand. Tillekeratne and de Silva slowly reasserted their command until bad light stopped play at 5.15 p.m. and, after a wet third morning, extended their partnership to 99. Tillekeratne's invaluable five-hour 74 finally ended with Sri Lanka 205 for six, growing more confident with every minute as the pitch eased. Vaas put together 36, while the debutant keeper Dunusinghe took command. The tailenders struggled to stay with him as he approached a century, but he was ninth out, for 91, after 323 minutes. In the closing stages he had a runner, though he was later able to take four catches.

Needing 427 to win in five sessions, New Zealand were baffled by Muralitharan's bounce and sharp off-spin. Though Murray and Greatbatch counter-attacked to take the score past 100 with only one wicket down, three quick wickets put New Zealand in trouble again. Rutherford and Thomson survived, not at all confidently, until stumps, when John F. Reid, the stand-in New Zealand coach, tastelessly claimed Muralitharan's action was suspect. Next morning, at 141, Rutherford was caught behind off Vaas and Muralitharan ended Thomson's struggle. Vaas ripped out the tail with merciful speed, for match figures of 45.3–13–90–10. No Sri Lankan had taken ten in a Test before.

Man of the Match: W. P. U. J. C. Vaas.

Close of play: First day, New Zealand 33-3 (S. P. Fleming 20*, K. R. Rutherford 8*); Second day, Sri Lanka 92-3 (P. A. de Silva 52*, H. P. Tillekeratne 16*); Third day, Sri Lanka 253-6 (C. I. Dunusinghe 50*, W. P. U. J. C. Vaas 12*); Fourth day, New Zealand 139-4 (K. R. Rutherford 20*, S. A. Thomson 2*).

Sri Lanka

A. P. Gurusinha b Walmsley	2	– lbw b Larsen	8
D. P. Samaraweera c Young b Walmsley	33	– run out	6
S. Ranatunga c Larsen b Nash	12	– lbw b Larsen	7
P. A. de Silva c Parore b Nash	0	– c Parore b Morrison	62
H. P. Tillekeratne lbw b Morrison	9	– c Young b Nash	74
*A. Ranatunga c Young b Walmsley	55	– b Morrison	28
†C. I. Dunusinghe c Rutherford b Larsen	11	– b Morrison	91
W. P. U. J. C. Vaas not out	33	– b Walmsley	36
G. P. Wickremasinghe c Fleming b Morrison	13	– c sub (M. N. Hart) b Larsen	16
M. Muralitharan c Nash b Larsen	8	– not out	10
K. R. Pushpakumara c Larsen b Morrison	1	– c Parore b Morrison	0
L-b 6	6	B 2, l-b 7, n-b 5	14
	183		**352**

1/15 (1) 2/40 (3) 3/40 (4) 4/54 (5) 5/64 (2) 6/88 (7) 7/137 (6) 8/166 (9) 9/178 (10) 10/183 (11)

1/14 (2) 2/21 (1) 3/22 (3) 4/121 (4) 5/165 (6) 6/205 (5) 7/294 (8) 8/323 (9) 9/352 (7) 10/352 (11)

Bowling: *First Innings*—Morrison 19–5–40–3; Walmsley 17–3–70–3; Nash 16–4–28–2; Larsen 17–6–39–2. *Second Innings*—Nash 36–12–87–1; Walmsley 38–7–112–1; Larsen 39–13–73–3; Thomson 6–3–10–0; Morrison 25.3–5–61–4.

New Zealand

B. A. Young c Dunusinghe b Wickremasinghe..	2	– c Samaraweera b Muralitharan..	14
D. J. Murray lbw b Vaas	1	– c Dunusinghe b Vaas..........	36
M. J. Greatbatch lbw b Wickremasinghe	1	– c Tillekeratne b Muralitharan..	46
S. P. Fleming c S. Ranatunga b Vaas	35	– c Tillekeratne b Muralitharan..	0
*K. R. Rutherford c Tillekeratne b Pushpakumara	32	– c Dunusinghe b Vaas..........	20
S. A. Thomson c Muralitharan b Vaas	8	– c Gurusinha b Muralitharan...	4
†A. C. Parore c Dunusinghe b Wickremasinghe	7	– c Tillekeratne b Muralitharan..	17
G. R. Larsen c Dunusinghe b Vaas............	0	– not out.....................	21
D. J. Nash lbw b Pushpakumara..............	0	– c Dunusinghe b Vaas..........	0
D. K. Morrison not out......................	7	– c Gurusinha b Vaas...........	0
K. P. Walmsley b Vaas......................	4	– c Dunusinghe b Vaas..........	4
B 5, l-b 1, w 1, n-b 5	12	B 6, l-b 11, n-b 6	23
	109		185

1/2 (1) 2/4 (3) 3/6 (2) 4/53 (4)   1/37 (1) 2/108 (3) 3/108 (2)
5/65 (6) 6/78 (7) 7/79 (8)   4/112 (4) 5/141 (5) 6/141 (6)
8/94 (9) 9/104 (5) 10/109 (11)   7/166 (7) 8/181 (9)
                                         9/181 (10) 10/185 (11)

Bowling: *First Innings*—Wickremasinghe 19–7–33–3; Vaas 18.5–3–47–5; Pushpakumara 5–1–23–2. *Second Innings*—Wickremasinghe 13–2–42–0; Vaas 26.4–10–43–5; Pushpakumara 9–2–19–0; Muralitharan 36–15–64–5.

Umpires: S. G. Randell (Australia) and D. B. Cowie.   Referee: B. N. Jarman (Australia).

NEW ZEALAND v SRI LANKA

Second Test Match

At Dunedin, March 18, 19, 20, 21, 22. Drawn. Toss: New Zealand.

The morale-sapping injuries which had afflicted New Zealand's seamers throughout this troublesome summer struck again. Morrison and Nash were ruled out, leaving the Auckland trio of Pringle, Su'a and Walmsley to head the attack. New Zealand gambled by putting Sri Lanka in. If anything, the pitch looked likely to take spin later, but off-spinner Thomson was omitted, mainly because of a decline in his batting.

The Sri Lankan openers looked solid enough for the first hour; in the second session New Zealand took the advantage when they claimed four wickets for 28. Though Tillekeratne and Vaas steadied the innings, when Tillekeratne, the last recognised batsman, was seventh out at 157, Sri Lanka had little hope of reaching 200. Then New Zealand's fielding went giddily astray. Wickremasinghe was dropped on six, while Pringle and Rutherford both missed high, slashed catches from Muralitharan – Rutherford split the webbing between two fingers in the process, ending his active service for the match. Faithful Vaas scored 51 in 134 minutes before he was last out, half an hour before stumps. But he was quickly into action once rain permitted a start on the second morning, removing Murray and Greatbatch for ducks at 26.

Fortunately for the New Zealanders, the rain closed in again just before lunch. Resuming, Young was dropped on 21, but he and Fleming struggled through 40 overs to the close and next morning achieved a rare landmark for New Zealand in 1994-95 – a century partnership. But Fleming was run out 14 runs later, and Vaas removed Parore and Young, who batted 381 minutes for his 84, before the total reached 200. A steady three-hour fifty from Patel helped New Zealand to 307, a lead of 74 – exactly the same as their first-innings deficit at Napier. Sri Lanka lost two wickets in drawing level and a third when only seven ahead; New Zealand scented victory again.

However, Gurusinha and Tillekeratne buckled down, adding 129 by stumps and offering only one chance, a very hard one to Young when Tillekeratne was 39. By the final morning the pitch had lost all menace, and the Test any hope of a result as the fourth-wicket pair extended their stand to 192. Gurusinha made a monumental 127, his sixth Test century, in 516 minutes with 11 fours and a six, while Tillekeratne scored his second in five and a half hours, with 14 fours. Arjuna Ranatunga looked likely to become the third century-maker until he was last out for a rapid 90. Sri Lanka led by 337; Vaas bowled one ball of New Zealand's second innings before the umpires agreed that the light was too bad. The draw ensured Sri Lanka's first overseas series win.

Man of the Match: W. P. U. J. C. Vaas.

Close of play: First day, New Zealand 7-0 (B. A. Young 6*, D. J. Murray 0*); Second day, New Zealand 95-2 (B. A. Young 44*, S. P. Fleming 39*); Third day, Sri Lanka 0-0 (A. P. Gurusinha 0*, D. P. Samaraweera 0*); Fourth day, Sri Lanka 210-3 (A. P. Gurusinha 92*, H. P. Tillekeratne 68*).

Sri Lanka

A. P. Gurusinha c Patel b Pringle	28	– b Su'a	127
D. P. Samaraweera b Su'a	33	– lbw b Su'a	5
S. Ranatunga c Young b Pringle	22	– c Parore b Patel	23
P. A. de Silva c Patel b Walmsley	18	– c Murray b Patel	13
*A. Ranatunga c Young b Larsen	0	– (6) c Parore b Larsen	90
H. P. Tillekeratne c Young b Patel	36	– (5) c Murray b Patel	108
†C. I. Dunusinghe lbw b Pringle	0	– c Fleming b Patel	11
W. P. U. J. C. Vaas c Fleming b Su'a	51	– c Parore b Walmsley	3
G. P. Wickremasinghe c Fleming b Patel	10	– c Parore b Walmsley	9
M. Muralitharan c Larsen b Patel	8	– run out	7
K. R. Pushpakumara not out	17	– not out	1
L-b 6, n-b 4	10	B 6, l-b 5, n-b 3	14

1/42 (1) 2/67 (2) 3/94 (4) 4/97 (5)   233   1/11 (2) 2/63 (3) 3/81 (4)   411
5/122 (3) 6/122 (7) 7/157 (6)   4/273 (5) 5/295 (1) 6/344 (7)
8/178 (9) 9/194 (10) 10/233 (8)   7/355 (8) 8/377 (9)
   9/405 (10) 10/411 (6)

Bowling: First Innings—Su'a 20.5-5-43-2; Walmsley 18-4-41-1; Pringle 15-1-51-3; Patel 21-3-62-3; Larsen 13-2-30-1. *Second Innings*—Walmsley 38-8-121-2; Patel 57-20-96-4; Su'a 26-3-97-2; Pringle 22-8-55-0; Larsen 25.4-14-31-1.

New Zealand

B. A. Young c Gurusinha b Vaas	84	– not out	0
D. J. Murray c Dunusinghe b Vaas	0	– not out	0
M. J. Greatbatch lbw b Vaas	0		
S. P. Fleming run out	66		
†A. C. Parore c de Silva b Vaas	19		
D. N. Patel b Muralitharan	52		
G. R. Larsen c Gurusinha b Muralitharan	16		
M. L. Su'a not out	20		
C. Pringle c S. Ranatunga b Vaas	4		
K. P. Walmsley b Vaas	0		
*K. R. Rutherford absent hurt			
B 3, l-b 28, n-b 15	46		

1/26 (2) 2/26 (3) 3/140 (4) 4/196 (5)   307   (no wkt) 0
5/197 (1) 6/244 (7) 7/291 (6)
8/303 (9) 9/307 (10)

Bowling: First Innings—Wickremasinghe 26-6-49-0; Vaas 40-9-87-6; Muralitharan 50-20-77-2; Pushpakumara 16-3-42-0; de Silva 1-0-11-0; Gurusinha 6-2-10-0. *Second Innings*—Vaas 0.1-0-0-0.

Umpires: V. K. Ramaswamy (India) and D. M. Quested.
Referee: B. N. Jarman (Australia).

†At Christchurch, March 24. Sri Lankans won by five wickets. Toss: Canterbury. Canterbury 164 for nine (50 overs) (C. Z. Harris 31; R. S. Kalpage three for 20); Sri Lankans 166 for five (39.1 overs) (S. T. Jayasuriya 46, P. A. de Silva 58 not out).

†NEW ZEALAND v SRI LANKA

First One-Day International

At Christchurch, March 26. New Zealand won by 33 runs. Toss: Sri Lanka. International debut: K. J. Silva.

The New Zealanders rediscovered their middle-order batting strength, so noticeably absent in the Tests, on a flat one-day pitch at Lancaster Park. Despite the customary bad start – both openers gone by 28 – Rutherford, with 65 in 75 balls, and Fleming lifted them to 122 by the halfway mark. Then Cairns, much missed during the Test series because of injury, stepped up the counter-attack with a run-a-ball 72 and New Zealand surged to 271 for six. Beating that looked simple when Jayasuriya and Gurusinha gave Sri Lanka a flying start of 83 in ten overs, but five wickets then fell for 49. Vaughan's military-medium bowling pegged down the second half of the innings and he took four wickets, his best return in one-day internationals.

Man of the Match: K. R. Rutherford.

New Zealand

M. J. Greatbatch b Pushpakumara	....	17
B. A. Young run out	....	3
*K. R. Rutherford c Gurusinha b Muralitharan	.	65
S. P. Fleming run out	....	46
C. L. Cairns c S. Ranatunga b Pushpakumara	.	72
†A. C. Parore b Vaas	....	31
D. N. Patel not out	....	23
J. T. C. Vaughan not out	....	1
B 2, l-b 5, w 5, n-b 1	....	13

1/5 2/28 3/122	(6 wkts, 50 overs) 271
4/177 5/235 6/265	

G. R. Larsen, M. L. Su'a and C. Pringle did not bat.

Bowling: Pushpakumara 10–0–53–2; Vaas 10–1–41–1; Gurusinha 4–0–19–0; Kalpage 8–0–54–0; Muralitharan 10–0–42–1; Silva 8–0–55–0.

Sri Lanka

A. P. Gurusinha c Greatbatch b Vaughan	.	33
S. T. Jayasuriya c Greatbatch b Vaughan	.	46
S. Ranatunga run out	....	11
P. A. de Silva c and b Vaughan	......	54
*A. Ranatunga run out	....	11
†H. P. Tillekeratne c Young b Pringle	.	10
R. S. Kalpage c Fleming b Vaughan	...	35
W. P. U. J. C. Vaas run out	....	27
M. Muralitharan c Parore b Cairns	....	8
K. R. Pushpakumara c Patel b Cairns	..	3
K. J. Silva not out	....	1
L-b 3, w 4, n-b 1	....	8

1/83 2/96 3/98	(47.5 overs) 238
4/105 5/132 6/193	
7/208 8/228 9/236	

Bowling: Pringle 9–1–47–1; Su'a 3–0–35–0; Cairns 7.5–0–49–2; Vaughan 10–1–33–4; Larsen 10–1–38–0; Patel 8–0–33–0.

Umpires: B. L. Aldridge and D. M. Quested.

†NEW ZEALAND v SRI LANKA

Second One-Day International

At Hamilton, March 29. New Zealand won on scoring-rate. Toss: New Zealand. International debut: J. C. Gamage.

New Zealand, who had not won any kind of series since December 1992, gained a decisive 2-0 lead by a technical knockout in the Hamilton rain. With their heaviest puncher, Greatbatch, lost to a back injury, New Zealand gambled by promoting Nathan Astle, a notional all-rounder, to open – and he virtually won the game himself. A free-stroking right-hander in his fourth international, Astle hit a solid 95 in 137 balls. With brief blasts from Rutherford and Cairns, followed by a brisk 61 from Parore, New Zealand reached 280. The Sri Lankan batting faded quickly – 16 for two, 46 for four, 111 for six – and they were well behind the rate when the arrival of rain presented a merciful end for everyone.

Man of the Match: N. J. Astle.

New Zealand

B. A. Young c Tillekeratne b Vaas	 4	†A. C. Parore not out	 61
N. J. Astle b Vaas	 95	S. A. Thomson b Jayasuriya	 1
*K. R. Rutherford c Kalpage		D. N. Patel not out	 22
b Muralitharan	. 34	L-b 9, w 6	 15
S. P. Fleming c Pushpakumara			
b Kalpage	. 6	1/23 2/83 3/94	(6 wkts, 50 overs) 280
C. L. Cairns c Gamage b Vaas	 42	4/173 5/242 6/245	

G. R. Larsen, J. T. C. Vaughan and C. Pringle did not bat.

Bowling: Pushpakumara 5–0–32–0; Vaas 10–1–36–3; Gamage 5–0–37–0; Kalpage 7–0–35–1; Muralitharan 10–1–62–1; Jayasuriya 10–0–47–1; A. Ranatunga 3–0–22–0.

Sri Lanka

A. P. Gurusinha c Larsen b Pringle	 7	R. S. Kalpage c Patel b Larsen	 11
S. T. Jayasuriya c Young b Patel	 6	W. P. U. J. C. Vaas not out	 1
S. Ranatunga run out	 15	B 1, l-b 2, w 1	 4
P. A. de Silva run out	 7		
*A. Ranatunga c Parore b Larsen	 27	1/8 2/16 3/30	(6 wkts, 31 overs) 117
†H. P. Tillekeratne not out	 39	4/46 5/80 6/111	

M. Muralitharan, K. R. Pushpakumara and J. C. Gamage did not bat.

Bowling: Pringle 7–1–22–1; Patel 10–1–31–1; Vaughan 3–0–18–0; Larsen 6–0–20–2; Thomson 5–0–23–0.

Umpires: B. F. Bowden and C. E. King.

†NEW ZEALAND v SRI LANKA

Third One-Day International

At Auckland, April 1. Sri Lanka won by 51 runs. Toss: Sri Lanka. International debut: C. Mendis.

Gaining first use of a flat, low-bouncing pitch that did not improve, Sri Lanka at last struck something like their best one-day form. They scored at a competitive five an over almost from the start: Gurusinha and Jayasuriya opened with 91 in 20 overs. Gurusinha then added 112 with Arjuna Ranatunga, on the way to his second one-day century, 108 from 149 balls. With the pitch remaining slow, the Sri Lankan spinners clamped down on New Zealand's batting. Greatbatch, Astle and Rutherford all reached 30 but the first five wickets brought only 139 and the second five a paltry 60; Sri Lanka strolled home when last man Pringle was dismissed with three and a half overs to spare.

Man of the Match: S. T. Jayasuriya.

Sri Lanka

A. P. Gurusinha b Cairns	108	C. Mendis not out	 3
S. T. Jayasuriya c and b Patel	 49	W. P. U. J. C. Vaas not out	 1
P. A. de Silva c and b Patel	 9	B 3, l-b 7, w 3, n-b 3	 16
*A. Ranatunga b Pringle	 39		
R. S. Kalpage c Rutherford b Cairns	... 9	1/91 2/106 3/218	(6 wkts, 50 overs) 250
†H. P. Tillekeratne c Fleming b Pringle	16	4/224 5/238 6/246	

S. Ranatunga, M. Muralitharan and J. C. Gamage did not bat.

Bowling: Pringle 10–0–56–2; Patel 10–1–28–2; Cairns 10–0–45–2; Vaughan 4–0–30–0; Larsen 10–0–49–0; Astle 6–1–32–0.

New Zealand

B. A. Young b Gamage	6	
M. J. Greatbatch c de Silva b Muralitharan	43	
N. J. Astle b Jayasuriya	35	
*K. R. Rutherford c Jayasuriya b de Silva	30	
C. L. Cairns c Gamage b Jayasuriya	15	
S. P. Fleming b Jayasuriya	18	
†A. C. Parore c Mendis b Kalpage	19	

D. N. Patel c Mendis b Kalpage	11	
J. T. C. Vaughan run out	5	
G. R. Larsen not out	2	
C. Pringle lbw b Kalpage	4	
B 1, l-b 5, w 4, n-b 1	11	

(46.3 overs) 199

1/13 2/80 3/104
4/135 5/139 6/173
7/178 8/192 9/192

Bowling: Vaas 8-0-34-0; Gamage 7-0-27-1; Muralitharan 10-0-32-1; Kalpage 9.3-0-47-3; Jayasuriya 10-0-35-3; de Silva 2-0-18-1.

Umpires: D. B. Cowie and R. S. Dunne.

THE COOPERS & LYBRAND RATINGS

Introduced in 1987, the Coopers & Lybrand Ratings (formerly the Deloitte Ratings) rank Test cricketers on a scale up to 1,000 according to their performances in Test matches. The ratings are calculated by computer and take into account playing conditions, the quality of the opposition and the result of the matches. A player cannot get a full rating until he has played 30 innings or taken 70 wickets in Tests.

The leading 20 batsmen and bowlers in the Ratings after the 1995 series between England and West Indies which ended on August 28 were:

	Batsmen	Rating			Bowlers	Rating
1.	S. R. Waugh (*Aus.*)	907		1.	C. E. L. Ambrose (*WI*)	862
2.	B. C. Lara (*WI*)	888		2.	Waqar Younis (*Pak.*)	859
3.	Inzamam-ul-Haq (*Pak.*)	868		3.	P. S. de Villiers (*SA*)	814
4.	G. P. Thorpe (*Eng.*)	783		4.	S. K. Warne (*Aus.*)	807
5.	J. C. Adams (*WI*)	781		5.	A. Kumble (*Ind.*)	797
6.	S. R. Tendulkar (*Ind.*)	774		6.	I. R. Bishop (*WI*)	781
7.	G. A. Hick (*Eng.*)	705		7.	H. H. Streak (*Zimb.*)	762†
8.	M. A. Atherton (*Eng.*)	698		8.	Wasim Akram (*Pak.*)	757
9.	M. J. Slater (*Aus.*)	690		9. {	C. A. Walsh (*WI*)	725
10.	M. E. Waugh (*Aus.*)	676			K. C. G. Benjamin (*WI*)	725
11.	W. J. Cronje (*SA*)	667		11.	S. L. V. Raju (*Ind.*)	705
12. {	H. P. Tillekeratne (*SL*)	647		12.	C. J. McDermott (*Aus.*)	691
	G. Kirsten (*SA*)	647*		13.	A. A. Donald (*SA*)	676
14.	R. A. Smith (*Eng.*)	637		14.	P. R. Reiffel (*Aus.*)	647†
15.	R. B. Richardson (*WI*)	634		15.	W. P. U. J. C. Vaas (*SL*)	646†
16.	D. C. Boon (*Aus.*)	632		16.	A. R. C. Fraser (*Eng.*)	634
17.	J. Stewart (*Eng.*)	622		17.	B. M. McMillan (*SA*)	599†
18.	M. Azharuddin (*Ind.*)	618		18.	D. G. Cork (*Eng.*)	554†
19.	M. A. Taylor (*Aus.*)	610		19.	D. K. Morrison (*NZ*)	545
20.	N. S. Sidhu (*Ind.*)	603		20.	C. R. Matthews (*SA*)	531†

* *Signifies the batsman has played fewer than 30 Test innings.*
† *Signifies the bowler has taken fewer than 70 wickets.*

The following players have topped the ratings since they were launched on June 17, 1987. The date shown is that on which they first went top; those marked by an asterisk have done so more than once.

Batting: D. B. Vengsarkar, June 17, 1987; Javed Miandad*, February 28, 1989; R. B. Richardson*, November 20, 1989; M. A. Taylor, October 23, 1990; G. A. Gooch*, June 10, 1991; D. L. Haynes, May 6, 1993; B. C. Lara, April 21, 1994; S. R. Tendulkar, December 5, 1994; J. C. Adams, December 14, 1994; S. R. Waugh, May 3, 1995.

Bowling: R. J. Hadlee*, June 17, 1987; M. D. Marshall*, June 21, 1988; Waqar Younis*, December 17, 1991; C. E. L. Ambrose*, July 26, 1992; S. K. Warne*, November 29, 1994.

THE AUSTRALIANS IN THE WEST INDIES, 1994-95

By ROBERT CRADDOCK

On May 3, 1995, the great wall crashed at last. After 15 years and 29 series, world cricket's longest-lasting dynasty was overthrown by the relentless, underestimated Australians – the most distinguished run of triumphant success gone with the Windies. The last time West Indies lost a series was in March 1980, when Clive Lloyd's tourists lost to Geoff Howarth's New Zealanders. Since then, they had won 20 and drawn nine (including two one-off Tests). Against Australia, the West Indians had won seven and drawn one since their defeat in 1975-76. It was 1972-73 when the last visiting team, Ian Chappell's Australians, had won a series in the Caribbean.

Mark Taylor led Australia to victory by 2-1, despite losing all four tosses. They had other problems: two leading pace bowlers, Craig McDermott and Damien Fleming, missed the series after injuries; only two batsmen – the Waugh twins – averaged over 26; the Australians had been thumped 4-1 in the one-day games; and during the First Test, Australian coach Bob Simpson developed a blood clot in his left leg and was admitted to hospital.

Against all expectations, ball dominated bat in the Tests, despite under-strength or outdated attacks. The Australian bowlers who had been belted to all parts of the Caribbean in the one-day series somehow restricted West Indies to three totals below 200 and a best of 265 in six completed innings. The cricket was like arm-wrestling, with white knuckles tilted back and forth until the strain told, the weaker man snapped and his arm was crunched into the table. It was strike-or-be-struck-down from the opening minutes of the series, when West Indies lost three batsmen for six, to the final wicket on the fourth afternoon of the last match. Two Tests were completed within three days and the winning margins were all landslides – ten wickets, nine wickets and an innings and 53 runs.

How did Australia do it? All discussion must start and finish with Steve Waugh, whose 429 runs at 107.25 represented the most courageous, passionate and decisive batting of his life. With his low-risk, keep-the-ball-along-the-ground game, Waugh scored 189 more than the next Australian – his brother, Mark – and 121 more than West Indies' most prolific batsman, Brian Lara. But his tour was laced with drama from the first day of the First Test, when he claimed a catch off Lara which, seemingly unbeknown to him, had touched the ground as he tumbled. As an unsavoury consequence, he was heckled every time he came to the crease, branded a cheat by local crowds, publicly chastised by Viv Richards and subjected to intimidatory phone calls in the small hours. In Trinidad, he had a verbal clash with Curtly Ambrose, who had to be restrained by captain Richie Richardson. During the final Test, he woke up to discover a security guard in search of some unsanctioned souvenirs. Weary but undeterred, he went in next morning to conjure one of the best innings by an Australian in decades, batting nearly ten hours for a maiden Test double-century. Every media critic in Australia had, at some stage, branded Steve Waugh gun-shy against short-pitched bowling. Yet at Kingston, he took more than six blows on the hands, arms and body; over the series, he absorbed more than 500 rib-rattlers by ducking or offering a straight defensive bat, sometimes with both feet six inches off the ground. Nineteen Australian wickets fell to the hook, but he refused to play the stroke, arguing it was too risky.

The only other batsman to enjoy much success for Australia was Waugh's brother, Mark, who shared with him in the glorious stand of 231 that decided the series. It sapped West Indian spirits so quickly that they had not put on 100 when Winston Benjamin was spotted in tears. The Waugh twins are opposites in many respects. Steve is the calculating percentage player, the student of cricket history, and Mark the free-spirited gambler, the risk-taker who breezes through life without a harsh thought. But at Sabina Park, where Mark was as tough as his brother, they became a perfect union. They acknowledged their twin centuries without histrionics, declining any show of brotherly emotion for the cameras.

No other Australian reached an aggregate of 200, though David Boon ticked off some more landmarks: at St John's, he reached 7,000 Test runs, overtaking Bradman's 6,996; at Port-of-Spain, he became the second Australian (after Allan Border) to play in 100 Tests; and finally, at Kingston, he pulled one run ahead of Greg Chappell, to finish on 7,111, more than any Australian apart from Border.

Meticulous planning was a key feature in Australia's success with the ball. Knowing they lacked the artillery to blast West Indies out, especially after McDermott tore his ankle ligaments falling off a sea wall in Georgetown, they attempted to suffocate them. The Australians had game plans for each batsman and a collective one of intimidation for the tail. They noted Lara's initial movement was back, so they baited him with full and wide balls. To Richardson, they angled the ball in, to stop him playing his famous off-side thrash; to Carl Hooper, they kept it tight, for they felt he was vulnerable under pressure. Quietly spoken Glenn McGrath made a personal commitment to bounce the West Indian tail and ensured that, of the last three, only Walsh reached double figures. McGrath also took 17 wickets, with hauls of five at Bridgetown and six at Port-of-Spain. He was well-supported by seamers Paul Reiffel, with 15, and Brendon Julian, called up to replace Fleming.

For once, Australia did not have to saddle up Shane Warne as a stock and shock bowler rolled into one. In fact, he was neither. Averaging barely 34 overs a Test, he took 15 wickets at 27.06; unlike the cement-footed batsmen of England and South Africa, the West Indians viciously attacked his bad balls ... and some of his good ones.

The home captain, Richardson, resumed control after several months recovering from mental fatigue. It was a greater challenge than expected, for many of the team's key components had changed character. Lara, an emerging star when Richardson left the fray, had become a world leader and Ambrose, the long-time pace champion, seemed to be in decline. There was no Desmond Haynes to fortify the top order – he was embroiled in a legal dispute with the West Indian board – and the rich well of fast bowling had run dry.

West Indies lost because they could not give adequate support to the redoubtable Courtney Walsh, their outstanding bowler with 20 wickets at 21.55, and because their batsmen, apart from Lara, underachieved. Richardson scored nearly half his runs in one innings, his century in Jamaica, and Jimmy Adams was the only other batsman to average over 30. Opener Stuart Williams always looked like falling early and middle-order men Hooper – a colossus in the one-day games – and Keith Arthurton managed only one Test fifty between them. Australia always sensed it was a case of "Lara out, all out".

Ambrose gave one great match-winning snarl in Trinidad, where he took nine of his 13 wickets. But that was on a pitch branded substandard by both sides, a seamer's heaven with grass an inch long. The tourists felt his pace, curtailed by a shoulder injury, had dropped substantially from his zenith in Australia two years before and he lacked the tricks to adapt to a more canny role. They also considered the West Indian bowling one-dimensional; the home side dished up so many short-pitched balls that Taylor wrote to the International Cricket Council claiming that the law on intimidatory bowling simply was not working.

Despite the humiliation of the historic series defeat, Richardson labelled Taylor's team – unchanged throughout the four Tests – "the weakest Australian side I have played" only minutes after surrendering the Frank Worrell Trophy. This caused a lot of anger and seemed out of tune with the facts.

AUSTRALIAN TOURING PARTY

M. A. Taylor (New South Wales) (*captain*), I. A. Healy (Queensland) (*vice-captain*), G. S. Blewett (South Australia), D. C. Boon (Tasmania), D. W. Fleming (Victoria), J. L. Langer (Western Australia), C. J. McDermott (Queensland), G. D. McGrath (New South Wales), T. B. A. May (South Australia), R. T. Ponting (Tasmania), P. R. Reiffel (Victoria), M. J. Slater (New South Wales), S. K. Warne (Victoria), M. E. Waugh (New South Wales), S. R. Waugh (New South Wales).

B. P. Julian (Western Australia) and C. G. Rackemann (Queensland) joined the tour as replacements for the injured Fleming and McDermott.

Manager: J. Edwards. *Coach:* R. B. Simpson.

AUSTRALIAN TOUR RESULTS

Test matches – Played 4: Won 2, Lost 1, Drawn 1.
First-class matches – Played 7: Won 3, Lost 1, Drawn 3.
Wins – West Indies (2), Guyana.
Loss – West Indies.
Draws – West Indies, West Indies Board President's XI, West Indies Board XI.
One-day internationals – Played 5: Won 1, Lost 4.
Other non-first-class match – Won v Barbados XI.

TEST MATCH AVERAGES

WEST INDIES – BATTING

	T	I	NO	R	HS	100s	Avge	Ct
B. C. Lara............	4	8	1	308	88	0	44.00	5
R. B. Richardson	4	8	1	229	100	1	32.71	4
J. C. Adams	4	7	2	160	42	0	32.00	7
C. L. Hooper	4	6	0	144	60	0	24.00	4
J. R. Murray..........	3	4	0	83	26	0	20.75	12
W. K. M. Benjamin....	4	6	0	109	51	0	18.16	2
S. C. Williams	4	8	1	120	42	0	17.14	2

	T	I	NO	R	HS	100s	Avge	Ct
K. L. T. Arthurton.....	3	4	0	61	26	0	15.25	1
C. A. Walsh..........	4	6	0	44	14	0	7.33	2
K. C. G. Benjamin	4	6	3	22	6	0	7.33	1
C. E. L. Ambrose......	4	6	1	25	7	0	5.00	0

Played in one Test: C. O. Browne 1, 31* (1 ct); S. L. Campbell 0, 6.

* Signifies not out.

BOWLING

	O	M	R	W	BB	5W/i	Avge
C. E. L. Ambrose......	100.1	25	258	13	5-45	1	19.84
C. A. Walsh..........	148.3	33	431	20	6-54	1	21.55
W. K. M. Benjamin....	97.2	16	291	9	3-71	0	32.33
K. C. G. Benjamin	93.4	9	359	10	3-32	0	35.90

Also bowled: J. C. Adams 15–0–54–0; K. L. T. Arthurton 6–1–18–1; C. L. Hooper 67–12–193–3.

AUSTRALIA – BATTING

	T	I	NO	R	HS	100s	Avge	Ct/St
S. R. Waugh	4	6	2	429	200	1	107.25	6
M. E. Waugh	4	6	0	240	126	1	40.00	3
I. A. Healy	4	6	1	128	74*	0	25.60	9/1
M. A. Taylor......	4	7	1	153	55	0	25.50	10
D. C. Boon	4	6	0	152	67	0	25.33	4
M. J. Slater	4	7	1	139	41	0	23.16	3
G. S. Blewett	4	6	0	132	69	0	22.00	5
P. R. Reiffel	4	6	2	76	23	0	19.00	3
B. P. Julian	4	6	0	67	31	0	11.16	1
S. K. Warne	4	5	0	28	11	0	5.60	2
G. D. McGrath....	4	5	2	7	4	0	2.33	0

* Signifies not out.

BOWLING

	O	M	R	W	BB	5W/i	Avge
S. R. Waugh	24	7	62	5	2-14	0	12.40
P. R. Reiffel	98.4	31	263	15	4-47	0	17.53
G. D. McGrath....	121.1	32	369	17	6-47	2	21.70
B. P. Julian	71	15	236	9	4-36	0	26.22
S. K. Warne	138	35	406	15	4-70	0	27.06

Also bowled: M. E. Waugh 14–3–48–1.

AUSTRALIAN AVERAGES – FIRST-CLASS MATCHES

BATTING

	M	I	NO	R	HS	100s	Avge	Ct/St
S. R. Waugh	6	8	3	510	200	1	102.00	7
M. E. Waugh	7	9	1	418	126	1	52.25	6
G. S. Blewett	7	9	0	353	116	1	39.22	5
M. J. Slater	7	10	1	291	90	0	32.33	4
I. A. Healy	7	9	2	202	74*	0	28.85	13/2
M. A. Taylor	7	10	1	222	62	0	24.66	11
D. C. Boon	6	8	0	190	67	0	23.75	4
P. R. Reiffel	6	7	2	80	23	0	16.00	5
B. P. Julian	6	7	0	80	31	0	11.42	2
S. K. Warne	6	6	0	51	23	0	8.50	5
G. D. McGrath	6	6	2	8	4	0	2.00	0

Played in two matches: J. L. Langer 55, 0 (4 ct); T. B. A. May 24*, 0. Played in one match: R. T. Ponting 19 (1 ct); C. G. Rackemann 0.

Signifies not out.

BOWLING

	O	M	R	W	BB	5W/i	Avge
S. R. Waugh	37	8	100	8	2-14	0	12.50
B. P. Julian	107	20	351	18	5-54	1	19.50
G. D. McGrath	168.4	45	515	24	6-47	3	21.45
S. K. Warne	178	46	553	23	4-70	0	24.04
P. R. Reiffel	129.4	36	374	15	4-47	0	24.93
T. B. A. May	67.1	17	194	6	4-73	0	32.33

Also bowled: G. S. Blewett 19-5-49-1; J. L. Langer 1-0-11-0; C. G. Rackemann 35-5-121-4; M. J. Slater 3-0-20-0; M. E. Waugh 37-7-146-4.

Note: Matches in this section which were not first-class are signified by a dagger.

†At Bridgetown, March 5. Australians won by 52 runs. Toss: Barbados XI. Australians 330 for seven (50 overs) (G. S. Blewett 78, S. R. Waugh 117 retired out, D. C. Boon 70; I. D. R. Bradshaw three for 62); Barbados XI 278 (48.2 overs) (S. L. Campbell 36, A. E. Proverbs 75, B. Morris 38; T. B. A. May four for 50).

†WEST INDIES v AUSTRALIA

First One-Day International

At Bridgetown, March 8. West Indies won by six runs. Toss: West Indies. International debut: V. C. Drakes.

Hooper's first act in a five-part *tour de force* was a run-a-ball 84. He was the well-oiled piston that pumped West Indies to 257, while Australia, despite runs from all the top six, were always a step or two behind. Returning after a bout of malaria, Hooper launched a vicious assault on Warne, designed to destabilise him before the Tests. Lara was beaten four times outside off stump by Reiffel, but added 68 in 69 balls with Hooper after Steve Waugh threw down Richardson's stumps from short fine leg. Richardson missed the next four games with an injured shoulder. Boon anchored Australia with 85 not out off 83 balls, but West Indies kept him out of strike for all but three deliveries of the final two overs.

Man of the Match: C. L. Hooper.

West Indies

P. V. Simmons c Taylor b Warne	37	V. C. Drakes c Warne b M. E. Waugh	9
S. C. Williams c Healy b Reiffel	11	C. E. L. Ambrose c Taylor	
*R. B. Richardson run out	9	b M. E. Waugh	0
C. L. Hooper c May b McDermott	84	C. A. Walsh not out	6
J. C. Adams c M. E. Waugh			
b McDermott	2	B 1, l-b 3, w 1, n-b 5	10
†J. R. Murray c Healy b M. E. Waugh	12		
W. K. M. Benjamin c May		1/26 2/69 3/87 (49.4 overs) 257	
b McDermott	22	4/155 5/158 6/191	
		7/241 8/242 9/246	

Bowling: McDermott 10–0–25–3; Reiffel 10–1–50–1; M. E. Waugh 6.4–0–42–3; Warne 10–1–56–1; Blewett 8–0–44–1; May 5–0–36–0.

Australia

*M. A. Taylor c Simmons b Walsh	41	†I. A. Healy run out	0
M. J. Slater c Adams b Benjamin	21	P. R. Reiffel not out	10
M. E. Waugh c Murray b Walsh	29	L-b 1, w 5	6
D. C. Boon not out	85		
S. R. Waugh b Drakes	26	1/50 2/94 3/94 (6 wkts, 50 overs) 251	
G. S. Blewett c Walsh b Ambrose	33	4/156 5/235 6/236	

T. B. A. May, S. K. Warne and C. J. McDermott did not bat.

Bowling: Ambrose 10–1–43–1; Walsh 10–1–52–2; Benjamin 6.1–0–24–1; Drakes 9.5–0–39–1; Hooper 5–0–46–0; Simmons 9–0–46–0.

Umpires: L. H. Barker and D. Holder.

†WEST INDIES v AUSTRALIA

Second One-Day International

At Port-of-Spain, March 11. Australia won by 26 runs. Toss: Australia.

Accurate seam bowling proved the tourists' passport to their only one-day triumph of the series; they dismissed West Indies in the 48th over. But Healy claimed the match award – a wooden trophy as tall as him – for a late flurry of 51 in 44 balls, after entering the fray at 163 for five. A target of 261 looked imposing, and Reiffel and McGrath hit a prudent length to suffocate the West Indian innings. But Warne was smacked about again, conceding 63 from ten: Hooper's footwork was too quick for him. Earlier, Hooper ran out Blewett with a direct hit from backward point – the first dismissal to be confirmed by video replay in the Caribbean, where the technology was being used for the first time. Healy and Adams were also given out by third umpire Ralph Gosein.

Man of the Match: I. A. Healy.

Australia

M. J. Slater c and b Hooper	55	P. R. Reiffel b Benjamin	14
*M. A. Taylor c Walsh b Ambrose	16	S. K. Warne not out	4
M. E. Waugh b Benjamin	0	L-b 3, w 6, n-b 1	10
D. C. Boon c Benjamin b Simmons	48		
S. R. Waugh b Walsh	58	1/37 2/39 3/93 (8 wkts, 50 overs) 260	
G. S. Blewett run out	4	4/153 5/163 6/207	
†I. A. Healy run out	51	7/252 8/260	

C. J. McDermott and G. D. McGrath did not bat.

Bowling: Ambrose 10–0–47–1; Walsh 8–0–59–1; Benjamin 10–0–49–2; Drakes 10–0–47–0; Hooper 7–0–33–1; Simmons 5–0–22–1.

West Indies

P. V. Simmons b McGrath	34	V. C. Drakes c Reiffel b McDermott	16
S. C. Williams lbw b Reiffel	0	C. E. L. Ambrose b McDermott	1
B. C. Lara c Healy b Blewett	62	*C. A. Walsh not out	0
C. L. Hooper c Blewett b Warne	55	L-b 8, w 4, n-b 1	13
J. C. Adams run out	15		
K. L. T. Arthurton c Boon b McDermott	35	1/5 2/79 3/121	(47.5 overs) 234
†J. R. Murray lbw b Reiffel	0	4/175 5/182 6/185	
W. K. M. Benjamin b Reiffel	3	7/191 8/232 9/234	

Bowling: McDermott 6.5–0–37–3; Reiffel 10–2–32–3; McGrath 9–1–36–1; Warne 10–0–63–1; Blewett 8–0–43–1; S. R. Waugh 4–0–15–0.

Umpires: S. A. Bucknor and C. E. Cumberbatch.

†WEST INDIES v AUSTRALIA

Third One-Day International

At Port-of-Spain, March 12. West Indies won by 133 runs. Toss: West Indies.
Lara's first century for West Indies in his native Trinidad revived the carnival which had finished two weeks earlier. His cover drives were breathtaking and he cut and pulled balls just short of a length in masterful fashion. He slashed 139 off 125 balls, with 15 fours and a six. West Indies had been pegged to 26 for two before he and Hooper put on 99 and then Adams joined the picnic, adding 135 in 19 overs with Lara. Challenged to score 283, Australia folded inside 35 overs. Simmons netted four for 18 with his unpretentious medium-pace. Australian spirits had already sagged to bootlace level when Fleming damaged a joint in his right shoulder after a high-class spell; it was to end his tour.

Man of the Match: B. C. Lara.

West Indies

P. V. Simmons c Healy b Fleming	6	†J. R. Murray not out	4
S. C. Williams run out	6		
B. C. Lara c Reiffel b Waugh	139	B 6, l-b 11, w 5, n-b 1	23
C. L. Hooper c Slater b Reiffel	41		
J. C. Adams not out	51	1/17 2/26 3/125	(5 wkts, 50 overs) 282
K. L. T. Arthurton c Boon b Waugh	12	4/260 5/276	

W. K. M. Benjamin, V. C. Drakes, C. E. L. Ambrose and *C. A. Walsh did not bat.

Bowling: Reiffel 10–0–36–1; Fleming 7.3–1–27–1; McGrath 10–0–57–0; Warne 10–1–52–0; Blewett 3–0–32–0; Waugh 9.3–1–61–2.

Australia

*M. A. Taylor run out	26	S. K. Warne b Simmons	12
M. J. Slater run out	0	D. W. Fleming not out	5
R. T. Ponting c Drakes b Simmons	43	G. D. McGrath b Simmons	0
D. C. Boon b Benjamin	4	L-b 4, w 4, n-b 2	10
S. R. Waugh c Hooper b Simmons	44		
G. S. Blewett st Murray b Hooper	0	1/12 2/50 3/59	(34.5 overs) 149
†I. A. Healy c Williams b Hooper	3	4/118 5/124 6/126	
P. R. Reiffel run out	1	7/127 8/129 9/147	

Bowling: Ambrose 6–1–8–0; Walsh 4–1–14–0; Benjamin 7–1–31–1; Drakes 7–0–36–0; Hooper 6–0–38–2; Simmons 4.5–0–18–4.

Umpires: S. A. Bucknor and C. E. Cumberbatch.

†WEST INDIES v AUSTRALIA

Fourth One-Day International

At St Vincent, March 15. West Indies won by seven wickets, their target having been revised to 206 from 46 overs. Toss: Australia.

West Indies' batting secured the series without the help of Lara, nursing a hip injury. Australia scrapped hard for a so-so total on a lively pitch at scenic Arnos Vale, where the neighbours are goats and ships. Slater fought his way to 68 and the Waugh twins and Boon chipped in. Rain pruned West Indies' target to 206 from 46 overs. At 61 for two after 20, they were vulnerable, and Warne seemed back to his best. But Taylor wanted to save him for the finale, replaced him with Blewett, and West Indies lashed out against his featureless medium-pace. Suddenly, Simmons was a new man, adding 96 in 15 overs with Hooper, whose 56 off 40 balls with Arthurton then provided the knockout punch.

Man of the Match: P. V. Simmons.

Australia

M. J. Slater b Arthurton	68	S. K. Warne not out		6
*M. A. Taylor c Simmons b Walsh	3	C. J. McDermott run out		11
M. E. Waugh c Murray b Benjamin	26	G. D. McGrath not out		1
D. C. Boon b Arthurton	33	L-b 5, w 6, n-b 1		12
S. R. Waugh c Arthurton b Simmons	25			
G. S. Blewett b Drakes	4	1/6 2/57 3/130	(9 wkts, 48 overs)	210
†I. A. Healy c Simmons b Walsh	12	4/137 5/152 6/171		
P. R. Reiffel c Murray b Walsh	9	7/190 8/190 9/209		

Bowling: Ambrose 8-0-22-0; Walsh 9-0-30-3; Benjamin 7-0-32-1; Drakes 7-0-36-1; Arthurton 10-0-45-2; Simmons 7-0-40-1.

West Indies

P. V. Simmons c Healy b Warne	86	K. L. T. Arthurton not out		22
S. L. Campbell st Healy b Warne	20	B 2, l-b 10, w 4, n-b 1		17
J. C. Adams b McGrath	3			
C. L. Hooper not out	60	1/47 2/56 3/152	(3 wkts, 43.1 overs)	208

B. C. Lara, †J. R. Murray, W. K. M. Benjamin, V. C. Drakes, C. E. L. Ambrose and *C. A. Walsh did not bat.

Bowling: McDermott 9-1-46-0; Reiffel 9-1-37-0; McGrath 10-1-40-1; Warne 9.1-3-33-2; Blewett 3-0-26-0; Boon 3-0-14-0.

Umpires: L. H. Barker and G. T. Johnson.

†WEST INDIES v AUSTRALIA

Fifth One-Day International

At Georgetown, March 18. West Indies won by five wickets. Toss: Australia.

Australia's euphoria on scoring their highest one-day total against West Indies did not last long. The home side reeled in 287 with 2.4 overs to spare, thanks to run-a-ball half-centuries from Adams, Simmons and Hooper. Mark Waugh's sublime 70 off 56 balls looked like a down payment on victory, but not even the willing support of Taylor could put Australia out of reach. On the flint-hard surface of his home ground, Hooper's sweet timing, from full-faced drives to rubber-wristed deflections, left the Australians wondering how they would contain him in the Tests. His straight six off Steve Waugh carried over the press box roof to smash the windscreen of a Mercedes outside the ground. Meanwhile, Simmons welcomed Julian to the tour with a brutal 6446 off successive balls.

Man of the Match: C. L. Hooper.

Australia

*M. A. Taylor c Adams b Hooper	66		B. P. Julian b Walsh		11
M. J. Slater c Holder b Drakes	41		T. B. A. May not out		3
M. E. Waugh run out	70				
S. R. Waugh c Benjamin b Hooper	11		B 2, l-b 11, w 4, n-b 3		20
R. T. Ponting b Hooper	0				
J. L. Langer run out	6		1/78 2/166 3/204	(9 wkts, 50 overs)	286
†I. A. Healy c Williams b Simmons	36		4/204 5/205 6/229		
P. R. Reiffel c Campbell b Benjamin	22		7/259 8/276 9/286		

G. D. McGrath did not bat.

Bowling: Simmons 10–0–54–1; Walsh 8–2–38–1; Benjamin 9–0–51–1; Drakes 6–0–46–1; Arthurton 7–0–48–0; Hooper 10–0–36–3.

West Indies

S. C. Williams c and b M. E. Waugh	45		R. I. C. Holder not out		34
S. L. Campbell b Reiffel	9				
P. V. Simmons c Slater b S. R. Waugh	70		L-b 10, w 3, n-b 6		19
C. L. Hooper c Slater b Reiffel	50				
J. C. Adams not out	60		1/17 2/108 3/172	(5 wkts, 47.2 overs)	287
K. L. T. Arthurton c M. E. Waugh b McGrath	0		4/192 5/193		

†J. R. Murray, W. K. M. Benjamin, V. C. Drakes and *C. A. Walsh did not bat.

Bowling: Reiffel 10–1–48–2; Julian 10–1–66–0; May 7–0–42–0; McGrath 8.2–0–51–1; M. E. Waugh 3–0–23–1; S. R. Waugh 9–0–47–1.

Umpires: C. R. Duncan and E. Nicholls.

GUYANA v AUSTRALIANS

At Georgetown, March 20, 21, 22. Australians won by an innings and 61 runs. Toss: Guyana.

The Australians' landslide victory was overshadowed by an off-field injury. McDermott, who was being rested, was jogging along Georgetown's sea wall when he jumped less than a metre to the cement walkway below, severely twisted his ankle and tore the ligaments. He wept as he prepared to return home from a major tour for the fourth time. On the pitch, Guyana were too weak for the good of an Australian side craving rugged match practice. They crumbled for 105 in three hours on the first day. McGrath gained a heartening five for 47 with his reverse swing, while recent arrival Julian bowled 11 overs for 23 runs in the first innings and picked up five wickets in the second. Blewett scored a sound 116 to heighten expectations of a prominent showing in the Test series.

Close of play: First day, Australians 204-4 (G. S. Blewett 82*, J. L. Langer 11*); Second day, Guyana 165-6 (A. R. Percival 20*, L. A. Joseph 4*).

Guyana

Sudesh Dhaniram lbw b McGrath	13	– (5) c Ponting b Julian	18
P. D. Persaud c Healy b Julian	8	– (1) c Waugh b McGrath	0
*K. F. Semple c Healy b Warne	6	– c Slater b Julian	67
N. A. DeGroot lbw b McGrath	23	– (2) b Julian	0
S. Chanderpaul c Healy b Warne	4	– (4) b Warne	31
R. A. Harper c and b Warne	2	– lbw b Julian	11
A. R. Percival lbw b McGrath	6	– not out	42
L. A. Joseph c Langer b Julian	18	– b Warne	14
M. V. Nagamootoo b McGrath	2	– (10) c Langer b Julian	3
†K. A. Wong not out	14	– (9) lbw b Warne	4
B. St A. Browne b McGrath	0	– lbw b McGrath	1
B 1, l-b 1, n-b 7	9	B 8, n-b 8	16

1/17 2/26 3/32 4/36 5/40	105	1/0 2/4 3/69 4/122 5/125	207
6/57 7/85 8/89 9/91		6/154 7/183 8/187 9/200

Bowling: *First Innings*—McGrath 15.5–6–47–5; Julian 11–2–23–2; Warne 11–6–21–3; May 7–3–12–0. *Second Innings*—McGrath 16.4–4–49–2; Julian 11–2–54–5; Blewett 3–1–3–0; Warne 15–5–42–3; May 13–3–51–0.

Australians

M. J. Slater b Joseph	2		S. K. Warne c Percival b Nagamootoo	23
*M. A. Taylor c Harper b Browne	4		T. B. A. May not out	24
G. S. Blewett c Chanderpaul b Harper	116		G. D. McGrath b Browne	1
M. E. Waugh c and b Harper	75			
R. T. Ponting c Persaud b Joseph	19		L-b 3, n-b 9	12
J. L. Langer c Semple b Dhaniram	55			
†I. A. Healy c and b Chanderpaul	29		1/7 2/7 3/126 4/183 5/255	373
B. P. Julian c Semple b Chanderpaul	13		6/303 7/321 8/327 9/372	

Bowling: Joseph 14–0–84–2; Browne 13.1–2–45–2; Harper 21–2–76–2; Nagamootoo 16–3–54–1; Chanderpaul 14–1–62–2; Dhaniram 12–0–49–1.

Umpires: C. R. Duncan and E. Nicholls.

WEST INDIES BOARD PRESIDENT'S XI v AUSTRALIANS

At St Lucia, March 25, 26, 27, 28. Drawn. Toss: West Indies Board President's XI.

It would have taken a brave man to back Australia's bowlers against West Indies on the strength of their final pre-Test workout. Warne sat alone outside the dressing-room, staring coldly into the distance, after a third-day mauling left him with figures of two for 84 at six an over. He was thumped unmercifully by the robust Dave Joseph and none of his colleagues looked Test-primed. The match's first and last days were lost to rain, but the Australian batsmen made a comfortable 322 for five on the second day. Dhanraj took two for 70 in 25 honest overs with some impressive leg-spin; the tourists were relieved when he was not called on in the Test series.

Close of play: First day, No play; Second day, Australians 322-5 (S. R. Waugh 73*, I. A. Healy 42*); Third day, West Indies Board President's XI 261-5 (K. L. T. Arthurton 75*, R. D. Jacobs 35*).

Australians

M. J. Slater st Jacobs b Dhanraj	90		†I. A. Healy not out	42
*M. A. Taylor c Joseph b Bishop	3			
D. C. Boon lbw b Cuffy	10		B 1, l-b 4, n-b 14	19
M. E. Waugh run out	73			
S. R. Waugh not out	73		1/23 2/58 3/174 (5 wkts dec.)	322
G. S. Blewett lbw b Dhanraj	12		4/207 5/226	

P. R. Reiffel, B. P. Julian, S. K. Warne and G. D. McGrath did not bat.

Bowling: Bishop 11–3–39–1; Cummins 16–1–70–0; Cuffy 12–1–51–1; Dhanraj 25–3–70–2; Chanderpaul 14–0–57–0; Arthurton 5–0–30–0.

West Indies Board President's XI

P. A. Wallace c S. R. Waugh b Julian	9		†R. D. Jacobs not out	35
R. G. Samuels lbw b Julian	12			
*R. I. C. Holder c and b Warne	29		N-b 16	16
K. L. T. Arthurton not out	75			
S. Chanderpaul c and b Warne	2		1/16 2/47 3/66 (5 wkts)	261
D. R. E. Joseph c Julian b S. R. Waugh	83		4/70 5/212	

A. C. Cummins, I. R. Bishop, R. Dhanraj and C. E. Cuffy did not bat.

Bowling: Julian 14–1–38–2; Reiffel 11–1–35–0; McGrath 15–3–50–0; Warne 14–0–84–2; M. E. Waugh 5–0–40–0; S. R. Waugh 4–0–14–1.

Umpires: D. Holder and L. Thomas.

WEST INDIES v AUSTRALIA

First Test Match

At Bridgetown, March 31, April 1, 2. Australia won by ten wickets. Toss: West Indies.

Australia swept to victory with two days to spare – West Indies' first three-day defeat for 30 years. The captain who beat them in 1964-65, Bobby Simpson, now the Australian coach, followed the closing stages from hospital, after succumbing to a thrombosis in his left leg on the second day. It was only West Indies' third defeat at Bridgetown – but their second in successive seasons.

The tone of a pulsating, intense series was set early. The former *Wisden* editor John Woodcock rated the first session one of the best mornings' play he had seen in six decades watching cricket. Australia's bare-boned pace attack, deprived of Fleming and McDermott, found a bouncy pitch at last and made the most of it. Julian and Reiffel reduced West Indies to six for three: Williams, Campbell and Richardson managed one run between them. It was the first of many occasions when they missed their bankable opening greats, Greenidge (retired) and Haynes (in dispute with the West Indies Board). But joyous Australian backslaps turned to pats of commiseration and concern as a withering counter-attack by Lara and Hooper lifted West Indies to 116 without further loss at lunch. The tide turned so quickly that Warne had a long-on posted in the first hour.

The drama intensified in the afternoon, when Steve Waugh four times juggled a cut shot by Lara as it bobbled beneath his tumbling body. Television replays confirmed the ball had hit the ground but Lara, after loitering a few seconds, trudged off for the most controversial – and perhaps the decisive – moment of the tour. "If I had doubts I would not have claimed it," Waugh said later. "I have called players back before." Setting the pattern for the remaining Tests, Lara's dismissal started a slide that the meek lower order could not arrest. The enigmatic Julian, his form as flukey as a Caribbean breeze, paid his way for the series with four top-order victims – just the injection of self-belief the novice seam attack craved. All ten wickets were caught, nine of them off edges.

Nevertheless, Australia were eyeing a marginal advantage at 194 for five, before Healy scored a stubborn 74 not out in three hours. His stand of 60 with Julian was priceless when runs were trading for gold bars and set up a lead of 151. In reply, West Indies' second innings was another limp effort, with the highest score an unbeaten 39 from Adams. That left a target of only 39, which Taylor and Slater knocked off inside seven overs. McGrath, who had primed himself to be the attacking fist of Australia's bowling in McDermott's absence, took his first five-wicket haul in Tests. But nothing embodied Australia's determination more than Steve Waugh's glorious interception of Murray at mid-wicket – running towards the boundary, glaring skywards and snaring the ball as he dived, never taking his eye off it.

Man of the Match: G. D. McGrath.

Close of play: First day, Australia 91-2 (M. A. Taylor 42*, M. E. Waugh 5*); Second day, West Indies 13-0 (S. C. Williams 6*, S. L. Campbell 4*).

West Indies

S. C. Williams c Taylor b Julian	1	– c Healy b McGrath	10
S. L. Campbell c Healy b Reiffel	0	– c S. R. Waugh b Warne	6
B. C. Lara c S. R. Waugh b Julian	65	– c Healy b McGrath	9
*R. B. Richardson c Healy b Julian	0	– (5) b Reiffel	36
C. L. Hooper c Taylor b Julian	60	– (4) c Reiffel b Julian	16
J. C. Adams c Warne b McGrath	16	– not out	39
†J. R. Murray c Taylor b McGrath	21	– c S. R. Waugh b Warne	23
W. K. M. Benjamin c Taylor b Warne	14	– lbw b McGrath	26
C. E. L. Ambrose c Blewett b McGrath	7	– c Blewett b McGrath	6
C. A. Walsh c S. R. Waugh b Warne	1	– b McGrath	4
K. C. G. Benjamin not out	0	– b Warne	5
B 3, w 1, n-b 6	10	L-b 1, n-b 8	9
	195		**189**

1/1 (1) 2/5 (2) 3/6 (4) 4/130 (5)   1/19 (1) 2/25 (1) 3/31 (3)
5/152 (6) 6/156 (3) 7/184 (8)   4/57 (4) 5/91 (5) 6/135 (7)
8/193 (9) 9/194 (10) 10/195 (7)   7/170 (8) 8/176 (9)
                                           9/180 (10) 10/189 (11)

Bowling: *First Innings*—Reiffel 11–4–41–1; Julian 12–0–36–4; Warne 12–2–57–2; McGrath 12.1–1–46–3; M. E. Waugh 1–0–12–0. *Second Innings*—Reiffel 11–6–15–1; Julian 12–2–41–1; Warne 26.3–5–64–3; McGrath 22–6–68–5.

Australia

M. J. Slater c Williams b W. K. M. Benjamin . .	18 – (2) not out	20
*M. A. Taylor c Hooper b K. C. G. Benjamin . .	55 – (1) not out	16
D. C. Boon c b W. K. M. Benjamin b Walsh	20	
M. E. Waugh c Murray b Ambrose	40	
S. R. Waugh c Murray b K. C. G. Benjamin . . .	65	
G. S. Blewett c Murray b Ambrose	14	
†I. A. Healy not out	74	
B. P. Julian c K. C. G. Benjamin b Hooper	31	
P. R. Reiffel b W. K. M. Benjamin	1	
S. K. Warne c Adams b Walsh	6	
G. D. McGrath b W. K. M. Benjamin	4	
L-b 13, n-b 5	18	N-b 3 3

1/27 (1) 2/72 (3) 3/121 (2) 4/166 (4)   346   (no wkt) 39
5/194 (6) 6/230 (5) 7/290 (8)
8/291 (9) 9/331 (10) 10/346 (11)

Bowling: *First Innings*—Ambrose 20–7–41–2; Walsh 25–5–78–2; K. C. G. Benjamin 20–1–84–2; W. K. M. Benjamin 23.2–6–71–3; Hooper 12–0–59–1. *Second Innings*—Walsh 3–0–19–0; K. C. G. Benjamin 2.5–1–14–0; Hooper 1–0–6–0.

Umpires: S. Venkataraghavan (India) and L. H. Barker.   Referee: Majid Khan (Pakistan).

WEST INDIES v AUSTRALIA

Second Test Match

At St John's, April 8, 9, 10, 12, 13. Drawn. Toss: West Indies.

The Second Test was a provocative teaser: both teams felt they could have snatched it but for rain. Nearly half the scheduled playing time on the final three days was lost. At stumps on the fourth day, Australia were 273 for seven, a tantalising 229 ahead, but heavy overnight rain kept them off until after lunch. They batted on to 300 and left West Indies a notional 257 from 36 overs. But Australian self-esteem was boosted; they had recovered from a poor first innings to be fractionally ahead on points at the bell.

West Indies dropped Campbell, shifted Richardson to open and re-introduced Arthurton to the middle order. They put Australia in on a firm, flat pitch, and Richardson's palms must have been sweating as the tourists breezed to 82 without loss. But in the over before lunch, Taylor skied an indiscreet pull shot off Ambrose to Walsh at fine leg. After the break, the middle order quivered and crumbled under an assault on their ribs from Walsh. Yet again, he was West Indies' get-out-of-jail card, grabbing six wickets as Australia folded for 216.

The epic innings that Lara had been threatening failed to materialise next day. On his return to the Recreation Ground, a year after his 375, he waltzed to 88 in 101 balls. Australian heads sagged under his whimsical mastery as he square-drove, swept and pulled; something freakish was needed to dislodge him. Boon provided it, leaping like a Tasmanian salmon to catch a dragged drive off Steve Waugh in his outstretched left hand. "It started out as a token attempt," Boon explained. "At my age it feels great to take catches like that." With Lara gone, the middle order failed to deliver under relentless pressure. They eclipsed Australia's total with five wickets down, but an eventual lead of 44 was well below expectations – if anything, it was a mental spur for the tourists.

Taylor must have felt like a piece of meat being tenderised as he was thumped on the body several times during nine fearsome overs from Ambrose and Walsh on the second evening. Next day, between showers, Mark Waugh was struck on the back by a Walsh beamer – one ball after hooking Walsh for six, his first scoring stroke. He went on to a patient half-century, as did his twin Steve and Boon, who had reached 7,000 Test runs to inch past Bradman in the first innings. But further rain made their fightback irrelevant.

Ambrose took only one wicket in the match and Richardson suggested he might have to be rested for the next Test. It was the cattle prod he needed.

Man of the Match: C. A. Walsh.

Close of play: First day, West Indies 14-0 (S. C. Williams 8*, R. B. Richardson 0*); Second day, Australia 16-0 (M. A. Taylor 4*, M. J. Slater 9*); Third day, Australia 134-2 (D. C. Boon 60*, M. E. Waugh 42*); Fourth day, Australia 273-7 (S. R. Waugh 52*).

Australia

M. J. Slater c Adams b Walsh	41	– (2) c Richardson b Walsh	18
*M. A. Taylor c Walsh b Ambrose	37	– (1) c Murray b Walsh	5
D. C. Boon b Walsh	21	– lbw b W. K. M. Benjamin	67
M. E. Waugh c Hooper b Walsh	4	– b W. K. M. Benjamin	61
S. R. Waugh b K. C. G. Benjamin	15	– not out	65
G. S. Blewett c Murray b W. K. M. Benjamin	11	– c Williams b Hooper	19
†I. A. Healy c Walsh b W. K. M. Benjamin	14	– c Hooper b Walsh	26
B. P. Julian b Walsh	22	– run out	6
P. R. Reiffel not out	22	– not out	13
S. K. Warne c Arthurton b Walsh	11		
G. D. McGrath c Murray b Walsh	0		
L-b 12, n-b 6	18	B 1, l-b 9, n-b 10	20

1/82 (2) 2/84 (1) 3/89 (4) 4/126 (3)　　　216　　1/22 (1) 2/43 (2)　　(7 wkts dec.) 300
5/126 (5) 6/150 (7) 7/168 (6)　　　　　　　　　3/149 (3) 4/162 (4)
8/188 (8) 9/204 (10) 10/216 (11)　　　　　　　5/196 (6) 6/254 (7)
　　　　　　　　　　　　　　　　　　　　　　　7/273 (8)

Bowling: *First Innings*—Ambrose 14–5–34–1; Walsh 21.3–7–54–6; K. C. G. Benjamin 16–3–58–1; W. K. M. Benjamin 15–2–40–2; Hooper 2–0–18–0. *Second Innings*—Ambrose 19–3–42–0; Walsh 36–7–92–3; W. K. M. Benjamin 24–2–72–2; K. C. G. Benjamin 15–1–51–0; Arthurton 1–0–1–0; Hooper 9–3–16–1; Adams 4–0–16–0.

West Indies

S. C. Williams c Boon b Warne	16	– not out	31
*R. B. Richardson c S. R. Waugh b Julian	37	– b Reiffel	2
B. C. Lara c Boon b S. R. Waugh	88	– b Julian	43
J. C. Adams lbw b Warne	22	– not out	3
C. L. Hooper c Julian b S. R. Waugh	11		
K. L. T. Arthurton c Taylor b Warne	26		
†J. R. Murray lbw b Reiffel	26		
W. K. M. Benjamin c Taylor b McGrath	4		
C. E. L. Ambrose c Taylor b Reiffel	0		
C. A. Walsh b Reiffel	9		
K. C. G. Benjamin not out	5		
B 6, l-b 3, w 1, n-b 6	16	N-b 1	1

1/34 (1) 2/106 (2) 3/168 (4) 4/186 (3)　　　260　　1/11 (2) 2/69 (3)　　(2 wkts) 80
5/187 (5) 6/240 (6) 7/240 (7)
8/240 (9) 9/254 (10) 10/260 (8)

Bowling: *First Innings*—Reiffel 17–3–53–3; Julian 10–5–36–1; Warne 28–9–83–3; McGrath 20.1–5–59–1; S. R. Waugh 6–1–20–2. *Second Innings*—Reiffel 6–2–12–1; Julian 5–2–15–1; Warne 7–0–18–0; McGrath 6–2–20–0; M. E. Waugh 6–2–15–0.

Umpires: D. R. Shepherd (England) and S. A. Bucknor. Referee: Majid Khan (Pakistan).

WEST INDIES BOARD XI v AUSTRALIANS

At St Kitts, April 15, 16, 17. Drawn. Toss: West Indies Board XI.

The match was of little consequence to either side, except to late arrival Rackemann, who made his only appearance of the tour, off-spinner May, who achieved a rare high point, and Blewett, who played himself into form. Rackemann's three for 68 in a steady first-innings display reassured Australia that he would be ready for a call-up should any of the front-liners fall. May was twice hoisted into the prison yard on the southern boundary, where the warders were watching eagerly – but took four for 73. After looking slightly fragile and unco-ordinated early on, Blewett displayed his best strokes after reaching 50 and fell only seven short of a second tour hundred.

Close of play: First day, West Indies Board XI 209-8 (N. O. Perry 52*, O. D. Gibson 14*); Second day, Australians 278-5 (D. C. Boon 24*, M. E. Waugh 4*).

West Indies Board XI

R. G. Samuels b May	31	– (2) c Langer b Rackemann	95
S. L. Campbell lbw b M. E. Waugh	5	– (1) c and b M. E. Waugh	53
K. F. Semple hit wkt b M. E. Waugh	3	– lbw b S. R. Waugh	39
D. R. E. Joseph c Langer b Rackemann	8	– c Taylor b May	1
S. Ragoonath c Reiffel b Rackemann	46	– not out	21
*†C. O. Browne c M. E. Waugh b May	17	– lbw b S. R. Waugh	0
V. C. Drakes c Healy b Rackemann	1	– c sub (S. K. Warne) b May	7
N. O. Perry c Reiffel b May	57	– not out	18
H. A. G. Anthony b Blewett	10		
O. D. Gibson st Healy b May	55		
D. Ramnarine not out	5		
B 4, l-b 8, w 1, n-b 10	23	B 4, l-b 11, n-b 4	19

1/22 2/30 3/39 4/80 5/107   261   1/135 2/194 3/201   (6 wkts) 253
6/110 7/132 8/178 9/214   4/203 5/203 6/214

Bowling: *First Innings*—Rackemann 19–3–68–3; Reiffel 16–4–44–0; M. E. Waugh 12–4–39–2; Blewett 10–2–25–1; May 24.1–6–73–4. *Second Innings*—Reiffel 4–0–32–0; Rackemann 16–2–53–1; May 23–5–58–2; S. R. Waugh 9–1–24–2; Blewett 6–2–21–0; M. E. Waugh 6–0–19–1; Slater 3–0–20–0; Langer 1–0–11–0.

Australians

*M. A. Taylor b Drakes	62	P. R. Reiffel lbw b Anthony	4
M. J. Slater b Gibson	60	T. B. A. May c Campbell b Gibson	0
G. S. Blewett c and b Semple	93	C. G. Rackemann b Gibson	0
J. L. Langer lbw b Anthony	0		
S. R. Waugh c Joseph b Anthony	8	B 2, l-b 9, w 1, n-b 17	29
D. C. Boon lbw b Anthony	28		
M. E. Waugh not out	30	1/119 2/159 3/171 4/187 5/269	317
†I. A. Healy lbw b Gibson	3	6/283 7/296 8/305 9/317	

Bowling: Gibson 18.4–3–45–4; Drakes 14–2–53–1; Perry 17–0–81–0; Anthony 19–4–70–4; Ramnarine 23–4–49–0; Semple 3–0–8–1.

Umpires: C. Mack and B. Morgan.

WEST INDIES v AUSTRALIA

Third Test Match

At Port-of-Spain, April 21, 22, 23. West Indies won by nine wickets. Toss: West Indies.

The Australians had a suspicion of trouble when they went looking for the pitch and could barely pick it out from the rest of the gumleaf-green square. It was covered by grass nearly an inch long, suspiciously damp and given only a token shave. Even the winning captain, Richardson, agreed it was unsatisfactory. Fast bowlers looked at it and grinned like fat men about to tackle Christmas dinner. It simply had to be their match, and it was. Ambrose, who had taken three wickets in two Tests, bounced back with nine for 65 on the site where he demolished England a year earlier, while McGrath ripped out six.

Only Steve Waugh reached 50; his unbeaten 63 on this pitch was as admirable as his 200 in the next Test. In Australia's first innings, no one else bettered Boon's 18 and they lost nine wickets to outside edges. West Indies had similar problems. "When the ball seams like that, it does not matter whether you are Brian Lara or Don Bradman; you are not going to get runs consistently, " said Australian coach Bob Simpson.

Rain, which cut the first day to 40 overs, hardly helped. Sent in, Australia lost Taylor and Slater with only two on the board. Mark Waugh, a debonair strokemaker under the most trying conditions, managed only two singles in 25 minutes before he tickled behind. When Boon edged to slip at 37, Australia seemed no certainty to make three figures. But by then Steve Waugh had entered the front line. He stood his ground like John Wayne when Ambrose engaged him in a verbal exchange of fire from two metres; the bowler had to be tugged away by Richardson. "It's Test cricket," the unrepentant Waugh said afterwards. "If you want an easy game, go play netball." Waugh suspected anything approaching 150 would prove competitive and even 128 looked reasonable as McGrath scythed down the West Indians for 136. He did more than let the pitch work for him: he swung the old ball and some of his team-mates rated the out-swinging yorker which Lara edged to slip the ball of the series.

Australia kept the deficit down to eight and their openers inched ahead on the second evening, but seizing the initiative proved beyond them. In the morning, the upper order struggled to 85 for three, then the last seven departed for 20, but to Ambrose, in a miserable procession that was not entirely the fault of the pitch. West Indies' target of 98 was small enough to clear in one hay-making assault. Richardson and Williams lashed out and Lara delighted his home crowd with the spectacular punchline, a six off Warne in the 21st over, to square the series and restore their confidence for the decider in Kingston. The match took less than 164 overs and, but for rain, might have finished earlier than tea on the third day.

Man of the Match: C. E. L. Ambrose.

Close of play: First day, Australia 112-7 (S. R. Waugh 54*, P. R. Reiffel 6*); Second day, Australia 20-0 (M. J. Slater 11*, M. A. Taylor 9*).

Australia

*M. A. Taylor c Adams b Ambrose	2	– (2) c Murray b K. C. G. Benjamin	30
M. J. Slater c Murray b Walsh	0	– (1) c Richardson b Walsh	15
D. C. Boon c Richardson b Ambrose	18	– c sub (S. Chanderpaul) b Walsh	9
M. E. Waugh c Murray b Ambrose	2	– lbw b Ambrose	7
S. R. Waugh not out	63	– c Hooper b K. C. G. Benjamin	21
G. S. Blewett c Murray b W. K. M. Benjamin	17	– c Murray b K. C. G. Benjamin	2
†I. A. Healy c Richardson b Walsh	8	– b Ambrose	0
B. P. Julian c Adams b K. C. G. Benjamin	0	– b Ambrose	0
P. R. Reiffel c Lara b Walsh	11	– c Hooper b Ambrose	6
S. K. Warne b Ambrose	0	– c Hooper b Walsh	11
G. D. McGrath c Murray b Ambrose	0	– not out	0
L-b 6, w 1	7	L-b 3, n-b 1	4

1/2 (2) 2/2 (1) 3/14 (4) 4/37 (3)   128   1/26 (1) 2/52 (2) 3/56 (3)   105
5/62 (6) 6/95 (7) 7/98 (8)   4/85 (5) 5/85 (4) 6/85 (7)
8/121 (9) 9/128 (10) 10/128 (11)   7/87 (6) 8/87 (8)
                                                                              9/105 (10) 10/105 (9)

Bowling: *First Innings*—Ambrose 16–5–45–5; Walsh 17–4–50–3; W. K. M. Benjamin 6–3–13–1; K. C. G. Benjamin 8–2–14–1. *Second Innings*—Ambrose 10.1–1–20–4; Walsh 13–4–35–3; W. K. M. Benjamin 5–0–15–0; K. C. G. Benjamin 8–1–32–3.

West Indies

S. C. Williams c Taylor b Reiffel	0	– c Warne b M. E. Waugh	42
*R. B. Richardson c Healy b McGrath	2	– not out	38
B. C. Lara c Taylor b McGrath	24	– not out	14
J. C. Adams c M. E. Waugh b Reiffel	42		
C. L. Hooper c Reiffel b S. R. Waugh	21		
K. L. T. Arthurton c M. E. Waugh b McGrath	5		
†J. R. Murray c Healy b McGrath	13		
W. K. M. Benjamin c Slater b Warne	7		
C. E. L. Ambrose c Slater b McGrath	1		
C. A. Walsh c Blewett b McGrath	14		
K. C. G. Benjamin not out	1		
L-b 4, n-b 2	6	B 4	4

1/1 (1) 2/6 (2) 3/42 (3) 4/87 (5)   136   1/81 (1)   (1 wkt) 98
5/95 (6) 6/106 (4) 7/113 (8)
8/114 (9) 9/129 (7) 10/136 (10)

Bowling: *First Innings*—McGrath 21.5–11–47–6; Reiffel 16–7–26–2; Julian 7–1–24–0; S. R. Waugh 3–1–19–1; Warne 12.5–5–16–1. *Second Innings*—McGrath 6–1–22–0; Reiffel 6–2–21–0; Julian 3–0–16–0; Warne 3.5–0–26–0; M. E. Waugh 2–0–9–1.

Umpires: D. R. Shepherd (England) and C. E. Cumberbatch.
Referee: Majid Khan (Pakistan).

WEST INDIES v AUSTRALIA

Fourth Test Match

At Kingston, April 29, 30, May 1, 3. Australia won by an innings and 53 runs. Toss: West Indies. Test debut: C. O. Browne.

The final Test was settled by a partnership to be cherished in Australian history, the pinnacle of the cricketing lives of Steve and Mark Waugh. In a series featuring only one other century, Steve scored 200 and Mark 126. They added 231 in 57 overs to bankroll the innings victory that regained the Frank Worrell Trophy, surrendered by Simpson's team in 1977-78, and ended West Indies' 15 years without a series defeat.

Batting was meant to be easy on a shiny pitch of rolled mud, as polished as a dance-room floor. When Richardson won his fourth consecutive toss it looked like a decisive advantage: West Indies' first 100 whistled by in 20 overs, with Lara running up a scorching fifty. Quite unexpectedly, he fell for 65, caught behind. It was the first time Warne had dismissed him in eight Tests. Richardson remained, patiently crafting the first hundred of the series before he was eighth out at 251. A moderate total of 265 was West Indies' best in the four Tests and next day Australia were teetering at 73 for three when Steve Waugh joined Mark. From then on, the home side spiralled towards oblivion.

The Waughs hit their stride almost immediately, smacking 67 from 11 overs after lunch. One by one they repelled the pace brigade; the buoyant West Indians were suddenly under siege. Winston Benjamin sat weeping during the drinks break and had to be cajoled to continue; Ambrose bowled only 11 overs in the day, amid whispers of team disunity, and underachieving Kenny Benjamin was hooted on arrival at the bowling crease. Sabina Park was stunned and some of the Waughs' best boundaries went unapplauded. They applauded each other's centuries (their eighth Test hundreds in both cases) reached by Mark in 146 balls and Steve in 183 – and shook hands, but no more. Mark had left behind his gambler's hat to play a low-risk game. His bravest stroke was a contemptuous laid-back dab off Walsh over the slips for four. He pulled and drove with great rhythm. As usual, Steve hit almost everything along the ground, displaying some attractive back-foot cover drives. He gave just one chance, on 42, when he was grassed by debutant wicket-keeper Courtney Browne (a late replacement for Murray, who was ill).

Mark fell on the second evening but Steve was 110 at stumps. He retired to his room to get some sleep, after being woken the previous night by a thief. Next day, supported by Blewett and the tail, he advanced to a maiden double-hundred in Tests. He was last out after batting for close on ten hours and 425 balls, more than 150 short-pitched, and had 17 fours, one six and six aching bruises at the end of his greatest innings.

West Indies faced 14 overs that night; their doom was all but certain when Reiffel dismissed three. Their last chance was the weather, and rain restricted itself to the rest day. Only night-watchman Winston Benjamin and Browne passed 20 and Warne took the last four wickets – his best return of the tour – to complete the West Indians' shattering defeat.

Man of the Match: S. R. Waugh.   *Man of the Series:* S. R. Waugh.

Close of play: First day, West Indies 265; Second day, Australia 321-4 (S. R. Waugh 110*, G. S. Blewett 6*); Third day, West Indies 63-3 (J. C. Adams 13*, W. K. M. Benjamin 1*).

West Indies

S. C. Williams c Blewett b Reiffel	0	– b Reiffel	20
*R. B. Richardson lbw b Reiffel	100	– c and b Reiffel	14
B. C. Lara c Healy b Warne	65	– lbw b Reiffel	0
J. C. Adams c Slater b Julian	20	– c S. R. Waugh b McGrath	18
C. L. Hooper c M. E. Waugh b Julian	23	– (6) run out	13
K. L. T. Arthurton c Healy b McGrath	16	– (7) lbw b Warne	14
†C. O. Browne c Boon b Warne	1	– (8) not out	31
W. K. M. Benjamin lbw b S. R. Waugh	7	– (5) lbw b Reiffel	51
C. E. L. Ambrose not out	6	– st Healy b Warne	5
C. A. Walsh c Boon b S. R. Waugh	2	– c Blewett b Warne	14
K. C. G. Benjamin c Healy b Reiffel	5	– c Taylor b Warne	6
B 1, l-b 9, w 1, n-b 9	20	B 13, l-b 8, n-b 6	27
	265		**213**

1/0 (1) 2/103 (3) 3/131 (4) 4/188 (5)   1/37 (2) 2/37 (3) 3/46 (1)
5/220 (6) 6/243 (7) 7/250 (8)   4/98 (4) 5/134 (5) 6/140 (6)
8/251 (9) 9/254 (10) 10/265 (11)   7/166 (7) 8/172 (9)
   9/204 (10) 10/213 (11)

Bowling: *First Innings*—Reiffel 13.4-2-48-3; Julian 12-3-31-2; McGrath 20-4-79-1; Warne 25-6-72-2; S. R. Waugh 4-1-11-0; M. E. Waugh 4-1-11-0. *Second Innings*—Reiffel 18.5-5-47-4; Julian 10-2-37-0; Warne 23.4-8-70-4; M. E. Waugh 1-0-1-0; McGrath 13-2-28-1; S. R. Waugh 4-0-9-0.

Australia

*M. A. Taylor c Adams b Walsh	8	B. P. Julian c Adams b Walsh	8
M. J. Slater c Lara b Walsh	27	P. R. Reiffel b K. C. G. Benjamin	23
D. C. Boon c Browne b Ambrose	17	S. K. Warne c Lara	
M. E. Waugh c Adams b Hooper	126	b K. C. G. Benjamin	0
S. R. Waugh c Lara		G. D. McGrath not out	0
b K. C. G. Benjamin	200	B 11, l-b 6, w 1, n-b 26	44
G. S. Blewett c W. K. M. Benjamin			
b Arthurton	69	1/17 (1) 2/50 (3) 3/73 (2) 4/304 (4)	**531**
†I. A. Healy c Lara		5/417 (6) 6/423 (7) 7/449 (8)	
b W. K. M. Benjamin	6	8/523 (9) 9/523 (10) 10/531 (5)	

Bowling: Ambrose 21-4-76-1; Walsh 33-6-103-3; K. C. G. Benjamin 23.5-0-106-3; W. K. M. Benjamin 24-3-80-1; Hooper 43-9-94-1; Adams 11-0-38-0; Arthurton 5-1-17-1.

Umpires: K. E. Liebenberg (South Africa) and S. A. Bucknor.
Referee: Majid Khan (Pakistan).

SINGER WORLD SERIES, 1994-95

By R. MOHAN

Sri Lanka's first four-nation tournament was badly disrupted by foul September weather. India lost a shortened opening game to the hosts, but came up trumps when they met again in a similarly rain-hit final. The planned floodlit match at the R. Premadasa (formerly Khettarama) Stadium, which is built on marshland, had to be shifted at the last minute to the Sinhalese Sports Club, where there were no lights. Indian captain Mohammad Azharuddin freely admitted that the toss was decisive: his bowlers dismissed Sri Lanka for 98 on a damp pitch and the batsmen got home as dusk fell.

Pakistan, who had just crushed Sri Lanka in Tests and one-day internationals alike, were clear favourites and Australia were highly rated. But Pakistan never won a match – their game with India was washed out – and Australia, about to tour Pakistan, appeared to regard the trip as practice. The home team romped into the final unbeaten; captain Arjuna Ranatunga was in rousing form and his 195 runs made him the first Sri Lankan to score 4,000 in limited-overs internationals. However, India lifted their game as the competition proceeded; and Sachin Tendulkar's maiden one-day hundred, against Australia, proved the turning point.

Crowds were reasonable and the day-night matches were scheduled at prime time on television in Asia, suggesting that a dollar-rich tournament with three visiting teams was a practical proposition. But the hazards of international cricket in the region were highlighted when an umpire consulted his colleague in the television replay box about a stumping, only to be told there was a power cut.

Note: Matches in this section were not first-class.

SRI LANKA v INDIA

At R. Premadasa Stadium, Colombo, September 5 (day/night). Sri Lanka won by seven wickets. Toss: Sri Lanka.

This match was scheduled for the previous day, when rain delayed the start and then washed out play after four overs. In that time, India were put in and reached 16 without loss (M. Prabhakar 3*, S. R. Tendulkar 11*, l-b 1, w 1), Wickremasinghe conceding nine runs in two overs and Vaas six. India were unchanged next day; Sri Lanka brought in Chandana for Sanjeeva Ranatunga. The tournament organisers declared that the original match should not stand in limited-overs international records. On the following day, play was further delayed, so that only 25 overs a side were possible. India, in rusty form a month before their home season began, failed to put enough runs together after Wickremasinghe removed both openers. Despite Azharuddin's brilliant run-out of Jayasuriya from point, Sri Lanka were not stretched in making 126. Mahanama's unbeaten fifty anchored the innings and Ranatunga increased the tempo with 41 in 48 balls.

Man of the Match: G. P. Wickremasinghe.

India

M. Prabhakar c Jayasuriya		V. G. Kambli not out	30
b Wickremasinghe	14	A. C. Bedade b Wickremasinghe	21
S. R. Tendulkar c Dharmasena		Kapil Dev not out	1
b Wickremasinghe	6	B 3, l-b 7, w 1	11
N. S. Sidhu c Mahanama b Jayasuriya	17		
*M. Azharuddin c Chandana		1/20 2/23 3/55 (5 wkts, 25 overs) 125	
b Dharmasena	25	4/87 5/122	

†N. R. Mongia, A. Kumble, R. K. Chauhan and J. Srinath did not bat.

Bowling: Wickremasinghe 5–0–28–3; Vaas 4–0–20–0; Dharmasena 5–0–22–1; Ranatunga 2–0–11–0; Jayasuriya 5–0–17–1; Kalpage 4–0–17–0.

Sri Lanka

R. S. Mahanama not out	50	R. S. Kalpage not out	3
S. T. Jayasuriya run out	3	L-b 12, w 2, n-b 1	15
P. A. de Silva c Mongia b Kumble	14		
*A. Ranatunga run out	41	1/7 2/31 3/119 (3 wkts, 24.2 overs) 126	

H. P. Tillekeratne, U. U. Chandana, †P. B. Dassanayake, H. D. P. K. Dharmasena, W. P. U. J. C. Vaas and G. P. Wickremasinghe did not bat.

Bowling: Prabhakar 4.2–0–17–0; Srinath 5–0–21–0; Kumble 5–0–17–1; Tendulkar 4–0–21–0; Kapil Dev 2–0–15–0; Chauhan 4–0–23–0.

Umpires: B. L. Aldridge (New Zealand) and K. T. Francis.

AUSTRALIA v PAKISTAN

At Sinhalese Sports Club, Colombo, September 7. Australia won by 28 runs. Toss: Pakistan.

Australia, in their first match since April, performed creditably to defeat a Pakistani team ending a triumphant tour of Sri Lanka. Though Mark Taylor, now captain in his own right, was one of four out for 49, the later batsmen fought back. Pakistan looked like extending their winning sequence while Saeed Anwar and Inzamam-ul-Haq were adding 75. But once Inzamam was stumped and Anwar forced off by a strained hamstring, they fell behind. Warne and Steve Waugh proved difficult to get away on a moist, sluggish pitch and Asif Mujtaba, who split his finger while fielding, batted only to prevent his side being bowled out.

Man of the Match: S. K. Warne.

Australia

*M. A. Taylor lbw b Wasim Akram	8	†I. A. Healy not out	30
M. J. Slater c Asif Mujtaba		S. K. Warne b Wasim Akram	30
b Wasim Akram	4	C. J. McDermott not out	2
D. C. Boon b Akram Raza	19		
M. E. Waugh st Rashid Latif			
b Mushtaq Ahmed	23	B 7, l-b 9, w 9	25
S. R. Waugh c Rashid Latif			
b Mushtaq Ahmed	1	1/11 2/34 3/48 (7 wkts, 50 overs) 179	
M. G. Bevan c Mushtaq Ahmed		4/49 5/85	
b Salim Malik	37	6/128 7/174	

T. B. A. May and G. D. McGrath did not bat.

Bowling: Wasim Akram 10–2–24–3; Waqar Younis 8–2–43–0; Mushtaq Ahmed 10–1–34–2; Akram Raza 10–1–26–1; Aamir Sohail 7–0–17–0; Salim Malik 5–0–19–1.

Pakistan

Saeed Anwar c McGrath b S. R. Waugh	46	Waqar Younis c Slater b Warne		2
Aamir Sohail b McGrath	0	Mushtaq Ahmed not out		2
Inzamam-ul-Haq st Healy b Warne	29	Asif Mujtaba not out		1
Basit Ali c and b Warne	0	B 2, l-b 5, w 6, n-b 3		16
*Salim Malik c Taylor b S. R. Waugh	22			—
†Rashid Latif c Taylor b S. R. Waugh	7	1/2 2/77 3/83	(9 wkts, 50 overs)	151
Wasim Akram b McGrath	16	4/94 5/124 6/129		
Akram Raza c Healy b McDermott	10	7/129 8/147 9/150		

Saeed Anwar, when 43, retired hurt at 80 and resumed at 124.

Bowling: McDermott 10-2-21-1; McGrath 10-3-25-2; May 10-0-53-0; Warne 10-1-29-3; S. R. Waugh 10-1-16-3.

Umpires: B. C. Cooray and W. A. U. Wickremasinghe.

AUSTRALIA v INDIA

At R. Premadasa Stadium, Colombo, September 9 (day/night). India won by 31 runs. Toss: India.

Tendulkar's maiden century in 78 one-day internationals was fashioned from a blazing assault in the first hour. He raced to 50 in 43 balls, knocking first the pace bowlers and then Warne – with two sixes in an over – out of the attack. His 110 from 132 balls should have been the platform for a huge total; India reached 100 in the 18th over. It never quite materialised after he played over a yorker from McDermott, but India won calmly, with Prabhakar challenging Tendulkar for the match award. He took a return catch off Taylor, two further wickets, another catch and two run-outs. Australia's only substantial partnership was 67 from Mark Waugh and Boon.

Man of the Match: S. R. Tendulkar.

India

M. Prabhakar c Slater b Warne	20	A. Kumble b S. R. Waugh		1
S. R. Tendulkar b McDermott	110	R. K. Chauhan not out		2
N. S. Sidhu c Boon b May	24			—
*M. Azharuddin c Healy b McDermott	31	L-b 2, w 5		7
V. G. Kambli not out	43			—
Kapil Dev run out	4	1/87 2/129 3/173	(8 wkts, 50 overs)	246
A. C. Bedade run out	1	4/211 5/216 6/217		
†N. R. Mongia c Healy b Warne	3	7/226 8/237		

S. L. V. Raju did not bat.

Bowling: McDermott 10-1-46-2; McGrath 6-0-41-0; Warne 10-0-53-2; May 10-0-35-1; S. R. Waugh 8-0-33-1; Bevan 2-0-17-0; M. E. Waugh 4-0-19-0.

Australia

M. J. Slater c Prabhakar b Kapil Dev	26	S. K. Warne b Raju		1
*M. A. Taylor c and b Prabhakar	4	T. B. A. May not out		1
M. E. Waugh b Chauhan	61	G. D. McGrath run out		1
D. C. Boon b Chauhan	40	B 2, l-b 10, w 2, n-b 2		16
S. R. Waugh b Prabhakar	22			—
M. G. Bevan c Sidhu b Kumble	26	1/22 2/56 3/123	(47.4 overs)	215
C. J. McDermott c Kumble b Prabhakar	2	4/143 5/181 6/183		
†I. A. Healy run out	15	7/209 8/212 9/213		

Bowling: Prabhakar 8-0-34-3; Kapil Dev 8-1-44-1; Raju 9.4-0-38-1; Kumble 9-0-31-1; Chauhan 10-0-41-2; Tendulkar 3-0-15-0.

Umpires: I. Anandappa and T. M. Samarasinghe.

SRI LANKA v PAKISTAN

At Sinhalese Sports Club, Colombo, September 11. Sri Lanka won by seven wickets. Toss: Sri Lanka.

Arjuna Ranatunga played the key role. He did not hesitate to put Pakistan in, counting on another rainy-season morning to help his bowlers. His own bowling was particularly effective, though Salim Malik, with a patient 53, helped squeeze out a few runs. The contest was still wide open when Ranatunga walked out to bat at 65 for three. Consistently sweeping the spinners, he handled the chase with aplomb. Mahanama withdrew with cramp when they had added 32 for the fourth wicket, but Tillekeratne helped Ranatunga extend the stand by 116. Pakistan missed Wasim Akram, who had strained his hamstring, but offered no excuses for losing to the team they had dominated so easily in August.

Man of the Match: A. Ranatunga.

Pakistan

Saeed Anwar c Jayasuriya b Vaas	24	†Rashid Latif not out	28	
Aamir Sohail run out	32	Akram Raza not out	9	
Inzamam-ul-Haq run out	2	L-b 2, w 4, n-b 2	8	
*Salim Malik c Tillekeratne b Kalpage	53			
Basit Ali c Mahanama b Jayasuriya	39	1/28 2/31 3/82	(6 wkts, 50 overs) 210	
Zahid Fazal run out	15	4/136 5/169 6/171		

Waqar Younis, Mushtaq Ahmed and Kabir Khan did not bat.

Bowling: Wickremasinghe 8–0–37–0; Vaas 8–0–38–1; A. Ranatunga 8–0–29–0; Dharmasena 8–0–39–0; Jayasuriya 10–0–33–1; Kalpage 8–0–32–1.

Sri Lanka

R. S. Mahanama retired hurt	39	*A. Ranatunga not out	82	
S. T. Jayasuriya c Salim Malik b Kabir Khan	4	H. P. Tillekeratne not out	39	
S. Ranatunga c Inzamam-ul-Haq b Akram Raza	16	B 5, l-b 10, w 6, n-b 1	22	
P. A. de Silva c and b Mushtaq Ahmed	11	1/9 2/44 3/65	(3 wkts, 47.2 overs) 213	

R. S. Mahanama retired hurt at 97.

R. S. Kalpage, †P. B. Dassanayake, H. D. P. K. Dharmasena, W. P. U. J. C. Vaas and G. P. Wickremasinghe did not bat.

Bowling: Waqar Younis 9–1–42–0; Kabir Khan 9.2–1–34–1; Akram Raza 10–0–49–1; Aamir Sohail 8–0–28–0; Mushtaq Ahmed 8–0–31–1; Salim Malik 3–0–14–0.

Umpires: B. L. Aldridge (New Zealand) and P. Manuel.

SRI LANKA v AUSTRALIA

At P. Saravanamuttu Stadium, Colombo, September 13. Sri Lanka won by six wickets, their target having been revised to 163 from 36 overs. Toss: Sri Lanka. International debut: G. R. Robertson.

Sri Lanka sailed on to a third straight win, after Ranatunga won the toss for the third time and kept a steady hand on the tiller in the run-chase, scoring 59 from 74 balls. Australia had a weakened team, omitting Boon, McDermott, McGrath and May to give other players match practice before the Pakistan tour. The rain gods certainly favoured Sri Lanka: a sharp shower adjusted their target to a simpler 163 off 36 overs. Having to face a full 50 overs in conditions suiting spin, the Australians did well to cobble together 225. Taylor batted nearly two hours, while Bevan pushed the innings along with a bright 47.

Man of the Match: A. Ranatunga.

Australia

*M. A. Taylor c de Silva b Kalpage . . .	41	
M. J. Slater run out	24	
M. E. Waugh st Dassanayake		
b Jayasuriya .	24	
J. L. Langer c Wickremasinghe		
b Kalpage .	9	
S. R. Waugh c Dassanayake		
b Jayasuriya .	30	

M. G. Bevan not out	47
†I. A. Healy run out	28
G. R. Robertson not out	5
L-b 11, w 5, n-b 1	17

1/61 2/90 3/100   (6 wkts, 50 overs) 225
4/116 5/144 6/204

S. K. Warne, J. Angel and D. W. Fleming did not bat.

Bowling: Wickremasinghe 7-0-29-0; Vaas 9-2-26-0; Ranatunga 2-0-14-0; Kalpage 9-0-42-2; Dharmasena 10-1-45-0; Jayasuriya 10-0-42-2; de Silva 3-0-16-0.

Sri Lanka

R. S. Mahanama b Warne	20	
S. T. Jayasuriya c Taylor b Angel	0	
P. A. de Silva st Healy b Warne	33	
*A. Ranatunga lbw b S. R. Waugh	59	
H. P. Tillekeratne not out	29	

R. S. Kalpage not out	9
L-b 10, w 3, n-b 1	14

1/4 2/48   (4 wkts, 34.4 overs) 164
3/102 4/141

U. U. Chandana, †P. B. Dassanayake, H. D. P. K. Dharmasena, W. P. U. J. C. Vaas and G. P. Wickremasinghe did not bat.

Bowling: Angel 7-1-29-1; Fleming 6.4-0-42-0; Warne 8-0-27-2; S. R. Waugh 6-0-32-1; Robertson 7-0-24-0.

Umpires: B. L. Aldridge (New Zealand) and T. M. Samarasinghe.

INDIA v PAKISTAN

At R. Premadasa Stadium, Colombo, September 15, 16. No result (abandoned).

Heavy rain washed out all play on the scheduled and reserve days. The points were shared, which was enough to see India through to the final ahead of Australia.

QUALIFYING TABLE

	Played	Won	Lost	No result	Points	Run-rate
Sri Lanka.	3	3	0	0	6	4.73
India	3	1	1	1	3	4.94
Australia	3	1	2	0	2	4.12
Pakistan.	3	0	2	1	1	3.61

FINAL

SRI LANKA v INDIA

At Sinhalese Sports Club, Colombo, September 17. India won by six wickets. Toss: India.

The tournament ended as it began, with a rain-affected 25-overs game between Sri Lanka and India. "Winning the toss was like winning the match," said Azharuddin, who did both. With no reserve day allowed, the fixture was moved from the waterlogged R. Premadasa Stadium. Even so, the captains felt conditions were too wet for an international, but the umpires ruled that they were not actually dangerous and play began at 1.55 p.m. Azharuddin needed no prompting to insert Sri Lanka, who struggled on a seaming pitch and suffered three run-outs on slippery ground. Chasing only 99, Azharuddin and Sidhu shrugged off the loss of the openers, adding 71 at five an over. But they perished in their hurry to get home while the light held. New batsmen Kambli and Bedade had difficulty sighting the ball – Kalpage even bowled a maiden. Amid the eerie light of paper torches in the crowd, bright against the tropical evening, Kambli finally chipped the ball teasingly over de Silva's head to seal victory.

Man of the Match: M. Azharuddin.　*Man of the Series:* A. Ranatunga.
Batsman of the Series: S. R. Tendulkar.　*Bowler of the Series:* S. R. Waugh.

Sri Lanka

R. S. Mahanama run out	2	
S. T. Jayasuriya c Bedade b Prabhakar	1	
P. A. de Silva c Prasad b Chauhan	10	
H. P. Tillekeratne c Kambli b Kapil Dev	7	
*A. Ranatunga c Chauhan b Kumble	13	
R. S. Kalpage c Mongia b Prasad	39	
U. U. Chandana run out	2	
†P. B. Dassanayake run out	1	
H. D. P. K. Dharmasena b Prabhakar	8	
W. P. U. J. C. Vaas not out	2	
G. P. Wickremasinghe not out	3	

L-b 2, w 5, n-b 3 10

1/5 2/5 3/24　(9 wkts, 25 overs) 98
4/28 5/64 6/74
7/76 8/91 9/95

Bowling: Prabhakar 5-0-19-2; Prasad 5-0-17-1; Kumble 5-0-22-1; Chauhan 5-0-21-1; Kapil Dev 5-0-17-1.

India

M. Prabhakar c Jayasuriya b Wickremasinghe	10	
S. R. Tendulkar c de Silva b Vaas	0	
N. S. Sidhu lbw b Wickremasinghe	24	
*M. Azharuddin c Mahanama b Vaas	45	
V. G. Kambli not out	8	
A. C. Bedade not out	4	

B 4, l-b 1, w 3 8

1/6 2/15　(4 wkts, 23.4 overs) 99
3/86 4/88

Kapil Dev, †N. R. Mongia, A. Kumble, R. K. Chauhan and B. K. V. Prasad did not bat.

Bowling: Wickremasinghe 5-0-13-2; Vaas 5-0-16-2; Dharmasena 5-0-22-0; Kalpage 5-1-23-0; Jayasuriya 3-0-15-0; de Silva 0.4-0-5-0.

Umpires: B. L. Aldridge (New Zealand) and K. T. Francis.
Series referee: C. W. Smith (West Indies).

OVERSEAS PLAYERS FOR 1996

Derbyshire	D. M. Jones (A)	Middlesex	D. J. Nash (NZ)*
Durham	S. L. Campbell (WI)	Northamptonshire	C. E. L. Ambrose (WI)
Essex		Nottinghamshire	C. L. Cairns (NZ)*
Glamorgan	O. D. Gibson (WI)	Somerset	S. Lee (A)
Gloucestershire	C. A. Walsh (WI)	Surrey	
Hampshire	W. K. M. Benjamin (WI)	Sussex	V. C. Drakes (WI)
Kent	C. L. Hooper (WI)	Warwickshire	S. M. Pollock (SA)
Lancashire	S. Elworthy (SA)	Worcestershire	T. M. Moody (A)*
Leicestershire	P. V. Simmons (WI)	Yorkshire	M. G. Bevan (A)*

* Overseas player for same county in 1995. All arrangements subject to alteration.

WILLS TRIANGULAR SERIES, 1994-95

By PETER DEELEY

Pakistan and Australia paused between Tests to contest a limited-overs tournament with South Africa, whose weakened team lost all six of their qualifying matches. Pakistan, with home advantage, entered the final as favourites, especially after their scintillating batting had beaten Australia eight days earlier. But they lost easily. The Australians' own fine form with the bat was complemented by Damien Fleming and Glenn McGrath, a new generation of pace bowlers. Their triumph in Lahore was the only tangible success of their tour.

Kepler Wessels's international swansong proved one tour too many for the retiring South African captain, while their new coach, Bob Woolmer, fresh from guiding Warwickshire to their unique triple success in England, now tasted the bitterness of repeated failure. South Africa's one consolation was the remarkable form of Hansie Cronje, Wessels's designated heir, who scored 354 at 88.50, more than any other batsman in the competition.

Large numbers watched the tournament, in sharp contrast to the accompanying Tests. Apart from crowd disturbances at Peshawar and Gujranwala, the competition was marred only by allegations of betting on the result; Pakistan's players had to swear their innocence before the final, but the story did not become public until several months later.

Note: Matches in this section were not first-class.

AUSTRALIA v SOUTH AFRICA

At Lahore, October 12. Australia won by six runs. Toss: Australia.

An opening stand of 98 between Taylor and Slater and then a half-century from Steve Waugh were crucial on a low pitch. South Africa were already missing Donald and Snell, and another of their quick bowlers, McMillan, bowled three overs for 24. He missed the rest of the competition through injury. Slow starts – here, 15 runs in ten overs – were to be the South Africans' problem throughout the tournament, yet Cronje almost stole the game. He finished only two short of his century, though more crucially South Africa were seven short of the 14 needed from McDermott's final over.

Man of the Match: S. R. Waugh.

Australia

*M. A. Taylor st Richardson b Shaw	56	†I. A. Healy not out		18
M. J. Slater st Richardson b Shaw	44	G. R. Robertson not out		1
M. E. Waugh c and b Cronje	3	L-b 1, n-b 5		6
D. C. Boon run out	8			
S. R. Waugh c Kirsten b Matthews	56	1/98 2/107 3/107	(6 wkts, 50 overs)	207
M. G. Bevan run out	15	4/128 5/160 6/202		

S. K. Warne, C. J. McDermott and D. W. Fleming did not bat.

Bowling: de Villiers 9-1-38-0; Matthews 10-1-41-1; McMillan 3-0-24-0; Simons 8-0-37-0; Shaw 10-0-34-2; Cronje 10-1-32-1.

South Africa

*K. C. Wessels c Healy b Fleming	....	6	C. R. Matthews b McDermott	1
G. Kirsten c Healy b Fleming	. . . .	4	T. G. Shaw not out	1
W. J. Cronje not out		98		
D. J. Cullinan c Slater b S. R. Waugh	.	12	B 4, l-b 7	11
J. N. Rhodes lbw b S. R. Waugh.		42		
B. M. McMillan b M. E. Waugh		3	1/8 2/15 3/50 (8 wkts, 50 overs) 201	
E. O. Simons b McDermott		19	4/126 5/143 6/182	
†D. J. Richardson b McDermott		4	7/194 8/200	

P. S. de Villiers did not bat.

Bowling: McDermott 10–2–32–3; Fleming 10–3–29–2; S. R. Waugh 10–0–35–2; Warne 10–0–39–0; Robertson 7–0–41–0; M. E. Waugh 3–0–14–1.

Umpires: Athar Zaidi and Mian Aslam.

PAKISTAN v AUSTRALIA

At Multan, October 14. Australia won by seven wickets. Toss: Pakistan.

In the heat and dust of this old city, Australia made a disastrous start, losing Slater and Mark Waugh without scoring. But Boon and Steve Waugh took up the fight, adding an unbroken 119 for the fourth wicket, to win with four overs to spare. Only the local hero, Inzamam-ul-Haq, with 59, showed any confidence against the pace of McDermott and especially Fleming, who removed both openers for the second match running and finished with four wickets, all bowled.

Man of the Match: D. C. Boon.

Pakistan

Saeed Anwar b Fleming	. . . .	22	Akram Raza not out	5
Aamir Sohail b Fleming	. . . .	5	Waqar Younis not out.	0
Inzamam-ul-Haq run out		59		
*Salim Malik c Healy b Warne	. . . .	32	B 6, l-b 1, w 3, n-b 1	11
Ijaz Ahmed c Healy b McDermott. . . .		21		
Aamer Malik c Healy b McDermott . . .		0	1/9 2/32 3/113 (8 wkts, 50 overs) 200	
Wasim Akram b Fleming	. . . .	9	4/132 5/164 6/166	
†Rashid Latif b Fleming	. . . .	16	7/184 8/199	

Mushtaq Ahmed did not bat.

Bowling: McDermott 10–1–34–2; Fleming 10–0–49–4; S. R. Waugh 10–1–37–0; Warne 10–1–29–1; Robertson 5–0–24–0; M. E. Waugh 5–0–20–0.

Australia

M. J. Slater lbw b Wasim Akram	. . . . .	0	S. R. Waugh not out	59
*M. A. Taylor b Akram Raza	. . . .	46		
M. E. Waugh c Rashid Latif			B 1, l-b 6, w 4, n-b 1	12
b Waqar Younis .		0		
D. C. Boon not out	. . . .	84	1/10 2/11 3/81 (3 wkts, 46 overs) 201	

M. G. Bevan, †I. A. Healy, G. R. Robertson, S. K. Warne, C. J. McDermott and D. W. Fleming did not bat.

Bowling: Wasim Akram 8–3–26–1; Waqar Younis 9–0–39–1; Akram Raza 10–0–35–1; Mushtaq Ahmed 9–0–48–0; Aamir Sohail 6–0–26–0; Salim Malik 4–0–20–0.

Umpires: Riazuddin and Saqib Qureshi.

PAKISTAN v SOUTH AFRICA

At National Stadium, Karachi, October 16. Pakistan won by eight wickets. Toss: South Africa. International debut: D. N. Crookes.

Another dismal South African batting performance – a meagre 163 for nine – left Pakistan with the easiest of tasks, which they accomplished with five overs in hand. But third umpire Atiq Khan shared the South Africans' embarrassment. Asked to rule on whether Richardson had been run out, he thought he had pressed the green button, signifying "not out", only for the red light to signal his dismissal. Inzamam-ul-Haq scored his second successive half-century and added a match-winning 115 with captain Salim Malik, who also took three catches.

Man of the Match: Salim Malik.

South Africa

A. C. Hudson lbw b Akram Raza	23	†D. J. Richardson run out	7
*K. C. Wessels c Salim Malik		D. N. Crookes b Wasim Akram	10
b Akram Raza	33	T. G. Shaw run out	0
W. J. Cronje run out	21	M. W. Pringle not out	13
D. J. Cullinan c Ijaz Ahmed		P. S. de Villiers not out	7
b Aamir Sohail	10	L-b 4, w 4, n-b 1	9
J. N. Rhodes c Salim Malik			
b Aqib Javed	16	1/49 2/70 3/90 (9 wkts, 50 overs)	163
E. O. Simons c Salim Malik		4/90 5/121 6/131	
b Wasim Akram	14	7/137 8/137 9/145	

Bowling: Wasim Akram 10-0-28-2; Aqib Javed 10-2-25-1; Waqar Younis 10-2-40-0; Akram Raza 10-0-30-2; Salim Malik 3-0-14-0; Aamir Sohail 7-1-22-1.

Pakistan

Saeed Anwar st Richardson b Cronje	20
Aamir Sohail c and b Simons	22
Inzamam-ul-Haq not out	51
*Salim Malik not out	62
L-b 2, w 4, n-b 5	11

1/41 2/51   (2 wkts, 44.4 overs) 166

Asif Mujtaba, Ijaz Ahmed, †Rashid Latif, Wasim Akram, Waqar Younis, Aqib Javed and Akram Raza did not bat.

Bowling: de Villiers 9.4-1-38-0; Pringle 8-0-35-0; Simons 10-2-39-1; Cronje 6-1-12-1; Shaw 7-1-23-0; Crookes 4-0-17-0.

Umpires: Feroz Butt and Salim Badar.

AUSTRALIA v SOUTH AFRICA

At Faisalabad, October 18. Australia won by 22 runs. Toss: Australia.

Warne took four tail-end wickets in six balls, three of them stumped by Healy, to thwart South Africa, after Cronje had hit 64 and given them a chance of meeting their target of 209 for a first win. Earlier, Bevan had completed Australia's innings with a flourish, hitting 36 in 31 balls.

Man of the Match: W. J. Cronje.

Australia

*M. A. Taylor c Richardson b de Villiers	4	†I. A. Healy c de Villiers b Simons	4
M. J. Slater b Eksteen	38	S. K. Warne not out	15
M. E. Waugh c Richardson b Cronje	38	B 1, l-b 2, w 3, n-b 1	7
D. C. Boon c Wessels b Pringle	43		
S. R. Waugh b Simons	23	1/6 2/69 3/95 (6 wkts, 50 overs)	208
M. G. Bevan not out	36	4/143 5/160 6/167	

C. J. McDermott, T. B. A. May and G. D. McGrath did not bat.

Bowling: de Villiers 9–2–41–1; Pringle 9–1–49–1; Simons 10–0–41–2; Cronje 10–1–31–1; Eksteen 8–0–26–1; Crookes 4–0–17–0.

South Africa

*K. C. Wessels c Bevan b May	30
A. C. Hudson run out	5
W. J. Cronje c S. R. Waugh	
b McDermott .	64
J. N. Rhodes c Boon b May	11
G. Kirsten b McGrath	24
†D. J. Richardson lbw b McGrath	10
E. O. Simons st Healy b Warne	11
D. N. Crookes not out	20

M. W. Pringle lbw b Warne 0
C. E. Eksteen st Healy b Warne 0
P. S. de Villiers st Healy b Warne 0

L-b 7, w 3, n-b 1 11

1/7 2/64 3/86　　　　　(48.2 overs) 186
4/124 5/138 6/156
7/176 8/176 9/186

Bowling: McDermott 9–2–34–1; McGrath 10–2–31–2; Warne 9.2–0–40–4; May 10–0–34–2; S. R. Waugh 10–1–40–0.

Umpires: Islam Khan and Khizar Hayat.

PAKISTAN v SOUTH AFRICA

At Rawalpindi, October 20. Pakistan won by 39 runs. Toss: South Africa.

Ijaz Ahmed answered criticism of his recall to the national team with a run-a-ball century – he hit 13 fours and a six and his last 60 runs took only 39 deliveries. With his captain and brother-in-law, Salim Malik, he added 125 in 25 overs. South Africa always struggled, with Wessels scoring 19 from as many overs, though Cronje reached his third half-century in four games before being run out. Cullinan and Rhodes were also run out, though Rhodes could plead grogginess; he had batted on for 20 minutes after ducking into a full toss from Aqib Javed.

Man of the Match: Ijaz Ahmed.

Pakistan

Saeed Anwar c Cullinan b Simons	42
Aamir Sohail c Richardson b Matthews	1
Inzamam-ul-Haq run out	10
*Salim Malik c Wessels b Eksteen	56
Ijaz Ahmed b Matthews	110
Wasim Akram b Matthews	12

†Rashid Latif not out 3
Akram Raza not out 4
B 4, l-b 4, w 1, n-b 2 11

1/2 2/39 3/61　　　　(6 wkts, 50 overs) 249
4/186 5/232 6/245

Asif Mujtaba, Waqar Younis and Aqib Javed did not bat.

Bowling: de Villiers 10–0–41–0; Matthews 10–2–50–3; Cronje 10–0–45–0; Simons 10–1–56–1; Eksteen 10–1–49–1.

South Africa

A. C. Hudson c Rashid Latif	
b Waqar Younis .	20
*K. C. Wessels lbw b Waqar Younis . . .	19
W. J. Cronje run out	53
D. J. Cullinan run out	36
J. N. Rhodes run out	33

G. Kirsten not out 20
†D. J. Richardson not out 10
B 2, l-b 12, w 3, n-b 2 19

1/35 2/61 3/130　　　　(5 wkts, 50 overs) 210
4/160 5/189

E. O. Simons, C. E. Eksteen, C. R. Matthews and P. S. de Villiers did not bat.

Bowling: Wasim Akram 10–1–40–0; Aqib Javed 10–0–36–0; Waqar Younis 10–0–35–2; Akram Raza 10–0–41–0; Salim Malik 5–0–24–0; Aamir Sohail 5–0–20–0.

Umpires: Javed Akhtar and Said Ahmed Shah.

PAKISTAN v AUSTRALIA

At Rawalpindi, October 22. Pakistan won by nine wickets. Toss: Pakistan.

Furious hitting by Pakistan's top three rushed them to their target of 251 with 11 overs to spare. Saeed Anwar and Aamir Sohail opened with 91 in 14 overs, then Anwar and Inzamam-ul-Haq added 160 in 25. Anwar hit 13 fours and a six in his seventh one-day international century, facing 119 balls, and Inzamam smashed three sixes and 11 fours in 80 balls. Even Mark Waugh's unbeaten 121, with eight fours off 134 deliveries, was overshadowed. Healy broke his thumb while keeping wicket; Langer stood in until New South Wales keeper Phil Emery could be flown in to complete the tour.

Man of the Match: Saeed Anwar.

Australia

M. J. Slater b Aqib Javed	4	M. G. Bevan b Waqar Younis	22
*M. A. Taylor c Akram Raza		†I. A. Healy run out	16
b Aqib Javed	14	S. K. Warne not out	11
M. E. Waugh not out	121	B 1, l-b 13, w 5, n-b 2	21
J. L. Langer c Saeed Anwar			
b Wasim Akram	27	1/14 2/50 3/114 (6 wkts, 50 overs) 250	
S. R. Waugh lbw b Salim Malik	14	4/140 5/206 6/234	

C. J. McDermott, T. B. A. May and G. D. McGrath did not bat.

Bowling: Wasim Akram 10-0-47-1; Aqib Javed 10-0-44-2; Waqar Younis 10-0-50-1; Aamir Sohail 5-0-25-0; Akram Raza 10-0-36-0; Salim Malik 5-0-34-1.

Pakistan

Saeed Anwar not out	104
Aamir Sohail c Bevan b May	45
Inzamam-ul-Haq not out	91
B 3, l-b 4, w 2, n-b 2	11
1/91 (1 wkt, 39 overs) 251	

*Salim Malik, Ijaz Ahmed, Basit Ali, Wasim Akram, †Rashid Latif, Akram Raza, Waqar Younis and Aqib Javed did not bat.

Bowling: McDermott 8-1-54-0; McGrath 6-1-37-0; May 9-0-65-1; Warne 9-1-47-0; S. R. Waugh 5-0-26-0; M. E. Waugh 2-0-15-0.

Umpires: Salim Badar and Siddiq Khan.

AUSTRALIA v SOUTH AFRICA

At Peshawar, October 24. Australia won by three wickets. Toss: South Africa.

Crowd trouble marred the game, with spectators pelting both sides on the field and the players' balconies. A firecracker exploded at Cullinan's feet, another landed by Boon and Warne was hit on the chest by a padlock. Amid these distractions, Cronje at last reached a deserved hundred when he hit McDermott's final delivery for four. Despite three run-outs, Australia reached the last two overs needing 17. Langer saw them most of the way with three fours (and four leg-byes) off de Villiers; Matthews then bowled Angel before McDermott took the winning single.

Man of the Match: W. J. Cronje.

South Africa

*K. C. Wessels c Bevan b McDermott	4	D. N. Crookes lbw b McGrath	0
G. Kirsten b McGrath	45	E. O. Simons not out	10
W. J. Cronje not out	100	B 12, l-b 9, w 3, n-b 4	28
D. J. Cullinan b Warne	36		
J. N. Rhodes c Taylor b Angel	3	1/7 2/92 3/157 (6 wkts, 50 overs) 251	
†D. J. Richardson c Slater b Waugh	25	4/167 5/207 6/207	

C. R. Matthews, T. G. Shaw and P. S. de Villiers did not bat.

Bowling: McDermott 9-0-48-1; Angel 10-1-37-1; McGrath 10-2-22-2; Waugh 6-0-39-1; May 5-0-33-0; Warne 10-0-51-1.

Australia

*M. A. Taylor c Richardson b de Villiers	17	J. Angel b Matthews 0
M. J. Slater run out	54	C. J. McDermott not out 1
M. E. Waugh c Rhodes b Shaw	43	L-b 5, w 2 7
D. C. Boon run out	39	
M. G. Bevan c Shaw b de Villiers	45	1/38 2/107 3/119　(7 wkts, 49.4 overs) 252
†J. L. Langer not out	33	4/186 5/223
S. K. Warne run out	13	6/239 7/251

T. B. A. May and G. D. McGrath did not bat.

Bowling: de Villiers 10–2–49–2; Matthews 9.4–1–43–1; Simons 8–0–46–0; Cronje 10–0–46–0; Shaw 10–0–49–1; Crookes 2–0–14–0.

Umpires: Mohammad Nazir and Shakeel Khan.

PAKISTAN v AUSTRALIA

At Gujranwala, October 26. No result (abandoned).

Rain forced officials to call off the game but, fearing for their safety when the large crowd rioted, they persuaded the teams to play a 12-a-side exhibition match of 15 overs an innings. The deputy commissioner of Gujranwala told Taylor, the Australian captain, "If you don't play some cricket they'll kill us." Taylor said he had never heard a more pressing reason to play. About sixty people were hurt in the disturbances. Conditions were so damp that bowling was possible only from one end; Pakistan reversed their batting order and won by four wickets.

PAKISTAN v SOUTH AFRICA

At Faisalabad, October 28. Pakistan won by six wickets. Toss: South Africa.

South Africa were given their best start of the tournament by Kirsten and Wessels, who opened with 125, in just under two hours, but it was still not enough to earn them victory. Ijaz Ahmed and Basit Ali hit off the final 148 required in less than 25 overs, though the winning run came as a disappointment to both sides; with the scores level and Ijaz two short of a second century in the tournament, Simons "bowled" him with a no-ball. Ijaz remained undefeated on 98 after 87 legitimate deliveries; he hit 11 fours and a six.

Man of the Match: Ijaz Ahmed.

South Africa

G. Kirsten run out	69	†D. J. Richardson not out 27
*K. C. Wessels c and b Wasim Akram	51	
W. J. Cronje b Salim Malik	18	B 1, l-b 2, w 2, n-b 3 8
D. J. Cullinan c Akram Raza		
b Waqar Younis .	4	1/125 2/130　(4 wkts, 50 overs) 222
J. N. Rhodes not out	45	3/138 4/166

E. O. Simons, C. R. Matthews, T. G. Shaw, C. E. Eksteen and P. S. de Villiers did not bat.

Bowling: Wasim Akram 10–0–36–1; Aqib Javed 10–0–35–0; Waqar Younis 10–0–55–1; Akram Raza 10–0–46–0; Salim Malik 8–0–37–1; Aamir Sohail 2–0–10–0.

Pakistan

Saeed Anwar c Cullinan b Matthews ...	14	Basit Ali not out 52
Aamir Sohail c Cullinan b Simons	25	B 1, l-b 4, w 1, n-b 2 8
Inzamam-ul-Haq c Eksteen b Simons .	19	
*Salim Malik b Simons	7	1/26 2/47　(4 wkts, 44.3 overs) 223
Ijaz Ahmed not out	98	3/66 4/75

Wasim Akram, †Rashid Latif, Akram Raza, Waqar Younis and Aqib Javed did not bat.

Bowling: de Villiers 8–0–46–0; Matthews 9–3–31–1; Cronje 2–1–10–0; Simons 8.3–0–49–3; Eksteen 10–1–52–0; Shaw 7–0–30–0.

Umpires: Afzal Ahmed and Salim Badar.

QUALIFYING TABLE

	Played	Won	Lost	No result	Points	Run-rate
Pakistan	6	4	1	1	9	4.76
Australia.........	6	4	1	1	9	4.55
South Africa......	6	0	6	0	0	4.11

FINAL

PAKISTAN v AUSTRALIA

At Lahore, October 30. Australia won by 64 runs. Toss: Pakistan. International debut: P. A. Emery.

New South Wales batting – represented by six of Australia's top seven – gave the tourists the initial advantage, and a seventh player from the state, the young fast bowler McGrath, ensured them the tournament prize. He took five for 52, including three wickets in ten balls in his second spell, after Fleming had dismissed both Pakistan openers. A run-a-ball 63 by Basit Ali failed to lift the home team. Salim Malik had the personal satisfaction of reaching 5,000 runs in his 199th limited-overs international, but was criticised for putting Australia in to bat on a good pitch. Slater and Taylor gave Australia the perfect start, with 121 at more than five an over, and Bevan scored an unbeaten 53 off 42 balls to take them to 269, the highest total of the series. Steve Waugh injured his shoulder and missed the final Test in Lahore.

Man of the Match: G. D. McGrath.

Australia

*M. A. Taylor c and b Salim Malik ... 56	M. G. Bevan not out 53
M. J. Slater st Rashid Latif	†P. A. Emery not out 11
b Salim Malik . 66	
M. E. Waugh b Salim Malik 38	B 1, l-b 16, w 4, n-b 2 23
D. C. Boon c Salim Malik	
b Waqar Younis . 21	1/121 2/146 3/188 (5 wkts, 50 overs) 269
S. R. Waugh b Aamir Sohail 1	4/191 5/226

S. K. Warne, C. J. McDermott, D. W. Fleming and G. D. McGrath did not bat.

Bowling: Wasim Akram 10-1-63-0; Aqib Javed 7-0-30-0; Waqar Younis 8-0-48-1; Akram Raza 10-0-45-0; Aamir Sohail 5-0-35-1; Salim Malik 10-0-31-3.

Pakistan

Saeed Anwar c Taylor b Fleming 0	†Rashid Latif not out 10
Aamir Sohail c S. R. Waugh b Fleming 21	Waqar Younis b McGrath 2
Inzamam-ul-Haq c Emery b McGrath .. 10	Aqib Javed b M. E. Waugh 17
*Salim Malik b Fleming 35	L-b 8, w 7, n-b 2 17
Ijaz Ahmed c Emery b McGrath 4	
Basit Ali lbw b McGrath 63	1/17 2/26 3/43 (46.5 overs) 205
Wasim Akram b McGrath 26	4/64 5/110 6/173
Akram Raza c Emery b M. E. Waugh . 0	7/174 8/176 9/178

Bowling: McDermott 9-0-32-0; Fleming 8-2-32-3; McGrath 10-0-52-5; Warne 10-2-32-0; S. R. Waugh 2-0-6-0; M. E. Waugh 7.5-0-43-2.

Umpires: Khizar Hayat and Mian Aslam. Series referee: J. R. Reid (New Zealand).

WILLS WORLD SERIES, 1994-95

By R. MOHAN

Sandwiched between matches in an India v West Indies one-day series, a triangular tournament provided India with further success and an enormous popular hit. The third side were New Zealand, who were *en route* for South Africa. Teams wore coloured clothing (the bilateral series continued in whites) and the competition culminated in a floodlit extravaganza at Calcutta. An enthusiastic audience, estimated at close to 100,000, watched India defeat West Indies. But large crowds assembled even at matches not involving the home team.

India added this title to the Singer Trophy they had won in Sri Lanka in September. They lost only once, to West Indies in controversial circumstances. Manoj Prabhakar, who scored a century, and Nayan Mongia were accused of "not making an effort to win the match" after stonewalling throughout the closing stages of the run-chase. The Indian authorities dropped the players, and referee Raman Subba Row went further, docking the team two points for not playing in the spirit of the game (it was thought that West Indies were India's preferred opponents for the final). India protested to ICC, who ruled that the referee had exceeded his authority. Subba Row also suspended West Indian vice-captain Brian Lara for one game, for arguing with an umpire, who he thought should have asked for a video replay before giving him out stumped. New Zealand did not record a win in four matches, though they were unlucky to be rained off after dismissing West Indies cheaply in their opening fixture.

Note: Matches in this section were not first-class.

INDIA v WEST INDIES

At Madras, October 23. India won by four wickets. Toss: India. International debut: S. L. Campbell.

West Indies seemed to be in absolute command while Lara and Hooper were adding 112 for the third wicket. But Lara was given out leg-before to Tendulkar, aiming an extravagant pull at a ball beyond off stump, and Adams and Hooper followed two runs later. An eventual total of 221 was inadequate. Still, the West Indian new-ball bowlers struck early to dismiss Sidhu and Tendulkar, who had made nought, nought and eight in successive matches. Azharuddin took charge with a fine 81, off 84 balls, to keep India ahead of the asking-rate. When he was out, 27 short of victory, Mongia guided them home.

Man of the Match: M. Azharuddin.

West Indies

P. V. Simmons b Srinath	2	K. C. G. Benjamin b Prasad	2
S. C. Williams c Mongia b Prasad	39	*C. A. Walsh not out	0
B. C. Lara lbw b Tendulkar	74	B. St A. Browne run out	0
C. L. Hooper c and b Kumble	58	L-b 5, w 1, n-b 2	8
†J. C. Adams c and b Tendulkar	0		
S. L. Campbell st Mongia b Tendulkar	3	1/29 2/64 3/176	(49.2 overs) 221
S. Chanderpaul b Prabhakar	19	4/178 5/178 6/202	
A. C. Cummins run out	16	7/204 8/209 9/221	

Bowling: Prabhakar 8–0–37–1; Srinath 7–0–24–1; Prasad 8.2–1–38–2; Chauhan 6–0–46–0; Kumble 10–1–35–1; Tendulkar 10–0–36–3.

India

M. Prabhakar lbw b Walsh	38	†N. R. Mongia not out		24
N. S. Sidhu c Lara b Walsh	3	A. Kumble not out		9
S. R. Tendulkar c Hooper b Cummins	8	L-b 1, w 4, n-b 14		19
*M. Azharuddin c Walsh b Cummins	81			
V. G. Kambli c Hooper b Benjamin	22	1/17 2/42 3/80	(6 wkts, 48.2 overs)	225
A. D. Jadeja c Campbell b Benjamin	21	4/136 5/178 6/195		

R. K. Chauhan, J. Srinath and B. K. V. Prasad did not bat.

Bowling: Walsh 10–1–33–2; Benjamin 10–0–42–2; Cummins 9.2–0–50–2; Browne 8–0–38–0; Simmons 6–0–29–0; Hooper 5–0–32–0.

Umpires: K. S. Giridharan and K. A. Parthasarathy.

NEW ZEALAND v WEST INDIES

At Margao, Goa, October 26. No result. Toss: West Indies. International debut: R. Dhanraj.

Misguidedly choosing to bat on an underprepared pitch, West Indies were all out for 123; only a downpour at lunch rescued them. Slow left-armer Hart bowled imaginatively to return five for 22, the best limited-overs analysis for New Zealand, while Parore became their first player to make five dismissals in a one-day international. But their first joint victim was the most significant. At 71 for one in the 14th over, umpire Murali, a newcomer at this level, gave Lara out stumped. Lara begged him to consult his colleague in the television replay box and showed some truculence when Murali refused. (The replay was indecisive, so Lara might have been reprieved.) ICC referee Raman Subba Row suspended Lara for one game and fined him half his match fee. West Indies' remaining eight wickets fell for 52 but the rain was to foil New Zealand.

West Indies

S. C. Williams run out	24	*C. A. Walsh c Parore b Hart		0
S. L. Campbell c Parore b Pringle	0	R. Dhanraj b Pringle		8
B. C. Lara st Parore b Hart	32	C. E. Cuffy not out		0
C. L. Hooper b Hart	22	B 4, l-b 7, w 9		20
P. V. Simmons c Young b Hart	0			
K. L. T. Arthurton run out	1	1/4 2/71 3/92	(39.1 overs)	123
†J. C. Adams st Parore b Hart	5	4/94 5/95 6/97		
A. C. Cummins c Parore b Harris	11	7/102 8/102 9/123		

Bowling: Pringle 4.1–0–19–2; Nash 8–1–25–0; de Groen 4–0–19–0; Hart 10–2–22–5; Thomson 10–5–19–0; Harris 3–0–8–1.

New Zealand

B. A. Young not out	13
B. R. Hartland hit wkt b Walsh	6
†A. C. Parore not out	3
W 2, n-b 1	3
1/14	(1 wkt, 9 overs) 25

*K. R. Rutherford, S. P. Fleming, C. Z. Harris, S. A. Thomson, M. N. Hart, D. J. Nash, C. Pringle and R. P. de Groen did not bat.

Bowling: Walsh 5–1–17–1; Cuffy 4–1–8–0.

Umpires: B. A. Jamula and K. Murali.

INDIA v NEW ZEALAND

At Baroda, October 28. India won by seven wickets. Toss: New Zealand.

A slow pitch at the small IPCL ground was ideal for batting: Rutherford reached his maiden hundred in his 103rd one-day international, only to be trumped when Tendulkar returned to form with 115. Rutherford scored at more than a run a ball and hit 13 fours, while Parore, who helped him add 180, made 96 without a boundary hit. Restored to open, Tendulkar was dropped on eight, bided his time in a 144-run stand with Prabhakar, and then broke out in a flurry of shots. He hit nine fours and three sixes in 136 balls. Though he was run out when Azharuddin's straight drive ricocheted off Nash's hands on to the stumps, victory was a near-formality.

Man of the Match: S. R. Tendulkar.

New Zealand

B. A. Young c Mongia b Srinath	5	S. A. Thomson not out		0
B. R. Hartland c Kumble b Prabhakar	8	B 5, l-b 8, w 3, n-b 3		19
†A. C. Parore c Kumble b Prabhakar	96			
*K. R. Rutherford run out	108	1/7 2/27	(4 wkts, 50 overs)	269
S. P. Fleming not out	33	3/207 4/268		

C. Z. Harris, D. J. Nash, M. N. Hart, C. Pringle and R. P. de Groen did not bat.

Bowling: Prabhakar 10-0-49-2; Srinath 10-1-41-1; Prasad 10-0-49-0; Raju 7-1-38-0; Kumble 10-0-53-0; Tendulkar 3-0-26-0.

India

M. Prabhakar c and b Hart	74	V. G. Kambli not out		12
S. R. Tendulkar run out	115	L-b 3, w 9		12
N. S. Sidhu c de Groen b Hart	11			
*M. Azharuddin not out	47	1/144 2/162 3/247	(3 wkts, 48.1 overs)	271

A. D. Jadeja, †N. R. Mongia, A. Kumble, J. Srinath, S. L. V. Raju and B. K. V. Prasad did not bat.

Bowling: Pringle 9.1-0-53-0; Nash 10-0-51-0; de Groen 9-0-52-0; Hart 10-0-56-2; Harris 5-0-31-0; Thomson 5-0-25-0.

Umpires: S. K. Bansal and S. Shastri.

INDIA v WEST INDIES

At Kanpur, October 30. West Indies won by 46 runs. Toss: India.

West Indies' victory was soured by the controversy surrounding India's sixth-wicket pair, Prabhakar and Mongia. They came together requiring 63 from nine overs, but their stonewalling defence produced only 16. Though Prabhakar completed an unbeaten century, the selectors dropped him and Mongia for the rest of the series, and ICC referee Raman Subba Row fined India two points, suspecting they were anxious for West Indies to join them in the final. His decision was later rescinded by ICC, who said it was not in his jurisdiction. The West Indians had played with sparkle. After Simmons and Williams opened with 115, Arthurton scored 72 from 62 balls. India were also given a bright start by Tendulkar, while Prabhakar anchored the innings. The loss of Azharuddin, to a brilliant outfield catch by Cummins, was a great setback, however, and the West Indian fielders also scored three direct hits to run out Sidhu, Kambli and Jadeja.

Man of the Match: K. L. T. Arthurton.

West Indies

P. V. Simmons c Srinath b Tendulkar	65	K. C. G. Benjamin not out		1
S. C. Williams c and b Tendulkar	45			
C. L. Hooper lbw b Raju	1	L-b 18, w 3, n-b 6		27
K. L. T. Arthurton run out	72			
R. I. C. Holder b Srinath	32	1/115 2/120 3/130	(6 wkts, 50 overs)	257
A. C. Cummins run out	14	4/219 5/250 6/257		

S. Chanderpaul, †J. C. Adams, *C. A. Walsh and C. E. Cuffy did not bat.

Bowling: Prabhakar 6-0-50-0; Srinath 9-0-31-1; Prasad 7-0-36-0; Kumble 10-0-50-0; Raju 10-1-41-1; Tendulkar 8-0-31-2.

India

M. Prabhakar not out	102	†N. R. Mongia not out	4
S. R. Tendulkar b Cummins	34		
N. S. Sidhu run out	2	L-b 9, w 5, n-b 4	18
*M. Azharuddin c Cummins b Cuffy	26		
V. G. Kambli run out	16	1/56 2/78 3/119 (5 wkts, 50 overs) 211	
A. D. Jadeja run out	9	4/169 5/195	

A. Kumble, J. Srinath, S. L. V. Raju and B. K. V. Prasad did not bat.

Bowling: Walsh 9-2-20-0; Cuffy 10-0-49-1; Simmons 2-0-19-0; Benjamin 10-1-39-0; Cummins 10-1-39-1; Hooper 8-0-36-0; Arthurton 1-1-0-0.

Umpires: Jasbir Singh and C. K. Sathe.

NEW ZEALAND v WEST INDIES

At Gauhati, November 1. West Indies won by 135 runs. Toss: West Indies.

The West Indian batsmen treated New Zealand's attack with contempt. Lara, returning from suspension, shared a rollicking stand of 111 in 21 overs with Hooper, who then breezed to 111 himself off 114 balls. With Arthurton and Cummins joining the run spree, West Indies passed 300. Despite perfect batting conditions, the New Zealanders might have lost by an even more crushing margin but for the last-wicket pair, Nash and Pringle; joining forces at 123 for nine, they batted out time and added 48. Leg-spinner Dhanraj, who had not bowled in his only previous international, the washout at Margao, hustled out the late middle order for the attractive figures of four for 26.

Man of the Match: C. L. Hooper.

West Indies

P. V. Simmons b Nash	0	R. I. C. Holder b Pringle	4
S. C. Williams lbw b Doull	25	†J. C. Adams not out	5
B. C. Lara c Hart b Nash	69	B 5, l-b 6, w 7	18
C. L. Hooper c Hartland b Pringle	111		
K. L. T. Arthurton b Nash	45	1/1 2/45 3/156 (6 wkts, 50 overs) 306	
A. C. Cummins not out	29	4/259 5/272 6/281	

*C. A. Walsh, R. Dhanraj and C. E. Cuffy did not bat.

Bowling: Nash 10-1-48-3; Pringle 9-1-71-2; Doull 9-0-65-1; Hart 5-0-34-0; Harris 10-0-43-0; Thomson 7-0-34-0.

New Zealand

B. R. Hartland b Walsh	9	D. J. Nash not out	20
B. A. Young c Williams b Dhanraj	33	S. B. Doull b Arthurton	4
†A. C. Parore run out	9	C. Pringle not out	34
*K. R. Rutherford b Hooper	13	B 4, l-b 8, w 1, n-b 2	15
S. P. Fleming c Simmons b Dhanraj	18		
S. A. Thomson st Adams b Dhanraj	2	1/15 2/33 3/60 (9 wkts, 50 overs) 171	
C. Z. Harris lbw b Arthurton	12	4/92 5/95 6/95	
M. N. Hart b Dhanraj	5	7/101 8/119 9/123	

Bowling: Walsh 6-1-18-1; Cuffy 6-0-13-0; Simmons 7-1-13-0; Cummins 4-0-18-0; Dhanraj 10-2-26-4; Hooper 10-1-28-1; Arthurton 5-0-26-2; Lara 2-0-17-0.

Umpires: S. Banerjee and M. R. Singh.

INDIA v NEW ZEALAND

At Delhi, November 3. India won by 107 runs. Toss: India. International debut: D. J. Murray.

After the chastening experience of Kanpur, the Indian batsmen were back in striking form, falling only ten short of their highest-ever limited-overs score, 299 against Sri Lanka in 1986-87. Jadeja, promoted to open in place of Prabhakar, and Tendulkar needed only 80 minutes to raise 100, while Azharuddin and Kambli rounded the innings off with 67 in 46 balls. Once reduced to 27 for three, New Zealand were hardly in the running. But there were flashes of brilliance from Fleming, who hit 56 off 48 balls; he and Parore took 23 runs off Chetan Sharma's only over and added 79 together before Tendulkar scotched their last hopes with two wickets.

Man of the Match: S. R. Tendulkar.

India

A. D. Jadeja c Hart b Nash	90	V. G. Kambli not out		36
S. R. Tendulkar b Hart	62	L-b 3, w 5		8
N. S. Sidhu c Hart b de Groen	35			
*M. Azharuddin not out	58	1/100 2/175 3/222	(3 wkts, 50 overs)	289

†V. S. Yadav, Chetan Sharma, A. Kumble, J. Srinath, B. K. V. Prasad and S. L. V. Raju did not bat.

Bowling: Nash 10–0–50–1; Doull 10–1–58–0; de Groen 9–0–67–1; Hart 9–0–36–1; Harris 2–0–24–0; Thomson 10–0–51–0.

New Zealand

B. A. Young c Yadav b Srinath	0	D. J. Nash b Kumble		3
D. J. Murray run out	3	S. B. Doull st Yadav b Kambli		8
†A. C. Parore lbw b Raju	51	R. P. de Groen not out		1
*K. R. Rutherford c Srinath b Prasad	8	L-b 4, w 4, n-b 3		11
S. P. Fleming lbw b Tendulkar	56			
S. A. Thomson c Raju b Tendulkar	9	1/0 2/12 3/27	(45.4 overs)	182
C. Z. Harris c Srinath b Raju	16	4/106 5/132 6/142		
M. N. Hart run out	16	7/168 8/172 9/173		

Bowling: Srinath 7–1–22–1; Prasad 7–0–26–1; Chetan Sharma 1–0–23–0; Kumble 10–1–41–1; Tendulkar 10–1–29–2; Raju 10–0–30–2; Kambli 0.4–0–7–1.

Umpires: T. K. Handu and R. C. Sharma.

QUALIFYING TABLE

	Played	Won	Lost	No result	Points
India	4	3	1	0	12
West Indies	4	2	1	1	10
New Zealand	4	0	3	1	2

FINAL

INDIA v WEST INDIES

At Calcutta, November 5 (day/night). India won by 72 runs. Toss: India.

There was a sense of *déjà vu* when West Indies fielded first in a day/night final against India at a packed Eden Gardens in November for the second year running. The only difference was that Richardson had chosen to bowl, whereas Walsh lost the toss. Once again, though, India outplayed their guests. Jadeja and Tendulkar opened with another century stand, Tendulkar providing the thrust with 66 in 68 balls, while Azharuddin and Kambli extended the torment. Kambli, after a more responsible start, still cut loose at the end to reach 58 off 40. Any hopes the West Indians had of chasing 275 took a near-fatal blow when Williams cut Srinath and Lara dragged a widish ball from Prasad into his stumps in successive overs. They were finally choked when Hooper cut high to point. Arthurton batted on for a while and Walsh hit Raju for three towering sixes. But West Indies's only consolation was to reduce the winning margin from 102 runs the previous year to 72.

Man of the Match: S. R. Tendulkar.   *Man of the Series:* S. R. Tendulkar.

India

A. D. Jadeja c Lara b Dhanraj	58	†V. S. Yadav lbw b Walsh 0
S. R. Tendulkar c Williams b Cuffy	66	A. Kumble not out.............. 1
N. S. Sidhu c Adams b Cummins	28	B 10, l-b 5, n-b 4.......... 19
*M. Azharuddin c Holder b Hooper	41	
V. G. Kambli not out	58	1/108 2/147 3/175 (6 wkts, 50 overs) 274
A. C. Bedade c Arthurton b Dhanraj	3	4/237 5/266 6/267

J. Srinath, S. L. V. Raju and B. K. V. Prasad did not bat.

Bowling: Walsh 10-0-46-1; Cuffy 10-1-53-1; Cummins 10-0-50-1; Hooper 10-0-55-1; Dhanraj 10-0-55-2.

West Indies

P. V. Simmons run out	21	*C. A. Walsh c Tendulkar b Raju 30
S. C. Williams c Azharuddin b Srinath	29	R. Dhanraj not out 0
B. C. Lara b Prasad	1	C. E. Cuffy c Kumble b Raju...... 0
C. L. Hooper c Azharuddin b Raju	30	B 2, l-b 14, w 5, n-b 1 22
K. L. T. Arthurton b Raju	42	
R. I. C. Holder c Jadeja b Tendulkar	5	1/46 2/49 3/68 (44 overs) 202
†J. C. Adams c Kumble b Jadeja	1	4/101 5/116 6/121
A. C. Cummins b Kumble	21	7/162 8/182 9/202

Bowling: Srinath 7-0-25-1; Prasad 7-3-23-1; Kumble 7-0-27-1; Raju 10-0-58-4; Tendulkar 8-2-35-1; Jadeja 5-0-18-1.

Umpires: V. K. Ramaswamy and S. Venkataraghavan.
Series referee: R. Subba Row (England).

BENSON AND HEDGES WORLD SERIES, 1994-95

By BRIAN MURGATROYD

The 1994-95 World Series, the first in the competition's 16 seasons to include a fourth side – Australia A – drew a mixed response from the players, public and critics.

The crowds by and large warmed to the idea, and if the purpose of the move was to generate extra interest, given the potentially weak drawing power of international newcomers Zimbabwe, then it succeeded. It also gave the home selectors an extra chance to assess emerging talent – they largely ignored the claims of experienced players, most notably Dean Jones, who reversed his decision to retire from international cricket in the hope of being picked.

But among the England and senior Australian players the concept was far from popular, with Mark Taylor arguing that it was wrong to ask an Australian crowd to choose between two home sides. No doubt the senior team feared an embarrassing defeat, but ultimately it was the credibility of the organisers that suffered. The A team matches were not recognised as one-day internationals by the International Cricket Council and the World Series finals became unofficial internationals contested by two sides from the same country. England and Zimbabwe, when they agreed to the idea, could hardly have envisaged players being swapped between the two Australian teams during the competition, as happened three times. The elevation of Paul Reiffel, the A side's best bowler in the qualifying matches, to the senior side for the finals, only for him then to be made twelfth man, was the final straw for some. The A team was dropped for the tournament in 1995-96.

Even allowing for team-tinkering, Australia were worthy winners. Their consistent batting was backed by fast bowler Craig McDermott, who was named International Cricketer of the Year. The A team's fielding was often breathtaking, and it managed to unearth Greg Blewett, a player full of self-confidence. England, plagued by injuries, were at a low ebb, and Zimbabwe, save their solitary success over England, never scored enough runs.

Notes: Matches in this section were not first-class. ICC ruled beforehand that matches involving Australia A, marked ‡, should not be regarded as official internationals.

AUSTRALIA v ZIMBABWE

At Perth, December 2 (day/night). Australia won by two wickets. Toss: Australia. International debut: S. G. Law.

Australia made hard work of the modest target of 167 set by Zimbabwe, making their first appearance in the World Series. Taylor and Slater opened at better than four an over; but, after both fell at 69, it required a pugnacious 40 from Healy, in company with Bevan, to ease Australia's nerves. Even then, three late wickets from occasional left-arm spinner Grant Flower forced Waugh, who had strained a groin muscle bowling, to come in with a runner to secure victory. Zimbabwe's batsmen had earlier failed to come to terms with the extra pace and bounce of the WACA pitch and some keen Australian out-cricket; debutant Stuart Law's medium-pace and Warne's leg-spin proved especially effective.

Man of the Match: S. K. Warne.   *Attendance:* 8,630.

Zimbabwe

*A. Flower c Warne b Fleming	29
G. W. Flower b McGrath	20
A. D. R. Campbell hit wkt b Warne . . .	22
D. L. Houghton run out	13
M. H. Dekker lbw b McGrath	16
†W. R. James run out	8
G. C. Martin b Law	16
P. A. Strang not out	17

E. A. Brandes c Healy b McDermott . . .	5
H. H. Streak c Fleming b Warne	7
D. H. Brain not out	1
L-b 9, w 3	12
1/49 2/56 3/83 (9 wkts, 50 overs) 166	
4/88 5/109 6/117	
7/144 8/151 9/164	

Bowling: McDermott 10-0-32-1; Fleming 10-0-45-1; McGrath 10-1-23-2; Waugh 1-0-3-0; Law 9-0-27-1; Warne 10-1-27-2.

Australia

M. J. Slater c A. Flower b Streak	18
*M. A. Taylor c G. W. Flower	
b Brandes .	45
D. C. Boon c Houghton b Strang	8
M. G. Bevan c James b Streak	30
S. G. Law c Houghton b Martin	7
†I. A. Healy c Campbell	
b G. W. Flower .	40
S. K. Warne c and b G. W. Flower	5
G. D. McGrath did not bat.	

C. J. McDermott c Dekker	
b G. W. Flower .	0
M. E. Waugh not out	6
D. W. Fleming not out	0
L-b 6, w 1, n-b 1	8
1/69 2/69 3/87 (8 wkts, 47.2 overs) 167	
4/96 5/156 6/161	
7/161 8/164	

Bowling: Brain 8.2-2-39-0; Streak 10-1-31-2; Brandes 10-1-29-1; Strang 10-1-30-1; Martin 5-0-17-1; G. W. Flower 4-0-15-3.

Umpires: T. A. Prue and W. P. Sheahan.

‡AUSTRALIA A v ZIMBABWE

At Perth, December 4. Australia A won by five wickets. Toss: Zimbabwe.

Darren Lehmann, whose career had stalled in the five seasons since he was twelfth man for Australia as a 20-year-old prodigy, finally hit something close to the big time, even though the match was not an official international. He hit a powerful run-a-ball 85 and secured a straightforward victory. This appeared unlikely when Zimbabwe's openers, Grant and Andy Flower, were scoring at almost a run an over. They were run in quick succession, however, and the innings then lost all momentum against tight bowling from Moody, Hughes and Robertson. Zimbabwe were further handicapped by the loss of pace bowler Brandes, who collapsed with a back injury after the toss, although Australia A captain Martyn generously allowed Martin to play instead.

Man of the Match: T. M. Moody.   *Attendance:* 7,287.

Zimbabwe

*†A. Flower c Reiffel b Hughes	44
G. W. Flower c Martyn b Moody	26
A. D. R. Campbell c Robertson	
b Moody .	29
D. L. Houghton run out	10
M. H. Dekker b Moody	4
G. J. Whittall run out	0
I. P. Butchart run out	21
P. A. Strang c Martyn b Robertson	0

G. C. Martin not out	25
H. H. Streak b Hughes	0
D. H. Brain not out	3
L-b 2, w 2	4
1/69 2/73 3/101 (9 wkts, 50 overs) 166	
4/106 5/106 6/121	
7/124 8/145 9/148	

Bowling: Angel 10-1-43-0; Reiffel 10-0-50-0; Hughes 10-1-21-2; Moody 10-5-16-3; Robertson 10-1-34-1.

Australia A

D. S. Lehmann st A. Flower b Strang	85	†P. A. Emery not out	1
M. L. Hayden c A. Flower b Streak	16		
*D. R. Martyn c Streak b Whittall	15	B 4, l-b 2, w 4	10
J. L. Langer c Butchart b Strang	24		
R. T. Ponting run out	0	1/30 2/56 3/108 (5 wkts, 35.1 overs) 167	
T. M. Moody not out	16	4/108 5/157	

G. R. Robertson, P. R. Reiffel, M. G. Hughes and J. Angel did not bat.

Bowling: Brain 8–2–40–0; Streak 9.1–0–32–1; Whittall 4–0–18–1; Butchart 2–0–9–0; Martin 2–0–16–0; Strang 8–2–32–2; G. W. Flower 2–0–14–0.

Umpires: S. J. Davis and T. A. Prue.

AUSTRALIA v ENGLAND

At Sydney, December 6 (day/night). Australia won by 28 runs. Toss: Australia.

England's middle order let them down after Atherton and Stewart laid the ideal foundations for victory, with 100 in 25 overs. Stewart departed to a disputed catch at backward point – he felt he played the ball into the ground, but umpire Hair disagreed, and television replays supported him. From then on Australia gradually took control. Pace bowlers McDermott and McGrath were outstanding, though Warne, facing England for the first time since taking 11 wickets at Brisbane, had a quiet match. His final ball effectively settled the outcome, however: he had Gooch caught at long-off. Off-spinners Udal and Hick had reined the home side back after Taylor and Slater started with 96 in 24 overs, but Boon's run-a-ball 64 provided late impetus. The England innings was interrupted three times by streakers, all male.

Man of the Match: D. C. Boon.   *Attendance:* 38,602.

Australia

*M. A. Taylor c and b Hick	57	S. G. Law not out	0
M. J. Slater c Hick b Udal	50	L-b 2, w 1	3
M. E. Waugh b Udal	4		
D. C. Boon not out	64	1/96 2/106 (4 wkts, 50 overs) 224	
M. G. Bevan c Gooch b Gough	46	3/126 4/218	

†I. A. Healy, S. K. Warne, C. J. McDermott, T. B. A. May and G. D. McGrath did not bat.

Bowling: Benjamin 6–0–25–0; DeFreitas 9–1–43–0; Gough 10–0–51–1; White 5–0–22–0; Udal 10–1–37–2; Hick 10–0–44–1.

England

*M. A. Atherton lbw b Law	60	D. Gough not out	8
A. J. Stewart c Law b May	48	S. D. Udal b McGrath	4
G. A. Hick c Boon b May	6	J. E. Benjamin b McDermott	0
G. P. Thorpe c Bevan b McDermott	21	L-b 7, w 6, n-b 1	14
G. A. Gooch c McDermott b Warne	21		
C. White b McDermott	0	1/100 2/112 3/133 (48.3 overs) 196	
†S. J. Rhodes c Warne b Law	8	4/147 5/149 6/164	
P. A. J. DeFreitas run out	21	7/180 8/187 9/195	

Bowling: McDermott 9.3–0–34–3; McGrath 9–4–22–1; Warne 10–0–46–1; Law 10–0–52–2; May 10.1–1–35–2.

Umpires: D. B. Hair and P. D. Parker.

AUSTRALIA v ZIMBABWE

At Hobart, December 8. Australia won by 84 runs. Toss: Australia.

Taylor dropped himself down the order to give others the chance of time at the crease, and Law responded to the unaccustomed challenge of opening by scoring a century. Dropped on 77, he reached 100 with a six. He added 159 in 33 overs with Boon, who finished unbeaten on 98. Faced with the daunting target of 255, Zimbabwe never threatened Australia's 100 per cent record, although their captain Andy Flower drove handsomely for 39. The interval between the innings was enlivened when Father Christmas arrived in a helicopter.

Man of the Match: S. G. Law.   *Attendance*: 7,472.

Australia

M. J. Slater c Whittall b Brain	10	M. G. Bevan not out	11
S. G. Law c G. W. Flower b Dekker	110	B 5, l-b 2, w 5, n-b 1	13
M. E. Waugh c G. W. Flower b Whittall	12		
D. C. Boon not out	98	1/12 2/55 3/214 (3 wkts, 50 overs)	254

*M. A. Taylor, †I. A. Healy, S. K. Warne, T. B. A. May, D. W. Fleming and G. D. McGrath did not bat.

Bowling: Brain 10–1–51–1; Streak 9–0–55–0; Whittall 7–1–22–1; Dekker 10–0–42–1; Strang 9–0–51–0; G. W. Flower 5–0–26–0.

Zimbabwe

*A. Flower c Healy b May	39	P. A. Strang not out	21
G. W. Flower c Healy b McGrath	8	H. H. Streak not out	12
A. D. R. Campbell b McGrath	1		
D. L. Houghton b May	4	L-b 6, w 7, n-b 1	14
M. H. Dekker run out	11		
G. J. Whittall c Healy b Fleming	35	1/15 2/24 3/47 (8 wkts, 50 overs)	170
†W. R. James c Healy b Warne	15	4/64 5/73 6/117	
I. P. Butchart b Fleming	10	7/129 8/136	

D. H. Brain did not bat.

Bowling: McGrath 8–2–18–2; Fleming 10–0–42–2; May 10–2–34–2; Law 10–1–25–0; Warne 9–0–23–1; Boon 2–0–11–0; Slater 1–0–11–0.

Umpires: A. J. McQuillan and S. G. Randell.

‡AUSTRALIA A v ZIMBABWE

At Adelaide, December 10. Australia A won by seven wickets. Toss: Zimbabwe.

Hayden's painstaking century, occupying three hours, steered Australia A to a comfortable victory over Zimbabwe, whose batting once again failed to perform. Andy Flower dropped down to No. 4 to try to shore up the middle order, but was one of three men out quickly. Though Campbell, Houghton and Whittall led a recovery and Zimbabwe topped 200 for the first time in four matches, that never looked likely to stretch Australia A on an easy-paced pitch. Hayden, dropped on 31 and 76, added 155 in 38 overs with Martyn and saw his team home with seven balls to spare.

Man of the Match: M. L. Hayden.   *Attendance*: 6,368.

Zimbabwe

A. D. R. Campbell c Martyn b Robertson	54	P. A. Strang c Emery b Reiffel	1
		G. C. Martin c Langer b Reiffel	5
G. W. Flower run out	9	H. H. Streak not out	8
†W. R. James c Moody b Rowell	0	L-b 9, w 1	10
*A. Flower c Lehmann b Hughes	4		
D. L. Houghton c Lehmann b Moody	48	1/23 2/23 3/33 (8 wkts, 50 overs)	201
G. J. Whittall not out	59	4/77 5/158 6/169	
M. H. Dekker c Martyn b Hughes	3	7/172 8/192	

D. H. Brain did not bat.

Bowling: Rowell 10–1–29–1; Reiffel 10–0–41–2; Hughes 9–0–22–2; Moody 10–1–37–1; Robertson 8–0–46–1; Martyn 3–0–17–0.

Australia A

D. S. Lehmann b Streak	1	R. T. Ponting not out	11
M. L. Hayden not out	101	B 1, l-b 6, w 4	11
*D. R. Martyn c A. Flower b Streak	69		
J. L. Langer lbw b Martin	9	1/2 2/157 3/172 (3 wkts, 48.5 overs) 202	

T. M. Moody, †P. A. Emery, G. R. Robertson, P. R. Reiffel, M. G. Hughes and G. J. Rowell did not bat.

Bowling: Brain 8–0–28–0; Streak 9–1–17–2; Whittall 6–1–25–0; A. Flower 3–0–12–0; Strang 10–1–57–0; Dekker 9.5–0–37–0; Martin 3–0–19–1.

Umpires: W. P. Sheahan and C. D. Timmins.

‡AUSTRALIA v AUSTRALIA A

At Adelaide, December 11. Australia won by six runs. Toss: Australia.

Backed by an increasingly vocal crowd, the A side were closing on a famous win, only for their lack of experience to scupper them: their last four fell for six runs in 11 balls, including three to McGrath. On a dry surface which made strokeplay difficult, Australia failed to hit a boundary after the 32nd over and owed much to the diligence of Taylor and Slater. In reply, Ponting – a rare talent, still eight days short of 20 – hoisted Warne for six on his way to 42. Afterwards Taylor, always an opponent of the A team concept, renewed his criticism, saying: "I don't like playing against my own players and I don't like it when the crowd does not support us when we are playing at home."

Man of the Match: G. D. McGrath.   *Attendance:* 20,470.

Australia

*M. A. Taylor b Robertson	44	C. J. McDermott not out	10
M. J. Slater c Hayden b Rowell	64	T. B. A. May run out	1
M. E. Waugh b Hughes	0	G. D. McGrath c Langer b Reiffel	0
D. C. Boon c Langer b Hughes	39	B 4, l-b 7, w 6	17
M. G. Bevan c Emery b Robertson	4		
S. G. Law b Moody	0	1/93 2/94 3/132 (48.3 overs) 202	
†I. A. Healy c Hayden b Reiffel	15	4/151 5/152 6/175	
S. K. Warne c Langer b Hughes	8	7/181 8/197 9/199	

Bowling: Rowell 10–0–41–1; Reiffel 9.3–2–34–2; Moody 7–0–36–1; Hughes 9–0–33–3; Martyn 3–0–20–0; Robertson 10–1–27–2.

Australia A

D. S. Lehmann c Healy b McGrath	4	P. R. Reiffel lbw b McGrath	0
M. L. Hayden c Taylor b Law	45	G. J. Rowell c Law b McGrath	0
*D. R. Martyn b Warne	37	M. G. Hughes c Law b McGrath	1
J. L. Langer c Law b Warne	1		
R. T. Ponting c Bevan b Warne	42	B 1, l-b 5, w 4, n-b 2	12
T. M. Moody c sub (D. W. Fleming) b May	5	1/10 2/71 3/77 (47.3 overs) 196	
†P. A. Emery run out	30	4/108 5/117 6/157	
G. R. Robertson not out	19	7/190 8/190 9/190	

Bowling: McDermott 9–0–33–0; McGrath 9.3–0–43–4; Waugh 4–1–17–0; Warne 10–1–40–3; May 10–0–29–1; Law 5–0–28–1.

Umpires: S. J. Davis and P. D. Parker.

‡AUSTRALIA A v ENGLAND

At Melbourne, December 13 (day/night). England won by 31 runs. Toss: England.

England, reduced to 12 fit men when Atherton pulled out with a sore back, recorded a morale-boosting first win two days after successive defeats by the Australian Cricket Academy. Former Academy pupil White, born in England but raised in nearby Bendigo, was at the heart of things. First, he rescued England from 97 for five with 43, and then he captured three wickets at lively medium-pace, after Australia A looked set for victory at 138 for three in the 38th over. But he paid for his heroics with a rib injury which ended his tour. Australia A's innings was held up when a drunken element of the crowd threw golf balls and beer cans on the field, and Tufnell was later fined $A700 by referee John Reid for throwing down the ball after an over when his appeal against Ponting was rejected and Fraser misfielded.

Man of the Match: C. White.   *Attendance*: 39,837.

England

G. A. Gooch c Emery b Hughes	6	S. D. Udal run out		9
*A. J. Stewart c Emery b Reiffel	5	P. C. R. Tufnell not out		0
G. A. Hick c Emery b Moody	32			
G. P. Thorpe run out	29	L-b 7, w 2		9
M. W. Gatting st Emery b Robertson	23			
C. White run out	43	1/9 2/23 3/55	(9 wkts, 50 overs)	188
†S. J. Rhodes run out	21	4/95 5/97 6/137		
P. A. J. DeFreitas c Martyn b Hughes	11	7/170 8/187 9/188		

A. R. C. Fraser did not bat.

Bowling: Hughes 10-3-22-1; Reiffel 10-0-45-1; Moody 10-0-33-1; Angel 9-1-45-0; Robertson 10-0-31-1; Martyn 1-0-5-0.

Australia A

D. S. Lehmann c Rhodes b Fraser	3	P. R. Reiffel c Rhodes b DeFreitas		1
M. L. Hayden c Rhodes b Fraser	12	M. G. Hughes b White		2
*D. R. Martyn c Gooch b Tufnell	40	J. Angel not out		3
J. L. Langer run out	55	L-b 2, w 1, n-b 1		4
R. T. Ponting b White	31			
T. M. Moody b White	2	1/7 2/20 3/79	(45.5 overs)	157
†P. A. Emery c Rhodes b DeFreitas	2	4/138 5/140 6/145		
G. R. Robertson run out	2	7/151 8/152 9/153		

Bowling: DeFreitas 10-2-24-2; Fraser 9-1-31-2; White 8.5-1-35-3; Udal 8-0-33-0; Tufnell 10-0-32-1.

Umpires: A. J. McQuillan and S. G. Randell.

ENGLAND v ZIMBABWE

At Sydney, December 15 (day/night). Zimbabwe won by 13 runs. Toss: Zimbabwe.

Zimbabwe made it two wins in two matches against England, having beaten them by nine runs in their only previous encounter, at Albury in the 1992 World Cup. It was their only win in this competition. They owed much to Grant Flower, who carried his bat for 84, his highest score in one-day internationals. He was fortunate when umpire Hair ruled he had not been run out on 26, without calling for the replay, which would have testified against him. With Houghton, Flower added 110 in 24 overs. But seven wickets then fell for 34 as the lively Gough took five for the first time in international cricket. England struggled against accurate bowling on a slow, low pitch, especially after Strang dismissed Gooch and Thorpe in his first over. The run-out of Zimbabwe-born Hick in the 47th over sealed their fate.

Man of the Match: G. W. Flower.   *Attendance*: 6,337.

Zimbabwe

*†A. Flower c Stewart b Fraser 12	H. H. Streak run out 1
G. W. Flower not out 84	S. G. Peall c Stewart b Gough 0
A. D. R. Campbell b Gough 23	D. H. Brain b Gough 7
G. J. Whittall c Stewart b Gough 0	L-b 7, w 1, n-b 1............. 9
D. L. Houghton c Stewart b Gough.... 57	
M. H. Dekker c DeFreitas b Fraser ... 5	1/24 2/61 3/61 (49.3 overs) 205
G. C. Martin b DeFreitas............ 7	4/171 5/179 6/192
P. A. Strang run out 0	7/192 8/197 9/198

Bowling: DeFreitas 10–2–27–1; Fraser 10–0–45–2; Gough 9.3–0–44–5; Tufnell 10–0–43–0; Udal 8–0–31–0; Hick 2–0–8–0.

England

G. A. Gooch c and b Strang 38	S. D. Udal run out................. 10
*M. A. Atherton c A. Flower b Whittall 14	A. R. C. Fraser b Dekker 2
G. A. Hick run out 64	P. C. R. Tufnell not out 0
G. P. Thorpe lbw b Strang 0	L-b 5, w 5 10
J. P. Crawley lbw b Dekker 18	
†A. J. Stewart b Streak 29	1/49 2/60 3/60 (49.1 overs) 192
P. A. J. DeFreitas run out 5	4/105 5/169 6/178
D. Gough b Streak 2	7/179 8/181 9/192

Bowling: Brain 8–1–27–0; Streak 8.1–1–36–2; Whittall 4–1–21–1; Strang 10–2–30–2; Peall 10–2–29–0; Dekker 9–0–44–2.

Umpires: D. B. Hair and C. D. Timmins.

ENGLAND v ZIMBABWE

At Brisbane, January 7. England won by 26 runs. Toss: England.

England secured a hard-fought win – their first over Zimbabwe – to keep alive their hopes of reaching the finals. In high humidity, two days after the back-to-back Melbourne and Sydney Tests, several of England's batsmen seemed jaded, while Fairbrother, who had just arrived to replace White, was run out as he carelessly jogged a single. Thorpe stood firm to make 89, his highest one-day international score, in 119 balls, but he later required hospital treatment for dehydration and heat exhaustion. In Zimbabwe's reply, only Andy Flower and Whittall established themselves against disciplined out-cricket. The match added another name to England's ever-growing injury list: Udal damaged a rib muscle, an injury which eventually ended his tour.

Man of the Match: G. P. Thorpe.   *Attendance:* 10,035.

England

G. A. Gooch b Brain................ 0	P. A. J. DeFreitas not out.......... 12
*M. A. Atherton lbw b Martin........ 26	S. D. Udal not out................. 11
G. A. Hick c A. Flower b Streak...... 8	
G. P. Thorpe c Brain b Strang........ 89	B 4, l-b 2, w 3............. 9
N. H. Fairbrother run out........... 7	
J. P. Crawley lbw b G. W. Flower 14	1/0 2/20 3/72 (8 wkts, 50 overs) 200
†S. J. Rhodes st A. Flower b Dekker .. 20	4/82 5/107 6/164
D. Gough c Campbell b Dekker 4	7/170 8/182

J. E. Benjamin did not bat.

Bowling: Brain 8–0–27–1; Streak 7–1–26–1; Whittall 5–0–19–0; Martin 5–1–15–1; Peall 5–0–19–0; Strang 10–0–42–1; G. W. Flower 3–0–16–1; Dekker 7–0–30–2.

Zimbabwe

G. W. Flower c Rhodes b Udal	19		D. H. Brain c Hick b Udal	2
A. D. R. Campbell c Fairbrother			H. H. Streak not out	9
	b DeFreitas	3	S. G. Peall run out	3
M. H. Dekker b Benjamin	5			
*†A. Flower c Rhodes b Gough	52		L-b 7, w 2	9
G. J. Whittall c Rhodes b DeFreitas	53			
I. P. Butchart run out	2		1/8 2/16 3/56 (48.1 overs) 174	
G. C. Martin st Rhodes b Hick	1		4/103 5/123 6/124	
P. A. Strang b Gough	16		7/149 8/156 9/169	

Bowling: Gough 9.1–3–17–2; DeFreitas 10–0–28–2; Benjamin 6–0–22–1; Udal 8–0–41–2; Hick 7–1–29–1; Gooch 8–0–30–0.

Umpires: A. J. McQuillan and C. D. Timmins.

‡AUSTRALIA v AUSTRALIA A

At Brisbane, January 8. Australia won by 34 runs. Toss: Australia.

Australia, already through to the finals, rested Warne but still beat their shadows comfortably. The match lacked the passion of the first encounter between the two, whose identities were blurred with Bevan and wicket-keeper Emery – deputising for the injured Healy – swapping sides. The moves damaged the competition's credibility. Australia looked set for a big score, thanks to Mark Waugh and Boon, but mustered only 52 from their final ten overs to leave the contest open. Blewett, in his first representative outing above Under-19 level, and Hayden opened with 104. But both perished trying to lift the scoring-rate as storm clouds threatened. The rain held off, and the later batsmen failed to gather any momentum.

Man of the Match: M. E. Waugh.   *Attendance:* 16,410.

Australia

M. J. Slater c Bevan b Reiffel	9		C. J. McDermott not out	5
*M. A. Taylor c Reiffel b Blewett	17			
M. E. Waugh c Blewett b Hughes	93		L-b 4, w 3	7
D. C. Boon not out	86			
S. R. Waugh c Hughes b George	23		1/17 2/65 3/163 (5 wkts, 50 overs) 252	
S. G. Law c Hayden b Reiffel	12		4/213 5/241	

†P. A. Emery, T. B. A. May, D. W. Fleming and G. D. McGrath did not bat.

Bowling: Hughes 10–0–55–1; Reiffel 10–0–46–2; George 10–0–54–1; Blewett 10–0–46–1; Robertson 10–0–47–0.

Australia A

M. L. Hayden b Law	51		G. R. Robertson not out	6
G. S. Blewett c M. E. Waugh b Law	63		†M. N. Atkinson b Law	11
R. T. Ponting run out	39		S. P. George b McDermott	4
M. G. Bevan run out	14			
J. L. Langer b McDermott	1		L-b 9, w 1	10
*D. R. Martyn c M. E. Waugh				
	b McGrath	12	1/104 2/131 3/166 (47.5 overs) 218	
M. G. Hughes b Fleming	3		4/172 5/176 6/180	
P. R. Reiffel c S. R. Waugh b Fleming	4		7/190 8/196 9/213	

Bowling: McDermott 8.5–1–29–2; Fleming 10–1–35–2; McGrath 10–0–62–1; May 6–0–20–0; Law 9–0–46–3; Boon 4–0–17–0.

Umpires: P. D. Parker and S. G. Randell.

AUSTRALIA v ENGLAND

At Melbourne, January 10 (day/night). England won by 37 runs. Toss: England.

England beat Australia for the first time on the tour to pull ahead of the A team in the qualifying table. But two more injuries took the gloss off the win. Gough, whose 45 in 49 balls revived England as he added 74 with Hick, broke down with a stress fracture of his left foot as he tried to bowl the first ball of Australia's innings. Then Fairbrother damaged shoulder ligaments as he dived in the field. That England still won was due to Hick, who followed up his three-hour 91 with his best bowling in one-day internationals, and Fraser, whose opening spell was three for seven in six overs. Australia hit only four boundaries in their lowest completed total of the series. Robertson became the third player to appear for both Australian sides while Chris Lewis, playing club cricket locally, substituted for Fairbrother as the fifth reinforcement to England's original party.

Man of the Match: G. A. Hick.   *Attendance:* 73,282.

England

G. A. Gooch c Taylor b McGrath	2	D. Gough b McGrath		45
*M. A. Atherton c S. R. Waugh		P. A. J. DeFreitas not out		2
	b M. E. Waugh	14	S. D. Udal not out	2
G. A. Hick c Fleming b Warne	91		B 4, l-b 10, w 6, n-b 2	22
G. P. Thorpe c Healy b M. E. Waugh	8			
N. H. Fairbrother c Healy b Warne	35	1/11 2/31 3/44	(8 wkts, 50 overs)	225
J. P. Crawley c Healy b McGrath	2	4/133 5/136 6/142		
†S. J. Rhodes lbw b McGrath	2	7/216 8/223		

A. R. C. Fraser did not bat.

Bowling: Fleming 10–1–36–0; McGrath 10–1–25–4; M. E. Waugh 10–1–43–2; Warne 10–0–37–2; Robertson 5–0–38–0; Law 5–0–32–0.

Australia

*M. A. Taylor c Rhodes b Fraser	6	S. K. Warne b Fraser		21
M. J. Slater b Fraser	2	D. W. Fleming not out		5
M. E. Waugh b Hick	41	G. D. McGrath b DeFreitas		10
S. R. Waugh c Rhodes b Fraser	0		W 3	3
S. G. Law c and b Udal	17			
D. C. Boon b Hick	26	1/3 2/16 3/19	(48 overs)	188
†I. A. Healy c Atherton b Hick	56	4/62 5/76 6/125		
G. R. Robertson run out	1	7/131 8/173 9/173		

Bowling: Fraser 10–2–22–4; DeFreitas 9–0–32–1; Gooch 10–0–50–0; Udal 9–1–43–1; Hick 10–1–41–3.

Umpires: P. D. Parker and S. G. Randell.

‡AUSTRALIA A v ENGLAND

At Sydney, January 12 (day/night). Australia A won by 29 runs. Toss: Australia A.

Australia A pipped England to a place in the finals by 0.01 on net run-rate in a frantic finish. Set 265 to win, England's previously superior net run-rate and two-point advantage meant they would qualify by scoring 237. But, needing three from Reiffel's final ball to achieve that target, Fraser could score only one. High-class Australia A ground-fielding and fine bowling from leg-spinner McIntyre had left England struggling, following brilliant centuries from Blewett and Bevan. Blewett faced 133 balls, Bevan 102, and they added 161 in 169 balls, with their aggressive running between the wickets testing England's fielders to the full. Emery reverted to the A team in this game after his brief elevation.

Man of the Match: G. S. Blewett.   *Attendance:* 38,152.

Australia A

M. L. Hayden c Gooch b DeFreitas	...	4	†P. A. Emery not out	0
G. S. Blewett c Thorpe b Lewis		113		
*D. R. Martyn c Thorpe b Lewis	...	13	L-b 7	7
M. G. Bevan c and b Udal		105		
J. L. Langer c Gooch b Udal	...	16	1/11 2/46 3/207 (5 wkts, 50 overs) 264	
R. T. Ponting not out	...	6	4/245 5/262	

P. R. Reiffel, M. G. Hughes, P. E. McIntyre and S. P. George did not bat.

Bowling: Fraser 10-1-36-0; DeFreitas 10-2-43-1; Lewis 6-0-48-2; Udal 10-0-56-2; Hick 8-0-40-0; Gooch 6-0-34-0.

England

G. A. Gooch c Emery b Hughes	...	17	P. A. J. DeFreitas b Blewett	12
*M. A. Atherton c Emery b Reiffel	...	20	S. D. Udal lbw b Reiffel	9
G. A. Hick b McIntyre	...	35	A. R. C. Fraser not out	1
G. P. Thorpe c Reiffel b McIntyre	...	24	L-b 13, w 7	20
J. P. Crawley c Emery b George	...	37		
M. W. Gatting lbw b Hughes	...	15	1/40 2/55 3/100 (9 wkts, 50 overs) 235	
†S. J. Rhodes c George b McIntyre	...	23	4/105 5/143 6/179	
C. C. Lewis not out	...	22	7/187 8/215 9/232	

Bowling: Hughes 8-0-43-2; Reiffel 10-2-42-2; Blewett 8-0-44-1; George 10-1-33-1; McIntyre 10-0-45-3; Martyn 4-0-15-0.

Umpires: D. B. Hair and T. A. Prue.

QUALIFYING TABLE

	Played	Won	Lost	Points	Net run-rate
Australia	6	5	1	10	0.42
Australia A	6	3	3	6	0.09
England	6	3	3	6	0.08
Zimbabwe	6	1	5	2	−0.59

Net run-rate was calculated by subtracting runs conceded per over from runs scored per over.

Player of the Preliminaries: D. C. Boon.

‡AUSTRALIA v AUSTRALIA A

First Final Match

At Sydney, January 15 (day/night). Australia won by five wickets. Toss: Australia A.

Australia narrowly avoided embarrassment in completing what should have been a straightforward success, with an edged four by Healy from the very last ball securing victory. In their 40th over they needed only 43, with eight wickets in hand but, after losing Slater and Boon within five balls, they entered the final over still requiring three. A succession of high-class yorkers by Rowell ensured only two came from five balls before Healy's winning blow. Earlier, Hayden and Bevan, who continued his fine form with 73 in 86 balls, helped Australia A set a target of 210, which might have been more testing but for high-class bowling at the death from McDermott. As if to illustrate that the final was no hollow showpiece, Hayden and McGrath clashed angrily in mid-pitch and both were reprimanded by referee John Reid. Before the start, the crowd booed when Reiffel, who had been transferred to the senior squad, was named only as twelfth man.

Attendance: 35,890.

Australia A

G. S. Blewett b McDermott	19	G. J. Rowell not out		1
M. L. Hayden c Slater b M. E. Waugh	50	P. E. McIntyre not out		1
*D. R. Martyn c Taylor b Warne	20			
M. G. Bevan b McDermott	73	B 6, l-b 2, w 1, n-b 1		10
J. L. Langer b McDermott	7			
R. T. Ponting b McGrath	19	1/28 2/69 3/105	(8 wkts, 50 overs)	209
†P. A. Emery run out	4	4/136 5/192 6/196		
G. R. Robertson c Taylor b McDermott	5	7/203 8/203		

S. P. George did not bat.

Bowling: McDermott 10–0–25–4; Fleming 10–2–38–0; McGrath 10–1–44–1; Warne 10–2–37–1; M. E. Waugh 5–0–30–1; Law 5–0–27–0.

Australia

M. J. Slater b Blewett	92	†I. A. Healy not out		9
*M. A. Taylor b George	16			
M. E. Waugh c Bevan b Blewett	16	B 2, l-b 2, w 5, n-b 1		10
D. C. Boon c Ponting b McIntyre	36			
S. R. Waugh not out	21	1/51 2/80 3/167	(5 wkts, 50 overs)	213
S. G. Law st Emery b McIntyre	13	4/167 5/190		

S. K. Warne, C. J. McDermott, D. W. Fleming and G. D. McGrath did not bat.

Bowling: Rowell 10–1–52–0; George 9–0–42–1; Blewett 10–2–25–2; Robertson 10–0–35–0; McIntyre 10–0–48–2; Martyn 1–0–7–0.

Umpires: P. D. Parker and T. A. Prue.

‡AUSTRALIA v AUSTRALIA A

Second Final Match

At Melbourne, January 17 (day/night). Australia won by six wickets. Toss: Australia A.
Steve Waugh's beautifully-paced 56, spanning 65 balls, steered Australia's senior team to victory with an over to spare, the first win for a side chasing over 200 under the MCG lights in the last four World Series tournaments. After Taylor and Slater opened with 107 in 25 overs, Australia appeared to lose their way, but Waugh hoisted Angel for six and added 57 in 50 balls for the fifth wicket with Law. Australia A looked capable of forcing the finals into a third-match decider when Blewett and Martyn produced some of the best batting of the summer, adding 99 in just 85 balls. Both men drove powerfully, with Martyn facing only 40 deliveries, but his fall to a dubious lbw decision cost the A side its momentum. With Fleming conceding under three an over as he picked up four wickets, Australia kept their target in bounds.

Player of the Finals: S. R. Waugh.　　　　*Attendance:* 53,765.

Australia A

G. S. Blewett c Taylor b McGrath	64	J. Angel not out		15
M. L. Hayden c Slater b Fleming	4	G. J. Rowell c Slater b McDermott		8
*D. R. Martyn lbw b Warne	58	S. P. George b Fleming		2
M. G. Bevan c Healy b McGrath	19	L-b 10, w 4, n-b 1		15
J. L. Langer c Healy b McGrath	14			
R. T. Ponting c M. E. Waugh b Fleming	13	1/12 2/111 3/144	(49.4 overs)	226
†P. A. Emery c Boon	10	4/158 5/174 6/191		
G. R. Robertson b Fleming	4	7/193 8/197 9/218		

Bowling: McDermott 10–1–38–1; Fleming 9.4–1–28–4; McGrath 10–0–41–3; Warne 10–0–55–1; Law 2–0–21–0; M. E. Waugh 3–0–20–0; Boon 5–0–13–1.

Australia

*M. A. Taylor c Langer b Blewett	50	S. G. Law not out		27
M. J. Slater run out	56	L-b 8, w 1, n-b 1		10
M. E. Waugh lbw b Blewett	3			
D. C. Boon c Martyn b Angel	27	1/107 2/111	(4 wkts, 49 overs)	229
S. R. Waugh not out	56	3/116 4/172		

†I. A. Healy, S. K. Warne, C. J. McDermott, D. W. Fleming and G. D. McGrath did
not bat.

Bowling: Angel 10–0–55–1; Rowell 10–1–40–0; George 8–0–34–0; Blewett 10–1–44–2;
Robertson 10–0–40–0; Martyn 1–0–8–0.

Umpires: D. B. Hair and S. G. Randell. Series referee: J. R. Reid (New Zealand).

ENGLAND UNDER-19 IN THE WEST INDIES, 1994-95

England Under-19 toured the West Indies in January and February 1995, playing 11 games.
They won six, lost two and drew three. West Indies Under-19 took the three-match
unofficial Test series 1-0 thanks to their victory in the second match at St Kitts; the
opening game at Port-of-Spain and the last at Georgetown were drawn. England Under-19
won the one-day series 2-1. England also played three three-day games against local Under-
19 teams, beating Trinidad & Tobago and Leeward Islands and drawing with Barbados,
and two one-day games, beating Barbados and Guyana. Anthony McGrath scored 290 runs
at 58.00 in the Test series and 604 at 46.46 in all matches; Vikram Solanki took 16 wickets
at 16.62 in the Tests and 30 at 16.80 in all. Lincoln Roberts and leg-spinner Dinanath
Ramnarine, both of Trinidad & Tobago, headed the West Indians' Test averages, with 250
runs at 50.00 and 17 wickets at 17.17 respectively.

The party of 15 originally named for the tour was: M. E. Trescothick (Somerset) *(captain)*,
U. Afzaal (Nottinghamshire), I. Dawood (Northamptonshire), M. Dimond (Somerset),
S. W. K. Ellis (Worcestershire), S. Lugsden (Durham), A. McGrath (Yorkshire), A. C.
Morris (Yorkshire), D. J. Sales (Northamptonshire), C. J. Schofield (Yorkshire), J. P. Searle
(Durham), O. A. Shah (Middlesex), A. Singh (Warwickshire), V. S. Solanki (Worcester-
shire), D. J. Thompson (Surrey).

A. Flintoff (Lancashire) and N. Killeen (Durham) replaced Lugsden and Shah.

Manager: G. J. Saville (Essex). *Coach:* D. Lloyd (Lancashire). *Physiotherapist:* D. O.
Conway (Glamorgan).

First Unofficial Test: At Port-of-Spain, January 12, 13, 14, 15. Drawn. Toss: England
Under-19. England Under-19 317 (A. McGrath 79, C. J. Schofield 83, D. J. Sales 70; R. D.
King four for 49, D. Ramnarine four for 74) and 199 for four dec. (M. E. Trescothick 106
not out, V. S. Solanki 40); West Indies Under-19 168 (A. N. Murphy 52, A. R. Percival 33;
A. Flintoff five for 39) and 152 for seven (A. N. Murphy 49, L. A. Roberts 37 not out; V. S.
Solanki four for 50).

Second Unofficial Test: At St Kitts, January 21, 22, 23, 24. West Indies Under-19 won by 34
runs. Toss: West Indies Under-19. West Indies Under-19 176 (A. N. Murphy 44; M.
Dimond three for 39, V. S. Solanki three for ten) and 240 (L. A. Roberts 45, G. R. Breese
42, A. R. Percival 39, Extras 31; M. Dimond five for 70, V. S. Solanki three for 50);
England Under-19 195 (A. McGrath 30, A. Singh 35, A. C. Morris 49, Extras 31; R. N.
Lewis three for 30, D. Ramnarine four for 63) and 187 (A. McGrath 31, A. Singh 52;
D. Ramnarine seven for 73).

Third Unofficial Test: At Georgetown, January 27, 28, 29, 30. Drawn. Toss: West Indies
Under-19. West Indies Under-19 277 (L. A. Roberts 32, A. R. Percival 37, R. N. Lewis 75,
M. I. Black 31; A. C. Morris three for 66) and 334 for eight (A. N. Murphy 35, L. A.
Roberts 114, A. R. Percival 35, D. Rampersad 64 not out, Extras 31; V. S. Solanki three for
73, J. P. Searle three for 56); England Under-19 267 (A. McGrath 133, V. S. Solanki 34;
R. D. King seven for 97).

MANDELA TROPHY, 1994-95

By PETER ROBINSON

South Africa staged a quadrangular one-day tournament, named after the country's president and sponsored by Benson and Hedges, in December 1994 and January 1995. It marked a change in their fortunes after losing ten successive limited-overs games between Test defeats by England and New Zealand; though Pakistan easily dominated the qualifiers, South Africa crushed them 2-0 in the best-of-three finals. For Pakistan, early success disintegrated as disagreement in the dressing-room over captain Salim Malik's tactics ultimately led to vice-captain Rashid Latif and Basit Ali announcing their retirement from international cricket (rescinded a few months later). Sri Lanka made a spirited attempt to reach the finals, hindered by bad weather in two matches, but New Zealand's season went into a nosedive as they failed to win any of their six games.

Note: Matches in this section were not first-class.

PAKISTAN v SRI LANKA

At Durban, December 2 (day/night). Pakistan won by six wickets. Toss: Sri Lanka.

Ranatunga played superbly for an unbeaten 101 from 108 deliveries, striking eight fours; surprisingly, it was his maiden century in 152 one-day games for Sri Lanka, though he had reached 50 on 29 previous occasions. But it could not keep Pakistan at bay, with Aamir Sohail (whose hundred, by comparison, was his third in 63 limited-overs internationals) and Salim Malik in equally commanding form. Malik, however, had a crucial let-off before reaching double figures. Third umpire Barry Lambson was asked to establish whether he had been stumped by acting-keeper Gurusinha off Kalpage, but the camera's view had been obscured and the batsman had the benefit of the doubt.

Man of the Match: A. Ranatunga.

Sri Lanka

R. S. Mahanama b Waqar Younis	24	R. S. Kalpage st Rashid Latif	
S. T. Jayasuriya c Akram Raza		b Salim Malik	29
b Aqib Javed	26	H. D. P. K. Dharmasena not out	23
A. P. Gurusinha lbw b Akram Raza	11	B 1, l-b 2, w 7, n-b 3	13
P. A. de Silva b Aqib Javed	10		
*A. Ranatunga not out	101	1/44 2/57 3/68 (5 wkts, 50 overs)	238
†H. P. Tillekeratne retired hurt	1	4/86 5/172	

W. P. U. J. C. Vaas, G. P. Wickremasinghe and K. R. Pushpakumara did not bat.

H. P. Tillekeratne retired hurt at 88.

Bowling: Waqar Younis 10-0-50-1; Aqib Javed 10-0-44-2; Ata-ur-Rehman 8-1-38-0; Akram Raza 10-1-26-1; Aamir Sohail 6-0-30-0; Salim Malik 6-0-47-1.

Pakistan

Saeed Anwar b Vaas	5	Basit Ali not out	22
Aamir Sohail c de Silva b Kalpage	100		
Inzamam-ul-Haq c Gurusinha		L-b 5, w 3	8
b Dharmasena	32		
*Salim Malik not out	65	1/22 2/110 (4 wkts, 47.5 overs)	239
Ijaz Ahmed c Mahanama b Jayasuriya	7	3/177 4/191	

†Rashid Latif, Akram Raza, Waqar Younis, Ata-ur-Rehman and Aqib Javed did not bat.

Bowling: Vaas 8–0–32–1; Pushpakumara 8–0–47–0; Wickremasinghe 6–0–28–0; Kalpage 10–0–40–1; Dharmasena 9.5–0–56–1; Jayasuriya 6–0–31–1.

Umpires: K. E. Liebenberg and D. L. Orchard.

PAKISTAN v SRI LANKA

At Verwoerdburg, December 4. Pakistan won by 12 runs. Toss: Sri Lanka.

An opening stand of 130 in 116 minutes between Saeed Anwar and Aamir Sohail provided the foundations of Pakistan's second victory over Sri Lanka in three days. Though both lost their wickets at that score, Inzamam-ul-Haq picked up the reins with 62 in 68 balls. A total of 245 was enough to withstand a ferocious onslaught by de Silva. He rushed to 95 in 105 balls, hitting Waqar Younis to all corners of the ground. Waqar went for seven an over, but Aqib Javed and Akram Raza suffocated the other batsmen and Sri Lanka's tempo was lost.

Man of the Match: Aamir Sohail.

Pakistan

Saeed Anwar c Muralitharan b Kalpage	57	Waqar Younis c Mahanama b Vaas ... 1
Aamir Sohail c and b Muralitharan ...	67	Ata-ur-Rehman c Mahanama
Inzamam-ul-Haq c Dassanayake b Vaas	62	b Wickremasinghe . 3
*Salim Malik run out	20	B 1, l-b 7, w 3, n-b 1 12
Ijaz Ahmed run out	1	
Basit Ali c de Silva b Kalpage	7	1/130 2/130 3/175 (9 wkts, 50 overs) 245
†Rashid Latif c Pushpakumara b Vaas .	7	4/184 5/198 6/229
Akram Raza not out	8	7/237 8/239 9/245

Aqib Javed did not bat.

Bowling: Vaas 8–0–46–3; Pushpakumara 10–0–39–0; Wickremasinghe 10–0–39–1; Muralitharan 8–0–49–1; Kalpage 10–0–41–2; Jayasuriya 4–0–23–0.

Sri Lanka

R. S. Mahanama run out	8	G. P. Wickremasinghe not out	13
S. T. Jayasuriya c Aamir Sohail		M. Muralitharan c sub (Manzoor Elahi)
b Waqar Younis .	4	b Aqib Javed . 1
A. P. Gurusinha c and b Aamir Sohail .	43	K. R. Pushpakumara not out	14
P. A. de Silva c and b Waqar Younis . .	95	
*A. Ranatunga b Aamir Sohail	24	L-b 8, w 3, n-b 1 12
R. S. Kalpage c Rashid Latif		
b Aamir Sohail .	4	1/16 2/36 3/95 (9 wkts, 50 overs) 233
†P. B. Dassanayake run out	8	4/140 5/146 6/167
W. P. U. J. C. Vaas run out	3	7/177 8/210 9/214

Bowling: Waqar Younis 10–0–73–2; Aqib Javed 10–2–31–1; Ata-ur-Rehman 10–0–53–0; Akram Raza 10–2–22–0; Aamir Sohail 10–0–46–3.

Umpires: W. Diedricks and R. E. Koertzen.

SOUTH AFRICA v NEW ZEALAND

At Cape Town, December 6 (day/night). South Africa won by 69 runs. Toss: South Africa.
International debut: M. J. R. Rindel.

With the ball swinging in the night air, New Zealand folded on a low, slow pitch which was later to become the subject of an official inquiry. Though Young launched the chase with a run-a-ball 25, no batsman on either side seemed comfortable, and Rutherford's 40 was the highest score of the game. Because Hart had broken a finger, Mark Priest took the field hours after flying in from New Zealand; he was asleep in the dressing-room by the time South Africa's debutant, Mike Rindel, received the match award for his 32 runs and two wickets. Rindel had changed his country's luck after ten successive one-day defeats.

Man of the Match: M. J. R. Rindel.

South Africa

A. C. Hudson lbw b Pringle	9	C. R. Matthews not out	4
G. Kirsten lbw b de Groen	19	P. S. de Villiers not out	0
*W. J. Cronje c Young b Priest	38		
D. J. Cullinan c Young b Doull	25	B 2, l-b 5, w 1	8
M. J. R. Rindel run out	32		
J. N. Rhodes b Pringle	21	1/23 2/35 3/83　　(8 wkts, 50 overs) 203	
†D. J. Richardson run out	23	4/104 5/145 6/153	
E. O. Simons run out	24	7/199 8/200	

C. E. Eksteen did not bat.

Bowling: Doull 7-0-35-1; de Groen 10-1-33-1; Pringle 10-3-29-2; Priest 10-0-42-1; Harris 10-0-45-0; Su'a 3-0-12-0.

New Zealand

B. A. Young c Rindel b Matthews	25	S. B. Doull not out	19
S. P. Fleming c Cronje b de Villiers	12	C. Pringle b Simons	1
M. D. Crowe c Richardson b Cronje	9	R. P. de Groen b Simons	0
*K. R. Rutherford c Cronje b de Villiers	40	L-b 3	3
†A. C. Parore run out	13		
C. Z. Harris c Richardson b Rindel	10	1/39 2/39 3/52　　　　(39.5 overs) 134	
M. L. Su'a run out	1	4/75 5/101 6/103	
M. W. Priest lbw b Rindel	1	7/106 8/124 9/134	

Bowling: de Villiers 8-2-36-2; Matthews 8-3-22-1; Cronje 5-1-10-1; Simons 8.5-1-28-2; Eksteen 5-1-20-0; Rindel 5-0-15-2.

Umpires: S. B. Lambson and C. J. Mitchley.

NEW ZEALAND v SRI LANKA

At Bloemfontein, December 8 (day/night). No result. Toss: Sri Lanka. International debut: L. K. Germon.

A thunderstorm denied Sri Lanka probable victory after an explosive innings from Jayasuriya. He took the New Zealand attack apart – with the exception of Pringle, who bowled with great intelligence – hammering six sixes, each sailing further than the last. Remarkably, he had been stranded on 21 for seven overs, but went on to his maiden hundred in one-day internationals, finishing with 140 in 143 balls, the highest ever limited-overs score for Sri Lanka. Century stands with Gurusinha and de Silva helped his team to 288. But torrential rain flooded Springbok Park an hour into New Zealand's innings.

Sri Lanka

R. S. Mahanama c Germon b Pringle	0	R. S. Kalpage not out	4
S. T. Jayasuriya c Crowe b Pringle	140	B 4, l-b 6, w 5, n-b 1	16
A. P. Gurusinha c and b Harris	53		
P. A. de Silva c Harris b Pringle	55	1/1 2/133　　　(4 wkts, 50 overs) 288	
*A. Ranatunga not out	20	3/235 4/278	

†P. B. Dassanayake, H. D. P. K. Dharmasena, W. P. U. J. C. Vaas, G. P. Wickremasinghe and K. R. Pushpakumara did not bat.

Bowling: Pringle 10-0-29-3; de Groen 10-0-75-0; Doull 10-1-66-0; Harris 10-0-54-1; Priest 10-0-54-0.

New Zealand

B. A. Young not out	22
S. P. Fleming b Pushpakumara	11
A. C. Parore not out	31
L-b 1, n-b 1	2

1/15　　　　(1 wkt, 14.3 overs) 66

M. D. Crowe, *K. R. Rutherford, C. Z. Harris, †L. K. Germon, M. W. Priest, S. B. Doull, C. Pringle and R. P. de Groen did not bat.

Bowling: Pushpakumara 5–0–18–1; Vaas 7–1–33–0; Wickremasinghe 2.3–0–14–0.

Umpires: W. Diedricks and R. E. Koertzen.

SOUTH AFRICA v PAKISTAN

At Johannesburg, December 10. South Africa won by seven wickets. Toss: Pakistan.

South Africa bowled impressively to restrict the opposition to 214 on an easy-paced pitch, despite a fluent 73 from Ijaz Ahmed, who had taken 110 and 98 not out off their attack in Pakistan in October. But only Inzamam-ul-Haq offered much support and once he was stumped, at 165, one batsman after another found ways to get out: the last seven wickets fell for 49 in ten overs. South Africa lost Kirsten early, but Hudson and Cronje added 145 for the second wicket, falling only when victory was well in sight.

Man of the Match: W. J. Cronje.

Pakistan

Saeed Anwar c Rindel b Snell	26	Waqar Younis b Snell		6
Aamir Sohail run out	23	Ata-ur-Rehman run out		2
Inzamam-ul-Haq st Richardson b Cronje	55	Aqib Javed not out		1
*Salim Malik c McMillan b Snell	5	L-b 3, w 4		7
Ijaz Ahmed c de Villiers b Snell	73			
Basit Ali run out	2	1/46 2/61 3/70	(49.1 overs)	214
†Rashid Latif c Snell b Cronje	13	4/165 5/176 6/196		
Akram Raza c Richardson b Matthews	1	7/199 8/205 9/211		

Bowling: de Villiers 10–1–25–0; Matthews 10–1–45–1; Snell 9.1–1–37–4; McMillan 10–0–51–0; Rindel 3–0–16–0; Cronje 7–0–37–2.

South Africa

A. C. Hudson lbw b Ata-ur-Rehman	74	M. J. R. Rindel not out		13
G. Kirsten b Waqar Younis	9	L-b 11, w 3, n-b 6		20
*W. J. Cronje c Rashid Latif b Waqar Younis	81			
D. J. Cullinan not out	18	1/18 2/163 3/185	(3 wkts, 45.4 overs)	215

J. N. Rhodes, †D. J. Richardson, B. M. McMillan, R. P. Snell, C. R. Matthews and P. S. de Villiers did not bat.

Bowling: Waqar Younis 9.4–1–38–2; Aqib Javed 10–0–39–0; Ata-ur-Rehman 10–0–57–1; Akram Raza 10–0–40–0; Aamir Sohail 2–0–13–0; Salim Malik 4–0–17–0.

Umpires: S. B. Lambson and C. J. Mitchley.

SOUTH AFRICA v NEW ZEALAND

At Verwoerdburg, December 11. South Africa won by 81 runs. Toss: South Africa.

South Africa recalled Callaghan and promoted him to open, with sensational effect: he thundered out the fifth-highest score in limited-overs internationals. Despite offering a chance in the first over, he devastated New Zealand's bowling in a sustained assault of 19 fours and four sixes. His unbeaten 169 took 143 balls and carried South Africa past 300 for the first time in one-day cricket. In reply, Parore hit 108 from 95 balls – like Callaghan's, his maiden hundred at this level – but, after he lost Thomson, New Zealand posed no threat and were bowled out with nearly ten overs left.

Man of the Match: D. J. Callaghan.

South Africa

A. C. Hudson c Priest b Doull	3	E. O. Simons c Rutherford b Su'a	10
D. J. Callaghan not out	169	R. P. Snell not out	1
*W. J. Cronje c Young b Thomson	68	L-b 14, w 1, n-b 3	18
D. J. Cullinan c Thomson b Su'a	38		
M. J. R. Rindel c Parore b Su'a	1	1/10 2/159 3/239 (7 wkts, 50 overs) 314
J. N. Rhodes c Parore b Su'a	2	4/261 5/263
†D. J. Richardson run out	4	6/282 7/294

C. R. Matthews and P. S. de Villiers did not bat.

Bowling: Pringle 10–0–40–0; Doull 9–0–70–1; Su'a 10–1–59–4; Harris 10–0–64–0; Priest 5–0–35–0; Thomson 6–0–32–1.

New Zealand

B. A. Young c Hudson b Matthews	27	M. L. Su'a lbw b Callaghan	1
S. P. Fleming c Rindel b Matthews	0	S. B. Doull c Richardson b Simons	13
†A. C. Parore c Cullinan b Callaghan	108	C. Pringle not out	1
*K. R. Rutherford c Matthews b Simons	14		
M. D. Crowe run out	6	L-b 2, w 4, n-b 2	8
S. A. Thomson c Richardson b Callaghan	39	1/0 2/37 3/60 (40.3 overs) 233
C. Z. Harris c Cronje b Rindel	3	4/82 5/188 6/195
M. W. Priest c and b Simons	13	7/215 8/216 9/232

Bowling: de Villiers 8–1–29–0; Matthews 6–1–28–2; Simons 6.3–0–46–3; Snell 4–0–32–0; Cronje 3–0–30–0; Rindel 7–0–34–1; Callaghan 6–0–32–3.

Umpires: K. E. Liebenberg and D. L. Orchard.

NEW ZEALAND v PAKISTAN

At Port Elizabeth, December 13 (day/night). Pakistan won by five wickets. Toss: Pakistan.

New Zealand's crisis of confidence was evident as their middle order squandered a bright start. Crowe and Parore had put on 101 for the second wicket in only 73 minutes, but after Crowe, who had hit eight fours and a six, was deceived by Salim Malik's gentle medium-pace, only Rutherford reached double figures. His dismissal at 173 began a collapse of eight wickets for 28, mostly to Waqar Younis and Aqib Javed. Aamir Sohail and Malik batted freely and Pakistan won with nearly four overs to spare.

Men of the Match: Aqib Javed and Waqar Younis.

New Zealand

B. A. Young lbw b Aqib Javed	13	M. L. Su'a b Waqar Younis	3
M. D. Crowe c and b Salim Malik	83	M. W. Priest not out	4
†A. C. Parore c Ijaz Ahmed b Salim Malik	59	C. Pringle b Aqib Javed	0
*K. R. Rutherford c Saeed Anwar b Akram Raza	16	R. P. de Groen b Aqib Javed	0
S. P. Fleming lbw b Waqar Younis	4	B 1, l-b 4	5
S. A. Thomson b Waqar Younis	8	1/41 2/142 3/173 (49.4 overs) 201
C. Z. Harris c Moin Khan b Waqar Younis	6	4/180 5/181 6/194
		7/195 8/200 9/201

Bowling: Waqar Younis 10–0–32–4; Aqib Javed 9.4–1–25–3; Manzoor Elahi 10–0–40–0; Akram Raza 8–0–36–1; Aamir Sohail 4–0–30–0; Salim Malik 8–0–33–2.

Pakistan

Saeed Anwar c Fleming b de Groen	... 17	Manzoor Elahi not out	 8
Aamir Sohail b Pringle	 75		
Inzamam-ul-Haq c Rutherford b Su'a	... 17	L-b 5, w 7, n-b 1	 13
*Salim Malik not out	 53		
Ijaz Ahmed c Parore b Pringle	 23	1/51 2/86 3/142	(5 wkts, 46.2 overs) 206
Basit Ali c Parore b Pringle	 0	4/182 5/182	

†Moin Khan, Akram Raza, Waqar Younis and Aqib Javed did not bat.

Bowling: Pringle 10–0–43–3; Thomson 6–0–31–0; de Groen 7.3–1–30–1; Su'a 10–2–30–1; Priest 6.3–1–26–0; Harris 6.2–0–41–0.

Umpires: R. E. Koertzen and C. J. Mitchley.

SOUTH AFRICA v SRI LANKA

At Bloemfontein, December 15 (day/night). Sri Lanka won by 35 runs. Toss: Sri Lanka. International debut: S. D. Jack.

Good fortune had eluded Sri Lanka in their first three matches, and their first victory of the tournament was thoroughly deserved. Though their innings seemed to have lost its way at 70 for three, a blistering 60 by Ranatunga from 52 balls revived it in thrilling fashion as he added 91 with de Silva. Hudson played several handsome drives and pulls, which brought him seven fours. But Sri Lanka's varied spin attack took charge and South Africa slid to 115 for seven, from which there was no escape.

Man of the Match: A. Ranatunga.

Sri Lanka

R. S. Mahanama c Hudson b Jack	 10	G. P. Wickremasinghe b Simons	 11
S. T. Jayasuriya c Rhodes b Jack	 23	M. Muralitharan not out	 0
A. P. Gurusinha c Rindel b Simons	... 14	L-b 3, w 3, n-b 4	 10
P. A. de Silva c Hudson b de Villiers	.. 73		
*A. Ranatunga run out	 60	1/33 2/44 3/70	(8 wkts, 50 overs) 226
†H. P. Tillekeratne b de Villiers	 21	4/161 5/201 6/214	
R. S. Kalpage c Jack b Simons	 4	7/226 8/226	

W. P. U. J. C. Vaas and K. R. Pushpakumara did not bat.

Bowling: de Villiers 10–1–31–2; Matthews 10–2–37–0; Jack 10–0–41–2; Simons 10–1–51–3; Callaghan 3–0–16–0; Rindel 4–0–24–0; Cronje 3–0–23–0.

South Africa

A. C. Hudson run out	 44	E. O. Simons c Ranatunga b Kalpage	.. 21
D. J. Callaghan c Ranatunga b Vaas	.. 9	C. R. Matthews not out	 15
*W. J. Cronje c Mahanama		P. S. de Villiers c Mahanama	
b Muralitharan	. 14	b Jayasuriya	. 20
D. J. Cullinan b Kalpage	 16		
M. J. R. Rindel run out	 8	B 3, l-b 12	 15
J. N. Rhodes b Muralitharan	 27		
†D. J. Richardson c Muralitharan		1/48 2/68 3/81	(47.5 overs) 191
b de Silva	. 1	4/96 5/109 6/113	
S. D. Jack run out	 1	7/115 8/152 9/154	

Bowling: Pushpakumara 3–0–20–0; Vaas 7–1–20–1; Wickremasinghe 6–0–16–0; Kalpage 10–0–42–2; Muralitharan 10–0–23–2; Jayasuriya 8.5–0–42–1; de Silva 3–0–13–1.

Umpires: S. B. Lambson and D. L. Orchard.

SOUTH AFRICA v PAKISTAN

At Durban, December 17. Pakistan won by eight wickets. Toss: Pakistan.

Ijaz Ahmed raised his average after five one-day innings against South Africa to 133.66 with a punishing exhibition of strokeplay. His unbeaten 114 – from 90 balls, featuring 17 fours and three sixes – swept Pakistan to victory, and a certain place in the finals, with 15 overs to spare. South Africa had collapsed to an abject 44 for five and only a spirited stand of 88 between Rhodes and Richardson enabled them to reach 200. With Ijaz in such irresistible mood, however, even 300 might not have been enough.

Man of the Match: Ijaz Ahmed.

South Africa

A. C. Hudson c Inzamam-ul-Haq	
b Waqar Younis .	1
D. J. Callaghan c Inzamam-ul-Haq	
b Aqib Javed .	9
*W. J. Cronje c Basit Ali	
b Waqar Younis .	2
D. J. Cullinan c Rashid Latif	
b Aqib Javed .	5
M. J. R. Rindel run out	10
J. N. Rhodes lbw b Aamir Sohail	61

P. S. de Villiers did not bat.

†D. J. Richardson c Ijaz Ahmed	
b Waqar Younis .	53
E. O. Simons b Waqar Younis	19
R. P. Snell not out	27
C. R. Matthews not out	3
L-b 4, w 8, n-b 4	16

1/2 2/10 3/20   (8 wkts, 50 overs) 206
4/27 5/44 6/132
7/174 8/178

Bowling: Waqar Younis 10-0-52-4; Aqib Javed 10-3-37-2; Manzoor Elahi 10-1-27-0; Akram Raza 10-0-39-0; Salim Malik 3-0-13-0; Aamir Sohail 7-0-34-1.

Pakistan

Saeed Anwar c Richardson b de Villiers	10
Aamir Sohail c Richardson b Snell	44
Ijaz Ahmed not out	114
*Salim Malik not out	36
W 3, n-b 1	4

1/13 2/72   (2 wkts, 35 overs) 208

Inzamam-ul-Haq, Basit Ali, Manzoor Elahi, †Rashid Latif, Akram Raza, Waqar Younis and Aqib Javed did not bat.

Bowling: Matthews 9-1-54-0; de Villiers 10-0-46-1; Simons 6-0-31-0; Snell 7-0-49-1; Callaghan 3-0-28-0.

Umpires: W. Diedricks and K. E. Liebenberg.

NEW ZEALAND v SRI LANKA

At East London, December 18. Sri Lanka won by five wickets. Toss: New Zealand.

Sri Lanka kept up their belated charge towards the finals with a splendid win. An adventurous 102 by Rutherford, off only 98 balls, set a demanding target. But they responded magnificently. Jayasuriya set the tone with a full-blooded onslaught on Pringle, previously New Zealand's most effective one-day bowler. He made the most of the short boundaries in hitting 52 off 31 balls, and the later batsmen lifted Sri Lanka to victory with nearly three overs to spare. ICC referee Burge fined Rutherford half his match fee for trying to influence the umpire over an appeal against Tillekeratne, and Ranatunga 25 per cent for dissent when given out caught behind.

Man of the Match: K. R. Rutherford.

New Zealand

B. A. Young c Tillekeratne		S. P. Fleming c Wickremasinghe b Vaas	5
b Wickremasinghe .	24	S. A. Thomson not out	11
B. R. Hartland b Kalpage	32	L-b 11, w 3	14
†A. C. Parore c Tillekeratne			
b Pushpakumara .	67	1/63 2/63 (4 wkts, 50 overs) 255	
*K. R. Rutherford not out	102	3/199 4/220	

C. Z. Harris, D. J. Nash, M. L. Su'a, M. W. Priest and C. Pringle did not bat.

Bowling: Pushpakumara 10–1–50–1; Vaas 10–1–33–1; Wickremasinghe 9–1–42–1; Kalpage 7–1–42–1; Muralitharan 9–1–50–0; Jayasuriya 5–0–27–0.

Sri Lanka

S. T. Jayasuriya c Parore b Pringle	52	R. S. Kalpage not out	43
R. S. Mahanama c Fleming b Nash	1		
A. P. Gurusinha c and b Thomson	47	B 3, l-b 4, w 3	10
P. A. de Silva c Hartland b Harris	4		
*A. Ranatunga c Parore b Nash	32	1/15 2/102 3/110 (5 wkts, 47.1 overs) 257	
†H. P. Tillekeratne not out	68	4/110 5/166	

K. R. Pushpakumara, W. P. U. J. C. Vaas, G. P. Wickremasinghe and M. Muralitharan did not bat.

Bowling: Pringle 8–1–73–1; Nash 10–0–52–2; Su'a 3.1–0–23–0; Thomson 10–1–37–1; Harris 10–0–40–1; Priest 6–0–25–0.

Umpires: C. J. Mitchley and D. L. Orchard.

NEW ZEALAND v PAKISTAN

At East London, December 19 (day/night). Pakistan won by five wickets. Toss: New Zealand.

Waqar Younis's first hat-trick at international level enlivened an otherwise forgettable match with nothing at stake – Pakistan had already qualified for the finals and New Zealand could not. In his ninth over, Waqar bowled Harris, Pringle and de Groen with inswinging yorkers to finish off New Zealand's innings at 172. Saeed Anwar and Aamir Sohail warmed up for the finals with an opening stand of 97, setting up victory with 11 overs in hand.

Man of the Match: Waqar Younis.

New Zealand

B. A. Young c Akram Raza		M. L. Su'a b Waqar Younis	2
b Kabir Khan .	17	M. W. Priest not out	17
B. R. Hartland b Akram Raza	44	C. Pringle b Waqar Younis	0
†A. C. Parore b Aqib Javed	1	R. P. de Groen b Waqar Younis	0
*K. R. Rutherford c Rashid Latif			
b Aamir Sohail .	30	L-b 1, w 7, n-b 1	9
S. P. Fleming b Aamir Sohail	19		
S. A. Thomson c Rashid Latif		1/36 2/38 3/83 (47.4 overs) 172	
b Kabir Khan .	15	4/108 5/132 6/136	
C. Z. Harris b Waqar Younis	18	7/145 8/172 9/172	

Bowling: Waqar Younis 8.4–1–33–4; Aqib Javed 10–2–31–1; Kabir Khan 10–1–32–2; Akram Raza 7–0–25–1; Salim Malik 5–0–30–0; Aamir Sohail 7–0–20–2.

Pakistan

Saeed Anwar c Parore b Thomson	41	†Rashid Latif not out	8
Aamir Sohail c Parore b Harris	52		
Basit Ali c Hartland b Priest	12	L-b 2, w 5, n-b 1	8
Inzamam-ul-Haq run out	15		
*Salim Malik c Su'a b Priest	14	1/97 2/102 3/122 (5 wkts, 38.5 overs)	175
Ijaz Ahmed not out	25	4/126 5/151	

Akram Raza, Waqar Younis, Kabir Khan and Aqib Javed did not bat.

Bowling: Pringle 8–0–36–0; Su'a 6–1–26–0; de Groen 4–0–30–0; Thomson 10–0–34–1; Harris 4–0–15–1; Priest 6–0–27–2; Fleming 0.5–0–5–0.

Umpires: W. Diedricks and S. B. Lambson.

SOUTH AFRICA v SRI LANKA

At Port Elizabeth, December 21 (day/night). South Africa won by 44 runs, Sri Lanka's target having been revised to 184 from 34 overs. Toss: South Africa.

South Africa squeezed past their opponents into the finals, when rain made a difficult task for Sri Lanka impossible. They were interrupted in the 29th over at 101 for five, 137 short of victory; when play resumed after a two-hour break (in which unruly spectators invaded the field to slide across the tarpaulin covers) a revised target left them less than five overs to score 83. But Sri Lanka were already down to their last recognised batsman, Tillekeratne, after Matthews reduced them to 34 for three. There were fifties for South Africa from Cullinan, who needed stitches in his lip after attempting a reverse sweep, and Rhodes.

Man of the Match: C. R. Matthews.

South Africa

A. C. Hudson lbw b Wickremasinghe	27	†D. J. Richardson c Ranatunga b Vaas	7
G. Kirsten b Dharmasena	20	E. O. Simons c Kalpage b Vaas	11
D. J. Cullinan c Gurusinha b Dharmasena	63	C. R. Matthews not out	11
		P. S. de Villiers not out	7
*W. J. Cronje c de Silva b Kalpage	5	B 3, l-b 7	10
J. N. Rhodes c Mahanama b Dharmasena	53		
D. J. Callaghan c Jayasuriya b Dharmasena	23	1/30 2/53 3/79 (8 wkts, 50 overs) 4/198 5/200 6/200 7/210 8/229	237

C. E. Eksteen did not bat.

D. J. Cullinan, when 62, retired hurt at 160 and resumed at 198.

Bowling: Wickremasinghe 8–0–44–1; Vaas 9–0–42–2; Dharmasena 10–0–37–4; Muralitharan 10–0–32–0; Kalpage 10–1–51–1; Jayasuriya 3–0–21–0.

Sri Lanka

R. S. Mahanama c Eksteen b Matthews	3	R. S. Kalpage b Callaghan	9
S. T. Jayasuriya c sub (M. J. R. Rindel) b Matthews	20	H. D. P. K. Dharmasena not out	12
A. P. Gurusinha lbw b Cronje	23	B 2, l-b 4, n-b 1	7
P. A. de Silva c Callaghan b Matthews	0		
*A. Ranatunga c and b Cronje	29	1/5 2/34 3/34 (6 wkts, 34 overs)	139
†H. P. Tillekeratne not out	36	4/55 5/84 6/112	

G. P. Wickremasinghe, W. P. U. J. C. Vaas and M. Muralitharan did not bat.

Bowling: de Villiers 7–1–24–0; Matthews 7–0–22–3; Simons 7–0–25–0; Cronje 8–0–27–2; Callaghan 3–0–19–1; Eksteen 2–0–16–0.

Umpires: R. E. Koertzen and K. E. Liebenberg.

QUALIFYING TABLE

	Played	Won	Lost	No result	Points	Run-rate
Pakistan..........	6	5	1	0	10	4.80
South Africa	6	4	2	0	8	4.69
Sri Lanka.........	6	2	3	1	5	4.72
New Zealand......	6	0	5	1	1	3.98

SOUTH AFRICA v PAKISTAN

First Final Match

At Cape Town, January 10. South Africa won by 37 runs. Toss: Pakistan.

South Africa bowled and fielded brilliantly to defend a moderate total after Salim Malik had made a puzzling decision to field first. From 193 for four they had lost their last six wickets for 22, including three run-outs. Then Aamir Sohail hit Jack out of the attack; he conceded 29 off his first two overs. Sohail went on to 71 in 74 balls, with 11 fours, but the home bowlers dried up the supply of runs at the other end. Pressure built up, Malik and Rashid Latif were senselessly run out and Pakistan fell far short. South Africa won with seven overs to spare, a far more comfortable margin than they could have expected.

Man of the Match: E. O. Simons.

South Africa

G. Kirsten lbw b Akram Raza........ 43	E. O. Simons c Inzamam-ul-Haq
D. J. Callaghan c Ijaz Ahmed	b Waqar Younis . 6
b Aqib Javed . 4	P. L. Symcox c sub (Asif Mujtaba)
*W. J. Cronje c Aamir Sohail	b Waqar Younis . 3
b Aqib Javed . 21	S. D. Jack b Waqar Younis 6
D. J. Cullinan run out.............. 64	P. S. de Villiers not out............. 0
J. N. Rhodes c Aamir Sohail	L-b 4, w 3, n-b 5............ 12
b Akram Raza . 21	
M. J. R. Rindel run out 31	1/6 2/54 3/89 4/121 5/193 (49.3 overs) 215
†D. J. Richardson run out 4	6/198 7/200 8/207 9/215

Bowling: Wasim Akram 10-0-43-0; Aqib Javed 10-1-51-2; Waqar Younis 9.3-0-32-3; Akram Raza 10-0-38-2; Salim Malik 4-0-22-0; Aamir Sohail 6-0-25-0.

Pakistan

Aamir Sohail run out................ 71	Akram Raza c Jack b Simons 12
Saeed Anwar b Simons 5	Waqar Younis c de Villiers b Cronje... 14
Inzamam-ul-Haq lbw b Simons 4	Aqib Javed not out 6
*Salim Malik run out............... 19	B 5, l-b 2 7
Ijaz Ahmed c Callaghan b Jack 5	
Basit Ali c Simons b Cronje 6	1/48 2/58 3/101 (42.5 overs) 178
†Rashid Latif run out 17	4/105 5/111 6/122
Wasim Akram c Jack b Simons 12	7/133 8/149 9/159

Bowling: de Villiers 8-0-23-0; Jack 8-0-45-1; Simons 8-0-42-4; Cronje 8.5-0-31-2; Symcox 10-0-30-0.

Umpires: C. J. Mitchley and D. L. Orchard.

SOUTH AFRICA v PAKISTAN

Second Final Match

At Johannesburg, January 12 (day/night). South Africa won by 157 runs. Toss: Pakistan.
Again, Salim Malik asked South Africa to bat, creating divisions in Pakistan's dressing-room. The home team thrived, especially Rindel, who had never opened before at any level higher than club cricket, waited 16 balls to get off the mark, but then took only 116 more balls to reach a maiden century in his seventh one-day international. He and Kirsten put on 190 in 38 overs. Requiring 267, Pakistan collapsed immediately. De Villiers took a wicket in each of his first three overs and Donald celebrated his return to international cricket with the next three wickets. No recovery was possible from 42 for six (four of them caught behind by Richardson, who later held a fifth) and South Africa took the finals 2–0.
Man of the Match: M. J. R. Rindel.

South Africa

G. Kirsten st Rashid Latif b Salim Malik . 87	D. J. Callaghan not out 7
M. J. R. Rindel run out 106	†D. J. Richardson not out 1
*W. J. Cronje c Aqib Javed b Wasim Akram . 37	
D. J. Cullinan b Waqar Younis 5	L-b 9, w 6, n-b 2 17
J. N. Rhodes run out 6	1/190 2/243 3/251 (5 wkts, 50 overs) 266
	4/257 5/260

E. O. Simons, B. M. McMillan, P. S. de Villiers and A. A. Donald did not bat.

Bowling: Wasim Akram 10–1–47–1; Aqib Javed 9–1–33–0; Waqar Younis 9–0–57–1; Akram Raza 8–0–44–0; Aamir Sohail 10–0–52–0; Salim Malik 4–0–24–1.

Pakistan

Aamir Sohail lbw b de Villiers 0	Akram Raza c McMillan b Simons 0
Saeed Anwar c Richardson b de Villiers 3	Waqar Younis c Cronje b Simons 6
Ijaz Ahmed c Richardson b de Villiers . 4	Aqib Javed not out 4
Inzamam-ul-Haq c Richardson b Donald 19	L-b 3, w 6, n-b 2 11
*Salim Malik c Richardson b Donald . . 12	
Asif Mujtaba c Richardson b Cronje . . . 24	1/1 2/7 3/14 (32.3 overs) 109
†Rashid Latif c McMillan b Donald . . . 0	4/37 5/42 6/42
Wasim Akram run out 26	7/97 8/98 9/98

Bowling: de Villiers 7–1–21–3; Donald 8–2–25–3; Simons 9.3–1–26–2; McMillan 5–0–25–0; Cronje 3–0–9–1.

Umpires: K. E. Liebenberg and C. J. Mitchley.
Series referee: P. J. P. Burge.

NEW ZEALAND CENTENARY TOURNAMENT, 1994-95

By TERRY POWER

Australia, India and South Africa visited New Zealand in February for a quadrangular one-day tournament to mark the centenary of the establishment of the New Zealand Cricket Council in Christchurch on December 27, 1894. Australia, who showed themselves good neighbours in coming during a busy season of three Test series and four limited-overs competitions, easily beat New Zealand in the final at Auckland. For the home country, the matches came in an overpacked season, after their tour of South Africa and between their unsuccessful clashes with West Indies and Sri Lanka. The centenary programme also included a one-off Test against South Africa; that was lost too.

Note: Matches in this section were not first-class.

AUSTRALIA v SOUTH AFRICA

At Wellington, February 15. Australia won by three wickets. Toss: South Africa. International debut: R. T. Ponting.

The pitch, on which New Zealand had just lost to West Indies inside four days, favoured the bowlers. Steve Waugh, whose 44 was easily the biggest and best innings of the day, said the spinners and slower seamers were more difficult than the pace attack; Warne's first spell was near-unplayable, though Reiffel had most profit. South Africa were 55 for five and even a recovery brought them only 123. But de Villiers led the counter-attack and Australia were five down for 56. It was nearly six: Rindel, dazzled by the sun, dropped Healy before he had scored. He survived and nearly doubled the total with Waugh. An Australian batting line-up featuring two Tasmanians, Boon and Ponting, was a novelty, but they scored only one each.

Man of the Match: S. R. Waugh.

South Africa

G. Kirsten c Healy b Reiffel	15	P. L. Symcox c M. E. Waugh b May	10
M. J. R. Rindel c Taylor b Reiffel	14	P. S. de Villiers b Reiffel	8
*W. J. Cronje c Taylor b Blewett	22	A. A. Donald b Reiffel	0
D. J. Cullinan st Healy b Warne	0	L-b 3, n-b 3	6
J. N. Rhodes b McGrath	25		
D. J. Callaghan c S. R. Waugh b Warne	1	1/20 2/48 3/52	(46.2 overs) 123
†D. J. Richardson not out	22	4/54 5/55 6/95	
E. O. Simons lbw b McGrath	0	7/95 8/111 9/121	

Bowling: McGrath 10–1–25–2; Reiffel 8.2–1–27–4; Blewett 10–0–30–1; Warne 10–3–18–2; May 8–0–20–1.

Australia

*M. A. Taylor c Cullinan b de Villiers	24	P. R. Reiffel c Rhodes b Cronje	8
G. S. Blewett run out	14	S. K. Warne not out	2
M. E. Waugh b Symcox	11	B 1	1
D. C. Boon lbw b de Villiers	1		
S. R. Waugh not out	44	1/38 2/38 3/39	(7 wkts, 43.2 overs) 124
R. T. Ponting b Simons	1	4/55 5/56	
†I. A. Healy lbw b Cronje	18	6/103 7/115	

T. B. A. May and G. D. McGrath did not bat.

Bowling: Donald 7–0–32–0; de Villiers 10–2–34–2; Simons 10–3–19–1; Symcox 10–1–23–1; Cronje 6.2–1–15–2.

Umpires: B. L. Aldridge and R. S. Dunne.

NEW ZEALAND v INDIA

At Napier, February 16. New Zealand won by four wickets. Toss: New Zealand.

New Zealand took their limited-overs record at Napier to eight out of eight, ending their sequence of 13 one-day defeats and three washouts since April 1994. Fleming, who scored 90 against the same team at Napier the previous season, hit a match-winning 59 not out from 60 balls, to cruise past India in the 33rd over. Gaining more lift than most, Srinath removed three in an over, but by then the target was only 17. India's only other success was Sidhu, who scored 73. He was one of four catches for Rutherford, a New Zealand record: John Bracewell took four against Australia in 1980-81 – but he was a substitute. The home team's only bad news was that Crowe, returning after injury, tore a thigh muscle in the field.

Man of the Match: S. P. Fleming.

India

A. D. Jadeja run out	7	J. Srinath run out	2
S. R. Tendulkar c Thomson b Morrison	13	B. K. V. Prasad lbw b Morrison	0
N. S. Sidhu c Rutherford b Su'a	73	S. L. V. Raju b Morrison	0
*M. Azharuddin c Rutherford b Thomson	28	B 1, l-b 4, w 3	8
V. G. Kambli c Rutherford b Vaughan	17		
M. Prabhakar c Rutherford b Cairns	2	1/20 2/22 3/79	(45.5 overs) 160
†N. R. Mongia c Greatbatch b Larsen	4	4/107 5/127 6/138	
A. Kumble not out	6	7/157 8/160 9/160	

Bowling: Morrison 7.5–1–22–3; Thomson 5–0–29–1; Su'a 10–1–35–1; Cairns 8–1–17–1; Larsen 10–2–28–1; Vaughan 5–0–24–1.

New Zealand

M. J. Greatbatch b Prabhakar	32	†A. C. Parore c Mongia b Srinath	0
M. D. Crowe c and b Srinath	7	J. T. C. Vaughan not out	5
*K. R. Rutherford c Kambli b Raju	25	B 2, w 3, n-b 4	9
S. P. Fleming not out	59		
C. L. Cairns c Azharuddin b Srinath	25	1/42 2/42 3/103	(6 wkts, 32.2 overs) 162
S. A. Thomson c Azharuddin b Srinath	0	4/144 5/144 6/144	

G. R. Larsen, M. L. Su'a and D. K. Morrison did not bat.

Bowling: Prabhakar 7–0–28–1; Srinath 9.2–1–52–4; Kumble 9–0–34–0; Prasad 2–0–11–0; Raju 5–0–35–1.

Umpires: D. B. Cowie and C. E. King.

INDIA v SOUTH AFRICA

At Hamilton, February 18. South Africa won by 14 runs. Toss: South Africa.

Though the margin was small, South Africa held the advantage throughout on an unusually bare, brown, slow pitch. Cullinan and Kirsten took South Africa to 167 for one before Kumble began a spell of four for 18 in five overs. Tight bowling meant that the South Africans did not capitalise, but neither did India when they replied. Jadeja took 91 deliveries over 29 and India slid far behind the needed rate; Srinath's 37 from 25 balls came too late. South Africa were boosted by superior fielding: Callaghan ran from long-on to take Sidhu left-handed as the ball fell behind him and de Villiers ran out Prabhakar with a superb sliding stop and throw at fine leg.

Man of the Match: G. Kirsten.

South Africa

A. C. Hudson b Srinath	24	†D. J. Richardson not out	11
G. Kirsten run out	80	E. O. Simons not out	7
D. J. Cullinan c Prasad b Kumble	65	B 1, l-b 7, w 4, n-b 5	17
*W. J. Cronje c and b Kumble	3		
J. N. Rhodes lbw b Kumble	0	1/47 2/167 3/174 (6 wkts, 50 overs) 223
D. J. Callaghan lbw b Kumble	16	4/174 5/201 6/201

P. L. Symcox, A. A. Donald and P. S. de Villiers did not bat.

Bowling: Prabhakar 6-0-24-0; Srinath 8-0-30-1; Prasad 7-0-32-0; Kumble 10-0-40-4; Raju 9-0-46-0; Tendulkar 10-0-43-0.

India

A. D. Jadeja c Kirsten b Symcox	29	A. Kumble lbw b de Villiers	1
S. R. Tendulkar c Symcox b Cronje	37	B. K. V. Prasad not out	5
N. S. Sidhu c Callaghan b Cronje	5		
*M. Azharuddin run out	20	B 2, l-b 3, w 10	15
V. G. Kambli c Richardson b Donald	30		
J. Srinath c Simons b Donald	37	1/61 2/73 3/76 (9 wkts, 50 overs) 209
M. Prabhakar run out	6	4/118 5/148 6/159
†N. R. Mongia run out	24	7/196 8/200 9/209

S. L. V. Raju did not bat.

Bowling: Donald 9-1-43-2; de Villiers 10-1-56-1; Simons 8-1-28-0; Cronje 10-0-34-2; Symcox 10-0-20-1; Callaghan 3-0-23-0.

Umpires: D. B. Cowie and E. A. Watkin.

NEW ZEALAND v AUSTRALIA

At Auckland, February 19. Australia won by 27 runs. Toss: Australia.

Though off-spinner Thomson removed Blewett in the second over, a brisk stand of 147 between Taylor and Mark Waugh gave Australia the ascendancy and earned them a place in the final. Taylor's 97 was his highest innings in 72 one-day internationals. New Zealand fought back through Greatbatch, who hit two sixes, and the stylish Fleming, and were ahead on run-rate until the 40th over. But Fleming's dismissal put the brakes on and the loss of Greatbatch and Cairns ended their hopes. The match was marred first by spectators throwing rubbish at Warne in the outfield and then by Rutherford's remark that New Zealand Cricket had announced the injured Crowe's chances of playing as 50-50 only to boost the attendance. This caused widespread public anger.

Man of the Match: M. A. Taylor.

Australia

G. S. Blewett c Fleming b Thomson	3	†I. A. Healy not out	4
*M. A. Taylor c and b Pringle	97		
M. E. Waugh c and b Vaughan	74	B 1, l-b 5, w 2, n-b 1	9
D. C. Boon c Larsen b Morrison	44		
S. R. Waugh b Pringle	13	1/3 2/150 3/214 (5 wkts, 50 overs) 254
R. T. Ponting not out	10	4/238 5/241

S. K. Warne, P. R. Reiffel, T. B. A. May and G. D. McGrath did not bat.

Bowling: Morrison 10-1-40-1; Thomson 10-1-43-1; Pringle 10-0-54-2; Cairns 3-0-21-0; Larsen 10-0-49-0; Vaughan 7-0-41-1.

New Zealand

B. A. Young b Reiffel	4	G. R. Larsen c Reiffel b M. E. Waugh	3
M. J. Greatbatch c Healy b Reiffel	74	C. Pringle b McGrath	4
*K. R. Rutherford st Healy b Warne	7	D. K. Morrison not out	3
S. P. Fleming c Warne b May	53	L-b 12, w 4, n-b 2	18
C. L. Cairns lbw b McGrath	22		
S. A. Thomson run out	9	1/19 2/42 3/124 (9 wkts, 50 overs) 227
†A. C. Parore not out	27	4/169 5/181 6/187
J. T. C. Vaughan c Healy b Reiffel	3	7/193 8/199 9/217

Bowling: McGrath 10–0–40–2; Reiffel 10–4–35–3; Warne 10–1–40–1; May 10–0–43–1; Blewett 2–0–18–0; Boon 4–0–20–0; M. E. Waugh 4–0–19–1.

Umpires: D. B. Cowie and D. M. Quested.

AUSTRALIA v INDIA

At Dunedin, February 22. India won by five wickets. Toss: Australia. International debut: P. S. Vaidya.

Australia's only defeat of the tournament and India's only win had no effect on their placings, with the one safely qualified for the final and the other out of the running. Ponting scored his maiden international half-century and Mark Waugh hit 48 in 32 balls to spearhead a solid Australian batting effort of five runs an over. But India's top order finally rediscovered their batting form to overhaul them with 13 balls to spare. Prabhakar and Tendulkar gave them a blazing start, Sidhu anchored the innings and Kambli brought up victory and his fifty off the 56th ball he received. The dreaded Warne cost more than six an over without picking up a wicket.

Man of the Match: N. S. Sidhu.

Australia

D. C. Boon c Kambli b Vaidya	32	*M. A. Taylor b Srinath	0
G. S. Blewett c Tendulkar b Tendulkar	46	S. K. Warne not out	5
R. T. Ponting c Vaidya b Prabhakar	62	B 2, l-b 3, w 2, n-b 6	13
S. R. Waugh c and b Kumble	23		
M. E. Waugh c Azharuddin b Srinath	48	1/56 2/103 3/158 (6 wkts, 50 overs) 250
†I. A. Healy not out	21	4/207 5/226 6/226

T. B. A. May, G. D. McGrath and J. Angel did not bat.

Bowling: Prabhakar 10–0–61–1; Srinath 9–0–49–2; Vaidya 7–0–36–1; Kumble 7–0–28–1; Kapoor 9–0–38–0; Tendulkar 8–0–33–1.

India

M. Prabhakar b Angel	50	†N. R. Mongia not out	6
S. R. Tendulkar c Taylor b Angel	47		
N. S. Sidhu run out	54	L-b 1, w 3, n-b 1	5
*M. Azharuddin c Healy b Blewett	25		
V. G. Kambli not out	51	1/97 2/100 3/144 (5 wkts, 47.5 overs) 252
S. V. Manjrekar c Healy b May	14	4/213 5/233

J. Srinath, P. S. Vaidya, A. Kumble and A. R. Kapoor did not bat.

Bowling: McGrath 9–1–45–0; Angel 10–1–47–2; Warne 10–0–61–0; May 10–0–51–1; Blewett 8.5–0–47–1.

Umpires: R. S. Dunne and C. E. King.

NEW ZEALAND v SOUTH AFRICA

At Christchurch, February 23, 24. New Zealand won by 46 runs. Toss: South Africa.

The contest to join Australia in the final was postponed a day, after rain prevented any play on February 23. Greatbatch scored 76 from 85 balls to take his aggregate in the tournament to 182 and looked more assured than Rutherford in a stand of 98. Cairns also hit out until, one ball after a beamer from Matthews, he hit a skimming cover drive, only for Kirsten to dive like a goal-keeper and stop the six with a superb right-handed catch. But Parore attacked successfully and later took a leg-side stumping off a wide to dismiss Cronje after he and Kirsten had reached 117 for two. South Africa offered little more resistance and were bowled out with three overs to spare.

Man of the Match: M. J. Greatbatch.

New Zealand

M. J. Greatbatch c and b Cronje	76
M. W. Douglas lbw b Matthews	8
*K. R. Rutherford c Callaghan b Cronje	61
S. P. Fleming c Cullinan b Matthews	21
C. L. Cairns c Kirsten b Matthews	33
S. A. Thomson c Richardson b de Villiers	6
†A. C. Parore not out	30
J. T. C. Vaughan run out	7
G. R. Larsen not out	2
L-b 2, w 1, n-b 2	5

1/28 2/126 3/167 (7 wkts, 50 overs) 249
4/172 5/190
6/227 7/246

C. Pringle and D. K. Morrison did not bat.

Bowling: de Villiers 10-0-39-1; Matthews 10-1-49-3; Donald 10-0-50-0; Cronje 10-0-50-2; Simons 6-0-33-0; Callaghan 4-0-26-0.

South Africa

A. C. Hudson c Douglas b Morrison	10
G. Kirsten c Fleming b Thomson	63
D. J. Cullinan c Vaughan b Larsen	13
*W. J. Cronje st Parore b Vaughan	34
J. N. Rhodes c Greatbatch b Morrison	14
D. J. Callaghan lbw b Larsen	23
†D. J. Richardson c Thomson b Vaughan	7
E. O. Simons c Greatbatch b Vaughan	7
C. R. Matthews b Larsen	16
P. S. de Villiers c Thomson b Pringle	7
A. A. Donald not out	0
B 1, l-b 4, w 4	9

1/28 2/67 3/117 (47 overs) 203
4/138 5/143 6/162
7/173 8/190 9/197

Bowling: Pringle 8-0-35-1; Morrison 8-1-30-2; Vaughan 10-0-37-3; Cairns 4-0-24-0; Larsen 10-0-39-3; Thomson 7-0-33-1.

Umpires: B. L. Aldridge and D. M. Quested.

QUALIFYING TABLE

	Played	Won	Lost	Points	Net run-rate
Australia	3	2	1	4	0.70
New Zealand	3	2	1	4	0.30
South Africa	3	1	2	2	−0.40
India	3	1	2	2	−0.59

FINAL

NEW ZEALAND v AUSTRALIA

At Auckland, February 26. Australia won by six wickets. Toss: New Zealand.

The home team's centenary celebrations came unstuck in a one-sided final, which Australia won with nearly 19 overs to spare. Stifled by the Australian bowling, which rendered Greatbatch impotent for half an hour, New Zealand totalled a feeble 137 on a tricky pitch. Rutherford, striving mightily by this stage of the ill-fated season, had virtually no support for his 46, with extras easily the next-biggest contributor on 28. Reiffel removed both openers and conceded just 1.4 an over; May and Warne cost barely two an over and shared five wickets. A week after they had added 147 against New Zealand, Taylor and Mark Waugh put on another 78, effectively settling the issue.

Man of the Match: T. B. A. May.

New Zealand

M. J. Greatbatch c McGrath b Reiffel .	8	G. R. Larsen run out..................	0
M. W. Douglas c Healy b Reiffel	2	C. Pringle b May	1
*K. R. Rutherford c Boon b May	46	D. K. Morrison not out	4
S. P. Fleming c Healy b M. E. Waugh .	0	B 1, l-b 10, w 13, n-b 4	28
C. L. Cairns c Taylor b May	17		
S. A. Thomson c and b Warne........	9	1/8 2/29 3/35 (9 wkts, 50 overs) 137	
†A. C. Parore c Taylor b Warne	2	4/81 5/102 6/106	
J. T. C. Vaughan not out	20	7/106 8/106 9/112	

Bowling: McGrath 9–1–25–0; Reiffel 10–3–14–2; M. E. Waugh 10–1–38–1; Warne 10–2–21–2; May 10–2–19–3; Blewett 1–0–9–0.

Australia

G. S. Blewett c and b Pringle.........	7	R. T. Ponting not out	7
*M. A. Taylor st Parore b Vaughan ...	44	L-b 3, w 3, n-b 3............	9
M. E. Waugh c Parore b Morrison	46		
D. C. Boon not out	24	1/15 2/93 (4 wkts, 31.1 overs) 138	
S. R. Waugh c Rutherford b Thomson .	1	3/116 4/121	

†I. A. Healy, P. R. Reiffel, S. K. Warne, T. B. A. May and G. D. McGrath did not bat.

Bowling: Morrison 9–1–31–1; Pringle 9.1–1–52–1; Thomson 5–0–22–1; Vaughan 6–1–18–1; Larsen 2–0–12–0.

Umpires: B. L. Aldridge and R. S. Dunne.

PETER SMITH AWARD, 1995

The Peter Smith Award, given by the Cricket Writers' Club in memory of its former chairman for services to the presentation of cricket to the public, was won in 1995 by Mark Taylor, the Australian captain, for "leading a team to the pinnacle of world cricket without losing sight of the need to play the game with flair and integrity and a concern for the game's traditions and image". The Award was instituted in 1992. Previous winners were David Gower, John Woodcock and Brian Lara.

PEPSI ASIA CUP, 1994-95

India ended the season as they began it, meeting Sri Lanka in a one-day final. As in Colombo in September, they were victorious, adding the Asia Cup (which they won for the fourth time in five tournaments) to the Singer Trophy. Their triumph would have been even sweeter had they overcome their traditional rivals, Pakistan, who beat them, as so often at Sharjah, in the qualifying rounds.

But the competition saw a major upset when Sri Lanka pushed past Pakistan to contest the final. Pakistan had appeared in every Sharjah final since 1988-89 and seemed certain to keep up that record after crushing India and Bangladesh. Their troubles in recent months finally caught up with them, however. They had survived the sacking of captain Salim Malik while he answered allegations of bribery, the dropping of several senior players and a squabble with all-rounder Wasim Akram about his wife's accommodation. But when the new captain, Moin Khan, succumbed to chicken-pox and Wasim's new-ball partner, Aqib Javed, was injured, they cracked. All three Test teams tied on points, but Sri Lanka, playing with forceful determination, edged out Pakistan on run-rate. The fourth side, Bangladesh, could never rise above their inexperience and provided easy wins for the others.

With four one-day titles, including two at home, in 1994-95, and a powerful batting line-up – Sachin Tendulkar, Navjot Sidhu and Mohammad Azharuddin all fired here – India looked forward with confidence to the 1996 World Cup, although their manager, Ajit Wadekar, announced at the final that he was retiring after three successful seasons.

Note: Matches in this section were not first-class.

BANGLADESH v INDIA

At Sharjah, April 5. India won by nine wickets. Toss: Bangladesh. International debuts: Anis-ur-Rahman, Khaled Masud, Mohammad Javed, Mohammad Rafiq, Sajjad Ahmed; U. Chatterjee.

Bangladesh's tenth full international, and their first since December 1990, ended in their tenth defeat. India had more than 22 overs in hand when they overhauled a modest 163, and lost only Tendulkar. He had already dazzled the crowd, dashing to 48 in 31 balls thanks to nine fours and a six. Sidhu then took up the charge, with 56 in 51 balls, while Prabhakar played the anchor role. When Bangladesh batted, Ather Ali Khan hit his first ball for four, but only Amin-ul-Islam reached 30 before he was caught at long leg off Chatterjee, the 30-year-old debutant left-armer.

Man of the Match: M. Prabhakar.

Bangladesh

Ather Ali Khan c Mongia b Srinath	17	†Khaled Masud lbw b Kumble	4
Mohammad Javed run out	18	Saif-ul-Islam not out	22
Sajjad Ahmed c Mongia b Prabhakar	4	Anis-ur-Rahman c Sidhu b Vaidya	2
Amin-ul-Islam c Vaidya b Chatterjee	30	L-b 7, w 1, n-b 3	11
Minhaz-ul-Abedin run out	21		
*Akram Khan c Chatterjee b Vaidya	24	1/30 2/40 3/51	(44.4 overs) 163
Enam-ul-Haque lbw b Prabhakar	8	4/93 5/99 6/114	
Mohammad Rafiq b Kumble	2	7/119 8/125 9/138	

Bowling: Prabhakar 10–0–43–2; Srinath 8–3–21–1; Chatterjee 10–0–28–1; Vaidya 8.4–1–41–2; Kumble 8–0–23–2.

India

M. Prabhakar not out 53
S. R. Tendulkar b Mohammad Rafiq .. 48
N. S. Sidhu not out 56
    L-b 1, w 5, n-b 1 7

1/72   (1 wkt, 27.5 overs) 164

*M. Azharuddin, V. G. Kambli, S. V. Manjrekar, †N. R. Mongia, A. Kumble, J. Srinath, U. Chatterjee and P. S. Vaidya did not bat.

Bowling: Anis-ur-Rahman 5–0–42–0; Saif-ul-Islam 5–0–31–0; Enam-ul-Haque 6–0–25–0; Mohammad Rafiq 5–0–15–1; Ather Ali Khan 3–0–22–0; Minhaz-ul-Abedin 3–0–19–0; Amin-ul-Islam 0.5–0–9–0.

Umpires: N. T. Plews (England) and I. D. Robinson (Zimbabwe).

BANGLADESH v SRI LANKA

At Sharjah, April 6. Sri Lanka won by 107 runs. Toss: Bangladesh. International debuts: Habib-ul-Bashar, Hasib-ul-Hassan.

After losing Gurusinha first ball and Mahanama in the fourth over, Sri Lanka were put back on course by Jayasuriya and de Silva, who added 71 before Jayasuriya left the field, suffering from dehydration. Ranatunga then reached 71 at a run a ball, putting on 93 with Tillekeratne. Both perished in the final assault and Bangladesh had the satisfaction of bowling out a Test side for the first time, with medium-pacer Saif-ul-Islam claiming four. But they made little attempt to pursue 234. No-one passed 26 and Vaas conceded only nine in seven overs.

Man of the Match: A. Ranatunga.

Sri Lanka

A. P. Gurusinha c Amin-ul-Islam	†C. I. Dunusinghe run out 1
b Saif-ul-Islam . 0	W. P. U. J. C. Vaas c Akram Khan
S. T. Jayasuriya c Khaled Masud	b Saif-ul-Islam . 11
b Saif-ul-Islam . 51	M. Muralitharan c Akram Khan
R. S. Mahanama b Hasib-ul-Hassan ... 2	b Mohammad Rafiq . 6
P. A. de Silva c Khaled Masud	J. C. Gamage not out 7
b Minhaz-ul-Abedin . 36	L-b 5, w 5 10
*A. Ranatunga b Saif-ul-Islam . 71	
H. P. Tillekeratne c Habib-ul-Bashar	
b Mohammad Rafiq . 37	1/0 2/8 3/101 (49.4 overs) 233
R. S. Kalpage run out 1	4/194 5/197 6/198
	7/203 8/213 9/220

S. T. Jayasuriya, when 51, retired ill at 79 and resumed at 194.

Bowling: Saif-ul-Islam 10–2–36–4; Hasib-ul-Hassan 6–2–29–1; Ather Ali Khan 7–0–28–0; Enam-ul-Haque 10–0–38–0; Minhaz-ul-Abedin 6–0–30–1; Mohammad Rafiq 8.4–0–50–2; Amin-ul-Islam 2–0–17–0.

Bangladesh

Ather Ali Khan run out 2	Mohammad Rafiq st Dunusinghe
Sajjad Ahmed c Jayasuriya	b Muralitharan . 13
b Muralitharan . 11	Saif-ul-Islam c Vaas b Muralitharan ... 5
Habib-ul-Bashar c de Silva b Gamage.. 16	Hasib-ul-Hassan not out 1
Amin-ul-Islam lbw b Gamage......... 0	
Minhaz-ul-Abedin c Dunusinghe	B 8, w 4 12
b Kalpage . 26	
*Akram Khan c Ranatunga b Vaas.... 24	1/4 2/32 3/32 (44.2 overs) 126
Enam-ul-Haque c Vaas b Jayasuriya ... 1	4/42 5/76 6/85
†Khaled Masud c and b Muralitharan.. 15	7/100 8/112 9/123

Bowling: Vaas 7–4–9–1; Gamage 7–2–17–2; Muralitharan 8.2–1–23–4; Ranatunga 5–0–24–0; Jayasuriya 7–0–19–1; Kalpage 10–1–26–1.

Umpires: C. J. Mitchley (South Africa) and N. T. Plews (England).

INDIA v PAKISTAN

At Sharjah, April 7. Pakistan won by 97 runs. Toss: Pakistan. International debuts: Naeem Ashraf, Zafar Iqbal.

Leaving their troubled cricket politics behind, Pakistan – under yet another captain, Moin Khan – secured their biggest ever win over India (in terms of runs) in 41 one-day games. Moin set India on the path to defeat by catching both openers off Aqib Javed, who added two more wickets as India struggled to 37 and finished with five for 19. Sidhu and Manjrekar rallied the innings, both reaching 50, but Manjrekar's dismissal started a terminal collapse of five wickets for 25. Pakistan had looked shaky in mid-innings, too, but Inzamam-ul-Haq and Wasim Akram, who hit 50 from 46 balls, turned them round and 91 came from their last ten overs.

Man of the Match: Aqib Javed.

Pakistan

Aamir Sohail c Tendulkar b Srinath	40	Naeem Ashraf not out	8
Saeed Anwar c Azharuddin b Kumble	25	Nadeem Khan run out	2
Ghulam Ali c Tendulkar b Chatterjee	13		
Inzamam-ul-Haq b Prasad	88	L-b 8, w 7, n-b 1	16
Asif Mujtaba run out	4		
*†Moin Khan b Chatterjee	2	1/58 2/73 3/104 (9 wkts, 50 overs) 266
Wasim Akram run out	50	4/122 5/133 6/214
Zafar Iqbal b Kumble	18	7/255 8/255 9/266

Aqib Javed did not bat.

Bowling: Prabhakar 10–0–64–0; Srinath 9–0–60–1; Prasad 8–0–43–1; Kumble 8–0–29–2; Tendulkar 7–0–27–0; Chatterjee 8–0–35–2.

India

M. Prabhakar c Moin Khan b Aqib Javed	0	J. Srinath c and b Aqib Javed	0
S. R. Tendulkar c Moin Khan b Aqib Javed	4	A. Kumble run out	0
N. S. Sidhu lbw b Zafar Iqbal	54	U. Chatterjee not out	3
*M. Azharuddin c Asif Mujtaba b Aqib Javed	11	B. K. V. Prasad c Moin Khan b Aamir Sohail	3
V. G. Kambli b Aqib Javed	0		
S. V. Manjrekar c Asif Mujtaba b Aamir Sohail	50	L-b 8, w 7, n-b 11	26
†N. R. Mongia hit wkt b Wasim Akram	18	1/2 2/11 3/37 (42.4 overs) 169
		4/37 5/106 6/144
		7/151 8/152 9/153

Bowling: Wasim Akram 8–0–23–1; Aqib Javed 9–1–19–5; Zafar Iqbal 8–0–34–1; Naeem Ashraf 6–0–40–0; Nadeem Khan 10–0–42–0; Aamir Sohail 1.4–0–3–2.

Umpires: C. J. Mitchley (South Africa) and I. D. Robinson (Zimbabwe).

BANGLADESH v PAKISTAN

At Sharjah, April 8. Pakistan won by six wickets. Toss: Bangladesh. International debut: Naim-ur-Rahman.

Pakistan beat Bangladesh with little exertion and 20 overs to spare. Wasim Akram reached the target of 152 with his second six – but the scoreboard showed only 151 so he edged another four, which did not count. On the official reckoning, he scored 30 from 25 balls, having added a rapid 45 with Inzamam-ul-Haq. Wasim also took two cheap wickets, despite a bad shoulder. He and Aamir Nazir had Bangladesh at 19 for four, though Amin-ul-Islam and captain Akram Khan put on 72 and enabled their team to bat out time. Akram Khan even had his score increased by three, as the third umpire had seen a fielder tread on the boundary. But that only just lifted Bangladesh above three an over.

Man of the Match: Wasim Akram.

Bangladesh

Ather Ali Khan c Moin Khan b Wasim Akram .	2	†Khaled Masud not out	27	
Mohammad Javed b Aamir Nazir	9	Enam-ul-Haque run out	7	
Habib-ul-Bashar b Wasim Akram	0	Saif-ul-Islam not out	3	
Amin-ul-Islam c and b Arshad Khan	42	L-b 1, w 9, n-b 4	14	
Minhaz-ul-Abedin c Moin Khan b Aamir Nazir .	0		—	
*Akram Khan run out	44	1/12 2/16 3/19 (8 wkts, 50 overs) 151		
Naim-ur-Rahman run out	3	4/19 5/91 6/97		
		7/119 8/133		

Hasib-ul-Hassan did not bat.

Bowling: Wasim Akram 10-0-25-2; Aqib Javed 10-0-29-0; Zafar Iqbal 5-1-8-0; Aamir Nazir 7-0-23-2; Arshad Khan 10-0-29-1; Aamir Sohail 8-1-36-0.

Pakistan

Aamir Sohail c Naim-ur-Rahman b Saif-ul-Islam .	30	Asif Mujtaba b Ather Ali Khan	0	
Saeed Anwar c Khaled Masud b Hasib-ul-Hassan .	18	Wasim Akram not out	30	
Ghulam Ali c and b Naim-ur-Rahman .	38	L-b 1, w 6	7	
Inzamam-ul-Haq not out	29	1/35 2/68 (4 wkts, 29.4 overs) 152		
		3/106 4/107		

*†Moin Khan, Zafar Iqbal, Aqib Javed, Aamir Nazir and Arshad Khan did not bat.

Bowling: Saif-ul-Islam 7-0-33-1; Hasib-ul-Hassan 8-0-43-1; Enam-ul-Haque 4-0-20-0; Naim-ur-Rahman 6.4-0-29-1; Ather Ali Khan 2-0-10-1; Minhaz-ul-Abedin 2-0-16-0.

Umpires: N. T. Plews (England) and I. D. Robinson (Zimbabwe).

INDIA v SRI LANKA

At Sharjah, April 9. India won by eight wickets. Toss: Sri Lanka.

Victory left India well-placed in the qualifying table, especially as they boosted their run-rate by passing their target inside 34 overs. They bowled well, fielded well, and Tendulkar batted superbly. He drove his way to an unbeaten 112 from 105 balls, including 15 fours and a six. His first 50 took just 44 balls but he then steadied himself to play a big innings; it was his fourth century in limited-overs internationals since September. Prabhakar supported him in an opening stand of 161, which settled the outcome. Sri Lanka had reached 60 for one before sliding to 113 for six, with three wickets falling to Prasad. Tillekeratne and Dharmasena then put on 71, but it was too late to set India a real challenge.

Man of the Match: S. R. Tendulkar.

Sri Lanka

A. P. Gurusinha c Mongia b Srinath	15	W. P. U. J. C. Vaas not out	10	
S. T. Jayasuriya b Kumble	31	C. P. H. Ramanayake b Prabhakar	0	
R. S. Mahanama c Azharuddin b Prasad	11	J. C. Gamage not out	1	
P. A. de Silva c Tendulkar b Prasad	21	L-b 12, w 12, n-b 5	29	
*A. Ranatunga lbw b Srinath	5		—	
H. P. Tillekeratne run out	48	1/25 2/60 3/70 (9 wkts, 50 overs) 202		
†R. S. Kaluwitharana c Jadeja b Prasad	1	4/76 5/105 6/113		
H. D. P. K. Dharmasena run out	30	7/184 8/196 9/199		

Bowling: Prabhakar 10-1-51-1; Srinath 10-1-35-2; Prasad 10-0-37-3; Kumble 10-0-37-1; Kapoor 10-0-30-0.

India

M. Prabhakar c Tillekeratne		J. Srinath not out	14
b Jayasuriya . 60		L-b 3, w 13, n-b 1	17
S. R. Tendulkar not out	112		
N. S. Sidhu c and b Jayasuriya	3	1/161 2/167 (2 wkts, 33.1 overs)	206

*M. Azharuddin, A. D. Jadeja, S. V. Manjrekar, †N. R. Mongia, A. Kumble, B. K. V. Prasad and A. R. Kapoor did not bat.

Bowling: Vaas 9-0-67-0; Gamage 3-0-23-0; Ramanayake 4.1-0-38-0; Dharmasena 5-0-16-0; Jayasuriya 10-0-42-2; de Silva 2-0-17-0.

Umpires: C. J. Mitchley (South Africa) and N. T. Plews (England).

PAKISTAN v SRI LANKA

At Sharjah, April 11. Sri Lanka won by five wickets. Toss: Sri Lanka. International debuts: Javed Qadir, Mahmood Hamid.

Against all expectations, Sri Lanka fought through to the final ahead of Pakistan. Victory alone was not enough: they had to keep Pakistan below 212 and win in 33 overs or less to beat them on run-rate. (They rejected the alternative of batting first and scoring nearly 300 to overtake India.) With his third ball, Vaas removed Aamir Sohail and, with Ramanayake following up, Pakistan were 38 for five by the 19th over. Though Inzamam-ul-Haq scored an heroic 73, the next-biggest contribution was 17 – from wides. Kaluwitharana, flown in because Dunusinghe was ill, made five dismissals. Sri Lanka now needed 179 at 5.42 an over. Jayasuriya blazed away with 30 from 15 balls, to set the pace for the later strokeplayers, while Mahanama acted as anchor; 13 balls inside the deadline Tillekeratne triumphantly struck Arshad Khan for six. In Pakistan's mitigation, they had lost Moin Khan to chicken-pox and Aqib Javed to injury, reducing the team to five established players.

Man of the Match: S. T. Jayasuriya.

Pakistan

Aamir Sohail c Kaluwitharana b Vaas .	0	Zafar Iqbal run out	13
*Saeed Anwar c Gurusinha		†Javed Qadir c Jayasuriya	
b Ramanayake .	4	b Ramanayake .	12
Asif Mujtaba c Kaluwitharana		Arshad Khan not out	9
b Ramanayake .	13	Aamir Nazir not out	9
Inzamam-ul-Haq c Kaluwitharana			
b Vaas .	73		
Mahmood Hamid run out	1	L-b 4, w 17, n-b 1	22
Wasim Akram st Kaluwitharana			
b Jayasuriya .	6	1/0 2/19 3/22 (9 wkts, 50 overs)	178
Naeem Ashraf c Kaluwitharana		4/25 5/38 6/74	
b Muralitharan .	16	7/117 8/156 9/158	

Bowling: Vaas 10-3-30-2; Ramanayake 10-1-25-3; Jayasuriya 10-1-31-1; Muralitharan 10-0-42-1; Kalpage 10-2-46-0.

Sri Lanka

R. S. Mahanama c Arshad Khan		*A. Ranatunga not out	23
b Aamir Sohail .	48	†R. S. Kaluwitharana b Wasim Akram.	17
S. T. Jayasuriya c Arshad Khan		H. P. Tillekeratne not out	8
b Aamir Nazir .	30	L-b 9, w 7, n-b 1	17
A. P. Gurusinha run out	14		
P. A. de Silva c Javed Qadir		1/34 2/65 3/118 (5 wkts, 30.5 overs)	180
b Aamir Sohail .	23	4/137 5/165	

R. S. Kalpage, W. P. U. J. C. Vaas, C. P. H. Ramanayake and M. Muralitharan did not bat.

Bowling: Wasim Akram 9-0-37-1; Aamir Nazir 5-0-47-1; Zafar Iqbal 5-0-25-0; Naeem Ashraf 1-0-12-0; Arshad Khan 5.5-0-29-0; Aamir Sohail 5-0-21-2.

Umpires: C. J. Mitchley (South Africa) and I. D. Robinson (Zimbabwe).

QUALIFYING TABLE

	Played	Won	Lost	Points	Run-rate
India..........	3	2	1	4	4.81
Sri Lanka.......	3	2	1	4	4.69
Pakistan........	3	2	1	4	4.58
Bangladesh......	3	0	3	0	2.93

FINAL

INDIA v SRI LANKA

At Sharjah, April 14. India won by eight wickets. Toss: India.

Azharuddin was back to his best with a wristy 90 from 87 balls. He and Sidhu, whose third half-century in four innings took him to 197 for twice out, shared an unbroken stand of 175 and swept India to victory with seven overs to spare (they had had one deducted for their slow over-rate). There was little chance of setting a defensible target against them in this mood. Sri Lanka must have sensed the worst once Jayasuriya, their own big hitter, was caught off Prasad for a 28-ball 22 and Ranatunga was run out for three. Only Gurusinha stood firm, for 85 including three sixes; the total would not have reached 200 without 37 extras. Tendulkar launched India with a run-a-ball 41 before Sidhu and the captain took control. Azharuddin finished the day with the Asia Cup, the winners' cheque of $US30,000 and, as a special tribute from his admirers, a steel sword in a gold-plated scabbard.

Man of the Match: M. Azharuddin.   *Man of the Series*: N. S. Sidhu.

Sri Lanka

R. S. Mahanama b Kumble 15	R. S. Kalpage not out 7
S. T. Jayasuriya c Mongia b Prasad.... 22	W. P. U. J. C. Vaas not out.......... 8
A. P. Gurusinha run out 85	L-b 23, w 10, n-b 4 37
P. A. de Silva c Mongia b Prabhakar .. 13	
*A. Ranatunga run out 3	1/46 2/46 3/81 (7 wkts, 50 overs) 230
H. P. Tillekeratne c Mongia b Prasad .. 22	4/89 5/150
†R. S. Kaluwitharana b Kumble 18	6/192 7/218

C. P. H. Ramanayake and M. Muralitharan did not bat.

Bowling: Prabhakar 10-0-45-1; Srinath 9-2-38-0; Prasad 10-1-32-2; Kumble 10-1-50-2; Kapoor 10-0-32-0; Tendulkar 1-0-10-0.

India

M. Prabhakar c Kaluwitharana b Vaas . 9	*M. Azharuddin not out 90
S. R. Tendulkar c Jayasuriya	L-b 1, w 7, n-b 1 9
b Ramanayake . 41	
N. S. Sidhu not out 84	1/48 2/58 (2 wkts, 41.5 overs) 233

A. D. Jadeja, S. V. Manjrekar, †N. R. Mongia, J. Srinath, A. Kumble, A. R. Kapoor and B. K. V. Prasad did not bat.

Bowling: Vaas 9-0-52-1; Ramanayake 8.5-0-52-1; Jayasuriya 6-0-38-0; Muralitharan 10-0-46-0; Kalpage 8-0-44-0.

Umpires: C. J. Mitchley (South Africa) and N. T. Plews (England).

ENGLISH COUNTIES OVERSEAS, 1994-95

Scorecards of matches granted first-class status, played by English counties on pre-season tours to other countries.

BOLAND v WARWICKSHIRE

At Paarl, April 1, 2, 3. Warwickshire won by 104 runs. Toss: Warwickshire. County debut: N. V. Knight.

Claude Henderson, the Boland leg-spinner, took a hat-trick at the end of the first day, dismissing Neil Smith, Piper and Small.

Close of play: First day, Warwickshire 321-9 (P. A. Smith 33*, R. P. Davis 0*); Second day, Boland 51-0 (W. N. van As 20*, J. M. Henderson 22*).

Warwickshire

A. J. Moles c Brink c C. W. Henderson	83	– c Brink b Holdstock		10
N. V. Knight c Villet b Bredell	15	– c Germishuys b Drew		27
T. L. Penney b Erasmus	10	– not out		77
*D. A. Reeve c Villet b C. W. Henderson	107			
G. Welch lbw b Drew	4	– (4) c Erasmus b C. W. Henderson		4
D. R. Brown c Germishuys b Bredell	22	– st Germishuys b Drew		16
P. A. Smith not out	33			
N. M. K. Smith c C. W. Henderson	31			
†K. J. Piper b C. W. Henderson	0	– (7) not out		1
G. C. Small lbw b C. W. Henderson	0			
R. P. Davis not out	0	– (5) lbw b Erasmus		0
B 8, l-b 1, w 3, n-b 4	16	B 3, l-b 3, w 1, n-b 1		8

1/24 2/55 3/143 4/162 5/242   (9 wkts dec.) 321   1/17 2/51 3/71   (5 wkts dec.) 143
6/275 7/321 8/321 9/321   4/72 5/138

Bowling: *First Innings*—Bredell 15-1-70-2; Holdstock 12-1-46-0; Jackson 5-2-21-0; Erasmus 9-1-30-1; C. W. Henderson 31-9-77-95-5; Drew 28-9-50-1. *Second Innings*—Bredell 6-0-24-0; Holdstock 6-1-14-1; C. W. Henderson 15-2-60-1; Drew 10-1-37-2; Erasmus 5-3-2-1.

Boland

W. N. van As b Small	0	– c Knight b Davis		22
J. M. Henderson c Reeve b Small	4	– c Piper b N. M. K. Smith		36
J. M. Villet b Welch	12	– b N. M. K. Smith		3
K. C. Jackson c Piper b Welch	6	– c Piper b Brown		40
†L-M. Germishuys c Piper b P. A. Smith	37	– (9) b Davis		47
M. M. Brink c Reeve b N. M. K. Smith	2	– (7) c Reeve b N. M. K. Smith		23
*M. Erasmus lbw b Davis	11	– (8) c Piper b N. M. K. Smith		54
A. T. Holdstock b Davis	0	– (5) c Welch b N. M. K. Smith		50
C. W. Henderson not out	7	– (10) c Reeve b Davis		12
M. S. Bredell lbw b P. A. Smith	0	– (6) b Brown		0
B. J. Drew c Knight b Davis	3	– not out		8
L-b 5, w 1	6	B 2, l-b 12, w 3		17

1/0 2/11 3/24 4/35 5/40   88   1/63 2/72 3/101 4/134 5/134   272
6/75 7/75 8/77 9/77   6/178 7/200 8/213 9/242

Bowling: *First Innings*—Small 5-2-9-2; Brown 5-3-8-0; Welch 7-2-15-2; N. M. K. Smith 7-0-28-1; Davis 4.5-0-11-3; P. A. Smith 2-1-7-2. *Second Innings*—Small 7-2-29-0; Brown 11-0-53-2; N. M. K. Smith 20-0-76-5; Davis 19.2-4-36-3; Welch 9-2-24-0; Reeve 3-0-17-0; P. A. Smith 5-0-11-0; Knight 2-0-12-0.

Umpires: W. Richards and A. van Wyk.

MASHONALAND SELECT XI v NORTHAMPTONSHIRE

At Harare Sports Club, Harare, April 4, 5, 6. Mashonaland Select XI won by six wickets.
Toss: Mashonaland Select XI.

Neil Mallender returned to Northamptonshire after eight seasons with Somerset. Evans,
having to attend a court hearing for a traffic offence, retired overnight on the first day and
returned at the fall of the ninth wicket. The next day, he scored 102 in 76 balls as
Mashonaland Select XI won with 8.1 overs to spare, recording the highest fourth-innings
total in Zimbabwean cricket history.

Close of play: First day, Mashonaland Select XI 14-2 (G. W. Flower 1*, C. N. Evans 4*);
Second day, Northamptonshire 166-6 (A. J. Lamb 44*).

Northamptonshire

R. R. Montgomerie c Gilmour b Evans	18	– c A. Flower b Strang	33
A. Fordham c Rudd b A. Flower	48	– c Wishart b Olonga	36
R. J. Bailey c A. Flower b Whittall	19	– c Gilmour b Olonga	21
M. B. Loye c Gilmour b Strang	3	– c and b Olonga	3
*A. J. Lamb c Whittall b G. W. Flower	62	– c Gilmour b Strang	72
J. N. Snape c Strang b Whittall	87	– (8) c Olonga b Strang	14
A. L. Penberthy c G. W. Flower b Olonga	13	– (6) c Gilmour b G. W. Flower	21
†D. Ripley not out	10	– (7) run out	0
J. G. Hughes (did not bat)		– c Gilmour b Whittall	11
N. A. Mallender (did not bat)		– c G. W. Flower b Strang	0
J. P. Taylor (did not bat)		– not out	0
B 11, l-b 2, w 1, n-b 2	16	B 6, l-b 2, w 3, n-b 1	12

1/73 2/73 3/94 4/96 5/221   (7 wkts dec.) 276   1/62 2/88 3/92 4/105 5/156   223
6/249 7/276   6/166 7/202 8/215 9/215

Bowling: *First Innings*—Strang 28-7-59-1; Olonga 16-2-40-1; Evans 12-1-39-1; Whittall
16.3-6-54-2; A. Flower 6-1-13-1; Rudd 3-0-20-0; G. W. Flower 12-5-28-1; Rennie
7-2-10-0. *Second Innings*—Strang 27-9-83-4; Olonga 18-3-53-3; Whittall 9.1-0-48-1;
Wishart 6-1-11-0; Evans 6-1-10-0; G. W. Flower 5-3-8-1; Rennie 1-0-2-0.

Mashonaland Select XI

G. W. Flower c Ripley b Taylor	1	– c Lamb b Snape	119
J. R. Craig b Taylor	4	– b Bailey	63
G. J. Rennie c Penberthy b Taylor	2	– c Fordham b Hughes	47
C. N. Evans not out	6	– c Hughes b Taylor	102
*A. Flower c Lamb b Penberthy	24	– not out	57
G. J. Whittall c Lamb b Mallender	6	– not out	10
C. B. Wishart c Taylor b Mallender	11		
†A. R. G. Gilmour c Snape b Hughes	10		
B. C. Strang c Snape b Penberthy	4		
H. K. Olonga b Mallender	0		
T. D. B. Rudd c Ripley b Taylor	9		
B 2, l-b 4	6	B 13, l-b 6	19

1/7 2/9 3/18 4/39 5/55   83   1/100 2/207 3/285 4/380 (4 wkts) 417
6/55 7/59 8/64 9/81

In the first innings C. N. Evans, when 4, retired at 14 and resumed at 81.

Bowling: *First Innings*—Taylor 15-8-28-4; Hughes 14.5-6-16-1; Penberthy 8-4-12-2;
Mallender 8-1-21-3. *Second Innings*—Taylor 21.5-1-99-1; Hughes 11-2-46-1; Penberthy
14-4-55-0; Mallender 11-3-47-0; Bailey 13.1-0-89-1; Snape 9.5-0-62-1.

Umpires: G. Evans and K. Kanjee.

MATABELELAND v GLAMORGAN

At Bulawayo Athletic Club, April 11, 12, 13. Matabeleland won by 159 runs. Toss: Glamorgan.

Close of play: First day, Glamorgan 14-1 (A. Dale 7*, D. L. Hemp 2*); Second day, Matabeleland 123-3 (G. J. Whittall 8*).

Matabeleland

J. R. Craig c Croft b Watkin	3	– b Dale	22
K. J. Davies c Maynard b Watkin	3	– b Croft	43
M. D. Abrams c Watkin b Thomas	64	– c Maynard b Thomas	50
G. J. Whittall c Maynard b Watkin	3	– c Morris b Watkin	12
M. H. Dekker b Dale	0	– (6) st Maynard b Croft	92
H. H. Streak c Hemp b Barwick	98	– (8) not out	11
*J. A. Rennie c Hemp b Barwick	31	– (9) not out	4
M. J. Hammett not out	40		
†T. N. Madondo lbw b Kendrick	48	– (7) st Maynard b Croft	36
G. Peck (did not bat)		– (5) b Kendrick	17
B 9, l-b 3	12	L-b 7	7

1/9 2/10 3/14 4/23 5/147   (8 wkts dec.) 302   1/33 2/112 3/123   (7 wkts dec.) 294
6/204 7/211 8/302   4/134 5/169
                                        6/261 7/282

H. K. Olonga did not bat.

Bowling: *First Innings*—Watkin 20-5-70-3; Thomas 22-2-79-1; Dale 7-0-24-1; Barwick 17-8-36-2; Butcher 4-0-18-0; Kendrick 18.1-6-45-1; Croft 12-4-18-0. *Second Innings*—Watkin 15-3-60-1; Thomas 8-1-30-1; Dale 8-1-27-1; Kendrick 15-2-60-1; Croft 24-8-82-3; Butcher 5-1-28-0.

Glamorgan

A. Dale b Olonga	26	– c Rennie b Olonga	15
*H. Morris c Madondo b Streak	2	– lbw b Whittall	12
D. L. Hemp c Madondo b Streak	11	– c Streak b Whittall	69
†M. P. Maynard c Olonga b Rennie	101	– (7) c Peck b Streak	12
P. A. Cottey run out	24	– (4) c Rennie b Whittall	21
R. D. B. Croft c Streak b Dekker	60	– (8) c Streak b Whittall	25
G. P. Butcher c Davies b Rennie	6	– (6) b Whittall	1
N. M. Kendrick not out	16	– (9) c Madondo b Streak	2
S. D. Thomas not out	0	– (5) c Streak b Whittall	0
S. L. Watkin (did not bat)		– not out	3
S. R. Barwick (did not bat)		– b Streak	1
B 7, l-b 1, w 5, n-b 7	20	L-b 6, w 2, n-b 2	10

1/4 2/28 3/68 4/138 5/203   (7 wkts dec.) 266   1/25 2/111 3/111 4/113 5/130   171
6/223 7/261   6/136 7/157 8/164 9/166

In the second innings H. Morris, when 7, retired hurt at 40 and resumed at 157.

Bowling: *First Innings*—Olonga 13-2-55-1; Streak 15-5-26-2; Rennie 14-3-47-2; Whittall 6-0-30-0; Peck 9-2-43-0; Abrams 5-2-19-0; Dekker 15-3-38-1. *Second Innings*—Olonga 6-2-30-1; Streak 11.1-0-47-3; Rennie 6-1-27-0; Whittall 15-4-56-6; Peck 3-1-5-0.

Umpires: K. Kanjee and R. Tiffin.

CRICKET IN AUSTRALIA, 1994-95

By JOHN MACKINNON

The best of the 1994-95 Australian season was kept until last. Queensland's first Sheffield Shield touched many more hearts than the exploits of an erratic, injury-prone English touring team or the precocious performances of Australia A in the World Series. That Australia prevailed over all opposition with something to spare was generally expected. Queensland's triumph, after 62 seasons without success, was less predictable, at least until their last league game in Hobart, where victory kept them on top of the table so that Brisbane hosted the final.

They tied on points with South Australia, but had a superior quotient (runs per wicket scored divided by runs per wicket conceded). Only once in the 13-year history of Shield finals have the visitors prevailed and South Australia never looked likely to do so. Home town celebrations were under way from the first day of the match and Queensland's victory, by an innings and 101, ended Australian sport's most famous losing streak and longest-running joke. It was just a pity that construction work to enlarge the Gabba was in progress, making the venue appear rather makeshift for such an auspicious occasion.

First-class cricket under lights made its debut in Perth, followed by games in Sydney and Melbourne, each team playing one floodlit match. The response was variable – only 6,689 at the inaugural match, down to 4,812 at the SCG, both for games played in indifferent weather. In much better conditions, 14,744 watched at the MCG, but this was pretty poor too. Those who were there complained that the yellow ball was virtually impossible to see. Some players seemed to overcome that problem, however, not least Dean Jones, who helped himself to a nocturnal 324 not out against South Australia, and Darren Lehmann, 202 not out in the same match. For 1995-96, the Australian Cricket Board planned six day/night games, with each side playing two, in an effort to lure more spectators back to the grounds. Whether further refinements to yellow balls and black sightscreens are required remains to be seen, but at least the players continued to dress in their traditional whites. In the limited-overs game, however, Victoria introduced an innovation: dark blue shorts were deemed both practical (except on cold days) and presumably sightly. There were no prizes for the best legs and certainly none from the anti-skin-cancer lobby, who saw the idea as an ill-advised publicity stunt.

Though they led the table for much of the season, Queensland's progress to their title had its fair share of setbacks, especially when they suffered heavy defeats by New South Wales in Sydney, by Western Australia in Brisbane, and South Australia in Adelaide a fortnight before they met in the final. John Buchanan, in his first year as coach, had a useful mix of youth in batting, plus Allan Border, and experience in bowling, mostly from local sources, which had not always been the case. The influence of Border, omnipresent after leaving international cricket, could not be overstated, especially in the middle-order batting, where Stuart Law, Martin Love and Jimmy Maher came of age. Many expected that, the Shield gained, Border would retire from the first-class game too, but in July, shortly before his 40th birthday, he announced his intention to carry on for another season.

Matthew Hayden could not quite repeat his phenomenal scoring feats of 1993-94, but he and the dashing Trevor Barsby formed a classic left-hand/right-hand opening pair. The top six in the order thus remained settled, an important ingredient of a successful campaign. The bowling had depth in seam, plus the dependable Paul Jackson with left-arm spin. Carl Rackemann and Dirk Tazelaar had wonderful seasons, with 99 wickets between them. Rackemann's reward for what was, especially for him, an emotional Shield win, was to fly out to the West Indies to replace Craig McDermott, play one inconsequential game and then hot-foot it to The Oval as Surrey's overseas player. Greg Rowell and Mike Kasprowicz have already done much for Queensland and on their shoulders will rest much responsibility for the future. But it was Andy Bichel, in his first Shield match of the season, who bowled out Tasmania in Hobart to sneak a place in the final. While Ian Healy was captain in name, he and McDermott could play only one Shield match each. Law proved a most able deputy and Wade Seccombe recovered from a broken collar-bone, sustained in a terrible collision with Tazelaar in the field, to keep wicket competently.

South Australia were worthy finalists, in both the Shield and Mercantile Mutual Cup. On their good days, and there were many of them, their batting was a delight; and their first-day collapse in the Shield final at Brisbane was a dreadful anticlimax. Even after Greg Blewett's deserved promotion to the Test team, they found an able replacement in Ben Johnson, not only as opening batsman but also as a medium-pace partnership-breaker. Jamie Siddons, the captain, had a vintage year, as did Lehmann, Jamie Brayshaw and Paul Nobes. Between them, they totted up nearly 4,000 runs and 14 hundreds, all at a rate of knots. There was a big improvement in their bowling, for which coach Jeff Hammond must take credit. The fastish left-armer, Mark Harrity, Shane George and Peter McIntyre not only bowled sides out but bowled themselves into the Young Australia tour of England. The selection of McIntyre as a secondary leg-spinning weapon in the Adelaide Test failed, but 40 wickets for the season put him on a level with Shane Warne as the country's most successful spinner.

Dean Jones was the focal point of Victoria's efforts. He topped the national averages, renounced his much-publicised international retirement and launched into television commentary. In all of this, his batting feats were quite the most convincing. Jones's early form was so good that nearly 30,000 turned up to his testimonial "farewell" at the MCG. Seeing a possible role as captain of Australia A, he then revoked his retirement, but the selectors remained unimpressed. His fellow-players, however, voted him their cricketer of the year, as did the umpires – proving him to be the man of the law and the people. Certainly he has achieved results. Victoria won all their matches in the limited-overs Mercantile Mutual Cup, triumphing – in their shorts – over South Australia in the final. Left-arm pace bowler Troy Corbett and Jason Bakker, both new to this level, undid South Australia's powerful batting line-up with four wickets each. Victoria also chalked up five Shield wins, normally more than enough to qualify for the final. This was no mean effort as injury played havoc with the bowling resources. Merv Hughes, predictably, fell into this category, as did Simon Cook and the admirable Corbett. In the final match, Tony Dodemaide was recalled to bolster a willing but very raw attack. Warne's international commitments permitted him only two Shield games. One player to benefit from Jones's example was the tall left-hander Matthew Elliott. Likened to Bill Lawry (for his build rather than his method), he became an opening batsman of genuine stature, on equal terms with Hayden as an understudy to Mark Taylor and Michael Slater in the Test team. But Brad Hodge's second season became an ordeal, after he had come close to 1,000 runs in 1993-94; the experience of lean times did not rest easily with him and next year will test his resolve.

Western Australia's season got off to a choppy start on and off the field. Geoff Marsh's decision to call it a day at 35 left them without a captain: Damien Martyn, all of 23 years old, took over. Then Tim Zoehrer's turbulent career was effectively concluded by the recruitment of young wicket-keeper/batsman Adam Gilchrist from New South Wales. Zoehrer was not amused and made no secret of his feelings towards his erstwhile employers. Three early defeats left Western Australia at the bottom of the table at Christmas, but they recovered so strongly, with three consecutive victories culminating in a win over Queensland at Brisbane, that they actually led the table for a week. A narrow defeat, when they fell nine short of a target of 407 in Adelaide, ended their chances. In spite of Mark Lavender's stout-hearted efforts, the batting was surprisingly brittle, with Martyn and Justin Langer both disappointing. Langer scored virtually half his runs in one innings against New South Wales, but (unlike Martyn) was selected for the senior tour of the West Indies and the junior tour of England. Tom Moody scored 272 on Hobart's feather-bed but otherwise did his best work with the ball. Jo Angel was Western Australia's key bowler but Brendon Julian returned to form in mid-season, his resurgence continuing when he was summoned to the Caribbean as a replacement. After the season ended, Daryl Foster resigned as coach to concentrate his efforts on Kent, and was replaced by the former Test bowler Wayne Clark.

New South Wales's early form gave little indication of the shambles that was to follow. Though they lost in Melbourne, first-innings points followed by wins against England and Queensland suggested another successful year for the Shield and one-day champions. In the event, they won none of their five Mercantile Mutual games and lost eight out of ten Shield games, to leave retiring coach Steve Rixon with bitter memories. Most players from the previous campaign were available, except injured left-arm pace bowler Phil Alley. But 26 players came and went in the Shield, partly because the first-choice top five were often playing for Australia. Apart from the Test players, none could look back on their season with satisfaction: even Greg Matthews, sporting a hair transplant and seemingly forgiven for past transgressions, failed to staunch the run of failures. The 14-man junior team in England contained not one representative of New South Wales. The new coach, Geoff Lawson, will have plenty to ponder with the Association's new chief executive Brian Hughes, appointed to take over from Bob Radford, who retired after a 25-year reign.

Tasmania dropped from being beaten Shield finalists to take the wooden spoon, partly due to the other states realising how much their previous year's success had owed to gratuitous declarations setting them achievable targets. Once opponents hardened their attitudes, Tasmania's bowling weakness was inevitably exposed. Their latest import, Leicestershire's David Millns, earned them a mere 18 wickets at 44. All-rounder Shaun Young had a splendid year with both bat and ball; he and the ubiquitous

Ricky Ponting toured England, Ponting having already cut his teeth with the senior side in New Zealand and the West Indies. David Boon appeared in the Shield – once – for the first time in two years.

FIRST-CLASS AVERAGES, 1994-95

BATTING

(Qualification: 500 runs)

	M	I	NO	R	HS	100s	Avge
D. M. Jones (*Vic.*)	11	21	3	1,251	324*	4	69.50
S. R. Waugh (*NSW*)	9	17	4	849	206	1	65.30
A. R. Border (*Qld*)	11	19	5	911	151*	2	65.07
R. T. Ponting (*Tas.*)	7	12	0	772	211	3	64.33
J. A. Brayshaw (*SA*)	12	22	6	1,012	134*	4	63.25
D. S. Lehmann (*SA*)	11	20	1	1,104	202*	3	58.10
G. S. Blewett (*SA*)	9	16	2	795	152	4	56.78
R. J. Tucker (*Tas.*)	11	19	7	673	140*	1	56.08
M. J. Slater (*NSW*)	9	17	0	896	176	3	52.70
S. Young (*Tas.*)	11	20	4	830	152*	2	51.87
T. M. Moody (*WA*)	11	20	2	919	272	1	51.05
M. A. Taylor (*NSW*)	8	15	0	751	150	2	50.06
M. T. G. Elliott (*Vic.*) . . .	11	21	0	1,029	171	3	49.00
M. E. Waugh (*NSW*)	9	17	0	827	140	3	48.64
J. D. Siddons (*SA*)	12	22	3	910	170	4	47.89
M. L. Hayden (*Qld*)	13	23	3	954	201*	2	47.70
M. L. Love (*Qld*)	13	23	0	1,097	187	3	47.69
S. G. Law (*Qld*)	12	20	1	894	145	4	47.05
M. P. Lavender (*WA*)	11	21	2	872	152	1	45.89
J. Cox (*Tas.*)	11	21	1	828	165	2	41.40
J. P. Maher (*Qld*)	13	22	5	700	100*	1	41.17
P. C. Nobes (*SA*)	12	22	0	896	110	3	40.72
B. A. Johnson (*SA*)	8	14	0	552	168	1	39.42
T. J. Barsby (*Qld*)	12	22	1	827	151	2	39.38
T. J. Nielsen (*SA*)	12	18	3	521	74*	0	34.73
M. J. Di Venuto (*Tas.*) . . .	11	20	0	656	119	1	32.80
G. B. Gardiner (*Vic.*)	11	19	0	596	64	0	31.36
D. R. Martyn (*WA*)	11	19	0	554	113	2	29.15
M. G. Bevan (*NSW*)	10	19	1	504	103	1	28.00
D. F. Hills (*Tas.*)	11	21	0	554	111	1	26.38

* Signifies not out.

BOWLING

(Qualification: 20 wickets)

	O	M	R	W	BB	5W/i	Avge
S. K. Warne (*Vic.*)	373.2	123	814	40	8-71	3	20.35
J. Angel (*WA*)	338.4	90	996	48	5-62	2	20.75
P. R. Reiffel (*Vic.*)	332.4	107	806	36	5-56	2	22.38
C. G. Rackemann (*Qld*) . . .	438.1	110	1,227	52	7-43	1	23.59
C. J. McDermott (*Qld*)	303.3	76	902	37	6-38	4	24.37
D. Tazelaar (*Qld*)	398.5	106	1,146	47	6-89	1	24.38

	O	M	R	W	BB	5W/i	Avge
M. S. Kasprowicz (*Qld*) ...	195.2	56	640	25	6-47	2	25.60
B. A. Reid (*WA*)	211.3	66	515	20	4-60	0	25.75
G. D. McGrath (*NSW*)....	218	68	613	23	5-50	1	26.65
T. M. Moody (*WA*)	319.1	93	766	28	4-42	0	27.35
B. P. Julian (*WA*)........	279	68	897	32	5-58	3	28.03
G. J. Rowell (*Qld*).......	355.2	104	952	33	4-17	0	28.84
P. W. Jackson (*Qld*)	374.4	115	905	28	3-54	0	32.32
S. P. George (*SA*)........	428.5	90	1,443	43	4-31	0	33.55
M. A. Harrity (*SA*)	238.1	54	767	22	5-92	1	34.86
P. E. McIntyre (*SA*)......	470.1	95	1,398	40	5-85	1	34.95
S. Young (*Tas.*)	381.3	97	1,128	32	5-56	2	35.25
T. F. Corbett (*Vic.*)	261.5	57	842	23	6-42	2	36.60
C. E. Coulson (*WA*).......	269	71	762	20	2-27	0	38.10

SHEFFIELD SHIELD, 1994-95

	Played	Won	Lost	Drawn	1st-inns Points	Points	Quotient
Queensland	10	6	3	1	2	38	1.317
South Australia	10	6	1	3	2	38	1.259
Victoria	10	5	4	1	4	33.1§	1.019
Western Australia	10	4	5	1	4	27.7§	1.086
New South Wales	10	2	8	0	6	16.8§	0.624
Tasmania	10	2	4	4	4	15.8§	0.849

Final: Queensland beat South Australia by an innings and 101 runs.

§ *Points deducted for slow over-rates.*

Outright win = 6 pts; lead on first innings in a drawn or lost game = 2 pts.
Quotient = runs per wicket scored divided by runs per wicket conceded.

Under Australian Cricket Board playing conditions, two extras are scored for every no-ball bowled whether scored off or not. Any runs scored off the bat are credited to the batsman, while byes and leg-byes are counted as no-balls, in accordance with Law 24.9, in addition to the initial penalty.

*In the following scores, * by the name of a team indicates that they won the toss.*

At Brisbane, October 13, 14, 15, 16. Drawn. Queensland 483 for eight dec. (T. J. Barsby 36, M. L. Love 187, S. G. Law 145, A. R. Border 33, Extras 33; C. D. Matthews four for 108) and 237 for six dec. (M. L. Love 116, J. P. Maher 49 not out; S. B. Oliver three for 36); Tasmania* 397 (J. Cox 79, M. J. Di Venuto 52, R. T. Ponting 119, S. Young 95, Extras 38; G. J. Rowell four for 83, D. Tazelaar three for 86) and 162 for seven (M. J. Di Venuto 51, R. T. Ponting 33). *Queensland 2 pts.*

In the first innings Love and Law added 326 for the third wicket, a Queensland record. C. G. Rackemann's second wicket made him Queensland's leading Shield wicket-taker, overtaking J. R. Thomson (328).

At Adelaide, October 19, 20, 21, 22. Drawn. Tasmania* 389 (J. Cox 59, M. J. Di Venuto 82, R. T. Ponting 45, R. J. Tucker 32, M. N. Atkinson 76 not out, C. R. Miller 34; M. J. Minagall seven for 152) and 262 (D. F. Hills 73, M. J. Di Venuto 33, S. Young 71; M. J. Minagall four for 111, P. E. McIntyre four for 62); South Australia 390 for nine dec. (G. S. Blewett 48, P. C. Nobes 43, J. A. Brayshaw 30, D. S. Lehmann 70, D. S. Webber 37, T. J. Nielsen 74 not out, Extras 36; M. A. Wasley three for 88) and 148 for three (P. C. Nobes 63, G. S. Blewett 32 not out). *South Australia 2 pts.*

At Brisbane, October 26, 27, 28. Queensland won by an innings and 202 runs. South Australia 139 (J. A. Brayshaw 46, D. S. Lehmann 30, D. S. Webber 31 not out; C. G. Rackemann seven for 43) and 147 (P. C. Nobes 38, D. S. Lehmann 48; G. J. Rowell four for 42, D. Tazelaar three for 76); Queensland* 488 for six dec. (T. J. Barsby 76, M. L. Hayden 80, M. L. Love 87, A. R. Border 151 not out, G. J. Rowell 42 not out). *Queensland 6 pts.*

At Melbourne, November 2, 3, 4, 5. Victoria won by eight wickets. New South Wales 256 (S. Lee 86, N. D. Maxwell 42; P. R. Reiffel five for 56) and 177 (K. J. Roberts 51; M. G. Hughes three for 42, P. R. Reiffel three for 39); Victoria* 255 (G. J. Clarke 48, D. M. Jones 94, G. B. Gardiner 36; W. J. Holdsworth five for 70, S. Lee three for 53) and 181 for two (D. M. Jones 103 not out, B. J. Hodge 42 not out). *Victoria 6 pts, New South Wales 2 pts.*
  Seven players made their first-class debuts – four for Victoria and three for New South Wales.

At Hobart, November 4, 5, 6, 7. Drawn. Tasmania* 457 for five dec. (M. J. Di Venuto 41, R. T. Ponting 211, R. J. Tucker 140 not out); Western Australia 502 for six (D. R. Martyn 113, T. M. Moody 272, G. B. Hogg 59 not out). *Western Australia 2 pts.*
  Ponting's 211, his maiden double-hundred, lasted 440 minutes and 401 balls and included 23 fours and one six; he and Tucker added 319 for the fifth wicket, a Tasmanian all-wicket record. T. M. Moody's career-best 272 lasted 404 minutes and 373 balls and included 34 fours and two sixes; he and Martyn added 279, a record for Western Australia's fourth wicket.

At Brisbane, November 11, 12, 13, 14. Queensland won by five wickets. Victoria* 224 (B. J. Hodge 49, G. B. Gardiner 39, M. G. Hughes 38 not out; C. G. Rackemann four for 31) and 349 for seven dec. (M. T. G. Elliott 76, B. J. Hodge 116, I. J. Harvey 62, P. R. Reiffel 32 not out; P. W. Jackson three for 83); Queensland 230 for nine dec. (S. G. Law 102, J. P. Maher 38; P. R. Reiffel five for 65) and 344 for five (M. L. Hayden 201 not out, J. P. Maher 61). *Queensland 6 pts, Victoria −0.9 pts.*
  Hayden's 201 not out, his maiden double-hundred, lasted 327 minutes and 239 balls and included 34 fours.

At Perth, November 12, 13, 14, 15. South Australia won by six wickets. Western Australia 254 (M. P. Lavender 152; T. B. A. May four for 77) and 266 (M. R. J. Veletta 66, T. M. Moody 31, B. P. Julian 51, Extras 31; T. B. A. May six for 80); South Australia* 272 (G. S. Blewett 152, T. B. A. May 36; J. Angel three for 90, B. A. Reid four for 60) and 250 for four (G. S. Blewett 71, D. S. Lehmann 41, J. A. Brayshaw 57 not out). *South Australia 6 pts, Western Australia −0.3 pts.*

At Melbourne, November 17, 18, 19, 20. Victoria won by 162 runs. Victoria 293 (D. M. Jones 126, G. B. Gardiner 64, S. K. Warne 34; C. D. Matthews three for 55, S. Young five for 68) and 283 (M. T. G. Elliott 58, D. M. Jones 76, I. A. Wrigglesworth 58; S. Young five for 56); Tasmania* 302 for seven dec. (D. F. Hills 40, M. J. Di Venuto 31, D. C. Boon 71, S. Young 30, M. A. Hatton 39 not out; S. K. Warne five for 104) and 112 (S. Young 45; T. F. Corbett six for 42). *Victoria 6 pts, Tasmania 2 pts.*

At Sydney, November 18, 19, 20, 21. New South Wales won by ten wickets. Queensland* 203 (T. J. Barsby 35, M. L. Love 42; A. J. Kershler five for 42) and 267 (T. J. Barsby 40, M. L. Love 38, A. R. Border 35, W. A. Seccombe 38, C. J. McDermott 52; G. R. J. Matthews three for 97); New South Wales 469 (M. A. Taylor 30, S. R. Waugh 64, M. E. Waugh 113, M. G. Bevan 103, G. R. J. Matthews 49, Extras 63; C. J. McDermott three for 96, C. G. Rackemann three for 82, A. Symonds three for 77) and two for no wkt. *New South Wales 6 pts.*

WESTERN AUSTRALIA v QUEENSLAND

At Perth, November 24, 25, 26, 27 (day/night). Queensland won by seven wickets. Queensland 6 pts, Western Australia 2 pts. Toss: Queensland.
  The inaugural first-class day/night match had little appeal for Western Australian players or spectators. The weather was untypically damp, the pitch helpful to seam; the home side, having gained a 45-run lead on first innings, collapsed in the dark, under lights, in their

second. Queensland then hit off the runs in daylight on the last day as Law and Border shared a decisive partnership of 122. Border's batting was also a feature of Queensland's first innings, but generally it was the pace bowlers, and especially Angel and Tazelaar, who dictated the terms.

Close of play: First day, Western Australia 279-8 (A. C. Gilchrist 51*, S. R. Cary 12*); Second day, Western Australia 31-4 (M. P. Lavender 5*); Third day, Queensland 54-1 (M. P. Mott 10*, M. L. Love 40*).

Western Australia

M. P. Lavender b Tazelaar	35	– lbw b Rackemann	20
M. R. J. Veletta c Hayden b Tazelaar	95	– c Mott b Tazelaar	4
J. L. Langer c Maher b Law	28	– b Tazelaar	12
*D. R. Martyn c Law b Rackemann	9	– (5) c Seccombe b Rackemann	0
T. M. Moody c Seccombe b Law	1	– (6) c Seccombe b Rowell	38
M. W. Goodwin b Rowell b Tazelaar	3	– (7) c Seccombe b Rackemann	17
†A. C. Gilchrist c Law b Rackemann	56	– (8) b Rowell	21
C. E. Coulson c sub b Tazelaar	10	– (9) lbw b Rowell	0
J. Angel c Seccombe b Tazelaar	7	– (4) lbw b Tazelaar	0
S. R. Cary b Rowell	12	– not out	4
B. A. Reid not out	0	– b Rowell	1
L-b 4, n-b 24	28	B 4, l-b 10, n-b 15	29

1/77 2/133 3/153 4/164 5/195   **284**   1/6 2/30 3/30 4/31 5/92   **146**
6/198 7/211 8/241 9/280   6/94 7/131 8/137 9/145

Bowling: *First Innings*—Rowell 28-8-74-1; Tazelaar 31.3-8-89-6; Rackemann 21-0-60-1; Law 17-2-43-2; Symonds 4-2-14-0. *Second Innings*—Rowell 20.3-11-17-4; Tazelaar 18-4-65-3; Rackemann 20-5-50-3.

Queensland

M. L. Hayden c Gilchrist b Angel	9	– c Gilchrist b Angel	2
M. P. Mott c Veletta b Coulson	9	– c Gilchrist b Angel	10
M. L. Love c Gilchrist b Cary	41	– c Moody b Angel	46
*S. G. Law c Veletta b Angel	7	– not out	62
A. R. Border c Gilchrist b Angel	73	– not out	54
J. P. Maher c Gilchrist b Coulson	40		
A. Symonds b Angel	26		
†W. A. Seccombe c Martyn b Reid	13		
G. J. Rowell c Gilchrist b Reid	3		
D. Tazelaar not out	1		
C. G. Rackemann c Moody b Reid	2		
L-b 7, n-b 8	15	L-b 6, n-b 12	18

1/20 2/24 3/34 4/96 5/180   **239**   1/2 2/58 3/70   **(3 wkts) 192**
6/205 7/232 8/234 9/237

Bowling: *First Innings*—Angel 22-10-53-4; Coulson 21-5-70-2; Reid 14.5-3-50-3; Cary 17-1-59-1. *Second Innings*—Angel 27-9-46-3; Reid 9-1-28-0; Cary 19.3-3-56-0; Coulson 16-7-36-0; Martyn 4-1-20-0.

Umpires: R. J. Evans and T. A. Prue.

At Sydney, December 9, 10, 11, 12 (day/night). Tasmania won by 51 runs. Tasmania* 350 for three dec. (D. F. Hills 30, J. Cox 122, M. J. Di Venuto 89, A. J. Daly 41 not out, S. Young 43 not out) and 238 for five dec. (D. F. Hills 53, M. J. Di Venuto 46, A. J. Daly 44, R. J. Tucker 32 not out); New South Wales 268 for five dec. (G. R. J. Matthews 34, S. Lee 100 not out, N. D. Maxwell 30 not out; S. Young three for 59) and 269 (R. J. Davison 44, S. R. Waugh 52, S. Lee 52; C. D. Matthews four for 65). *Tasmania 6 pts.*

At Adelaide, December 16, 17, 18, 19. South Australia won by 257 runs. South Australia* 428 (G. S. Blewett 50, B. A. Johnson 56, P. C. Nobes 97, D. S. Lehmann 109, P. E. McIntyre 30, J. D. Siddons 44; G. D. McGrath four for 90, G. R. Robertson five for 115) and 203 for four dec. (J. A. Brayshaw 73 not out, J. D. Siddons 60 not out); New South Wales 245 (M. J. Slater 51, M. A. Taylor 46, S. R. Waugh 43, M. E. Waugh 51; P. E. McIntyre three for 69, G. S. Blewett four for 39) and 129 (S. R. Waugh 42; S. P. George four for 41). *South Australia 6 pts.*

At Perth, December 16, 17, 18, 19. Victoria won by 28 runs. Victoria* 342 (M. T. G. Elliott 171, G. B. Gardiner 43, I. A. Wrigglesworth 31, D. S. Berry 39; J. Angel five for 87) and 161 (G. B. Gardiner 46; J. Angel four for 54, B. P. Julian three for 29); Western Australia 234 (M. P. Lavender 40, D. R. Martyn 35, T. M. Moody 55, M. W. Goodwin 31; D. W. Fleming four for 39) and 241 (M. P. Lavender 48, J. L. Langer 45, T. M. Moody 81, J. Stewart 31 not out; P. R. Reiffel three for 77, S. K. Warne four for 64). *Victoria 6 pts.*
   Western Australia's third consecutive home defeat.

At Perth, December 30, 31, January 1, 2. Western Australia won by ten wickets. New South Wales* 205 (R. J. Davison 35, B. E. McNamara 50, N. D. Maxwell 52, Extras 38; J. Angel five for 62, T. M. Moody three for 43) and 360 (R. J. Davison 33, P. A. Emery 92, N. D. Maxwell 91, Extras 38; J. Angel three for 112, B. P. Julian five for 58); Western Australia 542 for four dec. (M. P. Lavender 60, J. L. Langer 241 not out, D. R. Martyn 62, T. M. Moody 77, M. W. Goodwin 49 not out, Extras 52) and 26 for no wkt. *Western Australia 6 pts.*
   Langer's career-best 241 not out lasted 545 minutes and 456 balls and included 28 fours.

At Adelaide, December 31, January 1, 2, 3. South Australia won by an innings and 42 runs. South Australia* 524 for eight dec. (G. S. Blewett 112, P. C. Nobes 110, D. S. Lehmann 100, J. A. Brayshaw 134 not out, T. J. Nielsen 32; T. F. Corbett five for 108); Victoria 315 (M. T. G. Elliott 66, I. A. Wrigglesworth 43, D. M. Jones 33, P. R. Reiffel 49 not out; S. P. George three for 78, P. E. McIntyre five for 85) and 167 (D. M. Jones 43, W. G. Ayres 67; S. P. George four for 31, P. E. McIntyre four for 60). *South Australia 6 pts.*

At Perth, January 14, 15, 16, 17. Western Australia won by eight wickets. Tasmania* 236 (S. Young 45, C. R. Miller 47, Extras 38; B. P. Julian five for 63) and 236 (S. Young 51, D. J. Millns 51 not out; B. P. Julian five for 59); Western Australia 298 (M. R. J. Veletta 71, M. W. Goodwin 63, T. M. Moody 39, D. A. Fitzgerald 33 not out; D. J. Millns four for 81, S. Young four for 71) and 175 for two (M. P. Lavender 89, M. R. J. Veletta 32, M. W. Goodwin 39 not out). *Western Australia 6 pts.*

At Brisbane, January 20, 21, 22, 23. Western Australia won by 122 runs. Western Australia 214 (M. P. Lavender 38, M. W. Goodwin 37; G. J. Rowell four for 61) and 234 (J. Angel 41, J. L. Langer 43, M. W. Goodwin 37, G. B. Hogg 37; D. Tazelaar four for 71); Queensland* 204 (M. L. Hayden 47, T. J. Barsby 43, S. G. Law 30, J. P. Maher 30; J. Angel four for 70, B. P. Julian four for 51) and 122 (T. J. Barsby 35; J. Angel three for 25, T. M. Moody three for eight). *Western Australia 6 pts.*
   M. R. J. Veletta was fined $A500 for dissent when caught behind.

At Hobart, January 20, 21, 22, 23. New South Wales won by 97 runs. New South Wales* 487 for eight dec. (S. R. Waugh 206, M. G. Bevan 70, S. Lee 51, P. A. Emery 50 not out, G. R. Robertson 43; M. W. Ridgway three for 116) and 298 for two dec. (M. E. Waugh 132, M. J. Slater 70, S. R. Waugh 68 not out); Tasmania 446 for six dec. (M. J. Di Venuto 119, R. T. Ponting 58, A. J. Daly 37, S. Young 111 not out, R. J. Tucker 75; G. D. McGrath three for 99) and 242 (R. T. Ponting 134, M. N. Atkinson 32; G. D. McGrath five for 50, S. M. Thompson three for 67). *New South Wales 6 pts.*
   S. R. Waugh's 206 lasted 320 minutes and 257 balls and included 23 fours and one six.

At Sydney, January 27, 28, 29, 30. Victoria won by 254 runs. Victoria* 355 (M. T. G. Elliott 99, R. P. Larkin 35, G. B. Gardiner 42, I. J. Harvey 35, P. R. Reiffel 55, D. S. Berry 55; B. E. McNamara five for 72) and 299 for two dec. (R. P. Larkin 33, D. M. Jones 154 not out, B. J. Hodge 87 not out); New South Wales 250 (G. R. J. Matthews 59 retired hurt, S. Lee 46, P. A. Emery 34 not out; D. A. Emerson three for 62) and 150 (J. L. Arnberger 33, N. D. Maxwell 67; S. H. Cook three for 41, P. R. Reiffel three for 24). *Victoria 6 pts.*
   Victoria's first outright win in Sydney since January 1974.

At Hobart, January 27, 28, 29, 30. Drawn. South Australia* 352 (D. S. Webber 40, B. A. Johnson 47, J. A. Brayshaw 58, J. D. Siddons 105, T. J. Nielsen 71; M. W. Ridgway six for 79) and 284 for five dec. (B. A. Johnson 36, J. A. Brayshaw 100 not out, T. J. Nielsen 51 not out; D. J. Millns three for 67); Tasmania 354 for five dec. (D. F. Hills 36, J. Cox 165, R. T. Ponting 62, R. J. Tucker 35 not out; S. P. George three for 110) and 137 for four (M. N. Atkinson 59 not out, S. Young 38). *Tasmania 2 pts.*

At Melbourne, February 3, 4, 5, 6 (day/night). Drawn. Victoria* 572 for four dec. (M. T. G. Elliott 77, R. P. Larkin 69, D. M. Jones 324 not out, G. B. Gardiner 50); South Australia 363 (P. C. Nobes 72, D. S. Lehmann 48, P. E. McIntyre 32, J. A. Brayshaw 76, J. D. Siddons 45, T. J. Nielsen 36; P. R. Reiffel four for 61, I. J. Harvey three for 60) and 390 for six (D. S. Lehmann 202 not out, J. A. Brayshaw 104). *Victoria 2 pts.*
   Jones's 324 not out, his maiden triple-century, lasted 523 minutes and 448 balls and included 28 fours and two sixes; only W. H. Ponsford (four times) and H. S. T. L. Hendry have made higher scores for Victoria. When 132, he passed W. M. Lawry's Victorian record of 7,618 first-class runs. Lehmann's 202 not out lasted 263 minutes and 208 balls and included 31 fours and one six.

At Brisbane, February 8, 9, 10. Queensland won by ten wickets. Queensland 400 for eight dec. (M. L. Hayden 52, T. J. Barsby 37, M. L. Love 98, A. R. Border 94, W. A. Seccombe 35, Extras 31; S. M. Thompson three for 98, B. E. McNamara four for 95) and 34 for no wkt; New South Wales* 196 (K. J. Roberts 33, P. A. Emery 39 not out, N. D. Maxwell 30; G. J. Rowell three for 67, D. Tazelaar three for 74) and 237 (R. J. Davison 58, J. L. Arnberger 36, M. W. Patterson 39; G. J. Rowell three for 84, C. G. Rackemann four for 60). *Queensland 6 pts, New South Wales −0.6 pts.*
   In New South Wales's second innings, Seccombe was concussed and broke his collar-bone after colliding with Tazelaar, who nevertheless caught a skier off McNamara.

At Adelaide, February 15, 16, 17, 18. South Australia won by eight runs. South Australia* 397 (P. C. Nobes 101, B. A. Johnson 81, D. S. Lehmann 91, T. J. Nielsen 35, Extras 32; S. R. Cary three for 95, T. M. Moody four for 51) and 342 for six dec. (B. A. Johnson 168, D. S. Lehmann 78); Western Australia 333 (M. R. J. Veletta 42, T. M. Moody 75, A. C. Gilchrist 126, C. E. Coulson 30; M. A. Harrity five for 92, S. P. George three for 94) and 398 (M. P. Lavender 90, D. R. Martyn 89, T. M. Moody 79, A. C. Gilchrist 39; S. P. George four for 96). *South Australia 6 pts.*
   Chasing 407, Western Australia were 370 for nine; last pair Coulson and Cary managed 28.

At Melbourne, February 15, 16, 17, 18. Queensland won by six wickets. Victoria* 293 (M. T. G. Elliott 111, D. M. Jones 32, G. B. Gardiner 40, D. S. Berry 41; C. G. Rackemann three for 63) and 201 (D. M. Jones 76, D. S. Berry 30, Extras 30; M. S. Kasprowicz six for 47, P. W. Jackson three for 54); Queensland 294 for nine dec. (M. L. Hayden 89, T. J. Barsby 32, A. R. Border 38 not out, J. P. Maher 48; B. A. Williams five for 88, D. J. Saker three for 76) and 202 for four (T. J. Barsby 51, M. L. Love 63, A. R. Border 38 not out, J. P. Maher 41 not out; B. B. J. Doyle three for 59). *Queensland 6 pts.*
   Border chipped a bone in his arm in the first innings and needed pain-killers for the rest of the game.

At Sydney, March 9, 10, 11, 12. Western Australia won by four wickets. New South Wales 201 for five dec. (R. J. Davison 56, G. R. J. Matthews 58 not out) and 152 (M. G. Bevan 44; J. Angel three for 34, T. M. Moody four for 42); Western Australia* 150 for three dec. (M. P. Lavender 66 not out, T. M. Moody 71 not out; G. R. J. Matthews three for 35) and 204 for six (M. W. Goodwin 33, A. C. Gilchrist 45, G. B. Hogg 50 not out, B. P. Julian 32 not out; G. R. J. Matthews four for 72). *Western Australia 6 pts, New South Wales 1.4 pts.*
   In Western Australia's first innings, Matthews took three wickets in four balls.

At Adelaide, March 9, 10, 11. South Australia won by an innings and 88 runs. South Australia 543 (P. C. Nobes 70, J. D. Siddons 170, D. S. Lehmann 60, D. S. Webber 37, T. J. Nielsen 32, S. P. George 62, Extras 42; M. S. Kasprowicz five for 155); Queensland* 174 (S. G. Law 81; M. A. Harrity four for 39, P. E. McIntyre three for ten) and 281 (A. R. Border 31, J. P. Maher 41, G. A. J. Fitness 71, M. S. Kasprowicz 30; S. P. George four for 66, B. A. Johnson three for 16). *South Australia 6 pts.*

At Hobart, March 9, 10, 11, 12. Tasmania won by 57 runs. Tasmania 273 (D. F. Hills 30, R. J. Tucker 93, M. W. Ridgway 70; D. J. Saker three for 63, J. R. Bakker four for 40) and 413 for four dec. (J. Cox 86, A. J. Daly 48, S. Young 152 not out, R. J. Tucker 83 not out); Victoria* 325 (M. T. G. Elliott 140, D. M. Jones 43, G. B. Gardiner 37, D. S. Berry 47; M. W. Ridgway six for 29, S. Young three for 53) and 304 (R. P. Larkin 116, D. M. Jones 32, G. B. Gardiner 49; C. R. Miller three for 77, J. P. Marquet three for 53). *Tasmania 6 pts, Victoria 2 pts.*

At Sydney, March 16, 17, 18, 19. South Australia won by 122 runs. South Australia* 301 (B. A. Johnson 38, J. D. Siddons 30, D. S. Lehmann 40, J. A. Brayshaw 53, D. S. Webber 30, T. J. Nielsen 43; N. D. Maxwell three for 48) and 349 for four dec. (B. A. Johnson 34, J. D. Siddons 149 not out, D. S. Lehmann 61, D. S. Webber 78 not out); New South Wales 305 for nine dec. (M. G. Bevan 77, G. R. J. Matthews 80; M. A. Harrity three for 52) and 223 (J. L. Arnberger 63, N. D. Maxwell 41; P. E. McIntyre three for 96). *South Australia 6 pts, New South Wales 2 pts.*

At Hobart, March 16, 17, 18, 19. Queensland won by 221 runs. Queensland 234 (M. L. Hayden 44, S. G. Law 102, A. J. Bichel 42; G. J. Denton three for 44) and 397 for four dec. (T. J. Barsby 56, S. G. Law 138, A. R. Border 124 not out, J. P. Maher 33 not out); Tasmania* 155 (J. Cox 34, Extras 30; C. G. Rackemann three for 31) and 255 (D. F. Hills 111, A. J. Daly 45; A. J. Bichel six for 79). *Queensland 6 pts, Tasmania −0.2 pts.*

Queensland captain Law scored a century in each innings and ensured his team a home final. Bichel took three wickets in an over on his way to finishing off Tasmania's second innings.

At Melbourne, March 16, 17, 18, 19. Victoria won by 103 runs. Victoria* 280 (R. P. Larkin 60, J. R. Bakker 75; J. Angel three for 64) and 229 (D. S. Berry 35, A. I. C. Dodemaide 39, B. A. Williams 32 not out; T. M. Moody three for 30); Western Australia 221 (M. R. J. Veletta 45, G. B. Hogg 71, K. M. Harvey 41; D. J. Saker four for 39, J. R. Bakker three for 40) and 185 (M. P. Lavender 82; A. I. C. Dodemaide five for 42, B. B. J. Doyle three for 44). *Victoria 6 pts.*

FINAL

QUEENSLAND v SOUTH AUSTRALIA

At Brisbane, March 24, 25, 26, 27, 28. Queensland won by an innings and 101 runs. Toss: South Australia.

Queensland's victory was virtually settled from the moment Siddons chose to bat. South Australia's innings fell apart: they were 30 for four in just over an hour, and a total of 214 on a good pitch was quite inadequate. For the next three days, only spasmodic rain breaks held up Queensland's batting orgy. Hayden and Barsby were untroubled in opening with 144, then Love joined Barsby to add 192. Barsby showed rare restraint early on, but then reverted to his flamboyant style, batting in all for six hours and 151 runs and bringing the best out of his younger partners. Love responded with an emphatic hundred of his own and Border looked certain to follow suit, in what he had hinted might be his last match, until he dragged a wide ball on to his stumps. Queensland's 664 was the highest score in a Shield final and their highest at the Gabba. Resuming 450 behind, South Australia's second innings was little more than academic although Nobes and Webber showed some spirit. Near-capacity crowds attended the match and there was plenty of emotion when Law took the trophy to end Queensland's 68-year-long wait.

Close of play: First day, Queensland 36-0 (T. J. Barsby 11*, M. L. Hayden 14*); Second day, Queensland 409-3 (M. L. Love 114*, A. R. Border 26*); Third day, Queensland 501-4 (A. R. Border 76*, J. P. Maher 6*); Fourth day, South Australia 59-2 (P. C. Nobes 24*, D. S. Lehmann 14*).

South Australia

B. A. Johnson c Hayden b Bichel	4	– c Hayden b Jackson	10
P. C. Nobes c Law b Tazelaar	0	– b Tazelaar	100
*J. D. Siddons c Border b Rackemann	8	– c Seccombe b Rackemann	3
D. S. Lehmann c Seccombe b Tazelaar	12	– c Tazelaar b Bichel	62
J. A. Brayshaw run out	53	– c Seccombe b Rackemann	16
D. S. Webber c Seccombe b Bichel	33	– c and b Law	91
†T. J. Nielsen b Jackson	53	– lbw b Tazelaar	0
J. N. Gillespie c Seccombe b Rackemann	18	– c Rackemann b Jackson	39
P. E. McIntyre c Rackemann b Jackson	9	– c Law b Bichel	2
S. P. George b Rackemann	15	– c Bichel b Jackson	4
M. A. Harrity not out	0	– not out	0
B 1, n-b 8	9	B 4, l-b 8, n-b 10	22

1/4 2/6 3/26 4/30 5/93   214   1/31 2/34 3/142 4/194 5/253   349
6/126 7/179 8/189 9/210   6/253 7/314 8/335 9/347

Bowling: *First Innings*—Bichel 19-4-54-2; Tazelaar 20-3-45-2; Rackemann 18-6-54-3; Law 10-3-26-0; Jackson 14.4-5-34-2. *Second Innings*—Bichel 29-6-90-2; Tazelaar 21-6-65-2; Rackemann 30-10-86-2; Jackson 37.2-9-81-3; Border 1-0-1-0; Law 3-1-14-1.

Queensland

T. J. Barsby c Gillespie b Johnson	151	P. W. Jackson not out	11
M. L. Hayden c Nielsen b Harrity	74	D. Tazelaar b McIntyre	22
M. L. Love c Nielsen b Brayshaw	146	C. G. Rackemann lbw b McIntyre	7
*S. G. Law c Webber b George	11	B 1, l-b 14, w 3, n-b 34	52
A. R. Border b Johnson	98		
J. P. Maher c Nielsen b Gillespie	36	1/144 2/336 3/376	664
†W. A. Seccombe c Harrity b Gillespie	18	4/479 5/553 6/565	
A. J. Bichel c Nielsen b Gillespie	38	7/618 8/618 9/652	

Bowling: Harrity 46-12-129-1; George 33-8-102-1; Gillespie 35-10-112-3; McIntyre 49.5-10-176-2; Johnson 22-1-96-2; Brayshaw 14.5-5-34-1.

Umpires: D. B. Hair and P. D. Parker.

SHEFFIELD SHIELD WINNERS

1892-93	Victoria	1915-19	No competition
1893-94	South Australia	1919-20	New South Wales
1894-95	Victoria	1920-21	New South Wales
1895-96	New South Wales	1921-22	Victoria
1896-97	New South Wales	1922-23	New South Wales
1897-98	Victoria	1923-24	Victoria
1898-99	Victoria	1924-25	Victoria
1899-1900	New South Wales	1925-26	New South Wales
1900-01	Victoria	1926-27	South Australia
1901-02	New South Wales	1927-28	Victoria
1902-03	New South Wales	1928-29	New South Wales
1903-04	New South Wales	1929-30	Victoria
1904-05	New South Wales	1930-31	Victoria
1905-06	New South Wales	1931-32	New South Wales
1906-07	New South Wales	1932-33	New South Wales
1907-08	Victoria	1933-34	Victoria
1908-09	New South Wales	1934-35	Victoria
1909-10	South Australia	1935-36	South Australia
1910-11	New South Wales	1936-37	Victoria
1911-12	New South Wales	1937-38	New South Wales
1912-13	South Australia	1938-39	South Australia
1913-14	New South Wales	1939-40	New South Wales
1914-15	Victoria	1940-46	No competition

1946-47	Victoria	1971-72	Western Australia
1947-48	Western Australia	1972-73	Western Australia
1948-49	New South Wales	1973-74	Victoria
1949-50	New South Wales	1974-75	Western Australia
1950-51	Victoria	1975-76	South Australia
1951-52	New South Wales	1976-77	Western Australia
1952-53	South Australia	1977-78	Western Australia
1953-54	New South Wales	1978-79	Victoria
1954-55	New South Wales	1979-80	Victoria
1955-56	New South Wales	1980-81	Western Australia
1956-57	New South Wales	1981-82	South Australia
1957-58	New South Wales	1982-83	New South Wales
1958-59	New South Wales	1983-84	Western Australia
1959-60	New South Wales	1984-85	New South Wales
1960-61	New South Wales	1985-86	New South Wales
1961-62	New South Wales	1986-87	Western Australia
1962-63	Victoria	1987-88	Western Australia
1963-64	South Australia	1988-89	Western Australia
1964-65	New South Wales	1989-90	New South Wales
1965-66	New South Wales	1990-91	Victoria
1966-67	Victoria	1991-92	Western Australia
1967-68	Western Australia	1992-93	New South Wales
1968-69	South Australia	1993-94	New South Wales
1969-70	Victoria	1994-95	Queensland
1970-71	South Australia		

New South Wales have won the Shield 42 times, Victoria 25, Western Australia 13, South Australia 12, Queensland 1, Tasmania 0.

MERCANTILE MUTUAL INSURANCE CUP

Note: Matches in this section were not first-class.

At Brisbane, October 9. Queensland won by four wickets. Tasmania* 218 for six (50 overs) (J. Cox 75, R. T. Ponting 59, S. Young 30); Queensland 219 for six (46.5 overs) (T. J. Barsby 101, M. L. Love 46).

At Perth, October 14 (day/night). Victoria won by six wickets. Western Australia* 177 (44.1 overs) (D. R. Martyn 41, A. C. Gilchrist 31; T. F. Corbett three for 27); Victoria 178 for four (44 overs) (G. J. Clarke 39, M. T. G. Elliott 35, D. M. Jones 30; J. Stewart three for 49).

At North Sydney, October 16. South Australia won by five wickets. New South Wales* 272 for eight (50 overs) (R. Chee Quee 47, M. T. Haywood 87, K. J. Roberts 32, M. W. Patterson 36; S. P. George four for 58); South Australia 275 for five (48.4 overs) (D. S. Lehmann 106, P. C. Nobes 43, J. D. Siddons 77).

At Adelaide, October 23. South Australia won by ten wickets. Tasmania* 215 (48.1 overs) (M. J. Di Venuto 76, D. F. Hills 38; S. P. George four for 33); South Australia 217 for no wkt (37.1 overs) (D. S. Lehmann 142 not out, P. C. Nobes 64 not out).

At Hobart, October 29. Victoria won by 78 runs. Victoria 234 for six (50 overs) (G. J. Clarke 35, D. M. Jones 113, B. J. Hodge 37); Tasmania* 156 for nine (50 overs) (B. A. Robinson 59 not out; P. R. Reiffel four for 14, T. F. Corbett three for 21).

At Brisbane, October 30. Queensland won by three runs. Queensland 245 (50 overs) (T. J. Barsby 84, J. P. Maher 58; S. P. George three for 43); South Australia* 242 for eight (50 overs) (D. S. Lehmann 39, G. S. Blewett 42, T. J. Nielsen 57, J. C. Scuderi 35; S. G. Law four for 47).

At Melbourne, November 6. Victoria won by 55 runs, New South Wales's target having been revised to 177 from 45 overs. Victoria* 181 for eight (48 overs) (D. M. Jones 76); New South Wales 121 (40 overs) (R. Chee Quee 34; I. J. Harvey three for 18).

At Perth, December 9 (day/night). Western Australia won by one run. Western Australia* 242 for nine (50 overs) (M. P. Lavender 31, M. R. J. Veletta 49, A. C. Gilchrist 60, D. A. Fitzgerald 32; C. G. Rackemann three for 28); Queensland 241 for nine (50 overs) (T. J. Barsby 62, S. A. Prestwidge 33, W. A. Seccombe 64 not out; J. M. Allen three for 62, M. P. Atkinson three for 31).

At Sydney, February 3 (day/night). Western Australia won by six wickets. New South Wales* 116 (45.2 overs) (S. Lee 30; T. M. Moody three for 16); Western Australia 117 for four (35.3 overs) (M. R. J. Veletta 32 not out).

At Adelaide, February 11. Victoria won by 79 runs. Victoria* 236 for seven (50 overs) (R. P. Larkin 36, I. J. Harvey 43, P. R. Reiffel 35 not out, S. K. Warne 32); South Australia 157 (48.1 overs) (J. D. Siddons 33, J. C. Scuderi 51; D. J. Saker three for 19).

At Brisbane, February 12. Queensland v New South Wales. No result (abandoned).

At Hobart, February 12. Western Australia won by 31 runs. Western Australia* 240 for nine (50 overs) (T. M. Moody 36, M. P. Lavender 33, D. R. Martyn 57, J. L. Langer 34, G. B. Hogg 33; C. R. Miller four for 48); Tasmania 209 for six (50 overs) (J. Cox 68, S. Young 56).

At Hobart, February 18. Tasmania won by five wickets. New South Wales* 255 for seven (50 overs) (J. L. Arnberger 73, M. W. Patterson 62; C. R. Miller three for 48); Tasmania 256 for five (47.5 overs) (M. J. Di Venuto 33, S. Young 96, R. J. Tucker 42, Extras 31).

At Adelaide, February 19. South Australia won by four wickets. Western Australia* 213 (46.5 overs) (M. P. Lavender 100; P. J. Wilson three for 30, S. P. George three for 44); South Australia 214 for six (46.5 overs) (D. S. Lehmann 102, J. C. Scuderi 48 not out).

At Melbourne, February 19. Victoria won by eight wickets. Queensland 149 (49 overs) (T. J. Barsby 34; D. J. Saker four for 35, I. J. Harvey three for 27); Victoria* 151 for two (38.1 overs) (B. J. Hodge 78 not out, D. M. Jones 36).

Victoria 10 pts, South Australia 6 pts, Western Australia 6 pts, Queensland 5 pts, Tasmania 2 pts, New South Wales 1 pt.

Qualifying Final

At Perth, February 25. South Australia won by four wickets. Western Australia 280 for four (50 overs) (M. P. Lavender 80, D. R. Martyn 114 not out); South Australia* 281 for six (49.5 overs) (P. C. Nobes 140 not out, J. D. Siddons 46, D. J. Marsh 55 not out).

Final

At Melbourne, March 5. Victoria won by four wickets. South Australia* 169 (46.4 overs) (D. S. Webber 47; T. F. Corbett four for 30, J. R. Bakker four for 15); Victoria 170 for six (44.5 overs) (R. P. Larkin 45, D. M. Jones 35, M. T. G. Elliott 46 not out; J. C. Scuderi three for 36).

SHEFFIELD SHIELD PLAYER OF THE YEAR

The Sheffield Shield Player of the Year Award for 1994-95 was won by Dean Jones of Victoria. The Award, instituted in 1975-76, is adjudicated by the umpires over the course of the season. Each of the two umpires standing in each of the 30 Sheffield Shield matches (excluding the final) allocated marks of 3, 2 and 1 to the three players who most impressed them during the game. Jones earned 25 votes in his ten matches, eight ahead of Greg Blewett of South Australia. He also won the Player of the Year Award sponsored by the Lord's Taverners and decided by his fellow players, with 81 votes to 62 for Michael Slater of New South Wales.

CRICKET IN SOUTH AFRICA, 1994-95

By COLIN BRYDEN and ANDREW SAMSON

The emergence of fresh young talent was the most exciting feature of the South African season. Since South Africa's return to international cricket in 1991, the national side had coped admirably despite a shortage of quality batsmen. As recently as 1993-94, the selectors had struggled to fill the batting places in an A team to play England A. Happily, the reverse was the case when they picked an Under-24 team to visit Sri Lanka during August 1995. So many young batsmen had performed well that several with sound credentials were left behind.

The national team, now coached by the Englishman Bob Woolmer, won three Tests out of four against New Zealand and the one-off match with Pakistan, and an air of optimism prevailed at the end of the season. In addition to the Under-24 tour of Sri Lanka, an Under-19 team, including six black players, toured England during July and August 1995. Meanwhile South Africa's first full-time academy was launched in Johannesburg, with 23 young cricketers spending four months at the Rand Afrikaans University under the direction of former South Africa captain Clive Rice.

The trend towards youth was most notable in Natal and Western Province, though only one of them was rewarded with immediate success. Natal emerged from a period in the doldrums to win the Castle Cup for the first time since 1980-81. A team of enthusiastic youngsters, most with all-round ability, was inspired by the West Indian Malcolm Marshall. He led the side in five of their eight matches, in the absence of Jonty Rhodes, the appointed captain, and did such a fine job that Rhodes was happy to serve under him when he had completed his international duties. On the brink of his 37th birthday, Marshall no longer bowled at the pace that made him one of the world's leading fast bowlers in the 1980s, but remained a formidable competitor. He was Natal's leading bowler, taking 35 wickets at 16.17, was named Castle Cup Player of the Season and returned in 1995-96 to assist Natal in the defence of their title.

Among the other old hands, South Africa's opening batsman, Andrew Hudson, struggled at international level but scored 399 in five matches for Natal, and there were worthy contributions from the 37-year-old batsman Neville Wright and off-spinner Pat Symcox. But it was Natal's youngsters who carried the side to six victories in eight matches. Marshall shared the new ball with 21-year-old Shaun Pollock and 22-year-old Ross Veenstra. Pollock, son of the former Springbok opening bowler Peter, now convenor of the national selectors, is of average height, but generates considerable pace and possesses a well-disguised, effective bouncer. Veenstra, by contrast, is a tall and gangly left-armer, posing problems of line and swing for right-handed batsmen. Neil Johnson and Lance Klusener, 24 and 23 respectively, established themselves as genuine all-rounders – both fast-medium bowlers and competent top-order batsmen. Klusener, from Natal's country districts, was originally picked as a bowler but rose from No. 9 to No. 3 in the order and finished top of the Castle Cup batting averages, with 366 runs at 61.00. Mark Bruyns, who turned 21 during the season, improved so rapidly as a wicket-keeper that he displaced Errol Stewart, South Africa's reserve keeper only a year earlier. Other bright prospects for

Natal were opener Doug Watson, aged 21, middle-order batsman Dale
Benkenstein – who scored a double-hundred for the B team and was made
captain of the national Under-24 team at the age of 20 – and off-spinning
all-rounder Derek Crookes. Natal's depth of talent was confirmed when
their B side won both the first-class and one-day UCB Bowl competitions.
They beat Eastern Transvaal convincingly in the three-day final.

While Natal reaped the fruits of their youth policy, Western Province
won only two Castle Cup matches. They suffered from national calls on
Brian McMillan, Gary Kirsten and Craig Matthews, but they too could feel
confident about the future. The experience of West Indian Test batsman
Desmond Haynes provided the ideal foundation for the development of an
otherwise youthful top order. He and left-handed opener Sven Koenig often
gave Western Province a solid start and they were followed by Hylton
"H. D." Ackerman, aged 22, and the 19-year-old Jacques Kallis, both of
whom suggested international potential. Ackerman, son and namesake of
the former Western Province and Northamptonshire batsman, topped 500
runs and made a century against the touring Pakistanis. Kallis made fewer
runs but displayed an impressive temperament and technique, especially off
the back foot. Herschelle Gibbs has not yet fulfilled the promise he showed
as a teenager, but made a maiden Castle Cup hundred.

Northern Transvaal, after several seasons of disappointment, were
serious contenders for the Castle Cup until late January, when they lost a
top-of-the-table match to Natal, having led by 62 on first innings. The
captaincy of Joubert Strydom and the enthusiasm of a new coach, Anton
Ferreira, were important factors. Despite the loss of Test bowler Fanie de
Villiers for much of the season, an effective pace attack was spearheaded
by Steve Elworthy and Rudi Bryson while off-spinner Mark Davis proved a
capable all-rounder. Surprisingly, Greg Smith, a left-arm opening bowler,
was given fewer opportunities than his promise seemed to merit. Mike
Rindel and Roy Pienaar, who had lost their places the previous season, re-
established themselves as consistent run-scorers, with Rindel earning
national selection in the one-day team.

Orange Free State, Castle Cup champions in the previous two years, were
unable to repeat their success but finished third, though they did retain
their one-day title. The absence of Hansie Cronje and Allan Donald for
most of the matches was too great a handicap for a province with a small
playing base. The West Indian Franklyn Stephenson took 30 wickets at
16.40 but was one of several seam bowlers troubled by injury; only Nico
Pretorius remained fully fit. Left-arm spinner Nicky Boje continued to
impress, while all-rounder Chris Craven improved greatly. Rudolf Steyn
was the most consistent of the batsmen, and made his Test debut in
January.

Eastern Province struggled with a threadbare bowling attack, which was
carried by the experienced West Indian all-rounder Eldine Baptiste and
left-arm spinner Tim Shaw. In the closing weeks the return of left-arm
strike bowler Brett Schultz, who had missed the better part of two seasons
because of serious knee injuries, enabled them to make a strong finish and
reach the one-day final. Eastern Province's batting was anchored by Kepler
Wessels, who was second in the Castle Cup averages with 588 runs at
58.80, including three centuries. His decision to retire from international
cricket because of a chronic knee injury proved a blessing for his province:
immediately after giving up the captaincy he had a sequence of 102, 26 not

out, 104, 59 not out and 107. Wicket-keeper Dave Richardson had an outstanding season with the bat, heading the first-class averages with 608 at 67.55, while the hard-hitting Louis Koen showed a welcome return to form. Dave Callaghan and Philip Amm filled out one of the most consistent batting line-ups in the country.

The lack of such batting consistency was Border's enduring weakness, despite the constant presence of their captain, Peter Kirsten, whose international career seemed finally to be over. Their best batsman was Pieter Strydom, who hit two centuries, although Daryll Cullinan, who had moved from Transvaal, contributed some good innings when not required by South Africa. Frans Cronje, elder brother of the new national captain, Hansie, also shone. West Indian fast bowler Ottis Gibson had an outstanding match against Natal, taking 13 for 125, only to see his side surrender their last four wickets for 12 runs and lose by 12 to the eventual champions.

Once-mighty Transvaal had another disappointing season, finishing seventh out of eight. Mark Rushmere took over the captaincy from Jimmy Cook, who became player-coach. Cook phased himself out of the team, preferring to pick younger batsmen in the second half of the season, such as the 21-year-old opening batsman Adam Bacher, nephew of the United Cricket Board chief executive Ali. Despite having three Test bowlers in Snell, Jack and Eksteen, the Transvaal attack seldom fired together. The batting was variable, though the English left-hander, Neil Fairbrother, proved a good signing, especially in limited-overs matches.

Boland finished bottom after a season dogged by misfortune. John Commins, who became the first Boland cricketer to play a Test, finished the season injured, as did another reliable batsman, Salieg Nackerdien. The problems were compounded by the unreliability of the pitch at their home ground in Paarl; umpires stopped a match with the New Zealand tourists on the second morning because it was unsafe, and the Board threatened to take fixtures away from the ground. Although opener Lloyd Ferreira looked one of the most promising of the young South African batsmen, he had a series of failures and the side seldom started well. Kevin Curran, a late signing as the province's overseas player after the Pakistani spinner Abdul Qadir failed to turn up, was one of Boland's few consistent batsmen. The bowling lacked depth: seamer Henry Williams and spinner Claude Henderson had to shoulder a heavy load, though opening bowler Roger Telemachus could become a top-class performer. Despite their poor four-day form, Boland did win seven out of ten matches in the Benson and Hedges Series to top the league, only to lose in the semi-finals.

Eastern Transvaal, Western Transvaal and Griqualand West, who had previously combined to form the Impalas team in the Benson and Hedges night series, all played in their own right, with some success. Griquas beat Western Province in the first match to be played under floodlights in Kimberley, while Eastern Transvaal were responsible for one of the sensations of the season: they bowled out Transvaal for 61 at the Wanderers and then knocked off the required runs in 9.5 overs, to end the match before the lights were switched on.

The Benson and Hedges reached a controversial conclusion when a lack of clarity in the rules resulted in four teams contesting one place in the semi-finals. Boland, Western Province and Orange Free State qualified automatically but Transvaal, Natal, Northern Transvaal and Eastern Province had shared fourth place in the round-robin, finishing level on 24 points from five wins and two no-results. A committee could not decide whether to endorse Natal, going on results between the teams involved, or Transvaal on overall run-rate. An extra knockout series was staged to break the deadlock and to their own surprise Eastern Province went through, after losing fewer wickets against Transvaal when the scores were tied. Having already resigned themselves to being out of the competition, Eastern Province then knocked out table-toppers Boland, only to lose by a conclusive 113 runs to Orange Free State in the final. – C.B.

FIRST-CLASS AVERAGES, 1994-95

BATTING

(Qualification: 8 innings, average 40.00)

	M	I	NO	R	HS	100s	Avge
D. J. Richardson (*E. Province*)	8	13	4	608	109	2	67.55
D. N. Crookes (*Natal*)	8	10	1	600	123*	2	66.66
L. Klusener (*Natal*)	8	13	5	521	105	1	65.12
E. O. Simons (*W. Province*)	6	9	4	290	102*	1	58.00
K. C. Wessels (*E. Province*)	8	13	2	636	107	3	57.81
W. J. Cronje (*OFS*)	9	16	3	726	112	2	55.84
M. J. R. Rindel (*N. Transvaal*)	6	9	0	476	118	1	52.88
D. M. Benkenstein (*Natal*)	10	14	2	594	203*	1	49.50
G. K. Bruk-Jackson (*Zimbabwe Board XI*)	5	8	2	293	119*	1	48.83
B. M. McMillan (*W. Province*)	8	11	0	536	140	2	48.72
B. C. Baguley (*W. Province B*)	5	9	2	338	133*	1	48.28
D. J. Cullinan (*Border*)	9	18	4	674	150*	1	48.14
G. Kirsten (*W. Province*)	9	15	1	664	150	1	47.42
C. F. Craven (*OFS*)	7	13	3	473	107	1	47.30
N. Pothas (*Transvaal*)	8	14	4	472	76*	0	47.20
A. M. Bacher (*Transvaal*)	5	10	1	423	119*	1	47.00
C. Light (*OFS*)	5	10	0	468	121	2	46.80
S. J. Cook (*Transvaal*)	7	12	2	467	114	1	46.70
L. J. Koen (*E. Province*)	9	16	3	604	138*	1	46.46
H. A. Page (*Griqualand W.*)	6	10	2	461	95	0	46.10
C. Grainger (*Transvaal*)	8	14	1	588	233	1	45.23
N. R. Rhodes (*Transvaal B*)	5	8	1	314	141	1	44.85
M. L. Bruyns (*Natal*)	8	12	1	486	84	0	44.18
N. H. Fairbrother (*Transvaal*)	4	8	1	308	89	0	44.00
A. Moreby (*OFS B*)	5	10	0	436	115	2	43.60
P. S. de Villiers (*N. Transvaal*)	8	12	7	218	66*	0	43.60
C. R. Norris (*E. Transvaal*)	6	10	2	347	107	1	43.37
M. Michau (*Griqualand W.*)	5	9	2	302	95	0	43.14
Q. R. Still (*Border*)	6	10	2	345	111*	1	43.12
T. A. Marsh (*E. Transvaal*)	6	8	2	258	93	0	43.00
C. B. Lambert (*N. Transvaal*)	9	18	2	674	170	1	42.12
D. L. Haynes (*W. Province*)	5	8	0	337	96	0	42.12
C. B. Sugden (*Natal B*)	5	8	1	292	106	1	41.71
E. L. R. Stewart (*Natal*)	7	10	1	365	146	2	40.55
D. O. Nosworthy (*Border*)	6	11	1	405	94	0	40.50
H. D. Ackerman (*W. Province*)	9	14	0	562	118	1	40.14
G. C. Victor (*E. Province*)	5	9	1	321	139*	1	40.12

* *Signifies not out.*

BOWLING

(Qualification: 20 wickets)

	O	M	R	W	BB	5W/i	Avge
L. C. R. Jordaan (*E. Transvaal*) ..	247.4	67	601	38	6-59	6	15.81
M. D. Marshall (*Natal*)	263.3	98	566	35	4-40	0	16.17
F. D. Stephenson (*OFS*)	214	55	492	30	6-49	3	16.40
M. J. G. Davis (*N. Transvaal*)	247.5	67	585	35	8-37	1	16.71
S. M. Skeete (*E. Transvaal*)	129	22	401	23	5-27	1	17.43
P. S. de Villiers (*N. Transvaal*) ...	363.1	106	937	51	6-47	4	18.37
S. M. Pollock (*Natal*)	247.5	71	591	31	4-24	0	19.06
N. C. Johnson (*Natal*)	159.1	34	491	25	4-49	0	19.64
R. E. Veenstra (*Natal*)	186.5	48	525	26	4-36	0	20.19
O. D. Gibson (*Border*)	166.5	35	466	23	7-55	3	20.26
M. J. Vandrau (*Transvaal*)	225.5	42	713	34	6-49	4	20.97
D. Rossouw (*E. Province*)	141.5	18	483	23	4-33	0	21.00
D. G. Payne (*W. Province*)	222	57	623	29	4-50	0	21.48
M. Erasmus (*Boland*)	217.3	56	556	25	6-22	2	22.24
K. G. Storey (*Natal B*)	161.1	33	450	20	4-63	0	22.50
M. R. Hobson (*Transvaal*)	198.3	35	600	26	5-29	2	23.07
L. Klusener (*Natal*)	170.1	45	502	21	5-46	1	23.90
D. Q. MacHelm (*W. Province*)	231	77	552	23	5-57	1	24.00
R. E. Bryson (*N. Transvaal*)	218	52	682	28	5-25	1	24.35
E. A. E. Baptiste (*E. Province*)	280.5	79	673	27	5-62	3	24.92
P. A. N. Emslie (*Border*)	283.5	67	707	28	4-37	0	25.25
B. M. McMillan (*W. Province*)	266	66	634	24	4-65	0	26.41
M. W. Handman (*E. Province*)	224	45	638	24	4-55	0	26.58
H. S. Williams (*Boland*)	273.1	57	669	25	4-59	0	26.76
N. W. Pretorius (*OFS*)	312.4	48	1,079	40	5-96	2	26.97
J. A. Ehrke (*Border*)	205	54	626	23	4-85	0	27.21
A. C. Dawson (*W. Province*)	296.5	87	750	27	6-86	1	27.77
S. D. Jack (*Transvaal*)	251.5	59	757	27	4-60	0	28.03
S. Elworthy (*N. Transvaal*)	301	55	926	33	7-65	2	28.06
C. W. Henderson (*Boland*)	370.3	91	978	34	7-57	3	28.76
S. Abrahams (*E. Province*)	207.3	53	579	20	4-76	0	28.95
B. C. Fourie (*Border*)	278.3	66	767	26	6-91	2	29.50
G. J. Smith (*N. Transvaal*)	249.5	43	757	25	4-32	0	30.28
D. B. Rundle (*W. Province*)	415.3	105	1,109	36	6-51	2	30.80
T. G. Shaw (*E. Province*)	361.1	145	658	21	5-91	1	31.33
C. E. Eksteen (*Transvaal*)	458.2	169	891	26	5-84	2	34.26
R. P. Snell (*Transvaal*)	288.4	69	847	23	6-60	1	36.82
N. Boje (*OFS*)	357.3	100	958	25	5-38	2	38.32

CASTLE CUP, 1994-95

				Bonus points			
	Played	Won	Lost	Drawn	Batting	Bowling	Points
Natal.............	8	6	0	2	14	38	112
Northern Transvaal....	8	4	3	1	12	36	88
Orange Free State	8	3	4	1	8	35	73
Eastern Province	8	2	2	4	12	33	65
Border...............	8	2	2	4	7	33	60
Western Province	8	2	3	3	12	28	60
Transvaal	8	1	2	5	13	31	54
Boland	8	1	5	2	10	31	51

Outright win = 10 pts.
Bonus points are awarded for the first 100 overs of each team's first innings. One batting point is awarded for the first 200 runs and for every subsequent 50. One bowling point is awarded for the first wicket taken and for every subsequent two.

In the following scores, * *by the name of a team indicates that they won the toss.*

At Kingsmead, Durban, November 5, 6, 7. Natal won by nine wickets. Orange Free State 126 (N. Boje 49; S. M. Pollock four for 24, N. C. Johnson four for 49) and 250 (P. J. R. Steyn 46, P. J. L. Radley 37; M. D. Marshall four for 42, S. M. Pollock three for 64); Natal* 236 (N. E. Wright 39, E. L. R. Stewart 36, N. C. Johnson 39; F. D. Stephenson six for 49, N. W. Pretorius three for 54) and 141 for one (A. C. Hudson 73 not out, C. R. B. Armstrong 35). *Natal 16 pts, Orange Free State 5 pts.*

At Centurion Park, Verwoerdburg, November 5, 6, 7. Northern Transvaal won by ten wickets. Border* 286 (P. C. Strydom 127, S. J. Palframan 37; P. S. de Villiers four for 66) and 134 (P. N. Kirsten 51; P. S. de Villiers four for 37, R. E. Bryson four for 17); Northern Transvaal 357 (B. J. Sommerville 33, C. B. Lambert 43, R. F. Pienaar 37, M. J. R. Rindel 63, P. S. de Villiers 58 not out, R. E. Bryson 62; B. C. Fourie six for 91) and 64 for no wkt. *Northern Transvaal 17 pts, Border 7 pts.*
   De Villiers and Bryson added 108 for Northern Transvaal's tenth wicket.

At Wanderers Stadium, Johannesburg, November 5, 6, 7, 8. Drawn. Boland* 267 (J. B. Commins 77, L-M. Germishuys 35, M. Erasmus 59 not out; R. P. Snell six for 60, S. D. Jack four for 94) and 359 (L. D. Ferreira 71, W. J. Smit 52, J. B. Commins 93, M. Erasmus 33; S. D. Jack four for 60, C. E. Eksteen three for 93); Transvaal 316 (W. V. Rippon 57, N. H. Fairbrother 89, R. P. Snell 81, C. E. Eksteen 38; C. M. Willoughby three for 60, H. S. Williams four for 59) and 154 for four (B. M. White 35, S. J. Cook 75 not out). *Transvaal 8 pts, Boland 7 pts.*

At St George's Park, Port Elizabeth, November 11, 12, 13, 14. Drawn. Transvaal* 396 (B. M. White 120, M. W. Rushmere 31, N. H. Fairbrother 66, D. R. Laing 96; S. Abrahams three for 89) and 224 for nine dec. (B. M. White 68, M. W. Rushmere 37, N. H. Fairbrother 51; G. A. Roe three for 56, D. Roussouw three for 34); Eastern Province 325 (P. G. Amm 50, K. C. Wessels 44, D. J. Callaghan 62, D. J. Richardson 68, E. A. E. Baptiste 54; M. J. Vandrau four for 99) and 263 for six (K. C. Wessels 41, D. J. Richardson 72 not out, T. G. Shaw 84 not out). *Eastern Province 5 pts, Transvaal 5 pts.*
   Richardson and Shaw put on an unbroken 159 for the seventh wicket in the second innings, an Eastern Province record.

At Kingsmead, Durban, November 11, 12, 13, 14. Natal won by 12 runs. Natal 179 (N. E. Wright 50, N. C. Johnson 38, Extras 30; O. D. Gibson seven for 55, B. C. Fourie three for 58) and 183 (A. C. Hudson 78; O. D. Gibson six for 70, J. A. Ehrke three for 34); Border* 115 (M. D. Marshall four for 47, S. M. Pollock four for 32) and 235 (D. J. Cullinan 70, S. J. Palframan 56; M. D. Marshall three for 51, T. Bosch three for 47). *Natal 15 pts, Border 5 pts.*
   Border, set 248 for victory, were 223 for six before losing their last four wickets for 12.

At Newlands, Cape Town, November 11, 12, 13, 14. Orange Free State won by four wickets. Western Province* 105 (N. W. Pretorius three for 31, B. T. Player four for 34) and 386 (D. L. Haynes 96, G. Kirsten 50, H. D. Ackerman 58, B. M. McMillan 37, R. J. Ryall 39, D. B. Rundle 36 not out, M. W. Pringle 32; F. D. Stephenson five for 60, N. W. Pretorius three for 89); Orange Free State 215 (L. J. Wilkinson 74, J. F. Venter 36; C. R. Matthews five for 35) and 278 for six (P. J. R. Steyn 84, W. J. Cronje 111, G. F. J. Liebenberg 50; D. B. Rundle three for 77). *Orange Free State 16 pts, Western Province 5 pts.*

At Paarl CC, Paarl, November 18, 19, 20. Boland won by 75 runs. Boland* 239 (A. R. Wylie 31, J. B. Commins 86, M. Erasmus 32; G. A. Roe three for 38, M. W. Handman four for 55) and 149 (K. M. Curran 32; G. A. Roe three for 45, M. W. Handman three for 39); Eastern Province 118 (L. J. Koen 41; M. Erasmus three for 29) and 195 (P. G. Amm 39, D. J. Callaghan 34, L. J. Koen 92; C. W. Henderson seven for 57). *Boland 16 pts, Eastern Province 5 pts.*

At Buffalo Park, East London, November 18, 19, 20, 21. Drawn. Border 268 (M. P. Stonier 30, F. J. C. Cronje 42, D. J. Cullinan 42, P. C. Strydom 60; C. R. Matthews three for 51, D. B. Rundle three for 47) and 314 for seven (D. J. Cullinan 150 not out, P. C. Strydom 55); Western Province* 471 for nine dec. (S. G. Koenig 64, H. D. Ackerman 93, J. H. Kallis 46, E. O. Simons 73, M. W. Pringle 51 not out, Extras 37; P. A. N. Emslie three for 90). *Border 4 pts, Western Province 6 pts.*

At Centurion Park, Verwoerdburg, November 18, 19, 20, 21. Transvaal won by eight wickets. Transvaal* 360 (S. J. Cook 114, R. P. Snell 67, C. E. Eksteen 32, S. D. Jack 60 not out; P. S. de Villiers three for 96, M. J. G. Davis three for 71) and 72 for two; Northern Transvaal 193 (C. B. Lambert 30, R. F. Pienaar 73; R. P. Snell three for 35, S. Jacobs three for 52) and 238 (C. B. Lambert 63, L. P. Vorster 31, M. J. R. Rindel 62; C. E. Eksteen five for 84). *Transvaal 17 pts, Northern Transvaal 4 pts.*

At Paarl CC, Paarl, December 1, 2, 3. Northern Transvaal won by three wickets. Boland* 258 (A. R. Wylie 37, K. M. Curran 104, W. J. Smit 54, L-M. Germishuys 30; S. Elworthy three for 27, M. J. G. Davis four for 60) and 100 (A. R. Wylie 31; G. J. Smith three for 37, R. E. Bryson five for 25); Northern Transvaal 213 (C. B. Lambert 35, L. P. Vorster 64; C. W. Henderson three for 51, M. Erasmus five for 44) and 146 for seven (M. J. G. Davis 68 not out, D. J. van Zyl 31; C. W. Henderson four for 64). *Northern Transvaal 16 pts, Boland 7 pts.*

Lambert held seven catches in the match.

At Springbok Park, Bloemfontein, December 1, 2, 3, 4. Eastern Province won by seven wickets. Eastern Province 334 (P. G. Amm 82, K. C. Wessels 102, G. K. Miller 48, Extras 35; F. D. Stephenson four for 83, N. W. Pretorius five for 96) and 126 for three (L. J. Koen 30 not out); Orange Free State* 113 (L. J. Wilkinson 46; E. A. E. Baptiste three for 35, T. G. Shaw four for 16) and 346 (P. J. R. Steyn 115, G. F. J. Liebenberg 141; E. A. E. Baptiste five for 89). *Eastern Province 17 pts, Orange Free State 4 pts.*

At Newlands, Cape Town, December 10, 11, 12, 13. Drawn. Natal* 390 (D. J. Watson 60, N. C. Johnson 53, L. Klusener 50, P. L. Symcox 74 not out, S. M. Pollock 44; M. W. Pringle three for 100, D. B. Rundle three for 97) and 246 for five dec. (N. E. Wright 61, M. L. Bruyns 84); Western Province 303 (S. G. Koenig 89, D. L. Haynes 42, J. H. Kallis 39, R. J. Ryall 30 not out; M. D. Marshall three for 58, L. Klusener four for 62) and 193 for six (S. G. Koenig 73, D. L. Haynes 70). *Western Province 6 pts, Natal 4 pts.*

Klusener, Symcox and Pollock batted Nos 9, 10 and 11 in the Natal first innings; they had been 223 for eight.

At St George's Park, Port Elizabeth, December 15, 16, 17, 18. Drawn. Eastern Province 328 (P. G. Amm 65, K. C. Wessels 104, G. K. Miller 49, S. Abrahams 35 not out; S. Elworthy three for 65) and 268 for five dec. (P. G. Amm 58, L. J. Koen 55, K. C. Wessels 59 not out); Northern Transvaal* 306 (C. B. Lambert 43, K. J. Rule 36, D. J. van Zyl 36, R. C. Ontong 41, S. Elworthy 75, Extras 35; E. A. E. Baptiste five for 62) and 196 for seven (K. J. Rule 31, R. C. Ontong 75 not out, S. Elworthy 32 not out; E. A. E. Baptiste three for 69, M. W. Handman three for 42). *Eastern Province 6 pts, Northern Transvaal 6 pts.*

At Newlands, Cape Town, December 16, 17, 18, 19. Western Province won by an innings and 23 runs. Western Province* 500 for eight dec. (D. L. Haynes 54, H. H. Gibbs 102, H. D. Ackerman 45, B. M. McMillan 140, M. W. Pringle 54 not out, Extras 32; C. W. Henderson three for 93); Boland 206 (M. S. Nackerdien 49, J. B. Commins 83, M. Erasmus 38 not out; B. M. McMillan three for 28, A. C. Dawson four for 51) and 271 (L. D. Ferreira 52, M. S. Nackerdien 54, K. M. Curran 73; D. B. Rundle five for 76). *Western Province 17 pts, Boland 3 pts.*

Wicket-keeper L-M. Germishuys took six catches in Western Province's innings.

At Springbok Park, Bloemfontein, December 17, 18, 19, 20. Border won by 81 runs. Border* 380 (A. G. Lawson 41, P. N. Kirsten 47, P. C. Strydom 100, O. D. Gibson 58, B. C. Fourie 34; N. W. Pretorius three for 97) and 217 for eight dec. (M. P. Stonier 36, P. J. Botha 49 not out, S. J. Palframan 59; N. Boje five for 75); Orange Free State 294 (J. M. Arthur 39, G. F. J. Liebenberg 126, C. F. Craven 63; O. D. Gibson five for 96) and 222 (L. J. Wilkinson 77, F. D. Stephenson 52; I. L. Howell six for 62). *Border 16 pts, Orange Free State 6 pts.*

At Wanderers Stadium, Johannesburg, December 17, 18, 19, 20. Natal won by 244 runs. Natal* 339 (N. E. Wright 44, M. L. Bruyns 71, M. D. Marshall 82 not out, L. Klusener 35; T. C. Webster five for 93) and 244 (D. M. Benkenstein 32, M. L. Bruyns 49; R. A. Lyle three for 51, M. J. Vandrau three for 70); Transvaal 162 (N. H. Fairbrother 32; R. E. Veenstra four for 36) and 177 (N. H. Fairbrother 40, D. R. Laing 84 not out; R. E. Veenstra three for 40, N. C. Johnson three for 11). *Natal 18 pts, Transvaal 5 pts.*

Veenstra took a hat-trick with the final ball of Transvaal's first innings and the first two balls of the second over in the second.

At Centurion Park, Verwoerdburg, January 6, 7, 8, 9. Northern Transvaal won by eight wickets. Northern Transvaal* 455 (C. B. Lambert 170, R. F. Pienaar 108, L. P. Vorster 37, M. J. R. Rindel 48; N. W. Pretorius three for 118, J. E. Johnson four for 61) and 180 for two (C. B. Lambert 96, R. F. Pienaar 61 not out); Orange Free State 289 (J. M. Arthur 37, C. F. Craven 107, P. J. L. Radley 37; S. Elworthy five for 55) and 345 (G. F. J. Liebenberg 90, J. F. Venter 64, C. F. Craven 50, N. Boje 40, P. J. L. Radley 32 not out; R. E. Bryson three for 44). *Northern Transvaal 19 pts, Orange Free State 4 pts.*

Wicket-keeper K. J. Rule made six dismissals in Orange Free State's first innings.

At Buffalo Park, East London, January 13, 14, 15, 16. Drawn. Transvaal* 379 for eight dec. (N. Pothas 38, M. W. Rushmere 73, S. J. Cook 83, C. Grainger 54, D. R. Laing 83); Border 116 for three (F. J. C. Cronje 36). *Border 3 pts, Transvaal 4 pts.*

At St George's Park, Port Elizabeth, January 13, 14, 15, 16. Eastern Province won by five wickets. Western Province* 326 for five dec. (S. G. Koenig 149 not out, J. H. Kallis 77, R. J. Ryall 42 not out) and forfeited second innings; Eastern Province nought for nought dec. and 327 for five (K. C. Wessels 107, L. J. Koen 138 not out; D. G. Payne three for 64). *Eastern Province 13 pts, Western Province 2 pts.*

At Kingsmead, Durban, January 13, 14, 15, 16. Natal won by 111 runs. Natal 450 for eight dec. (A. C. Hudson 157, N. E. Wright 55, M. L: Bruyns 38, D. M. Benkenstein 71, S. M. Pollock 32; H. S. Williams three for 99) and 40 for one dec.; Boland* 250 (M. S. Nackerdien 69, K. M. Curran 85, M. Erasmus 36) and 129 (J. B. Commins 39; M. D. Marshall three for 17, S. M. Pollock three for 30). *Natal 18 pts, Boland 5 pts.*

At Kingsmead, Durban, January 26, 27, 28, 29. Natal won by five wickets. Northern Transvaal 270 (R. F. Pienaar 30, M. J. R. Rindel 118, S. Elworthy 33; M. D. Marshall three for 48, S. M. Pollock three for 33) and 159 (K. J. Rule 67; M. D. Marshall four for 40, S. M. Pollock three for 32); Natal* 208 (N. E. Wright 43, N. C. Johnson 71, L. Klusener 54; P. S. de Villiers three for 69, S. Elworthy seven for 65) and 223 for five (L. Klusener 43, M. L. Bruyns 59 not out, J. N. Rhodes 53). *Natal 16 pts, Northern Transvaal 7 pts.*

At Paarl CC, Paarl, January 27, 28, 29, 30. Drawn. Orange Free State* 403 for seven dec. (P. J. R. Steyn 36, J. M. Arthur 61, L. J. Wilkinson 101, W. J. Cronje 70, J. F. Venter 52 not out, C. F. Craven 44; H. S. Williams four for 93); Boland 227 (M. S. Nackerdien 36, K. C. Jackson 52, M. Erasmus 32; A. A. Donald four for 49, N. Boje three for 46) and 206 for five (J. M. Villet 30, K. C. Jackson 58, K. M. Curran 63 not out). *Boland 3 pts, Orange Free State 7 pts.*

At Buffalo Park, East London, January 27, 28, 29, 30. Drawn. Eastern Province* 281 (D. J. Callaghan 111, D. J. Richardson 105; J. A. Ehrke three for 49, P. A. N. Emslie three for 30) and 204 for four dec. (G. Morgan 45, K. C. Wessels 59); Border 182 (M. P. Stonier 31, D. J. Cullinan 32, P. C. Strydom 30, S. J. Palframan 34; A. G. Huckle six for 59) and 207 for eight (F. J. C. Cronje 70, P. N. Kirsten 33; A. G. Huckle four for 68). *Border 4 pts, Eastern Province 7 pts.*

At Wanderers Stadium, Johannesburg, January 27, 28, 29, 30. Drawn. Transvaal* 376 (M. W. Rushmere 134, G. A. Pollock 74, C. Grainger 54, S. J. Cook 37; A. C. Dawson six for 86) and 223 for five (D. R. Laing 42, G. A. Pollock 38, S. J. Cook 55 not out, N. Pothas 30 not out; D. G. Payne three for 42); Western Province 442 (G. Kirsten 150, B. M. McMillan 91, J. H. Kallis 52, A. C. Dawson 52; T. C. Webster three for 58, C. E. Eksteen five for 128). *Transvaal 4 pts, Western Province 5 pts.*

Lightning stopped play after a bolt hit close to the stadium, causing players to dive to the ground during E. O. Simons's run-up.

At Paarl CC, Paarl, February 3, 4, 5, 6. Border won by nine wickets. Boland* 228 (M. S. Nackerdien 77, K. M. Curran 39; B. C. Fourie three for 55) and 110 (L. D. Ferreira 30; B. C. Fourie three for 20, P. A. N. Emslie four for 37); Border 218 (M. P. Stonier 37, F. J. C. Cronje 35, S. J. Palframan 53; H. S. Williams three for 45, W. F. Stelling four for 12) and 121 for one (F. J. C. Cronje 36 not out, D. J. Cullinan 78 not out). *Border 15 pts, Boland 5 pts.*

It was reported that fried calamari stopped play when Cullinan hit a six off R. Telemachus into a frying pan. It was about ten minutes before the ball was cool enough for the umpires to remove the grease. Even then, Telemachus was unable to grip the ball and it had to be replaced.

At St George's Park, Port Elizabeth, February 3, 4, 5, 6. Natal won by ten wickets. Natal* 377 (A. C. Hudson 40, L. Klusener 75, D. M. Benkenstein 76, D. N. Crookes 123 not out; S. Abrahams four for 76) and 19 for no wkt; Eastern Province 218 (K. C. Wessels 38, D. J. Richardson 51, Extras 30; P. L. Symcox four for 47) and 175 (L. J. Koen 39, D. J. Richardson 54; M. D. Marshall three for 40, D. N. Crookes three for 26). *Natal 17 pts, Eastern Province 4 pts.*

At Springbok Park, Bloemfontein, February 3, 4, 5, 6. Orange Free State won by 179 runs. Orange Free State* 181 (P. J. R. Steyn 53, J. M. Arthur 30, W. J. Cronje 54 not out; M. J. Vandrau six for 49) and 332 (P. J. R. Steyn 40, J. M. Arthur 36, C. F. Craven 78 not out, N. W. Pretorius 33, Extras 30; S. D. Jack three for 61, M. J. Vandrau five for 79); Transvaal 184 (A. M. Bacher 37; N. Boje five for 38) and 150 (N. Pothas 46, R. P. Snell 39; A. A. Donald four for 36). *Orange Free State 15 pts, Transvaal 5 pts.*

At Newlands, Cape Town, February 3, 4, 5, 6. Western Province won by five wickets. Northern Transvaal 272 (R. F. Pienaar 42, K. J. Rule 102, J. P. Vorster 56; D. G. Payne four for 50, E. O. Simons three for 30) and 216 (M. J. R. Rindel 48, J. J. Strydom 46; D. G. Payne four for 56, D. B. Rundle four for 91); Western Province* 286 (H. H. Gibbs 79, H. D. Ackerman 44, J. H. Kallis 38, T. J. Mitchell 33; P. S. de Villiers six for 47) and 203 for five (G. Kirsten 85, H. D. Ackerman 62). *Western Province 16 pts, Northern Transvaal 5 pts.*

At Buffalo Park, East London, February 17, 18, 19, 20. Drawn. Natal* 303 (D. J. Watson 47, L. Klusener 30, N. C. Johnson 40, M. L. Bruyns 59, D. N. Crookes 47; B. C. Fourie five for 96, I. L. Howell three for 82); Border 202 (M. P. Stonier 57, P. N. Kirsten 60, S. J. Palframan 36; N. C. Johnson three for 30, D. N. Crookes three for 44). *Border 6 pts, Natal 8 pts.*

At Springbok Park, Bloemfontein, February 17, 18, 19, 20. Orange Free State won by five wickets. Western Province* 186 (H. D. Ackerman 55; N. W. Pretorius three for 72, F. D. Stephenson five for 61) and 287 (D. Jordaan 97, T. J. Mitchell 32, D. B. Rundle 33, M. W. Pringle 60 not out, Extras 43; N. W. Pretorius four for 93, F. D. Stephenson three for 37); Orange Free State 308 (J. M. Arthur 49, G. F. J. Liebenberg 81, C. F. Craven 46; D. G. Payne three for 91) and 168 for five (G. F. J. Liebenberg 42, F. D. Stephenson 37 not out, C. F. Craven 31 not out; M. W. Pringle three for 45). *Orange Free State 16 pts, Western Province 3 pts.*

At Wanderers Stadium, Johannesburg, February 17, 18, 19, 20. Drawn. Eastern Province* 344 (P. G. Amm 51, L. J. Koen 54, E. A. E. Baptiste 75, T. G. Shaw 45, M. W. Handman 31; R. A. Lyle six for 63) and 245 for eight dec. (P. G. Amm 118, L. J. Koen 74; R. P. Snell four for 84, R. A. Lyle four for 61); Transvaal 256 (A. M. Bacher 30, N. Pothas 47, R. P. Snell 45, M. J. Vandrau 59 not out; E. A. E. Baptiste five for 86, M. W. Handman four for 95) and 289 for nine (A. M. Bacher 70, D. R. Laing 30, G. A. Pollock 32, S. J. Cook 54, N. Pothas 40 not out; T. G. Shaw five for 91). *Transvaal 6 pts, Eastern Province 8 pts.*

At Centurion Park, Verwoerdburg, February 18, 19, 20, 21. Northern Transvaal won by one wicket. Boland 270 (K. C. Jackson 57, A. R. Wylie 54, M. M. Brink 45, C. W. Henderson 36, Extras 38; S. Elworthy three for 61, G. J. Smith three for 60) and 85 (R. E. Bryson four for 23); Northern Transvaal* 165 for seven dec. (R. F. Pienaar 66, M. J. G. Davis 38 not out; H. S. Williams three for 50, R. Telemachus three for 52) and 194 for nine (A. J. Seymore 84, C. B. Lambert 34; C. W. Henderson five for 57). *Northern Transvaal 14 pts, Boland 5 pts.*

CURRIE CUP AND CASTLE CUP WINNERS

The Currie Cup was replaced by the Castle Cup after the 1990-91 season.

1889-90	Transvaal	1962-63	Natal
1890-91	Kimberley	1963-64	Natal
1892-93	Western Province	1965-66	Natal/Transvaal (Tied)
1893-94	Western Province	1966-67	Natal
1894-95	Transvaal	1967-68	Natal
1896-97	Western Province	1968-69	Transvaal
1897-98	Western Province	1969-70	Transvaal/W. Province (Tied)
1902-03	Transvaal	1970-71	Transvaal
1903-04	Transvaal	1971-72	Transvaal
1904-05	Transvaal	1972-73	Transvaal
1906-07	Transvaal	1973-74	Natal
1908-09	Western Province	1974-75	Western Province
1910-11	Natal	1975-76	Natal
1912-13	Natal	1976-77	Natal
1920-21	Western Province	1977-78	Western Province
1921-22	Transvaal/Natal/W. Prov. (Tied)	1978-79	Transvaal
1923-24	Transvaal	1979-80	Transvaal
1925-26	Transvaal	1980-81	Natal
1926-27	Transvaal	1981-82	Western Province
1929-30	Transvaal	1982-83	Transvaal
1931-32	Western Province	1983-84	Transvaal
1933-34	Natal	1984-85	Transvaal
1934-35	Transvaal	1985-86	Western Province
1936-37	Natal	1986-87	Transvaal
1937-38	Natal/Transvaal (Tied)	1987-88	Transvaal
1946-47	Natal	1988-89	Eastern Province
1947-48	Natal	1989-90	E. Province/W. Province (Shared)
1950-51	Transvaal		
1951-52	Natal	1990-91	Western Province
1952-53	Western Province	1991-92	Eastern Province
1954-55	Natal	1992-93	Orange Free State
1955-56	Western Province	1993-94	Orange Free State
1958-59	Transvaal	1994-95	Natal
1960-61	Natal		

Transvaal have won the title outright 24 times, Natal 18, Western Province 14, Eastern Province and Orange Free State 2, Kimberley 1. The title has been shared five times as follows: Transvaal 4, Natal and Western Province 3, Eastern Province 1.

UCB BOWL, 1994-95

Section 1

	Played	Won	Lost	Drawn	Bonus points Batting	Bonus points Bowling	Points
Eastern Transvaal	5	3	0	2	11	25	66
Transvaal B	5	2	1	2	12	23	55
Eastern Province B	5	2	1	2	5	24	49
Border B	5	1	1	3	13	22	44*
Orange Free State B	5	1	1	3	12	20	42
Boland B	5	0	5	0	7	20	26*

One point deducted for slow over-rates.

Section 2

	Played	Won	Lost	Drawn	Bonus points Batting	Bonus points Bowling	Points
Natal B	5	3	0	2	13	21	64
Northern Transvaal B ...	5	2	2	1	7	25	52
Western Province B	5	2	1	2	10	20	50
Zimbabwe Board XI	5	1	1	3	12	22	44
Griqualand West	5	1	2	2	4	20	34
Western Transvaal	5	0	3	2	2	15	17

Final: Natal B beat Eastern Transvaal by five wickets.

Outright win = 10 pts.

Bonus points are awarded for the first 100 overs of each team's first innings. One batting point is awarded for the first 200 runs and for every subsequent 50. One bowling point is awarded for the first wicket taken and for every subsequent two.

In the following scores, * by the name of a team indicates that they won the toss.

Section 1

At Wanderers Stadium, Johannesburg, October 21, 22, 23. Drawn. Transvaal B* 467 for five dec. (H. Engelbrecht 100, G. M. Hewitt 36, C. Grainger 233, N. Pothas 76 not out) and 218 for three dec. (N. R. Rhodes 67, G. A. Pollock 101 not out); Orange Free State B 348 (F. P. Schoeman 36, S. G. Cronje 32, A. T. Hansen 79, A. Moreby 105; M. R. Hobson five for 85) and 299 for nine (F. P. Schoeman 65, C. Light 105, A. Moreby 40, S. G. Cronje 31 not out; M. R. Hobson four for 67, G. C. Yates three for 81). *Transvaal B 11 pts, Orange Free State B 6 pts.*

At Buffalo Park, East London, November 3, 4, 5. Border B won by two wickets. Boland B 264 (M. Brink 36, J. S. Roos 33, M. S. Nackerdien 64, M. S. Bredell 61, R. Telemachus 33; S. E. Fourie four for 71, P. A. N. Emslie three for 64) and 223 for six dec. (M. S. Nackerdien 106, A. T. Holdstock 42); Border B* 211 (L. M. Fuhri 31, S. E. Fourie 55, Extras 30; R. A. Smith four for 19) and 280 for eight (L. M. Fuhri 84, C. F. Spilhaus 62, F. J. C. Cronje 39; A. T. Holdstock four for 51). *Border B 16 pts, Boland B 7 pts.*

At Olympia Park, Springs, November 4, 5, 6. Eastern Transvaal won by ten wickets. Eastern Province B 131 (G. K. Miller 62; S. M. Skeete five for 27, J. R. Meyer three for 44) and 109 (L. C. R. Jordaan five for 40, C. R. Norris three for 23); Eastern Transvaal* 226 (C. R. Norris 37, A. Norris 33, T. Jamal 34, I. A. Hoffman 30, S. M. Skeete 32; M. W. Handman four for 64, S. C. Pope five for 30) and 17 for no wkt. *Eastern Transvaal 16 pts, Eastern Province B 5 pts.*

At St George's Park, Port Elizabeth, November 17, 18, 19. Drawn. Border B 254 (D. O. Nosworthy 94, A. C. Dewar 35, J. A. Ehrke 40; B. S. Forbes four for 83, G. K. Miller four for 57) and 347 for five dec. (L. M. Fuhri 39, A. G. Lawson 101, Q. R. Still 111 not out, D. O. Nosworthy 38); Eastern Province B* 318 (M. G. Beamish 48, M. C. Venter 30, G. C. Victor 139 not out, G. K. Miller 49; A. Badenhorst four for 67) and 63 for two. *Eastern Province B 8 pts, Border B 7 pts.*

At Buffalo Park, East London, November 30, December 1, 2. Drawn. Orange Free State B* 344 for eight dec. (F. P. Schoeman 62, C. Light 69, A. Moreby 87, C. C. van der Merwe 35, J. E. Johnson 37 not out; C. R. Ballantyne three for 51) and 189 (A. Moreby 34, J. E. Johnson 36, S. A. Cilliers 30; C. R. Ballantyne three for 28, Q. R. Still four for 56); Border B 300 for three dec. (Q. R. Still 82, A. G. Lawson 87, G. W. Thompson 48, D. O. Nosworthy 51 not out) and 176 for five (Q. R. Still 55, D. O. Nosworthy 35; S. G. Cronje four for 62). *Border B 7 pts, Orange Free State B 5 pts.*

At Grey High School, Port Elizabeth, December 1, 2, 3. Eastern Province B won by six wickets. Boland B* 302 (R. I. Dalrymple 31, M. S. Nackerdien 64, M. S. Bredell 99, J. H. Myers 37; D. Roussouw three for 82, B. S. Forbes five for 65) and 139 (J. S. Roos 74; Q. E. de Bruin three for 33, D. Roussouw four for 33); Eastern Province B 252 for six dec. (C. C. Wait 97, S. Abrahams 58 not out; M. S. Bredell five for 57) and 193 for four (W. Terblanche 52, G. C. Victor 74, G. Morgan 33 not out). *Eastern Province B 17 pts, Boland B 6 pts.*

At PAM Brink Stadium, Springs, December 2, 3, 4. Drawn. Eastern Transvaal* 337 (A. Norris 66, R. M. Loring 35, B. McBride 75, S. M. Skeete 80; A. G. Pollock three for 78, N. A. Fusedale three for 81); Transvaal B 171 (N. Pothas 33; S. M. Skeete three for 34) and 346 for eight (N. R. Rhodes 77, H. A. Manack 100, N. Pothas 72, Extras 31; L. C. R. Jordaan five for 69). *Eastern Transvaal 7 pts, Transvaal B 4 pts.*

At Brackenfell Sports Fields, Brackenfell, December 17, 18, 19. Transvaal B won by an innings and 21 runs. Boland B* 146 (W. S. Truter 34, S. B. Hockly 32; N. A. Fusedale four for 23) and 233 (S. B. Hockly 30, C. S. N. Marais 107, M. S. Bredell 45; A. V. Griffiths five for 78); Transvaal B 400 for nine dec. (N. R. Rhodes 141, C. Grainger 90, Extras 32; W. S. Truter four for 59). *Transvaal B 18 pts, Boland B 2 pts.*

At PAM Brink Stadium, Springs, December 17, 18, 19. Eastern Transvaal won by seven wickets. Orange Free State B* 111 (S. M. Skeete three for 35, L. D. Botha three for 39) and 282 (S. Nicolson 103, C. Light 121; L. C. R. Jordaan six for 93, T. A. Marsh four for 52); Eastern Transvaal 240 (W. R. Radford 30, A. Norris 35, T. A. Marsh 65, L. D. Botha 39, Extras 32; S. A. Cilliers four for 88) and 157 for three (W. R. Radford 32, C. R. Norris 51 not out). *Eastern Transvaal 16 pts, Orange Free State B 5 pts.*

At Springbok Park, Bloemfontein, January 5, 6, 7. Drawn. Orange Free State B* 450 for nine dec. (I. G. van Aswegen 92, A. T. Hansen 47, A. Moreby 115, N. S. Botha 70, S. G. Cronje 39; B. S. Forbes three for 100, G. B. Shaw four for 103) and 58 for five (D. Roussouw three for 21); Eastern Province B 173 (P. I. Barclay 40; S. G. Cronje four for 54, F. N. Botha five for 41) and 380 (M. C. Venter 73, M. G. Beamish 99, D. Roussouw 68 not out; P. Wille four for 67, S. G. Cronje four for 97). *Orange Free State B 9 pts, Eastern Province B 4 pts.*

At NFO Ground, Randjesfontein, January 5, 6, 7. Transvaal B won by six wickets. Border B* 303 for seven dec. (L. M. Fuhri 126, G. W. Thompson 36, D. O. Nosworthy 89; M. R. Hobson three for 43) and 198 (G. W. Thompson 60, C. F. Spilhaus 60; M. R. Hobson four for 45, G. A. Pollock three for 21); Transvaal B 272 for seven dec. (A. M. Bacher 73, H. A. Manack 57, G. A. Pollock 32, N. Pothas 39 not out; Q. R. Still three for 62) and 234 for four (A. M. Bacher 119 not out, C. Grainger 34; A. Badenhorst three for 27). *Transvaal B 16 pts, Border B 7 pts.*

At Brackenfell Sports Fields, Brackenfell, January 6, 7, 8. Eastern Transvaal won by 100 runs. Eastern Transvaal* 282 (C. R. Norris 44, B. McBride 44, T. A. Marsh 93; R. Telemachus three for 44) and 208 for nine dec. (S. M. Skeete 51, C. R. Norris 39; M. S. Bredell three for 52, R. I. Dalrymple five for 48); Boland B 160 (R. Telemachus 59; S. M. Skeete three for 72, L. C. R. Jordaan six for 59) and 230 (M. M. Brink 36, C. S. N. Marais 77, M. S. Bredell 39; L. C. R. Jordaan six for 89). *Eastern Transvaal 17 pts, Boland B 5 pts.*

At St George's Park, Port Elizabeth, January 26, 27, 28. Eastern Province B won by 37 runs. Eastern Province B* 117 (M. R. Hobson five for 29, M. J. Vandrau five for 46) and 336 (P. I. Barclay 52, M. C. Venter 110, G. C. Victor 35, S. C. Pope 39, C. C. Wait 42; M. J. Vandrau five for 76); Transvaal B 249 (A. M. Bacher 58, W. V. Rippon 115 not out; D. Roussouw three for 68) and 167 (W. V. Rippon 39, N. D. McKenzie 53; G. B. Shaw four for 53). *Eastern Province B 15 pts, Transvaal B 6 pts.*

At Springbok Park, Bloemfontein, January 26, 27, 28. Orange Free State B won by five wickets. Boland B* 257 (J. S. Roos 70, W. N. van As 43, M. S. Bredell 46, M. M. Brink 37; S. A. Cilliers three for 67) and 297 for three dec. (J. M. Henderson 122 not out, W. J. Smit 44, M. M. Brink 77); Orange Free State B 253 (S. Nicolson 43, I. G. van Aswegen 39, C. Light 35, B. T. Player 34; B. A. S. Chedburn three for 51) and 302 for five (I. G. van Aswegen 50, C. Light 84, A. T. Hansen 50 not out, B. T. Player 47). *Orange Free State B 17 pts, Boland B 6 pts.*

Henderson scored 122 not out on first-class debut.

At PAM Brink Stadium, Springs, January 27, 28, 29. Drawn. Border B 383 (Q. R. Still 50, A. G. Lawson 67, G. W. Thompson 34, M. L. Lax 90 not out, S. E. Fourie 44; J. R. Meyer four for 51) and 269 for six (A. C. Dewar 53, C. R. Wilson 101, M. L. Lax 32, S. E. Fourie 41 not out; C. R. Norris three for 100); Eastern Transvaal* 533 (C. R. Norris 107, I. A. Hoffmann 100, T. A. Marsh 33, S. M. Skeete 119, L. D. Botha 50; S. E. Fourie three for 124). *Eastern Transvaal 10 pts, Border B 7 pts.*

Wilson scored 101 on first-class debut.

Section 2

At Witrand Cricket Field, Potchefstroom, November 3, 4, 5. Northern Transvaal B won by 115 runs. Northern Transvaal B 271 (M. J. G. Davis 60, D. J. van Zyl 78; A. Cilliers four for 54) and 145 (M. J. G. Davis 46; A. Cilliers three for 25, D. J. van Schalkwyk four for 34); Western Transvaal* 164 (J. P. van der Westhuizen 48; M. J. G. Davis eight for 37) and 137 (H. W. D. Springer 43; G. J. Smith four for 32, M. J. G. Davis four for 47). *Northern Transvaal B 17 pts, Western Transvaal 5 pts.*

At Kimberley Country Club, Kimberley, November 4, 5, 6. Zimbabwe Board XI won by an innings and 19 runs. Zimbabwe Board XI 423 for nine dec. (M. G. Burmester 31, I. P. Butchart 99, E. A. Brandes 165 not out, Extras 32); Griqualand West* 121 (W. E. Schonegevel 34; E. A. Brandes seven for 38, P. A. Strang three for 39) and 283 (W. E. Schonegevel 34, M. I. Gidley 39, F. C. Brooker 33, R. A. Koster 69, H. A. Page 39; P. A. Strang five for 77). *Zimbabwe Board XI 20 pts, Griqualand West 5 pts.*

Brandes and D. J. Rowett added an unbroken 117 for the Zimbabwe Board XI's tenth wicket, a national record.

At Tigers CC, Parow, Cape Town, November 11, 12, 13. Western Province B won by nine wickets. Western Transvaal 242 (H. M. de Vos 35, H. G. Prinsloo 82, L. Botes 64; M. A. Meyer three for 41, D. Q. MacHelm four for 93) and 127 (L. van Wyk 33; T. J. Mitchell three for 15); Western Province B* 300 for eight dec. (B. C. Baguley 133 not out, H. H. Gibbs 60; L. Botes four for 67, H. G. Prinsloo three for 68) and 70 for one (B. C. Baguley 39 not out). *Western Province B 16 pts, Western Transvaal 4 pts.*

At Kingsmead, Durban, November 17, 18, 19. Natal B won by an innings and 62 runs. Western Province B* 157 (H. H. Gibbs 59; L. Klusener five for 46, R. E. Veenstra four for 40) and 246 (B. C. Baguley 72, D. Jordaan 31, F. B. Touzel 37, H. H. Gibbs 35; R. K. McGlashan six for 100); Natal B 465 for eight dec. (D. J. Watson 45, D. M. Benkenstein 69, D. N. Crookes 74, R. E. Veenstra 75, L. Klusener 105, U. H. Goedeke 44 not out). *Natal B 17 pts, Western Province B 3 pts.*

At Bulawayo Athletic Club, December 1, 2, 3. Drawn. Western Transvaal 248 (J. S. Olivier 34, H. W. D. Springer 34, A. Cilliers 42, L. Botes 61 not out; M. P. Jarvis four for 71) and 279 for seven (J. P. van der Westhuizen 51, H. G. Prinsloo 78, A. Cilliers 64 not out); Zimbabwe Board XI* 400 for seven dec. (S. V. Carlisle 97, K. J. Arnott 85, G. K. Bruk-Jackson 119 not out, J. A. Rennie 49; L. Botes three for 72). *Zimbabwe Board XI 6 pts, Western Transvaal 4 pts.*

At Northerns-Goodwood CC Oval, Goodwood, Cape Town, December 2, 3, 4. Western Province B won by an innings and two runs. Griqualand West* 208 (H. A. Page 89; G. Bramwell five for 74, T. J. Mitchell three for 23) and 176 (R. A. Koster 64, P. McLaren 33 not out; C. V. English four for 30, D. Q. MacHelm four for 38); Western Province B 386 (H. H. Gibbs 101, S. Conrad 32, T. J. Mitchell 85, A. C. Dawson 42, Extras 42; A. P. van Troost three for 81, P. McLaren three for 66). *Western Province B 18 pts, Griqualand West 4 pts.*

At Kingsmead, Durban, December 9, 10, 11. Natal B won by nine wickets. Northern Transvaal B 122 (W. M. Dry 51 not out) and 268 (A. J. Seymore 56, I. Pistorius 59; D. J. Pryke three for 35, R. K. McGlashan five for 99); Natal B* 362 for nine dec. (D. M. Benkenstein 203 not out, D. N. Crookes 37; C. van Noordwyk six for 100) and 29 for one. *Natal B 18 pts, Northern Transvaal B 5 pts.*

At Harare Sports Club, Harare, December 15, 16, 17. Drawn. Zimbabwe Board XI* 317 (K. J. Arnott 33, A. C. Waller 76, G. K. Bruk-Jackson 48, D. N. Erasmus 97; T. Bosch three for 39, K. G. Storey four for 63, D. N. Crookes three for 106) and 169 (S. V. Carlisle 60; T. Bosch four for 44, K. G. Storey three for 52); Natal B 265 (C. R. B. Armstrong 31, C. B. Sugden 40, D. N. Crookes 109; M. P. Jarvis six for 62) and 136 for five (C. B. Sugden 40, D. N. Crookes 30; B. C. Strang three for 45). *Zimbabwe Board XI 8 pts, Natal B 7 pts.*

At Centurion Park, Verwoerdburg, December 17, 18, 19. Drawn. Western Province B* 278 for nine dec. (F. B. Touzel 44, S. Conrad 61, H. H. Donachie 35, F. Davids 46; G. J. Kruis three for 57, N. Martin three for 63) and 181 (D. Jordaan 39, H. H. Donachie 66; M. C. Krug three for 38, D. J. J. de Vos three for 58); Northern Transvaal B 241 for seven dec. (P. H. Barnard 59, W. M. Dry 41, C. van Noordwyk 35 not out; D. Q. MacHelm three for 32) and 178 for nine (I. Pistorius 32, G. Dros 31; D. Q. MacHelm three for 70, G. Bramwell three for 49). *Northern Transvaal B 6 pts, Western Province B 6 pts.*

At Harare Sports Club, Harare, January 5, 6, 7. Northern Transvaal B won by 181 runs. Northern Transvaal B* 276 for nine dec. (P. H. Barnard 78, I. Pistorius 84, D. J. van Zyl 33, Extras 39; B. C. Strang four for 59) and 227 for seven dec. (A. J. Seymore 44, D. J. Smith 40, N. Martin 59 not out); Zimbabwe Board XI 205 (S. V. Carlisle 74; C. van Noordwyk three for 45, N. Martin four for 67) and 117 (M. C. Krug four for 23, D. J. van Zyl three for 16). *Northern Transvaal B 17 pts, Zimbabwe Board XI 4 pts.*

At Kimberley Country Club, Kimberley, January 6, 7, 8. Drawn. Natal B 476 for seven dec. (C. B. Sugden 106, E. L. R. Stewart 146, K. A. Forde 44, R. D. Allen 43, G. W. Bashford 76, D. J. Pryke 36 not out; M. I. Gidley three for 143); Griqualand West* 453 for seven (W. E. Schonegevel 76, M. I. Gidley 69, F. C. Brooker 63, R. A. Koster 30, H. A. Page 44, M. N. Angel 40 not out, J. Burger 54 not out, Extras 49; K. A. Forde three for 52). *Griqualand West 3 pts, Natal B 4 pts.*

At Kimberley Country Club, Kimberley, January 13, 14, 15. Drawn. Western Transvaal* 237 (A. J. van Deventer 57, H. W. D. Springer 31; H. A. Page three for 79, M. I. Gidley three for 79, M. N. Angel three for 29) and 143 for three dec. (A. J. van Deventer 68 not out); Griqualand West 79 for two dec. (W. E. Schonegevel 39) and 159 for six (M. Michau 39, R. A. Koster 40; D. J. van Schalkwyk three for 76). *Griqualand West 5 pts, Western Transvaal 2 pts.*

At Newlands, Cape Town, January 26, 27, 28. Drawn. Western Province B 284 for eight dec. (F. B. Touzel 77, C. V. English 108, G. Bramwell 30 not out; B. C. Strang four for 73) and 257 (B. C. Baguley 76, F. Davids 33; P. A. Strang five for 88, U. Ranchod three for 54); Zimbabwe Board XI* 260 (S. V. Carlisle 47, D. N. Erasmus 81; F. Davids three for 28, D. Q. MacHelm five for 57) and 86 for four (G. K. Bruk-Jackson 33 not out; F. Davids three for 20). *Western Province B 7 pts, Zimbabwe Board XI 6 pts.*
   Davids took a hat-trick spanning the Zimbabwe Board XI's two innings.

At Witrand Cricket Field, Potchefstroom, January 26, 27, 28. Natal B won by an innings and two runs. Western Transvaal* 184 (H. M. de Vos 31, H. G. Prinsloo 73 not out; G. M. Gilder four for 42, D. J. Pryke three for 36) and 208 (J. P. van der Westhuizen 105 not out; K. G. Storey three for 44); Natal B 394 for four dec. (D. J. Watson 47, C. R. B. Armstrong 112, E. L. R. Stewart 122 not out, K. A. Forde 57, P. L. Symcox 45). *Natal B 18 pts, Western Transvaal 2 pts.*

At Centurion Park, Verwoerdburg, February 3, 4, 5. Griqualand West won by six wickets. Northern Transvaal B 276 for nine dec. (P. H. Barnard 32, I. Pistorius 54, W. M. Dry 34, N. Martin 76; H. A. Page four for 49, M. I. Gidley three for 81) and 299 for five dec. (P. H. Barnard 62, A. J. Seymore 55, D. J. van Zyl 34, G. Dros 42, W. M. Dry 56 not out, N. Martin 44; M. I. Gidley three for 101); Griqualand West* 253 for nine dec. (F. C. Brooker 49, M. Michau 73, G. F. Venter 36; M. C. Krug four for 83) and 323 for four (M. I. Gidley 113, H. A. Page 95, M. Michau 40 not out). *Griqualand West 17 pts, Northern Transvaal B 7 pts.*

Final

At Kingsmead, Durban, February 17, 18, 19. Natal B won by five wickets. Eastern Transvaal* 212 (I. A. Hoffmann 40, T. A. Marsh 37 not out; D. J. Pryke four for 50) and 81 (B. N. Benkenstein four for 23); Natal B 150 (K. A. Forde 59; S. M. Skeete four for 51, L. C. R. Jordaan five for 44) and 144 for five (C. B. Sugden 44 not out, R. D. Allen 42).

OTHER FIRST-CLASS MATCH

The match between Boland and Warwickshire on April 1, 2, 3 may be found in English Counties Overseas, 1994-95.

BENSON AND HEDGES SERIES, 1994-95

Note: Matches in this section were not first-class.

Semi-finals

At Springbok Park, Bloemfontein, March 29. Orange Free State v Western Province. Abandoned.

At Newlands, Cape Town, March 31. Orange Free State won by 24 runs. Orange Free State* 253 for eight (50 overs) (P. J. R. Steyn 63, W. J. Cronje 101); Western Province 229 (49.3 overs) (D. L. Haynes 92; F. D. Stephenson three for 41, A. A. Donald three for 35).

At St George's Park, Port Elizabeth, April 5. Eastern Province won by 22 runs. Eastern Province* 262 for four (50 overs) (G. C. Victor 47, P. G. Amm 78, K. C. Wessels 67, D. J. Callaghan 49 not out); Boland 240 for nine (50 overs) (L. D. Ferreira 45, K. M. Curran 57, L-M. Germishuys 49; D. J. Callaghan three for 29).

At Boland Bank Park, Paarl, April 7. Eastern Province won by six wickets. *Boland 179 for eight (50 overs) (K. C. Jackson 39, K. M. Curran 68 not out; E. A. E. Baptiste three for 26); Eastern Province 183 for four (45 overs) (P. G. Amm 33, M. W. Handman 44, L. J. Koen 51 not out).

Final

At Springbok Park, Bloemfontein, April 13. Orange Free State won by 113 runs. Orange Free State 291 for eight (50 overs) (P. J. R. Steyn 53, W. J. Cronje 61, L. J. Wilkinson 83, F. D. Stephenson 36; B. N. Schultz four for 38, E. A. E. Baptiste three for 48); Eastern Province* 178 for eight (50 overs) (M. W. Handman 35 not out; N. Boje four for 39).

COCA-COLA CRICKET WEEK, 1994-95

The 52nd annual Cricket Week, formerly known as Nuffield Week, was held in Natal in a new format open to all Under-19 players instead of just schoolboys. At the end of the week a South African Under-19 XI was chosen to play Natal comprising: N. D. McKenzie (Transvaal, *captain*), M. V. Boucher (Border), Z. de Bruyn (Transvaal), B. K. Hughes (Natal), G. D. Jones (Natal), T. Ngxoweni (Border) A. M. Omar (Transvaal), J. September (Eastern Province), D. J. Terbrugge (Transvaal), I. G. van Aswegen (Orange Free State) and C. J. Vorster (Boland).

CRICKET IN THE WEST INDIES, 1994-95

By TONY COZIER

Immediately erasing the troubling memory of their barren season a year before, Barbados regained the Red Stripe Cup they last won in 1990-91 and qualified for the final of the revamped limited-overs tournament, the Shell/ Sandals Trophy.

It was the 13th time Barbados had secured the regional first-class title outright since it was inaugurated in 1965-66 as the Shell Shield. Their success was achieved by a young team – only the celebrated opening batsman Desmond Haynes and left-arm spinner Winston Reid were over 30 – and under a new captain, wicket-keeper Courtney Browne. It followed a disappointing 1993-94 when, for the first time in their history, Barbados failed to win a first-class match. Only the absence of the leading West Indies players, touring New Zealand, and a home defeat by Trinidad & Tobago in their final match, when the championship was already decided, took some of the sheen from the Barbados triumph.

It was the Trinidadians' first win at Kensington Oval since 1938-39. While they had to be satisfied with third place, they also had the satisfaction of beating the reigning champions, Leeward Islands, in a dramatic last-over finish to the opening match of the season. That was an immediate setback for the Leewards. But their title was finally lost when they conceded first-innings lead in a draw with Barbados, in the first first-class match ever played in Anguilla, where the Webster Park pitch was widely praised as the best in the Caribbean. Even with five Test players on tour of New Zealand, the Leewards emphasised the depth of their squad by innings victories over Guyana, Jamaica and the Windward Islands. Back to full strength for the Shell/Sandals Trophy, they retained the limited-overs championship, comfortably beating Barbados in the final on an unsatisfactory pitch at the Antigua Recreation Ground.

The Leewards were led by Richie Richardson, returning to his first competitive cricket since he left Yorkshire in July 1994, when his doctors ordered him to take a six-month break because of "acute fatigue syndrome". In the interim, Courtney Walsh had been appointed caretaker captain for the West Indian tours of India and New Zealand. Richardson's reappearance caused considerable interest. Although he sometimes batted in a helmet, a novel sight, he dispelled any doubts about his physical, and indeed psychological, condition by taking hundreds off Guyana, Barbados and the Windwards. He was the leading scorer in the Red Stripe Cup with 544 runs at 77.71, the first time he had passed 500 in the tournament.

Another Test player resuming his interrupted career was fast bowler Ian Bishop, inactive for nearly two years because of a second stress fracture in his lower back. He had been an integral part of the West Indian attack, with 83 wickets in 18 Tests before his injury, and his progress was monitored as carefully as Richardson's. As captain of Trinidad & Tobago in Brian Lara's absence, he restricted himself mostly to short spells. In only one innings did he bowl more than 20 overs but, though a groin strain kept him out of one game, he reported no recurrence of the injuries that had limited him to seven Tests in the preceding four years.

Another familiar name seeking reinstatement was Haynes. Approaching 39, he was the oldest player in the tournament and, having made his debut in 1976-77, also the longest-serving. Haynes had opted out of the tours of India and New Zealand, choosing instead a contract with the South African team, Western Province. He was keen, however, to regain his Test place for the home series against Australia. He broke off his season in South Africa to play in the Red Stripe Cup but, for reasons not entirely clear, arrived back two days late for the opening match against Jamaica. This meant he did not meet the rigid West Indies Cricket Board of Control rules on qualification for Test selection, which demand appearance in all five matches, barring injury or "special extenuating circumstances" – or absence with the international squad. In spite of two appeals for mitigation, the WICBC remained adamant that Haynes had disqualified himself, creating a public furore. Haynes brought a legal suit against them in the Barbados High Court, mainly on grounds of restraint of trade.

Though it looked likely to be his last first-class season in the West Indies, Haynes's experience was a bonus for Barbados. His 470 runs included an unbeaten 201, occupying almost ten hours, against the Windward Islands at Arnos Vale, St Vincent, the ground's highest individual score.

Roger Harper, the 31-year-old all-rounder in his 16th season, handed over the captaincy of Guyana he had held for nine years to Keith Semple, but was still in the thick of things, claiming 25 wickets with his off-spin, at 18.56 each, and reaching his highest score in regional cricket, 202 against the Windwards. The hard-hitting openers, Philo Wallace of Barbados and Robert Samuels of Jamaica, both kept their credentials in front of the selectors by passing 400 runs, as did the steady Dawnley Joseph, captain of the Windward Islands, who failed to win a match and were, yet again, bottom of the table. The seventh batsman to reach 400 in the Cup was the consistent Suraj Ragoonath, previously an irregular choice in the Trinidad & Tobago team, who did not score a hundred.

Some of the less familiar names came to the fore for the Leewards, including the Joseph brothers from Antigua, who might not have had any chance but for the many vacancies created by the West Indies selectors. Dave, a powerful, 25-year-old batsman, equalled his captain Richardson's three hundreds. His 514 runs, at an average of 102.80, were made aggressively and attractively. He had been a record-breaker in the Under-19 tournament in 1988-89 but had not maintained the fitness and commitment necessary at the higher level until now. His brother Jenson, three years older, generated lively pace from a deceptively short run to be the joint-highest wicket-taker, with 28, in his first season in the Red Stripe Cup – adequately filling the gap left by Ambrose and the Benjamins. The other bowler with 28 wickets was his team-mate, left-arm spinner Warrington Phillip, who took 13 for 123 in the innings victory over Jamaica on his native island of Nevis. Another slow left-armer, Reid of Barbados, collected 27 from 250.1 overs; only Harper bowled more. Jamaica, too, depended heavily on leg-spinner Robert Haynes and off-spinner Nehemiah Perry.

The search for new fast bowlers was not encouraging, although Reon King, of Guyana, showed distinct promise in the Under-19 series against England, which had first claim on players ahead of the Red Stripe Cup. The appropriately named Patterson Thompson, a powerfully built Barbadian, showed genuine pace, if not much control, in his first season and Nigel Francis, a tall Trinidadian, looked an interesting prospect in spite of his figures (15 wickets at 35.26). Otherwise, Vasbert Drakes and Ottis Gibson, the two Barbadians who had long since advanced their claims, demanded most attention. Drakes backed his 27 wickets with the innings of the season, an unbeaten 180 against the Leewards. It began with Barbados on shaky ground, at 144 for five in their second innings, and included seven sixes.

The domestic limited-overs tournament carried new sponsors, a new name and a new format, but produced the same champions as 1993-94. The Shell/Sandals Trophy, jointly sponsored by the oil company and the holiday resort group, replaced the Geddes Grant Shield and was contested after the Red Stripe Cup finished. The six teams were divided into two zones, and preliminary rounds, hosted in Guyana and Jamaica, saw each team play the other two twice over nine days. The top Cup sides, the Leewards and Barbados, qualified for the final, though Leewards were separated from Guyana only on net run-rate. But injury and confusion over the rules then deprived Barbados of three Test players, Haynes, Sherwin Campbell and Andy Cummins. Each squad was restricted to 14 players, although one change was allowed halfway through the preliminaries to accommodate those returning from New Zealand. Barbados unwittingly exhausted their changes, eliminating Haynes and Campbell from the final, when Cummins was injured. The match, played on a poor pitch, was an anticlimax: Hamish Anthony's record return of seven for 15 from seven overs, five of them clean bowled, proved decisive. It was the first regional match ever transmitted live on television throughout the Caribbean.

FIRST-CLASS AVERAGES, 1994-95

BATTING

(Qualification: 200 runs)

	M	I	NO	R	HS	100s	Avge
D. R. E. Joseph (*Leeward I.*)	7	10	2	606	131	3	75.75
D. L. Haynes (*Barbados*)	4	8	1	470	201*	1	67.14
S. Ragoonath (*T & T*)	6	11	2	516	97	0	57.33
R. G. Samuels (*Jamaica*)	7	13	2	615	159	1	55.90
R. B. Richardson (*Leeward I.*)	9	15	1	773	152	4	55.21
D. A. Joseph (*Windward I.*)	5	10	1	443	131	1	49.22
B. C. Lara (*West Indies*)	4	8	1	308	88	0	44.00
F. L. Reifer (*Barbados*)	5	10	3	308	85*	0	44.00
P. V. Simmons (*T & T*)	5	9	0	377	92	0	41.88
D. Williams (*T & T*)	5	9	1	318	112	1	39.75
C. O. Browne (*Barbados*)	7	12	4	316	74	0	39.50
P. A. Wallace (*Barbados*)	6	11	0	432	106	1	39.27
R. A. Harper (*Guyana*)	6	11	0	396	202	1	36.00
D. S. Morgan (*Jamaica*)	5	10	1	307	75*	0	34.11
Sudesh Dhaniram (*Guyana*)	6	11	0	369	100	1	33.54
V. C. Drakes (*Barbados*)	6	9	1	268	180*	1	33.50
R. D. Jacobs (*Leeward I.*)	6	8	1	233	83	0	33.28
P. D. Persaud (*Guyana*)	6	11	0	348	110	1	31.63
N. O. Perry (*Jamaica*)	6	10	1	270	89	0	30.00
L. K. Puckerin (*Barbados*)	5	9	0	269	55	0	29.88
M. D. Liburd (*Leeward I.*)	5	7	0	207	77	0	29.57
J. Eugene (*Windward I.*)	4	8	1	202	46	0	28.85
K. F. Semple (*Guyana*)	7	13	0	369	67	0	28.38

	M	I	NO	R	HS	100s	Avge
U. Pope (*Windward I.*)	5	9	0	251	91	0	27.88
K. Mason (*T & T*)	5	9	0	239	84	0	26.55
N. A. McKenzie (*Guyana*)	5	9	0	219	57	0	24.33
W. W. Lewis (*Jamaica*)	5	9	0	218	111	1	24.22
R. A. Marshall (*Windward I.*)	5	9	0	217	65	0	24.11

* *Signifies not out.*

BOWLING

(Qualification: 15 wickets)

	O	M	R	W	BB	5W/i	Avge
W. D. Phillip (*Leeward I.*)	167.1	48	434	28	8-92	2	15.50
J. E. S. Joseph (*Leeward I.*)	154.5	30	512	28	5-59	1	18.28
W. E. Reid (*Barbados*)	250.1	78	533	27	6-73	1	19.74
R. A. Harper (*Guyana*)	281.2	81	540	27	5-77	2	20.00
I. R. Bishop (*T & T*)	88.3	16	345	17	4-44	0	20.29
C. A. Walsh (*West Indies*)	148.3	33	431	20	6-54	1	21.55
N. O. Perry (*Jamaica*)	185.4	46	437	20	5-41	1	21.85
R. C. Haynes (*Jamaica*)	234.4	53	550	24	5-82	2	22.91
V. C. Drakes (*Barbados*)	183	23	661	28	7-47	2	23.60
B. St A. Browne (*Guyana*)	139.3	25	455	19	6-81	1	23.94
A. H. Gray (*T & T*)	126.2	19	447	17	4-40	0	26.29
M. Persad (*T & T*)	199.1	44	500	19	5-63	1	26.31
O. D. Gibson (*Barbados*)	200.1	27	703	26	4-45	0	27.03
H. A. G. Anthony (*Leeward I.*) . .	150.4	27	512	18	4-70	0	28.44
L. C. Weekes (*Leeward I.*)	116	7	470	16	4-15	0	29.37
C. E. Cuffy (*Windward I.*)	153.1	22	513	17	7-80	2	30.17
M. V. Nagamootoo (*Guyana*)	170.3	27	482	15	4-130	0	32.13
N. B. Francis (*T & T*)	130	20	529	15	4-57	0	35.26

RED STRIPE CUP, 1994-95

	Played	Won	Lost	Drawn	1st-inns Points	Points
Barbados	5	3	1	1	4	56
Leeward Islands	5	3	1	1	0	52
Trinidad & Tobago	5	2	0	3	4	48
Jamaica	5	1	3	1	9	29
Guyana	5	1	2	2	4	28
Windward Islands	5	0	3	2	4	12

Win = 16 pts; draw = 4 pts; 1st-innings lead in drawn match = 4 pts; 1st-innings lead in lost match = 5 pts.

In the following scores, * by the name of a team indicates that they won the toss.

At Sabina Park, Kingston, January 6, 7, 8, 9. Barbados won by four wickets. Jamaica* 282 (D. S. Morgan 39, R. C. Haynes 95, S. G. B. Ford 50, Extras 39; P. I. C. Thompson four for 46, W. E. Reid three for 43) and 225 (D. S. Morgan 46, M. D. Ventura 45; O. D. Gibson three for 46, W. E. Reid three for 47); Barbados 298 (P. A. Wallace 50, F. L. Reifer 85 not out, L. K. Puckerin 55, C. O. Browne 43; N. O. Perry five for 41, B. S. Murphy three for 65) and 210 for six (P. A. Wallace 71, F. L. Reifer 31, C. O. Browne 38 not out, V. C. Drakes 30). *Barbados 16 pts.*

At Guaracara Park, Pointe-à-Pierre (Trinidad), January 6, 7, 8, 9. Trinidad & Tobago won by 80 runs. Trinidad & Tobago* 405 (S. Ragoonath 67, K. Mason 43, D. Williams 112, M. Bodoe 35, A. H. Gray 44; W. D. Phillip three for 67, H. A. G. Anthony three for 61) and 226 (A. Balliram 54, S. Ragoonath 46; J. E. S. Joseph five for 59); Leeward Islands 288 (D. R. E. Joseph 131, W. D. Phillip 39; N. B. Francis four for 71) and 263 (M. D. Liburd 34, R. B. Richardson 86, H. A. G. Anthony 66; I. R. Bishop four for 44, M. Persad three for 68). *Trinidad & Tobago 16 pts.*

At Sabina Park, Kingston, January 13, 14, 15, 16. Drawn. Jamaica* 383 (D. S. Morgan 36, R. G. Samuels 41, W. W. Lewis 111, L. R. Williams 64, Extras 41; A. H. Gray three for 88, M. Persad three for 66) and 163 for no wkt (D. S. Morgan 75 not out, R. G. Samuels 77 not out); Trinidad & Tobago 311 (P. V. Simmons 83, S. Ragoonath 97, M. Bodoe 56 not out; J. B. Grant three for 43, R. C. Haynes four for 95). *Jamaica 8 pts, Trinidad & Tobago 4 pts.*

At Recreation Ground, St John's, January 13, 14, 15. Leeward Islands won by an innings and 84 runs. Leeward Islands 310 (R. B. Richardson 104, D. R. E. Joseph 77, Extras 31; B. St A. Browne six for 81); Guyana† 136 (L. C. Weekes three for 57, J. E. S. Joseph four for 32, W. D. Phillip three for 13) and 90 (J. E. S. Joseph four for 37, L. C. Weekes four for 15). *Leeward Islands 16 pts.*

At Arnos Vale, St Vincent, January 13, 14, 15, 16. Barbados won by eight wickets. Barbados 440 for five dec. (D. L. Haynes 201 not out, R. L. Hoyte 54, F. L. Reifer 81, L. K. Puckerin 44, Extras 38) and 26 for two; Windward Islands* 289 (D. A. Joseph 94, R. A. Marshall 44, Extras 32; W. E. Reid six for 73) and 175 (D. A. Joseph 80, Extras 30; O. D. Gibson three for 54). *Barbados 16 pts.*
Haynes's double-hundred was the first scored at Arnos Vale.

At Kensington Oval, Bridgetown, January 20, 21, 22, 23. Barbados won by six wickets. Guyana 160 (P. D. Persaud 52, K. F. Semple 54; V. C. Drakes seven for 47) and 227 (Sudesh Dhaniram 43, R. A. Harper 77, M. V. Nagamootoo 33; O. D. Gibson four for 52, W. E. Reid three for 58); Barbados* 230 (D. L. Haynes 74, P. A. Wallace 66, L. K. Puckerin 36; R. A. Harper five for 77, G. H. Nedd three for 42) and 158 for four (D. L. Haynes 48, F. L. Reifer 48 not out). *Barbados 16 pts.*

At Grove Park, Nevis, January 20, 21, 22. Leeward Islands won by an innings and 67 runs. Leeward Islands 425 (L. A. Harrigan 63, M. D. Liburd 32, R. D. Jacobs 47, D. R. E. Joseph 112 not out, H. A. G. Anthony 75; R. C. Haynes five for 95, N. O. Perry three for 72); Jamaica* 264 (R. G. Samuels 54, D. S. Morgan 33, N. O. Perry 89; W. D. Phillip eight for 92) and 94 (W. D. Phillip five for 31, J. E. S. Joseph four for 19). *Leeward Islands 16 pts.*

At Queen's Park Oval, Port-of-Spain, January 20, 21, 22, 23. Drawn. Windward Islands* 331 (K. K. Sylvester 73, R. A. Marshall 65, U. Pope 67, E. J. Warrican 44; A. H. Gray four for 67, M. Persad three for 62) and 177 for nine dec. (U. Pope 30, C. A. Davis 31 not out; N. B. Francis four for 57); Trinidad & Tobago 183 (K. Mason 84, Extras 37; C. E. Cuffy five for 60) and 183 for five (A. Balliram 75, S. Ragoonath 43). *Trinidad & Tobago 4 pts, Windward Islands 8 pts.*

At Albion, Berbice (Guyana), January 27, 28, 29, 30. Drawn. Trinidad & Tobago* 360 (P. V. Simmons 74, S. Ragoonath 37, K. Mason 30, D. Williams 56, M. Bodoe 53, I. R. Bishop 38; B. St A. Browne three for 52, R. A. Harper four for 94) and 104 for six (S. Ragoonath 55 not out; B. St A. Browne three for 42); Guyana 171 (N. A. McKenzie 57; A. H. Gray four for 40) and 340 (P. D. Persaud 85, Sudesh Dhaniram 100, N. A. McKenzie 41; I. R. Bishop four for 53). *Guyana 4 pts, Trinidad & Tobago 8 pts.*

At Webster Park, Anguilla, January 27, 28, 29, 30. Drawn. Barbados* 258 (D. L. Haynes 34, P. A. Wallace 106; L. C. Weekes three for 46, H. A. G. Anthony four for 73, J. E. S. Joseph three for 52) and 444 (D. L. Haynes 67, L. K. Puckerin 34, C. O. Browne 74, V. C. Drakes 180 not out; H. A. G. Anthony four for 112, W. D. Phillip three for 88); Leeward Islands† 222 (L. A. Harrigan 37, M. D. Liburd 36, C. M. Tuckett 33, R. B. Richardson 36; O. D. Gibson three for 63, V. C. Drakes four for 65, W. E. Reid three for 44) and 406 for five (R. B. Richardson 152, R. D. Jacobs 83, D. R. E. Joseph 85 not out). *Leeward Islands 4 pts, Barbados 8 pts.*
Anguilla's first first-class match at the West Indies' 33rd first-class venue.

At Mindoo Phillip Park, Castries (St Lucia), January 27, 28, 29, 30. Jamaica won by eight wickets. Jamaica* 342 (D. S. Morgan 30, R. G. Samuels 159, W. W. Lewis 31, Extras 30) and 17 for two; Windward Islands 141 (M. C. Thomas 39, J. Eugene 46; R. C. Haynes three for 45, N. O. Perry four for 29) and 217 (K. K. Sylvester 31, M. C. Thomas 37, D. Thomas 42 not out; R. C. Haynes five for 82). *Jamaica 16 pts.*

At Kensington Oval, Bridgetown, February 3, 4, 5, 6. Trinidad & Tobago won by 129 runs. Trinidad & Tobago 297 (P. V. Simmons 63, S. Ragoonath 96, D. Williams 61; O. D. Gibson three for 79, W. E. Reid three for 64) and 289 for nine dec. (P. V. Simmons 92, K. Mason 64, D. Williams 48; V. C. Drakes six for 75); Barbados* 220 (D. L. Haynes 34, P. A. Wallace 38, S. N. Proverbs 48; M. Persad five for 63) and 237 (P. A. Wallace 49, C. O. Browne 70 not out; I. R. Bishop three for 48, P. V. Simmons four for 52). *Trinidad & Tobago 16 pts.*

At Albion, Berbice (Guyana), February 3, 4, 5, 6. Guyana won by 74 runs. Guyana* 125 (Sudesh Dhaniram 42; L. R. Williams five for 41) and 349 (P. D. Persaud 110, K. F. Semple 57, N. A. McKenzie 48, R. A. Harper 54, Extras 35; L. R. Williams three for 74, N. O. Perry three for 58, R. C. Haynes three for 91); Jamaica 193 (D. S. Morgan 34, S. G. B. Ford 48 not out, R. C. Haynes 30; R. A. Harper three for 50, M. V. Nagamootoo three for 25) and 207 (R. G. Samuels 67, J. B. Grant 36 not out; B. St A. Browne three for 79, R. A. Harper four for 39, M. V. Nagamootoo three for 34). *Guyana 16 pts, Jamaica 5 pts.*

At Windsor Park, Dominica, February 3, 4, 5, 6. Leeward Islands won by an innings and 43 runs. Windward Islands 263 (D. A. Joseph 64, J. A. R. Sylvester 41, R. A. Marshall 39, D. Thomas 31; W. D. Phillip three for 54) and 151 (D. Thomas 55; J. C. Maynard four for 19); Leeward Islands* 457 (M. D. Liburd 77, J. Mitchum 42, R. B. Richardson 122, D. R. E. Joseph 102, J. E. S. Joseph 44, Extras 31; C. E. Cuffy seven for 80). *Leeward Islands 16 pts.*

At Bourda, Georgetown, February 10, 11, 12, 13. Drawn. Windward Islands* 414 (D. A. Joseph 131, A. L. Crafton 31, U. Pope 91, R. N. Lewis 53 not out, Extras 36; R. A. Harper five for 98, M. V. Nagamootoo four for 130) and ten for no wkt; Guyana 479 (Sudesh Dhaniram 79, K. F. Semple 67, R. A. Harper 202, Extras 39; R. A. Marshall four for 75). *Guyana 8 pts, Windward Islands 4 pts.*

SHELL SHIELD AND RED STRIPE CUP WINNERS

The Shell Shield was replaced by the Red Stripe Cup after the 1986-87 season.

1965-66	Barbados	1980-81	Combined Islands
1966-67	Barbados	1981-82	Barbados
1967-68	No competition	1982-83	Guyana
1968-69	Jamaica	1983-84	Barbados
1969-70	Trinidad	1984-85	Trinidad & Tobago
1970-71	Trinidad	1985-86	Barbados
1971-72	Barbados	1986-87	Guyana
1972-73	Guyana	1987-88	Jamaica
1973-74	Barbados	1988-89	Jamaica
1974-75	Guyana	1989-90	Leeward Islands
1975-76 {	Trinidad	1990-91	Barbados
	Barbados	1991-92	Jamaica
1976-77	Barbados	1992-93	Guyana
1977-78	Barbados	1993-94	Leeward Islands
1978-79	Barbados	1994-95	Barbados
1979-80	Barbados		

Barbados have won the title outright 13 times, Guyana 5, Jamaica 4, Trinidad/Trinidad & Tobago 3, Leeward Islands 2, Combined Islands 1. Barbados and Trinidad also shared the title once.

SHELL/SANDALS TROPHY, 1994-95

Note: Matches in this section were not first-class.

Zone A (In Guyana)

At Bourda, Georgetown, February 18. Leeward Islands won by 71 runs. Leeward Islands 275 for seven (50 overs) (M. D. Liburd 50, D. R. E. Joseph 94, R. Powell 48; C. L. Hooper three for 36); Guyana* 204 (38.2 overs) (P. D. Persaud 54, C. L. Hooper 59, N. A. McKenzie 35; L. C. Weekes four for 33).

At Enmore, Berbice, February 19. Guyana won on scoring-rate after Windward Islands had been set a revised target of 179 from 38 overs. Guyana 235 (49.3 overs) (C. L. Hooper 97, A. R. Percival 45; C. A. Davis three for 48, D. A. Joseph three for 25); Windward Islands* 132 (35.4 overs) (R. A. Marshall 42; C. L. Hooper three for 30).

At Hampton Court, Essequibo, February 21. Leeward Islands won by 75 runs. Leeward Islands* 258 for seven (45 overs) (M. D. Liburd 65, R. B. Richardson 84, D. R. E. Joseph 33); Windward Islands 183 for nine (45 overs) (A. L. Crafton 89).

At Hampton Court, Essequibo, February 23. Guyana won by 25 runs. Guyana 202 for nine (50 overs) (C. L. Hooper 51, R. A. Harper 38 not out; C. E. L. Ambrose three for 30); Leeward Islands* 177 (44.1 overs) (K. L. T. Arthurton 58; L. A. Joseph four for 26, S. Chanderpaul three for 53).

At Skeldon, Berbice, February 25. Guyana won by eight wickets. Windward Islands 112 (42.4 overs) (S. Chanderpaul three for 12, Sudesh Dhaniram three for 29); Guyana* 114 for two (18.2 overs) (Sudesh Dhaniram 50, P. D. Persaud 41 not out).

At Albion, Berbice, February 26. Leeward Islands won by six wickets. Windward Islands 208 for seven (50 overs) (D. A. Joseph 34, J. R. Murray 42, B. B. Stapleton 34 not out; W. D. Phillip three for 25); Leeward Islands* 210 for four (28.3 overs) (S. C. Williams 89 not out, R. B. Richardson 31).

Leeward Islands 6 pts, Guyana 6 pts, Windward Islands 0 pts. Leeward Islands qualified for the final on net run-rate.

Zone B (In Jamaica)

At Sabina Park, Kingston, February 18. Trinidad & Tobago won by virtue of losing fewer wickets. Jamaica 207 for nine (46 overs) (M. D. Ventura 73 not out, N. O. Perry 34; E. C. Antoine four for 50, P. V. Simmons three for 34); Trinidad & Tobago* 207 for eight (46 overs) (P. V. Simmons 54, S. Ragoonath 42, R. Mangalie 34).

At Sabina Park, Kingston, February 19. Trinidad & Tobago won by seven wickets. Jamaica 157 (47.4 overs) (M. D. Ventura 38, R. C. Haynes 31; H. R. Bryan three for 28); Barbados* 160 for three (42.1 overs) (P. A. Wallace 56, A. F. G. Griffith 32).

At Kaiser Sports Ground, Discovery Bay, February 21. Barbados won by six wickets. Trinidad & Tobago 159 for nine (50 overs) (P. V. Simmons 35; H. R. Bryan three for 30); Barbados* 164 for four (35.2 overs) (F. L. Reifer 34, L. K. Puckerin 52 not out).

At Jarrett Park, Montego Bay, February 23. Trinidad & Tobago won by six runs. Trinidad & Tobago 215 for nine (50 overs) (P. V. Simmons 44, S. Ragoonath 52, M. Bodoe 40; L. R. Williams five for 46, N. O. Perry four for 45); Jamaica* 209 (49 overs) (R. G. Samuels 59, Extras 33; E. C. Antoine four for 43).

At Sabina Park, Kingston, February 25. Barbados won on scoring-rate when rain ended play. Barbados* 293 for eight (50 overs) (P. A. Wallace 35, A. F. G. Griffith 44, R. I. C. Holder 60, F. L. Reifer 82; F. R. Redwood four for 59); Jamaica 172 for three (35 overs) (R. G. Samuels 45, D. S. Morgan 31 not out, M. D. Ventura 37 not out).

At Sabina Park, Kingston, February 26. Barbados won on scoring-rate after Trinidad & Tobago's target had been reduced to 194 off 38 overs. Barbados* 247 for six (48.3 overs) (S. N. Proverbs 92, C. O. Browne 60 not out); Trinidad & Tobago 169 (33 overs) (R. A. M. Smith 40; V. C. Drakes three for 40, H. R. Bryan four for 42).

Barbados 8 pts, Trinidad & Tobago 4 pts, Jamaica 0 pts.

Final

At Recreation Ground, St John's, March 4. Leeward Islands won by 78 runs. Leeward Islands 188 (49 overs) (K. L. T. Arthurton 53; D. R. Maynard three for 36, H. R. Bryan three for 41); Barbados* 110 (31 overs) (F. L. Reifer 30, L. K. Puckerin 30; H. A. G. Anthony seven for 15).

CRICKET IN NEW ZEALAND, 1994-95

By TERRY POWER

New Zealand Cricket's centenary got off to a happy start, with North v South Island matches for men and women – the first time the country's 50 top cricketers had gathered together, as chief executive Graham Dowling said – at the beautiful ground of Pukekura Park in New Plymouth. The men's Test team then left, via India, for South Africa, whom they defeated convincingly at Johannesburg. But from then on it all went downhill at electrifying speed, with Test defeats by South Africa, West Indies and Sri Lanka and a string of one-day failures.

The real storms broke on the team's return from South Africa. Michael Sandlant resigned as manager, citing the demands of his pharmacy. Soon after, it was revealed that Sandlant was not the only person in the drugs business and that he had fined Matthew Hart, Stephen Fleming and Dion Nash for smoking cannabis on tour. New Zealand Cricket thought Sandlant's penalty (R500 each) inadequate and the confidentiality he had promised them inappropriate; it suspended the three (rumour implicated several others) for a week, covering the one-day series against West Indies. Meanwhile, Chris Pringle was dropped; chairman Peter McDermott eventually said he had been suspended for a week too, for having failed to prepare himself properly for the Durban Test.

To the discomfort of other board members, McDermott had established a reputation for frankness. His remarks when announcing the suspensions thus rang true: "Often there is a temptation to sweep problems under the carpet in the belief that it is for the good of the game. New Zealand has always resisted that temptation . . . We will be open, we will be tough, we will be fair and accountable." Within a fortnight, however, New Zealand Cricket took out a gagging writ against a newspaper which published extracts from a confidential tour report. Cricket director Roddy Fulton had highlighted late-night drinking, of which Sandlant was unaware until a reporter told him; coach Geoff Howarth's failure "to maintain discipline, enthusiasm and general team harmony"; captain Ken Rutherford's absence from the social scene and alleged failure to discipline the team; and the need for "a vice-captain with the strength of character to support his captain, manager and coach" (Martin Crowe was Rutherford's deputy).

This episode overlapped with protracted efforts to dispense with Howarth, appointed national coach on a three-year contract in 1992-93. He had not gained nearly as many plaudits as he did for his Test batting; after the 1994 England tour, the majority of the players were reported to be against him. But the board confirmed him for the trip to South Africa, where he was matched against the precise and analytical Bob Woolmer. Howarth finally had to be bought out of his contract, reportedly for $220,000. John F. Reid, once his Test colleague, stood in until Glenn Turner, New Zealand's 1970s star, took over in June. Gren Alabaster, a retired headmaster as well as off-spinner, became manager and tightened discipline. The new vice-captain, from the West Indian series onwards, was strike bowler Danny Morrison; significantly, he had worked as an anti-drugs campaigner.

Dowling resigned as chief executive in April and was replaced by Christopher Doig, a well-known opera singer. Selection convenor Ross Dykes withdrew and former Test captain Bevan Congdon was pushed off the selection panel by Rick Pickard of Northern Districts, who never played first-class cricket. The climax, on June 22, was the sacking of Ken Rutherford. His successor, Canterbury captain Lee Germon, had played one limited-overs international in South Africa, but no Tests. Subsequently, Fulton was suspended and then dismissed as cricket director.

Consistent failure on the cricket field contrasted starkly with triumph at sea in the America's Cup, which New Zealand will defend in 1999-2000. By then, cricket may have lost its place as the national summer sport, unless the calibre of its stewardship improves. The incident which most riled fans in 1994-95 took place at Auckland, over a one-day match against Australia. Crowe had damaged a thigh muscle, but was announced as a 50-50 chance to play. He did not, and Rutherford said afterwards that he was never going to; the prediction was just an attempt to get more people into the ground. McDermott claimed Rutherford was joking. But Dowling acknowledged the comment arose from a remark by marketing manager Mike Dolden – who, unlike Rutherford, survived the season.

The most consistent of New Zealand's post-war cricket policies, until a few years ago, had been to increase the amount of first-class play. That is now heavily in reverse. The format has fluctuated season by season, but the number of days' play in the championship has dropped from 30 (ten three-day matches) in 1991-92 to 20 (five four-day games) scheduled for 1995-96, plus a final. Limited-overs games now outnumber first-class in both domestic and international programmes, and New Zealand has played 240 one-day internationals in the last 23 years compared with 237 Tests in 66.

Administrators cannot stop batsmen playing silly shots. But the board's enthusiasm for limited-overs cricket has affected the batting, much of which is talented but undisciplined. In South Africa, at least ten wickets were lost to injudicious pulls and hooks. In matches New Zealand might have drawn, there was a dismal lack of grit. There was another alarming trend: as Sri Lanka gained a deserved first Test win overseas, some of the New Zealand players appeared to be giving more than they got in unpleasant sledging.

The wall-to-wall international programme greatly diminished the significance of the Shell Trophy. The top players took little part and the final again clashed with a Test. Wellington were the best performers but finished with no prize. They topped the one-day and first-class tables comfortably but collapsed in both finals, to Northern Districts and Auckland respectively. The unspectacular Roger Twose batted soundly and made his Test debut in October 1995 once he had qualified as a New Zealander; fellow left-hander Mark Douglas was already in the one-day squad. Captain Gavin Larsen was an important bonus from the start, bowling to penetrate as well as contain. When on target, Heath Davis's speed was testing and he was the season's leading wicket-taker with 40. Less pacy but more controlled, Glenn Jonas looked like an international prospect.

Auckland won the Shell Trophy despite scoring no points before Christmas. Their batting was dominated by opening pair Andrew Reinholds and Craig Spearman. Willie Watson, ignored by the national selectors, was their player of the year, with 30 wickets at under two runs an over. Though less consistent, Dipak Patel had a good season; Pringle was rarely available but bowled tellingly in the Trophy final. Kerry Walmsley, as erratic as Davis but not as fast, was picked against Sri Lanka.

Northern Districts were hit hardest by national call-ups, though their Test players returned for the Cup final. But the biggest score that day came from Michael Parlane, a punishing opener. His partner was 17-year-old Matthew Bell, fresh from leading Whangarei Boys' High to victory in the national schools knockout. Bell resembled the teenaged Glenn Turner – slow against adult opposition but intelligent, sound and determined. Alex Tait successfully graduated to first-class cricket as a medium-pacer and hard hitter. Richard de Groen, dropped by New Zealand after the South African tour, topped his province's averages as a strong, persistent medium-fast bowler.

Canterbury had the next-biggest international contingent and again youngsters filled the gaps well. Nathan Astle, a medium-slow bowler and explosive batsman, made most runs, and batted decisively in the one-day series with Sri Lanka. Craig McMillan, at 18, was a spectacular strokemaker, though less impressive in defence. Rod Latham, in his final season, narrowly missed Paul McEwen's provincial batting aggregate record. Mark Priest continued to be the country's best left-arm spinner without adding to his one Test cap, though he was summoned to South Africa for the one-day games.

Otago's highlight was the emergence of slow left-armer Mark Richardson as a batsman. He was promoted to open, hit 122 in the first Trophy match, and later added 103 against the West Indies. The quicker bowling was led by Aaron Gale, who added a yard of pace, and Evan Marshall. Otago badly missed Jeff Wilson, who was preparing for the rugby World Cup. Mark Greatbatch, reappointed as Central Districts' captain, contributed two centuries and was easily their best batsman, despite uncertainty against real pace. But he had inadequate support, as did Warren Wisneski in the pace bowling department.

The season ended with a visit from the Australian Cricket Academy to play their New Zealand equivalents. The home team were older and more experienced; four had played for the senior national side. Yet several looked uninterested and they were crushed by ten wickets, showing an all-too-familiar inability to put their heads down and salvage a draw.

FIRST-CLASS AVERAGES, 1994-95

BATTING

(Qualification: 5 completed innings, average 35.00)

	M	I	NO	R	HS	100s	Avge
R. G. Twose (*Wellington*)	9	14	3	736	163*	3	66.90
M. W. Douglas (*Wellington*)	6	8	3	306	100*	1	61.20
N. J. Astle (*Canterbury*)	7	11	0	639	191	2	58.09
C. D. McMillan (*Canterbury*)	5	9	2	396	110	1	56.57
M. J. Greatbatch (*C. Districts*)	7	11	0	526	131	2	47.81
J. M. Aiken (*Wellington*)	8	15	1	628	138	2	44.85
C. M. Spearman (*Auckland*)	10	18	2	689	147	2	43.06
A. C. Parore (*N. Districts*)	5	8	1	293	100*	1	41.85
R. T. Latham (*Canterbury*)	6	10	1	367	90*	0	40.77

	M	I	NO	R	HS	100s	Avge
D. J. Murray (*Canterbury*)	9	17	1	629	182	2	39.31
G. R. Stead (*Canterbury*)	5	9	0	342	130	1	38.00
G. P. Burnett (*N. Districts*).	7	12	1	417	90	0	37.90
A. T. Reinholds (*Auckland*)	8	14	1	480	97	0	36.92
M. D. Bell (*N. Districts*)	6	10	0	357	78	0	35.70
M. H. Austen (*Wellington*)	8	14	2	423	166	2	35.25

* Signifies not out.

BOWLING

(Qualification: 20 wickets)

	O	M	R	W	BB	5W/i	Avge
J. T. C. Vaughan (*Auckland*) . . .	139.5	54	300	22	7-34	1	13.63
G. R. Larsen (*Wellington*)	240.1	82	495	25	6-37	1	19.80
R. P. de Groen (*N. Districts*). . . .	185.4	42	494	24	6-72	1	20.58
W. Watson (*Auckland*)	315.1	120	623	30	4-17	0	20.76
D. N. Patel (*Auckland*)	286.1	82	614	29	6-62	2	21.17
A. J. Gale (*Otago*)	194	54	429	20	6-42	1	21.45
G. R. Jonas (*Wellington*)	258.3	68	716	31	5-60	1	23.09
D. K. Morrison (*Auckland*)	245.1	60	647	28	6-69	2	23.10
W. A. Wisneski (*C. Districts*) . . .	191	53	486	21	5-21	2	23.14
H. T. Davis (*Wellington*)	254	57	971	40	5-46	2	24.27
S. J. Roberts (*Canterbury*)	172.3	25	513	21	5-56	1	24.42
E. J. Marshall (*Otago*)	220.2	35	663	26	6-53	2	25.50
M. W. Priest (*Canterbury*)	261.5	75	614	24	7-57	1	25.58
R. L. Hayes (*N. Districts*)	179.1	35	534	20	4-70	0	26.70
K. P. Walmsley (*Auckland*)	204.3	40	701	20	5-73	1	35.05
P. J. Wiseman (*Otago*)	352.4	86	943	23	4-122	0	41.00

SHELL TROPHY, 1994-95

	Played	Won	Lost	Drawn	1st-inns Points	Points
Wellington	7	5	1	1	22*	61†
Auckland	7	3	1	3	14*	38
Northern Districts	7	2	3	2	14*	30
Canterbury	7	2	3	2	12	28
Otago	7	2	5	0	12	28
Central Districts	7	2	3	2	10*	26

Final: Auckland beat Wellington by nine wickets.

Win = 8 pts; lead on first innings = 4 pts.
* Two points each where first innings not completed.
† One point deducted for slow over-rates.

In the following scores, * by the name of a team indicates that they won the toss.

At Lancaster Park, Christchurch, December 7, 8, 9, 10. Drawn. Canterbury* 351 (D. J. Boyle 31, B. Z. Harris 39, S. W. J. Wilson 74, N. J. Astle 96, S. J. Roberts 38; D. K. Morrison five for 100, J. T. C. Vaughan three for 42) and 203 (C. L. Cairns 64, S. J. Roberts 31; D. N. Patel six for 62); Auckland 299 (A. T. Reinholds 97, C. M. Spearman 39, R. A. Jones 36, J. T. C. Vaughan 60 not out; M. F. Sharpe three for 58, S. J. Roberts four for 82). *Canterbury 4 pts.*

At McLean Park, Napier, December 7, 8, 9, 10. Otago won by an innings and 12 runs. Otago* 449 for nine (M. G. Croy 61, M. H. Richardson 122, I. S. Billcliff 121, A. J. Gale 60; W. A. Wisneski three for 75, C. J. M. Furlong three for 101); Central Districts 247 (A. H. Jones 42, W. A. Wisneski 86, S. W. Duff 62; E. J. Marshall three for 36, P. J. Wiseman three for 80) and 190 (S. W. Duff 40, C. J. M. Furlong 48; R. J. Kennedy three for 18). *Otago 12 pts.*

While adding 192 for the fifth wicket, Richardson and Billcliff provided Otago's first Shell Trophy centuries since February 1992.

At Basin Reserve, Wellington, December 7, 8, 9, 10. Wellington won by seven wickets. Northern Districts* 202 (M. D. Bell 43, G. P. Burnett 36, A. J. Bradley 43 not out; G. R. Larsen six for 37) and 196 (M. D. Bell 60, A. J. Bradley 57; H. T. Davis four for 55, G. R. Jonas three for 29); Wellington 250 (J. M. Aiken 41, M. W. Douglas 100 not out; C. W. Ross four for 94, S. B. Styris five for 64) and 149 for three (J. M. Aiken 57, R. G. Twose 57). *Wellington 12 pts.*

At Eden Park, Auckland, December 14, 15, 16, 17. Central Districts won by one wicket. Auckland 152 (W. A. Wisneski five for 35, M. J. Pawson three for 55) and 147 (R. A. Jones 33, S. W. Brown 45 not out; D. C. Blake three for 37, M. J. Pawson four for 41); Central Districts* 166 (M. J. Greatbatch 48, T. E. Blain 32; D. K. Morrison four for 67, C. M. Brown four for 37) and 137 for nine (C. D. Ingham 40; J. T. C. Vaughan seven for 34). *Central Districts 12 pts.*

At Trust Bank Park, Hamilton, December 14, 15, 16, 17. Northern Districts won by four wickets. Canterbury* 160 (R. T. Latham 41, G. R. Stead 61; R. L. Hayes three for 29, S. B. Styris four for 38, A. R. Tait three for 57) and 330 (D. J. Boyle 59, N. J. Astle 175); Northern Districts 249 (M. E. Parlane 32, G. P. Burnett 59, G. E. Bradburn 50; N. J. Astle three for 49, H. J. Kember three for 44) and 242 for six (G. P. Burnett 52, M. D. Bailey 101 not out). *Northern Districts 12 pts.*

At Basin Reserve, Wellington, December 14, 15, 16, 17. Wellington won by an innings and 245 runs. Otago 139 (Extras 39; H. T. Davis three for 49, G. R. Larsen three for 23) and 110 (H. T. Davis four for 48); Wellington* 494 for three dec. (M. H. Austen 128, J. M. Aiken 138, R. G. Twose 113 not out, S. R. Mather 30, M. W. Douglas 52 not out, Extras 33). *Wellington 12 pts.*

Wellington's biggest win over Otago since 1899-1900.

At McLean Park, Napier, January 22, 23, 24, 25. Central Districts won by nine wickets. Central Districts* 360 (C. D. Ingham 76, L. G. Howell 45, M. J. Greatbatch 131, S. W. Duff 40; H. T. Davis three for 103, G. R. Jonas five for 60) and 45 for one; Wellington 178 (S. R. Mather 46, R. G. Petrie 31, J. D. Wells 35 not out; W. A. Wisneski five for 21) and 226 (S. R. Mather 43, R. G. Twose 79; C. J. M. Furlong three for 76, S. W. Duff three for 35). *Central Districts 12 pts.*

At Trust Bank Park, Hamilton, January 22, 23, 24, 25. Auckland won by ten wickets. Northern Districts 104 (G. P. Burnett 40; M. L. Su'a three for 39, C. M. Brown three for 48, W. Watson four for 17) and 318 (M. D. Bell 71, G. E. Bradburn 111, R. G. Hart 57 not out, M. E. Parlane 42; W. Watson three for 70, C. M. Brown three for 82, A. C. Barnes three for 23); Auckland* 394 (A. T. Reinholds 37, C. M. Spearman 147, R. A. Jones 42, M. L. Su'a 34; R. P. de Groen three for 86, A. J. Bradley three for 18) and 29 for no wkt. *Auckland 12 pts.*

At Centennial Park, Oamaru, January 22, 23, 24, 25. Otago won by 152 runs. Otago 172 (I. S. Billcliff 31, Extras 42; S. J. Roberts four for 69) and 177 (P. W. Dobbs 81 not out; M. B. Owens three for 45, S. J. Roberts five for 56); Canterbury* 94 (R. J. Kennedy four for 50, A. J. Gale three for 26) and 103 (A. J. Gale six for 42). *Otago 12 pts.*

At Eden Park Outer Oval, Auckland, January 27, 28, 29, 30. Drawn. Auckland* 485 for seven dec. (A. T. Reinholds 32, C. M. Spearman 115, A. C. Barnes 94, M. L. Su'a 52 not out, J. B. Cain 30, W. Watson 38 not out; S. J. Roberts three for 95) and 175 for six dec. (A. T. Reinholds 45, R. A. Jones 32, S. W. Brown 50 not out; G. R. Stead four for 58); Canterbury 338 for nine dec. (C. Z. Harris 60, C. L. Cairns 73, C. D. McMillan 110, M. W. Priest 55 not out; M. L. Su'a four for 82, W. Watson four for 64) and 226 for six (D. J. Murray 66, G. R. Stead 46, C. L. Cairns 31, C. D. McMillan 34 not out; M. J. Haslam three for 89). *Auckland 4 pts.*

At Pukekura Park, New Plymouth, January 27, 28, 29, 30. Drawn. Central Districts 421 for seven dec. (G. R. J. Hart 32, C. D. Ingham 102, M. J. Greatbatch 125, T. E. Blain 68; R. P. de Groen three for 97); Northern Districts* 195 for two (M. E. Parlane 94, M. D. Bell 78). *Central Districts 2 pts, Northern Districts 2 pts.*

At Carisbrook, Dunedin, February 3, 4, 5, 6. Wellington won by ten wickets. Otago 167 (P. W. Dobbs 65, I. S. Billcliff 60; H. T. Davis three for 67, G. R. Jonas three for 51, M. H. Austen three for 11) and 229 (M. H. Richardson 49, M. G. Croy 33, A. J. Gale 44 not out, Extras 40; H. T. Davis three for 62, G. R. Jonas three for 43, S. R. Mather three for nine); Wellington* 357 (R. G. Twose 163 not out, R. G. Petrie 30, M. C. Goodson 61; R. J. Kennedy three for 53, E. J. Marshall five for 85) and 44 for no wkt. *Wellington 12 pts.*

At Trust Bank Park, Hamilton, February 10, 11, 12, 13. Drawn. Northern Districts* 274 (M. E. Parlane 49, G. P. Burnett 90, J. E. Spice 30 not out; A. L. Penn four for 81) and 316 for five dec. (M. E. Parlane 44, M. D. Bell 66, G. P. Burnett 45, G. E. Bradburn 43, M. D. Bailey 45, A. R. Tait 50 not out); Central Districts 246 (G. R. J. Hart 55, M. J. Greatbatch 36, Extras 40; R. P. de Groen four for 73, R. L. Hayes four for 76) and 274 for seven (L. G. Howell 75, M. J. Greatbatch 89, W. A. Wisneski 56 not out; R. L. Hayes four for 70). *Northern Districts 4 pts.*

At Eden Park Outer Oval, Auckland, February 11, 12, 13, 14. Auckland won by seven wickets. Otago 277 (J. M. Allan 45, M. G. Croy 45, M. H. Richardson 86, P. J. Wiseman 35; K. P. Walmsley four for 101, C. Pringle three for 53) and 179 (I. S. Billcliff 58; D. N. Patel four for 59); Auckland* 239 (A. T. Reinholds 52, S. W. Brown 43, D. N. Patel 65; E. J. Marshall six for 53, P. J. Wiseman three for 41) and 218 for three (A. T. Reinholds 74, C. M. Spearman 41, R. A. Jones 54 not out). *Auckland 8 pts, Otago 4 pts.*

CANTERBURY v WELLINGTON

At Lancaster Park, Christchurch, February 11, 12, 13, 14. Wellington won by six wickets. Wellington 12 pts. Toss: Canterbury.

The match produced the fourth-highest match aggregate in first-class cricket and a world record for a four-day match – 1,945 runs for 18 wickets at 4.31 an over. Wellington's 475 for four was the highest fourth-innings winning score in New Zealand.

Close of play: First day, Canterbury 490-8 (M. W. Priest 96*, S. J. Roberts 1*); Second day, Wellington 443-2 (R. G. Twose 121*, M. D. Crowe 26*); Third day, Canterbury 476-2 (C. D. McMillan 86*, R. T. Latham 90*).

Canterbury

B. R. Hartland c Baker b Jonas	8	– c Wells b Hotter		150
G. R. Stead lbw b Larsen	24	– c Larsen b Davis		130
C. Z. Harris b Jonas	0			
R. T. Latham c Baker b Jonas	59	– not out		90
C. L. Cairns b Larsen	54			
N. J. Astle c Hotter b Davis	191			
C. D. McMillan c Larsen b Austen	11	– (3) not out		86
M. W. Priest not out	98			
*†L. K. Germon lbw b Austen	4			
S. J. Roberts b Hotter	5			
M. B. Owens c Baker b Hotter	0			
B 1, l-b 19, n-b 22	42	B 9, l-b 7, n-b 4		20

1/9 2/11 3/58 4/146 5/202   496   1/287 2/289   (2 wkts dec.) 476
6/228 7/469 8/481 9/496

Bowling: *First Innings*—Davis 19–0–106–1; Jonas 30–4–104–3; Hotter 22.3–3–101–2; Larsen 21–4–66–2; Austen 15–1–49–2; Twose 3–0–14–0; Wells 5–0–36–0. *Second Innings*—Jonas 4–0–29–0; Hotter 14–1–71–1; Davis 10–1–39–1; Larsen 16–3–59–0; Wells 41–2–164–0; Twose 5–0–18–0; Austen 4–0–25–0; Crowe 20–1–55–0.

Wellington

M. H. Austen c Harris b Priest 166	– c Latham b Priest	17
J. M. Aiken c McMillan b Astle 79	– c Germon b Roberts	116
R. G. Twose not out 150	– c Priest b Harris............	81
M. D. Crowe not out 50	– not out..................	193
M. W. Douglas (did not bat).................	– lbw b Harris	11
*G. R. Larsen (did not bat)	– not out	33
B 4, l-b 2, w 1, n-b 46 53	L-b 10, w 2, n-b 12.......	24

1/196 2/375	(2 wkts dec.) 498	1/53 2/183 (4 wkts) 475
		3/308 4/377

†G. R. Baker, J. D. Wells, G. R. Jonas, S. J. Hotter and H. T. Davis did not bat.

Bowling: *First Innings*—Owens 21–1–88–0; Roberts 16–1–94–0; Cairns 17–4–82–0; Harris 12–2–37–0; Priest 31–2–115–1; Astle 16.3–2–62–1; McMillan 4–0–14–0. *Second Innings*—Owens 12–0–60–0; Roberts 15–2–72–1; Cairns 13–0–58–0; Harris 10–0–44–2; Priest 25–2–112–1; Astle 25–1–92–0; McMillan 1–0–13–0; Latham 3–0–14–0.

Umpires: J. S. Crocker and D. M. Quested.

At Fitzherbert Park, Palmerston North, February 16, 17, 18, 19. Canterbury won by an innings and 136 runs. Central Districts* 242 (C. D. Ingham 41, A. H. Jones 78, S. W. Duff 44; M. W. Priest seven for 57) and 156 (C. D. Ingham 36, G. R. J. Hart 33; M. W. Priest five for 45, M. W. Priest four for 74); Canterbury 534 (B. R. Hartland 80, D. J. Murray 130, R. T. Latham 78, C. D. McMillan 58, C. Z. Harris 54, M. W. Priest 32, L. K. Germon 60; S. W. Duff three for 110, C. J. M. Furlong four for 204). *Canterbury 12 pts.*
Priest's 11 for 131 were the best match figures of the New Zealand season.

At Queens Park, Invercargill, February 16, 17, 18, 19. Northern Districts won by ten wickets. Otago 183 (I. S. Billcliff 58, R. P. Wixon 31; R. P. de Groen three for 28, G. E. Bradburn three for 64) and 163 (P. W. Dobbs 38, J. M. Allan 40; G. E. Bradburn three for 44); Northern Districts* 344 (M. D. Bailey 122, G. R. Hart 38, A. R. Tait 30, C. W. Ross 31 not out; P. J. Wiseman four for 132) and six for no wkt. *Northern Districts 12 pts.*

At Basin Reserve, Wellington, February 21, 22, 23, 24. Drawn. Auckland 260 (A. T. Reinholds 36, C. M. Spearman 46, S. W. Brown 76; S. J. Hotter three for 57); Wellington* 194 for eight (M. H. Austen 41, R. G. Twose 40, G. R. Baker 41, J. D. Wells 34 not out; C. M. Brown five for 54). *Wellington 2 pts, Auckland 2 pts.*

At Lancaster Park, Christchurch, March 3, 4, 5, 6. Canterbury won by one wicket. Northern Districts* 254 (G. P. Burnett 35, B. G. Cooper 72, R. G. Hart 43 not out, A. R. Tait 33; M. W. Priest three for 65, C. W. Flanagan four for 37) and 178 (A. R. Tait 40 not out; G. I. Allott three for 42, M. W. Priest four for 47); Canterbury 256 for nine dec. (D. J. Boyle 49, S. W. J. Wilson 60, L. K. Germon 37 not out) and 178 for nine (R. T. Latham 44, G. R. Stead 49; R. P. de Groen six for 72). *Canterbury 12 pts.*

At Carisbrook, Dunedin, March 3, 4, 5, 6. Auckland won by eight wickets. Auckland* 299 (J. T. C. Vaughan 59, C. D. Lee 111 not out, W. Watson 33; S. B. O'Conner three for 89, E. J. Marshall four for 76) and 99 for two; Otago 143 (W. Watson three for 12) and 254 (J. M. Allan 49, E. J. Marshall 52; W. Watson three for 40, M. W. Posa three for 62). *Auckland 12 pts.*

At Basin Reserve, Wellington, March 3, 4, 5, 6. Wellington won by ten wickets. Central Districts 225 (C. D. Ingham 40, W. A. Wisneski 56, G. R. Loveridge 38; S. J. Hotter four for 54) and 233 (S. W. Duff 59, M. A. Sigley 52, W. A. Wisneski 40; H. T. Davis five for 78, S. J. Hotter three for 50); Wellington* 441 (P. Chandler 33, S. R. Mather 126, J. D. Wells 96, R. G. Petrie 80, M. W. Douglas 44; A. L. Penn three for 99, G. R. Loveridge three for 116, S. W. Duff three for 42) and 20 for no wkt. *Wellington 12 pts.*

Final

At Basin Reserve, Wellington, March 14, 15, 16. Auckland won by nine wickets. Wellington 118 (C. Pringle four for 35, W. Watson three for 27) and 239 (J. M. Aiken 35, M. W. Douglas 75; D. N. Patel six for 75); Auckland* 257 (J. T. C. Vaughan 34, A. C. Barnes 43 not out; H. T. Davis three for 97, G. R. Jonas three for 66) and 101 for one (C. M. Spearman 58 not out).

     Auckland needed to win outright to take the Shell Trophy from Wellington, and did so before lunch on the third day.

PLUNKET SHIELD AND SHELL TROPHY WINNERS

The Plunket Shield was replaced by the Shell Trophy after the 1974-75 season.

1921-22	Auckland	1961-62	Wellington
1922-23	Canterbury	1962-63	Northern Districts
1923-24	Wellington	1963-64	Auckland
1924-25	Otago	1964-65	Canterbury
1925-26	Wellington	1965-66	Wellington
1926-27	Auckland	1966-67	Central Districts
1927-28	Wellington	1967-68	Central Districts
1928-29	Auckland	1968-69	Auckland
1929-30	Wellington	1969-70	Otago
1930-31	Canterbury	1970-71	Central Districts
1931-32	Wellington	1971-72	Otago
1932-33	Otago	1972-73	Wellington
1933-34	Auckland	1973-74	Wellington
1934-35	Canterbury	1974-75	Otago
1935-36	Wellington	1975-76	Canterbury
1936-37	Auckland	1976-77	Otago
1937-38	Auckland	1977-78	Auckland
1938-39	Auckland	1978-79	Otago
1939-40	Auckland	1979-80	Northern Districts
1940-45	No competition	1980-81	Auckland
1945-46	Canterbury	1981-82	Wellington
1946-47	Auckland	1982-83	Wellington
1947-48	Otago	1983-84	Canterbury
1948-49	Canterbury	1984-85	Wellington
1949-50	Wellington	1985-86	Otago
1950-51	Otago	1986-87	Central Districts
1951-52	Canterbury	1987-88	Otago
1952-53	Otago	1988-89	Auckland
1953-54	Central Districts	1989-90	Wellington
1954-55	Wellington	1990-91	Auckland
1955-56	Canterbury	1991-92	Central Districts / Northern Districts
1956-57	Wellington		
1957-58	Otago	1992-93	Northern Districts
1958-59	Auckland	1993-94	Canterbury
1959-60	Canterbury	1994-95	Auckland
1960-61	Wellington		

Wellington have won the title outright 18 times, Auckland 17, Otago 13, Canterbury 12, Central Districts 5, Northern Districts 3. Central Districts and Northern Districts also shared the title once.

AUSTRALIAN CRICKET ACADEMY TOUR

At Trust Bank Park, Hamilton, April 2, 3, 4, 5. Australian Cricket Academy won by ten wickets. New Zealand Academy XI* 240 (C. M. Spearman 75, C. D. McMillan 48; R. J. Baker six for 53) and 213 (M. E. Parlane 47, C. D. McMillan 30, L. K. Germon 40; B. Lee three for 71, C. Howard three for 54); Australian Cricket Academy 398 (N. W. Ashley 37, R. J. Baker 56, A. Symonds 115, K. M. Harvey 79; R. L. Hayes four for 59) and 56 for no wkt (R. M. Campbell 32 not out).

At Trust Bank Park, Hamilton, April 6 (not first-class). Australian Cricket Academy won by 70 runs. Australian Cricket Academy* 269 for nine (50 overs) (R. J. Baker 71, C. A. Glassock 72; S. R. Mather three for 39); New Zealand Academy XI 199 (42.1 overs) (L. K. Germon 43; R. J. Baker four for 39).

SHELL CUP, 1994-95

Note: Matches in this section were not first-class.

Play-offs

At Basin Reserve, Wellington, January 8. Northern Districts won by six wickets, their target having been revised to 154 from 44 overs. Wellington 171 for eight (50 overs) (S. R. Mather 40, R. J. Kerr 45; A. R. Tait three for 20, B. G. Cooper three for 24); Northern Districts* 156 for four (36.3 overs) (A. C. H. Seymour 62 not out, B. G. Cooper 33).

At Lancaster Park, Christchurch, January 9. Canterbury won by 67 runs. Canterbury* 274 for seven (50 overs) (C. D. McMillan 30, N. J. Astle 46, C. L. Cairns 143; W. Watson four for 60); Auckland 207 (48.3 overs) (J. T. C. Vaughan 80; M. F. Sharpe three for 34, M. W. Priest three for 38).
Cairns scored 143 in 123 minutes and 105 balls, with ten fours and nine sixes.

At Basin Reserve, Wellington, January 11. Wellington won by ten wickets. Canterbury 202 for nine (50 overs) (G. R. Stead 47, N. J. Astle 31, C. Z. Harris 35 not out); Wellington* 205 for no wkt (36.5 overs) (M. W. Douglas 93 not out, J. M. Aiken 101 not out).

Final

At Basin Reserve, Wellington, January 14. Northern Districts won by 148 runs. Northern Districts 256 for eight (50 overs) (M. E. Parlane 96, A. C. H. Seymour 44, B. G. Cooper 30); Wellington* 108 (29.2 overs) (S. R. Mather 34; D. J. Nash three for 28).

CRICKET IN INDIA, 1994-95

By R. MOHAN and SUDHIR VAIDYA

Priorities were misplaced in a season in which India had 21 one-day internationals scheduled and only three Tests. But there was one tangible gain for India from such a lopsided international timetable; for once, the top players were available for a major part of the domestic programme.

One of them certainly injected Indian cricket with a dose of much-needed class. Sachin Tendulkar was the toast of Bombay as he steered his team to their second successive triumph in the Ranji Trophy. He did it with style, too, with a century in each innings of the final, completing a prolific home season by scoring 856 Ranji runs from just 859 balls, with 23 sixes and 106 fours. The previous year, he had led Bombay to four wins in the West Zone league but had to leave on tour while Ravi Shastri took over the captaincy for the knockout stages. This time, at 21, he became the youngest captain to claim the Ranji Trophy in its 61 years. Tendulkar's presence from mid-January was a big fillip to Bombay, who hoped to extend their domination of the national scene – even if matching their 15 successive titles between 1958-59 and 1972-73 might prove impossible on today's more level playing field.

Punjab made a determined bid for the trophy, though at one time it looked as if they would be baulked in the semi-final, when Delhi ran up 554 in the first innings. At 298 for six in reply, Punjab seemed doomed, even in a land where Himalayan totals are the rule, not the exception. But a world record partnership of 460 between Bhupinder Singh, jun., who made 297, and wicket-keeper/batsman Pankaj Dharmani, who went on to an undefeated 202, sent them soaring into the lead. The stand was all the more commendable for being compiled in an away match, in a hostile environment made considerably worse by some senior Delhi players taking liberties with the code of conduct, with sledging to the fore.

Arriving in Bombay for the five-day final, Navjot Sidhu may have reckoned it was better to bowl first on the logic that the Wankhede Stadium pitch would offer help only for the first couple of hours. But his medium-pacers, the strength of the side for some years, could not test the seasoned Bombay batting line-up sufficiently. A second-wicket stand of 286 between Samir Dighe and Sanjay Manjrekar set the trend for another of those uniquely Indian bat-athons, with four batsmen making centuries and Manjrekar going on to a double. It seemed as if Punjab might repeat their semi-final performance while Vikram Rathore and Sidhu were adding 218 for the third wicket. Sidhu's dismissal just before the third-day close seemed to take the wind out of their sails, however, and they were dismissed 318 behind. Tendulkar did blot his copybook by choosing to bat again, rather than trying for an outright win by enforcing the follow-on. He argued that his bowlers were too tired. It gave him the chance to make his second century of the match, before lunch on the final morning, hitting 16 runs off the last five balls of the session.

If Bombay tightened their hold on the Ranji Trophy, so too did North Zone on the Duleep Trophy. They maintained an unbeaten record and topped the league table with 16 points, twice as many as their nearest rivals, South and West, to claim the title for the fifth year running. Though it was again staged mainly at remote venues with poor facilities, on dates clashing with the West Indians' tour, the Duleep tournament provided a platform for players outside the Test team to show their mettle in five-day first-class cricket. Docile pitches meant that only batsmen could be expected to benefit. With a personal best of 292 for West Zone against South, Surendra Bhave aggregated 651 in the competition, to lead the list of run-makers. Test reject Woorkeri Raman made three centuries, culminating in an unbeaten 250, for South Zone. In all, 19 batsmen made Duleep hundreds.

Ajay Sharma of North Zone scored 504 in five innings – exactly the same as his overall first-class record the previous year. But this time he went on to add 784 runs for Delhi in the Ranji Trophy, taking him to 1,288 for the season, 30 more than even Tendulkar managed. Vikram Rathore of Punjab passed 1,000 first-class runs for the second year running, with Amol Muzumdar, Tendulkar's 20-year-old Bombay colleague, and Rahul Dravid also achieving four figures. The season's leading wicket-takers represented the two Ranji finalists: medium-pacer Paras Mhambre of Bombay claimed 54 victims and Punjab's off-spinner, Aashish Kapoor, who made his way into the Test side, 52.

The twinning of the Deodhar Trophy limited-overs fixtures and the Duleep Trophy programme has never been appreciated by cricketers who have to play the instant game a day before or a day after their five-day match. That did not, however, deter Central Zone from winning all their fixtures to take the trophy after a gap of 17 seasons. A stand of 147 between Pravin Amre and Rizwan Shamshad for Central against North Zone virtually settled the issue; defending champions East Zone had a chance to finish level on points but went down by 22 runs to Central in the final game. The season concluded with the introduction of yet another limited-overs tournament – the third, following the Wills Trophy (for a selection of teams drawn from the zones and won in 1994-95 by Bombay) and the Deodhar. The India Challenger Series was intended to serve as a trial before the selection of the Indian team for the Asia Cup in Sharjah. Utpal Chatterjee, the Bengal left-arm spinner, was the principal beneficiary, forcing his way into the national side on the basis of his run-denying skills. Tailored for television, the event was a creature of the age. India's programme for 1995-96, in which they were again likely to play seven times as many one-day internationals as Tests, showed that times were not changing back. – R. M.

FIRST-CLASS AVERAGES, 1994-95

BATTING

(Qualification: 500 runs, average 40.00)

	M	I	NO	R	HS	100s	Avge
S. R. Tendulkar (*Bombay*)	8	13	0	1,258	179	6	96.76
Ajay Sharma (*Delhi*)	12	14	0	1,288	240	5	92.00
Bhupinder Singh, jun. (*Punjab*)	10	12	0	952	297	3	79.33
S. S. Bhave (*Maharashtra*)	9	13	2	855	292	2	77.72
P. Krishnakumar (*Rajasthan*)	7	12	4	607	208*	2	75.87
R. Lamba (*Delhi*)	8	10	0	744	312	3	74.40

	M	I	NO	R	HS	100s	Avge
S. S. Karim (*Bengal*)	9	12	3	641	160*	2	71.22
S. A. Shukla (*Uttar Pradesh*)	8	11	2	608	143*	2	67.55
P. Dharmani (*Punjab*)	9	12	3	605	202*	2	67.22
R. S. Dravid (*Karnataka*)	10	19	1	1,068	191	3	59.33
Robin Singh (*Tamil Nadu*)	10	16	1	851	155	1	56.73
Vikram Rathore (*Punjab*)	12	21	1	1,130	177	4	56.50
S. Sharath (*Tamil Nadu*)	11	18	4	753	121*	1	53.78
Abhay Sharma (*Railways*)	7	12	1	584	182	1	53.09
W. V. Raman (*Tamil Nadu*)	10	15	1	738	250*	3	52.71
Saurav C. Ganguly (*Bengal*)	8	14	1	677	200*	2	52.07
S. S. Sugwekar (*Maharashtra*)	10	13	2	560	160	1	50.90
A. A. Muzumdar (*Bombay*)	15	24	4	1,068	220	2	50.85
J. Arun Kumar (*Karnataka*)	8	14	2	582	117	1	48.50
N. R. Mongia (*Baroda*)	7	13	0	628	154	2	48.30
G. K. Khoda (*Rajasthan*)	10	18	1	815	237*	2	47.94
Bantoo Singh (*Delhi*)	12	16	0	765	214	1	47.81
V. V. S. Laxman (*Hyderabad*)	9	17	4	607	112	2	46.69
S. S. Dighe (*Bombay*)	13	19	4	658	137	2	43.86
A. R. Khurasia (*Madhya Pradesh*)	10	14	2	518	106	2	43.16
Rizwan Shamshad (*Uttar Pradesh*)	11	19	1	772	127	1	42.88
N. R. Odedra (*Saurashtra*)	8	14	0	592	142	1	42.28
S. V. Manjrekar (*Bombay*)	14	24	1	961	224	2	41.78

* *Signifies not out.*

BOWLING

(Qualification: 25 wickets)

	O	M	R	W	BB	5W/i	Avge
K. V. P. Rao (*Bihar*)	273.1	88	531	36	7-74	5	14.75
D. Vasu (*Tamil Nadu*)	240.5	49	610	34	8-114	4	17.94
A. Kumble (*Karnataka*)	292.5	77	770	41	8-41	2	18.78
D. Johnson (*Karnataka*)	159.3	42	480	25	5-28	3	19.20
S. A. Ankola (*Bombay*)	196.1	51	593	30	6-47	2	19.76
P. Krishnakumar (*Rajasthan*)	228.1	55	609	29	6-63	3	21.00
N. M. Kulkarni (*Bombay*)	249.5	52	694	33	6-80	3	21.03
Kanwaljit Singh (*Hyderabad*)	475.4	166	1,002	47	7-33	3	21.31
B. Ramaprakash (*Kerala*)	318.3	88	658	30	6-101	2	21.93
A. W. Zaidi (*Uttar Pradesh*)	238.2	57	627	28	5-89	2	22.39
A. S. Wassan (*Delhi*)	320.2	55	962	42	6-59	3	22.90
N. D. Hirwani (*Madhya Pradesh*)	461	103	1,114	48	7-83	3	23.20
A. Kuruvilla (*Bombay*)	200.1	35	628	27	5-42	1	23.25
P. L. Mhambre (*Bombay*)	478.2	113	1,264	54	5-46	4	23.40
Mohammad Aslam (*Rajasthan*)	224	40	682	29	5-66	2	23.51
K. N. A. Padmanabhan (*Kerala*)	295	88	666	28	6-26	3	23.78
M. Venkataramana (*Tamil Nadu*)	250	57	631	26	6-86	1	24.26
R. B. Biswal (*Orissa*)	308.4	73	769	31	7-38	2	24.80
Suresh Kumar (*Kerala*)	258.4	59	637	25	6-68	2	25.48
S. V. Bahutule (*Bombay*)	422.4	121	1,023	39	7-63	1	26.23
R. K. Chauhan (*Madhya Pradesh*)	336.5	82	857	32	6-87	3	26.78
Avinash Kumar (*Bihar*)	566.1	143	1,292	46	5-18	1	28.08
U. Chatterjee (*Bengal*)	524	125	1,277	40	5-117	1	31.92
Chetan Sharma (*Bengal*)	241.3	39	810	25	4-27	0	32.40
A. R. Kapoor (*Punjab*)	569.4	112	1,708	52	6-102	4	32.84
B. Vij (*Punjab*)	577.5	140	1,545	47	5-60	1	32.87
S. Subramaniam (*Tamil Nadu*)	521.4	149	1,174	34	7-68	1	34.52

In the following scores, * by the name of a team indicates that they won the toss.

IRANI CUP, 1994-95

Ranji Trophy Champions (Bombay) v Rest of India

At Wankhede Stadium, Bombay, October 12, 13, 14, 15, 16. Drawn. Bombay took the Irani Cup by virtue of their first-innings lead. Bombay* 424 (Z. Bharucha 164 not out, S. V. Manjrekar 117, S. S. Dighe 74; Iqbal Siddiqui four for 106, A. R. Kapoor four for 121) and 151 for four (S. V. Manjrekar 52, A. A. Muzumdar 55 not out); Rest of India 193 (Vikram Rathore 60, Ajay Mehra 46, R. S. Dravid 40; S. V. Bahutule seven for 63) and 485 for six dec. (Vikram Rathore 115, Ajay Mehra 32, Obaid Kamal 69, R. S. Dravid 72 not out, V. S. Yadav 111).

Bharucha carried his bat through the first innings.

DULEEP TROPHY, 1994-95

	Played	Won	Lost	Drawn	1st-inns Points	Points	Quotient
North Zone	4	2	0	2	4	16	3.05
South Zone	4	1	1	2	2	8	2.78
West Zone	4	1	0	3	2	8	2.72
Central Zone	4	0	2	2	4	4	2.84
East Zone	4	0	1	3	0	0	2.39

Outright win = 6 pts; lead on first innings in a drawn or lost game = 2 pts.
Quotient = runs scored per over.

At Burnpur Cricket Club Ground, Burnpur, October 25, 26, 27, 28, 29. Drawn. West Zone* 399 (S. S. Bhave 61, A. A. Muzumdar 144, S. S. Dighe 102 not out; Iqbal Thakur three for 64, N. D. Hirwani three for 65) and 241 for three (S. S. Bhave 107 not out, S. V. Jedhe 33, A. A. Muzumdar 77); Central Zone 449 (A. R. Khurasia 70, P. K. Amre 147, Rizwan Shamshad 127, R. P. Rathore 39; S. V. Bahutule four for 90). *Central Zone 2 pts.*

At Keenan Stadium, Jamshedpur, October 25, 26, 27, 28, 29. Drawn. South Zone* 454 (J. Arun Kumar 44, W. V. Raman 107, R. S. Dravid 67, S. Sharath 75, A. Vaidya 57; U. Chatterjee three for 144, Avinash Kumar four for 82) and 386 for five (J. Arun Kumar 68, R. S. Dravid 148, Robin Singh 64, S. Sharath 52 not out); East Zone 313 (S. S. Karim 83, R. B. Biswal 80; S. Subramaniam three for 100, Kanwaljit Singh six for 91). *South Zone 2 pts.*

At North-Eastern Frontier Railway Stadium, Gauhati, November 3, 4, 5, 6, 7. North Zone won by an innings and 84 runs. Central Zone* 205 (Abhay Sharma 73, P. K. Amre 51, Rizwan Shamshad 36; A. R. Kapoor five for 86) and 311 (Abhay Sharma 85, A. R. Khurasia 38, Rizwan Shamshad 70, G. K. Pandey 32; A. R. Kapoor five for 121, Ajay Sharma three for 46); North Zone 600 (Jitender Singh 31, Vikram Rathore 149, Ajay Sharma 202, R. Puri 100 not out, A. R. Kapoor 49; N. D. Hirwani four for 158, G. K. Pandey three for 119). *North Zone 6 pts.*

Ajay Sharma's 202 lasted 412 minutes and 292 balls and included 13 fours and three sixes; he and Vikram Rathore added 304 for the third wicket.

At Keenan Stadium, Jamshedpur, November 3, 4, 5, 6, 7. West Zone won by nine wickets. East Zone* 306 (P. R. Mohapatra 49, N. Haldipur 35, Saurav C. Ganguly 56, Snehashish C. Ganguly 80, Avinash Kumar 41; Iqbal Siddiqui four for 48) and 177 (S. S. Karim 42, S. T. Banerjee 51; S. V. Jedhe five for 68, S. V. Bahutule four for 66); West Zone 349 (N. R. Odedra 33, S. S. Bhave 45, S. V. Manjrekar 73, S. S. Sugwekar 84 not out, Extras 31; U. Chatterjee five for 117, R. B. Biswal three for 89) and 135 for one (S. S. Bhave 70 not out, S. V. Manjrekar 51 not out). *West Zone 6 pts.*

At Eden Gardens, Calcutta, November 12, 13, 14, 15, 16. South Zone won by ten wickets. Central Zone* 263 (V. Z. Yadav 35, G. K. Khoda 73, Abhay Sharma 40, Y. T. Ghare 58; K. N. A. Padmanabhan six for 78) and 156 (Y. T. Ghare 50, M. S. Doshi 30 not out; Kanwaljit Singh seven for 33); South Zone 313 (M. V. Sridhar 37, Robin Singh 63, W. V. Raman 107; N. D. Hirwani four for 78, M. S. Doshi five for 74) and 107 for no wkt (M. V. Sridhar 36 not out, J. Arun Kumar 65 not out). *South Zone 6 pts.*

Kanwaljit Singh's second-innings figures were 25–11–33–7.

At S. M. Dev Stadium, Silchar, November 12, 13, 14, 15, 16. Drawn. North Zone* 276 (R. Puri 33, P. Dharmani 50, Bhupinder Singh, sen. 38; S. A. Ankola three for 80, P. L. Mhambre five for 68) and 389 (Bhupinder Singh, jun. 91, Ajay Sharma 82, Bhupinder Singh, sen. 85 not out, B. Vij 35; S. A. Ankola five for 42, T. B. Arothe three for 137); West Zone 186 (S. S. Sugwekar 65; A. S. Wassan three for 65, B. Vij five for 60) and 318 for five (N. R. Odedra 90, S. S. Bhave 71, S. V. Jedhe 44, A. A. Muzumdar 58 not out; B. Vij three for 139). *North Zone 2 pts.*

At Eden Gardens, Calcutta, November 21, 22, 23, 24, 25. Drawn. Central Zone* 469 (G. K. Khoda 32, A. R. Khurasia 66, Rizwan Shamshad 86, G. K. Pandey 74, S. A. Shukla 132, P. V. Gandhe 30; U. Chatterjee three for 107, Avinash Kumar three for 101) and 106 for one dec. (Abhay Sharma 53 not out); East Zone 274 (N. Haldipur 30, Saurav C. Ganguly 37, S. S. Karim 103 retired hurt, Snehashish C. Ganguly 48; N. D. Hirwani six for 76) and 183 for five (Chetan Sharma 102 not out). *Central Zone 2 pts.*

At Moin-ul-Haq Stadium, Patna, November 21, 22, 23, 24. North Zone won by ten wickets. South Zone* 315 (Robin Singh 155, S. Sharath 44, S. Subramaniam 35; Obaid Kamal four for 100) and 157 (S. Sharath 54 not out; A. S. Wassan six for 81); North Zone 456 (Bhupinder Singh, jun. 31, Ajay Sharma 172, Bantoo Singh 41, A. R. Kapoor 79; S. Subramaniam four for 144, Kanwaljit Singh three for 100) and 20 for no wkt. *North Zone 6 pts.*

At Eden Gardens, Calcutta, November 30, December 1, 2, 3, 4. Drawn. East Zone* 250 (Saurav C. Ganguly 59, S. S. Karim 41, R. B. Biswal 58 not out, S. T. Banerjee 30; Bhupinder Singh, sen. three for 64, B. Vij four for 56) and 411 for seven (D. Gandhi 110, Saurav C. Ganguly 114, Chetan Sharma 71; A. R. Kapoor three for 116, B. Vij three for 133); North Zone 716 (Vikram Rathore 75, Bhupinder Singh, jun. 55, Ajay Sharma 42, Bantoo Singh 214, A. R. Kapoor 181, Bhupinder Singh, sen. 38, B. Vij 32; U. Chatterjee four for 176, Avinash Kumar three for 171). *North Zone 2 pts.*

Bantoo Singh's 214, his maiden double-hundred, lasted 574 minutes and 453 balls and included 18 fours and one six; he and Kapoor added 283, then an Indian seventh-wicket record.

At Ispat Stadium, Rourkela, November 30, December 1, 2, 3, 4. Drawn. South Zone* 233 (J. Arun Kumar 31, Robin Singh 61, S. Sharath 80 not out; M. S. Narula four for 24) and 531 for five (J. Arun Kumar 117, M. V. Sridhar 33, W. V. Raman 250 not out, R. S. Dravid 63, Robin Singh 30); West Zone 566 (S. S. Bhave 292, J. J. Martin 30, S. S. Sugwekar 43, T. B. Arothe 47, M. S. Narula 39; N. P. Singh three for 121). *West Zone 2 pts.*

Raman's 250 not out lasted 550 minutes and 426 balls and included 28 fours and four sixes; Bhave's career-best 292 lasted 739 minutes and 575 balls; he hit 34 fours and two sixes.

DULEEP TROPHY WINNERS

1961-62	West Zone	1973-74	North Zone	1985-86	West Zone
1962-63	West Zone	1974-75	South Zone	1986-87	South Zone
1963-64	West Zone	1975-76	South Zone	1987-88	North Zone
1964-65	West Zone	1976-77	West Zone	1988-89	{ North Zone
1965-66	South Zone	1977-78	West Zone		{ West Zone
1966-67	South Zone	1978-79	North Zone	1989-90	South Zone
1967-68	South Zone	1979-80	North Zone	1990-91	North Zone
1968-69	West Zone	1980-81	West Zone	1991-92	North Zone
1969-70	West Zone	1981-82	West Zone	1992-93	North Zone
1970-71	South Zone	1982-83	North Zone	1993-94	North Zone
1971-72	Central Zone	1983-84	North Zone	1994-95	North Zone
1972-73	West Zone	1984-85	South Zone		

RANJI TROPHY, 1994-95

Central Zone

At Karnail Singh Stadium, Delhi, December 20, 21, 22, 23. Madhya Pradesh won by an innings and 70 runs. Madhya Pradesh* 479 (A. R. Khurasia 100, C. S. Pandit 66, M. S. Sahni 75, D. K. Nilosey 128, Mohammad Saif 42; Iqbal Thakur three for 84); Railways 107 (S. S. Lahore three for 18, N. D. Hirwani four for 44) and 302 (P. S. Sheppard 51, R. Bora 145; N. D. Hirwani four for 80). *Madhya Pradesh 6 pts.*

At M. B. College Ground, Udaipur, December 20, 21, 22, 23. Uttar Pradesh won by 145 runs. Uttar Pradesh* 240 (P. Agarwal 67, Rizwan Shamshad 47; Mohammad Aslam five for 66) and 303 for six dec. (M. S. Mudgal 54, R. V. Sapru 106 not out, S. B. Yadav 52, A. W. Zaidi 30 not out); Rajasthan 202 (G. K. Khoda 57, A. D. Sinha 36, P. Krishnakumar 53 not out; A. W. Zaidi three for 69, S. Kesarwani four for 39) and 196 (R. J. Kanwat 41; A. W. Zaidi three for 45, Jasbir Singh three for 50). *Uttar Pradesh 6 pts.*

At BHEL Ground, Bhopal, December 28, 29, 30, 31. Madhya Pradesh won by ten wickets. Madhya Pradesh* 374 (K. K. Patel 93, C. S. Pandit 75, P. K. Dwevedi 40, D. K. Nilosey 92; R. P. Rathore three for 49, Mohammad Aslam four for 107) and 32 for no wkt; Rajasthan 168 (A. D. Sinha 74, A. S. Parmar 39; N. D. Hirwani seven for 83) and 237 (G. K. Khoda 36, A. S. Parmar 46, R. J. Kanwat 51, P. Krishnakumar 40; N. D. Hirwani five for 95, S. S. Lahore five for 92). *Madhya Pradesh 6 pts.*

At VCA Ground, Nagpur, December 28, 29, 30, 31. Uttar Pradesh won by 70 runs. Uttar Pradesh* 366 (R. V. Sapru 119, A. Gautam 56, S. B. Yadav 41, S. A. Shukla 71 not out; P. V. Gandhe four for 112) and 168 for six dec. (Rizwan Shamshad 88; P. K. Hedaoo three for 18); Vidarbha 216 (U. S. Phate 46, P. B. Hingnikar 33, Sangeet Rao 49; S. Kesarwani seven for 85) and 248 (P. K. Hedaoo 71, U. V. Gandhe 35; Jasbir Singh three for 45, R. V. Sapru three for 66). *Uttar Pradesh 6 pts.*

At Bhilai Steel Plant Ground, Bhilai, January 5, 6, 7, 8. Drawn. Vidarbha* 132 (U. S. Phate 44; N. D. Hirwani four for 42, R. K. Chauhan five for 43) and 42 for two; Madhya Pradesh 414 for nine dec. (Jai P. Yadav 34, K. K. Patel 168, C. S. Pandit 65, M. S. Sahni 65; P. K. Hedaoo six for 164). *Madhya Pradesh 2 pts.*

At Indira Gandhi Stadium, Alwar, January 5, 6, 7, 8. Drawn. Railways* 371 (V. Z. Yadav 42, Abhay Sharma 182, Extras 36; Mohammad Aslam five for 108); Rajasthan 392 for five (A. D. Sinha 51, G. K. Khoda 187, V. Joshi 44, P. Krishnakumar 59 not out; K. Bharathan three for 122). *Rajasthan 2 pts.*

At Karnail Singh Stadium, Delhi, January 13, 14, 15, 16. Drawn. Railways 256 (Yusuf Ali Khan 52, V. Z. Yadav 75, K. Bharathan 55, S. B. Bangar 44; P. B. Hingnikar three for 67, M. S. Doshi three for 77); Vidarbha* 271 for eight (U. S. Phate 84, K. S. M. Iyer 57, P. B. Hingnikar 61; R. Sanghvi four for 53, Iqbal Thakur four for 97). *Vidarbha 2 pts.*

At Gandhi Bagh Ground, Meerut, January 13, 14, 15, 16. Drawn. Madhya Pradesh 155 for three (Jai P. Yadav 35, K. K. Patel 54, A. R. Khurasia 50 not out) v Uttar Pradesh*. *Uttar Pradesh 1 pt, Madhya Pradesh 1 pt.*

At Green Park, Kanpur, January 22, 23, 24, 25. Railways won by four wickets. Uttar Pradesh* 150 (Rizwan Shamshad 78; Iqbal Thakur six for 22, Javed Alam three for 58) and 269 (Rizwan Shamshad 58, R. V. Sapru 33, S. A. Shukla 46, S. Kesarwani 42 not out; Iqbal Thakur four for 99, R. Sanghvi four for 52); Railways 175 (Abhay Sharma 33, R. Bora 54, A. Kapoor 31; A. W. Zaidi four for 44, R. V. Sapru three for 14) and 248 for six (P. S. Sheppard 107 not out, Abhay Sharma 44, S. B. Bangar 57 not out; M. Khalil three for 49). *Railways 6 pts.*

At VCA Ground, Nagpur, January 22, 23, 24, 25. Rajasthan won by one wicket. Vidarbha* 235 (K. S. M. Iyer 88, Y. T. Ghare 65; P. Krishnakumar six for 63, Mohammad Aslam three for 66) and 282 for eight dec. (U. S. Phate 84, P. B. Hingnikar 33, P. K. Hedaoo 69; P. Krishnakumar five for 101); Rajasthan 189 (V. Joshi 44; P. V. Gandhe four for 70, M. S. Doshi four for 53) and 330 for nine (G. K. Khoda 66, P. Krishnakumar 106 not out; P. V. Gandhe five for 143). *Rajasthan 6 pts, Vidarbha 2 pts.*

Chasing 329, Rajasthan were 290 for nine; Krishnakumar and D. P. Singh added 40 in 31 minutes to win a place in the knockout.

Madhya Pradesh 15 pts, Uttar Pradesh 13 pts, Rajasthan 8 pts, Railways 6 pts, Vidarbha 4 pts. Madhya Pradesh, Uttar Pradesh and Rajasthan qualified for the knockout stage.

East Zone

At Keenan Stadium, Jamshedpur, December 11, 12, 13, 14. Drawn. Orissa* 340 (S. S. Das 132, S. Raul 48, A. Khatua 44; Deepak Kumar four for 95) and 252 (M. Bhatt 62; Avinash Kumar three for 47, K. V. P. Rao six for 81); Bihar 217 (Sunil Kumar 36, S. T. Banerjee 32, Avinash Kumar 68 not out; R. Seth four for 38, P. Sushil Kumar three for 80, R. B. Biswal three for 53). *Orissa 2 pts.*

At Polytechnic Ground, Agartala, December 11, 12, 13. Assam won by 234 runs. Assam* 244 (Rajinder Singh 53, D. Bora 35, P. Dutta 33; C. Dey five for 70, S. Roy three for 64) and 220 for eight dec. (D. Bora 102, P. Dutta 75; C. Dey five for 74, S. Roy three for 91); Tripura 106 (P. Dutta four for 30) and 124 (Pawan Kumar 33; S. G. Chakraborty six for 35). *Assam 6 pts.*

Bora scored 102 on first-class debut after coming in when Assam were 39 for five.

At North-Eastern Frontier Railway Stadium, Gauhati, December 19, 20, 21, 22. Bengal won by nine wickets. Assam 269 (S. Saikia 97, G. Dutta 31) and 251 (Rajinder Singh 39, Z. Zuffri 65, G. Dutta 55; S. Sensharma three for 40, S. P. Mukherjee five for 70); Bengal* 503 for six dec. (Arun Lal 44, D. Gandhi 151, Ashok Malhotra 45, S. S. Karim 41, S. J. Kalyani 73, Chetan Sharma 101 not out) and 21 for one. *Bengal 6 pts.*

When 24, Ashok Malhotra became the leading run-scorer in the history of the Ranji Trophy, in his 108th match. He passed B. P. Patel of Karnataka, who scored 7,126.

At Polytechnic Ground, Agartala, December 19, 20, 21, 22. Orissa won by an innings and 89 runs. Orissa 379 (Ameya Roy 51, R. B. Biswal 126, S. Raul 80; A. Saha three for 82, R. Deb-Burman three for 67); Tripura* 102 (R. B. Biswal five for 33) and 188 (S. Dasgupta 47, S. Roy 35; R. B. Biswal seven for 38). *Orissa 6 pts.*

At North-Eastern Frontier Railway Stadium, Gauhati, December 27, 28, 29, 30. Drawn. Assam 339 (S. Saikia 55, Rajinder Singh 93, Z. Zuffri 39, N. Bordoloi 60, G. Dutta 41; R. B. Biswal four for 125, P. Sushil Kumar four for 104) and 242 for seven dec. (S. Saikia 44, N. Bordoloi 30, S. Limaye 34, P. Das 50 not out); Orissa* 295 (M. Bhatt 47, S. S. Das 38, Ameya Roy 30, R. B. Biswal 66, A. Khatua 36, R. Seth 32; Javed Zaman seven for 87) and 46 for two. *Assam 2 pts.*

At Eden Gardens, Calcutta, December 29, 30, 31. Bengal won by an innings and 172 runs. Bihar* 79 (Sunil Kumar 32, Deepak Kumar 31; Chetan Sharma four for 27, U. Chatterjee four for 13) and 167 (S. T. Banerjee 66 not out; S. Sensharma seven for 17, Chetan Sharma three for 61); Bengal 418 for four dec. (Saurav C. Ganguly 200 not out, Ashok Malhotra 63, S. S. Karim 67, S. J. Kalyani 33 not out). *Bengal 6 pts.*

Ganguly's 200 not out, equalling his career-best, lasted 437 minutes and 336 balls and included 20 fours and one six. Sensharma's second-innings figures were 11-5 17-5.

At Eden Gardens, Calcutta, January 5, 6, 7, 8. Drawn. Bengal 250 (Chetan Sharma 50, A. Singhla 66; R. Seth four for 84, R. B. Biswal four for 115) and 390 for five dec. (Arun Lal 113, S. J. Kalyani 85, Ashok Malhotra 42, Chetan Sharma 46, S. S. Karim 57 not out); Orissa* 244 (M. Bhatt 30, R. B. Biswal 54, A. Khatua 48; Chetan Sharma three for 51, A. Singhla three for 39) and 130 for four (S. Das 36 not out). *Bengal 2 pts.*

Kalyani was out obstructing the field. Batting with a runner, he scored a single. After it was completed his runner, D. Gandhi, was deemed to have put his hand down to pick the ball up – apparently to help the fielders – but then to have withdrawn it to attempt a second run.

At Keenan Stadium, Jamshedpur, January 5, 6, 7. Bihar won by ten wickets. Tripura* 223 (S. Roy 37, Arup Deb-Burman 35, S. Paul 39; K. V. P. Rao seven for 74) and 124 (R. Vals 30 not out; K. V. P. Rao six for 50); Bihar 309 (Z. Yaqeen 32, Sunil Kumar 67, Satish Singh 82, T. Rehman 36; A. Saha three for 61) and 39 for no wkt. *Bihar 6 pts.*

At Eden Gardens, Calcutta, January 12, 13, 14, 15. Bengal won by an innings and 22 runs. Tripura 129 (S. Roy 41, V. Prajapati 40 not out; S. Sensharma three for 38, A. Sarkar five for 36) and 125 (Chetan Sharma three for 43); Bengal* 276 for nine dec. (Arun Lal 60, S. J. Kalyani 78, S. S. Karim 36, S. P. Mukherjee 57 not out; C. Dey six for 95). *Bengal 6 pts.*

At DSA Ground, Hailalkandi, January 16, 17, 18. Bihar won by three wickets. Assam* 201 (P. Dutta 60, Rajinder Singh 75; Avinash Kumar three for 60, K. V. P. Rao five for 42) and 120 (G. Dutta 56; Avinash Kumar four for 33, K. V. P. Rao five for 53); Bihar 187 (Sunil Kumar 44, S. T. Banerjee 34, Avinash Kumar 36; G. Dutta five for 46, S. Limaye three for 59) and 135 for seven (V. Khullar 64; Javed Zaman three for 33). *Bihar 6 pts, Assam 2 pts.*

Bengal 20 pts, Bihar 12 pts, Assam 10 pts, Orissa 8 pts, Tripura 0 pts. Bengal, Bihar and Assam qualified for the knockout stage.

North Zone

At Feroz Shah Kotla Ground, Delhi, December 10, 11, 12, 13. Delhi won by 237 runs. Delhi* 261 (A. Dani 37, Bantoo Singh 62, Ajay Sharma 90; M. V. Rao three for 50) and 260 (A. Dani 44, R. Lamba 46, Bantoo Singh 34, S. Dogra 45; P. Maitreya four for 28); Services 213 (R. Vinayak 90 not out; A. S. Wassan six for 59) and 71 (A. S. Wassan five for 33, F. Ghayas four for 30). *Delhi 6 pts.*
  C. D. Thomson carried his bat for 26 in Services' second innings.

At Indira Stadium, Una, December 10, 11, 12, 13. Haryana won by an innings and ten runs. Himachal Pradesh 144 (R. Bittu 63, R. Nayyar 35; P. Thakur four for 55, P. Jain five for 35) and 280 (N. Gour 45, R. Nayyar 120; P. Jain five for 67); Haryana* 434 for six dec. (Jitender Singh 45, N. R. Goel 63, R. Puri 134, A. S. Kaypee 52, V. S. Yadav 79, Extras 38; Surinder Singh three for 73). *Haryana 6 pts.*

At Amritsar, December 10, 11, 12, 13. Jammu and Kashmir v Punjab. Abandoned.
  The Jammu and Kashmir players did not attend this or the game below, which were awarded to Punjab and Haryana. Later, however, the BCCI decided that no points should be awarded in any matches involving Jammu and Kashmir in 1994-95.

At Paddal Ground, Mandi, December 17, 18, 19, 20. Punjab won by ten wickets. Himachal Pradesh* 197 (R. Bittu 55, Shambhu Sharma 93 not out; B. Vij four for 68, A. R. Kapoor four for 46) and 258 (N. Gour 74, R. Nayyar 87; B. Vij four for 82, A. R. Kapoor four for 73); Punjab 451 for three dec. (R. Kalsi 179, Bhupinder Singh, jun. 153, Gursharan Singh 53 not out, Amit Sharma 54 not out) and six for no wkt. *Punjab 6 pts.*
  Kalsi and Bhupinder added 324 for Punjab's second wicket.

At Bhiwani, December 17, 18, 19, 20. Jammu and Kashmir v Haryana. Abandoned.

At Feroz Shah Kotla Ground, Delhi, December 23, 24, 25, 26. Delhi won by an innings and 132 runs. Jammu and Kashmir* 210 (Kanwaljit Singh 71, A. Gupta 43; F. Ghayas three for 41, Kartar Nath five for 53) and 157 (Vijay Sharma 36; A. S. Wassan four for 69, F. Ghayas five for 45); Delhi 499 for eight dec. (Bantoo Singh 67, Ajay Sharma 128, Akash Malhotra 136, G. Vadhera 70, F. Ghayas 47; Arun Sharma four for 122). *Points cancelled.*

At PCA Stadium, Mohali, Chandigarh, December 24, 25, 26, 27. Drawn. Punjab 376 (R. Kalsi 44, N. S. Sidhu 36, Bhupinder Singh, jun. 85, Gursharan Singh 33, Amit Sharma 82, Bhupinder Singh, sen. 35; Dhanraj Singh three for 79, P. Jain three for 98); Haryana* 189 (A. S. Kaypee 34; Bhupinder Singh, sen. three for 42, A. R. Kapoor five for 43) and 266 for seven (A. D. Jadeja 154 not out, R. Puri 33, Extras 31). *Punjab 2 pts.*

At Air Force Complex, Palam, Delhi, December 24, 25, 26, 27. Services won by an innings and 125 runs. Himachal Pradesh 182 (Shambhu Sharma 59, Jitender Jamwal 42 not out; M. V. Rao three for 61, J. P. Pandey four for 36) and 152 (R. Nayyar 45; J. P. Pandey six for 64); Services* 459 for eight dec. (S. Chopra 65, Suryaveer Singh 163, Chinmoy Sharma 115, Rashid Mohsin 55 not out; S. Thakur three for 108). *Services 6 pts.*

At Feroz Shah Kotla Ground, Delhi, December 31, January 1, 2. Delhi won by an innings and 310 runs. Himachal Pradesh 205 (N. Gour 32, R. Bittu 47, Virender Sharma 34, Shambhu Sharma 39; A. S. Wassan four for 79, Kartar Nath four for 59) and 122 (S. S. Sunder 32; F. Ghayas four for 39, Manoj Singh three for 26); Delhi* 637 for three dec. (R. Sehgal 216, R. Lamba 312, Bantoo Singh 87; Jitender Jamwal three for 174). *Delhi 6 pts.*

Sehgal's 216, his maiden hundred, lasted 441 minutes and 344 balls and included 23 fours; Lamba's 312 lasted 567 minutes and 392 balls and included 25 fours and two sixes. Their opening partnership of 464 was an Indian first-wicket record.

At Nehru Stadium, Gurgaon, January 6, 7, 8, 9. Drawn. Haryana* 167 (A. D. Jadeja 81, R. Manchanda 31; S. Chopra seven for 66) and 163 for three (R. Manchanda 31, N. R. Goel 35 not out, A. S. Kaypee 52 not out); Delhi 164 (A. S. Wassan 44, Akash Malhotra 32; P. Jain five for 46, Sonu Sharma three for 35). *Haryana 2 pts.*

At Air Force Complex, Palam, Delhi, January 6, 7, 8, 9. Drawn. Services* 101 (A. S. Bedi six for 26, Sandeep Sharma three for 40) and 46 for five; Punjab 318 (Gursharan Singh 73, K. Mohan 84, Sandeep Sharma 98; J. P. Pandey three for 91, S. Subramaniam five for 72). *Punjab 2 pts.*

At Indira Stadium, Una, January 7, 8, 9, 10. Drawn. Jammu and Kashmir* 579 for five (A. Bhatti 58, Kanwaljit Singh 46, A. Gupta 210 not out, V. Bhaskar 128, Ranjit Bali 61; Jaswant Rai three for 163) v Himachal Pradesh. *Points cancelled.*

Gupta's 210 not out lasted 476 minutes and 376 balls and included 11 fours; it was the first double-hundred for Jammu and Kashmir in the Ranji Trophy and their total was their first of 500.

At Feroz Shah Kotla Ground, Delhi, January 13, 14, 15, 16. Drawn. Punjab* 413 (Bhupinder Singh, jun. 137, Gursharan Singh 38, Amit Sharma 43, P. Dharmani 66, Bhupinder Singh, sen. 32, Extras 38; M. Prabhakar three for 118, A. S. Wassan four for 110); Delhi 310 (M. Prabhakar 43, R. Lamba 34, Akash Malhotra 62, R. Sehgal 66, Extras 33; B. Vij four for 86). *Punjab 2 pts.*

At Air Force Complex, Palam, Delhi, January 13, 14, 15, 16. Haryana won by eight wickets. Services 120 (S. Subramaniam 50; V. Jain four for 34, K. Batra three for 23) and 168 (Suryaveer Singh 67; V. Jain four for 55, P. Thakur four for 31); Haryana* 268 for six dec. (R. Manchanda 55, N. R. Goel 33, R. Puri 36, A. S. Kaypee 70) and 23 for two. *Haryana 6 pts.*

At Air Force Complex, Palam, Delhi, January 22, 23, 24, 25. Services won by an innings and 159 runs. Services* 543 for nine dec. (S. Chopra 152, R. Vinayak 75, Suryaveer Singh 63, Chinmoy Sharma 136, G. S. Thapa 55; Raj Kumar three for 70); Jammu and Kashmir 279 (A. Gupta 119 not out, V. Bhaskar 63; J. P. Pandey five for 96) and 105 (Vishal Sharma 40; S. Shirsat three for 21, S. Subramaniam five for 34). *Points cancelled.*

Haryana 14 pts, Punjab 12 pts, Delhi 12 pts, Services 6 pts, Himachal Pradesh 0 pts (all points in Jammu and Kashmir matches having been cancelled). Haryana, Punjab and Delhi qualified for the knockout stage.

South Zone

At Gymkhana Ground, Secunderabad, December 10, 11, 12, 13. Drawn. Hyderabad* 335 (G. A. Shetty 45, M. V. Sridhar 87, V. V. S. Laxman 39, Yuvraj Singh 40, N. David 30; M. Venkataramana four for 87) and 94 for two (G. A. Shetty 45 not out); Tamil Nadu 439 (V. B. Chandrasekhar 74, S. Ramesh 46, Robin Singh 63, D. Vasu 132, M. Venkataramana 60; V. Pratap four for 80). *Tamil Nadu 2 pts.*

At M. Chinnaswamy Stadium, Bangalore, December 10, 11, 12, 13. Karnataka won by an innings and 79 runs. Karnataka* 545 (J. Arun Kumar 42, R. S. Dravid 191, K. A. Jeshwant 126, S. Joshi 48, V. M. Parasuram 43 not out; P. Prakash four for 147); Andhra 187 (G. N. Srinivas 47, V. Vinay Kumar 53; R. Ananth six for 56) and 279 (V. Vinay Kumar 37, M. S. K. Prasad 48, B. S. Naik 103; D. Johnson three for 57, S. Joshi three for 110, R. Ananth three for 37). *Karnataka 6 pts.*

B. S. Naik scored 103 on first-class debut after Andhra were 52 for four.

At REC Ground, Kozhikode, December 10, 11, 12, 13. Kerala won by an innings and 48 runs. Kerala* 346 (V. Narayan Kutty 43, S. Shankar 52, S. Oasis 110, M. A. Satish 37; J. A. Fernandes three for 107, A. Shetty four for 80, S. V. Mudkavi three for 98); Goa 97 (N. Jayakumar three for 38, K. N. A. Padmanabhan six for 26) and 201 (Y. Barde 42, A. Shetty 30, S. V. Mudkavi 33, B. Misquin 35; N. Jayakumar three for 34, B. Ramaprakash five for 48). *Kerala 6 pts.*

At Dr Rajendra Prasad Stadium, Futardo, Margao, December 19, 20, 21, 22. Karnataka won by 243 runs. Karnataka* 428 (S. Somasunder 112, R. Nawali 32, S. Joshi 104, A. Vaidya 83; U. S. Naik five for 153, S. V. Mudkavi four for 114) and 226 for eight dec. (R. Nawali 48, K. A. Jeshwant 50, R. Vijay 33 not out; S. V. Mudkavi four for 79); Goa 308 (A. V. Mudkavi 33, S. V. Mudkavi 67, V. Jaisimha 32, M. M. Sawkar 51, Extras 36; J. Srinath three for 67, A. Kumble three for 45) and 103 (D. Johnson five for 28). *Karnataka 6 pts.*

At Gymkhana Ground, Secunderabad, December 19, 20, 21, 22. Drawn. Hyderabad* 227 (R. A. Swarup 56, V. V. S. Laxman 103; F. V. Rashid five for 29) and 210 (G. A. Shetty 102, N. David 32; S. Oasis three for 38, B. Ramaprakash three for 44); Kerala 248 (S. Shankar 45, V. Kamaruddin 36, Extras 34; V. Vardhan four for 62) and 93 for six (S. Oasis 31). *Kerala 2 pts.*

At M. A. Chidambaram Stadium, Madras, December 19, 20, 21, 22. Tamil Nadu v Andhra. Abandoned. *Tamil Nadu 1 pt, Andhra 1 pt.*

At Indira Stadium, Vishakhapatnam, December 28, 29, 30, 31. Drawn. Kerala* 252 (V. Narayan Kutty 35, S. Oasis 58, B. Ramaprakash 48; Chakradhar Rao five for 55, V. Vijayasarathy four for 48) and 241 for five dec. (S. Shankar 42, M. A. Satish 32, S. Oasis 81 not out, A. Kudva 32; Chakradhar Rao three for 102); Andhra 206 (M. F. Rehman 33, V. Vinay Kumar 70; Suresh Kumar three for 84, K. N. A. Padmanabhan five for 48) and 206 for nine (G. N. Srinivas 34, V. Vinay Kumar 61, V. Vijayasarathy 43; B. Ramaprakash three for 82, K. N. A. Padmanabhan four for 70). *Kerala 2 pts.*

At Gymkhana Ground, Secunderabad, December 28, 29, 30, 31. Hyderabad won by nine wickets. Goa* 302 (A. V. Mudkavi 55, N. Gautam 62, V. Jaisimha 58; N. P. Singh four for 71) and 157 (M. M. Sawkar 32, A. Shetty 31, Extras 34; Kanwaljit Singh four for 38, N. David three for 11); Hyderabad 310 (M. V. Sridhar 107, V. V. S. Laxman 112; N. D. Kambli four for 66) and 152 for one (M. V. Sridhar 102 not out, V. V. S. Laxman 44 not out). *Hyderabad 6 pts.*

At M. A. Chidambaram Stadium, Madras, December 28, 29, 30, 31. Drawn. Karnataka* 227 (S. Somasunder 65, P. V. Shashikanth 37, D. Johnson 31 not out; S. Subramaniam seven for 68) and 328 (P. V. Shashikanth 35, K. A. Jeshwant 154 not out, S. Joshi 53, A. Kumble 32; D. Vasu eight for 114); Tamil Nadu 411 (V. B. Chandrasekhar 64, S. Ramesh 55, W. V. Raman 43, S. Sharath 88, S. Subramaniam 40, Extras 31; A. Kumble three for 111, R. Ananth three for 102) and 106 for four (Robin Singh 64 not out). *Tamil Nadu 2 pts.*

At Arlem Breweries Ground, Margao, January 7, 8, 9, 10. Drawn. Andhra 176 (V. Vijayasarathy 45, Madhusudan Raju 45; S. Kamat three for 36, S. V. Mudkavi four for 29) and 337 for eight dec. (A. Pathak 45, V. Vinay Kumar 96, M. S. K. Prasad 50 not out, Madhusudan Raju 40, Extras 33; S. Kamat three for 89); Goa* 137 (S. Kamat 50 not out; Mallikarjuna Rao five for 55, Madhusudan Raju four for 38) and 241 for five (S. Y. Dhuri 38, A. Shetty 65, A. V. Mudkavi 71 not out, S. V. Mudkavi 42 not out). *Andhra 2 pts.*

At Dr Ambedkar Stadium, Bijapur, January 7, 8, 9, 10. Karnataka won by nine wickets. Hyderabad* 78 (A. Kumble three for 26) and 166 (G. A. Shetty 64, S. Riazuddin 39 not out; D. Johnson five for 48, R. Ananth three for 36); Karnataka 203 (J. Arun Kumar 31, A. Kumble 63, S. Somashekar 30; Mohammad Mohiuddin five for 69) and 43 for one (J. Arun Kumar 30 not out). *Karnataka 6 pts.*

At Govt Victoria College Ground, Palakkad, January 7, 8, 9, 10. Kerala won by 123 runs. Kerala* 241 (V. Narayan Kutty 38, B. Ramaprakash 46; M. Venkataramana four for 60) and 287 (B. Ramaprakash 56, P. G. Sunder 100, A. Kudva 46; D. Vasu four for 72, S. Subramaniam three for 81, M. Venkataramana three for 60); Tamil Nadu 258 (V. B. Chandrasekhar 35, W. V. Raman 93, Robin Singh 73; Suresh Kumar six for 96) and 147 (Robin Singh 33; Suresh Kumar six for 68, B. Ramaprakash three for 51). *Kerala 6 pts, Tamil Nadu 2 pts.*
  Kerala reached the knockout stage for the first time.

At Indira Gandhi Stadium, Vijayawada, January 15, 16, 17, 18. Andhra won by four wickets. Hyderabad* 240 (M. V. Sridhar 54, V. V. S. Laxman 96 not out; Mallikarjuna Rao three for 48, G. V. V. Gopalraju three for 88) and 195 for eight dec. (M. Azharuddin 74, V. V. S. Laxman 49; G. V. V. Gopalraju five for 63); Andhra 193 (A. Pathak 40, M. F. Rehman 69; Kanwaljit Singh five for 25) and 248 for six (A. Pathak 49, M. F. Rehman 59, V. Vijayasarathy 33, B. S. Naik 33 not out; R. Sridhar four for 70). *Andhra 6 pts, Hyderabad 2 pts.*
  Kanwaljit Singh's first-innings figures were 29.4–18–25–5.

At Nehru Stadium, Margao, January 15, 16, 17, 18. Tamil Nadu won by an innings and 69 runs. Tamil Nadu* 446 for six dec. (V. B. Chandrasekhar 45, S. Ramesh 45, W. V. Raman 40, Robin Singh 38, S. Sharath 121 not out, Arjan Kripal Singh 101; R. J. Kambli three for 162); Goa 175 (A. Amonkar 36, S. Upadhyaya 40; W. D. Balaji Rao four for 39, M. Venkataramana four for 47) and 202 (P. A. Amonkar 34, S. V. Mudkavi 45, M. M. Sawkar 45; M. Venkataramana six for 86). *Tamil Nadu 6 pts.*

At Municipal Stadium, Thalassery, January 15, 16, 17. Karnataka won by 270 runs. Karnataka* 269 (S. Somasunder 41, J. Arun Kumar 67, K. A. Jeshwant 32, S. Joshi 45, A. Vaidya 57; B. Ramaprakash six for 101) and 233 (P. V. Shashikanth 68, Y. Gouda 37, K. A. Jeshwant 33, S. Joshi 35; Suresh Kumar three for 84, B. Ramaprakash three for 63); Kerala 124 (B. Ramaprakash 39; A. Kumble eight for 58) and 108 (B. Ramaprakash 32; A. Kumble eight for 41). *Karnataka 6 pts.*
  Kumble's match figures of 33.2–9–99–16 were the best by any bowler in the history of the Ranji Trophy.

Karnataka 24 pts, Kerala 16 pts, Tamil Nadu 13 pts, Andhra 9 pts, Hyderabad 8 pts, Goa 0 pts. Karnataka, Kerala and Tamil Nadu qualified for the knockout stage.

West Zone

At Sardar Patel Stadium, Ahmedabad, December 23, 24, 25, 26. Drawn. Gujarat* 246 (N. S. Bakriwala 58, M. H. Parmar 38, P. H. Patel 66; R. Pandit five for 63, S. Pillai four for 59) and 358 (M. H. Parmar 32, K. R. Patadiwala 31, N. A. Patel 55, T. N. Varsania 37, P. H. Patel 53, B. Mehta 102; D. N. Chudasama four for 98, R. Pandit three for 113); Saurashtra 350 (N. R. Odedra 142, H. J. Parsana 84, P. Bhatt 31, Extras 33; M. H. Parmar four for 44) and 204 for six (S. S. Tanna 39, S. H. Kotak 67 not out; J. Pithawala three for 51). *Saurashtra 2 pts.*

At Indira Gandhi Stadium, Solapur, December 23, 24, 25, 26. Drawn. Bombay* 573 for nine dec. (S. S. More 166, A. A. Muzumdar 220, S. K. Kulkarni 38, S. S. Dighe 69, Extras 39; S. C. Gudge five for 140) and 123 for three (S. S. More 40 not out, S. K. Kulkarni 60); Maharashtra 361 (S. S. Bhave 37, S. S. Sugwekar 160, H. H. Kanitkar 44, S. C. Gudge 55; A. Kuruvilla three for 77, P. L. Mhambre five for 51). *Bombay 2 pts.*
  Muzumdar's 220 lasted 619 minutes and 442 balls and included 22 fours; he added 290 for the third wicket with More. When 139, he reached 1,000 first-class runs in his ninth match. S. V. Manjrekar was sent off the field by umpire V. N. Kulkarni for abusive language.

At Shastri Ground, Vallabh Vidyanagar, December 31, January 1, 2, 3. Drawn. Baroda* 568 for six dec. (R. B. Parikh 57, K. S. Chavan 109, N. R. Mongia 152, J. J. Martin 50, K. S. More 103 not out, T. B. Arothe 50); Gujarat 366 (N. S. Bakriwala 48, N. D. Modi 69, M. H. Parmar 109, N. A. Patel 40, P. H. Patel 45 not out; R. G. M. Patel four for 42, V. N. Buch four for 105) and 289 for nine (N. S. Bakriwala 32, M. H. Parmar 155 not out; T. B. Arothe three for 97). *Baroda 2 pts.*

Baroda's first, second, third and sixth wickets each added more than 100.

At Municipal Ground, Rajkot, December 31, January 1, 2, 3. Drawn. Maharashtra* 549 (H. A. Kinikar 138, S. S. Bhave 46, S. V. Jedhe 47, A. V. Kale 153, H. H. Kanitkar 38, S. M. Kondhalkar 48; D. N. Chudasama three for 156); Saurashtra 270 (S. S. Tanna 88, N. R. Odedra 47, Extras 38; M. S. Kulkarni three for 30, P. J. Kanade three for 51) and 237 for three (B. Dutta 76 not out, S. Pillai 109 not out). *Maharashtra 2 pts.*

At IPCL Sports Complex Ground, Baroda, January 7, 8, 9, 10. Drawn. Baroda 172* (J. J. Martin 45; M. S. Kulkarni six for 67, P. J. Kanade three for 44) and 256 (K. S. More 52, S. S. Hazare 38, N. R. Mongia 40, K. S. Chavan 47; M. S. Kulkarni four for 61); Maharashtra 272 (H. A. Kinikar 44, H. H. Kanitkar 74, S. S. Sugwekar 69, A. V. Kale 51; Sukhbir Singh five for 90, V. N. Buch three for 90) and 24 for one. *Maharashtra 2 pts.*

At University Ground, Bhavnagar, January 7, 8, 9, 10. Bombay won by four wickets. Saurashtra* 182 (S. S. Tanna 64, S. H. Kotak 51; P. L. Mhambre five for 46) and 206 (N. R. Odedra 54, S. H. Kotak 53, H. J. Parsana 40 not out; N. M. Kulkarni six for 80, S. M. Khartade four for 56); Bombay 253 (S. V. Manjrekar 86, A. A. Muzumdar 89; H. J. Parsana four for 34) and 138 for six (S. K. Kulkarni 35, V. G. Kambli 31; H. J. Parsana three for 44). *Bombay 6 pts.*

At Rashtriya Chemicals and Fertilisers Ground, Bombay, January 15, 16, 17, 18. Bombay won by five wickets. Baroda 302 (R. B. Parikh 67, J. J. Martin 39, T. B. Arothe 41, R. M. Naik 70; R. R. Gadiyar three for 79, B. R. Karnik three for 88, N. M. Kulkarni four for 104) and 330 (R. B. Parikh 38, N. R. Mongia 154, J. J. Martin 38, K. S. More 33; N. M. Kulkarni six for 119); Bombay* 348 (S. R. Tendulkar 175, V. G. Kambli 55, S. S. Dighe 34 not out; V. N. Buch four for 101, T. B. Arothe three for 89) and 289 for five (M. V. Joglekar 114 not out, S. R. Tendulkar 97, S. S. Dighe 36 not out; T. B. Arothe three for 82). *Bombay 6 pts.*

Tendulkar scored his 175 in 185 minutes and 141 balls, with eight sixes and 22 fours.

At Poona Club, Pune, January 15, 16, 17, 18. Maharashtra won by an innings and 71 runs. Gujarat* 199 (M. S. Kulkarni five for 36) and 274 (Umesh Patel 40, M. H. Parmar 56, U. S. Belsare 72; Iqbal Siddiqui three for 64, P. J. Kanade four for 65); Maharashtra 544 for eight dec. (S. S. Bhave 30, S. S. Sugwekar 44, S. C. Gudge 125, A. V. Kale 141, H. H. Kanitkar 100 not out; L. Patel three for 187, B. Patel five for 168). *Maharashtra 6 pts.*

Maharashtra's three centuries came from Nos. 5, 6 and 7.

At Wankhede Stadium, Bombay, January 21, 22, 23. Bombay won by an innings and 132 runs. Gujarat 198 (N. S. Bakriwala 66, H. Patel 31; A. Kuruvilla three for 67, P. L. Mhambre four for 60) and 161 (M. H. Parmar 56, N. S. Jhaveri 31; S. A. Ankola six for 47); Bombay* 491 for six dec. (M. V. Joglekar 51, S. V. Manjrekar 87, S. R. Tendulkar 30, V. G. Kambli 147, S. V. Bahutule 112 not out; H. Patel four for 168). *Bombay 6 pts.*

At IPCL Sports Complex Ground, Baroda, January 22, 23, 24, 25. Saurashtra won by 110 runs. Saurashtra* 285 (N. R. Odedra 50, S. H. Kotak 121, P. Bhatt 43, M. M. Parmar 30; M. S. Narula six for 80) and 223 (S. S. Tanna 54, N. R. Odedra 81, M. M. Parmar 39; V. N. Buch six for 75); Baroda 210 (J. J. Martin 94 not out; H. J. Parsana four for 58) and 188 (R. B. Parikh 59, N. R. Mongia 37, J. J. Martin 31; D. N. Chudasama three for 47). *Saurashtra 6 pts.*

Bombay 20 pts, Maharashtra 10 pts, Saurashtra 8 pts, Baroda 2 pts, Gujarat 0 pts. Bombay, Maharashtra and Saurashtra qualified for the knockout stage.

Pre-quarter-finals

At Feroz Shah Kotla Ground, Delhi, February 12, 13, 14, 15, 16. Drawn. Delhi were declared winners by virtue of their first-innings lead. Delhi 464 (Ajay Sharma 170, Akash Malhotra 152, Shakti Singh 37; A. Sarkar three for 110, Chetan Sharma four for 100) and 174 for three (V. Dahiya 76, Bantoo Singh 54); Bengal* 375 (S. P. Mukherjee 65, S. S. Karim 160 not out, Chetan Sharma 55, Extras 31; Shakti Singh six for 104).

At PCA Stadium, Mohali, Chandigarh, February 12, 13, 14, 15, 16. Drawn. Punjab were declared winners by virtue of their first-innings lead. Karnataka* 171 (S. Joshi 72 not out; A. S. Bedi four for 31) and 85 for two; Punjab 332 (Ajay Mehra 49, Bhupinder Singh, jun. 36, K. Mohan 98, P. Dharmani 39; D. Johnson five for 93, R. Ananth five for 99).

At M. B. College Ground, Udaipur, February 12, 13, 14, 15, 16. Rajasthan won by 482 runs. Rajasthan* 445 (A. D. Sinha 34, Dev Kumar 60, V. Joshi 67, A. S. Parmar 119, P. Krishnakumar 76; G. Dutta three for 63, S. Limaye three for 127) and 389 for five dec. (R. J. Kanwat 66, P. Krishnakumar 208 not out, A. S. Parmar 40); Assam 89 (P. Krishnakumar for 23, Mohammad Aslam four for 25) and 263 (S. Limaye 60, G. Dutta 73; R. P. Rathore five for 57).

Krishnakumar's 208 not out, his maiden double-hundred, lasted 350 minutes and 262 balls and included 20 fours and six sixes.

At Municipal Stadium, Rajkot, February 12, 13, 14, 15, 16. Bihar won by seven wickets. Saurashtra* 321 (S. S. Tanna 58, B. Dutta 74, P. Bhatt 65, H. J. Parsana 37; K. V. P. Rao three for 85, Avinash Kumar four for 76) and 52 (Avinash Kumar five for 18); Bihar 264 (Z. Yaqeen 32, V. Khullar 104, Avinash Kumar 43 not out; H. J. Parsana five for 84) and 110 for three (N. Ranjan 40, Sunil Kumar 30 not out, T. Rehman 31 not out).

At M. A. Chidambaram Stadium, Madras, February 12, 13, 14, 15, 16. Tamil Nadu won by ten wickets. Haryana* 165 (A. S. Kaypee 72; D. Vasu six for 47, S. Mahesh three for 63) and 290 (Parender Sharma 39, N. R. Goel 47, A. S. Kaypee 35, Avtar Singh 54, P. Thakur 60; D. Vasu six for 62, M. Venkataramana three for 91); Tamil Nadu 393 (W. V. Raman 35, Robin Singh 99, S. Sharath 56, D. Vasu 69 not out; V. Jain six for 138, K. Batra three for 131) and 63 for no wkt (V. B. Chandrasekhar 36 not out).

At K. D. Singh "Babu" Stadium, Lucknow, February 12, 13, 14, 15, 16. Drawn. Uttar Pradesh were declared winners by virtue of their first-innings lead. Kerala* 360 (F. V. Rashid 31, S. Oasis 52, B. Ramaprakash 94, P. G. Sunder 34, A. Kudva 34, Extras 33; A. W. Zaidi five for 89); Uttar Pradesh 472 for five (Jyoti P. Yadav 106, R. V. Sapru 32, G. K. Pandey 85, S. A. Shukla 143 not out, A. Gautam 39 not out).

Yadav scored 106 on his first-class debut.

At Nehru Stadium, Indore, February 13, 14, 15, 16, 17. Madhya Pradesh won by 287 runs. Madhya Pradesh* 291 (Jai P. Yadav 37, K. K. Patel 37, C. S. Pandit 122, Extras 33; P. Y. Chitale four for 69, S. V. Jedhe four for 54) and 451 (A. R. Khurasia 106, M. S. Sahni 118, Zuber Khan 39, H. S. Sodhi 75, Extras 30; M. S. Kulkarni four for 28); Maharashtra 239 (H. A. Kinikar 82, A. V. Kale 82; R. K. Chauhan six for 97, N. D. Hirwani three for 76) and 216 (H. A. Kinikar 36, S. S. Bhave 72, H. H. Kanitkar 37 not out; R. K. Chauhan six for 87, S. S. Lahore three for 58).

Quarter-finals

At Keenan Stadium, Jamshedpur, February 26, 27, 28, March 1, 2. Drawn. Delhi were declared winners by virtue of their first-innings lead. Delhi* 402 (R. Lamba 160, Bantoo Singh 68, Ajay Sharma 62; Avinash Kumar four for 129, Sanjay Singh four for 98) and 238 (Ajay Sharma 38, M. Prabhakar 116 not out; Avinash Kumar three for 54, Deepak Kumar three for 68); Bihar 229 (T. Rehman 83 not out, S. T. Banerjee 41, Extras 36; Ajay Sharma four for ten) and 156 for four (V. Khullar 49, T. Rehman 50 not out).

At Wankhede Stadium, Bombay, February 26, 27, 28. Bombay won by an innings and 22 runs. Tamil Nadu* 118 (S. A. Ankola three for 36, P. L. Mhambre five for 53) and 190 (Robin Singh 67; N. M. Kulkarni five for 71, S. V. Bahutule three for 26); Bombay 330 (M. V. Joglekar 67, S. R. Tendulkar 166; D. Vasu five for 107, S. Subramaniam three for 42).

Tendulkar scored his 166 in 220 minutes and 153 balls, with 27 fours and one six; Bombay won with more than two days to spare.

At PCA Stadium, Mohali, Chandigarh, February 26, 27, 28, March 1, 2. Drawn. Punjab were declared winners by virtue of their first-innings lead. Punjab 294 (N. S. Sidhu 51, P. Dharmani 114, B. Vij 37; D. K. Nilosey three for 67) and 353 for five (Ajay Mehra 41, Bhupinder Singh, jun. 34, K. Mohan 101 not out, A. R. Kapoor 59, P. Dharmani 55, Bhupinder Singh, sen. 30 not out); Madhya Pradesh* 189 (A. R. Khurasia 43; Obaid Kamal five for 39, A. R. Kapoor three for 40).

At OEF Ground, Kanpur, February 26, 27, 28, March 1, 2. Drawn. Uttar Pradesh were declared winners by virtue of their first-innings lead. Rajasthan* 237 (A. S. Parmar 79, R. P. Rathore 54; A. W. Zaidi five for 92, M. Khalil three for 74) and 417 for five (Dev Kumar 42, G. K. Khoda 237 not out, P. K. Amre 65; S. Kesarwani three for 125); Uttar Pradesh 487 (S. B. Yadav 141, Rizwan Shamshad 32, R. V. Sapru 104, S. A. Shukla 71, A. W. Zaidi 39; P. Krishnakumar three for 86, Mohammad Aslam four for 130).

Khoda's 237 not out lasted 484 minutes and 351 balls and included 22 fours and six sixes.

Semi-finals

At Wankhede Stadium, Bombay, March 12, 13, 14. Bombay won by an innings and 233 runs. Bombay 486 (S. R. Tendulkar 109, V. G. Kambli 64, A. A. Muzumdar 69, S. V. Bahutule 47, A. Kuruvilla 76; A. W. Zaidi four for 107); Uttar Pradesh* 144 (S. A. Shukla 72; S. A. Ankola three for 21, P. L. Mhambre three for 43) and 109 (S. B. Yadav 63; N. M. Kulkarni three for six).

DELHI v PUNJAB

At Feroz Shah Kotla Ground, Delhi, March 12, 13, 14, 15, 16. Drawn. Punjab were declared winners by virtue of their first-innings lead. Toss: Delhi.

Ajay Sharma's 240 lasted 650 minutes and 487 balls and included 22 fours and six sixes. Punjab were 298 for six – 57 short of saving the follow-on – when Dharmani joined Bhupinder Singh, jun. They added 460 in 563 minutes, a world record for the seventh wicket (previously held by D. St E. Atkinson and C. C. Depeiza, 347 for West Indies v Australia, Bridgetown, 1954-55) and easily secured the first-innings lead, which was decisive. Bhupinder's 297 lasted 785 minutes and 738 balls and included 35 fours and two sixes; Dharmani's 202 not out lasted 586 minutes and 385 balls and included 26 fours and one six.

Close of play: First day, Delhi 282-4 (Ajay Sharma 72, M. Prabhakar 0*); Second day, Delhi 505-8 (Ajay Sharma 216*, M. G. Chaturvedi 6*); Third day, Punjab 210-4 (Bhupinder Singh, jun. 19*, Bhupinder Singh, sen. 0*); Fourth day, Punjab 446-6 (Bhupinder Singh, jun. 116*, P. Dharmani 71*).*

Delhi

R. Sehgal b Obaid Kamal	11	G. Vadhera st Dharmani b Vij 39
*R. Lamba b Vij	165	Shakti Singh b Bhupinder Singh, sen. .. 8
Bantoo Singh c Dharmani b Kapoor	12	†M. G. Chaturvedi not out 18
Ajay Sharma lbw b Obaid Kamal	240	Kartar Nath c Vikram Rathore
A. S. Wassan b Vij	4	b Kapoor .. 11
M. Prabhakar c Dharmani		B 8, l-b 5, w 4, n-b 18 35
b Bhupinder Singh, sen. .	8	
Akash Malhotra c Bhupinder Singh, jun.		1/66 2/102 3/258 4/270 5/300 554
b Bhupinder Singh, sen. .	3	6/318 7/386 8/446 9/535

Bowling: Bhupinder Singh, sen. 35–6–101–3; Bedi 21–3–75–0; Obaid Kamal 25.2–2–84–2; Vij 57–12–123–3; Kapoor 54.1–7–147–2; Mohan 5–1–11–0.

Punjab

A. R. Kapoor c Sehgal b Wassan	52	K. Mohan lbw b Shakti Singh	31
Vikram Rathore c Ajay Sharma		†P. Dharmani not out	202
b Kartar Nath	74	Obaid Kamal lbw b Akash Malhotra	0
*N. S. Sidhu c Chaturvedi		B. Vij not out	10
b Kartar Nath	34		
Bhupinder Singh, jun. c and b Sehgal	297	B 5, l-b 9, w 2, n-b 28	44
Gursharan Singh c Prabhakar			
b Kartar Nath	17	1/86 2/159 3/176	(8 wkts) 780
Bhupinder Singh, sen. c Ajay Sharma		4/209 5/235 6/298	
b Prabhakar	19	7/758 8/759	

A. S. Bedi did not bat.

Bowling: Prabhakar 36–9–101–1; Wassan 24–10–113–1; Shakti Singh 23–5–64–1; Kartar Nath 66–9–195–3; Ajay Sharma 34–4–80–0; Sehgal 33–13–75–1; Akash Malhotra 16.2–3–78–1; Lamba 2–0–6–0; Bantoo Singh 6–0–42–0; Vadhera 4–0–12–0.

Umpires: A. V. Jayaprakash and S. Shastri.

Final

At Wankhede Stadium, Bombay, March 27, 28, 29, 30, 31. Drawn. Bombay were declared champions by virtue of their first-innings lead. Bombay 690 for six dec. (S. S. Dighe 137, S. V. Manjrekar 224, S. R. Tendulkar 140, V. G. Kambli 107 not out, S. V. Bahutule 36, Extras 38; Sandeep Sharma four for 155) and 513 for six dec. (A. A. Muzumdar 69, S. V. Manjrekar 32, V. G. Kambli 64, S. R. Tendulkar 139, S. V. Bahutule 103 not out, S. A. Ankola 35 not out; B. Vij three for 177); Punjab* 372 (Vikram Rathore 177, N. S. Sidhu 108) and 141 for two (Ajay Mehra 60 not out, P. Dharmani 65 not out).

Manjrekar's 224 lasted 545 minutes and 370 balls and included 29 fours; he added 286 for the second wicket with Dighe and 221 for the third with Tendulkar, who took 83 balls to reach 100; in the second innings Tendulkar needed only 66. All five Punjab bowlers conceded over 100 runs in the first innings.

RANJI TROPHY WINNERS

1934-35	Bombay	1955-56	Bombay	1976-77	Bombay
1935-36	Bombay	1956-57	Bombay	1977-78	Karnataka
1936-37	Nawanagar	1957-58	Baroda	1978-79	Delhi
1937-38	Hyderabad	1958-59	Bombay	1979-80	Delhi
1938-39	Bengal	1959-60	Bombay	1980-81	Bombay
1939-40	Maharashtra	1960-61	Bombay	1981-82	Delhi
1940-41	Maharashtra	1961-62	Bombay	1982-83	Karnataka
1941-42	Bombay	1962-63	Bombay	1983-84	Bombay
1942-43	Baroda	1963-64	Bombay	1984-85	Bombay
1943-44	Western India	1964-65	Bombay	1985-86	Delhi
1944-45	Bombay	1965-66	Bombay	1986-87	Hyderabad
1945-46	Holkar	1966-67	Bombay	1987-88	Tamil Nadu
1946-47	Baroda	1967-68	Bombay	1988-89	Delhi
1947-48	Holkar	1968-69	Bombay	1989-90	Bengal
1948-49	Bombay	1969-70	Bombay	1990-91	Haryana
1949-50	Baroda	1970-71	Bombay	1991-92	Delhi
1950-51	Holkar	1971-72	Bombay	1992-93	Punjab
1951-52	Bombay	1972-73	Bombay	1993-94	Bombay
1952-53	Holkar	1973-74	Karnataka	1994-95	Bombay
1953-54	Bombay	1974-75	Bombay		
1954-55	Madras	1975-76	Bombay		

Bombay have won the Ranji Trophy 32 times, Delhi 6, Baroda and Holkar 4, Karnataka 3, Bengal, Hyderabad and Maharashtra 2, Haryana, Madras, Nawanagar, Punjab, Tamil Nadu and Western India 1.

CRICKET IN PAKISTAN, 1994-95

By ABID ALI KAZI

Yet again, controversies surrounded Pakistan cricket in 1994-95, this time accompanied by failures on the field – a massive Test defeat by South Africa and an historic one by Zimbabwe. Rumours of revolt in the team were supplemented by charges of betting and bribery. The centre of attention was the Test captain, Salim Malik. In February, Australian spinners Tim May and Shane Warne claimed Malik had approached them before the First Test at Karachi in September and offered them $US50,000 each to throw the game. The Australian Cricket Board sent a report to the International Cricket Council and Javed Burki, then chairman of the ad hoc committee running Pakistan cricket, went to London to meet ICC chief executive David Richards.

By this time Malik, who was leading the national team in South Africa and Zimbabwe, was involved in other rumours about match-fixing to suit the requirements of bookmakers. Later, at the fag end of the Zimbabwean tour, Rashid Latif, the vice-captain, and Basit Ali suddenly announced their retirement from international cricket. It was believed they were disgusted with Malik. They returned three months later, but in the meantime, there were scores of allegations and counter-allegations levelled at each other by team members and other prominent cricketing personalities.

On their return to Pakistan, Malik and Intikhab Alam were sacked as captain and team manager. Malik was suspended from first-class cricket and given seven days' notice to answer the charges. After a six-and-a-half-hour meeting, the board decided he ought to have a chance to cross-examine his accusers and asked the Australian Cricket Board to send May and Warne to Pakistan. The invitation was declined, the ACB citing fears for their safety. Next time a Pakistan team was selected, for the Asia Cup in April, Malik and several others were not considered; wicket-keeper Moin Khan was named captain, only to catch chicken-pox.

The Asia Cup team was the first chosen by the reformed Pakistan Cricket Board, which finally replaced the Board of Control for Cricket in Pakistan after a 14-month interregnum, presided over by the three-man ad hoc committee. On March 20, 1995, state president Farooq Leghari, the board's patron, named Arif Ali Khan Abbasi – a member of the ad hoc committee – chief executive of the PCB. Syed Zulfiqar Ali Shah, a former senator and ambassador, was picked as chairman and Salman Taseer, a chartered accountant, treasurer.

In the domestic season, Karachi regained the crown they lost to Lahore the previous year when Karachi Blues beat Lahore City in the final of the Quaid-e-Azam Trophy. It was the 14th time a Karachi side had won this title, easily a record over its 37 seasons. Their total of 802 for eight was the fourth-highest in Pakistan's first-class history and contained double-centuries from Asif Mujtaba and Mahmood Hamid and centuries from Shoaib Mohammad and Moin Khan.

The Quaid-e-Azam was contested by ten teams, rather than eight. In 1993-94, Rawalpindi B had beaten Peshawar in the Grade II final to earn promotion, but it was ruled that only Karachi and Lahore could field more than one team at the top level. This decision was reversed, allowing Rawalpindi to enter their second string, but Peshawar were also retained. The tenth team were Bahawalpur, who had been scratched and relegated after failing to arrive for their final match in 1993-94 but were now reinstated.

In 1994-95, Sargodha were scratched and relegated. All points scored for and against them were cancelled after they did not turn up for their final game with Rawalpindi A. They had conceded a similar walkover to Bahawalpur in their first game, but then their explanation was accepted. Faisalabad also failed to attend a match against Karachi Blues: parents of some players were reluctant to let them travel to Karachi, because of the threat of violent political disturbances. Faisalabad's submissions were accepted and the match was rearranged later. Hyderabad were promoted to replace Sargodha.

Allied Bank won the Patron's Trophy at their first attempt after promotion to Grade I; they had been on the non-first-class circuit for ten years. Allied Bank were third in the league, but beat United Bank, the leaders with 64 points, on first-innings lead in the semi-final. Ata-ur-Rehman and Aamir Nazir bowled United out for 138 and Allied ran up 462; United's second-innings recovery came too late and Allied Bank beat PIA by ten wickets in the final. The Grade II final was won by Khan Research Laboratories, who beat Pakistan Customs. It was not immediately clear whether they would be promoted, as the Board had decided that promotions and relegations should take place at two-year intervals. But they had already reversed a similar decision on the Quaid-e-Azam Trophy, so Khan's elevation seemed likely.

The Pentangular Trophy was revived after a three-year gap and contested by the three top teams of the Patron's Trophy and the top two from the Quaid-e-Azam. The tournament was spoiled, however, by rain, which caused three of its ten games to be abandoned. The three Patron's teams tied on 14 points, but National Bank emerged as winners on run-rate. National Bank also won the 14th Wills Cup, Pakistan's 50-overs domestic competition. In the final, an opening partnership of 181 between Shahid Anwar and Sajid Ali paved the way for victory over PIA with more than six overs to spare. The Pepsi Junior Cup, for Under-19 players, was won by Karachi Whites, with Multan runners-up.

Asadullah Butt became the first bowler in Pakistan domestic cricket to be suspended for ball-tampering after a one-day match between Habib Bank and PIA. In the Quaid-e-Azam Trophy, three Bahawalpur players were suspended after a vehement argument with an umpire who turned down an appeal.

Salim Malik headed the overall first-class batting averages with 92.83 in three Tests against Australia, but he played no domestic first-class cricket. The leader on the domestic circuit was Ijaz Ahmed jun., of Faisalabad and Allied Bank, who averaged 87.38 over 24 innings. Third in the averages was Mazhar Qayyum, who had been banned for life for attacking an umpire the previous season but was reinstated after he "apologised unconditionally" and moved from Bahawalpur to Peshawar. The bowling averages were headed by Hasnain Kazim of Lahore City and United Bank, who took 38 wickets at 15.50 in ten matches. Arshad Khan of Peshawar and Railways was the leading wicket-taker, collecting 80 at 19.47 in 15 matches. For the second year running, Naved Anjum took nine wickets in an innings, the best return of the season; this time it was nine for 35 for Lahore City against Islamabad. Shafiq Ahmed of Bahawalpur took 11 for 204 – including eight for 111 in the first innings – on his first-class debut, against Karachi Blues. There were two hat-tricks, remarkably achieved in the same match and on the same day. Tauseef Ahmed, playing for United Bank in the Pentangular Trophy, finished off Karachi Blues in three balls but Ali Gauhar of Karachi then trumped him by taking United's first four with consecutive deliveries. He was the first Pakistani to take four in four balls, and only the seventh player since the Second World War. Rafaqat Ali of Allied Bank was the leading wicket-keeper, with 47 dismissals in 11 matches, and the most successful fielder was Sajid Ali, of Karachi Blues and National Bank, with 29 catches from 19 matches.

FIRST-CLASS AVERAGES, 1994-95

BATTING

(Qualification: 600 runs)

	M	I	NO	R	HS	100s	Avge
Ijaz Ahmed, jun. (*Faisalabad/Allied Bank*)	17	24	6	1,573	202*	7	87.38
Mansoor Rana (*Lahore City/ADBP*)	8	14	3	685	175*	2	62.27
Mazhar Qayyum (*Peshawar*)	8	14	2	641	201*	1	53.41
Mohammad Ramzan (*Faisalabad/United Bank*) . . .	19	30	5	1,286	203*	3	51.44
Mahmood Hamid (*Karachi Blues/United Bank*) . . .	20	30	6	1,183	208	3	49.29
Ghulam Ali (*Karachi Blues/United Bank*)	18	29	2	1,222	224	5	45.25
Ramiz Raja (*Allied Bank*)	11	18	1	754	300	1	44.35
Azam Khan (*Karachi Whites/Karachi Blues/PNSC*).	15	24	2	969	144	2	44.04
Mohammad Nawaz (*Sargodha/Allied Bank*)	17	30	4	1,140	202*	3	43.84
Manzoor Akhtar (*Karachi Blues/Allied Bank*)	21	31	3	1,220	249	3	43.57
Tahir Shah (*Lahore City/National Bank*)	12	18	3	646	84	0	43.06
Mohammad Javed (*Karachi Whites/National Bank*) .	15	24	4	842	169	3	42.10
Iqbal Imam (*Karachi Whites/United Bank*)	14	20	2	751	155	2	41.72
Sohail Jaffer (*Karachi Whites/Karachi Blues/PNSC*).	18	29	2	1,085	113	2	40.18
Moin Khan (*Karachi Blues/PIA*)	11	18	2	622	115*	3	38.87
Shoaib Mohammad (*Karachi Blues/PIA*)	13	23	1	816	201*	3	37.09
Sajid Ali (*Karachi Blues/National Bank*)	19	31	1	1,110	143	3	37.00
Shahid Anwar (*Lahore City/National Bank*)	19	32	1	1,128	110	1	36.38
Tariq Mahmood (*Lahore City/Railways*)	15	25	1	851	206*	1	35.45
Aaley Haider (*Rawalpindi B/Allied Bank*)	18	27	3	806	118	1	33.58
Sher Ali (*Peshawar/PNSC*)	14	23	1	623	110	1	28.31

* *Signifies not out.*

BOWLING

(Qualification: 30 wickets)

	O	M	R	W	BB	5W/i	Avge
Hasnain Kazim (*Lahore City/United Bank*)	188	34	589	38	7-54	4	15.50
Tauseef Ahmed (*United Bank*)	389.5	130	702	45	6-28	2	15.60
Aamir Nazir (*Islamabad/Allied Bank*)	331	57	1,163	68	6-52	8	17.10
Mohammad Aslam (*Rawalpindi A/Railways*) . . .	194.2	36	535	31	7-52	2	17.25

	O	M	R	W	BB	5W/i	Avge
Ali Gauhar (*Karachi Blues*)	173.3	34	549	31	7-92	2	17.70
Saqlain Mushtaq (*Islamabad/PIA*)	445	121	948	52	7-66	4	18.23
Arshad Khan (*Peshawar/Railways*)	676.4	163	1,558	80	8-115	8	19.47
Bilal Rana (*Allied Bank*)	266.4	84	591	30	4-31	0	19.70
Abdul Qadir (*Lahore City/Habib Bank*)	350.3	48	1,051	52	7-67	5	20.21
Masood Anwar (*Faisalabad/United Bank*)	289	87	660	32	8-72	2	20.62
Mohammad Hussain (*Lahore City*)	338.1	99	851	40	6-90	3	21.27
Nadeem Khan (*Karachi Blues/National Bank*)	502.4	134	1,196	56	5-28	5	21.35
Shahid Hussain (*Peshawar/United Bank*)	362	130	754	35	4-14	0	21.54
Zahid Ahmed (*PIA*)	359	97	755	35	6-82	1	21.57
Asadullah Butt (*Islamabad/Habib Bank*)	285.4	66	907	42	6-64	2	21.59
Zafar Iqbal (*Karachi Blues/National Bank*)	272.5	45	906	41	7-60	2	22.09
Raja Afaq (*Rawalpindi A/ADBP*)	387.5	66	975	41	7-55	4	23.78
Naeem Ashraf (*Lahore City/National Bank*)	421.1	69	1,265	53	7-53	5	23.86
Haaris Khan (*Karachi Blues*)	515.2	147	1,181	49	5-53	2	24.10
Imran Adil (*Bahawalpur/Railways*)	242.4	40	735	30	6-44	3	24.50
Mohammad Asif (*Lahore City/ADBP*)	665.5	168	1,453	59	5-40	2	24.62
Javed Hayat (*Lahore City/ADBP*)	337	86	739	30	4-40	0	24.63
Sajid Shah (*Peshawar/PNSC*)	252.2	44	813	33	7-77	2	24.63
Farrukh Zaman (*Peshawar*)	337.1	71	819	32	7-63	1	25.59
Ata-ur-Rehman, sen. (*Lahore City/Allied Bank*)	220.4	37	783	30	6-74	1	26.10
Athar Laeeq (*Karachi Blues/National Bank*)	471.1	85	1,616	60	8-65	2	26.93
Nadeem Afzal (*Faisalabad/PIA*)	360.3	52	1,251	43	6-63	3	29.09
Shahid Mahmood (*Sargodha/Habib Bank*)	335	30	1,224	31	4-76	0	39.48

QUAID-E-AZAM TROPHY, 1994-95

	Played	Won	Lost	Drawn	1st-inns Points	Points
Lahore City	8	5	2	1	8	48
Karachi Blues	9	4	1	4	12	42
Faisalabad	9	2	1	6	10	30
Islamabad	8	3	1	4	6	26
Rawalpindi A	8	3	2	3	6	26
Peshawar	9	3	3	3	6	26
Karachi Whites	8	2	3	3	6	26
Rawalpindi B	9	1	2	6	4	14
Bahawalpur	9	2	4	3	2	12
Sargodha	9	0	6	3	0	0

Note: Sargodha were disqualified from the competition after failing to turn up for their match against Rawalpindi A; all points earned by them and against them were cancelled. Sargodha had also failed to turn up to play Bahawalpur, but on that occasion their explanation was accepted by the board. Both matches were recorded as wins for Sargodha's opponents.

Semi-finals: Lahore City beat Faisalabad by virtue of their higher run-rate; Karachi Blues beat Islamabad by an innings and 270 runs.

Final: Karachi Blues beat Lahore City by an innings and 180 runs.

Outright win = 10 pts; lead on first innings in a won or drawn game = 2 pts.

In the following scores, * by the name of a team indicates that they won the toss.

At Bahawal Stadium, Bahawalpur, December 5, 6, 7, 8. Bahawalpur v Sargodha. Bahawalpur awarded match after Sargodha failed to turn up. *Points cancelled.*

At Iqbal Stadium, Faisalabad, December 5, 6, 7, 8. Drawn. Peshawar* 175 (Jahangir Khan, sen. 32, Zafar Sarfraz 69; Nadeem Afzal five for 60, Fazal Hussain three for 29) and 210 for four (Jahangir Khan, sen. 39, Mazhar Qayyum 70, Sher Ali 65 not out; Nadeem Afzal four for 69); Faisalabad 300 for six dec. (Mohammad Ramzan 126, Ijaz Ahmed, jun. 101 not out; Arshad Khan three for 70). *Faisalabad 2 pts.*

At Asghar Ali Shah Stadium, Karachi, December 5, 6, 7, 8. Karachi Blues won by 106 runs. Karachi Blues 241 (Manzoor Akhtar 113; Lal Faraz four for 43, Jaffer Qureshi three for 41) and 346 for four dec. (Sajid Ali 134, Shoaib Mohammad 110, Mahmood Hamid 50 not out; Jaffer Qureshi three for 110); Karachi Whites* 373 (Kamran Hussain 56, Sohail Jaffer 47, Iqbal Imam 45, Iqbal Saleem 74, Jaffer Qureshi 46, Jahangir Bakhsh 41 not out; Ghulam Ali three for 25) and 108 (Ameer-ud-Din 32, Kamran Hussain 33; Haaris Khan four for 24, Nadeem Khan four for 25). *Karachi Blues 10 pts.*

At LCCA Ground, Lahore, December 5, 6, 7. Islamabad won by ten runs. Islamabad* 69 (Naved Anjum nine for 35) and 287 (Abdul Basit 147, Ehsan Butt 35; Mohammad Asif three for 45, Abdul Qadir five for 86); Lahore City 194 (Babar Zaman 40, Tariq Mahmood 31, Sanaullah 35 not out; Aamir Nazir four for 104, Azhar Mahmood three for 64, Saqlain Mushtaq three for seven) and 152 (Aamir Nazir five for 75, Azhar Mahmood three for 53). *Islamabad 10 pts.*

At Rawalpindi Cricket Stadium, Rawalpindi, December 5, 6, 7, 8. Drawn. Rawalpindi B 219 for seven (Aamer Bashir 49, Tasawwur Hussain 89; Shakeel Ahmed three for 55) v Rawalpindi A*.
No play was possible after the first day.

At Bahawal Stadium, Bahawalpur, December 11, 12, 13, 14. Drawn. Faisalabad* 287 (Nadeem Arshad 42, Mohammad Ashraf 36, Iftikhar Hussain 43, Bilal Ahmed 52, Ijaz Mahmood 52; Imran Adil five for 70, Murtaza Hussain four for 90) and 174 (Mohammad Ramzan 83; Murtaza Hussain three for 44, Rehan Rafiq four for 28); Bahawalpur 286 (Aamir Sohail 98, Azhar Shafiq 74, Saifullah 30; Ijaz Mahmood three for 44, Wasim Hussain four for 99) and 27 for one. *Faisalabad 2 pts.*

At Marghzar Cricket Ground, Islamabad, December 11, 12, 13, 14. Drawn. Islamabad 178 (Ehsan Butt 60, Rizwan Bhatti 43; Shakeel Ahmed six for 75, Raja Afaq three for 65) and 136 for five (Tariq Rashid 50 not out, Tanvir Razzaq 35; Mohammad Akram four for 47); Rawalpindi A* 93 (Azhar Mahmood five for 36). *Islamabad 2 pts.*

At National Stadium, Karachi, December 11, 12, 13. Karachi Blues won by an innings and 349 runs. Karachi Blues 548 for two dec. (Ghulam Ali 224, Shoaib Mohammad 201 not out, Mahmood Hamid 51 not out, Extras 49); Sargodha* 106 (Zameer-ul-Hasan 38, Naeem Khan 31; Zafar Iqbal three for 26, Shoaib Mohammad three for 14) and 93 (Mohammad Saleem 33; Haaris Khan four for 26). *Points cancelled.*
Ghulam Ali and Shoaib Mohammad added 290 for the second wicket.

At LCCA Ground, Lahore, December 11, 12, 13. Lahore City won by seven wickets. Peshawar* 117 (Jahangir Khan, sen. 41; Abdul Qadir five for 31, Mohammad Asif three for 28) and 173 (Mazhar Qayyum 34; Abdul Qadir four for 78, Mohammad Asif three for 45); Lahore City 124 (Tariq Mahmood 68; Farrukh Zaman three for 57, Arshad Khan six for 30) and 170 for three (Javed Hayat 72 not out, Tariq Mahmood 33, Shahid Anwar 42). *Lahore City 12 pts.*

At Army Cricket Ground, Rawalpindi, December 11, 12, 13, 14. Drawn. Rawalpindi B 183 (Aamer Bashir 51, Tauqeer Hussain 38, Iftikhar Asghar 32; Naeem Tayyab six for 56) and 262 for nine dec. (Qayyum-ul-Hasan 71, Tasawwur Hussain 53, Masood Anwar 33; Jaffer Qureshi four for 69); Karachi Whites* 228 (Ameer-ud-Din 38, Sohail Jaffer 77, Kamran Hussain 46, Mohammad Javed 40; Sabih Azhar five for 13) and 38 for one. *Karachi Whites 2 pts.*

At Bahawal Stadium, Bahawalpur, December 17, 18, 19. Rawalpindi B won by eight wickets. Bahawalpur 127 (Saifullah 39; Tauqeer Hussain six for 53) and 114 (Tauqeer Hussain four for 43, Iftikhar Asghar three for 29); Rawalpindi B* 211 (R. Crosse 57, Tasawwur Hussain 51 not out; Murtaza Hussain seven for 65) and 32 for two. *Rawalpindi B 12 pts.*

At Marghzar Cricket Ground, Islamabad, December 17, 18, 19, 20. Islamabad won by 171 runs. Islamabad 232 (Masroor Hussain 51, Ghaffar Kazmi 56; Shahid Mahmood four for 89) and 253 (Masroor Hussain 56, Abdul Basit 57, Ghaffar Kazmi 45, Azhar Mahmood 30; Mohammad Hasnain four for 66); Sargodha* 139 (Mohammad Hasnain 56; Wali Ahmed four for 27) and 175 (Naved Latif 32, Mohammad Hasnain 47, Asad Mahmood 31 not out; Wali Ahmed six for 42). *Points cancelled.*

Sargodha wicket-keeper Ahsan Raza made five catches and one stumping in Islamabad's second innings.

At National Stadium, Karachi, December 17, 18, 19, 20. Peshawar won by three wickets. Karachi Blues* 294 (Wasim Arif 58, Malik Rasheed 52, Manzoor Akhtar 39, Munir-ul-Haq 62, Sohail Mehdi 35; Farrukh Zaman three for 103, Arshad Khan six for 100) and 140 (Sajid Shah four for 45, Arshad Khan four for 34); Peshawar 272 (Jahangir Khan, sen. 69, Wajahat Wasti 42, Mazhar Qayyum 44, Hameed Gul 52, Extras 34; Haaris Khan three for 82) and 165 for seven (Jahangir Khan, sen. 47, Mazhar Qayyum 58 not out; Ali Gauhar three for 35). *Peshawar 10 pts.*

At LCCA Ground, Lahore, December 17, 18, 19, 20. Lahore City won by an innings and 66 runs. Faisalabad* 132 (Shahid Nawaz 45; Mohammad Hussain four for 35, Mohammad Asif three for 38) and 272 (Mohammad Ramzan 40, Shahid Nawaz 43, Ijaz Mahmood 88; Mohammad Hussain six for 90); Lahore City 470 for three dec. (Babar Zaman 101, Sohail Idrees 63, Tariq Mahmood 206 not out, Tahir Shah 46 not out). *Lahore City 12 pts.*

At Army Cricket Ground, Rawalpindi, December 17, 18, 19, 20. Karachi Whites won by seven wickets. Rawalpindi A 278* (Majid Saeed 36, Nadeem Abbasi 105, Raja Afaq 55; Salman Fazal five for 77, Naeem Tayyab three for 49) and 161 (Shahid Javed 88; Salman Fazal six for 43); Karachi Whites 292 (Javed Sami 44, Iqbal Saleem 58, Iqbal Imam 63; Mohammad Akram four for 67, Raja Afaq five for 117) and 152 for three (Azam Khan 78 not out). *Karachi Whites 12 pts.*

At Marghzar Cricket Ground, Islamabad, December 23, 24, 25, 26. Islamabad v Karachi Whites. Abandoned.

At Arbab Niaz Cricket Stadium, Peshawar, December 23, 24, 25, 26. Drawn. Bahawalpur 168 (Rizwan Sattar 30, Saifullah 49; Farrukh Zaman seven for 63); Peshawar* 172 for nine (Sher Ali 39, Wajahat Wasti 42 not out; Murtaza Hussain six for 50, Mohammad Zahid three for 44). *Peshawar 2 pts.*

Murtaza Hussain, Mohammad Zahid and Imran Adil were suspended for arguing with the umpire.

At Rawalpindi Cricket Stadium, Rawalpindi, December 23, 24, 25, 26. Rawalpindi A v Lahore City. Abandoned.

At Sargodha Stadium, Sargodha, December 23, 24, 25, 26. Drawn. Sargodha* 173 (Mohammad Nawaz 68, Shahid Mahmood 45; Iftikhar Asghar six for 59) and 60 for one; Rawalpindi B 242 (Aaley Haider 118, Tauqeer Hussain 33; Mohammad Sarfraz three for 97, Naeem Khan three for 44, Sajjad Akbar three for 36). *Points cancelled.*

At Marghzar Cricket Ground, Islamabad, December 29, 30, 31, January 1. Drawn. Bahawalpur 160 (Saifullah 42 not out, Mohammad Khalid 34; Azhar Mahmood four for 26, Mohammad Ali five for 64); Islamabad* 161 for four (Masroor Hussain 37, Abdul Basit 32, Ehsan Butt 35 not out). *Islamabad 2 pts.*

At National Stadium, Karachi, December 29, 30, January 1. Drawn. Rawalpindi B* 242 (R. Crosse 43, Tauqeer Hussain 66, Pervez Iqbal 76; Athar Laeeq five for 52) and 189 for five (R. Crosse 73, Tasawwur Hussain 56 not out; Manzoor Akhtar three for 61); Karachi Blues 324 for eight dec. (Faisal Qureshi 80, Irfanullah 65, Aamer Iqbal 57, Athar Laeeq 55 not out, Extras 30; Pervez Iqbal five for 59). *Karachi Blues 2 pts.*

At Arbab Niaz Cricket Stadium, Peshawar, December 29, 30, 31, January 1. Drawn. Peshawar 178 (Sher Ali 58, Jahangir Khan, sen. 53; Naeem Tayyab six for 31); Karachi Whites* 128 (Arshad Khan five for 58). *Peshawar 2 pts.*

The first innings were restricted to 47 overs after the first two days were washed out, but Peshawar were bowled out in 46.3 overs and Karachi Whites in 38.5.

At Rawalpindi Cricket Stadium, Rawalpindi, December 29, 30, 31, January 1. Drawn. Rawalpindi A 212 for eight (Shahid Naqi 52; Fazal Hussain five for 65); Faisalabad* 148 (Mohammad Nawaz 30; Naeem Akhtar three for 37). *Rawalpindi A 2 pts.*

The first innings were restricted to 50 overs after the first two days were washed out.

At Sargodha Stadium, Sargodha, December 29, 30, 31, January 1. Lahore City won by ten wickets. Sargodha 203 (Mohammad Hasnain 39, Idrees Baig 34, Zahid Umar 59 not out; Mohammad Hussain five for 49, Mohammad Asif three for 36) and 147 (Mohammad Hasnain 42, Zahid Umar 35; Mohammad Hussain four for 44, Mohammad Asif five for 45); Lahore City* 343 (Sohail Idrees 39, Shahid Anwar 60, Iftikhar Hussain 101, Extras 32; Shahid Mahmood for 123) and nine for no wkt. *Points cancelled.*

At Boranwalla Ground, Faisalabad, January 4, 5, 6, 7. Faisalabad won by an innings and 40 runs. Karachi Whites 86 (Ameer-ud-Din 36; Wasim Hussain five for 50, Masood Anwar four for 31) and 290 (Azam Khan 77, Ameer-ud-Din 33, Mohammad Javed 113 not out; Masood Anwar three for 88, Fazal Hussain five for 78); Faisalabad* 416 for four dec. (Mohammad Ramzan 203 not out, Ijaz Ahmed, jun. 122, Extras 34). *Faisalabad 12 pts.*

At National Stadium, Karachi, January 4, 5, 6, 7. Drawn. Karachi Blues* 492 for seven dec. (Ghulam 108, Faisal Qureshi 107 retired hurt, Athar Laeeq 24, Manzoor Akhtar 109 not out); Islamabad 210 (Hasan Adnan 33, Tanvir Razzaq 30, Ghaffar Kazmi 32; Nadeem Khan three for 39) and 304 for six (Abdul Basit 57, Ghaffar Kazmi 110 not out, Tariq Rashid 30, Extras 39; Zafar Iqbal four for 71). *Karachi Blues 2 pts.*

At LCCA Ground, Lahore, January 4, 5, 6. Lahore City won by ten wickets. Lahore City* 308 (Shahid Anwar 53, Aleem Dar 34, Naeem Ashraf 74 not out, Mohammad Hussain 51; Shoaib Akhtar six for 69) and 64 for no wkt (Babar Zaman 34 not out); Rawalpindi B 152 (Aamer Bashir 54, Aaley Haider 38 not out; Abdul Qadir six for 31) and 219 (Aaley Haider 87, Aamer Bashir 49; Mohammad Hussain three for 44, Abdul Qadir four for 64). *Lahore City 12 pts.*

At Arbab Niaz Cricket Stadium, Peshawar, January 4, 5, 6, 7. Peshawar won by an innings and 14 runs. Sargodha 195 (Mohammad Nawaz 41, Asad Mahmood 44, Shahid Mahmood 35; Ijaz Elahi six for 65, Arshad Khan three for 43) and 216 (Naved Latif 70, Mohammad Hasnain 63, Mohammad Nawaz 35; Farrukh Zaman four for 77, Arshad Khan six for 63); Peshawar* 425 five dec. (Sher Ali 110, Mazhar Qayyum 201 not out, Wasim Yousufi 51 not out). *Points cancelled.*

At Rawalpindi Cricket Stadium, Rawalpindi, January 4, 5. Rawalpindi A won by seven wickets. Bahawalpur 123 (Azhar Shafiq 38 not out; Mohammad Aslam seven for 52) and 86 (Mohammad Akram five for 46, Mohammad Aslam four for 14); Rawalpindi A* 164 (Asif Mahmood 31, Nadeem Abbasi 37; Pervez Shah six for 77, Azhar Shafiq four for 50) and 46 for three. *Rawalpindi A 12 pts.*

At Bahawal Stadium, Bahawalpur, January 10, 11, 12, 13. Bahawalpur won by two wickets. Lahore City 169 (Naeem Mahmood 52 not out; Faisal Elahi five for 46) and 231 for nine dec. (Shahid Anwar 110, Naeem Ashraf 53 not out; Rizwan Sattar three for 29); Bahawalpur* 174 (Rehan Rafiq 34 not out; Naeem Ashraf five for 68, Aleem Dar three for 19) and 230 for eight (Aamir Sohail 34, Azhar Shafiq 70, Rizwan Sattar 57, Saifullah 43 not out; Javed Hayat four for 40). *Bahawalpur 12 pts.*

At Boranwalla Ground, Faisalabad, January 10, 11, 12. Faisalabad won by three wickets. Islamabad* 154 (Asif Ali 48, Zaheer Abbasi 31; Shahid Nawaz three for 35, Shahid Ali Khan four for 32) and 198 (Masroor Hussain 41, Ehsan Butt 40, Hasan Adnan 35, Ghaffar Kazmi 35; Masood Anwar eight for 72); Faisalabad 253 (Ahmed Siddiq 35, Ijaz Ahmed, jun. 33, Shahid Nawaz 43, Mohammad Nawaz 31, Extras 38; Mohammad Ali four for 48, Saqlain Mushtaq five for 100) and 101 for seven (Saqlain Mushtaq four for 21). *Faisalabad 12 pts.*

At National Stadium, Karachi, January 10, 11, 12, 13. Karachi Blues won by 149 runs. Karachi Blues* 258 (Manzoor Akhtar 37, Irfanullah 57, Zafar Iqbal 31, Athar Laeeq 32, Extras 31; Mohammad Akram three for 85, Mohammad Aslam four for 52) and 251 for four dec. (Sajid Ali 87, Haaris Khan 63, Manzoor Akhtar 88 not out); Rawalpindi A 154 (Shahid Javed 52; Athar Laeeq three for 34, Haaris Khan four for 44, Nadeem Khan three for 39) and 206 (Shahid Javed 73; Athar Laeeq eight for 65). *Karachi Blues 12 pts.*

At Arbab Niaz Cricket Stadium, Peshawar, January 10, 11, 12, 13. Peshawar won by five wickets. Rawalpindi B 160 (Aaley Haider 32; Farrukh Zaman three for 61, Arshad Khan four for 37) and 224 (Aaley Haider 72, Tauqeer Hussain 35, Iftikhar Asghar 34; Farrukh Zaman three for 94, Arshad Khan four for 61); Peshawar* 230 (Wajahat Wasti 71, Mazhar Qayyum 70; Shoaib Akhtar three for 38, Pervez Iqbal four for 46) and 156 for five (Jahangir Khan, sen. 71). *Peshawar 12 pts.*

At Sargodha Stadium, Sargodha, January 10, 11, 12, 13. Drawn. Karachi Whites 359 (Ahmed Kamal 87, Mohammad Javed 169; Ahmed Hayat six for 142, Shahid Mahmood three for 59) and 267 for five dec. (Ameer-ud-Din 42, Ahmed Kamal 47, Azam Khan 78 not out, Mohammad Javed 44; Shahid Mahmood four for 76); Sargodha* 241 (Mohammad Nawaz 135, Intikhab Alam 45; Naeem Tayyab six for 91) and 264 for six (Shahid Mahmood 59, Tanvir Hussain 31, Mohammad Nawaz 100 not out, Asad Mahmood 41; Jaffer Qureshi three for 62). *Points cancelled.*

At Marghzar Cricket Ground, Islamabad, January 16, 17, 18, 19. Drawn. Rawalpindi B 328 (Salman Ahmed 120, Aamer Bashir 37, Tasawwar Hussain 50, Tauqeer Hussain 31 not out; Saqlain Mushtaq seven for 105); Islamabad* 159 (Ehsan Butt 36; Raja Sarfraz three for 49, Tauqeer Hussain six for 62) and 47 for one. *Rawalpindi B 2 pts.*

At National Stadium, Karachi, January 16, 17, 18, 19. Drawn. Lahore City 222 (Tariq Mahmood 48, Javed Hayat 102 not out, Naeem Mahmood 33; Athar Laeeq four for 41, Ali Gauhar four for 47); Karachi Blues* 331 for nine (Ghulam Ali 32, Mahmood Hamid 63, Aamer Iqbal 94, Haaris Khan 41, Extras 51; Mohammad Hussain four for 59). *Karachi Blues 2 pts.*

At UBL Sports Complex, Karachi, January 16, 17, 18, 19. Karachi Whites won by nine wickets. Bahawalpur 201 (Aamir Sohail 37, Rizwan Sattar 64, Faisal Elahi 36 not out; Mohammad Hasnain four for 51, Mohammad Javed five for 53) and 162 (Lal Faraz five for 54); Karachi Whites* 298 for seven dec. (Mansoor Khan 38, Sohail Jaffer 55, Iqbal Imam 35, Mohammad Javed 61 not out, Shaheen Malik 52) and 69 for one (Mansoor Khan 39 not out). *Karachi Whites 12 pts.*

At Rawalpindi Cricket Stadium, Rawalpindi, January 16, 17, 18, 19. Rawalpindi A won by 75 runs. Rawalpindi A 190 (Shahid Naqi 61, Asif Mahmood 30; Sajid Shah six for 64, Arshad Khan three for 49) and 168 (Shahid Naqi 30, Asif Mahmood 37, Nadeem Abbasi 48; Ijaz Elahi three for 55, Sajid Shah seven for 77); Peshawar* 162 (Mohammad Akram four for 40, Naeem Akhtar four for 61) and 121 (Sajid Shah 41; Mohammad Akram three for 60, Mohammad Aslam five for 40). *Rawalpindi A 12 pts.*

At Sargodha Stadium, Sargodha, January 16, 17, 18, 19. Drawn. Sargodha* 356 (Mohammad Nawaz 202 not out, Sohail Maqbool 55; Masood Anwar five for 120, Ijaz Ahmed, jun. four for 97); Faisalabad 396 for seven (Mohammad Ramzan 32, Ijaz Ahmed, jun. 202 not out). *Points cancelled.*
Mohammad Nawaz scored his third century in successive innings.

At Boranwalla Ground, Faisalabad, January 21, 22, 23, 24. Drawn. Faisalabad* 479 for eight dec. (Mohammad Ramzan 71, Saadat Gul 113, Ijaz Ahmed, jun. 119, Mohammad Amin 107 not out; Tauqeer Hussain three for 152) and 47 for no wkt (Mohammad Ramzan 45 not out); Rawalpindi B 211 (Aaley Haider 46; Ijaz Ahmed, jun. three for 39). *Faisalabad 2 pts.*

At Asghar Ali Shah Stadium, Karachi, January 21, 22, 23, 24. Karachi Blues won by 217 runs. Karachi Blues* 216 (Haaris Khan 52, Aamer Iqbal 33, Zafar Iqbal 35; Shafiq Ahmed eight for 111) and 288 for seven dec. (Ghulam Ali 151 not out, Manzoor Akhtar 51, Haaris Khan 30; Shafiq Ahmed three for 93); Bahawalpur 120 (Saifullah 31; Nadeem Khan four for 46) and 167 (Mohammad Khalid 61; Zafar Iqbal seven for 60). *Karachi Blues 12 pts.*
Shafiq Ahmed took eight for 111 and 11 for 204 in the match on his first-class debut.

At UBL Sports Complex, Karachi, January 21, 22, 23, 24. Lahore City won by four wickets. Karachi Whites 146 (Sohail Jaffer 53 not out, Mohammad Javed 31; Naeem Ashraf seven for 53, Shehzad Butt three for 57) and 208 (Mansoor Khan 30, Azam Khan 30, Iqbal Imam 32; Naeem Ashraf four for 65); Lahore City* 237 (Iftikhar Hussain 52, Javed Hayat 32, Shahid Aslam 71; Lal Faraz five for 73, Mohammad Hasnain three for 55) and 118 for six (Javed Hayat 30 not out; Lal Faraz three for 45). *Lahore City 12 pts.*

At Arbab Niaz Cricket Stadium, Peshawar, January 21, 22, 23, 24. Islamabad won by six wickets. Islamabad* 299 (Hasan Adnan 72, Asadullah Butt 38, Mushtaq Ahmed 57, Azhar Mahmood 39 not out; Arshad Khan eight for 115) and 81 for four (Sajid Shah four for 39); Peshawar 140 (Wajahat Wasti 32; Asadullah Butt three for 33, Azhar Mahmood four for 18) and 239 (Mazhar Qayyum 63, Wajahat Wasti 103; Asadullah Butt three for 29, Mushtaq Ahmed four for 70). *Islamabad 12 pts.*

At Rawalpindi Cricket Stadium, Rawalpindi, January 21, 22, 23, 24. Rawalpindi A v Sargodha. Rawalpindi A awarded match after Sargodha failed to turn up. *Points cancelled.*

At National Stadium, Karachi, January 27, 28, 29, 30. Drawn. Faisalabad* 460 (Ahmed Siddiq 40, Ijaz Ahmed, jun. 194, Mohammad Nawaz 34, Nadeem Afzal 100); Karachi Blues 496 for four (Ghulam Ali 72, Manzoor Akhtar 249, Munir-ul-Haq 100 not out, Extras 39). *Karachi Blues 2 pts.*

Ijaz Ahmed, jun. and Nadeem Afzal added 211 for the eighth wicket.

Semi-finals

At Rawalpindi Cricket Stadium, Rawalpindi, March 7, 8, 9, 10. Drawn. Lahore City were declared winners by virtue of their higher run-rate. Faisalabad 461 for eight dec. (Mohammad Ramzan 114, Ahmed Siddiq 31, Ijaz Ahmed, jun. 168, Bilal Ahmed 43; Naeem Ashraf three for 127, Abdul Qadir three for 100); Lahore City* 366 for five (Aamir Sohail 105, Shahid Anwar 92, Aamer Manzoor 48, Tahir Shah 56 not out, Javed Hayat 38).

Ijaz Ahmed, jun. scored his fourth century in successive innings.

At MCC Ground, Multan, March 8, 9, 10. Karachi Blues won by an innings and 270 runs. Islamabad* 96 (Athar Laeeq three for 31, Nadeem Khan five for 28) and 128 (Nadeem Khan five for 32, Haaris Khan five for 53); Karachi Blues 494 for six dec. (Sajid Ali 75, Asif Mujtaba 166, Mahmood Hamid 55, Munir-ul-Haq 102 not out, Moin Khan 37).

Final

At Arbab Niaz Cricket Stadium, Peshawar, March 14, 15, 16, 17, 18. Karachi Blues won by an innings and 180 runs. Karachi Blues* 802 for eight dec. (Shoaib Mohammad 100, Manzoor Akhtar 44, Asif Mujtaba 208, Mahmood Hamid 208, Munir-ul-Haq 62, Moin Khan 107; Mohammad Hussain four for 231); Lahore City 302 (Aamir Sohail 35, Shahid Anwar 89, Ijaz Ahmed, sen. 32, Naeem Ashraf 30, Mohammad Hussain 39; Nadeem Khan five for 135, Haaris Khan four for 62) and 320 (Aamir Sohail 38, Shahid Anwar 43, Zulqarnain Haider 80 not out; Nadeem Khan five for 96).

Karachi Blues' 802 for eight, scored in 240.2 overs, was the fourth-highest total in first-class cricket in Pakistan.

QUAID-E-AZAM TROPHY WINNERS

1953-54	Bahawalpur	1970-71	Karachi Blues	1984-85	United Bank
1954-55	Karachi	1972-73	Railways	1985-86	Karachi
1956-57	Punjab	1973-74	Railways	1986-87	National Bank
1957-58	Bahawalpur	1974-75	Punjab A	1987-88	PIA
1958-59	Karachi	1975-76	National Bank	1988-89	ADBP
1959-60	Karachi	1976-77	United Bank	1989-90	PIA
1961-62	Karachi Blues	1977-78	Habib Bank	1990-91	Karachi Whites
1962-63	Karachi A	1978-79	National Bank	1991-92	Karachi Whites
1963-64	Karachi Blues	1979-80	PIA	1992-93	Karachi Whites
1964-65	Karachi Blues	1980-81	United Bank	1993-94	Lahore City
1966-67	Karachi Blues	1981-82	National Bank	1994-95	Karachi Blues
1968-69	Lahore	1982-83	United Bank		
1969-70	PIA	1983-84	National Bank		

Cricket in Pakistan, 1994-95

BCCP PATRON'S TROPHY, 1994-95

	Played	Won	Lost	Drawn	1st-inns Points	Points
United Bank	7	5	0	2	14	64
National Bank........	7	4	1	2	8	48
Allied Bank	7	4	2	1	8	48
PIA	7	2	3	2	6	26
ADBP	7	2	3	2	2	22
Habib Bank..........	7	2	3	2	2	22
PNSC................	7	0	3	4	4	4
Pakistan Railways......	7	0	4	3	4	4

Semi-finals: Allied Bank beat United Bank by virtue of their first-innings lead; PIA beat National Bank by eight wickets.

Final: Allied Bank beat PIA by ten wickets.

Outright win = 10 pts; lead on first innings in a won or drawn game = 2 pts.

In the following scores, * by the name of a team indicates that they won the toss.

At Municipal Stadium, Gujranwala, September 28, 29, 30, October 1. National Bank won by 105 runs. National Bank 312 (Shahid Anwar 40, Aamer Gul 88, Saeed Azad 60, Wasim Arif 33; Manzoor Elahi six for 102) and 167 (Sajid Ali 40; Manzoor Elahi four for 52, Ghayyur Qureshi three for 18); ADBP* 283 (Tariq Mohammad 32, Sabih Azhar 66, Atif Rauf 92, Extras 38; Naeem Ashraf six for 96) and 91 (Maqsood Rana six for 26, Athar Laeeq three for 53). *National Bank 12 pts.*

At UBL Sports Complex, Karachi, September 28, 29, 30, October 1. United Bank won by six wickets. Allied Bank* 143 (Raj Hans 33; Shahid Hussain three for 50, Tauseef Ahmed three for 34) and 264 (Ramiz Raja 83, Mohammad Nawaz 68, Manzoor Akhtar 53, Extras 34; Shahid Hussain four for 48, Tauseef Ahmed three for 80); United Bank 296 (Javed Sami 102, Ghulam Ali 38, Mansoor Akhtar 50; Aamir Nazir six for 58) and 112 for four (Mahmood Hamid 39 not out, Mansoor Akhtar 32). *United Bank 12 pts.*

At LCCA Ground, Lahore, September 28, 29, 30, October 1. Drawn. Habib Bank* 255 (Shakeel Ahmed 66, Shahid Javed 71, Shahid Mahmood 30 not out; Imran Adil five for 72, Mohammad Aslam three for 80) and 307 for seven dec. (Shaukat Mirza 39, Idrees Baig 60, Shahid Javed 75, Sohail Fazal 63 not out); Pakistan Railways 339 (Maqsood Akbar 52, Nadeem Younis 114, Majid Saeed 91; Shahid Mahmood three for 101, Abdul Qadir seven for 67) and 85 for five (Abdul Qadir four for 23). *Pakistan Railways 2 pts.*

At Asghar Ali Shah Stadium, Karachi, September 28, 29, 30. PIA won by an innings and 19 runs. PNSC* 190 (Sher Ali 48, Tahir Mahmood 34; Zahid Ahmed six for 82) and 125 (Ashfaq Ahmed three for 33, Zahid Ahmed four for 43); PIA 334 (Aamer Malik 56, Zahid Ahmed 61, Moin Khan 113; Sajjad Ali three for 78, Alauddin three for 91). *PIA 12 pts.*

At Jinnah Stadium, Sialkot, October 3, 4, 5, 6. ADBP won by an innings and 15 runs. Pakistan Railways 240 (Nadeem Younis 48, Tariq Mahmood 64; Javed Hayat three for 60) and 157 (Nadeem Younis 36; Raja Afaq five for 44, Javed Hayat three for 30); ADBP* 412 for seven dec. (Atif Rauf 200, Mansoor Rana 57, Ghaffar Kazmi 52, Manzoor Elahi 57; Arshad Khan five for 138). *ADBP 12 pts.*

At Municipal Stadium, Gujranwala, October 3, 4, 5. National Bank won by four wickets. Habib Bank 334 (Shaukat Mirza 124 not out, Tahir Rashid 48, Naved Anjum 45, Asadullah Butt 51, Extras 31; Maqsood Rana four for 72, Athar Laeeq three for 97) and 88 (Maqsood Rana six for 39, Athar Laeeq four for 46); National Bank* 223 (Saeed Azad 51, Naeem Ashraf 104; Naved Anjum three for 49, Asadullah Butt four for 62, Shahid Mahmood three for 57) and 201 for six (Saeed Azad 87, Tahir Shah 56; Asadullah Butt three for 60, Sohail Fazal three for 44). *National Bank 10 pts.*

At UBL Sports Complex, Karachi, October 3, 4, 5, 6. United Bank won by ten wickets. PNSC* 181 (Azam Khan 35, Sohail Jaffer 43; Shahid Hussain four for 74, Tauseef Ahmed three for 22) and 286 (Azam Khan 121, Sohail Jaffer 49, Aamer Ishaq 42; Iqbal Imam seven for 66); United Bank 406 for eight dec. (Ghulam Ali 128, Mansoor Akhtar 59, Mahmood Hamid 58, Extras 43; Sohail Farooqi three for 126) and 64 for no wkt (Ghulam Ali 32 not out). *United Bank 12 pts.*

At Asghar Ali Shah Stadium, Karachi, October 4, 5, 6, 7. Allied Bank won by eight wickets. PIA 149 (Babar Zaman 42, Asif Mohammad 40; Mohammad Zahid three for 29) and 208 (Sohail Miandad 41, Shoaib Mohammad 51, Nadeem Afzal 37; Aqib Javed three for 43); Allied Bank* 301 (Ramiz Raja 81, Manzoor Akhtar 53, Ijaz Ahmed, jun. 45, Bilal Rana 33 not out; Zahid Ahmed four for 110) and 58 for two. *Allied Bank 12 pts.*

At LCCA Ground, Lahore, October 9, 10, 11, 12. Drawn. PNSC 356 (Azam Khan 30, Sohail Jaffer 96, Sher Ali 37, Sajjad Akbar 81, Sajid Shah 32; Aamir Nazir four for 78, Mohammad Zahid three for 49) and 148 (Sajjad Akbar 37 not out, Naved Nazir 30; Bilal Rana four for 31); Allied Bank* 280 (Aaley Haider 32, Ijaz Ahmed, jun. 130, Rafaqat Ali 55; Sajjad Ali six for 92) and 209 for eight (Mohammad Nawaz 35, Ijaz Ahmed, jun. 94 not out, Rafaqat Ali 32; Tahir Mahmood four for 53). *PNSC 2 pts.*

At Railways Stadium, Lahore, October 9, 10, 11, 12. National Bank won by 195 runs. National Bank* 229 (Wasim Arif 65, Shahid Anwar 33, Athar Laeeq 31; Arshad Khan six for 88) and 286 for nine dec. (Sajid Ali 51, Ameer Akbar 88, Wasim Arif 69 not out; Aamer Wasim four for 70, Arshad Khan three for 115): Pakistan Railways 192 (Zahid Javed 31, Zahid Majid Saeed 57; Nadeem Khan five for 65, Hafeez-ur-Rehman three for 50) and 128 (Zahid Javed 32; Nadeem Khan three for 41, Hafeez-ur-Rehman four for 27). *National Bank 12 pts.*

At UBL Sports Complex, Karachi, October 9, 10, 11. United Bank won by 171 runs. United Bank* 220 (Aamer Bashir 32, Iqbal Imam 31; Nadeem Afzal three for 42, Tanvir Ali three for 40) and 131 (Mohammad Ramzan 38, Aamer Bashir 30; Zahid Ahmed three for 52, Tanvir Ali three for 15, Babar Zaman three for 22); PIA 115 (Tauseef Ahmed four for 38) and 65 (Asif Mohammad 30 not out; Shahid Hussain four for 35, Tauseef Ahmed five for 12). *United Bank 12 pts.*

At Bagh-e-Jinnah Ground, Lahore, October 10, 11, 12, 13. Habib Bank won by nine wickets. ADBP 232 (Sabih Azhar 31, Mansoor Rana 91; Asadullah Butt four for 48, Abdul Qadir four for 98) and 276 (Mansoor Rana 140 not out, Raja Afaq 46; Abdul Qadir five for 108); Habib Bank* 407 for nine dec. (Tahir Rashid 119, Mujahid Jamshed 53, Idrees Baig 107, Shahid Javed 38, Shaukat Mirza 58; Raja Afaq three for 118) and 102 for one (Shakeel Ahmed 42 not out, Tahir Rashid 48). *Habib Bank 12 pts.*

At MCC Ground, Multan, October 15, 16, 17, 18. Drawn. PIA* 459 for seven dec. (Rizwan-uz-Zaman 126, Shoaib Mohammad 88, Sagheer Abbas 68, Wasim Haider 70, Ayaz Jilani 45 not out; Mohammad Asif four for 141) and 134 for eight (Rizwan-uz-Zaman 41; Raja Afaq seven for 55); ADBP 357 (Sabih Azhar 34, Mansoor Rana 175 not out, Manzoor Elahi 50, Bilal Ahmed 33; Zahid Ahmed four for 97, Ayaz Jilani three for 60). *PIA 2 pts.*

At Bagh-e-Jinnah Ground, Lahore, October 15, 16, 17. Allied Bank won by an innings and 171 runs. Habib Bank 139 (Tahir Rashid 34; Aamir Nazir five for 67) and 242 (Tahir Rashid 45, Idrees Baig 58, Naved Anjum 48; Aamir Nazir five for 40, Manzoor Akhtar three for 75); Allied Bank* 552 (Ramiz Raja 300, Ijaz Ahmed, jun. 41, Aaley Haider 55, Ata-ur-Rehman, sen. 34; Abdul Qadir four for 175). *Allied Bank 12 pts.*

Ramiz Raja's 300 lasted 591 minutes and 415 balls.

At Railways Stadium, Lahore, October 15, 16, 17, 18. Drawn. PNSC* 267 (R. I. Alikhan 42, Sohail Jaffer 31, Sajjad Akbar 49, Mutahir Shah 31; Maqsood Rana four for 76, Nadeem Khan three for 81, Hafeez-ur-Rehman three for 61) and 325 for seven (Azam Khan 95, Sohail Jaffer 113, Sajjad Ali 31; Naeem Ashraf three for 92); National Bank 399 (Wasim Arif 90, Mohammad Javed 106, Ameer Akbar 75, Tahir Shah 37; Naved Nazir five for 133). *National Bank 2 pts.*

At LCCA Ground, Lahore, October 15, 16, 17. United Bank won by eight wickets. Pakistan Railways 111 (Majid Saeed 41; Hasnain Kazim five for 29) and 193 (Zahid Javed 34, Tariq Mahmood 66; Hasnain Kazim seven for 54); United Bank* 176 (Mansoor Akhtar 39, Wasim Yousufi 41; Imran Adil three for 54, Iqbal Zahoor five for 43) and 130 for two (Javed Sami 34, Mohammad Ramzan 30 not out). *United Bank 12 pts.*

At Army Sports Stadium, Rawalpindi, October 21, 22, 23. United Bank won by 66 runs. United Bank* 232 (Mohammad Ramzan 81, Mahmood Hamid 72; Raja Afaq six for 97, Mohammad Asif three for 42) and 119 (Mansoor Akhtar 35, Extras 30; Mohammad Asif four for 24, Javed Hayat four for 45); ADBP 181 (Zahoor Elahi 86; Tauseef Ahmed four for 37) and 104 (Masood Anwar three for 34, Tauseef Ahmed six for 28). *United Bank 12 pts.*

At MCC Ground, Multan, October 21, 22, 23, 24. Habib Bank won by 40 runs. Habib Bank* 191 (Shakeel Ahmed 61, Idrees Baig 30, Shahid Javed 45; Sajjad Akbar seven for 42) and 253 (Shakeel Ahmed 117, Shaukat Mirza 44; Naved Nazir four for 76); PNSC 196 (Sohail Jaffer 45, Sajjad Akbar 35, Sajjad Ali 55; Asadullah Butt four for 34, Nadeem Ghauri five for 63) and 208 (Sohail Jaffer 83, Sher Ali 37, Sajjad Akbar 34; Nadeem Ghauri six for 69). *Habib Bank 10 pts.*

At Railways Stadium, Lahore, October 21, 22, 23, 24. Drawn. Pakistan Railways* 270 (Zahid Javed 77, Tariq Mahmood 64, Majid Saeed 52; Saqlain Mushtaq seven for 66) and 231 (Tariq Shabbir 30, Shahid Saeed 104 not out, Aamer Wasim 31; Saqlain Mushtaq four for 60); PIA 135 (Wasim Haider 44; Imran Adil six for 44, Arshad Khan three for 40) and 274 for nine (Rizwan-uz-Zaman 57, Zahid Ahmed 110, Ayaz Jilani 36 not out). *Pakistan Railways 2 pts.*

At Bagh-e-Jinnah Ground, Lahore, October 22, 23, 24, 25. Allied Bank won by five wickets. National Bank 224 (Mohammad Javed 48, Tahir Shah 49, Extras 44; Aamir Nazir four for 64, Ata-ur-Rehman, sen. four for 46) and 254 (Sajid Ali 31, Aamer Gul 37, Saeed Azad 34, Ameer Akbar 53, Tahir Shah 44; Ata-ur-Rehman, sen. four for 65, Bilal Rana three for 55); Allied Bank* 249 (Ijaz Ahmed, jun. 50, Raj Hans 42, Rafaqat Ali 47; Zafar Iqbal three for 47) and 232 for five (Ramiz Raja 56, Mohammad Nawaz 45, Ijaz Ahmed, jun. 62 not out). *Allied Bank 12 pts.*

At Army Sports Stadium, Rawalpindi, October 27, 28, 29, 30. ADBP won by two wickets. Allied Bank* 185 (Ramiz Raja 49, Aaley Haider 41; Javed Hayat four for 49) and 163 (Shahid Naqi 43; Mohammad Asif five for 40, Raja Afaq three for 43); ADBP 174 (Zahoor Elahi 65; Aamir Nazir six for 53, Mohammad Nawaz four for 41) and 175 for eight (Sabih Azhar 59, Mansoor Rana 60 not out; Mohammad Nawaz three for 56). *ADBP 10 pts.*

At National Stadium, Karachi, October 27, 28, 29, 30. Drawn. United Bank 592 (Ghulam Ali 120, Aamer Bashir 82, Mansoor Akhtar 53, Mahmood Hamid 108, Iqbal Imam 155, Extras 39; Asadullah Butt six for 92) and 189 for two (Ghulam Ali 80, Mohammad Ramzan 57 not out); Habib Bank* 191 (Shakeel Ahmed 59, Naved Anjum 52; Hasnain Kazim six for 46, Mohammad Ali three for 63). *United Bank 2 pts.*

At UBL Sports Complex, Karachi, October 27, 28, 29, 30. National Bank won by eight wickets. PIA 169 (Shoaib Mohammad 52, Extras 36; Naeem Ashraf five for 53, Zafar Iqbal five for 32) and 293 (Rizwan-uz-Zaman 30, Zahid Fazal 65, Asif Mohammad 40, Moin Khan 65, Extras 35; Naeem Ashraf four for 86, Zafar Iqbal three for 65); National Bank* 369 (Shahid Anwar 73, Sajid Ali 79, Shahid Tanvir 88; Wasim Haider three for 98) and 97 for two (Shahid Anwar 39). *National Bank 12 pts.*

At Arbab Niaz Cricket Stadium, Peshawar, October 27, 28, 29, 30. Drawn. Pakistan Railways 501 for four dec. (Nadeem Younis 75, Haafiz Tahir 62, Tariq Mahmood 62, Majid Saeed 163 not out, Babar Javed 101 not out); PNSC* 318 for five (Azam Khan 60, Farrukh Bari 72, Sohail Jaffer 53, Sher Ali 70).

At Arbab Niaz Cricket Stadium, Peshawar, November 1, 2, 3, 4. Drawn. ADBP 235 (Atif Rauf 121; Sajjad Ali five for 76) and 321 for five (Tariq Mohammad 56, Zahoor Elahi 53, Atif Rauf 100 not out, Mansoor Rana 30, Manzoor Elahi 41); PNSC* 410 (Azam Khan 59, Sohail Jaffer 38, Nasir Wasti 99, Aamer Ishaq 106, Sajjad Akbar 42; Mohammad Asif four for 88). *PNSC 2 pts.*

At Army Sports Ground, Rawalpindi, November 1, 2, 3, 4. Allied Bank won by seven wickets. Pakistan Railways* 104 (Nadeem Younis 40; Raj Hans five for 31, Mohammad Nawaz three for 11) and 201 (Majid Saeed 37, Qayyum-ul-Hasan 46; Aamir Nazir for 52, Bilal Rana three for 31); Allied Bank 228 (Shahid Naqi 58, Aaley Haider 65; Iqbal Zahoor four for 52, Arshad Khan five for 107) and 83 for three (Ijaz Ahmed, jun. 36 not out). *Allied Bank 12 pts.*

At UBL Sports Complex, Karachi, November 1, 2, 3, 4. PIA won by 102 runs. PIA 196 (Rizwan-uz-Zaman 48, Hasnain Qayyum 80; Asadullah Butt six for 64, Shakeel Khan three for 21) and 291 (Zahid Fazal 44, Rizwan-uz-Zaman 37, Zahid Ahmed 33, Asif Mohammad 30, Wasim Haider 33, Saqlain Mushtaq 50 not out; Asadullah Butt four for 143, Shakeel Khan four for 76); Habib Bank* 126 (Idrees Baig 32 not out; Nadeem Afzal six for 63) and 259 (Mujahid Jamshed 93, Tahir Rashid 44, Asadullah Butt 38 not out; Wasim Haider five for 74, Zahid Ahmed three for 23). *PIA 12 pts.*

At National Stadium, Karachi, November 1, 2, 3, 4. Drawn. National Bank* 365 (Shahid Anwar 79, Sajid Ali 143, Mohammad Javed 35, Shahid Tanvir 35, Extras 32; Hasnain Kazim five for 65) and 298 for six (Aamer Gul 32, Sajid Ali 35, Mohammad Javed 70, Tahir Shah 84); United Bank 386 (Ghulam Ali 58, Mansoor Akhtar 41, Mahmood Hamid 59, Umar Rasheed 91, Wasim Yousufi 46, Extras 38; Habib Baloch five for 110, Shahid Tanvir three for 51). *United Bank 2 pts.*

Semi-finals

At Rawalpindi Cricket Stadium, Rawalpindi, November 20, 21, 22, 23. Drawn. Allied Bank were declared winners by virtue of their first-innings lead. United Bank 138 (Mahmood Hamid 48; Ata-ur-Rehman, sen. four for 41, Aamir Nazir four for 74) and 441 for four (Mohammad Ramzan 80, Umar Rasheed 62, Mahmood Hamid 145 not out, Iqbal Imam 107 not out, Extras 30); Allied Bank* 462 (Mohammad Nawaz 71, Manzoor Akhtar 97, Ijaz Ahmed, jun. 30, Aaley Haider 64, Raj Hans 94 not out, Rafaqat Ali 47, Extras 33; Tauseef Ahmed four for 124, Shahid Hussain three for 67).

At National Stadium, Karachi, November 20, 21, 22, 23. PIA won by eight wickets. National Bank 173 (Tahir Shah 55; Nadeem Afzal four for 44, Wasim Haider three for 56) and 282 (Shahid Anwar 33, Wasim Arif 32, Zafar Iqbal 63 not out; Nadeem Afzal five for 96, Saqlain Mushtaq three for 85); PIA* 423 (Rizwan-uz-Zaman 62, Asif Mujtaba 70, Zahid Fazal 59, Sagheer Abbas 36, Zahid Ahmed 35, Moin Khan 63, Extras 51; Naeem Ashraf three for 133, Mohammad Javed three for 47) and 33 for two.

Final

At National Stadium, Karachi, November 26, 27, 28, 29. Allied Bank won by ten wickets. PIA 165 (Sagheer Abbas 58; Shahid Mahboob three for 55, Bilal Rana three for 46) and 161 (Zahid Fazal 69, Asif Mohammad 33; Aamir Nazir six for 55); Allied Bank* 248 (Mohammad Nawaz 33, Manzoor Akhtar 71, Ijaz Ahmed, jun. 44, Shahid Mahboob 34; Zahid Ahmed three for 75, Saqlain Mushtaq five for 101) and 79 for no wkt (Mohammad Nawaz 48 not out).

AYUB TROPHY AND BCCP PATRON'S TROPHY WINNERS

The Ayub Trophy was replaced by the BCCP Trophy after the 1969-70 season and by the BCCP Patron's Trophy after the 1971-72 season.

1960-61	Railways-Quetta	1974-75	National Bank	1985-86	Karachi Whites
1961-62	Karachi	1975-76	National Bank	1986-87	National Bank
1962-63	Karachi	1976-77	Habib Bank	1987-88	Habib Bank
1964-65	Karachi	1977-78	Habib Bank	1988-89	Karachi
1965-66	Karachi Blues	1978-79	National Bank	1989-90	Karachi Whites
1967-68	Karachi Blues	†1979-80	IDBP	1990-91	ADBP
1969-70	PIA	†1980-81	Rawalpindi	1991-92	Habib Bank
1970-71	PIA	†1981-82	Allied Bank	1992-93	Habib Bank
1971-72	PIA	†1982-83	PACO	1993-94	ADBP
1972-73	Karachi Blues	1983-84	Karachi Blues	1994-95	Allied Bank
1973-74	Railways	1984-85	Karachi Whites		

† *The competition was not first-class between 1979-80 and 1982-83, when it served as a qualifying competition for the Quaid-e-Azam Trophy.*

BCCP PENTANGULAR TROPHY, 1994-95

	Played	Won	Lost	Drawn	1st-inns Points	Points
National Bank......	3	1	0	2	4	14
Allied Bank	2	1	0	1	4	14
United Bank	3	1	1	1	4	14
Karachi Blues	3	1	0	2	2	12
Lahore City	3	0	3	0	0	0

National Bank won the trophy by virtue of their higher run-rate.

Outright win = 10 pts; lead on first innings in a won or drawn game = 2 pts.

In the following scores, * by the name of a team indicates that they won the toss.

At Arbab Niaz Cricket Stadium, Peshawar, March 20, 21, 22, 23. Drawn. Allied Bank 345 (Mohammad Nawaz 62, Ramiz Raja 83, Manzoor Akhtar 37, Ijaz Ahmed, jun. 58, Aamer Hanif 58; Asif Mujtaba three for 64, Haaris Khan five for 108) and 28 for two; Karachi Blues* 298 (Asif Mujtaba 51, Sohail Jaffer 102, Munir-ul-Haq 72; Aqib Javed six for 77, Bilal Rana three for 63). *Allied Bank 2 pts.*

At Rawalpindi Cricket Stadium, Rawalpindi, March 20, 21, 22, 23. Drawn. United Bank 307 (Mohammad Ramzan 91, Mansoor Akhtar 73, Extras 42; Zafar Iqbal three for 89, Naeem Ashraf five for 55) and 62 for three (Athar Laeeq three for 23); National Bank* 208 (Saeed Azad 32, Tahir Shah 30, Extras 37; Hasnain Kazim three for 44, Umar Rasheed six for 64). *United Bank 2 pts.*

At Rawalpindi Cricket Stadium, Rawalpindi, March 25, 26, 27, 28. Allied Bank v National Bank. Abandoned.

At Arbab Niaz Cricket Stadium, Peshawar, March 25, 26, 27, 28. Karachi Blues v Lahore City. Abandoned.

At Rawalpindi Cricket Stadium, Rawalpindi, March 31, April 1, 2, 3. Allied Bank won by eight wickets. Lahore City 141 (Babar Zaman 62; Shahid Mahboob six for 22) and 154 (Babar Zaman 44, Sohail Idrees 30, Jamal Butt 35; Ata-ur-Rehman, sen. six for 74, Shahid Mahboob four for 58); Allied Bank* 288 (Mohammad Nawaz 50, Bilal Rana 80 not out; Inamullah Khan five for 90) and ten for two. *Allied Bank 12 pts.*

At Arbab Niaz Cricket Stadium, Peshawar, March 31, April 1, 2. Karachi Blues won by an innings and one run. United Bank* 222 (Mohammad Ramzan 44, Javed Sami 37, Mansoor Akhtar 35, Mahmood Hamid 38, Iqbal Imam 50 not out; Tariq Hussain eight for 97) and 122 (Iqbal Imam 47; Ali Gauhar six for 33); Karachi Blues 345 (Azam Khan 144, Saad Wasim 66, Sohail Jaffer 63; Tauseef Ahmed four for 99). *Karachi Blues 12 pts.*

On the third day, Tauseef Ahmed finished Karachi Blues' innings with a hat-trick and Ali Gauhar took United Bank's first four wickets with consecutive balls.

At Rawalpindi Cricket Stadium, Rawalpindi, April 5, 6, 7, 8. Drawn. Karachi Blues 221 (Irfanullah 34, Sarwat Ali 49 not out; Athar Laeeq three for 71) and 366 (Azam Khan 39, Sohail Jaffer 50, Tahir Rashid 99, Irfanullah 52; Mohammad Javed three for 78, Aleem Moosa three for 67); National Bank* 336 (Saeed Azad 39, Shahid Anwar 85, Tahir Shah 60, Shahid Tanvir 51; Ali Gauhar seven for 92, Lal Faraz three for 113) and 142 for five (Shahid Anwar 56, Ameer Akbar 68; Ali Gauhar three for 60). *National Bank 2 pts.*

At Arbab Niaz Cricket Stadium, Peshawar, April 5, 6. United Bank won by an innings and 99 runs. Lahore City* 139 (Tauseef Ahmed four for 26, Shahid Hussain four for 41) and 62 (Shahid Hussain four for 14, Iqbal Imam three for 16); United Bank 300 (Saifullah 52, Mansoor Akhtar 60, Iqbal Imam 68, Extras 31; Mohammad Hussain five for 88, Babar Zaman three for 51). *United Bank 12 pts.*

At Rawalpindi Cricket Stadium, Rawalpindi, April 10, 11, 12, 13. Allied Bank v United Bank. Abandoned.

At Arbab Niaz Cricket Stadium, Peshawar, April 10, 11, 12, 13. National Bank won by ten wickets. Lahore City 214 (Sohail Idrees 35, Habibullah 39, Tariq Humayun 32, Gulzar Awan 66; Hafeez-ur-Rehman five for 54) and 286 (Mohammad Hussain 46, Tariq Humayun 60, Inamullah Khan 60, Habibullah 32; Tahir Shah seven for 65); National Bank* 419 (Shahid Anwar 57, Sajid Ali 132, Saeed Azad 71, Tahir Shah 58; Inamullah Khan five for 149) and 85 for no wkt (Sajid Ali 54 not out). *National Bank 12 pts.*

PENTANGULAR TROPHY WINNERS

The competition was called the PACO Cup between 1980-81 and 1986-87, after sponsors Pakistan Automobile Corporation.

1973-74	PIA	1980-81	PIA	1985-86	PACO
1974-75	National Bank	1981-82	Habib Bank	1986-87	PIA
1975-76	PIA	1982-83	Habib Bank	1990-91	United Bank
1976-77	PIA	1984-85	United Bank	1994-95	National Bank

Note: Matches in this section were not first-class.

WILLS CUP, 1994-95

Semi-finals

At National Stadium, Karachi, November 16. PIA won by four wickets. Habib Bank 183 (43 overs) (Shakeel Ahmed 30, Mujahid Jamshed 31, Salim Malik 57; Adnan Naeem four for 50); PIA* 184 for six (43.4 overs) (Asif Mujtaba 67 not out; Nadeem Ghauri three for 32).

At Rawalpindi Cricket Stadium, Rawalpindi, November 16. National Bank won by five wickets. United Bank 185 (41.2 overs) (Inzamam-ul-Haq 61, Mahmood Hamid 31; Zafar Iqbal four for 32, Mohammad Javed three for 45); National Bank* 187 for five (39.4 overs) (Shahid Anwar 95 not out, Tahir Shah 55; Hasnain Kazim three for 51).

Final

At National Stadium, Karachi, November 18. National Bank won by eight wickets. PIA 211 (44.4 overs) (Sagheer Abbas 59, Asif Mohammad 38; Zafar Iqbal three for 44, Nadeem Khan three for 40); National Bank* 215 for two (43.2 overs) (Shahid Anwar 73, Sajid Ali 112 not out).

CRICKET IN SRI LANKA, 1994-95

By GERRY VAIDYASEKERA and SA'ADI THAWFEEQ

Sri Lankan cricket received great encouragement in March 1995 from the country's first overseas Test victory, in New Zealand, which was soon converted into victory in the series. It was very timely after two heavy home defeats by Pakistan and a dull drawn series in Zimbabwe. But much remained to be done to build a consistently successful national side. Though schools cricket in Sri Lanka is famously popular and competitive, too many promising players then fade, often hampered by economic difficulties. Hoping to bring the enthusiasm and high standards of their schoolboys to maturity, the Sri Lankan board set up a Cricket Academy, to be run by Anura Tennekoon. Meanwhile, they sought to raise the money to improve ground and coaching facilities throughout the country through Cricket Fund 2000, a campaign with the aim of making Sri Lanka world champions in five years. This initiative was closely associated with the board's new president, Ana Punchihewa. The local head of Coca-Cola, one of the principal sponsors of cricket in Sri Lanka, he represented a break from the line of politicians heading the board; his predecessor was the state presidential candidate Gamini Dissanayake, who was assassinated in October 1994.

The quantity of domestic first-class cricket exploded from 29 matches in 1993-94 to 73. The expansion was accounted for by the P. Saravanamuttu Trophy, whose first-class division had been cut from 14 teams to eight the previous season but swelled to 16 this time.

The Singer Inter-Provincial Tournament was played late, beginning a few days after the P. Sara final in February and running up to the start of April, thus coinciding with the national team's tour of New Zealand. But Western Province (City), fielding several players dropped from the Test team, retained the Trophy, beating Western Province (South) by an innings and 53 runs. Off-spinner Kumara Dharmasena took ten for 101 in the match and also made an unbeaten 68 to raise City's total to 498 for six declared. Varuna Waragoda scored 127, the only century, but all their batsmen contributed apart from Marvan Atapattu, with just nine. That counted as an upset: Atapattu entered the final with an average of 116.40, after scoring 582 in six innings; he had made three hundreds and never failed to reach 50. He and team-mates Waragoda, captain Chandika Hathurusinghe and Roshan Mahanama averaged over 70 to head the tournament's batting averages and Dharmasena led the bowling with 42 wickets at 13.09, a competition record. Those performances helped City to win the first three of their five league games by an innings and the last by ten wickets, and they took first-innings points in their previous encounter with South after scoring 545. Their lowest completed total was 438.

South were also unbeaten in the league, with three outright wins. Their captain, slow left-armer Don Anurasiri, took 31 wickets at 19.77; he and Suranjith Silva both took eight in an innings, against Central and Southern Provinces respectively. Wicket-keeper Romesh Kaluwitharana carried over his golden batting form from the P. Saravanamuttu Trophy; he scored three fifties and one hundred in four innings, following his six successive fifties for Galle, to equal the world record of ten shared by Ernest Tyldesley and Don Bradman.

In the P. Saravanamuttu Trophy, which ran from December to February, Bloomfield and Sinhalese shared the title after a high-scoring final – 929 runs for 14 wickets – ended in a draw. The captains agreed to call off the match in the final hour of the fourth day, when Bloomfield were still 89 behind with four first-innings wickets standing. Sanath Jayasuriya had displayed absolute patience and self-control for ten hours and five minutes and remained unbeaten on 130. After Bloomfield were in trouble at 207 for five, he shared century partnerships with Ruwan Kalpage and Mahanama. Mahanama, the captain, batted at No. 8 because of a long-standing injury and supported Jayasuriya for 48 overs in spite of severe pain. Sinhalese's massive 509 for eight, which occupied nearly seven sessions, centred on a third-wicket stand of 237 between Dhammika Ranatunga and Marvan Atapattu, who scored 181, while Test captain Arjuna Ranatunga made 125. It was the fifth time Sinhalese had had a share of the trophy in seven seasons since it became first-class; they had won it outright three times. Bloomfield's performance was more remarkable, however. They won their first five matches in Group A, all by large margins, and took first-innings points in the next two, remaining unbeaten throughout, under the guidance of a new coach, former Test leg-spinner Somachandra de Silva.

Both Sinhalese and Tamil Union won four matches in Group B, but Sinhalese were unbeaten while Tamil lost one. Tamil batsmen Damian Nadarajah and Upul Chandana added 285 for the fifth wicket against Kurunegala Youth, 16 short of the Sri Lankan record. This was the only innings in the tournament to top 500, until that of Sinhalese in the final. Jehan Jaymon made the highest individual score, 247, hitting 34 fours and two sixes. The fastest hundred came from Arjuna Ranatunga, who reached three figures in 98 balls and 123 minutes for Sinhalese against Sebastianites, and the slowest from his brother Sanjeeva, whose 124 for Bloomfield against Nondescripts took 371 balls and 508 minutes. Muttiah Muralitharan took eight for eight for Tamil Union against Burgher Recreation Club, and another spinner, his team-mate Niroshan Bandaratilleke, took 12 for 102 in their match against Sebastianites. Suranjith Silva of Sinhalese performed the hat-trick against Tamil Union.

Bloomfield also took the limited-overs Hatton National Bank Cricket Trophy, beating Tamil Union by three wickets when tailender Pulasthi Gunaratne hit a six with a ball to spare. The final of the P. Sara Trophy's second division was won by the Police, who beat the Navy by an innings. Nondescripts won the GTE Under-23 Yellow Pages Trophy on first-innings lead against Galle.

In schools cricket, Nimesh Perera of St Sebastian's took 131 wickets, surpassing Muttiah Muralitharan's record of 127 in 1990-91. He also scored over 750 runs. Several schoolboys scored 1,000 runs, including Tilan Samaraweera of Ananda, Chintaka Jayasinghe of Dharmapala, Thilina Asiri of Ananda Sastralaya, Sumedha Weerasiri of Sri Rahula College, who was the first boy from Kandy to achieve the feat, and Bathisha de Silva, captain of S. S. Senanayake College. De Silva also took 14 for 74 against Dharmarajah.

FIRST-CLASS AVERAGES, 1994-95

BATTING

(Qualification: 500 runs)

	M	I	NO	R	HS	100s	Avge
M. S. Atapattu (*WP City/Sinhalese*)	15	18	3	1,304	181	5	86.93
V. S. K. Waragoda (*WP City/Colombo*)	11	14	1	924	204	5	71.07
A. Ranatunga (*Sinhalese*)	7	9	1	538	209*	3	67.25
R. S. Kaluwitharana (*WP South/Galle*)	13	21	2	1,167	142	2	61.42
D. Ranatunga (*WP North/Sinhalese*)	13	19	2	1,027	166*	3	60.41
R. P. A. H. Wickremaratne (*WP North/Sinhalese*)	11	15	1	840	209	2	60.00
L. de Silva (*NWP/Kurunegala Youth*)	12	22	4	972	128	2	54.00
S. I. de Saram (*WP North/Tamil Union*)	12	20	2	952	226	2	52.88
M. N. Nawaz (*WP City/Bloomfield*)	11	13	1	615	152*	1	51.25
D. N. Nadarajah (*Tamil Union*)	12	20	1	889	170	2	46.78
U. U. Chandana (*WP City/Tamil Union*)	12	13	1	553	154*	3	46.08
J. Jaymon (*NWP/Burgher*)	9	18	0	768	247	2	42.66
U. C. Hathurusinghe (*WP City/Tamil Union*)	14	20	1	804	108	1	42.31
D. P. Samaraweera (*WP South/Galle*)	9	16	2	579	101*	2	41.35
P. B. Dassanayake (*CP/Bloomfield*)	10	16	1	612	144	2	40.80
H. D. P. K. Dharmasena (*WP City/Bloomfield*)	15	19	3	647	87	0	40.43
S. Jayantha (*SP/Singha*)	11	20	1	760	212*	2	40.00
R. P. Arnold (*WP City/Nondescripts*)	11	18	3	594	77*	1	39.60
V. S. Sittamige (*WP North/Antonians*)	12	19	1	712	140	1	39.55
D. D. Wickremasinghe (*SP/Galle*)	10	17	2	588	112*	1	39.20
S. I. Fernando (*CP/Colts*)	12	22	3	718	110*	1	37.78
H. S. S. Fonseka (*SP/Galle*)	12	22	2	752	190	1	37.60
S. Warusamana (*WP South/Nondescripts*)	13	22	3	668	91	0	35.15
H. Premasiri (*SP/Singha*)	12	23	1	752	147	3	34.18
C. Mahesh (*WP South/Sebastianites*)	12	19	2	553	109	1	32.52
R. Jaymon (*NWP/Kurunegala Youth*)	12	19	1	547	147	1	30.38
S. Jayawardene (*WP South/Panadura*)	10	18	0	511	118	1	28.38
J. Kulatunga (*NWP/Colts*)	12	20	1	507	69	0	26.68

* *Signifies not out.*

BOWLING

(Qualification: 20 wickets)

	O	M	R	W	BB	5W/i	Avge
M. Muralitharan (*Tamil Union*)	161.4	56	371	25	8-8	2	14.84
K. J. Silva (*Bloomfield*)	262	90	579	37	6-15	2	15.64
S. D. Anurasiri (*WP South/Panadura*)	618.5	172	1,263	80	8-90	8	15.78
J. C. Gamage (*Galle*)	245.4	61	718	45	7-69	5	15.95
H. D. P. K. Dharmasena (*WP City/Bloomfield*)	496.4	133	1,261	78	7-111	7	16.16
N. Bandaratilleke (*WP City/Tamil Union*)	275.5	69	774	43	7-47	4	18.00
N. Dabare (*Colombo*)	169.4	35	454	25	7-28	3	18.16
C. P. H. Ramanayake (*WP City/Tamil Union*)	297.3	93	816	37	6-88	1	22.05
P. W. Gunaratne (*WP City/Bloomfield*)	234.4	44	705	31	6-31	1	22.74
N. Ranatunga (*WP North/Colts*)	211	45	743	30	7-110	2	24.76
P. L. A. W. N. Alwis (*Antonians*)	247.5	54	771	29	4-30	0	26.58
K. G. Perera (*WP South/Moratuwa*)	503.3	104	1,330	50	8-60	7	26.60
P. M. Weragoda (*Antonians*)	418.5	103	1,066	39	7-102	4	27.33
A. Dalugoda (*WP North/Burgher*)	312.3	88	753	27	4-55	0	27.88
M. H. A. Jabbar (*WP South/Sebastianites*)	316.1	69	911	31	6-66	2	29.38
A. M. C. V. Kumara (*SP/Singha*)	268.3	43	969	32	6-91	2	30.28

	O	M	R	W	BB	5W/i	Avge
Suranjith Silva (*WP South/Sinhalese*)	596	102	1,968	64	8-130	3	30.75
A. W. Ekanayake (*NWP/Kurunegala Youth*) ...	489.3	114	1,419	46	7-35	3	30.84
M. J. H. Rushdie (*CP/Nondescripts*)	197	26	789	25	5-74	1	31.56
S. I. Fernando (*CP/Colts*)................	359.3	83	1,018	32	6-114	2	31.81
W. Labrooy (*WP North/Colombo*)	223.4	35	887	27	5-85	1	32.85
R. K. B. Amunugama (*NWP/Kurunegala Youth*)	222.5	23	930	28	5-60	1	33.21

*In the following scores, * by the name of a team indicates that they won the toss.*

SINGER INTER-PROVINCIAL TOURNAMENT, 1994-95

At Maitland Place, Colombo (NCC), February 22, 23, 24. Western Province (City) won by an innings and 134 runs. Southern Province 79 (M. Villavarayan four for 28, H. D. P. K. Dharmasena four for 17) and 225 (S. Jayantha 73; C. M. Hathurusinghe three for 65, N. Bandaratilleke three for 28); Western Province (City)* 438 for eight dec. (R. P. Arnold 68, M. S. Atapattu 71, U. U. Chandana 106, H. D. P. K. Dharmasena 80; S. T. R. Jayasekera three for 121, S. M. Faumi three for 66).

At Havelock Park, Colombo (BRC), February 22, 23, 24, 25. Western Province (North) won by four wickets. Western Province (North) 440 (S. I. de Saram 226, V. S. Sittamige 89; E. A. Upashantha three for 89, A. W. Ekanayake three for 110, A. H. Bandaranayake three for 74) and 229 for six (D. Ranatunga 45, W. T. de Silva 71 not out; A. H. Bandaranayake five for 74); North-Western Province* 231 (L. de Silva 43, E. A. Upashantha 69; W. Labrooy four for 63, D. Surendra four for 49) and 437 (L. de Silva 48, J. Kulatunga 31, E. A. Upashantha 58, R. Jaymon 73, A. W. Ekanayake 81; N. Ranatunga seven for 110).

At Tyronne Fernando Stadium, Moratuwa, February 22, 23, 24, 25. Western Province (South) won by three wickets. Central Province* 285 (K. Gunawardene 69, D. N. Nadarajah 34, U. H. Kodituwakku 58; S. D. Anurasiri three for 51) and 293 (S. I. Fernando 35, P. B. Dassanayake 96, K. Gunawardene 37, Extras 31; S. D. Anurasiri eight for 90); Western Province (South) 339 (T. M. Dilshan 126, R. S. Kaluwitharana 72, C. Mahesh 33; P. M. Weragoda three for 110, S. I. Fernando three for 66) and 242 for seven (S. Jayawardene 48, T. M. Dilshan 47, R. S. Kaluwitharana 92; T. Nonis three for 36).

At Maitland Crescent, Colombo (CCC), March 2, 3, 4. Western Province (City) won by an innings and 167 runs. North-Western Province 201 (J. Jaymon 36, L. de Silva 37, T. Herath 45, R. Jaymon 42; C. P. H. Ramanayake three for 61, C. M. Hathurusinghe four for 46, H. D. P. K. Dharmasena three for 35) and 74 (H. D. P. K. Dharmasena five for 13); Western Province (City)* 442 for eight dec. (M. S. Atapattu 112, V. S. K. Waragoda 160, U. U. Chandana 33, Extras 35; E. A. Upashantha three for 111, R. K. B. Amunugama four for 102).

At Air Force Ground, Katunayake, March 2, 3, 4. Western Province (North) won by an innings and 143 runs. Central Province 156 (P. Aluwihare 45; N. Ranatunga five for 61) and 90 (D. N. Nadarajah 43; W. Labrooy three for 45, N. Ranatunga four for 17); Western Province (North)* 389 (D. Ranatunga 166 not out, R. P. A. H. Wickremaratne 37, N. Ranatunga 37, Extras 36; S. I. Fernando six for 114).

D. Ranatunga carried his bat.

At Tyronne Fernando Stadium, Moratuwa, March 2, 3, 4, 5. Western Province (South) won by 115 runs. Western Province (South)* 249 (R. S. Kaluwitharana 145, D. K. Liyanage 30; M. de Silva five for 79) and 385 (N. S. Bopage 145, R. S. Kaluwitharana 70, C. Mahesh 41 not out; S. Sanjeeva three for 50, M. de Silva four for 122); Southern Province 346 (H. Premasiri 54, D. D. Wickremasinghe 112 not out, M. de Silva 83; Suranjith Silva eight for 130) and 173 (H. M. N. C. Dhanasinghe 37; Suranjith Silva four for 107, S. D. Anurasiri six for 35).

Kaluwitharana completed his tenth successive fifty, equalling the world record.

At Havelock Park, Colombo (Colts), March 9, 10, 11, 12. Southern Province won by six wickets. Central Province 385 (S. I. Fernando 62, K. Gunawardene 77, S. Liyanage 53, S. Madanayake 55, P. Aluwihare 31, Extras 39; S. Sanjeeva five for 86) and 203 (K. Gunawardene 55, H. M. Kodituwakku 32; S. M. Faumi four for 59, H. M. N. C. Dhanasinghe four for 17); Southern Province* 365 (H. S. S. Fonseka 80, H. Premasiri 107, H. M. N. C. Dhanasinghe 41, S. Sanjeeva 35 not out; P. M. Weragoda seven for 102) and 225 for four (H. M. N. C. Dhanasinghe 89, D. D. Wickremasinghe 82 not out).

At Reid Avenue, Colombo, March 9, 10, 11, 12. Western Province (City) won by an innings and 45 runs. Western Province (North)* 301 (D. Ranatunga 81, E. F. M. U. Fernando 32, W. T. de Silva 49, S. I. de Saram 42; H. D. P. K. Dharmasena five for 94) and 196 (E. F. M. U. Fernando 36, V. S. Sittamige 52, K. G. Priyantha 32; H. D. P. K. Dharmasena five for 68); Western Province (City) 542 (R. S. Mahanama 68, U. C. Hathurusinghe 108, M. S. Atapattu 174, H. D. P. K. Dharmasena 43, A. G. D. Wickremasinghe 39, N. Bandaratilleke 44; N. Ranatunga three for 119).

At St Sebastian's College Ground, Moratuwa, March 9, 10, 11. Western Province (South) won by five wickets. North-Western Province* 187 (J. Jaymon 39, E. A. Upashantha 62; K. G. Perera eight for 60) and 292 (J. Jaymon 73, J. Kulatunga 38, S. S. Guruge 39, T. Herath 39, Extras 43; K. G. Perera six for 92); Western Province (South) 235 (S. K. Silva 53, C. Mahesh 35; A. W. Ekanayake five for 43, A. W. R. Madurasinghe three for 31) and 249 for five (S. K. Silva 41, R. S. Kaluwitharana 32, S. Warusamana 73 not out, S. Kumara 66 not out).

At Maitland Place, Colombo (NCC), March 16, 17, 18, 19. North-Western Province won by five wickets. Central Province* 194 (S. I. Fernando 31, T. Nonis 66; R. K. B. Amunugama five for 60) and 187 (D. N. Nadarajah 71; A. W. Ekanayake six for 40); North-Western Province 168 (L. de Silva 38, J. Kulatunga 69; M. J. H. Rushdie five for 74) and 215 for five (L. de Silva 59, J. Kulatunga 39, A. W. R. Madurasinghe 32 not out, S. S. Guruge 35 not out).

At Tyronne Fernando Stadium, Moratuwa, March 16, 17, 18, 19. Drawn. Western Province (City)* 545 (R. S. Mahanama 102, U. C. Hathurusinghe 70, R. Peiris 56, M. S. Atapattu 50, U. U. Chandana 116, H. D. P. K. Dharmasena 37, C. P. H. Ramanayake 37; Suranjith Silva four for 183) and 177 for one (U. C. Hathurusinghe 80 not out, M. S. Atapattu 66 not out); Western Province (South) 330 (R. S. Kaluwitharana 57, D. K. Liyanage 95, Suranjith Silva 41, Extras 43; C. P. H. Ramanayake three for 48, P. W. Gunaratne three for 69).

At Air Force Ground, Katunayake, March 16, 17, 18, 19. Southern Province won by 22 runs. Southern Province 254 (G. Sanjeeva 38, A. Wewalwala 30, H. Rajapakse 33 not out; K. G. Priyantha three for 76, A. Dalugoda four for 59) and 219 (H. Premasiri 107; A. Dalugoda four for 55); Western Province (North)* 192 (V. S. Sittamige 36, A. Dalugoda 31, Extras 34; A. Wewalwala three for 69, M. de Silva three for 55) and 259 (D. Ranatunga 45, W. T. de Silva 34, R. P. A. H. Wickremaratne 40, A. Dalugoda 33; M. de Silva six for 87).

At Braybrooke Place, Colombo (Moors), March 23, 24, 25. North-Western Province won by seven wickets. Southern Province* 331 (S. M. Faumi 88, H. Rajapakse 73, S. Sanjeeva 66; R. K. B. Amunugama four for 125) and 181 (H. S. S. Fonseka 50, H. M. N. C. Dhanasinghe 41; A. W. Ekanayake four for 55, A. W. R. Madurasinghe four for 30); North-Western Province 395 (A. H. Bandaranayake 65, J. Jaymon 33, R. Jaymon 147, S. S. Guruge 59, R. K. B. Amunugama 33, Extras 34; S. Sanjeeva four for 98) and 121 for three (E. A. Upashantha 54 not out).

At Reid Avenue, Colombo, March 23, 24, 25. Western Province (City) won by ten wickets. Central Province* 201 (S. I. Fernando 82, Extras 36; H. D. P. K. Dharmasena three for 26, P. W. Gunaratne three for 42) and 283 (S. I. Fernando 77, D. N. Nadarajah 80, U. H. Kodituwakku 43; H. D. P. K. Dharmasena three for 67); Western Province (City) 457 for seven dec. (U. C. Hathurusinghe 78, R. Peiris 32, M. S. Atapattu 109, U. U. Chandana 56, H. D. P. K. Dharmasena 63, W. M. J. P. Weerasinghe 51 not out; P. Aluwihare three for 169) and 30 for no wkt.

Atapattu completed his seventh successive fifty.

At Panadura Esplanade, Panadura, March 23, 24, 25, 26. Drawn. Western Province (North)* 411 (D. Ranatunga 32, R. P. A. H. Wickremaratne 209, N. de Alwis 35, Extras 32; S. D. Anurasiri five for 103) and 234 (D. Ranatunga 96, S. I. de Saram 39, V. S. Sittamige 43; S. D. Anurasiri four for 50, Suranjith Silva three for 91); Western Province (South) 431 (S. Jayawardene 118, N. S. Bopage 86, C. Mahesh 82, Suranjith Silva 34, Extras 30; W. Labrooy three for 101) and 127 for five (R. S. Kaluwitharana 45, S. Warusamana 43).

Final

At Maitland Place, Colombo (SSC), March 30, 31, April 1. Western Province (City) won by an innings and 53 runs. Western Province (South) 179 (U. C. Hathurusinghe three for 20, H. D. P. K. Dharmasena five for 23) and 266 (S. K. Silva 30, N. S. Bopage 65, S. Warusamana 48, Suranjith Silva 44; H. D. P. K. Dharmasena five for 78); Western Province (City)* 498 for six dec. (R. S. Mahanama 41, U. C. Hathurusinghe 88, M. N. Nawaz 61, V. S. K. Waragoda 127, H. D. P. K. Dharmasena 68 not out, W. M. J. P. Weerasinghe 40 not out, Extras 39).

SINGER INTER-PROVINCIAL TROPHY WINNERS

1989-90	Western Province	1992-93	No competition
1990-91	Western Province (City)	1993-94	Western Province (City)
1991-92	Western Province (North)	1994-95	Western Province (City)

P. SARAVANAMUTTU TROPHY, 1994-95

Group A

At R. Premadasa Stadium, Colombo, December 9, 10, 11. Drawn. Moratuwa SC* 245 (C. Fernando 34, W. A. A. Wasantha 96; P. L. A. W. N. Alwis four for 79) and 260 (C. Fernando 56, W. A. A. Wasantha 64, S. Soysa 38; P. M. Weragoda five for 74, P. L. A. W. N. Alwis three for 98); Antonians SC 410 for nine dec. (M. Prasanga 69, N. Devarajan 48, V. S. Sittamige 140, K. Dharmasena 41, M. P. A. Cooray 32, Extras 44; K. G. Perera five for 103).

At Reid Avenue, Colombo, December 9, 10, 11. Drawn. Nomads SC 185 (D. Kanchana 38, A. Perera 34; A. M. C. V. Kumara three for 72, T. A. de Silva three for 25) and 244 (D. Kanchana 92, A. Jayasuriya 36; R. Priyantha three for 77); Singha SC* 316 (S. Jayantha 119, A. M. C. V. Kumara 76 not out, Extras 36; A. Perera five for 95) and 109 for six (S. Jayantha 32; B. Seneviratne four for 34).

At Braybrooke Place, Colombo, December 16, 17, 18. Antonians SC won by five wickets. Moors SC 199 (S. A. de Silva 32, A. Hettiarachchi 42, R. Ingram 31; K. Dharmasena three for 49, P. M. Weragoda five for 40) and 111 (M. P. A. Cooray five for 35, P. Wanasinghe three for 30); Antonians SC* 251 (W. A. M. P. Perera 35, P. Wanasinghe 80, V. S. Sittamige 69; T. Jeffry six for 89) and 61 for five (V. S. Sittamige 31 not out; D. Kolugala four for 29).

At Tyronne Fernando Stadium, Moratuwa, December 16, 17, 18. Bloomfield C and AC won by ten wickets. Bloomfield C and AC 407 (I. Batuwitarachchi 34, N. S. Bopage 105, M. N. Nawaz 84, N. A. C. P. Rodrigo 58, I. Galagoda 30; A. Mapatuna three for 110) and four for no wkt; Moratuwa SC* 232 (C. Perera 40, W. A. A. Wasantha 34, A. Mapatuna 44 not out; K. J. Silva six for 82) and 177 (S. Soysa 57; K. J. Silva three for 63).

At Panadura Esplanade, Panadura, December 16, 17, 18. Panadura SC won by five wickets. Singha SC* 205 (S. Gayan 59, T. A. de Silva 63; S. D. Anurasiri seven for 76); Panadura SC 320 (S. Gayan 95, T. A. de Silva 34; S. D. Anurasiri four for 41) and 211 (S. Jayawardene 91, N. Jayawardene 47, M. V. Deshapriya 42, S. Liyanage 54; R. Pushpakumara five for 83) and 100 for five (M. Jayasena 31 not out).

At Maitland Place, Colombo (NCC), December 30, 31, January 1. Nondescripts CC won by ten wickets. Nondescripts CC 290 (R. V. Hewage 54, S. Warusamana 55, L. Hannibal 82; C. de Silva five for 61) and 144 for no wkt (R. P. Arnold 77 not out, S. Warusamana 62 not out); Nomads SC* 127 (S. Wickremarachchi 46; M. J. H. Rushdie three for 21, R. P. Arnold five for 27) and 306 (D. Kanchana 76, N. Weerasinghe 51, C. de Silva 55 not out, Extras 35; M. J. H. Rushdie three for 66, R. P. Arnold three for 77).

At R. Premadasa Stadium, Colombo, January 6, 7, 8. Drawn. Antonians SC 361 (M. Prasanga 61, V. S. Sittamige 58, S. Sooriyarachchi 34, K. Dharmasena 76, Extras 36; R. Priyantha four for 93, L. Ranasinghe three for 87); Singha SC* 169 (H. Premasiri 53, S. Jayantha 48; K. Dharmasena four for 24, M. Prasanga four for 22) and 400 for eight (H. Premasiri 62, S. Jayantha 212 not out, T. A. de Silva 63; P. L. A. W. N. Alwis four for 145).

At Reid Avenue, Colombo, January 6, 7, 8. Bloomfield C and AC won by ten wickets. Bloomfield C and AC 337 (M. N. Nawaz 51, S. Perera 65, R. Palliyaguru 53, Extras 34; M. R. Farouk six for 87) and seven for no wkt; Moors SC* 156 (M. R. D. Hameen 54; P. W. Gunaratne six for 31) and 187 (K. T. de Silva 30, T. Jeffry 50; P. W. Gunaratne four for 47, K. J. Silva three for 40).

At Tyronne Fernando Stadium, Moratuwa, January 6, 7, 8. Nondescripts CC won by ten wickets. Moratuwa SC 137 (C. Perera 39; A. P. Weerakkody three for 53, R. P. Arnold three for nine) and 308 (M. Narayanage 50, R. Nonis 31, W. A. A. Wasantha 34, M. de Alwis 61, C. Perera 48; A. P. Weerakkody six for 89); Nondescripts CC* 351 (R. P. Arnold 47, C. P. Mapatuna 39, S. Warusamana 91, C. D. U. S. Weerasinghe 30, A. G. D. Wickremasinghe 39, Extras 35; K. G. Perera seven for 115) and 96 for no wkt (R. P. Arnold 45 not out, S. Weerasinghe 38 not out).

At Vihara Maha Devi Park, Colombo, January 6, 7, 8. Panadura SC won by nine wickets. Panadura SC* 384 (B. Perera 30, A. K. D. A. S. Kumara 119, M. V. Deshapriya 49, M. Jayasena 52, S. D. Anurasiri 32 not out; B. Rasanjana four for 68) and 47 for one (S. Kumara 38 not out); Nomads SC 164 (M. Jayasinghe 54; M. Jayasena five for 51) and 265 (M. Jayasinghe 43, C. de Silva 47, D. Kanchana 50, S. Umagiliyage 52 not out; M. V. Deshapriya four for 86).

At Reid Avenue, Colombo, January 13, 14, 15. Bloomfield C and AC won by 161 runs. Bloomfield C and AC 195 (M. N. Nawaz 81; A. M. C. V. Kumara five for 76, T. A. de Silva three for 51) and 311 (S. K. Perera 70, P. B. Dassanayake 46, S. T. Jayasuriya 32, R. S. Kalpage 51, H. D. P. K. Dharmasena 31; H. M. N. C. Dhanasinghe three for 29, S. Jayantha three for 76); Singha SC* 228 (T. A. de Silva 48, H. M. N. C. Dhanasinghe 60, W. M. J. Kumudu 32; P. W. Gunaratne four for 51) and 117 (K. J. Silva six for 15).

At Vihara Maha Devi Park, Colombo, January 13, 14, 15. Antonians SC won by six wickets. Nomads SC 294 (B. Seneviratne 103 not out, S. Ananda 86, A. Perera 32; M. P. A. Cooray three for 48, P. Wanasinghe three for 59) and 127 (M. P. A. Cooray three for 14, P. L. A. W. N. Alwis four for 53); Antonians SC* 156 (S. Sooriyarachchi 31, C. L. Dunusinghe 42; B. Rasanjana five for 70) and 267 for four (P. Wanasinghe 76, S. Sooriyarachchi 102 not out).

Nomads were 16 for six in their first innings; the last four wickets added 278.

At Maitland Place, Colombo (NCC), January 13, 14, 15. Nondescripts CC won by eight wickets. Moors SC 157 (P. Abeygunasekera 38; L. Hannibal five for 55) and 212 (U. I. Weerawarna 86; A. P. Weerakkody five for 64); Nondescripts CC* 256 (S. Ranatunga 93, C. D. U. S. Weerasinghe 84; D. Kolugala eight for 101) and 114 for two (S. Weerasinghe 42, R. P. Arnold 31).

At Panadura Esplanade, Panadura, January 13, 14, 15. Drawn. Panadura SC* 376 (B. Perera 45, N. Jayawardene 44, A. K. D. A. S. Kumara 57, M. V. Deshapriya 89, Extras 41; K. G. Perera six for 88) and 130 for four dec. (S. Jayawardene 45, A. K. D. A. S. Kumara 44); Moratuwa SC 229 (R. Nonis 68, Extras 36; S. D. Anurasiri four for 55) and 119 for five (D. Bodiyabaduge 31; S. D. Anurasiri three for 19).

At Reid Avenue, Colombo, January 20, 21, 22. Bloomfield C and AC won by an innings and 116 runs. Bloomfield C and AC 419 for four dec. (P. B. Dassanayake 74, M. N. Nawaz 152 retired hurt, S. Perera 87, S. T. Jayasuriya 74); Nomads SC* 119 (C. de Silva 35) and 184 (D. Kanchana 55, S. Ananda 30, N. Weerasinghe 44; H. D. P. K. Dharmasena four for 56, K. J. Silva four for 45).

At Braybrooke Place, Colombo, January 20, 21, 22. Drawn. Moratuwa SC* 189 (S. Soysa 50, M. de Alwis 30, P. Fernando 36; D. Kolugala four for 38, T. Jeffry three for 50) and 95 for three (C. Perera 45); Moors SC 337 (A. Hettiarachchi 31, T. Jeffry 124, U. I. Weerawarna 46, D. Kolugala 48; K. G. Perera seven for 134).

At Maitland Place, Colombo (NCC), January 20, 21, 22. Drawn. Nondescripts CC 382 (R. P. Arnold 68, C. P. Mapatuna 32, S. Warusamana 87, R. V. Hewage 35; R. Priyantha four for 132, A. M. C. V. Kumara three for 105, L. Ranasinghe three for 51) and 76 for five dec. (R. P. Arnold 33; T. A. de Silva three for 16); Singha SC* 261 (S. Jayantha 56, T. A. de Silva 84, W. M. J. Kumudu 46; A. P. Weerakkody three for 31) and 17 for two.

At Panadura Esplanade, Panadura, January 20, 21, 22. Drawn. Antonians SC* 276 (M. Prasanga 47, V. S. Sittamige 92, M. P. A. Cooray 50, Extras 33; S. D. Anurasiri seven for 90); Panadura SC 142 for eight (S. Jayawardene 33, S. Kumara 32; M. P. A. Cooray four for 29).

At Braybrooke Place, Colombo, January 27, 28, 29. Moors SC won by six wickets. Nomads SC 251 (N. Weerasinghe 35, C. de Silva 77 not out, P. Welagedera 45; M. R. Farouk five for 62, K. N. Waduge three for 21) and 234 (C. de Silva 42, P. Welagedera 89; P. Abeygunasekera four for 59); Moors SC* 326 (A. Hettiarachchi 40, M. R. D. Hameen 41, T. Jeffry 47, P. Abeygunasekera 65; S. de Silva four for 43) and 160 for four (P. Abeygunasekera 37, M. R. D. Hameen 38, T. Jeffry 33 not out).

At Tyronne Fernando Stadium, Moratuwa, January 27, 28, 29. Singha SC won by ten wickets. Singha SC* 408 for eight dec. (H. Premasiri 147, S. Gayan 83, S. Jayantha 38, T. A. de Silva 67, W. M. J. Kumudu 34; K. G. Perera five for 135) and 25 for no wkt; Moratuwa SC 188 (M. de Alwis 41, S. Soysa 39, D. Bodiyabaduge 36; S. Jayantha three for 24) and 241 (D. Bodiyabaduge 48, S. Soysa 30, W. A. A. Wasantha 53, P. Fernando 50; A. M. C. V. Kumara six for 91).

At Maitland Place, Colombo (NCC), January 27, 28, 29. Nondescripts CC won by 159 runs. Nondescripts CC 299 (R. P. Arnold 37, S. Ranatunga 59, S. Warusamana 34, C. P. Mapatuna 42, C. D. U. S. Weerasinghe 43; P. Wanasinghe three for 83) and 134 for nine dec. (R. P. Arnold 47; P. L. A. W. N. Alwis four for 30); Antonians SC* 186 (G. H. Perera 34, M. P. A. Cooray 47; C. D. U. S. Weerasinghe three for 34) and 88 (K. R. Pushpakumara six for 29).

At Panadura Esplanade, Panadura, January 27, 28, 29. Bloomfield C and AC won by an innings and 45 runs. Panadura SC* 150 (S. Kumara 41, A. K. D. A. S. Kumara 40; P. W. Gunaratne three for 36) and 129 (N. Jayawardene 38, S. Kumara 45; K. J. Silva three for 32, M. N. Nawaz five for 16); Bloomfield C and AC 324 (P. B. Dassanayake 144, H. D. P. K. Dharmasena 75; S. D. Anurasiri six for 84).

At Reid Avenue, Colombo, February 3, 4, 5. Drawn. Bloomfield C and AC* 303 (M. N. Nawaz 38, S. Perera 59, S. T. Jayasuriya 41, H. D. P. K. Dharmasena 38, R. Palliyaguru 54; P. Wanasinghe three for 67, P. M. Weragoda five for 93) and 273 for seven (P. B. Dassanayake 107, R. S. Kalpage 32, S. T. Jayasuriya 30; P. L. A. W. N. Alwis four for 105); Antonians SC 242 (W. A. M. P. Perera 79 not out, C. I. Dunusinghe 40; K. J. Silva four for 63).

W. A. M. P. Perera carried his bat through Antonians' innings.

At Braybrooke Place, Colombo, February 3, 4, 5. Drawn. Moors SC 347 (S. A. de Silva 38, K. N. Waduge 52, S. Dissanayake 39, M. R. D. Hameen 64, T. Jeffry 64 not out, Extras 32; H. M. N. C. Dhanasinghe three for 90); Singha SC* 237 (J. Nandakumara 79, A. M. C. V. Kumara 35; M. R. Farouk five for 86, K. N. Waduge three for 30).

At Tyronne Fernando Stadium, Moratuwa, February 3, 4, 5. Drawn. Moratuwa SC 435 for eight dec. (D. Bodiyabaduge 111, W. A. A. Wasantha 101, S. Soysa 43, R. Nonis 62 not out, A. Mapatuna 32, Extras 31; B. Rasanjana three for 81, P. Reginald three for 85) and 94 for three (S. Soysa 34, D. Bodiyabaduge 33); Nomads SC* 345 (C. de Silva 79, D. Kanchana 68, S. Wickremarachchi 35, S. Umagiliyage 47, B. Rasanjana 37, Extras 36; C. de Silva six for 69).

At Panadura Esplanade, Panadura, February 3, 4, 5. Drawn. Nondescripts CC 235 (S. Warusamana 40, P. A. de Silva 69; S. Jayawardene four for 102, S. D. Anurasiri four for 38) and 85 for two dec.; Panadura SC* 114 (P. A. de Silva seven for 24) and 154 for six (D. Prasanna 66 not out; M. J. H. Rushdie three for 20).
  C. P. Mapatuna held five catches in the field in Panadura's first innings.

At Braybrooke Place, Colombo, February 10, 11, 12. Moors SC won by five wickets. Panadura SC* 178 (S. Jayawardene 60, S. Kumara 53; P. Abeygunasekera three for 54, D. Schafter four for 33) and 141 (S. Jayawardene 31; P. Abeygunasekera five for 31); Moors SC 184 (T. Jeffry 40; S. D. Anurasiri four for 63, M. V. Deshapriya three for 35) and 139 for five (A. Hettiarachchi 34; M. V. Deshapriya three for 51).

At Maitland Place, Colombo (NCC), February 10, 11, 12. Drawn. Bloomfield C and AC 400 for eight dec. (S. K. Perera 44, M. N. Nawaz 36, S. Perera 69, H. D. P. K. Dharmasena 87, R. S. Kalpage 47, Extras 63; M. J. H. Rushdie three for 92); Nondescripts CC* 351 (R. P. Arnold 47, S. Weerasinghe 40, S. Ranatunga 124, P. A. de Silva 31, A. P. Weerakkody 47; R. S. Kalpage four for 83).
  Ranatunga's 124 lasted 508 minutes and 371 balls and included only five fours.

Group B

At Havelock Park, Colombo (Colts), December 9, 10, 11. Drawn. Colts CC 419 for six dec. (D. P. Samaraweera 53, C. Mendis 174, S. I. Fernando 110 not out, J. Kulatunga 33; R. K. B. Amunugama three for 67) and 96 for one (D. P. Samaraweera 31 not out, S. I. Fernando 38 not out); Kurunegala Youth CC* 325 (H. Liyanage 35, L. de Silva 128, K. Jayasinghe 56; J. Kulatunga three for 35).

At P. Saravanamuttu Stadium, Colombo, December 9, 10, 11. Tamil Union C and AC won by nine wickets. Colombo CC 246 (V. S. K. Waragoda 90; N. Bandaratilleke three for 59) and 221 (C. P. Handunettige 61, A. Perera 34, V. S. K. Waragoda 35; C. P. H. Ramanayake three for 41, N. Bandaratilleke three for 47, U. U. Chandana four for 54); Tamil Union C and AC* 323 (S. I. de Saram 87, D. N. Nadarajah 120, W. M. J. P. Weerasinghe 42; M. Villavarayan five for 90, S. Lokubalasuriya three for 49) and 147 for one (W. T. de Silva 55 not out, S. I. de Saram 56 not out).

At Havelock Park, Colombo (BRC), December 16, 17, 18. Colts CC won by 86 runs. Colts CC 300 (C. Mendis 30, N. Ranatunga 68, S. Alexander 60 not out; A. Dalugoda three for 57) and 124 for three dec. (C. Mendis 57, J. Kulatunga 35 not out); Burgher RC* 202 (W. K. D. J. D. K. Perera 46, A. Dalugoda 75; S. Alexander three for 58, D. Hettiarachchi five for 59) and 136 (W. K. D. J. D. K. Perera 83; S. I. Fernando three for 15, J. Kulatunga three for 15, D. Hettiarachchi three for 39).

At St Sebastian's College Ground, Moratuwa, December 16, 17, 18. Kurunegala Youth CC won by six wickets. Sebastianites C and AC* 119 (P. Salgado 31; A. W. Ekanayake seven for 35) and 210 (C. Mahesh 54, A. Perera 35, G. R. M. A. Perera 40; J. A. W. Kumara four for 53, A. W. Ekanayake three for 64); Kurunegala Youth CC 189 (L. Karunaratne 53, L. de Silva 67, R. Kariyawasam 33; G. R. M. A. Perera three for 35) and 145 for four (R. Jaymon 30, L. de Silva 81 not out).

At Maitland Place, Colombo (SSC), December 16, 17, 18. Sinhalese SC won by 138 runs. Sinhalese SC 408 for nine dec. (R. P. A. H. Wickremaratne 146, M. S. Atapattu 165; C. P. H. Ramanayake six for 88) and 128 (E. F. M. U. Fernando 37, M. S. Atapattu 42 not out; U. U. Chandana three for 29, N. Bandaratilleke seven for 47); Tamil Union C and AC* 260 (U. C. Hathurusinghe 46, R. Peiris 44, C. P. H. Ramanayake 40; Suranjith Silva five for 55) and 138 (S. I. de Saram 58, C. P. H. Ramanayake 50; M. Munasinghe three for 48, Suranjith Silva four for 40).

Wickremaratne and Atapattu added 278 for the fourth wicket in Sinhalese SC's first innings, a national record. Suranjith Silva took a hat-trick.

At Maitland Crescent, Colombo (CCC), December 30, 31, January 1. Galle CC won by an innings and 81 runs. Colombo CC 126 (M. A. R. Samarasekera 32; J. C. Gamage six for 48) and 166 (Y. N. Tillekeratne 53; J. C. Gamage five for 61, S. Jayasekera four for 64); Galle CC* 373 (H. S. S. Fonseka 66, R. S. Kaluwitharana 80, P. de Silva 39, H. Rajapakse 60 not out, Extras 48; M. Villavarayan three for 76).

Wicket-keeper Kaluwitharana held six catches in Colombo's first innings.

At Havelock Park, Colombo (BRC), January 6, 7, 8. Drawn. Burgher RC 259 (D. P. S. de Zoysa 34, A. Dalugoda 88, S. Tennakoon 37; D. Samarasinghe three for 41, M. H. A. Jabbar six for 66) and 327 for nine (J. Jaymon 112, S. Kodituwakku 36, A. Dalugoda 56, S. Tennakoon 35; C. Mahesh four for 63); Sebastianites C and AC* 273 (S. K. Silva 51, K. Anton 37, C. Mahesh 109, A. Perera 30; A. Dalugoda three for 92, U. Hettiarachchi four for 76).

At Welagedera Stadium, Kurunegala, January 6, 7, 8. Drawn. Galle CC 439 for nine dec. (N. Dharmasiri 98, R. S. Kaluwitharana 123, D. D. Wickremasinghe 77, E. A. R. de Silva 51; A. W. Ekanayake three for 108, V. Samarawickrama three for 37); Kurunegala Youth CC* 131 (A. W. Ekanayake 71; J. C. Gamage four for 44, S. Jayasekera three for 31) and 94 for one (L. Karunaratne 31 not out, L. de Silva 52 not out).

At Maitland Place, Colombo (SSC), January 6, 7, 8. Drawn. Sinhalese SC 264 (E. F. M. U. Fernando 36, M. S. Atapattu 35, U. N. K. Fernando 72 not out; W. Labrooy five for 85, M. A. R. Samarasekera three for 74) and 304 for five (D. Ranatunga 75, E. F. M. U. Fernando 42, R. P. A. H. Wickremaratne 58, M. S. Atapattu 60 not out; D. D. Madurapperuma three for 82); Colombo CC* 413 (C. P. Handunettige 74, V. S. K. Waragoda 101, A. M. de Silva 58, H. M. L. Sagara 34; H. Perera three for 65).

At P. Saravanamuttu Stadium, Colombo, January 6, 7, 8. Drawn. Colts SC 404 (S. I. Fernando 46, H. H. Devapriya 52, M. V. Perera 114, J. Kulatunga 47, D. K. Liyanage 53; S. de Silva four for 81) and 192 for four dec. (D. P. Samaraweera 101 not out, M. V. Perera 36); Tamil Union C and AC* 331 (R. Peiris 54, U. C. Hathurusinghe 46, S. I. de Saram 134; D. Hettiarachchi five for 88) and 28 for one.

At Havelock Park, Colombo (BRC), January 13, 14, 15. Drawn. Burgher RC 207 (J. Jaymon 31, S. Kodituwakku 37; S. Jayasekera three for 72, K. P. J. Warnaweera three for 26) and 382 for nine dec. (J. Jaymon 247, U. Hettiarachchi 41; J. C. Gamage three for 97, H. Rajapakse three for 56); Galle CC* 196 for nine dec. (H. S. S. Fonseka 31, J. C. Gamage 49, Extras 31; N. N. Amerasinghe eight for 79) and 71 for one (R. S. Kaluwitharana 54 not out).

Jaymon's 247 lasted 418 minutes and included 34 fours and two sixes.

At Maitland Crescent, Colombo (CCC), January 13, 14, 15. Drawn. Colombo CC 415 (C. P. Handunettige 33, V. S. K. Waragoda 204, D. D. Madurapperuma 40, M. Villavarayan 44, Extras 32; D. P. Samaraweera three for 20) and 95 for four; Colts CC* 402 (D. P. Samaraweera 79, C. Mendis 102, N. Ranatunga 92; H. M. L. Sagara three for 93, N. Dabare five for 98).

At Tyronne Fernando Stadium, Moratuwa, January 13, 14, 15. Tamil Union C and AC won by eight wickets. Sebastianites C and AC* 191 (S. K. Silva 44, C. Mahesh 43; N. Bandaratilleke six for 25) and 191 (A. Perera 55; M. Muralitharan three for 60, N. Bandaratilleke six for 77); Tamil Union C and AC 228 (U. C. Hathurusinghe 53, S. I. de Saram 52, W. T. de Silva 30; M. H. A. Jabbar four for 71, A. Perera three for 57) and 156 for two (R. Peiris 51, W. T. de Silva 50 not out).

At Maitland Place, Colombo (SSC), January 13, 14, 15. Sinhalese SC won by an innings and 78 runs. Kurunegala Youth CC 125 (R. Jaymon 50; C. N. Fernando five for 41) and 225 (L. de Silva 62, R. Jaymon 66; C. N. Fernando three for 29, Suranjith Silva four for 64); Sinhalese SC* 428 for six dec. (A. A. W. Gunawardene 56, A. Ranatunga 209 not out, M. S. Atapattu 62, C. N. Fernando 33; A. W. Ekanayake four for 148).

At Havelock Park, Colombo (BRC), January 20, 21, 22. Drawn. Burgher RC* 149 (S. Kodituwakku 61 not out; R. K. B. Amunugama four for 38) and 90 for four (D. P. S. de Zoysa 34); Kurunegala Youth CC 239 (L. de Silva 126 not out; W. K. D. J. D. K. Perera four for 41, A. Dalugoda three for 74).

At Maitland Crescent, Colombo (CCC), January 20, 21, 22. Colombo CC won by an innings and 92 runs. Colombo CC 324 (M. A. R. Samarasekera 38, C. P. Handunettige 79, A. C. Seneviratne 33, D. D. Madurapperuma 36, J. Jayaratne 32 not out; M. H. A. Jabbar four for 77); Sebastianites C and AC* 119 (P. Salgado 31; N. Dabare six for 25) and 113 (R. H. A. Silva 30; M. Villavarayan three for 48).

At Maitland Place, Colombo (SSC), January 20, 21, 22. Drawn. Colts CC 300 (D. P. Samaraweera 101, C. Mendis 72, D. K. Liyanage 30 not out, Extras 42; G. P. Wickremasinghe three for 42, Suranjith Silva five for 102); Sinhalese SC* 373 for seven (D. Ranatunga 135 not out, R. P. A. H. Wickremaratne 67 not out, M. S. Atapattu 58, C. Ranasinghe 52, Extras 31; N. Ranatunga three for 56).

At P. Saravanamuttu Stadium, Colombo, January 20, 21, 22. Drawn. Tamil Union C and AC* 206 (D. N. Nadarajah 79, M. Muralitharan 33; J. C. Gamage seven for 69) and 229 for seven dec. (R. Peiris 44, U. C. Hathurusinghe 70); Galle CC 139 (R. S. Kaluwitharana 55; C. P. H. Ramanayake three for 38, M. Muralitharan three for 11) and 30 for no wkt.

At Havelock Park, Colombo (BRC), January 27, 28, 29. Colombo CC won by ten wickets. Burgher RC* 223 (S. Kodituwakku 35, U. Hettiarachchi 67, W. K. D. J. D. K. Perera 44; H. M. L. Sagara four for 40) and 181 (M. Rajapakse 87 not out; H. M. L. Sagara five for 50); Colombo CC 355 (M. A. R. Samarasekera 60, A. M. de Silva 76, G. W. J. Bandara 132; A. Dalugoda three for 116, N. N. Amerasinghe three for 122) and 55 for no wkt (M. A. R. Samarasekera 30 not out).
Rajapakse carried his bat through Burgher RC's second innings.

At Havelock Park, Colombo (Colts), January 27, 28, 29. Colts CC won by nine wickets. Galle CC* 153 (H. S. S. Fonseka 39, E. A. R. de Silva 43 not out; W. P. U. J. C. Vaas four for 42, E. A. Upashantha four for 28) and 138 (S. I. Fernando five for 34); Colts CC 263 (D. P. Samaraweera 47, S. I. Fernando 31, J. Kulatunga 50, N. Ranatunga 36, H. H. Devapriya 36; J. C. Gamage four for 59, E. A. R. de Silva three for 71) and 32 for one.

At Maitland Place, Colombo (SSC), January 27, 28, 29. Sinhalese SC won by an innings and two runs. Sebastianites C and AC 273 (A. Perera 143 not out; A. Ranatunga five for 82) and 130 (R. H. A. Silva 36; S. Dodanwela three for 29, C. N. Fernando five for 28); Sinhalese SC* 405 for eight dec. (A. A. W. Gunawardene 140, M. S. Atapattu 40, A. Ranatunga 107, E. F. M. U. Fernando 44; M. H. A. Jabbar five for 153).
Ranatunga scored his century in 98 balls and 123 minutes.

At P. Saravanamuttu Stadium, Colombo, January 27, 28, 29. Tamil Union C and AC won by an innings and 137 runs. Tamil Union C and AC* 501 for five dec. (U. C. Hathurusinghe 34, R. Peiris 66, S. I. de Saram 39, D. N. Nadarajah 70, U. U. Chandana 154 not out); Kurunegala Youth CC 162 (L. de Silva 47, R. Kariyawasam 35; N. Bandaratilleke five for 25, M. Muralitharan three for 22) and 202 (L. Karunaratne 33, L. de Silva 45, R. Jaymon 43; M. Muralitharan five for 83, U. U. Chandana four for 52).
Nadarajah and Chandana added 285 for Tamil Union's fifth wicket.

At Maitland Crescent, Colombo (CCC), February 3, 4, 5. Colombo CC won by ten wickets. Kurunegala Youth CC 200 (L. Karunaratne 35, L. de Silva 57; W. Labrooy four for 82) and 175 (L. Karunaratne 43, A. H. Bandaranayake 70; N. Dabare seven for 28); Colombo CC* 320 (A. C. Seneviratne 37, V. S. K. Waragoda 100, Y. N. Tillekeratne 57, W. Labrooy 46 not out; J. A. W. Kumara five for 66) and 56 for no wkt (C. P. Handunettige 39 not out).

At Havelock Park, Colombo (Colts), February 3, 4, 5. Drawn. Colts CC 320 (S. I. Fernando 31, J. Kulatunga 52, H. H. Devapriya 33, D. K. Liyanage 47, E. A. Upashantha 58, W. P. U. J. C. Vaas 31; R. D. Nishantha three for 31) and 221 for six (D. P. Samaraweera 63, M. V. Perera 59, E. A. Upashantha 77); Sebastianites C and AC* 254 (R. H. A. Silva 37, C. Mahesh 38, B. Perera 50 not out; W. P. U. J. C. Vaas five for 50, S. I. Fernando three for 40).

At Maitland Place, Colombo (SSC), February 3, 4, 5. Drawn. Galle CC 288 (R. S. Kaluwitharana 52, E. A. R. de Silva 82 not out, Extras 54; G. P. Wickremasinghe three for 79, C. N. Fernando three for 59) and 263 (H. S. S. Fonseka 30, R. S. Kaluwitharana 65, D. D. Wickremasinghe 47, E. A. R. de Silva 35; H. Perera three for 76); Sinhalese SC* 300 (A. P. Gurusinha 72, M. S. Atapattu 67, U. N. K. Fernando 36, C. N. Fernando 68; J. C. Gamage four for 115, H. Rajapakse four for 40).

At P. Saravanamuttu Stadium, Colombo, February 3, 4, 5. Tamil Union won by an innings and 145 runs. Tamil Union C and AC 371 (U. C. Hathurusinghe 56, S. I. de Saram 82, D. N. Nadarajah 58, S. de Silva 50 not out; U. Hettiarachchi four for 79); Burgher RC* 138 (M. Rajapakse 45; M. Muralitharan eight for eight) and 88 (N. Bandaratilleke three for 28, U. U. Chandana four for 30).
   Muralitharan took eight for eight in 17.3 overs.

At Tyronne Fernando Stadium, Moratuwa, February 10, 11, 12. Drawn. Galle CC* 406 (H. S. S. Fonseka 190, R. S. Kaluwitharana 71, D. D. Wickremasinghe 56; D. Samarasinghe seven for 87) and 267 for seven (H. S. S. Fonseka 51, D. D. Wickremasinghe 80, R. S. Kaluwitharana 67; M. H. A. Jabbar four for 96); Sebastianites C and AC 257 (S. K. Silva 38, R. Martinesz 66, Extras 31; J. C. Gamage six for 51, H. Rajapakse three for 38).

At Maitland Place, Colombo (SSC), February 10, 11, 12. Sinhalese SC won by an innings and 25 runs. Burgher RC 220 (J. Jaymon 74, S. Tennakoon 34; G. P. Wickremasinghe four for 38, Suranjith Silva four for 51) and 156 (U. Hettiarachchi 54; G. P. Wickremasinghe three for 27, Suranjith Silva four for 38); Sinhalese SC* 401 for seven dec. (A. P. Gurusinha 45, R. P. A. H. Wickremaratne 95, D. Ranatunga 116, M. Munasinghe 59 not out, Extras 34; S. Chandrakantha four for 84).

Final

At Maitland Place, Colombo (SSC), February 15, 16, 17, 18. Drawn. Sinhalese SC 509 for eight dec. (D. Ranatunga 84, M. S. Atapattu 181, A. Ranatunga 125, R. P. A. H. Wickremaratne 64; R. Palliyaguru three for 131); Bloomfield C and AC* 420 for six (S. K. Perera 48, S. Perera 72, S. T. Jayasuriya 130 not out, R. S. Kalpage 51, R. S. Mahanama 39 not out, Extras 45; Suranjith Silva four for 159).

P. SARAVANAMUTTU TROPHY WINNERS

The competition was known as the Lakspray Trophy in 1988-89 and 1989-90.

1988-89 {	Nondescripts CC	1992-93 Sinhalese SC
	Sinhalese SC	1993-94 Nondescripts CC
1989-90	Sinhalese SC	1994-95 { Bloomfield C and AC
1990-91	Sinhalese SC	Sinhalese SC
1991-92	Colts CC	

CRICKET IN ZIMBABWE, 1994-95

By TERRY YATES-ROUND and JOHN WARD

At international level, Zimbabwe reached new heights in 1994-95. The highlight of the season was their first Test win, over Pakistan, on the back of a 269-run partnership between the Flower brothers, Andy and Grant. Grant Flower went on to add 233 with Guy Whittall and the seamers, led by Heath Streak, dismissed Pakistan twice with a day to spare. Though Pakistan came back to win the Tests 2-1, Zimbabwe shared the one-day series 1-1, with the first match tied. The Test victory was an enormous boost to morale and to public interest; 3,000 spectators – a substantial crowd in a country with no tradition of cricket-watching – witnessed the historic fourth day. It was encouraging to see black supporters coming to cheer on the team, perhaps prompted by the inclusion of Zimbabwe's first black player, pace bowler Henry Olonga.

Zimbabwe also hosted Sri Lanka, who drew all three Tests, and visited Australia to take part in the limited-overs World Series. But with a view to shoring up the Zimbabwe Cricket Union's ever-straitened finances, the best news was that South Africa would make a short tour in October 1995 to play an inaugural Test with their neighbours. During 1994-95, the ZCU benefited from a grant from the Sport and Recreation Commission, and the executive council made the most of what sponsorship they could raise from Zimbabwean companies. They also looked forward to a share of the proceeds from the World Cup.

Funding is badly needed to maintain grass-roots cricket. Playing and coaching facilities are not of a uniform standard throughout the country and in some areas have deteriorated. Predictably, the highest concentration is in Harare, where there are 70 grounds of acceptable standard; Matabeleland offers half that, with the distribution dwindling in other regions. The recently established Cricket Academy in Harare is in daily use. Three days a week children are bussed in, free of charge, from the main townships for coaching, and they have begun to show the benefits when selected for school and township teams. Private coaching is also popular. More than 158 secondary school teams, of varying ages, play cricket, about half of them in Harare, but more than 60 in the Country Districts and Matabeleland.

The second season of the first-class three-day competition, the Lonrho-Logan Cup, revealed another difficulty in building a strong domestic base: the problem of finding committed players. The Cup's three qualifying rounds stretched from September to March, by which time each of the four sides was struggling to raise a full-strength team. Although their league match was washed out, Mashonaland and reigning champions Mashonaland Under-24 won their other fixtures to head the table. Mashonaland triumphed in the final, thanks to a century from Gary Martin and an unbeaten double-hundred from Ali Shah, setting a target of 449 – too much for the Under-24s, though Grant Flower carried his bat for 145. The ZCU planned to stage the 1995-96 tournament over a shorter time-span in the hope of concentrating player enthusiasm.

There were similar problems raising competitive teams to play the tourists in the warm-up games before the internationals, resulting in some highly unequal contests. South Africa A toured early in the season and won all their three first-class matches, two of them by an innings. But the local players were capable of better: they beat English counties Northamptonshire and Glamorgan on pre-season tours in April. Mashonaland Select XI were dismissed for 83 in their first innings against Northamptonshire, but recovered to make a staggering 417 inside 81 overs – a Zimbabwean fourth-innings record – to win on the final day, with the Flowers and Craig Evans to the fore.

Grant Flower scored 983 first-class runs during the season, another Zimbabwean record, including four centuries, one of them his unbeaten 201 against Pakistan; Whittall also had four hundreds in an aggregate of 762, while Andy Flower made three in his 768. David Houghton still rode high in the averages at the age of 37. Eddo Brandes actually headed both batting and bowling averages, despite playing only two first-class games – he scored 165 not out and took nine wickets against Griqualand West in the UCB Bowl, but missed the international season because of injury. The leading wicket-takers were left-armer Bryan Strang, who made his first-class debut in October and his Test debut four months later; his brother, the leg-spinner Paul; Malcolm Jarvis, who made a brief but successful international return aged 39; and Streak, who bowled brilliantly in the Test series. Bryan Strang, Olonga and Darlington Matambanadzo went to the Madras pace bowling academy to be coached by former Australian star Dennis Lillee.

At club level, the Rothmans National First League was won by Old Georgians, who beat Harare Sports Club, and the National Second League, expanded from 13 teams to 16, by Bulawayo Athletic Club.

FIRST-CLASS AVERAGES, 1994-95

BATTING

(Qualification: 200 runs)

	M	I	NO	R	HS	100s	Avge
E. A. Brandes (*Mashonaland Country Districts*)	2	3	2	220	165*	1	220.00
D. L. Houghton (*Mashonaland*)	7	10	0	627	266	2	62.70
A. H. Shah (*Mashonaland*)	3	5	1	247	200*	1	61.75
A. Flower (*Mashonaland*)	10	15	2	768	156	3	59.07
G. W. Flower (*Mashonaland Under-24*)	12	20	3	983	201*	4	57.82
I. P. Butchart (*Mashonaland Country Districts*)	5	9	2	392	117	2	56.00
M. G. Burmester (*Mashonaland*)	4	5	0	232	67	0	46.40
W. R. James (*Matabeleland*)	8	13	1	510	127	2	42.50
G. J. Whittall (*Matabeleland*)	13	22	4	762	180*	4	42.33
S. V. Carlisle (*Mashonaland Under-24*)	7	11	2	378	97	0	42.00
G. K. Bruk-Jackson (*Mashonaland Country Districts*)	9	16	2	532	119*	1	38.00
G. C. Martin (*Mashonaland*)	5	10	1	301	117	1	33.44
A. C. Waller (*Mashonaland Country Districts*)	4	7	0	216	76	0	30.85
C. N. Evans (*Mashonaland*)	6	11	1	305	117	2	30.50
J. A. Rennie (*Matabeleland*)	9	14	4	299	67*	0	29.90
H. H. Streak (*Matabeleland*)	11	15	3	333	98	0	27.75
C. B. Wishart (*Mashonaland Under-24*)	11	20	1	481	75	0	25.31
D. N. Erasmus (*Mashonaland Under-24*)	9	17	1	404	97	0	25.25
P. A. Strang (*Mashonaland Country Districts*)	11	16	2	306	97	0	21.85
A. D. R. Campbell (*Mashonaland Country Districts*)	11	18	1	361	99	0	21.23
M. H. Dekker (*Matabeleland*)	11	18	0	338	92	0	18.77
G. J. Rennie (*Mashonaland Under-24*)	8	13	0	228	72	0	17.53
D. J. R. Campbell (*Mashonaland Country Districts*) .	9	16	1	226	60*	0	15.06

* *Signifies not out.*

BOWLING

(Qualification: 10 wickets)

	O	M	R	W	BB	5W/i	Avge
E. A. Brandes (*Mashonaland Country Districts*)	49.1	10	139	13	7-38	1	10.69
G. W. Flower (*Mashonaland Under-24*)	90.2	28	212	11	3-24	0	19.27
H. H. Streak (*Matabeleland*)	385.2	103	969	49	6-90	2	19.77
B. C. Strang (*Mashonaland Country Districts*) .	463.5	151	1,144	51	7-64	2	22.43
M. P. Jarvis (*Mashonaland*)	537	203	1,118	44	7-36	2	25.40
C. B. Wishart (*Mashonaland Under-24*)	91.5	19	305	11	5-24	1	27.72
G. C. Martin (*Mashonaland*)...............	120.1	36	322	11	4-66	0	29.27
P. A. Strang (*Mashonaland Country Districts*) .	395.5	96	1,177	40	7-75	4	29.42
G. J. Whittall (*Matabeleland*)	334.5	68	1,033	35	6-56	1	29.51
D. H. Brain (*Mashonaland*)...............	193.2	34	632	17	3-50	0	37.17
H. K. Olonga (*Matabeleland*)	175	27	604	15	3-53	0	40.26
J. A. Rennie (*Matabeleland*)	300	73	855	12	2-56	0	71.25

Note: These averages include performances for the Zimbabwe Board XI in the South African UCB Bowl.

LONRHO LOGAN CUP, 1994-95

	Played	Won	Lost	Drawn	Bonus points Batting	Bowling	Points
Mashonaland	2	2	0	0	14	20	53.4§
Mashonaland Under-24	2	2	0	0	12	17	47.3§
Matabeleland	3	1	2	0	17	20	46.1§
Mashonaland Country Districts	3	0	3	0	18.5	23.5	42

Final: Mashonaland beat Mashonaland Under-24 by 165 runs.
The league match between Mashonaland and Mashonaland Under-24 was abandoned.

Outright win = 10 pts.

Bonus points: One point is awarded for the first 100 runs in each innings and half a point for every subsequent 25 (restricted to the first 85 overs in the first innings). Half a point is awarded for every wicket taken throughout both innings.

§ Points deducted for slow over-rates.

*In the following scores, * by the name of a team indicates that they won the toss.*

At Harare South Country Club, Harare, September 16, 17, 18. Mashonaland Under-24 won by six wickets. Mashonaland Country Districts* 347 for four dec. (G. K. Bruk-Jackson 46, M. P. Stannard 47, A. C. Waller 53, I. P. Butchart 113 not out, D. J. R. Campbell 60 not out) and 160 (S. G. Peall 39; D. Matambanadzo four for 52, S. G. Davies three for 33); Mashonaland Under-24 259 (G. J. Rennie 72, G. B. Brent 40, D. D. Stannard 40; P. A. Strang seven for 75) and 250 for four (G. J. Rennie 33, G. W. Flower 91 not out, D. N. Erasmus 56 not out). *Mashonaland Under-24 23.3 pts, Mashonaland Country Districts 14.5 pts.*
  Butchart scored 113 not out, his maiden first-class hundred, from 109 balls. Waller became the first batsman to be given out handled the ball in Zimbabwean first-class cricket.

At Bulawayo Athletic Club, Bulawayo, September 16, 17, 18. Mashonaland won by nine wickets. Mashonaland* 344 for seven dec. (A. Flower 134 not out, D. H. Brain 126) and 76 for one (D. G. Goodwin 45 not out); Matabeleland 178 (G. J. Whittall 51, H. H. Streak 60 not out; H. J. Hira three for 24) and 241 (J. R. Craig 50, W. R. James 33, J. A. Rennie 67 not out, H. K. Olonga 34). *Mashonaland 23.9 pts, Matabeleland 9.5 pts.*

At Harare Sports Club, Harare, January 20, 21, 22. Mashonaland v Mashonaland Under-24. Abandoned, owing to a waterlogged ground. No points awarded.

At Harare South Country Club, Harare, January 20, 21, 22. Matabeleland won by seven wickets. Mashonaland Country Districts* 123 (G. K. Bruk-Jackson 30; J. E. Brinkley six for 35) and 336 (G. K. Bruk-Jackson 34, I. P. Butchart 117, P. A. Strang 97; H. H. Streak three for 30, H. K. Olonga three for 56); Matabeleland 127 (E. A. Brandes four for 46, P. A. Strang three for 24) and 335 for three (M. H. Dekker 43, G. J. Whittall 180 not out, W. R. James 71 not out). *Matabeleland 26.1 pts, Mashonaland Country Districts 13 pts.*

At Harare Sports Club, Harare, March 10, 11, 12. Mashonaland won by 266 runs. Mashonaland* 188 (M. G. Burmester 60, D. L. Houghton 38, G. C. Martin 42; B. C. Strang seven for 64) and 421 (M. G. Burmester 52, C. N. Evans 112, A. Flower 103, D. L. Houghton 40, G. A. Briant 48; A. D. R. Campbell four for 82); Mashonaland Country Districts 182 (G. K. Bruk-Jackson 87; M. P. Jarvis four for 74) and 161 (G. K. Bruk-Jackson 36, P. A. Strang 51; M. P. Jarvis seven for 36). *Mashonaland 29.5 pts, Mashonaland Country Districts 14.5 pts.*

At Alexandra Sports Club, Harare, March 10, 11, 12. Mashonaland Under-24 won by seven wickets. Matabeleland 194 (J. A. Rennie 40, G. Peck 51; C. B. Wishart four for 26) and 167 (W. R. James 30, G. C. Edwards 32; C. B. Wishart five for 24); Mashonaland Under-24* 240 for nine dec. (G. W. Flower 79, S. S. Prescott 35; M. Grainger five for 35) and 122 for three (S. S. Prescott 33 not out). *Mashonaland Under-24 24 pts, Matabeleland 10.5 pts.*

Final

At Harare Sports Club, Harare, March 24, 25, 26. Mashonaland won by 165 runs. Mashonaland* 258 (A. Flower 77, G. C. Martin 117; G. B. Brent three for 56, G. W. Flower three for 24) and 347 for six dec. (A. H. Shah 200 not out, E. A. Essop-Adam 69, G. A. Briant 40); Mashonaland Under-24 157 (D. R. Viljoen 39 not out; M. P. Jarvis three for 57) and 283 (G. W. Flower 145 not out, carrying his bat, S. D. Bean 48; G. C. Martin four for 66).

OTHER FIRST-CLASS MATCHES

South Africa A in Zimbabwe

At Old Hararians Sports Club, Harare, September 20, 21, 22, 23. South Africa A won by an innings and 70 runs. Mashonaland XI* 271 (A. D. R. Campbell 53, D. N. Erasmus 34, C. B. Wishart 73, G. C. Martin 50; N. Boje four for 65) and 158 (G. W. Flower 60; S. D. Jack three for 49, S. Elworthy five for 38); South Africa A 499 (G. F. J. Liebenberg 84, D. J. Callaghan 104, J. B. Commins 164, N. Boje 102; P. A. Strang five for 137).
   Commins and Boje added 268 for the ninth wicket, the second-highest partnership for that wicket in first-class cricket.

At Bulawayo Athletic Club, Bulawayo, September 27, 28, 29, 30. South Africa A won by six wickets. Matabeleland Select XI* 379 (G. J. Whittall 105, C. B. Wishart 63, W. R. James 107; H. S. Williams three for 72, S. Abrahams three for 89) and 308 (C. B. Wishart 44, W. R. James 127, H. H. Streak 49; H. S. Williams three for 42, S. Abrahams three for 114); South Africa A 471 for nine dec. (P. J. R. Steyn 51, M. W. Rushmere 49, D. J. Callaghan 154, N. Boje 57, Extras 39) and 219 for four (P. J. R. Steyn 35, J. M. Arthur 53, M. W. Rushmere 74 not out, S. J. Palframan 30).

At Alexandra Sports Club, Harare, October 4, 5, 6. South Africa A won by an innings and 179 runs. Zimbabwe A* 87 (S. Elworthy six for 47) and 143 (C. N. Evans 34, D. J. R. Campbell 33; S. D. Jack three for 29, S. Abrahams three for 13); South Africa A 409 (G. F. J. Liebenberg 107, M. W. Rushmere 90, L. J. Wilkinson 33, N. C. Johnson 30, S. D. Jack 65 not out; B. C. Strang five for 95).

Mashonaland Select XI v Northamptonshire (April 4, 5, 6) and Matabeleland Select XI v Glamorgan (April 11, 12, 13) may be found in English Counties Overseas, 1994-95.

CRICKET IN DENMARK, 1995

By PETER S. HARGREAVES

Victory over their Continental rivals Holland during a tournament in Scotland was the highlight of the Danish season. Playing a quadrangular tournament similar to the one organised in The Netherlands in 1994, which Denmark won so decisively, they beat Holland by 78 runs.

On turf, Denmark were unable to repeat their win over the Scots, but they made no bones about it in the last match, against Scotland B, when Steen Anker Nielsen scored an unbeaten 116, rounding off a season in which he had been a consistently heavy scorer.

Earlier, Denmark had easy wins, by 237 and 217 runs, in home matches against France, which suggested that the French were still a long way from the standard required of a country seeking ICC associate membership. The Danish captain, Søren Henriksen, thought they were about on a par with Sweden, who are normally easily beaten by Denmark Under-19.

Two matches in Central Jutland against MCC provided more worthwhile preparation. But Henriksen was absent getting married, and fast bowler Søren Vestergaard was injured early on, which tilted the advantage to MCC, who were well led by Paul Parker and won two tight contests by 43 runs and four wickets. It was refreshing to observe a very different approach by this MCC side from that of its two predecessors a generation ago, too many of whose members appeared to be along for the ride.

Before going to Scotland, Denmark played two matches in Durham, to settle on turf, against the county side and a Durham League XI. Both matches were lost, but 227 for five against the county was most creditable. Ole Mortensen, the national coach, was quietly positive about his team, saying "there was a hungry look in the eyes of every player". He helped put it there.

Of almost equal importance to the country's top cricket was the achievement of the Under-19 team in beating every opponent except England in the International Youth Cricket Tournament at The Hague.

On the domestic scene, the Svanholm side swept all before them, winning the knockout cup final against Esbjerg, and then going right through the league programme undefeated. Glostrup were runners-up with Esbjerg third, whilst at the foot of the scale the two promoted clubs, Køge and AB, could not make the grade and will be replaced by Husum and Skanderborg from the second division in 1996. In the youth divisions, the Pakistani clubs from Copenhagen were not as successful as they have been, but KB's successful junior side now consists almost entirely of Pakistani players.

Steen Anker Nielsen, who plays for the Chang club of Aalborg, produced a record batting aggregate of 1,538 runs, but he was edged out in the averages by the two Pakistani players, Aftab Ahmed – as yet unavailable for the national team – and Atif Butt. Among the bowlers, Morten Hedegaard, of Nykøbing Mors, topped the wickets with 61, but it was interesting that the young off-spinner, Anders Rasmussen, topped the averages. Søren Henriksen, captain of the national side, still looked the best all-rounder, with the Under-19 team captain, Thomas Hansen, impressing most among the younger players.

CRICKET IN THE NETHERLANDS, 1995

By DAVID HARDY

Dutch cricket had an intermediate year between the national team's historic qualification for the World Cup at the ICC Trophy in 1994 and participation in the World Cup itself in 1996. But 1995 was also a historic year in its own right: Holland became the first team from outside the British Isles to compete in an English domestic competition, when they played Northamptonshire in the NatWest Trophy.

Holland lost, but they scored 267 for nine and had one of the strongest counties worried, even though they were without all three of their players with experience of county cricket: Paul-Jan Bakker, now playing again in the Netherlands, was injured, and Roland Lefebvre and Andre van Troost were ineligible because they were still more contracted to counties. For the record, the Dutch team on the day contained more foreigners – five – than ever before, including South African newcomer Billy Stelling.

What followed was an anticlimax, as only one game out of nine was won, against Scotland, but Young Australia – who won by just one run in Haarlem on July 14 – were nearly added to the long list of impressive scalps. Earlier, the team had returned to Kenya for a triangular tournament with the other two qualifiers for the 1996 World Cup: Kenya and the United Arab Emirates. This time Holland came out on top, winning two games out of three against Kenya, and one out of two against the UAE. There was also a tour to India, which produced three wins out of six and invaluable experience in local conditions.

Following the match-fixing scandal of 1994, the domestic season was again blemished, this time by violence on the field. There was actual fighting between a player from Bloemendaal and one from Shaheen, and even between two from the same side, Sparta. On another occasion an elderly umpire was kicked, and the police had to be called to calm down a player from the Gandhi club. Unfortunately, cricket in the Netherlands is no longer immune from developments that are commonplace in other sports.

The shameful events of 1994, when HCC tried to achieve promotion by arranging a 702-run win over their own second team, led to the creation of a Reserve Premier League, in which the Second Elevens were separated from the rest. This league was promptly won by HCC Second Eleven, bowled out for one in the infamous 1994 match, who registered 17 wins out of 17.

In the Hoofdklasse, it was close all season before Excelsior won the Championship for the second time in their 75-year history. HCC were promoted ahead of Gandhi, their rivals in 1994 when Gandhi won a match by 797 runs before officials took action against everyone involved. VRA's New Zealand professional Darrin Murray was the leading scorer with 1,209. No one else managed 1,000. The leading amateurs were Excelsior's Erick Gouka, who topped the averages at 47.30, and Diederik Visee of HBS The Hague, who scored 824 runs. Excelsior's Australian professional Sean Cary again came top of the bowling averages with 57 wickets at 11.96. No one else took 50 wickets.

This may well have been the first season in history when "drought stopped play". Late in the season some matches were postponed because the outfields were too dry. What will happen after grass wickets are introduced this year if summers really do go on getting warmer?

CRICKET ROUND THE WORLD, 1995

ARGENTINA

The 96th annual North v South game, played over three days and the centrepiece of Argentine cricket, saw a reversal of the trend of the past 20 years with a 170-run victory for the North, who were helped by a re-drawing of the boundaries in their favour. Lomas won the First Division while Belgrano won the limited-overs championship. John Stephenson of Hampshire was employed as coach and a revitalised approach to the junior programme saw a new crop of under-10s taking up the game.

ASCENSION ISLAND

Plans are afoot to return cricket to one of the world's most distinctive grounds. The barren, volcanic rock of Ascension Island in the South Atlantic is believed to be the only place where "wedding stopped play" – to be resumed 40 minutes later as the last of the congregation left for the reception. The little Church of St Mary the Virgin is inside the boundary and, when it was restored in 1993, with a new slate roof, cricket moved to a new and larger ground at the island's RAF camp, where floodlit play is possible. However, the move has not been popular with the crowds (all things are relative – the total population is only 1,200) and Dr Sukhtanker, the resident surgeon and cricketing supremo, intends to take the game back to its traditional venue. Cricket on Ascension, uninhabited until the Royal Navy landed in 1815, took off when West Indian workers arrived in the mid-1960s to build a relay station. They started league cricket, which has been kept going by South Africans working for the cable company, and the RAF, who returned during the Falklands War. They have provided teaching input for the workers from St Helena who are employed here. Saint Helenians have a natural aptitude for the game, and have developed good technique, with two exceptions: the concrete strip offers little chance of spin, and the short boundaries – combined with American influence – have encouraged some towards the high baseball slog. The cricket field by the church, which used to be the army parade ground, is actually rolled volcanic ash, with not a blade of grass in sight, and the outfield is very fast. The ball used is a composite – a leather ball would be torn to shreds – and we need several per game there, to replace those which get stuck on the church roof or among the stores waiting to be loaded on the next ship. A dusty trade wind always blows across the pitch, but it is what people seem to prefer and it is indeed a fine setting, if you can find some shade: the four sides comprising the small, white church, a smooth, dark red, volcanic cone, the aging, arcaded barracks, and the dark blue ocean with its giant waves crashing in towards the anchorage below. – Canon Nicholas Turner, Vicar of Ascension.

AUSTRIA

A new purpose-built ground at Seebarn, 20 kilometres north of Vienna, opened with an artificial pitch provided by a joint grant from ICC, MCC and the TCCB. The only other cricket ground in Austria is at Kitzbühel but a new pitch is also being prepared at Velden, which should be ready in 1997. The Austrian Open League was won for the first time by Pakistan CC. More than 100 Under-19s have been introduced to the game, mainly in three Austrian schools where the game is now on the curriculum. – Andrew Simpson-Parker.

BANGLADESH

The major innovation in Bangladeshi cricket was the Office Cricket League, which was introduced to create employment opportunities for cricketers, and attracted 18 teams from a variety of local and multinational companies. The main League continues to be the Navana Premier Division. Although it only involves teams from Dhaka, it attracts the best players from all over the country as well as stars from elsewhere: Wasim Akram headed a group of six Indian and Pakistani international players who participated in 1994-95 in front of crowds up to 40,000. Abahani and Mohammedan SC finished as joint champions. The major event in Dhaka was the SAARC Tournament in December 1994, which included the Bangladeshi national team and the A teams of Pakistan, India and Sri Lanka. Bangladesh beat the Indian and Sri Lankan teams in the preliminaries, but lost the final to India A, led by Pravin Amre, by 52 runs. There are estimated to be 18,000 senior players in Bangladesh and 75,000 juniors. – Tanjeeb Ahsan Saad.

BELGIUM

The Belgian Championship was split into two divisions in 1995, with promotion and relegation. The Optimists of Luxembourg repeated their 1994 League success by winning the First Division. Mechelen Eagles, a true Flemish side, won the Second Division. Independent umpiring has been introduced into all championship games and has been an outstanding success, due especially to the work of Bryan Rouse. The national team drew the two-match series with France 1-1. The emphasis at national level is to develop native-born talent. – Colin Wolfe.

BERMUDA

The full Australian team visited Bermuda immediately after their historic win in the West Indies and proved to be perhaps the most popular tourists the island has hosted. They won all three of their matches but provided a full day's entertainment in each case and, even though they were relaxing, still played with pride and professionalism; most found time to visit local schools to talk cricket. Bermudan players achieved some success against a Jamaican national side which toured in September. The Jamaicans easily won their first four matches, but were beaten by St George's and by Bermuda in their final fixtures. Bermuda beat Jamaica again in a four-nation Christmas festival in Florida, which also involved Guyana and the US, while St George's held on to the trophy in Bermuda's special cricketing occasion, Cup Match, which was an uneventful draw. Western Stars won the 18-team Premier League. The national captain, Albert Steede, averaged 72 for them, scored 1,409 runs throughout the season and was named as Cricketer of the Year. – Maurice F. Hankey.

BRUNEI

Brunei lost the annual match against Sabah for the Borneo Cup by three wickets. Manggis, joint title holders in 1994, won the league outright, winning their last nine matches. But Manggis lost the knockout competition, the Galfar Cup, to the improving Yachties. – Derek Thursby.

CANADA

The left-handed opener Latchman Bhamsingh led Canada to an easy win against the United States, captained by former West Indian Test player Faoud Bacchus, in the annual two-day match. Bhamsingh scored 73 and 88 and, with support in both innings from captain Ingleton Liburd, was able to steer Canada to a 128-run victory. It was their seventh win in nine years, though the US still lead the series. The game, in Toronto, was watched by good crowds, and Liburd received the K. A. Auty Trophy from Sir Clyde Walcott. Loss of federal funding led to some events being cancelled, but a new tournament was held in Vancouver, with British Columbia beating Australian Police in the final. Canada's premier league, the Toronto & District, was won by Grace Church CC. – Ahmad Saidullah.

CAYMAN ISLANDS

The 1995 season was dominated by Wesley Gidson, captain of the Cayman Brac Second Division team, who scored 652 in six innings, averaging 217.33 with a top score of 237 not out – and took 21 wickets at seven each. Cayman Brac is the second-largest of the Cayman Islands and competition with the main island, Grand Cayman, only started in 1994. The highlight of the year was a festival involving several West Indian Test players who played a match with 27 sixes, watched by 2,000 spectators. Cricket began here in the 1960s; the pitch is a rubber mat laid on asphalt. – Jimmy Powell.

CHILE

There are about 30 players of various nationalities but only one cricket club in Chile. We are restricted to practice amongst ourselves for the matches against other South American countries, except when touring teams visit: Bath Schools played three matches here in 1994-95 before going to Argentina. Other teams would be assured of reasonably good opposition and excellent hospitality and facilities. The ground is at the exclusive Prince of Wales club in Santiago, which has a joining fee of $US500,000; fortunately the cricketers are exempt. – Ian Malcolm Scott.

CHINA

The highlight of the season was the Second Beijing International Sixes Tournament, co-sponsored by Allied Pickfords and Qantas. It featured ten teams, including sides from Japan, Hong Kong and Korea. The locally based England team were the winners. The tournament has rapidly gained momentum and will be held over two days in 1996. It is a far cry from the early 1980s when some of the small group of foreigners then in the city founded the Peking Cricket Club and selected a hard, dusty ground from the fields of the Beijing Physical Institute. The bounce remains unpredictable and helmets are essential: PCC's only woman player was knocked unconscious by a blow to the face in 1993 and last year a wicket-keeper received a badly cut lip. At present there is only one Chinese player playing for the PCC's four competing teams (England, Australia, India and Pakistan) and he learned his cricket in Australia. However, Chinese sports officials visited the Hong Kong Sixes this year and there are now plans to introduce the game into one of the Beijing universities. The Laws of Cricket have now been translated into Chinese. – Tony Fisher.

CUBA

A London pub team, including the former England batsman David Smith, played a side led by the British Ambassador in what was reported to be the first cricket match in Cuba since 1939.

EUROPEAN CLUB CHAMPIONSHIP

Pianoro of Italy, fielding seven natives, became European club champions by beating the holders Hassloch Cosmopolitans by 18 runs in the finals at Osnabrück, Germany. The Pianoro all-rounder Hemanthe Jayasena was Man of the Match with 74 and one for 27 off his ten overs. In 1996, all clubs will have to field at least two native-born players.

EUROPEAN NATIONS CUP

Portugal, competing for the first time, were unexpected winners of the Nations Cup at Oxford. They beat Germany in a high-scoring final by 61 runs – 317 to 256. Competition referee Don Oslear named Portugal's Muntazie Mehdi as Man of the Match for scoring an unbeaten 146 and taking four for 33. Germany beat holders France in one semi-final, while Portugal beat Austria. Belgium, Sweden, Malta and Greece also took part. Switzerland were barred for failing to pay their subscriptions on time.

FIJI

The highlight of the year was the challenge by Suva for the Dewar Shield, a magnificent trophy which dates back to 1913 and had been held since 1963 by Tubou from the island group of Lau. Tubou are very difficult to beat on their home ground, and repulsed the challenge in a three-day match in March. Tubou also won the annual Crompton Cup played over Easter. The Secondary Schools competition was won by Labasa from the northern island of Vanua Levu. This was a great achievement for Labasa, where cricket was revived only about three years ago, and a tribute to the main organiser there, Jone Salele; in a recent primary school competition he had 18 schools taking part. Cricket in Fiji has various problems. In Lau, one of the traditional strongholds of the game, it has been affected by an increase in population and consequent encroachment on the village greens. Our national coach, Seci Sekinini, recently came across a ground where the pitch had been moved to accommodate new buildings, and as a result the outfielders were required to stand in the sea. It was thought this might be the origin of deep mid-off. – Peter Knight.

FINLAND

Helsinki Cricket Club dominates the cricket scene in Finland, as it has done since its foundation in 1974. From time to time a few enthusiasts elsewhere in the country, notably in Lahti, have managed to put 11 men on the field. These efforts have not yet led to the establishment of formal associations – but two clubs have signalled their intention to constitute themselves properly for 1996. Helsinki won all their matches against the ad hoc teams in 1995, though some wins were by uncomfortably narrow margins. Regrettably, no fixture was arranged with the old enemy, Stockholm Cricket Club. John Cole, the regular opener for the past 18 years, continued to make a disproportionately large contribution to the team's totals; and the club made a special award to Francis Looby, a founder member, for his achievements on and off the field. – Richard Walker.

FRANCE

A seven-match visit from MCC, skippered by Jack Simmons, was the highlight of the French season. MCC won three matches and drew four, but their tour report was enough to persuade England (seconded by Zimbabwe) to back France's application for promotion to Associate status of ICC. After an official ICC inspection, the application was deferred to July 1996. Simmons, along with the ex-Leicestershire player Peter Hepworth, coached the national team. – Simon Hewitt.

GERMANY

Another busy year produced a signal that cricket is becoming accepted by the German sports authorities: the state sports federation agreed a £2,000 grant to the Hanau club towards an artificial pitch and a bowling machine. It is planned to follow this success with requests in other parts of Germany: the acquisition of more good pitches is a major priority and will add weight to German aspirations for ICC Associate status. The Pakistan Cricket Board has pledged its support as proposer for 1996. Berlin, a club in only its second year, became German champions. The German Cup, a regional competition reserved for German nationals, was won by the Eastern team from Berlin/Brandenberg. – Brian Fell.

GIBRALTAR

As anticipated, the cutback in the forces on the Rock meant the end of the dominance of the Combined Services, who had swept the senior competitions for the previous three seasons. Their place was taken by Gibraltar's oldest club, the Gibraltar Cricket Club, which took both senior league titles as well as the National Day trophy. The season was a triumph for Christian Rocca, captain of both the club and the national team: he scored 1,065 runs, averaging 66.56. The senior leagues were played on a 50-overs per side basis instead of the old 40-overs format to acclimatise players for future ICC Trophy matches. Youthful talent continues to be our top priority and a team of mainly young players had a successful tour of Birmingham in August. – T. J. Finlayson.

HONG KONG

Cricket in Hong Kong is going through a period of change: 1997, when Hong Kong reverts from British to Chinese sovereignty, looms as a threat to the future of the game. Already some grounds are being lost to cricket as the British forces continue their withdrawal and municipal councils reclaim facilities for sports which have greater Chinese representation. The Hong Kong Cricket Association has realised that if the game is to survive, it must cease to be an expatriate domain and be taken to the local Chinese. If they are to be attracted to the sport, bearing in mind Hong Kong's unique challenges, especially lack of space and time, this must mean shorter, faster versions of the game. The association is making strenuous efforts to expand the base of players and is having some success against a backdrop of resistance from certain sections of the expatriate community, intent on protecting their own patch. Mark Eames was the Player of the Year in 1994-95, scoring 1,700 runs in both the Saturday and Sunday Leagues; Rod Bannister averaged 127 on Sundays. The Hong Kong Sixes, held at Kowloon in October, was again a success and there was much delight when Eddie Tse, the first Chinese player to take part, dismissed Mohammad Azharuddin with his second ball in international cricket. At the 1995 AGM of the Hong Kong Cricket Club Rodney Miles was elected president at 6.45 p.m. Immediately after the AGM an EGM was held which approved a change in the structure, making the president a titular head and giving responsibility to the chairman. At 7.30 Miles became chairman. He thus ceased to be president after 45 minutes. This may be a record. – Russell Mawhinney.

ISRAEL

This was another significant year for cricket in Israel. Four local coaches were sent to Lilleshall in England to gain experience, and the fruits of their efforts can be seen during the youth league matches every week. The team from the Negev desert area includes children of English, Indian, Moroccan, Russian and Kurdish parentage, cutting across all levels of society. We hope these boys will soon be at the heart of Israeli cricket. The national team toured Italy, who had just been accepted as Associate Members of ICC. It was decided to overlook some of the stalwarts of the past decade to build the team for the 1997 ICC Trophy. The policy was a success, and there were several finds: the all-rounder Isaac Masil, the talented 18-year-old Raymond Ashton and the acrobatic wicket-keeper Paul Smith. A professional coach is soon to be appointed to take charge of the side. Lions Lod won the domestic trophy for the first time. The 1994 champions Neve Yonathan were bowled out for 11 in just 40 minutes by Tel Aviv; this was one of two games umpired by the ICC umpire Ian Robinson, who visited for a week in August. This survey would not be complete without a tribute to Yitzhak Rabin, the Prime Minister who was assassinated in November. All matches the next weekend were marked by a minute's silence. For cricketers, his legacy will be fulfilled when all the cricketing nations of the world welcome Israel. – Stanley Perlman.

ITALY

On July 13 the Associazione Italiana Cricket achieved its cherished goal of becoming an Associate Member – the 22nd – of ICC, thus gaining the right to take part in the 1997 ICC Trophy in Malaysia. The success on the field of the national side, coached by Doug Ferguson and captained by Andrea Pezzi, explained the reasons behind the elevation. Italy, at that time still an Affiliate Member, scored a historic win over Argentina at the Hurlingham Club in Buenos Aires. They also, not without a slice of luck, enjoyed the best of Israel's visit to Rome in September, easily winning the one-day game and saving the "Test", despite entering the last hour at 54 for eight, having been 103 behind on first innings. Pianoro's unexpected success in the European Club Championship was very pleasing, but their traditional rivals Cesena won the National Championship and Capanelle retained the Italian Cup, beating Pianoro by three runs at Punta Ala. – Simone Gambino.

KENYA

Kenya's success in reaching the World Cup enabled the game to blossom at all levels. The Kenya A team was created to provide a reservoir for the national squad, an Under-19 team took shape and, after a lapse of many years, a schools league was re-started. In August an Indian A team, under Ajay Jadeja and including five Test players, played five one-day games. Kenya lost the series 4-1 but in their sole win, by eight wickets, Steve Tikolo scored 74 not out off 62 balls, hitting Rajesh Chauhan for four sixes in two overs. Tikolo was also the star of the tour of South Africa later in the year when the team played ten matches on the country's major grounds. These included a drawn three-day game when Tikolo scored an unbeaten 131 against Border, who then signed him as their foreign professional. Kenya won two of the one-day matches and lost five. The local season was dominated by the Agakhan club, captained by the national captain Maurice Odumbe. They won the league by one point from the 1993 and 1994 champions Swamibapa. They also won the knockout tournament, beating Simba Union by six wickets in the final. – Jasmer Singh.

MALAYSIA

The 1995 season has been extremely hectic. The Malaysian Cricket Association had organised 197 senior matches up to the end of October, with a record number of visiting teams. The highlight was the visit of MCC, who played six matches. The match against Malaysia was halted six overs into the home team's innings by a thunderstorm that flooded the field and smashed the hospitality tents to pieces. The MCC did us proud and organised a quick indoor coaching session for the kids. Professionalism came into the National League, a total of seven pros coming from Australian Shield and grade cricket. This created very keen competition – sledging was the order of the day, though in good spirits – and helped raise the profile of the game. With the presence of other expatriates, Perak emerged as 1995 champions. In 1996 the League will include two-day matches for the first time. The idea of a regional off-season eight-a-side league, being put together by Australia, is very interesting, and Malaysia are keen to be part of this circuit. – Charlie Chelliah.

ST HELENA

Jamestown B won the championship and their left-hander Gavin George dominated the season, averaging 68 with the bat, taking 56 wickets at 7.94, and most catches as well. – Fraser M. Simm.

SINGAPORE

The results achieved by the national team have not matched the very real progress at junior level. Singapore lost its annual "Test" against Malaysia, the Saudara Cup, and fared indifferently in the Tuanka Ja'afar competition, which also involves Hong Kong and Thailand. But the campaign to re-introduce the game into the education system has produced a total of 40 schools and junior colleges now playing the game. There have been successful junior tours to Malaysia at every age group level and the Under-18 team won the junior Tuanka Ja'afar trophy. The domestic league, now comprising three divisions, was won by Singapore Cricket Club, who also won the annual knockout. The International Six-a-Side, sponsored by TNT, brought in teams from all the Test-playing countries. A crowd of 5,000 saw Sri Lanka win the final. – Joe Grimberg.

SOLOMON ISLANDS

Efforts are being made to revive cricket on the Solomon Islands, where the game has faltered against competition from football. Anyone visiting the country should contact Nick Constantine, PO Box 307, Honiara.

SOUTH KOREA

Korean cricket continued in 1995 with its regular two-season format. International highlights included enjoyable visits to both Kowloon and Beijing, where a combined Korea/Japan XI lost narrowly to the local club. Domestic highlights included the six that was deflected off the non-striking batsman, Adrian Stephens of the British Embassy, and the moment when Ron Burnes of the All Star team attempted to field the ball at mid-on and disappeared down the drain that is a feature of the ground in Seoul. He re-emerged covered in mud and became known as "the cricketer from the trench". – John Kaminsky.

SPAIN

Spain played their first two-day internationals in 1995, drawing with both Italy and Portugal. Off the field, it was also a year of important progress. After four years of negotiations, the Spanish Cricket Association was finally recognised by the Government in 1995, which should have far-reaching benefits for the development of the game. And there was also progress at a local level; Javea CC reached agreement with their local council, who will help finance the club's attempts to promote cricket in Spanish schools. Domestic cricket was dominated by Barcelona, who won both league and cup. In a 45-over play-off for the league against Costa del Sol at Javéa, Barcelona scored 507 for two, 97 runs coming in the last five overs. Nadeem Sarwar scored 203 not out and Zafar Ahmed 195. Barcelona won by 288 runs. Finance remains a problem. And the continual changing of qualifications for international competitions by ICC and the European Cricket Federation does little to help promote the game at the required level. – Clive Woodbridge.

SWITZERLAND

Alpine CC of Zurich again won the Swiss League, in which nine clubs participated. Teams from Austria, Germany, Italy and Switzerland took part in the Zuoz Festival in July; the final had to be abandoned in near-darkness, and Milan and Vienna were declared joint winners. – Bryan Pattison.

UGANDA

Uganda, which have 240 active senior players, won ten matches out of 12 on a tour of the UK in August, and efforts are being made to install turf wickets. Uganda are currently part of East and Central Africa for cricketing purposes, but are anxious to become directly associated to ICC.

UNITED ARAB EMIRATES

As the Emirates approached the World Cup, there was an upsurge in cricket activities at all levels, ranging from the international tournaments held at Sharjah to visits from English schools teams. There were 34 tournaments throughout the seven Emirates, of which six were under flood-lights, and a number of new grounds were added. We do not have the luxury of grass pitches and players have to make do with compacted sand. However, the grounds are of regular size and facilities such as spectator seating, dressing-rooms and practice areas are available at most of them. The A Division champions were: in Abu Dhabi, NMC; in Dubai, Emirates Bank; in Sharjah, Union Bank. The other A Division competition was the Auto Lease Gold Cup night tournament held in Sharjah during Holy Ramadan. One match was abandoned owing to rain and the "shoot-out" provision implemented. As per the tournament rules, six bowlers from one side had bowled one ball each at the unprotected stumps and five bowlers from the other side had also bowled one ball each. No one could hit the wicket; the players then objected to the rule. The organising secretary, Ali

Anwar, a former first-class player in Pakistan, promptly took the ball. Still wearing his coat and tie, he hit the stumps with a leg-break straight away. The final bowler, the sixth one of the other side, then tried. He missed. – Nasir F. M. Akram.

UNITED STATES

Cricket is now being played on a huge scale from New England to California, but the organisation remains far behind the potential. Yet again the USA Cricket Association came under attack for failing to foster the game's development, and there were no obvious signs of the problem being addressed. Cricket gained some publicity when community leader Ted Hayes and a British insurance broker, David Sentance, helped form a team called LA Kricketts from a group of homeless Los Angeles drop-outs. The team toured Britain and played at Hambledon. But this was an exception to the general failure to make the most of the game's possibilities. The feeling is that this may change only if the US qualify for the next World Cup.

VANUATU

There are 400 cricketers and 12 league teams in Vanuatu, the nation in the South-West Pacific that was formerly the Anglo-French New Hebrides. Eight of the teams play in the capital, Port Vila, and four in Luganville, the major town in the north of the island group. Cricket is also played at the two senior English-speaking secondary schools. About 70 per cent of the players are indigenous "Ni-Vanuatu", but a mainly expatriate team, Vila Refrigeration, won the Port Vila competition in 1995. The length of games in Vanuatu depends on when everyone turns up. We schedule starting times but invariably "island time" takes over. The game has been played here throughout the century, and there is no novelty effect for local people; this is illustrated by the fact that people take the shortest route across the ground while play is in progress. In Luganville the games are often played in a small park on the main street; shopkeepers on the other side put up their cyclone shutters to protect their windows from the big-hitters. – Mark Stafford.

WESTERN SAMOA

Local players in Apia, the capital of Western Samoa, challenged European players to a two-match series involving both the versions of cricket played here: Samoan "kirikiti", with four-foot bats and a flexible number of players, and the more familiar game. The scoring needed to be audited but pride was salvaged by both sides in their own codes. "English cricket" here continued through another retrenched year; the senior competition has been reduced from 14 teams to a group of just 30-50 regulars. There are hopes of a revival stimulated by Samoan men returning from Australasian cities, and the recent arrival of TV from New Zealand. The cost of equipment is a major constraint and there is a desperate need for visiting teams. The game, however, has survived the ravages of "wild women" – the local name for cyclones. Last time the island was hit, the ground was used as a relief base and taken over by helicopters and roofing iron. – Bob Barlow.

PART FIVE:
ADMINISTRATION AND LAWS

INTERNATIONAL CRICKET COUNCIL

On June 15, 1909, representatives of cricket in England, Australia and South Africa met at Lord's and founded the Imperial Cricket Conference. Membership was confined to the governing bodies of cricket in countries within the British Commonwealth where Test cricket was played. India, New Zealand and West Indies were elected as members on May 31, 1926, Pakistan on July 28, 1952, Sri Lanka on July 21, 1981, and Zimbabwe on July 8, 1992. South Africa ceased to be a member of ICC on leaving the British Commonwealth in May, 1961, but was elected as a Full Member on July 10, 1991.

On July 15, 1965, the Conference was renamed the International Cricket Conference and new rules were adopted to permit the election of countries from outside the British Commonwealth. This led to the growth of the Conference, with the admission of Associate Members, who were each entitled to one vote, while the Foundation and Full Members were each entitled to two votes, on ICC resolutions. On July 12, 13, 1989, the Conference was renamed the International Cricket Council and revised rules were adopted.

On July 7, 1993, ICC ceased to be administered by MCC and became an independent organisation with its own chief executive, the headquarters remaining at Lord's. The category of Foundation Member, with its special rights, was abolished. On October 1, 1993, Sir Clyde Walcott became the first non-British chairman of ICC.

Officers

Chairman: Sir Clyde Walcott. *Chief Executive:* D. L. Richards. *Administration Officer:* C. D. Hitchcock.

Constitution

Chairman: Elected for a three-year term from the date of the Council's annual conference. Normally, a new chairman will be chosen at the conference a year before the previous Chairman's term expires. Sir Clyde Walcott's term ends in 1997.

Chief Executive: Appointed by the Council. D. L. Richards has been given a contract until 1998.

Membership

Full Members: Australia, England, India, New Zealand, Pakistan, South Africa, Sri Lanka, West Indies and Zimbabwe.

Associate Members*: Argentina (1974), Bangladesh (1977), Bermuda (1966), Canada (1968), Denmark (1966), East and Central Africa (1966), Fiji (1965), Gibraltar (1969), Hong Kong (1969), Ireland (1993), Israel (1974), Italy (1995), Kenya (1981), Malaysia (1967), Namibia (1992), Netherlands (1966), Papua New Guinea (1973), Scotland (1994), Singapore (1974), United Arab Emirates (1990), USA (1965) and West Africa (1976).

Affiliate Members*: Austria (1992), Bahamas (1987), Belgium (1991), Brunei (1992), France (1987), Germany (1991), Greece (1995), Japan (1989), Nepal (1988), Spain (1992), Switzerland (1985), Thailand (1995) and Vanuatu (1995).

* *Year of election shown in parentheses.*

The following governing bodies for cricket shall be eligible for election.

Full Members: The governing body for cricket recognised by ICC of a country, or countries associated for cricket purposes, or a geographical area, from which representative teams are qualified to play official Test matches.

Associate Members: The governing body for cricket recognised by ICC of a country, or countries associated for cricket purposes, or a geographical area, which does not qualify as a Full Member but where cricket is firmly established and organised.

Affiliate Members: The governing body for cricket recognised by ICC of a country, or countries associated for cricket purposes, or a geographical area (which is not part of one of those already constituted as a Full or Associate Member) where ICC recognises that cricket is played in accordance with the Laws of Cricket. Affiliate Members have no right to vote or to propose or second resolutions at ICC meetings.

THE CRICKET COUNCIL

The Cricket Council, which was set up in 1968 and reconstituted in 1974 and 1983, acts as the governing body for cricket in England and Wales. It comprises the following.

Chairman: W. R. F. Chamberlain.
Vice-Chairman: J. D. Robson.
8 Representatives of the Test and County Cricket Board: J. R. T. Barclay, Sir Lawrence Byford, W. R. F. Chamberlain, D. J. Insole, M. P. Murray, H. J. Pocock, D. Rich, D. R. W. Silk.
5 Representatives of the National Cricket Association: F. H. Elliott, E. K. Ingman, J. G. Overy, J. D. Robson, M. J. K. Smith.
3 Representatives of the Marylebone Cricket Club: R. D. V. Knight, M. E. L. Melluish, The Hon. Sir Oliver Popplewell.
1 Representative (non-voting) of the Minor Counties Cricket Association: J. B. Pickup.

Secretary: A. C. Smith.

THE TEST AND COUNTY CRICKET BOARD

The TCCB was set up in 1968 to be responsible for Test matches, official tours, and first-class and minor county competitions. It is composed of representatives of the 18 first-class counties, Marylebone Cricket Club and Minor Counties Cricket Association (voting members); as well as Oxford University Cricket Club, Cambridge University Cricket Club, the Irish Cricket Union and the Scottish Cricket Union (non-voting members).

Officers

Chairman: D. R. W. Silk.

Chairmen of Committees: D. R. W. Silk (Executive); D. L. Acfield (Cricket); D. B. Carr (Pitches); B. G. K. Downing (Marketing); R. Illingworth (Selection); D. J. Insole (International); M. P. Murray (Finance); D. H. Newton (Test match grounds advisory); E. Slinger (acting) (Discipline); A. C. Smith (Appointment of Umpires); M. J. K. Smith (Development); Rev. M. D. Vockins (Second Eleven Competitions); A. Wheelhouse (Registration).

Chief Executive: A. C. Smith. *Cricket Secretary:* T. M. Lamb. *Administration Secretary:* A. S. Brown. *Accountant:* C. A. Barker. *Marketing Manager:* T. D. M. Blake. *Public Relations Manager:* R. E. Little. *England Team Manager:* R. Illingworth.

THE NATIONAL CRICKET ASSOCIATION

With the setting up of the Cricket Council in 1968 it was thought necessary to form a separate organisation to represent the interests of all cricket below the first-class game: the NCA comprises representatives from 51 county cricket associations and 19 national cricketing organisations. The following were in office in 1994-95:

Officers

President: M. J. K. Smith.
Chairman: J. D. Robson.
Vice-Chairman: F. H. Elliott.
Director of Finance: C. A. Barker.
Director of Coaching: M. J. Stewart.

Director of Administration
and Development: T. N. Bates.
Marketing Executive: D. A. Clarke.
Hon. Treasurer: D. W. Carter.

The above three bodies were due to merge in 1996 to form the English Cricket Board.

THE MARYLEBONE CRICKET CLUB

The Marylebone Cricket Club evolved out of the White Conduit Club in 1787, when Thomas Lord laid out his first ground in Dorset Square. Its members revised the Laws in 1788 and gradually took responsibility for cricket throughout the world. However, it relinquished control of the game in the UK in 1968 and the International Cricket Council finally established its own secretariat in 1993. MCC still owns Lord's and remains the guardian of the Laws. It calls itself "a private club with a public function" and aims to support cricket everywhere, especially at grassroots level and in countries where the game is least developed.

Patron: HER MAJESTY THE QUEEN

Officers

President: 1994-96 – The Hon. Sir Oliver Popplewell.

Treasurer: M. E. L. Melluish.   *Chairman of Finance:* D. L. Hudd.

Trustees: The Rt Hon. The Lord Griffiths, J. J. Warr, Field Marshal The Rt Hon. The Lord Bramall.

Hon. Life Vice-Presidents: Sir Donald Bradman, D. G. Clark, G. H. G. Doggart, D. J. Insole, F. G. Mann, C. H. Palmer, C. G. A. Paris, E. W. Swanton.

Secretary: R. D. V. Knight.

Assistant Secretaries: M. R. Blow (Finance), J. A. Jameson (Cricket), C. W. W. Rea (Marketing), J. R. Smith (Administration).   *Personal Assistant to Secretary:* Miss S. A. Lawrence.   *Curator:* S. E. A. Green.

MCC Committee, elected members 1994-95: The Rt Hon. The Lord Alexander, E. R. Dexter, D. A. Graveney, S. P. Henderson, C. B. Howland, A. R. Lewis, Sir Ian MacLaurin, Sir Tim Rice, M. O. C. Sturt, G. J. Toogood, J. A. F. Vallance.

Chairmen of main sub-committees: Sir Colin Cowdrey (Cricket); B. M. Thornton (Estates); R. V. C. Robins (General Purposes).   *Chairmen of specialist sub-committees:* J. R. T. Barclay (Indoor School Management); R. P. Hodson (Players and Fixtures); B. A. Sharp (Tennis and Squash); T. M. B. Sissons (Marketing); H. M. Wyndham (Arts and Libraries).

EUROPEAN CRICKET FEDERATION

The ECF was founded in Munich in 1989 by the national cricket associations of Austria, Germany, Italy and Switzerland to help promote and develop cricket in Europe. Spain became the 12th member country in 1995, joining the original four plus Belgium, France, Greece, Luxembourg, Malta, Portugal and Sweden.

Chairman: R. D. V. Knight.   *Secretary:* G. Lees.

ADDRESSES

INTERNATIONAL CRICKET COUNCIL

D. L. Richards, The Clock Tower, Lord's Cricket Ground, London NW8 8QN (0171-266 1818; fax 0171-266 1777).

Full Members

AUSTRALIA: Australian Cricket Board, G. W. Halbish, 90 Jolimont Street, Jolimont, Victoria 3002.

ENGLAND: Cricket Council, A. C. Smith, CBE, Lord's Ground, London NW8 8QZ.

INDIA: Board of Control for Cricket in India, J. Dalmiya, Dr B. C. Roy Club House, Eden Gardens, Calcutta 700 021.

NEW ZEALAND: New Zealand Cricket Inc., C. Doig, PO Box 958, 109 Cambridge Terrace, Christchurch.

PAKISTAN: Pakistan Cricket Board, Ghulam Mustafa Khan, Gaddafi Stadium, Lahore 54600.

SOUTH AFRICA: United Cricket Board of South Africa, Dr A. Bacher, PO Box 55009, Northlands 2116, Transvaal.

SRI LANKA: Board of Control for Cricket in Sri Lanka, A. P. B. Tennekoon, 35 Maitland Place, Colombo 7.

WEST INDIES: West Indies Cricket Board of Control, G. S. Camacho, Letchworth Complex, The Garrison, St Michael, Barbados.

ZIMBABWE: Zimbabwe Cricket Union, D. Arnott, PO Box 2739, Harare.

Associate and Affiliate Members

ARGENTINA: Argentine Cricket Association, B. C. Roberts, ACA Sede Central, J. M. Gutierrez 3829, 1425 Buenos Aires.

AUSTRIA: Austrian Cricket Association, A. Simpson-Parker, Benidikt-Schellingergasse 22/16, 1150 Vienna.

BAHAMAS: Bahamas Cricket Association, S. Deveaux, PO Box N-10101, Nassau.

BANGLADESH: Bangladesh Cricket Control Board, M. Aminul Huq Moni, National Stadium, Dhaka 1000.

BELGIUM: Belgian Cricket Federation, C. Wolfe, Rue de l'Eglise St Martin 12, B-1390 BIEZ.

BERMUDA: Bermuda Cricket Board of Control, W. Smith, PO Box HM992, Hamilton HM DX.

BRUNEI: Brunei Darussalam National Cricket Association, c/o Panaga Club, Seria 7082, Brunei Darussalam via Singapore.

CANADA: Canadian Cricket Association, Capt. J. Siew, 1650 Abbey Road, Ottawa, Ontario, K1G 0H3.

DENMARK: Danish Cricket Association, J. Holmen, Idraettens Hus, 2605 Brøndby.

EAST AND CENTRAL AFRICA: East and Central African Cricket Conference, T. B. McCarthy, PO Box 34321, Lusaka 1010, Zambia.

FIJI: Fiji Cricket Association, P. I. Knight, PO Box 300, Suva.

FRANCE: Fédération Française du Cricket, O. Dubaut, 73 Rue Curial, 75019 Paris.

GERMANY: Deutscher Cricket Bund, B. Fell, Luragogasse 5, 94032 Passau.

GIBRALTAR: Gibraltar Cricket Association, T. J. Finlayson, 21 Sandpits House, Withams Road.

GREECE: Greek Cricket Association, Y. Arvanitakis, Sossikleous 16, 116 32 Athens.

HONG KONG: Hong Kong Cricket Association, J. A. Cribbin, Room 1019, Sports House, 1 Stadium Path, So Kon Po, Causeway Bay.

IRELAND: Irish Cricket Union, D. Scott, 45 Foxrock Park, Foxrock, Dublin 18.

ISRAEL: Israel Cricket Association, S. Perlman, Ben Yosef Street 23/8, Tel-Aviv 61650.

ITALY: Associazione Italiana Cricket, S. Gambino, Via S. Ignazio 9, 00186 Roma.

JAPAN: Japan Cricket Association, R. G. Martineau, Shizuoka City, Chiyoda 736, Yamadai Corp. 305, Japan 420.

KENYA: Kenya Cricket Association, J. Rayani, PO Box 48363, Nairobi.

MALAYSIA: Malaysian Cricket Association, C. Chelliah, 1st Floor, Wisma OCM, Jalan Hang Jebat, 50150 Kuala Lumpur.

NAMIBIA: Namibia Cricket Board, L. Pieters, PO Box 457, Windhoek 9000.

NEPAL: Cricket Association of Nepal, Jaikumar N. Shah, Dasharath Stadium, PO Box 1432, Kathmandu.

NETHERLANDS: Royal Netherlands Cricket Board, A. de la Mar, Neuiwe Kalfjeslaan 21-B, 1182 AA Amstelveen.

PAPUA NEW GUINEA: Papua New Guinea Cricket Board of Control, W. Satchell, PO Box 83, Konedobu.

SCOTLAND: Scottish Cricket Union, R. W. Barclay, Caledonia House, South Gyle, Edinburgh EH12 9DQ.

SINGAPORE: Singapore Cricket Association, J. Grimberg, c/o The Ceylon Sports Club, 101 Balestier Road, Singapore 1232.

SPAIN: Asociacion Española de Cricket, C. E. Woodbridge, Apartado 269, 03730 Javea, Alicante.

SWITZERLAND: Swiss Cricket Association, P. Barnes, Spitzackerstrasse 32, 4103 Bottmingen.

THAILAND: Thailand Cricket League, T. Kamasuta, 17th Floor, Silom Complex Building, 191 Silom Road, Bangkok 10500.

UNITED ARAB EMIRATES: Emirates Cricket Board, Abdul Rahman Bukhatir, Sharjah Cricket Stadium, PO Box 88, Sharjah.

USA: United States of America Cricket Association, Naseeruddin Khan, 2361 Hickory Road, Plymouth Meeting, Pennsylvania 19462.

VANUATU: Vanuatu Cricket Association, M. Stafford, c/o Stafford and Associates, PO Box 734, Court Villa, Vanuatu.

WEST AFRICA: West Africa Cricket Conference, Mrs Tayo Oreweme, Tafawa Balewa Square, Surulere, Lagos, Nigeria.

UK ADDRESSES

TEST AND COUNTY CRICKET BOARD: A. C. Smith, Lord's Ground, London NW8 8QZ (0171-286 4405; fax 0171-289 5619).

MARYLEBONE CRICKET CLUB: R. D. V. Knight, Lord's Ground, London NW8 8QN (0171-289 1611; fax 0171-289 9100. Club office 0171-289 8979; fax 0171-266 3459).

First-Class Counties

DERBYSHIRE: County Ground, Nottingham Road, Derby DE21 6DA (01332-383211; fax 01332-290251).

DURHAM: County Ground, Riverside, Chester-le-Street, County Durham DH3 3QR (0191-387 1717; fax 0191-387 1616).

ESSEX: County Ground, New Writtle Street, Chelmsford CM2 0PG (01245-252420; fax 01245-491607).

GLAMORGAN: Sophia Gardens, Cardiff CF1 9XR (01222-343478; fax 01222-377044).

GLOUCESTERSHIRE: Phoenix County Ground, Nevil Road, Bristol BS7 9EJ (0117-924 5216; fax 0117-924 1193).

HAMPSHIRE: Northlands Road, Southampton SO9 2TY (01703-333788; fax 01703-330121).

KENT: St Lawrence Ground, Old Dover Road, Canterbury CT1 3NZ (01227-456886; fax 01227-762168).

LANCASHIRE: County Cricket Ground, Old Trafford, Manchester M16 0PX (0161-282 4000; fax 0161-282 4100).

LEICESTERSHIRE: County Ground, Grace Road, Leicester LE2 8AD (0116-283 1880/2128; fax 0116-244 0363).

MIDDLESEX: Lord's Cricket Ground, London NW8 8QN (0171-289 1300; fax 0171-289 5831).

NORTHAMPTONSHIRE: County Ground, Wantage Road, Northampton NN1 4TJ (01604-32917; fax 01604-232855).

NOTTINGHAMSHIRE: County Cricket Ground, Trent Bridge, Nottingham NG2 6AG (0115-982 1525; fax 0115-945 5730).

SOMERSET: County Ground, St James's Street, Taunton TA1 1JT (01823-272946; fax 01823-332395).

SURREY: The Oval, London SE11 5SS (0171-582 6660; fax 0171-735 7769).
SUSSEX: County Ground, Eaton Road, Hove BN3 3AN (01273-732161; fax 01273-771549).
WARWICKSHIRE: County Ground, Edgbaston, Birmingham B5 7QU (0121-446 4422; fax 0121-446 4544).
WORCESTERSHIRE: County Ground, New Road, Worcester WR2 4QQ (01905-748474; fax 01905-748005).
YORKSHIRE: Headingley Cricket Ground, Leeds LS6 3BU (0113-278 7394; fax 0113-278 4099).

Minor Counties

MINOR COUNTIES CRICKET ASSOCIATION: D. J. M. Armstrong, Thorpe Cottage, Mill Common, Ridlington, North Walsham NR28 9TY. (01692-650563).
BEDFORDSHIRE: D. J. F. Hoare, 5 Brecon Way, Bedford MK41 8DF (01234-266648).
BERKSHIRE: C. M. S. Crombie, Orchard Cottage, Waltham St Lawrence, Reading, Berkshire RG10 0JH (01734-343387 home, 01491-578555 business).
BUCKINGHAMSHIRE: S. J. Tomlin, Orchardleigh Cottage, Bigfrith Lane, Cookham Dean, Berkshire SL6 9PH (01628-482202 home, 016285-24922 business).
CAMBRIDGESHIRE: P. W. Gooden, The Redlands, Oakington Road, Cottenham, Cambridge CB4 4TW (01954-250429).
CHESHIRE: J. B. Pickup, 2 Castle Street, Northwich, Cheshire CW8 1AB (01606-74970 home, 01606-74301 business; fax 01606-871034).
CORNWALL: The Rev. Canon Kenneth Rogers, The Rectory, Priory Road, Bodmin, Cornwall PL31 2AB (01208-73867).
CUMBERLAND: D. Lamb, 42 Croft Road, Carlisle, Cumbria CA3 9AG (01228-23017).
DEVON: G. R. Evans, Blueberry Haven, 20 Boucher Road, Budleigh Salterton, Devon EX9 6JF (01395-445216 home, 01392-58406 business; fax 01392-411697).
DORSET: K. H. House, The Barn, Higher Farm, Bagber Common, Sturminster Newton, Dorset DT10 2HB (01258-473394).
HEREFORDSHIRE: P. Sykes, 5 Dale Drive, Holmer Grange, Hereford HR4 9RF (01432-264703 home, 01432-382684 business).
HERTFORDSHIRE: D. S. Dredge, "Trevellis", 38 Santers Lane, Potters Bar, Hertfordshire EN6 2BX (01707-658377 home, 0171-359 3579 business).
LINCOLNSHIRE: C. J. White, "Lyndonholme", Castle Terrace Road, Sleaford, Lincolnshire NG34 7QF (01529-302341 home, 01529-302181 business).
NORFOLK: S. J. Skinner, 27 Colkett Drive, Old Catton, Norwich NR6 7ND (01603-485940 home – weekend, 01354-59026 – midweek, 01733-412152 business).
NORTHUMBERLAND: A. B. Stephenson, Northumberland County Cricket Club, Osborne Avenue, Jesmond, Newcastle-upon-Tyne NE2 1JS (0191-281 2738).
OXFORDSHIRE: A. W. Moss, 14 Croft Avenue, Kidlington, Oxford OX5 2HU (01865-372399 home, 01865-226733/742277 business; fax 01865-226886).
SHROPSHIRE: N. H. Birch, 8 Port Hill Close, Shrewsbury, Shropshire SY3 8RR (01743-233650).
STAFFORDSHIRE: W. S. Bourne, 10 The Pavement, Brewood, Staffordshire ST19 9BZ (01902-850325 home, 01902-23038 business; fax 01902-714428).
SUFFOLK: Toby Pound, 94 Henley Road, Ipswich IP1 4NJ (01473-213288 home, 01473-232121 business).
WALES MINOR COUNTIES: Bill Edwards, 59a King Edward Road, Swansea SA1 4LN (01792-462233).
WILTSHIRE: C. R. Sheppard, 45 Ipswich Street, Swindon SN2 1DB (01793-511811 home, 01793-530784 business, 0831-565866 mobile).

Other Bodies

ASSOCIATION OF CRICKET UMPIRES AND SCORERS: G. J. Bullock, PO Box 399, Camberley, Surrey GU16 5ZJ (01276-27962).
BRITISH UNIVERSITIES SPORTS ASSOCIATION: J. Ellis, 8 Union Street, London SE1 1SZ (0171-357 8555).
CLUB CRICKET CONFERENCE: D. Franklin, 361 West Barnes Lane, New Malden, Surrey KT3 6JF (0181-949 4001).

COMBINED SERVICES: Major R. Ross-Hurst, c/o Army Sports Control Board, Clayton Barracks, Aldershot, Hampshire GU11 2BG.

ENGLISH SCHOOLS' CRICKET ASSOCIATION: K. S. Lake, 38 Mill House, Woods Lane, Cottingham, Hull HU16 4HQ.

EUROPEAN CRICKET FEDERATION: G. Lees, 56 Ashfield Road, Altrincham, Cheshire WA15 9QN (0161-929 5897).

LEAGUE CRICKET CONFERENCE: N. Edwards, 1 Longfield, Freshfield, Formby, Merseyside.

MIDLAND CLUB CRICKET CONFERENCE: D. R. Thomas, 4 Silverdale Gardens, Wordsley, Stourbridge, W. Midlands DY8 5NU.

NATIONAL CRICKET ASSOCIATION: Lord's Ground, London NW8 8QZ.

SCARBOROUGH CRICKET FESTIVAL: Colin T. Adamson, Cricket Ground, North Marine Road, Scarborough, North Yorkshire YO12 7TJ.

WOMEN'S CRICKET ASSOCIATION: Warwickshire County Cricket Ground, Edgbaston Road, Birmingham B5 7QX (0121-440 0520; fax 0121-446 6344).

CRICKET ASSOCIATIONS AND SOCIETIES

AUSTRALIAN CRICKET SOCIETY: D. Manning, Ravenstone, 240-246 Oban Road, North Ringwood, Victoria 3134, Australia.

BLACKLEY CRICKET SOCIETY: D. N. Butterfield, 7 Bayswater Terrace, Halifax, West Yorkshire HX3 0NB.

CHELTENHAM CRICKET SOCIETY: P. Murphy, 1 Colesbourne Road, Benhall, Cheltenham, Gloucestershire GL51 6DJ.

CHESTERFIELD CRICKET SOCIETY: J. S. Cook, 44 Morris Avenue, Newbold, Chesterfield, Derbyshire S41 7BA.

COUNCIL OF CRICKET SOCIETIES, THE: B. Rickson, 31 Grange Avenue, Cheadle Hulme, Cheshire SK8 5EN.

COUNTY CRICKET SUPPORTERS ASSOCIATION: W. Horsley, 10 Delamere Road, Northampton NN4 9QG.

CRICKET MEMORABILIA SOCIETY: A. Sheldon, 29 Highclere Road, Crumpsall, Manchester M8 4WH.

CRICKET SOCIETY, THE: D. H. A. Lodge, 2 Highfield Close, Amersham, Buckinghamshire HP6 6HG.

CRICKET STATISTICIANS AND HISTORIANS, ASSOCIATION OF: P. Wynne-Thomas, 3 Radcliffe Road, West Bridgford, Nottingham NG2 5FF.

CRICKET STATISTICIANS AND SCORERS OF INDIA, ASSOCIATION OF: T. Braganza, 63a Gokhale Road (North), Dadar, Bombay 400 028, India.

DERBYSHIRE CRICKET SOCIETY: O. Kinselle, 27 Wilstthorpe Road, Breaston, Derbyshire DE72 3EA.

DUKINFIELD CRICKET LOVERS' SOCIETY: B. Walker, 3 Bryce Street, Dukinfield, Cheshire SK14 4SJ.

EAST RIDING CRICKET SOCIETY: Mrs S. Forward, 121 Fairfax Avenue, Hull HU5 4QU.

ESSEX CRICKET SOCIETY: M. K. Smith, 321 Westbourne Grove, Westcliff-on-Sea, Essex SS0 0PU.

GLOUCESTERSHIRE CRICKET LOVERS' SOCIETY: M. Simpson, 318 Canford Lane, Westbury-on-Trym, Bristol BS9 3PL.

HAMPSHIRE CRICKET SOCIETY: J. Moore, 85 Kingsway, Chandlers Ford, Eastleigh, Hampshire SO53 1FD.

HERTFORDSHIRE CRICKET SOCIETY: W. Powell, The Shenley Cricket Centre, Radlett Lane, Shenley, Hertfordshire WD9 9DW.

HIGH PEAK CRICKET SOCIETY: G. K. Watson, Stubbins Lea, Stubbins Lane, Chinley, Stockport SK12 6ED.

INDIA, THE CRICKET SOCIETY OF: Sander Nakai, 1047 Pocket-B, Sector-A, Vasant Kunj, New Delhi 1120 030, India.

LANCASHIRE AND CHESHIRE CRICKET SOCIETY: H. W. Pardoe, "Crantock", 117a Barlow Moor Road, Didsbury, Manchester M20 2TS.

LINCOLNSHIRE CRICKET LOVERS' SOCIETY: C. Kennedy, 26 Eastwood Avenue, Great Grimsby, South Humberside DN34 5BE.

MERSEYSIDE CRICKET SOCIETY: W. T. Robins, 11 Yew Tree Road, Hunts Cross, Liverpool L25 9QN.

MIDLAND CRICKET SOCIETY: Miss H. Allen, 14 Merrions Close, Great Barr, Birmingham B43 7AT.

NATIONAL CRICKET MEMBERSHIP SCHEME: c/o Cricket Lore, 22 Grazebrook Road, London N16 0HS.

NEEDWOOD CRICKET LOVERS' SOCIETY: A. D. Campion, 45 Fallowfield Drive, Barton-under-Needwood, Staffordshire DE13 8DH.

NEW ZEALAND, CRICKET SOCIETY OF: J. H. Palmer, Eden Park, PO Box 2860, Auckland 1, New Zealand.

NORFOLK CRICKET SOCIETY: A. V. Burgess, 41 Ashby Street, Norwich, Norfolk NR1 3PT.

NORTHERN CRICKET SOCIETY: K. Harvey, 5 St Margaret's Drive, Gledhow Lane, Roundhay, Leeds, Yorkshire LS8 1RU.

NOTTINGHAM CRICKET LOVERS' SOCIETY: G. Blagdurn, 2 Inham Circus, Chilwell, Beeston, Nottingham NG9 4FN.

PAKISTAN ASSOCIATION OF CRICKET STATISTICIANS: Abid Ali Kazi, House No. 31, First Floor, Street No. 30, F-6/1, Islamabad, Pakistan.

ROTHERHAM CRICKET SOCIETY: J. A. R. Atkin, 15 Gallow Tree Road, Rotherham, South Yorkshire S65 3FE.

SCOTLAND, CRICKET SOCIETY OF: A. J. Robertson, 5 Riverside Road, Eaglesham, Glasgow G76 0DQ.

SOMERSET WYVERNS: G. Evison, 61 Welbeck Avenue, Bedgrove, Aylesbury, Buckinghamshire HP21 7BJ.

SOUTH AFRICA, CRICKET SOCIETY OF: Mrs J. Gleason, PO Box 78040, Sandton, Transvaal 2146, South Africa.

STOURBRIDGE AND DISTRICT CRICKET SOCIETY: R. Barber, 6 Carlton Avenue, Pedmore, Stourbridge, West Midlands DY9 9ED.

SUSSEX CRICKET SOCIETY: Mrs P. Brabyn, 4 Wolstonbury Walk, Shoreham-by-Sea, West Sussex BN43 5GU.

SWISS CRICKET ASSOCIATION: Dr B. Pattison, 9 Ch. du Bois Contens, 1291 Commugny, Switzerland.

WEST LANCASHIRE CRICKET SOCIETY: G. D. Anderson, 32 Dunster Road, Southport PR8 2EN.

WOMBWELL CRICKET LOVERS' SOCIETY: M. Pope, 59 Wood Lane, Treeton, Rotherham, South Yorkshire S60 5QR.

YORKSHIRE CCC SOUTHERN GROUP: D. M. Wood, 15 Rothschild Road, Linslade, Leighton Buzzard, Bedfordshire LU7 7SY.

ZIMBABWE, CRICKET SOCIETY OF: J. B. Stockwell, 6 Howard Close, Mount Pleasant, Harare, Zimbabwe.

THE LAWS OF CRICKET

(1980 CODE)

As updated in 1992. World copyright of MCC and reprinted by permission of MCC. Copies of the "Laws of Cricket" may be obtained from Lord's Cricket Ground.

INDEX TO THE LAWS

LAW 1.   THE PLAYERS

1. Number of Players and Captain

A match is played between two sides each of 11 players, one of whom shall be captain. In the event of the captain not being available at any time, a deputy shall act for him.

2. Nomination of Players

Before the toss for innings, the captain shall nominate his players, who may not thereafter be changed without the consent of the opposing captain.

Note

> **(a) More or Less than 11 Players a Side**
> A match may be played by agreement between sides of more or less than 11 players, but not more than 11 players may field.

LAW 2.   SUBSTITUTES AND RUNNERS: BATSMAN OR FIELDSMAN LEAVING THE FIELD: BATSMAN RETIRING: BATSMAN COMMENCING INNINGS

1. Substitutes

In normal circumstances, a substitute shall be allowed to field only for a player who satisfies the umpires that he has become injured or become ill during the match. However, in very exceptional circumstances, the umpires may use their discretion to allow a substitute for a player who has to leave the field for other wholly acceptable reasons, subject to consent being given by the opposing captain. If a player wishes to change his shirt, boots, etc., he may leave the field to do so (no changing on the field), but no substitute will be allowed.

2. Objection to Substitutes

The opposing captain shall have no right of objection to any player acting as substitute in the field, nor as to where he shall field; however, no substitute shall act as wicket-keeper.

3. Substitute not to Bat or Bowl

A substitute shall not be allowed to bat or bowl.

4. A Player for whom a Substitute has Acted

A player may bat, bowl or field even though a substitute has acted for him.

5. Runner

A runner shall be allowed for a batsman who, during the match, is incapacitated by illness or injury. The person acting as runner shall be a member of the batting side and shall, if possible, have already batted in that innings.

6. Runner's Equipment

The player acting as runner for an injured batsman shall wear the same external protective equipment as the injured batsman.

7. Transgression of the Laws by an Injured Batsman or Runner

An injured batsman may be out should his runner break any one of Laws 33 (Handled the Ball), 37 (Obstructing the Field) or 38 (Run Out). As striker he remains himself subject to the Laws. Furthermore, should he be out of his ground for any purpose and the wicket at the wicket-keeper's end be put down he shall be out under Law 38 (Run Out) or Law 39 (Stumped), irrespective of the position of the other batsman or the runner, and no runs shall be scored.

When not the striker, the injured batsman is out of the game and shall stand where he does not interfere with the play. Should he bring himself into the game in any way, then he shall suffer the penalties that any transgression of the Laws demands.

8. Fieldsman Leaving the Field

No fieldsman shall leave the field or return during a session of play without the consent of the umpire at the bowler's end. The umpire's consent is also necessary if a substitute is required for a fieldsman, when his side returns to the field after an interval. If a member of the fielding side leaves the field or fails to return after an interval and is absent from the field for longer than 15 minutes, he shall not be permitted to bowl after his return until he has been on the field for at least that length of playing time for which he was absent. This restriction shall not apply at the start of a new day's play.

9. Batsman Leaving the Field or Retiring

A batsman may leave the field or retire at any time owing to illness, injury or other unavoidable cause, having previously notified the umpire at the bowler's end. He may resume his innings at the fall of a wicket, which for the purposes of this Law shall include the retirement of another batsman.

If he leaves the field or retires for any other reason he may resume his innings only with the consent of the opposing captain.

When a batsman has left the field or retired and is unable to return owing to illness, injury or other unavoidable cause, his innings is to be recorded as "retired, not out". Otherwise it is to be recorded as "retired, out".

10. Commencement of a Batsman's Innings

A batsman shall be considered to have commenced his innings once he has stepped on to the field of play.

Note

(a) Substitutes and Runners
For the purpose of these Laws, allowable illnesses or injuries are those which occur at any time after the nomination by the captains of their teams.

LAW 3.   THE UMPIRES

1. Appointment

Before the toss for innings, two umpires shall be appointed, one for each end, to control the game with absolute impartiality as required by the Laws.

2. Change of Umpires

No umpire shall be changed during a match without the consent of both captains.

3. Special Conditions

Before the toss for innings, the umpires shall agree with both captains on any special conditions affecting the conduct of the match.

4. The Wickets

The umpires shall satisfy themselves before the start of the match that the wickets are properly pitched.

5. Clock or Watch

The umpires shall agree between themselves and inform both captains before the start of the match on the watch or clock to be followed during the match.

6. Conduct and Implements

Before and during a match the umpires shall ensure that the conduct of the game and the implements used are strictly in accordance with the Laws.

7. Fair and Unfair Play

The umpires shall be the sole judges of fair and unfair play.

8. Fitness of Ground, Weather and Light

(a) The umpires shall be the sole judges of the fitness of the ground, weather and light for play.

    (i) However, before deciding to suspend play, or not to start play, or not to resume play after an interval or stoppage, the umpires shall establish whether both captains (the batsmen at the wicket may deputise for their captain) wish to commence or to continue in the prevailing conditions; if so, their wishes shall be met.

    (ii) In addition, if during play the umpires decide that the light is unfit, only the batting side shall have the option of continuing play. After agreeing to continue to play in unfit light conditions, the captain of the batting side (or a batsman at the wicket) may appeal against the light to the umpires, who shall uphold the appeal only if, in their opinion, the light has deteriorated since the agreement to continue was made.

(b) After any suspension of play, the umpires, unaccompanied by any of the players or officials, shall, on their own initiative, carry out an inspection immediately the conditions improve and shall continue to inspect at intervals. Immediately the umpires decide that play is possible they shall call upon the players to resume the game.

9. Exceptional Circumstances

In exceptional circumstances, other than those of weather, ground or light, the umpires may decide to suspend or abandon play. Before making such a decision the umpires shall establish, if the circumstances allow, whether both captains (the batsmen at the wicket may deputise for their captain) wish to continue in the prevailing conditions; if so, their wishes shall be met.

10. Position of Umpires

The umpires shall stand where they can best see any act upon which their decision may be required.

Subject to this over-riding consideration, the umpire at the bowler's end shall stand where he does not interfere with either the bowler's run-up or the striker's view.

The umpire at the striker's end may elect to stand on the off instead of the leg side of the pitch, provided he informs the captain of the fielding side and the striker of his intention to do so.

11. Umpires Changing Ends

The umpires shall change ends after each side has had one innings.

12. Disputes

All disputes shall be determined by the umpires, and if they disagree the actual state of things shall continue.

13. Signals

The following code of signals shall be used by umpires who will wait until a signal has been answered by a scorer before allowing the game to proceed.

Boundary	– by waving the arm from side to side.
Boundary 6	– by raising both arms above the head.
Bye	– by raising an open hand above the head.
Dead Ball	– by crossing and re-crossing the wrists below the waist.
Leg-bye	– by touching a raised knee with the hand.
No-ball	– by extending one arm horizontally.
Out	– by raising the index finger above the head. If not out, the umpire shall call "not out".
Short Run	– by bending the arm upwards and by touching the nearer shoulder with the tips of the fingers.
Wide	– by extending both arms horizontally.

14. Correctness of Scores

The umpires shall be responsible for satisfying themselves on the correctness of the scores throughout and at the conclusion of the match. See Law 21.6 (Correctness of Result).

Notes

(a) Attendance of Umpires
The umpires should be present on the ground and report to the ground executive or the equivalent at least 30 minutes before the start of a day's play.

(b) Consultation between Umpires and Scorers
Consultation between umpires and scorers over doubtful points is essential.

(c) Fitness of Ground
The umpires shall consider the ground as unfit for play when it is so wet or slippery as to deprive the bowlers of a reasonable foothold, the fieldsmen, other than the deep-fielders, of the power of free movement, or the batsmen of the ability to play their strokes or to run between the wickets. Play should not be suspended merely because the grass and the ball are wet and slippery.

(d) Fitness of Weather and Light
The umpires should suspend play only when they consider that the conditions are so bad that it is unreasonable or dangerous to continue.

LAW 4.   THE SCORERS

1. Recording Runs

All runs scored shall be recorded by scorers appointed for the purpose. Where there are two scorers they shall frequently check to ensure that the score-sheets agree.

2. Acknowledging Signals

The scorers shall accept and immediately acknowledge all instructions and signals given to them by the umpires.

LAW 5. THE BALL

1. Weight and Size

The ball, when new, shall weigh not less than $5\frac{1}{2}$ ounces/155.9g, nor more than $5\frac{3}{4}$ ounces/163g; and shall measure not less than $8\frac{13}{16}$ inches/22.4cm, nor more than 9 inches/22.9cm in circumference.

2. Approval of Balls

All balls used in matches shall be approved by the umpires and captains before the start of the match.

3. New Ball

Subject to agreement to the contrary, having been made before the toss, either captain may demand a new ball at the start of each innings.

4. New Ball in Match of Three or More Days' Duration

In a match of three or more days' duration, the captain of the fielding side may demand a new ball after the prescribed number of overs has been bowled with the old one. The governing body for cricket in the country concerned shall decide the number of overs applicable in that country, which shall be not less than 75 six-ball overs (55 eight-ball overs).

5. Ball Lost or Becoming Unfit for Play

In the event of a ball during play being lost or, in the opinion of the umpires, becoming unfit for play, the umpires shall allow it to be replaced by one that in their opinion has had a similar amount of wear. If a ball is to be replaced, the umpires shall inform the batsman.

Note

    (a) Specifications
    The specifications, as described in 1 above, shall apply to top-grade balls only. The following degrees of tolerance will be acceptable for other grades of ball.

    (i) *Men's Grades 2–4*
        Weight: $5\frac{5}{16}$ ounces/150g to $5\frac{13}{16}$ ounces/165g.
        Size: $8\frac{11}{16}$ inches/22.0cm to $9\frac{1}{16}$ inches/23.0cm.

    (ii) *Women's*
        Weight: $4\frac{15}{16}$ ounces/140g to $5\frac{5}{16}$ ounces/150g.
        Size: $8\frac{1}{4}$ inches/21.0cm to $8\frac{7}{8}$ inches/22.5cm.

    (iii) *Junior*
        Weight: $4\frac{11}{16}$ ounces/133g to $5\frac{1}{16}$ ounces/143g.
        Size: $8\frac{1}{16}$ inches/20.5cm to $8\frac{11}{16}$ inches/22.0cm.

LAW 6. THE BAT

1. Width and Length

The bat overall shall be not more than 38 inches/96.5cm in length; the blade of the bat shall be made of wood and shall not exceed $4\frac{1}{4}$ inches/10.8cm at the widest part.

Note

    (a) The blade of the bat may be covered with material for protection, strengthening or repair. Such material shall not exceed $\frac{1}{16}$ inch/1.56mm in thickness.

LAW 7. THE PITCH

1. Area of Pitch

The pitch is the area between the bowling creases – see Law 9 (The Bowling and Popping Creases). It shall measure 5 feet/1.52m in width on either side of a line joining the centre of the middle stumps of the wickets – see Law 8 (The Wickets).

2. Selection and Preparation

Before the toss for innings, the executive of the ground shall be responsible for the selection and preparation of the pitch; thereafter the umpires shall control its use and maintenance.

3. Changing Pitch

The pitch shall not be changed during a match unless it becomes unfit for play, and then only with the consent of both captains.

4. Non-Turf Pitches

In the event of a non-turf pitch being used, the following shall apply:

(a) Length: That of the playing surface to a minimum of 58 feet/17.68m.

(b) Width: That of the playing surface to a minimum of 6 feet/1.83m.

See Law 10 (Rolling, Sweeping, Mowing, Watering the Pitch and Re-marking of Creases) Note (a).

LAW 8. THE WICKETS

1. Width and Pitching

Two sets of wickets, each 9 inches/22.86cm wide, and consisting of three wooden stumps with two wooden bails upon the top, shall be pitched opposite and parallel to each other at a distance of 22 yards/20.12m between the centres of the two middle stumps.

2. Size of Stumps

The stumps shall be of equal and sufficient size to prevent the ball from passing between them. Their tops shall be 28 inches/71.1cm above the ground, and shall be dome-shaped except for the bail grooves.

3. Size of Bails

The bails shall be each 4⅜ inches/11.1cm in length and when in position on the top of the stumps shall not project more than ½ inch/1.3cm above them.

Notes

(a) Dispensing with Bails
In a high wind the umpires may decide to dispense with the use of bails.

(b) Junior Cricket
For junior cricket, as defined by the local governing body, the following measurements for the wickets shall apply:

Width – 8 inches/20.32cm.
Pitched – 21 yards/19.20m.
Height – 27 inches/68.58cm.
Bails – each 3⅞ inches/9.84cm in length and should not project more than ½ inch/1.3cm above the stumps.

LAW 9. THE BOWLING, POPPING AND RETURN CREASES

1. The Bowling Crease

The bowling crease shall be marked in line with the stumps at each end and shall be 8 feet 8 inches/2.64m in length, with the stumps in the centre.

2. The Popping Crease

The popping crease, which is the back edge of the crease marking, shall be in front of and parallel with the bowling crease. It shall have the back edge of the crease marking 4 feet/1.22m from the centre of the stumps and shall extend to a minimum of 6 feet/1.83m on either side of the line of the wicket.

The popping crease shall be considered to be unlimited in length.

3. The Return Crease

The return crease marking, of which the inside edge is the crease, shall be at each end of the bowling crease and at right angles to it. The return crease shall be marked to a minimum of 4 feet/1.22m behind the wicket and shall be considered to be unlimited in length. A forward extension shall be marked to the popping crease.

LAW 10.   ROLLING, SWEEPING, MOWING, WATERING THE PITCH AND RE-MARKING OF CREASES

1. Rolling

During the match the pitch may be rolled at the request of the captain of the batting side, for a period of not more than seven minutes before the start of each innings, other than the first innings of the match, and before the start of each day's play. In addition, if, after the toss and before the first innings of the match, the start is delayed, the captain of the batting side may request to have the pitch rolled for not more than seven minutes. However, if in the opinion of the umpires the delay has had no significant effect upon the state of the pitch, they shall refuse any request for the rolling of the pitch.

The pitch shall not otherwise be rolled during the match.

The seven minutes' rolling permitted before the start of a day's play shall take place not earlier than half an hour before the start of play and the captain of the batting side may delay such rolling until ten minutes before the start of play should he so desire.

If a captain declares an innings closed less than 15 minutes before the resumption of play, and the other captain is thereby prevented from exercising his option of seven minutes' rolling or if he is so prevented for any other reason, the time for rolling shall be taken out of the normal playing time.

2. Sweeping

Such sweeping of the pitch as is necessary during the match shall be done so that the seven minutes allowed for rolling the pitch, provided for in 1 above, is not affected.

3. Mowing

(a) Responsibilities of Ground Authority and of Umpires
All mowings which are carried out before the toss for innings shall be the responsibility of the ground authority; thereafter they shall be carried out under the supervision of the umpires. See Law 7.2 (Selection and Preparation).

(b) Initial Mowing
The pitch shall be mown before play begins on the day the match is scheduled to start, or in the case of a delayed start on the day the match is expected to start. See 3(a) above (Responsibilities of Ground Authority and of Umpires).

(c) Subsequent Mowings in a Match of Two or More Days' Duration
In a match of two or more days' duration, the pitch shall be mown daily before play begins. Should this mowing not take place because of weather conditions, rest days or other reasons, the pitch shall be mown on the first day on which the match is resumed.

(d) Mowing of the Outfield in a Match of Two or More Days' Duration
In order to ensure that conditions are as similar as possible for both sides, the outfield shall normally be mown before the commencement of play on each day of the match, if ground and weather conditions allow. See Note (b) to this Law.

4. Watering

The pitch shall not be watered during a match.

5. Re-marking Creases

Whenever possible the creases shall be re-marked.

6. Maintenance of Foot-holes

In wet weather, the umpires shall ensure that the holes made by the bowlers and batsmen are cleaned out and dried whenever necessary to facilitate play. In matches of two or more days' duration, the umpires shall allow, if necessary, the re-turfing of foot-holes made by the bowler in his delivery stride, or the use of quick-setting fillings for the same purpose, before the start of each day's play.

7. Securing of Footholds and Maintenance of Pitch

During play, the umpires shall allow either batsman to beat the pitch with his bat and players to secure their footholds by the use of sawdust, provided that no damage to the pitch is so caused, and Law 42 (Unfair Play) is not contravened.

Notes

(a) Non-turf Pitches
The above Law 10 applies to turf pitches.
   The game is played on non-turf pitches in many countries at various levels. Whilst the conduct of the game on these surfaces should always be in accordance with the Laws of Cricket, it is recognised that it may sometimes be necessary for governing bodies to lay down special playing conditions to suit the type of non-turf pitch used in their country.
   In matches played against touring teams, any special playing conditions should be agreed in advance by both parties.

(b) Mowing of the Outfield in a Match of Two or More Days' Duration
If, for reasons other than ground and weather conditions, daily and complete mowing is not possible, the ground authority shall notify the captains and umpires, before the toss for innings, of the procedure to be adopted for such mowing during the match.

(c) Choice of Roller
If there is more than one roller available, the captain of the batting side shall have a choice.

LAW 11.   COVERING THE PITCH

1. Before the Start of a Match

Before the start of a match, complete covering of the pitch shall be allowed.

2. During a Match

The pitch shall not be completely covered during a match unless prior arrangement or regulations so provide.

3. Covering Bowlers' Run-up

Whenever possible, the bowlers' run-up shall be covered, but the covers so used shall not extend further than 4 feet/1.22m in front of the popping crease.

Note

(a) Removal of Covers
The covers should be removed as promptly as possible whenever the weather permits.

LAW 12.   INNINGS

1. Number of Innings

A match shall be of one or two innings of each side according to agreement reached before the start of play.

2. Alternate Innings

In a two-innings match each side shall take their innings alternately except in the case provided for in Law 13 (The Follow-on).

3. The Toss

The captains shall toss for the choice of innings on the field of play not later than 15 minutes before the time scheduled for the match to start, or before the time agreed upon for play to start.

4. Choice of Innings

The winner of the toss shall notify his decision to bat or to field to the opposing captain not later than ten minutes before the time scheduled for the match to start, or before the time agreed upon for play to start. The decision shall not thereafter be altered.

5. Continuation after One Innings of Each Side

Despite the terms of 1 above, in a one-innings match, when a result has been reached on the first innings, the captains may agree to the continuation of play if, in their opinion, there is a prospect of carrying the game to a further issue in the time left. See Law 21 (Result).

Notes

    (a) Limited Innings – One-innings Match
    In a one-innings match, each innings may, by agreement, be limited by a number of overs or by a period of time.

    (b) Limited Innings – Two-innings Match
    In a two-innings match, the first innings of each side may, by agreement, be limited to a number of overs or by a period of time.

LAW 13.   THE FOLLOW-ON

1. Lead on First Innings

In a two-innings match the side which bats first and leads by 200 runs in a match of five days or more, by 150 runs in a three-day or four-day match, by 100 runs in a two-day match, or by 75 runs in a one-day match, shall have the option of requiring the other side to follow their innings.

2. Day's Play Lost

If no play takes place on the first day of a match of two or more days' duration, 1 above shall apply in accordance with the number of days' play remaining from the actual start of the match.

LAW 14.   DECLARATIONS

1. Time of Declaration

The captain of the batting side may declare an innings closed at any time during a match, irrespective of its duration.

2. Forfeiture of Second Innings

A captain may forfeit his second innings, provided his decision to do so is notified to the opposing captain and umpires in sufficient time to allow seven minutes' rolling of the pitch. See Law 10 (Rolling, Sweeping, Mowing, Watering the Pitch and Re-marking of Creases). The normal ten-minute interval between innings shall be applied.

LAW 15.   START OF PLAY

1. Call of Play

At the start of each innings and of each day's play, and on the resumption of play after any interval or interruption, the umpire at the bowler's end shall call "play".

2. Practice on the Field

At no time on any day of the match shall there be any bowling or batting practice on the pitch.

No practice may take place on the field if, in the opinion of the umpires, it could result in a waste of time.

3. Trial Run-up

No bowler shall have a trial run-up after "play" has been called in any session of play, except at the fall of a wicket when an umpire may allow such a trial run-up if he is satisfied that it will not cause any waste of time.

LAW 16. INTERVALS

1. Length

The umpire shall allow such intervals as have been agreed upon for meals, and ten minutes between each innings.

2. Luncheon Interval – Innings Ending or Stoppage within Ten Minutes of Interval

If an innings ends or there is a stoppage caused by weather or bad light within ten minutes of the agreed time for the luncheon interval, the interval shall be taken immediately.

The time remaining in the session of play shall be added to the agreed length of the interval but no extra allowance shall be made for the ten-minute interval between innings.

3. Tea Interval – Innings Ending or Stoppage within 30 Minutes of Interval

If an innings ends or there is a stoppage caused by weather or bad light within 30 minutes of the agreed time for the tea interval, the interval shall be taken immediately.

The interval shall be of the agreed length and, if applicable, shall include the ten-minute interval between innings.

4. Tea Interval – Continuation of Play

If, at the agreed time for the tea interval, nine wickets are down, play shall continue for a period not exceeding 30 minutes or until the innings is concluded.

5. Tea Interval – Agreement to Forgo

At any time during the match, the captains may agree to forgo a tea interval.

6. Intervals for Drinks

If both captains agree before the start of a match that intervals for drinks may be taken, the option to take such intervals shall be available to either side. These intervals shall be restricted to one per session, shall be kept as short as possible, shall not be taken in the last hour of the match, and in any case shall not exceed five minutes.

The agreed times for these intervals shall be strictly adhered to, except that if a wicket falls within five minutes of the agreed time then drinks shall be taken out immediately.

If an innings ends or there is a stoppage caused by weather or bad light within 30 minutes of the agreed time for a drinks interval, there will be no interval for drinks in that session.

At any time during the match the captains may agree to forgo any such drinks interval.

Notes

(a) Tea Interval – One-day Match
In a one-day match, a specific time for the tea interval need not necessarily be arranged, and it may be agreed to take this interval between the innings of a one-innings match.

(b) Changing the Agreed Time of Intervals
In the event of the ground, weather or light conditions causing a suspension of play, the umpires, after consultation with the captains, may decide in the interests of time-saving to bring forward the time of the luncheon or tea interval.

LAW 17. CESSATION OF PLAY

1. Call of Time

The umpire at the bowler's end shall call "time" on the cessation of play before any interval or interruption of play, at the end of each day's play, and at the conclusion of the match. See Law 27 (Appeals).

2. Removal of Bails

After the call of "time", the umpires shall remove the bails from both wickets.

3. Starting a Last Over

The last over before an interval or the close of play shall be started provided the umpire, after walking at his normal pace, has arrived at his position behind the stumps at the bowler's end before time has been reached.

4. Completion of the Last Over of a Session

The last over before an interval or the close of play shall be completed unless a batsman is out or retires during that over within two minutes of the interval or the close of play or unless the players have occasion to leave the field.

5. Completion of the Last Over of a Match

An over in progress at the close of play on the final day of a match shall be completed at the request of either captain, even if a wicket falls after time has been reached.

If, during the last over, the players have occasion to leave the field, the umpires shall call "time" and there shall be no resumption of play and the match shall be at an end.

6. Last Hour of Match – Number of Overs

The umpires shall indicate when one hour of playing time of the match remains according to the agreed hours of play. The next over after that moment shall be the first of a minimum of 20 six-ball overs (15 eight-ball overs), provided a result is not reached earlier or there is no interval or interruption of play.

7. Last Hour of Match – Intervals between Innings and Interruptions of Play

If, at the commencement of the last hour of the match, an interval or interruption of play is in progress or if, during the last hour, there is an interval between innings or an interruption of play, the minimum number of overs to be bowled on the resumption of play shall be reduced in proportion to the duration, within the last hour of the match, of any such interval or interruption.

The minimum number of overs to be bowled after the resumption of play shall be calculated as follows:

(a) In the case of an interval or interruption of play being in progress at the commencement of the last hour of the match, or in the case of a first interval or interruption, a deduction shall be made from the minimum of 20 six-ball overs (or 15 eight-ball overs).

(b) If there is a later interval or interruption, a further deduction shall be made from the minimum number of overs which should have been bowled following the last resumption of play.

(c) These deductions shall be based on the following factors:

(i) The number of overs already bowled in the last hour of the match or, in the case of a later interval or interruption, in the last session of play.

(ii) The number of overs lost as a result of the interval or interruption allowing one six-ball over for every full three minutes (or one eight-ball over for every full four minutes) of interval or interruption.

(iii) Any over left uncompleted at the end of an innings to be excluded from these calculations.

(iv) Any over of the minimum number to be played which is left uncompleted at the start of an interruption of play to be completed when play is resumed and to count as one over bowled.

(v) An interval to start with the end of an innings and to end ten minutes later; an interruption to start on the call of "time" and to end on the call of "play".

(d) In the event of an innings being completed and a new innings commencing during the last hour of the match, the number of overs to be bowled in the new innings shall be calculated on the basis of one six-ball over for every three minutes or part thereof remaining for play (or one eight-ball over for every four minutes or part thereof remaining for play); or alternatively on the basis that sufficient overs are bowled to enable the full minimum quota of overs to be completed under circumstances governed by (a), (b) and (c) above. In all such cases the alternative which allows the greater number of overs shall be employed.

8. Bowler Unable to Complete an Over during Last Hour of the Match

If, for any reason, a bowler is unable to complete an over during the period of play referred to in 6 above, Law 22.7 (Bowler Incapacitated or Suspended during an Over) shall apply.

LAW 18. SCORING

1. A Run

The score shall be reckoned by runs. A run is scored:

(a) So often as the batsmen, after a hit or at any time while the ball is in play, shall have crossed and made good their ground from end to end.

(b) When a boundary is scored. See Law 19 (Boundaries).

(c) When penalty runs are awarded. See 6 below.

2. Short Runs

(a) If either batsman runs a short run, the umpire shall call and signal "one short" as soon as the ball becomes dead and that run shall not be scored. A run is short if a batsman fails to make good his ground on turning for a further run.

(b) Although a short run shortens the succeeding one, the latter, if completed, shall count.

(c) If either or both batsmen deliberately run short the umpire shall, as soon as he sees that the fielding side have no chance of dismissing either batsman, call and signal "dead ball" and disallow any runs attempted or previously scored. The batsmen shall return to their original ends.

(d) If both batsmen run short in one and the same run, only one run shall be deducted.

(e) Only if three or more runs are attempted can more than one be short and then, subject to (c) and (d) above, all runs so called shall be disallowed. If there has been more than one short run the umpires shall instruct the scorers as to the number of runs disallowed.

3. Striker Caught

If the striker is caught, no run shall be scored.

4. Batsman Run Out

If a batsman is run out, only that run which was being attempted shall not be scored. If, however, an injured striker himself is run out, no runs shall be scored. See Law 2.7 (Transgression of the Laws by an Injured Batsman or Runner).

5. Batsman Obstructing the Field

If a batsman is out Obstructing the Field, any runs completed before the obstruction occurs shall be scored unless such obstruction prevents a catch being made, in which case no runs shall be scored.

6. Runs Scored for Penalties

Runs shall be scored for penalties under Laws 20 (Lost Ball), 24 (No-ball), 25 (Wide-ball), 41.1 (Fielding the Ball) and for boundary allowances under Law 19 (Boundaries).

7. Batsman Returning to Wicket he has Left

If, while the ball is in play, the batsmen have crossed in running, neither shall return to the wicket he has left, even though a short run has been called or no run has been scored as in the case of a catch. Batsmen, however, shall return to the wickets they originally left in the cases of a boundary and of any disallowance of runs and of an injured batsman being, himself, run out. See Law 2.7 (Transgression by an Injured Batsman or Runner).

Note

(a) Short Run
A striker taking stance in front of his popping crease may run from that point without penalty.

LAW 19. BOUNDARIES

1. The Boundary of the Playing Area

Before the toss for innings, the umpires shall agree with both captains on the boundary of the playing area. The boundary shall, if possible, be marked by a white line, a rope laid on the ground, or a fence. If flags or posts only are used to mark a boundary, the imaginary line joining such points shall be regarded as the boundary. An obstacle, or person, within the playing area shall not be regarded as a boundary unless so decided by the umpires before the toss for innings. Sightscreens within, or partially within, the playing area shall be regarded as the boundary and when the ball strikes or passes within or under or directly over any part of the screen, a boundary shall be scored.

2. Runs Scored for Boundaries

Before the toss for innings, the umpires shall agree with both captains the runs to be allowed for boundaries, and in deciding the allowance for them, the umpires and captains shall be guided by the prevailing custom of the ground. The allowance for a boundary shall normally be four runs, and six runs for all hits pitching over and clear of the boundary line or fence, even though the ball has been previously touched by a fieldsman. Six runs shall also be scored if a fieldsman, after catching a ball, carries it over the boundary. See Law 32 (Caught) Note (a). Six runs shall not be scored when a ball struck by the striker hits a sightscreen full pitch if the screen is within, or partially within, the playing area, but if the ball is struck directly over a sightscreen so situated, six runs shall be scored.

3. A Boundary

A boundary shall be scored and signalled by the umpire at the bowler's end whenever, in his opinion:

(a) A ball in play touches or crosses the boundary, however marked.

(b) A fieldsman with ball in hand touches or grounds any part of his person on or over a boundary line.

(c) A fieldsman with ball in hand grounds any part of his person over a boundary fence or board. This allows the fieldsman to touch or lean on or over a boundary fence or board in preventing a boundary.

4. Runs Exceeding Boundary Allowance

The runs completed at the instant the ball reaches the boundary shall count if they exceed the boundary allowance.

5. Overthrows or Wilful Act of a Fieldsman

If the boundary results from an overthrow or from the wilful act of a fieldsman, any runs already completed and the allowance shall be added to the score. The run in progress shall count provided that the batsmen have crossed at the instant of the throw or act.

Note

(a) Position of Sightscreens

Sightscreens should, if possible, be positioned wholly outside the playing area, as near as possible to the boundary line.

LAW 20.   LOST BALL

1. Runs Scored

If a ball in play cannot be found or recovered, any fieldsman may call "lost ball" when six runs shall be added to the score; but if more than six have been run before "lost ball" is called, as many runs as have been completed shall be scored. The run in progress shall count provided that the batsmen have crossed at the instant of the call of "lost ball".

2. How Scored

The runs shall be added to the score of the striker if the ball has been struck, but otherwise to the score of byes, leg-byes, no-balls or wides as the case may be.

LAW 21.   THE RESULT

1. A Win – Two-innings Matches

The side which has scored a total of runs in excess of that scored by the opposing side in its two completed innings shall be the winner.

2. A Win – One-innings Matches

(a) One-innings matches, unless played out as in 1 above, shall be decided on the first innings, but see Law 12.5 (Continuation after One Innings of Each Side).

(b) If the captains agree to continue play after the completion of one innings of each side in accordance with Law 12.5 (Continuation after One Innings of Each Side) and a result is not achieved on the second innings, the first innings result shall stand.

3. Umpires Awarding a Match

(a) A match shall be lost by a side which, during the match, (i) refuses to play, or (ii) concedes defeat, and the umpires shall award the match to the other side.

(b) Should both batsmen at the wickets or the fielding side leave the field at any time without the agreement of the umpires, this shall constitute a refusal to play and, on appeal, the umpires shall award the match to the other side in accordance with (a) above.

4. A Tie

The result of a match shall be a tie when the scores are equal at the conclusion of play, but only if the side batting last has completed its innings.

If the scores of the completed first innings of a one-day match are equal, it shall be a tie but only if the match has not been played out to a further conclusion.

5. A Draw

A match not determined in any of the ways as in 1, 2, 3 and 4 above shall count as a draw.

6. Correctness of Result

Any decision as to the correctness of the scores shall be the responsibility of the umpires. See Law 3.14 (Correctness of Scores).

If, after the umpires and players have left the field in the belief that the match has been concluded, the umpires decide that a mistake in scoring has occurred, which affects the result, and provided time has not been reached, they shall order play to resume and to continue until the agreed finishing time unless a result is reached earlier.

If the umpires decide that a mistake has occurred and time has been reached, the umpires shall immediately inform both captains of the necessary corrections to the scores and, if applicable, to the result.

7. Acceptance of Result

In accepting the scores as notified by the scorers and agreed by the umpires, the captains of both sides thereby accept the result.

Notes

(a) Statement of Results
The result of a finished match is stated as a win by runs, except in the case of a win by the side batting last when it is by the number of wickets still then to fall.

(b) Winning Hit or Extras
As soon as the side has won, see 1 and 2 above, the umpire shall call "time", the match is finished, and nothing that happens thereafter other than as a result of a mistake in scoring (see 6 above) shall be regarded as part of the match.

However, if a boundary constitutes the winning hit – or extras – and the boundary allowance exceeds the number of runs required to win the match, such runs scored shall be credited to the side's total and, in the case of a hit, to the striker's score.

LAW 22.   THE OVER

1. Number of Balls

The ball shall be bowled from each wicket alternately in overs of either six or eight balls according to agreement before the match.

2. Call of "Over"

When the agreed number of balls has been bowled, and as the ball becomes dead or when it becomes clear to the umpire at the bowler's end that both the fielding side and the batsmen at the wicket have ceased to regard the ball as in play, the umpire shall call "over" before leaving the wicket.

3. No-ball or Wide-ball

Neither a no-ball nor a wide-ball shall be reckoned as one of the over.

4. Umpire Miscounting

If an umpire miscounts the number of balls, the over as counted by the umpire shall stand.

5. Bowler Changing Ends

A bowler shall be allowed to change ends as often as desired, provided only that he does not bowl two overs consecutively in an innings.

6. The Bowler Finishing an Over

A bowler shall finish an over in progress unless he be incapacitated or be suspended under Law 42.8 (The Bowling of Fast Short-pitched Balls), 9 (The Bowling of Fast High Full Pitches), 10 (Time Wasting) and 11 (Players Damaging the Pitch). If an over is left incomplete for any reason at the start of an interval or interruption of play, it shall be finished on the resumption of play.

7. Bowler Incapacitated or Suspended during an Over

If, for any reason, a bowler is incapacitated while running up to bowl the first ball of an over, or is incapacitated or suspended during an over, the umpire shall call and signal "dead ball" and another bowler shall be allowed to bowl or complete the over from the same end, provided only that he shall not bowl two overs, or part thereof, consecutively in one innings.

8. Position of Non-striker

The batsman at the bowler's end shall normally stand on the opposite side of the wicket to that from which the ball is being delivered, unless a request to do otherwise is granted by the umpire.

LAW 23. DEAD BALL

1. The Ball Becomes Dead

When:

    (a) It is finally settled in the hands of the wicket-keeper or the bowler.

    (b) It reaches or pitches over the boundary.

    (c) A batsman is out.

    (d) Whether played or not, it lodges in the clothing or equipment of a batsman or the clothing of an umpire.

    (e) A ball lodges in a protective helmet worn by a member of the fielding side.

    (f) A penalty is awarded under Law 20 (Lost Ball) or Law 41.1 (Fielding the Ball).

    (g) The umpire calls "over" or "time".

2. Either Umpire Shall Call and Signal "Dead Ball"

When:

    (a) He intervenes in a case of unfair play.

    (b) A serious injury to a player or umpire occurs.

    (c) He is satisfied that, for an adequate reason, the striker is not ready to receive the ball and makes no attempt to play it.

    (d) The bowler drops the ball accidentally before delivery, or the ball does not leave his hand for any reason other than in an attempt to run out the non-striker (See Law 24.5 – Bowler Attempting to Run Out Non-striker before Delivery).

    (e) One or both bails fall from the striker's wicket before he receives delivery.

    (f) He leaves his normal position for consultation.

    (g) He is required to do so under Law 26.3 (Disallowance of Leg-byes), etc.

3. The Ball Ceases to be Dead

When:

    (a) The bowler starts his run-up or bowling action.

4. The Ball is Not Dead

When:

    (a) It strikes an umpire (unless it lodges in his dress).

    (b) The wicket is broken or struck down (unless a batsman is out thereby).

    (c) An unsuccessful appeal is made.

    (d) The wicket is broken accidentally either by the bowler during his delivery or by a batsman in running.

    (e) The umpire has called "no-ball" or "wide".

Notes

(a) Ball Finally Settled
Whether the ball is finally settled or not – see 1(a) above – must be a question for the umpires alone to decide.

(b) Action on Call of "Dead Ball"
(i) If "dead ball" is called prior to the striker receiving a delivery, the bowler shall be allowed an additional ball.
(ii) If "dead ball" is called after the striker receives a delivery, the bowler shall not be allowed an additional ball, unless a "no-ball" or "wide" has been called.

LAW 24.   NO-BALL

1. Mode of Delivery

The umpire shall indicate to the striker whether the bowler intends to bowl over or round the wicket, overarm or underarm, right or left-handed. Failure on the part of the bowler to indicate in advance a change in his mode of delivery is unfair and the umpire shall call and signal "no-ball".

2. Fair Delivery – The Arm

For a delivery to be fair the ball must be bowled, not thrown – see Note (a) below. If either umpire is not entirely satisfied with the absolute fairness of a delivery in this respect he shall call and signal "no-ball" instantly upon delivery.

3. Fair Delivery – The Feet

The umpire at the bowler's wicket shall call and signal "no-ball" if he is not satisfied that in the delivery stride:

(a) The bowler's back foot has landed within and not touching the return crease or its forward extension; or

(b) Some part of the front foot whether grounded or raised was behind the popping crease.

4. Bowler Throwing at Striker's Wicket before Delivery

If the bowler, before delivering the ball, throws it at the striker's wicket in an attempt to run him out, the umpire shall call and signal "no-ball". See Law 42.12 (Batsman Unfairly Stealing a Run) and Law 38 (Run Out).

5. Bowler Attempting to Run Out Non-striker before Delivery

If the bowler, before delivering the ball, attempts to run out the non-striker, any runs which result shall be allowed and shall be scored as no-balls. Such an attempt shall not count as a ball in the over. The umpire shall not call "no-ball". See Law 42.12 (Batsman Unfairly Stealing a Run).

6. Infringement of Laws by a Wicket-keeper or a Fieldsman

The umpire shall call and signal "no-ball" in the event of the wicket-keeper infringing Law 40.1 (Position of Wicket-keeper) or a fieldsman infringing Law 41.2 (Limitation of On-side Fieldsmen) or Law 41.3 (Position of Fieldsmen).

7. Revoking a Call

An umpire shall revoke the call "no-ball" if the ball does not leave the bowler's hand for any reason. See Law 23.2 (Either Umpire Shall Call and Signal "Dead Ball").

8. Penalty

A penalty of one run for a no-ball shall be scored if no runs are made otherwise.

9. Runs from a No-ball

The striker may hit a no-ball and whatever runs result shall be added to his score. Runs made otherwise from a no-ball shall be scored no-balls.

10. Out from a No-ball

The striker shall be out from a no-ball if he breaks Law 34 (Hit the Ball Twice) and either batsman may be run out or shall be given out if either breaks Law 33 (Handled the Ball) or Law 37 (Obstructing the Field).

11. Batsman Given Out off a No-ball

Should a batsman be given out off a no-ball the penalty for bowling it shall stand unless runs are otherwise scored.

Notes

(a) Definition of a Throw

A ball shall be deemed to have been thrown if, in the opinion of either umpire, the process of straightening the bowling arm, whether it be partial or complete, takes place during that part of the delivery swing which directly precedes the ball leaving the hand. This definition shall not debar a bowler from the use of the wrist in the delivery swing.

(b) No-ball Not Counting in Over

A no-ball shall not be reckoned as one of the over. See Law 22.3 (No-ball or Wide-ball).

LAW 25. WIDE-BALL

1. Judging a Wide

If the bowler bowls the ball so high over or so wide of the wicket that, in the opinion of the umpire, it passes out of reach of the striker, standing in a normal guard position, the umpire shall call and signal "wide-ball" as soon as it has passed the line of the striker's wicket.

The umpire shall not adjudge a ball as being wide if:

(a) The striker, by moving from his guard position, causes the ball to pass out of his reach.

(b) The striker moves and thus brings the ball within his reach.

2. Penalty

A penalty of one run for a wide shall be scored if no runs are made otherwise.

3. Ball Coming to Rest in Front of the Striker

If a ball which the umpire considers to have been delivered comes to rest in front of the line of the striker's wicket, "wide" shall not be called. The striker has a right, without interference from the fielding side, to make one attempt to hit the ball. If the fielding side interfere, the umpire shall replace the ball where it came to rest and shall order the fieldsmen to resume the places they occupied in the field before the ball was delivered.

The umpire shall call and signal "dead ball" as soon as it is clear that the striker does not intend to hit the ball, or after the striker has made an unsuccessful attempt to hit the ball.

4. Revoking a Call

The umpire shall revoke the call if the striker hits a ball which has been called "wide".

5. Ball Not Dead

The ball does not become dead on the call of "wide-ball" – see Law 23.4 (The Ball is Not Dead).

6. Runs Resulting from a Wide

All runs which are run or result from a wide-ball which is not a no-ball shall be scored wide-balls, or if no runs are made one shall be scored.

7. Out from a Wide

The striker shall be out from a wide-ball if he breaks Law 35 (Hit Wicket), or Law 39 (Stumped). Either batsman may be run out and shall be out if he breaks Law 33 (Handled the Ball), or Law 37 (Obstructing the Field).

8. Batsman Given Out off a Wide

Should a batsman be given out off a wide, the penalty for bowling it shall stand unless runs are otherwise made.

Note

    (a) Wide-ball Not Counting in Over
    A wide-ball shall not be reckoned as one of the over – see Law 22.3 (No-ball or Wide-ball).

LAW 26. BYE AND LEG-BYE

1. Byes

If the ball, not having been called "wide" or "no-ball", passes the striker without touching his bat or person, and any runs are obtained, the umpire shall signal "bye" and the run or runs shall be credited as such to the batting side.

2. Leg-byes

If the ball, not having been called "wide" or "no-ball", is unintentionally deflected by the striker's dress or person, except a hand holding the bat, and any runs are obtained the umpire shall signal "leg-bye" and the run or runs so scored shall be credited as such to the batting side.

    Such leg-byes shall be scored only if, in the opinion of the umpire, the striker has:

    (a) Attempted to play the ball with his bat; or

    (b) Tried to avoid being hit by the ball.

3. Disallowance of Leg-byes

In the case of a deflection by the striker's person, other than in 2(a) and (b) above, the umpire shall call and signal "dead ball" as soon as one run has been completed or when it is clear that a run is not being attempted, or the ball has reached the boundary.

    On the call and signal of "dead ball" the batsmen shall return to their original ends and no runs shall be allowed.

LAW 27. APPEALS

1. Time of Appeals

The umpires shall not give a batsman out unless appealed to by the other side which shall be done prior to the bowler beginning his run-up or bowling action to deliver the next ball. Under Law 23.1 (g) (The Ball Becomes Dead), the ball is dead on "over" being called; this does not, however, invalidate an appeal made prior to the first ball of the following over provided "time" has not been called – see Law 17.1 (Call of Time).

2. An Appeal "How's That?"

An appeal "How's That?" shall cover all ways of being out.

3. Answering Appeals

The umpire at the bowler's wicket shall answer appeals before the other umpire in all cases except those arising out of Law 35 (Hit Wicket) or Law 39 (Stumped) or Law 38 (Run Out) when this occurs at the striker's wicket.

When either umpire has given a batsman not out, the other umpire shall, within his jurisdiction, answer the appeal or a further appeal, provided it is made in time in accordance with 1 above (Time of Appeals).

4. Consultation by Umpires

An umpire may consult with the other umpire on a point of fact which the latter may have been in a better position to see and shall then give his decision. If, after consultation, there is still doubt remaining the decision shall be in favour of the batsman.

5. Batsman Leaving his Wicket under a Misapprehension

The umpires shall intervene if satisfied that a batsman, not having been given out, has left his wicket under a misapprehension that he has been dismissed.

6. Umpire's Decision

The umpire's decision is final. He may alter his decision, provided that such alteration is made promptly.

7. Withdrawal of an Appeal

In exceptional circumstances the captain of the fielding side may seek permission of the umpire to withdraw an appeal provided the outgoing batsman has not left the playing area. If this is allowed, the umpire shall cancel his decision.

LAW 28.   THE WICKET IS DOWN

1. Wicket Down

The wicket is down if:

(a) Either the ball or the striker's bat or person completely removes either bail from the top of the stumps. A disturbance of a bail, whether temporary or not, shall not constitute a complete removal, but the wicket is down if a bail in falling lodges between two of the stumps.

(b) Any player completely removes with his hand or arm a bail from the top of the stumps, provided that the ball is held in that hand or in the hand of the arm so used.

(c) When both bails are off, a stump is struck out of the ground by the ball, or a player strikes or pulls a stump out of the ground, providing that the ball is held in the hand(s) or in the hand of the arm so used.

2. One Bail Off

If one bail is off, it shall be sufficient for the purpose of putting the wicket down to remove the remaining bail, or to strike or pull any of the three stumps out of the ground in any of the ways stated in 1 above.

3. All the Stumps Out of the Ground

If all the stumps are out of the ground, the fielding side shall be allowed to put back one or more stumps in order to have an opportunity of putting the wicket down.

4. Dispensing with Bails

If, owing to the strength of the wind, it has been agreed to dispense with the bails in accordance with Law 8, Note (a) (Dispensing with Bails), the decision as to when the wicket is down is one for the umpires to decide on the facts before them. In such circumstances and if the umpires so decide, the wicket shall be held to be down even though a stump has not been struck out of the ground.

Note

(a) Remaking the Wicket

If the wicket is broken while the ball is in play, it is not the umpire's duty to remake the wicket until the ball has become dead – see Law 23 (Dead Ball). A member of the fielding side, however, may remake the wicket in such circumstances.

LAW 29. BATSMAN OUT OF HIS GROUND

1. When out of his Ground

A batsman shall be considered to be out of his ground unless some part of his bat in his hand or of his person is grounded behind the line of the popping crease.

LAW 30. BOWLED

1. Out Bowled

The striker shall be out *Bowled* if:

(a) His wicket is bowled down, even if the ball first touches his bat or person.

(b) He breaks his wicket by hitting or kicking the ball on to it before the completion of a stroke, or as a result of attempting to guard his wicket. See Law 34.1 (Out Hit the Ball Twice).

Note

(a) Out Bowled – Not lbw

The striker is out bowled if the ball is deflected on to his wicket even though a decision against him would be justified under Law 36 (lbw).

LAW 31. TIMED OUT

1. Out Timed Out

An incoming batsman shall be out *Timed Out* if he wilfully takes more than two minutes to come in – the two minutes being timed from the moment a wicket falls until the new batsman steps on to the field of play.

If this is not complied with and if the umpire is satisfied that the delay was wilful and if an appeal is made, the new batsman shall be given out by the umpire at the bowler's end.

2. Time to be Added

The time taken by the umpires to investigate the cause of the delay shall be added at the normal close of play.

Notes

(a) Entry in Scorebook

The correct entry in the scorebook when a batsman is given out under this Law is "timed out", and the bowler does not get credit for the wicket.

(b) Batsmen Crossing on the Field of Play

It is an essential duty of the captains to ensure that the in-going batsman passes the out-going one before the latter leaves the field of play.

LAW 32.   CAUGHT

1. Out Caught

The striker shall be out *Caught* if the ball touches his bat or if it touches below the wrist his hand or glove, holding the bat, and is subsequently held by a fieldsman before it touches the ground.

2. A Fair Catch

A catch shall be considered to have been fairly made if:

    (a) The fieldsman is within the field of play throughout the act of making the catch.

        (i) The act of making the catch shall start from the time when the fieldsman first handles the ball and shall end when he both retains complete control over the further disposal of the ball and remains within the field of play.

        (ii) In order to be within the field of play, the fieldsman may not touch or ground any part of his person on or over a boundary line. When the boundary is marked by a fence or board the fieldsman may not ground any part of his person over the boundary fence or board, but may touch or lean over the boundary fence or board in completing the catch.

    (b) The ball is hugged to the body of the catcher or accidentally lodges in his dress or, in the case of the wicket-keeper, in his pads. However, a striker may not be caught if a ball lodges in a protective helmet worn by a fieldsman, in which case the umpire shall call and signal "dead ball". See Law 23 (Dead Ball).

    (c) The ball does not touch the ground even though a hand holding it does so in effecting the catch.

    (d) A fieldsman catches the ball, after it has been lawfully played a second time by the striker, but only if the ball has not touched the ground since being first struck.

    (e) A fieldsman catches the ball after it has touched an umpire, another fieldsman or the other batsman. However, a striker may not be caught if a ball has touched a protective helmet worn by a fieldsman.

    (f) The ball is caught off an obstruction within the boundary provided it has not previously been agreed to regard the obstruction as a boundary.

3. Scoring of Runs

If a striker is caught, no run shall be scored.

Notes

(a) Scoring from an Attempted Catch

When a fieldsman carrying the ball touches or grounds any part of his person on or over a boundary marked by a line, six runs shall be scored.

(b) Ball Still in Play

If a fieldsman releases the ball before he crosses the boundary, the ball will be considered to be still in play and it may be caught by another fieldsman. However, if the original fieldsman returns to the field of play and handles the ball, a catch may not be made.

LAW 33.   HANDLED THE BALL

1. Out Handled the Ball

Either batsman on appeal shall be out *Handled the Ball* if he wilfully touches the ball while in play with the hand not holding the bat unless he does so with the consent of the opposite side.

Note

(a) Entry in Scorebook

The correct entry in the scorebook when a batsman is given out under this Law is "handled the ball', and the bowler does not get credit for the wicket.

LAW 34. HIT THE BALL TWICE

1. Out Hit the Ball Twice

The striker, on appeal, shall be out *Hit the Ball Twice* if, after the ball is struck or is stopped by any part of his person, he wilfully strikes it again with his bat or person except for the sole purpose of guarding his wicket: this he may do with his bat or any part of his person other than his hands, but see Law 37.2 (Obstructing a Ball From Being Caught).

For the purpose of this Law, a hand holding the bat shall be regarded as part of the bat.

2. Returning the Ball to a Fieldsman

The striker, on appeal, shall be out under this Law if, without the consent of the opposite side, he uses his bat or person to return the ball to any of the fielding side.

3. Runs from Ball Lawfully Struck Twice

No runs except those which result from an overthrow or penalty – see Law 41 (The Fieldsman) – shall be scored from a ball lawfully struck twice.

Notes

(a) Entry in Scorebook
The correct entry in the scorebook when the striker is given out under this Law is "hit the ball twice", and the bowler does not get credit for the wicket.

(b) Runs Credited to the Batsman
Any runs awarded under 3 above as a result of an overthrow or penalty shall be credited to the striker, provided the ball in the first instance has touched the bat, or, if otherwise, as extras.

LAW 35. HIT WICKET

1. Out Hit Wicket

The striker shall be out *Hit Wicket* if, while the ball is in play:

(a) His wicket is broken with any part of his person, dress, or equipment as a result of any action taken by him in preparing to receive or in receiving a delivery, or in setting off for his first run, immediately after playing, or playing at, the ball.

(b) He hits down his wicket whilst lawfully making a second stroke for the purpose of guarding his wicket within the provisions of Law 34.1 (Out Hit the Ball Twice).

Notes

(a) Not Out Hit Wicket
A batsman is not out under this Law should his wicket be broken in any of the ways referred to in 1(a) above if:
(i) It occurs while he is in the act of running, other than in setting off for his first run immediately after playing at the ball, or while he is avoiding being run out or stumped.
(ii) The bowler after starting his run-up or bowling action does not deliver the ball; in which case the umpire shall immediately call and signal "dead ball".
(iii) It occurs whilst he is avoiding a throw-in at any time.

LAW 36. LEG BEFORE WICKET

1. Out lbw

The striker shall be out *lbw* in the circumstances set out below:

(a) Striker Attempting to Play the Ball
The striker shall be out lbw if he first intercepts with any part of his person, dress or equipment a fair ball which would have hit the wicket and which has not previously touched his bat or a hand holding the bat, provided that:

    (i) The ball pitched in a straight line between wicket and wicket or on the off side of the striker's wicket, or was intercepted full pitch; and

    (ii) The point of impact is in a straight line between wicket and wicket, even if above the level of the bails.

(b) Striker Making No Attempt to Play the Ball

The striker shall be out lbw even if the ball is intercepted outside the line of the off stump if, in the opinion of the umpire, he has made no genuine attempt to play the ball with his bat, but has intercepted the ball with some part of his person and if the other circumstances set out in (a) above apply.

LAW 37. OBSTRUCTING THE FIELD

1. Wilful Obstruction

Either batsman, on appeal, shall be out *Obstructing the Field* if he wilfully obstructs the opposite side by word or action.

2. Obstructing a Ball From Being Caught

The striker, on appeal, shall be out should wilful obstruction by either batsman prevent a catch being made.

    This shall apply even though the striker causes the obstruction in lawfully guarding his wicket under the provisions of Law 34. See Law 34.1 (Out Hit the Ball Twice).

Notes

    (a) Accidental Obstruction

    The umpires must decide whether the obstruction was wilful or not. The accidental interception of a throw-in by a batsman while running does not break this Law.

    (b) Entry in Scorebook

    The correct entry in the scorebook when a batsman is given out under this Law is "obstructing the field", and the bowler does not get credit for the wicket.

LAW 38. RUN OUT

1. Out Run Out

Either batsman shall be out *Run Out* if in running or at any time while the ball is in play – except in the circumstances described in Law 39 (Stumped) – he is out of his ground and his wicket is put down by the opposite side. If, however, a batsman in running makes good his ground he shall not be out run out if he subsequently leaves his ground, in order to avoid injury, and the wicket is put down.

2. "No-ball" Called

If a no-ball has been called, the striker shall not be given run out unless he attempts to run.

3. Which Batsman Is Out

If the batsmen have crossed in running, he who runs for the wicket which is put down shall be out; if they have not crossed, he who has left the wicket which is put down shall be out. If a batsman remains in his ground or returns to his ground and the other batsman joins him there, the latter shall be out if his wicket is put down.

4. Scoring of Runs

If a batsman is run out, only that run which is being attempted shall not be scored. If, however, an injured striker himself is run out, no runs shall be scored. See Law 2.7 (Transgression of the Laws by an Injured Batsman or Runner).

Notes

    (a) Ball Played on to Opposite Wicket

    If the ball is played on to the opposite wicket, neither batsman is liable to be run out unless the ball has been touched by a fieldsman before the wicket is broken.

(b) Entry in Scorebook

The correct entry in the scorebook when a batsman is given out under this Law is "run out", and the bowler does not get credit for the wicket.

(c) Run Out off a Fieldsman's Helmet

If, having been played by a batsman, or having come off his person, the ball rebounds directly from a fieldsman's helmet on to the stumps, with either batsman out of his ground, the batsman shall be "not out".

LAW 39. STUMPED

1. Out Stumped

The striker shall be out *Stumped* if, in receiving the ball, not being a no-ball, he is out of his ground otherwise than in attempting a run and the wicket is put down by the wicket-keeper without the intervention of another fieldsman.

2. Action by the Wicket-keeper

The wicket-keeper may take the ball in front of the wicket in an attempt to stump the striker only if the ball has touched the bat or person of the striker.

Note

(a) Ball Rebounding from Wicket-keeper's Person

The striker may be out stumped if, in the circumstances stated in 1 above, the wicket is broken by a ball rebounding from the wicket-keeper's person or equipment other than a protective helmet or is kicked or thrown by the wicket-keeper on to the wicket.

LAW 40. THE WICKET-KEEPER

1. Position of Wicket-keeper

The wicket-keeper shall remain wholly behind the wicket until a ball delivered by the bowler touches the bat or person of the striker, or passes the wicket, or until the striker attempts a run.

In the event of the wicket-keeper contravening this Law, the umpire at the striker's end shall call and signal "no-ball" at the instant of delivery or as soon as possible thereafter.

2. Restriction on Actions of the Wicket-keeper

If the wicket-keeper interferes with the striker's right to play the ball and to guard his wicket, the striker shall not be out except under Laws 33 (Handled the Ball), 34 (Hit the Ball Twice), 37 (Obstructing the Field) and 38 (Run Out).

3. Interference with the Wicket-keeper by the Striker

If, in the legitimate defence of his wicket, the striker interferes with the wicket-keeper, he shall not be out, except as provided for in Law 37.2 (Obstructing a Ball From Being Caught).

LAW 41. THE FIELDSMAN

1. Fielding the Ball

The fieldsman may stop the ball with any part of his person, but if he wilfully stops it otherwise, five runs shall be added to the run or runs already scored; if no run has been scored five penalty runs shall be awarded. The run in progress shall count provided that the batsmen have crossed at the instant of the act. If the ball has been struck, the penalty shall be added to the score of the striker, but otherwise to the score of byes, leg-byes, no-balls or wides as the case may be.

2. Limitation of On-side Fieldsmen

The number of on-side fieldsmen behind the popping crease at the instant of the bowler's delivery shall not exceed two. In the event of infringement by the fielding side the umpire at the striker's end shall call and signal "no-ball" at the instant of delivery or as soon as possible thereafter.

3. Position of Fieldsmen

Whilst the ball is in play and until the ball has made contact with the bat or the striker's person or has passed his bat, no fieldsman, other than the bowler, may stand on or have any part of his person extended over the pitch (measuring 22 yards/20.12m × 10 feet/3.05m). In the event of a fieldsman contravening this Law, the umpire at the bowler's end shall call and signal "no-ball" at the instant of delivery or as soon as possible thereafter. See Law 40.1 (Position of Wicket-keeper).

4. Fieldsmen's Protective Helmets

Protective helmets, when not in use by members of the fielding side, shall be placed, if above the surface, only on the ground behind the wicket-keeper. In the event of the ball, when in play, striking a helmet whilst in this position, five penalty runs shall be awarded as laid down in Law 41.1 and Note (a).

Note

(a) **Batsmen Changing Ends**
The five runs referred to in 1 and 4 above are a penalty and the batsmen do not change ends solely by reason of this penalty.

LAW 42.   UNFAIR PLAY

1. Responsibility of Captains

The captains are responsible at all times for ensuring that play is conducted within the spirit of the game as well as within the Laws.

2. Responsibility of Umpires

The umpires are the sole judges of fair and unfair play.

3. Intervention by the Umpire

The umpires shall intervene without appeal by calling and signalling "dead ball" in the case of unfair play, but should not otherwise interfere with the progress of the game except as required to do so by the Laws.

4. Lifting the Seam

A player shall not lift the seam of the ball for any reason. Should this be done, the umpires shall change the ball for one of similar condition to that in use prior to the contravention. See Note (a).

5. Changing the Condition of the Ball

Any member of the fielding side may polish the ball provided that such polishing wastes no time and that no artificial substance is used. No one shall rub the ball on the ground or use any artificial substance or take any other action to alter the condition of the ball.

In the event of a contravention of this Law, the umpires, after consultation, shall change the ball for one of similar condition to that in use prior to the contravention.

This Law does not prevent a member of the fielding side from drying a wet ball, or removing mud from the ball. See Note (b).

6. Incommoding the Striker

An umpire is justified in intervening under this Law and shall call and signal "dead ball" if, in his opinion, any player of the fielding side incommodes the striker by any noise or action while he is receiving a ball.

7. Obstruction of a Batsman in Running

It shall be considered unfair if any fieldsman wilfully obstructs a batsman in running. In these circumstances the umpire shall call and signal "dead ball" and allow any completed runs and the run in progress, or alternatively any boundary scored.

8. The Bowling of Fast Short-pitched Balls

The bowling of fast short-pitched balls is unfair if, in the opinion of the umpire at the bowler's end, it constitutes an attempt to intimidate the striker. See Note (d).

Umpires shall consider intimidation to be the deliberate bowling of fast short-pitched balls which by their length, height and direction are intended or likely to inflict physical injury on the striker. The relative skill of the striker shall also be taken into consideration.

In the event of such unfair bowling, the umpire at the bowler's end shall adopt the following procedure:

(a) In the first instance the umpire shall call and signal "no-ball", caution the bowler and inform the other umpire, the captain of the fielding side and the batsmen of what has occurred.

(b) If this caution is ineffective, he shall repeat the above procedure and indicate to the bowler that this is a final warning.

(c) Both the above caution and final warning shall continue to apply even though the bowler may later change ends.

(d) Should the above warnings prove ineffective the umpire at the bowler's end shall:

   (i) At the first repetition call and signal "no-ball" and when the ball is dead direct the captain to take the bowler off forthwith and to complete the over with another bowler, provided that the bowler does not bowl two overs or part thereof consecutively. See Law 22.7 (Bowler Incapacitated or Suspended during an Over).

   (ii) Not allow the bowler, thus taken off, to bowl again in the same innings.

   (iii) Report the occurrence to the captain of the batting side as soon as the players leave the field for an interval.

   (iv) Report the occurrence to the executive of the fielding side and to any governing body responsible for the match, who shall take any further action which is considered to be appropriate against the bowler concerned.

9. The Bowling of Fast High Full Pitches

The bowling of fast high full pitches is unfair.

A fast high full-pitched ball is defined as a ball that passes, or would have passed, on the full above waist height of a batsman standing upright at the crease. Should a bowler bowl a fast high full-pitched ball, either umpire shall call and signal "no-ball" and adopt the procedure of caution, final warning, action against the bowler and reporting as set out in Law 42.8.

10. Time Wasting

Any form of time wasting is unfair.

(a) In the event of the captain of the fielding side wasting time or allowing any member of his side to waste time, the umpire at the bowler's end shall adopt the following procedure:

   (i) In the first instance he shall caution the captain of the fielding side and inform the other umpire of what has occurred.

   (ii) If this caution is ineffective he shall repeat the above procedure and indicate to the captain that this is a final warning.

   (iii) The umpire shall report the occurrence to the captain of the batting side as soon as the players leave the field for an interval.

   (iv) Should the above procedure prove ineffective the umpire shall report the occurrence to the executive of the fielding side and to any governing body responsible for that match, who shall take appropriate action against the captain and the players concerned.

(b) In the event of a bowler taking unnecessarily long to bowl an over the umpire at the bowler's end shall adopt the procedures, other than the calling of "no-ball", of caution, final warning, action against the bowler and reporting as set out in 8 above.

(c) In the event of a batsman wasting time (See Note (e)) other than in the manner described in Law 31 (Timed Out), the umpire at the bowler's end shall adopt the following procedure:

(i) In the first instance he shall caution the batsman and inform the other umpire at once, and the captain of the batting side, as soon as the players leave the field for an interval, of what has occurred.

(ii) If this proves ineffective, he shall repeat the caution, indicate to the batsman that this is a final warning and inform the other umpire.

(iii) The umpire shall report the occurrence to both captains as soon as the players leave the field for an interval.

(iv) Should the above procedure prove ineffective, the umpire shall report the occurrence to the executive of the batting side and to any governing body responsible for that match, who shall take appropriate action against the player concerned.

11. Players Damaging the Pitch

The umpires shall intervene and prevent players from causing damage to the pitch which may assist the bowlers of either side. See Note (c).

(a) In the event of any member of the fielding side damaging the pitch, the umpire shall follow the procedure of caution, final warning and reporting as set out in 10(a) above.

(b) In the event of a bowler contravening this Law by running down the pitch after delivering the ball, the umpire at the bowler's end shall first caution the bowler. If this caution is ineffective the umpire shall adopt the procedures, other than the calling of "no-ball", as set out in 8 above.

(c) In the event of a batsman damaging the pitch the umpire at the bowler's end shall follow the procedures of caution, final warning and reporting as set out in 10(c) above.

12. Batsman Unfairly Stealing a Run

Any attempt by the batsman to steal a run during the bowler's run-up is unfair. Unless the bowler attempts to run out either batsman – see Law 24.4 (Bowler Throwing at Striker's Wicket before Delivery) and Law 24.5 (Bowler Attempting to Run Out Non-striker before Delivery) – the umpire shall call and signal "dead ball" as soon as the batsmen cross in any such attempt to run. The batsmen shall then return to their original wickets.

13. Player's Conduct

In the event of a player failing to comply with the instructions of an umpire, criticising his decisions by word or action, or showing dissent, or generally behaving in a manner which might bring the game into disrepute, the umpire concerned shall, in the first place, report the matter to the other umpire and to the player's captain, requesting the latter to take action. If this proves ineffective, the umpire shall report the incident as soon as possible to the executive of the player's team and to any governing body responsible for the match, who shall take any further action which is considered appropriate against the player or players concerned.

Notes

(a) **The Condition of the Ball**
Umpires shall make frequent and irregular inspections of the condition of the ball.

(b) **Drying of a Wet Ball**
A wet ball may be dried on a towel or with sawdust.

(c) **Danger Area**
The danger area on the pitch, which must be protected from damage by a bowler, shall be regarded by the umpires as the area contained by an imaginary line 4 feet/1.22m from the popping crease, and parallel to it, and within two imaginary and parallel lines drawn down the pitch from points on that line 1 foot/30.48cm on either side of the middle stump.

(d) Fast Short-pitched Balls

As a guide, a fast short-pitched ball is one which pitches short and passes, or would have passed, above the shoulder height of the striker standing in a normal batting stance at the crease.

(e) Time Wasting by Batsmen

Other than in exceptional circumstances, the batsman should always be ready to take strike when the bowler is ready to start his run-up.

REGULATIONS OF THE INTERNATIONAL CRICKET COUNCIL

Extracts

1. Standard Playing Conditions

In July 1995, ICC Full Members adopted standard playing conditions to apply to all Tests and one-day internationals for an initial three-year period. These include the following:

Duration of Test Matches

Test matches shall be of five days' scheduled duration. The two participating countries may:

(a) Provide for a rest day during the match.

(b) Play on any scheduled rest day, conditions and circumstances permitting, should a full day's play be lost on any day prior to the rest day.

(c) Make up time lost in excess of five minutes in each day's play owing to circumstances outside the game, other than acts of God.

Hours of Play and Minimum Overs in the Day in Test Matches

1. Start and cessation times shall be determined by the home board, subject to there being six hours scheduled for play per day (Pakistan a minimum of five and a half hours).

(a) Play shall continue on each day until the completion of a minimum number of overs or until the scheduled or rescheduled cessation time, whichever is the later. The minimum number of overs to be completed, unless an innings ends or an interruption occurs, shall be:

(i) on days other than the last day – a minimum of 90 overs.

(ii) on the last day – a minimum of 75 overs (or 15 overs per hour) for playing time other than the last hour when a minimum of 15 six-ball overs shall be bowled. All calculations with regard to suspensions of play or the start of a new innings shall be based on one over for each full four minutes. If, however, at any time after 30 minutes of the last hour have elapsed both captains (the batsmen at the wicket may act for their captain) accept that there is no prospect of a result to the match, they may agree to cease play at that time.

Subject to weather and light, except in the last hour of the match, in the event of play being suspended for any reason other than normal intervals, the playing time on that day shall be extended by the amount of time lost up to a maximum of one hour. The minimum number of overs to be bowled shall be in accordance with the provisions of this clause and the cessation time shall be rescheduled accordingly.

(b) When an innings ends, a minimum number of overs shall be bowled from the start of the new innings. The number of overs to be bowled shall be calculated at the rate of one over for each full four minutes to enable a minimum of 90 overs to be bowled in a day, and the time for close of play shall be rescheduled accordingly. The last hour of the match shall be excluded from this calculation (see (a) (ii)).

2. Either captain may decide to play 30 minutes (a minimum eight overs) extra time at the end of any day other than the last day if, in their opinion, it would bring about a definite result on that day. If it is decided to play such extra time, the whole period shall be played out even though the possibility of finishing the match may have disappeared before the full period has expired. The time by which play is extended on any day shall be deducted from the total number of hours of play remaining and the match shall end earlier on the final day by that amount of time.

The Bowling of Fast, Short-Pitched Balls: Law 42.8. Experimental Regulation for Test matches only for three years with effect from October 1, 1994

1. A bowler shall be limited to two fast, short-pitched deliveries per over.

2. A fast, short-pitched ball is defined as a ball which passes or would have passed above the shoulder height of the batsman standing upright at the crease.

3. In the event of a bowler bowling more than two fast, short-pitched deliveries in an over, either umpire shall call and signal "no-ball" on each occasion.

4. The penalty for a fast, short-pitched no-ball shall be two runs, plus any runs scored from the delivery.

5. The umpire shall call and signal "no-ball" and then raise the other arm across the chest.

Where a bowler delivers a third fast, short-pitched ball in one over which is also a no-ball under Law 24, e.g. a front-foot no-ball, the penalty will be two runs plus any runs scored from that delivery, i.e. the greater penalty will apply. The umpire shall also adopt the procedures of caution, final warning, action against the bowler and reporting as set out in Law 42.8.

The above Regulation is not a substitute for Law 42.8 (as amended below), which umpires are able to apply at any time:

The bowling of fast, short-pitched balls is unfair if the umpire at the bowler's end considers that, by their repetition and taking into account their length, height and direction, they are likely to inflict physical injury on the striker, irrespective of the protective clothing and equipment he may be wearing. The relative skill of the striker shall also be taken into consideration.

The umpire at the bowler's end shall adopt the procedures of caution, final warning, action against the bowler and reporting as set out in Law 42.8.

New Ball: Law 5.4

The captain of the fielding side shall have the choice of taking a new ball any time after 80 overs have been bowled with the previous ball.

Ball Lost or Becoming Unfit for Play: Law 5.5

In the event of a ball during play being lost or, in the opinion of the umpires, being unfit for play through normal use, the umpires shall allow it to be replaced by one that in their opinion has had a similar amount of wear. If the ball is to be replaced, the umpires shall inform the batsmen.

Practice on the Field: Law 15.2

At no time on any day of the match shall there be any bowling or batting practice on the pitch or the square, except in official netted practice pitch areas. In addition there shall be no bowling or batting practice on any part of the square or the area immediately parallel to the match pitch after the commencement of play on any day. Any fielder contravening this Law may not bowl the next over.

No practice may take place on the field if, in the opinion of the umpires, it could result in a waste of time.

Fieldsman Leaving the Field: Law 2.8

No fieldsman shall leave the field or return during a session of play without the consent of the umpire at the bowler's end. The umpire's consent is also necessary if a substitute is required for a fieldsman at the start of play or when his side returns to the field after an interval.

If a member of the fielding side does not take the field at the start of play, leaves the field, or fails to return after an interval and is absent from the field longer than 15 minutes, he shall not be permitted to bowl in that innings after his return until he has been on the field for at least that length of playing time for which he was absent. In the event of a follow-on, this restriction will, if necessary, continue into the second innings. Nor shall he be permitted to bat unless or until, in the aggregate, he has returned to the field and/or his side's innings has been in progress for at least that length of playing time for which he has been absent or, if earlier, when his side has lost five wickets. The restrictions shall not apply if he has suffered an external blow (as opposed to an internal injury such as a pulled muscle) while participating earlier in the match and consequently been forced to leave the field, nor if he has been absent for exceptional and acceptable reasons (other than injury or illness) and consent for a substitute has been granted by the opposing captain.

2. Classification of First-Class Matches

1. Definitions

A match of three or more days' duration between two sides of 11 players officially adjudged first-class shall be regarded as a first-class fixture.

2. Rules

   (a) Full Members of ICC shall decide the status of matches of three or more days' duration played in their countries.

   (b) In matches of three or more days' duration played in countries which are not Full Members of ICC:

      (i) If the visiting team comes from a country which is a Full Member of ICC, that country shall decide the status of matches.

      (ii) If the visiting team does not come from a country which is a Full Member of ICC, or is a Commonwealth team composed of players from different countries, ICC shall decide the status of matches.

Notes

   (a) Governing bodies agree that the interest of first-class cricket will be served by ensuring that first-class status is *not* accorded to any match in which one or other of the teams taking part cannot on a strict interpretation of the definition be adjudged first-class.

   (b) In case of any disputes arising from these Rules, the Chief Executive of ICC shall refer the matter for decision to the Council, failing unanimous agreement by postal communication being reached.

3. First-Class Status

The following matches shall be regarded as first-class, subject to the provisions of 2.1 (Definitions) being complied with:

   (a) **In Great Britain and Ireland:** (i) County Championship matches. (ii) Official representative tourist matches from Full Member countries unless specifically excluded. (iii) MCC v any first-class county. (iv) Oxford v Cambridge and either University against first-class counties. (v) Scotland v Ireland.

   (b) **In Australia:** (i) Sheffield Shield matches. (ii) Matches played by teams representing states of the Commonwealth of Australia between each other or against opponents adjudged first-class.

   (c) **In India:** (i) Ranji Trophy matches. (ii) Duleep Trophy matches. (iii) Irani Trophy matches. (iv) Matches played by teams representing state or regional associations affiliated to the Board of Control between each other or against opponents adjudged first-class. (v) All three-day matches played against representative visiting sides.

   (d) **In New Zealand:** (i) Shell Trophy matches. (ii) Matches played by teams representing major associations of the North and South Islands, between each other or against opponents adjudged first-class.

(e) **In Pakistan:** (i) Matches played by teams representing divisional associations affiliated to the Board of Control, between each other or against teams adjudged first-class. (ii) Quaid-e-Azam Trophy matches. (iii) BCCP Patron's Trophy matches. (iv) BCCP Pentangular Trophy matches.

(f) **In South Africa:** (i) Castle Cup competition four-day matches between Transvaal, Northern Transvaal, OFS, Western Province, Eastern Province, Border, Natal and Boland. (ii) The United Cricket Board Bowl competition three-day matches between Eastern Transvaal, Western Transvaal, Griqualand West, the Zimbabwe Board XI and the B teams of the Castle Cup provinces.

(g) **In Sri Lanka:** (i) Matches of three days or more against touring sides adjudged first-class. (ii) Singer Inter-Provincial Cricket tournament matches played over four days for the President's Trophy. (iii) Inter-Club Division I tournament matches played over three days for the P. Saravanamuttu Trophy.

(h) **In West Indies:** Matches played by teams representing Barbados, Guyana, Jamaica, Trinidad & Tobago, the Windward Islands and the Leeward Islands, either for the Red Stripe Cup or against other opponents adjudged first-class.

(i) **In Zimbabwe:** (i) Matches of three days or more against touring sides adjudged first-class. (ii) Logan Cup competition three-day matches between Mashonaland, Mashonaland Country Districts, Mashonaland Under-24 and Matabeleland.

(j) **In all Full Member countries represented on the Council:** (i) Test matches and matches against teams adjudged first-class played by official touring teams. (ii) Official Test Trial matches. (iii) Special matches between teams adjudged first-class by the governing body or bodies concerned.

3. Classification of One-Day International Matches

The following should be classified as one-day internationals:

(a) All matches played between the Full Member countries of ICC as part of an official tour itinerary.

(b) All matches played as part of an official tournament by Full Member countries. These need not necessarily be held in a Full Member country.

(c) All matches played in the official World Cup competition, including matches involving Associate Member countries.

(d) All matches played in the Asia Cup and Austral-Asia Cup competitions.

Note: ICC ruled that matches involving Australia A in the 1994-95 World Series should not be regarded as official internationals.

4. Qualification Rules for Test Matches and One-Day International Matches

Qualification by Birth

A cricketer is qualified to play in Tests, one-day internationals or any other representative cricket match for the country of his birth provided he has not played in Tests, one-day internationals or, after October 1, 1994, in any other representative cricket match for any other Member country during the two immediately preceding years.

Qualification by Residence

A cricketer is qualified to play in Tests, one-day internationals or in any other representative cricket match for any Full or Associate Member country in which he has resided for at least 183 days in each of the four immediately preceding years provided that he has not played in Tests, one-day internationals or, after October 1, 1994, in any other representative cricket match for any other Member country during that period of four years.

Notes: "Representative cricket match" means any cricket match in which a team representing a Member country at Under-19 level or above takes part, including Tests and one-day internationals.

The governing body for cricket of any Member country may impose more stringent qualification rules for that country.

ICC CODE OF CONDUCT

1. The captains are responsible at all times for ensuring that play is conducted within the spirit of the game as well as within the Laws.

2. Players and team officials shall not at any time engage in conduct unbecoming to an international player or team official which could bring them or the game into disrepute.

3. Players and team officials must at all times accept the umpire's decision. Players must not show dissent at the umpire's decision.

4. Players and team officials shall not intimidate, assault or attempt to intimidate or assault an umpire, another player or a spectator.

5. Players and team officials shall not use crude or abusive language (known as "sledging") nor make offensive gestures.

6. Players and team officials shall not use or in any way be concerned in the use or distribution of illegal drugs.

7. Players and team officials shall not disclose or comment upon any alleged breach of the Code or upon any hearing, report or decision arising from such breach.

8. Players and team officials shall not make any public pronouncement or media comment which is detrimental either to the game in general; or to a particular tour in which they are involved; or about any tour between other countries which is taking place; or to relations between the Boards of the competing teams.

9. Players and team officials shall not engage, directly or indirectly, in betting, gambling or any form of financial speculation on the outcome of any cricket match to which this Code applies and in which the player is a participant or with which a team official is associated or on any event which, in the opinion of the referee, shall be connected with any such cricket match the purpose (or pretended purpose) of which is to benefit such player or team official either directly or indirectly whether financially or otherwise. Players and team officials shall not accept any form of inducement which is considered by the referee to be likely to affect the performance of any player involved in any such cricket match adversely.

Application, Interpretation and Enforcement of the Code

1. The Code shall apply:

    (a) To players and, where applicable, to team officials of both teams for all Test matches and one-day international matches;

    (b) To players and, where applicable, to team officials of official touring teams for all matches, other than Test matches and one-day internationals ("other matches") with such modifications as ICC shall consider necessary in the absence of a referee for other matches.

2. The Code shall also apply to Associate and Affiliate members of ICC although its application, interpretation and enforcement shall be determined in the way deemed most suitable by those concerned with the running of the game at these levels.

3. Breaches of the Code shall be deemed also to include a breach of any ICC Regulation in force from time to time, including (without limitation) those relating to advertising on cricket clothing and equipment, and, in Test matches, those relating to minimum over-rates.

4. The Code, breach of which may render a player or team official liable to disciplinary action, shall be enforced:

    (a) In the case of Test matches and one-day internationals in accordance with procedures and guidelines laid down for the referee; and

(b) In the case of other matches, in such manner as ICC shall consider appropriate at the time when the incident occurs. This shall, so far as is practicable, follow the procedures and guidelines laid down for the referee.

Note: A breach of Clause 8 of the Code of Conduct (public pronouncements) should be dealt with by referees during a tour (except where related to a non-international match) and the home board of the player or official concerned in other circumstances.

ICC MATCH REFEREE

Extracts

1. Objective

To act on behalf of ICC:

(a) to see that the full implications of Law 42.1 are properly understood and upheld; and

(b) to ensure that the spirit of the game is observed and the conduct of the game maintained during Test matches and one-day internationals by players, umpires and team officials, either on or off the field, his responsibility being confined to the precincts of the ground.

2. Terms of Reference

(a) To be the independent representative of ICC (appointed by the Chairman or the Chief Executive, after consultation with the Boards concerned), at all Test matches and one-day internationals, the latter being part of a Test match tour, respecting the authority of the host country which is promoting a series, or the ground authority which is administering a match or series of matches.

(b) To liaise with the appointed umpires, but not in any way to interfere with their traditional role.

(c) To carry out the following duties:

(i) Observe and adjudicate upon breaches of the Code of Conduct.

(ii) Impose penalties for failure to maintain the minimum over-rate as set by ICC (at present 15 overs per hour).

(iii) Impose penalties for deliberate acts of unfair play, e.g. the deliberate slowing-down of over-rates and the deliberate speeding-up of overs to make up for any shortfall during a day's play.

(iv) Impose penalties for infringements of the ICC Regulation relating to advertising on cricket clothing and equipment.

(v) Impose penalties incurred under any other ICC Regulation which may be passed from time to time and which falls within the Terms of Reference.

(vi) Ensure the conduct of the game is upheld by the umpires in accordance with the Laws of Cricket and the ICC Standard Playing Conditions, and to give support to the umpires in this regard if required.

(vii) Report to ICC on matters relating to player safety at the ground; pitch and outfield preparations; adequacy of covers and equipment for pitch and outfield preparation; the condition and standard of facilities for players and umpires; the standard of practice facilities; adequacy of sight boards; and bowlers with suspect actions.

3. Method of Operation

The referee must be present within the precincts of the ground on all days of the match or matches assigned to him at least an hour before the start of play until after close of play, bearing in mind that reports can be submitted up to one hour after the end of the day's play. He must ensure, in conjunction with the ground authority, that he has a good view of the match and has access to a television monitor and, wherever possible, video equipment.

The referee must lay down the standards expected from the players, making it clear that the captains are responsible for their teams and for the good conduct of the game. The referee must make it clear that *no public criticism of umpires will be tolerated*.

The referee must not interfere with the traditional role of umpires but should urge umpires to be decisive in upholding the Law.

4. Disciplinary Procedures

Should an umpire decide to report a player for an alleged breach of the Code or other offence, he must inform the player's captain or manager and the referee of his intention at the earliest opportunity and complete a report form and hand it to the referee not later than one hour after the close of the day's play . . . the referee's decision is final.

5. Penalties

The referee may in his absolute discretion impose any penalty by way of reprimand and/or fine and/or suspension including a suspended fine or suspended suspension.

(a) Maximum fine to be imposed for breaches of the Code of Conduct and other ICC Regulations (excluding over-rates) – 75 per cent of a player's match fee.

When on tour, the fine shall be calculated on the last match fee paid to that player in his previous domestic season. If a player did not participate in an international match during his previous domestic season, that player shall be fined on the basis which would have applied had he played in an international match in his previous domestic season.

(b) Maximum suspension to be imposed for breaches of the Code of Conduct and other ICC Regulations – Tests: three matches; one-day internationals: three matches.

A referee may impose the maximum suspension over a combination of Tests and one-day internationals not exceeding three Tests, or two Tests and two one-day internationals, or one Test and four one-day internationals, or six one-day internationals in total. If any matches of international standard other than Tests or one-day internationals take place between matches, the suspension will also include these. If necessary, the suspension will carry over into another future series. A player's participation in his own domestic cricket during the period of any suspension imposed by the ICC referee will be up to his own Board to determine.

(c) Penalties for slow over-rates

(i) Test Matches

Over-rates shall be assessed on 15 overs per hour, i.e. a minimum of 90 overs in a six-hour day, subject to the following deductions:

Two minutes per wicket taken.
Actual time where treatment by authorised medical personnel is required on the ground, and also for a player leaving the field due to serious injury.
Four minutes for one drinks break per session.

Overs will be calculated at the end of the match. For each over short of the target number, five per cent of each player's match fee in the fielding side (including the twelfth man) is to be deducted for the first five overs and ten per cent per over thereafter.

(ii) One-Day International Matches

The target over-rate is to be 15 overs per hour. In the event of the target over-rate not being reached, for each over short of the number required to be bowled in the scheduled time, the fielding side (including the twelfth man) will be fined an amount equal to five per cent of each player's match fee for the first five overs and ten per cent per over thereafter. No deductions are to be made for wickets or drinks breaks.

(iii) A penalty may be reviewed by the referee if, after consultation with the umpires, he is of the opinion that events beyond the control of the fielding side, including time-wasting by the batting side, prevented that team from bowling the required number of overs. The batting side may be fined at the same rate as the fielding side if, in the opinion of the referee, the batting side is guilty of slowing down the over-rate.

6. Payment of Fines

Fines must be paid within one calendar month by the player(s) to his (their) Board who will, in turn, forward such fine(s) to the Chief Executive of ICC. Any player(s) failing to meet this requirement will be rendered unavailable for selection in any fixture under the control of his (their) own Board.

INTERNATIONAL UMPIRES' PANEL

On December 21, 1993, the International Cricket Council announced the formation of an international umpires' panel, backed by £1.1 million sponsorship over three years from National Grid. Each Full Member of ICC was to nominate two officials – apart from England, who named four, because of their large number of professional umpires and the fact that most Tests take place during the English winter. A third-country member of the panel was to stand with a "home" umpire, not necessarily from the panel, in every Test staged from February 1994. Teams would have no right of objection to appointments.

The following umpires were on the panel from January 1996:
B. L. Aldridge (New Zealand), L. H. Barker (West Indies), S. A. Bucknor (West Indies), B. C. Cooray (Sri Lanka), R. S. Dunne (New Zealand), K. T. Francis (Sri Lanka), D. B. Hair (Australia), Khizar Hayat (Pakistan), M. J. Kitchen (England), K. E. Liebenberg (South Africa), Mahboob Shah (Pakistan), C. J. Mitchley (South Africa), V. K. Ramaswamy (India), S. G. Randell (Australia), I. D. Robinson (Zimbabwe), G. Sharp (England), D. R. Shepherd (England), R. B. Tiffin (Zimbabwe), S. Venkataraghavan (India), P. Willey (England).

Note: Compared with the 1994-95 list, G. Sharp and P. Willey have replaced H. D. Bird and N. T. Plews, and R. B. Tiffin has replaced K. Kanjee.

REGULATIONS FOR FIRST-CLASS MATCHES IN BRITAIN, 1995

Hours of Play

1st, 2nd, 3rd days.... 11.00 a.m. to 6.30 p.m. or after 110 overs, whichever is the later.
4th day .... 11.00 a.m. to 6.00 p.m. or after 102 overs, whichever is the later.

Note: Minimum number of overs were due to be reduced to 104 (96 on the 4th day) in 1996.

Non-Championship matches:

1st, 2nd days........ 11.30 a.m. to 6.30 p.m. (11.00 a.m. to 6.30 p.m. in tourist matches and Oxford v Cambridge)
3rd day .... 11.00 a.m. to 6.00 p.m.

Note: The hours of play, including intervals, are brought forward by half an hour for matches scheduled to start in September.

(a) If play is suspended (including any interval between innings) the minimum number of overs to be bowled in the day to be reduced by one over for each $3\frac{1}{2}$ minutes or part thereof of such suspension or suspensions in aggregate (including the last hour).

(b) If at 5.00 p.m. on the final day, 19 overs or less remain to be bowled, the umpires shall indicate that play shall continue until a minimum of a further 20 overs has been bowled, or until 6.00 p.m., whichever is the later (a minimum of 16 overs must be bowled in tourist matches). Play may cease on the final day at any time between 5.30 p.m. and 6.00 p.m. by mutual agreement of the captains. Should an innings end between 4.50 p.m. and 5.00 p.m., the time at the end of the ten-minute interval to replace 5.00 p.m. (all timings brought forward by half an hour for matches in September).

(c) The captains may agree or, in the event of disagreement, the umpires may decide to play 30 minutes (a minimum ten overs, or eight in tourist matches) extra time at the end of the first and/or second day's play (and/or the third day of four) if, in their opinion, it would bring about a definite result on that day. In the event of the possibility of a finish disappearing before the full period has expired, the whole period must be played out. Any time so claimed does not affect the timing for cessation of play on the final day.

(d) The minimum number of overs remaining to be bowled in the day shall be shown on the scoreboard.

(e) If an innings ends during the course of an over, that part shall count as a full over so far as the minimum number of overs per day is concerned.

(f) Notwithstanding any other provision, there shall be no further play on any day, other than the last day, if a batsman is out, or retires, or if the players leave the field during the last minimum over within two minutes of the scheduled cessation time or thereafter.

(g) If play is suspended for the day in the middle of an over, that over must be completed next day in addition to the minimum overs required that day.

Intervals

Lunch: 1.15 p.m. to 1.55 p.m. (1st, 2nd [3rd] days) in Championship and tourist matches and Oxford v Cambridge, 1.30 p.m. to 2.10 p.m. in others
1.00 p.m. to 1.40 p.m. (final day)
In the event of lunch being taken early because of a stoppage caused by weather or bad light (Law 16.2), the interval shall be limited to 40 minutes.

Tea: (Championship matches) A tea interval of 20 minutes shall normally be taken at 4.10 p.m. (3.40 p.m. on final day), or when 40 overs or less remain to be bowled. The over in progress shall be completed unless a batsman is out or retires during that over within two minutes of the interval or the players have occasion to leave the field.

If an innings ends or there is a stoppage caused by weather within 30 minutes of the scheduled time, the tea interval shall be taken immediately. There will be no tea interval if the scheduled timing for the cessation of play is earlier than 5.30 p.m.

(Other matches) 4.10 p.m. to 4.30 p.m. (1st, 2nd [3rd] days), 3.40 p.m. to 4.00 p.m. (final day).

Substitutes

(Domestic matches only) Law 2.1 will apply, but in addition:
No substitute may take the field until the player for whom he is to substitute has been absent from the field for five consecutive complete overs, with the exception that if a fieldsman sustains an obvious, serious injury or is taken ill, a substitute shall be allowed immediately. In the event of any disagreement between the two sides as to the seriousness of an injury or illness, the umpires shall adjudicate. If a player leaves the field during an over, the remainder of that over shall not count in the calculation of the five complete overs.

A substitute shall be allowed by right immediately in the event of a cricketer currently playing in a Championship match being required to join the England team for a Test match (or one-day international). Such a substitute may be permitted to bat or bowl in that match, subject to the approval of the TCCB. The player who is substituted may not take further part in the match, even though he might not be required by England. If batting at the time, the player substituted shall be retired "not out" and his substitute may be permitted to bat later in that innings subject to the approval of the TCCB.

Fieldsman Leaving the Field

ICC regulations apply (see pages 1334-1335) but without mention of the follow-on, and adding the stipulation that the player must have been struck an external blow by an illegal ball (i.e. a no-ball) while batting and consequently been forced to retire hurt.

New Ball

The captain of the fielding side shall have the choice of taking the new ball after 100 overs (85 in tourist matches) have been bowled with the old one.

Covering of Pitches and Bowler's Run-up

The whole pitch shall be covered:

- (a) The night before a match and, if necessary, until the first ball is bowled; and whenever necessary and possible at any time prior to that during the preparation of the pitch.
- (b) On each night of a match and, if necessary, throughout any rest days.
- (c) In the event of play being suspended because of bad light or rain, during the hours of play.

The bowler's run-up shall be covered to a distance of at least ten yards, with a width of four yards, as will the areas ten feet either side of the length of the pitch.

Declarations

Law 14 will apply, but, in addition, a captain may also forfeit his first innings, subject to the provisions set out in Law 14.2. If, due to weather conditions, a County Championship match has not started when less than eight hours of playing time remains, the first innings of each side shall automatically be forfeited and a one-innings match played.

MEETINGS IN 1995

TCCB SPRING MEETING

The Test and County Cricket Board spring meeting on March 7 and 8 dismissed England team manager Keith Fletcher halfway through his five-year contract. It was reported that Fletcher would receive £100,000 compensation. Ray Illingworth, already chairman of the England committee and selection panel, was appointed to replace him for 12 months, with overall command on the 1995-96 tour of South Africa and for the World Cup. However, against Illingworth's wishes, Brian Bolus (61) was voted off a selection panel widely criticised as too old, and was replaced by David Graveney (42). Fred Titmus was re-elected; Jack Simmons stood unsuccessfully. The Board refined the system for docking penalty points from counties with unfit pitches, announcing, as well as the 25-point maximum, a sliding scale of penalties for pitches judged "poor", starting with a warning and progressing to ten points, then 15 for further offences within 12 months. The Board announced a five-year extension of sponsorship of the Benson and Hedges Cup. It did not discuss in detail a letter received from the Cricketers' Association before the meeting, asking for a £20,000 minimum salary for capped players and making suggestions on coaching and pitches. Micky Stewart was asked to research into footwear, following a spate of injuries to bowlers. A regional competition for Second Eleven players was announced for 1995 and an Under-17 competition for all counties in 1996. Second Eleven players, whether registered or not, were to be subject to random drug testing. Dennis Silk was re-elected chairman of the TCCB for another year from October 1.

MCC ANNUAL GENERAL MEETING

The 208th annual general meeting of the Marylebone Cricket Club was held on May 3. Sir Oliver Popplewell, in the first of his two years as President, took the chair. The annual report was adopted, mentioning in particular MCC's busy touring programme, at home and overseas. At a special general meeting after the AGM, approval was given for the development of new offices for the Test and County Cricket Board at the Nursery End of Lord's Ground. Membership of the club on December 31, 1994, was 19,669, made up of 17,016 full members, 1,996 associate members, 560 honorary members and 97 senior members. There were 9,960 candidates awaiting election. In 1994, 434 vacancies arose.

TCCB SPECIAL MEETING

At a special general meeting of the Test and County Cricket Board on May 31, its chief executive, A. C. Smith, presented the case for a unified body, bringing together the TCCB, the Cricket Council and the National Cricket Association, provisionally called the English Cricket Board. The Board agreed to move to a "detailed planning stage". It was proposed that the Minor Counties should take part in an ECB Championship, modelled on Australian grade cricket and providing a bridge between the league and first-class games. The Minor Counties would have to produce development plans for youth club cricket before receiving funding. Before the meeting, the so-called "Big Five" – Test ground counties Lancashire, Nottinghamshire, Surrey, Warwickshire and Yorkshire – had circulated their own plans to reform English cricket, including a Championship split into divisions, but these were not discussed.

ICC ANNUAL CONFERENCE

The International Cricket Council met on July 12 and 13 and continued the standardisation of playing conditions for all Tests and one-day internationals. From October 1, the minimum 90 overs in a Test day were to be played out in full and not recalculated at the end of each innings. Players failing to meet the 15 overs per hour requirement would be fined five per cent for every over short up to five overs, as before, and ten per cent for every over above five. The new ball would be available after 80 overs, instead of 85. One-day internationals in all countries were to last 50 overs a side, and only two men would be allowed outside the fielding circle in the first 15 overs. It was agreed that TV replays should be available in Tests wherever possible, and that the third umpire should signal out with a red light and not out with green. Match referees' reports were to be extended to cover pitches and ground facilities. A new clause was added to the Code of Conduct forbidding players and officials to bet on matches in which they were involved, or to accept inducements likely to affect their performances adversely. Umpires were asked to agree on a common interpretation of the Laws, especially Law 42 on intimidation. The Council accepted in principle an invitation for cricket to be included in the 1998 Commonwealth games in Kuala Lumpur. Italy were promoted to associate membership, while Greece, Thailand and Vanuatu became affiliates.

TCCB SUMMER MEETING

The summer meeting of the Test and County Cricket Board on August 22 approved the continuing plans for the English Cricket Board. It discussed the Edgbaston Test pitch, which was referred to the pitches committee, and crowd problems at Headingley during the NatWest semi-final. The Board agreed that England should visit Zimbabwe in December 1996, before touring New Zealand, and provisionally invited Zimbabwe to tour England in 2004. England A were to play The Rest, rather than the County Champions, in 1996. The Board discussed a letter from the county scorers arguing that England should employ one of them on tour, rather than an outsider, as announced for the forthcoming tour of South Africa. A £4,000 increase in the minimum salary of capped county players, taking them to £18,500, with similar rises for uncapped players, was reported to the Board by Michael Murray, chairman of finance. Edward Slinger was appointed acting-chairman of discipline, following the sudden death of Peter Bromage.

TCCB WINTER MEETING

At its winter meeting on December 13, the Test and County Cricket Board deferred the creation of the English Cricket Board from January to April 1996 at the earliest. It rejected the cricket committee's proposal that the chairman of selectors should have the right to withdraw England players from county matches, though the counties said they would be sympathetic to requests. The Board also rejected a proposal to ban all overseas players from 1999, though a moratorium on Sunday games, during the World Cup, was agreed. From 1996, players with dual nationality would have to sign a revised declaration asserting that they had no "desire or intention to play cricket for any country outside the European Community" and that they would not seek to do so. It was decided to retain the single-division Championship, but to offer prize money down to ninth place, rather than fifth, to encourage competition. Prize money was increased to £155,000. The minimum number of overs in a day was reduced from 110 to 104 (from 102 to 96 on the final day) and Wednesday starts were to be the general rule from 1997, to avoid interruption by Sunday games. The Benson and Hedges Cup was reduced to 50 overs a side and coloured clothing was approved for the next five years of the Sunday League. The regional competition for Second Eleven players was discontinued. The Board gave £1.9 million to the Cricket Foundation, to be distributed to grassroots cricket.

ICC CODE OF CONDUCT –
BREACHES AND PENALTIES IN 1994-95

J. Angel Australia v Pakistan, 1st Test at Karachi.
Dissent at disallowed appeal. Severely reprimanded by J. R. Reid.

G. J. Whittall Zimbabwe v Sri Lanka, 1st Test at Harare.
Dissent at dismissal. Fined 25 per cent of match fee by P. L. van der Merwe.

B. C. Lara West Indies v New Zealand, one-day international at Goa.
Dissent at dismissal. Fined 50 per cent of match fee, suspended for next game and severely reprimanded by R. Subba Row.

P. C. R. Tufnell England v Australia A, Benson and Hedges World Series at Melbourne.
Throwing ball in aggressive manner after disallowed appeal. Fined 30 per cent of match fee by J. R. Reid.

A. Ranatunga Sri Lanka v New Zealand, Mandela Trophy at East London.
Dissent at dismissal. Fined 25 per cent of match fee by P. J. P. Burge.

K. R. Rutherford New Zealand v Sri Lanka, Mandela Trophy at East London.
Attempted intimidation of umpire over appeal. Fined 50 per cent of match fee by P. J. P. Burge.

K. R. Rutherford New Zealand v South Africa, 3rd Test at Cape Town.
Dissent at dismissal. Fined 75 per cent of match fee and given suspended two-match ban by P. J. P. Burge.

D. J. Richardson South Africa v Pakistan, Mandela Trophy at Cape Town.
Demolished stump when given out. Severely reprimanded and given suspended fine of 20 per cent of match fee by P. J. P. Burge.

C. C. Lewis England v Australia, 4th Test at Adelaide.
Pointed batsman to pavilion. Fined 30 per cent of match fee by J. R. Reid.

D. L. Houghton Zimbabwe v Pakistan, 2nd Test at Bulawayo.
Public criticism of umpires and opposition. Fined 10 per cent of match fee and severely reprimanded by J. L. Hendriks.

Wasim Akram Pakistan v Zimbabwe, 2nd Test at Harare.
Abusive language and snatching hat from umpire after lbw appeal turned down. Severely reprimanded by J. L. Hendriks.

Salim Malik Pakistan v Zimbabwe, 3rd Test at Harare.
Accused umpire of interfering with ball. Fined 50 per cent of match fee, given suspended two-Test ban and severely reprimanded by J. L. Hendriks.

Aamir Sohail Pakistan v Zimbabwe, 3rd Test at Harare.
Accused umpire of interfering with ball. Severely reprimanded by J. L. Hendriks.

B. C. Strang Zimbabwe v Pakistan, 2nd one-day international at Harare.
Pointed batsman to pavilion. Cautioned by J. L. Hendriks.

G. S. Blewett Australia v India, New Zealand Centenary Tournament at Dunedin.
Logo on wristband. Fined 15 per cent of match fee by P. L. van der Merwe.

R. T. Ponting Australia v India, New Zealand Centenary Tournament at Dunedin.
Logo on wristband. Fined 10 per cent of match fee by P. L. van der Merwe.

S. K. Warne Australia v India, New Zealand Centenary Tournament at Dunedin.
Logo on wristband. Fined 25 per cent of match fee by P. L. van der Merwe.

K. P. Walmsley New Zealand v Sri Lanka, 1st Test at Napier.
Bad language. Reprimanded by B. N. Jarman.

Aamir Nazir Pakistan v Sri Lanka, Asia Cup at Sharjah.
Offensive gesture on dismissing batsman. Severely reprimanded by C. H. Lloyd.

N. R. Mongia India v Sri Lanka, Asia Cup at Sharjah.
Dissent and attempted intimidation of umpire after disallowed appeal. Fined 10 per cent of match fee by C. H. Lloyd.

PART SIX: MISCELLANEOUS

CHRONICLE OF 1995

JANUARY

5 Australia retain the Ashes by drawing the Third Test at Sydney. **17** Geoff Howarth resigns as New Zealand coach after media criticism. **19** Three New Zealand Test players are suspended after admitting smoking cannabis on their tour of South Africa. Aamir Nazir plays for Pakistan in a Test match 95 minutes after a 24-hour flight. **30** England beat Australia by 106 runs in Adelaide, their first Test win in Australia since 1986.

FEBRUARY

2 In Harare, Henry Olonga of Zimbabwe becomes the first serious bowler to be no-balled for throwing in a Test for 32 years. **4** Zimbabwe score their first Test win, beating Pakistan by an innings and 64. Dean Jones scores 324 not out for Victoria against South Australia in a day/night Sheffield Shield match. **6** Graham Gooch and Mike Gatting are out for four and eight in Perth, in what they said would be their final Test innings. **7** England lose the Perth Test by 329 runs and the Ashes series 3–1. **14** Canterbury v Wellington at Christchurch produces 1,945 runs, a world record aggregate for a four-day match. **15** Pakistan captain Salim Malik accused of trying to bribe Shane Warne and Tim May to lose Karachi Test in September 1994.

MARCH

7 Salim Malik sacked as Pakistan captain, and suspended from all cricket pending investigation of bribery allegations. **8** Keith Fletcher sacked as England team manager; Ray Illingworth to combine Fletcher's role with that of chairman of selectors. **15** Sri Lanka win their first overseas Test, at the 32nd attempt, against New Zealand in Napier. **16** Bhupinder Singh jun. and Pankaj Dharmani share world record seventh-wicket stand of 460 for Punjab against Delhi. **20** Salim Malik reinstated as a player to allow him to "confront his accusers". **22** Sri Lanka draw with New Zealand in Dunedin to win their first overseas series. **28** Queensland win the Sheffield Shield, at the 63rd attempt, thus ending Australian sport's longest-running joke. **29** Moin Khan named Pakistan captain for Sharjah one-day tournament.

APRIL

2 Ali Gauhar of Karachi Blues takes four wickets in four balls against United Bank. Australia beat West Indies in Bridgetown for the first time. **8** Graham Dowling resigns as chief executive of New Zealand Cricket. **20** Former England captain Bob Wyatt dies, aged 93. **21** David Boon becomes 15th player to appear in 100 Tests.

MAY

3 Australia win at Kingston to complete West Indies' first series defeat since March 1980, 2-1, and are acclaimed as unofficial world champions. **26** The 1,000th one-day international results in a 25-run win for England over West Indies at The Oval.

JUNE

15 Thirty wickets fall in a day at Luton, the most in a Championship match since 1960. **22** A video screen showing replays to the crowd used at Lord's for the first time. **26** England win a Lord's Test against West Indies for the first time since 1957; Dominic Cork takes seven for 43, the best figures by an England bowler on Test debut. **30** Winston Benjamin sent home from West Indies' tour of England on grounds of "fitness and discipline".

JULY

3 West Indies suffer their heaviest ever defeat against a county side: an innings and 121 runs against Sussex. **8** West Indies win the Edgbaston Test in two days 77 minutes, the quickest home defeat for England since 1921. **22** Former England fast bowler Harold Larwood dies, aged 90. **30** Dominic Cork becomes first England player to take a Test hat-trick since 1957.

AUGUST

25 Andrew Symonds of Gloucestershire hits a world record 16 sixes in a first-class innings against Glamorgan at Abergavenny. Courtney Walsh becomes tenth bowler to take 300 Test wickets. **26** Symonds hits four second-innings sixes to set a further record of 20 in a match. Brian Lara scores a century for the third successive Test. **27** West Indies score 692 for eight declared, their highest score against England, and the tenth-highest in Test history. Ramiz Raja appointed captain of Pakistan. **28** The Oval Test is drawn, leaving the England-West Indies series tied 2-2 and West Indies winners of the Wisden Trophy for the 12th consecutive time. Nottinghamshire's 527 at Northampton becomes the highest score ever by a team going down to an innings defeat; Northamptonshire's 781 for seven is the seventh-highest score in Championship history.

SEPTEMBER

3 Warwickshire win the NatWest Trophy, their fifth trophy inside two calendar years. **9** Anil Kumble of Northamptonshire becomes the first player to take 100 wickets in a season since the Championship was cut to 17 matches in 1993. **11** Andrew Symonds turns down place on England A tour to maintain his Australian qualification. **16** Warwickshire retain the County Championship. **17** Kent win the Sunday League, their first title since 1978. **26** Sri Lanka win a Test series abroad for the second time, beating Pakistan 2-1.

OCTOBER

18 Lee Germon of New Zealand becomes the first man since Tony Lewis of England in 1972-73 to captain his country on his Test debut. **21** Wasim Akram regains Pakistan captaincy for the tour of Australia. **22** Salim Malik included in Pakistan's tour party after being cleared of bribery allegations by Pakistani authorities. **27** The England touring team play the first ever first-class match in Soweto.

NOVEMBER

20 Australia secure victory in their home series against Pakistan to confirm their status as the world's leading Test team. **26** Nine people killed and 50 injured when a wall collapses during an India–New Zealand one-day international at Nagpur. **27** Brian Lara pulls out of West Indian squad for World Series after being fined for breach of discipline on the England tour.

DECEMBER

3 Jack Russell's 11th catch for England against South Africa in Johannesburg Test gives him world Test record. Naeem Aktar takes ten for 28, the best first-class figures in Pakistan, for Rawalpindi B against Peshawar. **4** Mike Atherton bats for 643 minutes to earn England draw at Johannesburg. **9** Sri Lankans formally warned during Perth Test for ball-tampering, although they were later cleared by ICC. Boland v England match at Paarl abandoned with a day to spare for being too boring. **12** Waqar Younis, 24, becomes youngest bowler to take 200 Test wickets. **26** Sri Lankan off-spinner Muttiah Muralitharan no-balled for throwing seven times by Darrell Hair in Melbourne Test. Paul Adams becomes South Africa's youngest Test player at 18 years 340 days.

The following were also among items reported in the media during 1995:

Blair Sellers, playing for South Melbourne in the Dowling Shield Under-16 competition, hit a lofted drive that was stopped by the back of a seagull's head, turning a certain four into two. He was not unduly upset by this until he was bowled for 98. The seagull recovered. (*Sunday Age*, Melbourne, February 5)

Elsecar Cricket Club in Yorkshire have failed in their attempt to get back the Wake Cup, which the club won in perpetuity in the 1880s. The trophy, said to be worth £25,000, has been bequeathed to a great-great-niece of the then-captain Willy Oates, who had it for safekeeping. She says it is a family heirloom, and the club's solicitors have advised them not to try and fight the case. (*Daily Mail*, February 7)

Sir Tim Rice, accepting an Oscar for Best Original Song – in the Disney film *The Lion King* – told the audience in Hollywood: "I'd also like to thank Denis Compton, a boyhood hero of mine." A spokesman for the Academy of Motion Picture Arts and Sciences said: "We don't know who Denis Compton is. He doesn't appear to be at Disney Studios or have anything to do with *The Lion King*." (*Daily Telegraph*, March 30)

Richard Blakey, the Yorkshire wicket-keeper, won a diploma of honour in the annual Pierre de Coubertin awards presented by the International Committee for Fair Play. Blakey admitted that a catch he took to dismiss James Whitaker of Leicestershire at Harrogate in 1994 hit the ground first. Whitaker, then on 35, went on to make 148. (*Daily Telegraph*, April 20)

Off-spinner Rob Jones conceded 48 in an over bowling for Durham University in a pre-season one-day friendly against Surrey at The Oval. David Ward hit the last over before lunch for six sixes and two fours; the first two balls of the over were no-balls, with two extra runs per ball counting against Jones under the prevailing regulations. "I basically just froze," the bowler said. (*Daily Telegraph*, April 20)

Police were called to a friendly village match between Brigstock and Wansford, after a Wansford batsman refused to walk when given lbw and the umpire shouted racial abuse. (*Northamptonshire Evening Telegraph*, April 26)

Graham Yallop, the former captain of Australia, was sacked from his post as manager of the Australian National Watersports Centre for playing club cricket at weekends. He was awarded $A12,500 compensation after an industrial relations court decided that his dismissal was "harsh, unjust and unreasonable". (*The Times*, May 20)

Detective John Bavister spotted his wife's stolen car while waiting to bat for Whittlesey Second Eleven at Crowland, Lincolnshire. His captain dropped him down the order to give him time to arrest two youths. (*Daily Mail*, May 29)

Slow left-armer James Didcote was no-balled twice under Law 40.1, playing for Glamorgan Colts against Llandovery College, because the wicket-keeper's peaked cap was protruding in front of the stumps. The keeper was Gareth Jones, 17, whose father Eifion kept for Glamorgan. (*Daily Telegraph*, June 3)

Father and son Mahindra and Ajoy Gokal both scored unbeaten centuries in the same innings for Luton Exiles against Langford Second Eleven. (*Independent on Sunday*, June 4)

Local doctors donated a vasectomy operation to a fund-raising auction organised by Newent Cricket Club, Gloucestershire. It was sold for £90. (*Gloucester Citizen*, June 5)

Greg Hobson, 21, became the first player to be killed in a cricket match in Canada when he was hit on the head while batting for North Vancouver against Vancouver Meralomas. He had taken off his helmet because of the heat. (*Associated Press*, June 6)

The Hawks, a Leeds-based club, advertised for "fun-loving" women in Bournemouth to meet them on their seaside tour. They received 30 replies. (*The Sun*, June 8)

Reports from Port-of-Spain say the land given to Brian Lara by the Trinidad Government for his new home has been cursed by an obeah man. Chicken entrails and black candles were reported to have been found at the site. (*Daily Telegraph*, June 8)

Thirty cardboard cut-out Mike Athertons, produced for a pub promotion, went missing from a warehouse in Leeds. (*Daily Express*, June 16)

Rick Sidwell, 33, of Fareham, Hampshire, smoked 12,800 cigarettes at a cost of £1,700 to win two free £20 tickets to the Benson and Hedges final. (*Daily Telegraph*, June 21)

Alan Clark, a maths student at the University of Hertfordshire, calculated that a throw returned on the bounce reached the wicket-keeper 0.05 of a second quicker than one returned on the full. (*Daily Telegraph*, June 24)

In a celebrity match, Bill Wyman of the Rolling Stones took what he claimed was the first televised hat-trick at The Oval. His victims were television news reader Trevor McDonald, cricket presenter Charles Colvile and Gary Lineker, the retired football star. (*The Times*, June 24)

Play in the village match at Chatburn, Lancashire, against Cowling, was stopped because of the noise coming from a nearby field. The Chatburn wicket-keeper then realised the commotion was caused by a farmer chasing his dog, which was chasing a herd of cows. He then angrily chased the farmer. What followed was described as "ten minutes of classic slapstick" before tempers cooled. Rodney Booth, the Chatburn captain, said the wicket-keeper then dropped three catches, which were probably responsible for his side's nine-run defeat. (*Clitheroe Advertiser*, June 29)

Graeme Parkinson, 33, hit a six through his parents' windscreen as they sat and watched him from their car in Darwen, Lancashire. (*The Sun*, July 6)

The *Diss Express* newspaper in Norfolk published a "Wanted" poster offering a £10 reward for "the capture of a reckless villain" who sent the paper bogus reports involving the village team at Bressingham. Two of them were published, one of which claimed a local businessman had taken six wickets in an over. (*Diss Express*, July 7/*Daily Telegraph*, August 5)

Bishop Auckland's West Indian professional Ricky Waldren was caught on the boundary when the ball ricocheted off the head of the umpire at the bowler's end, George Simpson. He needed ten stitches. "Luckily, these ex-miners are made of strong stuff," said Bishop Auckland chairman Keith Hopper. "George went to hospital but got back to the bar for last orders." (*The Sun*, July 8)

Joe Middleton, 13, took two hat-tricks in seven balls for Monks Park School, Bristol, against Fairfield. (*Bristol Evening Post*, July 12)

Prince Charles was bowled first ball by ten-year-old Wajid Khan at a Kwik Cricket demonstration at The Oval. (*The Sun*, July 15)

Local councillors in Ripon, Yorkshire, rejected an attempt to name the new by-pass after Sir Leonard Hutton Way. It will be called the Ripon By-Pass. (*The Times*, July 15)

Steve Dublin, the Montserrat-born professional with Kearsley of the Bolton League, hit 48 in an over off Rob Slater of Heaton to win a cup semi-final. Slater bowled three no-balls, all of which went for six. The one ball Dublin did not hit for six was dropped by the wicket-keeper. (*Bolton Evening News*, July 17)

The Bishop of Ludlow, the Right Reverend John Saxbee, has started wearing a baseball cap fitted with radio and earplugs so he can keep in touch with the Test score. "At a recent meeting of rural deans, I was obliged to wear the cap throughout to keep everyone informed," he said. (*Hereford Times*, July 20)

Johan van Niekirk, a 20-year-old South African, scored 102 and took ten for 46 playing for Marlow Park in Division Three of the Thames Valley League. He finished off the Stoke Green innings with a hat-trick. Van Niekirk, a former Western Province Under-19 player, said he was helped by a shower which freshened the pitch between innings. (*The Times*, July 22)

A boy falling out of a tree stopped play in a Winchester Evening League match between the city's fire service and the rugby club. An outfielder heard 11-year-old Thomas Wainwright's screams after he had fallen 30 feet and become trapped in the lower branches. The firemen then formed a human chain to take him to safety. The boy suffered a dislocated leg; the fire brigade lost. (*News of the World*, July 23)

Anton Joyce of Woodhouse in the Leeds League scored 109 in 20 minutes and 27 balls against Pool; he hit 11 sixes and lost eight balls in adjoining woodland. (*The Times*, July 29)

Bruce, a ten-year-old Labrador with a talent for sniffing out lost cricket balls, discovered his 500th ball in a cemetery at Sacriston, County Durham. His 88-year-old owner, Jack Moralee of Chester-le-Street, regularly gets calls from clubs asking for Bruce to comb fields near their grounds. (*Daily Telegraph*, August 7)

Graham Gooch was paid an undisclosed amount by a hair replacement studio to make personal appearances displaying his new hair graft. His new locks originated in Russia. Gooch said he would not try to stop his hair changing colour. "If it gets really grey, I might become chairman of the England selectors." (*Daily Telegraph*, August 10)

Robin Wightman was recorded in the scorebook as being "absent, huffed" when he failed to bat for Whiteleas against East Rainton in the North-east Durham League. Wightman had stormed off the pitch when his captain refused to let him bowl the last over, even though he had taken seven wickets. Then he went home. MCC assistant secretary John Jameson said the notation was quite legitimate and should count as a dismissal in the averages, as with "timed out". (*The Guardian*, August 10)

A match in Boddington, Gloucestershire, was abandoned because the pitch was engulfed by smoke from the Companion's Rest animal crematorium in nearby Elmstone Hardwicke. (*News of the World*, August 13)

The Royal Economic Society newsletter called for the eradication of cricket after a paper by Howard J. Wall of Birkbeck College claimed that baseball-playing countries had growth rates substantially higher than those in cricketing countries. "We are not yet convinced," a Treasury spokesman said. (*Sunday Telegraph*, August 20)

An Indian MP complained in Parliament that the Communication Department had refused to provide Sunil Gavaskar with an immediate telephone connection unless he produced a certificate proving his claim that he was a well-known sportsman. (*Indian Express*, August 23)

Paul Johnston made his debut for Blackhall Thirds against Preston in the North Yorkshire and South Durham League, aged six. The team were a man short and in danger of being fined before Paul was drafted in by his father. Wearing his own pad, gloves and helmet, he batted almost six overs in a last-wicket stand and scored a single. (*Daily Express*, August 25)

The former Pakistani international Parvez Mir was banned by the Carrow club in Norfolk for taking his mobile phone from the umpire and answering a call from his fiancée while he was bowling against Downham Market. (*The Times*, August 26)

Wayne Radcliffe was banned for five years by the Wakefield and District Cricket Union for urinating on the pitch while he was fielding in the covers for Newmillerdam. "By the time a wicket fell I was desperate. I turned towards some trees and answered the call of nature. Hardly anyone saw." (*Wakefield Express*, September 1)

David Winn, aged ten, saved Mirfield Parish Cavaliers from relegation in the Central Yorkshire League after being called in when the side were short. He shared a last-wicket stand of 28 to give his team victory over Thornhill. (*Daily Mail*, September 8)

Protesters from mining areas who invaded the garden of the Deputy Prime Minister, Michael Heseltine, in Northamptonshire to protest against opencast mining, played a Lancashire–Yorkshire match using coal shovels as bats before dispersing. (*The Guardian*, September 11)

Sukhinder Turner, Indian-born wife of former New Zealand Test player Glenn Turner, has been elected to a three-year term as mayor of the New Zealand city of Dunedin. (*Indian Express*, September 15)

Jack Swain, 73, collapsed and died seconds after bowling his final over in his retirement match at Cuckfield, Sussex. The match was abandoned but a planned farewell supper went ahead as a tribute to him. (*The Sun*, October 3)

The Conservative Party said ten thousand people a week were playing a game they had set up on the Internet, which involved trying to get the ball near John Major's bat. Winners got either a T-shirt showing the Prime Minister's face or a jigsaw depicting him and Mrs Major. (*News of the World*, October 29)

Seven people were arrested in Cuttack and charged with selling forged tickets for the India–New Zealand Test match. (*Indian Express*, November 11)

The South African Medical Journal reported that 49 per cent of schoolboy cricketers questioned in a survey were injured in a season. A third of the injuries were to back and trunk. (*The Star*, Johannesburg, November 15)

The North Zone players, on their way to play their Duleep Trophy fixture against Central Zone in Lucknow, had to bed down in the corridor of their sleeper train owing to a mix-up over bookings. Passengers were said to be angry because their kit was blocking all the gangways. (*Times of India*, November 26)

A calendar showing Mike Atherton replaced the picture of the local MP, Emma Nicholson, in the Devon Conservative headquarters when she defected to the Liberal Democrats. (*BBC Radio Four*, December 30)

Contributions from readers for this feature are very welcome, particularly from local or non-UK newspapers. Please send them to the editor, with the title and date of publication clearly marked.

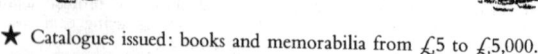

CRICKET BOOKS, 1995

By ALAN ROSS

Books about overseas tours and even home Test series have gone out of fashion. These are, in any case, not easy to make a success of, unless given a wider context than cricket. Neville Cardus understood this and so did John Arlott, though their differing merits did not always compensate for individual weaknesses. Cardus talked so much at matches that it was remarkable he saw any play at all, and grace of style did not disguise inattention to the matter at hand. Arlott was a robust and juicy radio commentator who sometimes seemed uncomfortable on the page with the techniques of the game. Both, however, had a relish and a feeling for character that makes the reading of the run of recent books a comparatively thin experience.

The one tour book of the year is, however, a very good one. **One Summer, Every Summer** by Gideon Haigh is a journal of the 1994-95 Ashes series, won comprehensively by Australia. Yet it is much more than an account of the actual matches, fairly and shrewdly described though they are. Haigh looks back rewardingly to previous series, offers many sharply focused portraits of players and journalists, and discusses the relative virtues of Border and Taylor. There is a final chapter in this generous, perceptive book about Australia's subsequent demolition of the West Indians.

There are high-class cricketing journalists around in Britain too: some of them former county players like Robin Marlar, Peter Roebuck, Mike Selvey and Vic Marks; but one who is not an ex-player, Alan Lee of *The Times*, has written perhaps the most interesting book of the year in his biography **Lord Ted: The Dexter Enigma**. Dexter has written his own account of his life and times, but as a general rule biographies are more rewarding than autobiographies, cricketing ones anyway, and especially ghosted ones. Lee had previously written several books about racing and one, with Dexter, about golf, so he was well suited for the present enterprise.

Dexter, one of the glories of English cricket in his time, had a rough ride as chairman of selectors at the hands of a sadistic tabloid press, and it is one of the great merits of Lee's book that he is able to deal shrewdly but sympathetically with Dexter's limitations as well as his virtues. The latter were many and often misunderstood. Lee was fortunate in that Dexter had an adventurous and varied life off the field, never afraid to try his hand at anything demanding skill and imagination. Politics, racing, religion, flying, motor-biking, golf, PR and greyhounds all engaged his attention at different times. Lee does justice to the highs and lows in a strange career, and he never loses sight of the fact – rarely acknowledged – that Dexter was a considerable student of cricket's real problems as well as a thrilling performer. He was often distracted in county cricket, but many Test cricketers share the same problem.

One of whom this was certainly true, even more so, was David Gower. In his **David Gower: A Man Out of Time** Rob Steen makes an articulate, slightly frenetic case for a cricketer in the Dexter class, all silken grace, whose career was amputated in the most brutal and unjustifiable fashion. Dexter, rather to his discredit, seemed unable to take on the puritans who were conniving at Gower's downfall and what had been, despite setbacks, an exhilarating career petered out miserably. Steen, with too many reckless cultural references – I never expected to see Cyril Connolly and Christopher Marlowe quoted in a book about cricket – has nevertheless told an interesting story very capably. The words "laid back" appear rather too often for comfort but he seems to understand Gower's seemingly flashy lifestyle. It is hard to give great credence to grown men who take champagne seriously as a regular drink, and the excess of it in this book perhaps accounts for the moments in Gower's life when the fizz went out of it. Both the Dexter and the Gower biographies are excellently illustrated. There appear to have been three previous books about Gower, but it would be surprising if this was not the best one.

In **Gooch: My Autobiography** Frank Keating has made a fair job of getting Gooch, the author, into gear: not exactly a sparkling innings but one not out of keeping with the moustachioed man with the heavy bat who more ruthlessly than Dexter or Gower was able to thump county bowlers into submission. He did the same to many Test bowlers too, after initial reverses, and it was unfortunate that his dedication to his own work ethic blinded him to the virtues of those like Gower cast in a different mould. Gooch looked like a Victorian cricketer should look, but Victorian views on the cricket fields of the late 1980s led to awkwardness. Gooch was always a super-patriot, keen for the national anthem to be played before Test matches, and it was obviously galling, when captain, to find his charges less enthusiastic. It is impossible not to like, respect and admire Gooch after reading this book, the frankness of which makes one less critical of the several grave misjudgments of his career. His plodding gait, drooping shoulders, impassive features and various degrees of whiskeriness made him more the embodiment of English cricket in the last 20 years than any of his contemporaries.

Wilf Wooller is probably remembered more as a powerful, long-striding centre threequarter for Cambridge and Wales, than as a rather dour, determined and dogmatic captain of Glamorgan at cricket. In **The Skipper** Andrew Hignell deals competently if not very stylishly with a career that embraced a spell as a Japanese prisoner of war that cost him his marriage and ended his rugby playing days. Wooller was in the first Wales side that beat England at Twickenham and the 1935 the All Blacks. He joined Glamorgan after the war, captained them to win the Championship, mainly through their fielding, and later as secretary ran the show for another 17 years until his retirement in 1977. A big man, he brought a formidable aggression to everything he did and brooked little opposition. A useful batsman, a fine bowler who twice took a hundred wickets in a season, he pressurised opponents by his mere presence. Hignell's book is largely based on taped conversations with his hero, so we get the Wooller view pretty much undiluted. But a surprising warmth emerges in the process and the final portrait of a man not much less endowed than C. B. Fry as a sportsman – Wooller also played soccer for Cardiff City and squash for Wales – is curiously endearing.

Brian Lara is still only 26 so **Beating the Field,** written with Brian Scovell and usefully introduced by Gary Sobers, has a modest number of years to deal with. It would be nice to think the words are mostly Lara's own, for he seems articulate enough, level-headed and without obvious conceit. Lara sees no merit in limiting bouncers – "There are no restrictions on the batsman so why should there be a restriction on the bowler?" – but what he

does not take into account is that nothing but short-pitched bowling, to the extent that West Indies indulged in during their heyday, makes for tedious watching. Intimidation is not the only vice: if batsmen are denied the variety of strokes that give cricket its charm and beauty, it will become a dull game indeed. Lara, as a West Indian and the greatest batsman of his day, has a rather cock-eyed view of what passes for entertainment in most places. This account of his life to date is factual, without frills, and understandably rather schoolboyish. The single-mindedness comes through and so does the necessary ambition.

Most people's routine run-through of the matches they have played in or watched has limited appeal, except perhaps to themselves and their families. Rowland Ryder's **Cricket Calling** is a horse of another colour, nearer to C. L. R. James and John Arlott in breadth of reference and clarity of recall. Ryder's father was secretary of Warwickshire for more than 40 years, and he himself, as Colin Cowdrey observes in a foreword, was born within the sound of the umpire's bell on the Edgbaston ground – a Warwickshire man through and through. This is an enthusiast's book, that of a man passionately in love with the cricket and cricketers of his own county. There are many enjoyable portraits of Warwickshire worthies: "Tiger" Smith, Canon Parsons – on Saturdays F. S. G. Calthorpe allowed him to field in the deep so that he could prepare his sermons – Len Bates, who was born in the pavilion at Edgbaston, his father being groundsman, and "Chico" Austin, scorer for the county for 52 years, from 1911 to 1963. There are entertaining chapters on Jessop, Armstrong's Australians, cricket and literature, class distinctions among cricketers, cricket and politicians. Lara gets a mention but only because he plays for Warwickshire. This is a book for connoisseurs of the game, up in the Robertson-Glasgow and Cardus league, with more anecdotes than statistics.

Women biographers of famous cricketers are rare but in **Masterclass** Bridgette Lawrence, ardent feminist, apparently, and teacher of history and politics, has done a better than routine job in dealing with George Headley. I don't know why she regards Headley, who lost nothing in comparison with Bradman in the decade before the war, as an "unsung" hero, but since she provides no bibliography it is unclear how much she is tilling virgin soil. She deals interestingly with Headley's Panamanian childhood – he was ten when his Jamaican mother took him to Kingston – and his subsequent rejection of baseball for cricket. A dandy and somewhat of a solitary from an early age, Headley at one time contemplated an American career in dentistry. A work permit failed to materialise and Headley, "bow-legged and bright-eyed", was soon getting his teeth into the bowlers of The Hon. L. H. Tennyson's visiting XI. He was 18 at the time and he made 211, the first of his nine double-centuries, two of them against England at Sabina Park.

Headley, who had soft hands, a legacy from baseball, played very late and mainly off the back foot, but his composure and stillness, combined with instinctive timing, made his great variety of strokes appear effortless. Like Hutton a decade later, he had to bear the burden of being responsible for most of his side's runs in match after match. In the 1930-31 series in Australia Headley made centuries at Brisbane and Sydney and, against England in 1933, 169 not out at Old Trafford, and six years later two hundreds in the Lord's Test. He was 30 then, and because of the war his Test career was virtually over. He did, belatedly, captain West Indies, the first black man to do so, but only as one of three captains in the 1947-48 series against England.

Cardus considered Headley a greater player on all wickets than Bradman and produced figures to prove it. Headley's last phase, as Jamaican celebrity and man of the people, was equally rewarding. He became a civil servant, read the Bible every day, married twice, fathered nine children, and gambled on everything in sight. He refused to learn to drive and sat happily behind his chauffeur. He died in 1983. *Masterclass* tells you everything, more or less, that you need to know about him.

Mark Ray in **Border and Beyond** deals with the tough Australian left-hander whose time as captain lasted slightly too long, and ended up in a muddle almost as unsatisfactory as Gower's. Ray observes, "Typically, Border was the ultimate players' man to the end, suspicious of officialdom, fearful of a hidden agenda that did not exist." He had more ups and downs than any of his contemporaries, and was, initially, a reluctant and not very inspiring captain, having inherited a debilitated team. In 1989, however, on the first day of the First Test at Headingley, Border threw off all his gloom and past inhibitions. His 66 in no time at all got Australia off to a flying start. Border had also changed from an amiable sort of bloke to a grim, surly opponent who exercised a fierce non-fraternisation policy. Ray writes understandingly about Border's various phases of mood and he gives a shrewd assessment of Australian cricket during his reign. On the field, Border did great things in terms of results, but his gracelessness both on and off it took the shine off his achievements in many people's eyes. Ray does not make light of this. He has an eye for character and is scathing about inadequacies of technique: "Lathwell lasted two matches . . . and displayed all the footwork of a drunken elephant."

A character as far removed from Border's as that of Brian Johnston it would be hard to imagine. Johnston's schoolboy, japish manner was not to everyone's taste and you had to be feeling strong to react adequately to the puns, jokes, nicknames and anecdotes. But as Tim Heald shows in his **Brian Johnston** there was a more serious side to this essentially good and caring man, for whom cricket was only one, if the most loved, of his various interests. As a broadcaster Johnston was knowledgeable without being technical, light-hearted and, most important of all, gave off an air of well-being and enjoyment. Tim Heald has previously written biographies of dukes, dames and Compton, as well as crime novels. In the present book he deals in relaxed fashion with prep school, Eton, the Grenadier Guards, coffee tasting, as well as steam radio. Johnston just failed to make the Eton XI through A. M. Baerlein staying on as wicket-keeper to an advanced age. Heald's book is not all jokes, though there are some excellent, well-rehearsed ones, and his crime-writing side must have been interested to learn about the sinister Scully, who failed to save Johnston's father from drowning and later married his mother, with whom it was rumoured he had been carrying on.

Indian cricketers have not hitherto found a writer to emulate the stylishness of their best players, but a book of high quality, **Spin and Other Turns,** has been produced by Ramachandra Guha, a 38-year-old historian from Dehra Dun who is a real enthusiast, but knowledgeable and sophisticated. His book starts by being a study of the comparative techniques and merits of India's three great spin bowlers of the seventies.

"Let us think of Bedi as Brahma the Creator, the deity who is everywhere but nowhere; of Prasanna as Vishnu the Preserver, the god who has numerous incarnations and variations in form; and of Chandrasekhar as Siva the Destroyer who with the wink of an eye, or turn of the wrists, would destroy any or all of his opponents." To these three is later added the highly intellectual and handsome Venkataraghavan, in relation to whom Bedi observed, "I would rather talk of the *four* Indian spinners of my time collectively. Technical correctness was our biggest asset; our side-on bowling action, the delivery stride and follow-through were all rhythmical. Each was different from the other and there was no hint of arrogance among us."

Guha, having traced the history of Indian spinners from the Untouchable Palwankar Baloo, who mowed down English batsmen in the summer of 1911 and whose only two words of English were "How's that?", to the later, rather lesser, purveyors of spin such as Doshi and Shastri, moves on no less eloquently to batsmen and all-rounders. He writes with proper admiration of Merchant, Gavaskar and Vengsarkar, lovingly of Viswanath, lyrically of Kapil Dev. He discusses wicket-keepers, quoting a colleague, Suresh Menon, who "interpreted the profusion of high-class wicket-keepers in India to be a consequence of the traditional Indian 'squatting' style of emptying the bowels". There is an appreciative portrait of the sociable Farokh Engineer, whose Irish Jesuit teachers encouraged him to keep goal rather than wicket, and who shared with Denis Compton the task of modelling for Brylcreem. Guha ranges widely over other matters than Indian cricket and his writing has a warmth and perception admirable in one whose early studies and adherences were of Marxism.

Intentionally comic books about cricket rarely last one through a single whisky and soda. Marcus Berkmann's **Rain Men** is an exception, at least when he gets down to serious cricket as opposed to the anarchic village variety. He is as genial as Brian Johnston on the surface, but has a savage, critical undertow which reveals a wish to wound and a skill in mimicry. Cricket on radio brings out the best and beast in him. He observes Laker's commentating style – "a awful spell of bowlin'" – and his fascination with little Harry Pilling "5 ft 3 in his stockin'ed feet", admires Benaud's way of bypassing interviewers, coruscates the "dreaded" Bannister for his lifeless carcass, meaningless hyperbole and fawning admiration for South Africa under apartheid. His observations extend to the *shape* of cricketers as they appear on or off the screen. As long as anyone can remember, England players have all had very large bottoms. "Ian Botham's is about as big a bottom as you can get without falling over." He suggests big bottoms catch the selectors' eyes more easily, enabling Lamb to play 79 Tests against Randall's 47. "Randall had no buttocks at all to speak of." If you want to know why Emburey played more Tests than Edmonds, "look at their trouser padding". Voices are another matter for comment. Compare, for example, Gooch's "Essex squeak" and Gatting's "uncanny Alan Ball impersonation" with the "deep brown proud and aristocratic tones of Imran Khan". In this instance, as opposed to small bottoms, thin, high-pitched squawks do not seem to put their owners at a disadvantage. Whether about playing at a knockabout level or watching the stars, this is a spirited book that could last you through a whole bottle.

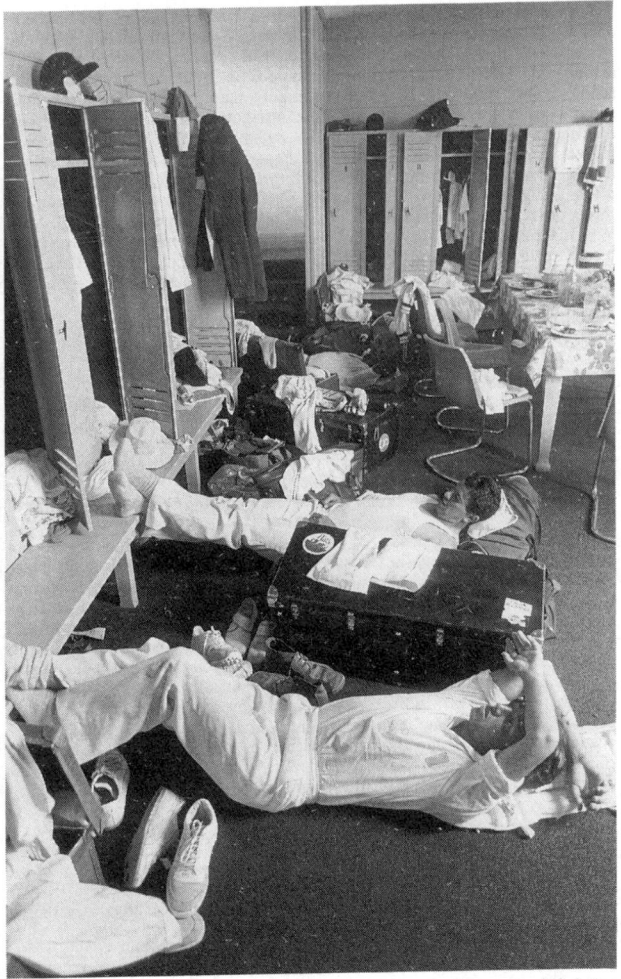

TEA-BREAK, FOURTH DAY: The visitors' dressing-room at Adelaide – South Australia v Tasmania, November 1984. One of many striking pictures in Mark Ray's *CRICKET, The Game Behind the Game*.

Jack Pollard begins his unusually informative book about left-handers, apparently known as "mollydookers", a term unfamiliar to me, with the statement: "Some scientists believe left-handers are more prone to alcoholism, bedwetting, attempted suicide, drug abuse, brain damage, school failure, schizophrenia and criminality than right-handers." There is some support for at least one of these attributes in the career of W. H. Scotton, a tedious but highly productive batsman for England in the 1880s. He was a large man, with a Merv Hughes-style moustache, and an appeal to both sexes. He did not bother to gain favour when batting, however, often going an hour without scoring. Nevertheless, he toured Australia three times, once contributed 34 in an opening partnership of 170 with W. G. Grace, and at the age of 37 was found in his nightshirt covered in blood, razor still in hand. His left-handed contemporary, Bobby Peel, was sacked by Lord Hawke a few years later for drunkenness, and for peeing on the pitch at Bramall Lane.

Mollydookers, a mine of bizarre facts distilled in rather school-report style, starts in the 1870s with such as John Hodges, who went in last in the first ever England-Australia Test and was later charged with indecent exposure. The great Clem Hill, it appears, took a wicket at Brighton with the first ball he bowled in England and followed it with a somersault and several handstands. Hill's new wife, Florrie, used to berate the official scorer if his total of Hill's runs failed to match her own tally. The last chapter takes us up to Border, Taylor, Bevan and Lara, and few eminent left-handers have been missed out on the way. Not all Pollard's entries are sparkling, but he has a deadpan manner in recording the more eccentric of his characters' habits.

Liberation Cricket consists of a series of essays examining the role of cricket in the culture of the West Indies. Its hero, not surprisingly, is the brilliantly articulate, sometimes intemperate, author of *Beyond a Boundary*, C. L. R. James. As well as one by him, four whole chapters are devoted to him, with such titles as "C. L. R. James's material aesthetic of cricket", "Cricket, literature and the politics of decolonisation: the case of C. L. R. James", and his name is scattered like confetti throughout the book. James, it is remarked by the editors, was "able to beautifully disguise his masterful examination of West Indies cricket culture as a semi-autobiography and political history of the modern region". That is certainly true, but the academic nature of most of the writing in *Liberation Cricket* does not provide for an easy read: "Dialectical analysis best explains the dichotomous development of the social culture of West Indies cricket," which may well be the case, but such sentences do not exactly warm one to the book.

All the same, there is much interesting comment, not only about James, buried here. The general aridity of the approach and its politicisation of the game, however, make it of appeal to critics of colonisation more than to cricketers. The trouble with analyses of this sort, however considered, is that they tend to lead further and further away from what actually takes place on the field. The editors, Hilary Beckles and Brian Stoddart, are respectively Professors of History and of Cultural Studies, and their desire to elaborate on the social context of Caribbean cricket is entirely admirable.

After that, **The Art of Wrist-Spin Bowling** comes as something of a relief, like facing, say, Richard Illingworth after Courtney Walsh. Peter Philpott

bowled for Australia and in 1981 became their first Test coach, specialising in leg-spin. If Philpott himself had never quite the fame of his fellow-Australian leg-spinners, Grimmett, Tribe, O'Reilly, Dooland, Benaud, and now Warne, he is the theorist of the movement. Not only that, but having divulged in the most lucid terms what wrist-spinners do, or attempt to do, he offers a final chapter advising how to deal with these devils. That is carrying generosity a long way, but knowing what to do and doing it is another matter. Philpott's book is essentially a text book, but one on a high level of sophistication, with excellent photographs and diagrams of how Warne, Qadir, Jenner and others set about it. His most valuable advice: "Remember you are not a slow bowler, you are a spin bowler. During the delivery your entire body will work just as hard putting spin onto the ball, as the fast bowler does putting pace on the ball."

Mike Atherton, collaborating with Pat Gibson in **A Test of Cricket,** has compiled a plain, no-nonsense, eminently sensible guide to various aspects of the game. He deals with captaincy, batting, bowling, though not fielding, with sub-headings on equipment, the press, intimidation, ball tampering, throwing (in bowlers), overseas players. Any youthful, or indeed any other, cricketer could not fail to benefit from Atherton's chattily expressed views. He is curiously tolerant on certain matters and appears to enjoy the hideous clothing, coal-coloured pads and look-alike tennis ball that make Sunday League cricket more like an amateurish pantomime than a contest. What on earth is wrong in playing in proper cricket clothes? There is a lot of useful information on aspects of the professional cricketer's life which ordinary members of the public are not likely to know about. A glossary, a chronology of historic dates and good photographs complete a well-conceived publication.

In 1932 the Australians toured North America, with Bradman among them. In **The Don Meets the Babe** Ric Sissons makes use of the Bradman scrapbook to describe a tour which involved 51 matches in 76 days, and in which Bradman scored 3,777 runs at an average of 102. Most of the party were either Test or Sheffield Shield players, though there were a couple of stockbrokers and a solicitor among them. Bradman met Babe Ruth, the baseball hero; there were meetings with film stars such as Boris Karloff, Clark Gable, Jean Harlow and Joan Crawford; and in Moose Jaw a man on a horse patrolled the boundary to retrieve Bradman's cover drives. Only 46 pages deal with the actual tour, but plenty of photographs and some evocative advertisements bulk up the text. There are facsimile scorecards and cartoons, and the book is nicely printed on good paper.

The Log of the "Old Un", produced in similar fashion, describes in even fewer pages the 1886 tour of Canada and America of a scratch side raised by E. J. Sanders. Sanders was a Devon man and secretary of the struggling county club. His team played nine matches, the two main ones against Philadelphia, where crowds of 5,000 attended each day. At the time of these matches, baseball had not definitively established itself as the major American sport. The *New York Commercial Advertiser* wrote: "It is believed by some Americans that cricket will very soon supersede the game of baseball, especially as a gentleman's game. It is conducted in a quiet manner and without the usual howling that marks the game of baseball." The matches were rather one-sided, K. J. Key, later captain of Surrey, hammering the American bowling. The author of the log, William Clulow

Sim, was a Haileyburian Indian civil servant. He volunteered to act as scorer to the team, but was more interested in describing the country than the actual play, much of which he missed because he was sightseeing and visiting his son.

Test Eleven is the account of 11 exciting Anglo-Australian matches, fairly predictably chosen by Bernard Whimpress and Nigel Hart. The first one is Melbourne 1877 and the last Nottingham 1993. The authors draw largely on contemporary accounts, but fill them out to give solid assessments of the players and tactics concerned, as well as discussions of more general issues, player dissent, "cronyism", and intimidatory bowling among them. Short of having been present at the actual matches these accounts are probably the next best thing.

The Journal of the Cricket Society, Golden Jubilee Edition, has a special feature, Captains All, containing thoughts on various aspects of leadership. Ted Dexter, Tony Lewis, Tom Graveney and M. J. K. Smith are main contributors, while Gooch provides a view of playing with Border, for Essex. "A tough nuggety sort of character, he had no qualms about bowling someone out in the side and could get very grumpy if things didn't go his way." Women's cricket is represented by articles from Netta Rheinberg and Rachael Heyhoe-Flint, who writes revealingly about her so far unsuccessful attempts to become an MCC member. Among the reasons offered for postponing such a possibility was that extra lavatories, baths and showers would have to be installed. Tim Rice offers as his "dream team" the 1953 England side that won back the Ashes under Leonard Hutton. Ned Sherrin pays a proper tribute, as a Somerset man, to the writings of R. C. Robertson-Glasgow and to the Somerset heroes of his youth – Gimblett, Walford, R. J. O. Meyer, Wellard, among others – and to the wicket-keeping of M. D. Lyon, described by Robertson-Glasgow as varying from "the brilliant to the blandly inattentive". Lyon objected to wide in-swingers on the leg-side, and as the ball sped to the flower border in front of the Taunton pavilion, he would remark casually: "Tut, tut; there go four more gerania." In the same entertaining issue E. W. Swanton deals with a choir of clerical cricketers, several of unusual talent. Among these was Canon F. B. R. Browne, nicknamed Tishy, because he bowled off the wrong foot, which gave him an action not unlike that of a contemporary racehorse.

Cricket at the Castle documents a hundred happy years of cricket at Arundel Castle, a ground made for pleasure at whatever level. Michael Marshall's account contains match details, scorecards, and numerous photographs. In **The Day of the "Demon"** Michael Dowsett has produced a nostalgic account of a strange match played at Maldon on June 19, 1878. The teams were Mr C. I. Thornton's XI v The Maldon Club. Thornton brought with him Spofforth, Hornby and Dr E. M. Grace; Maldon's star bowler was the 52-year-old John Hughes. The match itself was predictably one-sided. Hornby missed his train from Liverpool Street, arriving only after seven wickets were down. In the second innings he took five for 12. **Bound for Glory** and **Glory in the Cup,** two children's stories by Bob Cattell, relate the activities of Glory Gardens CC, who play in the North County Under-13 League. The writing is lively, the plots are full of action, and there are scoresheets, diagrams, and an appendix of technical terms.

Alan Ross is editor of the London Magazine. *He was cricket correspondent of* The Observer *from 1953 to 1972. He is the author of several cricket books and edited* The Cricketer's Companion.

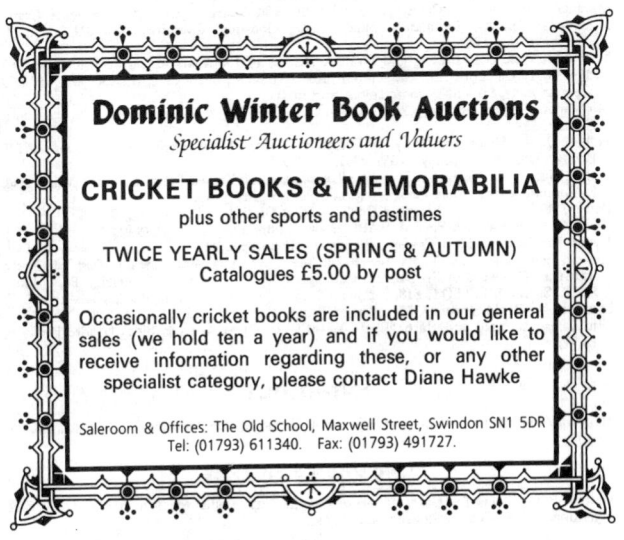

BOOKS RECEIVED IN 1995

GENERAL

Beckles, Hilary and Stoddart, Brian, eds. **Liberation Cricket: West Indies Cricket Culture** (Manchester University Press, £40 hardback, £12.99 paperback)

Berkmann, Marcus **Rain Men: The Madness of Cricket** (Little Brown, £16.99)

Craven, Nico **A Watching Brief** Foreword by Christopher Martin-Jenkins (from the author, The Coach House, Ponsonby, Seascale, Cumb. CA20 1BX, £5.55)

Das, D. K. **Cricket in America** and **Cricket for Baseball Players** (Cricket*USA* Inc., 4130 East Peakview Circle, Littleton, Colorado 80121-3250, $US7.95, $Can10.95, £5)

Dowsett, Michael **The Day of the "Demon": Maldon v C. I. Thornton's XI, June 19 1878** (from the author, 7 Lambs Close, Kidlington, Oxon. OX5 2YD, no price given)

Gooch, Graham and Keating, Frank **Gooch: My Autobiography** (Collins Willow, £15.99)

Guha, Ramachandra **Spin and Other Turns: Indian Cricket's Coming of Age** (Penguin India, 706 Eros Apartments, 56 Nehru Place, New Delhi 110019, Rs 100)

Haigh, Gideon **One Summer, Every Summer: An Ashes Journal** (Text Publishing, 171 La Trobe Street, Melbourne 3000, $A24.95)

Heald, Tim **Brian Johnston: The Authorised Biography** (Methuen, £14.99)

Hignell, Andrew **The Skipper: A Biography of Wilf Wooller** (Limlow Books, Blue Bell House, 2-4 Main Street, Scredington, Sleaford, Lincs. NG34 0AE, £16.99 + £1.50 p&p)

Knowles, Ray **South Africa versus England: A Test Cricket History** (New Holland, £19.99)

Lara, Brian with Brian Scovell **Beating the Field: My Own Story** Foreword by Sir Garfield Sobers (Partridge Press, £14.99)

Lawrence, Bridgette **Masterclass: The Biography of George Headley** (Polar Publishing, 2 Uxbridge Road, Leicester LE4 7ST, £7.99)

Lawrence, Ken **A Century of Cornhill Tests** Photographs by Patrick Eagar. Foreword by David Gower (Patrick Stephens, £14.99)

Lee, Alan **Lord Ted: The Dexter Enigma** (Gollancz/Witherby, £16.99)

Marshall, Sir Michael **Cricket at the Castle: 100 Years of Cricket at Arundel Castle** (Boundary Books, Southlands, Sandy Lane, Goostrey, Cheshire CW4 8NT, £13.95. Limited edition £80)

Midwinter, Eric ed. **Darling Old Oval: A History of 150 Years of Surrey Cricket at The Oval** (Cricket Lore, 22 Grazebrook Road, London N16 0HS, £22.50 UK, £24.50 overseas inc. p&p and 14 loose colour portraits)

Midwinter, Eric ed. **Surrey County Cricket Club 150 Years: A Celebration** (Surrey Youth Cricket, £5)

Pollard, Jack **Home and Away: A Complete Record of Australian Cricket Tours** (ABC Books, GPO 9994, Sydney, NSW 2001, $A49.95)

Pollard, Jack **Mollydookers: The World's Greatest Left-handed Batsmen** (Five Mile Press, 22 Summit Road, Noble Park, Victoria 3174, no price given)

Powell, William A. ed. **Aerofilms Guide: Cricket Grounds** (Dial House, £12.99)

Ray, Robin **Border and Beyond** (ABC Books, address above, $A19.95)

Ryder, Rowland **Cricket Calling** (Faber and Faber, £15.99)

Sissons, Ric **The Don Meets the Babe: the 1932 Australian Cricket Tour of North America** Foreword by Sir Donald Bradman (J. W. McKenzie, 12 Stoneleigh Park Road, Ewell, Surrey KT19 0QT, £18. Limited edition signed by Sir Donald and the author £55)

Steen, Rob **David Gower: A Man Out of Time** (Gollancz, £16.99)

Whimpress, Bernard and Hart, Nigel **Test Eleven: Great Ashes Battles** (Andre Deutsch, £8.99)

ANTHOLOGY

Rayvern Allen, David **More than a Game: A Classic Cricket Anthology** (Gollancz, £16.99)

CHILDREN'S FICTION

Cattell, Bob **Bound for Glory** and **Glory in the Cup** (Julia MacRae Books, £8.99 each hardback; Red Fox, £2.99 each paperback)

PHOTOGRAPHIC

Ray, Mark **Cricket: The Game Behind The Game** (Macmillan Australia; 31 Market Street, Sydney; obtainable from Sportspages, 94-96 Charing Cross Road, London WC2H 0JG and Barton Square, St Ann's Square, Manchester M2 7HA, £16.50)

TECHNICAL

Atherton, Mike with Pat Gibson **A Test of Cricket: Know the Game** (Hodder & Stoughton, £16.99)

Philpott, Peter **The Art of Wrist-Spin Bowling** (Crowood Press, £12.99)

STATISTICAL

Ambrose, Don ed. **Statistical Survey 1870** and **1871** (ACS, 3 Radcliffe Road, West Bridgford, Nottingham NG2 5FF, £4 each)

Association of Cricket Statisticians **Cricket Matches 1830-38** (ACS, address as above, £8.50) (ACS, address as above, £2.75 and £3.25)

Ayers, Michael **Surrey County Cricket Club First Class Records 1846-1994** (Limlow Books, Blue Bell House, 2-4 Main Street, Scredington, Sleaford, Lincs. NG34 0AE, £8 + 50p p&p)

Baggett, David **Derbyshire County Cricket Club First Class Records 1871-1994** (Limlow Books, address as above, £8.50 + 50p p&p)

Bailey, Philip J. comp. **Sri Lanka First Class Matches 1990-91** (ACS, address as above, £4)

Bartlett, C. J. **Paul Gibb:** His Record Innings-by-Innings (ACS, address as above, £4)

Croudy, Brian **Colin Blythe:** His Record Innings-by-Innings (ACS, address as above, £6.50)

Frindall, Bill **The Wisden Book of Test Cricket: Volume I 1877-1977** and **Volume II 1977-1994** (Fourth Edition) (Headline, £35 each)

Frindall, Bill ed. **Playfair Cricket World Cup Guide** (Headline, £4.99)

Heald, Brian **Essex County Cricket Club First Class Records 1894-1994** (Limlow Books, address as above, £8 + 50p p&p)

Isherwood, Robin, and Bailey, Philip **Transvaal Cricketers 1889-90 to 1993-94** (ACS, address as above, £3)

Ledbetter, Jim ed. **First-Class Cricket: A Complete Record 1935** (Limlow Books, address as above, £15.95 + £1.50 p&p)

Ledbetter, Jim **Frank Tyson:** His Record Innings-by-Innings (ACS, address as above, £4)

Lodge, Derek **P. B. H. May:** His Record Innings-by-Innings (ACS, address as above, £6)

Mubashir Ali Zaidi comp. **The Wills Record Book of One Thousand One-Day Internationals** Foreword by Zaheer Abbas (Cricket Research Consultants, 35 Ramzan Chambers, Dr Billimoria Street, Off I. I. Chundrigar Road, Karachi, Rs 100)

Sandiford, Keith **Everton Weekes:** His Record Innings-by-Innings (ACS, address as above, £4)

Ward, John comp. **Zimbabwean First Class Matches 1993-94** and **1994-95** (ACS, address as above, £2.75 and £3.25)

Woolgar, Jason **England: The Complete One-day International Record** (Eric Dobby Publishing, 12 Warnford Road, Orpington, Kent BR6 6LW, £14.99)

Woolgar, Jason **The Test Cricketers Almanac** (Eric Dobby, address as above, £6.99)

COUNTIES

Draper, Steven **Cricket Grounds of Yorkshire** (ACS, 3 Radcliffe Road, West Bridgford, Nottingham NG2 5FF, £4.50)

FIRST-CLASS COUNTY YEARBOOKS, 1995

Derbyshire (£4.50), Durham (£6), Essex (£6), Glamorgan (£5), Gloucestershire (£3), Hampshire (£6), Kent (£5), Lancashire (£6), Leicestershire (£4.95), Middlesex (£7.50), Northamptonshire (£7), Nottinghamshire (£4), Somerset (£6), Surrey (£5), Sussex (£6), Warwickshire (£4.50), Worcestershire (£4), Yorkshire (£8.50). 1996 prices may change. Some counties may add charges for p&p.

OTHER HANDBOOKS AND ANNUALS

Armstrong, David ed. **Minor Counties Cricket Annual and Official Handbook** (ACS, 3 Radcliffe Road, West Bridgford, Nottingham NG2 5FF, £4)

Bailey, Philip comp. **ACS International Cricket Year Book 1995** (ACS, address as above, £8)

Bryden, Colin ed. **Protea Assurance South African Cricket Annual 1995** (UCBSA/Protea Assurance, PO Box 646, Cape Town 8000, no price given)

The Cricketers' Who's Who, 1995 Statistics by Richard Lockwood (Lennard/Queen Anne Press, £12.99)

Frindall, Bill ed. **Playfair Cricket Annual 1995** (Headline, £4.50 paperback, £7.99 hardback)

Hatton, Les comp. **ACS First Class Counties Second Eleven Annual** (ACS, address as above, £4)

Leitch, Neil ed. **The W. H. Mann Guide to Scottish Cricket 1995** (Scottish Cricket Union, Caledonia House, South Gyle, Edinburgh, EH12 9DQ, £4 + 70p p&p)

Lemmon, David ed. **Benson and Hedges Cricket Year Fourteenth Edition.** Foreword by Graham Gooch (Headline, £19.99)

Menon, Mohandas ed. **Cricontrol Statistical Annual 1994-95** (Board of Control for Cricket in India, no price given)

Miller, Allan ed. **Allan's Australian Cricket Annual 1994-95** (from Allan Miller, PO Box 974, Busselton, WA 6280, $A29.95; available in UK from Sport in Print, 3 Radcliffe Road, West Bridgford, Nottingham NG2 5FF, £14.50 inc. p&p)

Salim Parvez ed. **England v West Indies Tour '95: Words on Sport Pocket Annual** (Words on Sport, PO Box 382, St Albans, Herts. AL2 3JD, £4.99)

REPRINTS AND UPDATES

Andrew, Keith **The Handbook of Cricket** Revised paperback (Pelham Books, £14.99)

Botham, Ian **My Autobiography** Paperback with extra chapter (Collins Willow, £5.99)

Brodribb, Gerald **Next Man In: A Survey of Cricket Laws and Customs** Updated edition of 1952 original (Souvenir Press, £18.50)

Gower, David with Martin Johnson **Gower: The Autobiography** Revised paperback (Collins Willow, £5.99)

James Lillywhite's Cricketers' Annual 1896 Facsimile edition (Cricket Lore, 22 Grazebrook Road, London N16 0HS, £11.95 UK, £13.95 overseas inc. p&p)

John Wisden's Cricketers' Almanack for 1898 and 1899 Facsimile editions (Willows Publishing, 17 The Willows, Stone, Staffs. ST15 0DE, £44 each inc. p&p UK, £46 inc. p&p overseas; £5 extra for version with facsimile of original hard cloth cover)

Manley, Michael **A History of West Indies Cricket** Revised paperback (Andre Deutsch, £15.99)

Martin-Jenkins, Christopher ed. **The Spirit of Cricket: A Personal Anthology** Paperback (Faber and Faber, £7.99)

Old English Cricket: Six Pamphlets by H. P. – T. Reprint of "A Collection of Evidences concerning the Game prior to the Days of Hambledon" published 1923-1929 by P. F. Thomas. Limited edition of 300 (Willows Publishing, address as above, £45 inc. p&p UK, £47 inc. p&p overseas surface, £49 inc. p&p airmail)

Pollard, Jack **The Complete History of Australian Cricket 1803-1995** Revised edition, five-volume boxed set (The Book Company, 9/9-13 Winbourne Road, Brookvale 2100, Sydney, NSW, $A49.95)

Pollard, Jack **The Complete Illustrated History of Australian Cricket** Revised edition (Viking Australia, $A50)

Sim, William Clulow **The Log of the "Old Un" from Liverpool to San Francisco 1886** Facsimile of 1887 edition (J. W. McKenzie, 12 Stoneleigh Park Road, Ewell, Surrey KT19 0QT, £15 inc. p&p)

PERIODICALS

Boundary (three a year) ed. Margot Butcher (14 Como Street, Takapuna, Auckland 10, NZ, $NZ9.95)

The Cricketer International (monthly) editorial director Richard Hutton (Beech Hanger, Ashurst, Tunbridge Wells, Kent TN3 9ST, £2.45)

The Cricketer Quarterly: Facts and Figures ed. Richard Lockwood (The Cricketer International, address as above, £2.75)

Cricket Lore (ten per volume, frequency variable) ed. Richard Hill (Cricket Lore, 22 Grazebrook Road, London N16 0HS, £35 per volume)

The Cricket Statistician (quarterly) ed. Philip J. Bailey (ACS, 3 Radcliffe Road, West Bridgford, Nottingham NG2 5FF, £1.50, free to ACS members)

Cricket World (monthly) editorial director Michael Blumberg (2a Chelverton Road, London SW15 1RH, £1.95)

The Indian Cricket Quarterly: Facts and Figures ed. Mohandas Menon (Valsa Publications, 2 Prem Jivan, Caesar Road, Amboli, Andheri (W), Bombay 400 058, Rs 70, annual subscription Rs 200; available in UK from Brian Croudy, 26 Harold Road, Deal, Kent CT14 6QH, annual airmail subscription £12.00)

Inside Edge (monthly) managing editor Norman Tasker (ACP Publishing, 54 Park Street, Sydney, NSW 2000, $A5.20)

The Journal of the Cricket Society (twice yearly) ed. Clive W. Porter (from Mr P. Ellis, 63 Groveland Road, Beckenham, Kent BR3 3PX, £5 to non-members)

Minor Counties News (four issues a year) (available from counties or from Mike Berry, Idsworth, 3 Fair Close, Frankton, Rugby, Warwicks. CV23 9PL, apply for subscription details)

Red Stripe Caribbean Quarterly ed. Tony Cozier (Cozier Publishing, PO Box 40W, Worthing, Christ Church, Barbados, annual subscription £12 Europe, BDS$22 Barbados, BDS$28/US$14 rest of the West Indies, US$18 US, Can$24 Canada, US$24 elsewhere)

SA Cricket Action (ten issues a year) (Cricket Action Subscriptions, Freepost JH 125, Private Bag X49, Auckland Park, SA 2006, R85 per annum)

SA Cricketer (monthly in season) ed. Ashley Lazarus (SA Cricketer, PO Box 146, Germiston, SA 1400, R5.70)

The Scottish Cricketer (three a year) ed. Brad Mann (145 Broomhill Drive, Glasgow GL11 7ND, £1.50)

Wisden Cricket Monthly (25 Down Road, Merrow, Guildford, Surrey GU1 2PY, £2.50)

MISCELLANEOUS

Cricket '95: The Official TCCB Sticker Collection (Panini Publishing, 2 Nevill Street, Tunbridge Wells TN2 5TT, 60p for album, £1.70 for ten stickers, £2.30 for 15)

Heavens, Roger **An Index to Frederick Lillywhite's/Haygarth's Cricket Scores and Biographies of Celebrated Cricketers Volumes One to Eight, 1746-1864** (Roger Heavens, 2 Lowfields, Little Eversden, Cambs. CB3 7HJ, £4.95 each inc. p&p)

Turner, F. M. ed. **Sources of Grant Aid for Cricket** (NCA, Lord's Ground, London NW8 8QZ, free to clubs)

PERSONAL ORGANISER

The Complete Cricket Companion (Gaymer's Guides, Russell House, Uxbridge Road, Hampton Hill, Middx TW12 3AD, £19.99 vinyl, £34.99 leather, £2 p&p – first three updates included)

THE CRICKET SOCIETY LITERARY AWARD

The Cricket Society Literary Award has been presented since 1970 to the author of the cricket book judged as best of the year. The 1995 award went to Rob Steen for **David Gower: A Man Out of Time**.

CRICKET VIDEOS, 1995

By STEVEN LYNCH

If the Monopolies Commission were interested in the relatively new industry of cricket videos, it might think the current situation in Britain worthy of investigation. Of the tapes received in 1995 which originated in this country, all bar one sprang from the producers of the **Cover Point** video magazine.

Previously the major player had been the BBC, with their huge cricket archive, but they seem to have largely given up on cricket – all sport, indeed – now, despite the *Botham's Ashes* tape (1981 Test series) being among the bestsellers of any video title. John Bodnar, the BBC's video producer, said that the explosion of live sport, especially on satellite TV, meant the demand for pre-recorded videos had dropped. He pointed out that any future BBC cricket videos would need to be assured of high sales, since the TCCB insisted on a minimum royalty payment of £10,000 for each title.

Cover Point buy in a lot of footage from the BBC, Australia's Channel 9 and elsewhere, and their monthly videos are well-produced, with the rare overseas footage being especially welcome. Sometimes there is almost too much to digest at one sitting, but there is always the pause button . . .

With the regular issues of *Cover Point* building up into a splendid visual record of recent seasons, their production company Sharp Focus Ltd is branching out into the realms of history. One such departure, the **Official History of Lancashire CCC** (narrated by the ubiquitous David Lloyd), traces the county club from its origins in 1864 – not much video footage then – to the present day; another is **Great Moments in English Cricket**, which starts with the 1952 Headingley Test, when the young Fred Trueman reduced India to nought for four. This tape is narrated by the *Daily Telegraph*'s Christopher Martin-Jenkins.

Even one of the year's comic offerings came from the Sharp Focus stable. **Rory Bremner: Creased Up** sees the popular TV impressionist run through his range of cricketing voices from A (Atherton) to B (Boycott) and beyond. Often humorous, it is perhaps best observed in small parts rather than as a whole. The same is true for **Botham & Lamb**, largely a collection of the best moments of their recent theatre tour: all the usual suspects are lampooned (Boycott, Illingworth, the Lord's ancients, etc).

The only coaching videos seen in 1995 were a set of four, produced in South Africa and featuring their successful national coach Bob Woolmer. The tapes cover straight-bat shots; cross-bat shots; bowling; and fielding, wicket-keeping and umpiring. As South Africa showed against England, doing things **The Bob Woolmer Way** does seem to work.

VIDEOS RECEIVED IN 1995

Australia v England: Highlights of the 1994-95 Ashes Tour (Sharp Focus/Cover Point; £12.99)

Botham & Lamb (Bespoke; £12.99)

Cover Point Video Magazine (Cover Point Cricket Ltd, 113 Upper Tulse Hill, London SW2 2RD; ten issues per year £79.99 inc. p&p)

Great Moments in English Cricket 1952-1994 (Sharp Focus/Cover Point; £12.99)

Official History of Lancashire CCC (Sharp Focus/Cover Point; £12.99)

Rory Bremner: Creased Up (Polygram/Sharp Focus; £12.99)

The Bob Woolmer Way (Sovereign; £49.99 for set of four)

Prices shown are Recommended Retail Prices

CRICKET AND THE MEDIA IN 1995

By TIM DE LISLE

At the end of 1994, Australia's Channel 9, the company which leads the way in cricket coverage, unveiled a new presenter: Shane Warne, the hottest property in Australian cricket. From the Second Test against England onwards, Warne was entrusted with fronting the eve-of-Test preview on the evening news, and took time off from the nets to interview his team-mates. The questions he lobbed up were jokey and anodyne (you would never have known he was a spinner). Viewers who tuned in to hear about the pitch, the weather or the line-ups were disappointed. The only thing to be learnt from Warne's first report was that Tim May had joined the fashion for goatee beards.

Cricketers have been going into the media for longer than the word "media" has been common currency. And stars of Warne's wattage have long had ghostwritten columns in popular newspapers. But this may have been the first case of a player acting as a reporter while still standing centre-stage. For Channel 9, the loss in information was evidently offset by the reflected celebrity. It was the way things seemed to be going. It ain't what is said, it's the person that's saying it.

During the English season, the trend blew up into a storm about who is better qualified to cover cricket, the ex-player or the lifelong journalist. The touchpaper was lit by Michael Henderson, a middle-order cricket writer on *The Times*. (This followed soon after Robert Henderson's racially inflammatory article in *Wisden Cricket Monthly*. The Beatles were on to something when they sang "the Hendersons will all be there".)

Michael Henderson was invited on *The Back Page*, a programme on BBC Radio 5 Live devoted to sports journalism. Asked what he thought of players-turned-writers, Henderson said some were good, and named names – Peter Roebuck, Mike Selvey, Mark Nicholas. Then he said some were bad, and named names. "Simon Hughes [one of the *Daily Telegraph's* regiment of cricket writers] can't write . . . He was a very poor player and he's an *execrable* writer." The stress on "execrable" was more than mere italics are capable of conveying. But there was more. "Vic Marks [cricket correspondent of *The Observer* since 1990] hasn't got a clue. He's palpably out of his depth and it's an embarrassment." Henderson then described Marks as "a lovely chap", to add compliment to injury.

There are not many new things under the sun, but one cricket writer savaging two others on national radio is probably among them. The victims reacted in different ways. Hughes let down one of the tyres of Henderson's car. Marks kept his own counsel, but was stoutly defended by his sports editor, Alan Hubbard. In his weekly column, Hubbard accused Henderson of bitterness, paranoia, bleating, pomposity, bitchery, prejudice, mean spirits, palpable ridiculousness, and sour grapes: he had been an *Observer* contributor, but a previous sports editor had felt that "he wrote pretentious twaddle and did not merit a place in *The Observer* 1st XI".

Fleet Street tradition holds that dog does not eat dog. But that presupposes that all journalists are members of the same species. Henderson's attack was intemperate, arrogant, and ill-directed; but it raised a legitimate issue. Former players, for years confined to column and sidebar, are now landing plum jobs.

But only on the broadsheets – with one exception, which proves the rule. David Gower joined the tabloid *Sunday Express* straight from Hampshire in 1993, dislodging the respected old-school reporter Pat Gibson. Gower found the job harder than either batting or television commentary, and in 1995 switched to writing a column, on the *Sunday Telegraph*. His experience points to the paradox of big-name reporting. The bigger the name, the keener editors will be to get him on board. But the bigger the name, the less opportunity he will have had to learn his new craft. All those winters that Gower was on tour all over the place with England, Roebuck spent in Australia, writing columns for the *Sydney Morning Herald*. Gower knows more about Test cricket; Roebuck knows more about journalism.

Sports writing is harder than it looks. The specialist correspondent regularly takes on what would be four jobs in, say, politics: news, comment, features and colour. (In politics, only one of these, comment, would normally be entrusted to a former practitioner, and then only if he or she wrote conspicuously well.) In Australia, the story of the year was the allegation of bribery made by three current Test players, including Channel 9's man, against the then Pakistan captain. It was broken by Phil Wilkins of the *Sydney Morning Herald*, another respected member of the old school. Journalistically, it had less in common with a match report than it did with Watergate. Would it have been published, let alone reported thoroughly, if the call from cricket's Deep Throat had been made to an ex-player?

The story touching on cricket that received most column inches in 1995 was nothing to do with the game at all. It was the marriage of a player-pundit, Imran Khan, to Jemima Goldsmith, student daughter of the British businessman Sir James Goldsmith. Excited by the good looks the couple shared, the papers were even more taken with the differences between them: age, race and, initially, religion. The story had little to do with cricket; Imran's fame had long been fanned by the gossip columnists as well as the sports writers. And it felt like a one-off. Certainly there was no obvious place for *Wisden* to record it. Births, Marriages and Deaths of Cricketers, anyone?

Meanwhile, cricket coverage continued to multiply. A new magazine, *Third Man* temporarily slotted in to the gap between the mainstream (*The Cricketer*, *Wisden Cricket Monthly*) and the fanzines (*Johnny Miller 96 Not Out*, *The Googly*), but though it looked handsome, it failed to see out the year. On television, the TCCB's new deal with the BBC and BSkyB brought magazine programmes and longer highlights. Sunil Gavaskar announced that he had secured the rights to publish scores from the 1996 World Cup on the Internet. A sharp increase in the cost of newsprint meant that Fleet Street pagination stopped growing, but sports pages, and budgets, were sometimes exempt. During the Ashes tour of 1994-95, the *Daily Telegraph* often had three reporters covering the same day's play, and published 3,000 words from them.

Some things didn't change. On November 22, the *Telegraph* scooped its rivals with details of the TCCB's proposal to turn itself into the English Cricket Board. It noted that these had been expressly excluded from general circulation, and that the counties and other organisations had been given only eight days to file comments. A TCCB official confirmed that the secrecy had been deliberate. "We don't want the press helping people make up their minds," he said. Perish the thought.

CRICKET AND THE LAW IN 1995

The following cricket-related court cases were reported during 1995:

The publishers of *Wisden Cricket Monthly* paid substantial damages and full legal costs to the England players Devon Malcolm and Phillip DeFreitas, following an article in the magazine which questioned their suitability to be selected for England, their patriotism and their loyalty. The publishers dissociated themselves from the article and accepted it should not have been printed.

The editor of the magazine, David Frith, had earlier apologised to everyone offended by the piece and admitted an error. An apology was also issued to Chris Lewis and a donation to charity made on his behalf. *Wisden Cricket Monthly* is under the ultimate ownership of John Wisden and Co., which publishes this almanack.

The decision by the Sydney Cricket Association to prevent the North Sydney club qualifying for the semi-finals of the Sydney First Grade competition was held to be unlawful by Mr Justice Grove of the New South Wales Supreme Court.

This followed a match between North Sydney and the University of NSW on March 18, 1995 in which the captains agreed to play for outright points by mutual declarations in order to give North Sydney a chance of qualifying for the semi-finals. Rain on the first Saturday of the match meant that had the game been played normally they would have had no chance of overhauling Waverley.

North Sydney won the match, but the association deducted the points on the grounds that the result was contrived. The judge said there was no evidence that either team was not trying and also ruled there had not been a fair hearing. North Sydney were reinstated and reached the final, where they lost to Bankstown.

Mark Glover, captain and groundsman of Over Wallop, Hampshire, was ordered to pay £175 compensation to two men he hit because he suspected them of vandalising the pitch and pavilion, which had been damaged in a series of attacks. All the windows had been smashed, the sightscreens wrecked and beer glasses broken over the wicket. Glover also had to pay £35 costs and was bound over to keep the peace. "I admit I snapped," he was quoted as saying. "It was a wallop for Over Wallop Cricket Club." The chairman of the parish council, Geoff Shadwell, said the punishment was an injustice.

The team at Jordans, Buckinghamshire, who won a court case in 1994 to remain on the village green despite objections from residents, decided that they would eventually move to a new pitch 150 yards away where there would be "a lot less hassle".

CRICKETANA IN 1995

By DAVID FRITH

In the game of cricketana collecting, the flow of sentiment and romance remains tolerably confluent with the relentless current of commerce. The auction-houses, the dealers and the vendors all ride high on the boom, while ambitious collectors mitigate their frustrations with the occasional hard-earned acquisition of note. More rather than fewer sales are staged. Prices continue to climb.

The biggest sale of this decade was at Phillips in January 1995, when the vast book collection of the late Hal Cohen was offered. The realisation was over £250,000 (to which had to be added 15 per cent buyer's premium). A run of *Wisden* from 1864 to 1985, sold piecemeal, made £41,492 all in, with the first edition fetching £3,176 and the 1869 £3,411. W. G. Grace's de luxe *Cricket*, signed by 81 cricketers of the Golden Age, made £7,646, and *Gilligan's Men* by M. A. Noble, signed by the Australian and England teams of 1924-25, sold for £1,118. Among the pictorial gems, J. C. Anderson's pencil/watercolour, *Surrey Cricketers* (1852), went for just under £10,000, a figure marginally exceeded for an original "Spy" portrait of Ranjitsinhji. Top price was £15,291, paid by MCC for Ponsonby Staples's *In the Pavilion Enclosure*, an enchanting pencil-and-gouache, which returned to Lord's after decades in exile.

It was a phenomenal sale, lasting six and a half hours, with collectors and dealers paying appreciably more than many had planned. But the hoard was of the highest quality. Of all the other fare, a medallion stood out: given to R. E. Foster to mark MCC's first Australian tour (1903-04), it was bought for £1,153, underlining the extra attraction of things once owned or worn by the famous. This was evident at other sales during the year. A cap of Jim Laker's fetched £1,090, one of Neil Harvey's (hardly worn) £918, both at Christie's. At Knight's, in Norwich, Kent caps that once perched on the heads of Frank Woolley and Colin Blythe each sold for £825, as surprising as the appearance of Geoff Boycott's Yorkshire blazer, which attracted a bid of £352.

The supreme prizes, however, were a 1934 Australian blazer and 1946-47 Test cap once worn by Sir Donald Bradman, both offered at the Christie's sale. The Bradman Museum in Bowral would have been the ideal home for them, but the budget would not stretch that far. Instead, Charlie Watts, the Rolling Stones' drummer, secured the blazer (£3,670), and a Western Australian schoolteacher bid £3,440 down the telephone line for the cap. Beside these items, a first-edition *Felix on the Bat* (£918) was scarcely noticed.

Highest price for any cricket item last year was £46,462, paid at Sotheby's for a version of Robert James's painting *Tossing for Innings*. The rarest book was possibly *Sidney Cohen's New South Wales Cricketers' Guide 1877-8* (only edition), which made £760. The most poignant item was a Christmas card sent by Harold Larwood from the 1932-33 Australian tour, sold for £300 at Vennett-Smith, Nottingham, several weeks after his recent death. The most satisfying news was that Duleepsinhji's archive of letters (some substantiating the suspicion that the 1929 South Africans objected to his selection for England) was now safely housed at West Sussex Record Office. Most remarkable instant inflation was a bat signed by both teams in the 1911-12 Ashes series, bought at auction in Sydney for $A2,640 in April and offered in a dealer's catalogue in October for $A6,000. The most special *Wisden* was one

from the 1870s, inscribed by editor W. H. Knight, which fetched over £3,000, though one which came close was sent c/o General Roberts to Major R. M. Poore, who was engaged in the Boer War. This 1900 *Wisden* recorded Poore's amazing batting for Hampshire, and drew a successful bid nearly a century later of £846.

And yet, if there was a gem of gems in 1995, it must have been what is reasonably thought to be the oldest cricket ball. Discovered, with an ancient little boot, behind a plaster wall in a house in Lewes, it has been dated as late 18th century. Scepticism was a deterrent, allowing a collector from Sussex (who had to accept the boot too) to get it at the bargain price of £860.

CRICKET SOCIETIES IN 1995

By MURRAY HEDGCOCK

The Cricket Society, London-based, but with members all over Britain and abroad, marked its 50th birthday with events culminating in a Golden Jubilee dinner, addressed by Sir Colin Cowdrey and Sir Tim Rice. It also raised £8,000 for Taverners' charities, with a special match at Arundel.

The South African society staged a tenth anniversary banquet for 380 guests, headed by ICC chairman Sir Clyde Walcott and Lady Walcott. In Australia, the Sydney branch annual dinner was addressed by Arthur Morris and Neil Harvey on the great 1948 Bradman tour of England. Journalist Mike Coward received the society literary award for his book on South Africa's return, *Australia v. The New South Africa – Cricket Contact Renewed*.

The Council of Cricket Societies, the umbrella body linking most societies, is again sponsored by Warwickshire County Cricket Club – a gesture of thanks from the professional game for the work of genuine enthusiasts like society members. Council's most appreciated function is its liaison on speakers, the movement being in constant need of visitors who have something fresh to offer about the game, express themselves clearly and wittily – and do not seek vast fees.

A welcome new voice on the circuit is that of former MCC Secretary Lt-Col. J. R. Stephenson, who made such an impact that societies are queuing to sign him for next winter. And Warwickshire's tireless pace bowler and vice-captain Tim Munton was warmly received when he spoke to the council's winter meeting, ensuring that he too can expect a very busy off-season over 1996-97.

A list of societies can be found on pages 1302-1303.

CRICKET EQUIPMENT IN 1995

By NORMAN HARRIS

When a plain bat – devoid of the normal markings or stickers that proclaim the maker's name – is used in first-class cricket, it usually announces to the world that its user is in dispute with his bat-supplier, or is available to be signed up by another.

Brian Lara was using such bats, and some of unknown provenance, in the first half of the summer of 1995. Switching between a number of different bats was hardly conducive to maintaining his form of 1994. His scores during last summer's first three Tests were, indeed, modest by his standards; and they were followed by the first "pair" of his career, against Kent.

What was clear, though, was that none of these bats was the "Scoop" with which he had made his record scores. Professional batsmen have developed a disagreeable reputation for taking money from one bat maker and putting that maker's livery on to a bat they prefer. That cannot credibly be done with a Scoop, because of its unique look, which has been ensured by the money spent by Gray-Nicolls on copyright-protection since they introduced the bat in 1974. Not that it would have been in Lara's character to resort to subterfuge. Indeed, during the period in which he and Grays could not agree new terms, there was nothing to have stopped him using the Scoop. Perhaps pride prevented him doing so.

In any case, Lara was on to something much bigger. Finally, came the breathtaking news that he had come close to emulating the shaver manufacturer in the TV adverts who liked the product so much he "bought the company". Lara International Ltd had contracted to get a special Scoop bat from Gray-Nicolls, marketing it under their own name. It would be known as the "375" (immortalising the Test record score) and the distinctive deep groove, now royal blue, would replicate the original shape rather than the maker's more recent modifications. If it was good news for Lara and his new company (his managers spoke of him becoming cricket's first millionaire) the deal also represented a considerable success for Gray-Nicolls.

Having announced the deal, Lara hesitated before switching back to his favourite Scoop. At Old Trafford he plastered his existing bat with labels announcing the new company that were rather too crude for the liking of agents. At any rate, hundreds in each of the last three Tests suggested that in his case the bat is a relatively minor factor in his success at the crease, though clearly he wanted to use the Scoop if he could. Should he ever change his mind, he – alone – is a man who need not be concerned about disloyalty to his bat sponsor.

"Switching the stickers" is a depressing feature of modern professional cricket. And ultimately it acts against the interests of the professionals. A manufacturer can produce a bat, glove or boot made of superior materials but may not be able to afford to pay players to use it. Instead, the company is likely to suffer the frustration of players using it with their own sponsor's sticker attached.

Further, the luckless firm may well find that within a year its product is being copied by a manufacturer in the subcontinent using cheaper materials. So the manufacturer follows the low-cost route or risks going bust.

The anguished cries of batsmen during the 1995 season only serve to underline the sad irony of this situation. Most would rather be paid a small sum for endorsing one firm's gloves, instead of paying for what would suit them best. While fingers were being broken with apparently unprecedented frequency, gloves with impressively resilient materials were being produced. One such product came from Hunts County, following a desperate plea from the Warwickshire batsman Paul Smith. Another was produced by Arcass, a company set up by the former Worcestershire wicket-keeper, Rodney Cass. Both gloves featured material that was much more dense and resilient, but just as light, as conventional "foam". Such material had been available for some time, and indeed was widely used in hockey gloves and pads.

But will batsmen – professionals who presumably need the best possible protective equipment – actively support such advancements? It is a question which should be addressed by the Cricketers Association. Interestingly, fast bowlers seem to have a different attitude from batsmen. Most receive free boots from manufacturers, and some are paid to wear them, yet, as reported here last year, many have beaten a path to the door of the Sutton Coldfield bootmaker Ian Mason, who does not discount his price of around £270 to anyone, be the customer's name Donald, Malcolm, Waqar or Bishop. And, remarkably, all of them have been prepared to pay.

Finally, back to broken fingers. The development of a hand guard that is attached to the bat handle (a product yet to catch on) has led to the idea of a smaller device that fits on the outside of the glove, almost encircling the first two fingers with a firm, shaped, sleeve made of orthopaedic plastic, preventing them being crushed but still allowing them contact with the handle. The device has been patented by the writer and broadcaster Ralph Dellor. No doubt professionals will want to try it. If he can persuade them to *buy* it, he might enter into professional cricket's hall of fame.

UMPIRING IN 1995

By JACK BAILEY

When the twenty international umpires met in London in August, they voted to restore their prerogative to decide for themselves what constitutes unfair bowling, without being hemmed in by the "two bouncers per over" regulation – which at first sight is a giant step in the right direction.

The ICC regulations for Test cricket currently in force are a licence for two up the batsman's nose in every over: a recipe for the bouncer forming the mainspring of the bowler's attack, rather than an occasional surprise weapon. Tell a fast bowler that he is allowed two bouncers an over and it becomes almost a point of honour to bowl them. This has worked to the detriment of the game in ways beyond counting, although not to the manufacturers of protective gear from head to waist.

The current ICC experimental regulation for Test match cricket was introduced in October 1994, for three years. Then a maximum of two bouncers an over superseded the previous one per over. Now the international umpires are in essence seeking a move back to Law 42.8 (as amended experimentally) which states: "The bowling of fast, short-pitched balls is unfair if the umpire at the bowler's end considers that, by their repetition and taking into account their length, height and direction, they are likely to inflict physical injury on the striker, irrespective of the protective clothing and equipment he may be wearing. The relative skill of the striker shall also be taken into consideration."

Before anyone gets too excited about this latest proposal, it should be noted that this is only the beginning of a long trail. The meeting of the full International Cricket Council in July 1996 would be the last stage in the process, after the captains of the World Cup teams and the ICC cricket committee have considered the proposals. Everyone will doubtless have in mind why the decision to nominate the number of short-pitched balls per over was adopted in the first place.

It was because the umpires at international level were taking no discernible action under Law 42, and the number of short-pitched, or "unfair", balls was increasing alarmingly. Given those circumstances, one or two per over was considered better than five or six. So what has changed?

David Richards, chief executive of ICC, says umpires are now a great deal more confident of their ability to implement the Laws. The arrival of referees on the international scene has made umpires feel more independent and has removed the reliance previously placed on reports given by captains with an axe to grind. The international panel of umpires – splendidly but somewhat quaintly supported by National Grid – has also gained confidence from contracts of reasonable length, the support of ICC as an institution and some improvement in the attitudes of individual Cricket Boards.

Should the latest proposal negotiate the various hurdles still in place, the general air of optimism will be put severely to the test. Consistency of interpretation of Law 42.8 has been as big a problem as the difficulty of framing it in a manner that can properly convey the wishes of the legislators. How to curb the bouncer without banning it altogether is the aim. As much would depend on the attitude of players as the skill of umpires.

CRICKET GROUNDS IN 1995

In the first century of Test cricket, between 1877 and 1977, 48 different cricket grounds round the world staged Test matches. But in the past couple of decades the number has exploded. There was an average of a new ground every year in the 1980s; in the 1990s the rate has been two a year. The list on pages 249-250 of this *Wisden* contains 74 grounds. But since the closing date for the Records section, the Arbab Niaz Stadium in Peshawar has become No. 75 and Centurion Park in South Africa No. 76.

The growth is partially explained by the arrival of two new Test-playing countries, Sri Lanka and Zimbabwe – especially Sri Lanka, with its confusing proliferation of stadiums in and around Colombo. But since 1977 there have been seven new grounds in both India and Pakistan, partly because new stadiums have been built, partly because the authorities have moved games into the hinterland to counter falling enthusiasm for the five-day game in the more sophisticated centres. Forty of the 76 are in the subcontinent and, like most of them, the Arbab Niaz Stadium is a featureless concrete bowl. There is said to be a distant view of the Khyber Pass on the rare occasions the smog lifts.

Centurion Park is altogether more attractive. Except for the one large stand, most of the ground comprises grass banks where spectators can gently fry sausages on the barbecues and themselves in the sun. At the inaugural Test, against England in November 1995, many people were being shaded by umbrellas for the first two days; the umbrellas had to fulfil a different function as the weather broke and the rest of the Test was rained off.

The ground is the headquarters of the Northern Transvaal Cricket Union and replaces the quaint, but hardly adequate, ground at Berea Park in Pretoria. When the province decided it needed a new HQ, the city authorities were unhelpful, but the local council in the suburban settlement of Verwoerdburg were more co-operative, and Centurion Park opened there in 1986. The city's name, however, became an embarrassment: it was called after Hendrik Verwoerd, the former prime minister and architect of apartheid – not the kind of person the new South Africa is anxious to honour. In 1995 the city council solved the problem by voting to change Verwoerdburg to Centurion, making it perhaps the first city in the world to be named after its cricket ground. The road leading to the stadium, however, is still John Vorster Drive, after Verwoerd's successor and the man whose ban on Basil D'Oliveira precipitated South Africa's cricketing isolation.

Among the other new Test grounds is the Queens Sports Club in Bulawayo. This was the traditional centre for cricket in the city, but it lost its status more than a decade ago following a financial dispute. The first Test Zimbabwe played in the city, in November 1992, was thus staged at the Bulawayo Athletic Club. However, facilities there were poor and Tests have now been switched to Queens Club. This is a much more attractive and practical ground, with a better playing surface and permanent stands. Its major drawback is that the clubhouse is actually behind the grandstand, making the game virtually invisible from the dressing-rooms which can be a problem for the next man in unless the game is on television.

Below Test level, new venues in 1995 included Webster Park, Anguilla, which became the West Indies' 33rd first-class ground when Leeward Islands played Barbados there in January. Afterwards, Richie Richardson, the Leewards' captain, said the pitch was the "fastest and best" in the Caribbean.

GROUNDSMEN IN 1995

By DAVID HOPPS

Rarely has the desire for central control been as apparent as in the Test and County Cricket Board's instructions in the past couple of years for the preparation of first-class pitches. At times it has been possible to imagine that the appearance of a single wormcast on a county square would bring an immediate edict on how it should be countered.

It can be argued that the attitude of some counties invited such unyielding guidelines. There is little point in having a four-day Championship designed to foster the long-term development of players if counties, with an eye to short-term gain, continue to produce three-day pitches. But groundsmen are a notoriously individualistic breed, resistant to the imposition of bureaucracy. Preparing pitches is more of an art than a science, and an inexplicable art at that. It is no surprise therefore that two of England's leading Test groundsmen, Ron Allsopp at Trent Bridge and Keith Boyce at Headingley, retired at the end of last season with an air of dissatisfaction.

Boyce laboured to combat the ground's unpredictability for 17 years, and his resignation to concentrate on the Rugby League side of the Headingley operation arose out of painful emotions. He was very upset that Yorkshire took him to task for his preparation of a Benson and Hedges Cup quarter-final strip against Worcestershire on the day of his wife's funeral.

"In my bleakest period in the mid-eighties, when they wouldn't let me dig up the square, Margaret was out there with me all hours of the night," he said. "I had to accept criticism as part of my life. Until I was allowed to re-lay the square in 1988, we had to keep moisture in to stop it cracking. Too little moisture, as in 1981, and the pitch would crack; too much, like for Pakistan in 1987, and it would seam too much on the first morning. Then we didn't re-lay deep enough, and we used over-light soils. I think we've begun to get it right."

It is Boyce's dissatisfaction with modern TCCB restrictions which will strike a chord with his fellow groundsmen. "Umpires should be the only people to judge a pitch," he said, "and their only criterion should be whether it has provided an even contest between bat and ball.

"Each groundsman has his specific problems and a way of dealing with them. We shouldn't be regimented. We shouldn't be fretting over moisture content, amount of grass or colour. Last season we were asked to fill in a detailed report before a ball was even bowled. It didn't half vex me."

Allsopp, who will be retained by Nottinghamshire as a consultant, retires without regret. He produced his first Test pitch in 1973 and after unveiling his final strip condemned the TCCB's marking system as "a complete shambles".

"They expect them to seam a little to begin with, flatten out into good batting tracks for two days and then turn, as if by magic, on the third afternoon. It's not always as simple as that," he said. Allsopp remained loyal to the memory of Clive Rice, the South African, who led the club in the 1980s to its first successes of the modern era. When Allsopp once resisted Rice's demands for a greentop, he got the response: "What's the matter – have you gone bloody religious?"

"The biggest compliment anyone ever paid me was to say that to play Notts was to face Rice, Hadlee and Allsopp," Ron concluded. "I was proud of that. Always will be."

CHARITIES IN 1995

THE LORD'S TAVERNERS raised around £1.7 million in 1995. The overall aim is "to give youngsters, especially the disadvantaged and disabled, a sporting chance". At least half the money distributed goes back into grassroots cricket, principally through the National Cricket Association and the English Schools Cricket Association. The other half is directed towards sporting opportunities for disabled youngsters, such as the New Horizons minibus programme.

Events in 1995 included the Tim Rice Golf Classic, at Forest of Arden GC, sponsored by Avesta Sheffield, which raised £85,000. The Taverners were nominated by the sponsors, Madagans, to be the official charity at the Guineas race meeting at Newmarket; this raised £45,000. There was a concert by Julian Bream in the Long Room at Lord's, staged jointly with MCC; this was so successful that a similar event is to be held on October 8, 1996 featuring the cellist Julian Lloyd-Webber.

The Director: Patrick Shervington, The Lord's Taverners, 22 Queen Anne's Gate, London SW1H 9AA. Telephone: 0171-222 0707.

THE JOHN ARLOTT MEMORIAL TRUST was launched in 1993 to help provide affordable housing and improve recreational facilities in rural areas, by raising funds for the Rural Housing Trust and the National Playing Fields Association. The first grants were made in 1995. In 1996 the Trust is planning to repeat its celebrity match at Kew, and the John Arlott Rioja Dinner. An England Seniors XI, featuring former Test players, is due to play a fund-raising match at Tilford, Surrey on September 1.

Janet Hart, John Arlott Memorial Trust, Hobart House, 40 Grosvenor Place, London SW1X 7AN. Telephone: 0171-235 6318.

THE BRIAN JOHNSTON MEMORIAL TRUST was launched in 1995. Its aims are to foster cricket (a) for young people, (b) in the community and (c) for people with disabilities. Its first priority is establishing scholarships for young players of potential who are in need of financial help, and the first of these was due to be awarded early in 1996. The Johnners Cricket Week is to be held from May 25 to June 2, 1996, and clubs everywhere are invited to stage fund-raising games.

Michael Elmitt, PO Box 3897, Lord's Cricket Ground, London NW8 8QG. Telephone: 0171-224 1005.

THE PRIMARY CLUB, one of the favourite charities of the late Brian Johnston, started at Beckenham Cricket Club in 1955. In 1995 it raised almost £70,000 for cricket and other sports for the visually handicapped. Most of the money goes to Dorton House School, Sevenoaks, where a £160,000 swimming pool for kindergarten children is now nearing completion, but equipment has been provided for schools for the blind throughout the country. Membership is nominally restricted to players who have been dismissed first ball in any form of cricket.

Mike Thomas, 6 Denbigh Close, Chislehurst, Kent BR7 5EB. Telephone: 0181-467 5665.

THE HORNSBY PROFESSIONAL CRICKETERS FUND was established in 1928, from the estate of J. H. J. Hornsby, who played for Middlesex, MCC and the Gentlemen. It provides money to assist "former professional cricketers [not necessarily first-class] or their wives, widows until remarriage, children and other dependents, provided the persons concerned shall be in necessitous circumstances". Assistance is given by monthly allowances, special grants or, in certain cases, loans. Donations, requests for help or information about potential recipients are all welcome.

Clerk to the Trustees: A. K. James, "Dunroamin", 65 Keyhaven Road, Milford-on-Sea, Lymington, Hampshire SO41 0QX. Telephone: 01590-644720.

THE CRICKETERS ASSOCIATION CHARITY was founded in 1983 to relieve financial hardship amongst present or former members of the Association, anyone who has played cricket for a first-class county or their "wives, widows, children, parents and dependents". It is becoming the custom for cricketers in their benefit year to donate half of one per cent of their proceeds to the fund. Donations are welcome; also requests for help and information about cricketers who may be in need.

Chairman of the Trustees: Harold Goldblatt, 60 Doughty Street, London WC1N 2LS. Telephone: 0171-405 9855.

GRANT AID FOR CRICKET, 1995

The establishment of the National Lottery in the UK meant that the opportunities for cricket clubs to obtain money for new projects dramatically increased in 1995. There are now numerous possible sources of funds available, including the Lottery, the Millennium Fund, the Foundation for Sports and the Arts, and the European Regional Development Fund. The best source of information is the booklet *Sources of Grant Aid for Cricket*, which is obtainable from the National Cricket Association at Lord's (London NW8 8QZ). Mike Turner, author of the booklet, is available to give advice to clubs on 0116-283 1615.

CRICKET FOR THE DISABLED

By GARETH A. DAVIES

The first international matches between England and Wales for cricketers with a disability were played in the summer of 1995. The two fixtures were a resounding success, with Wales winning by one wicket in the first, an indoor, eight-a-side game at Lord's, before England squared the series with a comfortable win by 58 runs in the second, played outdoors at Oswestry CC. They attracted a gratifying amount of support and media coverage and are set to continue in 1996.

The internationals came about through the formation of a new Cricket Federation for People with Disabilities, which aims to set up a league programme throughout the UK. Dick Wildgoose, founder of the Federation, was determined that the only league in the country, in Shropshire, should be extended: "The Shropshire league had people with a range of disabilities participating. By establishing a strong league set-up nationwide, and subsequent international matches, we'll find a way forward." Following the two internationals, the Federation gained many new members and a call from India: a tour there is planned, when funds allow. Roger Knight, secretary of MCC, added his support: "We have had disabled cricketers being coached in the indoor school for some time, and we're delighted that it has been taken a step further. We'll be giving it our full support."

Elsewhere, there is already a Great Britain side for deaf cricketers, who took on Australia in 1994 for a series of five three-day matches, of which Australia won two, with three drawn. Lord's was also the setting for the British Blind Sport's cricket final, in which White Rose of Yorkshire beat Metro of London, after ten teams had competed on a knockout basis. A league is due to be set up in 1996.

Contacts: Disabled cricket in Wales – Jim Phillips 01978-710332; Disabled cricket in England – Richard Furber 01939-290649; Blind cricket – Wally Kinder 0121-743 7991.

DIRECTORY OF BOOK DEALERS

AARDVARK BOOKS, "Copperfield", High Street, Harmston, Lincoln LN5 9SN. Tel: 01522 722671. Peter Taylor specialises in Wisdens. Send SAE for list. Wisden cleaning and repair service available. Wisdens purchased, *any* condition.

NEIL BARNARD, 7 St Georges Court, 23 St Georges Street, Cheltenham, Gloucestershire GL50 4AF. Tel: 01242 575719. Cricket booksearch service. Please send your "wanted" list. No search fee.

TIM BEDDOW CRICKET BOOKS, 62a Stanmore Road, Edgbaston, Birmingham B16 9TB. Tel: 0121-420 3466 (24-hour answerphone). Require antiquarian, modern and remainders. Highest price paid. Catalogues also available. (Send 1st/2nd class stamp.)

BOUNDARY BOOKS, Southlands, Sandy Lane, Goostrey, Cheshire CW4 8NT. Tel: 01477 533106. Second-hand and antiquarian cricket books, autographs and memorabilia bought and sold. Deluxe limited editions published. Catalogues issued.

PETER BRIGHT, 11 Ravens Court, Ely, Cambs. CB6 3ED. Tel: 01353 661727. Cricket books, Wisdens, autographs and printed ephemera bought and sold. Catalogues issued (stamp appreciated).

CRICKET BOOKS, "Headingley" 3 Pruiti Crescent, Lesmurdie, Western Australia 6076. Tel: (09) 291 8704; fax: (09) 291 8735. Second-hand and antiquarian cricket books and memorabilia bought and sold. Catalogues issued. Want-lists welcome.

IAN DYER, 29 High Street, Gilling West, Richmond, North Yorkshire DL10 5JG. Tel/fax: 01748 822786. Specialist in antiquarian, rare, second-hand books, Wisdens and annuals. Collections purchased. Please send stamp for catalogue.

EXTRA COVER, 101 Boundary Road, St John's Wood, London NW8 0RG. Shop premises with extensive opening hours, stocking huge range of books, prints, Wisdens etc. SAE for latest lists. **Tel: 0171-625 1191.**

A. R. HODGES, 4 Old Harrow Road, St Leonards-on-Sea, East Sussex TN37 7EG. Tel: 01424 434455. Dealing in second-hand cricket books by mail. Please send stamp for latest catalogue.

JONKERS BOOKS, 4 Ewin Court, Cherwell Drive, Oxford OX3 0NY. Tel/fax: 01865 247086. Specialist in rare cricket books, especially Wisdens. Catalogues issued. I exhibit each month at the Russell Hotel Book Fair, London.

E. O. KIRWAN, 3 Pine Tree Garden, Oadby, Leics. LE2 5UT. Tel: 0116 2714267 (evenings and weekends only). Second-hand and antiquarian cricket books, Wisdens, autograph material and cricket ephemera of all kinds.

J. W. McKENZIE, 12 Stoneleigh Park Road, Ewell, Epsom, Surrey KT19 0QT. Tel: 0181-393 7700; fax: 0181-393 1694. Specialists in antiquarian, second-hand cricket books, particularly Wisdens. Books and collections bought. Catalogues sent on request. Publisher of rare cricket books.

ROGER PAGE, 10 Ekari Court, Yallambie, Victoria 3085, Australia. Tel: (03) 435 6332; fax: (03) 432 2050. Dealer in new and second-hand cricket books. Distributor of overseas cricket annuals and magazines. Agent for Cricket Statisticians and Cricket Memorabilia Society.

RED ROSE BOOKS (BOLTON), 196 Belmont Road, Astley Bridge, Bolton BL1 7AR. Tel: 01204 598080. Antiquarian and second-hand cricket books. Please send stamp for latest catalogue.

CHRISTOPHER SAUNDERS, Orchard Books, Kingston House, High Street, Newnham on Severn, Gloucestershire GL14 1BB. Tel: 01594 516030; fax: 01594 517273. Full-time bookseller for 15 years. Second-hand/antiquarian cricket books and memorabilia bought and sold.

SPORTSPAGES, Caxton Walk, 94-96 Charing Cross Road, London WC2H 0JG. Tel: 0171-240 9604. Barton Square, St Ann's Square, Manchester M2 7HA. Tel: 0161-832 8530. New cricket books, audio and videotapes, including imports, especially from Australasia; retail and mail order service.

WISTERIA BOOKS, Wisteria Cottage, Birt Street, Birtsmorton, Malvern WR13 6AW. Tel: 01684 833578. Visit our family-run stall at county grounds for new, second-hand, antiquarian cricket books and ephemera, or contact Grenville Simons at the address above. Send SAE for catalogue.

MARTIN WOOD, 2 St John's Road, Sevenoaks, Kent TN13 3LW. Tel: 01732 457205. Martin Wood has been dealing in cricket books since 1970 and has now posted 20,000 parcels. For a copy of his 1996 catalogue listing 2,750 items, send 25p stamp to the address above.

AUCTIONEERS

CHRISTIE'S inaugural cricket sale was the MCC Bicentenary Sale of 1987. Since then sales have been held on a regular basis at London, South Kensington, with 28 June and 4 October as the planned dates for this year's sales.

PHILLIPS have held specialised cricket auctions since 1978, highlighted by the celebrated Hal Cohen Collection last year. Free valuations and collection undertaken by Mike Ashton on 01222 396453.

TREVOR VENNETT-SMITH, 11 Nottingham Road, Gotham, Notts. NG11 0HE. Tel: 0115 9830541. Chartered Surveyor and Auctioneer. Twice-yearly auctions of cricket and sports memorabilia. The cricket auction run by cricketers for cricket lovers worldwide.

DOMINIC WINTER, The Old School, Maxwell Street, Swindon SN1 5DR. Tel: 01793 611340; fax: 01793 491727. Book auctions, specialist auctioneers and valuers. Saleroom and offices at the above address. Specialist sales twice yearly. Valuations undertaken.

DIRECTORY OF CRICKET SUPPLIERS

CRICKET EQUIPMENT

CLASSIC BAT CO., 53 High Street, Keynsham, Bristol BS18 1DS. Tel: 0117-986 2714; fax: 0117-986 1753. Hand-made bats, balls, pads, gloves, helmets, coffins and clothing. Free colour catalogue available. League and Young Player Sponsorships considered.

DUNCAN FEARNLEY, 17 Vigo Place, Brickyard Road, Aldridge, Walsall WS9 8UG. Tel: 01922 57733; fax: 01922 52659. Makers of finest hand-made bats of today, and suppliers of a complete range of other cricket equipment.

GRAY-NICOLLS, Robertsbridge, East Sussex TN32 5DH. Tel: 01580 880357; fax: 01580 881156. The definitive range of products to cater for cricketers at all levels, from village green to Test arena.

GUNN & MOORE LTD, 119/121 Stanstead Road, Forest Hill, London SE23 1HJ. Tel: 0181-291 3344; fax: 0181-699 4008. Gunn & Moore, established in 1885, are the world's most comprehensive provider of cricket bats, equipment, footwear and clothing.

HUNTS COUNTY BATS, Royal Oak Passage, Huntingdon, Cambs. PE18 9DN. Tel: 01480 451234. Probably the best range of cricket bats, hand-made by craftsmen to your specification, plus full range of equipment, clothing, holdalls and coffins.

NOMAD BOX CO LTD. Tel: 01858 464878. Nomad are celebrating their 35-year history with a special edition "UNION JACK COFFIN" printed front and back for maximum impact.

ALFRED READER, Invicta Works, Teston, Maidstone, Kent ME18 5AW. Tel: 01622 812230. Contact: Graham Brown. England's largest manufacturer of cricket balls. Distributors of Albion head protection and Sovereign cricket clothing and equipment.

SLAZENGERS CRICKET, PO Box 8, Carr Gate, Wakefield, West Yorkshire WF2 0XB. Tel: 01924 828222. The first name for all cricket equipment, including hand-made bats, gloves and leg-guards, protective equipment, bags, clothing and balls.

BOWLING MACHINES

JUGS, 53 High Street, Keynsham, Bristol BS18 1DS. Tel: 0117-986 9519; fax: 0117-986 1753. The *original* bowling machine company. New machines from £895 + VAT. Used by Lancashire, Hampshire, Gloucestershire. Free colour catalogue and video available.

STUART & WILLIAMS (BOLA), 6 Brookfield Road, Cotham, Bristol BS6 5PQ. Manufacturers of bowling machines and ball throwing machines for all sports. Machines for recreational and commercial application. UK and overseas.

CLOTHING

CLASSIC CLUBWEAR, 53 High Street, Keynsham, Bristol BS18 1DS. Tel: 0117-986 9519; fax: 0117-986 1753. Fast, efficient embroidery and screenprinting service on cricket shirts, wool or acrylic sweaters, caps, sweatshirts, leisurewear. Free colour catalogue available.

LUKE EYRES, Freepost, Denny Industrial Estate, Pembroke Avenue, Waterbeach, Cambridge CB5 8BR. Tel: 01223 440501. 100% wool, cotton or acrylic sweaters as supplied to major county club, international cricket teams and schools.

MCM, The Old Granary, Floud Lane, West Meon, Nr Petersfield, Hants GU32 1JD. Tel: 01730 829686. Sweaters, shirts, caps, tracksuits, sweatshirts, rugby and T-shirts, polo shirts, numerous other personalised club items.

M. S. MICHAEL AND CO LTD, 4 Batchelor Street, Chatham, Kent ME4 4BJ. Tel: 01634 844994-5. County cricket caps made and embroidered to customers' specifications for over 70 years. Worn and tested by the best. Brochure available.

GROUND EQUIPMENT

COURTYARD DESIGNS – CLASSIC PAVILIONS, Suckley, Worcester WR6 5EH. Tel/fax: 01886 884640/884444. Designers, makers and erectors of beautiful, traditional timber pavilions. Request our brochure, together with prices and testimonials.

DECATHLON SPORTS EQUIPMENT, Ely, Cambs. CB6 3NP, England. Tel: 01353 668686. Manufacturers of quality sightscreens, scoreboxes and faces, net cages, synthetic wickets and wicket covers. Full colour catalogue available.

R. SPRING & CO. Tel: 0181-428 5919. Heavy rollers. Tandem rollers completely rebuilt to better than new, ballasted front and rear rolls. Widely used by clubs, schools and local authorities. Also all other grass machinery.

STUART CANVAS PRODUCTS (Props. Kenyon Textiles Ltd), Warren Works, Hardwick Grange, Warrington, Cheshire WA1 4RF. Tel: 01925 814525; fax: 01925 831709. Designers, manufacturers and suppliers of sports ground covering equipment.

TILDENET LTD, Longbrook House, Ashton Vale Road, Bristol BS3 2HA. Tel: 0117-966 9684; fax: 0117-923 1251. Mobile and static practice nets, perimeter and ballstop, netting, sightscreen, raincovers and germination, as used at Lord's.

MAIL ORDER/RETAIL CRICKET SPECIALISTS

FORDHAM SPORTS CRICKET EQUIPMENT SPECIALIST, 81 Robin Hood Way, Kingston Vale, London SW15. Tel: 0181-974 5654. 168-172 East Hill, Wandsworth, London SW18. Tel: 0181-871 2500. Largest range of branded stock in south of England at discount prices.

ROMIDA SPORTS, 18 Shaw Road, Newhey, Rochdale OL16 4LT. Tel: 01706 882444; fax: 01706 882160. Possibly the largest supplier of personal cricket equipment in the world. Ring for free colour catalogue.

PITCHES (NON-TURF)

CARPETITION LTD, 14 Kaffir Road, Edgerton, Huddersfield HD2 2AN. Tel: 01484 428777; fax: 01484 423251. Manufacturers of "Tufturf" artificial grass match and practice wickets in lengths to suit requirements.

DURA-SPORT, 42 Harvest Way, Broughton Astley, Leicester LE9 6WL. Tel: 01455 284929. Use our 15 years' experience within the industry to advise you on all aspects of synthetic cricket installations and maintenance.

NOTTS SPORT, Launde House, Harborough Road, Oadby, Leicester LE2 4LE. Tel: 0116-272 0222; fax: 0116-272 0617. Foremost in pitch technology. Write or telephone for visit to your club/school without obligation. New video and illustrated brochure available.

VERDE SPORTS (CRICKET) LTD, Cowling Mill, Chorley PR6 0QG. Tel: 01257 269069; fax: 01257 261064. Synthetic turf cricket pitch specialists. For excellent products and value for money contact Peter Dury.

PITCHES (TURF)

C. H. BINDER LTD, Moreton, Ongar, Essex CM5 0HY. Tel: 01277 890246; fax: 01277 890105. Suppliers nationwide of ONGAR LOAM for cricket squares, grass seed, fertilisers etc. Collections available.

SOCIETIES

CRICKET MEMORABILIA SOCIETY. Hon. Secretary, Tony Sheldon, 29 Highclere Road, Crumpsall, Manchester M8 4WH. Tel: 0161-740 3714. For collectors worldwide – meetings, speakers, auctions, magazines, directory, merchandise, but most of all friendship.

THE CRICKET SOCIETY. Tel: 0171-286 7054. An active, independent society for cricket lovers all over the world to share their passion through meeting, reading, playing or writing about the game. See advertisement on page 1442.

CRICKET TOURS (OVERSEAS)

MIKE BURTON SPORTS TRAVEL, Bastion House, Brunswick Road, Gloucester GL1 1JJ. Tel: 01452 412444; fax: 01452 527500. The number 1 in cricket, specialist in the arrangement of inbound and outbound sports tours for supporters, clubs and schools.

FSR SPORTS PROMOTIONS, 11 Croft Road, Chalfont St Peter SL9 9AE. Tel: 01753 888052; fax: 01753 891486. Tailor-made tours. South Africa, Zimbabwe, Kenya and Holland specialists.

KUONI TRAVEL, the official travel agent for the TCCB, arranges worldwide cricket tours. Follow the England team from Auckland to Zimbabwe with the acknowledged experts in long-haul holidays. For brochures, phone 01306 744 477.

JOHN SNOW TRAVEL, 2 Broadfield Barton, Broadfield, Crawley, Sussex RH11 9BA. Tel: 01293 440440. ABTA, ATOL and IATA bonded. Supporters' tours, retail and business house travel, groups.

SUN LIVING, 10 Milton Court, Ravenshead, Nottingham NG15 9BD. Tel: 01623 795365; fax 01623 797421. Since 1974 Sun Living have specialised in tours for cricketers at all levels, including our ever popular supporters' tours. ABTA and ATOL bonded.

CRICKET TOURS (UK)

MIKE BURTON SPORTS TRAVEL, Bastion House, Brunswick Road, Gloucester GL1 1JJ. Tel: 01452 412444; fax: 01452 527500. (Incorporating 3-D UK CRICKET TOURS) Specialist department in UK and Ireland. Cricket tours arranged, fixtures arranged, matches, hotels, transport, fixture bureau etc.

CLIFF VIEW HOTEL, Ventnor, Isle of Wight PO38 1SQ. Tel: 01983 852226. Hotel with coastal views and beach close by. Long experience with touring sides, open ended bar – evening bar snacks.

FORESTERS ARMS HOTEL, Williton, Somerset TA4 4QY. Tel: 01984 632508. 17th century coaching inn. Hosts to touring sides for many years. Good food. Real ales. Fixtures arranged; also golf, fishing and shooting.

FSR SPORTS PROMOTIONS, 11 Croft Road, Chalfont St Peter SL9 9AE. Tel: 01753 888052; fax: 01753 891486. Tailor-made tours to all parts of UK.

RIVERDALE HALL HOTEL, Bellingham, Northumberland NE48 2JT. Tel: 01434 220254. 16th year of organised tours, idyllic setting, award-winning restaurant, indoor pool and sauna, real ale, golf course opposite, all standards catered for.

OBITUARY

AGHA SAADAT ALI, who died on October 25, 1995, aged 66, was among the best fielders in the early years of Pakistan cricket. He appeared in one Test – against New Zealand at Dacca in 1955-56 – when he scored eight not out and took three catches. Otherwise he played only intermittently, mainly for Punjab and Lahore, between 1948-49 and 1961-62. Both his sons played first-class cricket.

ALLEN, MICHAEL HENRY JOHN, died on October 6, 1995, aged 62, after a long illness. Mick Allen made a sensational start to his career with Northamptonshire in 1956. He was unusual, anyway, because he was a public schoolboy (Bedford) and a professional. On his debut against Worcestershire, he scored 51 but did not bowl. In the next match he took eight successive Nottinghamshire wickets for 88. He rarely had such spectacular days again but settled into being a steady left-arm spinner, his orthodox, well-flighted style providing the foil for the fiercer bowling of the two Australians, George Tribe and Jack Manning. Allen had a smooth action and rarely bowled badly, and was a good close catcher. He made a habit of bowling well against Derbyshire – victims of his career-best eight for 48 – and they signed him after Northamptonshire let him go in 1963. This phase of his career was not a great success, and he retired in 1966.

ALLOM, MAURICE JAMES CARRICK, who died on April 8, 1995, aged 89, achieved cricketing glory at Christchurch in January 1930 when he became the first man to take a hat-trick on Test debut – and four wickets in five balls. He bowled Stewart Dempster with the second ball of his eighth over in Test cricket, then dismissed Tom Lowry, Ken James and Ted Badcock with the last three deliveries, reducing New Zealand to 21 for seven in their first ever Test match. Allom only played four further Tests, all overseas, but he was a highly effective amateur swing and seam bowler. Being almost 6ft 6in, he had the height to make the ball come sharply off the pitch; he regularly dismissed good players and sometimes frightened them. Alf Gover recalled Arthur Carr, the Nottinghamshire captain, complaining to Percy Fender, leading Surrey, when he was flattened by an Allom bouncer: "This is no way to play cricket, Percy." Carr had Larwood and Voce on his side at the time. Allom was a Cambridge Blue in 1927 and 1928 and played regularly for Surrey at first, but his appearances were gradually limited by the demands of his family business. His record speaks of quality: 179 matches and 605 wickets at 23.62. He was a skilful saxophonist who played with Fred Elizalde's band in the 1920s, and wrote two jolly books, *The Book of the Two Maurices* and *The Two Maurices Again*, with his friend and namesake Maurice Turnbull. Privately, he had a great sense of fun. This was less obvious when he found himself president of MCC in 1970, the year of the crisis over the South African tour, eventually called off after Government pressure. He followed this with eight less turbulent years as president of Surrey.

AMOS, GORDON STANLEY, who died on April 7, 1995, aged 90, was one of Queensland's stalwarts in their early years of Sheffield Shield cricket. He played in their very first Shield match in 1926-27 – but for New South Wales. By running out Leo O'Connor in the closing stages for 196, he ensured that his team won by eight runs, thus beginning Queensland's long run of failure in the Shield. He subsequently moved north and helped to mitigate the disasters in 20 matches, bowling fast-medium. Among his 49 first-class wickets was that of Bill Ponsford – caught and bowled for 437. Amos spent another season in New South Wales in 1931-32 and did not play first-class cricket again for another five years, when he turned out again for Queensland, and hit 93, his highest score, with five sixes. Ten days before his death, Queensland finally won the Shield; the news delighted him.

BARBER, ERIC GEORGE, who died on April 20, 1995, aged 79, was a professional batsman in the Coventry League and played two matches for Warwickshire in 1936.

BARBOUR, ROBERT ROY PITTY, who died on December 29, 1994, aged 95, was one of the last living first-class cricketers born in the 19th century and almost certainly the last man alive to have played a first-class match against M. A. Noble. This was on Barbour's debut, for Queensland v New South Wales in November 1919, when Noble was nearly 47, and playing his last match. Barbour was an opening bat, who played one subsequent match for Queensland, and four for Oxford University when he was a Rhodes Scholar. He became senior classics lecturer at Melbourne University.

BARRATT, ROY JAMES, died in February 1995, aged 52, after a heart attack. "Basher" Barratt was a slow left-arm bowler who played 70 matches for Leicestershire between 1961 and 1970; he acquired his nickname through his uninhibited tail-end batting. His bowling was characterised by a low, very round-armed action, and his attitude to the game was noticeably carefree – helped by the fact that his family had a prosperous building business. The firm's contracts included the new Grace Road pavilion; this went up in the midst of his playing career, with Barratt in the thick of the building work. He was a popular team man who continued playing village cricket until his sudden death.

BEE, AMIR, who died on January 26, 1995, aged 85, was the mother of four Pakistani Test players – Wazir, Hanif, Mushtaq and Sadiq Mohammad. A fifth son, Raees, was twelfth man in a Test and Hanif's son, Shoaib, has also played Tests. She was herself a local badminton champion, and brought up the family single-handed after the death of her husband in 1948.

BEESON, RONALD NEAVE, who died on August 9, 1995, aged 57, was Lincolnshire's wicket-keeper from 1957 to 1966. In his final season, he captained the county to their only Minor Counties Championship.

BENNETT, FREDERICK WILLIAM CECIL, OBE, who died on January 26, 1995, aged 79, was chairman of the Australian Cricket Board in the difficult years from 1983 to 1986, when Australian cricket struggled against the consequences of the mass defection of players to South Africa. He was a wicket-keeper for Balmain in Sydney grade cricket, and a good baseball player. However, he made his name as a hard-working administrator, first with Balmain, then with New South Wales, where he was chairman for nine years, and finally on the ACB, which he joined in 1967. He was manager of six Australian touring parties, including three to England: 1972, 1975 and 1981. After retiring from a management job with the Australian Broadcasting Corporation, he started his own business and regularly went to the office at 6 a.m. until shortly before his death; he continued jogging into his seventies. "He was one of those Australians who treated everyone equally," said David Richards, chief executive of ICC. "Always very affable at the start but very firm if he had to be. He was a wonderful friend to the game." Mike Gatting, who spent several seasons at Balmain, scored a century in the Adelaide Test the day after Bennett died, and dedicated the innings to him and the Middlesex scorer Harry Sharp.

BHAYA, JAMSHED NUSSERWANJI, who died on June 25, 1995, aged 87, was a prominent attacking batsman in the 1930s when India were emerging as a Test-playing country. He played in two unofficial Tests, and after the Indians beat the 1935-36 Australians in Lahore was borne aloft by the crowd – for his fielding, it was said. He made 106 against the same touring team for Central India.

BOUCHER, JAMES CHRYSOSTOM, who died on December 25, 1995, aged 85, was possibly Ireland's finest cricketer. Jimmy Boucher bowled big off-breaks from a medium-pacer's run-up and confounded good batsmen for over a quarter of a century. His 28 first-class matches, all for Ireland between 1930 and 1954, produced 168 wickets, at 14.04, a better average even than Hedley Verity. His figures included six for 30 and seven for 13 against successive touring teams, the 1936 Indians and the 1937 New Zealanders, and seven for 39 in a one-day match against the 1947 South Africans. He was top of the averages in *Wisden* in 1937 and 1948, though he would not have qualified under the modern system, which requires bowlers to bowl in ten innings. Boucher habitually bowled with three short legs and no extra cover, which he considered a sign of weakness, and refused to defend even on the rare occasions he was collared. The Irish belief that he could have played for England was not tested: he never left his clerk's job at the electricity board in Dublin. He was reputedly invited to join Lord Tennyson's 1937-38 tour of India, then heard no more. Boucher gave up playing in 1954 to become secretary of the Irish Cricket Union until 1973. He was a bachelor, obsessed with cricket and cricket talk, who loved every aspect of the game – except limited-overs cricket, which he abhorred.

BROMAGE, PETER ROBERT, who died suddenly on July 20, 1995, aged 61, was an important administrator in both cricket and rugby union, and had just been appointed chairman of the new Rugby Football Union executive. In cricket Bromage was chairman of the TCCB's disciplinary committee. He was a successful Birmingham solicitor who was on the Warwickshire committee for 13 years, and redrafted the club's' constitution.

BROWN, ALBERT, who died on April 27, 1995, aged 83, was a fast-medium bowler who played once for Warwickshire, against the Indians in 1932. He was a leading snooker player and reached the semi-finals of the world championship four times, but retired from the game in 1954 when snooker was so much in the doldrums he could not make a living.

CALDER, HARRY LAWTON, who died in Cape Town on September 15, 1995, aged 94, was both the youngest ever and the oldest surviving *Wisden* Cricketer of the Year. Calder was chosen as one of the "School Bowlers of the Year" in 1918 when there was no regular selection because of the war. He was in the Cranleigh XI for five years as a bowler of varied medium-paced spinners. But he played little cricket after leaving school, when he went to South Africa, and did not know he had ever been a Cricketer of the Year until he was tracked down in 1994. The Calder story appeared in the 1995 *Wisden*, page 275.

CAMERON, FRANCIS JAMES, died in February 1995, aged 71. Jimmy Cameron was a Jamaican batsman and off-spinner who was studying in North America when he was called to go on West Indies' tour of India and Pakistan in 1948-49. He played in all five Tests, scoring an unbeaten 75 at Bombay, but took only three wickets. He played league cricket in England for many years. His older brother, "Monkey" Cameron, also played for West Indies. Jimmy is not to be confused with the Francis James Cameron who played for New Zealand.

CARR, MICHAEL LEWIS, who died on September 29, 1995, aged 62, kept wicket for Cambridge University against Warwickshire at Fenner's in 1953.

CHILVERS, HUGH CECIL, who died on December 1, 1994, aged 92, was an Australian leg-spinner, born in Hertfordshire. He was unlucky that he was taken to a country where he would be a contemporary of both Grimmett and O'Reilly.

So he never played Test cricket but instead bowled regularly for New South Wales, taking 151 wickets at 26.39 between 1929-30 and 1936-37, including 11 instances of five or more in an innings. Chilvers had a bouncing approach to the wicket, suggesting the traditional leg-spinner's hopeful enthusiasm. He was indeed enthusiastic: he played Sydney grade cricket until he was in his late fifties.

CLARK, ARTHUR HENRY SEYMOUR, who died on March 17, 1995, aged 92, was an engine driver from Weston-super-Mare and one of the most improbable of all county cricketers. Seymour Clark never played the game at all before he was 25, when he was drafted in to keep wicket for a makeshift railwaymen's side. He turned out to be a brilliant natural wicket-keeper, with fantastic reflexes, and quickly became first choice for the Weston town club. Three years later, when the regular Somerset keeper Wally Luckes was ill, Clark was brought in and, though he had trouble getting time off from the railway, played five matches in 1930. He kept magnificently; however, he is mainly remembered for his batting, which was hopeless. Clark thought his highest score in club cricket was three, and two of them came from overthrows. He bought a new bat when he was picked for the county, but hardly ever made contact, failing to score a run in nine innings (though twice at Kettering his partner got out before he could). Peter Smith of Essex tried to give him one off the mark, and produced a ball that bounced twice before it reached him; Clark still got bowled. He was offered a contract for 1931 but thought the Great Western Railway offered more secure employment. "I got a tremendous kick out of playing for Somerset," he said later, "but it seemed sensible to go back to the locos."

COMMINS, KEVIN THOMAS, who died on October 3, 1995, aged 66, was captain of Border when they were bowled out for 16 and 18 by Natal at East London in 1959-60. He maintained that in the first innings it was a difficult wicket but admitted that second time round the batting was awful. On other days, he was a capable opening bat for both Western Province and Border. He later became Western Province's first full-time administrator. His son John has played for South Africa.

COOKE, NOEL HENRY, who died on February 28, 1995, aged 60, played in 12 first-class matches for Lancashire in 1958 and 1959 as a right-handed batsman and off-spinner. He played a lot of club cricket round Liverpool.

COPE, JOHN JAMES, died on January 28, 1995, aged 86. Jack Cope played three matches for Glamorgan in 1935 with no success. But he was a sound league and Minor Counties batsman, and also played soccer for Bury, Ipswich and Cardiff. He was picked to play football for Wales but had to withdraw because he was born in Ellesmere Port.

COVINGTON, FREDERICK ERNEST, who died on July 3, 1995, aged 82, was a left-hand bat who made 83 on his debut for Middlesex, against Warwickshire in 1936. He played five more matches that year without showing the same form. He captained Harrow in both 1931 and 1932 and made 1,000 runs over those two seasons. Though he appeared twice for Cambridge, he failed to win a Blue.

COX, SIDNEY RONALD, died on April 6, 1995, aged 79. Ronnie Cox was a former army captain who became secretary of Essex in 1972. During his six-year tenure the club slowly became a more commercially-minded operation. He was sometimes vague, but his old-fashioned charm was as effective at winning advertising and sponsorship as more scientific methods.

CRAIB, JAMES DEREK GRAHAM, who died on December 19, 1994, aged 77, scored 62 in 40 minutes against Nottinghamshire on his debut for Cambridge University in 1937. He took four wickets, bowling seamers, in the next match but, puzzlingly, never played again.

CRESSWELL, JAMES ARTHUR, who died on December 2, 1994, aged 91, made 21 appearances as a left-arm fast-medium bowler for Derbyshire between 1923 and 1927 without establishing himself. He later became a policeman.

DAVIES, CONRAD STEPHEN, died on May 9, 1995, aged 87. Con Davies played eight unspectacular matches as an amateur for Warwickshire between 1930 and 1936. But he was a legend as a club cricketer, and played for Alexandra Park for 50 years. In all, he scored 64,000 runs, with 126 centuries, and took 5,000 wickets with his left-arm spin. He became president of the Club Cricket Conference.

DAVIS, DAVID GRANT, who died on March 2, 1995, aged 93, had been the oldest surviving New Zealand first-class cricketer and the only player left alive who played a first-class match for Hawkes Bay. He appeared three times in 1920-21, the province's last year. Against Wellington, he scored 61 in half an hour.

DEPEIZA, CYRIL CLAIRMONTE, who died on November 10, 1995, aged 67, played five Tests for West Indies, four of them as wicket-keeper. He touched greatness when he shared an epic seventh-wicket stand of 347 with his captain Denis Atkinson in the Bridgetown Test against Australia in 1954-55, which remains a world record. It was a first-class record as well until surpassed in India in 1994-95. Depeiza walked in with the score 147 for six in reply to 668. The pair batted throughout the fourth day before Depeiza was out in the first over next morning, after 330 minutes batting, for 122. A large collection was taken for the two batsmen; Atkinson gave his share to his partner. Depeiza later came to Britain to play regular League cricket. He settled in Manchester and became a senior insurance official.

DEVERELL, SIR COLVILLE MONTGOMERY, who died on December 15, 1995, aged 89, played one first-class match, opening the batting with the playwright Samuel Beckett for Dublin University against Northamptonshire in 1926. Deverell made two and one. He was later Governor of the Windward Islands and then Mauritius, before becoming secretary-general of the International Planned Parenthood Federation.

DE ZOYSA, LUCIEN, who died on June 11, 1995, aged 78, represented Ceylon against various international touring teams and captured more than 500 wickets as a leg-spinner for Sinhalese Sports Club. He was also a successful cricket commentator, Shakespearean actor, writer and dramatist.

DRAKE, EDWARD JOSEPH, died on May 29, 1995, aged 82. Ted Drake was an apprentice at the Southampton Gasworks before he made his debut for Hampshire in 1931 and shared a vital stand of 86 with Phil Mead against Glamorgan. He made 45 but never reached this score again in the 15 further matches he played over the next six years, first as an amateur and then as a professional. However, he found greater glory in the winters, when Hampshire would have paid him ten shillings a week, as one of the great centre-forwards of his era, first with Southampton and then with Arsenal, where he was transferred in 1934 for £5,000. He only won five England caps, but scored 42 goals in the 1934-35 season, an Arsenal record, and went on to manage Chelsea to the 1955 League Championship. He married the girl he met at the gasworks dance, not a detail associated with modern football stars of his magnitude.

EASTERBROOK, BASIL VIVIAN, who died on December 15, 1995, aged 75, was cricket and football writer for Kemsley (later Thomson Regional) Newspapers from 1950 to 1983 and thus covered all the major domestic matches for many of Britain's largest regional papers. He was a regular writer for *Wisden* and contributed an article every year from 1971 to 1980. Easterbrook was a much loved member of the press corps with a puckish humour. He claimed that while covering a match from the old Lord's press box, he leaned out of the window to throw away his pencil shavings and the Nottinghamshire batsmen walked in, thinking it was the signal to declare. Once he phoned his office to dictate his copy, announced his name to the telephonist – "Basil V. Easterbrook" – to be greeted by the response "What league is that in?" When he retired he wrote: "The craft and practice of cricket writing was my personal window to the sky."

ELLIS, JOHN ALBERT, who died on October 17, 1994, aged 80, played in 22 matches for Queensland as an opening bowler on either side of the war, taking 71 wickets at 32.11. In another era he might easily have played for Australia, but he was already past 30 when he was picked for the Australian XI against MCC at Melbourne before the First Test in 1946-47, and he made no impact on Hutton and Washbrook.

ELMES, CEDRIC JAMES, died on March 9, 1995, aged 85. Ced Elmes was the only New Zealander ever to be out for 99 in first-class cricket and finish his career without scoring a hundred. The innings came against Errol Holmes's MCC team of 1935-36 in the unofficial Test at Auckland. Despite this, he remained a phlegmatic cricketer. He never played genuine Test cricket but was a regular for Otago from 1927-28 to 1940-41, batting left-handed and bowling slow to medium left-arm. Perhaps his best bowling performance also came against MCC, for Otago in 1929-30, when he took five wickets – the top five in the order – for 68.

EWART, GAVIN BUCHANAN, who died on October 23, 1995, aged 79, was a well-known poet and a lifelong cricket enthusiast. He produced many poems on cricket, penning *A Pindaric Ode* on the 1981 Headingley Test as well as shorter lyrics of wry nostalgia and a squib on the radio commentary team. His most substantial piece, *The Sadness of Cricket*, was a poignant elegy for the players of the Golden Age:

> We'd one at Wellington, that A. E. Relf,
> who'd bowled for England – long since on the shelf –
> in 1937 stalled and shot himself.
>
> Remembered bowling in the nets,
> a little irritable (I thought – but one forgets),
> doling out stumps to junior games, like doubtful debts,
>
> from the pavilion's mean back door.

FENN, MAURICE JOSEPH, who died on April 11, 1995, aged 83, was the best slow bowler produced by Fiji. He was particularly effective when he toured New Zealand in 1947-48, where he was able to add floating in-swing to his normal nagging accuracy, and he took 50 wickets, far more than any other Fijian, at 20.90 in the nine first-class matches he played.

FLACK, BERNARD IRVINE, who died on July 31, 1995, aged 81, was Warwickshire's head groundsman from 1955 to 1983. Test cricket returned to Edgbaston two years into his reign and the ground acquired a reputation for good, true wickets, if not quick ones. He was a conscientious groundsman and an early riser who believed in rolling with the dew. In later years, he became the TCCB's inspector of pitches. He was no relation to Bert Flack, the Old Trafford groundsman.

FRASER, THOMAS WILLIAM, who died on July 25, 1995, aged 83, was a South African-born slow left-armer who won a Cambridge Blue in 1937. He took eight for 71 for Orange Free State against Eastern Province in 1939-40.

GADSDEN, WILLIAM BELL, who died on March 18, 1995, aged 84, was a South African medium-pace bowler who took eight for 64 for Natal against Transvaal on his first-class debut as an 18-year-old in 1928-29. After a match return of seven for 47 against Border, he was selected for the tour of England but did not make the trip, apparently because his father said he was too young. Gadsden was included in the squad for the Third Test at Durban against England in 1930-31, but did not play. He played only nine first-class matches in all, but his record remained impressive: 35 wickets at 16.82.

GLOAK, RAYMOND LEONARD, who died on February 10, 1995, aged 62, represented Griqualand West in 33 first-class matches as a batsman and occasional off-spinner.

HARDIKAR, MANOHAR SHANKAR, who died on February 4, 1995, in Bombay, aged 58, was an all-rounder who played two Tests for India against West Indies in 1958-59. On his debut in Bombay, he took his only Test wicket (Kanhai, lbw) with his third ball and then helped save the game with 32 not out, having been out first ball in the first innings. In the next match at Kanpur, he was hit on the head, which badly affected his confidence. However, he remained a highly effective all-rounder for Bombay. He made his debut for them aged only 18 in 1955-56 and his slow to medium-paced bowling had its greatest day when he took eight for 39 against Bengal in the final of the Ranji Trophy that season. He played 14 seasons in all, captaining Bombay in the last two, and scored eight centuries, including 207 not out against Services in 1964-65.

HARVEY, MERVYN ROYE, who died on March 20, 1995, aged 76, was the eldest of four brothers who all played first-class cricket for Victoria. The most famous, Neil, said that Merv was the most talented of the four. Merv Harvey was a free-scoring right-handed opening bat whose opportunities were severely restricted by the war. When it ended he was 27, but he got his chance against England in 1946-47. After scoring a three-hour 136 for Victoria against New South Wales, he was picked for the Adelaide Test in place of the injured Sid Barnes. He did quite well, though not in his normal style, and scored 31 in the second innings, sharing a stand of 116 with Arthur Morris, who was on his way to his second hundred of the match. That was not enough for Harvey to keep his place. In 22 first-class matches he hit 1,147 runs at 38.23 with three centuries. He captained Victoria five times.

HENDERSON, WILLIAM ANDREW, who died on March 6, 1995, aged 77, was a South African fast bowler and one of only three men (along with Bill Copson and Pat Pocock) ever to take five wickets in six balls in first-class cricket. It happened in a Currie Cup match for North-Eastern Transvaal against Orange Free State at Bloemfontein in February 1938. Henderson had figures of 9.3–7–4–7, including four wickets in four balls. Free State were all out for 46.

HIDE, MARY EDITH, died in hospital on September 10, 1995, aged 81. Molly Hide was a farmer's daughter from Surrey (though she was born in Shanghai) who became one of the great pioneers of women's cricket in England. She played in the first ever women's Test in Brisbane in December 1934 and was England captain for 17 years. Tall and lithe, she could drive the ball beautifully, but her batting had a strength as well as a style that astonished sceptical male spectators, many of

Molly Hide: "the personification of women's cricket".

whom in her era thought women's cricket was like a dog on its hind legs. Her first great triumph came after the 1934-35 tour moved on to New Zealand, when she scored a century in the Christchurch Test, putting on 235 with Betty Snowball. England declared at 503 for five – New Zealand had been bowled out for 44, and lost by an innings and 337. She became captain for the home series against Australia two years later and held the post until her retirement in 1954. She would have missed the 1939-40 tour of Australia because her parents persuaded her to stay on the farm and not "go gallivanting". But the tour was cancelled anyway, and when it finally took place nine years later she scored five centuries, including 124 not out at the Sydney Cricket Ground, and her portrait was hung in the pavilion. In 15 Tests she scored 872 runs at 36.33, and took 36 wickets at 15.25, with the slowish off-cutters that she bowled only reluctantly. Her captaincy was firm, even stern, and she remained in touch with the game, as a selector and, in 1973, president of the Women's Cricket Association. Molly Hide also played lacrosse for England. She was something of a Joan Hunter Dunn figure but more than that, as Netta Rheinberg said, "she was the personification of women's cricket", doing an immense amount to give the game credibility.

HILL, WILLIAM AUBREY, who died on August 11, 1995, aged 85, was the last surviving Warwickshire player from the 1920s. Aubrey Hill was an opening batsman who played 169 times between 1929 and 1939 without ever being sure of his place. Though he was capped in 1933, he did not score his maiden century until 1936 and his best season came when he made 1,197 runs in 1947. After retiring he coached Oxford University.

HOLLINSHEAD, CYRIL, who died on November 25, 1995, aged 93, played his last cricket match in 1992 when he bowled six overs costing 16 runs for the Gloucestershire Gipsies, aged 90. This was the culmination of a life in which a love for cricket bordered on addiction. Hollinshead took 4,000 wickets in club matches as a left-arm bowler, fast in his day, over a span that began in 1911, 81 years before its conclusion. He made one first-class appearance, for Gloucestershire against Cambridge University in 1946. Between matches he edited the Cheltenham evening paper, the *Gloucestershire Echo*, from 1938 to 1967.

HOME OF THE HIRSEL, The Baron, KT, PC, who died at his home on October 9, 1995, aged 92, was the only British prime minister to have played first-class cricket. As Lord Dunglass, he was a useful member of the Eton XI. In the rain-affected Eton–Harrow match of 1922 he scored 66, despite being hindered by a saturated outfield, and then took four for 37 with his medium-paced out-swingers. He played ten first-class matches for six different teams: Middlesex, Oxford University, H. D. G. Leveson Gower's XI, MCC (with whom he toured South America under Pelham Warner), Free Foresters and Harlequins. His two games for Middlesex were in 1924 and 1925, both against Oxford University while he was actually an Oxford undergraduate; he did not represent the university until the following year. His cricket was gradually overtaken by politics, and he entered the Commons in 1931. After he succeeded to his father's title and became the 14th Earl of Home, he rose to be foreign secretary and then prime minister, when he emerged as a totally unexpected compromise choice as Harold Macmillan's successor. After renouncing his title (and becoming Sir Alec Douglas-Home until he returned to the Lords as a life peer) he remained in Downing Street for a year until the 1964 election. Despite all his honours, Alec Home never made an enemy and was much valued, in cricket as in politics, for his quiet charm and sagacity. He was president of MCC in 1966 and an important behind-the-scenes influence whenever the game was in difficulties. From 1977 to 1989 Lord Home was Governor of I Zingari. The general opinion is that, even if he had devoted himself to the game, he would not have been a regular county player, but then no one expected him to rise so high in politics either. H. S. Altham, in his review of public schools cricket in the 1923 *Wisden*, said Lord Dunglass was a better batsman on wet pitches – "he had the courage of his convictions and could hook and pull the turning ball effectively". Much the same could be said for his politics: he was always at his best on a sticky wicket.

HUDLESTON, Air Chief Marshal Sir EDMUND CUTHBERT, CBE, CB, KCB, GCB, who died on December 14, 1994, aged 85, played four first-class matches as a wicket-keeper/batsman for the RAF in 1929 and 1931. Hudleston was Commander-in-Chief, Allied Forces, Central Europe from 1964 to 1965.

HUDSON, Brig. REGINALD EUSTACE HAMILTON, DSO, who died on May 26, 1995, aged 90, was perhaps the best Services batsman of the inter-war period. He averaged 40.15 in 27 first-class matches for the Army and the Europeans in India, scoring five first-class centuries, including 217 in 225 minutes for the Army against the RAF at The Oval in 1932, the second hundred coming in 70 minutes. *Wisden* described his form as "brilliant". He scored 181 against the 1933 West Indians but was out for four when he and Bradman were opposing captains in the match against the Australians a year later. He won the DSO as commander of the 83rd Field Regiment, which he led from 1942 until VE Day. The new pavilion on the Royal Artillery ground at Woolwich is named after him.

INGELSE, DANIËL LODEWIJK, who died in June 1995, aged 77, was the first Dutchman to make a century against Denmark, in 1955.

INSHAN ALI, who died from throat cancer on June 24, 1995, aged 45, was a back-of-the-hand slow left-arm bowler who played in 12 Tests for West Indies in the 1970s. He was a slight figure who looked increasingly out of place in the team as the emphasis switched to non-stop fast bowling, and his inability to translate his first-class form to Test level was one of the factors that encouraged West Indies to transform their game. Inshan's 34 Test wickets cost 47.67, and he had limited success after taking five for 59 against New Zealand at Port-of-Spain in 1971-72. He made his debut for Trinidad aged only 16 and his unusual methods frequently troubled batsmen below top level. He had returned to playing club cricket in Trinidad shortly before his fatal illness.

JACQUES, THOMAS ALEC, died on February 23, 1995, aged 90. Sandy Jacques was said by Sir Len Hutton to have had the finest fast bowling action he had ever seen, but what might have been a famous career was curtailed by injury. Jacques made his debut for Yorkshire in 1927 and after only six matches was taking four for 53 in a Test trial at Lord's. His ability to maintain pace and length for long periods impressed observers and he turned professional, amid high expectations, the following year. But it became clear that his legs could not stand the strain of cricket six days a week; he even tried wearing five pairs of socks to try and lessen the pain. Thereafter, he appeared only intermittently, and devoted himself to League cricket, in which he was a demon, and his farm at Cliffe, near Selby, where he lived all his life. Jacques played 30 first-class matches in all, 28 for Yorkshire, and never finished on the losing side.

JAYASINGHE, SUNIL ASOKA, who died on April 20, 1995, aged 39, was Sri Lanka's wicket-keeper in the 1979 World Cup, and scored half-centuries against Nottinghamshire and Derbyshire on tour that summer. Before it was first-class, he scored 283 for Bloomfield in the P. Saravanamuttu Tournament. Jayasinghe reportedly poisoned himself while suffering from depression.

[*Ken Kelly*

Roly Jenkins, bowling – in a cap as ever – for Worcestershire against Somerset at
Kidderminster in 1949. He took nine for 216 in the match.

JENKINS, ROLAND OLIVER, died on July 21, 1995, aged 76. Roly Jenkins was one of the most popular, and skilful, county cricketers of the years just after the war. He will forever be associated with long afternoons at Worcester, running up to bowl his leg-breaks in his cap (though he batted without one) with a seaman's gait (though his furthest posting during the war was fire-watching at the top of Worcester Cathedral) and punctuating the game with a very mellow sort of humour. However, he was a fundamentally serious cricketer, indeed almost obsessive. He played nine Tests, but in the end his career may have been damaged by his constant search for perfection – as well as his propensity to make remarks that were not always appreciated by starchy authority.

Jenkins was the youngest of a family of ten, and was spotted playing in a knockabout on Worcester Racecourse. He made his debut in 1938, was capped in 1939 and, when cricket resumed, established himself as a gutsy middle-order batsman as well as a fierce spinner of the ball. He finished the 1948 season with 1,356 runs and 88 wickets and was just finalising plans for his wedding when he received a telegram asking him to replace Eric Hollies in the touring party for South Africa. The wedding was postponed and he had a hugely successful tour, dismissing Eric Rowan with his third ball in Test cricket, and topping the England bowling averages for the series. However, Jenkins did not play against New Zealand the following summer, though he took 183 wickets (including two hat-tricks in one match, against Surrey) and scored 1,183 runs: he may have made an ill-advised remark to someone important. Once, while batting with his captain, Bob Wyatt, who was alleged to be rather disdainful about calling, he said: "Say something, even if it's only goodbye." "I'll see you at lunch, Jenkins," came the stern reply.

Jenkins is said to have changed his grip after he came back from South Africa and switched to something more normal for a seamer; previously, he had been ripping both his fingers and the ball. But even after this change he still turned the ball prodigiously, possibly as much as Shane Warne, though at a slower pace. His googly was comparatively easy to pick: asked how many of the 183 victims in 1949 came through googlies, he replied: "About 14 – and they were all jazzhats." But he continued taking large quantities of wickets, was recalled by England in both 1950 and 1952, when he did the double again, and remained a force in county cricket until he retired in 1958. Still he worried constantly about his bowling. He was sometimes spotted in the nets at 7 a.m. and once remarked to Eric Hollies after he bowled Warwickshire out: "But I can't hear it fizzing." "I shouldn't worry about it, Roly," said Hollies. "Six of our blokes did." Tony Lewis said he was bowled out in Worcester by a ball that pitched in Hereford. Jenkins played on in the Birmingham League as the pro for West Bromwich Dartmouth until his mid-fifties. By then, he was a revered figure and one umpire insisted on letting him deliver a ten-ball over for the sheer pleasure of watching him bowl. He ran his own sweet shop next to Worcester bus station, before they moved the bus station and trade declined. Then he took a job as foreman in a canning factory. A manager once asked him why he was wearing two coats. "I'm doing two men's jobs," he told them, twinklingly, but pointedly all the same. For some years, he umpired village matches for Ombersley – and coached as he did so. He never lost his love of cricket, or cricket talk. "We're given memories so we can have roses in December," he once said.

JONES, HARRY OGWYN, who died on March 20, 1995, aged 72, was a seam bowler and appeared in two matches for Glamorgan in 1946. He played most of his cricket for Llangennech.

KELLEHER, DANIEL JOHN MICHAEL, was found dead at his home on December 12, 1995, aged 29. It was reported that a note was by the body. Danny Kelleher was a popular and extrovert medium-pacer who played 34 matches for

Kent between 1987 and 1991 without firmly establishing himself. He was later engaged on a match basis for Surrey but failed to reach the first team. His uncle, Harry Kelleher, played for Surrey and Northamptonshire.

KIDSON, HAYWARD CARY, died in hospital on April 26, 1995, aged 69, after undergoing his eighth hip operation. Kidson was South Africa's leading umpire in the period before isolation. He stood in 11 Test matches, including four on England's 1964-65 tour and all five of the series of matches against Australia two years later, when the Australians, heading for defeat, were inclined to blame him. He was an expert on the laws and a historian of the game.

LAMBERT, HENRY FRANCIS, who died in Adelaide on June 19, 1995, aged 77, was a left-arm fast-medium bowler for Victoria. In 33 first-class matches Harry Lambert took 76 wickets, 29 of them on the Commonwealth XI tour of India in 1949-50. He spent two seasons as professional for Ramsbottom in the Lancashire League.

LARWOOD, HAROLD, MBE, who died in hospital in Sydney on July 22, 1995, aged 90, was one of the great fast bowlers of all time. This will forever be overshadowed by his role in the cricketing controversy of the century, the Bodyline Affair. It is a dispute that retains its extraordinary potency even though nearly all the participants are now dead. It came close to rupturing cricket; indeed, it might have ruptured relations between Britain and Australia. But it was in the nature of cricket that Larwood should eventually settle happily in Australia, the country whose batsmen he once haunted.

Harold Larwood was a miner's son from Nuncargate outside Nottingham. He left school at 13; at 14 he was working with the pit ponies at Annesley Colliery near Nottingham and would doubtless have become a miner himself had he not already been showing promise at cricket; at 18 he had a trial at Trent Bridge. This was the classic instance of a county whistling down the nearest coal mine when they wanted a fast bowler. In 1924, at 19, Larwood was starring in the Second Eleven and making his Nottinghamshire debut; in 1925 he was a first-team regular; in 1926 he was in the England team at Lord's and, more significantly, the one that regained the Ashes at The Oval. In that match he took six wickets, all front-line batsmen, and consistently troubled everyone with pace and lift from short of a length. The word was already going round that "Lol" Larwood was the quickest bowler seen in years. In 1927 he came top of the national averages. By 1928 he was in harness with the left-armer Bill Voce and together they would become the world's most feared pair of opening bowlers.

Larwood began the 1928-29 series in Australia with a match-winning six for 32 on the old Exhibition Ground in Brisbane (in addition to scoring 70). The only batsman in the top seven that he did not get out in that match was the debutant D. G. Bradman, and though England comfortably retained the Ashes, Bradman asserted his authority as the series progressed. By the time he came to England in 1930, he was almost unassailable. Larwood played only three of the Tests that summer, and took just four wickets. Australia regained the Ashes. The combination of shirt-front wickets and the greatest batsman of all time was enough to break the spirit of any bowler. Larwood's urge to find something, *anything*, that would enable him to defeat Bradman, was crucial in rendering him a willing instrument in the crisis that was to come.

Bodyline, or leg-theory bowling, with bowlers aiming at the body with a ring of predatory leg-side fielders, was not unknown at this stage; Arthur Carr, the Nottinghamshire captain, would sometimes unleash Larwood in that manner in county matches. Several batsmen were carried off unconscious after being hit by Larwood even when he was bowling normally. Carr used Bodyline as a tactic. Douglas Jardine, who led England in Australia in 1932-33, elevated it into a strategy. But Larwood was not just his dupe. "The game had become so biased in favour of the batsmen, there was no pressure on them at all," he said in 1983. "If we got four wickets down in a day, we'd done a good day's work. If we got five we had an extra drink. Our way was the only way to quieten Bradman. I knew that if we eased up, we'd have to pay for it."

The controversy reached boiling point in the Adelaide Test when Larwood hit Bill Woodfull over the heart and Bert Oldfield over the temple. "Larwood again the unlucky bowler," as the newsreel commentator famously said. It was the feeling that Larwood, far from being unlucky, had achieved his side's objectives by inflicting injury that incensed the Australians. However, when he made 98 as a night-watchman in the final Test in Sydney he was, according to *Wisden*, "loudly cheered".

Larwood damaged his foot while bowling in that match, though Jardine made him stay on the field until Bradman was out. The foot injury meant he could bowl only ten overs in the 1933 season, and by the time the Australians came to England in 1934 the full implications of Bodyline had sunk in. A combination of poor communications, inadequate newspaper coverage and imperial arrogance, especially at Lord's, had prevented English cricket understanding immediately what had been going on in Australia. But once opinion had changed, Larwood is understood to have been given a letter of apology and told to sign. He refused and never played another Test match, alienating MCC once and for all by giving frank opinions on the subject to the *Sunday Express*. At the time he paid the penalty rather than Jardine, who captained MCC again in India in 1933-34. History has reversed the judgment, and Jardine is usually painted as the villain. Larwood's loyalty to his skipper remained unshaken until he died.

He continued to play county cricket to devastating effect and topped the national averages for the fifth time in 1936, two years before he finally retired. Bodyline had almost disappeared after Jardine's tour and was formally outlawed two years later. Larwood, though, was good enough, even if he was slowing down, to achieve success without it. He was only about 5ft 8in, less than 11 stone, and his training regime seemed to consist largely of beer and cigarettes. But he was stocky, and his technique was magnificent: "He ran in to bowl with a splendid stride," wrote Neville Cardus, "a gallop, and at the moment of delivery his action was absolutely classical, left side showing down the wicket, before the arm swung over with a thrillingly vehement rhythm." Later generations, observing only a few newsreel clips, have wondered whether Larwood threw; contemporary critics echoed the Cardus line – and in any case his Australian victims might just have raised the subject if there was any doubt at all. His bouncer was truly terrifying to unprotected batsmen, but it was employed only sparingly for most of his career. Of his 1,427 first-class wickets, more than half – 743 – were bowled. Larwood's average was 17.51, which was outstanding in a batsman's era; in his 21 Tests he took 78 at 28.35. His batting average was close to 20, and he scored three centuries.

After retirement, he went into eclipse and was living in Blackpool with his wife and five daughters, running a sweet shop, when he decided to emigrate to Australia. In 1949, he sailed on the *Orontes*, the ship which had taken him there, more famously, 17 years earlier. Encouraged by a former opponent, Jack Fingleton, and helped by a former Australian prime minister, Ben Chifley, Larwood settled in an obscure Sydney suburb, got a job on the Pepsi-Cola production line, and worked his way up – "not because I was a cricketer but because I could do the job" – to managing the lorry fleet.

It was possible to hear the noise of the Sydney Cricket Ground from his bungalow when the wind was right, and it became a place of pilgrimage for visiting Englishmen with a sense of history; Darren Gough delighted the old man by calling there in 1994-95. By then Larwood was blind, and long before that visitors were baffled by the idea that this shy, stooped, kindly man could ever have

terrorised cricket. There was never a hint of animosity in Australia, and Larwood had no regrets either, although he repented of his old view that Bradman was frightened of him. "I realise now he was working out ways of combating me." John Major signalled the British Establishment's forgiveness by awarding him the MBE in 1993. Larwood was most proud of the ashtray given him by Jardine: "To Harold for the Ashes – 1932-33 – From a grateful Skipper."
A special article appears on pages 31-33.

LAVERS, ALAN BRADEN, who died on October 25, 1995, aged 83, was an amateur who made 25 appearances for Essex between 1937 and 1953, as a batsman and off-spinner.

LEADER, JOHN VERNON, died on March 22, 1995, aged 86. Vern Leader was a left-hand bat and right-arm seam bowler who played irregularly for Otago between 1928-29 and 1940-41. He was a member of the team that won the Plunket Shield in 1932-33.

LEVETT, WILLIAM HOWARD VINCENT, died on November 30, 1995, aged 87. Howard "Hopper" Levett was in the great tradition of Kent wicket-keepers but his first-class career was hampered not only by the war but by the presence at Kent of the great Les Ames. However, he was brave and fearless and a genuine stumper – 195 of his 478 dismissals (in 175 matches) were stumpings – who stood up to almost everyone, and was good enough to win a Test cap in Calcutta in 1933-34. "Hopper" (the nickname reputedly came from his hop farm) was as famous as a character as a player. He supposedly emerged one morning, after a heavy night, to let the first ball through for four byes then dived to take a brilliant leg-side catch next ball. "Not bad for the first ball of the day," he said. He is also supposed to have bowled a bread roll when the 1938 Australians went in at Canterbury needing seven to win. After retirement in 1947, he became Kent's staunchest supporter, happily travelling to Second Eleven matches as a committee man to encourage young players. He had opinions on everyone in cricket, but they were always kindly expressed and secondary to his fund of stories. He was a magnificent talker, after dinner or at any other time, and was probably the most popular man in Kent.

LITTLE, RAYMOND CECIL JAMES, OAM, who died on April 28, 1995, aged 79, played in eight matches for New South Wales in 1934-35 and 1935-36; he was out for a king pair in his first match but later scored 360 runs at 24.00. He also made a powerful 117 against the 1932-33 MCC team, but this came for Northern New South Wales in the non-first-class match at Newcastle. Ray Little was a well-liked cricket administrator for more than 30 years, culminating in seven years on the Australian Cricket Board up to 1979.

LOCK, GRAHAM ANTHONY RICHARD, died on March 29, 1995, aged 65, in Perth, Western Australia where, in the 1960s, he enjoyed a career as rewarding as that pursued throughout the previous decade for Surrey and England. Tony Lock was an aggressive, attacking left-arm spinner, who complemented ideally the subtleties of Jim Laker's off-spin when Surrey were winning the County Championship every year from 1952 to 1958 and England regained, then retained, the Ashes; their names were twinned in cricket lore in a way usually associated with opening batsmen and fast bowlers. The final phase of his playing days saw him as a more orthodox slow bowler, relying on guile and flight as much as spin, and as a driving captain of Western Australia and Leicestershire.

Recommended to Surrey by H. D. G. Leveson Gower, Lock made his Championship debut in 1946, a week after his 17th birthday, against Kent at The

[*Popperfoto*

Tony Lock leaves The Oval in 1956 through a guard of honour after taking seven for 49 to give Surrey victory over the Australians.

Oval, and marked it with a hot catch at backward short leg off Alf Gover – the first of 830 in his career. In 1948, while doing National Service, he took six for 43 at Pontypridd, on a pitch "that afforded little assistance to bowlers", when the Combined Services beat Glamorgan, that summer's champions, and back at The Oval in 1949 he ousted the recently capped South Australian, John McMahon, as the left-arm spinner. Next year, when Surrey shared the Championship with Lancashire, his contribution was 72 wickets at 22.38 and his reward – belatedly in his opinion – was his county cap. In 1951 he took 100 wickets for the first time. But the 1952 *Wisden* said he would struggle to gain higher honours "unless he imparts more spin to his leg-break". After two winters working at an indoor school in Croydon, he emerged with a lower trajectory that produced vicious spin at around medium-pace. Now the ball spat from leg stump to hit the top of the off, or spun devilishly and jumped shoulder high. Gone were his original high-arm action and the classical spin bowler's loop, victims, it was said, of a low beam in those Croydon nets that had forced him to drop his arm. His new method was far more effective but produced mutterings about its legitimacy. In 1952 he was called up for the Old Trafford Test against India, and took four for 36 in the second innings. But a week later, when Surrey played the tourists at The Oval, he was no-balled three times in two overs for throwing his quicker ball. Raising the beam at the Croydon nets helped restore something of Lock's original action, but he was again called for throwing in the West Indies in 1953-54 and for a time he refrained from bowling his faster ball. It was this delivery which drew the legendary lament from Doug Insole, the Essex captain, to the square-leg umpire when he was bowled by Lock in fading light: "How was I out then – run out?"

Although picked for the First Test against Australia in 1953, he wore his spinning finger raw the day after selection and played in only the last two Tests. At Headingley, his resolute batting served England better than his bowling, but at The Oval his return of 21–9–45–5 on the third afternoon, along with Laker's four for 75, was instrumental in Australia's dismissal for 162. Next day, England regained the Ashes for the first time since 1932-33, and in the spring *Wisden* named him as one of the Five Cricketers of the Year.

It was a different story at Old Trafford in 1956, when Laker took 19 Australian wickets while Lock had to be content with the left-over, and economical match figures of one for 106 from 69 overs. He had enjoyed his own ten-wicket return three weeks earlier. After taking six for 29 in Kent's first innings at Blackheath, he demolished their second innings with figures of 29.1–18–54–10. In 1957 he had a match return of 11 for 48 from 37.4 overs in the Oval Test against West Indies, and in the wet summer of 1958 he was utterly ruthless against the weak New Zealanders, taking 34 wickets at just 7.47 apiece.

On overseas tours, he was not quite the same threat, except on the soft pitches of New Zealand in 1958-59. There he took 13 Test wickets at less than nine apiece, but also saw himself on film, and was genuinely shocked by the imperfection of his action. "Had I known I was throwing I wouldn't have bowled that way," he said later. So he remodelled his action once more, but he still took his 100 wickets every year until 1962, his penultimate year at The Oval. He was no longer such a fearsome proposition in England but emerged as a better bowler overseas. He was the leading wicket-taker on MCC's tour of India and Pakistan in 1961-62 and, when he was omitted from the side for Australia in 1962-63, he went instead to play for Western Australia, where he took 32 wickets in the Sheffield Shield and immediately became a fixture. In 1966-67, he was the first post-war bowler to take 50 or more Shield wickets in a season. He assumed the captaincy in 1967-68 and led Western Australia to only their second Shield. Meanwhile, he had been recruited by Leicestershire for mid-week games in 1965, and captained them in the next two seasons with such infectious enthusiasm that they rose from 14th in 1965 to second in 1967, then their highest position in the Championship.

There was an unexpected twist to this phase of his career when he was called to the Caribbean to replace the injured Titmus in 1967-68 and played in the last two Tests. In the final one, at Georgetown, his belligerent 89 in England's first innings surpassed his previous highest first-class score, and put England on course for the draw that gave them the series. He was, Trevor Bailey wrote, "the ideal person to walk out to the crease when the match seemed lost".

Lock continued as a coach in Perth and from 1987 to 1991 was cricket professional at Mill Hill School in north London. His final years were overshadowed by two allegations of sexual abuse involving young girls, the second only months before his death from cancer. Cleared of both charges, he was nevertheless forced to sell some of his cricket memorabilia to meet his legal costs, and while the second court case was pending his wife died of a heart attack. He said bitterly just before he died that he would be remembered only for the charges and not for his cricket, but he will be proved wrong. "There never has been a more aggressive spin bowler," wrote David Frith in *The Slow Men*, and the aggression came out in his captaincy, his famous full-throated appealing ("When Lock appeals at The Oval," as the old joke said, "someone's out at Lord's.") and his marvellous catching. "The spectacular ones, the sudden full-length dives, were the easy ones," recalled his Surrey team-mate Micky Stewart. "His best were when he took the rockets, close in, without anyone noticing." Only W. G. Grace and Frank Woolley have taken more catches. Lock is also ninth in the list of all-time wicket-takers with 2,844 at 19.23; 174 of those came in his 49 Tests, at 25.58. He was a volatile, vulnerable man but he was an astonishingly durable cricketer and the memory of that will endure too.

MALCOLM, HENRY JOHN JAMES, who died on January 6, 1995, aged 80, made 76 not out on his first-class debut for Middlesex against Cambridge University in 1948. He played only three more matches, but was an outstanding club batsman and medium-pace bowler for South Hampstead, and scored 105 not out for the Club Cricket Conference against the 1949 New Zealanders.

MALLETT, ANTHONY WILLIAM HAWARD, died in Cape Town on December 10, 1994, aged 70. Tony Mallett was an outstanding schoolboy player alongside Trevor Bailey at Dulwich, and an Oxford Blue in 1947 and 1948. He then became a schoolteacher and appeared irregularly for Kent – 33 matches between 1946 and 1953 – mostly during the holidays. When he played, he performed with gusto. His highest score, 97 against Sussex at Tunbridge Wells in 1946, was made in only 68 minutes. He bowled at a rapid pace and took six for 42 playing for the South against a strong North team in 1948. He emigrated to Southern Africa in 1957 and for 18 years was principal of Diocesan College, Cape Town. His son Nick, also an Oxford cricket Blue, played rugby for South Africa.

MAMA, BAPOO BURJORJI, who died on March 18, 1995, aged 71, was one of India's leading statisticians. He kept cricket records for almost 50 years and was a member of the Indian TV commentary team from 1973 to 1988.

MANSELL, PERCY NEVILLE FRANK, MBE, who died on May 9, 1995, aged 75, was one of the handful of Rhodesian cricketers to play for South Africa. Slightly built and bespectacled, he probably looked more at home in his other role – accountancy – than cricket. But he was a tennis champion as well as a cricketer and was a remarkable all-round player: forceful batsman, safe slip, skilful leg-spinner and, in emergency, a seamer as well. Mansell was born in Shropshire, but the family was already settled in Rhodesia and his mother took him back there as a baby. As a 16-year-old he played for Rhodesia against Transvaal and two years later scored 62 against MCC in Bulawayo in February 1939. He did not get a chance in Test cricket until picked to go to England in 1951. Brought in to bat at No. 7 for the Leeds Test, he got to 90 but, with the last man in, he was forced to attack and was caught at mid-on. It was the highest score of a generally disappointing tour (though he did bowl Freddie Brown, playing for MCC, with his first-ever ball at Lord's) and of his 13 Tests. But the following season, he became the second man, after A. E. E. Vogler, to do the 500 run/50 wicket double in a South African season. He was a member of the vibrant 1952-53 party to Australia, and returned to England in 1955, playing in four Tests with very little success. Mansell played his last first-class match in 1961-62, before retiring with a record of 4,598 runs at 29.66, 299 wickets at 26.08, and 156 catches in only 113 matches. In Tests he scored 355 runs at 17.75 and took 11 wickets at 66.90. On retirement, he was awarded the MBE for services for cricket and made a Freeman of Bulawayo. He was not a man for personal glory, though. In Rhodesia, he is reputed to have got into a situation where he needed to score two for victory and three for his century; he happily settled for the two.

MARLEY, ROBERT CECIL, who died in Florida on May 13, 1995, aged 85, was an opening batsman who captained Jamaica in one match in 1945-46. He later became a successful lawyer and a leading cricket administrator, serving as president of the West Indies Cricket Board of Control from 1971 to 1974.

MARSHALL, OLIVE, died in hospital in March 1995, aged 62. "Polly" Marshall was a stalwart of women's cricket in Yorkshire, whom she captained for many years. She played 13 Tests for England between 1954 and 1966, batting, bowling medium-paced and fielding magnificently: she once effected three run-outs in an innings at Auckland.

MIRZA, PARVAZ, who was found dead from natural causes at his home in Birmingham on September 24, 1995, aged 24, was a promising fast-medium bowler with Worcestershire. It is understood he had a heart condition, though this had not been regarded as a serious problem. He had played in seven Championship matches since his debut in 1994 and firmly established himself in the Sunday League side. The week before his death he was in the team for the match against Glamorgan that could have given Worcestershire the Sunday title. Mirza was a whippy bowler, willing to experiment, and was working on a useful fast off-break. He had delighted spectators by his fighting performance with the bat to save the match against Derbyshire at Kidderminster. "He was quiet, very popular, and absolutely thrilled to be playing county cricket," said Worcestershire secretary Mike Vockins.

MITCHELL, BRUCE, who died on July 1, 1995, aged 86, appeared for South Africa in all 42 Tests they played between 1929 and 1949. He nearly always opened the innings and acquired a reputation throughout the game as a dour and boring batsman. "The sad but brutal truth," wrote E. W. Swanton in 1949, after the last of his eight Test centuries, "is that any Test in which this ultra-patient cricketer makes a hundred is almost sure to end in a draw." This was not literally true: Mitchell's most famous innings was the unbeaten 164 that gave South Africa their first Test victory in England, at Lord's in 1935. But even he used to joke that he was not sure how he had time to make the runs, since the match lasted only three days.

The old-time South African wicket-keeper E. A. Halliwell is reputed to have predicted that Mitchell would play for South Africa when he coached him as a six-year-old, and he was immensely successful as a Johannesburg schoolboy. But he went into the Transvaal team as a 17-year-old for his bowling, and took five for 23 and six for 72 with his leg-breaks on his debut against Border. However, Mitchell soon worked his way up the batting order, and his bowling became more occasional. Aged 20, having played only one match on turf in his life, he was picked to tour England in 1929. He began the tour at No. 7, but the captain, H. G. Deane, chose him to open in the First Test at Edgbaston. Mitchell batted for seven hours, scoring 88, in the first innings. Even *Wisden* said the cricket was uninteresting, and the innings "featureless". He was in for a further two hours 35 minutes in the second innings, this time making 61 not out. By then the game was already doomed to be drawn, but Mitchell had made himself as much of an immovable fixture in the team as he was at the crease. His form fell away that series, to the relief of both opposition and spectators. But he topped the South African averages in the home series against England in 1930-31, scoring his maiden Test century in their first ever home Test on turf, at Cape Town, when he began the match with a stand of 260 with Jack Siedle that remains a South African first-wicket Test record. In Australia a year later, he was ill but still played in every Test and emerged as a brilliant slip fielder, taking six catches in the Third Test. Unfortunately, in the First Test, he put down Bradman on 15; it was supposedly the only time Mitchell had ever been heard to swear. Bradman went on to score 226.

Mitchell was the leading bowler in the 1934-35 Currie Cup, but when he came to England the following summer resumed his role as the linchpin of the batting. His great innings, which remains the highest for South Africa at Lord's, took five and a half hours and he off-drove beautifully to give his team-mate Xenophon Balaskas time to bowl England out. Mitchell was criticised in the last two Tests when South Africa successfully sat on their lead and squashed the series: he spent three and threequarter hours over 48 – a return to his form in Brisbane three years earlier when he went 70 minutes without scoring – at Manchester, and scored a risk-free hundred at The Oval. He struggled with the bat in the home series against Australia that followed too quickly after the tour of England, though he took some important wickets, and he returned to his best form before England toured in 1938-39. The Durban "Timeless" Test might have been made for him, though his second-innings 89 actually occupied less than four hours of the ten days.

Mitchell served with the Transvaal Scottish Regiment in the war, and was still South Africa's best batsman when he returned in 1947, scoring 120 and 189 not out at The Oval, batting for more than 13 hours and spending less than 15 minutes of the match off the field. He finished the 1948-49 series against England almost as strongly, with 99 and 56 in the last Test, and no one imagined that he would never play for South Africa again. But he was dropped, amid general astonishment, after failing in two preliminary matches against the 1949-50 Australians, and he retired at once. He remains South Africa's leading Test run-scorer, with 3,471 at 48.88. Mitchell was a quiet, modest man with a self-deprecating sense of humour. At his home he kept a cartoon that recalled not his triumphs but one of his rare failures: it showed a lone figure banished to a desert island and was captioned The Man Who Dropped Bradman. And he would chucklingly recall the spectator at Edgbaston in 1929 who, having watched him bat, asked him if he thought he was a war memorial.

MORRISBY, RONALD ORLANDO GEORGE, who died on June 10, 1995, aged 80, was Tasmania's leading run-getter in the days before the state was elevated to the Sheffield Shield. He made his first-class debut, against Victoria on Christmas Day 1931, 18 days before his 17th birthday, and went on to make 2,596 first-class runs as a back-foot opening batsman. He toured India with Frank Tarrant's team in 1935-36, and played in a Test trial at Sydney the following season.

MURRAY, ANTON RONALD ANDREW, who died on April 17, 1995, aged 72, after a long illness, played ten Test matches for South Africa as an all-rounder. He was a vigorous right-handed batsman, an accurate medium-paced stock bowler, and one of the most athletic members of the brilliant fielding team that toured Australia in 1952-53. He played four Tests, missing the Fourth because of appendicitis, the after-effects of which hampered him on his return; but his 51 in the Second Test was vital in helping put South Africa into position for their first win over Australia in 42 years. His only Test century came later that tour, at Wellington. He scored 109 and his seventh-wicket partnership of 246 with Jackie McGlew was then a world Test record. He toured England in 1955 but did not make the Test team. Murray played for Eastern Province from 1947-48 to 1955-56. He was a schoolteacher and founder of St Alban's College in Pretoria.

MURRAY-WILLIS, PETER EARNSHAW, who died on January 7, 1995, aged 84, was a brave and spirited cricketer who played briefly for Worcestershire before the war and was appointed captain of Northamptonshire in the confusion of 1946. Having helped organise wartime matches for the club, he was chosen in the hope that he would be an approximation of the county's popular pre-war captain, Robert Nelson, his school friend from St George's, Harpenden, who had been killed in the war. His appointment was not a success; there was criticism of his tactics and Murray-Willis's reputation failed to recover from the time his cap blew off while he was chasing the ball to the boundary, and he stopped to get the cap before returning for the ball – the batsmen were laughing too much to take advantage. He was obliged to resign in mid-season, and left the county game. But he continued playing club cricket until he was in his mid-fifties.

MUSSON, Maj.-Gen. ALFRED HENRY, CB, CBE, who died on August 6, 1995, aged 94, played for the Army against Cambridge University at Fenner's in 1925. His two brothers also played first-class cricket.

NORFOLK, LAVINIA, DUCHESS OF, who died on December 10, 1995, aged 79, was widow of the cricket-loving 16th Duke and enthusiastically developed the game at Arundel Castle, although she was personally more of a racing fan. Her daughter Lady Herries is married to Sir Colin Cowdrey.

PARKER, GRAHAME WILSHAW, OBE, who died on November 11, 1995, aged 83, was closely associated with Gloucestershire as player, administrator and historian, but was also one of the Renaissance men of English sport. It is said he came into cricket by fluke: at Cambridge he turned his back on the game but was pursued by the captain, on his bicycle, to fill a gap against Nottinghamshire. He agreed and scored 96 against Larwood and Voce. He went on to win a Blue that year and in 1935, when he was captain. Parker was already a rugby Blue and went on to win two England caps as a full-back; he was also offered professional terms by Gloucester City soccer club. He only played 70 cricket matches for Gloucestershire, being restricted by schoolteaching duties. But he was an attractive batsman, who made 210 in four hours against Kent at Dover in 1937. He was also a useful swing bowler and an athletic fielder. In the war he rose to the rank of major and then became a legendary figure at Blundell's School, where he was a housemaster for 15 years. In 1968 he left teaching to become Gloucestershire secretary, doing the job for eight years and helping revitalise the club. "He was not just a games player," said Tony Brown, then the county captain, "but a man of vision and ideas."

POWELL, LOUIS ST VINCENT, who died on June 6, 1995, aged 92, made ten appearances as one of Somerset's many amateurs at intervals between 1927 and 1938. He was an opening bowler who found himself forced to face Ted McDonald in full cry when he went out to bat No. 10 in his first match: the senior pro Tom Young noticed his pads were not good enough, loaned him his and Powell made 22. He played rugby for Bath and Somerset.

PRESTON, STEPHEN, who died on June 30, 1995, aged 89, was a medium-pace bowler who played five times between 1928 and 1930 for the strong Lancashire team, opening the attack with Ted McDonald on his debut.

RAO, Maj.-Gen. JOGINDER SINGH, died on October 3, 1994, aged 56. In 1963-64, he performed the hat-trick on his first-class debut, a feat achieved by only eight men in history. Five days later he took two hat-tricks in the second innings of his next match: he finished with seven for 30. Three hat-tricks in a player's first two matches is not merely unequalled; it may never be equalled. Rao was a fast-medium bowler, who was representing Services in the Ranji Trophy. His cricketing career was subsequently superseded by his military one; he served in the 1965 and 1971 wars against Pakistan.

RICHARDSON, JAMES VERE, who died on May 1, 1995, aged 91, was the oldest surviving Essex player. He won an Oxford Blue in 1925 as a middle-order batsman and medium-pace bowler and played 14 times for Essex. He won five England rugby caps.

RICKARDS, KENNETH ROY, who died on August 21, 1995, aged 71, scored 67 on his Test debut when he was part of the West Indies team that crushed England by ten wickets at Kingston in 1947-48. However, this was a difficult time to be a West Indian batsman whose surname did not begin with W, and Ken Rickards played only once more, at Melbourne on the tour of Australia in 1951-52. Rickards played for Jamaica from 1945-46 to 1958-59 and made his career-best 195 against British Guiana in 1950-51, which won him a place on the Australian tour. He came to England to be professional at Darwen in Lancashire; he also played twice for a Commonwealth XI in 1952, and against a similar team in 1953 for Essex. Supporters raised money in Jamaica to pay his fare home before the 1953-54 series against England, though scores of 75, 35, 0 and 1 in the two matches between Jamaica and MCC were not enough to win his selection.

RIGG, KEITH EDWARD, who died on February 28, 1995, aged 88, was Australia's senior Test cricketer before his death. Rigg was a strong, stylish batsman who flourished in the 1930s, though in an era of great batsmen he was often overshadowed. After making his Victorian debut in 1926-27, it took him a while to get established in the Shield side. In 1930-31 he was picked for the Test squad when he was supposed to be sitting his economics finals at Melbourne University; after getting special dispensation from his professor he was rather embarrassed to be made twelfth man, a position he maintained for three more Tests until he finally got his chance at Sydney. West Indies caught his side on a sticky wicket and achieved their first win over Australia: Rigg scored 14 and 16. On the same ground a year later he hit his only Test century, 127 against South Africa, made partly in tandem with Bradman. But Rigg was ignored for the Bodyline series of 1932-33, which was surprising since he was a fine hooker and cutter, and his eight Tests were all at home – he never toured, although in 1930, when Australia brought only 15 men to England, he was told by a selector he would have been the 16th. His final Test record was 401 runs at 33.41. In his 87 first-class games he scored 5,544 at 42.00. For 30 years, he worked for a large farm machinery company in Melbourne and became their public relations director. He was a Victorian selector for many years and remained a regular at the MCG into old age; he was a particular admirer of Steve Waugh's batting.

RIPPON, THOMAS JOHN, died in Swansea on December 29, 1994, aged 76. Jack Rippon was understudy to Glamorgan wicket-keeper Haydn Davies, but appeared in only three first-class matches in 1947 and 1948.

ROBERTS, HARRY EDMUND, committed suicide by throwing himself under a train in Coventry on September 26, 1995, aged 71. He was a left-handed opening batsman who made five appearances for Warwickshire in 1949 and 1950 and was a well-known club player round Coventry.

ROUGHT-ROUGHT, BASIL WILLIAM, who died on October 27, 1995, aged 91, was a left-hand amateur batsman who played for Norfolk for many years and made four first-class appearances for the Minor Counties and Gentlemen's XIs between 1933 and 1938. His two younger brothers both won Blues at Cambridge.

ROWE, CHARLES GORDON, died on June 9, 1995, aged 79. Gordon Rowe remains one of a select group of players who have made a pair in their only Test match. He batted No. 6 in the New Zealand team that lost by an innings to Australia at Wellington in 1945-46, a game given Test status only retrospectively. L. A. Butterfield, who followed him to the crease in that match, is the only other New Zealander to achieve this dubious feat. Rowe played for Wellington and later captained Central Districts.

ROWE, RAYMOND CURTIS, who died on May 14, 1995, aged 81, was a left-hand batsman who played ten matches for New South Wales. On his debut, against MCC in 1932-33, he scored 70.

SCOTT, Dr EDWARD KEITH, MRCS, died on June 3, 1995, aged 76. Keith Scott was a magnificently successful schoolboy leg-spinner, taking 244 wickets in five years at Clifton. He was an impressive batsman as well, and when he left in 1937 went straight into the Gloucestershire team. He played five times for Oxford in 1938, but did not show the same form. Most of his subsequent cricket was for Cornwall. He followed his father both into the England rugby team, winning five caps, and into his general medical practice near Truro.

SHARP, HARRY PHILIP HUGH, who died on January 15, 1995, aged 77, was an old-fashioned kind of cricketing stalwart who spent his entire adult life at Lord's except for the interruption of war, when he was an able seaman – which is why he was known as "The Admiral". He joined the Lord's groundstaff in 1934 and stayed on as player, coach, MCC umpire and Middlesex scorer for 60 years. He did not make his Middlesex debut until he was back on dry land in 1946, when he was already 28. At first he struggled to win a regular place in that dynamic batting side, but he did play in the famous match at Cheltenham in 1947 when his batting and his off-spin were vital in the win that decided the Championship for Middlesex. In 1948 he was capped, became the regular opener in 1950, and in 1953 scored five of his ten career hundreds. He was released in 1955, and became an MCC coach, a job he held for 17 years. For 20 years after that, he was Middlesex scorer, until retiring in 1993. In this post, he acquired an extra, unofficial, job as Mike Gatting's mentor. In all his roles he was genial, humorous, knowledgeable and helpful and he was a much loved figure on the circuit.

SHAW, Capt. ROBERT JOHN, MBE, who died on August 5, 1995, aged 95, appeared in seven first-class matches for the Royal Navy and the Combined Services between 1926 and 1937. He averaged 40.84 and hit 119 for the Services against the New Zealanders at Portsmouth in 1931. Aged 16, he served as a midshipman in the Battle of Jutland was awarded an MBE aged 19.

SITARAM, PONNUSWAMY, who died on September 13, 1995, aged 68, took 253 Ranji Trophy wickets for Services, Railways and Delhi. He then became a groundsman, working on several major grounds. His last big assignment was at Lucknow for the India–Sri Lanka Test in 1993-94. He was involved in preparing the World Cup pitch at Gwalior when he was taken ill.

SMITH, HARRY THOMAS OLIVER, died on July 13, 1995, aged 89. Tom Smith only played 23 matches for Essex, on holidays from the Midland Bank, but established a reputation as a useful amateur fast bowler. In his first season, 1929, he bowled three Middlesex batsmen in four balls: his last victim was Walter Robins, whose middle stump was broken. He took six for 56 against Derbyshire in 1930 and five for 38 against Kent in 1933. At club level, he scored more than 50 centuries.

SOLOMON, CYRIL MOSS, who died on July 15, 1995, aged 84, played 13 matches as a middle-order batsman for New South Wales between 1931-32 and 1939-40 (with a six-year gap) and scored 131 against South Australia at Adelaide in his last season.

STEVENSON, HUGH, who died on August 12, 1995, aged 60, was chairman of the Scottish international selectors. He died in Dublin from a heart attack immediately before the annual Ireland v Scotland first-class match, which was cancelled as a gesture of respect. He was also vice-chairman of the Scottish Cricket Union.

STRYDOM, WILLIAM THOMAS, died on February 22, 1995, aged 52, after being shot during a robbery on his business premises at Pietermaritzburg on February 20, 1995. He was one of four brothers who all played for Orange Free State, appearing in 80 first-class matches as a medium-pace bowler and lower-order batsman.

SURITA, PEARSON HARVEY ST REGIS, who died in October 1995, aged 82, was an Indian cricket commentator with a distinctive fruity voice. He commentated for the BBC on India's 1959 and 1967 tours.

TRICK, WILLIAM MERVYN STANLEY, died on October 27, 1995, aged 78. Stan Trick was an amateur left-arm spinner who came out of South Wales League cricket to play 19 matches for Glamorgan between 1946 and 1950. Seven of those games were in Glamorgan's Championship campaign of 1948; in his first match for two years, he bowled Glamorgan to victory over Somerset with match figures of 12 for 106. When he appeared again three weeks later he took a further ten wickets, for 71. To the disappointment of local headline-writers Trick was not quite as successful an author, and business commitments meant he could rarely play for the county, though he took plenty of wickets for Neath and Briton Ferry Steel.

VAULKHARD, PATRICK, who died on April 1, 1995, aged 83, was a hard-hitting Derbyshire amateur in the seven seasons after the war. He made only one century in his 122 first-class innings, but this was 264 at Trent Bridge in 1946, the highest score of that season and the third-highest score in cricket history by a player who never made another century (behind Pervez Akhtar's 337 not out in 1964-65 and C. R. N. Maxwell's 268 in 1935). Pat Vaulkhard's innings always created a sense of expectation, because he was a big six-hitter – he once lofted the ball over the football stand at Bradford – even though he had almost no backlift: his batting relied on the punched straight drive. He was a protégé of Sir Julien Cahn, and played nine times for Nottinghamshire before the war, without much success. But his cricket improved, as Nottinghamshire discovered. He batted seven hours for his 264 against them, and his partnership that day of 328 with Denis Smith remains a Derbyshire fourth-wicket record. Vaulkhard was Derbyshire captain in 1950, when they finished fifth.

WALCOTT, J. HAROLD, died in May 1995. Harold Walcott was one of West Indies' leading umpires, who stood in four Test matches, all in Barbados, between 1947-48 and 1957-58. "He was respected for his fairness and courage," wrote Tony Cozier, "the former epitomised when he gave his nephew, Clyde Walcott, out lbw for 98 in a Test against India, the latter when he no-balled Tony Lock for throwing in the MCC match against Barbados in 1953-54."

WARR, ANTONY LAWLEY, died on January 29, 1995, aged 81. Tim Warr was a wicket-keeper who played five first-class matches, four for Oxford in 1933 and 1934 and one for MCC in 1950. He won two rugby caps for England and taught at Harrow for 30 years.

WHARTON-TIGAR, EDWARD CLEMENT, MBE, who died on June 14, 1995, aged 82, was a benefactor to Kent, a committee member for ten years and president in 1977. He had the world's largest collection of cigarette cards – over a million in 45,000 sets; it has been bequeathed to the British Museum. During the war he was a saboteur for the Special Operations Executive.

WILSON, BEN AMBLER, who died early in 1995, aged 73, played for Warwickshire against Scotland at Edgbaston in 1951. He later played for Suffolk and coached at Blundell's School.

WRIGLEY, MICHAEL HAROLD, who died on January 13, 1995, aged 70, was a fast-medium bowler for Harrow, Combined Services and Oxford at a time of very strong university cricket: he won a Blue in 1949. Later he became a foreign intelligence officer in the Far East. His professional techniques were acquired earlier: he once burst into Vincent's Club as an undergraduate and announced that he had deceived the referee in a college soccer match and achieved a lifelong ambition by handling the ball into the net.

WYATT, ROBERT ELLIOTT STOREY, died on April 20, 1995, aged 93. The oldest living England player at the time of his death, Bob Wyatt led England in 16 of his 40 Tests, and in a first-class career spanning 35 years captained Warwickshire and then Worcestershire. Conservative as a captain, and technically correct rather than a dashing batsman in the amateur tradition, he was and remained throughout his long life an astute and perceptive thinker on the game. The change of the lbw law in 1935, which he deplored as inhibiting the glories of off-side strokes, remained a particular bone of contention.

Wyatt's family financial circumstances precluded his expected progress to Surrey, the county of his birth, via public school and Oxford or Cambridge. He was working and playing club cricket in Coventry when, aged 21, he was offered a 12-match trial by Warwickshire in 1923. F. S. G. Calthorpe, Warwickshire's captain, initially underestimated his batting potential, using him instead as a medium-pace swing bowler, but he went in No. 9 and scored a century against Worcestershire at Dudley in 1925, in a stand of 228 with A. J. W. Croom – still a county record for the eighth wicket – which led to his recognition as a batsman. When Calthorpe was away ill in 1926, Wyatt was promoted to open, with great success. He made the first of 14 consecutive appearances for the Gentlemen at Lord's and, passing 1,000 runs for the first of 17 times in England, finished the season eight wickets shy of the double.

Selection for MCC's 1926-27 tour of India, Burma and Ceylon followed, and with around 1,800 runs and an average of more than 50 he revealed the powers of concentration and endurance that put him in good stead for future tours. He played in all five Tests in South Africa in 1927-28 and, although his omission from the 1928-29 tour of Australia was a setback, and surprising in view of his 2,408 runs that season, he was a regular selection for MCC touring teams until the outbreak of war in 1939. In 1929 he was even more prolific, with 2,630 runs in all cricket. His maiden Test hundred, 113 against South Africa at Old Trafford, was the first century for England since the Great War by an amateur. Though he had command of all the attacking strokes, as he demonstrated on such occasions as the Scarborough Festival, he gave defence top priority and thrived on adversity. The sterner the struggle, the more he seemed at home. The secret of his success lay in his back-foot play and correct initial movement based on observation of Fry and Hobbs.

Wyatt's rise to the England captaincy, however, caused enormous controversy. He was chosen in place of Percy Chapman for the Oval Test of 1930. There were strong attacks in the press, and he received vitriolic, even threatening letters. The Ashes were at stake, and England lost by an innings. However, Wyatt was seen to have done a decent job with great dignity. And after the Bodyline tour of 1932-33, when he was vice-captain to Douglas Jardine, he was luckier when he next captained England: against Australia, at Lord's in 1934. A sticky wicket and Hedley Verity's 15 for 104 brought England their first Ashes win there since 1896 – and their last to date. It levelled the series at one apiece. But with Bradman again passing 200, the Ashes were once more lost at The Oval. There were further series defeats for Wyatt in the West Indies in 1934-35, when a short-pitched ball from Manny Martindale broke his jaw in four places in the Fourth and deciding Test, and by South Africa in 1935, though he scored 149, his only other Test hundred, against them at Trent Bridge. The captaincy then passed to Gubby Allen. Wyatt also lost the Warwickshire captaincy in 1937 after eight seasons of difficulties with a committee looking for something other than his methodical approach. Eventually the club turned to the lighter-hearted Peter Cranmer. The furore this caused was the mirror image of the one surrounding his England appointment and there was a widespread feeling that he had been treated churlishly. The club tried to keep Wyatt at Edgbaston after the war, but he accepted an offer to join Worcestershire and from 1949 to 1951 captained them to third, sixth and fourth in the Championship, their most successful phase at the time. Though aged 50 in 1951, his final summer of county cricket, he was not beyond hitting Somerset's Bertie Buse high into the pavilion when Worcestershire needed six off the last ball to win at Taunton. With occasional matches for MCC and Free Foresters, his first-class cricket continued until 1957.

Wyatt was an England selector from 1950 to 1954; in the first year he was chairman. Two books, *The Ins and Outs of Cricket* and the autobiographical *Three Straight Sticks*, demonstrated his candid and technical nature, and in later years, as a guest in Paul Getty's box at Lord's, he dispensed pithy analysis tempered with witty anecdotes while Mollie, his wife, dispensed the champagne. His longevity helped secure his reputation: the new R. E. S. Wyatt stand at Edgbaston was opened just after his death. In his own time, he was generally undervalued, because his cricket was efficient and brave rather than obviously glittering. His biographer Gerald Pawle wrote that Wyatt's qualities were always more likely to impress his colleagues than the public: "outstanding ability in every department, common sense, courage, and an abiding loyalty, both to companions who earned his respect and to the game itself." "No one," wrote Dudley Carew, "not even Sir Pelham Warner, has ever loved the game with such a concentrated single-mindedness."

A special article appears on pages 31-33.

INDEX TO TEST MATCHES

TEST MATCHES, 1995-96

Full details of these Tests, and the two between West Indies and New Zealand scheduled for April-May 1996, will appear in the 1997 edition of *Wisden*.

PAKISTAN v SRI LANKA

First Test: At Peshawar, September 8, 9, 10, 11. Pakistan won by an innings and 40 runs. Toss: Pakistan. Pakistan 459 for nine dec. (Saeed Anwar 50, Ramiz Raja 78, Inzamam-ul-Haq 95, Shoaib Mohammad 57, Wasim Akram 36, Moin Khan 51; W. P. U. J. C. Vaas five for 99, M. Muralitharan four for 134); Sri Lanka 186 (S. Ranatunga 33, H. P. Tillekeratne 44 not out; Wasim Akram five for 55) and 233 (U. C. Hathurusinghe 53, A. Ranatunga 76, H. P. Tillekeratne 48; Aamir Sohail four for 54).

Arbab Niaz Stadium became Test cricket's 75th venue and Peshawar's second, superseding the Services Ground. Ramiz Raja captained Pakistan in his first Test since May 1993. The teams went off on the first day after the Sri Lankans were pelted in the field, and a firecracker was thrown at Wasim Akram on the fourth.

Second Test: At Faisalabad, September 15, 16, 17, 18, 19. Sri Lanka won by 42 runs. Toss: Pakistan. Sri Lanka 223 (U. C. Hathurusinghe 47, H. P. Tillekeratne 115; Aqib Javed three for 34, Saqlain Mushtaq three for 74) and 361 (U. C. Hathurusinghe 83, P. A. de Silva 105, H. D. P. K. Dharmasena 49, W. P. U. J. C. Vaas 40; Aqib Javed five for 84); Pakistan 333 (Saeed Anwar 54, Saqlain Mushtaq 34, Ramiz Raja 75, Inzamam-ul-Haq 50, Moin Khan 30, Extras 32; M. Muralitharan five for 68) and 209 (Saeed Anwar 50, Moin Khan 50; W. P. U. J. C. Vaas four for 45, H. D. P. K. Dharmasena three for 43).

Sri Lanka won in Pakistan for the first time to level the series. De Silva scored his eighth Test century in his first match since arriving from England after a summer with Kent, and became the second Sri Lankan to pass 3,000 Test runs. Muralitharan became Sri Lanka's leading Test wicket-taker, passing R. J. Ratnayake's 73.

Third Test: At Sialkot, September 22, 23, 24, 25, 26. Sri Lanka won by 144 runs. Toss: Sri Lanka. Sri Lanka 232 (A. P. Gurusinha 45, H. D. P. K. Dharmasena 62 not out; Aqib Javed three for nine dec. (U. C. Hathurusinghe 73, A. Ranatunga 87, H. P. Tillekeratne 50, Extras 41; Mohammad Akram three for 39); Pakistan 214 (Aamir Sohail 48; M. Muralitharan four for 72) and 212 (Moin Khan 117 not out, Extras 34; G. P. Wickremasinghe four for 55, W. P. U. J. C. Vaas four for 37).

Sri Lanka took the series 2-1 after going one down – their second overseas series win and Pakistan's first home series defeat since 1980-81 by West Indies. Moin Khan came in at 15 for five in Pakistan's second innings and helped to add 197 for the next five wickets.

ZIMBABWE v SOUTH AFRICA

Only Test: At Harare, October 13, 14, 15, 16. South Africa won by seven wickets. Toss: Zimbabwe. Zimbabwe 170 (H. H. Streak 53; A. A. Donald three for 42, B. N. Schultz four for 54) and 283 (D. L. Houghton 30, A. Flower 63, G. J. Whittall 38, P. A. Strang 37; A. A. Donald eight for 71); South Africa 346 (A. C. Hudson 135, B. M. McMillan 98 not out, A. A. Donald 33; A. C. I. Lock three for 68, B. C. Strang five for 101) and 108 for three (W. J. Cronje 56 not out).

Schultz was warned by referee B. N. Jarman for his "unsportsmanlike gesture" on dismissing Houghton in the first innings, in which Streak's maiden Test fifty rescued Zimbabwe from 84 for seven. Donald's eight for 71 was the best innings return for South Africa since their return to Test cricket in 1992. It was South Africa's fifth successive Test win.

INDIA v NEW ZEALAND

First Test: At Bangalore, October 18, 19, 20. India won by eight wickets. Toss: New Zealand. New Zealand 145 (L. K. Germon 48; J. Srinath three for 24, A. Kumble four for 39) and 233 (S. P. Fleming 41, L. K. Germon 41; A. Kumble five for 81); India 228 (A. D. Jadeja 59, M. Azharuddin 87; D. K. Morrison three for 61, C. L. Cairns four for 44, D. J. Nash three for 50) and 151 for two (M. Prabhakar 43, A. D. Jadeja 73).

Germon became the first player to captain his country on Test debut since A. R. Lewis of England in December 1972, at Delhi. Kumble's first wicket – M. D. Crowe – was his 100th in 21 Tests, on his home ground.

Second Test: At Madras, October 25, 26, 27, 28, 29. Drawn. Toss: India. India 144 for two (M. Prabhakar 41 not out, N. S. Sidhu 33, S. R. Tendulkar 52 not out).

Only 71.1 overs were possible, on the first and fourth days; the other three were washed out.

Third Test: At Cuttack, November 8, 9, 10, 11, 12. Drawn. Toss: India. India 296 for eight dec. (A. D. Jadeja 45, N. S. Sidhu 41, M. Azharuddin 35, N. R. Mongia 45 not out, A. R. Kapoor 42; C. L. Cairns three for 95, D. J. Nash four for 62); New Zealand 175 for eight dec. (M. J. Greatbatch 50, R. G. Twose 36; N. D. Hirwani six for 59).

There was no play on the second or third days – water seeped through the plastic covers. Hirwani took six wickets in his first Test since November 1990. India took the series 1-0.

AUSTRALIA v PAKISTAN

First Test: At Brisbane, November 9, 10, 11, 13. Australia won by an innings and 126 runs. Toss: Australia. Australia 463 (M. A. Taylor 69, M. J. Slater 42, D. C. Boon 54, M. E. Waugh 59, S. R. Waugh 112 not out, G. S. Blewett 57; Waqar Younis three for 101); Pakistan 97 (Aamir Sohail 32; S. K. Warne seven for 23) and 240 (Aamir Sohail 99, Inzamam-ul-Haq 62; G. D. McGrath four for 76, S. K. Warne four for 54).

Wasim Akram was restored as Pakistan captain, while Salim Malik returned after being cleared by a Pakistani judge of attempted bribery. Malik injured his hand catching Taylor on the first day, and did not bat in the first innings; in the second he came in at No. 8 and was caught fourth ball off Warne, one of his accusers. S. R. Waugh scored a century in his first innings since his 200 in Kingston six months before. Warne's match figures of 11 for 77 were the best for Australia against Pakistan.

Second Test: At Hobart, November 17, 18, 19, 20. Australia won by 155 runs. Toss: Australia. Australia 267 (M. A. Taylor 40, D. C. Boon 34, M. E. Waugh 88, I. A. Healy 37; Wasim Akram three for 42, Mushtaq Ahmed five for 115) and 306 (M. A. Taylor 123, M. J. Slater 73; Wasim Akram three for 72, Mushtaq Ahmed four for 83); Pakistan 198 (Aamir Sohail 32, Ramiz Raja 59, Ijaz Ahmed 34 not out; G. D. McGrath three for 46, P. R. Reiffel four for 38) and 220 (Aamir Sohail 57, Inzamam-ul-Haq 40, Wasim Akram 33; G. D. McGrath five for 61, P. R. Reiffel three for 42).

In the first innings, the video replay system failed when umpire H. D. Bird asked for help; he gave Boon run out himself. S. K. Warne's toe was chipped by Waqar Younis and he did not bowl. Sohail was fined half his match fee and given a suspended two-match sentence by referee R. Subba Row for his reaction when caught in the second innings.

Third Test: At Sydney, November 30, December 1, 2, 3, 4. Pakistan won by 74 runs. Toss: Pakistan. Pakistan 299 (Ramiz Raja 33, Ijaz Ahmed 137, Inzamam-ul-Haq 39, Salim Malik 36; C. J. McDermott three for 62, S. K. Warne four for 55) and 204 (Ramiz Raja 39, Salim Malik 45, Inzamam-ul-Haq 59; C. J. McDermott five for 49, S. K. Warne four for 66); Australia 257 (M. A. Taylor 47, M. E. Waugh 116, S. R. Waugh 38; Wasim Akram four for 50, Mushtaq Ahmed five for 95) and 172 (M. A. Taylor 59, M. E. Waugh 34; Waqar Younis three for 15, Mushtaq Ahmed four for 91).

Pakistan won a Test in Australia for the first time since 1981-82 when Australia, chasing 247, lost their last seven wickets for 51 on the final morning, but Australia took the series 2-1.

SOUTH AFRICA v ENGLAND

First Test Match

At Centurion, November 16, 17, 18, 19, 20. Drawn. Toss: South Africa.

England

*M. A. Atherton c Donald b Pollock	78	D. Gough b McMillan	0
A. J. Stewart c Matthews b Schultz	6	R. K. Illingworth b Donald	0
M. R. Ramprakash c Richardson b Donald	9	A. R. C. Fraser not out	4
G. P. Thorpe c Richardson b Pollock	13	L-b 16, w 1, n-b 7	24
G. A. Hick lbw b Pollock	141		
R. A. Smith b McMillan	43	1/14 2/36 3/64 (9 wkts dec.) 381	
†R. C. Russell not out	50	4/206 5/290 6/320	
D. G. Cork c Matthews b McMillan	13	7/350 8/358 9/359	

Bowling: Donald 33–10–92–2; Schultz 16–5–47–1; Matthews 30–13–63–0; Pollock 29–7–98–3; McMillan 25–10–50–3; Cronje 8–5–14–0; Kirsten 2–1–1–0.

South Africa

A. C. Hudson, G. Kirsten, *W. J. Cronje, D. J. Cullinan, J. N. Rhodes, B. M. McMillan, †D. J. Richardson, S. M. Pollock, C. R. Matthews, A. A. Donald and B. N. Schultz.

Umpires: S. Venkataraghavan (India) and C. J. Mitchley.
Referee: C. H. Lloyd (West Indies).

Centurion (formerly Verwoerdburg), near Pretoria, became Test cricket's 76th venue. Pollock, whose father P. M., now chairman of the South African selectors, was bowling when England's last Test in South Africa was rained off in February 1965, removed three of England's top five on his Test debut. Richardson made his 100th dismissal in his 24th Test, equalling A. T. W. Grout's record; no other wicket-keeper has reached 100 without a stumping. Smith passed 4,000 runs in his 58th Test. After an electrical storm on the second day, the last three days were washed out; only 143 overs were bowled in the match.

SOUTH AFRICA v ENGLAND

Second Test Match

At Johannesburg, November 30, December 1, 2, 3, 4. Drawn. Toss: England.

South Africa

A. C. Hudson c Stewart b Cork	0	– c Russell b Fraser	17
G. Kirsten c Russell b Malcolm	110	– c Russell b Malcolm	1
*W. J. Cronje c Russell b Cork	35	– c Russell b Cork	48
D. J. Cullinan c Russell b Hick	69	– c Gough b Cork	61
J. N. Rhodes c Russell b Cork	5	– c Russell b Fraser	57
B. M. McMillan lbw b Cork	35	– not out	100
†D. J. Richardson c Russell b Malcolm	0	– c Ramprakash b Malcolm	23
S. M. Pollock c Smith b Cork	33	– lbw b Cork	5
C. E. Eksteen c Russell b Cork	13	– c Russell b Cork	2
M. W. Pringle not out	10	– c Hick b Fraser	2
A. A. Donald b Malcolm	0	– not out	9
B 1, l-b 14, w 2, n-b 5	22	B 5, l-b 12, w 1, n-b 3	21
	332	(9 wkts dec.)	346

1/3 2/74 3/211 4/221 5/260 6/260 7/278 8/314 9/331

1/7 2/19 3/116 4/145 5/244 6/296 7/304 8/311 9/314

Bowling: *First Innings*—Cork 32–7–84–5; Malcolm 22–5–62–4; Fraser 20–5–69–0; Gough 15–2–64–0; Hick 15–1–38–1. *Second Innings*—Cork 31.3–6–78–4; Malcolm 13–2–65–2; Fraser 29–6–84–3; Gough 12–2–48–0; Hick 15–3–35–0; Ramprakash 4–0–19–0.

England

*M. A. Atherton b Donald	9	– not out	185
A. J. Stewart c Kirsten b Pringle	45	– b McMillan	38
M. R. Ramprakash b Donald	4	– b McMillan	0
G. P. Thorpe c Kirsten b Eksteen	34	– lbw b Pringle	17
G. A. Hick c and b Eksteen	6	– c Richardson b Donald	4
R. A. Smith c and b McMillan	52	– c Pollock b Donald	44
†R. C. Russell c Rhodes b Eksteen	12	– not out	29
D. G. Cork c Cullinan b Pollock	8		
D. Gough c and b Pollock	2		
A. R. C. Fraser lbw b Pollock	0		
D. E. Malcolm not out	0		
B 6, l-b 1, n-b 21	28	B 4, l-b 7, n-b 23	34

1/10 2/45 3/109 4/116 5/125   200   1/75 2/75 3/134   (5 wkts) 351
6/147 7/178 8/193 9/200   4/145 5/232

Bowling: *First Innings*—Donald 15–3–49–2; Pringle 17–4–46–1; Pollock 15–2–44–3; McMillan 10.3–0–42–1; Eksteen 11–5–12–3. *Second Innings*—Donald 35–9–95–2; Pringle 23–5–52–1; Pollock 29–11–65–0; McMillan 21–0–50–2; Eksteen 52–20–76–0; Cronje 3–1–2–0; Kirsten 2–2–0–0.

Umpires: D. B. Hair (Australia) and K. E. Liebenberg.
Referee: C. H. Lloyd (West Indies).

Russell made 11 dismissals in the match, breaking R. W. Taylor's world record of 10 for England v India at Bombay in 1979-80. England were left to chase 479 in five sessions plus four overs; Atherton batted for 643 minutes, the fourth longest innings in Tests, facing 492 balls and hitting 28 fours in his highest Test score. He reached 4,000 Test runs (in his 53rd match) at 110 and 1,000 in a calendar year for the second year running at 173. Russell (29 not out) supported him for 277 minutes after coming in at 232 for five. Donald took his 100th Test wicket in his 22nd match. South African manager R. A. Woolmer was censured by referee Lloyd for criticising umpiring decisions.

SOUTH AFRICA v ENGLAND

Third Test Match

At Durban, December 14, 15, 16, 17, 18. Drawn. Toss: South Africa.

South Africa

G. Kirsten c Hick b Martin	8	S. M. Pollock not out	36
A. C. Hudson c Crawley b Illingworth	45	C. R. Matthews lbw b Ilott	0
*W. J. Cronje b Martin b Illingworth	8	A. A. Donald b Illingworth	32
D. J. Cullinan c Smith b Martin	10		
J. N. Rhodes lbw b Ilott	38	L-b 11, n-b 1	12
J. H. Kallis c Russell b Martin	1		
B. M. McMillan c Russell b Martin	28	1/54 2/56 3/73 4/85 5/89	225
†D. J. Richardson c Russell b Ilott	7	6/141 7/152 8/153 9/153	

Bowling: Cork 27–12–64–0; Ilott 15–3–48–3; Martin 27–9–60–4; Illingworth 29–12–37–3; Hick 2–0–5–0.

England

*M. A. Atherton c Hudson b Donald	2	D. G. Cork not out	23
A. J. Stewart c Hudson b Matthews	41		
G. P. Thorpe c Cullinan b Donald	2	L-b 4, n-b 7	11
R. A. Smith c McMillan b Matthews	34		
G. A. Hick not out	31	1/2 2/13 3/83	(5 wkts) 152
†R. C. Russell c Rhodes b Matthews	8	4/93 5/109	

J. P. Crawley, R. K. Illingworth, P. J. Martin and M. C. Ilott did not bat.

Bowling: Donald 12.1–1–57–2; Pollock 15–2–39–0; Matthews 12–5–31–3; McMillan 9–3–21–0.

Umpires: S. A. Bucknor (West Indies) and D. L. Orchard.
Referee: C. H. Lloyd (West Indies).

On the second morning, South Africa were 153 for nine, after Martin and Ilott took four wickets for 12 runs in nine overs, but Pollock and Donald added 72. During this stand, Crawley tore a hamstring which put him out of the tour. Television commentators suggested Matthews had tampered with the ball; referee Lloyd accepted that he was cleaning the seam with a thumbnail. The final two days, and most of the third, were lost to rain.

SOUTH AFRICA v ENGLAND

Fourth Test Match

At Port Elizabeth, December 26, 27, 28, 29, 30. Drawn. Toss: South Africa.

South Africa

A. C. Hudson c Russell b Cork	31	– c Russell b Martin	4
G. Kirsten c Thorpe b Ilott	51	– c Illingworth b Martin	69
*W. J. Cronje c Atherton b Martin	4	– c Russell b Martin	6
D. J. Cullinan c Russell b Cork	91	– st Russell b Illingworth	14
J. N. Rhodes c Smith b Cork	49	– lbw b Cork	0
B. M. McMillan c Russell b Illingworth	49	– c Hick b Cork	1
†D. J. Richardson c Russell b Illingworth	84	– c Russell b Cork	0
S. M. Pollock lbw b Cork	23	– c Cork b Illingworth	32
C. R. Matthews st Russell b Illingworth	15	– c and b Illingworth	5
A. A. Donald not out	12	– not out	12
P. R. Adams run out	0	– not out	0
L-b 11, n-b 8	19	B 8, l-b 7, w 1, n-b 3	19

1/57 2/85 3/89 4/207 5/251   428   1/6 2/18 3/60   (9 wkts dec.) 162
6/326 7/379 8/408 9/426   4/65 5/69 6/69
                 7/135 8/146 9/160

Bowling: *First Innings*—Cork 43.2–12–113–4; Ilott 29.4–7–82–1; Martin 33–9–79–1; Illingworth 39.5–8–105–3; Hick 12–2–32–0; Gallian 2–0–6–0. *Second Innings*—Cork 26.3–5–63–3; Martin 17–8–39–3; Illingworth 22–7–45–3.

England

*M. A. Atherton c Richardson b Adams	72	– lbw b Matthews	34
A. J. Stewart c Richardson b Pollock	4	– c Hudson b Donald	81
J. E. R. Gallian c Cullinan b Pollock	14	– lbw b Adams	28
G. P. Thorpe c Rhodes b Adams	27	– not out	12
G. A. Hick lbw b Donald	62	– not out	11
R. A. Smith b McMillan	2		
†R. C. Russell c Cullinan b Donald	30		
D. G. Cork c Richardson b Pollock	1		
R. K. Illingworth c Hudson b Donald	28		
P. J. Martin b Adams	4		
M. C. Ilott not out	0		
L-b 9, w 1, n-b 9	19	B 9, l-b 8, w 1, n-b 5	23

1/7 2/50 3/88 4/163 5/168   263   1/84 2/157 3/167   (3 wkts) 189
6/199 7/200 8/258 9/263

Bowling: *First Innings*—Donald 25.4–7–49–3; Pollock 22–8–58–3; Adams 37–13–75–3; Matthews 20–7–42–0; McMillan 15–6–30–1; Cronje 1–1–0–0. *Second Innings*—Pollock 10–4–15–0; Donald 19–4–60–1; Adams 28–13–51–1; McMillan 14–6–16–0; Matthews 19–10–29–1; Kirsten 2–1–1–0.

Umpires: S. A. Bucknor (West Indies) and C. J. Mitchley.
Referee: C. H. Lloyd (West Indies).

Adams became South Africa's youngest Test player at 18 years and 340 days; it was his sixth first-class match. Cork took three for nought in 17 balls on the fourth day, but was later called for a wide by umpire Mitchley after persistently bowling outside leg stump. England completed their seventh successive Test without defeat.

SOUTH AFRICA v ENGLAND

Fifth Test Match

At Cape Town, January 2, 3, 4. South Africa won by ten wickets. Toss: England.

England

*M. A. Atherton c Hudson b Donald	0	– c Richardson b Donald	10
A. J. Stewart b McMillan	13	– c Cullinan b Pollock	7
R. A. Smith b Adams	66	– (4) c Richardson b Adams	13
G. P. Thorpe c McMillan b Donald	20	– (5) run out	59
G. A. Hick c McMillan b Donald	2	– (6) lbw b Pollock	36
†R. C. Russell c McMillan b Pollock	9	– (7) c Hudson b Pollock	2
M. Watkinson lbw b Pollock	11	– (8) lbw b Adams	0
D. G. Cork b Donald	16	– (9) c Kallis b Pollock	8
P. J. Martin c Hudson b Donald	0	– (10) c Adams b Pollock	9
A. R. C. Fraser not out	5	– (3) c Adams b Donald	1
D. E. Malcolm b Adams	1	– not out	0
B 4, l-b 1, w 1, n-b 4	10	B 2, l-b 5, n-b 5	12

1/0 2/24 3/58 4/60 5/103   153   1/16 2/22 3/22 4/66 5/138   157
6/115 7/141 8/147 9/151   6/140 7/140 8/140 9/150

Bowling: *First Innings*—Donald 16–5–46–5; Pollock 14–6–26–2; McMillan 10–2–22–1; Adams 20.1–5–52–2; Kallis 4–2–2–0; Cronje 4–4–0–0. *Second Innings*—Donald 18–6–49–2; Pollock 15.5–4–32–5; Adams 22–6–53–2; McMillan 7–3–16–0.

South Africa

G. Kirsten c Atherton b Watkinson	23	– not out	41
A. C. Hudson lbw b Cork	0	– not out	27
*W. J. Cronje c Russell b Cork	12		
D. J. Cullinan c Russell b Martin	62		
J. N. Rhodes c Russell b Fraser	16		
B. M. McMillan run out	11		
J. H. Kallis lbw b Martin	7		
†D. J. Richardson not out	54		
S. M. Pollock c Smith b Watkinson	4		
A. A. Donald c Russell b Cork	3		
P. R. Adams c Hick b Martin	29		
L-b 22, n-b 1	23	L-b 1, n-b 1	2

1/1 2/19 3/79 4/125 5/125   244   (no wkt) 70
6/144 7/154 8/163 9/171

Bowling: *First Innings*—Cork 25–6–60–3; Malcolm 20–6–56–0; Martin 24–9–37–3; Fraser 17–10–34–1; Watkinson 15–3–35–2. *Second Innings*—Cork 4–0–23–0; Malcolm 2–0–12–0; Martin 4–2–3–0; Watkinson 4–0–24–0; Hick 1.4–0–7–0.

Umpires: S. G. Randell (Australia) and D. L. Orchard.
Referee: C. H. Lloyd (West Indies).

South Africa secured their first home series win over England since 1930-31. When Russell made his 27th dismissal of the series, one short of R. W. Marsh's world record of 28, South Africa were 171 for nine. But Richardson and Adams added 73 to take a first-innings lead of 91. In the second innings, umpire Orchard at first turned down a run-out appeal against Thorpe, then referred to the third umpire, who gave him out, after protests from South African captain Cronje; referee Lloyd fined Cronje half his match fee for demanding a video replay, against ICC regulations.

NEW ZEALAND v PAKISTAN

Only Test: At Christchurch, December 8, 9, 10, 11, 12. Pakistan won by 161 runs. Toss: New Zealand. Pakistan 208 (Aamir Sohail 88, Ramiz Raja 54, Ijaz Ahmed 30; C. L. Cairns four for 51) and 434 (Aamir Sohail 30, Ramiz Raja 62, Ijaz Ahmed 103, Inzamam-ul-Haq 82, Rashid Latif 39, Waqar Younis 34; C. L. Cairns three for 114); New Zealand 286 (C. M. Spearman 40, R. G. Twose 59, C. L. Cairns 76; Wasim Akram five for 53, Mushtaq Ahmed three for 115) and 195 (C. M. Spearman 33, R. G. Twose 51 not out; Mushtaq Ahmed seven for 56).

D. K. Morrison made his 23rd duck in Tests, equalling B. S. Chandrasekhar's record, but later took his 150th wicket in his 45th match. Ijaz Ahmed made his second Test hundred in 11 days, following his 137 at Sydney. Waqar Younis took his 200th Test wicket, in 38 matches; at 24 years and 26 days, he was the youngest bowler to achieve this feat.

AUSTRALIA v SRI LANKA

First Test: At Perth, December 8, 9, 10, 11. Australia won by an innings and 36 runs. Toss: Sri Lanka. Sri Lanka 251 (A. P. Gurusinha 46, A. Ranatunga 32, R. S. Kaluwitharana 50, H. D. P. K. Dharmasena 30; C. J. McDermott three for 44, G. D. McGrath four for 81, S. K. Warne three for 75) and 330 (R. S. Mahanama 48, A. Ranatunga 46, H. P. Tillekeratne 119, R. S. Kaluwitharana 40; G. D. McGrath three for 86, C. J. McDermott three for 73, S. K. Warne three for 96); Australia 617 for five dec. (M. J. Slater 219, M. A. Taylor 96, M. E. Waugh 111, R. T. Ponting 96, S. G. Law 54 not out).

Slater's 219, his seventh Test century and his first double, lasted 459 minutes and 321 balls; he hit 15 fours and five sixes and put on 228 with Taylor for the first wicket. Ponting made 96 on Test debut. Umpires Khizar Hayat and P. D. Parker informed Sri Lankan captain Ranatunga that the condition of the ball had been altered during Australia's innings; referee G. T. Dowling backed this up and warned Sri Lanka for ball-tampering, but ICC withdrew the charge a fortnight later and expressed regrets. In Sri Lanka's second innings, Warne took his 200th Test wicket in his 42nd match.

Second Test: At Melbourne, December 26, 27, 28, 29, 30. Australia won by ten wickets. Toss: Sri Lanka. Australia 500 for six dec. (M. J. Slater 62, D. C. Boon 110, M. E. Waugh 61, S. R. Waugh 131 not out, R. T. Ponting 71, I. A. Healy 41) and 41 for no wkt; Sri Lanka 233 (A. Ranatunga 51, R. S. Kaluwitharana 50; G. D. McGrath five for 40) and 307 (U. C. Hathurusinghe 39, A. P. Gurusinha 143, H. P. Tillekeratne 38; S. K. Warne four for 71).

Umpire D. B. Hair no-balled Sri Lanka's M. Muralitharan seven times in three overs for throwing; the bowler switched to the other end and was unchallenged, but ICC urged him to take corrective action to continue his career. M. A. Taylor took his 100th Test catch and Warne reached 50 wickets for the third successive calendar year. Australia ensured their fourth successive series win since they were beaten by Pakistan in November 1994.

Third Test: At Adelaide, January 25, 26, 27, 28, 29. Australia won by 148 runs. Toss: Australia. Australia 502 for nine dec. (D. C. Boon 43, M. E. Waugh 71, S. R. Waugh 170, I. A. Healy 70, P. R. Reiffel 56, S. K. Warne 33; G. P. Wickremasinghe three for 120) and 215 for six dec. (D. C. Boon 35, S. R. Waugh 61 not out, I. A. Healy 43; W. P. U. J. C. Vaas three for 44); Sri Lanka 317 (S. T. Jayasuriya 48, S. Ranatunga 60, R. S. Kaluwitharana 31, H. P. Tillekeratne 65; G. D. McGrath four for 91, P. R. Reiffel five for 39) and 252 (S. T. Jayasuriya 112, S. Ranatunga 65; G. D. McGrath three for 48, S. R. Waugh four for 34).

Boon announced his international retirement before this Test, his 107th; he finished it with 7,422 runs at 43.65. Only A. R. Border has played more Tests (156) and scored more runs (11,174) for Australia. S. R. Waugh became the tenth Australian to reach 5,000 Test runs, in his 81st Test, taking his average to 50.52. Sri Lanka reached 195 for two in their second innings but lost their last eight for 57.

NEW ZEALAND v ZIMBABWE

First Test: At Hamilton, January 13, 14, 15, 16, 17. Drawn. Toss: Zimbabwe. New Zealand 230 for eight dec. (R. G. Twose 42, S. P. Fleming 49, D. N. Patel 31, Extras 37; H. H. Streak four for 52) and 222 for five dec. (A. C. Parore 84 not out, N. J. Astle 32); Zimbabwe 196 (D. L. Houghton 31, G. J. Whittall 54, P. A. Strang 49; C. L. Cairns four for 56, R. J. Kennedy three for 28) and 208 for six (G. W. Flower 59, D. L. Houghton 31, A. Flower 58 not out).

After rain severely restricted the first three days, Germon challenged Zimbabwe to score 257 in 65 overs. Houghton became the first player to score 1,000 Test runs for Zimbabwe, in his 15th match. M. D. Crowe, ruled out of the series by his long-running injury, announced his retirement after 77 Tests; he had scored 5,444 runs at 45.36.

Second Test: At Auckland, January 20, 21, 22, 23, 24. Drawn. Toss: New Zealand. New Zealand 251 (C. M. Spearman 42, S. P. Fleming 84, C. L. Cairns 57; H. H. Streak three for 50, B. C. Strang three for 64) and 441 for five dec. (C. M. Spearman 112, R. G. Twose 94, A. C. Parore 76 not out, C. L. Cairns 120; H. H. Streak four for 110); Zimbabwe 326 (D. L. Houghton 104 retired hurt, A. Flower 35, P. A. Strang 44, E. A. Brandes 39; G. I. Allott three for 56) and 246 for four (G. W. Flower 71, S. V. Carlisle 58, A. Flower 45 not out, A. D. R. Campbell 34).

Houghton's foot was broken by R. J. Kennedy when he was 55; he batted on with a runner to his fourth Test century but retired overnight. A. Flower became the second Zimbabwean to reach 1,000 Test runs, in his 16th Test. Cairns scored a maiden Test hundred in 86 balls; in all, he hit 120 in 96 balls, with ten fours and nine sixes. Referee Nasim-ul-Ghani penalised Cairns and Parore for dissent when an appeal was turned down in Zimbabwe's second innings. The series was drawn 0-0.

INDEX OF UNUSUAL OCCURRENCES

FIXTURES, 1996

* Indicates Sunday play.   † *Not first-class.*

All County Championship matches are of four days' duration. Other first-class matches are of three days' duration unless stated.

Saturday, April 13

Oxford	Oxford U. v Leics.

Monday, April 15

Southampton	†Hants 2nd XI v England Under-19 (4 days)

Wednesday, April 17

Cambridge	Cambridge U. v Glam.
Oxford	Oxford U. v Durham

Thursday, April 18

Manchester	Lancs. v Yorks. ("friendly" match, 4 days)

Saturday, April 20

Chelmsford*	England A v The Rest
Cambridge*	Cambridge U. v Derbys.
Oxford	Oxford U. v Middx

Sunday, April 21

Manchester	†Lancs. v Yorks. (1 day)

Wednesday, April 24

Oxford	†British Univs. v Warwicks. (1 day)

Friday, April 26

†Benson and Hedges Cup (1 day)

Oxford	British Univs. v Kent
Chesterfield	Derbys. v Durham
Cardiff	Glam. v Essex
Bristol	Glos. v Sussex
Southampton	Hants v Ireland
Manchester	Lancs. v Minor Counties
Lord's	Middx v Somerset
Birmingham	Warwicks. v Leics.
Worcester	Worcs. v Northants
Leeds	Yorks. v Notts.

Sunday, April 28

†Benson and Hedges Cup (1 day)

Cambridge	British Univs. v Glam.
Chelmsford	Essex v Middx
Maidstone	Kent v Somerset
Manchester	Lancs. v Durham
Leicester	Leics. v Derbys.
Jesmond	Minor Counties v Warwicks.
Nottingham	Notts. v Scotland
The Oval	Surrey v Hants
Hove	Sussex v Ireland
Worcester	Worcs. v Yorks.

Tuesday, April 30

†Benson and Hedges Cup (1 day)

Chesterfield	Derbys. v Lancs.
Chester-le-Street	Durham v Warwicks.
Chelmsford	Essex v British Univs.
Cardiff	Glam. v Somerset
Southampton	Hants v Sussex
Canterbury	Kent v Middx
Jesmond	Minor Counties v Leics.
Nottingham	Notts. v Worcs.
Forfar	Scotland v Northants
The Oval	Surrey v Glos.

Wednesday, May 1

Lord's	†MCC v MCC Young Cricketers

Thursday, May 2

Derby	Derbys. v Leics.
Chester-le-Street	Durham v Northants
Cardiff	Glam. v Yorks.
Canterbury	Kent v Lancs.
Lord's	Middx v Glos.
Nottingham	Notts. v Sussex
Taunton	Somerset v Surrey
Worcester	Worcs. v Essex
Oxford	Oxford U. v Hants

Friday, May 3

Cambridge*	Cambridge U. v Warwicks.

Sunday, May 5

| Arundel | †Duke of Norfolk's XI v Indians (1 day) |

Monday, May 6

| Uxbridge | †England NCA v Indians (1 day) |

Tuesday, May 7

†Benson and Hedges Cup (1 day)

Chester-le-Street	Durham v Minor Counties
Chelmsford	Essex v Kent
Dublin (Clontarf CC)	Ireland v Glos.
Leicester	Leics. v Lancs.
Lord's	Middx v Glam.
Northampton	Northants v Notts.
Taunton	Somerset v British Univs.
Hove	Sussex v Surrey
Birmingham	Warwicks. v Derbys.
Leeds	Yorks. v Scotland

Wednesday, May 8

| Worcester | Worcs. v Indians |

Thursday, May 9

Southampton	Hants v Essex
Manchester	Lancs. v Leics.
Lord's	Middx v Durham
Northampton	Northants v Glam.
Taunton	Somerset v Notts.
The Oval	Surrey v Kent
Hove	Sussex v Warwicks.
Sheffield	Yorks. v Derbys.

Saturday, May 11

| Bristol* | Glos. v Indians |
| Oxford | †Oxford U. v Cambridge U. (1 day) |

Tuesday, May 14

†Benson and Hedges Cup (1 day)

Cambridge	British Univs. v Middx
Derby	Derbys. v Minor Counties
Bristol	Glos. v Hants
Eglinton	Ireland v Surrey
Canterbury	Kent v Glam.
Manchester	Lancs. v Warwicks.

Leicester	Leics. v Durham
Northampton	Northants v Yorks.
Edinburgh (Grange CC)	Scotland v Worcs.
Taunton	Somerset v Essex

Thursday, May 16

Chester-le-Street	Durham v Yorks.
Ilford	Essex v Kent
Cardiff	Glam. v Derbys.
Bristol	Glos. v Somerset
Leicester	Leics. v Worcs.
Nottingham	Notts. v Lancs.
Birmingham	Warwicks. v Hants
Hove	Sussex v Indians
Cambridge	Cambridge U. v Middx
Oxford	Oxford U. v Northants

Sunday, May 19

| Lord's | †Middx v Indians (1 day) |

Tuesday, May 21

| Luton | †Northants v Indians (1 day) |
| Lord's | †MCC v Club Cricket Conference |

Wednesday, May 22

| Horsham | Sussex v Middx |
| Lord's | †MCC v Midlands Club Cricket Conference |

Thursday, May 23

The Oval	†ENGLAND v INDIA (1st 1-day Texaco Trophy)
Derby	Derbys. v Essex
Abergavenny	Glam. v Worcs.
Gloucester	Glos. v Surrey
Portsmouth	Hants v Durham
Canterbury	Kent v Yorks.
Taunton	Somerset v Northants
Birmingham	Warwicks. v Leics.
Oxford	Oxford U. v Notts.

Saturday, May 25

| Leeds | †ENGLAND v INDIA (2nd 1-day Texaco Trophy) |

Sunday, May 26

| Manchester | †ENGLAND v INDIA (3rd 1-day Texaco Trophy) |

Tuesday, May 28

†Benson and Hedges Cup – Quarter-finals
(1 day)

Chelmsford or Cardiff	Essex or Glam. v Indians

Or Somerset if both Essex and Glam. in B&H Cup quarter-finals.

Thursday, May 30

Tunbridge Wells	Kent v Sussex
Manchester	Lancs. v Glos.
Lord's	Middx v Yorks.
Northampton	Northants v Warwicks.
Nottingham	Notts. v Durham
The Oval	Surrey v Derbys.
Worcester	Worcs. v Hants

Saturday, June 1

Leicester*	Leics. v Indians
Oxford	Oxford U. v Glam.

Wednesday, June 5

Leicester	Leics. v Kent

Thursday, June 6

Birmingham*	ENGLAND v INDIA (1st Cornhill Test, 5 days)
Chelmsford	Essex v Lancs.
Southampton	Hants v Derbys.
Lord's	Middx v Glam.
Nottingham	Notts. v Northants
Taunton	Somerset v Warwicks.
Hove	Sussex v Durham
Middlesbrough	Yorks. v Surrey
Oxford	Oxford U. v Worcs.

Tuesday, June 11

†Benson and Hedges Cup – Semi-finals
(1 day)

Thursday, June 13

Chester-le-Street	Durham v Lancs.
Chelmsford	Essex v Northants
Swansea	Glam. v Somerset
Bristol	Glos. v Sussex
Canterbury	Kent v Middx
The Oval	Surrey v Leics.
Worcester	Worcs. v Notts.
Leeds	Yorks. v Warwicks.
Derby*	Derbys. v Indians (4 days)

Friday, June 14

Cambridge*	Cambridge U. v Hants

Wednesday, June 19

Basingstoke	Hants v Northants
Bath	Somerset v Worcs.

Thursday, June 20

Lord's*	ENGLAND v INDIA (2nd Cornhill Test, 5 days)
Derby	Derbys. v Middx
Stockton-on-Tees	Durham v Surrey
Nottingham	Notts. v Glos.
Hove	Sussex v Glam.
Birmingham	Warwicks. v Kent
Bradford	Yorks. v Leics.

Friday, June 21

Cambridge*	Cambridge U. v Essex

Tuesday, June 25

†NatWest Bank Trophy – First Round
(1 day)

March	Cambs. v Kent
St Austell	Cornwall v Warwicks.
Carlisle	Cumb. v Middx
Chester-le-Street	Durham v Scotland
Chelmsford	Essex v Devon
Cardiff	Glam. v Worcs.
Southampton	Hants v Norfolk
Belfast (North of Ireland CC)	Ireland v Sussex
Leicester	Leics. v Berks.
Sleaford	Lincs. v Glos.
Northampton	Northants v Cheshire
Aston Rowant	Oxon. v Lancs.
Taunton	Somerset v Suffolk
Stone	Staffs. v Derbys.
The Oval	Surrey v Holland
Leeds	Yorks. v Notts.
Lord's	†Eton v Harrow (1 day)

Wednesday, June 26

Cambridge	British Univs. v Indians

Thursday, June 27

Chester-le-Street	Durham v Glos.
Southend	Essex v Surrey
Manchester	Lancs. v Somerset
Lord's	Middx v Warwicks.

Northampton	Northants v Derbys.
Worcester	Worcs. v Yorks.
Trowbridge	†England NCA v Pakistanis (1 day)

Saturday, June 29

Pontypridd*	Glam. v Pakistanis
Southampton*	Hants v Indians
Canterbury*	Kent v Oxford U.
Hove*	Sussex v Cambridge U.

Tuesday, July 2

| Lord's | Oxford U. v Cambridge U. |

Wednesday, July 3

Arundel	Sussex v Hants
Taunton	Somerset v Pakistanis
Leeds	Yorks. v South Africa A

Thursday, July 4

Nottingham	ENGLAND v INDIA (3rd Cornhill Test, 5 days)
Bristol	Glos. v Glam.
Maidstone	Kent v Durham
Manchester	Lancs. v Worcs.
Leicester	Leics. v Essex
The Oval	Surrey v Middx
Birmingham	Warwicks. v Notts.

Saturday, July 6

| Northampton* | Northants v Pakistanis |
| Chesterfield* | Derbys. v South Africa A |

Wednesday, July 10

†NatWest Bank Trophy – Second Round (1 day)

Truro or Birmingham	Cornwall or Warwicks. v Surrey or Holland
Chelmsford or Torquay	Essex or Devon v Durham or Scotland
Swansea or Worcester	Glam. or Worcs. v Hants or Norfolk
Leicester or Reading	Leics. or Berks. v Ireland or Sussex
Aston Rowant or Manchester	Oxon. or Lancs. v Northants or Cheshire
Taunton or Bury St Edmunds	Somerset or Suffolk v Lincs. or Glos.
Stone or Derby	Staffs. or Derbys. v Cambs. or Kent
Leeds or Nottingham	Yorks. or Notts. v Cumb. or Middx
Shenley Park	MCC v South Africa A

Thursday, July 11

| Stone | †Minor Counties v Pakistanis (1 day) |

Saturday, July 13

| Lord's | †BENSON AND HEDGES CUP FINAL (1 day) |

Monday, July 15

| Harrogate | †Costcutter Cup (3 days) |

Tuesday, July 16

| Lord's | †MCC v MCC Schools (1 day) |

Wednesday, July 17

Guildford	Surrey v Sussex
Birmingham	Warwicks. v Pakistanis
Cardiff	Glam. v South Africa A
Lord's	†MCC Schools v NAYC (1 day)
Wales	†Triple Crown Tournament (3 days)

Thursday, July 18

Chelmsford	Essex v Notts.
Cheltenham	Glos. v Leics.
Manchester	Lancs. v Derbys.
Northampton	Northants v Middx
Worcester	Worcs. v Durham
Harrogate	Yorks. v Hants
Chester-le-Street	†England Under-19 v New Zealand Under-19 (1st 1-day)
Lord's	†NCA Young Cricketers v Combined Services (1 day)

Saturday, July 20

Canterbury*	Kent v Pakistanis
Taunton*	Somerset v South Africa A
Nottingham	†England Under-19 v New Zealand Under-19 (2nd 1-day)

Wednesday, July 24

| Kidderminster | Worcs. v Northants |
| Cheltenham | †Glos. v South Africa A (1 day) |

Thursday, July 25

Lord's*	ENGLAND v PAKISTAN (1st Cornhill Test, 5 days)
Derby	Derbys. v Kent
Hartlepool	Durham v Essex
Cardiff	Glam. v Lancs.
Cheltenham	Glos. v Warwicks.
Southampton	Hants v Surrey
Leicester	Leics. v Sussex
Scarborough	Yorks. v Somerset

Friday, July 26

Nottingham*	Notts. v South Africa A (4 days)

Tuesday, July 30

†NatWest Bank Trophy – Quarter-finals (1 day)

Thursday, August 1

Derby	Derbys. v Glos.
Canterbury	Kent v Worcs.
Leicester	Leics. v Northants
Lord's	Middx v Essex
Worksop	Notts. v Glam.
Taunton	Somerset v Hants
Eastbourne	Sussex v Yorks.
The Oval*	Surrey v South Africa A (4 days)
Edinburgh (Grange CC)	†Scotland v Pakistanis (1 day)
Manchester*	†England Under-19 v New Zealand Under-19 (1st Unofficial Test, 4 days)

Saturday, August 3

Chester-le-Street*	Durham v Pakistanis

Tuesday, August 6

Chelmsford	†Essex v South Africa A (1 day)

Wednesday, August 7

Southport	Lancs. v Surrey
Lord's	†MCC v Scotland (2 days)

Thursday, August 8

Leeds*	ENGLAND v PAKISTAN (2nd Cornhill Test, 5 days)

Swansea	Glam. v Leics.
Southampton	Hants v Glos.
Northampton	Northants v Kent
Nottingham	Notts. v Middx
Taunton	Somerset v Essex
Hove	Sussex v Derbys.
Birmingham	Warwicks. v Durham

Friday, August 9

Worcester*	Worcs. v South Africa A (4 days)

Monday, August 12

Cambridge and Oxford	†NAYC Under-19 County Festivals (6 days)

Tuesday, August 13

†NatWest Bank Trophy – Semi-finals (1 day)

Wednesday, August 14

Leicester or Hove	Leics. or Sussex v Pakistanis

Thursday, August 15

Derby	Derbys. v Notts.
Bristol	Glos. v Yorks.
Canterbury	Kent v Somerset
Manchester	Lancs. v Hants
Lord's	Middx v Worcs.
Birmingham	Warwicks. v Glam.
Chester-le-Street*	TCCB XI v South Africa A (4 days)
Worcester*	†England Under-19 v New Zealand Under-19 (2nd Unofficial Test, 4 days)

†Bain Hogg Trophy Semi-finals (1 day)

Friday, August 16

†Bain Hogg Trophy Semi-finals (1 day) (if not played on August 15)

Saturday, August 17

Chelmsford*	Essex v Pakistanis
Linlithgow (Boghall CC)*	Scotland v Ireland

Tuesday, August 20

Lord's	†Lombard World Challenge Under-15 Final

Wednesday, August 21

Weston-super-Mare	Somerset v Durham

Thursday, August 22

The Oval*	ENGLAND v PAKISTAN (3rd Cornhill Test, 5 days)
Colchester	Essex v Glos.
Cardiff	Glam. v Kent
Leicester	Leics. v Hants
Northampton	Northants v Sussex
Nottingham	Notts. v Surrey
Worcester	Worcs. v Warwicks.
Leeds	Yorks. v Lancs.
Hove*	†England Under-19 v New Zealand Under-19 (3rd Unofficial Test, 4 days)

Wednesday, August 28

Chester-le-Street	Durham v Glam.
Portsmouth	Hants v Middx
Lord's	†Minor Counties Knockout Final (1 day)

Thursday, August 29

Manchester	†ENGLAND v PAKISTAN (1st 1-day Texaco Trophy)
Chesterfield	Derbys. v Worcs.
Bristol	Glos. v Northants
Tunbridge Wells	Kent v Notts.
Leicester	Leics. v Somerset
The Oval	Surrey v Warwicks.
Hove	Sussex v Lancs.
Leeds	Yorks. v Essex

Friday, August 30

Lord's	†National Club Championship Final (1 day)

Saturday, August 31

Birmingham	†ENGLAND v PAKISTAN (2nd 1-day Texaco Trophy)

Sunday, September 1

Nottingham	†ENGLAND v PAKISTAN (3rd 1-day Texaco Trophy)
Lord's	†National Village Championship Final (1 day)

Tuesday, September 3

Southampton	Hants v Glam.
Manchester	Lancs. v Middx
Nottingham	Notts. v Leics.
Taunton	Somerset v Derbys.
The Oval	Surrey v Northants
Birmingham	Warwicks. v Essex
Worcester	Worcs. v Sussex

Friday, September 6

Scarborough	†Yorks. v Tesco International XI (1 day)

Saturday, September 7

Lord's	†NATWEST BANK TROPHY FINAL (1 day)
Scarborough	†Yorks. v Durham (Northern Electric Trophy, 1 day)

Sunday, September 8

Scarborough	†Yorks. v Holland (McCain Challenge, 1 day)

Monday, September 9

†Bain Hogg Trophy Final (1 day).

Scarborough	†Tetley Bitter Festival Trophy (3 days)

Tuesday, September 10

Lord's	†MCC v Cricket Touring Club De Flamingos

Thursday, September 12

Derby	Derbys. v Warwicks.
Chester-le-Street	Durham v Leics.
Chelmsford	Essex v Sussex
Cardiff	Glam. v Surrey
Canterbury	Kent v Hants
Uxbridge	Middx v Somerset
Northampton	Northants v Lancs.
Worcester	Worcs. v Glos.
Scarborough	Yorks. v Notts.

Thursday, September 19

Derby*	Derbys. v Durham
Chelmsford*	Essex v Glam.
Bristol*	Glos. v Kent
Southampton*	Hants v Notts.
Leicester*	Leics. v Middx
Northampton*	Northants v Yorks.
The Oval*	Surrey v Worcs.
Hove*	Sussex v Somerset
Birmingham*	Warwicks. v Lancs.

INDIAN TOUR, 1996

MAY

5 Arundel	†v Duke of Norfolk's XI (1 day)
6 Uxbridge	†v England NCA (1 day)
8 Worcester	v Worcs.
11 Bristol*	v Glos.
16 Hove	v Sussex
19 Lord's	†v Middx (1 day)
21 Luton	†v Northants (1 day)
23 The Oval	†v ENGLAND (1st 1-day Texaco Trophy)
25 Leeds	†v ENGLAND (2nd 1-day Texaco Trophy)
26 Manchester	†v ENGLAND (3rd 1-day Texaco Trophy)
28 Chelmsford or Cardiff	v Essex or Glam.

Or Somerset if both Essex and Glam. in B&H Cup quarter-finals.

JUNE

1 Leicester*	v Leics.
6 Birmingham*	v ENGLAND (1st Cornhill Test, 5 days)
13 Derby*	v Derbys (4 days)
20 Lord's*	v ENGLAND (2nd Cornhill Test, 5 days)
26 Cambridge	v British Universities
29 Southampton*	v Hants

JULY

4 Nottingham	v ENGLAND (3rd Cornhill Test, 5 days)

PAKISTANI TOUR, 1996

JUNE

27 Trowbridge	†v England NCA (1 day)
29 Pontypridd*	v Glam.

JULY

3 Taunton	v Somerset
6 Northampton*	v Northants
11 Stone	†v Minor Counties (1 day)
17 Birmingham	v Warwicks.
20 Canterbury*	v Kent
25 Lord's*	v ENGLAND (1st Cornhill Test, 5 days)

AUGUST

1 Edinburgh (Grange CC)	†v Scotland (1 day)

3 Chester-le-Street*	v Durham
8 Leeds*	v ENGLAND (2nd Cornhill Test, 5 days)
14 Leicester or Hove	v Leics. or Sussex
17 Chelmsford*	v Essex
22 The Oval*	v ENGLAND (3rd Cornhill Test, 5 days)
29 Manchester	†v ENGLAND (1st 1-day Texaco Trophy)
31 Birmingham	†v ENGLAND (2nd 1-day Texaco Trophy)

SEPTEMBER

1 Nottingham	†v ENGLAND (3rd 1-day Texaco Trophy)

SOUTH AFRICA A TOUR, 1996

JULY

3 Leeds	v Yorks.
6 Chesterfield*	v Derbys.
10 Shenley Park	v MCC
17 Cardiff	v Glam.
20 Taunton*	v Somerset
24 Cheltenham	†v Glos. (1 day)
26 Nottingham*	v Notts. (4 days)

AUGUST

1 The Oval*	v Surrey (4 days)
6 Chelmsford	†v Essex (1 day)
9 Worcester*	v Worcs. (4 days)
15 Chester-le-Street*	v TCCB XI (4 days)

†AXA EQUITY & LAW LEAGUE, 1996

All matches are of one day's duration.

MAY

5–Derbys. v Leics. (Derby); Durham v Northants (Chester-le-Street); Glam. v Yorks. (Cardiff); Kent v Lancs. (Canterbury); Middx v Glos. (Lord's); Notts. v Sussex (Nottingham); Somerset v Surrey (Taunton); Worcs. v Essex (Worcester).

12–Hants v Essex (Southampton); Lancs. v Leics. (Manchester); Middx v Durham (Lord's); Northants v Glam. (Northampton); Somerset v Notts. (Taunton); Surrey v Kent (The Oval); Sussex v Warwicks. (Hove); Yorks. v Derbys. (Sheffield).

19–Durham v Yorks. (Chester-le-Street); Essex v Kent (Ilford); Glam. v Derbys. (Cardiff); Glos. v Somerset (Bristol); Leics. v Worcs. (Leicester); Notts. v Lancs. (Nottingham); Warwicks. v Hants (Birmingham).

26–Derbys. v Essex (Derby); Glam. v Worcs. (Ebbw Vale); Glos. v Surrey (Gloucester); Hants v Durham (Portsmouth); Kent v Yorks. (Canterbury); Somerset v Northants (Taunton); Sussex v Middx (Horsham); Warwicks. v Leics. (Birmingham).

JUNE

2–Kent v Sussex (Tunbridge Wells); Lancs. v Glos. (Manchester); Middx v Yorks. (Lord's); Northants v Warwicks. (Northampton); Notts. v Durham (Nottingham); Surrey v Derbys. (The Oval); Worcs. v Hants (Worcester).

9–Essex v Lancs. (Chelmsford); Hants v Derbys. (Southampton); Leics. v Kent (Leicester); Middx v Glam. (Lord's); Notts. v Northants (Nottingham); Somerset v Warwicks. (Taunton); Sussex v Durham (Hove); Yorks. v Surrey (Leeds).

16–Durham v Lancs. (Chester-le-Street); Essex v Northants (Chelmsford); Glam. v Somerset (Swansea); Glos. v Sussex (Bristol); Kent v Middx (Canterbury); Surrey v Leics. (The Oval); Worcs. v Notts. (Worcester); Yorks. v Warwicks. (Leeds).

23–Derbys. v Middx (Derby); Durham v Surrey (Stockton-on-Tees); Hants v Northants (Basingstoke); Notts. v Glos. (Nottingham); Somerset v Worcs. (Bath); Sussex v Glam. (Hove); Warwicks. v Kent (Birmingham); Yorks. v Leics. (Bradford).

30–Durham v Glos. (Chester-le-Street); Essex v Surrey (Southend); Lancs. v Somerset (Manchester); Middx v Warwicks. (Lord's); Northants v Derbys. (Northampton); Worcs. v Yorks. (Worcester).

JULY

7–Glos. v Glam. (Bristol); Kent v Durham (Maidstone); Lancs. v Worcs. (Manchester); Leics. v Essex (Leicester); Surrey v Middx (The Oval); Sussex v Hants (Arundel); Warwicks. v Notts. (Birmingham).

14–Derbys. v Durham (Derby); Essex v Glam. (Chelmsford); Glos. v Kent (Moreton-in-Marsh); Hants v Notts. (Southampton); Leics. v Middx (Leicester); Northants v Yorks. (Northampton); Surrey v Worcs. (The Oval); Sussex v Somerset (Hove); Warwicks. v Lancs. (Birmingham). *Note: Matches involving B&H Cup finalists to be played on July 16.*

21–Essex v Notts. (Chelmsford); Glos. v Leics. (Cheltenham); Lancs. v Derbys. (Manchester); Northants v Middx (Northampton); Surrey v Sussex (Guildford); Worcs. v Durham (Worcester); Yorks. v Hants (Leeds).

28–Derbys. v Kent (Derby); Durham v Essex (Hartlepool); Glam. v Lancs. (Swansea); Glos. v Warwicks. (Cheltenham); Hants v Surrey (Southampton); Leics. v Sussex (Leicester); Worcs. v Northants (Worcester); Yorks. v Somerset (Scarborough).

AUGUST

4–Derbys. v Glos. (Derby); Kent v Worcs. (Canterbury); Leics. v Northants (Leicester); Middx v Essex (Lord's); Notts. v Glam. (Nottingham); Somerset v Hants (Taunton); Sussex v Yorks. (Eastbourne).

11–Glam. v Leics. (Swansea); Hants v Glos. (Southampton); Lancs. v Surrey (Manchester); Northants v Kent (Northampton); Notts. v Middx (Nottingham); Somerset v Essex (Taunton); Sussex v Derbys. (Hove); Warwicks. v Durham (Birmingham).

18–Derbys. v Notts. (Derby); Glos. v Yorks. (Bristol); Kent v Somerset (Canterbury); Lancs. v Hants (Manchester); Middx v Worcs. (Lord's); Warwicks. v Glam. (Birmingham).

25–Essex v Glos. (Colchester); Glam. v Kent (Cardiff); Leics. v Hants (Leicester); Northants v Sussex (Northampton); Notts. v Surrey (Nottingham); Somerset v Durham (Weston-super-Mare); Warwicks. v Worcs. (Birmingham); Yorks. v Lancs. (Leeds).

SEPTEMBER

1–Derbys. v Worcs. (Chesterfield); Durham v Glam. (Chester-le-Street); Glos. v Northants (Bristol); Hants v Middx (Portsmouth); Kent v Notts. (Tunbridge Wells); Leics. v Somerset (Leicester); Surrey v Warwicks. (The Oval); Sussex v Lancs. (Hove); Yorks. v Essex (Leeds).

8–Hants v Glam. (Southampton); Lancs. v Middx (Manchester); Notts. v Leics. (Nottingham); Somerset v Derbys. (Taunton); Surrey v Northants (The Oval); Warwicks. v Essex (Birmingham); Worcs. v Sussex (Worcester). *Note: Matches involving NWT finalists to be played on September 10.*

15–Derbys. v Warwicks. (Derby); Durham v Leics. (Chester-le-Street); Essex v Sussex (Chelmsford); Glam. v Surrey (Cardiff); Kent v Hants (Canterbury); Middx v Somerset (Uxbridge); Northants v Lancs. (Northampton); Worcs. v Glos. (Worcester); Yorks. v Notts. (Scarborough).

†MINOR COUNTIES CHAMPIONSHIP, 1996

All matches are of two days' duration.

MAY

26–Devon v Dorset (Budleigh Salterton); Lincs. v Beds. (Sleaford); Northumb. v Herts. (Jesmond); Salop v Herefords. (Bridgnorth).

28–Bucks. v Suffolk (Beaconsfield); Cumb. v Herts. (Carlisle).

JUNE

2–Herefords. v Dorset (Colwall); Herts. v Suffolk (Bishop's Stortford); Lincs. v Staffs. (Bourne); Northumb. v Bucks. (Jesmond); Salop v Oxon. (Shrewsbury).

4–Cheshire v Oxon. (Neston); Cumb. v Bucks. (Barrow).

10–Cumb. v Norfolk (Millom).

12–Cambs. v Suffolk (Wisbech); Staffs. v Norfolk (Cannock).

16–Berks. v Herefords. (Falkland CC); Lincs. v Northumb. (Grimsby CC); Oxon. v Wales (Challow & Childrey); Salop v Wilts. (Wellington); Suffolk v Beds. (Ransomes, Ipswich).

17–Cornwall v Cheshire (Falmouth).

18–Cambs. v Northumb. (Saffron Walden).

19–Devon v Cheshire (Torquay).

23–Beds. v Herts. (Bedford Town); Berks. v Wales (Hurst CC).

JULY

3–Cambs. v Staffs. (Fenner's, Cambridge).

7–Beds. v Northumb. (Henlow); Berks. v Cornwall (Reading School); Herefords. v Devon (Hereford City); Lincs. v Cambs. (Lincoln Lindum); Wales v Salop (Pontypridd); Wilts. v Oxon. (S. Wilts. CC).

9–Oxon. v Cornwall (Thame); Staffs. v Bucks. (Old Hill).

14–Beds. v Norfolk (Southill Park); Cheshire v Berks. (Bowdon); Cornwall v Dorset (Truro); Herefords. v Wilts. (Brockhampton); Herts. v Bucks. (Shenley Park).

15–Lincs. v Cumb. (Grantham).

16–Bucks. v Norfolk (High Wycombe); Salop v Berks. (Oswestry).

17–Cambs. v Cumb. (Fenner's, Cambridge).

21–Wales v Devon (Colwyn Bay). *Note: To be played on July 22 if either Wales or Devon in MCC Trophy semi-finals.*

22–Northumb. v Staffs. (Jesmond).

24—Cambs. v Bucks. (Kimbolton School); Cumb. v Staffs. (Askam).

28—Bucks. v Beds. (Slough); Dorset v Salop (Weymouth); Norfolk v Lincs. (Lakenham); Oxon. v Devon (Thame); Suffolk v Northumb. (Ipswich School); Wales v Cornwall (Pontarddulais); Wilts. v Cheshire (Westbury).

29—Staffs. v Herts. (Longton).

30—Berks. v Devon (Reading CC); Dorset v Cheshire (Dorchester); Herefords. v Cornwall (Dales, Leominster); Norfolk v Northumb. (Lakenham).

AUGUST

1—Norfolk v Cambs. (Lakenham).

4—Cheshire v Wales (Boughton Hall, Chester); Cornwall v Wilts. (Camborne); Devon v Salop (Exmouth); Dorset v Oxon. (Dean Park).

5—Norfolk v Herts. (Lakenham); Suffolk v Lincs. (Bury St Edmunds).

6—Beds. v Cambs. (Wardown Park); Cornwall v Salop (St Austell); Devon v Wilts. (Bovey Tracey).

11—Beds. v Cumb. (Dunstable); Herts. v Lincs. (Hertford); Oxon. v Herefords. (Rover, Cowley); Wales v Dorset (Penarth); Wilts. v Berks. (Marlborough CC).

13—Cumb. v Suffolk (Netherfield).

15—Staffs. v Suffolk (Stone).

18—Cheshire v Herefords. (New Brighton); Dorset v Berks. (Dean Park); Wilts. v Wales (Trowbridge).

20—Berks. v Oxon. (Kidmore End); Bucks. v Lincs. (Marlow); Cheshire v Salop (Toft); Cornwall v Devon (Truro); Herefords. v Wales (Kington); Herts. v Cambs. (Long Marston); Northumb. v Cumb. (Jesmond); Staffs. v Beds. (Brewood); Suffolk v Norfolk (Mildenhall); Wilts. v Dorset (Trowbridge).

SEPTEMBER

8—Final.

†MCC TROPHY KNOCKOUT COMPETITION, 1996

All matches are of one day's duration.

Preliminary Round

May 19 Cumb. v Cheshire (Penrith); Herefords. v Wilts. (Brockhampton); Herts. v Dorset (Shenley Park); Staffs. v Norfolk (Walsall).

First Round

June 9 Beds. v Oxon. (Wardown Park); Bucks. v Devon (Aylesbury); Cumb. or Cheshire v Staffs. or Norfolk (Barrow or Nantwich); Herts. or Dorset v Herefords. or Wilts.

(Shenley Park or Sherborne School); Lincs. v Northumb. (Cleethorpes); Salop v Berks. (St Georges, Telford); Suffolk or Cambs. (Framlingham); Wales v Cornwall (Panteg, Newport).

Quarter-finals to be played on June 30.

Semi-finals to be played on July 21.

Final to be played on August 28 at Lord's.

†SECOND ELEVEN CHAMPIONSHIP, 1996

All matches are of three days' duration.

APRIL

21—Somerset v Notts. (Taunton).

22—Glos. v Leics. (Bristol); Kent v Lancs. (Canterbury); Warwicks. v Derbys. (Knowle & Dorridge).

28—Somerset v Derbys. (King's College, Taunton).

29—Glos. v Glam. (Bristol); Middx v Worcs. (Uxbridge CC); Surrey v Leics. (Cheam); Yorks. v Northants (Leeds).

30—Lancs. v Notts. (Manchester); Sussex v Kent (Hove).

MAY

5—Surrey v Durham (The Oval).

6—Derbys. v Yorks. (Abbotsholme School, Rocester); Lancs. v Worcs. (Manchester); Somerset v Northants (North Perrott); Sussex v Essex (Eastbourne).

7-Glos. v Hants (Bristol).

13-Essex v Glos. (Chelmsford); Glam. v Somerset (Pontypridd); Kent v Leics. (Maidstone); Lancs. v Sussex (Haslingden); Middx v Surrey (Uxbridge CC); Worcs. v Northants (Worcester); Yorks. v Notts. (Todmorden).

14-Hants v Warwicks. (Southampton).

20-Derbys. v Essex (Abbotsholme School, Rocester); Durham v Sussex (Boldon); Hants v Glam. (Southampton); Kent v Northants (Ashford); Leics. v Lancs. (Oakham Town CC); Surrey v Notts. (Oxted); Worcs. v Glos. (Worcester).

27-Derbys. v Notts. (Chesterfield); Glam. v Lancs. (Swansea); Northants v Durham (Campbell Park, Milton Keynes); Yorks. v Kent (Harrogate).

28-Hants v Somerset (Bournemouth SC); Middx v Essex (Southgate CC); Warwicks. v Sussex (Stratford-upon-Avon).

JUNE

3-Durham v Warwicks. (Chester-le-Street CC); Essex v Notts. (Southend); Glos. v Lancs. (Bristol); Northants v Middx (Old Northamptonians); Somerset v Worcs. (Taunton); Yorks. v Surrey (York).

10-Glam. v Middx (Pontarddulais); Hants v Durham (Portsmouth); Kent v Surrey (Maidstone); Lancs. v Essex (Fleetwood); Northants v Leics. (Campbell Park, Milton Keynes); Notts. v Warwicks. (Worksop CC); Sussex v Somerset (Horsham).

17-Durham v Derbys. (Ashbrooke); Glam. v Sussex (Ammanford); Lancs. v Yorks. (Manchester); Leics. v Essex (Leicester); Northants v Hants (Northampton); Worcs. v Kent (Ombersley).

19-Surrey v Glos. (The Oval).

24-Durham v Essex (Darlington); Glos. v Warwicks. (Tuffley Park, Gloucester); Kent v Hants (Canterbury); Lancs. v Somerset (Preston); Leics. v Middx (Hinckley); Surrey v Sussex (Cheam); Worcs. v Notts. (Barnt Green); Yorks. v Glam. (Sheffield).

JULY

1-Essex v Kent (Coggeshall); Glam. v Durham (Cardiff); Glos. v Somerset (Optimists CC, Bristol); Hants v Derbys. (Finchampstead); Leics. v Warwicks. (Egerton Park CC); Middx v Warwicks. (Southgate CC); Notts. v Northants (Collingham CC).

8-Derbys. v Worcs. (Trent College); Durham v Yorks. (Shildon); Essex v Surrey (Saffron Walden); Glam. v Leics. (Usk); Hants v Lancs. (Southampton); Sussex v Middx (Middleton-on-Sea); Warwicks. v Kent (Coventry & North Warwicks).

9-Northants v Glos. (Northampton).

15-Glam. v Derbys. (Swansea); Glos. v Middx (Bristol); Leics. v Warwicks. (Leicester); Northants v Sussex (Wellingborough School); Notts. v Durham (Nottingham); Somerset v Kent (Taunton); Surrey v Lancs. (The Oval); Worcs. v Hants (Halesowen).

22-Glos. v Durham (Bristol); Leics. v Derbys. (Hinckley); Middx v Yorks. (Harrow CC); Northants v Lancs. (Bedford School); Notts. v Glam. (Cleethorpes); Surrey v Hants (The Oval); Sussex v Worcs. (Hove); Warwicks. v Essex (Walmley CC).

29-Essex v Northants (Colchester); Glos. v Sussex (King's School, Gloucester); Kent v Glam. (Sittingbourne); Lancs. v Middx (Crosby); Leics. v Durham (Kibworth); Somerset v Surrey (Clevedon); Warwicks. v Worcs. (Moseley CC); Yorks. v Hants (Marske-by-Sea).

AUGUST

5-Derbys. v Glos. (Chesterfield); Durham v Lancs. (Seaton Carew); Glam. v Essex (Pontypridd); Hants v Sussex (Bournemouth SC); Middx v Kent (Harrow CC); Notts. v Leics. (Nottingham High School); Surrey v Northants (The Oval); Warwicks. v Somerset (Studley); Worcs. v Yorks. (Worcester).

8-Durham v Somerset (Riverside, Chester-le-Street).

12-Durham v Middx (South Shields CC); Essex v Yorks. (Wickford); Kent v Glos. (Folkestone); Lancs. v Derbys. (Liverpool); Leics. v Sussex (Oakham School); Notts. v Hants (Worksop College); Warwicks. v Surrey (Solihull CC).

19-Essex v Hants (Ilford); Glam. v Warwicks. (Swansea); Kent v Durham (British Gas, Eltham); Leics. v Somerset (Hinckley); Middx v Derbys. (Lensbury CC); Sussex v Notts. (Horsham); Worcs. v Surrey (Kidderminster); Yorks. v Glos. (Elland).

26–Durham v Worcs. (Felling); Hants v Middx (Southampton); Kent v Notts. (Canterbury); Sussex v Derbys. (Haywards Heath); Yorks. v Leics. (Park Avenue, Bradford).

27–Northants v Warwicks. (Northampton).

SEPTEMBER

2–Derbys. v Surrey (Derby); Essex v Worcs. (Chelmsford); Middx v Somerset (RAF Vine Lane, Uxbridge).

3–Northants v Glam. (Northampton); Warwicks. v Yorks. (Wardens CC, Kenilworth).

11–Derbys. v Kent (Chesterfield); Hants v Leics. (Southampton); Lancs. v Warwicks. (Manchester); Notts. v Middx (Nottingham); Somerset v Essex (Taunton); Surrey v Glam. (The Oval); Sussex v Yorks. (Hove).

16–Derbys. v Northants (Belper Meadows); Notts. v Glos. (Nottingham); Somerset v Yorks. (Taunton); Worcs. v Glam. (Barnt Green).

†BAIN HOGG TROPHY, 1996

All matches are of one day's duration.

MAY

2–Leics. v Middx (Leicester).

3–Essex v MCC Young Cricketers (Chelmsford); Lancs. v Notts. (Manchester); Sussex v Kent (Hove).

6–Glos. v Hants (Bristol).

9–Derbys. v Yorks. (Derby); Durham v Lancs. (Riverside, Chester-le-Street); Leics. v Warwicks. (Leicester); Sussex v Essex (Eastbourne).

10–MCC Young Cricketers v Kent (Shenley Park).

16–Middx v Leics. (Uxbridge CC); Yorks. v Notts. (Park Avenue, Bradford).

17–Durham v Notts. (Bishop Auckland); Worcs. v Somerset (Worcester).

23–Derbys. v Lancs. (Belper Meadows); Hants v Glam. (Southampton); Middx v Northants (Uxbridge CC); Minor Counties v Leics. (Walsall).

24–Kent v MCC Young Cricketers (Maidstone); Minor Counties v Warwicks. (Walsall).

30–Derbys. v Notts. (Derby).

31–Hants v Somerset (Southampton); MCC Young Cricketers v Surrey (Shenley Park); Middx v Minor Counties (Uxbridge CC).

JUNE

6–Glos. v Somerset (Bristol); MCC Young Cricketers v Sussex (Shenley Park); Northants v Middx (Northampton); Notts. v Yorks. (Worksop College).

7–Glam. v Glos. (Bridgend); Lancs. v Durham (Manchester); Surrey v Essex (The Oval); Warwicks. v Leics. (Old Edwardians).

13–Derbys. v Durham (Duffield); Hants v Glos. (Southampton); Kent v Surrey (Maidstone); Notts. v Lancs. (Nottingham).

14–MCC Young Cricketers v Essex (Shenley Park); Northants v Minor Counties (Campbell Park, Milton Keynes); Yorks. v Durham (Castleford).

20–Durham v Derbys. (Philadelphia CC); Lancs. v Yorks. (Manchester); Middx v Warwicks. (Southgate CC); Worcs. v Hants (Worcester).

21–Glam. v Somerset (Christ College, Brecon); Kent v Sussex (Canterbury); Leics. v Minor Counties (Leicester).

27–Minor Counties v Northants (Marlow); Surrey v Sussex (The Oval); Yorks. v Derbys. (Castleford).

28–Glos. v Glam. (Bristol); Minor Counties v Middx (Marlow); Somerset v Worcs. (Taunton); Surrey v MCC Young Cricketers (The Oval).

JULY

2—Yorks. v Lancs. (Bingley).

4—Essex v Kent (Coggeshall).

5—Glam. v Hants (Monmouth School);
Lancs. v Derbys. (Urmston); Sussex v
MCC Young Cricketers (Hove); Worcs.
v Glos. (Bromsgrove CC).

11—Durham v Yorks. (Durham City); Essex
v Surrey (Saffron Walden); Notts. v
Derbys. (Farnsfield CC).

12—Northants v Leics. (Campbell Park,
Milton Keynes); Somerset v Glos.
(Taunton); Sussex v Surrey (Hove);
Worcs. v Glam. (Worcester).

18—Leics. v Northants (Leicester); Notts. v
Durham (Welbeck CC).

19—Glam. v Worcs. (Panteg); Kent v Essex
(Maidstone); Warwicks. v Minor
Counties (Aston Unity CC).

25—Somerset v Hants (Taunton).

26—Hants v Worcs. (Bournemouth SC);
Northants v Warwicks. (Tring);
Somerset v Glam. (Taunton); Surrey v
Kent (The Oval).

AUGUST

1—Essex v Sussex (Chelmsford); Warwicks.
v Middx (Birmingham).

2—Glos. v Worcs. (Lydney); Warwicks. v
Northants (Birmingham).

Semi-finals to be played on August 15 or 16.

Final to be played on September 9 (reserve
day September 10).

---

†WOMEN'S CRICKET, 1996

MAY

25	Wellingborough	England trial match (3 days)

JUNE

8	Shenley Park	Audrey Collins XI v New Zealand (1 day)
9	Arundel	South of England v New Zealand (1 day)
11	Tunbridge Wells	England Under-21 v New Zealand (1 day)
13	Lord's	ENGLAND v NEW ZEALAND (1st 1-day international)
15	Leicester	ENGLAND v NEW ZEALAND (2nd 1-day international)
18	Chester-le-Street	ENGLAND v NEW ZEALAND (3rd 1-day international)
20	Morpeth	North of England v New Zealand (3 days)
24	Scarborough	ENGLAND v NEW ZEALAND (1st Test, 4 days)
29	Malvern College	WCA President's XI v New Zealand (3 days)

JULY

3	Worcester	ENGLAND v NEW ZEALAND (2nd Test, 4 days)
8	Christ Church, Oxford	Mid-West of England v New Zealand (3 days)
12	Guildford	ENGLAND v NEW ZEALAND (3rd Test, 4 days)
27	Cambridge	County Championship (5 days)

AUGUST

11	Colwall	Cricket Week (6 days)
31	National Club Knockout/Plate finals	

SEPTEMBER

8	Premier League final	

LOMBARD WORLD CHALLENGE

Under-15 Cricket World Championship

AUGUST 6-12 Group stage

Lensbury Club	**Group A** (Canada, England, India, West Indies, Zimbabwe)	Oundle School	**Group B** (Australia, Holland, Pakistan, South Africa, Sri Lanka)

SEMI-FINALS

AUGUST 15	Winner Group A v runner-up Group B at Nottingham.	**AUGUST 17**	Winner Group B v runner-up Group A at Leeds.

FINAL

To be played at Lord's on August 20.

ENGLAND IN ZIMBABWE, 1996-97

All fixtures subject to confirmation.

NOVEMBER

30 Harare South †v Districts XI (1 day)

DECEMBER

1 Harare	†v ZCU President's XI (1 day)
3 Harare	v Mashonaland (4 days)
8 Bulawayo	†v Matabeleland (1 day)
10 Bulawayo	v Matabeleland (4 days)

15 Bulawayo	†v ZIMBABWE (1st 1-day international)
18 Bulawayo	v ZIMBABWE (1st Test, 5 days)
26 Harare	v ZIMBABWE (2nd Test, 5 days)

JANUARY

1 Harare	†v ZIMBABWE (2nd 1-day international)
3 Harare	†v ZIMBABWE (3rd 1-day international)

England will tour New Zealand from January 5 to March 5. Details of their programme were not available when Wisden *went to press.*